D1345047

ii

Whitaker's Almanack 1900: Facsimile Edition © The Stationery Office 1999

This edition first published 1999 by
The Stationery Office Ltd
51 Nine Elms Lane, London SW8 5DR

First published 1899 by J. Whitaker and Sons Ltd

ISBN 0 11 702247 0

A CIP catalogue record for this book is available from the British Library

Facsimile photographed by ColourScript, Mildenhall, Suffolk
Jacket photographs: (*front*) *Four Generations at Osborne*, August 1899, by
Chancellor. Queen Victoria with Albert Edward, Prince of Wales (right), George,
Duke of York (left) and Prince Edward of York. The Royal Archives © 1998 Her
Majesty Queen Elizabeth II; (*inside flap*) Joseph Whitaker, reproduced by kind
permission of J. Whitaker and Sons Ltd
Jacket design by Bob Eames
Printed and bound in Great Britain by Clays Ltd, part of St Ives PLC, Bungay,
Suffolk

PREFACE TO THE FACSIMILE EDITION.

The first edition of *Whitaker's Almanack* was published in December 1868. Queen Victoria had been on the throne for 31 years, and Gladstone had just become Prime Minister. The *Almanack* was 382 pages long.

By December 1899, when the 1900 edition was published, Queen Victoria was 80 years old. By then she had appointed eight more Prime Ministers, including the Marquess of Salisbury for the third time in 1895. The *Almanack* had expanded to 928 pages.

In his preface to the 1900 edition, Cuthbert Whitaker, twelfth child of the *Almanack's* creator Joseph Whitaker, highlighted the book's growing diversity. As well as a list of charitable bequests and "eminent Octogenarians", this edition has an article on the growth of joint stock companies, an examination of the 1899 London Government Act, a complete revision of the material on mercantile fleets, and an article explaining the background to the Boer War in South Africa, which had begun a few months earlier.

The national budget for 1899–1900 had a deficit of £2,640,000, which would have been higher if the Chancellor of the Exchequer had not raised the duty on imported wines. Income tax ran at 8d. in the pound (just over 3p in today's decimal money), and the Bank of England's reserves were £3,136,776. The office of Prime Minister was still an unpaid position, although the Lord Chancellor received £4,000 a year. The section covering "Remarkable Occurrences, &c." noted that "Mr Rudyard Kipling, who had been very dangerously ill with double pneumonia, was reported to be on the road to recovery", and that Sheffield United won the FA Cup.

To anyone familiar with the modern *Whitaker's Almanack*, the 1900 edition is both recognizable and refreshingly different. The basic concept and organization have endured, but the contrasts are just as marked. The advertisements at the front and the back, the variations in type quality from page to page, the language – all make this Facsimile a unique child of its time, while the contemporary perspective on events and the sheer amount of detail have a charm and immediacy that no modern-day history of the period could ever capture.

The millennium mood encourages us to look back as well as forward. There is no better guide to how the 20th century began than *Whitaker's Almanack 1900*.

RUPERT PENNANT-REA
CHAIRMAN, THE STATIONERY OFFICE
51 NINE ELMS LANE, LONDON SW8 5DR

LANDMARKS IN THE HISTORY OF *WHITAKER'S ALMANACK*

1820   Joseph Whitaker born.

1868   First edition, *Whitaker's Almanack 1869*, published from 10 Warwick Square, London. It contained 382 pages and, even before publication, had attracted 36,000 subscriptions.

1870   Premises move to 12 Warwick Lane, London.

1878   *Whitaker's Almanack 1878* placed in a time capsule in the foundations of Cleopatra's Needle on the Embankment, London.

1884   With the book reaching 456 pages, Joseph Whitaker writes in his Preface: "Year by year the scope of the *Almanack* has widened, and its pages have increased in number; the limit has now been reached."

1895   Joseph Whitaker dies. He is succeeded as editor by his twelfth child, Cuthbert.

1914   In *The Valley of Fear*, Sherlock Holmes uses the Almanack to decode a message.

1927   The paperback Concise edition first published.

1931   For the first time, the *Almanack* exceeds 1,000 editorial pages.

1940   Premises in Warwick Lane destroyed by incendiary bombs, along with all of the *Almanack* records and reference library. Temporary refuge provided by Pitmans.

1948   *Whitaker's Almanack* moves to Bedford Square.

1950   Sir Cuthbert Whitaker dies, and is succeeded as editor by F. H. C. (Tom) Tatham.

1952   1953 edition first to include colour illustration – a portrait of HM Queen Elizabeth II as a frontispiece.

1953   1954 edition first to contain black and white photographs.

1959   1960 edition first to have a dust jacket.

1978   Premises move to Dyott Street, London.

1980   1981 edition first to be typeset by computer.

1981   Tom Tatham succeeded as editor by Richard Blake.

1986   Richard Blake succeeded as editor by Hilary Marsden.

1992   1993 edition introduces the first change in format since 1868. The new design includes a 16-page colour section.

1997   *Whitaker's Almanack* bought by The Stationery Office.

1998   Premises move to Nine Elms Lane, London.
            The first of a *Whitaker's Almanack* list of titles is published.

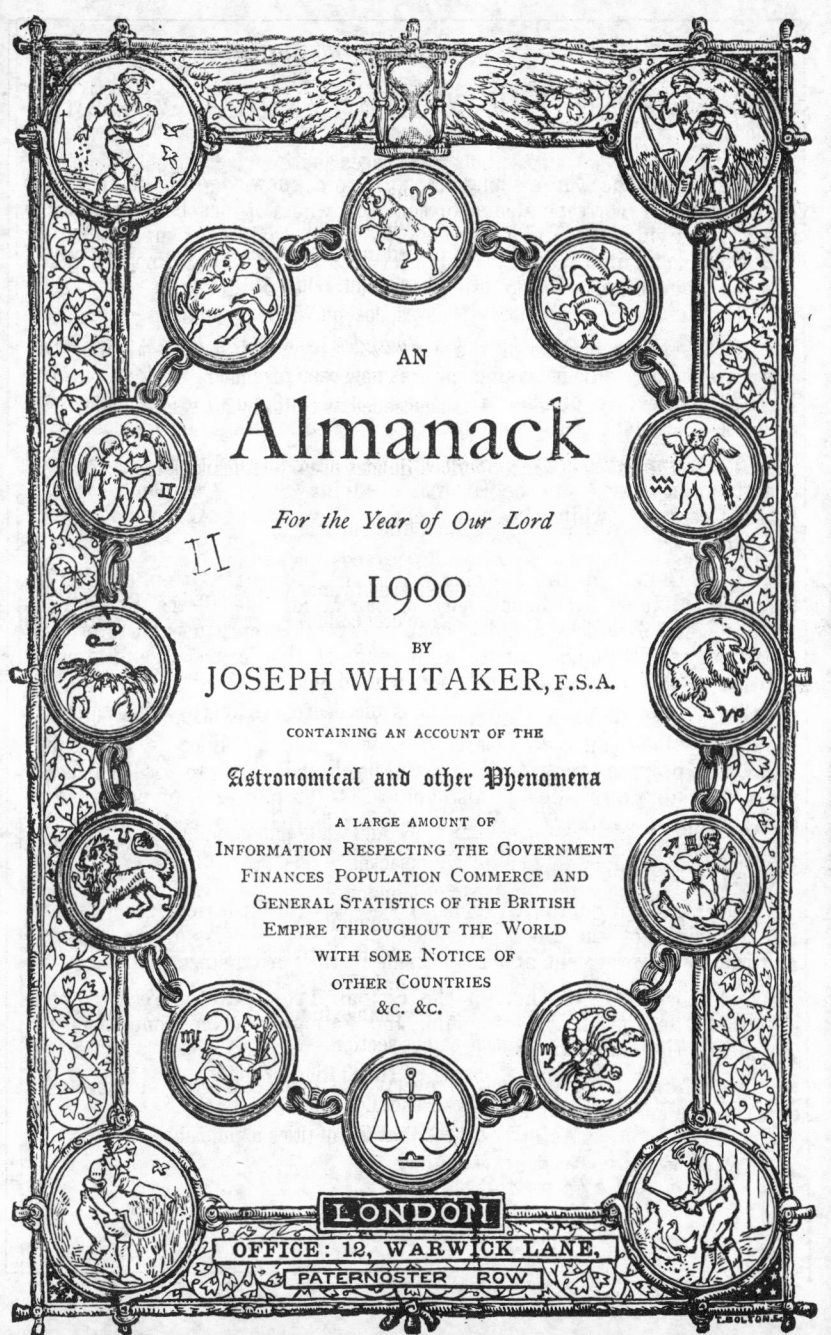

AN

Almanack

For the Year of Our Lord

1900

BY

JOSEPH WHITAKER, F.S.A.

CONTAINING AN ACCOUNT OF THE

Astronomical and other Phenomena

A LARGE AMOUNT OF

INFORMATION RESPECTING THE GOVERNMENT
FINANCES POPULATION COMMERCE AND
GENERAL STATISTICS OF THE BRITISH
EMPIRE THROUGHOUT THE WORLD
WITH SOME NOTICE OF
OTHER COUNTRIES
&c. &c.

LONDON

OFFICE: 12, WARWICK LANE,
PATERNOSTER ROW

PREFACE TO THE XXXIIND ANNUAL VOLUME.

It is again the Editor's pleasing duty to acknowledge his indebtedness to innumerable correspondents (to some of whom it has been impossible to reply individually), and to express his hearty thanks for suggestions for the Almanack's improvement. In order that full advantage may be taken of such suggestions, letters should reach the Editor not later than October.

In the earlier portion of the Almanack, every subject dealt with, with few exceptions, will be found in its accustomed place, while room has been found for a list of Charitable Bequests in 1899, and for the re-insertion of a list of eminent Octogenarians, which now occupies an entire page.

In the supplementary portion will be found, in addition to the usual contents, an article on the Growth of Joint Stock Companies in the present century; while the new London Government Act has also been treated.

"Our Ocean Mail" has this year been entirely rewritten, and is now incorporated in an article entitled "Ocean Mercantile Fleets, British and Foreign," which will be found to contain several interesting and informing statistical tables, in addition to an account of the formation and present position of all the great Ocean Lines in existence.

In the Geographical section some new maps have been inserted, to show the "Petersburg to Peking" railway, and a "Suez to Shanghai" route, as a proposed reply to that mainly political move in Eastern Asia; the "Cape to Cairo" line is also indicated for purposes of comparison. Other maps illustrate the Venezuela—British Guiana Settlement; the Anglo-German Agreement in West Africa; and the Anglo-French Convention in the Nile Valley.

The trouble in South Africa has necessitated a historical record showing the origin of the Boer grievances in the early years of the century, and the abuses prevalent under their rule in the period since 1882.

The history of Egypt and of the Soudan Provinces has received considerable attention, and the Colonial and Foreign section generally subjected to a rigid supervision.

The information given has in every case been corrected and brought down to the latest possible date.

Warwick Lane, Paternoster Row,
London, 26th November, 1899.

INDEX.

DURATION OF LIGHT AND DARKNESS.

THE second column of the first page of Calendar for every month contains a small diagram showing the amount of Darkness, or of Sun or Moonlight. These small figures represent the twelve hours from 6 P.M. to 6 A.M., and have four divisions, each representing three hours. For the first three and last six days of January there is no moonlight from 6 P.M. till 6 A.M., but from the 11th to the 17th it will be seen that there is moonlight. In the summer months the Sun comes to our aid.

THE DIAGRAMS USED ARE—

Six to 9	6 to 12	6 to 3	6 to 6:	Nine to 12	9 to 3	9 to 6:	Twelve to 3	12 to 6:	Three to 6

WHITAKER'S ALMANACK FOR 1900.

BEING THE FOURTH AFTER BISSEXTILE, AND 63 AND 64 OF QUEEN VICTORIA.

Common Notes for the Year.

Golden Number	I	*Ascension Day—Holy Thursday* ... ... May	24
Epact...	29	Birth of Queen Victoria (1819) ... ... ,,	24
Solar Cycle	5	*Pentecost—Whit Sunday* ... ... June	3
Roman Indiction	13	*Trinity Sunday* ... ... ,,	10
Dominical Letter	G	*Corpus Christi* ... ... ,,	14
Julian Period (Year of)	6613	Sundays after Trinity	24
Septuagesima Sunday ... ... Feb.	11	Accession of Queen Victoria (1837) ... ,,	20
Ash Wednesday ... ... ,,	28	Queen's Coronation (1838) ... ... ,,	28
Good Friday ... ... April	13	Birth of Prince of Wales (1841)... ... Nov.	9
Easter Day. (See p. 65) ... ,,	15	*St. Andrew's Day* ... ... ,,	30
St. George's Day ... ... ,,	23	*First Sunday in Advent* ... ... Dec.	2
Rogation Sunday ... ... May	20	CHRISTMAS DAY—Tuesday ... ... ,,	25

Beginnings of the Seasons.

	d. h.		d. h.
Spring, Sun enters Aries (0° long.) March	21 2M	Autumn, Sun enters Libra (180°) Sept.	23 0A
Summer ,, ,, Cancer (90°)... June	21 10A	Winter ,, ,, Capricornus (270°) Dec.	22 7M

The EQUINOXES occur when Spring and Autumn begin, and the SOLSTICES at Summer and Winter.

Law Sittings.

Hilary ....Begin Jan. 11 and end April 11	Trinity............ Begin June 12 and end Aug. 12
Easter .... ,, April 24 ,, June 1	Michaelmas...... ,, Oct. 24 ,, Dec. 21

INNS OF COURT LAW (DINING) TERMS.—*Hilary* begins Jan. 11, ends Jan. 31; CALL DAY, Jan. 29. *Easter* begins April 24, ends May 21; CALL DAY, May 9. *Trinity* begins June 12, ends July 2; CALL DAY, June 28. *Michaelmas* begins Nov. 2, ends Nov. 25; CALL DAY, Nov. 19.

University Terms.

OXFORD.	Begins.	Ends.	CAMBRIDGE.	Begins.	Ends.
Lent ....January 15		April 7	Lent ....January 8		March 27
Easter ....April 18		June 9	Easter ....April 24		June 25
Trinity ....June 2		July 7	Michaelmas......October 1		December 19
Michaelmas ......October 10		December 17			

Jewish Calendar. (A.D. 1900, A.M. 5660–61.)

The Year 5660 commenced September 5, 1899.

Jan. 1	New Moon ... ... Sebat	1	July 15	Fast of Tamuz ... Tamuz	18
,, 31	New Moon ... ... Adar	1	,, 27	New Moon ... ... Ab	1
Mar. 2	New Moon ... ... Veadar	1	Aug. 15	Fast of Ab ... ... ,,	10
,, 14	Fast of Esther ... ... ,,	13	,, 26	New Moon ... ... Elul	1
,, 15	Purim ... ... ,,	14	Sept. 24	First day of New Year, 5661 Tishri	1
,, 16	Shushan Purim ... ... ,,	15	,, 25	Fast of Gedliuah ... ... ,,	3
,, 31	New Moon ... ... :.. Nisan	1	Oct. 3	Fast of Expiation ... ... ,,	10
April 14	Festival of Passover ... ,,	15	,, 8	Feast of Tabernacles ... ,,	15
,, 15	,, ,, 2nd day ,,	16	,, 14	Hosana Raba... ... ,,	21
,, 20	,, ,, 7th day ,,	21	,, 15	Feast of the 8th day... ... ,,	22
,, 21	,, ,, ends ,,	22	,, 16	Rejoicing of the Law ... ,,	23
,, 30	New Moon ... ... Yiar	1	,, 24	New Moon ... ... Heshvan	1
May 17	Festival, 33rd day of Omer... ,,	18	Nov. 22	New Moon ... ... Kislev	1
,, 29	New Moon ... ... Sivan	1	Dec. 17	Dedication of the Temple... ,,	25
June 3	Festival of Weeks ... ,,	6	,, 23	New Moon ... ... Tebet	1
,, 3	,, ,, 2nd day ,,	7	Jan. 1, 1901 }	Fast, Siege of Jerusalem ... ,,	10
,, 28	New Moon ... ... Tamuz	1			

NOTE.—All the Jewish Sabbaths, Festivals, and Fasts commence the previous Evening at Sunset.

Mohammedan Calendar. (1317–1318.)

Year.	Name of Month.				Month begins.	Year	Name of Month.				Month begins.
1317.	Ramadán	...	...	...	January 3	1318.	Rabia I.	...	...	...	June 29
,,	Shawall	...	...	...	February 2	,,	Rabia II.	...	...	...	July 29
,,	Dulkaada	...	...	...	March 3	,,	Jomada I.	...	...	...	August 27
,,	Dulheggia	...	...	...	April 2	,,	Jomada II.	...	...	...	September 26
						,,	Rajab	...	...	...	October 25
1318.	Muharram	...	...	...	May 1	,,	Shaaban	...	...	...	November 24
,,	Saphar	...	...	...	,, 31	,,	Ramadán	...	...	...	December 23

A Calendar

For ascertaining Any Day of the Week for any given time within Two Hundred Years from the introduction of the New Style, 1752,¶ to 1952 inclusive.

YEARS 1753 TO 1952.

Years	Jan	Feb	Mar	Apr	May	Jun	July	Aug	Sep	Oct	Nov	Dec
1761 1767 1778 1789 1795 / 1801 1807 1818 1829 1835 — 1846 — 1857(1903) 1863(1914) 1874(1925) 1885(1931) — *1891(1942)	4	7	7	3	5*	1	3	6	2	4	7	2
1762 1773 1779 1790 / 1802 1813 1819 1830 — 1841 — 1847 — 1858(1909) 1869(1915) 1875(1926) 1886(1937) — 1897(1943)	5	1	1	4	6	2	4	7	3	5	1	3
1757 1763 1774 1785 1791 / 1803 1814 1825 1831 — 1842 — 1853 — 1859(1910) 1870(1921) 1881(1927) 1887(1938) — 1898(1949)	6	2	2	5	7	3	5	1	4	6	2	4
1754 1765 1771 1782 1793 1799 / 1805 1811 1822 1833 1839 1850(1901) — 1861(1907) 1867(1918) 1878(1929) 1889(1935) — 1895(1946)	2	5	5	1	3	6	1	4	7	2	5	7
1755 1766 1777 1783 1794 1800 / 1806 1817 1823 1834 1845 1851(1902) — 1862(1913) 1873(1919) 1879(1930) 1890(1941) — .. (1947)	3	6	6	2	4	7	2	5	1	3	6	1
1758 1769 1775 1786 1797 / 1809 1815 1826 1837 1843 1854(1905) — 1865(1911) 1871(1922) 1882(1933) 1893(1939) — 1899(1950)	7	3	3	6	1	4	6	2	5	7	3	5
1753 1759 1770 1781 1787 1798 / 1810 1821 1827 1838 1849 1855 1866(1906) 1877(1917) 1883(1923) 1894(1934) — 1900 1945 1951	1	4	4	7	2	5	7	3	6	1	4	6

LEAP YEARS.

Years	Jan	Feb	Mar	Apr	May	Jun	July	Aug	Sep	Oct	Nov	Dec
	..	29	..	..	..	..	..	..	..	..	..	..
1764 1792 1804 1832 1860 1888 .. 1928	7	3	4	7	2	5	7	3	6	1	4	6
1768 1796 1808 1836 1864 1892 1904 1932	5	1	2	5	7	3	5	1	4	6	2	4
1772 .. 1812 1840 1868 1896 1908 1936	3	6	7	3	5	1	3	6	2	4	7	2
1776 .. 1816 1844 1872 .. 1912 1940	1	4	5	1	3	6	1	4	7	2	5	7
1780 .. 1820 1848 1876 .. 1916 1944	6	2	3	6	1	4	6	2	5	7	3	5
1756 1784 1824 1852 1880 .. 1920 1948	4	7	1	4	6	2	4	7	3	5	1	3
1760 1788 1828 1856 1884 .. 1924 1952	2	5	6	2	4	7	2	5	1	3	6	1

NOTE.—To ascertain any day of the week, first look in the table for the year required, and under the months are figures which refer to the corresponding figures at the head of the columns of days below:—To know on what day of the week May 4 fell in the year 1891, in the table of years look for 1891, and in a parallel line, under May, is fig. 5, which directs to col. 5, in which it will be seen that May 4 fell on Monday.

¶ 1752 same as 1772 from Jan. 1 to Sept. 2. From Sept. 14 to Dec. 31 same as 1780 (Sept. 3–13 were omitted).

1	2	3	4	5*	6	7
Monday 1	Tuesday 1	Wednesd. 1	Thursday 1	Friday 1	Saturday 1	*Sunday* 1
Tuesday 2	Wednesd. 2	Thursday 2	Friday 2	Saturday 2	*Sunday* 2	Monday 2
Wednesd. 3	Thursday 3	Friday 3	Saturday 3	*Sunday* 3	Monday 3	Tuesday 3
Thursday 4	Friday 4	Saturday 4	*Sunday* 4	Monday 4	Tuesday 4	Wednesd. 4
Friday 5	Saturday 5	*Sunday* 5	Monday 5	Tuesday 5	Wednesd. 5	Thursday 5
Saturday 6	*Sunday* 6	Monday 6	Tuesday 6	Wednesd. 6	Thursday 6	Friday 6
Sunday 7	Monday 7	Tuesday 7	Wednesd. 7	Thursday 7	Friday 7	Saturday 7
Monday 8	Tuesday 8	Wednesd. 8	Thursday 8	Friday 8	Saturday 8	*Sunday* 8
Tuesday 9	Wednesd. 9	Thursday 9	Friday 9	Saturday 9	*Sunday* 9	Monday 9
Wednes. 10	Thursday 10	Friday 10	Saturday 10	*Sunday* 10	Monday 10	Tuesday 10
Thursday 11	Friday 11	Saturday 11	*Sunday* 11	Monday 11	Tuesday 11	Wednesd. 11
Friday 12	Saturday 12	*Sunday* 12	Monday 12	Tuesday 12	Wednesd. 12	Thursday 12
Saturday 13	*Sunday* 13	Monday 13	Tuesday 13	Wednesd. 13	Thursday 13	Friday 13
Sunday 14	Monday 14	Tuesday 14	Wednesd.14	Thursday 14	Friday 14	Saturday 14
Monday 15	Tuesday 15	Wednesd. 15	Thursday 15	Friday 15	Saturday 15	*Sunday* 15
Tuesday 16	Wednesd. 16	Thursday 16	Friday 16	Saturday 16	*Sunday* 16	Monday 16
Wednes. 17	Thursday 17	Friday 17	Saturday 17	*Sunday* 17	Monday 17	Tuesday 17
Thursday 18	Friday 18	Saturday 18	*sunday* 18	Monday 18	Tuesday 18	Wednesd.18
Friday 19	Saturday 19	*Sunday* 19	Monday 19	Tuesday 19	Wednesd. 19	Thursday 19
Saturday 20	*Sunday* 20	Monday 20	Tuesday 20	Wednesd. 20	Thursday 20	Friday 20
Sunday 21	Monday 21	Tuesday 21	Wednesd. 21	Thursday 21	Friday 21	Saturday 21
Monday 22	Tuesday 22	Wednesd. 22	Thursday 22	Friday 22	Saturday 22	*Sunday* 22
Tuesday 23	Wednesd. 23	Thursday 23	Friday 23	Saturday 23	*Sunday* 23	Monday 23
Wednesd.24	Thursday 24	Friday 24	Saturday 24	*Sunday* 24	Monday 24	Tuesday 24
Thursday 25	Friday 25	Saturday 25	*Sunday* 25	Monday 25	Tuesday 25	Wednesd 25
Friday 26	Saturday 26	*Sunday* 26	Monday 26	Tuesday 26	Wednesd. 26	Thursday 26
Saturday 27	*Sunday* 27	Monday 27	Tuesday 27	Wednesd. 27	Thursday 27	Friday 27
Sunday 28	Monday 28	Tuesday 28	Wednesd. 28	Thursday 28	Friday 28	Saturday 28
Monday 29	Tuesday 29	Wednesd. 29	Thursday 29	Friday 29	Saturday 29	*Sunday* 29
Tuesday 30	Wednesd. 30	Thursday 30	Friday 30	Saturday 30	*Sunday* 30	Monday 30
Wednesd. 31	Thursday 31	Friday 31	Saturday 31	*Sunday* 31	Monday 31	Tuesday 31

DAY OF			Fasts and Festivals. Remarkable Days—Events. SUN ENTERS AQUARIUS 20d. 0h. A.	THE SUN		DAYS	
M.	Light and Dark.	W.		Rises.	Sets.	of the Year.	to end of Year.
				H. M.	H. M.		
1	*	M	Circumcision. H.M. procl. Emp. of India, 1877.	8 8	4 0	1	364
2		Tu	Gen. Wolfe b. 1727; killed at Quebec, 13 Sept.	8 7	4 1	2	363
3		W	For Special High Tides see p. 22. [1759.	8 7	4 3	3	362
4		Th	* For use of this Column, showing Daily Darkness	8 7	4 4	4	361
5		F	and Moonlight, see note at end of p. 12.	8 7	4 5	5	360
6		S	Epiphany. Old Christmas Day. Twelfth Day.	8 6	4 6	6	359
7		S	First Sunday after Epiphany.	8 6	4 7	7	358
8		M	St. Lucian. Plough Monday. Camb. Term begins.	8 6	4 8	8	357
9		Tu	Lord Nelson buried at St. Paul's, 1806.	8 5	4 9	9	356
10		W	The Penny Post instituted, 1840.	8 5	4 11	10	355
11		Th	HILARY LAW SIT. BEGIN. Lord Curzon b. 1859.	8 4	4 12	11	354
12		F	Earl of Crewe b. 1858; Earl of Iddesleigh d. 1887	8 3	4 13	12	353
13		S	St. Hilary. Adm. Sir J. E. Commerell, VC, b. '29	8 3	4 15	13	352
14		S	Second S. aft. Epiph. Oxford Term begins.	8 2	4 16	14	351
15		M	British Museum opened, 1759.	8 2	4 18	15	350
16		Tu	Sir John Moore (Coruña), 1809.	8 1	4 19	16	349
17		W	Abu Klea, '85. Lord Rosse b. 1800; d. 31 Oct.,'67.	8 0	4 21	17	348
18		Th	St. Prisca. Lord Lytton d. 1873; b. 25 May, 1803.	7 59	4 23	18	347
19		F	Aden captured, 1839. Ciudad Rodrigo, 1812.	7 57	4 25	19	346
20		S	St. Fabian. Hong Kong ceded to G. Britain, 1841	7 56	4 26	20	345
21		S	3rd Sunday after Epiphany. St. Agnes. [1788.	7 54	4 28	21	344
22		M	St. Vincent. Rorke's Drift, 1879. Ld. Byron b.	7 53	4 30	22	343
23		Tu	Duke of Kent (Queen's father) died 1820.	7 53	4 31	23	342
24		W	Admiral Sir George Rooke d. 1709; born 1650.	7 52	4 33	24	341
25		Th	Conversion of St. Paul.	7 50	4 34	25	340
26		F	General Gordon killed at Khartoum, 1885.	7 49	4 36	26	339
27		S	William II. (German Emperor) b. 1859.	7 48	4 38	27	338
28		S	Fourth S. aft. Epiph. Sir H. M. Stanley, G.C.B.,	7 46	4 40	28	337
29		M	President McKinley, U.S.A., b. 1843. [b. '41	7 45	4 41	29	336
30		Tu	Walter Savage Landor, b. 1775; d. 17 Sept., 1864	7 43	4 43	30	335
31		W	Charles Edward, Young Pretender, died 1788.	7 42	4 45	31	334

PHASES OF THE MOON.

New Moon 1d. 1h. 52m. Afternoon.
First Quarter 8 5 40 Morning.
Full Moon 15 7 8 Afternoon.
Last Quarter 23 11 53 Afternoon.
New Moon 31 1 23 Morning.
Perigee 3d. 5h. A. 225,600 | Apogee 19d. 5h. A. 252,200

RAINFALL IN JANUARY, 1899.

In this month rain fell on 18 days. The total fall for the month was 2·53 inch; above the average of fifty years, 1841-90, by 0·54 inch.

MONTHLY NOTES.

January 1. All cases of infection to be notified to the Local Authorities.—The Sale of Food and Drugs Act, 1899, comes into force —Dog and establishment licences renewable. Queen's taxes due.

—. Parliamentary and Local Government Registers of Electors come into force.

2. Holiday on Stock Exchange; Bank Holiday in Scotland.

5. Dividends on Consols, &c., due.

9. Christmas Fire Insurances must be paid.

JANUARY FIRST MONTH.

THE SUN.

Day	After Clock. M. S.	Hrly Var. of Equa. of Time. S.	Right Ascension at Noon. H. M. S.	Hourly Var. of R.A. S.	Apparent Declination (8th.) at Noon. ° ' "	Hr.y Var. (☉)'s Declination. "	Sidereal Time at Noon. H. M. S.	Mean Time at Sidereal Noon. H. M. S.
1	3 40	1'19	18 46 24	11'05	23 1 23	12'3	18 42 44	5 16 25
2	4 9	1'18	18 50 49	11'04	22 56 15	13'4	18 46 40	5 12 29
3	4 37	1'16	18 55 13	11'02	22 50 40	14'5	18 50 37	5 8 33
4	5 4	1'14	18 59 37	11'00	22 44 38	15'7	18 54 33	5 4 37
5	5 31	1'12	19 4 1	10'98	22 38 9	16'8	18 58 30	5 0 41
6	5 58	1'10	19 8 24	10'96	22 31 12	17'9	19 2 26	4 56 45
7	6 24	1'08	19 12 47	10'94	22 23 50	19'0	19 6 23	4 52 49
8	6 50	1'06	19 17 9	10'92	22 16 0	20'1	19 10 19	4 48 53
9	7 15	1'04	19 21 31	10'90	22 7 45	21'2	19 14 16	4 44 57
10	7 40	1'01	19 25 52	10'87	21 59 4	22'3	19 18 13	4 41 1
11	8 4	0'99	19 30 13	10'85	21 49 57	23'3	19 22 9	4 37 5
12	8 27	0'96	19 34 33	10'82	21 40 24	24'4	19 26 6	4 33 9
13	8 50	0'94	19 38 52	10'80	21 30 27	25'4	19 30 2	4 29 14
14	9 12	0'91	19 43 11	10'77	21 20 5	26'5	19 33 59	4 25 18
15	9 34	0'88	19 47 29	10'74	21 9 18	27'5	19 37 55	4 21 22
16	9 55	0'85	19 51 46	10'71	20 58 6	28'5	19 41 52	4 17 26
17	10 15	0'82	19 56 3	10'68	20 46 31	29'5	19 45 48	4 13 31
18	10 34	0'80	20 0 19	10'65	20 34 32	30'5	19 49 45	4 9 34
19	10 53	0'77	20 4 34	10'62	20 22 10	31'4	19 53 42	4 5 38
20	11 11	0'73	20 8 49	10'59	20 9 24	32'4	19 57 38	4 1 42
21	11 28	0'70	20 13 3	10'56	19 56 16	33'3	20 1 35	3 57 46
22	11 45	0'67	20 17 16	10'53	19 42 46	34'2	20 5 31	3 53 50
23	12 0	0'64	20 21 28	10'50	19 28 53	35'2	20 9 28	3 49 54
24	12 15	0'61	20 25 40	10'47	19 14 39	36'1	20 13 24	3 45 59
25	12 30	0'58	20 29 50	10'43	19 0 4	36'9	20 17 21	3 42 3
26	12 43	0'54	20 34 0	10'40	18 45 7	37'8	20 21 17	3 38 7
27	12 56	0'51	20 38 10	10'37	18 29 50	38'6	20 25 14	3 34 11
28	13 8	0'48	20 42 18	10'34	18 14 13	39'5	20 29 11	3 30 15
29	13 19	0'44	20 46 26	10'30	17 58 16	40'3	20 33 7	3 26 19
30	13 29	0'41	20 50 33	10'27	17 42 0	41'1	20 37 4	3 22 23
31	13 38	0'38	20 54 38	10'23	17 25 25	41'9	20 41 0	3 18 27

METEOROLOGICAL OBSERVATIONS, JANUARY, 1899.

Day	TEMPERATURE. Maximum.	Minimum.	Avge. 50 Yrs.	BAROM. Mean.	RAIN-FALL.	SUN-SHINE.	WIND. Directn. (Pressure lbs. to foot.)	Prssure. lbs.
	°	°	°	inches.	inches.	hours.		
1	42'2	33'6	37	28'993	0'05	0'9	SW	7'7
2	42'0	35'6	37	28'832	0'15	2 3	WSW	22'5
3	44'2	39'2	37	29'688	...	0'7	WNW	9'9
4	53'0	41'3	36	29'844	0'01	1'6	WSW	3'7
5	50'6	31'3	36	30'175	...	0'1	W	1'7
6	45'8	30'2	36	30'039	...	...	SE	2'5
7	50'2	42'2	36	29'659	0'03	...	S	2'4
8	54'1	44'3	36	29'586	...	4'2	S	2'0
9	52'3	43'7	36	29'354	...	6'3	SSE	5'0
10	50'5	40'9	36	29'171	0'17	2'4	SSW	7'3
11	44'6	36'2	36	29'375	0'13	2'5	SW	4'0
12	54'5	37'6	36	29'128	0'28	0'8	SW	32'0
13	54'1	39'6	36	29'517	0'45	...	WSW	15'9
14	45'0	36'4	36	29'796	...	4'1	WSW	1'4
15	54'1	36'0	36	29'614	0'26	...	SW	12'0
16	53'1	42'6	37	29'245	0'28	0'8	WSW	17'0
17	43'3	34'2	37	29'833	0'09	2'3	WSW	7'8
18	52'7	41'0	37	29'650	0'04	...	WSW	11'5
19	53'0	45'5	37	29'472	0'07	...	SW	12'0
20	52'1	43'8	37	29'523	0'09	0'1	SSW	14'5
21	55'3	50'0	37	29'266	0'17	0'1	SSW	28'0
22	53'0	44'6	37	29'296	...	4'4	SW	22'3
23	44'6	37'2	38	29'745	0'08	...	N	8'8
24	41'8	31'4	38	29'250	...	3'6	NE	1'6
25	39'1	29'3	38	30'468	...	7'2	ENE	4'3
26	42'1	31'2	38	30'434	...	7'0	ENE	6'0
27	42'2	31'9	38	30'236	...	7'1	NE	4'1
28	39'4	30'2	38	30'070	...	8'5	NE	3'6
29	41'4	36'7	38	29'824	0'16	...	NNE	2'0
30	43'7	34'6	38	29'731	0'02	1'2	NE	2'2
31	39'0	31'2	38	29'491	...	...	NNE	0'0

MEMORANDA.

1₁ Lamps to be lighted (5.0)

2. (5.1)
3. (5.3)
4. (5.4)
5. (5.5)
6. (5.6)
7. S. (5.7)
8. (5.8)
9. (5.9)
10. (5.11)
11. (5.12)
12. (5.13)
13. (5.15)
14. S. (5.6)
15. (5.18)
16. (5.19)
17. (5.21)
18. (5.23)
19. (5.25)
20. (5.26)
21. S. (5.28)
22. (5.30)
23. (5.31)
24. (5.33)
25. (5.34)
26. (5.36)
27. (5.38)
28. S. (5.41)
29. (5.41)
30. (5.43)
31. (5.45)

JANUARY FIRST MONTH.

The Moon.

Day of M.	Rises Morning. H.	M.	Sets Afternoon. H.	M.	Souths Morning. H.	M.	Right Ascension at Noon. H.	M.	S.	Declination at Noon. °	′	″	Horizontal Parallax at Noon. ′	″	Semidiameter at Noon. ′	″	Age at Noon. D.	H.	Configuration of Jupiter's Satellites at 6h. A.M.
1	7	52	4	11	11	59	18	41	19	21	21	47s	59	48	16	19	29	11	32○41
2	8	32	5	33	aft.		19	42	17	18	23	26	60	14	16	26	0	22	1○324
3	9	4	6	57	1	55	20	41	20	14	12	54	60	24	16	29	1	22	○1234
4	9	31	8	23	2	50	21	38	4	9	10	22	60	20	16	28	2	22	21○34
5	9	54	9	46	3	42	22	32	43	3	38	30s	60	3	16	23	3	22	2○134
6	10	13	11	9	4	33	23	25	57	2	0	45n	59	37	16	16	4	22	31○24
7	10	35	mrn.		5	23	0	18	36	7	27	39	59	4	16	7	5	22	♃ ♃3○4
8	10	58	0	27	6	14	1	11	25	12	25	3	58	28	15	58	6	22	32○14
9	11	24	1	46	7	6	2	5	1	16	38	11	57	52	15	48	7	22	14○32
10	11	55	3	3	7	59	2	59	39	19	54	34	57	17	15	38	8	22	4○123
11	aft.		4	14	8	52	3	55	9	22	4	39	56	44	15	29	9	22	421○3
12	1	20	5	17	9	46	4	50	56	23	2	45	56	13	15	21	10	22	42○13
13	2	16	6	11	10	38	5	46	9	22	48	4	55	44	15	13	11	22	431○2
14	3	18	6	54	11	29	6	39	54	21	24	51	55	18	15	6	12	22	43○12
15	4	24	7	30	mrn.		7	31	34	19	1	38	54	55	14	59	13	22	432○1
16	5	33	7	57	0	17	8	20	54	15	49	23	54	34	14	54	14	22	413○2
17	6	41	8	19	1	3	9	7	59	11	59	58	54	18	14	49	15	22	4○123
18	7	47	8	38	1	46	9	53	15	7	44	46	54	7	14	46	16	22	12○43
19	8	52	8	56	2	28	10	37	16	3	14	10n	54	2	14	45	17	22	2○134
20	9	58	9	13	3	9	11	20	46	1	22	33s	54	4	14	46	18	22	13○24
21	11	4	9	28	3	49	12	4	32	5	56	43	54	16	14	49	19	22	3○124
22	mrn.		9	47	4	31	12	49	22	10	19	42	54	36	14	54	20	22	32○4●
23	0	12	10	6	5	14	13	36	4	14	22	6	55	7	15	3	21	22	31○4●
24	1	21	10	31	6	0	14	25	24	17	52	59	55	47	15	13	22	22	○1324
25	2	31	11	3	6	50	15	17	54	20	39	27	56	35	15	27	23	22	12○43
26	3	38	11	45	7	43	16	13	44	22	27	0	57	30	15	42	24	22	24○13
27	4	42	aft.		8	40	17	12	32	23	1	17	58	28	15	57	25	22	413○2
28	5	38	1	44	9	39	18	13	17	22	11	21	59	24	16	13	26	22	43○12
29	6	24	2	59	10	38	19	14	37	19	53	30	60	13	16	26	27	22	4321○
30	7	0	4	25	11	37	20	15	13	16	13	47	60	49	16	36	28	22	♃43○●
31	7	30	5	53	aft.		21	14	14	11	27	45s	61	8	16	41	0	11	4○132

Apparent Right Ascension of the Principal Planets at Mean Noon.

D.	☿ Mercury. H.	M.	S.	♀ Venus. H.	M.	S.	♂ Mars. H.	M.	S.	♃ Jupiter. H.	M.	S.	♄ Saturn. H.	M.	S.
1	17	15	16	20	39	24	19	2	20	15	57	7	17	50	23
6	17	44	9	21	4	45	19	19	3	16	1	7	17	52	52
11	18	15	9	21	29	31	19	35	43	16	4	59	17	55	20
16	18	47	36	21	53	43	19	52	17	16	8	43	17	57	44
21	19	21	2	22	17	23	20	8	44	16	12	18	18	0	5
26	19	55	9	22	40	32	20	25	3	16	15	43	18	2	21
31	20	29	43	23	3	16	20	41	14	16	18	56	18	4	33

Apparent Declination of the above Planets.

D.	☿ °	′	″	♀ °	′	″	♂ °	′	″	♃ °	′	″	♄ °	′	″
1	21	59	39s	20	9	51s	23	36	42s	19	37	14s	22	25	34s
6	23	2	11	18	29	38	23	10	19	19	48	40	22	26	16
11	23	41	1	16	36	36	22	37	22	19	59	22	22	26	47
16	23	51	12	14	32	20	21	58	1	20	9	19	22	27	7
21	23	29	33	12	18	30	21	12	28	20	18	30	22	27	17
26	22	33	47	9	56	43	20	20	58	20	26	56	22	27	17
31	21	2	22s	7	28	35s	19	23	49s	20	34	37s	22	27	9s

Eclipses, Occultations, and other Celestial Phenomena.

January 1. Day breaks at 6*h.* 2*m. morn.*, and Twilight ends at 6*h.* 6*m. aft.*, the length of the Day being 7*h.* 52*m.*

Jan. 2. Earth at least distance from the Sun, 6*h. morn.*

Jan. 3. Venus in conjunction with the Moon, 4*h. aft.*, ♀ 6° 0′ S.

Jan. 5. Mean time of Sun's semidiameter passing the meridian, 1*m.* 10·6*s.*

Jan. 6. Occultation of 19 Piscium, magnitude 5. The disappearance takes place at 7*h.* 12*m. aft.*, 63° from the vertex; the reappearance at 8*h.* 10*m. aft.*, 182° from the vertex.

Jan. 10. Occultation of τ^2 Arietis, magnitude 5. The disappearance takes place at 7*h.* 1*m. aft.*, 49° from the vertex; the reappearance at 7*h.* 59*m. aft.*, 295° from the vertex.

Jan. 11. Occultation of κ^1 Tauri; magnitude 4½. The disappearance takes place at 10*h.* 27*m. aft.*, 90° from the vertex; the reappearance at 11*h.* 34*m. aft.*, 205° from the vertex.

Jan. 17. Occultation of *a* Cancri, magnitude 4. The disappearance takes place at 5*h.* 17*m. morn.*, 136° from the vertex; the reappearance at 5*h.* 50*m. morn.*, 196° from the vertex.

Jan. 20. Mean time of Sun's semidiameter passing the meridian, 1*m.* 9·4*s.*

Jan. 28. Saturn in conjunction with the Moon, 8*h. morn.* ♄ 0° 2′ S.

In this month the Mornings increase 26 *m.*, and the Afternoons 45 *m.*

MORNING AND EVENING STARS.

☿ Mercury is a morning star; in Sagittarius, owing to its great southern declination cannot be well observed in this month.

♀ Venus is an evening star in Capricornus till the middle of the month, when it enters Aquarius.

♂ Mars is too near the Sun to be observed in this month.

♃ Jupiter is a morning star in Scorpio, near to β in early portion of month.

♄ Saturn is a morning star, in Sagittarius.

Horizontal Equatorial Parallax of Sun and Planets.

D.	☉ ″	☿ ″	♀ ″	♂ ″	♃ ″	♄ ″
5	9 0	7 3	6 1	3 7	1 5	0 8
15	9 0	6 7	6 3	3 7	1 5	0 8
25	9 0	6 3	6 6	3 7	1 5	0 8

Semidiameter of Sun and Planets.

D.	☉ ′	″	☿ ″	♀ ″	♂ ″	♃ ″	♄ ″
5	16	18	2 8	5 8	2 0	15 0	7 0
15	16	17	2 5	6 0	2 0	15 3	7 0
25	16	16	2 4	6 2	2 0	15 7	7 1

Time of High Water at the undermentioned Places—

Month.	Week.	LONDON BRIDGE Morn.	After.	LIVERPOOL. Morn.	After.	BRISTOL. Morn.	After.	HULL. Morn.	After.	GREENOCK. Morn.	After.	LEITH. Morn.	After.	DUBLIN (Bar.) Morn.	After.
		H. M.	H. M.	H. M.	H. M.	H. M.	H. M.	H. M.	H. M.	H. M.	H. M.	H. M.	H. M.	H. M.	H. M.
1	M	1 18	1 42	10 59	11 23	6 44	7 10	5 52	6 17	11 52	...	1 58	2 21	10 41	11 4
2	Tu	2 6	2 29	11 46	...	7 34	7 57	6 41	7 4	0 17	0 42	2 44	3 6	11 26	11 49
3	W	2 51	3 14	0 10	0 35	8 20	8 43	7 28	7 52	1 7	1 31	3 28	3 51	...	0 13
4	Th	3*37	4* 0	0 58	1 20	9 5	9 26	8 15	8 37	1 54	2 17	4 14	4 37	0 37	1 0
5	F	4 22	4 45	1 43	2 5	9 48	10 10	9 0	9 23	2 39	3 2	5 1	5 24	1 24	1 48
6	S	5 8	5 30	2 28	2 51	10 32	10 54	9 47	10 10	3 25	3 47	5 49	6 14	2 13	2 37
7	S	5 53	6 17	3 13	3 37	11 15	11 37	10 33	10 59	4 10	4 33	6 40	7 6	3 2	3 27
8	M	6 42	7 8	4 1	4 28	11 59	...	11 28	...	4 57	5 22	7 33	8 3	3 54	4 23
9	Tu	7 34	8 3	4 58	5 32	0 24	0 54	0 0	0 33	5 49	6 20	8 35	9 9	4 54	5 27
10	W	8 35	9 11	6 11	6 52	1 28	2 6	1 6	1 39	6 54	7 30	9 46	10 23	6 0	6 34
11	Th	9 50	10 30	7 32	8 10	2 47	3 29	2 13	2 48	8 9	8 48	10 59	11 35	7 9	7 45
12	F	11 9	11 47	8 46	9 18	4 9	4 47	3 24	4 0	9 26	10 0	...	0 10	8 21	8 55
13	S	...	0 21	9 45	10 10	5 20	5 49	4 34	5 1	10 30	10 57	0 41	1 7	9 25	9 53
14	S	0*49	1*15	10 33	10 54	6 16	6 41	5 26	5 49	11 22	11 45	1 31	1 54	10 17	10 37
15	M	1*39	2* 1	11 14	11 33	7 4	7 24	6 10	6 31	...	0 7	2 16	2 35	10 56	11 14
16	Tu	2 20	2 39	11 52	...	7 43	8 1	6 51	7 10	0 28	0 47	2 54	3 12	11 31	11 48
17	W	2 57	3 14	0 10	0 28	8 19	8 36	7 28	7 45	1 6	1 24	3 29	3 45	...	0 6
18	Th	3 30	3 46	0 44	1 1	8 52	9 8	8 2	8 18	1 41	1 58	4 1	4 18	0 23	0 40
19	F	4 3	4 19	1 17	1 33	9 24	9 39	8 34	8 50	2 14	2 29	4 35	4 51	0 57	1 14
20	S	4 35	4 50	1 48	2 3	9 53	10 8	9 5	9 21	2 44	2 59	5 7	5 22	1 30	1 47
21	S	5 5	5 21	2 18	2 34	10 23	10 38	9 37	9 53	3 15	3 30	5 38	5 55	2 2	2 19
22	M	5 37	5 53	2 50	3 6	10 53	11 8	10 9	10 26	3 46	4 2	6 14	6 33	2 37	2 55
23	Tu	6 10	6 28	3 24	3 43	11 24	11 42	10 46	11 9	4 20	4 39	6 53	7 14	3 14	3 35
24	W	6 49	7 13	4 6	4 33	...	0 3	11 36	...	5 0	5 25	7 39	8 9	3 59	4 28
25	Th	7 38	8 7	5 3	5 39	0 29	0 59	0 6	0 38	5 53	6 25	8 41	9 16	4 59	5 33
26	F	8 40	9 19	6 21	7 5	1 35	2 16	1 12	1 48	7 3	7 43	9 56	10 36	6 9	6 46
27	S	10 2	10 46	7 47	8 26	3 1	3 45	2 25	3 3	8 25	9 4	11 14	11 51	7 24	8 1
28	S	11 25	...	9 0	9 30	4 26	5 2	3 40	4 15	9 40	10 14	...	0 24	8 35	9 8
29	M	0 1	0 34	9 56	10 21	5 34	6 2	4 46	5 12	10 43	11 10	0 52	1 19	9 39	10 6
30	Tu	1 2	1 27	10 45	11 8	6 29	6 55	5 37	6 1	11 36	...	1 43	2 7	10 29	10 51
31	W	1 51	2 15	11 31	11 54	7 19	7 42	6 25	6 49	0 1	0 26	2 29	2 52	11 12	11 34

	ft. in.	ft. in.	ft. in.	ft. in.	ft. in.	ft. in.	ft. ft.
Springs rise	20 9	26 3	33 1	20 10	9 9	16 4	12 to 14
Neaps ,,	17 4	20 0	22 7	16 4	8 2	12 7	9 to 11

RISING, SOUTHING, and SETTING of the PRINCIPAL PLANETS at intervals of Seven Days.

	MERCURY ☿ Rises	Souths	Sets	VENUS ♀ Rises	Souths	Sets	MARS ♂ Rises	Souths	Sets	JUPITER ♃ Rises	Sths.	Sets	SATURN ♄ Rises	Sths.	Sets
D.	h. m.	h. m.	h. m.	h. m.	h. m.	h. m.	h. m.	h. m.	h. m.	h. m.	h. m.	h. m.	h. m.	h. m.	h. m.
1	6 30M	10 33M	2 36A	9 42M	1 57A	6 12A	8 28M	0 20A	4 12A	4 57M	9 15M	1 33A	7 8M	11 8M	3 8A
8	6 52M	10 46M	2 40A	9 36M	2 5A	6 34A	8 19M	0 15A	4 11A	4 36M	8 53M	1 10A	6 44M	1044M	2 44A
15	7 13M	11 3M	2 53A	9 26M	2 11A	6 56A	8 9M	0 11A	4 13A	4 16M	8 31M	0 46A	6 20M	1020M	2 2JA
22	7 29M	11 22M	3 15A	9 14M	2 17A	7 20A	7 58M	0 7A	4 16A	3 54M	8 8M	0 22A	5 55M	9 55M	1 55A
29	7 38M	11 43M	3 48A	9 0M	2 21A	7 42A	7 45M	0 2A	4 19A	3 32M	7 45M	11 58A	5 31M	9 31M	1 31A

APPARENT RIGHT ASCENSION AND DECLINATION OF THE POLE STAR.					ANGULAR DISTANCE OF THE MOON FROM POLLUX.			
	R. A.		DECL. N.		Position of Star.	6 P.M.	9 P.M.	Midnight.
D.	H. M. S.		° ′ ″	D.		° ′ ″	° ′ ″	° ′ ″
1	1 23 0·4		88 46 53	8	East	86 44 47	85 3 32	83 22 32
10	1 22 51·5		88 46 53	9	East	73 22 7	71 42 58	70 4 6
19	1 22 42·4		88 46 54	10	East	60 16 26	58 39 26	57 2 43
28	1 22 34·0		88 46 53	11	East	47 28 29	45 53 51	44 19 33

In the early part of the month the constellations Camelopardus, Lynx, Gemini, Monoceros, and Canis Major are on the meridian about midnight. In Gemini there is a fine compressed cluster of small stars in the right leg of Pollux, in R.A. 6h. 48m., and Decl. 18° 8′ N., nearly midway between γ and ζ Geminorum. This cluster is triangular in shape, and, in small telescopes, hardly distinguishable from a nebula. It can be best observed on the nights immediately after the 1st and those before and after the 30th. There is a very fine cluster in Canis Major, in R.A. 6h. 43m., and Decl. 20° 39′ S., about 4° South of Sirius. With a very small astronomical telescope the individual stars can be easily distinguished; and with a low-power eye-piece, on the larger instruments, the field appears full of stars of various magnitudes.

DAY OF			Fasts and Festivals. Remarkable Days—Events. Sun enters Pisces 19d. 2h. m.	THE SUN		DAYS	
M.	Light and Dark.	W.		Rises.	Sets.	of the Year.	to end of Year.
				H. M.	H. M.		
1		Th	Geo. Cruikshank died, 1878; born 27 Sept. 1792.	7 41	4 47	32	333
2		F	**Purification.** Candlemas. Scottish Quarter D.	7 39	4 49	33	332
3		S	*St. Blaize.* Marquess of Salisbury, K.G., b. 1830.	7 37	4 51	34	331
4		☉	**Fifth Sun. aft. Epiph.** Coomassie taken, 1874.	7 36	4 52	35	330
5		M	*St. Agatha.* Thomas Carlyle died, 1881.	7 34	4 54	36	329
6		Tu	Sir Henry Irving born, 1838.	7 32	4 56	37	328
7		W	Ann Radcliffe died 1823; born 9 July, 1764.	7 31	4 57	38	327
8		Th	Earl of Mayo assassinated, 1872; b. 21 Feb. 1822	7 29	4 59	39	326
9		F	General Sir Evelyn Wood, V⃝C, born, 1838.	7 27	5 1	40	325
10		S	Queen Victoria married, 1840. Sobraon, 1846.	7 25	5 3	41	324
11		☉	**Septuagesima Sunday.**	7 24	5 4	42	323
12		M	Field-Marshal Sir Lintorn Simmons, G.C.B., b. 1821	7 21	5 7	43	322
13		Tu	Warren Hastings trial, 1788; acquit. 23 Apr. 1795	7 19	5 9	44	321
14		W	*St. Valentine.* Battle of St. Vincent, 1797.	7 18	5 10	45	320
15		Th	*U.S.S. "Maine"* blown up in Havana Harb., 1898	7 16	5 12	46	319
16		F	Earl of Clarendon born 1608; died 9 Dec., 1674.	7 14	5 14	47	318
17		S	Duchess of Albany born, 1861.	7 12	5 16	48	317
18		☉	**Sexagesima Sunday.** Benin City captured, 1897	7 10	5 18	49	316
19		M	Duke of Bedford born, 1858. [Salmon b. 1835.	7 9	5 19	50	315
20		Tu	H.R.H. Duchess of Fife b. 1867; Adm. Sir N.	7 7	5 21	51	314
21		W	Battle of Goojerat, 1849.	7 4	5 24	52	313
22		Th	George Washington b. 1732; d. 14 Dec., 1799.	7 2	5 26	53	312
23		F	Samuel Pepys born, 1632; died 26 May, 1703.	7 0	5 28	54	311
24		S	**St. Matthias, Apostle and Martyr.**	6 58	5 29	55	310
25		☉	**Quinquagesima.** Shrove Sunday.	6 56	5 30	56	309
26		M	Lord Cromer born, 1841. Majuba Hill, 1881.	6 54	5 32	57	308
27		Tu	Shrove Tues. Transvaal convention signed, 1884.	6 52	5 34	58	307
28		W	**Ash Wednesday.** Tichborne Trial ended, 1874.	6 50	5 36	59	306

PHASES OF THE MOON.

☽ First Quarter 6d. 4h. 23m. Afternoon.
○ Full Moon 14 1 50 Afternoon.
☾ Last Quarter 22 4 44 Afternoon.

Perigee 1d. 0h. M. 222,700 | Apogee 16d. 1h. M. 252,600

IRON-MASTERS' QUARTERLY MEETINGS, 1900.

	Jan.	April.	July.	Oct.
Walsall ....Tu.	9	10	10	9
Wolverhampton ...W.	10	11	11	10
Birmingham ......Th.	11	12	12	11
Stourbridge ....F.	12	13	13	12
Dudley ....S.	13	14	14	13

MONTHLY NOTES.

Feb. 1. Partridge and pheasant shooting ends. Copies of Register of Voters to be sent to Secretary of State within three weeks.

11. Scottish general salmon-fishing begins.

19. Notice of Election of Borough Auditors to be published. Nominations must be delivered by the 22nd.

28. Hare-hunting ends.

RAINFALL IN FEBRUARY, 1899.

In this month rain fell on 12 days. The total fall for the month was 1·93 inches; *above* the average of fifty years, 1841-90, by 0·45 inch.

THE SUN.

Day.	After Clock.	Hrly Var of Equa. of Time.	Right Ascension at Noon.	Hourly Var. of R. A.	Apparent Declination (8th.) at Noon.	Hrly Var (⊙)'s declination.	Sidereal Time at Noon.	Mean Time at Sidereal Noon.
	M. S.	S.	H. M. S.	S.	° ' "	"	H. M. S.	H. M. S.
1	13 47	0·34	20 58 44	10·20	17 8 32	42·6	20 44 57	3 14 31
2	13 55	0·31	21 2 48	10·16	16 51 20	43·4	20 48 53	3 10 35
3	14 2	0·27	21 6 51	10·13	16 33 51	44·1	20 52 50	3 6 39
4	14 8	0·24	21 10 54	10·09	16 16 5	44·8	20 56 46	3 2 44
5	14 13	0·20	21 14 56	10·06	15 58 2	45·5	21 0 43	2 58 48
6	14 17	0·17	21 18 57	10·02	15 39 42	46·2	21 4 40	2 54 52
7	14 21	0·13	21 22 57	9·99	15 21 7	46·8	21 8 36	2 50 56
8	14 24	0·10	21 26 56	9·96	15 2 16	47·4	21 12 33	2 47 0
9	14 26	0·07	21 30 55	9·92	14 43 10	48·1	21 16 29	2 43 4
10	14 27	0·03	21 34 53	9·89	14 23 50	48·7	21 20 26	2 39 8
11	14 27	0·00	21 38 50	9·86	14 4 15	49·3	21 24 22	2 35 12
12	14 27	0·03	21 42 46	9·82	13 44 26	49·8	21 28 19	2 31 16
13	14 26	0·07	21 46 41	9·79	13 24 24	50·4	21 32 15	2 27 20
14	14 24	0·10	21 50 36	9·76	13 4 8	50·9	21 36 12	2 23 24
15	14 21	0·13	21 54 30	9·73	12 43 40	51·4	21 40 9	2 19 29
16	14 18	0·16	21 58 23	9·70	12 23 0	51·9	21 44 5	2 15 33
17	14 14	0·19	22 2 15	9·67	12 2 8	52·4	21 48 2	2 11 37
18	14 9	0·21	22 6 7	9·64	11 41 4	52·9	21 51 58	2 7 41
19	14 3	0·24	22 9 58	9·61	11 19 49	53·4	21 55 55	2 3 45
20	13 57	0·27	22 13 48	9·59	10 58 23	53·8	21 59 51	1 59 49
21	13 50	0·30	22 17 38	9·56	10 36 47	54·2	22 3 48	1 55 53
22	13 43	0·32	22 21 27	9·53	10 15 1	54·6	22 7 44	1 51 57
23	13 35	0·35	22 25 16	9·51	9 53 6	55·0	22 11 41	1 48 1
24	13 26	0·37	22 29 4	9·48	9 31 1	55·4	22 15 38	1 44 5
25	13 17	0·40	22 32 51	9·46	9 8 48	55·7	22 19 34	1 40 9
26	13 7	0·42	22 36 38	9·44	8 46 26	56·1	22 23 31	1 36 14
27	12 57	0·44	22 40 24	9·41	8 23 57	56·4	22 27 27	1 32 18
28	12 46	0·46	22 44 10	9·39	8 1 20	56·7	22 31 24	1 28 22

MEMORANDA.

1. Lamps to be lighted (5.47)
2. (5.49)
3. (5.51)
4. S. (5.52)
5. (5.54)
6. (5.56)
7. (5.57)
8. (5.59)
9. (6.1)
10. (6.3)
11. S. (6.4)
12. (6.7)
13. (6.9)
14. (6.10)
15. (6.12)
16. (6.14)
17. (6.16)
18. S. (6.18)
19. (6.19)
20. (6.21)
21. (6.24)
22. (6.26)
23. (6.28)
24. (6.29)
25. S. (6.30)
26. (6.32)
27. (6.34)
28. (6.36)

METEOROLOGICAL OBSERVATIONS, FEBRUARY, 1899.

Day.	TEMPERATURE. Maximum.	Minimum.	Avge. 50 Yrs.	BAROM. Mean.	RAIN-FALL.	SUN-SHINE.	WIND. Directn.	Pressure (lbs. to foot.)
	°	°	°	inches.	inches.	hours.		lbs.
1	39·1	32·8	38	29·281	...	...	W	0·3
2	39·8	29·4	38	29·375	...	2·3	N	2·7
3	37·3	27·5	38	29·708	...	0·2	N	0·6
4	40·4	21·9	38	29·750	...	3·7	S	4·5
5	37·8	33·8	39	29·421	0·41	...	E	1·0
6	40·2	34·6	39	29·562	0·20	...	E	4·1
7	54·8	37·2	39	29·328	0·01	2·8	SSW	5·0
8	53·2	47·2	39	29·258	0·43	...	SSW	15·3
9	57·6	47·9	39	29·323	0·13	0·6	SSW	10·0
10	63·9	50·3	39	29·380	...	5·8	SSW	12·0
11	54·6	48·0	39	29·324	0·01	1·3	SSW	16·0
12	48·9	42·8	39	29·155	0·21	3·0	SW	22·5
13	54·4	45·7	39	29·091	0·12	1·2	SSW	33·4
14	52·0	43·2	39	29·452	0·06	0·8	SSW	13·5
15	51·3	39·7	39	29·660	0·19	0·9	S	1·7
16	50·3	37·8	39	29·766	0·14	5·7	WSW	2·2
17	55·0	36·0	39	29·872	...	8·7	SE	0·2
18	49·8	34·4	39	29·893	...	1·7	E	0·0
19	47·2	38·7	39	30·008	0·02	...	SSW	0·6
20	46·4	42·8	39	30·038	...	...	E	6·2
21	45·5	36·4	39	30·154	...	8·3	E	7·6
22	49·0	32·9	39	30·179	...	8·9	E	2·6
23	52·1	29·2	39	30·103	...	8·6	ESE	1·2
24	52·8	28·0	39	30·127	...	5·6	ESE	0·6
25	44·1	29·7	40	30·180	...	7·5	ENE	2·3
26	44·7	26·2	40	30·210	...	7·6	E	1·6
27	43·3	22·0	40	30·375	...	7·0	ENE	0·2
28	46·7	22·8	40	30·499	...	7·1	SW	0·5

* The Meteorological Observations throughout the Almanack are those recorded at the Royal Observatory, Greenwich. They include the highest and lowest readings of the *Thermometer* with the average for 50 years; the mean of *Barometer* at a height of 159 feet above the mean level of the sea; the daily *Rainfall*, the daily *Sunshine* and the daily general direction and maximum force of the *Wind*.

THE MOON.

Day of M.	Rises Morning.	Sets Afternoon.	Souths Afternoon.	Right Ascension at Noon.	Declination at Noon.	Horizontal Parallax at Noon.	Semidiameter at Noon.	Age at Noon.	Configurations of Jupiter's Satellites at 5h. A.M.
	H. M.	H. M.	H. M.	H. M. S.	° ′ ″	′ ″	′ ″	D. H.	
1	7 56	7 20	1 30	22 11 27	5 57 34s	61 8	16 41	1 11	412○3
2	8 17	8 45	2 23	23 7 9	0 8 12s	60 50	16 36	2 11	42○13
3	8 39	10 10	3 16	0 1 58	5 36 3n	60 17	16 27	3 11	14○32
4	9 3	11 31	4 9	0 56 31	10 53 41	59 33	16 15	4 11	3○142
5	9 28	mrn.	5 1	1 51 21	15 27 0	58 44	16 2	5 11	321○4
6	9 59	0 50	5 55	2 46 42	19 2 23	57 54	15 48	6 11	32○14
7	10 35	2 4	6 49	3 42 30	21 30 28	57 7	15 35	7 11	○324●
8	11 19	3 10	7 42	4 38 16	22 46 22	56 24	15 24	8 11	1○234
9	aft.	4 6	8 35	5 33 19	22 49 47	55 46	15 13	9 11	2○134
10	1 12	4 54	9 26	6 26 57	21 44 51	55 15	15 5	10 11	1○234
11	2 17	5 30	10 14	7 18 38	19 39 8	54 49	14 58	11 11	3○142
12	3 22	6 0	11 0	8 8 8	16 42 27	54 29	14 52	12 11	3214○
13	4 29	6 25	11 44	8 55 31	13 5 36	54 14	14 48	13 11	423○1
14	5 36	6 45	mrn.	9 41 8	8 59 28	54 3	14 45	14 11	4○32●
15	6 42	7 2	0 26	10 25 29	4 34 24	53 58	14 44	15 11	♃4○23
16	7 48	7 20	1 7	11 9 11	0 0 11n	53 58	14 44	16 11	42○13
17	8 54	7 36	1 48	11 52 54	4 33 53s	54 3	14 45	17 11	41○3●
18	10 0	7 53	2 29	12 37 19	8 58 38	54 15	14 49	18 11	43○12
19	11 7	8 14	3 12	13 23 9	13 4 38	54 35	14 54	19 11	3412○
20	mrn.	8 37	3 56	14 11 1	16 41 47	55 3	15 2	20 11	324○1
21	0 15	9 5	4 43	15 1 27	19 38 52	55 39	15 11	21 11	1○24●
22	1 23	9 41	5 34	15 54 43	21 43 45	56 24	15 24	22 11	♃○234
23	2 26	10 26	6 27	16 50 41	22 44 10	57 15	15 38	23 11	2○134
24	3 23	11 24	7 23	17 48 49	22 29 31	58 12	15 53	24 11	1○34●
25	4 11	aft.	8 20	18 48 10	20 53 20	59 9	16 9	25 11	3○124
26	4 52	1 52	9 18	19 47 45	17 55 49	60 3	16 24	26 11	312○4
27	5 26	3 15	10 15	20 46 42	13 45 11	60 48	16 36	27 11	32○14
28	5 52	4 44	11 11	21 44 39	8 37 19s	61 18	16 44	28 11	1○42●

APPARENT RIGHT ASCENSION OF THE PRINCIPAL PLANETS AT MEAN NOON.

D.	☿ MERCURY. H. M. S.	♀ VENUS. H. M. S.	♂ MARS. H. M. S.	♃ JUPITER. H. M. S.	♄ SATURN. H. M. S.
5	21 4 33	23 25 38	20 57 15	16 21 58	18 6 39
10	21 39 30	23 47 43	21 13 5	16 24 46	18 8 39
15	22 14 24	0 9 34	21 28 45	16 27 20	18 10 32
20	22 48 51	0 31 18	21 44 14	16 29 39	18 12 19
25	23 21 52	0 52 58	21 59 32	16 31 42	18 13 57

APPARENT DECLINATION OF THE ABOVE PLANETS.

D.	☿ ° ′ ″	♀ ° ′ ″	♂ ° ′ ″	♃ ° ′ ″	♄ ° ′ ″
5	18 54 13s	4 55 46s	18 21 23s	20 41 33s	22 26 53s
10	16 8 55	2 19 52s	17 14 2	20 47 44	22 26 31
15	12 47 19	0 17 33n	16 2 8	20 53 11	22 26 3
20	8 53 9	2 55 1	14 46 6	20 57 56	22 25 30
25	4 36 36s	5 31 2n	13 26 19s	21 1 58s	22 24 55s

HORIZONTAL EQUATORIAL PARALLAX OF SUN AND PLANETS.

D.	☉ ″	☿ ″	♀ ″	♂ ″	♃ ″	♄ ″
5	9 0	6 3	6 9	3 7	1 6	0 8
15	9 0	6 6	7 2	3 7	1 6	0 8
25	8 9	7 4	7 6	3 8	1 7	0 8

SEMIDIAMETER OF SUN AND PLANETS.

D.	☉ ′ ″	☿ ″	♀ ″	♂ ″	♃ ″	♄ ″
5	16 15	2 4	6 5	2 0	16 1	7 2
15	16 13	2 5	6 8	2 0	16 6	7 2
25	16 11	2 8	7 2	2 0	17 1	7 3

Mean Longitude of Moon's Ascending Node, February 1, 257° 29′ ♐.

ECLIPSES, OCCULTATIONS, AND OTHER CELESTIAL PHENOMENA.

February 1. Day breaks at 5*h.* 42*m.* *morn.*, and Twilight ends at 6*h.* 46*m.* *aft.*, the length of the Day being 9*h.* 6*m.*

Feb. 2. Occultation of κ Piscium, magnitude 5. The disappearance takes place at 6*h.* 56*m.* *aft.*, 65° from the vertex; the reappearance at 7*h.* 43*m.* *aft.*, 172° from the vertex.

Feb. 5. Mean time of Sun's semidiameter passing the meridian, 1*m.* 7·6*s.*

Feb. 6. Occultation of δ Arietis, magnitude 4½. The disappearance takes place at 8*h.* 36*m.* *aft.*, 93° from the vertex; the reappearance at 9*h.* 24*m.* *aft.*, 175° from the vertex.

Feb. 9. Occultation of *n* Tauri, magnitude 5. The disappearance takes place at 3*h.* 50*m.* *morn.*, 99° from the vertex. At the reappearance the Star will be below the horizon at Greenwich.

Feb. 9. Mercury in superior conjunction with the Sun, 9*h.* *aft.*

Feb. 16. A near approach of the Moon, ε to Leonis magnitude 5 Least distance between Moon and star occurs at 7*h.* 51*m.* *aft.*, 242° from the vertex.

Feb. 20. Mean time of Sun's semidiameter passing the meridian, 1*m.* 6·0*s.*

Feb. 23. Jupiter in conjunction with the Moon, 4*h.* *morn.* ♃ 1° 31′ N.

In this month the Mornings increase 51*m.*, and the Afternoons 49*m.*

MORNING AND EVENING STARS.

☿ MERCURY too near the Sun for observation in the first half of the month: an evening star towards the end; in Aquarius.

♀ VENUS is an evening star throughout the month; in Aquarius till about the 5th, when it enters Pisces.

♂ MARS is a morning star, but still too near the Sun for observation.

♃ JUPITER is a morning star, in Scorpio.

♄ SATURN is a morning star; in Sagittarius.

Time of High Water at the undermentioned Places—

Month	Week	London Bridge Morn.	After.	Liverpool Morn.	After.	Bristol Morn.	After.	Hull Morn.	After.	Greenock Morn.	After.	Leith Morn.	After.	Dublin (Bar.) Morn.	After.
1	Th	2*37	2*59	...	0 19	8 5	8 27	7 12	7 36	0 50	1 14	3 14	3 36	11 57	...
2	F	3*22	3*44	0 42	1 4	8 49	9 10	7 59	8 21	1 37	2 0	3 58	4 20	0 20	0 43
3	S	4* 5	4*28	1 26	1 47	9 32	9 53	8 42	9 4	2 22	2 43	4 42	5 5	1 5	1 28
4	Su	4*50	5*11	2 8	2 29	10 13	10 33	9 26	9 48	3 5	3 26	5 28	5 49	1 51	2 13
5	M	5 31	5 53	2 50	3 11	10 54	11 14	10 9	10 30	3 46	4 6	6 12	6 36	2 36	2 58
6	Tu	6 15	6 37	3 32	3 55	11 33	11 53	10 53	11 20	4 28	4 51	7 0	7 26	3 21	3 46
7	W	7 1	7 28	4 21	4 54	...	0 18	11 52	...	5 16	5 45	7 55	8 31	4 15	4 49
8	Th	7 59	8 33	5 32	6 14	0 50	1 28	0 28	1 5	6 19	6 58	9 9	9 50	5 26	6 3
9	F	9 13	9 59	7 1	7 46	2 11	2 57	1 43	2 22	7 39	8 23	10 32	11 13	6 42	7 23
10	S	10 45	11 27	8 28	9 3	3 44	3 41	3 2	3 41	9 6	9 43	11 52	...	8 3	8 39
11	Su	...	0 4	9 33	9 58	5 4	5 35	4 18	4 49	10 16	10 44	0 27	0 55	9 11	9 40
12	M	0 36	1 3	10 21	10 41	6 3	6 27	5 14	5 37	11 9	11 33	1 19	1 42	10 5	10 26
13	Tu	1 26	1 47	10 59	11 16	6 49	7 9	5 57	6 16	11 51	...	2 3	2 22	10 43	10 58
14	W	2 7	2 23	11 32	11 48	7 26	7 43	6 33	6 50	0 9	0 26	2 38	2 53	11 13	11 28
15	Th	2 38	2 53	...	0 4	7 59	8 14	7 6	7 21	0 43	0 59	3 9	3 24	11 43	11 58
16	F	3 7	3 23	0 20	0 35	8 28	8 43	7 37	7 52	1 15	1 31	3 38	3 52	...	0 14
17	S	3 28	3 52	0 50	1 14	8 57	9 11	8 7	8 21	1 46	2 1	4 6	4 21	0 20	0 44
18	Su	4 7	4 21	1 19	1 34	9 26	9 40	8 36	8 51	2 16	2 30	4 36	4 51	0 59	1 14
19	M	4 36	4 51	1 49	2 3	9 54	10 8	9 6	9 21	2 45	3 0	5 7	5 23	1 30	1 46
20	Tu	5 6	5 20	2 18	2 34	10 23	10 38	9 37	9 53	3 15	3 30	5 39	5 56	2 2	2 19
21	W	5 35	5 53	2 51	3 9	10 54	11 11	10 10	10 29	3 47	4 5	6 15	6 36	2 37	2 57
22	Th	6 13	6 35	3 30	3 53	11 29	11 50	10 53	11 20	4 25	4 48	6 59	7 24	3 20	3 45
23	F	6 59	7 27	4 21	4 55	...	0 17	11 53	...	5 15	5 46	7 56	8 32	4 15	4 51
24	S	7 59	8 37	5 36	6 23	0 51	1 32	0 29	1 8	6 23	7 6	9 13	9 58	5 29	6 11
25	Su	9 23	10 11	7 14	7 57	2 19	3 10	1 50	2 32	7 51	8 35	10 43	11 24	6 53	7 34
26	M	10 55	11 36	8 36	9 10	3 55	4 37	3 12	3 50	9 15	9 51	...	0 1	8 11	8 46
27	Tu	...	0 12	9 38	10 3	5 11	5 42	4 25	4 54	10 23	10 50	0 33	0 59	9 18	9 46
28	W	0 42	1 8	10 25	10 47	6 9	6 34	5 19	5 42	11 15	11 39	1 24	1 48	10 10	10 31

* The days thus indicated throughout the Almanack are those on which High Tides may be expected. Strong northerly winds in the North Sea and a low barometer with heavy rains in the counties drained by the Thames, will probably cause a higher rise of the river, and the low-lying riverside districts to be flooded. See Tides, p. 74.

RISING, SOUTHING, and SETTING of the PRINCIPAL PLANETS at intervals of Seven Days

D.	Mercury ☿ Rises	Souths	Sets	Venus ♀ Rises	Souths	Sets	Mars ♂ Rises	Souths	Sets	Jupiter ♃ Rises	Souths	Sets	Saturn ♄ Rises	Souths	Sets
5	7 41M	0 4A	6 47A	8 46M	2 25A	8 4A	7 31M	11 57M	4 23A	3 10M	7 22M	11 34M	5 5M	9 6M	1 7A
12	7 39M	0 25A	5 11A	8 30M	2 28A	8 26A	7 16M	11 51M	4 26A	2 48M	6 58M	11 8M	4 41M	8 42M	0 43A
19	7 31M	0 45A	6 1A	8 15M	2 31A	8 47A	7 0M	11 45M	4 30A	2 24M	6 34M	10 44M	4 16M	8 17M	0 18A
26	7 19M	1 5A	6 51A	8 0M	2 34A	9 8A	6 43M	11 39M	4 35A	2 0M	6 9M	10 18M	3 50M	7 51M	11 52M

APPARENT RIGHT ASCENSION AND DECLINATION OF THE POLE STAR.

D.	R.A. H. M. S.	Decl. N.
1	1 22 29·5	88 46 53
10	1 22 21·9	88 46 52
19	1 22 13·9	88 46 51
28	1 22 7·5	88 46 49

ANGULAR DISTANCE OF THE MOON FROM ALDEBARAN.

D.	Position of Star	6 P.M.	9 P.M.	Midnight
11	West	43 5 20	44 35 13	46 5 2
12	West	55 2 34	56 31 55	58 1 12
13	West	66 55 35	68 24 26	69 53 14
14	West	78 44 57	80 13 25	81 41 50

In the early part of this month the constellations Ursa Major, Lynx, Cancer, and a part of Hydra are on the meridian about midnight. In Cancer there is a very beautiful cluster of stars situated in the Crab's southern claw, in R.A. 8h. 45m. 42s., and Decl. 12° 11' N., consisting of some 200 stars from the 8th to 13th magnitudes. The fine group of stars in Cancer, called "Præsepe," can be best observed in this month. It does not consist of a very great number of stars, but the components are, as compared with those of other clusters, of considerable magnitude. It is situated in R.A. 8h. 34m., and Decl. 20° 20' N., about 1° to the west of a line joining the stars δ and γ Cancri.

The triple star ζ in Cancer may be examined in this month: it will be found in R.A. 8h. 6m. 29s., and Decl. 17° 57' N. Two of the stars are only 1" apart, and the third about 5" from them.

MARCH XXXI DAYS.

Day of M.	Light and Dark	W.	Fasts and Festivals. Remarkable Days—Events. SUN ENTERS ARIES 21*d.* 2*h.* M. SPRING COMMENCES.	The Sun Rises. H. M.	The Sun Sets. H. M.	Days of the Year.	Days to end of Year.
1		Th	ST. DAVID'S DAY. F.-M. Sir D. Stewart b. '24.	6 48	5 38	60	305
2		F	*St. Chad.* Pope Leo XIII. born, 1810.	6 45	5 39	61	304
3		S	Rev. J. G. Wood, naturalist, died, 1889.	6 43	5 41	62	303
4		S	**Quadragesima. First Sunday in Lent.**	6 42	5 42	63	302
5		M	Covent Garden Theatre burnt, 1856.	6 40	5 44	64	301
6		Tu	Bishop Atterbury b. 1662; d. 15 Feb. 1732.	6 37	5 47	65	300
7		W	*St. Perpetua.* Adm. Lord Collingwood d. 1810.	6 35	5 48	66	299
8		Th	Battle of Aboukir, 1801. [Ember Day.	6 32	5 50	67	298
9		F	William I., German Emperor, d., 1888. Ember D.	6 30	5 52	68	297
10		S	Prince of Wales married, 1863. Ember Day.	6 28	5 54	69	296
11		S	**Second Sunday in Lent.**	6 25	5 55	70	295
12		M	*St. Gregory.* Torquato Tasso born, 1544.	6 23	5 57	71	294
13		Tu	Discovery of Uranus by Herschel, 1781.	6 21	5 59	72	293
14		W	Humbert, King of Italy, born, 1844.	6 18	6 0	73	292
15		Th	Lord Melbourne (Queen's first Premier) b. 1779.	6 16	6 2	74	291
16		F	Duchess of Kent, the Queen's mother, d. 1861.	6 14	6 4	75	290
17		S	ST. PATRICK'S DAY. Sir F. H. Jeune born, 1843.	6 12	6 6	76	289
18		S	**Third Sunday in Lent.** *Edward, K. W. S.*	6 9	6 7	77	288
19		M	David Livingstone born, 1813; died 1 May, 1873.	6 7	6 9	78	287
20		Tu	Louis Kossuth died, 1894; born 16 Sept. 1802.	6 5	6 11	79	286
21		W	*St. Benedict.* Princess Louise married, 1871.	6 2	6 12	80	285
22		Th	Goethe, German poet, d. 1832; b. 28 Aug., 1749.	6 0	6 14	81	284
23		F	Sir Thomas Smith, Bart., F.R.C.S., born 1833.	5 58	6 16	82	283
24		S	Qn. Elizabeth d. 1603. Loss of H.M.S. *Eurydice*, '78	5 56	6 17	83	282
25		S	**Fourth S. in Lent. Annunciation.** Lady D. Qr. D.	5 54	6 18	84	281
26		M	H.R.H. Duke of Cambridge born, 1819.	5 52	6 20	85	280
27		Tu	Cambridge Lent Term ends. Lincolnshire Hcp.	5 49	6 22	86	279
28		W	H.R.H. Duke of Albany d. 1884; b. 7 April, '53.	5 47	6 24	87	278
29		Th	Rev. John Keble d. 1866; b. 25 April, 1792.	5 45	6 25	88	277
30		F	Liverpool Grand National Steeplechase.	5 43	6 27	89	276
31		S	Andrew Lang b. 1844. Charlotte Brontë d. 1855.	5 40	6 29	90	275

PHASES OF THE MOON.

● New Moon	1*d.*	11*h.*	25*m.*	Morning.
☽ First Quarter	8	5	34	Morning.
○ Full Moon	16	8	12	Morning.
☾ Last Quarter	24	5	36	Morning.
● New Moon	30	8	30	Afternoon.

Perigee 1*d.* 0*h.* A. 221,700 Apogee 15*d.* 1*h.* M. 252,600
Perigee, 29*d.* 11*h.* A. 222,600.

RAINFALL IN MARCH, 1899.

In this month rain fell on 10 days. The total fall for the month was 0·53 inch; *below* the average of fifty years, 1841-90, by 0·88 inch.

MONTHLY NOTES.

March 1. Auditors of Boroughs to be elected.—Annual assembly of Parish Meetings in Rural parishes to take place during this month.

15. Close time for all wild birds till 1st August.

25. Lady Day. Quarter Day. Accounts of Overseers to be made up to this date; Parish Councils to 31st.

THE SUN.

Day.	After Clock.	Hrly Var. of Equa. of Time.	Right Ascension at Noon.	Hourly Var. of R. A.	Apparent Declination (8th.) at Noon.	Hrly Var. ⊙'s Declination.	Sidereal Time at Noon.	Mean Time at Sidereal Noon.
	M. S.	S.	H. M. S.	S.	° ′ ″	″	H. M. S.	H. M. S.
1	12 35	0·49	22 47 55	9·37	7 38 36	56·9	22 35 20	1 24 26
2	12 23	0·51	22 51 40	9·35	7 15 46	57·2	22 39 17	1 20 30
3	12 10	0·53	22 55 24	9·33	6 52 50	57·5	22 43 13	1 16 34
4	11 58	0·55	22 59 8	9·31	6 29 47	57·7	22 47 10	1 12 38
5	11 44	0·57	23 2 51	9·29	6 6 40	57·9	22 51 6	1 8 42
6	11 30	0·58	23 6 33	9·27	5 43 28	58·1	22 55 3	1 4 46
7	11 16	0·60	23 10 16	9·25	5 20 11	58·3	22 59 0	1 0 50
8	11 2	0·62	23 13 58	9·24	4 56 50	58·5	23 2 56	0 56 54
9	10 46	0·64	23 17 39	9·22	4 33 25	58·6	23 6 53	0 52 59
10	10 31	0·65	23 21 20	9·20	4 9 57	58·7	23 10 49	0 49 3
11	10 15	0·67	23 25 1	9·19	3 46 26	58·8	23 14 46	0 45 7
12	9 59	0·68	23 28 42	9·18	3 22 52	58·9	23 18 42	0 41 11
13	9 43	0·69	23 32 22	9·16	2 59 16	59·0	23 22 39	0 37 15
14	9 26	0·70	23 36 1	9·15	2 35 38	59·1	23 26 35	0 33 19
15	9 9	0·71	23 39 41	9·14	2 11 58	59·2	23 30 32	0 29 23
16	8 52	0·72	23 43 20	9·13	1 48 17	59·2	23 34 29	0 25 27
17	8 34	0·73	23 46 59	9·12	1 24 36	59·2	23 38 25	0 21 31
18	8 17	0·74	23 50 38	9·12	1 0 53	59·3	23 42 22	0 17 35
19	7 59	0·75	23 54 17	9·11	0 37 11	59·3	23 46 18	0 13 40
20	7 41	0·75	23 57 56	9·10	0 13 29	59·2	23 50 15	0 9 44
21	7 23	0·76	0 1 34	9·10	North.	59·2	23 54 11	0 5 48
22	7 5	0·76	0 5 13	9·10	0 33 54	59·1	23 58 8	0 1 52 / 23 57 56
23	6 46	0·76	0 8 51	9·09	0 57 34	59·1	0 2 4	23 54 0
24	6 28	0·76	0 12 29	9·09	1 21 12	59·0	0 6 1	23 50 4
25	6 10	0·76	0 16 7	9·09	1 44 48	58·9	0 9 58	23 46 8
26	5 51	0·77	0 19 46	9·09	2 8 22	58·9	0 13 54	23 42 12
27	5 33	0·76	0 23 24	9·09	2 31 54	58·7	0 17 51	23 38 16
28	5 15	0·76	0 27 2	9·09	2 55 22	58·6	0 21 47	23 34 20
29	4 56	0·76	0 30 40	9·10	3 18 47	58·4	0 25 44	23 30 25
30	4 38	0·76	0 34 19	9·10	3 42 8	58·3	0 29 40	23 26 29
31	4 20	0·76	0 37 57	9·10	4 5 24	58·1	0 33 37	23 22 33

MEMORANDA.

1.	Lamps to be lighted (6.38)
2.	(6.39)
3.	(6.41)
4. S.	(6.42)
5.	(6.44)
6.	(6.47)
7.	(6.48)
8.	(6.50)
9.	(6.52)
10.	(6.54)
11. S.	(6.55)
12.	(6.57)
13.	(6.59)
14.	(7.0)
15.	(7.2)
16.	(7.4)
17.	(7.5)
18. S.	(7.7)
19.	(7.9)
20.	(7.11)
21.	(7.12)
22.	(7.14)
23.	(7.16)
24.	(7.17)
25. S.	(7.18)
26.	(7.20)
27.	(7.22)
28.	(7.24)
29.	(7.25)
30.	(7.27)
31.	(7.29)

METEOROLOGICAL OBSERVATIONS, MARCH, 1899.

Day.	TEMPERATURE			BAROM. Mean.	RAIN FALL.	SUN SHINE.	WIND (Pressure lbs. to foot.)	
	Maximum.	Minimum.	Avge. 50 Yrs.				Directn.	Pressure.
	°	°	°	inches.	inches.	hours.		
1	54·0	33·2	40	30·454	...	0·5	WSW	lbs. 0·8
2	47·9	32·9	40	30·264	...	5·3	W	1·0
3	50·5	29·0	40	29·919	...	5·3	WSW	0·3
4	46·7	32·3	40	29·725	0·04	1·3	N	2·1
5	44·5	29·2	40	30·066	...	8·5	E	1·7
6	45·6	25·9	40	29·808	...	8·4	SSE	1·9
7	49·0	23·9	40	29·534	...	8·9	SW	0·6
8	51·0	35·2	40	29·305	0·01	4·9	SW	4·7
9	50·1	35·4	41	29·058	0·06	6·2	SW	6·8
10	54·2	32·3	41	29·795	...	6·8	WSW	1·6
11	51·4	35·7	41	30·147	...	...	SW	0·7
12	57·1	42·6	41	30·316	...	2·2	N	1·6
13	56·6	34·4	41	30·394	...	6·6	E	0·0
14	57·7	29·4	41	30·343	...	2·6	SE	0·0
15	59·1	28·7	41	30·262	...	7·6	ENE	0·0
16	44·5	32·3	41	30·276	...	...	ENE	1·0
17	45·2	37·1	41	30·157	...	...	SE	0·0
18	45·3	31·9	41	29·980	...	0·7	NE	4·4
19	41·6	28·7	41	29·829	...	6·1	NNW	2·5
20	41·0	27·6	41	29·612	...	6·0	N	4·7
21	37·8	20·3	41	29·554	0·04	2·1	SW	1·6
22	40·7	24·0	41	29·516	...	5·0	NW	7·2
23	37·3	23·1	41	29·636	...	2·4	NW	4·3
24	40·8	25·2	42	29·922	0·01	6·2	SSW	5·7
25	47·0	24·5	42	29·994	0·06	3·5	SSW	8·1
26	54·3	40·8	43	29·885	0·17	1·1	WSW	8·6
27	61·2	38·0	43	29·798	0·03	2·8	SW	4·4
28	55·1	43·6	43	29·801	0·02	2·4	SSW	14·0
29	59·9	46·3	44	29·841	...	8·9	WSW	15·5
30	57·8	42·8	44	30·092	...	1·5	N	2·0
31	60·5	41·8	44	29·959	0·14	0·1	SE	2·8

THE MOON.

Day of M.	Rises Morning. H. M.	Sets Afternoon. H. M.	Souths Afternoon. H. M.	Right Ascension at Noon. H. M. S.	Declination at Noon. ° ′ ″	Horizontal Parallax at Noon. ′ ″	Semidiameter at Noon. ′ ″	Age at Noon. D. H.	Configurations of Jupiter's Satellites at 4h. A.M.
1	6 18	6 12	0 7	22 41 39	2 54 1s	61 28	16 47	0 1	4○123
2	6 41	7 38	1 1	23 38 5	2 59 38n	61 18	16 44	1 1	42○3●
3	7 3	9 4	1 55	0 34 27	8 38 15	60 48	16 36	2 1	421○3
4	7 30	10 27	2 50	1 31 10	13 38 52	60 4	16 24	3 1	43○12
5	8 0	11 47	3 46	2 28 23	17 42 59	59 10	16 9	4 1	♃431○
6	8 34	mrn.	4 41	3 25 54	20 37 50	58 13	15 53	5 1	432○1
7	9 18	0 58	5 37	4 23 10	22 17 2	57 17	15 38	6 1	413○2
8	10 7	2 0	6 30	5 19 25	22 40 19	56 25	15 24	7 1	4○132
9	11 6	2 50	7 22	6 13 58	21 52 35	55 41	15 12	8 1	21○43
10	aft.	3 30	8 11	7 6 16	20 2 12	55 4	15 2	9 1	♃2○43
11	1 14	4 2	8 58	7 56 12	17 19 23	54 36	14 54	10 1	3○124
12	2 21	4 29	9 42	8 43 54	13 54 48	54 16	14 49	11 1	31○24
13	3 27	4 49	10 25	9 29 45	9 58 48	54 3	14 45	12 1	32○14
14	4 31	5 10	11 6	10 14 17	5 41 14	53 57	14 44	13 1	31○24
15	5 37	5 28	11 47	10 58 8	1 11 28n	53 57	14 44	14 1	○1324
16	6 43	5 44	mrn.	11 41 56	3 21 14s	54 2	14 45	15 1	21○43
17	7 51	6 1	0 28	12 26 21	7 47 29	54 12	14 48	16 1	2○143
18	8 58	6 20	1 11	13 12 0	11 57 29	54 27	14 52	17 1	4○32●
19	10 5	6 43	1 55	13 59 27	15 40 45	54 48	14 57	18 1	431○2
20	11 13	7 9	2 41	14 49 6	18 46 15	55 14	15 4	19 1	432○1
21	mrn.	7 42	3 30	15 41 9	21 2 34	55 46	15 13	20 1	431○●
22	0 16	8 24	4 21	16 35 28	22 18 48	56 24	15 24	21 1	4○312
23	1 14	9 16	5 15	17 31 36	22 25 50	57 7	15 35	22 1	412○3
24	2 5	10 18	6 10	18 28 48	21 17 59	57 55	15 49	23 1	42○13
25	2 46	11 31	7 5	19 26 18	18 54 22	58 46	16 2	24 1	4○32●
26	3 22	aft.	8 1	20 23 29	15 19 49	59 35	16 16	25 1	31○42
27	3 51	2 13	8 56	21 20 2	10 44 56	60 19	16 28	26 1	32○14
28	4 16	3 38	9 50	22 16 5	5 25 36s	60 52	16 37	27 1	31○4●
29	4 40	5 4	10 44	23 11 59	0 17 50n	61 10	16 42	28 1	○3124
30	5 4	6 29	11 38	0 8 17	6 1 58	61 9	16 41	29 1	12○34
31	5 28	7 56	aft.	1 5 27	11 22 14n	60 49	16 36	0 15	2○134

APPARENT RIGHT ASCENSION OF THE PRINCIPAL PLANETS AT MEAN NOON.

D.	☿ MERCURY. H. M. S.	♀ VENUS. H. M. S.	♂ MARS. H. M. S.	♃ JUPITER. H. M. S.	♄ SATURN. H. M. S.
2	23 51 26	1 14 39	22 14 41	16 33 28	18 15 27
7	0 14 17	1 36 25	22 29 39	16 34 57	18 16 49
12	0 26 52	1 58 19	22 44 29	16 36 7	18 18 1
17	0 27 18	2 20 23	22 59 10	16 36 58	18 19 4
22	0 17 20	2 43 39	23 13 44	16 37 29	18 19 57
27	0 2 58	3 5 7	23 28 11	16 37 41	18 20 40

APPARENT DECLINATION OF THE ABOVE PLANETS.

D.	☿ ° ′ ″	♀ ° ′ ″	♂ ° ′ ″	♃ ° ′ ″	♄ ° ′ ″
2	0 19 17s	8 4 9n	12 3 13s	21 5 18s	22 24 17s
7	3 24 11n	10 33 53	10 37 16	21 7 57	22 23 39
12	5 54 20	12 55 46	9 8 54	21 9 50	22 23 1
17	6 40 53	15 11 20	7 38 31	21 11 16	22 22 25
22	5 37 29	17 18 16	6 6 33	21 11 57	22 21 52
27	3 17 2n	19 15 15n	4 33 24s	21 11 59s	22 21 22s

ECLIPSES, OCCULTATIONS, AND OTHER CELESTIAL PHENOMENA.

March 1. Day breaks at 4*h*. 55*m*. *morn*., and Twilight ends at 7*h*. 31*m*. *aft*., the length of the Day being 10*h*. 50*m*.

Mar. 2. Mercury in conjunction with the Moon, 6*h*. *aft*. ☿ 4° 37′ S.

Mar. 4. Venus in conjunction with the Moon, 8*h*. *morn*. ♀ 3° 58′ S.

Mar. 5. Mean time of Sun's semidiameter passing the meridian, 1*m*. 4·9*s*.

Mar. 8. Mercury at greatest elongation (18°) East, 11*h*. *morn*.

Mar. 8. Occultation of Neptune. The disappearance takes place at 6*h*. 13*m*. *aft*., 107° from the vertex; the reappearance at 7*h*. 34*m*. *aft*., 249° from the vertex.

Mar. 11. Occultation of *f* Geminorum, magnitude 5. The disappearance takes place at 1*h*. 43*m*. *morn*., 57° from the vertex; the appearance at 2*h*. 40*m*. *morn*., 260° from the vertex.

Mar. 16. Occultation of ε Leonis, magnitude 5. The disappearance takes place at 3*h*. 20*m*. *morn*., 64° from the vertex. The reappearance at 4*h*. 25*m*. *morn*., 279° from the vertex.

Mar. 20. Mean time of Sun's semidiameter passing the meridian, 1*m*. 4·3*s*.

Mar. 21. Sun enters Aries: Spring commences, 2*h*. *morn*.

Mar. 22. Occultation of ρ Ophiuchi, magnitude 5½. The reappearance takes place at 5*h*. 33*m*. *morn*., 183° from the vertex.

Mar. 24. Occultation of Saturn. The disappearance takes place at 8*h*. 35*m*. *morn*., 56° from the vertex; the reappearance at 9*h*. 46*m*. *morn*., 225° from the vertex.

In this month the Mornings increase 1*h*. 8*m*., and the Afternoons 51*m*.

MORNING AND EVENING STARS.

☿ MERCURY is an evening star in the early part of the month; in Pisces.

♀ VENUS is an evening star; in Pisces till the 8th, when it enters Aries. Well placed for observation in this month.

♂ MARS is a morning star; in Aquarius.

♃ JUPITER is a morning star nearly in the same position as last month.

♄ SATURN is a morning star; in Sagittarius.

HORIZONTAL EQUATORIAL PARALLAX OF SUN AND PLANETS.

D.	☉ ″	☿ ″	♀ ″	♂ ″	♃ ″	♄ ″
5	8 9	8 9	7 9	3 8	1 7	0 9
15	8 9	12 0	8 4	3 8	1 8	0 9
25	8 9	14 7	9 0	3 8	1 8	0 9

SEMIDIAMETER OF SUN AND PLANETS.

D.	☉ ′ ″	☿ ″	♀ ″	♂ ″	♃ ″	♄ ″
5	16 9	3 3	7 5	2 0	17 5	7 4
15	16 6	4 5	8 0	2 0	18 1	7 6
25	16 3	5 5	8 6	2 0	18 6	7 7

Time of High Water at the undermentioned Places—

Month	Week	London Bridge Morn.	London Bridge After.	Liverpool Morn.	Liverpool After.	Bristol Morn.	Bristol After.	Hull Morn.	Hull After.	Greenock Morn.	Greenock After.	Leith Morn.	Leith After.	Dublin (Bar) Morn.	Dublin (Bar) After.
		H. M.	H. M.	H. M.	H. M.	H. M.	H. M.	H. M.	H. M.	H. M.	H. M.	H. M.	H. M.	H. M.	H. M.
1	Th	1 32	1 55	11 10	11 33	6 58	7 21	6 5	6 28	...	0 4	2 10	2 32	10 52	11 13
2	F	2 17	2 38	11 55	...	7 43	8 5	6 51	7 13	0 28	0 51	2 54	3 15	11 34	11 56
3	S	2 59	3 21	0 18	0 40	8 26	8 47	7 35	7 57	1 13	1 36	3 35	3 56	...	0 18
4	S	3 43	4 3	1 2	1 23	9 8	9 29	8 18	8 39	1 58	2 19	4 18	4 39	0 40	1 2
5	M	4 25	4 46	1 43	2 3	9 48	10 8	9 0	9 21	2 39	2 59	5 1	5 22	1 24	1 45
6	Tu	5 6	5 27	2 23	2 44	10 27	10 47	9 42	10 3	3 19	3 40	5 43	6 6	2 7	2 30
7	W	5 48	6 11	3 6	3 29	11 7	11 29	10 26	10 52	4 2	4 25	6 32	6 58	2 54	3 19
8	Th	6 34	7 1	3 54	4 26	11 53	...	11 22	11 58	4 50	5 19	7 26	8 0	3 46	4 20
9	F	7 31	8 6	5 2	5 46	0 22	0 57	...	0 36	5 52	6 31	8 38	9 22	4 57	5 38
10	S	8 46	9 30	6 32	7 21	1 40	2 27	1 16	1 57	7 13	7 58	10 6	10 49	6 19	6 59
11	S	10 18	11 3	8 3	8 40	3 17	4 1	2 38	3 18	8 41	9 19	11 30	...	7 39	8 15
12	M	11 40	...	9 11	9 36	4 41	5 12	3 54	4 25	9 52	10 20	0 4	0 35	8 47	9 15
13	Tu	0 13	0 41	9 57	10 16	5 40	6 2	4 52	5 13	10 43	11 3	0 59	1 18	9 39	10 0
14	W	1 2	1 21	10 33	10 49	6 22	6 41	5 32	5 49	11 22	11 40	1 37	1 55	10 18	10 34
15	Th	1 39	1 56	11 5	11 20	6 59	7 15	6 5	6 21	11 57	...	2 11	2 27	10 48	11 1
16	F	2 12	2 26	11 35	11 50	7 30	7 45	6 37	6 53	0 13	0 29	2 42	2 56	11 15	11 29
17	S	2 40	2 55	...	0 5	8 0	8 15	7 8	7 23	0 45	1 1	3 10	3 24	11 44	11 59
18	S	3 9	3 23	0 21	0 36	8 29	8 44	7 38	7 53	1 16	1 32	3 38	3 52	...	0 14
19	M	3 38	3 53	0 51	1 5	8 58	9 12	8 8	8 22	1 47	2 4	4 7	4 22	0 30	0 45
20	Tu	4 8	4 23	1 21	1 37	9 27	9 42	8 37	8 53	2 17	2 33	4 37	4 54	1 1	1 18
21	W	4 39	4 55	1 52	2 8	9 57	10 12	9 9	9 26	2 48	3 4	5 11	5 28	1 35	1 52
22	Th	5 10	5 28	2 25	2 45	10 29	10 47	9 44	10 4	3 21	3 40	5 47	6 9	2 11	2 32
23	F	5 48	6 11	3 6	3 30	11 6	11 28	10 27	10 54	4 2	4 25	6 33	6 59	2 55	3 23
24	S	6 35	7 4	3 57	4 32	11 54	...	11 27	...	4 52	5 24	7 30	8 2	3 50	4 27
25	S	7 38	8 15	5 12	5 58	0 28	1 8	0 5	0 46	6 1	6 43	8 49	9 35	5 7	5 48
26	M	8 59	9 46	6 49	7 33	1 54	2 44	1 28	2 9	7 27	8 10	10 20	11 0	6 30	7 10
27	Tu	10 30	11 10	8 11	8 44	3 29	4 11	2 48	3 25	8 50	9 25	11 36	...	7 46	8 20
28	W	11 46	...	9 12	9 37	4 45	5 15	3 59	4 28	9 55	10 23	0	0 35	8 51	9 19
29	Th	0 16	0 42	10 0	10 22	5 42	6 7	4 53	5 16	10 48	11 13	0 58	1 22	9 44	10 7
30	F	1 5	1 29	10 46	11 9	6 32	6 56	5 39	6 2	11 38	...	1 44	2 8	10 29	10 50
31	S	1 53	2 14	11 31	11 53	7 19	7 41	6 25	6 48	...	0 26	2 30	2 51	11 10	11 31

RISING, SOUTHING, and SETTING of the PRINCIPAL PLANETS at intervals of Seven Days.

D.	Mercury ☿ Rises	Mercury ☿ Souths	Mercury ☿ Sets	Venus ♀ Rises	Venus ♀ Souths	Venus ♀ Sets	Mars ♂ Rises	Mars ♂ Souths	Mars ♂ Sets	Jupiter ♃ Rises	Jupiter ♃ Souths	Jupiter ♃ Sets	Saturn ♄ Rises	Saturn ♄ Souths	Saturn ♄ Sets
	h. m.	h. m.	h. m.	h. m.	h. m.	h. m.	h. m.	h. m.	h. m.	h. m.	h. m.	h. m.	h. m.	h. m.	h. m.
5	7 1M	1 15A	7 29A	7 44M	2 37A	9 30A	6 27M	11 33M	4 39A	1 36M	5 44M	9 52M	3 25M	7 26M	11 27M
12	6 35M	1 8A	7 41A	7 30M	2 40A	9 34A	6 9M	11 26M	4 43A	1 11M	5 19M	9 27M		7 0M	11 1M
19	6 1M	0 38A	7 15A	7 13M	2 43A	10 13A	7 51M	11 19M	4 47A	0 44M	4 52M	9 0M	2 33M	6 33M	10 35M
26	5 29M	11 52M	6 15A	7 1M	2 47A	10 33A	7 32M	11 11M	4 50A	0 17M	4 25M	8 33M	2 7M	6 8M	10 9M

APPARENT RIGHT ASCENSION AND DECLINATION OF THE POLE STAR.

D.	R.A. H. M. S.	Decl. N.
1	1 22 6·7	88 46 48
10	1 22 2·0	88 46 46
19	1 21 57·7	88 46 43
28	1 21 55·3	88 46 41

ANGULAR DISTANCE OF THE MOON FROM REGULUS.

D.	Position of Star	6 P.M.	9 P.M.	Midnight
5	East	104 26 13	102 41 53	100 57 59
6	East	90 43 46	89 2 55	87 22 29
7	East	77 28 34	75 50 58	74 13 46
8	East	64 38 9	63 3 25	61 29 2

At midnight, in the beginning of March, the constellations Ursa Major, Leo, Crater, and Hydra are on the meridian. In Ursa Major is a large planetary Nebula, appearing as a mass of attenuated light, from 3½' to 4' in diameter; it is situated in R.A. 11h. 8m. 54s., and Decl. 55° 34' N. Its spectroscopic examination leads to the inference that it is mainly a mass of incandescent gas.

Virgo comes to the meridian about midnight towards the end of this month. Between Virgo and Coma Berenices is a large Nebula, one of the class known as "Spiral Nebulæ," situated in R.A. 12h. 13m. 34s., and Decl. 15° 0' N. With a large telescope of 8 inches aperture it appears to be resolvable in the centre into two bright star-like points. This constellation is thickly strewed with nebulæ, which may be best observed on the evenings immediately before and after the beginning and ending of the month.

DAY OF			Fasts and Festivals. Remarkable Days—Events. SUN ENTERS TAURUS 20d. 2h. A.	THE SUN		DAYS	
M.	Light and Dark.	W.		Rises.	Sets.	of the Year	to end of Year.
				H. M.	H. M.		
1		S	**Fifth Sunday in Lent.** All Fools' Day.	5 37	6 31	91	274
2		M	Léon Gambetta born, 1838 ; died 31 Dec., 1882.	5 35	6 32	92	273
3		Tu	*St. Richard.* Washington Irving born, 1783.	5 33	6 33	93	272
4		W	*St. Ambrose.* O. Goldsmith d. 1774; b. 10 Nov. 1728	5 31	6 35	94	271
5		Th	Pop. of U.K., 1891, 38,104,975. Ld. Lister b. '27.	5 29	6 37	95	270
6		F	John Francis (Athenæum) d. 1882; b. 18 July, '11.	5 27	6 39	96	269
7		S	Oxford Term ends. Old Lady Day.	5 24	6 40	97	268
8		S	**Palm Sunday.** Battle of the Atbara, 1898.	5 22	6 42	98	267
9		M	Ld. St. Alban's (Fr. Bacon) d. 1626; b. 22 Jan. 1560	5 20	6 44	99	266
10		Tu	Battle of Toulouse, 1814. Chartist demon., 1848.	5 18	6 45	100	265
11		W	HILARY LAW SIT. END. Treaty of Utrecht, 1713.	5 16	6 46	101	264
12		Th	Rodney's victory off Dominica, 1782.	5 14	6 48	102	263
13		F	**Good Friday.** Capture of Magdala, 1868.	5 11	6 50	103	262
14		S	Princess Beatrice b. 1857. Rangoon taken, '52.	5 8	6 52	104	261
15		S	**Easter Day.** Cardinal Vaughan born, 1832.	5 6	6 53	105	260
16		M	**Easter Monday.** Sir A. W. Woods, K.C.B., b. 1816.	5 4	6 55	106	259
17		Tu	**Easter Tuesday.** Heenan v. Sayers, 1860.	5 3	6 57	107	258
18		W	Camb. T. beg. Ox. T. beg. Relief of Chitral, '95.	5 1	6 58	108	257
19		Th	*St. Alphege.* Beaconsfield d. 1881. Primrose Day	4 58	7 0	109	256
20		F	Spanish Fleet destroyed by Blake, 1657.	4 56	7 2	110	255
21		S	Bishop Heber born, 1783 ; died 3 April, 1826.	4 54	7 4	111	254
22		S	**First Sunday after Easter.** Low Sunday.	4 52	7 6	112	253
23		M	ST. GEORGE'S DAY. Shakespeare b. 1564; d. 1616.	4 49	7 7	113	252
24		Tu	EASTER LAW SITTINGS BEGIN.	4 47	7 8	114	251
25		W	**St. Mark, E. and M.** Sir Robert Peel b. 1788	4 46	7 10	115	250
26		Th	Gabriel Rossetti d. 1854. [d. 2 July, '50	4 44	7 12	116	249
27		F	Edward Gibbon born, 1737; died 16 Jan. 1794.	4 42	7 14	117	248
28		S	Mutiny of the *Bounty*, 1789.	4 40	7 15	118	247
29		S	**Second Sunday after Easter.**	4 38	7 16	119	246
30		M	Duke of Argyll born, 1823.	4 36	7 18	120	245

PHASES OF THE MOON.

☽ First Quarter	6d.	8h.	55m.	Afternoon.
○ Full Moon	15	1	2	Morning.
☾ Last Quarter	22	2	33	Afternoon.
● New Moon	29	5	23	Morning.

Apogee 11d. 10h. M. 252,300.
Perigee 27d. 5h. M. 225,300.

RAINFALL IN APRIL, 1899.

In this month rain fell on 21 days. The total fall for the month was 2·99 inches; *above* the average of fifty years, 1841–90, by 1·33 inch.

MONTHLY NOTES.

April 1. Refreshment House Licenses to be renewed. Quarter Sessions to be held next week unless otherwise fixed.

5. Dividends on Consols, &c., due. Financial year, 1899–1900, for Imperial purposes ends to-day.

6. Clerks of the Peace and Town Clerks send registration precepts to Overseers before 15th inst.

9. Fire Insurances must be paid.

15. Parish Councils to hold their annual meeting on or within seven days after this date. There will be no Parish Council elections this year.

16. English Bank Holiday.

16. Edinburgh Spring Holiday.

THE SUN.

Day	After Clock. (M. S.)	Hrly Var of Eq'n of Time (S.)	Right Ascension at Noon (H. M. S.)	Hourly Var. of R. A. (S.)	Apparent Declination (Nth.) at Noon (° ' ")	Hrly Var of (+) s Declination (")	Sidereal Time at Noon (H. M. S.)	Mean Time at Sidereal Noon (H. M. S.)
1	4 2	0·75	0 41 35	9·10	4 28 37	57·9	0 37 33	23 18 37
2	3 44	0·75	0 45 14	9·11	4 51 44	57·7	0 41 30	23 14 41
3	3 26	0·74	0 48 53	9·11	5 14 40	57·5	0 45 27	23 10 45
4	3 8	0·74	0 52 31	9·12	5 37 43	57·2	0 49 23	23 6 49
5	2 51	0·73	0 56 10	9·12	6 0 33	57·0	0 53 20	23 2 53
6	2 33	0·72	0 59 49	9·13	6 23 17	56·7	0 57 16	22 58 57
7	2 16	0·72	1 3 29	9·14	6 45 55	56·4	1 1 13	22 55 1
8	1 59	0·71	1 7 8	9·15	7 8 25	56·1	1 5 9	22 51 5
9	1 42	0·70	1 10 48	9·16	7 30 48	55·8	1 9 6	22 47 10
10	1 26	0·69	1 14 28	9·17	7 53 4	55·5	1 13 2	22 43 14
11	1 9	0·68	1 18 8	9·18	8 15 11	55·1	1 16 59	22 39 18
12	0 53	0·66	1 21 49	9·19	8 37 10	54·8	1 20 56	22 35 22
13	0 37	0·65	1 25 29	9·20	8 59 1	54·4	1 24 52	22 31 26
14	0 22	0·64	1 29 10	9·22	9 20 42	54·0	1 28 49	22 27 30
15	0 7	0·62	1 32 52	9·23	9 42 15	53·6	1 32 45	22 23 34
16	Bef.	0·61	1 36 34	9·25	10 3 37	53·2	1 36 42	22 19 35
17	0 23	0·59	1 40 16	9·26	10 24 50	52·8	1 40 38	22 15 42
18	0 37	0·58	1 43 59	9·28	10 45 52	52·4	1 44 35	22 11 46
19	0 50	0·56	1 47 41	9·30	11 6 44	51·9	1 48 31	22 7 51
20	1 3	0·54	1 51 25	9·31	11 27 26	51·5	1 52 28	22 3 55
21	1 16	0·52	1 55 8	9·33	11 47 56	51·0	1 56 24	21 59 59
22	1 29	0·50	1 58 53	9·35	12 8 14	50·5	2 0 21	21 56 3
23	1 40	0·48	2 2 37	9·37	12 28 21	50·0	2 4 18	21 52 7
24	1 52	0·46	2 6 22	9·39	12 48 15	49·5	2 8 14	21 48 11
25	2 3	0·44	2 10 8	9·41	13 7 57	49·0	2 12 11	21 44 15
26	2 13	0·42	2 13 54	9·43	13 27 26	48·4	2 16 7	21 40 19
27	2 23	0·40	2 17 41	9·45	13 46 41	47·9	2 20 4	21 36 23
28	2 32	0·38	2 21 28	9·48	14 5 43	47·3	2 24 0	21 32 27
29	2 41	0·36	2 25 16	9·50	14 24 32	46·7	2 27 57	21 28 31
30	2 49	0·34	2 29 4	9·52	14 43 5	46·1	2 31 53	21 24 36

METEOROLOGICAL OBSERVATIONS, APRIL, 1899.

Day	TEMPERATURE Maximum	TEMPERATURE Minimum	TEMPERATURE Avge. 50 Yrs.	BAROM. Mean (inches)	RAIN-FALL (inches)	SUN-SHINE (hours)	WIND Directn.	WIND Pressure (lbs. to foot)
1	61·1	49·1	45	29·946	0·01	2·7	SW	1·2
2	58·0	47·7	45	29·920	...	1·6	SW	0·8
3	60·2	46·3	45	29·928	...	2·6	SW	3·3
4	56·1	45·2	45	29·902	0·06	0·5	SW	6·2
5	59·2	43·0	45	30·006	0·01	7·3	WSW	8·8
6	60·4	47·8	45	29·844	0·04	5·9	SW	5·7
7	51·8	43·4	45	29·101	0·25	0·7	W	15·0
8	47·1	34·8	45	29·456	0·13	6·7	NW	26·0
9	52·6	33·3	45	29·678	0·17	5·3	WSW	3·7
10	61·3	42·8	45	29·431	0·33	3·9	WSW	8·8
11	48·5	35·5	45	29·604	0·04	4·6	NW	15·2
12	53·8	31·2	45	29·565	0·28	5·6	SW	3·5
13	48·2	37·1	45	28·902	0·28	0·1	SSE	5·5
14	48·0	40·3	45	28·863	0·30	...	WNW	2·3
15	53·1	40·0	46	29·144	0·15	2·4	W	1·3
16	47·0	37·1	46	30·516	0·05	...	NNW	1·3
17	52·9	33·0	46	29·782	...	7·5	WSW	1·0
18	50·2	33·0	46	29·913	...	1·4	N	0·1
19	59·1	30·7	47	29·980	...	10·6	WSW	0·8
20	61·1	34·3	47	29·908	...	6·1	SW	1·1
21	47·2	40·1	47	29·734	0·38	...	ESE	3·3
22	48·8	34·5	47	30·095	...	0·9	NE	1·0
23	55·9	36·4	48	30·042	0·04	5·4	S	3·3
24	54·7	44·6	48	29·555	0·40	..	S	1·5
25	56·9	43·7	48	29·331	0·20	4·4	SW	5·6
26	54·1	43·5	48	29·495	0·09	2·5	NW	4·4
27	57·9	45·9	48	29·776	...	2·0	N	0·6
28	62·0	45·7	48	29·686	0·02	0·3	SW	2·0
29	59·7	48·8	49	29·496	0·04	3·2	WSW	7·7
30	51·9	36·5	50	29·991	...	9·1	N	3·5

MEMORANDA.

1. S. Lamps to be lighted (7.31)
2. .... (7.32)
3. .... (7.33)
4. .... (7.35)
5. .... (7.37)
6. .... (7.39)
7. .... (7.40)
8. S. .... (7.42)
9. .... (7.44)
10. .... (7.45)
11. .... (7.46)
12. .... (7.48)
13. .... (7.50)
14. .... (7.52)
15. S. .... (7.53)
16. .... (7.55)
17. .... (7.57)
18. .... (7.58)
19. .... (8.0)
20. .... (8.2)
21. .... (8.4)
22. S. .... (8.6)
23. .... (8.7)
24. .... (8.8)
25. .... (8.10)
26. .... (8.12)
27. .... (8.14)
28. .... (8.15)
29. S. .... (8.16)
30. .... (8.18)

THE MOON.

Day of M.	Rises Morning.	Sets Afternoon.	Souths Afternoon.	Right Ascension at Noon.	Declination at Noon.	Horizontal Parallax at Noon.	Semidiameter at Noon.	Age at Noon.	Configurations of Jupiter's Satellites at 2h. A.M.
	H. M.	H. M.	H. M.	H. M. S.	° ′ ″	′ ″	′ ″	D. H.	
1	5 56	9 19	1 30	2 3 40	15 55 43n	60 13	16 26	1 15	1○234
2	6 30	0 36	2 27	3 2 44	19 23 51	59 24	16 13	2 15	3○124
3	7 10	11 45	3 24	4 1 59	21 34 59	58 28	15 58	3 15	32○4●
4	7 59	mrn.	4 21	5 0 25	22 25 29	57 31	15 42	4 15	3421○
5	8 57	0 43	5 15	5 57 2	21 59 9	56 36	15 27	5 15	43○12
6	9 59	1 27	6 6	6 51 8	20 25 4	55 48	15 14	6 15	41○23
7	11 5	2 3	6 54	7 42 27	17 54 52	55 8	15 3	7 15	42○13
8	aft.	2 31	7 40	8 31 6	14 40 31	54 37	14 54	8 15	41○23
9	1 18	2 55	8 23	9 17 32	10 53 4	54 16	14 49	9 15	43○12
10	2 23	3 15	9 5	10 2 23	6 42 27	54 4	14 46	10 15	342○●
11	3 29	3 34	9 46	10 45 21	2 17 40n	54 1	14 45	11 15	3241○
12	4 35	3 50	10 27	11 30 9	2 12 36s	54 5	14 46	12 15	3○142
13	5 40	4 7	11 9	12 14 30	6 39 30	54 16	14 49	13 15	1○234
14	6 48	4 28	11 53	13 0 3	10 53 24	54 31	14 53	14 15	2○134
15	7 55	4 49	mrn.	13 47 24	14 43 42	54 51	14 58	15 15	1○234
16	9 3	5 13	0 38	14 36 56	17 58 52	55 15	15 5	16 15	3○124
17	10 8	5 45	1 27	15 28 50	20 26 56	55 41	15 12	17 15	321○4
18	11 9	6 24	2 18	16 22 53	21 56 34	56 11	15 20	18 15	♃32○4
19	mrn.	7 13	3 11	17 18 34	22 18 45	56 43	15 29	19 15	3○142
20	0 1	8 12	4 5	18 15 3	21 28 20	57 18	15 38	20 15	14○23
21	0 46	9 20	5 0	19 11 33	19 25 6	57 55	15 49	21 15	42○13
22	1 22	10 35	5 54	20 7 24	16 13 58	58 33	15 59	22 15	41○3●
23	1 51	11 53	6 47	21 2 24	12 4 24	59 10	16 9	23 15	43○12
24	2 17	aft.	7 39	21 56 42	7 9 29	59 44	16 18	24 15	4312○
25	2 41	2 36	8 31	22 50 47	1 45 26s	60 10	16 25	25 15	432○1
26	3 4	4 1	9 24	23 45 17	3 48 48n	60 26	16 30	26 15	43○2●
27	3 27	5 23	10 17	0 40 53	9 12 4	60 29	16 31	27 15	41○23
28	3 54	6 47	11 12	1 38 1	14 2 8	60 17	16 27	28 15	2○413
29	4 24	8 8	aft.	2 36 45	17 57 54	59 50	16 20	0 7	1○43●
30	5 2	9 23	1 7	3 36 35	20 42 31n	59 11	16 9	1 7	○3124

APPARENT RIGHT ASCENSION OF THE PRINCIPAL PLANETS AT MEAN NOON.

D.	☿ MERCURY.			♀ VENUS.			♂ MARS.			♃ JUPITER.			♄ SATURN.		
	H.	M.	S.	H.	M.	S.	H.	M.	S.	H.	M.	S.	H.	M.	S.
1	23	51	28	3	27	46	23	42	32	16	37	33	18	21	13
6	23	47	14	3	50	34	23	56	49	16	37	5	18	21	35
11	23	51	0	4	13	25	0	11	2	16	36	17	18	21	46
16	0	1	36	4	36	11	0	25	12	16	35	10	18	21	47
21	0	17	33	4	58	46	0	39	21	16	33	46	18	21	37
26	0	37	41	5	20	58	0	53	29	16	32	4	18	21	16

APPARENT DECLINATION OF THE ABOVE PLANETS.

D.	☿			♀			♂			♃			♄		
	°	′	″	°	′	″	°	′	″	°	′	″	°	′	″
1	0	42	59n	21	1	1n	2	59	29s	21	11	23s	22	20	57s
6	1	10	45s	22	34	26	1	25	15s	21	10	9	22	20	37
11	2	2	13	23	54	32	0	8	54n	21	8	19	22	20	23
16	1	51	51	25	0	32	1	42	37	21	5	52	22	20	15
21	0	48	1s	25	51	58	3	15	30	21	2	50	22	20	14
26	1	0	10n	26	28	36n	4	47	13n	20	59	14s	22	20	19s

ECLIPSES, OCCULTATIONS, AND OTHER CELESTIAL PHENOMENA.

April 1 Day breaks at 3*h*. 37*m*. *morn.*, and Twilight ends at 8*h*. 31*m*. *aft*., the length of the Day being 12*h*. 54*m*.

Apr. 4 Occultation of o Tauri, magnitude 5. The disappearance takes place at 9*h*. 30*m*. *aft.*, 29° from the vertex; the reappearance at 10*h*. 22*m*. *aft.*, 263° from the vertex.

Apr. 5. Mean time of Sun's semidiameter passing the meridian, 1*m*. 4·4*s*.

Apr. 6. A near approach of the Moon to ν Geminorum, magnitude 4. The least distance between Moon and star occurs at 0*h*. 34*m*. *morn.*, 155° from the vertex.

Apr. 8. Occultation of α Cancri, magnitude 4. The disappearance takes place at 11*h*. 46*m*. *aft.*, 53° from the vertex; the reappearance on April 9 at 0*h*. 45*m*. *morn.*, 277 from the vertex.

Apr. 17. A near approach of the Moon to δ Scorpii, magnitude 2½. The least distance between Moon and Star occurs at 10*h*. 45*m*. *aft.*, 224° from the vertex.

Apr. 20. Mean time of Sun's semidiameter passing the meridian, 1*m*. 5·0*s*.

Apr. 21. Occultation of ξ² Sagittarii, magnitude 3½. The disappearance takes place at 2*h*. 27*m*. *morn.*, 110° from the vertex; the reappearance at 3*h*. 42*m*. *morn.*, 267° from the vertex.

Apr. 22. Mercury at greatest elongation (27°) West, 3*h*. *morn.*

Apr. 24. Occultation of c¹ Capricorni, magnitude 5. The disappearance takes place at 3*h*. 23*m*. *morn.*, 45° from the vertex; the reappearance at 3*h*. 57*m*. *morn.*; 337° from the vertex.

Apr. 29. Venus at greatest elongation (45°, East, 0*h*. *morn.*

In this month the Mornings increase 1*h*. 1*m*., and the Afternoons 47*m*.

MORNING AND EVENING STARS.

☿ MERCURY is a morning star; in Pisces.

♀ VENUS is an evening star; well placed for observation, in Taurus.

♂ MARS is a morning star; in Pisces.

♃ JUPITER nearly stationary in Scorpio.

♄ SATURN in Sagittarius, a little north of λ.

HORIZONTAL EQUATORIAL PARALLAX OF SUN AND PLANETS.

D.	☉	☿	♀	♂	♃	♄
	″	″	″	″	″	″
5	8 8	13 9	9 9	3 8	1 9	0 9
15	8 8	11 8	10 8	3 9	1 9	0 9
25	8 8	9 8	11 9	3 9	2 0	0 9

SEMIDIAMETER OF SUN AND PLANETS.

D.	☉	☿	♀	♂	♃	♄
	′ ″	″	″	″	″	″
5	16 0	5 3	9 4	2 0	19 3	7 8
15	15 58	4 4	10 2	2 1	19 8	7 9
25	15 55	3 7	11 3	2 1	20 3	8 1

Mean Longitude of Moon's Ascending Node, April 1, 254° 22′ ♐.

Time of High Water at the undermentioned Places—

Month	Week	London Bridge Morn.	After.	Liverpool Morn.	After.	Bristol Morn.	After.	Hull Morn.	After.	Greenock Morn.	After.	Leith Morn.	After.	Dublin (Bar.) Morn.	After.
		H. M.	H. M.	H. M.	H. M.	H. M.	H. M.	H. M.	H. M.	H. M.	H. M.	H. M.	H. M.	H. M.	H. M.
1	S	2*36	2*56	...	0 15	8 2	8 24	7 10	7 33	0 48	1 11	3 11	3 32	11 53	...
2	M	3*18	3*39	0 37	1 0	8 45	9 6	7 55	8 17	1 34	1 56	3 54	4 16	0 16	0 39
3	Tu	4* 2	4*24	1 22	1 42	9 27	9 47	8 38	8 59	2 17	2 38	4 38	5 0	1 1	1 23
4	W	4 44	5 5	2 3	2 24	10 7	10 28	9 20	9 42	2 59	3 20	5 22	5 45	1 45	2 8
5	Th	5 26	5 49	2 45	3 7	10 48	11 8	10 4	10 28	3 41	4 3	6 9	6 35	2 32	2 56
6	F	6 12	6 38	3 31	4 0	11 29	11 57	10 56	11 31	4 27	4 54	7 3	7 34	3 22	3 54
7	S	7 7	7 39	4 34	5 11	...	0 30	...	0 7	5 24	5 59	8 10	8 49	4 29	5 6
8	S	8 13	8 54	5 53	6 40	1 7	1 49	0 45	1 23	6 38	7 18	9 30	10 11	5 44	6 22
9	M	9 35	10 19	7 21	7 56	2 35	3 17	2 1	2 37	7 58	8 35	10 49	11 23	6 59	7 33
10	Tu	10 56	11 29	8 28	8 56	3 55	4 29	3 11	3 42	9 7	9 37	11 53	...	8 3	8 31
11	W	11 58	...	9 19	9 39	4 57	5 22	4 11	4 35	10 2	10 24	0 20	0 42	8 56	9 18
12	Th	0 21	0 43	9 57	10 14	5 43	6 3	4 55	5 13	10 44	11 3	1 0	1 18	9 39	9 58
13	F	1 2	1 20	10 30	10 46	6 22	6 39	5 30	5 46	11 21	11 38	1 36	1 53	10 15	10 29
14	S	1 37	1 52	11 2	11 17	6 56	7 12	6 2	6 19	11 55	...	2 8	2 23	10 43	10 58
15	S	2 8	2 23	11 32	11 48	7 28	7 43	6 35	6 50	0 12	0 28	2 38	2 53	11 12	11 27
16	M	2 37	2 52	...	0 6	7 58	8 14	7 6	7 23	0 44	1 1	3 7	3 22	11 43	...
17	Tu	3 8	3 25	0 23	0 40	8 31	8 48	7 40	7 58	1 19	1 37	3 39	3 57	0 1	0 19
18	W	3 42	4 0	0 56	1 16	9 5	9 22	8 15	8 33	1 55	2 13	4 15	4 33	0 38	0 57
19	Th	4 18	4 36	1 34	1 53	9 39	9 57	8 51	9 10	2 31	2 49	4 52	5 12	1 16	1 35
20	F	4 55	5 14	2 12	2 33	10 16	10 36	9 31	9 52	3 9	3 29	5 33	5 56	1 56	2 19
21	S	5 35	5 59	2 55	3 20	10 56	11 17	10 15	10 44	3 51	4 16	6 22	6 50	2 44	3 11
22	S	6 26	6 56	3 49	4 22	11 47	...	11 18	11 55	4 44	5 15	7 22	7 58	3 42	4 17
23	M	7 28	8 3	4 59	5 41	0 18	0 55	...	0 34	5 49	6 27	8 36	9 18	4 54	5 33
24	Tu	8 43	9 25	6 26	7 7	1 37	2 21	1 13	1 50	7 6	7 45	10 0	10 36	6 11	6 46
25	W	10 5	10 41	7 42	8 15	3 3	3 41	2 25	2 58	8 21	8 54	11 9	11 39	7 19	7 50
26	Th	11 15	11 46	8 44	9 10	4 16	4 45	3 29	3 59	9 25	9 54	...	...	8 20	8 49
27	F	...	0 14	9 34	9 57	5 14	5 40	4 26	4 50	10 21	10 46	0 32	0 55	9 17	9 41
28	S	0 39	1 2	10 19	10 42	6 5	6 29	5 13	5 36	11 10	11 35	1 18	1 41	10 0	10 25
29	S	1 26	1*49	11 6	11 30	6 53	7 17	6 0	6 24	...	0 0	2 4	2 27	10 47	11 10
30	M	2*12	2*36	11 54	...	7 40	8 3	6 48	7 12	0 25	0 49	2 50	3 12	11 33	11 56

RISING, SOUTHING, and SETTING of the PRINCIPAL PLANETS at intervals of Seven Days.

D.	Mercury ☿ Rises h. m.	Souths h. m.	Sets h. m.	Venus ♀ Rises h. m.	Souths h. m.	Sets h. m.	Mars ♂ Rises h. m.	Souths h. m.	Sets h. m.	Jupiter ♃ Rises h. m.	Souths h. m.	Sets h. m.	Saturn ♄ Rises h. m.	Souths h. m.	Sets h. m.
2	5 4M	11 9M	5 14A	6 48M	2 51A	10 54A	5 13M	11 4M	4 55A	11 45A	3 57M	8 5M	1 40M	5 41M	9 42M
9	4 45M	10 40M	4 35A	6 38M	2 55A	11 12A	4 55M	10 56M	4 57A	11 17A	3 29M	7 37M	1 13M	5 14M	9 15M
16	4 30M	10 25M	4 20A	6 33M	3 0A	11 28A	4 37M	10 49M	5 1A	10 48A	3 0M	7 9M	0 45M	4 46M	8 47M
23	4 18M	10 21M	4 24A	6 27M	3 4A	11 41A	4 18M	10 41M	5 4A	10 17A	2 31M	6 40M	0 18M	4 19M	8 20M
30	6 M	10 24M	4 42A	6 24M	3 7A	11 50A	3 59M	10 33M	5 7A	9 46A	2 1M	6 11M	11 45A	3 50M	7 51M

APPARENT RIGHT ASCENSION AND DECLINATION OF THE POLE STAR.			ANGULAR DISTANCE OF THE MOON FROM POLLUX.				
	R. A.	Decl. N.	Position of Star.	6 P.M.	9 P.M.	Midnight.	
D.	H. M. S.		D.	° ′ ″	° ′ ″	° ′ ″	
1	1 21 54.8	88 46 39	10	West	42 57 20	44 23 7	45 49 1
10	1 21 54.8	88 46 37	11	West	54 27 1	55 53 45	57 20 35
19	1 21 56.8	88 46 33	12	West	66 3 57	67 31 34	68 59 19
28	1 21 59.5	88 46 31	13	West	77 48 14	79 16 49	80 45 32

At the latter part of April the constellations Draco, Boötes, and Libra will be on the meridian about midnight. An irresolvable double Nebula in Canes Venatici, near η Ursæ Majoris, can be observed in this month: it is situated in R.A. 13h. 25m. 37s., and in Decl. 47° 42′ N. The Southern Nebula is surrounded by a faint ring of nebulous light, and was called by Herschel, in his Catalogue, "the Halo Nebula." Later observations placed it among the "Spiral" Nebulæ. That this is not a true incandescent Nebula is shown by the absence of bright lines in its spectrum. In R.A. 15h. 13m. 27s., Decl. 2° 28′ N., is a very fine cluster of stars, condensed into great brilliancy towards the centre. Sir W. Herschel could distinguish over 200 stars in this group in the field of his 40-feet reflector, but found the middle portion so condensed that the individual stars could not be distinguished. Lord Rosse says that the stars range from the 12th to 15th mag. The evenings about the 1st and 28th are the best for observing these objects.

DAY OF		Fasts and Festivals. Remarkable Days—Events. SUN ENTERS GEMINI 21d. 1h. A.	THE SUN		DAYS	
M.	Light and Dark. / W.		Rises. H. M.	Sets. H. M.	of the Year.	to end of Year.
1	Tu	**SS. Philip & James.** Span. Fleet destroyed at	4 33	7 21	121	244
2	W	John Galt, Scot. novelist, b. 1779. [Manila, '98	4 32	7 22	122	243
3	Th	*Invention of the Cross.* Ld. Anson's victory, 1747.	4 30	7 24	123	242
4	F	Capture of Seringapatam, 1799.	4 29	7 25	124	241
5	S	Napoleon I. died, 1821; born 15 Aug. 1769.	4 27	7 27	125	240
6	**S**	**Third Sun. aft. Easter.** *St. John ante Port. Lat.*	4 25	7 28	126	239
7	M	Earl of Rosebery b. 1847. Roy. Academy opens.	4 23	7 29	127	238
8	Tu	John Stuart Mill d. 1873; b. 20 May, 1806.	4 22	7 30	128	237
9	W	Half-Quarter Day.	4 20	7 32	129	236
10	Th	Outbreak of the Indian Mutiny, 1857.	4 18	7 34	130	235
11	F	Spencer Perceval assassinated, 1812.	4 16	7 36	131	234
12	S	Earl Cadogan, K.G., b. 1840. Jubilee Stakes.	4 14	7 38	132	233
13	**S**	**Fourth Sunda after Easter.** [issued, 1842.	4 13	7 39	133	232
14	M	Old May Day. Illustrated London News first	4 11	7 41	134	231
15	Tu	Joseph Whitaker, F.S.A., d. 1895; b. 4 May, 1820.	4 10	7 42	135	230
16	W	Felicia D. Hemans d. 1835; b. 25 Sept. 1793.	4 8	7 44	136	229
17	Th	King of Spain born, 1886.	4 7	7 45	137	228
18	F	Nicholas II., Emperor of Russia, born, 1868.	4 6	7 46	138	227
19	S	*St. Dunstan.* W. E. Gladstone d. '98; b. 29 Dec. 1809	4 5	7 47	139	226
20	**S**	**Fifth Sunday after Easter.** Rogation Sunday.	4 4	7 48	140	225
21	M	Rogation D. H.M. open'd Manch. Ship Canal, 1894	4 2	7 50	141	224
22	Tu	Rogation Day. Dr. Conan Doyle born, 1859.	4 1	7 51	142	223
23	W	Rogation Day. Lord Loch born, 1827.	4 0	7 53	143	222
24	Th	**Ascension Day.** Holy Thurs. QUEEN'S BIRTHDAY,	3 59	7 55	144	221
25	F	Princess Christian born, 1846. [b. 1819.	3 58	7 56	145	220
26	S	*St. Augustin.* Duchess of York born, 1867.	3 56	7 58	146	219
27	**S**	**Sunday after Ascension.** *Venerable Bede.*	3 55	7 59	147	218
28	M	Gladstone buried in Westminster Abbey, 1898.	3 54	8 0	148	217
29	Tu	Constantinople taken by the Turks, 1453.	3 53	8 1	149	216
30	W	Derby Day. Alfred Austin born, 1835.	3 52	8 2	150	215
31	Th	General Lord Chelmsford, G.C B, born, 1827.	3 51	8 3	151	214

PHASES OF THE MOON.

☽ First Quarter	6d.	1h. 39m.	Afternoon.
○ Full Moon	14	3 37	Afternoon.
☾ Last Quarter	21	8 31	Afternoon.
● New Moon	28	2 50	Afternoon.

Apogee 9d. 2h. M. 251,600.
Perigee 24d. 6h. A. 228,400.

RAINFALL IN MAY, 1899.

In this month rain fell on 12 days. The total fall for the month was 1·64 inch; *below* the average of fifty years, 1841-90, by 0·36 inch.

MONTHLY NOTES.

May 1. Holiday at Bank Transfer Office and Stock Exchange.
—. Bank and general holiday in Scotland.
ENGLISH QUARTER DAYS.— These are —Lady Day, March 25; Midsummer, June 24; Michaelmas, Sept. 29; and Christmas, Dec. 25. Quarterly trade accounts are made up to the end of the months of March, June, Sept., and December.
SCOTTISH QUARTER DAYS or TERMS are:—Candlemas, Feb. 2; Whitsun, May 15; Lammas, Aug. 1; and Martinmas, Nov. 11. The Removal Terms in Scottish Burghs are, May 28; Nov. 28.

THE SUN.

Day.	Before Clock.	Hrly Var of Equa of Time	Right Ascension at Noon.	Hourly Var. of R. A.	Apparent Declination (Nth.) at Noon.	Hrly Var (·)'s Declination	Sidereal Time at Noon.	Mean Time at Sidereal Noon.
	M. S.	S.	H. M. S.	S.	° ′ ″	″	H. M. S.	H. M. S.
1	2 57	0·31	2 32 53	9·54	15 1 25	45·5	2 35 50	21 20 40
2	3 4	0·29	2 36 42	9·56	15 19 29	44·9	2 39 47	21 16 44
3	3 11	0·27	2 40 32	9·59	15 37 18	44·2	2 43 43	21 12 48
4	3 17	0·25	2 44 22	9·61	15 54 52	43·6	2 47 40	21 8 52
5	3 23	0·23	2 48 13	9·63	16 12 10	42·9	2 51 36	21 4 56
6	3 28	0·20	2 52 5	9·65	16 29 12	42·2	2 55 33	21 1 0
7	3 33	0·18	2 55 57	9·68	16 45 57	41·5	2 59 29	20 57 4
8	3 37	0·16	2 59 49	9·70	17 2 25	40·8	3 3 26	20 53 8
9	3 40	0·13	3 3 42	9·72	17 18 36	40·1	3 7 22	20 49 12
10	3 43	0·11	3 7 36	9·75	17 34 30	39·4	3 11 19	20 45 16
11	3 46	0·09	3 11 30	9·77	17 50 7	38·6	3 15 16	20 41 21
12	3 47	0·06	3 15 25	9·79	18 5 25	37·9	3 19 12	20 37 25
13	3 49	0·04	3 19 20	9·82	18 20 25	37·1	3 23 9	20 33 29
14	3 49	0·02	3 23 16	9·84	18 35 7	36·4	3 27 5	20 29 33
15	3 49	0·01	3 27 12	9·86	18 49 30	35·6	3 31 2	20 25 37
16	3 49	0·03	3 31 9	9·89	19 3 34	34·8	3 34 58	20 21 41
17	3 48	0·06	3 35 7	9·91	19 17 19	34·0	3 38 55	20 17 45
18	3 46	0·08	3 39 5	9·94	19 30 44	33·1	3 42 51	20 13 49
19	3 44	0·10	3 43 4	9·96	19 43 49	32·3	3 46 48	20 9 53
20	3 41	0·13	3 47 3	9·98	19 56 35	31·5	3 50 45	20 5 57
21	3 38	0·15	3 51 3	10·01	20 9 0	30·6	3 54 41	20 2 1
22	3 34	0·17	3 55 4	10·03	20 21 4	29·8	3 58 38	19 58 5
23	3 30	0·20	3 59 5	10·05	20 32 48	28·9	4 2 34	19 54 10
24	3 25	0·22	4 3 6	10·08	20 44 10	28·0	4 6 31	19 50 14
25	3 19	0·24	4 7 8	10·10	20 55 11	27·1	4 10 27	19 46 18
26	3 13	0·26	4 11 11	10·12	21 5 51	26·2	4 14 21	19 42 22
27	3 7	0·28	4 15 14	10·14	21 16 8	25·3	4 18 20	19 38 26
28	3 0	0·30	4 19 17	10·16	21 26 4	24·4	4 22 17	19 34 30
29	2 52	0·32	4 23 21	10·18	21 35 37	23·4	4 26 14	19 30 34
30	2 44	0·34	4 27 26	10·20	21 44 48	22·5	4 30 10	19 26 38
31	2 36	0·36	4 31 31	10·21	21 53 37	21·6	4 34 7	19 22 42

METEOROLOGICAL OBSERVATIONS, MAY, 1899.

Day.	TEMPERATURE.			BAROM.	RAIN-	SUN-	WIND.	
	Maximum.	Minimum.	Avge. 50 Yrs.	Mean.	FALL.	SHINE.	(Pressure lbs. to foot.)	
				inches.	inches.	hours.	Directn.	Pressure. lbs.
1	55·2	35·3	50	29·935	...	0·3	S	1·6
2	60·7	45·7	51	29·927	...	2·5	N	1·3
3	53·8	38·2	51	29·906	...	3·3	ENE	3·3
4	53·1	33·7	51	30·110	...	9·6	ENE	2·2
5	54·2	34·3	52	30·231	...	12·2	NE	1·6
6	58·2	36·5	52	30·227	...	12·7	ENE	3·1
7	61·8	37·7	52	30·101	...	13·8	NNE	3·8
8	62·0	41·7	52	29·843	0·01	9·5	NNE	4·3
9	57·7	44·6	52	29·686	...	0·6	SW	0·6
10	57·8	41·1	52	29·736	...	3·7	NNW	0·5
11	66·1	38·3	52	29·739	...	4·5	WSW	0·6
12	65·3	43·9	52	29·750	...	6·3	SW	0·9
13	63·7	44·4	52	29·624	...	4·6	SW	1·7
14	66·0	48·0	52	29·381	0·02	0·2	S	0·8
15	59·9	47·1	52	29·266	0·37	5·2	SW	4·3
16	61·9	46·5	53	29·539	0·24	8·3	SW	7·2
17	61·7	47·8	53	29·712	0·07	6·2	SW	23·2
18	70·2	49·2	53	29·700	...	8·6	SSW	11·2
19	62·1	45·9	54	29·788	0·04	3·2	SSW	5·6
20	63·1	52·8	54	29·590	0·23	2·2	SW	12·7
21	58·5	48·5	54	29·794	0·03	1·2	NE	2·2
22	54·7	47·6	54	29·845	0·06	...	ESE	0·4
23	64·2	44·0	55	29·768	0·02	7·9	SW	7·7
24	63·7	49·2	55	29·479	0·54	4·2	SW	2·7
25	51·9	39·8	55	29·776	0·01	2·0	NNE	4·7
26	51·1	36·8	55	29·969	...	4·7	N	2·2
27	55·5	36·2	56	30·158	...	9·3	NNE	4·5
28	60·3	37·9	56	30·283	...	13·8	N	3·6
29	63·8	37·1	56	30·237	...	14·2	NE	1·3
30	67·6	37·4	57	30·201	...	14·2	SE	0·3
31	72·7	41·0	57	30·162	...	15·0	S	0·2

MEMORANDA.

1. Lamps to be lighted (8.21)

2. (8.22)

3. (8.24)

4. (8.25)

5. (8.27)

6. S. (8.28)

7. (8.29)

8. (8.30)

9. (8.32)

10. (8.34)

11. (8.36)

12. (8.38)

13. S. (8.39)

14. (8.41)

15. (8.42)

16. (8.44)

17. (8.45)

18. (8.46)

19. (8.47)

20. S. (8.48)

21. (8.50)

22. (8.51)

23. (8.53)

24. (8.55)

25. (8.56)

26. (8.58)

27. S. (8.59)

28. (9.0)

29. (9.1)

30. (9.2)

31. (9.3)

THE MOON.

Day of M.	Rises Morning.	Sets Afternoon.	Souths Afternoon.	Right Ascension at Noon.	Declination at Noon.	Horizontal Parallax at Noon.	Semidiameter at Noon.	Age at Noon.	Configurations of Jupiter's Satellites at M'night.
	H. M.	H. M.	H. M.	H. M. S.	° ′ ″	′ ″	′ ″	D. H.	
1	5 48	10 28	2 6	4 36 30	22 6 23n	58 23	15 56	2 7	3 2○1 4
2	6 41	11 19	3 2	5 35 13	22 8 39	57 31	15 42	3 7	3 1○2 4
3	7 44	11 59	3 56	6 31 37	20 56 18	56 40	15 28	4 7	4 ○3 24
4	8 51	mrn.	4 47	7 25 5	18 41 13	55 53	15 15	5 7	2○1 34
5	9 58	0 31	5 34	8 15 29	15 36 58	15 13	15 4	6 7	1 2○4 3
6	11 6	0 57	6 19	9 3 11	11 56 25	54 42	14 56	7 7	4○3 12
7	aft.	1 18	7 1	9 48 49	7 50 46	54 21	14 50	8 7	4 3○1 2
8	1 18	1 37	7 43	10 33 8	3 29 31n	54 11	14 47	9 7	4 3 2○1
9	2 24	1 58	8 24	11 16 56	0 58 49s	54 10	14 47	10 7	4○3 12
10	3 29	2 12	9 5	12 1 2	5 26 1	54 18	14 49	11 7	4○3 12
11	4 35	2 30	9 48	12 46 13	9 43 20	54 33	14 53	12 7	4 2○3●
12	5 43	2 52	10 34	13 33 9	13 40 51	54 55	14 59	13 7	4 2 1○3
13	6 52	3 16	11 22	14 22 24	17 7 13	55 22	15 7	14 7	4○1 32
14	7 58	3 46	mrn.	15 14 9	19 49 53	55 51	15 15	15 7	3 1○2 4
15	9 2	4 22	0 12	16 8 23	21 36 18	56 22	15 23	16 7	3 2○1 4
16	9 59	5 8	1 6	17 4 30	22 15 47	55 53	15 32	17 7	3 1○2 4
17	10 45	6 5	2 1	18 1 36	21 41 45	57 23	15 40	18 7	1○2 4●
18	11 24	7 12	2 56	18 58 39	19 52 26	57 51	15 47	19 7	2○3 4●
19	11 56	8 24	3 50	19 54 48	16 56 9	58 18	15 55	20 7	2 1○3 4
20	mrn.	9 42	4 44	20 49 40	13 0 9	58 42	16 1	21 7	○1 3 24
21	0 22	11 1	5 35	21 43 18	8 19 0	5) 3	16 7	22 7	1 3○2 4
22	0 46	aft.	6 26	22 36 12	3 8 14s	59 21	16 12	23 7	3 2○4 1
23	1 7	1 41	7 17	23 29 3	2 15 19n	59 34	16 15	24 7	3 41○●
24	1 30	3 2	8 8	0 23 37	7 33 38	59 40	16 17	25 7	4 3○1 2
25	1 55	4 24	9 1	1 17 37	12 27 39	59 37	16 16	26 7	4 2 1○3
26	2 21	5 45	9 55	2 14 25	16 38 5	59 25	16 13	27 7	4 4 2○3
27	2 54	7 1	10 52	3 12 56	19 47 14	59 3	16 7	28 7	4○1 23
28	3 36	8 10	11 50	4 12 27	21 41 45	58 37	15 59	29 7	4 1 3○2
29	4 26	9 7	aft.	5 11 49	22 15 28	57 54	15 48	0 21	3 4 2○1
30	5 23	9 54	1 43	6 9 40	21 30 34	57 11	15 36	1 21	3 1 4 2○
31	6 32	10 30	2 36	7 5 0	19 36 19n	56 28	15 25	2 21	3○1 42

ECLIPSES, OCCULTATIONS, AND OTHER CELESTIAL PHENOMENA.

May 1. Day breaks at 2h. 3m. morn., and Twilight ends at 9h. 51m. aft., the length of the Day being 14h. 48m.

May 1. Occultation of ι Tauri, magnitude 4½. The disappearance takes place at 8h. 58m. aft., 71° from the vertex; the reappearance at 9h. 48m. aft.; 224° from the vertex.

May 2. Venus in conjunction with the Moon, 5h. aft. ♀ 4° 55′ N.

May 4. Mercury and Mars in conjunction, 4h. morn. ☿ 2° 10′ S

May 5. Mean time of Sun's semidiameter passing the meridian, 1m. 6·1s.

May 20. Mean time of Sun's semidiameter passing the meridian, 1m. 7·4s.

May 28. Total Eclipse of the Sun visible as a partial Eclipse at Greenwich. See p. 69.

May 30. Mercury in superior conjunction with the Sun, 7h. morn.

May 31. Mercury at least distance from the Sun, 11h. morn.

May 31. Venus in conjunction with the Moon, 10h. aft. ♀ 6° 5′ N.

In this month the Mornings increase 42m., and the Afternoons 42m.

APPARENT RIGHT ASCENSION OF THE PRINCIPAL PLANETS AT MEAN NOON.

D.	☿ Mercury.	♀ Venus.	♂ Mars.	♃ Jupiter.	♄ Saturn.
	H. M. S.	H. M. S.	H. M. S.	H. M. S.	H. M. S.
1	1 1 17	5 42 37	1 7 37	16 30 8	18 20 46
6	1 28 4	6 3 27	1 21 45	16 27 57	18 20 5
11	1 58 7	6 23 13	1 35 56	16 25 36	18 19 16
16	2 31 47	6 41 37	1 50 8	16 23 6	18 18 17
21	3 9 36	6 58 22	2 4 24	16 20 29	18 17 11
26	3 51 45	7 13 8	2 18 43	16 17 49	18 15 58
31	4 37 27	7 25 34	2 33 6	16 15 8	18 14 38

APPARENT DECLINATION OF THE ABOVE PLANETS.

	° ′ ″	° ′ ″	° ′ ″	° ′ ″	° ′ ″
1	3 24 43n	26 50 33n	6 17 22n	20 55 58s	22 20 30s
6	6 18 47	26 58 18	7 45 35	20 50 27	22 20 47
11	9 35 46	26 52 39	9 11 33	20 45 21	22 21 10
16	13 7 58	26 34 46	10 34 57	20 39 54	22 21 38
21	16 44 13	26 4 6	11 55 27	20 34 8	22 22 10
26	20 1 6	25 28 9	13 12 48	20 28 2	22 22 45
31	22 53 37n	24 42 57n	14 26 39n	20 22 48	22 23 23s

MORNING AND EVENING STARS.

☿ **Mercury** is a morning star; in Pisces. Enters Aries about the 8th, and Taurus about the 22nd.

♀ **Venus** is an evening star throughout the month; in Gemini, a little north of δ on the 27th.

♂ **Mars** is a morning star; in Pisces till about the 13th, when it enters Aries.

♃ **Jupiter** in Scorpio not far from β.

♄ **Saturn** may be found a little north of λ Sagittarii.

HORIZONTAL EQUATORIAL PARALLAX OF SUN AND PLANETS.

D.	⊙	☿	♀	♂	♃	♄
	″	″	″	″	″	″
5	8 8	8 4	13 4	3 9	2 0	0 9
15	8 8	7 3	15 2	3 9	2 0	1 0
25	8 7	6 8	17 5	4 0	2 0	1 0

SEMIDIAMETER OF SUN AND PLANETS.

	⊙	☿	♀	♂	♃	♄
	′ ″	″	″	″	″	″
5	15 53	3 2	12 7	2 1	20 6	8 2
15	15 51	2 8	14 2	2 1	20 9	8 3
25	15 49	2 5	16 6	2 1	21 0	8 4

Time of High Water at the undermentioned Places—

Month.	Week.	London Bridge Morn.	After.	Liverpool Morn.	After.	Bristol Morn.	After.	Hull Morn.	After.	Greenock Morn.	After.	Leith Morn.	After.	Dublin (Bar) Morn.	After.
		H. M.	H. M.	H. M.	H. M.	H. M.	H. M.	H. M.	H. M.	H. M.	H. M.	H. M.	H. M.	H. M.	H. M.
1	Tu	2*58	3*20	0 18	0 40	8 25	8 47	7 35	7 57	1 13	1 37	3 34	3 56	...	0 19
2	W	3 42	4 3	1 2	1 23	9 8	9 29	8 19	8 40	1 59	2 20	4 19	4 41	0 42	1 4
3	Th	4 26	4 47	1 44	2 5	9 49	10 9	9 2	9 24	2 41	3 2	5 3	5 25	1 26	1 49
4	F	5 7	5 29	2 27	2 49	10 30	10 51	9 46	10 9	3 23	3 45	5 49	6 14	2 13	2 37
5	S	5 53	6 17	3 12	3 36	11 12	11 34	10 34	11 3	4 8	4 32	6 40	7 8	3 2	3 28
6	S	6 43	7 9	4 3	4 33	11 59	...	11 34	...	4 57	5 24	7 38	8 10	3 57	4 29
7	M	7 38	8 11	5 7	5 44	0 29	1 3	0 7	0 41	5 55	6 28	8 44	9 21	5 2	5 35
8	Tu	8 44	9 20	6 22	7 0	1 40	2 18	1 14	1 47	7 3	7 38	9 57	10 30	6 8	6 40
9	W	9 58	10 32	7 33	8 3	2 56	3 31	2 19	2 49	8 11	8 42	11 0	11 29	7 10	7 39
10	Th	11 2	11 28	8 29	8 53	4 3	4 30	3 18	3 44	9 9	9 34	11 53	...	8 5	8 29
11	F	11 55	...	9 14	9 33	4 55	5 17	4 4	4 29	9 57	10 19	0 16	0 36	8 53	9 15
12	S	0 18	0 38	9 52	10 10	5 38	5 58	4 49	5 11	10 39	10 59	0 55	1 13	9 36	9 55
13	S	0 57	1 16	10 28	10 46	6 18	6 37	5 26	5 44	11 19	11 39	1 32	1 50	10 12	10 29
14	M	1 35	1 53	11 5	11 23	6 56	7 15	6 3	6 22	11 58	...	2 8	2 26	10 46	11 2
15	Tu	2 11	2 28	11 42	...	7 34	7 52	6 41	6 59	0 18	0 37	2 44	3 1	11 21	11 39
16	W	2 46	3 4	0 1	0 20	8 10	8 28	7 18	7 37	0 56	1 16	3 18	3 36	11 58	...
17	Th	3 22	3 42	0 39	0 58	8 46	9 5	7 56	8 16	1 36	1 55	3 55	4 17	0 18	0 39
18	F	4 1	4 22	1 19	1 40	9 25	9 45	8 36	8 57	2 15	2 36	4 37	4 59	1 0	1 22
19	S	4 42	5 4	2 2	2 25	10 6	10 28	9 20	9 43	2 58	3 21	5 22	5 47	1 46	2 10
20	S	5 27	5 51	2 48	3 13	10 50	11 13	10 7	10 34	3 44	4 9	6 13	6 41	2 35	3 2
21	M	6 18	6 46	3 40	4 10	11 38	...	11 6	11 41	4 36	5 5	7 11	7 44	3 31	4 4
22	Tu	7 17	7 49	4 44	5 21	0 7	0 40	...	0 18	5 36	6 9	8 20	8 58	4 39	5 16
23	W	8 24	8 59	6 0	6 37	1 17	1 56	0 55	1 28	6 43	7 16	9 35	10 9	5 49	6 19
24	Th	9 35	10 9	7 11	7 43	2 32	3 7	1 58	2 27	7 48	8 21	10 39	11 8	6 48	7 18
25	F	10 42	11 15	8 14	8 44	3 41	4 14	2 57	3 29	8 54	9 26	11 38	...	7 50	8 21
26	S	11 46	...	9 12	9 37	4 46	5 16	4 0	4 30	9 56	10 24	0 7	0 33	8 51	9 20
27	S	0 15	0 42	10 2	10 26	5 44	6 11	4 53	5 18	10 51	11 17	0 58	1 23	9 47	10 10
28	M	1 9	1 33	10 51	11 14	6 37	7 1	5 43	6 8	11 43	...	1 48	2 12	10 32	10 55
29	Tu	1 57	2 20	11 38	...	7 25	7 48	6 32	6 56	0 9	0 34	2 35	2 57	11 18	11 41
30	W	2 43	3 6	0 2	0 25	8 10	8 32	7 19	7 42	0 58	1 22	3 19	3 42	...	...
31	Th	3 27	3 49	0 47	1 8	8 54	9 15	8 4	8 25	1 44	2 5	4 4	4 26	0 26	0 48

RISING, SOUTHING, and SETTING of the PRINCIPAL PLANETS at intervals of Seven Days.

D.	Mercury ☿ Rises	Souths	Sets	Venus ♀ Rises	Souths	Sets	Mars ♂ Rises	Souths	Sets	Jupiter ♃ Rises	Souths	Sets	Saturn ♄ Rises	Souths	Sets
	h. m.	h. m.	h. m.	h. m.	h. m.	h. m.	h. m.	h. m.	h. m.	h. m.	h. m.	h. m.	h. m.	h. m.	h. m.
7	3 55M	10 34M	5 12A	6 23M	3 8A	11 53A	3 41M	10 25M	5 9A	9 16A	1 30M	5 40M	11 17A	3 22M	7 23A
14	3 47M	10 51M	5 55A	6 24M	3 7A	11 50A	3 22M	10 17M	5 12A	8 44A	0 59M	5 10M	10 49A	2 53M	6 53A
21	3 43M	11 15M	6 47A	6 27M	3 4A	11 41A	3 5M	10 10M	5 15A	8 12A	0 28M	4 40M	10 20A	2 24M	6 24A
28	3 45M	11 47M	7 49A	6 26M	2 56A	11 26A	2 47M	10 2M	5 17A	7 38A	11 52A	4 11M	9 51A	1 54M	5 54A

Apparent Right Ascension and Declination of the Pole Star.					Angular Distance of the Moon from Spica Virginis.						
	R. A.		Decl. N.			Position of Star.	6 P.M.		9 P.M.		Midnight.
D.	H. M. S.		° ′ ″		D.		° ′ ″		° ′ ″		° ′ ″
1	1 22 1·2		88 46 30		5	East	76 43 54		75 12 32		73 41 23
10	1 22 5·6		88 46 28		6	East	64 38 45		63 8 56		61 39 16
19	1 22 12·0		88 46 26		7	East	52 43 55		51 15 3		49 46 15
28	1 22 19·3		88 46 24		8	East	40 54 28		39 25 56		37 57 24

Towards the end of May we shall find the constellations Draco, Hercules, Ophiuchus, and Scorpio on the meridian about midnight.

Hercules contains a very splendid cluster of stars situated in R.A. 16h. 38m. 8s., and Decl. 36° 41′ N. This, like most of the star-clusters, is condensed in the centre, and may be easily seen with moderate telescopic aid; and a few days about the 1st and 28th, when the Moon is absent, it may, if the opportunity is taken of a very clear night, be seen with the naked eye, plainly, between the stars ζ and η Herculis, rather nearer to η. This cluster, discovered by Halley in 1714, is one of the most beautiful examples of these bodies to be seen in the heavens. With the great Refractor of the Lick Observatory the nebulous glow at the centre has been resolved into separate points.

Uranus can be observed well in this month, see p. 73.

DAY OF		Fasts and Festivals. Remarkable Days—Events. SUN ENTERS CANCER 21d. 10h. A. SUMMER COMMENCES.	THE SUN		DAYS	
M.	Light and Dark. / W.		Rises.	Sets.	of the Year.	to end of Year.
			H. M.	H. M.		
1	F	*St. Nicomede.* EASTER LAW SITT. END. Oxf. Term	3 51	8 5	152	213
2	S	Oxford Trinity Term begins. [ends.	3 50	8 6	153	212
3	☉	𝕎𝕙𝕚𝕥-𝕊𝕦𝕟𝕕𝕒𝕪. 𝕡𝕖𝕟𝕥𝕖𝕔𝕠𝕤𝕥. Duke of York b. 1865	3 49	8 7	154	211
4	M	𝕎𝕙𝕚𝕥𝕤𝕦𝕟 𝕄𝕠𝕟𝕕𝕒𝕪. Bank Holiday. Ld. Wolseley	3 48	8 8	155	210
5	Tu	𝕎𝕙𝕚𝕥𝕤𝕦𝕟 𝕋𝕦𝕖𝕤𝕕𝕒𝕪. *St. Boniface.* [b. 1833.	3 47	8 9	156	209
6	W	Ember Day. Admiral Lord Anson died, 1762.	3 47	8 9	157	208
7	Th	First Reform Bill passed, 1832.	3 47	8 10	158	207
8	F	Ember D. Charles Reade b. 1814; d. 11 Apr. 1884	3 46	8 11	159	206
9	S	Ember D. Charles Dickens d. 1870; b. 7 Feb. 1812	3 46	8 12	160	205
10	☉	𝕋𝕣𝕚𝕟𝕚𝕥𝕪 𝕊𝕦𝕟𝕕𝕒𝕪. Sir Edwin Arnold b. 1832.	3 45	8 13	161	204
11	M	𝕊𝕥. 𝔹𝕒𝕣𝕟𝕒𝕓𝕒𝕤. Sir John Franklin died, 1847.	3 45	8 14	162	203
12	Tu	TRINITY LAW SITTINGS BEGIN. Queen's Vase.	3 45	8 15	163	202
13	W	Dr. Arnold (Rugby) b. 1795. Hunt Cup.	3 45	8 15	164	201
14	Th	Corpus Christi. Marengo, 1800. Gold Cup.	3 44	8 16	165	200
15	F	Thomas Campbell d. 1844 ; b. 27 July, 1777.	3 44	8 16	166	199
16	S	Duke of Marlborough d. 1722; b. 24 June, 1650.	3 44	8 17	167	198
17	☉	𝔽𝕚𝕣𝕤𝕥 𝕊. 𝕒𝕗𝕥. 𝕋𝕣𝕚𝕟. *St. Alban, first Eng. Martyr.*	3 44	8 18	168	197
18	M	Battle of Waterloo, 1815. [destroyed, 1864.	3 44	8 18	169	196
19	Tu	Rev. C. H. Spurgeon b. '34; d. 31 Jan. '92. *Alabama*	3 44	8 18	170	195
20	W	𝕈𝕦𝕖𝕖𝕟'𝕤 𝔸𝕔𝕔𝕖𝕤𝕤𝕚𝕠𝕟 (1837). *Tr. of King Edward.*	3 44	8 18	171	194
21	Th	Marquess of Dufferin b. 1826. Vittoria, 1813.	3 44	8 19	172	193
22	F	QUEEN VICTORIA'S DAY (1897).	3 44	8 19	173	192
23	S	Clive's victory at Plassey, 1757.	3 45	8 19	174	191
24	☉	2nd 𝕊. 𝕒𝕗𝕥. 𝕋. 𝕊𝕥. 𝕁𝕠𝕙𝕟 𝔹. Ld. Kitchener, b. '50.	3 45	8 19	175	190
25	M	First Wesleyan Conf. 1784. Camb. T. ends. Q. day	3 45	8 19	176	189
26	Tu	Spithead Review (165 British Warships), 1897.	3 46	8 19	177	188
27	W	Harriet Martineau d. 1876 ; b. 12 June, 1802.	3 47	8 19	178	187
28	Th	CORONATION DAY (1838). Sir H. Lawrence b. 1806	3 47	8 19	179	186
29	F	𝕊𝕥. ℙ𝕖𝕥𝕖𝕣, 𝔸𝕡𝕠𝕤𝕥𝕝𝕖 & 𝕄𝕒𝕣𝕥𝕪𝕣.	3 47	8 19	180	185
30	S	Tower Bridge opened by Prince of Wales, 1894.	3 48	8 19	181	184

PHASES OF THE MOON.

☽ First Quarter	5d.	6h.	59m.	Morning.
○ Full Moon	13	3	38	Morning.
☾ Last Quarter	20	0	57	Morning.
● New Moon	27	1	27	Morning.

Apogee 5d. 9h. A. 251,300 | Perigee 19d. 2h. M. 229,600

RAINFALL IN JUNE, 1899.

In this month rain fell on 6 days. The total fall for the month was 0·76 inch ; *below* the average of fifty years, 1841-90, by 1·26 inch.

MONTHLY NOTES.

June 1. Overseers to give notice between this day and the 20th to Voters who have not paid all Poor Rates due on January 5th.
4. Eton celebration day.
15. Last day of the close season for freshwater fish.
19. 63 Victoria ends.
20. 64 Victoria begins. On or before this day Overseers to fix on church doors the register of persons qualified to vote for Counties.
24. Midsummer Day. Quarter Day. Sheriffs of City of London to be elected by the citizens.

THE SUN.

Day.	Before Clock.	Hrly Var. of Equa. of Time.	Right Ascension at Noon.	Hourly Var. of R. A.	Apparent Declination (Nth.) at Noon.	Hrly Var. ⊙'s Declination.	Sidereal Time at Noon.	Mean Time at Sidereal Noon.
	M. S.	S.	H. M. S.	S.	° ′ ″	″	H. M. S.	H. M. S.
1	2 27	0·37	4 35 36	10·23	22 2 2	20·6	4 38 3	19 18 46
2	2 18	0·39	4 39 42	10·25	22 10 5	19·6	4 42 0	19 14 50
3	2 8	0·40	4 43 48	10·26	22 17 44	18·7	4 45 56	19 10 55
4	1 59	0·42	4 47 54	10·28	22 25 0	17·7	4 49 53	19 6 59
5	1 48	0·43	4 52 1	10·29	22 31 53	16·7	4 53 49	19 3 3
6	1 38	0·44	4 56 8	10·30	22 38 22	15·7	4 57 46	18 59 7
7	1 27	0·45	5 0 16	10·31	22 44 27	14·7	5 1 43	18 55 11
8	1 16	0·47	5 4 23	10·33	22 50 8	13·7	5 5 39	18 51 15
9	1 5	0·48	5 8 31	10·34	22 55 25	12·7	5 9 36	18 47 19
10	0 53	0·49	5 12 39	10·35	23 0 18	11·7	5 13 32	18 43 23
11	0 41	0·50	5 16 48	10·36	23 4 46	10·7	5 17 29	18 39 27
12	0 29	0·51	5 20 56	10·36	23 8 51	9·7	5 21 25	18 35 31
13	0 17	0·51	5 25 5	10·37	23 12 31	8·7	5 25 22	18 31 35
14	0 5	0·52	5 29 14	10·38	23 15 46	7·6	5 29 19	18 27 40
15	After. 0 7	0·52	5 33 23	10·38	23 18 37	6·6	5 33 15	18 23 44
16	0 21	0·53	5 37 32	10·39	23 21 3	5·6	5 37 12	18 19 48
17	0 33	0·53	5 41 42	10·39	23 23 5	4·6	5 41 8	18 15 52
18	0 46	0·54	5 45 51	10·40	23 24 41	3·5	5 45 5	18 11 56
19	0 59	0·54	5 50 0	10·40	23 25 53	2·5	5 49 1	18 8 0
20	1 12	0·54	5 54 10	10·40	23 26 41	1·5	5 52 58	18 4 4
21	1 25	0·54	5 58 20	10·40	23 27 3	0·4	5 56 54	18 0 8
22	1 38	0·54	6 2 29	10·40	23 27 0	0·6	6 0 51	17 56 12
23	1 51	0·54	6 6 39	10·40	23 26 33	1·7	6 4 48	17 52 16
24	2 4	0·54	6 10 48	10·40	23 25 41	2·7	6 8 44	17 48 20
25	2 17	0·53	6 14 58	10·39	23 24 24	3·7	6 12 41	17 44 25
26	2 30	0·53	6 19 7	10·39	23 22 42	4·8	6 16 37	17 40 29
27	2 42	0·52	6 23 16	10·38	23 20 36	5·8	6 20 34	17 36 33
28	2 55	0·52	6 27 25	10·37	23 18 5	6·8	6 24 31	17 32 37
29	3 7	0·51	6 31 34	10·37	23 15 9	7·8	6 28 27	17 28 41
30	3 19	0·50	6 35 43	10·36	23 11 50	8·8	6 32 23	17 24 45

METEOROLOGICAL OBSERVATIONS, JUNE, 1899.

Day.	TEMPERATURE. Maximum.	Minimum.	Avge. 50 Yrs	BAROM. Mean.	RAIN-FALL.	SUN-SHINE.	WIND. Directn.	(Pressure lbs. to foot.) Prssure.
	°	°	°	inches.	inches.	hours.		lbs.
1	77·6	46·6	57	30·034	...	14·8	SE	1·9
2	80·5	54·1	57	29·933	...	11·6	WSW	3·2
3	73·2	50·8	57	30·017	...	12·3	NE	0·7
4	79·8	48·3	57	30·050	...	11·7	E	1·0
5	81·5	50·0	57	30·095	...	10·0	SSW	0·5
6	80·9	51·5	57	30·098	...	12·5	ENE	0·6
7	74·8	51·7	57	30·148	...	13·1	E	3·0
8	62·2	48·3	57	30·235	...	8·5	NE	2·8
9	65·7	47·3	58	30·204	...	6·2	NNE	2·4
10	68·0	46·4	58	30·125	...	10·1	NE	1·4
11	63·1	45·2	59	30·083	...	6·7	NE	0·8
12	75·8	47·5	59	29·943	...	10·1	NE	1·2
13	61·1	46·9	59	29·936	...	5·4	NNE	3·5
14	60·9	42·1	59	29·913	...	4·6	NNE	1·2
15	72·0	42·5	59	29·944	...	14·4	NNE	0·5
16	64·0	44·0	59	29·889	...	14·9	NE	0·8
17	77·1	47·8	59	29·829	...	11·9	ESE	0·7
18	75·0	50·4	59	29·611	0·07	7·2	SW	1·7
19	67·1	52·0	59	29·445	0·01	5·3	NW	2·9
20	71·9	56·0	60	29·240	0·25	2·9	SSE	4·7
21	73·0	53·4	60	29·413	...	6·3	S	1·7
22	65·2	55·0	61	29·519	0·18	...	N	1·8
23	64·7	54·9	61	29·722	...	...	NNE	0·5
24	71·1	54·0	61	29·890	...	4·5	NNW	2·6
25	65·1	51·2	62	30·009	...	1·2	WNW	1·3
26	80·8	57·4	62	30·052	0·01	10·5	W	2·1
27	71·1	52·8	62	30·124	...	3·1	NE	2·3
28	76·2	51·5	62	29·782	...	4·8	E	2·2
29	76·5	57·2	62	29·664	...	10·4	W	3·0
30	73·0	52·3	62	29·739	0·24	7·3	WSW	3·1

MEMORANDA.

1. Lamps to be lighted (9.5)
2. (9.6)
3. S. (9.7)
4. (9.8)
5. (9.9)
6. (9.9)
7. (9.10)
8. (9.11)
9. (9.12)
10. S. (9.13)
11. (9.14)
12. (9.15)
13. (9.15)
14. (9.16)
15. (9.16)
16. (9.17)
17. S. (9.18)
18. (9.18)
19. (9.18)
20. (9.18)
21. (9.19)
22. (9.19)
23. (9.19)
24. S. (9.19)
25. (9.19)
26. (9.19)
27. (9.19)
28. (9.19)
29. (9.19)
30. (9.19)

JUNE SIXTH MONTH.

The Moon.

Day of M.	Rises Morning. H.	M.	Sets Afternoon. H.	M.	Souths Afternoon. H.	M.	Right Ascension at Noon. H.	M.	S.	Declination at Noon. °	′	″	Horizontal Parallax at Noon. ′	″	Semidiameter at Noon. ′	″	Age at Noon. D.	H.	Configurations of Jupiter's Satellites at 11h. P.M.
1	7	40	10	59	3	26	7	57	19	16	46	1n	55	47	15	13	3	21	12○34
2	8	49	11	21	4	12	8	46	40	13	13	50	55	11	15	4	4	21	2○134
3	9	57	11	42	4	56	9	33	31	9	12	45	54	43	14	56	5	21	○234●
4	11	3	mrn.		5	38	10	18	3	4	53	47	54	24	14	51	6	21	13○24
5	aft.		0	0	6	19	11	2	37	0	26	13n	54	15	14	48	7	21	32○14
6	1	15	0	17	7	1	11	46	30	4	1	46s	54	16	14	49	8	21	312○4
7	2	20	0	35	7	43	12	31	6	8	22	3	54	28	14	52	9	21	3○142
8	3	28	0	55	8	27	13	17	12	12	25	52	54	48	14	57	10	21	♃14○3
9	4	36	1	17	9	14	14	5	28	16	2	59	55	16	15	5	11	21	42○13
10	5	43	1	45	10	3	14	56	24	19	1	32	55	50	15	14	12	21	41○23
11	6	49	2	17	10	55	15	50	8	21	8	28	56	28	15	25	13	21	41○32
12	7	49	3	0	11	51	16	46	20	22	11	14	57	6	15	35	14	21	432○1
13	8	41	3	54	mrn.		17	44	9	22	0	17	57	42	15	45	15	21	4321○
14	9	23	4	59	0	48	18	42	27	20	31	52	58	14	15	54	16	21	43○12
15	9	58	6	12	1	44	19	40	6	17	49	26	58	41	16	1	17	21	41○23
16	10	26	7	29	2	39	20	36	21	14	3	7	59	0	16	6	18	21	2○413
17	10	52	8	49	3	32	21	31	1	9	27	44	59	13	16	10	19	21	1○243
18	11	12	10	10	4	24	22	24	23	4	20	27s	59	20	16	12	20	21	♃○324
19	11	35	11	31	5	14	23	17	4	1	0	54n	59	20	16	12	21	21	32○14
20	11	58	aft.		6	5	0	9	49	6	18	31	59	15	16	10	22	21	321○4
21	mrn.		2	10	6	56	1	3	26	11	14	55	59	6	16	8	23	21	3○124
22	0	25	3	28	7	49	1	58	28	15	32	59	58	52	16	4	24	21	1○234
23	0	55	4	44	8	43	2	55	8	18	56	46	58	33	15	59	25	21	2○143
24	1	32	5	55	9	39	3	53	7	21	12	57	58	9	15	52	26	21	1○43●
25	2	17	6	57	10	35	4	51	36	22	13	9	57	41	15	45	27	21	4○132
26	3	13	7	47	11	32	5	49	25	21	55	41	57	9	15	36	28	21	432○●
27	4	16	8	27	aft.		6	45	26	20	25	57	56	34	15	26	0	11	4321○
28	5	23	8	59	1	17	7	38	54	17	54	44	56	0	15	17	1	11	43○12
29	6	32	9	25	2	5	8	29	34	14	35	31	55	27	15	8	2	11	41○2●
30	7	40	9	46	2	59	9	17	35	10	42	1n	54	58	15	0	3	11	42○13

Apparent Right Ascension of the Principal Planets at Mean Noon.

D.	☿ Mercury. H.	M.	S.	♀ Venus. H.	M.	S.	♂ Mars. H.	M.	S.	♃ Jupiter. H.	M.	S.	♄ Saturn. H.	M.	S.
5	5	24	25	7	35	8	2	47	32	16	12	29	18	13	12
10	6	9	48	7	41	26	3	2	3	16	9	55	18	11	43
15	6	51	22	7	43	57	3	16	37	16	7	29	18	10	10
20	7	28	2	7	42	21	3	31	15	16	5	12	18	8	36
25	7	59	22	7	36	32	3	45	57	16	3	7	18	7	0
30	8	25	14	7	26	52	4	0	41	16	1	15	18	5	25

Apparent Declination of the above Planets.

D.	☿ °	′	″	♀ °	′	″	♂ °	′	″	♃ °	′	″	♄ °	′	″
5	24	41	6n	23	52	32n	15	36	44n	20	16	0s	22	24	4s
10	25	20	21	22	59	0	16	42	49	20	10	4	22	24	45
15	24	57	18	22	4	16	17	44	41	20	4	24	22	25	27
20	23	45	49	21	9	55	18	42	6	19	59	6	22	26	10
25	22	1	4	20	17	13	19	34	53	19	54	18	22	26	51
30	19	57	3n	19	27	14n	20	22	51n	19	50	7s	22	27	32s

Horizontal Equatorial Parallax of Sun and Planets.

D.	☉ ″		☿ ″		♀ ″		♂ ″		♃ ″		♄ ″	
5	8	7	6	9	20	8	4	0	2	0	1	0
15	8	7	7	7	24	4	4	1	2	0	1	0
25	8	7	9	0	28	1	4	1	2	0	1	0

Semidiameter of Sun and Planets.

D.	☉ ′	″	☿ ″		♀ ″		♂ ″		♃ ″		♄ ″	
5	15	47	2	6	19	8	2	1	21	0	8	5
15	15	46	2	9	23	2	2	1	20	8	8	5
25	15	45	3	4	26	7	2	2	20	5	8	5

Mean Longitude of Moon's Ascending Node, June 1, 251°.8′ ♐.

Eclipses, Occultations, and other Celestial Phenomena.

June 1. There is no real night in this month, but either daylight or twilight; the length of the Day being 16*h.* 14*m.*

June 1. Venus at greatest brilliancy, 6*h. morn.*

June 2. Occultation of κ Cancri, magnitude 5. The disappearance takes place at 8*h.* 33*m. aft.*, 82° from the vertex; the reappearance at 9*h.* 35*m. aft.*, 247° from the vertex.

June 5. Mean time of Sun's semidiameter passing the meridian, 1*m.* 8·4*s.*

June 11. Jupiter in conjunction with the Moon, 8*h. aft.* ♃ 1° 29′ N.

June 13. A partial Eclipse of the Moon, partly visible at Greenwich. See p. 69.

June 13. Mercury in conjunction with ε Geminorum, 7*h. aft.*, ☿ 0° 3′ S.

June 13. Occultation of Saturn. The disappearance takes place at 9*h.* 40*m aft.*, 116° from the vertex; the reappearance at 10*h.* 52*m. aft.*, 283° from the vertex.

June 13. Saturn in conjunction with the Moon, 11*h. aft.* ♃ 0° 56′ S.

June 20. Mean time of Sun's semidiameter passing the meridian, 1*m.* 8·7*s.*

June 21. Sun enters Cancer. Summer commences, 10*h. aft.*

In this month the Mornings increase 3*m.*, and the Afternoons 14*m.*

MORNING AND EVENING STARS.

☿ Mercury is an evening star; in Taurus. Enters Gemini about the 8th, a little north of μ and η on the 10th. Enters Cancer about the 23rd.

♀ Venus is an evening star; in Germini.

♂ Mars is a morning star; in Aries till about the 13th, when it enters Taurus.

♃ Jupiter may be seen very near to β Scorpii at the end of the month.

♄ Saturn almost stationary in Sagittarius.

JUNE SIXTH MONTH.

Time of High Water at the undermentioned Places—

Month Day of	Week	LONDON BRIDGE Morn.	LONDON BRIDGE After.	LIVERPOOL Morn.	LIVERPOOL After.	BRISTOL Morn.	BRISTOL After.	HULL Morn.	HULL After.	GREENOCK Morn.	GREENOCK After.	LEITH Morn.	LEITH After.	DUBLIN (Bar.) Morn.	DUBLIN (Bar.) After.
		H. M.	H. M.	H. M.	H. M.	H. M.	H. M.	H. M.	H. M.	H. M.	H. M.	H. M.	H. M.	H. M.	H. M.
1	F	4 10	4 32	1 29	1 49	9 35	9 54	8 46	9 7	2 26	2 46	4 48	5 9	1 10	1 32
2	S	4 52	5 10	1 29	1 49	10 13	10 32	9 27	9 47	3 5	3 24	5 30	5 51	1 53	2 14
3	S	5 30	5 52	2 49	3 10	10 51	11 11	10 8	10 31	3 44	4 6	6 14	6 38	2 36	2 59
4	M	6 15	6 38	3 32	3 55	11 31	11 52	10 56	11 23	4 28	4 50	7 2	7 27	3 22	3 46
5	Tu	7 1	7 25	4 19	4 45	...	0 15	11 51	...	5 12	5 36	7 54	8 22	4 13	4 41
6	W	7 50	8 18	5 15	5 49	0 41	1 11	0 20	0 49	6 4	6 31	8 53	9 27	5 10	5 40
7	Th	8 49	9 23	6 25	6 59	1 45	2 20	1 19	1 49	6 58	7 37	9 59	10 29	6 10	6 39
8	F	9 57	10 27	7 29	7 58	2 54	3 27	2 18	2 45	8 7	8 37	10 57	11 24	7 7	7 34
9	S	10 57	11 25	8 25	8 51	3 58	4 27	3 13	3 40	9 5	...	11 50	...	7 57	8 27
10	S	11 53	...	9 14	9 36	4 53	5 17	4 5	4 29	9 57	10 22	0 14	0 36	8 52	9 18
11	M	0 17	0 41	9 58	10 19	5 41	6 4	4 52	5 14	10 46	11 9	0 57	1 19	9 42	10 3
12	Tu	1 3	1 25	10 40	11 1	6 27	6 49	5 35	5 56	11 32	11 54	1 41	2 2	10 23	10 43
13	W	1 47	2 7	11 22	11 43	7 11	7 33	6 18	6 40	...	0 17	2 22	2 43	11 3	11 23
14	Th	2 27	2 48	...	0 6	7 54	8 14	7 1	7 23	0 39	1 1	3 3	3 23	11 44	...
15	F	3 8	3 29	0 27	0 48	8 35	8 55	7 44	8 5	1 23	1 45	3 43	4 4	0 5	0 27
16	S	3 50	4 12	1 9	1 32	9 16	9 38	8 27	8 49	2 6	2 28	4 26	4 50	0 49	1 13
17	S	4 34	4 56	1 55	2 18	10 0	10 22	9 12	9 36	2 51	3 14	5 14	5 38	1 37	2 2
18	M	5 19	5 44	2 42	3 5	10 45	11 7	10 1	10 26	3 38	4 2	6 4	6 31	2 27	2 53
19	Tu	6 10	6 35	3 30	3 56	11 30	11 54	10 53	11 23	4 27	4 52	6 59	7 27	3 20	3 48
20	W	7 2	7 30	4 21	4 54	...	0 20	11 55	...	5 18	5 46	7 57	8 30	4 17	4 49
21	Th	7 59	8 29	5 28	6 4	0 50	1 24	0 28	1 1	6 16	6 48	8 55	9 40	5 22	5 54
22	F	9 5	9 39	6 41	7 16	2 0	2 36	1 33	2 3	7 21	7 54	10 13	10 44	6 24	6 54
23	S	10 13	10 47	7 49	8 19	3 12	3 47	2 33	3 4	8 27	9 1	11 15	11 46	7 25	7 57
24	S	11 22	11 56	8 53	9 22	4 22	4 55	3 36	4 8	9 35	10 7	...	0 16	8 30	9 2
25	M	...	0 26	9 49	10 15	5 26	5 55	4 38	5 8	10 37	11 5	0 44	1 11	9 32	10 0
26	Tu	0 55	1 21	10 40	11 4	6 23	6 50	5 31	5 56	11 32	11 58	1 37	2 2	10 24	10 46
27	W	1 47	2 10	11 27	11 49	7 15	7 37	6 21	6 45	...	0 22	2 26	2 47	11 7	11 27
28	Th	2 32	2 52	...	0 10	7 58	8 19	7 7	7 28	0 44	1 6	3 7	3 27	11 48	...
29	F	3 13	3 33	0 31	0 51	8 38	8 58	7 48	8 8	1 27	1 48	3 47	4 8	0 9	0 30
30	S	3 53	4 13	1 10	1 29	9 17	9 35	8 27	8 46	2 7	2 25	4 28	4 47	0 50	1 10

RISING, SOUTHING, and SETTING of the PRINCIPAL PLANETS at intervals of Seven Days.

D.	MERCURY ☿ Rises h. m.	MERCURY ☿ Souths h. m.	MERCURY ☿ Sets h. m.	VENUS ♀ Rises h. m.	VENUS ♀ Souths h. m.	VENUS ♀ Sets h. m.	MARS ♂ Rises h. m.	MARS ♂ Souths h. m.	MARS ♂ Sets h. m.	JUPITER ♃ Rises h. m.	JUPITER ♃ Sths h. m.	JUPITER ♃ Sets h. m.	SATURN ♄ Rises h. m.	SATURN ♄ Souths h. m.	SATURN ♄ Sets h. m.
4	4 1M	0 25A	8 49A	6 22M	2 43A	11 4A	2 30M	9 55M	5 20A	7 7A	1121A	3 40M	9 21A	1 26M	5 26M
11	4 31M	1 1A	9 31A	6 11M	2 24A	10 37A	2 15M	9 48M	5 21A	6 35A	1050A	3 9M	8 52A	0 56M	4 55M
18	5 6M	1 29A	9 52A	5 55M	1 58A	10 1A	1 57M	9 40M	5 23A	6 3A	1019A	2 40M	8 22A	0 26M	4 26M
25	5 40M	1 47A	9 54A	5 29M	1 24A	9 19A	1 42M	9 33M	5 24A	5 32A	9 49A	2 10M	7 52A	11 52A	3 57M

APPARENT RIGHT ASCENSION AND DECLINATION OF THE POLE STAR.			
	R. A.		DECL. N.
D.	H. M. S.		° ′ ″
1	1 22 22·6		88 46 23
10	1 22 30·8		88 46 22
19	1 22 39·4		88 46 21
28	1 22 49·1		88 46 21

ANGULAR DISTANCE OF THE MOON FROM REGULUS.				
D.	Position of Star.	6 P.M.	9 P.M.	Midnight.
		° ′ ″	° ′ ″	° ′ ″
7	West	45 13 25	46 42 35	48 11 57
8	West	57 12 27	58 43 18	60 14 22
9	West	69 25 57	70 58 46	72 31 51
10	West	81 56 8	83 31 9	85 6 28

In the last week of June the constellations Draco, Lyra, a portion of Hercules, Scutum Sobieski, and a part of Sagittarius will south about midnight.

In Sagittarius there is a notable and very extensive Nebula, known as the "Horse-shoe," from its peculiar shape. It will be found in R.A. 18h. 14m. 51s., and Decl. 16 15′ S. The spectroscope shows this Nebula to consist of a mass of incandescent gas. Professor Holden says that one arm of the Nebula has changed its position since Herschel's time. In shape it somewhat resembles the great Nebula in Andromeda.

In Sagittarius, a little West and North of λ, is a globular cluster of very small stars, densely crowded, to be seen only with difficulty in small telescopes. Owing to its great southern declination there is but little chance of seeing this Nebula except when southing. The evenings about the 27th will be the most favourable for observing it.

DAY OF			Fasts and Festivals. Remarkable Days—Events. SUN ENTERS LEO 23d. 8h. M.	THE SUN		DAYS	
M.	Light and Dark.	W.		Rises.	Sets.	of the Year.	to end of Year.
				H. M.	H. M.		
1		S	**Third Sunday after Trinity.** DOMINION DAY.	3 49	8 19	182	183
2		M	*Visitation.* Union of Gt. Britain and Ireland, 1800	3 49	8 19	183	182
3		Tu	Destruction of Spanish Fleet off Santiago, 1898.	3 50	8 18	184	181
4		W	Independence Day, U.S.A. (1776). Ulundi, '79	3 51	8 17	185	180
5		Th	Rt. Hon. C. J. Rhodes b. 1853. Bp. of London, b '43	3 51	8 17	186	179
6		F	Pcss. Victoria of Wales born 1868. D. of York	3 52	8 16	187	178
7		S	Oxford Trinity Term ends. [married, 1893.	3 53	8 16	188	177
8		S	**Fourth S. aft. Trin.** Rt. Hn. Joseph Chamberlain	3 54	8 16	189	176
9		M	Earl of Minto, G.C.M.G., born 1845. [b. 1836.	3 55	8 15	190	175
10		Tu	Sir William Blackstone b. 1723; d. 14 Feb. 1780.	3 56	8 14	191	174
11		W	Bombardment of Alexandria, 1882.	3 57	8 13	192	173
12		Th	Evacuation of the Crimea commenced, 1856.	3 58	8 12	193	172
13		F	Berlin Treaty, "Peace with Honour," signed, '78.	3 59	8 11	194	171
14		S	Storming of the Bastille, 1789.	4 1	8 11	195	170
15		S	**Fifth Sunday after Trinity.** *St. Swithun.*	4 2	8 10	196	169
16		M	Sir Joshua Reynolds, first P. R. A., born 1723.	4 3	8 9	197	168
17		Tu	France declared war against Prussia, 1870.	4 5	8 8	198	167
18		W	Bishop of Ely born, 1825. W. G. Grace b. 1848.	4 6	8 7	199	166
19		Th	H.R.H. the Duke of Albany, born 1884.	4 7	8 5	200	165
20		F	*St. Margaret.* Army purchase abolished, 1871.	4 8	8 4	201	164
21		S	Federal defeat at Bull Run, 1861.	4 10	8 2	202	163
22		S	**Sixth Sun. aft. Trinity.** *St. Mary Magdalene*	4 11	8 1	203	162
23		M	Duke of Devonshire born, 1833.	4 12	8 0	204	161
24		Tu	Gibraltar captd., 1705. Window Tax abolished, '51	4 14	7 58	205	160
25		W	**S. James, A. & M.** Rt. Hon. A. J. Balfour b. '48.	4 15	7 57	206	159
26		Th	*St. Anne.* The Irish Church disestablished, '69	4 16	7 56	207	158
27		F	Talavera 1809. Killiecrankie, 1689.	4 17	7 55	208	157
28		S	The *Alabama* sailed from the Mersey, 1862.	4 19	7 53	209	156
29		S	**Seventh S. aft. T.** Sir G. Faudel-Phillips b. '40	4 20	7 52	210	155
30		M	Prince Bismarck died, 1898; born 1 Apr. 1815.	4 21	7 51	211	154
31		Tu	Van Tromp, Dutch Admiral, killed, 1653.	4 23	7 49	212	153

PHASES OF THE MOON.

☽ First Quarter	5d.	0h.	14m.	Morning.
○ Full Moon	12	1	22	Afternoon.
☾ Last Quarter	19	5	31	Morning.
● New Moon	26	1	43	Afternoon.

Apogee 3d. 3h. A. 251,300 | Perigee 15d. 2h. A. 227,100
Apogee 31d. 9h. M. 251,900.

RAINFALL IN JULY, 1899.
In this month rain fell on 8 days. The total fall for the month was 1·74 inch; *below* the average of fifty years, 1841-90, by 0·73 inch.

MONTHLY NOTES.

July 1. Special Sessions for Licences to deal in Game to be held this month.—Quarter Sessions held this week.

5. Dividends due. 8. Old Quarter Day. 9. Fire Insurances to be paid.

14. Glasgow Fair Saturday.

20. Rates and Taxes due January 5th must be paid on or before this day by Voters to prevent disqualification.—Last day for County and Parochial Electors to send in their claims to vote.

THE SUN.

Day	After Clock.	Hrly Var. of Equa. of Time.	Right Ascension at Noon.	Hourly Var. of R.A.	Apparent Declination (Nth.) at Noon.	H.ly Var. (+)'s Declination.	Sidereal Time at Noon.	Mean Time at Sidereal Noon.
	M. S.	S.	H. M. S.	S.	° ′ ″	″	H. M. S.	H. M. S.
1	3 31	0·49	6 39 51	10·35	23 8 5	9·9	6 36 20	17 20 49
2	3 43	0·48	6 43 59	10·33	23 3 57	10·9	6 40 17	17 16 53
3	3 54	0·46	6 40 7	10·32	22 59 24	11·9	6 44 13	17 12 57
4	4 5	0·45	6 52 15	10·31	22 54 28	12·9	6 48 10	17 9 1
5	4 16	0·44	6 56 24	10·29	22 49 7	13·9	6 52 6	17 5 5
6	4 26	0·42	7 0 29	10·28	22 43 23	14·8	6 56 3	17 1 10
7	4 36	0·41	7 4 35	10·26	22 37 15	15·8	6 59 59	16 57 14
8	4 45	0·39	7 8 41	10·25	22 30 44	16·8	7 3 56	16 53 18
9	4 55	0·37	7 12 47	10·23	22 23 49	17·8	7 7 52	16 49 22
10	5 3	0·35	7 16 52	10·21	22 16 31	18·7	7 11 49	16 45 26
11	5 12	0·34	7 20 57	10·19	22 8 50	19·7	7 15 46	16 41 30
12	5 19	0·32	7 25 2	10·18	22 0 47	20·6	7 19 42	16 37 34
13	5 27	0·30	7 29 5	10·16	21 52 20	21·6	7 23 39	16 33 38
14	5 34	0·28	7 33 9	10·14	21 43 31	22·5	7 27 35	16 29 42
15	5 40	0·26	7 37 12	10·12	21 34 20	23·4	7 31 32	16 25 46
16	5 46	0·24	7 41 15	10·10	21 24 47	24·3	7 35 28	16 21 50
17	5 52	0·23	7 45 17	10·08	21 14 52	25·3	7 39 25	16 17 54
18	5 57	0·20	7 49 18	10·05	21 4 35	26·2	7 43 21	16 13 59
19	6 1	0·18	7 53 19	10·03	20 53 57	27·0	7 47 18	16 10 3
20	6 5	0·15	7 57 20	10·01	20 42 57	27·9	7 51 15	16 6 7
21	6 8	0·13	8 1 20	9·99	20 31 37	28·8	7 55 11	16 2 11
22	6 11	0·11	8 5 19	9·97	20 19 56	29·7	7 59 8	15 58 15
23	6 14	0·09	8 9 18	9·94	20 7 54	30·5	8 3 4	15 54 19
24	6 15	0·06	8 13 16	9·92	19 55 32	31·3	8 7 1	15 50 23
25	6 17	0·04	8 17 14	9·89	19 42 50	32·0	8 10 57	15 46 27
26	6 17	0·01	8 21 11	9·87	19 29 48	33·0	8 14 54	15 42 31
27	6 17	0·01	8 25 8	9·84	19 16 27	33·8	8 18 50	15 38 35
28	6 17	0·04	8 29 4	9·82	19 2 47	34·6	8 22 47	15 34 39
29	6 15	0·00	8 32 59	9·79	18 48 48	35·4	8 26 44	15 30 44
30	6 14	0·09	8 36 54	9·77	18 34 30	36·1	8 30 40	15 26 48
31	6 11	0·11	8 40 48	9·74	18 19 55	36·9	8 34 37	15 22 52

METEOROLOGICAL OBSERVATIONS, JULY, 1899.

Day	Temperature Maximum	Temperature Minimum	Temperature Avge. 50 Yrs.	Barom. Mean.	Rain-fall.	Sun-shine.	Wind Directn.	Wind Pressure. (Pressure lbs. to foot.)
	°	°	°	inches.	inches.	hours.		lbs.
1	68·7	53·9	62	29·354	0·49	6·6	SW	7·7
2	65·0	51·9	62	29·463	0·11	3·8	WSW	5·6
3	61·9	54·0	62	29·735	0·02	0·2	WNW	4·2
4	67·3	54·8	62	29·924	...	2·5	NW	4·6
5	73·1	52·4	62	30·052	...	10·6	NNW	0·7
6	77·0	57·5	62	30·055	...	1·8	V'ble	0·2
7	80·1	54·8	62	30·063	...	6·7	N	0·3
8	78·8	56·7	62	30·001	...	5·8	W	0·8
9	79·5	56·2	62	29·934	...	8·7	WSW	0·5
10	75·0	59·2	62	29·878	...	2·7	SW	2·1
11	83·1	59·1	62	29·729	0·09	11·8	S	2·2
12	82·3	59·2	62	29·650	...	6·9	SSW	1·8
13	75·1	56·5	62	29·819	...	4·9	WSW	1·4
14	75·1	50·9	63	29·940	...	6·9	SSW	2·3
15	74·0	57·5	63	30·010	..	7·5	WSW	1·3
16	76·7	52·9	63	30·015	...	4·8	SW	0·1
17	79·1	51·4	62	29·940	...	11·0	E	1·2
18	81·0	56·7	62	29·915	...	12·8	SE	0·7
19	88·1	59·5	62	29·793	...	13·8	S	2·0
20	86·0	60·1	62	29·786	...	11·8	E	2·0
21	83·5	62·4	62	29·836	...	10·7	WSW	1·0
22	81·8	62·3	62	29·768	0·06	6·1	NE	1·0
23	67·1	57·7	62	29·645	0·95	...	N	1·0
24	72·7	57·4	62	29·815	0·01	6·5	NNW	3·0
25	78·1	55·2	62	30·012	...	11·5	WNW	1·4
26	81·5	60·2	62	30·027	0·01	11·7	W	3·7
27	72·0	56·9	62	30·160	...	11·4	NNW	1·7
28	76·2	49·2	62	30·149	...	11·1	NNW	1·2
29	83·0	50·5	62	30·037	...	11·4	NW	2·1
30	82·2	60·8	62	30·115	...	14·2	NNE	1·0
31	74·9	56·5	62	30·284	...	11·5	E	2·9

MEMORANDA.

1. ☉. Lamps to be lighted (9.19)
2. (9.19)
3. (9.18)
4. (9.17)
5. (9.17)
6. (9.16)
7. (9.16)
8. ☽. (9.16)
9. (9.15)
10. (9.14)
11. (9.13)
12. (9.12)
13. (9.11)
14. (9.11)
15. ☽. (9.10)
16. (9.9)
17. (9.8)
18. (9.7)
19. (9.5)
20. (9.4)
21. (9.2)
22. ☽. (9.1)
23. (9.0)
24. (8.58)
25. (8.57)
26. (8.56)
27. (8.55)
28. (8.53)
29. ☽. (8.52)
30. (8.51)
31. (8.49)

THE MOON.

Day of M.	Rises Morning.	Sets Afternoon.	Souths Afternoon.	Right Ascension at Noon.	Declination at Noon.	Horizontal Parallax at Noon.	Semi-diameter at Noon.	Age at Noon.	Configuration of Jupiter's Satellites at 10h. P.M.
	H. M.	H. M.	H. M.	H. M. S.	° ' "	' "	' "	D. H.	
1	8 48	10 5	3 33	10 3 32	10 3 32n	6 26 37n	54 34	14 54	4 11	4 1 2 O 3
2	9 54	10 24	4 15	10 48 5	1 59 58n	54 19	14 50	5 11	4 O 1 3 2
3	11 0	10 40	5 1	11 32 1	2 28 54s	54 13	14 48	6 11	3 1 2 O 4
4	aft.	11 0	5 38	12 16 10	6 51 44	54 16	14 49	7 11	4 3 2 O 4
5	1 11	11 19	6 20	13 1 21	11 0 24	54 30	14 53	8 11	3 O 1 2 4
6	2 18	11 44	7 5	13 48 18	14 45 57	54 54	14 59	9 11	1 3 O 2 4
7	3 25	mrn.	7 53	14 37 41	17 58 1	55 28	15 8	10 11	2 O 1 3 4
8	4 32	0 15	8 44	15 29 53	20 24 43	56 8	15 19	11 11	1 2 O 3 4
9	5 34	0 52	9 38	16 25 11	21 53 18	56 53	15 32	12 11	O 1 2 3 4
10	6 30	1 41	10 35	17 22 17	22 12 8	57 40	15 45	13 11	4 3 1 O 2
11	7 18	2 42	11 32	18 21 0	21 13 28	58 25	15 57	14 11	4 3 2 4 O
12	7 57	3 51	mrn.	19 19 56	18 56 13	59 5	16 7	15 11	3 ₵ C 2 ●
13	8 29	5 9	0 29	20 18 10	15 24 41	59 35	16 16	16 11	4 1 3 O 2
14	8 55	6 30	1 24	21 14 39	11 0 8	59 53	16 21	17 11	4 2 O 1 3
15	9 20	7 54	2 18	22 9 50	5 53 25	60 0	16 23	18 11	4 1 2 O 3
16	9 42	9 1	3 10	23 3 56	0 27 19s	59 55	16 21	19 11	4 O 1 2 3
17	10 5	10 3	4 2	23 57 34	4 57 59n	59 41	16 17	20 11	4 3 1 2 O
18	10 30	11 57	4 53	0 51 27	9 59 50	59 20	16 12	21 11	3 1 2 O 1
19	10 58	aft.	5 46	1 46 11	14 31 58	58 54	16 4	22 11	3 4 O ●
20	11 32	2 34	6 39	2 42 2	18 8 20	58 25	15 57	23 11	3 1 O 4 2
21	mrn.	3 46	7 34	3 38 58	20 40 24	57 54	15 49	24 11	2 O 1 3 4
22	0 14	4 48	8 29	4 36 23	22 0 9	57 24	15 40	25 11	2 1 O 3 4
23	1 5	5 43	9 25	5 33 27	22 4 55	56 53	15 31	26 11	O 1 2 3 4
24	2 4	6 26	10 19	6 29 12	20 57 52	56 22	15 23	27 11	2 1 O 2 4
25	3 9	7 0	11 10	7 22 50	18 47 19	55 53	15 15	28 11	3 2 O 1
26	4 16	7 27	11 59	8 14 c	15 44 48	55 25	15 7	29 11	3 1 O 4 ●
27	5 27	7 50	aft.	9 2 43	12 3 11	54 59	15 0	0 22	4 2 3 O 2
28	6 34	8 11	1 29	9 49 20	7 55 3	54 37	14 54	1 22	2 4 O 1 3
29	7 39	8 30	2 11	10 34 23	3 31 47n	54 19	14 50	2 22	4 2 1 O 3
30	8 46	8 47	2 53	11 18 32	0 56 33s	54 4	14 47	3 22	4 O 1 2 3
31	9 52	9 5	3 34	12 2 32	5 21 0s	54 1	14 46	4 22	4 1 O 3 2

APPARENT RIGHT ASCENSION OF THE PRINCIPAL PLANETS AT MEAN NOON.

D.	☿ MERCURY.	♀ VENUS.	♂ MARS.	♃ JUPITER.	♄ SATURN.
	H. M. S.	H. M. S.	H. M. S.	H. M. S.	H. M. S.
5	8 45 22	7 14 25	4 15 27	15 59 39	18 3 51
10	8 59 19	7 0 47	4 30 15	15 58 20	18 2 21
15	9 6 22	6 48 23	4 45 2	15 57 19	18 0 54
20	9 5 51	6 38 46	4 59 49	15 56 36	17 59 32
25	8 57 48	6 32 55	5 14 34	15 56 11	17 58 16
30	8 44 19	6 31 12	5 29 16	15 56 0	17 57 7

APPARENT DECLINATION OF THE ABOVE PLANETS.

5	17 46 39n	18 41 19n	21 5 53n	19 46 38s	22 28 128
10	15 42 37	18 1 21	21 43 51	19 43 57	22 28 52
15	13 58 30	17 29 43	22 16 42	19 42 6	22 29 30
20	12 48 57	17 8 26	22 44 22	19 41 8	22 30 8
25	12 27 18	16 58 9	23 6 51	19 41 6	22 30 45
30	13 0 59n	16 57 49n	23 24 46	19 42 18	22 31 23s

ECLIPSES, OCCULTATIONS, AND OTHER CELESTIAL PHENOMENA.

July 1. There is no real night until after the 20th of this month.

July 2. Earth at greatest distance from the Sun, 1h. aft.

July 4. Mercury at greatest elongation (26°) East, 1h. aft.

July 5. Mean time of Sun's semidiameter passing the meridian, 1m. 8·4s.

July 8. Occultation of δ Scorpii magnitude 2½. The disappearance takes place at 11h. 24m. aft., 136° from the vertex; the reappearance at 11h. 54m. aft., 180° from the vertex.

July 12. Occultation of ξ² Sagittarii, magnitude 3½. The disappearance takes place at 0h. 19m. morn., 103° from the vertex; the reappearance at 1h. 18m. morn., 202° from the vertex.

July 14. Occultation of c¹ Capricorni, magnitude 5. The disappearance takes place at 9h. 43m. aft., 48° from the vertex; the reappearance at 10h. 17m. aft., 339° from the vertex.

July 17. Occultation of 19 Piscium, magnitude 5. The disappearance takes place at 5h. 1m. morn., 347° from the vertex; the reappearance at 5h. 35m. morn., 284° from the vertex.

July 20. Mean time of Sun's semidiameter passing the meridian. 1m. 7·4s.

July 23. Mars in conjunction with the Moon, 1h. morn. ♂ 0° 44' N.

July 27. Mercury in conjunction with the Moon, 7h. morn. ☿ 0° 16' S.

In this month the Mornings decrease 34m., and the Afternoons 30m.

MORNING AND EVENING STARS.

☿ MERCURY is an evening star till about the end of the month; in Cancer.

♀ VENUS too near the Sun for observation till towards the middle of the month, when it becomes a morning star; in Gemini.

♂ MARS is a morning star; in Taurus.

♃ JUPITER in Scorpio, near β.

♄ SATURN in Sagittarius.

HORIZONTAL EQUATORIAL PARALLAX OF SUN AND PLANETS.

D.	⊙	☿	♀	♂	♃	♄
	"	"	"	"	"	"
5	8 7	10 8	30 4	4 2	2 0	1 0
15	8 7	13 0	29 7	4 2	1 9	1 0
25	8 7	14 8	25 7	4 3	1 9	1 0

SEMIDIAMETER OF SUN AND PLANETS.

	⊙	☿	♀	♂	♃	♄
	' "	"	"	"	"	"
5	15 45	4 1	28 8	2 2	20 1	8 5
15	15 46	4 9	28 2	2 2	19 7	8 4
25	15 46	5 6	25 3	2 3	19 1	8 4

Mean Longitude of Moon's Ascending Node, July 1, 249° 33' ☋.

Time of High Water at the undermentioned Places—

Day of Month	Week	London Bridge Morn.	After.	Liverpool Morn.	After.	Bristol Morn.	After.	Hull Morn.	After.	Greenock Morn.	After.	Leith Morn.	After.	Dublin (Bar.) Morn.	After.
		H. M.	H. M.	H. M.	H. M.	H. M.	H. M.	H. M.	H. M.	H. M.	H. M.	H. M.	H. M.	H. M.	H. M.
1	S	4 31	4 49	1 47	2 5	9 52	10 10	9 5	9 23	2 43	3 1	5 6	5 24	1 29	1 48
2	M	5 7	5 25	2 23	2 40	10 27	10 43	9 41	9 59	3 19	3 36	5 43	6 3	2 7	2 26
3	Tu	5 42	6 1	2 58	3 17	11 0	11 17	10 18	10 38	3 54	4 13	6 24	6 45	2 46	3 6
4	W	6 22	6 42	3 36	3 57	11 35	11 54	11 0	11 25	4 33	4 53	7 6	7 29	3 27	3 49
5	Th	7 5	7 24	4 19	4 45	...	0 15	11 51	...	5 14	5 37	7 54	8 21	4 13	4 40
6	F	7 49	8 17	5 14	5 46	0 41	1 10	0 19	0 48	6 1	6 32	8 51	9 23	5 8	5 37
7	S	8 47	9 20	6 22	6 58	1 42	2 17	1 17	1 47	7 3	7 37	9 56	10 28	6 8	6 39
8	S	9 56	10 32	7 33	8 7	2 55	3 32	2 18	2 49	8 12	8 46	11 1	11 33	7 10	7 42
9	M	11 5	11 38	8 38	9 6	4 7	4 39	3 21	3 53	9 18	9 48	...	0 2	8 14	8 43
10	Tu	...	0 9	9 31	9 55	4 58	5 35	4 22	4 48	10 16	10 42	0 29	0 53	9 11	9 38
11	W	0 36	1 0	10 18	10 40	6 1	6 26	5 13	5 35	11 7	11 32	1 16	1 40	10 2	10 24
12	Th	1 24	1 48	11 3	11 26	6 50	7 13	5 57	6 20	11 56	...	2 3	2 25	10 45	11 6
13	F	2 9	2 31	11 49	...	7 36	7 59	6 43	7 6	0 20	0 44	2 46	3 8	11 28	11 50
14	S	2 52	3 13	0 12	0 34	8 21	8 43	7 29	7 51	1 7	1 30	3 29	3 50	...	0 12
15	S	3 36	3 58	0 56	1 19	9 9	9 25	8 13	8 36	1 53	2 15	4 12	4 35	0 35	0 58
16	M	4 21	4 44	1 42	2 4	9 47	10 9	8 59	9 22	2 38	3 0	4 59	5 23	1 22	1 46
17	Tu	5 6	5 23	2 26	2 48	10 31	10 52	9 45	10 8	3 23	3 45	5 47	6 12	2 10	2 34
18	W	5 51	6 15	3 11	3 35	11 13	11 35	10 32	10 57	4 7	4 31	6 37	7 3	2 59	3 25
19	Th	6 40	7 6	4 0	4 26	11 58	...	11 25	11 56	4 55	5 20	7 30	7 59	3 51	4 19
20	F	7 32	8 0	4 55	5 30	0 23	0 51	...	0 29	5 47	6 18	8 31	9 4	4 50	5 23
21	S	8 33	9 9	6 6	6 50	1 26	2 0	1 3	1 37	6 52	7 28	9 45	10 22	5 57	6 32
22	S	9 49	10 28	7 30	8 8	2 45	3 27	2 11	2 46	8 7	8 47	10 58	11 33	7 7	7 43
23	M	11 7	11 45	8 43	9 14	4 8	4 44	3 22	3 57	9 24	9 57	...	0 6	8 18	8 52
24	Tu	...	0 18	9 42	10 8	5 17	5 47	4 30	4 58	10 28	10 56	0 36	1 2	9 24	9 52
25	W	0 47	1 13	10 31	10 53	6 15	6 40	5 23	5 47	11 22	11 45	1 29	1 53	10 16	10 36
26	Th	1 38	2 1	11 14	11 34	7 3	7 24	6 10	6 31	...	0 8	2 15	2 35	10 55	11 14
27	F	2 20	2 39	11 53	...	7 44	8 2	6 51	7 10	0 29	0 48	2 54	3 11	11 32	11 49
28	S	2 56	3 13	0 12	0 30	8 19	8 36	7 28	7 44	1 8	1 25	3 28	3 45	...	0 7
29	S	3 31	3 49	0 47	1 5	8 54	9 11	8 4	8 21	1 43	2 0	4 3	4 21	0 26	0 44
30	M	4 6	4 24	1 21	1 36	9 27	9 42	8 37	8 53	2 17	2 33	4 38	4 54	1 1	1 17
31	Tu	4 39	4 54	1 52	2 7	9 57	10 12	9 9	9 25	2 48	3 3	5 10	5 26	1 34	1 50

Rising, Southing, and Setting of the Principal Planets at intervals of Seven Days.

D.	Mercury ☿ Rises h. m.	Souths h. m.	Sets h. m.	Venus ♀ Rises h. m.	Souths h. m.	Sets h. m.	Mars ♂ Rises h. m.	Sths. h. m.	Sets h. m.	Jupiter ♃ Rises h. m.	Souths h. m.	Sets h. m.	Saturn ♄ Rises h. m.	Sths. h. m.	Sets h. m.
2	6 6M	1 54A	9 42A	4 54M	0 42A	8 30A	1 29M	9 26M	5 23A	5 2A	9 19A	1 40M	7 23A	11 23A	3 27M
9	6 19M	1 49A	9 19A	4 14M	11 56M	7 38A	1 16M	9 20M	5 24A	4 31A	8 49A	1 11M	6 53A	10 53A	2 57M
16	6 11M	1 31A	8 46A	3 35M	11 11M	6 47A	1 3M	9 13M	5 23A	4 2A	8 20A	0 42M	6 23A	10 23A	2 28M
23	5 50M	0 59A	8 8A	2 58M	10 32M	6 1A	0 52M	9 6M	5 20A	3 34A	7 52A	0 14M	5 54A	9 54A	1 58M
30	5 3M	0 14A	7 25A	2 27M	10 1M	5 35A	0 42M	8 59M	5 16A	3 6A	7 24A	11 42A	5 25A	9 25A	1 29M

	Apparent Right Ascension and Declination of the Pole Star.				Angular Distance of the Moon from α Pegasi.			
	R.A.		Decl. N.		Position of Star.	6 p.m.	9 p.m.	Midnight
D.	H. M. s.		° ′ ″	D.		° ′ ″	° ′ ″	° ′ ″
1	1 22 51·9		88 46 21	9	East	100 9 24	98 33 25	96 57 4
10	1 23 1·7		88 46 21	10	East	87 11 21	85 32 31	83 53 21
19	1 23 10·8		88 46 22	11	East	73 52 12	72 11 5	70 29 45
28	1 23 20·0		88 46 23	12	East	60 17 59	58 35 37	56 53 12

In the middle of July the constellations Cygnus, Vulpecula, Aquila, and Sagittarius will be on the meridian about midnight.

The Annular Nebula in Lyra, situated between β and γ, is the best example of the Annular Nebulæ; the heavens containing, as far as is at present known, comparatively few examples of this class. It requires a rather good telescope to see it well; it is in R.A. 18h. 49m. 50s., and Decl. 32° 54′ N. It exhibits a spectrum as if composed of an incandescent gas. There is also a globular cluster in Lyra, as nearly as possible midway between γ Lyræ and β Cygni: it was formerly considered a Nebula, until resolved into stars by Sir William Herschel in 1784. It is in R.A. 19h. 12m. 41s., Decl. 30° 0′ N. The best nights for the observation of these objects are those just before and after the 26th.

Ceres and Pallas can be observed n this month, see p. 73.

DAY OF			Fasts and Festivals. Remarkable Days—Events. SUN ENTERS VIRGO 23d. 3h. A.	THE SUN		DAYS	
M.	Light and Dark.	W.		Rises.	Sets.	of the Year.	to end of Year.
				H. M.	H. M.		
1		W	*Lammas.* Battle of the Nile, 1798.	4 24	7 48	213	152
2		Th	Battle of Blenheim, 1704. Goodwood Cup.	4 26	7 46	214	151
3		F	Viscount Peel b. 1829. Eugène Sue d. 1857.	4 28	7 44	215	150
4		S	Shelley b. 1792. Adm. Lord Duncan d. 1804.	4 30	7 42	216	149
5		⦵	**Eighth Sunday after Trinity.**	4 32	7 40	217	148
6		M	*Transfiguration.* Lammas Holiday. R.A. closes.	4 33	7 39	218	147
7		Tu	*Name of Jesus.* First refmd. Parliament met, '32	4 34	7 38	219	146
8		W	George Canning died, 1827 ; born 11 Apr. 1770.	4 35	7 36	220	145
9		Th	Capt. Marryat died, 1848; born 10 July, 1792.	4 37	7 34	221	144
10		F	*St. Lawrence.* Rt. Hon. G. J. Goschen b. 1831.	4 38	7 32	222	143
11		S	Half Quarter Day. TRINITY LAW SITT. END.	4 40	7 30	223	142
12		⦵	**Ninth Sunday after Trinity.**	4 42	7 28	224	141
13		M	Grouse shooting begins.	4 44	7 26	225	140
14		Tu	Metz, 1870. Old Lammas Day. Lord Clyde, d. '63.	4 46	7 24	226	139
15		W	Sir Walter Scott born, 1771 ; d. 21 Sept. 1832.	4 47	7 22	227	138
16		Th	St. Roche's Day.	4 48	7 20	228	137
17		F	Admiral Robert Blake died, 1657.	4 50	7 18	229	136
18		S	Gravelotte, 1870. Emperor of Austria born, 1830.	4 52	7 16	230	135
19		⦵	**Tenth Sunday after Trinity.**	4 54	7 14	231	134
20		M	Lord Herbert of Cherbury died, 1648.	4 55	7 12	232	133
21		Tu	Vimeira, 1808. Taku Forts captured, 1860.	4 56	7 10	233	132
22		W	Bosworth, 1485. Warren Hastings died, 1818.	4 58	7 8	234	131
23		Th	Adm. of the Fleet, Lord John Hay, born, 1827.	5 0	7 6	235	130
24		F	*St. Bartholomew.* Huguenot massacre, 1572.	5 1	7 3	236	129
25		S	David Hume died, 1776; born 11 May, 1711.	5 3	7 1	237	128
26		⦵	**Eleventh S. aft. Trin.** Gen. Sir R. Biddulph b. '35	5 4	7 0	238	127
27		M	Algiers bombard. 1816. Zanzibar bombard. '96	5 5	6 57	239	126
28		Tu	*St. Augustin.* Household cavalry at Kassassin,'82	5 7	6 55	240	125
29		W	*Behead. St. John Bapt.* Loss of *Royal George*, 1782	5 9	6 53	241	124
30		Th	Plevna, '77. Adm. of Fleet, Sir A. M. Lyons b. '33	5 10	6 51	242	123
31		F	Queen of Holland b. 1880. John Bunyan d. 1688.	5 12	6 48	243	122

PHASES OF THE MOON.

☽ First Quarter 3d. 4h. 46m. Afternoon.
○ Full Moon 10 9 30 Afternoon.
☾ Last Quarter 17 11 46 Morning.
● New Moon 25 3 53 Morning.
Perigee12d.11h.M.224,100｜Apogee27d.10h.A.252,500

MONTHLY NOTES.

August 1. Borough and County Lists to be affixed to church doors and at Post Offices for two Sundays.—Claims of Lodgers to be sent in between this day and 20th. Lammas—Scottish Quarter Day.

5. Oyster Season commences. 6. Lammas Holiday.

20. Last day for service on Overseers of voting claims and objections in counties and boroughs.

25. Last day for publishing claims and objections to vote in elections, and for Overseers to deliver lists of Electors.

RAINFALL IN AUGUST, 1899.

In this month rain fell on 5 days. The total fall for the month was 0·26 inch ; *below* the average of fifty years, 1841–90, by 2·09 inches.

THE SUN.

Day	After Clock (M. S.)	Hrly Var. of Equa. of Time (S.)	Right Ascension at Noon (H. M. S.)	Hourly Var. of R. A. (S.)	Apparent Declination (Nth.) at Noon (° ' ")	Hrly Var. of ⊙'s Declination (")	Sidereal Time at Noon (H. M. S.)	Mean Time at Sidereal Noon (H. M. S.)
1	6 8	0·14	8 44 41	9·72	18 5 1	37·6	8 38 33	15 18 56
2	6 4	0·17	8 48 34	9·69	17 49 50	38·3	8 42 30	15 15 0
3	6 0	0·19	8 52 25	9·66	17 34 21	39·1	8 46 26	15 11 4
4	5 55	0·22	8 56 18	9·64	17 18 35	39·8	8 50 23	15 7 8
5	5 50	0·24	9 0 9	9·61	17 2 32	40·5	8 54 19	15 3 12
6	5 44	0·27	9 4 0	9·59	16 46 13	41·1	8 58 15	14 59 16
7	5 37	0·29	9 7 49	9·56	16 29 38	41·8	9 2 13	14 55 20
8	5 29	0·32	9 11 39	9·54	16 12 47	42·5	9 6 9	14 51 24
9	5 21	0·34	9 15 27	9·51	15 55 40	43·1	9 10 6	14 47 29
10	5 13	0·37	9 19 15	9·49	15 38 18	43·7	9 14 2	14 43 33
11	5 4	0·39	9 23 3	9·46	15 20 41	44·4	9 17 59	14 39 37
12	4 54	0·42	9 26 49	9·44	15 2 49	45·0	9 21 55	14 35 41
13	4 44	0·44	9 30 35	9·42	14 44 42	45·6	9 25 52	14 31 45
14	4 33	0·46	9 34 22	9·40	14 26 21	46·2	9 29 48	14 27 49
15	4 22	0·48	9 38 7	9·37	14 7 47	46·7	9 33 45	14 23 53
16	4 10	0·50	9 41 52	9·35	13 48 59	47·3	9 37 42	14 19 57
17	3 58	0·52	9 45 36	9·33	13 29 58	47·8	9 41 38	14 16 1
18	3 45	0·54	9 49 20	9·31	13 10 43	48·4	9 45 35	14 12 5
19	3 32	0·56	9 53 3	9·29	12 51 16	48·9	9 49 31	14 8 9
20	3 18	0·58	9 56 46	9·27	12 31 37	49·4	9 53 28	14 4 14
21	3 4	0·60	10 0 28	9·25	12 11 45	49·9	9 57 24	14 0 18
22	2 49	0·62	10 4 10	9·23	11 51 42	50·4	10 1 21	13 56 22
23	2 34	0·64	10 7 51	9·22	11 31 28	50·8	10 5 17	13 52 26
24	2 18	0·66	10 11 32	9·20	11 11 2	51·3	10 9 14	13 48 30
25	2 2	0·67	10 15 13	9·18	10 50 25	51·7	10 13 11	13 44 34
26	1 45	0·69	10 18 53	9·16	10 29 40	52·1	10 17 7	13 40 38
27	1 29	0·71	10 22 33	9·15	10 8 44	52·5	10 21 4	13 36 42
28	1 12	0·72	10 26 12	9·13	9 47 38	52·9	10 25 0	13 32 46
29	0 55	0·74	10 29 51	9·12	9 26 23	53·3	10 28 57	13 28 50
30	0 37	0·75	10 33 30	9·10	9 4 59	53·7	10 32 53	13 24 54
31	0 19	0·77	10 37 8	9·09	8 43 25	54·0	10 36 50	13 20 59

METEOROLOGICAL OBSERVATIONS, AUGUST, 1899.

Day	TEMPERATURE Maximum	TEMPERATURE Minimum	TEMPERATURE Avge. 50 Yrs.	BAROM. Mean (inches)	RAIN FALL (inches)	SUN SHINE (hours)	WIND Directn.	WIND Pressure (lbs. to foot)
1	79·5	53·5	62	30·224	...	12·1	E	1·8
2	78·1	52·1	62	29·965	...	10·7	E	2·5
3	79·6	59·0	62	29·832	...	13·0	ENE	3·5
4	77·2	59·8	62	29·800	...	9·3	ENE	4·0
5	79·8	59·1	62	29·811	...	9·9	E	4·4
6	73·8	61·9	62	29·816	0·02	2·4	ESE	1·7
7	71·0	59·4		29·839	...	0·9	E	1·2
8	75·0	57·3	62	29·831	...	7·0	NE	2·3
9	76·0	55·4	62	29·909	...	8·6	NE	2·5
10	76·4	52·5	62	30·035	...	12·9	ENE	1·4
11	74·8	51·2	62	30·107	...	10·7	NE	2·4
12	75·1	52·2	62	30·091	...	12·4	E	2·0
13	74·2	53·5	62	30·066	...	11·4	ENE	2·0
14	76·8	56·1	62	29·982	...	6·0	E	1·3
15	90·0	57·9	62	29·819	...	7·3	ENE	7·6
16	78·5	59·3	61	29·935	...	8·1	N	1·6
17	75·0	56·1	61	29·965	...	10·8	WNW	3·3
18	72·5	57·2	61	29·996	...	4·9	WNW	2·8
19	75·1	60·6	61	30·025	...	0·9	N	1·4
20	76·5	54·5	61	30·077	...	3·4	N	1·0
21	73·3	50·0	61	30·136	...	12·4	ENE	0·9
22	75·4	47·2	61	30·130	...	12·5	E	0·8
23	79·0	53·8	61	30·061	...	11·0	E	1·5
24	84·9	57·8	61	29·931	...	11·6	ESE	3·0
25	89·3	56·3	60	29·845	...	11·0	S	2·9
26	80·2	55·4	60	29·860	...	11·0	N	0·5
27	84·2	58·7	60	29·629	...	9·5	WSW	4·5
28	74·0	56·2	60	29·682	0·15	6·7	WSW	7·2
29	69·0	52·2	60	29·733	0·05	2·3	SW	2·7
30	74·1	57·7	60	29·663	0·01	9·4	SW	4·4
31	71·7	54·1	59	29·678	0·03	5·4	WSW	4·5

MEMORANDA.

1.	Lamps to be lighted	(8.48)
2.		(8.46)
3.		(8.44)
4.		(8.42)
5.	S.	(8.40)
6.		(8.39)
7.		(8.38)
8.		(8.36)
9.		(8.34)
10.		(8.32)
11.		(8.30)
12.	S.	(8.28)
13.		(8.26)
14.		(8.24)
15.		(8.22)
16.		(8.20)
17.		(8.18)
18.		(8.16)
19.	S.	(8.14)
20.		(8.12)
21.		(8.10)
22.		(8.8)
23.		(8.6)
24.		(8.3)
25.		(8.1)
26.	S.	(8.0)
27.		(7.57)
28.		(7.55)
29.		(7.53)
30.		(7.51)
31.		(7.48)

THE MOON.

Day of M.	Rises Morning.	Sets Afternoon.	Souths Afternoon.	Right Ascension at Noon.	Declination at Noon.	Horizontal Parallax at Noon.	Semidiameter at Noon.	Age at Noon.	Configurations of Jupiter's Satellites at 9h. P.M.
	H. M.	H. M.	H. M.	H. M. S.	° ′ ″	′ ″	′ ″	D. H.	
1	10 58	9 24	4 16	12 47 7	9 33 9s	54 11	14 47	5 22	432O1
2	aft.	9 47	4 59	13 32 56	13 24 34	54 27	14 52	6 22	43O12
3	1 8	10 15	5 43	14 20 47	16 46 8	54 54	15 0	7 22	42O3⊙
4	2 16	10 47	6 34	15 11 3	19 27 35	55 27	15 8	8 22	42O3⊙
5	3 18	11 30	7 25	16 4 0	21 17 42	56 11	15 20	9 22	21O43
6	4 17	mrn.	8 20	16 59 30	22 5 9	57 5	15 34	10 22	O1243
7	5 7	0 24	9 18	17 57 0	21 40 22	57 56	15 49	11 22	1O324
8	5 50	1 25	10 13	18 55 34	19 58 9	58 50	16 3	12 22	32O14
9	6 25	2 43	11 9	19 54 14	16 59 49	59 38	16 17	13 22	31O24
10	6 56	4 3	mrn.	20 52 13	12 54 24	60 17	16 27	14 22	3O124
11	7 22	5 26	0 5	21 49 11	7 57 29	60 41	16 34	15 22	41O34
12	7 46	6 52	1 0	22 45 11	2 29 46s	60 49	16 36	16 22	21O34
13	8 9	8 16	1 53	23 40 40	3 6 4n	60 40	16 33	17 22	O4213
14	8 35	9 42	2 47	0 36 8	8 27 33	60 17	16 27	18 22	41O32
15	9 3	11 1	3 40	1 31 14	13 14 15	59 43	16 19	19 22	423O1
16	9 35	aft.	4 35	2 28 46	17 9 3	59 3	16 7	20 22	4312O
17	10 16	1 36	5 30	3 26 6	19 59 8	58 18	15 55	21 22	4312O
18	11 3	3 42	6 28	4 23 37	21 36 46	57 37	15 43	22 22	4133O2
19	11 59	3 39	7 21	5 20 35	21 59 42	56 56	15 32	23 22	44 2O3
20	mrn.	4 26	8 15	6 16 10	21 11 4	56 16	15 21	24 22	4O13⊙
21	1 1	5 3	9 7	7 9 44	19 18 33	55 46	15 13	25 22	41O32
22	3 14	5 32	9 56	8 0 51	16 32 29	55 17	15 5	26 22	23O41
23	3 14	5 56	10 42	8 49 52	13 4 38	54 52	14 59	27 22	321O4
24	4 22	6 17	11 27	9 36 44	9 0 48	54 32	14 53	28 22	3O124
25	5 29	6 36	aft.	10 22 3	4 50 8	54 16	14 49	0 8	13O24
26	6 34	6 56	0 51	11 6 25	0 24 55n	54 8	14 46	1 8	2O134
27	7 41	7 11	1 32	11 50 27	3 59 19s	53 59	14 44	2 8	O34⊙⊙
28	8 51	7 33	2 14	12 34 49	8 13 39	53 59	14 44	3 8	1O234
29	9 50	7 53	2 56	13 20 7	12 9 20	54 7	14 46	4 8	23O14
30	10 56	8 18	3 41	14 6 57	15 37 29	54 23	14 51	5 8	321O4
31	aft.	8 50	4 28	14 55 45	18 28 47s	54 48	14 57	6 8	34O12

APPARENT RIGHT ASCENSION OF THE PRINCIPAL PLANETS AT MEAN NOON.

	☿ Mercury.			♀ Venus.			♂ Mars.			♃ Jupiter.			♄ Saturn.		
D.	H.	M.	S.	H.	M.	S.	H.	M.	S.	H.	M.	S.	H.	M.	S.
4	8	30	17	6	33	28	5	43	53	15	56	20	17	56	6
9	8	22	0	6	39	19	5	58	24	15	56	33	17	55	13
14	8	24	15	6	48	18	6	12	49	15	57	45	17	54	29
19	8	38	46	6	59	55	6	27	5	15	58	54	17	53	55
24	9	4	20	7	13	44	6	41	11	16	0	22	17	53	31
29	9	37	37	7	29	21	6	55	7	16	2	6	17	53	17

APPARENT DECLINATION OF THE ABOVE PLANETS.

4	14	13	15n	17	4	58n	23	36	19n	19	43	51s	22	32	1s
9	15	43	53	17	16	31	23	43	26	19	46	36	22	32	40
14	17	0	15	17	29	7	23	45	38	19	50	15	22	33	20
19	17	35	21	17	39	41	23	43	2	19	54	42	22	34	2
24	17	8	10	17	45	36	23	35	49	19	59	57	22	34	45
29	15	28	41n	17	44	42n	23	24	12n	20	5	56s	22	35	30s

HORIZONTAL EQUATORIAL PARALLAX OF SUN AND PLANETS.						SEMIDIAMETER OF SUN AND PLANETS.					
	⊙	☿	♀	♂	♃	♄	⊙	☿	♀	♂	♃	♄
D.		″	″	″	″	″	′ ″	″	″	″	″	″
5	8	7	14 1	22 6	4 4	1 8	1 0	15 48	5 3	21 5	2 3	18 5	8 3
15	8	7	11 0	19 3	4 5	1 7	0 9	15 49	4 2	18 4	2 4	18 0	8 2
25	8	8	8 3	16 0	4 7	1 7	0 9	15 51	3 9	15 9	2 4	17 5	8 0

Mean Longitude of Moon's Ascending Node, August 1, 247° 55′ ♐.

ECLIPSES, OCCULTATIONS, AND OTHER CELESTIAL PHENOMENA.

August 1. Day breaks at 1h. 31m. morn., and Twilight ends at 10h. 41m. aft., the length of the Day being 15h. 24m.

Aug. 5. Mean time of Sun's semidiameter passing the meridian, 1m. 6·1s.

Aug. 7. Saturn in conjunction with the Moon, 11h. morn. ♄ 0° 50′ S.

Aug. 13. Occultation of κ Piscium, magnitude 5. The disappearance takes place at 4h. 10m. morn., 15° from the vertex; the reappearance at 5h. 10m. morn., 236° from the vertex.

Aug. 14. Venus at greatest brilliancy, 8h. morn.

Aug. 19. Occultation of ι Tauri, magnitude 5. The disappearance takes place at 0h. 42m. morn., 81° from the vertex; the reappearance at 1h. 24m. morn., 346° from the vertex.

Aug. 19. Mercury at greatest elongation (19°) West, at 2h. aft.

Aug. 20. Mean time of Sun's semidiameter passing the meridian, 1m. 4·9s.

Aug. 23. Mercury in conjunction with the Moon, 5h. aft. ☿ 4° 59′ N.

Aug. 27. Mercury at least distance from the Sun, 10h. morn.

In this month the Mornings decrease 48m., and the Afternoons 60m.

MORNING AND EVENING STARS.

☿ Mercury is a morning star; in Cancer. Enters Leo about the 27th.

♀ Venus is a morning star; in Gemini.

♂ Mars is a morning star; in Taurus till about the 6th, when it enters Gemini.

♃ Jupiter almost stationary in Scorpio.

♄ Saturn in Sagittarius.

Time of High Water at the undermentioned Places—

Day of Month	Week	LondonBridge Morn.	After.	Liverpool Morn.	After.	Bristol Morn.	After.	Hull Morn.	After.	Greenock Morn.	After.	Leith Morn.	After.	Dublin (Bar.) Morn.	Aft.
1	W	5 9	5 25	2 23	2 38	10 27	10 42	9 41	9 57	3 19	3 34	5 43	6 1	2 7	2 24
2	Th	5 40	5 57	2 54	3 12	10 57	11 13	10 14	10 33	3 50	4 8	6 20	6 40	2 42	3 1
3	F	6 17	6 38	3 31	3 52	11 30	11 50	10 55	11 20	4 27	4 48	7 1	7 24	3 22	3 45
4	S	6 59	7 23	4 17	4 45	...	0 13	11 48	...	5 11	5 36	7 51	8 22	4 11	4 41
5	S	7 51	8 22	5 20	5 59	0 42	1 16	0 20	0 54	6 8	6 44	8 57	9 36	5 14	5 49
6	M	8 59	9 42	6 45	7 27	1 55	2 40	1 30	2 15	7 23	8 4	10 16	10 55	6 27	7 4
7	Tu	10 25	11 3	8 4	8 37	3 23	4 3	2 43	3 19	8 43	9 17	11 30	...	7 39	8 13
8	W	11 38	...	9 7	9 34	4 38	5 10	3 52	4 23	9 49	10 19	0 1	0 30	8 45	9 15
9	Th	0 10	0 38	9 58	10 21	5 38	6 4	4 50	5 14	10 46	11 11	0 55	1 19	9 42	10 6
10	F	1 3	1 28	10 45	11 8	6 26	6 54	5 37	6 0	11 36	...	1 43	2 6	10 28	10 49
11	S	1 51	2 14	11 31	11 53	7 18	7 41	6 24	6 48	0 1	0 25	2 29	2 51	11 10	11 31
12	S	2*35	2*56	...	0 16	8 3	8 24	7 11	7 33	0 48	1 12	3 12	3 33	11 53	...
13	M	3*18	3*39	0 38	1 1	8 46	9 8	7 56	8 18	1 35	1 57	3 55	4 18	0 16	0 40
14	Tu	4* 3	4*26	1 23	1 43	9 29	9 49	8 40	9 1	2 18	2 39	4 40	5 2	1 3	1 25
15	W	4*46	5* 7	2 4	2 26	10 10	10 30	9 22	9 44	3 0	3 22	5 24	5 47	1 47	2 10
16	Th	5 28	5 50	2 48	3 10	10 51	11 12	10 7	10 30	3 44	4 7	6 11	6 37	2 34	2 58
17	F	6 14	6 39	3 34	4 0	11 33	11 58	10 55	11 28	4 31	4 56	7 4	7 33	3 24	3 52
18	S	7 7	7 37	4 30	5 4	...	0 26	...	...	5 23	5 55	8 5	8 41	4 22	5 0
19	S	8 9	8 46	5 45	6 31	1 0	1 41	0 39	1 17	6 31	7 11	9 22	10 5	5 37	6 16
20	M	9 29	10 14	7 17	7 57	2 26	3 12	1 55	2 34	7 54	8 33	10 45	11 23	6 55	7 33
21	Tu	10 56	11 36	8 34	9 6	3 55	4 35	3 12	3 48	9 13	9 48	11 58	...	8 9	8 43
22	W	...	0 9	9 33	9 56	5 8	5 37	4 22	4 49	10 18	10 43	0 30	0 55	9 13	9 39
23	Th	0 38	1 1	10 17	10 37	6 2	6 25	5 12	5 33	11 6	11 28	1 17	1 38	10 1	10 21
24	F	1 22	1 43	10 56	11 14	6 47	7 7	5 53	6 12	11 49	...	1 58	2 17	10 39	10 55
25	S	2 3	2 20	11 31	11 47	7 24	7 40	6 31	6 48	0 8	0 26	2 35	2 51	11 10	11 26
26	S	2 35	2 51	...	0 4	7 56	8 12	7 4	7 21	0 43	0 59	3 6	3 21	11 42	11 58
27	M	3 6	3 22	0 20	0 35	8 28	8 43	7 37	7 52	1 16	1 32	3 37	3 52	...	0 14
28	Tu	3 37	3 53	0 50	1 6	8 58	9 13	8 7	8 23	1 47	2 2	4 7	4 23	0 30	0 46
29	W	4 8	4 23	1 21	1 35	9 27	9 40	8 38	8 52	2 17	2 31	4 38	4 53	1 1	1 16
30	Th	4 37	4 52	1 49	2 4	9 54	10 9	9 7	9 23	2 45	3 0	5 8	5 24	1 32	1 48
31	F	5 7	5 23	2 20	2 37	10 24	10 40	9 39	9 56	3 13	3 33	5 42	6 1	2 5	2 24

RISING, SOUTHING, and SETTING of the PRINCIPAL PLANETS at intervals of Seven Days.

	MERCURY ☿ Rises	Souths	Sets	VENUS ♀ Rises	Souths	Sets	MARS ♂ Rises	Sths.	Sets	JUPITER ♃ Rises	Souths	Sets	SATURN ♄ Rises	Sths.	Sets
	h. m.	h. m.	h. m.	h. m.	h. m.	h. m.	h. m.	h. m.	h. m.	h. m.	h. m.	h. m.	h. m.	h. m.	h. m.
6	4 6m	11 28m	6 50a	2 2m	9 37m	5 12a	0 34a	8 52m	5 10a	2 39a	6 57a	11 15a	4 56a	8 56a	1 0m
13	3 24m	10 57m	6 30a	1 45m	9 21m	4 57a	0 25m	8 44m	5 3a	2 14a	6 31a	10 48a	4 28a	8 27a	0 30m
20	3 11m	10 50m	6 29a	1 30m	9 4m	4 48a	0 18m	8 37m	4 56a	1 48a	6 5a	10 22a	4 0a	7 59a	11 58a
27	3 32m	11 3m	6 34a	1 22m	9 2m	4 42a	0 11m	8 29m	4 47a	1 25a	5 40a	9 55a	3 32a	7 31a	11 30a

APPARENT RIGHT ASCENSION AND DECLINATION OF THE POLE STAR.

D.	R. A. h. m. s.	DECL. N. ° ' "
1	1 23 23·9	88 46 24
10	1 23 32·7	88 46 26
19	1 23 41·0	88 46 28
28	1 23 47·8	88 46 30

ANGULAR DISTANCE OF THE MOON FROM SPICA VIRGINIS.

D.	Position of Star	6 P.M.	9 P.M.	Midnight
4	West	31 16 50	32 50 15	34 24 0
5	West	43 53 38	45 29 50	47 6 24
6	West	56 54 4	58 33 26	60 13 12
7	West	70 20 42	72 3 25	73 46 35

At the beginning of August Cepheus, Cygnus, Vulpecula, Delphinus, and Capricornus south at midnight.

In Vulpecula, nearly 4° due north of γ Sagittæ, is the famous "Dumb-bell" Nebula, generally considered irresolvable, although with the higher powers of Lord Rosse's telescope there seemed some trace of resolvability shown. It is situated in R.A. 19h. 55m. 17s., and Decl. 22° 27' N., and gives a spectrum of bright lines, according to Sir William Huggins.

There is a small bright globular cluster, 4° due south of ε Delphini, consisting of a mass of very small stars, not very easy for small telescopes: it is situated in R.A. 20h. 29m. 3s., and Decl. 7° 3' N. This cluster is a good one, according to Sir John Herschel, for testing the space-penetrating power of telescopes. This though a small is yet a bright cluster, and may be observed easily on the evenings immediately before and after the 25th. Ceres can be observed in this month, see p. 73.

DAY OF		Fasts and Festivals. Remarkable Days—Events. Sun enters Libra 23d. 0h. A. Autumn Commences.	THE SUN		DAYS	
M.	Light and Dark. W.		Rises H. M.	Sets H. M.	of the Year.	to end of Year.
1	S	*St. Giles.* Partridge Shooting begins.	5 14	6 46	244	121
2	S	**Twelfth S. aft. T.** Battle of Omdurman, 1898.	5 16	6 44	245	120
3	M	Battle of Dunbar, 1650. Cromwell died, 1658.	5 17	6 42	246	119
4	Tu	The French Republic declared, 1870.	5 18	6 40	247	118
5	W	Malta captured from the French, 1800.	5 20	6 37	248	117
6	Th	Scottish Rebellion commenced at Perth, 1745.	5 21	6 35	249	116
7	F	*St. Evurtius.* Loss of H.M.S. *Captain*, 1870.	5 23	6 33	250	115
8	S	*Nativity B. V. M.* Fall of Sevastopol, 1855.	5 25	6 31	251	114
9	S	**Thirteenth S. aft. Trinity.** Flodden, 1513.	5 26	6 28	252	113
10	M	Battle of Pinkie, 1547.	5 28	6 26	253	112
11	Tu	Battle of Malplaquet, 1709.	5 30	6 24	254	111
12	W	Siege of Vienna raised, 1683. St. Leger Day.	5 31	6 22	255	110
13	Th	Quebec, 1759. Tel-el-Kebir, '82. L.Pauncefote b.'28	5 33	6 19	256	109
14	F	*Holy Cross Day.* Duke of Wellington d. 1852.	5 35	6 17	257	108
15	S	Liverpool and Manchester Railway opened, 1830.	5 36	6 15	258	107
16	S	**Fourteenth Sunday after Trinity.**	5 38	6 12	259	106
17	M	*St. Lambert.* Lond. and B'ham Rail. op. 1838.	5 39	6 10	260	105
18	Tu	Dr. Samuel Johnson b. 1709; d. 13 Dec. 1784.	5 40	6 8	261	104
19	W	Ember Day. Battle of Poictiers, 1356.	5 42	6 6	262	103
20	Th	Battle of the Alma, 1854. Fall of Delhi, 1857.	5 44	6 3	263	102
21	F	**St. Matthew, Apostle, Evang. & M.** Emb. D	5 46	6 1	264	101
22	S	Ember Day. Sir Philip Sidney died, 1586.	5 47	5 59	265	100
23	S	**Fifteenth Sunday after Trinity.**	5 48	5 56	266	99
24	M	Dean Milman died, 1868; born 10 Feb. 1791.	5 50	5 54	267	98
25	Tu	LUCKNOW DAY (1857).	5 52	5 52	268	97
26	W	*St. Cyprian.* Marquess Wellesley died, 1842.	5 53	5 49	269	96
27	Th	Stockton and Darlington Railway opened, 1825.	5 55	5 47	270	95
28	F	Capitulation of Strasburg, 1870.	5 56	5 45	271	94
29	S	**St. Michael and all Angels.** Quarter Day.	5 58	5 42	272	93
30	S	**Sixteenth S. aft. T.** *St. Jerome.* Ld. Roberts b.'32	6 0	5 40	273	92

PHASES OF THE MOON.

☽ First Quarter 2d. 7h. 56m. Morning.
○ Full Moon* 9 5 6 Morning.
☾ Last Quarter 15 8 57 Afternoon.
● New Moon 23 7 57 Afternoon.
Perigee 9d.6h.A. 222,100 | Apogee 24d.4h.M. 252,600
* The Harvest Moon.

MONTHLY NOTES.

September 1. Declarations as to misdescription or other error in County or Burgess Lists to be delivered to the Town Clerks and Clerks of the Peace.—The lists of objections to County Electors, and claims and objections in Boroughs, to be open to inspection till 8th. Lists of Jurors to be affixed to church doors for the first three Sundays. Salmon close-time begins.

8. First day on which Revising Barristers may hold revision Courts. 17. Edin.: Autumn Holiday.

24. Sheriffs of City of London to be sworn in.

29. Accounts of Overseers to be made up to this date for the past half-year.

RAINFALL IN SEPTEMBER, 1899.

In this month rain fell on 15 days. The total fall for the month was 2·23 inches; *below* the average of fifty years, 1841-90, by 0·02 inch.

THE SUN.

Day.	Before Clock.	Hrly Var. of Equa. of Time.	Right Ascension at Noon.	Hourly Var. of R.A.	Apparent Declination (Nth.) at Noon.	Hrly Var. ⊙'s Declination.	Sidereal Time at Noon.	Mean Time at Sidereal Noon.
	M. S.	s.	H. M. S.	s.	° ′ ″	″	H. M. S.	H. M. S.
1	0 0	0·78	10 40 46	9·07	8 21 45	54·4	10 40 46	13 17 3
2	0 19	0·79	10 44 24	9·06	7 59 56	54·7	10 44 43	13 13 7
3	0 38	0·81	10 48 1	9·05	7 37 59	55·0	10 48 40	13 9 11
4	0 58	0·82	10 51 38	9·04	7 15 55	55·3	10 52 36	13 5 15
5	1 18	0·83	10 55 15	9·03	6 53 44	55·6	10 56 33	13 1 19
6	1 38	0·84	10 58 52	9·02	6 31 26	55·9	11 0 29	12 57 23
7	1 58	0·85	11 2 28	9·01	6 9 2	56·1	11 4 26	12 53 27
8	2 18	0·86	11 6 4	9·00	5 46 32	56·4	11 8 22	12 49 31
9	2 39	0·86	11 9 40	8·99	5 23 56	56·6	11 12 19	12 45 35
10	3 0	0·87	11 13 16	8·99	5 1 15	56·8	11 16 15	12 41 40
11	3 20	0·87	11 16 52	8·98	4 38 28	57·0	11 20 12	12 37 44
12	3 41	0·87	11 20 27	8·98	4 15 36	57·2	11 24 8	12 33 48
13	4 3	0·88	11 24 3	8·97	3 52 40	57·4	11 28 5	12 29 52
14	4 24	0·88	11 27 38	8·97	3 29 39	57·6	11 32 2	12 25 56
15	4 45	0·88	11 31 13	8·97	3 6 35	57·8	11 35 58	12 22 0
16	5 6	0·88	11 34 49	8·97	2 43 27	57·9	11 39 55	12 18 4
17	5 27	0·88	11 38 24	8·97	2 20 15	58·0	11 43 51	12 14 8
18	5 48	0·88	11 41 59	8·97	1 57 1	58·1	11 47 48	12 10 12
19	6 10	0·88	11 45 35	8·97	1 33 44	58·2	11 51 44	12 6 16
20	6 31	0·88	11 49 10	8·98	1 10 25	58·3	11 55 41	12 2 20
21	6 52	0·87	11 52 46	8·98	0 47 5	58·4	11 59 37	11 58 25
22	7 13	0·87	11 56 21	8·98	0 23 42	58·4	12 3 34	11 54 29
23	7 34	0·87	11 59 57	8·99	0 0 19	58·5	12 7 31	11 50 33
24	7 54	0·86	12 3 33	8·99	South	58·5	12 11 27	11 46 37
25	8 15	0·85	12 7 9	9·00	0 46 30	58·5	12 15 24	11 42 41
26	8 35	0·85	12 10 45	9·01	1 9 55	58·5	12 19 20	11 38 45
27	8 56	0·84	12 14 21	9·02	1 33 20	58·5	12 23 17	11 34 49
28	9 16	0·83	12 17 58	9·02	1 56 43	58·5	12 27 13	11 30 53
29	9 36	0·82	12 21 34	9·03	2 20 6	58·4	12 31 10	11 26 57
30	9 55	0·81	12 25 11	9·04	2 43 28	58·4	12 35 6	11 23 1

MEMORANDA.

1. Lamps to be lighted	(7.46)
2. S.	(7.44)
3.	(7.42)
4.	(7.41)
5.	(7.37)
6.	(7.35)
7.	(7.33)
8.	(7.31)
9. S.	(7.28)
10.	(7.26)
11.	(7.24)
12.	(7.22)
13.	(7.19)
14.	(7.17)
15.	(7.15)
16. S.	(7.12)
17.	(7.10)
18.	(7.8)
19.	(7.6)
20.	(7.3)
21.	(7.1)
22.	(6.59)
23. S.	(6.56)
24.	(6.54)
25.	(6.52)
26.	(6.49)
27.	(6.47)
28.	(6.45)
29.	(6.42)
30. S.	(6.40)

METEOROLOGICAL OBSERVATIONS, SEPTEMBER, 1899.

Day.	TEMPERATURE. Maximum.	Minimum.	Avge. 50 Yrs.	BAROM. Mean.	RAIN-FALL.	SUN-SHINE.	WIND. Directn.	Prssure (lbs. to foot).
				inches.	inches.	hours.		lbs.
1	73·5	55·2	59	29·580	0·01	8·8	WSW	3·6
2	72·3	52·1	59	29·600	0·04	11·3	WSW	4·0
3	76·6	47·9	58	29·913	...	11·3	SW	0·8
4	78·3	50·4	58	29·875	...	12·1	S	1·4
5	87·3	56·2	58	29·748	...	7·3	SW	3·0
6	78·7	60·3	58	29·761	0·42	1·7	ENE	8·0
7	72·1	59·3	58	29·778	0·12	1·2	ESE	0·1
8	73·9	58·2	58	29·840	...	5·1	N	1·7
9	68·3	54·3	58	29·993	...	8·8	NNW	2·1
10	64·0	48·9	58	29·973	...	1·5	NNW	3·2
11	65·4	42·2	58	30·006	...	...	WNW	1·2
12	69·0	51·1	58	29·969	...	4·3	N	0·6
13	71·2	45·4	57	29·904	...	2·9	V'ble	0·1
14	67·3	54·6	57	29·870	...	3·9	N	1·8
15	69·1	46·2	57	29·772	0·14	5·9	WSW	4·2
16	62·9	53·4	57	29·457	0·13	5·0	WNW	4·8
17	69·0	50·1	57	29·623	...	2·8	WSW	3·6
18	64·1	53·2	57	29·559	0·02	4·8	W	10·0
19	64·1	53·5	56	29·510	0·15	0·7	WSW	7·1
20	60·7	47·5	56	29·536	...	8·7	W	12·6
21	65·2	43·3	56	29·689	...	8·4	SW	1·3
22	60·5	47·4	55	29·653	0·17	8·3	W	14·2
23	61·2	43·2	55	29·788	0·02	4·6	WSW	7·1
24	61·9	45·3	55	29·777	0·02	8·1	WSW	6·0
25	66·7	54·5	55	29·567	0·02	4·8	WSW	3·9
26	63·1	49·0	55	29·380	...	5·8	WSW	10·5
27	60·5	46·3	54	29·338	0·16	3·3	SW	3·6
28	61·3	40·5	54	29·559	...	6·5	W	1·3
29	58·0	37·1	54	29·452	0·78	0·8	S	2·3
30	57·8	45·8	54	29·195	0·03	3·2	S	3·6

The Moon.

Day of M.	Rises Afternoon.	Sets Afternoon.	Souths Afternoon.	Right Ascension at Noon.	Declination at Noon.	Horizontal Parallax at Noon.	Semidiameter at Noon.	Age at Noon.	Configuration of Jupiter's Satellites at 7h. 30 P.M.
	H. M.	H. M.	H. M.	H. M. S.	° ′ ″	′ ″	′ ″	D. H.	
1	1 3	9 27	5 17	15 46 48	20 33 27s	55 22	15 7	7 8	431○2
2	2 3	10 13	6 8	16 40 8	21 41 41	56 5	15 18	8 8	42○13
3	2 55	11 12	7 2	17 35 26	21 44 40	56 55	15 32	9 8	421○3
4	3 41	mrn.	7 57	18 32 8	20 36 9	57 51	15 47	10 8	♃4○23
5	4 20	0 18	8 53	19 29 37	18 14 9	58 50	16 3	11 8	♃42○1
6	4 52	1 34	9 48	20 26 51	14 42 28	59 45	16 18	12 8	4321○
7	5 19	2 55	10 43	21 23 59	10 11 16	60 32	16 31	13 8	34○21
8	5 47	4 20	11 38	22 20 41	4 56 48s	61 5	16 40	14 8	31○42
9	6 10	5 44	mrn.	23 17 16	0 39 49n	61 21	16 45	15 8	2○314
10	6 36	7 12	0 33	0 14 8	6 14 41	61 16	16 43	16 8	21○34
11	7 3	8 37	1 28	1 11 40	11 23 32	60 53	16 37	17 8	○1234
12	7 36	10 1	2 24	2 10 3	15 44 36	60 14	16 26	18 8	♃○34●
13	8 15	11 19	3 21	3 9 4	19 0 58	59 26	16 13	19 8	321○4
14	9 0	aft.	4 19	4 8 10	21 2 18	58 32	15 59	20 8	3○214
15	9 55	1 32	5 15	5 6 28	21 45 33	57 39	15 44	21 8	31○24
16	10 56	2 23	6 11	6 3 6	21 14 15	56 49	15 30	22 8	24○1●
17	mrn.	3 2	7 3	6 57 25	19 36 49	56 4	15 18	23 8	421○3
18	0 0	3 34	7 53	7 49 8	17 4 16	55 26	15 8	24 8	4○123
19	1 8	4 1	8 41	8 38 20	13 48 28	54 56	15 0	25 8	41○23
20	2 15	4 20	9 25	9 25 24	10 0 49	54 32	14 53	26 8	4231○
21	3 21	4 43	10 8	10 10 50	5 51 58	54 14	14 48	27 8	43○1●
22	4 27	5 1	10 50	10 55 15	1 31 48n	54 2	14 45	28 8	431○2
23	5 32	5 19	11 31	11 39 19	2 50 26s	53 56	14 43	29 8	42○1●
24	6 37	5 39	aft.	12 23 37	7 5 38	53 55	14 43	0 16	214○3
25	7 41	6 0	0 55	13 8 45	11 4 46	54 0	14 44	1 16	○1423
26	8 46	6 24	1 39	13 55 13	14 38 36	54 10	14 47	2 16	1○234
27	9 51	6 53	2 25	14 43 24	17 37 44	54 26	14 52	3 16	♃23○4
28	10 55	7 27	3 13	15 33 30	19 52 45	54 50	14 58	4 16	3○14●
29	11 54	8 11	4 3	16 25 29	21 14 43	55 21	15 6	5 16	31○24
30	aft.	9 2	4 54	17 19 7	21 35 58s	55 59	15 17	6 16	23○14

Apparent Right Ascension of the Principal Planets at Mean Noon.

D.	☿ Mercury.	♀ Venus.	♂ Mars.	♃ Jupiter.	♄ Saturn.
	H. M. S.	H. M. S.	H. M. S.	H. M. S.	H. M. S.
3	10 14 17	7 46 25	7 8 51	16 4 7	17 53 13
8	10 50 56	8 4 41	7 22 21	16 6 24	17 53 20
13	11 25 56	8 23 53	7 35 38	16 8 56	17 53 38
18	11 58 54	8 43 51	7 48 41	16 11 42	17 54 6
23	12 30 6	9 4 21	8 1 27	16 14 42	17 54 44
28	12 59 55	9 25 16	8 13 58	16 17 54	17 55 33

Apparent Declination of the above Planets.

D.	☿	♀	♂	♃	♄
	° ′ ″	° ′ ″	° ′ ″	° ′ ″	° ′ ″
3	12 44 26n	17 35 13n	23 8 24n	20 12 35s	22 36 17s
8	9 16 11	17 15 47	22 48 39	20 19 48	22 37 6
13	5 25 35	16 45 23	22 25 13	20 27 32	22 37 56
18	1 28 19n	16 3 25	21 58 24	20 35 42	22 38 47
23	2 25 53s	15 9 43	21 28 28	20 44 13	22 39 28
28	6 11 6s	14 4 23n	20 55 47n	20 53 1s	22 40 29s

Horizontal Equatorial Parallax of Sun and Planets.

D.	☉	☿	♀	♂	♃	♄
	″	″	″	″	″	″
5	8 8	6 8	14 4	4 8	1 7	0 9
15	8 8	6 4	12 8	4 9	1 6	0 9
25	8 8	6 3	11 6	5 1	1 6	0 9

Semidiameter of Sun and Planets.

D.	☉	☿	♀	♂	♃	♄
	′ ″	″	″	″	″	″
5	15 54	2 6	13 7	2 5	16 9	7 9
15	15 56	2 4	12 2	2 6	16 5	7 8
25	15 59	2 4	11 0	2 7	16 1	7 6

Mean Longitude of Moon's Ascending Node, September 1, 246° 16′ ♐.

Eclipses, Occultations, and other Celestial Phenomena.

September 1. Day breaks at 3*h*. 7*m*. *morn*., and Twilight ends at 8*h*. 53*m*. *aft*., the length of the Day being 13*h*. 32*m*.

Sept. 1. Jupiter in conjunction with the Moon, 8*h*. *aft*. ♃ 0° 51′ N.

Sept. 3. Occultation of Saturn. The disappearance takes place at 7*h*. 16*m*. *aft*., 126° from the vertex; the reappearance at 8*h*. 11*m*. *aft*., 205° from the vertex.

Sept. 4. Occultation of ξ¹ Sagittarii, magnitude 5. The disappearance takes place at 7*h*. 35*m*. *aft*., 66° from the vertex; the reappearance at 8*h*. 50*m*. *aft*., 263 from the vertex.

Sept. 5. Mean time of Sun's semidiameter passing the meridian 1*m*. 4·0*s*.

Sept. 13. Occultation of 1, Tauri, magnitude 5½. The disappearance takes place at 9*h*. 43*m* *aft*., 99° from the vertex; the reappearance at 10*h*. 34*m*. *aft*., 314 from the vertex.

Sept. 17. Venus at greatest elongation (46°) West, 6*h*. *aft*.

Sept. 20. Mean time of Sun's semidiameter passing the meridian 1*m*. 3·8*s*.

Sept. 23. Sun enters Libra. Autumn commences, 0*h*. *aft*.

Sept. 24. Mercury in conjunction with the Moon, 8*h*. *aft*. ☿ 4° 59′ N.

In this month the Mornings decrease 46*m*., and the Afternoons 1*h*. 6*m*.

Morning and Evening Stars.

☿ Mercury is a morning star to the middle of the month, and in the latter half an evening star. In Leo; enters Virgo about the 15th.

♀ Venus is a morning star; enters Cancer early in the month.

♂ Mars in Gemini till about the 19th, when it enters Cancer.

♃ Jupiter is an evening star; in Scorpio.

♄ Saturn is an evening star; in Sagittarius.

Time of High Water at the undermentioned Places—

Day of Month	Week	London Bridge Morn.	After.	Liverpool Morn.	After.	Bristol Morn.	After.	Hull Morn.	After.	Greenock Morn.	After.	Leith Morn.	After.	Dublin (Bar.) Morn.	After.
		H. M.	H. M.	H. M.	H. M.	H. M.	H. M.	H. M.	H. M.	H. M.	H. M.	H. M.	H. M.	H. M.	H. M.
1	8	5 39	5 58	2 55	3 15	10 56	11 14	10 15	10 37	3 51	4 11	6 22	6 45	2 43	3 5
2	S	6 20	6 45	3 38	4 5	11 36	...	11 5	11 37	4 34	4 59	7 11	7 40	3 30	4 0
3	M	7 11	7 42	4 38	5 18	0 1	0 34	...	0 13	5 28	6 5	8 15	8 55	4 34	5 12
4	Tu	8 19	8 41	6 2	6 49	1 14	1 58	0 51	1 30	6 46	7 28	9 38	10 20	5 51	6 30
5	W	9 48	10 32	7 32	8 11	2 45	3 30	2 9	2 47	8 10	8 49	10 59	11 36	7 9	7 46
6	Th	11 11	11 45	8 44	9 11	4 11	4 45	3 24	3 58	9 24	9 55	...	0 7	8 29	8 50
7	F	...	0 15	9 36	9 59	5 14	5 41	4 27	4 53	10 22	10 48	0 33	0 57	9 18	9 44
8	S	0 41	1 4	10 21	10 43	6 7	6 31	5 16	5 38	11 12	11 36	1 21	1 44	10 6	10 26
9	S	1 28	1*50	11 6	11 28	6 54	7 16	6 0	6 23	...	0 0	2 6	2 27	10 46	11 7
10	M	2*12	2*33	11 50	...	7 38	7 59	6 46	7 8	0 23	0 45	2 48	3 8	11 28	11 50
11	Tu	2*54	3*15	0 13	0 35	8 21	8 43	7 30	7 52	1 8	1 31	3 29	3 51	...	0 13
12	W	3*37	4* 0	0 58	1 20	9 4	9 25	8 14	8 36	1 54	2 16	4 14	4 37	0 37	1 2
13	Th	4*22	4*43	1 41	2 3	9 46	10 8	8 58	9 21	2 37	2 59	5 0	5 23	1 23	1 47
14	F	5 5	5 28	2 26	2 48	10 30	10 51	9 45	10 8	3 22	3 44	5 47	6 13	2 11	2 36
15	S	5 53	6 16	3 11	3 36	11 12	11 34	10 33	11 3	4 7	4 32	6 39	7 8	3 3	3 28
16	S	6 42	7 12	4 7	4 42	...	0 3	11 39	...	5 1	5 33	7 42	8 19	4 2	4 38
17	M	7 47	8 25	5 24	6 11	0 38	1 20	0 17	0 56	6 10	6 52	9 1	9 45	5 17	5 57
18	Tu	9 9	9 55	6 57	7 38	2 6	2 53	1 36	2 15	7 35	8 16	10 26	11 5	6 36	7 14
19	W	10 35	11 14	8 14	8 45	3 36	4 15	2 53	3 28	8 53	9 27	11 39	...	7 49	8 22
20	Th	11 48	...	9 12	9 33	4 47	5 15	4 0	4 27	9 55	10 19	0 0	0 34	8 50	9 15
21	F	0 16	0 39	9 54	10 13	5 38	6 0	4 49	5 10	10 42	11 2	0 55	1 15	9 38	9 57
22	S	0 59	1 19	10 30	10 46	6 20	6 40	5 29	5 46	11 21	11 39	1 34	1 52	10 14	10 29
23	S	1 37	1 54	11 2	11 17	6 56	7 12	6 3	6 19	11 56	...	2 8	2 23	10 43	10 57
24	M	2 12	2 29	11 32	11 48	7 27	7 42	6 35	6 50	0 12	0 27	2 38	2 52	11 11	11 26
25	Tu	2 37	2 52	...	0 4	7 57	8 12	7 6	7 21	0 43	0 59	3 6	3 21	11 42	11 58
26	W	3 6	3 21	0 20	0 34	8 27	8 41	7 36	7 51	1 15	1 30	3 36	3 51	...	0 13
27	Th	3 36	3 51	0 49	1 5	8 55	9 10	8 6	8 21	1 45	2 1	4 6	4 21	0 28	0 44
28	F	4 7	4 23	1 20	1 36	9 26	9 41	8 37	8 54	2 16	2 32	4 37	4 55	1 1	1 18
29	S	4 38	4 54	1 51	2 8	9 56	10 12	9 10	9 27	2 48	3 5	5 12	30	1 35	1 53
30	S	5 10	5 29	2 27	2 47	10 29	10 48	9 46	10 8	3 23	3 43	5 51	6 15	2 14	2 36

RISING, SOUTHING, and SETTING of the PRINCIPAL PLANETS at intervals of Seven Days.

D.	Mercury ☿ Rises	Souths	Sets	Venus ♀ Rises	Souths	Sets	Mars ♂ Rises	Souths	Sets	Jupiter ♃ Rises	Souths	Sets	Saturn ♄ Rises	Souths	Sets
	h. m.	h. m.	h. m.	h. m.	h. m.	h. m.	h. m.	h. m.	h. m.	h. m.	h. m.	h. m.	h. m.	h. m.	h. m.
3	4 16M	11 26M	6 35A	1 20M	8 58M	4 36A	0 5M	8 20M	4 35A	1 0A	5 15A	9 30A	3 4A	7 3A	11 2A
10	5 6M	11 49M	6 32A	1 21M	8 56M	4 31A	11 59A	8 12M	4 23A	0 36A	4 50A	9 4A	2 37A	6 36A	10 35A
17	5 53M	0 9A	6 25A	1 26M	8 56M	4 26A	8 3M	8 3M	4 10A	0 15A	4 27A	8 39A	2 10A	6 9A	10 8A
24	6 37M	0 54A	6 13A	1 34M	8 57M	4 20A	11 48A	7 53M	3 56A	11 53M	4 3A	8 13A	1 45A	5 43A	41A

APPARENT RIGHT ASCENSION AND DECLINATION OF THE POLE STAR.		
	R.A.	Decl. N.
D.	H. M. S.	
1	1 23 51·1	88 46 31
10	1 23 56·8	88 46 34
19	1 24 2·2	88 46 37
28	1 24 6·2	88 46 40

ANGULAR DISTANCE OF THE MOON FROM α ARIETIS.			
D.	Position of Star	6 P.M.	9 P.M.	Midnight.
5	East	100 40 2	98 55 6	97 9 42
6	East	86 28 17	84 39 57	82 51 14
7	East	71 51 42	70 0 42	68 9 27
8	East	56 57 44	55 5 17	53 12 45

On the 1st of September, Cepheus, Pegasus, Aquarius, and Piscis Australis will be on the meridian at midnight.

In Pegasus, R.A. 21h. 25m. 8s., and Decl. 11° 43′ N., is a fine globular cluster of very small stars, 4½° north-west of ε Pegasi, much condensed towards the centre where the stars cannot be resolved : there are many telescopic and several rather bright stars in the field. Aquarius contains a fine cluster of stars, condensed in the centre, and presenting a true globular form, consisting of very small stars very much compressed. It is situated in R.A. 21h. 28m. 14s., and Decl. 1° 16′ S.

In the early evening, at the beginning of the month, the bright cluster in Capricornus, situated in R.A. 21h. 34m. 41s., and Decl. 23° 36′ S., can be observed : it is rather bright, with a central condensation, and does not require great telescopic power to see it well. The best evenings for observation are those immediately before and after the 23rd.

Juno can be observed in this month, see p. 73.

Day of M.	Light and Dark.	W.	Fasts and Festivals. Remarkable Days—Events. Sun enters Scorpio 23d. 9h. A.	Sun Rises H. M.	Sets H. M.	of the Year	to end of Year
1		M	*St. Remigius.* Pheasants. Camb. Term begins.	6 2	5 38	274	91
2		Tu	City of Glasgow Bank suspended payment, 1878.	6 3	5 35	275	90
3		W	Adm. of Fleet E. of Clanwilliam, G.C.B., b. 1832.	6 5	5 33	276	89
4		Th	Guizot, French Statesman and Historian, b. 1787.	6 7	5 31	277	88
5		F	B. W. Procter (Barry Cornwall), died 1874.	6 9	5 29	278	87
6		S	*St. Faith.* Tennyson d. 1892. Parnell d. 1891.	6 10	5 26	279	86
7		☉	**Seventeenth Sunday after Trinity.**	6 12	5 24	280	85
8		M	Henry Fielding d. 1754; b. 22 April, 1707.	6 14	5 22	281	84
9		Tu	*St. Denys.* Italian union established, 1870.	6 15	5 19	282	83
10		W	Oxford Term begins. Pres. Krüger born, 1825.	6 17	5 17	283	82
11		Th	Battle of Camperdown, 1797. Cesarewitch.	6 19	5 15	284	81
12		F	Old Michaelmas. Pekin occupied 1860. [1825.	6 21	5 13	285	80
13		S	*Trans. of K. Edward Conf.* Duke of Westminster b.	6 22	5 10	286	79
14		☉	**Eighteenth S. aft. T.** Battle of Hastings, 1066.	6 24	5 8	287	78
15		M	Prince Alfred of Edinburgh b. 1874; d. 16 Feb. '99	6 26	5 6	288	77
16		Tu	Sir H. Rose (Ld. Strathnairn) d. '85; b. 6 Apr. 1801.	6 27	5 4	289	76
17		W	*St. Etheldreda.* Duchess of Edinburgh b. '53.	6 28	5 2	290	75
18		Th	*St. Luke, Evangelist.* Whip-Dog Day.	6 30	5 0	291	74
19		F	Dean Swift died, 1745; born 30 Nov. 1667.	6 31	4 59	292	73
20		S	Ld. Palmerston b. 1784; d. 18 Oct. '65. Navarino, '27	6 33	4 57	293	72
21		☉	**Nineteenth S. after T.** Trafalgar Day (1805).	6 35	4 55	294	71
22		M	Abbé Liszt, pianist, b. 1811; d. 31 July, 1886.	6 38	4 52	295	70
23		Tu	Sir M. Hicks-Beach b. 1837. Lord Derby d. 1869.	6 39	4 49	296	69
24		W	Michaelmas Law Sittings begin. Cambridgeshire	6 41	4 47	297	68
25		Th	*St. Crispin.* Agincourt, 1415. Balaclava, 1854.	6 42	4 45	298	67
26		F	Count von Moltke b. 1800; d. 24 April, 1891.	6 44	4 44	299	66
27		S	Captain Cook born, 1728; died 14 Feb. 1779.	6 46	4 42	300	65
28		☉	**Twentieth S. after T.** *St. Simon & St. Jude.*	6 48	4 40	301	64
29		M	Sir Walter Raleigh beheaded, 1618.	6 49	4 39	302	63
30		Tu	Lord James of Hereford born, 1828. [1821.	6 51	4 37	303	62
31		W	Hallowmas Eve. John Keats b. 1795; d. 2 Feb.	6 53	4 35	304	61

PHASES OF THE MOON.
☽ First Quarter 1d. 9h. 11m. Afternoon.
○ Full Moon 8 1 18 Afternoon.
☾ Last Quarter 15 9 51 Morning.
● New Moon 23 1 27 Afternoon.
☽ First Quarter 31 8 17 Morning.
Perigee 8d.6h.M.221,900 | Apogee 21d.7h.M.253,000

RAINFALL IN OCTOBER, 1899.
In this month rain fell on 11 days. The total fall for the month was 2·35 inches; *below* the average of fifty years, 1841–90, by 0·46 inch.

MONTHLY NOTES.
Corrections for next year's Whitaker's Almanack should be sent some time this month.
October 1. Revising Barristers must complete revision of all lists of voters by 12th.—Pheasant shooting begins.—Common Lodging-houses to be whitewashed in the first week.
5. Dividends due. 9. Various Licences expire.
11. Quarter Sessions begin in the first *whole* week after this date.
14. Fire Insurances must be paid.
24. Borough Councillors to be nominated.

THE SUN.

Day	Before Clock.	Hrly Var of Equa. of Time	Right Ascension at Noon.	Hourly Var of R. A.	Apparent Declination (Sth.) at Noon.	Hrly Var (⊙'s) De-clination	Sidereal Time at Noon.	Mean Time at Sidereal Noon.
	M. S.	S.	H. M. S.	S.	° ′ ″	″	H. M. S.	H. M. S.
1	10 14	0·80	12 28 49	9·05	3 6 48	58·3	12 39 3	11 19 5
2	10 33	0·79	12 32 26	9·07	3 30 5	58·2	12 43 0	11 15 10
3	10 52	0·78	12 36 4	9·08	3 53 20	58·1	12 46 56	11 11 14
4	11 11	0·76	12 39 43	9·09	4 16 33	57·9	12 50 53	11 7 18
5	11 29	0·75	12 43 20	9·10	4 39 42	57·8	12 54 49	11 3 22
6	11 47	0·73	12 46 59	9·12	5 2 48	57·7	12 58 46	10 59 26
7	12 4	0·72	12 50 38	9·14	5 25 50	57·5	13 2 42	10 55 30
8	12 21	0·70	12 54 18	9·15	5 48 47	57·3	13 6 39	10 51 34
9	12 38	0·68	12 57 58	9·17	6 11 41	57·1	13 10 35	10 47 38
10	12 54	0·66	13 1 38	9·19	6 34 29	56·9	13 14 32	10 43 42
11	13 10	0·64	13 5 19	9·21	6 57 12	56·7	13 18 29	10 39 46
12	13 25	0·62	13 9 0	9·23	7 19 50	56·4	13 22 25	10 35 50
13	13 40	0·60	13 12 42	9·25	7 42 22	56·2	13 26 22	10 31 55
14	13 54	0·58	13 16 24	9·28	8 4 48	55·9	13 30 18	10 27 59
15	14 7	0·55	13 20 7	9·30	8 27 6	55·6	13 34 15	10 24 3
16	14 20	0·53	13 23 51	9·33	8 49 18	55·3	13 38 11	10 20 7
17	14 33	0·51	13 27 35	9·35	9 11 23	55·0	13 42 8	10 16 11
18	14 45	0·48	13 31 20	9·38	9 33 19	54·7	13 46 4	10 12 15
19	14 56	0·45	13 35 5	9·40	9 55 7	54·3	13 50 1	10 8 19
20	15 6	0·43	13 38 51	9·43	10 16 47	54·0	13 53 57	10 4 23
21	15 16	0·40	13 42 38	9·46	10 38 18	53·6	13 57 54	10 0 27
22	15 25	0·37	13 46 25	9·48	10 59 39	53·2	14 1 51	9 56 31
23	15 34	0·34	13 50 13	9·51	11 20 50	52·8	14 5 47	9 52 36
24	15 42	0·31	13 54 2	9·54	11 41 51	52·3	14 9 44	9 48 40
25	15 49	0·28	13 57 51	9·57	12 2 41	51·9	14 13 40	9 44 44
26	15 55	0·25	14 1 41	9·60	12 23 20	51·4	14 17 37	9 40 48
27	16 1	0·22	14 5 32	9·63	12 43 48	50·9	14 21 33	9 36 52
28	16 6	0·19	14 9 24	9·66	13 4 4	50·4	14 25 30	9 32 56
29	16 10	0·16	14 13 16	9·69	13 24 7	49·9	14 29 26	9 29 0
30	16 14	0·13	14 17 9	9·73	13 43 58	49·3	14 33 23	9 25 4
31	16 17	0·10	14 21 3	9·76	14 3 35	48·8	14 37 20	9 21 8

METEOROLOGICAL OBSERVATIONS, OCTOBER, 1899.

Day	TEMPERATURE.			BAROM.	RAIN-FALL	SUN-SHINE.	WIND	
	Maximum.	Minimum.	Avge. 50 Yrs.	Mean.			(Pressure lbs. to foot)	
	°	°	°	inches.	inches.	hours.	Directn.	Pressure.
1	63·0	43·4	54	29·077	0·11	0·3	SSE	lbs. 5·7
2	52·6	44·2	54	29·507	0·04	...	WSW	7·0
3	63·0	42·6	54	29·796	...	5·7	SW	12·5
4	57·6	48·3	54	29·715	0·31	...	NE	4·6
5	52·4	44·9	53	29·953	0·04	...	NNE	1·9
6	53·1	42·1	53	30·001	...	0·8	ENE	0·9
7	54·8	32·5	52	30·071	...	5·4	NNE	1·0
8	60·2	31·2	52	30·219	...	6·4	E	0·5
9	59·5	33·6	52	30·134	...	8·3	ESE	0·3
10	60·5	32·7	52	30·062	...	6·6	SW	0·1
11	62·9	35·5	51	29·737	...	6·3	SSW	0·5
12	61·9	45·3	51	29·373	0·12	1·1	SW	4·3
13	53·2	39·1	51	29·755	...	7·3	W	5·8
14	53·4	35·9	51	30·012	...	2·9	NE	1·0
15	53·5	39·5	50	29·955	...	9·0	E	6·3
16	56·3	40·7	50	29·764	...	7·0	E	1·8
17	60·0	42·1	50	29·945	...	9·1	ESE	1·4
18	62·2	36·7	50	30·150	...	8·6	E	1·6
19	58·3	37·0	49	30·224	...	5·4	E	1·0
20	59·9	38·1	49	30·190	...	4·2	ENE	0·7
21	46·0	42·0	49	30·232	...	...	SW	0·1
22	46·9	41·3	49	30·204	...	...	Calm	0·0
23	54·8	37·3	49	30·072	...	...	SW	0·5
24	58·2	43·2	48	30·175	...	0·9	NW	0·3
25	60·1	45·5	48	30·114	...	4·1	E	0·8
26	58·0	47·7	48	29·749	0·28	0·1	SSW	1·1
27	60·5	55·4	47	29·604	0·51	...	SW	3·7
28	63·6	51·1	47	29·697	0·51	2·7	SW	2·5
29	61·0	52·8	47	29·744	0·18	1·2	SSW	7·4
30	58·1	44·4	47	29·633	0·24	0·1	NNW	7·2
31	55·0	41·2	47	29·938	—	7·8	SW	4·6

MEMORANDA.

1.   Lamps to be lighted   (6.38)

2.   (6.35)

3.   (6.33)

4.   (6.31)

5.   (6.29)

6.   (6.26)

7. ☽   (6.24)

8.   (6.22)

9.   (6.19)

10.   (6.17)

11.   (6.15)

12.   (6.13)

13.   (6.10)

14. ☾   (6.8)

15.   (6.6)

16.   (6.4)

17.   (6.2)

18.   (6.0)

19.   (5.59)

20.   (5.55)

21. ☽   (5.57)

22.   (5.52)

23.   (5.49)

24.   (5.47)

25.   (5.45)

26.   (5.44)

27.   (5.42)

28. ☾   (5.40)

29.   (5.39)

30.   (5.37)

31.   (5.35)

THE MOON.

Day of M.	Rises Afternoon	Sets Afternoon	Souths Afternoon	Right Ascension at Noon.	Declination at Noon.	Horizontal Parallax at Noon.	Semidiameter at Noon.	Age at Noon.	Configurations of Jupiter's Satellites at 6h P.M.
	H. M.	H. M.	H. M.	H. M. S.	° ' "	' "	' "	D. B.	
1	1 34	9 5	5 47	18 13 53	20 51 10S	56 45	15 29	7 16	21○34
2	2 14	11 15	6 41	19 0 58	18 58 10	57 36	15 43	8 16	○2143
3	2 48	mrn.	7 34	20 4 48	15 58 54	58 32	15 58	9 16	14○23
4	3 16	0 30	8 24	20 41 0	15 11 59 47	59 25	16 13	10 16	4230I
5	3 44	1 53	9 21	21 55 39	11 11 56	60 17	16 27	11 16	4321○
6	4 7	3 12	10 15	22 51 20	1 51 14S	60 56	16 3S	12 16	4310○
7	4 33	4 38	11 10	23 47 44	3 42 1nN	61 20	16 45	13 16	4430I
8	5 0	6 0	mrn.	0 45 31	4 9 15	61 23	16 44	14 16	421○3
9	5 30	7 29	0 6	1 44 25	13 50 53	61 9	16 42	15 16	41○23
10	6 18	8 53	1 4	2 44 50	17 39 37	60 35	16 32	16 16	4 1○23
11	6 52	10 11	2 4	3 45 53	20 51 7	59 48	16 19	17 16	4 24○1
12	7 46	11 18	3 4	4 40 32	21 25 6	58 57	16 6	18 16	321○4
13	8 46	aft.	4 3	5 45 31	21 18 0	57 53	15 48	19 16	2I3○24
14	9 53	1 1	4 57	6 41 59	19 57 19	56 57	15 33	20 16	3○124
15	10 58	1 35	5 45	7 35 23	17 36 54	56 6	15 19	21 16	21○34
16	mrn.	2 4	6 37	8 25 41	14 39 58	55 24	15 7	22 16	0I34●
17	0 2	2 27	7 23	9 13 35	10 49 30	54 49	14 58	23 16	I○234
18	1 12	2 48	8 7	9 59 26	6 47 5	54 24	14 51	24 16	I○234
19	2 18	3 9	8 49	10 44 0	2 31 19nN	54 11	14 46	25 16	321○4
20	3 23	3 25	9 30	11 28 2	1 48 35S	53 59	14 44	26 16	34○12
21	4 28	3 44	10 11	12 12 14	6 4 2	53 57	14 44	27 16	4I○2
22	5 33	4 6	0 54	12 57 14	10 6 17	54 2	14 44	28 16	421○3
23	6 40	4 31	11 37	13 43 31	13 46 3	54 11	14 47	29 16	4○13●
24	7 43	4 57	aft.	14 31 34	16 53 36	54 25	14 51	0 23	41○23
25	8 46	5 29	0 21	15 21 29	19 18 50	54 44	14 56	1 23	4231○
26	9 48	6 10	2 6	16 13 13	20 52 54	55 7	15 3	2 23	4231○
27	10 45	6 59	2 51	17 6 24	21 27 39	55 33	15 10	3 23	423○12
28	11 32	7 43	3 43	18 0 28	0 58 1N	56 8	15 19	4 23	314○2
29	aft.	8 2	4 33	18 54 59	13 23 31	36 45	15 29	5 23	4 2○14
30	0 48	8 14	5 27	19 49 0	16 45 41	57 27	15 41	6 23	2○134
31	1 19	11 23	6 19	20 42 46	13 10 48S	58 12	15 53	7 23	I○234

APPARENT RIGHT ASCENSION OF THE PRINCIPAL PLANETS AT MEAN NOON.

D.	☿ MERCURY.	♀ VENUS.	♂ MARS.	♃ JUPITER.	♄ SATURN.
	H. M. S.	H. M. S.	H. M. S.	H. M. S.	H. M. S.
3	13 28 44	9 46 28	8 26 11	16 21 19	17 56 31
8	13 56 50	10 7 51	8 38 6	16 24 55	17 57 40
13	14 24 20	10 29 22	8 49 43	16 28 42	17 58 57
18	14 51 12	10 50 58	9 1 2	16 32 38	18 0 23
23	15 17 3	11 12 39	9 12 0	16 36 43	18 1 53
28	15 40 58	11 34 24	9 22 37	16 40 57	18 3 41

APPARENT DECLINATION OF THE ABOVE PLANETS.

D.	☿	♀	♂	♃	♄
	° ' "	° ' "	° ' "	° ' "	° ' "
3	9 43 29S	12 47 47nN	20 23 40N	21 2	22 41 19S
8	13 0 7	11 20 30	19 43 26	21 11 8	22 42 7
13	15 58 20	9 43 15	19 4 24	21 20 17	22 43 52
18	18 35 10	7 57 3	18 23 57	21 29 25	22 43 34
23	20 46 57	6 3 2	17 42 30	21 38 27	22 44 11
28	22 28 53S	4 2 27nN	17 0 20S	21 47 20S	22 44 43S

HORIZONTAL EQUATORIAL PARALLAX OF SUN AND PLANETS.						SEMIDIAMETER OF SUN AND PLANETS.					
D.	☉	☿	♀	♂	♃	♄	☉	☿	♀	♂	♃	♄
	"	"	"	"	"	"	' "	"	"	"	"	"
5	8 9	6 6	10 5	5 3	1 5	0 9	16 2	2 5	10 0	2 8	15 7	7 5
15	8 9	7 1	9 7	5 8	1 5	0 9	16 6	2 7	2 9	15 4	7 4
25	8 9	8 0	9 0	5 8	1 5	0 9	16 7	3 0	9 5	3 0	15 2	7 3

Mean Longitude of Moon's Ascending Node, October 1, 244° 40' ♐.

ECLIPSES, OCCULTATIONS, AND OTHER CELESTIAL PHENOMENA.

October 1. Day breaks at 4h. 8m. morn., and Twilight ends at 7h. 32m. aft., the length of the Day being 11h. 36m.

Oct. 5. Mean time of Sun's semidiameter passing the meridian, 1m. 4⋅3s.

Oct. 7. Occultation of κ Piscium, magnitude 5. The disappearance takes place at 1h. 35m. morn., 7° from the vertex; the reappearance at 2h. 29m. morn., 236° from the vertex.

Oct. 11. Occultation of ω² Tauri, magnitude 4½. The disappearance takes place at 8h. 47m. aft., 7° from the vertex; the reappearance at 9h. 25m. aft., 346° from the vertex.

Oct. 13. Occultation of ζ Tauri, magnitude 3. The disappearance takes place at 6h. 36m. morn., 16° from the vertex; the reappearance at 7h. 23m. morn., 280° from the vertex.

Oct. 14. Occultation of ν Geminorum, magnitude 4. The disappearance takes place at 3h. 0m. morn., 68° from the vertex; the reappearance at 3h. 43m. morn., 355° from the vertex.

Oct. 17. A near approach of α Cancri to the Moon, 1h. 17 n. morn.

Oct. 17. Occultation of κ Cancri, magnitude 5. The disappearance takes place at 5h. 28m. morn., 173° from the vertex; the reappearance at 6h. 30m. morn., 269° from the vertex.

Oct. 20. Mean time of Sun's semidiameter passing the Meridian 1m. 5⋅4s.

Oct. 29. Occultation of d Sagittarii, magnitude 5. The disappearance takes place at 8h. 27m. aft., 327° from the vertex; the reappearance at 8h. 46m. aft., 294° from the vertex.

Oct. 30. Mercury at greatest elongation (24°) East, 4h. morn.

In this month the Mornings decrease 51m. and the Afternoons 1h. 3m.

MORNING AND EVENING STARS.

☿ MERCURY is an evening star in Virgo.

♀ VENUS is a morning star; near Regulus, on the 7th.

♂ MARS is in Cancer.

♃ JUPITER is an evening star; in Scorpio.

♄ SATURN is an evening star; nearly stationary in Sagittarius.

Time of High Water at the undermentioned Places—

Day of Month	Week	LONDON BRIDGE Morn.	After.	LIVERPOOL Morn.	After.	BRISTOL Morn.	After.	HULL Morn.	After.	GREENOCK Morn.	After.	LEITH Morn.	After.	DUBLIN (Ba Morn.	After.
		H. M.	H. M.	H. M.	H. M.	H. M.	H. M.	H. M.	H. M.	H. M.	H. M.	H. M.	H. M.	H. M.	H. M.
1	M	5 52	6 16	3 10	3 37	11 9¾	11 34	10 34	11 6	4 6	4 32	6 41	7 10	3 1	3 30
2	Tu	6 43	7 15	4 9	4 48	...	0 5	11 43	...	5 2	5 37	7 45	8 25	4 4	4 43
3	W	7 51	8 34	5 33	6 20	0 44	1 29	0 22	1 3	6 17	6 59	9 9	9 52	5 25	6 4
4	Th	9 19	10 3	7 15	7 42	2 15	3 0	1 43	2 21	7 42	8 21	10 32	11 8	6 42	7 18
5	F	10 42	11 17	8 16	8 45	3 41	4 17	2 57	3 31	8 56	9 22	11 40	...	7 52	8 22
6	S	11 48	...	9 11	9 34	4 47	5 14	4 1	4 27	9 56	10 22	0 7	0 32	8 50	9 17
7	S	0 15	0 48	9 55	10 18	5 40	6 5	4 50	5 12	10 46	11 10	0 56	1 19	9 41	10 2
8	M	1 3	1*25	10 40	11 3	6 28	6 50	5 35	5 58	11 34	11 58	1 41	2 2	10 22	10 43
9	Tu	1*47	2° 8	11 26	11 50	7 13	7 36	6 21	6 44	...	0 22	2 23	2 45	11 5	11 28
10	W	2*31	2*54	...	0 14	7 58	8 21	7 7	7 30	0 46	1 10	3 7	3 30	11 52	...
11	Th	3*16	3*39	0 37	0 59	8 43	9 5	7 53	8 16	1 33	1 55	3 52	4 15	0 15	0 37
12	F	4° 1	4*24	1 22	1 43	9 27	9 48	8 39	9 1	2 17	2 39	4 39	5 2	1 1	1 25
13	S	4 45	5 7	2 5	2 27	10 9	10 30	9 24	9 47	3 1	3 23	5 25	5 50	1 49	2 13
14	S	5 29	5 54	2 50	3 15	10 51	11 14	10 12	10 40	3 46	4 16	6 17	6 46	2 39	3 6
15	M	6 21	6 50	3 44	4 17	11 40	...	11 14	11 51	4 38	5 9	7 17	7 53	3 37	4 12
16	Tu	7 22	7 58	4 56	5 38	0 13	0 52	...	0 30	5 45	6 23	8 33	9 15	4 50	5 28
17	W	8 38	9 21	6 23	7 3	1 34	2 18	1 8	1 45	7 2	7 40	9 55	10 31	6 8	6 41
18	Th	10 2	10 38	7 38	8 11	2 59	3 37	2 20	2 53	8 16	8 50	11 5	11 36	7 15	7 45
19	F	11 11	11 40	8 39	9 3	4 12	4 40	3 25	3 54	9 20	9 46	...	0 3	8 15	8 41
20	S	...	0 6	9 25	9 43	5 9	5 29	4 19	4 41	10 9	10 30	0 25	...	9 5	9 26
21	S	0*23	0 47	9 59	10 15	5 49	6 7	4 59	5 16	10 49	11 7	1 4	1 21	9 44	10 0
22	M	1 5	1 22	10 31	10 48	6 25	6 42	5 32	5 48	11 24	11 41	1 38	1 54	10 15	10 30
23	Tu	1 39	1 55	11 4	11 20	6 58	7 14	6 5	6 21	11 58	...	2 10	2 25	10 44	10 59
24	W	2 10	2 24	11 36	11 52	7 30	7 45	6 37	6 53	0 15	0 31	2 40	2 55	11 15	11 30
25	Th	2 40	2 55	...	0 8	8 0	8 16	7 9	7 26	0 47	1 4	3 10	3 25	11 46	...
26	F	3 10	3 26	0 24	0 41	8 32	8 48	7 42	7 58	1 21	1 38	3 41	3 58	0 0	0 20
27	S	3 44	4 1	0 58	1 16	9 4	9 24	8 15	8 33	1 55	2 12	4 15	4 33	0 38	0 57
28	S	4 18	4 35	1 33	1 51	9 38	9 55	8 51	9 9	2 29	2 47	4 52	5 11	1 16	1 35
29	M	4 52	5 12	2 10	2 31	10 13	10 32	9 29	9 51	3 6	3 27	5 32	5 57	1 55	2 19
30	Tu	5 34	5 59	2 55	3 21	10 54	11 19	10 17	10 48	3 51	4 19	6 24	6 53	2 45	3 13
31	W	6 28	6 58	3 52	4 27	11 48	...	11 23	...	4 45	5 17	7 26	8 4	3 46	4 23

RISING, SOUTHING, and SETTING of the PRINCIPAL PLANETS at intervals of Seven Days.

D.	MERCURY ☿ Rises	Souths	Sets	VENUS ♀ Rises	Souths	Sets	MARS ♂ Rises	Souths	Sets	JUPITER ♃ Rises	Souths	Sets	SATURN ♄ Rises	Souths	Sets
	h. m.	h. m.	h. m.	h. m.	h. m.	h. m.	h. m.	h. m.	h. m.	h. m.	h. m.	h. m.	h. m.	h. m.	h. m.
1	7 17M	0 38A	5 59A	1 45M	8 59M	4 13A	11 44A	7 43M	3 40A	11 31M	3 40A	7 49A	1 18A	5 16A	9 14A
8	7 53M	0 50A	5 47A	1 59M	9 1M	4 3A	11 38A	7 32M	3 24A	11 10M	3 18A	7 28A	C 52A	4 50A	8 48A
15	8 30M	1 1A	5 34A	2 13M	9 2M	3 55A	11 33A	7 20M	3 6A	10 50M	2 56A	7 2A	0 27A	4 25A	8 23A
22	8 56M	1 10A	5 24A	2 29M	9 6M	3 43A	11 27A	7 8M	2 48A	10 29M	2 34A	6 39A	0 1A	3 59A	7 57A
29	9 19M	1 16A	5 13A	2 47M	9 9M	3 31A	11 21A	6 55M	2 29A	10 8M	2 12A	6 16A	11 36M	3 34A	7 32A

APPARENT RIGHT ASCENSION AND DECLINATION OF THE POLE STAR.

D.	R. A. h. m. s.	DECL. N.
1	1 24 7·4	88 46 42
10	1 24 9·6	88 46 45
19	1 24 10·6	88 46 49
28	1 24 10·9	88 46 52

ANGULAR DISTANCE OF THE MOON FROM α AQUILÆ.

D.	Position of Star.	6 P.M.	9 P.M.	Midnight.
5	West	38 36 59	39 59 44	41 24 35
6	West	50 28 52	52 4 11	53 40 31
7	West	63 35 27	65 16 44	66 58 27
8	West	77 14 56	78 58 15	80 41 37

On the 1st of October, Cassiopeia, Andromeda, Pisces, and Cetus are on the meridian at midnight; while Cancer and Orion are rising, and Hercules and Capricornus setting.

In Andromeda, near to the 4th mag. star υ, is a large and irresolvable Nebula in the form of an elongated ellipse. It is situated in R.A. 0h. 37m. 20s., and Decl. 40° 43′ N. In Sept., 1885, a decided stellar nucleus was observed in R.A. 0h. 36m. 31s., Decl. 40° 38′ N., probably unconnected with the Nebula.

A splendid double group of stars may be observed in this month, situated midway on a line joining α Persei and γ Cassiopeiæ : the northern cluster is a magnificent collection of stars, much condensed towards the centre, and on a fine night, without moonlight, such as the nights about the 23rd, affords one of the most brilliant telescopic objects in the heavens. One of the stars near the middle of the group is of a fine ruby colour. Juno can be observed in this month, see p. 73.

DAY OF			Fasts and Festivals. Remarkable Days—Events. SUN ENTERS SAGITTARIUS 22*d.* 6*h.* A.	THE SUN		DAYS	
M.	Light and Dark.	W.		Rises. H. M.	Sets. H. M.	Of the Year.	to end of Year
1		Th	**All Saints' Day.** E. India Co. abolished, 1858.	6 55	4 33	305	60
2		F	All Souls' Day. Richard Hooker died, 1600.	6 57	4 31	306	59
3		S	Mutsuhito, Mikado of Japan, born, 1852.	6 59	4 29	307	58
4		☉	**Twenty-first Sunday after Trinity.**	7 1	4 27	308	57
5		M	Inkerman, 1854. Adm. Sir Harry Rawson, b. '43.	7 3	4 25	309	56
6		Tu	*St. Leonard.* Holborn Viaduct opened, 1869.	7 4	4 24	310	55
7		W	Sir Martin Frobisher died, 1594.	7 5	4 23	311	54
8		Th	John Milton died, 1674 ; born 9 Dec. 1608.	7 7	4 21	312	53
9		F	Lord Mayor's Day. Prince of Wales born, 1841.	7 9	4 19	313	52
10		S	Duke of Fife b. 1849. Oliver Goldsmith b. 1728.	7 11	4 17	314	51
11		☉	**Twenty-second Sunday after Trin.** *St. Martin.*	7 12	4 16	315	50
12		M	Sir John Hawkyns, navigator, died, 1595.	7 14	4 14	316	49
13		Tu	*St. Brice.* Arthur Hugh Clough died, 1861.	7 16	4 13	317	48
14		W	General Sir Hugh Gough, *VC*, born, 1833.	7 18	4 12	318	47
15		Th	*St. Machutus.* Queen's first parliament met, '37.	7 20	4 10	319	46
16		F	John Walter, founder of the *Times*, died, 1812.	7 21	4 9	320	45
17		S	*St. Hugh.* Suez Canal opened, 1869.	7 23	4 7	321	44
18		☉	**Twenty-third Sunday after Trinity.**	7 24	4 6	322	43
19		M	Charles I. born, 1600 ; beheaded, 30 Jan. 1649.	7 25	4 5	323	42
20		Tu	*St. Edmund.* Sir Wilfrid Laurier, G.C.M.G., b. '41.	7 28	4 4	324	41
21		W	Empress Frederic of Germany born, 1840.	7 29	4 3	325	40
22		Th	*St. Cecilia.* Lord Clive of Plassey born, 1774.	7 31	4 1	326	39
23		F	*St. Clement.* Richard Hakluyt died, 1616.	7 32	4 0	327	38
24		S	Laurence Sterne born, 1713; died 18 Mar. 1768.	7 34	3 59	328	37
25		☉	**Twenty-fourth Sun. after Trin.** *St. Catherine.*	7 36	3 58	329	36
26		M	Princess Charles of Denmark born, 1869.	7 37	3 57	330	35
27		Tu	Duchess of Teck b. 1833; died 27 Oct. 1897.	7 39	3 56	331	34
28		W	Mandalay occupied, 1885.	7 41	3 55	332	33
29		Th	F. C. Burnand, Editor of *Punch*, born, 1836.	7 42	3 54	333	32
30		F	**St. Andrew Ap. & M.** Arch. of Canterbury b. '21.	7 44	3 54	334	31

PHASES OF THE MOON.

○ Full Moon	6*d.* 11*h.* 0*m.*	Afternoon.
☾ Last Quarter 14	2 38	Morning.
● New Moon 22	7 17	Morning.
☽ First Quarter 29	5 35	Afternoon.

Perigee 5*d.* 4*h.* A. 223,500 | Apogee 17*d.* 7*h.* A. 252,000

RAINFALL IN NOVEMBER, 1898.
In this month rain fell on 13 days. The total fall for the month was 2·39 inches ; *above* the average of fifty years, 1841-90, by 0·12 inch.

An "Inch of Rain" means a gallon of water spread over a surface of nearly two square feet, or 3,630 cubic feet=100 tons upon an acre.

MONTHLY NOTES.

November 1. Latest day for receiving corrections for Whitaker's Almanack.

—. Salmon-fishing with rod and line ends.— Ordinary day of election of Borough Councillors —Holiday at Bank Transfer Office and Stock Exchange.—Fox-hunting begins.

9. Mayors and Aldermen of Boroughs to be elected and Sheriffs appointed.

11. Martinmas : Scottish Quarter Day.

13. County Sheriffs for next year nominated.

15. Solicitors', notaries', proctors', and sworn clerks' certificates expire. *See Note, Dec.* 15.

THE SUN.

Day	Before Clock	Hrly Var. of Equa. of Time	Right Ascension at Noon	Hourly Var. of R.A.	Apparent Declination (Sth.) at Noon	Hrly Var. (°) Declination	Sidereal Time at Noon	Mean Time at Sidereal Noon
	M. S.	S.	H. M. S.	S.	° ′ ″	″	H. M. S.	H. M. S.
1	16 19	0·07	14 24 57	9·79	14 22 59	48·2	14 41 16	9 17 12
2	16 20	0·04	14 28 53	9·82	14 42	47·6	14 45 13	9 13 16
3	16 20	0·00	14 32 49	9·86	15 1 4	47·0	14 49 9	9 9 21
4	16 20	0·03	14 36 45	9·89	15 19 45	46·4	14 53 6	9 5 25
5	16 19	0·07	14 40 40	9·92	15 38 11	45·8	14 57 2	9 1 29
6	16 17	0·10	14 44 42	9·96	15 56 21	45·1	15 0 59	8 57 33
7	16 14	0·14	14 48 41	9·99	16 14 15	44·4	15 4 55	8 53 37
8	16 10	0·17	14 52 42	10·03	16 31 53	43·7	15 8 52	8 49 41
9	16 6	0·21	14 56 43	10·06	16 49 14	43·0	15 12 49	8 45 45
10	16 0	0·24	15 0 45	10·10	17 6 18	42·3	15 16 45	8 41 49
11	15 54	0·28	15 4 48	10·14	17 23 5	41·6	15 20 42	8 37 53
12	15 47	0·31	15 8 51	10·17	17 39 34	40·8	15 21 38	8 33 57
13	15 39	0·35	15 12 56	10·21	17 55 44	40·1	15 28 35	8 30 1
14	15 30	0·39	15 17 1	10·24	18 11 36	39·3	15 32 31	8 26 6
15	15 21	0·42	15 21 7	10·28	18 27 9	38·5	15 36 28	8 22 10
16	15 10	0·46	15 25 15	10·32	18 42 22	37·7	15 40 24	8 18 14
17	14 59	0·49	15 29 23	10·35	18 57 15	36·8	15 44 21	8 14 18
18	14 46	0·53	15 33 31	10·39	19 11 48	30·0	15 48 18	8 10 22
19	14 33	0·56	15 37 41	10·42	19 25 1	35·1	15 52 14	8 6 26
20	14 19	0·60	15 41 52	10·46	19 39 52	34·2	15 56 11	8 2 30
21	14 4	0·53	15 46 3	10·49	19 53 22	33·3	16 0 7	7 58 34
22	13 49	0·67	15 50 15	10·53	20 6 30	32·4	16 4 4	7 54 38
23	13 34	0·70	15 54 28	10·56	20 19 16	31·5	16 8 0	7 50 42
24	13 15	0·73	15 58 42	10·59	20 31 39	30·5	16 11 57	7 46 46
25	12 57	0·76	16 2 50	10 62	20 43 40	29·0	16 15 53	7 42 51
26	12 39	0·79	16 7 11	10·65	20 55 17	28·6	16 19 50	7 38 55
27	12 19	0·82	16 11 27	10·68	21 6 31	27·6	16 23 47	7 34 59
28	11 59	0·85	16 15 44	10·71	21 17 21	26·6	16 27 43	7 31 3
29	11 38	0·88	16 20 1	10·74	21 27 47	25·6	16 31 40	7 27 7
30	11 17	0·91	16 24 19	10·77	21 37 48	24·6	16 35 36	7 23 11

MEMORANDA

1. Lamps to be lighted (5.33)
2. (5.31)
3. (5.29)
4. S. (5.27)
5. (5.25)
6. (5.24)
7. (5.23)
8. (5.21)
9. (5.19)
10. (5.17)
11. S. (5.16)
12. (5.14)
13. (5.13)
14. (5.12)
15. (5.10)
16. (5.9)
17. (5.7)
18. S. (5.5)
19. (5.5)
20. (5.4)
21. (5.3)
22. (5.1)
23. (5.0)
24. (4.59)
25. S. (4.58)
26. (4.57)
27. (4.56)
28. (4.55)
29. (4.54)
30. (4.54)

METEOROLOGICAL OBSERVATIONS, NOVEMBER, 1893.

Day	TEMPERATURE Maximum	Minimum	Avge. 50 Yrs.	BAROM.* Mean	RAIN-FALL	SUN-SHINE	WIND Direction	Prssure lbs.
			°	inches	inches	hours	(Pressure lbs. to foot.)	lbs.
1	53·4	38·0	46	29·851	...	7·3	SW	0·9
2	55·9	44·4	46	29·658	0·18	...	SSW	13·5
3	60·3	45·1	46	29·564	0·08	...	SW	7·0
4	55·1	40·4	45	29·741	...	5·9	SW	3·3
5	57·0	44·5	46	29·613	...	4·2	WSW	3·2
6	57·1	39·1	45	29·972	...	7·4	SSW	0·3
7	54·3	43·2	45	29·838	...	7·4	SSE	1·6
8	50·1	41·8	45	29·875	...	5·7	SE	0·6
9	58·6	47·7	45	29·697	...	1·4	ENE	0·8
10	56·4	47·2	44	29·885	...	1·3	ENE	0·5
11	51·5	45·5	44	29·845	...	3·7	E	0·2
12	53·5	43·4	44	29·562	0·02	...	ESE	1·1
13	55·0	41·2	44	29·814	...	1 6	WSW	0·5
14	50·1	35·6	43	30·136	...	1·8	SW	0·2
15	52·5	41·4	43	30·123	0·01	...	SW	0·9
16	55·8	50·0	43	30·071	0·01	...	SW	0·7
17	51·3	48·7	42	30·139	...	...	ENE	0·6
18	52·1	43·5	42	30·158	...	5·5	E	3·4
19	47·5	41·1	42	30·032	...	1·8	ENE	4·3
20	49·1	42·9	42	29·985	...	...	S	0·1
21	46·3	39·3	42	29·840	0·54	...	N	5·2
22	39·4	29·2	42	29·855	...	5·2	NNW	6·8
23	40·6	29·0	42	29·092	0·12	...	SSE	6·0
24	40·0	35·9	42	28·751	0·18	...	ESE	4·7
25	51·0	42·8	41	28·708	0·53	1·8	SE	3·2
26	41·8	41·7	41	28·851	0·51	...	V'able	1·4
27	44·9	37·0	41	29·030	...	...	NW	0·9
28	41·0	33·6	41	29·187	0·12	...	NNE	6·4
29	40·1	31·5	41	29·449	0·03	...	NNW	3·5
30	46·4	30·0	41	29·677	0·06	5·3	SW	2·2

THE MOON.

Day of M.	Rises Afternoon.	Sets Morning.	Souths Afternoon.	Right Ascension at Noon.	Declination at Noon.	Horizontal Parallax at Noon.	Semidiameter at Noon.	Age at Noon.	Configuration of Jupiter's Satellites at 5h. P.M.
	H. M.	H. M.	H. M.	H. M. S.	° ′ ″	′ ″	′ ″	D. H.	
1	1 44	....	7 10	21 36 13	8 48 6s	58 59	16 6	8 23	♃ O 134
2	2 8	0 48	8 1	22 49 49	3 49 53s	59 43	16 18	9 23	213 O 1
3	2 31	2 8	8 54	23 23 59	1 23 18n	60 20	16 28	10 23	3 O 214
4	2 58	3 33	9 48	0 19 33	6 47 23	60 47	16 35	11 23	31 O 24
5	3 25	4 54	10 45	1 17 1	11 45 59	60 58	16 39	12 23	23 O 14
6	4 0	6 20	11 44	2 16 36	16 0 30	60 52	16 37	13 23	42 O 3●
7	4 40	7 41	mrn.	3 17 55	19 10 4	60 29	16 30	14 23	41 O 23
8	5 30	8 57	0 44	4 19 50	20 59 51	59 50	16 20	15 23	4 O 213
9	6 29	9 59	1 44	5 21 20	21 24 35	59 0	16 6	16 23	4213 O
10	7 33	10 52	2 43	6 20 34	20 29 0	58 4	15 51	17 23	43 O 21
11	8 43	11 33	3 38	7 16 42	18 25 8	57 8	15 36	18 23	431 O 2
12	9 53	aft.	4 30	8 9 27	15 28 13	56 16	15 21	19 23	423 O 1
13	11 1	0 30	5 18	8 59 1	11 53 13	55 31	15 9	20 23	421 O 3
14	mrn.	0 51	6 3	9 46 3	7 53 11	54 54	14 59	21 23	1 O 423
15	0 7	1 13	6 46	10 31 17	3 38 53n	54 28	14 52	22 23	O 2143
16	1 13	1 31	7 28	11 15 33	0 40 38s	54 11	14 47	23 23	21 O 4
17	2 18	1 49	8 9	11 59 40	4 57 15	54 . 4	14 45	24 23	3 O 4
18	3 22	2 10	8 51	12 44 22	9 2 56	54 6	14 46	25 23	
19	4 28	2 31	9 34	13 30 18	12 49 7	54 15	14 49	26 23	
20	5 32	2 59	10 19	14 18 0	16 6 20	54 30	14 53	27 23	
21	6 37	3 29	11 6	15 7 46	18 44 24	54 51	14 58	28 23	
22	7 39	4 7	11 55	15 59 33	20 33 3	55 15	15 5	0 5	
23	8 39	4 55	aft.	16 53 33	21 23 20	55 41	15 12	1 5	
24	9 30	5 50	1 39	17 47 35	21 9 7	56 9	15 20	2 5	
25	10 14	6 55	2 32	18 42 23	19 48 23	56 38	15 28	3 5	
26	10 51	8 5	3 24	19 36 46	17 23 56	57 8	15 36	4 5	
27	11 21	9 19	4 15	20 30 19	14 2 28	57 39	15 44	5 5	
28	11 47	10 36	5 21	21 9 1	9 54 0	58 11	15 53	6 5	
29	aft.	11 53	5 56	22 15 14	5 10 40	58 43	16 1	7 5	
30	0 35	mrn.	6 46	23 7 32	0 6 21 8	59 12	16 10	8 5	

(column note spanning rows 18–30:) Owing to Jupiter's proximity to the Sun, the Satellites will be invisible to the end of the year.

ECLIPSES, OCCULTATIONS, AND OTHER CELESTIAL PHENOMENA.

November 1. Day breaks at 5h. 1m. *morn.*, and Twilight ends at 6h. 27m. *aft.*, the length of the Day being 9h. 38m.

Nov. 5. Mean time of Sun's semidiameter passing the meridian, 1m. 7ˑ1s.

Nov. 9. A near approach of the Moon to χ¹ Orionis, magnitude 5, at 9h. 53m. *aft.*, 220° from the vertex.

Nov. 10. A near approach of the Moon to χ⁴ Orionis, magnitude 5, at 2h. 51m. *morn.*, 184° from the vertex.

Nov. 13. Venus at least distance from the Sun, 6h. *morn.*

Nov. 20. Mercury in inferior conjunction with the Sun, 0h. *aft.*

Nov. 20. Mean time of Sun's semidiameter passing the meridian, 1m. 8ˑ9s.

Nov. 22. An Annular Eclipse of the Sun, invisible at Greenwich, see p. 69.

Nov. 23. Mercury at least distance from the Sun, 9h. *morn.*

Nov. 23. Jupiter in conjunction with the Moon, 5h. *aft.* ♃ 1° 3′ S.

Nov. 29. Mercury stationary in the Heavens, 7h. *aft.*

Nov. 30. Occultation of κ Piscium, magnitude 5. The disappearance takes place at 6h. 11m. *aft.*, 23° from the vertex; the reappearance at 7h. 7m. *aft.*, 277° from the vertex.

In this month the Mornings decrease 49m., and the Afternoons 39m.

MORNING AND EVENING STARS.

☿ MERCURY is an evening star till near the end of the month, when it becomes a morning star. In the early part of the month near to β and δ Scorpii.

♀ VENUS is a morning star; in Virgo.

♂ MARS is in Leo; near Regulus on the 17th.

♃ JUPITER is an evening star; between Scorpio and Sagittarius.

♄ SATURN is an evening star; in Sagittarius.

APPARENT RIGHT ASCENSION OF THE PRINCIPAL PLANETS AT MEAN NOON.

D.	☿ Mercury.	♀ Venus.	♂ Mars.	♃ Jupiter.	♄ Saturn.
	H. M. S.	H. M. S.	H. M. S.	H. M. S.	H. M. S.
2	16 1 21	11 56 13	9 32 53	16 45 19	18 5 31
7	16 13 51	12 18 9	9 42 46	16 49 47	18 7 27
12	16 14 10	12 40 14	9 52 16	16 54 21	18 9 30
17	15 58 1	13 2 32	10 1 21	16 59 0	18 11 39
22	15 32 24	13 25 5	10 9 59	17 3 45	18 13 53
27	15 15 26	13 47 56	10 18 7	17 8 33	18 16 12

APPARENT DECLINATION OF THE ABOVE PLANETS.

	☿	♀	♂	♃	♄
2	23 34 9s	1 56 38n	16 17 56n	21 55 59s	22 45 8s
7	23 52 11	0 13 58	15 35 38	22 4 20	22 45 25
12	23 5 47	2 25 17	14 53 50	22 12 21	22 45 34
17	20 56 29	4 38 26	14 13 0	22 19 58	22 45 43
22	17 52 0	6 51 0	13 33 35	22 27 9	22 45 25
27	15 39 54s	9 1 21s	12 56 4n	22 33 52s	22 45 5s

HORIZONTAL EQUATORIAL PARALLAX OF SUN AND PLANETS.

D.	☉	☿	♀	♂	♃	♄
	″	″	″	″	″	″
5	8 9	9 9	8 3	6 2	1 5	0 8
15	8 10	12 5	7 8	6 6	1 4	0 8
25	9 0	12 0	7 4	7 0	1 4	0 8

SEMIDIAMETER OF SUN AND PLANETS.

	☉	☿	♀	♂	♃	♄
	′ ″	″	″	″	″	″
	16 10	3 7	7 9	3 3	14 9	7 2
	16 12	4 7	7 6	3 1	14 7	7 1
	16 14	4 6	7 0	3 7	14 6	7 1

Mean Longitude of Moon's Ascending Node, November 1, 243° 2′ ♐.

Time of High Water at the undermentioned Places—

Month	Week	London Bridge Morn.	After.	Liverpool Morn.	After.	Bristol Morn.	After.	Hull Morn.	After.	Greenock Morn.	After.	Leith Morn.	After.	Dublin (Bar.) Morn.	After.
		H. M.	H. M.	H. M.	H. M.	H. M.	H. M.	H. M.	H. M.	H. M.	H. M.	H. M.	H. M.	H. M.	H. M.
1	Th	7 32	8 8	5 6	5 49	0 23	1 2	0 1	0 39	5 53	6 32	8 43	9 25	5 1	5 38
2	F	8 48	9 30	6 33	7 10	1 45	2 29	1 17	1 53	7 11	7 47	10 4	10 37	6 14	6 47
3	S	10 8	10 42	7 43	8 14	3 7	3 43	2 25	2 58	8 22	8 55	11 9	11 38	7 19	7 50
4	Su	11 16	11 46	8 43	9 8	4 15	4 45	3 29	3 58	9 26	9 53	...	0 5	8 20	8 48
5	M	...	0 12	9 31	9 53	5 12	5 37	4 24	4 47	10 18	10 43	0 29	0 57	9 14	9 38
6	Tu	0 37	0 59	10 16	10 41	6 1	6 26	5 10	5 33	11 8	11 34	1 15	1 38	9 59	10 21
7	W	1*22	1*47	11 6	11 30	6 51	7 16	5 58	6 23	...	...	2 2	2 26	10 45	11 9
8	Th	2*11	2*34	11 55	...	7 40	8 3	6 48	7 12	0 25	0 50	2 49	3 12	11 33	11 57
9	F	2*57	3*20	0 18	0 41	8 25	8 48	7 35	7 58	1 14	1 37	3 35	3 58	...	0 21
10	S	3*44	4 6	1 4	1 26	9 10	9 31	8 21	8 44	2 0	2 23	4 18	4 43	0 44	1 8
11	Su	4 28	4 51	1 48	2 11	9 53	10 14	9 7	9 30	2 45	3 7	5 8	5 33	1 32	1 56
12	M	5 13	5 36	2 33	2 56	10 35	10 56	9 53	10 17	3 29	3 52	5 58	6 24	2 20	2 45
13	Tu	6 1	6 25	3 20	3 45	11 18	11 43	10 45	11 17	4 16	4 41	6 51	7 20	3 11	3 40
14	W	6 52	7 22	4 16	4 49	...	0 12	11 50	...	5 7	5 37	7 52	8 26	4 11	4 44
15	Th	7 53	8 27	5 26	6 4	0 45	1 22	0 23	0 56	6 10	6 45	9 3	9 39	5 17	5 50
16	F	9 4	9 41	6 42	7 16	2 0	2 39	1 29	2 1	7 20	7 54	10 13	10 44	6 22	6 53
17	S	10 15	10 48	7 47	8 16	3 14	3 46	2 32	3 2	8 26	8 55	11 13	11 40	7 23	7 51
18	Su	11 16	11 43	8 40	9 3	4 16	4 42	3 30	3 56	9 22	9 46	...	0 4	8 17	8 42
19	M	...	0 6	9 24	9 43	4 56	5 28	4 19	4 40	10 9	10 30	0 25	0 45	9 5	9 27
20	Tu	0 28	0 48	10 1	10 18	5 49	6 4	4 59	5 17	10 50	11 9	1 4	1 23	9 46	10 3
21	W	1 7	1 26	10 36	10 54	6 28	6 46	5 35	5 53	11 28	11 47	1 41	1 58	10 19	10 35
22	Th	1 43	2 0	11 11	11 29	7 4	7 22	6 11	6 29	...	0 6	2 15	2 32	10 52	11 9
23	F	2 16	2 34	11 47	...	7 40	7 57	6 47	7 5	0 24	0 42	2 49	3 5	11 26	11 43
24	S	2 51	3 8	0 5	0 24	8 14	8 32	7 23	7 41	1 1	1 20	3 22	3 40	...	0 2
25	Su	3 25	3 45	0 43	1 1	8 49	9 7	7 59	8 18	1 39	1 57	3 59	4 19	0 22	0 42
26	M	4 3	4 23	1 20	1 41	9 25	9 45	8 38	8 59	2 16	2 37	4 39	5 0	1 3	1 24
27	Tu	4 43	5 4	2 2	2 24	10 6	10 27	9 21	9 43	2 59	3 20	5 23	5 47	1 47	2 10
28	W	5 26	5 50	2 46	3 10	10 48	11 10	10 6	10 32	3 42	4 4	6 13	6 40	2 34	3 0
29	Th	6 15	6 44	3 37	4 7	11 35	...	11 4	11 38	4 29	5 1	7 9	7 41	3 29	4 1
30	F	7 13	7 45	4 39	5 13	0 3	0 35	...	0 13	5 30	6 1	8 1	8 50	4 34	5 8

RISING, SOUTHING, and SETTING of the PRINCIPAL PLANETS at intervals of Seven Days.

D.	Mercury ☿ Rises	Souths	Sets	Venus ♀ Rises	Souths	Sets	Mars ♂ Rises	Souths	Sets	Jupiter ♃ Rises	Souths	Sets	Saturn ♄ Rises	Souths	Sets
	h. m.	h. m.	h. m.	h. m.	h. m.	h. m.	h. m.	h. m.	h. m.	h. m.	h. m.	h. m.	h. m.	h. m.	h. m.
5	9 23M	1 13A	5 3A	3 4M	9 12M	3 20A	...	6 42M	2 10A	9 48M	1 51A	5 54A	11 11M	3 9A	7 7A
12	8 54M	0 49A	4 44A	3 24M	9 16M	3 8A	11 12A	6 28M	1 13A	9 28M	1 30A	5 32A	10 47M	2 45A	6 43A
19	7 39M	11 56M	4 14M	3 44M	9 19M	2 54A	10 54A	6 13M	1 30A	9 9M	1 9A	5 32A	10 22M	2 20A	6 18A
26	6 18M	10 58M	3 38A	4 3M	9 23M	2 43A	10 44A	5 57M	1 8A	8 48M	0 48A	4 48A	9 58M	1 56A	5 54A

APPARENT RIGHT ASCENSION AND DECLINATION OF THE POLE STAR.

D.	R.A. H. M. S.	Decl. N.
1	1 24 10.0	88 45 53
10	1 24 8.5	88 46 45
19	1 24 4.7	88 46 59
28	1 24 0.2	88 47 2

ANGULAR DISTANCE OF THE MOON FROM ALDEBARAN.

D.	Position of Star	6 P.M.	9 P.M.	Midnight
2	East	87 36 18	85 48 1	83 59 25
3	East	73 1 48	71 11 16	69 20 31
4	East	58 11 57	56 20 0	54 27 57
5	East	43 14 42	41 22 33	39 30 29

On the 1st of November, Perseus, Aries, and Cetus are on the meridian at midnight.

An irresolvable Nebula 2½° to the East of γ Andromedæ may be observed in this month. It was discovered by Miss Herschel, with a small reflecting telescope of twenty-seven inches in local length. It is a very elongated Nebula, 15' long by 3' broad, with a cleft, dark in the middle, and suggests the idea of a flat ring seen obliquely. It is in R.A. 2h. 16m., and Decl. 41° 49' N. The best evenings for observing it are those immediately before and after the 22nd.

Neptune can be well observed in this month, see p. 73.

DAY OF			Fasts and Festivals. Remarkable Days—Events. SUN ENTERS CAPRICORNUS 22¼. 7¼ M. WINTER COMMENCES.	THE SUN		DAYS	
M.	Light and Dark.	W.		Rises.	Sets.	of the Year.	to end of Year.
				H. M.	H. M.		
1		S	Princess of Wales b. 1844 ; mar. 10 Mar. 1863.	7 45	3 54	335	30
2		S	First Sunday in Advent.	7 46	3 53	336	29
3		M	Bat. of Hohenlinden, 1800. Ld. Leighton, P.R.A.,	7 48	3 52	337	28
4		Tu	Suttee in India abolished, 1829. [b. 1830.	7 49	3 52	338	27
5		W	Alex. Dumas, père, d. 1870 ; b. 24 July, 1803.	7 50	3 52	339	26
6		Th	St. Nicolas. Rev. R. H. Barham (Ingoldsby) b. 1788.	7 51	3 51	340	25
7		F	Gen. Sir Redvers Buller, VC, born, 1839.	7 53	3 51	341	24
8		S	Conception B. V. M. Sir George Birdwood b. 1832.	7 54	3 50	342	23
9		S	Second Sun. in Advent. De Quincey d. 1859.	7 55	3 50	343	22
10		M	Sir Henry Ponsonby b. 1825 ; d. 21 Nov. 1895.	7 56	3 50	344	21
11		Tu	Richard Doyle died, 1883. John Gay died, 1732.	7 57	3 49	345	20
12		W	Fall of Plevna, 1877. Robert Browning d. 1889.	7 58	3 49	346	19
13		Th	St. Lucy. Fenian explosion at Clerkenwell, '67.	7 59	3 49	347	18
14		F	Prince Consort d. 1861. Princess Alice d. 1878.	8 0	3 49	348	17
15		S	Izaak Walton, "Compleat Angler," died, 1683.	8 1	3 49	349	16
16		S	Third Sunday in Advent.	8 2	3 49	350	15
17		M	Oxford Michaelmas Term ends.	8 3	3 49	351	14
18		Tu	Slavery abolished in U. S. A., 1862.	8 4	3 50	352	13
19		W	Ember Day. Cambridge Term ends.	8 4	3 50	353	12
20		Th	Battle of Suakin, 1888. [21st., Ember Day.	8 5	3 51	354	11
21		F	St. Thomas, Ap. and M. MICH. LAW SITT. END.	8 5	3 51	355	10
22		S	Ember Day. Sir Richard Webster born, 1842.	8 6	3 52	356	9
23		S	Fourth Sunday in Advent.	8 6	3 52	357	8
24		M	Christmas Eve. W. M. Thackeray died, 1863.	8 7	3 53	358	7
25		Tu	Christmas Day. William I. crowned, 1066.	8 7	3 53	359	6
26		W	St. Stephen. Bank Holiday. [b. 1847.	8 7	3 54	360	5
27		Th	St. John, Apostle and Evangelist. D. of Norfolk	8 8	3 55	361	4
28		F	Innocents' Day. Lord Macaulay died, 1859.	8 8	3 56	362	3
29		S	Capture of Canton, 1857.	8 8	3 57	363	2
30		S	First S. aft. Christmas. Rudyard Kipling, b. '65	8 8	3 58	364	1
31		M	St. Silvester. XIXth Century ends at midnight.	8 8	3 58	365	0

PHASES OF THE MOON.

○ Full Moon   6d. 10h. 38m. Morning.
☾ Last Quarter 13   10   42   Afternoon.
● New Moon   22   0   1   Morning.
☽ First Quarter 29   1   48   Morning.
Perigee 3d.8h. A. 226,700 · Apogee 15d. 1h. A. 251,500
        Perigee 30d. 4h. A. 229,800

RAINFALL IN DECEMBER, 1898.
In this month rain fell on 10 days. The total fall for the month was 2·22 inches; *above* the average of fifty years, 1841-90, by 0·45 inch.

MONTHLY NOTES.
Dec. 10. Grouse and Black Game Shooting ends.
15. Last day for renewing solicitors' certificates.
16. Notices to owners and occupiers affected by private bills in Parliament must be delivered.
21. Election of Common Councilmen in the City of London.
25. Quarter Day. Bills of exchange falling due this day must be provided for on the 23rd.
26. Bank and General Holiday. Bills of exchange falling due on 26th are not payable till the 27th. 31. Various Licences expire.

THE SUN.

Day.	Before Clock.	Hrly Var of Equa. of Time	Right Ascension at Noon.	Hourly Var. of R.A.	Apparent Declination (Sth.) at Noon.	Hrly Var ⊙'s De-clination	Sidereal Time at Noon	Mean Time at Sidereal Noon
	M. S.	S.	H. M. S.	S.	° ′ ″	″	H. M. S.	H. M. S.
1	10 55	0·93	16 23 38	10·79	21 47 25	23·5	16 39 33	7 19 15
2	10 32	0·96	16 32 57	10·82	21 56 36	22·5	16 43 29	7 15 19
3	10 9	0·98	16 37 17	10·84	22 5 22	21·4	16 47 26	7 11 23
4	9 45	1·01	16 41 38	10·87	22 13 43	20·3	16 51 22	7 7 27
5	9 20	1·03	16 45 59	10·89	22 21 37	19·3	16 55 19	7 3 31
6	8 55	1·05	16 50 20	10·91	22 29 6	18·2	16 59 16	6 59 35
7	8 30	1·08	16 54 42	10·94	22 36 8	17·1	17 3 12	6 55 40
8	8 4	1·11	16 59 5	10·96	22 42 44	15·9	17 7 9	6 51 44
9	7 37	1·12	17 3 28	10·98	22 48 53	14·8	17 11 5	6 47 48
10	7 10	1·13	17 7 52	10·99	22 54 55	13·7	17 15 2	6 43 52
11	6 43	1·15	17 12 15	11·01	23 0 31	12·6	17 18 53	6 39 56
12	6 15	1·17	17 16 40	11·03	23 4 58	11·4	17 22 55	6 35 0
13	5 47	1·18	17 21 5	11·04	23 8 58	10·3	17 26 52	6 32 4
14	5 18	1·20	17 25 30	11·06	23 12 50	9·1	17 30 48	6 28 8
15	4 49	1·21	17 29 55	11·07	23 16 15	8·0	17 34 45	6 24 12
16	4 20	1·22	17 34 21	11·08	23 19 12	6·8	17 38 41	6 20 16
17	3 51	1·23	17 38 47	11·09	23 21 40	5·6	17 42 38	6 16 20
18	3 21	1·24	17 43 13	11·10	23 23 41	4·5	17 46 34	6 12 25
19	2 51	1·24	17 47 39	11·10	23 25 13	3·3	17 50 31	6 8 29
20	2 22	1·25	17 52 6	11·11	23 26 18	2·1	17 54 27	6 4 33
21	1 52	1·25	17 56 32	11·11	23 26 54	0·9	17 58 24	6 0 37
22	1 21	1·25	18 0 59	11·11	23 27 2	0·3	18 2 21	5 56 41
23	0 51	1·25	18 5 26	11·11	23 26 41	1·4	18 6 17	5 52 45
24	0 21	1·25	18 9 52	11·11	23 25 52	2·6	18 10 14	5 48 49
25	After.	1·25	18 14 19	11·11	23 24 35	3·8	18 14 10	5 44 53
26	0 39	1·24	18 18 45	11·10	23 22 50	5·0	18 18 7	5 40 57
27	1 8	1·24	18 23 12	11·10	23 20 37	6·2	18 22 3	5 37 1
28	1 38	1·23	18 27 38	11·09	23 17 55	7·3	18 26 0	5 33 5
29	2 7	1·22	18 32 4	11·08	23 14 45	8·5	18 29 56	5 29 10
30	2 37	1·21	18 36 30	11·07	23 11 8	9·7	18 33 53	5 25 14
31	3 5	1·20	18 40 55	11·06	23 7 3	10·8	18 37 50	5 21 18

METEOROLOGICAL OBSERVATIONS, DECEMBER, 1898.

Day	TEMPERATURE. Maximum.	Minimum.	Avge. 50 Yrs	BAROM. Mean.	RAIN-FALL.	SUN-SHINE.	WIND. (Pressure lbs. to foot.) Directn.	Prssure
	°	°	°	inches.	inches.	hours.	Directn.	Prssure lbs.
1	52·0	46·4	41	29·764	...	0·2	WSW	6·4
2	54·5	50·1	41	29·524	...	...	WSW	14·8
3	54·1	47·8	41	29·744	0·05	0·1	WSW	5·5
4	57·8	52·6	41	29·824	...	3·9	SW	5·5
5	54·8	51·7	41	29·901	...	...	SSW	5·8
6	55·4	48·1	41	29·828	0·09	...	SW	6·4
7	50·0	40·0	41	29·561	1·20	...	WSW	3·8
8	45·9	38·0	41	29·908	...	...	NNW	3·1
9	51·4	42·4	41	29·658	0·05	2·7	WSW	7·4
10	53·8	42·7	41	30·090	...	0·1	WSW	14·0
11	51·6	50·4	41	30·333	...	...	WSW	2·6
12	51·0	49·8	40	30·074	...	...	SW	7·8
13	50·7	37·2	40	30·224	...	0·4	N	0·1
14	50·8	36·4	40	29·968	...	0·2	WSW	6·2
15	49·0	41·5	40	30·045	...	0·2	NW	3·4
16	52·0	37·0	40	30·072	...	...	WSW	3·7
17	52·4	49·0	40	30·093	...	..	SW	1·6
18	55·2	51·7	40	29·997	...	0·3	SW	2·9
19	53·1	38·6	39	29·976	...	0·7	WNW	4·4
20	39·2	24·2	39	30·239	...	1·2	NNW	2·5
21	41·3	29·2	39	30·274	0·02	...	NE	0·7
22	41·7	29·2	39	30·321	...	3·7	S	0·3
23	41·9	28·6	38	30·246	...	7·0	SSE	1·8
24	42·0	31·0	38	30·229	...	...	SSW	0·6
25	49·8	40·1	38	30·174	...	3·8	SW	2·0
26	50·2	41·9	37	29·909	...	1·2	SW	7·7
27	55·1	43·5	37	29·368	0·49	...	SW	29·8
28	44·6	35·1	37	29·457	0·05	4·7	WSW	3·5
29	50·7	37·5	37	28·997	0·14	...	SW	8·8
30	42·7	29·7	37	29·654	0·01	4·3	NNW	11·0
31	43 9	29·0	37	29·369	0·12	...	SSW	8·0

MEMORANDA.

1. Lamps to be lighted (4.54)
2. S. (4.53)
3. (4.52)
4. (4.52)
5. (4.52)
6. (4.51)
7. (4.51)
8. (4.50)
9. S. (4.50)
10. (4.50)
11. (4.49)
12. (4.49)
13. (4.49)
14. (4.49)
15. (4.49)
16. S. (4.49)
17. (4.49)
18. (4.50)
19. (4.50)
20. (4.51)
21. (4.51)
22. (4.52)
23. S. (4.52)
24. (4.53)
25. (4.53)
26. (4.54)
27. (4.55)
28. (4.56)
29. (4.57)
30. S. (4.58)
31. (4.58)

THE MOON.

Day of M.	Rises Afternoon	Sets Morning	Souths Afternoon	Right Ascension at Noon	Declination at Noon	Horizontal Parallax at Noon	Semidiameter at Noon	Age at Noon	Configurations of Jupiter's Satellites at 5h. P.M.
	H. M.	H. M.	H. M.	H. M. S.	° ' "	' "	' "	D. B.	
1	0 59	1 12	7 37	0 0 42	5 3 15n	59 39	16 17	9 5	
2	1 25	2 31	8 31	0 55 27	10 0 24	59 58	16 22	10 5	
3	1 54	3 52	9 26	1 52 22	14 25 32	60 7	16 24	11 5	
4	2 29	5 13	10 25	2 51 33	17 58 35	60 5	16 24	12 5	
5	3 15	6 31	11 25	3 52 33	20 21 53	59 49	16 20	13 5	
6	4 9	7 40	mrn.	4 54 9	21 24 0	59 21	16 12	14 5	
7	5 11	8 39	0 25	5 54 53	21 2 42	58 42	16 1	15 5	
8	6 22	9 25	1 22	6 53 19	19 25 11	57 56	15 49	16 5	
9	7 32	10 1	2 17	7 48 37	16 45 12	57 7	15 35	17 5	
10	8 44	10 31	3 8	8 40 34	13 18 57	56 19	15 22	18 5	
11	9 51	10 55	3 55	9 29 31	9 21 55	55 36	15 11	19 5	
12	10 58	11 16	4 40	10 16 8	5 7 12	55 0	15 1	20 5	
13	mrn.	11 36	5 23	11 1 12	0 45 29n	54 33	14 53	21 5	
14	0 4	11 55	6 1	11 45 34	3 34 29s	54 17	14 49	22 5	
15	1 8 aft.		6 46	12 30 3	7 44 49	54 11	14 47	23 5	
16	2 13	0 36	7 29	13 15 26	11 37 46	54 15	14 49	24 5	
17	3 19	0 59	8 13	14 2 22	15 4 56	54 24	14 52	25 5	
18	4 24	1 28	8 59	14 51 21	17 56 53	54 51	14 58	26 5	
19	5 28	2 4	9 48	15 42 35	20 3 24	55 18	15 6	27 5	
20	6 28	2 48	10 39	16 35 57	21 14 22	55 50	15 14	28 5	
21	7 24	3 41	11 32	17 30 54	21 21 30	56 23	15 23	29 5	
22	8 11	4 43 aft.		18 26 39	20 20 18	56 56	15 33	0 12	
23	8 51	5 54	1 19	19 22 38	18 11 27	57 28	15 41	1 12	
24	9 25	7 2	2 12	20 17 9	15 1 6	57 55	15 49	2 12	
25	9 53	8 24	3 3	21 10 55	10 59 56	58 19	15 55	3 12	
26	10 18	9 46	3 52	22 3 41	6 31 38	58 39	16 0	4 12	
27	10 41	10 59	4 43	22 55 54	1 21 6s	58 54	16 5	5 12	
28	11 5	mrn.	5 34	23 48 16	3 45 25n	59 3	16 8	6 12	
29	11 29	0 18	6 25	0 41 29	8 41 32	59 14	16 10	7 12	
30	11 56	1 36	7 18	1 36 15	13 10 16	59 17	16 11	8 12	
31	aft.	2 54	8 14	2 32 53	16 54 29n	59 15	16 10	9 12	

Owing to Jupiter's proximity to the Sun, the Satellites will not be visible in this month.

APPARENT RIGHT ASCENSION OF THE PRINCIPAL PLANETS AT MEAN NOON.

D.	☿ Mercury	♀ Venus	♂ Mars	♃ Jupiter	♄ Saturn
	H. M. S.	H. M. S.	H. M. S.	H. M. S.	H. M. S.
2	15 15 52	14 11 9	10 25 44	17 13 24	18 18 35
7	15 30 1	14 34 46	10 32 48	17 18 18	18 21 1
12	15 52 16	14 58 51	10 39 14	17 23 13	18 23 50
17	16 19 6	15 23 25	10 45 1	17 28 9	18 26 0
22	16 48 49	15 48 29	10 50 2	17 33 5	18 28 33
27	17 20 20	16 14 3	10 54 14	17 38 1	18 31 6

APPARENT DECLINATION OF THE ABOVE PLANETS.

D.	☿ Mercury	♀ Venus	♂ Mars	♃ Jupiter	♄ Saturn
2	15 23 35s	11 7 51s	12 20 55n	22 40 3s	22 44 34s
7	16 33 32	13 8 54	11 48 35	22 45 42	22 43 51
12	18 18 45	15 2 51	11 19 38	22 50 47	22 42 58
17	20 10 44	16 48 0	10 54 38	22 55 17	22 41 52
22	21 51 14	18 22 43	10 34 12	22 59 11	22 40 36
27	23 10 44s	19 45 26s	10 18 56n	23 2 29s	22 39 8s

HORIZONTAL EQUATORIAL PARALLAX OF SUN AND PLANETS.

	⊙	☿	♀	♂	♃	♄
	"	"	"	"	"	"
5	9 0	9 3	7 1	7 6	1 4	0 8
15	9 0	8 0	7 6	8 2	1 4	0 8
25	9 0	6 7	6 5	9 0	1 4	0 8

SEMIDIAMETER OF SUN AND PLANETS.

	⊙	☿	♀	♂	♃	♄
	' "	"	"	"	"	"
5	16 16	3 5	6 7	4 0	14 6	7 0
15	16 17	2 9	6 4	4 3	14 5	7 0
25	16 17	2 5	6 2	4 7	14 5	7 0

Mean Longitude of Moon's Ascending Node, December 1, 241° 27' ↑.

ECLIPSES, OCCULTATIONS, AND OTHER CELESTIAL PHENOMENA.

December 1. Day breaks at 5h. 41m. morn., and Twilight ends at 5h. 57m. aft., the length of the Day being 8h. 9m.

Dec. 5. Mean time of Sun's semidiameter passing the meridian, 1m. 10·4s.

Dec. 5. Occultation of ω² Tauri, magnitude 4½. The disappearance takes place at 6h. 11m. aft., 67° from the vertex; the reappearance at 6h. 46m. aft., 353° from the vertex.

Dec. 7. A near approach of the Moon to ζ Tauri, magnitude 3, at 3h. 27m. morn., 330° from the vertex.

Dec. 8. Mercury at greatest elongation (21°) West, at 3h. morn.

Dec. 10. Occultation of κ Cancri, magnitude 5. The disappearance takes place at 8h. 56m. aft., 148° from the vertex; the reappearance at 9h. 52m. aft., 317° from the vertex.

Dec. 13. Mars in conjunction with the Moon, 1h. morn. ♂ 8° 26' N.

Dec. 19. Venus in conjunction with the Moon, 7h. morn. ♀ 2° 19' N.

Dec. 20. Mean time of Sun's semidiameter passing the meridian, 1m. 11·0s.

Dec. 22. Sun enters Capricornus. Winter commences, 7h. morn.

Dec. 22. Mercury in conjunction with Uranus, 3h. aft. ☿ 0° 34' N.

Dec. 30. Mercury in conjunction with Jupiter, 4h. aft. ☿ 0° 43' S.

In this month the Mornings decrease 23m., and the Afternoons increase 4m.

MORNING AND EVENING STARS.

☿ Mercury is a morning star; in Libra till the 12th, when it enters Scorpio.

♀ Venus is a morning star; in Libra; enters Scorpio about the 23rd.

♂ Mars is in Leo.

♃ Jupiter too near the Sun for observation in this month.

♄ Saturn is an evening star; in Sagittarius.

Time of High Water at the undermentioned Places—

Day of Month	Week	London Bridge Morn.	After.	Liverpool Morn.	After.	Bristol Morn.	After.	Hull Morn.	After.	Greenock Morn.	After.	Leith Morn.	After.	Dublin (Bar.) Morn.	After.
		H. M.	H. M.	H. M.	H. M.	H. M.	H. M.	H. M.	H. M.	H. M.	H. M.	H. M.	H. M.	H. M.	H. M.
1	S	8 17	8 52	5 52	6 32	1 11	1 48	0 47	1 20	6 35	7 11	9 25	10 3	5 41	14
2	Su	9 30	10 6	7 9	7 42	2 27	3 5	1 52	2 24	7 46	8 20	10 36	11 7	6 46	7 17
3	M	10 40	11 13	8 12	8 41	3 40	4 14	2 56	3 27	8 53	9 24	11 37	...	7 48	8 19
4	Tu	11 45	...	9 9	9 35	4 44	5 13	3 57	4 25	9 54	10 23	0 5	0 31	8 50	9 19
5	W	0 14	0 39	10 0	10 20	5 41	6 8	4 51	5 16	10 50	11 18	0 56	1 22	9 45	10 9
6	Th	1 6	1 33	10 51	11 10	6 35	7 1	5 42	6 8	11 45	...	1 47	2 12	10 33	10 56
7	F	1 55	2 21	11 41	...	7 26	7 51	6 34	6 59	0 11	0 36	2 37	3 0	11 20	11 43
8	S	2 45	3 9	0 5	0 28	8 14	8 36	7 23	7 46	1 1	1 24	3 23	3 45	...	0 7
9	Su	3 30	3 52	0 50	1 12	8 57	9 18	8 8	8 29	1 46	2 8	4 7	4 29	0 30	0 52
10	M	4 14	4 36	1 34	1 55	9 39	10 0	8 51	9 13	2 30	2 51	4 52	5 14	1 15	1 38
11	Tu	4 56	5 17	2 15	2 36	10 20	10 39	9 34	9 55	3 12	3 32	5 36	5 59	2 0	2 22
12	W	5 38	5 59	2 57	3 16	10 57	11 16	10 16	10 39	3 52	4 12	6 22	6 45	2 44	3 6
13	Th	6 22	6 44	3 37	4 0	11 36	11 57	10 59	11 31	4 33	4 55	7 9	7 34	3 29	3 51
14	F	7 8	7 32	4 25	4 53	...	0 21	11 59	...	5 18	5 43	8 1	8 30	4 21	4 49
15	S	7 57	8 25	5 25	5 59	0 49	1 20	0 28	0 57	6 11	6 42	9 2	9 35	5 18	5 47
16	Su	8 58	9 35	6 36	7 11	1 55	2 32	1 27	1 57	7 15	7 48	10 8	10 39	6 17	6 43
17	M	10 10	10 41	7 43	8 13	3 7	3 41	2 28	2 58	8 21	8 52	11 10	11 38	7 19	7 48
18	Tu	11 12	11 42	8 41	9 5	4 13	4 42	3 27	3 55	9 21	9 48	...	0 4	8 16	8 43
19	W	...	0 9	9 28	9 49	5 8	5 32	4 20	4 43	10 13	10 36	0 28	0 49	9 8	9 32
20	Th	0 33	0 54	10 10	10 30	5 55	6 17	5 5	5 25	10 58	11 21	1 10	1 31	9 54	10 14
21	F	1 15	1 37	10 51	11 11	6 39	7 0	5 47	6 7	11 43	...	1 52	2 12	10 33	10 51
22	S	1 58	2 17	11 30	11 50	7 20	7 40	6 28	6 48	0 4	0 25	2 31	2 50	11 9	11 28
23	Su	2 35	2 53	...	0 11	7 59	8 19	7 8	7 28	0 45	1 6	3 8	3 27	11 48	...
24	M	3 13	3 33	0 31	0 51	8 39	8 53	7 48	8 8	1 27	1 48	3 47	4 8	0 9	0 30
25	Tu	3 53	4 14	1 12	1 32	9 18	9 38	8 28	8 49	2 8	2 28	4 29	4 50	0 51	1 13
26	W	4 34	4 55	1 53	2 14	9 58	10 19	9 11	9 33	2 49	3 11	5 12	5 35	1 36	1 59
27	Th	5 15	5 38	2 36	2 58	10 40	11 1	9 55	10 18	3 32	3 54	5 59	6 24	2 22	2 46
28	F	6 2	6 27	3 21	3 45	11 22	11 44	10 43	11 10	4 17	4 41	6 50	7 17	3 11	3 37
29	S	6 51	7 18	4 11	4 42	...	0 8	11 42	...	5 6	5 34	7 46	8 18	4 5	4 37
30	Su	7 47	8 19	5 15	5 52	0 38	1 11	0 16	0 50	6 5	6 38	8 52	9 29	5 10	5 42
31	M	8 53	9 31	6 33	7 11	1 43	2 28	1 23	1 56	7 13	7 49	10 6	10 40	6 17	6 50

RISING, SOUTHING, and SETTING of the PRINCIPAL PLANETS at intervals of Seven Days.

D.	MERCURY ☿ Rises h. m.	Souths h. m.	Sets h. m.	VENUS ♀ Rises h. m.	Souths h. m.	Sets h. m.	MARS ♂ Rises h. m.	Souths h. m.	Sets h. m.	JUPITER ♃ Rises h. m.	Sths h. m.	Sets h. m.	SATURN ♄ Rises h. m.	Souths h. m.	Sets h. m.
3	5 49M	10 31M	3 13A	4 24M	9 28M	2 32A	10 31A	5 40M	0 47A	8 29M	0 27A	4 25A	9 33M	1 1A	5 2A
10	5 58M	10 28M	2 58A	4 44M	9 34M	2 24A	10 17A	5 22M	0 25A	8 8M	0 6A	4 4A	9 9M	1 7A	5 5A
17	6 10M	10 36M	2 51A	5 6M	9 41M	2 16A	10 1A	5 3M	0 2A	7 49M	11 46M	3 43A	8 45M	0 43A	4 41A
24	6 50M	10 51M	2 52A	5 25M	9 48M	2 11A	9 41A	4 43M	11 41M	7 29M	11 25M	3 21A	8 20M	0 19A	4 18A
31	7 19M	11 9M	2 59A	5 46M	9 57M	2 8A	9 21A	4 20M	11 16M	7 9M	11 4M	2 59A	7 55M	11 55M	3 51A

APPARENT RIGHT ASCENSION AND DECLINATION OF THE POLE STAR.

D.	R.A. H. M. S.	Decl. N.
1	1 23 58·2	88 47 3
10	1 23 52·5	88 47 6
19	1 23 45·3	88 47 7
28	1 23 37·0	88 47 9

ANGULAR DISTANCE OF THE MOON FROM ALDEBARAN.

D.	Position of Star	6 P.M.	9 P.M.	Midnight
7	West	23 57 59	25 39 53	27 21 42
8	West	37 28 21	39 8 31	40 48 22
9	West	50 40 32	52 18 2	53 55 11
10	West	63 30 55	65 5 42	66 40 10

On the 1st of December, at midnight, the constellations Camelopardus, Taurus, and Eridanus will be on the meridian.

In Taurus is a fine resolvable Nebula of a pearly white colour 1¾° North-west of ζ Tauri, in R.A. 5h. 28m. 27s., and Decl. 21° 57' N. This Nebula is the one known as the "Crab."

About the middle of the month Orion souths at midnight, and can be best observed in this month, although favourably situated in both November and January. This magnificent constellation contains the grandest of all the Nebulæ, situate in the Sword-Scabbard. A line drawn from α Orionis through ζ, the third star of the belt, will pass over θ Orionis and the Nebula. It can be seen with the naked eye. Evenings before and after the 22nd of the month are the best for observing it.

M.	W.	Festivals, Phenomena, etc. ♑	Sun Rises H.M.	Sun Sets H.M.	After Clock M.S.	Moon Rises Aft. H.M.	Moon Sets Morn. H.M.	H.W. Morn. H.M.	H.W. After H.M.
1	Tu	XXth Century begins.	8 4	4 0	3 34	1 7	4 12	10 9	10 45
2	W		8 4	4 0	4 2	1 56	5 23	11 22	11 58
3	Th	☿ Rises 7h. 30m. morn.	8 4	4 1	4 30	2 43	6 26	...	0 29
4	F		8 4	4 2	4 58	3 59	7 16	0 58	1 25
5	S	○ Full Moon 0h. 14m. morn.	8 3	4 3	5 25	5 9	7 57	1 51	2 14
6	S	*Epiphany.*	8 2	4 5	5 52	6 21	8 30	2 36	2 57
7	M		8 2	4 6	6 18	7 32	8 57	3 17	3 38
8	Tu	♀ Rises 6h. 6m. morn.	8 1	4 8	6 41	8 40	9 21	3 58	4 18
9	W		8 0	4 9	7 9	9 46	9 41	4 36	4 53
10	Th		8 0	4 11	7 34	10 52	10 0	5 10	5 26
11	F	Hilary Law Sittings begin.	7 59	4 12	7 58	11 58	10 19	5 44	6 3
12	S	☾ Last Quarter 8h. 38m. aft.	7 58	4 13	8 21	mrn.	10 40	6 22	6 41
13	S	*First Sunday after Epiphany.*	8 2	4 15	8 44	1 4	11 2	7 2	7 24
14	M		8 2	4 16	9 7	2 8	11 27	7 50	8 18
15	Tu		8 1	4 17	9 29	3 10	aft.	8 51	9 20
16	W	♂ Rises, 8h. 21m. aft.	8 1	4 19	9 50	4 13	0 39	10 9	10 48
17	Th	* To find the time of high-water at the following ports, add for Bristol 5h. 15m., Hull 4h. 31m., Leith 0h. 19m., and for Dublin sub. 2h. 46m., Greenock 1h. 50m., Liverpool 2h. 35m.	8 0	4 21	10 10	5 12	1 28	11 24	11 57
18	F		7 59	4 23	10 30	6 2	2 27	...	0 26
19	S		7 57	4 25	10 49	6 47	3 35	0 52	1 15
20	S	*Second Sunday after Epiphany.*	7 56	4 26	11 7	7 24	4 47	1 37	1 59
21	M	[● New Moon 2h. 36m. aft.]	7 55	4 27	11 25	7 56	6 5	2 20	2 39
22	Tu		7 54	4 29	11 42	8 23	7 25	2 58	3 19
23	W		7 53	4 31	11 58	8 47	8 45	3 38	3 58
24	Th	♃ Rises 5h. 58m. morn.	7 52	4 32	12 13	9 11	10 7	4 20	4 42
25	F		7 51	4 33	12 28	9 35	11 25	5 2	5 23
26	S		7 50	4 35	12 41	10 1	mrn.	5 43	6 4
27	S	*Third Sunday after Epiphany.*	7 49	4 37	12 54	10 32	0 44	6 27	6 52
28	M	[) First Quarter, 9h. 52m. morn.]	7 47	4 39	13 6	11 7	2 1	7 20	7 50
29	Tu		7 46	4 41	13 17	aft.	3 12	8 23	9 0
30	W	♄ Rises 6h. 11m. morn.	7 44	4 43	13 27	0 46	4 15	9 42	10 26
31	Th		7 43	4 45	13 37	1 46	5 10	11 8	11 49

Common Notes for the Year 1901 (Fifth year after Bissextile).

Golden Number	II	Ascension Day—Holy Thursday	May 16
Epact	10	Birth of Queen Victoria (1819)	,, 24
Solar Cycle	6	Pentecost—Whit Sunday	,, 26
Roman Indiction	14	Trinity Sunday	June 2
Dominical Letter	F	Duke of York's Birthday (1865)	,, 3
Julian Period (year of)	6614	Corpus Christi	,, 6
Sundays after Trinity	25	Accession of Queen Victoria (1837)	,, 20
Russian New Year, Greek Calendar	Jan. 13	Summer Commences	,, 22
Septuagesima Sunday	Feb. 3	Queen's Coronation (1838)	,, 28
Queen Victoria married (1840)	,, 10	Jewish New Year, 5662	Sept. 14
Ash Wednesday	,, 20	Autumn Commences	,, 23
Spring Commences	March 21	Birth of Prince of Wales (1841)	Nov. 9
Good Friday	April 5	First Sunday in Advent	Dec. 1
Easter Day	,, 7	Birth of Princess of Wales (1844)	,, 1
Mohammedan New Year, 1319	,, 20	Winter Commences	,, 22
Rogation Sunday	May 12	CHRISTMAS DAY—Wednesday	,, 25

Tidal Constants,

WITH THE RISE OF TIDE AT SPRINGS AND NEAPS.

THE TIME OF HIGH WATER *at the undermentioned Ports and Places may be approximately found by taking the Time of High Water at London Bridge, and adding to or subtracting therefrom the quantities annexed.*

NOTE.—The time thus found will be Greenwich Time for British, Belgian and Dutch Ports; Dublin Time for Irish Ports, and Paris Time for French Ports.

PORT OR PLACE.	CONSTANTS.	h.	m.	SPNGS. ft.	NEAPS. ft.
Aberdeen Bar	sub.	0	50	12	10
Aberdovey	sub.	5	45	14¼	10
Aberystwyth	add	5	55	14¼	10
Aldborough	sub.	3	19	8	6½
Antwerp	add	2	9	15	
Arundel (Littlehmptn) Bar	sub.	2	36	16	11½
Banff	sub.	1	20	10½	8
Bantry Harbour	add	2	2	10	7½
Barnstaple Bridge	add	4	46	10½	
Barrow (Piel Harbour)	sub.	2	40	28	21
Beachy Head	sub.	2	39	20	15
Beaumaris	sub.	3	11	23¼	16½
Belfast	sub.	3	16	9½	8
Berwick	add	0	28	15	11½
Boulogne	sub.	2	27	25¼	19¾
Brest Harbour	add	2	16	19½	14½
Bridgwater Bar	add	5	4	35	26½
Bridport	add	4	18	11¼	7¾
Brielle, port for Rotterdam	add	0	45	5	
Brighton	sub.	2	42	19¾	16
Calais	sub.	2	8	21	17½
Cardiff (Penarth)	add	5	15	36½	27
Cardigan	add	5	22	12	9
Carnarvon	sub.	4	11	15¾	12
Cherbourg	sub.	5	42	17¾	13
Chichester Harbour	sub.	2	25	14	11
Christchurch Harbour	sub.	4	51	5	
Cowes (West)	sub.	3	38	12½	9½
Cromer	add	5	57	14¾	11
Dartmouth Harbour	add	4	32	14¼	10½
Deal	sub.	2	49	16	12½
Devonport Dockyard	add	4	2	15½	12
Dieppe	sub.	2	45	27½	21
Dingle Bay	add	2	9	10¾	7¾
Douglas Harbour	sub.	2	28	20¾	16
Dover	sub.	2	51	18¾	15
Dundalk Bar	sub.	3	1	15	11½
Dundee	add	0	46	14½	11½
Dungeness	sub.	3	17	21¾	19
Dunkerque	sub.	1	50	16¾	13½
Eddystone (off Plymouth)	add	3	44		
Exmouth	add	4	41	11	8½
Falmouth	add	3	19	16	12
Flamborough Head	add	2	32	16	12
Fleetwood	sub.	2	34	27	20½
Flushing	sub.	1	18	15	11
Folkestone	sub.	2	56	20	16½
Fowey	add	3	35	15	11¾
Galway Bay	add	2	48	14¾	11
Granville	add	4	27	37	27¼
Gravesend	sub.	0	54	18½	15
Guernsey, St. Peter Port	add	4	49	26	18¾
Hartlepool	add	1	35	15	11¾
Harwich	sub.	1	57	11½	9¾
Hâvre	sub.	4	31	22	18
Holyhead	sub.	3	29	16	12½
Honfleur Harbour	sub.	4	21	23	18
Ipswich	sub.	1	28	13½	
Jersey (St. Helier)	add	4	39	31½	23
Kingroad (Bristol)	add	5	25	40	31
Kingstown Harbour	sub.	2	46	11¼	8¾
Kinsale Harbour	add	2	54	11½	9
Lerwick Harbour	sub.	2	48	5¾	4½
Lynn Deep, Longsand	add	4	0	23	16¼
Margate Pier	sub.	2	19	15½	13
Milford Haven Entrance	add	4	29	21¾	16½
Minehead Pier	add	4	40	32¼	24½
Needles Point	sub.	4	6	7½	5
Newcastle-on-Tyne	add	1	40	15½	11¾
Newhaven	sub.	2	44	19	14
Newport (Bristol Channel)	add	5	24	38	29
Nore Light	sub.	1	31	15½	13
Ostend	sub.	1	45	17	13
Padstow	add	3	35	20½	16¼
Pembroke Dockyard	add	5	34	22½	17
Penzance	add	2	54	16¼	12½
Peterhead	sub.	1	17	11½	9¼
Poole	sub.	5	0	6½	4¾
Portland Breakwater	add	5	13	6¾	4½
Portsmouth Dockyard	sub.	2	13	13½	10¾
Queenstown	add	3	11	11¾	9
Ramsgate Harbour	sub.	2	20	15	12
St. Ives	add	3	8	21	15
St. Malo	add	4	24	36¼	25¾
Salcombe	add	3	58	15	11½
Scarborough	add	2	15	15¾	12½
Scilly Islands (St. Mary)	add	2	54	16	12
Selsea Bill	sub.	2	10	16½	12½
Sheerness Dockyard	sub.	1	24	16	13¼
Shoreham Harbour	sub.	2	23	18	13¼
Southampton	sub.	3	22	13	9½
Spithead (Anchorage)	sub.	2	32		
Spurn Head	add	3	27	18¾	15
Stromness	sub.	4	45	10	7½
Sunderland	add	1	29	14½	11
Swansea Bay	add	4	18	27¼	20¼
Tees River Bar	add	1	52	15	12¼
Torbay	add	4	16	13½	10
Tynemouth Bar	add	1	26	15¼	10¾
Valentia	add	2	1	11	8
Waterford Harbour	add	4	11	13½	10¾
Wexford	add	5	24	5	3½
Whitby	add	1	49	15	11½
Wisbech	add	5	31	15¼	
Yarmouth Road	sub.	4	50	6	4½
Ymuiden (pt. for Amstdm)	add	0	42	5¼	

EXAMPLE 1.—Required the time of high water at Aberdeen on *January 1st*:—

Time of high water at London Bridge	1*h.* 18*m.*	Morn.
Subtract tide interval	0 50	
Time of high water at Aberdeen	0 28	Morn.

EXAMPLE 2.—Required the time of high water at Scarborough on *January 24th*:—

Time of high water at London Bridge	6*h.* 49*m.*	Morn.
Add tide interval	2 15	
Time of high water at Scarborough	9 4	Morn.

It may happen that the "tide interval" to be subtracted is greater than the quantity from which it has to be taken, in which case 12 hours must be added to the London Bridge time; the resulting difference will be the preceding day's afternoon tide where the London morning tide was used. Sometimes the sum "high water at London Bridge"+"tide interval" will exceed 12 hours; in this case, the excess will be the time of high water after the noon or midnight following, according as the London high water was either morning or afternoon.

EXAMPLE 3.—Required the time of high water at Aberdeen, *January 28th aft.*:—

Time of high water at London Bridge on *January 29th*+12 hours	12*h.* 1*m.*	Morn.
Subtract tide interval	0 50	
Time of high water at Aberdeen, *Jan. 28th*	11 11	After.

A Table of Easter Days and Sunday Letters
FROM THE YEAR 1500 TO 2000.

		1500—1599.	1600—1699.	1700—1799.	1800—1899.	1900—2000.		
d	Mar. 22	1573	1668	1761	1818	……	d	Mar. 22
e	,, 23	1505-16	1600	1788	1845-56	1913	e	,, 23
f	,, 24	……	1611-95	1706-99	……	1940	f	,, 24
g	,, 25	1543-54	1627-38-49	1722-33-44	1883-94	1951	g	,, 25
A	,, 26	1559-70-81-92	1654-65-76	1749-58-69-80	1815-26-37	1967-78-89	A	,, 26
b	Mar. 27	1502-13-24-97	1608-87-92	1785-96	1842-53-64	1910-21-32	b	Mar. 27
c	,, 28	1529-35-40	1619-24-30	1703-14-25	1869-75-80	1937-48	c	,, 28
d	,, 29	1551-62	1635-46-57	1719-30-41	1807-12-91	1959-64-70	d	,, 29
e	,, 30	1567-78-89	1651-62-73-84	1746-55-66-77	1823-34	1902-75-86-97	e	,, 30
f	,, 31	1510-21-32-83-94	1605-16-78-89	1700-71-82-93	1839-50-61-72	1907-18-29-91	f	,, 31
g	April 1	1526-37-48	1621-32	1711-16	1804-66-77-88	1923-34-45-56	g	April 1
A	,, 2	1553-64	1643-48	1727-38-52(NS)	1809-20-93-99	1961-72	A	,, 2
b	,, 3	1575-80-86	1659-70-81	1743-63-68-74	1825-31-36	1904-83-88-94	b	,, 3
c	,, 4	1507-18-91	1602-13-75-86-97	1709-79-90	1847-58	1915-20-26-99	c	,, 4
d	,, 5	1523-34-45-56	1607-18-29-40	1702-13-24-95	1801-63-74-85-96	1931-42-53	d	,, 5
e	April 6	1539-50-61-72	1634-45-56	1729-35-40-60	1806-17-28-90	1947-58-69-80	e	April 6
f	,, 7	1504-77-88	1667-72	1751-65-76	1822-33-44	1901-12-85-96	f	,, 7
g	,, 8	1509-15-20-99	1604-10-83-94	1705-87-92-98	1849-55-60	1917-28	g	,, 8
A	,, 9	1531-42	1615-26-37-99	1710-21-32-52	1871-82	1939-44-50	A	,, 9
b	,, 10	1547-58-69	1631-42-53-64	1726-37-48-57	1803-14-87-98	1955-66-77	b	,, 10
c	April 11	1501-12-63-74-85-96	1658-69-80	1762-73-84	1819-30-41-52	1909-71-82-93	c	April 11
d	,, 12	1506-17-28	1601-12-91-96	1789	1846-57-68	1903-14-25-36-98	d	,, 12
e	,, 13	1533-44	1623-28	1707-18	1800-73-79-84	1941-52	e	,, 13
f	,, 14	1555-60-66	1639-50-61	1723-34-45-54	1805-11-16-95	1963-68-74	f	,, 14
g	,, 15	1571-82-93	1655-66-77-88	1750-59-70-81	1827-38	1900-06-79-90	g	,, 15
A	April 16	1503-14-25-36-87-98	1609-20-82-93	1704-75-86-97	1843-54-65-76	1911-22-33-95	A	April 16
b	,, 17	1530-41-52	1625-36	1715-20	1808-70-81-92	1927-38-49-60	b	,, 17
c	,, 18	1557-68	1647-52	1731-42-58	1802-13-24-97	1954-65-76	c	,, 18
d	,, 19	1500-79-84-90	1663-74-85	1747-67-72-78	1829-35-40	1908-81-87-92	d	,, 19
e	,, 20	1511-22-95	1606-17-79-90	1701-12-83-94	1851-62	1919-24-30	e	,, 20
f	April 21	1527-38-49	1622-33-44	1717-28	1867-78-89	1935-46-57	f	April 21
g	,, 22	1565-76	1660	1739-53-64	1810-21-32	1962-73-84	g	,, 22
A	,, 23	1508	1671	……	1848	1905-16-2000	A	,, 23
b	,, 24	1519	1603-14-98	1709-91	1859	……	b	,, 24
c	,, 25	1546	1641	1736	1886	1943	c	,, 25

Previous to 1752 the above dates are computed from the Old Style. Those printed in heavier type are leap-years. 1752 had E D up to September 2, but A from September 14 to December 31, the intermediate days being dropped for the change of Style. Its Easter was the last in Old Style. Until then also the years were considered to begin on March 25; but that, as it did not affect the date of Easter, is not noticed in this Table. The Table of Moveable Feasts in the Prayer-Book gives all the others after finding Easter in this. The Sunday Letters in the Calendar then enable any one to count days of the week from Sunday. The tables in modern Prayer-Books are calculated for the New Style only.

The French Republican Calendar.

THIS, although reckoned from the 22nd September, 1792, was not introduced until the 22nd November, 1793. It remained in use only till the 31st December, 1805. The Gregorian Calendar was restored January 1st, 1806 (Nivôse 10, Year XIV.). The months varied in different years, thus Nivôse 1 commenced December 21st in 1793, December 22nd in 1795, December 21st in 1796, December 22nd in 1799, December 23rd in 1803, and December 22nd in 1804 and 1805. The following are the dates for the year 1804, the last complete year of the Calendar:—

Vendémiaire	(Vintage),	23 Sept. to Oct. 22	Germinal	(Budding),	22 Mar. to Apr. 21
Brumaire	(Foggy),	23 Oct. to Nov. 22	Floréal	(Flowery),	21 April to May 20
Frimaire	(Sleety),	22 Nov. to Dec. 21	Prairial	(Pasture),	21 May to June 20
Nivôse	(Snowy),	22 Dec. to Jan. 20	Messidor	(Harvest),	20 June to July 19
Pluviôse	(Rainy),	21 Jan. to Feb. 20	Thermidor	(Hot),	20 July to Aug. 19
Ventôse	(Windy),	20 Feb. to Mar. 21	Fructidor	(Fruit),	19 Aug. to Sept. 18

The months were divided into three decades of ten days each, but to make up the 365, five were added at the end of September; (Primidi), dedicated to Virtue; (Duodi) to Genius; (Tridi) to Labour; (Quartidi) to Opinion; and the 5th (Quintidi) to Rewards. To Leap Year, called Olympic, a sixth day, the 22nd or 23rd September (Sextidi), "Jour de la Révolution," was added. This variation of dates has led to considerable confusion, but those who may wish to trace the fourteen years will find some very elaborate tables in the English edition of Bourrienne's "Life of Napoleon": Bentley.

APPOINTED FOR SUNDAYS AND OTHER HOLY DAYS THROUGHOUT THE YEAR.

The Athanasian Creed to be read on the days marked *.	MORNING PRAYER.		EVENING PRAYER		
	First Lesson.	Second Lesson.	First Lesson.		Second Lesson.
Jan. 1 Circumcision	Genesis .. 17, v. 9	Romans ..2, v. 17	Deuteron. 10, v. 12	.....	Col. ..2, v. 8 to 18
„ 6 *Epiphany	Isaiah 60	Luke 3, v. 15 to 23	Isaiah ..2, to v. 10		John ..2, to v. 12
„ 7 I.S. after Epiph.	Isaiah 51	Mat.4, v.23 to 5v.13	Isa. 52, v. 13, & 53 Or Isaiah...54		Acts ..14, to v. 32
„ 14 II. S. aft. Epiph.	Isaiah 55	Matt. ....8, v. 18	Isaiah ....57 Or Isaiah...61		Acts ....8, v. 26
„ 21 III.S. aft. Epiph.	Isaiah 62	Matt. ....12, v. 22	Isaiah ....65 Or Isaiah...66		Acts ..13, to v. 26
„ 25 Conv. of St. Paul	Isaiah 49, to v. 13	Galatians..1, v. 11	Jerem. 1, to v. 11		Acts ..20, to v. 21
„ 28 IV.S.after Epiph.	Job 27	Matt. ..15, v. 21	Job ....28 Or Job 29		Acts ..17, to v. 16
Feb. 2 Purification ...	Exodus 23, to v. 17	Mat.13, v.21, to19v.3	Haggai 2, to v. 10		Acts ..20, to v. 17
„ 4 V. S. after Epiph.	Proverbs 1	Mt. 19, v.27 to 20 v.17	Proverbs ....3 Or Proverbs 8		Acts ..21, to v. 17
„ 11 Septuagesima ..	Genesis 1, & 2 to v. 4	Rev. ..21, to v. 9	Genesis ..2, v. 4		Rev.21, v. 9 to 22 v.6
„ 18 Sexagesima ...	Genesis 3	Matt. ..26, v. 57	Genesis ....6 Or Genesis 8		Romans ..8, v. 17
„ 24 *St. Matthias ..	1 Sam. 2, v. 27 to 36	Mark ....1, v. 21	Isaiah....22, v. 15		Romans 8, to v. 18
„ 25 Quinquagesima .	Genesis 9, to v. 20	Mark 2, to v. 23	Genesis ....12 Or Genesis 13		Romans ..8, v. 18
„ 28 Ash Wednesday	Isaiah 58, to v. 13	Mrk. 2, v. 13 to 23	Jonah 3		Heb. 12, v. 3 to 18
Proper Psalms	Psalm ... 6, 32, 38	......	Psalm 102, 130, 143		
Mar. 4 I. Sun. in Lent.	Gen. 19, v. 12 to 30	Mk. 6, v. 14 to v.30	Genesis 22, to v. 20 Or Genesis 23		Romans 13
„ 11 II. Sun. in Lent.	Genesis 27, to v. 41	Mark ..10, to v. 32	Genesis ....28 Or Genesis 32		1 Cor. ..4, to v. 18
„ 18 III. Sun. in Lent	Genesis 37	Mark ..14, to v. 27	Genesis ....39 Or Genesis 40		1 Cor. 10 & 11, v. 1
„ 25 IV. Sun. in Lent	Genesis 42	......	Genesis ....43 Or Genesis 45		
„ 25 Annunciation ..	Genesis 3, to v. 16	Luke ......1, v. 26	Isaiah 52, v. 7 to 13		1 Cor. 15, to v. 35
April 1 V. Sun. in Lent.	Exodus 3	Luke ......5, v. 17	Exodus ....5 Or Exod. 6, to v. 14		2 Corinthians 5
„ 8 Palm Sunday ..	Exodus 9	Matthew 26	Exodus ....10 Or Exodus 11		Luke 19, v. 28, or [Lk.20, v.9 to v.21
„ 9 Mon. bef. Easter	Lament. 1, to v. 15	John ..14, to v. 15	Lament. ..2, v. 13		John ....14, v. 15
„ 10 Tues. bef. Easter	Lament. 3, to v. 34	John ..15, to v. 14	Lament. ..3, v. 34		John ....15, v. 14
„ 11 Wed. bef. Easter	Lament. 4, to v. 21	John ..16, to v. 16	Daniel ....9, v. 20		John ....16, v. 16
„ 12 Thur. bef. Easter	Hosea 13, to v. 15	John 17	Hosea 14		John ..13, to v. 36
„ 13 Good Friday ..	Genesis 22, to v. 20	John 18	Isa. 52, v. 13, & 53		1 Peter 2
Proper Psalms	Psalm .. 22, 40, 54	......	Psalm 69, 88		
„ 14 Easter Even..	Zechariah 9	Luke ..23, v. 50	Hos. 5, v. 8 to 6, v. 4		Rom. ..6, to v. 14
„ 15 *Easter Day ..	Exodus 12, to v. 29	Rev. ..1, v. 10 to 19	Exodus ..12, v. 29 Or Exodus 14		John 20, v. 11 to 19, [or Rev. 5
Proper Psalms	Psalm .. 2, 57, 111		Psalm 113, 114, 118		
„ 16 Mon.in East. Wk.	Exodus 15, to v. 22	Luke ..24, to v. 13	Exodus 16, to v. 16		Matt. 28, to v. 10
„ 17 Tues.in East. Wk.	2 Kgs. 13, v. 14 to 22	John ..21, to v. 15	Exodus 17, to v. 16		Canticles, 2, v. 10
„ 22 Low Sunday	Num. 16, to v. 36	Luke ....5, v. 29	Numbers 16, v. 36 Or Num. 17, to v. 12		Jn. 20, v.24 to v. 30
„ 25 St. Mark	Isaiah ....62, v. 6	Lk.18, v.31 to 19v.11	Ezekiel 1, to v. 15		Philippians 2
„ 29 II. S. after Easter	Num. 20, to v. 14	Lk.20, v.27 to 21, v.5	Nm.20, v.14 to 21, v.10 Or Num. 21, v. 10		Col. 1, v. 21 to 2 v. 8
May 1 SS. Philip&James	Isaiah 61	John ..1, v. 43	Zechariah 4		Coloss. 14, to v. 24
„ 6 III. S. aft. Easter	Numbers 16	Lk. 23, v. 26 to v. 50	Numbers ....23 Or Numbers 24		1 Thessalonians 3
„ 13 IV. S. aft. Easter	Deuter. 4, to v. 23	John ....3, v. 22	Deut. 4, v. 23 to 41 Or Deuteron. 5		1 Tim. 1, v. 18 & 2
„ 20 Rogation Sunday	Deuteronomy ..6	John ....6, v. 41	Deuteronomy ..9 Or Deuteron. 10		1 Timothy 3
„ 24 *Ascension Day	Dan. 7, v. 9 to 15	Luke ..24, v. 44	2 Kings 2, to v. 16		Hebrews 4
Proper Psalms	Psalm ... 8, 15, 21		Psalm 24, 47, 108		
„ 27 S. aftn. Ascension	Deuteronomy ..30	John ..10, v. 22	Deuteronomy 34 Or Joshua 1		Heb. 2 & 3, to v. 7
June 3 *Whitsun Day..	Deut. 16, to v. 18	Romans 8, to v. 18	Isaiah ....11 Or Ezek. 36, v. 25		Gal. 5, v. 16, or Acts [18, v. 24 to 19, v. 21
Proper Psalms	Psalm 48, 68		Psalm ..104, 145		1 Cor.12, to v. 14
„ 4 Mon.in Whit Wk.	Genesis 11, to v. 10	1 Cor. 12, to v. 14	Num. 11, v. 16 to 31		1 Cor.12, v. 27, & 13
„ 5 Tues.in Whit.Wk.	Joel ....2, v. 21	1 Thes. 5, v. 12 to 24	Micah ..4, to v. 8		1 John 4, to v. 14
„ 10 *Trinity Sunday	Isaiah..6, to v. 11	Rev. ....1, to v. 9	Genesis ....18 Or Gen. 1, & 2 to v.4		Eph. 4, to v. 17, or [Matt. 3
„ 11 St. Barnabas	Deut. 33, to v. 12	Acts ....4, v. 31	Nahum 1		Acts ......14, v. 8
„ 17 I. S. after Trin.	Josh. 3, v. 7 to 4, v. 15	Acts....2, to v. 22	Josh.5, v.13 to 6, v.21 Or Joshua 24		1 Pet.2, v. 11 to 3 v.8
„ 20 Queen'sAccession	Joshua 1, to v. 10	Romans 13	Ezra ..10, to v. 20		1 Peter 5
Proper Psalms	Psalm..20, 21, 101				
„ 21 II. S. after Trin.	Judges 4		Judges ....5 Or Judges 6, v. 11		
„ 24 *St. John Baptist	Malachi 3, to v. 7	Matthew 3	Malachi 4		Matt. ..14, to v. 13
„ 29 St. Peter	Ezek. 3, v. 4 to 15	John 21, v. 15 to 23	Zechariah 3		Acts..4, v. 8 to 23
July 1 III. S. after Trin.	1 Sam. 2, to v. 27	Acts ......9, v. 23	1 Samuel ....3 Or 1 Sam.4, to v.19		1 John ....4 ..v. 7
„ 8 IV. S. after Trin.	1 Samuel 12	Acts 12	1 Samuel ....13 Or Ruth 1		Matthew 3
„ 15 V. S. after Trin.	1 Sam. 15, to v. 24	Acts 18, v.24 to 19v.21	1 Samuel ....16 Or 1 Samuel 17		Matthew ..7, v. 7
„ 22 VI. S. after Trin.	2 Sam. 1	Acts 22, v.23 to 23v.12	2 Sam. 12, to v. 24 Or 2 Samuel 18		Matthew 9
„ 25 *St. James	2 Kings ..1, to v. 16	Luke 9, v. 51 to v. 57	Jerem. 26, v. 8 to v. 16		Matt. 13, to v. 24
„ 29 VII. S. after Trin.	1 Chronicles ..21	Acts ..28, to v. 17	1 Chronicles ....22 Or 1 Chr.28, to v.21		Matt. 15, to v. 21
Aug. 5 VIII. S. aft. Trin.	1 Chron.29, v. 9 to 29	Romans 9	2 Chronicles ....1 Or 1 Kings 3		Matt. 19, v. 3 to v.27
„ 12 IX. S. after Trin.	1 Kings 10, to v. 25	Romans 10	1 Kings 11, to v. 15 Or 1 Kings 11, v. 26		Mat.22, v.15 to 23 v.13
„ 19 X. S. after Trin.	1 Kings 18	Romans 16	1 Kings ....19 Or 1 Kings 17		Mat. 26, v. 31 to v.57
„ 24 *St. Bartholomew	Gen. 28, v. 10 to 18	1 Cor. 4, v. 18, & 5	Deut. ..18, v. 15		Matthew 28
„ 26 XI. S. after Trin.	1 Kings 22	1 Cor. ..7, to v. 25	2 Kings 19		Mark ..1, v. 21
Sept. 2 XII. S. after Trin.	1 Kings 22, to v. 41	1 Cor. 12, to v. 28	2 Kings 2, to v. 16 Or 2 Ks. 4, v. 8 to 38		Mark ..6, to v. 14
„ 9 XIII. S. after Trin.	2 Kings 5	2 Cor. ..1, to v. 23	2 Kings 6, to v. 24 Or 2 Kings 9		Mark ..9, v. 30
„ 16 XIV. S. aft. Trin.	2 Kings 9	2 Corinthians 3	2 Kings 10, to v. 32 Or 2 Kings 13		Mark ..13, v. 14
„ 21 *St. Matthew....	1 Kings ..19, v. 15	2 Cor. 12, v. 14, & 13	1 Chron. 29, to v. 20		Mark 15, v. 42, & 16
„ 23 XV. S. after Trin.	2 Kings 18	Galatians 3	2 Kings ....19 Or 2 Kgs. 23, to v.31		Lk. 1, v. 26 to v. 57
„ 29 St. Mich. & All An.	Genesis 32	Acts 12, v. 5 to 18	Daniel ....10, v. 4		Rev. ....14, to v. 14
„ 30 XVI. S. after Trin.	2 Chronicles 36	Ephesians 1	Nehem. 1, & 2 to v.9 Or Nehemiah ..8		Luke ....4, v. 16

The Athanasian Creed to be read on the days marked*.	MORNING PRAYER.		EVENING PRAYER.	
	First Lesson.	*Second Lesson.*	*First Lesson.*	*Second Lesson.*
Oct. 7 XVII. S. af. Trin.	Jeremiah 5	Philippians 1	Jeremiah 22	Or Jeremiah ...38	Luke ..8, to v. 26
,, 14 XVIII. S. af.Trin.	Jeremiah 36	Coloss. 3, to v. 18	Ezekiel 2	Or Ezek.13, to v. 17	Luke ..11, v. 29
,, 18 St. Luke	Isaiah 55	1 Thessalonians 3	Ezekiel 14	......	Luke ..13, v. 18
,, 21 XIX. S. aft. Trin.	Ezekiel 14	2 Thessalonians 3	Ezekiel 18	Or Ezek. 24, v. 15	Luke ..15, v. 11
,, 28 XX. S. af. Trin.	Ezekiel 34	......	Ezekiel 37	Or Daniel 1	......
,, 28 SS. Simon & Jude.	Isa ..28, v. 9 to 17	1 Timothy 5	Jer. 3, v. 12 to 19	......	Luke ..19, v. 28
Nov. 1 All Saints' Day..	Wisdom 3, to v. 10	Hb. 11, v33 & 12, to v7	Wisdom 5, to v. 17	......	Rev. ...19 to v. 17
,, 4 XXI. S. aft. Trin.	Daniel 3	Titus 1	Daniel 4	Or Daniel 6	Luke ...22, v. 54
,, 11 XXII.S.aft.Trin.	Daniel 6	Heb...4, v. 14 & 5	Daniel ...7, v. 9	Or Daniel ...12	John 1
,, 18 XXIII.S.af.Trin.	Hosea 14	Heb...11, to v. 17	Joel .....2, v. 21	Or Joel ...3, v. 9	John ...6, to v. 22
,, 25 XXIV. S. af. Trin.	Eccles. .....11 & 12	James 4	Haggai 2, to v. 10	Or Malachi, 3 & 4	John ..9, to v. 39
,, 30 *St. Andrew ...	Isaiah 54	John 1, v. 35 to 43	Isaiah 65, to v. 17	......	John 12, v. 20 to 42
Dec. 2 Advent Sunday..	Isaiah 1	1 Peter ...4, v. 7	Isaiah 2	Or Isaiah ..4, v. 2	John ...12, v. 20
,, 9 II. Sun. in Advt.	Isaiah 5	1 John ...2, v. 15	Isaiah 11, to v. 11	Or Isaiah 24	John ...13 to v. 21
,, 16 III. Sun. in Advt.	Isaiah 25	Jude	Isaiah 26	Or Isa.28, v.5 to 19	John 21
,, 21 St. Thomas ..	Job ...42, to v. 7	John 20, v. 19 to 24	Isaiah 35	......	John ...14, to v. 8
,, 23 IV. Sun. in Advt.	Isaiah 30, to v. 27	Revelation 11	Isaiah 32	Or Isa.33, v.2 to 23	Revelation 12
,, 25 *Christmas Day.	Isaiah ...9, to v. 8	Luke ..2, to v. 15	Isaiah 7, v. 10 to 17	......	Titus 3, v. 4 to v. 9
Proper Psalms	Psalm 19, 45, 85		Psalm 89, 110, 132		
,, 26 St. Stephen	Genesis 4, to v. 11	Acts 6	2 Chr. 24, v. 15 to 23	......	Acts ....8, to v. 9
,, 27 St. John Evang.	Exodus ...33, to v. 24	John 13, v. 23 to 36	Isaiah 6	......	Revelation 1
,, 28 Innocents' Day.	Jerem. 31, to v. 18	Revelation 16	Baruch 4, v. 21 to 31	......	Revelation 14
,, 30 I. Sun. aft. Xmas.	Isaiah 35	Revelation 19	Isaiah 38	Or Isaiah 40	Rev... 21, to v. 15

MEMORANDA FOR THE YEAR 1901.

January.
1 Tuesdays 8, 15, 22, 29.
1 Sunday after Xmas.
6 Epiphany.
13 1. Sunday after Epiph.
20 ii. Sunday ,, ,,
27 iii. Sunday ,, ,,

February.
1 Fridays, 8, 15, 22.
3 iv. Sunday after Epiph.
10 Sexagesima.
17 Quinquagesima.
20 Ash Wednesday.
24 i. Sunday in Lent.

March.
1 Fridays, 8, 15, 22, 29.
3 ii. Sunday in Lent.
10 iii. Sunday ,,
17 iv. Sunday ,,
24 v. Sunday ,,
31 Palm Sunday.

April.
1 Mondays, 8, 15, 22, 29.
5 Good Friday.
7 Easter Day.
14 Low Sunday.
21 ii. Sunday after Easter.
28 iii. Sunday ,, ,,

May.
1 Wednesdays 8, 15, 22, 29.
5 iv. Sunday after Easter.
12 Rogation Sunday.
16 Ascension Day.
19 Sunday after Ascension.
26 Whit Sunday.

June.
1 Saturdays 8, 15, 22, 29.
2 Trinity Sunday.
9 i. Sunday after Trinity.
16 ii. Sunday after Trinity.
20 Queen's Accession.
23 iii. Sunday after Trinity.
30 iv. Sunday ,, ,,

July.
1 Mondays 8, 15, 22, 29.
7 v. Sunday after Trinity.
14 vi. Sunday ,, ,,
21 vii. Sunday ,, ,,
28 viii. Sunday ,, ,,

August.
1 Thursdays 8, 15, 22, 29.
4 ix. Sunday after Trinity.
11 x. Sunday ,, ,,
18 xi. Sunday ,, ,,
25 xii. Sunday ,, ,,

September.
1 xiii. Sunday aft. Trinity.
8 xiv. Sunday ,, ,,
15 xv. Sunday ,, ,,
22 xvi. Sunday ,, ,,
29 xvii. Sunday ,, ,,

October.
1 Tuesdays, 8, 15, 22, 29.
6 xviii. Sunday aft. Trinity.
13 xix. Sunday ,, ,,
20 xx. Sunday ,, ,,
27 xxi. Sunday ,, ,,

November.
1 Fridays, 8, 15, 22, 29.
3 xxii. Sunday aft. Trinity.
10 xxiii. Sunday ,, ,,
17 xxiv. Sunday ,, ,,
24 xxv. Sunday ,, ,,

December.
1 Advent Sunday.
8 ii. Sunday in Advent.
15 iii. Sunday ,, ,,
22 iv. Sunday ,, ,,
25 Xmas Day. Tuesday.
29 Sunday aft. Christmas.
31 Tuesday.

MOON'S PHASES FOR 1901.

January.
Full Moon 5d 0h. 14m. Morn.
Lst. Quart 13 8 18 Aft.
New Moon 20 2 36 Aft.
Fst. Quart 27 9 52 Morn.

February.
Full Moon 3d 3h. 30m. Aft.
Lst. Quart 11 6 12 Aft.
New Moon 19 2 45 Morn.
Fst. Quart 25 6 38 Aft.

March.
Full Moon 5d 8h. 4m. Morn.
Lst. Quart 13 1 6 Aft.
New Moon 20 0 53 Aft.
Fst. Quart 27 7 39 Morn.

April.
Full Moon 4d 2h. 20m. Morn.
Lst. Quart 12 3 57 Morn.
New Moon 18 9 37 Aft.
Fst. Quart 24 4 15 Aft.

May.
Full Moon 3d 6h. 19m. Aft.
Lst. Quart 11 2 38 Aft.
New Moon 18 5 38 Morn.
Fst. Quart 25 5 40 Morn.

June.
Full Moon 2d 9h. 53m. Morn.
Lst. Quart 9 10 0 Aft.
New Moon 16 1 33 Aft.
Fst. Quart 23 8 59 Aft.

July.
Full Moon 1d 11h. 18m. Aft.
Lst. Quart 9 3 20 Morn.
New Moon 15 10 01 Aft.
Fst. Quart 23 1 58 Aft.
Full Moon 31 10 34 Morn.

August.
Lst. Quart 8d 8h. 2m. Morn.
New Moon 14 8 28 Morn.
Fst. Quart 22 7 52 Morn.
Full Moon 29 8 21 Aft.

September.
Lst. Quart 6d 2h. 27m. Aft.
New Moon 12 9 19 Aft.
Fst. Quart 21 3 33 Morn.
Full Moon 28 5 36 Morn.

October.
Lst. Quart 6d 8h. 52m. Aft.
New Moon 12 11 11 Aft.
Fst. Quart 20 5 58 Aft.
Full Moon 27 3 6 Aft.

November.
Lst. Quart 5d 7h. 24m. Aft.
New Moon 11 7 32 Morn.
Fst. Quart 19 8 23 Morn.
Full Moon 26 0 11 Morn.

December.
Lst. Quart 5d 9h. 50m. Aft.
New Moon 11 2 53 Morn.
Fst. Quart 18 8 35 Aft.
Full Moon 25 0 16 Aft.

TWELVE O'CLOCK NOON GREENWICH MEAN TIME,
AS COMPARED WITH THE CLOCK IN THE FOLLOWING PLACES:

	H. M.		H. M.		H. M.		H. M.
Adelaide	9 14 P.M.	Constantinople	1 56 P.M.	Melbourne, Aust	9 40 P.M.	Quebec	7 15 A.M.
Auckland (N. Z.)	11 39 P.M.	Dublin	11 35 A.M.	Moscow	2 30 P.M.	Rome	0 50 P.M.
Berlin	0 54 P.M.	Edinburgh	11 47 A.M.	Newfndlnd, S. Jns.	8 29 A.M.	Rotterdam	0 18 P.M.
Berne	0 30 P.M.	Florence	0 45 P.M.	New York	7 4 A.M.	San Francisco Port	3 52 A.M.
Bombay	4 51 P.M.	Glasgow	11 43 A.M.	Paris	0 9 P.M.	St. Petersburg	2 1 P.M.
Boston, U.S.	7 16 A.M.	Hobart, Tasmania	9 49 P.M.	Pekin	7 46 P.M.	Stockholm	1 12 P.M.
Brisbane, Qnslnd.	10 12 P.M.	Jerusalem	2 21 P.M.	Penzance	11 37 A.M.	Suez	2 10 P.M.
Brussels	0 17 P.M.	Lisbon	11 23 A.M.	Perth, W. Aust.	7 44 P.M.	Sydney	10 5 P.M.
Calcutta	5 53 P.M.	Madras	5 21 P.M.	Philadelphia	6 59 A.M.	Toronto	6 42 A.M.
Cape of Good Hope	1 14 P.M.	Madrid	11 45 A.M.	Port Moresby	10 4 P.M.	Vancouver	3 38 A.M.
Chicago	6 10 A.M.	Malta	0 58 P.M.	Prague	0 58 P.M.	Vienna	1 6 P.M.

Local Time depends upon Longitude; every Degree East of Greenwich is four minutes earlier, and every Degree West four minutes later. Note the variations in the U.S. or in British America.

Present Days of the Month.	March, May, July, October have thirty-one days.	January, August, December have thirty-one days.	April, June, September, November have thirty days.	February has twenty-eight days, and in Leap Year twenty-nine.
1	Kalendis.	Kalendis.	Kalendis.	Kalendis.
2	VI. ⎫ Ante Nonas.	IV. ⎫ Ante Nonas.	IV. ⎫ Ante Nonas.	IV. ⎫ Ante Nonas.
3	V. ⎬	III. ⎭	III. ⎭	III. ⎭
4	IV. ⎭	Pridie Nonas.	Pridie Nonas.	Pridie Nonas.
5	III.	Nonis.	Nonis.	Nonis.
6	Pridie Nonas.	VIII.	VIII.	VIII.
7	Nonis.	VII.	VII.	VII.
8	VIII. ⎫	VI. ⎫ Ante Idus.	VI. ⎫ Ante Idus.	VI. ⎫ Ante Idus.
9	VII. ⎬	V. ⎬	V. ⎬	V. ⎬
10	VI. ⎬ Ante Idus.	IV. ⎭	IV. ⎭	IV. ⎭
11	V. ⎬	III.	III.	III.
12	IV. ⎭	Pridie Idus.	Pridie Idus.	Pridie Idus.
13	III.	Idibus.	Idibus.	Idibus.
14	Pridie Idus.	XIX.	XVIII.	XVI.
15	Idibus.	XVIII.	XVII.	XV.
16	XVII.	XVII.	XVI.	XIV.
17	XVI.	XVI.	XV.	XIII.
18	XV.	XV.	XIV.	XII.
19	XIV.	XIV.	XIII.	XI.
20	XIII.	XIII.	XII.	X.
21	XII.	XII.	XI.	IX.
22	XI.	XI.	X.	VIII.
23	X.	X.	IX.	VII.
24	IX.	IX.	VIII.	VI.
25	VIII.	VIII.	VII.	V.
26	VII.	VII.	VI.	IV.
27	VI.	VI.	V.	III.
28	V.	V.	IV.	Pridie Kalendas Martias.
29	IV.	IV.	III.	
30	III.	III.	Pridie Kalendas (of the month following).	
31	Pridie Kalendas (of the month following).	Pridie Kalendas (of the month following).		

(In columns 2–4, the rows from the XVII/XIX/XVIII line downward are braced "Ante Kalendas (of the month following)." In column 5 the rows XVI down to III are braced "Ante Kalendas Martias.")

Greek and Russian Calendar.

A.D. 1899, A.M. 7407.

OLD STYLE	CERTAIN HOLY DAYS	NEW STYLE
Jan. 1	Circumcision	Jan. 13
" 6	Theophany (Epiphany)	" 18
Feb. 2	Hypapante (Purification)	Feb. 14
" 20	Carnival Sunday	Mar. 4
" 27	First Sunday in Lent	" 11
Mar. 9	Forty Martyrs	" 21
" 25	Annunciation of Theotokos	April 7
April 2	Palm Sunday	" 15
" 7	Great Friday (Good Friday) .	" 20
" 9	Holy Pasch (Easter Day)	" 21
" 23	St. George	May 6
May 9	St. Nicolas	" 21
" 14	Coronation of the Emperor *	" 27
" 18	Ascension	" 31
" 28	Pentecost (Whit Sunday)	June 10
" 29	Holy Ghost	" 11
June 29	Peter and Paul, Chief Apostles	July 12
Aug. 1	First day of Fast of Theotokos	Aug. 14
" 6	Transfiguration	" 19
" 15	Repose of Theotokos (Assumption)	" 28
" 30	St. Alexander Nevsky*	Sept. 12
Sept. 8	Nativity of Theotokos	" 21
" 14	Exaltation of the Cross	" 27
Oct. 1	Patronage of Theotokos*	Oct. 14
" 21	Accession of the Emperor*	Nov. 3
Nov. 15	First day Fast of the Nativity	" 28
" 21	Entrance of Theotokos	Dec. 4
Dec. 6	St. Nicolas	" 19
" 9	Conception of Theotokos	" 22
" 25	Nativity	Jan. 7

* Peculiar to Russia.

The Days of the Roman Month.

IN the Roman (Julian) Calendar the months corresponded exactly with our own, excepting that down to the time of the great Emperor Augustus, the fifth and sixth months of the year—which, with the Romans, began with March—were called Quintilis and Sextilis; afterwards they were named in honour of the emperors Julius and Augustus.

In reckoning the days of each month three fixed points were taken, and any particular day was said to be so many days *before* the next coming fixed day. These three points were (1) the Kalends, by which name the first of each month was known; (2) the Nones, which fell on the seventh day of the month in March, May, July, and October, and on the fifth day in each of the other months; and the Ides, which always fell eight days after the Nones.

For example, the 1st of January was the Kalends of January (*Kalendis Januariis*), the 31st of December was the day before the Kalends of January (*pridie Kalendas Januarias*); but Dec. 30th was the third day before the Kalends of January (*ante diem tertium Kalendas Januarias*), in this case both Jan. 1st and Dec. 31st being included in the reckoning. And so on back to Dec. 14th, which was the nineteenth day before the January Kalends (*ante diem undevicesimum Kal. Jan.*), Dec. 13th being *Idibus Decembribus*, the Ides of December. In Leap-year, both Feb. 24th and Feb. 25th were known as the sixth day before the March Kalends, being distinguished respectively as *prior* and *posterior*.

In the year 1900 there will be three Eclipses; two of the Sun, and one of the Moon.

I. A total Eclipse of the Sun, May 28, visible at Greenwich as a partial Eclipse.

At Greenwich.

Begins at	2h. 47m. aft.	} Greenwich
Greatest Phase	3 55 aft.	} Mean
Ends at	4 57 aft.	} Time.

The first contact takes place at 145° from the vertex, counting towards the *West*, and the last contact at 69° from the vertex towards the *East*. The magnitude of the Eclipse=0·68, taking the Sun's diameter=1.

At Edinburgh.

Begins at	2h. 41m. aft.	} Greenwich
Greatest Phase	3 46 aft.	} Mean
Ends at	4 47 aft.	} Time.

The first contact takes place at 144° from the vertex counting towards the *West*, and the last contact at 78° from the vertex towards the *East*. The magnitude of the Eclipse=0·60, taking the Sun's diameter=1.

At Dublin.

Begins at	2h. 13m. aft.	} Dublin
Greatest Phase	3 22 aft.	} Mean
Ends at	4 27 aft.	} Time.

The first contact takes place at 141° from the vertex counting towards the *West*, and the last contact at 71° from the vertex towards the *East*. The magnitude of the Eclipse=0·68, taking the Sun's diameter=1.

The line of central Eclipse passes from California across the northern portion of the Gulf of Mexico, and leaving the east coast of America near Charleston, crosses the Atlantic; striking the west coast of Portugal at Ovar, a little south of Oporto, passes across Spain to Alicante, thence over the Mediterranean Sea to Algiers, and across the north of Africa to near Assouan.

II. A partial Eclipse of the Moon, June 13, partly visible at Greenwich.

First contact with the Shadow	3h. 24m. morn.	} Greenwich
Last contact with the Shadow	3 31 morn.	} Mean Time.

It will be observed, on taking notice of the times of first and last contacts, that this is a very insignificant Eclipse; little more than mere contact of the Earth's shadow with the Moon's limb; the first contact with the shadow takes place at 176° from the north point of the Moon's limb, counting towards the *East*, and the last at 180°, in the same direction, from the same point. The whole of this portion of the Eclipse will be visible at Greenwich, as the Moon does not set there till 3h. 54m. morn.

III. An annular Eclipse of the Sun, November 22, invisible at Greenwich. Begins on the Earth generally 4h. 20m. morn., in longitude 21° East of Greenwich, and latitude 2° South. Central Eclipse begins generally at 5h. 27m. morn., in longitude 3° East of Greenwich, and latitude 6° South. Central Eclipse ends generally at 9h. 13m. morn., in longitude 135° East of Greenwich, and latitude 19° South. Eclipse ends on the Earth generally at 10h. 20m. morn., in longitude 117° East of Greenwich, and latitude 14° South. The line of Central Eclipse passes over the southern portion of Africa, so that there will be a partial Eclipse at the Cape and Natal.

At the Cape.

Begins at	6h. 14m.	} Cape
Greatest Phase	7 15	} Mean
Ends at	8 27	} Time.

The first contact takes place at 76° from the vertex towards the *East*, and the last contact at 165° from the vertex, towards the *West*.

Magnitude of the Eclipse=0·49, taking the Sun's diameter=1.

At Natal.

Begins at	6h. 54m.	} Natal
Greatest Phase	8 10	} Mean
Ends at	9 39	} Time.

The first contact takes place at 57° from the vertex towards the *East*, and the last contact at 153° from the vertex towards the *West*.

Magnitude of the Eclipse=0·72, taking the Sun's diameter=1.

IV. Eclipses of Jupiter's Satellites.

The following table contains *all* the Eclipses of the first Satellite, and *those only which are visible at Greenwich* of the second and third Satellites.

The Roman numerals indicate the Satellite eclipsed ; the letters D and R signifying respectively, Disappearance and Reappearance. Those Eclipses which are visible at Greenwich have an asterisk after the D or R in the second column.

Till May 27 the disappearances and reappearances will take place on the Western side of the Planet; from May 27 to November 17 on the Eastern side. If the phenomena are observed with an astronomical telescope (which inverts the image in the field of view), the Western limb of the planet will be on the observer's left hand, and the Eastern limb on the right, when looking south.

The mean time of Eclipse for any other place than Greenwich may be found by applying to the times given in the Table the difference of longitude, adding the difference if the longitude of the place is *East* of Greenwich, and subtracting if *West*.

JANUARY.

Day.	Satellite and Phase.	Greenwich Mean Time.		
		H.	M.	S.
2	I. D.	5	5	16 aft.
4	I. D.	11	33	46 morn.
6	I. D.*	6	2	10 morn.
8	I. D.	0	30	40 morn.
9	I. D.	6	59	2 aft.
11	I. D.	1	27	32 aft.
13	I. D.*	7	55	55 morn.
15	I. D.	2	24	24 morn.
16	III. R.*	2	20	32 morn.
16	I. D.	8	52	45 aft.

JANUARY—*continued*.

18	I. D.	3	21	14 aft.
20	I. D.	9	49	36 morn.
22	I. D.*	4	18	5 morn.
23	III. D.*	7	49	50 morn.
23	I. D.	10	46	23 aft.
25	I. D.	5	14	52 aft.
27	I. D.	11	43	14 morn.
29	I. D.*	6	11	41 morn.
31	I. D.	0	40	1 morn.

FEBRUARY.

1	I. D.	7	8	27 aft.
3	I. D.	1	36	48 aft.

FEBRUARY—*continued*.

5	I. D.	8	5	15 morn.
7	I. D.	2	33	34 morn.
8	I. D.	9	1	59 aft.
10	I. D.	3	30	20 aft.
12	I. D.	9	58	46 morn.
14	I. D.*	4	27	4 morn.
15	I. D.	10	55	29 aft.
17	II. R.*	2	31	45 morn.
17	I. D.	5	23	49 aft.
19	I. D.	11	52	15 morn.
21	I. D.	6	20	33 morn.
23	I. D.	0	48	57 morn.
24	II. D.*	2	48	36 morn.

FEBRUARY—continued.

Day.	Satellite and Phase.	Greenwich Mean Time. H. M. S.
24	II. R.*	5 7 59 morn.
24	I. D.	7 17 17 aft.
26	I. D.	1 45 42 aft.
28	I. D.*	3 36 35 morn.
28	III. R.*	5 10 5 morn.
28	I. D.	8 13 59 morn.

MARCH.

Day.	Satellite and Phase.	Greenwich Mean Time. H. M. S.
2	I. D.*	2 43 23 morn.
3	II. D.*	5 21 39 morn.
3	I. D.	9 10 42 aft.
5	I. D.	3 39 7 aft.
7	I. D.	10 7 24 morn.
9	I. D.*	4 35 48 morn.
10	I. D.	11 4 6 aft.
12	I. D.	5 32 31 aft.
14	I. D.	0 0 49 aft.
16	I. D.	6 29 12 morn.
18	I. D.*	0 57 31 morn.
19	I. D.	7 25 56 aft.
21	I. D.	1 54 14 aft.
23	I. D.	8 22 37 morn.
25	I. D.*	2 50 55 morn.
26	I. D.	9 19 21 aft.
28	I. D.	3 47 39 aft.
30	I. D.	10 16 2 morn.

APRIL.

Day.	Satellite and Phase.	Greenwich Mean Time. H. M. S.
1	I. D.*	4 44 22 morn.
2	I. D.	11 12 47 aft.
4	II. D.*	4 52 8 morn.
4	I. D.	5 41 6 aft.
5	III. R.*	1 1 49 morn.
6	I. D.	0 9 29 aft.
8	I. D.	6 37 50 morn.
10	I. D.*	1 6 15 morn.
11	I. D.	7 34 35 aft.
12	III. D.*	3 21 5 morn.
12	III. R.*	5 0 3 morn.
13	I. D.	2 2 59 aft.
15	I. D.*	8 31 20 morn.
17	I. D.	2 59 45 morn.
18	I. D.	9 28 9 aft.
20	I. D.	3 56 31 aft.
21	II. D.*	11 17 17 aft.
22	I. D.	10 24 53 morn.
24	I. D.*	4 53 20 morn.
25	I. D.	11 21 42 aft.
27	I. D.	5 50 8 aft.
29	II. D.*	1 51 48 morn.
29	I. D.	0 18 30 aft.

MAY.

Day.	Satellite and Phase.	Greenwich Mean Time. H. M. S.
1	I. D.	6 46 59 morn.
3	I. D.*	1 15 21 morn.
4	I. D.	7 43 48 aft.
6	I. D.	2 12 12 aft.
8	I. D.	8 40 41 morn.
10	I. D.*	3 9 5 morn.
11	I. D.	9 37 33 aft.
13	I. D.	4 5 58 aft.
15	I. D.	10 34 29 morn.
17	I. D.*	5 2 54 morn.
17	III. D.*	11 9 10 aft.
18	I. D.*	11 31 23 aft.
20	I. D.	5 59 50 aft.

MAY—continued.

Day.	Satellite and Phase.	Greenwich Mean Time. H. M. S.
22	I. D.	0 28 22 aft.
23	II. D.*	10 55 5 aft.
24	I. D.	6 56 49 morn.
25	III. D.*	3 7 31 morn.
26	I. D.*	1 25 19 morn.
29	I. R.	4 30 33 aft.
31	I. R.	10 59 2 morn.

JUNE.

Day.	Satellite and Phase.	Greenwich Mean Time. H. M. S.
2	I. R.	5 27 34 morn.
3	I. R.*	11 56 4 aft.
5	I. R.	6 24 38 aft.
7	I. R.	0 53 9 aft.
9	I. R.	7 21 42 morn.
11	I. R.*	1 50 14 morn.
12	I. R.	8 18 50 aft.
14	I. R.	2 47 22 aft.
16	I. R.	9 15 57 morn.
17	II. R.*	10 26 19 aft.
18	I. R.	3 44 30 morn.
19	I. R.*	10 13 7 aft.
21	I. R.	4 41 41 aft.
22	III. R.*	8 49 18 aft.
23	I. R.	11 10 17 morn.
25	II. R.*	1 3 23 morn.
25	I. R.*	5 38 51 morn.
27	I. R.*	0 7 29 morn.
28	I. R.	6 36 3 aft.
29	III. D.*	10 58 29 aft.
30	I. R.*	0 49 26 morn.
30	I. R.	1 4 41 aft.

JULY.

Day.	Satellite and Phase.	Greenwich Mean Time. H. M. S.
2	I. R.	7 33 17 morn.
4	I. R.*	2 1 56 morn.
5	I. R.*	8 30 33 aft.
7	I. R.	2 59 11 aft.
9	I. R.	9 27 48 morn.
11	I. R.	3 56 29 morn.
12	I. R.	10 25 7 aft.
14	I. R.	4 53 46 aft.
16	I. R.	11 22 24 morn.
18	I. R.	5 51 5 morn.
19	II. R.*	10 15 23 aft.
20	I. R.*	0 19 45 morn.
21	I. R.	6 48 24 aft.
23	I. R.	1 17 3 aft.
25	I. R.	7 45 45 morn.
27	I. R.*	2 14 25 morn.
28	I. R.*	8 43 6 aft.
30	I. R.	3 11 45 aft.

AUGUST.

Day.	Satellite and Phase.	Greenwich Mean Time. H. M. S.
1	I. R.	9 40 27 morn.
3	I. R.	4 9 9 morn.
4	III. R.*	8 48 41 aft.
4	I. R.	10 37 50 aft.
6	I. R.	5 6 30 aft.
8	I. R.	11 35 13 morn.
10	I. R.	6 3 55 morn.
11	III. D.*	10 50 29 aft.
12	I. R.	0 32 37 morn.
13	I. R.	7 1 18 aft.
15	II. R.*	7 27 11 aft.
15	I. R.	1 30 1 aft.
17	I. R.	7 58 44 morn.
19	I. R.	2 27 25 morn.

AUGUST—continued.

Day.	Satellite and Phase.	Greenwich Mean Time. H. M. S.
20	II. D.*	7 36 22 aft.
20	I. R.*	8 56 7 aft.
20	II. R.*	10 5 13 aft.
22	I. R.	3 24 50 aft.
24	I. R.	9 53 33 morn.
26	I. R.	4 22 15 morn.
27	I. R.	10 50 57 aft.
29	I. R.	5 19 39 aft.
31	I. R.	11 48 23 morn.

SEPTEMBER.

Day.	Satellite and Phase.	Greenwich Mean Time. H. M. S.
2	I. R.	6 17 5 morn.
4	I. R.	0 45 47 morn.
5	I. R.*	7 14 29 aft.
7	I. R.	1 43 13 aft.
9	I. R.	8 11 55 morn.
11	I. R.	2 40 37 morn.
12	I. R.	9 9 19 aft.
14	I. R.	3 38 4 aft.
14	II. R.*	7 18 38 aft.
16	I. R.	10 6 43 morn.
16	III. D.*	6 45 29 morn.
18	I. R.	4 35 27 morn.
19	I. R.	11 4 9 aft.
21	I. R.	5 32 54 aft.
23	I. R.	0 1 34 aft.
25	I. R.	6 30 17 morn.
27	I. R.	0 58 58 morn.
28	I. R.*	7 27 43 aft.
30	I. R.	1 56 23 aft.

OCTOBER.

Day.	Satellite and Phase.	Greenwich Mean Time. H. M. S.
2	I. R.	8 25 5 morn.
4	I. R.	2 53 46 morn.
5	I. R.	9 22 30 aft.
7	I. R.	3 51 11 aft.
9	I. R.	10 19 53 morn.
11	I. R.	4 48 33 morn.
12	I. R.	11 17 17 aft.
14	I. R.	5 45 57 aft.
16	I. R.	0 14 38 aft.
18	I. R.	6 43 18 morn.
20	I. R.	1 12 2 morn.
21	I. R.	7 40 41 aft.
22	III. R.*	4 51 18 aft.
23	I. R.	2 9 22 aft.
25	I. R.	8 38 1 morn.
27	I. R.	3 6 44 morn.
28	I. R.	9 35 23 aft.
30	I. R.	4 4 4 aft.

VEMBER.

Day.	Satellite and Phase.	Greenwich Mean Time. H. M. S.
1	I. R.	10 32 42 morn.
3	I. R.	5 1 25 morn.
4	I. R.	11 30 3 aft.
6	I. R.	5 58 43 aft.
8	I. R.	0 27 21 aft.
10	I. R.	6 56 3 morn.
12	I. R.	1 24 40 morn.
13	I. R.	7 53 20 aft.
15	I. R.	2 21 56 aft.
17	I. R.	8 50 38 morn.

The Satellites will be invisible to the end of the year, owing to Jupiter's proximity to the Sun.

MEAN RIGHT ASCENSION AND DECLINATION OF ONE HUNDRED FUNDAMENTAL STARS, VISIBLE AT GREENWICH, FOR JANUARY 1, 1900.

NAME OF STAR.	Mag.	Right Ascension.	Annual Precess.	Declination.	Ann Prec.
		H. M. S.	s.	° ′ ″	″
α Andromedæ	2	0 3 13.0	+ 3·08	+ 28 32 18	+20·1
γ Pegasi	3	0 8 5·1	+ 3·08	+ 14 37 39	+20·0
α Cassiopeiæ	2½	0 34 49·7	+ 3·37	+ 55 59 19	+19·8
β Ceti	2	0 38 34·2	+ 3·00	− 18 32 8	+19·8
α Piscium	4½	0 57 45·1	+ 3·12	+ 7 21 6	+19·4
θ Ceti	4	1 19 1·4	+ 3·00	− 8 48 58	+18·9
α UrsæMinoris (Pole St.)	2	1 22 33·1	+25·19	+ 88 46 27	+18·8
η Piscium	3½	1 26 7·8	+ 3·20	+ 14 49 49	+18·7
β Arietis	3	1 49 6·8	+ 3·30	+ 19 19 10	+17·8
α Arietis	2	2 1 32·0	+ 3·36	+ 22 59 23	+17·3
γ² Ceti	3	2 38 7·0	+ 3·11	+ 2 48 52	+15·5
α Ceti	2½	2 57 3·0	+ 3·13	+ 3 41 51	+14·4
α Persei	2	3 17 10·7	+ 4·26	+ 49 30 19	+13·1
η Tauri	3	3 41 32·3	+ 3·56	+ 23 47 45	+11·4
γ¹ Eridani	3	3 53 21·7	+ 2·79	− 13 47 35	+10·5
α Tauri (Aldebaran)	1	4 30 10·8	+ 3·43	+ 16 18 30	+ 7·7
ι Aurigæ	2½	4 50 28·8	+ 3·90	+ 33 0 29	+ 6·0
β Aurigæ (Capella)	1	5 9 18·0	+ 4·42	+ 45 53 47	+ 4·4
β Orionis	1	5 9 43·9	+ 2·88	− 8 19 1	+ 4·4
β Tauri	2	5 19 58·2	+ 3·79	+ 28 31 23	+ 3·5
α Orionis	2½	5 26 53·8	+ 3·06	+ 0 22 23	+ 2·9
α Leporis	2½	5 28 19·1	+ 2·65	− 17 53 38	+ 2·8
ε Orionis	2	5 31 8·3	+ 3·04	− 1 15 57	+ 2·5
α Columbæ	2½	5 36 1·7	+ 2·17	− 34 7 38	+ 2·1
α Orionis	1	5 49 45·4	+ 3·25	+ 7 23 19	+ 0·9
μ Geminorum	3	6 16 54·6	+ 3·63	+ 22 33 54	− 1·5
γ Geminorum	2	6 31 56·1	+ 3·46	+ 16 29 5	− 2·8
α Canis Majoris (Sirius)	1	6 40 44·5	+ 2·68	− 16 34 43	− 3·5
51 Cephei	5½	6 53 44·2	+29·70	+ 87 12 20	− 4·7
ε Canis Majoris	1½	6 54 41·7	+ 2·36	− 28 50 9	− 4·7
δ Geminorum	3½	7 14 9·0	+ 3·59	+ 22 9 59	− 6·4
α² Geminorum (Castor)	2	7 28 13·2	+ 3·85	+ 32 6 29	− 7·5
α CanisMinoris (Procyon)	1	7 34 4·1	+ 3·19	+ 5 28 52	− 8·0
β Geminorum (Pollux)	1	7 39 11·9	+ 3·73	+ 28 16 4	− 8·4
15 Argûs	3	8 3 17·1	+ 2·56	− 24 0 58	−10·3
ε Hydræ	3½	8 41 28·3	+ 3·19	+ 6 47 9	−13·0
ι Ursæ Majoris	3	8 52 21·8	+ 4·17	+ 48 26 4	−13·7
α Hydræ	2	9 22 40·4	+ 2·95	− 8 13 30	−15·5
θ Ursæ Majoris	3	9 26 10·3	+ 4·14	+ 52 7 59	−15·7
α Leonis	3	9 40 10·5	+ 3·43	+ 24 14 5	−16·4
α Leonis (Regulus)	1	10 3 2·8	+ 3·22	+ 12 27 22	−17·5
γ¹ Leonis	2½	10 14 27·6	+ 3·29	+ 20 20 51	−18·0
γ Ursæ Majoris	2	10 57 33·6	+ 3·76	+ 62 17 27	−19·3
δ Leonis	3	11 8 47·5	+ 3·19	+ 21 4 18	−19·6
δ Crateris	4	11 14 20·4	+ 3·01	− 14 14 15	−19·7
β Leonis	2	11 43 57·5	+ 3·10	+ 15 7 52	−20·0
γ Ursæ Majoris	2½	11 48 34·4	+ 3·17	+ 54 15 3	−20·0
ε Corvi	3	12 4 58·8	+ 3·08	− 22 3 50	−20·0
δ Virginis	4	12 14 47·3	+ 3·07	+ 0 6 40	−20·0
β Corvi	3	12 29 7·9	+ 3·14	− 22 50 38	−19·9
γ¹ Virginis	3½	12 36 35·4	+ 3·03	− 0 54 1	−19·8
α Canum Venaticorum	3	12 51 21·0	+ 2·83	+ 38 51 30	−19·6
α Virginis (Spica)	1	13 19 55·4	+ 3·16	− 10 38 22	−18·8
ζ Virginis	3½	13 29 35·8	+ 3·07	− 0 5 5	−18·5
η Ursæ Majoris	2	13 43 36·1	+ 2·38	+ 49 48 44	−18·0
η Boötis	3	13 49 55·4	+ 2·85	+ 18 53 56	−17·8
α Boötis (Arcturus)	1	14 11 6·0	+ 2·81	+ 19 42 11	−16·9
ε³ Boötis	2½	14 40 37·2	+ 2·62	+ 27 29 44	−15·3
α Libræ	3	14 45 20·7	+ 3·32	− 15 37 35	−15·1
β Ursæ Minoris	2	14 50 59·5	+ 0·21	+ 74 33 51	−14·7
β Libræ	2½	15 11 37·4	+ 3·23	− 9 0 51	−13·4
α Coronæ Borealis	2½	15 30 27·2	+ 2·53	+ 27 3 4	−12·5
α Serpentis	2½	15 39 20·5	+ 2·94	+ 6 44 24	−11·5
β¹ Scorpii	3	15 59 37·1	+ 3·48	− 19 31 55	−10·1
δ Ophiuchi	3	16 9 6·2	+ 3·14	− 3 26 13	− 9·3
η Draconis	3	16 22 38·2	+ 0·81	+ 61 44 26	− 8·3
α Scorpii (Antares)	1	16 23 16·4	+ 3·67	− 26 12 36	− 8·2
ζ Herculis	3	16 37 30·9	+ 2·30	+ 31 47 1	− 7·1

EXPLANATION OF THE ASTRONOMICAL TABLES.

Mean Right Ascension.

The Mean Right Ascension and Declination for any other date may be found from this table by multiplying the annual precession by the number of years elapsed, and applying the result to the quantities given in this table. If the required date be earlier than 1900, the *signs* of the annual variations must be changed. In applying the corrections, to reduce to any other date, to the Declinations, it must be borne in mind that N. Declination means +, and S. Declination means −, and that the corrections must be added *algebraically*.

Configuration of Jupiter's Satellites.

This column exhibits, at the particular hour mentioned, the respective position of Jupiter and his Satellites as seen in an inverting telescope. The white circles represent the Planet, and the numerals 1, 2, 3, and 4 the respective Satellites: a black circle is intended to show, either that the Satellite whose numeral it stands in the place of is in the shadow of the Planet (eclipsed), or else is behind the disc of Jupiter (occulted); the sign ♃ indicates that the Satellite in question is *on* the disc of the Planet.

Sidereal Time at Mean Noon.

This column indicates the Sidereal Time at Mean Noon on each day of the year, and is the time which the Observatory or Astronomical clock should show when the Mean Time clock points to Noon, and, in connection with the Table in the Appendix, serves to convert Sidereal into Mean Solar Time.

Mean Time at Sidereal Noon.

This column indicates the time which should be shown by the Mean Time Clock when the first point of Aries is on the meridian, or, in other words, when it is Sidereal Noon, and is useful for changing Mean

Name of Star.	Mag.	Right Ascension.			Annual Precess.	Declination.			Ann. Prec.
		H.	M.	S.	s.	°	′	″	″
κ Ophiuchi	3½	16	52	56·0	+ 2·86	+ 9	31	49	− 5·8
a¹ Herculis	3½	17	10	5·2	+ 2·74	+14	30	15	− 4·3
θ Ophiuchi	3½	17	15	52·0	+ 3·68	−24	54	0	− 3·8
β Draconis	3	17	28	10·3	+ 1·36	+52	22	31	− 2·8
δ Ophiuchi	2	17	30	17·5	+ 2·78	+12	37	58	− 2·6
μ Herculis	3½	17	42	32·6	+ 2·37	+27	46	45	− 1·5
γ Draconis	2½	17	54	16·9	+ 1·39	+51	30	2	− 0·5
Ursæ Minoris	4½	18	4	32·7	−19·51	+86	36	48	+ 0·4
μ Sagittarii	4	18	7	46·9	+ 3·59	−21	5	7	+ 0·4
α Lyræ (*Vega*)	1	18	33	33·1	+ 2·01	+38	41	26	+ 0·7
β¹ Lyræ (*var.*)	3½–4½	18	46	23·2	+ 2·21	+33	14	47	+ 2·9
ζ Aquilæ	3	19	0	48·8	+ 2·76	+13	42	53	+ 4·0
λ Ursæ Minoris	6½	19	22	30·8	−67·87	+88	59	16	+ 5·3
γ Aquilæ	3	19	41	30·3	+ 2·85	+10	22	10	+ 6·9
α Aquilæ (*Altair*)	1	19	45	51·2	+ 2·89	+ 8	36	14	+ 7·0
β Aquilæ	4	19	50	24·0	+ 2·94	+ 6	9	25	+ 8·9
a² Capricorni	4	20	12	30·4	+ 3·33	−12	51	18	+ 9·3
β Cygni	1½	20	38	1·3	+ 2·04	+44	55	22	+11·0
ζ Cygni	3½	21	8	40·8	+ 2·55	+29	49	0	+12·8
α Cephei	2½	21	16	11·5	+ 1·41	+62	9	43	+14·7
β Aquarii	3	21	26	17·7	+ 3·16	− 6	0	41	+15·1
S² Cephei	3½	21	27	22·2	+ 0·79	+70	7	18	+15·7
ε Pegasi	2½	21	39	16·4	+ 2·95	+ 9	24	59	+15·8
α Aquarii	3	22	0	38·8	+ 3·08	− 0	48	21	+16·4
γ Aquarii	4	22	16	29·4	+ 3·09	− 1	53	29	+17·4
ζ Pegasi	3½	22	36	28·4	+ 2·99	+10	18	33	+18·7
α Piscis Australis (*Fomalhaut*)	1½	22	52	7·5	+ 3·30	−30	9	8	+19·2
α Pegasi (*Markab*)	2½	22	59	45·7	+ 2·98	+14	40	2	+19·4
Piscium	4	23	11	5·8	+ 3·06	+ 2	44	9	+19·6
γ Cephei	3½	23	35	14·3	+ 2·44	+77	4	28	+19·9
ω Piscium	4	23	54	10·5	+ 3·07	+ 6	18	35	+20·0

Solar into Sidereal Time with the help of the Table in the Appendix.

Following the Phases of the Moon on the first page of each month there will be found, as well as the *times* of Apogee and Perigee, the corresponding distances from the Earth to the nearest 100 miles.

The mean distance of the Moon from the Earth is 238,840 miles.

Under the head "Eclipses, Occultations, and other Celestial Phenomena," in each month, will be found the "Mean Time of the Sun's Semidiameter passing the Meridian" for the 5th and 20th days. This will be useful in determining time by the Dipleidoscope or similar instrument, when, from the interference of clouds, &c., only one limb of the Sun is observed. From the values on the 5th and 20th, that for any other day can be easily inferred with sufficient accuracy, the change in the apparent diameter being very slow.

Mean Right Ascension and Declination of some of the Principal Fundamental Stars visible in the Southern Hemisphere, for January 1, 1900.

Name of Star.	Mag.	Right Ascension.			Annual Precess.	Declination.			Ann. Prec.
		H.	M.	S.	s.	°	′	″	″
β Hydri	2½	0	20	30·3		−77	49	2	+20·0
α Eridani (*Achernar*)	1	1	33	59·4		−57	44	41	+18·4
γ Hydri	3	3	48	47·1		−74	32	43	+10·9
α Argûs (*Canopus*)	1	6	21	43·9		−52	38	28	− 1·9
ι Argûs	2½	9	14	24·7		−58	51	19	−15·0
η Argûs	*Var.* 1–7½	10	41	10·8		−59	9	30	−18·9
β Chamæleontis	4½	12	12	28·4		−78	45	25	−20·0
a¹ Crucis	1½	12	21	1·9		−62	32	41	−20·0
a¹ Centauri	1	13	56	45·6		−59	53	26	−17·5
a² Centauri	1	14	32	49·0		−60	23	10	−15·7
α Trianguli Australis	2	16	38	4·3		−68	50	39	− 7·0
σ Octantis	6	18	59	43·3	+102·15	−89	15	16	+ 5·2
α Pavonis	2	20	17	44·2	4·77	−57	3	20	+11·3
α Gruis	2	22	1	55·9	3·79	−47	26	43	+17·5

α Centauri.

It is supposed that this star, one of the brightest in the Southern Hemisphere, is the nearest of the fixed stars to the Earth. Dr. Gill gives to it a parallax of 0″·75, which would make its distance from the Earth 275,000 times that of the Sun. At the rate at which light travels through space, it would require four years and four months to reach the Earth from this star.

THE ASTEROIDS, OR SMALL PLANETS.

Besides those Planets whose positions have already been given in the Calendar portions of the Almanack, there are a large number of small bodies revolving round the Sun in the space between Mars and Jupiter.

The first of these was discovered by Piazzi, in 1801, and called Ceres: the second in 1802, by Olbers, named Pallas: the third in 1804, by Harding, named Juno: the fourth in 1807, by Olbers, named Vesta. No more were discovered till 1845, when Hencke found Astræa, since which time many new members have been added annually, bringing the number up to 450.

1900 NOT A LEAP YEAR.

The intercalation of a day in every fourth year does not exactly correct the difference between the civil and tropical years, the outstanding difference amounting to about three days in 400 years.

To correct this, the intercalations on centenary years were ordered to be omitted, except when they were multiples of 400. Hence we see that, according to this rule, the years 1900, 2100, 2200, &c., are ordinary; and 2000, 2400, 2800, &c., are bissextile years.

This correction still leaves a small outstanding error which, however, only amounts to one day in about 3600 years.

RISING, SETTING, RIGHT ASCENSION, AND DECLINATION OF THE PLANETS URANUS, NEPTUNE, CERES, PALLAS, AND JUNO, 1900, ABOUT THE TIMES OF OPPOSITION AT MEAN NOON OF THE RESPECTIVE DAYS.

URANUS.

Day.	Rises. H. M.	Sets. H. M.	R.A. H. M. S.	Decl. ° ' "
May 6	9 42A	5 48M	16 39 54	22 7 35 S
" 15	8 59A	5 7M	16 38 18	22 4 35
" 26	8 17A	4 27M	16 36 36	22 1 17
June 5	7 35A	3 46M	16 34 50	21 57 53
" 15	6 54A	3 6M	16 33 7	21 54 24
" 25	6 13A	2 25M	16 31 29	21 51 7 S

In opposition June 1.

NEPTUNE.

Day.	Rises. H. M.	Sets. H. M.	R.A. H. M. S.	Decl. ° ' "
Nov. 11	6 24A	10 44M	5 55 0	22 11 57 N
" 21	5 44A	10 4M	5 54 3	22 11 39
Dec. 1	5 3A	9 23M	5 52 58	22 11 23
" 11	4 23A	8 43M	5 51 47	22 11 8
" 21	3 42A	8 2M	5 50 34	22 11 53
" 31	3 2A	7 22M	5 49 21	22 10 46 N

In opposition December 20.

CERES.

Day.	Rises. H. M.	Sets. H. M.	R.A. H. M. S.	Decl. ° ' "
July 6	10 52A	5 49M	21 16 50	26 55 35 S
" 16	10 15A	4 54M	21 10 21	28 4 1
" 26	9 31A	3 56M	21 2 11	29 9 35
Aug. 5	8 57A	3 0M	20 53 9	30 6 4
" 15	8 15A	2 6M	20 44 13	30 48 31
" 25	7 31A	1 14M	20 36 24	31 14 39 S

In opposition July 31.

PALLAS.

Day.	Rises. H. M.	Sets. H. M.	R.A. H. M. S.	Decl. ° ' "
June 14	5 35A	9 53M	19 13 36	22 0 6 N
" 24	4 47A	9 8M	19 6 15	22 13 57
July 4	4 0A	8 19M	18 59 4	22 0 39
" 14	3 18A	7 27M	18 49 54	21 19 20
" 24	2 39A	6 32M	18 42 19	23 12 37
Aug. 3	2 3A	5 37M	18 35 59	18 43 53 N

In opposition July 9.

JUNO.

Day.	Rises. H. M.	Sets. H. M.	R.A. H. M. S.	Decl ° ' "
Sept. 2	7 42A	8 8M	0 38 43	1 42 52 N
" 12	7 6A	7 16M	0 35 20	0 9 30 S
" 22	6 32A	6 21M	0 29 56	2 20 20
Oct. 2	5 57A	5 24M	0 23 26	4 35 58
" 12	5 23A	4 27M	0 17 3	6 41 31
" 22	4 47A	3 34M	0 11 58	8 24 32 S

In opposition September 27.

VESTA.

There will be no opposition of this Planet in the year 1900. The last opposition took place on October 14, 1899, and the next will occur on February 1, 1901.

The times of Southing may be obtained with sufficient accuracy by taking a mean between the times of Rising and Setting.

Astronomical and other Notes.

THE time used throughout this Almanack, with the one exception of that of High Water at Dublin, is Greenwich Mean Time, or the time which should be shown by a well-regulated clock ; the column headed "Sun before or after Clock" gives the difference between mean and apparent time, or the time as shown by the Sun.

SIGNS OF THE ZODIAC.

♈	Aries	The Ram.
♉	Taurus	The Bull.
♊	Gemini	The Twins.
♋	Cancer	The Crab.
♌	Leo	The Lion.
♍	Virgo	The Virgin.
♎	Libra	The Balance.
♏	Scorpio	The Scorpion.
♐	Sagittarius	The Archer.
♑	Capricornus	The Goat.
♒	Aquarius	The Water-Bearer.
♓	Pisces	The Fishes.

N. North. S. South. E. East. W. West.
h. Hours. ° Deg. of Arc, or Ther.
m. Minutes of time. ' Minutes of Arc.
s. Seconds of time. " Seconds of Arc.

Conjunction.—A Planet is said to be in Conjunction with another body when it has the same longitude, and is seen in the same direction in the heavens. It is obvious that in the case of the inferior Planets this Conjunction will be of two kinds : the one when the Planet is between the Earth and the Sun, called *inferior* Conjunction ; and the other when at the opposite point of its orbit, with the Sun between the Planet and the Earth, called *superior* Conjunction. The latter is the only kind of Conjunction that can happen to the *superior* Planets, Mars, Jupiter, Saturn, Uranus, and Neptune ; the *inferior* Planets, Mercury and Venus, being subject to both kinds.

Opposition.—A Planet is said to be in Opposition when it is distant from the Sun 180° of longitude, at which time it is most brilliant, souths about midnight, and is, generally, at its least distance from the Earth.

Elongation.—The inferior Planets, in their revolutions round the Sun, appear to an observer on the Earth to swing pendulum-like from side to side, being alternately east and west of the Sun ; the greatest Elongation is the termination of one of the swings, either east or west ; and at these times the Planet appears, when viewed through a telescope, like the Moon in her first quarter if the Elongation be in the east, and like her last quarter if west. Both Mercury and Venus exhibit these phases, passing from new to full while moving from inferior to superior Conjunction, and from full to new again while passing from superior to inferior Conjunction.

Occultation.—It often happens that the Moon in her orbital motion passes before, and hides from a spectator on the Earth, certain of the Fixed Stars, and occasionally one or other of the Planets; these occurrences are called *Occultations*. Among the "Celestial Phenomena" are given the times at which certain of these Occultations take place, as well as the exact point on the Moon's limb where the observer is to look for the phenomenon; this point is reckoned from the true vertex, or highest upper portion of the Moon's image, counting continuously towards the East from 0° to 360°. The disappearance always takes place on the left-hand side of the Moon, and the reappearance on the right, but *vice versâ* when viewed through an inverting or astronomical telescope. Stars to the fifth magnitude only have been included in this summary, excepting that, in one or two cases, fainter stars have been inserted, when the occultation takes place with the Moon in the first or fourth quarter; the times of disappearance or reappearance at the dark limb of the Moon only being noted.

Southing.—The *Time of Southing* is the time at which the heavenly bodies pass the Meridian, and is so called because they are then due south. The Meridian being a great circle passing through the Pole and Zenith of the place, the southing will also be the time when they attain their greatest altitude above the horizon.

TIDES AND TIDAL WAVES.

The great cause of our ocean tides is the Moon's nearness as compared with the Sun's distance. The Sun is 25¼ million times heavier than the Moon, but his attractive power acts upon our planet mainly as a whole; whereas the Moon, being in our immediate neighbourhood and much smaller in size, acts specially and more intensely upon that limited area of the Earth's surface which is nearest her and directly under her. Wherever the Moon may be in her course, if a great ocean lies immediately beneath, its waters are heaped up by what is termed her "lifting power," and the crest of that bulging and liquid mass constitutes *high water* for that part of the world.

In 24 hours and 50 minutes, owing to the Earth's rotation, plus the Moon's orbital motion, that same part of the world is exactly under the Moon again, and thus another similar tide must always occur after that interval of time. These, the primary tides, being accounted for, to what cause are the secondary tides due, which occur exactly half way between in point of time? Suppose Ocean A is exactly under the Moon, as in the case just discussed, and that Ocean B is on the opposite side of our planet, how is the latter affected by our satellite? Very slightly: because not only has she to lift up the waters of Ocean A, causing the primary tide there, but she has to exercise her attractive power on the great solid mass of the planet itself which separates the two oceans. Thus the Earth as a whole is drawn away from Ocean B, because the latter is so remote, and its waters, being left behind, bulge up at a point diametrically opposite to the primary tides of Ocean A, and form the secondary tides. It is manifest, therefore, that at every moment of the day and night two tides are being formed, on opposite sides of our planet, one directly under the Moon, the other at the point furthest from the Moon.

When a primary and the corresponding secondary tides are thus heaped up at two opposite points of the Earth's equator, then two other points half way between (*i.e.*, 90° distant in longitude) must be deprived of their waters, which have been ebb-

ing either East or West to make up the primary and secondary. In other words, at any moment *low water* occurs 90° East or West of high water: or, since the Moon revolves in 24*h.* 50*m.*, any particular meridian must not only have its secondary tide 12*h.* 25*m.* after the primary, but must have low water 6*h.* 12½*m.* after high water.

According to mathematicians, some of the greatest of whom have bestowed much attention on the theory of the tides, the lifting power of the Sun on our oceans is only from 33 to 44 per cent. of that of the Moon. Three points are notable as to the influence of the Sun during each lunar month:—(1) At New Moon he acts with the Moon upon the primary tide at that meridian; (2) at Full Moon he pulls against the Moon, and therefore helps to heap up the secondary tide; and (3) when the Moon is in her quarters, the influence of the Sun is at right angles to that of the Moon, counteracting it, and therefore both primary and secondary tides are lowered. The first and second cases constitute *Spring Tides;* the third, *Neap Tides.* Thus, the solar tides are practically of no account except for their modifying influence on the lunar or true tides.

If our planet had no land on its surface, and the shoreless ocean were of uniform depth, the tidal wave-crests, both primary and secondary, would travel in regular succession from East to West, following the Moon's course. With our actual geography many local complications arise: seas like the Mediterranean, Baltic, or Euxine offer so small an area that the Moon can only act upon each as a whole, and there is practically no tide. The disturbing action requires a very wide expanse of deep water, such as the great Southern Ocean, or the S. Pacific; and there accordingly is assigned the birthplace of our great tidal wave, to which many tides in distant seas are referred. One mighty pulse enters the Pacific in a N.W. direction, and another the Atlantic, both to be modified by the depth of water and the form of the coasts; and both extending to the bottom of the ocean. Owing to the islands of the Pacific the tides there become small, as the impulse travels north; but in the long deep trough of the Atlantic the tidal force attains a velocity of from 600 to 650 miles an hour. The western impulse across the S. Pacific reaches Tasmania in 12 hours, and in 12 hours more dashes against Hindostan and S. Africa. Another 12 hours and the tidal wave has reached Newfoundland on the West, and the African Cape Blanco on the East. Turning eastward across the N. Atlantic, the tide in four hours is split into two waves at Land's End, one of which goes slowly up the shallow English Channel, while the main branch is borne round the North of Scotland—to bring high water to Aberdeen and the coasts of Norway and Denmark—and finally reaches the mouth of the Thames in 48 hours after leaving the Antarctic Ocean. The Atlantic, being deep and free of islands, produces an independent tide, which helps to modify the tidal impulse from the South, one result being the famous high tides of the Bay of Fundy.

The tides are locally affected by the configuration of the coasts, and also to a slight extent by the changes of atmospheric pressure. Where the tidal wave enters gulfs or estuaries which open in its direction the difference between high and low water is much increased—*e.g.*, Bristol Channel, 40—60 ft.; St. Malo in the English Channel, 50 ft.; Chepstow, 60 ft.; Bay of Fundy, 70 ft. up to 100 ft.

in the highest spring-tides. The "bore" or "eagre" on certain rivers occurs when the advanced portion of the tidal wave moves so slowly, owing to shallowness or other circumstances, that the succeeding waters gather in a heap—*e.g.*, Severn, "head" 3 feet high; Hoogly, 5 ft.; Amazons, 12 to 15 ft.—that on the Tsien Tang in China has been estimated to flow up the river with a velocity of 25 miles an hour. Another curious local modification of the tides is seen at Southampton, Poole, Weymouth, &c., where two tides occur in 12 hours; a similar anomaly near Clackmannan on the Firth of Forth is known as the "leaky tides."

The following heights of tides on the Thames, with the distance of their respective stations from the mouth of the river, are from *Phil. Trans.* (23 iii. 204):—

	Height.	Distance.
	ft. in.	m.
London Docks	18 10	60
Putney	10 2	67½
Kew	7 1	73
Richmond	3 10	76
Teddington	1 4½	79

The lunar tides, according to the results of recent investigation, are by friction slowly interfering with the Earth's rotation, and therefore lengthening our day. This must go on through countless centuries till the Earth's time of rotation is equal to a lunation, when the lunar tides will no longer exist, and our seas are disturbed only by the weak action of the solar tides.

OUR SEASONS.

The revolution of the Earth in its annual orbit round the Sun has the effect of causing the latter body, seemingly, to describe a complete revolution among the Stars in the course of the year. If the plane of this apparent path had been parallel to the Earth's Equator, the Days and Nights would be equal all over the Globe, and each place on the Earth would have one constant Season, the character of which would depend on its geographical latitude. Instead of this coincidence of planes, the Equator and Ecliptic (as this apparent path of the Sun is called) are mutually inclined to each other at 23½°; consequently, the Sun is alternately seen above and below the Equator by this amount, causing the phenomena of summer and winter: giving long days and Summer to the Northern hemisphere when the Sun is North of the Equator, and short days and winter when South of it.

This inclination of the two planes will cause the Sun to cross the Equator twice in the year, viz., once in the Spring, and again in the Autumn, at which times the Days and Nights are equal all over the world; and we experience for a day or two what would be the constant state of our climate if the Sun moved in the plane of the Equator.

From Spring, through Summer to Autumn the Sun traverses exactly one half of the Ecliptic, and from Autumn, through Winter to Spring, the other half; but that these halves are not travelled over in equal times will be seen by an inspection of the times at which the different Seasons commence. It appears that the Sun is longer in performing the Summer than the Winter half; this is caused by the eccentricity of the Earth's orbit, and the Law of Areas, as it is called by Astronomers—a law which requires that an imaginary line, joining the Earth and Sun, shall sweep over equal areas in equal times. To do this, the Earth when nearer to the Sun, as at the Winter Solstice, must move more quickly than when farther away, at the Summer Solstice; because then the line joining the two bodies is shorter than in the latter case; the effect is to detain the Sun about eight days longer in the Northern than in the Southern Hemisphere.

The Earth's sensible atmosphere is generally supposed to extend some forty miles in height, probably farther, but becoming, at only a few miles from the surface, of too great a tenuity to support life. The condition and motions of this aërial ocean play a most important part in the determination of climate, modifying, by absorbing, the otherwise intense heat of the Sun; and when laden with clouds, hindering the Earth from radiating its acquired heat into space. The amount of heat absorbed in its passage through the atmosphere will depend upon the thickness of the stratum which the rays have to penetrate, and this on the meridian altitude of the Sun.

If the surface of the Globe were smooth, and consisted entirely of land or water, the mean temperature of our Seasons would depend solely on our geographical latitude, and we should then find that all places on the same parallel would enjoy the same temperatures; but being, as it is, made up of water and land very unequally distributed, the former occupying two-thirds of the entire surface of the Globe, the temperature of the Seasons at places on the same parallel of latitude is modified by the surrounding masses of land and water. The great capacity of water for heat, and its low power of radiation, make the great Ocean, extending from Pole to Pole, the reservoir which stores up for us the heat it has received from the Sun; while the land, radiating again its heat very quickly, would soon grow cold. The principal medium by which this heat is conveyed to the land is that of the Winds, which, receiving their warmth and moisture from the water, pass over the land, and compensate for the loss of heat which the latter suffers from radiation. From this cause it is that islands enjoy more equable Seasons than inland countries, being neither so cold in Winter nor so hot in Summer; since the same clouded skies that retard the cooling of the land by radiation also shield it from the rays of the Sun in Summer. But in the interior of continents, where the winds have lost their moisture on their passage from the coast, great extremes are known to prevail between the Summer and Winter temperatures. Moscow has a difference between its Summer heat and Winter cold of 82°, London of 57°, while in the Shetland Islands, and at Penzance, in Cornwall, the differences are only 46° and 48° respectively. Beyond the fact of the presence of water, we must not forget that the oceans and seas are traversed by currents of warm water from the Equatorial regions, which greatly promote the distribution of heat. The chief of these prevail in the North Atlantic Ocean, and it is to one of them—the Gulf Stream—that we probably owe the mildness of the western coasts of Europe. This remarkable current, issuing from the Gulf of Mexico, flows in a north-easterly direction along the shores of America, and on encountering the Banks of Newfoundland splits into two branches, one of which proceeds to the Azores, and the other to the British Isles.

VARIABLE STARS.

Although the Stars generally shine with uniform brightness, there are among them some remarkable exceptions to this general rule. The earliest known, and the most remarkable amongst this class of Stars, is one situated in the constellation Cetus, and known by the name of o Ceti, or Mira Ceti. It has a period of nearly 331·3 days; that is to say, it goes through its cycle of variations in that length of time, continuing for about twelve or fourteen days at its maximum brightness, which has, at some of its maxima, reached to the second order of magnitude; it then goes on decreasing for some three months until it becomes invisible, in which condition it remains for five more months, when it again goes on increasing to the end of the period, when the maximum is again reached; but the order of magnitude is not always the same at successive maxima. The month of October is the best time for observing it. It will be found in R. A. 2h. 14m. 18s. and South Declination 3° 25'. The maximum will occur about Aug. 3.

Another remarkable Variable Star is Algol, β Persei. This has a very short period, not quite three days—and ranges from the second to the fourth magnitude. It continues at its maximum for two days and a half, then begins to decrease very suddenly, and in rather more than three hours is reduced to a Star of the fourth magnitude; after remaining at this magnitude for a quarter of an hour, it again attains to its maximum in the same time that it took in passing from it to the minimum. This Star will be found in Right Ascension 3h. 1m. 38s. and North Declination 40° 34'. It can be well observed in October and November.

U Ophiuchi varies from the 6th to the 6¾ magnitude, with a period of 20h. 8m. It may be observed in June; southing about midnight on the 9th. Will be found in R. A. 17h. 11m. 27s. and North Declination 1° 19'.

The Variable Star β Lyræ is remarkable in having a double period, viz., two maxima and two minima—the double period being very nearly equal to thirteen days; the difference between the maximum and minimum is only one degree of magnitude. There is another peculiarity in the changes of this Star — that, although the two maxima are equal, the minima are unequal. It is situated in R.A. 18h. 46m. 24s. and North Declination 33° 15'. The best time for observing it is in the months of June and July. Bright lines are occasionally seen in the spectrum of this star.

The Star δ Cephei is also subject to considerable variations in magnitude, passing from the third to the fifth with a period of 5⅓ days. In passing from the minimum to the maximum it occupies less time than that required for it to reach the minimum again—in the proportion of 38 hours to 91. It is to be found in R. A. 22h. 25m. 26s. and North Declination 57° 54'. August and September are the best months in which to observe it.

There are two hypotheses suggested to explain the phenomena exhibited by the variable or periodical Stars; one of which endeavours to account for the variations in magnitude by supposing that opaque bodies are revolving around these particular Stars, and that at certain times they are interposed between the Earth and the Star, and so cut off from us a portion of the luminous rays of the latter. The other hypothesis suggests that the Stars themselves may have portions of their surface of unequal reflecting power, and that in their rotations they present to us in turns these more or less bright parts, and so cause the variations that we observe. This theory fails to explain the changes observed in the stars of the Algol type, and is only applicable to such as are quite regular in their fluctuations. Professor Pickering has shown that to account for the variability of the light of such stars as Algol no hypothesis will satisfy the observed changes, except that of an opaque satellite. Adopting this theory (which is now generally accepted) he finds theoretically such a satellite whose position and movements would agree with the observed facts.

The above-mentioned "variables" are but a very small portion of the Stars which are *known* to experience fluctuations of magnitude, but they are the most celebrated examples of their class. It is very likely that our knowledge concerning variable Stars and their distribution in space will be greatly increased when the examination of the photographic plates taken for the chart of the Heavens shall have been completed.

TERRESTRIAL MAGNETISM.

Magnetism is that property possessed by certain bars of steel, called Magnets, of attracting pieces of iron and also other magnets: beyond this idea very little, if any, meaning is popularly attached to the term Magnetism.

Every magnet has two poles, each pole having, as the term implies, exactly opposite properties, such that if we suspend one magnet by a thread free to move in any direction it will be found that on bringing another magnet, held in the hand, near to one end of the suspended magnet, if the opposing poles of each are of like properties, they will repel each other, but if of unlike, they will be attracted towards each other. By placing the magnet held in the hand in the proper position, the moveable magnet may be made to take up any required direction, as long as the magnetism in the magnets and their relative positions remain the same. In the Mariner's Compass we have a case of this kind, where the compass-needle is so suspended as to be free to move in the horizontal direction, the Earth itself being the other magnet, with its South Pole near to the Earth's North Pole, and its North Pole near to the Earth's South Pole; so that the North Pole of the compass will always point to the Magnetic South Pole of the Earth, differing from the true or Astronomical North by a quantity called the "Variation." The Variation of the compass is not only different for different places on the Earth, but is moreover liable to slow variation from year to year, causing it in the course of centuries to oscillate from East to West of the Astronomical meridian. In 1580, at London, the needle had an Eastern variation of about 11½°; between 1657 and 1662 its direction coincided with the plane of the Astronomical meridian; that is to say, the variation, or declination as it is generally called, was zero; since then it travelled westwards, and reached the maximum Western declination in 1815, and is at the present time (1900) approaching the zero, previously to again becoming Easterly.

The compass-needle being constructed to move in a horizontal direction only, exhibits that component of the total magnetic force which determines the declination; but if the needle had been mounted on a horizontal axis placed in the magnetic meridian, and been left free to move in a vertical plane, it would have been found to *Dip*, as it is technically called, or be inclined at an angle to the horizontal plane, the North Pole of the needle being depressed. The value of this *inclination* or *dip* varies also in different places on the globe, increasing towards the Poles, so that in the Northern Hemisphere, at the Magnetic Pole, we shall have the north end of the needle pointing directly downwards.

This North Magnetic Pole was found by Sir James Ross to be situate in 97° West longitude and 70° North latitude. The South Magnetic Pole is situated about 168° East longitude and 75° South latitude. Between these points there are found places of no *dip*; all such places are said to be situated on the Magnetic Equator, a plane not far removed from the terrestrial Equator. The *dip*, like the declination, is subject to secular and other variations, the true laws of which are not yet understood, but for the investigation of which Observatories have been established all over the world, and elaborate series of observations made on the motions of variously suspended magnets (their movements in most Observatories being automatically recorded by photography), furnishing a continuous record from hour to hour, and year to year, of the forces acting upon them.

FORECASTING THE WEATHER.

All outdoor pursuits, undertaken for profit or pleasure, depend so much upon the weather that we can imagine mankind to have taken an interest in its study from very early times; and, as a matter of fact, the popular ideas about weather prognostics are much the same as those which were in vogue in the earliest ages. Aristotle, in his book on Meteors (which, in his time, were supposed to have an atmospheric origin), collected all the then known prognostics of the weather, but in this work no serious attempt is made to explain the phenomena observed. In the cases where the attempt is made, the explanations offered are often very absurd, and show entire ignorance of the principles of physical science.

The observation of the state of the sky taught the meteorologists of early times when to expect good or bad weather, and the result of these observations, formulated into short and pithy sayings, made up, until quite recent times, the science of weather prognostics.

Birds and beasts are all more or less sensitive to coming changes in the weather, and by observation of their movements, sure warning of changes in the weather may be obtained. Among other instances it is observed that sea birds, as stormy weather comes on, fly inland in search of food; wild fowl leave the marshy grounds for higher localities; swallows and rooks fly low before and during bad weather; frogs are unusually noisy before rain; sheep huddle together near bushes and trees.

It was not until the discovery of the barometer, in 1643, that the first great step was made towards a knowledge of the nature of our atmosphere. We were then, by its help, enabled to ascertain the weight and pressure of the great aërial ocean which surrounds us, and to learn when and where it was in a state of calm or storm. The invention of the thermometer, shortly afterwards, gave the means of determining its temperature. The hygrometer for showing the amount of moisture it contained, and the anemometer for giving the direction and force of the wind, are also instruments of great importance to the meteorologist. The indications of these instruments, combined with the careful observation of atmospheric appearances, interpreted by the results of former observations, will enable the individual observer generally to predict the kind of weather that may be expected in his immediate locality for a day or sometimes longer in advance.

A strip of sea-weed forms a very useful hygrometer for practical purposes, provided it be not kept in a room warmed artificially. In fine weather it will keep dry and have a somewhat dusty feeling, but with an increase of moisture in the air will become limp and sticky, indicating a probable change of weather in the shape of rain.

Since the time of Admiral FitzRoy the science of weather forecasting has made much progress in its details, but, for the individual observer, the method remains much the same now as then. The principal rules in use for forecasting the weather at present may be briefly stated as follows:—

A rising barometer usually foretells less wind or rain, and a falling barometer more wind or rain, or both; a high barometer, fine weather, and a low one the contrary.

If the barometer has been *about* its ordinary height at the sea level, and is steady or rising, while the thermometer falls and the air becomes drier, north-westerly, northerly, or north-easterly wind, or less wind, may be expected; and, on the contrary, if a fall takes place with rising thermometer and increasing dampness, wind and rain may be looked for from the south-east, south, or south-west: a fall of the barometer, with low thermometer, foretells snow.

With the barometer *below* its ordinary height a rise foretells less wind, or change in the direction towards the north, or less wet; but when the barometer has been low, the first rising usually precedes strong wind or heavy squalls from the north-west, north, or north-east, and continued north-east rising foretells improving weather. If the barometer falls and warmth continues, the wind will probably *back*, and more southerly or south-westerly winds will follow.

In northern latitudes the heaviest northerly gales occur after the barometer first rises from a very low point. A rapid rise generally indicates unsettled weather; slow rise or steadiness, with little moisture in the atmosphere, fair weather. A considerable and rapid fall signifies stormy weather and rain. The barometer generally falls with a southerly and rises with a northerly wind; though sometimes the contrary happens, and then the southerly wind is dry and the weather fine, or the northerly wind wet and violent.

When the barometer sinks considerably, high wind and rain or snow will follow; wind from the northward, if the thermometer is low for the season; from the southward, if high.

When a gale sets in from the east or south-east, and wind *veers* by the south, the barometer will continue falling till the wind becomes south-west, when, after a lull, the gale will be renewed.

The north-east wind tends to *raise* the barometer most, and the south-west to lower it most.

Instances of fine weather often happen with a low barometer, and are generally followed by a duration of wind or rain, or both.

Predictions founded solely on the indications of the barometer and thermometer may be made with more certainty if combined with careful observation of the appearance of the sky, and the atmospheric effects peculiar to the particular locality.

A rosy sky at sunset, whether clouded or clear, a grey sky in the morning, a low dawn (that is when the first signs of the dawn appear on the horizon) all indicate fair weather. A red sky in the morning indicates bad weather, or much wind; and a high dawn (or when the first signs of the dawn are seen above a bank of clouds) presages wind.

From the clouds we may draw the following conclusions: soft-looking and delicate clouds foretell fine weather, with moderate breezes; hard-edged clouds, wind; rolled or ragged clouds, strong wind. A bright yellow sky at sunset also presages wind, and a pale yellow sky wet.

Dew and fog both indicate fine weather, while remarkable clearness of the atmosphere near the horizon (causing distant objects to appear very distinct and nearer than usual) is one of the most characteristic signs of coming wet.

At the present day, by the help of the electric telegraph, the meteorologist can obtain from as many stations as he desires the height of the barometer, direction and force of wind, &c., data which will inform him of the condition and movements of the aërial ocean at a definite time. He then marks on a map the height of the barometer at each place, and, drawing lines through all the places where the quicksilver stands at the same height, at any convenient interval he obtains a series of lines of equal pressure or weight, called shortly *isobars*, which show the height or depression at those places as the contour lines on a map show the different altitudes of the mountains and valleys. The thermometer readings, treated in the same way, are called *isotherms*. To make these synoptic charts (as they are called) complete, the force and direction of the wind, the amount of humidity, character of clouds, and other weather signs are also marked down, so that the chart may furnish a view of the weather at that particular time over the area from which reports have been obtained.

Supposing now that at the same time the next day a new set of data are received and marked on another chart, a comparison of the two will show the nature and direction of the change going on, and enable the meteorologist to predict, to a certain extent, what will be the immediately coming weather. This is a general description of the way in which the forecasts of weather, printed in the daily papers, are made. The interpretation of these synoptic charts may not appear to the reader to be a very difficult operation, but it must be remembered that meteorology is purely a science of observation, and, as such, will be most successfully handled by the observer of the greatest experience. From want of knowledge concerning the laws which govern the fluctuations of the weather, failures in the forecasts must happen now and again, and no reason can be given why certain states of the atmosphere, which previous observation would lead us to believe should be stable, suddenly break up without any apparent warning.

Attempts have been frequently made to connect the state of the weather with the aspects of the planets, the changes of the Moon, or some other astronomical occurrences. The idea that the weather is dependent on the Moon's phases still finds favour with the vulgar, although any appreciable connection has been repeatedly disproved.

Besides the meteorological instruments mentioned above, there is one often used to indicate weather changes which is known as the chemical weather-glass, camphor-glass, or storm-glass.

Though sold in London more than a hundred years ago, no scientific explanation of its indications seems to have been attempted till the late Admiral FitzRoy took it in hand. Up to the year 1825 these storm-glasses had been considered rather as curiosities than otherwise; nothing certain could be made of their variations; but lately, says the Admiral, writing in 1862, it was fairly demonstrated that if fixed undisturbed in free air —not exposed to radiation from fire or sun—but in the ordinary light of a well-ventilated room, or, preferably, in the outer air, the chemical mixture in the storm-glass varies in character with the *direction* of the wind—not its force, *specially* (though it *may* so vary in appearance only)—from *another* cause, electrical tension.

Admiral FitzRoy considered that these instruments had a scientific value, used in conjunction with the barometer and thermometer, in predicting local storms. Some other writers are at variance with the Admiral on this point—one affirming that the weather indications of the storm-glass are not to be relied on; another, that light and temperature are the agents that bring about the changes observed.

The instrument itself consists of a mixture of camphor, nitrate of potassium, and muriate of ammonia, partly dissolved in alcohol, with a little water. This solution is placed in a long glass vial or tube, with some air, and hermetically sealed. Some authorities say that a small hole should be left in the top to admit the external air.

At one time the upper part of the liquid in the tube will appear quite clear, the bottom portion being occupied by a shapeless mass like melting white sugar. Again, the liquid portion will be more or less filled with crystallizations like fern-leaves or hoar-frost, and under some circumstances like stars.

The general rules given for interpreting the readings of the storm-glass are as follow:—

(a) If the undissolved substance lies low and smooth at the bottom of the tube—fine weather.

(b) If it rises gradually in the shape of fern or feather-like crystallizations—rain.

(c) If it rises much higher than in (b), and if the liquid portion is less clear, with star-like crystals in motion, high wind or storm will follow.

RIGHT ASCENSION.

The Right Ascension of any heavenly body is its angular distance measured along the Equator from that point of intersection of the Equator and Ecliptic known as the Vernal Equinox. In the time of the ancient astronomers this point was situated in the constellation of Aries, and called by them the "First Point of Aries," but it has since then retrograded considerably behind that constellation, and is at present in the sign Pisces. Modern astronomers, however, still speak of this zero point, whence Right Ascensions are measured, as the "First Point of Aries." The Right Ascension and Declination are the two co-ordinates which define the position of any point on the celestial sphere with regard to the Equator as a fundamental plane, just as those of longitude and latitude define the position of any place on the terrestrial globe; the meridian of Greenwich being taken as the starting-point by geographers from which to reckon their longitudes, while the astronomer reckons his from the meridian of the First Point of Aries.

Since a well-regulated astronomical clock should show 0*h*. 0*m*. 0*s*. when the First Point of Aries is on the Meridian, the Right Ascension may be called the Sidereal time of Southing, and the approximate mean time corresponding to it may be easily found for any object whose Right Ascension is given in this Almanack by means of the column headed Sidereal Time at Mean Noon, printed on the second page of each month. The rule may be thus stated:—*From the given Right Ascension subtract the Sidereal Time at the preceding Noon, and further diminish the result at the rate of 10 secs. an hour.* If the Right Ascension should be smaller than the Sidereal time to be subtracted, then 24 hours must be added to it. As an example:—At what time will Regulus South on March 15!

R. A. of Regulus + 24*h*.	34*h*. 3*m*. 3*s*.
Sidereal Time at Mean Noon (sub.)	23*h*. 30*m*. 32*s*.
Diminish by the Acceleration for 10*h*. 32*m*. 31*s*. at 10*s*. per hour	10*h*. 32*m*. 31*s*.
	1*m*. 45*s*.
Approximate mean time of Southing, March 15	10*h*. 30*m*. 46*s*.

In a similar manner the Sidereal time corresponding to any mean time may be found. Suppose, for instance, that we wish to know approximately what the Sidereal time would be at 9.30 p.m. on November 5, we have merely to add Greenwich time to the time given in the column headed Sidereal Time at Mean Noon of that date, increasing the result by the amount of the acceleration in 9*h*. 30*m*. :—

Sidereal time at mean noon	14*h*. 57*m*. 2*s*.
Greenwich time (add)	9*h*. 30*m*. —
	0*h*. 27*m*. 2*s*.
Add for acceleration for 9*h*. 30*m*. at 10*s*. per hour	1*m*. 35*s*.
Sidereal time November 5 at 9*h*. 30*m*. P.M.	0*h*. 28*m*. 37*s*.

To observers who are not furnished with a Sidereal Clock the Sidereal times at Mean Noon will be found very useful for readily finding the approximate mean times of Southing of the Stars.

APPARENT DIMENSIONS OF SATURN'S RING, 1900.			ILLUMINATED PORTIONS OF THE DISCS OF VENUS AND MARS, 1900.		
Date.	Major Axis.	Minor Axis.	Date.	VENUS.	MARS.
Jan. 10	35″15	15″76	Jan. 15	0·873	1·000
Feb. 19	36·53	16·13	Feb. 14	0·801	0·998
Mar. 11	37·62	16·49	Mar. 15	0·708	0·993
April 20	40·18	17·52	April 15	0·576	0·985
May 30	42·21	18·56	May 15	0·402	0·975
June 19	42·61	18·87	June 15	0·144	0·962
July 29	41·78	18·75	July 15	0·018	0·948
Aug. 18	40·72	18·35	Aug. 15	0·280	0·932
Sept. 27	38·18	17·25	Sept. 15	0·493	0·915
Oct. 17	37·01	16·68	Oct. 15	0·637	0·902
Nov. 26	35·36	15·74	Nov. 15	0·751	0·896
Dec. 16	34·99	15·40	Dec. 15	0·836	0·907

The figures in the second and third columns of the above Table give the apparent dimensions of Saturn's Ring as seen from the Earth, and refer to the outer limit of the outer ring. In 1900 the northern surface will be visible. The ring will be invisible when its plane passes through either the centre of the Sun, centre of the Earth, or when the Sun and Earth are on opposite sides of the plane of the ring.

The figures in the fifth and sixth columns represent respectively the *versed sines* of the illuminated portions of the discs of Venus and Mars.

MAGNETIC ELEMENTS.

The following table of mean magnetic elements is derived from the observations made at Greenwich in the respective years, and apply to Greenwich only.

The diurnal variation of the magnetic declination at Greenwich is about 12′ in summer, and 7′ in winter. The needle occupies its mean position about 10*h*. a.m., and again about 6*h*. p.m., throughout the year. It reaches its most westerly position about 2*h*. p.m., and its most easterly position during the night or early morning, according to the season of the year. The inclination or dip also varies, from hour to hour, in a similar manner to the declination. The declination and dip are also subject to secular variations, the duration of which is not accurately known. Accidental perturbations, due to magnetic storms, affect the needles. These variations in the position of the magnets occur with great suddenness, deflecting the needle right and left with great rapidity, almost like ordinary telegraphic signalling, and are generally coincident with the passage of great outbursts of sun spots across the sun's central meridian.

Year.	Mean Magnetic Declination at Greenwich West.	Horizontal Magnetic Force in C. G. S. Units at Greenwich.	Mean Inclination or Dip of Needle at Greenwich.
1888	17° 40·4′	·1820	67° 25·4′
1889	17 34·9	·1821	67 24·9
1890	17 28·6	·1823	67 22·9
1891	17 23·4	·1825	67 21·4
1892	17 17·4	·1826	67 19·8
1893	17 11·4	·1829	67 17·8
1894	17 4·6	·1829	67 17·3
1895	16 57·0	·1832	67 14·7
1896	16 52·0	·1833	67 15·0
1897	16 46·0	·1836	67 13·0
1898	16 39·0	·1837	67 12·0

GREENWICH OBSERVATORY.

Founded 10th August, 1673.

ASTRONOMERS ROYAL.

John Flamsteed	1675
Edmund Halley	1719
James Bradley	1742
Nathaniel Bliss	1762
Nevil Maskelyne	1765
John Pond	1811
Sir George Biddell Airy	1835
William Henry Mahoney Christie, C.B.	1881

Name.	SAXONS AND DANES.	Access.	Died	Age.	Rgnd.
EGBERT	First King of all England	827	839	—	12
ETHELWULF	Son of Egbert	839	858	—	19
ETHELBALD	Son of Ethelwulf	858	860	—	2
ETHELBERT	Second Son of Ethelwulf	858	866	—	8
ETHELRED	Third Son of Ethelwulf	866	871	—	5
ALFRED	Fourth Son of Ethelwulf	871	901	52	30
EDWARD THE ELDER	Son of Alfred	901	925	55	24
ATHELSTAN	Eldest son of Edward	925	940	45	15
EDMUND	Brother of Athelstan	940	946	25	6
EDRED	Brother of Edmund	946	955	—	9
EDWY	Son of Edmund	955	958	18	3
EDGAR	Second son of Edmund	958	975	32	17
EDWARD THE MARTYR	Son of Edgar	975	979	—	4
ETHELRED II.	Half-brother of Edward	979	1016	48	37
EDMUND IRONSIDE	Eldest son of Ethelred	1016	1016	27	—
CANUTE	By conquest and election	1017	1035	40	18
HAROLD I.	Son of Canute	1035	1040	—	5
HARDICANUTE	Another son of Canute	1040	1042	—	2
EDWARD THE CONFESSOR	Son of Ethelred II.	1042	1066	62	24
HAROLD II.	Brother-in-law of Edward the Confessor	1066	1066	—	0
	THE HOUSE OF NORMANDY.				
WILLIAM I.	Obtained the Crown by conquest	1066	1087	60	21
WILLIAM II.	Third son of William I.	1087	1100	43	13
HENRY I.	Youngest son of William I.	1100	1135	67	35
STEPHEN	Third son of Stephen, Count of Blois, by Adela, fourth daughter of William I.	1135	1154	50	19
	THE HOUSE OF PLANTAGENET.				
HENRY II.	Son of Geoffrey Plantagenet, by Matilda, only daughter of Henry I.	1154	1189	56	35
RICHARD I.	Eldest surviving son of Henry II.	1189	1199	42	10
JOHN	Sixth and youngest son of Henry II.	1199	1216	50	17
HENRY III.	Eldest son of John	1216	1272	65	56
EDWARD I.	Eldest son of Henry III.	1272	1307	68	35
EDWARD II.	Eldest surviving son of Edward I.	1307	1327	43	20
EDWARD III.	Eldest son of Edward II.	1327	1377	65	50
RICHARD II.	Son of the Black Prince, eld. son of Edwd. III.	1377	Dep. 1399	34	22
	THE HOUSE OF LANCASTER.				
HENRY IV.	Son of John of Gaunt, fourth son of Edw. III.	1399	1413	47	13
HENRY V.	Eldest son of Henry IV.	1413	1422	34	9
HENRY VI.	Only son of Henry V. (Died 1471)	1422	Dep. 1461	49	39
	THE HOUSE OF YORK.				
EDWARD IV.	His grandfather was Richard, son of Edmund, fifth son of Edward III. ; and his grandmother, Anne, was great-granddaughter of Lionel, third son of Edw. III.	1461	1483	41	22
EDWARD V.	Eldest son of Edward IV.	1483	1483	13	0
RICHARD III.	Younger brother of Edward IV.	1483	1485	35	2
	THE HOUSE OF TUDOR.				
HENRY VII.	Son of Edmund, eldest son of Owen Tudor, by Katharine, widow of Henry V.; his mother, Margaret Beaufort, was great-granddaughter of John of Gaunt	1485	1509	53	24
HENRY VIII.	Only surviving son of Henry VII.	1509	1547	56	38
EDWARD VI.	Son of Henry VIII., by Jane Seymour	1547	1553	16	6
MARY I.	Daughter of Henry VIII. by Kath. of Arragon	1553	1558	43	5
ELIZABETH	Daughter of Henry VIII. by Anne Boleyn	1558	1603	70	44
	THE HOUSE OF STUART.				
JAMES I. (VI. of Scot.)	Son of Mary Queen of Scots, granddau. of James IV. and Margaret, dau. of Hen. VII.	1603	1625	59	22
CHARLES I.	Only surviving son of James I.	1625	Beh. 1649	48	24
COMMONWEALTH	Commonwealth declared May 19	1649	—	—	—
	Oliver Cromwell, Lord Protector	1653	1658	59	—
	Richard Cromwell, Lord Protector	1658	Res. 1659	—	—

Name.	THE HOUSE OF STUART—RESTORED.	Access.	Died.	Age.	Rgnd.
CHARLES II.	Eldest son of Charles I.	1660	1685	55	26
JAMES II.	Second son of Charles I. (died 16 Sept., 1701) (Interregnum, Dec. 11, 1688—Feb. 13, 1689.)	1685	Dep. 1688 Dec. 1701	68	*35 3
WILLIAM III. and	Son of William Prince of Orange, by Mary, daughter of Charles I.	1689	1702	51	13
MARY II.	Eldest daughter of James II.		1694	33	6
ANNE	Second daughter of James II.	1702	1714	49	12
	THE HOUSE OF HANOVER.				
GEORGE I.	Son of Elector of Hanover, by Sophia, daughter of Elizabeth, daughter of James I.	1714	1727	67	13
GEORGE II.	Only son of George I.	1727	1760	77	33
GEORGE III.	Grandson of George II.	1760	1820	82	59
	Regency commenced 5th February, 1811.				
GEORGE IV.	Eldest son of George III.	1820	1830	68	10
WILLIAM IV.	Third son of George III.	1830	1837	72	7
VICTORIA	Daughter of Edward, 4th son of George III.	1837	WHOM GOD PRESERVE.		

* Constitutionally, the regnal years of Charles II. date from 1649.

Sovereigns of Scotland from A.D. 1057 to the Union of the Crowns.

Names.	Began to Reign.	Names.	Began to Reign.	Names.	Began to Reign.
Malcolm (*Ceanmohr*)	1057, Apr.	Alexander III.	1249, July 8	James IV.	1488, June 11
Donald (*Bane*)	1093, Nov.	Margaret	1286, Mar. 19	James V.	1513, Sept. 9
Duncan	1094, May	John Baliol	1292, Nov. 17	Mary	1542, Dec. 16
Donald (*Bane*) rest.	1095, Nov.	Robert I. (Bruce)	1306, Mar. 27	Francis and Mary	1558, Apr. 24
Edgar	1097, Sept.	David II.	1329, June 7	Mary	1560, Dec. 5
Alexander I.	1107, Jan. 8	Robert II. (Stewart)	1371, Feb. 22	Henry and Mary	1565, July 29
David I.	1124, April 27	Robert III.	1390, April 12	Mary	1567, Feb. 10
Malcolm (*Maiden*)	1153, May 24	James I.	1406, April 2	James VI.	1567, July 29
William (*The Lion*)	1165, Dec. 9	James II.	1437, Feb. 20	(Ascended the throne of Eng. as James I., 24th March, 1603.)	
Alexander II.	1214, Dec. 4	James III.	1460, Aug. 3		

Welsh Sovereigns and Princes.

INDEPENDENT PRINCES, A.D. 840 to 1282.		ENGLISH PRINCES, A.D. 1284 to 1841.	
Roderick the Great	840	Edward of Cernarvon, afterwards King Edward II. of England; born	1284
Anarawd, son of Roderick	877	Created Prince of Wales	1301
Howel Dda, the Good	942	Edward the Black Prince, s. of Edwd. III.	1343
Jefan and Jago	948	Richard (Richard II.), s. of the Black Prince	1377
Howel ap Jefan, the Bad	972	Henry of Monmouth (Henry V.)	1399
Cadwallon, his brother	984	Edward of Westminster, son of Henry VI.	1454
Meredith ap Owen ap Howel Dha	985	Edward of Westminster (Edward V.)	1472
Idwal ap Meyric ap Edwal Voel	992	Edward, son of Richard III. (d. 1484)	1483
Llewelyn ap Sitsylht	1015	Arthur Tudor, son of Henry VII.	1489
Iago ap Idwal ap Meyric	1023	Henry Tudor (Hen. VIII.), s. of Henry VII.	1503
Griffith ap Llewelyn ap Sitsylht	1034	Henry F. Stuart, son of James I. (d. 1612)	1610
Bleddyn	1063	Charles Stuart (Charles I.), s. of James I.	1616
Trahaern ap Caradoc	1073	Charles (Charles II.), son of Charles I.	1630
Griffith ap Cynan	1079	George Augustus (Geo. II.), s. of George I.	1714
Owain Gwynedd	1136	Frederick Lewis, s. of George II. (d. 1751)	1727
David ap Owain Gwynedd	1169	George William Frederick (George III.)	1751
Llewelyn the Great	1194	George Augustus Frederick (George IV.)	1762
David ap Llewelyn	1240	Albert Edward, son of Queen Victoria	1841
Llewelyn ap Griffith, last Prince, 1246; slain	1282		

Presidents of the United States of America.

Declaration of Independence	4 July 1776	Millard Fillmore (elected as Vice-President)	1850
General Washington first President, 1789 and	1793	Franklin Pierce	1853
John Adams	1797	James Buchanan	1857
Thomas Jefferson	1801 and 1805	Abram. Lincoln (assas. 14 Apr. 1865) 1861 and	1865
James Madison	1809 and 1813	Andrew Johnson (elected as Vice-President)	1865
James Monroe	1817 and 1821	Ulysses S. Grant	1869 and 1873
John Quincy Adams	1825	Rutherford Burchard Hayes	1877
Andrew Jackson	1829 and 1833	James A. Garfield (died 19 Sept., 1881)	1881
Martin Van Buren	1837	Chester A. Arthur (elected as V.-Pres.)	1881
William Henry Harrison (died 4 April)	1841	Grover Cleveland	1885
John Tyler (elected as Vice-President)	1841	Benjamin Harrison (b. 20 Aug. 1833)	1889
James Knox Polk	1845	Grover Cleveland (b. 18 Mar., 1837) 1885 and	1893
Zachary Taylor (died 9 July, 1850)	1849	William McKinley (b. 29 Jan. 1843)... March	1897

Population in 1776, including slaves, 2,614,300. Population in 1881, all free, 50,152,866 ; 1890, 62,622,250

The Merovingians.

Clovis, "The Hairy," King of the Salic Franks ... 428
Childeric II., last of the race ... 737

The Carlovingians.

Pépin, "The Short," son of Charles Martel ... 752
Charlemagne, the Great, Emp. of the West ... 768
Louis V., "The Indolent," last of the race ... 986

The Capets.

Hugh Capet, "The Great" ... 987
Louis IX., "St. Louis" ... 1226
Philip, "The Hardy" ... 1270
Philip, "The Fair" ... 1285
Louis X. ... 1314
John I. ... 1316
Philip, "The Long" ... 1316
Charles IV., "The Handsome" ... 1322

The House of Valois.

Philip VI., de Valois, "The Fortunate" ... 1328
John II., "The Good" ... 1350
Charles, "The Wise" ... 1364
Charles, "The Beloved" ... 1380
Charles, "The Victorious" ... 1422
Louis XI. ... 1461
Charles VIII. ... 1483
Louis XII. ... 1498
Francis I. ... 1515
Henry II. ... 1547
Francis II. ... 1559
Charles IX. ... 1560
Henry III., last of the race ...

The House of Bourbon.

Henry IV., "The Great," King of Navarre ... 1589
Louis XIII., "The Just" ... 1610
Louis XIV., "The Great," Dieudonné ... 1643

Louis XV., "The Well-beloved" ... 1715
Louis XVI. (guillotined 21 January, 1793) ... 1774
Louis XVII. (never reigned) ... 1793

The First Republic.

The National Convention first sat 21 Sept. 1792
The Directory nominated ... 1 Nov. 1795

The Consulate.

Bonaparte, Cambacérès, and Lebrun 24 Dec. 1799

The First Empire.

Napoleon I. decreed Emperor ... 18 May 1804
Napoleon II. (never reigned) ... died 22 July 1832

The Restoration.

Louis XVIII. re-entered Paris ... 3 May 1814
Charles X. (dep. 30 July, 1830, d. 6 Nov. 1836) 1824

The House of Orleans.

Louis Philippe, King of the French ... 1830
(Abdicated 24 Feb., 1848, died 26 August, 1850.)

The Second Republic.

Provisional Government formed ... 22 Feb. 1848
Louis Napoleon elected President ... 19 Dec. 1848

The Second Empire.

Napoleon III. elected Emperor ... 22 Nov. 1852
(Deposed 4 Sept., 1870, died 9 Jan., 1873.)

Third Republic.

Committee of Public Defence ... 4 Sept. 1870
M. Thiers elected President ... 31 Aug. 1871
Marshal MacMahon elected Presdt. 24 May 1873
Jules Grévy, (first) elected President 30 Jan. 1879
Marie F. S. Carnot elected President 3 Dec. 1887
(Assassinated at Lyons 24 June, 1894.)
Jean Casimir Perier elected President 27 June 1894
François Félix Faure elected President 17 Jan. 1895
Emile Loubet elected President ... 18 Feb. 1899

Germany—Austria=Hungary.

Ferdinand III., Son of Emp. Ferdinand II. ... 1637
Leopold I., Son of Ferdinand ... 1658
Joseph I., Son of Leopold ... 1705
Charles VI., Brother of preceding ... 1711
Maria-Theresa of Hungary and Bohemia ... 1740
Charles VII., Elector of Bavaria ... 1742
Francis I., Husband of Maria-Theresa ... 1745
Joseph II., Son of preceding ... 1765
Leopold II., Brother of preceding ... 1790
Francis II. } as last Emperor of Germany ... 1792
Francis I. } as first Emperor of Austria ... 1804
Ferdinand (Abdicated 1848) ... 1835
Francis-Joseph (Nephew) ... 2 December 1848

Prussia—Germany.

Albert I., First Elector of Brandenburg ... 1134
John-Sigismund, Elector, Duke of Prussia ... 1616
George-William ... 1619
Frederick-William, "The Great Elector" ... 1640
Frederick, 1688; Crowned King of Prussia ... 1701
Frederick-William I. ... 1713
Frederick II., "The Great" ... 1740
Frederick-William II. ... 1786
Frederick-William III. ... 1797
Frederick-William IV. ... 1840
William I., First German Emperor (1871) ... 1860
Frederick (Second German Emperor) ... 1888
William II. (Third German Emperor) ... 1888

Emperors of Russia.

1689 Peter I. ... died 28 Jan. 1725
1725 Catherine I., Mistress of Peter, d. 17 May 1727
1727 Peter II., d. 1730; 1730, Ann, d. 29 Oct. 1740
1740 Ivan VI., imprisoned 1741, assassinated 1764
1741 Elizabeth ... died 5 Jan. 1762
1762 Peter III. ... assassinated 14 July 1762
1762 Catherine II., Wife of Peter III., d. 17 Nov. 1796

1796 Paul ... assassinated 24 March 1801
1801 Alexander I. ... died 1 Dec. 1825
1825 Nicholas I. ... died 2 March 1855
1855 Alexander II. ... assassinated 13 March 1881
1881 Alexander III. ... died 1 Nov. 1894
1894 Nicholas II. began to reign.

Popes of Rome.

St. Peter (first Bishop of Rome) ... 42
Adrian IV. (Nicholas Brakespeare, the only Englishman elected Pope) ... 1154
Innocent XIII. ... Conti ... 1721
Benedict XIII. ... Orsini ... 1724
Clement XII. ... Orsini ... 1730
Benedict XIV. ... Lambertini ... 1740
Clement XIII. ... Rezzonico ... 1758

Clement XIV. ... Ganganelli ... 1769
Pius VI. ... Braschi ... 1775
Pius VII. ... Chiaramonti ... 1805
Leo XII. ... della Genga ... 1820
Pius VIII. ... Castiglioni ... 1829
Gregory XVI. ... Cappellari ... 1831
Pius IX. ... Mastai-Ferretti ... 1846
Leo XIII. ... Pecci ... 1878

Country.	Ruler.	Born.		Acceded.	
Abyssinia (or Ethiopia) ...	Menelik II., of Shoa, G.C.M.G., *Emperor*		1843	12 March,	1889
Afghanistan	Abdur Rahman Khan, G.C.B., *Amir*		1843	22 July,	1880
Argentine Republic	Julio A. Roca, *President*			12 Oct.,	1898
Austria	Francis Joseph, *Emperor*	18 Aug.,	1830	2 Dec.,	1848
Baluchistan	Mir Mahmud, G.C.I.E., *Khan of Khelat*				1893
Belgium	Leopold II., *King of the Belgians*	9 April,	1835	10 Dec.,	1865
Bolivia	Severo Fernandez Alonzo, *President*			20 Aug.,	1896
Brazil (United States of) ..	Campos Salles, *President*			15 Nov.,	1898
Bulgaria	Ferdinand, *Prince*	26 Feb.,	1861	7 July,	1887
Chile	Federico Errázuriz, *President*			18 Sept.,	1896
China	Kuang Hsü: Queen (his aunt) *rules*	15 Aug.,	1871	12 Jan.,	1875
Colombia	Dr. L. Sanclemente, *President*				1898
Congo Free State	King of the Belgians, *Sovereign*	9 April,	1835		1885
Corea	Li Hsi, *Emperor* ...				1864
Costa Rica	Rafael Iglesias, *President*			8 May,	1898
Denmark	Christian IX., *King*	8 April,	1818	15 Nov.,	1863
Dominican Republic........	General Jimenez, *President*			Nov..,	1899
Ecuador	Eloy Medardo Alfaro, *President*				1895
Egypt	Abbas II., G.C.B., *Khedive*	14 July,	1874	7 Jan.,	1892
France	Emile Loubet, *President*	31 Dec.,	1838	18 Feb.,	1899
Germany	William II., *Emperor*	27 Jan.,	1859	15 June,	1888
Prussia	William II., *King*				
Bavaria	Otto, *King* (Prince Luitpold, *Regent*)	27 April,	1848	13 June,	1886
Saxony	Albert, *King*	23 April,	1828	29 Oct.,	1873
Würtemberg	William II., *King*	25 Feb.,	1848	6 Oct.,	1891
Baden	Frederick, *Grand Duke*	9 Sept.,	1826	5 Sept.,	1856
Hesse	Ernest Louis, *Grand Duke*	25 Nov.,	1863	13 March,	1892
Anhalt	Frederick, *Duke*	29 April,	1831	22 May,	1871
Brunswick	Prince Albrecht, *Regent*	8 May,	1837	21 Oct.,	1885
Mecklenburg-Schwerin..	Frederick Francis, *Grand Duke*	9 April,	1882	10 April,	1897
Mecklenburg-Strelitz	Frederick William, *Grand Duke*	17 Oct.,	1819	6 Sept.,	1860
Oldenburg	Peter, *Grand Duke*	8 July,	1827	27 Feb.,	1853
Saxe-Coburg and Gotha..	Alfred, *Duke* (*Duke of Edinburgh*)	6 Aug.,	1844	23 Aug.,	1893
Waldeck-Pyrmont........	Frederick, *Prince*	20 Jan.,	1865	12 May,	1893
Great Britain and Ireland.	Victoria, *Queen*	24 May,	1819	20 June,	1837
Greece	George, *King of the Hellenes*	24 Dec.,	1845	30 March,	1863
Guatemala	Manuel Estrada Cabrera, *President*			25 Sept.,	1898
Hayti	Tirésias Augustin Simon Sam, *President*...			31 March,	1896
Honduras	Terencio Sierra, *President*			1 Feb.,	1899
Hungary	Francis Joseph, *King*	18 Aug.,	1830	8 June,	1867
India	Victoria, *Empress*	24 May,	1819	1 Jan.,	1877
Italy	Humbert, *King*	14 March,	1844	9 Jan.,	1878
Japan	Mutsuhito, *Emperor* (or *Mikado*)	3 Nov.,	1852	13 Feb.,	1867
Liberia	William David Coleman, *President*			13 Nov.,	1896
Luxemburg	Adolphus, *Grand Duke*	24 July,	1817	23 Nov.,	1890
Mexico	Porfirio Diaz, *President* (4th time)			1 Dec.,	1896
Montenegro	Nicholas, *Prince*	7 Oct.,	1841	14 Aug.,	1860
Morocco	Muley Abdul Aziz, *Sultan*		1879	7 June,	1894
Nepal	Prithivi Bir Bikram Shamsher Jang Bahadur, *Maharaja*	8 Aug.,	1875	17 May,	1881
Netherlands	Wilhelmina, *Queen*	31 Aug.,	1880	23 Nov.,	1890
Nicaragua	José Santos Zelaya, *President*			June,	1893
Orange Free State........	M. T. Steyn, *President*			19 Feb.,	1896
Paraguay	Emilio Aceval, *President*			25 Nov.,	1898
Persia	Muzaffer-ed-Din, *Shah*	25 March,	1853	1 May,	1896
Peru	Señor Romana, *President*			8 Sept.,	1899
Portugal	Carlos, *King*	28 Sept.,	1863	19 Oct.,	1889
Roumania..	Charles, *King*	20 April,	1839	26 March,	1881
Russia	Nicholas II., *Emperor* (*Tzar*)	18 May,	1868	1 Nov.(n.s.) '94	
Salvador	General Tomas Regalado, *President*			19 Nov.,	1898
Sarawak	Sir Charles Johnson Brooke, G.C.M.G., *Raja*	3 June,	1829	11 June,	1868
Servia	Alexander (Obrenovitch), *King*	14 Aug.,	1876	6 March,	1889
Siam	Khoulalonkorn, *King*	21 Sept.,	1853	1 Oct.,	1868
Spain	Alfonso XIII. (a Minor), *King*	17 May,	1886	17 May,	1886
Sweden and Norway........	Oscar II., *King*	21 Jan.,	1829	18 Sept.,	1872
Switzerland	M. Müller, *President* (for 1898-99)			15 Dec.,	1898
Transvaal (S. A. Republic)	Stephanus J. Paul Krüger, *President*	10 Oct.,	1825	Feb..,	1898
Tripoli	Hashem Bey, *Governor-General*			March,	1899
Tunis	Sidi Ali Pasha, *Bey*		1817	28 Oct.,	1882
Turkey	Abdul Hamid II., *Sultan*	21 Sept.,	1842	31 Aug.,	1876
United States (America)	William McKinley, *President*	29 Jan.,	1843	4 March,	1897
Uruguay	Juan L. Cuestas, *President*			1 March,	1899
Venezuela	General Ignacio Andrade, *President*			28 Feb.,	1898
Zanzibar	Hamud bin Muhamad, *Sultan*			27 Aug.,	1896

Country.	British Representative.	Representative in Great Britain.
Argentine Republic	Hon. W. A. C. Barrington, *Minister* ...	Florencio L. Dominguez 16 Kensington Palace Gardens, W.
Austria-Hungary ...	Rt.Hn.SirH.Rumbold,Bt.,G.C.B.,*Amb.*...	Count Franz Deym, 18 Belgrave Sq. S.W.
Belgium	Hon. Sir F. K. Plunkett, G.C.M.G., *Min.*	Baron Whettnall, 18 Harrington Gardens, South Kensington, S.W.
Bolivia	(None)	Felix A. Aramayo, 3 Roland Houses, South Kensington, S.W.
Brazil..................	Edmund C. H. Phipps, C.B., *Minister* ...	A. de Souza Corrêa, 55 Curzon St.,W.
Bulgaria...............	F. E. H. Elliot, *Agent & Cons.-Gen.* ...	(None)
Central America......	{ George Francis Birt Jenner, *Minister and Cons.-Gen.* (Guatemala City).	{ Honduras / Nicaragua / Salvador / Costa Rica : John A. Le Lacheur, 58 Lombard St., E.C. / Guatemala : Col. José Saborio, 150 Leadenhall St., E.C.
Chile	Audley Charles Gosling, *Minister*........	Domingo Gana, 29 Queen's Gate Terr. S.W.
China..................	Sir C. M. MacDonald, K.C.B., *Minister*...	H. E. Sir Chichen Lofêngluh, K.C.V.O., 49 Portland Pl., W.
Colombia	George Earle Welby, *Minister*	Gen. Reyes, 53 Victoria Street, S.W.
Congo Free State ..	Lt.-Col., W.P.Pulteney,D.S.O.,*Vice-Con.*	M. Houdret, 21 Mincing Lane, E.C.
Denmark	Sir Edmd. D. V. Fane, K.C.M.G., *Minister*	F. E. de Bille, 24 Pont St., S.W.
Dominican Republic	Augustus Cohen, *Cons.-Gen.*............	Miguel Ventura, 17 Coleman St., E.C.
Ecuador...............	William N. Beauclerk (Lima), *Min.* ...	Celso Nevares, 3 Copthall Bldgs, E C.
Egypt..................	Visct. Cromer, G.C.B., *Min. & Cons.-Gen.*	
France	Rt. Hon. Sir E. J. Monson, G.C.B., *Amb.*	M. Paul Cambon, Albert Gate House, [Hyde Pk., W.
German Empire		
Prussia	{ Rt. Hon. Sir Frank Cavendish Lascelles, G.C.B., *Ambassador*........	
Bavaria............ } Würtemberg ... }	Victor A. W. Drummond, C.B., *Minister*	{ Graf von Hatzfeldt-Wildenburg, 9 Carlton House Terrace, S.W.
Saxony	Sir A. Condie Stephen, K.C.M.G., *Minister*	
Baden .... } Hesse............... }	G. W. Buchanan (Darmstadt), *Ch. d'A.*	
Saxe-Cob.-Goth. } Waldeck Pyrmt. }	Sir A. C. Stephen, K.C.M.G. (Dresden)..	
Greece	Sir Edwin H. Egerton, K.C.B., *Minister*	M. D. Metaxas, 31 Marloes Road, S.W.
Hayti..................	Augustus Cohen, *Consul-General*........	L. J. Janvier, 5 Albany Ct. Yd., W.
Italy	Rt. Hn. Lord Currie, G.C.B., *Ambassador*	Baron De Renzis, 20 Grosvenor Sq., W.
Japan..................	Sir Ernest Mason Satow, K.C.M.G., *Min.*	Takaaki Kato, 4 Grosvenor Gardens, W.
Liberia	William A. Ring, *Vice-Cons.*	H. Hayman, 3 Coleman St., E.C.
Luxemburg	SirH.Howard, K.C.B. (The Hague), *Envoy*	
Mexico	Sir H. Nevill Dering, Bt., C.B., *Envoy Ext.*	Sebastian Mier, 87 Cromwell Rd., S.W.
Montenegro	R. J. Kennedy, C.M.G., *Minister Resident*	
Morocco...............	Sir A. Nicolson, K.C.I.E., *Envoy Ext.* ...	
Netherlands...........	Sir Henry Howard, K.C.M G., *Minister*..	Baron van Goltstein van Oldenaller, 118 Eaton Square, S.W.
Paraguay	Hn. W. Barrington (Buenos Aires), *M.*	Alfred James, 18 Eldon St., E.C.
Persia	Sir H. M. Durand, K.C.S.I., *Env. Ext.*...	Gen. Mohamed-Ali-Khan, 30 Ennismore Gardens, S.W.
Peru	Wm. Nelthorpe Beauclerk, *Minister* ...	José F. Canevaro, 3 Park Place, S.W.
Portugal	Sir H. MacDonell, G.C.M.G., *Minister* ...	Luiz de Soveral, G.C.M.G., 12 Gloucester Place, W.
Roumania	John Gordon Kennedy, *Minister*	M. de Balaceano, 28 Victoria St., S.W.
Russia	Rt. Hon. Sir Chas. S. Scott, G.C.B., *Amb.*	Georges de Staal, Chesham House, S.W.
Servia	William Edward Goschen, *Minister* ...	M. Mijatovitch, 27 Pembroke Gardens, S.W.
Siam	George Greville, C.M.G., *Minister*	Marquis Visuddha, 23 Ashburn Pl., S.W.
Spain	Rt. Hon. Sir H. D. Wolff, G.C.B., *Ambas.*	Conde de Rascon, 1 Grosvenor Gardens, S.W.
Sweden and Norway	Hn. Sir Fras. J. Pakenham, K.C.M.G., *M.*	Count Lewenhaupt, 52 Pont St., S.W.
Switzerland	Frederick R. St. John, *Minister*	Charles D. Bourcart, 52 Lexham Garden, W.
Tripoli	Thomas S. Jago, *Consul-General*	Represented by Turkey.
Tunis	Ernest J. L. Berkeley, C.B., *Consul-Gen.*	Represented by France.
Turkey	Rt. Hon. Sir N. R. O'Conor, G.C.B., *Amb.*	Costaki Pacha, 1 Bryanston Sq., W.
United States	Rt. Hon. Lord Pauncefote, G.C.B., *Am.*	Joseph H. Choate, Carlton House Terrace, S.W.
Uruguay	Walter Baring, *Minister and Cons.-Gen.*	(Vacant) 87 Victoria St., S.W.
Venezuela...............	Wm. H. Doveton Haggard, *Min. Res.*...	José Andrade, 11 Montague St., W.C.

COUNTRY.	BRITISH REPRESENTATIVE.	REPRESNTVE. IN GT. BRITAIN.
INDIA, see pages (441-476)	Lord Curzon of Kedleston, *Viceroy & Gov. Gen.*	*India Office* — Lord George Hamilton, *Sec. of State.*
Madras (451)	Sir Arthur E. Havelock, G.C.M.G., *Governor*	
Bombay (452)	Sir H. S Northcote, Bart, G.C.M.G., *Governor*	
Bengal (452)	Sir John Woodburn, K.C.S.I., *Lieut.-Gov.*	
N.W. Prov. and Oudh (453) ...	Sir Antony P. MacDonnell, G.C.S.I., *Lieut.-Gov.* ...	
Punjab (453)	Sir W. Mackworth Young, K.C.S.I., *Lieut.-Gov.* ...	
Burma (454)	Sir Fredc. W. R. Fryer, K.C.S.I., *Lieut.-Gov.* ...	*Crown Agents for Colonies.*
Ceylon (477-478)	Colonel Rt. Hon. Sir J. West Ridgeway, K.C.B., *Gov.*	
Straits Settlements (478-479) ..	*Lieut.-Col.* Sir C. B. H. Mitchell, G.C.M.G., *Governor*	,, ,, ,, ,,
Hong Kong (480)	Sir Henry Arthur Blake, G.C.M.G., *Governor*	,, ,, ,, ,,
Borneo, Labuan (480-482)	Hugh Charles Clifford, *Governor*	,, ,, ,, ,,
Sarawak (481)	H.H. Sir Charles Johnson Brooke, G.C.M.G., *Raja*	,, ,, ,, ,,
*CANADA (483-491)	{ Earl of Minto, G.C.M.G., *Governor-General* ...... Rt. Hon. Sir Wilfrid Laurier, K.C.M.G., *Premier* }	Lord Strathcona and Mount Royal, G.C.M.G., *Agent-Gen.*
*Newfoundland (491-492)	{ Lt.-Col. Sir Hy. E. M'Callum, K.C.M.G., *Governor* Hon. Sir James S. Winter, K.C.M.G., *Premier* }	*Crown Agents for Colonies.*
British Guiana (492-493) ...	Sir Walter Joseph Sendall, K.C.M.G., *Governor*	,, ,, ,, ,,
British Honduras (493) ...	Colonel David Wilson, G.C.M.G., *Governor*	,, ,, ,, ,,
Bermuda (493-494)	Lieut.-Gen. George Digby Barker, C.B., *Governor* ...	,, ,, ,, ,,
AUSTRALASIA (495-508)		Sir Julian Salomons, *Agent-General.*
*New South Wales (497)	{ Earl Beauchamp, K.C.M.G., *Governor* ...... Hon. William John Lyne, *Premier* ...... }	Hon. Sir Andrew Clarke, G.C.M.G., *Agent-General.*
*Victoria (498-500)	{ Lord Brassey, K.C.B., *Governor* ...... Rt. Hon. Sir George Turner, K.C.M.G., *Premier* }	Hon. J. A. Cockburn, M.D., *Agent-General.*
*South Australia (500-501) ...	{ Lord Tennyson, *Governor* .... Rt. Hon. C. C. Kingston, *Premier* ...... }	Hon. Sir Horace Tozer, K.C.M.G., *Agent-General.*
*Queensland (501-502)	{ Lord Lamington, K.C.M.G., *Governor* ...... Hon. J. R. Dickson, C.M.G., *Premier* ...... }	Hon. E. H. Wittenoom, *Agent-General.*
*Western Australia (502-503) ...	{ Colonel Sir Gerard Smith, K.C.M.G., *Governor* .... Rt. Hon. Sir John Forrest, K.C.M.G., *Premier* }	Hon. W. P. Reeves, *Agent-General.*
*New Zealand (504-505)	{ Earl of Ranfurly, G.C.M.G., *Governor* ...... Rt. Hon. Richard John Seddon, *Premier* }	Sir Philip Oakley Fysh, K.C.M.G., *Agent-General.*
*Tasmania (505-506)	{ Viscount Gormanston, G.C.M.G., *Governor* ...... Rt. Hon. Sir E. N. C. Braddon, K.C.M.G., *Premier* }	*Crown Agents for Colonies.*
Fiji (506-507)	Sir George T. M. O'Brien, G.C.M.G., *Governor*	,, ,, ,, ,,
British New Guinea (507)	George Ruthven Le Hunte, C.M.G., *Lieut.-Governor*	,, ,, ,, ,,
Pacific Islands (507)	Sir G. T. M. O'Brien, K.C.M.G., *High Commissioner*	,, ,, ,, ,,
BRITISH WEST INDIES (509-514)	[Chief	
Jamaica (510)	Sir A. W. L. Hemming, K.C.M.G., *Capt.-Gen. & Gov. in*	,, ,, ,, ,,
Bahamas (510-511)	Sir Gilbert Thos. Carter, K.C.M.G., *Governor*	,, ,, ,, ,,
Leeward Isles (511-512)	Sir Francis Fleming, K.C.M.G., *Governor*	,, ,, ,, ,,
Windward Isles (512-513)	Sir Alfred Moloney, K.C.M.G., *Governor*	,, ,, ,, ,,
Barbados (513-514)	Sir James Shaw Hay, K.C.M.G., *Governor*	,, ,, ,, ,,
Trinidad and Tobago (514)......	Sir H. E. H. Jerningham, K.C.M.G., *Governor*	,, ,, ,, ,,
BRITISH AFRICA (515-530)		
1. *South Africa* (515-522)	{ Sir Alfred Milner, G.C.M.G., *Gov. & High Commr.* Hon. Wm. Philip Schreiner, C.M.G., *Premier...* }	Hon. Sir David Tennant, K.C.M.G., *Agent-General.*
*Cape Colony (516-518)		*Crown Agents for Colonies.*
Basutoland (518-519)	Sir Godfrey Yeatman Lagden, K.C.M.G., *Commr.*	,, ,, ,, ,,
Bechuanaland Protector. (519) ...	Major H. J. Goold-Adams, C.B., *Res. Commissioner*	
*Natal (519-521)	{ Hon. Sir W. F. Hely Hutchinson, G.C.M.G., *Gov.* Honble. Lt.-Col. A. H. Hime, K.C.M.G., *Premier* }	Sir W. Peace, K.C.M.G., *A.-Gen.*
Rhodesia (521-522)	Sir Marshal J. Clarke, *Res. Commissioner*	J. F. Jones, *Secretary.*
2. *West Africa* (523-527)		*Crown Agents for Colonies*
Gambia (523-524)	Sir Robert Baxter Llewelyn, K.C.M.G., *Administrator*	
Gold Coast Colony (524-525) ...	Sir Frederick Mitchell Hodgson, K.C.M.G., *Governor* ..	,, ,, ,, ,,
Sierra Leone (525)	Colonel Sir Frederick Cardew, K.C.M.G., *Governor* ..	,, ,, ,, ,,
Lagos (525-526)	Sir William McGregor, M.D., K.C.M.G., *Governor* ...	,, ,, ,, ,,
Nigeria, Southern (526)	Sir R. D. R. Moor, K.C.M.G., *H.M. Commr. & Cons.-Gen.*	,, ,, ,, ,,
Nigeria, Northern (526)	Lt.-Col. F. D. Lugard, C.B., D.S.O., *H.M. Commr.*	,, ,, ,, ,,
3. *East and Central* (527-530)		
Somaliland Protect. (527)	Lt.-Col. J. H. Sadler, *Cons. Gen.*	*Foreign Office.*
East Africa Protect. (527)	Sir A. H. Hardinge, K.C.M.G., *H.M. Commr. & Cons.-Gen.*	,, ,,
Uganda Protectorate (528-529)...	Sir H. H. Johnston, K.C.B., *H.M. Commr. & Cons.-Gen.*	,, ,,
Witu Protectorate (529)	{ Omari bin Hamed, *Sultan* A. S. Rogers, *Resident* }	
Zanzibar Protectorate (529)	{ Hamud bin Muhamad bin Said, *Sultan* Sir A. H. Hardinge, *H.M. Agent & C.-G.* }	
British Central Africa Protec. (529-530)	Alfred Sharpe, C.B., *H.M. Commissioner & Cons.-Gen.*	,, ,,
Mauritius (530-531)	Sir Charles Bruce, K.C.M.G., *Governor*	*Crown Agents for Colonies.*
Seychelles (531)	E. B. Sweet-Escott, C.M.G., *Administrator*	,, ,, ,, ,,
Ascension (531-532)	Captain G. N. A. Pollard, R.N., *Officer in Charge* ...	*H.M. Admiralty.*
Falkland Islands (532)	William Grey-Wilson, G.C.M.G., *Governor*	*Crown Agents for Colonies*
St. Helena (532-533)	Robert Armitage Sterndale, *Governor*	,, ,, ,, ,,
Cyprus (533-534)	Sir Wm. F. Haynes Smith, K.C.M.G., *High Commr.* ...	,, ,, ,, ,,
Malta (534-535)	Gen. Sir Fras. Wallace Grenfell, G.C.B., G.C.M.G., *Gov.*	,, ,, ,, ,,
Gibraltar (535)	General Sir R. Biddulph, G.C.B., *Gov. & C.-in-Ch.* ..	,, ,, ,, ,,
Statist. Table Brit. Emp. (535).		

* The figures in parentheses refer to the Appendix, where a descriptive account of each country will be found. The eleven self-governing colonies have an asterisk prefixed.

HER MAJESTY VICTORIA, by the Grace of God, of the United Kingdom of Great Britain and Ireland Queen, Defender of the Faith, Empress of India (in India, Kaisar-i-Hind), *born at Kensington Palace*, 24th May, 1819; *succeeded* to the Throne 20th June, 1837, on the death of her uncle, King William IV.; *crowned* 28th June, 1838; and *married*, 10th February, 1840, to his late Royal Highness Francis ALBERT Augustus Charles Emmanuel, PRINCE CONSORT, Duke of Saxony, Prince of Coburg and Gotha, who was *born* 26th August, 1819, and *died* 14th December, 1851. Her Majesty has had issue—

1. H.I.M. VICTORIA, Empress Frederick of Germany, Princess Royal, *b.* Nov. 21, 1840; *m.* Jan. 25, 1858, to *Frederick*, Crown Prince of Prussia, afterwards German Emperor (*b.* Oct. 18, 1831, *died* June 15, 1888), and has had issue—William, reigning German Emperor, *b.* Jan. 27, 1859, *m.* Feb. 27, 1881, to Princess Augusta of Schleswig-Holstein, and has six sons and a daughter; Charlotte, *b.* July 24, 1860, *m.* Feb. 18, 1878, to Hered. Prince of Saxe-Meiningen; Henry, *b.* Aug. 14, 1862, *m.* May 24, 1888, to his cousin, Princess Irene of Hesse; *Sigismund*, *b.* Sept. 15, 1864, *d.* June 18, 1866; Victoria, *b.* April 12, 1866, *m.* Nov. 19, 1890, to H.S.H. Prince Adolphe of Schaumburg-Lippe; *Waldemar*, *b.* Feb. 10, 1868, *d.* March 27, 1879; Sophia Dorothea, *b.* June 14, 1870, *m.* Oct. 27, 1889, to the Duke of Sparta; and Margaret, *b.* April 22, 1872, *m.* Jan. 25, 1893, to Prince Fredk. of Hesse-Cassel.

2. H.R.H. ALBERT EDWARD, Prince of Wales, *b.* November 9, 1841; *m.* March 10, 1863, to the Princess Alexandra (*b.* Dec. 1, 1844), eldest daughter of the King of Denmark, and has had issue—*Albert Victor*, Duke of Clarence, *b.* Jan. 8, 1864, *d.* Jan. 14, 1892; George Frederick, Duke of York, Captain R.N., *b.* June 3, 1865, *m.* July 6, 1893, Princess Victoria Mary ("May") of Teck (*b.* May 26, 1867), and has issue Edward, *b.* June 23, 1894, Albert, *b.* Dec. 14, 1895, and Victoria Alexandra, *b.* April 25, 1897; Louise, *b.* Feb. 20, 1867, *m.* July 27, 1889, to the Duke of Fife—issue Alexandra, *b.* May 17, 1891, and Maud, *b.* April 3, 1893; Victoria, *b.* July 6, 1868; Maud, *b.* Nov. 26, 1869; *m.* 22 July, 1896, to Charles, 2nd son of the Crown Prince of Denmark; and *Alexander*, *b.* April 6, *d.* April 7, 1871.

3. *H.R.H. Alice Maud Mary*, *b.* April 25, 1843; *m.* July 1, 1862, to H.R.H. *Louis IV.*, Grand Duke of Hesse (*b.* September 12, 1837, *d.* March 13, 1892); *d.* Dec. 14, 1878; her issue being—Victoria Alberta, *b.* April 5, 1863, *m.* April 30, 1884, to Prince Louis of Battenberg, R.N.; Elizabeth, *b.* Nov. 1, 1864, *m.* June 15, 1884, to the Grand Duke Serge of Russia; Irene, *b.* July 11, 1866, *m.* May 24, 1888, to her cousin, Prince Henry of Prussia, brother of the German Emperor; Ernest Louis, Grand Duke of Hesse, *b.* Nov. 25, 1868, *m.* April 19, 1894, to H.R.H. Princess Victoria Melita of Saxe-Coburg; *Frederick*, *b.* Oct. 7, 1870, *d.* June 29, 1873; Alix Victoria, *b.* June 6, 1872, *m.* Nov. 26, 1894, to H.I.M. the Czar of Russia, and has issue, Olga, *b.* Nov. 15, 1895, and Tatiana, *b.* June, 1897; and *Mary*, *b.* May 24, 1874, *d.* Nov. 15, 1878.

4. H.R.H. ALFRED Ernest Albert, Duke of Edinburgh and Duke of Saxe-Coburg-Gotha, *b.* August 6, 1844; Admiral of the Fleet; *m.* Jan. 23, 1874, to the Grand Duchess Marie of Russia (*b.* Oct. 17, 1853), and has issue—*Alfred*, *b.* Oct. 15, 1874, *d.* Feb 6, 1899, Marie, *b.* Oct. 29, 1875, *m.* Jan. 10, 1893, to Ferdinand, Crown Prince of Roumania, and has issue—Carol, *b.* Oct. 15, 1893, and a daughter; Victoria Melita, *b.* Nov. 25, 1876, *m.* April 19, 1894, to Ernest Louis, Grand Duke of Hesse, and has issue; Alexandra, *b.* Sept. 1, 1878, *m.* 1896, to Ernest, Hereditary Prince of Hohenlohe-Langenburg, and has issue; and Beatrice, *b.* April 20, 1884.

5. H.R.H. HELENA Augusta Victoria, *b.* May 25, 1846; *m.* July 5, 1866, to Prince Frederick Christian C. A. of Schleswig-Holstein (*b.* Jan. 22, 1831), and has had issue—Christian V., Maj. King's Roy. Rifles, *b.* April 14, 1867; Albert J., *b.* Feb. 26, 1869; Victoria L., *b.* May 3, 1870; Louise A., *b.* Aug. 12, 1872, *m.* July 6, 1891, to Pr. Aribert of Anhalt; and *Harold*, *b.* May 12, *d.* May 20, 1876.

6. H.R.H. LOUISE Caroline Alberta, *b.* March 18, 1848; *m.* March 21, 1871, to John, Marquess of Lorne (*b.* Aug. 6, 1845).

7. H.R.H. ARTHUR W.P.A., Duke of Connaught, *b.* May 1, 1850; General in command at Aldershot; *m.* March 13, 1879, Princess Louise Margaret (*b.* July 25, 1860), daughter of the late Prince Frederick Chas. of Prussia, and has issue—Margaret, *b.* Jan. 15, 1882; Arthur, *b.* Jan. 13, 1883; Victoria Patricia, *b.* March 17, 1886.

8. H.R.H. ARTHUR W.P.A., Duke of Albany, *b.* April 7, 1853; *m.* April 27, 1882, to Princess Helen (*b.* Feb. 17, 1861), daughter of the late Prince George of Waldeck, d. Mar. 28, 1884, his issue being—Alice Mary, *b.* Feb. 25, 1883; Leopold CHARLES EDWARD G. A., Duke of Albany, *b.* July 19, 1884.

9. H.R.H. BEATRICE Mary Victoria Feodora, *b.* April 14, 1857; *m.* July 23, 1885, to *Prince Henry Maurice of Battenberg* (*b.* Oct. 5, 1858; *d.* Jan. 20, 1896), and has issue—Alexander Albert, *b.* Nov. 23, 1886; Victoria Eugénie Julia Ena, *b.* Oct. 24, 1887; Leopold Arthur Louis, *b.* May 21, 1889; and Maurice Victor Donald, *b.* Oct. 3, 1891.

Descendants of H.R.H. the first Duke of Cambridge, Her Majesty's Uncle.

Field-Marshal H.R.H. GEORGE William Frederick Charles, 2nd Duke of Cambridge, *b.* Mar. 26, 1819.

AUGUSTA Caroline, *b.* July 19, 1822; *m.* June 28, 1843, Frederick, Grand Duke of Mecklenburg-Strelitz, and has issue—Adolphus Frederick, July 22, 1848, *m.* and has several children.

Mary Adelaide, *b.* Nov. 27, 1833; *m.* June 12, 1866, Francis, Duke of Teck (*b.* Aug. 27, 1837), *d.* Oct. 27, 1897. her issue being—Victoria Mary, *b.* May 26, 1867, *m.* July 6, 1893, to H.R.H. the Duke of York; Adolphus, *b.* Aug. 13, 1868, *m.* 1894, Lady Margaret Grosvenor, d. of the Duke of Westminster, and has issue; Francis, *b.* Jan. 9, 1870; and Alexander George, *b.* April 14, 1874.

Descendants of H.R.H. the Duke of Cumberland, King of Hanover, son of King George III.

H.R.H. ERNEST Augustus George, 3rd Duke of Cumberland, *b.* Sept. 21, 1845; *m.* Dec. 21, 1878, to Princess Thyra of Denmark; and has issue. His sisters—FREDERICA, *b.* Jan. 9, 1848; *m.* April 24, 1880, Freiherr von Pawel-Rammingen (issue—*Victoria*, *b.* Mar. 7, *d.* Mar. 27, 1881); and MARY Ernestine, *b.* Dec. 3, 1849.

PERSONAL.

Keeper of Her Majesty's Privy Purse, Lt.-Col. Rt. Hon. Sir Fleetwood Isham Edwards, K.C.B.

Private Secretary to Her Majesty, Lt.-Col. Sir Arthur John Bigge, K.C.B., C.M.G., R.A.

Assistant Keeper and Assistant Private Secretary, Capt. Frederick E. Grey Ponsonby, M.V.O.

Lectrices to H. M., Miss Bauer; Mdlle. Norèle.

Resid. Medical Attendant, Sir J. Reid, Bt., K.C.B., M.D.

German Secretary, Maurice Muther, M.V.O. [C.V.O.

Munshi and Indian Sec., Hafiz Abdul Karim, C.I.E.,

Commissioner at Balmoral, James Forbes.

Secretary to Privy Purse, Walter M. Gibson.

Clerks, F. R. Engelbach; H. K. Punshon; H. G. Sotheby   [Ism'ail Abdullah.

Indian Attendants, Shekh Chidda; Muhammad

Highland Attendant, Alexander Rankin.

Highland Servant, William Brown.

Land Steward, Windsor, W. Tait.

     ,,   *Osborne*, Andrew Slater.

Head Keeper, J. Overton.

LORD CHAMBERLAIN'S DEPARTMENT.—Office, Stable Yard, St. James's Palace.

Lord Chamberlain, Earl of Hopetoun, G.C.M.G.

Vice-Chamb., Hon. Ailwyn E. Fellowes, M.P.

Comptroller of Accounts, Hon. Sir Spencer Cecil Brabazon Ponsonby-Fane, G.C.B.

Chief Clerk Daniel Tupper.

Examiner of Accounts, Harry L. Hertslet, M.V.O.

Clerks, Cecil C. Marrable; R. G. March; Herbert A. P. Trendell; Frederic S. Osgood.

Examiner of Plays, George Alexander Redford.

Paymaster of Household, George T. Hertslet.

Lords in Waiting, Earl of Clarendon; Earl of Kintore, G.C.M.G.; Earl of Denbigh; Gen. Viscount. Bridport, G.C.B.; Lord Churchill; Lord Harris, G.C.S.I.; G.C.I.E.; Lord Lawrence; Lord Bagot.

Grooms in Waiting, Capt. W. D. S. Campbell, M.V.O.; Hon. Alex. Grantham Yorke, M.V.O.; Adm. of Fleet Sir John Edmund Commerell, G.C.B., Ṿℭ; Col. Lord William Cecil, M.V.O.; Capt. Malcolm Drummond (of Megginch); Maj. Hon. Chas. Harbord; Col. Henry Donald Browne; Gen. Godfrey Clerk, C.B.

Extra Grooms in Waiting, Col. Sir Walter George Stirling, Bart.; Major-Gen. Sir Thomas Dennehy, K.C.I.E.; Gen. Sir Michael A. Shrapnel Biddulph, G.C.B.

Master of the Ceremonies, Colonel Hon. Sir William James Colville, K.C.V.O., C.B.

Assistant Master, Lieut.-Col. Wm. Chaine.

Marshal of the Ceremonies, Hon. R. C. Moreton.

Gentlemen Ushers of Privy Chamber, Capt. Walter J. Stopford, C.B.; Conway F. C. Seymour; Col. Cuthbert Larking; Horace West; Capt. Wyndham Tufnell (*extra*).

Gentleman Usher of Black Rod, Gen. Sir Michael A. Shrapnel Biddulph, G.C.B.

Gentlemen Ushers Daily Waiters, Hon. Sir Spencer Cecil Brabazon Ponsonby-Fane, G.C.B.; Edward Hamilton Anson.

Assistant Gentleman Usher, Frederick Campbell.

Extra Gentleman Usher, Hon Alex. Nelson Hood.

Grooms of Privy Chamber, Col. Hon. C. G. C. Eliot, C.V.O.; Capt. Nath. G. Philips; Arnold Royle, C.B.; Capt. Hon. Otway Fredk. Seymour Cuffe.

Gentlemen Ushers Quarterly Waiters, Sir Francis Knollys, K.C.B., K.C.M.G.; Raglan G. H. Somerset; Hon. H. J. Stonor; Hon. A. Fitz-Clarence; Chas. J. Innes-Ker; Lt.-Col. A. Collins, C.B., M.V.O.; Brook Taylor; Capt. Hon. Arthur Hay.

Grooms of the Great Chamber, E. P. Collins; E. Goddard; John Martin; J. Ireland; William Collins; Henry Holloway; Leonard Collmann; J. B. Seymour; James Campbell; F. G. Vaughan.

LORD STEWARD'S DEPARTMENT.

Board of Green Cloth, Buckingham Palace.

Lord Steward, The Earl of Pembroke, G.C.V.O. £2,000

Treasurer, Viscount Curzon, M.P £904

Comptroller, Viscount Valentia, M.P. £904

Master of the Household, Colonel Lord Edward William Pelham-Clinton, K.C.B. £1,158

Secretary to the Board, George Augustus Courteux.

Chief Clerk, Col. E. L. F. Jennings.

Clerk, C. Gerald H. MacGill.

Paymaster, George Thomas Hertslet.

Gentleman of the Cellars, Thomas Kingscote.

Clerk Comptroller, A. F. W. Lloyd.

First Clerk of Kitchen, Edward Lawley.

Chief Cook, Louis Chevriot.

First Master Cook, G. F. Malsch.

First Gentleman Porter, Charles Michie.

Sergeant State Porter, Richard Hyem.

Coroner of the Verge, Arthur Walter Mills.

Electric Light Engineer, W. H. Massey, M.INST.C.E.

Librarian at Windsor, Richard R. Holmes, M.V.O.

Poet Laureate, Alfred Austin

Painter in Ordinary, James Sant, R.A.

Marine Painter, Edward de Martino, M.V.O.

Surveyor of Pictures, Sir Jno. Chas. Robinson.

Governor and Constable of Windsor Castle, Marquess of Lorne, K.T.

Deputy, Col. Lord E. W. Pelham-Clinton, K.C.B.

Bargemaster, J. A. Messenger

Keeper of the Swans, T. R. Abnett

Keeper of the Jewels, Tower, General Sir Hugh Henry Gough, G.C.B., Ṿℭ

Master of the Music, Sir Walter Parratt.

Conductor of the Band, Alfred Gibson.

Pages of the Back Stairs, Charles Thomson; G. Waite; Archibald Brown; F. Orchard

State Pages, Frederick Wagenreider; C. Robertson

Page of the Chambers, J. H. F. Harnack.

Pages of the Presence, J. Heir; Andrew Thomson; William Thomson; T. G. Shorter; J. Meredith

Pages, Men, W. Bovington; F. Gray; G. Woods.

Sergeants-at-Arms, George T. Hertslet; Maj. Jas. A. C. Gore; Richd. Edgcumbe; Lieut.-Col. Forbes Macbean; E. Hamilton Anson; Captain Sir W. B. Goldsmith, R.N.; Richard R. Holmes, M.V.O.; Maj. Evan Martin.

Her Majesty's Bodyguard of Yeomen of the Guard. Captain, Earl Waldegrave, £1,200; *Lieutenant*, Col. Sir Horatio Page Vance; *Ensign*, Col. Richard George Ellison; *Clerk of the Cheque & Adjutant*, Col. Reginald Hennell, D.S.O.; *Exons*, Lieut.-Col. Charles Doyle Patterson; Maj. Edmund Halburt Elliot, R.A.; Maj. Hon. Frank Colborne; Capt. Houston French. (See also p. 217.)

Her Majesty's Bodyguard of the Hon. Corps of Gentlemen at Arms. Captain, Col. Lord Belper, A.D.C., £1,200; *Lieutenant*, Col. Sir Henry Hugh Oldham; *Standard-Bearer*, Major Philip Limborch Tillbrook; *Clerk of the Cheque & Adjutant*, Col. Aubone George Fife; *Sub-Officer*, Lieut.-Col. John Glas Sandeman. (See also p. 217.)

Military Knights of Windsor. Governor, Capt. W. Maloney. (See also p. 217)

Inspector, Windsor—Leonard Collmann.

     ,,   *Buckingham Palace*—C. Taylor.

Sergeant Trumpeter, P. J. Paque

MEDICAL DEPARTMENT.

Physicians in Ordinary, Sir Edward Hy. Sieveking, M.D.; Sir James Reid, Bart., K.C.B., M.D.; Sir Richard Douglas-Powell, Bart., M.D.

Physicians Extraordinary, Sir Alf. Baring Garrod, M.D., F.R.S.; Sir Samuel Wilks, Bart., M.D., F.R.S.; Sir Wm. Henry Broadbent, Bart., M.D.; J. E. Pollock, M.D.; Thomas Barlow, M.D.

Serjeant Surgeon, Sir James Paget, Bart., F.R.C.S.

Surgeons Extraordinary, Lord Lister, P.R.S., M.D.; Sir Thomas Smith, Bart., F.R.C.S.; Thomas Bryant, F.R.C.S.

Physician to Household, Thomas Barlow, M.D.

Surgeon to Household, Rickman J. Godlee, F.R.C.S.

Surg. Apoth. to H.M. and Apothecary to the Household, Sir Fras. Henry Laking, K.C.V.O., M.D.

Surgeons and Apothecaries in Ordinary to the Household at Windsor, William Fairbank; and William Ellison (jointly).

Ditto at Osborne, William Hoffmeister, M.D., and H. E. W. Hoffmeister (jointly).

Surgeon Oculist, George Lawson, F.R.C.S.

Surg. Dentist, Sir Edwin Saunders, F.R.C.S.

Dentist to the Household, Edwin Truman.

Chemist and Druggist, Peter Wyatt Squire.

CHAPELS ROYAL.

Dean of the Chapels Royal, The Bishop of London.

Sub-Dean of the Chapels Royal, Rev. Edgar Sheppard, M.A.

Clerk of the Closet, The Bishop of Winchester.

Deputy Clerks of the Closet, Rev. William Rowe Jolley, M.A.; Very Rev. Dean Farrar, D.D.; Rev. Canon Dalton, C.M.G.

Organist and Composer, William Creser, MUS.D.

Organist of St. George's Chapel, Windsor, Sir Walter Parratt.

Domestic Chap., Very Rev. the Dean of Windsor.

Reader (Windsor) Rev. John H. Ellison, M.A.

　,, (Balmoral) Rev. S. J. R. Sibbald, B.D.

Chaplain (St. James's), Rev. Edgar Sheppard, M.A.

　,, *Hampton Court Palace*, Rev. Arthur George Ingram, M.A.

　,, *Kensington*, Rev. William G. Green, M.A.

　,, *German Chapel, St. James's*, Rev. Fredk. Frisius, D.D.

　,, *Savoy*, Rev. Paul Williams Wyatt, M.A.

ROYAL ALMONRY, 6, Craig's Court, S.W.

Hereditary Grand Almoner, Marquess of Exeter.

Lord High Almoner, Right Rev. Lord Alwyne Compton, D.D., Lord Bishop of Ely.

Sub-Almoner, Rev. Edgar Sheppard, M.A. (Sub-Dean of Chapels Royal).

Secretary, Hayward John Bidwell.

Assistant do., W. G. Hunt.

DEPARTMENT OF THE MASTER OF THE HORSE.
Office, Royal Mews, Pimlico.

Master of the Horse, The Duke of Portland, G.C.V.O.

Crown Equerry, and Secretary to Master of the Horse, Maj.-Gen. Sir H. P. Ewart, K.C.B., K.C.V.O.

Equerries in Ordinary, Maj.-Gen. Sir John C. McNeill, K.C.B., V.C.; Lieut.-Col. Sir Arthur J. Bigge, K.C.B.; Lieut.-Col. Hon. William H. P. Carington, C.B.; Lt.-Col. Hon. Henry Charles Legge, M.V.O.; Capt. Frederick Edward Grey Ponsonby, M.V.O.; Lt.-Col. Arthur Davidson, M.V.O.; Maj.-Gen. J. F. Brocklehurst, M.V.O.

Extra Equerries, Gen. Viscount Bridport, G.C.B.; Lt.-Col. Stanier Waller, R.E.; Lieut.-Col. Rt. Hon. Sir Fleetwood I. Edwards, K.C.B., R.E.; Major Count Gleichen, C.M.G.; Col. John Clerk, C.V.O., C.S.I.; Maj.-Gen. Sir Chas. Taylor Du Plat, K.C.B.

Honorary Equerry, Gen. the Duke of Grafton, K.G.

Pages of Honour, Hon. Ivan J. Lumley Hay; Harold E. Festing; Viscount Torrington; John Neville Biggs.

Supt. Royal Mews, London, Capt. J. Nicholas, M.V.O.

　　　,,　　　*Windsor*, Daniel Hickey.

Accountant, William Cullen.

Storekeeper, John Miller.

Clerk, Frederick Thomas Malleson.

Veterinary Surgeon, London, George H. Williams.

　　　,,　　　*Windsor*, R. C. Tennant.

Queen's Coachman, Thomas Burnham.

THE ROYAL HUNT.

Master of the Buckhounds, The Earl of Coventry.

Huntsman, John Comins.

Whippers-in, C. Strickland; C. Hoare.

Groom to the Hunters, Reuben Matthews.

Veterinary Surgeon, Sir Henry Lunnon Simpson.

Hereditary Grand Falconer, Duke of St. Albans.

DEPARTMENT OF THE MISTRESS OF THE ROBES.

Mistress of the Robes, The Duchess of Buccleuch.

Ladies of the Bedchamber, The Dowager Lady Churchill; Dowager Countess of Erroll; Dowager Lady Southampton; Dowager Lady Ampthill; Viscountess Downe; Countess of Antrim; Countess of Lytton, C.I.; Duchess of Roxburghe.

Extra Lady of the Bedchamber, Dowager Countess of Mayo.

Bedchamber Women, Viscountess Chewton; Hon. Lady Hamilton-Gordon; Hon. Mrs. Ferguson (of Pitfour); Hon. Horatia Charlotte Stopford; Mrs. Jno. Haughton; Hon. H. L. Phipps; Hon. Emily Cathcart; Hon. Ethel H. M. Cadogan.

Extra Bedchamber Women, Lady Elizabeth P. Biddulph; Hon. Mrs. Gerald Wellesley; Hon. Lady Biddulph; Lady Cowell; Hon. Caroline Cavendish; Hon. Mrs. Alaric Grant; Hon. Mrs. Bernard Mallet; Hon. Lady Ponsonby; Hon. Flora Clementina Isabella Macdonald.

Maids of Honour, Hon. Frances M. Drummond; Hon. Evelyn I. Moore; Hon. Bertha Lambart; Hon. Mary Florentia Hughes; Hon. Aline Majendie; Hon. Judith Harbord; Hon. Sylvia Gay Edwardes; Hon. Doris Vivian.

Extra Maid of Honour, Hon. Constance H. Kerr.

Groom of the Robes, H. D. Erskine (of Cardross).

Clerk of the Robes, Arnold Royle, C.B.

H.R.H. THE PRINCE OF WALES'S HOUSEHOLD.

Lord Warden of the Stannaries, Earl of Ducie.

Keeper of the Privy Seal, Earl of Leicester, K.G.

Attorney-Gen., Charles Alfred Cripps, Q.C., M.P.

Rec.-Gen., Col. Sir R. N. FitzH. Kingscote, K.C.B.

Sec. & Clerk of Council, Maurice Holzmann, C.B.

Auditor, Lesley Charles Probyn.

Groom of the Stole, Duke of Abercorn, K.G., C.B.

Lords in Waiting, Lord Suffield, K.C.B.; Earl of Gosford, K.P.

Comptroller and Treasurer, General Sir Dighton Macnaghten Probyn, G.C.V.O., V.C.

Grooms in Waiting, Sir Francis Knollys, K.C.B.; Hon. Henry Stonor.

Equerries, Maj.-Gen. Sir Stanley de A. Calvert Clarke, K.C.V.O.; Capt. George Lindsay Holford, C.I.E., M.V.O.; Comm. Hon. Seymour Fortescue, M.V.O., R.N.; Hon. S. Greville, C.B.

Extra Equerries, Col. Sir Robt. Nigel F. Kingscote, K.C.B.; Lt.-Col. Lord Wantage, K.C.B., V.C.; Maj.-Gen. John Cecil Russell; Capt. Hon. Alwyn Henry Fulke Greville; Vice-Admiral Sir Henry Frederick Stephenson, K.C.B.; Major-General Sir Arthur Ellis, K.C.V.O.

Honorary A.-de-C.'s, H.H. the Maharaja Sir Nripendra Narayan Bahadur, of Cooch Behar, G.C.I.E.; Lieut.-Col. Maharaj Dhiraj Sir Partab Singh, Bahadur, Regent of Jodhpore, G.C.S.I.
Orderly Native Officers, Ressaldar and Woordie-Major Ahmed Khan, Bahadur, Khan Sahib 11th P. W. O. Bengal Lancers.
Private Secretary, Sir Francis Knollys, K.C.B.
Domestic Chaplain, Rev. Canon Hervey, M.A.
Honorary Chaplains, Rev. Canon Robinson Duckworth, D.D.; Rev. A. Robins, M.A.; Rev. Canon J. Fleming, B.D.
Librarian, Maurice Holzmann, C.B.
Chief Clerk, Francis Morgan Bryant.
Second Clerk, Geo. B. Long. *Third,* E. W. Bryant.
Physicians in Ordinary, Sir Edward Henry Sieveking, M.D.; Sir Wm. H. Broadbent, Bart., M.D.; Sir James Reid, Bart.. M.D.
Surgeons in Ordinary, Sir Jas. Paget, Bt., M.D.; Sir William Mac Cormac, Bt., K.C.V.O., P.R.C.S.; Alfred Downing Fripp, M.V.O., F.R.C.S.
Surgeon to Household, Herbert Allingham, F.R.C.S.
Hon. Physicians, Sir Hy. W. Acland, Bt., K.C.B., M.D.; Surg.-Gen. Sir Joseph Fayrer, Bart., K.C.S.I., F.R.S., M.D.; John Lowe, M.D.; Sir Dyce Duckworth, M.D.; Fleet Surgeon A. G. Delmege, M.D., M.V.O.
Superintendent of Stables, Lord Suffield, K.C.B.
Surg. Apothecary, Sir Fras. Hy. Laking, K.C.V.O., M.D.
Surg. Apothecary, Sandringham, Alan R. Manby, M.D.
Surgeon Dentist, Sir E. Saunders, Knt., F.R.C.S.
Agent at Sandringham, Frank R. Beck.
House Steward, J. Blackburn.
Housekeeper, Mrs. R. Dodds.
Housekeeper at Sandringham, Mrs. E. Butler.

HOUSEHOLD OF H.R.H. THE PRINCESS OF WALES.
Chamberlain, Lord Colville of Culross, K.T., G.C.V.O.
Ladies of the Bedchamber, Dowager Countess of Morton; Lady Emily Kingscote; Lady Suffield.
Extra Lady of the Bedchamber, Countess of Macclesfield.
Bedchamber Women, Hon. Lady Hardinge; Miss Elizabeth C. Knollys; Hon. Mrs. C. Hardinge.
Extra Bedchamber Woman, Duchesse G. d'Otrante.
Private Secretary, Major-Gen. Sir Stanley de Astel Calvert Clarke, K.C.V.O.

HOUSEHOLD OF T.R.H. THE DUKE AND DUCHESS OF YORK.
Comptroller and Treasurer, Major-General Sir Francis Walter de Winton, G.C.M.G., C.B., R.A.
Equerries, Lieut. Sir Charles Leopold Cust, Bart., R.N.; Major Hon. Derek Wm. Geo. Keppel.
Ladies in Waiting, Lady Eva Dugdale; Lady Mary Lygon; Lady Kath. Grey Coke (*extra*).
Physician Accoucheur, Sir John Williams, Bt., M.D.
Surgeon in Ordinary, Frederick Treves, F.R.C.S.
Surgeon Apothecary, Alan Reeve Manby, M.D.
Physician in Ordinary, Robert W. Burnet, M.D.
Hon. Chaplain, Rev. (Canon) J. Neale Dalton, C.M.G.
Clerk and Accountant, Clifford Longden.
Auditor, Tansley Witt, F.C.A., J.P.

HOUSEHOLD OF H.R.H. DUKE ALFRED OF SAXE-COBURG-GOTHA (DUKE OF EDINBURGH).
Comptroller and Treasurer, Col. Monson, C.V.O.
Extra Equerries, Col. Hn. Sir W. J. Colville, K.C.V.O.; C.B.; Lt.-Col. Arthur B. Haig, C.M.G., R.E.; Col. John Clerk, C.V.O.; Capt. Hon. Maurice A. Bourke, R.N.; Maj.-Gen. F. H. Poore, R.M.A.; Capt. Colin Richard Keppel, C.B., D.S.O., R.N.
Acting Secretary, H. J. T. Joist.
Chaplain, Rt. Rev. Charles John Corfe, D.D., Missionary Bishop in Corea (*hon.*).

Physicians in Ordinary, Surg.-Gen. Sir Joseph Fayrer, Bart., K.C.S.I., M.D.; Dr. George Wilks.
Surgeon in Ordinary, Alfred Cooper, F.R.C.S.

HOUSEHOLD OF H.R. AND I.H. THE DUCHESS ALFRED OF SAXE-COBURG-GOTHA (DUCHESS OF EDINBURGH).
Ladies in Waiting, Lady Monson; Mrs. Colin Keppel; Lady Mary Wentworth-Fitzwilliam (*extra*).
Physician Accoucheur, Wm. Smoult Playfair, M.D.
Chaplain, Very Rev. E. Solvieviev, Archpriest.
Private Secretary, Baron Mengden.

HOUSEHOLD OF H.R.H. THE DUKE OF CONNAUGHT AND STRATHEARN.
Comptroller and Equerry, Col. Alfred Mordaunt Egerton, C.B.
Equerry, Capt. Malcolm McNeill.
Extra Equerries, Maj.-Gen. Ronald B. Lane, C.B.; Capt. Sir Maurice Fitzgerald, Bart., Knight of Kerry; Col. Arthur W. Reddie Becher; Col. Cuthbert Larking.
Physician, Sir Samuel Wilks, Bart., M.D., F.R.S.
Secretary, Andrew Wilson Murray.

HOUSEHOLD OF H.R.H. THE DUCHESS OF CONNAUGHT AND STRATHEARN.
Ladies in Waiting, Hon. Mrs. Alfred Egerton; Lady Elphinstone (*hon.*); Viscountess Downe (*hon.*); Lady Adela Larking (*hon.*)
Physician, Sir Samuel Wilks, Bart., M.D., F.R.S.
Physician Accoucheurs, William Smoult Playfair, M.D.; Sir Francis Henry Laking, M.D.
Secretary, Andrew Wilson Murray.

HOUSEHOLD OF H.R.H. THE DUCHESS OF ALBANY.
Comptroller, Sir Robert Hawthorn Collins, K.C.B.
Ladies in Waiting, Hon. Mrs. Richd. Moreton; Lady Collins; Miss E. Heron-Maxwell.

HOUSEHOLD OF H.R.H. PRINCE CHRISTIAN OF SCHLESWIG-HOLSTEIN.
Comptroller and Equerry, Col. the Hon. Charles George Cornwallis Eliot, C.V.O.
Equerry, Major James Evan B. Martin.
Extra Equerry, Col. Geo. Grant Gordon, C.V.O., C.B.
Physician in Ordinary, Thos. J. Maclagan, M.D.
Surgeons, William Fairbank; Wm. Hugh Beresford.

HOUSEHOLD OF H.R.H. PRINCESS CHRISTIAN, Cumberland Lodge, Windsor Great Park.
Bedchamber Women, Miss Emily Loch; Baroness von und zu Egloffstein.
Honorary Bedchamber Women, Lady Edward Cavendish; Lady Susan Leslie-Melville; Lady Agneta Montagu; Mrs. Geo. Gordon.

HOUSEHOLD OF H.R.H. PRINCESS LOUISE (MARCHIONESS OF LORNE).
Equerry, Lieut.-Colonel Arthur Collins, M.V.O.
Honorary Lady of the Bedchamber, Lady Sophia Macnamara.

HOUSEHOLD OF H.R.H. PRINCESS BEATRICE (PRINCESS HENRY OF BATTENBERG).
Comptroller and Treasurer, Col. Lord William Cecil, M.V.O.
Equerry, Maj. Hon. Fras. L. L. Colborne.
Ladies in Waiting, Miss Anne Annette Minna Cochrane; Miss E. Bulteel; Hon. Lady Biddulph.
Physician in Ordinary, Sir John Williams, Bt., M.D.

HOUSEHOLD OF H.R.H. PRINCESS CHARLES OF DENMARK (PRINCESS MAUD OF WALES).
Comptroller and Private Secretary, Col. Henry Knollys, R.A.

The Most Honourable Privy Council.

H.R.H. the Prince of Wales.
H.R.H. the Duke of Connaught.
H.R.H. the Duke of York.
H.R.H. the Duke of Cambridge.
H.R.H. Prince Christian (Schleswig-Holstein).
The Archbishop of Canterbury.
The Lord High Chancellor—Earl of Halsbury.
The Archbishop of York.
The Lord President (Duke of Devonshire).
The Lord Privy Seal—Viscount Cross.
Duke of Norfolk (*Postmaster-General*).
Duke of Richmond and Gordon.
Duke of Marlborough, *Paymaster-General*.
Duke of Rutland.
Duke of Argyll.
Duke of Portland (*Master of the Horse*).
Duke of Northumberland.
Duke of Westminster.
Duke of Fife.
Marquess of Huntly.
Marquess of Lothian.
Marquess of Lansdowne (*Secretary of State*).
Marquess of Salisbury (*Secretary of State*).
Marquess of Hertford.
Marquess of Londonderry.
Marquess of Ripon.
Marquess of Breadalbane.
Marquess of Dufferin and Ava.
Marquess of Zetland.
Marquess of Lorne.
Earl of Pembroke (*Lord Steward*).
Earl of Hopetoun(*Ld.Chamberlain*)
Earl of Derby.
Earl of Chesterfield.
Earl of Coventry.
Earl of Jersey.
Earl of Elgin and Kincardine.
Earl of Kintore.
Earl of Aberdeen.
Earl of Rosebery.
Earl of Dartmouth.
Earl of Tankerville.
Earl Cowper.
Earl Waldegrave.
Earl of Ilchester.
Earl of Radnor.
Earl Spencer.
Earl of Mount-Edgcumbe.
Earl Cadogan (*Ld. Lieut. Ireland*).
Earl of Cork and Orrery.
Earl of Cavan.
Earl of Kenmare.
Earl of Harrowby.
Earl Brownlow.
Earl of Morley.
Earl of Ducie.
Earl of Yarborough.
Earl of Kimberley.
Earl of Northbrook.
Earl of Cranbrook.
Earl of Ancaster.
Earl Carrington.
Earl of Crewe.
Lord Walter Gordon-Lennox.
Lord Henry Richard Somerset.
Lord Robert Montagu.
Lord George Hamilton (*Secretary of State*).
Viscount Peel.
Viscount Knutsford.
Viscount Llandaff.
Lord Henry Frederick Thynne.
Lord Arthur William Hill.
Lord Augustus Loftus.

The Bishop of London (Creighton)
Lord Windsor.
Lord Colville of Culross.
Lord Balfour of Burleigh (*Secretary for Scotland*).
Lord Suffield.
Lord Thurlow.
Lord Ribblesdale.
Lord Poltimore.
Lord Sudeley.
Lord Leigh.
Lord Belper.
Lord Tweedmouth.
Lord Penzance.
Lord Norton.
Lord Hobhouse.
Lord Ashbourne (*Ld. Chancellor Ireland*).
Lord Stalbridge.
Lord Macnaghten (*Ld. of Appeal*).
Lord Connemara.
Lord Morris (*Lord of Appeal*).
Lord Field.
Lord Rookwood.
Lord Shand.
Lord Ashcombe.
Lord Russell of Killowen (*Lord Chief Justice*).
Lord Davey (*Lord of Appeal*).
Lord Loch.
Lord Burghclere.
Lord James of Hereford(*D.of Lanc.*)
Lord Rathmore.
Lord Pirbright.
Lord Hencage.
Lord Ludlow.
Lord Curzon of Kedleston.
Lord Currie.
Lord Brampton.
Lord Pauncefote.
Lord Robertson (*Lord of Appeal*).
William Court Gully (*Speaker*).
Sir Matthew White Ridley, Bart. (*Secretary of State*).
Joseph Chamberlain(*Sec. of State*).
Hon. St. John Brodrick.
Hon. A. Evelyn M. Ashley.
Hon. Charles Robert Spencer.
Hon. Sir Henry George Elliot.
Hon. Sir Edmund John Monson.
Hon. Gerard James Noel.
Sir Frederick Peel.
George J. Goschen (*Admiralty*).
Sir James Fergusson, Bart.
Sir Edward Thornton.
George Young (*Lord of Session*).
Sir Michael E. Hicks-Beach, Bt. (*Chancellor of the Exchequer*).
Sir John C. Dalrymple-Hay, Bt.
Sir Richard Couch.
James Lowther.
Sir William Hart Dyke, Bart.
Sir William Vernon-Harcourt.
Sir Mountstuart E. Grant-Duff.
George John Shaw-Lefevre.
Sir Nathaniel Lindley (*Master of the Rolls*).
Sir George Otto Trevelyan, Bart.
Sir Charles Wentworth Dilke, Bt.
Sir Edward Fry.
John Blair Balfour (*Ld. Just. Gen.*)
Sir Henry Campbell-Bannerman.
Sir Edward Baldwin Malet.
Sir Henry Drummond Wolff.
Henry Chaplin (*President Local Government Board*).
Arthur James Balfour (*First Lord of the Treasury*).
Sir Arthur John Otway, Bart.
Sir William Thackeray Marriott.
Sir Massey Lopes, Bart.
John Hay Athol Macdonald (*Lord Justice Clerk*).

John Morley.
Sir John Tomlinson Hibbert.
John William Mellor.
Sir U. J. Kay-Shuttleworth, Bart.
Sir Henry Hartley Fowler.
Charles Thomson Ritchie (*President Board of Trade*).
Sir Richard Garth.
Leonard Henry Courtney.
Sir John Lubbock, Bart.
Sir John Eldon Gorst (*Vice-President Committee of Council*).
William Lawies Jackson.
Aretas Akers-Douglas (*First Commissioner of Works*).
William Lidderdale.
Sir C. J. Pearson (*Ld. of Session*).
Sir Francis Henry Jeune (*Pres. Probate,Divorce,and Admiralty*).
Sir Arch. L. Smith (*Lord Justice*).
Sir James Parker Deane.
Arnold Morley.
Herbert Henry Asquith.
Arthur Herbert Dyke Acland.
Jesse Collings.
Charles Scale-Hayne.
Christopher Palles.
Alexander Staveley Hill.
Sir Algernon Edward West.
Herbert John Gladstone.
Sir Frank Cavendish Lascelles.
Sir Arthur Divett Hayter, Bart.
Sir John Rigby (*Lord Justice*).
Cecil John Rhodes.
Robert William Hanbury.
Sir Bernhard Samuelson, Bart.
Sir Ralph Wood Thompson.
Walter Hume Long (*President Board of Agriculture*).
Sir Fleetwood Isham Edwards.
Sir Richard Horner Paget, Bart.
Francis John Savile Foljambe.
Sir Richard Temple, Bart.
Charles Beilby Stuart-Wortley.
Sir Nicholas Roderick O'Conor.
Friedrich Max-Müller.
Andrew Graham Murray (*Lord Advocate*).
Sir Horace Rumbold, Bart.
Sir John Henry Kennaway, Bart.
Sir Samuel James Way, Bart.
Sir John Henry de Villiers.
Sir Samuel Henry Strong.
Sir Wilfrid Laurier.
George Houston Reid.
Sir George Turner.
Richard John Seddon.
Sir Hugh Muir Nelson.
Sir John Gordon Sprigg.
Charles Cameron Kingston.
Sir William Vallance Whiteway.
Sir E. N. Coventry Braddon.
Sir John Forrest.
Harry Escombe.
William Edward Hartpole Lecky.
John Gilbert Talbot.
John Lloyd Wharton.
Sir Herbert Maxwell, Bart.
Sir Richd. H. Collins (*Ld. Just.*).
Sir Roland B. V. Williams (*Lord Justice*).
Sir George Taubman Goldie.
James Alexander Campbell.
James William Lowther.
Edmond Robert Wodehouse.
Sir Charles Stewart Scott.
Sir Charles Hall.
Edward James Saunderson.
William Kenrick.
Sir William Walrond, Bart.
Sir Robert Romer (*Lord Justice*).

Clerk of the Council, Almeric W. FitzRoy.   *Deputy Clerk*, James H. Harrison.
Members of the Privy Council are addressed as **The Right Honourable.**

The Lord Lieutenant and Her Majesty's Most Honourable Privy Council in Ireland.

His Excellency GEORGE HENRY, EARL CADOGAN, K.G., G.M.P.,
Lord Lieutenant-General and General Governor of Ireland.

H.R.H. the Prince of Wales.
H.R.H. the Duke of York.
H.R.H. the Duke of Cambridge.
H.H. Prince Edward of Saxe-Weimar.
The Lord Chancellor—Lord Ashbourne
Duke of Devonshire.
Duke of Abercorn.
Marquess of Londonderry.
Marquess of Dufferin and Ava.
Earl of Meath.
Earl of Fingall.
Earl of Belmore.
Earl of Dunraven and Mount Earl.
Viscount Powerscourt.
Viscount Wolseley.
Lord Morris (*Lord of Appeal*).
Lord Roberts, V.C. (*Commanding the Forces in Ireland*).
Lord Clonbrock.
Gerald W. Balfour (*Chief Sec.*).
Hedges Eyre Chatterton (*Vice-Ch.*).
Christopher Palles (*Chief Baron*).

Sir Michael Hicks-Beach, Bart.
James Lowther.
Gerald Fitzgibbon (*Lord Justice*).
Henry Bruen.
The O'Conor Don.
Wm. Moore Johnson (*Judge Q. B.*).
Sir George Otto Trevelyan, Bart.
Andrew Marshall Porter (*Master of the Rolls*).
Sir Henry Campbell-Bannerman.
Samuel Walker (*Lord Justice*).
Sir William Hart Dyke, Bart.
Hugh Holmes (*Lord Justice*).
John Morley.
John Young.
Arthur James Balfour.
John George Gibson (*Judge*).
General Sir Redvers H. Buller, V.C.
Sir Peter O'Brien, Bart. (*L. C. J.*).
Sir Henry Hervey Bruce, Bart.
Col. William Brownlow Forde.
Col. Sir Joseph West Ridgeway.

Dodgson H. Madden (*Judge*).
William O'Brien (*Judge*).
James Murphy (*Judge*).
William Lawies Jackson.
John Atkinson (*Attorney-General*).
The MacDermot.
Joseph Michael Meade.
Thomas Alexander Dickson.
Charles Hare Hemphill.
Sir Richard Martin, Bart.
Thomas Sinclair.
Arthur Hugh Smith-Barry.
Edward Henry Carson.
Hon. Horace Plunkett.
William D. Andrews (*Judge*).
William James Pirrie.
Lt.-Col. Edward Henry Cooper.

Clerk of the Council, James B. Dougherty (Dublin Castle).

Members of the Privy Council of Ireland, like those of England, are addressed as **The Right Honourable.**

Table of Precedency.

The Sovereign.
The Prince of Wales.
The Queen's younger Sons.
Grandsons of the Sovereign.
The Archbishop of Canterbury.
The Lord High Chancellor.
The Archbishop of York.
The Lord President of the Council.
The Lord Privy Seal.
The Lord Great Chamberlain.
The Earl Marshal.
The Lord Steward of Her Majesty's Household.
The Lord Chamberlain.
The last four rank above all Peers of their own degree.
Dukes, according to their Patents of Creation.
1. Of England; 2. Of Scotland; 3. Of Great Britain; 4. Of Ireland.
5. Those created since the Union.
Marquesses according to their Patents, in the same order as Dukes.
Dukes' eldest Sons.
Earls, according to their Patents, in the same order as Dukes.
Marquesses' eldest Sons.
Dukes' younger Sons.
Viscounts, according to their Patents, in the same order as Dukes.
Earls' eldest Sons.
Marquesses' younger Sons.
Bishops of London, Durham, and Winchester.
All other English Bishops, according to their seniority of Consecration.
Bishops of the Irish Church, created before 1869, according to seniority.
Secretaries of State, if of the degree of a Baron.
Barons, according to their Patents in the same order as Dukes.
Speaker of the House of Commons.
Treasurer of H.M.'s Household.
Comptroller of H.M.'s Household.
Master of the Horse.
Vice-Chamberlain of Household.
Secretaries of State under the degree of Barons.
Viscounts' eldest Sons.
Earls' younger Sons.

Barons' eldest Sons.
Knights of the Garter.
Privy Councillors.
Chancellor of the Exchequer.
Chancellor of the Duchy of Lancaster.
Lord Chief Justice Queen's Bench.
Master of the Rolls.
The Lords Justices of Appeal.
Lords of Appeal.
Judges according to seniority.
Viscounts' younger Sons.
Barons' younger Sons.
Sons of Life Peers.
Baronets of England, Scotland, Ireland, and United Kingdom, according to date of Patents.
Knights of the Thistle.
Knights of St. Patrick.
Knights Grand Cross of the Bath.
Knights Grand Commanders of the Star of India.
Knights Grand Cross of St. Michael and St. George.
Knights Grand Commanders of the Indian Empire.
Knights Grand Cross of the Royal Victorian Order.
Knights Commanders of the Bath.
Knights Commanders of the Star of India.
Knights Commanders of St. Michael and St. George.
Knights Commanders of the Indian Empire.
Knights Commanders of the Royal Victorian Order.
Commanders of the Royal Victorian Order.
Knights Bachelors.
Judges of County Courts.
Companions of the Bath.
Companions of the Star of India.
Companions of St. Michael and St. George.
Companions of the Indian Empire.
Members 4th Class of the Royal Victorian Order.
Companions of the Distinguished Service Order.
Members 5th Class of the Royal Victorian Order.

Eldest Sons of younger Sons of Peers.
Baronets' eldest Sons.
Eldest Sons of Knights —1. Garter. 2. Thistle; 3. St. Patrick; 4. The Bath; 5. Star of India. 6. St. Michael and St. George; 7. Indian Empire; 8. Royal Victorian Order; 9. Knights Bachelors.
Younger Sons of the younger Sons of Peers.
Baronets' younger Sons.
Younger Sons of Knights in the same order as eldest Sons.
Gentlemen entitled to bear arms.
Women take the same rank as their husbands or as their brothers; but the daughter of a peer marrying a Commoner retains her Title as Lady or Honourable. Daughters of Peers rank next immediately after the wives of their elder brothers, and before their younger brothers' wives. Daughters of Peers marrying Peers of lower degree take the same order of precedency as that of their husbands; thus the daughter of a Duke marrying a Baron *degrades* to the rank of Baroness only, while her sisters married to commoners retain their rank and take precedence of the Baroness. Merely official rank on the husband's part does not give any similar precedence to the wife.

There are three Orders confined to Ladies: the Order of Victoria and Albert, the Crown of India, and the Royal Red Cross. But members are entitled to no special precedence.

LOCAL PRECEDENCY.—No written code of county or city order of precedence has been promulgated, but naturally in the county the Lord Lieutenant stands first, and secondly the Sheriff. In London and other Corporations, the Mayor stands first, after him the Aldermen, Sheriff, Chief Officers, and Livery At Oxford and Cambridge the High Sheriff takes precedence of the Vice-Chancellor.

KNIGHTS OF THE MOST NOBLE ORDER OF THE GARTER (1349)—K.G.

Ribbon, Garter Blue.   **Motto**, Honi soit qui mal y pense (*Evil to him who evil thinks*).

THE SOVEREIGN.

H.R.H. the Prince of Wales.
H.R.H. the Duke of Saxe-Coburg-Gotha (Duke of Edinburgh).
H.R.H. the Duke of Connaught.
H.R.H. the Duke of York.
H.R.H. the Duke of Cambridge.
H.R.H. the Duke of Cumberland.
Austria, the Emperor of.
Belgians, the King of the.
Denmark, the King of.
German Emperor, the.
Hellenes, the King of the.
Italy, the King of.
Portugal, the King of.
Roumania, the King of.
Russia, the Emperor of.
Saxony, the King of.
Sweden and Norway, the King of.
Mecklenburg - Strelitz, Grand Duke of.

Hesse, Grand Duke of.
Schleswig - Holstein, H.R.H. Prince Christian of.
Prussia, H.R.H. Prince Albert William Henry of.
Naples, H.R.H. Prince of
Denmark, H.R.H. Crown Pr. of.
Fitzwilliam, Earl.
Spencer, Earl.
Cowper, Earl.
Richmond and Gordon, Duke of.
Ripon, Marquess of.
Westminster, Duke of.
Leicester, Earl of.
Salisbury, Marquess of.
Grafton, Duke of.
Argyll, Duke of.
Kimberley, Earl of.
Abergavenny, Marquess of.
Norfolk, Duke of.
Londonderry, Marquess of.

Rutland, Duke of.
Cadogan, Earl.
Devonshire, Duke of.
Abercorn, Duke of.
Rosebery, Earl of.
Breadalbane, Marquess of.
Lansdowne. Marquess of.
Derby, Earl of.
Buccleuch and Queensberry, Duke of.
Elgin, Earl of.
Northumberland, Duke of.
Prelate, Bishop of Winchester.
Chancellor, Bishop of Oxford.
Registrar, Dean of Windsor.
Garter Principal King of Arms, Sir Albert William Woods, K.C.B., F.S.A.
Usher of the Black Rod, General Sir Michael A. Shrapnel Biddulph, G.C.B.

KNIGHTS OF THE MOST ANCIENT AND MOST NOBLE ORDER OF THE THISTLE (1540, 1687)—K.T.

Ribbon, Green.   *Motto*, Nemo me impune lacessit (*No one annoys me with impunity*).

THE SOVEREIGN.

H.R.H. the Prince of Wales.
H.R.H. the Duke of Saxe-Coburg-Gotha (Duke of Edinburgh).
H.R.H. the Duke of Connaught.
H.R.H. the Duke of York.
H.R.H. the Duke of Cambridge.
Argyll, Duke of, K.G.
Stair, Earl of.
Atholl, Duke of.
Southesk, Earl of.
Lorne, Marquess of, M.P.
Colville of Culross, Lord.

Bute, Marquess of.
Buccleuch and Queensberry, Duke of, K.G.
Lothian, Marquess of.
Montrose, Duke of.
Fife, Duke of.
Galloway, Earl of.
Crawford and Balcarres, Earl of.
Rosebery, Earl of, K.G.
Tweeddale, Marquess of.
Home, Earl of.

Dean, Very Rev. James Cameron Lees, D.D.
Secretary, Maj. Sir Duncan Alexander Dundas Campbell, Bart.
Lyon King of Arms, James Balfour Paul.
Gentleman Usher of the Green Rod, Hon. Alan David Murray.

KNIGHTS OF THE MOST ILLUSTRIOUS ORDER OF ST. PATRICK (1783)—K.P.

Ribbon, Sky Blue.   *Motto*, Quis separabit ? (*Who shall separate?*)

THE SOVEREIGN.

The Lord-Lieutenant of Ireland, *Grand Master.*

H.R.H. the Prince of Wales.
H.R.H. the Duke of Saxe-Coburg-Gotha (Duke of Edinburgh).
H.R.H. the Duke of Connaught.
H.R.H. the Duke of York.
H.R.H. the Duke of Cambridge.
Saxe - Weimar, H.H. Prince Edward of.
Cork and Orrery, Earl of.
Dufferin and Ava, Marquess of.
Gosford, Earl of.
Powerscourt, Viscount.
Kenmare, Earl of.

Listowel, Earl of.
Dunraven, Earl of.
Carysfort, Earl of.
Howth, Earl of.
Monteagle of Brandon Lord.
Wolseley, *Field Marshal* Viscount (*Commander-in-Chief*).
Ormonde, Marquess of.
Erne, Earl of.
Kilmorey, Earl of.
Rosse, Earl of.
Inchiquin, Lord.
Cavan, Earl of.

Iveagh, Lord.
Roberts of Kandahar, V.C., *Field Marshal*, Lord.
Arran, Earl of.
Lucan, Earl of.
Chancellor, Chief Sec. for Ireland.
Ulster King of Arms, Sir Arthur E. Vicars, F.S.A.
Sec., G. Francis W. Lambart.
Usher of the Black Rod, Col. the Viscount Charlemont, C.B.

THE MOST HONOURABLE ORDER OF THE BATH (1399, 1725).

Ribbon, Crimson.   *Motto*, Tria juncta in uno (*Three joined in one*).

THE SOVEREIGN.

Great Master and Principal Knight Grand Cross, Field Marshal H.R.H. the Prince of Wales, K.G., K.T., K.P., G.C.S.I., G.C.M.G., G.C.I.E., G.C.V.O.

Military Knights Grand Cross. G.C.B.
Adye, *General* Sir John Miller.
Alison, *Gen.* Sir Archibald, Bart.
Biddulph, *Gen.* Sir Michael A. S.

Biddulph, *General* Sir Robert.
Browne, *Gen.* Sir Samuel J., V.C.
Brownlow, *Gen.* Sir Charles H.
Buller, *General* Rt. Hon. Sir Redvers Henry, V.C.

Cambridge, Fd.-Marshal H.R.H. the Duke of.
Chamberlain, *Gen.* Sir Neville B.
Chelmsford, *General* Lord.
Clanwilliam, *Ad.-Flt.* the Earl of.

MILITARY KNIGHTS, G.C.B.—*con.*

Commerell, *Admiral of the Fleet* Sir John Edmund, V.C.
Connaught, *General* H.R.H. the Duke of.
D'Aguilar, *General* Sir Chas. L.
Daubeney, *Gen.* Sir Henry C. B.
Dickson, *Gen.* Sir Collingwd., V.C.
Dowell, *Adm.* Sir Wm. Montagu.
Fanshawe, *Adm.* Sir Edward G.
Forbes, *General* Sir John.
Fremantle, *Admiral Hon.* Sir Edmund Robert.
Gough, *General* Sir C. J. S., V.C.
Gough, *Gen.* Sir Hugh H., V.C.
Graham, *Lt.-Gen.* Sir Gerald, V.C.
Greaves, *Gen.* Sir Geo. Richards.
Grenfell, *Gen.* Sir Francis W.
Grubbe, *Adm.* Sir W. J. Hunt-
Haines, *F.-M.* Sir Frederick Paul.
Hamilton, *Adm.* Sir Richd. Vesey.
Hay, *Adm.-Fleet* Lord John.
Hood of Avalon, *Admiral* Lord.
Hopkins, *Admiral* Sir John O.
Hoskins, *Adm.* Sir Anthony H.
Johnes, *Lt.-Gen.* Sir J. Hills-, V.C.
Keppel, *Admiral of the Fleet* Hon. Sir Henry.
Kerr, *General* Lord Mark.
Kitchener of Khartoum, *Maj.-Gen.* Lord (*Sirdar*).
Leiningen, *Adm.* H.S.H. Pr. of.
Lockhart, *General* Sir William Stephen Alexander
Low, *Lt.-Gen.* Sir Robert Cunliffe.
Lowe, *Lt.-Gen.* Sir D. C. Drury-
Lumsden, *Gen.* Sir Peter Stark.
Lyons, *Admiral of the Fleet* Sir Algernon M'Lennan.
M'Leod, *Lt.-Gen.* Sir J. Chetham.
Norman, *Gen.* Sir Henry Wylie.
Reid, *General* Sir Charles.
Richards, *Admiral of the Fleet* Sir Frederick William
Roberts of Kandahar, *Field Marshal* Rt. Hon. Lord, V.C.
Ross, *General* Sir John.
Salmon, *Admiral of the Fleet* Sir Nowell, V.C.
Saxe-Coburg-Gotha, *Admiral of the Fleet* H.R.H. the Duke of.
Saxe-Weimar, *Field-Marshal* H.H. Prince Edward of.
Seymour, *Admiral* Sir Michael Culme-, Bart., A.D.C.
Simmons, *F.-M.* Sir John L. A.
Stephenson, *General* Sir Frederick Charles Arthur.
Stewart, *F.-M.* Sir Donald M., Bt.
Stewart, *Adm.* Sir Wm. Houston.
Stransham, *Gen.* Sir Anthony B.
Taylor, *General* Sir Alexander.
Wellesley, *Adm.* Sir Geo. Greville
White, *Gen.* Sir Geo. Stewart, V.C.
Willes, *Admiral* Sir George O.
Willis, *Gen.* Sir George H. S.
Wolseley, *F.-M.* Rt. Hon. Viscount.
Wood, *General* Sir Evelyn, V.C.

CIVIL KNIGHTS GRAND CROSS. G.C.B.

Bannerman, Rt. Hon. Sir Henry Campbell- M.P.

Battenberg, *Capt.* H.S.H. Prince Louis of, R.N., A.D.C.
Bradford, *Col.* Sir Edward R. C.
Bridport, *General* Viscount.
Cromer, Viscount.
Cross, Rt. Hon. Viscount.
Currie, Rt. Hon. Lord.
Derby, Rt. Hon. the Earl of.
Dufferin and Ava, Marq. of.
Elliot, Rt. Hon. Sir H. George.
Fane, Hon. Sir S. C. Ponsonby-.
Haliburton, Lord.
Herbert, Hon. Sir Robert G. Wyndham.
Lascelles, Rt. Hon. Sir Frank C.
Loch, Rt. Hon. Lord.
Loftus, Rt. Hon. Lord Augustus William Frederick Spencer.
Malet, Rt. Hon. Sir Edward B.
Monson, Rt. Hon. Sir Edmund.
O'Conor, Rt. Hn. Sir Nicholas R.
Owen, Sir Hugh.
Pauncefote, Rt. Hon. Lord.
Rumbold, Rt. Hon. Sir H., Bt.
Rutland, Duke of.
Schleswig-Holstein, *Major* H.H. Prince Christian Victor of.
Scott, Rt. Hon. Sir Charles S.
Stanley, Sir Henry Morton, M.P.
Thornton, Rt. Hon. Sir Edward.
Welby, Lord.
Wolff, Rt. Hon. Sir Henry Drummond.

Hon. Knights Grand Cross.

Mecklenburg-Strelitz, the Reigning Grand Duke of.
Denmark, the King of.
Teck, H.H. the Duke of.
Hohenlohe-Langenburg, H.S.H. Prince of.
Mecklenburg-Strelitz, the Hereditary Grand Duke of.
Prussia, H.R.H. Prince Henry of.
Hesse, H.R.H. the G. Duke of.
Saxe-Coburg and Gotha, H.H. Prince Philippe of.
Russia, H.I.H. the Grand Duke Serge of.
Saxe-Meiningen, H.H. the Hereditary Prince of.
Denmark, H.R.H. the Crown Prince of.
H.I.H. Prince Akihito, of Komatsu (Japan).
Lambremont, Baron François Auguste.
Anhalt, H.H. Prince Aribert Joseph Alexander of.
Hesse, H.G.-D.H. Prince Henry Louis of.
Schaumburg - Lippe, H.S.H. Prince Adolphus Geo. of.
Egypt, H.H. the Khedive of.
Roumania, Prince Ferdinand of.
Afghanistan, H. H. Abdur Rahman Khan, Ameer of.
Greece, H.R.H. the Crown Pr. of.
Denmark, H.R.H. Pr. Carl of.
Hesse, H.H. Prince Frederick Charles of.
Hohenlohe-Langenburg, H.S.H. the Hereditary Prince of.

SECOND CLASS. K.C.B.

MILITARY KNIGHTS COMMANDERS.

Alderson, *Maj.-Gen.* Sir Henry James, R.A.
Ashburnham, *Maj.-Gen.* Sir C.
Baird, *Adm.* Sir John K. Erskine.
Barnard, *Gen.* Sir Charles Loudon.
Bedford, *Vice-Admiral* Sir Frederick George Denham.
Blood, *Maj.-Gen.* Sir Bindon.
Brackenbury, *Gen.* Sir Hy., R.A.
Bridge, *Vice-Adm.* Sir Cyprian Arthur George.
Browne, *Gen.* Sir James F. M.
Buller, *Admiral* Sir Alexander.
Bulwer, *General* Sir Edw. E. G.
Butler, *Lt.-Gen.* Sir William F.
Cameron, *Gen.* Sir Wm. Gordon.
Carrington, *Maj.-Gen.* Sir Fredk.
Chads, *Admiral* Sir Henry.
Clarke, *Lt.-Gen.* Sir C. M., Bart.
Clery, *Lt.-Gen.* Sir Cornelius F.
Cochrane, *Adm. Hon.* Sir Arthur Auckland Leopold Pedro.
Collett, *Colonel* Sir Henry.
Cox, *Lt.-Gen.* Sir John William.
Davis, *General* Sir John.
Dick, *Insp.-Gen.* Sir J. N., R.N.
Dillon, *Gen.* Sir Martin Andrew.
Domvile, *Vice-Admiral* Sir Compton Edward.
Donnet, *Insp.-Gen.* Sir James John Louis, R.N.
Doran, *General* Sir John.
Drysdale, *Lt.-Gen.* Sir William.
East, *Lt.-Gen.* Sir Cecil James.
Edwardes, *Gen.* Sir Stanley de B.
Elles, *Brig.-Gen.* Sir Edmond R.
Elliot, *Maj.-Gen.* Sir Alexr. J. H.
Elliot, *Admiral* Sir George.
Erskine, *Admiral* Sir James E.
Ewart, *Maj.-Gen.* Sir Hen. Peter.
Ewart, *General* Sir John Alex.
Fairfax, *Admiral* Sir Henry.
Farquhar, *Admiral* Sir Arthur.
Farren, *Gen.* Sir Richard Thomas.
Feilding, *General Hon.* Sir Percy Robert Basil.
Fisher, *Vice-Adm.* Sir John A.
Frankfort de Montmorency, *Maj.-General* Viscount.
Fraser, *General Hon.* Sir David Macdowall.
Galbraith, *Maj.-Gen.* Sir William.
Gaselee, *B.-Gen.* Sir Alfred, A.D.C.
Gatacre, *Maj.-Gen.* Sir William, D.S.O.
Gib, *Gen.* Sir William Anthony.
Gipps, *General* Sir Reginald.
Glyn, *Gen.* Sir Julius Richard.
Gordon, *Lt.-Gen.* Sir Benjamin L.
Gordon, *Gen.* Sir Jno. Jas. Hood.
Graham, *Admiral* Sir William.
Grant, *Lieut.-Gen.* Sir Robert.
Grove, *Maj.-Gen.* Sir Coleridge.
Hanbury, *Surg.-Maj.-Gen.* Sir James Arthur.
Harrison, *General* Sir Richard.
Hatt, *Brig.-Gen.* Sir Reginald C., V.C.

MILITARY KNIGHTS, K.C.B.—*con.*

Hay, *Adm.* Right Hon. Sir John Charles Dalrymple-, Bart.
Hay, *Lt.-Gen.* Sir Robt. J., R.A.
Heath, *Adm.* Sir Leopold Geo.
Heneage, *Admiral* Sir Algernon Charles Fieschi.
Higginson, *General* Sir George Wentworth Alexander.
Holdich, *Gen.* Sir Edward Alan.
Home, *Surg.-Gen.* Sir A. D., V.C.
Hotham, *Admiral* Sir Chas. F.
Howlett, *General* Sir Arthur.
Hughes, *Maj.-Gen.* Sir Robert J.
Hume, *Lieut.-Gen.* Sir Robert.
Hunter, *M.-Gen.* Sir Arch., D.S.O.
Innes, *Surg.-Gen.* Sir J. Harry Ker.
Jenkins, *Col.* Sir Francis Howell.
Jenkins, *Insp.-Gen.* Sir Jas., R.N.
Johnson, *Gen.* Sir Allen Bayard.
Johnson, *Gen.* Sir Chas. Cooper.
Jones, *Gen.* Sir Howard Sutton.
Kemball, *General* Sir Arnold B.
Kennedy, *Vice-Admiral* Sir Wm. Robert.
Kerr, *Adm.* Lord W. Talbot.
Luard, *Adm.* Sir Wm. Garnham.
Luck, *Maj.-Gen.* Sir George.
M'Clintock, *Adm.* Sir Francis L.
Macdonald, *Admiral* Sir Regd. J.
McNeill, *Maj.-Gen.* Sir John Carstairs, V.C.
McQueen, *Lt.-Gen.* Sir John W.
Maitland, *Maj.-Gen.* Sir James Makgill Heriot-.
Markham, *Lt.-Gen.* Sir Edwin.
Maunsell, *Gen.* Sir Fredk. Richd.
Meiklejohn, *Br.-Gen.* Sir Wm. H.
Molyneux. *Admiral* Sir Robert Henry More-.
Moore, *Lieut.-Gen.* Sir Henry.
Morris, *Commy.-Gen.* Sir Edward.
Murray, *Gen.* Sir John Irvine.
Newdegate, *Lt.-Gen.* Sir Edward Newdigate-.
Newdigate, *Lt.-Gen.* Sir Hy. R. L
Nicholson, *Admiral* Sir Hy. Fredk.
Nicholson, *Maj.-Gen.* Sir Wm. G.
Norbury, *Dir.-Gen.* Sir Hy. F., R.N.
Norman, *Lt.-Gen.* Sir F. Booth.
Norman, *Lt.-Gen.* Sir Henry R.
Olpherts, *Gen.* Sir William, V.C.
Palmer, *General* Sir Arthur P.
Penrose, *General* Sir Penrose C.
Perkins, *General* Sir Æneas.
Philips, *Maj.-Gen.* Sir Joseph.
Power, *Commy.-Gen.* Sir Wm. J. T.
Prendergast, *General* Sir Harry North Dalrymple-, V.C.
Raines, *Gen.* Sir Julius Aug. R.
Randolph, *Adm.* Sir G. Granville.
Rattray, *Lt.-Gen.* Sir James C.
Rawson, *Vice-Adm.* Sir Harry H.
Reid, *Insp.-Gen.* Sir John W., R.N.
Rice, *Adm.* Sir Edward Bridges.
Rogers, *Lt.-Gen.* Sir R. Gordon.
Rowlands, *Gen.* Sir Hugh, V.C.
Rundle, *Maj.-Gen.* Sir H. M. Leslie.
Russell, *Lieut.-Gen.* Sir Baker C.
Schneider, *Gen.* Sir John Wm.
Schomberg, *Gen.* Sir Geo. Aug.
Scott, *Admiral* Lord Charles Montagu-Douglas-.

Scott, *Maj.-Gen.* Sir Francis Cunningham.
Seymour, *Adm.* Sir E. Hobart.
Shute, *Gen.* Sir Chas. Cameron.
Smith, *Adm.* Sir N. Bowden-.
Sotheby, *Admiral* Sir Edward S.
Spurgin, *Lt.-Gen.* Sir John Blick.
Stephenson, *Vice-Admiral* Sir Henry Frederick.
Stewart, *Lt.-Gen.* Sir Richd. C.
Stirling, *Lt.-Gen.* Sir Wm., R.A.
Sullivan, *Adm.* Sir Fras. Wm., Bt.
Tanner, *Lieut.-Gen.* Sir Oriel V.
Taylor, *Gen.* Sir Rich. C. Hayes.
Thomson, *Surg.-Col.* Sir Geo., I.M.S.
Tracey, *Admiral* Sir Rd. Edwd.
Tuson, *Gen.* Sir Hy. B, R.M.A.
Tytler, *Gen.* Sir James Macleod Bannatyne Fraser-.
Vaughan, *Gen.* Sir John Luther.
Walker, *Lt.-Gen.* Sir Frederick William Edward Forestier-.
Walker, *Lt.-Gen.* Sir Mark, V.C.
Watson, *General* Sir John, V.C.
Westmacott, *Maj.-Gen.* Sir Richd.
White, *General* Sir Robert.
Wilbraham, *General* Sir Richard.
Wilkinson, *Lieut.-Gen.* Sir Hy. C.
Williams, *General* Sir John Wm. Collman, R.M.A.
Williams, *Lt.-Gen.* Sir Wm. John.
Wilson, *Maj.-Gen.* Sir Chas. Wm.
Wolseley, *Lieut.-Gen.* Sir George Benjamin.
Wood, *General* Sir H. Hastings A.
Wright, *General* Sir Thomas.

CIVIL KNIGHTS COMMANDERS.
K.C.B.

Abel, Sir Fred. Augustus, Bart.
Acland, Sir Henry W. Dyke, Bt.
Agnew, Sir Stair.
Austen, Sir Wm. C. Roberts-.
Banks, Sir John Thomas.
Barnaby, Sir Nathaniel.
Barry, Sir John W. Wolfe-.
Bigge, *Lt.-Col.* Sir Arthur John.
Blount, Sir Edward Charles.
Boyle, Sir Courtenay Edmund.
Brassey, Lord.
Buchanan, *Col.* Sir David Carrick Robert Carrick-.
Burdett, Sir Henry Charles.
Clinton, *Col.* Lord Ed. Pelham-.
Collins, Sir Robert Hawthorn.
Conyngham, *Col.* Sir Wm. F. Lenox-.
Craik, Sir Henry.
Davidson, *Col.* Sir David.
Desart, Earl of.
Digby, Sir Kenelm Edward.
Donnelly, *Maj.-Gen.* Sir John Fretcheville Dykes, R.E.
Du Cane, *Maj.-Gen.* Sir Edmd. F.
Du Plat, *Maj.-Gen.* Sir Chas. T.
Durston, *Ch.-Insp.-Mach.* Sir Albert John, R.N.
Edwards, *Lt.-Col.* Rt. Hon. Sir Fleetwood Isham.
Egerton, Sir Edwin Henry.
Engleheart, Sir Jno. D. Gardner.

Evans, Sir John, D.C.L.
Farquharson, *Col.* Sir John, R.E.
Foster, Sir Michael.
Fremantle, Hon Sir Chas. Wm.
Gairdner, Sir Wm. Tennant.
Giffen, Sir Robert.
Godley, Sir Arthur.
Halliday, Sir Frederick James.
Hamilton, Sir Edward Walter.
Harrel, Sir David.
Hassard, Sir John.
Hertslet, Sir Edward.
Hibbert, Rt. Hon. Sir John T.
Hill, *Col.* Sir Edward Stock, M.P.
Huggins, Sir William.
Humphery, *Col.* Sir Wm. Hy., Bt.
Jenkinson, Sir Edward George.
Jenkyns, Sir Henry.
Jeune, Right Hon. Sir Francis.
Johnston, Sir Harry Hamilton.
Kekewich, Sir George Wm.
Kingscote, *Colonel* Sir Robert Nigel FitzHardinge.
Kirk, Sir John, G.C.M.G.
Knollys, Sir Francis.
Knox, Sir Ralph Henry.
Knyvett, Sir Carey John.
Leach, *Lt.-Col.* Sir George Archb.
Lingen, Lord.
Lockyer, Sir Joseph Norman.
Longley, Sir Henry.
Lushington, Sir Godfrey, G.C M.G.
Lyall, Sir Alfred Comyns, G.C.I.E.
Lyte, Sir Henry C. Maxwell-.
MacDonald, *Maj.* Sir Claude M.
MacGregor, Sir Evan.
Mackenzie, Sir Kenneth Muir-.
M'Kerlie, *Col.* Sir John Graham.
Markham, Sir Clements Robert.
Martin, *Col.* Sir Richd. Rowley.
Martin, Sir Theodore.
Matheson, *Colonel* Sir Donald.
Milner, Sir Alfred, G.C.M.G.
Mitchell, Sir Arthur.
Moncrieff, *Colonel* Sir Alexander.
Morris, Sir George.
Mowatt, Sir Francis.
Murray, Sir George Herbert.
Murray, Sir Herbert Harley.
Murray, Sir John, F.R.S.
Nares, *Vice-Adm.* Sir George S.
Noble, Sir Andrew.
Olivey, *Colonel* Sir Walter Rice.
Palgrave, Sir Reginald Francis.
Palmer, Sir Elwin Mitford.
Pawel Rammingen, L.A.G. L.A. Baron von.
Pemberton, Sir Edward Leigh.
Preece, Sir William Henry.
Primrose, Sir Henry William.
Probyn, *General* Sir Dighton Macnaghten, G.C.V.O., V.C.
Reed, Sir Andrew.
Reed, Sir Edward James.
Reid, Sir James, Bart., M.D.
Richmond, Sir William B., R.A.
Ridgeway, *Col.* Right Hon. Sir Joseph West.
Robinson, Sir Frederic Lacy.
Ryan, Sir Charles Lister.
Sanderson, Sir Thomas Henry.
Sankey, *Lt.-Gen.* Sir Richard H.
Shaw, *Capt.* Sir Eyre Massey.
Simon, Sir John.
Smith, *Col.* Sir Chas. B. Euan-.

CIVIL KNIGHTS, K.C.B.—*cont.*

Smith, *Lieut.-Col.* Sir Henry.
Stephenson, Sir Aug. Keppel.
Stokes, *Lieut.-General* Sir John.
Suffield, *Colonel* Lord.
Taylor, Sir John.
Thackeray, *Col.* Sir Edwd. T., V.C.
Thompson, Sir Edwd. Maunde.
Thompson, Rt. Hon. Sir Ralph W.
Thomson, *Col.* Sir R. T. White.
Thorne, Sir Richard Thorne.
Thring, Lord.
Wallington, *Col.* Sir John W.
Walpole, Sir Horatio George.
Walpole, Sir Spencer.
Walter, *Captain* Sir Edward.
Wantage, *Lt.-Colonel* Lord, V.C.
Warren, *Lieut.-Gen.* Sir Chas., G.C.M.G.
West, Rt. Hon. Sir Algernon E.
Wharton, *Rear.-Adm.* Sir W. J.
White, Sir William Henry.
Wills, Sir Edward Payson.
Wilmot, *Col.* Sir Henry, Bt., V.C.
Wingfield, Sir Edward.
Woods, Sir Albert Wm. (*Garter*).

Honorary K.C.B., Raja Ram Singh (*Com.-in-Ch.* Kashmir Army).
Battenberg, H.S.H. Prince Francis Joseph, G.C.V.O.

THIRD CLASS.
C.B.
MILITARY COMPANIONS.

Abadie, *Maj.-Gen.* Henry Richard.
Abbott, *Lt.-Col.* Henry Alexius, I.S.C.
Adams, *Lt.-Col.* Robert Bellew, V.C., I.S.C.
Aglionby, *Colonel* Arthur Sisson.
Aitchison, *Gen.* Chas. Terrington.
Aitken, *Colonel* William, R.A.
Allen, *Capt.* Robert Calder, R.N.
Allgood, *Major-General* George.
Anderson, *Gen.* Horace Searle.
Andoe, *Rear-Admiral* Hilary G.
Appleyard, *Maj.-Gen.* Frederick Ernest.
Ardagh, *Maj.-Gen.* Sir John Chas., K.C.I.E.
Aynsley, *Vice-Adm.* C. Murray-.
Badcock, *Maj.-Gen.* Alex. Robt.
Baker, *Colonel* George.
Bannerman, *General* William.
Barchard, *Col.* Charles Henry.
Barker, *Lt.-Gen.* George Digby.
Barnard, *Brig.-Gen.* John Henry.
Barnes, *Colonel* Osmond.
Barrow, *Col.* Edmd. George, I.S.C.
Barton, *Maj.-Gen.* Geoffry.
Battye, *Maj.-Gen.* Arthur.
Bayly, *Colonel* Richard Kerr.
Beal, *Colonel* Henry.
Beamish, *Rear-Adm.* Henry H.
Beath, *Dep. Surg.-Gen.* John Hy.
Beatson, *Lt.-Col.* Stuart B., I.S.C.
Beckett, *Col.* Charles Edward.
Beckett, *Colonel* Stephen.
Begbie, *Maj.-Gen.* Elphinstone Waters, D.S.O.
Bell, *Col.* Mark Sever, V.C., A.D.C.
Bellairs, *Lt.-Gen.* Sir W., K.C.M.G.
Bengough, *Maj.-Gen.* Harcourt M.

Beresford, *Rear-Admiral* Lord Chas. William De la Poer, M.P.
Beville, *General* George Francis.
Bird, *Lieut.-Gen.* Sir Geo. Corrie, K.C.I.E.
Biscoe, *Maj.-Gen.* Wm. Walters.
Black, *Major-General* Wilsone.
Blair, *General* James, V.C.
Blane, *Lieut.-General* Sir Seymour John, Bart.
Blundell, *Col.* Henry B.- H.-, M.P.
Blundell, *Col.* John Eyles.
Blunt, *Maj.-Gen.* Chas. Harris.
Boardman, *Rear-Adm.* Frederick Ross.
Boileau, *Colonel* Francis William.
Bond, *Maj.-Gen.* William Dunn.
Borradaile, *Col.* George William.
Boswell, *Major-Gen.* John James.
Bourchier, *Lt.-Gen.* Eustace Fane.
Bowyear, *Vice-Adm.* G. Le Geyt.
Boyd, *Colonel* John Alexander.
Brabazon, *Major-General* John Palmer, A.D.C.
Brackenbury, *Rear-Adm.* John William.
Bradshaw, *Surg.-Maj.-Gen.* Alex. Frederick.
Bridge, *Colonel* Charles Henry.
Broadbent, *Col.* Jno. Edwd., R.E.
Broadfoot, *Col.* Archibald, R.A.
Bromhead, *Col.* Sir Benjamin Parnell, Bart.
Bromhead, *Col.* Charles James.
Browne, *Maj.-Gen.* Swinton John.
Brownlow, *Maj.-Gen.* Wm. Vesey.
Brownrigg, *Colonel* Henry John.
Buchanan, *Lt.-Gen.* Henry Jas.
Burnaby, *Maj.-Gen.* Eustace B.
Burne, *Gen.* Henry Knightley.
Burnett, *M.-Gen.* Charles John.
Burroughs, *Lieut.-Gen.* Frederick William Traill-.
Burton, *General* Fowler.
Bushman, *Maj.-Gen.* Henry Aug.
Byam, *Maj.-Gen.* William.
Bythesea, *Rear-Adm.* John, V.C.
Caldecott, *Maj.-Gen.* Francis Jas.
Cameron, *Col.* Aylmer Spicer, V.C.
Campbell, *Capt.* Chas., R.N., D.S.O.
Campbell, *Rear-Adm.* Hy. J. F.
Campbell, *Surg.-Maj.* John., I.M.S.
Campbell, *Maj.-Gen.* Sir John William, Bart.
Campion, *Rear-Admiral* Hubert.
Carew, *Colonel* Reginald Pole-.
Carey, *Colonel* William.
Carleton, *Gen.* Henry Alexander.
Carnegy, *General* Alexander.
Carr, *Colonel* George.
Castle, *Ch. Insp. Mach.* Wm., R.N.
Cave, *Admiral* John Halliday.
Chads, *Major-Gen.* Wm. John.
Chalmer, *Colonel* Reginald.
Chamier, *Lt.-Gen.* Stephen H. E.
Channer, *Gen.* Geo. Nicholas, V.C.
Chaplin, *Col.* John Worthy, V.C.
Chapman, *Gen.* Edward Francis.
Chatfield, *Admiral* Alfred John.
Chichester, *Maj.-Gen.* R. Bruce.
Chippindall, *Lieut.-Gen.* Edward.
Christopher, *Col.* Leonard W. I.S.C.
Clarke, *General* George Calvert.
Clarke, *Lt.-Gen.* S. M. Wiseman-.
Clerk, *General* Godfrey.

Clifford, *Lt.-Gen.* Robt. Cecil R.
Cochrane, *Col.* William F. D.
Coghill, *Col.* Kendal Josiah Wm.
Collen, *M.-G.* Sir E H. H., K.C.I.E.
Collingwood, *Col.* Cuthbert S.
Collinson, *Lt.-Col.* John.
Collis, *Maj.-Gen.* Francis Wm.
Colvile, *Lieut.-Gen.* Fiennes M.
Colvile, *M.-G.* Sir H. E., K.C.M.G.
Colville, *Capt.* Hon. Stanley Cecil James, R.N.
Colwell, *Maj.-Gen.* Geo. Harrie T.
Combe, *Maj.-Gen.* Boyce Albert.
Congleton, *Major-General* Lord.
Cook, *Colonel* James, I.S.C.
Cooke, *Lt.-Gen.* Anthony Chas.
Copland, *Colonel* Alexander.
Corbet, *Lt.-Col.* Arthur Domville.
Cowie, *Maj.-Gen.* Crombie, R.A.
Cox, *Col.* Alexander Temple.
Cox, *Maj.-Gen.* Chas. Vyvyan.
Creagh, *Col.* Arthur Gethin, R.A.
Crease, *Maj.-Gen.* John Frederick.
Crofton, *Col.* Mergan S., D.S.O.
Cuffe, *Surg.-Gen.* Charles McD.
Cumberland, *Maj.-Gen.* Chas. E.
Currie, *Lieut.-Col.* Thomas.
Dalgety, *Colonel* Reginald Wm.
Dalrymple, *M.-Gen.* Wm. Liston.
Dane, *Insp.-General* Richard.
Daunt, *Major-General* William.
Davis, *Col.* George McBride, I M S.
Dawson, *General* Francis.
Deane, *Colonel* Thomas, I.S C.
Degacher, *Maj.-Gen.* Henry Jas.
Delafosse, *Maj.-Gen.* Henry Geo.
De Renzy, *Surg.-Gen.* Annesley Charles Castriot.
Desborough, *Major-Gen.* John.
De Winton, *Maj.-Gen.* Sir Francis Walter, G.C.M.G.
D'Eyncourt, *Admiral* Edwin Clayton Tennyson-.
Dicken, *Col.* Wm. Popham, D.S O.
Dickson, *Maj.-Gen.* John Baillie Ballantyne.
Dixon, *Col.* Henry Grey, A.D.C.
Domville, *Capt.* Sir Wm. Cecil Henry, Bart., R.N.
Donnelly, *Dep. Surgeon-General* John M'Neale, M.D.
Douglas, *Admiral* Sholto.
Dowker, *Gen.* Howard Codrington.
Downes, *Commy.- Gen.* Arthur W.
Drage, *Col.* Thomas William.
Drew, *Maj.-Gen.* Francis Barry.
Duck, *Veterinary-Col.* Francis.
Dundonald, *Colonel* Earl of.
Dunne, *Col.* Walter Alphonsus.
Durand, *Col.* Algernon G. A.
Durnford, *Capt.* John, D.S.O., R.N.
Dyce, *Col.* George Hugh Coles.
Edwards, *Lt.-Gen.* Sir James B.
Egerton, *Maj.-Gen.* Charles C., D.S.O.
Egerton, *Capt.* George le Clerc, R.N.
Elliot, *Maj.-Gen.* Ed. Locke, D.S.O.
Elliott, *Colonel* John, R.M.L I.
Elrington, *Gen.* Fredk. Robert.
Elton, *Col.* Fredk. Coulthurst.
England, *M.-Gen.* Ed. Lutwyche.
Evans, *Lt.-Gen.* Horace Moule.
Ewart, *Lt.-Gen.* Chas. Brisbane.

MILIT. COMPANIONS, C.B.—*cont.*

Eyre, *Colonel* Edmund Henry.
Falmouth, *Maj.-Gen.* Viscount.
Farrington, *Col.* Malcolm Chas.
Feilden, *M.-Gen.* Henry Broom.
Fellowes, *Rear-Admiral* John.
Fellowes, *R.-Adm.* Thomas H. B.
Fisher, *Lieut.-Colonel* George.
FitzGerald, *Col.* C. J. Oswald.
Fit Hugh, *Maj.-Gen.* Alfred.
Flood, *Maj.-Gen.* Fred. R. Solly-
Forbes, *Lt.-Gen.* W. E. Gordon.
Forrest, *General* Wm. Charles.
Fraser, *Maj.-Gen.* Thomas, R.E.
Fremantle, *Gen.* Sir Arthur James Lyon, G.C.M.G.
French, *Maj.-Gen.* Arthur, R.M.A.
French, *Lieut.-General* William
Fryer, *Lieut.-General* John.
Furse, *Colonel* George Armand.
Gaitskell, *Major-Gen.* Frederick.
Gallwey, *Col.* Thos. J., R.A.M.C.
Garforth, *Rear-Adm.* Edm. St. J.
Garnett, *Colonel* Reginald.
Gatacre, *Maj.-Gen.* John, I S.C.
Geary, *Lieut.-Gen.* Henry Le Guay.
Gerard, *Maj.-Gen.* Sir M.G., K.C.S.I.
Glover, *Vet.-Lt.-Col.* Benj. L.
Glyn, *Lieut.-Gen.* Richard Thos.
Goldney, *Col.* Thos. Holbrow, I.S C.
Goodfellow, *General* Wm. West.
Gordon, *Col.* James Henry, D.S.O.
Gordon, *Gen.* Sir Thomas E., K.C.I.E.
Gordon, *Adm.* Wm. Everard A.
Gore, *Surg.-Gen.* Albert Aug.
Gosset, *Major-General* Matthev William Edward.
Gough, *Admiral* Frederick Wm.
Gough, *Col.* Hon. George Hugh.
Gough, *Colonel* Hugh Sutlej.
Grafton, *General* the Duke of.
Graham, *Lieut.-Gen.* Samuel Jas.
Graham, *Major-General* Thomas.
Grant, *Lieut.-Col.* Edward Long.
Grant, *Major-Gen.* Henry Fane.
Graves, *Col.* Benj. Chamney, I.S.C.
Green, *Col.* Malcolm Scrimshire.
Gregorie, *Maj.-Gen.* Chas. Fredk.
Haly, *Col.* Richard H. O'Grady-, D.S.O.
Hamilton, *Col.* Ian S. M., D.S.O.
Hammond, *Col.* Arthur George, V.C., A.D.C., D.S.O.
Handcock, *Maj.-Gen.* Arth. Gore.
Hanford, *Col.* John Compton.
Hankin, *Gen.* George Crommelin.
Hardy, *Lieut.-General* William.
Harley, *Col.* George Ernest.
Harness, *Maj.-Gen.* Arthur, R.A.
Harris, *Gen.* Philip Hy. Farrell.
Hart, *Maj.-Gen.* Arthur Fitztoy.
Harvey, *Surg.-Gen.* Robt., D.S O.
Hassard, *Maj.-Gen.* Fairfax Chas.
Hastings, *Rear-Adm.* Alex. P.
Hastings, *Maj.-Gen.* Fras. Eddowes
Hatton, *Colonel* Villiers.
Hawkes, *Lt.-Gen.* Henry Philip.
Hawkins, *Maj.-Gen.* A. Cæsar.
Hay, *Col.* Alexander S. Leith-.
Hay, *Colonel* James, I.S.C.
Heath, *Rear-Adm.* Wm. A. Jas.
Heffernan, *Chief Insp.-Mach.* John Harold, R.N.
Henderson, *Maj.-Gen.* Kennett G.

Henderson, *Capt.* Reginald Friend Hannam, R.N.
Hennessy, *Maj.-Gen.* G. Robertson
Herbert, *Col.* Ivor John Caradoc.
Higginson, *Colonel* Theophilus.
Hildyard, *Maj.-Gen.* Henry J. T.
Hill, *Gen.* Rowley Sale Sale-.
Hill, *Colonel* William, I.S.C.
Hills, *Major-General* John.
Hinde, *Surg.-Major-Gen.* Geo. L.
Hobday, *Maj.-Gen.* Thos. Fras.
Hogg, *Lieut.-Gen.* Adam G. F.
Hogg, *Maj.-Gen.* Geo. Crawford.
Hoggan, *Maj.-Gen.* John Wm.
Holdich, *Col.* Sir T.H., K.C.I.E.
Holland, *Maj.-Gen.* Henry Wm.
Holland, *Lt.-Col.* Trevenen Jas.
Holt, *Colonel* William John.
Hood, *General* John Cockburn-.
Hope, *Maj.-Gen.* Hugh Richard.
Hope, *Lt.-Col.* Lewis A., A.S.C.
Hopton, *Lieut.-Gen-ral* Edward.
Hoste, *Maj.-Gen.* Dixon Edward.
Howard, *Maj.-Gen.* Francis, A.D.C.
Howe, *General* Earl, G.C.V.O.
Howe, *Capt.* Hon. Assheton Gore Curzon-, A.D.C., R.N.
Hughes, *Col.* Charles Frederick.
Hughes, *Colonel* Emilius.
Hutchinson, *Maj.-Gen.* George.
Hutton, *Maj.-Gen.* Edward T. H.
Irvine, *Admiral* St. George Caulfield D'Arcy-.
Jackson, *Dep. Surg.-Gen.* Sir R.W.
Jeffreys, *Br.-Gn.* Patrick Douglas.
Jennings, *Maj.-Gen.* Robert M.
Jephson, *M.-Gen.* Sir S. William, Bart.
Jones, *Commy.-Gen.* Herb. S. H.
Jones, *Lt.-Col.* Morey Quayle.
Jopp, *Colonel* John.
Jordan, *Major-General* Joseph.
Kane, *Rear-Admiral* Henry Coey.
Keen, *Colonel* Frederick John.
Keighley, *Col.* Chas. Marsh, I.S.C.
Kelly, *Col.* James Graves, A.D.C.
Kelly, *Colonel* William Freeman.
Kenny, *Lt.-Gen.* Thomas Kelly-.
Keppel, *Capt.* Colin R., D.S.O., R.N.
Kerr, *Maj.-Gen.* Lord Ralph D.
Keyser, *Col.* Frederick Charles.
Kidston, *Col.* Alex. Ferrier.
King, *Maj.-Gen.* Aug. Henry, R.A.
Kingsley, *Col.* Wm. Henry Bell.
Kinloch, *Maj.-Gen.* Alex. Angus Airlie.
Knowles, *Maj.-Gen.* Chas. Benj.
Knox, *Col.* William George.
Lambert, *Vet.-Col.* J. Drummond-
Lambert, *Major-Gen.* William.
Lambton, *Lieut.-Gen.* Arthur.
Lance, *Lieut.-Gen.* Frederick.
Lane, *Maj.-Gen.* Ronald Bertram.
Laughton, *Col.* Arthur Fredk.
Law, *Maj.-Gen.* Fras. Towry A.
Lea, *Colonel* Samuel Job, A.S.C.
Leach, *Major-General* Edmund.
Leach, *Maj.-Gen.* Edward P., V.C.
Leach, *B.-Gen.* Harold Pemberton.
Le Mesurier, *Col.* Cecil Brooke.
Le Mesurier, *Col.* Fred. Augustus.
Leslie, *Col.* Sir Charles H., Bt.
Lewis, *Col.* David Francis.
Lindley, *Capt.* Geo. Robt., R.N.
Little, *Lieut.-Gen.* Hy. Alexander.

Lloyd, *Maj.-Gen.* Francis Thos.
Lloyd, *Rear-Ad.* Rodney Maclaine.
Lockhart, *Maj.-Gen.* Sir G. A. Bt.
Lovett, *Maj.-Gen.* Beresford.
Low, *General* Alexander.
Lowry, *Lieut.-Gen.* Robert Wm.
Lowth, *Lt.-Col.* Frank Robert.
Lyster, *Lt.-Gen.* Harry H., V.C.
Lyttelton, *Maj.-Gen.* Hon. Neville Gerald.
Macbean, *Gen.* George Scougall.
MacVail, *B.-Gen.* Hy. Blackwood.
MacCalmont, *Ma.-Gen.* Hugh.
MacDonald, *Col.* Hector Archibald D.S.O., A.D.C.
Macdonald, *Gen.* John A. Math.
Macdonnell, *Insp.-Gen.* Hy., R.N.
McDowell, *Surgeon-Col.* Edmund Greswold.
MacGill, *Capt.* Thomas, R.N.
Macgregor, *Col.* Chas. Reg., I.S.C.
MacGregor, *Col.* Henry Grey.
McInroy, *Colonel* Charles.
Mackenzie, *Col.* Alfred Robert Davidson.
Mackworth, *Col.* Sir Arthur W., Bart.
Maclean, *Maj.-Gen.* Chas. Smith.
McLeod, *Maj.-Gen.* Donald James Sim, D.S.O.
M'Nalty, *Lieut.-Col.* George William, A.M S
M'Namara, *Col.* Wm. Hy., R.A.M.C.
Macneill, *Maj.-Gen.* James G.R.D.
McQuhae, *Capt.* John M., R.N.
McRae, *Lt.-Col.* Hy. Napier, I.S.C.
Madden, *Surg.-Mj-Gn.* Chas. D.
Madden, *Lieut.-Col.* George Colquhoun, D.S.O.
Mahon, *Dep. Inspr.-Gen.* Edward Elphinstone, R.N.
Mainprise, *Capt.* Wm. Thos., R.N.
Maitland, *Colonel* Eardley.
Maitland, *Maj.-Gen.* Pelham Jas.
Malcolm, *Col.* Edward Donald.
Malcolmson, *Major-Gen.* John Henry Porter.
Malthus, *Colonel* Sydenham.
Manderson, *Major-Gen.* Geo. R.
Mangles, *Major-General* Cecil.
Manley, *Surg.-Gen.* William Geo. Nicholas, V.C.
Marston, *Surg.-Gen.* Jeffery Allen.
Martin, *Colonel* Cunliffe.
Martin, *Col.* George Blake N.
Martin, *Col.* Rowland Hill.
Mason, *Admiral* Thomas Henry.
Massy, *Lieut.-General* William Godfrey Dunham.
Master, *Col.* William Chester.
Mathias, *Col.* Henry H., A.D.C.
Maude, *Col.* F. Cornwallis, V.C.
Maunsell, *Major-Gen.* Thomas.
Maunsell, *Surg.-Gen.* Thomas.
Maurice, *Maj.-Gen.* J. Frederick, R.A.
May, *Capt.* Henry John, R.N.
May, *Lieut.-General* James.
Mayne, *Col.* Richd. Chas. G.
Methuen, *Lt.-Gen.* Lord, K.C.V.O.
Meyrick, *Insp. Vet.-Surg.* Jas. J.
Miller, *Maj.-Gen.* Geo. Murray.
Mills, *Col.* Herbert James.
Milman, *Lt.-Gen.* George Bryan.
Mollan, *Lt.-Col.* Wm. Campbell.

MILIT. COMPANIONS, C.B.—*con.*

Money, *Lt.-Col.* Chas. G. Colvin.
Money, *Col.* Elliott Alexander.
Money, *Col.* Gordon Lorn Campbell, D.S.O., A.D.C.
Montagu, *General* Horace Wm.
Montague, *Maj.-Gen.* Wm. Edwd.
Montgomerie, *Admiral* John E.
Montgomerie, *Captain* Robert Archibald James, R.N.
Moore, *Maj.-Gen.* A. Thos., V℃
Moore, *Rear-Adm.* Arthur Wm.
Morgan, *Col.* Alexander Brooke.
Morgan, *Col.* Harrison R. L., R.A.
Morton, *Major-Gen.* Sir Gerald de Courcy, K.C.I.E.
Mosse, *Dep.-Surg.-Gen.* Chas. B.
Mostyn, *Maj.-Gen.* Hon. Savage.
Murray, *Col.* Robt. Hunter, A.D.C.
Nation, *General* John Louis.
Nicholson, *Maj.-Gen.* Stuart Jas.
Nicolson, *Admiral* Sir Frederick William Erskine, Bt.
Nicolson, *Lieut.-Gen.* Malcolm H.
Nimmo, *Maj.-Gen.* Thos. Rose.
North, *Colonel* Dudley.
Northcott, *Lt.-Col.* Hy Ponting.
Nugent, *Colonel* Robert Arthur.
O'Callaghan, *Adm.* George W. D.
O'Callaghan, *Capt.* M. P., R.N.
Ogilvy, *Col.* W. Lewis Kinloch.
Ogle, *Maj.-Gen.* Fredc. Amelius.
Oldershaw, *Maj.-G.* Chas. Edward.
Ommanney, *Adm.* Sir Erasmus.
O'Nial, *Surgeon-General* John.
Paget, *Colonel* Harold.
Parker, *Colonel* George Hubert.
Parr, *Maj.-Gen.* Henry Hallam.
Patch, *Colonel* Robert.
Pearse, *General* George Godfrey.
Pearson, *Lt.-Gen.* Sir C.K., K.C.M.G
Pease, *Colonel* Thales.
Pemberton, *M.-Gen.* Wykeham L.
Pennington, *Lieut.-Gen.* Charles Richard.
Perceval, *Gen.* John Maxwell.
Peyton, *General* Francis.
Pipon, *General* Philip Gosset.
Poë, *Lt.-Col.* Wm. Hutcheson.
Poole, *Col.* Arthur James, A.D.C.
Powell, *Capt.* Francis, R.N.
Pratt, *Colonel* Henry Marsh.
Pretyman, *Maj.-Gen.* G. Tindal.
Prinsep, *Lieut.-General* Arthur Haldimand.
Pritchard, *Lieut.-Gen.* Gordon D.
Protheroe, *Maj.-Gen.* Montague.
Quirk, *Col.* John Owen, D.S.O.
Raby, *R.-Adm.* Henry Jas., V℃
Rainsford, *Lieut.-Gen.* Marcus E. R.
Rait, *Lieut.-Col.* Arthur John.
Ralston, *Maj.-Gen.* Wm. Henry.
Reade, *Surg.-Mj.-Gen.* John B.C.
Redmond, *Lt.-Gen.* John P., S.
Reeves, *Col.* Henry Spencer E.
Reid, *Brig.-Gen.* Alexr. J.F.,I.S.O.
Rennie, *Comm.* Jas. (Ind. Navy).
Rich, *Lt.-Gen.* Geo. W. Talbot.
Richardson, *Col.* Geo. L. R., I.S.O.
Richardson, *Maj.-Gen.* John S.
Richardson, *Maj.-Gen.* Joseph F.
Richardson, *Maj.-Gen.* William S.
Richardson, *Col.* Wodehouse D.
Riddell, *Major-General* Charles James Buchanan.

Robertson, *Col.* James Peter.
Robinson, *M.-Gen.* Chas. Walker.
Robinson, *Dep.-Controller* Henry.
Robinson, *Major-Gen.* Wellesley Gordon Walker.
Rocke, *Maj.-Gen.* Jas. Harwood.
Roe, *Dep. Surg.-Gen.* Sam. Black.
Roffey, *Chief Insp.* James, R.N.
Rogers, *Colonel* John, A.S.C.
Roife, *Rear-Adm.* Ernest N.
Rolland, *Vice-Adm.* Wm. Rae.
Rollo, *General* Hon. Robert.
Roome, *General* Frederick.
Ross, *Lieut.-Gen.* Alexander Geo.
Rowland, *Colonel* Thomas.
Russell, *Gen.* Lord Alexr. Geo.
Russell, *Colonel* Horatio Albert.
Salmond, *Maj.-Gen.* William, R.E.
Salusbury, *Maj.-G. F.* Octavius.
Sanford, *Lt.-Gen.* Geo. Edward Langham Somerset.
Sartorius, *M.-Gen.* EustonHy., V℃
Sartorius, *Col.* George Conrad.
Saumarez, *Admiral* Thomas.
Saunders, *Dep. Insp.-Gen.* Geo.
Saunders, *Col.* Wm. E., R.A.M.C.
Sayer, *Lt.-Gen.* Jas. R. Steadman.
Schomberg, *Col.* Herbt. St.George.
Schreiber, *Maj.-Gen.* Brymer F.
Scout, *Colonel* Chas. Henry, R.A.
Scott, *Col.* Douglas A., D.S.O.
Scott, *M.-Gen.* Jas. Woodward.
Scott, *Col.* Wm. Walter Hopton.
Settle, *Col.* Hy. H., R.E., D.S.O.
Seymour, *Gen.* William Henry.
Shaw, *Insp.-Gen.* Doyle M , R.N.
Shaw, *Major-Gen.* Hugh, V℃
Shone, *Col.* Wm. Terence, D.S.O.
Sibthorpe, *Surg.-Gen.* Chas., I M.S.
Simpson *Brigadier-Gen.* George.
Simpson, *Col.* Thos. Thomson.
Singleton, *Rear-Adm.* Uvedale C.
Skinner, *Col.* Edmund Grey.
Skinner, *Col.* James Tierney, D.S.O.
Slade, *Maj.-Gen.* Fredk. Geo.,R.A.
Slade, *Maj.-Gen.* John Ramsay.
Slatin Pacha, *Col.* Sir Rudolf C., K.C.M.G.
Smith, *M.-Gen.* Sir Chas. Holled., K.C.M.G.
Smith, *Surgeon-General* Colvin.
Smith, *General* John W. Sidney.
Smyth, *Col.* Charles Coghlan.
Smyth, *Col.* Etwall Walter.
Spencer, *Surg.-Gen.* Lionel Dixon.
Spragge, *Colonel* Charles Henry.
Stanton, *General* Sir E , K.C.M.G.
Stedman, *Maj.-Gen.* Sir E. K.C.I.E.
Steevens, *Major-General* John.
Stephen, *Colonel* FitzRoy.
Stephens, *Major-Gen.* Adolphus Haggerston.
Stevenson, *M.-Gen.* Thos. Rennie.
Stewart, *Major-General* George.
Stewart, *Maj.-Gen.* James Calder.
Stewart, *Maj.-Gen.* Robt. Crosse.
Stewart, *Maj.-Gen.* Robt. Mac-Gregor.
Stockley, *Colonel* Charles More.
Stopford, *Col.* Hon. Fredk. Wm.
Straghan, *Colonel* Abel.
Strong, *Major-General* Dawsonne Melancthon.
Swaine, *Col.* Charles Edward.
Swaine, *M.-Gen.* Leopold Victor.

Swinley, *Maj.-Gen.* George, R.A.
Sym, *Maj.-Gen.* John Munro.
Talbot, *Maj.-Gen.* Hon. Regd.
Tanner, *Major-General* Edward.
Taylor, *Surg.-Gen.* Wm , A.M.S.
Thackeray, *Colonel* Sir Edward Talbot, V℃ (*Civil* K.C.B.).
Thackwell, *Gen.* Joseph Edwin.
Thackwell, *Major-Gen.* Wm. de Wilton Roche.
Thomas, *Lt.-Gen.* J. Welledev.
Thornton, *D p-Surg.-Gen.* Jas H.
Thynne, *Maj.-Gen.* Reginald Thos.
Tillard, *Maj.-Gen.* John Arthur.
Toker, *M.-Gen.* AllistonChampan.
Tompson, *Maj.-Gen.* William D.
Tower, *Lieut.-General* Conyers.
Townsend, *Col.* Edmd., R A M C.
Townsend, *Surg.-Gen.* Stephen C.
Townshend, *Lt.-Col.* Charles V. F.
Tregear, *Maj.-Gen.* Vincent Wm.
Truell, *Maj.-Gen.* Robert Holt.
Tucker, *Colonel* Aubrey Harvey.
Tucker, *Maj.-Gen.* Charles.
Tucker, *Col.* Wm. Guise, R.M.A.
Tulloch, *Maj.-Gen.* Alex. Bruce.
Tulloh, *Maj.-Gen.* John Stewart.
Turner, *Maj.-Gen.* AlfredEdward.
Turner, *Col.* Augustus Henry.
Turner, *Colonel* Henry Fyers.
Turnour, *Admiral* Edward W.
Twentyman, *Col.* Augustus Chas.
Twynam, *Col.* Philip Alex. A.
Tyndall, *Major-General* Henry.
Upcher, *Maj.-Gen.* Russell, D.S.O.
Upperton, *Major-General* John.
Utterson, *Maj.-Gen.* Archibald H.
Van Straubenzee, *M.-G.* Turner.
Vandeleur, *Maj.-Gen.* J. Ormsby.
Vansittart, *Vice-Adm.* Edwd W.
Vaughan, *Maj.-General* Hugh Thomas Jones-.
Verner, *Col.* Thomas Edward.
Wace, *Maj.-General* Richard, R.A.
Walcott, *Col.* Edmund Scoori.
Walters, *Vety.-Lt.-Col.* William Barker.
Ward, *Colonel* Edward W. D.
Ward, *M.-Gen.* Francis William, R.A.
Ward, *Adm.* Thomas Le Hunte.
Wardrop, *Col.* Frederick Meyer.
Warren, *Maj.-Gen.* Arthur Fredk.
Warren, *Maj.-Gen.* Dawson S.
Waterfield, *Maj.-G.* Hy. Gordon.
Waters, *Brig.-Surg.* Robert, M.D.
Wauchope, *Maj.-Gen.* Andrew G.
Way, *Major-General* Nowell F. Sampson-.
Webber, *Maj.-Gen.* Chas. Edmd.
Webster, *Col.* Arthur George.
Welman, *Major-Gen.* William Henry Dowling Reeves.
Wemyss, *M.-Gen.* Henry Manley.
White, *Fleet-Surg.* Wm. Rogerson
Whitehead, *Maj.-Gen.* Robert C.
Wigram, *Maj.-Gen.* Godfrey Jas.
Wilkinson, *Major-Gen.* Osborn.
Williamson, *Col.* Robt. Fredk.
Wills, *Lt.-Col.* Caleb S , A M S.
Willson, *Col.* Mildmay Willson-.
Wilmot, *Maj.-Gen.* R. Eardley-.
Wilson, *Rear-Admiral* Arthur Knyvet, V℃
Wilson, *Colonel* Edward Hales.

MILIT. COMPANIONS, C.B.—*cont.*
Wilson, *Major-General* Francis Edward Edwards.
Winsloe, *Col.* Richd. Wm. Chas.
Wodehouse, *Maj.-G.* Josceline H.
Wood, *Colonel* Elliott, R.E.
Wood, *Colonel* Henry.
Woodgate, *M.-Gen.* Edward R.P.
Woodward, *Rear-Adm.* Robert.
Woolfryes, *Surg.-Gen.* John A.
Worsley, *Col.* Hy. Robt. Brown.
Wyndham, *Lieut.-Col.* Walter George Crole-.
Wynne, *Col.* Arthur Singleton.
Young, *Brig.-Gen.* Geo. Fredk.
Young, *Lt.-Gen.* George Samuel.
Younghusband, *Gen.* Robert R.

CIVIL COMPANIONS. C.B.

Abercorn, *Col.* the Duke of, K.G.
Abney, *Capt.* Wm. de Wiveleslie.
Adams, *Maj.* Hamilton J. Goold-.
Adrian, Alfred Douglas.
Alderson, Charles Henry.
Anderson, Robert.
Antrobus, Reginald L.
Ardagh, *Maj.-Gen.* Sir John Chas., K.C.I.E.
Armstrong, Lord.
Armstrong, Thomas.
Ashby, *Paym.-in-Chief* James William Murray, R.N.
Awdry, Richard Davis.
Badcock, Jasper Capper.
Bainbridge, *Col.* Edmond, R.A.
Baines, Frederick Ebenezer.
Ball, *Colonel* William Clare.
Barrington, *Hon.* Bernard Eric.
Barrington, Charles George.
Bateman, Edward Louis.
Baughan, William Frederick.
Bayly, *General* John.
Bell, James.
Bell, *Colonel* William.
Berkeley, Ernest J. Lennox.
Biliotti, Sir Alfred, K.C.M.G.
Blake, *Col.* Arthur Maurice.
Blake, *Col.* Maurice C. Joseph.
Blunt, John Elijah.
Bowring, Edgar Alfred.
Boxall, *Col.* Charles Gervais.
Boyce, Robert Henry.
Brabrook, Edward William.
Bramston, Sir John, K.C.M.G.
Brennan, Louis.
Bridgford, *Colonel* Robert.
Brise, Evelyn Ruggles-.
Brown, *Prof.* Sir George Thomas
Brown, Joseph, Q.C.
Brown, *Col.* William James.
Browning, *Col.* Montague Chas.
Buchanan, *Col.* Lewis Mansergh.
Bulwer, *Col.* W. E. G. Lytton.
Bunsen, Maurice W. Ernest de.
Butler, *Captain* Antoine Sloet.
Caborne, *Comm.* Warren F., R.N.
Cameron, Sir Charles, M.D.
Cardin, James Joseph.
Carington, *Lt.-Col.* Hon. William.
Cave, Basil Shillito.
Charlemont, Viscount.
Chermside, *Maj.-Gen.* Sir Herbert Charles, C.G.M.G.
Christie, Wm. H. Mahoney.
Clarke, *Colonel* Alexander Ross.

Clarke, *Lt.-Gen.* Hon. Sir Andrew.
Cleeve, *Fleet-Paym.* Frederick.
Cockburn, Henry.
Coll, Sir Patrick.
Collins, *Lt.-Col.* Arthur.
Colquhoun, *Col.* Alan John.
Colville, *Col.* Hon. Sir W. Jas., K.C.V.O.
Cookson, Sir Chas. A., K.C.M.G.
Couper, Sir Geo. E. Wilson, Bt.
Courthope, William John.
Cousins, William Henry.
Crawford, *Lt.* Lawrence H., R.N.R.
Cresswell, *Col.* Pearson Robert.
Creswick, *Col.* Nathaniel.
Cripps, Wilfred Joseph.
Cullinan, Sir Fred. Fitzjames.
Dalton, Cornelius Neale.
Dalyell, Ralph.
Dasent, John Roche.
Davidson, William E., Q.C.
Davie, William Aug. Ferguson-.
De la Bère, Henry Thomas.
Dering, Sir Henry Nevill, Bart.
Dicey, Edward.
Dingli, Sir Adriano, G.C.M.G.
Drummond, Victor A. W.
Dunbar, William Cospatrick.
Duncannon, Viscount.
Dundas, *Col.* Lorenzo George.
Durand, *Lieut.-Col.* Sir Edward Law, Bart.
Egerton, *Col.* Alfred Mordaunt.
Eliot, Charles Norton Edgcumbe.
Elliott, Thomas Henry.
Engelbach, Lewis William.
Esher, Viscount.
Eyre, *Colonel* Henry.
Fairfax, *Adm.* Sir Henry, K.C.B. (Mil.).
Fearon, Daniel Robert.
Fellows, *Col.* Robert Bruce.
Fergusson, John.
Field, *Adm.* Edward, M.P.
Finlaison, Alexander John.
FitzGeorge, *Col.* Augustus C. F.
Fleming, *Princ. Vet. Surg.* Geo.
Follett, Charles John.
Ford, *Col.* Arthur, R.A.
Forman, Harry Buxton.
Forsey, Charles Benjamin.
Franks, John Hamilton.
French, Edward H.
Fullerton, *Vice-Admiral* Sir John Reginald Thomas, K.C.V.O.
Gamble, *Colonel* Sir David, Bart.
Garnett, Richard.
Gibbons, James Samuel.
Gifford, Charles Edwin, R.N.
Gildea, *Colonel* James.
Gill, David, F.R.S.
Goldsmid, *Maj.-Gen.* Sir Fred. J., K.C.S.I.
Gordon, *Col.* George Grant, C.V.O.
Gosselin, Sir Martin le Marchant Hadsley, K.C.M.G.
Graham, Frederick.
Graham, Henry John Lowndes.
Green, *Maj.-Gen.* Sir Wm. H. R., K.C.S.I.
Greene, William Conyngham.
Greene, Wm. Graham
Greville, Hon. Sidney Robert.
Griffiths, Vincent.
Grimshaw, Thomas Wrigley, M.D.

Grove, Sir George, Knt.
Gubbins, Frederick Bebb.
Gurdon, Sir William Brampton, K.C.M.G., M.P.
Hall, *Colonel* Angus William.
Hamilton, *Colonel* Sir William Alexander Baillie-, K.C.M.G.
Hamley, *Com.-Gen.* Joseph O.
Hardinge, Sir Arthur Henry, K.C.M.G.
Hardinge, Hon. Charles.
Hay, *Col.* George Jackson.
Heberden, William Buller.
Helme, *Colonel* George Coope.
Henley, Joseph John.
Herbert, Chas. St. John Septimus.
Herbert, Hon. Michael Henry.
Herries, Edward.
Hervey, *Gen.* Chas. Robt. West.
Hervey, George William.
Hervey, Henry Arthur William.
Hill, Sir Clement L., K.C.M.G.
Hill, Edward Bernard L.
Hill, *Col.* William Alexander.
Hobart, Robert Henry.
Holmes, Robert Wm. Arbuthnot.
Holzmann, Maurice.
Hood, *Col.* Hon. Arthur Wellington Alexander Nelson.
Hooker, Sir Jos. Dalton, G.C.S.I.
Hope, Edward Stanley.
Hopwood, Charles Augustus.
Hopwood, Fras. John Stephens.
Howard, Sir Andrew Charles.
Howard, Sir Henry, K.C.M.G.
Howard, *Colonel* Samuel Lloyd.
Howland, Hon. Sir William Pearce, K.C.M.G.
Hozier, *Col.* Henry Montague.
Hume, Allan Octavian.
Hutchinson, *Maj.-Gen.* C. Scrope.
Hutton, *Col.* Geo. Morland.
Iddesleigh Earl of.
Jackson, Frederick John.
Jameson, *Surg.-Gen.* James.
Jameson, Leander Starr, M.D.
Jenkinson, Francis B.
Jones, John J. Casimir.
Jones, *Maj.-Gen.* Robert Owen.
Judd, John Wesley, F.R.S.
Julyan, Sir Penrose Goodchild, K.C.M.G.
Kaye, Sir Wm. Squire Barker.
Kennedy, Sir C. Malcolm, K.C.M.G.
Knocker, *Colonel* Edward W.
Knollys, William Edward.
Lamb, John Cameron.
Lambert, George Thomas.
Langevin, Hon. Sir Hector Louis, K.C.M.G.
Langley, Walter.
Laurie, *Colonel* Robert Peter.
Le Cornu, *Col.* Chas. Philip, A.D.C.
Lee, Henry Austin.
Leigh, Hon. E. Chandos, Q.C.
Lemmon, *Col.* Thomas Warne.
Lewis, *Col.* Somers Reginald.
Littler, Ralph Daniel Makinson.
Lloyd, *Col.* Morgan George.
Lloyd, *Col.* Thomas.
Locock, *Colonel* Herbert, R.E.
Ludlow, John Malcolm.
Lugard, *Lt.-Col.* F. J. D., D.S.O.
Lyttelton, Hon. George William Spencer.

CIVIL COMPANIONS, C.B.—*cont.*
Macdonald, *Col.* Rt. Hon. John Hay Athole (*Lord Justice Clerk*).
Macdonald, *Col.* John Andrew.
MacDonell, Sir H. Guion, K.C.M.G.
MacDonell, John, LL.D.
McDonnell, Hon. Schomberg Kerr.
Macdonnell, *Colonel* William.
Macdougall, Hon. William.
Macfie, *Col.* William.
Macgregor, Sir Wm., K.C.M.G.
Mackenzie, George Sutherland.
Maclean, *Col.* Sir Fitzroy D., Bt.
Macleay, *Col.* Alex. Caldcleugh.
MacLeod, Reginald.
Macleod, *Insp.-Gen.* William.
Malcolm of Poltalloch, *Col.* Lord.
Marshall, *Col.* Thomas Horatio.
Martindale, *Colonel* Ben Hay.
Masefield, *Col.* Robert Taylor.
Meyrick, *Col.* Sir T. Charlton-, Bt.
Milbanke, Ralph.
Miller, George.
Mills, *Colonel* Richard.
Milman, Archibald John Scott.
Mitford, Algernon B. Freeman-.
Molony, *Col.* Charles Mills.
Money, Sir Alonzo, K.C.M.G.
Monro, James.
Moore, *Col.* Charles Thos. John.
Moriarty, *Capt.* Henry A., R.N.
Murdoch, Charles Stewart.
Mure, William John.
Murton, Sir Walter.
Neale, Hy. Jas. Van Sittart.
Nepean, Sir Evan Colville.
Newell, Dr. William Homan.
Nicolas, Nicholas Harris.
Nicol, Henry.
Nicolson, David.
Niven, William Davidson.
Northcote, Hon. Sir Henry Stafford, Bart., M.P.
Norton, *Surg.-Lt.-Col.* Arthur T.
O'Dowd, James Cornelius.
Oram, Richard E. Sprague.
Orange, William.
Pattisson, Jacob Luard.
Patton, *Col.* Henry Bethune.
Pennefather, Alfred Richard.
Petre, Sir George Glynn, K.C.M.G.
Phipps, Edmund Constantine H.
Pickersgill, Wm. Clayton.
Pigott, Thomas Digby.
Pilkington, *Maj.* Henry, R.E.
Pilter, *Col.* William Frederick.
Pittar, Thomas J.
Plant, *Col.* Edmund Carter.
Platt, *Col.* Henry.

Porter, Alfred de Bock.
Provis, Samuel Butler.
Prowse, Richard T.
Purcell, John Samuel.
Ramsay, George Dalhousie.
Reed, *Colonel* Charles John.
Rice, Stephen Edward Spring-.
Richards, *Col.* Samuel S. C.
Ricketts, Geo. Henry Mildmay.
Ritchie, Richmond T. W.
Roberts, Samuel Ussher.
Robinson, Henry Augustus.
Rodd, Sir James Rennell, K.C.M.C.
Ross of Bladensburg, *Lieut.-Col.* John Foster George.
Rowton, Lord, K.C.V.O.
Royle, Arnold.
Ryder, George Lisle.
Samuel, Hon. Sir Saul, Bart., K.C.M G.
Sandwith, Thomas Backhouse.
Schaw, *Major-General* Henry.
Scott, *Admiral* Lord Chas. T. Montagu-Douglas-(*Mily.*K.C.B.)
Scott, *Colonel* John.
Scott, *Lieut.-Col.* Lothian Kerr.
Seccombe, Sir Thos. Lawrence, G.C.I.E.
Senior, *Col.* Thomas Palmer.
Seymour, Horace A. Damer.
Sharpe, Alfred.
Sharpe, Rev. Thos. Wetherherd.
Simpkinson, Henry Walrond.
Slacke, *Capt.* Sir Owen Randal.
Smiles, William.
Smith, John.
Somerset, *Col.* Alfred Plantagenet Frederick Charles.
Soulsby, William Jameson.
Stace, *Lt.-Col.* Edward Vincent.
Stainer, George Henry.
Standen, Edward James.
Stanhope, *Col.* Walter Spencer-.
Steele, John.
Stephen, Sir Alex. Condie, K.C.M.G.
Stephenson, *V.-Adm.* Sir H. F., K C.B. (*Mil.*).
Stewart, *Col.* Charles Edward.
Stopford, *Capt.* Walter James.
Strick, *Col.* John.
Talbot, George.
Taylor, *Col.* John L. du Plat-.
Taylor, *Colonel* Robert Lewis.
Thesiger, Hon. Edward Peirson.
Thompson, Prof. D'Arcy W.
Thomson, *Capt.* Anthony S., R.N.R.
Thynne, Sir Henry.
Tizard, *Capt.* Thomas Hy., R.N.

Trevor, Sir Charles Cecil.
Trotter, *Lieut.-Colonel* Henry.
Troup, Charles Edward.
Tucker, William.
Tulloch, *Major* Hector, R.E.
Tupper, Hn Sir Chas., Bt., G.C.M.G.
Turner, *Maj.-Gen.* Alfred E., R.A.
Turner, Charles George.
Turnor, Algernon.
Tynte, *Colonel* Fortescue Jos.
Vandeleur, *Col.* John Ormsby.
Vavasseur, Josiah.
Vetch, *Col.* Robert H., R.E.
Vickers, *Colonel* Thomas Edward.
Villiers, Hon. Francis Hyde.
Vincent, *Colonel* Sir Charles E. Howard, K.C.M.G., M.P.
Vivian, *Colonel* Arthur Pendarves.
Wake, Herwald Craufurd.
Wallace, Arthur Robert.
Waterfield, Sir Henry, K.C.S.I.
Watkin, *Lt.-Col.* Henry Spiller.
Watt, *Com.-Gen.* Fitzjas. Edwd.
Webb, *Col.* Walter George.
Welby, Sir Chas. Glynn Earle-, Bart.
Whitbread, *Col.* Howard.
Wilson, Sir Chas. Rivers, K.C.M.G.
Wilson, *Maj.-Gen.* Sir Chas. Wm.
Wilson, George.
Wilson, Guy Douglas Arthur Fleetwood.
Wilson, *Col.* John Gerald.
Wilson, *Col.* Thomas.
Wingate, *Col.* Sir F. R., K.C.M.G., D.S.C.
Wodehouse, Hon. Armine.
Wodehouse, Edmond Henry.
Wood, *Chief-Insp.* Alfred, R.N.
Wood, Charles Malcolm.
Wood, Sir Richard, G.C.M.G.
Wootton, *Chief-Insp.* James, R.N.
Wyndham, Sir Geo. H., K.C.M.G.
Yorke, Henry Fras. Redhead.
Young, Sir Allen William.

———

Dean of Order, Dean of Westminster.

Bath King of Arms, Maj.-Gen. Sir John Carstairs McNeill, K.C.B (*VC* (1898).

Registrar & Sec., Sir Albert Wm. Woods, K.C.B., F.S.A.

Gentleman Usher of the Scarlet Rod, Chas. Geo. Barrington, C.B.

THE MOST EXALTED ORDER OF THE STAR OF INDIA (1861).

Ribbon, Light Blue, with white stripes towards each edge.
Motto, Heaven's Light our Guide.

THE SOVEREIGN: EMPRESS OF INDIA.

Grand Master and First and Principal Knight Grand Commander, VICEROY AND GOV.-GEN. OF INDIA.

KNIGHTS GRAND COMMANDERS. G.C.S.I.
H.R.H. the Prince of Wales.
H.R.H. the Duke of Saxe-Coburg-Gotha.
H.R.H. the Duke of Connaught.
H.R.H. the Duke of Cambridge.

Baroda, H.H. the Gaekwar of.
Bhawuipore, H.H. the Nawab of.
Bhopal, H.H. the Begum of.
Chamberlain, *Gen.* Sir N. B.
Cranbrook, Rt. Hon. the Earl of.
Cross, Rt. Hon. Viscount, G.C.B.
Duff, Rt. Hon. Sir M. E. Grant-.

Dufferin and Ava, Most Hon. the Marquess of, K.P.
Elgin and Kincardine, the Rt. Hon. the Earl of, K.G.
Fergusson, Rt. Hon. Sir James, Bart., M.P.
Fowler, Rt. Hon. Sir H. H., M.P.

KTS. GRAND COMDS., G.C.S.I.—*con.*
Gwalior, *Col.* H.H. the Maharaja Sindia of.
Haines, *Fd.-M.*Sir Frederick Paul.
Harris, Lord.
Hooker, Sir Joseph Dalton.
Hyderabad, H.H. the Nizam of.
Indore, H.H. the Maharaja of.
Jeypore, H.H. the Maharaja of.
Kolhapur, H.H. the Raja of.
Lansdowne, Most Hon. the Marquess of, K.G.
Macdonnell, Sir Antony Patrick
Nabha, H.H. the Raja of.
Nahun, H.H. the Raja of.
Northbrook, Rt. Hon. the Earl of
Oodeypore, H.H.the Maharana of
Patiala, H. H. the Maharaja of.
Reay, Lord.
Rewa, H.H. Maharaja Sir Vyankatesh Raman Singh, Bahadur, Chief of.
Ripon, Most Hon. Marquess of, K.G.
Roberts of Kandahar, *Field-Marshal* Lord, K.P., V.C., R.A.
Shamsher Jang, H. E. Maharaja Sir Bir.
Singh, *Maj.-Gen.* H.H. Maharaja Sir Partab, of Jammu and Kashmir.
Singh, *Colonel* Maharaj Dhiraj Sir Partab, of Jodhpore.
Stewart *Fd.-M.* Sir D. M., Bt., G.C.B.
Strachey, Sir John.
Strachey, *Lt.-Gen.* Sir Richd., R.E.
Temple, Rt. Hon. Sir Richard, Bt.
Travancore, H.H. the Maharaja of.
Wenlock, Lord.
White, *Gen.* Sir George Stewart, G.C.B., V.C.

Honorary Knights Grand Commanders.

H.H. Mir Khodadad (Khelat).
H.H. Abdur Rahman Khan, Amir of Afghanistan, G.C.B.
H.R.H. Sultan Massoud Mirza, Yemin-ed-Dowleh, Zil-es-Sultan, of Persia.

KNIGHTS COMMANDERS. K.C.S.I.

Aiyar, Kumarapuram Sheshadri.
Akram Khan, Sir Nawab Muhammad (Chief of Amb).
Amar Singh, Rajah (Kashmir).
Arbuthnot, Sir Alexander John.
Barbour, Sir David Miller.
Bayley, Sir Steuart Colvin.
Bernard, Sir Charles Edward.
Brackenbury, *Gen.* Sir H., K.C.B.
Bradford, *Col.* Sir E. R. C., G.C.B.
Browne, *Gen.* Sir Samuel J., V.C, G.C.B.
Buck, Sir Edward Charles.
Burne, *Maj.-Gen.*Sir Owen Tudor, G.C.I.E.
Cochin, H.H. the Raja Rama Urma of.
Colvin, Sir Auckland.
Couper, Sir Geo. E. Wilson, Bart.
Cromer, Viscount, G.C.B.
Crosthwaite, Sir C. Haukes Tod.

Crosthwaite, Sir Robert Joseph.
Cuningham, Sir William John.
Dada Saheb, Sir Kasee Rao Holkar, of Indore.
Danvers, Sir Juland.
Datia, H.H. Maharaja Sir Lokindra Bhawani Singh, Bahadur of.
Davies, Sir Robert Henry.
Dhar, the Maharaja of.
Drangdra, H.H. the Raj Sahib of.
Durand, Sir Henry Mortimer.
Egerton, Sir Robert Eyles.
Elliott, Sir Charles Alfred.
Fayrer, *Surg.-Gen.* Sir Joseph, Bt.
FitzPatrick, Sir Dennis.
Fryer, Sir Fredc. W. Richards.
Gerard, *Maj.-Gen.* Sir Montagu.
Goldsmid, *Maj.-Gen.* Sir Fred. J.
Grant, Sir Charles.
Green, *Maj.-Gen.* Sir Wm. H. R.
Griffin, Sir Lepel Henry.
Hobhouse, Right Hon. Lord.
Hope, Sir Theodore Cracraft.
Hunter, Sir William Wilson.
Hutchins, Sir Philip Perceval.
Idar, H.H. the Maharaja of.
Ilbert, Sir Courtenay Peregrine.
Junagarh, the Nawab of.
Kapurthala, H.H. the Raja of.
Kemball, *Gen.* Sir Arnold B., K.C.B.
Lethbridge, *Lt.-Col.* Sir Alfred Swaine, M.D., I.M.S.
Lockhart, *General* Sir William Stephen Alexander, G.C.B.
Lyall, Sir Charles James.
Lyall, Sir Jas. Broadwood, G.C.I.E.
Macdonald, *Adm.* Sir Reginald J., K.C.B.
Mackenzie, Sir Alexander.
Melliss, *Col.* Sir Howard.
Morris, Sir John Henry.
Muir, Sir William.
Newmarch, *Maj.-Gen.* Sir O. R.
Palitana, Thakore Sahib of.
Peile, Sir James Braithwaite.
Plowden, Sir Trevor John Chichele Chichele-.
Plowden, Sir William Chichele.
Pollock, *Major - General* Sir Frederick R.
Price, Sir John Frederick.
Probyn, *Gen.* Sir Dighton Macnaghten, G.C.V.O., V.C.
Raghubir Singh Bahadur, H. H. Maharae Raja (Chief of Bundi).
Ridgeway, *Col.* Rt. Hon. Sir J. W., K.C.B.
Robertson, *Lieut.-Col.* Sir George Scott, I.M.S.
Russell, *General* Sir Edward L.
Scoble, Sir Andrew Richard, M.P
Seccombe, Sir Thos. Lawrence, G.C.I.E.
Sirobi, H.H. Maharao K. S.
Stevens, Sir Charles Cecil
Stokes, Sir Henry Edward.
Tagore, the Maharaja Sir Jotendro Mohun.
Trevor, Sir Arthur Charles.
Udny, Sir Richard.
Ward, Sir William Erskine.
Warner, Sir William Lee-.
Waterfield, Sir Henry.
Westland, Sir James.

Woodburn, Sir John.
Young, Sir William Mackworth.

COMPANIONS. C.S.I.

Akbar, Ali, Meer of Hyderabad.
Allyghur, the Raja of.
Anderson, Henry Aiken.
Arnold, Sir Edwin, K.C.I.E.
Arundel, Arundel Tagg
Asghur Ali Khan,the Nawab Sied.
Ashburner, Lionel Robert.
Badcock, *M.-Gen.* Alexr. R., C.B.
Baines, Jervoise Athelstane.
Baird, *Col.* Andrew Wilson.
Banganapalli, the Nawab of.
Barnes, Hugh Shakespear.
Barr, *Lt.-Col.* David Wm. K.
Birdwood, Sir George Christopher Molesworth, K.C.I.E.D.
Birdwood, Herbert Mills-, .M.
Bolton, Charles Walter.
Boughey, *Col.* Geo. F. Ottley·
Bourdilon, James Austin, I.C.S.
Bowring, Lewin Bentham.
Boyle, Richard Vicars.
Brackenbury, *Col.* Maule C., R.E.
Browne, Edward Raban Cave-.
Cadell, Alan.
Carmichael, Charles Paget.
Chalmers, Mackenzie Dalzell.
Chamberlain, *Gen.* Sir Crawford Trotter, G.C.I.E.
Chapman, Robert Barclay.
Cleghorn, *Surg.-Gen.* James.
Clerk, *Colonel* John, C.V.O.
Cockerell, Horace Abel.
Colvin, Clement Sneyd.
Cordery, John Graham.
Cotton, *Major-Gen.* F. Conyers.
Cotton, Henry John Stedman.
Cruickshank, Alex. Walmesley.
Cuningham, *Surg.-Gen.* Jas. M.
Davidson, Robert.
Deane, *Maj.* Harold Arthur.
Dickens, *Lieut.-Gen.* Sir Craven H.
Dickinson, *Lieut.-Col.* William.
Dillon, *General* Sir Martin, K.C.B.
Duncan, *Major-Gen.* Harvey T.
Edgar, Sir John Ware, K.C.I.E.
Ellis, *Major-General* Sir Arthur Edward Augustus. K.C.V.O.
Elsmie, George Robert (Punjab).
Etheridge, *Maj.-Gen.* Alfred T.
Evans, Henry Farrington.
Fanshawe, Arthur Upton.
Finlay, James Fairbairn.
Finucane, Michael.
FitzGerald, Sir Gerald S. Vesey.
Forbes, Arthur.
Ford, William.
Framjee, Dosabhoy (Karaka).
Fraser,Andrew Henderson Leith.
Garstin, John Henry.
Gordon, *Gen.* Sir Thos. Edward, K C.I.E.
Gracey, *Col.* Thomas.
Grey, *Col.* Leopold John Herbert
Gundah Singh, Sirdar Bakshi.
Henderson, *M.-G.* Philip Durham.
Henry, Edward Richard.
Hewett, John Prescott.
Hogg, Sir Fredk. Russell, K.C.I.E.
Holderness, Thomas William.
Home, *Col.* Fredk. Jervis, R.E.
Hooper, *Surg.-Gen.* Wm. Roe.

COMPANIONS, C.S.I.—*cont.*

Hopkinson, *General* Henry.
Hunter, *Lt.-Gen.* Jno. Muir, I.S.C.
Hutchinson, *Maj.-Gen.* Geo., C.B.
Hyat Khan, Mahomed.
Ibbetson, Denzil Charles Jelf.
Iyar, Kumarapuram Sheshadri.
James, Henry Evan Murchison.
Jasdan, Kachar Ala Chela, Chief of.
Jiwan Singh, Sirdar of Patiala.
Jones, William Brittain.
Kashi Rao San, Sardar Bahadur.
Keatinge, *General* Richard Harte, V.C.
Khoman Singh, Bakshi, of Indore.
King, Lucas White.
La Touche, James John Digges.
Lovett, *Major-General* Beresford.
Lumsden, *Gen.* Sir Peter Stark, G.C.B.
Lyall, David Robert.
M'Mahon, *Capt.* Arthur Henry.
Macnabb, Sir Donald Campbell, K.C.I.E.
Macpherson, John Molesworth.
Master, Charles Gilbert.
Maxwell, *Lieut.-Col.* Henry St. Patrick.
Melvill, Philip Sandys.
Merk, Wm. Rudolph Henry.
Merriman, *Gen.* Charles James.
Michael, *General* James.
Miley, *Col.* James Aloysius.
Miller, Sir Alexander E., Q.C.
Mingyi, Moung Kinwun.
Moncrieff, *Col.* Sir Colin C. Scott-, K.C.M.G.

Money, William James.
Monteath, James.
Mookerjee, Babu Peary Mohun.
Moule, Horace Frederick D'Oyly.
Muhammad Khan, Khan Bahadur Yar.
Naylor, James Richard.
Norton, David.
Nugent, John.
Obed Ulla Khan, Sahibzada.
O'Callaghan, Francis Langford.
Odling, Charles William.
Oliver, John O. Hercules Norman.
Ommanney, *Col.* Edward Lacon.
Parker, Joseph.
Pati, Rao Bahadur Chatr.
Pemberton, *Maj.-Gen.* Robert Charles Boileau, R.E.
Pennycuick, *Col.* John, R.E.
Powell, Eyre Burton.
Powlett, *Colonel* Percy William.
Pratab Singh, Raja Udai (Bhinga).
Prideaux, *Col.* Wm. Francis.
Primrose, Sir Henry Wm., K.C.B.
Pritchard, Sir Charles Bradley, K.C.I.E.
Pritchard, *Col.* Hurlock Galloway
Protheroe, *Maj.-Gen.* Montague, C.B.
Pyne, Sir Thomas Salter.
Ravenscroft, Edward William.
Renny, *General* Henry.
Reynolds, Herbert John.
Rice, *Surg.-Major-Gen.* William Roche, M.D.
Richey, Sir James Bellet, K.C.I.E.
Rivaz, Charles Montgomery.
Robertson, *Lt.-Col.* Donald, I.S.C.

Ross, *Col.* Sir Edward Charles.
Rundall, *Gen.* Francis Hornblow.
Sanford, *Lt.-Gen.* Geo. E.L.S., C.B.
Shashia Shastri, Dewan of Travancore.
Sherer, John Walter.
Sinclair, *Col.* David, M.B., I.M.S.
Smeaton, Donald Mackenzie.
Smith, Henry Babington.
Smith, *Col.* Sir Chas. B. Euan-, K.C.B.
Spence, James Knox, I.C.S.
Spurgin, *Lt.-Gen.* Sir John Blick.
Steel, Robert.
Stoker, Thomas.
Stokes, Whitley.
Sullivan, Henry Edward.
Tamburan, Kerala Varma V. K.
Tasadduk Rasul Khan Raja.
Tehri, H.H Raja Kirta Sah of.
Thornhill, George.
Thornton, Thomas Henry.
Thuillier, *Gen.* Sir Henry E. L.
Trevor, *Colonel* Geo. Herbert.
Tupper, Charles Lewis.
Tweedie, *Maj.-Gen.* William.
Ude Sanker, Azam Gowrisanker.
Walker, *Maj.-Gen.* Alexander, R.A.
Warburton, *Col.* Wm. P., M.D., I.M.S.
Willoughby, *Lt.-Gen.* Michael W.
Wylie, *Maj.-Gen.* Henry.
Yate, *Lieut.-Col.* Charles Edward.
Younghusband, *Major-General* J. William.
Registrar, Sir Albert Wm. Woods, K.C.B., F.S.A.
Secretary, The Foreign Secretary to the Government of India.

THE MOST DISTINGUISHED ORDER OF ST. MICHAEL AND ST. GEORGE (1818).

Ribbon, Saxon Blue, with a scarlet stripe. *Motto,* Auspicium melioris ævi (*A pledge of better times*).

THE SOVEREIGN.

Grand Master, and First and Principal Knight Grand Cross, F.-M. H.R.H. The Duke of Cambridge.

KNIGHTS GRAND CROSS. G.C.M.G. 65

H.R.H. the Prince of Wales.
H.R.H. the Duke of Saxe-Coburg-Gotha.
H.R.H. the Duke of Connaught.

Aberdeen, Rt. Hon. the Earl of.
Belmore, Rt. Hon. Earl of.
Biddulph, *Gen.* Sir Robert, G.C.B.
Blake, Sir Henry Arthur.
Brooke, *Rajah* Sir Chas. Anthony.
Bulwer, Sir Henry Ernest G.
Buxton, Sir T. Fowell, Bart.
Carrington, Rt. Hon. Earl.
Cartwright, Hon. Sir Richard J.
Chermside, *Maj.-Gen.* Sir Herbt. C.
Clarke, *Lt.-Gen.* Hon. Sir Andrew.
Cooper, Sir Daniel, Bart.
Cromer, Viscount, G.C.B.
Currie, Sir Donald, M.P.
Des Vœux, Sir George William.
De Winton, *Maj.-Gen.* Sir F. W.
Dingli, Sir Adriano.
Dufferin and Ava, Most Hon. the Marquess of, K.P.

Fremantle, *Gen.* Sir Arthur James Lyon.
Glasgow, Earl of.
Gormanston, Viscount.
Graham, *Lt.-Gen.* Sir Gerald, V.C.
Grenfell, *General* Sir F. W., G.C.B.
Griffith, Sir Samuel Walker.
Hampden, Viscount.
Hart, Sir Robert, Bart.
Havelock, Sir Arthur Elibank.
Hopetoun, Rt. Hon. Earl of
Hutchinson, Hon. Sir W. F. Hely-
Irving, Sir Henry Turner.
Jersey, Rt. Hon. Earl of.
Kintore, Rt. Hon. Earl of.
Kirk, Sir John, M.D.
Knutsford, Rt. Hon. Viscount.
Lansdowne, Most Hn. Mrq of, K.G.
Lascelles, Rt. Hon. Sir F.C., G.C.B.
Laurier, Rt. Hon. Sir Wilfrid.
Loch, Rt. Hon. Lord, G.C.B.
Lorne, Most Hn. Marq. of, K.T., M.P.
Low, Sir Hugh.
Lushington, Sir Godfrey.
MacDonell, Sir Hugh Guion.
Malet, Rt. Hon. Sir Edward B.

Milner, Sir Alfred.
Minto, the Earl of.
Mitchell, *Lt.-Col.* Sir C. B. H.
Monson, Rt. Hon. Sir Ed. J., G.C.B.
Mowat, Hon. Sir Oliver.
Norman, *Gen.* Sir Henry Wylie.
O'Conor, Rt. Hon. Sir Nicolas Roderick, G.C.B.
Onslow, Earl of.
Pauncefote, Rt. Hon. Lord, G.C.B.
Plunkett, Hon. Sir Francis R.
Reid, Sir Robt. Threshie, Q.C.
Robinson, Sir William.
Rumbold, Rt. Hon. Sir Horace, Bart., G.C.B.
Russell of Killowen, Rt. Hon. Lord (*Lord Chief Justice*).
Sackville, Lord.
St. John, Sir Spenser B.
Scott, Rt. Hon. Sir C. S., G.C.B.
Sendall, Sir Walter Joseph.
Simmons, *F.-M.* Sir John L. A.
Smith, Sir Cecil Clementi-.
Stafford, Sir Edward William.
Stanmore, Lord.
Strathcona and Mnt. Royal, Lord.

KNIGHTS GRAND CROSS, G.C.M.G.
    —continued.
Sutherland, Sir Thomas, M.P.
Tupper, Hon. Sir Charles, Bart.
Warren, Lt.-Gen. Sir Charles.
Webster, Sir Richd. E., Q.C., M.P.
Wilson, Sir Charles Rivers.
Wolff, Rt. Hon. Sir Henry D.
Wolseley, F.-M. Rt.Hn. Viscount.
Wood, Gen. Sir H. Evelyn, VC
Wood, Sir Richard.

Honorary Knights Grand Cross.
H.M. the King of Siam.
H. M. Menelek II., Negus of Abyssinia (Ethiopia).
H.E. Riaz Pacha (Egypt).
Vice-Adm. Baron von der Goltz.
H.H. the Khedive of Egypt.
Shahzada Habibulla Khan.
Shahzada Nasrulla Khan.
H.E. Sir Luiz de Soveral.
Sir Paul Honoré Vigliani.
H.E. Abulkasim Khan, styled Naor-ul-Mulk (Persia).
H.I.H. Prince Amir Khan Sirdar.
H.E. Chang Yen Hoon.
H.E. Mustapha Fehmy Pasha.

KTS.-COMMANDERS, K.C.M.G. 200
Abbott, Hon. Sir Joseph Palmer.
Adderley, Sir Augustus John.
Agnew, Hon. Sir Jas. Willson,M.D.
Akerman, Sir John William.
Alston, Sir Francis Beilby.
Anson, Maj.-Gen. Sir Arch. E. H.
Baker, Sir Benjamin, C.E.
Baker, Hon. Sir Richard Chaffey.
Barbour, Sir D. Miller, K.C.S.I.
Beauchamp, Earl.
Bellairs, Lieut.-Gen. Sir Wm.
Bergne, Sir John Henry Gibbs.
Berkeley, Sir George.
Berry, Hon. Sir Graham.
Biliotti, Sir Alfred.
Birch, Sir Arthur Nonus.
Boucaut, Hon. Sir James Penn.
Bourinot, Sir John George.
Bowell, Hon. Sir Mackenzie.
Bower, Comm. Sir Graham John.
Boyle, Sir Cavendish.
Braddon,Rt.Hn.SirE.N.Coventry
Bramston, Sir John.
Brett, Col. Sir Wilford.
Brown, Sir Charles Gage, M.D.
Bruce, Sir Charles.
Buller, General Right Hon. Sir Redvers Henry, VC, G.C.B.
Buller, Sir Walter Lawry.
Campbell, Sir Geo. Wm. Robert.
Carbone, Sir Giuseppe.
Cardew, Col. Sir Frederic.
Carling, Hon. Sir John.
Caron, Hon. Sir Joseph P. René A.
Carrington,Maj.-Gen.SirF.,K.C.B.
Carter, Hon.Sir Fredk. Bowker T.
Carter, Sir Gilbert Thomas.
Cassel, Sir Ernest.
Clanwilliam, Admiral of the Fleet the Earl of, G.C.B.
Clarke, Col. Sir G. Sydenham.
Clarke, Lt.-Col. Sir Marshal J.
Coles, Hon. Sir Jenkin.
Colomb, Capt. Sir John C. R., M.P.
Colton, Hon. Sir John.

Colvile, Maj.-Gen.Sir Hy.Edward.
Colvin, Sir Auckland, K.C.S.I.
Cookson, Sir Charles Alfred.
Crossman, Maj.-Gen. Sir Wm.
Cuthbert, Hon. Sir Henry.
Darley, Sir Frederick Matthew.
Davenport, Sir Samuel.
Davies,Lt.-Col. Sir H.D.,M.P.,V.D.
Davies, [Hon.] Sir Louis Henry.
Dawes, Sir Edwyn Sandys.
De Lotbinière,Hon.SirH.G.Joly-.
De Verteuil, Sir Louis A. Aim-.
De Villiers, Rt.Hon.Sir John Hy.
DeWet,Hon.SirJacobusAlbertus
Dent, Sir Alfred.
Dibbs, Hon. Sir George Richard
Donoughmore, Earl of.
Downer, Hon. Sir John William
Duffy, Hon. Sir Charles Gavan.
Dyer, Sir Wm. T. Thiselton-.
Edwards, Lieut.-Gen. Sir J. B.
Elliot, Maj. Sir Henry George.
Evans, Alderman Sir David.
Evans, Sir Francis Henry, M.P.
Everett, Col. Sir William.
Fane, Sir Edmund D. Veitch.
Faure, [Hon.] Sir Pieter Hendrik.
Fergusson, Right Hon. Sir J., Bart., M.P., G.C.S.I.
FitzGerald, Sir Gerald.
Fleming, Sir Francis.
Fleming, Sir Sandford.
Forrest, Rt. Hon. Sir John.
Fraser, Sir Malcolm.
Fysh, Hon. Sir Philip Oakley.
Gallwey, Sir Michael Henry.
Gallwey, Lt.-Gen. Sir Thos. L. J.
Garrick, Hon.Sir Jas.Francis,Q.C.
Garstin, Sir William Edmund.
Goldie,Rt.Hn.SirG.D.Taubman.
Goldsworthy, Sir Roger Tuckfield.
Gollan, Sir Alexander.
Gosselin,Sir Martin Le Marchant.
Grant, Sir James Alexander, M.D.
Greaves, Gen. Sir Geo. R., G.C.B.
Gurdon, Sir Wm. Brampton,M P.
Hall, Rt. Hon. Sir Chas., Q.C., M.P.
Hall, Hon. Sir John.
Hamilton, Sir Wm. Alex. Baillie-
Hardinge, Sir Arthur Henry.
Harris, Rear-Adm. Sir Robert H.
Hartley, Sir Charles Augustus.
Hay, Sir James Shaw.
Hector, Sir James, M.D.
Hemming, Sir Augustus Wm. L.
Hill, Sir Clement Lloyd.
Hillier, Sir Walter C.
Hodgson, Sir Arthur.
Hodgson, Sir Fredc. Mitchell.
Howard, Sir Henry, C.B.
Howland, Hon. Sir Wm. Pearce.
Hunter, Surg.-Gen. Sir Wm. G.
Jackson, Sir Henry Moore.
Jerningham, Sir Hubert Ed. Hen.
Julyan, Sir Penrose Goodchild.
Kennedy, Sir Charles Malcolm.
Kirkpatrick, Hon. Sir Geo.Airey.
Kitchener of Khartoum, Maj.-Gen. Lord, G.C.B. (Sirdar).
Knollys, Sir Francis, K.C.P.
Knollys, Sir Clement Courtenay.
Lackey, Hon. Sir John.
Lagden, Sir Godfrey Yeatman.
Lamington, Lord.
Lang, Sir Robert Hamilton.

Langevin, Hon. Sir Hector Louis.
Law, Maj. Sir E. FitzGerald.
Lister, Sir Thomas Villiers.
Llewelyn, Sir Robt. Baxter.
Lubbock, Sir Nevile.
McCallum,Lt.-Col.Sir H.Edward.
Macartney, Sir Halliday, M.D.
MacDonald, Maj. Sir C. Maxwell, K.C.B.
MacGregor, Sir William, M.D.
McIlwraith, Hon. Sir Thomas.
McNeill, Maj.-General Sir John Carstairs, VC, K.C.B.
Madden, Hon. Sir John.
Mansfield, Col. Sir Chas. Edward
Marindin, Col. Sir Francis A.
Marsh, Sir William Henry.
Marshall, Lieut.-Gen. Sir Fredk.
Martin, Col. Sir R. E. R., K.C.B.
Mathews, Gen. Sir Lloyd Wm.
Miéville, Sir Walter Frederick.
Moloney, Sir Cornelius Alfred.
Moncrieff, Col. Sir Colin C. Scott-
Money, Sir Alonzo.
Moor,SirRalphDenhamRayment.
Morice, Ferik Sir Geo., Pacha.
Naz, Sir Virgile.
Nelson, Rt.Hon. Sir Hugh Muir.
Nelson, Sir Edward Montague.
Noel, R.-Adm.Sir Gerd.H.Uctred.
Norton, Right Hon. Lord.
O'Brien, Sir Geo. Thos. Michael.
O'Brien, Lt.-Col. Sir John T N.
Ommanney, Sir Montagu Fredk.
Pakenham, Hon. Sir Francis.
Palmer, Sir Elwin Mitford,K.C.B.
Parsons, Col. Sir Charles S. B.
Peace, Sir Walter.
Pearson, Lt.-Gen. Sir Chas. K.
Peel, Rt. Hon. Sir Frederick.
Pelletier, [Hon.] Sir C. A. Pantaléon.
Perceval, Sir Westby Brook.
Petre, Sir George Glynn.
Porter, Sir Neale.
Ranfurly, The Earl of.
Robinson, Hon. Sir John.
Rodd, Sir James Rennell.
Rogers, Lt.-Col. Sir John Godfrey, Pacha, A.M.S., D.S.O.
Russell, Lt.-Gen. Sir Baker Creed.
Sadler, Col. Sir James Hayes.
Samuel, Hon. Sir Saul, Bart.
Sanderson, Hon. Sir Percy.
Sanderson, SirThos. Henry,K.C.B.
Sargood,Lt.-Col. Sir John Fred.T.
Satow, Sir Ernest Mason.
Saunders, Sir Frederick Richard.
Scanlen, Hon. Sir Thomas Chas.
Scott, Maj.-Gen. Sir F. C., K.C.B.
Scott, Sir John.
Shea, Hon. Sir Ambrose.
Shippard, Sir Sidney G. Alex.
Sivewright, Hon. Sir James.
Smith, Maj.-G. Sir Chas. Holled.
Smith, Sir Edwin Thomas.
Smith, Lt.-Col. Sir Gerard.
Smith, Maj.-Gen. Sir Robert M.
Smith, Sir T. B. Cusack-.
Smith, Sir Wm. Fredk. Haynes.
Smyth, Gen. Sir Henry Aug., R.A.
Southey, Hon. Sir Richard.
Sprigg, Rt.Hon.Sir John Gordon.
Stanton, General Sir Edward.
Stephen, Sir Alexander Condie.

KNIGHTS COMMS., K.C.M.G.—*con.*
Stout, Hon. Sir Robert.
Strickland, Sir Gerald B. S. (Count della Catena).
Swettenham, Sir Frank Athelstane.
Swettenham, Sir Jas. Alexander.
Tennant, Hon. Sir David.
Tennyson, Lord.
Thorburn, Hon. Sir Robert.
Todd, Sir Charles.
Tozer, Hon. Sir Horace.
Trutch, Sir Joseph William.
Tupper, Hn. Sir Chas. Hibbert, Q.C.
Turner, Rt. Hon. Sir George.
Twynam, Sir Wm. Crofton.
Vincent, *Colonel* Sir Charles E. Howard-, M.P.
Vincent, Sir Edgar, M.P.
Walker, Sir Edward Noel.
Walsham, Sir John, Bart.
Whiteway, Rt. Hon. Sir Wm. V.
Whitmore, *Major-Gen.* Hon. Sir George Stoddart.
Wilkin, Sir Walter Henry.
Wilson, *Maj.-Gen.* Sir Chas. Wm.
Wilson, *Col.* Sir David, V.D.
Wingate, *Col.*, Sir Francis R., D.S.O., A.D.C.
Winter, Hon. Sir J. Spearman, Q.C.
Woods, Sir Albert Wm., K.C.B.
Wrixon, Hon. Sir Henry John.
Wyndham, Sir George Hugh.
Youl, Sir James Arndell.
Young, Sir Frederick.
Zeal, Hon. Sir William Austin.

Honorary Knights Commanders.
His Excellency Réchad Pacha.
H.E. Chao Phya Bhanuwongse Maha Kosa Tibcditi Phraklang.
Mustapha Bey Yawer, Mudir of Dongola.
Major-Gen. Sir Edward Henry Zohrab Pacha, C.B.
Sir Zulfikar Pacha.
Sir Osman Pacha Orphi.
Medhi Kuli Khan, styled Majdud-Dowleh (Persia).
Muhammed Hasan Khan, styled Etimad-us-Sultaneh (Persia).
Sir Blum Pacha.
Count Jacq. Hen. E. de Lalaing.
H.H. the Sultan of Perak.
Vice-Adm. Jose de Carranza y de Echevarria (Ferrol).
Sir Wm. Cornelius Van-Horne.
H.H. the Sultan of Johore.
Chentung, Liang Cheng.
Col. Sir Rudolph Slatin (Pacha), C.B.
H.E. *Maj.* Sir Joaquim A. de Albuquerque.
Boutros Ghaly Pacha.

COMPANIONS. C.M.G. 342
Adams, *Maj.* Hamilton J. Goold-, C.B.
Adamson, William.
Adcock, Hugh.
Adeane, *Adm.* Edward Stanley.
Adrian, Frederick Obadiah.
Anderson, John.
Anthonisz, Peter Daniel, M.D.
Aplin, *Capt.* Jno. Geo. Orlebar.

Archer, Thomas.
Aslam Khan, Kazi Mahomed.
Aston, William George.
Aubert, Edgar (Port Louis).
Austin, John Gardiner.
Babtie, *Major* William, R.A M.C.
Barclay, George Head.
Barnard, *B.-Gen.* John Henry, C.B.
Barnham, Henry Dudley.
Barron, Sir Henry Page T., Bart.
Barrow, *Lieut.-Col.* Arthur Frederick, D.S.O.
Bateman, Alfred Edmund.
Bayly, *Col.* Zachary Stanley.
Beal, *Lt.-Col.* Robert.
Beech, *Capt.* John Robert, D.S.O.
Belilios, Emanuel Raphael.
Bernal, Frederic.
Bernays, Lewis Adolphus.
Bickford, *Rear-Adm.* A. Kennedy.
Bigge, *Lt.-Col.* Sir A. J., K.C.B.
Blennerhassett, *Lieut.-Col.* B. Montgomerie, R.A.M.C.
Blissett, *Commis.* Henry Fred.
Block, Adam Samuel James.
Booker, Sir William Lane.
Boothby, Josiah.
Boothby, William Robinson.
Bor, *Major* James Henry, R.M.A.
Borg, Raphael.
Bosisto, Joseph.
Bourke, *Capt.* Hn. Maurice A.-, R.N.
Bower, *Major* Robert Lister.
Brabant, *Col.* Edward Yewd.
Brackenbury, *R.-Adm.* J.W., C.B.
Brenan, Byron.
Bright, Charles Edward.
Brown, John M'Leavy.
Brown, Montagu Yeats-.
Brown, *Maj.* Robert Hanbury.
Burr, *Capt.* John Leslie, R.N.
Bushell, Stephen Wootton, M.D.
Caillard, Alfred.
Cameron, *Maj.-Gen.* Donald R.
Campbell, James Duncan.
Carr, *Lieut.* Geo. Shadwell Q., R.N.
Carrington, Sir John Worrell.
Cartwright, William Chauncy.
Casey, Hon James Joseph.
Chadwick, Osbert.
Chater, Catchick Paul.
Chichester, *Capt.* Sir Edward, Bart., A D.C., R.N.
Clarke, *Maj.-Gen.* Sir Stanley de A. Calvert, K.C.V.O.
Cloete, Henry.
Close, *Maj.* Charles F., R.E.
Collet, Wilfred.
Colmer, Joseph Grose.
Cornish, Josiah Easton.
Courtney, John Mortimer.
Cracknall, Walter Borthwick.
Crawford, Arthur Travers.
Crawfurd, Oswald John Fredk.
Creagh, Charles Vandeleur.
Creswell, *Capt.* Wm. Rooke, R.N.
Cumberbatch, Henry Alfred.
Curtis, *Col.* Francis G. Savage.
Dalton, Rev. Canon John Neale.
Dartnell, *Col.* John George.
Davis, *Capt.* Edward H. M., R.N.
Davis, Nicholas Darnell.
Dawkins, *Maj.* Chas. Tyrwhitt.
Dawson, *Lt.-Col.* Douglas F. R.

Dawson, George Mercer.
De Boucherville, Hon. C. E. Boucher.
De Laessöe, *Capt.* Albert Fredc.
De Piro, Giuseppe L., Marchese.
Dealtry, William.
Deane, Walter Meredith.
Denton, George Chardin.
Dicken, Charles Shortt.
Dickson, Hon James Robert.
Dodds, Hon. John Stokell.
Douglas, Hon. John.
Downes, *Maj.-Gen.* Major Francis.
Dredge, James.
Drew, Wm. Leeworthy Good.
Dunlop, *Colonel* Samuel.
Ellery, Robert Louis John.
Elliott, Chas. Bletterman, LL.B.
Elliott, *Colonel* John, C.B.
Escott, Ernest Bickham Sweet-.
Evans, Frederick.
Fabre, Hector.
Fairholme, *Maj.* Wm. Ernest, B.A.
Farnall, Harry de la Rosa Burrard.
Ferreira, P. J.
Fischer, Sir Henry Charles.
FitzGerald, *Fleet Surg.* Michael.
FitzGibbon, Edmund Gerald.
Fitzmaurice, Gerald Henry.
Fleming, And. Milroy, M.B.
Fletcher, *Lieut.-Colonel* John.
Foote, *Capt.* Randolph F. O., R.N.
Fortescue, *Lt.-Col.* Hon Chas. G.
Foster, Edward Wm. Percival.
Fowler, *Lieut.* Chas. Wilson, R.N.
Fraser, John.
Fraser, *Maj.-Gen.* Thomas, C.B.
Fréchette, Louis.
Freeman, *Col.* Alfred.
Fremantle, *Admiral* Hon. Sir E. R, G C.B.
French, *Maj.-Gen.* Geo. Arthur.
French, Somerset Richard.
Frost, Hon. John.
Froude, Ashley Anthony, B.A.
Gallwey, *Maj.* Henry L., D S O.
Gardner, Christopher Thomas.
Gascoigne, *Maj.-Gen.* Wm. Julius.
Gatt, *Major-General* Saverio.
Gifford, Hon. Maurice Raymond.
Gleadowe, George Edwd. Yorke.
Gleichen, *Major* Count Albert.
Glyn, *Lt.-Gen.* Richd. Thos , C.B.
Gordon, Arthur John Lewis.
Gough, *Col.* Hugh Sutlej, C.B.
Gowan, Hon. James Robt , LL.D.
Grace, Hon. Morgan Stanislaus.
Graham, John James.
Grant, William.
Graves, Robert Wyndham.
Gray, Samuel Brownlow.
Gregory, Hon. Augustus Charles.
Greville, George.
Grey, *Capt* Raleigh.
Grieve, Robert, M.D.
Griffin, William Henry.
Griffith, *Col.* Charles Duncan.
Gubbins, John Harington.
Haden, Francis Seymour.
Haig, *Lt.-Col.* Arthur Balfour.
Hamilton, Charles Boughton.
Harding, Colin.
Harman, Charles A. King-, M.A.
Harris, Walter Henry.
Harrison, *Gen.* Sir Richard, K C.B.

COMPANIONS, C.M.G.—*continued.*

Hatch, *Lt.-Col.* George Pelham.
Hatherton, *Colonel* Lord.
Hawtayne, George Hammond.
Heath, *Lieut.-Colonel* John M.
Heidenstam, Frederick Charles.
Henderson, Joseph.
Herbert, *Col.* Ivor J. C.
Hervey, Dudley Francis A.
Hilliard, *Major* George, R.A.M.C.
Hime, *Lieut.-Col.* Albert Henry.
Holborrow, *Col.* Wm. Hillier.
Hopwood, Fras. John Stephens.
Howard, *Maj.-Gen.* Francis, C.B., A.D.C.
Howe, *Capt.* Hon. Assheton Gore Curzon-, A.D.C., R.N., C.B.
Hughes, *Colonel* Emilius, C B.
Hunter, David.
Im Thurn, Everd. Ferdinand, M.A.
Innes, James Rose.
Irving, Charles John.
Jamieson, George.
Jarvis, *Maj.-Gen.* Samuel Peters.
Jekyll, *Colonel* Herbert, R.E.
Jelf, *Col.* Richard Henry, R.E.
Jenkins, George Henry.
Jordan, John Newell.
Jourdain, Henry John.
Justice, *Maj.-Gen.* William Clive.
Keefer, Thomas Coltrin.
Kennaway, Walter.
Kennedy, Robert John.
Kenney, *Maj.* Arth. Herbt., R.E.
Kerr, Thomas.
Kidd, John.
Knollys, *Major* Louis Frederick.
Kynnersley, Charle. W. Sneyd-.
Kynsey, Sir William Raymond.
Lamb, John Cameron, C.B.
Lang, *Capt.* John Irvine, R.E.
Larymore, *Capt.* Hy. Douglas.
Layard, Edgar Leopold.
Lazzarini, *Major-General* James.
Leclézio, Henri.
Le Hunte, George Ruthven.
Leverson, *Lieut.-Col.* Julian Jno., R.E
Levey, George Collins.
Lewis, Sir Samuel.
Leys, Peter.
Lockhart, Jas. Haldane Stewart
Lovell, Francis Henry.
MacBride, Robert Knox.
McCarthy, James Desmond, M.D.
McDougall, John Lorn.
McEachern, *Lt.-Col.* Archibald.
McFarlane, *Capt.* Ronald.
McInnis, *Lieut.-Colonel* Edward Bowater.
McKean, *Col.* Alexr. Chalmers.
McKinney, William James.
Maclean, *Kaid* Harry.
McLeod, *Maj.* Norman Magnus.
McNair, *Major* John Fredk. A.
Macpherson, James Simpson.
McTurk, Michael.
Mahony, *Lieut.-Colonel* John.
Mainwaring, *Lt.-Col.* Rowland B.
Maling, Irwin Charles.
Mann, *Maj.-Gen.* James Robert.
Mansel, *Commdt.* Geo. (Zululand).
March, George Edward.
Marinitch, Hugo.

Maxse, Ernest Geo. B.
May, Francis Henry.
Meares, George.
Meiklejohn, *Brig.-Gen.* Sir Wm. H., K.C.B.
Meldrum, Charles.
Melville, George.
Methuen, *Lt.-Gen.* Lord, K.C.V.O.
Milne, Alexander Roland.
Mitchell, Robert William Span.
Mitchell, William Wilson.
Moffat, Rev. John Smith.
Moffat, Robert Unwin, M.B.
Moore, *Rear-Adm.* Arthur W.
Moore, Noel Temple.
Morris, Daniel, D.SC.
Morris, *Col.* Wm. George, R.E.
Mosse, *Deputy Surgeon-General* Charles Benjamin.
Moysey, *Maj.-Gen.* Charles John.
Murray, *Col.* Robt. Hunter, C.B., A.D.C.
Murray, Hon. Thomas Keir.
Napier, *Colonel* William.
Nathan, *Maj.* Matthew, R.E.
Naudi, Sir Salvatore.
Newton, Francis James.
Nicholls, Hy. Alfred Alford, M.D.
Nicolson, Sir Arthur, K.C.I.E.
O'Connor, Charles Yelverton.
Odling, Tom Francis.
O'Donovan, Denis.
O'Halloran, Joseph Sylvester.
Oliver, *Maj.-Gen.* John Ryder.
Olivier, Sydney.
Ornstein, John Isidor Maurice.
Orpen, Hy. Martyn Herbert.
Owen, *Surg.-Lt.-Col.* Charles Wm.
Owen, Edward Cunliffe-.
Ozanne, John Henry.
Paget, *Capt.* Alfred W., R.N.
Panton, Joseph Anderson.
Parkin, George Robt., LL.D.
Parr, *Maj.-Gen.* Hy. Hallam, C.B
Parris, James William.
Paton, *Major-General* George.
Peacocke, *Col.* William.
Perry, Gerald Raoul de-Courcy-.
Peyton, *Capt.* Westropp Joseph.
Philips, *Maj.* Burton Henry
Pickering, William Alexander.
Pisani, Salvatore Luigi, M.D.
Preece, John Richard.
Price, *Col.* Adolphus James.
Rámá Náthan, Ponnambalam.
Rea, Edward Hugh.
Read, William Henry Macleod.
Richardson, Hon. Edward.
Rind, *Col.* Alexander Thos. S. A.
Roberts, *Colonel* Charles Fyshe.
Roberts, Hon. Charles James.
Roberts, John (Dunedin).
Robertson, *Capt.* C. Hope, R.N.
Robinson, William Valentine.
Rodger, John Pickersgill.
Rohrweger, Frank
Rolleston, Loftus John.
Ross, David Palmer, M.D.
Round, Francis Richard.
Rowell, Thomas Irvine.
Rowland, John William.
Rudolph, Gerhardus Martinus.
Rundle, *M.-G.* Sir H. M. L., K.C.B.
Russell, *M.-G.* Fras. Shirley, M.P.
Russell, Henry Chamberlaine.

Russell, Thomas.
Rutherford, George.
Sale, *Col.* Matt. Townsend.
Sami-ullah Khan. Moulvie M.
Sartorius, *Maj.-Gen.* Reginald W., V.C
Saunders, Charles J. Renault.
Sawyer, Robert Henry
Schreiber, Collingwood.
Schreiner, Hon. William Philip.
Scott, *Surg.-Col.* Fredk. Beaufort.
Selwyn, Alfred Richard Cecil.
Shelford, Thomas.
Shepstone, Henrique Charles.
Shepstone, John Wesley.
Shepstone, Theophilus.
Shipley, Hammond Smith.
Smith, Robert Murray.
Spalding, *Col.* Warner Wright.
Spreckley, John Anthony.
Stanford, Walter E. Mortimer.
Stavrides, Constantine George.
Steward, *Major-Gen.* Edward H.
Stewart, *Col.* Chas Edward, C.B.
Stewart, Donald William.
Stewart, James.
Stirling, Edward Charles, M.D.
Streatfeild, *Commdt.* Frank N.
Stuart, *Col.* J. Alex. Man-.
Sullivan, *Adm.* Sir Fras. Wm., Bt.
Swaine, *M.-Gen.* Leop. Vict., C.B.
Symonds, Edmund Stace.
Synge, Robert Follett.
Tanner, John Edwd. (Trinidad).
Taylor, Edwd. Barnett Anderson.
Taylor, William Thomas.
Tempier, Phillip Arthur.
Templeton, *Col.* Jno. Montgomery.
Thompson, Henry Langhorne.
Todd, John Spencer Brydges.
Treacher, William Hood.
Trendell, Arthur Jas. Richens.
Tresidder, *Capt.* Tolmie John.
Trotter, *Col.* Jas. Keith, R.A.
Tucker, James.
Tulloch, *Major-General* Alex. Bruce, C.B.
Vella, Francesco (Malta).
Villiers, Francis John.
Vine, Sir John Richard Somers.
Vroom, Hendrik.
Wagstaff, William George.
Wake, Chas. St. Aubyn.
Walker, *Capt.* Sir B. W., Bt., R.N.
Walker, *Lieut.-Gen.* Sir Fredk. Wm. E. Forestier-, K.C.B.
Walker, *Lieut. - Colonel* Robert Sandilands Frowd.
Walker, Richard C. Critchett.
Wallace. William.
Ward, Charles James.
Waring, Francis John, C.B.
Warren, *Col.* Falkland Geo. E.
Watson, *Col.* Charles Moore.
Wauchope, *Maj.-Gen.* A. G., C.B.
Webb, Frederick William.
Western, *Lt.-Col.* James Halifax.
White, *Lt.-Col.* William.
Willcocks, *Lt.-Col.* James, D S.O.
Willcocks, William.
Williams, *Maj.* John Hanbury-.
Williamson, Alexander.
Williamson, Victor Alexander.
Wilson, *Maj.* Edmond M., R.A.M.C.
Wilson, William Grey-.

COMPANIONS, C.M.G.—cont.	Wray, *Lieut.-General* Henry.	Chancellor, Hon. Sir R. G. W. Herbert.
Winter, Francis Pratt.	Wylde, Everard William.	
Wodehouse, Henry Ernest.	Wylde, *Colonel* William Henry.	Sec., Sir Edward Wingfield, K.C.B.
Wodehouse, *Maj.-Gen.* Josceline H , C.B.	Yardley, Samuel.	King of Arms, Sir Albert William Woods, K.C.B., F.S.A.
Woodgate, *Maj.-Gen.* E.R.P. C.B.	Vate, *Lieut.-Col.* Chs. Edw., C.S.I.	Registrar, Sir J. Bramston, K C M G.
Woolfryes, *Surg.-Gen.* J. A., C.B.	Young, *Capt.* Arthur Henderson.	Officer of Arms, Frederick Obadiah Adrian, C.M.G.
Wortley, *Maj.*E.J.Mont.-Stuart-.	Prelate, Archbp. of Rupertsland.	

THE MOST EMINENT ORDER OF THE INDIAN EMPIRE

Ribbon, Imperial blue. *Motto,* Imperatricis auspiciis (under auspices of the Empress.)

INSTITUTED 1st January, 1878. ENLARGED 1st June, 1887.

SOVEREIGN: HER MAJESTY QUEEN VICTORIA, EMPRESS OF INDIA.

Grand Master, THE VICEROY AND GOVERNOR-GENERAL OF INDIA FOR THE TIME BEING.

KNIGHTS GRAND COMMANDERS. G.C.I.E.

H.R.H. the Prince of Wales.
H.R.H. the Duke of Saxe-Coburg-Gotha (Duke of Edinburgh).
H.R.H. the Duke of Connaught.
H.R.H. the Duke of Cambridge.

Benares, H.H. the Maharaja of.
Burne, *Maj.-Gen.*Sir OwenTudor.
Chamberlain, *Gen.* Sir Crawford Trotter.
Connemara, Rt. Hon. Lord.
Cooch Behar, H.H. Maharaja of.
Dufferin and Ava, Most Hon. Marquess of, K.P.
Elgin and Kincardine, Rt. Hon the Earl of, K.G.
Gondai, H.H. Thakur, Sahib of.
Harris, Lord, G.C.S.I.
Havelock, Sir Arthur E., G.C.M.G.
Karauli, H.H. the Maharaja of.
Khairpur in Sind, H.H. the Mir of.
Khelat, H.H. the Khan of.
Kishengarh. H.H. Maharaja of.
Kutch, H.H. the Rao of.
Lansdowne, Most Hon. Marq. of.
Lyall, Sir Alfred Comyns.
Lyall, Sir James Broadwood.
Morvi, H.H. Thakur Sahib of.
Murshidabad, the Nawab of.
Palanpur, H. H. the Diwan of.
Phillips, Sir Geo. F. Faudel-, Bt.
Reay, Lord, G.C.S.I.
Roberts of Kandahar, *Field Marshal,* Lord, ♥♥, K.P.
Sandhurst, Lord.
Seccombe, Sir Thomas Lawrence.
Tonk, H.H. the Nawab of.
Wenlock, Lord, G.C.S.I.
White, *Gen.* Sir G. Stewart, ♥♥, G.C.B.

KNIGHTS COMMANDERS. K.C.I.E.

Aga Khan, H.H. Aga Sultan Muhammad.
Ajaigarh, the Maharaja of.
Ajudhya, Maharaja of.
Allen, Sir George William.
Amir Hassan, Raja of Mahmoodabad.
Areot, the Prince of.
Ardagh, *Maj.-Gen.* Sir John Chas.
Arnold, Sir Edwin.
Baksh Singh, Rana S. Bahadur.
Bamra, Chief of (Raja S. Deo).
Beresford, *Col.* Lord Wm. Leslie de la Poer, ♥♥
Bhownaggree Sir Mancherjee,M.P.
Bird, *Lt.-Gen.* Sir George Corrie

Birdwood, Sir George Christopher.
Bisset, *Lt.-Co'.* Sir W. S. Smith.
Bliss, Sir Henry William.
Bobbili, Raja of.
Brandis, Sir Dietrich.
Brooke, Sir William Robert.
Bundi, H.H. the Maharao Raja of.
Campbell, Sir James Macnabb.
Cappel, Sir Albert Jas. Leppoc.
Collen, *Maj.-Gen.*Sir Edwin H.H
Croft, Sir Alfred Woodley.
Cunningham, Sir Henry Stewart
Dacca, the Nawab Bahadur of.
Dennehy, *Maj.-Gen.* Sir Thomas.
Durand, Sir H. Mortimer, K.C.S.S.
Edgar, Sir John Ware.
Evans, Sir Griffith Humphry T.
FitzGerald, Sir Gerald S. Vesey.
Gidhaur, Maharaja of.
Gordon, *Gen.* Sir Thos. Edward.
Harnam Singh Kunwar, Sir Ahluwalia
Hatwa, Maharaja of.
Hext, *Rear-Adm.* Sir John.
Hogg, Sir Frederic Russell.
Holdich, *Col.* Sir T. Hungerford.
Howorth, Sir Henry Hoyle, M.P.
Hudson, *Lt.--Col.* Sir William Brereton, V.D.
Iman Baksh Khan, Nawab.
Jadu, Krishna Rao Bapu Saheb
Jah, Sir Asman (Ekbal ud Dowlah).
Janjiri, Nawab of.
Jardine, Sir John.
Jehan Kader Mirza Bahadur (Prince of Oudh).
Khem Singh Bedi Baba, of Kallar.
Khushed Jah Bahadur Nawab Shams - ul - Umara - Amir - i - Kabir.
King, Sir Henry Seymour, M.P.
King, *Brig.-Surg.- Lt.-Col.* Sir Geo., M.B.
Lambert, Sir John (Calcutta).
Leslie, Sir Bradford.
Lethbridge, Sir Roper.
Limri, Thakore Sahib of.
Loharu, Sir Armir ud Din, Chief of.
Lunawara, Raja of.
Mackay, Sir James Lyle.
Maclean, Sir Francis William.
Macnabb, Sir Donald Campbell.
Macpherson, Sir Arthur George.
Markby, Sir William.
Molesworth, Sir Guilford L.
Morton, *Maj.-Gen.* Sir G. de C.
Naoroz Khan, Sirdar, of Kharan.
Narendra Krishna Del Bahadur, Maharaja.

Nicolson, Sir Arthur.
Ollivant, Sir Edward Chas. Kayll.
Orchha, H.H. the Maharaja of.
Paul, Sir Gregory Charles.
Pontifex, Sir Charles.
Pritchard, Sir Charles Bradley.
Rendel, Sir Alexander Meadows.
Richey, Sir James Bellet. [abad].
Secundar Jung, Nawab (Hyderabad).
Simpson, *Surg.-Gen.* Sir Benj.
Stedman, *Maj.-Gen.* Sir Edward.
Talbot, *Lt.-Col.* Sir Adelbert C.
Thomas, Mgr. Sir Léon E. Clément (*Hon.*).
Thuillier, *Col.* Sir Hy. Ravenshaw.
Turner, Sir Charles Arthur.
Venkatagari, Raja of (Velugti Sir Krishna Yashendra).
Vikar ul Umrah H.E. Sir (Igbal ud Dowlah).
Wallace, Sir Donald Mackenzie.
West, Sir Raymond, LL.D.
Williams, *General* Sir Edward Charles Sparshott, R.E.
Wilson, Sir Arthur.
Wingate, Sir Andrew.

COMPANIONS. C.I.E.

Abdul Karim, *Munshi and Hafiz.*
Acworth, Harry Arbuthnot.
Adam, Sir Frank Forbes.
Adamson, *Lieut.- Col.* Charles Hen. E.
Afsur Dowlah, *Major* Nawab Ali Beg.
Ahmed Khan, Sirdar Shere.
Ahmed Khan Bahadur, Kazi Syud.
Aiyar Subbayar Subrahmanya Dewan Bahadur.
Ali Khan, Syud Wilayut, of Patna.
Ali Khan, H.H. Mir Hasan.
Ameer Ali, Syud.
Anderson, Alexander.
Anderson, Graham.
Anderson, *Brig.-Surgeon* John.
Arbuthnot. Sir Alex. John, K.C.S.I.
Arbuthnott, Jno. Campbell.
Aslam Khan, *Lt.-Col.*Muhammad, Sirdar Bahadur.
Aulad Husain, Khan B. Saiyad.
Ayangar, Dewan Bahadur Srinivasa Raghava, B.A.
Baghat, Rana Dhalip Singh, of.
Bahadur Khan, Raja Jung.
Baha-ud-din, Sheikh, Nawab-i-Umb (Junagarh).
Baha-ud-din Khan, *Rissaldar Major,* Sardar Bahadur.

COMPANIONS, C.I.E.—*cont.*
Bakir Ali Khan, Syud.
Balwant Singh, Raja of Awa.
Banerjee, Bahadur Rai Durga-
gati.
Barker, Rayner Childe.
Barnett, George Alfred.
Bayley, Sir Steuart Colvin, K.C.S.I.
Berkeley, *Maj.-Gen.* James Cavan.
Bhag Ram, Rai Bahadur Pandit.
Bhagat Sirdar Singh.
Bhandarkar, Ramkrishna Gopal.
Bhikaji Jatar, Rao Bahadur Sri
Ram.
Bichu Singh, Thakur of Dholpur.
Bidie, *Surgeon-General* George.
BipinKhrishnaBose, RaiBahadur.
Bir Bikram Singh, *Lt.* Kunwar.
Bishen Singh, Dewan of Nabha.
Blaney, Thomas (Bombay).
Bocquet, Roscoe.
Boppe, Lucien.
Branfoot, *Col.* Arthur Mudge,
M.B., I.M.S.
Brown, Thomas E. Burton-, M.D
Browne, *Lt.-Col.* Samuel H., I.M.S.
Browning, Colin Arrot R.
Browning, *Maj.* Winthrop B.,
I M S
Bruce, Richard Isaac.
Buckingham, *Col.* James.
Buckland, Charles Edward.
Bühler, Johann Georg.
Bullock, Frederick Shore.
Burgess, James.
Busteed, *Brig.-Surg.* Henry E.
Buyers, John Walker.
Bythesea, *Rear-Ad.* John, V.C., C.B.
Campbell, *Capt.* Alexander, D.S.O.
Campbell, *Col.* David W.
Cardozo, Henry O'Connell.
Carew, *Capt.* George O'Brien T.
Carey, Bertram Sausmarez.
Carlyle, Robert Warrand.
Carnac, *Col.* Jno. H. Rivett-.
Chandra Das, Baboo Sarat.
Chandra Nyaratna, Pandit M.
Charan Laha, Durga.
Charkhari, the Dewan of.
Chatterton, *Col.* Frank Wm.
Chitnavis, Rao Madhav.
Chitty, *Comm.* Arthur Whatley.
Christie, James Thomas.
Chunder Mukarji Bahadur, Rai
Kanta, Diwan of Jaipur.
Chunilal Venilal, Rao.
Church, *Maj.-Gen.* Thomas Ross
Clarke, *Lt.-Gen.* Hon. Sir And.,
G C.M.G.
Clarke, Caspar Purdon.
Clerk, *Captain* Claude.
Colvin, Sir Auckland, K.C.S.I.
Cook, Frank Henry.
Cooke, Theodore, LL.D.
Cooper, William Earnshaw.
Couper, Sir George E. W., Bart
Crawford, *Col.* Richmond Irvine.
Crole, Charles Stewart.
Cromer, Viscount, G.C.B.
Cumming, *Col.* Wm. Gordon, R.E.
Cunningham, Alex. Fredk. D.
Cunningham, *Br.-Surg.-Lieut.-
Col.* David Douglas, M.B.
Dad Khan (Gul Khan), Rai Baha-
dur Kadir.

Dallas, *Dep.-Surg.-Gen.* Alex. M.
Daly, *Captain* Hugh.
Daly, William Watt.
Dampier, Henry Lucius.
Dane, Richard Morris.
Darlington, Edwin.
Das Seth, Luchman, of Muttra.
Dastur, Bahmanji Jamasji.
Daukes, Frederick Clendon.
Daulat Ram, Rai Bahadur.
Davies, Sir Robert Henry, K C.S.I.
De Laessöe, *Capt.* Albert Fred.,
K C.M.G.
Dempster, Francis Erskine.
Dhaujibai Fakirji Commodore,
Khan Bahadur.
Dhanpat Rai, Rai Bahadur,
Sardar Bahadur.
Dhar, H.H. the Maharaja of.
Digby, William.
Dinshah, Edulji.
Dinshaw, Cowasjee (Aden).
Donald, John Stuart.
Downe, *Colonel* Viscount.
Drummond, *Major* Fras. H. R.
Duff, *Col.* Beauchamp.
Duff, Rt. Hon. Sir M. E. Grant-,
G.C.S.I.
Dulputram Dayabhoy.
Durand, *Col.* Alg. G. A., C.B.
Dutt, Romesh Chandra.
Dyer, Sir Wm. T. Thiselton-
K C.M.G.
Edgerley, Steyning William.
Egerton, Sir Robert Eyles, K.C.S I.
Eliot, John, F.R.S.
Elliot, Frederick Aug. Hugh.
Fenn, *Lt. - Col.* Ernest H.,
R.A.M.C.
Ferard, Henry Cecil.
Fergusson, Rt. Hon. Sir Jas., Bt.
Ffinch, Benjamin Traill.
Findlay, *Surgeon-Major* John.
Fleet, John Faithfull.
Forrest, George William.
Franklin, *Col.* Benjamin, I.M.S.
Franks, *Capt.* Norman.
Fuller, *General* John Augustus.
Fuller, Joseph Bampfylde.
Gajapati, R. G. Baba of Surat.
Gamble, James Sykes.
Ganpat Rai, Diwan.
George, Edwd. Claudius Scotney.
Ghose, Rash Behary.
Ghulam Ahmad, Mirza.
Gibbon, Thomas Mitchell.
Giles, Robert.
Grass, James George Henry.
Gohur Khan, Sirdar, of Khelat.
Gordon, *Lieut.-Col.* John C. F.
Gordon, *General* William.
Graham, Donald.
Greenstreet, Regd. Hawkins.
Grierson, George Abraham.
Griesbach, *Lt.-Col.* Carl Ludolph.
Griffith, Ralph Thos. Hotchkin.
Haffkine, Waldemar Mordecai.
Haines, *Field-Marshal* Sir Fred-
erick Paul, G.C.B.
Hellen, *Vet.-Lt.-Col.* James Her-
bert Brockencote.
Hamnett, George.
Hankin, Arthur Crommelin.
Hassan Khan, Mahomed.
Hastings, Charles G. W.

Hendley, *Col.* Thos. H., I.M.S.
Hennessey, James B. N.
Het Ram, Diwan.
Hewett, John Prescott, C.S.I.
Higgins, *Lt.-Col.* Andrew C. B.
Higham, Thomas.
Hildebrand, Arthur Hedding.
Hobhouse, Rt. Hon. Lord.
Hoernle, Augustus F. Rudolph.
Hogge, *Lieut.-Col.* John William.
Holdsworth, *Maj.* John Joseph.
Holford, *Capt.* George L, M V.O.
Hope, Sir Theodore Cracraft,
K.C.S.I.
Horsfall, Jeremiah Garnett.
Hossein, Syud Ameer.
Howell, Mortimer Sloper.
Hughes, Arthur John.
Hunter, Sir Wm. Wilson, K C.S.I.
Husband, Rev. John, D.D.
Husein Ali Khan, Mirza.
Ilbert, Sir Courtenay P., K.C.S.I.
Impey, *Col.* Eugene Clutterbuck.
Irwin, Henry.
Iyengar, Rao Bahadur Bashyam.
Izat, Alexander.
Jackson, *Colonel* Samuel.
Jacob, Edward Fountaine.
Jacob, *Col.* Samuel Swinton.
Jagat Singh, Sirdar Bahadur
(Kalawalla).
Jan Suddozaie, Shahzada Sultan.
Jarrett, *Col.* Henry Sullivan.
Jhujjhar Sing, Jee Dow.
Johnstone, Frederick John.
Joyner, Robert Batson.
Jubbar, Moulvi Abdul.
Kalooba, Kumar Shri.
Kanai Lal Dé, Rai Bahadur
Kandahar, Khan Bahadur Kazi
Jalul-ud Din Khan, Akhund-
zaza of.
Keene, Henry George.
Kennedy, Frederick Charles.
Khemchand Tahilram.
Kielhorn, Franz.
King, *Lt.-Col.* WalterGawen, I.M.S.
Kipling, John Lockwood.
Knight, James Blackburn.
Lafont, Rev. Eugene.
Lall Rai Munna Punna.
Lali Sijwar, Babu Chota.
Lane, *Col.* Clayton Turner.
Law, Joy Gobind.
Lawrence, *Col.* Alexander J.
Lawrence, Walter Roper.
Leigh, *Lieut.-Col.* Henry Percy.
Le Messurier, *Colonel* Augustus.
Linkedaw, Myo Wun.
Little, Thomas David.
Ludlow, *Col.* Edward Samuel.
Luke, Stephn. Paget W. Vyvyan.
Lyall, Sir Charles James, K.C.S.I.
Lyon, *Brig.-Surg.-Lt.-Col.* Isi-
dore Bernadotte.
MacCartie, Charles Falkiner.
MacCartie, *Lt.-Col.* Frederick
Fitzgerald, M.B., I.M.S.
McFerran, James.
McKay, *Lt.-Col.* Hy.Kellock, I.M.S.
Mackenzie, *Col.* Kenneth James
Loch.
Maclean, *Maj.-Gen.* Chas. Smith.
Macleod, *Lt.-Col.* James John.
McMahon, *Capt.* Arthur H., C.S.I.

COMPANIONS, C.I.E.—*cont.*

Macpherson, Chas. Gordon W.
Macpherson, Duncan James.
Mahendra Singh, Maharaja of Bhadawar.
Mahomed Hassan, Khalifa Syud.
Mainwaring, *Gen.* Wm. George.
Maitland, William James.
Man, Edward Horace.
Mance, Sir Henry Christopher.
Mancherjee Rustomji Dholu, Khan Bahadur.
Mangal Singh, Rai Bahadur Thakur.
Marshall, *M.-Gen.* G.F.Leycester.
Masson, *Lt.-Col.* David Parkes.
Mathew, George Felton.
Matthews, Henry Montagu.
Melitus, Paul Gregory.
Merriman, *Colonel* William.
Merwanji Mehta, Hon. Pheroze-shah.
Mij Pershad Singh, Heera Sahib Lal Rama.
Miller, Rev. William.
Milne, *Lt.-Col.* Alex. (Surma).
Minchin, *Lt.* Alfred Beckett, I.S.C.
Modak, Waman Abaji.
Mohendro, Lall Sircar.
Mohun Singh, Raja Jag.
Moore, *Lt.-Col.* Sir G. Montgomerie
Moore, *Lt.-Gen.* Sir Henry, K C.B.
MuhamedAbdulla Khan, Isakhel.
Muhammad Bakhtiyar Shah, Sahibzada.
Muir, *Col.* Charles Wemyss.
Muncherji Navasji Murzban, Khan Bahadur.
Murray, Charles Stewart.
Muzzaffar Khan, *Ressaldar-Major* Sirdar Bahadur.
Nabhi Bakhsh, Sirdar, of Kuppurtalla.
Nanquette, Pierre François H.
Naoroji Maneckjee Wadia.
Naoriji Pestonji Vakil, Khan Bahadur.
Napier, *Col.* Hon. George C.
Narain, Pandit Surup.
Narayan Singh, Maharaja Harhullub (Sombara).
Nawaz, Hak Khan.
Naylor, Henry Paul Todd-.
Needham, Francis Jack.
Neel, Edmund.
Nicholson, Fredk. Augustus.
Nisbet, *Colonel* Robert Parry.
Norman, *General* Sir Henry W.
Nulkar, R. B. Krishnaji L.
Nunn, *Vet.-Maj.* J. A., D.S.O.
O'Callaghan, Fraser Langford, C.S.I.
O'Conor, James Edward.
Oldham, Wm. Benjamin.

Ottley, *Col.* John Walter, R.E.
Owen, *Lieut.-Col.* Chas. W., C.M.G.
Palmer, Charles George.
Panap Dakham, Anandu Charlu.
Patterson, Alexander Bleakley.
Paul, Alfred Wallis.
Pennycuick, Alexander.
Pertab Narain Singh, Das of Jashpur, Raja.
Pestonji Jahangir, Khan Bahadur.
Petley, *Lieut.* Eaton Wallace, R.N.
Piagpur, Raja of.
Pitman, Charles Edward.
Playfair, Sir Patrick.
Plunkett, Arthur Henry.
Poona, Nursingharow Krishna.
Porteous, *Col.* Chas. Arkcol.
Powell, Baden Henry Baden-.
Prakash Lal, Rai Bahadur Jai (Dewan of Dumraon).
Puckle, Richard Kaye.
Pulford, *Col.* Russell Richard.
Punganur, Zemindar of.
Puntulu, Palle Chentsal Rao.
Raghanath Singh, Tika (Bashahr).
Raikes, *Lt.-Col.* Fredk. Duncan.
Ramachandra Vittal Rao, Raja of Sandur.
Ramaswami Mudaliar, Sir.
Ramsay, *Capt.* John, I.S.C.
Ranade, Mahadeo Govind, B.E.
Ranchonlal, Chotalal. B.B.
Ratlam, the Diwan of.
Rees, John David.
Reid, James Robert.
Reynolds, Charles Henry.
Ribbentrop, Berthold.
Rice, Benjamin Lewis.
Richardson, *Col.* Geo. L. R., C.B.
Ripon, Most Hon. Marquess of.
Risley, Herbert Hope.
Robertson, Benjamin.
Robertson, Frederick Ewart.
Robertson, *Colonel* John.
Robinson, Vincent Joseph.
Rose, George Pringle.
Royle, Joseph Ralph Edward J.
Rustamji Dhanjebhai, Mehta.
Sanderson, *Col.* Henry Bristow.
Scallon, *Lt.-Col.* Robt. I., D.S.O., I.S.C.
Schlieh, William, PH.D.
Scott, *Lieut.-Col.* Buchanan.
Scott, James George.
Shahab-ud-din, Kazi.
Shakespear, *Maj.* John, D.S.O.
Sime, John.
Singh, Sardar Ratan.
Singh, Raja Bhup Indra.
Singh, Rao Bahadur, Thakoor of Masuda.
Smith, George, LL.D.
Smith, *Capt.* John Manners, V.C.

Snow, Philip Chicheley H.
Spring, Francis Joseph Edward.
Stanyon, Henry John.
Stevens, Frederick William.
Stewart, *Col.* Charles Edward, C.B.
Stewart, *Fld.-Marshal* Sir Donald Martin, Bart., G.C.B.
Stewart, *Colonel* John.
Still, Charles.
Stokes, Whitley, LL.D., C.S.I.
Strachan, James.
Strachey, Sir John, G.C.S.I.
Suraj Kaul, Pundit.
Sutherland, Charles Leslie.
Symes, Edward Spence.
Tagore, Raja Sir Sourindro Mohun.
Tarapuraala, Meherjibhai E.
Tawney, Charles Henry.
Temple, Rt.Hon.Sir Richard, Bt.
Temple, *Lt.-Col.* Richard Carnac.
Tennant, *Lt.-Gen.* Jas. Francis.
Thibaw, Sawbwa of (Saw Saing).
Thompson, *Surg.-Maj.* Daniel R.
Thomson, *Surg.-Lt.-Col.* Samuel Jno., I.M.S.
Tomkins, *Gen.* W. Percival.
Travancore, the Diwan of.
Trichinopoly Rayalu Arakias-wamy Thumboo Chetty.
Tucker, *Maj.-Gen.* Louis H. Emile.
Turnbull, Robert.
Turner, Henry Blois Hawkins.
Tyler, Sir John William.
Tytler, Adam Gillis.
Van Someren, William Taylor.
Vasudeo Barvé, Mahadeo.
Vincent, Robt. Wm. E. Hampe.
Virchand Dipchand, of Ahmednagar.
Vishwanath Patankar Madhava Rao.
Visram, Fazlbhai.
Wadia, Naoroji Nasarvanji.
Wahab, *Col.* Robt. Alexr.
Walker, Ernest Octavius.
Walker, James Lewis.
Wallace, *Col.* William Arthur J.
Walsh, Langton Prendergast.
Walton, Frederick Thomas G.
Ward, *Col.* Henry Constantine E.
Watt, George, M.B.
Webster, Edmund Forster.
Weldon, *Colonel* Thomas.
White, Herbert Thirkell.
Wollaston, Arthur Naylor.
Wordsworth, William.
Wyllie, *Lt.-Col.* W. Hutt Curzon.
Yeilding, *Maj.* Wm. Richd., D.S.O.
Young, *Capt.* Frank Popham, I.S.C.
Younghusband, *Capt.* Fras. Edw.

Sec., Foreign Sec., Govt. of India.

Registrar, Sir Albert William Woods, K.C.B., F.S.A.

THE ROYAL VICTORIAN ORDER.

Ribbon, Dark blue with narrow edging of three stripes—red, white and red.
Instituted 21st April, 1896.

SOVEREIGN : HER MAJESTY QUEEN VICTORIA, EMPRESS OF INDIA.

KNIGHTS GRAND CROSS. G.C.V.O.

H.R.H. the Prince of Wales. K.G.
H.R.H. Duke of Saxe Coburg Gotha. K.G.
H.R.H. Duke of Connaught, K.G.
H.R.H. Duke of York, K.G.
H.R.H. Duke of Cambridge, K.G.
H.R.H. Prince Arthur of Connaught. ——
Colville of Culross, Lord, K.T.
Howe, *General* Earl.
Kelvin, *Lord.*
Mount Edgcumbe, Earl of.
Pembroke, Earl of.
Portland, Duke of.
Probyn, *General* Sir Dighton Macnaghten, 𝒱𝒞
Schleswig-Holstein, H.H. Prince Albert of.
Schleswig-Holstein, H.H. Prince Christian Victor of, G.C.B.
Teck, H.H. the Duke of.

Honorary Knights Grand Cross.

Arsène Henry.
Gen. Count Hilarion Vorontsov Dashkov.
General Otto de Richter.
Count Constantine Pahlen.
Prince Alexis Dolgorouky.
Maj.-Gen. Prince Dmitri Galitzin
H.E. Li Hung Chang.
Count Joachim Moltke.
Maj.-Gen. Count Paul Benkendorff.
H.E. Count G. Seckendorff.
H.H. Nicholas I. Prince of Montenegro.
H.M. Alfonso XIII., King of Spain.
Lieut.-Gen. Edward von Müller.

H.S.H. Prince Francis Joseph of Battenberg.
Count Arthur von Mensdorff Pouilly.
H.S.H. The Hereditary Prince of Leiningen.
General François de Négrier.
H.R.H. Prince Frederick Leopold of Prussia.

KNIGHTS COMMANDERS. K.C.V.O.

Acton, Lord.
Clarke, *Maj.-Gen.* Sir Stanley.
Colville, *Col.* Hon. Sir Wm. Jas.
De Ros, Lord.
Ellis, *Major-General* Sir Arthur.
Ewart, *Maj.-Gen.* Sir H. P., K.C.B.
Fullerton, *Vice-Admiral* Sir John Reginald Thomas.
Laking, Sir Francis Henry.
Mac Cormac, Sir William, Bart.
Martin, Sir Theodore, K.C.B.
Methuen, *Lt.-Gen.* Lord.
Rowton, Lord.
Teck, H.S.H. Prince Adolphus of.
Teck, H.S.H. Prince Alexander of.
Teck, H.S.H. Prince Francis of.
Von Pawel Rammingen, Freiherr Luitbert Alex. Geo. L. Alph.

COMMANDERS. C.V.O.

Abdul Karim, *Munshi and Hafiz.*
Bateson, *Lieut.-Gen.* Richard.
Clerk, *Col.* John.
Eliot, *Col.* Hon. Chas. Geo. C.
Gordon, *Col.* George Grant.
Harris, Sir James Charles.
Monson, *Capt.* Lord.
Watson, *Rear-Adm.* Burges, A.D.C.

MEMBERS, 4TH CLASS. M.V.O.

Bankart, *Surg.* Arthur R., M.B., R.N.
Brocklehurst, *Maj.-Gen.* John F.
Campbell, *Maj.-Gen.* Barrington Bulkley Douglas.
Campbell, *Capt.* Walter D. S.
Cecil, *Col.* Lord William.
Collins, *Lt.-Col.* Arthur, C.B.
Davidson, *Lt.-Col.* Arthur.
Delmege, Alfred Gideon.
Dundonald, *Col.* Earl of.
Falmouth, *Maj.-Gen.* Viscount.
Fortescue. *Com.* Hon. Seymour J.
Fripp, Alfred Downing.
Gilbert, Alfred.
Holford, *Capt.* Geo. Lindsay, C.I.E.
Holmes, Richard Rivington.
Hoskyns, *Capt.* Peyton, R.N.
Legge, *Lt.-Col.* Hon. Henry Chas.
Lockhart, *Lt.-Col.* Sir Simon, Bt.
May, *Capt.* Wm. Henry, R.N., A.D.C.
Miles, *Col.* Herbert Scott Gould.
Muther, Maurice.
Oliphant, *Maj.-Gen.* Laurence Jas.
Poë, *Capt.* Edmund S., R.N., A.D.C.
Ponsonby, *Capt.* Frederick E. G.
Smith, *Staff-Sg.* J. Lawrence, R.N.
Sturge, William Allan, M.D.
Sullivan, Sir Arthur.
Waters, *Lt.-Col.* Wallscourt Hely Hutchinson, R.A.
Woods, Henry Charles, M.D.
Yorke, Hon. Alexander G.

MEMBERS, 5TH CLASS. M.V.O.

Cook, Henry.
Hertslet, Harry Lester.
Nicholas, *Capt.* John, R.A.
Chancellor, The Ld. Chamberlain.
Secretary and Registrar, The Keeper of the Privy Purse.

THE DISTINGUISHED SERVICE ORDER, D.S.O.

Ribbon, Red with blue edge.

INSTITUTED 9th *November,* 1886.

SOVEREIGN : HER MAJESTY QUEEN VICTORIA, EMPRESS OF INDIA.

COMPANIONS. D.S.O.

Abbott, *Maj.* Herbert E. Stacy.
Airey, *Lt.-Col.* Henry Park.
Aldworth, *Lt.-Col.* William.
Annesley, *Capt.* Wm. Rd. Norton.
Arnold, *Lt.-Col.* Alfred James.
Austin, *Maj.* Herbert Henry.
Bacon, *Comm.* Regd. H. S., R.N.
Badcock, *Capt.* Francis Fredk.
Baldwin, *Major* Guy Melfort, I.S.C.
Barlow, *Capt.* Charles James, R.N.
Barratt, *Lt.-Col.* Wm. Cross, I.S.C.
Barrett, *Lt.-Col.* Alfred Lloyd.
Barrow, *Lt.-Col.* Arthur F., C.M.G.
Barton, *Lt.-Col.* Maurice C., R.E.
Bayly, *Major* Alfred Wm. L.
Beatty, *Lieut.* David, R.N.
Beech, *Capt.* John Robert, C.M.G.
Begbie, *Major-Gen.* Elphinstone Waters, C.B.
Benbow, *Ch. In. of Mach.* Hy., R.N.
Bennett, *Colonel* William.
Beynon, *Maj.* Wm. George L.
Biggs, *Maj.* Henry Vero, R.E.

Blakeney, *Lt.* Robt. B. Drury, R.E.
Blenkinsop, *Vety.-Capt.* L. J.
Blomfield, *Lt.-Col.* Chas. James.
Bond, *Engr.* Edmund E., R.N.
Borradaile, *Maj.* Harry Benn.
Bourke, *Lt.-Col.* Hy. Beresford.
Bowden, *Staff-Surg.* Walter, R.N.
Bowker, *Capt.* William Jas.
Brake, *Capt.* Herbert E. J.
Bretherton, *Capt.* Geo. Howard.
Brindle, *Rt. Rev.* Monsignor.
Brooke, *Capt.* Ronald George
Browne, *Col.* Arthur Geo. Fredk.
Browne, *Lieut.* Clement Lawrence Seton Seton-, I.S.C.
Browne, *Lt.-Col.* Geo. Fitzherbert.
Browne, *Com.* Godfrey Gore-, R.N.
Bunbury, *Maj.* Vesey Thomas.
Campbell, *Capt.* Alexander, G.I.E.
Campbell, *Capt.* Chas , C.B., R.N.
Campbell, *Col.* Colin Chas , I.S C.
Campbell, *Maj.* Fredk., I.S C.
Campbell, *Capt.* Kenneth J. R.
Carew, *Maj.* Geo. Albert Lade.

Carew, *Col.* Rd. Hugh, R.A.M.C.
Carpenter, *Capt.* Alfred, R.N.
Caulfeild, *Major* Algernon M.
Caulfeild, *Maj.* Gordon Napier.
Cecil, *Major* Lord Edward.
Chancellor, *Lt.* Jno. Robt., R.E.
Channer, *Col.* Bernard, I.S.C.
Clarke, *Lt.* Thos. Hy. Matthews, R.A.M.C.
Clements, *Col.* R. A. Penrhyn.
Climo, *Maj.* Skipton Hill, I.S.C.
Cockburn, *Major* George.
Coker, *Colonel* Edmund Rogers.
Cole, *Capt.* Henry Wells-.
Coles, *Lt.-Col.* Arthur Horsman.
Corbett, *Col.* R. de la C., R.A.M.C.
Couchman, *Lt.-Col.* Geo. Henry H.
Cowan, *Capt.* Jas. Wm. Alston.
Cowan, *Lieut.* Walter Hy., R.N.
Coxhead, *Capt.* Thos. Langhorne.
Crofton, *Col.* Morgan Samuel, C.B.
Cubitt, *Col.* William George 𝒱𝒞
Cummins, *Brig.-Gen.* Jas. Turner.
Cunningham, *Lieut.-Col.* Geo., G.

COMPANIONS, D.S.O.—*cont.*

Cure, *Major* Herbert Capel.
Daubeney, *Maj.* Edward Kaye.
Davie, *Capt.* A.F.Ferguson-,I.S.C.
Davies, *Maj.* Thos. A. Harkness.
Davis, *Col.* G. McBride,C.B.,I.M.S.
De Brett, *Capt.* Harry S., R.A.
Deedes, *Maj.-Gen.* William Hy.
De Lisle, *Capt.* Henry de Beauvoir.
De Moleyns, *Lt.-Col.* Hon. Frederick Rathmore W. Eveleigh-.
Dening, *Colonel* Lewis, C.B.
Deshon, *Col.* Charles John, R A.
Dicken, *Col.* Wm. Popham, C.B.
Digan, *Capt.* Augustin J.
Dimsey, *Staff-Surg.* E. R., R.N.
Dorrien, *Col.* Horace L. Smith-.
Dorward, *Col.* Arthur Robert F.
Downes, *Major* William Knox.
Doyle, *Maj.* Ignatius P., I.M.S.
Drage, *Lt.-Col.* William H., A.S.C.
Dugmore, *Capt.* William F.B.R.
Dundas, *Major* Laurence Chas.
Durnford, *Captain* John, C.B., R N
Earle, *Major* Henry.
East, *Capt.* Lionel Wm. Pellew.
Edlmann, *Capt.* Ernest E., R.A.
Edwardes, *Capt.* Stanley M., I.S.C.
Edwards, *Capt.* FitzjamesM.,I.S C
Edwards, *Major* John Burnard.
Egerton, *Maj.-Gen.* Chas. C., C.B.
Elliot, *M.-Gen.* EdwardLocke, C.B.
Evans, *Lt.-Col.* Charles Wm. Hy.
Everett, *Colonel* Edward.
Ewart, *Capt.* Richard Henry.
Fairtlough, *Capt.* Edward Charles D'Heilemer.
Fendall, *Major* Charles Pears.
Ferguson, *Capt.* Jno. D , R A M C
Fergusson, *Lt.-Col.* Charles.
Ferrier, *Lt.-Col.* Jas. Archibald.
Festing, *Maj.* Arthur Hoskyns.
Fisher, *Capt.* John, I.M.S.
Fitton, *Major* Hugh Gregory.
Fleming, *Capt.* Chas. G., R.A.M.C.
Forbes, *Lt.* Archibald Jones.
Fowler, *Maj.* Francis John.
Fowler, *Capt.* John Sharman, R.E.
Fraser, *Com.* Ian Mackenzie, R.N.
Fraser, *Capt.* Norman Warden.
Frere, *Major* Sir Bartle Compton Arthur, Bart.
Gallwey, *Maj.* Hy. Lionel, C.M.G.
Gascoigne, *Lieut.* Ernest F. O.
Gatacre, *Lt.-G.* Sir Wm. F.,K.C.B.
Girouard, *Col.* Edouard Percy C.
Glanville, *Major* Francis, R.E.
Godden, *Major* Henry Tufton.
Golightly, *Capt.* Robt. Edmund.
Goodwin, *Capt.* T.H.J.C.,R.A.M.C.
Goodwyn, *Major* Hy. Edward, R.E.
Gordon, *Colonel* James Henry,C.B.
Gordon, *Col.* Stannus Verner.
Gorringe, *Major* Geo. Frederick.
Graham, *Maj.* Herman W. Gore.
Griffith, *Vet.-Capt.* Geo. Richard.
Gurdon, *Capt.* Bertrand E. M.
Gwynn, *Lieut.* Chas. Wm., R.E.
Hadow, *Lt.-Col.* Regld. Campbell.
Haggard, *Capt.*Andrew C.Parker.
Haldane, *Capt.* Jas. A. Lowthrop.
Hale, *Maj.* Chas. Henry, R.A.M.C.
Hale, *Maj.* Geo. Ernest, R.A.M.C.
Hall, *Lieut.* Geo. C. Miller, R.E.
Hall, *Com.* Herbert G. King, R.N.

Hallett, *Lt.-Col.*Jas.W. Hughes-.
Haly, *Col.* R. H. O'Grady-, C.B.
Hamilton, *Major* Hubert I. W.
Hamilton, *Col.* Ian S. M., C.B.
Hamilton, *Major* Wm. George.
Hammond, *Col.* Arthur G., V C
Harley, *Major* Henry Kellett.
Harman, *Major* Richard.
Harrison, *Major* Edgar G.
Harvey, *Surg.-Gen.* Robert, C.B.
Hastings, *Lt.-Col.* Edward Spence.
Hayes, *Lt.-Col.* Aylmer E.
Henderson, *Lt.* Fras. Barkley, R.N.
Henegan, *Captain* John.
Hennell, *Colonel* Reginald.
Hepper, *Colonel* Albert James.
Herbert, *Capt.* Claude, I.S.C.
Heugh, *Com.* John George, R.N.
Heygate, *Maj.* Robt. Hy. Gage.
Hickman, *Lt.-Col.* T. Edgecomb.
Hickson, *Maj.* Samuel Arthur E
Hill, *Capt.* John, I.S.C.
Hobart, *Capt.* Claud V. Cavendish.
Holland, *Com.*GeraldEdwd ,R.I.M
Hornby, *Lt.* Montague L., I.S.C.
Huggins, *Lt.-Col.* Ponsonby G.
Hughes, *Lt.-Col.* G. A., R.A.M.C.
Hugo, *Lt.* James Hy., I.M.S.
Hunnard, *Capt.* Frank, A.S.C.
Hunter, *M.-G.* Sir Archd., K.C.B.
Hunter, *Maj.* G. Douglas, R.A.M.C.
Hutchinson, *Capt.* Geo. H. Ford-.
Ilderton, *Col.* Charles Edward.
Jackson, *Capt.*SydneyC.Fishburn.
Jacob, *Capt.* Arthur Le Grand.
Jenner, *Major* Albert Victor.
Jennings, *Capt.* Jas. W., R.A.M.C.
Jones, *Capt.* Herbert John.
Judge, *Capt.* Spencer Francis.
Keary, *Lt.-Col.* Henry D'Urban.
Keene, *Major* Alfred, R.A.
Keighley, *Col.* CharlesMarsh,C.B.
Keith, *Colonel* James, R.A.
Kempster, *Col.* Fras. Jas., A.D.C
Kennedy, *Lt.* Macdougall Ralston, R.E.
Keppel, *Capt.* Colin R., R.N., C.B.
Kerr, *Capt.* Frederick Walter.
Lambert, *Lt.-Col.* Walter Miller.
Lambton, *Major* Hon. Charles.
Lawrence, *Lt.* Freeling Ross.
Lawrie, *Major* Charles E., R.A.
Leach, *Brig.-Gen.* Harold P., C.B.
Legge, *Major* Norton.
Lewes, *Com.* Price Vaughan, R.N.
Lloyd, *Lt.-Col.* Francis.
Lloyd, *Lt.-Col.* George Evan.
Loch, *Lieut.* Hon. Edward D.
Lockhart, *Capt.* P.C. Eliott, I.S.C.
Low, *Capt.* Robert Balmain, I.S.C
Lucas, *Major* Fredc. Geo., I.S.C.
Lugard, *Capt.* Edward James.
Lugard, *Col.* F. J. Dealtry, C.B.
Lyle, *Major* Hugh Thomas.
MacBean, *Capt.* John A. E.
McCulloch, *Capt.*Robt.Hy.F.,R.A.
MacDonald, *Col.*H. A., C.B., A.D.C.
Macdonald, *Lt.-Col.* Regd. Percy.
MacGregor, *Col.* Chas. Regd., C.B.
Mackinnon, *Lt.-Col.* Hy. W. A. R.A.M.C.
McLeod, *Maj.-Gen.* Donald James
Sim, C.B.
McLoughlin, *Capt.* G. S., R.A.M.C.
McMahon, *Maj.* Sir H. W., Bart.

MacMunn, *Capt.* George F., R.A.
McMurdo, *Capt.*Arthur Montagu.
Maconchy, *Maj.*E. Wm.S.K.,I.S.C.
Macquoid, *Capt.* Chas. Edward Everny Francis Kirwan, I.S.C.
McSwiney, *Lt.-Col.* Edward F. H.
Madden, *Lieut.-Col.* Geo. C., C.B.
Mahon, *Lt.-Col.* Bryan Thomas.
Malcolm, *Capt.* Neill.
Mansel, *Lt.-Col.* Alfred, R.A.
Marriott, *Maj.* Reginald Adams.
Martin, *Dep.-Insp.-Gen.* Jas. H.
Martin, *Staff-Surg.* Jas. M., R.N.
Martyr, *Lt.-Col.* Cyril Godfrey.
Mathew, *Capt.* Charles Massy.
Mathias, *Maj.* Hugh B., R A M C.
Maxse, *Major* Frederick Ivor.
Maxwell, *Lt.* Fras. Aylmer, I.S.C.
Maxwel , *Col.* John Grenfell.
Merriman, *Opt.*Regd. Gordon, R.A.
Micklem, *Lt.* Henry Andrew.
Middleton, *Col.* Fras. Beckford.
Midwinter, *Lt.* Edward Colpoys.
Milne, *Lt.-Col.* Richard Louis.
Moberly, *Capt.* Fredk. Jas., I.S C
Molyneux, *Col.* G. H. More-, I.S.C.
Money, *Col.* Gordon L. C., C.B.
Morgan, *Maj.* Anthony H., I.M.S.
Morgan, *Maj.* Hill Godfrey, A.S.C.
Morris, *Major* Arthur Henry.
Morse, *Capt.* Frank Alexander.
Murphy, *Lt.-Col.* Wm. Reed,I.M.S.
Murray, *Colonel* Andrew.
Murray, *Colonel* Kenelm Digby.
Nason, *Lt.-Col.* Fortescue John.
Nicholson, *Maj.* Jno. Sanctuary.
Nicklin, *Insp.* of Mach. Wm , R.N.
Norris, *Major* Richard Joseph.
Nugent, *Maj.* Oliver S. W.
Nunn, *Vet.-Maj.* Joshua A.,C.I.E.
O'Donnell, *Lt.-Col.* Hugh.
Osborn, *Lieut.* Philip Barlow.
Paine, *Capt.* James Henry, R.A.
Patterson, *Lt.-Col.* T. W., A.M.S.
Payne, *Major* Richard Lloyd.
Penton, *Maj.*Richd.Hugh,R.A.M.C.
Peterson, *Capt.* Fredk. H., I.S.C.
Peyton, *Maj.* William Eliot.
Pigott, *Capt.* Grenville E., A.S.C.
Pink, *Lt.-Col.* Francis John.
Pirie, *Capt.* Arthur Murray.
Poyser, *Vet.-Lt.-Col.* Richard.
Pratt, *Lt.* Henry Roger E., I.S.C.
Presgrave, *Lt.-Col.* Edwd. R. J.
Preston, *Lt.-Col.* Jenico E , I.S.C
Price, *Maj.* C. H. Uve ale, I.S.C.
Pritchard, *Lt.* Harry Lionel, R.E.
Pulteney, *Lt.-Col.* Wm. Pulteney.
Quirk, *Col.* John Owen, C.B.
Radwan, *Maj.* Hassan (Egypt).
Radwan, *Lieut.* Said (Egypt).
Rattray, *Lt.* Haldane B., I.S.C.
Rawlins, *Lt.* Arth. Kennedy,I.S.C.
Rawlinson, *Lt.-Col.* Spencer R., I.S.C.
Rhodes, *Lt.-Col.* Elmhirst.
Rhodes, *Colonel* Francis William.
Robertson, *Capt.* Wm. Robt.
Roche, *Lt.-Col.* Thos. H. de M.
Rogers, *Major* Fred. Arth., I M S.
Rogers, *Col.* George Wm., I.S.C.
Rogers, *Lt.-Col.*Sir John Godfrey, A.M.S., K.C.M.G.
Romilly, *Major* Fredk. William.
Rose, *Col.* Henry Metcalfe, I.S.C.

COMPANIONS, D.S.O.—*cont.*

Rowcroft, *Maj.* Geo. Fras., I.S.C.
Royle, *Capt.* Henry Lucius Fanshawe, R.N.
Rundall, *Lt.-Col.* Frank M., I.S.C.
Rundle, *M.-G.* Sir H. M. L., K.C.B.
St. Leger, *Col.* Hy. Hungerford.
Scaife, *Capt.* George S. Garland.
Scallon, *Lt.-Col.* Robt. Irvin, C I.E.
Scott, *Col.* Douglas Alexr , C.B.
Scott, *Maj.* Thos. Edwin, I.S.C.
Scudamore, *Maj.* Charles Philip
Segrave, *Lt.* William Henry Erik.
Selby, *Capt.* William, I.M.S.
Settle, *Col.* Henry Hamilton.
Shakespear, *Major* John, C.I.E.
Shearer, *Maj.* Johnston, I.M.S.
Shephard, *Major* Chas. Sinclair.
Shepherd, *Col.* Charles Herbert.
Shone, *Col.* William Terence, C.B.
Shoubridge, *Lt.* Thos. Herbert.
Sinclair, *Lt.-Col.* Alfred L , I.S.C.
Sitwell, *Lt.-Col.* Claude Geo. Hy.
Skinner, *Col.* George John, I.S.C.
Skinner, *Col.* James Tierney, C.B.
Sladen, *Captain* David Ramsa y.
Smyth, *Lt.-Col.* Owen Stuart, R A
Spong, *Maj.* Chas. Stuart, R.A M.C.
Spragge, *Major* Basil Edward.
Stanton, *Major* Henry Ernest.
Stead, *Lieut.-Col.* Alfred James.
Steele, *Lt.-Col.* Fredk. William.
Stevenson, *Lt.* Alexr. Gavin, R.E.
Stewart, *Capt.* Cosmo Gordon, R.A.
Street, *Lt. Col.* Alfd. W. F., I.M.S.

Strickland, *Lieut.* Edwd. Peter.
Sunderland, *Col.* Marsden S. J.
Swayne, *Lt.-Col.* Chas. H., R.A M.C.
Sykes, *Major* Wm. Ainley, I.M.S.
Tanner, *Major* John Arthur, R.E.
Taylor, *Major* Hugh Neufville.
Teck, *Capt.* H.S.H. Prince Francis of, K.C.V.O.
Temple, *Col.* Charles Pilcher.
Ternan, *Col.* Trevor Patrick B.
Teversham, *Lt.-Col.* Richard K.
Thackwell, *Maj.* C. G. R., I.S.C.
Thompson, *Col.* William Oliver.
Tickell, *Maj.* Edward James.
Tighe, *Maj.* Michael Joseph.
Tighe, *Lieut.* Vincent John.
Tillard, *Lt.* Arthur Basil, I.S.C.
Tomkins, *Lt.* Harry Leith, I.S.C.
Topham, *Capt.* T. Harrison-, R.E.
Townshend, *Lt.-Col.* Charles Vere Ferrers, C.B., I.S.C.
Triscott, *Maj.* Chas. Prideaux, R.A.
Tullibardine, *Lt.* Marquess of.
Tweedie, *Colonel* John Lannoy.
Upcher, *Maj.-Gen.* Russell, C.B.
Vandeleur, *Major* Cecil F. S.
Van Someren, *Lt.* William Weymouth, I.S.C.
Vernon, *Capt.* Hubert Edward.
Wace, *Lt.-Col.* Ernest Charles, R.A.
Wake, *Lt.* Wm. St. Aubyn.
Wallnutt, *Major* C. C. Miller-.
Watson, *Major* James Kiero.
Way, *Capt.* Alfred Cotton.
Westlake, *Major* Almond P., I.S.C.

Westmacott, *Maj.-Gen.* Sir Richd., K.C.B.
Wheatley, *Lt.* Leonard L., I.S.C.
Wilkin, *Lt.* Henry Douglas, R.N.
Wilkins, *Lt.-Col.* Jas. Sutherland, i M.S.
Wilkinson, *Capt.* Henry Thos. D.
Wilkinson, *Major* Thomas Henry Des Vœux.
Willcocks, *Lt.-Col.* James, C.M G.
Wil iams, *Capt.* Weir de Lancy.
Williams, *Lt.* Wm. Art Glanmor.
Wilson, *Major* Edmond Monkhouse, C.M.G., R.A M.C.
Wingate, *Col.* Sir F. R., K.C.M.G.
Winsloe, *Capt.* Alfred R., R.E.
Wintle, *Colonel* Frank Graham.
Wood, *Maj.* Hastings St. Leger.
Wors' ip, *Lt.* Verelst Turner.
Wortley, *Major* Edward James Montagu- Stuart-, C.M.G.
Wright, *Lt.-Col.* Fred. Wm ,I.M.S
Wright, *Major* Hedley, I.S.C.
Wynter, *Capt.* Francis Arth. R.A.
Wynyard, *Capt.* Edwd. George.
Yaldwyn, *Lt.-Col.* Alfred G., I.S.C.
Yeilding, *Maj.* Wm. Richard, C.I.E.
Young, *Major* Norman E., R.A.

HONORARY D.S.O.

Miralai, *Col.* Fathy Bey (Egyptian Army).

Secretary and Registrar, Francis Albert Bayly, War Office, S.W.

THE ROYAL ORDER OF VICTORIA AND ALBERT, V.A.

Ribbon, White.

INSTITUTED 10th *Feb.* 1862. ENLARGED 10th *Oct.* 1864, 15th *Nov.* 1865, and 15th *Mar.* 1880

SOVEREIGN : HER MAJESTY QUEEN VICTORIA, EMPRESS OF INDIA.

FIRST CLASS.

H.I.M. the Empress Frederick of Germany (Princess Royal).
H.R.H. Princess Christian of Schleswig-Holstein (Helena).
H.R.H. the Princess of Wales.
H.R.H. Princess Louise (Marchioness of Lorne).
H.R.H. Princess Beatrice (Princess Henry of Battenberg).
H.R. & I.H. the Duchess Alfred of Saxe - Coburg - Gotha (Grand Duchess of Russia).
The Queen of Denmark.
The Queen Marie of Hanover.
The Queen of the Belgians.
H.R.H. the Duchess of Connaught and Strathearn.
Her Grand Ducal Highness Princess Louis of Battenberg.
H.R.H. the Duchess of Albany.
H.R.H. Princess Louise of Wales (Duchess of Fife).
H.R.H. Princess Victoria of Wales.
H.R.H. Prss. Charles of Denmark.
The Queen Regent of Spain.
H.R.H. Princess Louise Marie of Prussia (Gd. Duchess of Baden).
H.I.M. the Empress - Queen Augusta Victoria of Germany and Prussia.
H.M. the Queen of Roumania.

H.I.M. the Empress of Russia.
H.R.H. the Duchess of York.

SECOND CLASS.

H.I.H. Pss. Elizabeth of Hesse (Grand Duchess Serge of Russia).
H.R.H. Princess Charlotte of Saxe-Meiningen.
H.R.H. Prss. Henry of Prussia.
H.R.H. Prss. Victoria of Prussia (Princess Adolphe of Schaumburg-Lippe).
H.G.-D.H. Princess of Leiningen.
H.H. Princess Victoria of Schleswig-Holstein.
H.R.H. Prss. Sophie of Prussia (Crown Princess of Greece).
H.R.H. Prss. Margaret of Hesse.
H.H. Princess Louise of Schleswig-Holstein (Princess Aribert of Anhalt).
H.R.H. Princess Ferdinand of Roumania.
H.H. the Grand Duchess of Hesse (Victoria Melita).

THIRD CLASS.

Dowager Duchess of Wellington.
Dowager Lady Churchill.
Dowager Countess of Mayo.
Dowager Countess of Erroll.
Lady Abercromby.
Dowager Lady Southampton.

Dowager Duchess of Abercorn.
Duchess of Roxburghe.
Countess Spencer.
Duchess of Buccleuch.
Dowager Lady Ampthill.
Marchioness of Dufferin and Ava.
Viscountess Downe.
Countess of Antrim.
Marchioness of Lansdowne.
Countess of Lytton.

FOURTH CLASS.

Hon. Lady Hamilton-Gordon.
Viscountess Chewton.
Hon. Lady Biddulph.
Lady Eliz. Philippa Biddulph.
Hon. Flora C. I. Macdonald.
Hon. Mrs. George Ferguson.
Hon. Horatia C. F. Stopford.
Hon. Emily Sarah Cathcart.
Lady Cust.
Hon. Mrs. Gerald Wellesley.
Hon. Lady Ponsonby.
The Duchess of Argyll.
Lady Geraldine H. Somerset.
Hon. Harriet Lepel Phipps.
Hon. Caroline Fanny Cavendish.
Lady Cowell.
Hon. Mrs. Mallet.
Hon. Mrs. Jno. Haughton.
Registrar, Sir Albert William Woods, K.C.B., F.S.A.

THE IMPERIAL ORDER OF THE CROWN OF INDIA, C.I.

Ribbon, Light blue with white edge.

INSTITUTED 1st *January,* 1878.

SOVEREIGN: HER MAJESTY QUEEN VICTORIA. EMPRESS OF INDIA.

H.R.H. the Princess of Wales.
H.I.M. the Empress Frederick of Germany (Princess Royal).
H.R.H. Princess Christian of Schleswig - Holstein (Princess Helena).
H.R.H. Princess Louise (Marchioness of Lorne).
H.R.H. Princess Beatrice (Princess Henry of Battenberg).
H.R. &I.H. the Dchss. of Coburg-Gotha (Grand Duchess of Russia).
H.R.H. the Duchess of Connaught and Strathearn.
H.R.H. the Duchess of Albany.
H.R.H. Princess Louise Victoria of Wales (Duchess of Fife).
H.R.H. Princess Victoria Alexandra of Wales.
H.R.H. the Duchess of York.
H.R.H. the Grand Duchess of Mecklenburg-Strelitz (Princess Augusta of Cambridge).
H.R.H. the Dchs. of Cumberland.
H.R.H. Princess Frederica of Hanover (Baroness von Pawel-Rammingen).
H.R.H. Prss. Mary of Hanover.
H.R.H. Princess Ferdinand of Roumania.
H.R.H. the Grand Duchess of Hesse (Prss. Victoria Melita).

H.R.H. the Hereditary Princess of Hohenlohe-Langenburg.
H.R. Princess Victoria Louise of Schleswig-Holstein.
H.H. Nawab Shahjihan, Begum of Ehopal.
H.H. Maharanee Jumna Bai, Saheb Gaekwar of Baroda.
H.H. Princess Aribert of Anhalt.
H.H. the Maharanee Sahiba of Udaipur.
H.H. the Nawab Shamesi Jahan, Begum Sahiba of Murshidabad.
Maharanee Hai Shornomoyi of Cossimbazar.
Henrietta, Marchioness of Ripon.
Mary, Baroness Kinloss.
Blanche Julia, Countess Dowager of Mayo.
Mary Catherine, Lady Hobart.
Lady Jane Emma Crichton.
Anne, Baroness Napier and Ettrick.
Harriette, Baroness Lawrence.
Cecilia Frances, Countess Dowager of Iddesleigh.
Edith, Countess of Lytton.
Mary Augusta, Lady Temple.
Katherine Jane, Lady Strachey.
Mary Cecilia, Dowager Baroness Napier of Magdala.

H.H. Lakshmi Bhayie, Senior Rani of Travancore.
Emily Eliza, Lady Adam.
Anna Julia, Lady Grant-Duff.
Harriet Georgina, Marchioness of Dufferin and Ava.
Miss Edith Helen Fergusson.
Fanny Georgiana Jane, Lady Reay.
Lady Randolph S. Churchill.
Georgiana, Viscountess Cross.
H.H. Maharanee Sunity Devee, of Cooch Behar.
Maud Evelyn, Marchioness of Lansdowne.
Lucy Ada, Lady Harris.
Constance Mary, Lady Wenlock.
H. H. Maharanee Sahib Chimna Bai Gaikwar.
H.H. Lady Nundkooverbai Bhugvut Sinh Jareja, Ranee Saheb of Gondal.
H.H. the Maharani of Mysore.
Constance Mary, Countess of Elgin and Kincardine.
Lady Fowler.
Victoria, Lady Sandhurst.
Lady George F. Hamilton.
Lady Havelock.
Mary, Lady Curzon of Kedleston.

Registrar, Sir Albert William Woods, K.C.B., F.S.A.

THE ROYAL RED CROSS, R.R.C.

Ribbon, Dark blue with red edge.

(Instituted St.George's Day, 1883.)

FOR zeal and devotion in providing for and nursing sick and wounded sailors, soldiers, and others with the army in the field, on board ship, or in hospitals. Foreign as well as British subjects are eligible.

HER MAJESTY THE QUEEN.

H.R.H. The Princess of Wales.
H.I.M. The Empress Frederick.
H.M. The Queen of Greece.
H.R.H. The Princess Christian.
H.R.H. The Marchioness of Lorne.
H.R.H. The Princess Henry of Battenberg.
H.R.H. The Duchess of Connaught.
H.R.H. The Duchess of Albany.
H.R.H. The Baroness von Pawel Rammingen.
H.R.H. The Duchess of Sparta.
Airy, Miss Sybil.
Aloysius, *Sister* Mary.
Barker, Miss J. M. C.
Barker, *Sister* Mary E.
Benedetta, *Sister* Maria.
Burleigh, Miss R. M.
Byam, Miss C. L.

Camilla, *Sister* Maria.
Cannell, Miss E.
Carmela, *Sister* Maria.
Cator, Miss Susan.
Caulfeild, Miss A. E.
Cawley, Mrs. May.
Celestina, *Sister.*
Clarke, Miss Sarah.
Cole, *sister* Mary C.
Crisp, Miss A.
Damant, Mrs. C. R.
Deeble, Mrs. J. C.
Durham, Miss Eliza.
Ellis, *Sister* Mary H.
Ferguson, Miss C.
Forrest, Miss K.
Geddes, Miss Elizabeth.
Gildea, Mrs.
Gray, Mrs. J. A.
Gray, Miss J. M.
Grist, *Sister* Amy F.
Halford, Miss Emma.
Harper, *Sister* Mary E.
Hart, *Sister* Sarah F.
Hely, Mrs. Ann Eyre.
Holland, Miss A. B.
Holland, Miss A. K.
Hornor, Miss.

Huddon, *Sister* M. de Chantal.
Ireland, Miss S.
Jacoba, *Mother.*
Jerrard, *Sister* Julia J.
Jerrard, Miss M. C.
Jones, Miss M.
Jones, Miss Mary S.
Joseph, *sister* Mary E.
Kelly, *Sister* Mary.
King, Miss E.
King, Miss H.
King, Miss Jane.
King, Mrs. Janet.
Langlands, Miss.
Lickfold, *Sister* E. M.
Loch, *Sister* C. G.
Louise, *Sister.*
Ludovica, *Sister* Maria.
Lumley, Mrs. M. J. W.
McGrath, Miss Theresa.
Mackay, Miss L. J.
Makins, Mrs. M. A.
Mark, *Sister* Annie G.
Miller, Mrs. Ethel S.
Mowbray, *Sister* Cath. S.
Muller, *Sister* L. Maxwell-.

de Nightingale, Miss Florence.
Norman, *Sister* H. C.
Nutt, *Sister* Mary A. M.
Oram, *Sister* Sarah Elizabeth.
Orpheline, *sister* Camilla.
Parsons, Miss L.
Patrick, *Mother.*
Payne, *Sister* Gertrude M.
Pia, *Sister* Maria.
Powell, Miss Minnie.
Roberts, Norah, Lady.
Selby, Miss M.
Smith, Miss Isabella.
Stewart, Miss Henrietta Story, Miss B.
Terrott, Miss Sarah Anne.
Thomas, Miss M.
Tu'loh, *Sister* L. W.
Wantage, Harriet, Lady.
Webb, Miss Sara Emily.
Welchman, Miss Edythe.
Wheldon, Miss E.
Williams, Miss K.
Wilshaw, *Sister* Sarah L.
Yardley, Miss Amelia C.
Yorke, Mrs. Ada.

Ribbo, Crimson for Army; dark blue for Navy.

FOR CONSPICUOUS BRAVERY. INSTITUTED 29th January, 1856.

The following is a list of surviving recipients of the Victoria Cross. The decoration was instituted as a reward for conspicuous valour in the presence of the enemy.

n Adams, Rev. J. W. 1879
b Adams, Lieut.-Col. Robt. Bellew, C.B., I.S.C. 1897
a Arthur, Gunner T. 1855
n Ashford, Priv. Thos. 1880
u Aylmer, Lt.-Col. F. J.'91
g Bell, Private David 1867
k Bell, Col. Mark S., C.B.'74
m Beresford, Col. Lord W. De la Poer, K.C.I.E. 1879
b Blair, Gen. Jas., C.B. 1858
b Boisragon, Capt. G.H.'91
m Booth, Col.-Sergt. A.'79
b Boulger, Lt.-Col. A. 1857
m Browne, Lieut.-Col. E.S. 1879
b Browne, Col. H. G. 1857
b Browne, Gen. Sir Samuel James, G.C.B. ... 1858
m Buller, Gen. Rt. Hn. Sir Redvers Henry, G.C.B. 1879
b Butler, Maj. T. A. 1858
r Byrne, Trper. Thos. 1898
a Bythesea, Rear - Adm. John, C.B., C.I.E....1854
b Cadell, Col. Thomas 1857
b Cafe, Gen. Wm. M. 1858
b Cameron, Col. Aylmer Spicer, C.B. 1858
b Champion, Sgt.-Mj.J.'58
l Channer, General Geo. Nicholas, C.B. 1875
e Chaplin, Colonel John Worthy, C.B. 1860
n Chase, Maj.Wm.St.L.'80
b Coghlan, Sgt.-Maj.C.'57
b Colvin, Lieut. Jas. Morris Colquhoun, R.E. ...1898
a Commerell, Adm.-Fleet Sir John E., G.C.B. 1855
b Costello, Lieut. Edmond William, I.S.C. ...1897
n Creagh, Br.-Gen O'M.'79
s Grimmin, Maj. J., I.M.S. 1889
b Cubitt, Col. William George, D.S.O. 1857
n Cunyngham, Lieut.-Col. Wm. Henry Dick-1879
o Danaher, Sjt. John 1881
r De Montmorency, Capt. Hon. R. H. L. J. 1898
a Dickson, Gen.Sir C. 1854
a Dixon, Maj.-Gen. M. C. 1855
o Doogan, Priv. John 1881
g Douglas, Lt.-Col.C.M.'67
b Dowell, Lt.-Col.G.D.'55
r Edwards, Priv.Thos. 1884

q Edwards, Maj.W.M.1882
a Evans, Priv. Samuel 1855
p Farmer, Corp.Jos.J.1881
b Fincastle, Lieut. Visct. 1897
b Findlater, Piper G. 1898
o Fitzpatrick, Priv. F. 1879
o Flawn, Priv. Thos. 1879
b Fosbery, Lieut.-Col.Geo. Vincent............1863
o Fowler, Sergt. Edmd. '79
k Gifford, Major Lord 1874
b Goate, Corpl. Wm. 1858
b Goodfellow, Lieut.-Gen. Chas. Augustus1 ...1859
v Gordon, Corp. W. J. 1892
b Gough, Gen. Sir Charles J. Stanley, G.C.B....1857
b Gough, Gen. Sir Hugh Henry, G.C.B. 1857
a Graham, Lt.-Gen. Sir Gerald, G.C.B. 1855
t Grant, Maj. C.J.W. 1891
b Hale, Surg.-Maj.T. 1855
b Hall, Seaman Wm. 1857
a Hamilton, M.-G. Thos. de Courcy 1855
n Hammond, Col. Arthur Geo., C.B., D.S.O....1879
q Harding, Chief Gunner Israel 1882
n Hart, Brig. - Gen. Sir Reginald Clare, K.C.B. 1879
o Hartley, Surg.-Lt.-Col. Edmund Barron...1879
b Heathcote, Lt. A.S. 1857
y Henderson, Trumpeter Herbert Stephen 1896
b Heneage, Maj.C.W. 1858
o Hill, Maj. Alan R. 1881
e Hinckley, Seaman G. 1862
m Hitch, Priv.Fredk. 1879
b Home, Surg.-Gen. Anthony D., K.C.B. 1857
m Hook, Priv. Henry 1879
a Hope, Lt.-Col.Wm. 1855
b Innes, Lt.-Gen. James John McLeod 1858
b Jerome, Maj.-Gen. Hy. Edward............1858
b Johnes, Lieut.-Gen. Sir JamesHills-,G.C.B. 1857
b Jones, Lt.-Col.A.S.1857
a Jones, Capt. H. M. 1855
m Jones, Priv. Robert 1879
m Jones, Private Wm. 1879
b Keatinge, General Rd. Harte, C.S.I. 1858
b Kells, Tpt.-Maj. R. 1857

r Kenna, Capt.PaulA.1898
b Kerr, Lt. Wm. Alx. 1857
b Lawson, Private E. 1898
n Leach, Maj.-Gen. Edw. Pemberton, C.B. ...1879
s LeQuesne, Maj. Ferdnd. Simeon, R.A.M.C...1889
w Lloyd, Lt.-Col. Owen E. P., R.A.M.C.........1893
a Lucas, R.-Ad. C. D. 1854
o Lysons, Maj. Hy. ...1879
b Lyster, Lt.-Gen. Harry Hammon, C.B.......1858
f Macintyre, M.-G.D. 1872
f McKenna, Ensign Edw. 1864
f McNeill, Major-General Sir John Carstairs 1864
z Maillard, Staff-Surg. W. B. ...1898
c Malcolmson, Capt. John Graham...........1857
b Mangles, RossLewis1857
f Manley, Surg.-Gn. Wm. George N., C.B. ...1864
f Marling, Maj. P.S.1884
b Marshall, Capt. W. T. 1884
b Maude, Col. Francis Cornwallis, C.B.... 1857
c Moore, Maj.-Gn. Arthur Thomas, C.B. 1857
p Mullane, Sgt.-Mj.P.1880
b Murphy, Pvt. Thos. 1867
o Murray, Corp. Jas. 1881
f Murray, Sergt. John1864
b Napier, Sergeant W. 1858
y Nesbitt, Capt. R. C. 1897
a O'Connor, Major-Gen. Luke............1854
b Olpherts, General Sir William, K.C.B. ...1857
o Osborne, Priv. Jas 1881
m O'Toole, Sgt. Edm. 1879
a Owens, Sergt. James 1854
b Paton, Sergt. John...1857
b Pearson, Cpi. Jas. 1858
b Pennell, Lt. Hy. S. 1898
b Prendergast, General Sir Harry North Dalrymple, K.C.B. 1857
n Probyn, General Sir Dighton M.,G.C.V.O.'57
a Raby, Rr-Adm. Henry James, C.B. 1855
m Reynolds, Brig.-Surg.- Lt.-Col. Jas.Henry 1879
b Richardson, Priv.G. 1859
a Rickard, Ch.Off.of Coast Guard Wm., R.N. 1855

b Ridgeway, Lieut.-Col. Richard Kirby ... 1879
b Roberts of Kandahar, Fld-Marshal Lord, K.P. 1858
a Rowlands, General Sir Hugh, K.C.B. 1854
r Ruthven, Capt. Hon. A. G. A. Hore-.........1898
b Salmon, Admiral of the Fleet Sir Nowell, G.C.B. 1857
n Sartorius, Maj.-Gen. Euston Henry, C.B. 1879
k Sartorius, M.-Gen. Reg. Wm., C.M.G.........1874
m Scott, Lieut. R. G. 1879
f Seeley, Seam. Wm. 1864
f Shaw, Maj.-Gen.Hugh, C.B. ...1865
h Sleavon, Cpl. Mich. 1858
r Smith, Gunr. Albert 1895
u Smith, Capt. John Manners, C.I.E. ...1891
b Smith, Cpl. James 1807
a Smith, Cpl. Philip 1855
n Smyth, Capt. N. M. 1898
f Stagpoole, Drmr.D.1864
a Stancock, Priv.Wm. 1854
a Sylvester, Assist.-Surg. Henry Thomas ... 1855
t Temple, Lieut.-Colonel William, R.A.M.C. 1864
b Thackeray, Colonel Sir Edwd.Talbot, K.C.B.'57
h Trevor, Maj.-Gen. Wm. Spottiswoode 1867
a Trewavas, Seaman Jos. 1855
b Vickery, Corpl. S....1898
n Vousden, Col. W. J.1879
a Walker, Gen.SirM.1854
b Wantage, Colonel Lord, K.C.B. ...1854
m Wassall, Private Samuel 1879
b Watson, Gen. SirJ. 1857
b Watson, Capt. Thomas Colclough 1898
z Whitchurch, Captain HarryFredk.,I.M.S.1895
n White, Lt.-Gen. Sir Geo. Stewart, G.C.B. 1879
b Williams, Pvt.Jno. 1879
b Wilmot, Col. Sir Henry, Bart., K.C.B. ...1858
r Wilson, Rr-Adm. Arth. Knyvet, C.B. 1879
b Wood, Gen. Sir Henry Evelyn, G.C.B. 1858

The italic letter before each name stands for the country in which the Cross was won, viz.:—
a Russia; b India; c Persia; e China; f New Zealand; g Andamans; h Bhutan; i Abyssinia; j Looshai; k Ashanti; l Pérak; m Zululand; n Afghanistan; o South Africa; p Transvaal; q Egypt; r Soudan; s Burmah; t Manipur; u Hunza-Nagar; v Toniataba; w Kachin; x Chitral; y Rhodesia; z Crete.

THE ALBERT MEDAL. (Instituted March 7, 1866.)

For gallantry in saving or attempting to save life at sea ; and (since 1877) for similar acts ashore.

Ablett, G. ... 1877	Dineen, J. ... 1889	Macdonald, *Lt.*R.H. 1898	Sandilands, Henry
Adams, J. ... 1882	Dodd, J. ... 1872	MacGregor, Sir W.,	F. R. ... 1875
Addy, M. ... 1879	Dodd, W. ... 1895	K.C.M.G. ... 1884	Scullion, E. ... 1886
Barber, J., R.N. ... 1889	Donovan, J., R.N. ... 1867	McIntosh, E. B. ... 1879	Seed, *Insp.* W. ... 1891
Batist, J., R.N. ... 1867	Drubble, R. ... 1891	McKee, A. ... 1882	Sharp, P. ... 1879
Baynham, C. ... 1877	Evans, D. ... 1877	McLean, R. ... 1890	Shuttleworth, A. T. 1867
Beith, W. ... 1877	Farabuni (*Tindal*) 1880	McQuo, *Corpl.* A. . 1891	Simons, W. ... 1879
Borland, W. ... 1892	Forbes, *Capt.* W.B.,	Manley, A. ... 1885	Simpson, W., R.N. .. 1870
Bridges, W., R.N. ... 1879	R.N. ... 1871	Manley, A. ... 1885	Smallman, R. ... 1883
Burgess, W. ... 1878	Garrighty, A. R.M.L.I. 1878	Margary, A. R. ... 1871	Smith, I. ... 1889
Burt, W. K. ... 1881	Giles, E. ... 1870	Marsh, E. B. ... 1868	Smith, J. W. ... 1891
Carney, J. ... 1882	Gray, R. ... 1889	Marsh, F. S. ... 1883	Spruce, S. ... 1883
Carpenter, *Capt.* A.,	Green, C. ... 1879	Millett, W. ... 1867	Sprankling, C., R.N. 1867
R.N. ... 1876	Grier, *Lt.-Col.* Hy.,	Mitchell, J. ... 1878	Spring, J. ... 1888
Carter, W. ... 1889	R.A.M.C 1881	Montgomerie, *Capt.*	Stewart, W. ... 1878
Chapman, T. ... 1889	Harris, I. ... 1879	R. A. J., C.B., R.N. 1879	Stokes, A. H. ... 1883
Chetwynd, C. ... 1883	Harris, L. ... 1879	Morgan, C. ... 1879	Summers, J. S. ... 1876
Chetwynd, J. ... 1883	Hennessey, L., R.N. 1892	Morgan, W. ... 1877	Thomas, D. ... 1877
Christie, C. ... 1879	Herbert, T. ... 1879	Morris, W. ... 1883	Thomas, E. ... 1877
Clark, A. ... 1891	Hewinson, H. ... 1895	Moseley, M. ... 1879	Thomas, E. C. ... 1877
Cobb, Rev. C. ... 1867	Higson, G. ... 1885	Mottram, T. H. ... 1883	Thomas, I. ... 1877
Cole, W. ... 1885	Hindley, G. ... 1885	Nutman, *Cpt.* Wm. 1896	Thomas, T. ... 1877
Cooper, A. J. ... 1891	Hinton, W. ... 1882	Oatley, G., R.N. ... 1880	Thomas, W. ... 1877
Crook, J. ... 1885	Hoar, G., R.N. ... 1892	Oatridge, C. ... 1877	Thompson, Dr. E.C. 1885
Cropper, *Maj.* E.D.	Hood, H. ... 1883	Owens, E. W. ... 1877	Toman. *Engr.* Richard Wright, R.N. 1898
F. ... 1879	Hopkins, R. ... 1877	Parkinson, C. ... 1885	
Crowden, J., R.N. ... 1869	Howell, J. W. ... 1877	Pickering, W. ... 1883	Walters, W. ... 1879
David, E. ... 1877	Howells, R. ... 1877	Pickersgill, *Col.-*	Webster, C. ... 1874
Davies, D. ... 1877	Hudson, J. ... 1877	*Serg.* H. ... 1891	Wesley, C. ... 1880
Davies, H. ... 1879	Jaggers, F., R.N. ... 1882	Pitts, F., R.N. ... 1882	Whistler, *Lt.* T. A.,
Davis, T. G. ... 1877	Jones, D. ... 1877	Pochin, H. S. ... 1889	R.N.R. ... 1887
Davis, D. ... 1890	Jones, T. ... 1867	Popplestone, J. ... 1866	Williams, G , R.N. .. 1881
Davis, D. T. ... 1890	Jones, T. ... 1877	Pride, I. ... 1877	Williams, J. ... 1877
Day, C. ... 1888	Kemp, H. ... 1883	Rees, T. ... 1877	Williams, R. ... 1877
Dee, J. ... 1883	Kallan Khan ... 1898	Ricketts, J., R.N. ... 1867	Wilson, C. ... 1878
DeSausmarez, *Capt.*	Lake, S. ... 1867	Robinson, C.W. R.N. 1895	Wilson, *Col.-Serg.* W. 1891
L. A., R.N. ... 1868	Lawson, Dr. D. ... 1881	Rolleston, W. ... 1882	Wood, John Henry 1886
Dickins, *Captain* S.	Lees, D. ... 1877	Rosbotham, Miss H. 1882	Worrall, T. ... 1885
W. Scrase- ... 1896	Lewis, H. ... 1877	Samand, Abdul ... 1898	Yaldwyn, W. E. ... 1887

THE GRAND PRIORY OF THE ORDER OF THE HOSPITAL OF ST. JOHN OF JERUSALEM IN ENGLAND.

(INCORPORATED 14 MAY, 1888, WITH ADDENDA 1888 AND 1890.)

Sovereign ...	H.M. THE QUEEN.
Grand Prior ...	H.R.H. The Prince of Wales, K.G.
Sub Prior ...	H.R.H. The Duke of York, K.G.
Bailiff of Egle ...	H.R.H. The Duke of Connaught, K.G.

EXECUTIVE OFFICERS.

Prelate—His Grace the Archbishop of York.
Chancellor—Earl Egerton of Tatton.
Secretary General—Capt. Sir Alfred Jephson, R.N.
Receiver General—Edwin Freshfield, LL.D.
Almoner—The Rev. Canon Duckworth, D.D.
Registrar—Lieut.-Colonel Gould Hunter-Weston, F.S.A.

Genealogist—The Rev. W. K. R. Bedford, M.A.
Director-General of Ceremonies—Sir Albert W. Woods, K.C.B., K.C.M.G. (Garter),
Librarian—The Rev. W. K. R. Bedford, M.A.
Assistant Librarian—Edwin H. Freshfield.
Secretary—Colonel Sir Herbert C. Perrott, Bart.
Accountant—William R. Edwards, A.C.A.

AMBULANCE DEPARTMENT (ST. JOHN AMBULANCE ASSOCIATION).
Director and Chairman—The Right Hon. Viscount Knutsford, G.C.M.G.
Chief Secretary—Colonel Sir Herbert C. Perrott, Bart.

BRITISH OPHTHALMIC HOSPITAL, JERUSALEM.
Chairman—Earl Egerton of Tatton.
Honorary Secretary—R. Gofton-Salmond.

There are 60 *Knights of Justice*, 39 *Ladies of Justice*, 19 *Chaplains*, 124 *Knights of Grace*, 61 *Ladies of Grace*, and 45 *Esquires*.

Baronets of England, Gt. Britain, and United Kingdom.

(*With Dates of Creation.*) *Exclusive of those merged in the Peerage.*

Abdy, W. Neville...	1850	Bonham, Geo. Fras.	1852
Abel, Fredk. Aug...	1893	Boord, T. William...	1896
Acland, Charles		Boothby, Brooke ...	1660
Thomas Dyke	1644	Boreel, Jacob........	1644
Acland, Hy. W. D.	1890	Boswall, Geo. L. H.-	1836
Adair, Hugh Edwd.	1838	Boughey, Thos. F.	1798
Adam, Charles E.	1882	Boughton, C. H. R.-	1641
Affleck, Robert......	1782	Bowman, W. Paget	1884
Agnew, William ...	1895	Bowyer, Geo. Hen.	1660
Alexander, Lion. C.	1809	Boynton, Rev. G. H.	1618
Alexander, Claud..	1886	Brady, Francis W.	1869
Alison, Archibald ..	1852	Bramwell, Fred. J.	1889
Allan, Henry S. M.		Bridges, George T.	1718
Havelock-......	1858	Brinckman, T. H.	1831
Alleyne, John G. N.	1769	Brisco, Musgrave H.	1782
Amory, Jno. H. H.-	1874	Broadbent, Wm. H.	1893
Anson, Wm. R.,M.P.	1831	Brocklebank, Thos.	1885
Anstruther, W. R.		Brodie, Benj. V. S.	1834
Carmichael-	1798	Bromhead, Benj. P.	1806
Antrobus, Edmund	1815	Bromley, Henry ...	1757
Arbuthnot, Rbt. K.	1823	Brooke, Richard M.	1662
Armstrong, Rev. E.	1841	Brooke, A. R. de-C.-	1803
Armstrong, G. C. H.	1892	Brooke, Arthur D.	1822
Armytage, George J.	1738	Brooke, Thos........	1899
Arnott, John Alexr.	1896	Brooks, W. Cunliffe	1886
Arthur, Geo. C. A.	1841	Broughton, D. L....	1660
Ashburnham, A.....	1661	Brown, Wm. R. ...	1863
Austin, John, M.P...	1894	Brownrigg, Hy. M.	1816
Bacon, H. B. (Prem.)	1611	Bruce, Rt. Hn. Hy. H.	1804
Bagge, Alf. Thos....	1867	Brunner, J. T., M.P.	1895
Baillie, Robt. Alex.	1823	Buchanan, G. H. L.-	1775
Baird, David	1809	Buchanan, James...	1878
Baird, Alexander...	1897	Buckley, Edmund ...	1868
Baker, George S...	1796	Bulkeley, R. H. W.-	1661
Baker, Rev. T. H. B.	1802	Buller, Morton M.-	1866
Barlow, Richd. W.	1803	Bunbury, Hy. C. J.	1681
Barran, John	1895	Burdett, Francis ...	1619
Barrington, Chas. B.	1831	Burdett, Chas. G.	1665
Barron, Hen. P. T.	1841	Burgoyne, John M.	1641
Barrow, J. Croker.	1835	Burnaby, Henry ...	1767
Barry, F.Tress.,M.P.	1899	Burrard, Harry P...	1769
Barttelot, Walt. Geo.	1875	Burrell, Merrik R.	1774
Bates, Edward P...	1880	Burrows, Fredc. A.	1874
Bathurst, F.T.A.H.-	1818	Buxton, T. Fowell.	1840
Baynes, Chris. W.	1801	Call, W. G. Montagu	1791
Bazley, Thos. Seb.	1869	Cameron, Chas.,M.P.	1893
Beach, Rt. Hon. M.		Campbell, A. S. L.	1808
E. Hicks-, M.P...	1619	Campbell, Geo. Edwd.	1798
Beauchamp,R.W.P.-	1744	Campbell, Guy T...	1815
Beaumont, G. H. W.	1661	Campbell, Alex.T.C.-	1821
Becher, J. Wrixon-	1831	Campbell, A. Ava...	1831
Bedingfeld, H.G.P.-	1660	Campbell, D. A. D.	1831
Beevor, Hugh R. ...	1784	Campbell, G. Edw.	1831
Bell, IsaacLowthian	1885	Carbutt, Edward H.	1892
Bell, James	1895	Carden, Fredk. W.	1887
Bellew, H. Grattan-	1838	Carew, Henry Palk	1661
Bellingham, A. H..	1796	Carmichael, Jas. M.	1821
Berney, H. Hanson	1620	Carnac, J.H. Rivett-	1836
Biddulph, Theo. G.	1664	Cave, Charles D. ...	1896
Birkbeck, Edward	1886	Cave, M.C.-Browne-	1641
Blackett, Edwd. W.	1673	Chamberlain, H. E.	1828
Blackwood, Francis	1814	Chaytor, Wm. H. E.	1831
Blair, Rv. David H.-	1786	Chetwode, George...	1700
Blake, Patrick J. G.	1772	Chetwynd, George	1795
Blakiston, Horace N.	1763	Chichester, Edward	1641
Blane, Seymour J.	1812	Child, Smith Hill ...	1868
Blennerhassett, R.	1809	Cholmeley, H. A. H.	1806
Blois, Ralph B. M.	1686	Christison, Alexr...	1871
Blomefield, T. W. P.	1807	Clark, Jno. Forbes	1886
Blount, Walter de S.	1642	Clark,Jas.R.Andrew	1883
Blunt, William	1720	Clark, Thomas	1886
Blyth, James	1895	Clarke, C.M., K.C.B.	1831
Boehm, Edgar C. ...	1889	Clarke, Rupert T. H.	1882
Boevey, Thos. H. C.-	1784	Clay, Arthur T. F.	1841
Boileau, Frs.Geo.M.	1838	Clayton, Wm. Robt.	1732

Clerke, Wm. Fras.	1660	Duckett, Geo. F. ...	1791
Clifford,Geo.HughC.	1887	Duke, James........	1849
[Clifton, R., claimt.]	1611	Dunbar, Alex. Jas.	1814
Coats,Thos.G.Glen-	1894	Duncombe, E.D.P.-	1859
Coddington, W. M.P.	1896	Dundas, Sidney J...	1821
Codrington, Wm....	1721	Dundas, Robert ...	1898
Codrington, G.W.H.	1876	Dunn,William,M.P.	1895
Coghill, John J. ...	1778	Duntze, Geo. Alex.	1774
Colebrooke, Edwd.A.	1759	Durand, Edwd. Law	1892
Collet, Mark Wilks	1888	Durrant, Wm. R. E.	1784
Colleton, R. A. W.	1661	Dyer, T. Swinnerton	1678
Colquhoun, James	1786	Dyke,Rt. Hon.Wm.	
Colt, Rv.E.H.Dutton	1694	Hart, M.P........	1677
Conroy, John........	1837	Earle, Thomas	1869
Cook, Francis	1885	East, G. Aug. C.-...	1838
Cooke, Wm. H.C.W.	1661	Eden, William	1672
Cooper, Astley P.-	1821	Edmonstone, Arch.	1774
Cooper, Daniel	1863	Edwardes, H. H. ...	1644
Coote, Charles A. ...	1774	Edwards, J.H.P.C.	1865
Cope, Anthony	1611	Egerton, P. Grey-.	1617
Corbet, Walter C...	1808	Elliot, George	1874
Corbett, F. G. Ast-		Ellis, J. Whittaker	1886
ley-	1821	Elphinstone, H. W.	1816
Cornwall, Rev. G.	1764	Elphinst'n,G.D.-H.-	1828
Corry, William......	1885	Elton, Edm. Harry	1717
Cotterell, Geers H.	1805	Errington, George	1885
Couper, Geo. E. W.	1841	Erskine, Thomas ...	1821
Cowan, John	1894	Every, Edwd.Oswald	1641
Craig, J.H. Gibson-	1831	Ewart, Wm.Quartus	1887
Craufurd, Ch. W. F.	1781	Ewing, Wm. Orr-...	1885
Crewe, Vauncey H.	1666	Fagge,John W.Chas.	1660
Croft, Herb. Geo. D.	1671	Fairbairn, Arth. H.	1869
Croft, John Fredk	1818	Fairfax, W.G.H.R.-	1836
Crofton, Morgan G.	1801	Farmer, Richd. H.K.	1780
Crofton, Malby	1838	Farquhar, Walt. R.	1796
Crossley, Savile B.	1863	Farquhar, Robt. T.-	1821
Cumming, W.G.G.-	1804	Farrington, Wm. H.	1818
Cunard, Bache E....	1859	Fayrer, Joseph	1896
Cunliffe, Robert A.	1759	Feilden, William L.	1846
Currie, Rev. Fdk L.	1847	Fergusson, J. R. ...	1866
Curtis, Roger C. M.	1794	Ffolkes, Wm. H. B.	1774
Curtis, William M.	1802	Filmer, Robert M...	1674
Cust, Charles L. ...	1876	Fitzgerald, J. C. J.-	1801
Cuyler, Charles......	1814	Fitzgerald, Geo. C.	1822
Dale, David	1895	FitzGerald,Maurice	1880
Dalgleish,W.Ogilvy	1896	FitzGerald, R.U.-P.-	1896
Dallas, Geo. Edwd.	1798	FitzHerbert,Rv.Rd.	1783
Dalrymple, C., M.P.	1887	FitzWygram, F. W.	1805
Darell, Lionel Edw.	1795	Fleming, A.F.H. Le	1705
Dashwood, G. J. E.	1684	Fletcher, Hy., M.P..	1782
Dashwood, Robert J.	1707	Floyd, John	1816
Davie, John D. F.-	1847	Fludyer, Arthur Jn.	1759
De Bathe, Henry P.	1801	Forbes, Charles S....	1823
De Crespigny, C. C.-	1805	Ford, Francis C. R.	1793
De Hoghton, James	1611	Forrest, W. Chas....	1838
De la Rue, Thos. A.	1898	Forster, Charles ...	1874
De Trafford, H. F.	1841	Forwood, Dudley B.	1895
Denys, Fras. C. E...	1813	Foster, Aug. Vere...	1831
Dering, Hy. Nevill	1626	Foster, William ...	1838
Dilke,Rt.Hon.Chas.		Fothergill, R.Price...	1815
Wentworth, M.P.	1862	Fowke, Fredk. F. C.	1814
Dillon, John Fox ...	1801	Fowler, Thomas ...	1885
Dixie, Alex. B. C...	1660	Fowler, Jno.Edward	1890
Dodsworth, M.B.S.-	1784	Frankland, F. W....	1660
Domvile, Comp. M.	1815	Fraser, Keith A....	1806
Domville, Wm. C. H.	1814	Freake, Thos. Geo.	1882
Dorington, J.E.,M.P.	1886	Frederick, Chas. E.	1723
Douglas, Arthur P.	1777	Freeling, Harry ...	1828
Douglas, Geo. B. ...	1786	Frere, Bartle C. A.	1876
Douglas, Kenneth	1831	Fry, Theodore	1894
Doyle, Everard H...	1828	Gallwey, R. Payne-	1812
D'Oyly, Chas. W....	1663	Gamble, David, C.B.	1897
Drake, F. G. F.-E.-	1821	Geary, Wm. N. M.	1782
Drummond, J. W.-	1828	Gibbes, E. Osborne-	1774
Dryden, Alf. E......	1733	Gibbons, Charles ...	1752

Name	Date
Gilbey, Walter	1893
Gilmour, John	1897
Gladstone, John R.	1846
Glyn, Gervas Powell	1759
Glyn, Richard Geo.	1800
Goldney, Gabriel	1880
Gooch, Thos. Vere S.	1746
Gooch, Daniel F.	1866
Goold, Jas. Stephen	1801
Gordon, C. E. Duff	1813
Gordon, L. E. Smith-	1838
Goring, Harry Y.	1627
Grace, Percy R.	1795
Græme, G. E. W. H.-	1783
Graham, R. J. Stuart	1629
Graham, Regd. Hy.	1662
Graham, Rich. Jas.	1783
Grant, Geo. M'Ph.-	1838
Green, Edward	1886
Greenall, Gilbert	1876
Gresley, Robert	1611
Grey, Edward	1814
Griffith, Rich. J.W.-	1858
Grogan, Edw. Ion B.	1859
Grove, Walter Jno.	1874
Guise, Wm. F. Geo.	1783
Gull, Wm. C., M.P.	1872
Gunning, Geo. Wm.	1778
Haggerston, John de Marie	1643
Hamilton, Edw. A.	1776
Hamilton, Chas. E.	1892
Hammick, St. V. A.	1834
Hampson, Geo. F.	1642
Hanham, Jno. Alex.	1667
Hanmer, Wnd. C. H.	1774
Hanson, Reginald, M.P.	1887
Hardinge, Edmd. S.	1801
Hardy, Reginald	1876
Hare, Geo. R. Leigh	1818
Harington, Richd.	1611
Hart, Robt., G.C.M.G.	1893
Hartland, F.D.-,M.P.	1892
Hartopp, Chas. E.C.-	1796
Hartwell, Fras. H.	1805
Harty, Robert	1831
Harvey, Charles	1868
Harvey, Robert G.	1868
Hawkins, Rev. J. C.	1778
Hawley, Hen. Mich.	1795
Hay, Rt.Hn.J.C.D.-	1798
Hayter, Rt.Hn.A.D.	1858
Hazlerigg, A. Grey	1622
Head, Robert G.	1838
Heathcote, Wm. P.	1733
Henniker, B. Powell	1813
Hepburn, Arch. B.-	1815
Herschel, Wm. Jas.	1838
Hesketh,Thos.G.F.-	1761
Hewett, Harald G.	1813
Heygate, Fredk. G.	1831
Heywood, Arth. P.	1838
Hingley, Benjamin	1893
Hoare, Henry H. A.	1786
Hoare, Samuel, M.P.	1899
Hobhouse, Chas. P.	1812
Holden, Angus,M.P.	1893
Holder, Jno. Chas.	1898
Honyman,Rv.W.M.	1804
Honywood, Jno. W.	1660
Hood,A.F.-A-.,M.P.	1809
Hornby, W. H., M.P.	1899
Hort, Fenton Josiah	1767
Hoskyns, Rev. J. L.	1676
Hoste, Wm. H. C.	1814
Houldsworth,W.H., M.P.	1887
Hughes,A.Collgwd.	1773
Hulse, Edward Hy.	1739
Humphery, Wm. H.	1868
Hunt, F.Seager	1892
Hunter, Chas. Rod.	1812
Ingilby, Henry Day	1866
Ingram, Wm. Jas.	1893
Isham, Charles E.	1627
Jackson, Keith G.	1815
Jackson, H.Mather-	1869
Jaffray, John	1892
James,J.KingstonF.	1823
Jardine, Robert	1885
Jejeebhoy, Jamsetj.	1857
Jenkinson, Geo. B.	1661
Jenner, Walt. K. W.	1868
Jephson, S. W., C.B.	1815
Jervoise, Art. H. C.-	1813
Jessel, Charles Jas.	1883
Jodrell, Alfred	1783
Johnson, Wm. G.	1755
Johnson, Hy. A. W.	1818
Joicey, James, M.P.	1893
Jones, Lawrence J.	1831
Jones, Phil. Burne-	1894
Kay, Brook	1803
Kaye,Jno.P.Lister-	1812
Keane, John	1801
Kelk, John William	1874
Kellett, Wm.	1801
Kemp, Kenneth H.	1642
Kennard, C. A. F.	1891
Kennaway, Rt.Hon. J. H., M.P.	1791
Kennedy, J. Chas.	1836
Key, Kingsmill G.	1831
Kinahan, Edwd.H.-	1887
King,DudleyG.Alan Duckworth-	1792
King, Gilbert	1815
King, Charles S.	1821
King, James	1888
Kinloch,J.G.S.,M.P.	1873
Kitson, James, M.P.	1886
Knatchbull,Wndm.	1641
Knightley,Chs.Val.	1798
Knill, Ald. John	1893
Knowles, Chas. G.F.	1765
Lacon,Edm.B.F.H.	1818
Lake, St. Vincent A.	1711
Lamb, Archibald	1795
Lambert, H. Foley	1711
Lampson, Curtis G.	1866
Langham, Herb. H.	1660
Larcom, T. Perceval	1868
Laurie, Rev. J. R.	1834
Lawes, John Bennet	1882
Lawrence, Henry W.	1858
Lawrence, Jas. J.T.	1867
Lawrence, Edwin Durning-, M.P.	1898
Lawson, Edward	1892
Lawson, John	1841
Lawson, Wilfd.,M.P.	1831
Lea, Thomas, M.P.	1892
Lechmere, Edm. A.	1818
Leeds, Edwd. T.	1812
Lees, Harcourt Jas.	1804
Lees, Elliott, M.P.	1897
Legard, Charles	1660
Leighton, Bryan B.	1693
LeMarchant,Hy. D.	1841
Lennard, Thos. B-.	1801
Lennard,J.Farnaby	1880
Leslie, John	1375
Lethbridge, W. A.	1804
Lewis, Herbert E. F.	1846
Lewis, Wm. Thos.	1896
Leyland, Albert E. H. Naylor-	1895
Lindsay, Coutts	1821
Llewelyn, John Talbot Dillwyn-, M.P.	1890
Lloyd, M. Owen M.	1363
Lockhart,Simon M.	1806
Locock, Chas. Bird.	1857
Loder, Edmd. Giles	1887
Lopes, Rt. Hon. M.	1805
Loraine, Lambton	1664
Louis, Charles	1806
Lowther, Chas. B.	1824
Lubbock, Rt. Hon. John, M.P.	1806
Lucas, Thomas	1887
Lushington, A.P.D.	1791
Lusk, Andrew	1874
Lyell, Leonard, M.P.	1894
Mac Cormac, Wm.	1897
Macdonald, A. K.	1813
MacGregor, Malcm.	1795
Macgregor, Wm. G.	1828
M'Grigor, Jas. R. D.	1831
M'Iver, Lewis, M.P.	1896
Mackenzie,Alex.M.-	1805
Mackenzie, Allan R.	1890
Mackworth, A. W.	1776
Maclure, J. W.,M.P.	1898
MacMahon, W. S.	1815
M'Mahon, Hor. W.	1817
Macnaghten, F.W.-	1836
Magnay, William	1844
Mahon, Wm. Henry	1819
Mainwaring, P. T.	1804
Maitland, J. N.	1818
Malet, Hen. Chas. E.	1791
Mansel, C. Cecil	1622
Maple, J. Blundell	1897
Mappin, F. T., M.P.	1886
Marling, Wm. Hen.	1882
Marriott, W. S.	1774
Martin, Rd. Bryan	1791
Martin,Rt.Hon.Rd.	1885
Matheson, Ken. J.	1882
Maxwell, J.M.Stirling-, M.P.	1707
Maxwell, Wm. Fr.	1804
Medlycott, Edwd.B.	1808
Menteth,Jas.Stuart	1838
Metcalfe, Chs. H. T.	1802
Meux, Hen. Bruce	1831
Meyrick,Geo.T.-G.-	1791
Meyrick, Thos. C.-	1880
Middleton, Arth. E.	1662
Milbank, P.C.J.,M.P.	1882
Milbanke, Peniston	1661
Mildmay, H. St. J.-	1772
Miles, Henry R. W.	1856
Millais,Jno.Everett	1885
Miller,Chas Jno. H.	1705
Miller, Wm. Frede.	1788
Miller, Jas. Percy.	1874
Milman, Francis J.	1800
Milne, Archibald B.	1876
Milner, F. G., M.P.	1717
Molesworth, L. Wm.	1689
Montagu, Sam.,M.P.	1894
Monteiore, Fras. A.	1886
Montgomery, G. G.-	1801
Montgomery, Hugh Conyngham G.	1808
Moon, Rev. Edw. G.	1855
Moon, Cecil Ernest.	1887
Mordaunt, Osbert	16.1
Morris, R. Armine	1806
Morshead,Warw.C.	1784
Mosley, Oswald	1781
Moss, J. Edwards-	1868
Mostyn, Pyers Wm.	1670
Mowbray,Robt.G.C.	1880
Muir, John	1892
Munro, Thomas	1825
Musgrave, Rich. G.	1611
Musgrave, James	1897
Nanney,HughEllis-	1897
Napier, W. Lennox	1867
Neave, Thos. L. H.	1795
Neeld,Algern. Wm.	1859
Nepean, Rev. E. Y.	1802
Newman,R.H.S.D.	1836
Newnes, George	1895
Nicholson, Charles	1859
Nightingale, H. D.	1628
Northcote, Hon. Hy. Stafford, C.B.	1887
Nugent, Edmd. Ch.	1806
Nugent, John	1831
Nugent, Walter R.	1831
Oakeley, C. W. A.	1790
Oakes, Reginald L.	1815
O'Brien, Tim. C.	1849
O'Brien,Rt.Hn.Peb.	1891
Ochterlony, D. F.	1823
O'Connell, D. R.	1869
Ogle, Henry Asgill	1816
O'Loghlen, Bryan	1838
Onslow, Wm. W. R.	1797
Orde, Arthur John Campbell-	1790
Osborn, Alg. Kerr B.	1662
Otway, Rt. Hn.A.J.	1831
Outram, F. Boyd.	1858
Owen,Hugh C.Owen	1813
Oxenden, Percy D.-	1678
Paget, James, M.D.	1871
Paget,Rt.Hn.Rd.H.	1886
Paget, Geo. Ernest	1897
Palmer,Rev.Lew.H.	1660
Palmer, A. Robert	1761
Palmer, C. M., M.P.	1886
Parker, Rev. W. H.	1681
Parker, Melville	1797
Parker, William B.	1844
Parkyns, T. M. F.	1681
Pasley, T. E. Sabine	1794
Paul,AubreyE.Dean	1821
Pearce, Wm. Geo.	1887
Pearson, W. D.,M.P.	1894
Pease, Jos. W., M.P.	1882
Pechell,S.G.Brooke-	1797
Peek, Cuthbert E.-	1874
Peel, Robert	1800
Peel, Theophilus	1897
Peirse, Hy. M. De la Poer Beresford-	1814
Pelly, Harold	1840
Pender, James, M.P.	1897
Perring, Rev. Philip	1808
Perrott, Herbert C.	1716
Petit, Dinshaw M.	1890
Peto, Henry	1855
Peyton, Alg. Fras.	1776
Phillips,Geo.Faudel Faudel-, G.C.I.E.	1897
Philipps, Rev. J. E.	1621
Philipps, Chs. E. G.	1887
Phillimore,W.G.F.	1881

Pigot, George...... 1764	Rycroft, Rd. Nelson 1784	Stokes, Geo. Gabriel 1889
Pigott, Charles R... 1808	Salomons, David L. 1869	Stonhouse, E. Hay. 1628
Pocock, Geo. F. C. 1821	Salt, Shirley Harris 1869	Stracey, Edwd. P... 1818
Pole, Edm. R.T. de la 1628	Salt. Thomas 1869	Strachey, Edward .. 1801
Pole, Cecil P. Van N. 1791	Samuel, Saul 1898	Strickland, Ch. W. 1641
Pollen, Richard H. 1795	Samuelson, Rt. Hn. B. 1884	Stronge, Jn. Calvert 1038
Pollock, Frederick 1865	Sanderson, J. S. B.- 1899	Stuart, Simeon H.L. 1660
Pollock, M. F. M.- 1872	Sassoon, Edwd. Albt. 1890	Stuart, Charles J... 1841
Poore, Richard 1795	Savory, Rv Borradaile 1890	Stucley, George S... 1859
Porter, Wm. Henry 1889	Savory, Joseph, M.P. 1891	Style, Wm. H. M. 1627
Pottinger, Henry ... 1840	Sawle, Chas. B. G.- 1836	Sullivan, Fras. Wm. 1804
Powell, R. Douglas 1897	Schröder, Baron ... 1892	Sullivan. Edward... 1881
Powell, F. S. 1892	Scott, Edw. Dolman 1806	Sutton, Rd. Vincent 1772
Power, John E. Cecil 1836	Scott, F. D. Sibbald 1805	Swinburne, John ... 1660
Power, Jno. Talbot 1841	Scott, Samuel Edw. 1821	Sykes, Henry......... 1781
Poynder, John P.	Scott, John M. 1899	Sykes, Tatton 1783
Dickson-, M.P. ... 1802	Scourfield, O. H. P. 1876	Synge, Fras. R. M. 1801
Prescott, G. L. L. B. 1794	Seale, John Henry 1838	Tancred, Thos. S.... 1662
Preston, Jacob 1815	Sebright, Edgar R. 1626	Tate, Henry 1898
Prevost, Charles ... 1805	Seely, Charles 1896	Tempest, Robert T. 1827
Price, Chas. Rugge- 1804	Seymour, M. Culme- 1809	Temple, Grenv. L. J. 1611
Price, R. D. Green- 1874	Seymour, Alb. V. F. 1863	Temple, Rt. Hn. Rd. 1760
Pryse, Pryse 1866	Shakerley, Walt. G. 1838	Tennant, Charles ... 1885
Pulley, Joseph 1893	Shaw, John C. K... 1665	Thomas, Godfrey V. 1694
Quilter, Cuthbert ... 1897	Shaw, Frederick W. 1821	Thomas, Geo. S. M. 1766
Radcliffe, Joseph P. 1813	Sheffield, B. D. Geo. 1755	Thompson, Thos. R. 1806
Ramsay, Alex. E.... 1806	Shelley, John......... 1611	Thompson, Henry
Ramsden, John W. 1689	Shelley, Charles...... 1806	M. Meysey-, M.P... 1874
Rankin, Jas., M.P. 1895	Shiffner, Rev. G. C. 1818	Thompson, Rev.Peile 1890
Rashleigh, Colman B. 1831	Shuckburgh, S.F. D. 1660	Thompson, Henry . 1849
Rawlinson, Hy. S... 1891	Shuttleworth, Rt.Hn.	Thornhill, Thomas 1885
Reade, Geo. Compton 1660	U. J. Kay-, M.P... 1849	Thorold, Jno. Hen. 1642
Reckitt, James 1894	Simeon, J. S. B., M.P. 1815	Throckmorton, N.W. 1642
Reid, Henry V. Rae 1823	Simpson, Jas. W. M. 1866	Thursby, John H. 1887
Reid, James, K.C.B. 1897	Sinclair, John G. T. 1785	Tichborne, H. A. D. 1624
Renals, Joseph 1895	Sitwell, George R. . 1808	Travers, Guy F.T.C.- 1804
Rhodes, Fred. Edw. 1776	Skipwith, Grey H.E. 1622	Trelawny, Wm. S.- 1628
Rich, C. H. Stuart 1791	Slade, Cuthbert...... 1831	Trevelyan, Walt. J. 1662
Riddell, Rodney S. 1778	Smijth, W. Bowyer- 1661	Trevelyan, Rt. Hon.
Ridley, Rt. Hn. Mat-	Smith, Charles C.... 1804	Geo. O. 1874
thew White, M.P. 1756	Smith, Wm. Syd. W. 1809	Troubridge, T. H. C. 1799
Ripley, Edward 1880	Smith, Thomas 1897	Tupper, Charles ... 1888
Ripley, Frederick... 1897	Smyth, John H. G. 1859	Twysden, Louis J. F. 1611
Roberts, Howland 1809	Smythe, John W..... 1661	Tyler, Fre lk. Chas. 1894
Robinson, F. V. L. 1660	Soame, Chas. B.-H.- 1662	Usher, John 1809
Robinson, G. W. C. 1819	Spearman, J. L. E. 1840	Vane, Henry R. ... 1785
Robinson, E. Wm.- 1823	Stamer, Rt. Rv.L.T. 1809	Vavasour, Hen. M. 1801
Robinson, Fredk. A. 1854	Stapleton, Miles T. 1679	Vavasour, Wm. E. 1828
Roche, David V. ... 1838	Stephen, Herbert ... 1891	Verdin, Joseph 1896
Rose, William 1872	Stepney, Emile A.	Verner, Edwd. W. 1846
Rose, Philip Fredk. 1874	Arth. K. Cowell- 1871	Verney, Edmd. H... 1818
Rowley, Joshua T. 1786	Steuart, A.H.Seton- 1815	Vernon, Hy. Foley 1885
Rowley, Geo. C. E. 1836	Stewart, John M..... 1803	Vincent, William ... 1620
Rumbold, Rt. Hn. H. 1779	Stewart, Donald M. 1881	Vyvyan, Rev. V. D. 1645
Rushout, Chas. H. 1809	Stewart, M.M'T.-, M.P 1892	Wake, Herewald ... 1621
Russell, George, A.C. 1812	Stirling, Walter G. 1800	Wakeman, Offley .. 1828
Russell, William ... 1832	Stockenström, G. H. 1840	Walker, GeorgeF.F.- 1835

Walker, Baldwin W. 1856		
Walker, Jas. Heron 1868		
Walker, Pet. Carlaw 1886		
Walker, Fras. Ernest 1815		
Walrond, Rt. Hon.		
W. H., M.P. 1876		
Walsham,J.,K.C.M.G. 1831		
Warrender, George 1715		
Waterlow,SydneyH. 1873		
Watkin, Edw. Wm. 1880		
Watson, Wager Jos. 1760		
Watson, Arthur T. 1866		
Watson, John 1895		
Way,Rt.Hn.Saml.J. 1899		
Webster, Aug. F.W. 1703		
Webster, Richard... 1898		
Wedderburn,W.,M.P. 1803		
Welby, C. G. Earle 1801		
Wells, Arthur S. ... 1883		
Western,T.C.Callis 1864		
Wheler, Trevor...... 1660		
Whichcote, George 1660		
White, Thomas W. 1802		
Whitehead, James 1889		
Wigan, Fredk. 1898		
Wiggin,Henry Sam. 1892		
Wilks, Samuel 1897		
Williams,John,M.D. 1894		
Williams, Wm. G. 1798		
Williams, Wm.Rob. 1866		
Williamson, Hedw. 1642		
Willoughby, Jno. C. 1794		
Wills, Wm. H., M.P. 1893		
Wills, Frederick ... 1897		
Willshire, A. R. T. 1841		
Wilmot, Henry, V.C. 1759		
Wilmot, J. Eardley- 1821		
Wilmot, Robert R. 1772		
Wilson, S. Maryon- 1660		
Wilson, Hon. Ray-		
mond R. Tyrwhitt- 1808		
Wilson, Roland K. 1858		
Wilson, Mathew W. 1874		
Wilson, Alexander 1897		
Winnington, F. S. 1755		
Wiseman,W.G.Eden 1628		
Wolseley, Chas. M. 1628		
Wombwell, Geo. O. 1778		
Wood, Matthew ... 1837		
Wood, Lindsay 1897		
Worsley,Wm. H. A. 1838		
Wraxall,MorvilleN. 1813		
Wrey, Hn. B. Toke 1628		
Wynn, H.L.W.W.- 1688		
Young, William L. 1769		
Young, George 1813		
Young, W. M. Need 1821		

BARONETS OF SCOTLAND (AND NOVA SCOTIA) (88).

Abercromby, G. W. 1636	Campbell, J. Home-	Dalrymple,Wlt H.- 1698
Agnew, Andr. Noel 1629	Purves-Hume-. 1665	Dunbar, Uthred J.H. 1694
Anstruther, Ralph 1694	Campbell, James ... 1668	Dunbar, Drmnd. M. 1697
Anstruther, W. R.	Carmichael,Thomas	Dunbar, Archd. H. 1700
Carmichael- 1694	D. Gibson-, M.P. 1702	Eliott, Wm. F. A... 1666
Baird, Wm. Jas. G. 1695	Cathcart, Reg. A. E. 1703	Fergusson, Rt. Hon.
Bannerman, Geo.... 1682	Clerk, Geo. Douglas 1679	Jas., M.P............. 1703
Barclay, D. E. D.... 1668	Cuningham, A. E.	Forbes, William S. 1626
Broun, William ... 1686	Fairlie- 1630	Foulis, W. Liston- 1634
Bruce, W. Cuning-	Cuninghame,T.A.M. 1672	Gordon, Robert G. 1625
ham 1629	Cunyngham, Wm.	Gordon, Home B. 1631
Burnett, Thomas ... 1626	Dick- 1669	Gordon, William ... 1706
Campbell, Norman. 1628	Cunynghame, Fras.	Grant, Ludovic Jas. 1688
Campbell, John W. 1628	George Thurlow 1702	Grant, Arthur Hy. 1705
		Grierson, Alexr. D. 1685
		Halkett, Peter A.... 1697
		Hall, Basil Francis 1687
		Hamilton, F. H. A. 1646
		Hamilton, William
		Stirling- 1673
		Hay, D. Edwyn ... 1635
		Hay, Lewis John E. 1663
		Hay, Hector M. ... 1703
		Home, James......... 1671
		Hope, Alexander... 1628
		Innes, John 1628
		Jardine, William ... 1672
		Johnston, William 1626

BARONETS OF SCOTLAND (AND NOVA SCOTIA)—*continued.*

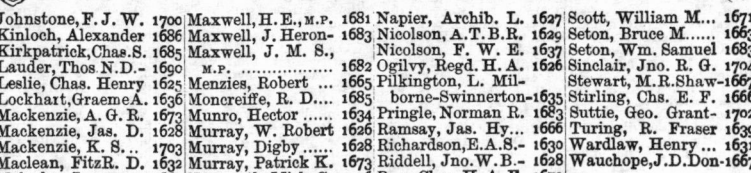

Johnstone, F. J. W.	1700	Maxwell, H. E., M.P.	1681	Napier, Archib. L.	1627	Scott, William M...	1671
Kinloch, Alexander	1686	Maxwell, J. Heron-	1683	Nicolson, A. T. B. R.	1629	Seton, Bruce M......	1663
Kirkpatrick, Chas. S.	1685	Maxwell, J. M. S.,		Nicolson, F. W. E.	1637	Seton, Wm. Samuel	1683
Lauder, Thos. N.D.-	1690	M.P.	1682	Ogilvy, Regd. H. A.	1626	Sinclair, Jno. R. G.	1704
Leslie, Chas. Henry	1625	Menzies, Robert ...	1665	Pilkington, L. Mil-		Stewart, M.R.Shaw-	1667
Lockhart, Graeme A.	1636	Moncreiffe, R. D....	1685	borne-Swinnerton-	1635	Stirling, Chs. E. F.	1666
Mackenzie, A. G. R.	1673	Munro, Hector	1634	Pringle, Norman R.	1683	Suttie, Geo. Grant-	1702
Mackenzie, Jas. D.	1628	Murray, W. Robert	1626	Ramsay, Jas. Hy...	1666	Turing, R. Fraser	1639
Mackenzie, K. S.	1703	Murray, Digby	1628	Richardson, E.A.S.	1630	Wardlaw, Henry ...	1631
Maclean, FitzR. D.	1632	Murray, Patrick K.	1673	Riddell, Jno.W.B.-	1628	Wauchope,J.D.Don-	1667
Malcolm, James ...	1665	Naesmyth, Mich. G.	1706	Ross, Chas. H. A. F.	1672	

BARONETS OF IRELAND (64).

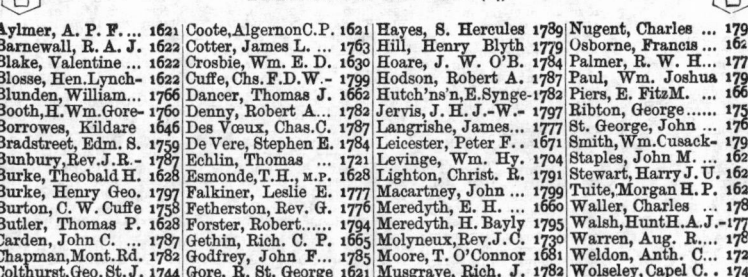

Aylmer, A. P. F. ...	1621	Coote, Algernon C.P.	1621	Hayes, S. Hercules	1789	Nugent, Charles ...	1795
Barnewall, R. A. J.	1622	Cotter, James L. ...	1763	Hill, Henry Blyth	1779	Osborne, Francis ...	1629
Blake, Valentine ...	1622	Crosbie, Wm. E. D.	1630	Hoare, J. W. O'B.	1784	Palmer, R. W. H. ...	1777
Blosse, Hen.Lynch-	1622	Cuffe, Chs. F.D.W.-	1799	Hodson, Robert A.	1787	Paul, Wm. Joshua	1794
Blunden, William...	1766	Dancer, Thomas J.	1662	Hutch'ns'n,E.Synge-	1782	Piers, E. FitzM. ...	1660
Booth, H.Wm.Gore-	1760	Denny, Robert A. ...	1782	Jervis, J. H. J.-W.-	1797	Ribton, George	1759
Borrowes, Kildare	1646	Des Vœux, Chas.C.	1787	Langrishe, James...	1777	St. George, John ...	1766
Bradstreet, Edm. S.	1759	De Vere, Stephen E.	1784	Leicester, Peter F.	1671	Smith, Wm.Cusack-	1799
Bunbury, Rev.J.R.-	1787	Echlin, Thomas ...	1721	Levinge, Wm. Hy.	1704	Staples, John M. ...	1628
Burke, Theobald H.	1628	Esmonde, T.H., M.P.	1628	Lighton, Christ. R.	1791	Stewart, Harry J. U.	1623
Burke, Henry Geo.	1797	Falkiner, Leslie E.	1778	Macartney, John ...	1799	Tuite, Morgan H.P.	1622
Burton, C. W. Cuffe	1758	Fetherston, Rev. G.	1776	Meredyth, E. H. ...	1660	Waller, Charles ...	1780
Butler, Thomas P.	1628	Forster, Robert......	1794	Meredyth, H. Bayly	1795	Walsh, HuntH.A.J.-	1775
Carden, John C. ...	1787	Gethin, Rich. C. P.	1665	Molyneux,Rev.J.C.	1730	Warren, Aug. R. ...	1784
Chapman, Mont.Rd.	1782	Godfrey, John F....	1785	Moore, T. O'Connor	1681	Weldon, Anth. C. ...	1723
Colthurst, Geo. St. J.	1744	Gore, R. St. George	1621	Musgrave, Rich. J.	1782	Wolseley, Capel C. .	1744

Knights Bachelors.

A LIST OF THE GENTLEMEN WHO HAVE RECEIVED THE HONOUR OF KNIGHTHOOD
(*Excluding those who have received the higher honour of the Bath, &c.*).

Ackroyd, Edward Jas.	1898	Bonython, John Langdon		Clarke, Ernest	1898	Duffey, Geo. Frederick	1897
Adam, Frank Forbes .	1890		1898	Clarke, Fielding	1894	Dumbell, Alured	1899
Agnew, Wm. Fischer .	1899	Booker, W. Lane	1897	Cochrane, Henry......	1887	Dunne, John	1887
Allen, John Campbell	1889	Boyd, Jno. Alexander	1899	Coll, Patrick, C.B.	1896	Eade, Peter, M.D.	1885
Altman, Albert Joseph	1894	Boyd, Thos. Jamieson	1881	Collins, Arthur J. H.	1885	Edgcumbe, E. R. P.—	1890
Anderson, Wm. John..	1890	Brady, Thos. Francis	1886	Collins, Rt. Hon. Rd. H.	1891	Edge, John............	1886
Armstrong, Walter ...	1899	Bridge, John	1890	Colnaghi, DominicEllis	1888	Edlin, Peter Henry ..	1888
Arnold, Arthur	1895	Bridge, Jno. F. MUS.D.	1897	Conway, Wm. Martin	1895	Edridge, Frederick T.	1897
Arrol, William, M.P. ..	1890	Brown, George T.,C.B...	1898	Cotton, George........	1897	Edwards, George Wm.	1888
Ashman, Rt. Hon. H..	1899	Brown, Wm. Roger ...	1887	Cotton, Wm. Jas. R. ..	1892	Ewart, Joseph, M.D. ..	1898
Bailey, William Henry	1894	Browne, Benj.Chapman	1887	Couch, Rt. Hon. Rich.	1866	Fairbairn, Andrew....	1865
Baker, John, M.P.	1895	Browne, Jas. Crichton	1883	Cox, William Henry..	1892	Fairfax, Jas. Reading	1898
Ball, Robert Stawell ..	1886	Bruce, Hon. Gainsford	1892	Craven, Rbt.M.,F.R.C.S.	1891	Falkner, Fred. R..q.o.	1890
Bancroft, Squire B. ..	1897	Bruce, George Barclay	1888	Crease, Henry P. P. ..	1896	Fanning, Rowland F.N	1886
Banks, W. Mitchell, M.D.	1899	Buckpill, Hon.Thos.T.	1899	Crookes,William, F.R.S.	1897	Fardell, T. George
Barnard, Herbert	1898	Bullard, Harry, M.P. ..	1887	Crosland, Joseph......	1892	M.P.	1897
Barnes, Hon. J. Gorell	1892	Burnside, Bruce L.....	1884	Cruise, Francis R.,M.D.	1896	Farmer, William	1891
Barrington,VincentK.-	1886	Burton, Frederic Wm.	1884	Crundall, William Hy.	1889	Farrant, Richard	1897
Barry, Jacob Dirk	1892	Burton, George Wm ..	1898	Cullinan, Fredc. Fitz-		Farrell, Thomas	1894
Barry, John	1899	Byrne, Edmd. Wm. ..	1897	james, C.B.	1897	Farrer, William James	1897
Bartlett,E. Ashmead-MP	1892	Caillard, Vincent		Currie, Edmund Hay	1899	Farwell, George......	1899
Bateman, Fredc., M.D.	1892	Henry P.............	1896	Cusack, Ralph Smith.	1873	Fenton, Myles	1889
Bayley, Lyttelton H.	1896	Cameron, Chas. Alex,		Cust, Reginald John..	1897	Findlater, William H.	1897
Bayliss, Wyke	1897	C.B.		Cuthbertson, John N.	1881	Finlay, Robt. B., q.c...	1895
Bell, William James ..	1892	Cameron, Rodk. Wm.	1883	Dalby, Wm. Bartlett	1886	Firth, Charles Henry.	1868
Bemrose, H. H., M.P.	1897	Canning, Samuel......	1866	Darling, Hon. Chas .J.	1897	Fischer, Hy.Chas.,C.M.G.	1898
Benjamin, Benjamin...	1889	Carrington, John W. .	1897	Davies, Matthew Hen.	1890	Fitch, Joshua G.......	1896
Berkeley, Hy. Spencer	1896	Casault, Louis Edel. N.	1888	Day,Hon.John Charles	1882	FitzGerald, Thos. N...	1897
Bertram, Geo. Clement	1895	Cayley, Richard	1884	De Wet, Jacobus P....	1883	Flannery, Jas. For-	
Besant, Walter	1895	Cayzer, Chas. W., M.P.	1897	Deane, Rt. Hon. Jas.		tescue, M.P.	1899
Bewley, Hon. Edmund		Chambers, Geo. Hen.		Parker	1885	Ford, Theodore Thos.	1888
Thos.	1894	Chambers, R. Newman	1897	Dease, Col. Gerald Rd.	1890	Forwood, Wm. Bower	1883
Bigham, Hon. John C.	1897	Channell, Hon. Arthur		Devereux, Joseph	1894	Foster, B. Walter, M.F.	1886
Binnie Alexr. R.	1897	M.	1897	Dias, Henry	1863	Fox, Charles Douglas	1886
Birt, William	1897	Charles, Arthur	1880	Dickeson, Richard	1886	Frost, Thos. Gibbons.	1885
Black, Samuel	1897	Charley, Wm. Thomas	1880	Dimsdale, J. Cockfield	1894	Frizelle, Joseph	1899
Blain, W. Arbuthnot	1897	Cheyne, John, q.c.	1896	Dixon, Daniel	1892	Fry, Rt. Hon. Edward	1877
Blaine Charles Fredk.	1890	Chubb, George Hayter	1885	Dixon, Rayrton	1890	Fulton, Forrest, q.c. ..	1892
Blaker, John George .	1897	Clarke, Campbell	1897	Drinkwater, Wm. L...	1897	Furley, John..........	1899
Bonser, John Winfield	1894	Clarke, Edw., q.c., M.P.	1886	Duckworth, Dyce	1886	Furness, Christopher.	1895

Galsworthy, Edwin H.   1887
Galt, Thomas   1888
Garrod, Alfred Baring   1887
Garth, Rt. Hn. Richd.   1875
Gaunt, Edwin   1887
Geddes, Wm. Duguid.   1892
Geikie, Archibald   1891
Gell, James   1877
Gilbert, J. Henry, F.R.S.   1893
Gillespie, John   1883
Gillespie, Robert   1891
Gilman, Charles R. ..   1897
Godson, Aug. Fredk. ..   1898
Goldney, J. Tankerville   1893
Goldsmith, *Staff-Capt.*
   William Burgess, R.N.   1897
Gorst, Rt. Hon. John
   Eldon, Q.C., M.P.   1885
Gourley, *Col.* E. T., M.P.   1895
Gowers, William R., M.D.   1897
Grantham, Hon Wm.   1886
Griffith, Wm. Brandford   1848
Grunlinton, John Joseph   1894
Grove, George   1883
Grubb, Howard   1887
Guinness, Reginald
   R. B.   1897
Gunn, John   1858
Haden, Fras. Seymour   1894
Hagarty, J. Hawkins   1897
Hamond, Chas E. M., M.P.   1896
Hannen, Nicholas J. ..   1895
Harben, Henry   1897
Harcourt Rt. Hon. W.
   Vernon-, Q.C., M.P. ..   1873
Hardy, Hon. H. H.
Cozens-   1839
Harris, George David   1888
Harris, James Charles   1896
Harris, Matthew   1899
Hart, Israel   1895
Harwood, John James   1888
Haslam, Alfred Seale.   1891
Haslett, Jas. H., M.P.   1897
Hay, Fras Ringler
   Drummond-   1881
Henderson, James   1899
Henderson, William ..   1893
Herron, Robert   1891
Hickman, Alfred, M.P.   1891
Hingston, Hn. W. H.,
   M.D.   1895
Hocking, Hy. Hicks..   1895
Hogg, Stuart Saunders   1876
Howard, A. Chas., C.B.   1897
Howard, Frederick ..   1897
Howard, Richard N...   1886
Hughes, Thomas   1898
Hunter, Robert   1894
Hutchinson, Joseph T.   1896
Hutton, John   1894
Irving, Henry B.   1895
Isaacs, Henry Aaron.   1889
Jackson, John   1895
Jackson, Robert Wm.   1882
Jackson, Thomas   1859
Jehanghir, Cowasjee..   1895
Jenkins, John J., M.P.   1882
Jenkins, Lawrence
   Hugh   1899
Jephson, *Capt.* A., R.N.   1897
Johnson, John Henry   1874
Johnson, Samuel Geo.   1897
Johnston, John B.   1899
Jones, Pryce Pryce-   1887
Jones, W. H. Quayle ..   1892
Juta, Henry H., Q.c.   1897
Karslake, William W.,
   Q.C.   1889
Kaye, William Squire B.   1885
Kekewich, Hon. Arthur   1886
Kennedy, Hon. W. Rann   1892
King, William David..   1887
Kirby, *Lt.-Col.* Alfred
   Knight. Henry Edmd.   1897
Knox, Edward   1898
Kynsey, W. Raymond   1897
Lack, Henry Reader..   1897
Lacoste, Alexandre ..   1891
Laing, James   1897
Laird, William   1897

Lakeman, Stephen B.   1853
Lawrance, Hon. John C   1890
Law.ence, Edward   1892
Lawson, Charles Allen   1895
Le Moine, Jas. McP...   1887
Lecky, Thomas   1887
Leclézio, Eugène P. J.   1897
Lee, Edward   1872
Leech, Bosdin Thomas   1894
Leese, Jos. F., Q.C., M.P.   1895
Leigh, Joseph   1894
Leng, John, M.P.   1893
Leng, Wm. Christopher   1887
Lewes, Samuel Wm. S.   1886
Lewis, George Henry..   1893
Lewis, Saml., C.M.G. ..   1895
Lindley, Rt. Hon. N...   1875
Linton, Jas. Dromole   1885
Lipton, Thomas John-
   stone   1898
Littlejohn, H. D., M.D.   1895
Lloyd, Horatio   1867
Logan, C. Bowman ..   1899
Long, George Henry ..   1897
Low, James   1855
Ludlow, Henry   1830
Lushington, Franklin   1899
MacCabe, Fras Xav. F.   1892
M'Causland, Rich. B.   1856
MacCullagh, Jas. A.,
   M.D.   1896
McDonald, Andrew ..   1897
Macdonald, William
   C.   1899
Macfarlane, Donald H.   1894
M'Intyre, Hon. Alfred   1895
M'Kenna, Joseph N...   1867
Mackenzie, A.C., MUS.D.   1895
Mackenzie, Felix C. ..   1896
Maclagan, Douglas...   1886
Maclean, Andrew   1899
Magnus, Philip   1886
Malcolm, Ormond D.,
   Q.C.   1898
Mance, Henry Christr.   1897
Manning, William Pat.   1894
Marriott, Right Hon.
   Wm. Thackeray, Q.C.   1888
Marshall, Anthony ..   1899
Marshall, *Col.* Arthur
   W.   1898
Marten, Alfred G., Q.C.   1895
Martin, George C   1895
Martin, (Thos.) Acquin   1895
Marwick, James David   1888
Mason, George Charles   1895
Mathew, Hon. Jas. Chas.   1881
Measom, Geo. Samuel   1897
Melvill, Wm. Henry .   1888
Meredith, James Creed   1890
Meredith, Wm. Ralph   1896
Micks, Robert   1894
Miller, Alex. Edward.   1895
Miller, William   1876
Milward, Christ. A. ..   1897
Mitter, RomeshChunder   1890
Moffett, Thos. Wm. ..   1896
Monckton, John B. ...   1880
Montefiore, Jos. Sebag-   1896
Moore, John Voce   1894
Moore, *Lt.-Col.* Geo. M.   1897
Morel, Thomas   1897
Morris, Lewis   1895
Mottram, Richard   1897
Moyers, George   1887
Mure, Andrew   1899
Murton, Walter, C.B..   1892
Nathan, Gustavus   1891
Naudi, Salvatore   1878
Neligan, James C.   1899
Nepean, Evan C., C.B..   1897
Nicholson, Richard...   1896
Nickalls, Patteson ...   1893
Nixon, Christopher J..   1895
North, Hon. Ford   1881
Oakel y, Hy. Evelyn   1896
Oakeley, Herbert S. ..   1876
Oakley, Henry, G.N.R   1892
O'Farrell, Geo. Plunkett   1899
Ogg, Wm. Anderson ..   1896
Oldfield, Richd. Chas.   1882
Oldham, *Col.* Henry ..   1897

O'Malley, Edwd. L. ..   1892
Onmanney, *Adm.* E...   1877
Onslow, Alex. Campb.   1880
Oppenheimer, Charles   1892
O'Rorke, Hn. Geo.
Maurice   1880
Paine, Thomas   1882
Parker, Geo. Arth   1896
Parratt, Walter   1892
Parry, Charles Hubert   1895
Paton, Joseph Noel ...   1867
Pearson, Right Hon.
   Charles Jno. (Lord P.)   1887
Penrose, George D. ...   1896
Perkins Frederick   1873
Petheram, Wm. Comer   1884
Phear, John Budd   1877
Phillipp, George   1882
Pile, George Clarke...   1893
Pilkington, Geo. A., M.P.   1843
Pink, William   1897
Pitman, Henry Alfred   1883
Playfair, Patrick, C.I.E.   1897
Plowden, Hy. Meredyth   1895
Poland, Harry Bodkin,
   Q.C.   1895
Pollitt, William   1899
Poole, James   1887
Powell, Francis   1893
Poynter, Edward John,
   P.R.A.   1896
Prendergast, James ..   1887
Prideaux, Walter S. ..   1893
Priestley, William
   Overend, M.D.   1893
Pringle, George   1882
Prinsep, Hy. Thoby ..   1894
Puleston, John Henry   1887
Pullar, Robert   1895
Pyne, Thos. Salter   1894
Radcliffe, David   1886
Rainals, Hy. Thos. A.   1882
Ramaswami Mudaliar,
   Rajah, C.I.E.   1887
Raper, Robert George   1886
Rattigan. Wm. Henry   1895
Rayner, Thos. Crossley   1888
Reeves, Wm. Conrad.   1889
Reid, Edward   1868
Reid, George, P.R.S.A.   1891
Reid, Hugh Gilzean- ..   1893
Reid, Thomas Wemyss   1894
Rennie, Richard T. ...   1884
Renwick, Hon. A., M.D.   1894
Richardson, Thos. M.P.   1897
Richmond, Hon. David   1883
Ridley, Hon. Edward   1897
Rigby, Rt. Hon. John   1892
Ritchie, Ald. James T.   1897
Roberts, Owen   1888
Robertson, Henry Beyer   1897
Robinson, John Chas.   1888
Robinson, John Richd.   1893
Roe, Chas. Arthur   1897
Roe, Thomas   1894
Rogers, Robert H.   1897
Rolleston, John F. L.   1897
Rollit, Albert Kaye,
   M.P.   1885
Romer, Rt. Hn. Robert   1890
Roscoe, Henry Enfield   1884
Ross, *Col.* Edwd. Chas.   1897
Rotton, John Francis,
   Q.C.   1899
Russell, Edward Rd...   1893
Russell, James Alex.   1894
Russell, Wm. Howard.   1895
Salomons, Julian E. ..   1891
Samuel, Marcus   1898
Sandison, Alfred   1897
Sargent, Charles   1898
Sarle, Allen Lanyon ..   1895
Saunders, Edwin   1883
Sawyer, James, M.D...   1885
Scholfield, Henry   1897
Scotland, Colley H....   1861
Scott, John Harley ...   1892
Scotter, Charles   1895
Selfe, His Hon. Wm. L.   1897
Semon, Felix   1897
Sexton, Ald. Robert ..   1892

Shenton, Hon. George   1863
Sibbald, John   1899
Sieveking, Edward H..   1886
Simpson, Henry L. ...   1887
Skelton, Chas. Thomas   1897
Slacke, *Capt.* Owen R.   1897
Smith, Rt. Hon. Archi-
   bald Levin   1883
Smith, Clarence   1895
Smith, Hon. F. Ville-
   neuve   1862
Smith, Hon. F. (Canada)   1894
Smith, George John ..   1897
Smith, James   1897
Smith, John Smalman   1896
Smith, Swire   1898
Smith, Wm. James ...   1896
Smyly, PhilipCrampton   1892
Snowden, Hon. Arthur   1895
Soundy, John Thos. ..   1899
Spokes, Peter   1872
Stainer, John, MUS.D..   1888
Steere, James G. Lee..   1888
Stephenson, Henry ...   1887
Stewart, David   1896
Stewart, Thos. G., M.D.   1894
Stirling, Hon. James..   1886
Stoker, W. Thornley,
   M.D.   1895
Stokes, William, M.D..   1886
Stone, John Benj., M.P.   1892
Strachey, Arthur   1899
Straight, Douglas, LL.D.   1892
Strong, Rt. Hon. S. H.   1893
Sullivan, Arthur S. ..   1883
Symes, Robert Henry.   1893
Szlumper, Jas. W., C.E.   1894
Ta'terna, L. Alma   1899
Tagore, Raja Sourindro
   Mohun   1884
Tait, Melbourne McT.   1897
Tangye, Richard   1894
Taylor, Robert Alex...   1899
Taylor, Thomas W. ..   1897
Tenniel, John   1893
Thompson, James   1897
Thomson, William, M.D.   1890
Thornton, Thomas ...   1894
Thuillier, *Gen.* H. E. L.   1879
Thynne, Henry, C.B. ..   1898
Trevor, Ch. Cecil, C.B.   1895
Tuke, John Batty, M.D.   1898
Turner, Llewelyn   1870
Turner, William   1886
Turney, John   1889
Tyler, Henry Whatley   1877
Tyler, John William..   1888
Vance, *Lt.-Col.* H. P.   1897
Vaughan, James   1897
Vezin, Arthur Edward   1898
Vine, John R. Somers   1888
Wade, Willoughby, M.B.   1896
Walpole, Charles Geo.   1897
Wardle, Thomas   1897
Waring, Henry John..   1891
Watson, Henry Edm.   1896
Watson, William   1897
Watson, Wm. Renny..   1892
Weber, Hermann   1899
White, Henry Arthur   1897
Whitney, Benjamin ..   1897
Whittall, Jas. William   1893
Williams, Edward L...   1894
Williams, Geo., Y.M.C.A.   1894
Williams, Hn. Hartley   1894
Williams, Rt. Hon. R.
L. B. Vaughan   1890
Willis, William   1885
Willox, Jno. A., M.P..   1897
Wills, Hon. Alfred....   1884
Wilson, Alexander   1887
Wilson, Jacob   1889
Wood, Henry Trueman   1890
Woodhouse, James T..   1895
Wragg, Walter Thos...   1891
Wrenfordsley, Hen. T.   1883
Wright, Hon. R. Samuel   1890
Wright, Thomas   1893
Wyatt, Richard Henry   1883
Wycherley, George Jos.   1885
Young, Allen William,
   C.B.   1877

HER MAJESTY QUEEN VIC-
TORIA, EMPRESS OF INDIA
(May 24, 1819) 81

90 YEARS AND UPWARDS.

Armstrong, Lord 90
Blount, Sir Edwd. C., K.C.B. ...91
Daubeney, Gen. Sir H., G.C.B. 90
De Verteuil, Sir L. A. A 93
Farquhar, Sir Walt. R., Bart....90
Gwydyr, Lord 90
Halliday, Sir Fredk. J., K.C.B. 94
Jephson, M.-Gen. Sir S. W., Bt.90
Keppel, Admiral of the Fleet,
  Hon. Sir H., G.C.B. 91
Lusk, Sir Andrew, Bart....... 90
McCausland, Sir Richd. B. ... 90
Mildmay, Sir H. St. J.-, Bt....90
Nicholson, Sir Chas., Bart. 92
Perth and Melfort, Earl of 93
Pitman, Sir Henry A., M.D.... 92
Southey, Hon. Sir R., K.C.M.G. 92
Stransham, Gen. Sir A.B.,G.C.B.95
Tankerville, Earl of 90
Wood, Sir Richard, G.C.M.G. ...94
Youl, Sir James A., K.C.M.G. ...90

85 YEARS AND UPWARDS.

Abraham, Rt. Rev. Bishop......86
Acland, Sir H. W., Bart. 85
Adair, Sir Hugh E., Bart. 85
Agnew, Hon Sir J.W.K.C.M.G.85
Aylmer, Lord 85
Bridport, Gen. Viscount, K.C.B. 86
Brocklebank, Sir Thos., Bart.. 85
Bromby, Rt. Rev. Bishop 86
Bunbury, Rev. Sir J. R.-, Bt...87
Courtenay, Rt. Rev. Bishop . 87
Cowan, Sir John, Bart. 86
Cranbrook, Earl of, G.C.S.I. ...86
Davidson, Sir David, K.C.B. ...86
Deane, Rt. Hon. Sir Jas. P. .. 88
De Vere, Sir Stephen E., Bart. 88
Devon, Rev. the Earl of 89
Drinkwater, Sir Wm. L. 88
Drummond, Hon. Fras. Chas...85
Duckett, Sir Geo. F., Bart. 89
Elliot, Adm. Sir Geo., C.B.....86
Fanshawe, Adm. Sir E., G.C.B. 86
Farquhar, Adm. Sir A., K.C.B. 86
Field, Lord 87
Fitzwilliam, Earl, K.G. 85
Fournier, Count 86
Galt, Sir Thomas 85
Goldney, Sir Gabriel, Bart. ...87
Harty, Sir Robt., Bart. 85
Howland, Sir Wm. P. .. 85
Key, Sir Kingsmill G., Bart....85
Lawes, Sir Jno. B., Bt., F.R.S. 85
McKerlie, Col. Sir Jno. G. 85
Maclagan, Sir Douglas, M.D. ...88
Masham, Lord 85
Nicolson, Sir Fredk. W. E., Bt. 85
Norton, Lord, K.C.M.G............86
Ommanney, Adm. Sir E., C.B. 86
Paget, Sir Jas., Bart., F.R.C.S. 86
Saunders, Sir Edwin...........86
Seccombe, Sir Th. L., G.C.I.E. 83
Sexton Sir Robert...........86
Sotheby, Adm. Sir E. S., K.C.B. 88
Strachey, Sir Edwd., Bart.....88
Stronge, Sir Jno. C., Bart. ... 88
Stucley, Sir Geo. S., Bart. ... 88
Thuillier, Gen. Sir H. E. L. .. 86
Vaughan, Sir James........... 86
Vavasour, Sir Henry M., Bart. 86
Vigliani, Sir P. H., G.C.M.G......86

Watson, Sir Henry E. 85
Wilbraham, Gen. Sir R., K.C.B. 89
Wellesley, Adm. Sir G. G. 86

80 YEARS AND UPWARDS.

Adye, Gen. Sir Jno. M., G.C.B. 81
Aldenham, Lord 80
Allen, Sir Jno. C. 82
Alleyne, Sir Jno. G. N., Bart...80
Alston, Sir Fras. B., K.C.M.G ..80
Baker, Rev. Sir T. H. B, Bt....80
Beckles, Rt. Rev. Bishop 84
Bell, Sir Lowthian, Bart. 84
Berkeley, Sir Geo., K.C.M.G. ...81
Blantyre, Lord 82
Boyd, Sir Thos. J............ 82
Bradstreet, Sir Edwd. S., Bart. 80
Brampton, Rt. Hon. Lord ... 83
Bramwell, Sir Fredk. J., Bart. 82
Bridges, Sir Geo. T., Bart 82
Brooks, Sir Wm. Cunliffe, Bt. 81
Brownrigg, Sir Henry M. Bart. 81
Bruce, Rt. Hn. Sir H. H., Bt...80
Cambridge, H.R.H., Duke of..81
Campbell, Sir Jas., Bart. 81
Carter, Hon Sir F., K.C.M.G. ...81
Cashel, Rt. Rev. Bishop of....81
Chads, Adm. Sir Henry, K.C.B. 80
Chamberlain, Gen. Sir N.,G C.B 80
Chambers, Sir Geo. H...........84
Collet, Sir Mark Wilks, Bart...84
Colville of Culross, Lord, K.T...82
Cook, Sir Francis. Bart. 83
Couch, Rt. Hon. Sir Richd......83
Davenport, Sir Sml., K.C.M.G. .83
De Montalt, Earl 83
Devereux, Sir Joseph 84
Dickson, Gen. Sir C, G.C.B. .82
Dingli, Sir Adriano, G.C.M.G...83
Donnet, Sir J. J.L., K.C.B..... 84
Drysdale, Lt.-G. Sir W., K.C.B 81
Duff, Sir Chas. Gavan, K C.M.G. 84
Earle, Sir Thomas, Bart. 80
Edlin, Sir Peter H., Q.C. 80
Edwards, Sir Geo. W. 82
Elliot, Rt. Hn. Sir H. G., G.C.B.83
Farren, Gen. Sir Rhd T., K.C.B.83
Forbes, Gen. Sir John, K.C.B...83
Fortescue, Earl 82
Frost, Sir Thos. Gibbons 80
Garrod, Sir Alfred B., M.D......81
Garth, Rt. Hon. Sir Richd......80
Gaunt, Sir Edwin 82
Gilbert, Sir J. Henry...........83
Gillespie, Sir Robert 82
Gloucester, Lord Bishop of ...81
Goldsmid, Maj.-Gen. Sir F. ...82
Gort, Viscount 80
Grimthorpe, Lord 84
Grove, Sir George, C.B...........80
Haden, Sir Francis S. 82
Haines, Field-Marshal Sir
  Frederick Paul, G.C.B. 81
Hamond, Sir Chas. F., M.P.....81
Harleca, Lord 81
Heath, Adm. Sir L. G., K.C.B...82
Heath, R.-Adm. W.A.J., C.B....80
Hobhouse, Lord, K.C.S.I. 81
Hobhouse, Rt. Rev. Bishop ...83
Hodgson, Sir Arthur, K.C.M.G...82
Honyman, Rev. Sir W. M., Bt...82
Hooker, Sir Jos. D., G.C.S.I. ...83
Hope, Sir Alexander, Bart. 81
Hoskyns, Rev. Sir Jno. L., Bt...83
Howlett, Gen. Sir A., K.C.B. ...81
Innes,Srg.-G.Sir J.H K.,K.C.B. 80

Isham, Sir Chas. E, Bart. 81
Jaffray, Sir John, Bart. 82
Jenkins, Sir Jas., K.C.B. 82
Jermyn, Rt. Rev. Bishop 80
Julyan, Sir P. G., K.C.M.G. ...83
Kay. Sir Brook, Bart...........80
Keane, Lord 84
Kemball, Gen. Sir A.B., K.O.B...80
Kennedy, Lord David 80
Kerr, Gen. Ld. Mark. G.C.B. ... 83
Kilmore, Rt. Rev. Bishop of....80
Leach, Sir Geo. A., K.C.B. 80
Lennard, Sir Jno. F., Bart. ...81
Lingen, Lord, K.C B. 81
Liverpool, Lord Bishop of 84
Lockhart, Maj.-Gen. Sir G.A....80
Loftus, Rt.Hon.Ld.A., G.C.B...83
Lopes, Rt. Hon. Sir M., Bart. 82
Louis, Maj.-Gen. Sir C., Bart. 82
Luard, Adm. Sir W. G., K.C.B.80
McClintock, Adm. Sir F. L. ...81
Macdonald, Sir A. K. Bart. ...80
Macdonald. Adm. Sir R. J. ...80
McKenna, Sir Joseph Neale ...81
Martin, Sir Theodore, K.C.B....84
Measom, Sir George S. 82
Menzies, Sir Robert. Bart......83
Montreal, Rt Rev. Bishop of...80
Mountgarret, Viscount 84
Muir, Sir William, K.C.S.I......81
Munro, Sir Thos. Bart. 81
Newburgh, Earl of 82
Norman, Lt.-Gen. Sir H. R. ...82
Oranmore and Browne, Lord 81
Palmer, Rev.SirLewis H., Bt...82
Penzance, Lord 84
Power, Sir Wm. Jas.T., K C B. 81
Rainals, Sir Henry T A. ... 84
Randolph, Adm. Sir G G. 82
Reid, Gen. Sir Charles, G.C.B...81
Reid, Sir Edward 81
Rice, Adm. Sir Edwd. B., K.C B. 81
Richmond & Gordon, Duke of 82
Russell, Gen. Sir Ed L.K.C.S.I...82
Russell, Sir Wm. Howard 80
Rutland, Duke of, K.G. 82
Samuel, Sir Saul, Bart. 80
Samuelson, Rt. Hon. Sir B. ...80
Sawle, Sir C. B. Graves, Bt. ...84
Scotland, Sir Colley H. 82
Shea, Hon. Sir A., K.C.M.G. 82
Shiffner, Rev Sir Geo. C., Bt...81
Shute, Gen. Sir. C. C., K.C.B. ...84
Sieveking, Sir Edwd H., M.D...84
Simon, Sir John, K.C.B., F.R.S. 84
Smith, Hon. Sir F. Villeneuve 81
Stafford, Hn. Sir E. W., G.C.M.G. 80
Stair, Earl of, K.T. 81
Stokes, Sir G. Gabriel, Bart. ...81
Strachey, Lt.-Gn.Sir R.,G C S I 83
Strathcona & Mount Royal, Ld 80
Strickland, Sir Chas. W. Bart...81
Tate, Sir Henry, Bart. 81
Taylor, Gen. Sir R. C. H., K.C.B. 81
Tenniel, Sir John 80
Thompson, Sir Henry Bart. ...80
Thornton, Rt. Hn. Sir E., G.C.B. 83
Thring, Lord, K.C.B. 82
Vaughan, Gen. Sir J. L., K.C.B.80
Watkin, Sir Edwd. Wm. Bt......81
Waring, Sir Henry J. 83
Wemyss and March, Earl of ...82
Woods, Sir Albert W., K.C.B....84
Young, Sir Fredk., K.C.M.G......83
Young, Rt. Hon. Lord............81

the *Magnum Concilium* of the early chroniclers, consists of the Spiritual Lords of England (the 2 Archbishops and 24 Bishops), the Temporal Peers of England, Great Britain, and the United Kingdom, and, in addition, 16 Hereditary Peers of Scotland elected to each Parliament, and 28 Hereditary or created Peers of Ireland elected for life. A large number of Scottish and Irish Peers have English titles, by virtue of which they are entitled to a seat, and 2 of the elected Peers of Ireland (viz. the Lords de Montalt and Powerscourt) have, since their election, been created Peers of the United Kingdom. No Peer can take his seat if he be under age, of unsound mind, or bankrupt. The *full* Assembly would consist of 6 Princes of the Blood, 2 Archbishops, 22 Dukes, 22 Marquesses, 121 Earls, 30 Viscounts, 24 Bishops, 319 Barons, 16 Scottish and 28 (26 besides the 2 above) Irish Representative Peers: total 588. See WHITAKER'S PEERAGE, page 21, for complete table, showing numbers of Life Peers, Minors, &c. There are also 11 Ladies who are Peeresses in their own right (9 of England and the United Kingdom, and 2 of Scotland), whose titles and names are given at pages 129, 132.
b. signifies born; *s.*, succeeded; *m.*, married; *w.*, widower or widow; *div.*, divorced; *M.*, minor.

SPEAKER.—Hardinge Stanley, Earl of Halsbury, Lord High Chancellor of England £4,000
Chairman of Committees.—The Earl of Morley ....
Deputy Speakers.—The Earl of Cork and Orrery, K.P., and the Earl de Montalt. £2,500

PRINCES OF THE BLOOD (6).—*Style*, His Royal Highness the Duke of ——. *Addressed as*, Sir, or more formally, May it please your Royal Highness.

1841	Albert Edward, Prince of Wales, Duke of Cornwall (1337), &c., *b.* 1841, *m.*		Eldest Son or Heir.
1866	Alfred Ernest Albert, Duke of Edinburgh, &c., *b.* 1844, *m.*		Duke of York, *b.* 1865
1874	Arthur William Patrick Albert, Duke of Connaught, &c., *b.* 1850, *m.*		(None).
1892	George Frederick Ernest Albert, Duke of York, &c., *b.* 1865, *m.*		Prince Arthur, *b.* 1883
1881	Leopold Charles Edward George, Duke of Albany, &c., *b.* & *s.* 1884, *M....*		Prince Edward, *b.* 1894
1801	George William Frederick Charles, Duke of Cambridge, &c., *b.* 1819, *s.* 1850., *w.*		(None)

ARCHBISHOPS (2).—*Style*, The Most Rev. His Grace the Lord Archbishop of ——. *Addressed as*, My Lord Archbishop; or, Your Grace.
Trans.

1896	*Canterbury*, Fredk. Temple, D.D., *b.* 1821. Consec. Bishop of *Exeter* 1869; *transl.* to London 1885.	
1891	*York*, William Dalrymple Maclagan, D.D., *b.* 1826. Consecrated Bishop of *Lichfield*, 1878.	

DUKES (22).—*Style*, His Grace the Duke of ——. *Addressed as*, My Lord Duke, or Your Grace. The eldest sons of Dukes and Marquesses take, by courtesy, their father's second title. The other sons and the daughters are styled Lord Edward, Lady Caroline, &c.

Created.		Family Name.	Heir Appar. or Presumpt.
1892	*Argyll*	G.D.Campbell, K.G., K.T.(*Sc.D.,Argyll*),*b.*'23,1stD.,*m.*	Marq. of Lorne, K.T., *b.* '45
1682	*Beaufort*............	Hy. A. W. FitzRoy Somerset, *b.* 1847, *s.* 1899, *m.*	Rt.Hn.Ld.H.Somerset,*b.*'49
1694	*Bedford*............	Herbrand Arthur Russell, *b.* 1858, *s.* 1893, *m....*	Marq. of Tavistock, *b.* 1888
1712	*Brandon*............	Alfred Douglas Douglas - Hamilton (*Scot. Duke, Hamilton*), *b.* 1862, *s.* 1895	Percy Seymour Douglas-Hamilton, *b.* 1875
1799	*Cumberland and Teviotdale*	Ernest Augustus W.A. G. F., K.G. (*Ir. Earl, Armagh*), *b.* 1845, *s.* 1878, *m.*	Earl of Armagh, *b.* 1880
1694	*Devonshire*	Spencer ComptonCavendish,K.G.,*b.*1833,*s.*1891,*m.*	Victor Cavendish,M.P.,*b.*'68
1889	*Fife*	Alexander William George Duff, K.T. (*Irish Earl, Fife*), *b.* 1849, 1st Duke, *m.*	
1675	*Grafton*	Aug. Chas. Lennox FitzRoy,K.G.,*b.*1821,*s.*1882,*w.*	(None)
1694	*Leeds*	G. G. Osborne (*S.Vis., Dunbiane*), *b.* 1862,*s.*1895, *m.*	Earl of Euston, *b.* 1848 [1864
1719	*Manchester*	Wm. Angus Drogo Montagu, *b.* 1877, *s.* 1892 ...	Lord Fras. Osborne,R.N., *b.*
1702	*Marlborough*	Chas.R.John Spencer-Churchill,*b.*1871,*s.*1892,*m.*	Ld. Chas. Montagu, *b.* 1860
1756	*Newcastle (u.Lyme)*	Henry P. A. Pelham-Clinton, *b.* 1864, *s.* 1879, *m.*	Marq. of Blandford, *b.* 1897
1483	*Norfolk*	Henry Fitzalan-Howard, K.G., *Earl Marshal*, *b.* 1847, *s.* 1860, *w.*	Lord Francis Hope, *b.* 1866
1766	*Northumberland* .	Henry George Percy, K.G., *b.* 1846, *s.* 1899, *m.* ...	E.of Arundel & Surrey,*b.*'79
1716	*Portland*............	W.J.Cavendish-Bentinck,G.C.V.O.,*b.*'57,*s.*'79,*m.*	Earl Percy, M.P., *b.* 1871
1675	*Richmond and Gordon* (1876)	Chas. H. Gordon-Lennox, K.G. (*Scot. Duke, Lennox*), *b.* 1818, *s.* 1860, *w.*	Marq. of Titchfield, *b.* 1893
1703	*Rutland*	John Jas. Robt. Manners, K.G., *b.* 1818, *s.* 1888, *w.*	Earl of March, *b.* 1845
1684	*St. Albans*	C. V. A. A. de Vere Beauclerk, *b.* 1870, *s.* 1898 ...	M. of Granby (a Peer) *b.*'52
1547	*Somerset*	Algernon St. Maur, *b.* 1846, *s.* 1894, *m.*	Lord O. Beauclerk, *b.* 1874
1833	*Sutherland*	Cromartie Sutherland-Leveson-Gower (*Scot. Earl, Sutherland*), *b.* 1851, *s.* 1892, *m.* ...	Lord Percy St. Maur, *b.*1847
1814	*Wellington*.........	Henry Wellesley (*Irish Earl, Mornington*), *b.* 1846, *s.* 1884, *m.*	Marq. of Stafford, *b.* 1888
1874	*Westminster*......	Hugh Lupus Grosvenor, K.G., *b.* 1825, 1st Duke, *m.*	Col. Lord Arthur Chas. Wellesley, *b.* 1849
			Viscount Belgrave, *b.* 1879

MARQUESSES (22).—*Style*, The Most Hon. the Marquess of ——. *Addressed as*, My Lord Marquess.

1790	*Abercorn*	James Hamilton, K.G., C.B. (*Irish Duke, Scot. Earl, Abercorn*), *b.* 1838, *s.* 1885, *m.*	Marq. of Hamilton, *b.* 1869
1876	*Abergavenny*......	William Nevill, K.G., *b.* 1826, 1st Marquess, *w.* .	Earl of Lewes, *b.* 1853
1821	*Ailesbury*	Hy. Aug. Brudenell-Bruce, *b.* 1842, *s.* 1894, *m.*	Earl of Cardigan, *b.* 1873
1831	*Ailsa*	Archibald Kennedy (*Scot. Earl, Cassillis*), *b.* 1847, *s.* 1870, *m.*	Earl of Cassillis, *b.* 1872
1815	*Anglesey*............	Henry Cyril Paget, *b.* 1875, *s.* 1898, *m.*	Chas. H. A. Paget, *b.* 1885

Created.	Family Name.	Eldest Son or Heir.
1789 *Bath*	Thomas Henry Thynne, *b.* 1862, *s.* 1896, *m.* ...	Visc. Weymouth, *b.* 1895
1885 *Breadalbane*	Gavin Campbell, K.G. (*Scot. Earl, Breadalbane*), *b.* 1851, 1st Marquess, *m.*	(None to English peerage)
1826 *Bristol*	Frederick William J. Hervey, *b.* 1834, *s.* 1864, *m.*	*Comm.* Fredk. Wm. Fane Hervey, R.N., *b.* 1863
1796 *Bute*	John Patrick Crichton-Stuart, K.T. (*Scot. Earl, Dumfries*), *b.* 1847, *s.* 1848, *m.*	Earl of Dumfries. *b.* 1881
1812 *Camden*	John Charles Pratt, *b.* & *s.* 1872, *m.*	Earl of Brecknock, *b.* 1899
1815 *Cholmondeley*	George Henry Hugh Cholmondeley (*Irish Viscount, Cholmondeley*), *b.* 1858, *s.* 1884, *m.*	Earl of Rocksavage, *b.* 1883
1888 *Dufferin & Ava.*	F. H.-Temple-Blackwood, K.P., G.C.B., G.C.S.I., G.C.M.G., G.C.I.E. (*Irish Baron, Dufferin & Clanehoye*), *b.* 1826, 1st Marquess, *m.*	Earl of Ava, *b.* 1863
1801 *Exeter*	Wm. Thos. Brownlow Cecil, *b.* 1876, *s.* 1898. ...	Ean Fras. Cecil, *b.* 1880
1793 *Hertford*	H. de G. Seymour (*I.B., Conway*), *b.* '43, *s.* '84, *m.*	Earl of Yarmouth, *b.* 1871
1784 *Lansdowne*	H.C.P.-Fitzmaurice, K.G., G.C.S.I., G.C.M.G., G.C.I.E. (*I. E., Kerry, S. B., Nairne*), *b.* '45, *s.* '66, *m.*	Earl of Kerry, *b.* 1872
1838 *Normanby*	Rev. Constantine Charles Henry Phipps (*Irish Baron, Mulgrave*), *b.* 1846, *s.* 1890	Geo. Alfred C. Phipps, *b.* 1875
1812 *Northampton*	William G. S. S. Compton, *b.* 1851, *s.* 1897, *m.*	Earl Compton, *b.* 1885
1871 *Ripon*	George Fredk. Samuel Robinson, K.G., G.C.S.I., C.I.E., *b.* 1827, 1st Marquess, *m.*	Earl De Grey, *b.* 1852
1789 *Salisbury*	Robert A. T. G.-Cecil, K.G., *b.* 1830, *s.* 1868, *w.* ...	Visc. Cranborne, M.P., *b.* 1861
1786 *Townshend*	James Dudley S. Townshend, *b.* 1866, *s.* 1899 ...	Chas. Townshend, C.B., *b.* '61
1551 *Winchester*	Augustus John Henry B. Paulet, *b.* 1858, *s.* 1887	Lord Henry Paulet, *b.* 1862
1892 *Zetland*	Lawrence Dundas, *b.* 1844, 1st Marquess, *m.*	Earl of Ronaldshay, *b.* 1876

EARLS (121).—Style, The Right Hon. the Earl of — . *Addressed as,* My Lord. The eldest sons of Earls take, by courtesy, their father's second title, the younger sons being styled the Hon. George, &c. The daughters, like those of Dukes and Marquesses, are called Lady Jane, &c. When the title and the surname are alike, the "of" is rarely used; but see WHITAKER'S PEERAGE, pp 8-9.

1682 *Abingdon*	Montagu Arthur Bertie, *b.* 1836, *s.* 1884, *m.* ...	Lord Norreys, *b.* 1860
1696 *Albemarle*	Arnold Allan Cecil Keppel, *b.* 1858, *s.* 1894, *m.* ...	Viscount Bury, *b.* 1882
1826 *Amherst*	William Archer Amherst, *b.* 1836, *s.* 1886, *m.*	Rev. Hon. P. Amherst, *b.* '39
1892 *Ancaster*	Gilbert Henry Heathcote-Drummond-Willoughby, *b.* 1830, 1st Earl, *m.*	Lord Willoughby de Eresby, *b.* 1867
1730 *Ashburnham*	Bertram Ashburnham, *b.* 1840, *s.* 1878, *m.*	Hon. J. Ashburnham, *b.* 1845
1714 *Aylesford*	Charles Wightwick Finch, *b.* 1851, *s.* 1885, *m.* ...	Lord Guernsey, *b.* 1883
1772 *Bathurst*	Seymour Henry Bathurst, *b.* 1864, *s.* 1892, *m.* ...	Lord Apsley, *b.* 1895
1815 *Beauchamp*	William Lygon, K.C.M.G., *b.* 1872, *s.* 1891 ...	Hon. E. Hugh Lygon, *b.* 1873
1679 *Berkeley*	Randal Mowbray Thos. Berkeley, *b.* '65, *s.* '88, *w.*	(None)
1815 *Bradford*	George C. Orlando Bridgeman, *b.* 1845, *s.* 1898, *m.*	Viscount Newport, *b.* 1873
1815 *Brownlow*	Adelbert W. B. Cust, A.D.C., *b.* 1844, *s.* 1867, *m.*	(None to Earldom)
1746 *Buckinghamshire*	Sidney Carr Hobart-Hampden, *b.* 1860, *s.* 1885, *m.*	Hn. C. Hob.-Hampden, *b.* '25
1800 *Cadogan*	Geo. Hen. Cadogan, K.G., G M P., *b.* 1840, *s.* 1873, *m.*	Visct. Chelsea, M.P., *b.* 1868
1878 *Cairns*	Herbert John Cairns, *b.* 1863, *s.* 1890	Hon. W. D. Cairns, *b.* 1865
1831 *Camperdown*	Robert A. H. P. Haldane-Duncan, *b.* 1841, *s.* 1867	Hon. G. A. H.-Duncan, *b.* '45
1661 *Carlisle*	George James Howard, *b.* 1843, *s.* 1889, *m.* ...	Viscount Morpeth, *b.* 1867
1793 *Carnarvon*	Geo. E. S. M. Herbert, *b.* 1866, *s.* 1890, *m.*	Lord Porchester, *b.* 1898
1895 *Carrington*	Charles Robert Wynn-Carrington, G.C.M.G. (*Irish Baron, Carrington*), *b.* 1843, 1st Earl, *m.*	Visct. Wendover, *b.* 1895
1814 *Cathcart*	A. F. Cathcart (*S.B., Cathcart*), *b.* 1828, *s.* 1859, *m.*	Lord Greenock, *b.* 1856
1827 *Cawdor*	Fredk. A. Vaughan Campbell, *b.* 1847, *s.* 1898, *m.*	Viscount Emlyn, *b.* 1870
1628 *Chesterfield*	Edwyn F. Scudamore-Stanhope, *b.* 1854, *s.* 1887	Hn. H.A.S.-Stanhope, *b.* '55
1801 *Chichester*	Walter John Pelham, *b.* 1838, *s.* 1886, *m.* ...	Rev. Hon. F.G. Pelham, *b.* '44
1776 *Clarendon*	Edward Hyde Villiers, A.D.C., *b.* 1846, *s.* 1870, *w.*	Lord Hyde, *b.* 1877
1850 *Cottenham*	Kenelm Chas. Edward Pepys, *b.* 1874, *s.* 1881 ...	Hon. Everard D. Pepys, *b.* '76
1697 *Coventry*	George William Coventry, *b.* 1838, *s.* 1843, *m.* ...	Visct. Deerhurst, *b.* 1865
1857 *Cowley*	Henry Arthur M. Wellesley, *b.* 1866, *s.* 1895, *div.*	Viscount Dangan, *b.* 1890
1718 *Cowper*	Francis Thomas De Grey Cowper, K.G. (*Scot. Baron, Dingwall*), *b.* 1834, *s.* 1856, *m.*	(None to Earldom)
1892 *Cranbrook*	Gathorne Gathorne-Hardy, G.C.S.I., *b.* 1814, 1st Earl, *w.*	Lord Medway, *b.* 1839
1801 *Craven*	Wm. George Robert Craven, *b.* 1868, *s.* 1883, *m.*	Visct. Uffington, *b.* 1897
1895 *Crewe*	Robt. O. A. Crewe-Milnes, *b.* 1858, 1st Earl, *m.*	(None)
1711 *Dartmouth*	William Heneage Legge, *b.* 1851, *s.* 1891, *m.* ...	Viscount Lewisham. *b.* 1881
1866 *Dartrey*	Vesey Dawson (*Irish Baron, Cremorne*), *b.* 1842, *s.* 1897, *m.* ...	Hon. Edward Stanley Dawson. *b.* 1843
1761 *De la Warr*	Gilbert G. R. Sackville, *b.* 1869, *s.* 1896, *m.*	Ld. Sackville, G.C.M.G., *b.* '27
1886 *De Montalt*	Cornwallis Maude (*Ir.V., Hawarden*), *b.* 1817, 1st Earl, *w.*	(None to Earldom)
1622 *Denbigh*	Rudolph Robert Basil Aloysius A. Feilding (*Irish Earl, Desmond*), *b.* 1859, *s.* 1892, *m.* ...	Viscount Feilding, *b.* 1885
1485 *Derby*	Frederick A. Stanley, K.G., G.C.B., *b.* 1841, *s.* 1893, *m.*	Lord Stanley, M.P., *b.* 1865
1553 *Devon*	Rev. Henry Hugh Courtenay, *b.* 1811, *s.* 1891, *w.*	Hn. Chas. P. Courtenay, *b.* '70

Created	Family Name.	Eldest Son or Heir.
1663 Doncaster	W.H.W.Mont.-Dougl.-Scott, K.G., K.T. (Sc. Duke, Buccleuch and Queensberry), b. 1831, s. 1884, m.	Earl of Dalkeith, M.P., b.'64
1837 Ducie	Henry John Moreton, b. 1827, s. 1853, w.	Lord Moreton, 1857
1860 Dudley	William Humble Ward, b. 1867, s. 1885, m......	Viscount Ednam, b. 1894
1833 Durham	John George Lambton, b. 1855, s. 1879, m.	Hon. F.W.Lambton, b.1855
1837 Effingham	Henry Alexr. Gordon Howard, b. 1866, s. 1898 ..	GordonF.H.Howard,b.1873
1897 Egerton of Tatton	Wilbraham Egerton, b. 1832, 1st Earl, m.	Hon. A. de T. Egerton, M.P., b. 1845 (to Barony)
1821 Eldon	John Scott, b. 1845, s. 1854, m.	Visct. Encombe, b. 1870
1846 Ellesmere	Francis C. Granville Egerton, b. 1847, s. 1862, m.	Viset. Brackley, b. 1872
1661 Essex	Geo. Devereux de Vere Capell, b. 1857, s. '92, m.	Viscount Malden, b. 1884
1711 Ferrers	Sewallis Edward Shirley, b. 1847, s. 1859, m......	Walter K. Shirley, b. 1864
1868 Feversham	Wm. Ernest Duncombe, b. 1829, 1st Earl, m.	Visct. Helmsley, b. 1879
1746 Fitzwilliam	Wm. Thos. S. Wentworth-Fitzwilliam, K.G. (Irish Earl, Fitzwilliam), b. 1815, s. 1857, w. ...	Visc. Milton, M.P., b. 1872
1789 Fortescue	Hugh Fortescue, b. 1818, s. 1861, w.	Visct. Ebrington, b. 1854
1841 Gainsborough ...	Chas. William Francis Noel, b. 1850, s. 1881, m.	Viscount Campden, b. 1884
1722 Graham	Douglas Beresford M. Ronald Graham, A.D.C., K.T. (Scot. Duke, Montrose), b. 1852, s. 1874, m.	Marq. of Graham, b. 1878
1833 Granville	Granville Geo. Leveson-Gower, b. 1872, s. 1891...	Hn.W.Leveson-Gower,b.'80
1806 Grey	Albert Henry George Grey, b. 1851, s. 1894, m...	Viscount Howick, b. 1879
1752 Guilford	Frederick George North, b. 1876, s. 1885	Dudley J. North, b. 1880
1898 Halsbury	Hardinge Stanley Giffard (Lord Chancellor), b. 1825, 1st Earl. m.	Viscount Tiverton, b. 1880
1754 Hardwicke	Albert Edward Yorke, b. 1867, s. 1897	Hon. J. M. Yorke, b. 1840
1812 Harewood	Henry Ulick Lascelles, A.D.C., b. 1846, s. 1892, m.	Viscount Lascelles, b. 1882
1742 Harrington	Chas. Augustus Stanhope, b. 1844, s. 1881, m....	Hn.F.W.W.Stanhope,b.'45
1809 Harrowby	Dudley Fras. Stuart Ryder, b. 1831, s. 1882, m...	Hon. Hy. D. Ryder, b. 1836
1772 Hillsborough	Arthur Wills J. W. Blundell Trumbull Hill (Irish Marquess, Downshire), b. 1871, s. 1874, m.	Earl of Hillsborough, b. 1894
1821 Howe	Richard William Penn Curzon-Howe, G.C.V.O., C.B., b. 1822, s. 1876, m.	Viscount Curzon, M.P., b. 1861
1529 Huntingdon	Warner Francis J. P. Hastings, b. 1868, s. 1885, m.	Hn. Osmond Hastings,b.'73
1885 Iddesleigh	W. Stafford Northcote, C.B., b. 1845, s. 1887, m.	Viscount St. Cyres, b. 1869
1756 Ilchester	Henry Edw. Fox-Strangways, b. 1847, s. 1865, m.	Lord Stavordale, b. 1874
1837 Innes	Henry John Innes-Ker (Scot. Duke, Roxburghe), b. 1876, s. 1892.	Lord Alastair Robt. Innes-Ker, b. 1880
1697 Jersey	Victor Albert George Child-Villiers, G.C.M.G. (Irish Viscount, Grandison), b. 1845, s. 1859, m.	Viscount Villiers, b. 1873
1866 Kimberley	John Wodehouse, K.G., b. 1826, 1st Earl, w.	Lord Wodehouse, b. 1848
1880 Lathom	Ed. Geo. Bootle-Wilbraham, b. 1864, s. 1898, m...	Lord Skelmersdale, b. 1895
1837 Leicester	Thomas William Coke, K.G., b. 1822, s. 1842, m.	Viscount Coke, b. 1848
1831 Lichfield	Thomas Francis Anson, b. 1856, s. 1892, m.	Viscount Anson, b. 1883
1626 Lindsey	Montague Peregrine A. Bertie, b. 1861, s. 1899, m.	(None)
1887 Londesborough ...	Wm. Hy. Forester Denison, b. 1834, 1st Earl, m.	Visct. Raincliffe, b. 1864
1807 Lonsdale	Hugh Cecil Lowther, b. 1857, s. 1882, m.	Hon. L. E. Lowther, b. 1867
1838 Lovelace	Ralph Gordon Noel Milbanke, b. 1839, s. 1893, m.	Hon. L. King-Noel, b. 1865
1880 Lytton	Victor Alexander Geo. Robert Lytton, b. 1876, s. 1891	Hon. Neville S. Lytton, b. 1879
1721 Macclesfield	George LovedenWm.Hy.Parker,b.1888,s.1895,M.	Hon. Cecil T. Parker,b.1845
1800 Malmesbury	James Edward Harris, b. 1872, s. 1899	Hn.Alex.Harris,b.'72 (twin)
1776 & 1792 Mansfield .	William David Murray (Scot. Viscount, Stormont), b. 1860, s. 1898	Hon. And. D. Murray, b.'63
1806 Manvers	Sydney Wm. H. Pierrepont, b. 1825, s. 1850, m.	Visct. Newark, M.P., b. 1854
1813 Minto	G.J.E.-M.-Kynynmond, G.C.M.G.,b.1845,s.1891,m.	Visct. Melgund, b. 1891
1815 Morley	Albert Edmund Parker, b. 1843, s. 1864, m......	Visct. Boringdon, b. 1877
1789 Mount Edgcumbe	WilliamHenry Edgcumbe,G.C.V.O.,b.1832,s.'61,w.	Visct. Valletort, b. 1865
1831 Munster	William Geo. FitzClarence, b. 1824, s. 1842, m...	Lord Tewkesbury, b. 1859
1805 Nelson	Horatio Nelson, b. 1823, s. 1835, m............	Visct. Trafalgar, b. 1854
1876 Northbrook	Thomas Geo. Baring, G.C.S.I., b. 1826, 1st Earl, w.	Viscount Baring, b. 1850
1801 Onslow	Wm. Hillier Onslow, G.C.M.G., b. 1853, s. 1870, m.	Viscount Cranley, b. 1876
1806 Orford	Robert Horace Walpole, b. 1854, s. 1894, m.	Clare H. Walpole, b. 1858
1551 Pembroke & Montgomery	(1605) Sid. Herbert, G.C.V.O., b.1853,s.1895,m.	Lord Herbert, b. 1880
1743 Portsmouth	Newton Wallop, b. 1856, s. 1891, m.	Hon. John F. Wallop, b.1859
1706 Poulett	(Claimed by Wm. T. T. and Wm. J. L. Poulett)	
1804 Powis	Geo. C. Herbert (Irish Baron, Clive), b.1862, s. 1891	Viscount Clive, b. 1892
1765 Radnor	William Pleydell-Bouverie, b. 1841, s. 1889, m....	Visct. Folkestone, M.P.,b.'68
1874 Ravensworth	Henry George Liddell, b. 1821, s. 1878, m.......	Hon. Atholl C. Liddell, b.'33
1801 Romney	Charles Marsham, b. 1841, s. 1874, m............	Visct. Marsham, b. 1864
1801 Rosslyn	Jas. Fras. H. St. Clair-Erskine, b. 1869, s.1890, m.	Lord Loughborough, b.'92
1861 Russell	John Francis Stanley Russell, b. 1865, s. 1878, m.	Hon.B.A.W. Russell, b.1872
1815 St. Germans	Henry Cornwallis Eliot, b. 1835 s. 1881, m.	Lord Eliot, b. 1885
1660 Sandwich	Edw. Geo. Henry Montagu, b. 1839, s. 1884	Hon. V. A. Montagu,b.1841
1690 Scarbrough	A.F.G.B.Lumley(I.V.,Lumley),b.1857, s. 84, m.	Hon. Oebert Lumley, b.'62

Created.	Family Name.	Eldest Son or Heir.
1883 Selborne	Wm. Waldegrave Palmer, *b.* 1859, *s.* 1895, *m.* ...	Viscount Wolmer, *b.* 1887
1672 Shaftesbury	Anthony Ashley-Cooper, *b.* 1869, *s.* 1886, *m.*...	Rt. Hon. E. M. Ashley, *b.*'36
1442 Shrewsbury and Talbot (1784) {	Charles Henry John Chetwynd-Talbot (*Irish Earl, Waterford*), *b.* 1860, *s.* 1877, *m.*	Viscount Ingestre, *b.* 1882 Hon. Lewis A. Milles, *b.*'56
1880 Sondes...............	George Edward Milles, *b.* 1861, *s.* 1894.	
1765 Spencer	John Poyntz Spencer, K.G., *b.* 1835, *s.* 1857, *m.*.	Rt. Hn. C. R. Spencer, *b.* 1857
1628 Stamford	William Grey, *b.* 1850, *s.* 1890, *m.*	Lord Grey of Groby, *b.* 1896
1718 Stanhope.........	Arthur Philip Stanhope, *b.* 1838, *s.* 1875, *m.*	Viscount Mahon, *b.* 1830
1821 Stradbroke	Geo. E. John Mowbray Rous, *b.* 1862. *s.* 1886, *m.*	Wm. John Rous *b.* 1833
1847 Strafford	Rev. Francis Edmund Cecil Byng, *b.* 1835, *s.* 1899, *m.*	Visc. Enfield, *b.* 1862
1786 Strange	John Jas. Hugh Henry Stewart-Murray, K.T. (*Scot. Duke, Atholl*), *b.* 1840, *s.* 1864, *m.*	[*b.* 1871. Marq. Tullibardine, D.S.O., Hon. J. K. E. Howard, *b.*'86
1603 Suffolk & Berks. (1626)	Henry M. Paget Howard, *b.* 1877, *s.* 1898 ...	
1714 Tankerville	Charles Bennet, *b.* 1810, *s.* 1859, *m.*	Lord Bennet, *b.* 1852
1822 Temple of Stowe	Wm. Stephen Gore-Langton, *b.* 1847, *s.* 1889, *m.*	Lord Langton, *b.* 1871
1823 Vane	Charles Stewart Vane-Tempest-Stewart, K.G. (*Irish Marq., Londonderry*), *b.* 1852, *s.* 1884, *m.*)	Viscount Castlereagh, *b.* 1878
1815 Verulam	James Walter Grimston (*Irish Visct., Grimston; Scot. Baron, Forrester*), *b.* 1852, *s.* 1895, *m.*)	Visct. Grimston, *b.* 1880
1729 Waldegrave	William Fredk. Waldegrave, *b.* 1851, *s.* 1859, *m.*.	Viscount Chewton, *b.* 1882
1759 Warwick & Brooke (1746)	Fras. R. C. Guy Greville, *b.* 1853, *s.* 1893, *m.*	Lord Brooke, *b.* 1882
1624 Westmorland	Anthony Mildmay Julian Fane, *b.* '59, *s.* 1891, *m.*	Lord Burghersh, *b.* 1893
1876 Wharncliffe	Francis John Montagu-Stuart-Wortley, *b.* 1856, *s.* 1899, *m.*	Visct. Carlton, *b.* 1892
1801 Wilton	Arthur Geo. Grey Egerton, *b.* 1863, *s.* 1898, *m.*...	Visct. Grey de Wilton, *b.* 1896
1628 Winchilsea & Nottingham (1681)	Henry Stormont Finch-Hatton, *b.* 1852, *s.* 1898, *m.*...	Visct. Maidstone, *b.* 1885
1859 Winton	George Arnulph Montgomerie (*Scot. Earl, Eglinton and Winton*), *b.* 1848, *s.* 1892, *m.*	Lord Montgomerie, *b.* 1880
1837 Yarborough	Chas. A. W. Anderson-Pelham, *b.* 1859, *s.* 1875, *m.*	Lord Worsley, *b.* 1887

VISCOUNTS (30).—*Style*, The Right Hon. the Viscount——. *Addressed as*, My Lord. The eldest sons of Viscounts and Barons have no distinctive title; they, as well as their brothers and sisters, are styled the Hon. Robert, Hon. Mary, &c.

1712 Bolingbroke & St. John (1715)	Rev. M. W. F. St. John, *b.* 1827, *s.* 1899, *m.*	Hon. Hy. P. St. John, *b.*'54
1868 Bridport	Alexander Nelson Hood, G.C.B. (*Irish Baron, Bridport*), *b.* 1814, 1st Viscount, *w.*	Hon. Arthur W. A. N. Hood, C.B., *b.* 1839
1835 Canterbury.........	Henry C. Manners-Sutton. *b.* 1839, *s.* 1877, *m.* ...	Hon. Henry F. W. Manners-[Sutton, *b.* 1879
1823 Clancarty	William Frederick Le-Poer-Trench (*Irish Earl, Clancarty*), *b.* 1868, *s.* 1891, *m.*	Lord Kilconnel, *b.* 1891
1718 Cobham	Charles George Lyttelton (*Irish Baron, Westcote*), *b.* 1842, *s.* 1889, *m.*	Hon. John Cavendish Lyttelton, *b.* 1881
1827 Combermere	Fras. L. W. Stapleton-Cotton, *b.* 1887, *s.* 1898, *M.*	Hon. R. S. G. S.-Cotton, *b.*'49
1899 Cromer	Evelyn Baring, G.C.B., G.C.M.G., K.C.S.I., C.I.E., *b.* 1841, 1st Viscount, *w.*	Hon. Rowland Thomas Baring, *b.* 1877
1886 Cross	Richard Assheton Cross, G.C.B., G.C.S.I., *b.* 1823, 1st Viscount, *m.*	Richard Assheton Cross, *b.* 1882
1897 Esher	Reginald Baliol Brett, C.B., *b.* 1852, *s.* 1899, *m.*..	Hon. Oliver Brett, *b.* 1881
1816 Exmouth	Edward Addington H. Pellew, *b.* 1890, *s.* 1899, *M.*	Hn. Wm. A. W. Pellew, *b.*'62
1720 Falmouth	Evelyn Edwd. T. Boscawen, C.B., M.V.O., *b.* 1847, *s.* 1889, *m.* (*also Baron Le Despencer*, 1264) ...	Hon. Evelyn Hugh John Boscawen, *b.* 1887
1814 Gordon	John Campbell Hamilton-Gordon, G.C.M.G. (*Scot. Earl, Aberdeen*), *b.* 1847, *s.* 1870, *m.*	Lord Haddo, *b.* 1879.
1849 Gough...............	Hugh Gough, *b.* 1849, *s.* 1895, *m.*	Hon. Hugh W. Gough *b.* 1892
1866 Halifax	Charles Lindley Wood, *b.* 1839, *s.* 1885, *m.*.......	Hon. E. F. L. Wood, *b.* 1881
1884 Hampden	Henry Robert Brand, G.C.M.G., *b.* 1841, *s.* 1892, *m.*	Hon. Thos. W. Brand, *b.* 1869
1846 Hardinge	Henry Charles Hardinge, *b.* 1857, *s.* 1894, *m.* ..	Hon. H. R. Hardinge, *b.* 1895
1550 Hereford	Robert Devereux, *b.* 1843, *s.* 1855, *m.*	Hon. R. C. Devereux, *b.* 1865
1842 Hill	Rowland Richard Clegg-Hill, *b.* 1863, *s.* 1895, *m.*	Hon. F. W. Clegg-Hill, *b.* 1866
1796 Hood	Francis Wheler Hood (*Irish Baron, Hood*), *b.* 1838, *s.* 1846, *m.*	Hon. G. A. A. Hood, *b.* 1868
1821 Hutchinson.........	John Luke George Hely-Hutchinson, K.C.M.G. (*Irish Earl, Donoughmore*), *b.* 1848, *s.* 1866, *m.*	Viscount Suirdale, *b.* 1875
1895 Knutsford	Henry Thurstan Holland, G.C.M.G., *b.* 1825, 1st Viscount, *m.*	Hon. S. G. Holland, *b.* 1855
1747 Leinster	M. FitzGerald (*I.D., Leinster*), *b.* '87, *s.* 1893, *M.*	Lord D. FitzGerald, *b.* 1888
1895 Llandaff	Henry Matthews, P.C., *b.* 1826, 1st Viscount......	(None).
1802 Melville	Henry Dundas, *b.* 1835, *s.* 1886, *m.*	Hon. C. S. Dundas, *b.* 1843
1895 Peel	Arthur Wellesley Peel, P.C., *b.* 1829, 1st Visct., *m.*	Hn. W. R. W. Peel, *b.* 1867
1873 Portman	Wm. Hy. Berkeley Portman, *b.* 1829, *s.* 1888, *w.*	Hon. E. W. B. Portman, *b.*'56
1801 St. Vincent	Carnegie Parker Jervis, *b.* 1855, *s.* 1885, obtd. div.	Hon. Ronald C. Jervis, *b.* 1859
1805 Sidmouth	William Wells Addington, *b.* 1824, *s.* 1864, *w.*	Hn. G. A. Addington, *b.* 1854
1721 Torrington.........	George Master Byng, *b.* 1886, *s.* 1889, *M.*	Hon. Sydney Byng, *b.* 1844
1885 Wolseley	Garnet Joseph Wolseley, K.P., G.C.B., G.C.M.G. (*Commander-in-Chief*), *b.* 1833, 1st Viscount, *m.*	Hn. Frances Wolseley, *b.* 1872

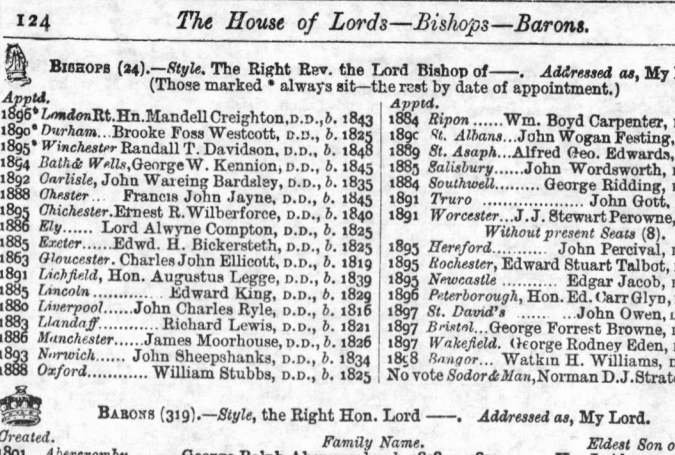

BISHOPS (24).—*Style.* The Right Rev. the Lord Bishop of——. *Addressed as*, My Lord.
(Those marked * always sit—the rest by date of appointment.)

Apptd.		
1896*	*London*..Rt.Hn.Mandell Creighton,D.D.,b. 1843	
1890*	*Durham*...Brooke Foss Westcott, D.D., b. 1825	
1895*	*Winchester* Randall T. Davidson, D.D., b. 1848	
1854	*Bath & Wells*,George W. Kennion, D.D.,b. 1845	
1892	*Carlisle*, John Wareing Bardsley, D.D., b. 1835	
1888	*Chester*.. Francis John Jayne, D.D., b. 1845	
1895	*Chichester*.Ernest R.Wilberforce, D.D., b. 1840	
1886	*Ely*.... Lord Alwyne Compton, D.D., b. 1825	
1885	*Exeter*......Edwd. H. Bickersteth, D.D., b. 1825	
1863	*Gloucester*. Charles John Ellicott, D.D., b. 1819	
1891	*Lichfield*, Hon. Augustus Legge, D.D., b. 1839	
1885	*Lincoln* .... Edward King, D.D., b. 1829	
1880	*Liverpool*....John Charles Ryle, D.D., b. 1816	
1883	*Llandaff* .... Richard Lewis, D.D., b. 1821	
1886	*Manchester*.... James Moorhouse, D.D., b. 1826	
1893	*Norwich*.... John Sheepshanks, D.D., b. 1834	
1888	*Oxford*............ William Stubbs, D.D., b. 1825	

Apptd.		
1884	*Ripon*......Wm. Boyd Carpenter, D.D., b. 1841	
189c	*St. Albans*...John Wogan Festing, D.D., b. 1837	
1889	*St. Asaph*...Alfred Geo. Edwards, D.D.,b. 1848	
1885	*Salisbury*......John Wordsworth, D.D., b. 1843	
1884	*Southwell*......... George Ridding, D.D., b. 1828	
1891	*Truro* .... John Gott, D.D., b. 1830	
1891	*Worcester*...J.J.Stewart Perowne,D.D.,b. 1823	
	Without present Seats (8).	
1895	*Hereford* .... John Percival, D.D., b. 1834	
1895	*Rochester*, Edward Stuart Talbot, D.D., b. 1844	
1895	*Newcastle* .... Edgar Jacob, D.D., b. 1844	
1896	*Peterborough*, Hon. Ed. Carr Glyn, D.D., b. 1843	
1897	*St. David's* .... John Owen, D.D., b. 1854	
1897	*Bristol*...George Forrest Browne, D.D., b. 1833	
1897	*Wakefield*. George Rodney Eden, D.D., b. 1853	
18c8	*Bangor*... Watkin H. Williams, D.D., b. 1845	
	No vote *Sodor&Man*, Norman D.J.Straton,D.D.1840	

BARONS (319).—*Style*, the Right Hon. Lord ——. *Addressed as*, My Lord.

Created.		*Family Name.*	*Eldest Son or Heir.*
1801	*Abercromby*	George Ralph Abercromby, b. 1838, s. 1852, m. .	Hn. J. Abercromby, b. 1841
1873	*Aberdare*	Henry Campbell Bruce, b. 1851, s. 1895, m.	Hon. H. L. Bruce, b. 1881
1835	*Abinger*	Jas. Yorke MacGregor Scarlett, b. 1871, s. 1892...	Shelley L. Scarlett, b. 1872
1869	*Acton*	J.E.E.Dalberg-Acton,K.C.V.O.,b.1834,1st Bar.,m.	Hn. R. M. D.-Acton, b. 1870
1887	*Addington*	Egerton Hubbard, b. 1842, s. 1889, m.	Hn.Jno.G.Hubbard, b.1883
1896	*Aldenham*	Henry Hucks Gibbs, o. 1819, 1st Baron, w.	Hon. A. Gibbs, M.P., b. 1846
1876	*Alington*	Henry Gerard Sturt, b. 1825, 1st Baron, m.	Hn. H. N. Sturt, M.P.,b.1859
1892	*Amherst of Hackney*	Wm. Amhurst Tyssen-Amherst, b. 1835, 1st B. m.	Lady William Cecil, b. 1857
1881	*Ampthill*	Arthur Oliver Villiers Russell, b. 1869, s. 1884, m.	Hon. J. H. Russell, b. 1896
1863	*Annaly*	Luke White, b. 1857, s. 1888, m.	Hon. Luke Hen. White, b. 1857
1880	*Ardilaun*	Arthur Edwd. Guinness, b. 1840, 1st Baron, m....	(None to peerage) [1885
1887	*Armstrong*........	Wm. Geo. Armstrong, C.B.,b. 1810, 1st Baron, w.	(None) [1834
1605	*Arundell of Wardour*	John Francis Arundell, b. 1831, s. 1862, m....	Rev. Hn. E. A. Arundell, b.
1885	*Ashbourne*	Edward Gibson, b. 1837, 1st B. (Ld. Ch. Irel.), m.	Hon. Wm. Gibson, b. 1868
1835	*Ashburton*	Francis Edw. Denzil Baring, b. 1866, s. 1889, m.	Hon. Alex. Baring, b. 1898
1892	*Ashcombe*	George Cubitt, b. 1828, 1st Baron, m.	Hon. H. Cubitt, M.P., b. 1867
1895	*Ashton*	James Williamson, b. 1842, 1st Baron, m.	(None)
1793	*Auckland*	Wm. M. Eden (I. B., Auckland), b. 1859, s.1890,m.	Hn.W. Morton Eden,b.1892
1780	*Bagot*	William Bagot, b. 1857, s. 1887	Hon. W. L. Bagot, b. 1864
1869	*Balinhard*	Jas.Carnegie,K.T.(S.E.,Southesk),b.1827,1stBar,m.	Lord Carnegie, b. 1854
1698	*Barnard*	Henry de Vere Vane, b. 1854, s. 1891, m.	Hon.Hen.Cecil Vane,b.1882
1887	*Basing*	G. Limbrey Sclater-Booth, b. 1860, s. 1894, m. ..	Hon. John S.-Booth, b. '90
1837	*Bateman*............	Wm. B. Bateman-Hanbury, b. 1826, s. 1845, m.	Hn.W.S.B.-Hanbury, b.'56
1892	*Battersea*	Cyril Flower, b. 1843, 1st Baron, m.	(None)
1856	*Belper*	Henry Strutt, b. 1840, s. 1880, m.	Hon. Algn. Strutt, b. 1883
1784	*Berwick*	Thomas Henry Noel-Hill, b. 1877, s. 1897	Rev. Chas. Noel-Hill, b.'48
1892	*Blythswood*	ArchibaldCampbellCampbell,b.1835,1stBaron,m.	Rv.S.Campb.-Douglas,b '39
1797	*Bolton*	William Thos. Orde-Powlett. b. 1845, s. 1895, m.	Hn.W.G.Orde Powlett,b.'69
1761	*Boston*	George Florance Irby, b. 1860. s. 1877, m.	Hon. Cecil S. Irby, b. 1862
1368	*Botreaux*	Charles Edw. H. Abney-Hastings (*Scot. Earl, Loudoun*,), b. 1855, s. 1874, m. ...	Hon. Paulyn F.C. Rawdon-Hastings, b. 1856
1887	*Bowes*	Claude Bowes-Lyon (*Scot. Earl, Strathmore & Kinghorne*), b. 1824, 1st Baron, m.........	Lord Glamis, b. 1855
1711	*Boyle*	Richd. Edmund St. Lawrence Boyle, K.P. (*Irish Earl, Cork & Orrery*), b. 1829, s. 1856,m.........	Visct. Dungarvan, b. 1861
1880	*Brabourne*	Edward Knatchbull-Hugessen. b. 1857, s. 1893,m.	Hon. W.K.-Hugessen,b.'85
1899	*Brampton*	Henry Hawkins, b. 1817, 1st Baron m.	(None)
1866	*Brancepeth*........	Gustavus Russell Hamilton - Russell (*Irish Viscount. Boyne*), b. 1830, s. 1872, m.............	Hon. G. H.-Russell, b. 1864
1886	*Brassey*	Thomas Brassey, K.C.B., b. 1836, 1st Baron, m.....	Hon. T. A. Brassey, b. 1863
1788	*Braybrooke*	Charles Cornwallis Neville, b. 1823, s. 1861, m....	Rev. Hon. L.Neville,b. 1827
1529	*Braye*	A. T. Townshend Verney-Cave, b. 1849, s. 1879, m.	Hn. A. Verney-Cave, b.1874
1796	*Brodrick*............	Wm. Brodrick (I.V.,Midleton), b. 1830, s. 1870, m.	Rt. Hon. St. J. Brodrick, M.P., b. 1856
1860	*Brougham & Vaux*	Henry Charles Brougham, b. 1836, s. 1886, m. ...	Hon. Hy. Brougham, b.1887
1895	*Burghclere*	Herbert Coulstoun Gardner, b. 1846, 1st Baron, m.	(None)
1886 & 1897	*Burton*	Michael Arthur Bass, b. 1837, 1st Baron, m.......	Hon. Mrs. Jas. Baillie, b. '73
1643	*Byron*	Geo. Frederick William Byron, b. 1855, s. 1870...	Rev. Hon. F. E. C. Byron, b. 1861
1796	*Calthorpe*	Augustus C. Gough-Calthorpe, b. 1829, s.1893,m.	Hn.W.G.-Calthorpe,b.1873

Created.		Family Name.	Eldest Son or Heir.
1383	Camoys	Ralph Francis Julian Stonor, *b.* 1884, *s.* 1897, *M.*...	Hon. Edw. M.Stonor,*b.*'85
1838	Carew	Robert Shapland George Julian Carew (*Irish Baron, Carew*), *b.* 1860, *s.* 1881, *m.*	Hon. G. P. J. Carew, *b.* '63
1786	Carleton	R. H. Boyle (*I.E., Shannon*), *b.* 1860, *s.* 1890, *m.* ...	Visc. Boyle, *b.* 1897
1801	Carysfort	Wm. Proby, K.P. (*I.E., Carysfort*), *b.* 1836, *s.* 1872, *m.*	(None)
1869	Castletown	Bern. Edw. Barnaby FitzPatrick, *b.*1848,*s.*1883, *m.*	(None)
1831	Chaworth	Reg. Brabazon (*I. E., Meath*), *b.* 1841, *s.* 1887, *m.*...	Lord Ardee, *b.* 1869
1858	Chelmsford	Fred. A. Thesiger, G.C.B., *b.* 1827, *s.* 1878, *m.*	Hon. F. J. Thesiger, *b.*'68
1858	Chesham	Charles Compton W. Cavendish, *b.* 1850, *s.* 1882, *m.*	Hn.C.W. Cavendish,*b.*'78
1815	Cheylesmore	William Meriton Eaton, *b.* 1843, *s.* 1891	Hon. Herbt. Eaton, *b.*1848
1815	Churchill	Victor Alb. F. Chas. Spencer, *b.* 1864, *s.* 1886, *m.*...	Hon. Victor Spencer, *b.*'90
1858	Churston	John Yarde-Buller, *b.* 1846, *s.* 1871, *m.*	Hon. J. Y.-Buller, *b.* 1873
1828	Clanwilliam	Richard Jas. Meade, G.C.B., K.C.M.G. (*Irish Earl, Clanwilliam*), *b.* 1832, *s.* 1879, *m.*	Lord Gillford, *b.*1868
1831	Clements	Chas. Clements (*I. E., Leitrim*), *b.* 1879, *s.* 1892, *M.*	Hon. F. P. Clements, *b.*'85
1672	Clifford of Chudleigh	Lewis H. Hugh Clifford, *b.* 1851, *s.* 1880, *m.* ...	Hon. W.H.Clifford,*b.*1858
1608	Clifton	E. H. S. Bligh (*Ir. Earl, Darnley*), *b.*1851,*s.*1896,*m.*	Hon. Ivo Bligh, *b.* 1859
1299	Clinton	C. H. Rolle H.-S.-F.-Trefusis, *b.* 1834, *s.* 1866, *m.*	Hon. C. Trefusis, *b.* 1863
1831	Cloncurry	V.F. Lawless (*Ir. Bar., Cloncurry*), *b.* 1840. *s.* 69, *w.*	Hon. E. Lawless, *b.* 1841
1817	Colchester	Reginald Chas. Edw. Abbot, *b.* 1842, *s.* 1867, *m.*...	(None) [1877
1874	Coleridge	Bernard John S. Coleridge, Q.C., *b.* 1851, *s.*1894, *m.*	Hon. G. D. Coleridge, *b.*
1885	Colville of Culross	Chas. John Colville, K.T.,G.C.V.O. (*Scot. Baron, Colville of Culross*), *b.* 1818, 1st Eng. Baron, *m.* ......{	Master of Colville, *b.* 1854
1841	Congleton	Henry Parnell, C.B., *b.* 1839, *s.* 1896, *m.*	Hon. H. B. F. Parnell,
1887	Connemara	Robert Bourke, G.C.I.E., *b.* 1827, 1st Baron, *w.* ...	(None) [*b.* 1830
1874	Cottesloe	Thomas Francis Fremantle, *b.* 1830, *s.* 1890, *m.* ...	Hon.T.F.Fremantle,*b.*'62
1899	Cranworth	Robert Thornhagh Gurdon, *b.* 1829, 1st Baron, *m.* ...	Hon. Bertr. Gurdon, *b.*'77
1892	Crawshaw	Thomas Brooks, *b.* 1825, 1st Baron, *m.*	Hon. Wm. Brooks, *b.* 1853
1899	Currie	Philip Hy. Wodehouse Currie, G.C.B., *b.*'34,1st B.,*m.*	(None)
1894	Davey	Horace Davey (*Lord of Appeal*), *b.* 1833. *m.*	Life Peerage.
1897	Dawnay	Hugh Richard Dawnay, C.I.E. (*Irish Viscount, Downe*), *b.* 1844, 1st Baron, *m.*	Hon.Jno.Dawnay,*b.* 1872
1299	De Clifford	Jack Southwell Russell, *b.* 1884, *s.* 1894, *M.*...	(Two co-heiresses)
1851	De Freyne	Arthur French, *b.*, 1855, *s.* 1868, *m.*	Hon. A. R. French,*b.*1879
1835	De L'Isle & Dudley	Philip Sidney, *b.* 1853. *s.* 1898	Hon.Algern. Sidney,*b.*'54
1838	De Mauley	Wm. Ashley Webb Ponsonby, *b.* 1843, *s.* 1896. ...	Rev. Hon. M. Ponsonby,
1299	De Morley	[*Claimant*—James Thorne Rowe.]	*b.* 1846
1887	De Ramsey	William Henry Fellowes, *b.* 1848, *s.* 1887, *m.*	Hon. C.C.Fellowes,*b.*1883
1254	De Ros	D. C. FitzGerald-de-Ros, K.C.V.O. *b.*1827, *s.* 1874, *m.*	Hon.MaryDawson,*b.*1854
1831	De Saumarez	James St. Vincent Saumarez, *b.* 1843, *s.* 1891, *m.*...	Hon. J. St. V. Broke Saumarez, *b.* 1889
1884	De Vesci	J. R. W.Vesey (*I.V., De Vesci*), *b.* 1844, 1st Bar., *m.*	(No net to Eng. title) [*b.*'52
1821	Delamere	Hugh Cholmondeley, *b.* 1870, *s.* 1887, *m.*	Capt. H.C.Cholmondeley,
1834	Denman	Thomas Denman, *b.* 1874, *s.* 1894	Hon.R.D.Denman, *b.*1876
1885	Deramore	R. Wilfrid de Yarburgh-Bateson, *b.* 1865, *s.*1893, *m.*	Hon. G. N. Bateson, *b.* '70
1881	Derwent	H. V.–Bempde-Johnstone, *b.* 1829, 1st Baron, *m.* ...	Hon. F. Johnstone, *b.*1851
1765	Digby	Edward Henry Trafalgar Digby (*Irish Baron, Digby*), *b.* 1846, *s.* 1889, *m.*	Hon. Edward Kenelm Digby, *b.* 1894
1615	Dormer	John Baptist Joseph Dormer, *b.* 1830, *s.* 1871, *m.*	Roland J. Dormer, *b.* '62
1875	Douglas	Charles Alexander Douglas-Home (*Scot. Earl, Home*), *b.* 1834, *s.* 1881, *m.*	Lord Dunglass, *b.* 1873
1892	Dunleath	Henry Lyle Mulholland, *b.* 1854, *s.* 1895, *m.*	Hon. Andrew E. S. Mul-
1831	Dunmore	Charles Adolphus Murray (*Scot. Earl, Dunmore*), *b.* 1841, *s.* 1845, *m.*	[holland, *b.* 1882 Viscount Fincastle,*b.*1871
1869	Dunning	J. R. Rollo (*Scot. Bar., Rollo*), *b.* 1835, 1st B., *m.*	Master of Rollo, *b.* 1860
1780	Dynevor	Arthur de Cardonnel Rice, *b.* 1836, *s.* 1878, *w.*	Hon. Walter Rice, *b.* 1873
1857	Ebury	Robert Wellesley Grosvenor, *b.* 1834, *s.* 1893, *m.* ...	Hn.R.V.Grosvenor,*b.*1868
1849	Elgin	Victor Alexander Bruce. K.G., G.C.S.I.,G.C.I.E. (*Scot. Earl, Elgin & Kincardine*), *b.* 1849, *s.* 1863, *m.* ...	Lord Bruce, *b.* 1881
1802	Ellenborough	Charles Towry Hamilton Law, *b.* 1856, *s.* 1890	Comm. E. D. Law, *b.* 1841
1885	Elphinstone	Sidney Herbert Elphinstone (*Scot. Baron, Elphinstone*), *b.* 1869, *s.* 1893	Hon. Mountstuart Wm. Elphinstone, *b.* 1871
1874	Emly	Thos. William Gaston Monsell, *b.* 1858, *s.* 1894, *m.*	(None.)
1806	Erskine	Wm. Macnaghten Erskine, *b.* 1841, *s.* 1882, *m.* ...	Hon. M. Erskine, *b.* 1
1872	Ettrick	Wm. J. G. Napier (*Scot. B., Napier*), *b.*'46, *s.*'98, *m.*	Master of Napier, *b.* 1867
1897	Fairlie	Dav. Boyle,G.C.M.G. (*Scot.E.Glasgow*) *b.*'33 1st B.*m.*	Visct Kelburne, *b.* 1874
1898	Farquhar	Horace B. Townsend-Farquhar, *b.* 1844, 1st B, *m.*	(None
1893	Farrer	Thomas Cecil Farrer, *b.* 1859, *s.* 1899, *w.*	Hon. Cecil Farrer, *b.* 1893
1876	Fermanagh	John Henry Crichton, K.P. (*Irish Earl, Erne*), *b.* 1839, *s.* 1885, *m.*	Viscount Crichton, *b.*1872
1890	Field	William Ventris Field, Q.C., *b.* 1813, 1st Baron, *w.*	(None)
1831	Fingall	A. J. Plunkett (*I. E., Fingall*), *b.* 1859, *s.* 1881, *m.*	Lord Killeen, *b.* 1896
1790	Fisherwick	George Augustus Hamilton Chichester (*Irish Marquess, Donegall*), *b.* 1822, *s.* 1889, *m.*	Lord Henry Fitzwarrine Chichester, *b.* 1834

Created.	Family Name.	Eldest Son or Heir.
1861	*Fitzhardinge* ...... Charles Paget Fitzh.Berkeley, *b.* 1830, *s.* 1896, *m.*	(None)
1776	*Foley* .... Henry Thomas Foley, *b.* 1850, *s.* 1869	Hon. Fitzal. Foley, *b.* 1852
1821	*Forester* .... Cecil Theodore Weld-Forester, *b.* 1842, *s.* 1894, *m.*	Hon. Geo. C. Beaumont
1815	*Foxford* .... William Henry E. de Vere Sheaffe Pery (*Irish Earl, Limerick*), *b.* 1863, *s.* 1896, *m.*	[Weld-Forester, *b.* 1867 Visct. Glentworth, *b.* 1894
1790	*Gage* .... Henry C. Gage (*Ir. Visct., Gage*), *b.*1854,*s.* 1877,*m.*	Hon. Henry R. Gage,*b.*1895
1806	*Gardner* .... (Vacant.)	
1876	*Gerard* .... Wm. Cansfield Gerard, *b.* 1851, *s.* 1887, *m.*......	Hon. F. J. Gerard, *b.* 1883
1824	*Gifford* .... Edric Frederick Gifford, ÞC, *b.* 1849, *s.* 1872, *m.*	Hon. E. B. Gifford, *b.*1857
1899	*Gianusk* .... Joseph Russell Bailey, *b.* 1840, 1st Baron, *m.* ...	Hon. Jos. Bailey, *b.* 1864
1895	*Glenesk* .... Algernon Borthwick, *b.* 1830, 1st Baron, *w.*	Hn. O. A. Borthwick,*b.*'73
1868	*Gormanston* ...... Jenico William Joseph Preston, G.C.M.G. (*Irish Viscount, Gormanston*), *b.* 1837, *s.* 1876, *m.*......	Hon. J. E. J. Preston,*b.*1879
1806	*Granard* .... Bernard Arthur William Patrick Hastings Forbes (*Irish Earl, Granard*), *b.*1874,*s.* 1889 ... }	Hon. Reginald George Benedict Forbes, *b.* 1877
1782	*Grantley* .... John Richd. Brinsley Norton, *b.* 1855, *s.* 1877, *m.*	Hon. R. H. B. Norton, *b.*'92
1869	*Greville* .... Algernon Wm. Fulke Greville, *b.* 1841, *s.* 1883, *m.*	Hon.R.H.F.Greville,*b.*1864
1324	*Grey de Ruthyn* .. Rawdon George Grey Clifton, *b.* 1858, *s.* 1887, *m.*	Hon. Cecil Clifton, *b.* 1862
1886	*Grimthorpe* ...... Edmund Beckett., Q.C., *b.* 1816, 1st Baron, *m.* ...	E. Wm. Beckett, M.P.,*b.*1856
1815	*Grinstead* .... Lowry E. Cole (*I. E., Enniskillen*), *b.*1845,*s.*1886,*m.*	Viscount Cole, *b.* 1876
1796	*Gwydyr* .... Peter Robert Burrell, *b.* 1810, *s.* 1870, *w.*	Hon. W. M. Burrell, *b.*1841
1880	*Haldon* .... Lawrence Hesketh Palk, *b.* 1846, *s.* 1883, *m.*...	Hon. L. W. Palk, *b.* 1869
1898	*Haliburton* ...... Arth. Laurence Haliburton, G.C.B., *b.*1832,1st B.*m.*	(None)
1886	*Hamilton of Dalzell* John G. Carter Hamilton, *b.* 1829, 1st Baron, *w.*	Hon. Gavin Hamilton, *b.*'72
1874	*Hampton* .... Herbt. P. Murray Pakington, *b.* 1848, *s.* 1893, *m.*	Hon. H. S. Pakington, *b.*'83
1869	*Hare* .... W. Hare, K.P. (*I.E.Listowel*),*b.*1833, 1st Baron, *m.*	Visct. Ennismore, *b.* 1866
1876	*Harlech* .... Wm. Richard Ormsby-Gore, *b.* 1819, *s.* 1876, *w.*	Hon. G. R. O.-Gore, *b.* 1855
1815	*Harris* .... G.R.Canning Harris, G.C.S.I.,G.C.I.E.,*b.*'51,*s.*'72,*m.*	Hon.G. St.V.Harris,*b.*1889
1866	*Hartismere*...... John Major Henniker-Major (*Irish Baron, Henniker*), *b.* 1842, *s.* 1870, *w.*......	Hon. A. E. H.-Major,*b.*1865
1264	*Hastings* .... George Manners Astley, *b.* 1857, *s.* 1875, *m.* ...	Hon. A. E. D. Astley, *b.* 1882
1835	*Hatherton* .... Edward Geo. P. Littleton, C.M.G., *b.*1842,*s.*1888,*m.*	Hon.E.C.R.Littleton,*b.*1868
1776	*Hawke* .... Martin Bladen Hawke, *b.* 1860, *s.* 1887	Hon. S. Hawke,R.N. *b.* 1863
1893	*Hawkesbury* ...... Cecil Geo. Savile Foljambe, *b.* 1846, 1st Bar., *m.*	Hon. A. S. Foljambe, *b.* 1870
1711	*Hay* .... A. F. G. Hay (*Sc. E., Kinnoull*), *b.* '55, *s.* '97, *m.*	Viscount Dupplin, *b.* 1879
1896	*Heneage* .... Edward Heneage, P.C., *b.* 1840, 1st Baron, *m.*	Hon. G. E. Heneage, *b.* 1866
1884	*Herries* .... Marmaduke Francis Constable-Maxwell (*Sc. Baron, Herries*), *b.* 1837, 1st Eng. Baron, *m.* ...	(None to English peerage
1886	*Herschell* ...... Richard Farrer Herschell, *b.* 1878, *s.* 1899 ...	(None)
1828	*Heytesbury* ...... Wm. Fredk. Holmes-A'Court, *b.* 1862, *s.* 1891, *m.*	Hn. L. Holmes-A'C., *b.* 1863
1886	*Hillingdon* ...... Charles William Mills, *b.* 1855, *s.* 1898, *m.*......	Hon. C. T. Mills, *b.* 1887
1886	*Hindlip* .... Charles Allsopp, *b.* 1877, *s.* 1897.	Hn. Wm. Hy.Allsopp,*b.*'43
1885	*Hobhouse* .... A. Hobhouse, K.C.S.I., C.I.E.,*b.*1819, 1st Baron, *m.*	(None)
1897	*HolmPatrick* ...... Hans Wellesley Hamilton, *b.* 1886, *s.* 1898, *M.* ...	(None)
1892	*Hood of Avalon* ... Arth. W. A. Hood, G.C.B., *b.* 1824, 1st Baron, *m.*	(None)
1809	*Hopetoun* .... J.A.L.Hope,G.C.M.G.(*Sc.E.Hopetoun*),*b.*'60,*s.*'73,*m.*	Lord Hope, *b.* 1887
1881	*Hothfield* ...... Henry James Tufton, *b.* 1844, 1st Baron, *m.*......	Hn. Jno. S.R.Tufton, *b.*1873
1597	*Howard de Walden* Thos. Evelyn Ellis, *b.* 1880, *s.* 1899, *M.*	Rev. Hn. Wm. C. Ellis, *b.* '25
1869	*Howard of Glossop* Francis E. Fitzalan-Howard, *b.* 1859, *s.* 1883, *m.*	Hn.B.Fitzln.-Howard,*b.*'85
1881	*Howth* .... W.U.T. St.Lawrence. K.P (*I.E.Howth*),*b.*'27,1st B.	(None)
1866	*Hylton* .... Hylton Geo. Hylton Jolliffe, *b.* 1862, *s.* 1899, *m.*,	Hn.Wm.G.H.Jolliffe, *b.*'58
1897	*Inverclyde* ...... John Burns, *b.* 1829, 1st Baron, *m.*	Hon. Geo. A. Burns, *b.* '61
1891	*Iveagh* .... Edward Cecil Guinness, K.P., *b.* 1847, 1st Baron, *m.*	Hon. Rpt. Guinness, *b.* 1874
1895	*James of Hereford* Henry James, P.C., Q.C., *b.* 1828, 1st Baron	(None)
1839	*Keane* .... John M. Arbuthnot Keane, *b.* 1816, *s.* 1882, *m.*...	(None)
1892	*Kelvin* .... William Thomson, G.C.V.O., *b.*1824, 1st Baron, *m.*	(None)
1831	*Kenlis* .... Geoff. T. Taylour (*I. M., Headfort*), *b.* 1878, *s.* 1894	E. H. H. Taylour, *b.* '86
1856	*Kenmare* .... Valentine Augustus Browne, K.P. (*Irish Earl, Kenmare*), *b.* 1825, *s.* 1871, *m.*.............	Visct. Castlerosse, *b.* 1860
1866	*Kenry* .... W.T.Wyndham-Quin,K.P.(*I.E.Dunraven*),*b.*'41,*s.*'71,*m.*	None to English title)
1886	*Kensington* ...... Wm. Edwardes (*I.B., Kensington*), *b.* 1868, *s.* 1896	Hon. H. Edwardes, *b.* 1873
1788	*Kenyon* .... Lloyd Kenyon, *b.* 1864, *s.* 1869	Hon. G. T. Kenyon, *b.* 1840
1821	*Ker* .... Schomberg Henry Kerr, K.T. (*Scot. Marquess, Lothian*), *b.* 1833, *s.* 1870, *m.*..............	Lord Jedburgh, *b.* 1874
1868	*Kesteven* .... John Henry Trollope, *b.* 1851, *s.* 1874	Hon. R. C. Trollope, *b.* 1852
1831	*Kilmarnock* ...... Chas. Gore Hay (*Sc. E., Erroll*), *b.* 1852,*s.*1891,*m.*	Lord Kilmarnock, *b.* 1876
1860	*Kinnaird* .... Arthur Fitzgerald Kinnaird (*Sc. B., Kinnaird*), *b.* 1847, *s.* 1887, *m.*	Master of Kinnaird, *b.*1879
1897	*Kinnear* .... Alexander Smith Kinnear, Q.C., *b.* 1833, 1st Baron	(None)
1838	*Kintore* .... Algernon H. Thomond Keith-Falconer, G.C.M.G. (*Scot. Earl, Kintore*), *b.* 1852, *s.* 1880, *m.*.........	Lord Falconer, *b.* 1879
1898	*Kitchener of Khartoum*	Horatio Herbert Kitchener, G.C.B., K.C.M.G., *b.* 1850, 1st Baron(*Sirdar of Egyptian Army*) ... }	(None)
1880	*Lamington* ...... C.W.A.N.Cochrane-Baillie,K.C.M.G.,*b.*'60,*s.*'90,*m.*	Hon. Victor C.-Baillie,*b.*'96

Created.	Family Name.	Eldest Son or Heir.
1869 *Lawrence*	John Hamilton Lawrence, *b.* 1846, *s.* 1879, *m.* ...	Hon. A. G. Lawrence, *b.* 1878
1859 *Leconfield*	Henry Wyndham, *b.* 1830, *s.* 1869, *m*	Hon. C. H. Wyndham, *b.* '72
1839 *Leigh*	William Henry Leigh, P.C., *b.* 1824, *s.* 1850, *m.* .	Hon. F. D. Leigh, *b.* 1855
1797 *Lilford*	John Powys, *b.* 1863, *s.* 1896, *m.* ...	Hon. Thos. A. Powys, *b.* 1896
1885 *Lingen*	Ralph R. W. Lingen, K.C.B., *b.* 1819, 1st Bar., *m.*	(None)
1897 *Lister*	Joseph Lister, P.R.S., *b.* 1827, 1st Baron, *w.*	(None)
1892 *Llangattock* ...	John Allan Rolls, *b.* 1837, 1st Baron, *m.*	Hon. J. M. Rolls, *b.* 1870.
1895 *Loch*	H. Brougham Loch, G.C.B., G.C.M.G., *b.* '27, 1st Bn., *m.*	Hon. Edwd. D. Loch, *b.* 1873
1801 *Loftus*	John Hen. Loftus (*Irish M., Ely*), *b.* 1851, *s.* '89, *m.*	Lord G. H. Loftus, *b.* 1854
1837 *Lovat*	Simon J. Fraser (*Sc. B., Lovat*), *b.* 1871, *s.* 1887	Hon. H. J. Fraser, *b.* 1874
1762 *Lovel & Holland*	Aug. A. Perceval (*I. E., Egmont*), *b.* '56, *s.* '97, *m.*	Chas. J. Perceval, *b.* 1858
1897 *Ludlow*	Henry Chas. Lopes, P.C., Q.C., *b.* 1828, 1st B., *w.*	Hon. Henry L. Lopes, *b.* 1868
1839 *Lurgan*	William Brownlow, *b.* 1858, *s.* 1882, *m.*	Hon. J. R. Brownlow, *b.* 1865
1859 *Lyveden*	Fitz-Patrick Henry Vernon, *b.* 1824, *s.* 1873, *m.*	Courtenay Vernon, *b.* 1857
1887 *Macnaghten*	Edwd. Macnaghten (*Lord of Appeal*), *b.* 1830, *m.*	Life Peerage.
1887 *Magheramorne* ...	Jas. Douglas M'Garel-Hogg, *b.* 1861, *s.* 1890, *m.*	Hon. D. S. M'G.-Hogg, *b.* '63
1896 *Malcolm of Poltalloch* John W. Malcolm, C.B., *b.* 1833, 1st B., *w.* ...		(None)
1807 *Manners*	John Thomas Manners, *b.* 1852, *s.* 1864, *m.* ...	Hon. J. N. Manners, *b.* 1892
1679 *Manners of Haddon* H.J.B Manners (*M.of Granby*), *b.* '52, *summ.* '96, *m.*		Ld. Roos of Belvoir, *b.* '86
1891 *Masham*	Samuel Cunliffe-Lister, *b.* 1815, 1st Baron, *w.* ...	Hon. Sam. C.-Lister, *b.* 1857
1815 *Meldrum*	Chas. Gordon (*Sc. Marq., Huntly*), *b.* '47, *s.* '63, *m.*	Lord Esmé Gordon, *b.* 1853
1794 *Mendip*	Thomas Charles Agar-Robartes (*I. V., Clifden*), *b.* 1844, *s.* 1899, *m.*	Hon. Thos. A.-Robartes, *b.* 1880
1866 *Meredyth*	James Herbert G. Meredyth Somerville (*Irish Baron, Athlumney*), *b.* 1865, *s.* 1873	(None to peerage)
1838 *Methuen*	Paul S. Methuen, K.C.V.O., C.B., C.M.G., *b.* '45, *s.* '91, *m.*	Hon. Paul Methuen, *b.* 1886
1711 *Middleton*	Digby W. Bayard Willoughby, *b.* 1844, *s.* 1877, *m.*	Capt. H. G. Willoughby, *b.* '47
1821 *Minster*	Victor George Henry Francis Conyngham (*Irish Marquess, Conyngham*), *b.* 1883, *s.* 1897, *M.*	Lord Frederick William Burton Conyngham, *b.* '90
1866 *Monck*	Henry Power Charles Stanley Monck (*Irish Visct., Monck*), *b.* 1849, *s.* 1894, *m.*	Hon. Chas. Henry Stanley Monck, *b.* 1876
1887 *Monckton*	George Edmund M. Monckton-Arundell (*I. V., Galway*), *b.* 1844, 1st Baron, *m.*	Hon. G. M.-Arundell, *b.* '82
1874 *Moncreiff*	Henry James Moncreiff (*Scot. Lord of Session*), *b.* 1840, *s.* 1895, *w.*	Rev. Hon. R. C. Moncreiff, *b.* 1843
1884 *Monk Bretton* ...	John William Dodson, *b.* 1869, *s.* 1897	(None)
1885 *Monkswell*	Robert Collier, *b.* 1845, *s.* 1886, *m.*	Hon. R. A. H. Collier, *b.* 1875
1728 *Monson*	Debonnaire Jno. Monson, C.V.O., *b.* 1830, *s.* 1898 (to V. Oxenbridge), *m.*	Hon. Aug. Monson, *b.* 1863
1885 *Montagu of Beaulieu* Henry John Douglas-Scott-Montagu, *b.* 1832, 1st Baron, *m.*		Hon. J. W. Douglas-Scott-Montagu, M.P., *b.* 1869
1806 *MontEagle*	Jno. T. Browne (*I. M., Sligo*), *b.* 1824, *s.* 1896 ...	Ld. Hy. Ulick Browne, *b.* '31
1839 *Monteagle of Brandon* Thos. Spring Rice, K.P., *b.* 1849, *s.* 1866, *m.* ...		Hon. S. Spring Rice, *b.* 1877
1889 *Morris*	Michael Morris (*Lord of Appeal*), *b.* 1827, *m.* ...	Life Peerage. [*b.* 1835
1831 *Mostyn*	Llewelyn N. V. Lloyd-Mostyn, *b.* 1856, *s.* 1884, *m.*	Hon. E. Ll. R. Ll.-Mostyn,
1891 *Mount Stephen* ...	George Stephen, *b.* 1829, 1st Baron, *m.*	(None)
1283 *Mowbray, Segrave* (1264), *and Stourton* (1448)	Chas. B. J. Stourton, *b.* 1867, *s.* 1893, *m.*	Hon. W. M. Stourton, *b.* 1895
1898 *Muncaster*	Josslyn Fras. Pennington (*I.B., Muncaster*), *b.* 1834, 1st Eng. Baron, *m.*	(None to English title)
1858 *Napier of Magdala* Robert William Napier, *b.* 1845, *s.* 1890, *m.*		Col. Hon. Geo. Campbell Napier, C.I.E., *b.* 1845
1898 *Newlands*	Wm. Wallace Hozier, *b.* 1825, 1st Baron, *w.* ...	Hn. J. H. C. Hozier, M.P., *b.* '5(
1892 *Newton*	Thomas Wodehouse Legh, *b.* 1857, *s.* 1898, *m.* ...	Hon. Rd. W. Legh, *b.* 1888
1554 *North*	Wm. Henry John North, *b.* 1836, *s.* 1884, *m.* ...	Hon. W. F. J. North, *b.* 1860
1884 *Northbourne*	Walter Henry James, *b.* 1846, *s.* 1893, *m.*	Hn. Walter J. James, *b.* 1869
1885 *Northington*	Fredc. Henley (*I. B., Henley*), *b.* 1849, *s.* 1898 ...	Hon A. E. Henley, *b.* 1858
1878 *Norton*	Chas. B. Adderley, K.C.M.G., *b.* 1814, 1st Bar., *w.*	Hon. C. L. Adderley, *b.* 1846
1870 *O'Hagan*	Thomas Towneley O'Hagan, *b.* 1878, *s.* 1885 ...	Hn. M. H. O'Hagan, *b.* 1882
1868 *O'Neill*	Edward O'Neill, *b.* 1839, *s.* 1883, *m.*	Hn. A. E. B. O'Neill, *b.* 1876
1821 *Oriel*	Clotworthy John E. Foster-Skeffington (*Irish Viscount, Massereene*), *b.* 1842, *s.* 1863, *m.* ...	Hon. Oriel J. C. Foster-Skeffington, *b.* 1871
1868 *Ormathwaite*	Arthur Walsh, *b.* 1827, *s.* 1881, *m.*	Hon. A. H. J. Walsh, *b.* 1859
1821 *Ormonde*	J.E.W.T. Butler, K.P. (*I.M., Ormonde*), *b.* '44, *s.* '54, *m.*	Lord Jas. A. Butler, *b.* 1849
1893 *Overtoun*	John Campbell White, *b.* 1843, 1st Baron, *m.* ...	(None)
1841 *Oxenfoord*	J.H. Dalrymple, K.T. (*Scot. E., Stair*), *b.* '19, *s.* '64, *w.*	Visct. Dalrymple, *b.* 1848
1899 *Pauncefote*	Julian Pauncefote, G.C.B., G.C.M.G., *b.* '28, 1st B., *m.*	(None)
1866 *Penrhyn*	George S. G. Douglas-Pennant, *b.* 1836, *s.* 1886, *m.*	Hon. Edward S. Douglas-Pennant, M.P., *b.* '64
1869 *Penzance*	James Plaisted Wilde, *b.* 1816, 1st Baron, *m.* ...	(None)
1603 *Petre*	Bernard Henry Philip Petre, *b.* 1858, *s.* 1893, *m.*	Hon. Philip Petre, *b.* 1864
1895 *Pirbright*	Henry De Worms, P.C., *b.* 1840, 1st Baron, *m.* ...	(None)
1892 *Playfair*	George Jas. Playfair, *b.* 1849, *s.* 1898, *m.*	Hn. L. G. H. Playfair, *b.* '88
1827 *Plunket*	William Lee Plunket, *b.* 1864, *s.* 1897, *m.*	Hon. Terence Plunket, *b.* '99
1831 *Poltimore*	A. F. Geo. Warwick Bampfylde, *b.* 1837, *s.* 1858, *m.*	Hon. C. Bampfylde, *b.* 1859
1749 *Ponsonby*	Rev. Walter William Brabazon Ponsonby (*Irish Earl, Bessborough*), *b.* 1821, *s.* 1895, *m.*	Viscount Duncannon, C.B., *b.* 1851

Created.	Family Name.	Eldest Son or Heir.
1885	Powerscourt	Mervyn Edward Wingfield, K.P., (Irish Viscount Powerscourt), b. 1836, 1st Baron, m......	Hon. Mervyn Richard Wingfield, b. 1880
1852	Raglan	Geo. FitzRoy Hy. Somerset, b. 1857, s. 1884, m..	Hon. F. R. Somerset, b. 1885
1875	Ramsay	Arthur George Maule Ramsay (Scot. Earl, Dalhousie), b. 1878, s. 1887	Hon. Patrick Wm. Maule Ramsay, b. 1879
1826	Ranfurly	Uchter John Mark Knox, K.C.M.G. (Irish Earl, Ranfurly), b. 1856, s. 1875, m......	Viscount Northland, b. 1882
1895	Rathmore	David Robert Plunket, Q.C., b. 1838, 1st Baron	(None)
1821	Rayleigh............	John William Strutt, b. 1842, s. 1873, m.	Hon. Rbt. J. Strutt, b. 1875
1881	Reay	Donald James Mackay, G.C.S.I., G.C.I.E. (Scot. Baron, Reay), b. 1839, 1st Engl. Baron, m......	(None to English title)
1894	Rendel	Stuart Rendel, b. 1834, 1st Baron, m.	(None)
1885	Revelstoke	John Baring, b. 1863, s. 1897	Hon. Cecil Baring, b. 1864
1797	Ribblesdale	Thomas Lister, b. 1854, s. 1876, m.	Hon. Thos. Lister, b. 1878
1892	Roberts of Kandahar	Frederick Sleigh Roberts, K.P., G.C.B., G.C.S.I., G.C.I.E. &c., b. 1832, 1st Baron, m......	Hon. Fred. Roberts, b. 1872
1899	Robertson	Jas. Patrick B. Robertson (Lord of Appeal), b. '45, m.	Life Peerage
1782	Rodney	Geo. B. Harley Dennett Rodney, b. 1857, s. 1864, m.	Hon. G. B. Rodney, b. 1891
1866	Romilly	John Gaspard LeM. Romilly, b. 1866, s. 1891, m.	Hon. — Romilly, b. 1899
1892	Rookwood	Henry J. Selwin-Ibbetson, b. 1826, 1st Baron, w.	(None)
1828	Rosebery	Archibald Philip Primrose, K.G., K.T. (Scot. Earl, Rosebery), b. 1847, s. 1868, w.	Lord Dalmeny, b. 1882
1896	Rosmead	Hercules A. Temple Robinson, b. 1866, s. 1897, m.	Hon. H. E. Robinson, b. '95
1838	Rossmore	Derrick Warner William Westenra (Irish Baron, Rossmore), b. 1853, s. 1874, m......	Hon. Wm. Westenra, b. 1892
1885	Rothschild	Nathaniel Mayer Rothschild, b. 1840, 1st Bn., m.	Hn. L. W. Rothschild, M P
1880	Rowton	Montagu W. Lowry-Corry, K.C.V.O., b. 1838, 1st B.	[b. 1868
1894	Russell of Killowen	Chas. Russell, G.C.M.G. (Ld. Chief Just.), b. '32, m.	Life Peerage. [West. b. '30
1876	Sackville..	Lionel S. Sackville-West, G.C.M.G., b. 1827, s. 1888	Hon. Wm. E. Sackville-
1555	St. John of Bletso	Beauchamp Moubray St. John, b. 1844, s. 1887, m.	Hon. Henry St. John, b. 1876
1852	St. Leonards	Edwd. Burtenshaw Sugden, b. 1847, s. 1875, m..	Hon. H. F. Sugden, b. 1850
1887	St. Levan	John St. Aubyn, b. 1829, 1st Baron, m.	Hon. J. T. St. Aubyn, b. 1857
1885	St. Oswald	Rowland Winn, b. 1857, s. 1893, m.	Hon. Rowland Winn, b. 1857
1796	Saltersford	James George Henry Stopford (Irish Earl, Courtown), b. 1823, s. 1858, w.	Viscount Stopford, b. 1853
1871	Sandhurst	William Mansfield, G.C.I.E., b. 1855, s. 1876, m..	Hon. J. W. Mansfield, b. 1857
1802	Sandys	Aug. Fredk. Arthur Sandys, b. 1840, s. 1863, m.	Hn. M. E. M. Sandys, b. '55
1888	Savile	John Savile Lumley-Savile, b. 1854, s. 1896, m...	(None)
1603	Saye and Sele ...	John F. T.-Wykeham-Fiennes, b. 1830, s. 1887, m.	Hon. G. C. Fiennes, b. 1858
1761	Scarsdale	Rev. Alf. N. Holden Curzon, b. 1831, s. 1856, m.	Ld. Curzon of Kdlstn., b. '50
1839	Seaton	John Reginald Upton Colborne, b. 1854, s. 1888, m.	Hon. F. L. Colborne, b. 1855
1831	Sefton	C. W. H. Molyneux (I. E. Sefton), b. 1867, s. 1897	Hon. O. Molyneux, b. 1871
1892	Shand	Alexander Burns Shand, b. 1828, 1st Baron, m.	(None)
1802	Sheffield	Hy. N. Holroyd (I. E., Sheffield), b. 1832, s. 1876	(None to English title)
1784	Sherborne	Edward Lenox Dutton, b. 1831, s. 1883, m.	Rev. Hon. F. Dutton, b. 1840
1880	Shute	Percy Barrington (Irish Viscount, Barrington), b. 1825, s. 1886, w.	Hon. Walter B. Barrington, b. 1848
1821	Silchester	Thos. Pakenham (I. E., Longford), b. 1864, s. 1887	Hn. E. M. Pakenham, b. 1866
1826	Somerhill	Hubert George De-Burgh-Canning (Irish Marquess, Clanricarde), b. 1832, s. 1874	(None to English title)
1784	Somers	Arth. Herb. Tennyson Cocks, b. 1887, s. 1893, W.	Rev. Hy. L. S. Cocks, b. 1862
1873	Somerton	Sidney James Agar (I. E., Normanton), b. 1865, s. 1896. m.	Hn. Fras. W. A. Agar, b. 1873
1780	Southampton	Charles Henry Fitzroy, b. 1867, s. 1872, m...... c	Hon. Edw. A. Fitzroy, b. 1869
1640	Stafford	Fitzherbert Edwd. S.-Jerningham, b. 1833, s. 1892	Francis E. Fitzherbert, b. '67
1886	Stalbridge	Richard de Aquila Grosvenor, b. 1837, 1st B., m.	Hon. H. Grosvenor, b. 1870
1839	Stanley of Alderley	Henry Edward John Stanley, b. 1827, s. 1869, m.	Hon. E. L. Stanley, b. 1859
1893	Stanmore	Arth. Hamilton-Gordon, G.C.M.G., b. '29, 1st Bar., m.	Hon. Geo. H.-Gordon, b. '71
1796	Stewart of Garlies	Alan Plantagenet Stewart, K.T. (Scot. Earl, Galloway), b. 1835, s. 1873, m.	Hon. Randolph Henry Stewart, b. 1836
1897	Strathcona and Mount Royal	Donald Alexander Smith, G.C.M.G., b. 1820, 1st Baron, m...	(None)
1836	Strathedon and Campbell (1841)	Hallyburton George Campbell, b. 1829, s. 1893, m.	Hon. John Beresford Campbell, b. 1866.
1884	Strathspey	James Grant-Ogilvie (Scot. Earl, Seafield), b. 1876, s. 1888	Hon. Trevor Grant-Ogilvie, b. 1879
1796	Stuart of Castle Stuart ...	Edmund Archibald Stuart (Scot. Earl, Moray), b. 1840, s. 1895, m.	Fras. Jas. Stuart-Gray, b. 1842
1838	Sudeley	C. Douglas R. Hanbury-Tracy, b. 1840, s. '77, m.	Hon. W. H.-Tracy, b. 1870
1884	Sudley............	Arthur Saunders William Charles Fox Gore (Irish Earl, Arran), b. 1839, 1st Baron, m......	Viscount Sudley, b. 1858
1786	Suffield	Charles Harbord, K.C.B., b. 1830, s. 1853, m......	Hon. Chas. Harbord, b. 1855
1893	Swansea............	Ernest Ambrose Vivian, b. 1848, s. 1894	Hon. Odo R. Vivian, b. '75
1856	Talbot de Malahide	Richard Wogan Talbot (I. B., Talbot of Malahide), b. 1846, s. 1883, w.	Hon. Jas. B. Talbot, b. 1854
1831	Templemore	Henry Spencer Chichester, b. 1821, s. 1837, m....	Hon. A. Chichester, b. 1854

Created	Family Name	Eldest Son or Heir
1884 Tennyson	Hallam Tennyson, K.C.M.G., b. 1852, s. 1892, m. .	Hon. L. H. Tennyson, b. 1889
1827 Tenterden	Charles Stuart Henry Abbott, b. 1865, s. 1882 ...	(None)
1616 Teynham	Henry John P. S. Roper-Curzon, b. 1867, s. 1892, m.	Hn. C. J. H. R.-Curzon, b. '96
1886 Thring	Henry Thring, K.C.B., b. 1818, 1st Baron, w......	(None)
1792 Thurlow	T. J. H.-T.-Cumming-Bruce, b. 1838, s. 1874, m.	Hon. James Bruce, b. 1867
1876 Tollemache	Wilbraham Fredc. Tollemache, b. 1832, s. 1890, m.	Hon. L. P. Tollemache, b. '60
1859 Tredegar	Godfrey Charles Morgan, b. 1831, s. 1875	Hon. F. Morgan, M.P., b. 1834
1880 Trevor	Arthur William Hill-Trevor, b. 1852, s. 1894. m.	Hon. G. E. Hill-Trevor, b. '59
1881 Tweeddale	W. M. Hay, K.T. (Sc. M., Tweeddale), b. 1826, 1st B. m.	Earl of Gifford, b. 1884
1881 Tweedmouth	Edward Marjoribanks, P.C., b. 1849, s. 1894, m. ...	Hon. D. C. Marjoribanks, [b. 1874
1786 Tyrone	Henry de la Poer Beresford (Irish Marquess, Waterford), b. 1875, s. 1895, m.	Ld. C. Beresford, C.B., M.P.,
1523 Vaux of Harrowden	Hubert Geo. Chas. Mostyn, b. 1860, s. 1883, w..	Three co-heiresses [b. 1846
1762 Vernon	Geo. F. A. Venables-Vernon, b. 1888, s. 1898, M.	Hn. Fras. V.-Vernon, b. '89
1841 Vivian	G. Crespigny Brabazon Vivian, b. 1878, s. 1893. ...	Hon. Claud Vivian, b. 1849
1780 Walsingham	Thomas De Grey, b. 1843, s. 1870, m.	Hon. J. A. De Grey, b. 1849
1895 Wandsworth	Sydney James Stern, b. 1845, 1st Baron	(None)
1885 Wantage	R. J. Loyd-Lindsay, K.C.B., V.C., b. 1832,1st Bar., m.	(None)
1894 Welby	Reginald E. Welby, G.C.B., b. 1832, 1st Baron...	(None)
1821 Wemyss	Francis Wemyss-Charteris-Douglas (Scot. E., Wemyss and March), b. 1818, s. 1883, w.	Lord Elcho, b. 1857
1839 Wenlock	Beilby Lawley, G.C.S.I., G.C.I.E., b. 1849, s. 1880, m.	Hon. R. T. Lawley, b. 1856
1861 Westbury	R. Luttrell Pilkington Bethell, b. 1852, s. 1875, m.	Hon. Richd. Bethell, b. 1883
1826 Wigan	James Ludovic Lindsay, K.T. (Scot. Earl, Crawford and Balcarres), b. 1847, s. 1880, m...	Lord Balcarres, M.P., b. 1871
1492 Willoughby de Broke	Henry Verney, b. 1844, s. 1862, w.	Hn. Rd. G. Verney, M.P., b. '69
1880 Wimborne	Ivor Bertie Guest, b. 1835, 1st Baron, m.	Hon. Ivor C. Guest, b. 1873
1529 Windsor	Robert George Windsor-Clive, b. 1857, s. 1869, m.	Hn. O. R. Windsor-Clive, b. '84
1869 Wolverton	Frederick Glyn, b. 1864, s. 1888, m.	Hon. G. E. D. Carr Glyn, b. [1896
1835 Worlingham	Archibald Brabazon Sparrow Acheson, K.P. (Irish Earl, Gosford), b. 1841, s. 1864, m.	Viscount Acheson, b. 1877
1838 Wrottesley	Arthur Wrottesley, b. 1824, s. 1867, w.	Hn Victor Wrottesley, b. '73
1829 Wynford	Henry Molyneux Best, b. 1829, s. 1899	Hon. Robt R. Best, b. 1834
1308 Zouche of Haryngworth	Robt. N. Cecil Geo. Curzon, b. 1851, s. 1873, w.	Hon. Darea Curzon, b. 1860

PEERESSES IN THEIR OWN RIGHT (9).

Created	Family Name	Eldest Son or Heir
1309 Beaumont	Mona Josephine T. Stapleton, Bss., b. 1894, s. 1895, M.	Hon. Ivy M. Stapleton, b. '95
1421 Berkeley	Louisa M. Milman, Baroness, b. 1840, s. 1893, m.	Hon. Eva M. F. Milman, b. '75
1455 Berners	Emma Harriet Tyrwhitt, Bs., b. 1835, s. 1871, w.	Hon. Sir Raymond Robert
1871 Burdett-Coutts	Angela Georgina Bartlett-Burdett-Coutts, 1st Baroness, b. 1814, m.	[Tyrwhitt-Wilson, b. 1855 (None)
1509 Conyers	Marcia Amelia Mary Anderson-Pelham (Countess of Yarborough), Baroness, b. 1863, m., title called out of abeyance 1892	Lord Worsley, b. 1887
1861 Cromartie	Sibell Lilian Mackenzie, Countess, b. 1878, title called out of abeyance 1895	Lady Constance Mackenzie, b. 1882.
1899 Dorchester	Henrietta Anne Carleton, 1st Bnss., b. 1846, m.	Hn. Dudley Carleton, b. '76
1891 Hambleden	Emily Smith, 1st Viscountess, b. 1828, w.	Hon. William F. Danvers Smith, M.P., b. 1868
1891 Macdonald of Earnscliffe	Susan Agnes Macdonald, 1st Baroness, b. '36, w.	(None)

SCOTTISH REPRESENTATIVE PEERS (16).

(Elected 24th July, 1895, to the Fourteenth Parliament of Queen Victoria.)

Earl of Mar.	Earl of Lauderdale.	Earl of Dundonald.	Lord Sinclair.
Earl of Morton.	Earl of Airlie.	Viscount Falkland.	Lord Torphichen.
Earl of Mar and Kellie.	Earl of Carnwath.	Lord Forbes.	Ld. Balfour of Burleigh.
Earl of Haddington.	Earl of Leven & Melville.	Lord Saltoun.	Lord Polwarth.

IRISH REPRESENTATIVE PEERS [*Elected for Life*] (28).

Earl of Drogheda.	Earl of Rosse.	Lord Inchiquin.	Lord Langford.
Earl of Lanesborough.	Earl of Kilmorey.	Lord Farnham.	Lord Ventry.
Earl of Portarlington.	Viscount Powerscourt	Lord Massy.	Lord Dunalley.
Earl of Mayo.	(Baron Powerscourt).	Lord Muskerry.	Lord Castlemaine.
Earl Annesley.	Viscount Bangor.	Lord Kilmaine.	Ld. Oranmore & Browne.
Earl of Lucan.	Viscount Hawarden	Lord Clonbrock.	Lord Rathdonnell.
Earl of Belmore.	(Earl de Montalt).	Lord Headley.	
Earl of Bandon.	Viscount Templetown.	Lord Crofton.	

SCOTTISH AND IRISH PEERS WITH OTHER TITLES IN THE ENGLISH PEERAGE.

Abercorn, D. & E. Abercorn, M.	Bessborough, E. Ponsonby, B.	Cassillis, E. ..... Ailsa, M.
Aberdeen, E. ... Gordon, V.	Boyne, V. .... Brancepeth, B.	Cathcart, B. ...... Cathcart, E.
Armagh, E. ...... Cumberland, D	Breadalbane, E. Breadalbane, M.	Cholmondeley, V. Cholmeley, M.
Arran, E. ...... Sudley, B.	Bridport, B. ...... Bridport, V.	Clancarty, E. ... Clancarty, V.
Athlumney, B... Meredyth, B.	Buccleuch, D. ... Doncaster, E	Clanricarde, M... Somerhill, B.
Atholl, D. .... Strange, E.	Carrington, B. ... Carrington, E.	Clanwilliam, E... Cianwilliam, B.
Barrington, V... Shute, B.	Carysfort, E. ... Carysfort, B.	Clifden, V. ...... Mendip, B.

SCOTTISH AND IRISH PEERS WITH OTHER ENGLISH TITLES—*continued.*

Clive, B. ...... Powis, E.	Galloway, E. ... Stewart of Gar-	Meath, E. .... Chaworth, B.
Conway, B. ...... Hertford, M.	lies, B.	Midleton, V....... Brodrick, B.
Conyngham, M. Minster, B.	Glasgow, E. ...... Fairlie, B.	Monck, V......... Monck, B.
Cork&Orrery, E. Boyle, B.	Gormanston, V. Gormanston, B.	Montrose, D. ... Graham, B.
Courtown, E. ... Saltersford, B.	Gosford, E. ...... Worlingham, B.	Moray, E......... Stuart, B.
Crawford, E. ... Wigan, E.	Granard, E. ...... Granard, B.	Mornington, E.. Wellington, D.
Cremorne, E. ... Dartrey, E.	Grandison, V. ... Jersey, E.	Mulgrave, B. ... Normanby, M.
Dalhousie, E. ... Ramsay, B.	Grimston, V. ... Verulam, E.	Naime, B .... Lansdowne, M.
Darnley, E. ...... Clifton, B.	Hamilton, D. ... Brandon, D.	Napier, B......... Ettrick, B.
De Vesci, V. ... De Vesci, B.	Hawarden, V. ... De Montalt, E.	Normanton, E. . Somerton, B.
Desmond, E. ... Denbigh, E.	Headfort, M. ... Kenlis, B.	Ormonde, M. ... Ormonde, B.
Dingwall, B. ... Cowper, E.	Henley, B.......... Northington, B.	Powerscourt, V. Powerscourt, B.
Donegall, M. ... Fisherwick, B.	Henniker, B. ... Hartismere, B.	Ranfurly, E. ... Ranfurly, B.
Donoughmore, E. Hutchinson, V.	Home, E............ Douglas, B.	Rollo, B. .... Dunning, B.
Downe, V. ...... Dawnay, B.	Hood, B. .... Hood, V.	Rosebery, E....... Rosebery, B.
Downshire, M... Hillsboro', E.	Hopetoun, E. ... Hopetoun, B.	Rothsay, D....... Wales, Pr. of.
Dufferin, B. ... Dufferin, M.	Howth, E. .... Howth, B.	Roxburghe, D.... Innes, E.
Dumfries, E. ... Bute, M.	Huntly, M. ...... Meldrum, B.	Seafield, E. ... Strathspey, B.
Dunblane, V. ... Leeds, D.	Kenmare, E. ... Kenmare, B.	Sefton, E. .... Sefton, B.
Dunmore, E. ... Dunmore, B.	Kerry, E. .... Lansdowne, M	Shannon, E. ... Carleton, B.
Dunraven, E. ... Kenry, B.	Kinnoull, E. ... Hay, B.	Sheffield, E. ... Sheffield, B.
Eglinton, E. ... Winton, E.	Kintore, E. ...... Kintore, B.	Sligo, M. .... MontEagle, B.
Egmont, E. ...Lovel&Holland, B.	Leinster, D. ... Leinster, V.	Southesk, E....... Balinhard, B.
Elgin, E. .... Elgin, B.	Leitrim, E. ...... Clements, B.	Stair, E............ Oxenfoord, B.
Ely, M. .... Loftus, B.	Lennox, E. ...... Richmond, D.	Stormont, V. ... Mansfield, E.
Enniskillen, E. . Grinstead, B.	Limerick, E. ... Foxford, B.	Strathmore, E... Bowes, B.
Erne, E. .... Fermanagh, B.	Listowel, E. ... Hare, E.	Sutherland, E. Sutherland, D.
Erroll, E. ...... Kilmarnock, B.	Londonderry, M. Vane, E.	Talbot of Mal., B. Talb.deMal., B.
Fife, E. .... Fife, D.	Longford, E. ... Silchester, B.	Tweeddale, M... Tweeddale, B.
Fingall, E. ...... Fingall, B.	Lothian, M. ... Ker, B.	Waterford, E. ... Shrewsbury, E.
Forrester, B. ... Verulam, E.	Loudoun, E...... Botreaux, B.	Waterford, M... Tyrone, E.
Gage, V. .... Gage, B.	Lumley, V. ...... Scarbrough, E.	Wemyss, E. ...... Wemyss, B.
Galway, V. ...... Monckton, B.	Massereene, V... Oriel, B.	Westcote, B....... Cobham, V.

Peerage of Scotland.

Those marked * are also Peers of the United Kingdom; † are Representative Peers.

DUKES (8).

Created.		*Family Names.*	Eldest Son or Heir.
1469	*Rothsay	H.R.H. Albert Edward (*Prince of Wales*), b. 1841, m.	
1701	*Argyll	George Douglas Campbell, K.G., K.T., *English Duke*, b. 1823, s. 1847, m.	Duke of York, K.G., b. 1865 Marquess of Lorne, K.T., M.P., b. 1845
1703	*Atholl	John Jas. Hugh Henry Stewart-Murray, K.T., *English Earl*, b. 1840, s. 1864, m.	[D.S.O., b. '71 Marquess of Tullibardine.
1663	*Buccleuch and Queensberry (1683)	Wm. Henry Walter Montagu-Douglas-Scott, K.G., K.T., *English Earl*, b. 1831, s. 1884, m. ...	Earl of Dalkeith, M.P., b. '64
1643	*Hamilton	Alfred D. D.-Hamilton, *E.D.*, b. 1862, s. 1895. ...	Percy D.-Hamilton, b. 1875
1675	*Lennox	C.H.Gordon-Lennox, K.G.,*E.D.*, b.1818, s.1860, w.	Earl of March, b. 1845
1707	*Montrose	Douglas Beresford MaliseRonaldGraham, A.D.C., K.T., *English Earl*, b. 1852, s. 1874, m.	Marq. of Graham, b. 1878
1707	*Roxburghe........	Henry John Innes-Ker, *E.E.*, b.1876, s.1892 ...	Lord Alastair Robert Innes-Ker, b. 1880.

MARQUESSES (4).

1599	*Huntly	Charles Gordon, *E.R.*, b. 1847, s. 1863, m.	Lord Esmé Gordon, b. 1853
1701	*Lothian	Schomberg H. Kerr, K.T., *E.B.*, b. 1833, s. 1870, m.	Lord Jedburgh, b. 1874
1682	*Queensberry	John Sholto Douglas, b. 1844, s. 1858, div.........	Lord Douglas of Hawick, b. 1868
1694	*Tweeddale	Wm. Montagu Hay, K.T., *E.B.*, b.1826, s.1878, m.	Earl of Gifford, b. 1884

EARLS (44).

1606	*Abercorn	Jas.Hamilton,K.G.,C.B., *E.M.,I.D.*, b.1838, s.1885, m.	Marq. of Hamilton, b. 1869
1682	*Aberdeen	J.C.Hamilton-Gordon, G.C.M.G., *E.V.*, b.'47, s.'70, m.	Lord Haddo, b. 1879
1639	*Airlie	David Stanley Wm. Ogilvy, b. 1856, s. 1881, m.	Lord Ogilvy, b. 1893
1677	*Breadalbane	Gavin Campbell, K.G., *E.M.*, b. 1851, s. 1871. m.	Hon. I. Campbell, b. 1859
1469	*Buchan	Shipley Gordon Stuart Erskine, b. '50, s. '98, m.	Lord Cardross, b. 1878
1455	*Caithness	John Sutherland Sinclair, b. 1857, s. 1891	Hon. Norman Sinclair, b.'62
1639	*Carnwath	Robt. Harris Carnwath Dalzell, b.1847, s.1887, tc.	Lord Dalzell, b. 1877
1509	*Cassillis	Archibald Kennedy, *E.M.*, b. 1847, s. 1870, m.	Earl of Cassillis, b. 1872

Created.	Family Name.	Eldest Son or Heir.
1398 *Crawford & Balcarres (1651) ...	Jas. Ludovic Lindsay, K.T., E.B., b. 1847, s. 1880, m.	Lord Balcarres, M.P., b. '71
1633 *Dalhousie	Arthur Geo. M. Ramsay, E.B., b. 1878, s. 1887 ...	Hon. P.W.M.Ramsay, b.'79
1633 *Dumfries & Bute (1703)	John Patrick Crichton-Stuart, K.T., E.M., b. 1847, s. 1848, m.	Earl of Dumfries, b. 1881
1669 †Dundonald	Doug.M.B.H. Cochrane, C.B., M.V.O., b.'52, s. '85, m.	Lord Cochrane, b. 1886
1686 *Dunmore	Chas. Adolphus Murray, E.B., b. 1841, s. 1845, m.	Visc. Fincastle, V.C., b. 1871
1643 *Dysart	Wm. John Manners Tollemache, b. 1859, s. 1878, m.	Lady Agnes Scott, b. 1855
1508 *Eglinton & Winton (1600)	G. A. Montgomerie, E.E., b. 1848, s. 1892, m.	Lord Montgomerie, b. 1880
1633 *Elgin & Kincardine (1647)	Victor Alex. Bruce, K.G., G.C.S.I., G.C.I.E., E.B., b. 1849, s. 1863, m.	Lord Bruce, b. 1881
1453 *Erroll	Charles Gore Hay, E.B., b. 1852, s. 1891, m.....	Lord Kilmarnock, b. 1876
1623 *Galloway	Alan P. Stewart, K.T., E.B., b. 1835, s. 1873, m.	Hon. R. H. Stewart, b. 1836
1703 *Glasgow............	David Boyle, G.C.M.G., E.B., b. 1833, s. 1890, m.	Viscount Kelburne, b. 1874
1619 *Haddington	Geo. Baillie-Hamilton-Arden, b. 1827, s. 1870, w.	Lord Binning, b. 1856
1605 *Home	C.A. Douglas-Home, K.T., E.B., b. 1834, s. 1881, m.	Lord Dunglass, b. 1873
1703 *Hopetoun	John A.L. Hope, G.C.M.G., E.B., b. 1860, s. 1873, m.	Lord Hope, b. 1887
1633 *Kinnoull	Archib. F. G. Hay, E.B., b. 1855, s. 1897, m......	Viscount Dupplin, b. 1879
1677 *Kintore	Algernon Hawkins Thomond Keith-Falconer, G.C.M.G., E.B., b. 1852, s. 1880, m.	Lord Falconer, b. 1879
1624 †Lauderdale	Frederick Henry Maitland, b. 1840, s. 1884, m..	Viscount Maitland, b. 1858
1641 *Leven & Melville (1690)	Ronald R. Leslie-Melville, b. 1835, s. 1889, m.	Lord Balgonie, b. 1886
1633 Lindsay	David Clark Fethune, b. 1832, s. 1894, m.........	Viscount Garnock, b. 1867
1633 *Loudoun	Chas. E. Abney-Hastings, E.B., b.1855, s.1874, m.	Hon. P. Rawdon-Hastings, b. 1855
1404 †Mar	John F. Erskine Goodeve-Erskine, b. 1836, s. 1866, m. Title confirmed by Act of Parliament, 1885	Lord Garioch, b. 1868
1565 †Mar & Kellie (1619)	Walter John Francis Erskine, b. 1865, s. 1888, m..	Lord Erskine, b. 1895
1562 *Moray	Edmund A. Stuart, E.B., b. 1840, s. 1895, m......	Fras. J. Stuart-Gray, b. 1842
1458 *Morton	Sholto George W. Douglas, b. 1844, s. 1884, m...	Lord Aberdour, b. 1878
1660 Newburgh	Sigismund Giustiniani-Bandini, b.1818, s.1877, w.	Viscount Kynnaird, b. 1862
1647 *Northesk.........	David John Carnegie, b. 1865, s. 1891, m.........	Hn. Douglas Carnegie, b. '70
1696 Orkney	Edmond Walter FitzMaurice, b. 1867, s. 1889, m.	Hon. A. E. FitzMaurice b. '74
1605 Perth &	George Drummond, b. 1807, s. 1840, claim to succession established 1853, w.	Visct. Strathallan, b. 1871
1686 Melfort		Lady E. Drummond, b. 1854
1703 *Rosebery	A. P. Primrose, K.G., K.T., E.B., b. 1847, s.1868, w.	Lord Dalmeny, b. 1882
1458 *Rothes	Norman Evelyn Leslie, b. 1877, s. 1893	Lady Mary E. Leslie, b. 1875
1701 *Seafield	James Grant-Ogilvie, E.B., b. 1876, s. 1889, m.	Hn.Trevor G.-Ogilvie, b.'79
1633 *Southesk	James Carnegie, K.T., E.B., b. 1827, s. 1855, m.	Lord Carnegie, b. 1854
1703 *Stair	J. Hamilton Dalrymple, K.T., E.B., b.1819, s.'64, w.	Visct. Dalrymple, b. 1848
1677 *Strathmore & Kinghorne (1606)	Claude Bowes-Lyon, E.B., b.'24, s.'65, m.	Lord Glamis, b. 1855
1228 *Sutherland.........	Cromartie S.-L.-Gower, E.D., b. 1851, s.1892, m.	Marq. of Stafford, b. 1888
1633 * Wemyss & March (1697)	Francis Wemyss-Charteris-Douglas, E.B., b. 1818, s. 1883, w.	Lord Elcho, b. 1857

VISCOUNTS (5).

1641 Arbuthnott.........	David Arbuthnott, b. 1845, s. 1895	Hn.HughArbuthnott, b.'47
1675 *Dunblane	George Godolphin Osborne, E.D., b. 1862, s. 1895, m.	Lord Francis Godolphin Osborne, R.N., b. 1864
1620 †Falkland	Byron Plantagenet Cary, b. 1845, s. 1886, m...	Master of Falkland, b. 1880
1621 *Stormont	W. D. Murray, E.E., b. 1860, s. 1898	Hon. And. Murray, b. 1863
1686 Strathallan	William Huntly Drummond, b. 1871, s. 1893 ...	Hon.J.E Drummond, b.'76

BARONS (25).

1607 †Balfour of Burleigh	Alexander Hugh Bruce, b. 1849, s. 1869, m......	Master of Burleigh, b. 1880
1647 Belhaven & Stenton	Alexander Chas. Hamilton, b. 1840, s. 1894, m...	Master of Belhaven, b. 1833
1606 *Blantyre............	Charles Stuart, b. 1818, s. 1830, w................	(None) [b. 1865
1452 Borthwick............	Archibald P. T. Borthwick, b. 1867, s. 1885	Hon. Gabrielle Borthwick,
1447 *Cathcart............	Alan Fredk. Cathcart, E.E., b. 1828, s. 1859, m..	Lord Greenock, b. 1856
1604 *Colville of Culross	C.J.Colville, K.T., G.C.V.O., E.B., b. 1818, s. 1849, m.	Master of Colville, b. 1854
1609 *Dingwall	Francis Thomas de Grey Cowper, K.G., E.E., b. 1834, s. 1871, m.	Auberon T. Herbert, b. 1876
1643 *Elibank	Montolieu Fox O. Murray, b. 1840, s. 1871, m....	Master of Elibank, b. 1870
1510 *Elphinstone	Sidney H. Elphinstone, E.B., b. 1869, s. 1893 ...	Hon. M. Elphinstone, b. '71
1627 Fairfax of Cameron	John Contée Fairfax, b. 1830, s. 1869, m...........	Hon. A. K. Fairfax, b. 1870
1442 *Forbes	Horace C. Gammell-Forbes, b. 1829, s. 1868	Hon. A. M. Forbes, b. 1841
1633 *Forrester	J. W. Grimston, F.R., I.V., b. 1852, s. 1895, m..	Viscount Grimston, b. 1852
1489 *Herries	M. F. Constable-Maxwell, E.B., b. 1837, s.1876, m.	Hn.Gwend. Maxwell, b. 1877
1682 *Kinnaird	Arthur F. Kinnaird, E.B., b. 1847, s. 1887, m.....	Master of Kinnaird, b. 1879
1539 *Lovat	Simon Joseph Fraser, E.B., b. 1871, s. 1887	Hon. H. J. Fraser, b. 1874
1681 *Nairne	H. C. K. P.-Fitzmaurice, K.G., G.C.S.I., G.C.M.G., G.C.I.E. (E.M., I.E.), b. 1845, s. 1895, m.....	Earl of Kerry, b. 1872
1627 *Napier	Wm. Jno. Geo. Napier, E.B., b. 1846, s. 1898, m.	Master of Napier, b. 1876

Created.	Family Name.	Eldest Son or Heir.
1690 +Polwarth	Walter Hugh Hepburne-Scott, b. 1838, s. 1867, m.	Master of Polwarth, b. 1864
1628 *Reay	Donald James Mackay, G.C.S.I., G.C.I.E., E.B., b. 1839, s. 1876, m	Baron Æneas Mackay, b.'38
1651 *Rollo	J. Rogerson Rollo, E.B., b. 1835, s. 1852, m....	Master of Rollo, b. 1860
1651 Ruthven	Walter Jas. Hore-Ruthven, b. 1838, s. 1864, m...	Master of Ruthven, b. 1870
1445 +Saltoun	Alexander Wm. Fredk. Fraser, b. 1851, s. 1886, m...	Master of Saltoun, b. 1886
1489 Sempill	William Forbes, b. 1836, s. 1884, m.....	Master of Sempill, b. 1863
1489 *Sinclair	Charles William St. Clair, b. 1831, s. 1880, m....	Master of Sinclair, b. 1875
1564 +Torphichen	James Walter Sandilands, b.1846, s.1869, obtd.div.	Master of Torphichen, b.'84
	BARONESSES (2).	
1445 Gray	Eveleen Smith-Gray, b. 1841, s. 1896, m.....	Master of Gray, b. 1854
1602 Kinloss	Mary Morgan-Grenville, C.I., b. 1852, s. 1889, w.	Master of Kinloss, b. 1887

Peerage of Ireland

Irish Peers have an advantage over those of Scotland inasmuch as (if not peers of Parliament) they are eligible for seats in the House of Commons. for constituencies in Great Britain *i.e.*, Viscount Valentia for Oxford City). Those marked * are also Peers of Great Britain or of the United Kingdom; † are Representative Peers.

DUKES (2).

1868 *Abercorn	James Hamilton, K.G., C.B., E.M., S.E., b.'38, s.'85, m.	Marq. of Hamilton, b. 1869
1766 *Leinster	Maurice FitzGerald, E.V., b. 1887, s. 1893, M...	Lord D. FitzGerald, b. 1888

MARQUESSES (10).

1825 *Clanricarde	Hubert G. De-Burgh-Canning, E.B., b. 1832, s.1874	Marq. Sligo, b.'24 (to Earld.)
1816 *Conyngham	V.G. H. F. Conyngham, E.B., b. 1883, s. 1897, M.	Ld.F.W.B.Conyngham, b.'90
1791 *Donegall	George Augustus Hamilton Chichester, E.B., b. 1822, s. 1889, m	Lord Henry Fitzwarrine Chichester, b. 1834
1789 *Downshire	A. W. J. W. B. T. Hill, E.E., b. 1871, s. 1874, m.	Earl of Hillsborough, b. '94
1800 *Ely	John Henry Loftus, E.B., b. 1851, s. 1889, m.	Lord Geo. H. Loftus, b. 1854
1800 *Headfort	Geoffrey Thos. Taylour, E.B., b. 1878, s. 1894	Edward H. Taylour, b. 1860
1816 *Londonderry	Charles Stewart Vane-Tempest-Stewart, A.D.C., K.G., E.E., b. 1852, s. 1884, m...	Visct. Castlereagh, b. 1878
1825 *Ormonde	James Edward William Theobald Butler, K.P., E.B., b. 1844, s. 1854, m............	Lord Jas. A. Butler, b. 1849
1800 *Sligo	Jno. Thos. Browne, E.B., b. 1844, s. 1896, m. ...	Lord Ulick Browne, b. 1831
1789 *Waterford	Hy. de la Poer Beresford, E.B., b. 1875, s. 1895, m.	Ld. Charles Beresford, C.B., M.P., b. 1846

EARLS (62).

1789 +Annesley	Hugh Annesley, b. 1831, s. 1874, m.	Viscount Glerawly, b. 1884
1785 Antrim	Wm. Randal M'Donnell, b. 1851, s. 1869, m.	Viscount Dunluce, b. 1878
1799 *Armagh	Ernest Augustus, E.D., b. 1845, s. 1878, m.	Earl of Armagh, b. 1880
1762 *Arran	Arthur S. W. C. Fox Gore, E.B., K.P., b. 1839, s. 1884, m ...	Viscount Sudley, b. 1868
1800 +Bandon	James Francis Bernard, b. 1850, s. 1877, m.	Percy B. Bernard, b. 1844
1797 +Belmore	S. R. Lowry-Corry, G.C.M.G., b. 1835, s. 1845, m.	Viscount Corry, b. 1870
1739 +Bessborough	Rev.W. W. B. Ponsonby, E.B., b. 1821, s. 1895, m.	Visct. Duncannon, C.B., b.'51
1800 Caledon	Erik James D. Alexander, b. 1885, s. 1898, M...	Hon. H.C.Alexander, b. '88
1748 Carrick	Somerset Arthur Butler, b. 1835, s. 1846	Maj. C. H. S. Butler, b. 1851
1789 *Carysfort	William Proby, K.P., E.B., b. 1836, s. 1872, m...	(None)
1800 Castlestewart	Hy. Jas. Stuart-Richardson, b. 1837, s. 1874, m.	Andrew J. Stuart, b. 1841
1647 Cavan	Frederick E. Gould Lambart, K.P., b.'39, s.'87, m.	Visct. Kilcoursie, b. 1865
1803 *Clancarty	Wm. F. Le-Poer-Trench, E.V., b. 1868, s.1891, m.	Lord Kilconnel, b. 1891
1776 *Clanwilliam	Rd. Jas. Meade, G.C.B., K.C.M.G., E.B., b.'32,s.'79,m.	Lord Gillford, b. 1868
1793 Clonmell	Rupert Charles Scott, b. 1877, s. 1898	Hon. L. G. Scott, b. 1850
1620 *Cork& Orrery(1660)	Rd. E. St. L. Boyle, K.P., E.B., b. 1829, s. 1856, m.	Visct. Dungarvan, b. 1861
1762 *Courtown	Jas. G. Henry Stopford, E.B., b. 1823, s. 1853, w.	Viscount Stopford, b. 1853
1725 Darnley	Edward Hy Stuart Bligh, E.B., b. 1851, s. 1845, m.	Hon. Ivo Bligh, b. 1859
1793 Desart	H. J. Agmondesham Cuffe, K.C.B., b. '48, s. '98, m.	Hon. Otway Cuffe, b. 1853
1622 *Desmond	Rudolph Robert Basil Aloysius A. Feilding, E.E., b. 1859, s. 1892, m.	Viscount Feilding, b. 1885
1800 *Donoughmore	J.L.Hely-Hutchinson, K.C.M.G., E.V., b.'48, s.'66, m.	Viscount Suirdale, b. 1875
1661 +Drogheda	Ponsonby William Moore, b. 1846, s. 1892, m.	Viscount Moore, b. 1884
1822 *Dunraven and Mount Earl.	Windham Thomas Wyndham-Quin, K.P., E.B., b. 1841, s. 1871, m.	Windham Henry Wyndham-Quin, M.P., b. 1857
1733 *Egmont	Augustus A. Perceval, E.B., b. 1856, s. 1897, m...	Chas. J. Perceval, b. 1858
1789 *Enniskillen	Lowry Egerton Cole, E.B., b. 1845, s. 1886, m...	Viscount Cole, b. 1876
1789 *Erne	John Hen. Crichton, K.P., E.B., b. 1839, s. 1885, m.	Viscount Crichton, b. 1872
1759 *Fife	Alexander William George Duff, K.T., E.D., b. 1849, s. 1879. m.	(None)
628 *Fingall	Arthur Jas. F. Plunkett, E.B., b. 1859, s. 1881, m.	Lord Killeen, b. 1856

Created.	Family Name.	Eldest Son or Heir.
1716 *Fitzwilliam	Wm. Thomas Spencer Wentworth-Fitzwilliam, K.G., *E.E.*, b. 1815, s. 1857, w......	Visct. Milton, M.P., b. 1872
1806 *Gosford	A. B. S. Acheson, K.P., *E.B.*, b. 1841, s. 1864, m.	Viscount Acheson, b. 1877
1684 *Granard	B. A. W. Patrick H. Forbes, *E.B.*, b. 1874, s. 1889	Hon. R. G.B. Forbes, b.1877
1767 *Howth	W.U.Tristram St.Lawrence, K.P., *E.B.*, b. 27, s. 74	(None)
1800 *Kenmare	Val. Aug. Browne, K.P., *E.B.*, b. 1825, s. 1871, m.	Visct. Castlerosse, b. 1860
1723 *Kerry and Shelburn (1753)	Hen.Chas.Keith Petty-Fitzmaurice, K.G. G.C.S.I., G.C.M.G. G.C.I.E., *E.M.*, *S.B.*, b 1845, s. 1866, m.	Earl of Kerry, b. 1872
1822 +Kilmorey	Francis Charles Needham, K.P., b. 1842, s. 1880, m.	Viscount Newry, b. 1883
1768 Kingston	Henry Edwyn King-Tenison, b. 1874, s. 1896, m.	Visct.Kingsborough, b.1897
1797 Landaff	[*Claimant* Arnold Harris Mathew, b. 1852, m.]	(None)
1756 +Lanesborough	Jno. Vansittart Danvers Butler, b. 39, s. 66, m.	LordNewtown-Butler, b. 65
1795 *Leitrim	Charles Clements, *E.B.*, b. 1879, s. 1892, M. ...	Hon. F. P. Clements, b.1895
1803 *Limerick	W. H. E. de Vere S. Pery, *E.B.*, b.1863, s.1896, m.	Visct. Glentworth, b. 1894
1776 Lisburne	Ernest E. H. Malet Vaughan, b. 1892, s. 1899, M	Geo. Aug. Vaughan, b. 1833
1822 *Listowel	William Hare, K.P., *E.B.*, b. 1833, s. 1856, m. ...	Visct. Ennismore, b. 1866
1785 *Longford	Thomas Pakenham, *E.B.*, b. 1864, s. 1887	Hon.E.M. Pakenham, b. 66
1795 +Lucan	George Bingham, K.P., b. 1830, s. 1888, m. ...	Lord Bingham, b. 1860
1785 +Mayo	Dermot R. Wyndham Bourke, b. 1851, s. 1872, m.	Hon. M. A. Bourke, b.1853
1627 *Meath	Reginald Brabazon, *E.B.*, b. 1841, s. 1887, m......	Lord Ardee, b. 1869
1766 Mexborough	John Horace Savile, b. 1843 s. 1899 m.	Hon. Jno. H. Savile, b. 1868
1763 Milltown	Claimed by both John and Robt. W. F. Leeson.	(Uncertain)
1760 *Mornington	Henry Wellesley, *E.D.*, b. 1846, s. 1884, m.	Lord A. C. Wellesley, b. 49
1781 MountCashell	Eawd. Geo. A. Harcourt Moore, b. 1829, s. 1898	(None)
1827 Norbury	Wm Brabazon Lindesay Graham-Toler, b. 62, s. 73	Hector Rob. G.-Toler, b. 47
1806 *Normanton	Sidney James Agar, *E.B.*, b. 1865, s. 1896, m	Hon. Fras. W.A.Agar, b.1873
1785 +Portarlington	L. G. H. Seymour Dawson-Damer, b. 58, s. 92, m.	Viscount Carlow, b. 1883
1831 *Ranfurly	U. J. Mark Knox, K.C.M.G., *E.B.*, b.1856,s.1875, m.	Viscount Northland, b.1884
1771 Roden	William Hy. Jocelyn, b. 1842, s. 1897	Hon. R J. Jocelyn, b. 1845
1806 *Rosse	Laurence Parsons, *E.B.*, b. 1840, s. 1867, m. ...	Lord Oxmantown, b. 1873
1771 *Sefton	Chas. Wm. H. Molyneux, *E.B.*, b. 1867, s. 1897	Hn. Osbert Molyneux, b. 71
1756 *Shannon	Richard Henry Boyle, *E.B.*, b. 1860, s. 1890, m	Viscount Boyle, b. 1883
1816 *Sheffield	Henry North Holroyd, *E.B.*, b. 1832, s. 1876 ...	Bn. Stanley, b. 27 (to I.B.)
1446 *Waterford	C. H. J. Chetwynd Talbot, *E.E.*, b.1860, s.1877, m.	Viscount Ingestre, b. 1882
1621 Westmeath	Anthony Francis Nugent, b. 1870, s. 1883	Hon. W. A. Nugent, b. 1870
1793 Wicklow	Ralph Francis Howard, b. 1877, s. 1891	Hon. Hugh Howard, b. 1883
1766 Winterton	Edward Turnour, b. 1837, s. 1879, m;.	Viscount Turnour, b. 1883

VISCOUNTS (36).

1751 Ashbrook	William Spencer Flower, b. 1830, s. 1882, m......	Hon. R. T. Flower, b 1830
1800 Avonmore	Algernon William Yelverton, b. 1855, s. 1885, m.	W. H. M.Yelverton, b. 1843
1781 +Bangor	Henry William Crosbie Ward, b. 1828, s. 1881, m.	Hon. Maxwell Ward, b.1868
1720 *Barrington	Percy Barrington, *E.B.*, b. 1825, s. 1886, w. ...	Hon. W.B.Barrington, b. 48
1717 *Boyne	G. R. Hamilton-Russell, *E.B.*, b. 1830, s. 1872, m.	Hon. G. H.-Russell, b. 1864
1665 *Charlemont......	James Alfred Caulfeild, C.B., b. 1830, s. 1892, m	James E. Caulfeild, b. 1880
1717 *Chetwynd	Richard Walter Chetwynd, b. 1823, s. 1879, w...	Hon. R. W. Chetwynd, b. 59
1661 *Cholmondeley......	Geo.Hy.H. Cholmondeley, *E.M.*, b. 58, s. 1884, m.	Earl of Rocksavage, b. 1883
1781 *Clifden	Thos.Chas.Agar-Robartes, *E.B.*, b.1844, s.1899, m.	Hn. Thos. A.-Robartes, b. 80
1776 *De Vesci	John Robt. Wm. Vesey, *E.B.*, b. 1844, s. 1875, m.	Yvo Richard Vesey, b. 1881
1622 Dillon	Harold Arthur Dillon-Lee, *E.B.*, b. 1844, s. 1892, m. ...	Hn. H. Lee-Dillon, b. 1874
1785 Doneraile	Edward St. Leger, b. 1866, s. 1891	Hon.Ralph St.Leger, b.1868
1680 *Downe	Hugh R. Dawnay, C.I.E., *E.B.*, b. 1844, s. 1857, m.	Hon. John Dawnay, b. 1872
1816 Frankfort de Montmorency ...	Raymond H. De Montmorency, K.C.B., b. 1835, s. 1889, m...	Hon. R. De Montmorency, *EC.*, b. 1857
1720 *Gage	Henry Charles Gage, *E.B.*, b. 1854, s. 1877, m...	Hon. Henry R. Gage, b. 1895
1727 *Galway	G.E.Monckton-Arundell, A.D.C. *E.B.*, b. 44, s. 76, m.	Hon. G. M.-Arundell, b. 82
1478 *Gormanston......	Jenico W.J.Preston, G.C.M.G., *E.B.*, b.1837, s. 76, m.	Hon. J.E.J.Preston, b.1879
1816 Gort	Standish P. Vereker, b. 1819, s. 1865, w.	Hon. J. G. P. Vereker, b. 49
1620 *Grandison	V.A.G.C.-Villiers, G.C.M.G., *E.E.*, b.1845, s.1859, m.	Viscount Villiers, b. 1873
1719 *Grimston	J. W. Grimston, *E.E.*, *S.B.*, b. 1852, s. 1895, m.	Viscount Grimston, b. 1880
1831 Guillamore......	Hardress Standish O'Grady, *E.B.*, b. 1841, s. 1877	Hon. F. S. O'Grady, b. 1847
1791 Harberton	James Spencer Pomeroy, b. 1836, s. 1862, m.	Hon.E.A.G Pomeroy, b. 67
1791 *+Hawarden	Cornwallis Maude, *E.E.*, b. 1817, s. 1856, w...	Lt.-Col. R. H. Maude, b.1842
1781 Liford	James Wilfrid Hewitt, b. 1837, s. 1887, m.	Hn. Arch Rbt. Hewitt, b. 44
1628 *Lumley	Aldred F. G. B. Lumley, *E.E.*, b. 1857, s. 1884, m.	Hn.O.V.G.A. Lumley, b. 62
1660 *Massereene and Ferrard (1797)	Clotworthy J. Eyre Foster-Skeffington, *E.B.*, b. 1842, s. 1863, m.	Hon. Oriel J. C. W.-M. F.-Skeffington, b. 1871
1717 *Midleton	William Brodrick, *E.B.*, b. 1830, s. 1870, m....	Rt. Hn.St.J.Brodrick, M.P., b. 56
1716 Molesworth......	Rev. Samuel Molesworth, b. 1829, s. 1875, m. ...	Hon.G.B.Molesworth, b. 67
1800 *Monck	Henry P. C. S. Monck, *E.B.*, b. 1849, s. 1894, m.	Hon. C. H. S. Monck, b.1876
1550 Mountgarret	Henry Edmund Butler, b. 1816, s. 1846, w...	Hon. H. E. Butler, b. 1844
1763 Mountmorres	Wm G. B. De Montmorency, b. 1872, s. 1880, m	Hn.F.DeMontmorency, b. 35
1744 *+Powerscourt	Mervyn Wingfield, K.P., *E.B.*, b. 1836, s. 1844, m.	Hon.M.R.Wingfield, b. 1880
1770 Southwell	Arthur Robt. Pyers Southwell, b. 1872, s. 1878, m.	Hon. Robt. Southwell, b. 98

Created.	Family Name.	Eldest Son or Heir.
1628 Taaffe	Henry Taaffe, b. 1872, s. 1895, m.	Hon. Ed. Taaffe, b. 1898.
1806 †Templetown	Henry E. M. D. C. Upton, b. 1853, s. 1890, m....	Hon. Eric Upton, b. 1885
1622 Valentia	Arthur Annesley, M.P., b. 1843, s. 1863, m..........	Hon. A. Annesley, b. 1880

BARONS (65).

Created.	Family Name.	Eldest Son or Heir.
1800 Ashtown	Frederick Oliver Trench, b. 1868, s. 1880, m......	Hon. F. S. Trench, b. 1894
1863 *Athlumney	J. H. G. M. Somerville, E.B., b. 1865, s. 1873 ...	(None to peerage)
1789 *Auckland	William Morton Eden, E.B., b. 1859, s. 1890, m.	Hon. W. Morton Eden, b.'92
1718 Aylmer	Udolphus Aylmer, b. 1814, s. 1858, w...........	Hon. Matthew Aylmer, b.'42
1848 Bellew	Charles Bertram Bellew, b. 1855, s. 1895, m......	Hon. G. L. Bryan, b. 1857
1794 *Bridport	A. Nelson Hood, G.C.B., E.V., b. 1814, s. 1868, w...	Hon. A. Hood, C.B., b. 1839
1715 Carbery	John Evans-Freke, b. 1892, s. 1838, M.	Hon. R. Evans-Freke, b.' 97
1834 Carew	Robt. Shapland Carew, E.B., b. 1860, s. 1881, m.	Hon. G. P. J. Carew, b. 1863
1796 *Carrington	C.R. Wynn-Carrington, G.C.M.G., E.E.,b.'43,s.'68, m.	Visct. Wendover, b. 1895
1812 †Castlemaine	Albert Edward Handcock, b. 1863, s. 1892, m....	Hon.R.A. Handcock,b.1864
1800 Clanmorris	John Geo. Barry Bingham, b. 1852, s. 1876, m....	Hon.A.M.R.Bingham, b.'79
1800 Clarina	Lionel Edwd. Butler-Massey, b. 1837, s. 1897, m.	Hon. Eyre N. Massey, b.'80.
1762 *Clive	George Charles Herbert, E.E., b. 1862, s. 1891, m.	Viscount Clive, b. 1892
1790 *Clonbrock	Luke Gerald Dillon, b. 1834, s. 1893, m.........	Hon. R. E. Dillon, b. 1869
1789 *Cloncurry	Valentine Fredk. Lawless, E.B., b.1840, s.1869, w.	Hon. E. Lawless, b. 1841
1712 *Conway	Hugh De Grey Seymour, E.M., b. 1843, s.1884, m.	Earl of Yarmouth, b. 1871
1797 *Cremorne	Vesey Dawson, E.E., b. 1842, s. 1897, m.	Hon. E. S. Dawson, b. 1843
1797 *Crofton	Edward Henry C. Crofton, b. 1834, s. 1869	Arth. E. L. Crofton,b. 1856
1898 Curzon of Kedleston	Geo. Nathaniel Curzon, P.C., G.M.S.I., G.M.I.E., Viceroy of India, b. 1859, 1st B., m.	(None)
1800 De Blaquiere ...	William de Blaquiere, b. 1855, s. 1889, m. ...	Hn. John de Blaquiere, b.'89
1812 Decies	W. M. de la Poer Horsley-Beresford, b.'65, s.'93	Hn.Jno.H.-Beresford,b.'66
1620 *Digby	E. H. Trafalgar Digby, E.B., b. 1846, s. 1889, m.	Hon. E. K. Digby, b. 1894
1800 *Dufferin and Claneboye	Fred. T. H.-Temple-Blackwood, K.P., G.C.B., G.C.S.I.,G.C.M.G.,G.C.I.E.,E.M.,b.1826,s.1841,m.	Earl of Ava, b. 1863
1300 †Dunalley	Henry O'Callaghan Prittie, b. 1851, s. 1885, m....	Hon.H.C.O'C.Prittie,b.'77
1541 Dunboyne	FitzWalter Robt.St. John Butler, b.1844, s.'59, m.	Hon. FitzW. Butler, b. 1874
1845 Dunsandle and ClanConal	James Frederick Daly, b. 1849, s. 1894 ...	(None)
1439 Dunsany	Edwd. Jno. M. Drax Plunkett, b. 1878, s. 1899 ..	Hn.Regd.A.Plunkett,b.'80
1756 †Earnham	Somerset H. Maxwell, b. 1849, s. 1896, w......	Hn. Arth. K. Maxwell,b.'79
1856 Fermoy	Edwd. FitzEdm. Burke Roche, b. 1850, s.1874, m.	Hn.J.B.B. Roche, M.P.,b.'52
1798 *Ffrench	Charles A. T. R. J. J. Ffrench, b. 1868, s. 1893, m.	Hon.Jno.M. Ffrench, b.'72
1800 *Gardner	(Vacant)	
1818 Garvagh	Chas. J. S. G. Canning, b. 1852, s. 1871, m.	Hn.L.E.S.G.Canning,b.'78
1794 Graves	Clarence Edward Graves, b. 1847, s. 1870, m. ...	Henry Cyril Graves, b. 1847
1797 †Headley	Chas. Mark Allanson-Winn, b. 1845, s. 1877, m.	Rowland G. A.-Winn, b.'55
1799 *Henley	Frederic Henley, E.B., b. 1849, s. 1898	Hon. A. E. Henley, b. 1858
1800 *Henniker	John M. Henniker-Major, E.B., b.1842, s.1870, w.	Hon.A.E.J.H.-Major,b.'65
1782 *Hood	Francis Wheler Hood, E.V., b. 1838, s. 1846, m.	Hon. G. A. A. Hood, b. 1868
1797 Hotham	John Hotham, b. 1838, s. 1872	Rev. J. H. Hotham, b. 1811
1796 Huntingfield	Joshua Charles Vanneck, b. 1842, s. 1897	Hn.Wm.A.Vanneck,b.1843
1543 *Inchiquin	Edward Donough O'Brien, K.P.b.'39, s. 1872, m.	Hon. L. W. O'Brien, b.1864
1776 *Kensington	William Edwardes, E.B., b. 1868, s. 1896	Hon. H. Edwardes, b. 1873
1789 *Kilmaine	Francis William Browne, b. 1843, s. 1873, m. ..	Hon. J. E. D. Browne, b.'75
1223 *Kingsale	Michael C. De Courcy, b. 1855, s. 1895, m.	Hon.M.W. De Courcy,b.'82
1800 †Langford	Hercules Edward Rowley, b. 1848, s. 1854, m. ...	Hon. H. Rowley, b. 1894
1758 Lisle	Geo. Wm. Jas. Lysaght, b. 1840, s. 1898, m.	Hon. Hor. Lysaght, b. 1873
1541 Louth	Randal Pilgrim R. Plunkett, b. 1868, s. 1883, m.	Hon.Otway Plunkett, b.'92
1776 Macdonald	Ronald Archibald Macdonald, b. 1853, s. 1874, m.	Hn.S.G.J.Macdonald, b.'76
1776 Massy	John Thos. Wm. Massy, b. 1835, s. 1874, w......	Hon. H. S. J. Massy, b.'64
1767 *Mulgrave	Rev. Constantine C. H. Phipps, E.M.,b.'46, s.'90	Geo. A. C. Phipps, b. 1875
1783 *Muncaster	Josslyn F. Pennington, E.B., b. 1834, s. 1862, m.	Hn.A.J. Pennington, b.'37
1781 *Muskerry	H. M. Fitzm. Deane-Morgan, b. 1854, s. 1868, m.	Hon.H.F.D.-Morgan,b.'73
1776 Newborough	William Charles Wynn, b. 1873, s. 1888	Hn.Thos. John Wynn, b.'78
1836 †Oranmore and Browne	Geoffrey Dominick Augustus Fredk. Browne-Guthrie, b. 1819, s. 1860, w................	Hon.G.H.B.-Guthrie, b.'61
1800 Radstock.........	Granv. A. W. Waldegrave, b. 1833, s. 1857, w...	Hn.G.G. Waldegrave, b.'59
1868 *Rathdonnell	T. Kane McClintock-Bunbury, b.1848, s.1879, m.	Hn.W.McC.-Bunbury,b.'74
1806 Rendlesham	F. W. Brook Thellusson, b. 1840, s. 1852, w......	Hon. F. Thellusson, b. 1868
1796 *Rossmore	Derrick W. W. Westenra, E.E., b. 1853, s. 1874, m.	Hon. Wm. Westenra, b.'72
1627 Sherard	Castel Sherard, b. 1849, s. 1886, m...........	Philip H. Sherard, b. 1851
1831 *Talbot of Malahide	Richd. Wogan Talbot, E.B., b. 1846, s. 1883, w.	Hon. J. B. Talbot, b. 1874
1797 Teignmouth	Charles John Shore, b. 1840, s. 1885, m.......	Hon. F. W. J. Shore, b.1844
1461 Trimlestown	Charles Aloysius Barnewall, b. 1861, s. 1891, m.	Hon. R. Barnewall, b. 1897
1800 †Ventry	D. B. Eveleigh-de-Moleyns, b. 1828, s. 1868, m.	Hon. F. R. Eveleigh-de-Moleyns, D.S O., b. 1851
1800 Wallscourt	Erroll Augustus J. H. Blake, b. 1841, s. 1849, m.	Hon.C.W.J.H.Blake,b.'75
1792 Waterpark........	Henry Anson Cavendish, b. 1839, s. 1863, m.....	Hon. C. Cavendish, b. 1883
1776 *Westcote	Chas. Geo. Lyttelton, E.V., b. 1842, s. 1876, m.	Hon. J.C. Lyttelton, b. 1881

The Houses of Parliament.—ii. The House of Commons.

THE constitution of Parliament, as it now exists, dates back almost eight centuries to the time of King John and Magna Charta. In this document there is a provision that "no scutage or aid shall be imposed in our realm save by the Commune Concilium of the realm," and to this Council were to be summoned the Prelates and Greater Barons individually, and the Lesser Barons and Tenants-in-chief collectively. From this groundwork the National Assembly has grown up through the reigns of the various Sovereigns until it has assumed its present shape. The principal landmarks of this growth are, the summons of citizens from Boroughs by Simon de Montfort, the assumption of the maxim "Grievances precede supply" under the Tudors and Stuarts; and the appearance of the office of Prime Minister, with the abolition of the custom of the Sovereign presiding at meetings of the Ministers, under the House of Hanover.

The representation in the Commons varied considerably until 1885, since which date it has stood at 670 :—465 members from England, 30 from Wales, 72 from Scotland, and 103 from Ireland. Previous to the Union with Scotland, in 1707, the House consisted of only 513 members; in that year 45 were added for the new Kingdom. In 1801, when Ireland became part of the Kingdom, 100 members were added, and in 1832 the Reform Act raised the representation of Ireland to 105, and that of Scotland to 53. Between this date and 1885 only one change was made, 7 members being added to Scotland in 1867. Many of the old abuses have been swept away by the different Acts of Reform, but much confusion still remains in the nomenclature of the various divisions and subdivisions of the constituencies, in consequence of which the members for Shoreditch, for instance, must be sought under the headings Haggerston and Hoxton.

The allotment of members to the great divisions of the Kingdom is shown in the following table, which also presents a view of the balance of parties as returned by each division at the General Election of 1895 :—

	DISTRIBUTION OF MEMBERS.				§ POSITION AS TO PARTIES (1895).		
	Counties.	Boroughs.	Universities.	Total Members.	Ministerial.	Opposition.	Majority.
England	234	226	5	465	349	116	233 *Min.*
Wales	19	11	—	30	8	22	14 *Opp.*
Scotland	39	31	2	72	33	39	6 *Opp.*
Ireland	85	16	2	103	21	82	61 *Opp.*
United Kingdom	377	284	9	670	411	259	152 *Min.*

More precisely, the parties stood as follows : Ministerialists, 411 (Conservatives 340; Liberal Unionists 71) ; Opposition, 259 (Liberals 177, Anti-Parnellites 71, Parnellites 11) ; the Labour Party being represented by 10 Liberals and 2 Anti-Parnellites.

The letters after the names are—*C.* Conservative, *U.* Liberal-Unionist, *L.* Liberal, *P.* Parnellite, *A.-P.* Anti-Parnellite, *S.* Socialist, *Ind.* Independent, *Lab.* Labour, and *Temp.* Temperance. Former Members who lost their seats at the General Election are denoted by an asterisk*, while those who contested or won constituencies other than they formerly represented are marked thus †.

The figures placed after the names of constituencies give the number of electors on the register in the year 1898; the figures after the names of candidates represent the votes polled at the General Election (unless otherwise stated) ; members are printed in italics.

The total number of Electors upon the register in 1899 is given below, together with the Registrar-General's estimate of the Population in the middle of the year :—

	ENGLAND AND WALES.		SCOTLAND.		IRELAND.		UNITED KINGDOM.	
	Total.	Per Member.	Total.	Per Member.	Total.	Per Member.	Total.	Per Member.
Electors	5,208,137	10,521	671,128	9,321	721,018	7,000	6,600,283	9,851
Estmd. Population	31,742,588	64,126	4,281,850	59,470	4,535,516	44,024	40,559,954	62,537

Between 1 Dec. 1898 and 25 Nov. 1899, 23 bye-elections took place—Aylesbury, N. Birmingham, Bow, Elland, Epsom, Exeter, Harrow, Hythe, the Kirkdale Division of Liverpool, Newton, N. Norfolk, Oldham, Osgoldcross, Oxford University, Rotherham, E. St. Pancras, and Southport in *England ;* Merionethshire in *Wales ;* E. and S. Edinburgh and N.W. Lanarkshire in *Scotland ;* and N.W. Antrim and Londonderry City in *Ireland.*

At the time of going to press there were 3 vacancies, Wells, Clackmannan & S. Mayo.

§ On December 1, 1898, the figures were, MINISTERIALISTS 403 (*England* 342, *Wales* 8, *Scotland* 32, *Ireland* 21). OPPOSITION 267 (*England* 123, *Wales* 22, *Scotland* 40, *Ireland* 82), MINISTERIAL MAJORITY, 136 (Labour Members, 15).

Speaker, The Right Hon. William Court Gully, M.P. for the City of Carlisle .... £5,000.
Chairman of Committees, Rt. Hon. James William Lowther, M.P. for Penrith Div. of Cumberland, £2,500.
Temporary Chairmen, Arthur O'Connor, Q.C.; James Edward Ellis; Rt. Hon. C. B. Stuart-Wortley, Q.C.;
J. Grant Lawson; and Rt. Hon. Edmond R. Wodehouse.

England.

465 Members; 4,917,980 Electors.

ABERCROMBY (L'pool), 8,340
Wm. Frederic Lawrence, C. unop.
ABINGDON DIV. (Berks), 8,617
Archie Kirkman Loyd, Q.C., C. 4,063
Charles Alfred Price, *L.* 3,019
ACCRINGTON DIV. (N. E. Lanc.), 13,956
Sir Joseph F. Leese, Q.C., L. 6,168
William Mitchell, *C.* 5,828
ALTRINCHAM D. (Cheshire), 12,789
Conyngsby R. Disraeli, C. 5,264
Alexander Mere Latham, *L.* 3,889
ANDOVER DIV. (Hants), 9,353
Wm. W. Bramston Beach, C. unop.
APPLEBY DIV. (Wstmld.), 6,556
Sir Herbert Savory, Bart., C. 2,950
Theodore W. Fry, *L.* 2,077
ASHBURTON DIV. (Devon), 9,710
Rt. Hon. C. Seale-Hayne, L. 4,380
John Ashburner Nix, *C.* 3,976
ASHFORD DIV. (Kent), 12,623
Lawrence Hardy, C. .... unop.
ASTON-UNDER-LYNE, 7,563
Herbert Whiteley, C. 3,436
William Woods, *C.* 2,680
James Sexton, *S.* (Lab.) ... 415
ASTON MANOR, 12,435
Capt. George William Grice-Hutchinson, C. 5,353
John Lawson, *L.* 1,675
ATTERCLIFFE (Sheffield), 13,144
Ald. Batty Langley, L. .... unop.
AYLESBURY DIV. (Bucks), 11,403
(Bye-election 6 Jan., 1899)
Hon. Lionel W. Rothschild, U. unop.
BANBURY DIV. (Oxon), 7,843
Albert Brassey, *C.* 4,057
Charles Thornton, *L.* 3,074
BARKSTON ASH DIV. (Yorks, W. R.), 9,296
Colonel Robert Gunter, C. .. unop.
BARNARD CASTLE DIVISION (Durham), 11,137
Sir Jos. W. Pease, Bt., L. ... 4,924
Capt. Hn. Wm. L. Vane, *C.* 3,848
BARNSLEY DIV. (Yorks, W. R.), 15,844
(Bye-election 28 Oct., 1897.)
Joseph Wolton, *L.* 6,744
Capt. James Blyth, *C.* 3,454
Pete Curran, *Ind.* (Lab.) ... 1,091
BARNSTAPLE DIV. (Devon), 11,889
Sir Wm. Cameron Gull, Bt., U. 4,825
Alfred Billson, L. 4,593
BARROW-IN-FURNESS, 7,522
Sir Chas. William Cayzer, C. 3,192
Woomes C. Bonnerji, *L.* ... 2,355
Pete Curran, *S.* (Lab.) 414
BASINGSTOKE DIV. (Hants), 10,293
Arthur Fredk. Jeffreys, C. unop.
BASSETLAW DIV. (Notts), 10,287
Sir Fredk. Geo. Milner, Bt., C. 4,874
Robt. Eadon Leader, *L.* ... 3,482
BATH (City of) (2), 7,218
Col. Chas. W. Murray, U. ... 3,445
Rt. Hon. E. R. Wodehouse, *U.* 3,358

Sir Wm. Martin Conway, *L.* 2,917
John M. Fleetwood Fuller, *L.* 2,865
BATTERSEA, 14,084
John Burns, *L.* (Lab., late S.) 5,019
Chas. Ridley Smith, *C.* (dec.) 4,766
BEDFORD (Borough), 4,591
Charles Guy Pym, C. 1,976
Sam. Howard Whitbread, L. 1,810
BEDFORDSHIRE: see Biggleswade, and Luton.
BERKS: see Abingdon, Newbury, and Wokingham.
BERMONDSEY (Southwark), 11,351
Alfred Lafone, *C.* 4,182
Reuben Vincent Barrow, L. 3,822
BERWICK-UPON-TWEED DIV. (Northumberland), 9,501
Sir Edward Grey, Bt., *L.* ... 4,378
Lord Warkworth, *C.* 3,593
BETHNAL GREEN (N.E.), 8,111
Sir Mancherjee Merwanjee Bhownaggree, K.C.I.E., C. 2,591
George Howell, L. (Lab.) ... 2,431
BETHNAL GREEN (S.W.), 8,158
Edwd. Hare Pickersgill, L. 2,603
Wm. Arnold Statham, *C.* 2,324
BEWDLEY DIV. (Worc.), 10,348
Alfred Baldwin, C. .... unop.
BIGGLESWADE DIV. (Beds), 13,671
Lord Alwyne Compton, *U.* 5,643
George W. E. Russell, L. 5,376
BIRKENHEAD, 15,158
Sir Elliott Lees, Bart., C. ... 6,178
Wm. Hesketh Lever, *L.* ... 5,974
BIRMINGHAM (Central), 11,767
Ebenezer Parkes, U. .... unop.
BIRMINGHAM (East), 12,668
Sir John Benjamin Stone, *C.* unop.
BIRMINGHAM (North), 10,168
(Bye-election 14 Feb., 1899.)
John T. Middlemore, U. .. unop.
BIRMINGHAM (South), 12,356
Joseph Powell Williams, C. 4,830
Walter Priestman, *L.* 1,257
BIRMINGHAM (West), 12,879
Rt. Hon. *Joseph Chamberlain, U.* (Colonial Sec.) ... 5,537
Dr. Bernard O'Connor, *A.-P.* 1,259
BIRMINGHAM: see also Bordesley, and Edgbaston.
BISHOP AUCKLAND DIVISION (Durham County), 11,157
James Mellor Paulton, L... 5,032
G. E. Markham, *C.* 3,735
BLACKBURN (2), 19,385
Sir Wm. Hy. Hornby, Bt., C. 9,553
Sir Wm. Coddington, Bart., C. 9,150
T. P. Ritzema, *L.* 6,840
BLACKPOOL D. (N. Lanc.), 16,017
Rt. Hn. Sir Matthew W. Ridley, Bart., C. (Home Sec.) ... unop.
BODMIN DIV. (Cornwall), 9,587
Rt. Hon. L. H. Courtney, U. 4,035
John M'Dougall, *L.* 3,492
BOLTON (2), 19,577
Herbert Shepherd-Cross, C. 8,494
George Harwood, L. 8,453
Col. Hn. F. C. Bridgeman, C. 7,901
Fred Brocklehurst, *S.* (Lab.) 2,694
BOOTLE D. (S. W. Lanc.), 16,936
Lt.-Col. T. Myles Sandys, C. unop.

BORDESLEY (Birmingham), 15,840
Ald. William Cook, *L.* ... 2,154
BOSTON, 3,451
William Garfit, C. 1,633
Sir Wm. Jas. Ingram, Bt., L. 1,237
BOSWORTH DIV. (Leic.), 11,478
Chas. B. Bright M'Laren, L. 5,327
Thomas Cope, *C.* 4,207
BOW AND BROMLEY (Tower Hamlets), 11,401
(Bye-election 27 Oct. 1899.)
Walter Murray Guthrie, C. 4,238
Harold Spender, *L.* 2,123
BRADFORD (Central), 10,488
Jas. M. Leslie Wanklyn, U. 4,024
Rt. Hon. George John Shaw-Lefevre, L. 3,983
BRADFORD (East), 14,001
(Bye-election 10 Nov. 1896.)
Capt. Hon. R. F. Greville, C. 4,921
Alfred Billson, *C.* 4,526
J. Keir-Hardie, *S.* (Lab.) ... 1,953
BRADFORD (West), 12,154
Ernest Flower, C. 3,936
John C. Horsfall, *L.* 3,471
Ben Tillett, *S.* (Lab.) 2,264
BRENTFORD DIV. (Midx.), 12,129
James Bigwood, C. .... unop.
BRIDGWATER D. (Somerset), 10,353
Edward James Stanley, C. unop.
BRIGG DIV. (Lincoln), 10,920
Harold James Reckitt, L. ... 4,886
John M. Richardson, C. ... 4,110
BRIGHTON (2), 17,973
Gerald W. Erskine Loder, C. 7,878
B. C. Vernon-Wentworth, C. 7,490
Sir Joseph Ewart, M.D.L. ... 5,082
BRIGHTSIDE (Sheffield), 11,649
(Bye-election 6 Aug. 1897.)
Fred. Maddison, L. (Lab.) 4,289
J. Fitzalan Hope, *C.* 4,106
BRISTOL (East), 12,777
Sir Wm. Henry Wills, Bt., L. 4,129
Samuel G. Hobson, *S.* (Lab.) 1,874
BRISTOL (North), 11,906
Lewis Fry, U. 4,702
Charles Townsend, L. ... 4,464
BRISTOL (South), 12,931
Sir Edward S. Hill, K.C.B., C. 5,190
John O'Connor Power, *L.* 4,431
BRISTOL (West), 8,316
Rt. Hon. Sir Michael Edward Hicks-Beach, Bart., C. ... 3,815
Hy. Hamilton Lawless, *C.* 1,842
BRIXTON (Lambeth), 10,559
(Bye-election 30 Jan., 1896.)
Hon. Evelyn Hubbard, C. ... 4,493
Edward W. Nunn, *C.* 2,131
BUCKINGHAM D. (Bucks), 11,723
Wm. Walter Carlile, C. ... 5,266
Herbert Samuel Leon, C. 4,830
BUCKINGHAMSHIRE: see Aylesbury. Buck'ham. and Wycombe.
BUCKROSE D. (Yorks, E.R.), 9,570
Sir Angus Holden, Bart., L. 4,078
Thos. Clarence Edwd. Goff, *C.* 3,986
BURNLEY, 14,209
Hon. Philip J. Stanhope, *L.* 5,454
Wm. Alexander Lindsay, *C.* 5,133
Hy. M. Hyndman, *S.* (Lab.) 1,498

BURTON DIV. (Stafford), 10,738
Sydney Evershed, L.... ...... unop.
BURY (Lancashire), 8,515
James Kenyon, C. 3,890
Jno. Fredk. Cheetham, L. 3,215
BURY ST. EDMUNDS, 2,574
Viscount Chelsea, C. ...... unop.
CAMBERWELL (North), 12,257
Maj. Philip Hugh Dalbiac, C. 4,009
*Edwd. Hodson Bayley, L. 3,316
Nelson Palmer, Ind. (Lab.) 32
CAMBERWELL: see also Dulwich and Peckham.
CAMBORNE D. (Cornwall), 7,513
Arthur Strauss, U. 3,166
*Chas. Aug. V. Conybeare, L. 2,704
CAMBRIDGE (Borough), 7,864
Sir R. Uniacke-Penrose-Fitz-gerald, Bt., C. 3,574
Alex. J. David, L. 2,920
CAMBRIDGESHIRE: see Chesterton, Newmarket, and Wisbech.
CAMBRIDGE UNIVERSITY (2), 6,838
Prof. Richard C. Jebb, C. }
Rt. Hn. Sir J. E. Gorst, Q.C. C. } unop.
CANTERBURY (City), 3,855
John Henniker-Heaton, C. .. unop.
CARLISLE (City), 7,153
Rt. Hon. William Court Gully,
Q.C., L. (Speaker) 3,167
Samuel Porter Foster, C.... 2,853
CHATHAM, 10,663
Ald. Sir H. Davies, K.C.M.G. C. 4,082
Robt. Hippisley Cox, L. 3,499
CHELMSFORD D. (Essex), 10,203
Thomas Usborne, C. ...... unop.
CHELSEA, 12,842
Chas. Algernon Whitmore, C. 5,524
Octavius Beatty, L. 3,604
CHELTENHAM, 7,465
Mj.-Gn. F. S. Russell, C.M.G. C. 3,409
Wilfrid Blaydes, L. 2,940
Alton W. Hillen, Indep. ... 23
CHERTSEY DIV. (Surrey), 11,752
(Bye-election, 18 Feb. 1897.)
Hy. Currie Leigh-Bennett, C. 4,845
Lawrence J. Baker, L. 3,977
CHESHIRE: see Altrincham, Crewe, Eddisby, Hyde, Knutsfd.. Macclesfield Northwich.and Wirral.
CHESTER (City), 7,182
Robt. Armstrong Yerburgh, C. unop.
CHESTER-LE-STREET DIVISION (Durham), 15,915
Sir James Joicey, Bart., L. 7,370
Viscount Morpeth, C. 4,113
CHESTERFIELD D. (Derby), 11,414
Thomas Bayley, L. 4,572
Augustus Wm. Byron, U... 4,325
CHESTERTON D. (Cambs), 10,439
Walter Raymond Greene, C. 4,432
*Hugh Edward Hoare, L. 4,012
CHICHESTER D. (Sussex), 9,624
Lord Edmund B. Talbot, C. unop.
CHIPPENHAM DIV. (Wilts), 8,294
Sir John D. Poynder, Bt., C. 3,898
John Thornton, L. 3,390
CHORLEY D. (N. Lanc.), 12,123
Lord Balcarres, C. .... unop.
CHRISTCHURCH, 7,889
Abel Henry Smith, C. 3,198
Hon. T. Allnutt Brassey, C. 3,114
CIRENCESTER DIV. (Glouc.), 9,501
Hon. Allen Benj. Bathurst, C. 4,509
*Harry L. W. Lawson, L. 4,294

CLAPHAM, 15,878
Percy Melville Thornton, C. 5,925
John Kempster, L. 3,904
CLERKENWELL (Finsbury, C.) 8,731
Hon. Wm. F. B. Massey-Mainwaring, C. 3,588
*Dadabhai Naoroji, L. 2,783
CLEVELAND D. (Yks. N. R.), 11,898
(Bye-election, 12 Jan. 1897.)
Alfred Edward Pease, L. 5,508
Lt.-Col. Robert Ropner, C. 4,080
CLITHEROE D. (N.E. Lanc.), 18,051
Rt. Hon. Sir Ughtred J. Kay-Shuttleworth, Bart., L. ... unop.
COCKERMOUTH D. (Cumb.), 10,591
Sir Wilfrid Lawson, Bt., L. 4,259
Thomas Milvain, Q.C., C. 4,018
COLCHESTER, 5,519
Sir Weetman D. Pearson, Bt. L. 2,475
Edward Samuel Norris, C. 2,270
COLNE VALLEY D. (Yorks, W.R.), 10,982
Sir James Kitson, Bt., L. 4,276
Harold Thomas, C. 3,737
Tom Mann, S. (Lab.) 1,245
CORNWALL: see Bodmin, Camborne, Launceston, St. Austell, St. Ives, and Truro.
COVENTRY (City), 11,657
Charles James Murray, C.... 4,974
*Wm. Hy. W. Ballantine, L. 4,624
CREWE D. (Cheshire), 13,093
Hon. Robt. Arthur Ward, C. 5,413
*W. S. Bright M'Laren, L. 4,863
CRICKLADE D. (N. Wilts), 12,249
(Bye-election 24 Feb., 1898.)
Lord Edm. Fitzmaurice, L. 5,624
Visc. Emlyn (E.Cawdor), C. 5,135
CROYDON, 17,992
Rt. Hon. C. Thomson Ritchie, C. 6,876
Christ. C. Hutchinson, L.... 4,647
CUMBERLAND: see Cockermouth, Egremont. Eskdale. & Penrith
DARLINGTON, 7,214
(Bye-election 17 Sept., 1898.)
Herbert Pike Pease, U. ... 3,497
Owen C. Philipps, L. 2,809
DARTFORD D. (N.W. Kent), 15,303
Rt. Hn. Sir W. H. Dyke, Bt., C. 5,699
Sir Patteson Nickalls, L. .. 4,557
DARWEN D. (N.E. Lanc.), 14,931
Ald. John Rutherford, C.... 7,058
*C. Philip Huntington, L. 6,217
DEPTFORD, 15,204
(Bye-election, 15 Nov., 1897.)
Arthur Hy. Aylmer Morton, C. 5,317
*Jno. Williams Benn, L. 4,993
DERBY (Borough) (2), 17,672
Ald. Sir Hy. Howe Bemrose, C. 7,907
Geoffrey Drage, C. 7,076
*Rt. Hon. Sir William Vernon Harcourt, L. 6,785
*Sir Thomas Roe, Knt., L. 6,475
DERBYSH. (Mid, or Belper), 11,122
James Alfred Jacoby, L. 4,926
William C. Bridgeman, C. 4,351
DERBYSHIRE (N.E., or Eckington), 12,477
Thomas Dolling Bolton, L. 4,737
Josiah Court, C. 4,210
DERBYS. (S., or Repton), 14,254
John Gretton, jun., C. 6,104
*Harrington E. Broad, L. 5,217

DERBYSH. (W., or Wirksworth), 11,023
Victor C. W. Cavendish, U. unop.
DERBYSHIRE: see also Chesterfield, High Peak, and Ilkeston.
DEVIZES DIV. (E. Wilts), 8,825
Edward Alfred Goulding, C. 4,114
*Chas. E. H. Hobhouse, L. 3,637
DEVONPORT (2), 8,207
Hudson E. Kearley, L. 3,570
Edwd. John C. Morton, L... 3,511
Pridham H. P.-Wippell, C. 3,302
Capt. T. Thynne, C. 3,262
DEVONSHIRE: see Ashburton, Barnstaple, Honiton, South Molton, Tavistock, Tiverton, Torquay, and Totnes.
DEWSBURY, 13,354
Mark Oldroyd, L. 5,379
Henry Strother Cautley, C. 3,875
Edwd. R. Hartley, L. (Lab.) 1,080
DONCASTER DIV. (Yorks, W.R.), 16,093
Frederick William Fison, C. 6,098
Joseph Walton, L. 5,957
DORSET (E., or Poole), 11,450
Hon. Humphrey N. Sturt, C. unop.
DORSET (N., or Shaftesbury), 8,393
John K. Wingfield-Digby, C. unop.
DORSET (S., or Dorchester), 8,893
William Ernest Brymer, C. unop.
DORSET (W., or Bridport), 7,437
Col. Robert Williams, C. ...unop.
DOVER, 5,865
George Wyndham, C. ...... unop.
DROITWICH D. (M. Worc.), 9,743
Rd. Biddulph Martin, C.... unop.
DUDLEY, 15,675
R. Brooke Robinson, C. 6,536
+Chas. Jas. Fleming, Q.C., L. 5,795
DULWICH (Camberwell), 12,535
SirJ.Blundell Maple, Bart.C. 5,258
Charles Goddard Clarke, L. 2,176
DURHAM (City), 2,587
(Bye-election 30 June, 1898.)
Hon. Arth. R. D. Elliot, U. 1,167
Hugh Fen. Boyd (decd.), L. 1,102
DURHAM (Mid, or Brancepeth), 12,813
John Wilson, L. (Lab.) 5,937
Anthony Wilkinson, C. ... 4,295
DURHAM (N.-W., or Lanchester), 13,505
Ll. A. Atherley-Jones, Q.C., L. 5,428
James Joicey, C. 3,869
DURHAM (S.-E., or N. Tees), 14,775
(Bye-election 3 Feb., 1898.)
Ald. Joseph Richardson, L. 6,286
Hon. Fredk W. Lambton, U. 6,111
DURHAM (County of): see also Barnard Castle, Bishop Auckland, Chester-le-Street, Houghton-le-Spring, and Jarrow.
EALING D. (Middlesex), 14,135
Rt. Hn. Ld. G. F. Hamilton, C. unop.
E. GRINSTEAD D. (Sussex), 9,645
George J. Goschen, jun., C. 3,731
Chas. J. H. Corbett, L....... 2,874
EASTBOURNE DIV. (Sussex), 10,961
Vice-Adm. Edw. Field, C.B. C. 4,139
Capt. Hon. Thos. Seymour Brand, R.N., C. 4,079
ECCLES D. (S. E. Lanc.), 14,258
Octavius Leigh Clare, C...... 5,722
*Henry John Roby, L. 5,302

ECCLESALL (Sheffield), 10,957
Sir Ellis Ashmead-Bartlett, C. unop.
EDDISBURY D. (Chesh.), 10,588
Henry James Tollemache, C. 5,176
Roger Bate, L............... 3,371
EDGBASTON (Birmingham). 11,658
(Bye-election 15 Feb : 1898.)
*Francis William Lowe, C. ... unov.
EGREMONT D. (Cumbrld.), 9,081
Hon. H. Val. Duncombe, C. 3,717
*David Ainsworth, L......... 3,586
ELLAND D. (Yorks. W.R.). 12,926
(Bye-election 8 March, 1899.)
*Charles Philips Trevelyan, L. 6,041
Philip Staveley Foster, C.... 5,057
ENFIELD D. (Middlesex), 16,216
Lt.-Col. Henry F. Bowles, C. unop.
EPPING DIV. (Essex, W.), 10,059
Lt.-Col. Mark Lockwood, C. unop.
EPSOM D. (Mid Surrey), 12,233
(Bye-election 23 Jan., 1899.)
*William Keswick, C. .... unop.
ESKDALE D. (Cumbrld.), 10,091
Robt. Andrews Allison, L.... 3,745
Henry Charles Howard, C. 3,598
ESSEX (S.E., or Tilbury), 14,653
Major Fredc. Carne Rasch, C. 5,460
D. Milne Watson, L............ 3,520
ESSEX; see also Chelmsford, Epping, Harwich, Maldon, Romford, Saffron Walden, and Walthamstow.
EVERTON (Liverpool), 10,241
Sir J. Archibald Willox, C. unop.
EVESHAM D. (Worcester), 9,937
Lt.-Col. C. Wigram Long, C. unop.
EXCHANGE (Liverpool), 6,812
(Bye-election 10 Nov., 1897.)
*Charles M'Arthur, C. 2,711
Russell Rea, L. 2,657
EXETER (City), 8,595
(Bye-election 6 Nov., 1899.)
Sir David Vincent, K.C.M.G., C., 4,030
Allan H. Bright, L. 3,371
EYE DIV. (Suffolk, N.E.), 10,148
Fras. Seymour Stevenson, L. 4,437
F. J. Wootton Isaacson, C. 3,603
FAREHAM DIV. (Hants, S.), 15,839
Lieut.-Gen. Sir Frederick W.
FitzWygram, Bart., C. ...unop.
FAVERSHAM D. (Kent), 13,582
Frederic Gorell Barnes, C. 5,738
Samuel Barrow, L............. 4,557
FINSBURY (East), 5,822
Henry Charles Richards, C. 2,260
*James Rowlands, L. (Lab.) 1,990
FINSBURY: see also Clerkenwell and Holborn.
FOREST OF DEAN D. (Gl.), 10,179
Rt. Hon. Sir C. W. Dilke, L. unop.
FROME DIV. (Somerset), 12,195
(Bye-election 2 June, 1896.)
John Emmott Barlow, L. ... 5,062
Lord Alexander Thynne, C. 4,763
FULHAM, 15,817
William Hayes Fisher, C. ... 5,378
Edwin Andrew Cornwall, L. 3,915
Wm. Parnell, S. (Lab.)...... 196
GAINSBOROUGH DIV.(Linc.),12,291
Emerson Bainbridge, L...... 5,077
Ald. Edward Pearson, C.... 4,301
GATESHEAD, 16,098
William Allan, L. 6,137
Ald. John Lucas, U.......... 5,654

GLOUCESTER (City), 7,278
Charles James Monk, U. ... 3,264
Arthur Spencer Wells, C. 2,791
GLOUCESTERSHIRE: see Cirencester, Forest of Dean, Stroud, Tewkesbury, and Thornbury.
GORTON D. (S. E. Lanc.). 14,403
Ernest Fredc. Geo. Hatch, C. 5,865
Rd. M. Pankhurst, S. (Lab.) 4,261
GRANTHAM, 2,896
Henry Yarde Buller Lopes, C. 1,507
Saml. Danks Waddy, Q.C., L. 1,167
GRAVESEND, 5,540
(Bye-election 13 July, 1898.)
Jno. H. Dudley Ryder, C.... 2,372
Walter Runciman, L. 1,955
GREENWICH, 11,894
Lord Hugh Cecil, C. 4,802
George Crispe Whiteley, L. 3,564
GRIMSBY, GREAT, 12,757
(Bye-election 2 Aug. 1898.)
George Doughty, U. 4,940
T. Wintringham, L. 3,189
R. D. Melhuish, Ind. C. 204
GUILDFORD D. (Surrey), 12,301
Rt.Hon. W. St. J. Brodrick, C. unop.
HACKNEY (Central), 8,831
Sir Andrew R. Scoble, Q.C.,
K.C.S.I., C................ 3,278
Hon. Charles Russell, L.... 2,966
HACKNEY (North), 11,442
Wm. Robt. Bousfield, Q.C., C. 4,725
Sylvain Mayer, L. 2,460
HACKNEY (South), 12,399
Thos. Herbert Robertson, C. 4,681
*J.FletcherMoulton, Q.C.,L. 4,362
HAGGERSTON (Shoreditch), 6,765
John Lowles, C. 2,269
*Wm. R. Cremer, L. (Lab.) 2,229
HALIFAX (2), 14,671
Alfred Arnold, C. (1895) ... 5,475
(Bye-election, 3 March, 1897.)
Alfred Billson, L............ 5,634
Sir Saville Crossley, C.... ... 5,252
Tom Mann, Ind. (Lab.)...... 2,000
HALLAM (Sheffield), 10,024
Rt.Hon.C.B. Stuart-Wortley,
Q.C., C...................unop.
HALLAMSH.D.(Yks.,W.R.),15,181
Sir Fredk.T. Mappin, Bt., L. 5,949
Frank S. U. Hatchard, C. 5,054
HAMMERSMITH, 13,227
Mj.-Gen. W. Goldsworthy, C. 5,017
Wm. C. Steadman, L. (Lab.) 3,238
HAMPSHIRE (or Hants): see Andover, Basingstoke, Fareham, New Forest, Petersfield, and Wight (Isle of).
HAMPSTEAD, 9,380
Edward Brodie Hoare, C. ... unop.
HANDSWORTH DIV. (Staff.), 20,478
Sir H. Meysey-Thompson, Bt., U.
HANLEY, 15,258 [unop.
William Woodall, L........ 5,653
Arthur Howard Heath, C. 5,367
HARBOROUGH D. (Leic.), 15,861
John William Logan, L.... 6,699
Lieut. Cecil Powney, C. ... 5,673
HARROW DIV. (Middx.), 18,444
(Bye-election, 5 April, 1899.)
Irwin Ed. Bainbridge Cox, O. 6,303
Corrie Grant, L............. 5,198
HARTLEPOOLS, The, 12,162
Sir Thomas Richardson, U. 4,853
*Sir Christopher Furness, L. 4,772

HARWICH DIV. (Essex), 11,890
James Round, C. 4,556
Robert Varty, L............. 2,685
HASTINGS, 7,817
Wm. Lucas Shadwell, C. ... 3,205
Cecil Bret Ince, L. 2,863
HENLEY DIV. (Oxon), 9,039
Robt. T. Hermon-Hodge, C. 3,831
Herbert Samuel, L. 3,470
HEREFORD (City), 3,441
Chas. W. Radcliffe Cooke, C. 1,669
Sir Edward Robert Pearce-
Edgcumbe, L. 1,356
HEREFORDSHIRE: see Leominster, and Ross.
HERTFORD DIV. (Herts), 10,538
(Bye-election 22 June, 1898.)
Evelyn Cecil, C. 4,118
Rt Hn.Chas.Robt.Spencer,L. 3,850
HERTFORDSHIRE (or Herts): see Hertford, Hitchin, St. Albans, and Watford.
HEXHAM D. (Northumb.), 10,259
Wentworth C.B. Beaumont, L. 4,438
Charles Edward Hunter, C. 4,003
HEYWOOD D. (S. E. Lanc.), 9,941
George Kemp, U............. 4,489
*Ald. Thomas Snape, L. ... 3,933
HIGH PEAK D. (Derbysh.), 10,655
Lt.-Col. Wm. Sidebottom, C. 4,671
Arthur Gibb Symonds, L. 4,164
HITCHIN D. (Herts), 9,269
Geo. Bickersteth Hudson, C. unop.
HOLBORN (Finsbury, W.), 11,116
Rt. Hon. Sir Charles Hall, C. unop.
HOLDERNESS D.(Yks.,E.R.), 10,029
Comr. G. R. Bethell, R.N., C. 4,512
Bourchier F. Hawkesley, L. 3,483
HOLMFIRTH D. (Yks.W.R.), 11,320
Henry Joseph Wilson, L... 5,001
G. E. Raine, C. 3,549
HONITON DIV. (Devon), 9,432
Sir J. H. Kennaway, Bt., C. unop.
HORNCASTLE D. (Lincoln), 9,547
Lord Willoughby de Eresby, C. 4,563
John Bruce Wallace, L. ... 3,022
HORNSEY DIV. (Middx.), 15,759
Henry Charles Stephens, C. unop.
HORSHAM DIV. (Sussex), 9,405
John Heywood Johnstone, C. unop.
HOUGHTON-LE-SPRING DIV. (Durham), 14,221
Robert Cameron, L............. 6,592
Vincent C.S. W. Corbett, C. 5,711
HOWDENSHIRE DIV.(Yorks,E.R.), 9,701
Capt. W. H.Wilson-Todd, C. unop.
HOXTON (Shoreditch), 8,085
James Stuart, L. 2,990
Hon.ClaudeGeo.D.-Hay,C. ,862
HUDDERSFIELD, 16,472
Sir Jas. T. Woodhouse, L. 6,755
*Sir Joseph Crosland, C.... 5,868
H. Russell Smart, L. (Lab.) 1,594
HULL (Central), 10,449
Sir Henry S. King,K.C.I.E.,C. 5,476
Fred Maddison, L. (Lab.)... 3,515
HULL (East), 11,546
Joseph Thomas Firbank, C. 4,305
*Sir Clarence Smith, L. ... 4,152
HULL (West), 16,687
Charles Henry Wilson, L.... 6,637
Tom M'Carthy, S. (Lab.)... 1,400

HUNTINGDON D. (Hunts), 5,262
Rt.Hn.A. H.Smith-Barry, C. .. 2,419
John J. Wilks, L. 2,068
HUNTINGDONSHIRE (or Hunts)
see Huntingdon, and Ramsey
HYDE DIV. (Cheshire), 10,480
Jos. Watson Sidebotham, C..
George Wood Rhodes, L.... 3,844
Geo. Smith Christie, S.(Lab.) 448
HYTHE, 5,224
(Bye-election, March, 1899.)
Sir Edwd. A. Sassoon, Bt., C. 2,425
Sir Israel Hart, L. 1,8q8
ILKESTON DIV. (Derby), 14,219
Sir B. Walter Foster, L. .. 6,215
Capt.Ed.P. Baumgarten, U. 5,251
INCE DIV. (S. W. Lanc.), 11,473
Col.H.B.-H.-Blundell,C.B...C.5,236
*Samuel Woods, L. (Lab.). 4,7⅞
IPSWICH (2), 10,450
Daniel Ford Goddard, L. 4,396
Sir Chas. Dalrymple, Bt., C. 4,293
Arth.Wellesley Soames, L. 4,250
*Lord Elcho, C. 4,219
ISLINGTON (East), 10,472
Benjamin Louis Cohen, C... 4,383
Thos. M'Kinnon Wood, L. 3,159
ISLINGTON (North), 11,775
Geo. C. Trout Bartley, C. .. 4,626
Thos. Bateman Napier, L. 3,317
ISLINGTON (South), 8,502
Sir Albert Kaye Rollit, C.... 3,563
Heber Leonidas Hart, L..... 2,342
ISLINGTON (West), 8,954
Thomas Lough, L. 3,494
George Barham, U. 3,031
JARROW DIV. (Durham), 15,348
Sir Chas. M. Palmer, Bt., L. unop.
KEIGHLEY D.(Yks.,W.R.), 12,415
Ald. John Brigg, L. 5,036
Walter Bairstow, C. 4,196
KENDAL D. (Westmorland), 6,063
Capt. J. FitzRoy Bagot, C. 2,771
Herbert Stephenson, L...... 2,049
KENNINGTON (Lambeth), 10,277
Frederick Lucas Cook, C. .. 3,764
*Mark Hanbury Beaufoy,L. 2,769
Wm. Wightman, L.(Temp.) 730
KENSINGTON (North), 9,494
Wm. E. Thompson Sharpe,C. 3,829
*Fredk.Charlwood Frye, L. 2,913
KENSINGTON (South), 8,914
(Bye-election, 28 Nov. 1895.)
Earl Percy, C. ....unop.
KENT (County of) : see Ashford,
Dartford, Faversham, Medway,
St. Augustine's, Sevenoaks,
Thanet (Isle of), & Tunbridge
KIDDERMINSTER, 4,185
Sir Augustus F. Godson, C. 2,008
Richard Eve, L. 1,713
KING'S LYNN, 3,119
Thos. Gibson Bowles, C...... 1,395
Herbert Beaumont, L. 1,326
KINGSTON (Surrey), 14,703
Ald. Thomas Skewes-Cox, C. 5,745
Alderman Charles Bart, L. 3,600
KINGSTON-UPON-HULL : see Hull.
KINGSWINFORD D. (Staff.), 12,163
Rt. Hon. A. S. Hill, Q.C., C. unop.
KIRKDALE (Liverpool), 10,395
(Bye-election, 9 Dec., 1898.)
David MacIver, U., unopposed.
KNUTSFORD D. (Cheshire)10,050
Hon. Alan de T. Egerton, U.unop.

LAMBETH (North), 6,976
Sir Henry Morton Stanley,
G.C.B., U. 2,878
Chas. Philips Trevelyan, L. 2,477
LAMBETH : see also Brixton, Ken-
nington, Norwood.
LANCASHIRE, North : see Black-
pool, Chorley, Lancaster, and
Lonsdale, North.
LANCASHIRE, North-East : see
Accrington, Clitheroe, Dar-
wen, and Rossendale.
LANCASHIRE, South-East : see
Eccles, Gorton, Heywood, Mid-
dleton, Prestwich, Radcliffe-
cum-Farnworth, Stretford,
and Westhoughton.
LANCASHIRE, South-West : see
Bootle, Ince, Leigh, Newton
Ormskirk, Southport, Widnes.
LANCASTER D. (N. Lanc.), 11,737
Col. Wm. Henry Foster, C. 5,028
Isaac Saunders Leadam, L. 4,394
LAUNCESTON D. (Cornwall), 9,485
(Bye-election 3 Aug., 1898.)
J. Fletcher Moulton, Q.C., L. 3,951
Sir Frederick Wills, Bt., U. 2,863
LEAMINGTON : see Warwick and
Leamington.
LEEDS (Central), 9,967
Rt.Hn. Gerald W. Balfour,C. 4,631
Leifchild Jones, L. 3,977
LEEDS (East), 9,326
Thomas Richmond Leuty, L. 3,856
John Danvers Power, C. ... 3,145
LEEDS (North), 16,355
Rt. Hon. Wm. L. Jackson, C. 5,992
Herbert S. Baines, L. 4,484
LEEDS (South), 13,205
J. Lawson Walton, Q.C., L. 4,608
Reginald Jas. Neville, C. .. 4,447
Arthur Shaw, S. (Lab.) ... 622
LEEDS (West), 16,387
Rt. Hon. H. J. Gladstone, L. 6,314
Col. Jno. T. North, C. 6,218
LEEK DIV. (Staffordsh.), 10,977
Robert Pearce, L. 4,091
LEICESTER (Boro') (2), 24,760
Henry Broadhurst, L. (Lab.) 9,792
Walter Hazell, L. 7,753
Jno. F. L. Rolleston, C. ... 7,654
Joseph Burgess, S. (Lab.) 4,009
LEICESTERSHIRE : see Bosworth,
Harborough, Loughborough,
and Melton.
LEIGH DIV. (S.W. Lanc.), 11,720
Charles Prestwich Scott, L... 5,130
Wm. W. A. FitzGerald, C. 4,453
LEOMINSTER D. (Hereford), 9,922
Sir James Rankin, Bart., C. unop.
LEWES DIV. (Sussex), 13,227
Sir Henry Fletcher, Bt., C. unop.
LEWISHAM, 14,172
John Penn, C. ....unop.
LICHFIELD D. (Staffordsh.), 9,424
(Bye-election, 26 Feb., 1896.)
Tho.Courtenay T.Warner,L. 4,483
*Maj. Leonard Darwin, U. 3,955
LIMEHOUSE (Tower H.), 7,165
Harry S. Samuel, C. 2,661
Wm.M.Thompson,L.(Lab.) 2,07...
LINCOLN (City), 8,595
Charles Hilton Seely, U...... 3,808
*William Crosfield, L. 3,590

LINCOLNSHIRE : see Brigg, Gains-
borough, Horncastle, Louth,
Sleaford, Spalding,& Stamford.
LIVERPOOL : see Abercromby,
Everton, Exchange, Kirkdale,
Scotland, Toxteth (E.), Toxteth
(W.), Walton, and West Derby.
LONDON (City) (2), 33,349
Sir Regd. Hanson, Bt., C. } unop.
Hon. Alban G.H.Gibbs,C. }
LONDON UNIVERSITY, 4,287
Rt. Hn. Sir J. Lubbock,Bt.,U.unop.
LONSDALE (NORTH) DIV.
(N. Lancashire), 9,609.
Richd. Fredk. Cavendish, U. 4,313
Baron Halkett, L. 3,010
LOUGHBOROUGH D. (Leic.) 11,097
J. E. Johnson-Ferguson, L. 4,732
Robert L. Tooth, C. 4,360
LOUTH D. (Lincolnsh.), 9,673
Robert William Perks, L.... 4,191
Lt.-Col. F. Alfred Lucas, C. 3,779
LOWESTOFT D. (Suffolk), 12,558
Harry Seymour Foster, C... 5,199
Alfred Sington, L. .... 3,8⍳0
LUDLOW D. (Shropshire), 10,395
Robert Jasper More, C...... unop.
LUTON DIV. (Beds), 13,167
Thomas Gair Ashton, L. ... 5,430
Col. Oliver Thos. Duke, U. 5,244
LYNN REGIS : see King's Lynn.
MACCLESFIELD D. (Chesh.), 8,590
Wm. Bromley-Davenport, U. unop.
MAIDSTONE, 5,003
(Bye-election, 26 March, 1898.)
Fiennes S. W. Cornwallis, C. 2,214
John Barker, L. 2,036
MALDON DIV. (Essex), 9,935
Hon. Chas. Hedley Strutt, C. 4,618
*Cyril J. S. Dodd, Q.C., L. 4,006
MANCHESTER (East), 12,613
Rt. Hon. Arth.J. Balfour, C. 5,386
Prof. Jos. E. C. Munro, L. .. 4,610
MANCHESTER (North), 10,874
Charles Ernest Schwann, L. 4,327
Arthur H. A. Morton, C.... 3,872
MANCHESTER (N.-E.), 10,032
Rt. Hon. Sir Jas. Fergusson,
Bart., G.C.S.I., C......... 3,961
Edwin Holt, L. 3,720
James Johnston, S. (Lab.) 546
MANCHESTER (N.-W.), 11,728
Sir William Henry Houlds-
worth, Bart., C. 4,997
Thomas Francis Byrne, L. 3,526
MANCHESTER (South), 11,624
Marquess of Lorne, K.T., U. 4,457
*Sir Hy. Enfld. Roscoe, L. 4,379
MANCHESTER (S. W.), 9,220
Wm. Johnson Galloway, C. 3,994
John Moir Astbury, Q.C., L. 3,495
MANSFIELD DIV. (Notts) 13,879
John Carvell Williams, L. ... 5,670
Col. Henry Eyre, C.B., C.... 4,285
MARYLEBONE (East), 6,971
Edmund Boulnois, C. 3,379
Col. Alan Gardner, L. 1,845
MARYLEBONE (West), 8,853
(Bye-election 3 Feb., 1898.)
Sir Samuel E. Scott, Bart. C. unop.
MEDWAY DIV. (Kent), 13,881
Maj. Chas. Edwd. Warde, C. unop.
MELTON D. (Leicester), 13,146
Lord Edward Manners, C. . 5,636
Arthur Wakerley, L. 4,283

MIDDLESBROUGH, 16,548
Jos. Havelock Wilson, L. (Lab) ... 6,755
Col. Saml. A. Sadler, v.D., C. 4,735
MIDDLESEX: see Brentford, Ealing, Enfield, Harrow, Hornsey, Tottenham, and Uxbridge.
MIDDLETON D. (S. E. Lanc.),13,487
(Bye-election, 4 Nov., 1897.)
Ald. James Duckworth, L..... 5,964
William Mitchell, C....... 5,664
MILE END (Tower Hamlets), 5,935
Spencer Charrington, C...... 2,38.
James Haysman, L. 1,514
MONMOUTH DISTRICT, 8,931
Albert Spicer, L. 3,743
E. M. Underdown, Q.C., C. 3,589
MONMOUTHSHIRE (N.), 11,184
Reginald M'Kenna, L. 4,965
W. Ellis Hume Williams, C. 4,203
MONMOUTHSHIRE (S.), 14,012
Col. Hon. Fredk. C. Morgan, C. 5,815
Clifford Cory, L. 5,203
MONMOUTHSHIRE (W.), 12,523
+ Rt. Hon. Sir Wm. Vernon Harcourt, L. 7,243
Wm. Edwin Williams, C. 1,955
MORLEY D. (Yorks,W.R.), 14,051
Alfred Eddison Hutton, L. ... 5,834
William Carr, C. 4,166
MORPETH, 8,358
Thomas Burt, L. (Lab.) 3,404
Maltman Barry, C. (Lab.) 1,235
NEW FOREST D. (Hants), 10,389
Hon. John W. E. Douglas-Scott-Montagu, C. ...... unop
NEWARK DIV. (Notts), 10,374
(Bye-election, 10 May, 1898.)
Viscount Newark, C. ...... unop.
NEWBURY DIV. (Berks), 10,604
William George Mount, C. ... 4,895
Sir John Swinburne, Bt., L. 3,770
NEWCASTLE-ON-TYNE (2), 34,210
Sir Chas. Fredc. Hamond, C. 12,833
Wm. Donaldson Cruddas, C.12,170
*Rt. Hon. John Morley, L.11,862
James Craig, L. 11,154
Fred. Hammill, S. (Lab.) ... 2,302
NEWCASTLE-UNDER-LYME, 8,694
William Allen, L. 3,510
Arthur Morrier Lee, U. ... 3,395
NEWINGTON (WEST), 9,489
Capt. Cecil Wm. Norton, L... 3,219
George Wm. Tallents, C... 2,769
NEWINGTON: see also Walworth.
NEWMARKET DIV. (Cambs.), 9,606
Harry L. B. M'Calmont, C. 4,210
*Sir George Newnes, Bt., L. 3,867
NEWPORT D. (Shropshire), 10,561
Col. Wm. Kenyon-Slaney, C. unop.
NEWTON D. (S.W. Lanc.), 12,075
(Bye-election, 16 Jan., 1899.)
Lt.-Col. Rich t. Pilkington, C., unop.
NORFOLK (E., or N. Walsham), 10,705
Robert John Price, L. 4,606
Henry Rider Haggard, C. ... 4,408
NORFOLK (M., or Dereham), 9,172
Frederick Wm. Wilson, L. 4,220
*Robert T. Gurdon, U...... 4,086
NORFOLK (N., or Aylsham), 10,017
(Bye-election, 16 March, 1899.)
Sir William B. Gurdon, K.C.M.G., L. 4,775
Sir Kenneth H. Kemp, Bt., C. 3,010

NORFOLK (N.-W., or Freebridge), 10,869
Joseph Arch, L. (Lab.) 4,817
Edwd. Kendrick B. Tighe, C. 3,520
NORFOLK (S., or Diss), 9,611
(Bye-election, 12 May, 1898.)
Arthur W. Soames, L. 4,625
t. Sancroft Holmes, U.... 3,296
NORFOLK (S.-W., or Thetford), 8,869
Thomas Leigh Hare, C...... 3,968
Ald. Richard Winfrey, L... 3,752
NORMANTON D.(Yks.,W.R.),12,966
Benjamin Pickard, L. (Lab.) 5,499
D'Arcy Wilson, C. 3,941
NORTHAMPTON (Boro') (2), 12,107
Henry Labouchere, L. 4,884
Adolphus Drucker, C. 3,820
Edward Harford, L. 3,703
Jacob Jacobs, C. 3,394
Fredk. G. Jones, S. (Lab.) 1,216
John M. Robertson, Ind.... 1,131
NORTHAMPTONSHIRE (East, or Wellingborough), 14,415
Fras. Allston Channing, L. 6,177
Herbt. Lush-Wilson, Q.C., C. 4,961
NORTHAMPTONSH. (Mid), 12,059
Sir James Pender, Bart., C. 5,084
*Rt. Hn. Chas. R. Spencer, L. 4,808
NORTHAMPTONSH. (N.), 10,191
Edward Philip Monckton, C. unop.
NORTHAMPTONSH. (South), 9,021
Hn. E. S. Douglas-Pennant, C. 4,553
*David Charles Guthrie, L. 3,324
NORTHUMBERLAND: see Berwick-upon-Tweed, Hexham, Tyneside, and Wansbeck.
NORTHWICH D. (Chesh.), 11,992
Sir John T. Brunner, Bt., L. 5,706
Thomas Ward, U. 4,068
NORWICH (City) (2), 18,586
Sir Samuel Hoare, Bart., C. 8,117
Sir Harry Bullard, C...... 8,035
Thomas C. Terrell, L. 7,329
Fredk. William Verney, L. 7,210
NORWOOD (Lambeth), 10,846
Charles Ernest Tritton, C... unop.
NOTTINGHAM (Boro')(East),12,352
Edward Bond, C...... 4,900
*Rt. Hn. Arnold Morley, L. 4,735
NOTTINGHAM (Boro') (S.), 12,211
Ld. H. Cavendish-Bentinck, C. 4,802
Fredk. William Maude, L. 4,369
NOTTINGHAM (Boro') (W.), 14,799
James Henry Yoxall, L. ... 6,080
Arthur G. Sparrow, U...... 5,575
NOTTINGHAMSHIRE (or Notts): see Bassetlaw, Mansfield, Newark, and Rushcliffe.
NUNEATON DIV. (Warwick),12,467
Fras. Alex. Newdigate, C... 5,572
James Tomkinson, L. 4,175
OLDBURY: see Worcester, N.
OLDHAM (2), 28,476
(Bye-election, 6 July, 1899)
Alfred Emmett, L. 12,976
Walter Runciman, L. 12,770
Winston L. S. Churchill, C. 11,477
James Mawdsley, C. 11,449
ORMSKIRK D. (S.W.Lanc.), 10,731
(Bye-election, 20 Oct., 1898.)
Hon. Arthur Stanley, C......unop.

OSGOLDCROSS D.(Yks.W.R.)14,009
(Bye-election, 5 July, 1899.)
Sir John Austin, Bart., L. ... 5,815
Charles Henry Roberts, L.
(T mp.) 2,873
OSWESTRY D. (Shropshire),10,032
Stanley Leighton, C. 4,605
Capt. Owen Thomas, L. ... 3,598
OTLEY DIV. (Yorks W.R.), 12,065
Marmaduke D'A. Wyvill, C. 4,670
*Sir John Barran, Bart., L. 4,622
OXFORD (City). 8,110
(Bye-election, 4 Nov., 1898.)
Viscount Valentia, C. ...... unop.
OXFORD UNIVERSITY (2), 6,186
Rt. Hon. J. Gilbert Talbot, C. unop.
(Bye-election, 11 May, 1899.)
Sir William Reynell Anson, Bart., U. u opposed.
OXFORDSHIRE: see Banbury, Henley, and Woodstock.
PADDINGTON (North), 8,178
John Aird, C...... 2,894
George Henry Maberly, L. 1,852
PADDINGTON (South), 5,668
Sir George T. Fardell, C. unop.
PECKHAM (Camberwell), 11,758
Fredk. George Banbury, C. 4,495
Ald. Chas. Clements, L. 3,472
PENRITH D. (Cumberland), 8,830
Rt. Hon. James W. Lowther, C. 3,868
Thos. Sadler Douglas, L... 3,268
PENRYN AND FALMOUTH, 2,763
Fredk. John Horniman, L. 1,150
*William George Cavendish-Bentinck, C...... 1,101
PETERBOROUGH (City), 5,105
Robert Purvis, C...... 2,259
*Alpheus C. Morton, L. ... 2,017
PETERSFIELD D. (Hants), 8,615
(Bye-election, 8 June, 1897.)
Wm. Graham Nicholson, C. 3,748
J. Bonham Carter, L 3,328
PLYMOUTH (2), 13,503
Sir Edward Clarke, C. 5,575
(Bye-election, 12 Jan., 1898.)
Sigismund Nerd. Mendl, L. 5,966
Hon. Ivor C. Guest, C...... 5,802
PONTEFRACT, 2,870
Thomas Willans Nussey, L. 1,245
James Fitzalan Hope, C..... 1,188
POPLAR (Tower Hamlets), 10,131
Sydney Charles Buxton, L. 3,938
Wm. Pelham Bullivant, C. 3,110
PORTSMOUTH (2), 26,095
Sir John Baker, L. 10,451
Walter Owen Clough, L. ...10,255
Alfred C. Harmsworth, C. 9,717
Rt. Hon. Evelyn M. Ashley, U. 9,5-7
PRESTON (2), 16,776
Rt. Hn. Robt. W. Hanbury, C. 8,928
Wm. E. M. Tomlinson, C... 7,622
Ald. J. T. Tattersall, S. (Lab.) 4,781
PRESTWICH D. (S.E.Lanc.), 15,259
Frederick Cawley, L. 6,039
*Robt. Gray C. Mowbray, C. 5,938
PUDSEY D. (Yorks, W.R.), 14,343
Briggs Priestley, L. 5,540
Sir Andrew Fairbairn, U... 5,070
RADCLIFFE-CUM-FARNWORTH DIV.
(S. E. Lanc.), 12,197
Col. J.   James Mellor, C. 5,525
Dr. Geo. Herb. Pollard, L. 4,923

RAMSEY DIV. (Hunts), 6,618
Hon. Ailwyn E. Fellowes, C. 3,012
Harry Heldmann, L...... 2,063
READING, 9,883
(Bye-election, 25 July, 1899.)
George William Palmer, L. 4,600
Charles E. Keyser, C. 3,906
H. Quelch, S.C............. 270
REIGATE DIV. (Surrey), 11,958
Hon. Henry Cubitt, C...... unop.
RICHMOND D. (Yks., N.R.), 10,562
John Hutton, C............ 4,535
Edmund R. Turton, C...... 3,971
RIPON DIV. (Yorks, W.R.), 10,814
Rt. Hn. J. Lloyd Wharton, C. 4,435
Robt. C. Phillimore, C...... 3,733
ROCHDALE, 12,730
Col. Clement M. Royds, C. 4,781
Wm. Leatham Bright, L... 4,359
Geo. N. Barnes, S. (Lab.)... 1,251
ROCHESTER, 4,785
Viscount Cranborne, C. 2,151
Cecil Grenfell, L........... 1,672
ROMFORD DIV. (Essex), 26,731
(Bye-election, 1 Feb., 1897.)
Louis Sinclair, C........... 8,156
Herbert Henry Raphael, L. 8,031
ROSS DIV. (Hereford), 10,622
Michael Biddulph, U...... 4,573
Arthur Withey, L.......... 2,824
ROSSENDALE D. (N.E.Lanc.) 12,147
John Henry Maden, L. .... unop
ROTHERHAM D. (Yorks, W.R.), 14,763
(Bye-election 23 Feb., 1899.)
+*William Henry Holland*, L. 6,671
R. H. Vernon-Wragge, C. 4,714
ROTHERHITHE (Southwark) 9,790
John Cumming Macdona, C. 4,092
Ambrose Pomeroy, L. 2,246
RUGBY D. (Warwickshire), 10,073
Hon. Richard G. Verney, C. 4,354
John Currie Grant, L. 4,070
RUSHCLIFFE D. (Notts), 14,472
John Edward Ellis, L. 5,752
Geo. Murray Smith, U...... 5,119
RUTLAND (County), 4,155
George Henry Finch, C...... unop.
RYE DIVISION (Sussex), 11,703
Arthur M. Brookfield, C..... unop.
SAFFRON WALDEN D. (Essex), 8,608
Charles Gold, L........... 3,805
Charles Wing Gray, C...... 3,381
ST. ALBANS DIV. (Herts), 10,756
Hon. Vicary Gibbs, C. ...unop.
ST. AUGUSTINE'S D. (Kent), 14,063
Right Hon. Aretas Akers-Douglas, C. .... unop.
ST. AUSTELL D. (Cornwall), 9,734
Wm. Alex. M'Arthur, L..... 4,193
Michael Williams, U. 3,094
ST. GEORGE, HANOVER SQ. 9,817
Rt. Hon. Geo. J. Goschen, C. unop.
ST. GEORGE (Tower Hamlets), 3,777
Harry Hananel Marks, C..... 1,581
*John Williams Benn, L. ... 1,570
ST. HELENS, 10,624
Henr. Seton-Karr, C. 4,700
John Forster, L. 4,091
ST. IVES D. (Cornwall), 8,067
Thos. Bedford Bolitho, U...... unop.
ST. PANCRAS (East), 7,191
(Bye-election 12 July, 1899.)
*Thomas Wrightson, U. 2,610
Benj. Francis Costelloe, L. 2,423

ST. PANCRAS (North), 7,660
Edwd. Robert Pacy Moon, C. 2,834
Herbert Henry Raphael, L. 2,623
John Leighton, Ind. 29
ST. PANCRAS (South), 5,643
(Bye-election 28 Jan., 1896.)
Capt. Herbt. Merton Jessel, U. 2,631
George Montagu Harris, L. 1,375
ST. PANCRAS (West), 7,118
Harry Robert Graham, C.... 3,104
Dr. Wm. Job Collins, L...... 2,273
SALFORD (North), 9,491
Fredk. Platt-Higgins, C. 3,787
*Wm. Henry Holland, L. 3,781
SALFORD (South), 9,403
Sir Hy. H. Howorth, K.C.I.E., C. 3,384
Alexander Forrest, L. 2,310
Hy. W. Hobart, S. (Lab.)... 813
SALFORD (West), 11,814
Lees Knowles, C............. 4,354
Vernon K. Armitage, L. ... 4,254
SALISBURY (City), 2,847
(Bye-election, 27 Jan., 1897.)
Augustus Henry Allhusen, C. 1,425
J. M. Fleetwood Fuller, L. 1,278
SCARBOROUGH, 5,595
Jos. Compton Rickett, L. ... 2,415
*Sir Geo. R. Sitwell, Bt., C. 2,391
SCOTLAND (Liverpool), 5,821
*Thos. Power O' Connor, A.-P. 2,089
+Wm. Ellison Macartney, C. 1,452
SEVENOAKS D. (Kent), 14,535
Henry William Forster, C...unop.
SHEFFIELD (Central), 10,167
Col. Sir H. Vincent, K.C.B., C. unop.
SHEFFIELD: see also Attercliffe, Brightside, Ecclesall, & Hallam.
SHIPLEY D. (Yorks, W.R.), 14,414
Sir Fortescue Flannery, U. 5,999
*Wm. Pollard Byles, L. 5,921
SHOREDITCH: see Haggerston and Hoxton.
SHREWSBURY, 4,535
Henry David Greene, Q.C., C. unop.
SHROPSHIRE: see Ludlow, Newport, Oswestry, & Wellington.
SKIPTON D. (Yorks, W.R.), 11,656
Walter Morrison, U. 4,902
Jas. Anson Farrer, L. 4,763
SLEAFORD D. (Lincoln), 9,878
Rt. Hon. Henry Chaplin, C. 4,653
Wm. Shearburn Fox, L. ... 2,687
SOMERSET (Eastern), 9,065
Henry Hobhouse, U. 4,408
J.C. Swinburne Hanham, L. 3,331
SOMERSET (Northern), 10,630
Evan Henry Llewellyn, C... 4,652
*Thos. Courtney Warner, L. 3,966
SOMERSET (S., or Yeovil), 9,406
Edward Strachey, L. 4,167
Henry Gribble Turner, C. 3,827
SOMERSET: see also Bridgwater, Frome, Wellington, and Wells.
SOUTH MOLTON D. (Devon), 8,676
George Lambert, L. 4,283
Prof. James Long, U. 2,923
SOUTH SHIELDS, 16,090
Wm. Snowdon Robson, Q.C., L. 5,057
Henry H. Wainwright, U. 4,924
SOUTHAMPTON (2), 16,014
(Bye-election, 22 Feb., 1896.)
*Sir John B. Simeon, Bt., U. 5,413
*Sir F. H. Evans, K.C.M.G., L. 5,557
George Candy, Q.C., C....... 5,522
C. A. Gibson, S. (Lab.)..... 273

SOUTHPORT D. (S.W. Lanc.), 12,656
(Bye-election 30 May, 1899.)
Sir Geo. Aug. Pilkington, L. 5,635
C. B. Balfour, C. 5,052
SOUTHWARK (West), 8,005
Richd. Knight Causton, C.... 2,989
Fredk. Wm. Horner, C. ... 2,870
SOUTHWARK: see also Bermondsey, and Rotherhithe.
SOWERBY D. (Yorks, W.R.), 11,981
Rt. Hn. John W. Mellor, Q.C., L. 5,328
J. C. Bailey, C. 3,754
SPALDING DIV. (Lincoln), 13,929
Harry Fredk. Pollock, U. ... 4,623
*Halley Stewart, L. 4,274
SPEN VALLEY D. (Yorks, W. R.), 10,869
Thos. Palmer Whittaker, L. 4,700
Frederick Ellis, C........... 3,879
STAFFORD (Borough), 3,468
Theodore F. Chas. E. Shaw, L. 1,568
Thomas Salt, C. 1,556
STAFFORDSHIRE (N.W.), 14,578
James Heath, C. 6,206
Leonard K. Shoobridge, L. 5,533
STAFFORDSHIRE (W.), 10,866
(Bye-election, 10 May, 1898.)
Alexander Henderson, U..... 4,725
W. Adams, L. 3,993
STAFFORDSHIRE: see also Burton, Handsworth, Kingswinford, Leek, and Lichfield.
STALYBRIDGE, 7,313
Tom Harrop Sidebottom, C.. 3,389
Joshua Macer Wright, L....... 2,757
STAMFORD D. (Lincoln), 9,589
William Younger, C. 4,203
Arthur Priestley, L. 3,814
STEPNEY (Tower Hamlets), 6,095
(Bye-election 9 March, 1898.)
Wm Chas. Steadman, L. (Lb.) 2,492
Maj. W.E. Evans-Gordon, C. 2,472
STOCKPORT (2), 12,261
George Whiteley, L. 5,410
Beresford V. Melville, C. ... 5,067
*Sir Joseph Leigh, L. 4,933
John Roskill, L. 4,562
STOCKTON-ON-TEES, 10,977
Jonathan Samuel, L. 4,786
*Thomas Wrightson, C. 4,314
STOKE-UPON-TRENT, 12,714
Douglas Harry Coghill, C. .. 4,396
*Geo. G. Leveson-Gower, L. 4,149
STOWMARKET DIV. (Suff.), 10,729
Ian Malcolm, C. 5,144
Henry Walker, L. 3,701
STRAND, 10,025
Hon. Wm. Fredk. D. Smith, C. unop.
STRATFORD-ON-AVON DIVISION (Warwickshire), 10,076
Col. Victor Milward, C. 4,598
Thomas Sadler, L. 2,827
STRETFORD D. (S.E.Lanc.), 18,058
Sir John Wm. Maclure, Bt., C. unop.
STROUD DIV. (Glouc.), 11,086
Chas. Alfred Cripps, Q.C., C. 5,175
Charles P. Allen, L. 4,514
SUDBURY DIV. (Suffolk), 10,364
Sir Cuthbert Quilter, Bart. U. unop.
SUFFOLK (County of): see Eye, Lowestoft, Stowmarket, Sudbury, and Woodbridge.

SUNDERLAND (2), 24,944
Wm. Theodore Doxford, C.   9,833
Sir Ed. Temperley Gourley, L. 8,232
Samuel Storey, L. 8,189

SURREY (County of): see Chertsey, Epsom, Guildford, Kingston, Reigate, and Wimbledon.

SUSSEX (County of): see Chichester, Eastbourne, East Grinstead, Horsham, Lewes, and Rye.

TAMWORTH D. (Warwick), 11,758
Philip Albert Muntz, C. ...... unop.

TAUNTON, 3,179
Lt.-Col. Alfred Cholmeley Earle-Welby, C. ...... unop.

TAVISTOCK D. (Devon), 12,332
Hugh C. Fownes-Luttrell, L. 4,970
Col. Sir R. W.-Thomson, C. 4,547

TEWKESBURY D. (Glouc.), 12,446
Sir John E. Dorington, Bt., C. unop.

THANET, ISLE OF, D. (Kent), 9,735
Rt. Hon. James Lowther, C. uncp.

THIRSK & MALTON DIVISION (Yorks, N. & W.R.), 12,502
John Grant Lawson, C. ...... unop.

THORNBURY D. (Glouc.), 12,352
Chas. Edwd. H. A. Colston, C. 5,727
Arthur Acland Allen, L. 4,638

TIVERTON D. (Devon), 9,078
Colonel Rt. Hon. Sir William Hood Walrond, Bart., C. unop.

TORQUAY DIV. (Devon), 9,113
Capt. Arthur S. Phillpotts, C. 4,205
Fras. Leyland Barratt, L. 4,030

TOTNES DIV. (Devon), 9,713
Fras. Bingham Mildmay, C. 4,630
Alfred J. Sparke, L. 2,264

TOTTENHAM D. (Middx.), 18,828
Joseph Howard, C. 6,388
Clem Edwards, L. (Lab.)... 3,817

TOWER HAMLETS: see Bow and Bromley, Limehouse, Mile End, Poplar, St. George, Stepney, and Whitechapel.

TOXTETH, EAST (L'pool) 9,239
(Bye-election, 29 Nov. 1895.)
Augustus Fredk. Warr, C. unop.

TOXTETH, WEST (L'pool) 8,443
Robt. Paterson Houston, C. 3,600
Wm. Mulholland, Q.C., L. 1,552

TRURO DIV. (Cornwall), 8,504
Sir E. Durning-Lawrence, Bart., U. 3,282
Henry Turner Waddy, L. 3,012

TUNBRIDGE DIV. (Kent), 13,044
A. S. T. Griffith-Boscawen, C. unop.

TYNEMOUTH, 7,773
Richard Sims Donkin, C. 3,168
Francis D. Blake, L. 2,959

TYNESIDE D. (Northumb.), 17,144
Joseph Albert Pease, L. 6,066
Arnold Henry White, U. 5,631

UXBRIDGE D. (Middx.), 13,280
Sir F. D. Dixon-Hartland, Bt., C. .... unop.

WAKEFIELD (City), 5,987
Viscount Milton, U. 2,864
Henry S. Lee Wilson, L. 2,165

WALSALL, 12,512
Sydney Gedge, C. 5,145
Rt. Hon. Sir Arthur D. Hayter, Bart., L. 4,828

WALTHAMSTOW D. (Essex), 22,161
(Bye-election, 3 Feb. 1897.)
+*Samuel Woods, L. (Lab.)*.. 6,518
Thomas Robert Dewar, C. .. 6,239

WALTON (Liverpool), 10,656
James Henry Stock, C. ...... unop.

WALWORTH (Newington), 7,823
James Bailey, C. 2,822
Russell Spokes, L. 2,269
George Lansbury, S. (Lab.) 203

WANDSWORTH, 19,588
Henry Kimber, C. 6,482
Marsh Mayhew, L. 3,246

WANSBECK D. (N'thumb.), 13,668
Charles Fenwick, L. (Lab.) 5,629
Jos. J. Harris, C. (Lab.)..... 2,422

WARRINGTON, 9,129
Robert Pierpoint, C. 4,001
Percival B. Scott, L. 3,326

WARWICK AND LEAMINGTON, 5,978
Hon. Alfred Lyttelton, C. .... unop.

WARWICKSHIRE: see Nuneaton, Rugby, Stratford-on-Avon, and Tamworth.

WATFORD DIV. (Herts), 13,151
Thomas Fredk. Halsey, C..... unop.

WEDNESBURY, 11,250
Walford Davis Green, C. 4,924
Charles R. R. Roberts, L..... 4,733

WELLINGTON D. (Salop), 8,393
Alex. Hargreaves Brown, U. unop.

WELLINGTON D. (Somerset), 9,730
Sir Alex. F. A. Hood, Bt., C. unop.

WELLS DIV. (Somerset), 11,095
(Bye-election, 1899.)

WEST BROMWICH, 9,919
James Ernest Spencer, C....... unop.

WEST DERBY (L'pool), 11,665
Rt. Hon. Walter Hume Long, C. 4,622
Oscar Browning, L. 1,681

WEST HAM (North), 15,461
Ernest Gray, C. 5,635
T. N. Archibald Grove, L. 4,931

WEST HAM (South), 18,042
Maj. George Edwd. Banes, C. 4,750
Jas. Keir-Hardie, S.(Lab.) 3,975

WESTBURY DIV. (Wilts), 9,732
Capt. Richard Godolphin Walmsley Chaloner, C..... 4,497
Geo. Pargiter Fuller, L..... 4,331

WESTHOUGHTON DIVISION (S.E. Lancs), 15,420
Lord Stanley, C. .... unop.

WESTMINSTER (City), 7,622
William Lehmann Burdett-Coutts, C. .... unop.

WESTMORLAND: see Appleby, and Kendal.

WHITBY D. (Yorks, N.R.), 10,832
Maj. Ernest Wm. Beckett, C. unop.

WHITECHAPEL (Tower H.), 5,297
Sir Samuel Montagu, Bt., L. 2,009
Sir Wm. Hy. Porter, Bt., C. 1,977

WHITEHAVEN, 2,850
Augustus Helder, C. 1,386
Thos. Shepherd Little, L. 1,114

WIDNES D. (S. W. Lanc.), 9,636
John Saunders Gilliat, C. 3,973
Henry Wade Deacon, L..... 3,456

WIGAN, 7,957
Sir Fras. Sharp Powell, Bt., C. 3,949
Thos. Aspinwall, L. (Lab.) 3,075

WIGHT, I. OF DIV. (Hants), 14,452
Sir Richard Everard Webster, Bart., Q.C., G.C.M.G., C..... 5,809
Hon. A. Wodehouse, C.B., L. 5,363

WILTON DIV. (Wilts), 8,299
Viscount Folkestone, C. 3,828
Lionel Edm. Pyke, Q.C., L. 3,565

WILTSHIRE (or Wilts): see Chippenham, Cricklade, Devizes, Westbury, and Wilton.

WIMBLEDON D. (Surrey), 18,821
Hy. Cosmo Orme Bonsor, C. unop.

WINCHESTER (City), 2,630
William Henry Myers, C..... unop.

WINDSOR, 3,103
Sir Fras. Tress Barry, B't. C. uncp.

WIRRAL D. (Cheshire), 14,236
Col. Edward T. Davenant Cotton-Jodrell, R.A. C...... unop.

WISBECH D. (Cambs), 10,144
Charles Tyrrell Giles, C. 4,368
Hon. Arthur G. Brand, L. 4,145

WOKINGHAM D. (Berks), 11,319
(Bye-election, 30 March, 1898.)
Comm. Oliver Young, R.N., C. 4,726
George Wm. Palmer, L. 3,690

WOLVERHAMPTON (E.), 9,053
Rt. Hon. Sir Henry Hartley Fowler, G.C.S.I., L. 4,011
Rupert E. Cooke Kettle, C. 2,977

WOLVERHAMPTON (S.), 9,302
(Bye-election, 3 Feb., 1898.)
John Lloyd Gibbons, U. 4,115
Geo. Rennie Thorne, L. 4,024

WOLVERHAMPTON (W.), 11,174
Sir Alfred Hickman, C. 4,770
George Rennie Thorne, L. 3,947

WOODBRIDGE DIV. (Suff.), 12,081
Capt. Ernest G. Pretyman, C. 5,410
Robert Lacey Everett, L. 4,778

WOODSTOCK D. (Oxford), 9,656
Geo. Herbert Morrell, C. ... 4,669
Godf. Rathbone Benson, L. 3,740

WOOLWICH, 14,289
Col. Edwin Hughes, C. 6,662
Benjamin Jones, L. (Lab.) 3,857

WORCESTER (City), 7,665
Hon. George H. Allsopp, C. 3,530
Jas. Thorpe Hincks, L. 2,328

WORCESTERSHIRE (E.), 13,111
Jos. Austen Chamberlain, U. unop.

WORCESTERSHIRE (N.), 12,336
John William Wilson, U. 5,012
Robert Waite, C. 4,024

WORCESTERSHIRE: see also Bewdley, Droitwich, and Evesham.

WYCOMBE D. (Bucks), 12,655
(Bye-election, 21 Feb. 1896.)
Viscount Curzon, C. .... unop.

YARMOUTH, GREAT, 8,407
Sir John Chas. R. Colomb, K.C.M.G., C. 3,543
Jas. M. Moorsom, Q.C., L. 2,907

YORK (City) (2), 12,402
John George Butcher, C..... 5,516
(Bye-election, 13 Jan. 1892.)
Rear-Adm. Ld. Chas. Beresford, C.B., C. 3,659
Sir Christopher Furness, L. 5,618

YORKSHIRE, East Riding: see Buckrose, Holderness, and Howdenshire.

---

* As before recount.

YORKSHIRE, North Riding : see Cleveland, Richmond, Thirsk and Malton, and Whitby.

YORKSHIRE, West Riding : see Barkston Ash, Barnsley, Colne Valley, Doncaster, Elland, Hallamshire, Holmfirth, Keighley, Morley, Normanton, Osgoldcross, Otley, Pudsey, Ripon, Rotherham, Shipley, Skipton, Sowerby, and Spen Valley.

Wales.

30 Members; 290,157 Electors.

ANGLESEY (County), 9,636
Ellis Jones Griffith, L. 4,224
Jno. Rice Roberts, C. 3,197
ARFON DIV. (Carnarvon), 9,405
William Jones, L. 4,480
Prof. Alfred Hughes, C. ... 2,861
BRECKNOCKSHIRE, 11,734
Charles Morley, L. 4,594
Col. Thomas Wood, C. 3,631
CARDIFF DISTRICT, 21,941
Jas. Mackenzie Maclean, C. 8,386
Sir Edw. J. Reed, K.C.B., L. 7,562
CARDIGANSHIRE, 13,272
Matt. L. Vaughan-Davies, L. 4,927
John Charles Harford, C. . 3,748
CARMARTHEN DISTRICT, 5,490
Sir John Jones Jenkins, U... 2,443
Maj. E. Rowland Jones, L. 2,391
CARMARTHEN (E.), 9,794
Abel Thomas, Q.C., L. 4,471
Ernald Edw. Richardson, C. 2,466
CARMARTHEN (W.), 9,394
John Lloyd Morgan, L. 4,143
Wm. Jos. Buckley, U. 3,103
CARNARVON DISTRICT, 5,157
David Lloyd-George, L. 2,265
Sir Hugh Ellis-Nanney, C. 2,071
CARNARVONSHIRE : see Arfon and Eifion.
DENBIGH DISTRICT, 4,057
William Tudor Howell, C. . 1,833
Ald. Walter H. Morgan, L. 1,604
DENBIGHSHIRE (East), 10,301
(Bye-election 28 Sept., 1897.)
Samuel Moss, L. 5,175
Hon. George T. Kenyon, C. 2,848
DENBIGHSHIRE (West), 9,366
John Herbert Roberts, L. ... 4,481
Capt. T. A. W.-Edwards, C. 2,878
EIFION DIV. (Carnarvon), 8,843
John Bryn Roberts, L. ...... unop.
FLINT DISTRICT, 3,632
John Herbert Lewis, L. 1,828
Philip P. Pennant, C. 1,663
FLINTSHIRE, 10,616
Samuel Smith, L. 4,376
Col. Henry R.L. Howard, C. 3,925
GLAMORGANSHIRE (E.), 15,258
Alfred Thomas, L. 6,055
C. Jas. Jackson, C. 3,509
GLAMORGANSHIRE (Mid) 13,012
Samuel Thomas Evans, L... 5,612
John Edwards Vaughan, C. 2,935
GLAMORGANSHIRE (S.), 16,713
Maj. W. H. Wyndham Quin, U. 5,947
Arthur John Williams, L. 4,922
GLAMORGANSHIRE : see also Gower, and Rhondda.
GOWER D., Glamorgan, W.,12,064
David Randall, L. 6,074
Chas. Hy. Glascodine, U. 2,256

HAVERFORDWEST : see Pembroke.
MERIONETHSHIRE, 9,371
(Bye-election 2 May, 1899.)
Prof. Owen Morg.Edwards,L...unop.
MERTHYR TYDFIL (2), 15,279
David Alfred Thomas, L. ... 9,250
Wm. Pritchard Morgan, L. 8,554
Herbert C. Lewis, C. 6,525
Allen Upward, L. (Lab.)... 659
MONTGOMERY DISTRICT, 3,144
Maj. Edward Pryce-Jones,C. 1,435
Owen Cosby Philipps, L. ...1,351
MONTGOMERYSHIRE, 7,954
Arth. C. Humphreys-Owen,L.3,442
Robt. W.Williams-Wynn,C.3,415
PEMBROKE AND HAVERFORDWEST DISTRICT, 6,530
Lt.-Gen.John W. Laurie, C. 2,719
Chas. F. Egerton-Allen, L. 2,550
PEMBROKESHIRE, 11,149
(Bye-election, 15 Feb., 1898.)
Jno. Wynford Philipps, L... 5,070
Viscount Emlyn, C. 3,400
RADNORSHIRE, 5,168
Sir Powlett C. J. Milbank, Bart., L. 1,949
Frank Edwards, L. 1,868
RHONDDA D. (Glamorg.), 11,711
William Abraham, L.(Lab.)..unop.
SWANSEA DISTRICT, 10,916
+Dav.Brynmor-Jones,Q.C.,L.3,850
E. Hall Headley, L. (Lab.) 2,018
Col. Jno. R. Wright, V.D.,C. 1,851
SWANSEA TOWN, 9,052
Sir J. T. D. Llewelyn, Bt., C. 3,977
Robt.J.Dickson-Burnie,L. 3,556

Scotland.

72 Members; 671,128 Electors.

ABERDEEN CITY (N.), 9,953
(Bye-election 1 May, 1896.)
Duncan Ver. Pirie, L. 2,909
Tom Mann, S. (Lab.) 2,479
ABERDEEN CITY (S.), 11,053
Rt. Hon. James Bryce, L. ... 3,985
David Stewart, U. 3,121
ABERDEENSHIRE (East), 12,183
Thos. Ryburn Buchanan, L. 4,723
William Smith, U. 3,308
ABERDEENSHIRE (West), 10,554
Dr. Robt. Farquharson, L. 4,187
Sir Arthur Hy. Grant, Bt., C. 3,967
ARGYLLSHIRE, 10,365
Donald Ninian Nicol, C. ... 3,970
*SirDonaldH.Macfarlane,L.*3,835
AYR DISTRICT, 6,813
CharlesLindsayOrr-Ewing,C.3,057
William Birkmyre, L. ... 2,722
AYRSHIRE (North), 13,479
Hon.T.H.A.E.Cochrane,U. 5,612
William Robertson, L. 4,902
AYRSHIRE (South), 15,734
Sir William Arrol, U. 6,875
Eugène Wason, L. 6,325
BANFFSHIRE, 7,875
Sir Wm. Wedderburn, Bt., L. 2,977
James Aug. Grant, U. 2,467
BERWICKSHIRE, 5,498
Harold John Tennant, L. ... 2,673
Chas.BarringtonBalfour,C. 2,166
BLACKFRIARS & HUTCHESONTOWN (Glasgow), 10,364
And. Dryburgh Provand, L. 3,107
Alexander Stuart, jun., C. 2,727
Shaw Maxwell, S. (Lab.)... 448

BRIDGETON (Glasgow), 11,208
(Bye-election, 15 Feb. 1897.)
+Sir Chas. Cameron, Bt., L. 4,505
Chas. Scott Dickson, C. 4,381
BUTESHIRE, 3,364
And. Graham Murray,Q.C., U. unop.
CAITHNESS-SHIRE, 4,254
Dr. Gavin Brown Clark, L... 1,828
John Cowper, C. 528
CAMLACHIE (Glasgow), 10,262
Alexander Cross, U. 3,198
Samuel Chisholm, L......... 2,197
Robert Smillie, S. (Lab.) 696
CLACKMANNAN AND KINROSS-SHIRES, 7,722
(Bye-election, 1899.)
COLLEGE (Glasgow), 15,893
SirJ.Stirling-Maxwell,Bt.,C.5,364
Sir Chas. Cameron, Bt., L. 4,219
DUMBARTONSHIRE, 13,340
Alexander Wylie, C. 5,375
Captain John Sinclair, L. 5,342
DUMFRIES DISTRICT, 3,731
Sir Robert T. Reid, Q.C., G.C.M.G., L. 1,785
William Murray, U. 1,185
DUMFRIES-SHIRE, 9,158
A. Robinson Souttar, L..... 3,989
Wm. Jardine Maxwell, U. 3,976
DUNDEE (City) (2), 18,384
Edmund Robertson, Q.C., L... 7,602
Sir John Leng, L. 7,592
Wm. Charles Smith, U. ... 5,390
Edward Jenkins, C. 4,318
James MacDonald, S.(Lab.) 1,313
EDINBURGH (City) (Central), 7,666
William M'Ewan, L. .... unop.
EDINBURGH (City) (East), 10,730
(Bye-election 23 June, 1899.)
George McCrae, L............ 4,891
Harry G. Younger, U. 2,961
EDINBURGH (City) (South), 13,891
(Bye-election 20 June, 1899.)
Arthur Dewar, L. 5,820
Maj.-Gen. A. G. Wauchope, C.B., C. 4,989
EDINBURGH (City) (West), 8,727
Sir Lewis M'Iver, Bart., U. unop.
EDINBURGH (8,253) AND ST. ANDREWS (1,483) UNIVERSITIES, 9,736
(Bye-election, 12 May, 1896.)
Sir Wm. Overend Priestley, C. unop.
EDINBURGHSHIRE (Midlothian), 13,940
SirT.D.G.Carmichael,Bart.,L. 6,090
Maj. Hon. North de Coigny Dalrymple, C. 5,631
ELGIN DISTRICT, 4,587
Alexander Asher, Q.C., L.... 1,853
Charles Thos. Gordon, U.... 1,161
ELGIN & NAIRN SHIRES, 5,929
Hn. John Edward Gordon, C. 2,147
John Seymour Keay, L. 2,019
FALKIRK DISTRICT, 9,958
John Wilson, L. 4,075
Harry Smith, L. 3,822
FIFESHIRE (East), 9,514
Ri.Hon.H.H.Asquith,Q.C.,L.4,332
John Gilmour, C. 3,616
FIFESHIRE (West), 11,058
Augustine Birrell, Q.C., L... 4,719
R. G. Erskine-Wemyss, U. 2,965

FORFARSHIRE, 12,663
(Bye-election, 30 Jan., 1897.)
Capt. J.hn Sinclair, L...... 5,423
Hon. C. Maule Ramsay, U. 4,965

GLASGOW (Central), 15,416
John Geo. Alex. Baird, C..... 5,621
Edwin A. Adam, L. 3,792
∴ See also Blackfriars and Hutchesntn, Bridgeton, Camlachie, College, St. Rollox, and Tradeston.

GLASGOW (5,541) AND ABERDEEN
(3 723) UNIVERSITIES, 9,264
Rt. Hon. J. Alex. Campbell,
C. .... unop.

GOVAN DIV. (Lanark), 14,016
John Wilson, L. 4,290
George Ferguson, U.......... 4,029
Alex. Haddow, S. (Lab.).... 430

GREENOCK, 7,522
Sir T. Sutherland, G.C.M.G., U. 3,751
Alfred Ewen Fletcher, L..... 2,753

HADDINGTON, 6,523
Rd. Burdon Haldane, Q.C. L. 2,774
The Master of Polwarth, L. 2,194

HAWICK DISTRICT, 5,976
Thomas Shaw, Q.C., L. 3,033
John Sanderson, C. 2,531

INVERNESS DISTRICT, 4,097
(Bye-election, 31 Aug. 1895.)
Sir Robt. B. Finlay, Q.C., U. unop.

INVERNESS-SHIRE, 9,294
James E. Bruce Baillie, C..... 2,991
Neil J. D. Kennedy, L....... 2,891

KILMARNOCK DISTRICT, 13,124
John M'Ausland Denny, C. 5,432
*Stephen Williamson, L..... 5,051

KINCARDINESHIRE, 6,319
John Wm. Crombie, L. 2,603
Hon. Chas. J. R. Trefusis, C. 2,040

KIRKCALDY DISTRICT, 6,924
James Henry Dalziel, L. ... 3,078
Chas. G. Kekewich, C........ 1,122

KIRKCUDBRIGHTSHIRE, 5,855
Sir Mark John Stewart, Bt., C. 2,664
Jno. Archd. Duncan, L. 2,494

LANARKSHIRE (Mid), 12,503
James Caldwell, L. 4,447
Charles K. Mackenzie, L... 4,376

LANARKSHIRE (N. East), 15,403
John Colville, L. 6,288
Alexander Whitelaw, C. ... 5,751

LANARKSHIRE (N. West), 13,337
(Bye-election, 21 Feb., 18 9.)
Charles Mackinnon Douglas, L. 5,723
*Græme Alex. Whitelaw, C. 5,364

LANARKSHIRE (South), 9,115
Hn. James Hy. Cecil Hozier, C. 4,053
Robert Lambie, L. 3,823
∴ See also Govan, and Partick.

LEITH DISTRICT, 15,185
R. C. Munro-Ferguson, L.... 5,819
John Wilson, U. 4,494

LINLITHGOWSHIRE, 9,115
Alexander Ure, Q.C., L...... 3,760
*Captain Thomas Hope, C. 3,753

LOTHIANS : EAST, see Haddington ; MID, see Edinburghshire ; WEST, see Linlithgowshire.

MONTROSE DISTRICT, 8,956
(Bye-election, 22 Feb., 1890.)
Rt. Hon. John Morley, L.... 4,565
John Wilson, U.............. 2,572

ORKNEY & SHETLAND, 7,584
Sir Leonard Lyell, Bart., L. 2,361
R. W. M. Fullarton, Q.C., U. 1,580

PAISLEY, 10,446
Sir William Dunn, Bart., L. 4,404
Alexander Moffat, U. 3,062

PARTICK D. (Lanark), 15,109
James Parker Smith, C. 5,551
Wm. Lyon Mackenzie, L..... 4,341

PEEBLES & SELKIRK SHIRES, 3,591
Walter Thorburn, U. 1,563
Master of Elibank, L. 1,509

PERTH (City), 4,839
Robert Wallace, Q.C., L...... 2,137
*William Whitelaw, C. ... 1,763

PERTHSHIRE (East), 7,550
Sir John G. S. Kinloch, Bt., L. 3,410
Wm. Lindsay Boase, C....... 2,535

PERTHSHIRE (West), 8,199
Sir Donald Currie, G.C.M.G., U. 3,379
John Deans Hope, L. 3,087

RENFREWSHIRE (East), 12,239
Michael H. Shaw-Stewart, C. unop.

RENFREWSHIRE (West), 9,134
Charles Bine Renshaw, C. 3,909
Duncan Vernon Pirie, L... 3,306

ROSS AND CROMARTY SHIRE, 8,130
Jas. Galloway Weir, L...... 3,272
Maj. Randle Jackson, C. ... 2,409

ROXBURGHSHIRE, 5,944
Earl of Dalkeith, C. 2,929
*Hon. Mark F. Napier, L. 2,368

ST. ANDREWS DISTRICT, 2,856
Hy. Torrens Anstruther, U. 1,185
John Paton, L. 989

ST. ROLLOX (Glasgow), 16,328
Ferd. Faithfull Begg, C..... 4,561
*Sir J. M. Carmichael, Bt., L. 4,200

STIRLING DISTRICT, 6,324
Rt. Hon. Sir Henry Campbell-Bannerman, G.C.B., L. ... 2,786
Stuart C. Macaskie, C....... 1,653

STIRLINGSHIRE, 15,731
James M'Killop, C.......... 5,916
*William Jacks, L......... 5,489

SUTHERLANDSHIRE, 2,550
John M'Leod, L. 1,085
James A. Swanston, U. 590

TRADESTON (Glasgow), 9,589
Archd. Cameron Corbett, U. 3,373
George Green, L. 2,568
Frank Smith, S. (Lab.)..... 368

WICK DISTRICT, 2,637
(Bye-election, 2 June, 1896.)
Thos. C H. Hedderwick, L. 1,054
William Charles Smith, U. 842

WIGTOWNSHIRE, 5,637
Rt. Hon. Sir H. E. Maxwell,
Bt., C. .... unop.

Ireland.

103 *Members*; 721,018 *Electors*

ANTRIM (East), 8,959
Col. Jas. M. M'Calmont, C. unop.

ANTRIM (Mid), 8,003
Hon. R. Torrens O'Neill, C. unop.

ANTRIM (North), 8,852
(Bye-election, 25 Feb. 18 9.)
William Moore, U. .... unop.

ANTRIM (South), 10,393
Wm. G. E.-Macartney, C.... unop.

ARMAGH (Mid), 7,292
(Bye-election, 21 Jan. 1898.)
Dunbar P. Barton, Q.C., C... unop.

ARMAGH (North), 11,282
Col. Rt. Hon. E. J. Saunderson,
C. .... unop.

ARMAGH (South), 6,985
Edward M'Hugh, A.-P. ... 3,373
William M'M. Kavanagh, C. 1,995

BELFAST (East), 15,511
Gustav Wilhelm Wolff, C. unop.

BELFAST (North), 10,179
(Bye-election, 22 Jan., 1896.)
Sir James H. Haslett, C. ... 3,595
Adam Turner, Ind. 3,424

BELFAST (South), 8,616
William Johnston, U....... unop.

BELFAST (West), 9,794
Hugh O. Arnold-Forster, U. unop.

BIRR DIV. (King's Co.), 4,739
Bernard C. Molloy, A.-P... unop.

CARLOW, 7,475
John Hammond, A.-P. 3,091
Stewart J. C. Duckett, C.... 685

CAVAN (East), 9,595
Samuel Young, A.-P....... unop.

CAVAN (West), 10,051
(Bye-election, 22 Aug. 1895.)
James Patrick Farrell, A.-P. unop.

CLARE (East), 10,491
Wm. H. K. Redmond, P. ... 3,315
+Patrick A. M'Hugh, A.-P. 3,257

CLARE (West), 10,294
Maj. J. Eustace Jameson, A.-P. 3,376
*Thos. Rochfort Maguire, P. 2,973

COLLEGE GREEN (Dublin), 9,380
(Bye-election, 6 April, 1896.)
James Laurence Carew, P. unop.

CONNEMARA D. (Galway), 6,452
William O'Malley, A.-P. ... unop.

CORK (City) (2), 13,471
Jas. F. Xavier O'Brien, A.-P. 5,327
Maurice Healy, A.-P....... 5,169
Ald. J. Roche, P. 4,994
Jeremiah C. Blake, P. 4,966

CORK (County) (East), 6,568
Anth. J. C. Donelan, A.-P. unop.

CORK (County) (Mid), 8,279
Dr. Chas. K. D. Tanner, A.-P. unop.

CORK (County) (North), 7,742
J. Christopher Flynn, A.-P. unop.

CORK (County) (N. East), 7,898
William Abraham, A.-P..... unop.

CORK (County) (South), 6,645
Edward Barry, A.-P. ...... unop.

CORK (County) (S. East), 7,859
Andrew Commins, A.-P. ... unop.

CORK (County) (South), 6,492
James Gilhooly, A.-P. ..... unop.

DERRY (North), 10,685
Rt. Hn. John Atkinson, Q.C. C. 4,763
Arthur Houston, Q.C., L... 2,538

DERRY (South), 8,567
Sir Thomas Lea, Bart., L.... 4,470
Serj. Wm. H. Dodd, Q.C., L. 4,018

DONEGAL (East), 6,556
Arthur O'Connor, Q.C., A.-P. 3,393
Emerson T. Herdman, U.... 2,731

DONEGAL (North), 6,542
+Thomas B. Curran, A.-P. unop.

DONEGAL (South), 6,311
J. G. Swift MacNeill, Q.C. A.-P. .3,614
Henry W. Stubbs, C. 1,313

DONEGAL (West), 6,775
Timothy D. Sullivan, A.-P. unop.

Down (East), 8,542
James Alex. Rentoul, Q.C., C. unop.

Down (North), 9,864
(Bye-election, 7 Sept. 1898.)
Jno. Blakison-Houston, C. ... 3,381
Thos. Lorimer Corbett, C. 3,107

Down (South), 8,662
Michael McCartan, A.-P. 4,051
James Rowan, C. 3,378

Down (West), 9,369
(Bye-election, 18 July, 1898.)
Capt. Arthur Hill, C. ....unop

DUBLIN CITY: see College Green
Dublin Harbour, St. Stephen's
Green, and St. Patrick's.

DUBLIN (County) (North), 11,276
John Joseph Clancy, P. 4,520
Danl. Jas. Wilson, C. 2,280

DUBLIN (County) (South), 10 481
Rt. Hon. Horace C. Plunkett, C. 4,501
Haviland Burke, P. .... 2,96.

DUBLIN HAR. (Dublin City), 9.323
Timothy C. Harrington, P... unop.

DUBLIN UNIVERSITY (2), 4,609
Rt. Hn.Ed. H. Carson, Q.C., U. unop.
(Bye-election, 6 Dec. 1895.)
Rt. Hn. Wm. E. H. Lecky, U. 1,751
Geo. Wright, U. 1,011

FERMANAGH (North), 5,129
(Bye-election, 1 Nov., 1898.)
Edwd. Mervyn Archdale, C. 2,568
Edwd. C. Thompson, M.D.,
C. (Ind.) 2,09

FERMANAGH (South), 5,470
†Jeremiah Jordan, A.-P. ... 2,79?
Sir Arthur D. Brooke, C. .. 2,098

GALWAY (City), 2,001
John Pinkerton, A.-P. 595
Edmund Leamy, P. 405
Martin H. P. Morris, C. 395

GALWAY (County) (East), 7,282
John Roche, A.-P. .... unop.

GALWAY (County) (North), 9,417
†Denis Kilbride, A.-P. 2,590
*Col. John Philip Nolan, P. 2,025

GALWAY (County) (South), 6,363
David Sheehy, A.-P. .... unop.

GALWAY Co.: see also Connemara

KERRY (East), 5,843
(Bye-election, 27 March, 1896.)
Hon. James B. Roche, A.-P. 1,561
John MacGillicuddy, C. ... 68.

KERRY (North), 5,613
(Bye-election, 24 April, 1896.)
Mich. Jos. Flavin, A.-P. unop

KERRY (South), 3,416
(Bye-election, 5 Sept. 1895.)
Thomas G. Farrell, A.-P... 1,209
Wm. Martin Murphy, A.-P. 474

KERRY (West), 5,563
Sir T.H.G.Esmonde, Bt., A.-P.unop

KILDARE (North), 5,569
Chas. John Engledow, P. ... 1,944
Jas. Laurence Carew, P. ... 1,712

KILDARE (South), 5,379
Matthew J. Minch, A.-P. unop

KILKENNY (City), 2,380
Patrick O'Brien, P. 681
James P. Farrell, A.-P. 667

KILKENNY (County) (N.), 5,342
Patrick McDermott, A.-P. ... unop

KILKENNY (County) (S.), 5,557
Patrick A. McHugh, A.-P. ... unop

KING'sCo.: see Birr, & Tullamore

LEITRIM (North), 5,822
Jasper Tully, A.-P. .... unop

LEITRIM (South), 6,527

LEIX DIV. (Queen's Co.), 5,068
Dr. M. A. MacDonnell, A.-P.unop

LIMERICK (City), 5,489
(Bye-election, 11 Sept., 1895.)
Fras. Arthur O'Keeffe, A.-P. 1,85
Joseph Nolan, P. 1,764

LIMERICK (County) (East), 7,628
John Finucane, A.-P. .... unop

LIMERICK (County) (West), 7,176
Michael Austin, A.-P. (Lab.) unop

LONDONDERRY (City), 4,723
(Bye-election, 16 Feb., 1899.)
Count Moore, A.-P. 2,343
Emerson Herdman, U....... 2,301

LONDONDERRYCo.:seeDerryN.&S

LONGFORD (North), 4,112
Justin McCarthy, A.-P. ... unop

LONGFORD (South), 4,274
Hon. Edward Blake, A.-P. .. unop.

LOUTH (North), 5,875
Timothy M. Healy, A.-P. ... 2,294
Joseph Nolan, P. 1,433

LOUTH (South), 5,174
(Bye-election, 19 March, 1896.)
Richard McGhee, A.-P. 1,626
Col. Jno. P. Nolan, P. 1,249
Philip Callan, Ind. 467

MAYO (East), 7,878
John Dillon, A.-P. .... unop

MAYO (North), 7,453
Daniel Crilly, A.-P. 2,037
B. Egan, P. 1,316

MAYO (South), 9,019
(Bye-election, 1899.)
Robert Ambrose, A.-P. ...... unop

MAYO (West), 9,917

MEATH (North), 5,463
James Gibney, A.-P. 2,324
John Sweetman, P. 2,292

MEATH (South), 5,886
John Howard Parnell, A.-P. 2,38c
†Jeremiah Jordan, A.-P. 2,337

MONAGHAN (North), 6,887
Daniel MacAleese, A.-P. 3,377
Capt.Hon.P.C.Westenra, C. 2,023

MONAGHAN (South), 6,622
James Daly, A.-P. 3,885
Major W. Tennison, C. ... 1,015

NEWRY, 1,734
Patrk. Geo. H. Carvill, A.-P. 987
Henry J. Thomson, C. 628

OSSORY D. (Queen's Co.), 5,200
Eugene Crean, A.-P. (Lab.) 2,986
Lt.-Col.Wm.H.Poë,C.B.,C. 630

QUEEN'S COUNTY: see Leix, and Ossory.

ROSCOMMON (North), 9,111
James J. O'Kelly, P. 9,311
†Thos. J. Condon, A.-P. ... 2,935

ROSCOMMON (South), 9,100
(Bye-election, 15 July, 1897.)
John Patrick Hayden, P. ... unop.

ST. PATRICK'S (Dub. City), 8,728
William Field, P. .... unop.

ST. STEPHEN'S GREEN (Dublin City), 7,452
(Bye-election 21 Jan., 1898.)
Jno H.M. Campbell, Q.C., C. 3,525
Count Plunkett, P. 3,387

SLIGO (North), 8,212
Bernard Collery, A.-P. 3,274
Henry Harrison, P. 1,281
Sir Malby Crofton, Bt., C. 771

SLIGO (South), 7,206
Thomas Curran, A.-P. 5,717
Lt.-Col. Jas. Campbell, C. 522

TIPPERARY (East), 6,152
Thomas Joseph Condon, A.-P.unop.

TIPPERARY (Mid), 6,525
James Francis Hogan, A.-P. unop.

TIPPERARY (North), 6,100
Patrick Jos. O'Brien, A.-P. unop.

TIPPERARY (South), 5,550
Francis Mandeville, A.-P. . 1,723
Count Moore, Ind. 1,222

TULLAMORE D. (King's Co.), 4,981
Joseph Fras. Fox, A.-P. ... unop.

TYRONE (East), 6,961
Patrick Chas. Doogan, A.-P. 3,413
Thos. Lorimer Corbett, C.. 3,261

TYRONE (Mid), 7,838
George Murnaghan, A.-P... 3,759
Edwd. C. Thompson, U....... 2,252

TYRONE (North), 5,597
Rt. Hon. Serjeant Charles
Hare Hemphill, Q.C., L...... 2,948
William Wilson, C. 2,857

TYRONE (South), 5,940
Thos. Wallace Russell, U.... 3,239
Thos. Shillington, L......... 3,096

WATERFORD (City), 3,907
John Edward Redmond, P. 1,730
Thomas G. Farrell, A.-P.... 1,229

WATERFORD (County) (E.), 4,681
Patrick Jos. Power, A.-P. .. unop.

WATERFORD (County) (West), 4,694
(Bye-election, 12 Sept., 1895.)
Nicholas K. Shee, A.-P. ... unop.

WESTMEATH (North), 5,094
James Tuite, A.-P. .... unop.

WESTMEATH (South), 5,060
Donal Sullivan, A.-P. ...... unop.

WEXFORD (North), 8,694
Thomas Joseph Healy, A.-P. 4,689
J. B. Falconer, U. 786

WEXFORD (South), 8,776
Peter ffrench, A.-P. .... unop.

WICKLOW (East), 4,528
Wm. Joseph Corbet, P. 1,295
Col. C. Geo. Tottenham, C. 1,208
Francis A. O'Keeffe, A.-P. 1,077

WICKLOW (West), 4,57
James O'Connor, A.-P... unop.

New Members are distinguished thus *; those representing new constituencies thus †.

Abraham, William (L) Rhondda
Abraham, W. (A-P) Cork Co., N.-E.
Aird, John (C) ... Paddington, S.
Allan, William (L) ... Gateshead
Allen, W. (L) Newcastle-under-L.
*Allhusen, Aug. H. (C) Salisbury
Allison, Robt. Andws. (L) Eskdale
Allsopp, Hn. Geo. H (C) Worcester
Ambrose, Robert (A-P) Mayo, W.
*Anson, Sir W. R., Bt. (C) Oxf. Un.
Anstruther, H.T. (U) St. Andrews
Arch, Joseph (L) Norfolk, N.W.
*Archdale, E.M. (C) Fermanagh, N
*Arnold, Alfred (C) ......Halifax
*Arrol, Sir Wm. (U) ... Ayrshire, S.
Asher, Alex., Q.C. (L) Elgin Dist.
*Ashton, Thos. Gair (L) ... Luton
Asquith, Rt.Hon. Herbert Henry Q.C., (L) Fife, E.
*Atkinson, Rt.Hn. J. (C) Derry, N.
Austin, Sir J., Bt. (C) Osgoldcross.
Austin, Michl. (A-P) Limerick, E.
Bagot, Capt. Joscine. F. (C) Kendal
Bailey, James (C) ...... Walworth
Baillie, J. E. B. (L) Inverness-shire
*Bainbridge, E. (L) ...Gainsboro'
Baird, JohnG.A. (C) Glasgw., Cent.
Baker, Sir John (L) ... Portsmouth
Balcarres, Lord (C) ...... Chorley
Baldwin, Alfred (C) ...... Bewdley
Balfour, Rt. Hon. Arthur James (C) Manchester, E.
Balfour, Rt.Hon. G. W. (C) Leeds, Cent.
Banbury, Fredk.Geo. (C) Peckham
*Banes, Mj. G.E. (C) West Ham, S
Bannerman, Rt. Hon. Sir Henry Campbell-, G.C.B. (L) Stirling Dist.
*Barlow, JohnEmmott (L) Frome
*Barnes, Fredc. G. (C) Faversham
Barry, Rt.Hn. Arth. HughSmith- (C) Huntingdon
Barry, Edwd. (A-P) CorkCounty, S.
Barry, Sir Fras T., Bt. (C) Windsor
Bartlett, Sir Ellis Ashmead- (C) Ecclesall, Sheffield
Bartley, Geo.C.T. (C) Islington, N.
Barton, D.P., Q.C., (C) Armagh, M.
*Bathurst, Hn. A. B. (C) Cirencsr.
Bayley, Thomas (L) Chesterfield
Beach, Rt. Hon. Sir Michael E. Hicks-, Bart. (C) ...Bristol, W.
Beach, Wm. W. B. (C) .. Andover
*Beaumont, W. C. B. (L) Hexham
Beckett, Mj.ErnestW. (C) Whitby
*Begg, F. F. (C) St. Rollox, Glasgow
*Benrose, Sir HenryH. (C) Derby
*Bennett, H.C.Leigh- (C) Chertsey
*Bentinck, Lord H.- (C) Nottingham, S.
†Beresford, Lord Chas. (C) York
Bethell, Commn. G.R. (C) Holdrns.
*Bhownaggree, Sir Mancherjee M., K.C.I.E. (C) Bethnal Gn. N.E.
Biddulph, Michael (U) ...... Ross
Bigwood, James (C) ... Brentford
Bill, Charles (C) .... Leek
†Billson, Alfred (L) ...... Halifax
Birrell, A., Q.C. (L) ... Fife, W.
Blake, Hon. Edwd. (A-P) Longford, S.

*Blundell, Col. H. B. H. (C) Ince
Bolitho, Thos.Bedford (U) St.Ives
Bolton, Thos. D. (L) Derbysh. N.E.
*Bond, Edwd. (C) Nottingham, E.
Bonsor, HenryC.O. (C) Wimbledon
Boscawen, A. S. T. Griffith- (C) Tunbridge
Boulnois, Ed. (C) Marylebone, E.
Bousfield, W. R. (C) Hackney, N.
Bowles, Maj. HenryF. (C) Enfield
Bowles, T.Gibson (C) King'sLynn
*Brassey, Albert (C) ... Banbury
*Brigg, John (L) .... Keighley
Broadhurst, Henry (L) ... Leicester
Brodrick, Rt. Hon. William St. John (C) Guildford
Brookfield, A. Montague (C) Rye
Brown, A.H. (U) Wellington, Salop
Brunner, Sir John T. (L) Northwich
Bryce, Rt.Hn.Jas. (L) Aberdeen, S.
Brymer, Wm.Ernest (C) Dorset, S.
Buchanan, T. R. (L) Aberdnsh., E.
Bullard, Sir Harry (C) Norwich
Burns, John (L) ...... Battersea
Burt, Thomas (L) ...... Morpeth
Butcher, JohnG., Q.C. (C) YorkCity
Buxton, Sydney Chas. (L) Poplar
Caldwell, James (L) Lanark, Mid.
†Cameron, SirC.Bt. (L) Bridgeton, Glasgow
*Cameron, R. (L) Houghton-le-Sp.
Campbell, Rt. Hon. James Alex. (C) Glasgow & Aberdeen Univ.
*Campbell, Jas. H. M. (C) St Stephen's Green
Carew, J.L. (P) College Gn., Dub.
*Carlile, Wm. W. (C) Buckingham
*Carmichael, Sir T. (L) Edinbrghs.
Carson, Rt.Hn. E., Q.c. (C) Dub. U.
Carvill, Patrk. G.H. (A-P) Newry
Causton, Rd. K. (L) Southwark, W.
*Cavendish, Rd. F. (U) N. Lonsdale
Cavendish, V. C. W. (U) Derby, W.
*Cawley, Fredk. (L) ...... Prestwich
Cayzer, Sir C. W. (C) Barrow-in-Furness
*Cecil, Evelyn (C) ...... Hertford
*Cecil, Lord Hugh (C) Greenwich
*Chaloner, Lt.-Cl. R. (C) Westbury
Chamberlain, Rt. Hon. Joseph (U) Birmingham, W.
Chamberlain, A. (U) Worcester, E.
Channing, F. A. (L) Northants, E.
Chaplin, Rt. Hn. Hy. (C) Sleaford
Charrington, Spencer (C) Mile End
Chelsea, Visc. (U) BurySt. Edmunds
Clancy, John Joseph (P) Dublin, N.
*Clare, Octavius L. (C) ... Eccles
Clark, Dr. Gavin B. (L) Caithness
Clarke, Sir Ed. Q.C. (C) Plymouth
Clough, Walt.Owen (L) Portsmouth
Cochrane, Hon.T. (U) Ayrshire, N.
Coddington, SirW.Bt (C) Blckbrn.
*Coghill, D. H. (C) Stoke-upon-Trent
Cohen, Benj.Louis (C) Islington, E.
Collery, Bernard (A-P) Sligo, N.
Collings, Rt. Hon. Jesse (U) Bordesley, Birmingham
*Colomb, Sir J.C.R. (C) Yarmouth

Colston, Chas. Ed. (C) Thornbury
*Colville, John (L) Lanark, N.E.
Commins, A. (A-P) CorkCo. S.E.
*Compton, Lord A. F. (U) Biggleswade
Condon, T.J. (A-P) Tipperary, E.
*Cook, F. Lucas (C) Kennington
Cooke, C. W. R. (C) ... Hereford
*Corbet, Wm.Jos. (P) Wicklow, E.
Corbett, A.C. (U) Tradeston, Glsgw.
Cornwallis, F.S.W. (C) Maidstone
Courtney, Rt. Hn. L. H. (U) Bodmin
Coutts, W.Burdett- (C) Westminstr.
*Cox, Irwin E. B. (C) Harrow
*Cox, Thos. Skewes- (C) Kingston
Cranborne, Viscount (C) Rochester
Crean, E. (A-P) Ossory, Queen's Co
Crilly, Daniel (A-P) ... Mayo, N.
*Cripps, Chas. A., Q.C. (C) Stroud
Crombie, John W. (L) Kincardine
Cross, Alex. (C) Camlachie, Glsgw.
Cross, Herbt. Shepherd- (C) Bolton
*Cruddas, W.D. (C) Newstle-on-T.
Cubitt, Hon. Henry (C) Reigate
Curran, Thomas (A-P) ...Sligo, S.
*Curran, Thos.B. (A-P) Donegl, N.
Currie, Sir D., G.C.M.G. (U) Perth W.
Curzon, Viscount (C) ... Wycombe
*Dalbiac, Maj. P. H. (C) Camberwell, N.
*Dalkeith, Earl of (C) Roxburgh
Dalrymple, SirCharles (C) Ipswich
*Daly, James (A-P) Monaghan, S.
Dalziel, Jas.H. (L) Kirkcaldy Dist.
Davenport, W.B.- (C) Macclesfield
*Davies, Sir H. D. (C) Chatham
Davies, M. V. (L) Cardiganshire
*Denny, J.M. (C) KilmarnockDist.
*Dewar, Arthur (L) Edinburgh, S.
Digby, John Kenelm Digby Wingfield (C) Dorset, N.
Dilke, Rt. Hon. Sir Charles Wentworth (L) Forest of Dean
Dillon, John (A-P) ....Mayo, E.
Disraeli, Coningsby (C) Altrincham
*Donalan, A. J. (A-P) CorkCo., E.
*Donkin, RichardS. (C) Tynemouth
*Doogn, P. C. (A-P) Tyrone, E.
Dorington, SirJ.E. (C) Tewkesbury
*Doughty, George (U) Gt. Grimsby
Douglas, Rt. Hon. Aretas Akers- (C) St. Augustine's, Kent
*Douglas, C.M. (L) Lanark, N.W.
*Doxford, Wm. T. (C) Sunderland
*Drage, Geoffrey (C) ....Derby
*Drucker, C.A.A. (C) Northampton
*Duckworth, Ald. J. (L) Middleton
*Duncombe, Hn.H.V. (C) Egremont
Dunn, Sir William, Bt. (L) Paisley
Dyke, Rt. Hon. Sir William Hart- (C) Dartford
*Edwards, Owen M. (L) Merioneth
Egerton, H. A. deT. (C) Knutsford
Elliot, Hon. Arthur (U) Durham
Ellis, John Edward (L) Rushcliffe
*Emmott, Alfred (L) ......Oldham
*Engledow, C.J. (A-P) Kildare, N.
Esmonde, Sir T. (A-P) Kerry, W.
Evans, Sir F. H. (L) Southampton
Evans, S. T. (L) Glamorgan, Mid.
*Evershed, Sydney (L) ......Burton

Ewing, Chas. L. Orr-, (C) Ayr D.
Fardell, Sir George T. (C) Paddington, S.
Farquharson, R. (L) Aberdsh., W.
*Farrell, Jas. P. (A-P) Cavan, W.
*Farrell, Thos. J. (A-P) Kerry, S.
Fellowes, Hon. A. E. (C) Ramsey
Fenwick, Charles (L) Wansbeck
Ferguson, J. E. Johnson- (L) Loughborough
Ferguson, R. C. Munro- (L) Leith
Fergusson, Rt. Hon. Sir James Bt., G.C.S.I. (C) Manchester, N.E
Ffrench, Peter (A-P) Wexford, S.
Field, Vice-Ad. E. (C) Eastbourne
Field, Wm. (P) St. Patrick's, Dublin
Finch, George Henry (C) Rutland
*Finlay, Sir Robert Bannatyne, Q.C. (U) Inverness D.
Finucane, John (A-P) Limerick, E.
*Firbank, Jos. Thomas (C) Hull, E.
Fisher, William Hayes (C) Fulham
*Fison, Fredk. Wm. (C) Doncaster
Fitzgerald, Sir Robert Uniacke-Penrose-, Bt. (C) Cambridge
†Fitzmaurice, Ld. E. (L) Cricklade
FitzWygram, Sir F. W. (C) Fareham
*Flannery, Sir F. (U) Shipley
*Flavin, M J. (A-P) N. Kerry
Fletcher, Sir Henry, Bt. (C) Lewes
*Flower, Ernest (C) Bradford, W.
Flynn, J. Christr. (A-P) Cork, N.
Folkestone, Viscount (C) Wilton
Forster, Henry Wm. (C) Sevenoaks
Forster, H. O. Arnold- (U) Belfast, W.
Foster, Sir B. Walter (L) Ilkeston
Foster, H. Seymour (C) Lowestoft
*Foster, Col. Wm. H. (C) Lancaster
Fowler, Right Hon. Sir Henry Hartley (L) Wolverhampton, E.
Fox, Jos. Francis (A-P) Tullamore
*Fry, Lewis (U) Bristol, N.
*Galloway, W.J. (C) Mch'ster, S.W
Garfit, William (C) Boston
*Gedge, Sydney, (C) Walsall
George, D. Lloyd- (L) Carnrvon D.
Gibbons, J. Ll. (U) W'hampton, S.
Gibbs, Hon. A. G. H. (C) London
Gibbs, Hon. Vicary (C) St. Albans
Gibney, James (A-P) Meath, N.
*Giles, Chas. Tyrrell (C) Wisbech
Gilhooly, James (A-P) Cork, W.
Gilliat, John Saunders (C) Widnes
Gladstone, Rt. Hon. Herbert John (L) Leeds, W.
*Goddard, Daniel F. (L) Ipswich
Godson, Sir A.F. (C) Kidderminster
*Gold, Chas. (L) Saffron Walden
Goldsworthy, Major-General W. (C) Hammersmith
*Gordon, Hn.J.E. (C) Elgin & Nairn
Gorst, Rt.Hn.SirJ. (C) Camb. Univ.
Goschen, Rt. Hon. Geo. Joachim (C) St. George, Hanover Sq.
*Goschen, G.J.,jr., (C) E. Grinstead
*Goulding, Edwd.A.,(C) Devizes
Gourley, Sir Edw.T.(L) Sunderland
Graham, H. R. (C) St. Pancras, N.
*Gray, Ernest (C) West Ham, N.
*Green, WalfordD.(C) Wedn'sb'ry
Greene, H. D., Q.C. (C) Shrewsbury
*Greene, Walter R. (C) Chesterton
*Gretton,J.A.,Jun.(C) Derbysh.S.

*Greville, Capt. Hon. Ronald Henry Fulke (C) Bradford, E.
Grey, Sir E. Bt. (L) Berwick-on-T.
*Griffith, Ellis (L) Anglesey
*Gull, Sir W. C. (C) Barnstaple
Gully, Rt. Hon. William Court, Q.C. (Speaker) (L) Carlisle
Gunter, Col. Robt. (C) Barkston Ash
Gurdon, Sir Wm.B. (L) Norfolk, N.
*Guthrie, W. M. (C) Bow and Bromley
Haldane, R. B. (L) Haddingtons.
Hall, Rt. Hn Sir C,Q.C. (C) Holborn
Halsey,Thomas Frdk. (C) Watford
Hamilton, Rt. Hn. Lord Geo. (C) Ealing
Hammond, John (A-P) Carlow
Hamond, Sir C.F. (C) N'c'stle-on-T.
Banbury, Rt. Hn. R. W. (C) Preston
Hanson, Sir Regd., Bt. (C) London
*Harcourt, Rt. Hon. Sir William Vern., Q.C. (L) Monmouthsh., W.
Hardy, Lawrence (C) Ashford
Hare, Thos. L. (C) Norfolk, S. W.
Harrington, Timothy (P) Dublin H.
Hartland, Sir F. Dixon- (C) Uxbridge
*Harwood, George, (L) Bolton
*Haslett, Sir James (C) Belfast, N.
*Hatch, Ernest F. G. (C) Gorton
*Hayden, Jnn.P., (P) Roscommon, S
Hayne, Rt. Hon. Charles Seale- (L) Ashburton
Hazell, Walter (L) Leicester
Healy, Maurice (A-P) Cork City
Healy, Thos. Jos., (A-P) Wexford, N.
Healy,Timothy M. (A-P) Louth, N.
Heath,Jas. (C) Staffordshire, N.
Heaton, J. Henniker- (C) Canterb'y
Hedderwick, T. C. H. (L) Wick D.
*Helder, Augustus (C) Whitehaven
*Hemphill, Rt. Hon. Charles Hare (L) Tyrone, N.
Henderson, Alexr. (U) Staff. W.
Hickman, Sir Alfred (C) Wolverhampton, W.
*Higgins, F. Platt- (C) Salford, N.
Hill, Rt. Hon. Alex.Staveley, Q.C. (C) Kingswinford
Hill, Capt. Arthur (C) Down, W.
Hill, Sir Edwd.Stock (C) Bristol, S.
Hoare, Edward B. (C) Hampstead
Hoare, Sir Samuel, Bt. (C) Norwich
Hobhouse, Henry (L) Somerset, E.
*Hodge, Rt. T. Hermon- (C) Henley
Hogan, Jas. Fras. (A-P) Tipperary, Mid.
Holden, Sir Angus, Bt. (L) Buckrose
*Holland, W. H. (L) Rotherham
Hood, Sir Alexander Fuller-Acland- (C) Wellington, Som.
Hornby, Sir Wm. Henry, Bt (C) Blackburn
*Horniman, F. J. (L) Penryn & Falm.
Houldsworth, Sir William Henry, Bart. (C) Manchester, N.W.
Houston, J. Blakiston- (C) Down, N.
Houston, R. P. (C) Toxteth, W.
Howard, Joseph (C) Tottenham
*Howell, Wm. T. (C) Denbigh Dist.
Howorth, Sir H. H. (C) Salford, S.
Hozier, Jas. H. J.C. (C) Lanark, S.

*Hubbard, Hon. E. (C) Brixton
Hudson, G. Bickersteth (C) Hitchin
Hughes, Col. Edwin (C) Woolwich
Hutchinson, Capt. G. (C) Aston Mr.
Hutton, Alfred Eddison (L) Morley
*Hutton, John (C) Richmond, Yks.
Jackson, Rt.Hn.W.L.(C) Leeds, N.
Jacoby, JamesA. (L) Derbyshire, M.
*Jameson, Maj. J. E., (A-P) Clare, W.
Jebb, Richard C. (C) Cambridge University
Jeffreys, Arthur F. (C) Basingstoke
*Jenkins, Sir John Jones (U) Carmarthen Dist.
*Jessel, Capt. H. M. (U) St. Pancras, S.
Jodrell,Col. Edward T. Davenant Cotton-, R.A. (C) Wirrall
Johnston, William (C) Belfast, S.
Johnstone, John H. (C) Horsham
Joicey, Sir Jas. (L) Chester-le-Street
*Jones, D. Brynmor (L) Swansea D.
*Jones, William (L) Arfon D.
Jones, L. Atherley- (C) Durham, N.W.
*Jones, E. Pryce- (C) M'tgom'ryD.
*Jordan, J. (A-P) Fermanagh, S.
Karr, Hy. Seton- (C) St. Helens
Kearley, Hudson E. (L) Devonport
*Kemp, George (U) Heywood
Kennaway, Rt. Hon. Sir John Henry, Bart. (C) Honiton
*Kenyon, James (C) Bury, Lanc.
*Keswick, Wm. (C) Epsom
*Kilbride, Denis (A-P) Galway, N.
Kimber, Henry (C) Wandsworth
King, Sir H. S. (C) Hull, Central
Kinloch, Sir J.G.S., Bt.(L) Perth, E.
Kitson, Sir Jas., Bt. (L) Colne Valley
Knowles, Lees (C) Salford, W.
Labouchere, H. L. (L) Northampton
*Lafone, Alfred (C) Bermondsey
Lambert, George (L) South Molton
Langley, B. (L) Attercliffe, Sheff'd.
*Laurie, Gen.J.W. (C) Pembroke D.
Lawrence, Sir E. Durning- (C) Truro
Lawrence, William Frederick Abercromby, Liverpool
Lawson, J. G. (C) Thirsk & Malton
Lawson, Sir W. (L) Cockermouth
Lea, Sir Thomas, Bt. (U) Derry, N.
*Lecky, Rt. Hon. William Edw. Hartpole (C) Dublin University
Lees, Sir Elliott, Bt. (C) Birkenhead
Leese, Sir J. F., Q.C. (L) Accrington
Leighton, Stanley (C) Oswestry
Leng, Sir John (L) Dundee
Leuty, Thos. R. (L) Leeds, E.
Lewis, John Herbt. (L) Flint Dist.
*Llewellyn, E. H. (C) Somerset, N.
*Llewelyn, Sir J.T.D. (C) Swansea Town
Lockwood, Lt.-Col. M. (C) Epping
Loder, Gerald W. E. (C) Brighton
Logan, John Wm. (L) Harborough
Long, Lt.-Col. C. W.(C) Evesham
Long, Rt. Hn. Walter Hume (C) W. Derby, Liverpool
Lopes, Hy. YardeB.(C) Grantham
*Lorne, Marq. of (U) Manchester, N.
Lough, Thomas (L) Islington, W.
Lowe, Francis Wm. (C) Edgbaston
*Lowles, John (C) Haggerston

Lowther, Rt.Hn.J.(C) I.of Thanet
Lowther, Rt. Hon. J. Wm. (C) Penrith
*Loyd,Archie K.,q.c.(C) Abingdon
Lubbock, Rt. Hon. Sir John (C) London University
Luttrell, Hugh C. F.(L) Tavistock
Lyell, Sir L , Bt.. (L) Orkney & S.
Lyttelton.Hn.A.,(U) Warwick & L.
*MacAleese, D. (A-P) Monaghan, N
*M'Calmont.Harry(C) Newmarket
M'Calmont, Col. J. (C) Antrim, E
M'Cartan, Michael (A-P) Down,S.
*M'Arthur, C. (C) Exchge., L'pool
M'Arthur, Wm. A. (L) St. Austel
M'Carthy, Justin (A-P) Longford, N
Macartney, William Grey Ellison- (C) Antrim, S.
*McCrae.George (L) Edinburgh,E.
M'Dermott,Patk.(A-P) Kilk'ny,N
Macdona, John C. (C) Rotherhith
MacDonnell,Dr.Mrk A.(A-P) Leix
M'Ewan,Wm.(C) Edinburgh, Cent.
*M'Ghee, Richard (A-P) Louth, S.
M'Hugh, Edwd.(A-P) Armagh, S.
M'Hugh, Patk. A.(A-P) Leitrim, N
*MacIver, D. (C)Kirksale, L'pool
M'Iver, SirL,.Bt..(U) Edinb'gh,W
*M'Kenna,Regd. (L) Monmouth, N
*M'Killop, Jas. (C) Stirlingshire
M'Laren, Chas. B. B.(L) Bosworth
*Maclean,J.Mackenzie(C) Cardiff
M'Leod, John (L) Sutherland
Maclure, Sir J. W., Bt. (C) Stretford
MacNeill, John George Swift, q.c. Donegal, S
*Maddison, Fred (L) . Brightside
Maden, John Henry(L) Rossendale
*Mainwaring, Hon.William F. B Massey-(C) .... Clerkenwell
*Malcolm, Ian (C) ...Stowmarket
Mandeville, F. (A-P) Tipperary,S
*Manners, Lord Edwd.(C) Melton
Maple,Sir J. B., Bt. (C) . Dulwich
Mappin, Sir F.T. (L) Hallamshire
*Marks, H. H. (C) St. George's, E.
Martin,R. Biddulph (L) Droitwich
Maxwell, Hon. Sir Herbert Eustace, Bart. (C) Wigtownsh.
*Maxwell, Sir John M. Stirling- Bart. (C) ....College, Glasgow
*Mellor, Col. John James (C) Radcliffe-cum-Farnworth
Mellor,Rt. Hon. J.W.(L) Sowerby
*Melville, B. V. (C) ...Stockport
*M ndl, Sigism. F. (L) Plymou h
*Middlemore, J. T. (C) B'ham.N.
Milbank, Sir P. C. J., Bt. (C) Radnor
Mildmay, Francis B. (U) Totnes
Milner, Sir Fred. G.(C) Bassetlaw
*Milton, Viscount (U) Wakefield
*Milward, Col. Victor (C) Stratford-on-Avon
Minch, Matt. J. (A-P) Kildare, S.
Molloy, Bernard Chas. (A-P) Bir
*Monckton. E. P.(C) Northants, N.
*Monk, Chas. Jas. (U) Gloucester
Montagu, Hon. J.W.E. Douglas-Scott- (C) ....New Fores!
Montagu,SirS.Bt.(L) Whitechapel
*Moon, E. R. P. (C) St.Pancras, N.
*Moore, Count (A-P) Londonderry
*Moore, Wm. (U)......Antrim, N.

More, Robert Jasper (U) Ludlow
Morgan,Hn.F.C.(C) Monmouth,S.
Morgan, J. Ll. (L) Carmarthen, W.
Morgan, W. Pritchard (L) Merthyr
*Morley, Chas. (L) Brecknockshire
+Morley, Rt. Hon. John (L) Montrose District
*Morrell, Geo. H. (C) Woodstock
Morris, Saml. (A-P) Kilkenny, S.
*Morrison, Walter (U) Skipton
Morton, Arthur H.A.(C) Deptford
Morton, Edwd. J.C.(L) Devonport
*Moss, Samuel (L) Denbighshire,E.
Moulton, J.F., q.c. (L) Launceston
Mount, Wm. George (C) Newbury
Muntz, P Albert (C) Tamworth
*Murnaghan, Geo. (L) Tyrone, M.
Murray, Rt. Hon. Andrew Graham, q.c., (C) ....But
*Murray, Chas. Jas. (C) Coventry
Murray, Col. C. Wyndham (C) Bath
Myers,Wm. Henry(C) Winchester
*Newark, Viscount (C)...Newark
Newdigate, Fras. A (C) Nuneaton
*Nicholson, W. G. (C) Petersfield
*Nicol, Donald N. (C) Argyllshire
Norton,Cecil W.(L) W. Newington
Nussey, T. Willans (L) Pontefract
+O'Brien, J. F. X. (A-P) Cork City
*O'Brien, Patrk. (P) Kilkenny City
O'Brien, P. J. (A-P) Tipperary, N.
O'Connor,Arth. (A-P) Donegal,E.
O'Connor, Jas. (A-P) Wicklow, W.
O'Connor, Thomas Power (A-P), Scotland, Liverpool
O'Keeffe,F.A.(A-P) Limerick City
*O'Kelly, J.J.(P) Roscommon, N.
Oldroyd, Mark (L) ..... Dewsbury
*O'Malley,Wm.(A-P) Connemara
O'Neill,Hon.R.T.(C) Antrim, Mid
Owen, Arthur Charles Humphreys-(L) Montgomeryshire
Palmer,Sir ChasM..Bt..(L) Jarrow
Palmer, Geo. Wm. (L) Reading
*Parkes, E. (U) Birmingham, C.
*Parnell, Jno. H. (P) ..Meath, S.
Paulton, Jas. M. (L) Bp. Auckland
Pearson, Sir W. D. (L) Colchester
+Pease,Alfd. E.(L) Cleveland, Yks.
*Pease, H. Pike (U) ..Darlington
Pease, Joseph Albert (L) Tyneside
Pease, Sir J.W.(L) Barnard Castle
*Pender,SirJ.Bt.(C) Northants, N.
Penn, John (C) ....Lewisham
*Pennant, Hon. Edward Sholto Douglas- (C) ..... Northants, S.
*Percy. Earl (C) Kensington, S.
Perks, Robert W. (L) Louth, Linc.
Philipps, J.W. (L) Pembrokeshire
*Philpotts, Capt. A. S., R.N.(C) Torquay
Pickard, Benjamin (L) Normanton
Pickersgill, Edward Hare (L) Bethnal Green, S.W.
Pierpoint, Robert (C) Warrington
+Pilkington,Sir G.A.(L) Southport
*Pilkington, Col. R. (C) Newton
Pinkerton, J. (A-P) Galway City
*Pirie, D. V. (L) Aberdeen, N.
Plunkett,Rt.Hon.H.(C) Dublin,S.
*Pollock, Harry F. (U) ..Spalding
Powell, Sir Francis S. (C) Wigan
Power, Pat.J.(A-P) Waterford,E.
Poynder,SirJ.D.(C) Chippenham

*Pretyman, Capt. Ernest G. (C) Woodbridge
Price Robert John (L) Norfolk, E.
Priestley, Briggs (L) ......Pudsey
*Priestley, Sir William (L) Edinburgh & St. Andrews Unw.
Provand,A.D.(L) Blkfriars., Glas.
Purvis, Robt. (U) ... Peterborough
*Pym, Chas. Guy (C) ....Bedford
Quilter, Sir Cuthbert, Bt. (C) Sudbury
Qu'n, Major Windham Henry Wyndham-(C) Glamorgan, S.
Randell, D. (L) Gower, Glamorgn
Rankin, Sir J., Bt. (C) Leominster
Rasch,Maj.Fred.C.(C) Essex,S.E.
*Reckitt, Harold James (L) Brigg
Redmond, J.E.(P) Waterford City
Redmond,Wm.H.K.(P) Clare, E.
Reid, Sir R.T.,q.c.(L) Dumfries D.
Renshaw,Chas.B.(C) Renfrew, W.
Rentoul, Jas. A., q.c. (C) Down, E.
*Richards, Hy.C.(C) Finsbury, E.
*Richardson, Jos. (L) Durham, S.E.
*Richardson, Sir T.(U) Hartlepool
*Rickett, J. C. (L) ..Scarborough
Ridley, Rt. Hon. Sir Matthew White, Bt. (C) .... Blackpool
Ritchie,Rt. Hon.C.T.(C) Croydon
Roberts, J. Bryn (L) Eifion, Carn.
Roberts, Jno. H. (L) Denbigh, W.
Robertson, Edmd., q.c.(L) Dundee
*Robertson, T. H. (C) Hackney, S.
Robinson, R. Brooke(C) ..Dudley
Robson, W. S., q.c. (L) S. Shields
*Roche,Hon.J.B (A-P) Kerry, E.
Roche, John (A-P) .Galway, E.
Rollit, Sir Albt. K.(C.) Islington, S.
*Rothschild, Hon. L. W. (U) Aylesbury
Round, James (C) ...... Harwich
*Royds, Col. C. M. (C) ..Rochdale
*Runciman, W. ( ) ......Oldham
*Russell, Maj.-Gen. F. S. (C) Cheltenham
Russell, Thomas W.(U) Tyrone, S.
*Rutherford, John (C) ..Darwen
*Ryder, J. H. D. (C) ..Gravesend
*Samuel, Harry S. (C) Limehouse
*Samuel, J. (L) ...Stockton-on-T.
Sandys, Lt.-Col. T. M. (C) Bootle
Sassoon, Sir E. A.(C) .... Hythe
Saunderson, Col.Rt.Hon.Edward James (C) .... Armagh, N.
Savory,SirJoseph,Bt.(C) Appleby
Schwann, C.E. (L) Manchester, N.
Scoble, Sir A. R (C) Hackney, C.
*Scott, Chas. P. (L) ....Leigh
*Scott, Sir Samuel E., Bart. (C) Marylebone, W.
*Seely, Charles H. (U) .. Lincoln
*Shadwell, Wm. L. (C) Hastings
*Sharpe,W.E.T.(C) Kensington,N
Shaw, Theo. F. C. E. (L) Stafford
Shaw, Thos.,q.c.(L.) Hawick Dist.
Shee, N.K.(A-P) Co. Waterf'd, W.
Sheehy, David (A-P) Galway, S.
Shuttleworth, Rt. Hon. Sir Ughtred Jas. Kay-,Bart.(L) Clitheroe
Sidebotham,Jos.Watson(C) Hyde
Sidebottom, T. H. (C) Stalybridge
Sidebottom, Lt.-Col. William (C) High Peak
*Simeon, Sir J. S.(U) Southampton

ALPHABETICAL LIST OF THE HOUSE OF COMMONS—*continued.*

*Sinclair, Capt. J. (L) Forfarshire
*Sinclair, Louis (C) ...Romford.
Slaney, Col. William Kenyon- (C) Newport, Salop
Smith, Abel Hnry. (C) Christchurch
Smith, Jas. Parker (U) ...Partick
Smith, Samuel (L) ...Flintshire
Smith, Hon. Wm. F.D. (C) Strand
Soames, A. W. (L) ...Norfolk, S.
*Souttar, A. R. (L) Dumfriesshire
Spencer, Jas.E.(C) West Bromwich
Spicer, Albert (L) Monmouth Dist.
Stanhope, Hon. Phil. J. (L) Burnley
Stanley, Lord (C) ..Westhoughton
*Stanley, Hon. A. (U) ...Ormskirk
Stanley, Edw. Jas. (C) Bridgwater
*Stanley, Sir H.M. (U) Lambeth, N.
*Steadman, Wm. C. (L) Stepney
Stephens, Henry C. (C) ...Hornsey
Stevenson. Fras. Seymour (L) Eye
Stewart, Sir M J. (C) Kirkcudbrigh
Stewart, M. H. Shaw- (C) Renfrew, E.
Stock, Jas. H. (C) Walton, L'pool.
*Stone, Sir J.B. (C) Birmingham, E.
Strachey, Edward (L) Somerset, S.
Strauss, Arthur (U) ...Camborne
*Strutt, Hon. Chas. H. (C) Maldon
Stuart, James (L) ......Hoxton
Sturt, Hon. Hn. N. (C) Dorset, E.
Sullivan, D. (A-P) Westmeath, N.
Sullivan, T.D. (A-P) Donegal, W.
Sutherland, Sir Thos. (U) Greenock
Talbot, Lord E. B. (C) Chichester
Talbot, Rt. Hn. J.G. (C) Oxford Un.
Tanner, Dr. Charles K. D. (A-P) Cork, Mid
Tennant, Harold J. (L) Berwicksh.
Thomas, A, q.c.(L) Carmarthen, E.

Thomas, Alfred (L) Glamorgan, E.
Thomas, Dvd. A. (L) Merthyr Tydfil
Thompson, Sir Henry Meysey- (U) Handsworth
Thorburn, Wltr. (U) Peebles & S.
Thornton, P. Melville (C) Clapham
Todd, Capt. W. H. Wilson- (C) Howdenshire
Tollemache, Hy. J. (C) Eddisbury
Tomlinson, W. E. M. (C) Preston
*Trevelyan, Chas. P. (L) Elland
Tritton, Chas. Ernest (C) Norwood
Tuite, Jas. (A-P) Westmeath, N.
Tully, Jasper (A-P) ...Leitrim, S.
*Ure, Alx. q.c. (L) Linlithgowshire
Usborne, Thomas (C) Chelmsford
Valentia, Visct. (C) ...Oxford City
Verney, Hon. Rich d.G. (C) Rugby
*Vincent, Sir Edgar, K.C.M.G. (C) Exeter
Vincent, Col. Sir H. (C) Sheffield
*Wallace, Robt., q.c. (L) Perth City
Walrond, Rt. Hon Sir W. H. B. (C) Tiverton
*Walton, John L., q.c. (L) Leeds, S.
*Walton, Joseph (L) ...Barnsley
Wanklyn, Jas. L. (U) Bradford, E.
Ward, Hon. R. A. (C) ...Crewe
Warde, Major C. E. (C) Medway
Warner, T.C.Theydon (L) Lichfield
*Warr, Aug. F. (C) ...E. Toxteth
Webster, Sir R. E., Bt. (C) I. Wight
Wedderburn, Sir W., Bt. (C) Banffs
Weir, J. G. (L) Ross & Cromarty
*Welby, Lt.-Col. A. C. Earle- (C) Taunton
Wentworth, Bruce Canning Vernon (C) ...Brighton
Wharton, Rt. Hon. J. Ll. (C) Ripon

Whiteley, George (L) ...Stockport
*Whiteley, Herbt. (C) Ashton-under-Lyne
Whitmore, Charles A. (C) Chelsea
Whittaker, Thos. P. (L) Spen Valley
Williams, J. Carvell (L) Mansfield
Williams, J.P. (U) Birmingham, S.
Williams, Col. Robt. (C) Dorset, W.
Willoughby de Eresby, Lord (C) Horncastle
Willox, Sir J.A. (C) Everton, L'pool
Wills, Sir Wm. H. (L) Bristol, E.
Wilson, Charles H. (L) Hull, W.
*Wilson, Fredk. W. (L) Norfolk, M.
Wilson, Hen. Joseph (L) Holmfirth
Wilson, John (L) Durham, Mid
*Wilson, John (U) Falkirk Dist.
Wilson, John (L) ......Govan
*Wilson, J.Wm. (U) Worcester, N.
Wilson, J.W. Havelock (L) Middlesbro
Wodehouse, Rt Hn. E. R. (U) Bath
Wolff, Gustav W. (C) Belfast, E.
Woodall, William (L) ...Hanley
*Woodhouse, Sir J.T. (C) Hddrsfld
Woods, Samuel (L) Walthamstow
Wortley, Rt. Hon. Charles Beilby Stuart-, q.c. (C) Hallam, Sheffield
*Wrightson, T. (C) St. Pancras, E.
*Wylie, Alx.J. (C) Dumbartonshire
Wyndham, George (C) ...Dover
*Wyvill, Marmaduke D'A. (C) Otley
Yerburgh, Robert A. (C) Chester
Young, Com. Oliver, R.N. (C) Wokingham
Young, Samuel (A-P) Cavan, E.
*Younger, Wm. (C) ...Stamford
*Yoxall, J.H. (L) Nottingham, W.

THE BALANCE OF PARTIES SINCE THE REFORM BILL OF 1832.

Year.	Ministry.	Opposition.	Majority.
1833	480 *Whigs.*	173 *Cons.*	307 *Whigs*
1835	380 "	273 "	107 "
1837	352 "	301 "	51 "
1841	367 *Cons.*	285 *Whigs.*	81 *Cons.*
1847	327 *Whigs.*	325 *Cons.*	1 *Whig.*
1852	333 *Lib.*	320 "	13 *Lib.*
1857	366 "	287 "	79 "
1859	348 "	305 "	43 "
1865	361 "	294 "	67 "
1868	393 "	265 "	128 "
1874	349 *Cons.*	303 {247 *Lib.* / 56 *Nat.*}	46 *Cons.*
1880	357 *Lib.*	295 {233 *Cons.* / 62 *Nat.*}	186 *Lib.*
1885	413 {331 *Lib.* / 82 *Nat.*}	247 *Cons.*	84 "
1886	395 {314 *Cons.* / 81 *L.U.*}	272 {188 *Lib.* / 84 *Nat.*}	123 *Cons.*
1892	354 {273 *Lib.* / 72 *A.-P.* / 9 *P.*}	315 {268 *Cons.* / 47 *L.U.*}	39 *Lib.*
1895	411 {340 *Cons.* / 71 *U.*}	259 {177 *Lib.* / 70 *A.-P.* / 12 *P.*}	152 *Un.*

SPEAKERS OF THE COMMONS SINCE 1660.

PARLIAMENT OF ENGLAND.

1660. Sir H. Grimston.
1661. Sir E. Turner.
1673. Sir J. Charlton.
1673. *Edwd. Seymour.
1678. Sir Robt. Sawyer.
1679. Serjeant William Gregory.
1680. W. Williams.
1685. +Sir John Trevor.
1688. H. Powle.
1694. Paul Foley.
1698. Sir T. Lyttleton.
1700. Robert Harley.
1702. John Smith.

PARLIAMENT OF GREAT BRITAIN.

1708. SirRichd.Onslow.
1710. Wm. Bromley.
1713. Sir Th. Hanmer.
1715. Spencer Compton.
1727. Arthur Onslow.
1761. Sir John Cust.
1770. Sir F. Norton.
1780. C. W. Cornwall.
1789. Hn.W. Grenville.
1789. ‡Hy. Addington.

PARLIAMENT OF UNITED KINGDOM.

1801. Sir John Mitford (*created Lord Redesdale*).
1802. Charles Abbot (*created Lord Colchester*).
1817. Charles M. Sutton (*cr. Visct. Canterbury*).
1835. James Abercromby (*cr. Lord Dunfermline*).
1839. Chas. Shaw-Lefevre (*cr. Visct. Eversley*).
1857. J. Evelyn Denison (*cr. Visct. Ossington*).
1872. Sir H. W. B. Brand (*cr. Visct. Hampden*).
1884. Arthur Wellesley Peel (*created Visct. Peel*).
1895. William Court Gully.

* Re-elected 1678, but King Charles II. refused to sanction election. † Re-elected 1689, but expelled for accepting a bribe, 1694. ‡ Created Viscount Sidmouth.

OFFICERS OF THE HOUSE OF LORDS.—£38,485.

Speaker—The Lord Chancellor (Earl of Halsbury), £4,000, who also receives £6,000 as a Judge.

Deputy Speakers, the Earl of Morley, the Earl of Cork and Orrery, K.P., the Earl De Montalt.

Chairman of Committees—The Earl of Morley, £2,500.

Private Secretary, Edmund Hall Alderson, £500.

Clerk of Parliamts., Hy. J. L. Graham, C.B. £2,000
Deputy do. (Clerk Assist.), Hon. Edward Pierson Thesiger, C.B. £1,500
Reading Clerk (vacant) £900
Counsel to Chairman of Committees, Albert Gray £1,500
Chief Clerk and Clerk of Public Bills, H. C. Malkin, £1,200
Principal Clerk and Taxing Officer, Private Bill Office, R. W. Monro £1,200
Do. attending the Table, Alfred Harrison £900
Principal Clerk and Taxing Officer, Judicial Department, E. F. Taylor £1,150
Clerk of the Journals, W. Austen-Leigh £900
Prin. Clerk, Private Committees, J. F. Symons-Jeune, £925

Other Clerks, F. Skene; W. H. H. Gordon; C. L. Anstruther; Hon. A. McDonnell; A. H. Robinson; H. P. St. John; V. M. Biddulph; Hon. E. A. Stonor; H. J. F. Badeley; C. Headlam; J. B. Hotham £100 to £600
Accountant and Receiver of Fees, G. Fulkes £600
Librarian, S. Arthur Strong £1,000
Assist. Librarian, A. H. M. Butler £340
Examiners to Standing Orders, Charles Walter Campion, £800; (vacant), £300.
Gentleman Usher of the Black Rod, General Sir Michael A. Shrapnel Biddulph, G.C.B. £1,000
Yeoman Usher and Secretary to Lord Great Chamberlain, Capt. T. D. Butler £500
Serjeant-at-Arms, Maj.-Gen. Sir Arthur E. A. Ellis, K.C.V.O. £1,000

OFFICERS OF THE HOUSE OF COMMONS.—£55,576.

Speaker—The Right Hon. William Court Gully, Q.C., M.P. for the City of Carlisle, £5,000.

Deputy Speaker and Chairman of Committees—Rt. Hon. Jas. Wm. Lowther, M.P., £2,500.

Private Secretary, Edward Gully, £500.

Temporary Chairmen—Arthur O'Connor, Q.C.; John Edward Ellis; Rt. Hon. Charles B. Stuart-Wortley, Q.C.; John Grant Lawson; and Rt. Hon. Edmond R. Wodehouse.

Clerk of the House of Commons, Sir Reginald F. D. Palgrave, K.C.B., Palace of Westminster £2,000
Clerk Assistant, Archibald J. S. Milman, C.B. £1,500
Second do., Francis B. G. Jenkinson, C.B. £1,000
Principal Clerk Public Bill Office, and Clerk of the Fees, Wm. Aug. Ferguson-Davie, C.B. £1,000
Principal Clerk of Committees, Reginald Dickinson £1,000
Clerk of the Journals, W. H. Ley £1,250
Principal Clerk Private Bill Office, John Henry William Somerset £1,000
Senior Clerks, Wm. Gibbons; F. G. St. Geo. Tupper; H. C. Tower; C. V. Frere; L. T. Le Marchant; G.C. Giffard £650 to £800
Assistant Clerks, A. W. Nicholson; Sir E. H. Doyle, Bart.; S. L. Simeon; A. I. Dasent; E. C. Howe-Browne; H. West; H. A. Ferguson-Davie; A. H. Ellis; P. W. Bull; F. R. Williams-Wynn; William E. Grey; F. C. Holland each £300 to £500
Junior Clerks, J. W. G. Bond; T. L. Webster; H. C. Dawkins; A. F. B. Williams; R. P. Colomb;

B. H. Fell; R. E. Childers; T. Scott Porter; F. C. Bramwell; R. Austen-Leigh; W. T. Legge; C. R. Turner each £100 to £250
Clerk in Charge of Accounts, C. L. Lockton £400
Office Clerk in Committee Office, T. F. Mitchell.
Vote Office—Chief Clerk, H.A. Milner Killick £650
Assistant Clerk, P. E. Smith, £350; H. O. Maine £100
Journal Office, Clerk, A. A. Taylor £210
Serjeant-at-Arms, Henry David Erskine £1,200
Deputy Serjeant, Francis R. Gosset £800
Assistant do., Col. Hon. Edwd. Henry Legge £650
Chaplain, Rev. Canon Basil Wilberforce, D.D. £400
Counsel to Speaker, Hon. Edw. C. Leigh, Q.C. £1,800
Referee of Private Bills, A. Bonham-Carter £1,000
Examiner for Private Bills and Taxing Officer, Charles Walter Campion £400
Librarian, R. C. Walpole £1,000
Assistant do., E. G. Harvey £500
Library Clerks, J. C. Crimp, Wm. Stewart.
Shorthand Writer, W. H. Gurney-Salter.

PARLIAMENTS OF QUEEN VICTORIA.

	Assembled.		Dissolved.		Duration.				Assembled.		Dissolved.		Duration.		
					Yrs.	M.	D.						Yrs.	M.	D.
1	Nov. 15,	1837	June 23,	1841	3	7	8	8	Dec. 10,	1868	Jan. 26,	1874	5	1	16
2	Aug. 19,	1841	July 23,	1847	5	11	4	9	March 5,	1874	March 23,	1880	6	0	20
3	Nov. 18,	1847	July 1,	1852	4	7	13	10	April 29,	1880	Nov. 18,	1885	5	6	20
4	Nov. 4,	1852	March 1,	1857	4	4	17	11	Jan. 12,	1886	June 26,	1886	0	5	14
5	April 1,	1857	April 23,	1859	1	11	23	12	Aug. 5,	1886	June 28,	1892	5	10	24
6	May 31,	1859	July 6,	1865	6	1	6	13	Aug. 4,	1892	July 8,	1895	2	11	5
7	Feb. 1,	1866	Nov. 11,	1868	2	9	10	14	Aug. 12,	1895	*Elected* July and Aug. 1895.				

THE PRESENT MINISTRY.		LD. SALISBURY'S 2ND MIN., 1886-92.
Marquess of Salisbury	*Prime Minister*	Marquess of Salisbury.
Earl of Halsbury	*Lord High Chancellor*	Lord (*now Earl of*) Halsbury.
Duke of Devonshire	*Lord President of Council*	Viscount Cranbrook.
Viscount Cross	*Lord Privy Seal*	Earl Cadogan.
Sir Michael E. Hicks-Beach, Bt.	*Chancellor of the Exchequer*	*Lord Randolph Churchill, dec.* George Joachim Goschen.
Sir Matthew White Ridley, Bt.	*Sec. of State Home Dept.*	Henry Matthews, Q.C.
Marquess of Salisbury	*Sec. of State Foreign Dept.*	*Earl of Iddesleigh, dec.* Marquess of Salisbury.
Joseph Chamberlain	*Sec. of State Colonial Dept.*	*Hon. Edward Stanhope, dec.* Lord Knutsford.
Marquess of Lansdowne	*Sec. of State War Dept.*	*William Henry Smith, dec.* Hon. Edward Stanhope, dec.
Lord George Francis Hamilton	*Sec. of State Indian Dept.*	Viscount Cross.
Lord Balfour of Burleigh	*Secretary for Scotland*	(Not in the Cabinet.)
George Joachim Goschen	*First Lord of the Admiralty*	Lord George Francis Hamilton.
Arthur James Balfour	*First Lord of the Treasury*	*Marquess of Salisbury.* *William Henry Smith, dec.* Arthur James Balfour.
Earl Cadogan	*Lord Lieutenant of Ireland*	(Not in the Cabinet)
Lord Ashbourne	*Lord Chancellor of Ireland*	Lord Ashbourne.
Charles Thomson Ritchie	*President Board of Trade*	*Lord Stanley of Preston.* Sir Michael E. Hicks-Beach, Bt.
Lord James of Hereford	*Chanclr. Duchy of Lancaster*	Duke of Rutland.
Henry Chaplin	*Pres. Local Government Bd.*	Charles Thomson Ritchie.
Walter Hume Long	*Pres. Board of Agriculture*	Henry Chaplin.
Aretas Akers-Douglas	*Works and Public Buildings*	(Not in the Cabinet.)

THE ABOVE FORM AND FORMED THE CABINET.

Gerald William Balfour	*Chief Secretary for Ireland*	Sir Michael E. Hicks-Beach, Bt. Arthur James Balfour. William Lawies Jackson.
Duke of Norfolk	*Postmaster-General*	Henry Cecil Raikes, dec. Sir James Fergusson, Bart.
Sir John Eldon Gorst, Q.C.	*V.-P. Committee of Council*	Sir William Hart Dyke, Bt.
(In the Cabinet)	*Works and Public Buildings*	Hon. David Robert Plunket, Q.C.
Henry Torrens Anstruther	} *Jun. Lords of the Treasury*	Hon. Sidney Herbert. Col. Sir Wm. Hood Walrond, Bt. Sir Herbert Eustace Maxwell, Bt.
William Hayes Fisher		
Lord Stanley		
Robert William Hanbury	*Financial Sec. to Treasury*	William Lawies Jackson. Sir John Eldon Gorst, Q.C.
Sir William Hood Walrond, Bt.	*Patronage Sec. to the Treasury*	Aretas Akers-Douglas.
Earl of Hopetoun Duke of Marlborough	} *Paymaster-General*	Lord Windsor.
Sir Francis Henry Jeune	*Judge-Advocate General*	Sir William Thackeray Marriott.
Adm. Lord Walter T. Kerr	} *Lords of the Admiralty*	Adm. Sir Anth. Hiley Hoskins. Vice-Adm. Henry Fairfax. Vice-Adm. John O. Hopkins. Rear-Adm.Fredk.Geo.D.Bedford Sir Ellis Ashmead-Bartlett (*Civ.*).
Rear-Adm. Archibald L. Douglas.		
Rear-Adm. A. K. Wilson, V.C.		
Rear-Adm. Arthur William Moore		
J. Austen Chamberlain (*Civil*)		
Wm. G. Ellison Macartney	*Secretary to the Admiralty*	Sir A. Bower Forwood, Bart., dec.
Jesse Collings	*Parliamentary Sec. Home Office*	Charles Beilby Stuart-Wortley, Q.C.
Hon. George Nathaniel Curzon Hon. St. John Brodrick	} *Parly. Sec. Foreign Office*	James William Lowther.
Earl of Selborne	*Parly. Sec. Colonial Office*	Bn. H. De Worms, *now* Ld. Pirbright.
Earl of Onslow	*Parly. Sec. India Office*	Hn. G. N. (*now* Ld.) Curzon (of Kedleston.)
George Wyndham	*Parly. Sec. War Office*	Earl Brownlow.
Earl of Dudley	*Parly. Sec. Board of Trade*	Lord Balfour of Burleigh.
Thomas Wallace Russell	*Parly. Sec. Local Gov. Bd.*	Walter Hume Long.
Joseph Powell Williams	*Financial Sec. War Office*	Hon. William St. J. F. Brodrick.
Sir Richard E. Webster, Bart., Q.C.	*Attorney-General*	Sir Richard Everard Webster, Q.C.
Sir Robert Bannatyne Finlay, Q.C.	*Solicitor-General*	Sir Edward Clarke, Q.C.

SCOTLAND.

(In the Cabinet)	*Secretary, Keeper of Gt. Seal*	Marquess of Lothian.
Andrew Graham Murray, Q.C.	*Lord Advocate*	Sir Charles John Pearson, Q.C.
Marquess of Lothian	*Keeper of the Privy Seal*	Marquess of Lothian.
Charles Scott Dickson, Q.C.	*Solicitor-General*	Andrew Graham Murray, Q.C.

IRELAND.

(In the Cabinet)	*Lord-Lieutenant*	Marquess of Londonderry. Earl (*now Marquess*) of Zetland Arthur James Balfour.
Gerald William Balfour	*Chief Secretary*	William Lawies Jackson.
Sir David Harrel	*Under-Secretary*	Col. Sir Joseph West Ridgeway.
Lord Ashbourne	*Lord Chancellor*	Lord Ashbourne.
John Atkinson, Q.C.	*Attorney-General*	John Atkinson, Q.C.
Dunbar Plunket Barton, Q.C.	*Solicitor-General*	Edward H. Carson, Q.C.

Administrations in the Present Century, 1809–1895.

Date.	Prime Minister.	Duration. Years.	Days.	Exchequer.	Home Secretary.	Foreign Secretary	Colonies and War.	Irish Secretary.	Bd. of Control, India
Dec. 4, 1809	Spencer Perceval	2	190	Spencer Perceval	Hon. Richd. Ryder	Wellesley	Liverpool	{ Robert Dundas.. / Wm. W. Pole.. }	Robert Dundas.
June 9, 1812	Earl of Liverpool	14	339	{ N. Vansittart.. / F. J. Robinson }	Sidmouth / Robert Peel	Castlereagh } / George Canning }	Bathurst	Sir Robert Peel / Hen. Goulburn }	E. of Buckingham. / George Canning. / Chas. W. W. Wyn. / Chas. W. W. Wyn.
April 44, 1827	George Canning	0	134	George Canning	Sturges Bourne	Dudley	Goderich	William Lamb..	Chas. W. W. Wyn.
Sept. 5, 1827	Viscount Goderich	0	144	J. C. Herries		Dudley		Lord F. L. Gower.	Viscnt. Melville.
Jan. 25, 1828	Dk. of Wellington	2	301	Henry Goulburn	Sir Robert Peel	{ Dudley / Aberdeen }		Sir H. Hardinge ..	Lord Ellenborough.
Nov. 22, 1830	Earl Grey	3	238	Althorp	Melbourne	Palmerston		E. G. Stanley..	Charles Grant.
July 16, 1834	Visct. Melbourne	0	161	Althorp	Duncannon	Palmerston		{ Sir J. Hobhouse / Sir J. Littleton	Charles Grant.
Dec. 26, 1834	Sir Robert Peel	0	113	Sir Robert Peel	H. Goulburn	Wellington		Sir H. Hardinge	LordEllenborough.
April 18, 1835	Visct. Melbourne	6	141	{ T. Spring Rice / F. T. Baring }	Lord J. Russell. / Normanby	Palmerston		Lord Morpeth	Sir J. C. Hobhouse.
Sept. 6, 1841	Sir Robert Peel	4	303	Henry Goulburn	Sir Jas. Graham	Aberdeen	Stanley / W. E. Gladstone	{ Lord Eliot...... / Earl of Lincoln.	Lord Ellenborough. / Lord Fitzgerald.
July 16, 1846	Lord John Russell	5	336	Sir Charles Wood	Sir George Grey	{ Palmerston / Granville.. / Clarendon }	Earl Grey	Earl of Ripon. / Sir W. Somerville / Lord Naas (Mayo).	Earl of Ripon. / Sir J. C. Hobhouse / Fox Maule.
Feb. 27, 1852	Earl of Derby	0	305	Benjamin Disraeli	S. H. Walpole	Malmesbury	{ Sir Jno. Pakington / Duke of Newcastle }	Lord Naas (Mayo).	J. C. Herries.
Dec. 28, 1852	Earl of Aberdeen	2	44	W. E. Gladstone	Palmerston	{ Lord J. Russell. / Clarendon }	War. / Newcastle / Colonies. / Sir Geo. Grey / Lord J. Russell	Sir John Young	Sir Charles Wood.
Feb. 10, 1855	Lord Palmerston	3	25	{ W. E. Gladstone / Sir G. C. Lewis }	Sir George Grey	Clarendon	Panmure. / Hon. S. Herbert / H. Labouchere.	{ Edwd. Horsman / H. A. Herbert }	Sir Charles Wood. / Robert V. Smith. / Earl of Ellenborough. / Secretary of State
Feb. 25, 1859	Earl of Derby	1	113	Benjamin Disraeli	{ S. H. Walpole / T. H. S. Estcourt }	Malmesbury	Gen. Peel / Sir E. B. Lytton.	Lord Naas (Mayo).	Lord Stanley
June 18, 1859	Lord Palmerston	6	44	W. E. Gladstone	{ Sir G. C. Lewis / Sir George Grey }	Lord J. Russell	Newcastle / Cardwell / Sir G. C. Lewis. / de Grey & Ripon	{ Edw. Cardwell.. / Sir Robert Peel }	Sir Charles Wood. / Sir de Grey & Ripon. / Viscnt. Cranborne.
Nov. 6, 1865	Earl Russell	0	235	W. E. Gladstone	Sir George Grey	Clarendon	Cardwell / Gen. Peel	C. P. Fortescue..	Sir Charles Wood.
July 6, 1866	Earl of Derby	1	236	Benjamin Disraeli	S. H. Walpole / Gathorne Hardy	Stanley	Carnarvon / Sir J. Pakington	Lord Naas (Mayo).	Visct. Cranborne.
Feb. 9, 1868	Benjamin Disraeli	0	286	Geo. Ward Hunt..	Gathorne Hardy	Stanley	Buckingham / sir J. Pakington	Col. Wilson Patten	Sir S. Northcote.
Dec. 9, 1868	W. E. Gladstone	5	74	{ Robert Lowe... / W. E. Gladstone }	Henry A. Bruce. / Robert Lowe	{ Clarendon / Granville. }	Granville / E. Cardwell	{ C. P. Fortescue.. / Marq. Hartington }	Duke of Argyll.
Feb. 21, 1874	Benjamin Disraeli / (Earl of Beaconsfield)	6	67	Sir S. Northcote	R. A. Cross	{ Derby / Salisbury }	Carnarvon / G. Hardy / Col F. A. Stanley	{ Sir M. H.-Beach / James Lowther / Sir M. H.-Beach }	Marq. of Salisbury. / Visct. Cranbrook.
April 28, 1880	W. E. Gladstone	5	57	{ W. E. Gladstone / H. C. E. Childers }	Sir W. Harcourt	Granville...	Kimberley / Derby	H. C. E. Childers / Hartington	Marq. Hartington. / Earl of Kimberley.
June 24, 1885	Marq. of Salisbury	0	227	Sir M.Hicks-Beach	Sir R. A. Cross	Salisbury	Col. F. A. Stanley	Ld. F. Cavendish / G. O. Trevelyan. / W. H. Smith	Lord R. Churchill.
June 4, 1886	W. E. Gladstone	0	178	Sir W. Harcourt	H. C. E. Childers	Rosebery	Granville	H. C. Bannerm'n / Sir W. Hart Dyke	Earl of Kimberley.
Aug. 3, 1886	Marq. of Salisbury	6	25	{ Lord R.Churchill / Geo. J. Goschen }	Henry Matthews	{ Iddesleigh / Salisbury }	E. Stanhope / Knutsford	Sir M. Hicks-Beach / Arth. Jas. Balfour	Viscount Cross.
Aug. 18, 1892	W. E. Gladstone	1	253	Sir W. Harcourt	Herbt. H. Asquith	Rosebery	Ripon	John Morley	Earl of Kimberley.
March 3, 1894	Earl of Rosebery	1	121	Sir W. Harcourt	Herbt. H. Asquith	Kimberley	Ripon	John Morley	Henry H. Fowler
July 2, 1895	Marq. of Salisbury			Sir M. Hicks-Beach	Sir M. W. Ridley	Salisbury	J. Chamberlain / Lansdowne	G. W. Balfour	Lord G. Hamilton.

ADMIRALTY, Whitehall, S.W.—£261,600.

LORDS COMMISSIONERS—

Rt. Hon. Geo. J. Goschen, M.P. *(First Lord)* £4,550
Private Sec., Capt.Hon.M.A.Bourke, C.M.G., R.N.
Assist. do., W. G. Greene, C.B.; O.A.R.Murray;
Viscount Encombe; G.J.Goschen,Junior, M.P.
Admiral Lord Walter T. Kerr, K.C.B. .. £1,500*
Rear-Adm. Archibald L. Douglas £1,200*
Rear-Adm.A.K.Wilson,C.B., V.C (*Contr.*)£1,700*
Rear-Adm. A. W. Moore, C.B ., C.M.G.. £1,200*
Civil Lord, Joseph Austen Chamberlain, M.P.£1,000
  †*Private Secretary,* Robert G. Hayes £50
Farliamentary and Financial Sec., William G.
  Ellison Macartney, M.P. £2,000
  †*Private Secretary,* William J. Evans........£150
  Assistant do., George Kemp, M.P. ....unp.
Permanent Sec., Sir Evan MacGregor, K.C.B. £2,000
  †*Private Secretary,* Sidney R. Marriott......£50
Assistant Sec., Hen.J.Van Sittart Neale, C.B.£1,200
Hydrographer, Rear-Adm. Sir William J. L.
  Wharton, K.C.B., F.R.S. £1,000
Director of Transports, Rear-Adm. Bouverie F.
  Clark £1,200
Director of Victualling, H. F. R. Yorke, C.B.
  ....£1,000 to £1,200
Director of Naval Construction, Sir William H.
  White, K.C.B., SC.D., LL.D., F.R.S........£2,500
Engin.-in-Chief, Sir A.John Durston, K.C.B. £1,800
Director of Dockyards, J. Williamson £2,000
Director of Stores, Gordon W.Miller £1,000 to £1,200
Storekeeper of Naval Ordnance, Col. Thales
  Pease, C.B. £1,450
Director of Ordnance, Rear-Adm. Edmund F.
  Jeffreys £1,000
Account.-General, Richard D. Awdry, C.B. £1,500
Director of Contracts, Tatham Gwyn £1,200
Medical Director-General, Sir Henry Norbury, M.D.,
  K.C.B., R.N. £1,500
Director of Works, Lt.-Col. E. Raban, R.E. £1,172*
Civil Engineer in Chief, Works Loan, Major H. Pil-
  kington, C.B., R.E. £2,000
Dir. of Naval Intelligence, Rear-Adm. Regd.
  N. Custance £1,500

(*Also see* NAVAL SERVICE, page 218.)

AGRICULTURE, BOARD OF
4 Whitehall Place; 3 St. James's Square—
£105,726.

President, Rt. Hon. Walter Hume Long, M.P. £2,000
  Private Secretary, Gerald A. Arbuthnot £300
  Assist. Priv. Sec., F. A. Fulford, G. Montagu,
    and Abel Henry Smith, M.P.............unp.
Secretary, Thomas Henry Elliott, C.B. £1,500
  Private Secretary, Thomas F. Husband £100
Assistant Secretaries, Major P. G. Cragie,
  Major John T. Tennant ......£800 to £1,000
Legal Adviser, James Wm. Clark £800 to £1,000
Assist. Legal Adviser, Fras. A. Jones £500 to £600
Assist. Commissioners and Inspectors, George Pem-
  berton Leach; Hon. Arthur Russell.
Director Land Divis. & Agricultural Adviser, Sir
  Jacob Wilson, Knt. £1,500
Chief Veterinary Officer, Alex.C.Cope, £800 to £1,000
  Assistant do., W. Duguid ....£600 to £800
Technical Adviser (vacant)..................£250
Chief Agr. Analyst, Prof.T.E.Thorpe, PH.D., F.R.S.
Superintending Inspectors, Major H. Landon and
  Capt. G. S. MacIlwaine, R.N. .... £500 to £600
Inspectors (Animals), E. G. H. Brown, Capt. W.
  H. Chamberlain, R.N.; Maj. E. H. St. L. Clarke,

* In addition to professional pay.
† The allowances made to those gentlemen who act
as private secretaries are in addition to their salaries as
clerks in the various offices.

F. H. Davenport, W. Dawson, F. A. Fulford,
A. Goddard, E. T. Kenyon, and Capt. G. R.
Spencer ....£300 to £400
  Do. (Educational), A. E B. Hunt £300 to £400
Chief Clerks, A. W. Anstruther, £400 to £700;
  John Robert Moore ....£400 to £750
Heads of Branches, Col. G. H. Bolland, R.E., R. F.
  Crawford, J. Graham, and Samuel Tomkins
  ....£400 to £600
1st Class Clerk, George Herbert Taylor £350 to £500
Assistants to Heads of Branches, J. N. Carey; B.C.
  Goulden; R. H. Hooker; Thos. F. Husband; G.
  W. Lloyd; R.S.Rew; A.G.L.Rogers £150 to £350
2nd Div. Clerks (Higher Grade), H. P. Attwater;
  J. Cornelius; W. Dishman; A. J. Rumbold;
  D. J. Tansley ....£250 to £350
Accountant, W. T. Taylor ....£400 to £500
Cashier, E. B. Wilson ....£250 to £350
Supg. Surveyor, J.J.Thomson,F.R I B.A.£500 to £600
Examiners, C. H. J. Clayton; J. Henderson; W.
  Webb ....£200 to £300
Assistant Surveyor, T. W. Pearson £270

Ordnance Survey Department, Southampton.

Director-General, Col. D. A. Johnston, R.E.
Executive Officer, Lt.-Col R. C. Hellard, R.E.
Assistant ditto, Captain W. C. Hedley, R.E.
Publication Branch, Col. E. R. Hussey, R.E.; Lieut.
  H. W. Gordon, R.E.
Engraving Branch, Lt. P. T. Denis de Vitré, R.E.
Revision Branch, Capt. C. de W. Crookshank, R.E.
Stores, Building and Trigonometrical Division, Capt.
  P. H. du P. Casgrain, R.E.; Hon. Lt. & Qr.
  Mr. H. Cripps, R.E.

Survey Divisions.

Officers: (Gt. Britain) Lt. G. E. Elkington,
  R.E., Bedford; Lieut. W. M. Thompson, R.E.,
  Carlisle; Capt G. F. A. Whitlock, R.E., Chester;
  Capt. E. P. Brooker, R.E., Redland, Bristol;
  Capt. R. J. B. Mair, R.E., Clifton; Capt. W. T.
  Digby, R.E., Derby; Major H. M. Jackson, R.E.,
  Capt. S. F. Williams, R.E., Edinburgh; Capt.
  A. C. Painter, R.E., Redhill, Surrey; Maj. R. A.
  P. O'Shee, R.E., York.
Officers: (Ireland) Maj. G. H. Sim, R.E., Capt.
  C. C. Perceval, R.E., Capt. W. H. Rotheram,
  R.E., Dublin; Lieut. G. S. Knox, R.E., Ennis, co.
  Clare; Capt. C. F. Close, R.E , Cork.

ARMS, COLLEGE OF, or HERALDS' COLLEGE,
  Queen Victoria Street, E.C.

Earl Marshal, His Grace the Duke of Norfolk, K.G.
Earl Marshal's Sec., Henry Edwd. Wilberforce.
Registrar, Edward Bellasis, Lancaster Herald.

KINGS OF ARMS.

Garter, Sir Albert Wm. Woods, K.C.B., K.C.M.G.,
  F.S.A.
Clarenceux, George Edward Cokayne, M.A., F.S.A.
Norroy, William Henry Weldon, F.S.A.

SIX HERALDS.

Chester, Henry Murray Lane.
Lancaster, Edward Bellasis.
York, Alfred S. Scott-Gatty, F.S.A.
Somerset, Henry Farnham Burke, F.S.A.
Richmond, Charles Harold Athill, F.S.A.
Windsor, Wm. Alex. Lindsay, Q.C., M.A., F.S.A.

Surrey Extraordinary, Charles Alban Buckler.
Maltravers Extr., Jos. J. Howard, LL.D., F.S.A.

FOUR PURSUIVANTS.

Rouge Croix, George Wm. Marshall, LL.D., F.S.A.
Bluemantle, Gordon Ambrose de Lisle Lee.
Rouge Dragon, Everard Green, F.S.A.
Portcullis, Thomas Morgan Joseph-Watkin.

Scotland, Lyon Court.

Lyon King of Arms, Jas. Balfour Paul, Adv...£500
Clerk & Keeper of Records, F. J. Grant, w.s., £250
Procurator-Fiscal, David Scott-Moncrieff, w.s.

Heralds:

Albany, Robert Spence Livingstone,
Marchmont, Andrew Ross, s.s c., }£25 each.
Rothesay, Francis James Grant, w.s.,

Pursuivants:

Unicorn, Stuart Moodie Livingstone,
Carrick, Wm. Rae Macdonald, f.f.a., }£16 13s. 4d. each.
Bute, James Keir Lamont, n.p.,

Ireland, Office of Arms.

Ulster King of Arms, Sir A. E. Vicars, f.s.a.£500
Athlone Pursuivant, Harry Blake.

CHARITY COMMISSIONERS for England and Wales (including Endowed Schools Dept.),

Gwydyr House, Whitehall, S.W.—£42,594
Chief Commissioner, Sir Hy. Longley, k.c.b.£2,000
   Private Sec., H. P. Morris £100
2nd Commissioner, Chas. H. Alderson, c.b. .. £1,500
3rd Commissioner, ...£1,200
4th Commissioner, J. Grant Lawson, m.p. ..... *unp.*
Secretary, Daniel Robert Fearon, c.b. £1,100
Assistant Secs., W. C. Lefroy, T. Allchin......£900
Official Trustees of Charitable Funds, W. T. Warry ; W. C. Lefroy ; T. Allchin.
Assist. Commrs., C. Archer Cook, £900: R. Durnford ; G. S. D. Murray ; T. Allchin, £700 to £800
Do. (under Endowed Schools Acts), W. C. Lefroy ; A. F. Leach ; Hon. W. N. Bruce ; A. C. Eddis ; R. E. Mitcheson ....£700 to £800
Do. (temp. employ.), A. Cardew; G. W. Wallace; L. A. Selby-Bigge ; W. A. Wigram ; A. C. Kay ; T. Marchant Williams ; G. B. M. Coore.
Principal Clerks, W. T. Warry ; F. T. C. Henry ; H. W. T. Bowyear ; John H. Allen .. each £800
Account., Off. Trustees' Dep., J. Messenger ..£700
1st Class Clerks, J. W. Owsley ; G. B. Bone : Chas. G. Drinan E. Gilbert ....£400 to £550
   Asst. do., C. T. Radcliffe ....£300 to £400
2nd Class Clerks, W. Endersby ; A. K. Kennedy-Purvis ; H. P. Morris ; H. Hodgkin : T. E. Wells ; G. C. Bower ; J. L. Casson ; C. F. Ritchie ; H. J. Simmonds ....£300 to £400
Recorder of Unreported Charities, W. W. Folkard. £360
Clerk in charge, Endowed Schools Dept., H. Kingdon £375
Lib. and Clk. to Sec., J. J. B. Petherbridge.
2nd Div. Clerks (Higher Grade), J. Ford ; F. F. Davy ; A. L. Guest ; J. W. Joyce...£250 to £350

CIVIL SERVICE COMMISSION,

68 Victoria St., Westminster, S.W.—£43,405
(Office hours 10 to 5.)
1st Commissioner, Wm. J. Courthope, c.b. .. £1,500
2nd Do., Lord Francis Hervey £1,200
Sec. and Registrar, J. S. Lockhart £900
Senior Clks., J. Hennell ; R. Howlett, E. A. Collier ; F. W. Jennings ; S. Cassan Paul.
Senior Examiner, J. Bonar.

COLONIAL OFFICE, Downing St., S.W.—£48,905

Colonial Secretary of State for the Colonies, Rt. Hon. Joseph Chamberlain, m.p. £5,000
   Priv. Sec., Lord Amphill £300
   Assist. do., G. E. A. Grindle £100 ; G. Craig Sellar, Hon. T. H. Cochrane, m.p. (parliamentary) ; Earl of Westmeath.........*unp.*

UNDER SECRETARIES.

Permanent, Sir Edward Wingfield, k.c.b. .. £2,000
   Priv. Sec., J. F. N. Green £150
Parliamentary, The Earl of Selborne £1,500
   Private Secretary, W. D. Ellis £150

Assist. Und.-Sec., Frederick Graham, c.b....£1,200
   Do. „   „   Charles Prestwood Lucas...£1,200
   Do. „   „   (Legal) Hugh B. Cox £1,000
   Do. „   „   Reginald L. Antrobus, c.b.£1,000
Chancellor of the Order of St. Michael & St. George, Sir Robt. George Wyndham Herbert, g.c.b.
Chief Clerk, Sir W. A. Baillie-Hamilton, k.c.m.g., c.b. £1,000
Principal Clerks, Arthur A. Pearson ; Francis Richard Round, c.m.g. ; Hartmann Wolfgang Just ; John Anderson, c.m.g. ; Wm. Hepworth Mercer ; Charles Alex. Harris ...£850 to £1,000
Legal Assistant, H. F. Wilson £1,000
1st Class Clerks, Geo. Wm. Johnson ; Sydney Olivier, c.m.g. ; H. J. Read ; Charles Strachey ; H. C. M. Lambert ; A. E. Collins £600 to £800
2nd Class Clerks, W. D. Ellis ; G. E. A. Grindle ; J. F. N. Green ; T. C. Macnaghten ; J. F. Perry ; E. H. Marsh ; C. T. Davis; F. G. A. Butler ; W. A. Robinson ; A. Fiddian ; H. E. Dale ; E. R. Darnley ; P. N. Ezechiel ; R. Geikie ; G. G. Robinson.........£200 to £500
Clerk for Legal Instruments, F.O. Adrian £550 to £600
Accountant, A. H. H. Engelbach.....£500 to £600
Asst. do., W. H. Eggett ....£300 to £450
Supt. of Library, C. Atchley ....£300 to £450
Do., Registry, W. F. Westbrook ....£300 to £450
Do., Printing, E. D. Rockett.........£300 to £400
Supt. of Copying, S. J. Meaney.......£200 to £450
Medical Adviser, Patrick Manson, m.d.

Emigrants' Information Office.—£1,500.

31 Broadway, S.W.—(10 to 5. Sat. 10 to 1.30.)
Chief Clerk, John Pulker.
Editor of Publications, Walter B. Paton, m.a.

COLONIES, CROWN AGENTS FOR THE.

Downing St., S.W.,& 1 Tokenhouse Buildings, E.C.
Crown Agents, Sir M. F. Ommanney, k.c.m.g. ; E. E. Blake ; Maj. M. A. Cameron, r.e.
Chief Clerk and Accountant, J. W. Leonard.
Registrar, T. S. Dunn.
Chief Cashier, L. Adams.
Engineering Clerk and Head of Contract Branch, T. R. Marsh, m.a.
Head of Shipping Branch, N. Hardingham.
Head of Correspondence Branch, G. Hodgson.

AGENTS FOR—

Antigua, Bahamas, Barbados, Basutoland, Bechuanaland Protectorate, Bermuda, British Guiana, British Honduras, Central Africa Protectorate, Ceylon, Cyprus, Dominica, East Africa Protectorate, Falkland Islands, Fiji, Gambia, Gibraltar, Gold Coast, Grenada, Hong Kong, Jamaica, Lagos, Leeward Islands, Malta, Mauritius, Montserrat, Newfoundland, Niger Coast Protectorate, Northern Nigeria, St. Helena, St. Kitts Nevis, St. Lucia, St. Vincent, Seychelles Islands, Sierra Leone, Somali Coast Protectorate, Straits Settlements (Singapore, Penang and Malacca, and Native States of Negri Sembilan, Pahang, Perak and Selangor), Tobago, Trinidad, Turks Island, Uganda, Virgin Islands, *and also for* The Uganda Railway and The West African Frontier Force.

CORNWALL, DUCHY OF, BuckinghamGate,S.W.

Lord Warden of the Stannaries, Earl of Ducie.
Keeper of Privy Seal, Earl of Leicester, k.g.
Attorney-Gen., Charles Alfred Cripps, q.c., m.p.
Rec.-Gen., Col. Sir R. N. FitzH. Kingscote, k.c.b.
Auditor, Lesley Charles Probyn.
Sec. & Keeper of Records, Maurice Holzmann, c.b.
Solicitor, Thornhill B. Heathcote.
Assistant Secretary, J. C. Pearce.
Clerk Accountant and Dep. Receiver, A. E. Gillett.
Land Stewards, George Herriot ; A. M. Webster.

CUSTOMS ESTABLISHMENT, E.C.

(Estimate for United Kingdom, £846 600.)
(Superintending Establishment, £60,295 .)
(Port Establishments, £625,172.)

Chairman, George L. Ryder, c.b. £2,000
Dep. Chairman, John Arrow Kempe £1,500
Commissioner, Lewis Wm. Engelbach, c.b. £1,200

SECRETARY'S OFFICE.

Secretary, Richard T. Prowse, c.b. £1,200
Assist. Secretary, John Courroux £1,000
Committee Clerks, Robert Robson; John Gatley;
  Victor Maslin £800
Principal Clerks of Old Establishment, Alfred H.
  Courroux; Alfred L. Hardy..................£700
Other Clerk, Upper Div., H. V. Reade, £100 to £500
Assist. to Committee Clerks, A. D. Greig, £250 to £450
Staff Clerks, A. S. Cranbrook; Fredk. Monk £220
Priv. Secs. to the Chairman, Herbert V. Reade;
  Albert D. Greig ....each £50
2nd Div. Clerks, Higher Grade, Wm. E. Young;
  Robert E. B. Saunders; E. H. Coombe; Wm. H.
  Ingmire; Charles Atkinson; E. E. Stonham
  ....£250 to £350
2nd Div. Clerks, E. Ford; A. E. Montague;
  A. J. Dyke; Wm. Young; J. W. Lishmund
  ....£70 to £250
Medical Insp., Thos. H. Dickson, M.B........£800

SOLICITOR'S OFFICE.

Solicitor, Charles John Follett, c.b., B.C.L. £2,000
Assistant Solicitor, Charles E. Thynne £800
Chief Clerk, ...£500 to £600
Second Clerk, James Macklin ....£350 to £450

SURVEYOR-GENERAL'S OFFICE.

Surveyors-General, Donald Fraser; James C.
  Thompson; William Muir....£800 to £1,000
Staff Clerks, Edward Bradbury; Alfred H. Knight;
  Ernest A. Harris ....£220 to £400

ACCOUNTANT AND CONTROLLER'S OFFICE.

Accountant and Cont.-Gen., Henry J. Gardner £1,000
Assistant, John W. de Grave £800
Principal Clerks, Geo. Martin Tait; Geo. W.
  Bennett; Charles H. Norman ....£520 to £620
Upper Div. Clerks, John R. Blackford; Alfred
  Brabner; James Burton; Geo. C. Calvert;
  Frederick Dyason; John W. Ellison; Daniel
  Ground; Isaac L. Meyers; Charles N. Potter;
  Wm. J. Reid ....(3 to £480) £100 to £430

STATISTICAL DEPARTMENT.

Principal, Thomas J. Pittar, c.b...........£1,100
Deputy do., Alfred J. Wood ....£650 to £750
Principal Clerks, old establishment, John Denney;
  Philip J. Le Sueur; R. Gibbings £520 to £620
Senior Clerks, Charles B. Pollard; John Channon;
  John R. Wildman ....£400 to £500
Upper Div. Clerks, old establishment, Jno. Cham-
  bers; John W. Flower ....£100 to £430
Clerks, John B. Boyle; Samuel Bozman; Alex-
  ander Hamilton; Charles L. Jones; Patrick
  Lynch; Edwin Marshall; Joseph C. O'Reilly;
  Wm. C. Tope. ....£230 to £400

LONG ROOM, PORT OF LONDON.

Collector & Chief Registrar of Shipping, Robert
  Henderson £1,000
Asst. Collector, C. J. Stebbing ....£600 to £700
Principal Clerks, Robert Mayhew; G. J. Kent;
  A. S. Roofe; J. S. Symon; John K. Williams
  ....£400 to £620
Upper Div. Clerks, William F. Adams; Joseph
  Hopson; John H. Jeffery; George M. Jenkings;
  Fras. W. Miller; George Munnion; John M.
  Newman..................(3 to £450) £100 to £430

2nd Div. Clerks employed in Outdoor Department,
  L. H. Snow; Edwin A. West; C. K. Gascoigne;
  Thomas Iverney ....£70 to £350

OUTDOOR DEPARTMENT, PORT OF LONDON.

Inspectors, James Fleming; George Excell; W.
  H. Sentance; W. Parker; J. C. Elliott
  ....£600 to £650 (1 to £700)
Assistant Inspector, Thos. Smith.....£490 to £550
1st Class Surveyors, John Cross; Charles A. Pyne;
  Thomas Rochford; William C. Samuel; Edwd.
  T. W. Semmens; Arthur Skelton; John Sell;
  Henry Surman; J. O. Maclean £490 to £550
2nd Class, James Cleugh; Joseph Flint; Francis
  G. Heath; William F. Hubbard; Samuel Long-
  man; Alexander McArthur; Pierce A. Rogan;
  Joseph T. Summerfield; Montague Yeomans;
  A. E. Rolt; J. W. Wakelin; W. H. Rowling;
  A. R. Ledger ....£430 to £480
3rd Class, Arthur B. Chalouer; Robert W. Gold;
  John P. Harding; Charles F. Jones; Richd.
  W. Joyner; Alexander McAra; Alexander
  Matthew; John Maxwell; Stephen Murphy;
  Aaron Richardson; Wm. T. Swanson; Thomas
  Williams; W. Gibson; M. Matthews; F. W.
  Scott; J. J. Shenton ....£350 to £420
Preventive Surveyors, Michael Reidy; James Tit-
  terton..................................£350 to £420

DURHAM, COUNTY PALATINE OF.

Temporal Chancellor, Thomas Milvain, Q.C.
Attorney-General, John Forbes, Q.C.
Solicitor-General, Edward Tindal Atkinson, Q.C.
Registrar of Chancery Court, A. O. Smith.
Steward & Clerk of Halmotes, A. de Bock Porter, c.b.
Deputy Steward and Clerk, F. A. Manley.
Manorial Surveyor and Local Dep., G. Young Wall.
Mining Surveyor, Sir Lindsay Wood, Bart.
Receivers, Smiths, Gore & Co.

ECCLESIASTICAL AND CHURCH ESTATES COMMISSIONERS, 10 Whitehall Place, S.W.

Ecclesiastical Commissrs., The two Archbishops,
  the 32 Bishops, 4 Cabinet Ministers, 4 Judges, 3
  Deans, and 12 eminent Laymen.
Church Estates Commissrs., Earl Stanhope £1,200
  Lees Knowles, M.P. ....unp.
  Rt. Hon. C. B. Stuart-Wortley, Q.C., M.P. £1,000
Auditor, Francis Phillips £450
*Secretary, Financial Adviser, and Steward of the
  Manors*, Alfred de Bock Porter, c.b. £1,700
  Private Secretary, J. A. Archer £100
Assistant Secretary and Assist. Financial Adviser,
  Robert C. Selfe ....£800 to £1,000
Accountant, M. P. Christie ....£700 to £800
Registrar, Francis Cobb ....£550 to £750
Asst. Steward of Manors, F. A. Manley £550 to £750
Principal Clerk, J. F. Pelham £700
Assistant Accountant, Edgar Blois Lawton
  ....£550 to £650
1st Class Clerks, Senior Div., J. W. Challis; J. L.
  Diplock George Dickins; G. J. Pearse
  ....£500 to £600
1st Class Clerks, Junior Div., T. Holford; J. Pope;
  Geo. Jas. White; H. H. Holford; J. C. Pearse;
  G. C. Harpour; H. S. Goodhart; A. Sturgeon;
  R. F. Meator ....£350 to £500
Legal Assistant (Manors), Hugh de Bock Porter
  ....£300 to £500
Junior Clerks, J. A. Archer; C. Hogg; G. H.
  Wheeler; F. Brereton; J. Kershaw; H. A.
  Gregg; G. A. Andrews; S. S. Brister; S. E.
  Downing; A. E. Palmer; J. H. Wisdom; W.
  Telfer; J. D. Howatson; C. M. T. Irving; F.
  C. Marillier; E. J. Davies; F. T. Barrett; S.
  Mills; R. W. Fowell; F. H. Glaister; F.

Walmsley; A. N. Allan; J. W. Lintott; W. H. Mouncey; E. H. B. Phillips .... £70 to £350

Solicitors, White, Borrett & Co., 6 Whitehall Pl.; Milles, Jennings-White & Foster, 8 Whitehall Pl.

Architects, Christian, Caroë & Purday, 8A Whitehall Place.

Surveyors, Messrs. Clutton, 9 Whitehall Place; Smiths, Gore, Ingram & Norton, 7 Whitehall Place.

EDUCATION, COMMITTEE OF COUNCIL ON.

Vote for Education, Science, and Art, for the United Kingdom, £12,207,860.

Cost of Administration, England and Wales, £81,830; Inspection, do., £211,885; Elementary Schools, do., £8,276,565; Training Colleges, &c., do., £180,819. Education, Ireland, £1,221,117; Do., Scotland, £1,391,851.

Education Department, Whitehall, S.W.—£81,880

Vice-President, Rt. Hon. Sir John Eldon Gorst, Q.C., M.P. £2,000
   Private Sec., William Loring £150
   Assist. do., Harold E. Gorst .... unp.
Secretary, Sir George Wm. Kekewich, K.C.B. £1,800
   Private Sec., W. H. Orange £150
   Assistant do., W. H. Bray £100
Principal Assistant Secretary, W. Tucker, C.B.
                £1,200 to £1,500
Assistant Secretaries, J. W. J. Stephenson; J. White; C. M. Cowie; H. F. Pooley
                £900 to £1,200
Senior Examiners, H. W. Hoare; W. I. Ritchie; H. M. Lindsell; J. R. Dasent, C.B.; R. M. Tabor; H. W. Simpkinson, C.B.; J. W. Mackail; C. L. Kingsford .... £650 to £800
Junior do., F. H. Trench; T. R. Walrond; E. K. Chambers; G. C. Sykes; J. G. Milne; H. W. Orange; W. Loring; R. J. G. Mayor; W. F. Sheppard; J. E. Talbot; G. N. Richardson; F. H. B. Dale; H. St. J. Thackeray; W. F. Sedgwick; H. J. Mordaunt; A. H. Wood; W. D. Bushell; W. R. Davies .... £250 to £600
Assistant Examiner, Drawing, J. A. D. Campbell
                £550
Advising Counsel, Henry Martin Lindsell £150
Consulting Architect, E. R. Robson, F.S.A. £850
Examinations Clerk, T. Lyle .... £400 to £550
1st Class Clerks, J. Pringle; C. Townsend; J. H. Levy; H. J. Gibbs; F. D. Fairman; J. R. Norton; G. M. Norris; A. M. Gilbert; W. G. Masham; A. R. Brewer; J. R. Smith; A. H. Reid; W. Collins; A. Bakewell; J. W. Edwards; A. J. Jennings; W. Pethybridge
                £360 to £500
2nd Class Clerks (holding Staff Appointments), W. Slater; E. Williams; T. Ground; E. E. Trathan .... £360 to £400
Permanent Staff Clerks, W. R. J. Maclean; A. J. Gibbs; G. R. Newton; W. H. Bray; A. Atwill; W. A. Sarjeant .... £360 to £400
Additional Staff Clerks, W. K. Roads; F. Bromwich; H. J. Ayliffe; H. J. Stich; G. F. Farmar; J. H. Ilott; F. G. Martyn; J. T. Ball; F. W. C. T. Jaffray; A. T. Shorey; A. Woodgate; J. W. Garden; J. N. Coombs; A. W. King; W. Wright; T. W. W. Whitnall; W. J. Moulton; W. E. Shoemack; A. T. Dingle; J. Rickard; F. Barber; W. W. Poole .... £250 to £350
2nd Div. Clerks (Higher Grade), J. Westrop; E. L. Eardley; J. P. Roberts; F. G. Emler
                £250 to £350

Her Majesty's Inspectors of Schools.—£211,885.

Senior Chief Inspector, T. King £1,100

Chief Inspectors, W. Scott Coward; Rev. C. H. Parez; Rev. F. F. Cornish; Rev. C. D. Du Port; T. W. Danby; W. P. Turnbull; A. Rankine; A. G. Legard; T. S. Aldis; W. E. Currey; J. A. Willis .... £700 and £900

Inspectors, Rev. C. Francis Routledge; Rev. H. G. Alington; Rev. F. Wilkinson; E. W. Colt; M. J. Barrington-Ward; F. W. H. Myers; J. P. Balmer; J. C. Ley; J. H. Wylie; J. G. FitzMaurice; E. M. Kenney-Herbert; W. H. Brewer; E. M. Sneyd-Kynnersley; R. P. A. Swettenham; H. W. Claughton; H. F. Dibben; G. H. Gordon; E. A. Helps; E. G. A. Holmes; T. Morgan-Owen; A. J. Swinburne; S. G. Tremenheere; W. B. S. Yarde; J. C. Colvill; A. P. Graves; R. S. Stevelly; E. H. Burrows; O. Airy; T. W. Greene; E. N. Wix; T. S. Gleadowe; H. E. B. Harrison; E. S. Mostyn Pryce; H. Cowie; R. M. Fowler; A. B. Fisher; F. B. De Sausmarez; C. H. R. Elliott; F. A. S. Freeland; W. Edwards; M. Pole; H. P. Henderson; J. Bancroft; G. Gardner; T. G. Rooper; E. L. Phelps; E. M. Field; W. C. G. Milman; R. D. M. Oliver; W. M. Hitchins; J. H. Davies; R. Holt-White; J. Wilson; F. B. Lott; C. T. Whitmell; C. G. Colson; S. R. Wilson; A. W. Newton; R. J. Alexander; A. Cartwright; F. T. Green; J. Tillard; L. T. Monro; R. F. Curry; F. S. Marvin; A. C. Iles; E. Joad; J. G. D. Campbell; W. Northrop; P. A. Barnett; John Foster Lewis; J. Roberts; Thomas Jones; H. Holman; Edwd. Roberts; H. Ward; E. F. Davidson; P. Worley; Frederick Dugard; Thomas Darlington; F. T. Howard; R. E. Hughes; E. H. Howard; A. Eichholz; B. S. Cornish; H. R. Mines; G. A. Turner; J. F. Leaf; E. C. Streatfeild; B. G. Ussher .... £400 to £800

Sub-Inspectors (1st class), William Taylor; T. Healing; C. Bilton; J. Hunter; E. Challens; A. Sharpe; J. Sparks; W. Morris; R. Barnes; W. H. Anstead; E. H. Short; R. Knight; J. R. Jarman; E. Ensor; W. T. Meggs; W. Martin; J. W. W. Burrage; J. W. Briggs; H. Brown; T. M. Morgan; T. Glover; A. Owen; C. Lewis; T. Eley; T. Williams; W. Dewse; D. Hamer; A. Seer; T. W. Pearce; W. Baldrey; J. Penber; G. Sedgwick; J. Rees; W. Turner; A. Finch; J. Gill; F. C. Mills; W. Kefford J. Hodges; J. Waite; T. Howlett; T. Hallam; S. Bush; H. Taylor; W. Mulhall; F. W. Parkes; W. Varnon; C. Beck; R. Gregson; G. Wade; J. Stacey; G. Hayward; J. S. Foister .... £300 to £500

Sub-Inspectors (Manual Instruction), R. Keate; P. L. Gray; S. Carrodus .... £300 to £500
Sub-Inspectors (Drawing), H. Tunaley; H. Allport; J. Lattimer; E. G. Baker; C. D. Fitz-Roy; Capt. F. D. Walker; A. W. Geffcken; C. W. S. Hudson; A. Taylor; J. C. Saltmarsh
                £300 to £500
Sub-Inspectors (Women), Miss R. A. Munday; Miss K. Bathurst; Miss C. L. Callis .... £150 to £300
Inspector of Music, Sir John Stainer, MUS.D.
Assistant do., William Gray M'Naught, MUS.D.
Directress of Needlework, The Hon. Mrs. R. E. Colborne £300
Inspectress, Cooking and Laundry Work, Miss H. M. Deane .... £250 to £350
Director, Special Enquiries, M. E. Sadler, M.A. £650 to £800
Assistant do., R. L. Morant .... £300 to £500

EDUCATION DEPARTMENT (SCOTCH),
Dover House, Whitehall, S.W.—£15,794.

Estimate for Public Education, Scotland, £978,228.
Grants in relief of fees, £323,633.

Secretary, Sir Henry Craik, K.C.B., LL.D. ...£1,500
   Private Secs., F. J. Armstrong; H. J. Macartney.
Assistant Secretary and Senior Examiner, T. Shute
   Robertson £1,000
Senior Examiner, J. Struthers .... £650 to £800
Junior Examiners, G. Todd, £700; R. A. Johnson; W. H. W. Cornish ....£250 to £600
Counsel (vacant) £250
Architect, E. R. Robson, F.S.A. £150
Assistant to Accounting Officer, H. G. Batley £600
Heads of Sections, J. Milne; A. Thomson; T.
   Hodgson; G. L. Apperson; P. H. Atkin ...£360
                                 to £550
Staff Clerk, J. W. Perks .... £360 to £400
Accountant, Edinb., Sir D. F. Ochterlony, Bt. £400

H.M. Inspectors of Schools.

Chief Inspectors, T. A. Stewart, LL.D. (Training
   Coll. and Southern Div.); Alexander Walker
   (Northern Div.); A. E. Scongall (Western
   Div.); J. L. Robertson (*acting*) ..... each £900
Inspectors, A. O. Barrie; J. Macleod; R. J. Muir;
   A. Dey; J. Smith, LL.D.; A. R. Andrew;
   J. Boyd; R. Calder; R. Harvey; W. W.
   Waddell; W. Bathgate; G. Dunn, LL.D.; A.
   Lobban; W. Y. King; D. M. Fraser; W.
   Whyte; Fras. R. Jamieson; J. M. Wattie;
   J. C. Smith; A. D. Thomson, D LITT... £400 to
                                  £800

Science and Art Inspectors.

Inspectors, R. Blair; D. S. Macnair, PH.D.
                             £400 to £600
Sub-Inspectors, 1st Cl., J. Binnie; J. W. Munro;
   D. Thompson; J. Galloway; S. D. Black; J.
   T. Ewen; J. M. Wilson ....£300 to £500

EDUCATION (NATIONAL), IRELAND.
Tyrone House, Marlborough St., Dublin.
£1,221,577—Administration, £28,793.

Resident Commissioner, William Joseph Miles
   Starkey, LITT. D. £1,500
Senior Secretary, M. S. Seymour £1,000
Junior do., Alexander Hamilton £800
Financial Assistant do., Peter Young £650 to £750
Chiefs of Inspection, E. Downing; A. Purser
                          £650 to £750
Bookkeeper, Morgan Donovan ......£315 to £530
Superintendent, Inspection Dept., Jas. J. Hand £580
Supt., Book Dept., William O'Byrne............ £530

EXCHEQUER AND AUDIT DEPARTMENT,
Somerset House, W.C.—£61,407.

Comptroller and Auditor-Gen., R. Mills, C.B. £2,000
   Private Secretary, James S. Francis £150
Assist. Comptroller & Auditor, Douglas Close Richmond £1,500
Chief Clerk, Francis Phillips £1,000
Legal Adviser, John Monsey Collyer.

DIRECTING BRANCH.

Principal Clerks, William Owen; Richard Lennox
   Woods; John Bromley; Henry Aloysius Stacke,
   J. C. King .... £775 to £900
1st Class Clerks, R. A. Hoblyn; A. C. M. M.
   Crichton; Clarence H Archibald; H. C. Purkis;
   T. J. Purchas, M. W. Whitmore £620 to £750
2nd Class Clerks (1st Section), R. E. Verburgh;
   Robert M. B. Otter-Barry; Hayward John
   Bidwell; William M. Martin; R. W. Reay; G.
   Y. Vanderzee; C. C. Glyn; Arthur R. Barrett;
   Alfred Hoskins Britton; J. Brand; C. W. A.

Trollope; J. S. Francis; H. J. W. Cox; Saml.
Butts; John Henry Fryday Brabner; Henry
Thomas Bellamy; Kenneth M. Macdonald
                          £420 to £600
2nd Class Clerks (2nd Section), Wm. H. Gallier;
   S. Waine; V. G. Crawley; F. W. A. Clarke;
   W. Fortescue Barratt; Ellis Wm. Davies;
   Benj. Horner .... £200 to £400

EXAMINING BRANCH.

Examiners (1st Sect.), Francis C. J. W. Dillon;
   Arthur Hy. Hallam Jesse; Robert Bell; Wm.
   Geo. Irwin; Sam. Geo. Fenton; Fredk. Wood;
   Sam. Davey Cray; Edmund Geo. Baker; Thos.
   Hy. Eagar; Fras. Nuttman Warman; Wm.
   Edwd. McKown; John Albert Barnes; Horatio
   Nelson Horton; Jno. Rd. Sowden; Jno. Tenney;
   Wm. Geo. Hunt; Henry Collot; Edwd. Merrick;
   F. C. Goldby; Samuel Stronge; James C. Hunt;
   Alfred Hawkes; Patrick J. D. Corbet; T. Orr;
   W. M. Taylor; F. W. Adams; C. M. Neale;
   W. W. Hunter .... £215 to £430
Examiners (2nd Sect.), A. Paterson; S. Wade; C.
   G. Poole; J. S. Lee; T. J. Bradley; C. H. Stoodley; C. W. Richardson .... £100 to £400
There are also 123 *2nd Div. Clerks* ...£70 to £350

Colonial Audit Branch.

Superintendent, J. W. Gullick ....£600 to £900
Asst. Supt., A. E. Stephenson .... £400 to £550
Clerks in charge of Accounts, C. P. Isaac; F. L.
   Francis ....£150 to £300

FOREIGN OFFICE, Downing St., S.W.—£74,482
               [Office hours 12 to 6.]

Principal Secretary of State for Foreign Affairs, The
   Most Hon. the Marquess of Salisbury, K.G.
   (*Prime Minister*) £5,000
Private Secretaries to Prime Minister, Hon.
   Schomberg K. McDonnell, C.B., £400; Visct.
   Newport £250; Evelyn Cecil, M.P. ....unp.
Private Sec. to Secretary of State for Foreign
   Affairs, Hon. Eric Barrington, C.B...........£300
Assist. do., Lord Monkbretton ....unpaid
Précis Writer Henry St. George Foley ...£300

UNDER SECRETARIES.

Permanent, Sir Thos. H. Sanderson, K.C.B. £2,000
   Private Sec., William George Tyrrell........£150
Parliamentary, Rt. Hon. St. John Brodrick
   M.P. £1,500
   Private Secs., Robert D. Norton, £150;
   Lord Edmund Talbot, M.P. ....unpaid
Asst. Under Secs., Hon. F. L. Bertie £1,500
   Hon. Francis Hyde Villiers, C.B. £1,200
   Sir Martin Gosselin, K.C.M.G., £1,000 to £1,200
Chief Clerk, Sir George Edward Dallas, Bart.
                          £1,000 to £1,200
Legal Adviser, Wm. Edward Davidson, C.B.,
   Q.C. £1,200
Senior Clerks, Sir Henry G. Bergne, K.C.M.G.
   (£1,200); Hon. Eric Barrington, C.B.; Sir
   Clement L. Hill, K.C.M.G.; Everard W. Wylde,
   C.M.G.; Wm. Acland Cockerell; Francis Alexander Campbell; Arthur Larcom . each £900 to
                                     £1,000
Assist. Clerks, Charles Augustus Hopwood, C.B.;
   Harry Farnall, C.M.G.; William Chauncy Cartwright, C.M.G.; Richard P. Maxwell; Walter
   L. F. G. Langley, C.B.; Wm. A. Law £700 to £800
Junior Clerks (1st Class), Edwd. A. W. Clarke;
   G. F. Fairholme; Eyre A. Crowe; Ph. Alphonso Somers-Cocks; H. St. G. Foley; William
   Geo. Tyrrell; Edw. R. E. Vicars; Robt. D.
   Norton; Beilby F. Alston; Lord Terence
   Blackwood; J. A. C. Tilley; Harry B. Brooke;

Hon. W. A. F. Erskine; Gerald S. Spicer;
Charles S. Somers-Cocks; Ronald J. Hamilton;
Wm. Edmund O'Reilly; Francis O. Lindley;
G. R. Clerk; M. A. Robertson ... £200 to £600
Junior Clerks (2nd Class) R. A. C. Sperling; E. G.
Lister; R. H. Greg; V. A. Wellesley... £100 to
£200
Assistant, Chief Clerk's Dept., E. B. Newman £750
Clerks in Chief Clerk's Department, Hanson Werry
Fraser; Frederick E. Ellis .... each £500
Staff Officer, Walter R. Wallis .... £300 to £450
Librarian, &c., Augustus Henry Oakes
£700 to £1,000
Assist. Librarian's Dept., F. H. T. Streatfeild
£550 to £650
Clerks in Librarian's Department, R. W. Brant;
G. J. de Bernhardt; Nicholas A. Ball; G. E. P.
Hertslet .... £100 to £500
Treaty Dept., Ch. Boyd Robertson £700 to £1,000
Assistant in do., W. R. D. Maycock £550 to £650
Clerks in do., R. Follett Synge, C.M.G.; E. G.
Wetherall .... £100 to £500
Oriental Translator, Charles Wells............ £175
Second Division Clerks, E. J. Cooper; W. L. Ber-
row; John Gritton (*Higher Grade*); F. H.
White; Harry L. Sherwood; Hugh Ritchie;
Frank Gritton; O.V. Blake; H. W. McQuown;
G. Badrick; E. Parkes; H. A. Slade; W. H.
Robinson; P. C. Rice; D. A. Leak; W. E.
Fuller; C. S. Nicoll; H. O. Baker; H. S.
Martin; J. H. Mears; B. Westell; L. G.
Brown; W. Weighell; J. W. Field £70 to £350
Queen's Foreign Service Messengers, Capt. P. H. M.
Wynter; Harry A. Taylor; J. Hicks Graves;
F. E. Raikes .... each £400
Do., Guy Ewen; Capt. H. K. Stewart; A. J.
Mounteney-Jephson; A. Herbert......each £325
Home Service Messengers, Murdoch Mackenzie;
Robert King Hall; William Boyle; Edward W.
Newberry, each £200. *2nd Class:* J. Wilson;
E. G. Pearson; A. E. Morbey; J. C. Veasey
each £150

FRIENDLY SOCIETIES' REGISTRY,
Central Office, 28 Abingdon Street, S.W.—£7,112
Chief Registrar, E. W. Brabrook, C.B., F.S.A. £1,500
Assist. Registrar, J. D. Stuart Sim............... £800
Chief Clerk, G. Brown............... £400 to £500
Clerks, G. Cheney; W. H. Tozer...£250 to £400
Actuarial Clerk, A. M. Leveaux ....£200 to £400

GENERAL REGISTER OFFICE,
Somerset House, W.C.—£39,884.
Registrar-General, Sir Br. P. Henniker, Bt. £1,200
Chief Clerk, Noel A. Humphreys £900
Sup. of Statistics, J. F. W. Tatham, M.A., M.D...£900
Do. of Records, James Lewis £750
Do. Accounts & Stores, R. Thompson............£720
Assist. Superintendents, G. W. Searle, £550; J. C.
B. Ellis £540
Inspectors of Registration, G. Micklewood £480 ;
J. H. Shoveller £426
Senior Clerks, T. H. Mayhew; T. B. Dore; A. J.
Mundy; A. C. Waters; H. B. H. Tytheridge;
E. Bacon........................£350 to £500

GEOLOGICAL SURVEY OF THE UNITED KINGDOM.
Museum of Practical Geology, Jermyn St., £3,839
Dir. of Museum, Sir Arch. Geikie, D.C.L., F.R.S.£800
Curator and Librarian, F. W. Rudler £500
Assistant Curator, A. Pringle, M.A., B.SC......£250
Assistant Librarian, C. V. Crook, B.A. £150

SURVEY OF ENGLAND.—£8,860.
Director-Gen., Sir Arch. Geikie, D.C.L., F.R.S.£800
Director, Gt. Britain (vacant) £700

District Surveyor, H. B. Woodward, F.R.S. ...£480
Geologists, English Survey, R. H. Tiddeman, M.A.;
C. Fox-Strangways; J. J. H. Teall, M.A., F.R.S.;
W. A. E. Ussher; A. C. G. Cameron; Clement
Reid, F.R.S.; Aubrey Strahan, M.A.£275 to £400
Asst. Geologists, J. H. Blake; C. E. Hawkins;
A. J. Jukes-Browne, B.A.; J. B. Hill, R.S.;
G. W. Lamplugh; W. Gibson; T. I. Pocock,
M.A.; T. C. Cantrill, B.SC.; W. Pollard, D.SC.;
C. B. Wedd, B.A.; F. E. L. Dixon, B SC.£127 to
£225
Palæontologist, E. T. Newton, F.R.S. £500
Assistant ditto, F. L. Kitchin, PH.D. £160
Curator of Fossils, H. A. Allen £170
General Assistant, H. J. Gray £183
Assistant Clerk, P. M. O'Connor ......£100 to £150
Assist. in Fossil Dept., J. Rhodes £120

SURVEY OF SCOTLAND.—£4,194.
District Surveyor, B. N. Peach, F.R.S. £500
Geologists, R. G. Symes, M.A.; S. B. Wilkinson;
J. Horne, F.R.S.E.; W. Gunn; C. T. Clough, M.A.
£275 to £400
Asst. Geologists, J. S. Grant-Wilson; G. Barrow;
Lionel Hinxman, B.A.; Alfred Harker, M.A.;
H. Kynaston, B.A.; E. H. Cunningham-Craig,
B.A. .... £127 to £255
Curator of Survey Collect., J. G. Goodchild...£350
Assist. in Fossil Dept., A. Macconochie £150
Resident Assistant, R. Lunn £183
Fossil Collector, D. Tait £73

SURVEY OF IRELAND.—£2,054.
Senior Geologist, J. Nolan £500
Geologists, F. W. Egan, B.A.; J. R. Kilroe; Alex-
ander McHenry.................£275 to £400
Assist. Geologist, H. J. Seymour, B.A. £146
Assist. in Fossil Dept., R. Clark £150

HOME OFFICE, Whitehall, S.W.—£35,109.
Principal Secretary of State for Home Affairs,
Rt. Hon. Sir M. White Ridley, Bt., M.P.£5,000
Private Sec., J. A. Longley.......................£300
Assist. do., J. Pedder (£100) ; Matthew White
Ridley ; and Capt. T. F. Bagot, M.P. ......unp

UNDER SECRETARIES.
Permanent, Sir Kenelm Edward Digby, K.C.B.£2,000
Private Secretary, G. A. Aitken £150
Parliamentary, Rt. Hon. Jesse Collings, M.P.£1,500
Private Sec., Robert F. Reynard £150
Assistant Under Secretaries, Hy. Hardinge S.
Cunynghame (*Legal*) £1,200 to £1,500; Chas.
Stewart Murdoch, C.B ... £1,000 to £1,200
Principal Clerks, Charles E. Troup, C.B.; Harry B.
Simpson; Wm. P. Byrne ......£900 to £1,000
Senior Clerks, Charles Deffell; F. J. Dryhurst;
Malcolm Delevigne ....£700 to £800
Junior Clerks, Robert F. Reynard; G. A. Aitken;
A. J. Eagleston; J. Pedder; C. Lubbock; W.
Wheeler; M. L. Waller; F. L. D. Elliott
£200 to £500
Clerk of Accounts, George H. Tripp..£400 to £700
Assistant Clerk of Accounts, S. M. Grünwald
£310 to £400
Clerk for Statist. Retns., W. J. Farrant £350 to £500
Clerk for Mineral Statistics, James B. Jordan £400
Superintendent of Registry, E. E. B. Boehmer
£353 to £600
Assist. do., C. A. Bradford ......£280 to £350
Second Division Clerks (Higher Grade), Gordon A.
Lewis ; A. H. Eggett; W. C. Platt; and W. W.
Ware ....£250 to £350
Senior Clerk to H.M. Chief Inspector of Factories,
W. Peacock.............................£250
Clerk in Charge of Factory Statistical Branch, L. W.
Thomas...............................£230

Second Assistant Superintendent of the Registry, A. Locke £220
Consulting Surveyor (Temporary), H. T. Steward.
Official Analysts, Thomas Stevenson, M.D., and Arthur Pearson Luff, M.D.

Factory Department, Home Office.—£53,912.
H.M.'s Ch. Insp., Arth. Whitelegge, M.D. £1,200
 H.M.'s Superintending Inspectors, W. D. Cramp, Birmingham; E. Gould, Whitehall; R. W. Cooke-Taylor, Glasgow; W. A. Beaumont, Leeds; J. A. Redgrave, Whitehall; H. S. Richmond, Manchester ....£550 to £700
Medical Inspr., T. M. Legge, M.D. £600 to £800
 H.M.'s Inspectors (1st Class), G. I. L. Blenkinsopp, Whitehall; J. Jones, Plymouth; Capt. H. W. Kindersley, Edinburgh; A. G. K. Woodgate, Whitehall; C. C. W. Hoare, Whitehall; J. S. Maitland, Bristol; Commander H. P. Smith, R.N., Sheffield; Capt. James F. Bevan, Southampton; S. H. Kuyvett, Birmingham; Major Eugène M. Roe, Manchester; Arthur Powis Vaughan, Whitehall; J. D. Prior, Huddersfield ......£410 to £550
J. A. Hine, Leeds; W. Williams, Blackburn; H.M. Robinson, Glasgow; Aug. Lewis, Swansea, 2nd Class; R. P. Arnold, Worcester; G. B. Snape, Belfast; J. Pearson, Lincoln; J. T. Birtwistle, Blackburn; Rowland Tinker, Manchester; G. Sedgwick, Leicester; C. W. Shaw, Whitehall; Jas. Hen. Walmsley, Stoke-on-Trent; D. Walmsley, Stockport; J. E. Ashworth, Wolverhampton; R. Johnson, Newcastle-on-Tyne; Joseph Law, Preston; R. E. Graves, Liverpool; Jas. Hen. Rogers, Derby; Gerald Bellhouse, Dublin; O. A. Shinner, Norwich; C. F. Wright, Northampton; C. R. Pendock, Whitehall; J. Jackson, Wolverhampton; H. J. Wilson, Dundee; K. H. Garvie, Halifax; W. H. Seal, Bradford; J. M. Arbuckle, Glasgow; G. A. Taylor, Burnley; F. J. Parkes, Nottingham; J. E. Harston, Whitehall; J. Dodgson, Manchester; T. O. Edwards, Swansea; J. H. Crabtree, Manchester; J. Hilditch, Wrexham; T. C. Butler, Whitehall ....£300 to £400
Junior Inspectors, A. Platt, Manchester; S. Shuter, Bristol; A. Newlands, Glasgow; Eliot F. May, Stoke-on-Trent; John Law, Leeds; Harry Verney, Leeds; W. S. Smith, Manchester; S. Eraut, Liverpool; J. H. Nicholl, Stourbridge; W. Buchan, Glasgow; W. F. Ireland, Whitehall; E. V. Clark, Newcastle-on-Tyne; James Kellett, Belfast; A. Wolfe, Birmingham; W. J. Bremner-Davis, Whitehall; H. J. Peacock, Bradford; W. J. Neely, Dublin; H. C. D. Fearon, Whitehall; W. Lauder, Liverpool; Thos. Taylor, Sheffield; A. F. Dunolly, Huddersfield; D. D. Kirkwood, Aberdeen & Dundee; E. S. Wilson, Southampton; L. P. Evans, Birmingham; T. Brown, Glasgow; W. H. Beverley, Manchester; T. Owen, Whitehall ....£200 to £300
H.M. Inspector under Clause 40 of the Factory & Workshop Act, 1895. T. Birtwistle, Accrington £400
 Assistants, H. Taylor, Huddersfield; E. J. Holmes, Accrington; J. T. Ashton, Oldham ..£150 to £250
H.M.'s Principal Lady Inspector, Miss A. M. Anderson, Whitehall; H.M. Lady Inspectors, Miss M. M. Paterson, Glasgow; Miss L. A. E. Deane, Whitehall; Miss R. E. Squire, Whitehall; Miss Anna Tracey, Whitehall; Miss E. Sadler, Whitehall; Miss M. Vines, Whitehall ......£200 to £300
Engineering Adviser, E. H. Osborn, Manchester.

Inspectors.
Of Explosives, Home Office.—£5,030.
Insp. (Chief), Capt. J. H. Thomson, late R.A. ....£800 to £1,000

Inspectors, Major A. McN. C. Cooper-Key, R.A.; Capt. M. B. Lloyd, R.A.; Capt. A. P. H. Desborough, R.A. ....£500 to £800
Chemical Adviser, Dr. Dupré, F.R.S.

Inspectors of Mines.—£35,430.
Of Coal and Metalliferous Mines.
Inspectors, Frank Newby Wardell, Wath, Rotherham, £1,000; Henry Hall, Rainhill, Lancs.; W. B. Scott, Handsworth, Birmingham, £900; J. M. Ronaldson, Athole Gardens, Glasgow, £900 J. S. Martin, Durdham Park, Bristol; J. T. Robson, Swansea, £900; A. H. Stokes, Greenhill, Derby; J. B. Atkinson, 10 Foremost Terrace, Glasgow; W. N. Atkinson, Barlaston, Stoke-on-Trent; J. L. Hedley, 2 Devonshire Ter., Newcastle-on-Tyne; J. Gerrard, Worsley, Manchester; R. D. Bain, Durham......£600 to £800
Assistant Inspectors, W. H. Pickering, Wolverhampton; R. McLaren, Uddingston, Glasgow; W. H. Hepplewhite, St. Anne's Hill, Nottingham; Jas. Mellors, Outwood, Wakefield; J. Plummer, Bishop Auckland; G. F. Bell, Newcastle-on-Tyne; F. A. Gray, Neath; Hugh Johnstone, 27 Montgomerie Street, Glasgow; W. Saint, Manchester; W. Walker, Durham; Thos. H. Mottram, 3 Beauly Terrace, Kelvinside, N. Glasgow; H. R. Makepeace, Stoke-on-Trent; Henry R. Hewitt, 23 Hartington Street, Derby; Edward E. V. Stokes, Truro; J. D. Lewis, 183 Richmond Road, Roath, Cardiff; A. Pearson, Rutherglen, Glasgow; D. H. F. Mathews, Hoole, Chester; J. R. R. Wilson, 1 St. Mary's Road, Leeds; George B. Harrison, Swinton, Manchester; George F. Adams Cardiff; Wm. Leck, Cleator Moor; Fredk. N. White, Mirador Crescent, Swansea; C. L. Robinson, Newport (Mon.); A. D. Nicolson, 25 Spencer Street, Carlisle ....£300 to £400
Of Metalliferous Mines.
Inspector, Dr. Clement Le Neve Foster, Llandudno £900
Assistant Inspectors, G. J. Williams, Coed Menai, Owen R. Jones, 5 Spring Gdns., Hoole, Chester. ....£300 to £40?

Of Burial Grounds.—Habitual Inebriates.—£1,00?
Medical Inspector, H. W. Hoffman, M.A., M.B.£6 00
Inspector of Certified Inebriate Reformatories (under the Inebriates Act, 1898) and Assist. Inspr. of Retreats, R. W. Branthwaite, L.R.C.P. ......£ 00
Assistant Inspr. of Burial Grounds, A. N. Weir, D.SC. (temporary)

Under Cruelty to Animals Act.—£522.
Inspector, Geo. D. Thane, junr., M.R.C.S. £315
Assistant do., Sir J. A. Russell, LL.D. £210

Of Anatomy, 30 Abingdon Street.—£1,00 7.
Metropolis, Wm. Henry Bennett, F.R.C.S. £100
Provinces, Thomas Pickering Pick, F.R.C.S. ...£100
Edinburgh, Sir Jas. Alexander Russell, LL.D. £100
Inspectors County & Boro' Constabulary.—£3,125.
Hon. Charles E. Legge; Capt. Francis Joseph Parry; Sir Herbert George Denman Croft, Bart. ....£750 to £850

Reformatory and Industrial Schools, Great Scotland Yard, S.W.—£7,625.
Inspector, J. G. Legge ....£800 to £1,000
Assist. Inspectors, T. D. M. T. Robertson; William Costeker; Hon. N. C. Walsh .....£420 to £620
Sub-Inspectors, A. G. S. Maule; L. J. Heath, £250 to £400; Lieut.-Col. C. Cunningham (temporary) £300

PRISON COMMISSION, Home Office, S.W. —£604,696.
Chairman, Evelyn John Ruggles-Brise, C.B. £1,800
Private Secretary, I. Turvey.....................£100

Prison Commissioners and Directors of Convict Prisons, R. S. Mitford, £1,100; Lt.-Col. M. Clare Garsia; H. B. Donkin, M.D. £1,000
Sec. & Insp., Major E. G. Clayton, R.E. £700 to £800
Surveyor, Lt.-Col. A. Beamish, R.E. £650 to £900
Clerk of Accounts, C. Crickmay........£550 to £650
Comptroller of Prison Industries, James Duncan
....£700 to £800
Insps., Capt. W. V. Harris: Capt. L. P. Penne-thorne; Maj. W. N. Darnell; Herbert Smalley, M.D. (*Medical Insp.*) ....£700 to £800
Assistant Surveyor, U. J. Wright......£300 to £350
1st Class Clerks, C. S. Joseph; W. B. Penny; T. R. Whiteley; H. H. Cribb; J. R. Bradshaw, £350 to £500; I. Turvey ....£280 to £480
2nd Class Clerks, H. E. Williams; C. H. Arnold; H. R. Bennett; J. N. Cole; J. Dawe; J. J. Griffith; W. Hoskins; J. Juleff; S. H. Roberts; F. J. Rhodes; E. Brine; W. S. Westland, £70 to £370; F. J. Price; C. Hall; A. T. Turpin; C. M. Overton; W. J. Pond; J. B. Scriven
....£70 to £300

MILITARY PRISON DEPARTMENT, Home Office, S.W.

Inspector-General, Colonel M. Clare Garsia.
Inspectors, Major E. G. Clayton; Capt. W. F. V. Harris; Capt. L. P. Pennethorne; Major W. N. Darnell.
Aldershot Prison—Governor, Major R. A. Hender-son; *Medical Officer*, Lt.-Col. W. F. Ruttledge.
Colchester Prison—Chief Warder in Charge, P. Prior.
Gosport Prison—Governor, Lt.-Col. H. Waring; *Medical Officer*, Capt. E. Chandler.
Kendal Prison—Governor, Major C. D. Johnstone.
York Prison—Chief Warder in Charge, A. Mason.
Cork Prison—Governor, Major R. W. Andrews; *Medical Officer*, Lt.-Col. U. A. Jenings.
Dublin Prison—Governor, Capt. G. S. Haines; *Medical Officer*, Lt.-Col. N. Alcock.
Malta Prison—Governor, Major G. A. P. Evans.
Chief Warders in Charge: Stirling; J. Martin; *Barbados*, J. B. Arnott: *Bermuda*, T. Curran; *Cairo*, W. H. Thacker; *Gibraltar*, J. Reynolds; *Halifax (Nova Scotia)*, J. Godfrey; *Kandy (Ceylon)*, J. Bird; *Wynberg (Cape Colony)*, H. Williams.

General Prisons Board, Ireland.—£8,914.

Chairman, J. S. Gibbons, C.B. £1,200
Vice-Chairman, John Mulhall £1,000
Medical Member, Dr. S. Woodhouse..£800 to £900
Inspectors, P. J. Joyce; W. V. Harrel each £600
Secretary, S. H. Douglass..................£350 to £450
Clerk of Accounts, R. Lewis ....£350 to £450

INDIA OFFICE, St. James's Park, S.W. £189,000.

Principal Secretary of State, Right Hon. Lord George Francis Hamilton, M.P. £5,000
Private Sec., Richmond T. W. Ritchie, C.B...£300
Parliamentary Do., Gerald Loder, M.P. ......unp.
Assist. Private Secretary and Précis Writer, F. T. C. Hastings..................................£150
Political A.-de-C., Sir Gerald Seymour Vesey-Fitzgerald, K.C.I.E. £800

UNDER SECRETARIES.

Permanent, Sir Arthur Godley, K.C.B. £2,000
Private Sec., John Edward Ferard £150
Parliamentary, The Earl of Onslow, G.C.M.G. £1,500
Private Sec., Frederick Arthur Hirtzel £150
Asst. Under Sec., Sir Horace G. Walpole, K.C.B.£1,200

COUNCIL.

Vice-President, Francis Charles Le Marchant.
Field-Marshal Sir Donald Martin Stewart, Bt.,

G.C.B.; Sir James Braithwaite Peile, K.C.S.I.; Sir Alfred Comyns Lyall, G.C.I.E.; Sir Chas. H, Tod Crosthwaite, K.C.S.I.; Sir Steuart Colvin Bayley, K.C.S.I.; Gen. Sir J. J. H. Gordon, K.C.B.; Sir James Lyle Mackay, K.C.I.E.; Sir Dennis Fitzpatrick, K.C.S.I.; Sir Philip Perceval Hutchins, K.C.S.I.; Sir John Edge; Sir James Westland, K.C.S.I. ....each £1,200
Clerk of the Council, Sir Horace Geo. Walpole, K.C.B.
Reading Clerk to the Council, Hermann A. Haines,£250
Res. Clks., M. C. C. Seton; A. R. B. Vaux, each £50

CORRESPONDENCE DEPARTMENT.

Financial, Sir Henry Waterfield, K.C.S.I. .. £1,200
Assistant, Stapleton C. Hogg......£800 to £1,000
Military, Maj.-Gen. Sir E. Stedman, K.C.I.E..£1,200
Assistant, Fras. Whitmore Smith £800 to £1,000
Revenue and Statistics, Sir Charles Edward Bernard, K.C.S.I...................................£1,200
Assist., Henry Hill ....£800 to £1,000
Political and Secret, Sir William Lee Warner, K.C.S.I...................................£1,200
Assistant, Colin G. Campbell ......£800 to £1,000
Public Works, Edmund Neel, C.I.E...............£1,200
Assistant, Fredk. C. Thompson...£800 to £1,000
Judicial and Public, Sir Charles James Lyall, K.C.S.I...................................£1,200
Assistant, W. Neville Sturt ......£800 to £1,000
Senior Clerks, Chas. N. B. Franks; Francis B. Armstrong; Jas. H. Seabrooke; Patrick H. C. Herbert; Francis W. Newmarch; Richmond T. W. Ritchie, C.B.; Hermann A. Haines; Francis C. Drake; Edward Franks; Henry L. Seccombe............................£600 to £800
Junior Clerks, B. Lionel Abrahams; John Edward Ferard; W. T. Bonson; W. Robin-son; F. A. Hirtzel; M. C. C. Seton; W. Stantiall.................................£200 to £600
Clerk specially attached to Political and Secret De-partment, F. T. C. Hastings ......£350 to £500
Clerk for Army Non-Effective Accounts, Walter James Greene ....£300 to £500
Staff Clerk, S. Keith ....£350 to £500

ACCOUNTANT-GENERAL'S DEPARTMENT.

Accountant-General, Edward Raban Cave-Browne, C.S.I...................................£1,200
Deputy do., Arthur Guillum Scott...£800 to £1,000
Senior Clerks, E. F. Bishop; A. M. Carter; J. Hewish; H. W. Badock; I. H. Humphrys; R. G. Jaquet; W. S. Durrant .....£500 to £700
Junior Clerks, F. Perrott; A. W. Housley; J. Johnson; S. G. Smith; J. H. F. Reed; G. H. Stoker
....£150 to £500
Staff Clerks, E. Owen, A. J. Pattle ..£350 to £500

FUNDS DEPARTMENT.

Director, Fredrick G. B. Trever ...£800 to £1,000
Senior Clerk, George F. Teague ...£500 to £700
Clerk, John Willis......................£200 to £450

STORE DEPARTMENT.

Director-General, Edwin Grant Burls £1,200
Deputy do., Robert George Crozier £800 to £1,000
Senior Clerks, William Lindsay; John M. Wigner; S. A. Taylor; William G. Butler; Frederick C. B. Wright; Henry J. W. Fry; George Herman Collier ....£500 to £700
Junior Clerk, Richard R. Howlett ..£150 to £500
Staff Clerk, F. T. Eades ....£350 to £500

BRANCH AT DÉPÔT, Belvedere Road, Lambeth.

Superintendent, Commander G. T. Wingfield, R.N...£800
Assistant do., William E. Phelps...................£600
Supervisors, 1st Grade, Gerald H. Talbot; W. Edgell; W. H. Hooker; J. Byatt...£350 to £500

Inspector, *Scientific Instruments*, Thomas Cushing
....£600
Examiner, *Surgical ditto*, Surg.-Maj. Nottidge
Charles Macnamara, F.R.C.S. £50
" *Medical Stores*, Charles J. H. Warden, M.D
....£300
Surveyor of Shipping, Capt. T. Coulter Kerr...£50

REGISTRY AND RECORD DEPARTMENT.

Registrar and Superintendent of Records, A. Naylor
Wollaston, C.I.E. £1,000
Principal Assistant, Percy J. Rowlands
....£500 to £700
Assistant, Chas. Morgan (*Despatch Clerk*), £350
to £650; M. S. Hall ....£350 to £500

MISCELLANEOUS APPOINTMENTS.

Government Director of *Indian Railway Companies*,
Col. Sir William S. S. Bisset, R.E., K.C.I.E. £1,000
Dep. Do., William James Maitland, C.I.E. £600
Assistant ditto, Henry Hill £100
Director in Chief of the *Indo-European Telegraph
Department*, B. T. Ffinch, C.I.E. £1,100
Clerk, C. E. J. Twisaday ....£320 to £500
Librarian, Charles Henry Tawney, C.I.E. ...£600
Assistant ditto, Fredk. W. Thomas............£350
Member of Committee for *Valuation of Military
Equipment*, Colonel G. A. Crawford, R.A. ...£500
Assistant ditto, W. J. Bowden .... £250 to £400

MEDICAL BOARD, for the Examination of Officers.
(Tuesday, at 1 o'clock.)

President, Surg.-Gen. William Roe Hooper, C.S.I.
....£600
Member, Brig.-Surg.-Lt.-Col. E. F. Drake-Brock-
man (I.M.S., retired) £300
Legal Adviser and Solicitor to Secretary of State,
Sir Arthur Wilson, K.C.I.E. £1,200
Assist. to Solicitor, Wm. H.Treasure £400 to £550
Actuary, Willis Browne, F.I.A. ......£600 to £800
Surv. and Clerk of the Works, T. H. Winny, A.R.I.B.A.
....£300 to £400
Ordnance Consulting Officer, Col. J. G. Stone, R.A.
....£500
Consulting Engineer, Sir Alex. M. Rendel, K.C.I.E.
Special Duty, *Paris Exhibition*, Sir Geo. C. M.
Birdwood, M.D., LL.D., K.C.I.E.
Stockbroker, Willie A. W. Scott, 57 Old Broad
Street, E.C.
Assistant Military Secretary for Indian Affairs at
the War Office, Col. Beauchamp Duff, C.I.E.
....£1,000
Official Agent to Administrators-General of India,
F. G. B. Trevor.

INDIA AUDIT OFFICE.—£6,133.

Auditor, William Godsell £1,000
Assistant to Auditor, F. C. Holiday £700 to £800
Senior Clerks, A. Benger; W. A. St. Quintin;
H. W. Harding; S. H. Everett ...£500 to £700
Junior Clerks, H. D. Poulton; H. A. Cooper
....£150 to £500
[The business of the Overland Troopship Service
is conducted by Rear-Admiral Bouverie F. Clark,
Director of Transport Services at the Admiralty.]

INLAND REVENUE OFFICES.—£1,966,232.
Somerset House, W.C.

Establishment Charges, England, £254,584.
Chairman, Sir H. W. Primrose, K.C.B., C.S.I. £2,000
Private Secretary, P. Williamson £100
Deputy Chairman, Sir F. Lacy Robinson, K.C.B.
....£1,500
Private Secretary, ...£50
Commissioners, Edmond Henry Wodehouse, C.B.;
Bernard Mallet............each £1,200

Special Commissioners of Income Tax.

Senior Commissioner, George Chew £800
Junior Commissioners, Walter Gyles; H. W. Page-
Phillips ....each £700

Secretaries' Department.

Joint Secretaries, T. N. Crafer (*Stamps & Taxes*);
James B. Meers (*Excise*) ....each £1,200
Assistant-Secretaries, E. E. N. Bower (also Regis-
trar of Land Tax) £1,000; H. Fogelstrom
Bartlett (*Stamps & Taxes*); J. P. Byrne;
Augustus H. Browne (*Excise*) .....£825 to £900
Chief of the Income Tax Repayments Branch, E. E.
Stoodley ....£825 to £900
Committee Clerks, M. S. Jackson; J. Mayhew;
J. E. Chapman; H. G. L. Shand...£725 to £800
Principal Clerks, J. A. Allanson; F. Atterbury;
C. Hallett; A. Spiller; P. Duncan; W. H.
Pascoe; J. P. Harding ....£600 to £700
Deputy Registrar of Land Tax, C. C. Atchison £750
Upper Division Clerks, C. S. West; C. A. Barrett;
C. S. Carter; E. E. Turnley; P. Williamson;
J. L. S. Smith; A. Grasemann; P. Thompson;
J. Jacob; H. A. A. Cruso; E. C. Cunningham;
W. J. Braithwaite, R. V. Vernon
at various personal salaries.
Chief Examiners of Income Tax Claims, F. H.
Baker; J. E. Bates ....each £550
Inspector of Railway Accounts, A. B. Samson £550
Inspector of Foreign Dividends, T. W. Roberts £550
Deputy Chief Examiners of Income Tax Claims,
C. Herbert; E. M. Tardif ...... £400 to £500
Examiners of Assessments, W. T. Coggins; E. O. H.
Fossey ....£400 to £500
Minor Staff Officers (*arranged alphabetically*), W.
J. Back; H. Birtles; J. Burns; E. E. Darke;
J. J. Edney; C. J. S. Gold; E. T. A. Kennedy;
E. H. Lambert; H. V. Osmond; A. Saker;
J. T. Sargent; J. Simpson; T. E. Swain; G.
Wells; W.H. Wright, £300 to £400; W.A.Collins;
E. C. Dodwell; W. N. Kennedy; G. T.
Nicholls; A. R. Reeves; J. A. Thompson
....£250 to £350
Superintendent of Stamps on the Stock Exchange,
W. Adams ....£600 to £800
Deputy Superintendent, W. Brown ...£300 to £400

Accountant and Comptroller-General's Department.

Account. & Comt.-Gen., Chas. G. Turner, C.B. £1,200
Assistant do., Alfred Stair £900
Principal Accountant, James Butler............£750
Accountants & Cashier, T. Trenery; J. Sansom;
G. A. Thompson; Geo. W. Maunder; Robert
L. Blachford; George T. Messervy; Henry F.
Clarke (*Cashier*) ....£550 to £700
Assistant Accountants & Assistant Cashier, Edmund
W. L. Ryves; Frederick Dutton; A. Millard;
Julius E. Pitcher (*Assistant Cashier*); H. C.
Strutt; Frederick A. Innell; Herbert C. King;
William H. Moore (Manchester); W. C.
Homersham ....£440 to £550
Clerks (*Old Establishment*), A. Baxter; George
Marshall; Henry Rice; at various personal
salaries.
Minor Staff Officers (*arranged alphabetically*), E.
Adams; B. Bramble; E. S. Chapman; J. E.
Howe; J. H. Maunder; J. Radforde; W. P.
Reynolds; J. Talbot; C. V. G. G. Yorke
....£300 to £400

Chief Inspector's Department—Excise.

Chief Inspector, F. L. Lambert ...£1,000 to £1,100
Assistant Chief Inspector, S. D. Leah £900
Superintending Inspectors, C. E. Langley; J.
Evans; T. Kelly; J. A. G. Sanders £725 to £800
1st Class Inspectors, J. N. Hobbs £700; C. F.
Cooke; J. Forrester; A. J. Eaton; R. D.

McGlasban; J. Robertson; J. W. Bailey; E. Russell; H. Magowan; J. B. Mant; D. A. Woozley; J. O'Halloran ....£550 to £650
2nd Class Inspectors, M. J. O'Loughlin; P. Hallaghan; H.E. Clifford; J. G. Cunningham; J. F. Mitchell; W. Gallagher; J. O'Hea; J. Duncan; J. Adams; J. Murphy; H. F. D. West; J. T. Mulqueen; W. H. Cogman £450
Detective Inspector, A. J. Llewellin £450

Chief Inspector's Department—Taxes.

Chief Inspector, W. H. Last £1,100
Superintending Inspectors, G. Fawcett; J. G. Musgrave (Edinburgh); G. J. Rawes; G. W. Wicker ....£725 to £800
Inspectors, W. Holtham; R. Compton; T. M. Jeans; W. L. Gough; W. N. Strangeways (*Ireland*); W. Gayler; W. Male; J. Russell (*Edinburgh*); A. Bain (*Edinburgh*); A. J. Apthorpe; S. G. Carter; G. C. Leslie; J. Scott; G. N. Moore ....£620 to £700
Surveyors attached to Chief Office, G. H. Blunden; E. Lambert; C. H. Rickman; T. Collins; E. Clark; J. J. Hoddinott; H. L. Loney; J. Jackson; J. Lawson; W. Webb; G. L. Williams; W. Emm; H. Wright.

Estate Duty Department.

Secretary, R. J. Wallace £1,400
Assistant Secretary, A. A. Aymard .. £825 to £900
Legal Adviser, G. B. Rosher £1,000
Chief Clerks, A. J. King; W. Sutherland; Samuel P. Platt; W. H. Harrison; C. O. Minchin ....£725 to £800
Principal Clerks, T. A. Routh; S. Smale; J. A. Miall; W. Filmer Vaughan; Wm. Heaton Jacob; Alfred W. Soward; Reginald J. Shebbeare; A. L. Gardner; A. W. Norman; E. N. Kilvert; L. S. Lloyd ....£600 to £700
1st Class Clerks, G. E. Dreaper; Ellis Harris; R. J. Dale; Wm. M. Chute; Wm. A. Nathan; Wm. George; Thos. C. Collett; Edmund West; A. W. Smyth; Fredk. W. Rose; George E. Hurt; Aug. Ff. Powell; J. E. Pitcairn; F. H. Warner; G. H. Heath; E. Heard; F. H. Duffield; W. Winter; C. A. Addison; A. J. Bird; E. Rosenfeld; T. Robinson; Hy. Catling; Alfred Craske; J. H. A. Reay; G. D. Fish; Henry A. Laurie; Frederic H. Mainwaring; Edwin C. Saunders ....£500 to £580
2nd Class Clerks, Herbert L. Bramall; Henry J. Wolfe; Harry F. Rising; Reginald D. Etheridge; J. C. Correll; H. H. Clare; W. J. Allen; Charles H. Lyon; J. F. D. Latham; J. H. Gunyon; C. E. Fletcher; J. C. Denmead; L. W. Browne; G. D. Callender; J. H. Taylor; J. W. Brown; A. Hewitt; J. Gaskill; J. R. Redhead; H. Dearden; M. W. Watson; E. Mather; P. J. Roper; S. T. Mimpries; T. W. McCormick; W. F. G. Roberts; J. H. P. Gilbertson; T. McIver; H. J. R. Herford; J. D. Pearson; T. A. Prest; J. Barber; H. D. Scott; W. L. Gane; G. S. White; H. P. Dunning; W. V. Palmer; J. Dales £320 to £450
3rd Class Clerks, W. E. Lockwood; A. E. Hodgson; W. G. Todhunter; H. W. Osborn; E. H. L. Jones; E. McGowan; A. E. Durrant; H. P. C. Skingley; E. J. Nicholson; P. W. G. Wratislaw; F. E. Jeram; C. J. H. Hutchins; L. H. C. Watson; J. F. Rhodes; J. Buckley; A. J. Doyle; R. G. Vaughton; G. H. Barnes; E. P. Rider; R. W. Ingram; R. R. Ricketts; I. Stack; H. P. Brown; F. H. Gorle; T. C. S. Smith; T. A. England; E. Welch; A. W.

Cooper; J. H. Eley; E. Whitaker; A. Veasey; J. W. Lumb; A. G. Stantiall; J. A. H. Daniell; H. G. Bell; J. J. Cowper; W. E. Willan; C. D. Knox; A. H. Troughton; F. C. Lambert; F. J. Colson; F. P. Clark; A. H. Farez; A. Robinson; R. Dymond; J. B. Birch; H. L. White; J. F. Tarrant; H. McIlquham; W. Addison; C. Beatty; J. Marshall; G. L. Price; H. C. Sword; C. W. L. Tytheridge ....£150 to £300
Minor Staff Officers (arranged alphabetically), T. F. Callum; J. W. Jackson; A. H. Locke, £300 to £400; G. A. Allin, S. T. Lock .... £250 to £350

Edinburgh Branch Office.

Dep. Controller, J. E. Hope, w.s. £900
Principal Clerks, A. Thompson; H. Glanvill ....£600 to £700
1st Class Clerks, W. E. Brand; G. Ford; W. A. Ross ....£500 to £580
2nd Class Clerks, A. W. Lomax; W. A. Wilson ....£320 to £450
3rd Class Clerks, H. Robinson; W. R. Morison; S. M. Findlay; W. E. Redding .. £150 to £300
Minor Staff Officer, J. Sime ....£300 to £400

Dublin Branch Office.

Deputy Controller, Evelyn Freeth £900
Principal Clerks, William Pitt Bremner; W. H. Maunder.........................£625 to £700
1st Class Clerks, M. Miller; C. J. Wilson; Arthur Whewell ....£500 to £580
2nd Class Clerks J. Roche; T. E. O'Connor ....£320 to £450
3rd Class Clerks, J. Quinn; B. Collins; H. H. Grace; P. Harding; M. Kelly; J. A. Carroll ....£150 to £300
Minor Staff Officers (arranged alphabetically), J. Barter; J. Maguire ....£300 to £400

The Government Laboratory.

Principal, Dr. T. E. Thorpe, F.R.S. £1,200
　　　　(*Inland Revenue Branch.*)
Deputy Principal, H. J. Helm £800
Superintend. Analysts, G. Lewin; J. Cameron ....£600 to £700
1st Class Analysts, G. N. Stoker; C. H. Burge; H. W. Davis; E. G. Hooper; Charles Proctor; John Woodward ....£400 to £550
2nd Class do., E. Jones; J. H. Robbins; J. Connah; T. J. Cheater; G. Stubbs; C. Simmonds; D. A. Gracey ....£160 to £350

Department of Controller of Stamps and Registrar of Joint Stock Companies, Newspapers, and Bank Returns.

Controller and Registrar, J. S. Purcell, C.B. £1,200
Assistant Controller and Assistant Registrar, Ernest Cleave £880
Principal Clerks, H. Gore; F. R. Johnson; James Barber; J. H. Neilson; H. Dowsett; J. Keates ....£540 to £640
Senior Clerks, Walter Walker; H. F. Molyneux; E. H. Douet; W. J. Richards; D. M. Mackay; M. Symes ....£420 to £500
1st Class Clerks, G. W. Cornelius; R. Humphrey; W. W. Hewitt; T. W. Beckwith; G. Martin ....£310 to £400
2nd Class Clerk, C. H. Bokenham £300
Minor Staff Officers (arranged alphabetically), W. Battersby; D. H. Blyth; L. H. Clark; G. H. Hillman; J. F. Oakeshott; G. J. Sargent; A. E. Taylor; A. P. Theobald ....£300 to £400

Stamping Department.

Inspector, T. A. Colls £830
Deputy Inspector, S. J. Bennett.........£475 to £600

Chief Superintendents, William G. Page, £500; John Smith Sworder £450
Superintendents, 1st *Class*, William Rose; E. Barnes; C. Laker; E. Richards ..£260 to £350

Solicitor's Department.—£14,540.
Solicitor, Francis Charles Gore £2,000
Assist. Solicitors, Nathaniel J. Highmore, £1,200 ; J. Mudie £1,000
Chief Clerks, G. Brooke; J. Edwin Piper ....£600 to £850
Assistant Clerks, G. H. Denniss; Frederick W. W. Kingdon; B. F. Brodie; A. Holt Freeth; T. C. Bates; John Allen Slater (at various personal salaries.)

Medical Officer.
G. A. Hamerton, M.D., F.R.C.S. £400

IRISH SECRETARY'S OFFICE,
Old Great George Street, S.W.—£22,236.
And The Castle, Dublin.
Chief Secretary to the Lord Lieutenant of Ireland, Rt. Hon. Gerald William Balfour, M.P. £4,425
Private Secretary, Laurence C. Dowdall.
Under Secretary, Sir David Harrel, K.C.B....£2,000
Private Secretary, W. P. J. Connolly.
Assist. Und. Sec., J. B. Dougherty £1,000
Principal Clerks, 1st *Div.*, Arthur Robert Wallace, C.B., D.L.; Sir Fredk. J. Cullinan, C.B. ....each £1,000
1st Class Clerks (1st Section), Thomas Alex. O'Dell; William Brent Neville; James Henry Davies; Laurence C. Dowdall ....£420 to £600
1st Class Clerks (2nd Section), T. P. Le Fanu; W. P. J. Connolly; J. J. Taylor; R. E. Beckerson; S. J. M. Power...............£100 to £400
Registrar, George Gilchrist.............£350 to £500
2nd Div. Clerks (*Higher Grade*), C. T. Beard; W. A. Boyle; C. W. Gibbs ....£250 to £350
2nd Div., R. H. Wright; W. P. Henry; S. W. Strange; G. R. Heaney; W. St. John Joyce ....£70 to £250
Chief Clerk, Irish Office, London, J. J. Taylor.
Draftsman of Parl. Bills, R. Manders, B.L.

LANCASTER, DUCHY OF.
Office, Lancaster Place, Strand, W.C.
Chancellor, Rt. Hon. Lord James of Hereford £2,000
Private Sec., Herbert E. Mitchell.
Vice-Chancellor, Samuel Hall, Q.C.
Attorney-Gen., Robert Alfred McCall, Q.C.
Receiver-Gen., Lt.-Col. Rt. Hon. Sir Fleetwood Isham Edwards, K.C.B., R.E.
Auditor, Francis Alfred Hawker.
Clerk of Council & Registrar, Wm. Rose Smith.
Clerk in Court and Solicitor, Francis Whitaker.
Seal Keeper, Arthur Shuttleworth.
Cursitor, Alfred T. Davies.
Surveyor and Dep. Receiv.-Gen., J. Leonard Bolden.
Coroner, Samuel Frederick Langham.
Chief Clerk, Edward L. C. P. Hardy.
1st Class, do., H. Sydney Seymour.
2nd Class, do., H. E. Mitchell; P. J. Lynch.
Registrar, Preston Dist., Alexander Pearce.
Do. Liverpool Dist., F. Willis Taylor.
Do. Manchester Dist., Hubert Winstanley.

LOCAL GOVERNMENT BOARD,
Whitehall, S.W.—£197,085.
President, Rt. Hon. Henry Chaplin, M.P. ...£2,000
Private Secretary, E. D. Court £300
Do. The Hon. G. Walsh....... unp.
Assistant Private Secs., E. A. Goulding, M.P.; Hon. R. A. Ward, M.P. ....unp.
Parliamentary Sec., T. W. Russell, M.P. ...£1,200
Private Sec., A. B. Lowry £150
Permanent Sec., S. B. Provis, C.B.............£1,600
Private Sec., C. Knight £150

Legal Adviser, A. D. Adrian, C.B.................£1,200
Assist. Sec., W. E. Knollys, C.B., *and Chief General Inspector* £1,200
Do. Horace Cecil Monro £1,050
Do. Thomas Pitts £1,050
Do. John Lithiby £1,000
Do. Noel Thomas Kershaw £1,000
Principal Clerks, F. Stevens; Robert Cranston; Howel Thomas; H. C. H. H. Houndle; Wm. Wellington Conolly; D. Dolton; John Alfred E. Dickinson; J. R. C. Hall; Geo. P. Beckley; G. E. Wainwright ....£625 to £850
1st Class Clerks, Thomas Lefevre Austin; Wm. Lewis Simner; Robert Montague Barton; C. W. Bellamy; E. A. Browne; Hamilton Pullen; W. W. Armstrong; A. J. A. Ball; W. H. Dumsday; A. E. Wood; F. J. Willis; A. Chapman ....£500 to £600
2nd Class Clerks, Joseph B. Edmd. Collings; Edward Geer; William H. Green; Edward Fleming; Charles R. Hicks; Walter R. Woollven; George Biddell; P. Handford; S. A. Hertzberg; E. D. Court; A. B. Lowry; R. H. A. G. Duff; C. Knight; H. O. Stutchbury; R. C. Maxwell; W. T. Jerred; E. T. Owen; A. B. McLachlan; F. Taylor; R. T. L. Parr; H. A. Leggett; E. H. Rhodes; Aubrey Vere Symonds; C. B. R. Ellis; T. E. Bettany; G. H. L. Barnsdale; R. J. Simpson; E. S. Mills; W. R. Frazer; C. F. A. Hore; J. Orchard; C. E. Royds; G. R. Snowden; H. J. Comyns.....................£150 to £500
Clerk of Accounts, John Jorden ......£400 to £600
Supert. Index Depart., R. W. Dingle £400 to £500
Supert. of Registry, J. W. Coles .....£400 to £500
Supert. of Deposit, Reference, and Binding Department, A. J. Mason ....£400 to £500
Statistical Assistant, G. W.B.McLeod £400 to £500
Staff Clerks, J. W. Colton; C. J. Huddart; T. Lawrance; J. W. Davidson; A. A. Kent; T. R. Johnson; G. H. Follows ....£300 to £400
Other Staff Posts, and Higher Grade 2nd Div., F. C. Allworth; T. E. Cartwright; A. J. Eves; A. G. R. Giller; E. F. Gits; W. G. W. Goodworth; L. J. Harding; A. O. Hobbs; W. E. Ivey; J. Langton; A. Newton; L. W. Shubrook; W. J. Sutton; J. W. Trickey; F. L. Turner; F. J. Welch; and M. Wicks ......£250 to £350
Redundant Clerk, Benjamin Marshall Wilson, £255
Architect, Percival G. Smith £800
Assistant Architects, B. T. Kitchin £200 to £300; H. J. Pearson ....£250 to £300
Parliamentary Agent and Legal Assistant, Herbert E. Boyce £900
Legal Assistant, I. W. Baines ....£500 to £600
General Inspectors, F. T. Bircham; H. Lockwood; Herbert Jenner-Fust, jun.; Henry George Kennedy ....each £1,000
Do., Baldwyn Fleming; T. L. M. Browne; R. I. Dansey; J. S. Davy; Henry Stevens; C. A. Dawson; H. Preston Thomas; J. W. Preston; P. H. Bagenal; E. B. Wethered..£600 to £900
Medical Inspectors for Poor Law Purposes, A. H. Downes, M.D. £900; A. Fuller.................£600
Inspector of Local Loans, Local Acts, and Bye-laws, E. P. Burd £800
Insp. under Canal Boats Acts, O. J. Llewellyn, £500
Assist. General Inspectors, S. Barrington Tristram; W. M. Moorsom; Nicholas Herbert; G. A. F. Hervey, each £500; Miss Ina Stansfeld ....£200 to £300
Senior Insp. of Boarded-out Children, Miss M. H. Mason £400; *Inspector*, Miss F. M. Chapman ....£200 to £300

Inspectors of Poor Law Schools, John R. Mozley ; Byam Martin Davies ....£400 to £600
Inspector of Audits and Auditor of Accounts of the London C.C., Hugh Lloyd Roberts........£1,100
District Auditors, John F. Adams ; A. F. P. Barton ; G. H. Brett ; J. A. B. B. Bruce ; William A. Casson ; A. G. Chamberlin ; T. B. Cockerton ; J. A. Cole ; A. H. D. Cunynghame ; H. C. Darlington ; A. W. Dolby ; E. G. Easton ; J. M. Evans ; W. D. Easterby ; R. M. Estcourt ; R. B. Fellows (*assist.*); F. Gaskell ; G. L. Gibson ; H. D. Gordon ; W. Griffith ; C. F. Jordison ; R. H. Harrington ; G. E. Haslehurst ; P. J. Hibbert ; C. L. Hockin ; C. Hunton ; D. S. Jerrold ; J. H. Lilly ; J. O'Neill ; H. W. Oliver ; E. B. Prest ; Sir R. D. Green-Price, Bart. ; A. C. Roberts ; T. H. K. Roberts ; E. Stevens ; L. H. Wraith ; H. H. Walrond ; H. R. Williams.
(and expenses £14,931) £350 to £800
Chief Engineering Inspector, Maj.-Gen. C. Phipps Carey, R.E..........................£1,100
Deputy do., Col. J. O. Hasted, R.E..............£900
2nd do., Rienzi Walton, M.I.C.E. £900
Engineering Inspectors, Col. C. H. Luard, R.E. ; Major-Gen. Henry D. Crozier, R.E. ; F. H. Tulloch, M.I.C.E. ; G. W. Willcocks, M.I.C.E. ; Col. J. T. Marsh, R.E. ; Col. W. L. Coke ; R. H. Bicknell, M.I.C.E. ; W. O. E. Meadeking, M.I.C.E. ; W. A. Ducal, A.M.I.C.E. ; H. H. Law, A.M.I.C.E. ; H. P. Boulnois, M.I.C.E. ; E. A. S. Fawcett, A.M.I.C.E......................£600 to £800
Medical Officer, Sir R. T. Thorne, K.C.B., M.B. £1,500
Assist. do. & Medical Inspector for Gen. Sanitary Purposes, William Henry Power £1,100
2nd Assist. Med. Officer, Henry F. Parsons, M.D. £900
Medical Inspectors, Robt. Bruce Low, M.D. ; Richard D. R. Sweeting, M.B. ; Theodore Thomson, M.D. ; S. A. Copeman, M.D. ; W. W. E. Fletcher, M.B. ; Herbert T. Bulstrode, M.D. ; Arnold Royle, C.B. ; Richard James Reece, M.D. ; G. Seaton Buchanan, M.D. ; Samuel W. Wheaton, M.D. ; F. St. George Mivart, M.D. ; L. W. Darra Mair, M.D. ; R. W. Johnstone, M.D. £500 to £800
Assist. Insp. of Vaccine Lymph, Alb. B. Farn...£500
Dir. of Animal Vaccine Stn., R. Cory, M.D. £400
Assistant Director, T. Stott.......................£300
Vaccinators, R. Cory, M.D. ; Joseph Loane each £150
Bacteriologist for Glycerinated Calf Lymph, F. H. Blaxall, M.D. £500
Assistant Bacteriologist, H. S. Fremlin £300
Laboratory Assistants, H. V. Jerram ; E. Sullivan ; H. C. Gates ; and W. Witts.
Laboratory Clerk, W. F. Mulcahy £250
Assistant Clerks (temporary), J. Hauley and J. J. Comyn.
Chief Insp. Alkali, &c., Works, R. F. Carpenter, £800
Inspectors, E. G. Ballard ; E. Jackson ; A. C. Fryer, PH.D.........................£420 to £550
Resident Inspector, John Affleck £600
Sub-Inspectors, F. N. Sutton ; E. M. Fletcher ; H. Porter ; J. W. Young ....£300 to £400

METROPOLIS WATER ACT DEPARTMENT.

Water Examiner (vacant) £850
Auditor, Allen Stoneham £650

LOCAL GOVERNMENT BOARD FOR IRELAND.
£139,773.

President, Chief Secretary to the Lord Lieutenant.
Vice-President, Henry A. Robinson, C.B. ...£2,000
Private Secretary, E. W. C. Leach £100
Commissioners, The Under Secretary for Ireland ; Wm. Lawson Micks £1,200
Medical do., Thos. J. Stafford £1,200

Secretary, H. M. Swaine...........................£900
Assistant Secretary, D. J. MacSheahan, B.A. £700
Heads of Branches, H. Courtenay ; G. A. Mahon ; A. R. Barlas ; M. O'Sullivan ; and J. E. Devlin
£400 to £600
Inspectors, A. Bourke ; E. Bourke ; Major Ruttledge Fair ; R. C. Lynch ; Robt. Agnew ; Col. Kirkwood ; C. R. Lynch-Staunton ; R. Kelly
£500 to £700
Medical Inspectors, T. J. Browne ; C. J. Clibborn ; W. Edgar Flinn ; Sir J. Acheson MacCullagh
£500 to £700
Chief Engineering Insp., P. C. Cowan, M.I.C.E. £800
Engineering Inspectors, R. O'Brien Smyth, £400 ; L. E. H. Deane........................£350
Auditors, Captain Gibson ; C. Croker ; J. W. Drury ; R. J. Newell ; W. E. Ellis ; J. H. Calvert ; D. B. Sheehan ; C. D. Barry ; G. O. R. Wynne ; K. Bourke ....£400 to £700
Legal Adviser, James Henry Monahan, Q.C.
Solicitors, T. Tighe Mecredy and Son.

LORD GREAT CHAMBERLAIN'S OFFICE.
Royal Court, House of Lords, S.W.—£4,519.
Joint Hereditary Great Chamberlains, Earl of Ancaster, Earl Carrington, G.C.M.G., and Marquess of Cholmondeley.
Secretary, Capt. T. D. Butler £200
Clerk, W. B. Paley.............................£100
Resident Supt. House of Lords, J. K. Williams, £300

METEOROLOGICAL COUNCIL.
63 Victoria Street, S.W.—£15,300.
Chief of Council, Lt.-Gen. Sir R. Strachey, R.E., G.C.S.I.
Secretary, Robert H. Scott, D.SC., F.R.S.
Marine Suptd., Capt. M. W. Campbell-Hepworth, R.N.R.
Chief Clerk, J. S. Harding.
Senior Clerks, J. E. Cullum (*Valencia Observatory*) ; J. A. Curtis ; R. H. Curtis ; F. Gaster ; C. Harding ; R. Strachan.

MINT, THE ROYAL, Tower Hill, E.
(Salaries £36,400.)
Master and Worker, Chancellor of the Exchequer.
Deputy Master, Horace A. D. Seymour, C.B. £1,500
Chief Clerk, Arthur J. Pope............£550 to £700
Senior Clerk & Registrar, F. L. D. Matthews
£300 to £450
Staff Clerk, John Roe..................£300 to £400
Supt. Operative Dep., Edward Rigg, M.A.
£800 to £900
Assistant do., T. R. Sacheverell ; A. W. Cobbold
£310 to £400
Chemist and Assayer, Sir William Chandler Roberts-Austen, K.C.B., D.C.L., F.R.S........£900
Assistant Assayers, F. W. Bayly ; T. K. Rose, D.SC. ....£350 to £450

MUSEUM, THE BRITISH,
Bloomsbury, W.C.—£127,670.
Director and Principal Librarian, Sir Edward Maunde Thompson, K.C.B., D.C.L., LL.D. £1,500
Assistant Secretary, John T. Taylor £690
Accountant, John Cleave £650
Assistants, 1st Class, Francis Ellis Tucker ; H. Louis Goertz ; A. R. Dryhurst £300 to £500
Assistant, 2nd Class, E. B. Nicholson, B.A.
£150 to £300
2nd Div. Clerks, James Knowles (Staff) ; C. P. Cooke ; J. H. Witney ....£70 to £250
Keeper of Printed Books, George K. Fortescue
£700 to £900
Assistant Keepers, Robert E. Graves, B.A. ; Arthur W. Kaye Miller, M.A. ; William R. Wilson ....£520 to £65₀

Superint. of Reading Room, Wm. R. Wilson.
Assistants, 1st Class, Stephen J. Aldrich; Edward Dundas Butler, F.R.G.S.; Gregory W. Eccles; Richard H. Caunter; Dorset Eccles, V.D.; Henry Jenner, F.S.A.; Henry M. Mayhew; George F. Barwick; Cyril J. Davenport, V.D., F.S.A.; Alf. W. Pollard, M.A. .....£300 to £500
Assistants, 2nd Class, Samuel van Straalen, £350; John P. Anderson; P. Nisbet Bain; F. B. Fitzgerald Campbell; John Macfarlane; Wm. B. Squire, B.A., M.A., F.R.G.S.; John Abraham J. de Villiers; Lawrence H. E. Taylor; Robert F. Sharp, B.A.; R. A. Streatfeild, B.A.; B. H. Soulsby, B.A.; R. G. C. Proctor, B.A.; F. D. Sladen, B.A.; Henry Symons, B.A.....................£150 to £300
Keeper of Manuscripts and Egerton Librarian, Edward J. L. Scott, M.A. ....£700 to £800
Assistant Keepers MSS., G. F. Warner, M.A.; F. G. Kenyon, D.LITT..............£520 to £650
Assistants, 1st Class, W. de Gray Birch, LL.D., F.S.A.; Henry John Ellis; Isaac H. Jeayes; Francis B. Bickley ....£300 to £500
Assistants, 2nd Class, A. Hughes-Hughes; John A. Herbert, B.A.; D. T. Baird Wood, M.A.; J. P. Gilson, B.A. ....£150 to £300
Keeper of Oriental Printed Books and MSS., Robert Kennaway Douglas ....£700 to £800
Assistant, 1st Class, Rev. G. Margoliouth, M.A. ....£300 to £500
Assistants, 2nd Class, A. G. Ellis, M.A.; Lionel D. Barnett, B.A.................£150 to £300
Keeper of Prints and Drawings, S. Colvin, M.A. ....£700 to £800
Assist. do., Freeman M. O'Donoghue, F.S.A. ....£520 to £650
Assistants, 2nd Class, Campbell Dodgson, M.A.; R. L. Binyon, B.A. ....£150 to £300
Keeper of Egyptian and Assyrian Antiquities, Ernest A. Wallis Budge, LITT.D. ....£700 to £800
Assistant, 1st Class, T. G. Pinches £450
Assistants, 2nd Class, L. W. King, M.A.; H. R. H. Hall, B.A.; R. Campbell Thompson, B.A. ....£150 to £300
Keeper of Greek and Roman Antiquities, Alexander Stuart Murray, LL.D. ....£700 to £800
Assistant Keeper, Cecil H. Smith, LL.D.£520 to £650
Assistant, 1st Class, A. H. Smith, M.A., F.S.A. ....£300 to £500
Assistant, 2nd Class, Hen. B. Walters, M.A., F.S.A. ....£150 to £300
Keeper of Brit. and Mediæval Antiquities and Ethnography, C. H. Read, F.S.A. ....£700 to £800
Assistants, 2nd Class, O. M. Dalton, B.A.; R. L. Hobson, B.A.; Regd. A. Smith, B.A. ....£150 to £300
Keeper of Coins & Medals, B. V. Head, D.C.L. ....£700 to £800
Assistant Keeper, H.A. Grueber, F.S.A.£520 to £650
Assistants, 1st Class, W. W. Wroth, F.S.A.; E. J. Rapson, M.A.................£300 to £500
Assistant, 2nd Class, G. F. Hill, M.A.£150 to £300
2nd Div. Clerk, Wm. E. Cox .....£70 to £250
Solicitors, Messrs. Warrens, 99 Gt. Russell Street.

MUSEUM, THE NATURAL HISTORY,
Cromwell Road, S.W.—£47,235.
Director and Keeper of Zoology, Professor E. Ray Lankester, LL.D., F.R.S.............£1,200
Assistant Secretary, Charles E. Fagan £600
Clerks, J. F. Isaac; W. H. R. Holl; W. J. Anderson...................£95 to £350
Assistant, 1st Class (Library), B. B. Woodward ....£300 to £500
Assistant Keepers, Dr. Arthur G. Butler; Edgar A. Smith; R. Bowdler Sharpe, LL.D.£520 to £650

Assistants, 1st Class, Charles Owen Waterhouse; George A. Boulenger, F.R.S.; Oldfield Thomas; Fras. Jeffrey Bell, M.A.; W. R. Ogilvie Grant; William Forsell Kirby; Reginald I. Pocock ....£300 to £500
Assistants, 2nd Class, Charles J. Gahan, M.A.; Randolph Kirkpatrick; Francis A. Heron, B.A.; Ernest E. Austen; Sir George Francis Hampson, Bart.; Gilbert J. Arrow ......£150 to £300
Keeper of Geology, Dr. H. Woodward, F.R.S.£925
Assistant do., Arthur Smith Woodward ....£520 to £650
Assistant, 1st Class, Richard Bullen Newton ....£300 to £500
Assistants, 2nd Class, George C. Crick; Francis A. Bather, M.A.; J. Walter Gregory, D.SC.; Charles W. Andrews, B.SC.............£150 to £300
Keeper of Mineralogy, L. Fletcher, M.A., F.R.S. ....£700 to £800
Assistants, 2nd Class, Geo. T. Prior, M.A.; L. J. Spencer, B.A.; G. F. Herbert Smith, B.A. ....£150 to £300
Keeper of Botany, Geo. R. M. Murray, F.R.S. ....£700 to £800
Assistants, 1st Class, James Britten, Antony Gepp, M.A. ....£300 to £500
Assistants, 2nd Class, E. G. Baker; A. B. Rendle, D.SC.; Vernon H. Blackman, B.A.£150 to £300

MUSEUM, THE VICTORIA AND ALBERT,
South Kensington,
and Branch Museum at Bethnal Green.—£12,569 (Purchases, &c., £14,710.)
Director of Science Museum, Maj.-Gen. Edward Robert Festing, F.R.S. (late R.E.) £700 to £900
Director of Art Museum, Caspar Purdon Clarke, C.I.E., F.S.A..............£700 to £900
Assistant Director, A. B. Skinner, B.A., F.S.A. ....£600 to £700
Keepers, W. I. Last; J. Barrett, B.A.; H. M. Cundall, F.S.A.; W. W. Watts, F.S.A.£500 to £600; H. E. Acton; G. H. Palmer, B.A.; A F Kendrick, B.A.............£410 to £500
Assist. Keepers, T. A. Lehfeldt; T. F. Parkinson (in Charge of Bethnal Green Museum); S. Wood, B.SC.; C. H. Wylde, M.R.A.S.; R. F. Martin; L. W. Fulcher, B.SC.; E. F. Strange; T. C. Grove; H. W. Dickinson; P. G. Trendell. ....£100 to £400

NATIONAL DEBT OFFICE Old Jewry.—£16,405
Comptroller-General, G. W. Hervey, C.B....£1,500
Private Sec., J. J. Bree....................£100
Assistant Comptroller, W. Taylor..............£1,000
Actuary, Alexander John Finlaison, C.B. £1,000
Chief Clerk, A. T. King £800
Principal Clerks, E. Dynham; W. G. Turpin; J. Blakey; F. M. Ashley..........£600 to £700
Assistant do., J. F. C. Burgess; C. von Berg; H. Manwaring; T. Gowland £400 to £500; G. F. Anseil ....£350 to £400
Brokers, Messrs. Mullens, Marshall, & Co....£1,000

NATIONAL GALLERY,
Trafalgar Square, S.W.—£12,749.
Director, Sir Edward J. Poynter, P.R.A. £1,000
Keeper and Sec., Hawes Turner £620

NATIONAL GALLERY OF BRITISH ART.
(The Tate Gallery.) Millbank, S.W.
Keeper, Charles Holroyd ....£350 to £600

NATIONAL PORTRAIT GALLERY.
St. Martin's Place, Charing Cross, W.C.—£5,481.
Director, Keeper, & Secretary, Lionel Henry Cust, M.A., F.S.A.............£500 to £600

NAUTICAL ALMANAC OFFICE,
3 Verulam Buildings, Gray's Inn, W.C.—£4,107
Superintendent, A.M.W. Downing, D.SC., F.R.S.£600

Chief Assist., Edward Roberts, F.R.A.S., F.S.S. £450
Assistants, F. B. Cooper; J. B. Jackman; P. L.
Davis, F.R.A.S.; T. Wright; J. H. Bell; W. H.
Walmsley, B.SC., F.R.A.S.; J. A. Sprigge; B. F.
Bawtree; W. F. Doak, M.A.; T. C. Hudson, M.A.
(and a vacancy) .... £100 to £300

OBSERVATORIES,
Royal Observatory, Greenwich—£9,000.
Astronomer Royal, William Henry Mahoney
Christie, C.B., M.A., F.R.S., F.R.A.S. £1,000
Chief Assistants, P. H. Cowell, M.A., F.R.A.S.;
Frank Watson Dyson, M.A., F.R.A.S. £500 to £600
1st Class Assistants, Edward W. Maunder, F.R.A.S.
(*Physical*); Thos. Lewis, F.R.A.S.; Wm. G.
Thackeray, F.R.A.S.; H. P. Hollis, B.A., F.R.A.S.;
Wm. C. Nash (*Magnetic & Meteorological*)
.... £320 to £450
2nd Class, Andrew C. D. Crommelin, B.A., F.R.A.S.;
W. W. Bryant, B.A., F.R.A.S. .... £200 to £300
Clerical Assistant, H. Outhwaite ... £250 to £350
Royal Observatory, Cape of Good Hope.—£7,017.
Astronomer, David Gill, C.B., LL.D., F.R.S. ... £850
Chief Assistant, S. S. Hough, M.A. ... £500 to £600
Assistant, Joseph Lunt, B.SC. .... £200 to £450
2nd Class do., R. T. Pett; W. H. Cox £200 to £300
Clerical Assist., R. T. A. Innes .... £200 to £300
Kew Observatory, Richmond.
Chairman of Committee, F. Galton, D.C.L., F.R.S. unp.
Superintendent, Charles Chree, SC.D., F.R.S
Chief Assistant, T. W. Baker.
Senior Assistants, E. G. Constable: W. Hugo; J.
Foster; T. Gunter; W. J. Boxall.

PATENT OFFICE (Hours 10 to 5).
[Subject to control of the Board of Trade.]
25 Southampton Buildings, W.C.—£60,383.
Comptroller-Genl., C. N. Dalton, C.B. £1,400
Registrar of Designs and Trade Marks, Ralph
Griffin £1,000
Chief Examiner, Henry Hatfield £1000
Chief Clerk, P. G. L. Webb £750
Principals, J. F. Flack; W. J. F. Tomlinson;
Arthur R. Wright .... £600 to £700
Librarian, E. Wyndham Hulme £500
Assist. do., and *Supt. of Publications*, J. Lowry-
Whittle £550
Examiners, Andrew Jas. Walke; Alfred Cliff;
William Martin .... £600 to £700
Deputy Examiners, H. J. Adams; F. Ogden;
P. H. Cathcart; W. H. D. Clark; W. Groves;
J. E. Needham; H. Seward ...... £500 to £580
Assistant Examiners, J. Gray; F. M. Sexton;
Alfred Sutton; A F. Ravenshear; Alfred S. A.
Ormsby; Frank Gossling; George Rutherford;
Richard P. Chope; H. F. Lowe; H. O. Minty;
Thomas E. Lones; John H. Tomlinson; Arthur
Whitwell; Robert Sandon; William A. Stiven;
William Sumner; Arthur W. Martiset; Rhys
Jenkins; Bowman H. Madden; James Layzell;
George Gibbens; Horace Newton; William
Martin; Chas. H. Powell; C. C. Starling; T. H.
Muras; L. Bolton; J. Reeves; F. J. Cheshire;
D. Mescal; J. T. Walls; A. E. Chippesfield;
W. Saxfield; T. H. Deaning; A. G. Page;
S. A. Willmott; H. G. Graves; F. W. Dunn;
R. Adams; W. S. Jarratt; H. C. Haycraft;
G. F. Hambly; R. W. Simmonds; F. Fisher;
E. A. Gere; W. A. Taylor; T. T. Bedford; A.
Nicholls; R. J. Sowter; T. Akroyd; J. W.
Barker .... £150 to £500
2nd Class Clerks, Samuel Sumner Tripp; George
Hurlstone Hardy .... £310 to £430
Staff Clerks, Trade Marks, F. W. Hodges; W. E.
Milliken; T. W. H. Davies ...... £300 to £500

Staff Clerks, Patents, H. S. H. Pegler; J. Maycock
.... £350 to £480
Superintendent Sale Branch, A. Harper Lobban £450
Clerk of Trade Marks Reg., J. Stringer £450
Clerk of Designs Register, E. H. Knight £400
Law Clerk, J. Watson £375
Index Clerk, Trade Marks, F. Newbery £285
Keeper of Cotton Marks (Manchester Branch),
Joseph Fry £640
2nd Div. Clerks, Higher Grade, T. Ridge; H. E.
D. Jones; J. G. Walker; T. Prees; J. B.
McLaren; F. W. Neale; J. H. H. Peake; H.
Lennane; T. F. Ordish; H. Clements; W. H.
Davies .... £250 to £350

PAYMASTER-GENERAL'S DEPARTMENT,
Whitehall, S.W., £18,293.
Paymaster-General, His Grace the Duke of Marl-
borough, P.C. .... unp.
Assist. Paym.-Gen., Charles J. Maude £1,100
Principal Clerks, J. M. Dunn; F. D'A. Willis
.... £700 to £900
1st Class Clerks, H. T. Robins; O. H. Pearson;
A. C. Read; G. Hereford; J. C. Aubourg; J.
Whitfield-Jackson; H. Davis; H. P. Hewitt;
J. L. F. H. Godfrey; A. D. F. Mills; A.
A. Dowty; H. E. Ward; A. P. Badcock;
R. E. Brine; H. Tomlinson; H. Kearns; H. W.
Warburton; A. Willcock .... £400 to £600

POST OFFICE—£8,552,885.
Post Office Packet Service—£780,915.
Telegraphs—£3,638,399.
Chief Office, St. Martin's-le-Grand, E.C.—
£2,671,855.
Postmaster-General, His Grace the Duke of Nor-
folk, E.M., K.G. £2,500
Private Secs., F. A. R. Langton £240
A. W. Coates £160
Parliamentary do., James F. Hope .... unp.

Secretary's Office.
Secretary to the Post Office, Sir G. H. Murray,
K.C.B. £2,000
Private Sec., L. T. Horne £120
Second Secs., John Cameron Lamb, C.B., C.M.G. £1,400
Comptroller & Accountant-General, J. J. Cardin, C.B.
.... £1,250 to £1,400
Assist. Secs., G. W. Smyth; H. Buxton Forman,
C.B.; Edwd. Yeld; J. Ardron; W. Roche; S.
Raffles Thomson .... £1,000 to £1,200
Principal Clerks, J. Swainson; R. L. Bridger;
C. G. Hall; C. H. Bundy; L. A. Marshall;
A. F. King; E. Crabb; E. W. Farnall; A. B.
Walkley .... £625 to £800
Clerks (1st Class), *T. Eardley-Wilmot; *C. F.
Cartwright; G. E. Salmond; G. A. Oakeshott;
J. Chambers; P. J. Beckley; H. S. Carey;
F. Podmore; A. M. J. Ogilvie; W. G. C.
Kirkwood; A. G. Ferard; B. Hoskyns-
Abrahall .... £500 to £600
Clerks (2nd Class), †C. G. Home; †E. Udny;
C. Eden; I. Richards; G. S. Edwards; A. H.
Norway; F. Martelli; R. J. Mackay; A. G.
Leonard; G. McLaren; T. G. Stuart-French;
H. W. Cardew; L. T. Horne; V. H. Stephens;
H. L. Kingsford; A. W. Coates; P. Z. Round;
A. E. W. Codrington; H. F. McClintock; E.
Raven; F. H. Williamson; J. Y. Bell £150 to £500
Clerk (2nd Class), Old Establishment, G. R. Tapp
.... £410

* Late Principal Clerks, Lower Section, of Old
Establishment.
† Late First Class Clerks of Old Establishment.

Supplementary Establishment.

Additional Staff Officers, F. A. R. Langton, £650;
W. Nops; P. G. Burrell...........£500 to £600
Deputy Staff Officers, F. J. Brown; W. Patrick;
C. Stevens; G. E. Pratt £450
Clerks (1st *Class*), R. Gilbert; J. R. Burr; M. B.
Mathias; W. F. Besant; W. Cann; J. T. Monk;
T. Beer; J. J. Summers; N. Hautrive; H. F.
Smart; E. H. Laurie; W. H. Sharland; B.
Masters; W. J. F. Apted; W. H. Harring-
ton; J. R. Weeks; J. Duff; C. J. Prout;
G. H. Jackson............ £310 to £400
Clerks (2nd *Class*), F. W. H. Preston; J. Wish; J.
Hodges; M. L. Gardiner; T. B. McDowell; W.
Price; A. L. Forrest; V. Corry; H. W. Charlton;
W. Hainworth; A. K. Langridge; J. I. De
Wardt; J. Hall; J. S. Stokes; W. H. Buck;
W. Newnam; F. E. Bunt; S. Granville; C.
Germain; E. W. Mills; W. Prime; J. P.
Leckenby; G. J. R. Scott; S. J. Ching; F.
E. James; H. Darby; J. D. Mackay; W. H.
A. Toomer; J. B. S. Engall; S. J. Holloway;
S. F. Lorden; H. Leeds; F. J. Barker; W. T.
Leech; E. A. Francis; J. B. H. Fleming;
G. S. Stow; H. J. Howard; R. E. Thornley;
J. W. Wissenden; D. A. Hogg; E. J. Gayes;
H. E. Heritage........................ £210 to £300

Confidential Enquiry Branch.

Director, J. Philips ....£600 to £800
Assistant ditto, W. G. Gates ....£500 to £600
Principal Clerks, A. P. Wakeman; W. T. White
...............................£400 to £500
Travelling Clerks (1st *Class*), W. McIntyre; E.
A. Kirby; A. G. Madder; F. W. Woodard;
F. W. Mann ....£400 to £500
Do. do. (2nd *Class*), J. Settle; J. Doubleday; F.
O. Wood; W. T. Edwards; W. Murray; J. H.
Shinner; J. Compton; J. G. Stevens; J. O.
Planck; J. A. B. Drummond; T. E. Tutton
...............................£150 to £350
Inspectors, Railway Business, Senior Inspector, H.
Cockerell (£300 to £400); *Inspectors,* E. Martin;
C. S. Stevens ....£175 to £280
Insp., Appointment Branch, G. C. Pike £175 to £280

Packet Services.

Controller, H. Buxton Forman, C.B. (*Assist. Sec.*)
Nautical Assistant, Commander F. Papillon, R.N.
...............................£260 to £380
Officers in charge of Indian Mails, H. B. Osborne;
H. B. R. Harvey; J. G. Wilmot
...............................£200 to £300, with allowances
*Superintendent Telegraph Business at Race Meetings,
&c.,* T. Mason ....£400 to £500
Assist. ditto, H. T. Toothill ....£275 to £375
Asst. Supts. (2nd *Class*), A. D. M. Swift; A.
Walker ....£200 to £250

Registry Branch.

Registrar, F. H. D. Bushnell ....£400 to £500
Deputy Registrar, E. Worthington ...£310 to £380
Assistant Registrars, Josiah Walker; W. L. A.
Smith; H. W. Hardcastle ....£220 to £300

ACCOUNTANT-GENERAL'S DEPARTMENT.

Comptroller and Accountant-General, James J.
Cardin, C.B.....................£1,250 to £1,400
Assistant Acct.-Gen., Philip Benton £800 to £1,000
Chief Clerk, Mark W. Ker ....£700 to £800
Chief Examiner, C. A. King ....£700 to £800
Principal Bookkeeper and Registrar of Bonds, F. E.
Smith ....£700 to £800
Cashier, C. W. Potter ....£650 to £750
Accountants, F. T. Swayne; C. Prall; C. E.
Gerahty; H. Davies; W. H. Miller; F. W.
Home; L. Incledon; W. D. Hepworth; L.
Barnes ....£550 to £650

Assistant do., A. Goodwin; A. J. Adams; E. B.
Parlour; E. W. Measor; H. J. Dickinson; E.
Solomon; W. D. Diplock; R. B. Hughes;
L. W. B. Maclean; A. G. Bowie; H. D.
Lewis ....£440 to £540
Examiners, J. Hartley; G. G. Knott; C. H.
Finch; H. Duesbury; W. A. Collard; H. W.
Mathias; A. Farmer; J. C. Wilson; C. T. M.
Martin; C. E. Yates; J. C. B. Middleton;
W. F. Mitchell; R. M. Rogers; C. R. Wickins;
H. A. L. Chetwynd; W. A. Shepherd; J.
Bunce ....£360 to £430

Former Telegraph Branch.

Accountants, A. C. Woodward; E. W. Chetwynd;
Ernest G. Richardson.............£550 to £650
Assistant do., A. M'Laren; E. H. J. Frost; W.
Bradfield ....£440 to £540
Examiners, W. Scott; G. V. Walshe; G. Mason;
E. E. Fowler; L. G. King; G. F. Lee; G. M.
Mann ....£360 to £430

Clearing House Branch—*Female Staff.*

Superintendent, Miss A. Boulton .....£250 to £400
Assist. Superin., Miss A. L. Powell ...£200 to £240
Principal Clerks, Misses F. Goddard; A. E.
Smith; E. W. Green; K. J. Wingrave; E. S.
Wingrave; H. M. Duret; A. M. Dent
...............................£140 to £190

Postal Order Branch—*Female Staff.*

Superintendent, Miss M. M. A. Brown £320 to £450
Senior Assistant Superintendent, Miss C. L. De
Renzi ....£250 to £300
Assist.-Supts., Misses E. I. Miles; R. Loch
...............................£200 to £240
Principal Clerks, Misses F. Parker; L. Macleod;
E. M. Ross; S. S. Allport; E. M. Semple;
S. A. M. Hawkins; E. J. Churchill; M. E.
Cather; A. E. Culley; A. Lacey; H. W.
Bindloss; B. M. Golden; E. E. Elliston; J. A.
Duncan ....£140 to £190

Central Telegraph Office.

Controller, E. May...................£800 to £1,000
Deputy Controller, T. Barlow.........£700 to £800
Assist. Controllers (1st *Class*), Joseph W. Eames;
J. Russell; A. E. Eames ....£525 to £600
Do. (2nd *Class*), A. Askins; W. Whight
...............................£400 to £500
Allowance of £50 to the Senior Assistant-
Controller.

Controller's Office.

Principal Clerk, J. F. Jelf £475
Clerks (1st *Class*), *L. Weaver; *R. Headland; J.
Willshire; R. D. Binsted ....£310 to £400
* To rise to £450.
Clerks (2nd *Class*), *R. J. Woodifield; F. P. Didden;
V. M. Dunford; A. W. Edwards; F. Goodheart
...............................£210 to £300
* To rise to £310.
Superintendents, *G. Gregory; *H. W. Brook-
man; *J. M. Maclachlan; *H. J. Smith; *W. G.
Gould; A. Stiles; C. Stanley; C. A. Morgan;
F. A. Pyne; A. J. S. Adams; H. A. Tre-
winnard; J. Gorton; W. Waterman; C. C.
Goodway; O. Rowland...........£310 to £400
* To rise to £450.
Matron, M. H. Greer ....£200 to £300
Female Supervisors, *M. A. Cooper; *M. A. Watts;
S. Chapman; *E. J. Black; M. Arundel; J. B.
Blance; E. Gloyns; S. S. Dowdey; E. P. F.
Moore ....£160 to £200
* To rise to £250.

Intelligence Department.

Superintendent, W. G. Faunch ....£310 to £450

Engineer-in-Chief's Office.
Engineer-in-Chief, J. Hookey......£1,000 to £1,200
Assist. Engineer-in-Chief and Electrician, J. Gavey ......£700 to £900
2nd Asst. Engin.-in-Chief, M. F. Roberts ......£500 to £800
Principal Technical Officer, M. Cooper £575 to £700
Technical Officers (1st Class), T. H. Stockwell; H. R. Kempe; P. Ennis; A. Eden; E. Hartnell; W. Slingo; A. J. Stubbs ...£420 to £550
Do. (2nd Class), A. W. Curra; J. G. Dalladay; F. Tremain; R. McIlroy; J. F. Lamb; A. L. De Lattre; J. H. Fossett; A. W. Martin; J. E. Taylor; W. Brown ......£200 to £400
Clerk (1st Class), R. C. Leversedge £310 to £400
Clerks (2nd Class), J. Smith; T. F. Purves; W. S. Mountain...... £210 to £300
Supt. to Electric Lighting, J. Probert £310 to £450
Submarine Superintendent (Woolwich), W. R. Culley £500 to £700
Do. (Dover), (vacant) ......£400 to £550
Assistant do. (Woolwich), H. Marsh £310 to £450
Assistant do. (Dover), F. Pollard ...£250 to £350
Superintending Engineer (Lond.), C. T. Fleetwood £500 to £700
Assistant do. (Lond.), S. M. Banker; G. W. Hook £360 to £450
Superintending Engineers, *J. Gibson; *W. Louth; E. Ashton; G. H. Comport (Senr.); A. W. Heaviside; H. Pomeroy; J. Jenkin; J. Walby; D. M. Stewart; G. N. Partridge (Senr.); G. M. Carr; J. W. Woods; H. Haskayne £440 to £650
* To rise to £700.

London Postal Service Department.
Controller's Office.
Controller, Jasper C. Badcock C.B.£1,000 to £1,200
Vice-Controller, Robert Bruce £800 to £900
Assist. Controllers, Edward Smith; J. W. Crawfurd £625 to £750
Chief Supts., A. Hunter; E. W. Helm; A. E. Adeney; J. E. T. O'M. Carew; J. Barnes; J. Dixon; R. G. Hitchcock; W. Roberts £500 to £600
Asst.Supt.(Old Estabmt.), L. R. Sealy £300 to £450
Principal Clerks, †A. H. Powell; F. J. Jones; W. J. Pounds (senr.); J. E. Gleed; F. G. Whitaker; H. Filmer; W. Howson; A. H. Reddrop; H. C. Somers...£400 to £500
† To rise to £550.
1st Class Clerks, *W. H. Hamlyn : *J. W. Standerwick; B. S. Hurman; R. H. W. Batley; H. F. Foster; W. Matthews; J. A. Walker; T. James; H. Norris; A. G. Atterbury; J. R. Edsall; J. W. Aston; W. T. Wheeler; J. Elder; H. Turrell £310 to £400
* Rise to £430.
Circulation Office.
Sub-Controller, Felix D. White......£700 to £800
Assistant Sub-Controller, T. Briggs..£600 to £700
Chief Clerk, F. Bray ......£520 to £600
Superintendents, C. P. Moginie; D. H. Rooney; T. P. Salt; H. Matthews; R. Ruffle; H. Naylor £450 to £550
Assistant Superintendents, J. S. D. Ford; W. Moran; G. Hopkins; B. Smith; E. Cane; J. Bell; W. E. Gould; H. W. Pym; G. Hine; R. Pascall; E. T. Woolley; J. G. Oakley; J. G. Elford; W. W. Robinson; C. Still; W. V. Inman; S. W. Lloyd; J. A. Hyde £300 to £450

Metropolitan District Offices.
West Central, New Oxford Street.
Postmaster, I. Naylor £600
Chief Clerk, W. D. Wheldon......£400 to £500

Assistant Superintendent, T. Napper...£300 to £400
Clerks, C. A. Wheeler; W. M. Frizell; W. J. Crothers ......£80 to £300
Western, 3 Vere Street.
Postmaster, Arthur H. Salmon......£600
Chief Clerk, A. H. Mann ......£400 to £500
Assistant Superintendent, W. Hodson £300 to £400
Clerks, R. H. Laurie; L. V. Cox; E. A. Martin £80 to £300
Paddington, 19 London Street.
Postmaster, W. D. Herbert......£650
Chief Clerk, H. E. Anderson......£400 to £500
Assistant Superintendent. C. Hood £300 to £400
Clerks, W. C. Waller; J. W. Campion; A. Wallwork; G. W. Wright ......£80 to £300
Eastern, 195 Whitechapel Road.
Postmaster, J. Lorrain...£600, after 5 years £650
Chief Clerk, J. Powell ......£400 to £500
Assistant Superintendent, J. Dwane £300 to £400
Clerks, A. E. Osler; J. Brennan; H. Wynne; W. J. Gow; H. H. Cannon......£80 to £300
South-Western, Howick Place, Victoria Street.
Postmaster, D. H. Somerville £700
Chief Clerk, C. A. Comber ......£400 to £500
Assistant Superintendent, J. F. Steel...£340 to £400
Clerks, A. R. Broad; J. Uprichard; W. A. Adams; A. Payne ......£80 to £300
P. M. House of Commons, E. W. Pike £300 to £400
Battersea, 202 Lavender Hill, S.W.
Postmaster, J. K. Gibson......£400 to £500
Assistant Superintendent, F. Harding £300 to £400
Clerk, F. W. D'Evelyn ......£80 to £300
South-Eastern, 239 Borough High Street.
Postmaster, W. J. Cooper £650
Chief Clerk, C. Exley ......£400 to £500
Assistant Superintendent, R. Foyle ..£300 to £400
Clerks, J. D. Biggs; W. W. Owen; C. E. Roe; J. W. F. Relph ......£80 to £300
Norwood, 35 Westow Street.
Postmaster, B. Pitt ......£400 to £500
Assistant Superintendent, H.T.Woods £300 to £400
Northern, 45 Essex Road.
Postmaster, J. Greer......£600
Chief Clerk, John H. Marriott ......£400 to £500
Assistant Superintendent, J. W. Bond £300 to £400
Clerks, L. T. Churley; W. F. Chessall; R. A. Moffatt; W. M. Hey......£80 to £300
North-Western, 28 Eversholt Street.
Postmaster (vacant) £600
Chief Clerk, E. F. Page ......£400 to £500
Assistant Superintendent, H.W. Mitten £300 to £400
Clerks, W. T. B. Young; J. Pryer; D. E. Ayling £80 to £300

Medical Department.
Chief Medical Officer, Arthur Huelin Wilson, L.R.C.P., M.R.C.S. ......£800 to £1,000
2nd Med. Officer, John Sinclair, M.R.C.P. £450 to £650
Female ditto, Miss Edith Shove, M.B. £350 to £500
Asst.do., Miss M. L. C.Madgshon, M.B. £200 to £300
1st Assistant, G.C.W.Wright,L.R.C.P.£300 to £400
2nd Assistant, S. Wicks, M.R.C.S., L.R.C.P. £200 to £300
Resident Assistant to Medical Officers, A. R. McLachlan £100
Dispensing Assistant, F. Freeman £225
Money Order Office.
Controller, J. Manson ......£700 to £900
Assistant ditto, F. Wickham ......£550 to £650
Principal Clerks, W. F. Evans; J. Fox £500 to £540
Asst. Principal Clerks, C. W. F. Welchman; H. Pearson ......£410 to £490

1st Class Clerks, *R. J. Sanderson; *F. J. White;
*H. Taylor; R. L. Frost .... £310 to £400
* To rise to £430.

Female Staff.
Superintendent, Miss N. Lankester ...£250 to £300
Asst. do., Miss M. H. Renwick ...... £200 to £240
Principal Clerk, Miss A. E. K. Fowler £140 to £190

Returned Letter Office.
Controller, Jonathan Downes............£550 to £700
Principal Clerks, J. R. Hay; H. F. McConnell
............................£440 to £540
1st Class Examiners, T. Purves; W. Howard; E.
G. Henshaw; P. H. Reid; Herbert J. Draper;
W. W. Berry; S. R. Hart; H. Burt £310 to £400
2nd Class do., J. Mahn; W. Schofield; R. E.
Brooks; W. G. Green; A. K. Chalk; N. L.
Hubert .... £210 to £300

Savings Bank Department.
Controller, Charles Dowson Lang ..£1,000 to £1,200
Assistant Controllers, E. H. Poole; J. H. R.
West ....£650 to £750
Sub-Controllers, I. J. Scaly; H. E. Carlyle; H.
Badcock; A. Belcher .... £570 to £640
Principal Clerks, J. A. J. Housden; W. E.
Kearns; W. F. Copeland; J. W. Unwin; E.
Nops; A. H. Sadler; E. H. Daniell; J. Williams;
W. Hill; G. R. Everitt; G. E. White; J. C. G.
Galton; F. W. Bundy; H. E. Charlton; C. C.
Sutch; J. C. E. Bridge; W. S. Thomas
.... £500 to £550
Assist. do., V. Shepperd; C. W. Treacher; H. P.
Cox; H. A. O'Molony; A. T. Woodward; A. H.
Thorns; W. E. Gifford; W. F. Lovell; T. Leach;
R. G. Grene; J. Kennett; G. A. F. Rogers;
J. C. Palmer; W. G. Trinder; M. Weeks; W.
A. E. Batchelor; B. I. J. W. Bowen; G.
Hockey; Wm. Johnson; H. J. Hancock; R.
T. G. Nevins .... £440 to £490
Clerks, 1st Class, W. W. Rishworth; R. Browne;
F. Paterson; H. E. Bayly; I. J. Dadd; J. A.
Parker; E. A. Loveday; G. P. Morris; E. S.
Coyne; J. T. McCallum; C. T. Hillier; E. P.
Hawkins; W. Wilkins; F. E. Walker; W.
W. Page; C. Russell; J. J. Curtayne; W. A.
Millington; E. H. J. Walliker; C. F. Nash;
J. P. White; W. R. Hudson; G. L. Brooks;
H. T. J. A. Rickeord; A. G. Gurr; E.
MacDonald; A. G. Duffield; R. Dudley;
F. Remington; T. Lyon; J. Pelham; M.
Wheeler; F. J. Venables; H. A. Sherburn;
R. H. A. B. Edwards ....£360 to £430

Female Staff.
Superintendent, Miss M. C. Smith......£320 to £500
Senior Assist. do.,Misses R. K.Corbould; F.Jaques;
E. F. Pearson; T. F. Haynes ....£250 to £300
Assistant Supts., Misses A. M. Haynes; E. G.
Edkins; M. M. J. Latham; J. E. Hume; M.
E. Haynes; K. Eyre; E. M. Stevens; H. G.
Young; A. E. Sharrock; E. E. Wyndham
.....................................£200 to £240
Principal Clerks, Misses E. S. Fullagar; E. Wyer;
J. W. Huddart; D. E. Michell; A. A. Michell;
E. A. Sheppard; A. Fullagar; S. S. Roberts;
F. E. Dale; J. A. Russell; E. A. Crowther;
E. C. Dean; M. F. L. Steuart; A. M. Foster;
F. S. M. West; K. A. Bumpus; F. L. Day;
E. M. Miller; A. M. M. Ritson; L. A. Sweet;
H. A. Scott; J. B. Lang; E. Mathews; M.
Phelan; M. G. Wyllie; A. E. Hooke; M.
Meggeson; R. F. Elliott; M. Dyke; L. E.
James; A. M. Weedon; D. L. Jones; C.
Tompkins; B. Southam............£140 to £190

Solicitor's Office.
The Solicitor, Sir Robert Hunter £1,500 to £2,000
Assist. do., ...£800 to £1,000
Principal Clerks, Zachary Brooke; Edwin Winter
£500 to £600 (additional allowance of £100 to
one).
Clerks, Herbert Goss; Samuel Budd; Edward
Arnold ....£200 to £500
Prof. Assists. (solicitors), Robert Noyes; H. Opie
Smith; J. Okell ....£200 to £375
Other Assistants to Solicitor, E. J. Armstrong; W.
McIntyre; W. C. E. Brignall; P. W. McIntyre.

Postal Stores Department.
Controller, S. C. Hooley ....£650 to £800
Assistant do., C. E. S. Poole ......£500 to £600
Superintendents, J. F. Aldridge; H. Ogden; D.
W. F. Foord; A. C. Day ....£300 to £450
Clerk, F. C. Lupton ....£250 to £350
Clerks, F. W. Fugeman; T. E. Rowland; W. S.
Landray; R. J. Fewings ....£210 to £300
Storekeeper, W. Curtis..............£300 to £400
Assist. Storekeepers, H. W. King; W. Holloway
...............................£200 to £290

Office of Controller of Stores (Telegraphs).
Controller, C. E. Stuart ....£700 to £900
Assistant Controller, A. F. Varley ...£500 to £700
Superintending Examiners, J. Day; H. J. Cox;
J. H. Ingram; G. Morgan ....£400 to £450
Assist. Superintending Examiners, W. J. Etheredge;
W. G. Hinton; John Bolton......£350 to £400
Examiners, 1st Class, S. W. Percy; J. Lofthouse;
R. W. Gudgeon; W. H. Allen; A. Garner;
W. B. Watkins; C. L. Barnes; H. A. Cheel;
H. Schramm; H. Sparkes; E. T. Gillett; A.
Dell; C. Ward; W. Nash; H. J. Langton
..................................£200 to £340
Examiners, 2nd Class, *J. B. Fulcher; J. H.
G. Taylor; W. J. Honnor; T. S. Filmer;
S. Busher; E. Banwell; A. Clegg; E. Ward;
E. G. Toby; F. Cody; F. G. Beak; F.
Shackleton; F. H. Horner; W. G. S. Gar-
land; L. W. Wright; C. Gellet; C. Wheeler;
R. G. Merrifield; J. H. Reeves; J. B.
Menzies; W. G. Potter; H. A. Mann; W. C.
J. Sawyer; A. J. White; T. B. Barker; D.
Williams; A. E. Foort; C. H. Crisp; J. J.
McCrory; R. J. Smith; A. G. Tydeman; T. L.
Adamson; J. Salter; J. R. Timson; J. Fraser;
T. H. Henderson; H. J. S. Bennett; J. M.
Rusk; S. M. Freeman; A. S. Manning; H. S.
Duncan; H. A. Somers; Robert Fanshawe;
G. T. Hensel; E. F. Nunns; C. S. Gulliver;
J. Mare; H. E. Willmott; M. Dixon; G. H.
McGregor; A. H. Betjemann; H. J. Hall; A.
Young..............................£75 to £200
* To rise to £320.

Factories.
Superintendents, (Holloway) J. W. Willmot;
(Mount Pleasant) W. Bosomworth £500 to £650
Assistant do., (Holloway) R. Britton; (Mount
Pleasant) W. A. Rylands ....£350 to £450
Surveyors' Establishment (United Kingdom).
Surveyors, E. P. W. Redford; B. W. Seton; G.
Anson Yeld; W. S. Rushton; W. J. Roe; P.
P. V. Turner; P. M. Berkeley; R. J. H.
Mahon; C. S. Court; R. O'C. N. Deane; W.
A. D. Evanson; T. P. Barnard; D. W. O.
Harkness; A. Mellersh; J. Muir; W. M.
Gattie ....£550 to £800
Assist. Surveyors, 1st Class, C. M. Hibberd; W.
F. Webber; J. L. McDonald; J. F. Brown;
M. J. Gardiner; G. A. Whiteman; W. Castell;
F. Pullen; G. G. Kent; H. S. Wooster; W.
Dickinson; H. R. Telford; A. Dowling; E. C.
Griffith; H. W. Austin ....£425 to £525

Assistant Surveyors, 2nd Class, E. T. R. Merewether; J. G. Chichester; E. S. Forrest; E. J. A. Doyle; W. Cooper; W. Brown; Daniel J. Moore; P. F. Richardson; E. D. Shawfield; R. L. Hammond; J. E. Wernham; E. F. A. Burckhardt; W. W. Halliburton; J. J. Thompson; J. G. Hamilton; T. R. Ling; J. S. Harvey; D. A. Macphee; G. P. B. Hallowes; T. Kelly; G. L. Harding; F. J. W. Oakley; J. F. Horn; G. E. M. Forrest; F. W. Le Fèvre; W. M. Simpson; A. S. Ayton; C. Carwithen; W. Benson; E. W. Wedlake; C. White; F. C. Luke; G. N. Merrefield; J. G. Mellersh; G. Wallace; J. M. Stephenson; W. Hallowes; R. M. Longland; J. G. Maddan; R. Ramsay; F. L. Freeling; F. Makepeace; F. W. Rhodes; R. F. Bradford; H. V. Orr; T. W. Davis; J. H. Irish; W. S. Harrison; D. Dunlop £150 to £400

PRIVY COUNCIL OFFICE,
Whitehall, S.W.—£11,900.
Lord President of the Council, His Grace the Duke of Devonshire, K.G., P.C. £2,000
Private Sec., T. Riversdale Walrond £300
     ,,   ,,   John Dunville ....*unp.*
Clerk of the Council, Almeric W. FitzRoy... £1,500
Deputy do. & Chief Clerk, J. H. Harrison
                                 £1,100 to £1,200
Senior Clerk, William Robert Walkes £600 to £800
Junior do., Chas. J. Dalrymple Hay £150 to £250
2nd Div. Clerk, Higher Grade, H. E. Moon £250 to £350

PRIVY SEAL OFFICE,
3 St. James's Square, S.W.
Lord Privy Seal, Right Hon. Viscount Cross, G.C.B.
Private Secretary, A. W. Williams-Wynn £100

PUBLIC WORKS LOAN BOARD,
3 Bank Buildings, E.C.
Secretary, R. Philpot.
Chief Clerk, B. Allen.
Solicitor, Herbert Barnes.
Chief Clerk to do., Chas. Hy. Davis.
Princ. Clerk, R. F. Shattock.

QUEEN ANNE'S BOUNTY, 3 Dean's Yard, S.W.
Secretary & Treasurer, Joseph Keech Aston.
Chief Clerk, William R. Le Fanu.
Senior Clerks, George Fenn Aston; Wm. Vincent Prior; Wm. Lipscomb; Chas. Fredk. Howell; George Simpson.
Solicitors, The Secretary; The Chief Clerk; and F. G. Hughes.
Architect, William Alfred Hughes.
Auditor, H. C. Garlant, 33 Nicholas Lane.
Counsel, E. P. Wolstenholme, 2 Stone Bldgs., W.C.

RECORD OFFICE, THE PUBLIC,
Chancery Lane, W.C.—£24,300.
Keeper of the Records, The Master of the Rolls.
Deputy Keeper, Sir H. C. Maxwell-Lyte, K.C.B.
                                 £1,100
Secretary, James Joel Cartwright £600
Assistant Keepers, C. T. Martin; L. O. Pike; S. R. Scargill-Bird; R. D. Trimmer; J. M. Thompson; John E. E. Sharp ....£520 to £700
Clerks, G. F. Handcock; G. H. Overend; R. A. Roberts; F. Isaacson; G. J. Morris; E. G. Atkinson; E. Salisbury; R. H. Brodie; H. Hall; H. Rodney; J. G. Black; A. Hughes; C. G. Crump; A. St. J. Story-Maskelyne; R. C. Fowler; J. V. Lyle; M. S. Giuseppi; C. Johnson; A. E. Stamp; H. E. Headlam; H. W. B. Chapman ....£150 to £500

ROYAL BOTANIC GARDENS, KEW (under the control of H.M. Office of Works).—£32,630.
Director, Sir William Turner Thiselton-Dyer, K.C.M.G., F.R.S. £1,200
     Private Sec., S. T. Dunn, B.A. £150

Keeper of Herbarium & Library, W. B. Hemsley, F.R.S. £600
Principal Assistants, G. Massee; O. Stapf, PH.D.; I. H. Burkill, M.A. ....£300 to £400
Assistant for India, H. W. W. Pearson
                                 £150 to £200
Keeper of Museums, J. R. Jackson ...£300 to £400
Curator of Gardens, George Nicholson
                                 £300 to £400
Assistant Curator, William Watson ...£80 to £250
Hon. Keeper, Jodrell Laboratory, D. H. Scott, PH.D., F.R.S.
Assistants, John Aikman; W. N. Winn (*Office*); N. E. Brown; R. A. Rolfe; C. H. Wright; J. M. Hillier; S. A. Skan ....£80 to £250

ROYAL PARKS AND PLEASURE GARDENS
(under the control of H.M. Office of Works).
—£119,000.
St. James's, Green, and Hyde Parks—Ranger, H.R.H. the Duke of Cambridge, K.G. ...... *nil.*
  Do.   *Supt. Ranger*, Lt.-Gen. R. Bateson... £191
  Do.   ,, *Works*, William Browne £300
Bailiff of Royal Parks, &c., Colonel Moreton John Wheatley, R.E. £900
Assist. Bailiff, Major W. C. Hussey, R.E. £300 to £400
Richmond—Ranger, Duke of Cambridge, K.G. £110
  Do. *Deputy do.*, Rear-Ad. A. A. F. FitzGeorge £57
  Do. *Superintendent*, H. G. Sawyer £346
Greenwich—Superintendent, A. D. Webster... £135
Bushy—Keeper, J. Halliday £190
Hampton Court Gardens—Supt., J. Gardiner £140
Regent's Park—Supt., C. Jordan £200

SALFORD HUNDRED COURT OF RECORD,
Town Hall, Manchester.
High Steward, Rt. Hon. the Earl of Sefton.
Judge, Henry Gordon Shee, Q.C.
Registrar, William Henry Talbot (*Town Clerk*).
Deputy Registrar, John Mountain.
Chief Clerk, Harry Eltoft.
Clerks, B. R. Davis; J. S. Adamson; P. Dale; J. W. Davis.
Head Bailiff, James Simpson.
Assistant Bailiffs, G. Mountain; J. G. Ireland; James Thornley (Bolton).

SCIENCE AND ART DEPARTMENT.
(Administration, South Kensington, S.W.£60,481).
Secretary, Sir George W. Kekewich, K.C.B. £
Principal Assistant Secretary, Capt. W. de W. Abney, C.B., D.C.L., F.R.S. £1,200
   Private Secretary to Do., J. Bailey.........£100
Assist. Sec., A. J. R. Trendell, C.M.G. £850 to £1,000
Chief Clerk, Edward Belshaw ....£550 to £650
Clerk of Upper Div. A. F. E. Torrens.. £500 to £550
Clerks of the Higher Division, A. E. Thomas, M.A.; E. Wilkinson; H. Graves, B.A.; A. E. Garrard; A. E. Cooper ....£150 to £500
Clerk in Charge of Accounts, E. Harris £550 to £650
Assistant to ditto, C. McEnroe ....£400 to £525
Storekeeper, J. Saltmarsh ....£350 to £550
Deputy do., J. W. Emler ....£300 to £450
Superintendent of Registry, L. Finding £400
Second Division Clerks, Higher Grade, W. Burtt (*Postal*); W. H. R. Dahm (*Book-Keeper*); F. J. Hodgkinson; A. Maslen; G. Stringer; H. Tipper; T. Wright ....£250 to £350
Do., holding staff posts, F. H. Bate; A. Burch; T. Davies; C. K. Eley; J. F. Hubert; H. A. Josland; A. J. Pitman; G. B. Stubbs £250 to £350

Science Division.
Assistant Director, Frank R. Fowke £600 to £750
Official Examiner, T. Healey ....£550 to £650
Assist. do., J. Bailey; E. E. Freehill £250 to £550
Science Exam. Clerk, H. W. Etheridge £350

Royal College of Science, S. Kensington.—£18,388.
Dean and Professor of Geology, John Wesley
Judd, C.B., LL.D., F.R.S. £1,000
Assist. Prof. of Mineral., C. G. Cullis, D.SC.
Mechanics & Math., J. Perry, M.E., D.SC., F.R.S. £800
Assistant Professor, A. R. Willis, M.A., D.SC. £400
Instructors, P. T. Wrigley, M.A.; J. Harrison,
M.INST.M.E. .... each £360
Physics, A. W. Rücker, D.SC., F.R.S. (*Sec.*) ...£800
Assistant Professor, W. Watson, B SC. £400
Astronomical Physics, Sir J. N. Lockyer, K.C.B.,
F.R.S. £800
Chemistry, W. A. Tilden, D.SC., F.R.S. £800
Assistant Professor, W. P. Wynne, D.SC., F.R.S.
£400
Conjoint Professors of Biology, G. B. Howes, LL.D.,
F.R.S. (£600); J. B. Farmer, M.A. (£400).
Metallurgy, Sir W. Chandler Roberts-Austen,
K.C.B., F.R.S. £800
Instructor, Assaying, A Stansfield, D.SC. ...£300
Mining, C. Le Neve Foster, D.SC., F.R.S. £300
Instructor, Mine Surveying, L. H. Cooke ...£300
Regis. and Supt. of Discipline, F. Fladgate .. £300
Clerk and Librarian, A. Tillott ......£70 to £250

Art Division.
Director (vacant) ....£750 to £950
Assist. do., Alan S. Cole ......£600 to £750
Official Examiner (vacant) ....£550 to £650
Assist., H. A. Bowler ......£450 to £550
Examination Clerk M. Webb........ ......£400

Royal College of Art.—£8,726
Principal (vacant) ....£700 to £800
Registrar, J. A. Grant ......£300 to £350

Inspection.
Chief Senior Insp., Gilbert R. Redgrave £600 to £800
Senior Inspectors, C. A. Buckmaster, M.A.; T. B.
Shaw; H. H. Hoffert, D.SC. ......£600 to £800
Inspectors, E. J. Ball, PH.D.; T. Preston, D.SC.,
F.R.S.; S. F. Dufton, D.SC.; D. E. Jones, B.SC.;
H. W. T. Wager, M.A.; F. Pullinger, B.SC.; Hugh
Gordon, M.A.; W. B. D. Edwards; A. E. Tutton,
B.SC., F.R.S.; G. Fletcher; S. J. Cartlidge
£400 to £600
Junior Inspectors, W. R. Swain, B.SC.; J. Brill,
M.A.; A. Dufton, D.SC.; M. A. Fenton, M.A.;
W. B. Haas, B.A.; J. P. Laws, F.I.C.; J. W.
Hartley, M.A.; B. B. Skirrow, M.A.; F. W.
Westaway .... each £300 to £500

SCIENCE AND ART DEPARTMENT, DUBLIN.
Royal College of Science, Dublin.—£23,020.
Director, Lt.-Col. G. T. Plunkett, R.E. £700 to £800
Chief Clerk & Secretary to the Board, H. B. White,
M.A. £350
Professors:—Descriptive Geometry and Engineering,
James Lyon, M.A. (*Dean*) £400; *Applied Math.,*
W. McF. Orr, M.A.; *Botany,* T. Johnson, D.SC.;
Chemistry, W. N. Hartley, F.R.S.; *Physics,* W.
F. Barrett, F.R.S.E., each £500; *Zoology,* A. C.
Haddon, D.SC., £200; *Geology & Mineralogy,*
Grenville A. J. Cole, F.G.S. £400

Librarian, National Library, T. W. Lyster, M.A.
£450 to £550
Keeper, Science & Art Museum, Thomas H. Long-
field, F.S.A. ....£350 to £500
Keeper, Natural History Collection, E. F. Scharff,
PH.D. ....£350 to £500
Keeper, Botanical Collection, Professor T. John-
son, D.SC.
Keeper of the Minerals, Professor Cole.
Keeper, Royal Botanic Gardens, Glasnevin, F. W.
Moore, M.R.I.A. ....£200 to £400

Edinburgh Museum of Science and Art.
∴(See p. 325.)

SECRETARY FOR SCOTLAND'S OFFICE,
Dover House, Whitehall, S.W.—£13,358.
Edinburgh, Parliament Square.
Sec., Rt. Hon. Lord Balfour of Burleigh ...£2,000
Private Secretary, G. A. J. Lee £300
Under Secretary, Permanent, Sir Colin Scott-
Moncrieff, K.C.M.G., C.S.I. £1,500
Private Sec., J. H. Gascoigne......................£100
Asst. Und. Sec., W. Cospatrick Dunbar, C.B. £1,000
Senior Clerk, James M. Dodds ......£600 to £800
Junior Clerks, J. H. Gascoigne; H. M. Conacher
£200 to £500
Clerk of Accounts & Statistics, E. D. Berkeley £600
Assistant do., P. B. Moodie ......£300 to £400
Staff Clerk, R. Penny........................£250
2nd Div. Clerks, W. Hogg; T. C. Gilbert; C.
Weatherill; A. S. Cotton; W. G. Turner
£70 to £250

See also SCOTTISH SECTION, page 325.

STATIONERY OFFICE, Prince's Street, Storey's
Gate, S.W.—£570,535 (Salaries, £29,210).
Controller, Thomas Digby Pigott, C.B. £1,500
Private Sec., Wm. George Newton......*extra* £50
Assistant Controller, E. P. Plowman £650 to £750
Accountant, J. M. Galer ......£500 to £600
Registrar, F. Hayward ....£450 to £550
Storekeeper, William H. Harrison ......£450 to £550
Clerk of Publications, J. J. Anderson..........£500
Clerk in charge in Dublin, Herbert Taylor.....£500
Clerks, Assistants to Staff Officers, E. Bryan; C. H.
Dyason; C. Paull (Dublin); L. Pender
max. £450
Clerks, R. Barton; W. F. Gorin; W. G. Newton
(£470) ....max. £420
Clerks, J. T. Brooks; J. Lofts; T. A. Wilson
max. £400
2nd Div. Clerks, C. H. Balmain; E. G. Beck; J.
Brooks; E. H. Chapman; W. R. Codling; A. J.
Ellis*; C. Green*; L. W. Hill; D. W. Judge
(Dublin); A. E. Lacey; E. W. E. Liddington; G.
McIsaac; H. E. Pitman*; H. Proctor; A. L.
Screech; G. H. Thwaites*; I. A. H. Watson*;
H. M. Welch; G. H. Wright ......£70 to £250
Supt. of Printing, Robt. W. Moffrey £450 to £550
Assist. do., J. T. Bullock ......£350 to £440
Assist. Exam. of Printing and Binding in Dublin,
J. C. Rowden ....£200 to £300
Receiver of Job-work Printing, E. J. H. Stallybrass
£125 to £275
Examiners of Printers' Accounts, T. D. Dutton; C.
W. Howard, £260 to £400; A. G. Bishop
£260 to £375

* Temporary Staff Officers.

Exam. of Binding, F. J. Williamson £350 to £450
Assist. do., J. B. Crane ......£200 to £300
Exam. of Binders' Accts., G. D. Rose £150 to £300
Exam. of Paper, W. G. Wightman ...£400 to £500
Assistant ditto, George F. Whiles......£200 to £350

THAMES CONSERVANCY.
Victoria Embankment, E.C.
Chairman, Sir F. D. Dixon-Hartland, Bart., M.P.
Secretary, James H. Gough.
Engineer, Charles James More, C.E.
Solicitor, James Hughes.
Chemist, C. E. Groves, F.R.S.
Harbour Master, London, Captain L. W. E. Bowen.
Deputy Harbour Masters, Capt. A. W. Wilson;
Capt. R. S. Pasley.

TRADE, BOARD OF, Whitehall Gardens, S.W.—£68,042.

President, Rt. Hon. Charles T. Ritchie, M.P. £2,000
 Private Sec., Garnham Roper £300
 ,, ,, Lees Knowles, M.P. ....*unp.*
Parliamentary Sec., The Earl of Dudley ...£1,200
 Private Sec., J. G. Willis £100
Permanent Sec., Sir C. Boyle, K.C.B. £1,500 to £1,800
 Private Secs., E. G. Moggridge, £80; J. K. Grebby £70

Four Assistant Secretaries.

Railway Dept., F. J. S. Hopwood, C.B., C.M.G. £1,200
Finance Depart., Cosmo Monkhouse £1,200
Fisheries & Harbour Depart., Hon. T. H. W. Pelham £1,150
Marine Depart., Walter J. Howell £1,150
Principals, Hy. A. Dobson; E. Roscoe; Walter J. Howell; Sir Thomas Blomefield, Bart.; R. P. P. Bingham ....£650 to £800
1st Class Clerks, T. E. Price; J. W. Martyn; Henry R. Bence-Jones; R. C. Heron-Maxwell; John Taylor; Samuel Waddington; G. J. Stanley ....£400 to £600
2nd Class do., J. G. Willis; J. M. Nicolle; G. Roper; E. G. Moggridge; E. T. Griffith; E. C. Stoneham; W. F. Marwood; C. Hipwood; A. Barnes; O. Jones; H. S. Carllll ....£150 to £400
Chief Bookkeeper, G. S. Fry ....£500 to £600
Supt. of Registry, Thomas Anderson £500
Clerk in Charge of Work under Electric Lighting Acts, H. Booth.........................£400 to 500
Librarian, R. J. Lister ....£350 to £400
Do., in charge of Railway Plans, R. S. Lendrum £350
Assist. Clerks (1st *Class*), S. Bullock (£550); F. W. Haine; F. C. Pike; Frank Hardy; Henry Jolliffe; Lewis Browne; E. Portch; J. M. Spencer; John Peake; A. Hill ....£300 to £430
Assist. Clks. (2nd *Class*), T. Thorpe; P. H. Thomas; G. W. Sellar; Jas. Quick; G. E. Norman; A. Neeves; F. A. Fahy; P. J. Descours; J. G. Hargreaves; W. Greig ....£160 to £350
Supernumerary, Ditto, R. Broom; R. J. Sheldon £350
Second Div. (*Higher Grade*), J. C. Toovey; E. Andrews; G. W. Irons; J. L. Bendall; W. P. Scogings; R. E. Martyr; L. Goldie; S. R. Miles; A. C. W. Gay; T. Inch; G. Thornton; and W. Stanley, £250 to £350; and 47 second division clerks.

COMMERCIAL, LABOUR & STATISTICAL DEPARTMENT.—Labour Branch, 43 Parliament Street; Statistical, 1 Whitehall; Commercial Intelligence, 50, Parliament Street.—£19,708.
Controller-General, A. E. Bateman, C.M.G. £1,200 to £1,500
Deputy do. & Labour Commissioner, H. Llewellyn Smith ....£750 to £900
Assistant Labour Commissioner, A. Wilson Fox
Principal for Statistics, G. H. Simmonds ...£800
Principal for Commercial Intelligence, T. Worthington £800
Staff Clerks (for ditto), F. Barley; G. H. Sherton; and W. J. Glenny ...£720 to £1,050
Chief Labour Correspondent, J. Burnett £500
Labour Correspondents, Miss Clara E. Collett; C. J. Drummond; J. J. Dent ...£300 to £400
Translator, Edmund Gosse £400
Senior Investigator, F. H. McLeod £450 to £500
Investigators, D. F. Schloss and H. Fountain £700

LEGAL BRANCH.—£22,700.

Solicitor, Sir Walter Murton, C.B. £1,800
Assistant Solicitor, Edmund Potter ...£600 to £800
Principal Clerk, K. E. K. Gough.

Clerks, Edwin Gillett; G. C. Vaux; Hon. N. M. Farrer; J. Hutchins.
Clerk in Charge of Bankruptcy Sub-Department, H. E. Burgess; *Clerks,* W. T. Kaye; E. J. Merryweather; F. Wildey Wright.

PROFESSIONAL DEPARTMENT.

Professional Member of Marine Dept. (7 Whitehall Gardens), Capt. A. J. G. Chalmers...£800 to £1,000
Fisheries & Harbour Department, Capt. Hon. F. C. P. Vereker, R.N. £1,000
Inspector of Life-Saving Apparatus, Commander William Francis Edgar Freeland, R.N. £300
Chief Inspector of Fisheries, W. E. Archer. ...£800
Inspectors of Fisheries, Henry N. Malan; Charles Edward Fryer ....each £500

Office of Inspector of Railways, 8 Richmond Terrace, Whitehall, S.W.

Senior Insp., Col. Sir Francis Arthur Marindin, K.C.M.G.; *Inspectors,* Lt.-Col. Horatio Arthur Yorke, R.E.; Lt.-Col. P. G. Von Donop, R.E. £3,285
Electric Adviser, A. P. Trotter £800
Electrician, J. Rennie £300

BANKRUPTCY DEPARTMENT, Horse Guards Avenue, Whitehall, S.W.—£134,885.

Inspect.-Gen. in Bankruptcy, John Smith, C.B. £1,800
Inspectors, F. Wreford; E. Hough; W. Evans £2,800
Auditor, A. G. W. Gavin £650
Chief Bankruptcy Clerk, F. L. Clark £600 to £700
Examiners, R. C. Klyne; C. Keeble; H. N. Oakeshott £1,700
Junior Do., W. C. Taylor; J. F. Bird; C. Wright; F. A. Clarke; A. Mills; H. C. Watson; W. G. Knight; J. R. J. Johnston £310 to £400; A. H. S. Miller ....£300 to £350
Companies Clerk, E. W. Humphreys. £400
Staff Officers, A. A. Taylor; H. V. Bate; W. A. Clark; C. C. G. Stonhouse; R. F. Price; W. J. Walker; F. W. Pote; W. W. Coombs £2,040

Official Receivers in Bankruptcy, Bankruptcy Buildings, W.C.

Official Receivers, E. Leadam Hough (*senior*), £1,200; Alfred Henry Wildy; George Walter Chapman ....£800 to £1,000
Assist. Receivers (*senior*), W. P. Bowyer, £800; E. S. Grey; C. A. Pope; H. Ll. Howell £500 to £600

Official Receivers under Companies Winding-up Act, 1890.—Office, 33 Carey St., W.C.

Senior Off. Rec., G. S. Barnes £1,200
Official Receiver, H. De V. Brougham...........£1,000
Assistant ditto, A. S. Cully, £700; W. J. Warley; H. M. Winearls ....each £400 to £600

Receivers.

Birmingham, &c., Luke J. Sharp £1,075
Bristol, E. G. Clarke £1,000
Carmarthen and Swansea, Thomas Thomas ...£800
Hull, &c., Arthur Stewart Maples £1,000
Liverpool, F. Gittins £1,200
London and Northern Suburban, C. Mercer; A. Ewen; H. W. Cox £2,000
London & Southern Suburban, A. Mackintosh; E. W. J. Savill £1,450
Manchester, Christopher Jenkins Dibb £1,200
 Assistant, A. B. Potter.........................£500
Newcastle-on-Tyne, J. Grant Gibson £500
Nottingham, Henry Roby Thorpe £800
Newcastle-under-Lyme and Shrewsbury, &c., Thomas Bullock...................................£700

GENERAL REGISTER AND RECORD OFFICE OF SHIPPING AND SEAMEN, Custom House, E.C.—£14,103.

Registrar-General, John Clark Hall £900
Assist. Registrar-General, F. W. Gardner ...£700

Staff Clerks, C. H. Jones G. A. Hooke £900
Supernumerary, J. S. Home £400
Clerks, G. Cruickshank ; R. Denniford ; W. H.
Norton ; P. C. H. Jay ; J. M. Curtis ; R. A.
Mountjoy ; A. Clatworthy ; R. Hughes ; J. B.
Gaunt ; S. Kett ; H. Nicole £5,056

OFFICERS APPOINTED UNDER METROPOLITAN GAS
ACTS.
Referees, Augustus G. Vernon-Harcourt, F.R.S. ;
C. V. Boys, F.R.S. ; J. S. Haldane, F.R.S.
Chief Gas Examiner, Dr. Alexander William
Williamson, F.R.S.

STANDARDS DEPARTMENT, 7 Old Palace Yard,
S.W.—£2,877.
Superintendent, Henry J. Chaney £600

MARINE CONSULTATIVE BRANCH,
17-19 Bedford Street, W.C.
*Engineer Surveyor-in-Chief, and Inspector Chain
Cables and Anchor Proving Establishments*, P.
Samson, M.I.N.A. ....£600 to £800
Assistants to do., D. G. Watson ; W. T. Seaton ;
T. Carlton ; S. A. Houghton.
Clerks, G. T. Monson ; W. Taborn ; C. E. C.
Stead ; J. Tagg.
Princ. Shipwright Surv., W. D. Archer
......................£600 to £700
Prin. Surv. Tonnage, W. H. Laslett...£520 to £600
Assistants to do., J. T. Wilkins ; E. W. Colvill ;
A. J. Daniel ; T. Walton.
Clerks, W. Kent ; F. C. E. Steuart ; W. S.
Abbott ; E. J. Roddis.
Principal Examiner of Engineers, Jno. A. Rowe*
......................£420 to £500
 „ „ *in Navigation*, Capt. G. Beall £600
Assistant Examiner, Capt. J. Massey Harvey
......................£315 to £400
Assistant to Principal Examiner, Comm. F. Hay
Chapman, R.N.
Clerk, G. H. Keene.
*Survey for Passenger Certificates, Admeasurement
of Tonnage, Emigration Office, Detention of
Unseaworthy Vessels*, 79 Mark Lane, E.C.
Principal Officer, C. P. Wilson £700

BOARD OF TRADE, DUBLIN.
Princ. Off., Captain C. Johnson ; *Engineer Sur-
veyor*, J. J. Rose ; *Shipwright Surveyor*, Walter
Jubb ; *Clerk*, W. H. T. P. St. Austin.
BELFAST.— *Engineer Surveyors*, W. Fair ; J.
Mackellar ; *Shipwright Surveyors*, W. H. Chant-
ler ; J. W. Larcombe ; *Clerk*, J. H. Thomas.
LONDONDERRY.—*Engineer Surveyor*, Geo. Shott.
CORK.—*Engineer Surveyor*, C. O. Weeks ; *Ship-
wright Surveyor*, A. F. Weir.
QUEENSTOWN.—*Nautical Surveyor*, W. H. Wil-
loughby ; *Sanitary Surveyor*, F. W. Exham, M.B.

TREASURY, Whitehall, S.W.—£60,784.
FIRST LORD OF THE TREASURY—
The Rt. Hon. Arthur James Balfour, M.P. £5,000
Private Sec., J. S. Sandars ; Fred. S. Parry £300
CHANCELLOR OF THE EXCHEQUER—
Rt. Hon. Sir Michael E. Hicks-Beach, M.P. £5,000
Private Sec., Lawrence N. Guillemard £300
Assist. do., W. A. Mount £100
 „ „ W. C. Bridgeman ....*unp.*
 „ „ A. Griffith Boscawen, M.P. ......*unp.*
JUNIOR LORDS—
Henry Torrens Anstruther, M.P. £1,000
William Hayes Fisher, M.P. £1,000
Lord Stanley, M.P. £1,000

JOINT SECRETARIES—
Financial, Rt. Hon. R. W. Hanbury, M.P. ...£2,000
Private Sec., R. F. Wilkins £150
Do. (*P. O. business*) Henry Higgs £100
Patronage, Rt. Hon. Sir William Hood Walrond,
Bart., M.P. £2,000
Priv. Secs., Reginald Lucas, £200 ; John Wes-
terman Cawston £150
PERMANENT SECRETARY—
Sir Francis Mowatt, K.C.B. £2,500
Private Sec., Charles Ll. Davies £150
Assistant Sec., Sir Edw. W. Hamilton, K.C.B. £1,500
Auditor of the Civil List, Stephen E. Spring-Rice,
C.B. £1,500
Principal Clerks, F. A'Court Bergne ; George E.
Yorke Gleadowe, C.M.G. ; Robert Chalmers
each £1,000 to £1,200
1st Class Clerks, Ronald N. R. Ferguson ; Wm. A.
Dalrymple Hay ; Thomas L. Heath ; J. P.
Crowly ; F. S. Parry ; L. N. Guillemard
......................£700 to £900
2nd Class Clerks, Charles Ll. Davies ; J. W.
Cawston ; W. Blain ; T. Ll. Davies ; R. F.
Wilkins ; L. J. Hewby ; C. A. Phillimore ;
J. S. Bradbury ; M. G. Ramsay ; G. L. Barstow ;
M. F. Headlam ; H. Higgs ...... £200 to £500
Parliamentary Clerk, R. N. K. Ferguson.
Treasury Officers of Accounts, Sir E. W. Hamilton,
K.C.B. ; Percy Woods ....£850 to £1,000
Accountant, G. Pearson ....£600 to £900
Assistant do., George H. Hunt £600
Clerk for Wreck Inquiry Business, W. E. S. Thom-
son £600
Assist. Auditor of Sheriffs' Accounts, G. W.
Couch ....£200 to 400
Superintendent of Registry, F. C. Stephenson £500
Clerk in Charge of Paper Room, A. J. Hiscock
......................£300 to £400
Assistant to Parly. Clerk, E. Tigar ...£300 to £400
Clerks, J. Davies, £385 ; C. Waters £425
2nd Div. Clerks, Higher Grade, F. G. Clarke ;
J. Fry ; R. J. Luff ; T. Sibley ; E. Usher
......................£250 to £350

Parliamentary Counsel, 3 Whitehall Gardens, S.W.
Counsel, Sir Courtenay P. Ilbert, K.C.S.I., C.I.E. £2,500
Assist. do., Mackenzie D. Chalmers, C.S.I. .. £2,000
Clerks, Frederick Wm. Gardiner ; Albert Prince
Bishop ; Edward Gardiner............£100 to £400

*Department of Solicitor to the Treasury, Director
of Public Prosecutions and Queen's Proctor*,
Treasury Chambers, Whitehall—£23,442.
Solicitor, and Director of Public Prosecutions, The
Earl of Desart, K.C.B. £2,500
Assistant Solicitors, J. Francis Chance, £1,500 ;
Barnard Thomas, £1,200 ; John P. Mellor, £1,000
Assistants, Wm. Brown, £1,000 ; Frederick William
Hayden ; Henry E. F. Comyn ....£600 to £900
1st Class Clerks, H. M. Warne ; A. S. Lewis ; W.
de G. Iamotte ; F. J. Sims ; F. G. Frayling ;
C. H. E. Fletcher ....£350 to £500
Clerk in charge of Accounts, W. C. B. Ravn
......................£350 to £500
Supplementary Clerk, W. F. Addey..............£320
Professional Clerks, R. H. Gardner ; C. E. Stred-
wick ; F. J. Williamson ; S. Pearce ; R. M.
Greenwood ; W. Lewis ; A. F. Rowe ; H. A.
Weeks ; A. E. Wade ; G. H. Morrell ; G. C. J.
Crispin ; P. F. W. Le Breton.
Clerks, Account Branch, C. H. Hunt ; W. J.
Hagon.
Clerks, A. Browning ; A. C. Crane ; H. S. Free-
stone ; W. G. Hawkins ; A. E. Lamb ; T. H.
Lentz ; W. J. Rider ; W. C. Rudge ; W. F.
Sewel ; R. J. Wilson.

* Office : 79 Mark Lane, E.C.

Queen's Proctor's Department—
Queen's Proctor, The Earl of Desart, K.C.B.
Assistant Queen's Proctor, Wm. Brown.
Clerks, F. Burnay ; C. E. Stredwick.

Law Courts Branch.

Principal, A. T. Hare £1,200
Assistant for Chancery and Charity Business, J. Rye
                    £400 to £650

County Court Department.—£39,714.

Rating of Government Property.—Office £2,505
Treasury Valuer & Insp., R. J. Thompson
            £1,000 to £1,200
Clerk, Arthur Paxon £600
2nd Div. Clerk, Upper Grade, W. A. Walker £310
  (Rates on Government Property, £434,800.)
Fines and Penalties, 30 Abingdon Street, S.W.
Receiver, Thomas Edward Kebbel, M.A.

TRINITY HOUSE, Tower Hill, E.C.
Master, H.R.H. the Duke of York, K.G., elect. 1894.
Deputy do., Capt. George R. Vyvyan, R.N.R.
Secretary, Charles A. Kent.
Principals, E. Price Edwards ; Arthur Owen ;
  Horace Smith (*Accountant*).
Senior Clerks, H. G. Willett ; H. A. Measor ;
  E. G. Weller ; W. K. Bowen.
Engineer-in-Chief, Thomas Matthews, M.INST.C.E.
Principal Pilotage Clerk, D. Keigwin.

WALLACE COLLECTION, Hertford House, W.—
        £12,000.
Keeper and Sec., Claude Phillips ......£500 to £600

WAR OFFICE, Pall Mall, S.W.—£248,300.
Secretary of State for War, Most Hon. the
  Marquess of Lansdowne, K.G. £5,000
  Private Sec., H. P. Harvey £300
  Assistant do., H. W. W. McAnally £150,
    and H. Morrison .... unp.
  Extra do., Sir C. G. E. Welby, Bt., C.B..... unp.
Financial Sec., J. Powell Williams, M.P. £1,500
  Private Sec., W. L. McArthur £150

UNDER SECRETARIES.
Parliamentary, G. Wyndham, M.P. £1,500
  Private Sec., P. H. Hanson £150
Permanent, Sir Ralph Henry Knox, K.C.B. £2,000
  Private Sec., N. F. B. Osborn £150
Assistant, G. D. A. Fleetwood Wilson, C.B £1,200
Accountant-Gen., F. T. Marzials £1,500
Deputy do., Thomas Cave-Browne-Cave .. £1,200
Assist. do., W. Seed ; A. Higgins and A. à
  Beckett (acting) .... each £1,000
Director of Army Contracts, Alfred Major.. £1,200
Director of Army Clothing Factory, H. D. de la
  Bère £1,000
Chaplain-Gen., Rev. John Cox Edghill, D.D. £1,000
Chief Superintendent Ordnance Factories, Col.
  E. Bainbridge, C.B. £1,800
  (*See also* MILITARY DEPARTMENT, *page* 192.)

WOODS, FORESTS, AND LAND REVENUES,
  1 and 2 Whitehall Place, S.W.—£21,400.
Commissioners, Edward Stafford Howard ; John
  Francis Fortescue Horner ....each £1,200
Principal Clerk, Frederick Hellard ...£600 to £900

Do., Charles E. Howlett..............£600 to £800
Senior Clerks, Charles B. Stableforth; Stuart
  Futcher....................................£420 to £580
First Class Clerks, Algernon M. Hart.£300 to £430;
  Morton Evans ; W. Dawson Ainger ; F. J.
  Wardale ; D. R. C. Smith ; J. R. Maple
                 £300 to £400
Second Class do., H. J. Eyles ; E. Blanford;
  W. Lee-Nash ; G. H. Burnett ; J. Whyte;
  T. A. Cochrane ; G. P. Best ; H. Clarke
             £100 to £275
Receiver-General, J. Murray Duncan £900
Chief Mineral Insp., Thomas Forster Brown £700
Bookkeeper, Edward Burrough ....£400 to £600
      OFFICE IN DUBLIN.
Senior Clerk, J. Harper Scaife, LL.B. £420 to £580
First Class do., W. Fidler ....£300 to £400
      SOLICITORS' BRANCH.
Solicitor, Thomas William Gorst £1,500
Clerks, D. Westmacott; F. J. Kent; E. S. Grant;
  W. C. Martin ; E. W. Welley £1,560
Solicitor, Scotland, Thomas Carmichael, S.S.C.
Do., Ireland, Hallowes & Hamilton, Dublin.
      WOODS AND FORESTS.
New Forest, Alice Holt, Bere, Parkhurst & Woolmer—
  Deputy Surveyor, Hon. Gerald William Lascelles.
Dean—Gaveller, Edward Stafford Howard.
  Do. Deputy do., Thomas Forster Brown.
  Do. Dep. Surv. & Crown Receiver, Philip Baylis.
Windsor—Ranger, H.R.H. Prince Christian, K.G.
  Do. Deputy do., Captain Walter Campbell.
  Do. Bailiff, S. Collard.
  Do. Deputy Surveyor, Frederick Simmonds.
New Forest—Official Verderer, Rt. Hon. Evelyn
  Ashley.

Land Revenue Records and Enrolments.
St. Stephen's House, Westminster, S.W.—£1,377.
Keeper of Records, Maurice H. Hewlett £700
Assistant, W. J. Green ....£250 to £350

WORKS AND PUBLIC BUILDINGS,
  12 Whitehall Place, S.W.—£55,333.
First Commissioner, Right Hon. Aretas Akers-
  Douglas, M.P. £2,000
Private Secs., H. J. Hapgood, £200 ; R. Ford £100
Secretary, Viscount Esher, C.B. £1,200
Principal Clerks, J. Willis ; H. R. Potter each £900
Clerk of Accounts, F. Woodfall. £600
Senior Clerks, J. Fitzgerald ; M. Hooper ; W. J.
  Downer ; H. M. Paull ....each £600
1st Class Clerks, H. Wordley ; W. R. Kerr ; J. R.
  Bradford ; W. Torpy ; T. G. Elliott ; H. J.
  Hapgood ; W. H. David ; F. O. Drew, each £400
Consulting Surveyor, Sir John Taylor, K.C.B.
Principal Surveyors W. W. Robertson (Edin.),
  £1,000 ; H. Tanner £1,200
Surveyors, E. G. Rivers ; J. Wager ; W. Cowan
  (acting) ; J. B. Westcott ; W. T. Oldrieve ; H.
  N. Hawks ....£500 to £700
Inspector of Ancient Monuments, Gen. Augustus
  Henry Pitt-Rivers, F.R.S.
Controller of Stores, R. Bailey £700
  Do. Deputy, J. H. Hillier £400
Do. of Contracts for Coals, &c., E. Price......£350

GREAT LAW OFFICERS OF THE CROWN.

Lord High Chancellor, Right Hon. Hardinge Stanley, Earl of Halsbury £10,000
 Private Secretary, Edmund Hall Alderson £500
Attorney-General, Sir Richard E. Webster, Bt., G.C.M.G., Q.C., M.P. £7,000 and fees (in 1897-98 £8,183)
Solicitor-General, Sir Robert Bannatyne Finlay, Q.C. M.P. ...... £6,000 and fees (in 1897-98 £6,029)

SCOTLAND.
Lord Advocate, Right Hon. Andrew Graham Murray, Q.C., M.P. £5,000
Solicitor-General, Charles Scott Dickson, Q.C. £2,000

IRELAND.
Lord Chancellor, Right Hon. Lord Ashbourne £8,000
 Private Secretary, M. L. O'Connor Morris £500
Attorney-General, Right Hon. John Atkinson, Q.C., M.P. £5,000
Solicitor-General, Dunbar P. Barton, Q.C., M.P. £2,000

APPELLATE TRIBUNALS.
HOUSE OF LORDS.
The Lord High Chancellor.
The Right Hon. Hardinge Stanley, Earl of Halsbury £10,000

Lords of Appeal in Ordinary.
The Right Hon. Lord Macnaghten £6,000
The Right Hon. Lord Morris £6,000
The Right Hon. Lord Davey £6,000
The Right Hon. Lord Robertson £6,000
And such Peers of Parliament as are holding, or have held, high judicial office.

JUDICIAL COMMITTEE OF THE PRIVY COUNCIL.
Downing Street, S.W.

The Committee is composed of Members of the Privy Council qualified under 3 & 4 Wm. IV. cap 41; 3 & 4 Vict. cap. 86; 34 & 35 Vict. cap. 91; 39 & 40 Vict. cap. 59; and 50 & 51 Vict. cap. 70. The members usually attending are the Lord Chancellor, the Lords of Appeal in Ordinary (Macnaghten, Morris, Davey, Robertson); Lord Hobhouse, K.C.S.I.; Lord Ashbourne; Lord Shand: Lord James of Hereford; Sir Richard Couch.

Registrar, Edward Stanley Hope, C.B. £1,200
Chief Clerk (Judicial), G. P. Wheeler, B.A. ...£600
Record Clerk, Thomas Preston, F.S.A. £400
3rd Clerk, James C. Ledlie, M.A. £400
Registrar in Ecclesiastical and Maritime Causes, J. G. Smith, M.A. (Admiralty Registry, Royal Courts).

SUPREME COURT OF JUDICATURE.
COURT OF APPEAL.

EX-OFFICIO JUDGES.
The Lord High Chancellor, the Lord Chief Justice of England, the Master of the Rolls, and the President of the Probate, Divorce, and Admiralty Division.

MASTER OF THE ROLLS.
The Rt. Hon. Sir Nathaniel Lindley £6,000

LORDS JUSTICES.
The Rt. Hon. Sir Archibald Levin Smith... £5,000
The Rt. Hon. Sir John Rigby £5,000
The Rt. Hon. Sir Richard Henn Collins ...£5,000
The Rt. Hon. Sir Roland Vaughan Williams £5,000
The Rt. Hon. Sir Robert Romer £5,000

Officers of the MASTER OF THE ROLLS.—£1,125.
Secretary, Walter B. Lindley £500
Principal Clerk. N. Butcher.
Junior Clerk, W. Vere.

HIGH COURT OF JUSTICE.
CHANCERY DIVISION.
Justice, The Rt. Hon. Lord High Chancellor.
The Hon. Sir Ford North £5,000
The Hon. Sir James Stirling £5,000
The Hon. Sir Arthur Kekewich £5,000
The Hon. Sir Edmund W. Byrne £5,000
The Hon. Sir H. H. Cozens-Hardy £5,000
The Hon. Sir George Farwell £5,000

QUEEN'S BENCH DIVISION.
Lord Chief Justice of England, The Rt. Hon. Charles, Lord Russell of Killowen, G.C.M.G. ...£8,000
 Secretary, Hon. Arthur Russell £500
 Chief Clerk, Robert John Block £400
Justices—
The Hon. Sir James Charles Mathew £5,000
The Hon. Sir John Charles Day £5,000
The Hon. Sir Alfred Wills £5,000
The Hon. Sir William Grantham £5,000
The Hon. Sir John Compton Lawrance £5,000
The Hon. Sir Robert Samuel Wright £5,000
The Hon. Sir Gainsford Bruce £5,000
The Hon. Sir William Rann Kennedy £5,000
The Hon. Sir Edward Ridley £5,000
The Hon. Sir John Charles Bigham £5,000
The Hon. Sir Charles John Darling £5,000
The Hon. Sir Arthur Moseley Channell ...£5,000
The Hon. Sir Walter Phillimore. Bart. £5,000
The Hon. Sir Thomas T. Bucknill £5,000

PROBATE, DIVORCE, & ADMIRALTY DIV.
President, Rt. Hon. Sir Fras. H. Jeune, K.C.B. £5,000
Justice, The Hon. Sir John Gorell Barnes ...£5,000

BANKRUPTCY DIVISION.
Justice, The Hon. Sir Robt. Saml. Wright £5,000

COURT OF ARCHES.
Judge, Sir Arthur Charles.

COURTS, OFFICERS, &c.
CROWN OFFICE, House of Lords.—£1,133.
Chief Clerk, Adolphus Geo. Chas. Liddell ...£60?

LORD CHANCELLOR'S OFFICE, House of Lords.—£3,296.
Permanent Sec. and Clerk of the Crown, Sir Kenneth A. Muir-Mackenzie, K.C.B., Q.C. £1,800
Assist. Sec. and Priv. Sec. for Ecclesiastical Patronage, Adolphus George Charles Liddell £100
Private Sec. and Sec. of Commissions of the Peace, Edward Hall Alderson £500
Sergeant-at-Arms, Sir Arthur Ellis, K.C.V.O.
Deputy do., Samuel Hand.
Clerk of the Chamber, Edward Preston £400
Clerk, Henry Robert White £400
Messenger of the Great Seal, Richard Davis ...£350

CHANCERY COURTS.—£39,467.

Justice, The Hon. Sir Ford North.
Principal Clerk, John Seymour................£400
At Chambers.—Masters of the Supreme Court, A to
F, Spencer Whitehead ; *G* to *N,* Edmd. W.
Walker ; *O* to *Z,* J. C. Fox ....each £1,500
Justice, The Hon. Sir James Stirling.
Principal Clerk, C. F. Williams £400
At Chambers.—Masters of the Supreme Court, A to
F, Wm. Binns-Smith ; *G* to *N,* S. M. Satow ;
O to *Z,* T. A. Romer ....each £1,500
Justice, The Hon. Sir Arthur Kekewich.
Principal Clerk, Charles G. Weller £400
At Chambers.—Masters of the Supreme Court, A to
F, W. O. Hewlett, £1,200 ; *G* to *N,* Edw.
Lionel Clarke ; *O* to *Z,* Richard John Villiers
each £1,500
Justice, The Hon. Sir Edmund W. Byrne
Principal Clerk, Edward Carter £400
At Chambers.—Masters of the Supreme Court, A to
F, Charles Burney ; *G* to *N,* John Wm. Hawkins ;
O to *Z.* George Augustus Crowder ..each £1,500
Justice, The Hon. Sir H. H. Cozens-Hardy.
Principal Clerk, William P. Mara £400
Justice, The Hon. Sir George Farwell.

CHANCERY REGISTRARS' OFFICE.—£28,262.
Registrars, Loftus L. Pemberton £2,000 ; Herbert
Innes Jackson ; Charles Carrington ; G. Lavie ;
Warren Pugh ; Charles Beal ; Richard H. W.
Leach ; Robert S. Godfrey ; C. E. Farmer ; W.
Tindal King ; W. E. Church ; R. F. K. Greswell................................£1,250 to £1,800
Principal Clerks, W. F. Leach ; A. G. Theed ;
W. O. Goldschmidt ; Charles Merivale ; A. H.
Borrer ; Frederick T. Bloxam ; Francis J.
Synge ; H. S. Jolly ; G. W. Lavie £300 to £800

TAXING-MASTERS, Chancery Division, Royal
Courts of Justice.—£16,877.
Markham Spofforth ; Henry Skipper Ryland ;
Wm. Frederick Baker ; Edwd. Shearme ; T. H.
Bolton ; A. Rawlinson ; H. R. T. Alexander
each £1,500
Principal Clerks, Robert G. Laybourn ; Charles
William Scott ; James R. Howes ; E. G. Box ;
W. J. Bannehr ; J. B. Dunning ; J. W. Malyon
£500 to £600
Clerks, C. Baylis ; C. Hunt ; W. C. Brett ; H. F.
Blake ; C. Atherton ; E. Corley ; H. P. C. De
Lisle ....£100 to £400

OFFICERS OF THE SUPREME COURT.—£5,060.
Referees, Henry Wm. Verey ; George Wirgman
Hemming, Q.C. ; Edward Pollock ..each £1,500
Official Solr., Wm. Howard Winterbotham £1,100

SUPREME COURT PAY OFFICE.—£22 729.
Asst. Paym.-Gen., Thomas Lewis................£1,200
Deputy do., William Hugh Rowe £900
Principal Clerks, W. Oliver ; C. J. A. Meijer ; T.
H. Sharp ; J. Headland ; H. N. Colville ...£800
Stockbroker, William Mortimer £700

CENTRAL OFFICE OF THE SUPREME
COURT.—£42,980.
Senior Master and Queen's Remembrancer, George
Frederick Pollock.

MASTERS OF THE SUPREME COURT.
Marcus Hy. Johnson (a) ; Charles Manley Smith ;
Joseph Kaye ; Chas. Henry Walton ; Lord
Dunboyne ; James Robert Mellor ; John
Macdonell, C.B., LL.D. ; Edward Wilberforce ;
Wm. Fred. Alphonse Archibald ...each £1,500
(a) Mr. Johnson is the prescribed officer under the Municipal Elections Petitions Act.

Assistant Masters, Hon. Gilbert J. D. Coleridge ;
Egerton Baring Lawford ; W. H. Macnamara
each £800 to £1,000
WRIT, APPEARANCE, AND JUDGMENT DEPARTMENT.*
Head Clerk, Francis A. Stringer (Room 75) ......‡
Deputy Head Clerk, N. A. Aldridge ....‡
Clerks, A to *K,* G. A. Stonhouse ; B. E. Hodgson ;
P. Richards ; W. T. Cooke ; J. Johnston ; R.
E. Ross ; R. Macgregor ; R. O. Roberts ; *L* to
Z, W. G. Chapman ; E. V. Methold ; S. P.
Ilbert ; H. P. Cottam ; F. C. S. S. Booty ; A.
Brocklesby ; H. J. Matthews ; P. Clark ....‡

SUMMONS AND ORDER DEPARTMENT.†
Head Clerk, P. E. Vizard ....‡
Clerks, E. H. Hallett ; J. F. Townesend ; W. H.
Waugh ; G. G. Lacey ; J. C. Watson ; P. A.
Quinn ; G. E. L. Coulson ....‡

FILING AND RECORD DEPARTMENT.*
(Including *Affidavits*) Swearing Affidavits, Room 85.
Head Clerk, C. H. Murray ....‡
Clerks, E. J. Oram ; A. T. Pask ; W. Harrison ;
J. H. Bradley ; W. Higgs ; C. Timms ; T. D.
Salter ; A. J. Penny ; W. W. Melville ; T. A.
Hanlon ; E. Hicks-Beach ....‡
Book Shewer, H. F. Taylor.

TAXING DEPARTMENT.*
Head Clerk, Alfred Vincent ....‡
Clerks, R. E. Mackinnon ; George A. N. Kitson ‡
Election Petitions, E. C. Cooke.

INROLMENT DEPARTMENT.
Clerks, Edwin Morgan ; Fred. G. Woodall........‡
QUEEN'S REMEMBRANCER'S, JUDGMENTS, AND
ACKNOWLEDGMENTS DEPARTMENT.*
Queen's Remembrancer, Master Geo. F. Pollock £300
Registrar of Married Women's Acknowledgments,
Master Joseph Kaye.............................£200
Clerks, Richard Hankins ; Herbert Radcliffe ; J.
J. Harris ; Herbert A. Hance ; Hugh M. Drake ‡
BILLS OF SALE AND DEEDS OF ARRANGEMENT
DEPARTMENT.*
Head Clerk, Edward L. Hill ....‡
Deputy Head Clerk, W. J. Weller.
Clerks, A. S. Frayling ; S. Hall ; C. H. Barnes...‡
Book Shewer, E. T. Welch.

CROWN OFFICE DEPARTMENT.*—£923.
Queen's Coroner and Attorney and Master of Crown
Office, James Robert Mellor £100
Assistant Master, Hon. Gilbert Coleridge.
Clerks, Frederick H. Short ; E. H. D. Image ;
John L. B. Short ; F. Hullah ....‡
Associates' and Court Order Department of the
Crown Office.†
Assistant Master of the Crown Office, Egerton C. B.
Lawford.
Clerks, John B. Davis ; Joseph Davis ; John
Baines ; Thomas W. Reed ; J. E. Bentley ; L.
Bolton ; James Kenyon ; A. H. Gipps ; Adolphus St. J. W. Wriford ; H. M. W. Baynes ;
W. J. Field ; A. O. Thomas ; W. E. Davis .....‡
COURTS OF JUSTICE SCRIVENERY DEPARTMENT.
Superintendent, F. A. Stringer (Room 75).
Distributor and Auditor, F. Wortham.
Bookkeeper, Benj. Heasman.
Assistant, C. W. Peachey.

PROBATE, DIVORCE, & ADMIRALTY DIV.
President, Rt. Hon. Sir Francis Hy. Jeune, K.C.B.
Secretary, Hon. Sydney Peel £300
Clerk, Philip Dyke £400

_____
* Office hours, 10 to 4 ; Saturdays and Vacation, 10 to 2.
† Office hours, 11 to 5 ; Saturdays and Vacation, 11 to 3.
‡ The salaries of clerks in the Central Office range from, 1st class, £500 to £800 ; 2nd class, £250 to £500 ; 3rd class, £100 to £300.

Judge, Hon. Sir John Gorell Barnes £5,000
Clerk, George Tait £400
Admiralty Advocate, Rt. Hon. Sir James Parker
    Deane, Q.C., D.C.L.
Queen's Proctor, The Earl of Desart, K.C.B. £2,000

PRINCIPAL PROBATE REGISTRY, Somerset House.—
    £37,485.
Registrars, David H. Owen (*Senior*), £1,600; Robt.
    Albion Pritchard, D.C.L.; James Chitty Hannen;
    Alfred Musgrave ....£1,200 to £1,500
Record Keeper, T. W. Simons £600
Sealer, Amyatt Edmund Ray £300

ADMIRALTY REGISTRY AND MARSHAL'S OFFICE,
    Royal Courts of Justice.—£7,387.
Registrar, J. G. Smith, M.A. £1,500
Assistant Registrar, E. S. Roscoe £1,200
Marshal and Chief Clerk, C. M. Callow
                      £700 to £800
Clerks, G. M. Cockell; W. T. Rolfe; J. H. John-
    son; J. Pope; R. Incledon (also in charge of
    Slave Trade matters): E. S. Davison; F. A.
    Wright; H. W. Lovell; A. E. J. Harris
                      £100 to £600
Messengers, T. Ellis; H. Crease.

BANKRUPTCY DEPARTMENT,
    Carey Street, Lincoln's Inn Fields.—£14,732.
Judge, Hon. Sir Robert Samuel Wright £5,000
**Clerk of the Court,* £500
Senior Registrar, Jas. Rigg Brougham £1,500
Registrars, Harry Stanley Giffard; John E. Link-
    later; Herbert James Hope; Henry J. Hood.
                  £1,200 to £1,500
*Chief Clerk (*Senior Registrar's Department*),
    Samuel R. Stockton £600
Taxing-Master, John A. Chas. Tanner, M.A. £1,500
Senior Official Receiver, E. Leadam Hough £1,200
Official Receivers, George Walter Chapman;
    Alfred H. Wildy.
Assistant do., Egerton S. Grey; H. L. Howell;
    Charles A. Pope; W. P. Bowyer.
    **Affidavits may be sworn before these officers.*

COMPANIES (WINDING-UP),
    Bankruptcy Buildings, Carey Street, W.C.
Judge, Hon. Sir Robert Samuel Wright.
Registrar, Henry John Hood £1,200
Principal Clerk, Thomas Barnes.*
Second Class Clerks, Frank E. W. Nichols *; W. T.
    Roberts.
Third do., Alfred Paget; Audley R. G. Wil-
    loughby; C. Samuels; J. R. Bull; M. Johnson.
Senior Official Receiver, G. S. Barnes.
Official Receiver, Harold de Vaux Brougham.
Assistant do., A. S. Cully; W. J. Warley; H. M.
    Winearls.
    * Commissioners for Oaths.

CROWN CASES RESERVED COURT.
Judges.—The Judges of the High Court of Justice.
Clerk, John B. Davis £100

ECCLESIASTICAL COURTS.
Judge, Sir Arthur Charles.
    [Judge of the Provincial Courts of Canterbury
    and York under "The Public Worship Regu-
    lation Act, 1874," and as such is also Dean of
    the Arches and Master of the Faculties.]
COURT OF ARCHES (REGISTRY, 1, The Sanctuary).
Dean of the Arches, Sir Arthur Charles.
Registrar, Frederick Hugh Lee.
Clerk and Record Keeper, Kenneth Munro.

COURT OF FACULTIES (Registry and Office for Mar-
    riage Licences. &c.), 23 Knightrider Street,
    Doctors' Commons, E.C. Office hours 10 to 4;
    Saturdays, 10 to 2.
Master, Sir Arthur Charles, D.C.L.
Registrar, William Price Moore.
    Deputy do., Edmund Charles Currey.
Clerk and Record Keeper, Henry Tayler.
    Assistant, B. B. Bull.
Seal Keeper, Cyrus Waddilove.
    Sealer, Edwin Pitt.

VICAR-GENERAL'S OFFICE for Granting Marriage
    Licences, and COURT OF PECULIARS, 3 Creed
    Lane, Ludgate Hill, E.C. Office hours 10 to 4;
    Saturdays 10 to 2.
Vicar-General, The Rt. Hon. Sir James Parker
    Deane, D.C.L., Q.C.
Registrar, Sir John Hassard, K.C.B.
Chief Clerk and Record Keeper, Thomas G. Ryder.
    Assistant, Arthur Ryder.
    DEAN AND CHAPTER OF ST. PAUL'S COURT.
Commissary, Arthur Milman.
Chapter Clerk and Registrar, H. W. Lee, 1 The
    Sanctuary, Westminster.
Receiver, G. J. Murray.
THE BISHOP OF LONDON'S CONSISTORY COURT, 1
    Dean's Court, E.C.
Judge, Thomas Hutchinson Tristram, Q.C., D.C.L.
Registrar, Harry Wilmot Lee.
Apparitor-General, W. A. Ryder.
Record Keeper, H. E. Tayler.
    Assistant, A. C. Cross.

LUNACY COMMISSION,
    19 Whitehall Place, S.W.—£14,446.
Chairman, Rt. Hon. Earl Waldegrave.
Commissioners, Sir John Edward Dorington, Bt.,
    M.P.; John Davies Cleaton, M.R.C.S. ....unp.
Commissioners (paid): *Legal,* Charles Samuel
    Bagot; William Edward Frere; George Harold
    Urmson; *Medical,* Fredk. Needham, M.D.;
    Edward Marriott Cooke, M.B.; Sidney Coup-
    land, M.D. ....each £1,500
Secretary, Hardinge Frank Giffard £800 to £1,000
Chief Clerk, Charles Deans ....£500 to £600

MASTERS IN LUNACY AND VISITORS IN
LUNACY.
    Royal Courts of Justice.—£15,985.
Masters, Thomas Halhed Fischer, Q.C.; William
    Ambrose, Q.C. ....each £2,000
Chief Clerk, T. A. Southwell Keely £800
Visitors in Lunacy, Ralph Charlton Palmer (*Legal*);
    Sir James Crichton-Browne, M.D., LL.D., F.R.S.;
    David Nicolson, M.D., C.B. ....each £1,500
Secretary, O. E. Dickinson £300

RAILWAY AND CANAL COMMISSION,
    Rooms 106 and 108 Royal Courts.—£6,970.
Ex-officio Commissioners. The Hon. Mr. Justice
    Wright (*England*); The Hon. Lord Stormonth-
    Darling (*Scotland*); The Rt. Hon. Mr. Justice
    Gibson (*Ireland*) ....unp.
Commissioners, Right Hon. Sir Frederick Peel,
    K.C.M.G.; Viscount Cobham £3,000
Registrar, Walter Henry Macnamara
Clerk, Thomas Whittall £300

LIGHT RAILWAY COMMISSION.
    54 Parliament Street, S.W.—£2,200.
Commissioners, The Earl of Jersey, G.C.M.G. (*Chair-
    man*); Gerald A. R. FitzGerald, *unpaid*; Col.
    George F. Ottley Boughey, R.E., C.S.I. ...£1,000
Secretary, Henry Allan Steward £400

Assist. Secs., Alan D. Erskine; Viscount Emlyn;
Hon. G. Gathorne-Hardy.
Clerks, Ralph P. Stoneham : W. W. W. Stevens ;
A. H. Dawson ; W. G. Adams.

LAND REGISTRY OFFICE,

34 Lincoln's Inn Fields, W.C.—Office hours, 10 to
4 ; Saturdays, 10 to 12 ; in vacation, 11 to 2.
Registrar, Robert Hallett Holt £1,800
Chief Assist. do., Chas. Fortescue Brickdale £900
Examiners of Titles, Arthur Burrows ....*Fees*
Chief Clerk, George Abbott £400
Solicitor Clerk, G. Irving Holt £400

Registration of Title Department.
Assist. Registrars, Hugh Pollock ; T. S. Drury.
1st Class *Clerks*, W. L. Spofforth ; E. J. Harvey.
Clerks, H. Spink ; G. W. Falkner ; H. S. Jolly.

Survey and Map Department,
Director of Surveys, Col. F. P. Washington, R.E.
Chief Surveyor, James R. Burnage.
Surveyors, W. S. Tratman ; A. Fraser ; R. R.
Baterden.
Land Charges Registration and Search Department,
34 Lincoln's Inn Fields.
Clerks, Ernest W. Eaton ; J. P. Purcell £490

Middlesex Deeds Department.
33 Lincoln's Inn Fields.
Chief Clerk, J. E. Ansell £400
Second Clerks, E. Buckland ; E. H. Foird..£300
Senior Examiner, G. T. Hills £200
Clerks, G. Golding ; G. A. H. Robson ; J. D.
Dart; E. Sheffield; E. W. Braine; G. H. Abbott,
each £200

YORKSHIRE LAND REGISTRY.

East Riding, *Beverley*—G. A. Thompson.
West   ,,   *Wakefield*—William Pickard.
North   ,,   *Northallerton*—C. E. L. Ringrose.

SHERIFFS' OFFICES AND OFFICERS,

SHERIFFS' AND SECONDARY'S OFFICE,
Guildhall, E.C.
Secondary and Under Sheriff of the City of London,
Thomas Roderick.
Officers to Sheriffs of London ["Sergeants at Mace."]
—Samuel Heywood ; Edgar T. Odell ; David
Hibbard; W. Holland.

SHERIFF OF ESSEX' OFFICE.
London Agents, Gepp & Sons, 107 Temple Chambers,
Temple Avenue, E.C.

SHERIFF OF HAMPSHIRE'S OFFICE,
11 Bedford Row, W.C.
London Agents, Prior, Church & Adams.

SHERIFF OF HERTS' OFFICE, 25 Lincoln's Inn Fields,
W.C.
Agents, Patersons, Snow, Bloxam, and Kinder.

SHERIFF OF KENT'S OFFICE, 24 Bedford Row.
London Agents, Palmer & Bull.

SHERIFF OF MIDDLESEX' OFFICE,
29 Essex Street, Strand, W.C.
Under Sheriff, William Ruston.
Officer to Sheriff, B. G. Pring, 33 Chancery Lane.

SHERIFF OF OXFORDSHIRE, DURHAM, & GLAMORGAN-
SHIRE, 48 Chancery Lane, W.C.
London Agents, Cunliffes and Davenport.

SHERIFF OF SUFFOLK'S OFFICE, 35 John Street,
Bedford Row, W.C.
London Agents, Belfrage and Co.

SHERIFF OF SURREY'S OFFICE, 31 Lincoln's Inn
Fields, W.C.
Under Sheriff, Charles Wigan.

SHERIFF OF SUSSEX' OFFICE, 24 Bedford Row, W.C.
Under-Sheriff, Walter Bartlett.

CITY COURTS.

LORD MAYOR'S COURT, Guildhall.
Judges, The Lord Mayor and Aldermen.
The Recorder, The Rt. Hon. Sir Charles Hall,
     K.C.M.G., Q.C., M.P..................£4,000
Common Serjeant, Sir Forrest Fulton, Q.C. £3,000
Assistant Judge, Francis Roxburgh, LL.M...£1,500
Registrar, Frank Stather Jackson £1,000
Assistant Registrar, David Harrison £500
Sergeant at Mace, Christopher Fitch £500
Deputy do., John Fitch £375
Chief Clerk, Alfred Henry White..................£400

CITY OF LONDON COURT, Guildhall.
Judge, Robert Malcolm Kerr, LL.D............£2,400
Assistant do., Julian Robins.
Treasurer, The Chamberlain of London.
Registrar, James Anstey Wild, jun. £1,700
Assist. do., Evelyn Brooksbank Tattershall...£600
High Bailiff, J. Edward Sly £600

COUNTY COURTS.

Treasury County Court Department—£25,000.
Treasury, Whitehall (11 to 5).
Superintendent, B. J. Bridgeman......£650 to £850
Clerk of Accounts, F. Arthy £400
Deputy do., F. W. J. Kemp ....£250 to £400
Examiners of Accounts, W. G. Heppel; W. A.
Slade ; W. Biles ; H. B. Moore ; G. H.
Bowkett ; H. Cautherley ; J. Andrew; W.
Morgan ; G. J. Whitehouse ; E. B. Goodwin;
H. Baber ; T. Stinton ; W. Massey ; J. F.
Jones ; A. F. F. Wright; G. T. Thompson;
F. Edge; E. Hopkins; F. W. Brook; J. R.
Folkes ; J. E. H. Burnet .... £200 to £400
Abstractor, T. H. Essex ....£80 to £180

Registry of County Court Judgments, &c.
Treasury, Whitehall, S.W. Hours, 10 to 5; 11 to 3
for searches.
Registrar, F. A'Court Bergne, *unp.*
Chief Clerk, Henry Allen £215
Abstractor, G. E. Goodrich ....£55 to £150

COUNTY COURT JUDGES (each £1500).

[*All the County Court Judges are addressed as* "*His
Honour.*"]
Addison, John, Q.C. (32), Greenwich & Woolwich.
Austin, James Valentine (54), Bristol, Wells, &c.
Bacon, Francis Hy. (42), Bloomsbury, &c.
Bagshawe, Wm. H. G., Q.C. (35), Cambridgeshire.
Beresford, Cecil H. W. (57), Devon & Somerset.
Bishop, John (31), Carmarthenshire, &c.
Bompas, Henry Mason, Q.C. (11), Bradford, &c.
Cadman, John Heaton (12), Halifax, &c.
Collier, John Francis (5), Liverpool, &c.
Coventry, Millis (4), Preston, Blackburn, &c.
Edge, James Broughton (41), Clerkenwell, &c.
Ellicott, Arthur Becher (53), Gloucester, &c.
Emden, Alfred (46), West Kent, &c.
Evans, William (28), Mid Wales.
Ffoulkes, William Wynne (7), Birkenhead, &c.
French, D. O'C. (40), Bow and Shoreditch.
Gardiner, Wm. Dundas (52), Bath, Devizes, &c.
Granger, Thomas Colpitts (56), Cornwall, &c.
Greenhow, Wm. T. (14), Leeds and Wakefield.
Greenwell, Francis John (1), Northumberland.
Gye, Percy (51), Winchester, &c.
Harington, Sir Richard, Bart. (21-3), Worcester, &c.
Ingham, Robert Wood (22), Coventry, Warwick, &c.
Jones, Edwin (5), Bolton, Bury, &c.

Lea, Geo. Harris (27), Hereford, Shrewsbury, &c.
Lee, Lawford Yate- (9), Macclesfield, &c.
Lloyd, Sir Horatio (29), Chester and North Wales.
Lushington, V., Q.C. (45), Croydon & Wandsworth.
Marten, Sir Alfred, Q.C. (37), Uxbridge, &c.
Martineau, Alfred (50), Brighton, Sussex, &c.
Masterman, W. (18), Notts and Yorkshire.
Meynell, Edgar John (2), Durham, &c.
Mulholland, Wm., Q.C. (26), North Staffordshire.
Owen, William Stevenson (24), Cardiff, &c.
Parry, Edward (8), Manchester.
Paterson, William (38), Edmonton.
Philbrick, F. A., Q.C. (55), Wilts and Dorset.
Raikes, Fras. Wm., Q.C. (16), Hull, Malton, &c.
Selfe, Sir William Lucius (49), E. Kent, Dover, &c.
Shand, Charles Lister (6), Liverpool, &c.
Shortt, John (17), Lincolnshire, &c.
Smith, Lumley, Q.C. (44), Westminster, &c.
Smyly, William Cecil, Q.C. (19), Derbyshire, &c.
Snagge, Thomas William (36), Oxford, &c.
Steavenson, D. F. (3), Cumberland & Westmorland.
Stonor, Henry James (43), Marylebone, &c.
Templer, Fredk. Gordon (15), York, Ripon, &c.
Waddy, Samuel Danks, Q.C. (13), Sheffield, &c.
Whitehorne, James Chas., Q.C. (21), Birmingham.
Williams, Gwilym (30), Glamorganshire.
Willis, William, Q.C. (32), Cambs. & Norfolk.
Wilmot, Hugh E. Eardley- (33), Norfolk & Suffolk.
Wood, Wm. Wightman (20), Leicestershire.
Woodfall, Robert (58), Exeter, &c.
Young, Alfred (25), Wolverhampton.
** The figures within parentheses show the number of the Circuit.

METROPOLITAN COUNTY COURTS.
BLOOMSBURY, Great Portland Street, W.
WHITECHAPEL, Great Prescot Street, E.
Judge, His Honour Francis Henry Bacon...£1,500
Bloomsbury.—*Registrar,* Edward Huelin.
  "   *High Bailiff,* Robert Wright.
Whitechapel.—*Registrar,* Matthew R. Webb, J.P.
  "   *High Bailiff,* Frederic White.

BROMLEY; DARTFORD; GRAVESEND; LAMBETH.
Judge, His Honour Alfred Emden £1,500
Bromley.—*Registrar,* A. E. Willett.
Dartford.—*Registrar,* W. B. Pritchard.
Gravesend.—*Registrars and High Bailiffs,* George Edward Sharland and Charles Edward Hatten.
Lambeth.—*Joint Registrars,* H. D. Pritchard; F. W. Englefield.
Maidstone.—*Registrar,* G. D. Warner.
Sevenoaks.—*Registrar,* W. W. Knocker.
Tonbridge.—*Registrar,* C. E. Warner.
Tunbridge Wells.—*Registrar,* F. W. Stone.
CLERKENWELL, 33 Duncan Terrace, Islington, N.
Judge, His Hon. James Broughton Edge...£1,500
Registrar, Basil Upton Eddis.
High Bailiff, William Young Hucks.

CROYDON, Surrey.   KINGSTON, Surrey.
WANDSWORTH, South Street.
Judge, His Honour Vernon Lushington, Q.C. £1,500
Croydon.—*Registrar and High Bailiff,* J. E. Fox.
Kingston.—*Registrar and High Bailiff,* James Bell.
Wandsworth—*Registrar and High Bailiff,* W. A. Willoughby.

EDMONTON; WALTHAM ABBEY; ROMFORD.
Judge, His Honour Wm. Paterson £1,500
Edmonton.—*Registrar,* William Pulley.
  "   *High Bailiff,* William Pulley.
Waltham Abbey, Essex.—*Registrar,* W. J. Bruty.
  "   *High Bailiff,* W.J.Bruty (act.).
Romford, Essex.—*Registrar,* Wm. Comyns Clifton.
  "   *High Bailiff,* C. Godfrey.

LAMBETH, Camberwell New Road.
Judge, His Honour Alfred Emden £1,500
MARYLEBONE, 179 Marylebone Road, N.W.
BROMPTON, Whitehead's Grove, Chelsea, S.W.
BRENTFORD. Town Hall, W.
Judge, His Honour Henry James Stonor ...£1,500
Marylebone.—*Registrar,* James Curtis.
  "   *Assist. Registrar,* W. G. Watson.
  "   *High Bailiff,* Lambton Young.
Brompton.—*Registrar,* Richard Wright.
  "   *Assist. Registrar,* E. Kemp Taylor.
  "   *High Bailiff,* Reginald S. Boddington.
*Brentford.—*Regist. and High Bailiff,* Wm. Ruston.
Bow Bow Rd., E.; Shoreditch, 221 Old St., E.C.
Judge, His Honour D. O'C. French, Q.C....£1,500
Shoreditch.—*Registrar,* E. E. Wickham.
  "   *High Bailiff,* Robert J. Hackshaw.
Bow.—*Registrar,* F. W. R. Hore.
  "   *High Bailiff,* Charles J. R. Tijou.
SOUTHWARK, Swan Street.
GREENWICH, Burney St.; WOOLWICH, Brewer St.
Judge, His Honour John Addison, Q.C. £1,500
Southwark.—*Registrar,* Thomas Kemmis Bros.
  "   *High Bailiff,* Geo. J. K. Richards.
Greenwich and Woolwich.—*Registrar and High Bailiff,* C. Pitt Taylor.

UXBRIDGE; BARNET; WATFORD.
Judge, His Honour Sir Alfred Marten, Q.C., £1,500
Uxbridge.—*Registrars and High Bailiffs,* Charles Woodbridge, Thomas H. Riches Woodbridge.
Barnet.—*Registrar and High Bailiff,* William Osborn Boyes.
Watford.—*Registrar and High Bailiff,* Henry Morten Turner.

WESTMINSTER, 82 St. Martin's Lane, W.C.
Judge, His Honour Lumley Smith, Q.C.......£1,800
Registrars, Christopher Robert Cuff; Chas. Ernest Cuff.
High Bailiff, John Arthur Bayley.

CORONERS FOR THE COUNTY OF LONDON.
County of London: Western District, Clifford Luxmore Drew.
  Deputy, Henry Robert Oswald.
  Coroner's Office, 49 Leinster Square, W.
Central District, George Danford Thomas, M.D.
  Deputy, Walter Schröder.
  Coroner's Office, 87 Euston Road, N.W.
Westminster and Duchy of Lancaster Savoy District, John Troutbeck.
  Deputy, Harold Oxley Chamberlain Smith.
  Coroner's Office, 21 Great Smith Street, S.W.
North-Eastern District, Wm. Wynn Westcott.
  Deputy, George Eugène Yarrow.
  Coroner's Office, 396 Camden Road, N.
Eastern and Liberty of Tower District, Wynne E. Baxter.
  Deputy, Edmund King Houchin.
  Coroner's Office, 170 Church Street, Stoke Newington, N.
City of London and Borough of Southwark, Samuel Frederick Langham.
  Deputy, Arthur Cuthbert Langham.
  Coroner's Office, City Mortuary, Golden Lane, E.C.
South-Western District, A. Braxton Hicks.
  Deputy, Henry Robert Oswald.
  Coroner's Office, 20 Lupus Street, S.W.
Southern District, George Perceval Wyatt.
  Deputy, Arthur Wellesley Wyatt.
  Coroner's Office, 66 Tulse Hill, S.W.

*Additional Judge at Brentford, His Honour Wm. H. G. Bagshawe, Q.C.

South-Eastern District, E. A. Carttar.
   Deputy, Edward Negus Wood.
   Coroner's Office, 31 Blackheath Road, S.E.
Penge District, Edward R. Carr.
   Deputy, F. C. Morrison.
   Coroner's Office, Redhill, Surrey.

Chief Officer, Public Control Dept. L.C.C., Alfred
   Spencer £950

METROPOLITAN POLICE OFFICE
New Scotland Yard, S.W.

Commissioner, Colonel Sir Edward Ridley Col-
   borne Bradford, G.C.B., K.C.S.I. £2,500
   Private Secretary, G. H. Gardner.
Assistant Commissioners, Alexander Carmichael
   Bruce; Robt. Anderson, LL.D., C.B.; Sir Charles
   Howard, C.B. .... each £1,350
Chief Clerk, C. L. Bathurst £850
Surgeon-in-Chief, Alex. O. Mackellar, M.D. ... £600
Clerk of Accounts, Lewis J. Fry £600
Clerks, 1st Class, C. M. L. Hallward; A. W. Hall-
   ward; W. H. Kendall.................. £500 to £600
Clerk, 1st Class (2nd Sect.), G. H. Gardner ... £460
Temporary Staff Officer, F. H. Underwood ... £400
Staff Officers, C. B. Hopkins; D. H. North
                                        £300 to £400
Clerks, 2nd Class (1st Sect.), G. H. Edwards; B.
   T. Earle .... £300 to £360
Clerks, 2nd Class (2nd Sect.), W. C. Grenside; W.
   S. Mylius; H. Ravenscroft; C. Annesley; E.
   Napier; G. H. Atkinson; C. Macartney-Filgate;
   F. C. Barchard; M. B. Frere; Hon. Eric R.
   Thesiger; C. E. Ruck; J. E. Simpson; C. E.
   Browne .... £90 to £300
Assistant Clerks, W. Raw; E. L. S. Power; H.
   W. Staples; W. G. Galley.
Solicitors to the Commissioner, Wontner & Sons.
Chief Constables, Lt.-Col. Bolton J. A. Monsell;
   Major Walter Edward Gilbert; Capt. George
   Henry Dean; Melville Leslie Macnaghten.
                                        £600 to £800
Superintendent Executive and Statistical Branches,
   William Davis.
Superintendents of the Crim. Investigation Dept.,
   Percy Neame; Donald Swanson.
*Supt. Public Carriage Branch and Lost Property
   Office*, William Beavis.

Superintendents of Divisions.

A WHITEHALL.—Frederick Beard; Charles Fraser,
   in attendance upon H.M. the Queen.
B CHELSEA.—Denis Neylan.
C ST. JAMES'S.—George E. Smith.
D ST. MARYLEBONE.—John Warner.
E HOLBORN.—Thomas Cole.
F PADDINGTON.—Henry Ferrett.
G FINSBURY.—William Hammond.
H WHITECHAPEL.—John Mulvany.
J BETHNAL GREEN.—Frederick Weston.
K Bow.—Cresswell Wells.
L LAMBETH.—Walter T. Wren.
M SOUTHWARK.—Henry Wyborn.
N ISLINGTON.—John McFadden.
P CAMBERWELL.—George Carr.
R GREENWICH.—Onslow Wakeford.
S HAMPSTEAD.—Charles Dodd.
T HAMMERSMITH.—Charles Hunt.
V WANDSWORTH.—David Saines.
W CLAPHAM.—Stephen T. Lucas.
X KILBURN.—James Cuthbert.
Y HIGHGATE.—Louis Vedy.
   THAMES.—William Robinson.
   WOOLWICH.—Josiah Hobbins.
   PORTSMOUTH.—James W. Carter.
   DEVONPORT.—Edwin Smith.
   CHATHAM.—George Hornsby.
   PEMBROKE DOCK.—James Last (*Chief Insp.*)

OFFICE OF THE RECEIVER
FOR THE METROPOLITAN POLICE DISTRICT.

Receiver, Alfred Richard Pennefather, C.B....£1,500
Chief Clerk, H. A. Everest .... £650 to £750
1st Class Clerks, M. H. Festing; John P. Mann;
   F. J. Rose .... £400 to £550
Accountant, W. J. Wilby .... £400 to £550
2nd Class Clerks (1st Section), G. H. Pryce; C. E.
   Gipps; A. E. Hall, B.A. .... £300 to £360
Do. (2nd Section), E. Eraut; G. H. Lufkin; A.
   Flower; F. B. Delavoye; H. de L. Anderson;
   H. H. Comyn; R. K. O'Neill ...... £90 to £300
Assistant Clerks, O. Bower, £70 to £240; G. A.
   Bracey; E. H. Hinson; W. T. Brattle; F. G.
   Morley; J. B. Reynolds; C. A. Palmer; R.
   J. Hayward; W. Blomefield; W. P. Paynter
                                        £70 to £190
Solicitors, Messrs. Ellis & Ellis, 5 DelahaySt., S.W.
Surveyor, J. Dixon Butler £600
2nd do., F. King .... £360 to £500
Assist. do., A. Howell; S. A. Braam £210 to £300
Draughtsmen, A. Hodges; A. Ferris; J. Tharp
                                        £150 to £210
Clerks of the Works, 1st Class, G. Eraut; T.
   Greengrass .... £250 to £300
Do., 2nd Class, N. Baker; T. Longstreeth; J. R.
   McIntosh .... £150 to £220
Storekeeper, D. McG. Guthrie ...... £250 to £300
Insp. Clothing and Equipments, G. Burton ...£275

CITY POLICE OFFICE, 26 Old Jewry, E.C.

Commissioner, Lt.-Col. Sir Henry Smith, K.C.B.
                                        £1,500
Assist. Commissioner, Major E. F. Wodehouse £750
Superintend. & Chief Clerk, John Whatley ...£327
Receiver, John W. Carlyon-Hughes £600
Surgeon, Fredk. Gordon Brown, M.R.C.S. £500

POLICE COURTS, CITY OF LONDON.
MANSION HOUSE JUSTICE ROOM.

Magistrate, The Lord Mayor, or one of the
   Aldermen.
Chief Clerk, Cecil George Douglas £1,050
Assistant Clerk, J. G. Trotter £500
Cashier, Robert Arthur Warren £300
Marshal (vacant) £350

GUILDHALL.

Magistrate, An Alderman (in rotation).
Chief Clerk, Herbert George Savill £1,000
Assistant Clerk, Silvester Richards £500
Cashier, John Herbert Major £200
Clerk of Special Sessions, C. F. Monckton ... £500
Assistant Do., Charles Fitch £250

METROPOLITAN POLICE COURTS.
BOW STREET, Covent Garden.

Magistrates, Sir Franklin Lushington £1,800
   Albert de Rutzen £1,500
   Robert H. B. Marsham £1,500
Chief Clerk, Harry Cavendish £650

CLERKENWELL, King's Cross Road.

Magistrates, James Reader White Bros......£1,500
   Cecil M. Chapman £1,500
Chief Clerk, Oliver Wheeler £600

NORTH LONDON, Stoke Newington Road.

Magistrate, Edward Snow Fordham £1,500
Chief Clerk, F. G. Nott-Bower £600

LAMBETH, Lower Kennington Lane, S.E.

Magistrates, Arthur Autwis Hopkins £1,500
   Charles King Francis £1,500
Chief Clerk, Temple C. Martin £600

GREAT MARLBOROUGH STREET.

Magistrates, Edward N. Fenwick Fenwick, £1,500
   George Lewis Denman £1,500
Chief Clerk, John Ronaldson Lyell, M.A. ...£600

MARYLEBONE, Seymour Place.
Magistrates, Henry Curtis Bennett £1,500
Alfred Chichele Plowden £1,500
Chief Clerk, Wilfred Tate £600

SOUTHWARK, Borough High Street.
Magistrates, Wyndham Slade £1,500
G. Paul Taylor £1,500
Chief Clerk, Henry Nairn £600

THAMES, Arbour Street East, Stepney.
Magistrates, Frederick Mead £1,500
John Dickinson £1,500
Chief Clerk, Stanley Savill ......*(and fees)* £600

WESTMINSTER, Vincent Square.
Magistrates, James Sheil £1,500
Horace Smith £1,500
Chief Clerk, A. Herbert Safford £600

WORSHIP STREET, E.C.
Magistrates, Haden Corser £1,500
Albert Rowland Cluer £1,500
Chief Clerk, Harry Titterton £600

WEST LONDON, Vernon Street, West Kensington.
Magistrates, John Rose £1,500
Richard Ouseley Blake Lane, Q.C. £1,500
Chief Clerk, Francis E. Lewris, LL.B. £600

GREENWICH AND WOOLWICH.
Magistrates, Gilbert George Kennedy £1,500
E. C. Tennyson-D'Eyncourt £1,500
Chief Clerk, H. P. Newton £600

SOUTH WESTERN. Lavender Hill, S.W.
Magistrate, Edmund William Garrett £1,500
Chief Clerk, George A. Bird £600

WEST HAM, West Ham Lane, Stratford.
Magistrate, Ernest Baggallay £1,000
Chief Clerk, W. H. Fowler £900

INNS OF COURT.
THE TEMPLE CHURCH.
Master, Rev. Canon Ainger, D.D., 1894.
Reader, Rev. S. A. Alexander, M.A.
Organist, Dr. H. Walford Davies.
Custodian, A. F. Stone.

INNER TEMPLE.
Treasurer, William Patchett, Q.C.
Master of Library, Sir Harry B. Poland, Q.C.
Sub-Treasurer, Sir Hon. Waldemar Lawrence, Bt.
Librarian, J. E. Latton Pickering.
Sub-Librarian, Walter T. Rogers.
Clerk, J. H. Milton.

MIDDLE TEMPLE.
Treasurer, William Ambrose, Q.C.
Under Treasurer, J. W. Waldron.
Librarian, John Hutchinson.

LINCOLN'S INN.
Treasurer, Hon. Sir John Compton Lawrance.
Master of the Library, Hon. Sir James C. Mathew.
Preacher, Rev. Hastings Rashdall, D.C.L.
Chaplain, Rev. Charles James Ball, M.A.
Steward, A. Weatherley Marriott.
Clerks, J. A. Clark; F. W. Corn; N. Y.
Marriott.
Librarian, A. F. Etheridge.
Sub-Librarian, W. F. Charles Suter.
Assist. Librarian, H. I. Whitaker.

GRAY'S INN.
Treasurer, John A. Russell, Q.C.
Master of Library, W. Bowen-Rowlands, Q.C.
Preacher, Rev. Joseph Hirst Lupton, D.D.
Reader, Rev. Reginald J. Fletcher, M.A.
Steward, Dennis W. Douthwaite.
Chief Clerk, Standley W. Bunning.
Librarian, W. Ralph Douthwaite.

CENTRAL CRIMINAL COURT.—OLD BAILEY.
The following days have been appointed for
holding the Sessions for the jurisdiction of the
Central Criminal Court, for 1899-1900 :—

1899.	20 November.	1900.	30th April.
,,	11 December.	,,	21st May.
1900.	15th January.	,,	25th June.
,,	12th February.	,,	23rd July.
,,	12th March.	,,	23rd September.
,,	2nd April.	,,	22nd October.

Clerk of the Court, Henry Kemp Avory, Sessions
House, Old Bailey.
Deputy, Henry A. Read.
Judges, Rt. Hon. Sir Charles Hall, K.C.M.G.,
Q.C., M.P., *Recorder;* Sir Forrest Fulton, Knt.,
Common Serjeant; Robert Malcolm Kerr, LL.D.,
Commissioner.

GENERAL QUARTER SESSIONS.

London.		Southwark.	
3rd Jan.	4th Apr.	5th Jan.	6th April.
4th July.	17th Oct.	6th July.	19th Oct.

Clerk of the Peace, Alfred Read, Sessions House,
Old Bailey.

COUNTY OF LONDON SESSIONS.
(North side of the Thames.)
SESSIONS HOUSE, Clerkenwell Green.
Custos Rotulorum & Lord Lieutenant, The Duke of
Westminster, K.G.
Chairman, Wm. Robert M'Connell, Q.C., D.L. £2,000
Deputy do., R. Loveland-Loveland, Q.C.,
D.L. £1,500
Clerk of the Peace, Sir Richard Nicholson.
Deputy do., John Dix.
Solicitor Conducting Criminal Prosecutions, George
Allen.
Clerk to the Lieutenancy, Sir Richard Nicholson.
(South side of the Thames.)
SESSIONS HOUSE, Newington Causeway, S.E.
Chairman, William Robert M'Connell, Q.C., D.L.
Deputy do., R. Loveland-Loveland, Q.C., D.L.
Clerk of the Peace, Sir Richard Henry Wyatt.
Deputy do., Alfred H. Lefroy.

SURREY SESSIONS.
County Hall, Kingston-on-Thames.
Chairman, George Cave.
Deputy Chairmen, H. C. Leigh Bennett, M.P.; Sir
William Vincent, Bart.
Clerk of the Peace, Sir R. H. Wyatt, J.P., D.L.,
County Hall, Kingston-on-Thames.
Deputy Clerk of the Peace, Thos. W. Weeding.
County Treasurer, Francis H. Beaumont.
Clerk to the Lieutenancy, Sir Richard H. Wyatt.
Chief Constable, Capt. M. L. Sant, Guildford.
County Surveyor, F. G. Howell, County Hall.

MIDDLESEX QUARTER SESSIONS.
GUILDHALL, Broad Sanctuary, Westminster, S.W.
Custos Rotulorum and Lord Lieutenant, The Duke
of Bedford, 1 Belgrave Sq., S.W.
Chairman of Quarter Sessions, Ralph Makinson
Littler, C.B., Q.C.
Deputy do., Montagu Sharpe.
Clerk of the Peace,
Clerk of the County Council,
Clerk to the Lieutenancy,
{ Sir Rd. Nicholson,
Guildhall, Broad
Sanctuary, West-
minster.
*Deputy Clerk of the Peace and
of the County Council* ......
{ W. G. Austin,
Guildhall, West-
minster.

QUARTER SESSIONS IN COUNTIES.

These are to be held in the first whole weeks after March 31, June 24, Oct. 11, and Dec. 28; the magistrates determining the day of the week on which the sessions shall commence at each place. Any of the above days falling on Sunday, the sessions will be held in the ensuing and not in the same week. BREWSTER SESSIONS are held in the first ten days of the month of March for Middlesex and Surrey, and for all other counties between Aug. 20 and Sept. 14.

HER MAJESTY'S PRISONS.

AYLESBURY FEMALE CONVICT PRISON.
Gov. and Med. Off., G. E. Walker, L.R.C.P., £545

BEDFORD.
Gov., A. G. Western.

BIRMINGHAM.
Gov., Rear-Adm. Arthur R. Tinklar.

BODMIN.
Gov., W. R. Shenton.

BORSTAL.
Gov., Capt. C. Eardley-Wilmot £318

BRECON.
Gov., J. Cranston.

BRISTOL.
Gov., Major C. D. Cottrell.

CAMBRIDGE.
Gov., W. E. Burkinshaw.

CANTERBURY.
Gov., J. R. Farewell.

CARDIFF.
Gov., Capt. E. E. S. Schuyler.

CARLISLE.
Gov., A. H. Hollingdale.

CARMARTHEN.
Gov., W. J. Barnes.

CARNARVON.
Gov., John Dillon.

CHELMSFORD.
Gov., (vacant).

DARTMOOR.
Gov., W. H. O. Russell £700

DERBY.
Gov., Capt. C. E. Farquharson.

DEVIZES.
Gov., J. L. Smith.

DORCHESTER.
Gov., H. J. Hellier.

DURHAM.
Gov., Capt. R. D. G. H. Burgoyne.

EXETER.
Gov., Maj. D. Matheson.

GLOUCESTER.
Gov., J. Finn.

HEREFORD.
Gov., B. Charles.

HOLLOWAY, for Prisoners awaiting trial, Female convicted Prisoners, Debtors, &c., for London and Middlesex. Also THE QUEEN'S PRISON.
Gov., Lt.-Col. Everard S. Milman, R.A....£700

HULL.
Gov., W. R. Chidley.

IPSWICH.
Gov., S. Gorsuch.

KNUTSFORD.
Gov., Capt. H. L. Conor.

LANCASTER.
Gov., W. Stevens.

LEEDS.
Gov., J. H. Shepherd.

LEICESTER.
Gov., Capt. C. V. Gunning.

LEWES.
Gov., Lt.-Col. H. B. Isaacson.

LINCOLN.
Gov., Major E. W. Briscoe.

LIVERPOOL.
Gov., Capt. F. G. Firth.

MAIDSTONE.
Gov., William Green.

MANCHESTER.
Gov., R. D. Cruikshank £700

NEWCASTLE.
Gov., Maj. J. O. Nelson.

NEWGATE
(Staff same as Holloway).

NORTHALLERTON.
Gov., H. Bartle.

NORTHAMPTON.
Gov., Basil Thomson.

NORWICH.
Gov., Capt. J. F. Bell.

NOTTINGHAM.
Gov., Maj. O. E. M. Davies.

OXFORD.
Gov., J. Pullan.

PARKHURST.
Gov., Lt.-Col. H. Plummer £752

PENTONVILLE.
Gov., Capt. Frank Johnson £700

PLYMOUTH.
Gov., James H. Duncan.

PORTLAND.
Gov., Lt.-Col. S. R. B. Partridge £624

PORTSMOUTH.
Gov., G. E. Northey.

PRESTON.
Gov., Capt. Percy Green.

READING.
Gov., Capt. C. W. B. Farrant.

RUTHIN.
Gov., E. Parry Jones.

ST. ALBANS.
Gov., E. Lloyd.

SHEPTON MALLET.
Gov., J. G. Barrow.

SHREWSBURY.
Gov., N. G. Mitchell-Innes.

STAFFORD.
Gov., H. Gibson.

SWANSEA.
Gov., Capt. J. J. C. Smail, R.N.

USK.
Gov., F. W. Gibson.

WAKEFIELD.
Gov., Capt. G. A. Crickitt.
Dep., Capt. R. H. D'Aeth.

WANDSWORTH.
Gov., Major James Knox £700

WARWICK.
Gov., Maj. W. A. Campbell.

WINCHESTER.
Gov., Lt.-Col. F. Lodge.

WORCESTER.
Gov., Capt. W. M. T. Synge.

WORMWOOD SCRUBS.
Gov., Capt. H. T. Price, R.N............£700
Dep., Lieut. Lionel Sanders, R.N. £260

YORK.
Gov., E. Taylor.

FELTHAM INDUSTRIAL SCHOOL, Feltham, Middlesex (under London County Council).
Superintendent, T. B. Beuttler, M.A.

BROADMOOR CRIMINAL LUNATIC ASYLUM, Crowthorne, Berks.—£32,812.
Med. Superintendent, Richard Brayn, L.R.C.P. £900

The dates of the Assizes are respectively about the middle of February (Winter), July (Summer), and November (Autumn). Except in Lancashire and Glamorganshire, the Autumn assizes are for criminal business only. There is an additional assize, for Lancashire and Yorkshire only, in May.

SOUTH-EASTERN, OR HOME.

Herts (Hertford)—Summer, Autumn and Winter.
Essex (Chelmsford) — Summer, Autumn and Winter.
Sussex (Lewes)—Summer, Autumn and Winter.
Kent (Maidstone)—Summer, Autumn and Winter.
Surrey (Guildford) — Summer, Autumn and Winter.
Clerk of Assize for Home Division, Arthur Denman, 1 Hare Court, Temple........................£300
Clerk of Indictments for the whole Circuit, Henry Avory Read, Old Bailey £400
Huntingdonshire (Huntingdon) — Summer and Winter.
Cambridgeshire (Cambridge)—Summer, Autumn. (Chesterton) Winter (for Assize County No. 3).
Suffolk (Ipswich or Bury St. Edmunds)—Summer, Autumn and Winter.
Norfolk (Norwich)—Summer, Autumn and Winter.
Clerk of Assize for Norfolk Division, Charles Platt, 1 Harcourt Buildings, Temple, E.C. £900
Associate for the whole Circuit, William Collisson, 27 Bedford Row..........................£400

MIDLAND.

Beds (Bedford)—Summer, Autumn and Winter.
Bucks (Aylesbury)—Summer, Autumn and Winter.
Derbyshire (Derby)—Summer, Autumn and Winter.
Leicestershire (Leicester)—Summer, Autumn (for Assize County No. 2), and Winter.
Lincolnshire (Lincoln)—Summer, Autumn and Winter.
Northants (Northampton) —Summer, Autumn and Winter.
Notts (Nottingham) — Summer, Autumn and Winter.
Rutlandshire (Oakham)—Summer and Winter.
Warwickshire (Warwick Div.)—Summer, Autumn and Winter.
Do. (Birmingham Div.)—Summer, Autumn and Winter.
Clerk of Assize, Arthur Duke Coleridge, 3 Harcourt Buildings, Temple £850
Clerk of Arraigns, George A. Cockburn........£400
Associate, Spencer Langton Holland £400

NORTHERN.

Cumberland (Carlisle) —Summer, Autumn and Winter (for Assize County No. 1).
Westmorland (Appleby)—Winter and Summer.
Lancashire, Northern Division (Lancaster)—Summer, Autumn and Winter.
Salford Division (Manchester)—Spring, Summer, Autumn and Winter.
Liverpool—Spring, Summer, Autumn and Winter.
Clerk of Assize, Sir Herbert Stephen, Bart., 4 Paper Buildings, Temple, E.C. £1,000
Associate, Arthur Shuttleworth, Preston £400
Clerk of Indictments and Taxing Officer, John Gifford, Preston.........................£300

NORTH-EASTERN.

Durham (Durham)—Summer, Autumn and Winter.
Northumberland and City of Newcastle (Newcastle) —Summer, Autumn and Winter.
Yorkshire, N. & E. Riding, and City of York (York) —Summer, Autumn and Winter.
West Riding Div. (Leeds) — Spring, Summer, Autumn and Winter.
Clerk of Assize, Edward Bromley, 1 Paper Buildings, Temple, E.C. £900

Deputy Clerk of Assize and Clerk of Arraigns, Robert Holtby, York £400
Associate, Claude F. Wade, 3 Pump Court ...£400
Bailiff, W. Budd, 1 Paper Buildings.

OXFORD.

Assizes are held three times a year at *Reading, Oxford, Worcester, Gloucester, Monmouth, Hereford, Shrewsbury, Stafford.*
Clerk of Assize, James L. Mathews......£800
Associate and deputy do., Archer C. Hemp. ...£400
Clerk of Indictments, Francis W. Jones £300
Clerk & Bailiff, H. J. Curtis.
Office, 13 King's Bench Walk, Temple.

WESTERN CIRCUIT.

GENERAL ASSIZES.—*Hants* (Winchester) S., A. and W.; *Wilts* (Devizes) W., (Salisbury) S., (Devizes and Salisbury alternately) A., 1900 *Salisbury, Devizes; Dorset* (Dorchester) S., A. and W.; *Devon* (Exeter) S., A. and W.; *City of Exeter* (The Guildhall) S., A. and W.; *Cornwall* (Bodmin) S., A. and W.; *Somerset* (Taunton) W., (Wells) S. (Taunton and Wells alternately) A.; 1900 *Taunton, Wells, Bristol* (The Guildhall) S., A. and W.
Clerk of Assize, James Read; *Office,* 39 Temple £800
Associate, A. Read £300
Clerk of Arraigns, C. J. Tennant Dunlop.....£200

NORTH WALES AND CHESTER.

Merionethshire (Dolgelly) —Winter and Summer.
Montgomeryshire (Welshpool) —Winter; (Newtown) —Summer.
Carnarvonshire (Carnarvon)—Winter, Summer and Autumn.
Anglesey (Beaumaris)—Winter and Summer.
Denbighshire (Ruthin)—Winter, Summer and Autumn.
Flintshire (Mold)—Winter and Summer.
Cheshire (Chester Castle)—Winter, Summer and Autumn.
Clerk of Assize, Henry Crompton, 42 Mecklenburgh Square, W.C. £500
Clerk of Indictments and Deputy Clerk of Assize, Henry Lister Reade, Congleton £300
Associate, Arthur Andrew, Congleton £150
Agents, G. F. Hudson, Matthews & Co., 32 Queen Victoria St., E.C.

SOUTH WALES DIVISION.

Pembrokeshire (Haverfordwest) — Winter and Summer.
Cardiganshire (Lampeter)—Winter and Summer.
Carmarthenshire (Carmarthen)—Winter, Summer, and Autumn (for Assize County No. 6).
Glamorganshire (Cardiff)—Winter and Autumn alternately with Swansea; (Swansea) Summer.
Brecknockshire (Brecon)—Winter, Summer, and Autumn (for Assize County No. 7).
Radnorshire (Presteign)—Winter and Summer.
Clerk of the Crown, Clerk of Assize, and Associate, Hon. Stephen W. B. Coleridge, M.A., Room 474, Royal Courts of Justice £500
Princ. Assist., T. M. Williams, 353 Camden Rd., N. £300.
Second Assist. & Clerk of Indictments, G. J. Walter Rigley, Room 474, Royal Courts of Justice £150

At the Autumn Assizes held at Carmarthen and Brecon, Criminal business only is taken; but at the Glamorgan Assize, Civil and Criminal business are taken.

| Year. | REVENUE. | | | | | (4) Expenditure. | Surplus of Deficit. |
	(1) Taxes.	(2) P. Office, &c.	Crown Lands.	(3) Suez Canal.	(4) Total.		
	£	£	£	£	£	£	£
1881–2	70,580,518	3,248,704	580,000	198,829	74,209,222	73,859,496	+ 349,726
1882–3	73,128,000	3,287,307	380,000	198,829	76,795,327	75,697,129	+ 58,178
1883–4	71,856,000	2,901,440	380,000	198,829	75,147,440	74,941,820	+ 205,620
1884–5	73,745,000	2,931,728	380,000	—	77,167,728	78,157,500	– 1,019,772
1885–6	74,927,000	2,687,343	380,000	377,776	78,294,343	80,936,886	– 2,642,543
1886–7	76,115,000	2,631,107	370,000	178,946	79,124,107	78,348,101	+ 775,006
1887–8	75,660,000	2,950,455	390,000	198,829	79,000,455	76,621,846	+ 2,378,609
1888–9	73,597,000	3,335,701	430,000	198,829	77,362,701	76,573,718	+ 788,983
1889–90	73,414,000	3,524,003	430,000	238,595	77,388,000	74,147,001	+ 3,221,002
1890–1	73,578,000	3,649,311	430,000	198,829	77,657,311	75,901,054	+ 1,756,257
1891–2	75,340,000	3,355,686	430,000	198,829	79,125,686	78,058,673	+ 1,067,013
1892–3	74,800,000	3,062,940	430,000	198,829	78,292,940	78,272,929	+ 20,011
1893–4	75,427,000	2,908,156	420,000	198,829	78,755,156	78,924,592	– 169,436
1894–5	78,655,000	3,091,196	410,000	394,995	82,551,191	81,785,850	+ 765,341
1895–6	85,116,000	3,766,552	415,000	673,418	89,970,020	85,761,448	+ 4,209,472
1896–7	86,974,000	3,601,000	415,000	694,076	92,115,885	89,642,669	+ 3,373,216
1897–8	88,548,000	3,615,000	415,000	698,684	95,049,004	91,370,994	+ 3,678,010
1898–9	89,450,000	3,663,000	430,000	678,856	96,139,193	95,953,235	+ 185,858

Nota Bene.—(1) Taxes include Excise, Customs, Property, and Income Tax, Estate Duty, Stamps, Land Tax, and House Duty.

(2) The Post Office returns are net—*i.e.*, exclusive of the cost ; and refer to Telegraph and Packet Services also.
(3) Up to July 1, 1894, interest was paid on the purchase-money, and since that date on the shares held.
(4) The totals do not include Post Office expenses, as these have already been deducted.

IN the Financial Statement or **Budget** for the Financial Year 1899-1900 (1 April to 31 March) the **Revenue** was estimated at £110,287,000 on the then basis of taxation, and the **Expenditure** at £112,927,000, leaving an estimated **Deficit** of £2,640,000. To meet this deficit additional duties were imposed on imported wines which were estimated to produce £420,000, and alterations made in the Stamp Duties to produce an increase of £400,000 ; whilst the Expenditure was reduced by £2,000,000, that amount being deducted from the sum annually set aside for the service and redemption of the National Debt. The final balance sheet thus showed an estimated Revenue of £111,157,000 and an Expenditure of £110,927,000, leaving a balance of £230,000 for Contingencies.

The following tables show the total amounts of the **Exchequer Receipts and Issues** in the Financial Year 1898-99 :—

RECEIPTS.

	£
Balance at Banks of England and Ireland, 31 March, 1898	10,918,422
Total Revenue (as detailed below)	108,336,193
Repayment of Advances—	
(1) By Mint	840,000
(2) By Italian Government for Sardinian Loan	69,863
Raised by the Renewal of Bills, &c.—	
For Supply Purposes	8,133,000
Raised by the creation of additional Debt (Terminable Annuities), for the purposes of the Barracks Act (1890), Telegraph Acts (1892, 1896 & 1898), Uganda Railway Act (1896), and (Public Offices Acts (1895 & 1897)	3,932,336
Amount temporarily borrowed :— On deficiency of the Consolidated Fund in October, 1898 and Jan. 1899	3,300,000
Casual Receipts (Suez Canal shares paid off)	3,476
Total Receipts	**£135,533,290**

ISSUES.

	£
Total Expenditure (as detailed below)	108,150,236
To meet other Expenditure—	
(1) Barracks Act (1890)	200,000
(2) Telegraphs (1892, 1896 & 1898)	133,336
(3) Uganda Railway Act (1896)	1,005,000
(4) Public Offices Act (1895)	30,000
(5) Public Offices Act (1897)	475,000
Advance for Purchase of Bullion for Coinage	850,000
Bills and Bonds paid off—	
For Supply Purposes	8,133,000
Temporary Advances Repaid	2,171,990
For Redemption of Debt	1,128,010
Surplus Revenue 1895-96 applied under Naval Works Act (1896 and 1897)	1,080,000
Surplus Revenue 1896-7 applied under Military Works Act (1897)	630,000
Surplus Revenue 1897-8 applied under Public Buildings Expenses Act (1899)	2,550,000
Suez Canal shares realized and applied to Redemption of Debt under Finance Act (1898)	77,546
Balance at Banks of England and Ireland, 31 March, 1899	8,919,172
Total Issues	**£135,533,290**

THE NATIONAL INCOME

is mainly derived from the following sources:—
(I.) EXCISE, (II.) CUSTOMS, (III.) PROPERTY and INCOME TAX, (IV.) ESTATE DUTY, (V.) the POST OFFICE, and (VI.) STAMPS. The amount derived from Taxes being £89,450,000 in 1898-9, the remaining £18,885,193 being Non-Tax Revenue.

NATIONAL INCOME FOR THE LAST TWO YEARS.

	1897-98.	1898-99.
Excise	£28,300,000	29,200,000
Customs	21,798,000	20,850,000
Property & Income Tax	17,250,000	18,000,000
Estate Duty	11,100,000	11,400,000
Post Office	12,170,000	12,710,000
Telegraph Service	3,010,000	3,150,000
Stamps (excluding Fee, &c., Stamps)	7,650,000	7,630,000
Land Tax	940,000	770,000
House Duty	1,510,000	1,600,000
Crown Lands (net)	415,000	430,000
Interest on Suez Shares	698,684	678,856
Miscellaneous	1,772,320	1,882,639
Total National Income	£106,614,004	£108,336,193

Of the sources of Income mentioned in the above Table:—

(I.) EXCISE is derived mainly from Intoxicants, which account for £28,747,474 (*Spirits* £17,109,273, and *Beer* £11,638,201), the remainder accruing from *Licences (£247,015) and Railway Duty (£308,975).

(II.) CUSTOMS: The contributory articles are Beer (£16,988), Chicory (£52,108), Cocoa (£193,844), Coffee (£173,590), Currants (£120,635), Dried Plums (£31,494), Figs (£25,700), Prunes (£7,127),

Raisins (£196,989), Spirits (£4,236,159), Tea (£4,023,504), Tobacco and Snuff (£10,993,796), Wine (£1,399,099).

(III.) PROPERTY and INCOME TAX: To this PROPERTY contributes £5,129,000, which is made up of £4,979,000 from Lands and Tenements, and £150,000 from the Occupation of Land; the share from INCOME TAX (at 8*d*. in the £) is £12,913,311, being £1,171,000 from Annuities and Dividends; £10,396,311 from Trades and Professions, and £1,346,000 from Public Offices, Annuities from Public Revenues, &c.

(IV.) ESTATE DUTY: The total amount payable to the Exchequer is made up of £7,719,943 from the estates of persons dying after August 1, 1894; and £57,617 from those who died before that date; £2,837,091 from Legacy, £751,227 from Succession, and £41,432 from Corporation Duty.

(V.) The POST OFFICE and TELEGRAPH contributions are made up of £13,297,228 from the Sale of Postage Stamps, £301,080 collected in cash for Postage of Letters, &c., and £451,538 poundage on Money and Postal Orders, while £3,608,422 was received for transmission of Telegrams, of which £404,026 was refunded to Cable Companies.

(VI.) STAMPS: Under this heading are included Deeds £4,182,377, Bills of Exchange £667,311, and Receipts, Drafts, and other 1*d*. stamps £1,381,835.

One of the remaining items, the SUEZ CANAL SHARES (£658,505, interest and dividend on 173,001 ordinary shares, and £10,351 on 3,601 Actions de Jouissance), is worthy of mention; the estimated market value of these shares (for which £4,080,000 was paid) was £26,451,000 on March 31, 1899.

* The total amount produced by the Licence Duties in 1898-9 was £4 015,667 (Publicans' Licences accounting for £1,688,925, Dog Licences £532,275, and Carriage Licences £511,016; of this total £3,798,952 was paid to the Local Taxation Accounts and £217,015 to the Exchequer.

THE NATIONAL EXPENDITURE.

The main headings under which the Expenditure is accounted for are as follow:—

I.—CONSOLIDATED FUND SERVICES:

	1897-98.	1898-99.
A The National Debt (see pp. 186-87)	£25,000,000	£25,000,000
B Civil List	408,289	428,774
Annuities to the Royal Family (p. 188)	172,049	168,000
Annuities and Pensions, various	119,059	113,567
Salaries and Allowances	79,560	79,113
Courts of Justice	512,483	517,069
Miscellaneous Services	344,553	305,330
Payments to Local Taxation Accounts	—	452,382
Expenses under Coinage Acts 1891 and 1893	250,000	—
	£26,885,994	£27,044,235

II.—SUPPLY SERVICES:

	1897-98.	1898-99.
Navy	£20,850,000	£24,068,000
Army (including Ordnance Factories)	19,330,000	20,000,000
Miscellaneous Civil Services	21,560,000	22,025,000
Customs and Inland Revenue Departments	2,745,000	2,816,000
Post Office	7,592,000	8,030,000
Telegraph Service	3,226,000	3,347,000
Post Office Packet Service	747,000	820,000
	£76,050,000	£81,106,000
Total Expenditure	£102,935,994	£108,150,235

PAYMENTS TO LOCAL TAXATION ACCOUNTS.

1898-99.	England.	Scotland.	Ireland.	Total.
	£	£	£	£
LOCAL TAXATION (Customs and Excise) DUTIES:				
Additional Beer Duty (CUSTOMS)	463	64	52	579
Additional Spirit Duty "	162,476	22,376	18,309	203,431
Additional Beer Duty (EXCISE)	361,403	50,180	38,420	450,003
Additional Spirit Duty "	672,745	92,139	77,996	843,180
LICENCES (including Penalties)	3,432,685	358,679	......	3,791,364
SHARE OF ESTATE DUTY:—				
Under Finance Act, 1894	2,117,438	285,648	237,711	2,640,797
Under Agricultural Rates Act, &c.	1,333,433	183,347	75,023	1,591,803
	8,080,912	992,735	447,513	9,251,160

The National Debt.*

THE NATIONAL DEBT amounted on 31 March, 1899, to £635,040,965 *Gross*, and £598,966,831 *Net*. This amount is the remanent of the growth of many years, and nearly all was raised for foreign wars. There was a trifling sum (£664,263) due when the "glorious revolution" of 1688 brought over the Dutch King William to save the country from Popery, arbitrary government, and other evils, but in carrying out these projects he succeeded in adding to the Debt nearly sixteen millions during the twelve years of his reign. Under Queen Anne, Marlborough added to the glories of the country, and helped to swell the Debt, which at the time of the Queen's death had increased by nearly thirty-eight millions. Under King George I. the Debt decreased slightly; but George II. in a reign of 33 years, left the country nearly eighty-seven millions worse off than he found it. During the first twelve years of George III. the Debt was again reduced by about ten millions, and at the time of the revolt of the American Colonies it was under one hundred and thirty millions, an amount which frightened all the political economists of that day. The cost of the American War was very heavy, and one hundred and twenty-one millions were added to the permanent Debt. On the conclusion of the disastrous war, which had all along been unpopular, there was a considerable outcry at the waste; some efforts were made to reduce the amount, and in the nine years from 1784 to 1793, ten and a half millions were paid off, no less than £2,421,681 of this sum disappearing in one year—1792.

The French revolutionary war began in 1793, and with a short interval of exhaustion, called "Peace," lasted till 1815, when Bonaparte was sent to St. Helena, and the forty years' real peace commenced. During these twenty-three years of war money was borrowed in the most extravagant manner. From 1793 to 1801 the average price of £100 three per cent. stock was £57 17s. 6d., and from 1803 to the conclusion of the war, £60 17s. 6d. In 1815 a loan of £36,000,000 was negotiated, every subscriber receiving £174 three per cent. stock, and £10 four per cent. The following loans were raised from 1793 to 1816:—

Year.	£	Year.	£	Year.	£
1793...	4,877,956	1801...	27,305,271	1809...	12,298,375
1794...	6,998,389	1802...	14,638,254	1810...	7,792,444
1795...	30,464,831	1803...	8,752,761	1811...	19,143,953
1796...	22,244,982	1804...	14,570,763	1812...	24,790,697
1797...	30,356,873	1805...	16,649,801	1813...	39,649,282
1798...	16,858,503	1806...	13,035,344	1814...	34,563,603
1799...	21,714,863	1807...	10,432,934	1815...	20,241,807
1800...	23,030,529	1808...	12,095,044	1816...	514,059

In 1816 our indebtedness was over nine hundred millions sterling. Within a few years this was reduced by one hundred millions, and after that by a comparatively small sum nearly every year. In 1816 the debt amounted to £45 a head of the population; but in 1899, taking the population from the Registrar General's estimate, the *Net* total only amounted to £14 15s. 4d. for each of the 40,559,954 inhabitants of the United Kingdom. The *nominal* amount of debt in January, 1816, was £885,186,323; but by adopting the present method of capitalizing the Annuities then outstanding as three per cent. stock, the following figures will represent the actual state of the Debt on that date. Reckoned in this manner, it stood as follows:—

Funded Debt	£816,312,000
Unfunded Debt	44,727,000
Terminable Annuities capitalized...	39,397,000
	£900,436,000

With peace secured efforts were made to reduce the Debt; but this was no easy matter. In 1813, the national expenditure had reached the unprecedented amount of £108,397,645, of which £68,748,363 was raised by taxation, and £39,640,282 by loans. In 1815, the Waterloo year, the amount raised by taxation had increased to £72,210,512; but in 1817, the war being finished, taxation was reduced to £52,055,913, and out of this the sum of £1,826,814 was applied to the reduction of Debt. The following amounts were paid off from 1817-37:

Year.	£	Year.	£	Year.	£
1817...	1,826,814	1824...	7,456,559	1831...	2,673,858
1818...	1,624,606	1825...	9,900,725	1832...	5,696
1819...	3,163,130	1826...	1,195,531	1833...	1,023,784
1820...	1,918,019	1827...	2,023,028	1834...	1,776,378
1821...	4,104,457	1828...	4,667,965	1835...	1,270,050
1822...	2,962,564	1829...	2,760,003	1836...	1,590,727
1823...	5,261,725	1830...	1,935,465	1837...	1,985,885

The abolition of slavery (1833) led to an increase of the debt, and the Crimean War added over £3,000,000, so that the total in March, 1857, was £838,918,443. In the 42 years since that date the sum of £203,877,478 has been paid off.

Decreases from 1888-1899:—

Year.	£	Year.	£	Year.	£
1888...	32,051,595	1892...	5,412,351	1896...	7,620,502
1889...	7,426,812	1893...	6,894,203	1897...	7,630,258
1890...	8,636,931	1894...	4,543,540	1898...	6,643,365
1891...	4,709,820	1895...	8,943,417	1899...	6,873,119

The gross Liabilities of the State on March 31, 1899, were as follows:—

I. THE FUNDED DEBT:—		
(a) Permanent	£583,185,305	
(b) Annuities	36,243,280	
II. The Unfunded Debt	8,133,000	
III. Other Capital Liabilities	7,478,380	
Total Debt	£635,040,965	

From this total must be deducted the following assets:—

Value of Suez Canal Shares	£26,451,000
Unrepaid Loans	505,359
Moiety of estimated capital value of Red Sea and India Telegraph Company's Annuity, repayable by Indian Government	140,727
Present value of Annuity from Australasian Colonies	57,875
Exchequer Balances at the Banks of England and Ireland	8,919,173
Total Assets	£36,074,134

leaving the net Liabilities at £598,966,831.

* See also article "The Growth of National Indebtedness," p. 595 of 1899 issue.

The Debt is of three descriptions:—I. Funded (a) Permanent, (b) Terminable; II. Unfunded; III. Certain other Liabilities.

I. FUNDED DEBT.—(a) PERMANENT.
That is, Debt which the Government is not under obligation to pay off at any fixed time. This consisted of the following stock on March 31, 1899:—

2¾ per cent. Consols	£520,154,149
2¾ per cent. 1905	4,635,991
2½ per cent.	31,750,295
Bank of England Debt	11,015,100
Bank of Ireland do.	2,630,769
Book Debt 2¾ per cent	13,000,000
	£583,185,305

(b) TERMINABLE ANNUITIES.
These are a description of Sinking Fund by means of which a considerable portion of debt is paid off every year, and after a certain time the capitalized sum entirely extinguished. It may be shortly explained that the Treasury is empowered to give an Annuity for a certain number of years in exchange for permanent stock. Thus A transfers to the Treasury £1,000 of 2¾ per cent. stock on which he is receiving £27 10s. a year; the Treasury in return undertakes to pay A £55 a year for twenty years or thereabouts. The Treasury cancels the £1,000 stock, and thus reduces, say, Consols by that amount; but during twenty years it pays a much larger sum than it would have paid if it had left matters alone.

The following is a list of these terminable annuities with the dates when they expire, and their capitalized value as on March 31, 1899:—

(1) Annuities for Life and Terms of years	£12,383,230
(2) Red Sea and India Telegraph Companies (1908)	281,454
(3) Converted Annuities (1904)	2,924,197
(4) Chancery Funds (1904)	13,808,188
(5) Savings Banks (1901-2)	6,032,145
(6) Trustee Savings Banks (1908)	657,086
(7) Annuity of 1884 (1903)	151,980
	£35,243,280

II. UNFUNDED DEBT.
The Unfunded Debt consists of loans, money borrowed for short periods, which the Government is bound to pay off at certain dates, and is repre-sented by certain loans having currency for periods varying from a few months to five or more years. On March 31, 1899, these consisted of three- six- and twelve-months Treasury Bills (for supply purposes) to the amount of £8,133,000.

III. OTHER CAPITAL LIABILITIES.
These sums are not included in the Capital on which Interest is arranged for in the Permanent charge.

On March 31, 1899, these sums stood as follows:—

Imperial Defence Act (1888) Annuities	£187,893
Russian Dutch Loan Annuity	312,441
Under Barracks Act, 1890	2,829,029
„ Telegraph Act, 1892	1,222,276
„ Uganda Railway Act, 1896	1,969,722
„ Public Offices Act, 1895	455,381
„ „ „ (Whitehall Site) Act, 1897	501,638
Total	£7,478,380

There are also sundry Contingent or Nominal Liabilities which the State is not likely to be called upon to any material extent to discharge. On March 31, 1899, these amounted to the following sums:—

Liability to Suitors (Chancery)	£2,331,884
„ „ Bankrupts' Estates	1,114,577
„ „ Suitors (Ireland)	259,151
Fee and other Funds „	163,285
Court of Bankruptcy „	35,042
Unclaimed Dividends (B. of England)	211,669
„ South Sea Annuities, &c.	39,788
„ Dividends (Bank of Ireland)	1,459
Life Annuities, &c. (Nat. Debt Office)	20,000
Uncl. Dividend acct. „	72,191
Total	£4,249,046

The Permanent Charge of the Debt for the last two years is detailed below:—

DEBT:	1897-8.	1898-9.
Funded Debt (Interest)	£16,063,925	£16,009,557
Terminable Annuities	7,251,159	7,281,703
Unfunded (Interest)	139,300	139,254
Cost of management	174,309	175,027
New Sinking Fund	1,361,307	1,394,459
Total Charge for Debt	£25,000,000	£25,000,000

GROSS AMOUNT AND FIXED ANNUAL CHARGE OF THE DEBT (1888-1899).

Year.	Gross Amount of the Debt.					Cost of Interest and Management.		
	Funded Debt.		Unfunded Debt.	Other Liabilities.	Gross Total.	Funded Debt.		Unfunded Interest & Management, &c.
	Permanent.	Annuities.				Permanent.	Annuities.	
	£	£	£	£	£	£	£	£
1887	637,437,640	81,123,148	17,517,900	2,500,488	738,779,176	18,771,838	8,131,218	462,311
1888	609,740,743	78,449,230	17,385,100	1,152,508	706,727,581	18,187,386	6,614,704	1,197,910
1889	507,057,811	75,279,438	16,093,322	870,198	699,300,769	18,361,288	5,907,495	1,731,217
1890	585,959,852	71,731,869	32,252,305	619,812	690,663,838	16,836,000	6,555,596	1,607,938
1891	579,472,082	68,458,798	36,140,079	1,834,059	685,954,018	15,998,486	6,549,871	2,451,643
1892	577,944,665	64,421,912	35,312,994	2,862,196	680,541,767	15,893,049	6,557,637	2,549,314
1893	589,533,082	60,761,490	20,748,270	2,594,722	673,647,564	16,052,835	6,350,401	2,796,764
1894	587,631,096	57,076,898	20,696,300	2,949,730	669,110,024	16,132,688	6,393,504	2,473,608
1895	586,015,919	53,582,722	17,400,300	3,161,666	660,160,607	16,069,869	6,422,410	2,507,721
1896	589,146,878	49,351,465	9,975,800	4,065,962	652,540,105	16,110,274	6,422,138	2,437,588
1897	587,698,732	44,941,947	8,133,000	4,136,168	644,909,847	16,108,037	7,149,743	1,742,220
1898	585,787,622	40,515,080	8,133,000	3,830,778	638,266,482	16,063,925	7,261,159	1,535,716
1899	583,185,305	35,243,280	8,133,000	7,478,380	635,040,965	16,009,557	7,281,703	1,708,740

Income Tax Rates
FROM 1853 TO THE PRESENT TIME.

From and to April 5th	Free under	On £100 to £150	On £150 and upwards.	Chancellor of the Exchequer.	Premier.
	£	Rate in the £			
1853 to 1854	100	5d.	7d.	William E. Gladstone.	Earl of Aberdeen.
1854 ,, 1855	Do.	10d.	1s. 2d.	Do.	Do.
1855 ,, 1857	Do.	11½d.	1s. 4d.	Sir G. Cornewall Lewis.	Viscount Palmerston.
1857 ,, 1858	Do.	5d.	7d.	Do.	Do.
1858 ,, 1859	Do.	5d.	5d.	Do.	Do.
1859 ,, 1860	Do.	6½d.	9d.	Benjamin Disraeli.	Earl of Derby.
1860 ,, 1861	Do.	7d.	10d.	William E. Gladstone.	Viscount Palmerston.
1861 ,, 1863	*100	6d.	9d.	Do.	Do.
1863 ,, 1864	Do.	7d.		Do.	Do.
1864 ,, 1865	Do.	6d.		Do.	Do.
1865 ,, 1866	Do.	4d.		Do.	Do.
1866 ,, 1867	Do.	4d.		Do.	Earl Russell.
1867 ,, 1868	Do.	5d.		Benjamin Disraeli.	Earl of Derby.
1868 ,, 1869	Do.	6d.		George Ward Hunt.	Benjamin Disraeli.
1869 ,, 1870	Do.	5d.		Robert Lowe.	William E. Gladstone.
1870 ,, 1871	Do.	4d.		Do.	Do.
1871 ,, 1872	+Do.	6d.		Do.	Do.
1872 ,, 1873	Do.	4d.		Do.	Do.
1873 ,, 1874	Do.	3d.		Do.	Do.
1874 ,, 1876	Do.	2d.		Sir Stafford Northcote.	Benjamin Disraeli.
1876 ,, 1878	‡150	3d.		Do.	Earl of Beaconsfield.
1878 ,, 1880	Do.	5d.		Do.	Do.
1880 ,, 1881	Do.	6d.		William E. Gladstone.	William E. Gladstone.
1881 ,, 1882	Do.	5d.		Do.	Do.
1882 ,, 1883	Do.	6½d.		Do.	Do.
1883 ,, 1884	Do.	5d.		Hugh C. E. Childers.	Do.
1884 ,, 1885	Do.	6d.		Do.	Do.
1885 ,, 1886	Do.	8d.		Sir Michael Hicks-Beach.	Marquess of Salisbury.
1886 ,, 1887	Do.	8d.		Sir William Harcourt.	William E. Gladstone.
1887 ,, 1888	Do.	7d.		George J. Goschen.	Marquess of Salisbury.
1888 ,, 1892	Do.	6d.		Do.	Do.
1892 ,, 1893	Do.	6d.		Sir William Harcourt.	William E. Gladstone.
1893 ,, 1894	Do.	7d.		Do.	Do.
1894 ,, 1895	¶160	8d.		Do.	Earl of Rosebery.
1895 ,, 1898	Do.	8d.		Sir Michael Hicks-Beach.	Marquess of Salisbury.
1898 ,, 1900	aDo.	8d.		Do.	Do.

* Differential rate upon scale of incomes abolished. Incomes under £100 exempt; and incomes of £100 and under £200 per annum received an abatement of £60 from the assessment:—thus £100, paid on £40; £160 upon £100; £190 upon £139; but £200 paid on £200.   † £80 allowed if under £300.   ‡ Under £150 exempt; if under £400 the tax is not chargeable upon the first £120.   ¶ Under £160 exempt; not exceeding £400 the tax is not chargeable on first £160: not exceeding £500 the tax is not chargeable on first £100.   a Incomes under £700 subject to special rebate on £70.

ANNUITIES TO THE ROYAL FAMILY.

Her Majesty:—

Privy Purse	£60,000	£
Salaries of Household	131,260	
Expenses of Household	172,500	
Royal Bounty, &c.	13,200	
Unappropriated	8,040	—385,000
Prince of Wales		40,000
Princess of Wales		10,000
For the children of Their Royal Highnesses		*36,000
Dowager German Empress		8,000
Duke of Edinburgh (Saxe-Coburg)		+10,000
Princess Christian of Schleswig-Holstein		6,000
Princess Louise (Marchioness of Lorne)		6,000
Duke of Connaught		25,000
Princess Beatrice (Henry of Battenberg)		6,000
Duchess of Mecklenburg-Strelitz		3,000
Duke of Cambridge		12,000
Duchess of Albany		6,000
Civil List Pensions, only £1,200 granted annually, as opposite		23,773

* For the proper disposal of this money, which will continue to be paid till six months after Her Majesty's decease, certain trustees have been appointed.
† Has surrendered £15,000.

CIVIL LIST PENSIONS, 1898-99.

Alabaster, Laura Abbie, Lady, widow of Sir Chaloner Alabaster, K.C.M.G.	£100
Armstrong, Miss Emma C. } daughters of the late Dr. Archibald Armstrong, A.R.A. } Armstrong, Miss Julia A. } Lexicographer.	25
Ashton, Charles (Welsh Literature)	40
Bates, Mrs., widow of Mr. Harry Bates, A.R.A.	60
Burton, Miss Eliza, daughter of Dr. Burton, Scottish Historian	65
Dalziel, Edward (Wood Engraving)	100
Kanthack, Mrs. Lucie, widow of the Eminent Pathologist	60
Kingsford, Mrs., wid. of the Canadian Historian	100
Malleson, Mrs., wid. of the Eminent Historian	100
Payne, John (Oriental Literature)	100
Robinson, Mrs., widow of the Musician	40
Steingass, Dr. (Oriental Scholar)	25
Taylor, Mrs. Mary } daughters of Dr. Eldersh-im, Theologian } Tyndale, Mrs. Maria } and Biblical Critic }	25 25
Walker, Mrs. Rawson, widow of Mr. Consul Walker	100
White, Mrs., widow of Mr. Gleeson White	35
Wright, Dr. Joseph (English Dialect Dict.)	200

Year.	Gross Estimate.	Supplement-ary Estimate.	Estimated Receipts, &c.	Appropria-tions in Aid.	Net Estimate.	Actual Grant.	Revenue Departments.
	£	£	£	£	£	£	£
1888-89	18,145,293	201,637	1,845,276		16,300,017	18,872,986	11,094,031
1889-90	15,739,092	93,849	2,008,466		13,824,516	15,589,990	10,999,598
1890-91	15,660.959	37,734	1,950,693		13,948,000	15,901,513	11,307,358
1891-92	16,516,029	264,358			17,500,709	11,747,897
1892-93	17,310,920	118,955	1,100,294		16,210,626	17,626,875	12,299,471
1893-94	18,129,929	315,105	1,146,082		16,983,847	18,143,561	12,970,785
1894-95	20,021,785	402,689	1,149,934		17,538,285	18,841,038	13,619,982
1895-96	20,647,410	86,000	1,142,016	1,349,666	19,297,744	18,155,728	13,761,322
1896-97	21,214,703	551,266	1,120,312	1,419,663	19,795,040	20,045,000	14,152,246
1897-98	21,590,686	923,713	1,313,572	1,422,718	20,167,968	21,045,000	14,543,166
1898-99	23,191,384	126,218	1,290,931	1,398,738	21,792 646	21,918,064	15,433,697
1899-1900	23,680,461		1,399,750	1,500,796	22,179,665		16,191,071

CIVIL SERVICE, GROSS, £23,680,461 ; REVENUE DEPARTMENTS, £16,191,071. TOTAL, £39,871,532.

In the following divisions the gross and net totals of each vote are given for the years 1898-99 and 1899-1900, the net amount being arrived at by deducting " (a) Appropriations in Aid " :—

CIVIL SERVICE.	1898—99		1899—1900	
	Gross.	Net.	Gross.	Net.
	£	£	£	£
I. Public Works and Buildings	1,988,651	1,910,431	1,977,050	1,895,622
II. Salaries and Expenses	2,624,681	2,180,616	2,675,594	2,160,715
III. Law and Justice	4,426,583	3,757,592	4,501,275	3,809,088
IV. Education, Science, and Art	12,042,356	11,965,790	12,286,515	12,207,860
V. Foreign and Colonial Services	1,345,576	1,221,956	1,585,138	1,458,840
VI. Non-effective & Charitable Services	711,721	711,539	592,185	592,040
VII. Miscellaneous	51,816	44,716	62,704	55,500
Total Civil Service	23,191,384	21,792,646	23,680,461	22,179,665
REVENUE DEPARTMENTS.				
Customs	900,050	855,600	895,840	846,600
Inland Revenue	1,998,323	1,980,323	1,981,232	1,956,232
Post Office	8,118,425	8,002,250	8,677,585	8,552,885
Post Office Packet Service	1,007,424	824,350	955,289	780,915
Post Office Telegraphs	3,409,475	3,364,635	3,681,025	3,638,390
Total Revenue Departments	15,433,697	15,027,158	16,191,071	15,785,022
Grand total	38,625,081	38,619,804	39,871,532	37,964,687

DUCHY OF LANCASTER.

The revenue of the Duchy was £29,000 in 1847 and £94,788 net in 1898. £60,000 was paid to Her Majesty ; £6,684 laid out for the benefit of the estate ; £4,505 deducted under various Acts of Parliament ; £6,123 to defray the cost of management ; and £2,000 to the Chancellor, leaving a balance of £12,257. Capital account, December, 1897, £20,562 in cash, and £16,319 in securities.

DUCHY OF CORNWALL.

Income, 1898. £108,970. £61,243 was paid to the Prince of Wales ; £13,046 the benefit of the estate ; deductions under various Acts of Parliament, £12,928 ; superannuations, &c. £1,347 ; expenses of management, £9,685 ; leaving a balance in favour of 1899 of £10,124. Capital account, December, 1898, £22,412 in cash, and £283,184 in securities.

(a) *Appropriations in Aid.*—Under CLASS II.—Fees for Private Bills, &c. (House of Lords), £32,000 ; House of Commons, £30,000 ; Board of Trade fees, £10,515 ; Mercantile Marine Department Office fees, £49,826 ; Bankruptcy Department, £136,000 ; Royal Mint profit on coinage, £530,000 ; Sales by Stationery Office, £91,155. CLASS III.—Supreme Court fees, £53,130 ; County Court fees, £435,000 ; Scottish Court fees, &c., £36,500. CLASS IV.—London University fees, £17,940 ; fees and books, National Schools (Ireland), £38,750 ; Queen's College (Ireland) fees, £6,740. CLASS V.—Consular Court fees, £68,500. CLASS VII.—Fees for honours and dignities, £5,204.

Year.	Gross Estimate.	Net Estimate.	Expended.	No. of Men.	Secretary of State for War.
	£	£	£	‡	
1886-87	21,172,936	18,233,200	18,564,742	151,867	{ Rt. Hon. H. C. Bannerman, L.
					{ Rt. Hon. W. H. Smith, C.
1887-88	21,485,018	18,393,900	17,614,031	149,391	Rt. Hon. Edward Stanhope, C.
1888-89	19,458,205	16,700,300	16,553,611	149,667	,,
1889-90	20,006,362	17,335,800	17,335,812	152,282	,,
1890-91	20,582,357	17,897,900	17,611,969	153,483	,,
1891-92	20,550,507	17,545,300	17,441,293	153,696	,,
1892-93	20,664,962	17,631,200	17,587,772	154,073	,,
1893-94	20,750,651	17,802,800	17,813,293	154,442	Rt. Hon. H. C. Bannerman, L.
1894-95	21,004,390	18,080,900	17,935,920	155,347	,,
1895-96	20,805,758	17,983,800	17,770,095	155,403	,,
1896-97	20,938,978	18,042,100	18,156,520	156,174	The Marquess of Lansdowne, C.
1897-98	21,362,422	18,340,500	19,330,000	158,774	,,
1898-99	22,359,599	19,220,500	20,000,000	180,513	,,
1899-1900	23,822,333	20,617,200	—	184,853	,,

‡ *Exclusive of those serving in India (73,157 in 1899-1900).*

NET INCREASE, 1899-1900, £1,396,700; ORDNANCE FACTORIES, GROSS, £3,319,100; NET, £100.

THE Army Expenditure in 1898-99 amounted to about five twenty-sevenths of the whole expenditure of the country, and was at the rate of about 10s. per head of the estimated population. In the following table, the gross and net totals of each vote are given for the purpose of comparison, the net amount of each vote being arrived at by deducting " (a) Appropriations in Aid":—

EFFECTIVE SERVICES.	1898-9.		1899-1900.	
	Gross.	Net.	Gross.	Net.
	£	£	£	£
1. Pay, &c., of the Army	7,246,400	6,266,400	7,703,000	6,509,000
2. Medical Establishments: Pay, &c.	297,100	295,800	307,100	305,800
3. Militia, Pay, &c.	568,600	553,000	586,600	571,000
4. Yeomanry, Pay, &c.	75,010	75,000	75,010	75,000
5. Volunteers, Pay, &c.	614,700	614,200	624,700	624,200
6. Transport and Remounts	733,100	710,400	813,300	790,000
7. Provisions, Forage, &c.	3,392,200	3,352,600	3,465,100	3,425,500
8. Clothing Establishments, &c.	1,295,600	862,000	1,506,500	1,090,000
9. Warlike and other Stores	2,373,900	1,972,000	2,939,000	2,531,000
10. Works, Buildings, and Repairs	1,175,645	1,020,700	1,380,575	1,211,900
11. Military Education : Pay, &c.	182,300	118,200	178,200	111,100
12. Miscellaneous Effective Services	61,600	54,300	69,800	60,200
13. War Office : Salaries and Charges	245,250	245,200	248,400	248,300
Total of Effective Services	18,441,405	16,139,800	19,897,285	17,553,000
NON-EFFECTIVE SERVICES.				
14. Retired Pay, Half-pay, &c., for Officers	1,938,206	1,567,800	1,948,264	1,555,000
15. Pensions for Warrant Officers, &c.	1,802,535	1,335,600	1,793,035	1,325,500
16. Superannuation, &c. Allowances	177,453	177,300	183,749	183,700
Total	22,359,599	19,220,500	23,822,333	20,617,200

ORDNANCE FACTORIES ESTIMATE, 1899-1900.

The gross amount of the estimate is £3,319,100, against £2,922,000 in 1898-99 and the items are:—Establishment pay £26,878; wages and police £1,615,588; materials and stores £1,511,000; machinery obtained by contract £41,900; buildings £85,034; miscellaneous £29,200; non-effective charges £9,500. Of the gross total £1,395,000 is chargeable to the Army for stores, £1,265,000 to the Navy, £100,000 to India, £70,000 is covered by sale of old stores, £12,000 by miscellaneous receipts, and £22,000 transferred from Suspense Account. This leaves £100 as the net amount of the vote, as in 1898-99. Materials and stores for Woolwich cost £1,314,000, for Enfield £47,000, for Waltham Abbey £140,000, and for Birmingham £10,000. The machinery obtained by contract is in addition to that made by the factory, and is valued at £41,900. Buildings include the cost of new works £53,034, the maintenance and repairs being £32,000.

(a) *Appropriations in Aid*:—These consist of contributions from India £729,700 and the Colonies, £283,000 (Ceylon, £117,800; Mauritius, £21,500; Hong Kong, £47,000; Straits Settlements, £87,700; Malta, £5,000; and Natal, £4,000), and of £87,000 paid by Egypt, while £42,000 is derived from the purchase of Discharges and £42,000 from Hospital Stoppages. The sum of £14,000 is derived from the sale of horses, &c.; £24,000 from the sale of provisions, &c.; £60,000 from the sale of old arms, &c.; £132,975 from the sale and rents of land, &c.; and £66,100 from fees payable by Gentlemen Cadets at Woolwich and Sandhurst.

Year.	Gross Estimates.	Net Estimate.	Expended.	No. of Officers & Men. Seamen.	No. of Officers & Men. Marines.	First Lord of the Admiralty.
	£	£	£			
1886-87	13,650,626	12,993,100	13,265,401	48,500	12,900	Marquess of Ripon.
1887-88	13,162,247	12,476,800	12,325,357	49,600	12,900	Lord George Hamilton.
1888-89*	13,776,572	13,082,800	12,999,895	49,634	12,766	,,
1889-90	14,361,810	13,685,400	13,842,241	51,526	13,874	,,
1890-91	14,557,856	13,786,600	14,125,358	54,918	13,882	,,
1891-92	15,210,620	14,215,100	14,150,000	56,995	14,005	,,
1892-93	15,256,811	14,240,200	14,302,000	49,133	14,379	,,
1893-94	15,267,674	14,240,100	14,048,000	51,428	14,865	Earl Spencer.
1894-95	18,371,713	17,366,100	17,642,000	57,026	15,365	,,
1895-96	19,613,821	18,701,000	19,637,238	61,945	15,363	,,
1896-97	22,774,318	21,823,000	22,271,902	65,757	15,861	George J. Goschen.
1897-98	23,280,473	22,238,000	22,170,000	70,472	16,841	,,
1898-99	24,733,832	23,778,400	24,068,000	75,709	17,807	,,
1899-1900	27,578,039	26,594,500	—	79,322	18,290	,,

* The sum of £1,717,561 was this year transferred from the Army Estimates, and £205,980 to the Army Estimates.

Net Increase 1899-1900, £2,816,100.

The Naval Expenditure in 1898-9 amounted to about six twenty-sevenths of the whole expenditure of the country, and was at the rate of about 12s. per head of the estimated population.

The gross and net totals of the several votes for the last two years are shown in the following abstract for the purpose of comparison, the net amount being derived by deducting " (a) Appropriations in Aid " :—

Effective Services.	1898-9. Gross.	1898-9. Net.	1899-1900. Gross.	1899-1900. Net.
	£	£	£	£
1. Wages to Officers, Seamen, &c.	5,105,185	4,988,000	5,361,017	5,242,700
2. Victualling and Clothing	1,921,325	1,491,700	2,051,712	1,606,700
3. Medical Establishments & Services	190,900	167,000	197,890	176,600
4. Martial Law	11,427	11,400	12,232	12,200
5. Educational Services	116,027	86,600	119,756	90,600
6. Scientific Services	79,629	67,200	82,341	69,500
7. Royal Naval Reserves	257,113	257,000	271,113	271,000
8. Shipbuilding, Repairs, Maintenance, &c.—				
I. Personnel	2,230,915	2,218,000	2,429,815	2,417,000
II. Matériel	3,132,000	2,971,000	3,960,000	3,799,000
III. Contract Work	5,649,440	5,612,000	6,638,460	6,601,000
9. Naval Armaments	2,584,700	2,549,200	2,755,585	2,710,800
10. Works, Buildings, and Repairs	657,100	650,100	806,830	795,100
11. Miscellaneous Effective Services	243,127	232,900	258,645	248,200
12. Admiralty Office	256,700	247,700	270,600	261,600
Total Effective Services	22,435,588	21,549,800	25,215,996	24,302,000
Non-Effective Services.				
13. Half-pay, Reserved & Retired Pay	764,803	752,500	786,914	774,700
14. Pensions, Gratuities, and Compassionate Allowances	1,104,808	1,082,900	1,137,936	1,116,000
15. Civil Pensions and Gratuities	333,323	332,900	341,893	341,500
Total, Non-Effective Services	2,202,934	2,168,300	2,266,743	2,232,200
Services in connection with the Colonies.				
16. Additional Naval Force in Australasian Waters, Annuity payable under	95,300	60,300	95,300	60,300
Grand Total	24,733,822	23,778,400	27,578,039	26,594,500

(a) *Appropriations in Aid.*—These consist of sums paid by India, £144,138; Australasian Colonies, £74,900; Canada, £3,500; and in addition by Queensland, for survey of her coast, £2,750; and £10,800 is derived from the purchase of discharges, £15,000 from stoppages in pay, £372,000 from stoppages from pay for uniforms and extras £27,702 from proceeds of sales of old stores, &c., and £12,590 from the sale of charts The fees paid for training a Naval Cadets in H.M.S. *Britannia* amount to £18,500.

ARMY AGENTS.

1. Cox & Co., 16 Charing Cross, S.W.
2. Holt & Co., 3 Whitehall Place, S.W.

3. M'Grigor, Sir Charles R., Bart., & Co., Charles Street, St. James's Square, S.W.

The Military Administration.

War Office, Pall Mall, S.W. Hours, 10 to 5.

Secretary of State, The Most Hon. the Marquess of Lansdowne, K.G., G.C.S.I., G.C.M.G., G.C.I.E.

MILITARY DEPARTMENT—HEADQUARTERS STAFF OF THE ARMY.—*Salaries, &c.,* £248,300.

Commander-in-Chief, Field-Marshal Rt. Hon. Viscount Wolseley, K.P., G.C.B., G.C.M.G. £4,500
Private Sec., Col. J. Davidson £600
Aides-de-Camp, Maj. Hon. W. Coke, £50c; Maj. A. A. Weldon; Maj. Hon. T. F. Fremantle; Col. Sir S. M. Lockhart, Bart., M.V.O. £500
Military Secretary, Major-Gen. Sir Coleridge Grove, K.C.B. £1,500
Assist. Military Sec., Col. A. M. Delavoye (*Education*); Col. J. C. Dalton; Col. W. E. Franklyn (*temp.*) ...... each £800
A.-A.-G (Mobiln.), Lt.-Col. P. H. N. Lake. £800
A.-A.-G. Staff-Capt ., Capt. W. T. Furse, R.A.; Capt. W. G. Gwatkin ...... each £500

Director of Military Intelligence, Major-Gen. Sir John Charles Ardagh. K.C.I.E., C.B. ...£1,500
A.A.G., Col. Sir Wm. Everett, K.C.M.G. ... £800
D.A.A.G., Capt. E. H. Hills, R.E. (*temp.*); Maj. T. Capper (*temp.*) ...... each £650
Staff Captains, Lieut. C. W. Gwynn, D.S.O.; Maj. N. W. Barnardiston; Capt. W. R. Robertson, D.S.O.; Capt. E. Peach, I.S.C.; ...... each £500
Librarian, Capt. W. H. Cromie, LL.B £300 to £450
Map Curator, A. Knox. ...... £300 to £450

Adjutant-General to the Forces, General Sir Evelyn Wood, V.C., G.C.B., G.C.M.G. £2,400
D.A.G. Maj.-Gen. Sir H. M. Leslie Rundle, K.C.B., C.M.G., D.S.O., R.A. (*temp.*) £1,500
A.A.G., Col. E. O. Hay; Col. J. H. Laye (*temp.*) ...... each £800
D.A.A.G., Lt.-Col. F. S. Robb; Capt. L. A. M. Stopford ...... each £650
Inspector-Gen. of Auxiliary Forces and Recruiting, Major-Gen. H. C. Borrett (*temp.*) ... £1,500
A.A.G. do., Col. A. G. Wavell £800
D.A.A.G do., Lt.-Col. C. Crutchley £700
D.A.A.G., R.E., Maj.-Gen. W. Salmond, C.B. £1,500
A.A.G., do., Col. E. Dickinson £800
Director of Army Schools, Col. D. F. Jones £800
Quartermaster-General to the Forces, Lt.-Gen. Sir Charles Mansfield Clarke, Bart., K.C.B. £2,100
A.Q.M.G., Col. J. T. Skinner, C.B., D.S.O. £1,472; Col. A. G. Raper; Col. R. Auld ...... each £800
D.A.Q.M.G., Col. J. A. Boyd, C.B., £922; Maj. F. B. Buist; Maj. J. S. Cowans ...... each £650
Inspector-General of Remounts, Maj.-Gen. W. R. Truman £1,200
Staff Paymaster, Lt.-Col. J. E. Kitson, A.P.D. £700
Inspector-General of Fortifications, General Sir R. Harrison, K.C.B., C.M.G., R.E. £2,100
Deputy Inspects.-Gen. do., Col. C. M. Watson, C.M.G.; Col. G. Hildebrand; Col. C. H. Bagot ...... each £1,200
Assistant do., Col. R. M. Hyslop, R.E.; Col. G. Barker, R.E.; Lt.-Col. N. M. Lake, R.E.; Lt.-Col. H. W. Smith-Rewse, R.E.; Lt.-Col. R. Thompson, R.E.; Lt.-Col. C. H. Darling, R.E.; Lt.-Col.W.J.Mackenzie,R.E. each £850

Artillery Adviser, Maj. A. C. Hansard, R.A. £500
Inspector of Submarine Defences, Major F. Rainsford-Hannay, R.E £500
Assist. do., Maj. P.R.Burn-Murdoch, R.E. £450
Inspector of Iron Structures, Capt. C. H. H. Nugent, R.E. (*temp.*) £500
Director - General of Ordnance, Gen. Sir H. Brackenbury, K.C.B., K.C.S.I., Col. Commdt., R.A. £2,100
Deputy do., Col. R. A. Montgomery, R.A. £900
Assist. do., Lt.-Col. C. W. H. Tate; Col. W. F. Vetch (*temp.*) £800
Deputy-Assist. do., Lt.-Col. C. G. Jeans; Maj. G. H. Bitt'eston, R.A.; Lt.-Col. F. B. Elmslie, R.A.; Maj. T. F. Bushe, R.A. ...... each £650
Staff Captain, Capt. L. R. Kenyon, R.A. £500
Inspector-Gen. of Cavalry, Maj.-Gen. Henry Fane Grant, C.B. £1,200
A.-de-C., Capt. George Langworthy.
A.A.G., the Earl of Erroll £800
Chaplain-General, Rev. J. Cox Edghill, D.D. £1,000
Director-General Army Medical Service, Surg.-Gen. James Jameson, C.B., M.D., LL.D. £1,500
Deputy do., Surg.-Gen. H. S. Muir, M.D. £1,300
Assist. Director, Lt.-Col. W. L. Gubbins, M.B., R.A.M.C. £750
Deputy do., Maj. G. W. Macpherson, M.B., R.A.M.C.; Maj. E. M. Wilson, C.M.G., D.S.O., R.A.M.C. ...... each £650
Director-General Army Veterinary Department, Vety.-Col. Francis Duck, C.B. £850

CLERICAL STAFF (arranged alphabetically).

Principals, F. A. Bayly; G. W. Bevan; R. H. Brade; J. M. Bull; J. A. Flynn; R. Freeth; H. J. Gibson; J. Gray; R. H. Hobart, C.B.; W. P. Perry; D. R. C. Robinson; F. J. Sewell; G. W. Stevens; F. R. Thomas; G. P. Wight ...... £700 to £900
Seniors, G. E. Allen; J. G. Ashley; W. A. Bland; J. A. Corcoran; B. B. Cubitt; H. H. Fawcett; C. Harris; H. P. Harvey; F. Jackson; F. Leach; A. F. Major; C. J. Maxwell; C. Morton; F. G. Sills; W. J. T. Sheean; A. C. Strange; H. Strong; E. C. Syms; F. E. Vandeleur; T. H. Wyatt ...... £450 to £650
Clerks, A. H. B. Allen; G. A. Breading; C. C. Chapman; J. P. Crosland; H. E. Davies; S. Dannreuther; B. M. Draper; E. V. Fleming; H. G. Goligher; P. H. Hanson; L. D. Holland; P. F. Law; H. W. W. McAnally; W. L. McArthur; E. J. Norman; N. F. B. Osborn; W. J. D. Rich; C. Vere; C. F. Watherston; W. L. Wilkinson.
Staff-Clerks, F. J. Arnold; F. W. Askham; D. M. Boardman; W. Bussell; A. D. L. Cary; C. W. Cooper; H. G. Duneher; F. W. Dunn; E. G. Easton; H. J. Edwards; W. Evans; F. T. Freeman; H. J. Green; W. C. Grove; W. T. H. Harris; R. S. Harrison; S. Herbert; J. W. Hickey; D. Hurley; A. Martinelli; C. R. Moir; W. H. Nicoll; J. Paterson; W. Pear-

son ; A. C. Pedley ; G. Piper ; E. J. Riley ; M. Roche ; R. de M. Rudolf ; G. Smith ; W. H. Thomas ; W. Trathan ; H. A. Venables ; F. H. Warren ; H. O. Williams.

Supplementary Clerks, J. Barry ; H. Bower ; W. W. Browning ; A. Carter ; E. M. Cavenaugh ; G. H. Copping ; J. I. Farrant ; T. Larcombe ; J. P. McCleland ; J. J. Macken ; E. C. Minter ; R. Q. Moody ; T. Oldis ; W. Y. P. Pyne ; F. G. Russell ; J. Sharpe ; A. G. Thorn ; W. J. Turnbull ; R. Ward.

Higher Grade Clerks, 2nd Div., A. A. Barge ; H. J. Barlow ; H. Boulton ; M. J. Fenelon ; W. H. Glasson ; R. Hawkins ; J. M. Minards ; J. S. Pettitt ; J. Phillips ; J. A. Rochford ; O. H. Taylor.

There are also 183 clerks of the 2nd Division, 80 abstractors and assistant clerks, and about 100 boy clerks and copyists.

JOINT NAVAL AND MILITARY COMMITTEE ON DEFENCE.

President, The Purly. Under Sec. of State for War.
Secs., Col. G. Hildebrand ; Capt. Hon. W. G. Stopford, R N.

ORDNANCE COMMITTEE, Woolwich.—£10,800.
President, Lieut.-Gen. Henry Le G. Geary, C B., R.A. £1,500
Vice-Pres., Rear-Adm. A. B. Jenkings ...£1,150
Secretary, Maj. H. P. Hickman, R.A. £750
Assist. Sec., Commr. A.W.Waymouth, R.N.£650
Specially Employed, Lt. J. G. M. Watson, R.A.

WORKS BRANCH, Horse Guards.
Chief Surveyor, N. B. McDermott.

ARMY SANITARY COMMITTEE.—£600.
President, Lt.-Gen. Sir C. M. Clarke, Bart., K.C B.
Secretary, C. E. Innes.

ROYAL ENGINEER COMMITTEE.—£350.
President, Maj.-Gen. Thos. Fraser, C.B., C.M.G.
Secretary, Maj. Edward Druitt, R.E.

DRESS AND EQUIPMENT COMMITTEE, Aldershot.
President, Col. C. W. H. Douglas, A.D.C.
Secretary, Maj. G. F. Ellison.

ESTABLISHMENTS & LOADS COMMITTEE, Aldershot.
President, Col. C. W. H. Douglas, A D.C.
Secretary, Maj. G. F. R. Ellison.

ARMY PURCHASE COMMISSION (7, Victoria St., S W.).
Commissioner, James Cornelius O'Dowd, C.B.

ARMY RAILWAY COUNCIL.
President, Col. D. A. Scott, C.B., D.S.O.
Secretary, Maj. D. Henderson.

JUDGE-ADVOCATE-GENERAL'S OFFICE.
7, Victoria Street, S.W.
Judge-Advocate-General, Rt. Hon. Sir F. H. Jeune, K.C B.
Deputy do., Sir J. Scott, K.C.M G.
Deputy Judge-Advocate,

MILITARY PRISON DEPARTMENT.
(*See* Home Office p. 158.)

ROYAL ARMY CLOTHING FACTORY, Grosvenor Road, S.W.
Director, H. D. De la Bere £1,000
Medical Officer, Lt.-Col. J. H. Reynolds, V.C., M.B.

BRENNAN TORPEDO FACTORY.
Consulting Engineer, L. Brennan, C.B.
Supt., Capt. W. MacAdam, R.E.

BALLOON FACTORY, Aldershot.
Supt., Lt.-Col. J. L. B. Templer.

ORDNANCE FACTORIES.
Chief Superintendent, Col. Edmond Bainbridge, C.B., late R.A.
Secretary to do., Maj. H. W. W. Barlow, R.A.
Chief Mechanical Eng., H. F. Donaldson, M.I.C.E.
Civil Assistant, G. M. Tapp.

ROYAL ARSENAL, WOOLWICH.
Royal Carriage Factory.
Supt., Col. Sir G. S. Clarke, K.C.M.G., R.E.
Asst. do., Capt. F. T. Fisher, R.A.
Civil Manager of Railway Traffic, R. Birt.
Medical Officer, Maj. J. R. Dodd, M.B. R.A.M.C.
Royal Laboratory.
Supt., Maj. J. S. Douglas, R.A.
Asst. do., Capt. H. C. W. Eteson, R.A.
Officers in charge of Danger Buildings, Capt. C. J. Blunt, R.A.; Lt. C. J. D. Freeth, R.A.
Royal Gun Factory.
Supt., Maj. H. C. L. Holden, R A.
Asst. do., Lieut. C. R. Acklom, R.N.
Building Works.
Supt., Col. M. T. Sale, C.M.G., late R.E.
1st Asst : Maj. H. Huleatt, R.E.
2nd do., Capt. E. R. B. Stokes-Roberts, R.E.
ROYAL SMALL ARMS FACTORY, Enfield Lock.
Supt., Col. H. S. S. Watkin, C.B.
ROYAL SMALL ARMS FACTORY, Birmingham.
Supt., Col. Francis Wm. J. Barker.
ROYAL GUNPOWDER FACTORY, WALTHAM ABBEY.
Supt., Colonel John Becher Ormsby.
Asst do., Maj. F. L. Nathan, R.A.
Officer in charge of Danger Buildings, Lt. W. B. Anley, R.A.

DISTRICT COMMANDS.
HOME.
ALDERSHOT.—Maj.-Gen. T. Kelly-Kenny, C.B. (*temp.*) £2 000
EASTERN (*Colchester*).—Maj.-Gen. H. R. Abadie, C.B. (*temp.*) £1,095
GUERNSEY AND ALDERNEY.— Lieut.-Governor, Maj.-Gen. Michael Henry Saward, R.A. £1,700
HOME.—Maj.-Gen. Henry Trotter £1,095
JERSEY.—Lt.-Gov., Lt.-Gen. E.Hopton, C.B. £1,600
N.E. (*York*).—Maj.-Gen. R. T. Thynne, C.B. £1,095
N. W. (*Chester*).—Maj.-General Leopold Victor Swaine, C.B., C.M.G. £1,095
SCOTTISH (*Edinburgh*).—Gen. Edward Francis Chapman, C.B., R.A. £2,007
SOUTH-EASTERN (*Dover*).— £1,095
SOUTHERN (*Portsmouth*).—Lieut.-Gen. Sir Baker Creed Russell, K.C.B. £2 007
THAMES (*Chatham*).—Maj.-Gen. Thomas Fraser, C.B., C.M.G., R.E. £1,95
WESTERN (*Devonport*).—Lieut.-Gen. Sir William Francis Butler, K.C.B. £2,007
WOOLWICH.—Maj.-Gen. J. F. Maurice, C.B., R.A. £1,095

Staff in Ireland.
Commanding the Forces.—Field-Marshal Rt. Hon. Lord Roberts of Kandahar, V.C., K.P., G.C.B., R.A. £2,920
Asst. Mil. Sec., Maj. H. V. Cowan, R.A. (*temp.*) £383
D. A.-G., Col. Wm. Freeman Kelly, C.B. ...£750
A. A.-G., Col. Ed. Jas. Courtenay............£416
D. A. A.-G., Col. S. J. Lea, A.S. Corps ...£383
Dist. Insp. of Musketry, Capt. H. R. Hardy £333
D.A.A.-G.,R.A., Maj. J.T.Johnston, R A. £83
Chief Engineer, Col. C. F. C. Beresford £913
D. A. A.-G., Roy. Eng., Capt. G. M. W. Macdonogh, R.E. £383
P. M. O., Surg.-Gen. A.F. Preston, M.B. £1,004
Chief Ord. Officer, Col. E. G. Skinner, C.B. £767
Chief Paymaster, Col. F. Treffry, A.P.D. £550
BELFAST.—Maj.-Gen. Sir F. Carrington, K.C.B. £1,095
CORK.—Maj.-Gen. Hugh McCalmont, C.B. £1,095
CURRAGH.—Maj.-Gen. Sir Herbert C. Chermside, G.C.M.G. £1,095
DUBLIN.—Maj.-Gen. M.W.E. Gosset, C.B. £1,095

FIRST ARMY CORPS, SOUTH AFRICA.

General Commanding in Chief, Rt. Hon. Sir Redvers Buller, V.C., G.C.B., K.C.M.G.

Military Secretary, Col. Hon. F.W. Stopford, C.B.; *Chief of the Staff*, Maj.-Gen. Sir A. Hunter, K.C.B., D.S.O.; *D.A.G.*, Col. A. S. Wynne, C.B.; *Commg. R.A.*, Maj.-Gen. G. H. Marshall; *Chief Engineer*, Maj.-Gen. E. Wood, C.B.

FIRST DIVISION :—Lieut.-General Lord Methuen, K.C.V.O., C.B., C.M.G.
1st *Brig.*, Maj.-Gen. Sir H. E. Colville, C.B.; and *Brig.*, Maj.-Gen. H. J. T. Hildyard, C.B.
SECOND DIVISION :—Lieut.-General Sir C. F. Clery, K.C.B.
3rd *Brig.*, Maj.-Gen. A. G. Wauchope, C.B.; 4th *Brig.*, Maj.-Gen. Hon. N. G. Lyttelton.
THIRD DIVISION :—Lieut.-General Sir W. F. Gatacre, K.C.B., D.S.O.
5th *Brig.*, Maj.-Gen. A. F. Hart, C.B.; 6th *Brig.*, Maj.-Gen G. Barton, C.B.
FIFTH DIVISION :—Lieut.-General Sir Charles Warren, G.C.M.G.
9th *Brig.*, Maj.-Gen. E. R. P. Woodgate, C.B., C.M.G.; 10th *Brig.*, Maj.-Gen. J. T. Coke.
CAVALRY DIVISION :—Lieut.-General J. D. P. French.
1st *Brig.*, Maj.-Gen. J. M. Babington; and *Brig.*, Maj.-Gen. J. P. Brabazon, C.B., A.D.C.

NATAL FIELD FORCE.

Lieut.-on-General, Sir George S. White, V.C., G.C.B., G.C.S.I., G.C.I.E.
Asst. Military Sec., Col. B. Duff, C.I.E.; *Chief of the Staff*, Col. I. S. M. Hamilton, C.B., D.S.O.
FOURTH DIVISION :—Lieut.-General
7th *Brig.*, Maj.-Gen. F. Howard ; 8th *Brig.*, Maj.-Gen J. H. Yule.
3rd *Cavalry Brigade*, Maj.-Gen. J. F. Brocklehurst, M.V.O.

FIELD-MARSHALS.

H.R.H. Duke of Cambridge, K.G., K.T., K.P., G.C.B., G.C.S.I., G.M.M.G., G.C.I.E., G.C.V.O., Gren. Gds.. 17 Lancers, R.A., R.E., Middx. Regt., K.R.R.C., Hon. Col.-in-Chief to the Forces, Chief Pers. A.D.C.
H.R.H. Prince of Wales, K.G., K.T., K.P., G.M.B., G.C.S.I., G.C.M.G., G.C.I.E., G.C.V.O., Col. 10 Hussars, and Col.-in-Chief 1 Life Guards, 2 Life Guards, Royal Horse Guards, and Gord. Highrs., A.D C.
Sir John Lintorn Arabin Simmons, G.C.B., Colonel Commandant of the Royal Engineers.
Sir Frederick Paul Haines, G.C.B., G.C.S.I., C.I.E., Colonel of the Royal Scots Fusiliers.
Sir Donald Martin Stewart, Bart., G.C.B., G.C.S.I., C.I.E., Ind. Staff Corps, Governor of Chelsea Hospital.
Right Hon. Garnet Joseph, Viscount Wolseley, K.P., G.C.B., G.C.M.G., Col. R.H.G., Col.-in-Ch. Roy. Irish Regt., and Commander-in-Chief.
V.C., Right Hon. Frederick Sleigh, Lord Roberts of Kandahar, K.P., G.C.B., G.C.S.I., G.C.I.E., Col. Comdt. Royal Artillery, Commanding the Forces in Ireland.
H.H. Prince William Augustus Edward of Saxe-Weimar, K.P., G.C.B., Col. 1 Life Guards.

GENERALS.—Active List (14).

Schleswig - Holstein, H.R.H. Prince Christian of, K.G., A.D.C.
Biddulph, Sir Robert, G.C.B., G.C.M.G., Col. Comdt. R.A. (*Gov. Gibraltar*).
Connaught & Strathearn, H.R.H. the Duke of, K.G., Scots Gds., 6 Dragns., Rifle Brig., A.D.C.
Dunne, John Hart, Wilts Regt.
V.C., Wood, Sir Henry Evelyn, G.C.B., G.C.M.G., (*Adjt.-Gen.*).
Harrison, Sir Richd., K.C.B., C.M.G., R.E. (*Insp.-Gen.of Fortificatns.*).
Chapman, Edward Francis, C.B., R.A. (*Commdg. Scottish District*).
Lyon-Fremantle, Sir Arthur J., G.C.M.G., C.B.

V.C., Buller, Rt. Hon. Sir Redvers Henry, G.C.B., Col. Comdt. K.R.R.C. (*Comdg. 1st Army Corps*).
Montgomery-Moore, Alexander George, Col. 18 Hussars.
Lockhart, Sir Wm. Stephen Alexander, G.C.B., K.C.S.I., Indian Army (*C.-in-Ch., India*).
Anderson, Horace S., C.B., I.S.C.
Jones, Sir Howard S., K.C.B., R.M.L.I.
Tomkins, Wm. Percival, C.I.E., Col. Comdt. Royal Engrs.
Stevenson, Nathaniel.

Cumberland&Teviotdale, H.R.H. the Duke of, K.G.
Clerk, Godfrey, C.B. (*Tower*).
V.C., Channer, George Nicholas, C.B., I.S.C.
Le Grand, Fredk. Gasper, R.M.L.I.
Palmer, Sir Arthur Power, K C.B., I.S.C. (*Punjab Command*).
Tuson, Sir Hv. B., K.C.B., R.M.A. (*D.A.-G., Royal Marines*).
Suther, Cuthbert C., R M A.

Brackenbury, Sir Henry, K.C.B., R.A. (*Dir. Gen. Ordnance*).
Grenfell, Sir Francis Wallace, G.C.B., G.C.M.G. (*Gov. Malta*).

LIEUTENANT-GENERALS.—Active List (30).

Stirling, Sir William, K.C.B., R.A.
Hall, Julian Hamilton.
Barker, G. Digby, C.B. (*Bermuda*).
Stewart, Sir Richard Campbell, K.C.B., Indian Army.
Markham, Sir Edwin, K.C.B., R.A. (*Governor R.M.C.*).
V.C., White, Sir George Stewart, G.C.B., G.C.S.I., G.C.I.E., Gord. Highrs. (*Natal*).
Moncrieff, George Hay.
Forster, Bowes Lennox, R.A.
Forestier-Walker, Sir Frederick W. E., K.C.B., C.M.G. (*Lines of Communications, S. Africa*).
Clarke, Sir Chas. Mansfield, Bart., K.C.B. (*Q.M.G.*).
East, Sir Cecil Jas., K.C.B.
Seymour, Lord Wm. Frederick Ernest (*Commdg. in Canada*).
Low, Sir Robert Cunliffe, G.C.B., Indian Army (*Bombay Comd.*).

Russell, Sir Baker Creed, K.C.B., 13 Hussars (*Comdg.at Portsmouth*).
Graham, Samuel James, C.B.
Grant, Sir Robert, K.C.B., R.E.
Warren, Sir Charles, G.C.M.G., R.E. (*5th Division, S. Africa*).
Glyn, John Plumptre Carr.
Methuen, Lord, K.C.V.O., C.B. (*1st Divn., S. Africa*).
Sanford, George Edwd. Langham Somerset, C.B., C.S.I., R.E.
Geary, Henry Le Guay, C.B., R.A. (*President, Ordnance Cmttee.*).
Fryer, John, C.B.
Hopton, Edward, C.B. (*Jersey*).
Lance, Frederick, C B , I.S.C.
Bird, Sir George Corrie, K.C.I.E., C.B., I.S.C.
Clifford, Robt. Cecil Richd., C.B., I.S.C.
Owen, John Fletcher, R.A.
Barnes, Ardley H. F., R.M.L.I.

Pennington, Chas. Richd., C.B., I.S.C.
Nicolson, Malcom H., C.B., Ind. Army (*Mhow*).
Evans, Horace M., C.B., I.S.C.
French, Arthur, C.B., R.M.A.
Wolseley, Sir G.B., K.C.B. (*Madras*).
Butler, Sir Wm. Francis, K.C.B. (*Devonport*).
Luck, Sir George, K.C.B. (*Bengal Command*).
Clery, Sir Cornelius F., K.C.B. (*2nd Divn., S. Africa*).
Kelly - Kenny, Thomas, C.B. (*Aldershot*).
Gatacre, Sir Wm. Forbes, K.C.B., D.S.O. (*3rd Divn., S. Africa*).
French, John D. P. (*Cavalry Divn., S. Africa*).

MAJOR-GENERALS.—ACTIVE LIST (110).

Munro, Gustavus Fras., R.M.L.I.

Cairncross, John, R.M.L.I.

Gore, Ed. Arthur (*Remounts*).

Congleton, Lord, C.B. (*Inf.,Malta*).

Teck, H.H. the Duke of, G.C.B.

Thynne, Reg. Thos., C.B. (*York*).

Tucker, Chas., C.B. (*Secunderabd.*).

Carrington, Sir Fredk., K.C.B., K.C.M.G. (*Belfast*).

Walker, Alexander, C.S.I., R.A.

Walker, Albert Lancelot.

Biscoe, William Walters, C.B., Indian Army.

Montgomery, William Edward.

Dalrymple, Wm. Liston, C.B.

Elliott, Edward Draper, R.A.

Trotter, Henry (*London Comd.*).

Moore, Chas. Alfred, Ind. A.

Hazlerigg, Thomas Maynard, R.A.

Ward, Francis Wm., C.B., R.A.

Jennings, Robert Melvill, C.B., Ind. Army (*Dist. Comd., Bengal*).

Gascoigne, Wm. Julius, C.M.G. (*Comdg. at Hong Kong*).

Bushman, Henry Augustus, C.B.

Morris, Robert, Indian Army.

Burnett, Chas. John, C.B. (*Poona*).

Maurice John F., C.B. (*Woolwich*).

Combe, Boyce A., C.B.

Prior, George Upton.

Gosset, Matthew Wm. Edwd., C.B. (*Comdg. at Dublin*).

Saward, Michael Henry, R.A. (*Guernsey*).

McCalmont, Hugh, C.B. (*Cork*).

Grove, Sir Coleridge, K.C.B. (*Mil. Sec., Headqrs.*).

Swaine, Leopold Victor, C.B., C.M.G. (*Comdg. at Chester*).

Sterling, John Barton.

Kitchener of Khartoum, Lord (Pasha), G.C.B., K.C.M.G., R.E. (*Sirdar, Egyptian Army*).

Sym, John Munro, C.B., I.S.C.

Handcock, Arthur G., C.B., I.S.C.

Halliday, George Thomas, Indian Army.

Hunter, Sir Archbd., K.C.B., D.S.O. (*Chief of the Staff, S. Africa*).

Rundle, Sir H. M. Leslie, C.B., D.S.O., R.A. (*D.-A.-G., Hdqrs.*).

Strahan, Charles, R.E. (*Surv.-Gen., India*).

Badcock, Alexander Robert, C.B., C.S.I., L.S.C. (*Q.-M.-G., India*).

Gerard, Sir Montagu Gilbert, K.C.S.I., C.B. (*Hyderabad Contgt.*).

Stedman, Sir Edwd., K.C.I.E., C.B., Ind. Staff Corps.

Protheroe, Montague, C.B., C.S.I., I.S.C. (*Burma*).

Toker, Alliston C., C.B., I.S.C.

Parker, Neville Fraser, Ind. Army.

Colwell, Geo. Harrie T., C.B., R.M.

Moysey, Charles John, C.M.G., R.E.

Pretyman, Geo. Tindal, C.B., R.A.

Salis-Schwabe, Geo. (*Lt.-Gov. and Sec., Roy. Hospital, Chelsea*).

Stewart R. MacGregor, C.B. (*Comdg. Arty., Portsmouth*).

Tregear, Vincent W., C.B., Indian Army.

Berkeley, Fredk. George.

Hogg, Geo. Crawford, C.B., Ind. Army (*District Staff, Bombay*).

Hobson, Fredk. Taylor (*Ceylon*).

ⓋⒸ, Leach, Edwd. P., C.B., R.E.

Lloyd, Francis Thomas, C.B. (*Roy. Mil. Acad., Woolwich*).

Vanderzee, Francis Hy., I.S.C.

Abadie, Henry Richard, C.B. (*Eastern Dist.*).

Lawrence, Wm. Alex., I.S.C.

Gatacre, John, C.B., I.S.C.

Hutchinson, Wm. Francis Moore (*Staff College*).

Butler, Robert Fowler (*Barbados*).

Rose, Edward Lee, R.M.L.I.

Hallowes, Hy. Jardine (*Jamaica*).

Borrett, Herbert Charles (*Insp. Gen. Aux. Fces. & Recruiting*).

Boughey, John.

Colvile, Sir Hy. Edward, K.C.M.G., C.B. (*1st Brig., S. Africa*).

Ardagh, Sir John Charles, K.C.I.E., C.B. (*Dir. Mil. Intelligence*).

Fraser, Thomas, C.B., C.M.G., R.E. (*Thames Dist.*).

Brownlow, William Vesey, C.B.

Brook, Edmund Smith.

Paton, George, C.M.G.

Falmouth, Viscount, C.B., M.V.O.

Blood, Sir Bindon, K.C.B., R.E. (*Meerut*).

Campbell, Barrington D., M.V.O.

Cooke, Thomas Arthur.

Salmond, Wm., C.B. (*D.-A.-G., Roy. Eng.*).

Begbie, Elphinstone Waters, C.B., D.S.O., Indian Army.

Elton, Henry Strachan, I.S.C.

Smalley, Frederick, Indian Army.

Waterfield, Henry Gordon, C.B., I.S.C.

Morton, Sir Gerald de Courcy, K.C.I.E., C.B. (*Adjt.-Gen., India*).

Holley, Edmund Hunt, R.A.

Upcher, Russell, C.B., D.S.O.

Talbot, Hon. Reginald Arthur James, C.B. (*Cairo*).

Campbell, Frederick Lorry.

Turner, Alfred Edwd., C.B., R.A.

Barton, Geoffrey, C.B. (*6th Brig., S. Africa*).

Lyttelton, Hon. Neville Gerard, C.B. (*4th Brig., S. Africa*).

Wauchope, Andrew G., C.B. (*3rd Brig., S. Africa*).

Hunter, Woodburn, R.A.

Chermside, Sir Herbert Charles, G.C.M.G., C.B., R.E. (*Curragh*).

Oliphant, Laurence James, M.V.O.

Hart, Arthur FitzRoy, C.B. (*5th Brig., S. Africa*).

Lane, Ronald Bertram, C.B. (*Alexandria*).

Cox, George.

Boyes, John Edward.

Cuningham, Charles Alex., I.S.C.

Clifford, Richard Melville.

Stewart Hopton Scott, I.S.C.

McLeod, Donald James Sim, C.B., D.S.O., Indian Army (*Bangalore*).

Slade, Frederick George, C.B., R.A. (*Gibraltar*).

ⓋⒸ, Sartorius, Euston Henry, C.B.

Percy-Smith, Percy Wyndham, Indian Army.

Wodehouse, Joscelyn Heneage, C.B., C.M.G., R.A. (*Fort William*).

Slade, John Ramsay, C.B., R.A.

Hildyard, H. John Thoroton, C.B. (*2nd Brig., S. Africa*).

Morris, John Ignatius, R.M.L.I.

Westmacott, Sir Richd., K.C.B., D.S.O., I.S.C.

Waterhouse, James, I.S.C.

Parr, Henry Hallam, C.B., C.M.G. (*Shorncliffe*).

Truman, Wm. Robinson (*Remounts*).

Fagan, James Lawtie, I.S.C.

Shakespear, Geo. R. J., I.S.C.

Pengelley, George Faquharson, R.M.A.

Eaton, Hon. Herbert Francis Wylie Henry, C.S.I., Ind. Army. *Local and Temporary Rank.*

Smith, Sir Charles Holled, K.C.M.G., C.B. (*Comdg. Forces, Victoria*).

French, George Arthur, C.M.G., (*Comdt., New South Wales*).

Hutton, Edward Thos. Hy., C.B., A.D.C. (*Comdg. Militia, Canada*).

Gunter, Howel (*Comdt. in Queensland*).

Egerton, Chas. Comyn, C.B., D.S.O., A.D.C., I.S.C. (*Abbottabad, India*).

Howard, Fras., C.B., A.D.C. (*7th Brig., S. Africa*).

Brocklehurst, Jno. F., M.V.O. (*3rd Cav. Brig., S. Africa*).

Wood, Elliott, C.B., R.E. (*Ch. Engr., S. Africa*).

Brabazon, Jno. P., C.B., A.D.C. (*2nd Cav. Brig., S. Africa*).

Marshall, Geo. Hy. (*Comg. R.A., S. Africa*).

Babington, Jas. M. (*1st Cav. Brig., S. Africa*).

Yule, Jas. H. (*8th Brig., S. Africa*).

Woodgate, E. R. P., C.B., C.M.G. (*9th Brig., S. Africa*).

Coke, J. T. (*10th Brig., S. Africa*).

Hobday, Thos. Francis, C.B. (*Commy.-Gen.-in-Chief, India*).

Collen, Sir Edwin Henry Hayter, K.C.I.E., C.B. (*Indian Council*).

Maitland, Pelham James, C.B. (*Sec. Govt. India, Mily. Dept.*).

Wace, Richard, C.B., R.A. (*Dir.-Gen. of Ord., India*).

Tyler, Trevor Bruce (*Insp.-Gen. of Arty., India*).

Elliot, Edward Locke, C.B., D.S.O. (*Insp.-Gen. of Cavalry, India*).

Coke, John Talbot (*Mauritius*).

Grant, Henry Fane, C.B. (*Insp.-Gen. Cavalry*).

Nicholson, Sir Wm. G., K.C.B., A.D.C., Indian).

Turner, Samuel Compton, R.E. (*Col. W..., India*).

Dickson, John Baillie Ballantyne, C.B (*Straits Settlements*).

O'Callaghan, Desmond D. T. (*Comg. R.A., Malta*).

BRIGADIER-GENERALS.

Young, George Fredk., K.C.B. (D.-A.-G., Bengal).

Lugard, Edward Jno. (Madras).

Elles, Sir Edmond Roche, K.C.B. (Punjab).

Simpson, Geo., C.B. (D.-A.-G., Madras).

Cummins, Jas. Turner, D.S.O. (Madras).

V.C., Hart, Sir Reginald Clare, K.C.B. (Madras).

Pipon, Henry, R.A. (Comdg. R.A. Bengal).

Barnard, Jno. Hy., C.B., C.M.G., A.D.C. (Madras).

Rolland, Stuart Erskine, I.S.C. (Madras).

Curtis, Wm. Fredk. de Hubbenet, R.A. (Punjab).

Ventris, Francis (Bombay).

Jeffreys, Patrick Douglas, C.B. (Bengal).

Gaselee, Sir Alfred, K.C.B. (Bengal).

Meiklejohn, Sir William Hope, K.C.B. (Bengal).

Reid, Alexr. Jno. Forsyth, C.B. (Bengal).

Barlow, Jno. Arthur, (D.-A-G., India).

V.C., Creagh, O'Moore (Aden).

MacCall, Hy. Blackwood (D.-A.-G., India).

Michell, St. John Fancourt (Bengal).

Blaksley, Edward (Bombay).

Stewart, Norman Robert (Hyderabad).

Murray, Jas. Wolfe, R.A. (Communications, S. Africa).

Hemming, Fredk. Wm. (Cav. Brig., Canterbury).

MILITARY AIDES-DE-CAMP TO THE QUEEN.

Chief Personal Aides-de-Camp, Field-Marshal H.R.H. the Duke of Cambridge, K.G., K.T., K.P., Hon. Colonel-in-Chief to the Forces.

Personal Aides-de-Camp { Field-Marshal H.R.H. the Prince of Wales, K.G., K.T., K.P.
General H.R.H. the Duke of Connaught and Strathearn, K.G., K.T., K.P., G.C.B.
General H.R.H. Prince Christian of Schleswig-Holstein, K.G.

Aides-de-Camp.

Bell, Col. William, C.B.

Derby, Col. Rt. Hon. Earl of, K.G., G.C.B.

Wemyss, Col. Earl of.

Westminster, Cl. Duke of, K.G.

V.C., Bell, Col. Mark S., C.B.

Brabazon, M.-Gen. J.P., C.B.

V.C., Hammond, Colonel Arthur George, C.B., D.S.O.

Barnard, Br.-Gen. J. H., C.B.

Rivett-Carnac, Col. J. H., C.I.E.

Cavendish, Col. James Chas.

Suffield, Col. Rt. Hn. Lord, K.C.B.

Northumberland, Col. the Duke of.

Hutton, M.-Gen. E.T.H., C.B.

Gaselee, Br.-Gen Sir A., K.C.B.

Campbell, Col. Wm., R.M.A.

Ogilvy, Col. Sir R. H. A., Bt.

Haddington, Col. Earl of.

Belper, Col. Rt. Hon. Lord.

Blythswood, Col. Lord.

Davies-Cooke, Col. Bryan G.

Money, Col. G. L. C., D.S.O.

Howard, Maj.-Gen. F., C.B.

Crosbie, Col. Adolphus B., R.M.

Kelly, Col. Jas. Graves, C.B.

Davis, Col. John.

March, Col. Earl of.

Stevenson, Col. James.

Kempster, Col. Fras.J.,D.S.O.

Ezerton, Maj.-Gen. C., C.B.

Clements, Col. R. A. P., D.S.O.

Wood-Martin, Col. Wm. G.

Bashford, Col. Chas. Brome.

Montrose, Col. Duke of, K.T.

Clarendon, Col. Earl of.

Harewood, Col. Earl of.

Galway, Col. Viscount.

Londonderry, Col. the Marquess of, K.G.

Brownlow, Col. Earl of.

Le Cornu, Col. Chas. P., C.B.

Aitken, Col. William, C.B., R.A.

Wingate, Col. Sir Fras. R., C.B., D.S.O., R.A.

Douglas, Cl. Chs. W. Horsley.

Dixon, Col. Hy. Grey, C.B.

Matthias, Col. H.H., C.B. (ext.)

Murray, Col. R. H., C.B. (ext.)

Cooper, Col. Harry (extra).

MacDonald, Col. H. A., C.B., D.S.O. (extra).

Cawdor, Col. the Earl of.

Beaufort, Col. the Duke of.

Roberts, Col. C. F., C.M.G. (hon.).

❧ Cavalry (HOUSEHOLD, £60,900 ; LINE, £400,500).

[The figures in parentheses refer to the list of Army Agents at page 192.]

1ST LIFE GUARDS. (1)
Windsor.

Col.-in-Ch., H.R.H. Prin. of Wales

Col., H.H. Prince Edward of Saxe-Weimar, K.P., G.C.B., f.m.

Lt.-Col., C. N. Miles.

Majors, T. C. P. Calley (2nd) ; G. Carter ; Hon. C. E. Bingham.

Adjt. P. B. Cookson, lt.

2ND LIFE GUARDS. (1)
Regent's Park.

Col.-in-Ch., H.R.H. Prin. of Wales

Col., Earl Howe, G.C.V.O., C.B., g.

Lt.-Col., A. D. Neeld.

Majors, J. A. Smith-Cuninghame (2nd) ; C. F. St. C. Anstruther-Thomson ; M. J. C. Longfield.

Adjt., R. T. Ellison, capt.

ROYAL HORSE GUARDS
(The Blues). *Hyde Park.* (1)

Col.-in-Ch., H.R.H. Prin. of Wales

Col., Visct. Wolseley, K.P., G.C.B., G.C.M.G., f.m. (Comm.-in-Chief).

Lt.-Col., Lord Binning.

Majors, H. T. Fenwick (2nd) ; W. Anstruther-Thomson.

Adjt.,

1ST (KING'S) DRAGOON GUARDS. *Dublin.* (1)

Col.-in-Chief, H. I. M. Francis Joseph, Emperor of Austria and King of Hungary, K.G. ('96).

Col., J. R. S. Sayer, C.B., l.g.

Lt.-Col., H. M. Owen.

Adjt.,

2ND D. GUARDS (Queen's Bays). *York.* (1)

Col., Wm. Henry Seymour, C.B., g.

Lt.-Col., J. A. Lambert.

Adjt., E. W. L. Urquhart, capt.

3RD D. GUARDS (Prince of Wales's). *Dundalk.* (2)

Colonel, Conyers Tower, C.B., l.g.

Lt.-Col., U. G. de Burgh.

Adjt., A. Burt, lt.

4TH D. GUARDS (Roy. Irish). *Rawal Pindi, Punjab Comd.* (2)

Col., Sir H. C. Wilkinson, K.C.B., l.g.

Lt.-Col., G. D. F. Sulivan.

Adjutant, W. Belk, capt.

5TH D. G. (Princ. Charlotte of Wales's). *Natal.* (1)

Col., Hon. S. J. Gough-Calthorpe, l.g.

Lt.-Col., R. S. S. Baden-Powell, c.

Adjt., W. Q. Winwood, lt.

6TH D. GUARDS (Carabiniers). *S. Africa.* (1)

Col., Sir A. J. H. Elliot, K.C.B., m.g.

Lt.-Col., T. C. Porter.

Adjt., Hon. L. R. D. Gray, lt.

7TH D. G. (Princess Royal's). *Colchester.* (1)

Colonel, Andrew Nugent, l.g.

Lt.-Col., H. W. M. Lowe.

Adjt., H. A. Lempriere, capt.

1 (ROYAL) DRAGOONS. (1)
S. Africa.

Col.-in-Chief, H.M. William II., Germ. Emp., King of Prussia.

Col., Sir F. Marshall, K.C.M.G., l.g.

Lt.-Col., J.F. Burn-Murdoch.

Adjt., G. F. Steele, capt.

2 DRAGOONS (Royal Scots Greys). *S. Africa.* (1)

Colonel-in-Chief, H.I.M. Nicholas II., Emperor of Russia.

Col., Geo. Calvert Clarke, C.B., g.

Lt.-Col., Hon. W. P. Alexander.

Adjt., A. D. Miller, cap.

3 (KING'S OWN) HUSSAR. *Lucknow, Bengal Comd.* (1)

Col., Edwd. Howard Vyse, l.g.

Lt.-Col., **F. W. N.** Wogan-Browne.
Adjt., J. S. Roche, *capt.*

4 (**Queen's Own**) **HUSSARS.** *Lucknow, Bengal Comd.* (1)
Colonel, Alexander Low, C.B., *g.*
Lt.-Col., W. A. Ramsay.
Adjt., R. W. R. Barnes, *lt.*

5 (**Roy. Irish**) **LANCERS.** (1) *Natal.*
Colonel, W. G. D. Massy, C.B., *l.g.*
Lt.-Col., J. F. M. Fawcett.
Adjt., H. H. Hulse, *lt.*

6 (**Inniskilling**) **DRAGOONS.** *S. Africa.* (1)
Col.-in-Chief, H.R.H. Duke of Connaught, K.G., G.C.B., *g.*
Col., Sir C. C. Shute, K.C.B., *g.*
Lt.-Col., H. C. Page-Henderson.
Adjt., G. K. Ansell, *lt.*

7 (**Queen's Own**) **HUSSARS.** *Norwich.* (1)
Colonel, Robert Hale, *m.g.*
Lieut.-Col., Hon. R. T. Lawley.
Adjt., C. E. Graham Norton, *capt.*

8 (**King's Royal Irish**) **HUSSARS** *Curragh, Ireland.* (1)
Col., William Mussenden, *m.g.*
Lieut.-Col., P. L. Clowes.
Adjt., P. A. T. Jones.

9 (**Queen's Royal**) **LANCERS.** *S. Africa.* (1)
Col., Sir Wm. Drysdale, K.C.B., *l.g.*
Lt.-Col., B. Gough.
Adjt., E. F. Bell, *lt.*

10 (**Pr. of Wales's Own Roy.**) **HUSSARS.** *S. Africa.* (1)
Colonel, H.R.H. Prince of Wales, K.G., K.T., K.P., &c., *f.m.*
Lt.-Col., R. B. W. Fisher.
Adjutant, Hon. J. Dawnay, *capt.*

11 (**Prince Albert's Own**) **HUSSARS.** *Egypt.* (1)
Col., Wm. Chas. Forrest, C.B., *g.*
Lt.-Col., E. R. Courtenay.
Adjt., R. M. Yorke, *lt.*

12 **LANCERS** (**Pr. of Wales's Royal**). *S. Africa.* (1)
Col., A.L. Lyttelton-Annesley, *l.g.*
Lieut.-Col., Earl of Airlie.
Adjt., W. J. Greenly, *lt.*

13 **HUSSARS.** *S. Africa.* (1)
Colonel, Sir Baker Creed Russell, K.C.B., K.C.M.G., *l.g.*
Lt.-Col., H. J. Blagrove.
Adjt., J. H. Tremayne, *capt.*

14 **HUSSARS** (**King's**). *S. Africa.* (1)
Col., Hon. C. W. Thesiger, *l.g.*
Lt.-Col., G. H. C. Hamilton.
Adjt., *lt.*

15 (**King's**) **HUSSARS.** *Meerut, Bengal.* (1)
Col., Sir Fredk. Wellington J. FitzWygram, Bart., M.P., *l.g.*
Lt.-Col., J. R. P. Gordon.
Adjt., P. O. Hambro, *capt.*

16 (**Queen's**) **LANCERS.** *Umballa, Punjab Comd.* (1)
Col., Wm. Thomas Dickson, *l.g.*
Lt.-Col., H. L. Aylmer.
Adjt., , *capt.*

17 (**Duke of Cambridge's Own**) **LANCERS.** *Ballincollig.* (1)
Col.-in-Chief, H.R.H. Duke of Cambridge, K.G., A.D.C., *f.m.*
Col., Sir D. C. Drury-Lowe, G.C.B., *l.g.*
Lt.-Col.,
Adjt., V. S. Sandeman, *capt.*

18 **HUSSARS.** *Natal.* (1)
Col., A. G. Montgomery-Moore.
Lt.-Col., B. D. Möller.
Adjt., W. M. P. Pollok, *capt.*

19 (**Princess of Wales's Own**) **HUSSARS.** *Natal.* (1)
Col., Coote Synge Hutchinson, *l.g.*
Lt.-Col., C. B. H. Wolseley-Jenkins.
Adjt., M. Archer-Shee, *lt.*

20 **HUSSARS.** *Mhow, Bombay Comd.* (1)
Col., Sir Roger William Henry Palmer, Bart., *l.g.*
Lieut.-Col., H. G. P. Beauchamp.
Adjt., A. O. Jacob, *capt.*

21 (**Empress of India's**) **LANCERS.** *Curragh—Canterbury.* (1)
Col., Sir Robert White, K.C.B., *g.*
Lt.-Col., W. G. Crole Wyndham., C.B.
Adjutant, C. J. Clerk, *capt.*

CAVALRY BRIGADES.

1ST. .... *Aldershot.*
Maj.-Gen.,
Brigade Major,

2ND. .... *Canterbury.*
Col. on Staff, F. W. Hemming, C.B., A.D.C., *br.-gen.*
Adjt.,

3RD. .... *Curragh.*
Col. on Staff, Viscount Downe, C.I.E.
Adjt., E. H. H. Allenby, *maj.*

4TH. .... *Colchester.*
Col. on Staff,
Adjt.,

CAVALRY DEPOT.
Canterbury.

Lt.-Col., E. Hegan.
Maj. (2nd) R. C. Cokayne-Frith.
Adjt., J. G. Fair, *capt.*
Rg. Mr., J. J. Matthews, *hon. m.*
Qr. Mr., J. W. Humphrey, *hon. capt.*

REMOUNT ESTABLISHMENT.

66, *Victoria St., S.W.*
Insp.-Gen., W. R. Truman, *m.g.*;
Asst. Insprs., B. L. Tollner, *c.*;
J. C. Hanford, C.B., *c.*
D.A.A.G., J. W. P. Peters, *m.*
Staff Capt., C. G. Mackenzie, *capt.*; H.S.H. Prince Francis of Teck, K C.V.O., D.S.O., *capt.*

YEOMANRY CAVALRY.—(£73,000)—*List of Regiments, with Names of Lieutenant-Colonels.*

Ayrshire—Robt. Morris Pollok, *c.*
Berks—Hon. Osbt. Wm. Craven, *c.*
Bucks—Lord Chesham, *c.*
Cheshire—Earl of Harrington.
Denbighshire—H. R. L. Howard, *c.*
Derbyshire—R. W. Chandos-Pole.
Devon (Royal 1st)—Sir John Shelley, Bart., *c.*
  (Royal N.)—Visct. Ebrington, *c.*
Dorset—J. R. P. Goodden, *c.*
Gloucestershire—D. of Beaufort, *c.*
Hampshire—William Woods.
Herts—Earl of Clarendon, A.D.C.
Kent (Royal East)—Lord Harris, G.C.S.I., G.C.I.E.
  (West)—C. E. Warde.
Lanarkshire—Sir S. M. Lockhart, Bt., M.V.O., *c.*; J. Addie.
Lanarkshire (Queen's Own)—James Neilson, *c.*

Lancashire (D. of Lancaster's Own)—Clement Molyneux Royds, *c.*
Lancs (Hussars)—Lord Gerard, *c.*
Leicestershire—Fredk. G. Blair, *c.*
Lothians and Berwickshire—Sir W.A.B.Hamilton, K.C.M.G.,C.B.
Middlesex—W. Kenyon Mitford, *c.*
Montgomeryshire—Sir Herbert L. W. Williams-Wynn, Bart.
Northumberland—J. B. Cookson, *c.*
Nottinghamshire (S.)—L. Rolleston, *c.*
Nottinghamshire (Sherwood Rangers)—Visct. Galway, A.D.C., *c.*
Oxfordsh.—Visct. Valentia, M.P., *c.*
Pembroke—Sir Charles Edward Gregg Philipps, Bart., *c.*
Shropshire—E. H. Baldock, *c.*
Somerset (North)—Viscount Dungarvan.

Somerset (West)—F. W. Forester.
Staffordshire—James Heath, *c.*
Suffolk—Alfred George Lucas, *c.*
Warwickshire—Lord Willoughby de Broke, *c.*
Westmorland and Cumberland—Earl of Lonsdale, *c.*
Wiltshire (Royal)—Rt. Hon. Walter Hume Long, M.P., *c.*
Worcestershire—Lord Windsor, *c.*
Yorkshire (Hrs.)—Lord Bolton, *c.*
Yorkshire (Das.)—Earl of Scarbrough, *c.*

LIGHT HORSE VOLUNTEERS.
Fifeshire—Sir J. Gilmour, Bt., V.D.

Royal Regiment of Artillery (£858,270 ; Militia, £53,030). (1).

Colonel-in-Chief, Duke of Cambridge, K.G., A.D.C., *f.m.*

Colonels Commandant, Sir Collingwood Dickson, G.C.B., *VC., g.*; Sir Arnold Burrowes Kemball, K.C.B., K.C.S.I. (*late Bombay*); Sir Chas. Lawrence D'Aguilar, G.C.B., *r.h.a., g.*; Sir Jn. Miller Adye, G.C.B., *g.* (*late Bengal*); Sir Henry Edward Landor Thuillier, C.S.I., *g.* (*late Beng.*); Sir Michael Anthony Shrapnel Biddulph, G.C.B., *g.*; Napier Geo. Campbell, *g.* (*late Madras*); Robert Parker Radcliffe, *l.g.*; George Godfrey Pearse, C.B., *g.* (*late Madras*), *r.h.a.*; Sir William Olpherts, *VC., K.C.B.* (*late Bengal*); Hon. Sir David Macdowall Fraser, K.C.B., *g., r.h.a.*; Geo. Vanderheyden Johnson, *l.g.*; Philip Gossett Pipon, C.B., *g.*; Charles Bowdler Fuller, *g.* (*late Bomb.*); James Edward Cordner, *g.* (*late Beng.*); Francis William Hastings, *g.*; Sir Henry Augustus Smyth, K.C.M.G., *g.*; Sir Robert Biddulph, G.C.B., *g.* (*Gov. Gibraltar*); Sir Wm. Stirling-Hamilton. Bart., *g.* (*late Beng.*); Thomas Nicholl, *g.* (*late Beng.*); Gaspard Le Marchant Tupper, *l.g.*; Right Hon. Lord Roberts of Kandahar, *VC., G.C.B., f.m.* (*late Beng.*); Geo. H. J. Alex. Fraser, *l.g.*; Walter d'Oyly Kerrich, *g.* (*late Madras*); Aug. Abingdon Bayly, *g.* (*late Bomb.*); Sir Henry Brackenbury, K.C.B., *l.g.*; Sir Robert John Hay, K.C.B., *l.g.*; Sir Wm. John Williams, K.C.B., *l.g.*; Patrick John Campbell, *m.g.*; Duncan John McGrigor, *g.* (*late Madras*).

ROYAL HORSE AND ROYAL FIELD ARTILLERY.

Lieut.-Cols., H. T. S. Yeats, *c.*; R. Purdy, *c.*; P. H. Hammond; J. Leach, *c., r.h.a.*; L. J. H. Chapman, *c.*; W. L. Davidson, *r.h.a.*; R. G. W. Hepburne; J. W. T. Spencer; F. J. W. Eustace, *r.h.a.*; E. B. Coke, *r.h.a.*; C. J. Long, *c.,*; L. W. Parsons; H. W. Brackenbury; H. V. Hunt; A. N. Rochfort, *r.h.a.*; J. Hotham, *r.h.a.*; F. T. M. Beaver; S. Watson; P. C. E. Newbigging; H. H. Pengree; G. R. Challenor; M. W. Saunders (*r.g.a.*); W. H. Suart, *r.h.a.*; F. H. Hall; E. M. Flint; A. J. Montgomery; J. W. H. Potts, *r.h.a.*; F. M. Banister; J. McDonnell; J. Temple; J. A. Coxhead; J. S.

Barker; A. H. Hewat, *r.h.a.*; H. B. Jeffreys; W. B. Fletcher; J. W. Hawkins; F. M. Bland; E. H. Pickwoad; A. H. C. Phillpots (*r.g.a.*); T. S. Baldock; E. Gunner; H. Burton (*r.g.a.*); F. Waldron; W. G. de Jersey.

ROYAL GARRISON ARTILLERY.

Lieut.-Cols., G. M. Stevens, *c.*; H. T. Curling, *c.*; W. J. Fowler, *c.*; H. T. Lugard, *c.*; F. O. B. Foote, *c.*; C. M. Western; A. R. Fraser; G. D. Fanshawe; Lord Playfair; G. G. Monck-Mason; J. V. V. Baker; F. A. Aylmer; R. W. P. Robertson; L. E. Coker; J. H. Rosseter; W. H. Frith; H. C. M. Woods; G. P. Owen; N. P. Fowell; A. L. Lane; F. A. Bowles; W. S. Walford; W. F. Graham; C. L. Casey; C. R. W. Henry; H. A. Scott; R. Oakes; E. N. Henriques; R. F. Johnson; E. C. Wace, D.S.O.; A. Mansel, D.S.O.; H. G. Weir; H. J. Lyster; A. M. Murray; P. Saltmarshe; B. L. Eman; O. S. Smyth, D.S.O.; W. F. Cleeve; F. C. Farmer; R. A. Rigg; E. U. Blackett; E. J. K. Priestley; A. H. W. Brett; M. O. Hopkins.

ROYAL HORSE ARTILLERY.

22 Batteries, 1 Depôt.
(£70,500.)

Headquarters, *Woolwich.*

Lieut.-Cols., (S. Africa) C. J. Long, F. J. W. Eustace, W. L. Davidson.
(Home) A. N. Rochfort, *c., Aldershot*; E. B. Coke, *Ipswich.*
(India) J. Leach, *c., Secunderabad*; A. H. Hewat, *Umballa*; J. Hotham, *Bangalore*; J. W. H. Potts, *Meerut*; W. H. Suart, *Kirkee.*

BATTERIES.

A *Meerut,* E. A. Burrows, *m.*
B *Lucknow,* F. Houlton Ward, *m.*
C *Mhow,* C. B. Watkins, *m.*
D *Umballa,* J. W. Stirling, *m.*
E *Kirkee,* E. A. Lambert, *m.*
F *Sialkote,* F. L. Cunliffe, *m.*
G *S. Africa,* R. Bannatine-Allason, *m.*
H *Meerut,* E. A. Fanshawe, *m.*
I *Umballa,* C. A. Anderson, *l.c.*
J *Bangalore,* J. M. S. Brunker, *m.*
K *Rawal Pindi,* C. F. Blane, *m.*
L *Secunderabad,* A. Eardley-Wilmot, *m.*
M *Woolwich,* E. C. F. Holland, *m.*
N *Woolwich,* J. W. Dunlop, *m.*
O *S. Africa,* Sir J. H. Jervis-White-Jervis, Bart., *m.*
P *S. Africa,* Sir G. V. Thomas, Bt., *m.*
Q *Newbridge,* E. J. Phipps-Hornby, *m.*
R *S. Africa,* B. Burton, *m.*
S *Hom-,* J. L. Keir, *m.*
T *Ipswich,* F. B. Lecky, *m.*
U *Newbridge,* P. B. Taylor, *m.*
Dépôt, Woolwich.—Major, H. F. Mercer.

ROYAL FIELD ARTILLERY.

95 Batteries, 1 Depôt, and Riding Establishment.

(£265,120.)

Headquarters, *Woolwich.*

Lieut.-Cols., (S. Africa) F. H. Hall, E. H. Pickwoad, J. A. Coxhead, H. V. Hunt, P. C. E. Newbigging, J. S. S. Barker, L. W. Parsons, H. B. Jeffreys.
(Home) S. Watson, *Weedon*; E. M. Flint, *Shorncliffe*; H. T. S. Yates, *c.*; *Newcastle-on-Tyne*; J. McDonnell, *Exeter*; G. R. Challenor, *Colchester*; A. J. Montgomery, *Athlone*; L. J. A. Chapman, *Hulsea*; H. H. Pengree, *Woolwich*; P. H. Hammond, *Limerick*; W. B. Fletcher, *Cahir*; T. S. Baldock, *Leeds.*
(India) R. Purdy, *Jhansi, c.*; R. G. W. Hepburne, *Meean Meer*; H. W. Brackenbury, *Campbellpore*; F. M. Banister, *Mhow*; J. Temple, *St. Thomas's Mount*; J. W. Hawkins, *Allahabad.*

BATTERIES.

1	*Kirkee,* C. D. King, *m.*	
2	*Shorncliffe,* A. Bell-Irving, *m.*	
3	*Campbellpore,* A. Capel-Cure, *m.*	
4	*Aldershot,* A. E. A. Butcher, *m.*	
5	*Fermoy,* J. R. Foster, *m.*	
6	*Cawnpore,* A. G. Creagh, C.B., *c.*	
7	*S. Africa,* C. G. Henshaw, *m.*	
8	*Christchurch,* H. Chance, *m.*	
9	*Limerick,* A. S. Wedderburn, *m.*	
10	*Woolwich,* S. W. Lane, *m.*	
11	*Meean Meer,* J. P. Langley, *m.*	
12	*Jullundur,* F. E. Johnson, *m.*	
13	*Natal,* J. W. G. Dawkins, *m.*	
14	*S. Africa,* A. C. Bailward, *m.*	
15	*Meerut,* E. Pollock, *m.*	
16	*Kirkee,* C. T. Robinson, *m.*	
17	*Woolwich,* T. K. E. Johnston, *m.*	
18	*Natal,* A. B. Scott, *m.*	
19	*S. Africa,* A. W. B. Gordon, *m.*	
20	*S. Africa,* C. H. Blount, *m.*	
21	*Natal,* W. E. Blewitt, *m.*	
22	*Mhow,* Bombay, W. Hanna, *m.*	
23	*Secunderabad,* C. N. Simpson, *m.*	
24	*Peshawar,* C. M. Haggard, *m.*	
25	*Bangalore,* A. H. Carter, *m.*	
26	*Shorncliffe,* H. S. Dawkins, *m.*	
27	*Neemuch,* D. E. Dewar, *m.*	
28	*S. Africa,* A. Stokes, *m.*	
29	*Kirkee,* R. G. Strange, *m.*	
30	*Fyzabad,* C. H. S. Vores, *m.*	
31	*Hyderabad,* A. P. Longfield, *m.*	
32	*Jhansi,* R. F. X. McG. Bond, *m.*	

33 *St. Thomas's Mount,*

34 *Ahmedabad,* A. C. Daniell, *m.*
35 *Kurrachee,* *m.*

36 *Nusserabad,* J. H. Jellett, *m.*
37 *Woolwich,* R. A. K. Montgomery, *m.*
38 *S. Africa,* H. E. Oldfield, *m.*
39 *Hilsea,* *m.*
40 *Bangalore,* H. M. Campbell, *m.*
41 *Lucknow,* C. C. Sankey, *m.*
42 *Natal,* C. E. Goulburn, *m.*
43 *Shorncliffe,* *m.*
44 *Colchester,* B. F. Drake, *m.*
45 *St. Thomas's Mt.,* W. E. Fairholme, C.M.G., *m.*
46 *Dinapore,* F. W. Boteler, *m.*
47 *Ferozepore,* S. D. Rainsford, *m.*
48 *Barrackpore,* A. J. Hughes, *m.*
49 *Belgaum,* R. E. Boothby, *m.*
50 *Agra,* C. M. T. Western, *m.*
51 *Rawal Pindi,* L. Forde, *m.*
52 *Jubbulpore,* W.J.A. Beatson, *m.*
53 *Natal,* A. J. Abdy, *m.*
54 *Meerut,* J. E. Harvey, *m.*
55 *Sangor,* P. H. Enthoven, *m.*
56 *Egypt,* D. G. Prinsep, *m.*
57 *Meean Meer,* A. B. Helyar, *m.*
58 *Kamptee,* F. T. Oldham, *m.*
59 *Woolwich,* H. O'B. Owen, *m.*
60 *Allahabad,* *m.*
61 *Woolwich,* A. Hamilton-Gordon, *m.*
62 *S. Africa,* E. J. Granet, *m.*
63 *S. Africa,* W. L. H. Paget, *m.*
64 *S. Africa,* C. E. Coghill, *m.*
65 *Woolwich,* W. Tylden, *m.*
66 *S. Africa,* W. Y. Foster, *m.*
67 *Natal,* J. F. Manifold, *m.*
68 *Hilsea,* *m.*
69 *Natal,* F. D. V. Wing, *m.*
70 *Bareilly,* *m.*
71 *Mooltan,* A. S. Tyndale-Biscoe, *m.*

72 *Bellary,*
73 *S. Africa,* C. M. Barlow, *m.*
74 *S. Africa,* R.G. McQ. McLeod, *m.*
75 *S. Africa,* W.F.L. Lindsay, *m.*
76 *Athlone,* R. A. G. Harrison, *m.*
77 *S. Africa,* E. M. Perceval, *m.*
78 *Woolwich,* D. C. Carter, *m.*
79 *Cahir,* E. H. Armitage, *m.*
80 *Nowgong,* A. L. Hibbert, *m.*
81 *Trowbridge,* H. A. Chapman, *m.*
82 *Exeter,* A. S. Pratt, *m.*
83 *Colchester,* G. R. Darley, *m.*
84 *Newcastle,* E. Guinness, *m.*
85 *Clonmel,* H. K. Jackson, *m.*
86 *Newcastle,* C. D. Guinness, *m.*
87 *Seaforth,* *m.*
88 *Weedon,* *m.*
89 *Hilsea,* *m.*
90 *Longford,* *m.*
91 *Waterford,* H. A. D. Curtis, *m.*
92 *Birmingham,* H. A. Bethell, *m.*
93 *Cahir,* W. H. Williams, *l.c.*
94 *Leeds,* R. M. Rodwell, *m.*
95 *Leeds,* Hn.H.M. Addington, *m.*

DÉPÔT, *Woolwich.*

Lt.-Col., J. W. T. Spencer.
Adjt., E. H. T. Parsons, *capt.*
Rg. Mr., E. Rock, *hon. lt.*

Qr. Mr., J. Scott, *hon. lt.*
1 Sec., S. E. G. Lawless, *m.*
2 Sec., E. W. Blunt, *m.*

ROYAL GARRISON ARTILLERY.

Mountain Division.

10 Batteries.

Lieut.-Cols., O. S. Smyth, D.S.O., *Quetta;* E. Gunner, *Murree Hills;* M. W. Saunders, *Quetta.*
Adjt., R. A. Kaye, *capt., Quetta.*
District Off., J. Rowley, *lt., Newport.*

BATTERIES.

1 *Landi Kotal,* G. F. A. Norton, *m.*
2 *Khyra Gali,* C.P. Fendall, D.S.O.;

3 *Bara Gali,* G. B. Smith, *m.*
4 *Newport* (*Mon.*), H. C. C. D. Simpson, *m.*
5 *Kalabagh,* R. W. Fuller, *m.*
6 *Jutogh,* A. Keene, D.S.O., *m.*
7 *Quetta,* M. F. Fegen, *m.*
8 *Darjeeling,* A. H. C. Birch.
9 *Mandalay,* F. H. J Birch, *m.*
10 *Natal,* G. E. Bryant, *m.*

Eastern Division.

Headquarters.............*Dover.*
29 Service Companies.
2 Depôts.

Lt.-Cols., (Home) W. F. Cleeve, *Harwich;* R. A. Rigg, *Sheerness;* H. T. Curling, *c., Dover;* N. P. Fowell, *Shoeburyness.*
Adjt., C. W. Clark, *capt.*
(Abroad) A. H. C. Phillpotts and H. A. Scott, *Gibraltar;* G. M. Stevens, *c., Bombay.*

COMPANIES.

1 *Calcutta,* E. P. A. Tawney, *m.*
2 *St. Helena,* C. C. Wiseman-Clark, *m.*
3 *Rangoon,* G. R. Townshend, *m.*
4 *Kurrachee,*
5 *Malta,*
6 *Dover,* A. B. Shute, *m.*
7 *India* (*S.T.*), G. N. H. Barlow, *m.*
8 *Aden,* T. R. Harkness, *m.*
9 *Allahabad,* A. B. N. Churchill, *m.*
10 *Shoeburyness,* C. E. Jervois, *m.*
11 *Gibraltar,* H. M. Slater, *m.*
12 *Mooltan,* A. B. Purvis, *m.*
13 *Bombay,*
14 *Golden Hill,* W. H. Darby, *m.*
15 *Dover,* O. Rowe, *m.*
16 *Egypt,* J. H. L. Dallas, *m.*
17 *Malta,* J. F. Craig, *m.*
18 *Gibraltar,* D'A. B. Preston, *m.*
19 *Gibraltar,* W. H. Cummings, *m.*
20 *Gibraltar,* W. C. Anderson, *m.*
21 *Sheerness,* F. W. G. Tothill, *m.*
22 *Sheerness* (*H.*), F.B.R. Toms, *m.*
23 *Shoeburyness,* M. A. Inglis, *m.*
24 *Delhi,* A. H. Callwell, *m.*
25 *Hong Kong,* M. M. Morris, *m.*
26 *Bombay,* A. Handley, *m.*
27 *Sheerness,* H. B. Brownlow, *m.*
28 *Landguard Fort,* J.H. Balguy, *m.*
29 *Leith Fort,* G. T. Kelaart, *m.*

DÉPÔTS.—Lt.-Cols., F. T. Beaver, *Woolwich;* J. V. V. Baker, *Dover;* F. A. Aylmer, *Great Yarmouth.*

1 *Depôt Co.,* R. C. Carr, *m.*
2 *Depôt Co.,* G. E. Weigall, *m.*
Adjt., R. G. Merriman, D.S.O., *capt., Dépôt, Dover;* Hon. F. R. Bingham, *capt., Great Yarmouth.*

Kent (*Dover*)—Lt.-Col., E. L. F. Jennings, *c.*
Norfolk (*Great Yarmouth*)—Lt.-Col., Viscount Coke, *c.*
Suffolk (*Ipswich*) — Lieut.-Col., Lionel Tillotson, *c.*
Sussex (*Eastbourne*) — Lt.-Col., A. R. Margary, *c.*

VOLUNTEER.

Cinque Ports (1st) (*Dover*)—Lt.-Col., A. H. Daniel, V.D.
Cinque Ports (2nd) (*St. Leonards*)—Lt.-Col., H. C. Wilson.
City of London (1st) (*Staines House, Barbican*) — Lt. - Col. - Comdt., C. H. Coles, V.D., *c.*
Essex (1st) (*Artillery House, Stratford*)—Lt.-Col., A. Bianchi, V.D.
Kent (1st) (*Gravesend*)—Lt.-Col., R. H. Simpson.
Kent (2nd) (*Plumstead*)—Lt.-Col., E. T. Hughes, V.D., *c.*
Kent (3rd) (*Royal Arsenal, Woolwich*)—Lt.-Col., H. M. Hozier, C.B., V.D., *c.*
Middlesex (2nd) (*City Rd., London*)—Lt.-Col., M. B. Pearson, V.D., *c.*
Middlesex (3rd) (*Charing Cross, London*) — Lt. - Col. - Comdt., F. H. Hoskier.
Norfolk (1st) (*Great Yarmouth*)—Lt.-Col. Comdg., Earl of Stradbroke.
Suffolk and Harwich (1st) (*Harwich*)—Lt.-Col. A. I. H. Ward.
Sussex (1st) (*Brighton*)—Lt.-Col., E. N. Edwards, V.D., *c.*
Sussex (2nd) (*Eastbourne*) — Lt.-Col., W. A. Cardwell, V.D., *c.*

Southern Division.

Headquarters.........*Portsmouth.*
41 Service Companies.
3 Depôts.

Lt.-Cols., (Home) J. H. Rosseter and A. Mansel, D.S.O., *Portsmouth;* F. A. Bowles, *Weymouth;* W. S. Walford, *Golden Hill, I. of W.;* E. C. Wace, D.S.O., *Londonderry;* E. N. Henriques, *Gosport;* R. Oakes, *Cork Harbour;* E. V. Blackett, *Leith.*
(Abroad) G. D. Fanshawe, *Ceylon;* M. O. Hopkins, R. W. P. Robertson, and W. F. Graham, *Malta;* C. L. Casey, *Singapore;* G. P. Owen, *Roorkee;* W. H. Frith, *Aden;* A. R. Fraser, *Hong Kong;* R. F. Johnson, *Rangoon;* A. H. W. Brett, *Aden.*

COMPANIES.

1 *Malta,* N. B. Inglefield, *m.*
2 *Gibraltar,* T. W. Powles, *m.*
3 *Portsmouth,* M. W. P. Block, *m.*
4 *Portsmouth,* G. W. R. Fulton, *m.*
5 *Agra,* Hon. R. Tyrwhitt, *m.*

6 *Roorkee*, A. J. Mullins, m.
7 *Weymouth*, C. A. Howard, m.
8 *Bermuda*, C. E. English, m.
9 *Roorkee*, J. J. MacMahon.
10 *Portsmouth*, R. Wynyard, m.
11 *Roorkee*, H. C. Molesworth, m.
12 *Singapore*, J. Lewes, m.
13 *Golden Hill*, W. C. Hunter-Blair, *l.c.*
14 *Cork Harbour*, W. L. Brook-Smith, m.
15 *Gosport (S. T.)*, J. R. H. Allen, m.
16 *Malta*, C. E. Callwell, m.
17 *Malta*, J. de W. Lardner-Clarke, m.
18 *Aden*, J. O. English, m.
19 *Malta*, C. H. Alexander, m.
20 *Fareham*, T. H. J. Woodrow, m.
21 *Portsmouth*, E. D. H. Buckley, m.
22 *Jamaica*, F. A. L. Powell, m.
23 *Quetta*, W. W. T. Duban, m.
24 *Campbellpore*, H. O. Piers, m.
25 *Hong Kong*, W. W. Griffin, m
26 *Gibraltar*, L. P. Carden, m.
27 *Malta*, R.E.F.Goold-Adams,m.
28 *Weymouth*, A. Tracey, m.
29 *Barrackpore*, T. E. Carte, m.
30 *Portsmouth*, W. S. Churchward, m.
31 *Malta*, W. H. F. Taylor, m.
32 *Cork Harbour*, E. A. Gartside-Tippinge, m.
33 *Thobba*, J. M. Burt, m.
34 *Ceylon*, W. R. W. James, m.
35 *Singapore*, P. B. Hanham, m.
36 *Gibraltar*, R. C. Foster, m.
37 *Ceylon*, F. F. Minchin, m.
38 *Hong Kong*, H. H. Rich, m.
39 *Golden Hill*, J. Labalmondiere, m.
40 *Cork Harbour*, F. J. Græme, m.
41 *Portsmouth*, T. Ff. Chamberlain, m.

Dépôts.—*Lt.-Cols.*, H. G. Weir, *Fort Rowner* ; A. M. Murray, *Cork* ; Lord Playfair, *Aberdeen* ; E. Gunner, *Leith Fort* ; P. Saltmarshe, *Seaforth.*

1 *Dépôt Co.*, A. Matthews, m., *Gosport.*
2 *Dépôt Co.*, J. O. Hodgson, m., *Liverpool.*

Militia.

Antrim (*Carrickfergus*)—*Lt.-Col.*, E. T. Pottinger, *c.*
Clare (*Ennis*) — *Lt.-Col.*, G. O'Callaghan-Westropp.
Cork (*Fort Elizabeth*)—*Lt.-Col.*, T. A. Lunham, *c.*
Donegal (*Letterkenny*)—*Lt.-Col.*, T. E. Batt, *c.*
Dublin City (*Dublin*)—*Lt.-Col.*, W. C. Dickenson, *c.*
Duke of Edinburgh's Own (*Edinburgh*) — *Lt.-Col.*, A. J. Colquhoun, C.B., *c.*
Fife (*Cupar*) — *Lt.-Col.*, G. M. Boothby, *c.*
Forfar and Kincardine (*Montrose*)—*Lieut.-Col.*, Lord Carnegie, *c.*

Hampshire and Isle of Wight (*Sandown*)—*Lt.-Col.*, M. Moore-Lane, *c.*
Lancashire (*Seaforth*)—*Lt.-Col.*, S. Arnold, *c.*
Limerick City (*Limerick*) — *Lt.-Col.*, W. D. Maunsell, *c.*
Londonderry (*Londonderry*)—*Lt.-Col.*, S. A. M. Bruce.
Mid-Ulster (*Dungannon*) — *Lt.-Col.*, R. J. P. Saunders, *c.*
Sligo (*Sligo*) — *Lt.-Col.*, W. G. Wood-Martin, A.D.C., *c.*
S.E. of Scotland (*Dunbar*)—*Lt.-Col.*, T. A. Houstoun-Boswall-Preston, *c.*
Tipperary (*Templemore*) — *Lt.-Col.*, F. J. S. Lecky, *c.*
Waterford (*Waterford*)—*Lt.-Col.*, H. W. F. Chapman, *c.*
West of Scotland (*Maryhill Barracks, Glasgow*) — *Lt.-Col.*, J. Younger, *c.*
Wicklow (*Wicklow*)—*Lt.-Col.*, H. E. W. de Robeck.

Volunteer.

Aberdeenshire (1st) (*Aberdeen*)—*Lt.-Col. Comdt.*, J. Ogston, V.D., *c.*
Argyll and Bute (1st) (*Rothesay*)—*Lt.-Col. Comdt.*, F. Campbell, V.D., *c.*
Ayrshire and Galloway (1st) (*Kilmarnock*)—*Lt.-Col.*, J. G. Sturrock, V.D., *c.*
Banff (1st) (*Castle St., Banff*)—*Lt.-Col.* (vacant).
Berwickshire (1st) (*Eyemouth*)—(Attached to 1st Edinburgh).
Caithness (1st) (*Thurso*) — *Lt.-Col.*, Sir J. R. G. Sinclair, Bart.
Cheshire and Carnarvonshire (1st) (*Chester*)—*Lt.-Col.*, H. T. Brown, V.D., *c.*
Cumberland (1st) (*Carlisle*)—*Lt.-Col.*, W. H. Atkinson, V.D., *c.*
Dorsetshire (1st) (*Weymouth*)—*Lt.-Col.*, A. Maclean, V.D.
Edinburgh City (1st) (*York Place, Edinburgh*) — *Lt.-Col.*, J. F. Mackay, V.D., *c.*
Fifeshire (1st) (*St. Andrews*) — *Lt.-Col. Comdt.*, J. W. Johnston, V.D., *c.*
Forfarshire (1st) (*Dundee*)—*Lt.-Col. Comdt.*, T. Couper, jun., V.D., *c.*
Hampshire (1st) (*Southampton*)—*Lt.-Col.*, J. MacLauchlan, V.D., *c.*
Hampshire (2nd) (*Southsea*) —*Lt.-Col.*, C. L. Reynolds, V.D.
Highland (The) (*Inverness*)—*Lt.-Col. Com.*, J. E. B. Baillie.
Lanarkshire (1st) (*Crown Halls, Glasgow*) — *Lt.-Col. Com.*, A. B. Grant, V.D., *c.*
Lancashire (1st) (*Low Hill, Liverpool*)—*Lt.-Col.*, T. Gee.
Lancashire (2nd) (*Windsor Barracks, Liverpool*)—*Lt.-Col.*, T. Royden, V.D.
Lancashire (3rd) (*Blackburn*)—*Lt.-Col.*, W. J. Thom, V.D., *c.*

Lancashire (4th) (*Edge Hill, Liverpool*) — *Lt.-Col.*, G. J. Williams, V.D., *c.*
Lancashire (5th) (*Preston*)—*Lt.-Col.*, W. H. Hunt, V.D., *c.*
Lancashire (6th) (*Liverpool*) — *Lt.-Col.*, H. J. Robinson, V.D., *c.* Adjt., Geo. Neal, *capt.*
Lancashire (7th) (*Manchester*)—*Lt.-Col.*, R. K. Birley, V.D., *c.*
Lancashire (8th) (*Toxteth Park, Liverpool*) — *Lt.-Col.*, R. C. Rathbone.
Lancashire (9th) (*Bolton*)—*Lt.-Col.*, H. E. Musgrave, V.D., *c.*
Midlothian (1st) (*Edinburgh*)—*Lt.-Col.*, J. A. Dalmahoy, V.D.
Orkney (1st) (*Kirkwall*)—*Lt.-Col.*, R. Bailey, *c.*
Renfrew and Dumbarton (1st) (*Greenock*) — *Lt.-Col.*, F. G. Gemmill, V.D., *c.*
Shropshire and Staffordshire (1st) (*Stoke-upon-Trent*)—*Lt.-Col.*, J. Strick, C.B., V.D., *c.*
Worcestershire and Warwickshire (1st) (*Worcester*)—*Lt.-Col.*, J. B. Maybury, V.D., *c.*

Western Division.

Headquarters.........Devonport.

29 Service Companies.
2 Depôts.

Lt.-Cols., (Home) B. L. Eman, W. J. Fowler, *c.*, and L. E. Coker, *Devonport* ; F. M. Bland, *Cardiff* ; C. M. Western, *Pembroke Dock* ; A. L. Lane, *Falmouth.*

(Abroad), E. J. K. Priestley, *Cape* ; F. C. Farmer, *Halifax, N.S.* ; H. C. M. Woods, *Bermuda* ; C. R. W. Hervey, *Kurrachee* ; G. G. Monck-Mason, *Barrackpore* ; H. J. Lyster, *Mauritius.*

Companies.

1 *St. Lucia*, A. L. Molesworth, m.
2 *Pembroke Dock*, F. A. Curteis, m.
3 *Halifax, N.S.*, E. B. Anderson, m.
4 *Ferozepore*, N. B. Heffernan, m.
5 *Rawal Pindi*, A. H. Browne, m.
6 *Dunbar*, G. J. F. Talbot, m.
7 *Jhansi*, F. R. Thackeray, m.
8 *Mauritius*, A. L. Carroll, m.
9 *Secunderabad*, A. H. Block, m.
10 *Devonport*, F. E. Kent, m.
11 *Fort St. George*, J. R. B. Davidson, m.
12 *Jersey*, H. C. G. Taylor, m.
13 *Devonport*, H. W. Morrieson, m.
14 *Cape*, W. H. E. Dobie, m.
15 *Plymouth*, E. G. Nicolls, m.
16 *Aden*, G. R. M. Church, m.
17 *Devonport*, W. F. Cockburn, m.
18 *Bombay*, H. T. Butcher, m.
19 *Esquimalt*,
20 *Halifax, N.S.*, W. A. Plant, m.
21 *Bermuda*, H. de T. Phillips, m.
22 *Rangoon*, S. V. Thornton, m.
23 *Cape*, G. D. Chamier, m.
24 *Malta*, G. D'A. Alexander, m.
25 *Quetta*, N. W. H. Du Boulay, m.

26 *Mauritius*, H. S. Nelson, m.

27 *Pembroke Dock*, M. B. G. Jackson, m.

28 *Londonderry*, G. Wright. m.

29 *Plymouth*, C. H. Milward, m.

DÉPÔTS—*Lt.-Cols.*, H. T. Lugard, *Scarborough* ; L. E. Coker, *Devonport*.

1 *Dépôt Co.*, P. de S. Burney, m., *Plymouth*.

2 *Dépôt Co.*, A. Ff. Powell, m., *Scarborough*.

MILITIA.

Cardigan (*Aberystwith*) — *Lt.-Col.*, T. Lloyd, C.B., c.

Carmarthen (*Carmarthen*)—*Lt.-Col.*, Earl of Cawdor, A.D.C., c.

Cornwall and Devon Miners (*Falmouth*)—*Lt.-Col.*, T. M. A. Horsford, c.

Devon (*Devonport*)—*Lt.-Col.*, W. G. Lowther, c.

Durham (*Sunderland*)—*Lt.-Col.*, H. P. Ditmas, c.

Glamorgan (*Swansea*)—*Lt.-Col.*, J. R. Wright, c.

Northumberland (*Berwick-on-Tweed*) — *Lt.-Col.*, H. B. H. Hamilton, c.

Pembroke (*Milford Haven*)—*Lt.-Col.*, F. P. Edwardes, c.

Yorkshire (*Scarborough*)—*Lt.-Col.*, J. D. Legard, c.

VOLUNTEER.

Berwick - on - Tweed (1st) (*attached to* 2nd *Northumberland Vol. Art.*)—*Capt. Comdt.*, A. T. Robertson, V.D., m.

Cornwall (1st) (*Falmouth*)—*Lt.-Col.*, T. W. Field, V.D., c.

Devonshire (1st) (*Exeter*)—*Lt.-Col.*, W. Brock, V.D., c.

Devonshire (2nd) (*Devonport*)—*Lt.-Col.*,

Durham (1st) (*Sunderland*) - *Lt.-Col.*, E. Vaux, V.D., c. Adjt. (vacant).

Durham (2nd) (*Seaham*)—*Lt.-Col. Comdt.* Marq. of Londonderry, K.G., A.D.C.

Durham (3rd) (*South Shields*)—*Lt.-Col.*, W. J. Dawson, V.D., c.

Durham (4th) (*West Hartlepool*)—*Lt.-Col.*, R. Lauder, V.D., c.

Glamorganshire (1st) (*Swansea*) — *Lt.-Col. Comdg.* Sir E. S. Hill, K.C.B., M.P., c. *Lt.-Col.*, J. W. Williams.

Glamorganshire (2nd) (*Cardiff*), —*Lt.-Col.*, H. O. Fisher, V.D., c. Adjt., Frank Wilkinson Dent, capt.

Gloucestershire (1st) (*Bristol*)—*Lt.-Col. Comdt.*, F. C. Ord, c.

Lincolnshire (1st) (*Grimsby*)—*Lt.-Col.*, A. Bannister, V.D., c.

Monmouthshire (1st) (*Newport*)—*Lt.-Col.*, C. T. Wallis.

Newcastle-on-Tyne (1st) (*Newcastle*)—*Lt.-Col.*, W. M. Angus, V.D., c.

Northumberland (1st) (*Newcastle-on-Tyne*)—*Lt.-Col.*, P. Watts.

Northumberland (2nd, *Percy*) (*Alnwick*) — *Lt.-Col.*, J. G. Hicks, V.D., c.

Tynemouth (*Tynemouth*) — *Lt.-Col.*, R. F. Kidd, c.

Yorkshire, East Riding of (1st) (*Scarborough*) — *Lt.-Col.*, W. F. Sutton, V.D., c.

Yorkshire, East Riding of (2nd) (*Hull*)—*Lt.-Col. Comdg.*, H. F. Pudsey, V.D., c. *Lt.-Col.*, W. L. White, V.D., c.

Yorkshire, North Riding of (1st) (*Middlesbrough*) — *Lieut.-Col.*, C. L. Bell, V.D., c.

Yorkshire, West Riding of (1st) (*Leeds*)—*Lt.-Col.*, C. Coghlan, V.D., c.

Yorkshire, West Riding of (2nd) (*Bradford*)— *Lt.-Col.*, G. J. J. Hoffmann, V.D., c.

Yorkshire, West Riding of (4th) (*Sheffield*)—*Lt.-Col.*, C. Allan.

ROYAL MALTA ARTILLERY.

£10,100.

Lieut.-Colonel, P. Bernard.

Majors, A. Gatt, (2nd) A. Mattei, A. Trapani, R. Briffa, A. Vella, W. Savona, I. E. Savona, H. A. Balbi.

Paymaster, Louis Monreal, capt.

Adjt., Joseph Fras. Bernard, capt.

HON. ARTILLERY COMPANY OF LONDON.

(The Armoury House, Finsbury, E.C.)

Capt.-General and Col., H.R.H. Prince of Wales, K.G., f.m.

Lt.-Col. Comdg., Earl of Denbigh and Desmond.

Lt.-Col. (2nd in comd.), L. R. C. Boyle.

Majors, G. McMicking, W. E. Williams, W. Evans, F. B. Bell.

Adjt., capt. R.A.

BERMUDA MILITIA ARTILLERY.

Commdt. & Adjt. W. C. A. Nicholson, capt. R.A.

Corps of Royal Engineers (£297,360). (1)

Col.-in-Chief, Duke of Cambridge, K.G., f.m.

Cols. Comm. (£990 each), Sir John Linton Arabin Simmons, G.C.B., f.m.; Francis Hornblow Rundall, C.S.I. (*late Madras*); Wm. Charles Hadden, g.; Sir Frederick Richard Maunsell, K.C.B., g. (*late Bengal*); Horace William Montagu, C.B., g.; Sir Edward Chas. Sparshott Williams, K.C.I.E., g. (*late Bengal*); Charles Fanshawe, g.; Sir James Frankfort Manners Browne, K.C.B., g.; John Bayly, C.B., g.; Sir Thos. Lionel John Gallwey, K.C.M.G., l.g.; Sir Æneas Perkins, K.C.B., g. (*late Bengal*); Wm. West Goodfellow, C.B., g. (*late Bombay*); Richard Dyott, l.g.; Charles Aug. Goodfellow, VC, l.g. (*late Bombay*); Wm. Percival Tomkins, C.I.E., g. (*late Bengal*); Sir Gerald Graham, VC, G.C.B., l.g.; George Warren Walker, g. (*late Madras*).

Lieutenant-Colonels, R. M. Hyslop, c., *War Office*; H. Dove, c., *Jersey*; J. C. Barker, c., *Shorncliffe*; J. Cameron, c., *Malta*; R. T. Orpen, *Madras*; G. R.R. Savage, c., *Ceylon*; P. Haslett. c., *Newcastle*; A. Porcelli, c., *Bengal*; J. W. Thurburn, c., *Punjab*; F. Gossett, c., *Perth*; C. Hoskyns, c., *Bombay*; E. R. Hussey, c., *Southampton*; St. G. C. Gore, c., *Bengal*; R. O. Lloyd, c., *Bombay*; C. R. Conder, c., *Weymouth*; W. G. Du Boulay, *Ryde*, I. of W.; E. W. Creswell, c., *Bengal*; T. R. Main, c., *Plymouth*; C. W. Sherrard, c., *Chatham*; W. Pitt, c., *Aldershot*; C. Wilkinson, c., *Halifax, N.S.*; H. H. Hart, c, *Punjab*; O. V. Boddy, *Madras*; C. B. Wilkieson, *Madras*; C. A. Rochfort-Boyd, *S. Africa*; M. W. Skinner, *Guernsey*; W. T. Shone, C.B., D.S.O., c., *Madras*; W. H. White, *Bengal*; J. M. T. Badgley, *Bengal*; H. W. Puperier, *Punjab*; F.W. Bennet, *S. Africa*; A. Heathcote, *Madras*; R. Thompson, *War Office*; E. J. T. Ross of Bladensburg, *Liverpool*; S. McM. Maycock, *Gosport*; E. J. Dewing, *Gibraltar*; T. N. M. Lake, c., *War Office*; E. Raban, *Admiralty*; M. Martin, *Aden*; B. Scott, C.I.E., *Bengal*; S. Grant, *Madras*; S. H. Exham, *Portsmouth Dockyard*; E. Glennie, *Bombay*; G. F. Wilson, *Bengal*; H. H. Muirhead, *Pmbrke Dock*; M. L. Jessep, *Mauritius*; R. M. Ruck, *Malta*; H. P. Leach, C.B., D.S.O., c., *Bengal*; W. H. Chippindall, *Singapore*; E. W. Cotter, *Cork*; E. J. Bor, *Bermuda*; Sir H. E. McCallum, K.C.M.G., *Newfoundland*; J. H. C. Harrison (*unposted*); J. Kellie, *Punjab*; P. G. Von Donop, *B. of Trade*; W. L. C. Baddeley, *Madras*; H. D. Olivier, *Bombay*; H.W. Smith-Rewse, *War Office*; J.

E. Blackburn, *Gibraltar*; H. D'A. Breton, *Shoeburyness*; H. P. Knight, *Gravesend*; W. H. Goldney, *Portsea*; F. S. Leslie, *Exeter*; C. L. Young, *Aldershot*; J. J. Leverson, C.M.G., *Barbados*; R. L. Hippisley, *Cairo*; R. C. Hellard, *Southampton*; J. C. L. Campbell, *Alexandria*. C. K. Wood, *S. Africa*; G. H. W. O'Sullivan, *Bombay*; E. Blunt, *Bombay*; C. C. Ellis, *Bengal*; J. B. Sharpe, *S. Africa*; T. Digby, *Madras*; M. C. Barton, D.S.O., *Bengal*; R. C. Maxwell, *Chatham*; H. D. Love, *Madras*; J. W. Sill, *Chatham*; R. Mackean, *Belfast*; A. H. Bagnold, *Jamaica*; W. V. Constable, *Bengal*; R. H. Jennings, *Bombay*; A. C. Foley, *Curragh*; C. H. Darling, *War Office*; H. E. Rawson, *S. africa*; W. J. Mackenzie, *War Office*; H. S. Andrews-Speed, *Aden*; P. T. Buston, *Dover*; J. C. Tyler, *Colchester*; G. H. Sim, *Dublin*. *Adjt., R.E. Troops, Aldershot,* G. P. Scholfield, *capt.* *Adjt. Training Bn., Chatham,* T. A. H. Bigge, *capt.*

Head Quarters of Companies.
1st Co.—Cork Harbour (Fortress).
2nd—Egypt (Fortress).
3rd—Bermuda (Fortress).
4th—Gosport (Submarine Miners).
5th—Portsmouth (Fortress).
6th—Gibraltar (Fortress).
7th—South Africa (Field).
8th—South Africa (Railway).
9th—Chatham (Fortress).
10th—S. Africa (Railway).
11th—S. Africa (Field).
12th—Aldershot (Field).
13th—Clifton, Bristol (Survey).
14th—Dublin (Survey).
15th—Gibraltar (Fortress).
16th—Bedford (Survey).
17th—S. Africa (Field).
18th—Halifax, N.S. (Fortress).
19th—Southampton (Survey).
20th—Gibraltar (Fortress).
21st—Felixstowe (Sub. Miners).
22nd—I. of Wight (Sub. Miners).
23rd—Natal (Field).
24th—Malta (Fortress).
25th—Hong Kong (Fortress).
26th—S. Africa (Field).
27th—Bermuda (Sub. Miners).
28th—Malta (Submarine Miners).
29th—Cape Town (Fortress).
30th—Plymouth (Sub. Miners).
31st—S. Africa (Fortress).
32nd—Gibraltar (Fortress).
33rd—Cork Harb. (Sub. Miners).
34th—Gravesend (Sub. Miners).
35th—Pembroke Dk.(Sub.Minrs)
36th—Bermuda (Fortress).
37th—S. Africa (Fortress).

38th—Shorncliffe (Field).
39th—Sheerness (Sub. Miners).
40th—Halifax, N.S. (Sub.Miners).
41st—Ceylon & Singapore (Fort.).
42nd—Malta (Fortress).
43rd—Mauritius (Fortress).

Dépôts—A, B, C, D, E, F, G, M (Sub. Miners), and N Companies, Chatham; H Co., Army Headquarters, India.

Telegraph Battalion.
1st Division—Natal.
2nd Division—London (27 Newgate Street, E.C.)

Bridging Battalion.
A and B Troops, S. Africa.
Field Troop, S. Africa; Field Dépôt R. E. Troops—Aldershot.
1st Field Park—S. Africa.
Balloon Dépôt Aldershot, and Section. S. Africa.
Coast Battalion (Submarine Miners), 1 N. Shields, 2 Cardiff, 3 Greenock, 4 Paull, 5 Middlesbrough, 6 Broughty Ferry, 7 Leith. 8 Liverpool, 9 Falmouth, 10 Weymouth.

ROYAL ENGINEERS MILITIA—£6,740.
Fortress Forces.
Anglesey (*Beaumaris*)—Lieut.-Col. Sir R. H. Williams - Bulkeley, Bart.
Monmouthshire (*Monmouth*)—Lt.-Col., W. E. C. Curre, *c.*
Submarine Miners.
Portsmouth—T. E. A. Jones, *lc.*
Needles—L. N. Barrow, *m.*
Plymouth—R. P. Pilgrim, *l.c.*
Thames—C. P. Boyd, *l.c.*
Medway—E. W. Guinness, *m.*
Harwich—F. Gumley, *m.*
Milford Haven—H. Davis, *m.*
Plymouth (*Western*)—C. S. Baker, *l.c.*
Humber—W. H. Wellsted, *l.c.*
Falmouth—C. H. L. Baskerville, *m.*

VOLUNTEER ENGINEERS.
Aberdeenshire (*Hardgate, Aberdeen*)—Lt.-Col., R H. Anstice, *c.*
Cheshire (1st) (*Birkenhead*)—Lt.-Col., F. T. S. Hamilton.
Cheshire (2nd) (*Railway, Crewe*)—Lt.-Col., E. T. D. Cotton-Jodrell, M.P., *c.*
Devon and Somerset (1st) (*Exeter*)—Lt.-Col., T. J. Scoones, V.D., *c.*
Durham (1st) (*Jarrow-on-Tyne*)—Lt.-Col., J. B. Furneaux.
Flintshire (1st) (*Buckley*)—attached to 1st Cheshire.
Gloucestershire (1st) (*Cheltenham*)—Lt.-Col. R. Rogers, V.D., *c.*
Gloucestershire (2nd) (*College Green, Bristol*)—Lt.-Col., E. C. Plant, O.B., V.D., *c.*

Hampshire (1st) (*Portsmouth*)—Major, F. N. Maude, *l.c.*
Lanarkshire (1st) (*Kelvinside, Glasgow*)—Lt. - Col., E. R. Crawford V.D., *c.*
Lancashire (1st) (*Edge Hill, Liverpool*)—Lt.-Col., S. W. Doyle, V.D., *c.*
Lancashire (2nd) (*St. Helens*)—Lt.-Col. W. H. Pendlebury, V.D., *c.*
London (1st) (*Barnsbury Park, Islington*) — Lt. - Col., W. F. Wood, V.D.
Middlesex (1st) (*Fulham Road, London*)—Lt - Col., F. Josselyn, V.D., *c.*
Newcastle-on-Tyne (1st)—Lieut.-Col., A. S. Palmer, V.D., *c.*
Northamptonshire (1st) (*Peterborough*)—attached to 2nd Tower Hamlets.
Sussex (1st) (*Eastbourne*)—Major, F. W. Savage.
Tower Hamlets (2nd) ("*East London*," *Victoria Park Square*)—Lt.-Col. Comdt., W. Whetherly.
Yorkshire West Riding (1st) (*Sheffield*)—Lt.-Col., J. E. Bingham.
Yorkshire (2nd) (*Leeds*)—Lt.-Col., W. C. Dawson, V.D., *c.*

Submarine Miners.
Clyde (*Greenock*), D.F.D. Neill, *m.*
Forth (*Leith*), F. G. Ogilvie, *m.*
Mersey (*Liverpool*), A. H. Knight, *m.*
Severn (*Cardiff*), J. A. Hughes, *m.*
Tay (*Broughty Ferry*), W. H. Fergueson, *m.*
Tees (*Middlesbrough*), T. Belk, *m.*
Tyne (*N. Shields*), W. Johnson, V.D., *l.c.*

Electrical Engineers—Victoria St., S.W.—R. E. B. Crompton, *m.*

ENGINEER AND RAILWAY VOLUNTEER STAFF CORPS (*Gt. George St., Westminster*).
Lieut.-Col. Comdt., J. C. Hawkshaw.
Lt.-Cols., J. S. Forbes, V.D., *c.*; Geo. F. Lyster, C.E.; Sir W. Birt, V.D., *c.*; Sir J. Thompson; Sir C. Scotter, Sir W. Pollitt, *c.*; Sir J. W. Wolfe-Barry, K.C.B.; G. B. Newton, Sir B. Baker, K.C.M.G.; W. R. Galbraith, C.E.; G. S. Gibb, J. Conacher, G. H. Turner, F. Harrison, J. L. Wilkinson, Sir F. A. Marindin, K.C.M.G., *c.*; A. J. Barry, J. F. S. Gooday, C. Steel, C. J. Owens, J.C. Inglis, J. A. McDonald.

The Foot Guards (£221,700).

GRENADIER GUARDS. (1)
Regtl. Hdqrs., Horse Gds. Whitehall.
Col., Duke of Cambridge, K.G. *f.m.*
Regtl. Comdt., H. Ricardo *c.*
Regtl. Adjt., Visct. Kilcoursie, *capt.*

1st Battalion, *Windsor.*
Lt.-Col., Villiers Hatton, C.B., *c.*
Majors, Hon. J. T. St. Aubyn (2nd), W. A. L. Fox-Pitt, R. J. Cooper, Count Gleichen, C.M.G.
Adjt., E. F. O. Gasgoigne, D.S.O. *lt.*
Medical Officer, Surg.-Maj. C. R. Kilkelly, M.B.

2nd Battalion, *Wellington Bks.*
Lieut.-Col., Francis Lloyd, D.S.O.
Majors, R. G. Gordon-Gilmour (2nd), H. Streatfeild, Hon. G. Legh, H. Scott-Kerr.
Adjutant, ——, *lt.*
Medical Officers, Surg.-Maj. E. N. Sheldrake; Capt. R. M. Le H. Cooper, R.A.M.C.

3rd Battalion, *S. Africa.*
Lt.-Col., Eyre M. Stewart Crabbe.
Majors, D. A. Kinloch (2nd), C. Ferguson, D.S.O., *l.c.;* H. R. Crompton-Roberts; F.J.Davies.
Adjt., F. L. Fryer, *lt.*
Medical Officers, Brig.-Surg. Lt.-Col. C. E. Harrison, M.B.; Capt. H. W. Vaughan-Williams, R.A.M.C.

COLDSTREAM GUARDS. (1)
Regtl. Hdqrs., Horse Gds., Whitehall, S.W.

Col., Sir Fredk. Charles Arthur Stephenson, G.C.B., *g.,* Constable of Tower of London.
Regtl. Comdt., Hon. H. W. L. Corry, *c.*
Regtl. Adjt., J. R. Hall, *capt.*
Solicitor, R. J. P. Broughton.

1st Battalion, *S. Africa.*
Lt.-Col., Alfd. Edwd. Codrington.
Majors, H. C. Surtees (2nd), G. G. F. Smith, Hon. W. Lambton, J. A. G. Drummond-Hay.
Adjt., T. G. Matheson *lt.*
Medical Officers, Surg.-Maj. W. R. Crooke-Lawless, M.D.; Capt. A. W. Hooper, R.A.M.C.

2nd Battalion, *S. Africa.*
Lt.-Col., H. R. Stopford.
Majors, Hon. A. H. Henniker-Major (2nd); Marquess of Winchester, H. G. D. Shute; Sir H. S. Rawlinson, Bt., *l.c.*
Adjt., J. McC. Steele, *lt.*
Medical Officers, Surg.-Lt.-Col. J. Magill, M.D.; Capt. A. F. Heaton, R.A.M.C.

3rd Battalion, *Tower.*
Lieut.-Col., Vesey John Dawson.
Majors, G. Pleydell-Bouverie. (2nd), F. I. Maxse, D.S.O.; F. S. Maude.
Adjt., Hon. G. A. C. Crichton, *lt.*
Medical Officers, Surg.-Maj. A. C. Alexander; Lieut. A. C. Lupton, R.A.M.C.

SCOTS GUARDS. (1)
Regimental Headquarters, Horse Guards, Whitehall, S.W.
Colonel, H.R.H. Duke of Connaught, K.G., G.C.B., *g.*
Regtl. Comdt., Henry Fludyer, *c.*
Reg. Adj., J. W. Marten-Neill, *lt.*

1st Battalion, *S. Africa.*
Lt.-Col., A. H. Paget, *c.*
Majors, Hon. N. deC. Dalrymple-Hamilton (2nd), L. G. Drummond, W. P. Pulteney, D.S.O.; G. J. Cuthbert, B. F. S. Baden-Powell.
Adjt., H. C. Lowther, *capt.*
Medical Officers, Surg.-Maj. W. C. Beevor, M.B.; Capt. S. G. Moores, R.A.M.C.

2nd Battalion, *Chelsea Barracks.*
Lt.-Col., Inigo Richmond Jones, *c.*
Majors, F. W. Romilly, D.S.O., (2nd); Hon. C. Harbord, E. Milner, E. E. Hanbury.
Adjt., J. C. Heriot-Maitland, *lt.*
Medical Officers, Surg.-Maj. G. S. Robinson; Capt. F. McDowell, R.A.M.C.

3rd Battalion (*not yet formed*).

GUARDS DÉPÔT (Caterham).
Comdg., C. A. A. Frederick, *maj.* (Coldstreams).
Adjt., F. H. de Kierzkowski Steuart, *capt.* (Scots Guards).

Territorial Regiments of the Line.

WITH THEIR AFFILIATED VOLUNTEER BATTALIONS (£2,263,700).

Arranged alphabetically by the titles directed to be used in official correspondence. The former designations of the Regiments are given in parentheses.]

ARGYLL AND SUTHERLAND HIGHLANDERS. (Princess Louise's). (1)
District No. 91.—*Stirling.*
Colonel, Sir J. A. Ewart, K.C.B., *g.*
Comg. Regtl. District, P. D. Trotter, *c.*
1st Batt. (91st Foot), *S. Africa.*
Lt.-Col., G. L. J. Goff.
Adjt., D. J. Glasfurd, *lt.*
2nd Batt. (93rd Ft.), *Rhaniket, Bengal Command.*
Lt.-Col., J. H. Campbell.
Adjt., J. Campbell, *lt.*
3rd Batt. (Highlnd. Mil.), *Stirling.*
Lt.-Col., Duke of Montrose, K.T., *c.*
4th Batt. (Renfrew Mil.) *Paisley.*
Lt.-Col., A. C. D. Dick, *c.*
1st (Renfrewsh.) Vol. Batt., *Greenock.*
Lt.-Col., W. Lamont, V.D., *c.*
2nd (Renfrewsh.) Vol. Batt., *Paisley.*
Lt.-Col., Sir T. G. Glen-Coats, Bart., V.D., *c.*
3rd (Renfrewsh.) Vol. Batt., *Pollockshaws.*
Lt.-Col., D. Hamilton.

4th (Stirlingshire) Vol. Batt., *Stirling.*
Lt.-Col., D. McFadyen, V.D., *c.*
5th Vol. Batt., *Dunoon.*
Lt.-Col., D. Campbell.
1st Dumbartonshire Volrs., *Helensburgh.*
Lt.-Cols., J. McA. Denny, *c.* (comdg.), A. Denny.
7th (Clackmannan and Kinross) Vol. Batt., *Alloa.*
Lt.-Col., A. T. Moyes, V.D., *c.*

BEDFORDSHIRE REGT. (2).
District No. 16.—*Bedford.*
Col., Sir John Wm. Cox, K.C.B., *l.g.*
Comg. Regtl. District, W. H. Young, *c.*
1st Batt. (16th Ft.), *Mooltan. Punjab Command.*
Lt.-Col., W. H. Riddell.
Adjt., W. E. C. Hood, *lt.*
2nd Batt. (16th Ft.), *Dublin.*
Lt.-Col., W. O. Cavanagh.
Adjt., C. R. J. Griffith, *capt.*
3rd Batt. (Militia), *Bedford.*
Lt.-Col., Duke of Bedford.

4th Batt. (Militia), *Hertford.*
Hon. *Col.,* Marq. of Salisbury, K.G.
Lt.-Col., Viscount Cranborne, M.P.

1st (Herts) Vol. Batt., *Hertford.*
Lt.-Col., A. M. Blake, C.B., V.D., *c.*

2nd (Herts) Vol. Batt. *Gt. Berkhamstead.*
Lt.-Col., Earl Brownlow, A.D.C., V.D., *c.*

3rd Vol. Batt., *Bedford.*
Lt.-Col., E. R. Green, V.D., *c.*

BERKSHIRE REGT. (ROYAL). (Princess Charlotte of Wales's). (1)
District No. 49.—*Reading.*
Col., Robt. Wm. Lowry, C.B., *l.g.*
Comg. Regtl. District, E. T. Dickson, *c.*

1st Batt. (49th Foot), *Portsmouth.*
Lt.-Col., F. C. Carter.
Adjt., W. R. P. K. Betty, *capt.*
2nd Batt. (66th Ft.), *King William's Town, Cape Colony.*
Lt.-Col., C. Evans-Gordon.
Adjt., H. M. Finch, *capt.*
3rd Batt. (Militia), *Reading.*
Lt.-Col., T. J. Bowles, *c.*

1st Vol. Batt., *Reading.*
Lt.-Col. Comdt., A. F. Walter, v.d., c.

BLACK WATCH, The.—See "Royal Highlanders."

BORDER REGIMENT. (1)
District No. 34.—*Carlisle.*
Colonel, Sir Henry Chas. Barnston Daubeney, g.c.b., g.
Comg. Regtl. District, C. G. Brind, c.
1st Batt. (34th Foot), *S. Africa.*
Lt.-Col., J. H. E. Hinde, c.
Adjt., C. L. Macnab, lt.
2nd Batt. (55th Foot), *Bareilly.*
Lt.-Col., J. S. Wood.
Adjt., A. S. W. Moffat, capt.
3rd Batt. (Militia), *Carlisle.*
Lt.-Col., J. R. Bain, c.
4th Batt. (Militia), *Carlisle.*
Lt.-Col., A. W. D. Lewis.
1st (Cumberland) Vol. Batt., *Carlisle.*
Lt.-Cols., J. S. Ainsworth, c. (comdg.) ; T. R. Riddell, v.d.
2nd (Westmorland) Vol. Batt., *Kendal.*
Lieut.-Colonel, J. W. Weston.

CAMERON HIGHLANDERS
(The Queen's Own). (2)
District No. 79.—*Inverness.*
Colonel, Sir Richard Chambré Hayes Taylor, k.c.b., g.
Comg. Regtl. District, R. H. Murray, c b., c.m.g., a d c.
1st Batt. (79th Foot), *Egypt.*
Lt.-Col., T. F. A. Watson-Kennedy.
Adjt., J. Campbell, maj.
2nd Batt., *Gibraltar.*
Lt.-Col., J. M. Hunt.
Adjt., L. O. Græme, capt.
3rd Batt. (Highland Mil.), *Inverness.*
Lt.-Col., A. D. Mackintosh of Mackintosh, c.
1st Vol. Batt. (Inverness-shire Highland), *Inverness.*
Lt.-Col., A. Macdonald, v.d., c.

CAMERONIANS, THE (Scottish Rifles). (1)
District No. 26.—*Hamilton, N.B.*
Col., Sir J C. Rattray, k c.b., l.g.
Comg. Regtl. District, H. de C. Rawlins, c.
1st Batt. (26th Foot), *Lucknow.*
Lt.-Col., S. H. Lomax.
Adjt., J. G. Chaplin, lt.
2nd Batt. (90th Foot), *S. Africa.*
Lt.-Col., E. Cooke.
Adjt., F. Murray, capt.
3rd and 4th Batts. (Lanark Militia), *Hamilton, N.B.*
Lt.-Col. Comdt., A. H. Courtenay, c. (4).
Lt.-Col., G. Farie, c. (3).
1st Lanarkshire Volrs., *Glasgow.*
Lt.-Cols., J. A. Reid, v.d., c. (comdg) ; H. A. Ker, v.d., c.

2nd Vol. Batt. *Hamilton, N.B.*
Lt.-Col., J. Scott.
3rd Lanarkshire Volrs., *Victoria Road, Glasgow.*
Lt.-Col. Comdt., H Morton, v.d., c.
4th Vol. Batt. (4th Lanarkshire), *Stirling Road, Glasgow.*
Lt.-Col., J. F. Newlands, v.d.

CHESHIRE REGIMENT. (1)
District No. 22.—*Chester.*
Colonel, David Anderson, g.
Comg. Regtl. District A. W. Sheringham, c.
1st Batt. (22nd Foot), *Secunderabad, Madras Command.*
Lt.-Col., F. W. Bromfield.
Adjt., W. Martin-Leake, lt.
2nd Batt. (22nd Foot), *Limerick.*
Lt.-Col., W. F. Curteis.
Adjt., W. V. Moul, capt.
3rd Batt. (Militia), *Chester.*
Lt.-Col. A. Hill, c.
4th Batt. (Militia), *Macclesfield.*
Lt.-Col., J. M. Read, c.
1st Vol. Batt., *Birkenhead.*
Lt.-Col., F. W. Blood.
2nd Vol. Batt., (Earl of Chester's), *Chester.*
Lt.-Col., T. J. Smith, v.d. c.
3rd Vol. Batt., *Knutsford.*
Lt.-Col., W. Mothersill, v.d., c.
4th Vol. Batt., *Stockport.*
Lt.-Cols., W. T. Carrington, v.d., c. (comdg.) ; C. E. Wilkinson, v.d.; J. Wood, v.d., c.
5th Vol. Batt., *Congleton.*
Lt.-Col., Sir W. G. Shakerley, Bt., c.

CITY OF LONDON REGT.—
(The Royal Fusiliers.) (1)
District No. 7.—*Hounslow.*
Colonel, Sir Richard Wilbraham, k.c.b., g.
Comg. Regtl. District. G. F. Guyon, c.
1st Batt. (7th Foot), *Nusserabad, Bombay Command.*
Lt.-Col., R. P. B. Rodick.
Adjt., A. V. Johnson, capt.
2nd Batt. (7th Foot), *S. Africa.*
Lt.-Col., C. G. Donald.
Adjt., H. A. S. Wright, capt.
3rd Batt. (1898), *Gibraltar.*
Lt.-Col., G. E. Briggs.
Adjt., A. H. Sanders, capt.
4th Batt. (not yet raised).
5th Batt. (Roy. Westminster Mil.), *Hounslow.*
Lt.-Col., C. E. Lang, c.
6th Batt. (Militia), *Finsbury.*
Col., L. G. Dundas, c.b.
Lt.-Col. H. N. B. Good, c.
7th (Middlesex Mil.), *Hounslow.*
Col., G. Dibley.
1st Vol. Batt. *Fitzroy Square, W.*
Lt.-Col., A. J. Bolton, v.d., c.

2nd Vol. Batt., *Great Smith Street, S.W.*
Lt.-Col., A. L. Keller, v.d., c.
3rd Vol. Batt., *Hampstead Road, N.W.*
Lt.-Col., T. J. Long, v.d., c.

CONNAUGHT RANGERS. (1)
District No. 88.—*Galway.*
Col., Joseph E. Thackwell, o.b., g.
Comg. Regtl. District, A. S. Woods, c.
1st Batt. (88th Foot), *S. Africa.*
Lt.-Col., L. G. Brooke, c.
Adjt., P. T. Horton, lt.
2nd Batt. (94th), *Meerut, Bengal.*
Lt.-Col., C. E. Harman.
Adjt., G. L. Hobbs. capt.
3rd (Mayo Militia), *Castlebar.*
Lt.-Col., G. L. Bence-Lambert, c.
4th Batt. (Militia), *Galway.*
Lt.-Col., R. L. Staunton.
5th (Roscommon Mil.), *Boyle.*
Lt.-Col., T. Y. L. Kirkwood, c.

DERBYSHIRE REGIMENT.
(The Sherwood Foresters). (1)
District No. 45.—*Derby.*
Col., Lord Chelmsford, g.c.b., g.
Comg. Regtl. Dist., J.G. Sparkes, c.
1st Batt. (45th Foot), *Malta.*
Lt.-Col., H. L. Smith-Dorrien, d.s.o., c.
Adjt., F. Casswell, lt.
2nd Batt. (95th Foot), *Malta.*
Lt.-Col., A. D. Bulpett.
Adjt., T. H. M. Green, capt.
3rd Batt. (Militia), *Derby.*
Lt.-Col., J. H. Moore, c.
4th Batt. (Militia), *Newark.*
Lt.-Col., J W. Keyworth, c.
1st Vol. Batt., *Derby.*
Lt.-Col., G. Gascoyne, v.d., c. (comdg.) ;
2nd Vol. Batt., *Chesterfield.*
Lt.-Col. E. Hall, v.d., c.
1st Notts (Robin Hood) Volrs. *Nottingham.*
Lt.-Cols., A. C. Cantrell-Hubbersty, c. (comdg.); J. Wright, v.d., c.
4th Vol. Batt. (Notts), *Newark.*
Lt.-Col., E. H. Nicholson, v.d., c.

DEVONSHIRE REGIMENT. (1)
District No. 11.—*Exeter.*
Colonel, Sir Edward Newdigate-Newdegate, k.c.b., l.g.
Comg. Regtl. Dist., D. T. Kinder, c.
1st Batt. (11th Foot), *Natal.*
Lt.-Col., J. H. Yule, c.
Adjt., H. S. L. Ravenshaw, capt.
2nd Batt. (11th Foot), *S. Africa.*
Lt.-Col., G. M. Bullock.
Adjt., L. J. Bols, capt.
3rd Batt. (Militia), *Plymouth.*
Lt.-Col., F. H. Mountsteven, c.

4th Batt. (Militia), *Exeter.*
Lt.-Col., Hon. J. S. Trefusis, *c.*

1st (Exeter and S. Devon) Vol. Batt., *Exet·r.*
Lt.-Col. Sir D. G. A. Duckworth-King, Bart., *c.*

2nd (Prince of Wales's) Vol. Batt., *Plymouth.*
Lt.-Col., P. S. Snell.

3rd Vol. Batt., *Exeter.*
Lt.-Col., Rt. Hon. Sir J. H. Kennaway, Bart., V.D., *c.*

4th Vol. Batt., *Barnstaple.*
Lt.-Col., E. S. Walcott, C.B., *c.*

5th (The Hay Tor) Vol. Batt., *Newton Abbot.*
Lt.-Col. Lord Clifford, V.D., *c.*

DORSETSHIRE REGIMENT. (1)
District No. 39.—*Dorchester.*
Colonel, Henry Ralph Browne, *g.*
Comg. Regtl. District, C. P. Egerton, *c.*

1st Batt. (39th Foot), *Nowshera, Punjab Command.*
Lt.-Col., H. J. J. Kentish.
Adjt., R. T. Roper, *it.*

2nd Batt. (54th), *S. Africa.*
Lt.-Col., C. H. Law.
Adjt., R. H. K. Butler, *lt.*

3rd Batt. (Militia), *Dorchester.*
Lt.-Col., J. H. Austen, *c.*

1st Vol. Batt., *Dorchester.*
Lt.-Col., R. Williams, V.D., *c.*

DUBLIN FUSILIERS (ROY.). (4)
District No. 102.—*Naas.*
Col., Sir John B. Spurgin, K.C.B., *l.g.*
Comg. Regtl. Dist., A. M. Paterson, *c.*

1st Batt. (102nd Foot), *S. Africa.*
Lt.-Col., G A. Mills.
Adjt., P. Maclear, *lt.*

2nd Batt. (103rd Foot), *Natal.*
Lt.-Col., C. D. Cooper, *c.*
Adjt., M. Lowndes, *capt.*

3rd Batt. (Kildare Mil.), *Naas.*
Lt.-Col., F. J. Tynte, C.B., *c.*

4th (City Militia), *Dublin.*
Lt.-Col., R. J. Morrison, *c.*

5th (County Militia), *Dublin.*
Lt.-Col., H. C. Gernon, *c.*

DUKE OF CORNWALL'S LIGHT INFANTRY. (1)
District No. 32.—*Bodmin.*
Colonel, John Thomas Hill, *g.*
Comg. Regtl. Dist., C. E. Knox, *c.*

1st Batt. (32nd Foot), *Lucknow.*
Lt.-Col., C. F. A. Turnbull, *c.*
Adjt., L. P. H. Bliss, *capt.*

2nd Batt. (46th Foot), *S. Africa.*
Lt.-Col., W. Aldworth, D.S.O.
Adjt., E P. Wardlaw, *capt.*

3rd Batt. (Militia), *Bodmin.*
Lt.-Col., T. E. J. Lloyd, D.L., *c.*

1st Vol. Batt., *Falmouth.*
Lt.-Col., W. E. Rosewarne, V.D., *c*

2nd Vol. Batt., *Bodmin.*
Lt.-Col., B. Childs, V.D., *c.*

DURHAM LIGHT INF.
District No. 68.—*Newcastle.*
Col., Sir Reginald Gipps, K.C.B., *g.*
Comg. Regtl. Dist., A. A. Garstin, *c.*

1st Batt. (68th Foot), *S. Africa.*
Lt.-Col., A. L. Woodland.
Adjt., B. McMahon, *capt.*

2nd Batt. (106th), *Mandalay.*
Lt.-Col., A. de B. V. Paget.
Adjt., C. C. Luard, *capt.*

3rd Batt. (Militia), *Barnard Castle.*
Lt.-Col., R. B. Wilson, *c.*

4th Batt. (Militia), *Newcastle.*
Lt.-Col., M. H. Lambert, *c.*

1st Vol. Batt., *Stockton-on-Tees.*
Lt.-Col., R. Burdon, V.D., *c.*

2nd Vol. Batt., *Bishop Auckland.*
Lt.-Col., D. Armstrong, V.D., *c.*

3rd (Sunderland) Vol. Batt., *Sunderland.*
Lt.-Col., A. Peters.

4th Vol. Batt., *Durham.*
Lt.-Col., C. Perkins, V.D., *c.*

5th Vol. Batt., *Gateshead.*
Lt.-Col., W. B. Proctor, V.D., *c.*

ESSEX REGIMENT. (1)
District No. 44.—*Warley.*
Colonel, The Hon. John Jocelyn Bourke, *l.g.*
Comg. Regtl. District, E. H. G. Ravenhill, *c.*

1st Batt. (44th Foot), *Warley.*
Lt.-Col., T. E. Stephenson, *c.*
Adjt., F. C. Winter, *lt.*

2nd Batt. (56th), *Shwebo, Burma.*
Lt.-Col., T. Stock.
Adjt., C. G. Lewes, *lt.*

3rd Batt. (Militia), *Warley.*
Lt.-Col., A. T. D. Neave.

4th Batt. (Militia), *Warley.*
Lt.-Col., F. S. Walker, *c.*

1st Vol. Batt., *Brentwood.*
Lt.-Col., F. Landon, V.D., *c.*

2nd Vol. Batt., *Colchester.*
Lt.-Col., W. Howard, V.D., *c.*

3rd Vol. Batt., *West Ham.*
Lt.-Col., H. Palmer.

4th Vol. Batt., *Silvertown.*
Lt.-Col., J. W. Beningfield.

GLOUCESTERSHIRE REGT. (1)
District No. 28.—*Bristol.*
Colonel, John Patrick Redmond, C.B., *l.g.*
Comg. Regtl. Dist., F. J. Curtin, *c.*

1st Batt. (28th Foot), *Natal.*
Lt.-Col.—
Adjt., W. L. B. Hill, *lt.*

2nd Batt. (61st Foot), *Aldershot.*
Lt.-Col., R. F. Lindsell.
Adjt., E. D'A. Le Mottée, *lt.*

3rd Batt. (Militia), *Bristol.*
Lt.-Col., W. A. Hill, *c.*

4th Batt. (Militia), *Cirencester.*
Lt.-Col., Earl Bathurst.

1st Vol. Batt. (City of Bristol).
Lt.-Col., C. L. Methuen, *c.*

2nd Vol. Batt., *Gloucester.*
Lt.-Col., M. Holland, V.D., *c.*

GORDON HIGHLANDERS. (2)
District No. 75.—*Aberdeen.*
Col.-in-Chief, H.R.H. Prince of Wales, K.G., *f.m.*
Col., Sir George Stewart White, V.C., G.C.B.
Comg. Regtl. Dist., H. H. Mathias, C.B., *c.*

1st Batt. (75th Foot), *S. Africa.*
Lt.-Col., G. T. F. Downman.
Adjt., W. E. Gordon, *capt.*

2nd Batt. (92nd Foot), *Natal.*
Lt.-Col., W. H. Dick-Cunyngham, V.C.
Adjt., E. Streatfeild, *capt.*

3rd (Aberdeensh. Mil.), *Aberdeen.*
Lt.-Cols., J. A. Man-Stuart C.M.G., *c.*; Earl of Kintore, G.C.M.G., *c.*

1st Vol. Batt., *Aberdeen.*
Lt.-Col., D. Duncan, V.D., *c.*

2nd Vol. Batt., *Old Meldrum.*
Lt.-Col., J. Rae, V.D., *c.*

3rd (Buchan) Vol. Batt., *Peterhead.*
Lt.-Col., A. D. Fordyce, V.D., *c.*

4th (Donside Highland) Vol. Batt., *Aberdeen.*
Lt.-Col., G. Jackson, V.D., *c.*

5th (Deeside Highland) Vol. Batt., *Banchory.*
Lt.-Col., J. Johnston, V.D., *c.*

6th Vol. Batt. (1st Banff), *Keith.*
Lt.-Col., G. S. Grant, V.D., *c.*

HAMPSHIRE REGIMENT. (1)
District No. 37.—*Winchester.*
Col., John W. Thomas, C.B., *l.g.*
Comg. Regtl. Dist., W. H. Moberly, *c.*

1st Batt. (37th), *Cherat, Punjab Command.*
Lt.-Col., J. R. Parkinson.
Adjt., B. H. Boucher, *capt.*

2nd Batt. (67th Foot), *Cork.*
Lt.-Col., W. E. Briggs.
Adjt., M. de Montmorency, *capt.*

3rd Batt. (Militia), *Winchester.*
Lt.-Col., Earl of Selborne, *c.*

1st Vol. Batt., *Winchester.*
Lt.-Cols., T. S. Cave, V.D., *c.* (comdg.); R. H. Simonds.

2nd Vol. Batt., *Southampton.*
Lt.-Col., E. K. Perkins, V.D., *c.*

3rd Vol. Batt. (Duke of Connaught's Own), *Portsmouth.*
Lt.-Cols., A. R. Holbrook, V.D., *c.* (comdg.); G. E. Kent, jun., V.D., *c.*

4th Vol. Batt., *Bournemouth*
Lt.-Col., J. O. Vandeleur, C.B., V.D., *c.*

5th Vol. Batt. (Isle of Wight, Princess Beatrice's), *Newport, I.W.*
Lt.-Col., E. W. Cradock, *c.*

HIGHLAND LIGHT INF. (4)
District No. 71.—*Hamilton, N.B.*
Col., W. D. P. Patton-Bethune, *g.*
Comg. Regtl. Dist., H. de C. Rawlins, *c.*

1st Batt. (71st Foot), *S. Africa.*
Lt.-Col., F. M. Reid, *c.*
Adjt., J. W. A. Cowan, D.S.O., *capt.*

2nd Batt. (74th Foot), *Ceylon.*
Lt.-Col., R. D. B. Rutherford.
Adjt., F. M. Sandys-Lumsdaine, *capt.*

3rd and 4th Batts. (Lanark Mil.), *Hamilton, N.B.*
Lt.-Cols., J. W. Thackeray, *c.* (4) comdt.; W. F. Story, *c.* (3).

1st Vol. Batt., *Glasgow.*
Lt.-Col., R. C. Mackenzie, V.D., *c.*, comdt.; J. Outram, V.D., *c.*

2nd Vol. Batt., *Overnewtown.*
Lt.-Col., J. D. Young, V.D., *c.*

3rd (Blythswood) Vol. Batt., *Glasgow.*
Lt.-Cols., W. Clark, V.D., *c.* (comdt.); R. S. Murray, V.D., *c.*

9th Lanarkshire Volrs., *Lanark.*
Lt.-Col., J. Stevenson, A.D.C., V.D., *c.*

h (Glasgow Highland) Vol. Batt. (10th Lanarksh.), *Glasgow.*
Lt.-Col., C. M. Williamson, V.D., *c.* (comdt.); J. Menzies, V.D., *c.*

INNISKILLING FUSILIERS (The Royal). (1)
District No. 27.—*Omagh, Irela.*
Colonel, William Roberts, *l.g.*
Comg. Regtl. Dist., M. Churchill, *c.*

1st Batt. (27th Foot), *S. Africa.*
Lt.-Col., T. M. G. Thackeray.
Adjt., E. J. Buckley, *capt.*

2nd Batt. (108th Foot), *Dalhousie, Punjab Command.*
Lt.-Col., R. M. Greenfield.
Adjt., T. E. Clarke, *capt.*

3rd Batt. (Fermanagh Militia), *Enniskillen.*
Lt.-Col., H. H. Stewart.

4th Batt. (Tyrone Mil.), *Omagh.*
Lt.-Col., C. M. Alexander, *c.*

5th Batt. (Donegal Mil.), *Ballyshannon.*
Lt.-Col., B. J. Barton, *c.*

IRISH FUSILIERS (ROYAL). (Princess Victoria's). (1)
District No. 87.—*Armagh.*
Col., T. R. Stevenson, C.B., *m.g.*
Comg. Regtl. Dist., W. Wood, *c.*

1st Batt. (87th Foot), *S. Africa.*
Lt.-Col., F. R. C. Carleton.
Adjt., F. H. B. Connor, *capt.*

2nd Batt. (89th Foot), *S. Africa.*
Lt.-Col., J. Reeves.
Adjt., C. Dick, *lt.*

3rd Batt. (Militia), *Armagh.*
Lt.-Col., J. R. Jameson, *c.*

4th Batt. (Militia), *Cavan.*
Lt.-Col., Sir R. A. Hodson, Bart., *c.*

5th Batt. (Militia), *Monaghan.*
Lt.-Col., J. Leslie, *c.*

IRISH REGIMENT (ROY.). (1)
District No. 18.—*Clonmel.*
Col.-in-Chief, Viscount Wolseley, K.P., G.C.B., P.M. (Comr.-in-Chief.
Col., C. F. Gregorie, C.B., *m.g.*
Comg. Regtl. Dist., J. H. A. Spyer, *c.*

1st Batt. (18th Foot), *Buttevant, Ireland.*
Lt.-Col., H. W. N. Guinness.
Adjt., H. J. Downing, *capt.*

2nd Batt. (18th Foot), *Mhow, Bombay Command.*
Lt.-Col., J. B. Forster.
Adjt., H. N. Kelly, *capt.*

3rd Batt. (Militia), *Wexford.*
Lt.-Col., M. G. Lloyd, C.B., *c.*

4th (N. Tipperary Mil.), *Clonmel.*
Lt.-Col., F. Trant, *c.*

5th Batt. (Militia), *Kilkenny.*
Lt.-Col., R. C. Knox, *c.*

IRISH RIFLES (The Royal). (1)
District No. 83.—*Belfast.*
Col., Wilmot Hen. Bradford, *g.*
Comg. Regtl. Dist., F. J. Graves, *c.*

1st Batt. (83rd Foot), *Dum Dum, Bengal.*
Lt.-Col., C. Haggard.
Adjt., O. C. Baker, *lt.*

2nd Batt. (86th Foot), *S. Africa.*
Lt.-Col., H. A. Eagar.
Adjt., D. Wilmot-Sitwell, *lt.*

3rd Batt. (N. Down Militia), *Newtownards.*
Lt.-Col., R. G. Sharman-Crawford, *c.*

4th Batt. (Antrim Mil.), *Belfast.*
Lt.-Col., H. D. A. Cutbill, *c.*

5th (S. Down Mil.), *Downpatrick.*
Lt.-Col., R. H. Wallace.

6th Batt. (Louth Mil.), *Dundalk.*
Lt.-Col., H. W. Jameson, *c.*

KENT (EAST) REGIMENT (The Buffs). (1)
District No. 3.—*Canterbury.*
Colonel, Sir Julius Augustus Robert Raines, K.C.B., *g.*
Comg. Regtl. Dist., W. E. R. Kelly, *c.*

1st Batt. (3rd Foot), *Kamptee, Bombay Command.*
Lt.-Col., A. E. Ommanney, *c.*
Adjt., R. F. Pearson, *capt.*

2nd Batt. (3rd Foot), *Brighton.*
Lt.-Col., R. A. Hickson, *c.*
Adjt., A. D. Geddes, *capt.*

3rd Batt. (Militia), *Canterbury.*
Lt.-Col., T. F. Brinckman.

1st Vol. Batt. *Canterbury.*
Lt.-Col., E. W. Knocker, C.B., V.D., *c.*

2nd (Weald of Kent) Vol. Batt. *Cranbrook, nea Staplehurst.*
Lt.-Col., E. W. Hussey, V.D., *c.*

KENT (WEST) REGT. (ROYAL) (The Queen's Own). (1)
District No. 50.—*Maidstone.*
Colonel, Fowler Burton, C.B., *g.*
Comg. Regtl. Dist., T. H. Brock, *c.*

1st Batt. (50th Foot), *Aden.*
Lt.-Col., C. W. H. Evans, D.S.O.
Adjt., C. G. Pack-Beresford, *lt.*

2nd Batt. (97th Foot), *Egypt.*
Lt.-Col., E. A. W. S. Grove.
Adjt., M. P. Buckle, *capt.*

3rd Batt. (Militia), *Maidstone.*
Lt.-Col., J. Bonhote, *c.*

1st Vol. Batt., *Tunbridge.*
Lt.-Col, G. Henderson, *c.*

2nd Vol. Batt., *Blackheath.*
Lt.-Cols., E. Satterthwaite, V.D., *c.* (comdg.); F. W. Frigout, V.D., *c.*

3rd Vol. Batt.. *Woolwich Arsenal.*
Lt.-Col., W. Hunt, V.D., *c.*

KING'S OWN SCOTTISH BORDERERS. (1)
Dist. No. 25.—*Berwick-on-Tweed.*
Col., W. Craig Emilius Napier, *g.*
Comg. Regtl. Dist., H. G. Dixon, C.B., A.D.C., *c.*

1st Batt. (25th Foot), *Dublin.*
Lt.-Col., J. W. Godfray.
Adjt., H. G. M. Amos, *lt.*

2nd Batt. (25th Foot), *Cawnpore. Bengal Command.*
Lt.-Col., G. T. W. Hewat.
Adjt., A. E. Haig, *m.*

3rd Batt. (Militia), *Dumfries.*
Lt.-Col., K. M. Witham.

1st Vol. Batt. (Roxburgh and Selkirk, the Border), *Newtown St. Boswells.*
Lt.-Col., Sir R. J. Waldie-Griffith, Bt.

2nd V.B. (Berwickshire), *Duns.*
Lt.-Col., C. Hope, *c.*

3rd Vol. Batt., *Dumfries.*
Lt.-Col., R. F. Dudgeon, *c.*

4th V.B. (Galloway), *Castle Douglas.*
Lt.-Col., J. M. Kennedy, V.D., *c.*

KING'S ROY. RIFLE CORPS. (1)
Rifle Depôt.—*Gosport (tempy.).*
Colonel-in-Chief, H.R.H. the Duke of Cambridge, K.G., *f.m.*
Colonels — Commandant, Rt. Hon. Sir Redvers Henry Buller, VC, G.C.B., *g.*; Sir Francis Grenfell, G.C.B., *g.*
Comg. Rifle Depôt, H. R. Mends, *c.*

1st Batt. (60th Foot), *Natal.*
Lt.-Col., H. Gore-Browne.
Adjt., H. R. Blore, *capt.*

2nd Batt. (60th Foot), *Natal.*
Lt.-Col., G. G. Grimwood, *c.*
Adjt., H. C. R. Green, *lt.*

3rd Batt. (60th Foot), *S. Africa.*
Lt.-Col., R. G. Buchanan-Riddell.
Adjt., C. W. Wilson, *capt.*

4th Batt. (60th Foot), *Cork.*
Lt.-Col., E. W. Herbert.
Adjt., W. H. L. Allgood, *capt.*

5th Batt. (Militia), *Huntingdon.*
Lt.-Col., Earl of Sandwich, *c.*

7th Batt. (Middlesex Militia), *Barnet.*
Lt.-Col., G. Astell, *c.*

8th Batt. (Militia), *Carlow.*
Lt.-Col., G. W. L'Estrange, c.
Adjt., St. John D. T. Loftus, capt.

9th Batt. (N. Cork Mil.), *Mallow.*
Lt.-Col., W. Cooke-Collis, c.

1st Middx. Volrs. (Victoria and St. George's), *Davies St., Berkeley Square.*
Lt.-Col., C. Bird, v.d., c.

2nd (S. Middx.) Volrs., *Beaufort House, Walham Green.*
Lt.-Col., H. W. Gray, v.d., c., (comdt.), C. B. Dimond, v.d., c.

4th (W. London) V.B., *Kensington.*
Lt.-Col., A. S. Daniell.

5th V.B. (West Middlesex), *Park Road, Regent's Park, N.W.*
Lt.-Col., H. Harris, v.d.

12th (Civil Service) V.B., Pr. of Wales's Own, *Somerset House.*
Lt.- :l., Earl of Albemarle, c.

13th (Queen's Westminster) V.B., *James St., Buckingham Gate.*
Lt.-Cols., Sir C. E. Howard Vincent, c.b., m.p., c. (comdt.), G. H. Trollope, v.d., c.

21st (Finsbury Rifle Vol. Corps), *Penton Street, Pentonville.*
Lt.-Col., H. Byrne, v.d., c.

22nd (Central London Rangers), *South Square, Gray's Inn.*
Lt.-Col., W. J. Alt., v.d., c.

25th (Bank of Eng.), *Somerset House*—attached to 12th Middx. Vol. Rifle Corps.

1st (City of London) R.V.B., *Bunhill Row, E.C.*
Lt.-Cols., H. C. Cholmondeley, c. (comdt.) : E. Matthey, v.d., c.

2nd (City of Lond.) R.V.B., *Farringdon Road, E.C.*
Lt.-Col., R. G. Grene, v.d., c.

3rd (City of Lond.) R.V.B., *Farringdon Street, E.C.*
Lt.-Cols., M. Hancock, v.d., c. (comdg.); E.C. Stevenson, v.d., c.

LANCASHIRE FUSILIERS. (1)
District No. 20.—*Bury, Lancs.*
Colonel, Sir Edward Alan Holdich, k.c.b., g.
Comg. Regtl. Dist., J. L. Ross, c.

1st Batt. (20th Foot), *Crete.*
Lt.-Col., G. L. E. May.
Adjt., A. R. Lempriere, capt.

2nd Batt. (20th Foot), *S. Africa.*
Lt.-Col., C. J. Blomfield, d.s.o.
Adjt., R. B. Blunt, lt.

3rd Batt. (raised in 1898), *Malta.*
Lt.-Col., R. G. Bruxner-Randall.
Adjt., J. F. V. Thorne, lt.

4th Batt.—(*not yet formed*).
5th and 6th Batts. (Militia), *Bury, Lancs.*
Lt.-Cols., F. F. Mackenzie (5) comdt.; F. C. Romer (6).

1st Vol. Batt., *Bury.*
Lt.-Col., T. P. Young, c.

2nd Vol. Batt., *Rochdale.*
Lt.-Col., T. R. Philippi, v.d., c.

3rd Vol. Batt. (17th Lanc.), *Salford.*
Lt.-Col., F. Haworth, v.d., c.

LANCASHIRE (EAST REG. (1)
District No. 30.—*Burnley.*
Col., Thos. Hen. Pakenham, l.g.
Comg. Regtl. Dist., M. S. Brown-rigg, c.

1st Batt. (30th Foot), *Jersey.*
Lt.-Col., A. J. A. Wright.
Adjt., L. St. G. Le Marchant, capt.

2nd Batt. (59th Foot), *Rhaniket. Bengal Command.*
Lt.-Col., A. G. Watson.
Adjt., A. C. M. Alington, lt.

3rd Batt. (Militia), *Burnley.*
Lt.-Col., J. E. Butler-Bowdon, c.

1st Vol. Batt., *Blackburn.*
Lt.-Col., H. J. Robinson, v.d., c.

2nd Vol. Batt., *Burnley.*
Lt.-Cols., T. Mitchell, v.d. c. (comdt.); J. H. Hardman.

LANCASHIRE REGIMENT (Loyal North). (1)
District No. 47.—*Preston.*
Cmg. Regtl. Dist., M. S. Brown-rigg, c.

1st Batt. (47th Foot), *Cape.*
Col., Sir Richd. T. Farren, k.c.b., g.
Lt.-Col., R G. Kekewich.
Adjt., J. G. Lowndes, lt.

2nd Batt. (81st Foot), *Malta.*
Colonel, Henry Renny, c.s.i., g.
Lt.-Col., B. A. Satterthwaite.
Adjt., W. R. Lloyd, capt.

3rd Batt. (Militia), *Preston.*
Lt.-Col., L. Bonhôte, c.

1st Vol. Batt., *Preston.*
Lt.-Col., P. Widdows, v.d., c.

2nd Vol. Batt., *Bolton.*
Lt.-Col., G. Hesketh, v.d., c.

LANCASHIRE (S.) REGT.— Pr. of Wales's Volunteers. (1)
District No. 40.—*Warrington.*
Col., A. H. L. Fox-Pitt-Rivers, l.g.
Comg. Regtl. Dist., E. J. H. Spratt, c.

1st Batt. (40th Foot), *S. Africa.*
Lt.-Col., W. McCarthy-O'Leary.
Adjt., A. H. Bailey, lt.

2nd Batt. (82nd Foot), *Jubbulpore. Bengal Command.*
Lt.-Col., A. F. G. Richardson.
Adjt., F. A. Dudgeon, capt.

3rd Batt. (Militia), *Warrington.*
Lt.-Col., R. I. Blackburne.

1st Vol. Batt., *Warrington.*
Lt.-Col., J. C. Ridgway.

2nd Vol. Batt., *St. Helens.*
Lt.-Col., W. W. Pilkington, v.d., c.

LANCASTER REGT. (ROY.) The King's Own. (1)
District No. 4.—*Lancaster.*
Colonel, Sir William Gordon Cameron, k.c.b., g.
Comg. Regtl. Dist., E. H. Fitz-herbert.

1st Batt. (4th Foot), *Singapore.*
Lt.-Col., J. Rowlandson.
Adjt., J. H. Lloyd, lt.

2nd Batt. (4th Foot), *S. Africa.*
Lt.-Col., M. E. Crofton.
Adjt., A. McN. Dykes, lt.

3rd and 4th Battalions (Militia), *Lancaster.*
Lt.-Cols., J. L. Whalley, c. (4) comdt.; B. N. North (3).

1st Vol. Batt., *Ulverston.*
Lt.-Col., A. H. Strongitharm, v.d., c.

LEICESTERSHIRE REGT. (1)
District No. 17.—*Leicester.*
Colonel, Sir John Ross, g.c.b., g.
Comg. Regtl. Dist., E. R. P. Wood-gate, c.b., c.m.g., c.

1st Batt. (17th Foot), *Natal.*
Lt.-Col., G. D. Carleton.
Adjt., H. M. Welstead, capt.

2nd Batt. (17th Foot), *Curragh.*
Lt.-Col., A. W. McKinstry.
Adjt., A. H. Wilkinson, capt.

3rd Batt. (Militia), *Leicester.*
Lt.-Col., Lord Braye.

1st Vol. Batt., *Leicester.*
Lt.-Cols., J. E. Sarson (comdg.) ; L. L. Powell, v.d., c.

LEINSTER REGIMENT (Roy. Canadians)—Pr. of Wales's. (1)
District No. 100.—*Birr.*
Col., Alastair McI. Macdonald, l.g.
Comg. Regtl. Dist., G. W. N. Rogers, c.

1st Batt. (100th Foot), *Halifax, Nova Scotia.*
Lt.-Col., H. Martin.
Adjt., F. R. Dugan, lt.

2nd Batt. (109th Foot), *Barbados.*
Lt.-Col., J. G. Glancy, c.
Adjt., F. E. Whitton, lt.

3rd Batt. (King's Co. Mil.), *Birr.*
Lt.-Col., J. H. G. Smyth, c.

4th Batt. (Queen's County Mil.), *Maryborough.*
Lt.-Col., Lord Castletown.

5th Batt. (Meath Mil.), *Navan.*
Lt.-Col., C. Pepper, c.

LINCOLNSHIRE REGT. (1)
District No. 10.—*Lincoln.*
Col., Sir Julius R. Glyn, k.c.b., g.
Comg. Regtl. Dist., T. E. Verner, c.b., c.

1st Batt. (10th Foot), *Secunderabad, Madras Command.*
Lt.-Col., F R. Lowth, c.b.
Adjt., J. R. M. Marsh, m.

2nd Batt. (10th Foot), *Aldershot.*
Lt.-Col., H. R. Roberts.
Adjt., F. W. Stringer, *lt.*
3rd Batt. (Militia), *Lincoln.*
Lt.-Col., E. W. Willson, *c.*
4th Batt. (Militia), *Grantham.*
Lt.-Col., Lord Wm. Cecil, M.V.O.,*c.*
1st Vol. Batt., *Lincoln.*
Lt.-Col., J. G. Williams, V.D., *c.*
2nd Vol. Batt., *Grantham.*
Lt.-Col., J. Hutchinson, V.D., *c.*

LIVERPOOL REGIMENT (The   (1)
     King's).
    District No. 8.—*Warrington.*
Col., Robert S. Baynes, *l.g.*
Comg. Regtl. Dist., E. J. H. Spratt, *c.*
1st Batt. (8th Foot), *Natal.*
Lt.-Col., L. S. Mellor.
Adjt., L. M. Jones, *lt.*
2nd Batt. (8th), *Enniskillen.*
Lt.-Col., S. H. Harrison.
Adjt., C. H. Harington, *lt.*
3rd and 4th Battalions (Lanc. Mil.), *Warrington.*
Lt.-Cols., C. C. Woodward, *c.* (4) comdt.; J. M. Batten, *c.*
1st Vol. Batt., *St. Anne St., Liverpool.*
Lt.-Cols., C. F. Smith, V.D., *c.*, comdt.; C. Alder, V.D., *c.*
2nd Vol. Batt., *Prince's Park, Liverpool.*
Lt.-Col., C. Spencely, V.D., *c.*
3rd Vol. Batt. (13th Lanc.), *Southport.*
Lt.-Col., W. Macfie, C.B., V.D., *c.*
4th V.B., *Shaw St., Liverpool.*
Lt.-Col., J. W. De Silva, V.D., *c.*
5th (Irish) V.B., *Everton Brow, Liverpool.*
Lt.-Col., R. Carruthers.
6th Vol. Batt., *Everton Road, Liverpool.*
Lt.-Col., A. L. Watts, V.D., *c.*
7th (Isle of Man) Vol. Batt., *Douglas* (attached to 6th Vol. Batt.).

LOTHIAN REGIMENT (The   (1)
     Royal Scots).
    District No. 1.—*Glencorse, N.B.*
Col., Edward Andrew Stuart, *m.g.*
Comg. Regtl. Dist., W. Gordon, *c.*
1st Batt. (1st Foot), *S. Africa.*
Lt.-Col., E. P. Morgan-Payler.
Adjt., A. J. G. Moir, *lt.*
2nd Batt. (1st Foot), *Poona, Bombay Command.*
Lt.-Col., T. F. Ross, *c.*
Adjt., F. J. Duncan, *capt.*
3rd Batt. (Edinburgh Light Inf. Militia), *Glencorse, N.B.*
Lt.-Col., E. J. Grant, *c.*
Queen's Rifle V. Brig., *Edinburgh.*
Lt.-Cols., H. R. Macrae, V.D., *c.*, comdt.; R. Cranston, V.D., *c.*, L. Bilton, V.D., *c.*; G. W. Young, V.D., *c.*

4th Vol. Batt., *Edinburgh.*
Lt.-Col., W. U. Martin, V.D., *c.*
5th Vol. Batt. (1st Midlothian), *Leith.*
Lt.-Col., J. R. Bertram, V.D., *c.*
6th Vol. Batt., *Penicuik.*
Lt.-Col., R. G. Wardlaw-Ramsay, *c.*
7th Vol. Batt., *Haddington.*
Lt.-Col., J. D. Watson, V.D., *c.*
8th Vol. Batt., *Linlithgow.*
Lt.-Col., T. Hope, *c.*

MANCHESTER REGT.   (1)
   Dist. No. 63.—*Ashton-under-Lyne.*
Col., Sir H. R. Norman, K.C.B., *l.g.*
Comg. Regtl. Dist., R. C. Hare, *c.*
1st Batt. (63rd Foot), *Natal.*
Lt.-Col., A. E. R. Curran.
Adjt., W. P. E. Newbigging, *capt.*
2nd Batt. (96th). *Manchester.*
Lt.-Col., C. P. Ridley, *c.*
Adjt., E. Vaughan, *capt.*
3rd and 4th Batts. (Lancashire Militia). *Ashton-under-Lyne.*
Lt.-Cols., C. D. Leyden (4), comdt.; J. B. Irving (3).
1st V.B., *Patricroft, Manchester.*
Lt.-Cols., Earl of Crawford, K.T., V.D., *c.* comdt.; J. Higson, V.D., *c.*
2nd V.B., *Hulme, Manchester.*
Lt.-Cols., R. Bridgford, C.B., V.D., *c.*, comdt.; W. W. Clapham, V.D., *c.*
3rd V.B., *Ashton-under-Lyne.*
Lt.-Col., J. Eaton, V.D., *c.*
4th V.B., *Manchester.*
Lt.-Cols., W. A. Lynde, V.D., *c.*, comdt.; E. R. Walker, V.D., *c.*
5th (Ardwick) V.B., *Manchester.*
Lt.-Cols., J. B. Lloyd, V.D., *c.* comdt.; H. Moore.
6th V.B., *Oldham.*
Lt.-Col., J. C. Lees, V.D., *c.*

MIDDLESEX REGIMENT
   (Duke of Cambridge's Own). (1)
    District No. 57.—*Hounslow.*
Col.-in-Ch., H.R.H. the Duke of Cambridge, K.G , F.M.
Comg. Regtl. Dist., G. F. Guyon, *c.*
1st Batt. (57th Foot), *Wellington, Madras Command.*
Lt.-Col., J. G. White.
Adjt., H. W. E. Finch, *lt.*
2nd Batt. (77th Foot), *S. Africa.*
Lt.-Col., A. W. Hill.
Adjt., H. F. Mac Ewan, *lt.*
3rd Batt. (Militia), *Hounslow.*
Lt.-Col., V. Rolleston.
4th Batt. (Militia), *Hounslow.*
Lt.-Col., G. C. Helme, C.B., *c.*
1st Vol. Batt., *Hornsey.*
Lt.-Col., R. Hennell, D.S.O., *c.*
2nd Vol. Batt., *Whitton Park, Hounslow.*
Lt.-Col., H. Bott.

17th Middx. Volrs. (N. Middx.), *High Street, Camden Town.*
Lt.-Col., C. St. J. K. Roche, *c.*

MUNSTER FUSIL. (ROYAL). (2)
    District No. 101.—*Tralee.*
Col., William Rickman, *l.g.*
Comg. Regtl. Dist., D. G. Johnston, *c.*
1st Batt. (101st Foot), *Cape.*
Lt.-Col., E. S. Evans.
Adjt., G. D. Crocker, *capt.*
2nd Batt. (104th Foot), *Dinapore, Bengal Command.*
Lt.-Col., P. S. Druitt.
Adjt., E. P. Thomson, *lt.*
3rd Batt. (S. Cork Mil.), *Kinsale.*
Lt.-Col., F. W. Bell, *c.*
4th Batt. (Kerry Mil.), *Tralee.*
Lt.-Col., Viscount Castlerosse.
5th (County Militia), *Limerick.*
Lt.-Col., J. Massy-Westropp.

NORFOLK REGIMENT.   (2)
    District No. 9.—*Norwich.*
Col., Hny. J. Buchanan, C.B., *l.g.*
Comg. Regtl. Dist., C. H. Shepherd, D.S.O., *c.*
1st Batt. (9th Foot), *Bombay.*
Lt.-Col., J. L. Gowan.
Adjt., W. F. L. Gordon, *lt.*
2nd Batt. (9th Foot), *Fermoy.*
Lt.-Col., L. H. Phillips.
Adjt., F. de B. Bell, *lt.*
3rd Batt. (Militia), *Norwich.*
Lt.-Col., F. H. Custance, *c.*
4th Batt. (Militia), *Norwich.*
Lt.-Col., Sir Chas. Harvey, Bt., *c.*
1st Vol. Batt., *Norwich.*
Lt.-Col., S. G. Hill.
2nd Vol. Batt., *Gt. Yarmouth.*
Lt.-Col., H. J. Harteup, V.D., *c.*
3rd Vol. Batt., *East Dereham.*
Lt.-Col., H. E. Hyde, V.D., *c.*
4th Vol. Batt., *Norwich.*
Lt.-Col., H. T. S. Patteson, V.D., *c.*

NORTHAMPTONSH. REGT. (1)
    District No. 48.—*Northampton.*
Col., Robt. C. Whitehead, C.B., *m.g.*
Comg. Regtl. Dist., T. C. O. Powlett, *c.*
1st Batt. (48th Foot), *Fyzabad, Bengal Command.*
Lt.-Col., W. B. Capper.
Adjt., F. J. Parker, *capt.*
2nd Batt. (58th Foot), *S. Africa.*
Lt.-Col., H. C. Denny.
Adjt., J. Little, *capt.*
3rd Batt. (Militia). *Northampton.*
Lt.-Cols., S. G. Stopford-Sackville, *c.* (3); comdt. J. Hill, *c.* (4).
1st Vol. Batt., *Northampton.*
Lt.-Col., Earl of Euston, V.D., *c.*; comdt.

NORTHUMBERLND. FUSIL. (1)
    District No. 5.—*Newcastle.*
Col., Geo. Bryan Milman, C.B., *l.g.*

Comg. Regtl. District, A. A. Garstin, *c.*

1st Batt. (5th Foot), *S. Africa.*
Lt.-Col., C. G. C. Money, *c.*
Adjt., C. E. Fishbourne, *it.*

2nd Batt. (5th Foot), *S. Africa.*
Lt.-Col., R. L. A. Pennington.
Adjt., C. Yatman, *capt.*

3rd Batt. (Militia), *Alnwick.*
Lt.-Col., Lord Algernon Percy, *c.*

1st Vol. Batt., *Hexham.*
Lt.-Col., R. Weddell, v.d., *c.*

2nd Vol. Batt., *Newcastle-on-Tyne.*
Lt.-Col., H. F. Swan, v.d., *c.*

3rd Vol. Batt., *Newcastle-on-Tyne.*
Lt.-Col., E. Downing, v.d., *c.*

OXFORDSH. LIGHT INF. (1)
District No. 43.—*Oxford.*
Col., Fredk. Green Wilkinson, *l.g.*
Comg. Regtl. Dist., J.A.Strachan,*c.*

1st Batt. (43rd Foot), *Devonport.*
Lt.-Col., Hon. A. E. Dalzell.
Adjt., C. H. Cobb, *capt.*

2nd Batt. (52nd Foot), *Ferozepore, Punjab Command.*
Lt.-Col., F. H. Plowden, *c.*
Adjt., R. M. Feilden, *lt.*

3rd (Bucks Mil.), *High Wycombe.*
Lt.-Col., Earl of Orkney.

4th Batt. (Militia), *Oxford.*
Lt.-Col., C. R. Bulkeley, *c.*

1st (Oxford Univ.) V.B., *Oxford.*
Lt.-Col., G. C. Bourne.

2nd Vol. Batt., *Oxford.*
Lt.-Col., H. S. Hall, v.d., *c.*

1st Bucks V.B., *Great Marlow.*
Lt.-Col., Lord Addington, v.d.,*c.*

4th (Eton Coll.) V.B., *Eton.*
Major-Comdt., C. Lowry.

RIFLE BRIGADE (The Prince Consort's Own). (1)
Rifle Dépôt—*Gosport (tempy.).*
Col.-in-Chief, H.R.H. Duke of Connaught,K.G.,G.C.B.,A.D.C.,*g.*
Ocmg. Rifle Dépôt, H. R. Mends,*c.*

1st Battalion, *S. Africa.*
Colonel Commandant, Lord Alexander George Russell, C.B., *g.*
Lt.-Col., C. H. B. Norcott.
Adjt., S. C. Long, *capt.*

2nd Battalion, *S. Africa.*
Colonel Commandant, Frederick Robert Elrington, C.B., *g.*
Lt.-Col., C. T. E. Metcalfe.
Adjt., Hon. H. Dawnay, *lt.*

3rd Batt., *Kuldana.*
Lt.-Col., W. R. Kenyon-Slaney.
Adjt., Hon. G. H. Morris, *capt.*

4th Battalion, *Dublin.*
Lt.-Col., A. R. Pemberton.
Adjt., H. E. Vernon, D.S.O.,*capt.*

5th Batt. (Tower Hamlets Mil.), *Woolwich.*
Lt.-Col., J. W. Lee, *c.*

6th Batt. (Militia), *Mullingar.*
Lt.-Col., J. R. Malone, *c.*

7th Batt. (Tower Hamlets Mil.), *Dalston.*
Lt.-Col., Viscount Hardinge, *c*

7th V.B. (London Scottish), *James Street, Buckingham Gate, S.W.*
Lt.-Col., E. J. A. Balfour.

14th V.B. (Inns of Court), *Lincoln's Inn.*
Lt.-Col., S.H.S.Lofthouse,v.d.,*c*

15th V.B. (Customs and Docks), *Custom House.*
Lt.-Cols., A. W. Chambers, v.d., *c.* (*comdt.*); H. W. Hummel, v.d., *c.*

16th V.B. (London Irish), *Duke St., Charing Cross, W.C.*
Lt.-Cols., H. Roberts, v.d., *c.* (*comdt.*); E. G. K. P. Lloyd, v.d., *c.*

18th V.B., 207, *Harrow Road, W.*
Lt.-Co's., P. H. Dalbiac, *c.,* *comdg.*; A. G. Pawle, *c.*

19th V.B. (Bloomsbury), *Chenies Street, Bedford Sq., W.C.*
Lt.-Col., B. W. Hardcastle.

20th V.B (Artists') *Duke's Road, Euston Road.*
Lt.-Col., R. W. Edis, v.d., *c.*

24th V B (G.P.O.)
Lt.-Cols., S. R. Thompson, v.d., *c.* (*comdt.*); E. M. Hale, v.d.

26th V.B. (Cyclists), *Queen's Rd., Chelsea* (attached to 12th Mid. R. V. Corps).
Maj. Comdt., C. E. Liles.

1st (Tower Hamlets Rifle Vol. Brig.), *City Road.*
Lt.-Cols., E. T. R. Wilde, v.d., *c. comdt.*; H. Coningham, *c.*

2nd (Tower Hamlets), *Tredegar Road, Bow.*
Lt.-Col., W. B. Bryan, v.d., *c.*

ROSS-SHIRE BUFFS—See "Seaforth Highlanders."

ROYAL FUSILIERS—See "City of London Regt."

ROYAL HIGHLANDERS (The Black Watch). (1)
District No. 42.—*Perth, N.B.*
Col., Hon. Robert Rollo, C.B., *g.*
Comg. Regtl. Dist., R. H. L. Brickenden, *c.*

1st Batt. (42nd Foot), *Sitapur, Bengal Command.*
Lt.-Col., E. G. Grogan.
Adjt., J. G. Collins, *lt.*

2nd Batt. (73rd Foot), *S. Africa.*
Lt.-Col., J. H. C. Coode.
Adjt., W. MacFarlan, *capt.*

3rd Batt. (Militia), *Perth.*
Lt.-Col., Hon. Wm. Chas. Wordsworth Rollo (Master of Rollo).

1st Vol. Batt., *City of Dundee.*
Lt.-Col., J. Rankin, v.d., *c.*

2nd (Angus) Vol. Batt., *Arbroath.*
Lt.-Cols., W. A. Gordon, v.d., *c., comdt.*; A. McHardy, v.d., *c.*

3rd (Dundee Highland) Vol. Batt., *Dundee.*
Lt.-Col., W. Smith, v.d., *c.*

4th (Perthsh.) Vol. Batt., *Perth.*
Lt.-Col., Sir R. D. Moncreiffe, Bt.

5th (Perthsh. Highland) Vol. Batt., *Birnam.*
Lt.-Col., Marq. of Breadalbane, K.G., *c.*

6th (Fifeshire) Vol. Batt. (late 1st), *St. Andrews.*
Lt.-Cols., Ff. W. Erskine, *c.* (*comdt.*); J. T. Cathcart.

ROYAL SCOTS, THE
See "Lothian Regiment."

SCOTS FUSILIERS (ROY.). (1)
District No. 21.—*Ayr, N.B.*
Colonel, Sir Fredk. Paul Haines, G.C.B., G.C.S.I., C.I.E., *f.m.*
Comg.Regtl.Dist., E. C. Browne, *c.*

1st Batt. (21st Foot), *Peshawar, Punjab Command.*
Lt.-Col., A. H. Abercrombie.
Adjt., W. D. Smith, *capt.*

2nd Batt. (21st Foot), *S. Africa.*
Lieut.-Col., E. E. Carr.
Adjt., C. P. A Hull, *capt.*

3rd (Ayr and Wigtown Mil.),*Ayr.*
Lt.-Col., W. H. Campbell, *c.*

1st Vol. Batt., *Kilmarnock.*
Lt.-Col., R. M. McKerrell, v.d., *c.*

2nd Vol. Batt., *Ayr.*
Lt.-Col., R.P.Robertson-Glasgow.

SCOTTISH BORDERERS—See "King's Own Scottish Borderers."

SCOTTISH RIFLES—See "Cameronians."

SEAFORTH HIGHLAND'RS,
(Ross-shire Buffs, The Duke of Albany's). (1)
District No. 72.—*Fort George.*
Colonel, Sir Archibald Alison, Bart., G.C.B., *g.*
Comg. Regtl. Dist., R. H. Murray, C.B., C.M.G., A.D.C., *c.*

1st Batt. (72nd Foot), *Egypt.*
Lt.-Col., J. A. Campbell.
Adjt., N. C. Maclachlan.

2nd Batt. (78th Foot), *S. Africa.*
Lt.-Col., J. W. Hughes-Hallett, D.S.O.
Adjt., A. W. M. Brodie, *capt.*

3rd Batt. (Highland Militia), *Dingwall.*
Lt.-Col., Sir H. Munro, Bart.

1st (Ross Highland) Vol. Batt., *Dingwall.*
Lt.-Col., A. R. B. Warrand.

1st Sutherland (Highland) V B., *Golspie.*
Lt.-Col., J. MacKintosh, v.d.

3rd (Morayshire) V.B., *Elgin.*
Lt.-Col., C. J. Johnston, v.d., *c.*

SHERWOOD FORESTERS, THE
—See "Derbyshire Regiment."

SHROPSHIRE LIGHT INF.
(The King's).   (1)
District No. 53.—*Shrewsbury.*
Col., Sir Hen. P. de Bathe, Bt., *g.*
Comg. Regtl. Dist., F. W. Robinson, *c.*

1st Batt. (53rd Foot), *Poona.*
Lt.-Col., C. H. Collette.
Adjt., H. L. Smyth, *lt.*

2nd Batt. (85th Foot), *S. Africa.*
Lt.-Col., J. Spens.
Adjt., C. P. Higginson, *capt.*

3rd Batt. (Militia), *Shrewsbury.*
Lt.-Col., Sir T. Meyrick, Bt., C.B., *c.*

4th Batt. (Militia), *Hereford.*
Lt.-Col., E. S. Lucas, *c.*

1st Vol. Batt., *Shrewsbury.*
Lt.-Col., J. A. Anstice, V.D., *c.*

2nd Vol. Batt., *Newport.*
Lt.-Col., R. T. Masefield, C.B., V.D., *c.*

1st Herefordsh. V.B., *Hereford.*
Lt.-Col., M. J. G. Scobie, V.D.

SOMERSETSHIRE LIGHT INF
(Prince Albert's).   (1)
District No. 13.—*Taunton.*
Col., Lord Mark Kerr, G.C.B., *g.*
Com. Regtl. Dist., R. B. Cotton, *c.*

1st Batt. (13th Foot), *Rawal Findi, Punjab Command.*
Lt.-Col., H. A. Walsh.
Adjt., E. F. Cooke-Hurle, *lt.*

2nd Batt. (13th Foot), *S. Africa.*
Lt.-Col., E. J. Gallwey.
Adjt., E. H. Swayne, *capt.*

3rd Batt. (Militia), *Taunton.*
Lt.-Col., Hon. H. P. Gore-Langton.

4th Batt. (Militia), *Taunton.*
Lt.-Col., W. Long, *c.*

1st Vol. Batt., *Bath.*
Lt.-Col., H. F. Clutterbuck.

2nd Vol. Batt., *Taunton.*
Lt.-Cols., M. L. Blake, V.D., *c.*
(*comdt.*); T. F. Barham, V.D., *c.*

3rd Vol. Batt., *Weston-super-Mare.*
Lt.-Col., V. U. Langworthy, *c.*

STAFFORDSHIRE (N.) REGT.
(The Prince of Wales's).   (1)
District No. 64.—*Lichfield.*
Col., Chas. Algernon Lewis, *g.*
Comg. Regtl. Dist., J. E. H. Prior, *c.*

1st Batt. (64th Foot), *Subathu, Punjab Command.*
Lt.-Col., T. Currie, C.B.
Adjt., R. S. Hutchison, *capt.*

2nd Batt. (98th Foot), *Newry.*
Lt.-Col., C. E. Bradley.
Adjt., V. W. de Falbe, *capt.*

3rd Batt. (Militia), *Lichfield.*
Lt.-Col., J. H Monckton, *c.*

4th Batt. (Militia), *Lichfield.*
Lt.-Col., R. Mirehouse.

1st Vol. Batt., *Stoke-upon-Trent.*
Lt.-Cols., R. Clive, V.D., *c.* (*comdg.*);
W. W. Dobson.

2nd Vol. Batt., *Burton-on-Trent.*
Lt.-Col., C. J. Goer, V.D., *c.*

STAFFORDSHIRE (S.) REG. (1)
District No. 38.—*Lichfield.*
Colonel, John William Sidney Smith, C.B., *g.*
Comg. Regtl. Dist., J. E. H. Prior, *c.*

1st Batt. (38th Foot), *Kinsale.*
Lt.-Col., H. C. Savage.
Adjt., E. Layton, *capt.*

2nd Batt. (80th Foot), *Thayetmyo, Burma.*
Lt.-Col., N. S. Allen.
Adjt., G. N. Deans, *lt.*

3rd and 4th Batts. (Militia), *Lichfield.*
Lt.-Cols., M. A. W. Broun, *c.*
(*comdt.*); F. Charrington.

1st V. B., *Handsworth, nr. Birmingham.*
Lt.-Col., J. B. Cochrane, V.D., *c.*

2nd V. B., *Walsall.*
Lt.-Col., T. T. Fisher, V.D., *c.*

3rd V. B., *Wolverhampton.*
Lt.-Cols., J. B. Morgan, V.D., *c.*
(*comdt.*); E. H. Thorne, V.D., *c.*

SUFFOLK REGIMENT.   (1)
Dist. No. 12.—*Bury St. Edmunds.*
Colonel, John M. Perceval, C.B. *g.*
Comg. Regtl. Dist., R. T. E. Dowse, *c.*

1st Batt. (12th Foot), *Dover.*
Lt.-Col., A. J. Watson.
Adjt., F. A. P. Wilkins, *lt.*

2nd Batt. (12th Foot), *Quetta.*
Lt.-Col., C. R. Townley, *c.*
Adjt., E. C. Doughty, *lt.*

3rd Batt. (Militia), *Bury St. Edmunds.*
Lt.-Col., R. Norton, *c.*

4th Batt. (Cambridge Mil.), *Ely.*
Lt.-Col., H. D. Fryer, *c.*

1st Vol. Batt., *Ipswich.*
Lt.-Col., H. A. Collins.

2nd Vol. Batt., *Bury St. Edmunds.*
Lt.-Col., G. L. Andrewes, V.D., *c.*

3rd (Cambridgesh.) Vol. Batt., *Cambridge.*
Lt.-Col., C. T. Heycock, V.D., *c.*

4th (Camb. Univ.) Vol. Batt., *Cambridge.*
Lt.-Col., (Rev.) H. S. Cronin.

SURREY (EAST) REGT.   (1)
District No. 31.—*Kingston.*
Col., Sir George Richard Greaves, G.C.B., K.C.M.G., *g.*
Comg. Regtl. Dist., R. W. F. Phillips, *c.*

1st Batt. (31st Foot), *Jhansi, Bengal Command.*
Lt.-Col., W. J. H. Frodsham.
Adjt., W. H. Paterson, *capt.*

2nd Batt. (70th Foot), *S. Africa.*
Lt.-Col., R. H. W. H. Harris.
Adjt., F. W. King-Church, *lt.*

3rd Batt. (Militia), *Kingston.*
Lt.-Col., Sir G. D. Clerk, Bart., *c.*

4th Batt. (Militia), *Kingston.*
Lt.-Col., B. G. Haines, *c.*

1st Surrey Volrs. (South London), *Camberwell.*
Lt.-Col., E. Villiers, *c.*

2nd Vol. Batt., *Wimbledon.*
Lt.-Col., E. H. Bailey, V.D., *c.*

3rd Vol. Batt., *Kingston-on-Thames.*
Lt.-Col., J. L. G. Powell, V.D.

4th Vol. Batt., *Upper Kennington Lane, S.E.*
Lt.-Col., T. Tully, V.D.

SURREY REGIMENT (ROYAL WEST) (The Queen's).   (1)
District No. 2.—*Guildford.*
Colonel, Granville Geo. Chetwynd Stapylton, *l.g.*
Comg. Regtl. Dist., A. H. Nourse.

1st Batt. (2nd Foot), *Gharial, Punjab Command.*
Lt.-Col., J. S. Collins, *c.*
Adjt., W. J. T. Glasgow, *capt.*

2nd Batt. (2nd Foot), *S. Africa.*
Lt.-Col., E. O. F. Hamilton.
Adjt., G. G. Whiffin, *capt.*

3rd Batt. (Militia), *Guildford.*
Lt.-Col., F. H. Fairtlough.

1st Vol. Batt., *Croydon.*
Lt.-Col., J. P. Fearon, V.D., *c.*

2nd Vol. Batt., *Guildford.*
Lt.-Col., G. Drewitt, V.D., *c.*

3rd Vol. Batt., *Bermondsey, S.E.*
Lt.-Col., S. B. Bevington, V.D., *c.*

4th V. B., *New Street, Kennington Park.*
Lt.-Col., J. Davies-Jenkins.

SUSSEX REGT. (ROYAL). (1)
District No. 35.—*Chichester.*
Col., Geo. Samuel Young, C.B., *l.g.*
Comg. Regtl. Dist., W. F. Cavaye, *c.*

1st Batt. (35th Foot), *Malta.*
Lt.-Col., B. D. A. Donne.
Adjt., E. W. B. Green, *capt.*

2nd Batt. (107th Foot), *Sialkot, Punjab Command.*
Lt.-Col., J. C. Young.
Adjt., W. L. Osborn, *capt.*

3rd Batt. (Militia), *Chichester.*
Lt.-Col. Comdt., Earl of March, A.D.C., *c.*

1st Vol. Batt., *Brighton.*
Lt.-Col., C. S. Clarke.

2nd Vol. Batt., *Worthing.*
Lt.-Col., W. H. Campion, V.D., *c.*

1st Cinque Ports Volrs., *Hastings.*
Lt.-Col., A. M. Brookfield, *c.*

WALES (S.) BORDERERS. (2)
District No. 24.—*Brecon.*
Colonel, Richard Thomas Glyn, C.B., C.M.G., *l.g.*
Comg. Regtl. Dist., E. S. Browne, V.C., *c.*

1st Batt. (24th Foot), *Chakrata,*
Bengal Command.
Lt.-Col, H. G. Mainwaring.
Adjt., W. E. B. Smith, *capt.*

2nd Batt. (24th Foot), *Dublin.*
Lt.-Col., Ralph Arthur Penrhyn
Clements, D.S.O., A.D.C., *c.*
Adjt., C. L. Taylor, *lt.*

3rd Batt. (Militia), *Brecon.*
Lt.-Col., C. Healey.

4th Batt. (Militia), *Welshpool.*
Lt.-Col., C. E. Ramsbottom-
Isherwood, *c.*

1st (Brecknockshire) Vol. Batt.,
Brecon.
Lt.-Col., F. R. D. A. Gough.

2nd V.B., *Stow Hill, Newport, Mon.*
Lt.-Col., R. H. Mansel, *c.*

3rd Vol. Batt., *Pontypool.*
Lt.-Col., J. A. Bradney, *c.*

4th Vol. Batt., *Pontypool.*
Lt.-Col., W. H. Williams, V.D., *c.*

5th Vol. Batt., *Newtown, Montgomeryshire.*
Lt.-Col., E. Pryce-Jones, M.P.

**WARWICKSHIRE REGIMENT
(ROYAL).** (1)
District No. 6.—*Warwick.*
Colonel, Frederick William Traill-
Burroughs, C.B., *l.g.*
Comg. Regtl. Dist., E. Nesbitt, *c.*

1st Batt. (6th Foot), *Madras.*
Lt.-Col., W. E. G. Forbes, C.B.
Adjt., F. A. Earle, *m.*

2nd Batt. (6th Foot), *S. Africa.*
Lt.-Col., M. Q. Jones, C.B.
Adjt., G. D. Armstrong, *capt.*

3rd Batt. (1898), *Malta.*
Lt.-Col., A. W. F. Jackson.
Adjt., H. R. Vaughan, *capt.*

4th Batt. (*not yet formed*).

5th Batt. (Militia), *Warwick.*
Lt.-Col., W. A. Pennington, *c.*

6th Batt. (Militia), *Warwick.*
Lt.-Col., I. L. B. McCalmont.

1st Vol. Batt., *Thorpe St.,
Birmingham.*
Lt.-Cols., W. S. Jervis, *c.* (comdg.);
W. Cox, V.D., *c.*

2nd Vol. Batt. (2nd Warwicksh.),
Coventry.
Lt.-Col., W. F. Wyley, V.D., *c.*

WELSH FUSILIERS (ROY.). (1)
District No. 23.—*Wrexham.*
Colonel, Sir Edward Gascoigne
Bulwer, K.C.B., *g.*
Comg. Regtl. Dist., E. S. Creek, *c.*

1st Batt. (23rd Foot), *S. Africa.*
Lt.-Col., C. C. H. Thorold.
Adjt., W. G. Braithwaite, *capt.*

2nd Batt. (23rd Foot), *Hong Kong.*
Lt.-Col., Hon. R. H. Bertie.
Adjt. C. M. Dobell, *m.*

3rd Batt. (Militia), *Wrexham.*
Lt.-Col., S. Sandbach, *c.*

4th Batt. (Militia), *Carnarvon.*
Lt.-Col., H. Platt, C.B., *c.*

1st Vol. Batt., *Wrexham.*
Lt.-Col.,

2nd Vol. Batt., *Hawarden.*
Lt.-Col., J. S. Roberts.

3rd Vol. Batt., *Carnarvon.*
Lt.-Col., C. H. Rees, V.D., *c.*

WELSH REGIMENT. (1)
District No. 41.—*Cardiff.*
Colonel, Francis Peyton, C.B., *g.*
Comg. Regtl. Dist., J. O. Quirk,
C.B., D.S.O.

1st Batt. (41st Foot), *S. Africa.*
Lt.-Col., R. J. F. Banfield.
Adjt., D. A. N. Lomax, *capt.*

2nd Batt. (69th Foot), *Ahmednagar,
Bombay Command.*
Lt.-Col., F. S. L. Penno.
Adjt., L. Brandreth, *lt.*

3rd Batt. (Militia), *Cardiff.*
Lt.-Col., A. T. Perkins, *c.*

1st (Pembrokeshire) Vol. Batt.,
Haverfordwest.
Lt.-Col., W. P. Evans, V.D., *c.*

2nd Vol. Batt., *Bridgend, Glam.*
Lt.-Col., H. R. Homfray, *comdt.*

3rd Vol. Batt., *Cardiff.*
Lt.-Cols., P. R. Cresswell, C.B.,
V.D., *c.* (comdt.) ; D. R. Lewis,
V.D., *c.* ; J. Gaskell, V.D., *c.*

3rd Glamorgan Volrs., *Swansea.*
Lt.-Col., J. C. Richardson, V.D., *c.*

**WEST RIDING REGIMENT
(The Duke of Wellington's).** (1)
District No. 33.—*Halifax.*
Col., Sir Hugh Rowlands, V.C., *g.*
Comd. Regtl. Dist., H.B. LeMottée.

1st Batt. (33rd Foot), *Dover.*
Lt.-Col., G. E. Lloyd, D.S.O.
Adjt., W. E. M. Tyndall, *lt.*

2nd Batt. (76th Foot), *Rangoon.*
Lt.-Col., H. E. Belfield.
Adjt., P. A. Turner, *capt.*

3rd Batt. (Militia), *Halifax.*
Lt.-Col., A. K. Wyllie, *c.*

1st Vol. Batt., *Halifax.*
Lt.-Col.,

2nd Vol. Batt., *Huddersfield.*
Lt.-Col., E. H. Carlile.

3rd Vol. Batt., *Skipton-in-Craven.*
Lt.-Col., W. Bairstow.

**WILTSHIRE REGIMENT
(The Duke of Edinburgh's).** (1)
District No. 62.—*Devizes.*
Colonel, John Hart Dunne, *g.*
Comg. Regtl. Dist., W. B. Williams,
c.

1st Batt. (62nd Foot), *Quetta,
Bombay Command.*
Lt.-Col., H. M. Carter.
Adjt., J. R. Wyndham, *capt.*

2nd Batt. (99th Foot), *Aldershot.*
Lt.-Col., H. C. Harford.
Adjt., E. Evans, *lt.*

3rd Batt. (Militia), *Devizes.*
Lt.-Col., E. C. A. Sanford.

1st Wiltshire Volrs., *Warminster.*
Lt.-Col., Duke of Somerset.

2nd Vol. Batt., *Chippenham.*
Lt.-Col., E. B. Merriman, V.D., *c.*

WORCESTERSHIRE REGT. (1)
District No. 29.—*Worcester.*
Col., Sir Geo. Wentworth Alex.
Higginson, K.C.B., *g.*
Comg. Regtl. Dist., H. J. de B. de
Berniere, *c.*

1st Batt. (29th Foot), *Guernsey.*
Lt.-Col., O. H. Oakes.
Adjt., B. F. B. Stuart, *lt.*

2nd Batt. (36th Foot), *Halifax, N.S.*
Lt.-Col., F. S. Allen.
Adjt., E. C. F. Wodehouse, *lt.*

3rd and 4th Batts. (Militia),
Worcester.
Lt.-Cols., A. W. Hooper, *c.* (3),
comdt. ; E. H. Bearcroft, *c.* (4).

1st Vol. Batt., *Kidderminster.*
Lt.-Cols., R. T. Watson, V.D., *c.*
(comdt.) ; E. V. V. Wheeler, *c.*

2nd Vol. Batt., *Worcester.*
Lt.-Col., Viscount Deerhurst.

YORK & LANCAST. REGT. (1)
District No. 65.—*Pontefract.*
Col., Jas. H. Craig Robertson, *g.*
Comg. Regtl. Dist., W. Clark, *c.*

1st Batt. (65th Foot), *S. Africa.*
Lt.-Col., W. J. Kirkpatrick.
Adjt., T. T. Gresson, *lt.*

2nd Batt. (84th Foot), *Agra, Bengal.*
Lt.-Col., H. Boughey, *c.*
Adjt., F. F. W. Daniell, *capt.*

3rd Batt. (Militia), *Pontefract.*
Lt.-Col., J. G. Wilson, C.B., *c.*

1st (Hallamsh.) V. B., *Sheffield.*
Lt.-Col., H. Hughes, V.D.

2nd Vol. Batt., *Doncaster.*
Lt.-Col., E. A. Johnson, V.D., *c.*

**YORKSHIRE LIGHT INF.
(The King's Own).** (1)
District No. 51.—*Pontefract.*
Col., Sir Robert Hume, K.C.B., *l.g.*
Comg. Regtl. Dist., W. Clark, *c.*

1st Batt. (51st Foot), *Sheffield.*
Lt.-Col., Sir H. A. W. Johnson, Bt.
Adjt., W. T. Potts, *capt.*

2nd Batt. (105th Foot), *S. Africa.*
Lt.-Col., C. St. L. Barter.
Adjt., H. Wells-Cole, D.S.O., *capt.*

3rd Batt. (Militia), *Pontefract.*
Lt.-Col., T. H. Skinner, *c.*

1st Vol. Batt., *Wakefield.*
Lt.-Col., A. S. Lee, V.D., *c.*

YORKSHIRE REGIMENT
(The Princess of Wales's Own). (2)
District No. 19.—*Richmond.*
Col., Edward Chippindall, C.B., *l.g.*
Comg. Regtl. Dist., A. Wilkinson, *c.*
1st Batt. (19th Foot), *S. Africa.*
Lt.-Col., H. Bowles.
Adjt., G. Christian, *capt.*
2nd Batt. (19th Foot), *Dagshai.*
Punjab Command.
Lt.-Col., C. J. Spottiswoode, *c.*
Adjt., R. D'A. Fife, *capt.*
3rd Batt. (Militia), *Richmond.*
Lt.-Col., J. Hoole, *c.*
4th Batt. (Militia), *Richmond.*
Lt.-Col., J. W. Richardson, *c.*
1st Vol. Batt. *Northallerton.*
Lt.-Col., A. F. Godman, *c.*
2nd Vol. Batt., *Scarborough.*
Lt.-Col., W. Scoby, V.D., *c.*

YORKSHIRE (EAST) REGT. (1)
District No. 15.—*Beverley.*
Colonel, William Hardy, C.B., *l.g.*
Comg. Regtl. Dist., D.C.DeWend.*c.*
1st Batt. (15th Foot), *Belgaum,*
Madras Command.
Lt.-Col., C. F. Garnett.
Adjt., T. A. Headlam, *lt.*
2nd Batt. (15th Foot), *Templemore.*
Lt.-Col., W. W. Ward.
Adjt., J. A. Unett, *capt.*
3rd Batt. (Militia), *Beverley.*
Lt.-Col., J. H. Burstall, *c.*
1st Vol. Batt., *Hull.*
Lt.-Col., A. Thorney, V.D., *c.*
2nd Vol. Batt., *Beverley.*
Lt.-Col., J. A. Staveley, V.D., *c.*

YORKSHIRE (WEST) REGT.
(The Prince of Wales's Own). (1)
District No. 14.—*York.*
Col., Sir Martin Andrew Dillon,
K.C.B., C.S.I., *g.*
Comg. Regtl. Dist., A. W. Noyes, *c.*
1st Batt. (14th Foot), *Karachi,*
Bombay Command.
Lt.-Col., G. Grant-Dalton.
Adjt., A. F. Stewart, *lt.*
2nd Batt. (14th Foot), *S. Africa.*
Lt.-Col., F. W. Kitchener, *c.*
Adjt., A. C. Daly, *capt.*
3rd Batt. (Militia), *York.*
Hon. Col., H.R.H. Duke of York.
Lt.-Col., G. J. Hay, C.B., *c.*
4th Batt. (Militia), *York.*
Lt.-Col., C. R. Prideaux-Brune, *c.*
1st Vol. Batt., *York.*
Lt.-Col., G. Kearsley, V.D., *c.*
2nd Vol. Batt., *Bradford.*
Lt.-Col., G. H. Müller, *c.*
3rd V.B., *Carlton Barracks, Leeds.*
Lt.-Col., E. Wilson, V.D., *c.*

PROVISIONAL BATTALION.
Shorncliffe.
Lt.-Col., C. H. Kelly.
Adjt., F. W. Towzey, *capt.*

WEST INDIA REGIMENT. (1)
(£73,000). *Dépôt, Jamaica.*
Col., Wm. John Chamberlayne, *g.*
Comg. Dépôt
1st Batt., *Bermuda.*
Lt.-Cols., A. L. Bayley (*comdg.*) ;
J. W. A. Marshall.
Adjt., B. Faunce, *capt.*

2nd Batt., *Jamaica.*
Lt.-Cols., D. M. Allen (*comdg.*) ;
R. Egerton.
Adjt., J. P. Bliss, *capt.*
3rd Batt., *Sierra Leone.*
Lt.-Cols., A. Bor (*comdg.*) ; H.
B. Bourke, D.S.O.
Adjt., E. J. Pomeroy, *lt.*

HONG KONG REGIMENT.
(£16,300).
Hong Kong.
Comdt., J. M. A. Retallick, *l.c.*
Adjt., A. L. Barrett, *lt.*

BRITISH CENTRAL AFRICA
RIFLES. (2)
1st Batt., *Central Africa.*
Comdt., W. H. Manning, *l.c.*
Adjt.,
2nd Batt., *Mauritius.*
Comdt., H. E. J. Brake, *m.*
Adjt., A. F. Gordon, *capt.*

WEST AFRICAN REGIMENT.
(1)
Comdt., G. G. Cunningham,
D.S.O., *l.c.*
Adjt., H. T. Manley, *lt.*

CHINESE REGIMENT. (1)
1st Batt., *Wei-Ha-Wei.*
Comdt., H. Bower, *l.c.,* I.S.C.
Adjt.,

MILITARY MOUNTED
POLICE.
Quartermasters, J. W. M. Wood,
m., *Aldershot;* C. Burroughs,
l., *S. Africa.*

Army Service Corps (£169,000). (3)

Colonels, J. T. Skinner, C.B., D.S.O., *War Office;* W. D. Richardson, C.B., *S. Africa;* W. A. Dunne, C.B., *N.-E. Dist.;* R. A. Nugent, C.B., *Malta;* L. A. Clutterbuck, *Dublin District;* M. E. R. Rainsford, C.B., *c., S. District.*
Lieut.-Colonels, C. H. Bridge, C.B., *c., S. Africa;* J. G. Y. Wilson, *c., Cork Dist.;* A. W. Collard, *c., Nova Scotia;* J. Whitley, *Straits Settlements;* E. W. D. Ward, C.B., *c., S. Africa;* J. A. Boyd, C.B., *c., Head Qrs., War*
Office; S. J. Lea, C.B., *c., Head Qrs., Ireland;* E. P. B. Smith, *c., Egypt;* W. F. Moore, *Cork;* J. W. B. Parkin, *c., Aldershot;* M. Graham, *c., Malta;* S. H. Winter, *S. Africa;* A. G. Hipwell, *S. Africa;* G. G. Challice, *Woolwich;* W. R. Winter, *S. Africa* G. Stanley, *S. Africa;* R. B. McComb, *S. Africa;* L. A. Hope, *c., Egypt;* W. Dunne, *Woolwich Dockyard;* K. Arnold, *Gibraltar;* M. J. Godfery, *S. Africa;* F. S. C. Hare, *S. Africa;* H. G. Rice, *Southern*
Dist.; J. Stoneman, *S. Africa;* G. H. Jessop, *Capetown;* S. H. Lynn, *Gibraltar;* F. A. Le-Poer-Trench, *S. Africa;* R. V. Day, *c., Pembroke Dock;* F. F. Johnson, *c., S. Africa;* C. A. Edes, *Colchester;* E. Gaussen, *Bermuda;* C. E. Heath, *South-Eastern Dist.;* C. G. Knocker, *Devonport;* C. A. Hadfield, *Dublin;* J. C. Oughterson, *Woolwich;* F. T. Clayton, *S. Africa;* G. P. Bourcicault, *Woolwich Arsenal;* J. A. W. Falls, *S. Africa.*

Army Medical Service (£305,800). (2)

Office, 18, Victoria Street, Westminster, S.W.
Director-General, J. Jameson, M.D., C.B., *s.g.*

ARMY MEDICAL STAFF.
Surgeon Generals, W. Taylor, M.D., C.B., *India;* A. F. Preston, M.B., *Ireland;* T. F. O'Dwyer, M.D.,
Aldershot; W. Nash, M.D., *Netley;* C. McD. Cuffe, M.D., *Portsmouth;* H. S. Muir, M.D., *War Office;* W. A. Catherwood, M.D.,
Bengal; W. D. Wilson, M.B., *Devonport;* W. S. M. Price, *Bombay;* T. O'Farrell, M.D., *Malta.*

ROYAL ARMY MEDICAL CORPS.

Colonels, C. A. Maunsell, M.D., *Mhow*; C. F. Churchill, M.B., *Mussoorie*; W. E. Riordan, *Cork*; J. H. Hughes, M.D., *Quetta*; J. Maturin, *Colchester*; R. H. Carew, D.S.O., *Rawalpindi*; G. J. H. Evatt, M.D., *; W. McWalters, Nova Scotia*; J. L. Notter, *Netley*; H.Comerford, M.D., *Dover*; J. P. Rooney, *Edinburgh*; W. F. Stevenson, M.B., *S. Africa*; R. C. Eaton, *Poona*; W. F. Burnett, *Mandalay*; N. B. Major, *Secunderabad*; E. Townsend, M.D., C.B., *S. Africa*; J.F.Supple, *Cape*; J. H. Moore, *Bombay*; R. de la C. Corbett, M.D., D.S.O., *Lucknow*; W. H. Macnamara, M.D., C.B., *Gibraltar*; T. J. Gallwey, M.D., C.B., *S. Africa*; A. W. Duke, M.D., *S. Africa*; J. M. Beamish, M.D. *Allahabad*; J. A. Clery, M.B., *S. Africa*; W. J. Fawcett, M.B., *Egypt*; W. E. Saunders, c.b., *York*; W. J. Charlton, *Aldershot*.

Lieut.-Colonels, A. H. Anthonisz, M.B., *S.Africa*; R. Ezham, *Netley*; J. McNamara, M.D., *Malta*; G. D. N. Leake, *Bermuda*; M. D. O'Connell, M.D., *Punjab*; E. H.

Joynt, M.D., *Jamaica*; J. D. Edge, M.D., *S. Africa*; R. Blood, M D., *Punjab*; H. J. W. Barrow, *Punjab*; W. Donovan, *S. Africa*; R. H. Quill, M.B., *Ceylon*; B. M. Blennerhassett, C.M.G., *Bombay*; W. B. Slaughter, *Binga*; H. B. Stokes, M.B., *Curragh*; W. S. Pratt, M.B., *Gibraltar*; W. B. Allin, M.B., *Aldershot*; W. E. Webb, M.D., *Netley*; R. W. Mapleton, *S. Africa*; W. L. Gubbins, M.B., *War Office*; R. G. Thomsett, *Belfast*; C. W. M. Keys, M.D., *Mauritius*; O. G. Wood, M.D., *S. Africa*; J. Martin, *Aldershot*; J. A. Gormley, M.D., *Shorncliffe*; C. H. Swayne, D.S.O., *Bengal*; F. W. Trevor, M B, *Bombay*; S. H. Carter, M B, *S. Africa*; W. A. May, *Devonport*; W. B. Miller, M D., *Punjab*; G. D. Bourke, *Punjab*; H. Charlesworth, *Portsmouth*; J. C. Dorman, M.B., *Dublin*; G. H. Le Mottée, M.D., *Bombay*; W.L.Chester, M.B., *Netley*; E.A. Mapleton, M.B., *Punjab*; E. H. Fenn, C.I.E, *India*; W.O.Wolseley, *Madras*; A. T. Sloggett, *Egypt*; M. R Ryan, M D, *; J. J. Morris, M.D.,*

Bengal; J. F. Williamson, M.B., *Gosport*; W. J. R. Rainsford, *Bengal*; P. H. Johnston, M.D., *Cape*; I. B. Emerson, *Madras*; E. A. Roche, *Barbados*; U. J. Bourke, *Woolwich*; J. L. Peyton, M.B., *Limerick*; A. W. Carleton, M.B., *Bengal*; G. A. Hughes, M.B., D S.O., *Netley*; B. W. Somerville-Large, *Portsmouth*; R. C. Gunning, *Chester*; R. Drury, M.D., *Bengal*; J. T. Care, M.B., *Bengal*; W. H. Allen, *Parkhurst*; W.T.Johnston,M.D. *Bengal*; A. W. Browne, *Malta*; R. D. Hodson, *S. Africa*; H. C. Kirkpatrick, M.D., *Bombay*; J. Armstrong, *Fermoy*; W. W. Kenny, M.B., *Dublin*; P. M. Ellis, *Bengal*; W. Keays, *Punjab*; R. T. Beamish, M.D., *Punjab*; J. Anderson, M.B., *Sheerness*; J. I. Routh, *Bengal*; H. Grier, *S. Africa*; H. R. Whitehead, *Punjab*; W. L. Lane, M.B., *Bombay*; P. J. Dempsey, M.D., *Bengal*; J. W. H. Flanagan, *Bengal*; O. E. P. Lloyd, VC, *Madras*; J. G. MacNeece, *Bermuda*; M. D. O'Connell, *S.Africa*; J. J. Falvey, *Weedon*; C. Seymour, M.B., *Bengal*; G. W. Robinson, *Punjab*.

Channel Islands Militia (£6,900). Malta Militia (£3,100).

ROYAL JERSEY.

Lt.-Gov. Comg., E. Hopton, C.B., l.g.

D.-A.-A.-G., M. H. F. Le Gallais, m.

ARTILLERY.

Lt.-Cols., C. P. Le Cornu, C.B., A.D.C., c.; J. Bichard.

Adjt., E. L'E. Whitehead, capt., R.A.

LIGHT INFANTRY.
1st (West) Regiment.
Lt.-Col.,
Adjt., J. H. Gideon, capt.
2nd (East) Regiment.
Lt.-Col., E. E. Nicolle.
Adjt., G. P. Stewart, capt.

3rd (South) Regiment.
Lt.-Col., E. Esnouf.
Adjt., E. B. Blennerhassett, capt.

ROYAL GUERNSEY.

Lt.-Gov. Comg., M. H. Saward, l.g.

D.-A.-A.-G., J. E. Le Mottée, c.

ARTILLERY.
Lt.-Col., P. Groves.
Adjt., W. H. Carey, capt., R.A.

LIGHT INFANTRY.
1st (East) Regiment.
Lt.-Col., T. W. M. de Guérin.
Adjt., C. Conyers, lt.

ROYAL ALDERNEY.

ARTILLERY.
Lt.-Col. Com., P. T. Herivel.
Adjt., J. Christian, capt. (lt., R.A.).

ROYAL MALTA.
1st and 2nd Battalions.
Lt.-Cols., R. R. Samut; J. L. de Piro, C.M.G.
Adjts., G. L. Beaumont, m., R.M.A. (2); A. J. S. Maunsell, capt. (1).

BERMUDA VOLUNTE R RIFLES.
Maj., Sir J. Rees.
Adjt., C. S. B. Evans-Lombe, capt.

Indian Staff Corps.

Field Marshal, Sir D. M. Stewart, Bart., G.C.B., G.C.S.I., C.I.E. (*Gov. of Chelsea Hospital*).

Generals, H. S. Anderson, C.B.; G. N. Channer, V.C., C.B.; Sir A. P. Palmer, K.C.B. (*Punjab Command*).

Lieut.-Generals, F. Lance, C.B.; Sir G. C. Bird, K.C.I.E., C.B.; R. C. R. Clifford, C B.; C. R. Pennington, C.B.; H. M. Evans, C.B.

Major-Generals, J. M. Sym, C.B.; A G Handcock, C.B.; A. R. Badcock, C B., C.S.I. (*Q.-M.-G., India*); Sir M. G. Gerard, K.C.S.I., C.B.; Sir E. Stedman, K C.I.E., C.B.; M. Protheroe, C.B., C.S.I. (*Burma District*); A. C. Toker, C.B.; F. H. Vanderzee; W. A. Lawrence; J. Gatacre, C B.; H. S. Elton; H. G. Waterfield, C.B.; C. A. Cuningham; R. M. Clifford;

H. S. Stewart; Sir R. Westmacott, K C.B., D.S.O.; J. Waterhouse; J. L. Fagan; G. R. J. Shakespear.

Lieut.-Colonels, E. Swinton Skinner, c.; Walter Scott, c.; T. R. Cowie, c.; E. A. Money, C.B., c.; G. R. J. Shakespear, c.; M. J. King-Harman, c.; C. E. Shepherd, c.; R. G. E. Dalrymple, c.; A. H. Turner, C B., c.; A. G. Hammond, V.C.,

C.B., D.S.O., A.D.C., c.; J. E. Sandeman, c.; C. F. Hughes, C.B., c.; C. C. Brownlow, c.; J. Cook, C.B., c.; J. T. Cummins, D.S.O., c. (temp. Brig.-Gen.); H. S. Tandy, c.; A. L. McNair, c.; G. Simpson, C.B., c. (temp. Brig.-Gen.); A. M. Hogg, c.; W. V. Ellis, c.; A. Clark-Kennedy, c.; J. P. D. Vanrenen, c.; G. W. Rogers, D.S.O., c.; H. Paterson, c.; E. B. Bishop, c.; Sir A. Gaselee, K.C.B., A.D.C., c. (temp. Brig.-Gen.); W. O. Thompson, D.S.O., c.; J. Davidson, c.; Sir E. H. H. Collen, K.C.I.E., C.B., c. (Member of Council of Gov. Gen. of India) (temp. Maj.-Gen.); J. B. Hutchinson; L. R. H. D. Campbell, c.; H. V. Hunt, c.; C. H. Stoddart, c.; J. G. Kelly, C.B., A.D.C., c.; W. Hailes, c.; J. R. Burlton-Bennet, c.; W. J. Vousden, V.C., c.; A. Fishe, c.; H. H. Harvey-Kelly, c.; H. De la M. Hervey; G. W. Sawyer, c.; F. W. V. Leckie, c.; W. H. D. Jones; S. V. Gordon, D.S.O., c.; D. W. K. Barr, C.S.I.; G. H. C. Dyce, C.B., c.; A. E. Gordon; C. F. Massy; R. A. Swetenham, c.; G. F. Young, C.B., c. (Brigadier-General, India); Sir H. Melliss, K.C.S.I., c.; J. Grant, c.; F. C. Burton, c.; J. A. Miley, C.S.I., c.; T. F. Hobday, C.B., c. (temp. Maj.-Gen.); E. H. Wilson, C.B., c.; R. A. Gilchrist, c.; D. Robertson, C.S.I.; J. N. S. Kirkwood, c.; D. S. Cuninghame, c.; A. K. Macpherson; W. Hill, C.B., c.; W. C. Black, c.; W. H. Salmon, c.; B. C. Graves, C.B., c.; W. A. Wetherall, c.; J. Butler, W. Loch; L. T. Bishop; G. L. R. Richardson, C.B., C.I.E., c.; A. C. G. Lydiard; P. J. Maitland, C.B., c. (temp. Maj.-Gen.); C. W. H. Sealy; F. R. Begbie, c.; O'M. Creagh, V.C., c. (temp. Brig.-Gen.); W. H. Lyster, c.; F. C. Maltby; W. H. C. Wyllie, C.I.E., c.; A. W. Jamieson, c.; S. E. Rolland, c. (temp. Brig.-Gen.); H. A. Vincent, c.; J. P. C. Neville, c.; Sir C. H. Leslie, Bt., C.B., c.; G. W. Arson; B. T. M.

Gompertz; Sir A. C. Talbot, K.C.I.E.; A. J. F. Reid, C.B., c. (temp. Brig.-Gen.); T. Greenaway; B. Channer, D.S.O., c.; E. B. Anderson, c.; H. M. Rose, D.S.O., c.; L. W. Christopher, C.B., c.; W. G. W. Macbay; C. M. Keighley, C.B., D.S.O., c.; F. G. T. Welch, c.; L. Dening, D.S.O., c.; C. Egerton, C.B., D.S.O., A.D.C., c. (Maj.-Gen., India); C. A. Mercer, c.; T. H. Goldney, C.B., c.; G. W. Martin; H. D. Hutchinson, c.; F. R. Ditmas; G. H. H. Elliott, c.; J. N. Walker, c.; J. A. L. Montgomery; A. P. Thornton; A. J. Brander, c.; C. E. Yate, C.S.I., C.M.G.; R. K. Ridgeway, V.C., c.; G. L. Eliot, c.; F. B. Peile; J. B. Lynch, c.; R. Gordon, c.; H. E. Penton, c.; E. L. Elliot, C.B., D.S.O., c. (temp. Maj.-Gen.); C. W. J. Hingston, c.; A. McL. Mills, c.; H. A. Abbott, C.B., c.; H. B. Ternan; F. D. Raikes, C.I.E.; C. R. Macgregor, C.B., D.S.O., c.; W. F. H. Grey; C. G. Mansel; C. T. Bingham, D.D. Pryce; C. A. R. Sage, c.; F. F. R. Burgess; C. Dempster, c.; E. Bruce, c.; T. E. Spencer; F. Abbott, c.; A. Howlett, c.; S. H. P. Graves, c.; W. A. Broome, c.; M. A. Gray; J. R. Hobday; G. W. Deane; F. W. Snell; T. H. Mackenzie; J. F. D. Fordyce; H. St. P. Maxwell, C.S.I.; H. R. D. Thomas, c.; A. J. P. Nuthall; E. D. Newnham-Smith; W. B. Wilson; E. V. P. Monteith; H. C. Lamb, c.; V. A. Schalch, c.; G. S. Eyre; E. Balfe, p.s.c.; W. J. Orr, c.; A. W. C. Bell, c.; G. C. Dobbs, c.; B. L. P. Reilly, c.; C. W. Muir, C.I.E., c.; T. R. M. Macpherson; E. D. F. Bignell; G. B. Austin, c.; G. E. Money; J. Clibborn; W. B. Ferris; A. F. Barrow, C.M.G., D.S.O., p.s.c.; H. C. E. Lucas, c.; A. R. Porter; E. C. Kellie; J. C. F. Gordon, C.I.E.; C. H. V. Garbett; A. W. Proudfoot; St. J. F. Michell, c. (temp. Brig.-Gen.); A. de V. Alexander;

R. F. Trotter; E. A. Young; G. H. More-Molyneux, D.S.O., c., p.s.c.; L. L. Fenton; W. P. Kennedy; H. M. Mason; F. Stevenson; A. A. Pearson; G. Hawkes; R. C. Hadow, D.S.O.; E. A. Barclay; C. O. Nicholetts; J. E. Mein; M. E. H. O. Welch; H. S. Wheatley; H. H. Young; E. E. Kenny; G. D. C. Gastrell; G. L. Garstin; W. R. Le G. Anderson; J. W. E. Angelo; G. F. Francis; J. W. Wray; A. Masters; H. P. P. Leigh, C.I.E.; R. C. Temple, C.I.E.; F. G. Vivian; H. N. McRae, C.I.E.; F. C. Maisey; C. Hogge; G. Wingate; J. W. Hogge, C.I.E., p.s.c.; O. C. Radford; A. Montanaro; W. H. F. Macmullen; C. Pulley, c.; L. J. Browne; F. Jameson; A. G. F. Browne, D.S.O., c.; A. Wapshare; G. H. B. Coats; W. J. B. Bird; N. R. Stewart, c. (temp. Brig.-Gen.); A. W. D. Campbell; C. S. Wheler; E. G. Barrow, C.B., c.; W. G. Mansel; M. S. Cooke-Collis; W. S. Hewett; F. G. L. Mainwaring; A. B. Mein; M. I. Gibbs; C. M. FitzGerald; H. Des Vœux, c.; R. Fulton; F. M. Rundall, D.S.O.; F. S. Gwatkin, c.; G. B. Renny; P. A. Buckland; E. C. C. Sandys; C. W. Ravenshaw; W. C. F. Field; T. C. Pears; H. M. Temple; H. H. R. Heath; R. E. D. Reilly; W. W. Lean; G. A. Money; L. J. Torrie; R. W. MacLeod; W. F. C. C. Plowden; P. R. Bairnsfather; R. C. S. Macausland; J. Monteith; H. R. Marrett; H. M. P. Hawkes; A. G. A. Durand, C.B., C.I.E., p.s.c., c.; R. C. G. Mayne, C.B.; A. Pringle; E. J. F. Wood; H. Read; C. J. Robarts; W. A. D'O. O'Malley; E. H. Molesworth; R. R. N. Sturt; H. B. Thornhill; E. H. H. Montresor; F. P. L. White; R. F. Gartside-Tipping; V. C. Tonnochy; M. J. Mead; J. de C. D. Meade; H. E. Passy; E. E. M. Lawford; F. W. Egerton; E. M. Needham; S. B. Beatson, C.B.; G. H. Robinson; A. W. T. Radcliffe.

Indian Army.

BENGAL.

General, Sir W. S. A. Lockhart, G.C.B., K.C.S.I. (Commander-in-Chief, India).
Lieut.-General, Sir R. C. Low, G.C.B., cav. (Bombay Comd.).
Major-Generals, W. W. Biscoe, C.B., cav.; R. M. Jennings, C.B., cav. (Lucknow); R. Morris, cav.; G. T. Halliday, cav.; N. F. Parker; V. W. Tregear, C.B., P. W. Percy-Smith; H. Wylie, C.S.I.
Lieut.-Colonels, W. W. H. Scott, C.B., c.; Sir W. H. Meiklejohn, K.C.B., C.M.G., c. (temp. Brig.-Gen.) W. Loch; B. Wemyss, c.

MADRAS.

Lieut.-General, Sir R. C. Stewart, K.C.B., cav.

Major-Generals, E. W. Begbie, C.B., D.S.O.; F. Smalley; D. J. S. McLeod, C.B., D.S.O., cav (Bangalore).

BOMBAY.

Lieut.-General, M. H. Nicolson, C.B. (Mhow).
Major-Generals, C. A. Moore, cav.; G. H. Hogg, C.B., cav. (Deesa).
Lieut.-Colonel, R. A. Prideaux, c.

Royal Marines (£539,542).

(Head Quarters, Portsmouth.)

Hon. Col., H.R.H. the Duke of Saxe-Coburg-Gotha (Duke of Edinburgh), K.G., &c., Adm. Fl.
D.-A.-G., Sir H. B. Tuson, K.C.B., g.
A.-A.-G., W. P. Wright, col. comdt.
D.-A.-A.-G., J. H. Bor, C.M.G., m.
Quarter-Masters, T. W. Davies, m.; R. J. Waldron, lt.

ROYAL MARINE ARTILLERY.

Generals, Sir H. B. Tuson; C. C. Suther.
Lt.-Gen., A. French, C.B.
Maj.-Gen., F. Pengelley.
Col. Comdt., W. G. Tucker, C.B.
Col. 2nd Com., W. Campbell, A.D.C.
Lt.-Cols., J. B. Leefe; A. L. S.

Burrows; A. S. Le Quesne; W. C. Nicholls.
Adjt., E. McCarthy, capt.

ROYAL MARINE LIGHT INFANTRY.

Generals, Sir H. S. Jones, K.C.B.; F. G. Le Grand.
Lieut.-Gens., S. J. Graham, C.B.; A. H. F. Barnes.
Major-Gens., G. F. Munro; J. Cairncros; G. H. T. Colwell, C.B.; E. L. Rose; J. J. Morris.

1ST DIVISION—Chatham.

Col. 1st Com., F. V. G. Bird.
Col. 2nd Com., F. Baldwin.
Lieut.-Cols., A. E. Chapman, c.; W. T. Adair; A. F. Gatliff. E. A. Wylde.
Adjt., W. E. G. Connolly, capt.

2ND DIVISION—Portsmouth.

Col. Com., C. S. F. Fagan.
Col. 2nd Com., R. B. Kirchhoffer.
Lt.-Cols., C. G. Gordon; T. J. P. Evans; T.H. de M. Roche, D.S.O.; G. T. Onslow.
Adjt., F. W. Luard, capt.

3RD DIVISION—Plymouth.

Col. Com., C. H. Scafe.
Col. 2nd Com., H. St. G. Schomberg, C.B.
Lt.-Cols., R. P. Coffin, c.; T. F. D. Bridge; H. E. Eagles.
Adjt., R. N. Bendyshe, capt.

DÉPÔT—Walmer.

Col. Com., W. P. Wright.
Lt.-Col., A. D. Corbet, C.B., c.
Adjt., H. D. Palmer, capt.

Army Chaplains' Department (£62,350). (3)

Chaplain General (ranking as Major-General), Rev. John Cox Edghill, D.D.

Chaplains to the Forces, 1st Class (ranking as Colonels): Rev. W. H. Bullock, M.A., Halifax, N.S.; Rev. F. Sadleir, M.A., Cork; Rev. A. J. Townend, B.A., R.M.C.; Rev. J. H. S. Moxly, B.A., Chelsea Hosp.; Rev. G. Kirkwood, P., London; Rev. T. Foran, R.C., Shorncliffe; Rev. A. Malim, M.A., Malta; Rev. E. H. Goodwin, B.A., S. Africa; Rev. R.F. Collins, R.C., Gibraltar; Rev. F. J. Bateman, Warley; Rev. W. H. Milner, Aldershot; Rev. J. K.

Lethbridge, M.A., Plymouth; Rev. R. Morrison, Gosport; Rev. D. Nickerson, M.A., Malta; Rev. E. J. Hardy, M.A., Dublin; Rev. T. P. Mullins, LL.D., Netley; Rev. W. Le Grave, R.C., Bermuda; Rev. J. Hackett, B.D., Gibraltar; Rev. H. H. Beattie, LL.D., P., Aldershot; Rev. H. A. Darnell, London; Rev. A. S. Norfolk, Egypt; Rev. F. A. Darnell, M.A., Hilsea.
Chaplains to the Forces, 2nd Class (ranking as Lieut.-Colonels): Rev. G. Smith, Preston; Rev.

O. A. W. O'Neill, M.A., Chatham; Rev. E. M. Morgan, R.C., S. Africa; Rev. C. J. Hort, London; Rev. T. F. Falkner, M.A., S. Africa; Rev. P. F. Raymond, M.A., Gibraltar; Rev. C. W. Keatinge, R.C., Egypt; Rev. W. S. Randall, B.A., London; Rev. S. P. H. Statham, B.A., Dover; Rev. J. M. Simms, P., Egypt; Rev. A. W. B. Watson, M.A., Aldershot; Rev. C. F. O'Reilly, Dublin; Rev. W. B. L. Alexander, R.C., Dover.

. Chaplains to the Forces 3rd Class rank as *Majors,* and 4th Class as *Captains.* Presbyterian and Roman Catholic chaplains are distinguished by the letters P. and R.C.

Indian Medical Service.

BENGAL.

Surgeon-Generals, R. Harvey, M.D., C.B., D.S.O.; L. D. Spencer, M.D., C.B.
Colonels, J. H. Newman, M.D.; J. C. G. Carmichael, M.D.; G. Hutcheson, M.D.; B. Franklin, C.I.E.; G. McB. Davis, M.D., C.B., D.S.O.; T.H. Hendley, C.I.E.; C. W. Carr-Calthrop; A. S. Reid.
Lieut.-Colonels, R. C. Sanders, M.D.; W. H. Gregg; W. A. C. Roe; A. Deane, M.D.; W. F. Murray; C. H. Joubert; E. G. Russell; G. C. Hall; J. T. B. Bookey; J. Young; R. L. Dutt, M.D.; J. Duke; J. McConaghey, M.D.; H. Hamilton, M.D.; E. Palmer; E. Lawrie; J. M. Zorab; M. D. Moriarty; E.

Bovill; B.O'Brien, M.D.; Z.A. Ahmed, M.D.; W. E. Griffiths; D. Wilkie; D. P. Macdonald, M.D.; F. W. Wright, D.S.O.; A. J. Willcocks, M.D.; H. K. McKay, C.I.E.; F. R. Swaine, M.D.; S. H. Browne, M.D., C.I.E.; E. Mair; J. Armstrong; J. C. Fullerton; C. J. H. Warden; R. N. Stoker; G. Bomford, M.D.; C. J. McCartie, M.D.; G. S. A. Ranking; R. D. Murray; D. W. D. Comins; P. F. O'Connor; J. Moran, M.D.; W. A. Simmonds; R. Macrae; T. E. L. Bate; S. Borah; P. A. Weir; P. de H. Haig; J. Lewtas, M.D.; W. A. Mawson; S. H. Dantra, M.D.; B. Doyle; R. Cobb; W. H. Cadge; C. W. Owen, C.M.G.,

C.I.E.; G. S. Griffiths; C. H. Beatson; W. Owen, M.D.; G. J. Kellie; D. Basú; A. W. Mackenzie; D. ffrench-Mullen, M.D.; J. A. Nelis; A. M. Crofts; J. Crofts, M.D.; W. Coates, M.D.; S. J. Thomson, C.I.E.; R. N. Campbell; E. S. Brander; G. A. Emerson; J. ffrench-Mullen, M.D.; E. Cretin; A. Duncan, M.D.; S.F. Bigger; Sir G. S. Robertson, K.C.S.I.; T. Grainger, M.D.; T. H. Sweeny; D. F. Barry, M.D.; G. F. A. Harris; J. Anderson; C. J. Bamber; F. F. Perry; S. Little, M.D.; G. H. D. Gimlette, M.D.; C. B. Hunter; J. C. C. Smith.

MADRAS.

Surgeon-Generals: C. Sibthorpe, C.B., ; C. E. McVittie.

Colonels: T. J. McGann; D. Sinclair, M.B., C.S.I.; A. M. Branfoot, C.I.E.; W. E. Johnson, M.D.

Lieut.-Colonels: E. Fawcett; G. F. Bevan; A. F. Dobson; C. Little, M.D.; A. N. Rogers-Harrison; H. FitzL. P. F. Esmonde - White; W. R. Browhe, M.D.; A. H. Leapingwell; H. Allison, M.D.; T. J. H. Wilkins; H. D. Cook; P. H. Benson, M.B.; J. Lancaster, M.B.; W. G. King M.B., C.I.E.; W. O'Hara; G. T. Thomas;

A. J. Sturmer; A. Adams, M.D.; E. Fetrand; J. Maitland, M.D.; G. L. Walker, M.P.; C. L. Swaine; W. A. Lee; M. S. Eyre; H. A. F. Nailer; N. Chatterjie; C. H. Bennett, M.D.; M. E. Reporter; T. H. Pope, M.D.; R. Pemberton; D. P. Warliker; W. A. Quavle, M.D.; H. Armstrong; E. M. Damla; H. St. C. Carruthers; W. F. Thomas; H. G. L. Wortabet, M.D.; E. P. Frenchman; R. James; S.C. Sarkies; D. S. E. Bain.

BOMBAY.

Surgeon-General: G. Bainbridge, M D.

Colonels: S.O'B. Banks; G. W. R. Hay, M.D.; W. McConaghy, M.D.

Lieut.-Colonels: F. C. Barker, M.D.; G. Walters; T. S. Weir; M. L. Bartholomeusz; J. S. Wilkins, D.S.O.; A. H. C. Dane, M.D.; J. P. Greany, M.D.; A.S.G. Jayakar; J. McCloghry; J. W. Clarkson; J. Parker, M D.; W. G. H. Henderson; K. A. Dalal; H. W. B. Boyd; O. H. Channer; W. K. Hatch; K. R. Kirtikar; A. W. F. Street, D.S.O.; H. P. Jervis; D. C. Davidson; K. S. Nariman; C. Monks; G. H. Bull, M.D.; F. F. MacCarbie, C.I.E.; H. B. Briggs; W. P. Carson.

Army Ordnance Department (£154,600). (3)

Principal Ordnance Officer, **John Steevens,** C.B., c. (ranking as Maj.-Gen.), *Woolwich Arsenal.*

HEAD QUARTERS OF COMPANIES' ARMY ORDNANCE CORPS.

1 *Woolwich;* 2 *Aldershot;* 3 *Aldershot;* 4 *Na.al;* 5 *Dublin;* 6 *Curragh;* 7 *Egypt;* 8 *Gibraltar;* 9 *York;* 10 *Devonport and Portsmouth;* 11 *Aldershot*—DepôtCo., *Woolwich.*

Ordnance Officers 1st class, E. G. Skinner, C.B., c. *Ireland;* A. W. Bridgman, c. *Malta;* F. G. Wintle, D.S.O., *Woolwich Arsenal;* F. E Mulcahy, c. *R. A. Clothing Dept.;* E. E. Markwick, c. *Western Dist.;* R. F. N. Clarke, c. *South Africa.*

Ordnance Officers 2n I class, R. T. Stainforth, l.c. *Bermuda;* W. B. Cooke, l.c. *Weedon;* F. O. Leggett, l.c. *Egypt;* J. L. Wheeler, l.c. *China;* C. W. H. Tate, l.c. *War Office;* E. Heath, l.c. *Ceylon;* C. G. Jeans, l.c. *War Office;* G. R. Hobbs, l.c.

S. Africa; C. Purchas, l.c. *S. Africa;* G. R. Atkinson, l.c. *Halifax, N.S.;* A. Sadler, l.c. *Woolwich Arsenal;* T. Heron, l.c. *N.W. District;* H. W. Barrett, l.c. *Woolwich Arsenal;* W. G. Collingwood, l.c. *S.E. District;* E. B. Appelbe, l.c. *Natal;* T. P. Battersby, l.c. *Eastern District.*

Ordnance Officers 3rd class, **20.**

Ordnance Officers 4th class, **41.**

Army Pay Department (£100,570).

Colonels A. P. D., (*Chief Paymasters*), T. B. Senior, C.B., *Western Dist.:* T. W. Drage, C.B., *Home Dist.;* E. Roberts, *Southern Dist.;* E. H. Gorges, *Hong Kong;* G. H. Anson, *Scottish Dist.;* F. Treffry, *Ireland;* R. O. Richmond, *Eastern Dist.;* H. W. Bateman, *Woolwich Dist.;* W. B. Wade, *Cape;* W. H. Mortimer, *Natal;* J. H. Jackson, *Malta;* C. F. Carey, *Gibraltar;* H. W. Phillips, *Egypt;* S. D. Crookenden, *N.E. Dist.;* W. B. Caulfeild-Stoker, *S. E. Dist.*

Lieut.-Colonels A. P. D. (*Staff Paymasters*), W. C. Kennedy, *Dover;* R.M. Ireland, *Natal;* A. Longley, *Devizes;* J. C. Stockley, *Cape Town;* T. S. Coppinger, *Cape Town;* G. W. Barnes, *London;* O. M. Johnston, *Barbados;* J. E. Kitson, *War Office;* C. Ward, *J.S. D'Aguilar, Canterbury;* G. H. Moor - Lane, *Shorncliffe;* J. Bromfield, *Pontefract;* E. Orange, *Preston;* L. R. Dowdall, *Preston;* S. Churchill, *Discharge Depôt, Gosport;* C. E. Souper, *Warley;* G. H. Ferrier, *Hounslow;* J. Pearson, *Lichfield;* De la P. Robinson,

Sts. Settlements; R. R. B. Ternan, *Mala;* R. O'S. Brooke, *Netley Hosp.;* J. C. T. Humfrey, *York;* F. H. Haynes, *Newcastle - on - Tyne;* G. H. Singer, *Gibraltar;* G. Dewar, *Cork Dist.;* H. H. Gilbert, *N. W. Dist.;* J. O'B. Drury, *Tralie;* E. R. Reid, *Thames Dist.;* F. F. Parkinson, *Portsmouth;* H. R. Rathborne, *Dorchester;* J. A. R. Bell, *Jamaica;* J. Angus, *Rifle Depôt, Gosport;* W. Montgomery, *Clonmel;* W. Mackie, *Guildford;* H. C. Cowell, *Exeter.*

Army Veterinary Department (£25,900). (2)

Director-General, **Francis Duck,** C.B., *vety. col.,* 66, *Victoria Street, S.W.*

Veterinary Lieut.- Colonels, C. Clayton, *Aldershot;* H. Thomson, *vety. col. Bengal;* A. E. Queripel, *vety. col., Civil Vety.*

Dept., India; W. S. Adams, *Bombay;* J. Reilly, *Madras;* B. L. Glover, C.B, *Punjab;* G.

Durrant, London; I. Matthews, *S. Africa;* G. J. R. Rayment, *Woolwich.*

DAILY PAY OF THE ARMY.

STAFF.—General, £8; Lieutenant-General, £5 10s.; Major-General, £3; Brigadier-General, £2 10s.; Colonel on staff, £2; D.A.G. or Military Secretary, £1 10s.; A.A.G., £1 5s.; Brigade-Major, D.A.A.G., or Asst. Mil. Sec., £1 1s.; Aides-de-Camp to General, 15s.; Staff Captains, 15s.; Garrison and Camp Quartermasters, 9s. to 15s.

REGIMENTAL DAILY PAY (BRITISH ESTABLISHMENT).

	R. Horse Artillery		Royal Field Artillery		Royal Garrison Artillery		Royal Engineers *		Household Cavalry		Line Cavalry		Foot Guards †		Infantry and A.S.C.	
	s.	d.	s.	d.	s.	d.	s.	d.	s.	d.	s.	d.	s.	d.	s.	d.
Colonel or Lieutenant-Colonel	24	9	18	0	18	0	18	0	23	6	21	6	18	0	18	0
Major	18	5	16	0	16	0	16	0	15	6	15	0	13	7	13	7
Captain	15	0	11	7	11	7	11	7	13	6	13	0	11	7	11	7
Lieutenant	8	10	6	10	6	10	6	10	9	0	7	8	6	6	6	6
Second Lieutenant	7	8	5	7	5	7	5	7	6	8	6	8	5	3	5	3
‡Adjutant, if Captain	2	6	2	6	2	6	2	6	2	6	2	6	2	6	2	6
" if Lieutenant	3	6	3	6	3	6	3	6	3	6	3	6	3	6	3	6
Riding-Master	10	6	10	6			10	6	10	6	10	6				
Quartermaster	10	6	9	6	9	6	9	6	10	6	10	6	9	0	9	0
Sergeant (Corporal) Major	6	0	5	10	5	6	5	6	5	10	5	4	5	2	5	0
Bandmaster					6	0	6	0	5	6	5	6	5	0	5	0
Quartermaster Sergeant (Corp.-Major)	4	4	4	2	4	2	4	6	4	6	4	4	4	0	4	0
Sergeant (Corporal) Instructor	4	2	4	0	4	0			3	3	3	3	3	3	3	3
Battery Sergeant-Major, do. Q.-M. Sergt.	4	4	4	2												
Squad. Sergt. Maj. (Corp. Maj.)									4	6	4	4				
Troop & Company Sergt. (Corporal) Major					4	3	3	9	4	0	3	10				
Farrier Quartermaster Sergeant (Corp.)	4	5			4	3	3	9	4	3	4	0				
Wheeler Quartermaster Sergeant	3	11			3	9										
Collar-Maker & Saddler Q.M. Serg. (Corp.)	3	11			3	9			4	0	3	8				
Orderly-room Sergeant (Corporal)	2	8	2	8	3	2			3	0	2	8	2	6	2	6
Sergt. (Corp.) Trumpeter, Sergt. Bugler.	3	4	3	2	3	2	4	6	3	2	2	8				
Sergeant (Corporal) Cook	3	4	3	2	3	2	3	3	3	0	2	8	2	4	2	4
Sergeant (Corporal of Horse)	3	4	3	2	3	2	3	3	3	0	2	8	2	4	2	4
Sergt. (Corp.) Farrier and Carriage Smith	3	9	3	7	3	7	3	3	3	4	2	10				
Paymaster Sergeant (Corporal)					3	2			3	0						
Kettle-Drummer, Sergeant Drummer					3	2			2	4			2	6	2	4
Corporal Artificer, Colour Sergeant							2	11					3	2	3	0
Corporal	2	8	2	6	2	6	2	6	2	8	2	0	1	9	1	8
Bombardier, Second Corporal	2	5	2	3	2	3	2	2								
Collar-Maker, Wheeler, Saddler, Artificer	2	5	2	3	2	3	1	11	2	4½	1	9½				
Shoeing and Carriage Smith	2	2	2	0	2	0			2	3	1	8				
Trumpeter, Bugler, Drummer and Fifer	2	0	1	2½	1	2½	1	1½	1	11	1	4	1	2	1	1
Gunner, Sapper, Private	1	4	1	2½	1	2½	1	1½	1	9	1	2	1	1	1	0
Driver	1	3	1	2½	1	2½	1	1½								

* In addition to "Engineer's pay": Lt.-Col., 14s.; Maj., 9s.; Capt., 6s.; Lt. and 2nd Lt., 4s.
† In addition to "Guard's pay": Col., £250; Lt.-Col., £200; Maj., £170; Capt., £140; Lt. and 2nd Lt., £70 pr. ann.
‡ In addition to regimental pay.

MILITARY KNIGHTS OF WINDSOR.

Royal Foundation.
Maloney, Capt. W., (Governor).
Pickworth, Capt. John Atkins.
Dickens, Major Robert Vaughan.
Meredyth, Sir Edward H. T., Bt.
Marsh, Capt. Henry Dyke.
Deacon, Lt. Col Wm E. Durand

FitzGerald, Capt. M. G. Beaufoy.
Swinfen, Col. Frederick Hay.
Bolton, Major H. F. Somerset.
Watson, Major Stephen.
Atkinson, Capt. William.
Maguire, Lieut.-Col. John Thos.
Maude. Col. Cornwallis, V.C.

Lower Foundation.
Molesworth, Major R.
Tighe, Lt.-Col. John Aug.
Battye, Lt.-Col. Montague McP.
Somerset, Col Henry Geo E.
Muter, Col. Dunbar Douglas.

HER MAJESTY'S BODYGUARD OF THE HON'BLE. CORPS OF GENTLEMEN-AT-ARMS.

Captain, Col. Lord Belper, A.D.C.
Lieutenant, Col. Sir Henry Hugh Oldham.
Standard Bearer, Major P. L. Tillbrook.
Colonels, Morrison, Stewart, Master, C.B.; Cooch, Brown, Dumbar, Owen, Gore. Kelsey, Murray.
Lt.-Cols., Wemyss, Lowndes, Pockington, Mildmay, Rogers, Davidson, Hill, Fletcher, Holbech, Tufnell, Keppel, Horns-by-Drake, Kennett, Gore, Brooke Hunt.

Majors, Granville Wyatt Brackenbury, Hume, Gubbins, Rowley, Edwards, V.C.
Captains, Douglas-Willan, Bourke, Wallack, Clarke, Cuninghame, Pavy, Wingfield, Clement, Liddell.
Lieutenants, Malcolmson, V.C., Waller.
Civilian, Stapleton C. Cotton.
Clerk of Cheque & Adjutant, Col. Aubone George Fife.
Sub-Officer, Lieut.-Col. John Glas Sandeman.

HER MAJESTY'S ROYAL BODYGUARD OF YEOMEN OF THE GUARD.

Captain, Rt. Hon. Earl Waldegrave.
Lieutenant, Lt.-Col. Sir Horatio Page Vance.
Ensign, Col. R. G. Ellison. *Exons,* Lt.-Col. C. D.

Patterson; Major E. H. Elliott; Major Hon. F. L. L. Colborne; Capt. H. French. *Clerk of Cheque & Adjutant,* Col. R. Hennell, D.S.O.

Amount Estimated for 1899-1900, £27,578,039 (*gross*). Voted in 1898-99, £24,733,822 (*gross*).

ADMIRALTY OFFICE (£261,600). Naval Department—Whitehall. Hours, 10 to 5.

LORDS COMMISSIONERS (£13,950):—*First Lord*, Rt. Hon. Geo. Joachim Goschen, M.P. (*with house*) £4,550
Private Secretary to the First Lord, Captain Hon. Maurice A. Bourke, C.M.G., R.N. ... £801
Assistant Private Secretaries to First Lord, W. G. Greene, C.B., £100; and O. A. R. Murray £50
Senior Naval Lord, Vice Admiral Lord Walter Talbot Kerr, K.C.B. ....(*with house*) £1,500
Private Secretary, Charles H. R. Stansfield ... £50
Second Naval Lord, Rear-Admiral Archibald Lucius Douglas ... £1,200
Private Secretary, James H. Brooks ... £50
Third Naval Lord and Controller, Rear-Admiral Arthur Knyvet Wilson, C.B., V.C. ... £1,700
Secretary, Frederick Brown ... £700 to £900
Junior Naval Lord, Rear-Admiral Arthur William Moore, C.B., C.M.G. ... £1,200
Private Secretary, Henry F. V. Negus ... £50
Civil Lord, Austen Chamberlain, M.P. £1,000. *Private Sec.*, Robert G. Hayes ... £50
Parliamentary and Financial Secretary, William Grey Ellison-Macartney, M.P. ... £2,000
Private Secretary, William J. Evans ... £150
Permanent Secretary, Sir Evan MacGregor, K.C.B., £2,000. *Private Sec.*, Sidney R. Marriott ... £50
Counsel, and Judge Advocate of the Fleet, Rt. Hon. Alex. Staveley Hill, D.C.L., Q.C., M.P. (*besides fees*) £100

Secretary's Department—£19,538.

Assistant Secretary, H. J. Van Sittart Neale, C.B.
£1,200
Principal Clerks, Claude C. Birch, John H. Giffard, Charles I. Thomas ...£850 to £1,000
Assistant Principals, C. J. Adams, W. P. Feiling, W. G. Greene, C.B., G. H. Hoste, H. N. Stuart
£600 to £800
Clerks, J. W. S. Anderson, V. W. Baddeley, J. H. Brooks, A. J. Clayton, W. J. Evans, R. G. Hayes, O. A. R. Murray, W. F. Nicholson, C. Norwood, C. H. R. Stansfield, and C. Walker (and a vacancy) ...£150 to £500
Staff Clerks, W. Arthur Chapman, Richard J. Falkus, Arthur E. Piper, Arthur E. S. Roberts
£350 to £450
Clerks, 2nd Div. Higher Grade, B. D. Atkinson, Ferd. Brand, S. R. A. Marriott, J. W. H. Sherrington, J. Stewart ...£250 to £350
Clerks, 2nd Div., P. D. Bussell, J. E. Collins, G. F. Cotton, F. K. Crossley, E. E. Hawes, W. E. Llewellyn, C. G. Madin, A. Main, G. J. Main, G. R. Mascall, A. Mottley, H. F. V. Negus, J. Northam, W. G. Perrin, W. A. T. Shorto, H. O. Simmons, V. T. Simpson, F. G. C. Young
£70 to £250

Hydrographic Depart., Whitehall.—£13,582.

Hydrographer, Rear-Adm. Sir Wm. James Lloyd Wharton, K.C.B., F.R.S. ...£1,000
Assist. ditto, Capt. T. H. Tizard, C.B., R.N., F.R.S. £800
Chief Civil Asst., Comr. George C. Frederick, R.N.
£550 to £650
Naval Assists., Captain J. C. Richards, R.N.: Capt. Charles H. C. Langdon, R.N.: Staff-Capt. W. U. Petley, R.N.: Com. Arthur Havergal, R.N.: Com. C. V. Smith, R.N.: Lieut. V. B. Webb, R.N.: Com. Cecil F. Oldham, R.N., and Staff-Com. Herbert J. Dockrell ...£500 to £600
Surveying Officer (special business), Commander William V. Howard, R.N. ...£500 to £600
Superintendent of Compasses, Captain Ettrick William Creak, R.N., F.R.S. ...£750
Assistant do., Staff-Capt. J. Henderson, R.N. £600
Surv. Officer, Chart Brnch., Capt. G. Stanley R.N.
£650 to £750
Chief Draughtsman, Augustin J. Boyle £415 to £500
Draughtsmen, Charles O'N. Clark, T. H. Briggs, C. Sancroft Webber, Alexander Gibson, B.SC.; Hugh H. Underhill, A. W. Codd. B.A.; F. H. Sharbau, J. E. McGegan, J. W. Atherton, L. De Ville ...£120 to £400
Staff Clerk, J. P. Sadler ...£350 to £450
Clerks, 2nd Div. W. D. Barber, A. G. Thorn. H. Moody ...£70 to £350

Transport Department, Whitehall.—£10,760.

Director, Rear-Adm. Bouverie F. Clark ...£1,200
Assistant Director, Stephen J. Graff £700 to £900
Naval Assist., Capt. Fras. J. Pitt, R.N. £700 to £800
Superintending Clerk, J. A. Strong ...£600 to £800
Senior Clerks and Clerks, W. McC. Hill, J. W. W. Peake, F. S. White, and a vacancy £150 to £650
Staff Clerk, F. M. Duplock ...£350 to £450
Clerks, 2nd Div., E. Buxton, Robert Gear, J. J. Hayes, A. S. Hurst, F. Mallinson, C. J. Olver, F. E. Parker, W. J. Sargeaunt, J. Spear, W. Youngman ...£70 to £350
Chief Insp. of Shipping, Edwd. G. Farrell £350 to £500
Asst. Inspector, H. E. Parlett ...£150 to £200

Victualling Department.—£7,177.

Director, Henry F. R. Yorke, C.B., £1,000 to £1,200
Assistant-Director, J. A. Peil ...£800 to £900
Superintending Clerks, J. B. Hickman, H. Morris
£600 to £800
Deputy Store Officers, F. J. A. Arch, J. W. H. Culling, Uriah King ...£350 to £500
Assist. Store Officers, J. M. Bailey, A. A. Bakewell, A. N. Clothier, G. C. L. Grant, F. J. Gelsthorpe, F. H. Lambourn, C. R. Lane, J. R. Tapp, G. W. Wildman ...£100 to £350

Controller's Department.—£88,754.

Controller of the Navy, Rear-Admiral Arthur Knyvet Wilson, C.B., V.C. ...£1,700
Director of Naval Ordnance & Torpedoes, Rear-Admiral Edmund Frederick Jeffreys ...£1,000
Assistant Director of Torpedoes, Capt. Alexander W. Chisholm Batten, R.N. ...£950
Insp. of Warlike Stores, Comm. Barrington H. Chevallier, R.N. ...£800
Assistants to Director of Naval Ordnance, Commanders Alfd. E. A. Grant, R.N., J. F. Murray-Aynsley, R.N., Robert S. H. Hornby, R.N., E. L. Vaughan-Lee, R.N., each £485, Lieut. Philip Francklin, R.N. ...£321

Constructive Branch.

Assistant Controller and Director of Naval Construction, Sir William Henry White, K.C.B., SC.D., LL.D., F.R.S. ...£2,500
Chief Constrs., Henry E. Deadman (*senior*)
£850 to £1,000 with allowance.
W. E. Smith, W. H. Whiting
each £700 to £850 and allowance.
Constructors, J. H. Cardwell, J. Cotsell, W. Main (*overseeing*), A.E. Richards ... £400 to £550 and allowance.
Assistant Constructors, 1st Class, E. R. Bate, W. J. Berry, C. H. Croxford (*actg.*) J. J. Ellis (*overseeing*), S. W. F. Morrish, C. F. Munday, J. H. Narbeth, V. B. Paige (*actg.*), P. L. Pethick, W. T. Pine (*overseeing*) ...£300 to £450

Assist. Constrs., 2nd Class, W. H. Carter, R. J. Dennis (*Haslar*), W. J. Martin, A. M. Worthington .... £160 to £240

Assist. Constructors, 3rd Class, E. L. Attwood, N. J. McDermaid, C. G. Hall, E. H. Mitchell, F. W. Raven (*Haslar*), J Smith.

Curator of Drawings, J. R. Deatler £200 to £250

Confidential Clerk, J. G. J. Luffnau £200 to £300

Confidential Shorthand Writers, J. F. Phillips £200 to £250

R. E. Andrews .... £150 to £250

Engineering Branch.

Eng.-in-Chief, Sir A. J. Durston, K.C.B., R.N. £1,800

Chief Engineer Inspector of Mach., R. J. Butler £850 to £1000 *and allowance.*

Senior Engineer Inspector, H. J. Oram, R.N. £600 to £750 *and allowance.*

Engineer Inspector, David Edward Smith, R.N. (*for gun mountings*) £500 to £550 *and allowance.*

Engineer Inspctors, Joseph H. W. H. Ellis, R.N., P. Marrack, R.N., A. Spyer, E. A. Linnington (*acting*) (*oversee-ing*) £400 to £500 *and allowance.*

Fleet-Engineer, William H. Riley, R.N. £512

Staff Engineer, William J. Anstey, R.N. £300 to £400 *and allowance.*

Assistant Engineers, 1st Class, Howard Bone (*actg.*), Wm. McK. Wisnom, R.N., C. W. Bryant, R.N. (*gun mountings*), William H. Wood, R.N. .... £300 to £450

Ditto, 2nd Class, C. W. J. Bearblock, R.N., James Maewell, R.N., James Mountifield, R.N. £160 to £240 & *allow.*

Dockyard Branch.

Director of Dockyards, J. Williamson £2,000

Chief Constructor, J. B. Marshall, £850 to £1,000 *and allowance.*

Constructors, E. Beaton and H. J. Webb £400 to £550 *and allowance.*

Eng. Assist., Chas. Rudd, R.N. £650 to £800 & *allow.*

Staff Engineers, George G. Goodwin, R.N. and C. W. Gregory, R.N. ...£400 to £500 *and allowance.*

Examrs. Dockyd. Wk., J Humphreys, F. Logan, J. Shillinglaw, H.G.Williams (*acting*) £350 to £450

Clerical Staff.

Secretary to Controller, Fredk. Brown £700 to £900

Superintending Clerks, W. D. Legg, L. C. Thomson, W. J. Waymouth ...... £600 to £800

Clerks, H. W. Brown, A. W. Smallwood, augustus Williams... .... £150 to £500

Staff Clerks, A.H. Purchase, E.J.Tozer. £350 to £450

Clerks, 2nd Div., H. Akhurst, J. R. Brotherton, J. A. Champion, P. E. Couratin, F. F. Fisher, W. Sowray, W. T. Jones, C. H. Kendall, W. G. Kynvin, E. Lee, E. Leefe, J. C. Martin, C. R. Ogle, R. W. Waterhouse. £70 to £350

Naval Store Branch.

Director of Stores, Gordon W. Miller £1,000 to £1,200

Assist. Direct. of Stores, P.H.S.Desprez £700 to £900

Superintending Clerks, F. W. Black, George Lyon, John Wilson, A. F. Wootton... .....£600 to £800

Deputy Store Officers, W. Bonny, E. A. S. Hayward, and a vacancy .... £350 to £500

Assist. Store Officers, E. H. Codling, A. W. Grundy, J. C. Kell, H. G. Lowe, R. A. Pitcher, E. C. Sands, F. Weston, and two vacancies .... £100 to £350

Chief Exam. of Store Accts., B. Donald £350 to £500

Examiners of Store Accounts, Hon. Lieut. Wm. H. Bound, R.N.; and B. J. Thomas . £250 to £350

Examiner ditto (*employed as Inspector of Furniture*), J. R. Hughes .... £250 to £350

Assistant Examiners of Store Accounts, T. G. Crassweller, A. Eason, J. Puddicombe, and W. Riggs £200 to £250

Accounts Branch.

Inspector of Expense Accounts, Gordon B. Voules £850 to £1,000

Assistant, Philip Francis.......... £600 to £800

Professional Assist. do., John Ryan ..£350 to £500

Assist. Expense Accts. Officer, F.W.Cary £100 to £250

Naval Ordnance Store Department.

Storekeeper-General of Naval Ordnance, Colonel Thales Pease, C.B. £1,450

Civil Assistant do., David Evans ......£700 to £900

Deputy Naval Ordnance Officer, Lt.-Col. Charles Heinekin Ozanne .... £500 to £600

Staff Clerks, J. C. Escott, J. Fathers, and A. F. Taylor .... £300 to £400

Examiners, J. Gledhill, J. G. Morgan, J. Reeves, F. Ward, and G. E. Woodward £200 to £300

Account.-Genl.'s Depart., Spring Gdns. – £47,117.

Accountant-Gen., Richd. Davis Awdry, C.B. £1,500

Private Secretary, Ernest Nicks £50

Deputy Acct.-General, Williams Cuming £1,200

Assistants, W. F. King and G. M. Blandford £850 to £1,000

Superintending Clerks, J. G. Best, A. F. Dyer, Alfred Eyles, J. R. Mosse, C. J. Naef, W. H. H. Simmons, J. F. Taylor, F. Trafford, A. J. P. Webb ....£600 to £800

Paymaster of Contingencies, Henry Ashley Travers Cummins, R.N. .... £350 to £450

Assist. Supng. Clerks and Clerks, R. R. Bannatyne, W. R. V. Brade, C. M. Bruce, J. J. E. Butler, Philip Butt, E. S. Croft, J. F. Freeburn, F. G. Gordon, T. D. James, A. Northwood, Harold Roper, Wm. Sarger, W. S. Sarel, Osmund Seager, Frank Storr ....£150 to £500

Staff Clerks, J. B. B. Bailey, Edward Bilcliffe, W. H. Boar, John Cronin, Sidney Edwards, G. E. Foot, J. M. Henry, R. E. Nash, H. F. Painter, Thos. Platts, W. G. Ralph, A. G. Smith, E. W. Stafford, A. E. Tippen, A. E. Watling ....£350 to £450

Contract and Purchase Department, £7,697.

Director of Navy Contracts, Tatham Gwyn ..£1,200

Assistant Director, Wm. C. B. Hall £700 to £900

Superintending Clerks, C. A. Oliver, H. Sotham £600 to £800

Clerks, G. B. Cobb, W. St. D. Jenkins, Percy Minter, H. Morris ....£150 to £500

Staff Clerk, R. W. Wilson ....£350 to £450

Clerks, 2nd Div., H. J. Allen, J. F. Ford, G. W. Hall, W. H. Judson, H. W. Pillow, A. E. Rule, H. T. Sampson, F. G. Young ......£70 to £350

Medical Department,

Craven House, Northumberland Avenue.—£7,297.

Director-Genl., Sir Henry F. Norbury, M.D ; K.C.B., R.N. £1,300

Dep. Insp.-Gen., J. C. B. Maclean, M.B., R.N. £922

Staff-Surg., Geo. Welch £570

Senior Clerks, F. M. Clark, (*in charge*) ....£650 Robert G. Breaks £566

Staff Clerk, H. W. Temple ...... £350 to £450

Clerks, 2nd Div., W. A. F. Armstrong, H. S. Barlow, G. F. Bristow, F. W. Crawford, W. H. Gane, J. F. Golden, W. Innes, T. E. Kennedy, W. A. Montford, T. H. Perolz ......£70 to £350

Director of Works, Department, 21 Northumberland Avenue, W.C.—£17,348

Dir. of Works, Lt.-Col. E.Raban, R.E. £1,300 to £1,500

Assistant Director, D. C Leitch £850 to £1,000

Supg. Engrs ., Lt.-Col. S. H. Exham, R.E., (*Portsmouth*) ; Major E. R. Kenyon, R.E., (*Devonport*) ....£8oo and £700

Sup. Civil Eng ., W. J. Clarke, J. B. Hunt (*acting*), T. C. Hunter, F. W. Kite, L. Parr (*acting*), T. Sims ....£600 to £700 *and allowance.*

Chief Surveyor, G. Brighton £800
Surveyors, F. W. Harrison, P. P. Caldecott Smith,
    H. T. Matthews... .... £400 to £500
Assist. Survs., 1st G., J. Biden, F. H. Goadby, A. B.
    Holmes, H. H. Skipper £250 to 350. *and allow.*
Assist. Surveyors, 2nd Grade, E. J. Baker, M. T.
    James, J. A. Jones, F. C. Leest. T. Parker,
    J. L. Westland ... £125 to £250, *and allowance.*
Surv. of Coastgrd. Bldgs., J.M.Maxfield£500 to £700
Clerk of Works, F. R. Oglesby ....£215 to 300
Surveyor of Lands, J. W. Stone ....£500 to £600
Clerk, 2nd Div. J. W. Lamprell ......£70 to £350
Draughtsmen, W. F. Crisp, H. F. Wootton, £215
    to £400

Civil Engineer-in-Chief, Works Loan,
47, Victoria Street, S.W.

Civil Engineer-in-Chief, Major Henry Pilkington,
    O.B.,R.E. £1,000
Deputy do., C. Colson £1,000
Chief Draughtsman, H. Fidler.
Temporary Assistant Surveyors, H. M. Hodgson
    and H. Davis.
Architect (*temporary*), J. C. T. Murray.

Admiral Superintendent of Naval Reserves.
Admiralty, Whitehall.—£4,732.

Admiral Superintendent, Vice-Admiral Sir Comp-
    ton Edward Domvile, K.C.B. £1,984
Assist., Capt. Charles John Norcock, R.N. ..£1,000
Secretary, Fredk. J. Krabbé R.N...............£625
Clerk to Adm. Supt., Chas. H. Rowe, R.N.£200 to £269
Staff Clerk, F. W. Danter ....£350 to £450

Clerks, 2nd div., G. A. Neilson, G. J. Prentice
    £70 to £350

Royal Marine Office,
Craven House, Northumberland Avenue, W.C.

Deputy Adjutant-General, Lieutenant-General Sir
    Henry Brasnel Tuson, K.C.B...........£1,500
Assistant ditto, Col. Wm. Purvis Wright £800
Deputy-Asst. Adjt.-Gen. (*also Judge-Advocate*),
    Major James Henry Bor, C.M.G. £600
Quartermasters, Major T. W. Davies, Lieut. R. J.
    Waldron.

Naval Intelligence Department—£8,054.

Director, Rear-Adm. Regd. N. Custance £1,500
Assistant Directors, Captain H.S.H. Prince Louis
    of Battenberg, G.C.B., A.D.C., R.N., £800 ; Capt.
    Robert S. Lowry, R.N. £700
Naval Staff, Commrs. C. E. E. Carey, A. W. Ewart,
    G.E.Patey, W.C.Pakenham,E.R.Pears each £500
Marine Staff, Maj. Archibald Paris, R.M.A. . ; £500
    Capts. Pryce Peacock, R.M.A., Maj.H.W.L. Hol-
    man, R.M.L.I., Capt. J. E. Crowther, R.M.L.I.
    each £400
Clerk, (vacant).
Staff Clerk, G. J. Rickman................£350 to £450
Clerks, 2nd div., H. Broadbent, J. T. Cotton. R.
    Gordon, W. H. Hancock ....£70 to £350

Greenwich Hospital Department.

Director of Hospital, George T. Lambert, C.B. £1,000
Clerk in Charge, George H. H. Carrington....£600
Accountant, John Burrell ....£350 to £450
Clerks, 2nd div., L. Setacci, A. A. Rutter, £70 to £350

FLAG OFFICERS ON THE ACTIVE LIST. (80)

ADMIRALS OF THE FLEET. (3)
H.R.H. Prince of Wales (*hon.*).
H. I. M. William II., German
    Emperor,King of Prussia(*hon.*).
Keppel, Hon. Sir Henry, G.C.B.

ADMIRALS. (12)
Culme-Seymour, Sir Michael, Bt.,
    G.C.B. (*C.-in-C. Portsmouth and
    First and Principal* A.D.C.).
Fremantle, Hon. Sir Edm. Robt.,
    K.C.B., C.M.G.
Fairfax, Sir Henry, K.C.B. (*C.-in-
    C., Plymouth*).
Erskine, Sir J. Elphinstone, K.C.B.
Adeane, Edward Stanley, C.M.G.
Tracey, Sir Richd. Edward, C.B.
    (*Pres. R. N. Coll.*)
Hotham, Sir Charles Frederick
    K.C.B.
Scott, Lord Chas. Montagu-
    Douglas, K.C.B.
More-Molyneux, Sir R. H., K.C.B.
Bowden-Smith, Sir Nathaniel,
    K.C.B. (*C.-in-C., Nore*).

VICE-ADMIRALS. (22)
Kerr, Lord Walter Talbot, K.C.B.
    (*Senior Naval Lord*).
Morant, George Digby.
Seymour, Sir Edw. Hobart, K.C.B.
    (*C.-in-C., China*).
St. John, Henry Craven.
Kennedy, Sir Wm. Robert, K.C.B.

Fisher, Sir John Arbuthnot,
    K.C.B.(*C.-in-C.,Mediterranean*).
Stephenson, SirHenryFdk.,K.C.B.
    (*Extra Equerry to Pr. of Wales*)
Fane, Charles George.
Domvile, Sir Compton Edward,
    K.C.B. (*Supt. of Naval Reserves*).
Bedford, Sir Fredk. Geo. Denham,
    K.C.B. (*C.-in-C., N. America*).
Markham, Albert Hastings.
Dale, Alfred Taylor.
Buckle, Claude Edward.
Rawson, Sir Harry Holdsworth,
    K.C.B. (*C.-in-C. Channel*).
Bridge, Cyprian Arthur George.
Drummond, Edmund Charles.
Cardale, Charles Searle.
Fullerton, Sir John Regd. Thos.,
    A.D.C., K.C.V.O., C.B.
Rice, Ernest.
Vander-Meulen, Fredk. Samuel

REAR-ADMIRALS (43)
Andoe. Hilary Gustavus, C.B.
Powlett, Armand Temple.
Hastings, Alex. Plantagenet, C.B
Lloyd, Rodney Maclaine, C.B
    (*Supt. Malta Dockyard*).
Oxley, Chas. Lister.
Harris, Sir Robert Hastings,
    K.C.M.G. (*C.-in-C., Cape and
    West Africa*).
Pearson, Hugo Lewis (*C.-in-C.,
    Australia*).
Fellowes, John, C.B.
Penrose - FitzGerald, Charles
    Cooper
Wilson, Arthur Knyvet, C.B., V☰
    (*Controller of the Navy*).
Douglas, Archibald Lucius
    (*Second Naval Lord*).

St. Clair, Wm. Home Chisholme.
Lake, Atwell Peregrine Macleod
    (*Coast of Ireland*).
Noel, Sir Gerard Henry Uctred,
    K.C.M.G. (*2nd. Mediterranean*).
Brackenbury,JohnW.,C.B.,C.M.G.
Jackson,Thomas Sturges (*Devon-
    port*).
Fanshawe, Arthur Dalrymple,
    2nd, Channel).
Bosanquet, Day Hort (*C.-in-C.
    East Indies*).
Beaumont,Lewis Anthony (*C.-in-
    C. Pacific*)
Beresford, Lord Chas. Wm. Dela-
    poer, C.B., M.P.
Jenkings, Albert Baldwin (*V.-P.
    Ordnance Committee*).
Bruce, James Andrew T. (*2nd,
    China*).
Rose, Henry.
Aldrich, Pelham (*Portsmouth
    yard*.)
Holland, Swinton Colthurst
    (*Chatham yard*)
Rolfe, Ernest Neville, C.B.
Moore, Arthur William, C.B.,
    C.M.G.. (*Junior Naval Lord*).
Bickford. Andrew Kennedy, C.M.G.
Acland, William Allison Dyke.
Mann, Wm. Fredk. Stanley.
Bainbridge, John Hugh.
Drury. Charles Carter.
Jeffreys, Edmund Fredk. (*Direc-
    tor of Naval Ordnance and
    Torpedoes*).
Custance, Regd. Neville (*Naval
    Intelligence*).
W tson, Hu ges, C.V.O.
Pattisson, Jno. Robert E.

NAVAL AIDES-DE-CAMP TO THE QUEEN.

Admiral of Fleet H.R.H. Duke of Saxe-Coburg-Gotha K.G. (*personal*).

Captain H.R.H. Duke of York, K.G. (*personal*).

Culme - Seymour, *Admiral Sir* Michael, Bart., G.C.B. (*first and principal*).

Fullerton, *Vice-Adm.* Sir John R. T., K.C.V.O., C.B. (*Royal Yacht*).
Captains :
Fawkes, Wilmot H.
Atkinson, George L.
May, William H., M.V.O.
Parr, Alfred A. C.
Metaxa, Count Frederick C.
Curzon-Howe, Hon. Assheton G., C.B., C M.G.

Macleod, Angus.
Poë, Edmund S., M.V.O.
Campbell, Charles, C.B., D.S.O.
Chichester, Sir Edward, Bart., C.M.G.
H.S.H. Prince Louis A. of Battenberg, G.C.B. (*hon.*).
Marine—
Campbell, *Colonel* William, R.M.A.
Crosbie, *Colonel* Adolphus Brett.

FLAG OFFICERS IN COMMISSION, AND THEIR SECRETARIES.

Nore	*Admiral* Sir N. Bowden-Smith, K.C.B.	Wildfire	*Sec.*, F.G.W Taylor.
Portsmouth...............	*Adm.* Sir Mich.Culme-Seymour, Bt.,G.C.B.	Nelson'sVictory	*Sec.*, Hy. H. Rickard.
Plymouth.................	*Adm* Sir Henry Fairfax, K.C.B.	Vivid	*Sec.*, F. H. Smith.
Queenstown, Ireland	*Rear-Adm.* Atwell Peregrine M. Lake ..	Howe	*Sec.*, Chas. Meredyth.
Channel Squadron...	{ *Vice-Adm.* Sir Harry H. Rawson, K.C.B.	Majestic	*Sec.*, Wm. H. Rowe.
	{ *Rear-Adm.* Arthur D. Fanshawe, (2nd)	Magnificent......	*Sec.*, C.M.Luckham.
Mediterranean........	{ *Adm.* Sir John A. Fisher, K.C.B.	Renown	*Sec.*, D.B.L Hopkins.
	{ *Rear-Ad.* Sir Gerard Noel, K.C.M.G.	Revenge	*Sec.*, Alfd.R. Parker.
North America and	{ *Vice-Adm.* Sir Fred.G D.Bedford,K.C.B.	Crescent	*Sec.*, Chas. E. Byron.
West Indies	{ *Commodore* Wm. H.Henderson, *Jamaica*	Urgent	*Sec.*, T. H. Millet.
Pacific	*Rear-Adm.* Lewis A. Beaumont	Warspite	*Sec.*, H. H. Share.
China	{ *Vice-Adm.* Sir Edward H.Seymour,K.C.B.	Centurion	*Sec.*, Fras. C. Alton.
	{ *Rear-Adm.* James A. T. Bruce (2nd) ...	Grafton	*Sec.*,R.CluttonBaker.
	{ *Commodore*,Fran.Powell,C.B.,*Hong Kong*	Tamar	*Sec.*, F. G. Motton.
East Indies	*Rear-Adm.* Day Hort Bosanquet	Eclipse	*Sec.*, Ed. F. E. Gipps.
Australia	*Rear-Adm.* Hugo Lewis Pearson	Royal Arthur..	*Sec.*, Chas. Ferguson.
Cape and WestAfrica	*Rear-Adm.* Sir Robt. H. Harris, K.C.M.G.	Doris	*Sec.*, Chas. Woolley.
S.E.Coast of America	*Commodore* Robert Leonard Groome	Flora	*Sec.*, Victor Weekes.
Training Squadron...	*Commodore*, Edmund Samuel Poë, M.V.O.	Raleigh	*Sec.*,W. E. R. Martin.
Portsmouth Dockyd.	*Rear-Admiral* Pelham Aldrich (Supt.)..	Asia	*Sec.*, E. Curtler.
Devonport Dockyard	*Rear-Adm.*Thom.SturgessJackson(Supt.)	Indus	*Sec.*, W. T. Sanders.
Chatham Dockyard .	*Rear-Adm.* Swinton C. Holland (Supt.)	Algiers	*Sec.*, George Egan.
MaltaDockyd.(Supt.)	*Rear-Adm.* Rodney Maclaine Lloyd (Supt.)	Hibernia	*Sec.*, F. R.Waymouth.
Supt.,NavalReserves	*Vice-Adm.* Sir Cmptn. E. Domvile, K.C.B.	Alexandra	*Sec.*,Fredk.J.Krabbe.

A LIST OF THE SQUADRONS AFLOAT, 1 NOV. 1899.

MEDITERRANEAN AND RED SEA. *Commander-in-Chief*, Adm. Sir John A. Fisher, K.C.B. (Renown). *Battleships*, Anson, Cæsar, Devastation (*Port guardship, Gibraltar*), Empress of India, Hood, Illustrious, Ramillies, Renown, Revenge, Royal Oak, Royal Sovereign. *Cruisers*, Andromeda, Astræa, Barham, Dido. Fearless, Isis, Theseus, Thetis, Venus. *Torpedo-boat destroyers*, Ardent, Banshee, Boxer, Bruizer, Dragon, Earnest, Griffon. *Torpedo-boats*, Harrier, Hazard, Hebe, Hussar. *Gunboats*, Cockatrice, Halcyon, Salamander. *Sloops*, Melita, Nymphe ; with the Hibernia (*flagship, Malta Dockyard*), Rupert, Polyphemus (*torpedo ram*) Surprise, (*despatch vessel*), Tyne (*troopship*), Imogene (*sp. service*), Cruiser (*training-ship*).

CHANNEL. *Senior Officer in Command*, Vice-Admiral Sir Harry H. Rawson, K.C.B. (Majestic). *Battleships*, Hannibal, Jupiter, Magnificent, Majestic, Mars, Prince George, Repulse, Resolution. *Cruisers*, Arrogant, Diadem, Furious, Niobe, Pactolus, Pelorus.

NORTH AMERICA AND WEST INDIES. *Commander-in-Chief*, Vice-Admiral Sir Frederick G. D. Bedford, K.C.B. (Crescent). *Coast Defence*, Hotspur(Bermuda).*Cruisers*,Comus,Crescent,Hermes, Indefatigable, Pearl, Proserpine, Psyche, Talbot, Tribune. *Sloops*, Alert, Buzzard. *Floating battery*, Terror (Bermuda). *Port Guardship*, Hotspur (Bermuda). *Depôt ship*, Urgent (Jamaica). *T.B.D.*, Quail. *Special Service*, Columbine.

SOUTH EAST COAST OF AMERICA. *Captain* (Commodore), Robert Leonard Groome, (Flora). *Cruisers*, Flora, Pegasus. *Sloops*, Beagle, Swallow.

PACIFIC. *Commander-in-Chief*, Rear-Admiral Lewis A. Beaumont (Warspite). *Cruisers*, Arethusa, Leander, Phaeton, Warspite. *Sloop*,

Icarus. *Gunboat*, Pheasant. *T. B. D.*, Virago. *Store-ship*, Liffey (Coquimbo).

CAPE AND WEST COAST OF AFRICA. *Commander-in-Chief*, Rear-Admiral Sir Robert Hastings Harris, K.C.M.G. (Doris). *Battleship*, Monarch (*guardship*, Cape). *Cruisers*, Barracouta, Barrosa, Doris, Forte, Magicienne, Philomel, Powerful, Tartar, Terrible. *Gunboats*, Dwarf, Partridge, Sparrow, Widgeon, *River service*, Herald, Mosquito.

EAST INDIES. *Commander-in-Chief*, Rear-Admiral Day Hort Bosanquet (Eclipse). *Cruisers*, Eclipse, Marathon, Melpomene, Pomone, Racoon. *Gunboats*, Lapwing, Pigeon. *Special service*, Sphinx. *Coast defence*, Assaye and Magdala (Bombay).

CHINA. *Commander-in-Chief*, Vice-Admiral Sir E. Hobart Seymour, K.C.B. (Centurion). *Battleships*, Barfleur. Centurion, Victorious. *Cruisers*, Aurora, Bonaventure. Brisk, Endymion, Hermione, Iphigenia, Orlando, *Terrible*, Undaunted. *Gun-boats*, Esk, Linnet, Peacock, Pigmy, Plover, Rattler, Redpole. *Torpedo-boats*, Fame, Whiting. *Sloops*, Algerine, Daphne, Phœnix. *Receiving ship*, Tamar, (Hong Kong). *Despatch-vessel*, Alacrity. *Storeship*, Humber. *Shallow draught steamers for river service*, Sandpiper, Woodcock, Woodlark.

AUSTRALIA. *Com.-in-Chief*, Rear-Adm. Hugo Lewis Pearson (Royal Arthur). *Cruisers*, Katoomba, Mildura, Mohawk, Porpoise, Pylades, Royal Arthur, Tauranga, Wallaroo. *Sloop*, Torch. *Gun-boats*, Lizard, Ringdove. *Torpedo-boat*, Karrakatta.

TRAINING SQUADRON. *Commodore*, Edmund Samuel Poë, M.V.O. (Raleigh). *Cruisers*, Champion, Cleopatra, Raleigh, Volage.

WITH DATE OF LAUNCHING, GUNS, TONNAGE, HORSE POWER (*N.D.*), AND RATE OF SPEED,

Armoured vessels have their names printed in CAPITALS; those ships in commission on Nov. 1, 1899, have an asterisk * prefixed, and the names of their commanding officers attached; those marked † are sailing vessels, and those with a ‡ are paddle steamers.

ABYSSINIA (1870), 4, 2900 tons (900 h.-p.), Coast Defence ship, 9 kts., for India's naval defence, Bombay Harbour.

ACHILLES (1864), 16, 9820 (4000), 1st cl. cruiser, 12·7 kts., Portsmouth.

Active (1869). 12. 3080 (2400), 2nd cl. cruiser, 15·10 kts., Portsmouth.

Æolus (1892), 8. 3600 (7000), 2nd cl. cruiser, 19¾ kts., Devonport.

AGAMEMNON (1883), 6, 8660 (4500), 2nd cl. battleship, 12·1 kts., Devonport.

AGINCOURT (1868), 17, 10690 (4000), 1st cl. cruiser, 12 kts., depôt for boys, Portland. *Comm.* Drury St. Aubyn Wake.

AJAX (1883), 4, 8660 (4500), 2nd cl. battleship, 12·1 kts., Chatham.

Alacrity (1885), 1700 tons (2000). despatch vessel, 17 kts., China. *Comm.* Arthur H. Smith-Dorrien.

Alarm (1892). 2, 810 (2500), 1st cl. torpedo gunboat, 19¼ kts, Hull. *Lieut. & Comm.* Herbert Powley

Albacore (1883), 4, 560 (500), 2nd cl. gunboat, 11 kts., particular service. *Lieut. and Comm.* Walter J. W. Steward.

Albatross 1899, 6, 360 (7500 *f.d.*), t.b.d., 32 kts., completing at Chiswick.

‡*Alberta* (1863), 370 (1000), tender to Royal yacht, Portsmouth. *Staff-Capt.* George A. Broad.

ALBION (1898), 16, 12950 (13500), 1st cl. battleship, armoured, complement 700, 18¼ kts., completing at Blackwall.

Alert (1894), 6, 960 (1100), sloop, 13¼ kts., N. Amer. and W. Indies. *Comm.* Henry Savile.

*ALEXANDRA (1877), 18, 9490 (7000), 2nd cl. battleship, 14·3 kts., Coastguard, Portland. *Vice-Adm.* Sir Compton Edward Domvile, K.C.B. (Naval Reserves); *Capt.* Count Frederick C. Metaxa A.D.C.; *Comm.* Henry F. Aplin.

Algerine (1895), 6, 1050 (1100), sloop, 13 kts., China. *Comm.* Edmond J. W. Slade.

Algiers late Anson (1860), 5260 tons, flag-ship, Chatham Dockyard. *Rear-Adm.* Swinton C. Holland; *Capt.* Geo. Lambart Atkinson, A.D.C.

Amelia (late *Hawk*), 416 tons (150). Coastguard, screw, tender to *Collingwood*, Bantry.

Amphion (1883), 10, 4300 (5000), 2nd cl. cruiser, 16·6 kts., Pacific. *Capt.* Frank Finnis.

Amphitrite (1898, 16, 11000 (18,000, 1st cl. cruiser, complement 677, 20¾ kts., Chatham.

Andromache (1890), 8, 3400 (7000), 2nd cl. cruiser, 20 kts., Chatham.

Andromeda (1897). 16, 11000 (16500), 1st cl. cruiser, 20 kts., Mediterranean. *Capt.* John L. Burr, C.M.G, *Comm.* Charles A. Christian.

Angler (1898), 310 tons (5700 *f.d.*), t.b.d., 30¼ kts., Chatham.

*ANSON (1889), 10, 10600 (7500), 1st cl. battleship. 16·9 kts., Mediterranean. *Capt.* Wm. Wilson; *Comm.* Richard F. Philimore

Ant (1873), 1, 254 (110), 3rd cl. gunboat, Portsmouth.

Antelope (1893, 2, 810 (2500). 1st cl. torpedo gunboat, 19¼ kts., employed for training of R.N.R. Portishead. *Comm.* Oliver A. Stokes.

Apollo (1891), 8, 3400 (7000), 2nd cl. cruiser, 20 kts., Chatham.

Archer (1885), 6, 1770 (2200), 3rd cl. cruiser, 16·5 kts., China.

Ardent (1894), 6, 265 (4300 *f.d.*), t.b.d., 27·97 kts., tender to *Renown*, Mediterranean. *Lieut.-Comm.* Francis E. Walters.

Arethusa (1882), 10, 4300 (5000), 2nd cl. cruiser, 16·6 kts., Chatham.

Argonaut (1898), 16, 11000 (18000), 1st cl. cruiser, 20·5 kts., Chatham.

Argus (1864), 2, 300 (150), Coastguard service, screw, tender to *Collingwood*, Bantry.

Ariadne (1898), 16, 110·0 (18000), 1st cl. cruiser, complement 677, 20¾ kts., Chatham.

Ariel (1898), 8·0 tons (5400 *f.d.*), t.b.d., 30½ kts., Chatham.

Arrogant (1896), 10, 5750 (10000), 2nd cl. cruiser, 19·5 kts., Channel Squadron. *Capt.* Arthur W. E. Prothers; *Comm.* John de M. Hutchinson.

Arrow (1871), 1, 254 (110), 3rd cl. gunboat, Portsmouth.

*† Asia (1824), 3594 tons, flag-ship, Portsmouth Dockyard. *Rear-Adm.* Pelham Aldrich; *Capt.* Alfred A. C. Parr, A.D.C

*Assaye (1891), 2, 735 (2500), 1st cl. torpedo gunboat, 19 kts., for India's naval defence, Bombay Harbour. *Lieut.-Comm.* O. U. Coates.

Astræa (1893), 10, 4360 (7000), 2nd cl. cruiser, 19¾ kts., Mediterranean. *Capt.* A. W. Paget, C.M.G.

AUDACIOUS (1869), 18, 6010 (3300), 3rd cl. battleship, 11·6 kts., Chatham.

*AURORA (1889), 12, 5600 (5500), 1st cl. cruiser, 18 kts., China. *Capt.* Edward H. Bayly; *Comm.* Henry J. L. Clarke.

*AUSTRALIA (1888), 12, 5600 (5500), 1st cl. armoured cruiser, 18 kts, Coastguard, Southampton Water. *Capt.* John Mackenzie McQuhae, C.B.; *Comm.* Montague G. Cartwright.

Avon (1898), 6,330 (6000 *f.d.*), t.b.d., 30 kts. Chatham.

Badger (1872), 1, 254 (110), 3rd cl. gunboat, Devonport.

Banshee (1854), 6, 295 (4400 *f.d.*), t.b.d., 27·97 kts., Mediterranean (tender to *Royal Sovereign*). *Lieut. and Comm.* Hector L. Watts-Jones.

*BARFLEUR (1894), 14, 10500 (9000), 1st cl. battleship, 18·5 kts., Flagship of Second in command, China. *Rear-Adm.* James A. T. Bruce. *Capt.* Hon. Stanley C. J. Colville, C.B.; *Comm.* David Beatty, D.S.O.

*Barham (1889), 6, 1830 (3200), 3rd cl. cruiser, 18·6 kts., Mediterranean. *Comm.* Henry L. Tottenham.

*Barracouta (1889), 6, 1580 (1750), 3rd cl. cruiser, 16·5 kts., Cape and West Africa. *Comm.* Richard Henry Peirse.

*Barrosa (1889), 6, 580 (1750), 3rd cl. cruiser, 16·5 kts., Cape and West Africa. *Comm.* Wm. Francis Tunnard.

Basilisk (1889), 8, 1170 (1400), sloop, 14·7 kts., Sheerness.

Bat (1897). 360 tons (5900 *f.d.*), t.b.d., 30 kts., Devonport (tender to *Vivid*). *Comm.* Alexander L. Duff.

Beagle (1889). 8, 1170 (1400), sloop, 14·7 kts., S. E. Coast of America. *Comm.* Hon. H. A. S. Stanhope.

BELLEISLE (1878), 4. 4870 (2600), armoured Coast Defence ship, 11·9 kts., Devonport.

BELLEROPHON (1866), 20, 7550 (4000), 3rd cl. battleship, 12·4 kts., Devonport.

Bellona (1890). 6, 1830 (3200), 3rd cl. cruiser, 17·8 kts., Portsmouth.

*BENBOW (1888), 12, 10600 (7500), 1st cl. battleship 16·75 kts, Coastguard, Greenock. *Capt.* Richd. P. Humpage; *Comm.* Ralph Hudleston.

Bittern (1898), 6, 330 tons (6000 *f.d.*), t.b.d., 30 kts., Chatham.

*BLACK PRINCE (1861), 28, 9210 (4000), 1st cl. cruiser, training-ship for boys, Queenstown. *Comm.* William J. Grogan.

Blake (1889), 12, 9000 (13000), 1st cl. cruiser, 21·5 kts., Devonport.

Blanche (1889), 6, 1580 (1750), 3rd cl. cruiser, 16·5 kts., Devonport.

Blazer (1870), 2, 254 (110), 3rd cl. gunboat, Portsmouth.

Blenheim (1890), 12, 9000 (13000), 1st cl. cruiser, 21·5 kts., Chatham.

*Blonde (1889), 6, 1580 (1750), 3rd cl. cruiser, 16·5 kts., Fishery Duties. *Comm.* Charles H. Dare.

Bloodhound (1871), 2, 254 (110), 3rd cl. gunboat, Portsmouth.

Boadicea (1875), 14, 4140 (4500), 2nd cl. cruiser, Portsmouth.

*Bonaventure (1892), 10, 4360 (7000), 2nd cl. cruiser, 19·5 kts., China. *Capt.* R. A. J. Montgomerie, C.B.

Bonetta (1871), 1, 254 (110), 3rd cl. gunboat, Devonport.

Boomerang (1889), 2, 735 (2500), 1st cl. torpedo gunboat, 20 kts., for protection of floating trade in Australasian waters, Sydney, New South Wales.

*Boscawen (1841), 4579 tons, training-ship for boys, Portland. *Capt.* Thomas H. M. Jerram ; *Comm.* Wm. G. Van Ingen.

Bouncer (1881), 1, 265 (110), 3rd cl. gunbt., Sheerness.

*Boxer (1894), 6, 265 (4300 f.d.), t.b.d., 27·17 kts., Mediterranean (tender to *Revenge*). *Lieut. and Comm.* Cecil J. Twisleton-Wykeham-Fiennes.

Bramble (1898), 6, 700 (900). 1st cl. gunboat, 13½ kts., completing at Liverpool.

Brazen (1896), 6, 300 (5800 f.d.), t.b.d., 30 kts., Glasgow (completing for sea).

Brilliant (1891), 8, 3600 (7000), 2nd cl. cruiser, 19·7 kts., Chatham.

*Brisk (1886), 6, 1770 (2200), 3rd cl. cruiser, 16·5 kts., China. *Comm.* R. B. S. Wrey.

*Britannia (1860), 6201 tons, training-ship for naval cadets, Dartmouth. *Capt.* Hon. Assheton G. Curzon-Howe, C.B., C.M.G., A.D.C. ; *Comm.* Christopher G. F. M. Cradock.

Briomart (1899), 6, 700 (900), 1st cl. gunboat, 13½ kts., completing at Liverpool.

*+Briton (1814), 1408 tons, drill-ship, R.N. Reserve, Inverness, N.B. *Lt. & Comm.* Alexr. Y. C. M. Spearman.

*Bruizer 1895), 6, 265 (4300 f.d.), t.b.d., 27·97 kts., Mediterranean (tender to *Hood*). *Lieut.-Comm.* Montague Lister Hulton.

Bulldog (1872), 2, 254 (110), 3rd cl. gunboat, Devonport.

Bullfinch (1899), 6, 300 tons (5800 f.d.), t.b.d., 30 kts., Portsmouth.

BULWARK (1899), 16, 15000 (15000) 1st cl. battleship, 18 kts., completing at Devonport.

Bustard (1871), 1, 254 (110), 3rd cl. gunbt., Sheerness.

*Buzzard (1887), 8, 1140 (1400), composite sloop. 14·50 kts., N. America and West Indies. *Com.* Leicester F. G. Tippinge.

*CÆSAR (1896), 16, 14500 (10000), 1st cl. battleship, 17·5 kts., Mediterranean. *Cap.* Edward H. Gamble ; *Comm.* Charles E. Madden.

*Caledonia (1810) 388o tons, training-ship for boys, Queensferry, N.B. *Comm.* John G. Hewitt.

Calliope (1884), 16, 2770 (2700), 3rd cl. cruiser, 14·6 kts., particular service. *Capt.* H. P. Routh.

Calypso (1883), 16, 2770 (2700), 3rd cl. cruiser, 14·6 kts., Devonport.

Cambrian (1893), 10, 4360 (7000), 2nd cl. cruiser, 19·5 kts., China.

*Cambridge (1858), 4971 tons, gunnery school ship, Devonport. *Capt.* Robert Wm. Craigie : *Comm.* Herbert C. C. Da Costa.

CAMPERDOWN (1889), 10, 10600 (7500), 1st cl. battleship, 16·9 kts., Portsmouth.

CANOPUS (1897), 16, 12950 (13500), 1st class battleship, Portsmouth. *Comm.* Arthur C. Leveson.

*CENTURION (1893), 14, 10500 (9000), 1st cl. battleship, 18·51 kts., flag-ship, China. *Vice-Adm.* Sir Edward Hobart Seymour, K.C.B. ; *Capt.* John R. Jellicoe ; *Comm.* Chas. D. Granville.

Charon (1896), 6, 360 (6200 f.d.), t.b.d., 30¼ kts., Portsmouth.

*Champion (1878), 12, 2380 (2000), 3rd cl. cruiser, 12¾ kts., Training Squadron. *Capt.* F. O. Pike.

Charger (1894), 6, 250 (3100 f.d.), t.b.d., 27·98 kts., Portsmouth.

Charybdis (1893), 10, 4360 (7000), 2nd cl. cruiser, 19·5 kts., Devonport.

Cheerful (1897), 6, 308 (5800 f.d.), t.b.d., 30 kts., Chatham.

Circe (1892), 2, 810 (2500), 1st cl. torpedo gunboat, 19¼ kts., tender to *Severn*, Harwich. *Lieut.-Comm.* George S. Q. Carr, C.M.G.

*Cleopatra (1878), 12, 2380 (2000), 3rd cl. cruiser, 13 kts., Training Squadron. *Capt.* R. K. McAlpine.

*+Clyde (1849), 1447 tons, drill-ship, R. N. Reserve, Aberdeen. *Comm.* James Pipon Montgomery.

*Cockatrice late *Bramble* (1883), 6, 715 (600), 1st cl. gunboat, Mediterranean (for Danube). *Comms.* Herbert Neville Rolfe, John B. Stevenson.

Cockchafer (1881), 4, 465 (360), 2nd cl. gunboat, 9·8 kts., Coastguard Cruiser, tender to *Rodney*, Queensferry, N.B.

*COLLINGWOOD (1886), 10, 9500 (7000), 1st cl. battleship, 16½ kts., Coastguard, Bantry. *Capt.* Henry C. Bigge ; *Comm.* Edmund Hyde Smith.

*COLOSSUS (1886), 9, 9420 (5500), 2nd cl. battleship, 14·2 kts., Coastguard, Holyhead. *Capt.* Samuel A. Johnson ; *Comm.* Edmund M. C. Cooper-Key.

*Columbine (late *Hiaria*), 270 tons (200), tender to *Crescent*, Newfoundland Fisheries. *Lieut.-Comm.* Adolphus Huddlestone Williamson.

Comet (1870), 2, 254 (110), 3rd cl. gunboat, Portsmouth.

*Comus (1878), 10, 2380 (2000), 3rd cl. cruiser, 12¾ kts., N. America and W. Indies. *Capt.* George A. Giffard (*Commodore, 2nd cl.*).

Condor (1898), 5, 980 (1400), screw sloop, 13 kts., Sheerness.

Conflict (1894), 6, 270 (4500 f.d.), t.b.d., 27·21 kts., Portsmouth.

CONQUEROR (1882), 6, 6200 (4500), 3rd cl. armoured battleship 15·3 kts., Devonport.

Contest (1894), 6, 295 (4400 f.d.), t.b.d., 27·4 kts., Chatham.

Coquette (1898) 6, 285 (5400 f.d.), t.b.d. 30 kts., Chatham.

Cordelia (1881), 10, 2380 (2000), 3rd cl. cruiser, 12¾ kts., Portsmouth.

Cossack (1886), 6, 1770 (2200), 3rd cl. cruiser, 16·5 kts., Chatham.

Crane (1896) 6, 360 (5900 f.d.), t.b.d., 30 kts., Portsmouth (tender to *Victory*). *Comm.* Cecil Gledstanes Treherne.

*Crescent (1892), 13, 7700 (10000), 1st cl. cruiser, 19·7 kts, Flag-ship N. America and W. Indies. *Vice-Adm* Sir Fdk. G. D. Bedford, K.C.B ; *Capt.* Chas. J. G. Sawle ; *Comm.* Hy. H. Campbell.

*+Cressy (1874), 1130 tons, training-ship for ordinary seamen, Mediterranean. *Comm.* L.G.Tufnell.

Cuckoo (1873), 1, 254 (110), 3rd cl. gunboat, Devonport.

*Curaçoa (1878), 12, 2380 (2000), 3rd cl. cruiser, 13 kts., seagoing training-ship for boys, particular service *Comm.* Herbert Lyon.

Curlew (1885), 4, 950 (850), 1st cl. gun-vessel, 14·5 kts., Devonport.

CYCLOPS (1871), 4, 3560 (1200), Coast Defence ship, 9·9 kts., Sheerness.

Cygnes (1898), 6, 300 (5400 *f.d.*), t.b.d., 30 kts., tender to Pembroke, Chatham. *Comm.* Mk. E. F. Kerr.

Cynthia (1898), 6, 300 tons (5400 *f.d.*), t.b.d., 30 kts., Chatham.

†Dædalus (1828), 1447 tons, drill-ship, R. N. Reserve, Bristol. *Lieut. & Comm.* Basil C. Barber.

Daphne (1888), 8, 1140 (1400), sloop, 14 kts., China. *Comm.* Charles W. Winnington-Ingram.

Daring (1893), 4, 260 (4200 *f.d.*), t.b.d., 27·70 kts., Portsmouth.

Dart (1882), 470 tons (250), 8.7 kts., Surveying service. *Comm.* John Franklin Parry.

Dasher (1895), 6, 250 (3800 *f.d.*), t.b.d., 26·21 kts., Portsmouth.

Decoy (1894), 4, 260 (4200 *f.d.*), t.b.d., 27·76 kts., Devonport.

Dee (1877), 3, 363 (200), 3rd cl. gunboat, for torpedo instruction, Malta.

Defiance (1861), 5270 tons, torpedo school ship, Devonport. *Capt.* Fredk. Tower Hamilton; *Comm.* Wm. C. M. Nicholson.

Desperate (1895), 6, 310 (5700 *f.d.*), t.b.d., 30 kts., Chatham.

DEVASTATION (1873), 4, 9330 (5500), 2nd cl. battleship, 14 kts., port guardship, Gibraltar. *Capt.* Frederick S. Inglefield; *Comm.*, Charles H. Umfreville.

Diadem (1896), 16, 11000 (16500), 1st cl. cruiser, 20·5 kts., Channel Squadron. *Capt.* Harry S. F. Niblett; *Comm.* B. J. D. Yelverton.

Diana (1895), 11, 5600 (8000), 2nd cl. cruiser, 19·5 kts., Chatham.

Dido (1896), 11, 5600 (8000), 2nd cl. cruiser. 19·5 kts., Mediterranean. *Capt.* George Neville; *Comm.* Seymour E. Erskine.

+*Dolphin* (1882), 925 tons, training-ship for boys, Portland.

Don (1877), 3, 363 (200), 3rd cl. gunboat, Malta.

Doris (1897), 11, 5600 (8000), 2nd cl. cruiser, 19·5 kts., flagship, Cape and West Africa. *Rear-Adm.* Sir Robert H. Harris, K.C.M.G.; *Capt.* Reginald C. Prothero; *Comm.* Wm. L. Grant.

Dove (1899), 6, 300 tons (5800 *f.d.*), t.b.d., 30 kts., completing for sea, Hull.

Dragon (1894), 6, 295 (4400 *f.d.*), t.b.d., 27·14 kts., Mediterranean (tender to *Royal Oak*). *Lieut.-Comm.* Randal Methven Lambert.

DREADNOUGHT (1875), 4, 10820 (6500), 2nd cl. battleship, 13·7 kts., Chatham.

Dryad (1893), 2, 1070 (2500), 1st cl. torpedo gunboat, 19 kts., Chatham.

Duke of Wellington (1852), 6071 tons, general depôt ship, Portsmouth. *Capt.* J. L. Hammet (*in command of Fleet Reserve*); *Comm.* Godfrey H. B. Mundy.

+Durham (1845), 1815 tons, drill-ship, R. N. Reserve, Leith. *Lt. & Comm.* Wilford F. Forrest.

Dwarf (1898), 6, 710 (900), 1st class gunboat, 13¾ kts., W. Africa. *Lieu. & Com.* Hastings F. Shakespear.

+Eagle (1804), 2340 tons, drill-ship, R.N. Reserve, Liverpool. *Comm.* Charles E. Gladstone.

Earnest (1895), 6, 360 (6300 *f.d.*), t.b.d., 30 kts., tender to *Cæsar*, Mediterranean. *Lieut. & Comm.* Edward A. Baird.

Eclipse (1894), 11, 5600 (8000), 2nd cl. cruiser, 19·5 kts., flag-ship, East Indies. *Rear-Adm.* Day Hort. Bosanquet; *Capt.* Paul Warner Bush; *Comm.* Charles H. H. Moore.

Edgar (1890), 12, 7350 (10000), 1st cl. cruiser, 20·5 kts., Devonport.

EDINBURGH (1886), 9, 9420 (5500) 2nd cl. battleship, 14·2 kts., Chatham.

Egeria (1873) 4, 940 (700), surveying vessel, 11·3 kts., Surveying Service. *Comm.* Morris Henry Smyth.

Electra (1899), 6, 300 (5800 *f.d.*) t.b.d., 30 kts., completing at Glasgow.

‡*Elfin* (1849), 93 tons (170), tender to Royal yacht, Portsmouth. *Staff-Comm.* James E. Tully.

EMPRESS OF INDIA (1893), 14. 14150 (9000), 1st cl. battleship, 17·5 kts., Mediterranean. *Capt.* Henry H. Dyke; *Comm.* Reginald H. S. Bacon, D.S.O.

‡Enchantress (1865), 1000 tons (1100) Admiralty Yacht, Portsmouth. *Staff-Comm.* in command, Philip Daniel Ouless; *Staff-Comm.* Frederick W. E. H. Smith.

Endymion (1891), 12, 7350 (10000), 1st cl. cruiser, 20·5 kts., China. *Capt.* George A. Callaghan; *Comm.* William O. Boothby.

Esk (1877), 3, 363 (200), 3rd cl. gunboat, coast defence, China. *Lieut. & Comm.* Charles Chadwick.

Europa (1897), 16, 11000 (16500), 1st cl. cruiser, Portsmouth.

+Excellent (1883), 1, 508 (380), gunnery ship, Whale Island, Portsmouth. *Capt.* William Henry May, M.V.O.; *Comm.* Thomas B. S. Adair.

Express (1899), 6, 300 (9250 *f.d.*), t.b.d, 33 kts., completing at Birkenhead.

Fairy (1897), 6 (6500 *f.d.*), t.b.d., 32 kts., Devonport.

Fame (1896), 6, 300 (5700 *f.d.*), t.b.d., 30 kts., China. *Lieut. and Comm.* Roger J. B. Keyes.

Fawn (1897), 6, 324 (5900 *f.d.*), t.b.d., 30 kts., Portsmouth.

Fearless (1886), 4, 1580 (2100), 3rd cl. cruiser, 16·7 kts., Mediterranean. *Comm.* Henry C. Kingsford.

Ferret (1893), 4, 280 (4400 *f.d.*), t.b.d., 27·62 kts, Devonport (tender to *Vivid*). *Lieut. & Comm.* Herbert J. T. Marshall.

Fervent (1895), 6, 270 (3850 *f.d.*), t.b.d., 27 kts., completing for sea.

Fidget (1872), 1, 254 (110), 3rd cl. gunboat, Portsmouth.

Firebrand (1877), 4, 455 (360), 2nd cl. gunboat, 10·17 kts., Hong Kong.

Fire Queen (1881), 446 tons (500), special service vessel, tender to *Victory*, Portsmouth. *Staff-Capt.* Thomas Hawkins Smith.

Flirt (1897), 6, 324 (5500 *f.d.*), t.b.d., 30½ kts., Portsmouth. *Lieut. & Com.* Edward A. Thomas.

Flora (1893), 10, 4360 (7000), 2nd cl. cruiser, 19·5 kts., Senior Officer's ship, S.E. Coast of America. *Capt.* (*Commodore*, 2nd cl.) Robert L. Groome; *Comm.* George Couper.

Flying Fish (1897), 6, 360 (6200 *f.d.*), t.b.d., 30¼ kts., Portsmouth. *Comm.* Arthur G. M. Meredyth.

Foam (1895), 6, 300 (5700 *f.d.*), t.b.d., 30 kts., Malta.

FORMIDABLE (1898), 16, 15000 (15000), 1st class battleship, complement 750, 18 kts., Portsmouth.

Forte (1893), 10, 4360 (7000), 2nd cl. cruiser, 19·5 kts., Cape and West Africa. *Capt.* E. P. Jones.

Forth (1886), 12, 4050 (3800), 2nd cl. cruiser, 16·8 kts., Devonport.

Fox (1893), 10, 4360 (7000), 2nd cl. cruiser, 19·5 kts., Devonport.

Furious (1896), 10, 5750 (10000), 2nd cl. cruiser, 19 kts., Channel Squadron. *Capt.* Lewis Edmund Wintz; *Comm.* Joseph R. Bridson.

Gadfly (1879), 1, 265 (110), 3rd cl. gunboat, coast defence, Cape of Good Hope.

GALATEA (1889), 12, 5600 (5500), 1st cl. cruiser, 18·1 kts., coastguard ship, Hull. *Capt.* Charles

Henry Cross; *Comm.* Reginald A. Cave-Browne-Cave.

Ganges, 3594 tons, training-ship for boys, Falmouth. *Comm.* Walter V. Anson.

Gibraltar (1892), 12, 7700 (10,000), 1st cl. cruiser, 19·7 kts., Portsmouth.

Gipsy (1897), 6, 300 (6500 *f.d.*), t.b.d., 32 kts., Devonport.

Gladiator (1896), 10, 5750 (10000), 2nd cl. cruiser, 19 kts., Portsmouth.

GLATTON (1872), 2, 4910 (2000), armoured coast defence ship, 11 kts., Portsmouth.

Gleaner (1890), 2, 735 (2500), 1st cl. torpedo gunboat, 19 kts., for training of R.N.R., Gravesend. *Comm.* Frank H. Peyton.

Glory (1899), 16, 12250 (13500), 1st cl. battleship, 18¼ kts., completing at Birkenhead.

Goldfinch (1889), 6, 805 (720), 1st cl. gunboat, 13 kts., Australia.

GOLIATH (1898), 16, 12950 (13500), 1st cl. armoured battleship, 18¼ kts., Chatham.

GORGON (1872), 4, 3560 (1200), armoured coast defence ship, 9·9 kts., Devonport.

Gossamer (1890), 2, 735 (2500), 1st cl. torpedo gunboat, 19 kts., Kingstown (tender to *Melampus*). *Lieut. and Comm.* Francis G. T. Cole.

Grafton (1892), 12, 7350 (10000), 1st cl. cruiser, 20 kts., Chatham. *Capt.* Frederick W. Fisher ; *Comm.* Edmund P. E. Jervoise.

Grasshopper (1887), 1, 525 (1600), 1st cl. torpedo gunboat, 17 kts., Chatham.

Griffon (1896), 6, 360 (6300 *f.d.*), t.b.d., 30 kts., tender to *Illustrious*, Mediterranean. *Lieut. & Comm.* Hon. Hubert George Brand.

Griper (1879), 1,265 (110), 3rd cl. gunboat, coast defence, Cape of Good Hope.

Halcyon (1894), 2, 1070 (2500), 1st cl. torpedo gunboat, 19 kts., Mediterranean. *Comm.* Scott W. A. H. Gray.

Handy (1895), 6, 275 (4000 *f.d.*), t.b d., 27 kts., Hong Kong. *Lieut. & Comm.* (J. A. Moreton (*tempy.*)

Hannibal (1897), 16, 14900 (10000), 1st cl. armoured battleship, 17·5 kts., Channel Squadn. *Capt.* Sir Baldwin Wake Walker, Bart., C.M.G.; *Comm.* Frederick C. T. Tudor.

Hardy (1895), 6, 290 (4200 *f.d.*), t.b.d., 26 kts., Portsmouth.

Harrier (1894), 2, 1070 (2500), 1st cl. torpedo gunboat, 19 kts., Mediterranean (Crete). *Lieut. and Comm.* Philip Walter.

Hart (1895), 6, 275 (4000 *f.d.*), t.b.d., 27 kts., Hong Kong.

Hasty (1894), 6, 250 (3100 *f.d.*), t.b.d., 26 kts., Portsmouth.

Haughty (1895), 6, 290 (4200 *f.d.*), t.b.d., 27 kts., Chatham.

Havock (1893), 4, 240 (3000 *f.d.*), t.b.d., 26¾ kts., Portsmouth.

Hawk (1884), 520 tons (400), tender to *Alexandra*, for Coastguard, Portland.

Hawke (1891), 12, 7350 (10000), 1st cl. cruiser, 20 kts., Chatham.

Hazard (1894), 2, 1070 (2500), 1st cl. torpedo gunboat, 19 kts., Mediterranean. *Lieut. and Comm.* Price Vaughan Lewes, D.S.O.

Hearty, 2, 1300 (2100), special service, North Sea Fisheries. *Comm.* Herbert G. King Hall, D.S.O.

Hebe (1892), 2, 810 (2500), 1st cl. torpedo gunboat, 19¼ kts., Mediterranean. *Lieut. and Comm.* Arthur Trevelyan Taylor.

HECATE (1872), 4, 3560 (1200), coast defence ship, 9·9 kts., Devonport.

Hecla (1878), 6, 6400 (2400), torpedo depôt ship, 13 kts., Portsmouth. *Comm.* (*for service with Fleet Reserve*) William Jabez Scullard.

‡Herald (1890), 82 tons (80), river service (Zambesi). *Lieut. & Comm.* John Harvey.

HERCULES (1868), 20, 8680 (7000), 3rd cl. battleship, 14·6 kts., Portsmouth.

Hermes (1898), 11, 5600 (10000), 2nd cl. cruiser, 20 kts., North America and West Indies. *Comm.* Fredk. K. C. Gibbons.

Hermione (1893), 10, 4360 (7000), 2nd cl. cruiser, 19·5 kts., China. *Capt.* Robert S. D. Cumming.

HERO (1888), 6, 6200 (4500), 3rd cl. armoured battleship, 15·2 kts., Portsmouth. *Comm.* William De Salis.

‡Hibernia (1804) 2nd rate, 4149 tons, flag-ship, Malta Dockyard. *Rear-Adm.* Rodney Maclaine Lloyd, C.B.; *Comm.* William Ricketts.

Highflyer (1898), 11, 5600 (10000), 2nd cl. cruiser, 20 kts., Devonport.

HOGUE (1898), 14, 12000 (21000), 1st cl. cruiser, 21 kts., completing at Barrow.

Hood (1893), 14, 14150 (9000), 1st cl. battleship, 17·5 kts., Mediterranean. *Capt.* Alvin C. Corry ; *Comm.* John B. Eustace.

Hornet (1893), 4, 240 (3800 *f.d.*), t.b.d., 27 kts. Portsmouth.

Hotspur (1871), 4, 4010 (2500), port guard ship, 11·25 kts., Bermuda. *Comm.* Charles Sinclair Elliot.

Howe (1889), 10, 10300 (7500), 1st cl. battleship, 16·8 kts., flag-ship and port guard, Queenstown. *Rear-Adm.* Atwell P. M. Lake; *Capt.* Edward H. M. Davis, C.M.G.; *Comm.* Alfred E. Tizard.

Humber (1878), 1640 tons (800), store-ship, China. *Comm.*, Henry Jocelyn Davison.

Hunter (1895), 6, 275 (4000 *f.d.*), t.b.d., 27 kts., Portsmouth. *Lieut. and Comm.* Robert G. Corbett.

Hussar (1894), 2, 1070 (2500), 1st cl. torpedo gunboat, 19 kts., Mediterranean. *Lieut.-Comm.* Marcus R. Hill.

Hyacinth (1898), 11, 5600 (10000), 2nd cl. cruiser, 20 kts., completing at Glasgow.

Hyæna (1873), 1, 254 (110), 3rd cl. gunboat, tender to *Wildfire*, Sheerness.

HYDRA (1872), 4, 3560 (1200), armoured coast defence ship, 9·9 kts., Sheerness.

Icarus (1885), 8, 970 (850), sloop, 12·2 kts., Pacific. *Comm.* George F. S. Knowling.

Illustrious (1896), 16, 14900 (10000), 1st cl. armoured battleship, 17·5 kts., Mediterranean. *Capt.* Sir Richard Poore, Bart.; *Comm.* William H. Baker-Baker.

IMMORTALITÉ (1889), 12, 5600 (5500), 1st cl. armoured cruiser, 18 kts., Sheerness.

Imogene (1882), 460 tons (390), special service, Mediterranean. *Comm.* Edward Joseph Bain.

IMPÉRIEUSE (1886), 14, 8400 (8000), 1st cl. cruiser, 16.7 kts., Portsmouth.

+*Implacable*—see *Lion*.

IMPLACABLE (1899), 16, 15000 (15000), 1st cl. battleship, 18 kts., Devonport.

+Impregnable, late *Bulwark* (1860), 6557 tons, training-ship for boys, Devonport. *Capt.* Arthur C. B. Bromley ; *Comm.* Robt. H. J. Stewart.

Indefatigable (1891), 8, 3600 (7000). 2nd cl. cruiser, 19¾ kts., North America and West Indies. *Capt.* Frederick L. Campbell.

+Indus, late *Defence* (1861) armour-plated, 6270 tons, Guardship of Reserve and flagship of Admiral Supt. R.N.R., Devonport Dockyard. *Rear-Adm.* Thos. S. Jackson. *Capt.* William Marrack.

INFLEXIBLE (1881), 12, 11880 (6500), 2nd cl. armoured battleship, 12·8 kts., Portsmouth.

Insolent (1881), 1, 265 (110), 3rd cl. gunboat, Portsmouth.

Intrepid (1891), 8, 3600 (7000), 2nd cl. cruiser, 19¾ kts., Portsmouth.

INVINCIBLE (1870), 16, 6010 (3300), 3rd cl. battleship, 12·5 kts., Portsmouth.

*Iphigenia (1891), 8, 3600 (7000), 2nd cl. cruiser, 19¾ kts., C'iina. *Capt.* Horatio Nelson Dudding.

Iris (1877), 13, 3730 (6000), 2nd cl. cruiser, 18 kts., Portsmouth.

IRON DUKE (1871), 14, 6010 (2500), 3rd cl. battleship, 12·5 kts., Portsmouth.

IRRESISTIBLE (1899), 16, 15000 (15000), 1st cl. battleship, 18 kts., Chatham.

*Isis (1896). 11, 5600 (8000), 2nd cl. cruiser, 19·5 kts., Mediterranean. *Capt.* Geo. M. Henderson; *Comm.* Geo. Alexr. Ballard.

*Jackal, late *Woodcock* 750 tons (1200), Scottish Fisheries. *Lieut. & Comm.* James C Tancred.

Janus (1895), 6, 280 (3900 *f.d.*), t.b.d., 27¾ kts., tender to *Pembroke*, Chatham.

Jaseur (1892), 2, 810 (2500), 1st cl. torpedo gunboat, 19·25 kts., Portsmouth (tender to *Vernon*). *Comm.* Walter Carey.

*Jason (1892). 2, 810 (2500), 1st cl. torpedo gunboat, 19·25 kts., particular service. *Lieut. & Comm.* Henry Hervey Bruce.

Juno (1895), 11, 5600 (8000), 2nd cl. cruiser, 19·5 kts., Devonport.

*JUPITER (1896), 16. 14900 (10000), 1st cl. battleship, 17·5 kts., Channel Squadron. *Capt.* John Durnford, C.B., D.S.O.; *Comm.* Archibald P. Stoddart.

*Karrakatta (1890), 2, 735 (2500), 1st cl. torpedo gunboat, 20 kts., Australasian waters (Sydney. N.S.W.). *Lieut. and Comm.* Richard Morden Harbord.

*Katoomba (1889), 8, 2575 (4000), 3rd cl. cruiser, 19 kts., Australasian waters (Sydney, N.S.W.). *Capt.* Herbert W. S. Gibson.

*Kestrel (1899), 6, 300 tons (5800 *f.d.*), t.b.d., 30 kts., completing at Glasgow.

Kite (1871), 2, 254 (110), 3rd cl. gunboat, tender to *Excellent*, Portsmouth. *Lieut. & Comm.* Geo. Price Webley Hope.

Landrail (1886), 4. 950 (850), 1st cl. gun-vessel, 14·5 kts., tender to *Wildfire*. Sheerness.

*Lapwing (1889). 6, 805 (720), 1st cl. gunboat, 13 kts., East Indies. *Lieut. & Comm.* Cecil Foley Lambert.

Latona (1890), 8, 3400 (7000), 2nd cl. cruiser, 20 kts., Portsmouth.

Leander (1882). 10, 4300 (5000), 2nd cl. cruiser, 16·6 kts., Pacific. *Capt.* Fredk. Fogarty Fegen.

Leda (1892), 2, 810 (2500), 1st cl. torpedo gunboat, 19¾ kts., Southampton Water (tender to *Australia*). *Lieut. & Comm.* Vernon Maud.

Lee (1899). 6. 335 (6000 *f.d.*), t.b.d., 30 kts., completing at Sunderland.

Leopard (1897), 6, 300 (6000 *f.d.*), t.b.d., 30 kts., Devonport.

Leven (1899), 6, 300 (6000 *f.d.*), t.b.d., 30 kts., completing at Glasgow.

+*Liberty* (850), 447 tons, sailing brig, Devonport (tender to *Lion*). *Lieut. & Comm.* Charles H. Morgan.

*Liffey. (1856), 3915 tons, store and depôt ship, Coquimbo. *Staff-Comm.* Philip H. Wright.

Lightning (1895), 6, 280 (3900 *f.d.*), t.b.d., 30 kts., tender to *Victory*, Portsmouth. *Lieut. & Comm.* Loftus C. O. Mansergh.

*Linnet (1880), 2, 756 (870), 2nd cl. gun-vessel, 11·80 kts., China. *Comm.* Wm. Wyatt Smythe.

*Lion (1847). 3842, and *Implacable* (1803), 3223 tons, training-ships for boys, Devonport. *Comm.* Edward George Shortland.

*Lizard (1886). 6, 715 (600), 1st cl. gunboat, 13 kts., Australia. *Lieut. & Comm.* John C. Watson.

Locust (1896), 6, 360 (6300 *f.d.*), t.b.d., 30 kts., Devonport.

LONDON (1899), 16, 15000 (15000), 1st cl. battleship, 18 kts., completing at Portsmouth.

Lynx (1894), 4, 280 (4400 *f.d.*), t.b.d., 27 kts., Devonport. *Lieut. & Comm.* Hubert H. Holland.

*MAGDALA (1870), 4, 3340 (1400), coast defence ship, 10 kts., for India's naval defence, Bombay Harbour. *Capt.* Henry Louis Fleet.

* *Magicienne* (1888). 6, 2950 (5500), 3rd cl. cruiser, 19 kts., Cape and West Africa. *Capt.* William B. Fisher.

*Magnet (1883), 430 tons (650), special-service vessel, Portsmouth. *Lieut. & Comm.* James Webber.

*MAGNIFICENT (1895), 16, 14900 (10000), 1st cl. battleship, 17·5 kts (flag-ship, Second-in-Command), Channel Squadron. *Rear-Adm.* Arthur D. Fanshawe; *Capt.* John Ferris; *Comm.* Francis G. Eyre.

Magpie (1889). 6, 805 (720), 1st cl. gunboat, 13 kts., Devonport.

*MAJESTIC (1895), 16, 14900 (10000), 1st cl. battleship, 17·5 kts. (flagship). Channel Squadron. *Vice-Adm.* Sir Harry H. Rawson, K.C.B.; *Capt.* George Le Clere Egerton, C.B.; *Comm.* Dudley R. de Chair.

*Mallard (1896). 6, 275 tons (5700 *f.d.*), t.b.d.,30 kts., Chatham. *Lieut. & Comm.* Godfrey G. Webster.

*Marathon (1888), 6, 2950 (5500), 3rd cl. cruiser, 19 kts., East Indies. *Capt.* John G. M. Field.

*MARS (1897), 16. 14900 (10000), 1st cl. battleship, 17·5 kts., Channel Squadron. *Capt.* Henry J. May, C.B.; *Comm.* Harry H. Stileman.

+*Martin (1890), 508 tons, sailing brig, Portsmouth. *Lieut. & Comm.* Samuel M. Agnew.

Mastiff (1871), 3, 254 (110), 3rd cl. gunboat, Portsmouth.

* *Medea (1888), 6, 2800 (5000), 3rd cl. cruiser, 19 kts., drill-ship for R. N. Reserve, Southampton. *Comm.* Charles G. May.

Medina (1876), 3, 363 (200),3rd cl. gunboat, Bermuda.

*Medusa (1888), 6, 2800 (5000), 3rd cl. cruiser, 19 kts., drill-ship for R. N. Reserve, North Shields. *Comm.* Augustus L. K. Knapton.

Medway (1876), 3, 363 (200), 3rd cl. gunboat, Bermuda.

*Melampus (1890), 8, 3400 (7000), 2nd cl. cruiser, 20 kts., Coastguard, Kingstown. *Capt.* Richard N. Gresley; *Comm.* Reginald R. Growse.

*Melita (1888), 8, 970 (850), sloop, 12·50 kts., Mediterranean. *Comm.* Ian M. Fraser, D.S.O.

*Melpomene (1888), 6, 2950 (5500), 3rd cl. cruiser, 19 kts., East Indies. *Capt.* John Denison.

*Mercury (1878), 13, 3730 (6000), 2nd cl. cruiser, 16·8 kts., Portsmouth.

*Mermaid (1898), 6, 300 tons (5800 *f.d.*), t.b.d., 30 kts., Chatham. *Comm.* John M. de Robeck.

Mersey (1885), 12, 4050 (4000), 2nd cl. cruiser, 17·3 kts., Chatham.

*Mildura (1889), 8, 2575 (4000), 3rd cl. cruiser, 19 kts., Australasian waters. *Capt.* Henry Leah.

*Minerva (1895), 11, 5600 (8000), 2nd cl. cruiser, 19·5 kts., Chatham.

MINOTAUR (1867), 21, 10690 (4000), 1st cl. cruiser, 12 kts., training-ship for boys, Portland (tender to *Boscawen*). *Comm.* Ernest Gillbe Barton.

*Mohawk (1886), 6, 1770 (2200), 3rd cl. cruiser, 16·5 kts., Australia. *Comm.* Fredk. H.P.W. Freeman.

*MONARCH (1869), 7. 8930 (6500), 3rd cl. battleship, 15 kts., guardship, Simon's Bay, Cape. *Capt.* Robert D. Barwick Bruce; *Comm.* Spencer V. Y. de Horsey.

*‡ Mosquito (1890), 82 tons (80), stern wheel steel vessel, (river service, Zambesi). *Lieut. & Comm.* Lancelot C. Cox.

*Naiad (1890), 8, 3400 (7000), 2nd cl. cruiser, 20 kts., Portsmouth.

NARCISSUS (1889), 12, 5600 (5500), 1st cl. cruiser, 18·1 kts., Portsmouth.

†*Nautilus* (1879), 501 tons, sailing brig, Devonport (tender to *Impregnable*). *Lieut. and Comm.* Hugh H. D. Tothill.

NELSON (1880), 16, 7630 (5500), 1st cl. cruiser, Portsmouth.

NEPTUNE (1878), 6, 9310 (6000), 2nd cl. battleship, 13·4 kts, Portsmouth.

Niger (1892), 2, 810 (2500), 1st cl. torpedo gunboat, 19¼ kts., Queensferry, N.B. (tender to *Rodney*). *Lieut. & Comm.* Regd Henry Curteis

Nightingale (1898), 85 tons (240), shallow-draught steamer for river service, Chatham.

*NILE (1890), 10, 11940 (7500), 1st cl. battleship, 16·7 kts., port guard, Devonport. *Capt.* Gerald C. Langley; *Comm.* Hon. Fras. C. B. Addington.

**Niobe* (1897), 10, 11000 (16500) 1st cl. cruiser, 20¼ kts., Channel Squadron. *Capt.* Alfred L. Winsloe; *Comm.* Resslyn E. Wemyss.

*NORTHAMPTON (1878), 12, 7630 (4500), 1st cl. armoured cruiser, 12·6 kts., seagoing training-ship for boys, Home Station. *Capt.* Herbert A. W. Onslow; *Comm.* Robert J. Prendergast.

NORTHUMBERLAND (1868), 35, 10780 (4000), 1st cl. cruiser, 13·3 kts., depôt ship for stokers, Chatham (tender to *Pembroke*). *Comm.* Cyril Everard Tower.

**Nymphe* (1888), 8, 1140 (1400), sloop, 14 kts., Mediterranean (Constantinople). *Comm.* Richd. B. Farquhar.

OCEAN (1899), 16, 12950 (13500), 1st cl. battleship, Devonport.

Onyx (1892), 2, 810 (2500), 1st cl. torpedo gunboat, 19¼ kts., tender to *Severn* Harwich. *Lieut. & Comm.* Gerald Oliver.

Opossum (1895), 6, 295 (4000 *f.d.*), t.b.d., 28¼ kts., Devonport.

ORION (1882), 4, 4870 (2600), 2nd cl. coast defence ship (armoured), 11·9 kts., Malta.

*ORLANDO (1888) 12, 5600 5500), 1st. cl. cruiser, 18·1 kts., China. *Capt.* James H. T. Burke; *Comm.* Edward F. B. Charlton.

Orwell (1899), 6, 300 (6000 *f.d.*), t.b.d., 30 kts., completing at Birkenhead.

*‡*Osborne* (1870), 1850 tons (3000), Royal yacht, Portsmouth. *Capt.* Charles Windham.

Osprey, (1898), 6, 300 (6500 *f.d.*), t.b.d., 32 kts., Devonport.

Otter (1896), 6, 300 (6300 *f.d.*), t.b.d., 30 kts., completing at Barrow.

**Pactolus* (1898), 8, 2135 (5000), 3rd cl. cruiser, 20½ kts., Channel Squadron. *Capt.* Francis J. Foley.

Pallas (1890), 8, 2575 (4500), 3rd cl. cruiser, 19 kts., Portsmouth.

Panther (1897), 6, 300 (6300 *f.d.*), t.b.d., 30 kts., Devonport. *Comm.* John I. Graham.

**Partridge* (1880), 6, 75 (720), 1st cl. gunboat, 13¼ kts., Cape and West Africa. *Lieut. and Comm.* Allen T. Hunt

**Peacock* (1888), 6, 755 (720), 1st cl. gunboat, 13¼ kts., China. *Lieut. & Comm.* Sholto G. Douglas

**Pearl* (1890), 8, 2575 (4500), 3rd cl. cruiser, 19 kts., North America and West Indies (Bermuda). *Capt.* James E. C. Goodrich.

**Pegasus* (1897), 8, 2135 (5000), 3rd cl. cruiser, 20 kts., S. E. Coast of America. *Capt.* Charles H. Cochran.

Pelican (1872), 8, 1130 (800), sloop, 10·6 kts., Devonport.

**Pelorus* (1896), 8, 2135 (5000), 3rd cl. cruiser, Channel Squadron. *Capt.* Henry C. B. Hulbert.

*†*Pembroke*, late *Duncan* (1859), 5724 tons, depôt ship, Chatham. *Capt.* Angus MacLeod, A.D.C. *Comm.* Ernest H. Grafton.

**Penguin* (1876), 2, 1130 (700), sloop, 11 kts., Surveying service, Australia. *Comm.* James W. Combe.

Perseus (1898), 8, 2135 (5000), 3rd cl. cruiser, Sheerness.

**Phaeton* (1883), 10, 4300 (5000), 2nd cl. cruiser, 16·6 kts., Pacific. *Capt.* Francis George Kirby.

**Pheasant* (1888), 6, 755 (720), 1st cl. gunboat, 13¼ kts., Pacific. *Lieut. and Comm.* Herbert Granville Smith.

**Philomel* (1890), 8, 2575 (4500), 3rd cl. cruiser, 19 kts., Cape and West Africa. *Comm.* Jno. Edwd. Bearcroft.

**Phœbe* (1890), 8, 2575 (4500), 3rd cl. cruiser, 19 kts., Devonport.

**Phœnix* (1895), 6, 1050 (1100), sloop, 13 kts., China. *Comm.* Reginald P. Cochran.

Pickle (1872), 1, 254 (110), 3rd cl. gunboat, Portsmouth.

**Pigeon* (1888), 6, 755 (720), 1st cl. gunboat, 13¼ kts., East Indies. *Lieut. & Comm.* Edward H. Moubray.

**Pigmy* (1888), 6, 755 (720), 1st cl. gunboat, 13¼ kts., China. *Lieut. & Comm.* Jno. Frederick Ernest Green.

Pike (1872), 1, 254 (110), 3rd cl. gunboat, coast defence, Portsmouth.

†*Pilot* (1879), 501 tons, sailing brig, Devonport. *Lieut. & Comm.* William J. S. Alderson.

Pincher (1879), 1, 265 (110), 3rd cl. gunboat, Portsmouth.

Pioneer (1899), 8, 2200 (5000) 3rd cl. cruiser, 20 kts., Chatham.

Pique (1890), 8, 3600 (7000), 2nd cl. cruiser, 19¾ kts., Devonport.

Plassy (1890), 2, 735 (2500), 1st cl. torpedo gunboat, 19 kts., for India's Naval Defence, Bombay Harbour.

**Plover* (1888), 6, 755 (720), 1st cl. gunboat, 13¼ kts., China. *Lieut. and Comm.* Carlton V. de M. Cowper.

Plucky (1870), 2, 195 (90), 3rd cl. gunboat, Portsmouth.

**Polyphemus* (1881), 2640 (3000), special torpedo vessel (protected ram), 18 kts., Mediterranean. *Comm.* Edward Lewis Lang.

**Pomone* (1898), 8, 2135 (5000), 3rd cl. cruiser, E. Indies. *Capt.* Ernest A. Simons.

Porcupine (1895), 6, 280 (3900 *f.d.*), t.b.d., 28 kts., Chatham.

**Porpoise* (1886), 6, 1770 (2200), 3rd cl. cruiser, 16·5 kts., Australia. *Comm.* Arthur H. D. Ravenhill.

**Powerful* (1895), 14, 14200 (25000), 1st cl. cruiser, 21·8 kts., China (on passage home *viâ* Cape Town). *Capt.* Hon. Hedworth Lambton; *Comm.* Alfred P. Ethelston.

*†*President* (1830), 1969 tons, drill-ship for R. N. Reserve, West India Docks, London. *Comm.* Arthur Charles Woods.

*PRINCE GEORGE (1896), 16, 14900 (10000), 1st cl. battleship, 17·5 kts., Channel Squadron. *Capt.* Arthur Barrow; *Comm.* Montague E. Browning.

Prometheus (1898), 8, 2135 (5000), 3rd cl. cruiser, 20 kts., Sheerness.

**Proserpine* (1897), 8, 2135 (5000), 3rd cl. cruiser, 18·1 kts., North America and West Indies. *Capt.* John Locke Marx.

**Psyche* (1898), 8, 2135 (5000), 3rd cl. cruiser, North America and West Indies. *Capt.* Francis R. Pelly.

**Pylades* (1884), 14, 1420 (950), 3rd cl. cruiser, 12·6 kts., Australia. *Comm.* Reginald G. O. Tupper.

Pyramus (1898), 8, 2135 (5000), 3rd cl. cruiser, 20 kts., Chatham.

Quail (1895), 6, 360 (6300 *f.d.*), t.b.d., 30¼ kts., North America and West Indies (tender to *Crescent*). *Lieut. and Comm.* Edward H. Rymer.

Racer (1884), 8, 970 (850), sloop, 11 kts., Dartmouth (for instruction of naval cadets, tender to *Britannia*).

Racoon (1887), 6, 1770 (2500), 3rd cl. cruiser, 17·5 kts., East Indies. *Comm.* Geo. Hayley Hewett.

Rainbow (1891), 8, 3600 (7000), 2nd cl. cruiser, 19·7 kts., Devonport.

Raleigh (1873), 24, 5200 (4200), 2nd cl. cruiser, 13·9 kts., Training Squadron. *Capt.* (*Commodore 2nd cl.*) Edmund Samuel Poë, M.V.O., A.D.C.; *Comm.* Claud A. W. Hamilton.

*Rambler (1880), 2, 835 (650), surveying vessel, 10·66 kts., on surveying service. *Comm.* Herbert E. P. Cust.

*RAMILLIES (1893), 14, 14150 (9000), 1st cl. battle-ship, 17·5 kts., Mediterranean. *Capt.* Wm. Des Vœux Hamilton; *Comm.* James de C. Hamilton.

Ranger (1895), 6, 295 (4000 *f.d.*), t.b.d., 27 kts., Portsmouth.

Rapid (1883), 12, 1420 (950), 3rd cl. cruiser, 12·6 kts., Devonport.

*Rattler (1886), 6, 715 (600), 1st cl. gunboat, 13·6 kts., China. *Lieut. and Comm.* Hon. George A. Hardinge.

Rattlesnake (1886), 1, 550 (1600), 1st cl. torpedo gunboat, 18·5 kts., Portsmouth.

*Raven (1882), 4, 465 (360), 2nd cl. gunboat, 9·5 kts., Channel Islands. *Comm.* Alex. Meldrum.

Recruit (1858), 6, 300 (5800 *f.d.*), t.b.d., 30 kts., Glasgow (completing for sea).

Redbreast (18·8), 6, 805 (720), 1st cl. gunboat, 13 kts., Haulbowline.

*Redpole (1888), 6, 805 (720), 1st cl. gunboat, 13 kts., China. *Lieut. & Comm.* Francis F. Haworth-Booth.

Redwing (1880), 2, 461 (360), 2nd cl. gunboat, 9·68 kts., Coastguard, Queensferry, N.B.—tender to *Rodney*.

Renard (1892), 2, 810 (2500), 1st cl. torpedo gun-boat, 19¼ kts., Holyhead—tender to *Colossus*. *Lieut. and Comm.* Wm. Henry Eyre.

*RENOWN (1895), 14, 12350 (10000), 1st cl. battle-ship, 18 kts., flagship, Mediterranean. *Vice-Adm.* Sir John Arbuthnot Fisher, K.C.B.; *Capt.* Daniel McNab Riddel; *Comm.* Archibald G. H. W. Moore.

*REPULSE (1894), 14, 14150 (9000), 1st cl. battle-ship, 17·5 kts., Channel Squadron. *Capt.* Randolph F. O. Foote, C.M G.; *Comm.* Arthur D. Ricardo.

*‡Research (1888), 520 tons (450), surveying service, Portsmouth. *Capt.* Wm. Usborne Moore.

*RESOLUTION (1893), 14, 14150 (9000), 1st cl. battle-ship, 17·5 kts., Channel Squadron. *Capt.* Chas. Ramsay Arbuthnot; *Comm.* William O. Story.

Retribution (1891), 8, 3600 (7000), 2nd cl. cruiser, 19¾ kts., Devonport.

*REVENGE (1895), 14, 14150 (9000), 1st cl. battle-ship, 17·5 kts. (flagship, 2nd in command), Mediterranean (Crete). *Rear-Adm.* Sir Gerald Henry Uctred Noel, K.C.M G.; *Capt.* Chas. John Briggs; *Comm.* Ernest C. T. Troubridge.

Ringarooma (1890), 8, 2575 (4000), 3rd cl. cruiser, 19 kts., Australasian waters, Sydney, N.S.Wales.

*Ringdove (1889), 6, 805 (720), 1st cl. gunboat, 13 kts., Australia. *Lieut. and comm.* Ralph Fearon Ayscough.

Robin (1898), 85 (240), shallow-draught steamer for river service, Chatham.

Rocket, (1899) 6, 280 (4100 *f.d.*), t.b.d., 27¼ kts., Bermuda.

*RODNEY (1888), 10, 10300 (7500), 1st cl. battle-ship, 16¾ kts., Coastguard, Queensferry, N.B. *Capt.* Gerald Walter Russell; *Comm.* Charles H. Dundas.

Rosario (1898), 6, 980 (1400), screw sloop, 13 kts., Sheerness.

*Royal Arthur (1891), 13, 7700 (10000), 1st cl. cruiser, 18½ kts., flagship, Australia. *Rear-Adm.* Hugo Lewis Pearson; *Capt.* Chas. Gauntlett Dicken; *Comm.* Bernard Currey.

*ROYAL OAK (1894), 14, 14150 (9000), 1st cl. battle-ship, 17·5 kts., Mediterranean. *Capt.* Walter H. B. Graham; *Comm.* Henry W. Thierens.

*ROYAL SOVEREIGN (1892), 14, 14150 (9000), 1st cl. battleship, 17·5 kts., Mediterranean. *Capt.* Michael Pelham O'Callaghan, C.B.; *Comm.* Sir Robert Keith Arbuthnot, Bart.

*Royalist (1883), 12, 1420 (950), 3rd cl. cruiser, 12·6 kts., Devonport. *Capt.* Arthur Ward Torlesse.

*RUPERT (1874), 4, 5440 (4500), coast defence ship, 14 kts., Mediterranean; *Comm.* Algernon B. G. Grenfell.

Sabrina (1876), 3, 363 (200), 3rd cl. gunboat, Devon-port.

St. George (1892), 12, 7700 (10000), 1st cl. cruiser, 19·7 kts., Portsmouth.

*†St. Vincent (1815), 4672 tons, training-ship for boys, Portsmouth. *Comm.* Cecil F. Thursby.

*Salamander (1889), 2, 735 (2500) 1st cl. torpedo gunboat, 17 kts., Mediterranean. *Lieut. and Comm.* Edward Cecil Villiers.

Salmon (1895), 6, 280 (3600 *f.d.*), t.b.d., 27½ kts., Chatham.

Sandfly (1887), 1, 525 (1600) 1st cl. torpedo gun-boat, 19 kts., Malta.

*Sandpiper (1897), 85 tons (240), shallow-draught steamer for river service, China. *Lieut. and Comm.* Henry Cecil Carr.

*SANS PAREIL (1889), 15, 10470 (7500), 1st cl. battleship, 17·2 kts. Sheerness (port guard). *Capt.* John Robt. E. Pattisson; *Comm.* H. Jones.

Sappho (1891), 8, 3400 (7000), 2nd cl. cruiser, 20·47 kts., Chatham.

Satellite (1881), 8, 1420 (950), 3rd cl. cruiser, 12·6 kts., Sheerness.

SCORPION (1865), 4, 2750 (1000), coast defence ship, 8·5 kts., Bermuda.

Scourge (1871), 1, 254 (110), 3rd cl. gunboat, Devonport.

Scout (1885), 4, 1580 (2100), 3rd cl. cruiser, 15·7 kts., Portsmouth.

Scylla (1892), 8, 3400 (7000), 2nd cl. cruiser, 20·62 kts., Sheerness.

†Seaflower (1873), 454 tons, sailing brig, Portland (tender to *Boscawen*). *Lieut. and Comm.* Edgar G. H. Gamble.

*Seagull (1889), 2, 735 (2500). 1st cl. torpedo gun-boat, 20 kts., Portsmouth. *Comm.* Hubert Grant-Dalton.

*Seahorse (1880), 670 tons (1100), special surveying service. *Staff-Comm. in comd.* Geo. Stephen Keigwin.

Seal, (1897), 6, 360 tons (6300 *f.d.*), t.b.d., 30 kts., Devonport. *Lieut. and Comm.* Arthur J. Payne.

Seamew (1880), 376 tons (150), tender to *Severn*, for Coastguard service, Harwich.

*Severn (1885), 12, 4050 (4000), 2nd cl. cruiser, 17·3 kts., Coastguard service, Harwich. *Capt.* William L. B. Browne; *Comm.* Henry V. W. Elliott.

*Shark, (1894) 6, 280 (4100 *f.d.*), t.b.d., 27½ kts., tender to *Vivid*, Devonport. *Lieut. and Comm.* Godfrey E. Corbett.

Sharpshooter (1888), 2, 735 (3000), 1st cl. torpedo gunboat, 20 kts., Devonport (tender to *Vivid*, for instruction of engineer students). *Lieut. and Comm.* John Innes Pocock.

Sheldrake (1889), 2, 735 (2500), 1st cl. torpedo gunboat, 20 kts., Devonport.

Sirius (1890), 8, 3600 (7000), 2nd cl. cruiser, 19¾ kts., Devonport.

Skate (1895), 6, 270 (4000 *f.d.*), t.b.d., 27 kts., Devonport.

Skipjack (1889), 2, 735 (2500), 1st cl. torpedo gunboat, 20 kts., Sheerness.

Skylark (1855), 6, 284 (180), gunboat, Portsmouth.

Slaney (1877), 3, 363 (200), 3rd cl. gunboat, Sheerness.

Snake (1871), 1, 254 (110), 3rd cl. gunboat, Portsmouth.

Snap (1872), 1, 254 (110), 3rd cl. gunboat, Devonport.

Snapper (1895), 6, 280 (3600 *f.d.*), t.b.d., 28 kts., Chatham.

*Snipe (1898), 85 tons (240), shallow-draught steamer for river service, on Yantze-Kiang. *Lieut. and Comm.* Arthur H. Oldham.

Spanker (1889), 2, 735 (3500 *f.d.*), 1st cl. torpedo gunboat, 20 kts., Portland. *Lieut. and Comm.* Hy. E. F. Worthington.

*Sparrow (1889), 6, 805 (720), 1st cl. gunboat, 13 kts., Cape and West Africa. *Lieut. and Comm.* Henry Douglas Wilkin, D.S.O.

Sparrowhawk (1895), 6, 360 (6300 *f.d.*), t.b.d. 30·2 kts., Esquimalt.

Spartan (1891), 8, 3600 (7000), 2nd cl. cruiser, 19¾ kts., Devonport.

Spartiate (1898), 16, 11000 (18000), 1st cl. cruiser, 20½ kts., Pembroke.

Speedwell (1889), 2, 735 (2500), 1st cl. torpedo gunboat, 20 kts., Devonport.

Speedy (1893), 2, 810 (3150), 1st cl. torpedo gunboat, 20·21 kts., Sheerness.

Spey (1876), 3, 363 (200), 3rd cl. gunboat, Portsmouth.

*‡Sphinx (1882), 5, 1130 (1100), special service vessel, East Indies. *Comm.* Henry Arthur Philipps.

Spider (1887), 1, 525 (1500), 1st cl. torpedo gunboat, 19 kts., Devonport.

Spiteful (1899), 6, 360 (5900 *f.d.*), t.b d., 30 kts., Portsmouth.

Spitfire (1895), 6, 295 (4500 *f.d.*), t.b.d. 27½ kts., Chatham.

Stag (1899) 6, 312 tons (5800 *f.d.*), t.b.d , 30 kts , completing at Chiswick.

Star, (1896) 6, 360 (5900 *f.d.*), t.b.d., 30½ kts., Portsmouth. *Lieut. and Comm.* F. W. Kinahan.

Starfish, (1894) 6, 270 (4000 *f.d.*), t.b.d., 28 kts , Portsmouth.

Starling (1882), 4, 465 (360), 2nd cl. gunboat, 9·5 kts., Greenock.

Staunch (1867), 1, 180 (60), 3rd cl. gunboat, Portsmouth.

*Stork (1882), 465 tons (360), 2nd cl. gunboat, 9·5 kts., surveying service. *Comm.* Herbert James Gedge.

Sturgeon (1894), 6, 275 (4000 *f.d.*), t.b.d., 27 kts., Sheerness. *Lieut. and Comm.* John Luce.

Sultan (1871), 16, 9290 (6500), 3rd cl. battleship, 14 kts., Portsmouth (recovered after shipwreck near Malta, 1889).

Sunfish (1895), 6, 295 (4000 *f.d.*), t.b.d., 27½ kts., Devonport.

Superb (1880), 22, 9170 (6000), 2nd cl. battleship, 15 kts., Chatham.

Surly (1894), 6, 280 (4100 *f.d.*), t.b.d., 28 kts., Portsmouth.

Surprise (1885), 4, 1650 (2000), despatch vessel, 17 kts., Mediterranean. *Comm.* Frederick W. F. Hervey.

Swallow (1885), 8, 1130 (1030), sloop, 13·5 kts., S. E. Coast of America. *Comm.* Edward F. Inglefield.

Swift (1879), 2, 756 (870), 2nd cl. gun-vessel, 11·81 kts., China.

Swiftsure (1872), 18, 6910 (3500), 3rd class battleship, 12·6 kts., Portsmouth.

Swordfish (1895), 6, 295 (4500 *f.d.*), t.b.d., 27 kts., Chatham. *Lieut. and Comm.* Charles Tibbets.

Sybille (1890), 8, 3400 (7000), 2nd cl. cruiser, 20 kts., Portsmouth. *Lieut.* Hon. Lionel J. O. Lambart.

Sylvia (1898), 6, 283 (6000 *f.d.*), t.b d., 30 kts., Portsmouth.

*Talbot (1895), 11, 5600 (8000), 2nd cl. cruiser, 20 kts., Devonport.

*Tamar, 4650 tons, receiving-ship, Hong Kong. *Capt.* (*Commodore, 2nd cl.*), Francis Powell, C.B.; *Comm.* Claude W. M. Plenderleath.

Tartar (1886), 6, 1770 (2200), 3rd cl. cruiser, 16·5 kts., Cape and West Africa. *Comm.* Frederick R. W. Morgan.

*Tauranga (1889), 8, 2575 (4000), 3rd cl. cruiser, 19 kts., for service in Australasian waters, Sydney, New South Wales. *Capt.* Leslie C. Stuart.

Tay (1876), 3, 363 (200), 3rd cl. gunboat, Devonport.

Teazer (1895), 6, 270 (4500 *f.d.*), t.b.d., 27 kts., Portsmouth.

Tees (1876), 3, 363 (200), 3rd cl. gunboat, Portsmouth.

Téméraire (1877), 14, 8540 (6500), 2nd cl. battleship, 13·8 kts., Devonport.

Terpsichore (1890), 8, 3400 (7000), 2nd cl. cruiser, 20 kts., Chatham.

*Terrible (1895), 14, 14200 (25000), 1st cl. cruiser, 22·4 kts., on passage to China *via* Cape Town. *Capt.* Percy M. Scott; *Comm.* Arthur H. Limpus.

*Terror (1856), 1844 tons, floating battery (armourplated), receiving ship, Bermuda. *Captain* Thomas MacGill, C.B.; *Staff-Comm.* Arthur R. Phipps Bawden.

Thames (1885), 12, 4050 (3800), 2nd cl. cruiser, 16·8 kts., Devonport.

Theseus (1892), 12, 7350 (10000), 1st cl. cruiser. 20 kts., Mediterranean. *Capt.* Vernon A. Tisdall ; *Comm.* John H. Robertson.

*Thetis (1890), 8, 3400 (7000), 2nd cl. cruiser, 20 kts., Mediterranean. *Capt.* William Stokes Rees.

Thistle (1899), 6, 710 (700), 1st cl. gunboat, 13½ kts., Devonport.

*Thrasher (1895), 6, 360 (6300 *f.d.*), t.b.d., 30 kts., Devonport. *Lieut. & Comm.* Thomas D. Pratt.

Thrush (1889), 6, 805 (720), 1st cl. gunboat, 13 kts., Simons Bay.

*Thunderer (1877), 4, 9330 (5500), 2nd cl. battleship, 14 kts., port guard, Pembroke Dock. *Capt.* John E. Blaxland ; *Comm.* Edward Duke Hunt.

Tickler (1879), 1, 265 (110), 3rd cl. gunboat, coast defence, Cape of Good Hope.

*Torch (1894), 6, 960 (1100), sloop, 13¼ kts., Australia. *Comm.* Henry Preedy.

*Trafalgar (1890), 10, 11940 (7500), 1st cl. battleship, 16·7 kts., port guard, Portsmouth. *Capt.* Henry L. F. Royle, D.S.O.; *Comm.* Henry L. D. Pearce.

Traveller (1883), 700tns. (1100), special-service vessel, Devonport. *Lieut. & Comm.* Richd. A. Cathie.

Trent (1877), 4, 363 (200), 3rd cl. gunboat, Sheerness.

*Tribune (1891), 8, 3400 (7000), 2nd cl. cruiser, 20 kts., N. America and West Indies. *Capt.* Robert S. Rolleston.

*‡Triton (1882), 410 tons (350), surveying service, Sheerness. *Capt.* George E. Richards.

Triumph (1873), 14, 6640 (3500), 3rd cl. battleship, 12·6 kts., Devonport.

Tweed (1877), 3, 363 (200), 3rd cl. gunboat, Hong Kong.

Tyne (1878), 3560 tons (1200), troop-ship, Mediterranean. *Comm.* Keppel Wade.

*Undaunted (1886), 12, 5600 (5500), 1st cl. cruiser, 18·1 kts., China. *Capt.* Arthur C. Clarke ; *Comm.* Cresswell J. Eyres.

*+Unicorn (1824), 1447 tons, drill-ship, R. N. Reserve, Dundee. *Lieut. & Comm.* E. L. Austen.

*+Urgent (1855), 2 guns, 2801 tons, depôt ship, Jamaica. *Capt.* (*Comm.. 2nd cl.*) Wm. Hannam Henderson ; *Comm.* Frank Alexr. Garforth.

Vengeance (1899), 16, 12950 (13500). 1st cl. battleship. 18¼ kts., completing at Barrow.

Venerable (1899), 16, 15000 (1·000), 1st cl. battleship, 18 kts., completing at Chatham.

*Venus (1895). 11, 5600 (8000), 2nd cl. cruiser, 20·1 kts., Mediterranean. *Capt.* Sir Archibald B. Milne, Bart. ; *Comm.* Cuthbert G. Chapman.

*+Vernon, late *Donegal* (.858), 5481 tons, torpedo school ship, Portsmouth. *Capt.* Charles G. Robinson ; *Comm.* Stuart Nicholson.

Vesuvius (1874), 245 tons (350), special torpedo vessel, Portsmouth (tender to *Vernon*). *Lieut. & Comm.* Frederick C. U. V. Wentworth.

*+Victoria and Albert (1855), 2470 tons (2400), Royal yacht, Portsmouth. *Rear-Adm.* Sir John R. T. Fullerton, K.C.V.O., C.B., A.D.C. (in command) ; *Comm.* Richard P. Fitzgerald.

Victoria and Albert (1899), 4700 tons (11000), Royal yacht, 20 kts., completing at Pembroke.

*Victorious (1897), 16, 14900 (10000), 1st cl. battleship, 17·5 kts., China. *Capt.* Anson Schomberg ; *Comm.* Robert H. Travers.

*+Victory (May 7, 1765), 26 guns, 2184 tons, flagship, Portsmouth. *Adm.* Sir Michael Culme-Seymour, Bart., G.C.B. ; *Capt.* Fras. C. B. Bridgeman. *Comm.* Julian C. A. Wilkinson.

Vindictive (1898), 10, 5750 (10000), 2nd cl. cruiser, 19·5 kts., Chatham.

Viola (1898), 6, 283 (6000 f.d.), t.b.d., 30 kts., tender to *Victory*, Portsmouth. *Lieut. and Comm.* John B. Sparks.

Viper (1899), 6, 312 (10000 f.d. turbine), t.b.d., 35 kts., completing at Newcastle.

Virago (1896), 6, 360 (6300 f.d.), t.b.d., 30 kts., tender to *Warspite*, Pacific. *Lieut. and Comm.* Gerald T. F. Pike.

*Vivid (1882), 550 tons (425), iron schooner, 11¼ kts., flag-ship, Devonport. *Adm.* Sir Henry Fairfax, K.C.B. ; *Staff-Comm.* (in command) Wm. Way.

*Volage (1874), 12, 3080 (2400), 2nd cl. cruiser, 12·8 kts., Training Squadron. *Capt.* Geo. H. Cherry.

*Vulcan (1889), 8, 6620 (7200), torpedo depôt ship, 20 kts., particular service. *Capt.* Richard Wm. White.

Vulture (1899), 6, 300 (5800 f.d.) t.b.d., 30 kts., Portsmouth.

*Wallaroo (1889), 8, 2575 (4000), 3rd cl. cruiser, 19 kts., Australasian waters. *Capt.* Arthur N. Farquhar.

+Wanderer, 925 tons, training-ship for boys, Portland. *Lieut. and Comm.* Lawrence de W. Satow.

Warrior (1860), 32, 9210 (4000), 1st cl. cruiser, Portsmouth.

*Warspite (1888), 14, 8400 (8000), 1st cl. cruiser. 16·7 kts., flagship, Pacific. *Rear-Adm.* Lewis A. Beaumont ; *Capt.* Thomas P. Walker ; *Comm.* Aylmer H. G. Williams.

*Waterwitch (1878) 620 tons (450), surveying vessel, China station. *Comm.* Willoughby P. Dawson.

Weasel (1873), 1, 254 (110), 3rd cl. gunboat, Portsmouth.

*Whiting (1895), 6, 350 (5900 f.d.), t.b.d., 30 kts., tender to *Centurion*, China. *Lieut. and Comm.* Edward Kelly.

*Widgeon (1889), 6, 805 (720), 1st cl. gunboat, 13 kts., Cape and West Africa. *Lieut. in comd.* Anthony Francis Gurney.

*Wildfire, 453 tons (360), flag-ship, Sheerness. *Vice-Adm.* Sir Nathaniel Bowden-Smith, K.C.B.; *Staff-Comm.* (in command) Edwin Wm. Geo Hilliard.

Wild Swan (1876), 8, 1130 (800), sloop, Devonport.

Wivern (1865), 4, 2750 (1000), coast defence ship, 8·5 kts., Hong Kong.

Wizard (1895), 6, 270 (4500 f.d.), t.b.d., 27 knots, Portsmouth.

Woon (1897), 6, 300 (6000 f.d.), t.b.d., 30 kts, Devonport. *Lieut. and Comm.* R. C. Kemble-Lambert.

*Woodcock (898), 150 tons (550), shallow-draught steamer for riv-rservice, China. *Lieut. and Comm.* Hugh Dudley R. Watson.

*Woodlark 1898 , 150 tons (550), shallow-draught steamer for river service, China. *Lieut. and Comm.* Ion P. Barton.

*Wye (1893), 1370 tons (700), store-ship, particular service. *Staff-Comm. in comd.* C. R. H. Robinson.

Zebra, (1895) 6, 310 (4800 f.d.), t.b.d., 27 knts., Chatham.

Zephyr (1895), 6, 280 (3850 f.d.), t.b.d., 27 kts. Paisley (completing for sea).

Ships building for the Royal Navy (November 1, 1899)

Government Dockyards have an asterisk * prefixed.

Aboukir, 14, 12000 (21000), 1st cl. cruiser, Fairfield, Glasgow.

Africa, 18, 14100 (30000), 1st cl. cruiser, Fairfield, Glasgow.

Arab, t.b.d., Clydebank, Glasgow.

Bacchante, 14, 12000 (21000), 1st cl. cruiser, Clydebank, Glasgow.

Bedford, 14 9800 (22000), 1st cl. cruiser. Fairfield. Glasgow.

Cornwallis, 16, 14000 18000), 1st cl. battleship, Blackwall.

Cressy, 14, 12000 (21000), 1st cl. cruiser, Fairfield, Glasgow.

*Drake, 18, 14 00 (30000), 1st cl. cruiser, Pembroke.

Duncan, 16, 14000 (18000), 1st cl. battleship, Blackwall.

*Espiègle, sloop, Sheerness.

*Essex, 14, 9800 (22000), 1st cl. cruiser, Pembroke.

Euryalus, 14, 12000, (21000), 1st cl. cruiser, Barrow-in-Furness.

Exmouth, 16, 14300 (18000), 1st cl. battleship, Birkenhead.

Falcon, t.b.d. Fairfield, Glasgow.

*Fantome, sloop, to be built at Sheerness.

Grafton, d.t.b.d. Newcastle-on-T.

Hogue, 14, 12000 (21000), 1st cl. cruiser, Barrow-in-Furness.

*Kent, 14, 9800 (21000), 1st cl. cruiser, Portsmouth.

King Alfred, 18, 14100 (30000), 1st class cruiser, Barrow.

Leviathan, 18, 14100 30000), 1st cl cruiser, Clydebank, Glasgow.

Loveg, t.b.d., Birkenhead.

Monmouth, 14, 9800 (22000), 1st cl. cruiser, Glasgow.

Mutine, 6, 980 (1400), sheathed sloop, Birkenhead.

Myrmidon, t.b.d., Jarrow.

Ostrich, t.b.d., Fairfield, Glasgow.

*Pandora, 2200 (7000), 3rd cl. cruiser, Portsmouth.

Perel, t.b.d., Jarrow.

Racehorse t.b.d , Newcastle-on-T.

Rinaldo, 6, 980 (1100), sheathed sloop, Birkenhead.

Roebuck, t.b.d., Newcastle-on-T.

Russell, 16, 14000 (18000), 1st cl. battleship, Jarrow.

Shearwater, 6, 980 (1400), sloop, Sheerness.

Sprightly, t.b.d., Birkenhead.

Success, t.b.d., Sunderland.

Sutlej, 14, 12000 (21000), 1st cl. cruiser Clydebank, Glasgow.

Syren, t.b.d., Jarrow.

Ves al, 6, 980 (1400), sloop, Sheerness Dockyard.

Vixen, t.b.d., Barrow.

The amounts in brackets represent the sums estimated in 1899-1900 under the head of Salaries and Allowances.

ASCENSION (£2,281).

Naval Off. in Ch., G. N. A. Pollard, R.N.
Fleet Paymaster, A. Turner, R.N.

BERMUDA (£9,051).

Naval Off. in Ch , Capt. T. MacGill, C.B., R.N.
Staff Commander, T. Maclean, R.N.
Ch. Constructor, C. P. Lemon.
Ch. Engineer, J. A. Lemon, R.N.
Naval & Virtualling Store Off. & Cashier, W. Smith.
Chaplain, Rev. R. V. Wilson, B A., R.N.
Staff Surgeon, J. M. Rogers, R.N.

BOMBAY (£433).
(*Royal Indian Marine.*)

Asst. Direc or, Capt. W. Chandler, R I.M.
St ff Off., Comm. G. E. Holland, R.I M , D S O.
Ch. Constructor, R. Watson.
Ch. Inspr. of Machinery, F. O. Gadsden, R.I.M.

CALCUTTA.
(*Royal Indian Marine.*)

Deputy Director, Capt. A Gwyn, R.I.M.
Staff Off., Comm T. A. L. de Berry, R.I.M.
Constructor, T. Avery.
Inspr. of Machine y, C. Fuller, R.I.M.

CAPE OF GOOD HOPE (£4,197).

Staff Commander F. Roberts, R.N.
Naval Store Off. & Acct., H. Baker.
Ch. Engineer, G. Elbrow, R.N.
Civil Engr., E. A. W. Barnard.
Chaplain, Rev. A. P. Hill, M.A., R.N.

CHATHAM YARD (£36,742).

Adml. Supt., Swinton C Holland.
Civil Asst., J. G. Wildish.
Sec., G. Egan.
Staff Capt. & Queen's Harbour Master, A.G. Douglas, R.N.
Ch. Constructor, W. James.
Ch. Engineer, W. G. Littlejohns, R.N.
Supg Civil Engr., W. J. Clarke.
Naval Store Off., H. J. Laslett.
Expense Accts., W. J. Roff.
Cashier, T. Watson.
Chaplain. Rev. W. Oxland, B.A., R.N.
Fleet Surgeon, A. W. Russell, R.N.

DEVONPORT YARD (£39,465).

Adml. Supt., Thomas S. Jackson.
Civil Asst., G. Crocker.
Secy , W. T. Sanders.
Staff Capt. & Queen's Harbour Master of the Hamoaze, H. E. Wood, R.N.
Ch. Constructor, H. R. Champness.
Ch. Engineer, R. Mayston, R.N.
Surg. Engineer, Maj. E. R. Kenyon, R.E.
Asst. Staff Capt., R. G. Roe, R.N.
Queen's Harb. Master, J. B. Johnson, R.N.
Naval Store Off., E. Besant.
Cashier, P. Bascen-Smith.
Expense Accts., D. C. Simpson.
Chaplain, Rev. J. M. Clarkson, M.A., R.N.
Fleet Surgeon, J. Dudley, M.B., R.N.

ESQUIMALT (£3,640).

Naval & Victual ing Store Off & Acct., W. H. Lobb.
Ch. Engineer, J. Langmaid, R.N.

GIBRALTAR (£4,064).

Naval Officer in Charge, Capt. W. H. Pigott, R.N.
Ch. Engineer, G. A. Haddy, R.N.

HALIFAX (£2,580).

Naval Store Off., N. A. Hay.
Ch. Engineer, C. G. Taylor, R.N.

HAULBOWLINE (£1,090).

HONG KONG (£11,018).

Naval Off. in Ch , Commodore F. Powell, C.B.
Comma der, L. F. Blackburn, R.N.
Ch. Constructor, J. Black.
Ch. Engineer S J. Robins, R.N.
Naval St re Off. & Cashier, H. Simmins.
Supg Civil Engr., O. Ordish (tempy.).
Expense Accts., J. J. O'Neill.
Chaplain, Rev. F. Flynn, M.A., R.N.

JAMAICA (£3,952).

Naval Off. in Ch., Commodore W.H.Henderson,R.N.
Master Attendant, Staff Com J. D. Moulton, R.N.
Naval & Vict. Store Officer & Acct., J. Dean.
Ch. Engineer, M. Onyon, R.N.

MALTA (£17,195).

Adml. Supt., Rodney M. Lloyd, C.B.
Secy.,
Staff Capt. & Queen's Harb. Master, W.J.Symons,R.N.
Ch. Constructor, W. H. Gard.
Ch Engineer, R J. Trench.
Su g. Civil Engr., T. C. Hunter.
Naval Store Off. & Cashier, J. Forsey.
Chaplain, Rev. R. D. Lewis, M.A., R.N.
Fleet Surgeon, R. D. White, M.D., R.N.

PEMBROKE DOCKYARD (£12,607).

Capt. Supt., Charles J. Barlow, D.S.O.
Secy.,
Queen's Harbour Master, A. J. W. Neville, R.N.
Ch. Constructor, Henry Cocks, M.V.O.
Store Off. & Cashier, E. A. de Ridder.
Civil Engr., C. H. Colson.
Chaplain, Rev. J. W. Longrigg, M.A., R.N.
Fleet Surgeon, E. W. Luther, R.N.

PORTLAND (£235).

Supg. Civil Engr., D. Macfarlane.

PORTSMOUTH YARD (£47,404).

Adml. Supt., Pelham Aldrich.
Civil Asst., L. G. Davies.
Secy., M. E. P. Frost.
Staff Capt. & Queen's Harbour Master, T. H. J. Rapson, R.N.
Ch. Constructor, J. A. Yates.
Ch Engineer, J. T. Corner, R.N.
Supg. Engineer, Lt.-Col. S H. Exham, R.E.
Asst. Staff-Capt., B. E. W. Gwynne, R.N.
Naval Store Off., W. Tarn.
Expense Accts., W. R. Thomas.
Cashier, W. R. Ternan.
Chaplain, Rev. W. Law, B.SC., R.N.
Fleet Surgeon, W. E. Breton, M.D., R.N.

SHEERNESS YARD (£18,986).

Capt. Supt., R. F. H. Henderson, C.B.
Secy., H. M. Dixon.
Staff Capt. & Deputy Queen's Harbour Master, W. S. Chambré, R.N.
Ch. Constructor, H. H. Ash.
Ch. Engineer, R. H. Andrews.
Naval Store Off., J. E. Rattenbury.
Chaplain, Rev. John Brabazon, M.A., R.N.
Fleet Surgeon, C. Pearson, M.D., R.N.

SYDNEY (£5,180).

Naval Off. in Ch., Capt. H W. S. Gibson, R.N.
Naval Store Off., G. H. Ashdown.
Inspr. of Warlike Stores, Lieut. H. G. Grenfell, R.N.
Ch. Engineer, W. F. Hinchcliff, R.N.

TRINCOMALEE (£1,449).

Naval & Victualling Store Officer & Accountant, W. M. Millett.

WEST INDIA DOCKS (£4,485).
(*Naval Store Depôt.*)

Naval Store Off. & Inspr. of Naval Stores, W. P. S. Burton.

VICTUALLING YARDS (£18,834).

BERMUDA.
Store Officer, W. Smith.

CAPE OF GOOD HOPE.
Store Officer, H. G. Arnold.

DEPTFORD.
(Royal Victoria.)
Supt., E. C. Capel.

ESQUIMALT.
Store Officer, W. H. Lobb.

GIBRALTAR.
In charge, Capt. W. H. Pigott, R.N.

GOSPORT.
(Royal Clarence.)
Supt., W. H. Hopper.

HALIFAX.
In charge, W. E. Clayton.

HAULBOWLINE.
Store Officer, H. M. Miller.

HONG KONG.
Store Officer, H. S. Vaughan.

JAMAICA.
Store Officer, J. Dean.

MALTA.
Supt., W. E. Turner.

PLYMOUTH.
(Royal William.)
Supt., W. A. Moore.

SYDNEY.
Store Officer, W. Hogarth.

TRINCOMALEE.
Store Officer, M. W. Millett.

MEDICAL ESTABLISHMENTS (£36,358).

ASCENSION.
Staff Surg., C. W. Sharples, R.N.

BERMUDA.
Dep. Insp. Gen., R. Hay, M.D., R.N.

CAPE OF GOOD HOPE.
Fleet Surg., H. A. W. Richardson, R.N.
Chaplain, Rev. A. P. Hill, B.A., R.N.

CHATHAM.
(Royal Hospital.)
Dep. Insp. Gen., R. Grant, M.B., R.N.

COQUIMBO.
Staff Surg., G. E. Kennedy, R.N.

DARTMOUTH.
(R.N. Cadets Sick Qrs.)
Fleet Surg., H. L. Crocker, R.N.

ESQUIMALT.
Staff Surg., P. B. Handyside, R.N.

GIBRALTAR.
Staff Surg., W. H. Norman, R.N.

HALIFAX, N.S.
Store Off., W. E. Clayton.

HASLAR.
(Royal Hospital.)
Insp. Gen., H. D Stanistreet, R.N.
Dep. Insp. Gen., T. L. Horner, R.N.; E. E. Mahon, C.B., R.N.

Storekeeper & Cashier, W. H. E. Mitchell, R.N.
Chaplain, Rev. F. A. J. Gace, B.A., R.N.

HAULBOWLINE.
(Royal Hospital.)
Fleet Surg., E. R. H. Pollard, R.N.

HONG KONG.
Dep. Insp. Gen., T. Bolster, R.N.

JAMAICA.
Dep. Insp. Gen., R. W. Coppinger, M.D., R.N.

MALTA.
Dep. Insp. Gen., R. S. P. Griffiths, R.N.
Chaplain, Rev. R. D. Lewis, M.A., R.N.

PLYMOUTH.
(Royal Hospital.)
Insp. Gen., J. W. Fisher, M.D., R.N.
Dep. Insp. Gen., C S. Godding R.N.
Storekeeper & Cashier, H.F.Roe, R.N.
Chaplain, Rev.C.J.Todd, M.A., R.N.

PLYMOUTH.
(R.M. Barrack Dispensary.)
Fleet Surg., R. Bentham, R.N.

PORTLAND.
(R.N. Sick Quarters.)
Staff Surg., E.R.Dimsey, D S.O., R.N.

PORTSMOUTH.
(R.M.A. Infirmary.)
Fleet Surg., H. M. Ellis, R.N.

PORTSMOUTH.
(R.M. Infirmary.)
Fleet Surg., J. H. Anderson, M.D., R.N.

SHEERNESS.
(Barracks Dispensary.)
Fleet Surg., C. Pearson, M.D., R.N.

SYDNEY.
(Medical Depôt.)
Staff Surg., J. H. Thomas, R.N.

TRINCOMALEE.
Store Off., M. W. Millett.

WALMER.
(R.M. Infirmary.)
Fleet Surg., W. B. Drew, R.N.

YARMOUTH.
(Royal Hospital.)
Fleet Surg., S. T. O'Grady, R.N.

YOKOHAMA.
(R.N. Sick Quarters.)
Staff Surg., D.T. Hoskyn, M.B., R.N.

ANNUAL PAY OF EFFECTIVE OFFICERS AND SEAMEN.

Exclusive of Allowances to Flag Officers.

ADMIRAL OF THE FLEET, £2,190. Admiral, £1,825. Vice-Admiral, £1,460. Rear-Admiral, £1,095. Commodore (1st class), £1,095; (2nd class), £410 to £602; extras. £365 to £730. Captain of H.M.S. Excellent, £850; of H.M.S. Britannia, £750 to £821. Captain, £410 to £602; extras, £91 to £328. Staff-Captain, £511; extras, £84 to £141. Commander, £365; extras, nil to £141. Staff-Commander £219 to £401; extras, £84 to £159. Lieutenant in command, £201 to £274; extras, £84 to £141. Lieutenant, £182 to £256; extras, nil to £73. Chief Officer, £201; extras. nil to £38. Sub-Lieutenant, £91; extra for navigating duties, £25. Senior Mate, £119 to £137. Second Mate, £91 to £100. Midshipman, £32. Naval Cadet, £1. Chief Gunner Chief Boatswain and Chief Carpenter £182 to £219. Gunner, Boatswain and Carpenter, £100 to £164. Petty Officer, and leading Seaman, £32 to £181. Various Ratings, £9 to £136. Able, ordinary, and 2nd class ordinary Seaman, £24 to £106. Boy, £9 to £18.

Chief Inspector of Machinery afloat, £730. Inspector ditto, £638. Fleet, Staff and Chief Engineer, £256 to £475; extras, £18 to £255. Engineer, £164 to £219; extras, £18 to £164. Assistant Engineer, £110 to £137; extras, £18. Artificer Engineer, £155 to £192. Stoker, £30 to £91.

Chaplain, £210 to £401. Secretary, £274 to £548. Paymaster, £236 to £602; extras, £45 to £91. Assistant ditto, £91 to £210. Clerk, £73. Assistant Clerk, £46.

Naval Instructor, £219 to £401. Head Schoolmaster, £137 to £155.

Fleet-Surgeon, £493 to £602; extras, £46 to £91. Staff-Surgeon, £383 to £438; extras, £46 to £91. Surgeon, £210 to £283.

NAVY AND PRIZE AGENTS.

Banton, Mackrell, & Co., 3 Gt. Winchester St., E.C.
Burnett & Co., 123 Pall Mall, S.W.
Stilwell & Sons, 43 Pall Mall, S.W.
Woodhead & Co., 44 Charing Cross, S.W.

* RELATIVE RANK IN ARMY AND NAVY.

	Rank with		Rank with
Field Marshals	Admirals of the Fleet.	Majors, according to date of Commission or Order.	Lieutenants, and Navigating Lieutenants of 8 years' standing.
Generals	Admirals.		
Lieut.-Generals	Vice-Admirals.		
Major-Generals	Rear-Admirals.		
Brigadier-Gens.	Commodores, 1st and 2nd Class.	Captains, according to date of Commission or Order.	Lieutenants, and Navigating Lieutenants under 8 years' standing.
Colonels	Captains of 3 years.		
Lieut.-Colonels	Captains under 3 years and Staff Captains.		
Lieut.-Colonels but Senior to	Commanders & Staff Commanders.	Lieutenants, according to date of Commission or Order.	Sub-Lieutenants.

(Field Marshals to Lieut.-Colonels: according to date of Commission.)

* The title and rank of officers of the Royal Indian Marine are similar to those of the Royal Naval Reserves, but senior to those officers in their respective ranks.

EFFECTIVE FIGHTING FLEETS OF THE NATIONS (1898-9.)

CLASSIFICATION.	U. KINGDOM.		U. S. A.		JAPAN.		GERMANY.		FRANCE.		RUSSIA.		ITALY.	
	Built	Bldg.	Built	Bldg.	Built	Bldg.	Built	Bldg.	Built	Bldg.	Built	Bldg.	Built	Bldg.
Battleships—														
1st Class	18	16	4	8	2	4	5	4	8	3	4	6	3	4
2nd ,, ...	11	...	...	...	...	...	...	...	9	1	10	...	5	...
3rd ,, ...	12	...	1	...	1	...	7	...	15	...	1	...	2	...
Total........	41	16	5	8	3	4	12	4	32	4	15	6	10	4
Coast Defence	23	...	6	4	1	...	19	...	16	...	15	1	3	...
Cruisers—														
1st Class	21	12	4	...	1	5	2	...	3	11	4	11	2	4
2nd ,, ...	57	3	11	...	9	...	8	...	21	4	7	...	5	...
3rd ,, ...	41	3	5	...	3	...	10	...	11	2	2	4	10	...
Total........	119	18	20	...	13	5	20	...	35	17	13	15	17	4
Gunboats— 1st Class or Torpedo Gunboats...	34	...	...	...	...	...	4	...	21	...	9	...	15	...
T.-B.-D.	50	46	...	20	...	8	...	1	...	8	...	28	...	1
Torpedo Boats..........	93	...	8	22	44	13	113	9	211	38	174	...	142	2

THE CHURCH of ENGLAND is "that pure and reformed part of Christ's Holy Catholic Church which is established within this Realm." The word "established" implies that a certain relation exists between it and the Realm itself; and the Church of England is "established" in its recognition as the national organisation for the maintenance of Christian belief and practice. Its clergy are an estate of the realm; the Sovereign is one of its members, and its supreme governor on earth; the free exercise of its inherent rights as a Church is guaranteed, and its authority, when lawfully exercised, is enforced. The Church has taken a large share in the promotion of civilisation, education, and philanthropic enterprise, and has exercised a powerful moral influence towards order, peace, and national progress.

Christianity was introduced into these islands before the close of the second century. It soon found a home amongst the Britons of the Roman provinces, and gradually spread amongst the Celtic tribes outside the sphere of Roman influence. We know that Alban, the first British martyr, was put to death about the beginning of the fourth century, and that three British bishops took part in the Council of Arles in 314 We read also of British bishops attending the Council of Ariminum in 359, and there is much other evidence with regard to the wide-spread Christianity of the Celtic peoples. When however the pagan English tribes landed in Britain, they drove the inhabitants into the mountainous regions of the west; and their faith went with them.

The English Church, as distinguished from the earlier British Church which the pagan English had expelled from their kingdoms, took its rise in 597, when Ethelbert, the pagan King of Kent, was baptized by missionaries sent by Gregory, the Bishop of Rome. The Italians only converted, permanently, the small kingdom of Kent; but they made the first beginning of the Church of England. East Anglia and Wessex were converted by other foreigners. The great impetus to the spread of the faith was given by two English Northumbrian Kings, who had been taught by the Scotic (Celtic) Church from its centre at Iona. By their influence the new faith was established in by far the largest part of the country.

The Church of the Britons continued a separate existence in its mountainous retreats, and took no part in the conversion of the English. It had merged its organisation in that of the English Church as early as the Norman times; and thus the Church of England and Wales is one.

About the years 660 to 680, the principal Kings of the English Heptarchy learned to take united action in Church matters, and that was the beginning of the unity of England. It was not till 150 years later that England became in any sense one kingdom. At that time, A.D. 828, the Archbishoprics of Canterbury and York had long been in existence, and the Bishoprics of London, Rochester, Winchester, Lichfield, Worcester, Hereford, and the originals of the Sees now called Chester, Lincoln, Salisbury, Norwich, Chichester, Durham, as also four Bishoprics since merged in others. Thus, to speak generally, the present organization and geographical arrangement of the Church of England is older by a century and a half, in some parts by two centuries and more, than the Kingdom of England.

The Church of England passed unbroken through the Norman Conquest. Lanfranc was consecrated the first Norman Archbishop of Canterbury by nine English Bishops. The Reformation which began under Henry VIII. is the most important landmark in its existence. All care was taken to preserve the continuous life of the English Church, and many important changes were made with a view to purifying that life by the light of Holy Scripture and the primitive fathers. In 1541 the Bishoprics of Chester, Oxford, Peterborough, Bristol, and Gloucester were formed. In the present century, to meet the wants of the growing populations, the sees of Ripon, Manchester, St. Albans, Liverpool, Wakefield, Truro, Newcastle and Southwell have been created. There are now two Archbishops, 33 diocesan Bishops (of whom 24 have seats in the House of Lords), and 17 Bishops Suffragan. The Anglican Episcopate has spread far and wide. There are 90 colonial and missionary bishoprics, the first being that of Nova Scotia in 1787; and 80 American bishoprics, the first in 1784. The growth in modern times may be seen from the invitations to the Lambeth Conference of Bishops in communion with the Church of England: in 1867, 144; 1878, 173; 1888, 211; in 1897, 247.

The Convocations of Canterbury and York are the deliberative bodies of the Church of the Southern province and the Northern province respectively. The archbishops and bishops, the deans and archdeacons, sit in Convocation *ex officio*, and there are elected representatives of the Cathedral Chapters and the beneficed clergy. In accordance with ancient custom, Convocation cannot make ecclesiastical laws or canons without the permission of the Sovereign.

There are about 14,000 parishes, and in half of these the income of the incumbent is less than £130 a year. The estates of the Bishoprics and Cathedrals are in the main managed by the Ecclesiastical Commissioners, who pay the incomes of the bishops, &c., and spend the balance in improving the endowments and buildings of parishes, providing funds for additional clergy, and endowing new parishes. The whole number of clergy, beneficed and not beneficed, is about 23,000; the Archdeacons (90 in number) and Rural Deans (810) are the officers through whom the bishop of the diocese regulates their proceedings. Each diocesan bishop has a Court with legal officials, for the trial of cases that arise.

The sums raised by voluntary contribution during the year 1895, or the alternate period from Easter 1895 to Easter 1896, as given in the "Church Year Book" for 1897, amounted to nearly £5,750,000, exclusive of offerings by Churchmen made direct to societies and independently of the parochial clergy (or for the general maintenance of hospitals and similar institutions). In the 25 years from 1860 to 1884, £35,000,000 was given for Church building and work of that kind; £7,000,000 for Home Mission work, £10,000,000 for Foreign Missions, £22,000,000 for Elementary Education, £4,000,000 for Charitable Work, and £2,000,000 for Clergy Charities; with a total of £81,000,000. In the ten years from 1884 to 1893, £13,500,000 was given for church building, &c. Some of the most important items are exclusive of the action of Societies, and a vast amount of charity is never put on record.

*The Dean and Chapters of certain Dioceses (marked * in the following pages) preferred several years ago to take, in lieu of fixed annual money payments, estates estimated at that time to produce the same annual income; they are consequently suffering more or less from the present agricultural depression.*

*Canterbury. £15,000.

Archbishop and Primate of All England, Rt. Hon. and Most Rev. Frederick Temple, D.D. ......1896 (Lambeth Palace, S.E.) [Signs F. Cantuar.]

PROVINCE OF CANTERBURY.
Provincial Dean, The Bishop of London.
Provincial Chancellor, The Bishop of Winchester.
Provinc. Vice-Chancellor, The Bishop of Lincoln.
Provincial Precentor, The Bishop of Salisbury.
Provincial Chaplain, The Bishop of Rochester.
Bishop of Dover, Rt. Rev. William Walsh, D.D. (appointed 1898)
Dean, Very Rev. F. Wm. Farrar, D.D. (1895) £1,400.
  Canons Residentiary (each £700).
G. Rawlinson, M.A. 1872 | W. P. Roberts, M.A. 1895
F. J. Holland, M.A. 1882 | A. J. Mason, D.D. 1895
Archd. Smith, M.A. 1887 | Bishop of Dover, 1897
  Organist, H. J. Perrin, MUS. BAC.
  Archdeacons.
Ven. Benj. Fredk. Smith, M.A., *Maidstone*......1887
Rt. Rev. William Walsh, D.D., *Canterbury* ...1897
  Beneficed Clergy, 427 ; *Curates, &c.*, 199.
Vicar-Gen. of Province and Diocese, Rt. Hon. Sir James Parker Deane, Q.C., D.C.L.
Commissary of Diocese, T. H. Tristram, Q.C., D.C.L.
Domestic Chaplain, Rev. E. L. Ridge, M.A.
Principal Reg. of Province and Diocese, Sir John Hassard, K.C.B., 3, Creed Lane, Ludgate Hill, E.C.
Apparitor-General, Sir John A. Hanham, Bart.
Legal Secs., H. W. & F. H. Lee, 1, Sanctuary, S.W.

* York. £10,000.

Archbishop and Primate of England, Right Hon. and Most Rev. Wm. Dalrymple Maclagan, D.D. '91 (Bishopthorpe, York.) [Signs Willelm: Ebor.]
Bishop Suffragan of Beverley, Rt. Rev. Robert Jarratt Crosthwaite, D.D. (Bolton Percy, York) 1889
Bp. Suff. of Hull, Rt. Rev. R. F. L. Blunt, D.D. 1891 (St. Mary's Vicarage, Scarborough.)
Dean, Very Rev. A.P. Purey-Cust, D.D. (1880) £2,000
Canons Resident. (each £700, red. temp. to £400).
Jas. Fleming, D.D. 1877 | Henry Temple, M.A. 1895
Bishop Blunt, D.D.1882 | John Watson. M.A. 1896
  Organist, Thomas Tertius Noble.
  Archdeacons (each £200).
Rt. Rev. Robert J. Crosthwaite, D.D., *York* ...1884
Ven. William Hy. Hutchings, M.A., *Cleveland* 1897
Ven. John Rashdall Eyre, *Sheffield* 1897
Ven. Charles Coleridge Mackarness, M.A., *East Riding* 1898
  Beneficed Clergy, 632 ; *Curates, &c.*, 250.
Vicar-General of the Province, and Chancellor of the Diocese, Lord Grimthorpe, Q.C., LL.D.
Registrar, Henry Arthur Hudson, York.
Secretary, Thos. Shepherd Noble, Lendal, York.

London. £10,000.

Bishop, Rt. Hon. and Rt. Rev. Mandell Creighton, D.D. (Provincial Dean of Canterbury) 1897 (St. James's Square ; Fulham Palace, S.W.) [Signs M. London.]

  Bishops Suffragan.
Marlborough, Rt. Rev. Alfred Earle, D.D. ... 1888 (St. Botolph's Rectory, Bishopsgate, E.C.)
Stepney, Rt. Rev A.F Winnington Ingram, D.D.,1897 (2, Amen Court, E C.)
Islington, Rt. Rev. C. H. Turner, D.D. .... 1898 (West Hill, Highgate.)
Bp. Assistant for Northern and Central Europe, Right Rev. Thomas Edw. Wilkinson, D.D. ...1886 (42 Norfolk Square, Hyde Park, W.)

Dean of St. Paul's, Very Rev. Robert Gregory, D.D. (1891), Deanery, Doctors' Commons, £2,000
  Canons Residentiary (each £1,000).
Henry Scott-Holland, | W.C.E.Newbolt, M.A.1890
  M.A. .... 1884 | Bishop Ingram, D.D. 1897
Achd. Sinclair, D.D. 1889|
  Organist, Sir George Clement Martin, MUS.D.
  Archdeacons.
Ven. William M. Sinclair, D.D., *London* (1889).
Ven. Robinson Thornton, D.D. *Middlesex* (1893)£333
  Beneficed Clergy, 561 ; *Curates, &c.*, 1015.
Chancellor of Dioc., Thos. H. Tristram, Q.C., D.C.L.
Registrar, H. W. Lee, 1, Dean's Court, E.C.
Secs. & Chapter Clerk, Harry Wilmot Lee and Frederic Hugh Lee, 1, The Sanctuary, S.W.

Westminster. £2,000.

Dean, Very Rev. Geo. Granville Bradley, D.D. 1881
  Canons Residentiary (each £1,000).
R. Duckworth, D.D. 1875 | B. Wilberforce, D.D. 1894
Ven.C.W.Furse.M.A.'83 | Charles Gore, M.A. 1894
  Joseph Armitage Robinson, M.A....1899.
  Organist, Sir John Frederick Bridge, MUS.D.
Sub-Dean, Rev. Canon Duckworth, D.D.
Archdeacon, Ven. Charles W. Furse, M.A.........1895
Receiver-General, John Charles Thynne.
Chapter Clerk, Charles St. Clare Bedford
Precentor, Rev. H. G. Daniell-Bainbridge, M.A.

Durham. £7,000.

Bishop, Rt. Rev. Brooke Foss Westcott, D.D. 1890 (Auckland Castle, Bishop Auckland.) [Signs B. F. Dunelm.]
Assist. Bp., Rt. Rev. Dan. Fox Sandford, D.D. 1889
Dean, Very Rev. G. W. Kitchin, D.D. £2,000 1894
  Canons Residentiary (each £1,000).
Dr. H. B. Tristram 1873 | Archden. Hamilton 1882
Dr. A. S. Farrar ...1878 | Dr. George Body ...1883
Archden. Watkins 1880 | Dr. H. Kynaston ...1889
  Organist, P. Armes, MUS.D.
  Archdeacons (each £200).
Ven. Henry Wm. Watkins, D.D., *Durham*......1882
Ven. Robert Long, M.A., *Auckland* 1882
  Beneficed Clergy, 243 ; *Curates, &c.*, 207.
Chancellor, Lewis Tonna Dibdin, D.C.L. 1891
Registrar, J. B. Lazenby, Durham.
Secretary, John George Wilson, M.A. Durham.
London Sec., H. W. Lee, 1, The Sanctuary, S.W.

*Winchester. £6,500.

Bishop, Rt. Rev. Randall Thos. Davidson, D.D. 1895 (Farnham Castle, Surrey.) [Signs Randall Winton.]
Bishop of Guildford, Rt. Rev. George Henry Sumner, D.D. 1888
Bishop Suffragan of Southampton, Rt. Rev. Hon. Arthur Lyttelton, D.D. 1898
Dean, Very Rev Wm. Rd. Wood Stephens,B.D.,1894
Canons Res., each £420 to £450 (*nominally* £910).
W.P.Warburton, M.A.'84 | Archd. Sapte, M.A.,1888
Bishop Sumner, D.D.1885 | Archd. Haigh, M.A., 1890
  Arthur S. Valpy, M.A. ... .1895
  Organist, G. B. Arnold, MUS.D.
  Archdeacons (each £200).
Rt. Rev. George H. Sumner, D.D., *Winchester* 1885
Ven. Henry Haigh, M.A., *Isle of Wight* 1886
Ven. John Henry Sapte. M.A., *Surrey* 1888
  Beneficed Clergy, 563 ; *Curates, &c.*, 450.
Chancellor, Harold Carlyon Gore-Browne, M.A.
Hants & I. of W. Registrar, Charles Wooldridge, Winchester.
Surrey Regist. W.P. Moore, Doctors' Commons, E.C.
Secretaries, H. W. & F. H. Lee, 1 Sanctuary, S.W.

Bangor. £4,200.

Bishop, Rt. Rev. Watkin Hbt. Williams, D.D. 1899
(Palace, Bangor, Carnarvonshire.)
Dean, Very Rev. Evan Lewis, M.A. (1884) ...£700
Canons Residentiary (each £350).
Arch. Williams, D.D.1889 | E. Williams, B.A....1888
Archdeacon Pryce 1884 | D. W. Thomas, M.A.1891
Organist, T. Westlake Morgan.
Archdeacons (Canonries attached).
Ven. John Pryce, M.A., *Bangor* 1887
Ven. Thomas Williams, M.A., *Merioneth* 1891
Beneficed Clergy, 147; *Curates, &c.,* 70.
Chancellor, James Edmund Vincent, M.A. ... 1891
Regist.Sec.& Chapter Clk., R. Hughes Pritchard, M.A.
London Sec., H. W. Lee, 1 The Sanctuary, S.W.

Bath and Wells. £5,000.

Bp., Rt. Rev. Geo. Wyndham Kennion, D.D. 1894
(The Palace, Wells.) [Signs G. W. Bath: & Well:]
Dean, Very Rev.T.W. Jex-Blake,D.D. (1891)£1,000
Canons Residentiary of Wells (each £600).
T. D. Bernard, M.A. 1868 | Geo. Buckle, M.A....1887
C. M. Church, M.A.1879 | Archd. Ainslie, LL.D. '95
Organist, Rev. T. H. Davies, MUS.B.
Archdeacons.
Ven. Hilton Bothamley, M.A., *Bath* 1895
Ven. Alexander C. Ainslie, LL.D., *Taunton* ...1896
Ven. Frederick A. Brymer, M.A., *Wells* 1899
Beneficed Clergy, 493; *Curates, &c.,* 136.
Chancellor, Thomas Englesby Rogers, M.A.
Registrar, Sec. & Chapt. Clerk, Rd. Harris, Wells.
London Sec., H. W. Lee, The Sanctuary, S.W.

Bristol. £3,000 (reconstituted 1897).

Bishop, Rt. Rev. Geo. Forrest Browne, D.D... 1897
Dean, Very Rev. Francis Pigou, D.D. (1891)£1,400
Canons Residentiary (each £650).
H. Robeson, M.A....1884 | Jas. G. Tetley, M.A. 1892
Alf. Ainger, LL.D....1887 | S. A. Barnett, M.A. 1893
Organist, G. Riseley.
Archdeacon, Ven. H. Robeson, M.A. (1892) ...£180
Chancellor, Arthur Becher Ellicott, M.A., 1891.
Registrar and Secretary, William Hurle Clarke.
London Sec., H. W. Lee, The Sanctuary, S.W.

*Carlisle. £4,500.

Bishop, Rt. Rev. J. Wareing Bardsley, D.D....1892
(Rose Castle, Carlisle, Cumberland.)
Bp. Suffragan of Barrow-in-Furness, Right Rev.
Henry Ware, D.D. (The Abbey, Carlisle) ...1889
*Dean,*Very Rev.W.G.Henderson, D.D. (1884)£1,225
Canons Residentiary (each £600).
Archd. Prescott,D.D. '70 | Bp. of Barrow, D.D.1888
T.K.Richmond,M.A.1883 | Archd. Diggle, M.A.1896
Organist, H. E. Ford, MUS.D.
Archdeacons.
Ven. John Eustace Prescott, D.D., *Carlisle* ...1883
Ven. Thompson Phillips, M.A., *Furness* (1893) £200
Ven. J. W. Diggle, M.A., *Westmorland* (1896) £200
Beneficed Clergy, 291; *Curates, &c.,* 95.
Chancellor, Richard Saul Ferguson, M.A.
Registrar and Sec., A. N. Bowman, Carlisle.
London Secretary, Sir John Hassard, K.C.B.,3 Creed
Lane, Ludgate Hill, E.C.

*Chester. £4,200.

Bishop, Rt. Rev. Francis John Jayne, D.D. ...1889
(The Palace, Chester.) [Signs F. J. Cestr.]
Dean, Very Rev. J. L. Darby, D.D. (1886)...£1,000
Canons Residentiary (each £500).
Archd. Barber, M.A.1886 | G. R. Feilden, M.A.1888
A. J.Blencowe, M.A.1886 | Arthur Gore, D.D. 1893
Organist, Joseph C. Bridge, M.A., MUS.D.
Archdeacons (each £200).
Ven. Edward Barber, M.A., *Chester* 1886
Ven. Chas. M. Woosnam, M.A., *Macclesfield* ...1893

Beneficed Clergy, 270; *Curates, &c.,* 197.
Chancellor, Rev. Thomas Espinell Espin, D.D.
Registrar, John Gamon, Chester.
Deputy Registrar, Richard Farmer, Chester.
Bishop's Secretaries, Gamon, Farmer & Co., Chester;
and H. W. Lee, Sanctuary, Westminster, S.W.

*Chichester. £4,060.

Bishop, Rt. Rev. Ernest R. Wilberforce, D.D. 1895
(The Palace.) [Signs Ernest R. Cicestr.]
Dean, Very Rev. R. W. Randall, D.D. (1892) £500
Canons Residentiary (each £250).
Archd. Mount, M.A.1887 | R.E.Sanderson,D.D.1889
Jos. S. Teulon, M.A.1888 | A. M. Deane, M.A. 1897
Organist, F. J. Read, MUS.D.
Archdeacons (each £200).
Ven. Francis John Mount, M.A., *Chichester* ...1887
Ven. Robert Sutton, M.A., *Lewes* 1888
Beneficed Clergy, 377; *Curates, &c.,* about 188.
Chancellor, Thos. H. Tristram, Q.C., D.C.L.
Registrar (Lewes), Edmund Charles Currey.
*Secretary to the Bishop, Chapter Clerk, and Regis-
trar,* Sir Robert George Raper, Chichester.
London Secretary, Sir John Hassard, K.C.B., 3
Creed Lane, Ludgate Hill, E.C.

Ely. £5,500.

Bishop, Rt. Rev. Lord Alwyne Compton, D.D. 1886
(Palace, Ely; & Ely House, Dover St., Piccadilly.)
Dean, Very Rev. C. W. Stubbs, D.D. (1894) £1,320
Canons Residentiary (each £600).
Ven.W.Emery, D.D. 1870 | A.F.Kirkpatrick,D.D.'82
E. C. Lowe, D.D. 1873 | V. H. Stanton, D.D. 1889
Ven.Chapman,M.A. 1879 | Bp. Macrorie, D.D. 1892
Organist, Percy Allen, MUS. DOC.
Archdeacons.
Ven. William Emery, B.D., *Ely* (1864) £600
Ven. F. R. Chapman, M.A., *Sudbury* (1870) ...£200
Ven. Fredk. Bathurst, M.A., *Bedford* (1873)...£200
Ven. Fras. Gerald Vesey, LL.D., *Hunts* (1874) £200
Beneficed Clergy, 565; *Curates, &c.,* 230.
Chancellor, George J. Talbot, M.A.
Registrar & Secretary, Wm. Johnson Evans, Ely.
Lond. Secretary, H. W. Lee, The Sanctuary, S.W.

Exeter. £4,200.

Bishop, Rt. Rev. Edw. Hy. Bickersteth, D.D. 1885
(The Palace, Exeter.) [Signs E. H. Exon.]
Bishop Suffragan of Crediton, Rt. Rev. Robert
Edward Trefusis, D.D. 1897
Dean, Very Rev. B. M. Cowie, D.D. (1883) £2,000
Canons Residentiary (each £1,000).
Arch.Sandford,M.A.1888 | Bishop Trefusis......1889
C. I. Atherton, M.A. 1889 | W. J.Edmonds,B.D.1890
Organist, Daniel Joseph Wood, MUS. DOC.
Archdeacons.
Ven. Ernest Grey Sandford, M.A., *Exeter* (1888), £50
Ven.Chas.Thos.Wilkinson,D.D., *Totnes* (1888), £200
Ven. A. E. Seymour, M.A., *Barnstaple* (1890), £200
Benefices, 515; *Incumbents,* 495; *Curates, &c.,* abt. 300.
Chancellor, Lewis Tonna Dibdin, D.C.L. (1888).
Registrar and Secretary, Arthur Burch, Exeter.
London Secretary, Sir John Hassard, K.C.B., 3
Creed Lane, Ludgate Hill, E.C.

*Gloucester. £5,000.

Bishop, Rt. Rev. Charles John Ellicott, D.D....1863
(Palace, Gloucester, and 55 Great Cumberland
Place, W.)
Assist. Bishop, Rt. Rev. Saml. Edwd. Marsden, D.D.
Dean, Very Rev. H. D. M. Spence, D.D. (1886) £1,500
Canons Residentiary (each £200).
M. F. St. John, B.D.1884 | J. P. A. Bowers,M.A. '90
Archd. Sheringham 1889 | Archdn. Hayward, 1893
Bishop Mitchinson, D.C.L., 1899.

Organist, Herbert Brewer, MUS.B., £250.
Archdeacons (each £200).
Ven. John W. Sheringham, M.A., *Gloucester*...1881
Ven. Henry Rudge Hayward, *Cirencester* ...1882
Beneficed Clergy (Glo. & Br.), 498; *Curates, &c.,* 190
Chanc. & Vicar-Gen., Arthur B. Ellicott, M.A. 1891
Regist. & Sec., T. Hannam Clark (Gloucester).

Hereford. £4,200.

Bishop, Right Rev. John Percival, D.D. 1895
(The Palace, Hereford.)
Dean, Very Rev. Hon. James Wentworth Leigh,
D.D. (1894) £1,000
Canons Residentiary (each £500).
Sidn. L. Smith, M.A.1877 | Chas.S.Palmer,M.A.1892
Archd. Bather, M.A.1892 | F.M.Williams,M.A., '96
Organist, George Robertson Sinclair, MUS. DOC.
Archdeacons (each £200).
Ven. Hon. Berkeley L.S. Stanhope,M.A.,*Heref.*1887
Ven. Henry Francis Bather, M.A., *Ludlow* ...1892
Beneficed Clergy, 352 ; *Curates, &c.,* 81.
Chancellor, Thomas H. Tristram, Q.C., D.C.L.
Registrar, James Beresford Atlay, M.A.
Dep. do. and Sec., Henry Child Beddoe, Hereford.
Lond. Sec., H. W. Lee, Sanctuary, Westminster.

Lichfield. £4,200.

Bishop, Right Rev. and Hon. Augustus Legge,
D.D. (The Palace, Lichfield) 1891
Bishop Suffragan of Shrewsbury, Right Rev. Sir
Lovelace Tomlinson Stamer, Bart., D.D. ...1888
(Edgmond Rectory, Salop.)
Dean, Very Rev. H. M. Luckock, D.D. (1892) £1,000
Canons Residentiary (each £500).
J.G.Lonsdale, M.A.1855 | C. Mortimer, M.A.....1890
Chas. Bodington ......1888 | Bishop Anson, D.D. 1898
Organist, J. B. Lott, MUS.B.
Archdeacons (each £200).
Ven. Ernald Lane, M.A., *Stoke-on-Trent*.........1888
Ven. Robert Hodgson, M.A., *Stafford* 1898
Ven. Charles Bulmer Maude, M.A., *Salop* ...1896
Beneficed Clergy, 480 ; *Curates, &c.,* 279.
Chancellor, Hon. Robert Charles Herbert, M.A.
Registrar, Hubert Courtney Hodson, Lichfield.
Sec., R. R. Redmayne, B.A., The Close, Lichfield.

Lincoln. £4,500.

Bishop, Right Rev. Edward King, D.D. 1885
(The Old Palace, Lincoln.)
*Dean,*Very Rev.Edw.C.Wickham,D.D. (1894) £2,000
Canons Residentiary (each £1,000).
Archden.Kaye,M.A. 1863 | H. R. Bramley,M.A.1895
E. T. Leeke, M.A.....1877 | J. H. Crowfoot,M.A.1898
Organist, George J. Bennett, MUS. DOC.
Archdeacons.
Ven. Wm. Fredk. John Kaye, M.A., *Lincoln*...1863
Ven. John Bond, M.A., *Stow* (£200)...............1897
Benefices, 581 ; *Curates, &c.,* 122.
Chancellor Geo. John Talbot, 4 Eaton Terrace,S.W.
Registrar, John Swan, Lincoln.
Secretary, William Walker Smith, Lincoln.

Liverpool. £4,200.

Bishop, Right Rev. John Chas. Ryle, D.D. 1880
(Palace, 19 Abercrombie Square, Liverpool.)
*Assist.Bishop,*Rt.Rev.Peter Sorenson Royston,D.D.
Archdeacons (each £200).
Ven. Wm. Francis Taylor, D.D., *Liverpool*......1895
Ven. Thos. John Madden, M.A., *Warrington*...1895
Beneficed Clergy, 203 ; *Deaneries,* 11 ; *Curates,&c.,*229.
Chancellor, Rev. Thomas Espinell Espin,D.D., D.C.L.
Regists, J. Gamon & R. Farmer, 53 Lord St.,Lpl.
Secretaries, Gamon, Farmer, & Gamon, 53 Lord St.
London Secretary, Sir John Hassard, K.C.B., 3 Creed
Lane, Ludgate Hill, E.C.

Llandaff. £4,200.

Bishop, Right Rev. Richard Lewis, D.D. 1883
(The Palace, Llandaff.)
Dean, Very Rev. Wm. Harrison Davey, M.A.
(1897) £700
Canons Residentiary (each £350).
Archdeacon Bruce 1885 | Griff. Roberts, M.A.1889
Archden.Edmondes1897 | H. R.Johnson,M.A. 1896
Organist, George G. Beale, MUS.B., £140.
Archdeacons (Canonries attached).
Ven. Frederick Wm Edmondes,M.A., *Llandaff* 1897
Ven. Wm. Conybeare Bruce, M.A., *Monmouth* 1886
Beneficed Clergy, 246 ; *Curates, &c.,* 228.
Chancellor, Joseph Earle Ollivant, M.A.
Secretary, Arthur G. P. Lewis, M.A., Cardiff.
Registrar & Apparitor-General, Fred. J. Smith.
Chapter Clerk, John Ernest Gladstone, Cardiff.
Hon. London Sec., H. W. Lee, The Sanctuary, S.W.

Manchester. £4,200.

Bishop, Right Rev. James Moorhouse, D.D. 1886
(Bishop's Court, Higher Broughton, Manchester.)
Assistant Bishop, Right Rev. Francis A. Randal
Cramer-Roberts, D.D.,Vicarage,Blackburn,1888.
Dean, Very Rev. Edward Craig Maclure, D.D.
(1890)...£
Canons Residentiary (each £).
Wm. Crane, M.A. .....1871 | Jas. D. Kelly, M.A.1884
C.W.Woodhouse,M.A.'74 | Ewd.L.Hicks, M.A. 1892
Organist, James Kendrick Pyne.
Archdeacons (each £200).
Ven. James Maurice Wilson, M.A., *Manchester* 1890
Ven. Robert A. Rawstorne, M.A., *Blackburn*...1885
Ven. Arthur Frederick Clarke, M.A., *Lancaster* 1896
Beneficed Clergy, 525 ; *Curates, &c.,* about 360.
Chancellor, Philip Vernon Smith, LL.D.
*Registrar and Secretary,*Edward P. Charlewood,M.A.
Diocesan Registry and Office for Marriage Licences,
51 South King Street, Manchester.

Newcastle. £3,500.

Bishop, Right Rev. Edgar Jacob, D.D. 1896
(Benwell Tower, Newcastle-upon-Tyne.)
Archdeacons.
Ven. G. H. Hamilton, D.D., *Northumberland*...1882
Ven. Henry John Martin, M.A., *Lindisfarne* ...1882
Organist, John E. Jeffries, F.C.O.
Beneficed Clergy, 170 ; *Chaplains,* 8 ; *Curates,* 130.
Chancellor, Alfred Bray Kempe, M.A., F.R.S.
Registrar and Sec., J. B. Lazenby, Newcastle.
London Secretary, H. W. Lee, The Sanctuary, S.W.

*Norwich. £4,500.

Bishop, Rt. Rev. John Sheepshanks, D.D........1893
(The Palace, Norwich.) [Signs Joh. Norvic.]
Bishop Suffragan of Thetford, Right Rev. Arthur
Thomas Lloyd, D.D. (North Creake, Faken-
ham) 1894
Bishop Suffragan of Ipswich, Rt. Rev. George
Carnac Fisher, D.D. (*cons.* '96) 1899
Dean, Very Rev. Wm. Lefroy, D.D. (1889)...£1,300
Canons Residentiary (each £650).
C.K.Robinson, D.D.1861 | Arthur B. Crosse 1893
Archdeacon Nevill 1873 | F.A.J. Hervey,M.A.1897
Organist, F. A. Bates, MUS.D., £200
Archdeacons.
Ven. T. T. Perowne, B.D., *Norwich* (1878) ...£200
Ven. H. Ralph Nevill, M.A., *Norfolk* (1873)...£200
Ven. Richard H. Gibson, M.A., *Suffolk* (1892) £184
Rt.Rev.Arthur T. Lloyd, D.D., *Lynn* (1894) ..£200
Beneficed Clergy, 924 ; *Curates, &c.,* 180.
Chancellor, Thomas Calthorpe Blofeld, M.A.
*Regis. and Sec.,*Wm. Thos.Bensly, LL.D., Norwich.
London Sec., Harry W. Lee, The Sanctuary, S.W.

Orford. £5,000.

Bishop, Right Rev. William Stubbs, D.D. 1889
(Cuddesdon Palace, Oxon.) [Signs W. Oxon.]
Bishop Suffragan of Reading, Right Rev. James
Leslie Randall, D.D. (Ch. Ch., Oxford) 1889
Dean of Christ Church, Very Rev. Francis Paget,
D.D. (1892) £3,000
Canons Residentiary (£1,200—£1,500).

William Bright, D.D. 1885 | R. C. Moberly, D.D. 1892
William Ince, D.D. 1878 | W. Sanday, D.D. ...1895
S. R. Driver, D.D. .... 1882 | Bishop Randall, D.D. 1895
Organist, Basil Harwood, MUS.B., £300.
Archdeacons.

Ven. Alfred Pott, B.D., *Berks* (1869) £200
Rt. Rev. Jas. L. Randall, D.D., *Oxford* (1895)
Ven. Cecil F.J. Bourke, M.A., *Buckingham* (1895) £300
Beneficed Clergy, 651; *Curates, &c.*, 233.
Chancellor, Sir Wm. Reynell Anson, D.C.L., M.P.
Sec. & Registrar, T. M. Davenport, M.A., Oxford.
London Sec., H. W. Lee, 1 The Sanctuary, S.W.

Windsor. £2,000.

Dean, Very Rev. Philip Frank Eliot, D.D. 1891
Canons Residentiary (each £1,000).

J. Neale Dalton, D.D. 1885 | Marq. Normanby, M.A.'91
Bishop Barry, D.D. 1890 | Richard Gee, D.D. ...1894
Chapter Clerk, Richard Cope.
Organist, Sir Walter Parratt, MUS.D.

*Peterborough. £4,500.

Bishop, Rt. Rev. Hon. Edwd. Carr Glyn, D.D. 1897
(Palace, Peterborough.) [Signs E. C. Petriburg.]
Assist. Bishop, Rt. Rev. John Mitchinson, D.C.L.
Bishop Suffragan of Leicester, Rt. Rev. Francis
Henry Thicknesse, D.D. (Precincts, Peterboro.) 1888
Dean, Very Rev. W. Clavell Ingram, D.D. (1893) £686
Canons Residentiary (each £343).

Bishop Thicknesse 1875 | Lewis Clayton, M.A. 1887
J.C. MacDonnell, D.D.'83 | F.Cecil Alderson, M.A.'90
Organist, Haydn Keeton, MUS.D.
Archdeacons.

Rt.Rev.F.H. Thicknesse, D.D., *Northamp.* (1875) £80
Ven. Reg. P. Lightfoot, M.A., *Oakham* (1884) £200
Ven. Jno. Edwd. Stocks, M.A., *Leicester* (1899) £200
Beneficed Clergy, 582; *Curates, &c.*, 152.
Chancellor, George Holmes Blakesley, M.A. ...1891
Registrar, Charles Smith Magee, M.A.
Sec. and Dep. Registrar, Henry Wm. Gates, N.P.
London Secretary, Sir John Hassard, K.C.B., 3 Creed
Lane, Ludgate Hill, E.C.

Ripon. £4,200.

Bishop, Right Rev. Wm. Boyd Carpenter, D.D. 1884
(The Palace, Ripon.)
Bp. Suffragan of Richmond, Rt. Rev. John James
Pulleine, D.D. (Stanhope Rectory, Darlington) '88
Dean, Very Rev. the Hon. W. H. Fremantle, D.D.
(1895)..£1,000
Canons Residentiary (each £500).

Wm. W. Gibbon, M.A. 1879 | Archd. Waugh, M.A. 1891
M. MacColl, M.A. .... 1884 | Archd. Danks, M.A. 1896
Organist, E. J. Crow, MUS. DOC., £200.
Archdeacons.

Ven. William Danks, M.A., *Richmond* (1894)...£200
Ven. Arthur T. Waugh, M.A., *Ripon* (1894) ... nil
Ven. Francis Chas. Kilner. M.A., *Craven* (1896) £200
Beneficed Clergy, 347; *Curates*, 192.
Chancellor, Thomas H. Tristram, Q.C., D.C.L. £250
Regist. and Country Sec., F. Dickson Wise, Ripon.
London Secretary, H. W. Lee, The Sanctuary, S.W.

*Rochester. £3,800.

Bishop, Rt. Rev. Edward Stuart Talbot, D.D. 1895
(Bishop's House, Kennington Park, S.E.)
[Signs Edw. Roffen.]

Bishop Suffragan of Southwark, Rt. Rev. Huyshe
Wolcott Yeatman-Biggs, D.D. 1891
(Dartmouth House, Blackheath, S.E.)
Dean, Very Rev. S. R. Hole, D.D. (1887) ...£1,500
Canons Residentiary (each £600).

Geo. E. Jelf, M.A....1880 | Professor Cheyne, D.D.'86
Arch. Cheetham, D.D.'83 | Herbt. C. Pollock, M.A.'92
Organist, J. Hopkins.
Archdeacons.

Ven. Samuel Cheetham, D.D., *Rochester* 1882
Ven. John Richardson, D.D., *Southwark* (£200) 1882
Ven. Charles Burney, M.A., *Kingston* (£200)...1879
Beneficed Clergy, 342 ; *Curates, &c.*, 386.
Chancellor, Lewis Tonna Dibdin, D.C.L.
Registrar, A. A. Arnold, Rochester.
Secs., Day & Son, 28 Gt. George St., S.W.

St. Saviour's, Southwark.

Dean, Rt. Rev. the Lord Bishop of Rochester.
Sub-Dean, Rt. Rev. the Lord Bishop of Southwark.
Canons Residentiary.

W. Thompson, D.D. | R. Rhodes Bristow, M.A.
S. M. Taylor, M.A. | Allen Edwards, M.A.
Organist, A. M. Richardson, MUS. DOC.
Succentor and Sacristan, Rev. E. C. B. Philpot, B.A.
Chapter Clerk, Henry Langton.
Treasurer, Sir Fredk. Wigan, Bart.

St. Albans. £3,200.

Bishop, Rt. Rev. John Wogan Festing, D.D....1890
(21 Endsleigh Street, Tavistock Square, W.C.)
[Signs J. W. Alban.]
Bishop Suffragan of Colchester, Rt. Rev. Henry
Frank Johnson, D.D. (Rectory, Chelmsford) 1894
Organist, C. Gaffe, F.C.O.
Archdeacons.

Ven. W.J. Lawrance, M.A., *St. Albans* (1883) £200
Bishop of Colchester, D.D., *Colchester* (1894) £600
Ven. Thos. Stevens, M.A., *Essex* (1894) £450.
Beneficed Clergy, 627; *Curates*, 225.
Chancellor, Alfred Bray Kempe, M.A., F.R.S. (1891).
Registrar, Arthur Day, 28 Gt. George St., S.W.
Secretaries, Day & Son 28, Great George St., S.W.

St. Asaph. £4,200.

Bishop, Rt. Rev. Alfred Geo. Edwards, D.D....1889
(Palace, St. Asaph.) [Signs A. G. Asaph.]
Dean, Very Rev. Shadrach Pryce, M.A. (1899) £700
Canons Residentiary (each £350).

Arch. Thomas, M.A. 1886 | Archd. Evans, M.A. 1897
W.H. Fletcher, M.A. 1897 | Archd. Jones, M.A. 1897
Organist, A W. Wilson, MUS. DOC.
Archdeacons.

Ven. David Evans, M.A., *St. Asaph* 1897
Ven. David Rd. Thomas, M.A., *Montgomery* ...1886
Ven. LL. Wynne Jones. M.A., *Wrexham*........1897
Beneficed Clergy, 205 ; *Curates, &c.*, 106.
Chancellor, Wm. Trevor Parkins, M.A.
Registrar, Henry Asaph Cleaver, St. Asaph.
Secretary, John Pryse Lewis, Solicitor, Denbigh.

St. Davids. £4,500.

Bishop, Rt. Rev. John Owen, D.D. 1897
(Abergwili Palace, Carmarthen.)
Bishop Suffragan of Swansea, Rt. Rev. John Lloyd,
D.D. (St. Peter's, Carmarthen) 1890
Dean, Very Rev. David Howell, B.D. (1897) . £700
Canons Residentiary (each £350).

Bishop Lloyd, D.D. 1890 | Jas. A Smith, M.A. 1897
W. Williams, B A. 1893 | R. C. Williams...... 1899
Organist, Herbert C. Morris, F.C.O.
Archdeacons.

Ven. Geo. C. Hilbers, M.A., *St. David's* (1888) £279
Ven. J. H. Protheroe, M.A., *Cardigan* (1893) £200

Ven. Wm. Latham Bevan, M.A., *Brecon* (1895) £400
Ven. David Lewis, M.A., *Carmarthen* (1899)...£200
   Beneficed Clergy, 360 ; *Curates, &c.*, 130.
Chancellor, Joseph Earle Ollivant, M.A. (1891).
Registrar and Sec., J. Hoyes Barker, Carmarthen

Salisbury. £5,000.

Bishop, Right Rev. John Wordsworth. D.D....1885
   (The Palace, Salisbury.) [Signs John Sarum.]
Dean, Very Rev. Geo. David Boyle, M.A. (1880) £703
   Canons Residentiary (each £351).
Archd. Lear, M.A. 1862 | A. Buchanan, M.A. 1895
Ed. R. Bernard, M.A.1889 | E. S. Bankes, M.A. 1898
   Organist, Charles F. South.
   Archdeacons (each £200).
Ven. Thos. Boughton Buchanan, M.A., *Wilts*..1874
Ven. Francis Lear, M.A., *Sarum*......................1875
Ven. Francis Briggs Sowter, M.A., *Dorset* 1889
   Beneficed Clergy, 490 ; *Curates, &c.*, 227.
Chancellor, Rt.Hon. Sir J.Parker Deane, Q.C., D.C.L.
Registrar and Secretary to the Bishop, Clifford
   Wyndham Holgate, M.A., Palace, Salisbury.

Sodor and Man. Net £1,500.

Bishop, Rt. Rev. Norman D. J. Straton, D.D. 1892
   (Bishop's Court. Isle of Man.)
Domestic Chaplain, Rev. W. I. Moran, M.A.
Archdeacon, Ven. Hugh Stowell Gill (1895)...£550
   Beneficed Clergy, 28 ; *Curates, &c.*, 34.
*Chancellor and Vicar-General and Registrar and
   Sec.*, Samuel Harris, Douglas.
London Secretary, Sir John Hassard, K.C.B., 3 Creed
   Lane, Ludgate Hill, E.C.

Southwell. £3,500.

Bishop, Right Rev. George Ridding, D.D. 1884
   (Thurgarton Priory, Southwell, Notts.)
Bishop Suffragan of Derby, Rt. Rev. Edward Ash
   Were, D.D. (St.Werburgh's Vicarage, Derby)1889
   Archdeacons (each £200).
Ven. Thomas Henry Freer, M.A., *Derby* 1891
Ven. John Gray Richardson, M.A., *Notts* 1894
   Beneficed Clergy, 493 ; *Curates, &c.*, 200.
Domestic Chaplain and Sec., Rev. A. N. Bax.
Chancellor, Alfred Bray Kempe, M.A., F.R.S.
Registrar, John Borough, Derby.
Deputy Registrar, D'Oyley B. Ransom, Nottingham.
Secretaries, John Borough: D'Oyley Scott Ransom.
London Secretary, Sir John Hassard, K.C.B., 3 Creed
   Lane, Ludgate Hill, E.C.

Truro. £3,000.

Bishop and Dean, Rt. Rev. John Gott, D.D. 1891
(Trenython, Par Station.) [Signs John: Truron:]
   Canons Residentiary.
A. B. Donaldson, M.A.'85 (Under 50 & 51 Vict.)
A.J.Worlledge, M.A.1887 | B. G. Hoskyns, M.A. 1895
 (Each of above £400.) | F. E. Gardiner, M.A. 1897
   Archdeacons (each £200).
Ven. John Rundle Cornish, M.A., *Cornwall* (1888).
Ven. Henry H. Du Boulay, M.A., *Bodmin* (1892).
   Organist, M. J. Monk, MUS.D.
Beneficed Clergy, 231 : *Curates*, 91 ; *other Clergy*, 38.
Chancellor, Robert Macleane Paul, M.A. (1888) Truro.
Registrar and Sec., Arthur Burch, Principal
   Registry, Palace Gate, Exeter.
London Secretary, Sir John Hassard, K.C.B., 3 Creed
   Lane, Ludgate Hill, E.C.

Wakefield. £3,000.

Bishop, Rt. Rev. George Rodney Eden, D.D. (cons.
   1890) (Bishopgarth, Wakefield) 1897
   Archdeacons.
Ven. Joshua I. Brooke, M.A., *Halifax* (1888) £200
Ven. William Donne, M.A., *Huddersfield* (1892) £200
   Organist, J. N. Hardy, F.C.O.
   Beneficed Clergy, 170 ; *Curates, &c.*, 136.
Chancellor, T. H. Tristram, Q.C., D.C.L.
Registrar and Sec., W.F.L. Horne, B.A., Wakefield.

Worcester. £5,000.

Bishop, Right Rev. John James Stewart Perowne,
   D.D. (Hartlebury Castle, Kidderminster) ...1890
Bishop Suffragan of Coventry, Rt. Rev. Edmund Ar-
   buthnott Knox (St. Philip's, Birmingham) 1894
Dean, Very Rev. R. W. Forrest. D.D. (1891) £1,450
   Canons (each £800).
David Melville, D.D.1881 | T.L.Claughton, M.A. 1886
W. Knox-Little, 1881 | T.Teignmouth Shore1891
   Organist, Ivor Atkins. MUS.B.
   Archdeacons (each £200).
Ven. William Bree, D.D., *Coventry* 1887
Ven. William Walters, M.A., *Worcester* 1889
Rt. Rev. Edmund A. Knox, D.D., *Birmingham*...1894
Beneficed Clergy, 493 ; *Curates*, 253 ; *non-parochial
   Clergy*, 180.
Chancellor, John Stratford Dugdale, M.A., Q.C.
*Bishop's Sec., Registrar of Diocese, and Archdeacon-
   ries of Worcester, Birmingham, and Coventry*,
   John Harvey Hooper, M.A., Worcester.
London Sec., Sir John Hassard, K.C.B., 3 Creed
   Lane, Ludgate Hill, E.C.

BISHOPS WHO HAVE RESIGNED.

Name.	Diocese.	Cons.	Res.
Chas. Jno. Abraham...	*Wellington* ...	1858	1870
[1] Hon. A. J. R. Anson...	*Qu'Appelle* ...	1884	1892
[2] Alfred Barry	*Sydney,N.S.W.*	1884	1889
Edwd. H. Beckles	*Sierra Leone.*	1860	1870
Chas. Hy. Bromby	*Tasmania* ..	1864	1882
Jno. Shaw Burdon ...	*Victoria,China*	1873	1895
Henry Cheetham ...	*Sierra Leone.*	1870	1882
Robt. Kestell-Cornish	*Madagascar*	1874	1895
Reginald Courtenay...	*Kingston, W.I.*	1856	1879
Frederick Gell	*Madras*	1861	1898
Octavius Hadfield ...	*Wellington,N.Z.*	1870	1893
Isaac Hellmuth	*Huron*	1871	1883
Edmund Hobhouse ...	*Nelson, N. Z.*	1858	1865
Wilfrid Bird Hornby .	*Nyasaland* ...	1892	1894
Ernest G. Ingham	*Sierra Leone..*	1883	1896
Edward R. Johnson ...	*Calcutta*	1876	1898
[3] Wm Kenne'h Macrorie	*Maritzburg* ...	1868	1892
[4] Samuel E. Marsden ...	*Bathurst*	1869	1885
[5] John Mitchinson	*Barbados*......	1873	1881
Louis George Mylne	*Bombay*	1876	1897
[6]-F A R. Cramer-Roberts	*Nassau*.........	1878	1886
[7] Peter S. Royston	*Mauritius* ...	1872	1890
[8] Daniel F. Sandford ...	*Tasmania* ...	1883	1889
EdmundCraig Stuart...	*Waiapu*	1877	1893
[9] William Walsh	*Mauritius* ...	1891	1897
Wm.Pakenham Walsh	*Ossory*	1878	1897
Allen Beecher Webb...	*Grahamstown*	1883	1898

1 Now Canon Res. of Lichfield ; 2 Canon Res. of Windsor ; 3 Canon Res. of Ely ; 4 Asst. Bp. of Gloucester ;
5 Master of Pemb. Coll. Oxford and Canon Res. of Gloucester ; 6 Asst. Bp. of Manchester ; 7 Asst. Bp. of Liverpool ;
8 Asst. Bp. of Durham ; 9 Bp. of Dover and Archdeacon and Canon Res. of Canterbury.

MEMBERS OF CONVOCATION.

In theory the Church of England is governed by means of its Convocations of Bishops and Clergy: there is a House of Convocation for each province, Canterbury and York. Each Convocation consists of two Houses, the upper confined to the archbishops and bishops, the lower composed of the dean of every cathedral, the archdeacons, with proctors elected from every cathedral chapter, and two more elected by the clergy of every diocese in the province of Canterbury, and by every archdeaconry in the province of York. A fresh election is made with every new Parliament.

PROVINCE OF CANTERBURY.
Upper House.

President.—The Most Rev. the Lord Archbishop. The Right Rev. the Lords Bishops of London; Winchester; Bangor; Bath and Wells; Chester; Ely; Exeter; Gloucester; Bristol; Hereford; Lichfield; Lincoln; Llandaff; Norwich; Oxford; Peterborough; Rochester; Salisbury; Southwell; St. Albans; St. Asaph; St. Davids; Truro; Worcester.

Lower House.

Prolocutor, The Rt. Rev. Bishop Sumner, D.D.
The Very Rev. the Deans.
The Venerable the Archdeacons.

Also the following Proctors:
Bangor.—*Chapter,* Canon Thomas.
  Clergy, T. Edwards; E. Hughes.
Bath & Wells.—*Chapter,* Canon Buckle.
  Clergy, W. Michell; F. Augustus Brymer.
Bristol.—*Chapter,* Canon Tetley.
  Clergy, H. Procter; Hon. M. J. G. Ponsonby.
Canterbury.—*Chapter,* Canon F. J. Holland.
  Clergy, F. H. Murray; H. Bartram.
Chichester.—*Chapter,* Canon Sanderson, D.D.
  Clergy, A. H. S. Barwell; J. J. Hannah.
Ely.—*Chapter,* Canon E. C. Lowe, D.D.
  Clergy, J. H. Macaulay; W. Cunningham.
Exeter.—*Chapter,* Canon Edmonds.
  Clergy, H. Tudor; R. Martin.
Gloucester.—*Chapter,* Canon St. John.
  Clergy, F. V. Mather; S. J. Jones.
Hereford.—*Chapter,* W. Poole.
  Clergy, E. F. Clayton; C. S. Palmer.
Lichfield.—*Chapter,* Rt. Rev. Sir L. T. Stamer, Bt.
  Clergy, C. N. Bolton; E. Philips.
Lincoln.—*Chapter,* Canon J. H. Overton.
  Clergy, G. W. Jeudwine; A. S. Wilde.
Llandaff.—*Chapter,* Prebendary C. J. Thompson.
  Clergy, John T. Harding; S. F. H. Nicholl.
London.—*Chapter,* Rt. Rev. C. H. Turner; Canon Duckworth (*Westminster*). *Clergy,* Preb. A. J. Ingram; H. W. Villiers.
Norwich.—*Chapter,* Canon C. K. Robinson.
  Clergy, Constantine Frere; W. M. Hoare.
Oxford.—*Chapter,* Canon William Bright.
  Clergy, Edmund Savory; H. Barter.
Peterborough.—*Chapter,* Canon L. Clayton.
  Clergy, W. Yates; H. L. Watson.
Rochester.—*Chapter,* Canon Jelf.
  Clergy, Canons Clarke and Bristow.
St. Albans.—*Chapter* (none).
  Clergy, J. W. Irvine; J. M. Procter.
St. Asaph.—*Chapter,* Canon W. H. Fletcher.
  Clergy, David Evans; W. Ll. Nicholas.
St. David's.—*Chapter,* The Bishop of Swansea.
  Clergy, T. R. Walters; D. Jones.
Salisbury.—*Chapter,* Canon T. L. Kingsbury.
  Clergy, R. S. Hutchings; Canon E. S. Bankes.
Southwell.—*Chapter* (none).
  Clergy, Charles Gray; C. J. Hamilton.

Truro.—*Chapter,* A. J. Worlledge.
  Clergy, A. C. Thynne; J. S Tyacke.
Winchester.—*Chapter,* Canon W. P. Warburton.
  Clergy, Vernon Musgrave; W. Durst.
Windsor—*Chapter,* Rt. Rev. Bishop Barry.
Worcester—*Chapter,* Canon Knox Little.
  Clergy, E. A. Waller; C. A. Dickins.
  Vicar-Gen., The Rt. Hon. Sir Jas. Parker Deane,
  Registrar, Sir John Hassard, K.C.B. [D.C.L., Q.C.
  Actuary, Francis Cobb.
  Apparitor-General, Sir John A. Hanham, Bart.
  Clerk, Arthur Ryder.

PROVINCE OF YORK.
Upper House.

President.—The Most Rev. the Lord Archbishop. The Right Rev. the Lords Bishops of Durham; Ripon: Chester; Carlisle; Manchester; Liverpool; Newcastle; Wakefield; Sodor and Man.

Lower House.

Prolocutor, T. E. Espin, D.D.
The Very Reverend the Deans of the Province.
The Venerable the Archdeacons.

And the following Proctors:
York.—*Chapter,* Canon C. S. Wright; Bishop Blunt. *Clergy,* Canon Faber; Canon Argles. *Clergy of Cleveland,* Rev. C. N. Gray; Canon H. Temple. *Of E. Riding,* Canon Watson; Canon Stanbridge. *Of Sheffield,* J. Gilmore; H. J. Sale.
Carlisle. — *Chapter,* Bishop Ware. *Clergy,* Canon Bower; E. A. Askew. *Clergy of Westmorland,* Canon Stock; Canon Sherwin. *Clergy of Furness,* Canon Ayre; Canon Bell.
Chester.—*Chapter,* Canon Feilden. *Clergy,* Canon A. M. Wood; W. E. Torr. *Clergy of Macclesfield,* Canon Gore; S. A. Boyd.
Durham.—*Chapter,* Canon Tristram. *Clergy,* Canon J. Baily; Canon H. E. Savage. *Clergy of Auckland,* Chancellor T. E. Espin; Canon D. R. Falconer.
Liverpool. — *Chapter* (none). *Clergy,* Canons Jones and Blundell. *Clergy of Warrington,* Canons O. H. L. Penrhyn and G. H. Spooner.
Manchester.—*Chapter,* Canon Crane. *Clergy,* C. H. Lomax; Canon E. J. Russell. *Lancaster,* Canon Hawkins; S. Hastings. *Blackburn,* Bishop Cramer-Roberts; Canon Rogers.
Newcastle.—*Chap.* (none). *Clergy of Northumberland,* Canons J. M. Lister; *Clergy of Lindisfarne,* Canons J. Waite and H. F. Long.
Ripon.—*Chapter,* Canon Wynter-Gibbon. *Clergy of Richmond,* R. P. Daniell-Bainbridge; V. J. Ryan. *Of Craven,* Canon Eddowes; A. J. G. Nash. *Of Ripon,* Canons Owen and Wood.
Sodor and Man.—*Chapter,* Canon F. J. Moore. *Clergy,* Canon B. P. Clarke.
Wakefield.—*Chapter* (none). *Clergy of Halifax,* Canons Ivens and Grenside. *Clergy of Huddersfield,* Canons J. W. Bardsley and W. F. Norris.
Archbishop's Commissioners.—Bishop of Beverley; the Dean and Canons Residentiary of York.
Synodal Secretary.—Rev. Canon Wright, Rectory, Stokesley, Yorkshire.
Registrar.—Hen. A. Hudson, Minster Yard, York.

THE HOUSES OF LAYMEN.

The House of Laymen for the Province of Canterbury, as also for that of York, consists of members elected by the various Diocesan Conferences, who are themselves elected by the Laity of their respective Parishes or Rural Deaneries. The members are elected with every fresh Parliament.

BISHOPS SUFFRAGAN OF THE CHURCH OF ENGLAND.

Title.	Diocese.	Name.	Title.	Diocese.	Name.
Barrow-in-F.	(Carlisle)	Rt. Rev. Henry Ware.	Leicester......	(Peterb.)	Rt. Rev. F. H. Thicknesse.
Beverley......	(York)	„ Robt. J. Crosthwaite.	Marlborough	(London)	„ Alfred Earle.
Colchester ...	(St. Alb.)	„ Henry F. Johnson.	Reading	(Oxford)	„ Jas. Leslie Randall.
Coventry	(Worc.)	„ Edmund A. Knox.	Richmond ...	(Ripon)	„ Jno. Jas. Pulleine.
Crediton......	(Exeter)	„ Robt. Edwd. Trefusis.	Shrewsbury ...	(Lichfd.)	„ Sir Lovelace Stainer, Bt.
Derby.........	(Southw.)	„ Ash Were	Southampton	(Winch.)	„ Hon. Alfred Lyttelton
Hull	(York)	„ Richd. F. L. Blunt.	Stepney	(London)	„ A. F. W.--Ingram.
Ipswich	(Norw'h)	„ Geo. Carnac Fisher,	Swansea......	(St. Dav.)	„ John Lloyd.
Islington ...	(London)	„ Charles Hen. Turner.	Thetford ...	(Norwh.)	„ Arthur Thos. Lloyd.

COLONIAL AND MISSIONARY BISHOPS OF THE CHURCH OF ENGLAND.

PROVINCE OF CANADA.

Sees.	Colonial Bishops.	Apptd.	Clgy.
Algoma ...	George Thorneloe, D.C.L.	1897	27
Fredericton	H. Tully Kingdon, D.D.	1892	82
Huron	Maurice S. Baldwin, D.D.	1883	140
Montreal ...	Wm. B. Bond, D.D.	1879	103
Niagara ...	John P. DuMoulin, D.D.	1896	70
Nova Scotia	Fredk. Courtney, S.T.D.	1888	122
Ontario......	Jno. T. Lewis, D.D., LL.D. Archbishop and Metrop.	1862	126
Ottawa	C. Hamilton, D.D. (cons.'85)	1896	
Quebec	Andrew H. Dunn, D.D.....	1892	65
Toronto ...	Arthur Sweatman, D.D.	1879	188

PROVINCE OF RUPERTSLAND.

Athabasca	Richard Young, D.D....	1884	8
Mackenzie River	Wm. Day Reeve, D.D.	1891	6
Moosonee ...	J. A. Newnham, D.D. ...	1893	11
Qu'Appelle	John Grisdale, D.D.	1897	21
Rupertsland	Robert Machray, D.D., Archbp. of Rupertsland and Primate of All Canada	1865	83
Saskatchewan and Calgary	W. Cyprian Pinkham, D.D.	1887	43
Selkirk ...	W. C. Bompas, D.D. (Cons.'74)	1891	2
British Columbia,	W. W. Perrin, D.D.	1893	22
New Westminster	...John Dart, D.C.L.	1895	24

PROVINCE OF INDIA AND CEYLON.

Bombay ...	James Macarthur, D.D. ...	1898	73
Calcutta ...	J. E. C. Welldon, D.D. Met.	1898	124
Chota Nagpur	Jabez C. Whitley, D.D.	1890	30
Colombo ...	Regd. S. Copleston, D.D.	1875	81
Lahore......	George A. Lefroy. D.D. ...	1899	100
Lucknow ...	Alfred Clifford, D.D.......	1893	77
Madras ...	Henry Whitehead, D.D. ...	1899	26½
Rangoon ...	J. M. Strachan, D.D.......	1882	39
Tinnevelly	Samuel Morley, D.D.	1896	
Travancore & Cochin	Edward Noel Hodges, D.D.	1890	39

PROVINCE OF NEW ZEALAND.

Auckland...	Wm. G. Cowie, D.D. (Prim.)	1869	77
Christchurch	Churchill Julius, D.D. ...	1890	61
Dunedin...	Saml. Tarratt Nevill, D.D.	1871	25
Melanesia	Cecil Wilson, M.A.	1894	12
Nelson......	Chas. Oliver Mules, D.D.	1892	21
Waiapu ...	Wm. Leonard Williams...	1895	44
Wellington	Frederick Wallis, D.D. ...	1895	34

AUSTRALIA.
Province of New South Wales.

Bathurst ...	Chas. E. Camidge, D.D. ...	1887	41
Goulburn...	William Chalmers, D.D....	1892	40
Grafton & Armidale	Arthur Vincent Green, LL.D.	1894	34
Newcastle...	G. H. Stanton, D.D. (cons.'78)	1891	41
Riverina ...	Ernest A. Anderson, D.D.	1895	17
Sydney ...	W. Saumarez Smith, B.D., Abp.; Primate of Australia, & Metrop. N.S.W.	1890	158
Adelaide ...	John Reg. Harmer, D.D.	1895	79
Ballarat...	Samuel Thornton, D.D.	1875	60
	H. E. Cooper (Coadj.)...	1895	

AUSTRALIA --continued.

Sees.	Colonial Bishops.	Apptd.	Clgy.
Brisbane...	Wm. T. T. Webber, D.D.	1885	50
	J. F. Stretch, LL.D. (Coadj.)	1895	
Melbourne...	Field Flowers Goe, D.D.	1887	179
New Guinea	M. J. Stone-Wigg	1898	
N. Queensland,	Chris. Geo. Barlow, D.D.	1891	25
Perth	Chas. Owen L. Riley, D.D.	1894	33
Rockhampton	N. Dawes, D.D. (cons. '89)	1892	
Tasmania...	H. H. Montgomery, D.D.	1889	63

PROVINCE OF SOUTH AFRICA.

Bloemfontein,	John Wale Hicks, D.D.	1892	43
Capetown...	W. W. Jones, D.D., Abp.	1874	78
	A. G. S. Gibson (Coadj.)	1894	
Grahamstown	Chas. E. Cornish. D.D. ..	1899	85
Lebombo...	Wm. Edm. Smyth, M.A.	1893	
Mashonaland	William Thos. Gaul....	1895	9
Natal	A. H. Baynes, D.D.	1893	40
Pretoria......	Henry B. Bousfield, D.D.	1878	30
St. Helena .	J. Garraway Holmes, D.D.	1899	4
St. John's...	Bransby L. Key, D.D. ...	1886	33
Zululand ...	Wm. M. Carter, D.D. ...	1891	22

PROVINCE OF THE WEST INDIES.

Antigua ...	Herbert Mather, D.D.......	1897	32
Barbados, &c.,	, D.D....	1899	71
Guiana	Wm. Proctor Swaby, D.D.	1893	42
Honduras...	George A. Ormsby, D.D.	1893	18
Jamaica ...	E. Nuttall, D.D. Abp. Prim.	1880	107
Assistant,	Chas. Fredk. Douet, D.D.	1888	
Nassau......	Edward T. Churton, D.D.	1886	21
Trinidad ...	Jas. Thos. Hayes, D.D. ...	1889	27

DIOCESES UNDER THE ARCHBISHOP OF CANTERBURY.

Caledonia......	William Ridley, D.D.	1879	13
*China, Mid-	Geo. Evans Moule, D.D.	1880	27
*China, North...	C. Perry Scott, D.D. ...	1880	11
*China, West	W. Wharton Cassells, D.D.	1895	5
*Corea	Charles J. Corfe, D.D....	1889	7
*Equatorial Africa (Western Niger, &c.)	Herbert Tugwell, D.D.	1894	13
„ „ Asst.-Bps.	C. Philipps	1893	
	I. Oluwole	1893	
Falklands......	Waite H. Stirling, D.D.	1869	17
Gibraltar......	C. W. Sandford, D.D....	1874	90
Hokkaido (Japan),	P. K. Fyson, D.D.	1896	9
*Honolulu ...	Alfred Willis, D.D.......	1872	7
*Jerusalem...	Geo. F. P. Blyth, D.D.	1887	54
Kiushiu (S. Japan),	Hy. Evington, D.D.	1894	
*Likoma	John E. Hine, D.D., M.D.	1896	
*Madagascar	Geo. Lanchester King...	1899	27
Mauritius......	Walter R. Pym, D.D....	1898	23
Mombasa ...	Wm. George Peel, D.D.	1899	
Newfoundland and Bermuda,	Llewellyn Jones, D.D.	1878	54
Osaka (Japan),	Hugh Jas. Foss, D.D.	1899	16
Sierra Leone...	John Taylor Smith, D.D.	1897	60
Singapore, &c.,	Geo. Fredk. Hose, D.D.	1881	24
*South Tokyo	William Awdry, D.D.	1898	28
Uganda......	A. R. Tucker, D.D.......	1890	19
Victoria, Hong Kong,	Joseph C. Hoare	1898	30
*Zanzibar......	W. M. Richardson, D.D.	1895	25

* Missionary Bishops.

THE CHURCH OF IRELAND (DISESTABLISHED).

Sees.	ARCHBISHOPS.	Apptd.	Ch. Pop. (1891.)	Benefices.	Curates.	Income of See.
Armagh...	Most Rev. W. Alexander, D.D. (*cons.*1867)	1896	... 62,593	... 92	... 18	... £3,115
Dublin ...	Most Rev. J. F. Peacocke, D.D. (*cons.*1894)	1897	... 99,372	... 155	... 82	... 2,500
	BISHOPS.					
Meath......	Most Rev. James Bennett Keene, D.D. ...	1897	... 11,892	... 73	... 10	... 1,500
Clogher ...	Right Rev. Charles Maurice Stack, D.D..	1886	... 43,410	... 73	... 16	... 1,273
Tuam ...	Right Rev. James O'Sullivan, D.D.........	1890	... 11,563	... 62	... 11	... 1,493
Down......	Right Rev. Thomas James Welland, D.D.	1892	... 186,958	... 167	... 63	... 1,800
Cork	Right Rev. William Edward Meade, D.D.	1894	... 35,889	... 105	... 32	... 1,703
Derry......	Right Rev. George Alex. Chadwick, D.D.	1896	... 55,424	... 110	... 26	... 1,600
Killaloe ..	Right Rev. Mervyn Archdall, D...........	1897	... 10,619	... 61	... 10	... 1,500
Kilmore..	Right Rev. Alfred George Elliott, D.D ..	1897	... 36,297	... 106	... 23	... 1,506
Ossory ...	Right Rev. John Baptist Crozier, D.D. ...	1897	... 25,157	... 110	... 32	... 1,535
Limerick :	Right Rev. Thomas Bunbury, D.D..........	1899	... 11,271	... 56	... 12	... 1,358
Cashel ..	Right Rev. (vacant)	1899	... 10,258	... 62	... 17	... 1,396

ST. PATRICK'S NATIONAL CATHEDRAL, DUBLIN.—*Dean and Ordinary*, Very Rev. Henry Jellett, D.D.

GENERAL SYNOD.

Consisting of House of Bishops (13) and House of Representatives (viz., 208 clerical and 416 lay).

Honorary Secretaries, Ven. J. George Scott, D.D.; Ven. Wm. Colquhoun, M.A.; Sir J. C. Meredith, LL.D.; Gordon E. Tombe, J.P.

Sec. to the REPRESENTATIVE CHURCH BODY (INCOR. 1870), T. Greene, M.A., 52 St. Stephen's Grn. E., Dublin.

THE CHURCH OF IRELAND, founded by St. Patrick in the fifth century, existed as a separate Church for nearly 1,200 years. From 1152 to 1560 she was in alliance with the Church of Rome. This ceased when, only two Bishops dissenting, she accepted the Reformation. By the Act of Union, 1800, she was united with the Church of England. By the Act of 1869 this union was severed, and on Jan. 1, 1871, the Church of Ireland resumed her ancient position. The Act of 1869 not only disestablished the Irish Church, but also took away her property, nothing being left but the right to the life services of the Annuitant Bishops and Clergy, the right to claim churches in use for divine service, the right to buy the See and Glebe Houses (with garden and curtilage) built by the clergy at their own cost, and £500,000 in lieu of private endowments.

The supreme governing body of the Church of Ireland is the GENERAL SYNOD, which meets annually.

Subject to the General Synod are 23 *Diocesan Synods*, which are assisted by smaller elected bodies called Diocesan Councils.

The Bishop of the Diocese is chosen by the clerical and lay members of the *Diocesan Synod*. The Primate is chosen by the bench of Bishops from amongst their own number.

The incumbent of the Parish is appointed by a *Board of Nomination*, consisting of 7 persons, viz.:—The Bishop, 3 diocesan nominators (2 clerical and 1 lay) appointed by the Diocesan Synod, and three parochial nominators (lay) appointed by the registered vestrymen of the parish.

The financial trustees of the Church are the REPRESENTATIVE BODY, composed of the Archbishops and Bishops, 13 clergymen and 26 laymen, chosen by the Diocesan Representatives in the General Synod, with 13 co-opted members (clerical or lay). This body holds the property of the Church, and administers its funds, subject to the General Synod.

The first property it held was the capital sum £7,581,075, representing the life annuities of the Bishops and Clergy paid over as commutation money by the Church Commissioners, and also £500,000 compensation for private endowments. The commutation capital now amounts only to £1,308,608, charged with annuities to 253 annuitants, £45 667. The funds, however, in the custody of the Representative Body amount in all to £7,973,976, made up of *Commutation* £1,308,603, *Parochial Sustentation* £4,563,570, *Episcopal Sustentation* £565,404, *Glebes purchase* £337,268, *Miscellaneous purposes* £1,199,131.

Since 1869, members of the Church have paid in to the Representative Body a total sum of £5,185,876. The interest of the Parochial Sustentation Fund is £183,640. The total amount of assessment for stipend paid by parishes, 1898, was £133,613, and the total amount paid for stipends under Diocesan Schemes was £250,242.

The number of members of the Church of Ireland by the Census of 1891 was 602,300.

THE EPISCOPAL CHURCH IN SCOTLAND.

Sees.	THE RT. REV. BISHOPS.	Cons.	Cley.	Stipd.	Sees.	THE RT. REV. BISHOPS.	Cons.	Cley.	Stipd.
Aberdeen ..	Hn. A. G. Douglas, D.D.1883	...47...	£722		*Edinburgh..*	John Dowden, D.D.....1886	84...	£914	
Argyll	James Robt. A. Chinnery-Haldane, D.D.1883..	19 ..	633		*Glasgow ..*	Wm. T. Harrison, D.D.1888..	80 ..	706	
Brechin.....	Most Rev. Hugh W.				*Moray ....*	James B. Kelly, D.D....1867 ..23...	859		
	Jermyn, D.D., *Primus* (1886)1871 ..35		835		*St. Andrews*	G. H. Wilkinson, D.D. 1883 ...47...	786		

Registrar to Primus, W. Roberton, S.S.C., 14 Young St., Edinburgh.

Churches, Mission Stations, &c., 354. Parsonages, 151. Clergy, 335. Communicants, 45,384.

The ESTABLISHED CHURCH OF SCOTLAND is Presbyterian in constitution, and is governed by Kirk Sessions, Presbyteries, Synods, and the General Assembly, which consists of both clerical and lay representatives from each of the Presbyteries, and also from the universities and royal burghs. It is presided over by a Moderator (chosen annually by the Assembly), and the Sovereign is represented by a Lord High Commissioner (appointed each year by the Crown), who receives the sum of £2,000 for his services. The country, for Church purposes, is divided into 16 synods and 84 presbyteries, and there are about 1,800 ministers and licentiates engaged in ministerial work. The Church population exceeds that of all the other Presbyterian bodies united, and is estimated at about half the whole population of Scotland; the number of communicants in 1897 was 641,803. The sum of £485,695 was raised in 1897 for home and missionary purposes. Within the last 50 years 405 chapels, at a cost of £1,477,833, have been endowed and erected into parishes *quoad sacra*. The original parishes were 924, in addition to which there were in 1898, 405 new and 42 Parliamentary parishes, also 203 unendowed churches and 184 mission stations; a total of 1,758 The Presbyterian form of Church government as first set up in Scotland was superseded in 1662 by the Episcopal Church under the Stuarts; but at the Revolution in 1688, Presbyterianism regained the legal establishment, which it still preserves. In consequence of the action of the civil courts in certain cases of disputed settlements, confirmed by a decision of the House of Lords in 1842, about 289 parish ministers resigned their preferments and in 1843 founded the *Free Church*. LORD HIGH COMMISSIONER, The Earl of Leven and Melville. MODERATOR, 1899, Rt. Rev. J. Pagan, D D.

PRESBYTERIANISM HAS SEVERAL SUBDIVISIONS.

(1) *The Free Church of Scotland*, founded in 1843, is based on the great principle of the independence of the Church in its spiritual action, and holds as a consequence the right of each congregation to elect its own minister. The circumstances that led to the formation of this Church have been already mentioned. The sum of £367,000 was raised in the first year of the disruption, and by 1853 850 congregations had been formed. At the present day the Free Church is a fully organised body, consisting of a General Assembly, 16 synods, and 75 presbyteries. There

are 1,165 ministers, with 1,094 congregations meeting in well-appointed churches built for them, of which about 50 are preaching stations. The General Assembly meets every year at the same time as that of the Established Church. Having no endowments, the clergy are mainly supported by the Sustentation Fund, which along with congregational supplements gives on an average £245 to each minister, three-fourths of whom are also provided with manses. The sum of £713,742 was raised in 1898–99 for the various purposes of the Church, including Missions. MODERATOR for 1900 the Rev. Dr. Walter Ross Taylor, of Glasgow.

(2) *The United Presbyterian Church*, which has 29 presbyteries, 589 churches, 631 ministers, and 197,476 members in Scotland and Ireland, who raised £443,106 in 1898 for all purposes. It has 1,017 missionaries, evangelists, and teachers in the East and West Indies, in Africa, China, and Japan. MODERATOR, 1899–1900, the Rev. John Robson, D.D., Edinburgh.

(3) *The Presbyterian Church in Ireland.*—According to the Census of 1891, the members of the various Presbyterian churches in Ireland were 446,687. The largest of these, under the superintendence of the General Assembly, consists of 36 home presbyteries, 656 ministers, 569 congregations, with 106,424 communicants, 84,379 families, 9,216 Sabbath-school teachers, and 105,046 scholars. During the year 1898–99 this branch contributed by congregational effort £190,855 for religious, charitable, and missionary purposes. The total income for the year for all purposes was £261,135. It possesses two Colleges, with power to confer Theological Degrees, comprising a staff of 14 professors, and has 30 ordained with 5 medical missionaries in foreign parts. MODERATOR, 1899–1900, Rev. David A. Taylor, M.A., Belfast. *Clerk*, Rev. W. J. Lowe, M.A., Londonderry.

(4) *The Presbyterian Church of England* has 12 presbyteries, 311 congregations, 13 preaching stations, and 71,444 communicants. It has a Theological College (Westminster Coll., Cambridge), and supports 54 missionaries abroad, including 22 women In 1896 the amount raised for all purposes was £270,577. MODERATOR of Synod for 1899–1900, Rev. Charles Moinet, D.D., Bromley, Kent.

(5) The less numerous divisions are: the Reformed Presbyterian Synod, the Eastern Reformed Synod, the United Original Seceders, the Secession Presbytery in Ireland, and the Synod of the Church of Scotland in England.

Other Religious Denominations.

The INDEPENDENTS, or CONGREGATIONALISTS, in England come next to the Methodists; they are the most ancient community of Dissenters. They maintain that each church is its own ruler, and thus dispense with both episcopacy and presbytery. They first appeared in the time of Elizabeth, under whom they were very harshly treated; in consequence, great numbers repaired to North America; but their principles triumphed under the Commonwealth. In 1831 the majority of their churches were formed into the Congregational Union. There are 51 county and other Associations in England and Wales, with 4,569 churches and preaching stations containing 1,634,327 sittings; the number of ministers in the British Isles is 3,122. Of these 288 are temporarily without pastoral charge, 63 are engaged in collegiate and tutorial duties, 54 are occupied in secretarial work, and 321 by reason of age or ill-health have retired from pastoral duty. CHAIRMAN, 1900,

J. Carvell Williams, M.P. *Sec.*, Rev. W. J. Woods, B.A. (Memorial Hall, Farringdon St.).

The *Countess of Huntingdon's Connexion*, with 36 chapels. Its tenets are expressed in XV articles, founded on the XXXIX articles and Westminster Confession, but in some chapels the prayers of the Church of England are read.

The BAPTISTS are, in all respects but one, similar to the Independents; they have the same form of Church government, and differ but in one point of practice—viz., the Baptism by immersion of believers only. Like the Congregationalists, they are for the most part grouped in Associations of churches, and the majority of these belong to the Baptist Union, which was formed in 1813. In the British Isles these were, in 1898, 3,845 chapels and 1,951 pastors. The members numbered 355,218, and Sunday scholars 525,533. In addition to the members in this country, the Baptists have numerous chapels and several hundred ministers in the Colonies. In the United States they form one of the most numerous religious bodies there, the "members" alone numbering somewhere about 4,000,000. Their missionaries are employed in India, Ceylon, China, Palestine, the West Indies, Africa, Brittany, and Italy. *Secretary,* 1899-1900, Rev. J. H. Shakespeare, M.A.

The WELSH CALVINISTIC METHODIST CONNEXION is the only Church of purely Welsh origin, and embraces a very large section of the Welsh-speaking population. The form of Church government is presbyterian. At the present time the body numbers—churches, 1,339; chapels and places of worship. 1,523; ministers and preachers, 1,200; deacons. 5,506; communicants. 153,712; on probation, 2,547; Sunday-school teachers, 25,716; scholars and teachers, 246,365; number belonging to the congregations (including communicants), 316,053. A sum amounting to £246,365 was collected for various religious purposes in 1898. One of the features of the Welsh churches is the Sunday-school, which is attended by adults as well as children : the vernacular is the language generally used in these schools. There are 257 English congregations with 17,027 communicants ; all the rest are Welsh. MODERATOR of General Assembly, 1899-1900, Rev. Evan Phillips, Newcastle-on-Tyne ; *Sec.*. Rev. J. Evans, Denbigh.

The SALVATION ARMY is one of the most recent religious denominations, and one of the most successful. In Dec. 1898, the number of *Officers* was 13,894, of *Corps* and *Outposts* 6,822, *Local Officers* 36,224. The number of countries occupied was 45, and of languages used 28. Connected with the Salvation Army are numerous philanthropic institutions under various denominations including 92 Rescue Homes for Fallen Women, 116 Slum Posts, 12 Prison Gate Homes, 112 Shelters and Cheap Food Depôts for the Homeless, 54 Workshops and Factories, 34 Labour Bureaux, 11 Farms, &c. "GENERAL," William Booth.

MINOR RELIGIOUS DENOMINATIONS.—The chief are the Unitarians, with about 350 ministers, 343 chapels, and other places of worship. The Society of Friends, which consists of 17,031 members in Great Britain and 2,586 in Ireland, has 375 recorded ministers. including 156 women; their places of worship in 1898 numbered 409. *Central Office*, 12 Bishopsgate St. Without, E.C. The Moravians have about 50 congregations and preaching stations. The Catholic Apostolic Church have above 80 churches ; the New Jerusalem Church (Swedenborgians), 75 societies, with 6,063 registered members ; the Latter-Day Saints (Mormons) have 82 churches. Among the inhabitants of the United Kingdom are about 120,000 Jews, mainly in London and other large towns, who possess 80 synagogues, with about 100 ministers and readers (*Chief Rabbi*, Dr. Hermann Adler, Chief Rabbi's House, Finsbury Square, E.C.). The Jews support their own poor, and raise about £150,000 annually for religious and benevolent purposes. Their number throughout the world is computed at various totals, ranging between 8 and 9 millions. The Brethren, or Plymouth Brethren, have 23 places of worship in London and the suburbs. The Greeks have churches in London, Manchester, and Liverpool. The Armenians have churches in London and Manchester ; the French, Dutch, Swedes, and Swiss in London, Norwich, and Canterbury ; and a mosque has been opened for Moslems.

The Methodist Churches.

UNDER the general designation of METHODISTS are included all those religious bodies which owe their existence, directly or indirectly, to the efforts of the Revds. John and Charles Wesley. The most numerous and influential of them are—

Wesleyan Methodists, the original body founded in 1739 by these two brothers. While students at Oxford, in 1729, they gathered a number of young men together for purposes of study and devotion, who were nicknamed, first, "The Holy Club," and afterwards "The Methodists." In 1739 John Wesley founded the "Religious Societies," in which the first beginnings of Methodism are to be found. The number of members rapidly increased, until a more definite and extensive organisation than Wesley at first gave them was imperatively demanded. The first *Conference*, consisting of six clergymen and four laymen, was held in 1744. The Conference is now composed in its Representative Session of 240 ministers and 240 laymen with a ministerial president and secretary at its head, elected year by year ; by semi-annual meetings of the ministers in each district, over which a chairman is appointed by the Conference; and by quarterly meeting of the ministers and lay officers of each circuit. The authority of both these last meetings is subordinate to the Conference, which has the supreme legislative and judicial power in Methodism. When Wesley died the number of members was 76,968, and since then the increase has been so great that about 18,000,000 people are now receiving Methodist instruction in various parts of the world. At Washington in October, 1891, it was reported that there were more than 30,000,000 Methodists. This statement has been recently repeated by leading Wesleyans; but no evidence is forthcoming to establish its accuracy, which is more than doubtful. *Pres.* Rev. F. W. Macdonald ; *Sec.* Rev. M. Hartley. Various distinct bodies of Methodists have been formed, the most important being—

1. *The Methodist New Connexion,* which was formed in 1797 by the Rev. Alexander Kilham, one of the early itinerating Wesleyan preachers. He demanded that the members of the societies, and not the Conference, should be constituted the source of all power in Methodism ; and that the Conference should consist of lay as well as ministerial members, all of whom should be elected by the members of the various societies as their delegates. He was expelled by the Conference and at once founded a new community.—*President,* Rev. J. E. Radcliffe.

2. *The Primitive Methodists,* who sprang up in Staffordshire, in 1810. under the leadership of Hugh Bourne and William Clowes. Owing to the excesses attending certain outdoor services called "camp meetings" the Wesleyan Conference prohibited the continuance of the practice. Bourne and Clowes refused to comply with this decision, and were in consequence expelled. They and their sympathisers banded together in a new body, with enlarged powers for the laity. Next to the Wesleyans they are the most numerous of all the denominations which have arisen out of the Methodist movement.—*President,* Rev. W. Goodman.

3. *The Bible Christians,* founded in 1815 by William O'Bryan, a Wesleyan lay preacher in Cornwall. They exist principally in the West of England.—*President,* Rev. T. Braund.

4. *The United Methodist Free Churches,* which

are an amalgamation of three different secessions —the Protestant Methodist, formed in 1828; the Wesleyan-Methodist Association, which sprang out of a controversy in 1834, concerning the training of ministers; and the Wesleyan Reform Association, founded in 1849, during a great agitation. A strong opposition to leading Wesleyan officials was organised, which found expression in the Conference debates, but more strongly in anonymous pamphlets, on suspicion of being the authors and circulators of which three ministers were expelled. They found so many sympathisers that over 100,000 members seceded to found a new denomination.—*President*, Rev. J. C. Brewitt.

Finances.—The *Wesleyans* raised in 1898-99 £126,163 to sustain their very extensive mission-

ary operations. At the same time their Home missionary income was £29,796; £19,343 were expended on the education of ministers' children at the Connexional schools; £2½5,156 were expended in Great Britain for chapel-building; and £8,296 for the training of candidates for the ministry, of whom there are 186 in the four theological colleges. By the *Methodist New Connexion* the following sums were raised: For chapel fund, £554; for missions, £8,425. The *Primitive Methodists* raised £34,196 for new chapels, and the *United Methodist Free Churches* £12,794 for their missions. During the past year the *Wesleyans* have begun to raise a Twentieth Century Fund of one million guineas to be applied to their Evangelistic Educational and Philanthropic work.

The number of Members is for the United Kingdom; of Chapel and scholars, Great Britain only.	Ministers	Lay Preachrs.	Members	On Probation.	Chapels.	Sunday Scholars.
Wesleyan Methodists	2,377	18,283	474,737	33,625	7,166	969,484
Methodist New Connexion	202	1,101	32,322	4,647	441	83,481
Primitive Methodists	1,102	16,617	198,930	...	4,257	467,884
Bible Christians	168	1,479	27,625	333	605	42,495
United Methodist Free Churches	385	3,011	71,910	5,806	1,258	189,795
Independent Methodists (1885)	...	412	8,544	369	146	26,025
Wesleyan Reformers	14	412	7,035	348	194	20,191

The Roman Catholic Church.

In *England*, from 1623 to 1850, Catholics were under Bishops, as Vicars-Apostolic, with first 1, then 4, and afterwards 8 Districts or Vicariates; in 1850 the Hierarchy was restored, by the erection of one Archiepiscopal and 12 Episcopal See, now increased to 15. In *Scotland*, Catholics were under Bishops, as Vicars Apostolic, from 1694 to 1878, with first 1, then 2, and afterwards 3 Districts or Vicariates; in 1878 the Hierarchy was restored, by the erection of 2 Archiepiscopal and 4 Episcopal Sees. In *Ireland*, the Hierarchy consists of 4 Archiepiscopal and 23 Episcopal Sees.—Besides the United Kingdom, Hierarchies are established in British America, India, and Australasia. There are now in the British Empire 28 Archiepiscopal and 105 Episcopal Sees; and 28 Vicariates and 11 Prefectures Apostolic. Including 10 Coadjutors and 5 Bishops Auxiliary, the number of Archbishops and Bishops now holding office in the British Empire is 172, distributed as follows:—

ENGLAND AND WALES.

Archbishops.

		Cons.	Clergy.
Westminster...	Herbert, Cardinal Vaughan	1872	414
	Robert Brindle, D.S.O. Bishop-Auxiliary...	1899	

Bishops.

Birmingham...	Edward Ilsley	1879	257
Clifton	Wm. R. Brownlow	1894	102
Hexham and Newcastle	Thomas W. Wilkinson	1888	175
Leeds	William Gordon	1890	121
Liverpool	Thomas Whiteside	1894	401
Middlesbrough	Richard Lacy	1879	76
Newport	John C. Hedley	1873	75
Northampton...	Arthur G. Riddell	1880	72
Nottingham	Edward G. Bagshawe	1874	122
Plymouth ...	William Vaughan	1856	103
	Chas. Graham, Coadj.	1891	
Portsmouth	John Vertue	1882	125
Salford	John Bilsborrow	1892	269
Shrewsbury	Samuel Webster Allen	1897	80
Southwark ..	Francis Bourne	1897	319
Wales, Menevia	Francis Mostyn	1895	58

SCOTLAND.

Archbishops.

St. Andrews & Edinburgh...	Angus Macdonald	1878	68
Glasgow	Charles Eyre	1869	211
	J. Maguire, Bp. Aux.	1894	

Bishops. Cons. Clergy.

Aberdeen	Donald Chisholm	1899	68
Argyll & Isles	George J. Smith	1893	23
Dunkeld	James A. Smith	1890	43
Galloway	William Turner	1893	30

IRELAND.

Archbishops.

Armagh	Michael Card. Logue	1879	181
Dublin	William J. Walsh	1885	532
	N. Donnelly, Bp. Aux.	1883	
Cashel	Thomas W. Croke	1870	118
Tuam	John MacEvilly	1857	120

Bishops.

Achonry	John Lyster	1888	49
Ardagh	Joseph Hoare	1895	96
Clogher	Richard Owens	1894	104
Clonfert	John Healy	1884	52
Cloyne	Robert Browne	1894	137
Cork	Thomas O'Callaghan	1884	190
Derry	J. Keys O'Doherty	1890	109
Down & Connor	Henry Henry	1895	141
Dromore	Thomas MacGivern	1887	53
Elphin	John Clancy	1895	102
Ferns	James Browne	1884	134
Galway and Kilmacduagh	Francis MacCormack	1872	65
Kerry	John Coffey	1889	130
Kildare and Leighlin	Patrick Foley	1896	155
Killala	John Conmy	1892	36
Killaloe	Thomas McRedmond	1890	158

IRELAND. *Bishops—continued.*

		CON·	CLERGY
Kilmore........	Edward Magennis ...	1888	102
Limerick......	Edward T. O'Dwyer .	1886	161
Meath	Matthew Gaffney ...	1899	140
Ossory	Abraham Brownrigg .	1884	117
Raphoe........	Patrick O'Donnell ...	1888	71
Ross	Denis Kelly	1897	27
Waterford & Lismore.	R. A. Sheehan.	1892	162

BRITISH COLONIES AND DEPENDENCIES.

EUROPE.

Bishops. CONS.

Malta............	Peter Pace	1877
Gozo	John Camilleri	1889
Gibraltar	James Bellord, Vic. Ap.	1899

AMERICA.

Delegate-Apostolic of Canada, Abp. Falconio.

Archbishops.

Quebec	Louis Bégin	1888
Halifax........	Cornelius O'Brien	1883
Kingston......	C. H. Gauthier	1898
Montreal	Paul N. Bruchesi	1897
Ottawa	Joseph Thomas Duhamel ...	1874
Port of Spain	Vincent Flood	1887
Toronto........	Denis O'Connor	1899
St. Boniface..	Louis Philip Langevin	1895

Bishops.

Alexandria ...	Alexander Macdonell	1890
Antigonish ...	John Cameron......	1870
Charlottetown...	Charles McDonald	1890
Chatham, N.B.	James Rogers	1860
Chicoutimi ...	Michael Labrecque	1892
Hamilton	Joseph Thomas Dowling ...	1887
Harbour-Grace,	Ronald McDonald ...	1881
London........	F. P. McEvay	1899
New Westminster,	{ Paul Durieu	1875
	A. Dontenville, Coadj.	1897
Nicolet	Elphege Gravel	1885
Peterborough...	Richard O'Connor	1889
Pontiac	N. Z. Lorrain	1882
Rimouski	Andrew Blais	1890
Roseau	Michael Naughten......	1890
St. Albert	{ Vitalis Grandin	1859
	E. Légal, Coadj.	1897
St. Hyacinth	{ Louis Moreau	1876
	Maximus Decelles, Coadj.	1893
St. John, N. Brunswick,	John Sweeny ...	1860
St. John, Newfoundland,	Michael Howley ...	1892
Sherbrooke ...	Paul Stanislas La Rocque ...	1893
Three Rivers..	F. X. Cloutier	1899
Valleyfield ...	Joseph Emard	1892
Vancouver ...	Vacant	
Athabasca-Mackenzie	{ E. Grouard, Vic. Ap.	1891
	Isidore Clut, Auxil.	1867
Demerara......	Antony Butler, Vicar Apost.	1878
Honduras	Vicariate, vacant.	
Jamaica........	Chas. Gordon, Vicar Apost...	1889
St. George, N.F.	Neil MacNeil, Vic. Ap. ...	1895
Saskatchewan	Albert Pascal, Vicar Apost.	1891

AFRICA.

Bishops.

Port Louis ...	Peter Austin O'Neill......	1896
Cape Colony	{ East...H MacSherry, V. A.	1896
	West { J. Leonard, Vic. Ap.	1872
	J. Rooney, Coadj.	1886
Lagos........	Paul Pellet	1895
Natal........	Charles Jolivet	1874
Orange Free State, &c.,	A. Gaughran, Vic. Ap.	1886
Orange River,	J. Simon, Vic. Ap.	1898
Port Victoria, Seychelles,	Mark Hudrisier.....	1890
Uganda, Upper Nile	Henry Hanlon, Vic. Ap.	1894
Victoria Nyanza,	H. Streicher, Vic. Ap....	1897

ASIA.

Delegate-Apostolic of India, Abp. Zaleski.

Archbishops. CONS.

Agra	Charles Gentili	1897
Bombay........	Theodore Dalhoff	1892
Calcutta	Paul Goethals	1878
Colombo	{ Andrew Theophilus Melizan.	1880
	A. Coudert, Coadj.	1898
Cyprus	N. Seluan, Maronite Rite ...	1892
Madras	{ Joseph Colgan	1882
	Theoph. Mayer, Bp. Auxil.	1894
Verapoly ...	B. Arguinzonis, Abp.	1896

Bishops.

Aden	Louis Lasserre. Vicar Apost.	1888
Allahabad ...	Victor Sinibaldi	1899
Burma, East	R. Tornatore, Vicar Apost...	1890
Burma, North	Antony Usse, Vicar Ap....	1894
Burma, South	Alexander Cardot, Vicar Ap.	1893
Changanacherry...	Matthew Makil, V.A.	1896
Cochin	Matthew d'Oliveira	1897
Coimbatore ...	Joseph L. Bardou	1874
Dacca	Peter J. Hurth	1894
Ernakolam ...	Aloysius Pareparambil, V. A.	1896
Galle	Joseph van Reeth	1894
Hong Kong ...	Louis Piazzoli, V. A.	1895
Hyderabad ...	Peter A. Vigano	1897
Jaffna	Henry Joulain	1893
Kandy	Clement Pagnani	1879
Kishnagur ...	Francis Pozzi	1887
Kumbaconum	H. Bottero	1899
Lahore	Godfrey Pelckmans	1893
Malacca	René M. Fey	1896
Mangalore ...	Claudius Cavadini	1896
Meliapur	Theotonia E. de Castro ...	1899
Mysore	Louis Eugene Kleiner ...	1890
Nagpur	Charles Pelvat......	1893
Poona	Bernard Beiderlinden ...	1887
Quilon	Ferdinand Ossi	1883
Trichinopoly	John Mary Barthe......	1890
Trichur	John Manacherry, Vic. Ap.	1896
Trincomalee ...	Charles Lavigne	1887
Visagapatam..	John Mary Clerc......	1891

AUSTRALASIA.

Archbishops.

Sydney........	Patrick F. Cardinal Moran ...	1872
Adelaide	John O'Reilly	1888
Brisbane	Robert Dunne	1882
Hobart........	{ Daniel Murphy	1846
	Patrick Delany, Bp. Coadj.	1893
Melbourne ...	Thomas Carr	1883
Wellington ...	Francis Redwood	1874

Bishops.

Armidale	Elzear Torregiani	1879
Auckland	George M. Lennihan	1896
Ballarat	James Moore	1884
Bathurst	Joseph Patrick Byrne ...	1885
Christchurch ...	John J. Grimes	1887
Cooktown	Dominic Murray, Vic. Ap.	1898
Dunedin	Michael Verdon	1896
Fiji Islands ...	Julian Vidal, Vic. Apost.	1887
Geraldton......	W. B. Kelly	1898
Goulburn ...	{ William Lanigan	1867
	John Gallagher, Coadj.	1895
Grafton........	Jeremiah Doyle	1887
Maitland	{ James Murray......	1865
	Patrick Dwyer, Coadj.	1897
New Norcia ...	R. Salvado, Abbot.	1849
Perth	Matthew Gibney	1886
Port Augusta	James Maher	1895
Rockhampton	Joseph Higgins	1883
Sale	James Corbett......	1887
Sandhurst ...	{ Martin Crane	1874
	Stephen Reville, Coadj.	1885
Wilcannia	John Dunne......	1887

In the Middle Ages the term "University" could be applied to any organised body of men. There could thus be a "university" of persons engaged in any particular occupation. The term came, however, to be appropriated exclusively to bodies of persons engaged in the occupation of teaching and study. Such Universities or guilds of teachers and students, when they had attained some definite organisation, naturally secured the right of granting licences to teach. As time went on it became the custom to grant these licences not only to persons who actually wished to teach, but to all who demanded them and who fulfilled certain requirements, and thus they became what we now understand by the term "degrees."

The earlier Universities grew so imperceptibly from small beginnings, that it is impossible to say who were their founders or in what year they were founded. Bologna (the earliest) and Paris (the most important) first rose into notice in the twelfth century, Oxford and Cambridge in the thirteenth. The system of degrees and the names of the chief officers of the University were introduced into England, as well as into other countries, from Paris. The distinguishing characteristic of the Universities of Oxford and Cambridge undoubtedly is the existence of a number of separate corporations, or Colleges, of which the names are given below.

There have been and are Colleges at many Universities, but nowhere have they reached anything like the same influence and importance as at Oxford and Cambridge. The origin of the Colleges was due to benevolent persons who desired to relieve a certain number of poor scholars from some of the hardships of their life at the mediæval Universities, and in order to do this provided a building in which such scholars could live a common life, and also an endowment for their maintenance. University and Balliol Colleges at Oxford were established in a somewhat rudimentary form in the middle of the thirteenth century; but the establishment of Merton College at Oxford, in 1274, by Walter de Merton, was the real beginning of the English college system. In the foundation of Peterhouse, the first Cambridge college, ten years later, "the rule of Merton" was closely followed.

The early College consisted of a Head and scholars, endowed with board and lodging by means of the buildings and revenues provided by the founder. The scholars were divided into senior scholars engaged in giving instruction, and junior scholars engaged in receiving it; the senior scholars were each other's "fellows;" and gradually the term "Fellow" became appropriated to the senior or governing members of the College, while the term "Scholar" was restricted to the junior members. It was not till long after the establishment of Colleges that it became the custom for them to take in paying boarders—"commoners" at Oxford, "pensioners" at Cambridge. At first the class which corresponds to the commoners and pensioners of the present time continued to live (as the whole University did before the establishment of Colleges) in lodgings, kept by townsmen or graduates. One of the old lodging-houses, or "Halls" kept by graduates still remains at Oxford; but under the regulations of the Commission of 1882, it will disappear on the next vacancy in the office of Principal. But a statute of the same year provided for the existence of Private Halls: of these there at present are three, with 45 undergraduates. Twenty years ago the pre-college era was to some small extent restored by the admission of "non-collegiate students" to Oxford and Cambridge.

THE UNIVERSITY OF OXFORD at present numbers upwards of 12,000 members. Of these about 3,000 are in residence in Oxford; the remainder, with a few exceptions, have finished their academical course, taken a degree, and are scattered over the country following various professions. The resident members of the University consist of undergraduates going through a course of instruction and study, and of graduates giving instruction or engaged in research. The resident graduates are 400 or 500 in number, and the undergraduates in residence are about 2,500.

The government of the University is in the hands of three bodies :—1. Convocation, which consists of all Masters of Arts and Doctors of Civil Law, Medicine, or Divinity, who remain members of the University, whether resident or non-resident; 2. Congregation of the University, which consists of resident members of Convocation; 3. The Hebdomadal Council, which consists of certain officers and 18 members elected by Congregation. The Hebdomadal Council alone has the power of initiation; Congregation can amend, confirm, or reject its proposals; Convocation can only confirm or reject them; it may, however, amend certain proposals relating to money. The election of the University representatives in Parliament is vested in the members of Convocation. The Ancient House of Congregation, which must not be confounded with the Congregation of the University, has now nothing to do with legislation in any form, but confines itself to granting degrees and electing examiners. In order to " matriculate," or become a member of the University, it is necessary to be admitted into one of the Colleges or Halls, or into the body called Non-Collegiate Students. A candidate may be admitted into a College as a scholar, as an exhibitioner, or as a commoner. Most of the scholarships are now open to competition for youths under 19, and are chiefly of the value of £80 per annum for (practically) four years. Some of the exhibitions are scarcely distinguishable in any important respect from open scholarships, but election to an exhibition is, as a rule, subject to the satisfaction of the electors that the candidate is in necessitous circumstances. Besides the open scholarships and exhibitions, there are still a few "close" ones confined to particular localities, or particular schools. To be admitted into a College as a commoner, or to become a member of a Hall, or a non-collegiate student, it is necessary to pass an examination held by the College or Hall, or by the delegates of non-collegiate students, or to have passed some test accepted in lieu of this examination. The degree of Bachelor of Arts, the ordinary University degree, cannot be obtained in less than 2 years and 8 months from matriculation, nor without residing in Oxford for twelve terms, which need not be continuous; there are 4 terms in each year. Members of the University who wish to proceed to a degree must first pass Responsions or one of the examinations accepted as equivalent. The path of undergraduates then divides: those aiming at Honours in Natural Science take the science preliminary, and then the final schools; to the rest three courses are open, (a) to read Pass Moderations and Pass Finals; (b) to read Pass Moderations (or, what is reckoned as the equivalent for the schools of Law and Modern History, the Law Prelim.), and one of the final honour schools of Litt. Hum., Mathematics, Natural Science, Law, Modern History, Theology, Oriental Studies, and English Literature; (c) to read Honour Moderations in Classics or Mathematics, and any one of the above-mentioned Honour Schools or the Pass final School. After passing these examinations the under-graduate is entitled to take the degree of Bachelor of Arts (or Medicine). For a musical degree a special course is prescribed. For the higher degrees of Bachelor or Doctor in Civil Law, Medicine, and Divinity no more residence is necessary, but for the baccalaureate in Civil Law and Medicine there is an examination prescribed. For the degree of B.Litt. or B.Sc., a special course of study is prescribed by the statutes of the University; for the baccalaureate in Divinity a thesis is at present required. For the M.A. degree the only requirement is that the candidate should have taken the B.A. degree and had his name on the books for twenty-six terms since his matriculation. The bulk of the instruction at Oxford is given by the college tutors and lecturers under a system which allows members of one College to attend lectures given in any other. The remainder of the instruction is given by the University Professors and Readers. The chief University institutions are the Bodleian Library, the second library in the Kingdom; and the Museum, which is furnished with all that is necessary for teaching natural science and medicine.

In 1880 a statute was passed by which "any College or Institution within the United Kingdom, or in any part of the British dominions, being a place of education in which the majority of the students are of the age of 17 at least, may, under certain conditions, be admitted to the privilege of affiliated Colleges." A list of such affiliated Colleges and Universities is given on p. 252.

In 1884 a statute was passed allowing the delegates of local examinations to use the several honour schools of the University for the purpose of the examination of women. Somerville College, Lady Margaret Hall, St. Hugh's Hall, and St. Hilda's Hall, are now established in Oxford for the higher education of women, and some of the members avail themselves of this statute, and are also admitted to the lectures of some of the University professors. and to certain of the College lectures.

The semi-official guide to the University is the "Student's Handbook to the University of Oxford."

THE UNIVERSITY OF CAMBRIDGE is an incorporation of students in all and every of the liberal arts and sciences. It consists of seventeen Colleges, one public, and one private, hostel, founded "for the study of learning and knowledge, and for the better service of Church and State." These are maintained by the endowments of their several founders and benefactors; each of them is a corporate body, and is bound by its own statutes, but is likewise controlled by the paramount laws of the University. A new Code of Statutes for the University was approved by the Queen in Council in 1882. In each of the Colleges there are eight separate orders: these are (1) Head (2) Fellows; (3) Noblemen graduates, doctors in the several faculties, bachelors of divinity, masters of arts and masters of law, who are not upon the foundation; (4) Bachelors of Arts, Physic, and Law (5) Fellow-commoners; (6) Scholars; (7) Pensioners, forming the great bulk of the students; and (8) Sizars, students of narrow means, and in receipt of various emoluments. The head of each College has supreme disciplinary authority in

educational matters; and he, together with the foundation fellows, or a council elected by them, form the governing body. The great legislative assembly of the University is called the Senate: it is composed of all those who have obtained the degree of Doctor or Master, and whose names are still on the register. There is a Council of the Senate (consisting of the Vice-Chancellor and sixteen members of the Senate, of whom eight vacate their office every second year, the office being held for two years), by whom every University "grace" or decree must be approved before it is offered to the Senate. A residence of nine terms is required from each student before taking the B.A. degree, and "honours" may be obtained in any of the following: — Mathematics, Classics, Moral Sciences, Natural Sciences, Mechanical Sciences, Law, History, Theology, Semitic, Indian, and Modern Languages. The University possesses a library of more than 200,000 printed volumes, besides MSS., the Fitzwilliam Museum, the Observatory, the Botanical Garden, the Museum of Biological and Physical Science, and the Divinity School. James I. granted to the University the privilege of sending two Members to Parliament, which it has ever since enjoyed. In 1896–97, the number of students who matriculated was 887, while the members on the boards amounted in 1897 to 13,079. The University has powers with regard to the admission of affiliated students similar to those possessed by the University of Oxford, and privileges of affiliation are also granted under certain conditions to students and local lecture centres. A list of the Colleges and Institutions admitted to the privileges of affiliation is given on p. 254.

The University also admits persons as Advanced Students. Each applicant must submit (1) a diploma or other certificate of graduation; (2) a statement as to the course or courses of (a) advanced study or (b) research which he desires to pursue, with such evidence of qualification, attainments, and previous study as he may be able to submit; (3) a certificate or declaration that he has attained the age of 21 years. When the application has been approved by the Special Board connected with the applicant's studies, he must be admitted a member of a College or a Non-Collegiate Student. An Advanced Student who has kept by residence at least six terms, and has obeyed the regulations as to examinations, &c., may proceed to the degree of B.A., as also may an Advanced Student who has obtained a certificate of research.

DUBLIN UNIVERSITY, which is, for most purposes, identical with Trinity College, Dublin, was incorporated by Royal Charter in 1591 Oxford and Cambridge recognise each other's degrees, and those granted by Dublin University, but no others. There are schools of Divinity, Law, Medicine and Surgery, and Engineering. It is represented in Parliament by two members.

SCOTLAND possesses four Universities, namely, those of St. Andrews, Aberdeen, Edinburgh, and Glasgow, and the general regulations as to graduation are common to all. THE UNIVERSITY OF EDINBURGH was founded in 1582 by a charter granted by James VI. of Scotland, and in 1621 the Scottish Parliament granted to it all the privileges enjoyed by other Universities in the kingdom. This grant was confirmed in the Treaty of Union between England and Scotland, and again in the Act of Security. The constitution was, however. modified by the Act (1858) relating to the Scottish Universities, and again by the Universities Act of 1889, with numerous ordinances issued by the Commissioners appointed under the latter Act. The University of Edinburgh is a Corporation consisting of a chancellor, rector, principal, 40 professors, and 100 lecturers, &c., 8,500 registered graduates, and about 2,800 matriculated students. The essential qualification for graduation at this, as at other Scottish Universities, is attendance at certain series of lectures or classes and passing of the required examinations. There are now six faculties in the University, viz., Arts, Science, Divinity, Law, Medicine, and Music. The University confers the following degrees after examination, viz.:—M.A., D.Litt., D.Phil., B.Sc., D.Sc., B.D., B.L., LL.B., M.B., Ch.B., M.D., Ch.M., Mus. B. and Mus. D. It also confers the honorary degrees of D.D., LL.D., and Mus. Doc. The buildings have been more than doubled in extent within the last 20 years, and the magnificent McEwan hall is now completed. The library contains about 250,000 volumes and 7,500 MSS., and there is also a theological library of 10,000 volumes. In the various faculties there are bursaries, prizes, scholarships, and fellowships, tenable from one to four years, and ranging in value from £10 to £160, their total value being about £17,800 per annum.

THE UNIVERSITY OF ST. ANDREWS was founded by Henry Wardlaw, Bishop of the diocese, in 1411, and was confirmed by a Bull of Pope Benedict XIII. in 1413. During the 15th and 16th centuries three Colleges were established in connection with it, viz., St. Salvator (1450), St. Leonard (1512), and St. Mary (1537). All the Colleges had originally teachers both in philosophy (or arts) and in theology, but in 1579 the two older of them were confined to philosophy, and that of St. Mary to theology. In the year 1747, the Colleges of St. Leonard and St. Salvator were united by Act of Parliament. The Universities of Edinburgh and St. Andrews unite in sending a representative to Parliament.

The UNIVERSITY OF GLASGOW was founded by a Bull of Pope Nicholas V. (1450-51), with the power of creating doctors and masters, and enrolling readers and students, the whole of whom were to enjoy the same rights and privileges as the University of Bologna. At first it had neither property nor endowment, but in 1460, James, Lord Hamilton, bequeathed to the then Regent and his successors a tenement in the High Street, with four acres of land adjoining, for the "use of the College of Arts." Between 1577, when a new charter was issued, and the Restoration, the University flourished in every way but the re-establishment of episcopacy detached from it a large part of its revenues, and many of its professorships were abandoned. After the Revolution prosperity set in and in the present century there has been great expansion. In 1864 the old buildings were sold for £100,000, and a Government grant of £120,000 was obtained; these amounts, together with public subscriptions and college funds, were laid out in the new buildings now to be seen at the west end of the city. The University of Glasgow includes five faculties, viz., Arts, Theology, Law, Medicine, and Science: it was reconstituted and received further endowments under the Acts of 1858 and 1889 the latter Act providing for the admission of women to Graduation. Conjointly with the University of Aberdeen, it sends one member to Parliament.

The present UNIVERSITY OF ABERDEEN derives its origin from two distinct foundations, viz., the University and King's College of Aberdeen, founded in 1494 by William Elphinstone, Chancellor of Scotland and Bishop of Aberdeen, under the authority of a Papal Bull; and the Marischal College and University of Aberdeen, founded (1593) by George Keith, 5th Earl Marischal, under a charter afterwards ratified by Act of Parliament. In 1860, by another Act of Parliament, the two foundations were united and incorporated into one University and College, under the title of the University of Aberdeen. The five faculties are Arts, Science, Divinity, Law, and Medicine. Bursaries, Scholarships, Fellowships, and Prizes (exclusive of the ordinary class prizes and medals) to the number of 350, and annual value of £7,800, are awarded to students in the various faculties. The University Library contains upwards of 125,000 volumes.

Of the modern Universities of the United Kingdom the most important is the UNIVERSITY OF LONDON, which was first incorporated by Royal Letters Patent dated November 28, 1836. The present Charter was issued in 1863; and a supplemental charter, opening all degrees to women, was granted in 1878. This University is simply an examining body which, by reason of its unquestionable integrity and its severely high standard, has gained an excellent reputation. The fees are moderate, ranging from £2 to £10. The various faculties are Arts, Science, Law, Medicine, and Music, and all faculties (except Medicine) are open to candidates irrespective of the place or manner of their education. The Matriculation, the Pass examinations in Arts and some in Science, are held at a large number of provincial Colleges, while the Matriculation, B.A., and LL.B. examinations may be held at colonial centres. The corporate body of the University includes the Chancellor, Vice-Chancellor, fellows, and graduates. In 1898, the total number of candidates at all the examinations was 6,319.

The remaining modern Universities are DURHAM, established by the Dean and Chapter of Durham under the authority of an Act of Parliament passed in 1831; the VICTORIA UNIVERSITY, which received a Royal Charter in 1880, and combines Owens College, Manchester, University College, Liverpool, and the Yorkshire College, Leeds; the ROYAL and CATHOLIC UNIVERSITIES OF IRELAND; and the UNIVERSITY OF WALES. Efforts are also being made to raise a sufficient sum for the establishment and endowment of a University at Birmingham and when the amount required is obtained application for a Charter will be made.

UNIVERSITY EXTENSION.

Of late years much has been done in the way of extending University teaching and advantages. Both Oxford and Cambridge now hold what are called "Local" Examinations, senior and junior, in many parts of the country, and the certificates granted to the successful candidates are accepted as evidence of competency from an educational point of view. They have also organised "University Extension Lectures," which are given in all parts of the kingdom by arrangement with local committees, who apply for a course of lectures and guarantee the small expenses (see also p. 268).

The University of London, too, has arranged a definite scheme, which is now in full working, and a scheme has been started by the Victoria University Manchester and by the "London Society for the Extension of University Teaching."

	Elect.
Chancellor, Most Hon. the Marquess of Salisbury, K.G., D.C.L., *All Souls*	1869
High Steward, Right Hon. the Earl of Halsbury, D.C.L., *Merton*	1896
Vice-Chancellor, T. Fowler, D.D., President of *Corpus*	1899
Pro-Vice-Chancellors, J. R. Magrath, D.D., Provost of *Queen's*; W. W. Merry, D.D., Rector of *Lincoln*; D. B. Monro, M.A., Provost of *Oriel*	1899
Proctors, W. C. Allsebrook, M.A., *Jesus*; H. E. D. Blakiston, M.A., Fellow of *Trinity*	1898
Burgesses, Rt. Hon. John G. Talbot, D.C.L., *Ch. Ch.*... 1878; Sir William Reynell Anson, D.C.L., Warden of *All Souls*	1899
Assessor of the Chancellor's Court, Thomas Erskine Holland, D.C.L., *All Souls*	1876
Deputy Steward, A. S. Hill, D.C.L., *St. John's*	1874
Public Orator, W. W. Merry, D.D., *Lincoln* .	1880
Member of the Medical Council of the United Kingdom, John F. Payne, D.M., *Magdalen*	1899
Bodley's Librarian, Edward Williams Byron Nicholson, M.A., *Trinity*	1882
Sub-Librarians, A. Neubauer, M.A., *Exeter.* Falconer Madan, M.A., *Brasenose*	1873
	1880
Keeper of Archives, T. V. Bayne, M.A., *Ch. Ch.*	1885
Keeper of Museum, Edward Burnett Tylor, M.A., *Balliol*	1883
Radcliffe's Librarian, Sir Henry Wentworth Acland, Bart., M.D., *Ch. Ch.*	1851
Keeper of the Ashmolean Museum, A. J. Evans, M.A., *Brasenose*	1884
Keeper of the Indian Institute,	
Registrar of the University, T. H. Grose, M.A., *Queen's*	1897
Radcliffe Observer, A. A. Rambaut, M.A., *Qns.*	1897
Bampton Lecturer for 1901 (not yet appointed).	

Secretary to the Curators of the University Chest, William B. Gamlen, M.A., *Exeter* 1873
Secretary to the Boards of Faculties, C. Leudesdorf, M.A., *Pembroke.*
Registrar of the Chancellor's Court, Frederic Parker Morrell, M.A., *St. John's* 1870
Coroners of University, F. P. Morrell, M.A., *St. John's* 1853; W. T. Brooks, M.A., *Ch. Ch.* 1899
Univ. Counsel, Sir R. T. Reid, B.A., *Balliol*... 1899
Solicitor, Frederic Parker Morrell, M.A., *St. John's.*
Bedels, G. Shelton, *Law*; E. Parker, *Medicine*; W. Moon, *Arts*; E. H. Bellamy, *Divinity.*
Organist, James Taylor, Hon. MUS.D., *New College.*
Clerk of the University, George Parker.
Keeper of University Galleries, A. Macdonald, M.A.

HEBDOMADAL COUNCIL.

Official Members, The Chancellor; Vice-Chancellor; ex-Vice Chancellor; Proctors.
Heads of Houses, Dean of *Ch. Ch.*; Master of University; Rector of *Lincoln*; Principal of *Brasenose*; President of *St. John's*; Warden of *All Souls.*
Professors, The Reader in Ancient History; the Professor of Exegesis; the Camden Professor of Ancient History; the Hope Professor of Zoology; the Waynflete Professor of Chemistry, the Regius Professor of Divinity.
Members of Convocation, A. Sidgwick, M.A.; L. R. Phelps, M.A.; A. J. Butler, M.A.; H. T. Gerrans, M.A.; P. E. Matheson, M.A.; H. A. Wilson, M.A.

1. PUBLIC EXAMINERS:—*Final Honour Schools.*
In *Literis Humaniorious,* G. Wood, M.A., *Pembroke;* S. Ball, M.A., *St. John's;* W. W. How, M.A., *Merton;* E. G. Hardy, M.A., *Jesus;* W. H. Hadow, M.A., *Worcester*

In *Scientiis Math. et Phys.,* A. L. Dixon, M.A., *Merton;* E. B. Elliott, M.A., *Magdalen;* S. L. Loney, M.A. (*Sid. Sussex Coll.,* Camb.).
In *Scientiâ Naturali, Preliminary,* W. Ramsden M.A., *Pembroke;* C. E. Haselfoot, M.A., *Hertford;* P. Elford, M.A., *St. John's;* S. G. Mostyn, M.A., *Exeter;* C.H.H. Walker, M.A., *Univ.;* P. Groom, M.A., *Exeter.*
— *Final,* A. L. Selby, M.A., *Merton;* J. A. Gardner, M.A., *Magdalen;* W. Ramsden, M.A., *Pembroke;* E. H. Hayes, M.A., *New;* H. B. Dixon, M.A., *Merton;* W. D. Halliburton, D.M. (*Lond.*).
In *Jurisprudentiâ, Preliminary,* H. W. C. Davis, M.A., *All Souls;* R. W. Leage, M.A., *Brasenose;* R. W. Lee, M.A., *Balliol.*
In *Jurisprudentiâ, Final,* A. T. Carter, D.C.L., *Christ Church;* E. Jenks, M.A., *Balliol.*
In *Historiâ Modernâ,* A. H. Johnson, M.A., *All Souls;* H. A. L. Fisher, M.A., *New College;* O. M. Edwards, M.A., *Lincoln;* G. H. Wakeling, M.A., B.N.C.; S. M. Leathes, M.A., *Cambridge;* R. L. Ottley, M.A., *Magdalen.*
In *Sacrâ Theologiâ,* F. E. Brightman, M.A., *University;* W. C. Allen, M.A., *Exeter;*

Final Pass Schools.

H. B. Cooper, M.A., *Keble;* J. L. Myves, M.A., *Ch. Ch.;* C. N. Jackson, M.A., *Hertford;* G. McN. Rushforth, M.A., *St. John's;* W. H. Hughes, M.A., *Jesus;* C. Cookson, M.A., *Magdalen;* H. B. George, M.A., *New College;* F. Armitage, M.A., *Worcester;* F. Urquhart, M.A., *Balliol;* J. B. Baker, M.A., *Non-Coll.;* J. A. R. Marriott, M.A., *New College;* A. J. Carlyle, M.A., *University;* A. A. Prankerd, D.C.L., *Brasenose;* F. E. Smith, B.C.L., *Merton;* A. E. W. Hazel, M.A., *Jesus;* C. F. Burney, M.A., *St. John's;* C. E. Plumb, M.A., *Worcester;* H. J. White, M.A., *Merton.*

2. MODERATORS:—*Honour Schools.*
In *Literis Græcis et Latinis,* A. Sedgwick, M.A., *Corpus;* A. B. Poynton, M.A., *University;* H. S. Jones, M.A., *Trinity;* S. G. Owen, M.A., *Ch. Ch.;* F. J. Leys, M.A., *Worcester.*
In *Disciplinis Mathematicis,* C. E. Haselfoot, M.A., *Hertford;* A. L. Pedder, M.A., *Magdalen;* J. W. Russell, M.A., *Merton.*

Pass School.

In *Literis Græcis et Latinis,* C. H. Sampson, M.A., *Brasenose;* H. L. Wild, M.A., *Exeter;* W. R. Inge, M.A., *Hertford;* J. Tracey, M.A., B.N.C.; H. N. Bate, M.A., *Magdalen;* F. C. Brabant, M.A., *Corpus.*

3. MASTERS OF THE SCHOOLS.
R. L. Abbott, M.A., *Non-Coll.;* R. H. Ferard, M.A., *Exeter;* A. E. Cowley, M.A., *Wadham;* F. W. Hall, M.A., *St. John's;* D. H. Nagel, M.A., *Trinity;* F. J. Haverfield, M.A., *Ch. Ch.*

PROFESSORS, &c.	Elect.
Anglo-Saxon, John Earle, M.A., *Oriel*	1876
Anthropology, E. B. Tylor, M.A., *Balliol*	1895
" (*Romanes*)	1899
Arabic (*Laud's*), D. S. Margoliouth, M.A., *New*	1889
" (*Ld. Almoner's*), G. F. Nicholl, M.A., *Ball.*	1878
Archæology (*Linc.*), P. Gardner, M.A., *Lincoln*	1887
Assyriology, A. H. Sayce, M.A., *Queen's*	1891
Astronomy (*Savilian*), H. H. Turner, M.A., *New*	1893
Botany (*Sherard*), S. H. Vines, M.A., *Magd.*	1888
Celtic, John Rhys, M.A., Principal of *Jesus*	1877
Chemistry (*Waynflete*), W. Odling, M.A., *Worc.*	1872
Chinese, T. L. Bullock, M.A., *New Coll.*	1898
Civil Law (*Regius*), H. Goudy, D.C.L., *All Souls*	1893

	Elect.
Comparative Anatomy (Linacre), W. F. R. Weldon, M.A., *Corpus*	1899
Comparative Philology, Rt. Hon. Friedrich Max Müller, M.A., *All Souls*	1866
Deputy, J. Wright, M.A., *Exeter*	1891
Dante (Lect. in), E. Moore, D.D., *Principal of St. Edm. Hall*	1896
Diplomatic (Lect. in), R. L. Poole, M.A., *Magdalen*	1896
Divin. (Margaret), W. Sanday, D.D., *Ch. Ch.*	1895
Divinity (Regius), William Ince, D.D., *Ch. Ch.*	1878
Eccles. Hist. (Reg.), W. Bright, D.D., *Ch. Ch.*	1868
English History (Ford), Lect. in, J. H. Wylie, M.A., *Pembroke.*	
English Language and Literature (Merton), Arthur S. Napier, M.A., *Merton*	1885
Exegesis (Ireland), Walter Lock, D.D., *Keble*	1895
Exp. Phil., R. Bellamy Clifton, M.A., *Merton*	1865
Fine Art (Slade), H. E. Wooldridge, M.A. *Trin.*	1895
Foreign Hist. (Rdr.),	
Geogr. (Rdr.), H. J. Mackinder, M.A., *Ch. Ch.*	1887
Geology, W. J. Sollas, M.A., *Queen's*	1897
Geometry (Savilian), W. Esson, M.A., *New College*	1897
Greek (Regius), I. Bywater, M.A., *Ch. Ch.*	1893
„ (Reader), A. Sidgwick, M.A., *Corpus*	1894
Hebrew (Regius), S. R. Driver, D.D., *Ch. Ch.*	1882
History, Ancient (Camden), H. F. Pelham, M.A., *President of Trinity*	1889
„ (Reader), R. W. Macan, M.A., *Univ.*	1890
Human Anatomy, A. Thomson, M.A., *Exeter*	1885
Indian Hist. (Rdr.), S. J. Owen, M.A., *Ch. Ch.*	1862
Indian Law (Rdr.), Sir W. Markby, D.C.L., *All Souls*	1878
International Law (Chichele), Thomas Erskine Holland, D.C.L., *All Souls*	1874
Interpretation of Holy Scripture (Oriel), Thomas Kelly Cheyne, M.A., *Oriel*	1885
Jurisprudence (Corp.), Sir Frederick Pollock, Bt., M.A., *Corpus*	1883

	Elect.
Latin Literat. (Corp.), R. Ellis, M.A., *Corpus*	1893
„ „ (Reader), (Vacant).	
Law (Vinerian), A. V. Dicey, M.A., *All Souls*	1882
„ „ (Rdr.), E. Jenks, M.A., *Balliol*	1896
Logic (Wykeham), J. Cook Wilson, M.A., *New*	1889
Mechanics (Lect.) F. J. Jervis-Smith, M.A., *Trinity*	1888
Mediæval Palæography (Lecturer), F. Madan, M.A., *Brasenose*	1889
Medicine (Reg.), Sir John S. Burdon Sanderson, Bart., M.A., *Magdalen*	1895
Clinical Lecturers, Medicine, W. Collier, M.A., M D. Camb., *Exeter*; Surgery, A. Winkfield, F.R.C.S.	
Mineralogy, Henry A. Miers, M.A., *Magdalen*	1895
Modern History (Chichele), Montagu Burrows, M.A., *All Souls*	1862
Modern Hist. (Reg.), F. York Powell, M.A., *Oriel*	1894
Moral Philosophy (Waynflete), T. Case, M.A., *Magdalen*	1889
Moral Philos. (Whyte), J. A. Stewart, M.A., *Ch. Ch.*	1897
Music, (Vacant).	
Natural Philos. (Sedleian), A. E. H. Love, M.A., *Queen's*	1899
Pastoral Theology (Reg.), Robert Campbell Moberly, D.D., *Christ Church*	1891
Physiology (Waynflete), Francis Gotch, M.A., *Magdalen*	1895
Poetry, William J. Courthope, M.A., C.B., *New College*	1895
Political Econ., F. Y. Edgeworth, M.A., *Balliol*	1891
Rabbinical Lit. (Rdr.), A. Neubauer, M.A., *Ex.*	1884
Rural Economy (Sibthorp), (Vacant).	
Russian, &c. (Reader), W. R. Morfill, M.A., *Oriel*	1889
Sanskrit, (Vacant).	
„ Teacher in, A. A. Macdonell, M.A., *Corpus*	1899
Septuagint, Ll. J. M. Bebb, M.A., *Brasenose*	1897
Zend Philology, L. H. Mills, Hon. M.A.	1898

Fnded.	COLLEGES.	HEADS.	Elect.	Income from Endowments.	Members on the Books.	Undergrads.	Members of Convocation.
1437	All Souls	Sir W. R. Anson, Bt., D.C.L., *Warden*	1881	£14,653	117	5	87
1262	Balliol	Edward Caird, M.A., *Master*	1893	6,578	943	245	426
1509	Brasenose	Charles B. Heberden, M.A., *Principal*	1889	10,083	559	138	324
1532	Christ Church	Francis Paget, D.D., *Dean*	1892	31,055	1,404	316	733
1516	Corpus	Thomas Fowler, D.D., *President*	1881	10,693	379	85	229
1314	Exeter	William W. Jackson, D.D., *Rector*	1887	3,689	872	177	540
1874	Hertford	Henry Boyd, D.D., *Principal*	1877	—	347	98	147
1571	Jesus	John Rhys, M.A., *Principal*	1895	9,988	340	120	130
1869	Keble	Walter Lock, D.D., *Warden*	1897	—	677	222	203
1427	Lincoln	William Walter Merry, D.D., *Rector*	1884	4,657	364	81	179
1456	Magdalen	Thomas H. Warren, M.A., *President*	1885	26,773	717	173	304
1270	Merton	Hon. G. C. Brodrick, D.C.L., *Warden*	1881	12,157	509	118	257
1386	New College	James Edwards Sewell, D.D., *Warden*	1860	17,782	885	289	347
1326	Oriel	David Binning Monro, M.A., *Provost*	1882	5,199	420	134	230
1624	Pembroke	Rt. Rev. John Mitchinson, D.C.L., *Master*	1899	3,592	316	85	173
1340	Queen's	John Richard Magrath, D.D., *Provost.*	1878	13,024	501	108	266
1555	St. John's	James Bellamy, D.D., *President*	1871	13,608	650	158	330
1554	Trinity	Henry Francis Pelham, M.A., *President*	1897	4,875	664	178	320
1249	University	James Franck Bright, D.D., *Master*	1881	5,767	637	173	305
1613	Wadham	George Earlam Thorley, M.A., *Warden*	1881	2,558	417	112	231
1714	Worcester	William Inge, D.D., *Provost.*	1881	2,132	394	95	240
	HALLS.						
1269	St. Edmund	Edward Moore, D.D., *Principal*	1864	—	100	37	35
	St. Mary Hall	Drummond Percy Chase, D.D.	1857	—	60	10	40
	Grindle's	Edward Samuel Grindle, M.A.		—	14	12	0
	Marcon's	Charles Abdy Marcon, M.A.		—	49	34	2
	Clarke's	Richard Edward Clarke, M.A.		—	10	9	0
1868	Non-Coll. Stu.	Richard Wm. M. Pope, D.D., *Censor.*	1887	—	435	200	103
		Total (Oxford Calendar, 1899)			12,780	3,412	6,185

Zoology, E. B. Poulton, M.A., *Jesus*............ 1893
TEACHERS.—Hindustani, Robert St. John, M.A.;
Telugu, G. U. Pope, M.A.; Persian, J. T. Platts,
M.A.; German, A. A. Macdonell, M.A., *Corpus*;
French, H. E. Berthon; Italian, Carlo Felice
Coscia, M.A.; Spanish, F. de Arteaga, M.A.;
Bengali, J. F. Blumhardt, M.A.; Burmese, R. F.
St. Andrew St. John, M.A.
PRIZEMEN, &c., 1899.—THE CHANCELLOR'S.
English Essay—W. R. Barker, *Worcester*.
Latin Verse—R. C. K. Ensor, *Balliol*.
Latin Essay—C. A. Du Pontet, *Trinity*.
GAISFORD.
Greek Verse—H. T. Baker, *New College*.
Greek Prose—F. H. Williamson, *Balliol*.
NEWDIGATE.
English Verse—H. E. Butler, *New College*.
COBDEN, 1899.
F. W. Hirst, *Hertford*.
CONINGTON, 1897.
F. G. Kenyon, *Magdalen*.

Arnold—J. L. Myres, *Christ Church*.
Lothian—C. T. Atkinson, *Exeter*.
Stanhope—R. S. Rait, *New College*.
Ellerton—A. F. Gaskell, *Hertford*.
Sacred Poem (1899)—Rev. W. O. Peile, *Magdalen*.
SCHOLARS, &c., 1898-9.
Craven (Fellow) (1899)—J. H. Hopkinson, *Univ.*
Eldon—V. M. Coutts-Trotter, *Balliol*.
Derby (1896)—G. S. Robertson, *New College*.
Vinerian—[No Election].
Hertford (1899)—H. W. Garrod, *Balliol*.
Ireland (1898)—E. E. Genner, *Balliol*.
Craven (1893)—R. Asquith, *Balliol*.
  ,, ,, A. S. Ward, *Balliol*.
  ,, ,, W. F. Nicholson, *Balliol*.
Taylorian (1897) (German)—D. de S. Bray, *Balliol*.
 ,, (1899) (Italian)—E. F. W. Welch, *Pembroke*.
 ,, (1898) (French)—P. Galec, *Magdalen*.

John Locke (1899)
Sanskrit—[No Election.]
Chinese—G. Scott, *Christ Church*.
Burdett-Coutts (1899)—J. B. Scrivenor, *Hertford*.
Senior (and Johnson) Mathem.—H. Hilton, B.A., *Magdalen*.
Junior ,, I. O. Griffiths, *Balliol*.
      Exh., [No Election].
Kennicott (1899) (senior).
  ,, (1899) (junior), C. A. B. Brockwell, *Wadham*.
Pusey and Ellerton (1899), G. G. V. Stonehouse, *Exeter*; G. H. Vasey, *St. John's*.
Denyer and Johnson, F. H. Dudden, *Lincoln*; B. H. Streeter, *Pembroke*.

AFFILIATED COLLEGES.
Lampeter, St. David's 1880
Nottingham, University 1882
Sheffield, University College 1886
Reading, Reading College 1899
AFFILIATED UNIVERSITIES.
Cape of Good Hope, 1888; Sydney, 1888;
Calcutta, 1889; Punjaub, 1889; Bombay, 1889;
Adelaide, 1891; Madras, 1894; Melbourne, 1894;
New Zealand, 1894; Allahabad, 1894; Toronto,
1895; Tasmania, 1899; Montreal, 1889.
MATRICULATION ...1865, 524; 1875, 718; 1897, 852.
DEGREES. 1865 1875 1898 DEGREES. 1865 1875 1898

	1865	1875	1898		1865	1875	1898
M.A.	343	294	345	*D. Mus.	4	2	6
B.A.	297	394	554	B.D.	7	—	8
*D.D.	5	2	8	B.C.L.	4	2	6
*D.C.L.	15	11	13	B. Med.	3	5	10
D. Med.	1	2	8	B. Mus.	6	11	13

* Including Honorary Degrees.

University Receipts and Expenditure, 1897:
Receipts £59,779
Deficit 2,127
           £61,906

University of Cambridge.

Chancellor, His Grace the Duke of Devon- Elect.
 shire, K.G., LL.D., *Trin*.................... 1892
High Steward, Lord Walsingham, LL.D., *Trin*. 1891
Vice-Chancellor, Wm. Chawner, M.A., *Emm*. 1899
Representatives in Parliament, Prof. Richard
 Claverhouse Jebb, LITT.D., *Trin*.......... 1895
 Right Hon. Sir John Eldon Gorst, M.A., Q.C.,
 St. John's 1895
Commissary, Wm. Forsyth, M.A., Q.C., *Trin*. 1893
Deputy High Steward, Hon. Alf. Lyttelton,
 M.A., *Trin*. 1899
Public Orator, J. E. Sandys, LITT.D., *St. John's* 1876
Registrary, J. Willis Clark, M.A., *Trin*. 1891
Librarian, F. J. H. Jenkinson, M.A., *Trin*... 1889
Counsel, Arthur Cohen, M.A., Q.C., *Magdalene* 1879
Esquire Bedells, A. P. Humphry, M.A., *Trin*. 1877
 W. A. Gill, M.A., *Magdalene* 1893
Director of the Observatory, Sir Robert
 Stawell Ball, M.A., *King's*.
Superintendent of the Museum of Zoology,
 S. F. Harmer, SC.D., *King's* ....
Director of the Fitzwilliam Museum, M. R.
 James, LITT.D., *King's*.
Strickland Curator, H. Gadow, M.A., *King's*.
Curator in Zoology, D. Sharp, M.A. ....
Curator of the Museum of Archæology and Eth-
 nology, Baron A. von Hügel, M.A., *Trin*.
Curator of the Botanic Garden, R. I. Lynch...
COUNCIL OF THE SENATE.
The Chancellor; the Vice-Chancellor; the Provost
 of *King's*; the Master of *Downing*; the Master
 of *Christ's*; the Master of *Emmanuel*; Prof-

Kirkpatrick, *Trin*.; Prof. Jebb, *Trin*.; Prof.
 Forsyth, *Trin*.; Prof. Ewing, *King's*; Dr.
 Keynes, *Pemb*.; W. L. Mollison, *Clare*; A. E.
 Shipley, *Christ's*; Dr. Langley, *Trin*.; Dr. D.
 MacAlister, *John's*; Mr. Whitting, *King's*; Mr.
 R. T. Wright, *Christ's*; Mr. Dale, *Tr. Hall*.
Sex Viri, Mr. C. Smith, *Sid*.; Dr. Peile, Dr. Bond,
 Mr. Austen Leigh, Dr. Clark, Dr. Kenny.
Court of Discipline, Dr. Atkinson, Dr. Butler, Mr.
 C. Smith, Mr. Austen Leigh, Dr. Ryle, Mr. W.
 Chawner.
Auditors of the Chest, Dr. Keynes, *Pemb*.; Mr.
 Innes, *Trin*.; Mr. Shipley, *Christ's*.
Proctors, G. B. Shirres, M.A., *Trin. H.*; W. W.
 Buckland, M.A., *Cai*.
Moderators, Dr. Routh, A. N. Whitehead, M.A.,
 Trin.

PROFESSORS.   Elect.
Agriculture, W. Somerville........................ 1899
Anatomy, A. Macalister, M.D., *St. John's* ... 1883
Anglo-Saxon, W. W. Skeat, LITT.D., *Christ's* 1878
Arabic, C. Rieu, M.A. 1894
 ,, (Ld. Alm.), A. A. Bevan, M.A., *Trin*. 1893
Arch. (Disney), W. Ridgeway, M.A., *Caius*.. 1892
Astro. (Lowndes), Sir R. S. Ball, M.A., *King's* 1892
Astronomy (Plumian), G. H. Darwin, M.A., *Trin*. 1883
Botany, Harry Marshall Ward, SC.D., *Christ's* 1895
Chemistry, G. D. Liveing, M.A., *St. John's* .. 1861
Chinese, H. A. Giles, LL.D. 1898
Civil Law (Regius), E. C. Clark, LL.D., *St.
 John's* 1872
Divinity (Regius), H. B. Swete, D.D., *Caius*. 1890

	Elect.
Divinity (Marg.), A. J. Mason, M.A., Trin...	1895
" (Hulsean), H. E. Ryle, D.D., King's ...	1887
" (Norrisian), H. C. G. Moule, D.D., Trin.	1899
" (Ely), V. H. Stanton, D.D., Trin.	1886
Ecclesiastical History (Dixie), Henry Melville Gwatkin, M.A., Emmanuel	1891
Expl. Physics, J. J. Thomson, M.A., Trin....	1884
Fine Art (Slade), C. Waldstein, LITT.D., King's	1895
Geology (Woodwardian), T. McK. Hughes, M.A., Clare.	1873
Greek (Reg.), R. C. Jebb, LITT.D., M.P., Trinity	1889
Hebrew, A. F. Kirkpatrick, D.D., Trinity ...	1882
Latin, J. E. B. Mayor, M.A., St. John's	1872
Law (Down.), F. W. Maitland, LL.D., Down.	1888
International Law, J. Westlake, LL.D., Trin.	1888
Mathematics (Lucasian), Sir George Gabriel Stokes, Bart., M.A., F.R.S., Pembroke	1849
Mechanism and Applied Mechanics, J. A. Ewing, M.A., Trinity	1890
Medicine (Downing), J. B. Bradbury, M.D., Down.	1894
Mineralogy, W. J. Lewis, M.A., Trinity	1881
Modern History, Lord Acton, M.A., Trin. ...	1895
Moral Philos., H. Sidgwick, LITT.D., Trin...	1883
Music, Charles V. Stanford, MUS.D., Trin....	1887
Natural Philosophy (Jacksonian), James Dewar, M.A., Peterhouse	1875
Pathology, G. S. Woodhead, M.A., Trin. H...	1899
Physic (Regius), T. C. Allbutt, M.D., Caius...	1892
Physiology, Sir M. Foster, M.A., Trinity...	1883
Pol. Econ., Alfred Marshall, M.A., St. John's	1884
Sadlerian, A. R. Forsyth, SC.D., Trin.	1895
Sanskrit, E. B. Cowell, M.A., Corpus	1867
Surgery (vacant).	
Zoology, &c., Alfred Newton, M.A., Magdalene	1866

	Elect.
Hulsean Lect., A. J. Mason, D.D., Jes.	1899
Lady Marg. Preacher, Ven. J. M. Wilson, M.A., St. John's	1899

READERS.

Classical Archæology, C. Waldstein, LITT.D., King's	1884
Comparative Philology, P. Giles, M.A., Emm.	1891
Botany, F. Darwin, M.A., Christ's	1888

	Elect.
English Law, C. S. Kenny, LL.D., Down	1888
Animal Morphology, A. Sedgwick, M.A., Trin.	1890
Talmudic, S. Schechter, LITT.D., Christ's	1892
Surgery, J. Griffiths, M.A., King's	1898
Geography, H. Y. Oldham, M.A., King's....	1898
Sandars in Bibliography, J. W. Clark, M.A., Trin.	1899

UNIVERSITY LECTURERS.

Comparative Philology, E. S. Roberts, M.A., Caius.
Sanskrit, R. A. Neil, M.A., Pemb.
Mathematics, Dr. Hobson, Chr.; J. J. Larmor, M.A., St. John's; R. T. Pendlebury, M.A., St. John's; H. F. Baker, M.A., St. John's; H. M. Macdonald, M.A., Cla.
Experimental Physics, W. N. Shaw, M.A., Emm.
Botany, A. C. Seward, M.A., St. John's; F. F. Blackman, M.A., St. John's.
Organic Chemistry, S. Ruhemann, M.A., Caius.
Advanced Morphology of Vertebrates, H. Gadow, M.A., King's.
Advanced Morphology of Invertebrates, A. E. Shipley, M.A., Christ's.
Advanced Physiology, Dr. Gaskell, Dr. Shore.
Physiological and Experimental Psychology, W. H. Rivers, M.A., St. John's.
Advanced Human Anatomy, Dr. Hill.
Medical Jurisprudence, Dr. Anningson.
Medicine, Dr. D. MacAlister.
Midwifery, A. F. Stabb, M.B., B.C., Down.
Surgery, G. E. Wherry, M.A., Down.
Histology, Dr. Langley.
Geology, J. E. Marr, M.A., St. John's.
History, O. Browning, M.A., King's; B. E. Hammond, M.A., Trin.; T. Thornely, M.A., Trin. Hall; J. B. Mullinger, M.A., St. John's.
Ancient History, L. Whibley, M.A., Pemb.
Moral Science, Dr. Keynes.
Harmony and Counterpoint, C. Wood, MUS.D. Caius.
French, E. G. W. Braunholtz, M.A., King's.
German, K. H. Breul, LITT.D., King's.
Persian, E. G. Browne, M.A., Pemb.
Palæography, J. R. Harris, M.A., Clare.
Aramaic, R. H. Kennett, M.A., Queens'.

Founded.	COLLEGES.	HEADS.	Elected.	Gross income of Coll.	Under-Grads.	Members of the Senate.	Members on the Boards.
				£			
1473	Catharine	Charles Kirkby Robinson, D.D., Master	1861	5,650	72	101	229
1505	Christ's	John Peile, LITT.D., Master	1887	13,600	157	358	719
1326	Clare	Edward Atkinson, D.D., Master	1856	14,834	181	285	576
1352	Corpus Christi	Edward Henry Perowne, D.D., Master	1879	8,684	69	260	404
1800	Downing	Alex Hill, M.D., Master	1888	5,852	54	103	221
1584	Emmanuel	William Chawner, M.A., Master	1895	13,165	178	363	745
1348	Gonville & Caius	Norman Macleod Ferrers, D.D., Master	1880	24,044	193	413	884
1496	Jesus	Henry Arthur Morgan, D.D., Master	1885	11,151	116	219	431
1441	King's	Augustus Austen Leigh, M.A., Provost	1889	32,815	140	301	675
1519	Magdalene	Hon. and Rev. Latimer Neville, M.A., Master	1853	4,069	58	127	223
1347	Pembroke	Charles Edward Searle, D.D., Master	1880	11,541	203	313	801
1257	Peterhouse	James Porter, D.D., Master	1876	7,519	61	203	315
1448	Queens'	Herbert Edward Ryle, D.D., President	1896	5,742	99	143	317
1595	Sidney-Sussex	Charles Smith, M.A., Master	1890	10,248	69	133	291
1511	St. John's	Charles Taylor, D.D., Master	1881	36,643	255	994	1,563
1546	Trinity	Henry Montagu Butler, D.D., Master	1886	72,130	653	2,162	3,638
1350	Trinity Hall	Henry Latham, M.A., Master	1888	9,923	206	232	636
	HOSTELS.						
1882	Selwyn College	A. F. Kirkpatrick, D.D., Master	1898		99	53	275
1869	Non-Coll. Stdnts.	Tristram Fredk. Croft Huddleston, M.A., Censor	1890		113	18	176
		Members of Senate not on College Boards.				209	209
		Total (Cambridge Calendar, 1898)...			6,995	3,016	13,413

English, I. Gollancz, M.A., *Christ's.*
Chemical Physiology, F. G. Hopkins.
Physical Anthropology, W.L.H.Duckworth,M.A.,*Jes.*
Gilbey Lecturer in Agriculture, Sir Ernest Clarke, M.A., *St. John's.*
Hausa Lecturer, C. H. Robinson, M.A., *Trin.*

SIR ROBERT REDE'S LECTURER.
Prof. A. Cornu, Professeur de Physique à l'École Polytechnique, Paris.

AFFILIATED COLLEGES.
Lampeter, St. David's 1882
Sheffield, Firth College 1886
Aberystwith, Univ. College of Wales 1892
Nottingham, Univ. College 1894
Ware, St. Edmund's College... 1895

AFFILIATED UNIVERSITIES.
New Zealand, 1886; Adelaide, 1891 : Cape of Good Hope, 1892; Calcutta, 1895; Allahabad, 1895; Bombay, 1896; Punjab, 1896; Toronto,1896.

MATRICULATIONS.
1889-90	1,027	1894-95	918
1890-91	952	1895-96	935
1891-92	934	1896-97	887
1892-93	941	1897-98	931
1893-94	935	1898-99	946

UNIVERSITY SCHOLARSHIPS, 1898-99.
Abbott, W. S. Ostle, *Jes.*; W. H. Smith, *Jes.* (equal).
Barnes, A. P. Thompson, *Pemb.*
Battie, J. Toplis, *Trin.*
Bell, R. Morrice, *Trin.*; E. A. Edghill, *King's.*
Browne (Sir Wm.), A. E. A. W. Smyth, *Trin.*
Clerk Maxwell, J. S. E. Townsend, B.A., *Trin.*
Craven, A. E. A. W. Smyth, *Trin.*
Crosse, C. E. Garrad, *Jes.*; W. Outram, B.A., *Pemb.*
Davies, A. D. Nightingale, *Trin.*
Harkness, H. H. Thomas, *Sid.*
Lightfoot (not awarded).
Pitt, J. A. Nairn, *Trin.*
Porson, J. F. Dobson, *Trin.*
Stewart of Rannoch, C.T. Carr, *Trin.*; C. B. Tayler, *Corp.* (Classics); G.T. Shaw, *Gonv. & Cai.*; F. E. E. Harvey, Non-Coll.(Sacred Music); A. S. B. Jones, *Gonv. & Cai.*; C.R. Bull, *Cath.*; A. Hood, *Chr.* (Hebrew).
Tyrwhitt (Hebrew). No candidates.
Waddington, G. C. Armstrong, *Trin.*
Whewell, J. E. R. De Villiers, *St. John's*; H. M. Adler, *St. John's.*

UNIVERSITY STUDENTSHIPS, 1898-99.
Arnold Gerstenberg, C. F. G. Masterman, B.A., *Christ's.*
Balfour, J. Stanley Gardiner, M.A., *Gonv. & Cai.*
Craven, J. C. Lawson, B.A., *Pemb.*
Isaac Newton, G. W. Walker, B.A., *Trin.*
John Lucas Walker, W. Myers, M.A., *Gonv. & Cai.*; E. S. St. B. Sladen, M.A., *Gonv. & Cai.*
Prendergast, C. D. Edmonds, B.A., *Em.*

UNIVERSITY PRIZES, 1898-99.
Adam Smith, W. H. Austin, B.A., *Trin.*; G. W. Walker, B.A., *Trin.*

Adams, J. Larmor, M.A., *St. John's*; G. T. Walker, M.A., *Trin.*
Bhaunagar, A. C. Chatterjee, B.A., *King's.*
Browne (Sir Wm.) Medals, T. G. Johnson, *Jes.* (Greek Elegiacs); R. K. Gaye, *Trin.* (Greek Epigram); E. Harrison *Trin.* (Latin Epigrams); not awarded (Latin Ode.)
Burney, C. F. G. Masterman, B.A., *Christ's.*
Carus, C. E. Garrad, B.A., *Jes.*; R. R. Smith, *Selwyn.*
Chancellor's Medals : Classics, J. Toplis, B.A., *Trin.* English Verse, A. C. Pigou, *King's.* English Law (not awarded).
Cobden, S. J. Chapman, B.A., *Trin.*
Evans (not awarded.)
George Long (not awarded).
George Williams, T. B. Panther, *Jes.*
Hare (vacant).
Harness (no essays sent in).
Hebrew, C. H. Druitt, B.A., *Corp.*
Hebrew Mason, T. H. Hennessy, B.A., *Trin.*
Hulsean (not awarded).
Jeremie, C. T. Wood, B.A., *Pemb.*; C. H. Druitt, B.A., *Corp.*
Kaye (not awarded.)
Le Bas (no essays sent in).
Maitland, R. A. Thomas, B.A., *Trin. Hall.*
Members, F. A. C. Morrison, B.A., *Jesus.* (English Essay) ; not awarded (Latin do.).
Norrisian, E. H. Askwith, M.A., *Trin.*
Porson, J. E. C. Jukes, *Pemb.*
Powis (Medal) (not awarded.)
Prince Consort, J. H. Clapham, B.A., *King's.*
Scholefield (not awarded).
Seatonian, G. W. Rowntree, M.A., *Cla.*
Sedgwick (not awarded).
See.ey (Medal) (no essay sent in).
Smith, E. W. Barnes, B.A., *Trin.*; W. A. Houston, B.A., *St. John's.*
Thirlwall (no essay sent in).
Tyson (not awarded).
Walsingham (Medal), J. Graham Kerr, B.A., *Christ's.*
Winchester, C. R. Buxton, B.A., *Trin.*; V. M. Ferrers, B.A., *Trin.*, H. W. Haworth, *Trin. Hall* (equal).
Yorke, R. C. Maclaurin, B.A., *St.*

SENIOR WRANGLER.
W. H. Austin, *Trin.*

UNIVERSITY RECEIPTS AND EXPENDITURE.
Receipts for the year 1898.
Receipts, 1898 .... £44,139 14 10

Expenditure for the year 1898.
Total payments	£41,619	19	2
Balance due from chest. 1897	1,032	14	7
Balance due to chest, 1898	1,487	1	1
	£44,139	14	10

University of London (£17,460)* 1836.
Burlington Gardens, W.

Chancellor, The Rt. Hon. Earl of Kimberley, K.G, D.C.L.
Vice-Chancellor, Sir Henry Enfield Roscoe, D.C.L.
The Senate, Visct. Llandaff, Q.C. ; Lord Acton ; Lord Lister ; J. Anstie, Q.C. ; Rt. Hon. A. J. Balfour, M.P. ; Rt. Hon. J. Bryce, M.P. ; E. H. Busk ; W. J. Collins ; Hon. Sir H. H. Cozens-Hardy ; Rt. Hon. Sir M. E. Grant Duff, G.C.S.I. ; Sir J. G. Fitch ; Prof. G. C. Foster ; Rt. Hon. Sir E. Fry ; Rt. Hon. G. J. Goschen, M.P. ; V. A. H. Horsley ; Prof. R. C. Jebb ; W. Leaf ; Rt. Hon. Sir J. Lubbock ; Sir P. Magnus ; A. Milman ; J. F. Moulton, Q.C., M.P. ; T. B. Napier ; T.S.Osler ; Sir J.Paget, Bt.; Sir C.H.H. Parry ; J. F. Payne ; P. H. Pye-Smith ; Sir A. K. Rollit, M.P. ; E. J. Routh ; Prof. A. W. Rücker ; Prof. T.E.Thorpe ; Prof.W.A. Tilden ; Prof. S. H. Vines ; Prof. W. F. R. Weldon ; Sir S. Wilks, Bart. ; Prof. A. W. Williamson.

* The amounts named in this list are the sums nominally voted by Parliament for the current year.

Representative n Parliament, Right Hon. Sir John Lubbock, Bart., D.C.L.

Representative on Medical Council, Philip Henry Pye-Smith, M.D., F.R.S.

Registrar, F. V. Dickins, M.B. £942

Assist. do. and Librarian, H. F. Heath, PH.D. £557

Clerk to Senate, Alfred Milnes, M.A. £429

Assistant do., Edwin Brewer £319

Chairman of Convocation, E. H. Busk, M.A.

Clerk of do., Henry E. Allen, LL.B. £250

EXAMINERS.

Anatomy, G. D. Thane; A. H. Young, M.B., each £150

Botany and Vegetable Physiology, F.W. Oliver, D.SC.; J. W. H. Trail, M.A., F.R.S. .... each £135

Chemistry, Percy F. Frankland, PH.D., F.R.S.; Wm. Ramsay, LL.D., F.R.S. .... each £240

Common Law and Evidence, Hugh Fraser, LL.D.; W. Blake Odgers, LL.D., Q.C. .... each £50

Comparative Anatomy & Zoology, F. E. Beddard, M.A., F.R.S.; G. B. Howes, LL.D., F.R.S. .. each £120

Constitutional History of England, S. H. Leonard, B.C.L.; F. C. Montague, M.A. .... each £25

English Language, and Literature, J. W. Hales, M.A.; A. H. Napier, PH.D. .... each £150

Equity and Real and Personal Prop., E. J. Elgood, B.C.L.; T. Cyprian Williams, LL.B. ...... each £50

Experimental Philos., G. F. Fitzgerald, M.A., F.R.S.; Silvanus Thomson, D.SC., F.R.S. .... each £210

Forensic Med., J. D. Mann, M.D.; Thomas Stevenson, M.D. .... each £80

French Language and Lit., James Boïelle, B.A.; Frederick Spencer, PH.D. .... each £130

Geology and Physical Geog., Prof. Lapworth, F.R.S.; T. G. Bonney, D.SC., F.R.S. .... each £75

German, E. L. Milner-Barry, M.A.; A. W. Schüddekopf, PH.D. .... each £80

Greek, G. E. Marindin, M.A.; R. Y. Tyrrell, D.LITT. each £120

Hebrew Text of the Old Test., Greek Text of the New Test., Evidence of Christian Religion and Scripture History, Rev. C. F. Burney, M.A.; J. F. Stenning, M.A. .... each £50

History, S. R. Gardiner, D.C.L.; F. York Powell, M.A. .... each £100

Jurisprudence, Roman Law, &c., J. P. Bate, D.C.L.; E. Robertson, Q.C., LL.D., M.P. each £100

Latin, J. P. Postgate, LITT.D.; J. S. Reid, LL.D. each £50

Materia Medica, &c., D. J. Leech, M.D.; Sidney Phillips, M.D.

Mathematics and Nat. Phil., E. W. Hobson, D.SC., F.R.S.; Joseph Larmor, D.SC., F.R.S....each £200

Mental and Moral Science, S. Alexander, M.A.; G. F. Stout, M.A. .... each £120

Mental Physiology, T. Claye Shaw, M.D.; S. Alexander, M.A. .... each £25

Music, C. H. Lloyd, MUS.DOC.; Sir Walter Parratt, MUS.DOC. .... each £50

Obstetric Medicine, Peter Horrocks, M.D.; G. Ernest Herman, M.A. .... each £105

Physiology, J. G. M'Kendrick, M.A., F.R.S.; E. A. Schäfer, F.R.S. .... each £140

Political Economy, C. F. Bastable, M.A.; W. A. S. Hewins, M.A. .... each £50

Practice of Medicine, W. H. Allchin, M.D.; Frederick Taylor, M.D. .... each £210

State Medicine, Edward Seaton, M.D.; Arthur Newsholme, M.D. .... each £30

Surgery, W. Anderson, F.R.C.S.; W. W. Cheyne, M.B. .... each £200

Teaching (Art, Theory and History of), F. Storr, B.A.; James Sully, LL.D. .... each £25

UNIVERSITY COLLEGE, Gower St., W.C., 1826.

President, Rt. Hon. Lord Reay, G.C.S.I., LL.D.

Vice-Pres., Rt. Hon. Sir U. J. K. Shuttleworth, Bt.; M.P.

Treasurer, W. Arthur Sharpe.

Secretary, J. M. Horsburgh, M.A.

Cashier, Walter Brown.

Lady Superintendent, Miss Rosa Morison.

PROFESSORS.

Faculties of Arts and Laws, and of Science.

Ancient and Modern History, F. C. Montague, M.A.

Arabic, S. A. Strong, M.A.

Archæology (Yates), E. A. Gardner, M.A.

Architecture, T. Roger Smith, F.R.I.B.A.

Botany (Quain), F. W. Oliver, D.SC.

Burmese, R. F. St. A. St. John, M.A.

Chemistry, &c., William Ramsay, LL.D., F.R.S.

Civil Engin. & Survey., L. F. Vernon-Harcourt, M.A.

Comparative Philology, J. P. Postgate, LITT.D.

Constitutional Law & Hist., A. T. Carter, M.A.

Drawing, Painting, and Sculpt. (Slade), F. Brown.

Elec. Eng. (Pender), J. A. Fleming, D.SC., F.R.S.

Egyptology (Edwards), W. M. F. Petrie, D.C.L.

English Lang. and Lit. (Quain), W. P. Ker, LL.D.

Fine Arts (Slade), Frederick Brown.

French, Henri Lallemand, B. ès SC.

Geology & Mineral., Rev. T. G. Bonney, D.SC., F.R.S.

German, R. Priebsch, PH.D.

Greek, J. A. Platt, M.A.

Gujerati, S. A. Kapadia, M.D.

Hebrew (Goldsmid), S. Schechter, LITT.D.

Hindustani, J. F. Blumhardt, M.A.

History, F. C. Montague, M.A.

Hygiene, &c., W. H. Corfield, M.D.

Italian, A. J. Butler, M.A.

Indian Law and Marathi, J. W. Neill.

Jurisprudence, J. Pawley Bate, LL.D.

Latin, A. E. Housman, M.A.

Law (Quain), Augustine Birrell, Q.C., M.P.

Pure Mathematics, M. J. M. Hill, D.SC., F.R.S.

Applied Mathematics, K. Pearson, M.A., F.R.S.

Mechanical Engineering, T. H. Beare, B.SC., M.I.C.E.

Pali and Buddhist Lit., T. W. Rhys Davids, LL.D.

Pathological Chemistry, V. Harley, M.D.

Pathology, Sidney Martin, M.D., F.R.S.

Persian, E. Denison Ross, PH.D.

Philosophy of Mind, &c. (Grote), J. Sully, LL.D.

Physics (Quain), H. L. Callendar, M.A., F.R.S.

Physiology (Jodrell), E. H. Starling, M.D., F.R.S.

Political Economy, H. S. Foxwell, M.A.

Roman Law, A. F. Murison, LL.D.

Sanskrit, Cecil Bendall, M.A.

Tamil, R. W. Frazer, LL.B.

Zoology (Jodrell), E. A. Minchin, M.A.

Faculty of Medicine.

Anatomy, George Dancer Thane.

Botany, F. W. Oliver, D.SC.

Chemistry, &c., W. Ramsay, LL.D., F.R.S.

Clinical Dental Surgery, S. Spokes, M.R.C.S.

Clinical Medicine (Holme), S. Ringer, M.D.

Clinical Surgery (Holme), Chris. Heath, F.R.C.S.

Clinical Surgery, R. J. Godlee, F.R.C.S.

Hygiene and Public Health, W. H. Corfield, M.D.

Materia Medica, J. Rose Bradford, M.D., F.R.S.

Medical Jurisprudence and Clinical Medicine, G. V. Poore, M.D.

Mental Physiology, W. J. Mickle, M.D.

Obstetric Medicine, H. R. Spencer, F.R.C.P.

Operative Surgery, B. Pollard, F.R.C.S.

Ophthalmic Medicine, &c., John Tweedy, F.R.C.S.

Medicine, F. T. Roberts, M.D.; T. Barlow, M.D.

Pathology, Sidney Martin, M.D., F.R.S.

Physiology & Zoology (Jodrell), see above.

Practical Surgery, B. Pollard, F.R.C.S.; R. Johnson, F.R.C.S.
Surg. & Clinical Surg., A. E. Barker, F.R.C.S.

KING'S COLLEGE, Strand, W.C., 1828.

Principal of College, Rev. A. Robertson, D.D.
Vice-Principal & Chaplain, Rev. G. E. Newsom, M.A.
Vice-Principal, Ladies' Dept., Miss L. M. Faithfull.
Secretary, Walter Smith.
Librarian, F. W. Walton, M.A.

PROFESSORS.

Theological Faculty, The Principal, Rev. R. J. Knowling, D.D.; Rev. S. Leathes, D.D.; Rev. H. C. Shuttleworth, B.A.; Rev. W. E. Collins, M.A.; Rev. G. E. Newsom, M.A.
Classical Literature, G. C. W. Warr, M.A.
English Lang., John W. Hales, M.A.
Modern History, J. K. Laughton, M.A.
Mathematics, W. H. H. Hudson, M.A.
Natural and Experimental Philosophy, W. G. Adams, D.SC., F.R.S.
Law and Jurisprudence, J. Gault; H. J. H. Mackay, LL.B.; W. N. Hibbert, LL.D.; C. M. Neale.
Logic and Metaphysics, Rev. A. Caldecott, B.D.
Political Economy, W. A. S. Hewins, M.A.
Geography, Mineral., & Geology, H. G. Seeley, F.R.S.
Architecture (vacant).
Hebrew, Rev. Stanley Leathes, D.D.
Colloquial Arabic, Habib Anthony Salmoné.
Sanskrit and Persian, G. F. Nicoll, M.A.
Indian Jurisprudence, A. McMillan, M.A.
Chinese, Robert K. Douglas.
French, Victor Spiers, M.A.
Spanish, Ricardo Ramirez.
German, C. A. Buchheim, PH.D.
Italian, Napoleone Perini.
Vocal Music, J. E. Vernham.
Geometrical Drawing, F. E. Hulme, F.S.A.
Mechanical Engineering and Workshops, D. S. Capper, M.A.
Metallurgy, A. K. Huntingdon, M.I.M.E.
Civil Engineering, H. Robinson, M.INST.C.E.
Electrical Engineering, E. Wilson.
Fine Art, A. W. Holden.
Commerce, James Gault.

Medical School.

Anatomy, A. W. Hughes, M.B., *Dean.*
Anæsthetics, J. F. W. Silk, M.D.
Aural Surgery, Urban Pritchard, M.D.
Bacteriology, E. M. Crookshank, M.B.
Botany, W. B. Bottomley, B.A.
Chemistry, J. M. Thomson, F.R.S.
Clinical Medicine, John Curnow, M.D.
Clinical Surgery, W. Rose, F.R.C.S.
Dental Surgery, A. S. Underwood; F.R.C.S.
Diseases of the Skin, A. Whitfield, M.D.
Forensic Medicine, W. R. Smith, M.D.
Hygiene, W. J. R. Simpson, M.D.
Materia Medica, N. I. C. Tirard, M.D.
Medicine, Isaac Burney Yeo, M.D.
Midwifery, T. C. Hayes, M.D.; J. Phillips, M.D.
Neuro-Pathology, David Ferrier, M.D., F.R.S.
Ophthalmology, M. M. McHardy, F.R.C.S.
Pathological Anatomy, N. Dalton, M.D.
Physiology, Dr. W. D. Halliburton, F.R.S.
Psychological Medicine, E. W. White, M.B.
Surgery, W. W. Cheyne, F.R.S.
　　,, *Operative*, A. Carless, M.S.

Dean, Civil Service Dept., W. Bragington, M.A.

State Medicine Laboratory, W. R. Smith, M.D.

University of Durham, 1831.

TERMS (1900).—*Epiphany*, Jan. 9 to March 12. *Easter*, April 28 to June 19. *Mich.*, Oct. 9 to Dec. 11.
Governors, The Dean and Chapter of Durham.
Warden, Very Rev. the Dean of Durham.
Sub-Warden, Rev. Alfred Plummer, D.D.

PROFESSORS.

Divinity & Eccles. Hist., Rev. A. S. Farrar, D.D.
Greek and Classical Lit., Rev. H. Kynaston, D.D.
Mathematics, R. A. Sampson, M.A.
Hebrew, Ven. H. W. Watkins, D.D.
Medicine, G. H. Philipson, M.D.
Surgery (vacant).
Physiology, T. Oliver, M.D.
Anatomy, R. Howden, M.B.
Comparative Pathology, G. R. Murray, M.D.
Music, P. Armes, MUS.D.
Tutors, Rev. A. Plummer, D.D.; F. B. Jevons, D.LITT.; Rev. Dawson Walker, M.A.
Registrar, W. K. Hilton, M.A.
[*Affiliated Colleges*—Codrington, Barbados; Fourah Bay, Sierra Leone.]

UNIVERSITY COLLEGE.

Master, Rev. A. Plummer, D.D.
Censor and Bursar, W. K. Hilton, M.A.

HATFIELD HALL.

Principal, F. B. Jevons, D.LITT.
Bursar, Arthur Robinson, B.C.L.

COLLEGE OF MEDICINE.

Newcastle. 1832.

President, George Hare Philipson, D.C.L.
Registrar, Frederick Page, M.D.
Treasurer, William Christopher Arnison, M D.
Secretary, Robert Howden, M.B.

DURHAM COLLEGE OF SCIENCE,

Newcastle, 1871.

President, Very Rev. the Dean of Durham.
Principal, Rev. H. P. Gurney, D.C.L.
Secretary, F. H. Pruen.

PROFESSORS.

Mathematics, The Principal; C. M. Jessop, M.A.
Physics, H. Stroud, D.SC.
Chemistry, P. Phillips Bedson, D.SC.
Geology, G. A. Lebour, M.A.
Natural History, G. S. Brady, LL.D., F.R.S.
Botany, M. C. Potter, M.A.
Classics, J. W. Duff, M.A.
English Language and Literature, Charles E. Vaughan, M.A.
Agriculture and Forestry, Thomas H. Middleton, B.SC.
Engineering and Naval Architecture, R. L. Weighton, M.A.
Mining, Henry Louis, M.A.
Normal Education, Mark R. Wright, M.A.
Head master, School of Art, R. G. Hatton.

The Victoria University.

Manchester, 1880.

TERMS (1899).—*Mich.*, Oct. 3 to Dec. 20.
　　(1900).—*Lent*, Jan. 9 to March 27.
　　Easter, April 17 to June 30.
Chancellor, Earl Spencer, K.G., LL.D.
Vice-Chancellor, N. Bodington, LITT.D.
Treasurer, Alfred Neild.
Registrar, Alfred Hughes, M.A.
Chairm. of Board of Studies, T. F. Tout, M.A.
Deputy Chairman, Alfred Hopkinson, M.A., Q.C.
Chairman of Convocation, A. Smithells, B.SC.
Clerk of Convocation, A. E. Steinthal, M.A.

COLLEGES OF THE UNIVERSITY—Owens College, Manchester; University College, Liverpool; Yorkshire College, Leeds.

I.—OWENS COLLEGE, Manchester. 1851.

President, The Duke of Devonshire, K.G., LL.D.
Principal, Alfred Hopkinson, Q.C.
Registrar, Sydney Chaffers.

PROFESSORS.
Arts, Science, and Law Department.
Greek & Comp. Philology, J. Strachan, M.A.
Latin & Greek Testament, A. S. Wilkins, LL.D.
English Language, T. N. Toller, M.A.
French, Victor Kastner, B. ès L.
German, Arwid Johannson, M.A.
History, T. F. Tout, M.A.
Logic & Moral Philosophy, S. Alexander, M.A.
Political Economy, A. W. Flux, M.A.
Law, W. A. Copinger, LL.D.; J. S. Beaton, M.A.; The Principal.
Education, H L. Withers, M.A.
Mathematics, Horace Lamb, LL.D., F.R.S.
Physics, A. Schuster, PH.D., F.R.S.; T. H. Core, M.A.
Engineering, O. Reynolds, LL.D., F.R.S.
Chemistry & Metallurgy, H. B. Dixon, M.A., F.R.S.
Organic Chemistry, W. H. Perkin, PH.D., F.R.S.
Zoology, S. J. Hickson, D.SC., F.R.S.
Botany, F. E. Weiss, B.SC.
Geology, W. B. Dawkins, M.A., F.R.S.
Physiology, W. Stirling, M.D.

DAY TRAINING COLLEGE (for Men and Women).
Master of Method, H. T. Mark, B.A. (*acting*).
Mistress of Method, Miss C. I. Dodd.

Medical Department.
Anatomy, A. H. Young, M.B., F.R.C.S., *Dean*.
Physiology, Biology and Zoology, Chemistry, Organic Chemistry, Botany, see Arts Department.
Medicine, J. Dreschfeld, M.D.
Surgery (*Systematic*), T. Jones, F.R.C.S.
      "   (*Clinical*), W. Whitehead, F.R.C.S.E.
Pathology, A. Sheridan Delépine, M.B.
Obstetrics & Gynæcology, W. J. Sinclair, M.D.
Medical Jurisprudence, J. Dixon Mann, M.D.

Department for Women.
(29A Dover Street.)
The Professors and Lecturers of the College.
Tutor, Miss Edith C. Wilson.
Assistant do., Miss Alice M. Cooke, M.A.

Department of Evening Classes.
The Professors and Lecturers of the College, and some additional Lecturers.

II.—THE YORKSHIRE COLLEGE, Leeds, 1874.
President, The Marquess of Ripon, K.G.
Principal, N. Bodington, LITT.D.
Dean of Dept. of Medicine, T. Scattergood, M.R.C.S.
Registrar and Secretary, W. F. Husband, LL.B.

PROFESSORS.
Department of Science, Technology and Arts.
Mathematics, L. J. Rogers, M.A.
Physics, W. Stroud, D.SC.
Chemistry, Arthur Smithells, B.SC.
Mining, E H. Liveing, A.R.S.M.
Biology, L. C. Miall, F.R.S.
Engineering, John Goodman, M.I.M.E.
Greek, N. Bodington, LITT.D.
History, Arthur J. Grant, M.A.
French, P. H. M. du Gillon.
Teutonic Languages, A. W. Schüddekopf, PH.D.
Textile Industries, Roberts Beaumont.
Dyeing, J. J. Hummel, F.I.C.
Education, J. Welton, M.A.
Leather Industries, H. R. Procter, F.I.C.
Agriculture, J. R. Campbell, B.SC.

Medical Department.
Medicine, A. G. Barrs, M.D.
Surgery, E. Ward, M.B.
Anatomy, T. Wardrop Griffith, M.D.
Physiology and Histology, De Burgh Birch, M.D.
Pathology, E. F. Trevelyan. M.D.
Midwifery, Charles J. Wright, M.R.C.S.
Materia Medica, Pharmacology, Therapeutics, C. M. Chadwick, M.D.
Hygiene and Public Health, R. N. Hartley, M.B.

III.—UNIVERSITY COLLEGE, Liverpool, 1881.
President, Rt. Hon. the Earl of Derby, K.G.
Principal, Richard T. Grazebrook, M.A., F.R.S.
Registrar, Chevalier E. Londini, D.C.L.

PROFESSORS.
Faculties of Art, Science and Law.
Greek, Gilbert A. Davies, M.A.
Latin, Herbert A. Strong, LL.D.
Teutonic Languages, Kuno Meyer, PH.D.
Modern Literature, Walter Raleigh, M.A.
Economic Science, E. G. K. Gonner, M.A.
History, J. M. Mackay, M.A.
Natural Philosophy, The Principal.
Philosophy, John MacCunn, LL.D.
Mathematics, F. S. Carey, M.A.
Physics, Prof. O. J. Lodge, D.SC., F.R.S.
Engineering, H. S. Hele Shaw, LL.D., F.R.S.
Law, G. H. Emmott, LL.M.
Architecture, F. M. Simpson.
Chemistry, James Campbell Brown, D.SC.
Natural History, William A. Herdman, D.SC., F.E.S.
Botany, R. J. Harvey Gibson, M.A.
Education, W. H. Woodward, M.A.

Faculty of Medicine.
Anatomy, A. Melville Paterson, M.D. (*Dean*).
Medicine, T. Robinson Glynn, M.D.
Surgery, Rushton Parker, F.R.C.S.
Pathology, Robert Boyce, M B.
Physiology, C. S. Sherrington, M.D., F.R.S.
Midwifery and Gynæcology, W. Briggs, M.D.
Materia Medica, W. Carter, LL.B., M.D.
Medical Jurisprudence, F. T. Paul, F.R.C.S.
Public Health, E. W. Hope, M.D.

GRESHAM COLLEGE, Basinghall St., E.C.
Clerk to the Joint Gresham Committee, Mercers' Hall, London, E.C., John Watney.

Provincial Colleges.
BIRMINGHAM—MASON UNIVERSITY COLLEGE. 1875.
Chairman of Council, Alderman F. C. Clayton, J.P.
Principal, R. S. Heath, D.SC.
Librarian, W. H. Cope.
Secretary and Registrar, G. H. Morley.

PROFESSORS.
Faculties of Arts and Science.
Mathematics, The Principal.
Physics, J. H. Poynting, D.SC., F.R.S.
Chemistry & Metallurgy, P. F. Frankland, PH.D., F.R.S.
Zoology, T. W. Bridge, D.SC.
Botany, W. Hillhouse, M.A.
Physiology, E. W. Wace Carlier, M.D.
Geology & Physiography, C. Lapworth, LL.D., F.R.S.; W. W. Watts, M.A.
Civil, Mech., & Electr. Eng., F. W. Burstall, M.A.
Greek and Latin, E. A. Sonnenschein, M.A.
English Lang. and Lit., W. Macneile Dixon, LITT.D.
Mental and Moral Philosophy, and Political Economy, J. H. Muirhead, M.A.
French and Italian, Clovis Bévenot, M.A.
German, Hermann G. Fiedler, PH.D.
Brewing, Adrian J. Brown, F.I.C.

Queen's Faculty of Medicine.

Dean, B. C. A. Windle, M.D.
Sub-Dean, G. Barling, F.R.C.S.
Medicine, R. Saundby, M.D. ; A. H. Carter, M.D.
Surgery, Bennett May, F.R.C.S.; G. Barling, F.R.C.S.
Anatomy, B. C. A. Windle, D.SC.
Elementary Biology, T. W. Bridge, SC.D.
Therapeutics, A. Foxwell, M.D.
Forensic Medicine, J. T. J. Morrison, F.S.C.S.
Hygiene and Public Health, A. Bostock Hill, M.D.
Midwifery, Edward Malins, M.D.
Gynæcology (vacant).
Pathology, R. F. C. Leith, F.R.C.P.
Lunacy & Mental Diseases, E. B. Whitcombe, M.R C.S.
Operative Surgery, Jordan Lloyd, F.R.C.S.
Ophthalmology. Priestley Smith, M.R.C.S.
Dental School, J. Humphreys, L.D.S.I. *Hon. Sec.*
Physiology, Chemistry & Physics, see above.

DAY TRAINING DEPARTMENT.

Head Mistress, Miss A. H. Joyce.
Master of Method (men), C. O. Tunstall, B.A.

BRISTOL—UNIVERSITY COLLEGE. 1876.

President, The Lord Bishop of Hereford.
Principal, C. Lloyd Morgan, F.R.S.
Lady Tutor, Miss M. R. Earle.
Secretary, James Rafter.

PROFESSORS.
Arts and Science.

Chemistry, Sydney Young, D.SC.
Mathematics, Frank R. Barrell, M.A.
Experimental Physiology, A. P. Chattock, M.I.E.E.
Engineering, John Ryan, D.SC.
Geology and Zoology, The Principal ; S. H. Reynolds, M.A.
Modern History & Eng. Lit., J. Rowley, M.A.
Greek & Latin, Reginald Fanshawe, M.A.

Medicine.

Medicine, E.M. Skerritt, M.D. (*Dean*) ; J.E. Shaw, M.B.
Surgery, Charles A. Morton, F.R.C.S.
Anatomy, Edward Fawcett M.B.
Physiology & Histology, A. F. Stanley Kent, M.A.
Midwifery, A. E. Aust Lawrence, M.D.
Pathology, J. Michell Clarke, M.D.

EXETER—ROYAL ALBERT MEMORIAL COLLEGE.

Principal, A. W. Clayden, M.A.
Secs., G. R. Shorto ; J. D. Montgomery.

NEWCASTLE-ON-TYNE—RUTHERFORD COLLEGE. 1878.

Chairman, Dr. V. H. Rutherford, M.A.
Principal, A. M. Ellis.
Hon. Sec. & Treas., H. Crawford Smith, J.P.

DURHAM COLLEGE OF SCIENCE.

(See University of Durham.)

NOTTINGHAM—UNIVERSITY COLL. 1880.

Principal, Rev. J. E. Symes, M.A.
Secretary, P. H. Stevenson.

PROFESSORS.

History, Literature, & Political Economy, The Principal.
Latin, Greek, and Philosophy, F. S. Granger, LITT.D.
French, E. Weekley, M.A.
Chemistry and Metallurgy, F. S. Kipping, D.SC., F.R.S.
Natural Sciences, J. W. Carr, M.A.
Mathematics & Physics, W. H. Heaton, M.A.
Engineering, William Robinson, M.E.

DAY TRAINING COLLEGE;

Normal Master, A. Henderson, B.A.
Normal Mistress, Miss Bird, LL.A.

READING COLLEGE.

Principal, H. J. Mackinder, M.A.
Registrar, F. H. Wright.

SHEFFIELD—UNIVERSITY COLLEGE, 1897.

Principal, W. M. Hicks, D.SC.
Registrar, Ensor Drury.

PROFESSORS.

Mathematics, A. H. Leahy, M.A.
Physics, The Principal.
Chemistry, W. C. Williams, B.SC.
Latin and Greek, W. C. F. Anderson, M.A.
History, H. W. Appleton, M.A.
English Lang. and Lit., G. C. Moore Smith, M.A.
Biology, A. Denny, F.L.S.
Pol. Econ. and Philosophy, G. H. Lloyd, B A.

Technical Department.

Civil and Mech. Engineering, W. Ripper, M.INST.C.E.
Mining do., F. W. Hardwick, M.A.
Metallurgy, J. O. Arnold.

Medical Department.

Anatomy, C. Addison, F.R.C.S.
Physiology, Practical Physiology, and Histology, C. F. Myers-Ward.
Medicine, W. Dyson, M.D.
Practical do., W. T. Cocking, M.D.
Surgery, R. J. Pye-Smith, F.R.C.S.
Pathology, Duncan Burgess, M.B.
Practical Bacteriology, Andrew Walker, M.D.
Diseases of Women, Richard Farell, F.R C.S.
Materia Medica, &c., W. T. Cocking, M.D.
Ophthalmology, Simeon Snell, F.R.C.S.E.
Public Health, John Robertson, M.D.

SOUTHAMPTON—HARTLEY COLLEGE.

Principal, R. Wallace Stewart, D.SC.
Clerk, D. Kiddle.

WALES.

The University of Wales, 1893.
"PRIFYSGOL CYMRU."

Chancellor, H.R.H. The Prince of Wales, K.G.
Vice-Chancellor, Principal Reichel, M.A.
Senior Dep. Chancellor, Dr. Isambard Owen.
Registrar, Ivor James (Brecon).

I. UNIVERSITY COLLEGE OF WALES—Aberystwyth (1872).

Principal, Thomas Francis Roberts, M.A.
Registrar, T. Mortimer Green.
Librarian, E. P. Jones, M.A.

PROFESSORS.

Greek, The Principal ; J. W. Marshall, M.A.
Latin & Comparative Philology, J. M. Angus, M.A.
Oriental, German, & Italian Languages, H. Ethé, PH.D.
English Lang. and Lit., C. H. Herford, LITT.D.
History and Pol. Econ., Edward Edwards, M.A.
Math., Nat. Philos., & Astron., R. W. Genese, M.A.
Logic and Philosophy, J Brough, LL.D.
Chemistry, H. Lloyd Snape, D.SC.
Physics, D. Morgan Lewis, M.A.
Biology and Geology, J. R. Ainsworth Davis, B.A.
Botany, J. H. Salter, D.SC.
Welsh, Edward Anwyl, M.A.
French, W. Borsdorf, PH.D.
Education, Foster Watson, M.A.

HALL OF RESIDENCE FOR WOMEN.

Lady Principal, Miss E. A. Carpenter.

II. UNIVERSITY COLLEGE OF NORTH WALES—Bangor (1884).

Principal, Henry R. Reichel, M.A.
Secretary and Registrar, J. Edward Lloyd, M.A.

PROFESSORS.

History, The Principal.
Greek, W. Rhys Roberts, M.A.
Latin, Edward V. Arnold, LITT.D.
French & German, Frederic Spencer, PH.D.
English Language & Literature, W. L. Jones, M.A.
Logic and Philosophy, James Gibson, M.A.

Mathematics, G. H. Bryan, sc.d., f.r.s.
Physics, Andrew Gray, ll.d., f.r.s.
Chemistry and Geology, James J. Dobbie, d.sc.
Botany, R.W. Phillips, d.sj.
Welsh, J. Morris Jones, m.a.
Agriculture, T. Winter, m.a.
Zoology, Philip J. White, m.b., f.r.s.e.

HALL OF RESIDENCE FOR WOMEN.
Lady Superintendent, Miss Mary Maude.

III UNIVERSITY COLL. OF SOUTH WALES AND MONMOUTHSHIRE—Cardiff (1883).
Principal, J. Viriamu Jones, m.a., f.r.s.
Registrar and Sec., J. Austin Jenkins, b.a.
PROFESSORS.
Greek, R. N. Burrows, m.a.
Latin, R. S. Conway, litt.d.
Logic and Philosophy, J. S. Mackenzie, m.a.
English Lang. & Literature, H. Littledale, m.a.
History, A. G. Little, m.a.
Mathematics and Astronomy, H. W. Lloyd Tanner, m.a., f.r.s.
Celtic, Thomas Powel, m.a.
Physics, The Principal and A. L. Selby, m.a.
Chemistry, C. M. Thompson, d.sc.
Engineering, A. C. Elliott, d.sc.
Biology, W. N. Parker, ph.d.
Mining, W. Galloway, m.e.
Anatomy, A. Francis Dixon, d.sc.
Physiology, J. B. Haycraft, m.d.

LAMPETER—ST. DAVID'S COLLEGE. 1828.
TERMS : 1899 - *Michaelmas*, 11 Oct to 13 Dec.
1900— *Lent*, 17 Jan. to 21 March.
Easter, 25 April to 29 June.
Principal, Rev. Ll. J. M. Bebb, m.a.
Steward, Prof. Williams.
PROFESSORS
Theology and Greek, The Principal.
Hebrew and Theology, Rev. E. T. Green, m.a.
Mathemat. and Physical Science, A. W. Scott, m.a.
Latin, Rev. G. W. Wade, m.a.
English and Philosophy, H. Walker, m.a.
Welsh and History, Rev. R. Williams, m.a.
[Lampeter possesses the exceptional privilege of conferring degrees, b.a. and b.d., and has been affiliated to Oxford and Cambridge.]

SCOTLAND.
University of St. Andrews, 1411
(£10,800).
Number of Students (1898-9), 254.
Winter Session (1899-1900), 10 Oct. to 21 March.
Summer Session (1900), 24 April to 29 June.
Chancellor, Duke of Argyll, k.g., k.t., ll.d.
Vice-Chancellor, Principal Donaldson, ll.d.
Rector, James Stuart, ll.d., m.p.
Principal, James Donaldson, ll.d.
Representative in Parliament, Sir William Overend Priestley, ll.d.
Registrar & Secretary, John E. Williams.

UNITED COLLEGE OF ST. SALVATOR AND ST. LEONARD.
Principal, James Donaldson, ll.d. 900
Clerk and Factor, Charles Stuart Grace, w.s.
PROFESSORS.
Humanity, Wallace M. Lindsay 96
Logic & Metaphysics, D. G. Ritchie, ll.d. 615
Greek, John Burnet, m.a. (*Dean : Arts*) 734
Mathematics, P. R. Scott Lang, m.a. £709
Moral Philosophy, Wm. A. Knight, ll.d. 615

Nat. Philosophy, Arthur Stanley Butler, m.a.£709
Natural History, W. C. McIntosh, m.d. 615
Medicine, J. Bell Pettigrew, m.d. 578
Chemistry, Thos. Purdie, b.sc. (*Dean : Science*) 615
Education, John M. D. Meiklejohn. m.a. 523
English Literature, Alexander Lawson, m.a. 555
Clerk and Factor, Charles Stuart Grace, w.s.

COLLEGE OF ST. MARY.
Principal, Very Rev. A. Stewart, d.d. (*Dean : Theology*.)
Secretary and Factor, Charles Stuart Grace, w.s.
PROFESSORS.
Primarius Prof. of Divinity, The Principal ...£633
Biblical Criticism, Rev. Allan Menzies, d.d. ... 534
Ecclesiastical History, Rev. John Herdess, d.d. 540
Oriental Languages, Rev. John Birrell, d.d. ... 615

UNIVERSITY COLLEGE, DUNDEE. 1880.
Principal, John Yule Mackay, m.d.
Secretary, R. N. Kerr, f.e.i.s.
PROFESSORS.
Mathematics, J. E. A. Steggall, m.a. £463
Natural Philosophy, J. P. Kuenen, ph.d. 432
Chemistry, James Walker, d.sc. 476
Natural History, D'Arcy W. Thompson, b.a. 430
Botany (*White's*), Patrick Geddes, f.r.s.e. ... 227
Anatomy (*Cox's*), J. Yule Mackay, m.d. 395
Physiology, E. W. Reid, b.a. (*Dean : Medicine*) 359
Engin. and Drawing, T. C. Fidler, m.i.c.e. ... 477
English Literature, Wm. S. M'Cormick, m.a.. 409
Modern Languages, H. Durlac. 50
Pathology, L. R. Sutherland 350
Surgery, D. MacEwan, m.d. 120

University of Glasgow, 1450 (£20,880).
Number of Students (1898-9), 1,953.
TERMS (1899-1900), 19 Oct. to 23 Mar. ; 900)
24 April to 1 July.
Chancellor, Earl of Stair, k.t.
Vice-Chancellor, The Principal.
Rector, Earl of Rosebery, k.g., k t.
Principal, Very Rev. Robt. H. Story, d.d ..*£1,100
Represent. in Parl., Rt. Hon. James A. Campbell, ll.d.
PROFESSORS.
Humanity, George G. Ramsay, ll.d. *£1,430
Greek, John S. Phillimore, m.a. *1,000
Civil Engineering & Mechanics, Archibald Barr, b.sc. 900
Logic and Rhetoric, Robert Adamson, ll.d. ... *800
Moral Philosophy, Henry Jones, ll.d. *1,000
Natural Philosophy, A. Gray, ll.d., f.r.s. .. *1,000
Mathematics, William Jack, ll.d. (*Dean : Arts*) *1,440
English Lang. & Lit., A. C. Bradley, m.a .. 900
History, Dudley J. Medley, m.a. 900
Astronomy, Ludwig Becker, ph.d. 600
Naval Architecture, J. Harvard Biles 800
Divinity, William Hastie, d.d. *554
Church History, James Cooper, d.d. *483
Biblical Criticism, W. Stewart, d.d. (*Dean : Divinity*) 625
Hebrew & Semitic Lang., Jas.Robertson,d.d. *700
Scots Law, A. Moody Stuart, ll.d. *800
Conveyancing, James Moir (*Dean : Law*)... 600
Materia Medica, Ralph Stockman, m.d., f.r.s. 700
Chemistry, John Ferguson, ll.d. 1,300
Surgery, William Macewen, m.d., f.r.s. 800
Practice of Medicine, Sir William T. Gairdner, k.c.b., m.d., f.r.s. *800
Midwifery, Murdoch Cameron, m.d.......... 700

* The sums appended to the various Chairs are those received in the year 1897-98 ; each of those marked
has an official residence in addition.

Anatomy, John Cleland, M.D., F.R.S. (*Dean:
  Medicine*) *£1,645
Natural History, John Young, M.D. (*Dean:
  Science*) 806
Botany, Frederick O. Bower, D.SC., F.R.S. 830
Physiology, J. G. McKendrick, M.D., F.R.S. .. 1,100
Forensic Medicine, John Glaister, M.D. 600
Clinical Surgery, Geo. Buchanan, M.D. 320
Clinical Medicine, T. McCall Anderson, M.D. .. 432
Pathology, Robert Muir, M.D. 1,100
Clerk of Senatus, Professor W. Stewart, D.D.
Assistant do., W. Innes Addison.
Keeper of Hunterian Mus., Prof. Young, M.D.
Curator of the Library, Prof. Dickson, D.D.
Librarian, James Lymburn.
Registrar of Gen. Council, Jas. Coutts, M.A.
Clerk to Gen. Council, Archibald Craig, LL.B.
Sec. to Univ. Court, A. E. Clapperton, B.L.

University of Aberdeen, 1494.

Number of Matriculated Students (1898-9). 808.
TERMS (1899), 16 Oct. to 22 Dec.; (1900) 8 Jan.
  to 16 March; 24 April to 6 July.
Chancellor, Duke of Richmond and Gordon, K.G. 1861
Rector, Lord Strathcona and Mount Royal... 1899
Vice-Chancellor and Principal, Sir William Duguid
  Geddes, LL.D. *£800
Represent. in Parl., Rt. Hon. J. A. Campbell, LL.D.
Registrar and Sec. of Univ. Court, R. Walker, M.A.
Secretary of the Senatus, Donaldson R. Thom, M.A.
Librarian, P. J. Anderson, LL.B.

PROFESSORS.

Greek, John Harrower, M.A. *£770
Humanity, Wm. M. Ramsay, D.C.L. *775
English, Herbert J. C. Grierson, M.A. 631
Logic & Metaphysics, Rev. W. L. Davidson, LL.D. 631
Mathematics, Rev. George Pirie, LL.D. *725
Moral Philosophy, Wm. Ritchie Sorley, M.A. .. 631
Natural Philosophy, Charles Niven, M.A., F.R.S. 916
Systematic Theol., Rev. Wm. P. Paterson, D.D. *388
Church History, Rev. Henry Cowan, D.D. .. *488
Biblical Criticism, Rev. Thomas Nicol, D.D. *415
Heb. & Sem. Lang., Rev. James Gilroy, B.D. 540
Law, John Dove Wilson, LL.D. 540
Physiology, John Alex. McWilliam, M.D. *811
Medicine, David White Finlay, M.D. 540
Chemistry, Fras. R. Japp, LL.D., F.R.S. *811
Anatomy, Robert William Reid, F.R.C.S. .. †1,300
Surgery, Alexander Ogston, C.M. 600
Materia Medica, John Theod. Cash, M.D., F.R.S. 631
Midwifery, William Stephenson, M.D. 540
Forensic Medicine, Matthew Hay, M.D. 540
Botany, James W. H. Trail, M.D., F.R.S. *745
Pathology, D. J. Hamilton, M.B., F.R.C.S.E. *811
Natural History, J. Arthur Thomson, M.A.... 700

University of Edinburgh, 1582.

(£25,870.)

Number of Students (1898-9), 2,846.
WINTER SESSION, Oct., 1899-March, 1900;
  SUMMER SESSION, May to July, 1900.
Chancellor, Rt. Hon. Arthur J. Balfour, M.P., D.C.L.
Rector, Marquess of Dufferin and Ava, K.P.
Vice-Chancellor and Principal, Sir William Muir,
  K.C.S.I., D.C.L.
Representative in Parliament, Sir William Overend
  Priestley, LL.D.
Sec. of Univ. Court, Rev. Professor Taylor, D.D.
Secretary of Senatus, Sir L. J. Grant, Bart., B.A.

Clerk to the Senatus and Secretary and Registrar of
  the General Council, Thomas Gilbert.
Librarian, Hugh A. Webster.

PROFESSORS.

Humanity, W. R. Hardie, M.A. £1,100
Greek, Samuel Henry Butcher, LL.D. 1,176
Mathematics, Geo. Chrystal, LL.D. (*Dean:
  Arts*) 1,343
Logic & Metaphysics, Andrew Seth Pringle
  Pattison, LL.D. 900
Moral Philosophy, James Seth 900
Natural Philos., Peter Guthrie Tait, D.SC. ... 1,028
Rhetoric & Eng. Lit., Geo. Saintsbury, M.A. . 900
Astronomy, Ralph Copeland 400
Agriculture & Rural Economy, Robt. Wallace. 600
Music, Frederick Niecks 621
Sanskrit & Comp. Philology, Julius Eggeling,
  PH.D. 600
Engineering, G. F. Armstrong, M.I.C.E., M.A. 800
Geology, James Geikie, LL.D. (*Dean: Science*) 830
Commercial and Political Economy and Mer-
  cantile Law, Joseph S. Nicholson, D.SC. ... 800
Education, Simon S. Laurie, LL.D. 700
Fine Art, G. Baldwin Brown, M.A. 600
Celtic Languages & Lit., D. Mackinnon, M.A. 600
Divinity, Robert Flint, D.D. 604
Ecclesiastical History, Malcolm Campbell
  Taylor, D.D. (*Divinity*) 443
Hebr. & Semitic Lang., Rev. A. R. S. Kennedy 800
Biblical Criticism, John Patrick, D.D. ....
Public Law, Sir L. J. Grant, Bt. (*Dean: Law*) 650
Civil Law, James Mackintosh, B.A. 700
Constitut. Law & Hist., J. Kirkpatrick, LL.D. 600
History, Richard Lodge, M.A. 900
Scots Law, John Rankine, LL.D. 955
Conveyancing, John Philp Wood, W.S.......... 700
Materia Medica, Thomas Richard Fraser,
  M.D. (*Dean: Medicine*) 1,390
Forensic Med., Sir Hen. D. Littlejohn, M.D. . 800
Chemistry, Alexander Crum Brown, M.D. ... 1,828
Surgery, John Chiene, M.D. 1,209
Medicine, Sir T. Grainger Stewart, M.D. 1,058
Anatomy, Sir William Turner, M.B. 2,012
Pathology, William Smith Greenfield, M.D. . 1,482
Midwifery, Alexander R. Simpson, M.D. 875
Clinical Medicine, Drs. Sir T. G. Stewart, Thomas R.
  Fraser, W. S. Greenfield, Alexander R. Simpson.
Clinical Surgery, Thomas Annandale, M.D.... 823
Botany, Isaac Bayley Balfour, M.D. 1,515
Physiology, Edward A. Schäfer 1,734
Zoology, James Cossar Ewart. M.D. 1,615
Public Health, &c., C. Hunter Stewart, D.SC.... 600

IRELAND.

University of Dublin, 1591.

[Students in 1898, 1,090; TERMS, 1900:—*Hilary*,
  Jan. 10—March 25; *Trinity*, April 15—June 30;
  Michaelmas, Oct. 10—Dec. 17.]   Elected
Chancellor, Earl of Rosse, K.P., F.R.S 1885
Vice-Chancellor, Rt. Hon. D. H. Madden ... 1885
Represent. in Parl., Rt.Hon.E.H.Carson,Q.C. 1895
  „   Rt. Hon. W. E. H. Lecky, LL.D. 1896
Provost, Rev. George Salmon, D.D., F.R.S. ... 1888
Vice-Provost, Rev. J. W. Barlow, M.A......... 1899
Deans, A. Traill, M.D., and E. J. Gwynn, M.A. 1898
Registrar and Secretary to Senate, Rev. P.
  Mahaffy, D.D. 1899
Bursar, Rev. T. T. Gray, M.A. 1898
Senior Lecturer, B. Williamson, M.A. 1898
Auditor, Rev. R. M. Connor, D.D. 1898

* The sums appended to the various Chairs are the amounts received in the year 1897-98 ; each of those marked
* has an official residence in addition ; the salaries marked † are fixed on the understanding that the Professors
do not engage in private practice.

	Elected
Librarian, Rev. Thomas K. Abbott, B.D. ...	1887
Curator of Anatomical & Pathological Museum,	
H. W. Mackintosh, M.A.	1879

REGISTRARS.

Law School, Robert Russell, M.A.	1891
School of Physic, Hen. W. Mackintosh, M.A.	1879
School of Engineering, G. F. FitzGerald, M.A.	1886
School of Music, Rev. J. P. Mahaffy, MUS.D.	1896

PROFESSORS.

Divinity (Regius), Rev. John Gwynn, D.D....	1888
(Archbp. King's), Rev. J. H. Bernard, D.D.	
Pastoral Theol., Very Rev. H. H. Dickinson	1894
Law, Civil (Regius), H. B. Leech, LL.D.	1888
" *Feudal and English (Regius),* George	
Vaughan Hart, LL.D., Q.C.	1891
" *Crim. & Consti.,* J. S. Baxter	1899
History, Modern, John B. Bury, M.A.	1893
" *Eccles.,* Rev. Hugh J. Lawlor, D.D.	1898
" *Ancient,* Rev. J. P. Mahaffy, D.D....	
German, A. M. Selss, LL.D.	1866
Greek (Regius), J. B. Bury, M.A.	1899
Greek, Biblical, Rev. R. H. Charles, M.A. ...	1898
Hebrew, Rev. T. K. Abbott, M.A.	1879
Irish, Rev. J. E. H. Murphy, M.A.	1896
Latin, (vacant)	1898
Romance Languages, Robt. Atkinson, LL.D.	1867
Sanskrit, Robert Atkinson, LL.D.	1863
Royal Astronomer, Charles Joly, M.A.	1898
Mathm. (Erasmus Smith), W. S. Burnside, M.A.	1879
Natural Philosophy, F. A. Tarleton, LL.D....	1890
Natural & Experimental Philosophy (Erasmus	
Smith), George Francis FitzGerald, M.A....	1881
Oratory and Eng. Lit., Edw. Dowden, LL.D.	1867
Political Economy, C. F. Bastable, LL.D.	1882
Moral Philosophy, S. P. Johnstone, M.A. ...	1848
Anat. & Surg., Dan. Jno. Cunningham, M.D.	1883
University Anatomist, Charles B. Ball, M.A.	1895
Physics (Regius), Thomas Little, M.D.	1898
Surgery (Regius Prof.), Chas. B. Ball, M.CH.	1896
Botany, Edward Perceval Wright, M.D.	1869
Chemistry, J. Emerson Reynolds, M.D.	1875
Civil Engineering, Thos. Alexander, M.E. ...	1887
Geology & Mineralogy, John Joly, M.A.	1897
Music, Ebenezer Prout, MUS.D.	1894
Comp. Anat. & Zoology, H.W. Mackintosh, M.A.	1879
Public Orator, Robert T. Tyrrell, M.A.	1898

Royal University of Ireland, 1880.

Earlsfort Terrace, Dublin.

Visitor, Her Majesty THE QUEEN.
Chancellor, Marquess of Dufferin and Ava, K.P.
Vice-Chancellor, Lord Morris, LL.D.
Secretaries, Sir James C. Meredith, LL.D.; J. McGrath, LL.D.
Librarian, John E. Oram, M.A.
Curator, W. E. Adeney, D.SC.
Clerk of Convocation, Thomas J. Wall, LL.D.

FELLOWS AND EXAMINERS.

Classics, Rev. Henry Browne, M.A.; T. W. Dougan, M.A.; James MacMaster, M.A.; D'Arcy W. Thompson, M.A.; Charles H. Keene, M.A.; Rev. T. P. O'Nowlan, M.A.; P. Semple, M.A.
Modern Languages, E. Cadic; V. Steinberger, M.A.; W. F. Butler, M.A.; Katherine Hogan, M.A.; Mary Ryan, M.A.
English, George F. Savage-Armstrong, M.A.; Thomas Arnold, M.A.; Rev. Joseph Darlington, M.A.; S. I. MacMullan, M.A.; Mary T. Hayden, M.A.
History, W. J. Carbery, M.A.; Rev. R. J. Semple, M.A.
Mathematics, A. C. Dixon, M.A.; J. Purser, LL.D.; H. McWeeney, M.A.; J. J. Gibney, M.A.; W. A. Houston, M.A.

Natural Philosophy, Alexander Anderson, M.A.; J. Huston Stewart, B.A.; T. Preston, M.A.; J. A. McClelland, M.A.; W. B. Morton, M.A.
Mental and Moral Sciences, Rev. T. A. Finlay, M.A.; John Park, M.A.; W. Magennis, M.A.; Rev. George Woodburn, M.A.; P. J. Hogan, M.A.
Political Economy, C. F. Bastable, LL.D.; W. P. Coyne, M.A.
Chemistry, E. A. Letts, D.SC.; W. D. Donnan, M.A.; Hugh Ryan, M.A.
Natural Sciences, Robert O. Cunningham, M.D.; Marcus M. Hartog, D.SC.; George Sigerson, M.D.; Alexander J. Blaney, M.A.
Geology, Joseph P. O'Reilly, C.E.
Celtic, Rev. E. Hogand, D.LIT.; D. Hyde, LL.D.
Hebrew, Rev. R. H. F. Dickey, M.A.
Engineering, E. Townsend, D.SC.; A. Jack, M.A.
Music, J. Smith, MUS.D.; T. R. G. Joyé, MUS.D.
Law, J. Donaldson, M.A.; C. F. Doyle, M.A.

In the Faculty of Medicine.

Anatomy, Joseph P. Pye, M.D.; Joseph Symington, M.D.; A. E. I. Birmingham, M.D.
Physiology, J. J. Charles, M.D.; D. J. Coffey, M.B.
Medicine, J. I. Lynham, M.D.; J. F. O'Carroll, M.D.
Surgery, Patrick J. Hayes, M.D.; Sir W. Thornley Stoker, M.D.
Ophthalmic Surgery, Arthur W. Sandford, M.D.; Louis Werner, M.B.
Midwifery, J. W. Byers, M.D.; A. J. Smith, M.B.
Medical Jurisprudence, A. Roche, F.R.C.S.I.; C. Y. Pearson, M.D.
Materia Medica, F. J. B. Quinlan, M.D.; William Whitla, M.D.
Sanitary Science, Sir Charles Cameron, M.D.
Pathology, E. J. McWeeney, M.D.; J. Lorrain-Smith, M.D.
(This is the only University in Ireland in which all Degrees are open to Women.)

BELFAST—QUEEN'S COLLEGE, 1845.

President, Rev. Thomas Hamilton, D.D.
Registrar, John Purser, LL.D.
Bursar, William Wylie.

PROFESSORS.

Greek Language, Samuel Dill, M.A.
Latin Language, Thomas Wilson Dougan, M.A.
Mathematics, John Purser, LL.D.
Natural Philosophy, William Blair Morton, M.A.
Hist. and English Lit., Samuel J. MacMullan, M.A.
Logic and Metaphysics, John Park, D.LIT.
Chemistry, Edmund A. Letts, D.SC., F.R.S.E.
Natural History, R. O. Cunningham, M.D.
Modern Languages, Albert L. Meissner, PH.D.
Jurisprudence and Political Economy, W. Graham, M.A.
English Law, William N. Watts, LL.D.
Anatomy, Johnson Symington, M.D., F.R.S.E.
Physiology (Dunville), W. H. Thompson, F.R.C.S.
Medicine (vacant.)
Surgery, Thomas Sinclair, F.R.C.S.
Materia Medica, William Whitla, M.D.
Midwifery, John W. Byers, M.D.
Civil Engineering, Maurice F. Fitzgerald, B.A.
Agriculture, John F. Hodges, M.D.

CORK—QUEEN'S COLLEGE, 1845.

President, Sir Rowland Blennerhassett, Bart.
Bursar, Lt.-Col. W. R. Jenney (retired).
Registrar, Alexander Jack, M.A.
Librarian, W. F. T. Butler, M.A.

PROFESSORS.

Greek Language, Charles Haynes Keene, M.A.
Latin Language, Bunnell Lewis, M.A., F.S.A.
Mathematics, Arthur H. Anglin, M.A.
Natural Philosophy, William Bergin, M.A.
History & English Literature, G. F. Savage-Armstrong, LITT.D.

Mental and Social Science, Geo. J. Stokes, M.A.
Chemistry, A. E. Lixon, M.D.
Natural History, Marcus M. Hartog, D.SC.
Modern Languages, W. F. T. Butler, M.A.
English Law, R. W. Brereton Barry, B.A.
Anatomy and Physiology, J. J. Charles, M.D.
Medicine, W. E. Ashley Cummins, M.D.
Surgery, Stephen O'Sullivan, F.R.C.S.I.
Materia Medica, C. Yelverton Pearson, F.R.C.S.E.
Midwifery, Henry Corby, M.D.
Engineering, Alexander Jack, M.A.

GALWAY—QUEEN'S COLLEGE, 1845.

President, Alexander Anderson, M.A.
Registrar, E. Townsend, D.SC.
Bursar, J. A. Lynham, M.D.

PROFESSORS.

History, English Lit. & Mental Science, Wilbraham FitzJohn French, M.A.
Greek, D'Arcy W. Thompson, M.A.
Latin, Philip G. Sandford, M.A.
Mathematics, Alfred Cardew Dixon, SC.D.
Natural Philosophy, The President.
Chemistry, Alfred Senier, PH.D.
Natur. Hist., &c., R. J. Anderson, M.A., M.D.
Modern Languages, Valentine Steinberger, M.A.
Jurisprud. & Polit. Econ., C. F. Bastable, LL.D.
English Law, Wm. B. Campion, M.A.
Anatomy & Physiology, Joseph P. Pye, M.D.
Medicine, John I. Lynham, M.D.
Surgery, W. Westropp Brereton, L.R.C.S.I.
Materia Medica, Nicholas W. Colahan, M.D.
Midwifery, Richard John Kinkead, M.D.
Civil Engineering, Edward Townsend, D.SC.

Roman Catholic Colleges.

Supreme Governing Body, the Catholic Archbishops and Bishops: with a *Rectorial Council,* consisting of the Rector, and Heads of Colleges.
Rector, Right Rev. Monsignor Molloy, D.D.
The University now consists of the following six colleges :

ST. PATRICK'S COLLEGE (Maynooth).—*President,* Right Rev. Monsignor Gargan, D.D.
UNIVERSITY COLLEGE (St. Stephen's Green, Dublin).—*President,* Very Rev. Wm. Delany, S.J., LL.D.
UNIVERSITY COLLEGE (Blackrock).—*Superior,* Very Rev. Jules Botrel.
. PATRICK'S COLLEGE (Carlow).—*President,* Very Rev. J. Foley, D.D.
HOLY CROSS COLLEGE (Clonliffe).—*President,* Very Rev. Michael Walsh.
MEDICAL SCHOOL OF THE CATHOLIC UNIVERSITY (Cecilia Street, Dublin).— *Dean of the Faculty,* Sir C. J. Nixon, M.D., *Registrar,* A. Binningham, M.D.

Professional Education.

AGRICULTURE.

ASPATRIA AGRICULT. COLL., near Carlisle

President, Sir Wilfrid Lawson, Bart., M.P.
Vice-President, H. Howard, J.P.
Principal, J. Smith Hill, B.A. (*Botany & Zoology*).
Practical Agric. and Agric. Eng., H. F. Hill.
Chemistry and Bookkeeping, D. D. Williams.
Mathematics, J. P. Wilton, P.A.S.I.
Agricultural Law, The Principal.
Practical Surv., D. Burns, C.E.; J. P. Wilton, P.A.S.I.
Veterinary Science, H. Thompson, M.R.C.V.S.

CIRENCESTER ROYAL AGRICULT. COLL.

President, Duke of Richmond and Gordon, K.G.
Chairman of Governing Body, Earl of Ducie.
Principal, Rev. John B. McClellan, M.A.
Agriculture, E. Blundell.
Dairy Farming, E. Blundell ; A. Kay.
Estate Management & Forestry, R. Anderson, F.S.I.
Chemistry, E. Kinch, F.C.S.; W. James.
Geology, Botany, Bacteriology, & Natural Hist., T. T. Groom, D.SC.; G. S. West, B.A.
Physics and Mechanics, G. T. Locke, M.A.
Land Surv. & Prac. Engineering, G. Paton, C.E.
Veterin. Science, &c., H. A. Woodruff, M.R.C.V.F.
Building, F. W. Waller, F.R.I.B.A.
Agricultural Law, E. B. Haygarth.
Bookkeeping, G. Paton, C.E.
Architectural Drawing, C. Stolle.

COLONIAL COLLEGE, Hollesley Bay, Suffolk.

Resident Director, Robert Johnson.
Agricultural Science, &c., C. G. F. Thonger, M.B.A.C.
Practical Agriculture, George J. Goodwyn.
Nat. Hist. & Laboratory, C. M. Hutchinson, B.A.
Hygiene, Ambulance, &c., F. R. P.-Sims, M.R.C.S.
Engin., Surveying, &c., F. Dahne, A.R.I.G.A.
Veterinary Science, &c., R. G. Saunders, M.R.C.V.S.
Horticulture, J. Wolton.

DOWNTON—COLLEGE OF AGRICULTURE.

President, Prof. Wrightson, F.C.S.
Agriculture, The President; J. F. H. Wrightson, F.A.S.I.
Chemistry, J. M H. Munro, D.SC.
Veterinary Science, W. A. Edgar, *Vice-Pres.* R.C.V.S.
Estate Management Survey, C. E. Curtis.
Mathematics, Bookkeeping, and Building Construction, C. E. Curtis, B.A.

SOUTH EASTERN AGRIC. COLL., Wye, Kent

(Under the County Councils of Kent and Surrey).
Chairman, E. J. Halsey.
Clerk to the Governors, J.T. Welldon, B.A. (Ashford).
Principal, A. D. Hall, M.A.
Agriculture & Estate Management, F. B. Smith, F.S.I.
Chemistry, The Principal ; H. H. Cousins, M.A.
Botany, J. Percival, M.A.
Zoology & Economic Entomology, F.V. Theobald, M.A.
Surveying, Building, &c., T. J. Young, P.A.S.I.
Veterinary Science, J. Wortley Axe, M.R.C.V.S.
Dairy and Poultry Keeping, T. R. Robinson, F.S.I.

UCKFIELD AGRICULTURAL COLLEGE.

(East Sussex County Council.)
Principal and Prof. of Agriculture, W. J. Malden, A.S.I.
Agric. Sciences, S. A. Woodhead, B.SC.
Land Agency, Surveying, &c., R. E. C. Burder, P.A.S.I.
Veterinary Hygiene, H. Sessions, F.R.C.V.S.
Horticulture, W. Goaring, F.R.H.S.
Poultry Farming, B. Taylor.

WEST OF SCOTLAND AGRIC. COLL. (1899).

6o John St., Glasgow.
Chairman, Rev. John Gillespie, LL.D.
Secretary,
Agriculture, Robert Patrick Wright, F.R.S.C.
Senior Assistant, James Wood, M.A.

ARCHITECTURE.

The examination of Architects is conducted by the Royal Institute of British Architects in London and at various Provincial Centres. The diplomas granted are A.R.I.B.A., M.R.I.B.A., and F.R.I.B.A.

ARCHITECTURAL ASSOCIATION, 56 Great Marlborough St., W.

BIRMINGHAM, Municipal School of Art.—*Head Master*, Edward R. Taylor; *Sec.*, E. Preston Hytch.

DUBLIN, Metropolitan School of Art.—Cecil Orr, A.R.I.B.A.

GLASGOW, School of Art.—Wm. J. Anderson, A.R.I.B.A.

GLASGOW, Technical College.—See p. 256.

LEEDS, Yorkshire College.—See p. 257.

LIVERPOOL, School of Architecture and Applied Art.—Prof. F. M. Simpson.

MANCHESTER, Municipal School of Art. — R. Glazier, A.R.I.B.A.

NOTTINGHAM, University College.—See p. 258.

ROYAL ACADEMY SCHOOL, Burlington House, W. *Master*, R. Phené Spiers, F.R.I.B.A., F.S.A.

UNIVERSITY COLLEGE, London.—See p. 255.

ENGINEERING.

ROYAL INDIAN ENGINEERING COLLEGE, COOPERS HILL, STAINES, 1871.

President Col. J. W. Ottley, C.I.E., R.E.

Secretary, Lt.-Col. W. J. Boyes.

Bursar, J. P. Pasco, R.N.

Chaplain, Rev. H. Bowden Smith, M.A.

Medical Officer, H. E. Giffard.

PROFESSORS.

Engineering & Surveying Construction, A. W. Brightmore, D.SC.

Hydraulic Engineering, T. A. Hearson, M.I.C.E.

Assist. Prof. of Eng., A. H. Heath, A.M.I.C.E.

Drawing, Geometrical, A. Hicks.

Assist. do., and Freehand, C. B. McElwee.

Mathematics (Applied), G. M. Minchin, M.A., F.R.S.

Pure Mathematics, A. Lodge, M.A.

Chemistry, H McLeod, F.R.S.; F.E.Matthews, PH.D.

Do. Organic, A. H. Church, M.A., F R.S.

Analytical Chemist, F. W. Harbord, F.I.C.

Physics, W. N. Stocker, M.A.

Do. and Electrical Engineering, T. Shields, M.A.

Geology and Mineralogy, Prof. H. G. Seely, F.R.S.

Forestry, W. Schlich, PH.D., C.I.E.; W.R.Fisher, B.A.

Botany, C. A. Barber, M.A.

French, J. A. Perret. *German*, T. H. Dittel.

CRYSTAL PALACE COMPANY'S SCHOOL OF PRACTICAL ENGINEERING.—*Principal*, J. W. Wilson, A.M.INST.C.E.; *Vice-Princ.* M. Wilson, A.M.INST.C.E.

ELECTRICAL AND GENERAL ENGINEERING COLLEGE, 2 & 4, Penywern Road, Earl's Court. *President*, G. W. de Tunzelmann.

ELECTRICAL STANDARDIZING, TESTING AND TRAINING INSTITUTION, Faraday Ho., Charing Cross Rd., W.C. *Principal*, H. E. Harrison, B.SC.

POLYTECHNIC SCHOOL OF ENGINEERING (Electrical, Civil, Marine, Mechanical, and Colonial), 307, 311, Regent St., W. *Director*, Prof. Henry Spooner, M.I.M.E., F.G.S.

LEGAL.

INNS OF COURT.

[Joint Board of Examiners appointed by the Four Inns of Court for conducting the Examination of Students previous to Admission at an Inn of Court.]

Middle Temple.—Edmd. Macrory, Q.C.; George Pitt-Lewis, Q.C.; Charles Grey Wotherspoon; Edmund Russell Roberts.

Inner Temple.—Robt. Henville Simonds; James Edward Aldous; Arthur Llewelyn Davies; Herbert Chitty.

Lincoln's Inn.—Sir G.Sherston Baker, Bart.; James Williams, D.C.L.; J. Samuel Green; Lionel Horton-Smith.

Gray's Inn.—William E. Ball, LL.D.; Ferdinand L. Firminger; A. G. Jeffreys Hall, M.A.; Cecil H. Walch.

Secretary to the Board, Thomas Purdue, Oak of Honour Hill, S.E.

COUNCIL OF LEGAL EDUCATION.
(Lincoln's Inn Hall, W.C.)

[Established by the four Inns of Court to superintend the Education and Examination of Students for the Bar.]

Chairman, Rt. Hon. Lord Macnaghten.

Vice-Chairman, C. M. Warmington, Q.C.

Chairman of the Board of Studies, His Hon. Judge Sir Alfred G. Marten, Q.C.

Clerk of the Council, Frederick Dapp.

READERS.

Jurisprudence, &c., J. Pawley Bate.

Assistant, S. H. Leonard.

Equity, J. A. Scully.

Assistant, Walter Ashburner.

Real and Personal Property, A. Underhill.

Assistant, J. Andrew Strahan.

Constitutional Law, A. T. Carter.

Procedure, Civil and Criminal, W. B. Odgers, Q.C.

Common Law, Hugh Fraser.

Assistant, A. Llewellyn Davies.

GENERAL COUNCIL OF THE BAR.
2 Hare Court, E.C.

[The Council is the accredited representative of the Bar, and its duty is to deal with all matters affecting the profession, and to take such action thereon as may be deemed expedient.]

Chairman, Joseph Walton, Q.C.

Vice-Chairman, C. M. Warmington, Q.C.

Secretary, H. C. A. Bingley.

INNS OF COURT BAR LIBRARY.
(Royal Courts of Justice.)

Secretary & Librarian, R. Riches.

INCORPORATED LAW SOCIETY
(of the United Kingdom), Chancery Lane, W.C.

[The Society controls the examination of articled clerks, the admission of solicitors, and the discipline of the profession. Number of members, 7,852.]

President, 1899-1900, Henry Manisty.

Vice-President, Robert Ellett.

Secretary, Edward Walter Williamson.

Assist. Secretary, S. P. B. Bucknill.

Librarian, F. Boase.

MEDICAL.

MEDICAL AND DENTAL REGISTRATION.

GENERAL MEDICAL COUNCIL, 299 Oxford Street, W.—*President*, Sir William Turner, M.B., F.R.S.; *Registrar of General Medical Council and Branch Council for England*, H. E. Allen, LL.B.; *Registrar of Branch Council for Scotland*, James Robertson, 1 George Square, Edinburgh; *Registrar for Ireland*, S. Wesley Wilson, 35 Dawson Street, Dublin.

Any person falsely assuming the title of Physician, Surgeon, Doctor, or Apothecary, is liable to a heavy penalty under the Medical Act; and to a further fine under the Apothecaries Act. There is a similar penalty for Dentists.

CHARING CROSS HOSPITAL MEDICAL COLLEGE, —Entrance fee for *General* students, 110 guineas. or 121 guineas in five instalments. For *Dental* students, 54 guineas, or 60 guineas in two equal instalments. Number of beds, 180. *Dean*, Montague Murray, M.D.

GUY'S HOSPITAL.—Average number of beds in

occupation, 554. The various appointments and offices are filled by students, selected according to merit. Some of the scholarships are of the value of £150. *Composition* fee, £157 10s. in one sum, or £163 in four instalments. *Dean,* Dr. Shaw.

KING'S COLLEGE HOSPITAL.—Fees, £135. Number of beds, 217. *Dean,* Alfred W. Hughes, F.R.C.S.

LONDON HOSPITAL AND MEDICAL COLLEGE.—This is the largest general hospital in Great Britain, and contains nearly 800 beds. 60 resident appointments are made annually, as well as numerous clinical clerkships, dresserships, &c. Holders of resident appointments are provided with rooms and board entirely free of expense. Fee £126 or by instalments; 15 guineas less to sons of medical men; 38 prizes and scholarships are awarded annually. *Warden of the College,* Munro Scott, Turner Street, Mile End.

LONDON SCHOOL OF TROPICAL MEDICINE (Under Government Auspices). Connected with Seamen's Hospital Society, *Dreadnought.* Seamen's Hospital, Albert Dock, E.—Weekly fee £1 10s. 6d.; a travelling scholarship of £300 per annum is offered. *Sec.,* P. Michelli.

MIDDLESEX HOSPITAL.—Entrance fee, £141 15s. Number of beds 321. Two scholarships, value £100 and £60, and one of £60 for students of Oxford or Cambridge, are awarded annually. *Dean,* W. Pasteur, M.D.

ST. BARTHOLOMEW'S HOSPITAL AND COLLEGE.—The clinical practice of this hospital comprises a service of 674 beds, besides 70 beds for convalescent patients at Swanley, in Kent. The resident appointments, 34 in number, as well as all the students' appointments—clinical clerkships, dresserships, &c.—are chosen from the students, without fee. Scholarships and prizes to the value of nearly £900 are awarded annually. A college is attached, where students may reside. Number of patients, 1898—in, 6,405; out, 145,789. Entrance fee, for lectures and hospital practice, 150 guineas, *perpetual.—Warden of the College,* Dr. James Calvert.

ST. GEORGE'S HOSPITAL.—Perpetual fee £150, or £160 in four yearly instalments. Number of beds 351. *Dean,* Isambard Owen, M.D.

ST. MARY'S HOSPITAL.—Perpetual fee, £139; or by instalments, £144. Number of beds 281.—*Dean,* George P. Field.

ST. THOMAS'S HOSPITAL. (Founded 1228.)—In this hospital, which contains 572 beds, the prizes and scholarships are numerous. More than 20 house appointments are open to students who have obtained their diplomas. Clinical clerkships and dresserships may be held without extra fees. The School buildings are among the most complete in London. *Composition* fee, £150.—*Medical Secretary,* G. Rendle, M.R.C.S.

UNIVERSITY COLLEGE HOSPITAL.—Entrance fees varying from £57 15s. to £141 15s.; or by instalments £147. Number of beds, 210. *Dean,* H. R. Spencer, F.R.C.P.

WESTMINSTER HOSPITAL.—Entrance fee, £115 10s.; or by instalments, £126 to £141 15s. Number of beds, 212.. *Dean,* Dr. Tubby.

All the above Hospitals have Schools of Medicine attached to them. Application in every instance to be made to the *Medical Secretary.*

LONDON (ROYAL FREE HOSPITAL) SCHOOL OF MEDICINE FOR WOMEN, 8, Hunter Street, Brunswick Sq., W.C.—Perpetual fee £125, or by instalments £135. *Dean,* Mrs. Garrett-Anderson, M.D. *Sec.,* Miss Douie, M.A.

PROVINCIAL MEDICAL SCHOOLS.

Birmingham, General and Queen's Hospitals.
Birmingham, Mason College. see p. 257.
Bristol, Royal Infirmary and General Hospital.
Bristol, University College, see p. 258.
Cambridge, Addenbrooke's Hospital.
Cardiff, University College, see p. 259.
Leeds, Yorkshire College, see p. 257.
Liverpool, Royal Infirmary.
Liverpool, Royal Southern Hospital.
Manchester, Owens College, see p. 257.
Newcastle, Durham College of Medicine, see p. 256.
Northampton, School of Medicine.
Norfolk and Norwich Hospital, Norwich.
North Staffordshire Infirmary, Hartshill.
Sheffield, University College, see p 258.
Wolverhampton and Stafford General Hospital.

MILITARY.

WOOLWICH—ROYAL MILITARY ACADEMY, 1741.

Governor & Comm., Maj.-Gen. F.T. Lloyd, C.B., R.A.
Assist. Commdt. and Sec., Col. F. A. Yorke, R.A.
Adjt. and Q.-M., Capt. A. E. J. Perkins, R.A.
Surgeon, Lt.-Col. W. C. Gasteen, M.B., late A.M.S.
Mathematics and Mechanics, H. Hart, M.A.
Fortification, Major Wm. Daniel Conner, R.E.
Artillery, Major S. B. Von Donop, R.A.
Military Topography, Col. L. G. Fawkes, R.A.
Tactics, Major B. St. J. Barter.
French, Albert Barrère. *German,* A. Weiss, PH.D.
Landscape Dwng., Lt.-Col. Dacres T. C. Belgrave.
Chemistry and Physics, Dr. W. R. E. Hodgkinson.
Electricity, Capt. W. P. Brett, R.E.

SANDHURST—ROYAL MILITARY COLLEGE, 1799.

Governor & Commandant, Lt.-Gen. Sir Edwin Markham, K.C.B., R.A.
Asst. Commdt. and Sec., Lt.-Col. J. S. Talbot.
Quartermaster, Capt. Thomas King Bunting.
Riding Master, Major Hugh Ernest Elliott.
Surgeon, Lt.-Col. Alfred F. S. Clarke, M.D., R.A.M.C.
Assist.-Surg., Lt.-Col. F. Gillespie, M.D., R.A.M.C.
Chaplain, Rev. Alfred J. Townend, B.A.

PROFESSORS (£500), INSTRUCTORS (£350).

Fortification, Major W. Huskisson, R.E.
　Instructors, Capt. F. W. D. Quinton, R.A.; Capt. J. L. Armitage; Capt. Chas. Moore; Capt. Sir C. Cuyler, Bart.; Capt. W. H. P. Plomer.
Military Topography, Lt.-Col. W. W. C. Verner.
　Instructors, Maj. A. F. Mockler-Ferryman; Capt. T. R. R. Ward; Maj. Lewis Conway-Gordon, R.M.A.; Capt. L. A. H. Hamilton; Maj. N. W. Cuthbertson; Capt. C. B. Fitz Henry; Capt. A. Foster; Capt. H. V. Benett.
Tactics, Military Administration and Law, Col. John Adam Fergusson.
　Instructors, Capt. P. Wildman-Lushington; Capt. S. T. Banning; Capt. J. S. Knox; Capt. C. M. De Gruyther; Maj. J. E. Cauter.
French, M. Deshumbert.
　Instructors, B. L. O'Donnell, L. Lassimonne; E. de Tuetey.
German Instructor, J. A. Liebmann.

STAFF COLLEGE, CAMBERLEY.

[Officers who pass through the college have the letters *p.s.c.* after their names in Service Lists.]
Commandant, Col. H. S. G. Miles, M.V.O., *p.s.c.*
Military Art & History, Lt.-Col. G. F. R. Henderson.
Fortification, &c., Lt.-Cl. Hy. C. C. Walker, R.A., *p.s.c.*
Topography, Col. R. C. B. Lawrence, *p.s.c.*
　Capt. E. S. Heard Northd. Fus. (*Instructor*).
Staff Duties, &c., Lt.-Col. E. W. Fleming, R.A., *p.s.c.*

French, Monsieur M. Deshumbert.
German, Dr. H. Oskar Sommer.
Military Law, James Cornelius O'Dowd, C.B.

ORDNANCE COLLEGE,
Red Barracks, Woolwich.
[Officers who pass through the advanced class of the college have the letters *p.o.c.* after their names in Service Lists.]
Director, Col. J. R. J. Jocelyn, R.A.
Adjutant, Lieut. E. S. de V. Bland-Hunt, R A.
Artillery, Maj. H. C. Dunlop, R.A.; Maj. C. P. Martel, R.A.; Capt. J. W. Ormiston, R.A.; Instructors, Capt. C. R. B. Owen, R.A.; Lt. J. T. Dawson, R.A.; Capt. T. H. Crozier, R.A.
Applied Mathematics, A. G. Greenhill, M.A., F.R.S.
Chemistry & Physics, W. R. E. Hodgkinson, PH.D.
Metallurgy, H. Bauerman, F.G.S.
Armour Plates, Capt. C. O. Browne, late R.A.
Practical Mechanics, H. W. Jones.

MISCELLANEOUS.
COLLEGE OF PRECEPTORS, Bloomsbury Square, W.C.
President, Very Rev. Thomas Wm. Jex-Blake, D.D.
Dean, H. Weston Eve, M.A.
Treasurer, Edward Pinches, B.A.
Secretary, C. R. Hodgson, B.A.
Teachers, after passing certain examinations, are granted diplomas of F.C.P., L.C.P., and A.C.P., and are authorized to wear gowns and hoods.

GILCHRIST EDUCATIONAL TRUST,
17 Victoria Street, Westminster.
Trustees, Rt. Hon. Sir U. J. Kay-Shuttleworth, Bart., M.P., Chairman; Hon. Alfd. Lyttelton, M.P.; Alderman James Stuart, M.P.; Rt. Hon. Lord Reay, G.C.S.I.; Walter Leaf, LITT.D.
Secretary, R. D. Roberts, D.SC.

Founded by the late Dr. Gilchrist (died 1841) for "the benefit, advancement, and propagation of education and learning in every part of the world, as far as circumstances will permit." The income is applied to the maintenance of Scholarships, to the carrying on of lectures on scientific subjects for artizans, and to the assistance of approved Educational objects.

LONDON PAROCHIAL CHARITIES
(Trustees of the), 3 Temple Gardens, E.C.
Chairman of Governors, Sir J. Savory, Bart., M.P.
Vice-Chairman, Sir Owen Roberts.
Clerk, H. Howard Batten.

MUSIC.
ROYAL ACADEMY OF MUSIC (1822),
Tenterden Street, Hanover Square, W.
[The R.A.M. was founded in 1822 by Lord Burghersh (afterwards Earl of Westmorland) for the cultivation of the science of music. The average number of students attending in 1899 was about 500. There are 83 Fellows (F.R.A.M.), 334 Associates (A.R.A.M.), and 1,174 Licentiates (L.R.A.M.), of whom 4 Fellows, 15 Associates, and 192 Licentiates were elected in 1899.]
President, H.R.H. Duke of Saxe-Coburg, K.G.
Chairman of Committee, Thomas Threlfall.
Principal, Sir A. C. Mackenzie, MUS.D., F.R.A.M.
Lady Superintendent, Miss Riedl.
Secretary, F. W. Renaut.

ROYAL COLLEGE OF MUSIC,
Prince Consort Road, South Kensington, S.W.
President, H.R.H. the Prince of Wales, K.G.
Director, Sir C. Hubert H. Parry, D.C.L., MUS. DOC.
Hon. Secretary, Charles Morley, M.P.
Registrar, Frank Pownall, M.A.

GUILDHALL SCHOOL OF MUSIC (£30,747).
Principal, William Hayman Cummings......£1,000
Secretary, Hilton Carter 400
Lady Superintendent, Mrs. C. P. Smith 200
Professors, 120 in number.

LONDON COLLEGE OF MUSIC,
Gt. Marlborough Street, W.
Principal, Frederick J. Karn, MUS.B.
Director of Examns., G. Augustus Holmes.
Secretary, T. Weekes Holmes.

TRINITY COLLEGE, 1872.
Mandeville Place, Manchester Square, W.
President, Lord Coleridge, Q.C.
Warden, Edmund Hart Turpin, MUS.D.
Secretary, Shelley Fisher.

ROYAL COLLEGE OF ORGANISTS,
Bloomsbury Hall, Hart Street, W.C.
President, Sir C. Hubert H. Parry, D.C.L., MUS. DOC.
Registrar, T. Shindler, LL.B.

ROYAL MILITARY SCHOOL OF MUSIC,
Kneller Hall, Hounslow.
Commandant, Col. Farquhar Glennie.
Adjutant, Capt. F. H. Mahony.
Director of Music, Lieut. A. J. Stretton.

ROYAL MANCHESTER COLLEGE OF MUSIC, 1893. Ducie Street, Manchester.
President, Sir W. H. Houldsworth, Bart.
Principal, Adolph Brodsky.
Registrar, Stanley Withers.

NAVAL.
GREENWICH—ROYAL NAVAL COLLEGE.
President, Vice-Admiral Sir Richard E. Tracey, K.C.B.
Director of Studies, W. D. Niven, C.B., M.A., F.R.S.
Captain of College, Capt. Spencer H. Login, R.N.
Professors: Mathematics, Carlton J. Lambert, M.A.; W. Burnside, M.A., F.R.S.; Applied Mechanics, S. Dunkerley, M.SC.; Physics, A. W. Reinold, M.A., F.R.S.; J. W. W. Waghorn, D.SC. (Assist.); Chemistry, Vivian B. Lewes; Fortification, Maj. Henry D. Drake, R.M.A.; Capt. Charles L. Brooke, R.M.A.; Capt. Harry D. Farquharson, R.M.L.I.; Lieut. A. S. Morse, R.M.L.I. (Assistants).
Instructors: Mathematics, William Gleed, M.A.; Nicholas Fletcher, B.A.; Rev. J. L. Robinson, M.A., R.N. (Chaplain); H. H. Holland, B.A., R.N.; Applied Mechanics, J. G. Liversedge, Chief Engineer R.N.; Physics and Mathematics, Thos. H. Blakesley, M.A., C.E.; Nautical Astronomy and Navigation, James R. Clark, M.A., R.N.; Navigation and Mathematics, J. R. Walker, B.A., R.N.; Steam, John Yeo, F.S.N.A., Fleet Engineer, R.N.; J. McLaurin, Engineer, R.N.; Nautical Surveying, &c., and Meteorology, Staff-Comm. William R. Martin, R.N.; Lieut. Stuart V. S. C. Messum, R.N.; Naval Architecture, C. F. Munday; A. W. Johns; Marine Engineering, F. H. Lister, Chief Engineer R.N.; Freehand Drawing, A. Ackland Hunt, J. E. Goodall; French, M. Henri Testard, A. Huguenet, A. E. Vasselier; German, H. G. Attkins.
Assist. to Director, George Williams, R.N.
Chaplain, Rev. John Lovell Robinson, M.A., R.N.
Med. Officers, G. W. Armstrong; Wm. Willes.
Storekeeper, Cashier, &c., James G. Matthews, R.N.
Senior Clerk and Secretary, Isaac T. Oliver.
Civil Engineer, C. S. A. Richardson.
Curator of Museum, Lieut. Thomas Pratt, R.N.

Training Ships.

Royal Navy.

FOR NAVAL CADETS :—See *H.M.S. Britannia* (Navy List, p. 223).

FOR BOYS :—See Marine Society's ship *Warspite* (Societies, p. 282).

Mercantile Marine.

THAMES NAUTICAL TRAINING COLLEGE (INCORPORATED).—H.M.S. *Worcester*, off Greenhithe. *Capt. Supt.*, D. Wilson Barker, R.N.R., F.R.S.E.

CADET SCHOOL SHIP *Conway*, Rock Ferry, Birkenhead. *Comm.* Lieut. A. T. Miller, R.N.

Hospital Training Ship.

METROPOLITAN ASYLUMS BOARD *Exmouth* (see p. 290).

SHORTHAND.

PITMAN'S METROPOLITAN SCHOOL, Southampton Row, W.C.

Principal, B. de Bear.

TECHNICAL.

CITY AND GUILDS OF LONDON INSTITUTE. Gresham College, E.C.

President, H.R.H. the Prince of Wales, K.G.

Chairman of Council, The Lord Chancellor.

Treasurer, E. L. Beckwith.

Chairman Exec. Committee, Sir F. Abel, Bt., K.C.B.

Hon. Secretary, John Watney.

Assistant Secretary, A. L. Soper.

Superintendent of Technological Examinations throughout the Country, Sir Philip Magnus.

The following Technical Schools and Colleges are maintained and managed by the City and Guilds Institute :—

CENTRAL TECHNICAL COLLEGE, Exhibition Road, S.W.

Dean, W. E. Ayrton, F.R.S.

Secy., *Board of Studies*, A. L. Soper.

TECHNICAL COLLEGE, Leonard St., Finsbury, E.C.

Principal, Prof. Silvanus P. Thompson, D.SC., F.R.S.

Registrar, K. Dove.

SOUTH LONDON TECHNICAL ART SCHOOL, 122 & 124 Kennington Park Road, S.E.

Superintendent of Studies, J. C. L. Sparkes.

LEATHER TRADES SCHOOL, 42 Bethnal Green Road, E.

Head Master, F. Y. Golding.

BRADFORD TECHNICAL COLLEGE.

Head Master of Day-School, James Spencer, B.SC.

Secretary, John Nutter.

BRIGHTON (MUNICIPAL SCHOOL OF SCIENCE AND TECHNOLOGY).

Principal, C. H. Draper, D.SC.

BRIGHTON (MUNICIPAL SCHOOL OF ART.)

Headmaster, W. M. Alderton.

BRISTOL MERCHANT VENTURERS' TECHNICAL COLLEGE.

Principal, Prof. J. Wertheimer, B.SC.

Treasurer and Secretary, G. H. Pope, M.A.

Registrar and Librarian, J. W. Jubb.

Professors.

Appl. Physics and Elect. Eng., A. Philip, B.SC.

Chemistry and Metallurgy, The Principal.

Civil and Mech. Eng., John Munro, M.I., MECH. E.

DERBY MUNICIPAL TECHNICAL SCHOOL.

Principal, F. W. Sherlock, B.SC.

GLASGOW AND WEST OF SCOTLAND TECHNICAL COLLEGE, 1796.

Andersonian Buildings—204 George Street.

Science and Arts Buildings—38 Bath Street.

Young Laboratory Buildings—60 John Street.

Industrial Arts Rooms—4 West Regent Street.

Allan Glen's School—68 North Hanover Street.

Secretary, H. F. Stockdale, 38 Bath St., Glasgow.

Professors.

Mathematics, George A. Gibson, M.A.

Natural Philosophy, James Blyth, M.A.

Architecture, Charles Gourlay, A.R.I.B.A.

Chemistry, G. G. Henderson, D.SC.

Electrical Engineering, Magnus Maclean, D.SC.

Machine Design, Alex. MacLay, B.SC.

Technical Chemistry, Edmd. J. Mills, D.SC., F.R.S.

Applied Mechanics, William T. Rowden, B.SC.

Metallurgy, A. H. Sexton, F.C.S.

Steam and Steam Engines, W. H. Watkinson, M.I.M.E.

HEROLDS INSTITUTE (Leather Sellers' Company's Tanning School, Drummond Rd., S.E ; *Director*, J. G. Parker, PH.D.

HUDDERSFIELD TECHNICAL COLLEGE.

Principal, S. G. Rawson, D.SC.

Secretary, Thomas Thorp.

Librarian, F. Blackburn.

MANCHESTER (Municipal Technical School, 1883). —*Director and Secretary*, J. H. Reynolds. *Ass. Director*, F. C. Forth, A.R.C.S. *Registrar*, H. Williams.

NORTHAMPTON AND COUNTY MODERN AND TECHNICAL SCHOOL, NORTHAMPTON.—*Head Master*, R. Elliot-Steel, M.A.

SHEFFIELD TECHNICAL SCHOOL (see p. 258).

SOUTH-WESTERN POLYTECHNIC, Manresa Rd., Chelsea. *Principal*, H. Tomlinson, B.A., F.R.S.

[There are also Technical Schools at Bideford (see p. 269) ; Chester (College School, see p. 270) ; Coventry ; Crofton-on-the-Solent, Hants (Seafield College) ; Exeter (see p. 270) ; Leamington ; Mansfield ; Plymouth ; Swansea (see p. 275) ; and Tenby.

THEOLOGICAL, &c.

Church of England.

ABERDARE (St. Michael's).—*Warden*, Rev. Canon Johnson, M.A.

BIRKENHEAD (St. Aidan's).—*Principal*, Rev. Edwin Elmer Harding, M.A.

BIRMINGHAM (Queen's College).—*Warden*, Rev. Wm. H. Poulton, M.A.

BURGH (St. Paul's Missionary Coll.).—*Principal*, Rev. T. H. Dodson, M.A.

CAMBRIDGE (Ridley Hall). — *Principal*, Rev. Thomas Wortley Drury, M.A.

CANTERBURY (St. Augustine's Missionary College). —*Warden*, Rev. Canon Geo. Fredk. Maclear, D.D.

CHICHESTER.—*Princ.*, Rev. H. Rickard, M.A.

CUDDESDON.—*Princ.*, Rev. J. O. Johnston, M.A.

DORCHESTER (Foreign Missionary).—*Princ.*, Rev. Darwell Stone, M.A.

ELY.—*Principal*, Rev. Canon B.W. Randolph, M.A.

HIGHBURY, St. John's Hall (London College of Divinity). — *Principal*, Rev. A. W. Greenup, M.A.

ISLE OF MAN (Bp. Wilson's).—*Principal*, Rev. W. I. Moran, M.A.

ISLINGTON (Church Missionary College).—*Principal*, Rev. John Alfred Lightfoot, M.A.

LEEDS (Clergy School).—*Principal*, Rev. Winfrid Oldfield Burrows, M.A.

LICHFIELD.—*Princ.*, Rev. H. B. Southwell, M.A.

LINCOLN.—*Princ.* Rev. Chancellor Crowfoot, M.A.

LONDON (King's College, W.C.).—*Principal*, Rev. Archibald Robertson, D.D.

OXFORD (Wycliffe Hall).—*Principal*, Rev. Francis James Chavasse, M.A.

„	(St. Stephen's House).—*Principal*, Rev. Charles E. Plumb, M.A.

SALISBURY.—Rev. Canon Whitefoord, B.D.
TRURO.—Rev. Chancellor A. J. Worlledge, M.A.
WARMINSTER (St. Boniface Missionary College).—Rev. J. F. Welsh, M.A.
WELLS.—*Principal,* Rev. Hugh Penton Currie, M.A.

Methodist.

BELFAST.—*President,* Rev. Wm. Nicholas, D.D.
„ McArthur Hall (Ladies). *Lady Prin.,* Miss Shillington.
DIDSBURY.—*Governor,* Rev. Richard Green.
HANDSWORTH.—*Governor,* Rev. Thomas Allen.
HEADINGLEY.—*Governor,* Rev. G. S. Rowe.
MANCHESTER, Victoria Park (Free Methodist Coll.).—*Principal,* Rev. T. Sherwood.
MANCHESTER, Alexandra Rd. (Primitive Methodist).—*Principal,* Rev. G. Parkin, B.D.
RANMOOR, SHEFFIELD (Method. New Connexion).—*Principal,* Rev. J. S. Clemens, B.D.
RICHMOND (Surrey).—*Governor,* Rev. G. Fletcher.

Congregational.

BALA-BANGOR (Bangor).—*Princ.,* Rev. L. Probert, D.D.
BRADFORD, YORKS (United College).—*Principal,* Rev. D. W. Simon, D.D.
BRECON.—*Principal,* Rev. David Rowlands, B.A.
CHESHUNT (Countess of Huntingdon's). — *President,* Rev. O. C. Whitehouse, M.A.
EDINBURGH (George Sq.).—*Principal,* Rev. J. M. Hodgson, D.D.
HACKNEY, Hampstead.—*Princ.,* Rev. A. Cave, D.D.
MANCHESTER (Lancashire Independent College).—*Principal,* Rev. Caleb Scott, D.D.
NEW COLLEGE, HAMPSTEAD.—*Principal,* Rev. R. Vaughan Pryce, M.A.
NOTTINGHAM.—*Principal,* Rev. J. A. Mitchell, B.A.
OXFORD—MANSFIELD COLLEGE (1886).—*Principal,* Rev. A. M. Fairbairn, D.D.
PLYMOUTH (Western College).—*Principal,* Rev. C. Chapman, LL.D.

Roman Catholic.

BLAIRS, Aberdeen (St. Mary's).
President, Rev. James McGregor.
DRUMCONDRA (All Hallows, for Foreign Missions).
President, Rev. J. Moore, C.M.
HEREFORD (St. Michael's Priory).
Prior, Right Rev. P. Wilfrid Raynal, O.S.B.
LEEDS (St. Joseph's Seminary).
Rector, Rt. Rev. Dr. Gordon.
LIVERPOOL (St. Edward's, Everton).
President, Very Rev. Evan Canon Banks, B.A.
MILL HILL, N.W. (St. Joseph's for Foreign Missions). *Rector,* Very Rev. F. Henry.
OSCOTT, Birmingham (St. Mary's).
Rector, Right Rev. Monsignor Parkinson, D.D.
ST. ASAPH (St. Beuno's).
Rector, Rev. John Rickaby, S.J.
ST. PATRICK'S COLLEGE (Maynooth).—*President,* Right Rev. Monsignor Gargan, D.D.

Baptist.

ABERYSTWYTH.—*Pres.,* Rev. J. A. Morris, D.D.; T. A. Williams, B.A.
BANGOR.—*Principal,* Rev. Silas Morris, M.A.
BRISTOL (1685).—*Pres.,* Rev. W. J. Henderson, B.A.
GLASGOW.—*Chairman,* (vacant).
MANCHESTER.—*Pres.,* Rev. J. T. Marshall, M.A.
NOTTINGHAM (Midland Coll.).—*Prin.,* Rev. S. W. Bowser, M.A.
PASTORS' COLLEGE (Newington, S.E.)—*President,* Rev. Thomas Spurgeon.
RAWDON, Leeds.—*Pres.,* Rev. T. V. Tymms, D.D.
REGENT'S PARK.—*Pres.,* Rev. G. P. Gould, M.A.

Presbyterian.

ABERDEEN (Free Church Coll.).—*Princ.,* Stewart D. F. Salmond, D.D.

BELFAST (Presbyterian Coll.).—*Pres.,* Rev. W. D. Killen, D.D.
CAMBRIDGE (Westminster Coll.).—*Princ.,* Rev. J. Oswald Dykes, D.D.
DERBY (Magee Coll.).—*Pres.,* J. R. Leebody, D.SC.
EDINBURGH (Free Church New Coll.).—*Principal,* Rev. Robert Rainy, D.D.
EDINBURGH (United Presbyterian Coll.).—*Principal,* Rev. George Clark Hutton, D.D.
GLASGOW (Free Church Coll.).—*Principal,* Rev. George C. M. Douglas, D.D.

Calvinistic Methodists.

BALA.—*Principal,* Rev. T. C. Edwards, D.D.
TREVECCA TALGARTH.—*Princ.,* Rev. Owen Prys, M.A.

Unitarian.

MANCHESTER.—*Princ.,* Rev. Alex. Gordon, M.A.

Theology Unfettered by Dogma.

CARMARTHEN PRESBYTERIAN COLLEGE. — *Principal,* Walter J. Evans, M.A.
OXFORD (Manchester Coll.).—*Principal,* Rev. Jas. Drummond, LL.D.

JEWS' COLLEGE, Tavistock Squar., W.C.

President, Rev. Dr. Hermann M. Adler, Chief Rabbi.
Principal, Dr. M. Friedländer.

TRAINING COLLEGES.
CHURCH OF ENGLAND.
National Society.

BATTERSEA.—*Prin.,* Rev. H. Wesley Dennis, M.A.
Vice-Principal, Rev. E. B. Hugh Jones, M.A.
CHELSEA (St. Mark's College).—*Principal,* Rev. R. Hudson, M.A. *Vice-Principal,* Owen Breden.
Sec., T. Gunning.
CHELSEA, Whitelands (Women).
Principal, Rev. J. P. Faunthorpe, M.A., F.R.G.S.
Lady Supt., Miss Lane. *Sec.,* Miss Denning.
Head Governess, Miss Stanley.
CARMARTHEN.—*Principal,* Rev. Preb. Brown, B.A.
TOTTENHAM (Women).—Rev. E. Hobson, M.A.

Home and Colonial School Society,
344 Gray's Inn Road, W.C.

GRAY'S INN ROAD, ELEMENTARY (Women).—*Prin.,* Rev. D. J. Thomas, M.A.; *Lady Sup.,* Mrs. Thornbury. *Head Governess,* Miss Young.
HIGHBURY HILL, N., SECONDARY (Women).—*Princ.,* Rev. D. J. Thomas, M.A.; *Vice-Princ.,* Miss Penstone.

Diocesan, &c.

BANGOR.—*Principal,* Rev. John Fairchild, M.A.
BRIGHTON (Women).—Rev. G. Corfield, M.A.
BRISTOL (Women).—Rev. E. Compton Gill, B.SC.
CHELTENHAM (for both sexes).—*Principal,* Rev. H. A. Bren, M.A.
CHESTER.—Rev. John D. Best, M.A.
CHICHESTER (Women), Bishop Otter Memorial College.—*Principal,* Rev. E. Hammonds, M.A.
CULHAM.—Rev. A. R. Whitham, M.A.
DERBY (Women).—Rev. A. B. Sater, M.A.
DURHAM (Bede Coll.).—Rev. G. H. S. Walpole, D.D. (Women).—Rev. J. Haworth, M.A.
EXETER.—Rev. James Geo. Dangar, D.D.
HOCKERILL, BISHOP'S STORTFORD (Women).—Rev. A. E. Vinter, M.A.
LINCOLN (Women).—Rev. Canon Rowe, M.A.
NORWICH AND ELY, Norwich (Women).—Rev. J. A. Hannah, M.A.
OXFORD (Women).—Rev. H. D. De Brisay, M.A.
Lady Principal, Miss Simpson.
PETERBOROUGH.—*Prin.,* Rev. Thomas Ward, M.A.
RIPON (Women).—Rev. George W. Garrod, B.A.
SALISBURY (Women).—Rev. Canon Steward, M.A.
„ The Hostel (Women).—Miss Pickersgill-Cunliffe.

SALTLEY (B'gham.).—Rev. F. W. Burbidge, M.A.
TRURO (Women).—The Ven. Archd. Cornish, M.A.
WARRINGTON (Women).—Rev. M. Stevenson, M.A.
WINCHESTER.—Rev. Canon Martin, M.A.
YORK.—*Principal*, Rev. E. E. Nottingham, M.A.

British and Foreign School Society.
115 & 116 Temple Chambers, E.C.
BANGOR.—*Principal*, John Price.
DARLINGTON (Women).—*Pr.*, W. A. Spafford, M.A.
ISLEWORTH (Borough Road Coll.).—*Principal*, H. L. Withers, M.A.
SAFFRON WALDEN (Women).—*Pr.*, Miss Dunlop.
STOCKWELL (Women).—*Principal*, Miss Manley.
SWANSEA (Women).—*Prin.*, David Salmon.

For Teachers of the Deaf.
CASTLEBAR HILL, EALING.—*Lady Superintendent and Secretary*, Mrs. Arthur Kinsey.
TRAINING COLLEGE FOR TEACHERS OF THE DEAF AND DUMB (Pure Oral System), 11 Fitzroy Square, W.—*Director*, William van Praagh.

Wesleyan.
BATTERSEA, Southlands (Women).—Rev. James Chapman.
WESTMINSTER.—*Principal*, Rev. J. H. Rigg, D.D.

Roman Catholic.
HAMMERSMITH (Men).—Rev. William Byrne, C.M.
LIVERPOOL, Mt. Pleasant (Women).—Miss Lescher.
WANDSWORTH, West Hill (Women).—Mrs. Moran.

Undenominational.
BEDFORD COLL. (Women).—Miss Robertson, B.A.
BIRMINGHAM (Mason Coll.).—See p. 257.
BRISTOL (Univ. Coll.—See p. 258.
EDGE HILL, LIVERPOOL (Women).—Miss Hale.
MANCHESTER (Owens Coll.).—See p. 257.
NOTTINGHAM (Univ. Coll.).—See p. 258.

VETERINARY.

Any person falsely assuming the title of Veterinary Surgeon is liable to a penalty under the Veterinary Surgeons Act (1881). Debts incurred in treatment of animals by such persons are not recoverable at law.

ROYAL COLLEGE OF VETERINARY SURGEONS, 10 Red Lion Square.
President, James Fraser, F.R.C.V.S.
Secretary, A. W. Hill.
Diplomas granted, M.R.C.V.S. and F.R.C.V.S.

ROYAL VETERINARY COLLEGE, CAMDEN TOWN.
Pathology and Bacteriology, J. McFadyean, M.B. (*Principal and Dean*).
Veterinary Medicine, J. Penberthy.
Chemistry, J. Bayne. *Physiology*, H. Power.
Anatomy, E. S. Chave. *Surgery*, J. Macqueen.
Histology, D'Arcy Power.
Biology, W. B. Bottomley.
Materia Med. and Hygiene, F. T. Hobday.
Secretary, Richard A. N. Powys.

ROYAL (Dick) VETERINARY COLLEGE, Clyde St., Edinburgh. *Principal*, Professor Dewar.
NEW VET. COLL., Leith Walk, Edinburgh. *Princ.* W. Williams, F.R.C.V.S., F.R.S.E.

VETERINARY COLLEGE, Buccleuch St., Glasgow.
Principal, Prof. M'Call, F.R.C.V.S.

UNIVERSITY EXTENSION.

EXTRA-MURAL WORK OF THE UNIVERSITIES OF OXFORD AND CAMBRIDGE.—This work falls under three heads: (1) Local Examinations; (2) The

Examination of Schools; (3) University Extension. The purpose of the latter is to provide the higher education of persons of all ranks and of both sexes. The Extension authorities organise proposals for the establishment of lectures and classes in all parts of England and Wales, and for this purpose are authorised to appoint lecturers and examiners for the purpose. Each lecture is preceded or followed by a class for more detailed instruction. Written exercises are set and corrected, and at the conclusion of each course a voluntary examination is held. The average charge for a series of twelve lectures and classes, together with examinations, &c., and the use of a travelling library containing the books recommended, is £42 12s. exclusive of travelling expenses. A "summer meeting" is held annually at Oxford or Cambridge to give students the advantages of a brief residence in the university town. In 1900 the meeting will be held in Cambridge, and in 1901 in Oxford. Further particulars may be obtained from J. A. R. Marriott, M.A. (Oxford), and R. D. Roberts, M.A. (Cambridge).
The VICTORIA UNIVERSITY, Manchester, also provides lecturers in the same way as the above; full particulars may be obtained from P. J. Hartog, B.SC., the Victoria University, Manchester. A fourth authority is the "London Society for the Extension of University teaching." *Sec.*, C. W. Kimmins, D.SC., The Charterhouse, E.C.

COLLEGES WITH EVENING CLASSES.

BIRKBECK LITERARY AND SCIENTIFIC INSTITUTION, Bream's Buildings, Chancery Lane, and Fetter Lane, E.C.—*Principal*, G. Armitage Smith, M.A. *Secretary*, W. H. Congreve.
BOROUGH POLYTECHNIC INSTITUTE, 103 Borough Road, S.E.—*Sec.*, W. M. Richardson.
CARLYON COLLEGE, 55 and 56, Chancery Lane, W.C. *Principal*, R. C. B. Kerin, B.A.
CITY OF LONDON COLL., White St., Moorfields. *Principal*, Sidney Humphries, LL.B. *Secretary*, D. Savage.
EAST LONDON TECHNICAL COLL., People's Palace, Mile End Road.—*Director of Studies*, J. L. S. Hatton, M.A.; *Engineering*, D. A. Low, M.I.M.E.; *Chemistry*, J. T. Hewitt, D.SC.; *Electrical Engineering*, J. T. Morris; *Art*, R. Christie; *Physics*, R. A. Lehfeldt, D.SC.; *Clerk*, C. Brandon.
GOLDSMITHS' COMPANY'S (Technical and Recreative) INSTITUTE, New Cross, S.E., with branch at Sayes Court, Deptford, S.E. *Sec.*, J. S. Redmayne, B.A.
KING'S COLLEGE, Strand. See page 256.
MANCHESTER (Owen's Coll.). See p. 257.
MORLEY MEMORIAL COLLEGE (for Working Men and Women), Waterloo Road, S.E.—*Princ.*, Miss C. A. Martineau; *Vice-Prin.*, Miss Sheepshanks.
NORTHAMPTON INSTITUTE, St. John St. Rd., E.C. *Principal*, R. Mullineux Walmsley, D.SC., F.R.S.E. *Clerk*, Sydney Axford.
POLYTECHNIC (Professional, Technical, Commercial, and Continuation), 309 Regent Street, W.—*Director of Education*, Robert Mitchell.
SOUTH WESTERN POLYTECHNIC, Manresa Road, Chelsea.—*Principal*, H. Tomlinson, B.A., F.R.S.
UNIVERSITY TUTORIAL COLLEGE (for London University Examinations), (Oral Branch of University Correspondence College), 32 Red Lion Square, W.C.—*Principal*, William Briggs, LL.B.
WORKING MEN'S COLLEGE, 46 Great Ormond St.—*Secretary*, Charles S. Colman, B.A.

"MR. WOODROW'S CLASSES," 97, Buckingham Palace Road, S.W.—F. J. Woodrow, M.A.

A LIST OF THE SECONDARY SCHOOLS OF GREAT BRITAIN AND IRELAND WITH THE NAMES OF THE HEADMASTERS.

*** *The Head Masters of Schools marked * were members of the Head Masters Conference in 1899.*

ABBOTSHOLME (New Sch.)—C. Reddie, PH.D.
ABERGAVENNY (Henry VIII.)—T. H. Sifton, M.A.
ABINGDON (Roysse's).—Rev. T. Layng, M.A.
ACCRINGTON (Municipal).—F. Bastow, B.SC.
ACKWORTH, Pontefract (Friends).—F. Andrews, B.A.
*ALDENHAM (Herts).—Rev. John Kennedy, M.A.
ALFORD.—Rev. William Horn, M.A.
ALMONDBURY, Huddersfield (King James's Gr. Sch.)—L. F. Griffiths, B.A.
ALNWICK.—W. Smith, M.A.
„ (Duke's School).—F. E. Skinner-Jones, M.A.
ALTON (Eggar's).—George Johnston Poole, M.A.
AMERSHAM.—E. H. Wainwright, M.A.
AMPLEFORTH (York, R.C.).—Very Rev. J. O. Smith.
ANDOVER.—Rev. J. C. Witton, B.SC.
APPERLEY BRIDGE (Leeds).—A. Vinter, LL.D.
APPLEBY (Leictrshre.).—Rev. R. H. Armitage, M.A.
APPLEBY (Westmorland).—R. E. Leach, M.A.
ARDINGLY (College).—Rev. F. K. Hilton, M.A.
ARMAGH (Royal Sch.).—A. C. McDonnell, M.A.
„ (Cathedral Gr. Sch.)—James Fanning.
ASHBOURNE (Queen Eliz.).—W. J. Butcher, B.SC.
ASHBY-DE-LA-ZOUCH.—Rev. L. W. Lloyd, M.A.
ASHFORD (Kent).—Benjamin Snell, M.A.
ASHTON-IN-MAKERFIELD.—W. E. McClure, M.SC.
ASKE's, Hatcham (Haberdashers').—A. Barker, M.A.
ATHERSTONE.—Rev. Smith W. Churchill, M.A.
ATHLONE (Ranelagh School).—R. Baile, M.A.
AYLESBURY.—Rev. C. Ridley, B.A.
BAKEWELL (Derby).—Charles Jodrell Mansford, [B.A.
BARNARD CASTLE (N. E. Co.).—Rev. F. L. Brereton, M.A.
BARNET (Qn. Elizabeth).—Rev. J. B. Lee, M.A.
BARNSLEY (Holgate's).—Rev. C. Stokes Butler, M.A.
BARNSTAPLE (Gr. School).—C. C. Cox.
BARROW-ON-SOAR (Loughborough).—Rev. C. K. Gimson, B.A. [M.A.
BASINGSTOKE (Q. Mary's).—Rev. J. H. Chadwick.
*BATH COLLEGE.—Rev. W. Yorke Fausset, M.A.
„ (King Edw.).—E. W. Symons, M.A.
„ (Kingswood, Wesl.).—W. P. Workman, M.A.
BATLEY.—Rev. Langton Samuel Calvert, M.A.
BATTERSEA.—Wm. Henry Bindley, M.A.
„ (St. John's).—W. Taylor.
BEAMINSTER.—Thomas Brown, B.A.
BECCLES (Fauconberge).—Rev. J. H. Raven, M.A.
„ (Leman's).—Henry Boyce.
BEDALE (Queen Eliz.).—
*BEDFORD GRAMMAR SCHOOL (1552).—J. Surtees Phillpotts, B.C.L.
„ MODERN SCHOOL.—Rev. R. B. Poole, D.D.
„ (County Sch.)—Rev. C. F. Farrar, M.A.
BELFAST (Royal Academy).—T. R. Collier, M.A.
„ (Roy. Acad. Institn.).—R. M. Jones, M.A.
„ (Campbell Coll.).—J. A. McNeill, M.A.
„ (Methodist Coll.).—H. S. MacIntosh, M.A.
*BERKHAMSTED.—Rev. T. C. Fry, D.D.
BERWICK-UPON-TWEED.—G. Hartley Ballard, M.SC.
BEVERLEY.—T. B. Williams, M.A.
BEWDLEY (Gr. School).—Rev. A. Hodgson, M.A.
BIDEFORD (Gr. & Tech.).—Rev. J. Faulkner, M.A.
BINGLEY.—J. Sutcliffe, B.A.
BIRKENHEAD (Sch.).—F. Griffin, M.A.
„ (Institute).—W. S. Connacher, M.A.
*BIRMINGHAM (King Edward's Sch.).—Rev. Albert Richard Vardy, M.A.
„ (Five Ways).—Rev. E. F. M. MacCarthy, M.A.

BIRMINGHAM (Camp Hill).—Rev. A. Jamson-Smith, M.A.
„ (Aston).—E. W. Floyd, M.A.
„ (Bourne Coll.).—T. J. S. Hooson, B.A.
BISHOP AUCKLAND (James I.).—R. Bousfield, M.A.
BISHOP STORTFORD.—R. Geare, B.A.
„ (Nonconformist).—Rev. R. Alliott, M.A.
BLACKBURN.—F. Allcroft, M.A.
*BLACKHEATH (Prop.).—H. R. Woolrych, M.A.
„ (Missionary).—W. B. Hayward, M.A.
BLANDFORD (Milton Abbas School).—Rev. F. T. Harrison, M.A.
BLOXHAM (Banbury).—Rev. G. H. Ward, M.A.
BOLTON-LE-MOORS.—L. W. Lyde.
BORDEN.—J. W. Thurnham, M.A.
*BOSTON.—W. White, M.A.
BOVEY TRACEY.—Rev. R. Wellington Menneer, B.A.
BOW, E. (Coopers' Co.).—Rev. H. Pinder, B.A.
BRACKLEY (Magd. Co. Sc.).—Rev.
*BRADFIELD COLLEGE.—Rev. H. B. Gray, D.D.
*BRADFORD (1662).—Rev. William H. Keeling, M.A.
BRAUNTON (Chaloner's).—J. L. Ralph, B.A.
BRECON (Christ Coll.).—Rev. R. H. Chambers, M.A.
BRENTWOOD.—Rev. Edwin Bean, M.A.
BREWOOD.—T. E. Rhodes, M.A.
BRIDGNORTH.—H. V. Dawes, B.A.
BRIDGWATER (Morgan's).—Rev. C. E. Lucette, B.A.
BRIDLINGTON.—Arthur Thornton, M.A.
BRIGG.—Richmond Flowers, M.A.
BRIGHOUSE (Rastrick).—Rev. E. N. Langham, M.A.
*BRIGHTON COLL.—Rev. A. F. Titherington, M.A.
„ (Grammar Sch.).—T. Read, B.S.C.
BRISTOL GR. Sch.—R. L. Leighton, M.A.
„ (Cathed. Sch.).—Rev. H. W. Pate, M.A.
*BROMSGROVE SCHOOL.—Herbert Millington, M.A.
BROMYARD (Queen Eliz.).—A. S. Waterfield, M.A.
BRUTON (King's).—David Evans Norton, M.A.
„ (Sexey's).—W. A. Knight, F.C.S.
BUCKINGHAM (Lat. Sch.).—W. Matthew-Cox.
BUNGAY.—Rev. William Boyce.
BURFORD.—H. F. Piggott, M.A.
BURNLEY.—H. L. Joseland, M.A.
BURTON-ON-TRENT.—Rev. T. W. Beckett, M.A.
BURY (Lanc.).—Rev. W. H. Howlett, M.A.
BURY ST. EDMUNDS.—Rev. A. W. Callis, M.A.
BUXTON (Derbyshire).—R. A. Little, LL.D.
CAISTOR.—A. F. Glover, B.A.
CAMBERWELL (Wilson's).—Rev. F. McDowell, D.D.
CAMBRIDGE (Leys).—Rev. W. T. A. Barber, B.D.
„ *(Perse, Gr.)—H. C. Barnes-Lawrence, M.A.
*CANTERBURY (King's, 7th century & 1541).—Rev. A. J. Galpin, M.A.
„ *(St. Edmund's).—Rev. A. W. Upcott, M.A.
„ (Kent Coll.)—Frank M. Facer, B.A.
„ (Langton Schs.).—Wm. P. Mann, B.A.
*CARLISLE.—F. J. R. Hendy, M.A.
CARTMEL (Dual Sch.)—Joseph S. Cooper, M.A.
CATERHAM (Congregational).—Rev. H. E. Hall, M.A.
CATFORD BRIDGE, Lewisham (St. Dunstan's Coll.).—C. M. Stuart, M.A.
CAVAN (Royal School).—J. H. Hampton, B.A.
CHARD.—Rev. C. E. Lucette, B.A.
*CHARTERHOUSE SCHOOL, Godalming (1611).—Rev. G. H. Rendall, LITT.D.
CHELMSFORD.—F. W. Rogers, M.A.
CHELSEA (St. Mark's).—J. W. Jarvis.
*CHELTENHAM COLLEGE (1841).—Principal, Rev. R. Waterfield, M.A.
„ (Gr. School).—J. Style, B.A.

CHELTENHAM COLLEGE *(Dean Close School).— Rev. W. H. Flecker, D.C.L.
*CHESTER (King's Sch.).—Rev. J. T. Davies, M.A.
,, (College School).—A. E. Lovell, M.A.
CHESTERFIELD.—James Mansell, B.A.
,, (Mount St. Mary's, *R. C.).* — Rev. G. Huggins, S.J.
*CHIGWELL.—Rev. R. D. Swallow, M.A.
CHIPPING CAMPDEN (Glos.).—F. B. Osborne.
CHIPPING SODBURY.—Rev. J. Dumas, B.A.
CHORLEY.—John Roberts.
*CHRIST'S HOSPITAL (The Bluecoat School), -Newgate St., E.C. (1552).—Rev. Richard Lee, M.A.
CIRENCESTER (Gr. & Tech).—S. Elford, B.A.
*CITY OF LONDON SCHOOL (1442), Embankment, E.C.—Arthur Tempest Pollard, M.A.
CLAPHAM (High Sch.).—F. Kettle, B.A.
CLEE (Gt Grimsby).—Rev. A. Abbott, M.A.
CLEOBURY MORTIMER (Salop).—J. Davis, M.A.
*CLIFTON COLLEGE, Bristol (1862).—Rev. M. G. Glazebrook, M.A.
CLITHEROE.—Rev. S. H. Haslam, M.A.
CLONGOWES WOOD (Co. Kildare—*R. C.).*—Very Rev. M. Devitt, S J.
COATHAM (Redcar)—Arthur Pryce, M.A.
COLCHESTER.—G. J. Yates, M.A.
COLERAINE (London lerry).—T. G. Houston, M.A.
COLESHILL.—F. Reginald Mayou, B.A.
CONGLETON.—Rev. W. Bevern Grix, M.A.
CORK.—Rev. Ralph Harvey, M.A.
*COVENTRY (Henry VIII.).—Rev. C. R. Gilbert, M.A.
COWBRIDGE.—Rev. W. F. Evans, M.A.
COWPER St., City Road, E. (Central Foundation Sch.).—F. Collins, M.A.
CRANBROOK (Kent).—Rev. C. F. Forbes-Muller, M.A.
CRANLEIGH (Surrey).—Rev. G. C. Allen, M.A.
CREDITON.—J. E. Burton, M.A.
CREWKERNE.—Rev. Frederic Weller, M.A.
CROYDON (Whitgift Gr. Sch.).—Robt. Brodie, M.A.
,, (Middle).—W. Ingrams.
DARLINGTON (Queen Eliz.).—Philip Wood, M.A.
DARTFORD.—Lewis Philip Harris, F.R.G.S.
DAVENTRY.—Rev. H. W. Johnson, M.A.
DENBIGH (County Sch.).—D. H. Davies, B.A.
DENMARK HILL, S.E. (St. Joseph's, *R. C.).*—Brother Attale.
DENSTONE (Coll.).—Rev. D. Edwardes, M.A.
DEPTFORD (Addey and Stanhope, New Cross Rd., S.E.)—A. E. Salter, B.SC.
*DERBY.—P. K. Tollit, M.A.
DEWSBURY (Wheelwright Sch.).—A. E. Holme, M.A.
DOLGELLY.—G. W. Kinman, M.A.
DONCASTER.—Rev. Townsend Storrs, M.A.
DONINGTON (Linc.).—Rev. W. H. Judd, M.A.
DORCHESTER.—S. A. Rootham, B.A.
*DOVER COLL.—Rev. W. C. Compton, M.A.
DOWNSIDE, Bath (St. Gregory's, *R. C.).*—Very Rev. H. E. Ford.
DROGHEDA.—Rev. F. S. Aldhouse, M.A.
DRONFIELD.—C. C. Baggaley, B.A.
DUBLIN (High School).—W. Wilkins, M.A.
,, (St. Andrews).—W. W. Haslett, M.A.
DUDLEY.—Rev. J. Shapland Veysey, M.A.
*DULWICH COLLEGE, S.E. (1619).—A. H. Gilkes, M.A.
,, (Alleyn's).—Rev. J. H. Smith, B.A.
DUNGANNON (Co. Tyrone; Royal School).—R. F. Dill, M.A.
DUNSTABLE.—L. C. R. Thring, M.A.
*DURHAM SCHOOL.—Rev. A. E. Hillard, M.A.
EASINGWOLD.—G. Sandham, M.A.
*EASTBOURNE (Coll.).—Rev. M. A. Bayfield, M.A.
EDGBASTON, Birmingham (Oratory, *R. C.).*—Rev. J. Norris.

*EDINBURGH ACADEMY (1824).—*Rector,* R. J. Mackenzie, M.A.
,, (High School).—J. Marshall, LL.D.
,, *(Merchiston).—George Smith, M.A.
,, (Inst.).—G. O. Turner, M.A.; T. G. McNaughton, M.A.
EDINBURGH MERCHANT COMPANY SCHOOLS.—
1. Ladies' College; 2. G. Watson's Coll. (Ladies')—(see p. 275).
3. G. Watson's Coll.—W. L. Carrie, M.A.
4. Daniel Stewart's.—W. Wallace Dunlop, M.A.
5. James Gillespie's Schs.—Wm. Jenkins, M.A.
EDMONTON (Latymer's).—W. A. Shearer, M.A.
ELLAND (Yorks).—J. Stewart Ross, B.SC.
ELLESMERE.—Rev. R. Beviss Thompson, M.A.
ELTHAM (Roy. Nav. 1840).—Rev. A. E. Rubie, M.A.
ELY (King's School).—Rev. F. W. Hawes, M.A.
ENFIELD.—W. S. Ridewood, B.SC.
ENNISKILLEN (Portora).—Richard Biggs, LL.D.
*EPSOM COLLEGE.—Rev. T. N. Hart-Smith, M.A.
*ETON COLLEGE (1441).—*Provost,* Rev. James J. Hornby, D.D. *Headmaster,* Rev. Edmond Warre, D.D.
*EXETER.—W. Allison Cunningham, M.A.
,, (Cathedral).—Rev. H. de V. Welchman, M.A.
,, (Hele's).—Edward H. Shorto.
EYE (Suffolk).—W. G. Watkins, M.A.
FALMOUTH.—A. Newland Deakin, B.A.
FAREHAM (Modern).—W. S. Beard.
FARNHAM (Surrey).—Rev. Samuel Priestley, M.A.
FARNWORTH (near Bolton).—Rev. F. Adams, M.A.
,, (near Widnes).—Frank Chantler, M.A.
FAVERSHAM.—Rev. F. M. Crapper, M.A.
,, (Wright's).—A. Telfer, M.A.
*FELSTED SCHOOL, Essex.—Rev. H. A. Dalton, M.A.
*FETTES COLLEGE, Edinburgh (1870).—Rev. William Augustus Heard, M.A.
FINCHLEY, N. (Christ's Coll.).—J. T. Phillipson, M.A.
FOLKESTONE (Harvey Gr. Sch.).—R. Stead, B.A.
FOREST SCHOOL (Walthamstow). — Rev. Ralph Courtenay Guy, M.A.
FORMBY.—Rev. W. J. G. Lasseter, M.A.
FRAMLINGHAM.—Rev. O. D. Inskip, LL.D.
GAINSBOROUGH.—Rev. J. R. U. Elliot, M.A.
GALWAY.—Alexander Eraut, M.A.
GATESHEAD.—G. S. Smart, M.A.
*GIGGLESWICK SCHOOL.—Rev. George Style, M.A.
*GLENALMOND, Perthshire (1841).—*Warden,* Rev. Canon Skrine, M.A.
GLOUCESTER (King's Sch.).—Rev. A. E. Fleming, M.A.
,, (Crypt Gr. Sch.).—Rev. C. Naylor, M.A.
,, (Rich's).—J. Crofts.
GOSPEL OAK (Ellis's).—E. B. Cumberland, B.A.
GRANTHAM.—Rev. W. R. Dawson M.A.
GRAYS (Palmer's).—George H. Silverwood, LL.B.
GREENWICH (Roan).—C. M. Ridger, M.A.
*GUERNSEY (Eliz. Coll.).—Rev. W. C. Penney, M.A.
GUILDFORD (K. Elwd.).—J. C. Honeybourne, M.A.
GUILSBOROUGH.—Rev. F. W. Kingston, M.A.
GUISBORO' (Yorksh.).—Rev. T. T. Lee-Jones, M.A.
HACKNEY (Grocers' Co.).—Rev. C. G. Gull, M.A.
*HAILEYBURY COLLEGE (1862).—*Master,* Rev. the Hon. Canon Edward Lyttelton, M.A.
HALESOWEN.—T. Disney, M.A.
HALIFAX (Crossley & Porter Sch.).—W. C. Barber, M.A.
,, (Heath).—A. W. Reith, M.A.
HALSTEAD, Essex.—S. Savery, B.A.
*HAMMERSMITH (Godolphin).—Rev. G. E. Mackie, M.A.
,, (Latymer Sch.).—Rev. C. J. Smith, M.A.
HAMPSTEAD, Haberdashers' (temporarily at Cricklewood, N.W.).—R. W. Hinton, B.A.
HAMPTON (Middlesex).—W. A. Roberts, M.A.
HANDSWORTH.—S. R. Hart, M.A.
HANLEY CASTLE (Worcestershire).—A. James, M.A.

HARROGATE.—G. M. Savery, M.A.
   ,, (Ashville).—J. Bowick, LL.D.
*HARROW SCHOOL (1571).—Rev. Joseph Wood, D.D.
   ,, (John Lyon's).—Ernest Young.
HARTLEBURY (Worc.).—E. W. Hopewell, B.A.
HARTLEPOOL.—F. H. R. Alderson, M.A.
HASTINGS.—W. H. La Touche, M.A.
HAWKSHEAD (Ambleside).—Rev. R. M. Samson, M.A.
HENLEY-ON-THAMES.—C. E. Chambers, LL.B.
*HEREFORD (SCHOOL).—Rev. W. H. M. Ragg, M.A.
HERTFORD.—J. B. Wohlmann, B.A.
HEVERSHAM.—Rev. J. Price, M.A.
*HIGHGATE SCHOOL.—Rev. A. E. Allcock, M.A.
HINCKLEY.—Rev. Alex. Law Watherston, M.A.
HINDLEY (Wigan).—E. Law.
HINGHAM (Attleboro').—G. K. Dobbs.
HIPPERHOLME.—H. Hancock, M.A.
HITCHIN.—Jabez King, M.A.
HOLBORN ESTATE GR. SCH. (St. Clement Dane's', Houghton St., W.C.).—W. J. Addis, B.A.
HOLT (Gresham).—Rev. R. J. Roberts, M.A.
HONITON (Allhallows).—Rev. R. A. Byrde, M.A.
HORNCASTLE.—Rev. A. G. Madge, LL.D.
HORNSEY (Stationers').—Henry Chettle, M.A.
HORSHAM.—Rev. G. A. Thompson, LL.D.
HOUGHTON-LE-SPRING.—F. Lyon Gaul, M.A.
HOWDEN (Yorks).—C. S. Fosbery, M.A.
HULL.—J. E. Forty, M.A.
   ,, (Hymers Coll.).—C. H. Gore, M.A.
HUNTINGDON.—Roland Bell, B.A.
HURSTPIERPOINT (Coll.).—Rev. C. E. Cooper, M.A.
ILKLEY (Yorks).—F. Swann, B.S?.
ILMINSTER.—R. J. W. Davison, B.A.
*IPSWICH.—Rev. P. E. Raynor, M.A.
   ,, (Middle School).—T. E. Cattell.
*ISLE OF MAN (King William's Coll.).—(Vacant.)
   ,, (Castletown Gr. Sch.), J. T. W. Wicksey, MUS.BAC.
ISLEWORTH (County High S.). H. M. Richards, M.A.
*JERSEY (Victoria Coll.).—L. V. Lester, M.A.
KEIGHLEY.—Denis Barrett, M.A.
KENDAL.—Rev. George H. Williams, M.A.
KETTERING.—James H. Gill, B.A.
KIBWORTH (Leices.).—Rev. A. P. Dawson, M.A.
KIDDERMINSTER (Charles I.).—Rev. H. de B. Gibbins, LITT.D.
KINGSBRIDGE.—Rev. William Watson, M.A.
KING'S COLLEGE SCHOOL, Wimbledon Common.—Rev. C. W. Bourne, M.A.
KING'S LYNN.—Rev. Walter Boyce, M.A.
KINGSTON-ON-THAMES.—Rev. W. E. Inchbald, M.A.
   ,, (Tiffin's).—C. J. Grist, M.A.
KIRKBY LONSDALE.—E. A. C. Stowell, B.A.
KIRKBY RAVENSWORTH.—Rev. R. Gifford Wood, B.D.
KIRKBY STEPHEN.—J. Nicholson, B.A.
KIRKHAM.—Rev. E. Spry Leverton, M.A.
KIRTON (Boston).—C. Elliott, B.A.
KNUTSFORD (Cheshire).—Rev. T. J. Evans, B.A.
LAMPETER (Coll. Sch.).—Rev. T. M. Evans, M.A.
*LANCASTER (Royal).—G. A. Stocks, M.A.
*LANCING COLLEGE (Shoreham) (1848). — Rev. Ambrose J. Wilson, D.D.
LANGPORT.—S. G. Day, M.A.
LAUNCESTON (Dunheved Coll.).—B. B. Hardy, M.A.
   ,, (Horwell).—C. D. Rosling, B.A.
*LEAMINGTON (Coll.).—Rev. A. Rnold Edgell, M.A.
*LEATHERHEAD (St. John's).—Rev. A. F. Rutty, M.A.
*LEEDS.—Rev. J. H. Dudley Matthews, M.A.
   ,, (Modern).—W. H. Barber, B.A.
   ,, (Middle).—F. G. Harmer.
*LEICESTER (Wyggeston).—Rev. J. Went, M.A.
LEICESTER SQUARE (Tenison's).—J. F. Arnold.
LEIGH (Lancs.).—W. H. Leek, B.A.

LEWISHAM (Colfe's Gr. Sch.).—F. W. Lucas, B.SC.
LEYLAND (Balshaw's).—J. D. Wilde, M.A.
LICHFIELD (Edward VI.).—H. S. Cooper, M.A.
*LINCOLN.—Rev. Canon W. W. Fowler, M.A.
   ,, (Middle Sch.).—Rev. R. M. Hill, M.A.
LIVERPOOL (Institute).—Wm. Chas. Fletcher, M.A.
   ,, *(College).—Rev. Frank Dyson, M.A.
   ,, *Crosby (M.T.S.).—Rev. Canon Armour, D.D.
LLANDAFF (Cathedral Sc.).—Rev. J. E. S. Moore, M.A.
*LLANDOVERY COLL.—Rev. Owen Evans, M.A.
LLANBYTHER.—T. Wallis Thomas.
LONDONDERRY (Foyle Coll.).—J. C. Dick, M.A.
LONGTON (Staffs).—E. Haigh, M.A.
LORETTO SCHOOL, Musselburgh, N.B. (1830).—Hely H. Almond, LL.D.
LOUGHBOROUGH.—Cecil W. Kaye, M.A.
LOUTH.—Rev. Canon W. W. Hopwood, M.A.
LUCTON (Herefords.).—Rev. Wm. Ireland, M.A.
LURGAN (Coll.).—James Cowan, M.A.
MACCLESFIELD.—Rev. Darwin Wilmot, M.A.
MAIDENHEAD (Modern Sch.).—F. Fairman, M.A.
MAIDSTONE.—Rev. C. G. Duffield, M.A.
*MALVERN COLLEGE (1863).—Rev. Sydney Rhodes James, M.A.
*MANCHESTER (Grammar Sch.).—J. E. King, M.A.
   ,, (Hulme Gr. Sch.).—Joseph Hall, M.A.
   ,, (St. Bede's, *R. C.*).—Very Rev. Dr. Casartelli.
MANSFIELD (Notts.).—Rev. Edwin Johnson, M.A.
MARCH (Gr. Sch.).—W. W. Cole, M.A.
MARKET BOSWORTH.—Rev. L. H. Pearson, B.A.
MARKET DRAYTON.—F. C. Woodforde, B.A.
MARKET HARBOROUGH.—F. Hammond, M.A.
MARKET RASEN.—Rev. Arthur Temperley, M.A.
*MARLBOROUGH COLLEGE (1843). — *Master*, Rev. George C. Bell, M.A.
MARLOW (Gr.) (Sir W. Borlase's).—E. W. Clark, M.A.
MASHAM (Yorks).—H. W. Marshall.
MERCERS' (Barnard's Inn, Holborn, E.C.).—Rev. D. L. Scott, LL.D.
*MERCHANT TAYLORS' SCHOOL, Charterhouse Sq., E.C. (1561).—Rev. William Baker, D.D.
MERTON (Surrey).—A. N. Disney, M.A.
MIDDLESBROUGH (High Sch.).—John Sewell, B.A.
MIDHURST (Sussex).—H. Byatt, M.A.
MILE END (People's Palace).—J. L. S. Hatton, M.A.
*MILL HILL SCHOOL, N.W.—J. D. McClure, LL.D.
MIRFIELD (Yorks).—Rev. C. T. Raynham, M.A.
*MONMOUTH.—E. Hugh Culley, M.A.
MORPETH (Edward VI., 1551).—G. D. Dakyns, M.A.
MOTTRAM-IN-LONGDENDALE (Cheshire).—E. J. Salmons, B.A.
MOULTON (Lincs.).—A. S. Hatt.
NAVAN.—Rev. James B. Keene, M.A.
NEEDHAM MARKET (Theobald's, 1632).—T. Normandale, B.A.
NEWARK.—Rev. E. Spencer Noakes, M.A.
NEWBURY.—Rev. John Atkins, LL.B.   [M.A.
*NEWCASTLE (Staff. High Sch.).—G. W. Rundall, M.A.
NEWCASTLE-ON-TYNE (Royal).—S. C. Logan, M.A.
   ,, (Allan's Endowed).—F. W. Brewer, M.A.
NEWCHURCH (Lancs.).—T. E. Jackson, M.A.
NEWPORT (Essex).—W. Waterhouse, M.A.
   ,, *(Salop).—Thomas Collins, M.A.
   ,, (Isle of Wight).—C. D. Vibert, B.A.
NEWTON ABBOT.—J. R. Wo thams, B.A.
   ,, (Prop.).—Rev. C. A. C. Bowlker, M.A.
NORTH WALSHAM.—Rev. Henry W. Wimble, M.A.
NORTHAMPTON (Mod. & Tech.).—R. E. Steel, M.A.
NORTHLEACH.—Frederick Godwin, A.K.C., J.P.
NORTHWICH (Witton).—Rev. A. C. Whitley, M.A.
NORWICH.—Rev. Eustace F. Gilbard, M.A.
   ,, (Ed. VI, Middle).—W. R. Gurley, M.A.

NOTTING HILL, W. (St. Charles's).—Rev. R. Butler, D.D.

*NOTTINGHAM HIGH SCH.—James Gow, LITT.D.

NUNEATON (Edward VI.).—Rev. S. G. Waters, M.A.

OAKAMOOR (St. Wilfrid's, R. C.).—Very Rev. Walter Ireland.

*OAKHAM.—Rev. Edward Vere Hodge, M.A.

OCKBROOK (Derby, Moravian).— Rev. J. M. Mallalieu.

ODIHAM (Hants).—Rev. J. T. Thorburn, LL.D.

OLDHAM.—S. O. Andrew, M.A.

ORMSKIRK.—Harold J. R. Murray, M.A.

OSWESTRY.—John J. Lloyd Williams, M.A.

*OUNDLE SCHOOL.—F. W. Sanderson, M.A.

OWEN'S, Islington (Brewers' Co.).—J. Easterbrook, M.A.

OXFORD (Magdalen Coll. School).—Rev. William Edward Sherwood, M.A.   [M.A.
  ,, (Cathedral).—Rev. J. Howard Swinstead,
  ,, (St. Edward's).—Rev. T. W. Hudson, M.A.
  ,, *(High Sch.).—A. W. Cave, M.A.

PEMBROKE DOCK.—T. R. Dawes, M.A.

PENGE.—W. J. Gerrans, B.A.

PENISTONE (Yorks).—J. W. Fulford, M.A.

PENKETH, Warrington (Friends).—A. Pollard.

PETERBOROUGH.—Rev. E. J. Bidwell, M.A.
  ,, (Deacon's School).—J. Wheeler.

PETERSFIELD (Churcher's).—Rev. W. H. Bond, M.A.

PHILOLOGICAL (Marylebone Road, N.W.).—Wm. Moore, B.A.

*PLYMOUTH (College).—F. H. Colson, M.A.
  ,, (Corp. Gr. Sch.).—J. Kinton Bond, B.A.

*POCKLINGTON.—Rev. Charles F. Hutton, M.A.

PONTEFRACT (King's School).—Rev. T. Howey Nichols, M.A.

POPLAR (George Green's: Boys).—J. T. Ashby.

*PORTSMOUTH.—J. C. Nicol, M.A.

POULTON-LE-FYLDE, Lancs. (Baines').—T. D. Whittington, B.A.

PRESTON.—H. C. Brooks, M.A.

QUORN (The Rawlins).—E. W. Hensman, M.A.

*RADLEY COLLEGE (1847).—Rev. T. Field, D.D.

RAINES (St. George in the East).—R. S. Taylor.

RAMSEY (I. of M.).—Rev. A. S. Newton, B.A.

RAMSGATE (St. Augustine's, R. C.).—Rt. Rev. F. T. T. Bergh, O.S.B.

RATCLIFFE (Leicester).—Rev. J. Cremonini.

RATHFARNHAM (S. Columba's).— Rev. P. S. Whelan, M.A.

RAWDON (Leeds Friends').—J. A. Barringer.

*READING.—Rev. W. Charles Eppstein, M.A.
  ,, (Kendrick).—Rev. E. Priestley, B.A.
  ,, (Friends').—John Ridges, M.A.

REIGATE.—Robert S. Ragg, B.A.

*REPTON SCHOOL (1556).—Rev. Wm. Mordaunt Furneaux, M.A.

RETFORD.—Rev. T. Gough, B.SC.

RICHMOND (Surrey).—A. E. Buckhurst, M.A.
  ,, (Yorks).—D. R. Smith, M.A.

RIPON.—C. S. S. Bland, M.A.

RISHWORTH (Yorks).—R. H. Elliott, M.A.

RISLEY (Derbyshire).—Rev. C. W. Groves, M.A.

RIVINGTON and BLACKROD (Lancs.).—R. T. Johnson, M.A.

ROCHESTER (King's).—Rev. J. B. Lancelot, M.A.
  ,, (Mathematical Sch.).—Charles Bird, B.A.

*ROSSALL SCHOOL, Fleetwood (1844).—Rev. J. P. Way, D.D.

ROTHERHAM.—Rev. Hargreaves Heap, B.SC.

RUABON.—Rev. Alfred Lee Taylor, M.A.

*RUGBY (1567).—Rev. Herbt. Armitage James, D.D.

RUTHIN.—Rev. Watkin P. Whittington, M.A.

RYDE (I. W. Coll.).—Rev. W. G. Whittam, M.A.

ST. ALBANS.—Rev. Frank Willcox, M.A.

*ST. BEES.—Rev. W. T. Newbold, M.A.

ST. HELEN'S (Cowley).—E. J. Simpson, M.A.

ST. IVES (Hunts).—Rev. John Clegg, B.A.

*ST. OLAVE'S (Tower Bridge, S.E.).—W. G. Rushbrooke, M.L.

*ST. PAUL'S SCHOOL, Hammersmith Rd., W. (1509).
  —High Master, Fredk. W. Walker, M.A.
  ,, (Cathedral Choir School, 34 Carter Lane, E.C.).—Rev. N. M. Morgan-Brown.

SAFFRON WALDEN (Edw. VI.).—H.B.Stanwell, M.A.
  ,, (Friends').—J. E. Walker.

SALISBURY.—Rev. J. C. Alcock, M.A.
  ,, (Choristers').—Rev. E. E. Dorling, M.A.

SANDBACH.—S. W. Finn, M.A.

SANDWICH, Kent (1563).—E. H. Blakeney, M.A.

*SEDBERGH SCHOOL.—H. G. Hart, M.A.

SEDGEBROOK (Lincs.).—F. Upton, M.A.

SEVENOAKS.—G. H. Heslop, M.A.

SHAFTESBURY.—P. T. Taylor, M.A.

SHEBBEAR (Devon).—Thomas Ruddle, B.A.

SHEFFIELD (Royal).—Rev. A. B. Haslam, M.A.
  ,, (Wesley Coll.).—Rev. V. W. Pearson, B.A.

SHEPTON MALLET.—William Aldridge, B.A.

*SHERBORNE SCH. (1550).—Rev. F. B. Westcott, M.A.

SHIPLEY (Salt Schools).—W. B. Pimlott, M.A.

*SHREWSBURY (1551).—Rev. H. W. Moss, M.A.

SIBFORD, Banbury (Friends').—R. B. Oddie.

SIDCOT, Somersetshire (Friends').—E. Ashby.

SILCOATES (Wakefield).—J. A. Yonge, M.A.

SKIPTON.—E. Tomson Hartley, M.A.

SLIGO.—W. C. Eades, M.A.

SNETTISHAM, Norf. (Hall's).—Rev. F. W. H. Palmer, M.A.

SOLIHULL.—Rev. Robert Wilson, LL.D.

*SOUTH EASTERN COLL. (Ramsgate).—C. Morris, M.A.

SOUTHAMPTON (Edward VI.).—J. Fewings, B.A.
  ,, (Taunton Trade).—S. J. Gubb, B.A.

SOUTHPORT.—W. Ross, B.A.

SOUTH SHIELDS (Marine Sch.).—A. T. Flagg, M.A.

SOUTHWELL.—Rev. J. S. Wright, M.A.

SPALDING (Lincs.).—Rev. E. M. Tweed, M.A.

SPILSBY (Lincs.).—W. M. Ellis.

STAFFORD (Edward VI.).—A. E. Layng, M.A.

STAMFORD.—Rev. Dennis J. J. Barnard, LL.D.

STEPNEY (Coopers' Co.).—

STEVENAGE.—C. R. Edwards, B.A.

STEYNING.—Rev. Alfred Harre, B.A.

STOCKPORT.—Rev. W. A. Pemberton, M.A.

STOCKTON-ON-TEES (Gr. Sch.).—E. J. Vie, B.A.

STOKESLEY (Yorks.).—H. Fawcett, M.A.

STONE (Alleyne's).—W. J. Harding, M.A.

*STONYHURST (Blackburn, R.C.). — Rev. J. Browne, S.J.

STOURBRIDGE (Edwd. VI.).—Rupert Deakin, M.A.

STRATFORD-ON-AVON (Edward VI.).—Rev. E. J. W. Houghton, M.A.

STROUD (Marling End).—W. J. Greenstreet, M.A.

SUDBURY.—W. G. Normandale, B.A.

SUNDERLAND (High S.).—Rev. E. M. Adamson, M.A.

SUTTON-COLDFIELD.—Rev. Albert Smith, M.A.

*SUTTON VALENCE (Kent).—G. L. Bennet, M.A.

TAMWORTH (High Sch.).—F. W. Richardson, B.A.

TAUNTON (King's Coll.).—Rev. E. B. Vincent, M.A.
  ,, (School).—C. D. Whittaker, M.A.
  ,, (Queen's Coll.).—Arthur S. Haslam, M.A.

TAVISTOCK (Kelly Coll.).—Rev. W. H. David, M.A.
  ,, (Gr. Sch.).—J. J. Alexander, M.A.

TENBURY (St. Michael's).—Rev. E. Hinchcliff, M.A.

THAME (Lord Williams's).—Rev. A. E. Shaw, M.A.

THETFORD.—Rev. Benjamin Reed, B.A.

THORNBURY.—G. Nixon, LL.B.

THORNTON.—J. Latham, M.A.

TIDESWELL (Buxton).—W. G. Boul, LL.D.

*TIVERTON, BLUNDELL'S.—A. L. Francis, M.A.

*TONBRIDGE SCH. (1553).—Rev. C. C. Tancock, D.D.

TOTNES (Edward VI.).—C. F. Rea, B.SC.
TOTTENHAM.—J. T. Cohen, B.A.
TOWCESTER.—J. Wetherell, M.A.
TRENT (Coll.), Derbyshire.—Rev. J. S. Tucker, M.A.
TRURO.—Rev. F. G. E. Field, M.A.
TUNBRIDGE WELLS (Skinners' Middle School).—Rev. F. G. Knott, M.A.
UCKFIELD.—J. Montgomery, B.A.
UFFCULME (Devon).—H. C. Prideaux, M.A.
*UNIVERSITY COLL. SCH., Gower St., W.C.—J. L. Paton, M.A.
UPHOLLAND (Wigan).—D. S. Rennard, B.A. [B.D.
*UPPINGHAM (1584).—Rev. Edwd. Carus Selwyn,
USHAW (Durham, *R. C.*).—Rt. Rev. Bp. Wilkinson.
UTTOXETER (Alleyne's).—J. F. Acheson, M.A.
VICTORIA PARK (Parmiter's).—R. P. Scott, LL.D.
WAINFLEET (Magdalen).—Rev. W. Gerrish.
*WAKEFIELD (Qn. Eliz.).—M. H. Peacock, M.A.
WALLASEY (Liscard, Chesh.).—A. F. Mead, B.A.
WALLINGFORD.—G. S. Morgan.
WALSALL (Qn. Mary).—H. Bompas Smith, M.A.
WALSINGHAM.—W. Shaw Hayler.
WALTHAMSTOW (Monoux).—Rev.H.A.Allpass,B.A.
WANTAGE (King Alfred's).—F. Shervill, M.A.
WARE.—Walter New, M.A.
   ,,   (St. Edmund's).—Rev. B. Ward.
WARMINSTER.—W. F. Blaxter, M.A.
WARRINGTON.—Rev. E. J. Willcocks, M.A.
*WARWICK (King's Sch.).—Rev. R.P. Brown, M.A.
   ,,   (Middle).—H. S. Pyne, B.SC.
WATFORD.—W. R. Carter, M.A.
   ,,   (Lond. Orphan), Rev. O. C. Cockrem, LL.D.
WELLINGBOROUGH.—H. E. Platt, LL.D.
WELLINGTON, Som. (County Sch.).—G. Corner, M.A.
*WELLINGTON COLLEGE, Berks (1859).—*Master*, Rev. B. Pollock, M.A.
WELLS (Cathedral Sch.).—Rev. W. H.Creaton, M.A.
WEM (Salop).—J. Ohm, M.A.
WEST BUCKLAND.—J. B. Challen, M.A.
WEST KIRBY (Cheshire).—Rev. W. Hollowell, B.A.
WEST LAVINGTON (Gr. School).—J. C. Everett.
WESTMINSTER, S.W. (1560).—Rev. W. Gunion Rutherford, LL.D.

WESTMINSTER CITY.—Robert E. H. Goffin.
WESTWARD HO!—Rev. F. W. Tracy.
WEYBRIDGE (St. George's).—Rev. A.De Vuyst,C.J.
*WEYMOUTH COLLEGE.—Rev. John A. Miller, B.D.
WHALLEY (Lancs.).—J. Ulrick Ransom, B.A.
WHITCHURCH (Salop).—E. Sharwood-Smith, M.A.
WHITECHAPEL (Foundation).—H. Carter, B.A.
WIGAN.—Rev. G. C. Chambres, M.A.
WIGTON, Cumb. (Gr. Sch.)—T. P. W. Meyer-Warlow, LL.D.
   ,,   (Friends').—J. J. Jopling, B.A.
WIMBORNE.—E. Fynes-Clinton, M.A.
WINCHCOMBE.—Thomas C. Webb.
*WINCHESTER COLLEGE (1387).— Rev. William Andrewes Fearon, D.D.
WINDERMERE.—Rev. Edward Mears, M.A.
WIRKSWORTH.—A. Berridge, M.A.
WISBECH.—A. W. Poyser, M.A.
WOLSINGHAM (Durham).—Rev. F. H. Eales, M.A.
*WOLVERHAMPTON.—J. H. Hichens, M.A.
   ,,   (Tettenhall Coll.).—J. H. Haydon, M.A.
WOODBRIDGE.—Rev. P. E. Tuckwell, M.A.
WOODFORD (Bancroft's).—Rev. J. E. Symns, M.A.
   ,,   (S. Francis' Coll.).—C. S. Millard, M.A.
WOOD GREEN, N. (Masonic).—Rev.H.A.Hebb,M.A.
WOODSTOCK.—Rev. J. Bell, M.A.
WOOLHAMPTON (Reading, *R. C.*).—Rev. Canon Scannell, D.D.
*WORCESTER (Cathedral, King's).—Rev. W. H. Chappel, M.A.
   ,,   (Roy. Gr. Sch.).—F. A. Hillard, M.A.
   ,,   (Blind College).—Rev. J. B. Nicholson, B.A.
WORKSOP (St.Cuthbert's).—Rev.F.A.Hibbert,M.A.
WOTTON-UNDER-EDGE.—Rev. F. W. Morris, M.A.
WYMONDHAM (Norfolk).—J. W. Burnside, B.A.
   ,,   (Oakham).—Rev. E. T. Glasspool, M.A.
YALDING (Cleaves Endowed Sch.).—S. Williams.
YARM (Yorks.).—W. H. Hill, B.SC.
YARMOUTH.—Rev. Herbert A. Watson, M.A.
*YORK (St. Peter's).—Rev. G. T. Handford, M.A.
   ,,   (Abp. Holgate's).—Rev. W. Johnson, M.A.
   ,,   (Bootham, Friends').—A. Rowntree, B.A.
YORKSHIRE SOCIETY'S (Westminster Bridge Road, S.E.).—R. C. Norton, B.SC.

PRIMARY DAY SCHOOLS IN GREAT BRITAIN AND IRELAND.

YEAR.	ENGLAND.			SCOTLAND.			IRELAND.		
	No. of Schools Inspected.	No. on Registers.	Average Attendance.	No. of Schools Inspected.	No. on Registers.	Average Attendance.	No. of Schools Open.	Pupils on Rolls.	Average Attendance.
1884	18,761	4,337,321	3,273,124	3,131	587,945	448,242	7,832	1,089,079	492,928
1885	18,895	4,412,148	3,371,325	3,081	592,266	455,655	7,936	1,075,604	502,454
1886	19,022	4,505,825	3,438,425	3,092	615,498	476,890	8,024	1,071,791	490,484
1887	19,154	4,635,184	3,527,381	3,111	631,865	491,735	8,112	1,071,768	515,388
1888	19,221	4,687,510	3,614,967	3,105	641,540	496,239	8,196	1,060,895	493,883
1889	19,310	4,755,835	3,682,625	3,116	648,089	503,100	8,251	1,053,399	507,865
1890	19,419	4,804,149	3,717,917	3,076	664,465	512,690	8,298	1,037,102	489,144
1891	19,508	4,824,683	3,749,956	3,105	677,948	538,365	8,346	1,022,361	506,336
1892	19,515	5,005,979	3,870,774	3,030	656,992	538,678	8,403	1,019,624	495,254
1893	19,577	5,126,373	4,100,030	3,004	664,838	542,851	8,459	1,032,287	527,060
1894	19,709	5,198,741	4,225,834	3,054	686,335	567,442	8,505	1,028,281	525,547
1895	19,739	5,299,469	4,325,030	3,034	692,202	575,305	8,557	1,018,408	519,515
1896	19,848	5,387,959	4,422,911	3,083	709,478	592,934	8,606	808,939	534,957
1897	19,958	5,507,039	4,488,543	3,086	716,893	605,389	8,631	798,972	521,141
1898	19,937	5,576,865	4,554,165	3,057	717,747	605,776	8,651	794,818	518,799

ENGLAND.

Bristol.

UNIVERSITY COLLEGE.
Lady Tutor, Miss M. Rosamund Earle.

Cambridge.

GIRTON COLLEGE.
Mistress, Miss Welsh.
Vice-Mistress, Miss C. Jones.
Resident Lecturers.—Miss Jex-Blake; Miss Classics. Miss Meyer, *Mathematics*. Miss Hensley, *Mediæval and Modern Languages*. Miss Bentinck-Smith, *Moral Science*. Miss D. Marshall, *Natural Science.*
Head Lecturers.— Rev. C. E. Graves, M.A., *Divinity.* Rev. A. H. Cooke, M.A., *Latin.* Rev. E. S. Roberts, D.D., F.R.S., *Greek.* Rev. N. M. Ferrers, D.D., LITT.D., *Mathematics.* R. T. Glazebrook, M.A., F.R.S., *Physics.* Prof. G. D. Liveing, M.A., F.R.S., *Chemistry.* Prof. Sir Michael Foster, M.A., F.R.S., *Physiology.* B. E. Hammond, M.A.; Miss E. A. McArthur, *History.* J. N. Keynes, SC.D., *Logic.*
Bursar, Miss M. Pickton, 13, Leinster Square, Bayswater, W.
Hon. Sec., Miss Davies, 12, York Street, W.
Secretary, Miss Shore Nightingale, 11, Queensborough Terrace, W.
Junior Bursar, Miss E. M. Allen.
Registrar and Librarian, Miss M. Fletcher.

NEWNHAM COLLEGE.
Principal, Mrs. Henry Sidgwick.
Vice-Principals, Miss Katherine Stephen; Miss Mary Rickett; Miss B. A. Clough.
Hon. Sec., Miss M. G. Kennedy, Shenstone, Cambridge.

Cheltenham.

LADIES' SCHOOL AND UNIVERSITY COLLEGE.
Principal, Miss Beale.

Egham.

ROYAL HOLLOWAY COLLEGE.
Principal, Miss Penrose.
Vice-Principal, Miss E. M. Guinness.
Lecturers and Professors—Classics, E. H. Donkin, M.A.; Miss M. E. J. Taylor; T. W. Allen, M.A. *Mathematics*, S. L. Loney, M.A.; Miss C. Frost; Miss E. M. Powell. *Mental and Moral Science* J. Solomon, M.A. *Physics*, W. Cassie, M.A. *Chemistry*, Miss E. E. Field. *Botany*, Miss M. Benson, D.SC. *History*, Miss M. W. Hayes-Robinson. *English Lang. and Lit.*, Miss K. S. Block. *French*, Miss M. Péchinet, B.A. *German*, Miss A. G. Corry. *Philology*, Miss H. M. R. Murray. *Music*, Miss J. M. Crawford.
Secretary, Miss Sim.

Hampstead.

WESTFIELD COLLEGE.
Resident Mistress, Miss C. L. Maynard.
Resident Lecturers, Miss A. W. Richardson, B.A., Miss M. T. Beloe, B.A., Miss L. Whitby, B.A., Miss Strudwick and Miss Caroline Steel.
Secretary, Miss S. M. Smee.

London.

BEDFORD COLLEGE, York Place, Baker St., W.
Principal, Miss Ethel Hurlbatt.
KING'S COLLEGE (see p. 256).

Manchester.

OWEN'S COLLEGE (see p. 257).

Oxford.

LADY MARGARET HALL.
Principal, Miss Wordsworth.
Vice-Principals and Resident Tutors, Miss Pearson; Miss Sellar; Miss Lodge.
Resident Bursar, Miss Holgate.
Hon. Sec., Mrs. A. H. Johnson, 8, Merton Street.
ST. HILDA'S HALL.
Lady Principal, Mrs. Burrows.
ST. HUGH'S HALL.
Principal, Miss C. A. E. Moberly.
Vice-Principal, Miss D. Wylie.
SOMERVILLE COLLEGE.
Principal, Miss Agnes Maitland.
Vice-Principal, Hon. Alice Bruce.
Resident Tutors, Miss Lees, Miss M. Pope, Miss Lorimer. Miss P. Sheavyn.
Librarian, Miss S. M Fry.
OXFORD HOME STUDENTS.
Principal, Mrs. A. H. Johnson, 8, Merton Street.

WALES.

Aberystwyth.

UNIVERSITY COLLEGE.
Lady Principal, Miss E. A. Carpenter.

Bangor.

UNIVERSITY COLLEGE.
Lady Superintendent, Miss Mary Maude.

Cardiff.

ABERDARE HALL.
Principal, Miss Kate Hurlbatt.

SCOTLAND.

Glasgow.

GLASGOW UNIVERSITY (see p. 259).

St. Andrews.

ST. ANDREWS UNIVERSITY (see p. 259).

IRELAND.

Dublin.

THE ROYAL UNIVERSITY (see p. 260).

GIRLS' PUBLIC SECONDARY SCHOOLS.

ASHBY-DE-LA-ZOUCH.—Miss E. J. Hogg.
ASHFORD (Welsh Girls' Sch.) Miss A. H. Jones.
BANGOR (County).—Miss Mason, B.A.
BATH (Royal Sch.).—Miss C. M. Blake.
BEDFORD (High).—Miss Collie.
  ,, (Modern).—Miss E. E. Dolby.
BERKHAMSTED.—Miss Beatrice Harris.
BIDEFORD (Edgehill Sch.).—Rev. W. B. Reed.
BIRKENHEAD (High).—Miss Waldron.
  ,, (Wallasey High Sch.).—Miss Vyner.
BIRMINGHAM (Edgbaston High).—Miss G. Tarleton-Young.
  ,, (Aston, Kg. Edwd's.).—Miss Nimmo, B.A.
  ,, (Kg. Edwd's. Gr.).—Miss Parmiter.
  ,, (New Street).—Miss Creak, B.A.

BLACKBURN (High).—Miss Tate.
BOLTON (High).—Miss O. Dymond, B.A.
BRADFORD (Gr.).—Miss M. E. Roberts.
BRIGHTON (St. Mary's Hall).—Miss Birrell.
BRISTOL (Clergy Daughters' School).—Miss A. J. Billing.
  ,, (Colston's).—Miss G. A. Smith.
  ,, (Redland).—Miss Cocks.
BURTON-ON-TRENT.—Miss K. Rutty.
BURY (High School).—Miss Kitchener.
BUSHEY (St. Margaret's, Clergy Orphan).—Miss Baylee.
CAMBORNE (Redbrook Coll.).—Miss Pratt.
CAMBRIDGE (Perse High Sch.).—Miss Street.
CANTERBURY (Langton)—Miss Proudfoot.
CARDIFF (County).—Miss Collin, B.A.

CARMARTHEN (County).—Miss Holme.
CAVERSHAM (Queen Anne's).—Miss Holmes.
CHELTENHAM, 1854 (Ladies' Coll.).—Miss Dorothea Beale.
CHESTER (Queen's).—Mrs. H. Sandford.
CLIFTON (High School).—Miss Burns.
COLWYN BAY (Denbighshire).—Miss R. Hovey, B.A.
CORK (High).—Miss H. A. Martin.
COWBRIDGE (County).—Miss Collin, B.A.
DARLINGTON (High).—Miss Twose.
DEWSBURY (Wheelwright).—Mrs A. E. Holme.
DUDLEY (Proprietary).—Miss Burke, B.A.
EALING (Princess Helena).—Miss Williamson.
EDGBASTON (Calthorpe Rd.).—Miss L. L. Thomas.
EDINBURGH (Ladies' Coll.).—R. Robertson. M.A.
  „ 'G. Watson's).—Alex. Thomson.
EXETER (High).—Miss Caroline Turner.
FALMOUTH (High School).—Miss Todds.
FOLKESTONE (Kent Coll.).—Miss Brunyate.
GRAVESEND (Milton Mt.).—Miss Conder.
GRAYS (Palmer's Endowed).—Miss H. Berk.
GREAT CROSBY (M. T. S.).—Miss I. Bolton.
GUERNSEY (Ladies' Coll.).—Miss Gilbert.
HAVERFORDWEST (Taskers).—Miss Waddy, B.A.
HEREFORD (High).—Miss E Krabbé.
HITCHIN (Gr.).—Miss Gosnell, B.A.
HUYTON (Liverpool Coll.).—Miss S. G. Anthony, B.A.
ILMINSTER (Gr.).—Miss Sumner, LL.A.
JERSEY (Ladies' Coll.).—Miss Roberts.
  „ (High School).—Miss Royce and Miss Wilson.
KEIGHLEY (Gr.).—Miss Atkinson, B.A.
KIDDERMINSTER (High).—Miss Bennett.
KINGSTON-ON-THAMES (Tiffin's).—Miss Flavell.
KIRKBY LONSDALE (Clergy).—Miss Williams.
LEAMINGTON (High).—Miss M. L. Huckwell.
LEEK (High).—Miss E. A. Brierley.
LEEDS (High).—Miss Powell.
  „ (Modern).—Miss E Garbutt, M.A.
LEICESTER (Wyggeston).—Miss Leicester.
LICHFIELD (High School).—Miss Hawkins.
LINCOLN (High).—Miss Body.
LIVERPOOL (Coll.).—Miss D. C. E. Clark.
  „ (Blackburne House).—Miss Coombe.
LLANDAFF (Howell's).—Miss Kendall.
LLANELLY (Intermediate).—Miss C. Davies.
LONDON (Ch. of Eng. High Schools).—Baker St., N.W.. Miss L. B. Strong ; Graham St., Miss Wolseley Lewis, B.A.
  „ (Coborn Sch. Bow).—Miss Cawthorne.
  „ (Datchelor Sch. Camberwell).—Miss Rigg.
  „ (Camden Sch.).—Miss Lawford.
  „ (Catford).—Miss Ashworth.
  „ (Central Foundation Sch., E.C.).—Miss Hanbidge, M.A.
  „ (Charing Cross, St. Martin's High Sch., W.C.).—Miss Pullée.
  „ (City of London Sch.).—Miss Blagrave, B.A.
  „ (James Allen's, Dulwich).—Miss Coulter.
  „ (Greenwich, Roan Sch.).—Miss Walker, B.A.
  „ (Haberdashers', Acton).—Miss E. Millar.
  „ („ Hatcham).—Miss Connolly.
  „ (Hackney, Lady Holles's).—Miss A. R. Clarke, B.A.
  „ (Harley St., Queen's College School, 1838).—Miss C. G. Luard.
  „ (Islington, Owen's).—Miss Armstrong.
  „ (Langham Place, W., Polytechnic Sch.).—Miss Pelter.
  „ (N. London Collegiate School, Camden Rd.).—Mrs. Bryant, D.SC.
  „ (Poplar, George Green's).—Miss Chaffer.

LONDON (St. Clement Danes, Endowed).—Miss Cocking.
  „ (Stamford Hill, Skinner's).—Miss M. H. Page.
  „ (Westminster, Grey Coat).—Miss E. Day.
LOUGHBOROUGH (Gr.).—Miss Walmsley.
MACCLESFIELD (High).—Miss Field.
MAIDSTONE (Gr.).—Miss Hailey.
MANCHESTER (High).—Miss Burstall, B.A.
  „ NORTH (High).—Miss E. M. Clarke.
  „ (Pendleton, High).—Miss Butcher.
MANSFIELD (Qn. Elizabeth's).—Miss Macrae, B.A.
MIDDLESBROUGH (High).—Miss Bedford, M.A.
MONMOUTH (High).—Miss Lückes.
NEWCASTLE-ON-TYNE (Allan's Endowed).—Miss Dobson.
  „ Staffs. (Orme Girls' Sch.).—Miss M. Powell.
NEWPORT, MON. (Intermediate).—Miss Vivian.
NORTHWICH (High).—Miss E. M. Clark.
OLDHAM (Hulme Gr. Sch.).—Miss A. B. Clark, B.A.
PENZANCE (W. Cornwall Coll.).—Miss E. C. Hanna, B.A.
PLYMOUTH (High).—Miss Turnbull.
PRESTON (High).—Miss L. C. Dodd.
READING (Kendrick).—Miss Rundell.
REDHILL (St. Anne's).—Miss Freeman.
RETFORD (High).—Miss Arblaster.
ROCHESTER (Gr.).—Miss Easton.
RUGELEY (St. Anne's).—Miss M. A. Dugdale.
ST. ANDREWS (St. Leonards).—Miss Grant.
  „ (St. Katharines).—Miss F. R. Gray.
ST. HELEN'S (Cowley Schools).—Miss Walker, B.A.
ST. LEONARD'S (Ladies' Coll.).—Miss F. Bishop.
SALE (High).—Miss E. B. Bower.
SALISBURY (Godolphin).—Miss M. A. Douglas.
SHIPLEY (Salt Schools).—Miss Byles.
STAMFORD (High).—Miss Monro.
STOCKPORT (High Sch.).—Miss E. M. Sewell.
SWANSEA (County Sch.).—Miss L. M. Benger.
TOTTENHAM (High).—Miss Beggs.
TRURO (High).—Miss Morison.
TWICKENHAM (Royal School for Daughters of Naval Officers).—Miss Leys.
WAKEFIELD (High).—Miss McCroben.
WALLINGTON (County).—Miss E. Williams, B.A.
WALSALL (Queen Mary's).—Miss Foxley.
WALTHAMSTOW (High).—Miss Hewett, B.SC.
WARWICK (King's High School).—Miss Lea.
WATFORD (Gr.).—Miss Coles.
WELLS (Blue Sch.).—Miss Orme.
WEST HAM (High).—Miss Atkins.
WINCHESTER (High).—Miss Mowbray.
WORCESTER (High).—Miss Ottley.
WYCOMBE ABBEY (Bucks).—Miss Dove.

Church Schools Company.

Secretary, W. D. Grant M.A. Assist. Sec., H. F. Wyatt, B.A. Offices, Church House, Dean's Yard, Westminster, S.W.
§BOURNEMOUTH (Ellerslie).—Miss James.
§BRIGHTON (18 Gloucester Place).—Miss Graham.
BURY ST. EDMUNDS (Northgate St.).—Miss Scott.
§DERBY (Osmaston Road).—Miss Tuke.
§DEWSBURY (Eightlands House).—Miss Page.
§DURHAM (3 South Bailey).—Miss F. Lefroy.
§GLOUCESTER (College Green).—Miss Woodward.
GUILDFORD (London Road).—Miss Morton.
§HULL (Park Street).—Miss Cochrane.
§KENDAL (Ellerbank).—Miss Smallpiece.
KENSINGTON PARK (Colville Sq.).—Miss Heppel.
§LEICESTER (Beausite).—Miss Ackerley.
§NEWCASTLE-ON-TYNE (Tankerville Terrace).—Miss Siddall.

§ A Kindergarten department is attached.

§NORTHAMPTON (Clevedon School).—Miss Straker.
§READING (Blenheim House).—Miss Haigh.
§REIGATE (Somers Road).—Miss Nicholson.
§RICHMOND (Surrey) (Church Rd.).—Miss Johnson.
§ST. ALBANS (Holywell Hill).—Miss Lee.
STREATHAM (High Road).—Miss A. C. Lefroy.
§STROUD GREEN (Albany Road).—Miss Metcalfe.
§SUNDERLAND (Mowbray Road).—Miss Hay.
§SURBITON (Surbiton Park Crescent).—Miss Proctor.
§WIGAN (19 New Market Street).—Miss Syson.
§YARMOUTH (G.) (Albert Sq.).—Miss Sallitt.
YORK (Minster Yard).—Miss Symons.

Girls' Public Day Schools Company.

Sec., A. McDOWALL, B.A.   *Offices,* 21 Queen Anne's Gate, S.W.

§BATH (5 Portland Place).—Miss Shekleton.
§BLACKHEATH (Wemyss Road).—Miss F. Gadesden.
§BRIGHTON & HOVE (Montpelier Rd.).—Miss Mayhew
§BROMLEY (Elmfield Road, Kent).—Miss Heppel.
§CARLISLE (19 Castle Street).—Miss Beevor.
CLAPHAM (Clapham Common).—Mrs. Woodhouse.
§CLAPHAM MODERN SCHOOL (Clapham Common). — Miss Wheeler.
§CROYDON (Wellesley Road).—Miss Neligan.
§DOVER (Maison Dieu Road).—Miss Sheldon.
§DULWICH (Thurlow Park Road).—Miss Cooper.

§GATESHEAD (Windmill Hill).—Miss Tooke.
§HIGHBURY (Canonbury Place).—Miss Minasi.
§IPSWICH (Northgate Street).—Miss Kennett.
§KENSINGTON (S. Alban's Rd.).—Miss Hitchcock.
§LIVERPOOL (Prince's Park).—Miss Cannings.
§   ,,   (Newsham Drive).—Miss Silcox.
§MAIDA VALE (Elgin Avenue).—Miss Skeel.
§NEWCASTLE-ON-TYNE (Central).—Miss Moberly.
§NORWICH (Theatre Street).—Miss L. Gadesden.
§NOTTINGHAM (Arboretum Street).—Miss Clark.
§NOTTING HILL (Norland Square).—Miss Jones.
§OXFORD (Banbury Road).—Miss Leahy.
§PORTSMOUTH (Kent Rd., Southsea.—Miss Ledger.
§PUTNEY (18 Carlton Rd.).—Miss Huckwell.
§SHEFFIELD (Rutland Park).—Miss Escott.
§SHREWSBURY (College Hill).—Miss Gavin.
§SOUTH HAMPSTEAD (Maresfield Gds.).—Miss Benton
§STREATHAM HILL AND BRIXTON (Wyatt Park). —Miss Oldham.
SUTTON (Cheam Road).—Miss Duirs.
§SYDENHAM (West Hill, Syden.) — Miss Thomas.
§TUNBRIDGE WELLS (Mount Sion).—Miss Julian.
§WIMBLEDON (Mansell Road, Wimbledon).—Miss Hastings.
§YORK (Fishergate House).—Miss Phillimore.

§ A Kindergarten department is attached.

Primary Education and the Decrease of Crime.

The following table gives the average attendance in Primary Schools in England and Wales, Scotland and Ireland, respectively, for the twenty years from 1879-1898 and the number of persons convicted of indictable offences in the same period. The population of England and Wales at the 1881 census was 25,974,439; Scotland 3,735,573; Ireland 5,174,836; and at the 1891 census 29,002,525 for England and Wales, 4,025,647 for Scotland, and 4,704,750 for Ireland.

YEAR.	ENGLAND AND WALES.		SCOTLAND.		IRELAND.	
	Average Attendance in Schools.	Criminal Convictions.	Average Attendance in Schools.	Criminal Convictions.	Average Attendance in Schools.	Criminal Convictions.
1879	2,594,995	12,525	385,109	2,091	435,054	207
1880	2,750,916	11,214	404,618	2,046	468,557	2,333
1881	2,863,534	11,353	409,966	1,832	453,567	2,698
1882	3,015,151	11,699	421,255	1,944	439,192	2,255
1883	3,187,214	11,347	433,137	1,914	467,704	1,740
1884	3,273,124	11,134	448,242	2,077	492,928	1,546
1885	3,371,325	10,500	455,655	1,956	502,454	1,573
1886	3,438,425	10,686	476,890	1,838	499,484	1,619
1887	3,527,381	10,338	491,735	1,843	515,388	1,411
1888	3,614,967	10,561	496,239	1,853	493,883	1,220
1889	3,682,625	9,348	503,100	1,737	507,865	1,225
1890	3,717,917	9,242	512,690	1,825	489,144	1,193
1891	3,749,956	9,055	538,365	1,823	506,336	1,255
1892	3,870,774	9,607	538,678	1,773	495,254	1,196
1893	4,100,030	9,797	542,851	1,903	527,060	1,378
1894	4,225,834	9,634	567,442	1,937	525,547	1,469
1895	4,325,030	9,169	575,305	1,652	519,515	1,096
1896	4,422,911	8,856	592,934	1,704	534,957	1,310
1897	4,488,513	8,992	625,383	1,795	521,141	1,242
1898	4,554,165	9,273	605,776	1,877	518,791	1,367

PRIMARY EVENING SCHOOLS IN GREAT BRITAIN.

YEAR.	NUMBER OF SCHOOLS INSPECTED.			NUMBERS ON REGISTERS.			AVERAGE ATTENDANCE.		
	England.	Scotland.	TOTAL.	England.	Scotland.	TOTAL.	England.	Scotland.	TOTAL.
1894	3,318	669	3,987	266,683	67,200	333,883	115,530	32,934	148,464
1895	3,421	953	4,374	270,285	91,898	362,183	129,523	45,487	175,010
1896	3,742	1,063	4,805	298,724	96,247	394,971	147,023	50,822	197,845
1897	4,226	1,019	5,245	358,628	94,595	453,223	179,600	51,967	231,567
1898	4,626	998	5,624	435,600	90,450	526,050	211,095	53,340	263,636

ACADEMY, ROYAL, Burlington House, W.—*President*, Sir Edward John Poynter, 1896. *Keeper*, E. Crofts. *Treasurer*, Alfred Waterhouse. *Lib.*, W. F. Yeames. *Sec.*, Fred. A. Eaton. *Reg.*, C. McLean.

ROYAL ACADEMICIANS. R.A.

1898 Aitchison, George	1893 MacWhirter, John
1879 Armstead, Hy. H.	1877 Orchardson, W. Q.
1896 Boughton, Geo. Hy.	1881 Ouless, Walter W.
1891 Brock, Thos.	1876 Poynter, Sir E. J.
1867 Cooper, Thos. Sid.	1894 Prinsep, Val. Cn.
1896 Crofts, Ernest.	1896 Richmond, Sir Wm.
1877 Davis, Hen. W. B.	B., K.C.B.
1891 Dicksee, Frank.	1881 Riviere, Briton.
1887 Fildes, S. Luke.	1869 Sant, James.
1895 Ford, Edwd. Onslow	1897 Sargent, John S.
1892 Gilbert, Alf., M.V.O.	1877 Shaw, Rd. Norman.
1863 Goodall, Frederick.	1887 Stone, Marcus.
1891 Gow, Andrew C.	1879 Tadema, Sir
1881 Graham, Peter.	Laurence Alma-
1890 Herkomer, Hubert.	1888 Thornycroft, W. H.
1860 Hook, Jas. Clarke.	1885 Waterhouse, Alf.
1896 Jackson, Thos. G.	1895 Waterhouse, J. W.
1898 Leader, Benj.	1870 Wells, Henry Tan.
Williams.	1893 Woods, Henry.
1876 Leslie, G. Dunlop.	1878 Yeames, Wm. F.
1898 Lucas, John Seymour.	

HON. RETIRED ACADEMICIANS.

1864 Faed, Thomas.	1857 Pickersgill, F. Rd.
1853 Frith, Wm. Powell.	1867 Watts, Geo. Fredk.
1864 Horsley, J. Callcott.	

HON. FOREIGN ACADEMICIANS.

1898 Breton, Jules.	1869 Guillaume. C. J.
1896 Dubois, Paul.	1882 Knaus, Ludwig.
1869 Gérôme, Jean Léon.	1896 Menzel, Adolf.

ASSOCIATES. A.R.A.

Abbey, Edwin Austin.*	La Thangue, Henry H.
Bodley, Geo. Fred.	Macbeth, Rbt. Walker.
Bramley, Frank.	Morris, Philip Richard.
Brett, John.	Murray, David.
Clausen, George.	North, John W.
Cope, Arthur Stockdale.	Parsons, Alfred.
Crowe, Eyre.	Shannon, James J.
East, Alfred.	Smythe, Lionel P.
Forbes, Stanhope A.	Solomon, J. Solomon.
Frampton, Geo. Jas.	Storey, Geo. Adolphus.
Gregory, Edward John.*	Swan, John M.
Hacker, Arthur.	Waterlow, Ernest Albt.
Hemy, Charles N.	Webb, Aston.
Hunter, Colin.	Wyllie, W. L.
John, Wm. Goscombe.	

* R.A. Elect.

HON. RETIRED ASSOCIATES.

Le Jeune, Henry.	Stacpoole, Frederic.
Nicol, Erskine.	

FORMER PRESIDENTS.

1 Sir Joshua Reynolds, 1768.	5 Sir Charles Eastlake, 1850.
2 Benjamin West, 1792.	6 Sir Francis Grant, 1866.
3 Sir Thomas Lawrence, 1820.	7 Sir Frederic (Lord) Leighton, 1878.
4 Sir Martin A. Shee, 1830.	8 Sir John Everett Millais, Bt., 1896.

ACADEMY, ROYAL IRISH, 19 Dawson Street, Dublin. —*Pres.*, Earl of Rosse, K.P. *Treas.*, Rev. M. H. Close, M.A. *Sec. Rev.* J. H. Bernard, D.D.; *Sec. of Council*, R. Atkinson, LL.D. *For. Sec.*, R. F. Scharff, PH.D. *Librarian*, G. A. J. Cole, F.G.S. *Resident Sec.*, R. Macalister, LL.B.

ACCOUNTANTS AND AUDITORS, SOCIETY OF, 4 King Street, Cheapside.—*Sec.*, James Martin.

ACCOUNTANTS, INSTITUTE OF CHARTERED, in England and Wales, Moorgate Place, E.C.—*President*, Ernest Cooper. *Sec.*, Hon. George Colville.

ACTORS' ASSOCIATION, 36 St. Martin's Lane, W.C. —*Pres.*, Sir H. Irving. *Sec.*, Chas. Cruikshanks.

ACTUARIES, INSTITUTE OF, Staple Inn Hall, Holborn, W.C.—*Pres.*, H. W. Manly. *Hon. Secs.*, A. F. Burridge; E. Woods. *Asst. Sec.*, A. G. Wiggins.

ADDITIONAL HOME BISHOPRICS FUND AND POOR CLERGY HOLIDAY FUND.— *Hon. Sec.*, Rev. Prebendary Arthur J. Ingram, M.A., St. Margaret's Rectory, Ironmonger Lane, E.C.

AERONAUTICAL SOCIETY, 8 St. George's Place, S.W.—*Hon. Sec.*, Major B. F. S. Baden Powell.

AFTER CARE ASSOCIATION, for assisting poor persons discharged from Asylums for the Insane. Offices: Church House, S.W.—*Sec.*, H.T. Roxby.

AGRICULTURAL BENEVOLENT INSTITUTION, ROYAL, 26 Charles St., St. James's.— *Pres.*, Duke of Richmond and Gordon, K.G. *Sec. & Act. Treas.*, C. B. Shaw.

AGRICULTURAL SOCIETY, ROYAL, 13 Hanover Sq.— *Pres.*, H.R.H. Prince of Wales, K.G. *Sec.*, Sir Ernest Clarke. Country Meeting, 18-22 June, 1900, at York.

AGRICULTURE, CENTRAL CHAMBER OF, Broad Sanctuary Chambers, Westminster, S.W.—*Sec.*, Ernest H. Godfrey.

ALBERT, ROYAL, ORPHAN ASYLUM, near Bagshot (non-canvassing).—*Sec.*, H. W. Tatum, 62 King William Street, London Bridge.

ANALYSTS, SOC. OF PUBLIC, 4 New Court, Lincoln's Inn, W.C. *Hon. Secs.*, E. J. Bevan; A. C. Chapman.

ANCIENT BUILDINGS, SOCIETY FOR THE PROTECTION OF, 10 Buckingham St., W.C.—*Sec.*, T. Turner.

ANTHROPOLOGICAL INSTITUTE, 3 Hanover Square, W.—*President*, C. H. Read, F.S.A. *Sec. (acting)*, J. A. Webster.

ANTIQUARIES, SOCIETY OF, Burlington House.— *Pres.*, Viscount Dillon. *Treas.*, Philip Norman. *Director*, F. G. Hilton Price. *Sec.*, Chas. H. Read. *Assist. Sec.*, W. H. St. John Hope, M.A. *Clerk*, George Clinch. F.S.A.

ANTI-SLAVERY SOC., BRITISH AND FOREIGN (1839), 55 New Broad St., E.C. *Sec.*, Travers Buxton, M.A.

ANTI-VACCINATION LEAGUE, 50 Parliament Street, S.W. *Sec.*, Arthur Trobridge.

ANTI-VIVISECTION SOCIETY, LONDON, 32 Sackville Street, W. *Sec.*, Sidney G. Trist.

ANTI-VIVISECTION SOCIETY, NATIONAL, 92 Victoria Street, S.W.—*Hon. Sec.*, Hon. Stephen Coleridge. *Sec.*, Robert Stewart.

APOTHECARIES, SOCIETY OF, Water Lane, Blackfriars.—*Clerk*, J. R. Upton. *Sec. to Examiners*, Frank Haydon, L.R.C.P. L.S.A.

ARCHÆOLOGICAL ASSOCIATION, BRITISH, 32 Sackville Street, W.—*Pres.*, Marquess of Granby. *Treasurer*, T. Blashill. *Sub-treas.*, S. Rayson. *Secs.*, Rev. H. J. D. Astley, M.A.; G. Patrick.

ARCHÆOLOGICAL INSTITUTE, ROYAL, 20 Hanover Square, W.—*Pres.*, Sir H. Howorth, K.C.I.E. *Treas.*, J. Hilton, F.S.A. *Hon. Sec.*, A. H. Lyell, F.S.A.

ARCHITECTS, THE ROYAL INSTITUTE OF BRITISH, 9 Conduit Street, W.—*Secretary*, W. J. Locke, B.A. F.R.I.B.A., and A.R.I.B.A.

ARCHITECTS, SOCIETY OF, St. James's Hall, Piccadilly.—*Pres.*, T. Walter L. Emden, J.P. *Hon. Sec.*, Ellis Marsland. *Sec.*, C. McArthur Butler.

ARCHITECTURAL ASSOCIATION, 56 Gt. Marlborough Street, W.—*Pres.*, G. H. Fellowes Prynne. *Hon. Secs.*, G. B. Carvill; R. S. Balfour. *Sec.*, D. G. Driver.

ARMY AND NAVY LABOUR CORPS. For the Civil Employment of Discharged Soldiers and Sailors of H.M.'s Forces, 21 Regent Street, W.—*Secretary*, Captain N. Sp. Perceval.

ARMY SCRIPTURE READERS' AND SOLDIERS' FRIEND SOCIETY, 112 St. Martin's Lane, W.C.—*Sec.*, Col. G. Philips.

ARTILLERY ASSOCIATION, NATIONAL, 24 Bedford Street, W.C.—*Pres.* H.R.H. the Duke of Cambridge, K.G. *Pres. of Council*, Lieut.-Col. the Earl of Stradbroke. *Sec.*, Major H. Vane Stow.

ARTISTS' BENEVOLENT FUND, 5A Pall Mall East, S.W.—*Sec.*, Percy Edsall.

ARTISTS' GENERAL BENEVOLENT INSTITUTION (AND ORPHAN FUND), 3 Soho Square, W.—*Treas.*, A. Waterhouse, R.A. *Sec.*, D. Gordon.

ARTISTS, ROYAL SOCIETY OF BRITISH, Suffolk St., S.W.—*Pres.*, Sir Wyke Bayliss, F.S.A. *Hon. Sec.*, T. F. M. Sheard, M.A. *Act. Sec.*, Carew Martin.

ARTS, SOCIETY OF, 18 John St.. Adelphi.—*Sec.*, Sir H.T.Wood,M.A.*Assist.Sec.*,H.B.Wheatley,F.S.A.

ART-UNION OF LONDON, 112 Strand.—*President*, The Marquess of Lothian, K.T. *Hon. Secs.*, John Sparkes; T. B. Morrish,J.P. *Sec.*, F. L. Marriott.

ASIATIC SOCIETY, ROYAL, 22 Albemarle Street.—*Pres.*, Right Hon. the Lord Reay, G.C.S.I. *Sec.*, Prof. T. W. Rhys-Davids, LL.D. *Hon. Sec.*, R. N. Cust, LL.D. **R.A.S.**

ASIATICS, STRANGERS' HOME FOR, West India Dock Road, E. *Hon. Sec.*, Major-Gen. F. E. A. Chamier.

ASSOCIATED BOARD, THE, OF THE ROYAL ACADEMY OF MUSIC AND THE ROYAL COLLEGE OF MUSIC, for Local Examinations in Music, 32 Maddox St.—*Pres.*, H.R.H. the Prince of Wales, K.G. *Chair.*, T. Threlfall. *Hon. Sec.*, Saml. Aitken.

ASTRONOMICAL ASSOCIATION, BRITISH. *Office*, 26 Martin's Lane, Cannon Street, E.C. Meetings at Sion College, E.C.—*Pres. and Treas.*, W. H. Maw, F.R.A.S. *Secs.*, Jas. C. Petrie, F.R.A.S.; Wm. Schooling, F.R.A.S.

ASTRONOMICAL SOCIETY, ROYAL, Burlington House.—*Pres.*, Prof. G. H. Darwin, F.R.S. *Treas.*, E. B. Knobel. *Secs.*, F. W. Dyson, M.A.; H. F. Newall, M.A. *Foreign Sec.*, Sir W. Huggins, K.C.B., F.R.S. *Assist. Sec.*, W. H. Wesley. **F.R.A.S.**

AUCTIONEERS' INSTITUTE OF THE UNITED KINGDOM (INCORPORATED), Founded 1886, 57 & 58 Chancery Lane, W.C.—*Sec.*, Charles Harris.

AUTHORS, INCORPORATED SOCIETY OF, 4 Portugal Street, Lincoln's Inn Fields.—*Sec.*, G. H. Thring.

BAND OF HOPE UNION, UNITED KINGDOM, 60 Old Bailey.—*Sec.*, Charles Wakely.

BANKERS, INSTITUTE OF, 34 Clement's Lane, Lombard Street.—*President*, Lord Hillingdon. *Secretary*, W. Talbot Agar.

BAPTIST MISSIONARY SOCIETY(1792),19 Furnival St., Holborn.—*Sec.*, Alfred Henry Baynes, F.R.A.S.

BAPTIST UNION CORPORATION, LIMITED, 19 Furnival St., E.C.—*Sec.*, Rev.J.H.Shakespeare,M.A.

BARNARDO'S (DR.) HOMES FOR ORPHAN WAIFS. *Chief Offices*, 18 to 26 Stepney Causeway, E.—*President*, Lord Brassey, K.C.B. *Treas.*, Wm. Fowler. *Founder and Director*, Thomas John Barnardo, F.R.C.S.E. *Gen. Sec.*, John Odling.

BARONETAGE, HONOURABLE SOCIETY OF THE, 58 Coleman St., E.C.—*Registrar*, Francis W. Pixley, F.S.A.

BIBLE SOCIETY, BRITISH AND FOREIGN (1804), 146 Queen Victoria Street.—*Pres.*, Earl of Harrowby; *Secs.*, Rev. John Sharp, M.A.; (a vacancy). *Editorial Superintendent*, Rev. J. G. Watt, M.A. *Literary Sup.*, Rev. T. H. Darlow,

M.A. *Home Sup.*, Rev. H. B. Macartney, M.A. *Publishing Sup.*, J. J. Brown.

BIBLICAL ARCHÆOLOGY, SOCIETY OF, 37 Gt. Russell St., W.C.—*Sec.*, W. Harry Rylands, F.S.A.

BIBLIOGRAPHICAL SOCIETY, 20 Hanover Square, W.—*Hon. Sec.*, A. W. Pollard.

BIMETALLIC LEAGUE (London, Manchester, Bristol and Dublin). *London Office*, 4 St. George St., S.W.—*President*, Lord Aldenham. *General Sec.*, Henry McNiel, F.S.S.

BISHOP OF LONDON'S FUND, 46A Pall Mall, S.W.—*Secretary*, Rev. H. Kirk, M.A.

BLIND ASSOCIATION, BRITISH AND FOREIGN, for promoting the Education and Employment of the Blind, 33 Cambridge Square, W.—*Hon. Sec.*, Mrs. T. R. Armitage. Communications to G. R. Boyle.

BLIND PENSION SOCIETY, ROYAL, 237 Southwark Bridge Road.—*Sec.*, W. Elliott Terry.

BLIND, SOCIETY FOR GRANTING ANNUITIES TO THE POOR ADULT, *Office*, St. George's Circus, Southwark. — *Treasurer*, Stuart Johnson. *Hon. Secretary*. Rev. St. Clare Hill, M.A.

BLIND TO READ, SOCIETY FOR TEACHING THE, 10 Upper Avenue Road, N.W.—*Sec.*, Capt. G. G. Webber, R.N.

BLUES, BENEVOLENT SOCIETY OF, FOR THE RELIEF OF PERSONS EDUCATED AT CHRIST'S HOSPITAL, THEIR WIDOWS AND ORPHAN CHILDREN.—*Pres.*, Rev. William Haig Brown, LL.D. *Treas.*, Ald. Vaughan Morgan. *Sec.*, Geo. Wilkins, Lyndhurst, Greenhill Park, Harlesden, N.W.

BOTANIC SOCIETY, ROYAL, Regent's Park.—*Sec. and Supt.*, J. Bryant Sowerby, F.L.S.

BRIDEWELL HOSPITAL (KING EDWARD'S) SCHOOLS —for Girls, St. George's Road, Southwark, S.E.; for Boys, Witley, Surrey.—*President*, Sir G. Faudel Phillips, Bt. *Treas.*, Leicester M. Reed.

BRITISH ASSOCIATION FOR THE ADVANCEMENT OF SCIENCE, Burlington House.—*Pres. Elect*, Sir W. Turner, F.R.S. *General Secs.*, Prof. E. A. Schäfer, F.R.S.; Sir W.C. Roberts-Austen, K.C.B. *Asst. Gen. Sec.*, G. Griffith, M.A. *Gen. Treas.*, Prof. G. Carey Foster, F.R.S. *Clerk*, H. C. Stewardson. In 1900 will meet at Bradford (Sept. 5) ; in 1901, at Glasgow.

BRITISH MEDICAL ASSOCIATION, 429 Strand.—*President*, John Ward Cousins, M.D. *President Elect*, William Alfred Elliston, M.D. *Gen. Sec.*, Francis Fowke.

BRITISH ORPHAN ASYLUM, Mackenzie Pk., Slough. *Office*, 62 Bishopsgate St. Within.—*Sec.*, Charles T. Hoskins.

BUILDERS, INSTITUTE OF (Incorporated), 31 Bedford Street, Strand, W.C.—*Sec.*, T. Costigan.

BUREAU VERITAS. International Registry of Shipping, British Committee, 155 Fenchurch Street, E.C.—*Sec.*, P. L. Breslauer.

CALEDONIAN ASYLUM, ROYAL, Caledonian Road, Holloway, N.—*Sec.*, P. D. Graham.

CAMBRIAN ACADEMY OF ART, ROYAL, Plâs Mawr, Conway.—*Hon. Sec.*, W. J. Slater.

CAMBRIDGE ASYLUM FOR SOLDIERS' WIDOWS, ROYAL, Kingston-on-Thames. *Office*, 20 Cockspur Street.—*Sec.*, Lt.-Col. F. W. James.

CAMBRIDGE FUND FOR OLD AND DISABLED SOLDIERS, ROYAL, War Office, Pall Mall.—(This fund is personally administered by the Commander-in-Chief.) *Sec.*, W. Sheean.

CARRIAGE MANUFACTURERS, INCORPORATED INSTITUTE OF BRITISH, Town Hall, Westminster.—*Sec.*, A. W. Barr, 30 Moorgate Street, E.C.

CHARITY ORGANISATION SOCIETY, 15 Buckingham Street, Strand.—*Sec.*, C. S. Loch.

CHEMICAL INDUSTRY, SOCIETY OF, Palace Chambers, Westminster.— *Gen. Sec.,* C. G. Cresswell.

CHEMICAL SOCIETY, Burlington House.— *President,* T. E. Thorpe, LL.D., F.R.S.; *Hon. Secs.,* Wyndham R. Dunstan, F.R.S.: Alexander Scott, F.R.S.; *Asst. Sec. and Lib.,* Robert Steele. F.C.S.

CHEMISTRY, INSTITUTE OF, OF G. BRITAIN AND IRELAND, 30 Bloomsbury Sq., W.C.— *Pres.,* Dr. Thomas Stevenson, F.R.C.P. *Regist.,* Prof. J. Millar Thomson, F.R.S. *Resident Sec.,* Richard B. Pilcher. F.I.C. and A.I.C.

CHILDREN'S HOME AND ORPHANAGE and Training School for Christian Workers. *Chief Office,* Bonner Road, London, N.E.— *Prin.,* Rev. T. B. Stephenson, D.D.; *Sec.,* J. Pendlebury, M.A.

CHOLMONDELEY CHARITIES, 2 Bloomsbury Place, W.C.— *Treas. and Sec.,* Sir Paget Bowman, Bt.

CHRISTIAN EVIDENCE SOCIETY, 26 Charing Cross, S.W.— *Pres.,* Archbp. of Canterbury. *Secs.,* Revs. C.L.Engström, M.A.; T. T.Waterman, B.A.

CHRISTIAN KNOWLEDGE, SOCIETY FOR PROMOTING, Northumberland Avenue.— *Treasurers,* Rev. H. Wace, D.D., W. H. Clay; J. C. Salt; Hon. Alban Gibbs, M.P. *Secs.,* Rev. W. O. B. Allen; Rev. E. McClure. *Organising Secs.,* South, Rev. W. B. Taylor; North, Rev. W. Robinson, 26 St. Andrew's Place, Bradford. *Accountant,* G. Wilkins. *Coll.,* H. W. Orchard.

CHURCH ARMY, 130 Edgware Rd.— *Hon. Chief Sec.,* Rev. W. Carlile.

CHURCH ASSOCIATION, 14 Buckingham Street, W.C.— *Sec.,* Henry Miller. *Organising Secs.,* R. Stewart Clough; Rev. T. H. Sparshott; Rev. E. G. Bowring. *Parl. Agents,* J. W. B. Barrow, J.P.; W. Fraser.

CHURCH BUILDING SOCIETY, LONDON DIOCESAN, 46a, Pall Mall, S.W.— *Hon. Sec.,* J. H. Nelson.

CHURCH COMMITTEE FOR CHURCH DEFENCE AND CHURCH INSTRUCTION, Church House, Westminster.— *Secretary,* T. Martin Trip.

CHURCH EMIGRATION SOCIETY, 34 Newark Street, Stepney, E.— *President,* Rt. Rev. the Bishop of London. *Hon. Sec.,* Rev. E. Sheppard, M.A.

CHURCH HOUSE, Dean's Yard, Westminster, S.W. — *Sec.,* Sydney W. Flamank.

CHURCH MISSIONARY SOC., Salisbury Sq.— *Pres.,* Rt. Hon. Sir John Kennaway, Bt., M.P. *Treas.,* Col. Robert Williams, M.P. *Secs.,* Rev. H. E. Fox, M.A. (*Hon.*); Rev. B. Baring-Gould, M.A.; Rev. F. Baylis, M.A.; Rev. G. Furness Smith, M.A.; Rev. G. B. Durrant, M.A.; Rev. D. H. D. Wilkinson, M.A.; Rev. W. E. Burroughs, B.D.; Eugène Stock (*Editorial*); D. M. Lang (*Lay*).

CHURCH OF ENGLAND BOOK SOCIETY, 11 Adam St., Strand, W.C.— *Hon. Sec.,* John Shrimpton. *Sec.,* C. R. Ray.

CHURCH OF ENGLAND INCORPORATED SOCIETY FOR PROVIDING HOMES FOR WAIFS AND STRAYS, Savoy House, W.C. — *Sec.,* Rev. E. de M. Rudolf.

CHURCH OF ENG. SCRIPTURE READERS' ASSOC., 56 Haymarket, S.W.— *Sec.,* Reuben G. Kestin.

CHURCH OF ENG. SOLDIERS' INSTITUTES, Church Ho., Westminster.— *Sec.,* Col. E. Hughes, C.B.

CHURCH OF ENGLAND S. S. INSTITUTE, 13 Serjeants' Inn, Fleet St.— *Sec.,* J. Palmer. *Organ. Sec.,* Rev. H. Dawson.

CHURCH OF ENGLAND TEMPERANCE SOCIETY. Deansgate, Westminster.— *Sec.,* F. Eardley-Wilmot, R.N.; *Asst. Sec.,* A. F. Harvey.

CHURCH OF ENG. ZENANA MISSION, 27 Chancery Lane, W.C.— *Secs.,* Rev. G. Tonge; R. G. Macdonald.

CHURCH PASTORAL AID SOCIETY, Falcon Court, 32 Fleet Street.— *Sec.,* Rev. R. G. Fowell, M.A.; *Asst. Sec.,* Rev. H. M. Sanders, M.A. *Lay Sec.,* Col. H. S. Clarke.

CITY OF LONDON GENERAL PENSION SOCIETY, 34 Finsbury Circus.— *Sec.,* J. Slater-Spence.

CITY OF LONDON TRUSS SOCIETY, 35 Finsbury Square, E.C.— *Sec.,* John Whittington.

CIVIL ENGINEERS, THE INSTITUTION OF, Gt. George Street, S.W.— *President,* Sir Douglas Fox. *Sec.,* J. H. T. Tudsbery, D.SC. M.Inst.C.E.

CLERGY FRIENDLY SOCIETY.— *Sec.,* Rev. George Howard, 29 Cambridge Road, Bromley, Kent.

CLERGY ORPHAN CORPORATION, 35 Parliament Street, S.W.— *President,* Archbishop of Canterbury. *Sec.,* Rev. Wm. Charles Cluff, M.A.

CLERGY PENSIONS INSTITUTION, 11 Norfolk Street, Strand, W.C.— *Sec. and Actry,* J. Duncan, F.I.A.

CLINICAL SOCIETY, 20 Hanover Square, W.— *Hon. Secs.,* Percy Kidd, M.D.; C. J. Symonds, M.S.

COAL SMOKE ABATEMENT SOC., 59 Chancery Lane, W.C.— *Pres.,* Sir William Richmond, K.C.B. *Sec.,* Owen B. Thomas.

COLONIAL AND CONTINENTAL CHURCH SOCIETY, 9 Serjeants' Inn, Fleet St.— *Sec.,* Rev. Canon Hurst, B.D.

COLONIAL INSTITUTE, ROYAL, Northumberland Avenue.— *President,* H.R.H. the Prince of Wales. *Sec.,* J. S. O'Halloran, C.M.G. *Lib.,* J. R. Boosé. *Chief Clerk,* W. Chamberlain. (4,168 Fellows.) F.R.C.I.

COMMERCE, ASSOCIATED CHAMBERS OF, OF THE UNITED KINGDOM.— *President,* Sir Stafford Northcote, Bart., M.P.; *Sec.,* Ed. W. Fithian, 1 Gt. College St., S.W.

COMMERCE, LONDON CHAMBER OF (Incorporated), 10 Eastcheap.— *Pres.,* Albert G. Sandeman. *Sec.,* Kenric B. Murray.

COMMISSIONAIRES, CORPS OF (1859). Headquarters, Exchange Court, 419 Strand. Discharged soldiers and sailors of good character can be obtained for almost any sort of employment.— *Founder and Commanding Officer,* Sir E. Walter, K.C.B. *Sec.,* Major F. E. Walter.

COMMONS AND FOOTPATHS PRESERVATION SOC., 1 Great College St., S.W. *Sec.,* L. W. Chubb.

CONGREGATIONAL CHURCH AID AND HOME MISSIONARY SOCIETY, Memorial Hall, Farringdon Street.— *Treasurer,* Gerard N. Ford (Manchester). *Secs.,* J. Edward Flower, M.A.

CONSERVATIVE CENTRAL OFFICE, St. Stephen's Chambers, Westminster.— *Principal Agent,* R. W. E. Middleton. *Secs.,* Hon. FitzRoy Stewart; E. Solbé.

CORPORATION OF SONS OF THE CLERGY, 2 Bloomsbury Pl., W.C.— *Regis.,* Sir Paget Bowman, Bt.

CREMATION SOCIETY OF ENGLAND, 324 Regent St., W.— *Pres.,* Sir Hy. Thompson, Bt., F.R.C.S. *Hon. Sec.,* J. C. Swinburne Hanham, J.P.

CRUELTY TO ANIMALS, ROYAL SOCIETY FOR PREVENTION OF, 105 Jermyn Street, S.W. — *Pres.,* H.R.H. the Duke of York, K.G. *Sec.,* J. Colam.

CRUELTY TO CHILDREN, NATIONAL SOCIETY FOR THE PREVENTION OF (Incorporated), Central Office, 7 Harpur Street, W.C.— *Director,* Rev. Benjamin Waugh.

CURATES' AUGMENTATION FUND, 2 Dean's Yard, S.W.— *Sec.,* Rev. J. R. Humble.

CYMMRODORION, THE HONOURABLE SOCIETY OF, 54 Chancery Lane.— *Pres.,* The Marquess of Bute, K.T. *Sec.,* E Vincent Evans.

DEACONESSES' INSTITUTION (Evangelical Protestant), Tottenham. *Director*, Edwin A. White. *Lady Sup. Deaconess*, E. Greenwood.

DEAF AND DUMB, ASSOCIATION FOR THE ORAL INSTRUCTION OF THE, 11 Fitzroy Square (School for Children and Training College for Teachers of the Deaf on the German or pure oral system).—*Director*, William Van Praagh.

DEAF AND DUMB, ASYLUM FOR. Old Kent Road and Margate. For the Support and Education of Children of the Poor. *Office*, 93 Cannon Street, E.C.—*Sec.*, Frederic H. Madden.

DEAF AND DUMB FEMALES, British Asylum for, Lower Clapton. *Office*, 5 Bloomsbury Square, W.C.—*Sec.*, W. T. Hillyer.

DEAF AND DUMB, ROYAL ASSOCIATION IN AID OF, 419 Oxford Street, W.— *Sec.*, Thomas Cole.

DEEP SEA FISHERMEN, ROYAL NATIONAL MISSION TO, Bridge House, 181 Queen Victoria Street, E.C.—*Sec.*, F. H. Wood.

DIOCESAN CONFERENCES, CENTRAL COUNCIL OF, National Societies' House, Westminster, S.W.— *Hon. Secs.*, Lord Cranworth; Archdeacon Emery; S. Leighton, M.P.; *Lay Sec.*, G. H. F. Nye.

DISCHARGED PRISONERS' AID SOCIETY (METROPOLITAN), 10 Freegrove Road, Holloway; 15 Buckingham St., Strand.—*Chairman*, G. Melville Dale. *Secretary*, T. R. Price.

DISCHARGED PRISONERS, ROYAL SOCIETY FOR THE ASSISTANCE OF, 32 Charing Cross, S.W.—*Sec.*, Lt.-Col. H. B. Buchanan.

DRAWING SOCIETY, ROYAL, 50 Queen Anne's Gate, S.W.—*Hon. Sec.*, T. R. Ablett.

DUBLIN SOCIETY, ROYAL, Leinster House, Kildare Street.—*Pres.*, Rt. Hon. Lord Ardilaun. *Hon. Secs.*, Hon. Mr. Justice Boyd, Dr. J. Joly, F.R.S. *Registrar*, Richard J. Moss, F.C.S.

EARLY CLOSING ASSOCIATION, 21 New Bridge St., E.C.—*Sec.*, Jas. A. Stacey; *Asst. Sec.*, Albert Larking.

EAST INDIA ASSOCIATION, 3 Victoria Street, S.W. —*Sec.*, C. W. Arathoon.

EAST LONDON CHURCH FUND, 26 St. Mary Axe, E.C. —*Joint Presidents*, The Bishops of Stepney and Islington. *Sec.*, Rev. G. N. Walsh, M.A.

EGYPT EXPLORATION FUND, 37 Gt. Russell Street, W.C.—*Sec.*, Emily Paterson.

ELECTRICAL ENGINEERS, INSTITUTION OF, 28 Victoria Street, S.W.—*Sec.*, W. G. McMillan, F.I.C.

ENGINEERS, SOCIETY OF (1854), 17 Victoria St., S.W.—*Sec.*, Perry F. Nursey.

ENGLISH CHURCH UNION, 35 Wellington Street, Strand.—*Pres.*, Viscount Halifax. *Sec.*, Col. John B. Hardy. *Organising Secs.*, Rev. T. O. Marshall ; H. W. Hill. 33 Bishops, 4,400 Clergy, and 34,000 Lay Communicants. Total, 38,400.

ENTOMOLOGICAL SOCIETY, 11 Chandos Street, Cavendish Square, W.—*Pres.*, G. H. Verrall. *Hon. Secs.*, J. J. Walker, R.N.; C. J. Gahan, M.A. *Hon. Lib.*, G. C. Champion, F.Z.S.; *Res. Lib.*, W. R. Hall.

EPIDEMIOLOGICAL SOC., 11 Chandos Street, W.— *Pres.*, Franklin Parsons, M.D. *Hon. Secs.*, H. T. Bulstrode, M.D.; J. W. Washbourn, M.D.

EVANGELICAL ALLIANCE, 7 Adam Street, Strand. —*Treas.*, Donald Matheson. *Sec.* E. J. Field.

FEMALE ORPHAN ASYLUM, ROYAL, Beddington, Surrey. *Office*, 32 Essex St., Strand.—*Pres.*, H.R.H. the Duke of Cambridge, K.G. *Chairman*, Sir John B. Monckton, F.S.A. *Sec.*, Brough Maltby.

FEMALE ORPHANS, HOME FOR, WHO HAVE LOST BOTH PARENTS, Grove Road, St. John's Wood. —*Hon. Sec.*, Maj. G. Deane. *Matron*, Miss Laver.

FIELD LANE REFUGES AND RAGGED SCHOOLS, Vine Street, Clerkenwell.—*Sec.*, Peregrine Platt.

FIRE BRIGADES UNION, NATIONAL.—*Pres.*, Duke of Marlborough. *Chairman*, Lt.-Col. Seabroke, Rugby. *Hn. Sec.*, H. S. Folker, F.A.I., Guildford.

FOLK-LORE SOCIETY.—*Sec.*, F. A. Milne, 11 Old Square, Lincoln's Inn, W.C. Meets at 22 Albemarle Street, W.

FOUNDLING HOSPITAL, Guilford Street. Inquiries to be made between 10 and 4 at the Secretary's office; Saturdays, between 10 and 1. *Sec.*, W. S. Wintle, M.A.

FREEMASONS, United Grand Lodge, Freemasons' Hall, Great Queen Street.—*Grand Sec.*, Edward Letchworth, F.S.A. *Assist. Gd. Sec.*, W. Lake.

FRIEND OF THE CLERGY CORPORATION, 17 King William Street, Strand.—*Sec.*, Rev. H. Jona.

FROEBEL SOCIETY OF GREAT BRITAIN AND IRELAND, 4 Bloomsbury Square, W.C.—*Sec.*, Miss Noble.

FROEBEL UNION, NATIONAL, 4 Bloomsbury Square, W.C.—*Sec.*, Miss Maclean.

GAS ENGINEERS, INSTITUTION OF (Incorporated), 11 Victoria St., S.W.— *Sec.*, Thos. Cole, A.M.I.C.E.

GEOGRAPHICAL SOCIETY, ROYAL, 1 Savile Row, W. —*Pres.*, Sir Clements R. Markham, K.C.B., F.R.S. *Hon. Secretaries*, Major L. Darwin, R.E.; J. F. Hughes. *Foreign Secretary*, Sir John Kirk, K.C.B. *Sec.*, J. Scott Keltie, LL.D. *Curator of Maps*, John Coles, F.S.A. *Librarian*, Dr. H. R. Mill. *Chief Clerk*, S. J. Evis. F.R.G.S.

GEOLOGICAL SOCIETY, Burlington House. — *Pres.*, W. Whitaker, F.R.S. *Secs.*, R. S. Herries, M.A.; W. W. Watts, M.A. *Foreign Sec.*, Sir J. Evans, F.R.S. *Treas.*, W. T. Blanford, F.R.S. *Assist. Sec. and Lib.*, L. L. Belinfante, M.SC. F.G.S.

GORDON BOYS' HOME, West End, Woking. *Office*, 20 Cockspur Street, S.W.—*Treas.*, Gen. Sir Dighton Probyn, G.C.V.O., V.C. *Sec.*, Lt.-Col. G. A. Beaty-Pownall.

GOSPEL IN FOREIGN PARTS, SOCIETY FOR THE PROPAGATION OF THE, 19 Delahay St., Westminster. —*Sec.*, Rev. H. W. Tucker, M.A. *Assist. Secs.*, W. F. Kemp, M.A.; Rev. Ernest Sketchley, M.A. Income, 1898, £132,355 ; missionaries, 787.

GOVERNESSES' BENEVOLENT INSTITUTION, 32 Sackville Street, W.—*Sec.*, Chas. W. Klugh.

GUILD OF CHURCH MUSICIANS, 42, Berners Street, W.— *Warden*, J. H. Lewis, MUS.D., D.C.L.

HAKLUYT SOCIETY. — *Agent*, B. Quaritch, 15 Piccadilly, W. *Hon. Sec.*, W. Foster, Bordean, Holly Road, Wanstead, N.E.

HARLEIAN SOCIETY, 140 Wardour Street, W.— *Sec.*, J. Paul Rylands, F.S.A.

HARVEIAN SOCIETY, Stafford Rooms, Titchborne Street, W. — *Hon. Secs.*, J. Jackson Clarke, F.R.C.S.; Leonard G. Guthrie, M.D.

HEAD MASTERS' CONFERENCE.—*Sec.*, A. R. S. Hallidee, 1 New Sq., Lincoln's Inn, W.C.

HEAD MASTERS, INCORPORATED ASSOCIATION OF. —*Assistant Sec.*, H. Bendall, 37 Norfolk St., Strand, W.C.

HEAD MISTRESSES ASSOCIATION. — *Sec.*, Miss Louisa Brough, 25 Craven St., W.C.

HEALTH SOCIETY, NATIONAL, 53 Berners St., W. —*Sec.*, Miss Lankester.

HELLENIC STUDIES, SOCIETY FOR THE PROMOTION OF, 22 Albemarle Street.—*Pres.*, Prof. R. C. Jebb, M.P. *Hon. Sec.*, George A. Macmillan.

HENRY BRADSHAW SOCIETY, for editing Rare Liturgical Texts. — *Hon. Sec.*, Rev. H. A. Wilson, M.A., Magdalen College, Oxford.

HISTORICAL SOCIETY, ROYAL, 115 St. Martin's Lane, W.C.—*Pres.*, A. W. Ward. *Sec.*, H. Hall, F.S.A. *Lib.*, T. Mason, LL.D. F.R.Hist.S.

HOME AND COLONIAL SCHOOL SOCIETY, Gray's Inn Road, W.C., and Highbury Hill House, N.—*Principal*, Rev. D. J. Thomas, M.A. *Hon. Sec.*, Thomas Robertson.

HOMELESS AND DESTITUTE CHILDREN, NATIONAL REFUGES FOR, 164 Shaftesbury Avenue, W.C.—*Sec.*, H. Bristow Wallen.

HOME MISSIONS OF CHURCH OF ENGLAND; ADDITIONAL CURATES SOCIETY, Albany Buildings, 39 Victoria St.. S.W.—*Sec.*, Rev. P. Petit, M.A.

HOME READING UNION, NATIONAL, Surrey Ho., Victoria Embankment, W.C.—*Sec.*, Miss MOLDY.

HOMES OF HOPE, 4-6 Regent Square, Gray's Inn Road, W.C.—*Treas.*, Alfred Hoare. *Sec.*, William Hornibrook.

HOMES FOR LITTLE BOYS, Farningham and Swanley. *Offices*, 25 Holborn Viaduct, E.C.—*Sec.*, W. Robson.

HOMES FOR WORKING BOYS IN LONDON, 12 Buckingham St.. Strand.—*Sec.*, William Denham.

HOMES FOR WORKING GIRLS IN LONDON, 3 Victoria Street, S.W. — *Founder and Director*, John Shrimpton.

HORTICULTURAL SOCIETY, ROYAL, Chiswick Gardens. Open every day. Offices, 117 Victoria Street, S.W.—*Pres.*, Sir Trevor Lawrence, Bt. *Sec.*, Rev. W. Wilks, M.A. *Treas.*, Philip Crowley, F.L.S. *Chief Clerk*, Frank Reader. F.R.H.S.

HOSPITAL SATURDAY FUND, 54 Gray's Inn Road, W.C.—*Sec.*, W. G. Bunn.

HOSPITAL SUNDAY FUND (METROPOLITAN), Mansion House and 18 Queen Victoria Street, E.C.—*Pres.*, The Lord Mayor. *Sec.*, H. N. Custance.

HOSPITALS ASSOCIATION, 28 Southampton Street, Strand, W.C.—*Hon. Sec.*, Sydney Phillips, B.A.

HOWARD ASSOCIATION, for the Promotion of the best Methods of Treatment and Prevention of Crime, Pauperism, &c., 5 Bishopsgate Street Without.—*&c.*, William Tallack.

HUGUENOT SOCIETY OF LONDON.—*Hon. Sec.*, R. S. Faber, 90 Regent's Pk. Road, N.W.

HUMANE SOCIETY, ROYAL, 4 Trafalgar Square, W.C.—*Sec.*, Maj. F. A. C. Claughton.

HUMANITARIAN LEAGUE, 53 Chancery Lane, W.C.—*Hon. Sec.*, Henry S. Salt.

HUNTERIAN SOCIETY, THE LONDON INSTITUTION, Finsbury Circus, E.C.—*President*, J. S. E. Cotman, M.R.C.P.E. *Secs.*, A. T. Davies, M.D.; J. H. Targett, M.S.

IMPERIAL INSTITUTE OF THE U.K., COLONIES, AND INDIA, South Kensington, S.W.—*Pres.*, H.R.H. the Prince of Wales, K.G. *Hon. Sec. and Director*, Sir F. Abel, Bart., K.C.B., F.R.S. *Director of Scientific Dept.*, Prof. Wyndham R. Dunstan, F.R.S. *Assist. Sec.*, Lt. G. K. Maltby, R N., 1et.

INCORPORATED FREE AND OPEN CHURCH ASSOCIATION, Church House, S.W.—*Hon. Sec.*, F. C. Dobbing, J.P.

INDIGENT BLIND, SCHOOL FOR (1799), St. George's Circus, Southwark.—*Treas.*, Col. B. T. Bosanquet. *Resid. Chaplain & Sec.*, Rev. St. Clare Hill, M.A.

INDIGENT BLIND VISITING SOCIETY, 27 Red Lion Square, W.C.—*Sec.*, T. A. Wallis.

INEBRIATES REFORMATORY FUND, to help in the establishment of voluntary Reformatories and generally promote the operation of the Act of 1898.—*Sec.*, A. J. S. Maddison.

INEBRIETY, SOCIETY FOR THE STUDY OF, 11 Chandos Street, Cavendish Square, W.—*Pres.*, W. WYNN Westcott, M.D. *Hon. Sec.*, E. T. Aydon Smith.

INFANT ORPHAN ASYLUM, Wanstead. *Office*, 63 Ludgate Hill, E.C.—*Sec.*, Henry W. Green.

INVALID CHILDREN'S AID ASSOC., 18 Buckingham Street, Strand, W.C.—*Sec.*, H. G. Evered.

IRISH CHURCH MISSIONS TO THE ROMAN CATHOLICS, 11 Buckingham Street, W.C.—*Secs.*, Rev. N. F. Duncan, M.A.: William Pasley.

IRISH DISTRESSED LADIES' FUND, 17 North Audley Street, W.—*Sec.*, Gen. W. M. Lees.

IRISH LITERARY SOCIETY, 8 Adelphi Terrace, W.C.—*Hon. Sec.*, A. P. Graves, M.A.

IRISH SOCIETY, 32 Sackville Street, W.—*Sec. and Treas.*, Rev. Thomas Keane.

IRON AND STEEL INSTITUTE, 28 Victoria Street, S.W.—*Pres.*, Sir William C. Roberts-Austin, K.C.B. *Sec.*, Bennett H. Brough.

IRON TRADE ASSOCIATION, BRITISH, 165 Strand, W.C.—*Pres.*, Sir J. J. Jenkins. M.P. *Sec.*, J. S. Jeans.

JAPAN SOCIETY, 20 Hanover Square, W.—*Hon. Secs.*, C. Holme ; Y. Yamashita. *Asst. Sec.*, A. B. Brice.

JOURNALISTS, INSTITUTE OF, 78 Fleet Street.—*Sec.*, Herbert Cornish.

JUNIOR ENGINEERS, INSTITUTION OF, Westminster Palace Hotel, Victoria St.. S.W. *Pres.*, Hon. C. A. Parsons, F.R.S. *Sec.*, W. T. Dunn.

KYRLE SOCIETY, 49 Manchester Street, W.—*Hon. Secs.*, Miss L. James ; C. W. ELLDRON.

LABOUR PROTECTION ASSOCIATION, 7 Victoria St., S.W.—*Sec.*, Frederick Millar.

LABOURING CLASSES, SOCIETY (INCORPORATED 1850) FOR IMPROVING THE CONDITION OF THE, 4 Bloomsbury Mansions, Hart Street, W.C.—*Sec.*, Alfred Humphreys.

LAND NATIONALISATION SOC., 432 West Strand, W.C.—*Sec.*, Joseph Hyder.

LAW ASSOCIATION (1817), 55 Lincoln's Inn Fields, W.C. — *President*, Sir Richard E. Webster, G.C.M.G., Q.C., M.P. *Sec.*, E. E. Barrow.

LIBERAL CENTRAL ASSOCIATION, 41 Parliament Street, S.W.—*Hon. Sec.*, Robert A. Hudson.

LIBERAL FEDERATION, NATIONAL, 42 Parliament St., S.W.—*Sec.*, Robert A. Hudson.

LIBERATION OF RELIGION FROM STATE PATRONAGE, SOCIETY FOR, 2 Serjeants' Inn.—*Chairman*, J. Carvell Williams, M.P. *Secs.*, J. Fisher; S. Robjohns.

LIBERTY AND PROPERTY DEFENCE LEAGUE, 7 Victoria Street, S.W.—*Sec. and Parliamentary Agent*, Frederick Millar.

LIBRARY ASSOCIATION, 20 Hanover Square, W.—*Pres.*, Ald. J. W. Southern (Chairman Manchester Pub. Lib. Committee). *Hon. Sec.*, F. Pacy.

LICENSED VICTUALLERS' ASYLUM, Asylum Road, Old Kent Road, S.E. — *Sec.*, A. L. Annett. Offices, 17 New Bridge Street, E.C.

LICENSED VICTUALLERS' SCHOOL, Kennington Lane, S.E.—*Sec.*, Edward Grimwood.

LIFEBOAT INSTITUTION, ROYAL NATIONAL, 14 John Street, Adelphi.—*Sec.*, Charles Dibdin, F.R.G.S.

LIFE FROM FIRE, ROYAL SOCIETY FOR THE PROTECTION OF, 20 New Bridge Street, E.C.—*Sec.*, George Cooke.

LIFE SAVING SOCIETY, 8 Bayley Street, Bedford Square, W.C.—*Hon. Sec.*, Wm. Henry.

LINNEAN SOCIETY, Burlington House. — *Pres.*, Albert L. G. Günther, F.R.S. *Secs.*, B. D. Jackson ; G. B. Howes. *Assist. Sec.*, J. E. Harting. *Lib.*, A. W. Kappel.

LITERARY FUND, ROYAL, 7 Adelphi Terrace.—*Pres.*, Earl of Crewe. *Sec.*, Llewelyn Roberts, B.A.

LITERATURE, ROYAL SOCIETY OF, 20 Hanover Sq., W.—*President*, Earl Halsbury. *Treas.*, E. W. Brabrook, C.B., F.S.A. *Sec. and Lib.*, Percy W. Ames, F.S.A. F.R.S.L.

LLOYD'S REGISTER OF BRITISH AND FOREIGN SHIPPING, 2 White Lion Court, Cornhill.—*Chairman*, John Glover. *Sec.*, A. G. Dryhurst. Publication Office of *Lloyd's Register Book, Yacht Register, &c.*

LLOYD'S, Royal Exchange.—*Secretary*, Col. H. Hozier, C.B.

LONDON CITY MISSION, 3, Bridewell Pl., E.C.—*Secs.*, Rev. R. Dawson, B.A.; Rev. T. S. Hutchinson, M.A.

LONDON DIOCESAN COUNCIL, for Preventive Rescue and Penitentiary Work, Church House, S.W.—*Sec.*, Rev. George Brett, M.A.

LONDON FEMALE GUARDIAN SOC., Training Home, 191 High St., Stoke Newington; Probational Home, 21 Old Ford Road, Bethnal Green.—*Secretary*, W. Edwin Page.

LONDON FEMALE PREVENTIVE AND REFORMATORY INSTITUTION, 200 Euston Road, N.W.—*Sec.*, Wm. J. Taylor.

LONDON INSTITUTION, Finsbury Circ., E.C.—*Principal Librarian & Secretary*, R. W. Frazer, LL.B.

LONDON LIBRARY, St. James's Sq., S.W.—*Secretary and Librarian*, C. T. Hagberg Wright, LL.D.

LONDON MATHEMATICAL SOCIETY, 22 Albemarle Street, W.—*Pres.*, Lord Kelvin, F.R.S. *Secs.*, R. Tucker, M.A.; A. E. H. Love, F.R.S.

LONDON MISSIONARY SOCIETY, 14 Blomfield St., London Wall, E.C.—*Treas.*, Albert Spicer, M.P. *Foreign Secs.*, Revs. R. Wardlaw Thompson; Geo. Cousins. *Home Sec.*, Rev. A. N. Johnson.

LONDON ORPHAN ASYLUM, Watford. *Office*, 21 Great St. Helen's, E.C.—*Sec.*, H. C. Armiger.

LONDON SOCIETY FOR EXTENSION OF UNIVERSITY TEACHING, Charterhouse, E.C.—*Pres.*, Rt. Hon. Sir John Lubbock, Bart., M.P. *Sec.*, C. W. Kimmins, D.SC. *Assist. Sec.*, P. M. Wallace, M.A.

LONDON SOCIETY FOR PROMOTING CHRISTIANITY AMONGST THE JEWS (1809), 16 Lincoln's Inn Fields.—*Sec.*, Rev. W. Fleming, LL.B. *Assist. Sec.*, Rev. W. T. Gidney, M.A.

LONDON SOCIETY FOR TEACHING THE BLIND TO READ AND TRAINING THEM IN INDUSTRIAL OCCUPATIONS, Upper Avenue Road, Swiss Cottage.—*Sec.*, Capt. G. G. Webber, R.N.

LORD'S DAY OBSERVANCE SOCIETY, 20 Bedford Street, W.C.—*Sec.*, Rev. Frederic Peake, LL.D.

MAGDALEN HOSPITAL, Streatham, S.W.—A home for penitent females, who are maintained entirely gratis; application may be sent to the Head Matron, or to the *Warden*, Rev. W. Watkins.

MARINE ENGINEERS, INSTITUTE OF, 58 Romford Road, Stratford (Centres at Cardiff and Southampton).—*Pres.*, Sir James Lyle Mackay, K.C.I.E. *Hon. Sec.*, J. Adamson, Stopford Rd., Upton Manor, E.

MARINE SOCIETY FOR THE EQUIPMENT, MAINTENANCE, AND INSTRUCTION OF DESTITUTE BOYS FOR THE ROYAL NAVY AND MERCHANT SERVICE, Clark'n Place, Bishopsgate Street Within, E.C. (Training Ship, *Warspite*).—*President*, Earl of Romney. *Sec.*, Albert E. Poland, R.N.

MARK MASTER MASONS, GRAND LODGE OF, Mark Masons' Hall, Great Queen St., W.C.—*Grand Sec.*, C. F. Matier.

MASONIC BENEVOLENT INSTITUTION, ROYAL, 4 Freemasons' Hall, W.C.—*Sec.*, James Terry.

MASONIC DEGREES, GRAND COUNCIL OF ALLIED, Mark Masons' Hall, Great Queen St., W.C.—*Grand Sec.*, C. F. Matier.

MASONIC INSTITUTION FOR BOYS, ROYAL (Instituted 1798), Wood Green, N.—*Sec.*, J. Morrison McLeod, 6 Freemasons' Hall, W.C.

MASONIC INSTITUTION FOR GIRLS, ROYAL (Instituted 1788), St. John's Hill, Battersea Rise, S.W.—*Offices*, 5 Freemasons' Hall, W.C. *Sec.*, F. R. W. Hedges.

MECHANICAL ENGINEERS, INSTITUTION OF, Storey's Gate, Westminster, S.W.—*Pres.*, Sir W. H. White, K.C.B. *Sec.*, E. Worthington, B.SC. **M.I.Mech.E.**

MEDICAL AND CHIRURGICAL SOCIETY, ROYAL, 20 Hanover Square, W.—*Pres.*, Thomas Bryant, F.R.C.S. *Hon. Secs.*, T. Barlow, M.D.; A. Pearce Gould, M.S. *Libr.*, J. Y. W. MacAlister, F.S.A.

MEDICAL EDUCATION AND REGISTRATION, GENERAL COUNCIL OF, 299 Oxford Street.—*Pres.*, Sir William Turner, M.B., F.R.S. *Regist.*, Henry E. Allen, LL.B.

MEDICAL MEN (WIDOWS AND ORPHANS OF), SOCIETY FOR RELIEF OF, 11 Chandos Street, Cavendish Square. W.—*Sec.*, J. B. Blackett.

MEDICAL OFFICERS OF HEALTH, SOCIETY (Incorporated) OF, 197 High Holborn, W.C.—*Pres.*, Arthur Newsholme, M.D. *Hon. Secs.*, F. J. Allan, M.D.; J. Mitchell Wilson, M.D.

MEDICAL SOCIETY OF LONDON, 11 Chandos Street, Cavendish Square.—*Pres.*, Fredk. Roberts, M.D. *Hon. Secs.*, J. Calvert, M.D.; F. C. Wallis, F.R.C.S. *Reg. and Res. Lib.*, W. R. Hall.

MENDICITY SOCIETY, 9 Red Lion Square, W.C.—*Assist. Manager & Sec.*, Eric A. Buchanan.

MERCHANT SEAMEN'S ORPHAN ASYLUM, Snaresbrook. *Office*, 1 Fen Court, Fenchurch St., E.C. *Pres.*, H.R.H. Duke of York. *Treas.*, E. S. Norris. *Sec.*, F. W. Rawlinson, F.R.G.S.

MERCY, LEAGUE OF.—*Pres.*, H.R.H. Prince of Wales. *Hon. Secs.*, Lord Wolverton; Dr. W. J. Collins; J. Harrison.

METEOROLOGICAL SOCIETY, ROYAL, 70 Victoria Street, Westminster.—*Pres.*, F. C. Bayard, LL.M. *Secs.*, E. Mawley, F.R.H.S.; G. J. Symons, F.R.S. *For. Sec.*, R. H. Scott, F.R.S. *Assist. Sec.*, Wm. Marriott. F.R.Met.Soc.

METROPOLITAN AND CITY POLICE PENSIONERS' EMPLOYMENT ASSOCIATION, 7 Victoria Street, S.W.—*Secretary*, Frederick Nelson.

METROPOLITAN DRINKING FOUNTAIN AND CATTLE TROUGH ASSOCIATION, 70 Victoria Street, Westminster, S.W.—*Sec.*, Capt W. Simpson.

METROPOLITAN FEDERATION OF EVANGELICAL FREE CHURCHES, 26 Memorial Hall, E.C.—*Sec.*, Joseph Fletcher.

METROPOLITAN VISITING AND RELIEF ASSOC., 45A Pall Mall, S.W. *Sec.* Grant Marston.

MICROSCOPICAL SOCIETY, ROYAL, 20 Hanover Sq., W.—*Pres.*, E. M. Nelson. *Secs.*, Rev. W. H. Dallinger, F.R.S.; R. G. Hebb, M.A., M.D. *Libr. and Assist. Sec.*, F. A. Parsons. **F.R.M.S.**

MORDEN COLLEGE FOR DECAYED MERCHANTS, Blackheath.—*Treas.*, H. E. Rivers. *Chaplain*, Rev. Henry Lansdell, D.D. *Lib.*, H. L. Hall.

MUNICIPAL AND COUNTY ENGINEERS, INCORPORATED ASSOCIATION OF, 11 Victoria Street, S.W.—*Sec.*, Thomas Cole, A.M.I.C.E.

MUSICIANS OF GREAT BRITAIN, ROYAL SOCIETY OF, 12 Lisle Street, W.—*Treas.*, W. H. Cummings, F.S.A. *Sec.*, Stanley Lucas, 84 New Bond St.

NATIONAL BENEVOLENT INSTITUTION, 65 Southampton Row, W.C.—*President*, Marquess of Bristol. *Sec.*, Henry C. Latreille.

NATIONAL PORTRAIT GALLERY, Merrion Square, Dublin.—*Director*, Sir Walter Armstrong; *Regist.*, W. G. Strickland.

NATIONAL RIFLE ASSOCIATION, 12 Pall Mall East, S.W.—*Pres.*, H.R.H. the Duke of Cambridge, K.G.—*Treas.*, Lord Kinnaird. *Sec.*, Col. C. R. Crosse; *Assist. Do.*, Capt. M. C. Matthews.

NATIONAL SOCIETY FOR AID TO THE SICK AND WOUNDED IN WAR (British Red Cross Society). 5 York Bldgs., Adelphi. *Sec.*, James G. Vokes.

NATIONAL SOCIETY FOR PROMOTING THE EDUCATION OF THE POOR IN THE PRINCIPLES OF THE ESTABLISHED CHURCH, Broad Sanctuary, Westminster. - *Treas.*, Very Rev. Dean Gregory. *Sec.*, Rev. Canon Brownrigg, M.A. *Organis Secs.*, Rev. F. J. Chandler; Rev. C. H. Spurrell. *Depôt Sues.*, G. Roberts. *Dep*²*t Account tnt*, F. C. Badrick.

NATIONAL TRUST (for Places of Historic Interest or Natural Beauty), 1 Great College St., S.W. —*Sec.*, Hugh Blakiston, B.A.

NAVAL AND MILITARY BIBLE SOCIETY, 32 Sackville Street, W.—*Sec.*, Samuel Rayson.

NAVAL ARCHITECTS, INSTITUTION OF, 5 Adelphi Terrace, W.C.—*Sec.*, George Holmes.

NAVAL FUND, ROYAL (1893). 9 Craig's Court, S.W. For the relief of Widows, Orphans, &c., of Seamen and Marines dying in the service of the Crown.—*Sec.*, J. F. Phillips.

NAVY LEAGUE, 13. Victoria St., S.W.—*Pres.*, Earl of Drogheda. *Chairman of Executive Committee*, H. Seymour Trower. *Secretary*, Commr. W. Caius Crutchley, R.N.R.

NEWSPAPER PRESS FUND, 11 Garrick St., W.C.—*Pres.*, Lord Glenesk. *Treas.*, Sir John A. Willox, M.P. *Sec.*, W. Thornton Sharp, B.A.

NEWSVENDORS' BENEVOLENT AND PROVIDENT INSTITUTION, Memorial Hall Buildings, Farringdon Street, E.C.—*Sec.*, W. W. Jones.

NUMISMATIC SOCIETY, 22 Albemarle St., W.—*Pres.*, Sir John Evans, K.C.B. *Treasurer*, Alfred E. Copp. *Hon. Secs.*, H. A. Grueber, F.S.A.; E. J. Rapson, M.A. *For. Sec.*, G. F. Hill, M.A. *Librarian*, O. Codrington, M.D.

NURSES, ROYAL NATIONAL PENSION FUND FOR, 28 Finsbury Pavemt., E.C.—*President*, H.R.H. the Princess of Wales. *Sec.*, Louis H. M. Dick.

OBSTETRICAL SOCIETY OF LONDON. 20 Hanover Square, W.—*Hon. Secs.*, John Phillips, M.D.; H. R. Spencer, M.D.

OIL PAINTERS, SOCIETY OF, Piccadilly. — *Pres.*, Frank Walton, R.I. *Vice-Pres.*, S. Melton Fisher. *Treas.*, T. B. Kennington. *Sec.*, W. T. Blackmore.

OPIUM TRADE, SOCIETY FOR SUPPRESSION OF THE, Finsbury House, Blomfield Street, E.C.—*Hon. Sec.*, Joseph G. Alexander, LL.B. *Sec.*, Rev. George A Wilson.

ORCHESTRAL ASSOCIATION, 39 Gerard Street, W.—*Sec.*, F. Orcherton.

ORDINATION CANDIDATES' EXHIBITION FUND, Albany Buildings, 39 Victoria St., Westminster. —*Hon. Sec.*, Rev. Paul Petit, M.A.

ORGANISTS, GUILD OF (Incorporated), 24 Queen Victoria Street, E.C.— *Hon. Sec.* Fred. B. Townend, Brentwood, Essex. *Warden*, P. Rideout, MUS.D.

ORPHAN HOME, NATIONAL, for Fatherless Girls, Ham Common, Richmond. — *Office*, 12 Pall Mall, S.W. *Sec.*, E. Evans Cronk.

ORPHAN WORKING SCHOOL, Haverstock Hill; Alexandra Orphanage. Hornsey Rise; and Convalescent Home, Harold Rd., Margate. *Offices*, 73 Cheapside.—*Sec.*, Algernon C. P. Coote, M.A.

OXFORD AND CAMBRIDGE SCHOOLS EXAMINATION BOARD, *Offices*, Caius College, Cambridge, and 74 High Street, Oxford. — *Secs.*, E. J. Gross, M.A., Caius College, Cambridge; P. E. Matheson, M.A., New College, Oxford.

PAINTER - ETCHERS AND ENGRAVERS. ROYAL SOCIETY OF. 5A Pall Mall East, S.W.—*Sec.*, Cloudesley Brereton, M.A.

PAINTERS IN WATER COLOURS, ROYAL INSTITUTE OF, Piccadilly. — *Pres.*, E. J. Gregory, R.A. *Vice-Pres.*, E. M. Wimperis. *Tre.s.*, Yeend King. *Sec.*, W. T. Blackmore.

PAINTERS IN WATER COLOURS. ROYAL SOCIETY OF, 5A Pall Mall East.—*Sec.*, Percy E Isall

PALESTINE EXPLORATION FUND, 38 Conduit Street, W.—*Sec.*, George Armstrong.

PARENTS' NATIONAL EDUCATIONAL UNION, 26 Victoria Street, S.W.—*Sec.*, Miss F. Blogg.

PATENT AGENTS, CHARTERED INSTITUTE OF. 19 Southampton Buildings, Chancery Lane, W.C.—*Secretary and Registrar*, H. Howgrave Graham.

PATHOLOGICAL SOCIETY, 20 Hanover Sq., W.—*Hon. Secs.*, H. D. Rolleston, M.D.; C. A. Ballance, M.S.

PATRIOTIC FUND, ROYAL COMMISSION OF THE (1854), 53 Charing Cross. For the administration of Funds for the benefit of Widows, Children, and other dependents of deceased Soldiers, Sailors and Marines.—*Secretary*, Col. J. S. Young.

PEABODY DONATION FUND, 64 Queen Street, Cheapside, E.C.—*Sec.*, J. Crouch.

PEACE SOCIETY, 47 New Broad Street, E.C.—*Sec.*, W. Evans Darby, LL.D.

PHARMACEUTICAL SOCIETY, 17 Bloomsbury Sq., W.C.—*Pres.*, William Martindale. *Sec. and Registrar*, Richard Bremridge.

PHILHARMONIC SOCIETY, Queen's Hall, Langham Place, W.—*Hon. Sec.*, Francesco Berger, 6 York Street, Portman Square, W.

PHONOGRAPHIC SOCIETY (Incorporated), Eccleston House, 100 Mattison Road, Harringay, N.—*Pres.*, Alfred Pitman. *Sec.*, H. W. Harris.

PHOTOGRAPHIC SOCIETY, ROYAL, 66 Russell Sq., W.C.—*Pres.*, Earl of Crawford, K.T. *Assist. Sec.*, A. W. W. Bartlett.

PHRENOLOGICAL SOCIETY. BRITISH (Incorporated), 63 Chancery Lane, W.C.—*Hon. Sec.*, F. R. Warren.

PHYSICAL RECREATION SOCIETY, NATIONAL, *Office*, Exeter Hall, Strand.— *Hon. Sec.*, Eugene Sully.

PHYSICAL SOCIETY, Burlington House, W.—*Pres.*, Prof. J. Lodge, F.R.S. *Hon. Secs.*, H. M. Elder, M.A.; W. Watson, B.SC.

PHYSICIANS, ROYAL COLL. OF, Pall Mall East.—*President*, W. S. Church, M.D. *Treas.*, Sir Dyce Duckworth, M.D. *Registrar*. E. Liveing, M.D. *Bedell & Act. Sec.*, Wm. Fleming.

PHYSICIANS, IRELAND, ROYAL COLLEGE OF.—*Pres.*, John William Moore, M.D. *Vice Pres.*, W. J. Smyly, M.D. *Regist.*, James Craig. M.D

POOR CLERGY RELIEF CORPORATION (1856), 38 Tavistock Place, W.C.—*Sec.*, M. B. Phillips.

POST OFFICE ORPHAN HOMES INSTITUTION, for Children of Deceased Sorters, Postmen, &c. *Chief Offices*, General Post Office, and 125 Copthall House, Copthall Avenue, E.C.—*Treas.*, C. J. Stevens. *Sec.*, J. Avery.

PRIMROSE LEAGUE, 64 Victoria Street, Westminster. — *Chancellor*, Lord Glenesk. *Vice-Chanc.*, G. Lane Fox. *Treas.*, Sir F D. Dixon-Hartland, Bt., M.P.

PRINCE OF WALES'S HOSPITAL FUND, *Offices*, Bank of England, E.C. *Hon. Secs.*, Sir Savile Crossley, Bart.; J. G. Craggs, F.C.A.

PRINCESS LOUISE HOME FOR THE PROTECTION OF YOUNG GIRLS. *Office*, 32 Sackville St., W.—*Sec.*, Reginald Drake.

PRINTERS' PENSION CORPORATION, Gray's Inn Chambers, 20 High Holborn. Almshouses at Wood Green.—*Sec.*, Joseph Mortimer.

PROTESTANT ALLIANCE, 430 Strand, W.C. — *Sec.*, S. W. Brett. *Asst. do.*, H. Fowler.

PROTESTANT LEAGUE, NATIONAL, 14 Buckingham Street, Strand, W.C.—*Registrar*, H. Miller.

PUBLIC HEALTH, ROYAL INSTITUTE OF, 197 High Holborn, W.C.—*Pres.*, Prof. Wm. R. Smith, M.D. *Chairman of Council*, Sir James R. Andrew Clark, Bart. *Hon. Sec.*, Henry C. Jones.

PURE LITERATURE SOCIETY, 11 Buckingham Street, Strand, W.C.—*Sec.*, Richard Turner.

RAGGED SCHOOL UNION AND SHAFTESBURY SO-CIETY.—HOLIDAY HOMES FUND.—POOR CHIL-DREN'S AID SOCIETY.—BAREFOOT MISSION.—CRIPPLE CHILDREN'S MISSION, 37 Norfolk St., Strand.—*Sec.*, John Kirk.

RAILWAY BENEVOLENT INSTITUTION (supported by voluntary contributions), for the Relief of disabled Railway Officers and Servants, their Orphans, Widows, and Children, when left in distressed circumstances, 133 Seymour Street, Euston Square, N.W.; Railway Orphan-age, Derby. *Income*, 1898-9, £63,639.—*Gen. Sec.*, A. E. Mills, M.A.

RAINE'S SCHOOLS, Cannon Street Road, St. George-in-the-East.— *Chairman*, J. Ashbridge Telfer. *Headmaster*, R. S. Taylor.

RECREATIVE EVENING SCHOOLS ASSOCIATION, 37 Norfolk St., Strand. — *Hon. Secs.*, Rev. Dr. Paton; R. A. Yerburgh, M.P.

RED CROSS SOCIETY (see NATIONAL SOC. FOR AID TO SICK AND WOUNDED).

REEDHAM ORPHANAGE, Purley, Surrey. *Office*, 35 Finsbury Circus.—*Treas.*, H. C. O. Bonsor, M.P. *Sec.*, J. Rowland Edwards.

REFORMATORY AND REFUGE UNION, 32 Charing Cross.—*Sec.*, Arthur J. S. Maddison.

RELIGIOUS TRACT SOCIETY, 56 Paternoster Row. —*Treasurer*, Edward Rawlings. *Hon. Secs.*, Rev. Canon Fleming, B.D.; Rev. T. Monro Gibson, D.D. *Secs.*, Rev. Preby. L. B. White, D.D.; Rev. R. Lovett, M.A. *Cashier*, G. T. Betts. *Lay Sec. and Gen. Manager*, James Bowden. *Publisher*, Richard Bradshaw.

RESERVE SOLDIERS, NATIONAL ASSOCIATION FOR THE EMPLOYMENT OF, 12 Buckingham St., Strand, W.C. Office hours 10 to 4.—To assist men of good character in obtaining employment after leaving the Colours.—*Chairman*, Lt.-Gen. Sir W. Drysdale, K.C.B. *Sec.*, Col. A. M. Handley.

RÖNTGEN SOCIETY.—*Hon. Sec.*, — Low, M.D., 12 Sinclair Gdns., W. Kensington.

ROYAL ALFRED AGED MERCHANT SEAMEN'S INSTI-TUTION, Belvedere, Kent. *Office*, 58 Fenchurch St., E.C.—*Sec.*, J. Bailey Walker.

ROYAL COMMISSION FOR THE EXHIBITION OF 1851, 18, Victoria Street, S.W.—*Sec.*, Maj.-Gen. Sir Arthur Ellis, K.C.V.O.

ROYAL INSTITUTION OF GREAT BRITAIN, 21 Albe-marle Street.—*Pres.*, Duke of Northumberland, K.G. *Hon. Sec.*, Sir Fredk. Bramwell, Bart., F.R.S. *Asst. Sec. & Libr.*, H. Young.

ROYAL NAVAL BENEVOLENT SOCIETY, 18 Adam Street,Strand.—*Pres.*, The Duke of Saxe-Coburg and Gotha, K.G. *Sec.*, R. H. Clark, R.N.

ROYAL NAVAL SCRIPTURE READERS' SOCIETY, 112 St. Martin's Lane, W.C.—*Sec.*, Col. M. H. Farquharson, R.M.L.I.

ROYAL SOCIETY, Burlington House.—*Pres.*, Lord Lister. *Treasurer*, Alfred B. Kempe, M.A. *Secs.*, Sir Michael Foster, K.C.B.; Arthur Wm. Rücker, D.C.L. *For. Sec.*, (vacant). *Assist. Sec. and Lib.*, Robert Harrison. *Clerk*, T. James. F.R.S.

SAILORS' SOCIETY, BRITISH AND FOREIGN, SAILORS' INSTITUTE, Shadwell, E.—*Treasurer*, Ald. Sir J. C. Dimsdale. *Sec.*, Rev. E. W. Matthews.

ST. ANDREW'S WATERSIDE CHURCH MISSION for Sailors, Fishermen and Emigrants. 65 Fenchurch Street, E.C.—*Sec.*, Comr.W.F.Caborne,C.B.,R.N.R.

ST. ANNE'S SOCIETY SCHOOLS, ROYAL ASYLUM OF, Redhill, Surrey. *Office*, 58 Gracechurch St.—*Sec.*, R. H. Evans.

ST. JOHN AMBULANCE ASSOC., St. John's Gate Clerkenwell. *Ch. Sec.*, Col. Sir H. C. Perrott, Bt.

ST. JOHN OF JERUSALEM, Grand Priory of the Order in England, St. John's Gate, Clerkenwell. *Sec.-Gen.*, Capt. Sir Alfred Jephson, R.N. *Secretary*, Col. Sir Herbert C. Perrott, Bart.

ST. PATRICK, BENEVOLENT SOCIETY OF, 61 Stamford St., Blackfriars Road, S.E.—*Pres.*, Rt. Hon. Lord Justice Henn-Collins. *Sec.*, A. F. R. Daniel.

SALVATION ARMY, International Headquarters:—101 Queen Victoria Street; Central Offices of the Social Wing and Labour Bureau, 20 & 22 Whitechapel Road, E.; Deposit Bank, 107 Queen Victoria Street; International Training Home for Officers, Congress Hall, Clapton, N.E.; Publishing Office, 98 and 100 Clerkenwell Road; Bookbinding Factory, Rawstorne St., Goswell Road; Boys' Home (for waifs and strays), Fetter Lane, E.C.; Office for Rescue Work. Missing Friends Enquiry Office, Laundry, &c., 259 Mare Street, Hackney; Bakery, Hawthorn St., Ball's Pond, N.; Farm Colony, Hadleigh, Essex.—"*General*," William Booth. *Bankers*, The Bank of England (Law. Courts Branch). *Auditors*, Knox, Burbidge & Co.

SANITARY INSTITUTE, with which is incorporated the Parkes Museum, Margaret Street, W.—*Sec.*, E. White Wallis, F.S.S.

SCHOOLMASTERS, SOCIETY OF, 7 Adelphi Terrace.—*Chairman*, Rev. R. Lee. *Treas.*, Rev. Dr. Baker. *Sec.*, Llewelyn Roberts, B.A.

SCHOOL S., BRITISH AND FOREIGN, Temple Cham-bers, Temple Avenue, E.C.—*Sec.*, A. Bourne,B.A.

SCOTTISH HOSPITAL, ROYAL (for the relief of Scot-tish poor), 7 Crane Court. Fleet Street.—*President*, H.R.H. the Prince of Wales, K.G. *Treas.*, the Earl of Rosebery, K.G. *Sec.*, T. R. Moncrieff.

SCRIPTURE GIFT MISSION AND CRYSTAL PALACE BIBLE STAND 15 Strand, W.C.—*Hon. Sec.*, W. Walters.

SEA FISHERMEN, ROYAL PROVIDENT FUND (Incorporated by Royal Charter), Fishmongers' Hall,E.C.—*Chairman*,Marquess of Ormonde,K P. *Sec.*, Edward Cunliffe-Owen.

SEAMEN, THE MISSIONS TO, 11 Buckingham St., Strand, W.C.—*Clerical Sec.*, Rev. E. B. Back-house. *Lay do.*, Capt. W. Dawson, R.N.

SHIPMASTERS' SOCIETY, 60 Fenchurch St., E.C.—*Sec.*, Capt. A. G. Froud, Lieut. R.N.R.

SHIPWRECKED FISHERMEN AND MARINERS' ROYAL BENEVOLENT SOC., 26 Suffolk St., Pall Mall East, S.W.—*Sec.*, G. E. Maude.

SION COLLEGE, Victoria Embankment, E.C.—*Librarian*, Rev. W. H. Milman, M.A. *Treas.*, Rev. Blomfield Jackson, M.A.

SOCIÉTÉ NATIONALE DES PROFESSEURS DE FRAN-ÇAIS EN ANGLETERRE, for promoting Study of the French Language and Literature, 329 Vaux-hall Bridge Rd., S.W.— *Hon. Sec.*, A. P. Huguenet.

SOLDIERS AND SAILORS FAMILIES' ASSOCIATION, and "The Serpent." "Edgar," and "North West Frontier" Funds, 23 Queen Anne's Gate, Westminster.—*Chairman & Treas.*, Col. James Gildea, C.B. *Sec.*, Capt. G. E. Wickham Legg.

SONS OF THE CLERGY, SOCIETY OF THE FESTIVAL OF THE, 2 Bloomsbury Place.—*Treas.*, Sir Paget Bowman, Bart.

South African Association.—*Chairman of Committee*, Geoffry Drage, M.P.

South American Missionary Society, 1 Clifford's Inn, Fleet Street.—*Secs.*, Rev. E. P. Cackemaille, M.A.; Capt. E. Poulden, R.N.

Stationers' Hall, Stationers' Hall Court, for copyright registry.—*Regist.*, Chas. R. Rivington, F.S.A.

Statistical Society, Royal, 9 Adelphi Terrace.—*Pres.*, Rt. Hon. Sir H. H. Fowler, G.C.S.I., M.P. *Hon. Secs.*, Noel A. Humphreys; J. A. Baines. *Foreign Sec.*, Maj. P. G. Craigie. *Asst. Sec.*, B. W. Ginsburg, LL.D. *Lib.*, J. A. P. Mackenzie. F.S.S.

Stock Exchange, Throgmorton Street, E.C.—*Sec.*, Edward Satterthwaite.

Sunday League, National, 34 Red Lion Square, High Holborn, W.C.—*Sec.*, Henry Mills.

Sunday School Association, Essex Street, Strand.—*Pres.*, Stephen S. Tayler. *Treas.*, W. Blake Odgers, Q.C. *Hon. Sec.*, Ion Pritchard. *Manager*, B. C. Hare.

Sunday School Union.—*Benevolent Department*, 56 Old Bailey.—*Secs.*, W. H. Groser, B.SC.; J. Edmunds. *Business Department*, 57 Ludgate Hill, *Trade Manager*, A. Melrose.

Sunday Society, to Open Museums on Sundays, and repeal Lord's Day Act, 7 Pall Mall, S.W.—*Hon. Sec.*, Mark H. Judge, A.R.I.B.A.

Surgeons, Royal College of, 40 Lincoln's Inn Fields.—*Pres.*, Sir W. MacCormac, Bart., K.C.V.O *Vice-Pres.*, H. G. Howse; J. Tweedy. *Sec.*, Edw. Trimmer, M.A. *Assist. Sec.*, S. Cowell, B.A. *Conserv. of Museum*, Prof. Chas. Stewart, F.R.S. *Lib.*, Victor G. Plarr, M.A.

Surgeons in Ireland, Royal College of.—*Pres.*, R. L. Swan. *Vice-Pres.*, T. Myles. *Sec. to Council*, J. Barton. *Curator of Museum*, J. A. Scott. *Registrar*, G. F. Blake.

Surgical Aid Society, Salisbury Square, Fleet Street.—*Secretary*, Richard C. Tresidder.

Surgical Appliance Society (Provident), 12 Finsbury Circus, E.C.—*Sec.*, J. Slater Spence.

Surveyors' Institution, 12 Great George Street, S.W.—*Sec.*, J. C. Rogers.

Teachers' Benevolent and Orphan Funds, 71 Russell Square, W.C.—*Sec.*, J. H. Yoxall, M.P.

Teachers' Guild of Great Britain and Ireland, 74 Gower St., W.C.—*Chairman*, the Rev. Canon the Hon. E. Lyttelton, M.A. *General Secretary*, Herbert B. Garrod, M.A.

Teachers, National Union of, 71 Russell Square, W.C.—*President*, T. Clancy, M.A. *Sec.*, J. H. Yoxall, M.P. *Assist. Sec.*, C. James.

Technical and Secondary Education, National Association for the Promotion of, 10 Queen Anne's Gate, S.W. — *Hon. Sec.*, Sir H. E. Roscoe, F.R.S. *Sec.*, Frederick Oldman.

Temperance League, National, 34 Paternoster Row, E.C.—*Secretary*, Robert Rae.

Thames Church Mission, 31 New Bridge St., E.C.—*Treas.*, Sir Samuel Hoare, Bart., M.P. *Sec.*, F. Penfold, R.N.

Theatrical Fund, Royal General, 8 Catherine Street, Strand.—*Sec.*, C. J. Davies.

Toynbee Trust.—*Trustees*, The Council of the Universities Settlements Association. *Chairman*, Lord Herschell, Toynbee Hall, E.

Travellers' Aid Society (for Girls and Women), 3 Baker St., W.—*Sec.*, Miss Jessie Gordon.

Trinitarian Bible Society, 25 New Oxford St., W.C.—*Sec.*, Rev. E. W. Bullinger, D.D.

Unitarian Association, British and Foreign, Essex Hall, Essex St., W.—*Sec.*, Rev. W. C. Bowie.

United Kingdom Railway Officers' and Servants' Assoc., 21 Finsbury Pavement, E.C. *Sec.*, Alfred James.

United Service Institution, Royal, Banqueting House, Whitehall, S.W.—*Sec. & Curator*, Lieut. Col. R. Holden, F.S.A. *Editor & Libr.*, Capt. Hubert J. G. Garbett, R.N.

Universities Mission to Central Africa, 9 & 10 Dartmouth Street, S.W. — *Sec.*, Rev. Duncan Travers. *Lay Sec.*, C. J. Viner.

Veterinary Surgeons, Royal College of, 10 Red Lion Square, W.C.—*Pres.*, Prof. James Fraser, F.R.C.V.S.

Victoria Institute, 8 Adelphi Terrace.—*Pres.*, Sir G. G. Stokes, Bart., F.R.S. *Hon. Sec.*, Capt. F. W. H. Petrie, F.G.S.

Volunteers, Institute of Commanding Officers of, 31 Bedford St., Strand.—*Hon. Sec.*, Col. S. G. Bird.

Waterworks Engineers, British Association of, 54 Parliament Street, S.W.—*Sec.*, W. H. Brothers.

Weights and Measures, Incorporated Society of Inspectors of.—*Sec.*, William Crabtree, 43, Bridge Gate, Retford.

Welsh Girls' School "of the Most Honourable and Loyal Society of Ancient Britons," Ashford, Middlesex.—*Treas.*, Lord Llangattock. *Head Mistress*, Miss A. Hildred Jones. *Sec.*, Rev. Canon Brownrigg.

Wesleyan Conference Office, and Publishing House of the Wesleyan Methodist Church, 2 Castle St., 25 City Road, and 26 Paternoster Row.—*Princ.*, Rev. C. H. Kelly.

Wesleyan Missionary Society, 17 Bishopsgate St. Within.—*Treas.*, Williamson Lamplough; Rev. Jas. H. Rigg, D.D. *Secs.*, Rev. G. W. Olver, B.A.; Rev. F. W. Macdonald; Rev. W. Perkins; Rev. M. Hartley. *Hon. Sec.*, Rev. E. E. Jenkins, LL.D. (*Income*, 1898, £129,573.)

Widows, Society for the Relief of Distressed (applying within the first month of widowhood), 32 Sackville Street, W.—*Sec.*, Samuel Rayson.

Williams's (Dr.) Theological Library, Gordon Sq., W.C.—*Lib.*, Rev. F. H. Jones, B.A. Open 10 to 5, Sat. 10 to 1. Closed in August.

Women and Children, Associated Societies for the Protection of, 36 St. Martin's Lane, W.C.—*Sec.*, Arthur L. McIlwaine.

Women's Local Government Soc., 17 Tothill St., Westminster. *Pres.*, Countess of Aberdeen. *Sec.*, Mrs. Stanbury.

Women's Suffrage, Society for (Central and East of England), 20 Great College Street, S.W. —*Sec.*, Miss E. Palliser.—(Central and Western) 39 Victoria St., S.W. *Sec.*, Mrs. Charles Baxter.

Working Men's Club and Institute Union (a union of 700 clubs), Club Union Bdgs., Clerkenwell Rd., E.C. — *Sec.*, B. T. Hall.

Yacht Register—Lloyd's Register of Shipping, 2 White Lion Court, Cornhill.—*Chairman*, John Glover. *Sec.*, A. J. Dryhurst.

Young Men's (Central) Christian Association, Headquarters, Exeter Hall. *Branches*, 186 Aldersgate St. ; 59 Cornhill.—*Gen. Sec.*, John H. Putterill. *Financial Sec.*, Clarence Hooper.

Young Women's Christian Association. *Head Offices*, 25 and 26 George St., Hanover Sq., W.—*Hon. Secs. for London*, Hon. E. Kinnaird; Miss Morley. *Sec.*, H. Kidner.

Zoological Society, 3 Hanover Square, W.—*Pres.*, Duke of Bedford. *Treas.*, Charles Drummond. *Sec.*, Dr. P. L. Sclater, M.A., F.R.S. *Libr.*, F. H. Waterhouse. *Supt. of Gardens*, C. Bartlett.

Many of the following Hospitals admit paying In-Patients, the charges being varied in proportion to the means and the requirements of persons applying for admission. Some of the Hospitals also receive paying Out-Patients.

General Hospitals.

ST. BARTHOLOMEW'S HOSPITAL, West Smithfield. Ordinary cases admitted from 9 to 10 daily; accidents at all times. Out-patients daily, 1.30; ear, Tu. and F., at 2; throat, Mon. and Th., 2; women, Wed. and Sat., at 9; dental, Tu and F., 9; orthopædic, Tu., at 1.30; skin, Tu., at 9; eye, Mon. and Th., at 9, and Wed. and Sat., at 2.30; electrical, Mon., Tu., Th., and F., at 1.30; operations daily at 1.30. Visiting-days: Sun., and 3, Wed., 3 to 4 p.m. *Clerk*, W. H. Cross. *Steward*, A. Watkins. *Matron*, Miss Stewart.

ST. THOMAS'S HOSPITAL, Albert Embankment, S.E. In and out-patients daily at 12 o'clock; accidents and urgent cases at all times; ear, M.; throat, Th.; skin, F.; women, W. and Sat.; children under 7, Wed. 9.30; eye, daily, except Sat. 1; dental, Tu. and F., 9.30; mental, Th., 9.30; vaccination, W., 11.30; X-rays, Tu. and F., 2; whooping-cough, Sat., 9.30; electrical, Th., 2. Visiting-days: Sundays 3 to 4.30 p.m.; Wednesdays, 3.30 to 4 30. Paying patients are admitted to "The Home." Terms, 9s. per day. *Steward*, Sydney Phillips, B.A. *Matron*, Miss Gordon. The Nightingale Nursing School is attached to the Hospital.

[*The above Hospitals being endowed, receive no aid from the Metropolitan Hospital Sunday Fund.*]

CHARING CROSS HOSPITAL, Agar Street, Strand. Urgent cases at all times; others at 1.30 daily. Out-patients daily at 1. *Sec.*, A. E. Read.

GUY'S HOSPITAL, St. Thomas' Street, Borough, S.E. Accidents and urgent cases at all times. Taking-in days, Wednesdays at 10. *Treasurer*, H. Cosmo Bonsor, M.P. *Superintendent*, E. C. Perry, M.D. *Clerk of Hospital*, Henry Williams. *Matron*, Miss Nott Bower.

KING'S COLLEGE HOSPITAL, Portugal Street, Lincoln's Inn Fields. Urgent cases at all times. Surgical out-patients, daily at 1.30. Medical—Men, Tu., Th., and Sat.; Women, M., Wed., and Fri. Children Mon. 10.30, Wed. and Sat. 1.30; throat, Tu.; eye, Mon. and Th.; ear, Th.; skin, Mon. 10; dental, Tu. and Tn. 9.30. *Warden*, Rev. N. Bromley, A.K.C., and *Sister-Matron*, Miss Katherine Monk.

LONDON HOSPITAL, Whitechapel Road, E. Urgent cases and accidents at all hours; out-patients daily. *Hous. Gov. and Sec.*, G. Q. Roberts, M.A. *Matron*, Miss E. C. E. Lückes.

MIDDLESEX HOSPITAL, Mortimer St., Berners St. Urgent and ordinary cases at all times, with or without a Governor's or subscriber's letter. Cancer patients without letter in order of application. *Resident Medical Officer*, E. A. Fardon. *Secretary Supt.*, F. Clare Melhado.

NORTH LONDON, or UNIVERSITY COLLEGE HOSPITAL, Gower Street. W.C In-patients daily at 11 a.m.; out-patients daily, at 1.30, diseases of women, Mon. and Fri., at 1.30; dental cases, Tues. and Fri., at 9.30 a.m.; skin, Tues. and Fri., 2; eye, Mondays, Wednesdays, at 1.30; ear and throat, Mondays and Thursdays at 9. *Sec.*, N. H. Nixon.

ROYAL FREE HOSPITAL, Gray's Inn Road. For relief without letters of recommendation. Accidents and urgent cases received at all hours. Out-patients daily at 12.30 p.m.; diseases of women, Tu. and Sat. at 9; diseases of the

eye, M. and F. at 9; throat, nose and ear, W. at 9.30; skin, Th. at 9.30 a.m. Visiting-days: Sun. 2 to 4; Thur. 3.30 to 4.30. *Sec.*, C. W. Thies.

ST. GEORGE'S HOSPITAL, Hyde Park Corner, S.W. Open at all times for accidents. *Resident Medical Officer*, F. J. Marshall. *Sec.*, C. L. Todd. *Matron*, Miss Smedley.

ST. MARY'S HOSPITAL, Praed Street, Paddington. In-patients at 1. Accidents and urgent cases at all times. Out-patients, daily at 12.45; diseases of women, M. and Th. at 1 p.m.; eye, Tues. and Fri. at 9; ear, M. and Th. at 9, dental, W. and Sat. at 9. skin, M. and Th. at 9; throat, Tu. and Fri lay at 3. Patients relieved, 1898 In-patients, 3,710. Out-patients, 34,217—Maternity cases attended, 1,609. Visiting-days: Sun., 3 to 4, Thur. and Sat., 4 to 5. *Sec.*, Thomas Ryan.

SEAMEN'S HOSPITAL SOCIETY, GREENWICH, FOR SEAMEN OF ALL NATIONS. Formerly on board the Hospital Ship "Dreadnought," Greenwich, for seamen suffering from disease or accident, who are admitted daily without any recommendation. BRANCH HOSP.—Roy. Victoria and Albert Docks, E. *The London School of T. opi al Medicine* is attached to this. DISPENSARIES for out-patients, 5, East India Dock Road, E., and Gravesend. *Sec.*, P. Michelli.

WESTMINSTER HOSPITAL, near Westminster Abbey. In-patients with Governor's letter, to apply on Tuesdays, at 12.30 o'clock. Urgent cases admitted without a letter on any day at any hour. Visiting-days: Sundays, between 2 and 3; Thursdays, 3.30 to 4.30 p.m. *Sec.*, Sidney M. Quennell. *Matron*, Miss Cave.

[*At the preceding have Medical Schools attached.*]

FRENCH HOSPITAL AND DISPENSARY, open to all Foreigners, 172 Shaftesbury Avenue, W.C. Out-patients daily at 10. The Convalescent Home at Brighton contains 32 beds. *Hon. Treas.*, E. Lazarus. *Hon. Sec.*, Ernest Ruffer. *Sec. and Collector*, G. Pondepeyre.

GERMAN HOSPITAL, Dalston. In-patients daily, 10 a.m. to 4 p.m., except Sundays. Out-patients, males, Tu. and Th.; females, Mon., Wed., and Fri., at 2 p.m. Oculist, M. and Fri., 2.30. Visiting-days: Wed., 3 to 5; Sun., 2.30 to 4.30 p.m. *Supt. & Sec.*, H. Gülich.

ITALIAN HOSPITAL, Queen's Square, Devonshire Street, W.C. *Treasurer*, Comm. G. B. Ortelli. *Secretary*, Giovanni Ferrari.

GREAT NORTHERN CENTRAL HOSPITAL, Holloway Road, N. In-patients every day between 12 and 4 p.m.; accidents and urgent cases admitted at all times. Out-patients, 12 daily; medical, M., Tu., W., Th., and Fri.; surgical, M., Tu., Th., and F., dental Wed.; ear, Tu. and Fri., skin, Fri.; eye, M. and Th.; throat, Th. Visiting-days—Sun., 2 to 3.30; Th., 1 to 2.30. *Secretary*, Lewis H. G. Kerr. *Matron*, Miss M. Hull.

HAMPSTEAD HOSPITAL AND NURSING INSTITUTE, Parliament Hill, N.W. Free to the poor of the neighbourhood. Paying wards from 12s. to 105s. weekly. Provides trained lady nurses to private families. *Hon. Sec.*, R. A. Owthwaite.

LONDON HOMŒOPATHIC HOSPITAL. Founded 1849. Great Ormond St., W.C. Accidents and urgent cases admitted at all hours. *Pres.*, Earl of Wemyss and March. *Treas.*, Earl Cawdor. *Sec. Supt.*, G. A. Cross.

LONDON TEMPERANCE HOSPITAL, Hampstead Road, N.W. *Sec.*, A. W. Bodger. *Hon. Sec.*, Dawson Burns, D.D.

METROPOLITAN HOSPITAL, Kingsland Road, N.E. Accidents and urgent cases admitted at all times. *Out-patients*, M., Tu., W., Th., F., 1.30, Sat., 9. Dental, Tu., Th., F., 9; Women, W., 1.30; throat and ear, Th., 3.30; eye, M., 1.30. *Out-Patient's Provident Department*, 7.30 every evening except Sat. Visiting days, Th., 3 to 4; Sun., 3 to 4.30. *Sec.*, Chas. H. Byers. *Matron*, Miss J. C. Bennett.

NORTH-WEST LONDON HOSPITAL, Kentish Town Road. Physicians, Saturday, 10 a.m.; other days, 2 p.m. Surgeons, Wednesday, 10 a.m.; other days, 2 p.m.; no attendance on Sunday. Urgent cases at all times. *Treas.*, George Herring. *Sec.*, Alfred Craske.

POPLAR HOSPITAL FOR ACCIDENTS, Poplar, E. Open free at all hours. Visiting days, Tu. and Fri. 3 to 4, Sun. 2 to 4. *Sec. and House Gov.*, Lieut.-Col. Edward Feneran.

TOTTENHAM HOSPITAL. The Green, South Tottenham. *Supt. of Nurses*, Miss M. Fox.

WEST LONDON HOSPITAL, Hammersmith Road, W., 153 beds. Accidents and urgent cases at all times; other cases on Monday at 10.30. Out-patients at 10.45 and 2; dental cases at 9.30 Tu. and Fri.; throat, nose, and ear, Tu. at 2, and Sat. at 10; electric, 3.15, Mon. and Th.; eyes, 2, Tu. and Th.; orthopædic, 2, Wed. Women's cases, 2, Wed. and Sat. Skin diseases, 2, Mon. and Fri. *Sec. & Supt.*, R. J. Gilbert.

Special Hospitals.

CANCER.

CANCER HOSPITAL (Free), Brompton. Poor persons admitted free without letter of recommendation. Out-patients seen daily at 2 p.m., except Sundays. *Visiting days*, Th. and Sun. 2 to 4. *Sec.*, Fred. W. Howell. *Matron*, Miss A. Rogers.

CHILDREN.

ALEXANDRA HOSPITAL FOR CHILDREN WITH HIP DISEASE, Queen Sq., W.C. *Sec.*, Stanley Smith.

BELGRAVE HOSPITAL FOR CHILDREN, 79 Gloucester Street, Pimlico. Out- and in-patients admitted on recommendation of subscribers, Mondays, Tuesdays, Thursdays, Fridays, and Saturdays, at 9 a.m. *Lady-Supt.*, Miss F. E. Barwell.

CHEYNE HOSPITAL FOR SICK AND INCURABLE CHILDREN, Cheyne Walk, Chelsea, S.W. No out-patients. Weekly payment, 4s.; a few free and half-payment cots. Admission forms on application to the *Secretary*, Reginald Blunt.

EAST LONDON HOSPITAL FOR CHILDREN AND DISPENSARY FOR WOMEN, Shadwell, E. Open daily. *Treasurer*, Charles Creston. *Sec.*, Thomas Hayes.

EVELINA HOSPITAL FOR SICK CHILDREN, Southwark Bridge Road. Patients to attend at 1 P.M., Sat. at 9 a.m. Visiting days: Sundays 2 till 4. *Lady-Supt.*, Miss Alice Cross. *Sec.*, T.S. Chapman.

HER MAJESTY'S HOSPITAL (Dr. Barnardo's). Admission free, but only to destitute children or youths. 13 to 19 Stepney Causeway, E. *Founder and Director*, T. J. Barnardo, F.R.C.S.E. *Medical Officer*, Robert Milne, M.D., 32 Bow Road, E. *Hon. Surgeon*, Watson Cheyne, F.R.S., King's College Hospital. *Secretary*, John Odling.

HOME AND INFIRMARY FOR SICK CHILDREN, Lower Sydenham, S.E. *Matron*, Miss Meadows. *Hon. Secs.*, E. M. Stone, S. R. Boag.

HOSPITAL AND HOME FOR INCURABLE CHILDREN, 2 Maida Vale, W. Visiting hours, 3 to 5 daily. *Matron*, Mrs. Bruce. *Hon. Sec.*, H. Sewell.

HOSPITAL FOR CHILDREN WITH HIP OR SPINE DISEASE, "The Vine," Sevenoaks. Paying cases received. *Lady-Supt.*, Miss E. Jackson. *Hon. Sec.*, Miss M. Rose.

HOSPITAL FOR SICK CHILDREN, Great Ormond Street, Bloomsbury, and Convalescent Branch, Cromwell House, Highgate. *Matron*, Miss G. Payne. (*Highgate*), Miss Mandell Bell. *Sec.*, Adrian Hope. *Assist. do.*, J. McKay.

NORTH-EASTERN HOSPITAL FOR CHILDREN, Hackney Road, Shoreditch, N.E. In- and out-patients daily at 12.30. Surgical cases, W. and Sat. 12.30; Eye, Wed. 9.30; Dental, Tu. and Fri. 9.30. *Matron*, Miss Curno. City Office, 27 Clement's Lane, E.C. *Sec.*, T. Glenton-Kerr.

PADDINGTON GREEN CHILDREN'S HOSPITAL, London, W. 46 cots. Free to all necessitous patients without letter of recommendation. Convalescent Home, Harrow. *Treasurer*, George Hanbury. *Secretary*, W. H. Pearce. *Matron*, Miss E. A. Anderson.

ROYAL HOSPITAL FOR CHILDREN AND WOMEN, Waterloo Bridge Road. Letter of Governor required. *Secretary and Supt.*, T. S. Conisbee.

ROYAL SEA-BATHING HOSPITAL, Margate. Admission on a Governor's recommendation, and payment of 5s. to 6s. per week. *Treas.*, M. Biddulph, M.P., 30 Charing Cross, S.W.

ST. MARGARET'S HOME FOR INVALID AND INCURABLE CHILDREN, Seymour Villas, Anerley, Surrey (near the Crystal Palace). *Hon. Sec.*, F. Lloyd-Palmer.

VICTORIA HOSPITAL FOR CHILDREN, Queen's Road, Chelsea, and Victoria Home, Broadstairs. Out-patients daily at 12.30 and 9.30 a.m., on Mon., Wed., and Th. *Chairman of Committee*, Martin R. Smith. *Sec.*, A. C. Skinner.

WEST END HOSP. FOR DIS. OF NERVOUS SYSTEM, PARALYSIS, and EPILEPSY, 73 Welbeck St., W. *Sec.*, B. Heckstall-Smith.

CONSUMPTION AND CHEST DISEASES.

BROMPTON HOSPITAL FOR CONSUMPTION. Visiting-days: Tuesday and Friday, 2 to 3; Sunday, 2 to 4. *Res. Med. Officer*, H. J. Felkin, M.D. *Sec.*, Wm. H. Theobald.

CITY OF LONDON HOSPITAL FOR DISEASES OF THE CHEST, Victoria Park, E. Out-patients daily at 2. *Secretary*, Henry T. Dudley Ryder.

INFIRMARY FOR CONSUMPTION AND DISEASES OF THE CHEST AND THROAT, 26 Margaret St., W. *Secretary*, William Henry Johnson.

NATIONAL HOSPITAL FOR CONSUMPTION (on the separate principle), at Ventnor. *London Office*, 34 Craven Street, Strand. *Sec.*, Ernest Morgan.

NORTH LONDON HOSPITAL FOR CONSUMPTION AND DISEASES OF THE CHEST, Mount Vernon, Hampstead (the "Open-air" Hospital). Out-patients' Departments and Office, 41 Fitzroy Square, W. *Sec.*, W. J. Morton.

ROYAL HOSPITAL FOR DISEASES OF THE CHEST, City Road, E.C. Open daily for admission of in- and out-patients: Mondays to Fridays at 1; Saturdays, 9 a.m. *Secretary*, John Harrold.

DENTAL.

DENTAL HOSPITAL OF LONDON, Leicester Square, W.C. Free. For extraction under gas, or stopping, a subscriber's letter is required. Open daily, 9 till 11 a.m., and 1.30 to 3 p.m. *Sec.*, J. Francis Pink.

NATIONAL DENTAL HOSPITAL, Gt. Portland St., and Devonshire St., W. *Sec.*, C. Lumley Cator, M.A.

FEVER.

LONDON FEVER HOSPITAL, Liverpool Road, Islington, N. *Secretary*, Major W. Christie.

FISTULA.

GORDON HOSPITAL, Vauxhall Bridge Road (1884). Special Wards for paying patients. Patients daily at 2; Tu. at 8 p.m. *Sec.*, Charles A. Harrison.

ST. MARK'S HOSPITAL, City Road. Males on Sat., at 2 p.m., Females on Wed., at 9.30 a.m. Operations on Tuesdays at 2.30, Thurs. at 2, open to the Profession and Students. *Matron*, Mrs. Hepper. *Sec.*, Edgar Penman.

HEART DISEASE.

HEART DISEASES AND PARALYSIS, 32 Soho Square. *Sec.*, Capt. F. Handley.

INCURABLES.

BRITISH HOME FOR INCURABLES, Streatham, S.W. *Office*, 72 Cheapside, E.C. *Sec.*, Robert G. Salmond.

FREE HOME FOR THE DYING, 82 The Chase, Clapham, S.W. Apply to Sister-in-charge.

HOSPITAL OF ST. JOHN AND ST. ELIZABETH, 20 Grove End Road, N.W. For women suffering from advanced and long-standing disease.

ROYAL HOSPITAL FOR INCURABLES, Putney Heath. *Offices*, 105 Queen Victoria Street, E.C. *Sec.*, F. Andrew.

ST. CYPRIAN'S HOME FOR INCURABLE YOUNG WOMEN, 31 The Grove, Hammersmith. *Lady-Sup. and Hon. Sec.*, Miss Thorman.

LOCK HOSPITAL.

LOCK HOSPITAL. Female Hospital and Rescue Home, Harrow Road, W. Admission daily from 11 a.m. to 1 p.m. Male Hospital and Out-patient department, 91 Dean St., Soho. Admission for In-patients daily from 10 to 4; Out-patients, Males, M., 1 to 2 and 6 to 8; Tu., 6 to 8; W., 6 to 8; Sat., 2 to 4; Females, Friday, 2 to 3. *Sec.*, A. W. Cruikshank.

LUNATICS, &c.

BETHLEM ROYAL HOSPITAL, Lambeth Road, S.E. Visiting-days: males, 1st and 3rd Monday; females, 2nd and 4th Monday in the month. *Resid. Physician*, Theo. Hyslop, M.D. *Assist. Med. Officers*, Maurice Craig, M.D.; W. H. B. Stoddart, M.D. *Steward*, A. H. Martin.

ST. LUKE'S, Old Street. *Res. Med. Sup.*, W. Rawes, M.D., F.R.C.S. *Assist. Med. Off.*, H. Pulford, M.B. *Sec.*, W. H. Baird.

ASYLUM FOR IDIOTS AND IMBECILES, Earlswood, Redhill; office, 36 King William St., E.C. *Sec.*, H. Howard. [*Admis. to above by elec. or pay.*]

The following are for *pauper* lunatics from the Poor Law Unions in the Home Counties:—

COUNTY OF LONDON.

Banstead.—*Med. Sup.*, T. Claye Shaw, M.D., F.R.C.P.
Cane Hill.—*Med. Sup.*, J. M. Moody.
Claybury.—*Med. Sup.*, Robt. Jones, M.D., F.R.C.S.
Colney Hatch.—*Med. Sup.*, W. J. Seward, M.B.
Hanwell.—*Med. Sup.*, R. R. Alexander, M.D.

CITY OF LONDON.

Dartford.—*Med. Sup.*, E. W. White, M.B., M.R.C.P. (*Private patients received at £1 1s. weekly.*)

MIDDLESEX.

Wandsworth.—*Med. Sup.*, H. Gardiner Hill, M.R.C.S.

SURREY.

Brookwood.—*Med. Sup.*, J. E. Barton, L.R.C.P.

KENT.

Barming Heath.—*Med. Sup.*, F. Pritchard Davies, M.D.
Chartham.—*Med. Sup.*, G. C. FitzGerald, M.D.

LYING-IN HOSPITALS.

BRITISH LYING-IN HOSPITAL, Endell Street, St. Giles's. Patients to apply to subscribers for recommendation. *Secretary*, A. C. Wickens.

CITY OF LONDON HOSPITAL, City Road, E.C. (with training school for nurses and midwives). In-patients on Wednesdays at 10; out-patients at 12. *Secretary*, R. A. Owthwaite.

EAST END MOTHERS' HOME (late Mothers' Lying-in Home, Shadwell), 396 Commercial Rd., E. *Resident Lady-Supt.*, Miss Blomfield. *Sec.*, A. W. Lacey.

GENERAL LYING-IN HOSP., York Road, Lambeth. Patients present subscriber's letter on any day between 11.30 and 12.30. Training school for midwives and nurses. *Matron*, Miss Atkinson.

QUEEN CHARLOTTE'S LYING-IN HOSPITAL, AND MIDWIFERY TRAINING SCHOOL, Marylebone Road, N.W. For married women and for the reception of unmarried women with their first child; married women are also attended at their own homes. Medical pupils, nurses, and midwives are trained. *Secretary*, Arthur Watts.

ROYAL MATERNITY CHARITY, 31 Finsbury Square. *Secretary*, J. W. Long.

NERVOUS DISEASES, EPILEPSY, PARALYSIS, &c.

BRITISH HOSPITAL FOR MENTAL DISORDERS AND BRAIN DISEASES, "Forbes Winslow Memorial," 203 Euston Road, N.W. *Sec.*, W. J. Whelan.

HOSPITAL FOR EPILEPSY AND PARALYSIS, AND OTHER DISEASES OF THE NERVOUS SYSTEM, Portland Terrace, Regent's Park, near St. John's Wood Road Station. Paying patients are received and treated. *Sec.*, H. Howgrave Graham.

NATIONAL HOSPITAL FOR THE PARALYSED AND EPILEPTIC, Queen Sq., Bloomsbury. 200 beds. Country branch, East Finchley. Special wards for middle-class patients in straitened circumstances at a charge of 21s. per week. Out-patients, M., Tu., W., and F., at 1.30. Visiting-days: Th. and Sun., 2 to 4. *Sec. & Gen. Director*, B. Burford Rawlings.

WEST END HOSPITAL FOR DISEASES OF THE NERVOUS SYSTEM, PARALYSIS, AND EPILEPSY, 73 Welbeck Street, Cavendish Square, W. Special wards for children. Out-patients, M., W., and Th., 1.30; Tu. and F., 5.30. Visiting day, Sun., 2 to 4. *Treas.*, H. A. Dowell. *Secretary*, B. Heckstall-Smith.

OPHTHALMIC.

CENTRAL LONDON O. H., 238A Gray's Inn Road. Attendance daily, at 1 p.m. Accidents and urgent cases seen at all hours. *Chairman*, Col. A. Woodroffe Boyce. *Sec.*, John Griggs Bryant.

LOYAL LONDON OPHTHALMIC HOSPITAL, City Rd., E.C. Open free daily (except Bank Holiday). to the poor, from 8 to 10 a.m. Visiting-days to in-patients, M. and Th. from 3 to 4. *Sec.*, Robt. J. Bland. *Lady-Supt.*, Miss Richards.

ROYAL EYE, OR SOUTH LONDON OPHTHALMIC H., St. George's Circus, Southwark, S.E. Out-patients daily at 2. *Sec.*, Edwin Easton.

ROYAL WESTMINSTER OPHTHALMIC, King William St., Strand, W.C. Attendance daily at 1 p.m. Accidents at any time. Free to the poor on their own application. *Sec.*, T. Beattie-Campbell.

WESTERN O. H., 155 Marylebone Road. Free to the deserving poor. *Treas.*, Sir R. Hanson, Bt., M.P. *Secretary*, H. A. Dunn.

ORTHOPÆDIC (CLUB FOOT, SPINAL AND OTHER DEFORMITIES).

CITY ORTHOPÆDIC HOSPITAL, Hatton Garden. For the absolute poor suffering from Club Foot, Contractions and Distortions of the Limbs, Curvatures of the Spine, or other bodily deformities, and the surgical treatment of diseased and sickly children. New cases, Females M. and Tu., and Males Th. and Fri. at 2. *Sec.,* Ernest D renth.

NATIONAL ORTHOPÆDIC H. (FOR THE DEFORMED), 234 Gt. Portland St., Regent's Park, W. Surgeons attend M., Tu., Th., and F. at 2 p.m., and Tu. at 10 A.M. *Sec.,* H. J. Tresidder.

ROYAL ORTHOPÆDIC HOSPITAL, 297 Oxford St., and 15, Hanover Sq., W. *Sec.,* Tate S. Mansford. *Matron,* Mrs. Willicombe.

PAY HOSPITALS.

BOLINGBROKE HOSPITAL, Medical and Surgical Home for Children and Adults, Wandsworth Common. Accidents and emergencies free. *Res. Med. Off. and Hon. Sec.,* Cecil R. C. Lyster.

ST. SAVIOUR'S HOSPITAL (for Ladies of limited means), 10, Osnaburgh Street, Regent's Park, N.W. From 15s. to £3 3s. weekly. *Secretary,* A. B. Harding.

ST. THOMAS'S HOME, ST. THOMAS'S HOSPITAL, Albert Embankment, S.E. Terms £3 3s. a week. Applications for admission by letter to the Steward, or personally to the Res. Med. Officer, at 12 daily.

ST. MARYLEBONE HOME (for Incurables), 61, Weymouth St., W. *Hon. Sec.,* Miss E. Underwood.

HOME FOR CONFIRMED INVALIDS, 36 Aubert Park, Highbury Terrace, N. For invalid ladies of limited incomes. *Hon. Sec.,* John Hollnay. [*Many other Institutions also admit paying patients.*]

SKIN.

BRITISH HOSPITAL FOR DISEASES OF SKIN, 29 Euston Road, N.W. Out-patients—Tu., W, Fri., and Sat. at 2 and Mon. and Th. at 7 p m. Female in-patients admitted. *Hon. Sec.,* Albert Wills.

HOSPITAL FOR DISEASES OF THE SKIN, 52 Stamford St., Blackfriars, S.E. Out-patients, M. and Th. at 2; on Tu., W. and F. at 1. Free and paying patients received. *Sec.,* G. A. Richardson.

LONDON SKIN HOSPITAL, 40 Fitzroy Sq., W.—Out-patients treated every week-day at 2 and 7 p.m. Application for admission to be made to the *Secretary,* H. Montague Duncan.

ST. JOHN'S H. FOR DISEASES OF S., 1 Leicester Square, W.C. (1863). Out-patients daily, except Sunday, 2 to 4; and, except Sat. and Sun. 6 to 8 p.m. Free and paying in-patients are received at 238 Uxbridge Road. Visiting-days, Wed. and Sun., 2 to 4. *Supt.,* J. Dunlop Costine.

WESTERN SKIN HOSPITAL, 179 Great Portland Street. *Sec.,* Arthur W. Adeney.

STONE.

ST. PETER'S HOSPITAL FOR STONE, STRICTURE, AND URINARY DISEASES. Henrietta St., Covent Garden. 26 beds. Ward for paying patients. Out-patients M., Tu., and Th., at 2; M., W., and Sat. at 5; Women and Children, F. at 2. *Sec.,* Irwin H. Beattie.

THROAT, NOSE, AND EAR.

CENTRAL LONDON THROAT AND EAR HOSP., 330 Gray's Inn Rd., W.C. *Sec.,* Richard Kershaw.

HOSPITAL FOR DISEASES OF THE THROAT, EAR, AND NOSE, Golden Sq., W. Open daily, 1.30; Tuesday and Friday evenings, 6.30. Monday, 9 a.m., for children only. *Sec.,* W. Holt.

LONDON THROAT HOSPITAL, for Diseases of the Throat, Nose, and Ear, 204 Gt. Portland St., W., and 72 Bolsover St., W. Daily, 1.30 to 3; Tu. and Fri. 6 to 8 p.m. *Sec.,* L. Hellis.

METROPOLITAN EAR, NOSE AND THROAT HOSPITAL, 64 Grafton St., Fitzroy Sq., W. *Sec.,* J. Mackinna.

ROYAL EAR HOSPITAL, Frith Street, Soho. Out-patients seen Tu. and F., 9 to 11 A.M.; W. 2.30 to 3; M. and Sat., 3 to 5 P.M.; Th. 7.30 to 8.30 P.M.; in-patients daily. *Sec.,* M. C. Puddy.

WOMEN.

CHELSEA HOSPITAL FOR WOMEN, Fulham Road; (Convalescent Home at St. Leonards, *not limited to Hospital patients*). In-patients admitted free with subscriber's letter, or by weekly payments of from 10s. 6d. to 42s. Visiting-days: Wednesdays and Sundays, 3 to 4.30. Out-patients admitted by subscriber's letter, or upon payment of 1s. per weekly attendance; seen daily at 2. *Hon. Treas.,* H. E. Wright. *Secretary,* Herbert H. Jennings.

GROSVENOR HOSPITAL FOR WOMEN AND CHILDREN, Vincent Square, Westminster. Women only as In-patients. Out-patients seen daily at 2 p.m. *Superintendent,* Miss Phillips. *Secretary,* H. Wilkinson.

HOSPITAL FOR WOMEN, 29 Soho Square, W. Open free to out-patients Mon. and Th. 9 to 1; other days, 12 to 2. Paying patients received. *Sec.,* David Cannon. *Matron,* Miss Squier.

NEW HOSPITAL FOR WOMEN, 144 Euston Road, N.W. The physicians are all women. Out-patients seen daily at 1 o'clock. A charge of 6d. or 1s. is made on entrance, and 2d. each visit afterwards. *Treasurer,* Mrs. Westlake. *Secretary,* Margaret M. Bagster.

SAMARITAN FREE HOSPITAL, Marylebone Road, N.W. Out-patients' department entrance, 171 Marylebone Road. *Sec.,* George Scudamore *Matron,* Miss Butler.

DISPENSARIES.

METROPOLITAN ASYLUMS BOARD.

Office—Norfolk House, Norfolk St., Strand, W.C. (*after March,* 1900: Victoria Embankment, E.C.) *Clerk to the Board,* T. Duncombe Mann. *Stores Dept.,* Mermaid Court, Borough, S.E. *Sup.,* F. Howgate; *Asst. Clerk,* J. Mallett.

ASYLUMS FOR IMBECILES :—
Leavesden, near King's Langley, Herts. *Med. Sup.,* F. A. Elkins, M.D., C.M.

Caterham, Surrey. *Med. Sup.*, G. S. Elliot, M.R.C.P., F.R.C.S.

Darenth, near Dartford, Kent. *Med. Sup.*, F. R. P. Taylor, M.D.

Darenth Schools and Pavilions (for Children). *Med. Sup.*, F. R. P. Taylor, M.D., B.S.

Tooting Bec, S.W. (for Infirm Cases). Will be erected shortly.

FEVER HOSPITALS:—

Eastern, The Grove, Homerton, N.E. *Med. Sup.*, E. W. Goodall, M.D.

North-Eastern, St. Ann's Rd., Tottenham, N. *Med. Sup.*, H. E. Cuff, M.D., B.S.

North-Western, Lawn Rd., Hampstead, N.W. *Med. Sup.*, W. Gayton, M.D., M.R.C.P.

Western, Seagrave Rd., Fulham, S.W. *Med. Sup.*, R. M. Bruce, M.R.C.S.

South-Western, Landor Rd., Stockwell, S.W. *Med. Sup.*, F. F. Caiger, M.D., B.S.

South-Eastern, Avonley Road, New Cross, S.E. *Med. Sup.*, F. M. Turner, M.D., B.S.

Fountain, Tooting Grove, S.W. *Med. Sup.*, C. E. Matthews, M.D.

Brook, Shooters Hill, Kent. *Med. Sup.*, J. MacCombie, M.D.

Park, Hither Green, Lewisham, S.E. *Med. Sup.*, R. A. Birdwood, M.D.

Grove, Tooting Grove, S.W. *Act. Med. Sup.*, F. F. Caiger, M.D., B.S.

Northern (for Convalescing Patients), Winchmore Hill, N. *Med. Sup.*, F. N. Hume, M.R.C.S.

Southern (for Convalescing Patients), Carshalton, Surrey. Will be erected shortly.

SMALL POX HOSPITALS:—

Hospital Ships, moored in the river Thames at Long Reach, near Dartford, Kent. *Med. Sup.*, T. F. Ricketts, M.D., B.S.

Gore Farm (for Convalescing Patients), Darenth, near Dartford, Kent. *Med. Sup.*, F. H. Thomson, M.B.

Joyce Green, near Dartford, Kent. Will be erected shortly.

LAND AMBULANCE STATIONS:—

Eastern, adj. Eastern Hospital. *Sup.*, E. Robinson.

North-Western, adj. N.-Western Hospital, *Sup.*, G. Hyatt.

Western, adj. Western Hospital. *Sup.*, W. Craig.

South-Eastern, adjoining South-Eastern Hospital. *Superintendent*, J. Carter.

South-Western, adjoining S.-Western Hospital. *Superintendent*, W. A. Cockrell.

Brook, adj. Brook Hospital. *Sup.*, J. Blake.

River Ambulance Service—*Sup.*, Chas. Thomson, R.N., M.I.N.A.

North Wharf, Managers' Street, Blackwall, E.

South Wharf, Trinity Street, Rotherhithe, S.E.

West Wharf, Townmead Rd., Fulham, S.W.

CHILDREN'S HOMES:—

Seaside:

S. Anne's Home, Herne Bay, Kent. *Matron*, Miss E. Turton ; *Medical Officer*, C. K. Bowes, M.D.

East Cliff House, Margate, Kent. *Matron*, Miss E. K. Jacob ; *Medical Officer*, W. G. Sutcliffe, F.R.C.S.

Millfield, Rushington, near Littlehampton. Will be erected shortly.

Ophthalmia:

Highwood School, Brentwood, and White Oak School, Swanley. Will be erected shortly.

Defective Children:

Lloyd House, Lloyd St., Pentonville. *Matron*, Miss Algreen.

16 Elm Grove, Peckham, S.E. Will be erected shortly.

Remand Children:

36-38 Camberwell Green. Will be opened shortly.

TRAINING SHIP:—

The "Exmouth," moored off Grays, Essex. *Capt.-Sup.*, W. S. Bourchier, R.N.

AMBULANCE SERVICE FOR LONDON.

Office, St. Mary's Hospital, Praed Street, W. *Hon. Sec.*, Thos. Ryan.

THE METROPOLITAN HOSPITAL SUNDAY FUND.

THIS excellent charity was started, under the presidency of the LORD MAYOR, in 1873, the total receipts in that year amounting to £27,700. They have since risen as high as £60,301 in the year of greatest prosperity, 1895, when a special donation of £10,000 was received. The total for the year ending Oct., 1899, stood at £53,504.

The BALANCE SHEET for the year ending 31st October, 1899, shows the following results:—

RECEIPTS.—Collections made at various places of worship, £38,188 16s. 9d. ; collections at schools £20 ; donations (including £16 14s. for surgical appliances), £14,043 ; dividend on £45,346, invested in 2¾ Consols, per executors to the will of the late W. A. Guesdon, £1,247 ; balance in hand, £723.

EXPENDITURE.—*Awards to* one hundred and thirty-one hospitals (including 30 General Hospitals, 5 Chest Diseases, 17 Children's, 5 Lyingin, 6 Hospitals for Women, 25 other special hospitals, 29 Convalescent, and 14 Cottage Hospitals), £47,397 ; seven Institutions, £700 ; fifty-five Dispensaries, £2,096 ; Surgical Appliances £2,255 ; office expenses, printing and stationery, advertising, postage, &c., £1,702.

SPECIAL EXPENSES.—Special Church and Chapel Appeals, £64.

THE HOSPITAL SATURDAY FUND.

THE twenty-fifth Annual Report (1899) shows a slight decrease on its immediate predecessor, the receipts being £990 less than those for 1897. The BALANCE SHEET for the year ending 10th January, 1899, is as follows:—RECEIPTS.—Balance brought forward, £905 ; Special and Workshop Collections, £18,765 ; special Donations, £333, making a total of £20,113.

EXPENDITURE.—General expenses (including rent, salaries, printing, postage, local committees, £2,381 ; awards to Hospitals, Dispensaries, &c., £14,583 ; grants to Distribution Committee, £1,360 ; to Surgical Appliance Committee, £1,020 ; Ambulance, £64 ; leaving a balance of £115.

THE PRINCE OF WALES'S HOSPITAL FUND.

THE account of Receipts and Expenditure from 1st January to 31st Dec., 1898, shows the total receipts for that period to have been £39,472 ; the total expenses amounting to £2,461. The sums disbursed to Hospitals were as follows :— Grants to Hospitals, £31,500 ; Grants to Convalescent Homes, £1,000 ; total, £32,500. The Funds in Hand after payment of the 1898 distribution were £171,333.

THE BANK OF ENGLAND, FOUNDED 1694.

Capital, £14,553,000.   **Rest, or Reserve, on 4th October, 1899, £3,136,776.**

The Total Dividends for the year ending 31st August, 1899, were at the rate of £10 per cent. The Price of Bank Stock, 4th October, 1899, was £344.

NOTES in circulation, 4th Oct., 1899, £28,841,715.   Notes unemployed, £18,917,965.

GOLD and SILVER Coin and Bullion, Head Office and all Branches, £32,692,932.

THE GOVERNOR, DEPUTY GOVERNOR, AND OTHER OFFICERS FOR THE YEAR   —1900.

Governor, Samuel Steuart Gladstone (£2,000).—*Deputy Governor*, Augustus Prevost (£1,500).

DIRECTORS, each £500.

Aldenham, The Rt. Hon. Lord.	Currie, James Pattison.	Johnston, Reginald Eden.
Arbuthnot, Charles George.	Gilliat, John Saunders, M.P.	Lidderdale, The Rt. Hon. Wm.
Bonsor, Hy. Cosmo Orme, M.P.	Goschen, Charles Hermann.	Morley, Samuel Hope.
Brooks, Herbert.	Greene, Benjamin Buck.	Newman, Robert Lydston.
Campbell, William Middleton.	Grenfell, Henry Riversdale.	Revelstoke, the Rt. Hon. Lord.
Cole, Alfred Clayton.	Hambro, Everard Alexander.	Sandeman, Albert George.
Collet, Sir Mark Wilks, Bart.	Hoare, William Douro.	Smith, Hugh Colin.
Cunliffe, Walter.	Jackson, Frederick Huth.	Wallace, Alexander Falconer.

PRINCIPAL OFFICERS.

Chief Acct., Geo. F. Stutchbury.	*Joint Auditors*, E. M. Harvey,	*Do. Accts.' Bk. Note Off.*, C. Fenn.
Deputy do., John D. Farrell.	and W. H. Clegg.	*Do. B.Sk., &c., do.*, F.E.Blaiklock.
Assistant do., T. A. Stephens.	*Contr. of Stk. & Cash Offs.*, H.B.	*Do. Consols Office*, E. D. Pyne.
Chief Cashier, H. G. Bowen.	Orchard.	*Do. £2 10s. p. c. Off.*, A. Bridger.
Deputy do., John G. Nairne.	*Princ., Bullion Off.*, N.D. Livesay.	*Do. Div. Office*, J. H. Sheppy.
Assistant do., T. Askwith.	*Do. Priv. Draw. Off.*, G. Sander.	*Do. India do.*, D. Hotson.
Secretary, K. Grahame.	*Do. Public do.*, A. A. de Steiger.	*Do. Register do.*, W. J. Halsey.
Deputy do., C. E. Edlmann.	*Do. Bill Office*, H. S. Sclater.	*Do.Power of Att.do.*, E.J.Wheeler.
Assistant do., S. M. Ward.	*Do. Issue Office*, L. Napper.	*Do. Post. Warrt. do.*(Vacant.)
Insp. of Branches and Principal	*Do. Securities Office*, F. G. Allan.	*Do. Dividend Accounts do.*, W. P.
Branch Banks Office, E. Edye.	*Do. Intellers' do.*, H. W. Tilly.	Saffery.
Prin., Dist. Off., R. W. Searcn.	*Princ. Div. Pay do.*, E. E. Gaute.	*Supt. of Printing Offi.*, W. J. Coe.

Western Branch, Burlington Gardens.	*Law Courts Branch.*
Agent, Sir Arthur Nonus Birch, K.C.M.G.	*Agent*, Sir C. W. Baynes, Bart.

COUNTRY BRANCHES AND AGENTS.

Birmingham, H. A. N. Smith.	*Leeds*, R. J. West.	*Newcastle*, H. A. Erskine.
Bristol, M. A. Shee.	*Liverpool*, T. F. A. Agnew.	*Plymouth*, A. S. Adair.
Hull, J. Dyce Nicol.	*Manchester*, C. G. Ross.	*Portsmouth*, W. B. Molyneux.

BANKS AND BANKERS IN LONDON AND SUBURBS.

BANKS printed in heavier type are *Limited*, those with † are registered at Somerset House, those with an asterisk * are Clearing Bankers, and those with ‡ are Army Agents.

1 †Agra Bank, 35, Nicholas Lane.
1A African B. Corp., 43, Threadneedle St., E.C.
2 †Alexander, Fletcher & Co., 2, St. Helen's Place.
3 †Alexanders & Co., 24, Lombard Street.
4 †Allan (T. H.) & Co., 17, Gracechurch Street.
5 American Express Co., 3, Waterloo Place, S.W.
6 Anglo-Argentine Bank, 14 Austin Friars.
7 Anglo-Austrian Bank, 31, Lombard Street.
8 †Anglo-Californian, 18, Austin Friars, E.C.
9 Anglo-Egyptian, 27, Clement's Lane.
10 Anglo-Foreign Bg. Co., 2, Bishopsgate St. Withn.
11 †Anglo-Italian, 9, St. Helen's Place, E.C.
†Armstrong & Co., 93 Bishopsgate St. Within.
13 Australian Joint-Stock, 2, King William St.
12 Bank of Adelaide, 11, Leadenhall St., E.C.
15 Bank of Africa, 113, Cannon Street, E.C.
16 †Bank of Australasia, 4, Threadneedle Street.
17 Bank of British Columbia, 60, Lombard St., E.C.
18 Bank of British N. America, 3, Clement's Lane.
14 Bank of China & Japan, 36, Nicholas Lane.
20 Bank of Egypt, 26, Old Broad Street.
21 *†Bank of England (*see above*).
19 Bank of Mauritius, George Yd., Lombard St.
22 †Bank of Montreal, 22, Abchurch Lane.
23 Bank of New South Wales, 64, Old Broad St.
24 Bank of New Zealand, 1, Queen Victoria St.
25 Bank of Roumania, 7, Great Winchester St.
26 †Bank of Scotland, 19, Bishopsgate St. Within, E.C.

28 †Bank of Tarapacá & London, 123, Bishopsgate St. Within.
29 Bank of Victoria (Austr.), 28, Clement's Lane.
30 *†Barclay & Company, 54, Lombard St., 1, Pall Mall East; 27, Cavendish Sq., 19, Fleet St., and 171, Brompton Road, S.W.
31 Baring Bros. & Co., 8, Bishopsgate St. Within.
Barker (G.) & Co., *in liquidation.*
34 †Biggerstaff, W. and J., 18, West Smithfield; 6, Bank Buildings, Metrop. Cattle Market; Foreign Cattle Market, Deptford.
35 †Birkbeck, Southampton Buildings, Holborn.
36 Blake, Boissevain & Co., 11, Copthall Court.
38 Blydenstein(B.W.)&Co.,55 & 56, Threadndle.St.
British E. of Australia, *in liquidation.*
39 British B. of South America, 2A, Moorgate St.
40 British Linen Co., 41, Lombard Street.
41 †British Mutual Banking Co., Ludgate Circus.
42 †Brooks & Co., 81, Lombard Street.
43 *†Brown, Janson, and Co., 32, Abchurch Lane.
44 †Brown (John) and Co., 25, Abchurch Lane.
45 Brown, Shipley & Co., Founders Ct., Lothbury.
46 †Burt (Fredk.) and Co., 80, Cornhill.
49 *†Capital & Counties, 39, Threadneedle St.; 25, Ludgate Hill; 125, Oxford St.; 195, Edgware Road; 35, King St.,W.C.; 50, Upper St., N.; 151 & 153, Newington Causeway; 35, Piccadilly, W.; 145, High St., Shoreditch; 89

& 90, York St., Westminster; 115, Fore St.; and 216, Commercial Rd., E.
52†Charing Cross Bank, 23, Bedford St., W.C.
53†Chartered Bank of India, Australia, and China, Hatton Court, Threadneedle Street.
55†Cheque Bank, 93, Bishopsgate St. Within, E.C.; 14, Cockspur St., S.W.
56 Chick (Alfred Y.) & Co., 52, Old Broad Street.
57†Child and Co., 1, Fleet Street, Temple Bar.
58†*City Bank (now 136, *London City & Midland*).
59†Civil Service Bank, 10, Charing Cross Road.
†Clare & Harvey, 4, Hercules Passage, Threadneedle Street.
60†Clydesdale Bank, 30, Lombard Street.
61†Cocks, Biddulph, and Co., 43, Charing Cross.
64†Cohn (Maurice), and Co., 27, Throgmorton St.
65 Colonial Bank, 118, Bishopsgate St. Within.
65†Commercial B. of Scotland, 62, Lombard Street.
69†Comm. B. Co. of Sydney, 18, Birchin Lane.
70 Commercial B. of Australia, 1, Bishopsgate Street Within, E.C.
71 Comptoir National d'Escompte de Paris, 52, Threadneedle Street.
73†‡Cook (Thomas) & Son, Ludgate Circus; 99, Gracechurch Street; 33, Piccadilly; 82, Oxford St.; 13, Cockspur St.; Charing Cross Station, and 21, High St., Kensington.
75†Coutts and Co., 59, Strand.
76†‡Cox & Co., 16, Charing Cross, S.W.
77†Crédit Lyonnais, 40, Lombard St.; and 4, Cockspur Street, Charing Cross.
78†Cripplegate Bank, 116, Fore St. & 1, Whitecross Street, E.C.
81†Cunliffe (Roger), Sons, & Co., 22, Finch Lane.
82†Delhi and London B., 123, Bishopsgate St. Wn.
83†Dresdner Bank, 65, Old Broad St.
84†Deutsche Bank, 4, George Yard, Lombard St.
87†Dobree (Samuel) & Sons, 6, Tokenhouse Yard.
88†Drummond, Messrs., 49, Charing Cross, S.W.
89 Duff (Wm.) and Co., 113, Cannon Street, E.C.
Economic Bank, 34, Old Broad Street.
93 English, Scottish, & Australian, 38, Lombard St.
94†Erlanger (Emile) and Co., 20, Bishopsgate Street Within.
96†Forbes, Forbes, & Co., 9, King Wm. St., E.C.
Freehold Investmt. B. Co. of Aust., *in liquidation.*
98†German B. of London, 34, Old Broad Street.
99†Gillett Bros. and Co., 53, Lombard Street, E.C.
100*†Glyn, Mills, Currie, and Co., 67, Lombard St.
101 Gordon, Smith, and Co., 139, Cannon Street.
Goslings and Sharpe, now *Barclay & Co.*
103†Grant, Maurice, 61, Old Broad Street.
104†Green, Tomkinson, & Co., 32, Nicholas Lane.
105†Grindlay and Co., 54, Parliament Street, S.W.
106 Haarbleicher & Schumann, 144, Leadenhall St., E.C.
108†Hickie, Borman and Co., 14, Waterloo Place.
109†Hill and Sons, 56, West Smithfield; 2, Bank Bdgs., Metrop. Cattle Market; Bank Bdgs., Foreign Cattle Market, Deptford.
110†Hoare (Charles) & Co., 37, Fleet Street.
111†‡Holt and Co., 3, Whitehall Place.
112 Hongkong and Shanghai Banking Corporation, 31, Lombard Street.
115 Imperial Bank of Persia, 25, Abchurch Lane.
117 Imperial Ottoman B., 26, Throgmorton St.
118 International Bank of London, Winchester House, 50, Old Broad Street.
119 Ionian Bank, Palmerston Buildings, 93, Bishopsgate Street.
123 Ironmonger & Co., 75, Old Broad Street.
125 Keizer (N.) & Co., 23, Threadneedle St.
126†Keyser (A.) & Co., 21, Cornhill.
125†King (Hen. S.) & Co., 45, Pall Mall; 65, Cornhill.
127 Ladenburg (W.) & Co., 10, Angel Court.

131 Lazard Brothers & Co., 40, Threadneedle St.
132*†Lloyds Bank, *Gen. Manager*, Howard Lloyd; *City Office*, 72, Lombard St., E.C.; *Managers*, J. P. Benwell and H. B. Francis; 16, St. James's Street, S.W.; Law Courts, 222, Strand, W.C.; 95, Leadenhall Street; Holborn Circus, E.C.; 33, Belgrave Road, S.W.; 35, Cambridge St., W.; 34, Hammersmith Road; Rosslyn Hill, Hampstead; Finchley Road, ditto; Entfield; and Caterham Valley.
133†London & Brazilian Bank, 7, Tokenhouse Yd.
135*†London and County B. Co., *Head Office Manager*, H. Dean; *Deputy do.*, G. J. Rodolph; *Country Manager*, J. B. James, 21, Lombard St.; 21, Hanover Square; 0, Albert Gate; 4 & 5, Upper St., Islington; 134, Aldersgate St.; 1, Connaught St., Edgware Road; 109 & 111, New Oxford St.; 34, Borough High St.; Sussex Place, Queen's Gate; Kensington High St.; 217, Lavender Hill, Clapham Junction; 180, 181 & 182, High St., Shoreditch; 74, Westbourne Grove; 0, Henrietta St., Covent Garden; 165, Westminster Bridge Road; Deptford Broadway; Stratford Broadway; 324 & 325, High Holborn; Amhurst Road, Hackney; 52, East India Dock Road; 18, Newington Butts; 173, Victoria St., S.W.; 266 & 268, Pentonville Rd.; Beckenham; Blackheath; Croydon; Greenwich; Hammersmith; Norwood; Woolwich; 369, Brixton Road; 334, Harrow Road; 74, High St., Kingsland; 100, High St., Wandsworth; High St., Putney; West End Lane, West Hampstead; Ealing; 490, Holloway Road; High Road, Chiswick; 4, High St., Wimbledon; Richmond; Finchley; 128 & 130, Balham High Rd., S.W.; 51 & 53, Barking Rd., Canning Town; 3, The Broadway, W. Norwood; Ilford Broadway; and Forest Gate.
55†London & District Bank, 58, Old Broad St., E.C. London and General Bank, *in liquidation.*
137†London and Hanseatic Bank, 38, Lombard St.
138 London & Northern, 84, Cheapside, E.C.
139†London and Provincial Bank, *General Manager*, J. W. Cross, 7, Bank Buildings; 83, Commercial St.; 163, Edgware Road; Queen's Gate, South Kensington; 1, High St., Kingsland; 56, Old Kent Rd., S.E.; 383, Essex Rd., N.; Anerley; Beckenham; Bermondsey; Bexley Heath; Blackheath; Canning Tn.; Carshalton; Catford; Chingford; Edmonton (Upper and Lower); Egham; Enfield; Erith; Ewell; Green Lanes; Hackney; Hampstead; Hampton Hill; Harringay; Highbury; Hither Green; Hornsey; Ilford; Kew; Ladywell; Lea Bridge Rd.; Lee Green; Lewisham; Leytonstone; Manor Park; Mitcham; Munster Park; Muswell Hill; New Cross Gate; Newington Gn.; New Southgate; Penge; Plumstead; Ponder's End; Richmond; St. Margaret's; Sidcup; S. Tottenham; Southgate; Staines; Stamford Hill; Stoke Newington; Stratford; Sunningdale; Surbiton; Surbiton Hill; Sutton; Sydenham; Teddington; Thornton Heath; Tottenham (Upper and Lower); Tufnell Park; Twickenham; Walham Gn.; Walthamstow (Hoe Street, St. James' St. and Wood St.); Westcombe Pk.; West End Lane; Wood Green; Woolwich.
140†London and River Plate Bk., 7, Princes St., E.C.
141†London & San Francisco B., 71, Lombard St.

142*†**London & South-Western B.**, 170. Fenchurch St.; *General Managers*, John Williams and Robert Woodhams; Acton; Addiscombe; Anerley; Balham; Barking; Barnes; Battersea; Battersea Park; Belgravia; Bermondsey; Bloomsbury; Bow; 256, Brixton Hill; 275 & 465, Brixton Rd.; 295, High Rd., Kilburn (Brondesbury): Bushey; Camberwell Grn.; Park St., Camden Town; Catford; Charlton; Chelsea; Chiswick; Clapham; Clapham Junction; Clapton; Clerkenwell; Cricklewood; Crofton Park, Brockley; Croydon; Croydon, South; Dulwich; Dulwich, East; Ealing; Ealing Dean; 183, Earl's Court Rd.; East Ham; Edgware; Finchley, Church End; Finchley, East; 82, Finsbury Pavement; Finsbury Park; 78, Fleet St.; Forest Gate; Forest Hill; Fulham; 56, Gt. Portland St.; Hackney; Hammersmith; Hampstead; Hampstead, South; Hanwell; Harlesden; Harrow; 416, Harrow Rd.; Hendon; Highgate; Holland Park; 403, Holloway Rd.; Hornsey; Kennington; 230, Kentish Town Rd.; Kew Bridge; Kilburn; Kingston-on-Thames; Lavender Hill; Leyton; Merton; Mile End (236, Whitechapel Rd.); Minories; Mortlake; New Barnet; New Cross; New Cross Gate: New Malden; Norbiton; Norwood, South, Upper, and West; Notting Hill; Oxford St.; High St., Peckham; Poplar (187, East India Dock Rd.); Putney; 27, Regent St.; Richmond; St. John's Wood; Shepherd's Bush; Shoreditch; Southwark; Stanmore; Stepney; Stockwell (256, Clapham Rd.); Strand; Streatham; Streatham Common; Stroud Green; Sutton; Sydenham; Tooting; Tulse Hill; Twickenham; Upton Park; Vauxhall; Walham Green; Wallington; Walthamstow (Hoe St., St. James St.); 260, Walworth Road; Wandsworth; Wanstead; Watford; Wembley; W. Brompton; W. Kensington; Whetstone; Willesden Grn.; Wimbledon; Wimbledon Common.

London and Universal Bank, *in liquidation*.

144*†**London and Westminster Bank**, *Manager*, H. Smith; *Country Manager*, T. J. Russell; and *Secretary*, A. E. Mann: 41, Lothbury; 1, St. James's Square; 214. High Holborn; 6, Borough High Street; 130, High St., Whitechapel; 1, Stratford Place, W.; 112 & 114, Oxford St.; 217, Strand; 91, Westminster Bridge Rd.; 1, Brompton Sq.; 62, Victoria St., S.W.; 269 & 270, Upper St., Islington, N.; 133, Westbourne Grove; 8, Holborn Circus; 44 & 46, Hampstead Rd., N.W.; 106, Finchley Road, N.W.; 94, High Street, Kensington, W.; Broadway, Crouch End, Hornsey, N.: 77 & 79, King Street West, Hammersmith; 106A, High Road, Kilburn: 79, Ebury St., Belgravia; 5, St. Paul's Churchyard; 1, Streatham High Rd., S.W.; 504, Brixton Rd., S.W.; 4, Mincing Lane, E.C.; 9, Harewood Avenue, N.W.; 3, The Market, Uxbridge Rd., W.; 8, Victoria Parade, Balham Hill, S.W.; 161, Bow Road, E.; 45, Uxbridge Road, Ealing, S.W.; 1, Bank Buildings, Herne Hill, S.E.; 98 & 100, City Road, E.C.; 3, Anson Parade, Cricklewood.

145 **London Bank of Mexico and South America**, 94, Gracechurch Street.

146†**London and Yorkshire Bk.**, Drapers' Gardens.

147 **London Bank of Australia**, 2, Old Broad St.

136*†**London City and Midland**, *Managing Director*, E. H. Holden; *Joint Gen. Managers*, D. G. H. Pollock, J. M. Madders, S. B. Murray; *Secretary*, E. J. Morris; *Head Office*, 5, Threadneedle St.; *Registered Office*, 52, Cornhill; 45 & 47, Ludgate Hill; 34, Old Bond St.; 159-60. Tottenham Court Road; 219, Edgware Road; 6, Sloane Street; 94, Fenchurch St.; 34, Holborn Viaduct; 93, Great Eastern St.; 71A, Queen Victoria St.; 100, Fore St.; 134. Shaftesbury Av.; 44, Theobald's Rd.; 28 Old Kent Road; 196, Oxford Street; 20, Eastcheap; 193, Streatham Hill; 140, Bishopsgate Street Without; 20, Bow St., Covent Garden; 29, Woodgrange Rd., Forest Gate; 21, Hill St., Richmond; North End, Croydon; 271, High Road, Balham; Beckenham; 488, Bethnal Green Rd.; Blackfriars Rd.; 58, Jamaica Rd., Bermondsey; 10, Charterhouse Buildings, Clerkenwell; 91, Newgate St.; 49, Rye Lane, Peckham; 196, Lower Road, Rotherhithe; 50, Shaftesbury Avenue; 30 & 31, High Street, Shoreditch; 150, High St., Stoke Newington; 90, Tooley St.; 60, West Smithfield; 449, Strand, Charing Cross; 110, High St., Whitechapel; 237, Tottenham Court Rd.; 91, Mile End Rd.; 43, High St., Deptford; Islington (Metropolitan Cattle Market); Broadway, Ealing; 129, New Bond St.; 19, Coleman St.; Mayfair; 110, High St., Lewisham; 327, High Road, Chiswick; Mare St., Hackney; 324, High Road, Leyton; The Parade, Loughborough Junction; 19, High St., Marylebone: 157, Hackney Road, N.E.; 32, Grand Parade, Harringay; 646. High Road, Leytonstone; North End Road, Walham Green.

148*†**London Joint-Stock Bank**, *General Manager*, Charles Gow; 5, Princes Street; 6, Lothbury; 59, Pall Mall; 123, Chancery Lane; 89, Charterhouse Street; 2, Craven Rd., W.; 28, Borough High St.; 98, Gt. Tower St.; 113, Wood St.; 144, Leadenhall St.; 55, Old Broad St.; 5, Bank Bldgs., Gloucester Road; 44, Fenchurch Street; 680, Commercial Road, E.; 22, Victoria St., S.W.; 137, Buckingham Palace Rd.; 1, Sydney Pl., Onslow Sq.; 15. Wigmore St., W.; 52, Lordship Lane: 69, High St., Peckham; The Broadway, Tooting; Buckhurst Hill; Cheshunt; Enfield Highway; Loughton; Waltham Abbey; Waltham Cross; Woodford; Muswell Hill; Lower Edmonton; Winchmore Hill; Palmer's Green.

149†**London, Paris, & American Bank**, 40, Threadneedle St.

150†**London Trading Bank**, 12, Coleman St., E.C.

151†**Macfadyen (P.) & Co.**, Winchester House, E.C.

152†‡**McGrigor (Sir C. R.) & Co.**, 25, Charles Street, St. James Square.

153†**Manchester & L'pool Dist. Bkg. Co.**, 75, Cornhill.

154*†**Martin's Bank**, 68, Lombard Street, E.C.

159 **Melville, Fickus & Co.**, 75, Lombard Street.

160†**Mercantile B. of India**, 40, Threadneedle St.

161 **Mercantile Bank of London**, 6, Old Jewry, E.C.

162*†**Metropolitan Bank (of England and Wales)**, 60, Gracechurch Street.

163 **Merchant Banking Co.**, 112, Cannon Street.

164†**Middlesex Bkg.. Co.**, 89 & 90, Leadenhall St., E.C.

166†**Morris, Robert**, 8, Regent Street, S.W.

167 **Natal Bank**, 18, St. Swithin's Lane.

168*†**National Bank**, 13, Old Broad Street; 68, Gloucester Gardens: 9, Charing Cross: 189, High St., Camden Town; 286, Pentonville

Road; 158, High St., Notting Hill; 21, Grosvenor Gardens; 276, Oxford Street; 2, Elgin Avenue, Harrow Road; 361 & 363, Goswell Road; St. Mary's Road, Harlesden; 180, Strand; and 23, Baker Street.
169 **Nat. B. of Australasia,** 123, Bishopsgate St. Within, E.C.
170+National Bank of China, 61, Old Broad St.
170A National Bank of Egypt, 92, Cannon St.
171+**National Bank of India,** 47, Threadneedle St.
172 **National B. of New Zealand,** 15, Moorgate St.
173+**National Bank of Scotland,** 37, Nicholas Lane.
173A **National Bank of the South African Republic,** 73, Cornhill, E.C.
174 **National Discount Company,** 35, Cornhill, E.C.
175*+**National Provincial Bank of England,** 112, Bishopsgate St.; 291B Oxford St., W.; 208 & 209, Piccadilly; 53, Baker St.; 218 Upper St., Islington; Carey St., Lincoln's Inn; 88, Cromwell Road, S.W.; South Audley St., W.; 185, Aldersgate Street, E.C.; 128, Finchley Rd., N.W.; 55 & 57, High St., Kensington; 494, Brixton Rd., S.W.; and Lancaster Gate, Hyde Park.
New English Bank of the River Plate, *in liq.*
New Oriental Bank, *in liquidation.*
177*+Parr's Bank, Bartholomew La., 52, Threadneedle St.; 77, Lombard St.; 1, Cavendish Sq.; 88, Kensington High St.; 239, Regent Street; 9 & 10, St. Martin's Place, W.C.; 164 & 166, High Street, Camden Town; 14, Sloane Sq., Chelsea; 74, High Road, Kilburn; Kingston-on-Thames, Norbiton, Cobham, and Teddington; 30, Victoria Road, Battersea Park; 201, Earl's Court Rd.; 820, Holloway Road; 138, High Road, Streatham; 333, High Rd., Brondesbury; 74, High St., Notting Hill; 53, High St., Clapham; 415, High St., Stratford, E.; George Lane, Woodford; 1, Finsbury Square; 126, High Holborn; 2, Grand Parade, Highgate, N.; and 8, Station Parade, Willesden Green.
182*+**Prescott, Dimsdale & Co.,** 50, Cornhill, E.C.; 3, Regent St.; & 22, London St., Paddington.
183+**Provincial B. of Ireland,** 8, Throgmorton Av.
184 **Queensland National Bank,** 8, Princes St., E.C.
185+Quin, Cope, & Co., 29, Royal Exchange, E.C.
186+Reeves, Whitburn, & Co., 27, Clement's Lane.
188+Richardson and Co., 25, Suffolk Street, S.W.
189*+Robarts, Lubbock, and Co., 15, Lombard St.
190+Ross (Geo.) & Co., 55, Bishopsgate St. Within.
191 Rothschild (N. M.) & Sons, St. Swithin's Lane.
192 **Royal B. of Queensland,** 25, Abchurch Lane.
193+Royal B. of Scotland, 123, Bishopsgate Street.
194+Rüffer (A.) and Sons, 39, Lombard Street.
195 Russian Bank, 61 & 62 Gracechurch St.
196+Samuel Montagu and Co., 60, Old Broad St.
197+**Robinson S. African,** 1 Bank Bdgs., Lothbury.
198+Seyd and Co., 38, Lombard Street.
200+Silver (S. W.) and Co., 67, Cornhill, E.C.
201*+Smith, Payne, and Smiths, 1, Lombard St.
202+Société Générale, 53, Old Broad Street, E.C.
203 **Standard Bk. of S. Africa,** 10, Clement's Lane.
204+Stilwell & Sons, 42, Pall Mall, S.W.
205 Swiss Bankverein, 40, Threadneedle St., E.C.
208+**Union Bank of Australia,** 71, Cornhill.
209*+**Union Bank of London,** *Manager,* R. H. Nunn; 2, Princes Street, E.C.; 14, Argyll Place, Regent Street; 66, Charing Cross; 95, Chancery Lane; Holborn Circus; 67, Bishop's Rd., Bayswater; 116, Fenchurch St.; 97, Tottenham Court Road; 74, Sloane St.; High St., Croydon; 12, Southwark St.; 12, Mount St., Mayfair; 18, Cromwell Pl., S.W.; 76, High St., S. Norwood; 33, High St., Bromley; 8, High St., Notting Hill, W.; 111, South End, Croydon; and 54, Theobald's Road.
210+**Union Bank of Scotland,** 62, Cornhill, E.C.
Union B. of Spain and England, 21, Old Broad St., *in liquidation.*
212+Union Deposit B., 17, King William St., W.C.
213 **Union Discount Co. of London,** 39, Cornhill, E.C.
214 **United States Exchange,** 9, Strand, W.C.
217+Watson (Wm.) & Co., 7, Waterloo Place, S.W.
220+**Whadcoat Brothers & Co.,** Crown Court, E.C.
221+White and Shaxson, 8, George Yard, E.C.
222+Whiteley, William, 39, Westbourne Grove, W.
223*+**Williams Deacon and Manchester and Salford Bk.,** 20, Birchin Lane., E.C.; 2, Cockspur St., S.W.; and Marylebone Road.
Wynne & Son, *in liquidation.*
225 **Yokohama Specie B.,** 120, Bishopsgate St. Within

Joint-Stock Banks

Name of Bank.	When Established.	Capital.			Shares.			Dividend for last complete year.
		Subscribed.	Paid-up.	Reserve Fund.	Of £	Paid per Share.	Price, Oct. 1899	
		£	£	£	£	£	£	Per cent.
African Banking Corp. ...L.	1890	800,000	400,000	60,000	10	5	5	5
Agra Bank (1833) ...L.	1867	600,000	600,000	20,000	6	6	3¼	3½
Alexanders & Co. ...L.	1891	900,000	500,000	50,000	10	10 & 5	..	...
Anglo-Argentine ...L.	1889	450,000	350,000	15,000	9	7	6¾	5
Anglo-Austrian Bank	1863	2,000,000	2,000,000	350, 40	fl. 120	fl. 120	14	6⅔
Anglo-Californian ...L.	1873	600,000	300,300	130,000	20	10	12	6
Anglo-Egyptian Bank ...L.	1864	1,200,000	400,000	150,000	15	5	7¼	8
Anglo-Foreign Bkg. Co. ...L.	1872	420,000	420,000	105,000	7	7	8½	6¼
Anglo-Italian ...L.	1866	50,000	50,000	13,755	5	5	6½	6
Ashton, Hyde & Glossop B., L.	1836	250,000	50,000	20,000	20	4	9½	10
Australian Joint-Stk. Bk., L.	1853	1,566,020	1,168,041	52,000	10	7½	...	*nil.*
Bank of Adelaide	1865	500,000	400,000	165,000	5	4	5	7
Bank of Africa ...L.	1879	2,250,000	750,000	465,000	18¾	6¼	10¾	12
Bank of Australasia	1835	1,600,000	1,600,000	800,000	40	40	...	6
Bank of British Columbia ...	1862	600,000	600,000	100,000	20	20	...	5
Bk. of British North America	1836	1,000,000	1,000,000	300,000	50	50	62	5
Bank of Egypt ...L.	1856	500,000	250,000	125,000	25	12½	23½	9&bs.5/-
Bank of Ireland	1783	3,000,000	2,769,230	1,034,000	Stock	Stock	400	12
Bank of Liverpool ...L.	1831	8,000,000	1,000,000	588,532	100	12½	...	13
Bank of Mauritius ...L.	1894	125,550	125,550	20,000	10	10	10	5

NAME OF BANK	When Established.	CAPITAL. Subscribed.	Paid-up.	Reserve Fund	SHARES. Of £	Paid per Share.	Price, Oct. 1899	Dividend for last complete year.
		£	£	£	£	£	£	Per cent.
Bank of Montreal	1817	2,465,753	2,465,753	1,232,876	$200	$200	$522	10
Bank of New South Wales	1817	2,000,000	1,950,000	1,200,000	20	20	...	9
Bank of New Zealand	1861	500,000	412,354	23,174	...	...	...	
Bank of Roumania	1865	1,000,000	300,000	158,294	20	6	7⅛	8½
Bank of Scotland	1695	1,875,000	1,250,000	700,000	Stock	Stock	...	12
Bank of Tarapacá & L'don, L.	1888	1,000,000	500,000	40,000	10	5	4	5
Bank of Victoria (Austr.)...L.	1852	2,816,760	1,476,805	70,000	10 & 10	10 & 5	10 17/20 & 2	P. 5, O. *nil.*
Bank of Whitehaven ......L.	1837	295,590	98,530	90,000	30	10	47	11¼
Barclay & Company ....L.	1896	5,793,000	2,317,200	1,000,000	20	8		...
Belfast Banking Co. ....L.	1827	2,000,000	400,000	400,000	125	25	126½, 51	20 & 8
Birm., Dist. & Cnties. B. Co., L.	1836	3,062,500	612,500	460,625	20	4	11	12½
Bolitho, Williams & Co. ...L.	...	1,500,000	300,000	279,500	50	10	33	13
Bradford Banking Co. ......L.	1827	1,360,000	408,000	165,000	10	3	7½	11⅔
Bradford Com. Jt.-Stk. B., L.	1833	1,300,000	325,000	115,000	100	25	42	8
Bradford District Bank ..L.	1862	860,000	344,000	200,000	10	4	9½	4/3 pr. sh.
Bradford Old Bank ....L.	1864	1,250,000	500,000	175,000	50	20	39½	9
British Bank of S. Am. ...L.	1863	1,000,000	500,000	300,000	20	10	...	6
British Linen Co. Bank	1746	1,250,000	1,250,000	1,600,000	Stock	Stock	493	18
British Mutual Bkg. Co....L.	1857	150,000	52,080	27,000	5	£1 10	35/-	5
Bucks & Oxon Union Bk., L.	1866	400,000	80,000	39,000	25	5	22	17½
Caledonian Banking Co. ...L.	1838	750,000	150,000	78,500	12½	2½	5	8
Capital & Counties Bank...L.	1834	5,000,000	1,000,000	750,000	50	10	39	16
Carlisle & Cumbld. Bg. Co., L.	1836	400,000	100,000	85,000	20	5	22⅛	17
Chartered Bk. of India, &c.....	1853	800,000	800,000	500,000	20	20	...	10
Cheque Bank ....L.	1873	217,200	83,822	5,000	5 & 1	1 & 1	...	...
Civil Service Bank...........L.	1892	42,015	20,017	350	1	10/-	10/-	4⅛
Clydesdale Bank, The ......L.	1838	5,000,000	1,000,000	540,000	50	10	23	10
Colonial Bank (Chartered)	1836	2,000,000	600,000	150,000	20	6	...	6
Commercl. B. of Australia, .L.	1893	4,800,000	3,113,724	*nil.*	6 & 10	4½ & 10	Pf. 58/-	Pref. 2
Commercl. B. of Scotland, .L.	1810	5,000,000	1,000,000	900,000	100	20	..	18
Commrcl. B. Co. of Sydney, .L.	1834	2,000,000	1,000,000	1,010,000	25	12½	25¼	8
Comptoir Nat. d'Escp. de Paris	1889	4,000,000	4,000,000	361,613	20	20	595 fr.	5¼
Cornish Bank ....L.	1879	500,000	150,600	90,000	50	15 & 25	40	12½
Craven Bank ....L.	1880	900,000	210,000	150,000	30	7	26	15
Crédit Lyonnais	1863	8,000,000	8,000,000	2,400,000	20	20	...	8
Cripplegate ....L.	1819	25,000	5,000	13,290	5	1	2	10 & B. 5
Crompton & Evans Union, L.	1877	1,250,000	250,000	265,000	20	4	17	18⅛
Cumberland Union B. Co., L.	1829	600,000	250,000	160,000	30	12½	23⅝	8
Delhi & London Bank......L.	1844	337,625	337,625	none	25	25	12.10/-	4
Deutsche Bank ....L.	1870	7,500,000	7,500,000	2,322,906	30 & 60	30 & 60	201 p.c.	10½
Devon & Cornwall Bg. Co., L.	1832	1,500,000	206,250	318,750	100	20	100½	20
Dresdner Bank	1872	6,500,000	6,500,000	1,700,000	60 & 30	60 & 30	160	9
Dumbells Bkg. Co ...... L.	1874	150,000	50,000	40,000	6	2	8⅛	18
Eng. Scot. & Australian ...L.	1852	1,078,875	539,438	...	25	12½	...	...
Glyn, Mills, Currie & Co.	1885	1,000,000	1,000,000	500,000	...	..	...	...
Grant & Maddisons U. B. Co., L.	1888	350,000	112,000	39,000	50	16	33	10
Guernsey Banking Co. .....L.	1827	250,000	50,000	30,000	50	10	...	14/-
Guernsey Com. Bkg. Co. ...	1835	80,000	28,000	42,000	100	35	120	22¾
Halifax Commi. Bkg. Co., L	1836	400,000	200,000	95,000	20	10	18	8
Halifax & Huddersfield Un. L.	1836	1,200,000	300,000	90,000	40	10	18½	8
Halifax Jt.-Stk. Bkg. Co...L.	1829	750,000	300,000	305,000	25	10	25	10
Hibernian Bank.............L.	1825	2,000,000	500,000	55,000	20	5	6¼	5
Hongkong and Shanghai......	1865	$10000000	$10000000	$11000000	$125	$125	61 1/9	65/- pr. sh. &Bs. £1/-
Imperial Bank of Persia.	1889	650,000	650,000	72,458	6 10/-	6 10/-	..	...
Imperial Ottoman Bank ...	1863	10,000,000	5,000,000	616,140	20	10	12	5
Internat. Bk. of London...L.	1880	400,000	300,000	15,000	20	15	12½	4
Isle of Man Banking Co... L.	1865	150,000	30,000	50,000	10	2	12¼	25
Knaresbro' & Claro B. Co., L.	1831	213,700	42,740	45,000	25	5	20¼	17½
Lancashire & Yorksh. Bk., L.	1872	1,200,000	600,000	385,000	20	10	33	12
Lancaster B. Co. (1st J.S.B.) L.	1826	1,925,000	302,500	300,000	35	5½	34¾	27s. pr. sh.
Leicestershire Bankg. Co., L.	1829	1,100,000	440,000	200,000	25	10	30	10 & 2% Bs.
Lincoln & Lindsey Bg. Co., L.	1833	400,000	140,000	225,930	200, 50	70, 17½	295, 75	18
Liverpool Union Bank ....L.	1835	3,000,000	600,000	400,000	100	20	57½	12½
Lloyds Bank ....L.	1865	13,750,000	2,200,000	1,300,000	50	8	31⅝	17½
Lond. B. of Mexico & S. Am. L.	1864	500,000	400,000	200,000	10	5	6	8
London and Brazilian ..L.	1862	1,500,000	750,000	600,000	20	10	...	14
London Bank of Australia, .L.	1893	1,643,020	914,860	...	30	15	...	...
London & County Bkg. Co., L.	1836	8,000,000	2,000,000	1,275,000	80	20	104	22

NAME OF BANK.	When Estab-lished.	CAPITAL.			SHARES.			Dividend for last complete year.
		Subscribed.	Paid-up.	Reserve Fund.	Of £	Paid per Share.	Price, Oct. 1899	
		£	£	£	£	£	£	Per cent.
London and Hanseatic B., L.	1873	800,000	400,000	120,000	20	10	12	7
London & Northern Bank L.	1898	579,760	278,417	...	10 & 10	10 & 2½	...	...
London City & Midland . L.	1836	10,571,520	2,202,400	2,202,400	60	12½	52	17 & Bs. 1%
London Joint-Stock Bank, L.	1836	12,000,000	1,800,000	1,200,000	100	15	...	10½
Lond., Paris, & Americn. B., L.	1884	500,000	400,000	170,000	20	16	25	7
London & Provincial Bk., L.	1864	1,400,000	700,000	1,045,000	10	5	...	18
Lond. & San Francisco B., L.	1865	490,000	490,000	...	7	7	6	3½
London & Sth. Western B., L.	1862	2,000,000	800,000	660,000	50	20	77 & 77½	16
London & Westminster B., L	1834	14,000,000	2,800,000	1,600,000	100	20	62½	14½
London & Yorkshire Bk.... L	1872	983,000	260,000	145,000	9½	2½	6$\frac{13}{16}$	10
Manchester & County B....L	1862	5,460,000	873,632	910,000	100	16	61	15
Manchstr. & Lp'lDst. B.Co., L.	1829	6,000,000	1,000,000	1,130,000	60	10	52	20
Manx Bank L	1882	75,000	25,000	10,800	6	2	3½	7
Martin's Bank (1570) ..... L.	1891	1,000,000	500,000	85,000	20	10	14½	7
Mercantile Bank of India. L	1892	1,125,000	562,500	20,000	25	12½	...	5 & 3
Mercantile Bk. of London L.	1891	46,800	42,072	3,450	10	10	...	2½
Mercantile Bk.of Lancash., L.	1890	921,500	200,000	47,000	20	3 & 10	& 10	7½
Merchant Banking Co. L	1888	675,000	300,000	none	9	4	2¾	5
Met. Bk. (of Eng. & Wales), L.	1866	5,000,000	500,000	350,000	50	5	15	13¾
Midland Counties Dis. Bk..L	1889	701,880	116,930	23,792	30	5	7¼	5½
Moore & Robinson's Notts B.L.	1836	507,750	203,800	100,000	10	4	8⅞	10
Munster and Leinster B....L	1885	500,000	200,000	202,500	5	2	5$\frac{5}{8}$	11½
Natal Bank L	1854	878,110	284,437	110,000	...	...	...	10
National Bank L	1835	7,500,000	1,500,000	410,000	50	10	22,$\frac{5}{8}$	10
National B.of Australasia ..L	1858	4,000,000	1,669,674	50,000	10	7 & 10	...	*nil.* & 5
National Bank of Egypt...L	1898	1,500,000	1,500,000	..	10	10	...	...
National Bank of India ...L	1863	1,000,000	500,000	300,000	25	12½	20½	8
National B. of N. Zealand, L.	1872	750,000	250,000	60,000	7½	2½	1	7
National Bk. of Scotland, L.	1825	5,000,000	1,000,000	1,000,000	Stock	Stock	404	18
Nat. B. of S. African Rep., L.	1891	1,002,000	1,002,000	48,900	10	10	...	...
Nat. Prov. B. of England, L.	1833	15,900,000	3,000,000	2,150,000	75 & 60	10½ 12	55, 63½	20
Northamptonshire Union, L.	1836	900,000	300,000	250,000	30	10	29¼	12
North & South Wales B., L.	1836	2,400,000	600,000	400,000	40	10	36⅝	15
North Eastern Bkg. Co. ...L	1872	1,020,000	306,000	115,000	20	6	17⅛	11⅜
North of Scotland Bank...L	1836	2,000,000	400,000	135,000	20	4	10⅜	8¾
Northern Banking Co......L	1824	2,500,000	482,064	300,000	50	10	26¾	11 & 5½
Nottingham Jnt.-Stk. B....L	1865	1,000,000	200,000	164,000	50	10	29½	12½
Nottingham & Notts B.Co., L.	1834	1,200,000	300,000	67,500	20	5	10½	8
Pares's Leicestersh. B. Co., L	1836	1,000,000	350,000	175,000	25	12½ & 5	36¾, 14¾	12½
Parr's Bank ... . L.	1865	6,850,000	1,370,000	1,370,000	100	20	93½	19
Prescott,Dimsd.,Cave&Co.L.	1890	1,274,700	407,994	203,952	25	8	...	...
Provincial Bk. of Ireland, L.	1825	4,080,000	540,000	280,000	100, 20	12½, 10	30	10
Queensland National Bk. ..L	1872	800,000	412,644	9,000	5	3	...	...
Robinson S. Afr. Bkg. Co., L	1895	3,000,000	3,000,000	28,720	4	4	...	5
Royal Bank of Ireland. L.	1836	1,500,000	300,000	200,000	50	10	...	12 & B. 1
Royal Bank of Queensland, L.		750,000	386,264	41,000	9	5⅙	...	2½
Royal Bank of Scotland ...	1727	2,000,000	2,000,000	803,554	Stock	Stock	230	8
Sheffield Banking Co. .....L.	1831	955,500	334,425	157,732	50	17½	54 10/-	12½, 1½ B.
Sheffield & Hallamshire...L.	1836	1,200,000	300,000	206,530	20	10	14¾	12½
Sheff. & Roth. Jt. St. B.Co., L.	1836	1,200,000	192,000	120,325	50	8	28½	15
Sheffield Union Bkg. Co...L	1843	720,000	180,000	65,000	40	10	29	10 & B. 2/6
Société Générale	1861	6,400,000	3,200,000	740,000	20	8	24	5
Stamf., Spal., & Bost.B.Co., L.	1832	883,770	294,590	118,000	30	10	23½	10
Standard Bk. of S. Africa, L.	1862	4,959,100	1,239,775	1,164,820	100	25	65¼	16
Stuckey's Banking Co. ...L	1826	2,040,000	408,000	350,000	60	12	65	23½
Town & Cy. Bk. (Aberdn.), L.	1825	1,260,000	252,000	146,000	35	7	21$\frac{1}{16}$	12½
Ulster Bank.................. L	1836	2,700,000	450,000	550,000	15	2½	11½	20
Union Bank of Australia...L	1837	4,500,000	1,500,000	750,000	75	25	33½	5½
Union Bank of London L	1839	11,000,000	1,705,000	850,000	100	15½	33	13
Union Bk. of Manchester, L.	1836	1,250,000	550,000	375,000	25	11	30	24/- pr.sh.
Union Bank of Scotland ...L	1830	5,000,000	1,000,000	625,000	50	10	26¾	12
Wakefield & Barnsl.Un.B., L	1832	500,000	135,000	147,000	50	13¼	36¾	12½
West Riding Un. Bkg. Co., L	1832	1,580,000	316,060	57,153	50	10	18¾	8
Whitehaven Jt. Sk. B. Co., L.	1829	401,040	60,150	60,150	50	7½	42	24
Williams Deac. & M. & S. B.L.	1836	6,250,000	1,000,000	525,000	50	8	27⅜	13¾
Wilts & Dorset Bkng. Co., L.	1835	3,250,000	650,000	750,000	50	10	51½	21
York City & County Bk....L	1830	2,000,000	600,000	660,000	10	3	13⅜	18½
York Union Banking Co...L	1833	1,260,000	262,500	173,000	60	12½	53	18
Yorkshire Banking Co. ...L	1843	1,500,000	375,000	307,500	10	2½	9¾	16

LIST OF COUNTRY BANKS IN ENGLAND AND WALES,
WITH THEIR BRANCHES (EXCLUSIVE OF THOSE NOT OPEN DAILY), AND THEIR LONDON AGENTS.

(H.O.) *signifies the Head Office of a Joint Stock Banking Company; the* **Numbers refer to the London Agents in List, pages 291-94.**

Aberavon, Capital & Counties 49
Aberayron, National Provincial ...175
Aberdare, Lloyds Bank 132
  ,, London and Provincial 100
  ,, Metrop. Bank of Eng. & Wales162
Abergavenny, Birm.Dist.& Coy.B.Co.30
  ,, Capital and Counties 49
  ,, Lloyds Bank 132
  ,, National Provincial 175
Abergele, North & South Wales B. 144
Abertillery, Capital and Counties 49
Aberystwyth, National Provincial..175
  ,, North and South Wales B. ..144
  ,, London and Provincial 100
Abingdon, London and County 135
  ,, Gillett & Co. 100
Accrington, Lanc. & Yorkshire ...144
  ,, Manchester and County ...200
  ,, Manchest. & L'pool. Dist. B.Co.153
  ,, Union Bank of Manchester ..100
Acocks Green, Met.B.of Eng. & W...162
Addlestone, T. Ashby & Co. 223
Adlington, Williams Deacon Bk. 223
Aintree, Bank of Liverpool.......100
  ,, N. & S. Wales Bk. 144
Alcester, Capital and Counties .. 49
  ,, Metrop. B. of Eng. & Wales ..162
Aldeburgh (Suffolk), Barclay & Co. 30
  ,, London & Provincial 100
Alderley Edge, Union B. of Manch.100
  ,, Manchester & L'pool Dis.B.Co.153
Alderney, Capital and Counties .. 49
Aldershot, London and County 135
  ,, Capital and Counties 49
Alford (Linc.), Capital and Counties 49
  ,, Lincoln and Lindsey 182
  ,, Stamford, Spald. & Bos. B. Co. 30
Alfreton, Crompton & Evans'Union100
  ,, Nottingham Joint-Stock 209
Allendale Town, Cumb.Union B. Co. 30
Alnwick, Hodgkin, Barnett, & Co. 132
  ,, Lambton & Co. 30
  ,, North Eastern Banking Co. ..100
  ,, Barclay & Co. (Woods) 30
Alresford, Prescott, Dimsdale & Co.182
  ,, Capital and Counties 49
Alston, Carlisle & Cumberld. B. Co.193
  ,, London City and Midland ...136
Alton (Hants), Prescott & Co. 182
  ,, Capital and Counties 49
Altrincham, Cunliffes, Brooks,& Co. 42
  ,, Lancashire and Yorkshire...144
  ,, Merc. B'nk of Lancashire ...148
  ,, Parr's Bank 177
  ,, Williams, Deacon,& Co. ...223
Alverstoke, Capital and Counties .. 49
Amble, North-Eastern B. Co. 100
  ,, Hodgkin, Barnett, & Co. ..132
Ambleside, Lancaster Banking Co. .. 30
  ,, Bank of Liverpool 100
  ,, London City and Midland ...136
Amersham, Capital & Counties .. 49
Amlwch, National Provincial 175
  ,, Lloyd's Bank 132
Ampthill, Barclay & Co. 30
Ancoats, Man. & L'pool Dis. B. Co. 153
Andover, Capital and Counties .. 49
  ,, London and County 135
Annfield Plain, Hodgkin, Barnett & Co. ..132
  ,, N. Eastern B. Co. 100
Appleby, Carlisle & Cumblnd. B. Co.193
  ,, Cumberland Union Bankg. Co. 30
Arundel, Capital and Counties .. 49
  ,, London and County 135
Ascot, T. Ashby & Co. 223
Ashbourne, Birm. & Counties Bk. Co. 30
  ,, Lloyds Bank 132
  ,, Crompton & Evans Union Bk.100
Ashburton, Devon & Cornwall B.Co. 30
  ,, Capital and Counties 49
Ashby-de-la-Zouch, Leicstrsh. B. Co.201
  ,, Pares's Leicestershire Bkg. Co.201

Ashford, London and County......135
  ,, Pomfret, Burra, & Co. 201
Ashington, Hodgkin, Barnett & Co. 132
  ,, North-East. Banking Co. ...100
Ashton-in-Makerfield, Parr's Bank..177
  ,, Union Bank of Manchester. 100
Ashton-under-Lyne, Ashton, Stalybridge, Hyde & Glossop Bk. (H.O.) 100
  ,, Manchester & County 209
  ,, Manch. & Liverpool Dist.B.Co.153
  ,, Union Bank of Manchester .100
Aspatria, Bank of Whitehaven....100
  ,, Cumberland Union Bkg. Co. .. 30
Astley Bridge,Williams Deacon Bk.223
  ,, Manchester and County 209
Aston Cross, B'ham Dis. & Cties. .. 30
  ,, London, City, & Midland ...136
  ,, Metropolitan Bank 162
Astwood Bank,Capital and Counties 49
  ,, Lloyds Bank 132
Atherstone, Leicestershire Bnkg.Co.144
  ,, Lloyds Bank 132
Atherton, Manchester & County .209
  ,, Williams Deacon Bank 223
Attleborough, Barclay & Co. 30
Auldenshaw, London City and Mid.136
Aulum, Birmingham Dist. & Cties. 30
Avonmouth, Capital and Counties.. 49
  ,, Prescott & Co. 182
Axbridge, Stuckey's Banking Co. ..189
  ,, Wilts and Dorset B. Co. ...144
Axminster, Wilts and Dorset B. Co.223
  ,, Stuckey's Banking Co. 189
  ,, Devon and Cornwall B. Co...30
Aylesbury, Bucks & Oxon Union B.144
  ,, Cobb, Bartlett & Co. 144
  ,, London and County 135
  ,, Thomas Butcher & Sons 182
Aylsham, Barclay & Co. 30
Bacup, Lancashire and Yorkshire .144
  ,, Manchester and County Bankg.200
Baildon, Bradford Old Bank 182
Bakewell, Crompton & Evans' Un. B.100
  ,, Sheffield &Rotherham B.Co.30,144
Bala, National Provincial Bk. 175
  ,, North and South Wales Bk. ..144
Baldock, Capital & Counties 49
Balsall Heath, Lond. City & Mid .136
Bampton (Devon), Stuckey's B. Co.189
  ,, (Oxon), Metrop. Bk. of E. & W.162
Banbury,Bucks and Oxon Union B.144
  ,, Cobb & Son 144
  ,, Gillett & Co. 100
  ,, London and County 135
  ,, Metrop. B. of Eng. & Wales .162
Bangor, Metrop. B. of Eng. & Wales162
  ,, National Provincial 175
  ,, Lloyd's Bank 132
Banwell, Fox, Fowler, & Co. 30
Barking, London & South Western144
Barmouth, North and South Wales144
  ,, Metrop. Bank of Eng. & Wales162
Barnard Castle, Barclay & Co. 30
  ,, North East. Bkg. Co. 100
  ,, National Provincial 175
  ,, York City and County Bkg. Co.132
Barnet, London and County 135
  ,, Barclay & Co. 30
Barnoldswick, Craven Bk. 182
Barnsley, York City and County ..132
  ,, London & Yorkshire Bk. 146
  ,, Wakefield & Barnsley Un. Bk. 132
  ,, London, City & Midland ...136
Barnstaple, Devon & Cornwall B. Co. 30
  ,, Fox, Fowler, & Co. 30
  ,, National Provincial Bank ..175
  ,, Wilts. & Dorset B. Co. 144
Barrow-in-F'ness, Lancaster Bk. Co. 30
  ,, Cumberland Union Bankg.Co. 30
  ,, Bank of Liverpool 100
Barry, London and Provincial ...100
Barry Docks, London & Provincial 100

Barry Docks, Lloyds Bank 132
  ,, Metrop. Bank of Eng. & Wales162
  ,, National Provincial Bank . 175
  ,, London City & Midland ...136
Barton-on-Humber, York City & County Bankg. Co. 132
Basford, Samuel Smith & Co. 201
  ,, Nottingham Joint Stock ...209
Basingstoke, Capital and Counties 49
  ,, London and County 135
  ,, J. & C. Simonds & Co. 223
Baslow, Sheff. & Rotherham Bk. Co.144
Bath, National Provincial 175
  ,, Stuckey's Banking Co. 189
  ,, Prescott, Dimsdale & Co. ...182
  ,, Wilts and Dorset Bg. Co. ...144
  ,, Lloyds Bank 132
  ,, Metrop. Bank of Eng. & Wales162
  ,, Capital & Counties 49
  ,, London City & Midland ...136
Batley, London City and Midland..136
  ,, West Riding Union Bnkg. Co.144
  ,, London and Yorkshire Bank 146
Battle, London and County 135
  ,, Barclay & Co. 30
Beaminster, Wilts & Dorset Bg. Co.223
Beaumaris, National Provincial ..175
Beccles, Barclay & Co. 30
  ,, Lacons, Youell, & Kemp....100
Beckenham, London and County ..135
  ,, London and Provincial 100
  ,, London City & Midland ...136
Bedale, York City & County 132
Bedford, Thomas Barnard & Co. ..201
  ,, London and County 135
  ,, Northamptonshire U. Bank .223
  ,, London City and Midland ...136
Bedlington, North-East. Bankg. Co.100
Bedminster (Glos.), Nat. Pro. 175
  ,, Prescott, Dimsdale & Co. ...182
Bedworth, Leicestershire Bnkg. Co.144
  ,, Birm District & Counties ...30
Beeston, Nottingham Jt. St. 209
Belford, North-Eastern Bankg. Co.100
Belgrave, Stamf Spalding & Boston 30
Bellingham, North-Eastern B. Co. 100
  ,, Hodgkin, Barnett & Co. ...132
Belper, Crompton & Evans' Un. Bk.100
  ,, Parr's Bank 177
Berkeley, National Provincial ...175
Berkhampstead, Gt., Lond. & Cnty.135
Berwick-on-Tweed, British Linen Co. 40
  ,, Com. Bank of Scotland 68
  ,, National Bank of Scotland ..173
  ,, North-Eastern Banking Co. ..100
  ,, Barclay & Co. 30
  ,, Hodgkin, Barnett, & Co. ...132
Beswick, Man. & L'pool Dist. B. Co.153
Bethesda, National Provincial 175
  ,, Metrop. Bank of Eng. & Wales162
Beverley, Beckett & Co. 100
  ,, York City & County B. Co. ..132
  ,, Yorkshire Banking Co. 223
  ,, York Union Banking Co. 100
Bewdley, London City & Midland..136
Bexhill, Lloyds Bank 132
  ,, London and County 135
Bexley & B. Heath. Martin's Bank154
  ,, London and Provincial 100
Bicester, Tubb & Co. 144
Bideford, Devon & Cornwall B. Co. 30
  ,, Fox, Fowler, & Co. 30
  ,, National Provincial 175
  ,, Wilts & Dorset B. Co. 144
Bidford (Warw.), Lloyds Bank ...132
Biggleswade, Capital and Counties 49
Billericay, Barclay & Co. 30
Bilston, Birm'ham D. & Counties B. 30
  ,, Metrop. Bank of Eng. & Wales162
Bingley, Bradford Old Bank 182
  ,, Craven Bank 182
Birkdale, Parr's Bank 177
  ,, (exc.Sat.) Williams Deacon Bk.223

Birkdale, Bank of Liverpool 100
Birkenhead. North & S. Wales Bank144
  „ Parr's Bank 177
  „ Bank of Liverpool 100
  „ Liverpool Union 132
  „ Hill & Sons 100
  „ Man. & L'pool Dis. B. Co. ... 2 1
Birmingham, Lloyds Bank (H.O.)..132
  „ Birmingham District & Counties Banking Co. (H.O.) .. 30
  „ Bank of England 21
  „ London City and Midland 136
  „ Capital and Counties 49
  „ T. Cook & Son 73
  „ Goode, Marr, & Co. 115
  „ Metrop. Bank of Eng. & Wales162
  „ National Provincial 175
  „ London & Northern 138
Birtley, Hodgkin, Barnett & Co. ..132
Bishop Auckland, Barclay & Co. .. 30
  „ National Provincial 175
  „ North Eastern Bank Co. 100
  „ York City and County B. Co.132
  „ Birmingham & Counties B. Co. 30
Bishops Castle, N. & S. Wales Bank144
  „ Birmingham & Counties B. Co. 30
Bishop Stortford, Foster & Co. 182
  „ Barclay & Co 30
  „ London and County 135
Bishop's Waltham, Gunner & Co. 30
  „ Capital & Counties 49
Bishopston, Capital and Counties.. 49
Blackburn, Cunliffes, Brooks & Co.. 42
  „ Lancashire and Yorkshire 144
  „ Manchester and County 209
  „ Manchester&Lpool, Dis. B.Co.153
  „ Mercantile Bk. of Lancashire148
  „ London City & Midland 136
  „ T. Cook and Son 73
Blackheath, Birmingham & C'ties. 30
Blackhill, North-East. Banking Co. 100
Blackley, Union Bank of Manchester,100
Blackpool, Lancaster Banking Co 30
  „ Manchester and County 209
  „ London City and Midland 136
  „ Lancs. and Yorks. Bank 144
  „ Manch. & L'pool Dis. B. Co. 153
  „ Williams Deacon Bank 223
Blaenau-Festiniog, Met.B. of E.&W.162
  „ North and South Wales Bank 144
Blaenavon, Met. B of Eng. & Wales 162
Blandford, National Provincial 175
  „ Wilts & Dorset Banking Co. ..100
Blaydon-on-Tyne, Lambton & Co. .. 30
Bloxwich. Met. B. of Eng. & Wales 162
Blundellsands, Bank of L'pool 100
  „ Parr's Bank 177
Blyth, Hodgkin, Barnett & Co. 132
  „ Lambton & Co. 30
  „ Barclay & Co. (Woods) 30
Bodmin, Bolitho, Williams, &Co.30, 223
  „ Capital and Counties Bank .. 49
  „ Devon and Cornwall B. Co. .. 30
Bognor, London and County 135
Bolton, Manchester & County 209
  „ Manchester & Lpool. Dis. B.Co.153
  „ T. Cook & Son 73
  „ Merc. Bk of Lancashire 148
  „ Parr's Bank 177
  „ London City and Midland 136
  „ Union Bank of Manchester ...100
  „ Williams Deacon Bank 223
Bolton-on-Dearne, Shef. B. Co. 210
Boothstown, Un. Bk. Manchester ..100
Bootle (Cumb.), Bank of Liverpool..100
Bootle (Lancs.), Bank of Liverpool..100
  „ Parr's Bank 177
  „ N. & S. Wales Bank 144
  „ London City & Midland 136
  „ Lancashire & Yorkshire 144
Boroughbridge, York Cy.& Cy. Bk.Co.132
Boro'bridge, Knaresbro'& Claro B.Co.132
Boscombe, Capital Counties 49
  „ Wilts & Dorset Bkg Co. 100
Boston, Capital and Counties 49
  „ Lincoln and Lindsey Bank ...182
  „ National Provincial 175
  „ Stamford, Spaldg.&Bost'n B.Co. 30
Boston Spa (Yks.) York City & Cy.132
Botesdale, Barclay & Co. 30
Bourne, Peacock, Willson & Co. ...132
Bourne, Stmfd., Spalding & Boston
  B. Co. 30

Bournemouth, Capital & Counties .. 49
  „ National Provincial 175
  „ Wilts & Dorset Bg Co 223 & 100
  „ London City and Midland 136
Bourton-on-the-Water, Cap. & C'ties. 49
Bowness, Bank of Liverpool 100
  „ London City and Midland 136
  „ Lancaster Banking Co. 30
Brackley, Gillett & Co. 30
  „ Bucks and Oxon Union Bk. ..144
Bracknell, Lloyds Bank 132
  „ I. & C. Simonds & Co. 30
Bradford Bradford Bnkg.Co.(H.O.)144
  „ Brdfd C'm.Jt.-Sk.Bg.Co.(H.O.)100
  „ Bradford District Bank (H.O.)201
  „ Bradford Old Bank (H.O.) 132
  „ Beckett & Co. 30
  „ London City and Midland 136
  „ T. Cook & Son 73
  „ Craven Bank 182
  „ Halifax Commercial Bkg. Co. 223
  „ Halifax & Hudd. Un. B. Co.100
  „ Halifax Joint Stock Bkg. Co.144
  „ London and Yorksh're Bank..144
  „ Yorkshire Banking Co. 223
Bradford-on-Avon, Cap. & Counties 49
  „ Wilts and Dorset Bkg. Co. ...144
Brailes, Metrop. B. of Eng.& Wales162
Braintree, London and County 135
  „ Barclay & Co. 30
Bramley (Leeds), Lond. City & Mid.136
Brampton, London City and Mid...136
  „ Cumberland Union Bank 30
Brecon, Birm. Dist. & Cnts. Bk. Co. 30
  „ National Provincial 175
  „ Lloyds Bank 132
Brent (Devon), Cornish Bk. 201
Brentford, London and County 135
  „ Woodbridge, Lacy, H.H. & Co. 100
Brentwood, London and County ...132
  „ Barclay & Co. 30
Bridgend, London and Provincial 100
  „ National Provincial 175
  „ Metrop. Bank of Eng. & Wales162
Bridgnorth, Lloyds Bank 132
  „ Metr'p. Bank of Eng. & Wales162
  „ Eyton, Burton & Co. 189
Bridgwater, Fox, Fowler & Co. 30
  „ Stuckey's Banking Co. 189
  „ Devon & Cornwall Bnkng. Co. 30
Bridlington, York Union Bkg. Co.100
  „ York City and County Bkg.Co.132
Bridlington Quay, York Union B. Co.100
  „ York City & County Bkg. Co. 132
  „ Barclay & Co. 30
Bridport, Wilts & Dorset Bg Co.144&223
  „ Devon & Cornwall Bkg. Co. .. 30
  „ Union Bank of Manchester ...100
Brierley Hill, Met. B. of Eng. & W. 162
  „ London City and Midland 136
Brigg, Smith, Ellison & Co. 182
  „ Lincoln and Lindsey Bank ...182
Brighouse, Halifax Comm. Bkg. Co. 223
  „ Halifax & Hudd. Un. B. Co.100
  „ Halifax Joint-Stock Bkg. Co. 144
  „ London and Yorkshire Bank..144
Brighton, Capital and Counties 49
  „ Barclay & Co. 30
  „ T. Cook & Son 73
  „ London and County 135
  „ London and South-Western .. 142
  „ London City and Midland 136
  „ Lloyds Bank 132
  „ National Provincial 175
Bristol, Bank of England 21
  „ Capital and Counties 49
  „ T. Cook & Son 73
  „ Lloyds Bank 132
  „ London and Provincial 100
  „ Lond. and South-Western Bk.142
  „ Prescott, Dimsdale & Co. 100
  „ Metrop. Bank of Eng. & Wales162
  „ National Provincial 175
  „ Stuckey's Banking Co. 189
  „ Wilts and Dorset B. Co. 144
  „ London City and Midland 136
Briton Ferry, Capital & Counties .. 49
  „ London and Provincial 100
  „ Metrop. Bk. of Eng. & Wales162
Brixham, Devon & Cornwall B. Co. 30
Brixham, National Provincial 175

Broadstairs, Lloyds Bank 132
Broadway Worc.),Cap.& Cnties.Bk. 49
Bromley (Kent), London & County135
  „ Martin's Bank 154
  „ London City and Midland 136
  „ Union Bank of London 209
Bromsgrove, Lloyds Bank 132
  „ Metrop. Bank of Eng. & Wales162
Bromyard, Berwick&Co.(Lechmere)189
  „ National Provincial 175
Broseley, Lloyds Bank 132
Broughton Bridge, Manch. & L'pool
  District B. Company 201
Broughton-in-Furness. Cumberl'd.
  Union Banking Co. 100
  „ Bank of Liverpool 100
Bruton, Stuckey's Banking Co. 189
Brynmawr, Capital and Counties.. 49
Buckingham, Bucks and Oxon Union
  Bank (H.O.) 144
  „ Bartlett & Co. 144
  „ London and County 135
Bude, Devon & Cornwall Bkg. Co. 30
  „ Bolitho, Williams & Co. ..30, 223
  „ Dingley & Co. 209
Budleigh Salterton, Wilts & Dorset144
  „ Sanders & Co. 30
Builth, London & Provincial 100
  „ National Provincial 175
Bulwell, Samuel Smith & Co. 201
  „ Nottingham Joint Stock 209
Sunbury, Birm. Dist. & Counties B. 30
Sungay, Barclay & Co. 30
  „ London and Provincial 100
Burford, Lloyds Bank 132
Burgess Hill, Capital & Counties .. 49
  „ Barclay & Co. 30
Burnley-in-Wharfdale, Bradf'dold B 132
Burnham (Som.), Stuckey's Bkg.Co.189
  „ Wilts and Dorset Bkg. Co. ...144
Burnley, Craven Bank 182
  „ Lanc. and Yorkshire Bk. 144
  „ Manchester and County Bk. ..209
  „ Union Bank of Manchester ...100
  „ London City and Midland 136
  „ T. Cook & Son 73
Burslem, Manch. & Liv. Dis. B. Co.153
  „ Birm. and Counties Bkg. Co. 30
  „ Lloyds Bank 132
Burton-on-Trent, Lloyds Bank 132
  „ Leicestershire Banking Co. ...144
  „ National Provincial 175
  „ London, City and Midland 136
Burwash, Barclay & Co. 30
Bury (Lanc.), Lancashire & York.B.144
  „ Manch. & L'pool Dist. B. Co. 153
  „ Union Bank of Manchester ...100
  „ Williams Deacon Bk. 100
Bury St. Edmunds, Nat. Provincial 175
  „ Barclay & Co. 30
  „ Oakes, Bevan, Tollemache ... 30
Bushey, London & South Western ..142
Buxton, Crompton & Evans Un. B.100
  „ Manchester and County Bank 209
  „ Sheffield and Rotherham. .30, 144
Byker, North-Eastern Bank. Co. ...100
  „ Lambton & Co. 30
  „ Hodgkin, Barnett & Co. 132
Caddishead, Lancashire & Yorksh. 144
Cadoxton, London & Provincial ...100
  „ Metrop. Bank of Eng.& Wales162
Caerphilly. London and Provincial 100
  „ Capital & Counties 49
  „ Lloyds Bank 132
Caistor, Smith, Ellison & Co. 182
Callington, Bolitho, Williams ..30, 223
  „ Capital and Counties Bank .. 49
  „ Dingley & Co. 209
  „ Cornish Bank 201
Calne, Wilts and Dorset Bankg. Co.144
  „ Capital and Counties 49
Calstock, Dingley & Co. 209
Camborne, Bolitho, Williams ..30, 223
  „ Cornish Bank 201
  „ Devon & Cornwall Banking Co. 30
Cambridge, Barclay & Co. 30
  „ Foster & Co. 182
  „ London and County 135
Camelford, Dingley & Co. 209
  „ Bolitho, Williams, & Co. ..30, 223
  „ Capital and Counties B. 49
Campden, Capital and Counties .. 49

Cannock, Lloyds Bank 132
Canterbury, Hammond & Co.....10c
  ,, London and County 13c
  ,, Lloyds Bank 122
Canton, Lloyds Bank 132
  ,, Metropolitan Bank 162
Cardiff, Lloyds Bank 132
  ,, London and Provincial 100
  ,, Metrop. B. of Eng. & Wales 162
  ,, National Provincial 175
  ,, Wilts and Dorset Bkg. Co..144
  ,, London City and Midland ..136
  ,, Capital & Counties 49
Cardigan, Lloyds Bank 132
  ,, National Provincial 175
  ,, Metrop. Bank of Eng. & Wales162
Carlisle, Carl. & Cumb. B. Co. (H.O.)193
  ,, Cumb. Union Bkg. Co (H.O.) 30
  ,, London City & Midland 136
  ,, Clydesdale Bank 117
Carmarthen, Lloyds Bank 132
  ,, London and Provincial 100
  ,, National Provincial 175
Carnarvon, Met. B. of Eng. & Wales162
  ,, N. & S. Wales Bank 144
  ,, Lloyds Bank 132
Carnforth, Lancaster B. Co 30
  ,, Bank of Liverpool 10c
Carshalton, London and Provincial100
  ,, London & South Western ..142
Castle Cary, Stuckey's Banking Co. 180
Castleford, London City and Mid...136
  ,, Leatham, Tew, & Co. 30
  ,, Yorkshire Banking Co 223
Castleton, London City and Mid. ..136
  ,, Manch. & L'pool Dist. 153
Castletown, Dumbell's Banking Co. 10c
  ,, Isle of Man Banking Co. ..144
  ,, Manx Bank 175
Caterham Valley, Lloyds Bank ..132
Chaddorton, Manch. & County Bank 209
  ,, Lond. City and Mid.......136
Chineford, Dingley, Pearse, & Co. 136
Chapel-en-le-frith, Manch. & City. B.209
Chard, Stuckey's Banking Co. ...180
  ,, Wilts and Dorset Bkg. Co. 144
Charlbury, Metrop. B. of Eng. & W.162
Chatham, London and County 13c
  ,, London and Provincial 100
  ,, Capital & Counties 30
Chatteris, Barclay & Co. 30
Cheadle(Staff.), Birm. & Counties B. 30
  ,, Manchester & Liverpool Dist.153
Cheetham, Lancashire & Yorkshire144
Chelmsford, London and County ..135
  ,, Barclay & Co. 30
Cheltenham, Capital and Counties . 40
  ,, Lloyds Bank 132
  ,, National Provincial 175
  ,, Wilts & Dorset Bkg Co ...144
  ,, London City & Midland ...136
Chepstow, London and Provincial..100
  ,, Metrop. B. of Eng. & Wales.162
  ,, London City and Midland ..136
Chertsey, London and County 135
  ,, T. Ashby & Co. 30
Chesham, Thomas Butcher & Sons189
  ,, Bucks. & Oxon Un. Bank ..144
Chester, National Provincial 175
  ,, North and South Wales Bank144
  ,, Parr's Bank 177
  ,, Lloyds Bank 132
  ,, Liverpool Union Bank 132
  ,, Bank of Liverpool 100
Chesterfield, Crompton & Evans Un.100
  ,, Sheffield Banking Co. 201
  ,, Sheffield Union Banking Co..182
  ,, London City and Midland ..136
Chester-le-Street, Lambton & Co. .. 30
  ,, North-Eastern Banking Co. 100
  ,, Hodgkin, Barnett & Co. ...100
Chichester, Capital and Counties .. 49
  ,, Milbanke Woodbridge & Co...132
  ,, London and County 135
Chippenham, Capital and Counties 49
  ,, Wilts and Dorset Banking Co.144
  ,, Prescott, Dimsdale and Co..182
Chipping Campden, Metrop. Bk. of
    England and Wales 62
Chipping Norton, Gillett & Co......100
  ,, Metrop. B. of Eng. & Wales..162
Chipping Ongar, Barclay & Co. 30

Chipping Sodbury, Nat. Provincial 175
Chislehurst, Martin's Bank 154
Chorley, Lancaster Banking Co.... 30
  ,, London City & Midland ...136
  ,, Williams Deacon Bank 223
Chorlton-cum-Hardy, Wms. Deac.B.223
  ,, Manchester & County 203
  ,, Manch. & L'pool Dist. B. Co. 153
Chorlton-upon-Medlock, Williams
    Deacon Bank 223
Christchurch, Wilts & Dorset Bg. Co.144
  ,, Capital and Counties 49
Church, Manch. & Lpool. Dis. B. Co. 153
  ,, Union Bank of Manchester .100
Cinderford, Capital & Counties Bk. 49
  ,, Lloyds Bank 132
Cirencester, Capital & Counties Bk. 49
  ,, Lloyds Bank 132
  ,, Wilts and Dorset 144
Clacton-on-Sea, Barclay & Co. 30
  ,, London and County 135
Clare, Barclay & Co. 30
  ,, Oakes Bevan, T. & Co 30
Clayton-le-Moors, Manchester and
    Liverpool District..........153
Cleator Moor, Bank of Whitehaven 100
  ,, Whitehaven Joint Stock ...148
Cleckheaton, York Banking Co.....223
  ,, West Riding Union Bkng. Co.144
  ,, London City and Midland ..136
Clevedon, Wilts & Dorset Bnkg. Co. 144
  ,, Stuckey's Banking Co. 189
Clifton Prescott, Dims. Cave & Co.182
  ,, Lloyds Bank 132
  ,, National Provincial 175
  ,, Capital & Counties Bank .. 49
  ,, Stuckey's Banking Co.......189
  ,, Wilts and Dorset Banking Co.144
  ,, London City & Midland ...136
Clitheroe, Craven Bank 182
  ,, Manchester & County 200
  ,, London City & Midland ...136
Coalville, Leicestersh. Bkg. Co.....144
  ,, Lloyd's Bank 132
Cockermouth, London City & Mid..136
  ,, Carlisle and Cumberland B.Co.193
  ,, Cumberland Union Bnkg. Co. 30
Coggeshall, Barclay & Co. 30
Colchester, London and County ...135
  ,, Barclay & Co. 30
  ,, Parr's Bank 177
Coleford, Capital and Counties 49
Coleshill, London City and Mid. ..136
  ,, Lloyds Bank 132
Colne (Lanc.), Craven Bank 182
  ,, Manchester and County Bk. 209
  ,, Union B. of Manchester 100
Colwyn Bay, Met. B. of Eng. & W. 162
  ,, National Provincial 175
  ,, North & South Wales B. ...144
Colyton, Wilts and Dorset 223
Combe Down, Prescott D. & Co. ..182
Congleton, Manch. & L'pool. Dist. .153
  ,, Parr's Bank 177
Coniston, Bank of Liverpool 100
Consett, Hodgkin, Barnett, & Co. ..132
  ,, North-Eastern Banking Co. 100
Conway, Met. B. of Eng. & Wales 162
  ,, National Provincial 175
Corbridge, North Eastern Bk. Co..100
Cornbrook, Lancs. & Yorks. B. ...144
Corsham, Capital and Counties 49
  ,, Wilts and Dorset Banking Co.144
Corwen, North & South Wales Bk..144
Coshan, Capital and Counties 49
  ,, Grant & Maddison 100
Coventry, Birm. & Counties Bk. Co. 30
  ,, London City and Midland ..136
  ,, Lloyds Bank 132
  ,, Midland Counties Dist. 148
Cowbridge, London and Provincial 100
  ,, National Provincial 175
  ,, Metrop. B. of Eng. & Wales. 162
Cowes, Capital and Counties 49
  ,, London and County 135
Cradley Heath, Birm. & Counties Bk. 30
  ,, Metrop. B. of Eng. & Wales.162
Cranbrook, London and County ...35
Crawley, London and County 135
Crawshawbooth, Manchester and
    County.....................209
Crediton, Devon & Cornwall B. Co. 30

Crediton, Fox, Fowler, & Co. 30
  ,, National Provincial 175
Crewe, Birm. and Counties Bkg. Co. 30
  ,, Manch. & L'pool. Dist. B. Co. 153
  ,, Parr's Bank 177
Crewkerne, Stuckey's Banking Co..189
  ,, Wilts and Dorset Banking Co.144
Crickhowell, National Provincial ..175
Cricklade, Capital and Counties.... 49
Cromer, Barclay & Co. 30
  ,, Lacons, Youell, & Kemp....100
Crook, Barclay & Co. 30
  ,, North Eastern Banking Co. 100
Crumlin, London & Provincial 100
Cullompton, Devon&Cornwall B. Co. 30
  ,, Stuckey's Banking Co. 189
Dalton-in-Furness, Cumbrland Union 30
  ,, Lancaster Banking Co. 30
  ,, Bank of Liverpool 100
Darlaston, Lloyds Bank 132
  ,, Metrop. B. of Eng. & Wales .162
Darley Dale, Sheff. & Rotherham ..144
Darlington, Barclay & Co. 30
  ,, National Provincial 175
  ,, J. & J. W. Pease.........182
  ,, York City and County Bkg. Co.132
  ,, North Eastern Bank. Co. ..100
Dartford, London and County 135
  ,, Martin's Bank 154
Dartmouth, Harris, Bulteel, & Co. 189
  ,, Lloyds Bank 132
  ,, National Provincial 175
Darwen, Cunliffes, Brooks, & Co. .. 42
  ,, Lancashire & Yorkshire Bank144
  ,, Manchester and County Bk. .209
  ,, Manch.&Liverpool Dist. B.Co.153
Daventry, Northants Union Bank ..223
  ,, Capital and Counties Bank . 49
Dawlish, Capital and Counties 49
  ,, Devon and Cornwall Bkg. Co. 30
Deal, National Provincial 175
  ,, Lloyds Bank 132
Deeptale, Williams Deacons Co. ...223
Delabole, Bolitho, Williams & Co. 30,223
Denbigh, National Provincial 144
  ,, North and South Wales Bank 144
Denton, Manchester and County ...209
  ,, Manchester & Liverpl. Dist. 153
Derby, Crompton & Evans Union
    Bank (H.O.) 100
  ,, London City & Midland ...136
  ,, Samuel Smith & Co. 201
  ,, Parr's Bank 177
  ,, Birm. and Counties Bk. Co. .30
  ,, Lloyds Bank 132
  ,, Midland C'ties District 148
Devizes, Capital and Counties 49
  ,, Wilts and Dorset Banking Co.144
Devonport, Bolitho, Williams ...30, 223
  ,, Capital and Counties 49
  ,, Devon and Cornwall Bkg. Co. 30
  ,, Harris, Bulteel, & Co. 189
  ,, National Provincial 175
Dewsbury, London City & Mid. ...136
  ,, Lancashire & Yorkshire Bank144
  ,, London and Yorkshire Bank 146
  ,, West Riding Union Bnkg. Co. 144
Didsbury, Union B. of Manchester 100
  ,, Mercantile B. of Lanc. 148
Diss, Barclay & Co. 30
  ,, London and Provincial 100
Dobcross, Manchester & County B. 209
Dolgelly, National Provincial 175
  ,, North and South Wales Bank 144
Doncaster, Beckett & Co. 100
  ,, London and Yorkshire Bank..146
  ,, York City and County Bkg. Co. 132
  ,, Yorkshire Banking Co. 223
Dorchester, Capital & Counties 49
  ,, Stuckey's Banking Co. 189
  ,, Wilts & Dorset Bkg Co. 144 & 223
  ,, Devon & Cornwall B. Co....80
Dorking, Capital and Counties 49
  ,, London and County 135
Douglas (Isle of Man), Dumbell's
    Banking Co. (H.O.) 100
  ,, Isle of Man Bkg. Co. (H.O.)144
  ,, Manx Bank (H.O.).........175
  ,, Liverpool Union Bank 132
Dover, London and County 135
  ,, National Provincial 175

Dover, Lloyds Bank	132
" Capital & Counties	49
Dowlais, Lloyds Bank	132
" Metrop. Bk. of Eng. & Wales	162
Downham Market, Barclay & Co.	30
" London and Provincial Bank	100
Driffield, Beckett & Co.	100
" London and Yorkshire Bank	146
" York Union Banking Co.	100
" York City and County Bkg. Co.	132
Droitwich, Lloyds Bank	132
Bromfield, Sheff. & Rotherham	30, 144
Droylsden, Manch. & Liv. Dis. B. Co.	153
Dudley, Birm. and Counties Bank.	30
" Lloyds Bank	132
" Metrop. B. of Eng. & Wales	162
Dudley Hill, Yorkshire Bkg. Co.	223
Dukinfield, Manch. & Liverpool Dis.	
Banking Co.	153
Dulverton, National Provincial	175
Dunmow, Barclay & Co.	30
Dunstable, Barclay & Co.	30
" London and County	135
Dunster, Stuckey's Banking Co.	180
Dunston, North East B. Co.	100
Durham, Barclay & Co.	30
" National Provincial	175
" North Eastern Bank. Co.	100
" York City and County B. Co.	132
" Hodgkin, Barnett & Co.	132
Dursley, Lloyds Bank	132
" National Provincial	175
Eardisley, Birm. Dist. & County	30
Earlestown, Parr's Bank	177
" Man. & Liverpool Dist. B. Co.	153
Earls Colne, Barclay & Co.	30
Easingwold, Yorkshire Banking Co.	223
" York Union Banking Co.	100
East Dereham, Barclay & Co.	30
" Lacons, Youell & Kemp	100
" London and Provincial	100
" National Provincial	175
East Grinstead, Lloyds Bank	132
" Barclay & Co.	30
" Capital and Counties	49
East Molesey, T. Ashby & Co.	223
" London & S. Western	142
Eastbourne, London and County	135
" Capital and Counties	49
" London City and Midland	136
" London and Provincial	100
" Barclay & Co.	30
Eastleigh, Capital and Counties	49
" Wilts and Dorset Bankg. Co.	144
Eastwood, Nottingham Jt.-St.	209
" Midland C'ties Dist.	148
Ebbw Vale, London and Provincial	100
" Met. B. of Eng. & W.	162
Eccles, Manchester & County Bank	209
" Williams Deacon Bank	223
" Parr's Bank	177
Eccleshall, Manch. & Liverpl. Dist.	153
Eckington, London and Yorkshire.	146
Edenbridge, Capital and Counties	49
" Lloyds Bank	132
Edgware, L. and S. West	142
Egham, Thomas Ashby & Co.	223
" London & Provincial Bank	100
Egremont, Cumberland Un. Bk. Co.	30
" Whitehaven Jt.-Stk. Bkg. Co.	248
" London City & Midland	136
" Bank of Whitehaven	100
" North & South Wales	144
" Bank of Liverpool	100
Elland, Halifax & Hudd. Un. B. Co.	100
" Lancashire & Yorkshire Bank	144
" London and Yorkshire B.	146
" Halifax Joint Stock Bkg. Co.	148
Ellesmere, Eyton, Burton, & Co.	189
" Lloyds Bank	132
Ellesmere Port, Parr's Bank	177
" Bank of Liverpool	100
" Liverpool Union Bank	132
Elsecar, London and York	146
Elswick, North-Eastern Bankg. Co.	100
" Lambton & Co.	30
Eltham, Martin's Bank	154
Ely, Foster & Co.	182
" Barclay & Co.	30
Emsworth, Capital and Counties	49
Enfield, Lloyds Bank	132
" London and Provincial	100

Englefield Green, T. Ashby & Co.	223
Epping, Barclay & Co.	30
Epsom, Capital and Counties	49
" London and County	135
Erdington, Lond. City & Midland	136
" Lloyds Bank	132
Eton, Woodbridge, Lacy, H.H. & Co.	100
" London and County	135
Everton, London City & Mid.	136
" North & South Wales Bank	144
Evesham, Capital and Counties	49
" Lloyds Bank	132
Exeter, Devon & Cornwall Bkg. Co.	30
" Fox, Fowler, & Co.	30
" Milford, Snow, & Co.	180
" National Provincial	175
" Sanders & Co.	30
" Wilts and Dorset Banking Co.	144
Exmouth, Devon & Cornwall B. Co.	30
" Wilts and Dorset Banking Co.	144
" Sanders & Co.	30
Eye, Barclay & Co.	30
" London and Provincial	100
Failsworth, Manchester & County	209
Fairford, Capital and Counties	49
" London and Provincial	100
Fakenham, Barclay & Co.	30
" London and Provincial	100
Fallowfield, Manchester & Liverpool	
Dis. B. Co.	153
Falmouth, Capital & Counties	49
" Bolitho, Williams, & Co.	30, 223
" Cornish Bank	201
" Devon and Cornwall Bkg. Co.	30
Fareham, Capital and Counties	49
" Wilts & Dorset B. Co.	144
Faringdon, Lloyds Bank	132
Farnham (Sur.), Capital & Counties	49
" London & County	135
Farnworth, Manchester & County	209
" Union Bank of Manchester	100
" Williams Deacon Bank	223
" Manchester & Liverpool Dist.	
B. Co.	201
Faversham, Hilton, Rigden&Rigden	182
" London and County	135
Featherstone, Leatham, Tew, & Co.	30
Felixstowe, Barclay & Co.	30
" Bacon, Cobbold, & Co.	88, 100
Felling, North-Eastern B. Co.	100
Feltham, T. Ashby & Co.	223
Felton, North-Eastern Banking Co.	100
Fenton, Manch. & L'pool. District	153
" Lloyds Bank	132
Festiniog, N. and S. Wales Bank	144
" Metrop. Bk. of Eng. & Wales	162
Filey, York City & County B. Co.	132
Finchley, Lon. and South Western	142
" London and County	135
Fishguard, Lloyds Bank	132
" London and Provincial	100
Fishponds, Lloyds Bank	132
Fleet (Hants), Capital and Counties	49
Fleetwood, Lancaster Banking Co.	30
" London City & Midland	136
" Manchester & County	209
" Williams Deacon Bank	223
Flint, N. & S. Wales B.	144
Flixton, Williams Deacon Bk.	223
Foleshill, Lon. City & Mid.	136
Folkestone, National Provincial	175
" Lloyds Bank	132
" Capital and Counties	49
Fordingbridge, Wilts & Dorset	144
Formby, Williams Deacon Bank	223
Foulsham, Lacons, Youell & Kemp	100
Fowey, Bolitho, Williams, & Co.	30, 223
" Cornish Bank	201
" Devon & Cornwall B. Co.	30
Framlingham, Barclay & Co.	30
Freshwater, Wilts and Dorset	144
Frodsham, Parr's Bank	177
Frome, Stuckey's Banking Co.	180
" Wilts & Dorset Banking Co.	144
" Capital and Counties	49
Gainsborough, Lincln. & Lindsey B.	182
" Smith, Ellison, & Co.	201
" Sheffield Banking Co.	201
Garston, Parr's Bank	177
" Bank of Liverpool	100
Gateshead-on-Tyne, Lambton & Co.	30
" National Provincial	175
" North-Eastern Banking Co.	100

Gateshead-on-Tyne, Hodgkin, Barnett & Co.	132
" York City & County	132
" London City & Midland	136
Gillingham (Dorset), Wilts & Dorset	100
" Stuckey's Bnkg. Co.	180
Girlington, Bradford Old Bank.	132
Glastonbury, Stuckey's Banking Co.	180
" Wilts & Dorset Banking Co.	144
Glossop, Manch. & L'pool. Dist. B. Co.	153
" Manchester and County	209
Gloucester, Capital and Counties	49
" Lloyds Bank	132
" National Provincial	175
" Wilts and Dorset Bkg. Co.	144
" London City and Midland	136
Godalming, London and County	135
" Capital and Counties	49
Godstone, Lloyds Bank	132
Goole, Beckett & Co.	100
" London City and Midland	136
" Leatham, Tew, & Co.	30
" York City and County Bkg. Co.	132
Goring-on-Thames, Metro. Bank	162
Gorton, Union Bank of Manchester	100
" Manchester & County	209
Gosforth, Cumberland Union	30
" North-Eastern Banking Co.	100
Gosport, Capital and Counties	49
" Grant & Maddison's Union B.	100
" London and Provincial	100
Grantham, Stamfd. Spalding, & Bost.	30
" Smith, Ellison & Co.	201
" Leicestershire Banking Co.	144
Gravesend, London & County Bk.	135
" London and Provincial	100
Grays (Essex), London & Provincial	100
Grayshott, Capital & Counties	49
Great Bridge, Lloyds Bank	132
Great Crosby, Parr's Bank	177
Great Heywood, Lanc. & Yorksh.	144
" Manchester and County	209
Great Horton, Bradford Old Bank	132
Great Marlow, Lloyds Bk.	132
Gt. Missenden, Bucks and Oxon	144
Greenacres, London City & Mid.	135
Grimsby, Lincoln & Lindsey B. Co.	182
" Stamford, Spalding, & Bost.	30
" Smith, Ellison, & Co.	201
" York City and County Bkg. Co.	132
Guernsey, Capital and Counties	49
" Commercial Banking Co.	144
" Lond. City & Midland	136
" Guernsey Bkg. Co.	135
Guildford, Capital and Counties	49
" London and County	135
Guisborough, National Provincial	175
" York City & County Bkg. Co.	132
Guiseley, Yorkshire Banking Co.	223
Gunnislake, Dingley & Co.	209
Hadfield, Manchester & L'pool Dist.	153
" Manchester & County	209
Hadleigh, Barclay & Co.	30
Hailsham, Barclay & Co.	30
Halesowen, Lloyds Bank	132
Halesworth, Barclay & Co.	30
" Lacons, Youell, & Kemp	100
" London & Provincial	100
Halifax, Halifax Joint-Stock Banking Co. (H.O.)	148
" Halifax Commercial Banking Co. (H.O.)	223
" Halifax & Huddsfield. Union Banking Co. (H.O.)	100
" London and Yorkshire Bank.	146
" Lancashire and Yorkshire.	144
" Mercantile of Lancashire	148
" Yorkshire Banking Co.	223
Halstead, London and County	135
" Barclay & Co.	30
Haltwhistle, London City & Mid.	136
" Cumberland Union Bankg. Co.	30
" Lambton & Co.	30
Hampton, T. Ashby & Co.	223
Handsworth, Lloyds Bank	132
" London City & Midland	136
Hanley, Birm. Dis. & County B. Co.	30
" Lloyds Bank	132
" Manch. & Liverpl. Dist. B. Co.	153
" National Provincial	175
Hanwell, London & South Western	142
Harborne, Lloyds Bank	132

Harleston, Barclay & Co. 30
„ London and Provincial 100
Harpenden, Marten, Part & Co. 201
Harrington, Cumberld. Un. B. Co. .. 30
„ Whitehaven Joint Stock B.Co. 148
Harrogate, Knaresbro' and Claro Banking Co. (H.O.) ... 132
„ Bradford Old Bank 132
„ York City and County B. Co. 132
„ Yorkshire Banking Co. 223
„ Beckett & Co. 103
Harrow, London and County 135
„ London and South Western ... 142
„ York City and County 132
Hartlepool, Barclay & Co. 30
„ National Provincial 175
„ York City and County 132
Harwich, Bacon, Cobbold & Co. 88, 100
Haslingden, Manch. & L'pool. Dist. 153
„ Lancashire & Yorkshire Bank 144
Hastings, Lloyds Bank 132
„ Capital and Counties 49
„ London and County 135
„ London City & Midland ... 136
Hatherleigh, Dingley, Pearse, & Co. 136
Hatherstock, London City & Mid... 130
Havant, Capital and Counties...... 49
Haverfordwest, Lloyds Bank 132
„ London and Provincial 100
„ National Provincial 175
„ Metrop. B. of Eng. and Wales 102
Haverhill, Oakes, Bevan, T. & Co. 30
„ London & County 135
Hawkhurst, London and County ... 135
Hawkshead, Bank of Liverpool ... 100
Hay, National Provincial 175
„ Birm. and Counties Bank ... 30
„ Mills, Birmingham District & Counties ....
Hayle, Bolitho, Williams, & Co. 30, 223
Haywards Heath, Cap. & Cnties. B. 49
„ Barclay & Co. 30
Headingley, York City & County ... 132
Heanor, Nottm Joint-Stock Bank... 209
„ Crompton & Evans' Un......
Heaton (Nthmb.), Hodgkin, B. & Co. 132
Heaton Chapel, Lanc. & Yorkshire 144
Hebburn, North-Eastern Bkng. Co. 100
Hebden Bridge, Halifax Jt.-St.B.Co. 144
„ Lancs. and Yorks. Bank ... 144
„ Manch. & Liverpool Dist. ... 153
Heckmondwike, Lond. City and Mid. 133
„ Yorkshire Banking Co. 223
„ West Riding Union Bkg. Co. 144
Hednesford, Lloyds Bank 132
„ Metrop. Bk. of Eng. & Wales.. 102
Heeley, Sheffield & Hallamshire Bk. 146
„ Sheffield Banking Co. ......
„ Sheffield Union Banking Co. ...
Helmsley, York Union Banking Co. 100
Helston, Bain, Field, Hitchins, & Co. 115
„ Bolitho, Williams, & Co... 30, 223
„ Cornish Bank 201
Hemel Hempstead, Bucks & Oxon. U. 144
„ Cobb, Bartlett & Co. ......
Hemsworth, Leatham, Tew & Co. ... 30
Hendon, Lond. and S. West. 142
Henley-in-Arden, Met. B. of E.&W. 102
Henley-on-Thames, J. & C. Simonds 223
„ London & County 135
Hereford, Birm. & Count. Bk. Co.... 30
„ Capital and Counties 49
„ Lloyds Bank 132
„ National Provincial 175
Herne Bay, London & County 135
„ Parrs Bank 177
Hertford, London & County 135
„ Barclay & Co. 70
Heswall, Liverpool Union B. 30
Hetton-le-Hole, North-Eastern B.Co. 100
„ Barclay & Co. 30
Hexham, Cumberland Un. Bkg. Co. 30
„ Lambton & Co. 30
„ North-Eastern Bank 100
„ Hodgkin, Barnett & Co. ... 132
„ London City and Midland ... 130
Heywood, Lanc. & Yorkshire Bank 144
„ Manchester & Liverpool Dist. 153
„ Union Bank of Manchester ...
High Wycombe, London & County ... 135
„ Capital and Counties 49
„ J. & C. Simonds & Co. 223
Highbridge, Stuckey's Banking Co. 189

Highbridge, Wilts & Dorset B. Co. 144
Higher Broughton, WilliamsDeacon 223
Higher Buxton, Crompton & Evans 100
Higher Openshaw, Williams Deacon 223
Hillsborough York City and County 132
„ Sheffield Union Banking Co. ... 182
Hill Top. B'nam Dis. & Counties .. 30
Hinckley, Leicestershire Bkg. Co. ... 144
„ Pares Leicestersh. Bkg. Co. ... 201
Hindley, Parr's Bank 177
„ Williams Deacon B. 223
Hipperholme, Halifax Com. B. Co. 24
Hitchin, London and County 135
„ Barclay & Co. 30
Hockley, B'nam Dis. & Counties ... 30
Hoddesdon, Barclay & Co. 30
„ London & County 135
Holbeach, Barclay & Co. 30
„ Samuel, Spldg. & Bost. Bkg. Co. 30
Hollinwood, Manchester & Cnty. B. 209
„ London City & Midland ... 130
Holmes Chapel, Union Bank of Manca. 100
Holmrook, Bank of Whitehaven ... 100
Holsworthy, Devon and Cornwall... 30
„ Dingley & Co. 209
„ Fox, Fowler, & Co. 132
Holt, Barclay & Co. 30
„ Lacons, Youell, & Kemp.... 100
Holyhead, National Provincial ... 175
„ North and South Wales Bank 144
Holywell, National Provincial ... 175
„ North and South Wales Bank 144
Honiton, London & S.-Western Bk. 144
„ National Provincial 175
„ Devon & Cornwall B. Co ... 30
Horbury, Wakefield & Barnsley Un. 100
Horley, Capital & Counties 49
„ Lloyds Bank 132
Horncastle, Capital and Counties .. 49
„ Lincoln & Lindsey Bk. 104
„ Smith, Spald. & Boston B. Co. 30
Horsforth, York City & County ... 132
Horsham, Capital & Counties...... 49
„ London and County 135
Horwich, Manchester and County... 30
„ Union Bank of Manchester ... 100
„ Williams Deacon Bank 223
Houghton-le-Spring, N.-East B. Co. 100
„ Barclay & Co. (Woods) ... 30
Hounslow, London and County ... 135
„ Woodbridge, Lacy, H. H. &Co. 100
Hove, Barclay & Co. 30
„ Capital and Counties 49
„ London and County 135
„ Nat. Provincial 175
„ Lloyds Bank 132
Howden, York City & County B. Co. 132
„ Yorkshire Banking Co. 223
Hoylake, North and South Wales B. 144
„ Bank of Liverpool 100
„ Parr's Bank 177
Hucknall Torkard, Nottm. Jt. Stk. 209
Huddersfield, West Riding Union Co. (H.O.) ... 144
„ Halifax & Huddersfd.U.B.Co. 144
„ Halifax Joint-Stock Bkg .Co. 144
„ London City and Midland ... 130
„ Yorkshire Banking Co. 223
„ London and Yorkshire 140
„ London & Northern ......
Hull, Bank of England 21
„ Barclay & Co. 30
„ London City and Midland ... 130
„ London and Yorkshire Bank 140
„ National Provincial 175
„ Samuel Smith Bros. & Co. ... 201
„ York City and County B. Co. 132
„ York Union Banking Co. ......
„ Yorkshire Banking Co. 223
„ T. Cook & Son 73
„ Halifax Com. Bkg. Co. 24
Hulme, Williams Deacon Bank... 223
„ Union Bank of Manchester ... 100
„ Manch. & L'pool. Dist. Bkg. Co. 153
„ Lancashire & Yorkshire 144
Hungerford, Capital & Counties Bk. 49
„ London and County 135
Hunslet, Beckett & Co. 100
„ York Union Co. ......
„ London City and Midland ... 136
Hunstanton, Barclay & Co. 30

Hunstanton, London & Prov. 100
Huntingdon, London and County ... 135
„ Barclay & Co. 30
Hyde, Manch. & Liverpl. Dis.Bkg.Co. 153
„ London City & Midland ... 130
„ Lancashire & Yorkshire ... 144
Hyde's Cross, Parr's Bank 177
Hythe, London and County 135
Idle, Bradford Old Bank 132
„ London and Yorkshire Bank 140
Ilford, London and County 135
„ London and Provincial 100
„ London & S. Western 142
Ilfracombe, Devon & Cornwall B.Co. 30
„ Fox, Fowler & Co. 30
„ National Provincial 175
Ilkeston, Nottingham Joint-Stock 209
„ Midland C'ties District 148
„ Samuel Smith & Co. 201
„ Crompton & Evans' Union .. 100
Ilkley, Bradford Old Bank 132
„ Craven Bank 182
„ York City & County 132
Ilminster, Stuckey's Banking Co. 189
„ Wilts and Dorset Banking Co. 144
Ipswich, Bacon, Cobbold & Co. 88, 100
„ Barclay & Co. 30
„ National Provincial 175
Irlams-o'th-Height, U.B.M'chester 100
Ironbridge, Lloyds Bank 132
Isleworth, Woodbridge, Lacy, H.&Co. 100
Ivy Bridge, Harris, Bulteel & Co. ... 189
Jarrow, Hodgkin, Barnett & Co. ... 132
„ North-Eastern Banking Co .. 100
„ Barclay & Co. (Woods)...... 30
Jersey, Capital and Counties 49
„ London City and Midland ... 130
„ Commercial B. (Robin Bros.) ... 177
Keighley, Bradford District Bank... 30
„ Bradford Old Bank 132
„ Craven Bank 182
„ London City & Midland ... 136
„ London & Yorkshire Bank ... 140
„ Yorkshire Banking Co. 223
Kemp Town, Capital & Counties .. 49
Kendal, Lancaster Banking Co. 30
„ Bank of Liverpool 30
„ London City & Midland ... 130
Kenilworth, Lond. City & Midland 130
„ Lloyds Bank 132
Keswick, Cumberland Un. Bkg. Co. 30
„ Carlisle & Cumb'land B. Co... 193
„ Bank of Liverpool 100
Kettering, Capital and Counties ... 49
„ Leicestershire Banking Co. ... 144
„ Northamptonshire U. B. 223
„ Stamford, Spald. & Bost. B. Co. 30
„ Nottingham Joint Stock 209
Keynsham, Prescott & Co. 182
Kidderminster, Bir. & Cties. B. Co. 30
„ Lloyds Bank 132
„ Metrop. B. of Eng. & Wales ... 102
Ridgrove, Birmingham & Counties 30
Kimberley, Nottingham Joint Stk. 209
Kineton, Lloyds Bank 132
„ Metrop. B. of Eng. & Wales ... 102
King Cross, Halifax Com. B. Co. ... 24
King's Heath, London City & Mid. 131
„ B'nam D. & Counties 30
King's Norton, Lloyds Bank 132
Kingsbridge, Lloyds Bank 132
„ Devon and Cornwall Bkg.Co... 30
„ Wilts and Dorset Bkg. Co. ... 144
„ Harris, Bulteel & Co. 189
Kingston (Pismth.),Grant &M.B.Co. 100
Kingston (Surrey),London & County 135
„ London and South Western ... 142
„ Parr's Bank 177
Kingswood (Glos.), Stuckey's B. Co. ...
„ Lloyds Bank 132
Kington, Birm. & Counties B. Co. ... 30
„ Davies, Banks, & Co. 189
Kirby Moorside, York Union B. Co. 100
Kirkby-in-Ashfield, Midland C'ties District Bank ... 148
„ Nottingham and Notts B. Co. 209
Kirkby Lonsdale, Lancaster Bkg.Co. 30
„ Bank of Liverpool 100
„ London City & Midland ... 136
Kirkby Stephen, Bank of Liverpool 100
„ London City & Midland ... 136
Kirkley, Natl. Prov. Bk 175

Kirkoswald, Cumberland Union .. 30
Kirkstall, London City & Midland .136
Knaresborough, Bradford Old Bank 132
" Knaresborough & Claro. B. Co. 132
Knighton, North & S. Wales Bank 144
" Birm. & Counties B. Co. .. 30
Knot Mill, Parr's Bank 177
Knottingley (West Riding Bank),
Leatham, Tew & Co. ....
Knowle, London City & Midland.. 136
Knutsford, Parr's Bank 177
" Union Bank of Manchester .. 100
Laisterdyke, London City & Mid..136
" Yorkshire Banking Co. 223
Lampeter, National Provincial .. 175
" David Jones & Co. 189
" London & Provincial 100
Lancaster, Lancaster B. Co. (H.O.) 30
" London City & Midland .. 136
" Bank of Liverpool 100
Landport, Capital and Counties .. 49
" Grant & Maddison's Union .. 100
" National Provincial 175
" London & Provincial 100
Langport, Stuckey's Bkg. Co. (H.O.)148
Lansdowne Wilts and Dorset 102
Launceston, Bolitho, Williams 30, 223
" Devon and Cornwall Bkg. Co. 30
" Dingley & Co. 209
" Fox, Fowler, & Co. 132
Laxey, Dumbells Bg. Co. 100
" Isle of Man Bg. Co. 144
Leamington, London City & Mid.. 136
" Lloyds Bank 132
" Metrop. Bk. of Eng. & Wales..102
" Midland Counties Dist. 148
Leatherhead, Capital & Counties .. 49
Lechlade, Capital & Counties Bank 49
Ledbury, Capital & Counties Bank 49
" National Provincial 175
Lee-on-Solent, Capital & Counties.. 49
Leeds, Yorkshire Bkg. Co. 223
" Yorkshire Penny Bk. (H.O.) .. 21
" Bank of England 21
" Beckett & Co. 100
" London City & Midland 136
" London and Yorkshire 146
" National Provincial 175
" Wm. Williams, Brown & Co. 43
" York City & County Bkg. Co..132
" Halifax Com. Bkg. Co. 223
" T. Cook & Son 73
" West Riding Union 144
" London & Northern 144
Leek, Manch. & L'pool. Dist. B. Co.153
" Parr's Bank 177
Lees, Manch. & L'pool. Dist. B. Co.153
" Union Bank of Manchester .. 100
Leicester, Leicestersh. B. Co. (H.O.)144
" Pares's Leicestersh B. C.(H.O.)201
" Lond. City & Midland 136
" National Provincial 175
" Northamptonshire Union B. ..223
" Midland C'ties & District 148
" Lloyds Bank 132
" Stamford, Spald. & Bost. Co. 30
" T. Cook & Son 73
Leigh, Parr's Bank 177
" Manch. & Liverpool Dist. B.Co.153
" Union Bank of Manchester .. 100
" Manchester and County 209
" Williams Deacon Bank 223
Leigh-on-Sea, London & Provincial 100
Leighton Buzzard, London & County125
" Barclay & Co. 30
Lemington, Hodgkin, Barnett & Co.132
Leominster, Lloyds Bank 132
" National Provincial 175
" Birmingham Dist.&Counties B. 30
Levenshulme, Man. & L. Dis. B. Co.153
" Lancashire & Yorkshire 144
Lewes, London and County 135
" Barclay & Co. 30
Leyburn, York City & County B.Co.132
" Barclay & Co. 30
Lichfield, Lloyds Bank 132
" National Provincial 175
" London City & Midland 136
Lightcliffe, Halifax Com. B. Co. ..223
Linacre, Bank of Liverpool 100
Lincoln, Lincoln & Lindsey Banking
Co. (H.O.) 182

Lincoln, Capital and Counties 49
" Smith, Ellison, & Co. 201
" Stamfd.,Spald.,& Boston B.Co.30
" Peacock, Willson & Co. 132
" National Provincial 175
Liscard (Chesh.), N. & S. Wales B. 144
Liskeard, Bolitho, Williams, & Co. 30, 223
" Capital and Counties Bank .. 49
" Cornish Bank 201
" Devon and Cornwall Bkg. Co. 30
Litchurch, Parr's Bank 177
Littleborough, Union Bk. of Manch.100
" Manch. & L'pool Dist. B. Co. ..153
Littlehampton, Capital & Counties 49
" London & County 135
Liverpool, Bank or Liverpool (H.O.)100
" Liverpool Union Bank (H.O.) 132
" North & South Wales B. (H.O.)144
" Bank of England 21
" Philip Barnett & Nephew .. 148
" Biggerstaff, W. & I. 34
" L. Benas & Son 59
" Comptoir D'Escompte 71
" T. Cook & Son 73
" Forbes, Forbes & Co. 96
" Hill & Son 100, 109
" J. E. Kneeshaw & Co. 142
" Lancashire & Yorkshire 144
" Leyland & Bullins 144
" London City and Midland 136
" Manch. & Livpl. Dist. Bkg. Co.201
" National Provincial 175
" Parr's Bank 177
" W. Watson & Co. 217
" Edward W. Yates & Co. ..190, 209
Llanberis, Met. B. of Eng. & Wales 162
Llanbrynmair, Nat. Prov. 175
Llandilo, David Jones & Co. 189
" Capital and Counties 49
" London & Provincial 100
Llandovery, David Jones & Co. .. 189
" National Provincial 175
" London & Provincial 100
Llandrindod, London & Provincial 100
" Davies, Banks & Co. 189
Llandudno, Met. B. of Eng. & Wales162
" National Provincial 175
" Lloyds Bank 132
Llandyssil (Cardigan), Lloyds Bk. 132
" Metrop. B. of Eng. & Wales ..162
Llanelly, Lloyds Bank 132
" London and Provincial Bank 100
" Metrop. B. of Eng. & Wales ..162
" Capital and Counties 49
Llanfair Caereinion, N. & S. Wales144
Llanfyllin, North & South Wales B.144
Llangefni, National Provincial .. 175
" Metrop. B. of Eng. & Wales.. 162
Llangollen, North & S. Wales Bank144
" Richards & Co. 175
Llanidloes, North & S. Wales Bank144
" London and Provincial 100
Llanrwst, North & S. Wales Bank 144
" Metrop. B. of Eng. & Wales.. 162
Loddon, Barclay & Co. 30
Loftus, National Provincial 175
" North-Eastern Bank ....
Long Eaton, Nottm.Joint-Stock Bk.209
" Samuel Smith & Co. 201
" Parr's Bank 177
Long Sutton, National Provincial.. 175
" Barclay & Co. 30
Longsight, Parr's Bank 177
Longton, Birm. & Counties Bk. Co. 30
" Lloyds Bank 132
" Man. & L'pool. Dist. Bkg. Co.153
Longtown, Carlisle & Cumbrld.B.Co.193
Looe, Bolitho, Williams, & Co. 30, 223
" Capital and Counties Bank .. 49
" Cornish Bank 201
Lostwithiel, Bolitho, Willms., & Co. 30, 223
" Cornish Bank 201
Loughborough, Pares's Leicestersh. B.201
" Midland Counties Dist. B. 148
" Nottingham & Notts Bkg. Co. 144
" Leicestershire B. Co. 144
Louth, Lincoln & Lindsey Bank ..182
" Capital and Counties ....
" Stamfd.,Spald.,&Boston B.Co. 79
Low Fell, North East B. Co. 100
Lowestoft, National Provincial .. 175
" Barclay & Co. 30

Lowestoft, Lacons, Youell, & Kemp 100
" London & Provincial 100
Ludlow, Birm. & Counties Bk. 30
" Eyton Burton & Co. 189
" Lloyds Bank 132
Luton, London and County 135
" Barclay & Co. 30
" Capital and Counties ....
Lutterworth, Pares's Leictrsh. B. Co.201
" Midland Counties Dist. 148
Lydney, Capital & Counties Bk. 49
Lye, London City & Midland 136
" Metrop. Bk. of Eng. & Wales..162
Lyme Regis, Wilts and Dorset 223
Lymington, Wilts & Dorset Bkg. Co.144
" Capital & Counties 49
Lymm, Lanc. & Yorks. Bank 144
" Parr's Bank 177
Lynn (King's), Barclay & Co. 30
" Lacons, Youell, & Kemp 100
" London and Provincial 100
Lynton, Devon & Cornwall Bkg. Co. 30
" Fox, Fowler, & Co. 132
Lytham, Lancaster Banking Co. .. 30
" Manchester and County B. ..209
" London City & Midland 136
" Williams Deacon Bank 223
Mablethorpe, stamf., Spald. & Boston 30
" Lincoln and Lindsey B. Co. ..182
Macclesfield, Lancashire & Yorks. 144
" Manch. & Liverpol. Dist. Bg. Co.153
" Parr's Bank 177
Machynlleth, National Provincial.. 175
" London and Provincial 100
Maesteg, Metropolitan Bank 162
Maiden Newton, Wilts & Dorset.. ..
Maidenhead, London and County.. 135
" Lloyds Bank ....
" Metrop. of England & Wales..102
Maidstone, London and County 135
" Wigan & Co. (Kentish Bank)..201
" Lloyds Bank ....
Maldon, London and County 135
" Barclay & Co. 30
Malmesbury, Capital and Counties 49
" Wilts & Dorset Bkg. Co. 144
Malton, Beckett & Co. ....
" York City and County B. Co. ..132
" York Union Banking Co. 100
" London and Yorkshire Bank .. 146
Malvern, Berwick & Co.(Lechmere)189
" Lloyds Bank 132
Malvern Link, Lloyds Bank 132
" Berwick & Co. (Lechmere) .. 199
(Lechmere)
Malvern Wells, Berwick & Co.
(Lechmere) 199
Manchester, Un. B. of Manch.(H.O.)100
" Lancashire & Yorks. (H.O.) .. 144
" Williams Deacon & Manch.
& Salford Bank (H.O.) 223
" Manch. & Liverpool District
Banking Co. (H.O.) 153
" Mercantile B. of Lancs. (H.O.)148
" Bank of England 21
" Comptoir D'Escompte 71
" Coryton's Exchange Bank 148
" Cunliffes, Brooks, & Co. 42
" Lomas, Jackson, & Co. 100
" London City & Midland 136
" Manchester and County Bank209
" National Provincial 175
" Parr's Bank 177
" John Stuart & Co. ....
" T. Cook & Son 73
Manningham, Craven Bank 132
" Manningham, Barclay & Co. .. ..
Mansfield, Nottm. and Notts B. Co.144
" Nottingham Joint Stock ....
" Samuel Smith & Co. 201
" Crompton & Evans' Un. Bk. ..100
Marazion, Bolitho, Williams&Co. 30, 223
March, Barclay & Co. 30
" National Provincial 175
Margate, Lloyds Bank 132
" London & County Banking Co. 135
" London, City & Midland 136
" Parr's Bank 177
Market Drayton, Manch. & L'pool.153
" Birm. & Counties Bnkg. Co. .. 30
Market Harboro', Leicestersh. B. Co.144
" Stamford, Spald. & Bost. B. Co. 30
Market Rasen, Lincoln. & Lindsey B.182

Market Weighton, York Un. B. Co. 100
Marlboro', Wilts & Dorset Bkg. Co. 144
" Capital and Counties 49
Martock, Wilts and Dorset Bkg. Co.144
" Stuckey's Banking Co. 189
Maryport,Cumberland Un. Bkg. Co. 30
" London City & Midland 136
" Whitehaven Joint-Stock Bank
Co.............................143
Masham, Knaresboro' & Claro B. Co. 100
" Barclay & Co. 30
Matlock Bath, Crompton and E. Un.100
" Parr's Bank 177
Matlock Bridge, Sheff. & Rothm.30,144
" Parr's Bank 177
" Crompton & Evans' U. Bank ..100
Meals, London & County 135
Melbourne (Derby), Parr's Bank 177
Melksham, Capital and Counties .. 49
" Wilts and Dorset Banking Co.144
Melton Mowbray, Leicestrsh. B. Co. 144
" Stamfd., Spaldg., & Bost. B. Co. 30
Menai Bridge, National Provincial175
Mere, Wilts and Dorset Bkg. Co. .144
Merthyr Tydvil, Lloyds Bank 132
" London and Provincial 100
" Metrop. B. of Eng. & Wales ..162
Mevagissey,Bolitho,Willms.&Co.30,212
" Cornish Bank 201
Mexborough, Sheffield Banking Co.201
" York City & County B. Co. ..132
Middlesbrough, Barclay & Co. 30
" National Provincial 175
" North-Eastern Banking Co. ..100
" York City and County Bkg. Co.132
" Yorkshire Banking Co. 223
Middleton, Manchester & County .. 209
" Union Bank of Manchester ..209
" Williams Deacon Bk. 223
Middlewich, Union Bank of Manch.100
Midhurst, London and County 135
Midsomer Norton, Stuckey's B. Co.189
Milborne Port, Stuckey's Bkg. Co..189
Mildenhall, Oakes, Bevan, T. & Co. 30
" Barclay & Co. 30
Milford Haven, London and Prov...100
" Metropolitan Bank 162
Milnthorp, Cumberland U. Bkg. Co. 30
" Lancaster Banking Co. 30
" Bank of Liverpool 100
Milnrow, Manch. & L'pool. Dist. ..153
" London City & Midland......130
Milnsbridge, Halifax Jt.-Sta. B. Co.148
" Halifax & Hudd. Un. Bkg. Co.100
" London City and Midland 136
" West Riding Union Bkg. Co.144
" York Banking Co. 223
Milverton, Stuckey's Banking Co.. 189
Minehead, Stuckey's Banking Co.. 189
" Fox, Fowler & Co. 30
" Devon and Cornwall Bkg. Co. 30
Mirfield, London City and Mid....136
" London & Yorkshire Bk. 146
" West Riding Union Bkg. Co.144
Modbury Harris, Bulteel, & Co. .. 189
" Devon and Cornwall Bkg. Co. 30
Mold, North and South Wales Bk. .144
" National Provincial 175
Monkwearmouth, Barclay & Co. .. 30
" North Eastern Banking Co. ..100
Monmouth, Capital and Counties .. 49
" National Provincial 175
" Lloyds Bank 132
Montgomery, North & South Wales144
Montpellier, Lloyds Bank 132
Morecambe, Lancaster Bankg. Co. 30
" London City & Midland 136
" Bank of Liverpool 100
Moreton Hampstead, Dingley,
Pearse & Co. 136
Moreton-in-Marsh, Capital & Cos. 49
" Metrop. B. of Eng. and Wales162
Morley, London and Yorkshire Bk.146
" London City and Midland ...136
" Yorkshire Banking Co. 223
Morpeth, Hodgkin, Barnett, & Co.132
" Lambton & Co. 30
" North-Eastern Bkg. Co. 100
" Barclay & Co. (Woods)....... 30
Morriston, Capital and Counts. ... 49
" Metrop. B. of Eng. & Wales ..162
Moseley, Lloyds Bank 132

Moss Side, Williams Deacon Bk. ..223
" Manchester & County 209
" London City & Midland 136
Mossley, Manch.& L'pool Dist. B.Co.153
" Manchester and County 209
Mossley Hill, Bank of Liverpool ..100
" Liverpool Union Bk. 132
Mountain Ash, Lloyds Bank 132
" Metrop. B. of Eng. & Wales ..162
Much Wenlock, Met. B. of E. & Wales162
Mutley, Harris, Bulteel & Co. 189
Nailsworth, Capital and Counties.. 49
" Wilts and Dorset 144
Nantwich, Manch. & L'pool Dist..153
" Birm. and Counties Bkg. Co. 30
" Downes & Co. 144
" Parr's Bank 177
Narberth, National Provincial 175
" London and Provincial 100
Neath, Capital and Counties 49
" London and Provincial 100
" Metrop. B. of Eng. & Wales ..162
Needham Market, Barclay & Co. .. 30
Nelson, Craven Bank 182
" Lancashire & Yorks. Bank ..144
" Manchester and County Bank209
" Union Bank of Manchester ..100
Neston, North and S. Wales 144
Netherfield, Lloyds Bank 132
Netherton, Lloyd's Bank 132
Nevin, Metrop. B. of Eng. & Wales162
New Barnet, Barclay & Co. 30
" London & South Western 142
New Brighton, Nth & Sth. Wales B.144
" Bank of Liverpool 100
New Brompton,London & Provincial100
" London & County 135
New Ferry, N. & S. Wales B. 144
" Parr's Bank 177
New Malden, London & S. Western142
New Mills, Manch. & County Bk. .. 209
New Quay Bolitho, Williams &Co.30,212
" Cornish Bank 201
" Devon & Cornwall Bkg. Co. .. 30
New Radnor, B'nham Dis. & Cties. 30
New Swindon,Wilts & Dorset B. Co.144
" Capital and Counties 49
" Lloyds Bank 132
Newark-on-Trent, Saml. Smith &Co.201
" Peacock, Willson, & Co. 132
" Nottingham and Notts Bkg.Co144
Newbiggin-by-Sea,North-Eastern B.100
" Hodgkin, Barnett, & Co. 132
Newbury, Capital and Counties ... 49
" London & County Banking Co.13,
Newcastle (Staff.), Lloyds Bank ...132
" Manchester and Liverpool Dis.153
" National Provincial 175
Newcastle Emlyn. National Prov. ..175
" Metrop. B. of Eng. & Wales ..162
Newcastle-on-Tyne, North-Eastern
Banking Co. (H.O.) 100
" Bank of England 21
" Hodgkin, Barnett, & Co. 132
" T. Cook & Son 73
" Lambton & Co. 30
" National Provincial 175
" Barclay & Co. (Woods)....... 30
" York City and County B. 132
" London City & Midland 136
Newent, Capital and Counties 49
Newhaven, London and County 135
" Barclay & Co. 30
Newlyn, Bolitho, Wms. & Co. ..30, 212
Newmarket, Foster & Co. 182
" Hammond & Co. 61
" Lacons, Youell & Kemp 100
Newnham, Capital and Counties .. 49
Newport (I. of W.), Cap. and Cties.
" London and County Bkg. Co. .135
" National Provincial 175
" (Mon.) Birmingham Dist &Cties.30
" Lloyds Bank 132
" London City and Midland....136
" London & Provincial 100
" Metrop. B. of Eng. & Wales ..162
" National Provincial 175
" (Pem.), Lloyds Bank 132
" (Salop), Lloyds Bank 132
" National Provincial 175
Newport Pagnell, Barclay & Co. .. 30

Newton Abbot, Capital & Counties 49
" Devon & Cornw. B. Co. 30
" Harris, Bulteel, & Co. 189
" Wilts and Dorset Bkg. Co. ..144
Newton Heath, Williams Deacon Bk.223
" Parr's Bank 177
Newtown, National Provincial 175
" North and South Wales Bk. ..144
" B'ham District & Counties .. 30
Norbiton, London & S. Western ..142
" Parr's Bank 177
Norden, Union B. of Manchester ..100
Normanton, Leeman, Tew & Co. .. 30
North Ernington, Stamford, Spalding 30
North Ormesby, North Eastern Bk. 100
North Shields, Hodgkin, Barnett, &
Co.............................132
" Lambton & Co. 30
" National Provincial 175
" Barclay & Co. 30
" York City and County 132
North Walsham, Barclay & Co. ... 30
" Lacons, Youell & Kemp 100
" London and Provincial 100
Northallerton, Barclay & Co. 30
" York City & County Bkg. Co.132
" Yorkshire Banking Co. 223
Northampton, Northamptonshire
Union Bank (H.O.) 223
" London City & Mid. 136
" Capital and Counties 49
" Leicestershire Banking Co. .144
" Lloyds Bank 132
" Stamfd., Spaldg., & Bost. B.Co. 30
Northfield, B'nham. D. & Counties .30
Northleet, London and Provincial 100
" Parr's Bank 177
Northwich, Parr's Bank 177
" Manchester and County 209
" Union Bank of Manchester ..100
Norton (Yorks), Beckett & Co. 100
Norwich, Barclay & Co. 30
" Lacons, Youell, & Kemp. 100
" London and Provincial 100
" National Provincial 175
" Stamf., Spald., and Bost.B.Co. 30
Nottingham, Moore & Robinson's
Nottinghams. B. Co. (H.O.)100
" Nott'ham & Notts B. Co.(H.O.)144
" Nottingham Jt. St. Bk. (H.O.)209
" Midl'. Cties Dist. Bk. (H.O.)148
" Lloyds Bank 132
" Capital & Counties 49
" Samuel Smith & Co. 201
" T. Cook & Son 73
" London City & Midland 136
Nuneaton, Birmingham & Cnties. B.30
" Leicestershire Banking Co. .144
" London City & Midland 136
Oakengates, Birmingham D. & Cties.30
" Lloyds Bank 132
Oakham, Stamfd., Spaldg., & Bos. B.Co. 30
Odiham, Capital and Counties ... 49
Okehampton, National Provincial ..175
" Dingley, Pearse, & Co. 136
" Devon and Cornwall Bkg. Co. 30
Old Basford, Nottingham Jt. stk. 209
Oldbury, Lloyds Bank 132
" Birmingham & Counties Bk... 30
Oldham, Manch. & L'pool Dist. B.Co.153
" Manchester and County Bank209
" London City & Midland 136
" Union Bank of Manchester ..100
" T. Cook & Son 73
" Mercantile B. of Lancs. 148
Ollerton, Beckett & Co. 100
Openshaw, Williams Deacon Bank 223
" Manch. & L'pool Dist. Bkg.Co.153
Ordsall (Salford), Manch. & Lpl. ..153
Ormskirk, Manchester & Liverpool
Dist. B. Co 153
" Parr's Bank 177
" London City & Midland 136
" Williams Deacon Bank 223
Orpington, Martin's Bank 154
Ossett, London City and Midland ..136
" Wakefield & Barns. Un. Bank100
Oswaldtwistle, Manch. & Cty. Bank 209
Oswestry, Lloyds Bank 132
" North and South Wales Bank144
" Parr's Bank (The Old Bank) ..177
Otley, Yorkshire Banking Co. 223
" Bradford Old Bank 132

St. George's (*Bristol*), Lloyds Bank 132
„ St. Helens, Parr's Bank 177
„ London City & Midland......136
„ Williams Deacon Bank 223
„ Manchester and County......209
St.Ives(Corn.)Bolitho, Wms.,&Co.30,223
„ Cornish Bank 201
„ Devon & Cornwall Bank. Co.. 30
St. Ives (*Hunts*), Foster & Co.......132
„ Barclay & Co. 30
St. John's Chapel, Barclay & Co. ... 30
St.Just,Bolitho,Williams,& Co....30,243
„ Cornish Bank 201
St. Leonards, London and County 135
„ Lloyds Bank 132
„ Capital and Counties Bank.. 49
St. Mary Church, Dev. & Corn. B. Co. 30
„ Wilts and Dorset Bkg. Co. ...144
St. Neots, Barclay & Co. 30
St. Sampson's (*Guernsey*), Guernsey
Banking Co. 135
Sale (*Cheshire*), Parr's Bank 177
„ Cunliffes, Brooks, & Co. 42
„ Manchester & County 209
Salford, Manches. & L'pool Dis. Bnk 153
„ Union Bank of Manchester ...100
„ Parr's Bank 177
„ Williams Deacon Bank 223
Salisbury,Wilts&Drst.Bk.Co.(H.O.)144
„ National Provincial 175
„ Capital and Counties 49
Saltash, Harris, Bulteel & Co. 189
„ Bolitho, Williams & Co. ..30, 223
Saltburn, York City & County B. Co. 132
Saltley, Metrop. B. of Eng. & W. ...162
Sandbach, Manch. & L'pool D. Bk.Co.153
„ Parr's Bank 177
Sandgate Snnclif. (Op.), Lloyds Bk.132
Sandiacre, Crompton & Evans Un. 100
Sandown, Capital and Counties....... 49
Sandwich, London & County 135
Sawbridgeworth, Barclay & Co. ... 30
Saxmundham, Barclay & Co. 30
Scarboro', London & Yorkshire Bk. 146
„ Barclay & Co. 30
„ York City and County B. Co. 132
„ York Union Banking Co. ...100
„ Beckett & Co. 100
„ London and Northern 138
Scilly Islands, Bolitho, Wms.,&Co.30,223
„ Capital and Counties 49
„ Cornish Bank 201
Scunthorpe,Smith, Ellison & Co.......201
Seacombe, North & S. Wales Bank. 144
„ Parr's Bank 177
Seaford, Barclay & Co. 30
Seaforth, Parr's Bank 177
„ London City & Midland......136
Seaham Harbour, Barclay & Co. ... 30
„ North-Eastern Banking Co....100
„ York City and County.......132
Seascale, Whitehaven Jt. St. B. Co.148
Seaton, Wilts & Dorset B. Co.......144
„ Devon & Cornwall Bkg. Co. ..30
Sedbergh, Bank of Liverpool.......100
„ London City and Midland ...136
„ Lancaster Banking Co. 30
Sedgefield, North-Eastern B. Co. ...100
Selby, York City and County B. Co.132
„ Yorkshire Banking Co. 223
„ York Union Banking Co. ...100
Selly Oak, Lloyds Bank 132
„ Birmingham Dist. & Countis.. 30
Settle, Craven Bank 182
„ Yorkshire Banking Co. 223
Sevenoaks, London & County 135
„ Lloyds Bank 132
Shaftesbury, National Provincial ...175
„ Wilts and Dorset Banking Co.144
Shanklin, Capital and Counties ... 49
Sharpness Docks, Capital & Counties 49
Shaw, London City and Midland ...136
„ Union Bk. of Manchester ...100
Sheerness, London and County 135
Sheffield, Sheffield Bankng. Co. (H.O.)201
„ Sheffield & Hallamsh. B.(H.O.)100
„ Sheffield & Rotherham Joint-
Stock Banking Co.(H.O.)30, 244
„ Sheffield Union Bkg. Co.(H.O.)132
„ Birmghm. & Counties Bkg. Co. 30
„ London City and Midland ...136
„ London and Yorkshire Bank. 146

Sheffield, York City & County B. Co.132
„ T. Cook & Son 73
„ National Provincial 175
Shepton Mallet, Wilts and Dorset 144
„ Stuckey's Banking Co. 189
Sherborne, National Provincial ...175
„ Wilts and Dorset Banking Co.144
Sherburn, York City & County ... 132
„ Barclay & Co. 30
Shildon, York City & County ... 132
„ Barclay & Co. 30
„ London City & Midland......136
„ Yorkshire Banking Co. 223
Shipston, Lloyds Bank 132
„ Metrop. B. of Eng. & Wales ...162
Shipton-under-Wychwood, Metrop.
Bk. of Eng. and Wales 162
Shirehampton, Capital and Cnties.. 49
Shirley, Capital and Counties 49
Shoreham, Capital and Counties ...49
„ Barclay & Co. 30
Shotley Bridge, Hodgkin, B., & Co..132
„ North-Eastern Banking Co....100
Shrewsbury, National Provincial ...175
„ Birm. and Counties B. Co.... 30
„ Eyton, Burton, & Co. 189
„ Lloyds Bank 132
Sidcup, Martin's Bank 154
„ London & Provincial.........100
Sidmouth, Devon & Cornwall Bk.Co. 30
„ London and S.-Western 142
Silloth, London City and Midland 136
„ Cumberland Union Bkg. Co... 30
Silsden, Craven Bank 182
Sittingbourne, London and County 135
„ Martin's Bank 154
Skegness, Capital and Counties ... 49
„ Stamford, Spald., & Bos. B. Co. 30
Skipton, Craven Bank (H.O.)........182
„ London City and Midland......136
„ Yorkshire Banking Co. 223
Slaithwaite, Halifax Joint Stock 148
Sleaford, Lincoln & Lindsey Bank 182
„ Peacock, Willson, & Co. 132
„ Stamford, Spald. & Bost. B.Co. 30
„ Smith, Ellison & Co. 201
Slough, London and County 135
„ Woodbridge, Lacy,H.H. & Co.100
„ Metropolitan Bank 162
Small Heath, Lloyds Bank 132
„ London City & Midland......136
Smethwick, Birm. & Counties B. Co. 30
„ Lloyds Bank 132
„ London City & Midland......136
Snaith, Leatham, Tew & Co. 30
Solihull, Lloyds Bank 132
Somerton, Stuckey's Banking Co....189
„ Wilts and Dorset Banking Co.144
South Bank, Barclay & Co. 30
„ York City and County B. Co. 132
South Cave, Yorkshire Bank. Co. ...223
South Molton, Devon & Cornwall 30
„ Fox, Fowler, & Co. 30
„ National Provincial 175
South Petherton, Stuckey's Bkg. Co.189
Southshields, Hodgkin,Barnett&Co.132
„ National Provincial 175
„ Barclay & Co. (Woods) 30
„ North Eastern Bank 100
„ York City and County Bank...132
South Wigston, Leicestershire B. Co.144
Southam, Woodbridge, Lacy H.& Co.100
„ London City & Midland......136
„ Lloyds Bank 132
Southampton, Capital and Counties 49
„ Grant & Maddison's Union ...132
„ National Provincial 175
„ Wilts & Dorset Banking Co...144
„ London City & Midland......136
„ T. Cook & Son 73
„ Docks, Grant & M. Union ...100
„ „ Wilts & D.B. Co. 144
„ „ Capital & Counties......49
„ „ National Provincial ...175
Southend, London & Co. 135
„ Capital and Counties 49
„ Barclay & Co. 30
„ London and Provincial.......100
Southminster, Barclay & Co. 30
Southport, Manch. & L'pool Dist. 153
„ Mercantile of Lancs. 148
„ Parr's Bank 177

Southport, London City & Midland 136
„ Williams Deacon Bank 223
„ Union Bank of Manchester ...100
„ Lancs. & Yorkshire Bank ...144
„ Manchester & County......209
Southsea, Capital and Counties ... 49
„ Grant & Maddison Union Bk. 100
„ National Provincial 175
„ Wilts and Dorset 144
Southwell, Nottnghm. & Nts.Bkg.Co.144
„ Samuel Smith & Co. 201
Southwold, Barclay & Co. 30
„ Lacons, Youell, & Kemp......100
Sowerby Bridge,Halifax J't.St.B.Co.148
„ Halifax & Hudd. Un. B. Co. 100
„ Lancashire and Yorkshire...144
Spalding, Capital and Counties ... 49
„ National Provincial 175
„ Stamford, Spalding, & Boston 30
Spennymoor, Nat. Prov............175
„ Barclay & Co. 30
„ North-Eastern Bank 100
Spilsby, Capital and Counties 49
„ Lincoln and Lindsey Bank......182
„ Stamfd. Spldng. & Bostn. B. Co. 30
Stacksteads,Lancashire & Yorkshire
Bank 144
Stafford, Birm. & Counties Bnkg. Co. 30
„ Lloyds Bank 132
„ Manch. & L'poolDist.Bkg.Co....153
Staines, Thomas Ashby & Co. 223
„ London and Provincial.......100
Stalybridge,Manch.andCountyBnk.209
„ Manch. & Li'pool Dist. Bkg. Co.153
„ Merc. B. of Lancaster 148
Stamford, Stamford, Spalding &
Boston Banking Co.(H.O.).. 30
„ Capital & Counties Bank ... 49
Stanley, Hodgkin, Barnett & Co. ...132
„ North-Eastern Banking Co....100
Stanmore, L. and S. West 144
Stanningley, Bradford Old Bank ... 32
„ London City & Midland......136
Stansted, Barclay & Co. 30
Staple Hill, Lloyds Bank 132
Stevenage, Barclay & Co. 30
Steyning, Capital and Counties ... 49
„ Barclay & Co. 30
Stirchley, Lloyds Bank 132
Stockport, Manchstr. & L'pool Dist. 153
„ Manchester and County......209
„ Mercantile of Lancashire ...148
„ Williams Deacon Bank 223
„ Union Bank of Manchester ...100
Stockton-on-Tees, Barclay & Co. ... 30
„ National Provincial 175
„ North Eastern Banking Co....100
„ York City & County Bank....132
Stoke-upon-Trent, Manch. & L'pool153
„ Birmingham Dist. & Counties 30
„ National Provincial 175
Stokes Croft, Stuckey's Banking Co.189
„ Lloyds Bank 132
„ National Provincial 175
Stokesley, National Provincial.......175
„ York City and County Bk. Co.132
Stone (*Staff.*), National Provincial 175
„ Manch. & Liv. Dis. Bkg. Co. 153
Stonehouse (*Devon*), Cornish Bank ..201
„ Devon & Cornwall Bank. Co... 30
„ Harris, Bulteel, & Co. 189
Stony Stratford, Bartlett & Co. 144
„ Bucks and Oxon Union Bank 144
Stourbridge, Lon. City & Mid. Bk. 136
„ Metrop. B. of Eng. & Wales..162
Stourport, Met. B. of Eng.& Wales..162
Stowmarket, Barclay & Co. 30
„ Oakes, Bevan, T. & Co. 30
Stow-on-the-Wold, Capital & Co. ... 49
Strangeways, Williams Deacon Bk.223
„ Union Bank of Manchester ...100
Stratford-on-Avon, Lloyds Bank ..132
„ Metrop. B. of Eng. & Wales ..162
Stratton, Bolitho, Williams,& Co.30,223
„ Dingley & Co. 209
Street, Wilts & Dorset Bankg. Co. ..144
Stretford, Williams Deacon Bank ..223
„ Manchester & Liverpool......153
Stroud, Capital and Counties 49
„ Lloyds Bank 132
„ Wilts and Dorset 144
Sturminster, Wilts and Dorset 223

Sudbury, Barclay & Co. 30
Sudbury, Oakes, Bevan, T. & Co. .. 30
Sunbury, Thomas Ashby & Co. ...223
Sunderland, Barclay & Co. 30
  ,,   Lambton & Co. 30
  ,,   National Provincial 175
  ,,   North Eastern Banking Co. ..100
  ,,   Barclay & Co. (Woods) 30
  ,,   York City & County Bkg. Co. 132
  ,,   London and Northern 138
  ,,   London City and Midland ..136
Surbiton, London & County 135
  ,,   London and Provincial 100
Sutton (Surrey), London and Prov.100
  ,,   London & S. Western 142
Sutton-in-Ashfield, N.& Notts B. Co.144
  ,,   S. Smith & Co. 201
  ,,   Crompton & Evans' Un. Bk. 100
Sutton Bridge (Linc.), Barclay & Co. 30
Sutton Coldfield, Lloyd's Bank ...132
  ,,   London City & Midland ...136
Swadlincote, Leicestrsh. Bankg. Co. 144
  ,,   Lloyd's Bank 132
Swaffham, Barclay & Co. 30
Swanage, Wilts and Dorset 223
Swansea, Capital and Counties ... 49
  ,,   Lloyds Bank 132
  ,,   London and Provincial 100
  ,,   Metrop. B. of Eng. & Wales 162
  ,,   London City and Midland ..136
Swindon, Capital and Counties ... 49
  ,,   Lloyds Bank 132
  ,,   Wilts and Dorset Bk. Co. ..144
Swinton, Lanc. & York. B. 144
  ,,   Sheffield Bkg. Co. 201
  ,,   Williams Deacon Bank 223
Tadcaster, Bradford Old Bank ...132
  ,,   Yorkshire Banking Co. 223
Tamworth, National Provincial ...175
  ,,   Lloyds Bank 132
  ,,   London City and Midland ..136
Taunton, Stuckey's Banking Co. ..189
  ,,   Devon and Cornwall Bkg. Co. 30
  ,,   Fox, Fowler, & Co. 30
  ,,   Wilts and Dorset Bkg. Co. ..144
Tavistock, Devon &CornwallBkg.Co. 30
  ,,   Dingley & Co. 209
  ,,   Fox, Fowler, & Co. 132
Teams, Hodgkin, Barnett & Co. ..132
Teddington, London & Provincial ..100
  ,,   Parr's Bank 177
Teignmouth, National Provincial...175
  ,,   Devon and Cornwall Bkg. Co. 30
  ,,   Capital and Counties 49
Tenbury, Berwick & Co. (Lechmere)189
  ,,   Lloyds Bank 132
Tenby, London and Provincial ...100
  ,,   National Provincial 175
Tenterden, London and County ...135
  ,,   Lloyds Bank 132
Tetbury, Lloyds Bank 132
Tewkesbury, Capital & Counties .. 49
  ,,   Lechmere & Co. (Berwick) ..189
Thame, Bucks and Oxon Union B. 144
  ,,   Cobb, Bartlett, & Co. 144
Thetford, Oakes, Bevan, T. & Co. .. 30
  ,,   Barclay & Co. 30
Thirsk, Yorkshire Banking Co. ...223
  ,,   York Union Banking Co. ...100
  ,,   York City & County Bkg. Co. 132
Thornaby-on-Tees, Nat. Provin. B. 175
  ,,   Barclay & Co. 30
Thornbury, Prescott, Dimsdale & Co.144
Thornton (Bradford), Bradf'd Old B.132
Thornton Heath, Lond. & Prov. ...100
Thrapston, Northamptonsh. Un. B.223
  ,,   Stamfd.,spaldg., & Bost. B.Co. 30
Tideswell, Manchester & County B. 209
Tintagel, Bolitho, Williams ...30, 223
Tipton, Birm. & Counties Bkg. Co. 30
  ,,   Metropolitan Bank 102
Tiverton, National Provincial ...175
  ,,   Stuckey's Banking Co. 189
  ,,   Devon and Cornwall Bkg. Co. 30
  ,,   Fox, Fowler & Co. 30
Todmorden, Man.& Liv. Dis. Bkg.Co.153
  ,,   Lancashire & Yorksh. Bank 144
  ,,   Halifax Joint Stock Bank ..148
Tollesbury, Barclay & Co. 30
Tonbridge, Lloyds Bank 132
  ,,   London & County 135
Torquay, Devon & CornwallBkg.Co. 30

Torquay, Lloyds Bank 132
  ,,   National Provincial 175
  ,,   Vivian, Kitson, & Co. 182
  ,,   Wilts & Dorset Bkng. Co. ..144
Torre, Vivian, Kitson & Co. 182
Torrington, National Provincial ...175
  ,,   Fox, Fowler, & Co. 30
  ,,   Devon & Cornwall Bkg. Co. .. 30
Totnes, National Provincial 175
  ,,   Devon & Cornwall Bkg. Co. .. 30
  ,,   Harris, Bulteel, & Co. 144
Totterdown, Lloyds Bank 132
Towcester, Northants Union Bk. ..223
Towlaw, Barclay & Co. 30
  ,,   North Eastern B. 100
Tredegar, London & Provincial ...100
  ,,   Metrop.Bank of Eng.&Wales 162
Tring, Thomas Butcher & Sons ...144
Trowbridge, Capital & Counties .. 49
  ,,   Wilts & Dorset Banking Co...144
Truro, Cornish Bank (H.O.) 201
  ,,   Bolitho, Williams, & Co. ..30, 223
  ,,   Devon & Cornwall Bkg. Co. .. 30
Tunbridge Wells, London & County 135
  ,,   Lloyds Bank 132
  ,,   Barclay & Co. 30
Tunstall, Manch.&Liv.Dist. B. Co.153
  ,,   National Provincial 175
  ,,   B'ham Dis. and Counties ... 30
Twickenham, London & Fr'vincial100
  ,,   London & South Western ... 142
Tyldesley, Union B. of Manchester 100
  ,,   Parr's Bank 177
  ,,   Manchester and County ...209
Uckfield, Barclay & Co. 30
Ulverston, Lancaster Banking Co. .. 30
  ,,   Bank of Liverpool 100
  ,,   London City & Midland ...136
  ,,   Cumberland U. B. 30
Upper Brighton (Chesh.), Parr's Bk.177
Uppermill, Manch. & County Bk 209
Uppingham, Stamfd.,Spald.,& Bost. 30
  ,,   Leicestershire Banking Co. .. 144
Upton-on-Severn, Cap. & Counties.. 49
  ,,   Lechmere & Co. (Berwick) ..189
Urmston, Williams Deacon 223
Usk, London & Provincial Bk. 100
  ,,   Capital & Counties 49
Uttoxeter, Birm. & Counties B. Co. 30
  ,,   Lloyds Bank 132
  ,,   Crompton and Evans Union.100
Uxbridge, London & County 135
  ,,   Woodbridge,Lacy, H.H.,&Co 100
Ventnor, Capital & Counties 49
  ,,   National Provincial 175
Wadebridge, Bolitho, Williams. 30, 223
  ,,   Cornish Bank 201
  ,,   Capital and Counties 9
Wainfleet, Capital and Counties .. 49
Wakefield, Wakefield and Barnsley
    Union Bank (H.O.) 100
  ,,   Leatham, Tew, & Co. 30
  ,,   London City & Midland ...136
  ,,   York City & County Bkg. Co. 132
Walkden, Manchester & County ..209
  ,,   Williams Deacon Bank 223
Wallasey, N. & S. Wales 144
Wallingford, Hedges, Wells, & Co. 144
  ,,   London & County 135
Wallington, London & Sth. West. 142
Wallsend, Hodgkin, Barnett, & Co.132
  ,,   York City and County 132
Walsall, London, City & Midland ..136
  ,,   Lloyds Bank 132
  ,,   Metrop. Bk. of Eng. & Wales 132
  ,,   Birm. Dist. Cnties. Bkg. Co. 30
  ,,   T. Cook & Son 73
Walton (L'pool), Bk. of Liverpool. 100
  ,,   North & South Wales 144
Walton-on-Thames, T. Ashby & Co. 30
  ,,   London & S. Western 142
Wanstead, L. & S. West. 142
Wantage, London & County 135
Ware, London & County 135
  ,,   Barclay & Co. 30
Wareham, National Provincial ...175
  ,,   Wilts and Dorset 223
Warkworth, North Eastern Bk. Co. 100
Warminster, Capital & Counties .. 49
  ,,   Wilts & Dorset Bkg. Co. ...144
Warrington, Lancash. & Yrksh. Bk. 144
  ,,   Manch. & Liverp. Dist. B. Co. 153

Warrington, Parr's Bank 177
  ,,   Union Bank of Manchester ..100
  ,,   National Provincial 175
Warwick, Lond. City & Midland ..136
  ,,   Lloyds Bank 132
  ,,   Metrop. Bk. of Eng. & Wales 162
Washington, Hodgkin, Barnett & Co.132
Watchet, Stuckey's Banking Co. ..189
Waterfoot, Lanc. & Yorkshire Bk. 144
  ,,   Manchester & County 209
Waterloo (Liverpool), Parr's Bk. ..177
  ,,   Bank of Liverpool 100
  ,,   Lond. City & Mid. 135
Watford, London & County 135
  ,,   London & South Western ..142
  ,,   Bucks & Oxon Union Bank 144
Watton (Norfolk), Barclay & Co. .. 30
Wavertree, Bank of Liverpool 100
Wealdstone, Bucks and Oxon. 144
Wednesbury, Lond. City & Midland 136
  ,,   Lloyds Bank 132
  ,,   Metrop. B. of Eng. & Wales .162
Wellingboro', Leicestershire Un. Co. 144
  ,,   Northamptons. Un. B. 223
  ,,   Capital & Counties B. 49
Wellington(Salop),Bir.Dis.&Cos.Bk. 30
  ,,   Lloyds Bank 132
  ,,   (Som.), Stuckey's B. Co. ...189
  ,,   Fox, Fowler, & Co. 30
Wells (Norfolk), Barclay & Co. ... 30
  ,,   London & Provincial 100
  ,,   (Somerset), Stuckey's B. Co. 189
  ,,   Wilts & Dorset Banking Co. 144
Welshpool, N. & S. Wales Bank ..144
  ,,   Lloyds Bank 132
Wem, National Provincial 175
  ,,   Birm. & Counties Bkg. Co. .. 30
Wembley, L. & S. West. 142
Wendover, Bucks & Oxon Un. ...144
Weobley, Capital & Counties 49
  ,,   Lloyds Bank 132
Werneth, Manch.& Liv.Dist. B. Co. 153
West Bromwich, Birm. & Counties 30
  ,,   Lloyds Bank 132
  ,,   Metrop. B. of Eng. & Wales .162
West Corn'th, N. East Bk. Co. ...100
West Hartlepool, N.-Eastn. Bk. Co.100
  ,,   Barclay & Co. 30
  ,,   National Provincial Bank ..175
  ,,   York City & County Bkg. Co. 132
West Kirby, N. & S. Wales B. 144
  ,,   Bank of Liverpool 100
West Mersea, Barclay & Co. 30
*Westbourne*Wilts&Dorset Bkg.Co. 100
  ,,   National Provincial 175
Westbury, (Wilts) Wilts & Dorset ..144
  ,,   Capital & Counties. 49
Westbury-on-Trym, Prescott & Co. 182
Westerham, London & County ...135
Westgate-on-Sea, Lloyds Bank ...132
Westhoughton, Manch. & County ..209
  ,,   Parr's Bank 177
Weston-super-Mare,Stuckey's B.Co.189
  ,,   Capital & Counties 49
  ,,   Fox, Fowler, & Co. 30
  ,,   Wilts & Dorset Banking Co. 144
Wetherby, Yorkshire Banking Co. .223
  ,,   Knaresbro & Claro Bkg. Co.132
Weybridge, London & County 135
Weymouth, Capital & Counties ...49
  ,,   Stuckey's Banking Co. 189
  ,,   Wilts & Dorset Bkng. Co. 144, 223
  ,,   Devon & Cornwall B. Co. ... 30
Whaley Bridge, Manch.& County ..209
Whetstone, L. & S. West. 142
Whitby, National Provincial 175
  ,,   York City & County Bkg. Co. 132
Whitchurch (Salop), Nat. Provincial 175
  ,,   Birm. & Counties Bk. Co. ... 30
  ,,   Lloyds Bank 132
Whitefield, Lanc. & Yorks. Bank .144
Whitehaven, Whitehaven Joint
    Stock Banking Co. (H.O.) ..148
  ,,   B. of Whitehaven (H.O.) ...100
  ,,   Cumberland Union Bkg. Co. .. 30
  ,,   Clydesdale Bank. 60
Whitley, Barclay & Co. 30
  ,,   York City and County 132
Whitstable, Hammond & Co. 132
Whittlesea, Barclay & Co. 30
Whitworth, Manch. & L'pool. Dist. 153

Whitworth, Un. Bk. of Manchester 100
Widnes, Parr's Bank 177
　,, Mercantile B. of Lanc. 148
Wigan, Parr's Bank 177
　,, Manch. & L'pool Dist. B. Co. ... 153
　,, Manch. & County Bk. 205
　,, Williams Deacon Bk. 223
Wigton, Bank of Whitehaven 100
　,, Carlisle & Cumberland B. Co. 193
　,, Cumberland Union Bk. Co. .. 30
Willenhall, Lloyds Bank 132
　,, Metrop. B. of Eng. & Wales .. 162
Willington, North Eastern Bkg. Co. 100
Williton, Stuckey's Bkg. Co. 189
Wilmslow, Union B. of Manch. ... 100
　,, Manch. and U'p of Dist. B Co 201
Wilsden, Bradford Old Bank 232
Wimborne, Wilts & Dorset Bkg. Co. 100
　,, National Provincial 175
Wincanton, Stuckey's Bkg. Co. ... 18
　,, Wilts & Dorset Banking Co. .. 100
Winchcomb, Capital & Counties ... 49
　,, Lloyds Bank 132
Winchester, London & County 135
　,, Capital & Counties 4
　,, Prescott, Dimsdale, & Co. ... 180
Windermere, Lancaster Bnkng. Co. 30
Windermere, Bank of L'pool 100
Windsor, London & County 135
　,, Nevile Reid & Co. 223
　,, Woodbridge Lacy, H. H.,& Co. 100
Winsford, Union Bk. of Manch. ... 100
　,, Parr's Bank 177
Winslow, Bartlett & Co. 100
　,, Bucks & Oxon Union Bank .. 144
Winton, Wilts & Dorset Bkg. Co. .. 100
Wirksworth, Moore & Robinson's B. 201
　,, Crompton & Evans' Union Bk. 100
Wisbech, Barclay & Co. 30

Wisbech, National Provincial 175
Witham, Barclay & Co. 3
Wittington, Manch. and County B. 209
Withy Grove, Man. & L. Dis. B. Co. 153
　,, Manchester & County 209
Witney (Oxon), Gillett & Co. 100
　,, Metrop. B. of Eng. & Wales ... 162
Wiveliscombe, Stuckey's Bkg. Co. ... 189
　,, Wilts & Dorset Banking Co. .. 144
Woking, Thomas Ashby & Co. 223
　,, Capital & Counties 49
Wokingham, J. & C. Simonds & Co. 223
Wolsingham, Barclay & Co. 30
　,, North East Banking Co. 100
Wolverhampton, Birm.&Ctics. B. Co. 30
　,, Lloyds Bank 132
　,, National Provincial 175
　,, London City & Midland 13
　,, Metrop. B. of Eng. & Wales ... 162
　,, T. Cook & Son 73
Wombwell, Lloyd in a Yorks 100
　,, Wakefield & Barnsley Union 100
Woodbridge,Bacon,Cobbold&Co. 36,100
　,, Barclay & Co. 30
Woodley, Un. Bank of Manchester 100
Woodstock, Gillett & Co. 100
Woolacombe Bay,Dev.& Corn.B.Co. 30
Wooler, British Linen Co. 40
　,, North-Eastern Bank 100
Woolton, Bank of Liverpool 100
Woolwich, Capital and Counties ... 49
　,, London and Provincial 100
　,, London & County 135
Wootton-Bassett, Capital and Cties. 49
　,, Wilts and Dorset Bkg. Co. ... 144
Worcester, Berwick & Co.(Lechmere)100
　,, Lloyds Bank 132
　,, Met. Bk. of Eng. & Wales ... 162
　,, National Provincial 175

Workington, Bank of Whitehaven 100
　,, London City & Midland 136
　,, Clydesdale Bank 100
　,, Cumberland Union Bkg. Co. 30
Workson, Beckett & Co. 100
　,, York City and County 132
　,, Nottingham & Notts Bkg. Co. 214
　,, Mid. Cities District Bank ... 148
　,, Capital and Counties 49
Worthing, Capital and Counties ... 49
　,, London and County 135
Wotton-an-Edge, Lloyds Bank 132
　,, National Provincial 175
Wrentham, Barclay & Co. 30
Wrexham, National Provincial 175
　,, North & South Wales Bank .. 144
　,, Parr's Bank 177
　,, Bank of Liverpool 100
　,, Lloyds Bank 132
Yarmouth (Norfolk), Barclay & Co. 30
　,, Lacons, Youell, & Kemp..... 100
　,, London & Provincial 100
　,, National Provincial 175
　,, (I. of W.), Wilts and Dorset.. 144
Yeadon, Bradford Old Bank 232
Yeovil, Stuckey's Banking Co. 189
　,, Capital and Counties 49
　,, Devon and Cornwall B. Co. .. 30
　,, Wilts and Dorset Banking Co. 144
York, York City & County Banking
　　　　Co. (H.O.) 132
　,, York Union Brg. Co. (H.O.).. 100
　,, Beckett & Co. 100
　,, National Provincial 175
　,, Yorkshire Banking Co. 2,3
　,, London and Northern 100
York Town (Surrey), J.& C.Sim'nds 223
Ystalyfera, Metropolitan Bank of
　　　　England and Wales 162

BANKS AND THEIR BRANCHES IN SCOTLAND.

Bank of Scotland —*Head Office*, Edinburgh, Bank-st (9 branches). *London Branch*, 19 Bishopsgate-st. Within, E.C. *Branches*: Aberdeen, Aberfeldy, Airdrie, Annan, Arbroath, Ardrossan, Auchterarder, Auchtermuchty, Ayr, Barrhead, Beauly, Bellshill, Blackford, Blairgowrie, Bucklyvie, Callander, Campbeltown, Carnoustie, Castle-Douglas, Coldstream, Corstorphine, Coupar-Angus, Crieff, Cumnock, Denny, Dingwall, Dumfries, Dunbar, Dunblane, Dundee, Dunfermline, Dunkeld, Duns, Dysart, Elgin, Eskdaim (Dalkeith), Falkirk, Forfar, Fort William, Fraserburgh, Galashiels, Gatehouse, Glasgow (21 branches), Govan, Grangemouth, Greenock, Haddington, Hamilton, Helensburgh, Innerleithen, Inverness, Jedburgh, Kelso, Killin, Kilmarnock, Kirkcaldy, Kirkcudbright, Kirkwall, Kirriemuir, Lamlash, Lasswade, Lauder, Leith, Lockerbie, Lossiemouth, Milnegavie, Moffat, Montrose, Motherwell, New Cumnock, Oban, Paisley, Peebles, Perth, Pitlochrie, Port Glasgow, Rothesay, St. Andrews, Saltcoats, Slamannan, Stirling, Stonehaven, Strathaven, Tain, Thurso, Uddingston, West Linton. Wick

Royal Bank of Scotland.—*Head Office*, in Edinburgh, 36, St. Andrew-sq. (9 branches). *London Branch*, 123, Bishopsgate street Within. *Branches*: Aberdeen, Airdrie, Alloa, Alyth, Arbroath, Ardrossan, Ayr, Ayton, Bathgate, Biggar, Blairgowrie, Borrowstounness, Bowmore (Islay), Brechin, Broughty-Ferry, Buckhaven, Campbeltown, Campsie, Catrine, Coatbridge, Cumbernauld, Cumnock, Cupar, Dalkeith, Dalmellington, Doune, Drymen, Dumfries, Dundee (& 5 branches), Dunfermline, Duns, Ecclefechan, Elgin, Eyemouth, Fairlie, Falkirk, Forfar, Forres, Galashiels, Girvan, Glamis, Glasgow(&17branches), Govan, Grangemouth (2 branches),

Granton (near Edinburgh), Grantown, Greenlaw, Greenock, Haddington, Hamilton, Hawick, Inverness, Irvine, Jedburgh, Johnstone, Kinaldcoln, Kilmarnock, Kilsyth, Kinross, Kirkcaldy, Lanark, Largs, Larkhall, Leith (2 branches), Lesmahagow, Leven, Lochee, Lockerbie, Markinch, Maryhill, Maybole, Meigle, Melrose, Monifieth, Montrose, Musselburgh, Nairn, Newhaven (Edinb.), Newmilns, Newtown St. Boswells, Oban, Paisley, Partick, Perth (2 branches), Port Ellen (Islay), Port Glasgow, Portobello, Prestonpans, Rothesay, St. Andrews, Saltcoats, Sanquhar, Shettleston, Stewarton, Stirling, Strathaven, Tayhuilt, Tighnabruaich, Tranent, Wishaw.

British Linen Company Bank.— *Head Office*, 38, St. Andrew-square, Edinburgh (9 branches). *London Office*, 41, Lombard - street, E.C. *Branches*: Aberdeen, Airdrie, Alexandria (Dumbartonshire), Annan, Arbroath, Ayr, Balfron, Berwick, Brechin, Broxburn, Carluke, Castle-Douglas, Coatbridge,Coldstream, Crieff, Cupar (Fife), Dairy (Ayrshire), Dumbarton, Dumfries, Dunbar, Dundee (3 branches) Dunfermline, Dunoon, Duns, Elgin, Falkirk, Falkland, Forfar, Forres, Fort William, Galashiels, Gaiston, Girvan, Glasgow (24 district branches), Gorspie Greenock, Haddington, Hamilton, Hawick, Helmsdale, Inverness, Irvine, Jedburgh, Kelso, Kilmarnock, Kingussie, Kinross, Kirkcaldy, Kirriemuir, Lanark, Langholm, Largs, Leith, Lesmahagow, Leven, Linlithgow, Loanhead, Melrose, Moffat, Montrose, Motherwell, Nairn, Newcastleton, Newton-Stewart, North Berwick, Paisley, Peebles, Perth, Port William, Renfrew, Sanquhar, Selkirk, Stirling, Stornoway, Stranraer, Tain, Thornhill, Thurso,

Troon, Uddingston, Wick, Wigtown, Wishaw, Wooler (2 sub-branches)
Commercial Bank of Scotland, Limited.—*Head Office*, Edinburgh, George-st. (21 City branches). *Branches*: 62, Lombard street. *Branches*: Aberdeen, Aberfeldy, Abington, Alloa, Alness, Annan, Anstruther, Arbroath, Armadale, Ayr, Ayton, Ballantrae, Balmacara (Lochalsh), Banff, Beauly, Beith, Berwick-on-Tweed, Biggar, Blairgowrie, Bonhill, Bonnybridge, Buckhaven, Burntisland, Callander, Cambuslang, Campeltown, Carnwath, Castletown (Caithness), Chirnside, Coatbridge, Colinsburgh, Comrie, Crail, Crieff, Cromarty, Cupar, Dalbeattie, Dalkeith, Douglas (Lanarkshire), Dumbarton, Dumfries, Dunbar, Dundee, Dunfermline, Earlston, Elgin, Eyemouth, Falkirk, Forfar, Galashiels, Girvan, Glasgow (and 12 branches), Grahamston, Grangemouth, Greenock (2 branches), Haddington, Hamilton, Hawick, Invergordon, Inverness, Jedburgh, Juniper Green, Kelso, Kilmarnock, Kilwinning, Kirkcaldy (2 branches), Kirkcudbright, Kirkintilloch, Kirkwall, Kyle (Lochalsh), Lanark, Leith (2 branches), Lenzie, Lerwick, Leven, Linlithgow, Lochwoisate (South Uist), Lockerbie, Lybster, Markinch, Mauchline, Maybole, Melrose, Methil, Montrose, Motherwell, Musselburgh, Newburgh (Fifeshire), Newton-Stewart, Oban, Paisley (2 branches), Partick, Pathhead (Kirkcaldy), Peebles, Perth, Peterhead, Pitlochrie, Pollokshaws, Rutherglen, St. Andrews, Selkirk, Shotts, Stirling, Stranraer, Stromness, Tain, Thurso, Turriff, West Calder, West Kilbride, Whitburn, Wick. Wishaw.
National Bank of Scotland, Limited. —Edinburgh, 42, St. Andrew-sq. (10 branches); *London Office*, 37, Nicholas lane. *Branches*: Aberdeen, Airdrie, Alloa, Anstruther, Arbroath,

Ayr, Banff, Barrhead, Bathgate, Berwick-on-Tweed, Biggar, Brechin, Burntisland, Carluke, Castle-Douglas, Cellardyke, Clydebank, Coatbridge, Coupar-Angus, Cowdenbeath, Cupar, Dalkeith, Dingwall, Dumfries, Dundee, Dunfermline, East Linton, Elie, Falkirk, Fauldhouse, Forfar, Forres, Fort William, Galashiels, Girvan, Glasgow (and 15 branches), Glenluce, Gourock, Govan, Grantown, Greenock, Hawick, Inveraray, Inverness, Islay, Jedburgh, Johnstone, Kelso, Kilmarnock, Kilsyth, Kirkcaldy, Pathhead (Kirkcaldy), Kirkcudbright, Kirkintilloch, Kirkwall, Kirriemuir, Langholm, Largo, Leith, Leven, Lochmaben, Lochwinnoch, Montrose, Motherwell, Musselburgh, Nairn, Newton-Stewart, Oban, Paisley, Partick, Perth, Pittenweem, Portobello, Portree, Rutherglen, Selkirk, Stirling, Stornoway, Stranraer, Stromness, Thurso, Ullapool, Whithorn, Wigtown, Wishaw.

Union Bank of Scotland, Limited.— *Head Offices:* in Glasgow, 101, Ingram-st. (15 branches); in Edinburgh, George-st. (10 branches). *London Office:* 62, Cornhill. *Branches:* Aberdeen (3 branches), Aberfeldy, Aberlour, Alloa, Alva, Ardrishaig, Ardrossan, Auchterarder, Auchtermuchty, Ayr, Ballater, Banchory, Banff, Barrhead, Barrhill, Bathgate, Beith, Blair-Athole, Blairgowrie, Bo'ness, Braemar, Brechin, Bridge of Allan, Buckie, Campbeltown, Castle-Douglas, Clydebank, Coatbridge, Coupar-Angus, Crieff, Cullen, Dalbeattie, Dalry (Galloway), Darvel, Doune, Dumbarton, Dumfries, Dunblane, Dundee, Dunkeld, Dunning, Dunoon, Edzell, Elgin, Ellon, Errol, Fochabers, Forfar, Fraserburgh, Galston, Gatehouse, Girvan, Gourock, Govan, Greenock, Hamilton, Helensburgh, Huntly, Inveraray, Inverness, Inverurie, Irvine, Johnstone, Keith, Killin, Kilmarnock, Kincardine, Kirkcaldy, Kirkwall, Kirriemuir, Ladybank, Largs, Larkhall, Leith, Lerwick, Leslie, Lochgelly, Lochgilphead, Macduff, Maybole, Mearns, Millport,

Moffat, Moniaive, New Aberdour, New Pitsligo, Paisley, do. Willmeadow, Partick, Perth, Peterhead, Pitlochrie, Port-Glasgow, Portsoy, Renfrew, Rosehearty, St. Margaret's Hope (Orkney), Scalloway (Shetland), Shettleston, Stewarton, Stirling, Stonehouse, Strachur (Lochfyne), Stranraer, Strathaven, Stromness, Tarbert, Tarland, Thornhill, Tillicoultry Tollcross, Troon, Turriff, Wick.

Clydesdale Bank, Limited.— *Head Office,* St. Vincent-place, Glasgow (17 branches). *London Office:* 30, Lombard-street, E.C. *Branches:* Airdrie, Alexandria, Alloa, Anstruther, Arbroath, Ardrishaig, Ardrossan, Auchinleck, Ayr, Baillieston, Beith, Bellshill, Blantyre, Borrowstounness, Bothwell, Brechin, Bridge of Weir, Cameton, Campbeltown, Carlisle, Castle Douglas, Coatbridge, Crieff, Cumnock, Cupar, Dalkeith, Dalry, Darvel, Denny, Dollar, Dumbarton, Dumfries, Dundee, Dunfermline, Dunlop, Dunoon, Eaglesham, East Kilbride, Edinburgh (6 branches), Falkirk, Garliestown, Greenock, do. East End, Hamilton, Helensburgh, Holytown, Innellan, Inverkeithing, Irvine, Kilbarchan, Kilbirnie, Kilmarnock, Kilwinning, Kinross, Lanark, Larbert, Leith, Lochgilphead, Lockerbie, Midcalder, Milnathort, Motherwell, Muirkirk, Neilston, New Galloway, Newmilns, Newport (Fifeshire), Newton - Stewart, North Berwick, Oban, Paisley, Partick, Penicuik, Perth, Pittenweem, Pollokshaws, Port Glasgow, Portobello, Prestwick, Renton, Rothesa', St. Andrews, South Queens ferry, Stewarton, Stirling, Stranraer, Strone, Tarbert Tillicoultry, Tobermory, Wemyss Bay, West Kilbride, Whitehaven, Whithorn, Wigtown, Wishaw, Workington.

Town and County Bank, Limited.— *Head Office,* Aberdeen, 62, Union-st (6 branches). *Branches:* Alford, Alyth, Auchinblae, Auchnagatt, Badenscoth, Ballater, Banchory, Banff, Bervie, Brora, Buckie, Castletown (Caithness), Craigellachie, Cumines-

town, Dingwall, Dornoch, Dufftown, Dundee, Durno-Pitcaple, Echt, Elgin, Ellon, Fochabers, Fraserburgh, Fyvie, Golspie, Hatton (Aberdeen), Hopeman, Huntly, Insch, Inverness, Inverurie, Keith, Kemnay, Kildrummy, Laurencekirk, Lybster, Mintlick, Mintlaw, Montrose, Newburgh (Aberdeen), New Deer, Newmill (Keith), Old Meldrum, Perth, Peterhead, Rhynie, Rothes, Stonehaven, Strathdon, Strichen, Tarland, Tarves, Thurso, Tomintoul, Torphins, Turriff, Udny, Wick, Woodside (Aberdeen). *London Agents:* Joint Stock Bank, Limited.

North of Scotland Bank, Limited. *—Head Office,* Aberdeen (6 branches). *Branches:* Aberchirder, Aberlour, Aboyne, Alford, Arbroath, Auchinblae, Ballater, Banchory, Banff, Bervie, Blairgowrie, Bridge of Allan, Broughty Ferry, Buckie, Carnoustie, Crieff, Cullen, Dufftown, Dundee, Dunfermline, Elgin, Ellon, Fettercairn, Fife-Keith, Forres, Fraserburgh, Friockheim, Gardenstown, Glenlivet, Huntly, Insch, Invergordon, Inverness, Inverurie, Keith, Kintore, Kirkcaldy, Laurencekirk, Lerwick, Lossie, Longside, Lonmay, Lumphanan, Lumsden, Macduff, Methlick, Montrose, Nairn, New Deer, New Maud, Oban, Old Deer, Old Meldrum, Perth, Peterhead, Port Erroll, Portree, Portsoy, Rhynie, Rothes, Sauchen (Cluny), Stirling, Stonehaven, Strichen, Tain, Tayport, Tobermory, Turriff, Wick. *Agents in London:* Barclay & Co., Limited, and the Union Bank of London, Limited.

Caledonian Banking Co., Limited.— *Head Office,* Inverness. *Branches:* Avoch, Bonar-Bridge, Burghead, Cromarty, Dingwall, Dornoch, Elgin, Forres, Fort Augustus, Fortrose, Gairloch, Garmouth, Glen-Urquhart, Grantown, Halkirk, Hopeman, Invergarry, Kingussie, Lairg, Lochcarron, Lochmaddy, Nairn, Portree, Rothes, Stornoway, Strathpeffer. *Agents in London,* Bank of Scotland.

BANKS AND THEIR BRANCHES IN IRELAND.

PRIVATE BANKS IN DUBLIN.

BOYLE, LOW, MURRAY & Co.—35, College-green. *London Agents:* Williams Deacon & Manchester & Salford.

GUINNESS, MAHON, & Co.—College-green. *London Agents,* Parr's Bank, Limited.

JOINT-STOCK BANKS.

Bank of Ireland.—*Head Office,* College-green, Dublin. *Branches:* Arklow, Armagh, Bagnalstown, Ballibay, Ballina, Ballinasloe, Ballinrobe, Banagher, Bandon, Belfast (3 branches), Boyle, Callan, Carlow, Castlebar, Castleblayney, Cavan, Charleville, Clonakilty, Clones, Clonmel, Cork, Derry, Drogheda, Dundalk, Ennis, Enniscorthy, Galway, Gorey, Kilbeggan, Kilkenny, Limerick, Listowel, Longford, Mallow, Maryborough, Midleton, Mitchelstown, Mountbellew, Mountmellick, Mullingar, Navan, Newry, New Ross, Omagh, Portadown, Queenstown, Roscommon, Roscrea, Skibbereen, Sligo, Thurles, Tipperary, Tralee, Tullamore, Waterford, Westport, Wexford, Youghal. 8 *Sub-Branches. London Agents:* Bank of England, Coutts & Co.

Hibernian Bank, Limited.—*Head Office,* Dublin, 27, College-green. (3 branches). *Branches:* Abbeyleix, Ardee, Armagh, Athy, Ballaghaderin, Ballybofey, Bray, Cookstown, Cork,

Drogheda, Dundalk, Edenderry, Fintona, Granard, Kells, Kilkenny, Letterkenny, Londonderry, Loughrea, Mohill, Monaghan, Monasterevan, Mullingar, Naas, Navan, Newbridge, Oldcastle, Parsonstown, Portumna, Rathfriland, Strabane, Swinford Thomastown, Tubbercurry, Tullamore, Wicklow. 26 *Sub-Branches. London Agents:* Lloyds Bank.

Royal Bank of Ireland, Limited.—*Head Office,* Foster-place, Dublin. *Branches,* 23 and 24, Arran-quay, 63 and 64, Upper Sackville-street, 54, Lower Baggot-street, 14 and 15, Cornmarket, 102, Upper George-street, Kingstown, 46, North Wall, 76, Rathmines-road, and Dalkey (Tu. & Fri.). *London Agents:* The London and Westminster Bank, Limited.

Munster and Leinster Bank, Limited. *—Head Office,* Cork. *Branches:* Bandon, Bantry, Bruff, Buttevant, Cahirciveen, Castletown Bere, Charleville, Drogheda, Drumcollogher, Dublin (3 branches), Dungarvan, Dunlavin, Dunmanway, Fermoy, Fethard (Co. Tipperary), Hospital, Kenmare, Kildysart, Kilfinane, Killarney, Killmallock, Kinsale, Limerick, Lismore, Macroom, Maryborough, Midleton, Mitchelstown, Mountrath, Naas, Nenagh, Newmarket (Co. Cork), Rathdowney, Rathkeale, Skibbereen, Tallow, Tarbert, Thurles, Tipperary,

Tralee, Waterford. 12 *Sub-branches. London Agents:* Union Bankot London.

Provincial Bank of Ireland, Lim.—*Head Office,* 8, Throgmorton-avenue, London. *Dublin Offices,* 5, College-street, and 96, Capel-street. *Branches:* Armagh, Athlone, Ballina, Ballymena, Ballyshannon, Banbridge, Bandon, Bantry, Belfast, Carrick-on-Shannon, Carrick-on-Suir, Cavan, Clogheen, Clonmel, Coleraine, Cootehill, Cork, Drogheda, Dungannon, Dungarvan, Ennis, Enniscorthy, Enniskillen, Fermoy, Galway, Kanturk, Kilkenny, Killaloe, Kilrush, Kinsale, Limerick, Listowel, Londonderry, Mallow, Monaghan, Nenagh, Newcastle (Co. Lime ick), Newry, Omagh, Parsonstown, Skibbereen, Sligo, Strabane, Swinford, Templemore, Tipperary, Tralee, Waterford, Wexford, Youghal. 12 *Sub-branches.*

National Bank.—*Head Office,* 13, Old Broad-street, London. *Dublin Offices,* 34, College-green, Great Britain Street, Pembroke & Rathmines. *Branches:* Abbeyfeale, Athlone, Athy, Ballaghaderreen, Ballina, Ballinasloe, Ballymahon, Baltinglass, Belfast, Boyle, Bruff, Cahir, Cahirciveen, Carlow, Carrickmacross, Carrick-on-Suir, Cashel, Castlebar, Castlecomer, Castleisland, Castlerea, Charleville, Claremorris, Clifden, Clonakilty, Clonmel, Cork, Dingle

Doneraile, Dundalk, Dungarvan, Dunmore (co. Galway), Ennis, Enniscorthy, Ennistymon, Fermoy, Galway, Gorey, Gort, Graigue-na-Managh, Headford, Kanturk, Kells, Kilkenny, Killarney, Killorglin, Kilrush, Kingstown, Limerick, Lismore, Listowel, Longford, Loughrea, Macroom, Mallow, Midleton, Millstreet (Co. Cork), Miltown - Malbay, Mitchelstown, Moate, Mountmellick, Mullingar, Nenagh, Newbridge, Newcastle (Co. Limerick), New Ross, Newtownbarry, Parsonstown, Portarlington, Rathkeale, Roscommon, Roscrea, Scariff, Strokestown, Templemore, Thurles, Tipperary, Tralee, Tuam, Tullow, Waterford, Wexford, Wicklow. 11 Sub-branches.

Northern Banking Company, Lim.— Head Office, Belfast (4 branches). Branches: Armagh, Ballieborough, Balbriggan, Ballinamore, Ballybay, Ballybofey, Ballycarry, Ballycastle, Ballyclare, Ballymena, Ballynahinch, Banbridge, Bray, Carndonagh, Carrickfergus, Carrick-on-Shannon, Castle- wellan, Claudy, Clones, Coleraine, Comber, Cushendall, Downpatrick, Dromore (Co. Down), Dublin (2 branches), Dungiven, Dungloe, Fintona, Fivemiletown, Hillsborough, Irvinestown, Keady, Kilrea, Larne, Limavady, Lisburn, Londonderry, Lurgan, Magherafelt, Mohill, Newry, Newtownstewart, Oldcastle, Ramelton, Randalstown, Raphoe, Strokestown, Virginia. 40 Sub-branches. London Agents: Glyn, Mills & Co., and Barclay & Co., Limited.

Belfast Banking Company, Limited.—Head Office, Belfast (4 branches). Branches: Antrim, Armagh, Ballymena, Ballymoney, Ballyshannon, Bangor (co. Down), Bushmills, Castleblayney, Coleraine, Cookstown, Crossmaglen, Donegal, Drogheda, Dublin (2 branches), Dundalk, Dunfanaghy, Dungannon, Enniskillen, Kilkeel, Larne, Letterkenny, Limavady, Londonderry, Lurgan, Magherafelt, Monaghan, Moville, Navan, Newry, Newtownards, Portadown, Portaferry, Portrush Rathfriland, Rathgar, Saintfield, Sligo, Strabane, Tandragee. 25 Sub-branches. London Agents: Union Bank of London, Limited.

Ulster Bank, Limited.—Head Office. Belfast (5 branches). Branches: Antrim, Ardee, Armagh, Arva, Athboy, Aughnacloy, Ballina, Ballinrobe, Ballyhaunis, Ballyjamesduff, Ballymena, Ballymoney, Ballynure, Banbridge, Belturbet, Blackrock, Carrickmacross, Castlederg, Castlepollard, Castlerea, Cavan, Clones, Cookstown, Cootehill, Donegal, Downpatrick, Dromore (co. Tyrone), Dublin (3 branches), Dundalk, Edenderry (King's Co.), Enniskillen, Garvagh, Glenties, Granard, Killybegs, Larne, Letterkenny, Lisburn, Lisnaskea, Londonderry, Longford, Lurgan, Maghera, Manorhamilton, Monaghan, Mullingar, Naas, Newtownards, Omagh, Portadown, Sligo, Strabane, Trim, Tuam, Tullamore, Westport. 68 Sub-branches. London Agents, London & Westminster Bank, Ld., and Prescott, Dimsdale & Co., Ld.

AVERAGE PRICE OF CONSOLS FOR THE PAST HUNDRED AND SEVEN YEARS, WITH THE AMOUNT OF INTEREST PRODUCED.

Year	Price	£	s	d	Year	Price	£	s	d
1792	84¾	3	10	9	1819	71⅞	4	3	5
1793	75¼	3	19	2	1820	67⅝	4	8	5
1794	67¼	4	8	10	1821	73¾	4	1	4
1795	65¾	4	11	3	1822	79⅛	3	15	10
1796	61⅞	4	16	11	1823	78⅞	3	16	1
1797	52	5	15	4	1824	90¾	3	6	1
1798	52⅝	5	14	0	1825	84⅝	3	10	11
1799	60¾	4	18	9	1826	79⅛	3	15	10
1800	63⅝	4	14	3	1827	83⅛	3	12	2
1801	62⅛	4	16	7	1828	84⅞	3	10	11
1802	72½	4	2	9	1829	89⅞	3	6	9
1803	61⅝	4	17	4	1830	85⅞	3	9	10
1804	56¼	5	6	8	1831	79¾	3	15	3
1805	59⅛	5	0	9	1832	83⅝	3	11	9
1806	61½	4	17	7	1833	87¾	3	8	4
1807	61	4	18	9	1834	90¾	3	6	1
1808	65⅜	4	11	1	1835	91	3	5	11
1809	66⅞	4	9	8	1836	89⅜	3	7	1
1810	67⅛	4	9	4	1837	90⅞	3	6	0
1811	64¼	4	13	4	1838	92⅞	3	4	7
1812	59	5	1	8	1839	91½	3	5	7
1813	61	4	18	9	1840	89⅜	3	7	1
1814	67	4	9	7	1841	88⅞	3	7	6
1815	59¾	5	0	4	1842	91¼	3	5	4
1816	62	4	16	9	1843	94⅝	3	3	5
1817	73⅛	4	2	0	1844	98⅛	3	0	8
1818	77½	3	17	4	1845	98¼	3	0	6

Year	Price	£	s	d	Year	Price	£	s	d
1846	95½	3	2	10	1873	92½	3	4	10
1847	86¾	3	9	5	1874	92½	3	4	10
1848	85	3	10	7	1875	93¾	3	4	0
1849	93¾	3	4	4	1876	95	3	3	2
1850	96⅝	3	2	1	1877	95¾	3	3	0
1851	97¾	3	1	4	1878	95⅜	3	3	10
1852	98⅞	3	0	8	1879	97½	3	1	6
1853	95⅞	3	2	6	1880	98⅜	3	1	0
1854	90½	3	6	3	1881	100	3	0	0
1855	90	3	6	8	1882	100½	2	19	8
1856	90¾	3	6	1	1883	101⅛	2	19	2
1857	90¾	3	6	1	1884	101	2	19	4
1858	96⅜	3	2	2	1885	99½	3	0	2
1859	92⅛	3	4	8	1886	100½	2	19	8
1860	94½	3	3	5	1887	101⅛	2	19	0
1861	91¾	3	5	4		Reduced to 2¾ per cent.			
1862	93¾	3	4	4	1888	97¼⅛	2	16	4½
1863	92⅝	3	4	9	1889	96⅞	2	16	3
1864	90⅛	3	6	6	1890	96½	2	17	3
1865	89⅜	3	7	0	1891	95¾	2	17	7½
1866	87⅜	3	8	7	1892	95⅛	2	17	6
1867	93	3	4	6	1893	98½	2	15	10¾
1868	93¾	3	4	0	1894	101⅜	2	14	5
1869	92⅜	3	4	7	1895	106	2	11	9
1870	93¼	3	4	10	1896	110¾	2	9	7¾
1871	93¾	3	4	0	1897	112⅜	2	8	11⅞
1872	93¼	3	4	10	1898	110⅛	2	9	6¾

BANK OF ENGLAND MINIMUM RATE OF DISCOUNT, 1884 TO 1898

Months	1884	1885	1886	1887	1888	1889	1890	1891	1892	1893	1894	1895	1896	1897	1898
January	3	5	3½	5	3½	4 3/16	6	4¼	3⅓	3 2/10	3		2	3⅞	3
February	3½	5	2¾	4	2½	3	5⅜	3	3	2½	2⅜		2	3⅜	3
March	3⅝	3¼	2¾	3½	2¼	3	4½	3	3	2½	2	2	2⅞	2¾	3¼
April	2½	3½	2½	2⅔	2	2½	3	4½	2½	3½	2	2	2¼	3⅞	
May	2½	2¼	2½	2	2½	2½	3	3¾	2	2½	2	2	2	2½	
June	2½	2	2½	2	2½	2½	3¼	2½	2	2½	2	2	2	2½	
July	2	2	2½	2	2	2½	4⅜	2½	2	4	2	2	2	2½	
August	2	2	2½	2¼	2½	3	4⅜	2½	2	4¼	2	2	2	2½	
September	2	2	3½	4	4	4 1/10	4½	2½	2	4¼	2	2 7/16	2½	2⅝	
October	2¾	4	4	5	5	5	5	4	2½	4	3	3⅓	2½	3⅝	
November	4¾	2¼	4½	4	4	5 1/16		3¾	3	4	4	3	4	4	
December	5	3¼	4½	4	4	5 1/16		3¾	3	4	4	3	4	4	
Average	2 13/16	3	3	3½	3½	3½	4½	3½	2½	3 1/16	2½	2½	2½	2⅞	3¼

For the rate of Discount and price of Consols in 1898–99 see pages 362 to 367.

COLONIAL AND FOREIGN BANKS, WITH THEIR LONDON AGENTS.

.*. *The numbers given in the following List refer to the London Office or to Banks in London on which the Colonial or Foreign Banks draw. See List of London Bankers, pages 291-4. The addresses there given are the Head Offices in London. Bankers in the United Kingdom issue drafts on all the leading Colonial and Foreign Banks.*

Aalesund.—Aalesund Kreditbank, 118.
Abbeville.—Monchaux & Bignon, 71.
Aberdeen (Cape).—St. B. of S. Afr., 203.
Acapulco.—London B. of Mexico, 145.
Accra.—Bk. of Brit. W. Africa.
Adalia.—Imp. Ottoman Bank, 117.
Adana.—Imp. Ottoman, 117.
Adelaide (Cape).—St B. of S. Af., 203.
Adelaide (S. Aus.).—B. of Australasia, 16; Eng. Scot. & Aust. B., 93; Bk. of N.S.W., 23; Nat. Bk. of Australasia, 169; Union B. of Aust., 208; B. of Adelaide, 12; B. of N. Zea., 24; Com. Bk. of Aust., 70; Laycock, Goodfellow & Bell, 134.
Adelong.—Bk. of New S. Wales, 23.
Aden.—National Bank of India, 171.
Adrianople.—Imp. Ottoman B., 117.
Agen.—Société Gén. 202; B.de France; Compt. Nat., 71.
Agra.—Agra Bk., 1; Bk. of Bengal, 75.
Aguas Calientes.—Lon. B. of Mex, 145
Ahmedabad.—Bk. of Bombay, 75.
Aidin.—Imp. Ottoman Bank, 117.
Aillevillers.—Soc. Gén., 202.
Aix-en-Provence (Bouches-du-Rhône).—Crédit Lyonnais, 77; Compt. Nat., 71; Soc. Gén., 202.
Aix-la-Chapelle.—Aachener Dis.Co.,84
Aix-les-Bains.—Crédit Lyonnais, 77.
Ajaccio.—J. Bozzo Costa.
Akaroa.—Bank of New Zealand, 24.
Akola.—Bk. of Bombay, 75.
Ayab.—Bank of Bengal, 75.
Alais.—Soc. Gén. 202; Créd. Lyon., 77
Albany (W. Aust.).—Un. Bk. of Aust. 208; Nat. Bk. of Australasia, 169; West. Aust. Bk., 12.
Albany (N.Y.).—State Nat. Bank, 45.
Albi.—Société Générale, 202.
Albion Park (N.S.W.).—E., S., & A. 93.
Albion (Queens.).—Qnsld. Nat. B., 184
Albury.—B. of New S. Wales, 23; Com. B. Co. of Sydney, 69; B. of Australasia, 16; Australian J. S. B., 13; Union Bank of Aust., 208.
Aldinga.—Bk. of Adelaide, 12.
Alençon.—Société Générale, 202.
Aleppo.—Imp. Ottoman B., 117.
Alexandra (N.Z.).—Bank of N.Z., 24; Bank of N. S. Wales, 23.
Alexandra (Vic.).—Un. B. of Aust.,208; Nat. B. of Aust., 169.
Alexandria.—B. of Egypt, 20; Crédit Lyon.,77; Anglo-Egyptian B., 9; Imp. Ottoman B., 117; L. Müller, 52; Thomas Cook & Son (Egypt), 73. National Bank of Egypt, 170A.
Alexandria (Ont.).—U. B. of Canada, 177; B. of Ottowa, 177.
Algiers.—Crédit Lyonnais, 77 hos. Cook & Son, 73.
Alicante.—Carey & Co.
Alica.—Stand. Bank of S. Africa, 203.
Aliwal, North (Cape).—Bk. of Africa, 15; Stand. B. of South Africa, 203.
Allahabad.—Bank of Bengal, 75; Allahabad Bank, 209.
Allendale.—Nat. Bk. of Aust., 169.
Alliston (Ont.).—Ontario Bk., 177.
Allora.—Australian Joint St. Bk., 13; Queensland Nat. B., 184.
Almonte (Ont.).—B. of Montreal, 22.
Amberley.—Bk. of N. S. W., 23.
Amherst.—Bank of Nova Scotia, 193; Halifax Banking Co., 177; Bk. of Montreal, 22.
Amiens. Crédit Lyonnais, 77; Société Générale, 202; Comptoir Nat , 71.
Amoy.—Hongkong & Shanghai, 112; Nat. B. of China, 170.
Amrasti.—Bk. of Bombay, 75.
Amsterdam.—Determeyer Weslingh & Son, 135; B. de Paris et Pays B., 148; Netherland Trading Soc., 209;

Lipmann, Rosenthal & Co.. 118; Amsterdamsche B.. 135; T. Cook and Son, 73; Blydenstein & Co., 38.
Ancona.—L. Classen, 209; R. Almagia, 190; Bk. of Adelaide, 12.
Angaston.—Nat. B. of Australasia, 169; Bk. of Adelaide, 12.
Angers.—Créd. Lyon , 77; Soc.Gén.,202
Angora.—Imperial Ottoman Bk., 117.
Angoulême.—Societe Générale, 202; Crédit Lyon., 77; Compt. Nat., 71.
Annapolis.—Union Bk. of Halifax, 144; Bank of Nova Scotia, 193.
Annecy.—Soc.Gén.,202; Créd. Lyon.,77
Annonay.—Créd. Lyon., 77; Soc. Gén., 202.
Aussig.—Anglo-Austrian, 7.
Antigonine.—Merchants' Bank, 26 ; Halifax Banking Co., 177.
Antigua.—Colonial Bank, 65
Antofagasta.—London Bk. of Mexico, 145; Bank of Tarapacá & Lond., 28.
Antwerp.—H. . de Bary & Co., 209; B. d'Anvers, 144; B. Centrale Anversoise, 148; C. de Browne & Co., 154.
Appila Yarrowie. - Enq.,Sc.,&Aus.,93
Apt.—Soc. Générale, 202.
Aramac.—Bk. N. Wales, 23.
Ararat (Vic.).—B. of N.S.W.,23; Lon B. of Aust., 147; B. of Victoria, 29.
Aratapu.—Nat. Bk. N. Zea., 172.
Arcachon.—Eng. Bk Fredk. Undap,71.
Archangel.—Russian Bank, 195.
Arequipa.—Lond. B. of Mexico, 145.
Argentan, Soc. Générale, 202.
Arica.—London B. of Mexico, 145.
Arles.—Société Générale, 202.
Armentières.—Crédit Lyonnais, 77.
Armidale.—Bk. of New South Wales 23; Australian Joint Stock Bk., 13 Com. Bk. of Sydney, 69.
Arnprior.—Bank of Ottawa, 177.
Arras.—Société Générale, 202; Crédit Lyonnais, 77
Arrowtown.—Bk. of New Zealand, 24.
Ascot Vale.—Bk. of Soot.,and Aust.,93
Ashburton (N. Z.).—Un. Bk. of Aust. 208; Bk. of N. Zealand, 24; Bk. of Australasia, 16; B. of N. S. W., 23.
Ashcroft (B.C.)—Bk. B. N. Amer., 18.
Ashfield.—B. of N. S. W., 23.
Ashurst.—B. of N. Zealand, 24.
Asnières.—Soc. Générale, 202.
Astrakhan.—Russian Bk., 195.
Athens.—Ionian B., 119 ; Société Ottomane, 206 ; Thos. Cook & Son, 73.
Atkin (S.C.).—Bk. B. N. Amer., 18.
Aubervilliers.—Société Générale, 202.
Auburn.—Nat. B. of Australasia, 169.
Auch.—Société Générale, 202.
Auckland.—B. of Australasia 16; B. of N. S. W., 23; Bk. of N. Z., 24; Nat. B. of N. Z., 172; Union B. of Australia, 208; Thos. Cook & Son, 73.
Augsburg.—Friedr. Schmid & Co., 118.
Auray.—Soc. Générale, 202.
Aurillac.—Société Générale, 202.
Aurora (Ont.).—Ontario Bk., 177.
Austin (Canada).—Bank of Austin, 8.
Autun.—Soc. Générale, 202.
Auxerre.—Société Générale, 202.
Avenel.—Com. B. of Australia, 70.
Avignon.—Soc. Gén., 202; Créd. Ly., 77
Avoca.—Bank of Victoria, 29.
Aylmer (Ontario).—Molson's Bk., 177; Traders Bank of Canada, 173.
Bacchus Marsh.—N. B.Australasia,169.
Baden (Suisse).—Bank of Baden.
Baden-Baden.—Oberrheinische B., 75; F. S. Meyer, 75; Meyer & Diss, 209.
Bagdad.—Imp. Ott., 117.
Bagnères de Luchon.—Compt. Nat., 71.
Bahia.—London&Brazil Bk., 133; Banco Mercantile de Bahia, 135; Brit. B. of S. Am. 39; B. de Bahia, 135.
Bairnsdale.—B. of Victoria, 29; Bk. of

Australasia, 16; Bk. of N. S. W., 23; Nat. B of Australasia, 169; Col. B. of Australasia, 148.
Balclutha.—Nat. Bk. New Zealand, 172; Bank of New Zealand, 24.
Balian.—Com. Bank of Australia, 70.
Ballarat (Victoria).—B. of Australasia, 16; B. of New S. Wales, 23; Union B. of Australia, 208; B. of Victoria, 29; Lon. B. of Australia, 147; Col. B. of Australasia, 148; Nat. Bk. of Australasia, 169; Com. B of Australia, 70; Eng., Scot., & Aust., 93.
Ballina (N. S. W.).—Australian Jt. St. Bk., 13; Comm. Bkg. Co. Sydney, 69.
Balmain.—B. of New South Wales, 23; Eng., Scot., & Aust. Bk., 93.
Balranald.—Australian Jt. Stock, 13.
Baltimore.—Alex. Brown & Sons, 45; Hambleton & Co., 173; Nat. Exchge. Bk., 196.
Bangalore.—B.of Madras,21; Agra B., 1.
Bangkok.—Hongkong & Shanghai B. Corp., 112; Ch. B. of India, &c., 53.
Bar-le-duc.—Société Générale, 202; Crédit Lyonnais, 77
Barbados.—Colonial Bank, 65.
Barberton.—Bank of Africa, 15; Stand. Bank of S. A., 202; Natal Bk., 167; National Bank, 173a.
Barcaldine.—Queensland Nat. Bk.,184; B. of N. S. W., 23.
Barcelona.—Crédit Lyon., 77.
Bareilly.—B. of Upper India, 209.
Barkly East.—Stand. Bk. S. Afr., 203.
Barmen.—Barmer Bk. Verein, 10.
Barraba (N. S. W.).—Com. Bkg. Co. of Sydney, 69.
Barrie.—B. of Toronto, 136 ; Canad. B. of Commerce, 26.
Barrington (N.S.).—Halifax B. Co., 177.
Basle.—Banque Fédérale, 77 ; Swiss Bankverein, 209.
Batavia.—Ch. B. of India, 53; Merc. Bk. of India,160; Hongkong & Shanghai B., 112; Netherlds. Trad. Soc., 209.
Bathurst (N. S. W.).—Australian J.S. B., 13; B. of N. S. Wales, 23; Com. B. of Sydney, 60; City B. of Sydney, 148 ; B. of Australasia, 16.
Bayonne.—Société Générale, 202.
Beaconsfield.—Stand. B. of S. Af., 203.
Beaudesert—Queens Nat. B., 184; (Tasmania), Nat. B. of Tas., 68.
Beaufort (Victoria).—B. of Victoria, 29.
Beaufort West (S. Africa).—Stand. Bk. of S. Africa, 203.
Beaune.—Créd. Ly. 77 ; Compt. Nat.,71; Soc. Générale, 202.
Beauvais.—Société Générale, 202.
Bedford (S.Afr.).—Std. Bk. S. Afr. 203.
Beeac.—Lon. B. of Aust., 147.
Beechworth (Vic.).—B. of Australasia, 16; B. of N. S. W., 23; B. of Vic., 29.
Bega.—B. of N. S. Wales, 23; Coml. B. of Sydney, 69; Aust. J. S. B. 13.
Beira (East Africa).—B. of Afr., 15; Stand. Bank S. Africa, 203.
Belfast.—National Bank, 173a.
Belport.—Société Générale, 202.
Bellary.—Bank of Madras, 21.
Belleville.—Bnk. of Montreal, 22; Merchants' Bank of Canada, 60; Bk. of Commerce, 26; Dominion B., 173.
Belleville-sur-Saône.—Crédit Lyon., 77.
Bellingen.—Com. Bank of Sydney, 69.
Benalla.—B. of N. S. Wales, 23; Nat. B. of Australasia, 169; Colonial Bank of Australasia, 148.
Benares.—Bank of Bengal, 75.
Bendigo or Sandhurst (Vic.).—B. of Vic., 29; Bk. of Austria, 16; Union B. of Aust., 208; B. of New S. Wales, 23; Col. B. of Aust. 148; Nat

Bk.of Austlsia.,169 ; Lond.Bk.Aust., 147; Com. Bk. of Aust., 70.

Bennett (B.C.)—Bk. B. N. Amer., 18.

Benoni.—National Bank, 173a.

Berbice—British Guiana Bank, 201 ; Colonial Bank, 65.

Bergen—Bergens Kredit B., 84 ; Thos. Cook & Son, 73.

Bergerac.—Soc. Gén. 202 ; Comptoir National, 71.

Berhampore.—Bank of Madras, 21.

Berlin—Möser & Co., 209 ; Deutsche Bk., 84 ; Schickler Frères, 30 ; B. für Handel & Ind., 77 ; S. Bleichröder, 201 ; Dresdner Bank, 83.

Berlin (Ontario)—M.B. of Canada, 60 ; B. of Hamilton, 175 ; B. of Commerce. 26.

Berne.—Banque Fédérale, 77.

Berrigan.—Com. B. Co. of Sydney, 69; Union Bank of Aust., 208.

Berry (N.S. W.).—Eng., Scot., & Aust. B., 93 ; Com. B. Co. of Sydney, 69.

Berwick (Vict.).—Com.Bk. of Aust., 70.

Berwick (N.S.).—Com. B. of Windser, 209.

Besançon.—S.Gén.,202; Créd. Lyon.,77.

Bothlehem (S. Afr.).—Bk. of Africa, 15. Com. Bank of Aust., 169.

Beulah (Vic.)—Nat Bank of Aust 169; Com. Bank of Aust., 70.

Beverley.—West. Aus. Bk., 12.

Beyrout.—Imp. Ottoman Bank, 117 ; Henry Heald & Co., 75 ; Thos. Cook & Son, 73.

Béziers.—Créd.Lyon.,77; Soc. Gén.,202; Compt. Nat., 71.

Bhavnagar.—Bank of Bombay, 75.

Biarritz.—E. H. W. Bellairs, 148 ; Soc. Générale, 202 ; Cred. Lyon, 77.

Bilbao.—B. de Bilbao, 77.

Bimlipatam.—Bank of Madras, 21.

Bingara (N.S.W.).—Cm. B. Sydney, 69; Birchip.—Nat. Bk. Australasia, 169 ; Com. B. Aus. 70.

Birregurra.—Col. B. of Aust., 148.

Blackall (Queensland).—Q. Nat. Bank, 184 ; Bk. of N. S. Wales, 23.

Black Flag.—West Aust. Bank, 12.

Blayney (N. S. W.).—Com. Bkg. Co. of Sydney, 69 ; Austral. Jt. Stock, 13.

Blenheim (N. Z.).—Bk. of New Zeal., 24 ; Nat. B. of N. Z., 172 ; Bk. of N. S. Wales, 23.

Blenheim (Ont.).—B. of Comm., 26.

Bloemfontein.—B. of Africa, 15 ; Nat. Bank of Orange Free State, 209.

Blois.—Créd. Lyon, 77 ; Soc. Gén. 202.

Bluff.—B. of New Zealand, 24.

Blumberg—Bk. of Adelaide, 16.

Boggabri (N.S.W.).—Aust. Jt. St. B.,13.

Bogotá.—Lond. B. of Mexico, 145.

Boissevain(Man.).—U.B.of Canada,177.

Boksourg (Trans.).—Std. Bank of Sth. Africa, 203 ; Nat. Bank, 173a.

Bolbec.—Soc. Générale, 202.

Bologna.—L. Gavaruzzi & Co.

Bombala.—B. of N. S. W.,23 ; Com. B. Co. of Sydney, 69 ; Aust. J. S. B., 13.

Bombay.—Agra B., 1 ; Merc. B. of India, 160 ; Comptoir d'Escompte, 71; Grindlay, Groom & Co., 105 ; Hongkong & Shanghai B. Corp., 112; Nat. Bk. of India, 171; King, King & Co., 123 ; Char. B. of India, 53 ; W. Watson & Co., 217; Thos. Cook & Son,73; Imp. B. of Persia, 116 ; Yokohama Specie B. 225; Forbes & Co. 96 ; Bk. of Bombay,75 ; B.of China & Japan,14.

Bonn.—Jonas Cahn, 209.

Booleroo Centre.—Eng., Scot., & Aust Bank, 93.

Boonah.—Queen's Nat. Bk., 184.

Boort.—Nat. Bk. of Australasia, 169.

Bordeaux.—J. Violett & Cie., 209 ; Crédit Lyonnais, 77 ; Société Gén., 202; Comptoir Nat.d'Escompte, 71.

Bordighera.—Edwd. E. Berry, 235.

Boshof.—Nat.B.Orange Free State, 209.

Boston (U.S.).—Brown Bros. & Co.,45; Foote & French, 159 ; Thos. Cook & Son, 73 ; Express Co., 5 ; Mass. Nat. B., 8 Merchants Nat. B., 22.

Boulogne-sur-Mer.—Adam & Co., 5 ; Société Générale, 202.

Boulogne-sur-Seine.—Soc. Gén., 202.

Bourg.—Crédit Lyonnais, 77.

Bourges.—Société Générale, 202.

Bourke.—Com. B. Co. of Sydney, 69 ; Australian J.S. B., 13; B. of N. S. W., 23; Lon. B. of Australia, 147; Com. Bk. of Aust., 70.

Bowen (Queensland).—B. N. S. Wales, 23; Aust. Jt. Stock B., 13.

Bowmanville. — Ontario Bank, 177 ; Stand. B. of Canada, 173.

Bowral (N.S.W.).—Com. B. of Sydney, 69 ; Eng., Scot., & Aust B., 93.

Box Hill.—Eng., Scot., & Aust., 93.

Bracebridge (Ont.).—B. of Ottowa, 177.

Bradford (Ontario).—Standard Bk., 173.

Braidwood (N.S.W.).—Bk. of N. S. W., 23; Com. Bkg. Co. of Sydney, 69.

Braila.—Bank of Roumania, 25.

Brampton (Ontario).—Mrchnts' B.,60; Dominion B., 173.

Brandon (Can.).—Imp. B. Canada,132; Merchants' B.. 60 : B. of Brit. N. America, 18 ; B. of Hamilton, 175.

Brantford.—Bk. B. N. America, 18 ; B. of Montreal, 22; B. of Commerce, 26 ; Standard B. of Canada, 173.

Bremen.—Deutsche B., 84; Bremer B., 209; Dresdner Bank, 83.

Bremersdorf.—National Bank, 173a.

Breslau.—Eichborn & Co.

Brest.—Société Générale, 202.

Brewarrina (N. S. W.).—Com. B. of Sydney, 69 ; B. of N.S. W., 23 ; Aust. Jt. St. Bk., 13.

Bridgetown—Bk. of Nova Scotia, 193.

Bridgewater (Canada).—Merch. Bk. of Halifax, 26 ; Halifax B. Co., 177.

Bridgewater (Vic.).—Nat. B. of Aust., 169.

Bright (Vic.).—B. of Australasia, 16; Nat. Bank of Australasia, 169.

Brighton (Vic.).—Eng., Scot., & Aust Bk., 93 ; Com. B. of Aus., 70.

Brighton—Standard B. of Canada,173.

Brindisi.—E. Dionisi, 123 ; Thos. Cook & Son, 73 ; Banco d'Italia, 196.

Brinkworth (S. A.).—Eng., Scot., & Aust., 93.

Brisbane.—B. of Australasia, 16 ; Australian J. St. B., 13; B. of New S. Wales, 23; Union B. of Australia, 208; Com. B. Co. of Sydney, 69; Queensland National Bank, 184; London Bank of Australia, 147 ; Com. Bank of Australia, 70 ; Royal Bank of Queensland, 192; B. of N. S. Queensland, 27; Eng., Scot., & Aust. B., 93.

Britstown.—Stand. B. of S. Af., 203.

Brives.—Société Générale, 202.

Broach.—Bk. of Bombay, 75.

Broad Arrow.—Western Aust. B., 12 ; Bank of Aust., 16.

Brockville (Ont.).—B. of Montreal, 22; Molson's B., 177; B. of Toronto, 58.

Broken Hill (N.S.W.).—B. of Australasia, 16; Un. B. of Aust., 208; Lon. B. of Aust., 147 Nat. B. of Aust., 169 ; B. of N.S. W., 23.

Broussas.—Imperial Ottoman Bk., 117.

Bruges.—English Bank, 154

Brünn.—Anglo-Austrian Bank, 7.

Brunswick.—Brunswick Bank, 84.

Brunswick (Vic.).—Col.Bk.of Austlsia., 148; Un. B. of Aust., 208 ; Com. B. of Aust., 70.

Brussels.—Bigwood & Morgan, 209 ; B. de Paris et des Pays Bas, 148; Thos. Cook & Son, 73 ; Crédit Lyonnais, 77 ; Cassel & Co., 148.

Brussels (Canada).—Stand. Bk., 173.

Kruthen.—Bk. of Victoria, 29.

Bucharest.—Bank of Roumania, 25.

Buckingham (Queb.), Ontario Bk., 177.

Budapest. — Anglo - Austrian B., 7 ; Thos. Cook & Son, 73.

Buenos Ayres.—Lond. & River Plate, 140 ; Banco del Comercio, 177 ; Brit.

B. of S. Amer. 39 ; Lond. & Brazilian, 133; Anglo-Arg. B., 6.

Buffalo (U. S. A.).—German Bank of Buffalo, 177 ; Bank of Buffalo, 209.

Bulli.—Eng., Sc., & Aust. Bk., 93.

Bulls.—B.of N.Zeal. 24 ; B.of N.S.W.23.

Bulong—West. Aust. Bk. 12.

Bulawayo (South Africa).—St. B. of S. Af., 203 ; B. of Africa, 15 ; African Bank Corporation, 1A.

Bunbury.—U. B. of Aust., 208 ; Westn. Australian Bk., 12

Bundaberg.—Queensland Nat. B., 184 ; B. of N. S. Wales, 23 ; Com. B. Co.of Sydney, 69 ; Union B. of Aust., 208; Royal B. of Queensland, 192.

Bungendore.—B. of New S. Wales, 23.

Buninyong.—Nat. B. of Austlsia., 169.

Burghersdorp.—Stan. B. S. Africa, 203.

Burketown (Queensld.).—Q.Nat.B., 184.

Burnie (Tasmania).—B. Australasia, 16 ; Nat. B. of Tas., 68.

Burnley.—Bk. of Australasia, 16.

Burrawang.—Eng., Scot., & Aust 93.

Burrowa (N.S.W.).—B. of N. S. Wales. 23 ; Union B. of Aust., 208.

Burwood.—B. N. S.Wales, 23 ; Aust. Joint Stock Bank, 13.

Bushire.—Imp. B. of Persia, 116.

Busselton.—W. Aust. Bank, 12.

Byron Bay.—Eng., Scot., & Aust., 93.

Cadiz.—B. of Spain, 191 ; J. E. Gomez, 209.

Caen. — Soc. Générale, 202 ; Crédit Lyon., 77 ; Compt. Nat. d'Esc., 71.

Cahors.—Société Générale, 202.

Cairns.—Queensland Nat. Bk., 184 ; Bank of Australasia, 16 ; Bank of N. S.W.,23; B. of N. Queensld., 27.

Cairo.—Bk. of Egypt, 20; Imp. Ottoman Bk., 117; Anglo-Egypt. B., 9 ; Crédit Lyonnais, 77 ; L. Müller, 72; Thomas Cook & Son (Egypt), 73 ; National Bank of Egypt, 170A.

Cala.—Stand. B. of S. Africa, 203.

Calais.—Créd Lyon. 77; Compt.Nat.71.

Calcifer.—Bank of Aust., 16.

Calcutta.—Agra B., 1 ; B. of Bengal, 75; Ch. B. of India, &c., 53 ; Merc. B. of Ind., 160 ; Land Mortgage Bk. of I., 129 ; Comptoir d'Escompte, 71 ; Delhi & Lond. B., 82 ; Nat. B. of India, 171; Gillanders & Co., 75 ; Grindlay & Co., 105 ; King, Hamilton & Co., 123 ; Hongkong & Shanghai B. Corp., 112 ; Thos. Cook & Son. 73 ; W. Watson & Co., 217 ; Bk. of China & Japan, 14.

Caledon.—Stand. B. of S. Africa, 203.

Calgary (N. W. T.).—B. of Montr., 22 ; Impl. B. of Canada, 132; Union B. of Canada, 177.

Calicut.—B. of Madras, 21.

Callao.—London Bk. of Mexico and S. America. 145.

Caltowick.—Bank of Adelaide, 16.

Camberwell (Victoria).—Eng., Scot., & Aust. Bk. 93 ; Com. of Aust., 70.

Cambrai.—Société Générale, 202.

Cambridge.—Bk. of New Zealand, 24.

Camden.—Bank of New South Wales, 23 ; Com. B. Co. of Sydney, 69.

Campbell Town (N. S. W.).—B. of New S. W., 23 ; Com. Bkg. Co. of Syd., 69.

Campbelltown(N.B.)—B.of N.Scotia,193.

Campeche.—Lond. B. of Mexico, 145.

Camperdown.—Col. Bank of Australasia, 148 ; Bank of Victoria, 29 ; Union Bk. of Aust., 208.

Campinas.—London & Brazilian, 133.

Candelo.—Com. B. Co. of Sydney, 69.

Cannes — Taylor & Riddett, 209 ; Crédit Lyonnais, 77; Soc. Générale, 202; Thos. Cook & Son, 73.

Canning.—Halifax Bkg. Co., 177.

Cannington (Canada).—Stand. B. 173.

Canowindra (N.S.W.).—Comm. Bkg. Co. of Sydney, 69.

Canso (N.S.).—People's Bk., 209.

Capetown.—Stand.B. of S. Af., 203 ; B. of Af., 15 ; African Bkg. Corp., 1A ; Nat. Bk. 173A.

Diamond Creek (*Vict.*).—Comm. Bk. of Aust., 70.

Dieppe.—Soc. Gén., 202; L. Delarue, 209; Duval, Blainville & Co., 75; F. Chapman, 144; Comptoir Nat., 71.

Digby.—Nova Scotia Bank, 193.

Dijon.—Crédit Lyonnais, 77; Société Générale, 202; Compt. Nat., 71.

Dimboola.—Col. B. of Austlsia., 148; Nat. Bk. of Australasia, 169.

Dinan.—Soc. Generale, 202.

Dinard.—E. O'Rorke, 144.

Dominica.—Colonial Bank, 65.

Donald.—Bank of Victoria, 29; Col. Bank of Australasia, 148; Com. B. of Australia, 70.

Dongara.—West. Aust. Bk., 12.

Dookie.—Nat. Bk. of Australasia, 169

Dorchester.—Merch. B. of Halifax, 26.

Dordrecht (*S. Afr.*).—Stand. B. S. A. 203

Douai.—Société Gén., 202; Créd. Lyon., 77.

Draguignan.—Soc. Générale, 202.

Dresden.—Dresdner Bk., 83; Deutsche Bank, 84.

Dresden (*Ont.*).—B. of Commerce, 26.

Drontheim.—Trondhjem Privatbank.

Drouin (*Victoria*).—B. of Austlsia., 16.

Drysdale.—Col. B. of Australasia, 148.

Dubbo.—B. of N. S. Wales, 23; Com B. Co. of Sydney, 69; Aust. Jt St Bk., 13; Bank of Australasia, 16.

Dundas (*Can.*).—Bk. of Commerce, 26

Dundee (*Natal*).—St. B. of S. Africa, 203; Natal Bank, 167.

Dunedin (*Otago*).—Union Bk. of Australia, 208; Bank of Australasia, 16 Bk. of N. S.W., 23; Bk. of N. Z., 24; Nat. Bk. of New Zealand, 172.

Dunedin (*North*).—B. of N. Zealand, 24; Nat. Bank of New Zealand, 172.

Dungog.—Com. B. Co. of Sydney, 69; Bank of N. S. Wales, 23.

Dunkeld.—Col. Bk. of Austral., 148.

Dunkerque.—Soc. Générale, 202; Crédit Lyon., 77; A. Petyt & Co., 209; Compt. Nat., 71.

Dunnville (*Can.*).—Bk. of Commerce, 26

Dunolly.—Bank of Victoria, 29; Lond. Bank of Australia, 147.

Durango.—London B. of Mexico, 145.

Durban (*Natal*).—Bk. ofAfrica, 15; Natal B., 167; Standard B. of S. Africa, 203 Af. Bkg. Corp., 1A.; Nat. Bk., 173A.

Durham.—St. B. of Canada, 173.

Düsseldorf.—BergischeMark.Bank,148

Eaglehawk (*Vic.*).—B. of New Sout. Wales, 23; Bk. of Victoria, 29; Com. Bk. of Aust., 70.

East Collingwood.—Nat. B.of Aust.,169; Bk. N. S. Wales, 23.

East London (*S. Arrica*).—Stand. B. S. Africa, 203; Bk. of Africa, 15; African Bkg. Corp., 1A.

Echuca (*Vic.*).—B. of N. South Wales, 23; London Bk. of Australia, 147; Com. Bk. of Aus., 70; Col. Bk. of Australasia, 148.

Edithburg.—Bk. of Adelaide, 12.

Edmon'on.—Impl. B. of Canada, 132.

Eisenach.—S. Ziegler.

Eiberfeld.—Bergische Märk. Bank, 148

Eketahuna.—Bk. N. Zea., 24.

Elbeuf.—Soc. Gén., 202; Créd.Lyon., 77

Elmira (*Ont.*).—Traders Bk., 173.

Elmore Victoria.—Bk. of New South Wales, 23; Bank of Victoria, 29.

Eltham (*Vict.*).—Comm. B. of Aust., 70

Elthnm. (*N. Z.*).—Bk. N. Zea., 24; Bk. N. S Wales, 23.

Emden.—Y. & B. Brons, 135.

Emerald.—Com. of Sydney 69.

Ems.—L. J. Kirchberger, 209.

Epernay.—Société Générale, 202; Crédit Lyonnais, 77.

Epinal.—Créd. Lyon., 77; Soc.Gén., 202.

Ermelo (*S.A.R.*)—Natal Bk., 167; Nat. Bk., 173A.

Eshowe (*Zululand*).—Natal Bank, 167

Esperance.—W. Australian Bank, 12; Com. Bk. of Aust., 70.

Essendon.—Eng., Scot. & Aust., 93.

Essex (*Ont.*).—Impl. B. of Can., 132.

Estcourt (*Natal*).—St. B. S. Africa, 203.

Etampes.—Soc. Générale, 202.

Eu.—Soc. Générale, 202.

Eudunda.—Nat. B. of Australasia, 169.

Eurôa.—Nat. B. of Australasia, 169.

Evreux.—Soc. Générale, 202.

Exeter (*Ontario*).—Molson's Bank, 177.

Falmouth (*Jamaica*).—Col. Bk., 65

Faversmith (*S. Af.*).—Bk. of Africa, 15.

Featherston (*N. Zealand*).—B. of Australasia, 16; B. of New Zealand, 24.

Fecamp.—Crédit Lyonnais, 77.

Feilding (*N. Z.*).—B. of Austlsia., 16; B. of N. Z., 24; Bk. N. S. Wales, 23.

Fergus (*Canada*).—Imperial Bk., 132.

Fingal (*Tas.*).—B. of Australasia, 16.

Finley.—Com. B. of Sydney, 69.

Firminy.—Compt. Nat., 71.

Fitzroy.—B. of Victoria, 29; Lon. Bk. of Australia, 147; B. of N. S. Wales, 23; Eng., Scot. & Aust. Bk., 93; Un.B.of Aus.,208; Nat. B. of Aust.169.

Fleche, La.—Soc. Générale, 202.

Flers.—Crédit Lyon.,77; Compt. Nat.71

Florence.—French & Co., 100; Macquay & Co., 209; Thos.. Cook & Son, 73; Anglo-Italian, 5.

Flushing.—Netherlds. Trade Co., 209.

Foix.—Soc. Générale, 202.

Fontainebleau.—Société Générale, 202

Fontenay-le-Comte.—Soc. Générale,202.

Foochow.—Hongkong and Shanghai B. Corp., 112; Chartered Bank of India, 53.

Footscray.—Nt.B.ofAustlsia., 169; Col. B.of Austlasia, 148; Com.of Aust., 70; Bk. of N. S. Wales, 23.

Forbes (*N. S. W.*).—Aus. Jt St., 13; B. of N. S. W., 23; Com. B. of Sydney, 69; Un. Bk. of Australia, 208

Forest.—Stand. B of Canada, 173.

Fordsburg.—Nat. Bk. 173A.

Fort Beaufort.—Stand. B. S. Afr., 203.

Fort William.—Bk. of Montreal, 22.

Fortitude Valley.—Queens. Nat., 184 Com. Bk.ofSydney,69; B.ofN.S.W.,23

Fortrose.—B. of N. Z., 24.

Foster (*Vic.*).—Bank of Australasia, 16.

Fougerolles.—Soc. Générale, 202.

Foxton (*N. Zealand*).—Bank of New Zealand, 24.

Francis Town.—African B. Corp., 1A.

Frankfort-on-M.—Schuster Bros., 209 ; Sachs & Hochheimer, 209; Deutsche B., 84; Deutsche Vereinsbank, 209.

Fraserville.—People's B. of Halifax, 209.

Fredericton (*N. B.*).—B. of Brit. North Amer., 18; Merchants' B.of Hal., 148

Freiburg (*Baden*).—J. A. Krebs, 209.

Fremantle.—Un. B. of Aust., 208; Nat. B. of Austlsia, 169; W. Aust. B., 12; Com.B.of Aust.,70; B.of Austlsia, 16; Bk. N. S. Wales, 23.

Fresno (*California*).—Farmers' Bk., 14; Bank of Central California, 8.

Fribourg (*Switz.*).—F. Vogel.

Fürth.—Dresdner Bank, 83.

Gaillac.—Société Générale, 202.

Galle (*Ceylon*).—Merc. B. of India, 160; Nat. B. of India, 171.

Galt.—B. of Comm., 26; Merch. B. of Canada, 60; Imperial Bk., 132.

Galveston (*Texas*).—Adoue & Lobit,209

Gananoque (*Canada*).—Merchants' B. of Can., 60; B. of Toronto, 53.

Gatton.—Royal B. of Queensland, 192.

Gawler.—Nat. B. of Australasia, 169; Union B. of Aust., 208.

Geelong (*Victoria*).—B. of Australasia, 16; B. of N. S. Wales, 23; Col. B. of Australia, 148; London Bk. of Aust., 147; Com. Bk. of Aust., 70; Union Bk. of Aust., 208; B. of Victoria, 29; Nat. B. of Australasia, 169.

Geneva.—B. de Paris et des Pays Bas, 143; Crédit Lyonnais, 77; Lombard Odier & Co., 144; T. Cook & Son, 73.

Genoa.—BancaGen., 209, RussianB.195; Thos. Cook & Son, 73.

Georgestreet (*Qld.*)—R.B. of Qnsld., 192

George (*Cape*).—Stand. B.of S.Afr., 203.

George Town (*Can.*)—B.of Hamilton, 175.

George Town (*Qnsld.*).—B. of N. S. W., 23; R. of Adelaide, 12.

George's Bay.—Com. Bk. of Tasm., 23.

Geraldine (*N. Zealand*).—B. of New S. Wales, 23.

Geraldton (*W. Aust.*).—Queensld. Nat. Bk., 184; Union Bk. of Aus 208; Nat Bk. of Austlsia., 169; West. Aust. B., 12; Com. B. of Sydney, 69.

Germanton.—Com. B. Co. of Sydney,69

Germiston.—Stand. Bk. of Africa, 203; African B. Corp., 1A.; Nat. Bk., 173A.

Gerringong.—Eng., Scot. & Aust.B.,93

Ghent.—Bank of Ghent, 144.

Gibraltar.—Anglo-Egyptian, 9; Thos. Cook & Son, 73; T. Mosley & Co., 135.

Gisborne.—B. of N. Zealand, 24; Un. B. of Australia, 208; Bk. of New S. Wales, 23; Com. B. of Aust., 70; Bank of Australasia, 16.

Glace Bay.—Un. of Halifax, 144.

Gladstone (*S.A.*).—Nat. Bk. Aust., 169.

Gladstone (*Qnsld.*).—Aust. Jt. Stk.,13; Com. Bk. of Sydney, 69.

Glenboro.—Un. B. of Canada, 177.

Glen Innes.—Aust. Jt. St. B., 13; B. of N. S. W., 23; Com. B. C. of Sydney 69.

Goderich (*Ont.*).—Bk. of Montreal, 22; Bank of Commerce, 26.

Goondiwindi (*Qnsld.*).—B.of N.S.W.,23.

Gordon (*Vic.*).—Lon. B. of Aust., 147.

Gore (*N.Z.*).—Un. B. of Australasia, 16; B. of N. Z., 24; B. of N. S. Wales, 23.

Gormanston.—Nat. B. of Tas., 18.

Gorz.—M. Vervega, 177.

Gosford.—Com. B. of Sydney, 69.

Gotha.—B.M. Strupp.

Gothenburg.—Scand. Cred. Co., 175; Aktiebolaget, Köpmans Bank, 209.

Göttingen.—Klettwig & Reibstein

Goulburn (*N. S. W.*).—Australian Jt. St. B., 13 B. of N. S. Wales, 23; Com B. of Sydney, 69; Eng., Scot., & Aust B., 93; Lon. B. of Aust., 147; Bk. of Australasia, 16.

Graaf Reinet.—Std. B. of S.Africa, 203 : African Bkg. Corp., 1A.

Grafton.—Com. B. Co. of Sydney, 69 ; B. of N.S.W., 23 ; Australian Jt. St., 13 ; Eng., Scot. & Aust. B., 93.

Grahamstown (*S. Africa*).—Stand. Bk. of S. Afr., 203; B. of Afr., 15; African Bkg. Corp., 1A.

Granada.—B. of Spain, 191.

Grand Canary.—Bk. of Brit. W. Africa.

Granville.—Soc. Générale, 202.

Granville (*N. S. W.*).—Com. Bk. Co. of Sydney, 69.

Grass.—Crédit Lyon., 77.

Gritz.—Steirmärkische Escompte

Gray (*France*).—Soc. Gén., 202 ; Créd. Lyon., 77.

Greenock.—B. of Adelaide, 12.

Greenwood (*B.C.*).—Bk. B. N. Amer., 18.

Grenada.—Colonial Bank, 65.

Grenfell.—B. of N. S. W., 23; Aus. Jt. St. B. 13;B.ofAust., 16; Un. B.of Aust.,208.

Grenoble.—Créd.Lyon.,77;Soc.Gén.,202.

Grenville (*Grenada*).—Colon. B., 65.

Gretna.—Un. B. of Canada, 177.

Greymouth.—B. of N. S. Wales, 23; B. of N. Zealand, 24; Nat. B. of N. Zealand, 172 ; Un. B. of Aus., 208.

Greytown (*S. Afr.*).—Stan. B.S. Afr.,203.

Greytown (*N.Z.*).—B. of N. Zealand, 24.

Grimsby (*Can.*).—B. of Hamilton, 175.

Guadalajara.—Lon. B. of Mexico, 145; Banco Nacional de Mexico, 100.

Guanajuato.—Lon. B. of Mexico, 145.

Guatemala.—B. de Guatemala, 77.

Guayaquil.—Lond. B. of Mexico, 145.

Guaymas.—London B. of Mexico, 145.

Guelph (*Ont.*).—B. of Montreal, 22; Bk. of Commerce, 26; Dominion Bk., 173; Traders' Bk., 173.

Guingamp.—Soc. Générale, 202.

Gulgong.—Australian Joint Stock, 13; Bk. of N. South Wales, 23.

Gumeracha.—Bank of Adelaide, 12.

Gundagai.—Com. B. Co. of Sydney, 69; B. of N. S. W., 23; Aust. Jt. St.B.,13.

Gunnedah.—Bk. of New S. Wales, 23 Commercial Bk. Co. of Sydney, 69.

Gunning.—Com. Bk. Co. of Sydney, 69.

Gwelo.—Stand. Bk. S. Africa, 203.

Gympie (Queensland).—B. of N. S. Wales, 23; Queensld. Nat. B., 184; Austral. Jt. Stock, 13; Union B. of Aust., 208; Roy. Bk. of Queensld.,192.

Prague, The. Schoeller & Sons, 75; P. J. Landau, 176.

alcombe.—Bk. of New Zealand, 24.

Halifax (Nova Scotia).—Bk. of Brit. N. America, 18; B. of Nova Scotia, 193; Merchants B., 26; People's B., 209; Union B. of Halifax, 44; Halifax B. Co., 177; Bk. of Montreal, 22.

Halifax (Q.).—Queensld. Nat. Bk., 184.

Halle-a.-S. Hallescher B. Verein, 118.

Hamburg.—Berenberg, Gossler & Co., 209; Verein Bank, 118; L. Behrens 118; Deutsche B., 81; H. C. Schmidt, 136; Hongkong B. Corp., 112; Dresdner Bank, 83; Lond. & Hanseatic,137.

Hamilton (N. Z.).—Bank of N. Z., 24.

Hamilton (Ont.).—B. of Hamilton, 175; B. of Montreal, 22; B. of Brit. North America, 18; Merchants' Bk. of Can., 60; Bank of Commerce, 26; Molson's Bank, 177; Traders' B., 173.

Hamilton (Victoria).—Bk. of Vict., 29; Nat. B. of Austlsia., 169; Col. B. of Aus.,148; Comml.Bk.of Australia,70.

Hamiota.—Un. B. of Canada, 177.

Hammond.—Bank of Adelaide, 12.

Hampden.—Bank of N. Zealand, 24.

Hankow.—Chartd. Bk. of India, 53; Hongkong and Shanghai B. Corp.,112.

Hanover.—Hannoversche Bank, 84; H. Bartels, 118; Dresdner Bank, 83.

Hanover (S. Africa).—St. B. of S. A., 203.

Harrismith.—Nat. B. Or. Free St. 203; Bk. of Africa, 15.

Harriston (Canada).—Standard B.,173.

Harrow.—Bank of Victoria, 29.

Hastings.—Bk. of New Zealand, 24; Un. B. of Aust., 208; B. of N.S.W., 23.

Hastings (Ont.).—Un. B. of Can., 177.

Havana.—Borjes & Co., 148; M. Falk & Co.,118.

Havre.—Crédit Havrais, 209; Crédit Lyonnais, 77; Société Générale, 202; Comptoir d'Escompte, 71.

Hawaii.—Yokohama Specie Bk., 225.

Hawera (N. Z.).—B. of New Zealand, 24; B. of Australasia, 16; B. of New S. Wales, 23.

Hawker.—Bank of Adelaide, 12.

Hawkesbury.—B. of Ottawa, 177.

Hawthorn.—Eng., S., & Aust. B., 93; Nat. B. of Australasia, 169; Com. B. of Aust., 70; B. of Victoria, 29.

Hay.—Australian Jt. St.,13; Union B. of Australia, 208; London B. of Australia, 147; Com. B. Co. of Sydney, 69; Bk. of New South Wales, 23.

Haymarket (Vic.).—Com. Bk. Aust., 70.

Hazebrouck.—Compt. Nat. d'Esc., 71.

Heathcote.—Bk. of Victoria, 29; Com. Bank of Australia, 70.

Heidelberg (Germ.).—Köster's Bank.

Heidelberg (Vic.).—Com. B.of Aust., 70.

Heidelberg (S. Af.)—Standard Bank of South Africa, 203; Natal B., 167; Natl. Bk., 173A.

Heilbron.—Nat. B. Orange Free St., 203.

Helena (Montana).—Merchants' Nat. Bank, 8; First Nat. Bank, 159.

Helsingborg.—Skanes Enskilda, 118.

Helsingfors (Finl.).—Forenings B., 84.

Henley (N. Z.).—B. of N. Z., 24.

Henty.—B. of N. S. Wales, 23.

Herberton.—Queens. Nat. B., 184; B. of Australasia, 16; B. of N. Queens., 27.

Heyfield (Vic.).—Bank of Victoria, 29.

Hillston (N.S.W.).—Aust.Jt.Stk.B., 13.

Hindmarsh (S. Aust.).—Nat. Bank of Australasia, 169; B. of Adelaide, 12.

Hiogo.—Hongkong & Shang. B. Cor., 112.

Hobart.—Bk. of Australasia, 16; Commercial Bk., 23; Un. Bk. of Aus., 208.

Hokitika.—B. of N. S. W., 23; B. of N. Z., 24; Nat. B. of N. Zeal., 172.

Homburg.—J. & W. Goldschmidt, 209.

Honfleur.—Société Générale, 202.

Hongkong.—Mercantile Bk. of Ind., 160; Chartered Bk. of India, &c., 53; Hongkong and Shanghai, 112; B. of China and Japan, 14; Nat. B. of China, 170; Yokohama Specie Bk., 225.

Honolulu.—First American Bank of Hawaii, 8; Bishop & Co., 8; Yokohama Specie, 225.

Hometown.—Com. of Aust. 70.

Hopetoun.—Stand B. of S. Africa, 203.

Horsham (Vict.).—Lond. B. of Austr. 147; Nat. Bk. of Australasia, 169; B. of Victoria, 29; Com. B. of Australia, 70; Col. B. of Australasia, 148.

Howlong.—Bank of Australasia, 16.

Hughenden.—Queensland Nat. Bk., 184; Bank of Australasia, 16; Bank of N. S. W. 23.

Humansdorp.—Stnd. B. S. Africa, 203.

Hunterville.—B. of N. Zealand, 24.

Hutt.—Bank of New Zealand, 24.

Hyderabad.—Bank of Bengal, 75.

Hyères.—English Bk., 175; Soc. Gén., 202; Créd. Lyon., 77.

Ica.—London B. of Mexico, 145.

Iloilo.—Char. Bk. of India, 53.

Indore.—Bk. of Bombay, 75.

Indwe.—Stand. Bk. S. Africa, 203.

Ingersoll.—Imprl. Bk., 132; Merch. B. of Canada, 60; Traders' B., 173.

Ingham.—Queensland Nat. Bank, 184; Com. B. of Sydney, 69.

Inglewood (N. of N. Zeald.., 24; B. of N. S. Wales, 23.

Inglewood (Victoria.—Bank of New S. Wales, 23; Bank of Victoria, 29.

Innsbruck.—M. Löwe, 209.

Interlaken.—Thos. Cook & Son, 73.

Invercargill (N. Z.).—Un. B. of Aust., 208; B. of N. S. W., 23; B. of N. Z., 24; Nat. Bk. of N. Z., 172; B. of Australasia, 16.

Inverell.—Com. B. Co. of Sydney, 69; Aust. Jt. St., 13; Bk. of N. S. W., 23.

Ipswich (Queensland).—B. of Australasia, 16; Aust. Jt. St. B., 13; Bk. of N.S.W., 23; Queensland Nat. B.,184; Roy. B. of Queensland, 192.

Iquique.—Tarapacá & Lond., 28; Bank of Chile, 98; Lon. B. of Mexico, 145.

Iroquois.—Un. B. of Canada, 177.

Isfahan.—Imp. B. of Persia, 116.

Isisford.—Queen's National B., 184.

Ismailia.—T. Cook & Son (Egypt), 73.

Issoire.—Créd. Lyon., 77.

Ithaca.—Roy. B. of Queensland, 192.

Jacksonville.—1st Nat. B.of Florida,75.

Jaffa.—Thos. Cook & Son, 73.

Jalapa.—Lond. B. of Mexico, 145.

Jamberoo.—Eng., Scot., & Aust. B., 93.

James Town (S. Aust.).—Nat. Bank of Australasia, 16; Un B. of Aust.,208.

Jamieson.—Col. B. of Australasia, 148.

Jansenville.—Stand. Bk. S. Africa, 203.

Jarnac.—Créd. Lyon., 77.

Jena.—Julius Elkan

J.parit.—Nat. Bk. of Aust., 169.

Jeppestown.—Natl. Bk., 173A.

Jerilderie (N. S. W.).—Bk. of Australasia, 16; Bk. of N. S. Wales, 23.

Jerusalem.—Thos. Cook & Sons, 73.

Johannesburg.—Bk. of Afr., 15; Stand. Bk. of S. Afr., 203; Af. Bkg. Corp.,1A; Natal B., 167; Robinson S. Af. B. 197; Natl. Bk., 173A.

Joliette(Can.).—Banq. d'Hochelaga, 60.

Jonee.—Union Bk. of Australia, 208 ; Bk. of N. S. Wales, 23.

Kadina.—Nat. B. of Australasia, 169; Union B. of Australia, 208.

Kaiapoi (N. Z.).—B. of N. Zeald., 24.

Kaikoura (N.Z.).—B. of N. Zeald., 24.

Kaitangata.—B. of N. Z., 24 ; Nat. B. of N. Z., 172.

Kalgoorlie.—W. Austral. Bk., 12; Bk. N. S. Wales, 23; Bk. of Australia,

16; Nat. Bk. of Aust., 169; Com. Bk. of Aust., 70; Un. Bk. of Aust., 208.

Kamloops.—Bk. of B. Columbia, 17.

Kandy (Ceylon).—Merc. Bk. of Ind., 160; Nat. Bnk of India, 177.

Kangaroo Valley.—Eng., Sc.,&Aus.,93.

Kaniva.—Com. Bank of Australia, 70; Bank of Victoria, 29.

Kanowna.—West Australian Bk., 12; Union Bk. of Aust., 208.

Kansas City (Mo.).—Nat. B.of Com., 8.

Kanonga.—Bank of N. Zealand, 24.

Kapunda.—B. of Adelaide, 12; Nat. Bank of Australasia, 169.

Karachi.—Bk. of Bombay, 75; W. Watson & Co., 217; Forbes, Forbes & Co. Ld., 96.

Karahissar, Imp. Ottoman, 117.

Kaslo (B. C.).—Bk. B. N. Amer., 18.

Katamatitet (Vict.)—B.of Austrlsia.,16.

Katoomba (N.S.W.).—Aust. Jt. St. B.,13.

Kelso (N. Z.).—B. of New Zealand, 24.

Kempsey.—Com. B. Co. of Sydney, 69; Australian Joint Stock, 13; Eng., Scot., and Australn. Bk., 93.

Kentville.—Bank of Nova Scotia, 193.

Kerang.—Nat. B. of Australasia, 169; B. of Vic., 29; Lon. B. of Aus., 147.

Kew (Vic.).—Eng., Scot., & Aust. B., 93; Nat. B. of Australasia, 169.

Kiama.—Eng., Sco., & Austral. Bk., 93; Com. Bankg. Co. of Sydney, 69; City Bank, Sydney, 148.

Kieff.—Russian Bank, 195.

Kiel.—Vereins Bank, 98.

Killarney.—Australia Jt. Stk. B., 13.

Kilmore.—B. of Victoria, 29; Col. B. of Australasia, 148.

Kimberley.—Stand. B. of S. Africa, 203; B. of Africa, 15; African Bkg. Corp.,

Kindolton.—Bk. of N. Zealand, 24.

Kincardine (Ont.).—Merchants' B., 60.

King Williamstown.—Stan. Bk. S. Af., 203; B. of Afr., 15; African Bkg. Corp., 1A.

Kingston (Jamaica).—Colonial B., 65.

Kingston (Ont.).—Bk. of Montreal, 22; Merchants' B. of Canada, 60; Bank of B. N. America, 18; Ont. Bk., 177.

Kingston (Vic.).—B. of Australasia, 16.

Klerksdorp (Transv.).—Standard B. of South Africa, 203; Natl. Bk., 173A.

Knysna (S. Afr.).—Std. B. of S. A., 203.

Kobi (Japan).—Yokohama Specie, 225; Chart. Bk. of India, 53; Nat. Bk. of China, 170.

Kogarah.—Bk. of Australia, 16.

Kokstad.—Stand. B. of S. Africa, 203.

Koniah.—Imperial Ottoman Bk., 117.

Kooringa (S. Aust.).—Bk. of Australasia, 16; Nat. Bk. of Austlsia., 169.

Koroit (Victoria).—Nat. B. of Australasia, 169; Col. B. of Australasia, 148.

Korongvale (Vic.).—B. of Austlsia., 16.

Korumburra.—Bk. of Australasia, 16; Nat. Bk. of Australasia, 169.

Kroonstad.—Bank of Africa, 15.

Krugersdorp (Trans.).—Stand. Bk. of South Africa, 203; Natl. Bk., 173A.

Kumara (N. Z.).—B. of N. Zea., 24.

Kurow.—Nat. B. of N. Z., 172.

Kurrachee.—Agra Bank, 1; National B. of India, 171.

Kwala Lumpor.—Ch. Bk. of India, 53.

Kyabram (Vict.).—Bk. of Victoria, 29; Com. Bk. of Australia, 70.

Kyneton (Victoria).—Bank of New S. Wales, 23; Nat. B. of Austlsia., 169; B. of Victoria, 29; Col. B. Aust., 148.

Lady Grey.—Stand. B. of S. Afr., 203.

Ladybrand.—Nat. Bk. Orange Free State, 203; Bk. of Africa, 15.

Ladysmith (Natal).—Natal B., 167; Stand. Bk. of S. Afr., 203.

Lagos.—Bk. of Brit. W. Africa.

Lagos (Mex.).—Lond. B. of Mexico,145.

Lahore.—Agra B., 1; B. of Bengal, 75; Punjab B.,68; Alliance B.of Simla,177.

Laidley.—Queensland Nat., 184; Roy. Bank of Queensland, 192.

Laigle.—Soc. Générale, 202.

Laingsburg.—St. Bk. S. Africa, 203.
Lancefield.—Com. B. of Australia, 70 ; Nat. Bank of Australasia, 169.
Landskrona.—Skanes Enskilda B., 118.
Larnaca (Cyprus).—Imp.Ottoman,117.
Latrobe (Tasmania).—B. of Australasia, 16; Com. Bk., 23.
Launceston (Tasmania).—Bk. of Australasia, 16 ; Commercial Bank, 23 ; Union B. of Aust., 208 ; Nat. B. of Tas., 63.
Laura.—Union B. of Aust., 208.
Lausanne.—B. Fédérale, 77 ; Thos. Cook & Son, 73 ; Galland & Co., 77.
Laval.—Société Gén., 202 ; Créd. Lyon., 77.
Laverton.—West Aust. Bk., 12.
Lawlers.—Union B. of Aust., 208.
Lawrence (N. Z.).—B. of N. Z., 24 ; Bk. N. S. Wales, 23.
Learmonth.—Nat. B. of Austlsin., 169.
Leesburg (Flo.).—County & State B.,199
Leeston (N. Z.).—B. of New Zeal., 24.
Lefroy (Tasmania).—Com. Bank, 23.
Leghorn.—C. Fremura, 209 ; Maccean & Co., 75.
Leichhardt.—Bank of Australasia, 16.
Leipsic.—Leipziger Bank,84 ; Knauth, Nachod, & Kühne, 177.
Leon.—London Bk. of Mexico, 145.
Leongatha (Vic.).—B. of Austrlsia., 16.
Leonora.—West Australia B., 12.
L'Epiphanie (Queb.).—B.Ville Marie 22
Lerdo.—London Bk. of Mexico, 145.
Lethbridge.—Bk. of Montreal, 24.
Levin.—Bk. of New Zealand, 24.
Levis (Queb.).—People Bk., 109.
Lewiston (U. S. A.).—Union Bk. of Aust., 208.
Leuuka (Fiji).—Bk. of New Zeal., 24
Libourne.—Compt. Nat. d'Esc., 71.
Liège.—De Sauvage, Vercour & Co.
Lijdenburg.—Nat. Bk., 173A.
Lille.—Soc. Gén., 202 ; Créd. Lyon., 77.
Lima.—Banco del Peru, 145.
Limasol (Cyprus).—Imp.Ottmn.B.,117.
Limoges.—Créd Lyon.,77; Soc.Gén.,202
Lindsay (Ont.).—B. of Montreal, 22 ; Ontario Bk., 177 ; Dominion B., 173.
Linton (Victoria).—B.of N.S.Wales,23
Lisbon.—Lond. & Brazil. B., 133 ; B. de Portugal, 135 ; W. P. Custance, 209.
Lisieux.—Société Générale, 202.
Lismore (N. S. W.).—B. of N. S. W., 23 ; Com. B. Co. of Syd., 69 ; Aust. Jt. St., 13 ; Eng., Scot. & Aust. Bk., 93.
Listowel (Canada).—B.ofHamilton,175.
Lithgow.—Com. B. Co. of Sydney, 69 ; Eng., Scot., & Aust. B., 93.
Liverpool (N. S. W.).—B.of N.S.W.23 ; Commercial Bkg. Co. of Sydney, 69.
Liverpool(Can.).—B.of Nova Scotia,193.
Lobethal.—Bk. of Adelaide, 12.
Lockeport (N.S.).—Halifax Bkg.Co.,177.
Lockhart.—Com. B. of Sydney, 69.
Lodève.—Société Générale, 202.
London (Ont.).—Merchants' B. of Can. 60; Bk. of B. N. America, 18 ; Bk. of Commerce, 26 ; Molson's B., 100; B. of Montreal, 22 ; Toronto B., 58.
Longreach.—Qnsld. Nat. B., 184; B. of N. S. W., 23 ; Com. Bk. of Sydney, 69; B. of Australia, 16.
Lorient.—Société Générale, 202.
Los Angeles (Cal.).—First Nt. B., 30 ; Los Angeles Nat. B., 209; S. Cal. Nat. B., 8.
Loudun.—Soc. Générale, 202.
Louisville.—Louisville Bnkg. Co., 159
Lourenço Marques.—See *Delagoa Bay.*
Louvires.—Soc. Générale, 202.
Lübeck.—Commercial Bank, 178.
Lucerne.—B. Fédérale, 77 ; Thos. Cook & Son, 73.
Lucknow.—B. of Bengal, 75; Delhi & Lon. B., 82 ; B. of Upper India, 209.
Lugano.—Swiss-Italian Bank
Lund.—Skanes Enskilda Bank, 118
Lunenburg (Can.).—Merchants' B. of Halifax, 26; Halifax B. Co., 177.
Lure.—Soc. Générale, 202.
Luxeuil.—Soc. Générale, 202.
Lydenburg (Transv.).—St. B. S. Africa, 203.

Lyell (N. Z.).—Nat. B. of New Zea..172
Lyons.—Hongkong and Shanghai B. Corp., 112 ; Comptoir d'Escompte,71: Crédit Lyonnais, 77 ; Société Générale, 202; Yokohama Specie, 215.

Lyttelton (N.Z.).—Bank of New Zealand, 24; Union B. of Australia, 208.
Macarthur.—Nat. B. of Australasia, 169
Mackay (Queensland).—Australian Jt. Stock, 13 ; Union Bank of Australia, 208 ; Comm. B. Co. of Sydney 69; Queensland National Bank, 184.
McLaren Vale.—B. of Adelaide, 12.
Maclean (N. S. W.).—B. of N.S. Wales, 23 ; Aust. J. St., 13 ; Comm. B. Co. of Sydney, 69.
Macon.—Soc.Gén., 202 ; Créd.Lyon.,77
Madeira.—Bk. of Portugal, 135.
Madras.—Agra Bank, 31 ; Arbuthnot & Co. 151 ; Merc. Bank of India, 160 ; Commer.& Land Mortgage Bank,177 Binny & Co., 105; Nat. Bk. of India 171 ; B.of Madras,21 ; Parry&Co.,178
Madrid.—A. Bayo, 209 ; Crédit Lyonnais, 77 ; Un. B. of Spain & Eng., 211; Thos. Cook & Son, 73.
Mafeking (Bechuana.)—St.B.of S.A. 203
Mafra.—Nat. Bk. of Australasia, 169
B. of Vic. 29; Com B. of Australia,70
Magog (Can.).—E. Townships B., 173.
Maitland (N.S.).—Merchants' Bk., 26.
Maitland (N. S. W.).—B. of Australasia 16 ; B. of N. S. W. 23 ; Com. B. Co. of Sydney, 69 ; Aust. Jt. St. Bk., 13 : Union of Aust., 208.
Maitland (S. A.).—Un. B. of Aust., 208.
Majorca.—Lond. Bk. of Aust., 147.
Majunga (Madag.).—Compt. Nat. d'Esc., 71.
Malaga.—Clemens & Co., 148.
Maldon (Victoria).—Bk. of New South Wales, 23 ; Bank of Victoria, 29 ; London Bank of Aust., 147.
Malmesbury(S.Afr).—Stand. B. of S A.,203; African Bkg. Corp., 11.
Malmö.—Skanes Enskilda Bank, 118
Malta.—J.Bell&Co., 209; Anglo-Egypt B.9; C. B. Eynaud & Co., 72; anglo-Maltese, 175 ; Coppini & Bro., 123 ; Thos. Cook & Son, 73.
Malvern (Vict.).—Eng., S. & Aust., 93 ; Nat. B. of Australasia, 169.
Mamers.—Soc. Générale, 202.
Manaia (N.Z.).—Bank of New Zealand 24 ; Bank of Australasia, 16.
Manakau.—B. of New Zealand, 24.
Manaos (Brazil).—B. de Manáos, 75.
Mandalay.—Nat. Bank of India, 171.
Manawuka.—Bank of N. Zea., 24.
Manila.—Hongkong and Shanghai B. Corp., 112 ; J. M. Tuason & Co., 209 ; Chartered Bank of India, 53.
Manilla.—Com. B. of Sydney, 69.
Manly.—Aust. Jt. Stk., 13.
Mannheim.—Koster's Bk. ; Dresdner Bk., 83.
Manonia.—Bank of Adelaide, 12.
Manoora.—Eng., Scot., & Aust. B., 93.
Manosque.—Compt. Nat. d'Esc., 71.
Mans(Le).—Soc. Gén.,202;Créd Lyon.,77.
Mansfield (Vic.).—Bank of New South Wales, 23 ; Col. B. of Austlsia., 148.
Mantes.—Soc. Générale, 202.
Maraisburg.—Stand. Bk. S. Af., 203.
Markham (Canada).—Standard B., 173.
Marmande.—Société Générale, 202.
Marrickville.—Bank of Australasia,16.
Marseilles.—Société Générale, 202 ; Comptoir d'Escompte,71;Créd.Lyon., 77 ; Thos. Cook & Son, 73 ; W. Watson & Co., 209.
Martinique.—Colonial Bank, 65.
Marton (New Zealand).—B. of Australasia, 16 ; Bk. of New Zealand, 24.
Maryborough (Queensland).—Bank of New South Wales, 23 ; Com. Bk. of Sydney, 69; Australian Jnt. Stk. 13 ; Union Bank of Australia, 208 ; Qnsld. Nat. B., 184; B.of Austlas., 16.
Maryborough (Vict.).—Lond. Bk. of

Aust., 147 ; B. of Victoria, 29 ; U. B. of Aust., 208.
Masterton (N.Z.).—B. of Austlas.,16: B. of N. Zeald., 24 ; B. of N.S. Wales, 23.
Matamoros.—Lond. Bk. of Mexico, 145.
Matatiele.—Stand. B. S. Africa, 203.
Mataura (N.Z.).—B. of N. Zeald., 24.
Matehuala.—Lond. Bk. of Mexico, 145.
Matosfontein.—African B. Corpn., 11A.
Maubeuge.—Soc. Générale, 202.
Mauritius.—See *Port Louis.*
Maynee (Saints).—G. L. Kayser 209.
Mazamet.—Compt. Nat. d'Esc., 71.
Mazatlan.—London B. of Mexico, 145.
Meaford (Ontario).—Molson's Bk., 177
Medan.—Char. Bk. of India, 53.
Meerut.—Bank of Upper India, 209.
Melbourne.—Bank of Australasia, 16: Eng., Scot., &c. Bk., 93 ; Bk. of N. S. W., 23 ; B. of Victoria, 29 ; Col. B. of Australasia, 148 ; London B. of Aust., 147; National Bk. of Australasia. 169; Union Bk., 208; B. of New Zeal., 24 ; Comptoir d'Escompte, 71; Com. Bk. of Australia, 70 ; Land Mortgage B. of Vict., 130 ; Thos. Cook & Son, 73; Laycock, Goodfellow, & Bell, 134.
Melrose.—Union B. of Aust., 208.
Melton.—Nat. B. of Aust ; 169.
Melun.—Soc. Générale, 202.
Memphis (U. S. A.).—Un. & Planters' Bk., 45.
Mentone.—Créd. Lyon., 77 ; Thos. Cook & Son, 73.
Mendoza.—London & River Plate, 140.
Menzies.—Bank of Austlsia., 16 ; West Aust. Bk., 12 ; Un Bk. of Aust., 208.
Merced.—Merced Savings Bank, 8.
Meriden(C.Amer).—Lond.B.ofMex.,145.
Merriwa (N. S. W.).—Aust. Jt. St., 13.
Mersina.—Imper Ottoman Bk., 117.
Meshed.—Imp. Bank of Persia, 116.
Messina.—Cailler, Walker & Co.
Metz.—Banque de Metz.
Meulan.—Soc. Générale, 202.
Meursault.—Soc. Générale, 202.
Mexico.—Lon. B. of Mex. & S. Am., 145 ; Nat. Bank of Mexico, 100.
Middleburg(Cape).—Stan.B.ofS.Af.,203
Middleburg (Trans.).—St. B. of S. A., 203 ; Nat. Bk., 173A.
Middleton (N.S.).—Com. B. of Windsor, 209.
Midhirst.—B. of New Zealand, 21.
Midland (Ont.).—Bk. B. N. Amer., 18.
Milan.—Vonwiller & Co., 209; Thos. Cook & Son, 73.
Mildura.—Nat. Bk. of Austlsia., 169.
Millar's Flat.—Bk. of New Zeald., 24.
Millau.—Soc. Générale, 202.
Millicent.—Eng., Sco. & Austln. B., 93 ; Union B. of Aust., 208.
Millthorpe.—B. of N. S. Wales, 23.
Milton(Canada).—B. of Hamilton, 175.
Milton (N. S. W.).—Com. B. Co. of Sydney, 69; Eng.,Scot., & Aust. Bank, 93.
Milton (N. Z.).—Nat. B. of N. Z., 172; B. of New Zeal., 24.
Minlaton (S. A.).—B. of Adelaide, 12.
Minneapolis(Minn.).—N.W.Nat.Bk.,40.
Minyip.—Col. B. of Australasia, 148 ; Com. B. of Australia, 70.
Mirboo North.—Bk. of Australasia, 16.
Mitchell (Ont.).—Merchants' B., 60.
Mittagong.—Com. B. Co. of Sydney, 69.
Moama (N. S. W.).—Bk. of N. S.W., 23.
Mobile (Alabama).—First Nat. Bk., 45.
Moissac.—Soc. Générale, 202.
Molong.—Australian Jt. stock Bank, 13 ; Commerc. Bk. Co. of Sydney, 69.
Molteno (Cape).—Bk. B. of S. Africa,203; African Banking Corporation, 11A.
Mombasa.—Nat. Bk. of India, 171.
Moncton (N. B.).—Bk. of Montreal, 22; Bk. of N. S., 193 ; Merchants' B., 26.
Mont de Marsan.—Compt. Nat. d'Esc., 71 ; Soc. Générale, 202.
Montague.—African Bkg. Corp., 1A.
Montargis.—Soc. Générale, 202.
Montauban.—Soc.Gén.,202;Créd.Ly.,77.
Monte Carlo.—Crédit Lyonnais, 77.

Montego Bay.—Colonial Bank, 65.
Montélimar.—Soc. Générale, 202.
Montereau.—Soc. Générale, 202.
Monterey.—London B. of Mexico, 145.
Monte Video.—Lndn. & River Plate B., 140; London and Brazilian, 133; British Bank of South America, 39; Anglo-Arg. Bk., 6.
Montlucon.—Société Générale, 202.
Montpellier.—Soc. Gén., 202; Crédit Lyon., 77; Compt. Nat. d'Esc., 71.
Montreal (Canada).—B. of Brit. N. Am., 18; Merc. B. of Can., 60; B. of Mont. 22; Ont. B., 177; Bk. of Toronto, 58; Union B., 177; Molson's B., 177; Quebec Bk., 26; B. of Commerce, 26; Banque Nationale, 173; D'Hochelaga, 60.
Montreux.—B. of Montreux, 144; Thos. Cook & Son 73.
Moonee Ponds.—Nat. B. of Aust., 169.
Booroia(S.Australia).—National Bank of Australasia, 169; U.B. of Aust.,208.
Mooroopna (Victoria).—B. of Australasia, 16; Com. Bk. of Australia, 70.
Morden (Manit.).—Un. B. of Can., 177
Moree (N. S. W.).—B. of N.S. Wales,23; Com. Bkg. Co. of Sydney, 69.
Moretia.—London Bk. of Mexico, 145.
Morlaix.—Soc. Générale, 202.
Mornington(Vict.).—Col. B.of Aust.,148.
Morpeth.—Com. B. Co. of Sydney, 69.
Morrisburg (Ontario).—Molson's, 177.
Mortlake.—Bank of Victoria, 29.
Moruya (N. S. W.).—Bank of New S. Wales, 23; Com. B. Co. of Australasia, 16.
Morwell (Vic.).—B. of Australasia, 16.
Moscow.—J. W. Junker & Co.; Volga Kama Com. B., 191; Russian B., 195.
Mosgiel (N. Z.).—National Bank of N. Zeald., 172; Bank of New Zeald., 24.
Moss Vale.—Com. Bkg. Co. of Sydney, 69; Eng., Scot., & Aust. Bk., 93.
Mossel Bay.—Stan. B. of S. Africa, 203
Motueka (N.Z.).—B. of N. Zeald., 24.
Moulins.—Créd.Lyon.,77; Soc.Gén., 202
Moulmein.—Bank of Bengal, 21, 75.
Mount Barker.—B. of Australasia, 16; Nat. B. of Australasia, 169.
Mount Forest (Can.)—Ontario Bk., 177
Mount Gambier.—Eng., Scot., & Australian Bk., 93; Nat. Bk. of Australasia, 169; Com. B. of Aust., 70; Un. Bk. of Aust., 208.
Mount Leonora.—Nat. B. of Aust., 169.
Mount Magnet.—West. Aust. Bk., 12.
Mount Malcolm.—Nat. Bk. of Aust., 169; West Aust. Bk., 12
Mount Morgan.—Queensland Nat., 184.
Mount Pleasant.—Bk. of Adelaide, 12.
Mount Torrens.—B. of Adelaide, 12.
Mudgee.—B. of N. S. Wales, 23; Aust. Jt. St., 13; Com. B. Co. of Sydney, 69.
Mulhouse (Alsace).—B. d'Alsace et Lorraine.
Munich.—Bayerische Handelsbk., 202; Deutsche B., 84.
Murchison.—Bk. of Victoria, 29; Com. Bank of Australia, 70.
Murraysburg.—Stand. B. of S. Af., 203
Murree.—Alliance Bank of Simla, 172.
Murrumburrah.—Commercial B. Co. of Sydney, 69.
Murrurundi.—Com. B. of Sydney, 69.
Murtoa.—Comm. Bk. of Australia, 70.
Murwillumbah.—Com. B. Co. of Sydney, 69; Aust. Joint Stock, 13.
Mussoorie.—Delhi & London B., 82; Mussoorie Bank, 209.
Muswellbrook.—Com. B. Co. of Sydney, 69; Bank of Australasia, 16.
Muttaburra.—Queen's Nat. B., 184.
Nagambie.—Com. Bk. of Australia, 70; Colonial Bank of Australasia, 148.
Nagasaki.—Hong Kong & Sh., 112; Yokohama Specie, 225.
Nagpore.—Bank of Bengal, 21, 75.
Nanaimo.—Bk. of Brit. Columbia, 17.
Nancy.—Soc. Gén., 202; Créd. Lyon., 77.
Nannine.—West Aust. B., 12
Nantes.—Société Générale, 202; Comp. d'Escompte, 71; Crédit Lyonnais, 77.

Napanee (Can.).—Merchants' Bk. of Canada, 60; Dominion Bk., 173.
Napier (N. Z.).—Union Bk. of Australia, 208; B. of N. Z., 24; Nat. B. of N. Z., 172; B. of Austlsia., 16; B. of N. S. W., 23.
Naples.—W. J. Turner & Co., 209; A. Auverny & Co., 118; Thos. Cook & Son, 73.
Varandera.—Aust. Joint Stock, 13; Commercial B. Co. of Sydney, 69; B. of N. S. W., 23.
Narbonne.—Créd. Lyon. 77; Soc. Gén., 202; Compt. Nat. d'Esc., 71.
Varrabri.—Com. B. Co. of Syd., 69; B. of Austlsia., 16; B. of N. S. W., 23.
Narracoorte.—Nat. B. of Austlsia., 169; Union Bk. of Aust, 203.
Narromine.—Com. B. of Sydney, 69.
Naseby (N.Z.).—B. of N. Z., 24; B. of N. S. W., 23.
Nathalia.—B. of Australasia, 16; Com. Bk. of Aust., 70; B. of Victoria, 29.
Natimuk.—Col. B. of Australasia, 148; Nat. B. of Australasia, 169.
Neepawa.—Un. B. of Canada, 177.
Neerim, South.—Com. of Aust., 70.
Nelson (B.C.).—B. of Brit. Columbia, 17; B. of Montreal, 22.
Nelson (N. Z.).—Union Bk. of Australia, 208; Bk. of N. Z., 24; Bk. of N. South Wales, 23; Nat. Bk.of N.Z.,172
Neuchatel.—Pury & Co.; Dupasquier & Co.
Neuilly-sur-Seine.—Soc. Générale, 202.
Nevada.—Citizen's Bank, 8.
Nevers.—Soc. Gén., 202; Cr. Lyon., 77.
New Denver.—B. of Montreal, 22.
New Glasgow (N. S.).—Nova Scotia Bank, 193; Halifax Bk., 167.
New Orleans.—Citizen's Bank, 148; Canal & Bankg. Co., 148; State Nat. Bank, 148; Hibernia Nat. Bk., 72; Compt. Nat. d'Escompte, 71.
New Plymouth (N. Z.).—B. of N. Z., 24; Nat. Bk. of N. Z., 172; Bk. of N. S. W., 23; Bk. of Australasia, 16.
New Westminster.—B. of Br. Columb., 17; B. of Montreal, 22.
New York.—Brown Brothers & Co.,45; B.of Brit. N.Amer., 18; Thos.Cook & Son 73; Hongkong & Shang., 112; Kelly, 72; Kessler, 190; Knauth, Nachod, & Kuhne, 177; Lond. & Brazilian Bk., 133; Maitland, Coppell & Co., 201; Merchants' Bank of Canada, 60; Bank of Montreal, 22; Yokohama Specie, 225; J. Munroe & Co., 33; Nat. B. of Commerce, 100; B. of N. Y., 209; Ninth Nat. Bk., 30; C. B. Richard & Co., 177; Wells, Fargo, & Co., 209; White & Co., 136; Winslow & Co., 100; Colonial Bank 65; Lond., Par., & Amer., 149; L. & R. Plate, 140; Lazard Bros., 131; African B. Corp., 1a; Baring, Magoun, & Co., 31; Blair & Co., 41.
Newcastle (Natal).—Standard Bank of South Africa, 203; Natal Bank, 167.
Newcastle (N.B.).—B. of Nova Scotia, 193; Merchants' Bk. of Halifax, 26.
Newcastle, (N. S. W.).—B. of Australasia, 16; B. of N. S. W., 23; Australian Jt. St. Bk.,13; Com. Bkg. Co. of Sydney, 69; Union Bk. of Australia, 208; Lon. B. of Australia, 147; Com. B. of Australia, 70; West. Aust. Bk., 12.
Newera Eliya.—Nat. B. of India, 171.
Newmarket.—Ontario Bank, 177.
Newport (Vict.).—Com. B. of Aust., 70
Newstead (Vict.).—B. of Aust.,169
Newton (Auckland).—Bk. of N. Z., 24; Nat. Bank of N. Zealand, 172.
Newton (Kansas).—Harvey Cnty. B.
Newtown (N.S.W.).—Bk. of Austlia.,16; Eng., Scot., & Aust., 93; Bk. of N.S. Wales, 23; Com. B. of Sydney, 69.
Ngaruawahia.—B. of New Zeal., 24.
Nhill (Victoria).—Bk. of Victoria, 29; Com. B. of Aus., 70; Nat. B. Aus.,169
Niagara (Ont.).—Impl. B. of Can., 132.

Nice.—Carlone & Co., 209; F. Crossa, 61; Société Générale, 202; Crédit Lyon., 77; Thos. Cook & Son, 73.
Nicolajeff.—Russian Bank, 195.
Nigel, Natal Bk., 167.
Nijni Novgorod.—Russian Bk., 195.
Nikosia (Cyprus).—Imp. Ottom. B.,117.
Nîmes.—Société Générale, 202; Crédit Lyonnais, 77; Compt. Nat. d'Esc., 71.
Niort.—Soc. Gén. 202; Créd. Lyon., 77.
Noarlunga.—B. of Adelaide, 12.
Nogent-sur-Marne.—Soc. Générale, 202
Normanton.—Queens. Nat. B., 184; B. of N. S. W., 23.
Norrkoping.—Scand. Cred. Co., 175.
Norseman.—West. Australia Bank, 12; Union Bk. of Aust., 203.
North Adelaide.—Nat. B. of Aust., 169.
North Carlton.—Eng., Sc., & Aus., 93;
North Sydney.—B. of Nova Scotia, 193.
Northam.—Nat. B. of Australasia, 169; West. Aust. Bk., 12.
Northcote (Vic.).—Nat. B. of Australasia, 169; Lon. B. of Aust., 147.
Norwich (Ont.).—Molson's Bk., 177.
Nowra (N.S.W.).—Eng., Scot., & Aust. B., 93; Com. Bkg. Co. of Syd., 69.
Numurkah.—B. of Australasia, 16; Com. of Australia, 70; B. of Vic., 29.
Nuremberg.—M.C. Huber, 100; Dresdner Bank, 83.
Nuriootpa.—Nat. B. of Austlsia, 169; Bk. of Adelaide, 12.
Nymagee.—Com. B. of Sydney, 69.
Nyngan.—Aust. Jt. Stk., 13; Com. Bkg. Co. of Sydney, 69.
Oakland (U. S. A.).—1st Nat. B., 149; Savings B., 8.
Oakleigh(Vict.).—Eng., Sc.&Aust.B.93.
Oamaru (N. Z.).—B. of N. Z., 24; Nat. B. of N. Z., 172; Union Bk. of Aust., 208; Bk. of N. S. W., 23.
Oatlands (Tas.).—Comm. B.ofTasm.,23.
Oaxaca.—London Bk. of Mexico, 145.
Oberon (N.S.W.).—Aust. Jt. Stk. Bk.,13.
Odessa.—Russian B.,195; Créd.Lyon,77
Ohinemuri (N. Z.).—B. of New Zea., 24.
Oloron.—Soc. Générale, 202.
Omeo (Vict.).—Col. B. of Australasia, 148; Com. B. of Australia, 70.
Onehunga.—Nat. Bk. of N. Z.; 172.
Ootacamund.—B. of Madras, 21; Agra Bk., 1.
Ophir.—Bk. of New Zealand, 24; Bank of New South Wales, 23.
Oporto.—B. Commercial do Porto; London and Brazilian Bk., 133; Merc. Bk., 209; Banco de Portugal, 135; J. W. Burmester, 75.
Opotiki (N. Z.).—Bk. of New Zea., 24.
Opunake (N. Z.).—B. of New Zeal., 24.
Oran.—Crédit Lyonnais, 77.
Orange (N.S.W.).—Bk. of New South Wales, 23; Com. B. Co. of Sydney, 69; Aust. Jt. Stk., 13; B. of Australasia, 16; Un. B. of Aust., 208.
Orangeville (Canada).—B.of Comm.,26.
Orbost.—Com. B. of Aust., 70.
Oregnik.—Nat.B.ofN.Z.,172; B N.Z.24.
Orillia (Canada).—Traders' Bk., 173; Dominion Bk., 173.
Orizaba.—Lond. B. of Mexico, 145.
Orleans.—S. Gén., 202; Créd. Lyon., 77.
Orroroo.—Nat. Bk. of Australasia, 169; Union B. of Aust., 208.
Orvieto.—Whitby & Co., 209.
Oshawa (Ont.).—Dominion B., 173.
Ostend.—Crédit Ostendais.
Otaki.—Bank of Australasia, 16.
Otautau.—B. of New Zeal., 24.
Ottawa (Ont.).—Bank of British N. America, 18; Bank of Montreal, 22; Quebec B., 26; Merchants' B., 60; Molson's Bk., 177; Union B., 177; Bk. of Ottawa, 177; Ontario Bk., 177; Bk. of Commerce, 26; Banque Nationale, 173.
Ouchak.—Imp. Ottoman Bank, 117.
Oudtshoorn (S. A rica).—Stan. Bk. S. Africa, 203; Bk. of Africa, 15.
Outram (N.Z.).—Bk. of Zealand, 24; Nat. B. of New Zealand, 172.

Owen Sound.—Molson's Bk., 177; Merchants' Bk. of Canada, 60.

Oxford (N. Z.).—B. of N. Zealand, 24

Oxford (Ont.).—B. of Nova Scot., 193.

Paarl (S. Afr.).—St. B. of S. Afr., 203; Bk. of Af., 15; Afrn. Bkg. Corp., 1A.

Pachuca.—Lond. B. of Mexico, 145.

Padua.—Banca Veneta, 77.

Paddington (N. S. W.).—Eng., S., & A., 93; Com. B. of Sydney, 69.

Paeroa.—Nat. B. of N. Z., 172.

Pahiatua.—B. of N. Zealand, 24.

Pakenham.—Com B. of Aust., 70.

Palermo.—W. B. Gardiner, 144.

Palmerston (Otago).—B.of N. Zeald.,24

Palmerston,N.(Wellington).—Union of Australia, 208; B. of Australasia, 16 ; B. of N. Z., 24.

Pambula.—Aust. Joint St. Bank, 13.

Panniers.—Soc. Generale, 202.

Panama.—London B. of Mexico, 145.

Pará (Brazil).—L. & Brazil. B., 133; Comm. B. of Para, 209; B.of Para.,177; Brit. Bk. of S. America, 39 ; L. & R. Plate, 140.

Paris.—Anglo-Egyptian B., 9; Comptr. d'Esc., 71; Imp. Ottoman B., 117; Mallet Bros., 75; André, Neuflize, & Co.,148; Soc.Gén., 202; Soc.Ottomane, 206; Créd. Lyon., 77 ; Munroe & Co., 3; Demachy & F. Seillière, 75 ; Thos. Cook & Son, 23; Lond. and B. Plate B., 140; Russian Bk., 195; Lond.,Par., & Amer.,131; Robinson S.Afr.B., 197; Lazard Brs. & Co., 131 ; Nat. Bk. S. A. R., 173A ; Bk. of Roumania, 25 ; Jordaan, Conen & W., 101 ; Eugène Chartier, 131.

Paris (Canada).—Bk. of Commerce, 26.

Parkdale (Ont.).—St. B. of Canada, 173.

Parkes.—Comm. B. Co. of Sydney, 69; Australian Joint Stock Bank, 13 ; U.B.of Aus.,208 ; Bk.of Austlasia.,16.

Parramatta.—Bk. of N. S. Wales, 23 ; Com. B. Co. of Sydney, 69 ; Aus. Jt. St. B., 13.

Parrsboro (Canada).—Halifax B., 177.

Pasadena.—San Gabriel Valley Bk., 8.

Patea (N.Zealand).—B.of Australasia, 16 ; B. of N. Z., 24 ; B. of N. S.W., 23.

Paterson.—Com. B. Co. of Sydney, 69.

Patna.—Bank of Bengal, 21, 75.

Patras.—Ionian B., 119.

Pau.—English B., 209 ; Soc. Gén., 202.

Paysandu.—Lond. and R. Plate, 140.

Pearston.—Stand. Bk. S. Africa, 203.

Peking.—Hongkong & Shanghai, 112.

Pelotas.—London & Brazilian B., 133.

Pembroke (Canada).—B. of Ottawa, 177, Quebec Bank, 26.

Penang.—Merc. Bk. of India, 160 ; Ch. B. of India, Aust., & China, 53; Hongkong & Shang., 112; Bank of India and Japan, 14.

Penola.—Nat. Bk. of Australasia, 169.

Penrith.—Com. B. Co. of Sydney, 69 ; Bk. of N. S. W., 23.

Penshurst.—Bank of Victoria, 29; Nat Bank of Australasia, 169.

Pera.—Imp. Ottoman Bank, 117.

Perigueux.—Société Générale, 202; Credit Lyonnais, 77; Compt. Nat.,71.

Pernambuco.—London and Brazilian Bank, 133 ; B. of Pernambuco, 135 Lond. & R. Plate, 140.

Perpignan.—Société Générale, 202 Credit Lyonnais, 77; Compt. Nat.,71.

Perth (Ont.).—Merch. Canada, 60 ; Bk. of Montreal, 22.

Perth (W. Aust.).—Un. B. of Aust., 208 Western Aust. Bk., 12 ; Nat. Bk. of Australasia, 169 ; Bk. of N. S. W., 23 ; Com.B.of Aus.,70; B. of Austlsia., 16.

Pertuis.—Soc. Générale, 202.

Perugia.—Whitby & Co., 209.

Peterboro' (Ont.).—Ontario Bk., 177 Bk. of Montreal, 22; Bk. of Toronto, 58; Bank of Commerce, 26.

Petersburg (S.Aust.).—E.,S., & A.B.,93.

Petersham.—Bank of Australasia, 16.

Petone.—B. of N. Zealand, 24.

Pezenas.—Soc. Générale, 202.

Philadelphia.—Brown Bros. & Co., 45; Thos. Cook & Son, 73; Centenn. Nat. B., 136; Johnson & Co., 75 ; J. M. Shoemaker & Co., 159; Dunn Bros., 209; Bank of Brit. N. Amer., 18.

Philippopolis.—Imp. Ottom. Bk., 117.

Picton (N.S.W.).—Com. B. of Syd., 69

Picton (N. Z.).—Bk. of New Zeal., 24

Picton (Ontario).—B. of Montreal, 22.

Picton.—Nova Scotia Bk., 193 ; Merch. of Halifax, 26.

Pietermaritzburg.—Stan. B. S. Africa, 203; Natal B., 107 ; Bk. of Africa, 15.

Pietersburg (S.A.R.).—Natal Bk., 107 ; Nat. Bk., 173A.

Piet-Retief.—Natl. Bk., 173A.

Pilgrim's Rest.—Nat. Bk., 173A.

Pilsen.—Böhmische Escpte. Bk., 209.

Pisa.—Whitby & Co., 209.

Pisagua.—B. of Tarapaca & Lond., 28.

Pitfield.—Com. Bk. of Aust., 70.

Pittsburgh(Pa).—Tradesm. Nat. B.,58.

Pittsworth.—Queensland Nat. B., 184; Un. Bank of Australia, 208.

Piura.—London Bank of Mexico and S. America, 145

Poitiers.—Soc.Gen.,202; Créd.Lyon.,77.

Pont Audemer.—Soc. Générale, 202.

Pontoise.—Soc. Générale, 202.

Poona.—Bank of Bombay, 72.

Port Adelaide (So. Aust.).—Union Bk. of Aust., 208 ; B. of Australasia, 16 ; Nat. B. of Australasia, 169 ; B. of Adelaide, 12 ; B. of N. S. Wales, 23; Com. B. of Aust., 70.

Port Arthur.—Ontario Bank, 177.

Port-au-Prince.—Otto Bieber & Co., 169; Bk. of Adelaide, 12.

Port Augusta.—Nat. B. of Australasia, 169; Bk. of Adelaide, 12.

Port Chalmers(N.Z.).—Nat. Bank of New Zealand, 172; Bk. of N. Z., 24.

Port Colborne (Canada).—Imp.Bk.132.

Port Darwin.—Eng., Scot. & Aust., 93; Com. Bank of Aust., 70.

Port Douglas.—QueenslandNat.B.,184.

Port Elgin (Can.).—B.of Hamilton,175.

Port Elizabeth.—St. B. South Africa, 203; Bank of Africa, 15; African Bkg. Corp., 1A ; Nat. Bk., 173A.

Port Fairy.—Bk. of Victoria, 29; Bk. of Australasia, 16.

Port Germein.—Nat. Bk. Australia, 169.

Port Hope.—Toronto Bk., 58 ; Traders' Bank, 173.

Port Lincoln.—Bk. of Australasia, 16.

Port Louis (Mauritius).—Commercial B., 132; B. of Mauritius, 19.

Port Macquarie.—B. N. S. Wales, 23 ; Comm. Bkg. Co. of Sydney, 69.

Port Melbourne.—Nat. B. of Australasia, 169; Bk. of Australasia, 16.

Port Pirie (S. Australia).—Nat. Bk. of Australasia, 169 ; Bank of Adelaide, 12; B. of Austlsia., 16; Un. B. of Aust., 208.

Port Said.—Imp. Ottoman B., 117 ; B. of Egypt, 20 ; Créd. Lyonnais, 77 ; W. Watson & Co., 217; T. Cook & Son (Egypt), 73.

Port St. John.—S and. B. of South Africa, 203.

Port Victor.—Union B. of Aust., 208

Port Wakefield.—Nat. B. Austlas., 169.

Portage la Prairie.—Imperial Bk.,132.

Portld. (Maine).—First Nat. B., 159.

Portland (Oregon).—Bank of British Columbia, 17 ; Ladd & Tilton, 159 London & San Francisco, 141.

Portland (Victoria).—Un. B. of Aust., 208 ; B. of Vict., 29.

Porto Alegre.—Lond.& Brazil. Bk.,133.

Potchefstroom.—Stand.Bk.of S.Af.203; Nat. Bank, 173A.

Prague.—Oesterreich. Credit Anstalt, 209; Moritz Zdekauer, 209 ; Anglo-Austrian B., 7; Böhmische Escompte Bank, 209.

Prahran (Vict.).—Nat. B. of Austlsia. 169; B.of Vic.,29; Com.B. of Aus.,70; Bk. of Australasia, 16.

Prescott (Ont.).—Merchants' Bank of Canada, 60.

Prescott (Ariz.).—Bank of Arizona, 8.

Pretoria (Transvl.).—St. Bk. of South Africa, 203; Bank of Africa, 15; Natal Bank, 107; African Bkg. Corp., 1A ; National Bank, 173A.

Providence (R.I.).—First Nat. Bk., 45.

Puebla.—Lond. B. of Mex.& S.Am.,145.

Puerto Gallegos.—Tarapaca & Lon., 28.

Punta Arenas.—Tarapaca & Lond., 28.

Pury (Le).—Société Générale, 202.

Pyramid Hill.—Nat. B. of Aust., 169.

Pyrmont(N.S.W.).—Eng.,Scot.,& Aus. Bank, 93.

Queanbeyan.—Bank of New S. Wales, 23 ; Com. Bkg. Co. of Sydney, 69.

Quebec.—Bk. of British N. America, 18; Bk. of Montreal, 22; Quebec Bk., 26; D'Hochelaga, 60; Un. Bk. of Canada, 177; Banque Nat., 173; Merchants' Bk. of Canada, 60.

Queenscliff (Vic.).—Bank of Victoria, 29.

Queenstown (N. Z.).—B. of N. Z., 24.

Queenstown (S. Africa).—St. B. of S. Africa, 203; B. of Africa, 15 ; African Bkg. Corp., 1A.

Queenstown (Tas.).—Nat. B. of Tas., 69.

Queretaro.—London B. of Mexico, 145.

Quimper.—Soc. Générale, 202.

Quirindi.—Com. B. Co. of Sydney, 69; Aust. Joint Stock Bank, 13.

Quito.—Com. Bk. of Agriculture.

Quorn.—Nat. B. of Australasia, 169 ; Bk. of Adelaide, 12.

Rakaia (N.Z.).—B. of New Zealand, 24.

Randfontein.—Natl. Bk., 173A.

Randwick (N.S. W.).—Aust. Jt. St., 13.

Rangiora (N.Z.).—B. of New Zealand, 24; Union Bank of Australia, 208.

Rangoon.—Thos. Cook & Son, 73; Ch. B. of India, Aust., & China. 53 ; Bk. of Bengal, 75 ; Nat. B. of India, 171; Hongkong & Shang., 112 ; Agra B., 1.

Ratisbon.—Haymann & Co.

Rat Portage.—B. of Ottawa, 177.

Ravenswood (Queensland).—Queensland Nat., 184.

Rawa. Piadi.—Alliance B.of Simla,177.

Raymond Terrace.—Australian J.S.,13; Com. B. Co. of Sydney, 69.

Redfern.—Com. B. of Sydney, 69.

Red Hill.—Nat. Bank of Austlsia., 169.

Reefton (N.Z.).—Bk. of New Zeal., 24 ; Nat. Bank of New Zealand, 172.

Regina (N.W.T.).—B. of Montreal, 22.

Renfrew (Canada).—Merchts'. B. 60.

Rennes.—Soc.Gén.,202; CréditLyon.,77.

Resht.—Imp. Bank of Persia, 116.

Revelstoke.—Impl. B. of Canada, 132.

Rheims.—Soc. Gén.,202; Créd. Lyon.,77.

Richmond (Canada).—Eastern Townships Bank, 173.

Richmond (Indiana).—FirstNat. B.,155.

Richmond (N. S. W.).—B. of New S. Wales, 23; Com. B. Co. of Sydney, 69; Aust. Joint Stock Bank, 13.

Richmond (S.Afr.).—St.B.of S.Afr.203.

Richmond (Vic.).—B. of N. S. W., 23 ; Eng., Scot. & Aust. Bank, 93; Nat. B. of Aus., 169.

Ridgetown (Ontario).—Molson's B., 177.

Riga.—Jacobs & Co.; Hill Bros.

Rio de Janeiro.—London & Brazilian B., 133; Brit. B. of S. Amer., 39; Com. B., 135; Banco do Commercio, 58; London & River Plate, 140.

Rio Grande do Sul.—Lon.& Braz.B.,133.

Riverdale(S.Afr.).—St.B.of S.Afr.,203

Riverton (N.Z.).—B. of N. Zealand, 24 ; Nat. Bank of New Zealand, 172.

Riverton (S.A.).—Nat. B. of Australasia, 169; Eng., Scot., & Aust., 93.

Roanne.—Soc. Gén., 202; Créd. Lyon.,77.

Robertson(S.A.).—Stand.B.S. Africa,203

Robertson (N.S.W.).—Com. Bkg. Co. of Sydney, 69.

Rochefort-sur-Mer.—Soc. Générale, 202.

Roche-sur-Yon (La).—Soc. Gén., 202.

Rochelle (La).—Société Générale, 202 ; Créd. Lyon., 77.

Rochester (N. Y.).—Powers' Bank, 177.

Rochester (Victoria).—Bank of New S. Wales, 23; Union B. of Aust., 208.

Rockhampton.—Queensland Nat. Bk., 184; Union B. of Australia, 203; Australian Jt. Stk. Bk., 13; Bk. of Australasia, 16; Bk. of N. S. Wales, 23; Com. B. Co. of Sydney, 69; Bk. of N. Queensland, 27; Royal Bank of Queensland, 192.

Rockley (N.S.W.).—Austr. Jt.Stk.B.,13.

Rodez.—Société Générale, 202.

Roebourne (Aust.).—Un.B.of Aust.,208.

Rokewood.—Com. of Aust., 70.

Roma.—Qnslnd. Nat. Bk.,184; B.of N. S. Wales, 23; B. of Australasia, 16.

Romans.—Crédit Lyonnais, 77

Rome.—Plowden & Co., 209; Vansittart & Co., 77; Thos. Cook & Son, 73; Alexander R. Franz, 75.

Romsey (Victoria).—Nat. B. of Australasia, 169; Com. Bk. of Australia, 70.

Rongotea.—Bk. N. Zea., 24.

Roodepoort.—National Bank, 173A.

Rosario (Arg.).—Lon. & Riv. Plate, 140; Lon. & Braz., 133.

Rosario S. Fé.—Brit.B.of S. Amer.,39.

Rosedale—Bank of Australasia, 16.

Ross (N.Z.).—Bk. of New Zealand, 24.

Rossland (B.C.).—Bk. of B. N. America, 18; Bk. of Montreal, 22; Bk. of B.C. 17.

Rostock.—Edward Burchard, 209

Rotterdam.—B. of Rotterdam, 209; De Wissel en Effecten Bank, 38; The Handels Bank, 181.

Roubaix.—Soc. Gén., 202; Créd. Lyon., 77; Compt. Nat. d'Escompte, 71.

Rouen.—H. Pécuchet & Co.; Soc. Gén., 202; Créd. Lyon., 77; Compt. Nat. d'Escompte, 71.

Rozburgh (N.Z.).—Bk. of N. Zland., 24.

Rozelle.—Eng., Scot., & Aust. Bk., 93; Bk. N. S. Wales, 23.

Ruffec.—Compt. Nat. d'Escompte, 71; Soc. Gén. 202.

Rupanyup.—Com. B. of Australia, 70; Union B. of Aust., 208.

Rushworth.—Bk. of Victoria, 29; Com. Bk. of Aust., 70.

Rustchuk.—Imp. Ottoman Bk., 117.

Rustenburg.—Nat. Bk., 173A.

Rutherglen.—Bank of Victoria, 29; B. of Aust., 16

Ryde(N.S. W.).—Bk. of N. S. Wales, 23.

Rylstone.—Australian Jt. Stk. Bk., 13.

Sackville.—Hanf'x B. Co., 177.

Sacramento.—Calif. State Bk., 8.

Saddleworth.—Eng., Scot. & Aus., 93.

Saigon.—Hongkong Bkg. Corp., 112.

St. Andrews.—B. of Nova Scotia, 193.

St. Arnaud (Vic.).—B.of N.S.W.,23;B. of Vic., 29; Col. Bk. of Australasia, 148; London B. of Aust., 147.

St. Augustine.—T. Cook & Son, 73.

St. Bathans.—Bk. of New S. Wales,23; Bank of New Zealand, 24.

St. Brieuc.—Société Générale, 202.

St. Catharine's.—B. of Com., 26; Imprl. B. of Canada, 132; B. of Toronto, 58.

St. Chaumond.—Créd. Lyon., 77; Compt. Nat. d'Escompte, 71; Soc. Gén., 202.

St. Croix (W.I.).—Colonial Bank, 65.

St. Denis.—Soc.Gén.,202; Cred.Lyon,77

St. Dié.—Soc. Géne.,202; Compt.Nat.71

St. Dizier.—Crédit Lyonnais, 77.

St. Étienne.—Société Générale, 202; Crédit Lyonnais, 77; Compt. Nat., 71.

St. Fernando.—Colonial Bank, 65.

St. Galle.—B. Suisse de l'Un., 209; Swiss Bankverein, 205.

St. Gaudens.—Société Générale, 202.

St. George.—Bk. of N. S. Wales, 23.

St. Germain-en-Laye.—Société Générale, 202; Crédit Lyonnais, 77

St. Hyacinthe (Queo.).—B. Nacle., 173.

St. James (Vic.).—Bank of Australasia, 16; Nat. Bk. of Australasia, 169.

St. Jean D'Angely.—Soc. Générale, 202.

St.John(New Brunswick).—B. of Brit.N. America, 18; B. of N. Brunswick, 223; Bk. of Nova Scotia, 193; B. of Montreal, 22; Halifax Bg. Co., 177.

St. John's(Newfdld).—B.of Montreal,22.

St. John's (Quebec).—Merchants' B., 60.

St. Kilda (Vict.).—Com. B.of Australia, 70; Col. Bk. of Australasia, 148; Nat. Bk. of Austlsia., 169; Bk. of Aust.,16.

St. Kitts—Colonial Bk., 65.

St. Leonards.—Bk. N. S. Wales, 23.

St. Lô.—Société Générale, 202.

St. Louis (Missouri).—Nat. B. of Com., 8; Third Nat. Bk., 159; State Bk., 201

St. Loup-sur-Semouse.—Soc. Gén., 202

St. Lucia.—Colonial Bk., 65.

St. Malo.—Société Générale, 202.

St. Mary's (Ont.).—B. of Montreal, 22; Traders' Bank, 173.

St. Mary's N.S.W.—Aust. Jt. Stk. B., 13; Nat. B. of Tas., 68.

St. Nazaire.—Soc. Générale, 202.

St. Omer.—Deneuville & Co., 209.

St. Paul (Minn.).—Merch. Nat. Bk., 58; First Nat.B.,159; B.of Minnesota,159

St. Petersburg.—St. P. Disct.Bk., 209; Russian Bank, 195; Créd. Lyon., 77.

St. Quentin.—Société Générale, 202; Crédit Lyonnais, 77.

St. Servan.—A. O'Rorke, 144; Société Générale, 202.

St. Stephen (N. B.).—St. Stephen Bk. 100; Bank of Nova Scotia, 193.

St. Thomas.—Impl. B. of Canada, 132; Merchants' B. of Can., 60; Molson's Bank, 177.

St. Thomas (W. I.).—Colonial B., 65; Bk. of St. Thomas, 209.

St. Vincent.—Colonial Bank, 65.

Salamanca.—Banco de España, 191.

Sale (Vic.).—Bk. of Australasia, 16; B. of Vic., 29; Nat. B. of Australasia, 169; Comm. Bk. of Australia, 70.

Salisbury (South Africa).—St. Bk. of S. Africa, 203; Bank of Africa, 15; African Bkg. Corporation, 1A.

Salon.—Compt. Nat. d'Escompte, 71.

Salonica.—Imperial Ottoman Bk., 117.

Salt Lake City.—Deseret Nat. Bk.,152; Wells, Fargo, & Co., 209.

Saltillo.—Lond. Bk. of Mexico, 145.

Salzburg.—F. Berger; C. Spangler, 209.

Samsoun.—Imp. Ottoman Bk., 117.

San Antonio (Texas).—Lockwood Nat. Bank, 75.

San Bernardino.—B.of San Bern.,149; Farmers' Exch. B., 8.

San Francisco.—B.of Brit. N. America, 18; Bk. of Brit. Columbia, 17; L. & San Francisco, 141; Wells, Fargo, & Co., 209; B. of California, 191; Donohue, Kelly B. Co., 201; Hongkong & Shanghai B., 112; Canadian B'k of Commerce, 71; Anglo-Californian Bk., 8; Nevada Bk., 209; Lond., Paris, and Amer., 149; Yokohama Specie, 225; Thos. Cook & Son, 73.

San José.—Comm. & Savings Bk., 72; Safe Depos. B., 72; Un. Savings B., 8.

San Luis Obispo (Cal.).—County B., 8.

San Luis Potosi (Mex.).—Lon. B. of Mexico, 145

San Remo.—A. Rubino, 144.

San Sebastian.—Banco de España, 191.

Sandgate.—Queensland Nat., 184.

Sandhurst (Vict.). See Bendigo.

Sandon (B. C.).—Bk. of B. Columb.,17

Sarason (N. Z.).—B. of New Zealand, 24.

Santa Cruz(Cal.).—Bk. of Santa Cruz,8.

Santander.—Banco de España, 191.

Santiago.—Bk. of Chile, 58; L'n. Bk. of Mexico, 145; Tarapaca & London, 28.

Santos.—Brit. B. of S. Amer., 39; Lon. & Braz., 133; Merc. B., 209; London and River Plate, 140.

Sao Paulo.—Lon. & Brazil. Bank, 133; Brit. B. of S. Amer., 39; Lon. & R. Plate, 140.

Saragossa.—Villarova y Castellanos, 209.

Saratof.—Russian Bank, 195.

Sarlat.—Soc. Générale, 202.

Sarnia (Ont.).—Bk. of Montreal, 22; B. of Commerce, 26; Traders' B., 173.

Saumur.—Société Générale, 202.

Savannah (Geo.).—Southern Bank, 72

Sav-la-Mar.—Colonial Bk., 65.

Sceaux.—Société Générale, 202.

Schaffhausen.—Zundel & Co.

Schwalbach.—Bernhard Berlé & Co.,77.

Scone(N. S. W.).—B. of N. S. Wales, 23; Aust. Joint Stock Bank, 13

Seaforth (Can.).—Dominion Bk., 173.

Sea-Lake.—Com. B. of Aust., 70

Seattle (Wash.).—Dexter, Horton, & Co., 159; Boston Nat. B., 8.

Sedan.—Soc. Gén., 202; Créd. Lyon., 77.

Semur.—Société Générale, 202.

Sens.—Société Générale, 202.

Serajpunga.—Bank of Bengal, 21, 75.

Serena.—Bank or Chile, 58.

Seville.—Bank of Seville.

Sèvres.—Société Générale, 202.

Seymour.—Col. B. of Austral., 148; B. of Vic., 29

Shanghai.—Merc. Bank of India, 160; Hongkong & Shanghai B. Corp., 112; Chart. Bk. of India, Aust. & China; 53; Yokohama Specie, 225; Bk. of China and Japan, 14; National B. of China, 170.

Sheep Hills (Vic.).—Com. B.of Aus., 70.

Sheffield (Tas.).—B. of Australasia, 16; Nat. B. of Tas., 68

Shellharbour.—B. of Sydney, 69.

Shepparton (Vic.).—B. of Austlsia., 16; B. of Vic., 29; Nat. Bk. Austlsia., 169; Comm. Bank of Australia, 70.

Sherbrooke (Canada).—Eastern Townships B., 173; Banque Nationale 173; Merchants' Bk., 60; Un of Halifax, 144; D'Hochelaga, 209.

Shiras.—Imp. B. of Persia, 116

Sidi-Bel-Abbes.—Cred. Lyon., 77.

Siena (Italy).—Whitby & Co. 209.

Sierra Leone.—Bk. of Brit. W. Af.

Silao.—Lond. B. of Mexico, 145.

Simcoe (Canada).—Hamilton B., 175; Bank of Commerce, 26.

Simla.—Alliance Bank of Simla, 177; Delhi & London, 81.

Simons Town.—Stand. B. S. Afr., 203.

Singapore.—Merc. Bk. of India, 160; Hongkong & Shanghai B. Corp., 112; Chart. B. of Ind., Aus. & China, 53; B. of China & Japan, 11; Nat. Bk. of China, 170.

Singleton.—Com.B.of Sydney, 69; Aust. Jt. Stock B., 13; B. of N. S. W., 23.

Smeatoni(Vic.).—Nat.B.of Austlsia.,169.

Smith's Falls.—Un. of Canada, 177.

Smyrna.—Imp. Ottoman B.,117; Paterson & Co., 175; Crédit Lyonnais, 77.

Snowtown.—Eng., S. & Aust. Bk., 93.

Soissons.—Soc. Générale, 202.

Solsesberg.—Skanes Enskilda Bk., 118.

Somerset, East (S. Afr.).—Standard Bank of S. Africa, 203.

Somerset. West.—Stand. Bk. S. Af., 203.

Sorel (Canada).—Molson's B., 177.

Sourabaya.—Chart. B. of India, 53; Hongkong & Shanghai, 112

Souris.—Un. B. of Canada, 177.

Sousa (Tunis).—Compt. Nat. d'Esc.,71.

South Brisbane.—Queensland Nat. B. 184; Bk. of N. S. Wales, 23; Royal B. of Queensland, 192.

South Yarra.—Eng., Scot., & Aust., 93.

Southbridge (N. Z.).—Bk. N. Zeald., 24.

Southern Cross.—Com. Bk. Aust., 70; Western Australian Bk., 12.

Spa.—Henry Hayemal, 209.

Springs (S.A.R.).—Nat. Bk., 173A.

Stambout.—Imp. Ottoman Bk., 117.

Standerton (S.A.R.).—Nat. Bk., 173A.

Stanley (Tas.).—Nat. B. of Tas., 68.

Stanstead (Canada).—Eastern Townships Bank, 173.

Stanthorpe(Qnsld.).—Aust. Jt Stk.,13.

Stawell.—Un. B. of Aust., 208; Lon. B. of Aust., 147; B. of Australasia, 16.

Steamer Point (Aden).—Nat. Bank of India, 171.

Steiglitz.—Eng., Scot. & Aust., 93.

stellenbosch (S. Afr.)—St. B. S. Af., 203.

Sterkstroom.—Stand. B. of S. Af. 203.

Stettin.—Wm. Schlutow, 209.

Steynsburg.—Stand. Bk. S. Africa, 203

Stockholm. — Stockholm's Handels bank, 201; Scandinavian Credit Co. 175; Stockholm's Enskilda Bank, 144.

Stockton (Cal.).—Savings B., 8.

Strahan (Tas.)—Nat. B. of Tas., 68.

Strasburg.—Staehling, Valentin & Co.

Stratford (N.Z.).—Bk. of Australasia, 16; B. of N.Z.,24; Nat. B. of N.Z., 172.

Stratford (Ont.).—Bk. of Montreal, 22; Merchants' B., 60; Commerce, 26.

Stratford (Vict.).—Comm. B.or Aust.,70.

Strathalbyn.—Nat. B. of Austlas, 169.

Strathmerton.—Bk. of Austrlsa., 16.

Strathroy (Canada).—Commerce, 26.

Stroud (N.S.W.).—Bk. Australasia, 16.

Stuttgart.—Stahl & Federer, 209.

Summerhill.—Aust. Jt. S. B., 13.

Summerside (P. E. I.)—Merchants', of Halifax, 26; B. of N. Scotia, 193.

Surat.—Bk. of Bombay, 75.

Suva (Fiji).—Bk. of New Zealand, 24

Swan Hill (Vic.).—Nat. B. of Austlsia., 169; London Bank of Australia, 147.

Sweetendam(S.Afri.)—St. B.S. Afr., 203.

Sydney (C.B.).—Bk. B. N. Amer., 18.

Sydney (N. S. W.).—Australian Jt. St. B., 13; Bk. of Australasia, 16; B. of N. S. W., 23; City B., 148; Com. B. Co. of Sydney, 69; Eng., Scot., & Aus. Bank, 93; Lond. Bank of Aust., 147; Union Bank of Australia, 208; B. of N. Zea., 24; Queensld. Nat. B., 184; Compt. d'Escompte, 71; Com. B. of Aust. 70; Nat. Bk. of Australasia, 169; B. of N. Queensld., 27; Laycock, Goodfellow & Bell, 134; Thos. Cook & Son, 73.

Tabris.—Imp. B. of Persia, 116.

Tacna.—London Bank of Mexico, 145.

Tacoma.—Lond. & San Francisco, 144.

Talbot (Victoria). — London Bk. of Aust., 147; Bk. of Australasia, 16.

Talca.—Bank of Chile, 58.

Tallangatta.—Bk. of N. S. W., 23; Bk. of Australasia, 16.

Tamatave.—Comp. Nat. d'Escompte,71.

Tampico.—London B. of Mexico, 145.

Tamworth (N. S. W.).—B. of N. S. W., 23; Com. B. Co. of Sydney, 69; B. of Australasia,16; Aust. Joint Stock,13.

Tananarive.—Comp. d'Escompte, 71.

Tangier.—M. Pariente, 209.

Tanunda.—Eng.,Scot., & Aust. Bk., 93.

Tapanui (N. Z.).—B. of New Zealand, 24; Nat. Bk. of New Zealand, 172.

Taradale.—Nat. B. Aust., 169.

Taralga.—Bk. of N. S. W., 23.

Tarascon Beaucaire.—Soc. Gen., 202.

Tarbes.—Société Générale, 202.

Taree (N. S. W.).—Com. B. Co. of Syd., 69; B. of N. S. W., 23.

Tarkastad.—Stand. Bk. S. Africa, 203.

Tarles(S.Aus.)—Eng.,Scot.&Aust.,93

Tarnagulla.—Un.B. of Australia, 208.

Tarragona.—Carey Bros. & Co., 67.

Tatura (Victoria).—Com. Bk. of Australia, 70; Bank of Victoria, 29.

*Taurangα (N. Z.)—B. of New Z., 24.

Te Aro (N. Z.).—B. of New Zealand, 24; Nat. Bank of New Zealand, 172.

Te Awamutu.—Bk. of New Zeal., 24.

Teheran.—Imp. B. of Persia, 116.

Temora (N.S.W.).—Aust. Jt. St. B., 13. B. of N. S. W., 23; Un. B. Aust. 208.

Temuka (N.Z.).—Bk. of New Z., 24.

Teneriffe.—Bk. of Brit. W. Africa.

Tenerife(Santa Cruz).—Hamilton&Co.

Tenterfield.—Australian Joint St., 13; Bank of New South Wales, 23.

Tepic.—Lond. B. of Mexico, 145.

Teplitz.—Anglo-Austrian, 7.

Terang.—Col. B. of Australasia, 148; Bk. of Austria, 16; Bk. Victoria, 29.

Terowie.—Eng., Scott., & Aust., 93.

Thaiping.—On. Bk. of India, Aust., & China, 53.

Thames (N.Z.).—B. of N. Z., 24; B. of New South Wales, 23.

Thargomindah (Queensland).—Comm. Bkg. Co. of Sydney, 69; Q. Nat. B.,184.

Thiers.—Soc. Générale, 202.

Thornbury(N.Z.).—Nat. B. of N. Z.,172.

Thorold (Canada).—Bk. of Commerce, 26; Bank of Quebec, 26.

Three Rivers.—Bank of Quebec, 26 D'Hochelaga, 60.

Thursday Island.—Queensld. Nat.,184 B. of North Queensland, 27.

Tientsin.—Hongkong & Shang., 112 Chart. B. of India, &c., 53; Yokohama Specie, 225.

Tilsonburg (Canada).—Traders B., 26

Timaru (New Zealand).—Union B. of Australia, 208; B. of N. Z., 24; Nat. B. of N. Z., 172; B. of N. S. W., 23.

Tocumwal.—Com. B. Co. of Sydney, 69

Tokio.—Yokohama Specie, 225.

Toluca.—Lond. B. of Mexico, 145.

Tomsk.—Russian Bank, 195.

Toowoomba.—Aust. Jt.St., 13 Queensland Nat. B., 184; Un. B. of Aust. 208; Com. B. Co. of Sydney,69; Roy B. of Queensland, 192; Bk. N. S. Wales, 23; Bk. of Aust., 16.

Toronto.—B. N. Amer., 18; B. of Toronto, 48; B. of Montreal, 22; Traders' B., 173; Can. B. of Commerce, 26; Merchants' B., 60; Ontario B., 177; Quebec Bank, 26; Imperial B., 132; Domin. B., 173; Molson's B. 177; Standard, 173; Union B., 177.

Toulon.—Soc.Gen.,202; Créd. Lyon., 77

Toulouse.—Soc.Gén.,202;Créd.Lyon.,77. Compt. Nat. d'Escompte, 71.

Tourcoing. — Crédit Lyonnais, 77 Compt. Nat. d'Escompte, 71.

Tours.—Goüin Bros., 75; Soc. Gén., 202

Townsville (Queensland).—B.ofN.S.W. 23; Australian Jt. St., 13; Un. B. of Australia,208; Queensld. Nat. B.,184 B. of Australasia, 16; London B. of Aust., 147; B. of N. Queensland, 27; Com. of Sydney, 69.

Trail (B.C.).—Bk. B. N. Amer., 18.

Traralgon (Vic.).—B. of Austlsia., 16.

Trebizonde.—Imp. Ottoman Bk., 116.

Trentham (Vic.).—Nat. B. of Aust.,16;.

Treves.—Reverchon & Co.

Trieste.—Anglo-Austrian, 7.

Trinidad.—Colonial Bank, 65.

Trondhjem.—See Drontheim.

Trouville.—Comptoir Nat., 71.

Troyes.—Soc.Gén.,202; Créd. Lyon.,77

Trujillo.—L'don Bk. of Mexico, 145.

Truro (Nova Scotia).—Merchants' Bk. of Halifax, 26; Halifax Bg. Co., 177.

Truro (S.Aust.).—Bk. of Adelaide, 12.

Tulle.—Soc. Général., 202.

Tumut (N.S.W.).—B. of N. S. W., 23; Commercial Bkg. Co. of Sydney, 69.

Tingamah.—Col. B.o. Australasia,148 B. of Australasia, 16.

Tunis.—Compt. Nat. d'Escompte, 71.

Turin.—J. de Fernex & Co., 209.

Tuticorin.—Bank of Madras, 27; Nat. Bank of India, 171; Agra Bank, 1.

Uitenhage.—Stand. Bk. of S. Afr., 203.

Uleaborg.—Finlands Bank, 191.

Ulverston (Tas.).—B. of Australasia, 16; Com. Bank, 23.

Umballa.—Alliance Bk. of Simla, 177.

Umtata (S.A.)—Stan. B. of S. Africa 203; Af. Bkg. Corp., 12.

Unstad.—Stand. B. of S. Africa, 203; Bk. of Africa, 15.

Upsala.—Malare Enskilda Bk., 182.

Uralla.—B. of N. S. W., 23.

Urana.—Bk. of New South Wales, 23. *Utrecht.*—Vlaer & Kol.

Utrecht (S.A.R.).—Nat. Bk., 173a.

Uxbridge (Can.).—Dominion Bk., 173.

Vaidivia.—Bank of Chile, 58.

Valence.—Soc.Gén.202; Créd.Lyon.,77

Valencia.—Dart & Co., 209.

Valenciennes.—Société Générale, 202; Crédit Lyonnais, 77.

Valleyfield (Que.).—D'Hochelaga, 60

Valparaiso.—Bank of Chile, 58; A. Edwards & Co., 100; London Bank of Mexico,145; Tarapacá & Lond., 28.

Vancouver (B.C.). — Bk. of British Columbia, 17; Bk. of Montreal, 22 Bk. of B. N. A., 18; B. of Commerce

2; Comml. B., 8; Impl. Bk. of Canada, 132; Molson' Bk., 177.

Vannes.—Société Générale, 202.

Vegetable Creek.—Bk. of N. S. W., 23.

Venice.—S S A. Blumenthal & Co., 209; J S. h & Son, 73.

Vera Cruz.—London Bk. of Mexico, 145; Nat. B. of Mex., 100.

Vermon.—Soc. Generale, 202.

Vernon (B. C.).—Bk. of Montreal, 22.

Versailles.—Société Générale, 202.

Verwins.—Soc. Generale, 202.

Vesoul.—Soc. Générale, 202.

Viareggio.—Whitty Co., 209.

Vichy.—Soc. Gén., 202; Compt.Nat., 71.

Victoria(B.C.).—B. of Brit.N.America, 18; B. of Brit. Columbia, 17; B. of Montreal, 22 ;Merchants' of Halifax, 26 Molson's B., 177.

Victoria, West.—Stand. B. of S. Afr., 203

Vienna.—Anglo-Austrian Bank, 7; Aust. Crea. Anstalt, 209; B. of the Lower Austrian Escompts Co., 144; Societ-Autrichienne de Crédit, 144; Thos. Cook & Son, 73.

Vigo.—Banco de España, 191.

Villeneuve-sur-Lot. — Comptoir Nat. d'Esc., 71; Soc. Générale, 202.

Vincennes.—Société Générale, 202.

Violet Town.—Nat. B. of Austlsia, 169.

Virden.—Un. of Canada, 177.

Virginia (U.S.).—Nevada Bank of San Francisco, 209.

Vitoria.—Banco de España, 191.

Volksrust (S.A.R.).—Natal Bk., 167; National B., 173a.

Vryheid (Trans.).—Bank o 15; Nat. Bk., 173a.

Vryburg.—Stan. Bk. S. Africa, 203.

Waggu-Wagga.—B. of N. S. Wales, 23; Australian Jt. Stk., 13; Com. Bk. of Sydney, 69; Union B. of Aust., 208; Bk. of Australasia, 16.

Waikaia.—Nat. B. of N. Zealand, 172.

Waikouaiti (N.Z.).—B. of N. Zeal., 24.

Waimatei (N.Z.).—B. of New Zealand, 24; Union Bank of Australia, 208.

Waipawa (N. Zealand)—Bk. of Australasia, 16; B. of New Zealand, 24.

Waipukurau (N.Z.).—B. of N. Zeal., 24.

Waitahuna (N.Z.).—Bk. of N. Z., 24.

Waitara (N.Z.).—B. of N. Z., 24.

Wakkerstroom (S.A.R.).—Nat. B.,173a.

Walcha (N.S.W.).—Com. Sydney, 69.

Walgett (N.S.W.).—Com. B. Co. of Syd., 69; B. of N. S. W., 23; Australian Jt. Stock, 13.

Walhalla (Vict.).—B. of Austlsia., 16; B. of Victoria, 29.

Walkerton (Canada).—Merchants'B.60.

Walla Walla (Wash.).—Baker-Boyer Nat. Bk., 8.

Wallaceburg (Ont.).—Bk. of Montr...22.

Wallaroo.—B. of Australasia, 169.

Wallerawang.—Com. Bk.of Sydney, 69.

Wallsend (N.S.W.).—B. of Australasia, 16; Australian Jt. Stk. Bank, 13.

Wanganui (N. Z.).—B. of Australasia, 16; Bk. of N.S.W.,23; B. of N.Z.,24; Nat. Bk. of N. Z., 172.

Wangaratta (Vic.).—B. of N.S.W., 23; London Bk of Aust., 147 Nat. Bank of Australasia, 169.

*Waratah, Nat. B. of Tas., 68.

Warialda (N.S.W.).—B. of N. S. W., 23; Com. B. Co. of Sydney,69.

Warrackmabeal (Vic.). – Com Bk. of Aust., 70; Un. Bk. of Aust.,208.

Warragul (Victoria).—Bk. of Australasia, 16; Com. Bk. of Australia, 70 B. of N. S. W., 23; Lon. B.of Aus.,147.

Warren (N.S.W.).—Com. B.Co. of Syd., 69; B. of N. S. W., 23.

Warrnambool (Vic.).—Bk.of Austlsia, 16; Bk. of Vic., 29; Nat. B. of Austlsia.,169; Col. B. of Austlsia.,148; B. of N.S.W.,23; Cm. B. of Aus., 70.

Warsaw.—Disconto Bank; Bank o Poland.

Warwick (Queensland).—B. of N.S.W. 23; Qnsl. Nat. B., 184; Aus. Jt. S,. 13; Roy. B. of Queensland, 192.

Washington.—Lewis Johnson & Co.,45; Lon. & San Fran., 141.

Waterloo (Ont.).—Molson's Bank, 177.

Waterloo (Quebec).—E. Towns. B., 173.

Waverley (N.S.W.).—Eng.. Scot., & Aust. B., 93 ; B. of N. S. W., 23.

Waverly (N. Z.).—Bk. Australasia, 16.

Wedderburn (Vic.).—B. of Austlas., 16.

Wee Waa.—Com. B. Co. of Sydney, 69.

Weimar.—Julius Elkan ; Imperial Bank of Germany.

Welland (Canada).—Imperial Bk., 132.

Wellington (Cape).—St. B. of S. Africa, 203.

Wellington (N. S. W.).—Com. B. Co. of Sydney,69; Bk. of N. S. Wales, 23; Thos. Cook & Son, 73.

Wellington (N.Z.).—Union B. of Aust., 208 ; B. of N. Zeal., 24 ; Bk. of N.S.W. 23; Bk. of Australasia, 16 ; Nat. Bk. of N. Z., 172.

Wentworth (N.S.W.).—Aus.Jt. Stk.,13.

Werribee.—Com. Bk. of Aust., 70.

West Melbourne.—Eng. Scot. & Aust. 93 ; Bk. N. S. Wales, 23.

Westbury.—Com. Bk. of Tas., 23.

Westport (N.Z.).—Bk. of N. S. W., 23 ; B. of N. Z., 24.

Wexio.—Skanes Enskilda Bank, 118.

Whangarei.—Bk. of New Zealand, 24.

Whitby (Ontario).—Dominion Bk., 173.

Whitton (N.S.W.).—Aust. Jt. Stk. B., 13.

Wiborg.—Finlands Bank, 101.

Wickham (N.S.W.).—Aust.Jt.St.B.,13.

Wiesbaden.—Bernhard Berlé & Co., 77; Imper. Bk. of Germany.

Wilcannia (N.S.W.).—London Bk. of Aust., 147 ; Aust. Jt. Stk. Bk., 13 ; Com. B. Co. of Sydney, 69.

Williamstown (Vic.).—Com. B. of Aus., 70; Eng., Scot., & Austrl. Bk. 93 ; B. of Australasia, 16.

Willow (Cal.).—B. of Willow, 8.

Willowie.—Bk. of Adelaide, 12.

Willowmore (S. Af.).—Stand. Bk. S Af. 203.

Willunga.—Bk. of Adelaide, 12.

Wilmington (S. Aust.).—Nat. Bk. of Australasia, 169.

Winburg (S. Af.).—Bank of Africa, 15;

Windsor (N.S.W.).—B. of N. S. W., 23; Com. Bkg. Co. of Sydney, 69.

Windsor (N. Scotia).—Halifax B. Co., 177; Com. B. of Windsor, 209.

Windsor (Ont.).—Merchants' B., 60 ; B. of Com., 26 ; Traders' B., 173 ; Un B. of Canada, 1,7.

Windsor (Vict.).—Eng., Scot., & Aust Bk., 93.

Wingham.—Com. B. Co. of Sydney, 69.

Winnipeg.—Bk. of Montreal, 22 ; B. of Ottawa 177 Imp. Bk. of Can., 132 ; Un. B. of Can., 177; Merchants' Bk., 60 ; Bk. of Brit. N. Amer., 18; Banque D'Hochelaga, 60 ; Molson's Bk., 177 ; Dominion Bank, 173 ; Canadian B. of Commerce, 26 ; B. of Hamilton, 175 ; Alloway & Champion, 30.

Winterthur.—Bk. of Winterthur, 100.

Winton (N.Z.).—Bk. of N. Zeal., 24.

Winton (Queens.).—Queensland Nat Bk., 184; Bk. of New South Wales, 23; B. of Australia, 16.

Wirrabara(S.A.).—En.,Sc&Aust.B.93.

Wodonga.—B.ofVic.,29;B.ofN.S.W.,23.

Wolfville (N.S.).—People's Bank, 209.

Wollongong.—Eng.,Scot.,&Aust.B.,93; Ccml. B. Co. of Sydney, 69; B. of N. S. Wales, 23; Australian Jt. Stck., 13.

Woodburn (N.S.W.).—Aus. J. S. B., 13.

Woodend (Vic.).—Com. B. of Aus., 70.

Woodland (Cal.).—B. of Woodland, 8.

Woodside.—B. of Adelaide, 12.

Woodstock (N.B.).—B. of Nova Scot., 193; Merch. Bk. of Halifax, 26.

Woodstock (Ont.).—Imp. B. of Canada, 132 ; B. of Com., 26 ; Molson's B., 177.

Woodville (N.Z.).—B. of N. Zeal., 24.

Woolloomooloo.—Eng.Scot.&Aust.,93

Woonona.—Eng., Scot.,& Aust. Bk., 93.

Worcester (S.Afr.).—St. B. S. Afr.,203; African Bkg. Corp., 14.

Worms.—Pfalzische Bk., 84.

Wunghnu.—Bk. of Australasia, 16.

Wurzburg.—Oehninger's Son & Co.

Wyalong.—B. of N. S. Wales, 23; Un. B. of Australia, 208.

Wycheproof.—Com. Bk. of Aust., 70 : Bk. of Australasia, 16.

Wynberg.—Af. B. Co., 1a.

Wyndham (N.Z.).—B. of N. Zeal., 24.

*Wynyard, Nat. B. of Tas., 68.

Wynyard (Tas.).—B.of Australasia, 16.

Wyong.—Com. B. of Australia, 70.

Yackandandah.—B. of Austlsia., 16.

Yankalilla.—Bk. of Adelaide, 12.

Yarmouth (Nova Scotia).—Yarm. Bk., 209 ; Nova Scotia B., 193.

Yarram-Yarram.—Bk.ofAustralasia, 16 ; Bk. of Victoria, 29.

Yarraville. Nat. B. Aust., 169.

Yarrawonga.—B. of Austlasia.,169 ; Nat. B.ofAustlsia,169 ; Com.B.ofAust.,70.

Yass.—Com. B.Co.of Sydney, 69 ; Aust. Joint Stock B., 13 ; B. of N. S. W., 23.

Yea.—Com. Bk. of Australia, 70.

Yead.—Imp. Bank of Persia, 116.

Yoilo.—Hongkong & Shanghai, 112.

Yokohama.—Chart. Bk. of India, 53 ; Hongkong & Shanghai, 112 ; Yokohama Specie, 225; B. de China & Japan, 14; Comptoir Nat. d'Escompte, 71 ; National Bk. of China, 170.

Yongala.—Nat. B. of Australasia, 169.

York (W.A.).—Union Bank of Aust., 208 ; Western Aust. B., 12.

Yorketown.—Bk. of Adelaide, 12.

Young.—B. of N. S. W., 23 ; Com. B. Co. of Sydney, 69; City B., Sydney, 148 ; Union Bk. of Australia, 208 ; Bk. of Australasia, 16.

Yreka (Cal.).—Siskiyou B. Co., 8.

Ystad.—ChristianstadsEnskildaB.,118

Zacatecas.—Lond. Bk. of Mexico, 145; Banco de Zacatecas, 8.

Zamora.—Lond. Bk. of Mexico, 145.

Zante.—Ionian Bank, 119.

Zanzibar.—Nat. Bk. of India, 171.

Zeehan (Tas.).—Bk. of Australasia, 16 ; Com. Bk. of Tas., 23 ; Nat. B. of Tas., 68.

Zeerust (S.A.R.).—Nat. Bk., 173a.

Zermatt.—Galland & Co.

Zurich.—Swiss Credit Co., 100; Banque Fédérale, 77 ; Kugler & Co., 154 ; Swiss Bankverein, 206.

The Bankers' Clearing-House.

THE BANKERS' CLEARING-HOUSE, in Post Office Court, Lombard Street, is the medium through which Bankers obtain the amount of Cheques and Bills in their hands for collection from other Bankers. Instead of presenting their cheques at each Banking House, and receiving cash and notes in payment, Clearing Bankers settle the whole amount delivered during the day at this establishment by receiving or paying the difference in their amount by a single cheque on the Bank of England. As every Bank in London and the Country is represented by Clearing Bankers, who, as agents, send through the Clearing House all drafts payable in the City and in the Country, the amount passing through this channel is enormous. The total for the year ending December 31st, 1898, was £8,097,291,000 an increase of £606,010,000 as compared with the year 1897 and the largest amount on record. [The previous highest total was in 1890, when over £7,801,000,000 were dealt with ; and the amount as recently as 1879 was only £4,886,000,000.] On Stock Exchange days the payments were £1,231,847,000, an increase of £118,165,000 on the year 1897. [The highest total under this head was £1,417,000,000 in 1890 ; in 1879 the amount was £843,000,000.] The payments on Consols account days for the same period have amounted to £402,861,000, an increase of £40,251,000 as compared with 1897 [the highest total ever reached—in 1879 the amount was £225,000,000], and on the 4ths of the months the payments for 1898 amounted to £331,267,000, an increase of £29,144,000 as compared with 1897 [also the highest amount on record—in 1879 the total under this head was £213,000,000]. The establishment is managed by a Committee, the officers of which are—*Chairman*, The Rt. Hon. Sir John Lubbock, Bart., M.P., F.R.S. ; *Deputy Chairman*, Bonamy Dobree ; *Hon. Sec.*, J. Herbert Tritton ; *Acting Managers*, John C. Pocock (*Chief Inspector*); Philip W. Matthews (*Deputy Inspector*).

THE British Isles consist of Great Britain (England and Wales, and Scotland) and Ireland, and lie between the 49th and 61st degrees of N. latitude, and the 2nd degree of East and the 11th degree of West longitude. The total area is 121,115 sq. miles or 77,477,781 acres, with a population in 1891 of 37,740,283 (estimated at 40,559,954 in 1899), an increase of 2,855,435 in ten years, in addition to the 604,182 who had emigrated. In 1898 there were 1,159,192 births, 712,856 deaths, and 309,491 marriages in the United Kingdom. Of the total area 47,668,183 acres were under cultivation in 1898; of this total 8,791,276 acres were under corn crops; 4,238,496, green crops; 6,164,239, grass, &c.; 226,059, orchards; and 3,033,777 acres were preserved woods, coppices, &c. The live stock included 1,517,160 horses; 6,622,364 cattle; 26,743,194 sheep; and 2,451,595 pigs.

ENGLAND,

which may be roughly said to be divided from Scotland on the north by the Cheviot Hills and the Rivers Tweed and Solway, and from Wales by the Severn and Dee, has an area of nearly 51,000 square miles, and a population (census, 1891) of 27,501,362. Except in the west and the north, England is for the most part a level country, so cultivated as to be highly productive. The other districts have mineral riches, including iron, tin, lead, zinc, slate, and coal, which make abundant amends for the poverty of their surface.

The southern and eastern parts of England have a population mainly derived from Belgic Gaul, whilst the western districts and Wales have been peopled from the West of France and the North of Spain, while Ireland and Scotland are believed to have been peopled by a race originally Belgic. When the Romans first came to our shores the inhabitants might have been roughly divided into two sections: those who lived inland, and who may with some reason be called Celtic colonists, were a race of hunters and shepherds, dressed in the skins of beasts, and inhabiting huts made of rude wickerwork and covered with rushes; whereas the coast-dwellers were, probably, of Gallic origin, with some approach towards civilisation, and holding intercourse, for purposes of trade, with foreign merchants visiting the island. Neglecting the Romans, who were no more than mere military garrisons, and mingled little with the natives —much like Europeans in the East at the present day—we have the Saxons and Jutes established from Kent to Devonshire, and the Angles (and subsequently the Norsemen) from the Thames to the Tweed. The Norman Conquest brought in a mixed multitude from the Continent; the wars of Stephen introduced a numerous body of Flemings, who were settled by Henry II. in Wales; and the commercial views of Edward III. led to the establishment of a still larger body of the same people as clothworkers in Kent. Political and religious dissensions have had a great share in bringing in new races, for Dutch, French, and other refugees and their descendants exist among us in such numbers as perceptibly to modify the national character. The western part of England was known to the Phœnicians, and was resorted to by them for its tin, four centuries or more B.C.; hence the whole country received the name of the Cassiterides, or Tin Islands. When invaded by Cæsar (B.C. 55) it was called Britain (perhaps derived from Prydain, the name of an early chief of great power), or sometimes Albion, that is, the *White Land*, from the white cliffs on the S. E. coast.

The Romans subdued all England, and parts of Scotland and Wales, but did not reach Ireland, though its existence was known to them. About A.D. 410, the Romans abandoned the island after a rule of about 350 years, traces of which still remain in every quarter. These may best be observed in the names of many of our most ancient towns, in the great roads that reach from end to end of the country, and in the remains of Roman buildings and architecture from time to time unearthed in different places. For example, every town whose name consists wholly, or in part, of *cester*, *caster*, or *chester* (derived from Latin *castra*, a camp) marks the site of one of those wonderful entrenched camps for which the Roman armies were famous. The military roads, straight, broad, and splendidly made, are still to be traced; Watling Street, from the coast of Kent by way of London, to Carnarvon; the Foss—or Fosdyke —from Cornwall to Lincoln; Ikenild Street, from the mouth of the Tyne, through York and Derby, to St. David's; and Irmin Street, from the last-named spot to Southampton. The Britons, being divided into as many hostile States as they had cities, were unable to resist the fresh hordes (now called Saxons and Angles) that poured into the island, and about A.D. 457 the kingdom of Kent was founded. The Britons still fought stubbornly, but were gradually driven westward, and by the year 584 the kingdom of Mercia (meaning the march-land, or frontier State) was established, being the last of the seven kingdoms founded by the invaders—whence the whole is usually styled the Heptarchy. The kings of the Heptarchy made war on each other, but at last, in 827, Egbert of Wessex obtained the supremacy of the whole, and styled himself King of England. His descendants, of whom Alfred the Great was the most illustrious, held the throne for more than 200 years, but the country suffered greatly during the time from the ravages of the Danes, who, under Canute and his sons, became its rulers for 25 years (1017-1042). The Saxon line was restored in the person of Edward the Confessor, to whom Harold succeeded; but his death in the Battle of Hastings, on the 14th October, 1066, gave England into the hands of the Norman kings, who reigned from 1066 to 1154. Then came the Plantagenets (1154-1485), the Tudors (1485-1603), and the Stuarts (1603-1714), to whom the House of Hanover succeeded on the death of Queen Anne. Her present Majesty is the sixth sovereign of that line, and on June 22, 1897, celebrated the completion of the 60th year of her reign.

THE entire population of England and Wales is here given for 1891 (29,002,525), with the gross estimated rental as settled by the Assessment Committees in the Valuation Lists in 1898, the amount collected for the Poor Rate for the year ending Lady-Day, 1898, and the number of paupers who were actually in receipt of relief on Jan. 1st, 1899. The total number of persons in England and Wales receiving relief on Jan. 1st, 1899, was 821,066, as against 836,913 on Jan. 1st, 1898. The total cost of Relief to the Poor for the year ended Lady-Day 1898 (the last information published), was £10,828,276, as against £10,432,189 for the year ended Lady-Day, 1897.

The sum raised by Poor Rates in England and Wales during the year ended Lady-Day, 1898, was £21,410 311; the receipts in aid, inclusive of grants from County and Borough Councils, and grants under the Agricultural Rates Act, 1896, amounted to £3,150,385, forming a total receipt of £24,560.696; considerably over one-half of this amount was expended for other purposes than the relief of the Poor; the payments towards the County, Borough, and Police Rate, for instance, amounted to £8,930,672; to Rural District Councils, £1,541,963; and to School Boards, £1,321,502. The actual relief to the poor for the year ended Lady-Day, 1898, amounted to 7s. 0d. per head of the estimated population, while the sum levied as Poor Rate during the same period was equal to a rate of 13s. 9d. per head. The total amount raised as Poor Rates and the total payments therefrom to other local authorities were less during the year ended Lady-Day, 1898, than during the preceding year, the decrease being due to the operation of the Agricultural Rates Act, 1896. (For statistics and other particulars as to Wales, see next page.)

*COUNTIES.	Population.	No. of Acres	Gross Rental	Poor-Rate.	Paupers.	LORDS LIEUTENANT.
	1891.	1891.	1898.	1898.	1899.	
Bedford	165,999	309,989	£1,129,877	£108,982	5,724	Earl Cowper, K.G.
Berks	268,357	574,298	1,989,843	160,734	6,692	Lord Wantage, K.C.B., V.C.
Bucks	164,442	410,242	1,111,644	97,772	6,149	Lord Rothschild.
Cambridge	196,269	565,737	1,449,791	121,446	6,795	Alexander Peckover.
Chester	707,978	643,791	4,916,537	363,239	16,151	Duke of Westminster, K.G.
Cornwall	318,583	886,372	1,529,502	156,585	11,438	Earl of Mount-Edgcumbe.
Cumberland	266,549	970,161	1,887,986	128,117	6,849	Lord Muncaster. [G.C.V.O.
Derby	432,414	557,768	2,668,823	244,853	11,154	Duke of Devonshire, K.G.
Devon	636,225	1,650,705	4,069,134	370,296	24,527	Lord Clinton.
Dorset	188,995	616,403	1,274,750	135,824	8,512	Earl of Ilchester.
Durham	1,024,369	764,783	5,566,654	476,121	24,064	Earl of Durham.
Essex	761,191	904,642	5,036,009	692,492	26,073	Lord Rayleigh, F.R.S.
Gloucester	548,886	714,763	3,601,099	326,615	20,9·3	Earl of Ducie.
Hants.	666,250	1,047,223	4,488,941	421,664	22,444	Earl of Northbrook, G.C.S.I.
Hereford	113,346	535,846	964,830	88,339	4,657	Lord Bateman.
Hertford	215,179	443,787	1,581,827	163,201	8,075	Earl of Clarendon.
Huntingdon	50,289	207,569	395,683	31,157	1,372	Earl of Sandwich.
Kent	806,297	969,879	5,833,732	589,887	22,948	Earl Stanhope.
Lancaster	3,957,906	1,306,777	24,941,537	2,416,466	82,548	Earl of Derby, K.G.
Leicester	379,286	551,845	2,641,209	164,164	11,758	Earl Howe, G.C.V.O.
Lincoln	467,281	1,659,930	3,505,074	302,683	16,817	Earl Brownlow.
London	4,211,743	74,672	44,633,649	6,029,874	123,665	Duke of Westminster, K.G.
Middlesex	574,999	178,754	4,9·7,219	500,320	12,465	Duke of Bedford.
Monmouth	275,242	394,424	1,675,745	193,828	10,884	Lord Tredegar.
Norfolk	460,362	1,291,170	2,545,057	297,483	19,850	Earl of Leicester, K.G.
Northampton	308,072	641,925	2,058,698	174,263	9,510	Earl Spencer, K.G.
Northumberland	506,030	1,289,756	3,616,288	210,774	10,859	Earl Grey.
Nottingham	505,311	616,285	3,112,113	231,280	14,109	Duke of Portland, G.C.V.O.
Oxford	188,220	490,146	1,341,009	88,997	6,901	Earl of Jersey, G.C.M.G.
Rutland	22,123	110,190	224,936	14,511	733	Earl of Dysart.
Salop	254,765	952,842	2,074,424	130,669	5,963	Earl of Powis.
Somerset	510,076	1,061,614	3,630,289	317,055	17,179	Earl of Cork and Orrery, K.P.
Stafford	1,103,452	767,102	5,802,919	564,141	35,471	Earl of Dartmouth.
Suffolk	353,758	931,134	1,813,553	167,948	13,141	Marquess of Bristol.
Surrey	572,092	452,733	5,177,443	453,855	12,790	Viscount Midleton.
Sussex	554,542	947,564	4,639,348	406,304	17,775	Marq. of Abergavenny, K.G.
Warwick	801,738	621,833	4,981,984	578,110	17,300	Lord Leigh.
Westmorland	66,215	503,073	659,531	30,013	1,414	Lord Hothfield.
Wilts	255,119	811,367	1,630,651	171,293	9,898	Marq. of Lansdowne, K.G.
Worcester	422,530	441,510	2,631,170	275,936	12,918	Earl of Coventry.
York, E. Riding	400,085	695,431	2,671,166	268,113	11,977	Lord Herries.
North Riding	354,382	1,253,974	2,686,478	192,890	10,808	Marquess of Ripon, K.G.
West Riding	2,464,415	1,775,298	14,282,649	1,541,4·7	47,936	Earl of Scarbrough.
Total	27,501,362	32,595,312	197,431,816	20,415,911	769,165	

* POPULATION OF COUNTIES.—The county population is that given in the Census of 1891, as the population of each Registration County. The Registration Counties do not precisely correspond with the area of ordinary counties, but with Poor Law areas to which the figures in this table relate. In 1861 the amount levied for poor rates was at the rate of 7s. 11½d. per head; in 1891 the amount levied was at the rate of 10s. 9¾d. In 1861 the officials employed received but £660,370; in 1891 this had increased to £1,452,810, and in 1898 to £1,879,659.

THE Principality of Wales, with an extreme length of 135 miles, and a breadth varying from 35 miles to 95 miles, lies in the S.W. of Great Britain, and has an area of 7,378 square miles, or about 4,720,000 acres. The Principality is rich in minerals; slate, coal, and iron being among the more important; while of its manufactures, flannel, cloth, and hosiery alone are worthy of mention. The native inhabitants are almost wholly of the Cymric stock of the Celtic race; and a large number of them belong to the religious body known as the Calvinistic Methodists.

At what time Christianity was introduced it is impossible to tell, but certainly not later than A.D. 400. When the British Christians were driven from their homes, such of them as did not seek refuge beyond the seas, found in the rocky fastnesses of the Welsh mountains a secure retreat from their enemies. There they immediately set about dividing the country into ecclesiastical divisions for administrative purposes, and the present sees of Wales represent those leading centres of religious thought that became famous in the sixth century.

The four bishoprics still remain as of old, and the numbers of beneficed clergy now to be found in them are as follows: St. David's, 360; Llandaff, 246; St. Asaph, 206; and Bangor, 147. The sees of St. David's and Llandaff were united with the Southern province in the year 1107, and those of Bangor and St. Asaph in the years 1092 and 1143 respectively.

When the Saxon pirates began to visit and ravage the eastern shores of Britain, the Celtic inhabitants were gradually pressed westward by the invading hordes, and finally found secure shelter in the wilds of Wales, Devon, and Cornwall. The border-lands, or marches, between England and Wales were long in a state of at least guerilla warfare; and it was not until about 850 A.D. that one Roderick (Rhodi Mawr) contrived to unite the whole country into one Principality, dividing it afterwards among his sons into three smaller ones, named, severally, Gwynedd, Dyved and Ceredigion, and Powis. This was followed by the incursions of the Danes, after which Howel once more (in the 10th century) succeeded in re-uniting the country. Later, when England was tending in the same direction of unity, Athelstane received a tribute from the Welsh in recognition of his nominal sovereignty over them. William I. and his son Rufus both tried the plan of granting fiefs to their more adventurous Norman knights, on condition of their conquering the land, while Henry I. introduced into the Principality a colony of Flemish wool-workers. Henry II., too, and John, endeavoured, with doubtful success, to effect a final subjugation of the troublesome province. A combination of fortuitous circumstances led to its lasting conquest. Llewellyn, who succeeded David, had been implicated in the Montfort rebellion, but, on the accession of Edward I., managed to get included in the general amnesty granted to those who had joined the Leicester faction. In 1276, however, Edward, having been repeatedly refused the homage due to him from Llewellyn, raised an army to enforce his commands. Internal dissensions among the Welsh greatly aided the English, and Llewellyn, at length cooped up and almost starved to death among the Snowdon mountains, was forced to submit at discretion, and accept the terms offered by the victor (1277). By the grace of Edward the Welsh prince was allowed to return to the Principality; but trouble arising again, in which both Llewellyn and his brother David were concerned, a war arose, and the independence of Wales was for ever shattered. Llewellyn was slain in battle in 1282, with two thousand of his followers; and in the following year David, being betrayed to the English, was sent in chains to Shrewsbury, and at last put to a painful and ignominious death as a traitor. The Welsh nobility then submitted in a body, and King Edward invested his son Edward (who had been born at Carnarvon) with the Principality, which very soon afterwards was fully annexed to the Crown. In later days the history of Wales has been almost identical with the history of England, the Principality and country marching side by side in sure and steady progress.

In education the Principality has made great strides of recent years, and possesses a University (Prifysgol Cymru) consisting of the three university colleges of Aberystwyth, Bangor, and Cardiff, in addition to St. David's College at Lampeter.

The following table of statistics contains some interesting information with reference to the various individual counties of Wales. In addition to those named, Monmouth is, not without good reason, claimed as a Welsh county; if admitted, it would add another quarter of a million to the population of the Principality, thus making it larger than that of Scotland in the early part of the century. The Welsh is a distinct nationality, with a language and literature of its own.

COUNTIES.	Population.	No. of Acres	Gross Rental	Poor-Rate	Paupers.	LORDS LIEUTENANT.
	1891.	1891.	1898.	1898.	1899.	
Anglesey	34,219	120,199	£152,015	£	1,552	Sir R. H. Williams Bulkeley, Bt.
Brecon	52,872	458,652	344,324	34,756	1,784	Sir Jos. Russell Bailey, Bt.
Cardigan	86,383	595,285	380,809	43,159	2,780	Herbert Davies-Evans.
Carmarthen	118,624	478,717	650,407	68,044	4,244	Sir J.H. Williams-Drummond,
Carnarvon	125,585	322,135	708,369	72,283	4,928	John Ernest Greaves. [Bt.
Denbigh	116,698	386,416	702,570	59,709	3,597	Col. Wm. Cornwallis West.
Flint	42,565	73,380	232,995	25,060	1,979	Hugh Robert Hughes.
Glamorgan	693,072	576,308	4,984,759	536,296	22,863	Lord Windsor.
Merioneth	64,726	525,802	350,211	45,701	2,277	Wm. Maurice Rt. Wynne.
Montgomery	67,297	589,846	496,078	36,779	2,193	Sir H. L. W. Williams-Wynn, Bt.
Pembroke	82,003	357,118	435,349	43,561	3,116	Earl Cawdor. Sir C. E. Gregg Philipps, Haverfordwest.
Radnor	17,119	238,715	127,122	11,790	617	Sir Powlett Milbank, Bt., M.P.
Total	1,501,163	4,722,573	9,564,968	994,400	51,930	

THE most northerly part of the island, divided from the south by the River Tweed, the Cheviot Hills, and the Solway Firth, is the ancient Caledonia or modern Scotland, a mountainous country, and to a great extent bleak and barren, but inhabited by a race of men who have made the country productive, wealthy, and prosperous. It contains nearly 30,000 square miles, or 19,084,659 acres, of which not quite 4,500,000 are in a state of cultivation, with a population in 1881 of 3,735,573, and of 4,025,647 in 1891.

After the Union with England in the year 1707, and the suppression of the Rebellion of 1745, the Scottish people generally awoke to the fact that the loss of their separate nationality was a gain; and being united to a wealthy neighbour, they with one accord determined to derive all possible benefit from the change. By means of an admirable banking system, capital was utilised. With wonderful ingenuity and perseverance a great commercial port, Glasgow, was opened in the west, Scottish citizens flocked south and into the British colonies, everywhere carrying with them their habits of industry and thrift. India especially became the scene of their operations, and notwithstanding any narrow feelings of national jealousy, it was seen that they were creators of commerce and producers of wealth. Education was widely diffused throughout the masses, while the Calvinistic religion, even if it did not in all instances produce piety, helped to promote thought and mental activity. At the Union the Scottish Church and Judiciary were left intact, and so, with slight modifications, have remained to the present day; both England and Scotland borrowing something from each other and gradually assimilating.

POPULATION, AREA, VALUATION AND PAUPERS OF COUNTIES.

* The valuation of lands and heritages is only approximate: it is that furnished by the Inspectors of the Poor to the Local Government Board for Scotland. The number of Paupers is that chargeable on May 14, 1896.

County.	Population.	Acres.	Acres Cultivated.	Gross Valuation 1896.	Paupers including Dependents.	Lords Lieutenant.
	1891.	1891.	1891.	£	1896.	
Aberdeen	284,036	1,251,451	573,189	1,609,573	6,710	The Lord Provost of Aberdeen.
Argyll	74,998	2,056,400	120,522	511,585	2,374	Duke of Argyll, K.G., K.T.
Ayr	226,386	722,229	293,859	1,356,478	5,654	Earl of Eglinton & Winton.
Banff	61,684	410,110	157,353	254,290	1,736	Duke of Richmond, K.G.
Berwick.............	32,290	294,805	184,211	311,260	686	Earl of Lauderdale.
Bute	18,404	139,440	22,966	130,837	344	Marquess of Bute, K.T.
Caithness	37,177	438,878	100,853	150,453	708	Duke of Portland, G.C.V.O.
Clackmannan ...	33,140	30,477	14,562	153,629	432	Earl of Mar and Kellie.
Dumbarton	98,014	154,542	41,877	576,750	1,991	Sir James Colquhoun, Bart.
Dumfries	74,245	680,217	213,784	598,270	1,681	Duke of Buccleuch, K.G., K.T.
Edinburgh	433,994	231,724	127,669	3,463,305	9,554	Earl of Rosebery, K.G., K.T.
Elgin or Moray...	43,471	304,606	104,149	239,390	1,549	Duke of Fife, K.T.
Fife	190,365	314,952	229,752	1,130,122	3,679	Earl of Elgin and Kincardine.
Forfar	277,735	560,087	235,613	1,580,522	5,870	Earl of Strathmore.
Haddington	37,377	173,298	107,420	310,865	1,075	Earl of Haddington.
Inverness	89,847	2,616,498	114,986	439,217	3,385	Donald Cameron of Lochiel.
Kincardine	35,492	245,346	116,912	244,415	613	Sir Alexander Baird of Urie, Bt.
Kinross	6,673	46,485	33,874	66,457	149	Sir G. G.-Montgomery, Bart.
Kirkcudbright ...	39,985	574,587	164,221	346,645	1,100	Lord Herries.
Lanark	1,091,644	564,284	227,218	6,557,356	26,294	Earl of Home.
Linlithgow	53,532	76,806	53,612	348,624	1,235	Earl of Rosebery, K.G., K.T.
Nairn	8,516	114,400	24,494	47,593	277	Major James Rose.
Orkney	30,453	280,352	84,328	75,843	896	Malcolm Laing, junr.
Peebles	14,750	226,899	37,053	136,187	240	Lord Elibank.
Perth	122,185	1,617,808	333,845	1,061,803	2,579	Duke of Atholl, K.T.
Renfrew	245,067	156,785	90,224	1,388,808	5,454	Sir M. R. Shaw-Stewart, Bart.
Ross and Cromarty ...}	78,727	2,003,065	122,248	306,852	3,529	Sir Hector Munro, Bt.
Roxburgh.........	53,500	425,657	174,199	434,921	1,011	Lord Reay, G.C.S.I., G.C.I.E.
Selkirk	27,270	164,545	20,308	150,504	401	Lord Polwarth.
Shetland	28,711	312,000	51,884	43,455	1,027	Malcolm Laing.
Stirling	118,021	286,338	104,228	696,619	2,657	Duke of Montrose, K.T.
Sutherland	21,896	1,297,846	23,126	100,819	971	Duke of Sutherland.
Wigtown	36,062	310,742	133,598	241,148	1,141	Earl of Stair, K.T.
Total......	4,025,647	19,083,659	4,438,137	25,063,675	98,002	

Expenditure on relief and management of poor in 1880, £849,064; in 1881, £853,348; in 1882, £844,782; in 1883, £834,657; in 1884, £832,115; in 1885, £830,641; in 1886, £838,035; in 1887, £843,290; in 1888, £844,830; in 1889, £842,726; in 1890, £841,952; in 1891, £841,645; in 1892, £871,306; in 1893, £873,947, in 1894, £894,500; in 1895, £926,759; and in 1896, £942,037.

Paupers of all classes in 1880, 103,186; in 1881, 102,306; in 1882, 99,341; in 1883, 97,097; in 1884, 94,642; in 1885, 95,516; in 1886, 97,504; in 1887, 96,536; in 1888, 96,226; in 1889, 74,836; in 1890, 92,824; 1891, 91,063; 1892, 90,792; 1893, 92,004; 1894, 93,682; 1895, 95,868; and 1896, £98,002.

SCOTLAND.—OFFICERS OF STATE, ROYAL HOUSEHOLD, Etc.

Great Steward of Scotland, H.R.H. Prince of Wales, K.G. (Duke of Rothsay).

OFFICERS OF STATE.

The Secretary for Scotland, and Keeper of the Great Seal, Rt. Hon. Lord Balfour of Burleigh.
Keeper of the Privy Seal, The Marquess of Lothian, K.T.
Lord Clerk Register, Duke of Montrose, K.T.
Lord Advocate, Rt. Hon. A. G. Murray, Q.C., M.P.

ROYAL HOUSEHOLD.

Hereditary High Constable, Earl of Erroll.
Hereditary Master of Household, Duke of Argyll, K.G.
Hereditary Standard-Bearer, Earl of Lauderdale.
Hereditary Royal Standard-Bearer, Henry Scrymgeour-Wedderburn.
Hereditary Armour-Bearer, Sir Alan Henry Seton-Steuart, Bart.
Hereditary Carver, Sir Windham Robert Carmichael-Anstruther, Bart.
Heredi ary Cup-Bearer, Earl of Southesk, K.T.
Hereditary Keeper of Holyrood Palace, Duke of Hamilton and Brandon.
Do., Rothsay; Falkland, Marquess of Bute, K.T.

Hereditary Keeper of Dunstaffnage; Dunoon; Carrick, Duke of Argyll, K.G., K.T.
Domestic Chaplain,
Historiographer, David Masson, LL.D. £184
Geographer, George Harvey Johnston, F.R.G.S.
Physicians in Ordinary, Sir William T. Gairdner, K.C.B., M.D.; Sir Thos. Grainger Stewart, M.D.
Surgeons in Ordinary, Patrick Heron Watson, M.D.; Alexander Ogston, M.D.
Limner, Sir Noel Paton, R.S.A.
Composer, Sir Herbert S. Oakeley, D.C.L.
Dean of the Chapel Royal and of the Order of the Thistle, Very Rev. James Cameron Lees, D.D.
QUEEN's BODY GUARD, *Royal Company of Archers.*
—*Captain-General,* Marquess of Lothian, K.T.
President of the Council, Earl of Stair, K.T.
Vice-Pres., Lord Balfour of Burleigh.
Joint Secretaries, Sir J. Gillespie and H. Cook.
Treasurer, Harry Cheyne, W.S.
Chaplain, Rev. Norman Macleod, D.D.

COURT OF SESSION (1532).

Lord President of the whole Court, Lord Balfour (Right Hon. John Blair Balfour).

INNER HOUSE.—First Division.

Rt. Hon. the Lord President £5,000
Lord Adam, James Adam £3,600
Lord M'Laren, John M'Laren £3,600
Rt. Hon. Lord Kinnear (a peer) £3,600

Second Division.

Lord Kingsburgh, C.B. (Rt. Hon. J. H. A. Macdonald), *Lord Justice Clerk* £4,800
Lord Young, Right Hon. George Young £3,600
Lord Trayner, John Trayner £3,600
Rt. Hon. Lord Moncreiff (a peer) £3,600

OUTER HOUSE.

Lord Pearson, Rt. Hon. Sir C. J. Pearson. £3,600
Lord Kyllachy, William Mackintosh £3,600
Lord Kincairney, William Ellis Gloag £3,600
Lord Stormonth-Darling, Moir Tod Stormonth Darling £3,600
Lord Low, Alexander Low £3,600
Principal Clerks of Court, Charles Tennant Couper, Adv.; P.W. Campbell, W.S. each £1,000
Inner House Depute Clerks, John Paton, B.S.C.; M. M. Prain .... each £550

Outer House Depute Clerks, John Moir; James McCaul, S S.C.; Graham Marrable, S.S.C.; Robert Brown; William Veitch .... each £550
Outer House Assistant Clerks, And. Ross, S S.C.; Chas. Taylor; John Cairns; Hugh Watt; Wm. Brown .... each £475

High Court of Justiciary (1672).

Lord Justice Gen., Rt. Hon. John Blair Balfour.
Lord Justice Clerk, Rt. Hon. Lord Kingsburgh, C.B.
Lords Comm. of Justiciary, all the other Judges.
Lord Advocate, Rt. Hon. A. G. Murray, Q.C., M.P.
Solicitor-General, Charles Scott Dickson, Q.C.
Clerk of Justiciary, G. L. Crole, LL.B., Advocate.
Assistant and Depute, George A. Slight.
Circuit Clerks, A. D. Veitch; Geo. A. Slight.
Advocates Depute, C. Kincaid Mackenzie; James A. Fleming; John Wilson; A. L. McClure.
Crown Agent, W. J. Dundas, W.S.

Court of Lords Commissioners for Teinds.

The Judges of the Inner House, and Lord Low, *Lord Ordinary on Teinds.*
Clerk of Teinds & Extractor, N. Elliot, S.S.C.....£500
Keeper of Records and Assist. Clerk, Alex. Logan.

SECRETARY FOR SCOTLAND'S OFFICE.

Dover House, Whitehall, S.W., and 6 Parliament Square, Edinburgh.—£12,111.
Sec., Rt. Hon. Lord Balfour of Burleigh ...£2,000
Private Secretary, G. A. J. Lee £300
(For Staff, see p. 171.)

Local Government Board.

125, George Street, Edinburgh.
(Office hours 9 30 to 4.30, Saturdays 9.30 to 1.)
Ex-officio Members, Rt. Hon. Lord Balfour of Burleigh (*Secretary for Scotland*), President; Col. Sir C. C. Scott-Moncrieff, K.C.M.G. (*Under-Secretary for Scotland*); Charles Scott Dickson, Q.C. (*Solicitor-General for Scotland*).
Appointed Members.—*Vice-President,* Malcolm McNeill; *Legal Member,* J. Patten MacDougall, M.A. (Advocate); *Medical Member,* James Burn Russell, M.D., LL.D.

OFFICERS OF BOARD.

Secretary, George Falconar-Stewart.
Chief Clerk, Abijah Murray.
General Superintendents of Poor and Inspecting

Officers under Public Health Act, Robert B. Barclay; Kenneth Mackenzie; William Penney; Alexander Stuart, junior.
Medical Officer under Public Health Act, Professor Sir Henry Duncan Littlejohn, M.D., LL.D.
Superintendent of Vaccine Institution, W. Husband, M.D.
First Class Clerks in Charge of Departments:—
A. Murray, *Local Government Department.*
David Brown, *Poor Law Department.*
John T. Maxwell, *Statistical Department.*
Arthur Grant, *Public Health Department.*
Lord Advocate's Office.—£15,036.
Lord Advocate, Rt. Hon. Andrew Graham Murray, Q.C., M.P. £5,000
Legal Secretary, T. Rutherfurd Clark £500
Solicitor-Gen., Charles Scott Dickson, Q.C. £2,000
Clerk to Lord Advocate, R. W. Hepburn £400
Crown Agent, W. J. Dundas, W.S. £1,300
Museum of Science and Art, Chambers Street. —£13,166.
Director, Major-Gen. Sir Robert Murdoch Smith, K.C.M.G. £800

Keeper Natural History Department, Ramsay Heatley Traquair, M.D., F.R.S. £500
Curator, David J. Vallance £500
Assist. Industrial and Art Dept., W. Clark ...£250
" C. N. B. Muston.......................£250
" T. W. Nash £250
Assist. Nat. History Dept., W. Eagle Clarke..£245

Geological Survey of Scotland.—£5,106.
Sheriff Court Buildings, George IV. Bridge.
District Surveyor, B. N. Peach, F.R.S. £500
Geologists, R. G. Symes, M.A.; S. B. Wilkinson; J. Horne, F.R.S.E.; W. Gunn; C. T. Clough, M.A.; G. Barrow ....£275 to £400
Asst. Geologists, J. S. Grant Wilson; Lionel Hinxman, B.A.; H. Kynaston; A. Harker, M.A.; E. H. C. Craig £1,095
Curator of Survey Collect., J. G. Goodchild ..£350
Assistant in Fossil Dept., A. Macconochie £150
Resident Assistant, R. Lunn £183
Fossil Collector, D. Tait £73

REVENUE OFFICES.
Office of Inland Revenue, Waterloo Place.
Solicitor of Inland Revenue, P. J. H. Grierson, Advocate £1,200
Chief Clerk, Thomas Robertson £700
First Class Clerks, Thomas C. Addis; Wm. Andrew ....each £500
Second Class Clerks, Michael Pithie; Percival Waugh ....each £400
Third Class Clerks, Wm. Jamieson; Thomas J. Boyd; John McNiel ....each £270

Stamps and Taxes.
Comptroller, Alfred C. Trevor £1,000
Principal Clerks, T. W. Nowers (*Senior*) £600; J. K. Stewart £500
Minor Staff Officers (*alphabetically*), D. A. Abernethy; W. Carmichael; W. Gardner; J. A. Hearne; J. Mullineux ......£300 to £400

Collector's Office.
Collector of Inland Revenue, R. M. Douglas.
Principal Clerks, 1st Class, H. A. P. Sarah; D. Morgan.
Principal Clerks, 2nd Class, A. C. Gregory; A. G. Cogman.

Legacy and Succession Duty Department.
Deputy-Controller (for Scotland) and Registrar of Inventories, James Edward Hope, W.S. £900
Prin. Clks., A. Thompson; H. Glanvill £600 to £700
First Class Clerk, Upper Sect., W. E. Brand £580
" *Lower Sect.,* G. Ford; W. A. Ross £500 to £550
2nd Class do., A. M. Lomax; W. A. Wilson ....£320 to £450
3rd Class Clerks, H. Robinson; W. R. Morison; S. M. Findlay; W. E. Redding ...£150 to £300
Minor Staff Post, J. Sime ....£300 to £400

H.M. Customs, Scotland.
COLLECTORS.
Glasgow, C. Edwards, £1,000. *Leith,* J. Bladon, £800. *Aberdeen,* Henry de Moulpied, £500. *Dundee,* H. P. Devereux, £500. *Greenock,* J. W. Hay, £500. *Grangemouth,* J. Dodsworth, £450. *Ayr,* W. H. Bignold; *Inverness,* W. M. Callander; *Kirkcaldy,* W. Hedges, each £300. *Granton,*

G. Owen; *Wick,* T. G. Mitchell; *Berwick,* W. R. Twichett; *Borrowstounness,* J. Mortished; *Ardrossan,* Wm. Stevenson ....each £250 to £320
H.M. Post Office, General Post Office Buildings.
Secretary, Henry Louis Creswell £1,200
Chief Clerk, E. D. Thomson £800
Princ. Clerks, H. A. R. Chancellor ; R. Scott £540
Counsel, J. A. Fleming, Advocate.
Solicitor, John S. Pitman, W.S....................£500
Medical Officer, Dr. K. M. Douglas...............£675

Receivers of Crown Rents, Scotland.
Crown Receiver, Holmes Ivory, W.S., New Register House, Edinburgh £600
Bishopric of Orkney, J. W. Foy, Kirkwall.
Lordship of Dunbar, A. J. Napier, W.S., Edinburgh.
" *of Strathearn,* Earl of Ancaster.

Exchequer, 1 Parliament Square.
Lord Ordinary, Lord Stormonth-Darling.
Queen's Remembrancer, Reginald MacLeod, C.B.
Chief Clerk, R. R. MacGregor.
First Class Clerks, P. P. Sealy ; W. E. Snell ; R. Mackinlay.
Joint-Stock Companies Registry Office, Exchequer Chambers, 1 Parliament Square.
Registrar, Reginald MacLeod, C.B.

Commissary Office, 2 Parliament Square.
Sheriff, Andrew Rutherfurd.
Sheriff-Substitutes, Hubert Hamilton ; T. H. Orphoot ; Charles C. Maconochie............£3,150
Commissary Clerk, Ralph Richardson, W.S....£600
Depute Commissary Clerk, James G. Currie ...£480
Chief Clerk, John Smith.

Justiciary Office, 2 Parliament Square.
Clerk of Justiciary, G. L. Crole, M.A., LL.B., Adv. £700
Depute Clerk, A. D. Veitch £450
Assistant & Depute Clerk, George A. Slight ...£275
Sheriff Clerk of Chancery's Office, 2 Parliament Sq.
Sheriff of Chancery, John Chisholm, LL.B., Adv. £500
Sheriff Clerk of Chancery, John Macmillan, S.S.C.
Depute Sheriff Clerk, Alexander Macmillan, L.A.
Macer, William Allan.

H.M. Office of Works, 3 Parliament Square.
Surveyor for Scotland, W. W. Robertson.
Assistant Surveyors, J. Rutherford ; W. Harris ; W. Gilruth.
Clerk, G. W. Jupp.
Junior Clerk, G. C. Anderson.
Clerks of Works, G. L. Davis ; R. Kennedy.
Draughtsmen, W. Steell ; W. H. A. Ross ; T. Smith ; G. M. Wilson.
Solicitor, T. Carmichael, S.S.C., 10 Duke Street.

Crown Office, 9 Parliament Square.
Crown Agent, W. J. Dundas, C.B. £1,300
Chief Clerk, Hugh Milroy, S.S.C.
Second, W. D. Smart.
Other Clerks, H. Weaver ; W. Glegg ; W. Edgar ; James Kyd Young.
Crofters Commission ; Office, 6 Parliament Square.
Commissioners, David Brand, Advocate (Sheriff of Ayr), *Chairman* (£1,200) ; Wm. Hosack and P. B. Macintyre ....£800 each
Secretary and Principal Clerk, Wm. Mackenzie £700
Assistant Clerk, Arthur Morgan £260
Junior do., Peter Macintyre £150

GOVERNMENT OFFICES IN H.M. GENERAL REGISTER HOUSE, EDINBURGH.
Lord Clerk Register, The Duke of Montrose, K.T.
Keeper of the Records & Registrar-General for Scotland, Sir Stair Agnew, K.C.B., Advocate £1,200
GENERAL RECORD DEPARTMENT.
Deputy Keeper of the Records, M. Livingstone £600

First Clerk, William Sharpe £385
Second Clerks, A. Clark ; P. M. Robertson.

HISTORICAL AND ANTIQUARIAN DEPARTMENT.
Curator, John Maitland Thomson, M.A. £400 to £600
" *Assistant,* Rev. John Anderson £150 to £250

General Registry Births, Deaths, and Marriages.
Registrar-General, Sir Stair Agnew, K.C.B....£1,200
Secretary and Chief Clerk, Daniel Stewart ...£550
Clerks, J. C. Fyfe; John W. Dodd; Thos. McGregor; R. E. Barbour.
Super. Statist. Dep., Dr. R. J. Blair Cunynghame£500
Statistical Clerks, Wm. Ralph; J. J. Cossar; A. W. Carruthers.
Index Clerks, P. Macglashan; John J. Blyth; James Findlay.
Registration Examiners, John Liddell; W. H. Dick Lowe; Grant B. Gibson; R. H. Gray; G.T. Bisset Smith.

Lyon Court.
Lyon King of Arms, James Balfour Paul, F.S.A. Scot., *Advocate*......................£500
Clerk & Keeper of Records, Fras. J. Grant, W.S. £250
Procurator-Fiscal, David Scott-Moncrieff, W.S.

Heralds.
Albany, Robert Spence Livingstone. ⎫
Marchmont, Andrew Ross, S.S.C. ⎬ £25 each.
Rothesay, F. J. Grant. W.S., F.S.A. Scot. ⎭

Pursuivants.
Unicorn, Stuart Moodie Livingstone ⎫
Bute, James K. Lamont, N.P. ⎬ £16 13s. 4d.
Carrick, Wm. Rae Macdonald, F.F.A. ⎭ each.

H.M. Chancery.
Interim Director, J. C. Strettell Miller £300
Interim Depute Do., Colin J. Stalker £350

Extractor's Office.
Principal Extractor, William B. Glen, S.S.C. ...£750
Assistant Extractor D. K. B Whyte £400
Clerk of the Records, Jas. Walker *(and fees)*...£200

Bill Chamber, New Register House.
Principal Clerk of Bills, Petitions, and Sequestrations, D. Antonio ....£600 to 700
Assistant Clerk, James D. Fraser £400
Clerk, C. Edgar Glennie £150
Indexing Clerk, David Duncan £60

Minute Book Office, Parliament Square.
Edictal Citations Office, 16, New Register House.
Keeper of Minute Book, Colin G. Macrae, W.S. £300
Depute Keeper, Alexander R. Forbes £200

Rolls of Court and Calling Lists.
Keepers of Inner House Rolls, J. S. Saunders;
William Gilchrist Roy, S.S.C. ....each £450
Keeper of the Seal of Court, J. S. Saunders.

The Sasine Office.
Keeper of the General Register of Sasines, John Hope Finlay, W.S. £1,000
Chief Assistant Keeper, John A. Ewart £600
Assistant Keepers, J. R. Campbell; R. A. Ireland;
John Maclagan; James Barr; W. Menzies, each £550
Accountant, William McCulloch £400
First Class Clerks, David D. Brown; G. McP. Duffes; C. S. McCabe; E. McGlade; Wm. Leask; Jas. McL. Marr; W. Riach; And. Robertson; W. G. Robertson; E. Steele; Alex. Wilson; T. S. Miller; P. Mortimer; J. Urquhart £400

Hornings, Inhibitions, and Adjudications.
Keeper of the Registers of Hornings, Inhibitions, and Adjudications, John Hope Finlay, W.S.

Register of Deeds and Protests.
Keeper, James Cameron.
Assistants, G. D. Balfour; James Watson.
Chief Clerk, Robt. D. Gray.

Record of Entails Office.
Keeper of the Record, David Winter £50

Accountant of Court (Judicial, Factories, and Bankruptcy).
Accountant, J. Campbell Penney, C.A. £1,200

Chief Clerk, R. M. Rose, A.C.A.
Chief Clerk Bankruptcy Dept., J. U. Anderson.
  „   *Factory Dept.,* J. Henderson, C.A.

Registry of Friendly Societies, 3a Howe Street.
Registrar, R. Addison Smith, S.S.C.
Clerk, Thomas Davie.

PRISON COMMISSIONERS FOR SCOTLAND, 11 Rutland Square, Edinburgh, £6,929. — Lt.-Col. Alex. Burness McHardy, R.E., *Chairman*; R. Mure McKerrell, £1,000; *Secretary,* David Crombie, £450; *Inspector,* Major Willis.

BOARD OF LUNACY, 51 Queen Street, Edinburgh.— *Chairman,* Hon. W. G. Scott (Master of Polwarth); *Secretary,* T. W. L. Spence.

FISHERY BOARD, 101 George Street, Edinburgh.— *Chairman,* Angus Sutherland; *Sec.,* Wm. C. Robertson; *Chief Clerk,* David T. Jones; *Insp. of Salmon Fisheries,* Wm. Leadbetter Calderwood, F.R.S.E.; *Scientific Supt.* T. Wemyss Fulton, M.D., F.R.S.E.; *Gen. Insp. of Sea Fisheries,* Alex. Miltikin.

CONGESTED DISTRICTS BOARD, 6, Parliament Square, Edinburgh.—*Sec.,* R. R. MacGregor.

BOARD OF MANUFACTURES, &c., Royal Institution, Edinburgh.—*Sec.,* A. W. Inglis. (This Board controls the School of Art in the Royal Institution, the National Gallery of Scotland, and the Scottish National Portrait Gallery, Queen Street, Edin.)

ROYAL SCOTTISH ACADEMY, Mound, Edinburgh. *Pres.,* Sir George Reid; *Sec.,* Geo. Hay; *Treas.,* John Hutchison; *Lib.,* W. D. McKay; *Clerk,* James Hastings.

ROYAL SCOTTISH ACADEMICIANS. R.S.A.

1897 Adam, P. W.	1896 Leiper, William.
1888 Alexander, Robt	1878 Lockhart, W. E.
1884 Beattie-Brown, W.	1877 McDonald, J. B.
1896 Blanc, Hippolyte J.	1889 Macgregor, Robt.
1869 Cameron, Hugh.	1883 McKay, W. D.
1882 Gibb, Robert.	1870 McTaggart, Wm.
1892 Guthrie, James.	1892 Noble, J. C.
1895 Hardie, C. M.	1850 Paton, Sir Noel.
1876 Hay, George.	1877 Reid, Sir George.
1889 Hole, William.	1898 Reid, Geo. Ogilvy.
1896 Honeyman, John.	1886 Stevenson, D. W.
1867 Hutchison, John.	1895 Stevenson, W. G.
1895 Johnstone, G. W.	1881 Vallance, W. F.
1896 Lavery, John.	1886 Wingate, J. L.

HON. RETIRED ACADEMICIANS.
Faed, John; Archer, Jas.; Nicol, Erskine.

ASSOCIATES.   A.R.S.A.

Aikman, George.	Michie, J. Coutts.
Bell, R. P.	Murray, David.
Brown, A. K.	Nisbet, Pollok S.
Brown, T. Austen.	Nisbet, R. B.
Browne, G. Washington	Noble, Robert.
Burnet, J. J.	Paterson, James.
Farquharson, David.	Rattray, A. Wellwood.
Henry, George.	Reid, A. D.
Kerr, Henry W.	Reid, R. Payton.
Kinross, John.	Rhind, W. Birnie.
Lorimer, J. H.	Robertson, David.
MacGeorge, W. S.	Roche, Alexander.
Macgillivray, Pittendreigh.	Ross, J. Thorburn.
Mackenzie, A. Marshall.	Scott, Thomas.
Macgregor, W. Y.	Steell, David G.
Melville, Arthur.	Walton, Edward A.

COMMISSIONERS OF NORTHERN LIGHTHOUSES, 84 George Street, Edinburgh.—*Sec.*, Jas. Murdoch. *Engineer*, D. A. Stevenson.

CONVENTION OF ROYAL, PARLIAMENTARY, AND POLICE BURGHS. (Instituted 1150, 1487; Meets at Edinburgh first Tu. of April.)—*Pres.*, The Lord Provost of Edinburgh; *Chaplain*, The Rev. A. Wallace Williamson, M.A.; *Counsel*, R. Vary Campbell, LL.B.; *Clerk*, D.W. Walker, B.L. S.S.C.; *Agent and Treas.*, Wm Officer, S.S.C.; *Convention Officer*, Jas. Russell.

EDINBURGH MEDICAL COLLEGE FOR WOMEN, 20 Chambers Street, Edinburgh; in connection with Royal Infirmary.—*Sec.*, Miss H. F. Mackay. (27 Lecturers are attached to this College.)

EDUCATIONAL INSTITUTE OF SCOTLAND (Incorporated).—*Sec.*, John Laurence, Coatbridge.

EXAMINERS UNDER LAW AGENTS(SCOTLAND) ACTS, 1873 and 1891.—*Chairman*, John Cowan, W.S. Edin.; John Carment, LL.D., S.S.C., Edin.; T. C. Young, LL.B., Glasgow; George Ogilvie, M.A., Dundee; Prof. Moody Stuart, LL.D., Glasgow; Chas. B. Davidson, LL.D., Aberdeen; Prof. J. Dove Wilson, LL.D., Aberdeen; and Prof. Rankine, LL.D., Edin. *Registrar*, John Moir, D.C.S., New Register House, Edin.; *Sec.*, G. S. Donaldson, S.S.C., 15 Hanover Street, Edin.

FACULTY OF ACTUARIES IN SCOTLAND.—*Hall*, 24 George Street, Edinburgh; *Pres.*, David Deuchar; *Vice-Pres.*, James Meikle; *Hon. Sec.*, Thomas Wallace; *Hon. Treas.*, Colin McCuaig, C.A.; *Acting Secretary*, Hy. Moir, 19 St. Andrew Sq.

FACULTY OF ADVOCATES, EDINBURGH.—*Dean of Faculty*, Alex. Asher, Q.C., M.P.; *Vice-Dean*, Sir John Cheyne,Q.C.; *Treas.*, J.Balfour Paul; *Librarian*, J. T. Clark; *Agent*, Geo. M. Paul, W.S.

HIGHLAND AND AGRICULTURAL SOCIETY, 3 George IV. Bridge, Edinburgh.—*Pres.*, Lord Balfour of Burleigh; *Treas.*, Sir James H. Gibson-Craig, Bart.; *Hon. Sec.*, Sir John Gilmour, Bart.; *Sec.*, James Macdonald, F.R.S.E.

INCORPORATED SOCIETY OF LAW AGENTS IN SCOTLAND.—*Pres.*, Jas. W. Barty, LL.D.; *Vice-Pres.*, John P. Kyd; *Sec.*, Robert MacLuckie, Stirling. **L.A.**

INSTITUTE OF BANKERS IN SCOTLAND (1876), 27 Queen Street, Edinburgh.—*Pres.*, T. Hector Smith; *Vice-Pres.*, Robert Blyth, Adam Tait, and George Anderson; *Sec. and Treasurer*, William Baird, Clydesdale Bank, Portobello.

METEOROLOGICAL SOCIETY FOR SCOTLAND (1855), 122 George Street.—*Pres.*, Duke of Richmond and Gordon, K.G.; *Hon. Sec. and Chairman of Medico-Climatological Committee*, Sir Arthur Mitchell, K.C.B.; *Sec.*, Alex. Buchan, LL.D., F.R.S.; *Treas.*, W. B. Wilson, W.S.

NATIONAL PORTRAIT GALLERY, SCOTTISH, Queen Street, Edinburgh.—*Curator*, Jas. L. Caw.

ROYAL COLLEGE OF PHYSICIANS OF EDINBURGH (1681).—*Pres.*, James Andrew, M.D.; *Vice-Pres.*, Sir John Batty Tuke M.D.; *Treas.*, P. A. Young, M.D.; *Sec. & Regist.*, R. W. Philip, M.D.

ROYAL COLLEGE OF SURGEONS OF EDINBURGH (1505).—*President.* James Dunsmure, M.D.; *Vice-President*, Prof. John Chiene; *Treas. and Sec.*, Francis Cadell, M.B.; *Clerk*, James Robertson, Solicitor.

ROYAL OBSERVATORY.—*Astronomer Royal*, Prof. Ralph Copeland, PH.D., F.R.S.E., Prof. of Astronomy in the University of Edinburgh; *First Class Assistants*, T. Heath, B.A.; J. Halm, PH.D.; *Second Assistant*, G. Clark, M.A.

ROYAL PHYSICAL SOCIETY OF EDINBURGH (founded 1771, instituted by Royal Charter, 1788).—*Pres.*, Benj. N. Peach, F.R.S.; *Treas.*, G. Lisle, C.A.; *Sec.* R. H. Traquair, M.D., F.R.S.; *Assist. Sec.*, W. S. Bruce; *Offices*, 3 India Buildings, Edinburgh.

ROYAL SCOTTISH GEOGRAPHICAL SOCIETY (1884).—*Pres.*, The Marquess of Lothian, K.T.; *Hon. Secs.*, Ralph Richardson, F.R.S.E.; J. G. Bartholomew, F.R.S.E.; *Sec.*, Lt.-Col. Bailey, late R.E.; *Hon. Treasurers*, John Cockburn, Edinburgh; Robt. Gourlay, Glasgow; *Hon. Lib.*, James Burgess, C.I.E.,LL.D.; *Hon. Editor*, Prof. Jas. Geikie,D.C.L., F.R.S.; *Acting Editor*,W.A. Taylor, M.A., F.R.S.E.

ROYAL SOCIETY OF EDINBURGH (1783).—*Pres.*, Rt. Hon. Lord Kelvin, G.C.V.O.; *General Sec.*, Prof. Tait, M.A.; *Treas.*, Philip R. D. Maclagan; *Curator of Library and Museum*, Alex. Buchan, LL.D. **F.R.S.E.**

SOCIETY OF ACCOUNTANTS IN EDINBURGH (Chartered).—*Pres.*, David Pearson; *Sec. and Treas.*, Richard Brown; *Auditor*, Francis A. Bringloe; *Law Agent*, David Wardlaw, W.S. **C.A.**

SOCIETY OF ANTIQUARIES, SCOTLAND (1780).—*Pres.*, Marquess of Lothian, K.T.; *Secs.*, David Christison, M.D.; Robert Munro, M.A., M.D.; *Treasurer*, J. H. Cunningham; *Keeper of the National Museum of Antiquities*, Queen Street, Edinburgh, Joseph Anderson, LL.D. **F.S.A., Scot.**

SOCIETY OF WRITERS TO THE SIGNET, EDINBURGH.—*Keeper of the Signet*, The Duke of Montrose, K.T.; *Dep. Keeper*, Sir Charles Logan, LL.D.; *Sub-keeper and Clerk*, John Milligan; *Asst.-Clerk*, J. H. Notman; *Treas.*, Jno. Cowan; *Fiscal*, Robert L. Stuart; *Professor of Conveyancing*, John P. Wood; *Collector of Widows' Fund*, Charles Cook; *Libn.*,T. G. Law, LL.D. **W.S.**

SOLICITORS BEFORE THE SUPREME COURTS, EDINBURGH.—*Pres.*, Wm. White Millar; *Vice-Pres.*, Wm. Drummond; *Treas.*, J. Knox Crauford; *Fiscal*, D. Forbes Dallas; *Collector of Widows' Fund*, Robt. Cumming; *Librarian*, D. A. Scott; *Acting Do.*, Wm. Black; *Sec.*, A. Ellison Ross. **S.S.C.**

LEADING GLASGOW INSTITUTIONS.

ARCHÆOLOGICAL SOCIETY (Instd. 1856), 207 Bath Street.—*Pres.*, Archbishop Eyre, D.D.; *Vice-Pres.*, J. O. Mitchell, LL.D.; Very Rev. Principal Story; Geo. Neilson; *Hon. Secs.*, J. D. Duncan and W. G. Black; *Hon. Treas.*, George J. Walker, C.A.

CHAMBER OF COMMERCE AND MANUFACTURES (Incorp. 1783).—*Pres.*, John Galloway; *Vice-Pres. and Hon. Treas.*, G. Handasyde Dick; *Sec. and Dep. Treas.*, W. H. Hill, LL.D.; *Libr.*, W. Hurst.

FACULTY OF PHYSICIANS AND SURGEONS.—*Pres.*, Dr.H.C. Cameron; *Visitor*,Dr. James Finlayson; *Treas.*, Dr. J. D. Maclaren; *Clerk*, W. H. Hill,

LL.D.; *Sec. and Lib.*, Alex. Duncan, B.A., LL.D. (Faculty Hall, 242 St. Vincent Street.)**L.F.P.S.G.**

FACULTY OF PROCURATORS.—*Dean of Faculty*, Joseph Macintyre Taylor; *Clerk*, *Treas. and Fiscal*, John Fraser Orr, 83 St. Vincent Street.

INSTITUTE OF ACCOUNTANTS AND ACTUARIES (Incorporated), 218 St. Vincent Street.—*Pres.*, John Wilson, C.A.; *Treas.*, W. A. Guild, C.A.; *Auditor*, J. R. Strong, C.A.; *Sec.*, Alexander Sloan, C.A.

INSTITUTION OF ENGINEERS AND SHIPBUILDING IN SCOTLAND, 207 Bath Street.—*Pres.*, Robert Caird, F.R.S.E.; *Vice-Pres.*, James Gilchrist;

Prof. W. H. Watkinson ; Prof. A. Barr, D.SC. ; *Hon. Treas.*, J. M. Gale ; *Sec. and Editor*, E. H. Parker.

PHILOSOPHICAL SOCIETY (Instd. 1802), 207 Bath Street.—*Pres.*, Ebenezer Duncan, M.D. ; *Vice-Presidents*, F. T. Barrett, Gilbert Thomson, M.A. ; *Hon. Libn.*, John Robertson ; *Hon. Sec.*, F. Fergus, M.D. ; *Hon. Treas.*, John Mann, C.A.

ROYAL INFIRMARY.—*Sec.*, Henry Lamond, 93 W. Regent Street ; *Superintendent*, Dr. M. Thomas.

SHERIFF COURT OF LANARKSHIRE.—*Sheriff of County*, Robert Berry, advocate ; *Sheriff Substitutes*, Wm. Guthrie, W. C. Spens, D. D. Balfour, R. U. Strachan, and John Boyd, advocates (Glasgow) ; W. L. Mair, advocate (Airdrie), Mark G. Davidson, advocate (Hamilton), T. A. Fyfe (Lanark) ; *Sheriff-Clerk*, John Downie ; *Procurator Fiscal*, J. N. Hart.

TRUSTEES OF THE CLYDE LIGHTHOUSES.—*Chairman*, George J. Kidston ; *Clerk*, James F. Anderson, 137 St. Vincent Street ; *Treas.*, Thomas Adam, 16 Robertson St.

TRUSTEES OF THE CLYDE NAVIGATION, 16 Robertson Street. — *Chairman*, The Hon. the Lord Provost of Glasgow ; *Deputy Do.*, John Ure, LL D. ; *Sec.*, T. R. Mackenzie ; *Treas.*, Thomas Adam ; *Engineer*, James Deas ; *Harbour-Master*, Robert White ; *Collector*, Walter Macfarlane ; *Mechanical Engineer*, George H. Baxter ; *Pilot Master*, Capt. Morris ; *General Traffic Supt.*, William Stewart.

VICTORIA INFIRMARY.—*Chairman*, Sir Renny Watson ; *Hon. Treas.*, W. B. Crawford ; *Hon. Sec.*, John Laing ; *Sec. and Treas.*, F. Bisset, 22 Carlton Place, S.S. ; *Sup.*, Dr. W. Nicholson, M.B. ; *Matron*, Miss M. M. McFarlane.

WESTERN INFIRMARY (Incorporated) —*Chairman* James H. Dickson ; *Vice-do* Matthew Arthur ; *Sec. and Cashier*, Henry Johnston, 125 Buchanan Street ; *Sup.*, Dr. Donald J. Mackintosh.

ANDERSON'S COLLEGE MEDICAL SCHOOL.—*Pres.*, A. Malloch Bayne ; *Vice-Presiden*, Chas. M. King ; *Sec.*, J. B. Kidston, 50 West Regent Street ; *Dean of Faculty of Medicine*, Dr. T. Kennedy Dalziel.

GLASGOW ATHENÆUM, LIMITED (Instd. 1847), St. George's Place.—*Pres.*, Sir J. Stirling-Maxwell, Bt., M.P. ; *Chair. of Directors*, Dr. T. Lapraik ; *Vice-Do.*, Maj. J.Cassells ; *Sec.*, J. Lauder, F.R.S.L.

GLASGOW SCHOOL OF ART. 167 Renfrew Street.—*Chairman of Governors*, Jas. Fleming ; *Sec. and Treasurer*, E. R. Catterns ; *Head-Master*, Francis H. Newbery.

ST. MUNGO'S COLLEGE.—*Pres.*, Hugh Brown ; *Vice-Pres.*, Robt. Ramsey ; *Sec.*, Hy. Lamond, 93 W. Regent St.

TERM DAYS IN SCOTLAND.

Candlemas, 2nd Feb. ; Whitsunday, 15th May ; Lammas, 1st Aug. ; Martinmas, 11th Nov. ; Removal Terms, 28 May, 28 November.

When a Scottish Term falls on a Sunday, the day after is held as Term Day.

LAW TERMS.—Sittings, 15th October to 20th March ; 12th May to 20th July.

BANK HOLIDAYS.—New Year's Day, 1st Jan. ; Christmas Day [if either of the preceding falls on a Sunday, the Monday following shall be the Bank Holiday] ; Good Friday ; First Monday in May ; First Monday in August.

The above, with the addition of Her Majesty's Birthday, are also the holidays observed in Customs and Inland Revenue Offices.

CONVENERS AND SHERIFFS OF SCOTTISH COUNTIES.

CONVENER OF COUNTY.	COUNTY.	SHERIFF-PRINCIPAL.	
A. M. Gordon of Newton	*Aberdeen*	Donald Crawford	£1,000
Lord Malcolm, C.B., of Poltalloch	*Argyll*	James Ferguson, M.A.	700
R. M. Pollok of Middleton	*Ayr*	David Brand	700
Sir G. M. Grant of Ballindalloch, Bt.	*Banff*	Donald Crawford	
Sir Geo. H. Boswall of Blackadder, Bt.	*Berwick*	Richard Vary Campbell, LL.D.	750
Thomas Russell of Ascog	*Bute*	Sir John Cheyne, B.A., Q.C.	950
John Miller of Scrabster	*Caithness*	Christopher N. Johnston	775
Lord Balfour of Burleigh	*Clackmannan*	J. M'Kie Lees, M.A.	800
Lord Overtoun of Overtoun	*Dumbarton*	J. M'Kie Lees, M.A.	
(Vacant)	*Dumfries & Galloway*	Charles Rampini	700
Sir Robert Dundas of Arniston, Bart.	*Edinburgh*	Andrew Rutherfurd	1,800
		(Sheriff of The Lothians and Peebles.)	
J. G. Peterkin of Grange	*Elgin or Moray*	William Ivory	800
Earl of Elgin and Kincardine	*Fife*	Æneas J. G. Mackay, LL.D., Q.C.	800
Earl of Camperdown	*Forfar*	Henry Johnston, B.A., Q.C.	1,000
Earl of Wemyss and March	*Haddington*	(Included in The Lothians.)	
Donald Cameron of Lochiel	*Inverness*	William Ivory	800
Jas. Badenoch Nicolson of Glenbervie	*Kincardine*	Donald Crawford.	
Sir Charles Adam of Blairadam, Bart.	*Kinross*	Æneas J. G. Mackay, LL.D.,Q.C.	
W. J. Maxwell, yngr., of Munches	*Kirkcudbright*	Charles Rampini	
Lord Hamilton of Dalzell	*Lanark*	Barns Graham (Glasgow)	2,000
Thomas Hope of Bridgecastle	*Linlithgow*	(Included in The Lothians.)	
Col. M. A. Clark of Achareidh	*Nairn*	William Ivory	
Col. J. W. Balfour of Balfour	*Orkney*	Christopher N. Johnston	775
Sir G. Graham-Montgomery, Bart.	*Peebles*	Andrew Rutherfurd	
Col. Home Drummond	*Perth*	Andrew Jameson, M.A., Q.C.	852
Sir Michael R. Shaw-Stewart, Bart.	*Renfrew*	Sir John Cheyne, B.A., Q.C.	962
Sir Kenneth Smith Mackenzie, Bart.	*Ross and Cromarty*	William Charles Smith	812
Lord Polwarth	*Roxburgh*	Richard Vary Campbell, LL.D.	750
Hugh M. Lang of Broadmeadows	*Selkirk*	Ronald Bailie.	
John Bruce of Sumburgh	*Shetland*	Christopher N. Johnston.	
(Vacant)	*Stirling*	J. M'Kie Lees, M.A.	800
Rev. John Murray, Brora	*Sutherland*	William Charles Smith.	
Earl of Stair, K.T.	*Wigtown*	James Wallace, M.A.	

The Sheriff-Principal of Lanark resides in Glasgow, all the others reside in Edinburgh.

IRELAND is an island lying between 51° 26′ and 55° 23′ N. lat. and 5° 20′ and 10° 26′ W. long. It is about 60 miles to the west of England. On three sides it is washed by the Atlantic Ocean, and on the east by the Irish Sea and St. George's Channel. Its greatest length is, from north to south, 306 miles, and from east to west from 120 to 180, with an area of about 31,759 square miles, or 20,326,209 acres. The greater part of the surface is a plain, interspersed with low hills, the highest mountain being 3,414 feet above the sea-level. The rivers are numerous, the Shannon, 254 miles in length, being the principal; but the chief water feature of the country is the beautiful series of lakes or (as they are called) loughs, the largest, Lough Neagh, covering a surface of 98,255 acres. The harbours are among the finest in the world. The climate is temperate, and many plants which can only be grown in hot-houses in England flourish in the open air in Ireland; while the great moisture which generally prevails is so favourable to vegetation that the country early received the name of the Green or Emerald Isle.

The population of Ireland on April 3, 1891, was 4,704,750, a decrease of 470,086—equal to 9·1 per cent. since the preceding Census of 1881. It was not till 1821 that the first complete census was taken, and the numbers were then found to be 6,801,827; in 1831 they had increased to 7,767,401, and in 1841 to 8,175,124. The highest point was reached in 1845, when the entire population was estimated at 8,295,061. The potato crop, upon which all the agricultural and many of the manufacturing poor depended for their subsistence, having failed for two successive years, produced famine and disease, which carried off large numbers, and

gave a great impulse to emigration, so that from 1845 the population rapidly decreased.

The conquest of Ireland was begun in the year 1170, but can hardly be regarded as completed until the surrender of Limerick in 1691, and was declared a kingdom in 1542; and this kingdom was united to that of Great Britain by the Act of Union, on Jan. 1st, 1801, the empty title of "King of France," which the English kings had borne since the time of Edward III., being abandoned.

The government is semi-independent. A Lord-Lieutenant, appointed by each successive Ministry, exercises almost regal sway. He has a salary of £20,000, but being usually a nobleman of large private fortune, his expenditure is frequently much more than the amount received. The peerage consists of 176 members, who are represented in the Imperial Parliament by 28 of their number; and 103 members represent the country in the House of Commons.

The prevailing religion is Roman Catholic, 75 per cent. of the population professing that form of faith. Until the year 1871 the Established Church was a branch of that of England, with two archbishops and ten bishops, although the members of this communion were but 12 per cent.—9 per cent. of the remaining Protestants being Presbyterians.

Ireland is well supplied with educational establishments, having two universities, a large number of secondary schools, indirectly endowed under the Intermediate Education Board, and an admirable system of Primary Schools under the National School Commissioners.

The legal establishment is similar to that of England, and is presided over by a Lord Chancellor.

THE LORD LIEUTENANT.

His Excellency the Right Honourable George Henry, 5th Earl Cadogan, K.G., G.M.P., *born* 12th May, 1840; succeeded his father 8th June, 1873; *married*, 16th May, 1865, Lady Beatrix, 4th daughter of 2nd Earl of Craven; Lord Lieutenant General and General Governor of Ireland; sworn in 8th July, 1895 .... £20,000

Chief Secretary and Keeper of Privy Seal—Right Hon. Gerald William Balfour, M.P. £4,425	*Perm. Under Sec.*, Sir David Harrel, K.C.B....£2,000
Private Secretary, Laurence C. Dowdall.	*Private Secretary*, W. P. J. Connolly.
	Assistant Under Secretary, J. B. Dougherty.

LORD LIEUTENANT'S HOUSEHOLD.—£4,764.

Private Sec., Sir William Squire Barker Kaye, Q.C., C.B. £829
Additional Private Sec., Algernon Robert Peel.
Asst. Private Secs., Herbert Fetherston-Haugh; J. McCraw (*financial*).

Ulster King of Arms, Sir Arthur E. Vicars ...	300
State Steward, Lord Lurgan	506
Comptroller, Lord Langford..........................	414
Gentleman Usher, John Olphert	200
Chamberlain, Col. Sir Gerald Richard Dease	200
Master of the Horse, Col. F. R. Forster	200

Gentlemen in Waiting, Herbert Fetherston-Haugh; Capt. Hon. O. F. S. Cuffe; Capt. J. Harrison 129
Aides-de-Camp, Major Lord Athlumney; Capt.

the Hon. Murrough O'Brien; Capt. Hon. G. O. Cadogan; Lieut. Sir John Keane, Bt., R.A. each £200
Extra Aides-de-Camp, Capt. Wm. Van de Weyer; Capt. F. Wise; Capt. Lord George Scott; Capt. C. W. Feilden; Capt. W. A. Tilney; Lieut. the Earl of Granard; Lieut. W. H. B. Long.
Physician in Ordinary, Walter G. Smith, M.D.
Surgeons in Ordinary, Edward Hamilton, M.D.; Sir William Thomson, M.D.
Surgeon to Household, J. Lentaigne, F.R.C.S.I., £100
Surgeon Oculist, Archibald H. Jacob, M.D.
Surg.-Dentist in Ord., Robt. H. Moore, F.R.C.S.I.
First Chaplain, Very Rev. Hercules H. Dickinson, D.D. (Dean of Chapel Royal) 335
Sub-Dean, Rev. R. G. M. Webster, M.A. ....

SUPREME COURT OF JUDICATURE.
COURT OF APPEAL.

Ex-Officio Judges.—The Lord Chancellor, the Lord Chief Justice, the Master of the Rolls, the Chief Baron of the Exchequer.
Lords Justices of Appeal.—Rt. Hon. Gerald Fitz-Gibbon: Rt. Hon. Hugh Holmes; Rt. Hon. Samuel Walker (*additional*) .... each £4,000

HIGH COURT OF JUSTICE.
CHANCERY DIVISION.

Lord Chancellor, Rt. Hon. Ld. Ashbourne . £8,000

Master of the Rolls, Rt. Hon. A. M. Porter £4,000
Vice-Chancellor, Rt. Hon. H. E. Chatterton £4,000
Land Judge, Hon. John Ross, Q.C. £3,500

QUEEN'S BENCH DIVISION.

Ld. Ch. Justice, Rt. Hon. Sir Peter O'Brien, Bt., £5,000
Chief Baron, Rt. Hon. Christopher Palles....£4,600
Judges, Rt. Hon. Wm. O'Brien; Rt. Hon. William Drennan Andrews (*Probate*); Rt. Hon. Wm. Moore Johnson (*Admiralty*); Rt. Hon. James Murphy; Rt. Hon. John G. Gibson; Rt. Hon.

Dodgson H. Madden: Hon. Walter Boyd (*Bankruptcy*); Hon. William Kenny each £3,500
Masters, D. R. Pigot; W. R. Bruce; A. H. Courtenay ....each £1,200
Chief Probate Registrar, H. C. Warren, B.A. £1,100
Judge's Registrar, Robert Travers, B.L. £700
Assistant Registrar, Jacob T. Geoghegan £700
Accountant Genl. Supreme Court, Luke Teeling.
Chief Registrar, Bankruptcy, W. H. S. Monck £800
Chief Clerk, Hugh Doyle £800
Registrars, A. F. Lloyd £500
Deputy Do., H. F. Gibson £368
Senior Clerk, T. Hamilton £318
Official Assignees, J. Arthur Maconchy, and A. K. McEntire .... fees

IRISH LAND COMMISSION.—£112,431.

Jud. Commr., Hon. Mr. Justice Meredith ...£3,500
Commissioners, Hon. Gerald Fitzgerald, Q.C.; Frederick S. Wrench, each £3,000; S. J. Lynch, £2,500; Morrough O'Brien £2,000
Secretary, John H. Franks, C.B.

LAW OFFICERS.

Attorney-General, The Rt. Hon. John Atkinson, Q.C., M.P. £5,000
Solicitor-Gen., Dunbar P. Barton, Q.C., M.P. £2,000
Crown Solicitor, Sir Patrick Coll, C.B.

PAYMASTER-GENERAL'S DEPARTMENT.
Castle, Dublin.

Treasury Remembrancer and Deputy Paymaster in Ireland, R.W. Arbuthnot Holmes, C.B.... £1,200
Principal Clerk. Henry Hitchins £700 to £800
Clerk, A. Ormsby .... £350 to £500

Local Government Board, Custom House, Dublin; *Vice-President*, Hy. Aug. Robinson, C.B. £2,000
Secretary, H. M. Swaine.

Board of Public Works, Custom House, Dublin; *Chairman*, Thomas Robertson £2,500
Commissioners, Richard O'Shaughnessy; George A. Stevenson. *Secretary*, Henry Williams.

General Register Office, Charlemont Ho., Dublin. *Registrar-General*, Thomas W. Grimshaw, C.B.,M.D.
Secretary and Assist. Registrar-General, Robert E. Matheson, B.L.

STATISTICS OF IRISH COUNTIES, WITH NAMES OF LIEUTENANTS.

*The total number of Emigrants who left Ireland from 1st May, 1851, to 31st Dec., 1897, was 3,760,531.

PROVINCES AND COUNTIES.	Population.	Extent in Acres.	Rateable Valuation of Property.	*Irish Emigrants.	Poor Rate lodged in year ended 29 Sept.	Number in receipt of Poor Relief on 24 Sept.	LIEUTENANTS AND CUSTODES ROTULORUM.
LEINSTER.	1891.	1891.	1898.	1897.	1897.	1898.	
Carlow	40,936	221,295	£165,234	16	£12,984	1,024	Lord Rathdonnell.
Dublin	419,216	226,821	1,567,496	747	120,725	11,030	Earl of Meath.
Kildare	70,206	418,496	339,557	170	22,322	1,902	Robert Kennedy.
Kilkenny	87,261	507,254	358,717	272	28,666	2,376	Marq. of Ormonde, K.P.
King's	65,563	493,263	244,158	185	19,464	1,437	Earl of Rosse, K.P.
Longford	52,647	257,770	153,067	343	15,081	1,325	Earl of Longford.
Louth	71,038	201,619	243,266	216	26,015	3,588	Lord Bellew.
Meath	76,987	578,298	550,091	346	35,173	2,458	Simson Mangan.
Queen's	64,883	424,853	260,637	279	12,713	1,094	Viscount de Vesci.
Westmeath	65,109	434,017	318,167	184	21,263	1,457	Lord Castlemaine.
Wexford	111,778	573,200	377,400	256	30,815	3,306	Ld. Maurice FitzGerald.
Wicklow	62,136	499,822	277,841	51	19,078	1,555	Earl of Carysfort, K.P.
MUNSTER.	1,187,760	4,836,708	4,855,631	3,210	364,299	31,552	
Clare	124,483	768,265	319,620	1,164	33,422	3,514	Lord Inchiquin, K.P.
Cork	438,432	1,838,921	1,253,485	5,840	125,834	13,661	Earl of Bandon.
Kerry	179,136	1,159,356	296,522	2,850	38,388	4,756	Earl of Kenmare, K.P.
Limerick	158,912	662,973	536,686	722	64,844	5,979	Earl of Dunraven, K.P.
Tipperary.........	173,188	1,048,968	683,105	1,380	61,023	5,385	Earl De Montalt.
Waterford........	98,251	456,198	320,305	842	29,085	3,030	Duke of Devonshire,K.G.
ULSTER.	1,172,402	5,934,681	3,409,123	12,798	352,596	36,325	
Antrim	428,128	711,276	1,534,984	978	77,038	7,417	[Bart. Sir F. E.W. Macnaghten,
Armagh	143,289	313,036	444,411	494	12,327	1,026	Earl of Gosford, K.P.
Cavan	111,917	467,025	278,583	1,074	14,766	1,450	Earl of Lanesborough.
Donegal	185,635	1,190,268	302,643	983	15,801	1,271	Duke of Abercorn, K.G.
Down	267,059	611,927	930,431	472	26,644	2,855	Marq. of Dufferin, K.P.
Fermanagh	74,170	417,665	240,968	419	8,071	452	Earl of Erne, K.P. [Bt.
Londonderry	152,009	513,388	407,851	602	16,167	938	Rt. Hon. Sir H.H. Bruce,
Monaghan	86,206	318,805	274,707	425	11,013	801	Lord Rossmore.
Tyrone	171,401	778,043	457,664	819	24,055	1,729	Earl of Belmore,G.C.M.G.
CONNAUGHT.	1,619,814	5,322,334	4,932,242	6,265	206,892	7,940	
Galway	214,712	1,502,362	478,311	3,166	43,395	3,421	Lord Clonbrock.
Leitrim	78,618	376,510	137,947	644	9,985	1,136	Lord Harlech.
Mayo	219,034	1,318,130	318,419	3,995	26,653	2,960	Earl of Arran.
Roscommon	114,397	585,407	297,204	1,249	16,897	1,793	Rt.Hn.TheO'Conor Don
Sligo	98,013	451,815	219,069	1,207	13,927	1,358	Rt.-Hon. E. H. Cooper.
	724,774	4,234,224	1,459,750	10,261	110,857	10,668	
Total, IRELAND	4,704,750	20,327,947	14,647,746	32,535	1,034,644	96,485	

ISLE OF MAN (MONA),

an island in the Irish Sea, in lat. 54° 3'—54° 25' N. and long. 4° 18'—4° 47' W., nearly equidistant from England, Scotland, and Ireland. It is about 34 miles long, and from 10 to 12 broad, containing an area of 145,325 acres, with a population of 55,598. Curiously enough the history of the island is intimately linked with that of the Hebrides and the kingdoms of Scotland and Norway. In the ninth century a body of malcontents from Norway emigrated to the western isles of Scotland, and their prosperity drew upon them the anger of the Norwegian monarch Harold, who in the year 870 set forth a great expedition, conquered the Orkneys and the Shetlands, the Western Isles, and Man, and added them to the kingdom already beneath his sway. For three centuries the Norwegian rule remained intact, but when, in 1263, Alexander III. defeated the famous Haco, at the Battle of Largs, all these islands fell under Scottish rule. On his accession to the English throne, Henry IV. seized on the Isle of Man, and in 1406 bestowed it on the Stanley family. In 1736 James, 10th Earl of Derby, died without issue male; the earldom went to his next male heir, but the sovereignty of the island went, with the Barony of Strange, to his heir general, James, Duke of Athole, on whose death the island descended to his daughter Charlotte, from whom, in 1765, Parliament purchased the sovereignty for £70,000. In 1827 the Crown purchased it for the sum of £417,144. The land is rich in minerals, lead, iron, blende, and slate, and exports large quantities of agricultural produce. About 50 miles of railway have been constructed, and about 23 miles of electric tram roads. The natives of this island belong to a mingled race of Celts and Norwegians, and the language, in which the Celtic element is predominant, is known as the Manx.

Man is governed by an independent Legislature called the Tynwald, consisting of two branches—the Governor and Council, and the House of Keys. Bills after having passed both Houses are signed by the Members, and then sent for the Royal Assent. Unless signed by the legal quorum of each House a Bill is not sent for the Royal Assent, the quorum of the Upper House or Council being the Governor and two Members, and of the Lower House or Keys thirteen Members, the majority of the whole number (24). After receiving the Royal Assent, it does not become law until promulgated in the English and Manx languages on the Tynwald Hill. On the promulgation taking place a certificate thereof is signed by the Governor and the Speaker of the House of Keys.

CAPITAL: Douglas, pop. 19,525 (Castletown, pop. 2,178, is the ancient capital); the other towns are Peel, pop. 3,5 , and Ramsey, pop. 4,866.

Public revenue, 1898-99	£78,111
Public expenditure, 1898-99	71,425
Public debt, 1899	276,852

Lieut.-Governor, The Rt. Hon. Lord Henniker	(*with house*)	£1,800
Clerk of the Rolls, Sir A. Dumbell, Kt.		1,000
First Deemster, Sir James Gell, Kt.		1,000
Second Deemster, Thomas Kneen		1,000
Attorney-General, George Alfred Ring		1,000
Receiver-General, Colonel W. J. Anderson		230
Sec. to Govt. & Treasr., A. B. Herbert-Story		500
Speaker, House of Keys, A. W. Moore, M.A.		unp.

THE CHANNEL ISLANDS

comprise the bailiwicks of Jersey and Guernsey (in the latter of which are comprehended the small islands of Alderney, Sark, and Herm, and the Minquiers and Ecréhou Rocks), situated off the north-west coast of France, at distances of from ten to thirty miles. They are the only portions of the Dukedom of Normandy now belonging to England, to which they have been attached ever since the Conquest. The area altogether is about 73 square miles; and the population in 1891 was 92,272—Jersey, 54,518, Guernsey with Herm and Jetou 35,243, Alderney, 1,857, and Sark, 570. The land under cultivation in Jersey amounts to 20,000 acres, under about 2,500 proprietors, and more than 700 varieties of flowering plants and ferns, including many species not to be found among British flora, may be obtained there. The principal officer is the Lieut.-Governor, who represents Her Majesty. French is the official language of the local legislature, called the *States,* and of the Royal Court, but the old Norman dialect is still spoken by the people. The Bailiff, appointed by the Crown, presides over the *States* and over the Royal Court. The royal court is the judicial body, and is composed of twelve jurats elected by the people. The States consist of fifty members (excluding the president), viz., the twelve jurats, twelve rectors, twelve constables, and fourteen deputies, three for St. Helier and one for each of the eleven country parishes. The climate of these islands is mild, and the soil exceptionally productive. An abundance of early potatoes are grown for the London markets, 63,040 tons (value £330,421) being exported in 1899, and the famous Jersey and Guernsey breed of cows has earned a well-deserved celebrity. The islands being all but exempt from taxation, they possess a very large trade. The chief town of Jersey is St. Helier, on the south side, where there is excellent sea-bathing; the principal town of Guernsey is St. Pierre, on the east coast. In 1896 an act was passed removing certain impediments to marriage with a deceased wife's sister.

Imports from United Kingdom, 1898	£1,299,111
Exports to United Kingdom, 1898	1,553,065

JERSEY.— *Lieut.-Governor,* Lieut-General
    Edward Hopton, C.B. £1,700
Govt. Sec., Lieut.-Col. A. Ward-Simpson.
Bailiff, William Henry Venables-Vernon.
Dean, Very Rev. George Orange Balleine, M.A.
Procurator-Gen., Adolphus Hilgrove Turner, M.A.
Viscount, Reginald Raoul Lemprière.
Solicitor-Gen., Henry Edward Le Vavasseur.
Receiver-General, A. Le Gallais.

Revenue, 1896, £108,303; Expenditure ..		100,499
Public debt, 1896		310,000

GUERNSEY AND DEPENDENCIES (INCLUDING ALDERNEY).

Lieut.-Gov., Maj.-Gen. M. H. Saward... .. £1,700
Government Sec., Col. W. Bell, C.B., A.D.C.
Bailiff, Thomas Godfrey Carey.
Dean, Very Rev. Thomas Bell, M.A.
Attorney-General, Edward C. Ozanne.
Solicitor-General, Arthur W. Bell.
Receiver-General, Hilary M. Carré 300
Supt. of Education, J. A. Munday.

Judge and Acting Attorney-General (Alderney), Nicholas Barbenson. *Receiver,* W. Gauvin.

Revenue, 1896, £62,823; Expenditure, £64,451	
Public debt, 1896	135,684

LONDON was a place of importance under the Romans, and was famed for its vast conflux of traders and its abundant commerce even in the first century of the Christian era. From the Romans it received municipal institutions, which have endured in their main features to the present day. In Saxon times it was in reality a small independent State, and its burgesses maintained their independence even after the Battle of Hastings. William the Norman only gained possession of their city by means of a treaty with them; and about eight years after he granted a charter, which is still preserved. It is addressed to William the Bishop, Godfrey the Portreeve, and all the Burgesses, and promises that they shall be "law worthy" (i.e., possessed of privileges) as they were in the days of Edward the Confessor. The Portreeve, however, received the Norman title of Bailiff, which, in 1189, was changed to Mayor; the first holder under the new name being Henry Fitzalwyn, who filled the office for 24 years. On his death a new charter was granted by King John in 1214, which directed the Mayor to be chosen annually, which has ever since been done, though in early times the same individual often held the office more than once. A familiar instance is that of "Whittington, thrice Lord Mayor of London" (in reality, four times, A.D. 1397, 1398, 1406, 1409); and modern cases occur with Alderman Wood, 1815, 1816; Sir John Key, 1830, 1831; Alderman Cubitt, 1861, 1862; and Alderman Sir R. N. Fowler, 1883, 1885. The title of Lord Mayor was first bestowed in 1354 on Sir Thomas Legge, by Edward III.

Aldermen were first appointed by a charter of Henry III. in 1242, and were elected annually until 1394, when a charter of Richard II. directed them to be chosen for life. The Common Council was at an early date substituted for a popular assembly called the Folkmote. At first only two representatives were sent from each ward, but the number has since been greatly increased, some wards having as many as 16 members, and none less than 4. Sheriffs (as well as aldermen) were Saxon officers, who usually had charge of a large district. The time of their appointment for London is uncertain, but it is commonly placed in A.D. 1189. At first they were only the officers of the Crown, and were named by the Barons of the Exchequer; but Edward IV., whose cause was favoured by the citizens of London, gave them, in the first year of his reign, permission to choose their own Sheriffs. The citizens, however, lost this privilege as far as the election of Sheriff of Middlesex is concerned, by the Local Government Act, 1888, but they continue as heretofore to choose the Sheriffs of the City of London. They are appointed on Midsummer Day, and enter on office at Michaelmas, on which day the Lord Mayor is elected. He is sworn into office on November 8, and on the following day presented to the Lord Chief Justice at the Royal Courts of Justice, to take the final declaration of office—the pageant, conducted with some degree of civic state, being popularly known as the Lord Mayor's Show. The Recorder was first appointed in 1298. The Chamberlain is mentioned as a royal officer in 1195; when he became a civic official is not known; but the Town Clerk (called Common Clerk) and Common Serjeant (now appointed by the Crown) are mentioned as "ancient" officers in the Charter of Edward II. (A.D. 1319).

The Lord Mayor, Aldermen, and Principal Officers of the City of London.

Lord Mayor. £10,000.
The Rt. Hon. Alfred James Newton .... { Bassishaw .... }
Private Secretary, William Jameson Soulsby, C.B.. { Mansion House, E.C. }

Aldermen.	Ward.	Address.	Ald. 1890	Shff. 1888	Mayor. 1899
Sir John Whittaker Ellis, Bart.	Broad Street	29 Fleet Street, E.C.	1872	1874	1881
Sir Henry Edmund Knight, Kt.	Cripplegate	41 Hill St., Mayfair, W.	1874	1875	1882
Sir Reg. Hanson, Bt., LL.D., M.P.	Billingsgate	4 Bryanston Square, W.	1880	1881	1886
Sir Joseph Savory, Bart., M.P.	Bridge Without	31 Lombard Street, E.C.	1883	1882	1890
Sir David Evans, K.C.M.G.	Castle Baynard	24 Watling Street, E.C.	1884	1885	1891
Sir Joseph Renals, Bart.	Aldersgate	108 Fore Street, E.C.	1888	1892	1894
Sir Walter Hny. Wilkin, K.C.M.G.	Lime Street	43 Gloucester Square, W.	1888	1892	1895
Sir G. Faudel-Phillips, Bt., G.C.I.E.	Farringd. Within	Balls Park, Hertford	1888	1884	1896
Sir Horatio D. Davies, K.C.M.G., M.P.	Bishopsgate	21 Bishopsgate St., Without	1889	1887	1897
Sir John Voce Moore, Kt.	Candlewick	35 King William Street, E.C.	1889	1893	1898

All the above have passed the Civic Chair.

Frank Green	Vintry	74 Belsize Park Gardens, N.W.	1891	1897	......
Sir J. Cockfield Dimsdale, Kt.	Cornhill	50 Cornhill, E.C.	1891	1893	......
Sir Marcus Samuel, Kt.	Portsoken	20 Portland Place, W.	1891	1894	......
Sir James Thomson Ritchie, Kt.	Tower	6 Lime Street, E.C.	1891	1896	......
John Pound	Aldgate	84 Leadenhall Street, E.C.	1892	1895	......
Walter Vaughan Morgan	Cordwainer	Christ's Hospital, E.C.	1892	......	......
William Purdie Treloar	Farringd. Without	Ludgate Hill, E.C.	1892	1899	......
John Charles Bell	Coleman St.	95 Finsbury Pavement, E.C.	1894	......	......
George Wyatt Truscott	Dowgate	3 Suffolk Lane, E.C.	1895	......	......
Frederick Prat Alliston	Bread Street	46 Friday Street, E.C.	1895	1898	......
Samuel Green	Walbrook	28 St. Swithin's Lane, E.C.	1897	......	......
Sir John C. Knill, Bart.	Bridge Within	5 Adelaide Place, E.C.	1897	......	......
Thomas Vezey Strong	Queenhithe	196, Upper Thames Street, S.E.	1897	......	......
Harry George Smallman	Cheap	2 Queen Street. E.C.	1898	......	......
Thomas Boor Crosby, M.D.	Langbourne	13 Fenchurch Street, E.C.	1898	......	......

OFFICERS OF THE CITY OF LONDON.
Appointed by the Court of Aldermen.

	Elect.		Elect.

RECORDER—The Right Hon. Sir Charles Hall, K.C.M.G., Q.C., M.P. £4,000 1892
High Steward of Southwark, The Recorder £79 7 0 1892
Clerk to Lord Mayor, Cecil G. Douglas £1,150 1887
Assistant, J. G. Trotter £550 1887

Cashier, R. A. Warren £300 1893
Clerk to Sitting Justices (Guildhall) Herbert George Savill £1,000 1887
Assistant, S. Richards £500 1888
Cashier and Account., John H. Major ...£200 1895

Appointed by the Court of Common Council.

TOWN CLERK—Sir John Braddick Monckton, Knt., F.S.A. £3,500 1873
Com. Serjeant, Sir Forrest Fulton, Q.C.£3,000 1892
Judge of City of London Court (and other offices), Robert Malcolm Kerr, LL.D.£3,200 1859
Assistant Judge of the Mayor's Court, Francis Roxburgh £1,500 1887
Commissioner of Police, Lieut.-Col. Sir Henry Smith, K.C.B. £1,500 1890
Comptroller, Edgar Alexander Baylis £2,000 1898
Remembrancer, Gabriel P. Goldney ...£2,000 1882
Solicitor, H. Homewood Crawford £2,250 1885
Secondary and High Bailiff of Southwark, Thomas Roderick £1,500 1884
Medical Officer and Public Analyst, Wm. Sedgwick Saunders,M.D.,F.I.C.,F.S.A.£1,700 1874
Coroner, Samuel Fred. Langham £1,155 1884
Clerk of the Peace, Alfred Read £210 1896
Surveyor, Andrew Murray,A.R.I.B.A...£1,250 1891
Head Master of City of London School, Arthur Tempest Pollard, M.A. £1,250 1889

2nd Master, Frederick Wm. Hill, M.A. ...£500 1890
Head Master of Freemen's Orphan School, R. E. Montague, M.A. £350 1890
Registrar of Mayor's Court, F. S. Jackson... ....£1,000 1890
Deputy Registrar, David Harrison........£500 1890
Sword-Bearer, George J. W. Winzar ...£500 1874
Common Crier, Col. Eustace B. Burnaby£400 1889
Marshal (vacant).......................£350
Principal Clerk to the Chamberlain, G. A. Pickering £1,000 1854
Registrar City of London Court, James Anstey Wild, jun. £1,700 1889
High Bailiff of do., J. E. Sly £600 1892
Prothonotary, Edgar Alexander Baylis £100 1879
Librarian, Charles Welch, F.S.A. £750 1888
Keeper of Guildhall, James Gannon ...£550 1880
Medical Officer Port of London, Wm. Collingridge, M.D.,M.R.C.S. £1,000 1880
Principal of the Guildhall School of Music, William Hayman Cummings ...£1,000 1896

CHAMBERLAIN—Sir Wm. J. R. Cotton, Knt., £2,000. Elected by the Livery, 1893.
Sheriffs, William Purdy Treloar (Ald.), Ludgate Hill, E.C. and Alfred Henry Bevan, 39 Queen's Gate, S.W.
Under-Sheriffs, William Henry Cortlandt Mahon, 33 Ely Place, E.C., and Joseph David Langton, 12 New Inn, Strand, W.C.
Chaplain to the Lord Mayor, Rev. James Stephen Barrass (St. Lawrence Jewry, E.C.).

RECEIPTS AND EXPENDITURE for the year ending 31st December, 1898.

Dr. INCOME.	£	Cr. EXPENDITURE.	£
Balance in hand 31st Dec., 1897	11,209	Expenses of Civil Government	67,308
Rents and Quit-rents	181,153	Donations, Pensions, &c.	23,761
Renewing Fines.............................	622	Educational Expenses......................	14,598
Interest on Government Securities.........	1,209	Administration of Justice (Criminal) ...	8,146
Do. on City Bonds and India Stock .	2,259	Office of Coroner (gross)	2,904
Income Tax Retained.......................	3,204	City Library, Museum, Art Gallery	8,946
Markets, viz.:—		Collection and Management, Rates, &c....	45,233
Metropolitan Cattle Market, Islington	21,937	Charges on Markets, viz.:—	
London Central Markets, Smithfield...	128,541	Billingsgate	20,620
Leadenhall	7,562	Metropolitan Cattle Market, Islington	28,325
Billingsgate	24,122	London Central Markets, Smithfield...	87,341
Metage of Corn, Fruit, &c.	691	Other Markets, &c.	6,255
Mayor's Court Fees (Gross)	6,986	Charges : Metage	1,237
Judiciary Fees	2,079	Expenses of Magistracy and Police	47,163
Reimbursement on Office of Coroner	1,200	City Pauper Lunatic Asylum	1,424
,, Wages to Workmen, &c.	2,414	Sanitary Expenses, Port of London	6,964
Officers' Surplus Fees and Profits	10,097	City of London Grain Duty Loans Sinking Fund Account	3,021
Transfers, Expenses in Parliament, Remembrancer's Suspense Account ...	3,897	Remembrancer's Office Suspense Account	4,450
Sale of Catalogues, &c., Art Gallery Loan Exhibition	612	Expenses of Sirdar Reception	272
Securities realised	1,000	Guildhall School of Music Extension ...	15,278
Sale of Freehold Sites. &c.	2,370	Debenture Stock Redemption	15,000
Commutation of Renewing Fines for Leases	1,508	Erection of new Police Station, Minories	2,716
Balance overpaid on General Account ...	15,181	Supply of Gas and Water to Citizens ...	3,356
Loans raised, viz.:—		Investments	1,234
Leadenhall Market	44,400	Loans discharged, viz.:—	
Metropolitan Cattle Market............	154,200	Metropolitan Cattle Market............	154,200
Billingsgate Market Extension	67,500	Holborn Valley (Money) Act	42,400
London Central Markets	783,400	Leadenhall Market	44,400
Holborn Valley (Money) Act	42,400	London Central Markets	783,400
Holborn Valley and Farringdon Market	1,000	Lunatic Asylum	8,000
(Sundry small sums omitted on both sides are included in the totals.)		Expenses of West Ham Park, &c.	3,356
		Miscellaneous Expenditure	5,130
Total...£1,532,302		Total...£1,532,302	

Offices—**Victoria Embankment, E.C.** Hours 10 to 5 (Sat. 10—1). Board Meetings Thursday, at 3 p.m.

Was instituted (in accordance with Mr. Forster's Elementary Education Act) in 1870, and the first election took place on Nov. 29, 1870. From that date to Lady Day, 1899, accommodation in permanent schools had been provided for 519,273 children, and schools with accommodation for 47,837 are in process of erection. At Lady Day last there were upon the rolls of the Board Schools (including certain schools transferred, and temporary schools), 533,855 children. The staff of teachers comprised 9,890 adult, and 2,204 pupil-teachers and probationers.

When the census of all efficient and non-efficient schools in London was taken in 1871, the number of children on the roll was 320,143; the number upon the roll of efficient schools was (1899) 758,337; the number sent to industrial schools at the instance of the Board, up to Lady Day, 1899, being 27,066. In addition, many other cases had been referred to various voluntary agencies, &c., to be dealt with. The precepts for the year 1899-1900 amount to £2,049,582, which is at the rate of 13·37*d*. in the pound.

MEMBERS (elected Nov. 25, 1897, for 3 years).
Chairman—Lord Reay. G.C.S.I., G.C.I.E.
Priv. Sec., T. A. Spalding, £400.
Vice-Chairman—Hon. E. Lyulph Stanley.
City of London.—Miss E. McKee (*P.*); W. H. Key (*M.*); Canon Ingram (*M.*); Francis W. Buxton.
Chelsea.—Frederick Davies (*M.*); Thomas Huggett (*M.*); *Mrs. Emma Knox Maitland (*P.*); *Viscount Morpeth (*P.*); A. R. Fordham.
Finsbury.—Miss Margaret Anne Eve (*P.*); *Chas. Bowden (*P.*); *Mrs. R. W. Dibdin (*M.*); Jas. Wilson Sharp (*I.M.*); Rev. R. F. Hosken, M.A. (*M.*); Anthony John Mundella (*P.*).
Greenwich.—George S. Warrington (*P.*); Rev. John Wilson (*P.*); *Rev. F. Storer Clark M.A (*M.*); *Mrs. Bridges Adams (*Lab.*).
Hackney.—*Miss V. H. Morten (*P.*); Rev. Stewart D. Headlam, B.A. (*P.*); Graham Wallas (*P.*); *W. C. Bridgeman, M.A. (*M.*); *John Lobb, F.R.G.S. (*I.P.*).
* Elected for first time.

Lambeth (East).—Rev. Arthur Jephson, M.A.(*P.*); George Crispe Whiteley, M.A, (*P.*); *Henry C. Gooch (*M.*); Thomas Gautrey (*P.*).
Lambeth (West).—Thomas Jas. Macnamara (*P.*); Rev. Wm. Hamilton (*I.*); *Mark Mayhew (*P.*); John Sinclair (*P.*); Rev. Canon Allen Edwards, M.A. (*M.*); William Henry Kidson, F.C.A. (*M.*).
Marylebone.— Edmund Barnes, J.P. (*I.*); Hon. E. L. Stanley (*P.*); *Rev. Hy. R. Wakefield (*P.*); Alfred Jas. Shepheard (*P.*); *J. A. Murray Macdonald (*P.*); *W. W. Thompson, M.A., LL.B. (*M.*); John Cator (*M.*).
Southwark.—*Rev. J. Lidgett, M.A. (*P.*); *Rev. W. Copeland Bowie (*P.*); Rev. W. F. Brown (*R. C.*); John M. T. Dumphreys (*M.*).
Tower Hamlets.—Mrs. Francis Homan (*P.*); Sir Charles Elliott, K.C.S I. (*M.*); Rev. Edward Schnadhorst M.A. (*P.*); *B. F. C. Costelloe, M.A., L.C.C. (*R. C.*); *E. Flower, M.P. (*M.*).
Westminster.—*H. Morgan-Browne (*P.*); Major Skinner (*M.*); Wm. Winnett, J.P. (*M.*); David Hope Kyd (*M.*); Hon. Agnes Maude Lawrence (*P.*).

OFFICERS OF THE BOARD.

Clerk of the Board—George H. Croad, B.A. ... £1,400
Assistant Clerk of the Board—C. W. Isitt £600
Accountant of the Board—G. Attenborough .. £750
Minuting Clerk and Principal Clerk, General Purposes Department—E. H. Bramley...£600
Principal Clerk, Works Dept.—G. C. Harcourt £500
School Management Department—F. Wiles....£500
Principal Clerk Industrial Schools, A.E.Garland £405
Store Superintendent—G. Frater £500
Architect—T. J. Bailey............................£1,100
Land Surveyor and Valuer—W. S. Cooke £600
Inspectors of Schools—G. Ricks, £500; R. McWilliam; F. G.Landon; W. L. Clague; T. Nickal; G. Girling, each £475; J. Murray, £350; W. H. Winch £375
Singing Instructor—A. L. Cowley................£260
Drawing Instructors—A. W. F. Langman, £350; A. Wilkinson £345
Assistant Superintendent of Drawing and Suitable Occupations—J. Vaughan........£205
Organising Physical Exercises for Boys—T. Chesterton, £200; G. O. H. Smails....£185

Do. Girls & Infants—Mrs. Strachan-Matthews, £200; Miss Kingston £180
Deaf Superintendent—W. Nelson................£350
Exams. of Needlework—Miss Loch, £200; Miss M.A. Christiansen..........................£195
Superintendent of the Blind—Miss Greene ..£200
Superintendents of Cookery—Miss Matthews; Miss Briggs, £200; Miss Tattersall, £195; Miss Oslar, £185; Miss Borthwick, £175; and Miss Cade £160
Science Demonstrators—W. H. Grieve, £200; A. Hubble, S. R. Todd, each £200; J. H. Howitt £185
Superintendents of Laundry Work—Mrs. Lord, £195; Miss Jones, £175; and Mrs. Kirby..£155
Organiser & Instructor of Manual Training—S. Barter £340
Superintendent of Schools for Special Instruction—Mrs. Burgwin........................£350
Organising Superintendent of the Instruction of Ex-Pupil Teachers, W. T. Goode £400

Medical Officer of the Board—Prof. William R. Smith, M.D., D.SC., F.R.S.ED., £600.
Solicitor—Charles Edward Mortimer, 22 Surrey Street, W.C.

RECEIPTS AND EXPENDITURE FOR THE YEAR ENDING 25TH MARCH, 1899.

INCOME.	£	EXPENDITURE.	£
Balance in hand 25th March, 1898	517,542	Day Schools, £1,829,627 ; Evening Continuation Schools, £73,340	1,902,967
Day Schools (Government grants, Fee grants, &c.)	671,985	Enforcement of Compulsion	49,577
Deaf and Blind Classes	5,485	Indus.Schls., £57,507; Office Exp. £43,330	100,937
Evening Continuation Schools (Government grants, School fees, &c.)	18,010	Bldgs.£28,462; Deaf. & Bld.Cl., £13,971	42,433
Industrial Schools (Treasury grants), &c.	6,129	Leans: Repaymt. £230,157 ; Int. £320,968	551,125
Loans raised	500,000	Legal Expenses	665
Precepts	1,835,656	Stamp Duty and Charges on Loans	710
Scholarships Fund	1,935	Purchase of Land	175,138
Sundries	4,528	Erection of Buildings and Furniture	381,507
		Sundries(£2,256) Schlrshps.(£1,810)Fund	4,066
		Balance in hand 25th March, 1899	352,305
Total..............£3,561,430		Total..............£3,561,430	

Offices, Spring Gardens, S.W.; Hours 9.30 to 5; (Saturday 9.30 to 2).—Meets on Tuesday at 3 p m.

THE London County Council was constituted, in common with county councils throughout England and Wales, under the Local Government Act of 1888. The main principle of the Act is that it adapts to counties that form of municipal government which had previously pertained only to English boroughs.

London is an *administrative* county, covering an area of 121 square miles, with boundaries conterminous with those of the area over which the late Metropolitan Board of Works exercised its jurisdiction under the Metropolis Management Act of 1855; so that it has absorbed, so far as *rateable value* is concerned, about seven-eighths of Middlesex, about two-thirds of Surrey, and nearly one-third of Kent. Under the London Government Act, 1899, there is to be some re-arrangement of the county boundaries.

The City of London is an electoral division of the county and was not much affected by the Act. The County of the City of London is a county for *non-administrative* purposes, such as quarter sessions, justices, &c.; and the Metropolis outside the City is a county for *non-administrative* purposes, by name the County of London, in which the justices continue their judicial duties. Such matters as necessitate the consideration of both the *administrative* county and the *non-administrative* county are referred to "The Standing Joint Committee" of the London County Council and the London Quarter Sessions.

The Administrative County of London has no jurisdiction over the police, in that respect differing from other counties.

The Council comprises a chairman, 19 aldermen, and 118 councillors, together 138, or, if the chairman be also an elected member or alderman (as at present), 137. The term of office for aldermen is 6 years, and 10 or 9 retire every 3 years. The councillors are elected for 3 years, and will all retire in March, 1901, the fourth council having been elected in March, 1898. The councillors are elected directly by the ratepayers, and the councillors elect the aldermen. The positions of aldermen and councillors are the same except as to the term of office. The first meeting of the London County Council was held on the 21st March, 1889, under the presidency of Lord Rosebery.

The powers, duties, and liabilities of the Council are: *First*, those formerly belonging to the Metropolitan Board of Works in connection with the raising and loaning of money, and the sanctioning of loans required by vestries; main-drainage, and the sanctioning of local sewers; fire brigade; parks and open spaces; works for prevention of floods by the Thames; bridges over the Thames within the county (but outside the City), and other Thames crossings, including the new tunnel under the Thames at Blackwall and the free ferry at Woolwich; street improvements; controlling the width of new streets, the building line, and the naming and numbering of streets; maintaining subways under streets for gas and water mains, &c.; supervising buildings and district surveyors; dangerous structures; buildings unfit for habitation; structure of theatres and music-halls; artizans' dwellings; cattle diseases; offensive businesses; dairies and cowsheds; explosive substances and petroleum storage; infant life protection; tramways; locomotives for roads; gas, gas-meter, and electric-meter testing; and constant supply of water.

Secondly, those transferred from former county justices in connection with the granting of music and dancing licences in the Metropolis, including the City; asylums for pauper lunatics; reformatory and industrial schools; testing weights and measures; county buildings; coroners, and other minor matters. *Thirdly*, powers transferred from various authorities with regard to highways; licensing of houses or places for the performance of stage-plays beyond the limits of the Lord Chamberlain's authority; licensing of slaughter-houses and of cow-houses; and the supervision of common lodging-houses. *Fourthly*, new powers conferred by recent Acts with respect to technical education; Bills in Parliament, and actions at law; registration of electors; medical officers of health; inspection of factories to secure means of escape from fire; suppression of nuisances and regulation of overhead wires; and the appointment of inspectors under the Shop Hours Acts. As the central representative body in London, the Council also interests itself in the thousand and one things affecting the welfare of the people of London as a whole, and has delegates on the Thames and Lea Conservancy Boards, and numerous other boards, charities, &c.

The Council meets weekly, and receives reports from its 28 committees. The Finance Committee have important statutory powers. The Council is the principal money-raising body for all the local authorities of the Metropolis, and has a gross debt of £41,900,000, a Sinking Fund of £20,400,000, and an annual expenditure of about seven millions. The Asylums Committee have special powers under the Lunacy Acts, and manage Hanwell, Colney Hatch, Banstead, Cane-hill, and Claybury Asylums. The last-named was opened during 1893, and two further asylums, each for 2,000 patients, are in process of building, one at Bexley and one near Epsom. Temporary buildings to accommodate 700 patients are also being built on the Epsom site, and the provision of a working colony for 300 male epileptic patients has been approved as an experiment. The Industrial Schools are under the care of another Committee: the schools at Feltham and Mayford accommodate 780 boys. A great deal of attention has been given to the organisation of the schools. The Housing of the Working Classes Committee perform the duties cast upon the Council by the Housing of the Working Classes Acts; they have recently formulated schemes for the clearance of insanitary areas in Clerkenwell, Holborn, Southwark, St. Luke's and Poplar, at an estimated net cost of £505,900; 3,767 persons will be displaced, and at least as many are to be re-housed. The Committee has in hand the clearance of several smaller areas, and the building of working-class dwellings. The Council has established a model municipal lodging-house for 324 men, at Parker Street, Drury Lane. The Bridges Committee are chiefly concerned with Thames crossings. The Blackwall Tunnel was opened in May, 1897, the opening ceremony being performed by H.R.H. the Prince of Wales on behalf of Her Majesty the Queen. The Woolwich Free Ferry is used by 4,500,000 passengers and 380,000 vehicles per annum. The rebuilding of Vauxhall Bridge is proceeding; and a foot-tunnel is being constructed under the Thames at Greenwich. Powers are to be sought in the next session of Parliament for the construction of a 30 feet (external measurement) tunnel to connect the districts of Rotherhithe and Shadwell. The cost is estimated approximately at £1,400,000 plus £798,250 for property, including sites for re-housing people to be displaced. The Improvements Committee are engaged upon the formation of a new street 100 feet wide between Holborn and the Strand authorised by Act of 1899), new approaches to the Tower Bridge, and several smaller improvements; and the Council has resolved to apply to Parliament in the forthcoming session for powers to embank the Thames from the Houses of Parliament to Lambeth-bridge and to widen Millbankstreet, also to widen Mare-street, Hackney, and several other thoroughfares in various localities. The Fire Brigade, directed by the Fire Brigade Committee, has been much increased since the Council came into existence: the authorised staff now numbers over 1,100 men, and several new stations are being built, while old stations are being improved and enlarged.*

Perhaps the most popular work of the Council is that connected with its parks and open spaces: 2,656 acres were taken over from the late Board, and 1,100 acres have since been added. Bands are employed by the Council to play during the summer months.

The disposal of sewage is the work of the Main Drainage Committee. All the sewage of London is conveyed by 87½ miles of main intercepting sewers to the outfalls at Barking and Crossness, and there the solid matters held in suspension are precipitated, the harmless effluent being allowed to flow into the river, and the sludge, amounting to upwards of 2,300,000 tons in a year, being carried out to sea by a fleet of six specially-constructed vessels. The great improvement in the condition of the river observed in late years has been maintained. The engineering experts who advise the Committee are, however, of opinion that extensive works are still needed to prevent the discharge of crude sewage into the river at the storm overflows in times of heavy rain, and a comprehensive scheme involving the outlay of three millions sterling has recently been brought before the Council. Experiments in the treatment of sewage are constantly being made, the more recent being in the direction of filtration through coke filters.

In 1893 a "Works Department" was formed for the purpose of carrying out building, painting, sewer construction, paving, and other works, without the intervention of contractors. £105,000 has been expended on the purchase of premises and the erection of workshops, &c., at Belvedere-road, Lambeth, and a subsidiary depot at Battersea bridge. Works are carried out by the Manager of the Department, who is responsible to the Spending Committees in the same way as a contractor would be; the finances of the department are under the control of the Finance Committee. During the year ended the 31st March last the department executed works to the value of £2:6,844.

In the 1898 Almanack, particulars were given of the purchase by the Council of the tramways of the London Street Tramways Company, and those of the North Metropolitan Tramways Company within the county, comprising in all about 50 miles of tramway lines, and the depots, stables, &c., connected therewith. These are leased to the North Metropolitan Company until Midsummer, 1910, at rents amounting to nearly £50,000 a year, together with 12½ per cent.

of the increase in gross receipts over those for the year 1895. On the 31st December, 1898 the Council purchased the undertaking of the London Tramways Company, which is the largest of the systems south of the Thames, extending over 24 miles. These tramways are worked by the Council. Night services have been started on certain routes.

The Council has decided to seek powers in the next session of Parliament for the conversion of the southern system, now partly horse and partly cable traction, to electrical traction, and for numerous extensions of both the northern and southern systems. Application is also to be made to the Light Railway Commissioners for orders to construct light railways connecting with the tramways. Altogether some 25 miles of new lines (mostly double track) are contemplated within the county. These will all be laid for electrical traction.

Upwards of £600,000 has been expended by the Council on the provision of working class dwellings, which are, generally speaking, selfsupporting. The Council is pressed to take up the problem of providing suitable healthy dwellings for the poorer classes and in congested districts, but financial difficulties have hitherto barred the way, it being held by many to be economically unsound to build such dwellings except they are self-supporting.

The Council is seeking powers to purchase and manage the Spitalfields market.

The question of water supply is still engaging serious attention. The Council has resolved to again promote bills for the purchase of the undertakings of the eight London Water Companies, and also for the introduction of a new supply from the valleys of the Wye and the Towy in South Wales. The new supply is estimated to cost £17,000,000.

Twenty members of the Council, together with fifteen representatives (nominated by the Council) of other bodies or interests, constitute the Technical Education Board, charged with the performance of duties under the Technical Instruction Acts.

The expenditure of the Council is met by two chief sources of supply—capital money raised by the issue of Stock, and current income raised in a county rate. Certain contributions are also received from the Imperial Exchequer. The capital disbursements for the year ended 31 March, 1899, amounted to £1,992,035, including street improvements, £369,231; parks and open spaces, £63,656; housing of the working classes, £221,831; main drainage, £88,567; fire brigade, £38,738; lunatic asylums, £287,400; and the purchase of tramways, £809,579. The maintenance of such works, the sinking fund to pay off debt, and the interest on the debt, together with all recurring disbursements of every kind, are paid out of rates. Some idea of the nature and amount of this class of disbursements will be gathered from the statement on page 338.

The Council's powers to expend capital money and raise Stock, or, as they are called, "borrowing powers," are conferred by its annual Money Act. The Act of last session sanctioned, for the year ending March, 1900, expenditure on various improvements and services not exceeding £4,625,575, but a large proportion of this amount was a regrant of unexercised powers contained in previous Acts. The Act also conferred powers to lend during the year to the School Board, vestries, and other public bodies not exceeding £2,502,500. The Council issued a further £1,750,000 of the new 2½ per cent. London County Consolidated

* For further particulars, see "Metrop. Fire Brigade."

Stock last July. This stock is not to be redeemed at any fixed date, but the Council reserves power to redeem at any time after the 19th March, 1920, and a sinking fund has to be provided, under Treasury approval, sufficient to repay all expenditure within a period of 60 years. The tenders amounted to £5,823,780, and the average price obtained was £92 4s. 10½d. per cent. The total stock now outstanding amounts to £41,761,638. During 1899, three issues of London County bills were made, £600,000 in February, £400,000 in May and £600,000 in November, all with a six months currency. The gross debt of the Council, including liabilities transferred from the former counties of Middlesex, Surrey, and Kent, stood, on 31st March last, at £41,941,322; against this there were loans owing to the Council from the School Board, vestries, and other public bodies amounting to £16,760,479. Property was held to the extent of £2,540,263, and there were also other assets bringing down the net liability to £21,562,018.

The rating for the year 1899-1900 amounts to 11½d. in the pound over the whole county, including the City, and a further rate over the county outside the City of 2d. in the pound, together 13½d.; in 1898-99 and 1897-98 the rate was 14d.: in 1896-97 and 1895-96, it was 15d.; in 1894-95 14d.; in 1893-94 13d.; in 1892 93 12½d.; in 1891-92 11¾d.; in 1890-91 13¼d.; and in 1889-90 12½d. The assessable value of the County of London on 6th April, 1899, was £37,008,733 — a 1d. rate producing £154 203.

In considering the question of rating, the grants paid by the Council in relief of local rates (indoor paupers, registration of electors, &c.) must be borne in mind; they tend to lighten the burden in some parishes and increase it in others; generally speaking, the effect is to materially benefit the poorer parishes. Each parish pays an equal rate in the £1 on its rateable value, but receives back, for instance, 4d. per day per head of the indoor paupers; the City receiving ½d., and St. George-in-the-East about 11¼d. in the pound under this head alone. A still more important step towards the equalisation of London rates was effected by the London (Equalisation of Rates) Act, 1894, under which the Council is to levy half-yearly a rate of 3d. in the £ to make an "equalisation fund"; and then to distribute the fund on the basis of population.

The amount raised by county rate for the year to 31st March, 1899, is made up as follows:—

ESTIMATED RECEIPTS.

1. CASH BALANCE on 1 April, 1899 ...		£392,013
2. RECEIPTS in aid of expenditure:—		
Exchequer Contribution	£562,500	
Interest on loans advanced, on cash balances, &c.	619,545	
Rents	100,025	
Sundry contributions, fees, fines, &c.	127,810	
		1,409,880
3. TRANSFER from Tramways Account		78,935
4. GRANT from Local Taxation Account under the Agricultural Rates Act, 1896		931
5. COUNTY CONTRIBUTIONS required to be raised:—		
For General County purposes, equal to a rate of 11½d.	£1,773,336	
For Special County purposes, equal to a rate of 2d.	270,484	
		2,043,820
[Total rate, 13½d.]		
		£3,925,579

ESTIMATED EXPENDITURE.

1. DEBT:—		
Redemption	£582,040	
Dividends on Stock (less income-tax)...............	1,215,010	
Interest on sundry liabilities	19,427	
Income Tax	18,500	
Management of stock, &c.	26,375	
		£1,861,352
2. GRANTS:—		
To Guardians for indoor paupers.....................	£326,809	
To Guardians and others out of the Exchequer contribution	243,962	
Registration of Electors	15,050	
Main roads.....................	10,955	
		596,785
3. PENSIONS (including Superannuation and Provident Fund).........		47,680
4. ESTABLISHMENT CHARGES		137,185
5. JUDICIAL EXPENSES		45,925
6. SERVICES:—		
Main Drainage.............	£227,675	
Fire Brigade.............	196,810	
Parks and Open Spaces	114,515	
Bridges, Tunnel and Ferry	53,561	
Embankments	13,295	
Pauper Lunatics	85,640	
Industrial Schools	28,815	
Coroners	31,495	
Weights and Measures.	14,635	
Miscellaneous	67,442	
		833,883
7. TECHNICAL EDUCATION.............		170,000
8. PARLIAMENTARY EXPENSES, Inquiries, Rating Appeals, Election of Councillors, &c.............		33,075
Total Expenditure		3,725,886
9. ESTIMATED CASH BALANCE on 31 March, 1900		199,693
		£3,925,579

The Fourth London County Council.

Chairman .... Lord Welby, G.C.B. *Alderman.*
Vice-Chairman .... Richard Strong. J.P., *North Camberwell.*
Deputy-Chairman........ Thomas L. Corbett, J.P., *Clapham.*

BATTERSEA, 13,298
*William Davies, P. **5,284**
*John Burns, M.P., P. **5,126**
*Earl of Denbigh, M. 3,715
A. T. Quicke, M. 3,670

BERMONDSEY, 10,592
*Dr. George J. Cooper, P. 2,977
[*Joseph Thornton, P. ..... 2,843]
(Bye-election 24 June, 1899.)
Arthur Acland Allen, P.
(*vice* Joseph Thornton *resigned*).

BETHNAL GREEN (N.E.), 7,772
*Charles Freak, P. 2,733
*Edwin A. Cornwall, P. ... 2,580
J. A. Nix, M. 1,611
Sir Edward Sassoon, M. ... 1,599

BETHNAL GREEN (S.W.), 8,801
*James Branch, P. 2,275
*Benjamin F. C. Costelloe, P. 2,155
Percy Braby, M. 1,397
H. H. Finch, M. 1,374
A. D. Jones, I. 54

BOW & BROMLEY, 10,848
*Wm. Wallace Bruce, P. ... 3,082
*Benjamin Cooper, P. 3,018
V. J. Hussey-Walsh, M. 2,112
A. a'Becket-Terrell, M. 1,992

BRIXTON, 10,855
*William Haydon, P. 2,941
*Charles Jerome, M. 2,853
Rev. J. W. Horsley, P. ... 2,339
*S. Barclay Heward, P. 2,323

CAMBERWELL (NORTH), 11,955
*Richard Strong, P. 3,477
*Henry R. Taylor, P. 3,318
Guy Lushington, M. 1,834
F. R. Anderton, M. 1,773

CHELSEA, 13,043
James Jeffery, P. 4,044
E. J. Horniman, P. 3,675
*C. Chapman, M. 3,673
E. L. Meinertzhagen, M. 3,315

CITY OF LONDON, 25,307
Sir Joseph C. Dimsdale, M. 5,893
Duke of Leeds, M. 5,785
*Beaj. L. Cohen, M.P., M. ... 5,780
*Henry Clarke, M. 5,780
(Bye-election 27 March, 1899.)
Lord Alexr. Thynne, M.
(*vice* Duke of Leeds *resigned*).

CLAPHAM.
*Lt.-Col. Arthur Rotton, M. 4,785
*Thomas L. Corbett, M. 4,757
D. Martineau, P. 3,929
H. Gosling, P. 3,842

DEPTFORD.
*Sidney Webb, P. 4,512
Robert C. Philimore, P. ... 4,497
H. S. A. Foy, M. 3,218
*J. M. T. Dumphreys, M. 2,865
J. Yallop, L. 233

DULWICH, 13,502
(Bye-election 29 May, 1899.)
Bryce Grant, M. 3,028
J. Ratcliffe Cousins, M. ... 3,011
H. E. Ramsey, P. 2,521
A. A. Allen, P. 2,465

FINSBURY (Central).
Philip J. Rutland, M. 2,392
*Richard M. Beachcroft, M. 2,286
*W. F. Blake, P. 2,267
Rt. Hon. Sir A. Hayter, P 1,987
J. E. Woolacott, I. L. 582

FINSBURY (East).
*Joseph A. Baker, P. 2,114
Joseph Benson, P. 2,038
Walter Smith, M. 1,391
W. W. Grantham, M. 1,338

FULHAM, 15,757
Lord Wolverton, M. 4,494
Edward G. Easton, P. 4,407
T. Sadler, P. 4,148
Beaumont Morice, P. 4,043

GREENWICH, 11,604
Richard S. Jackson, P. 3,898
John Peppercorn, P. 3,249
Lord Skelmersdale, M. ... 3,194
Dr. W. E. Ball, M. 3,190
J. M. M'Carthy, I. L. 689

HACKNEY (Central), 8,615
*Thos. McKinnon Wood, P. 3,162
*James Stuart, M.P., P. 3,125
*T. B. Westacott, M. 2,369
Hon. Claude Hay, M. 2,291

HACKNEY (North), 12,236
*Dr. Elijah B. Forman, M. 3,507
George Lampard, P. 2,783
M. Shaw, P. 2,566
J.V. Fitzgerald, Q.C., M. 2,274
E. Reynolds, I. 1,779

HACKNEY (South), 12,150
*Alfred Smith, P. 3,360
Edward Browne, P. 3,174
C. Steel, M. 2,484
F. B. Oldfield, M. 2,452
J. R. Macdonald, I. L. ... 379

HAGGERSTON, 6,784
*Lord Monkswell, P. 2,057
*Rt. Hon. G. J. Shaw-
Lefevre, P. 2,069
Stanley Boulter, M. 862
C. F. Shallard, M. 839

HAMMERSMITH, 13,974
*William J. Bull, M. 4,168
*E. A. Goulding, M.P., M. ... 4,121
*Earl Russell 3,197
Sir R. G. Head 3,163

HAMPSTEAD, 10,033
*John S. Fletcher, M. 2,344
*Edward Bond, M.P., M. ... 2,277
F. Debenham, P. 1,878
H. Wilberforce, P. 1,873

HOLBORN, 12,815
*James F. Remnant, M 3,117
Sir John Dickson-Poynder,
Bart., M.P., M. 3,011
*A. Hoare, P. 1,320

HOXTON, 8,209
*Henry Ward, P. 2,179
Henry T. Sowell, P. 2,151
A. Arter, M. 1,567
T. W. Shaw, M. 1,545

ISLINGTON (East), 10,541
*Andrew M. Torrance, P. ... 3,015
*James Larghband, P. 2,717
G. F. Mortimer, M. 2,495
Colonel Alt, M. 2,306

ISLINGTON (North), 11,292
*Dr. T. B. Napier, P. 3,525
*Wm. C. Parkinson, P. 3,228
G B. Clough, M. 2,880
Lord Alexr. Thynne, M. ... 2,801

ISLINGTON (South), 7,954
*George S. Elliott, I. 2,377
Howell J. Williams, P. ... 2,172
F. Kimber Bull, M. 1,543

ISLINGTON (West), 7,783
*William Goodman, P. 2,456
*George H. Radford, P. 2,361
G. J. Chatterton, M. 1,421
D. H. Kyd, M. 1,361

KENNINGTON, 9,859
*Thomas A. Organ, P. 2,672
*John W. Benn, P. 2,661
*J. Dixon, M. 2,526
J. R. Cousins, M. 2,471
N. P. Palmer, Lab. 68

KENSINGTON (North), 10,168
*George E. S. Fryer, M. ... 2,319
*James B. Porter, M. 2,293
J. Lloyd, P. 2,285
R. B. Doake, M. 2,209

KENSINGTON (South), 10,848
*Charles H. Campbell, M. ... 3,078
*Richard A. Robinson, M. 3,056
S. Mayer, P. 648
I. A. Symmons, P. 639

LAMBETH (North), 7,372
*Lt.-Col. Charles Ford, P. ... 1,849
Francis Samuel Smith, P. 1,557
Charles Ansell, M. 1,252
R. Mortimer, M. 1,072

LEWISHAM, 15,431
George E. Dodson, M. 4,061
*Theophilus W. Williams, M. 4,025
J. E. Matthews, P. 3,037
A. C. Arnold, P. 3,021

LIMEHOUSE, 6,838
*William Pearce, P. 2,336
*Arthur L. Leon, P. 2,142
J. R. Pascoe, M. 1,726
Sir W. H. Porter, M. 1,553

MARYLEBONE (East), 8,119
*Lord Farquhar, M. 2,182
*Edmund Boulnois, M.P., M. 2,089
J. F. Little, P. 1,516
T. Slater, P. 1,419

MARYLEBONE (West), 10,344
*Earl of Hardwicke, M. ... 3,035
*Edward White, M. 2,892
Sir Algernon West, P. 2,028
Hon. J. Wallop, P. 2,015

MILE END, 5,813
John Renwick Seager, P. ... 1,711
Betram Straus, P. 1,663
Major L. Darwin, M. 1,535
*G. Bicker Caarten, M. ... 1,492

NEWINGTON (West), 8,282

James D. Gilbert, P. 2,639
John Piggott, P. 2,598
Dr. Lansdale, M. 1,383
A. A. Bethune, M. 1,368
W. Langley, Soc. 194

NORWOOD, 12,007

*Col. Frederick Campbell, M. 4,051
*Dr. James White, M. 4,025
J. E. Matthews, P. 3,037
A. C. Arnold, P. 3,021

PADDINGTON (North), 8,277

*William Urquhart, M. 2,142
Henry P. Harris, M. 2,088
A. White, P. 1,842
W. Stevenson, P. 1,816

PADDINGTON (South), 6,462

*Sir George D. Harris, M. 2,190
Henry A. Harben, M. 2,146
C. G. Paddon, P. 620
H. C. Biron, P. 614

PECKHAM, 11,998

Charles Goddard Clarke, P. 3,201
Frederick W. Verney, P. ... 2,849
W. Scott-Scott, M. 2,664
W. L. Dowton, M. 2,356
J. E. Dobson, I.L. 268

POPLAR, 9,874

*William Crooks, P. 3,632
*John McDougall, P. 3,310
J. B. Atlay, M. 1,585

ROTHERHITHE, 9,556

Ambrose Pomeroy, P. 2,778
Harold J. Glanville, P...... 2,650
*W. H. C. Payne, M. 2,427
A. Radford, M. 2,344

ST. GEORGE'S, HANOVER SQ., 10,457

*R. Crawford Antrobus, M. 3,143
*Col. Hon. H. Legge, M. 3,086
L. V. Biggs, P. 1,039
C. L. Heywood, P. 1,032
NOTE.—Mr. Antrobus was elected an Alderman, and at the consequent bye-election (18 March, 1898), Mr. W. H. C. Payne was returned.

ST. GEORGE'S-IN-THE-EAST, 3,867

Charles Barrett, P. 1,510
Christopher Balian, P. 1,450
J. Abrahams, M. 1,232
*Dalby Williams, M....... 1,227

ST. PANCRAS (EAST), 7,470

*Nathan Robinson, P......... 2,952
Frederick Purchese, P. 2,741
E. W. Sinclair-Cox, M. 1,698
A. F. Calvert, M. 1,595

ST. PANCRAS (North), 6,783

*Thomas H. W. Idris, P. ... 2,334
David S. Waterlow, P. ... 2,112
*W. J. Wetenhall, M. ... 2,001
R. J. Willis, M............ 1,607
J. Leighton, I. 144
A. E. Lucas, I. 65

ST. PANCRAS (South), 6,504

*Sir John Hutton, P. 2,036
*Sir J. Blundell Maple, M.P.M. 1,830
J. Macdonald, Soc. 494

ST. PANCRAS (West), 7,137

*Dr. Wm. Job Collins, P. ... 2,404
*Earl Carrington, P. 2,236
G. Barham, M. 2,017
Lord Elcho, M. 2,002

SOUTHWARK (West), 8,421

*Thomas Hunter, P. 2,578
*Edric Bayley, P............... 2,575
Oscar Berry, M............ 1,201
W. C. Copeland, M....... 1,193

STEPNEY, 6,244

*Wm. C. Steadman, M.P., P. 1,955
*Walter B. Yates, P. 1,855
Maj. Evans-Gordon, M. 1,648
H. T. A. Chidgey, M..... 1,534

STRAND, 10,526

*Lieut.-Col. C. Probyn, M... 2,697
*Thomas Walter Emden, M. 2,343
Rev. A. W. Oxford, P.... 1,664
C. Charington, P. 1,356
E. C. Keevil, I. 327

WALWORTH, 7,668

*Russell Spokes, P. 2,172
*Richard Parker, P. 2,163
Hugh F. S. Hole, M. ... 1,299
T. H. Brooke-Hitching, M. 1,292

WANDSWORTH, 20,758

*Dr. G. Blundell Longstaff, M. 6,378
[*Earl of Dunraven, M.... 5,493]
R. Steven, P. 4,583
A. R. Gridley, P. 3,954

WESTMINSTER, 7,958

*Louis H. Hayter, M........ 2,212
R. W. Granville-Smith, M. 2,190
T. Bremner, P. 789

WHITECHAPEL, 5,925

*H. L. Webster Lawson, P. 1,917
William C. Johnson, P. ... 1,768
L. Campbell-Johnson, M. 1,322

WOOLWICH, 14,230

*Col. Edwin Hughes, M.P., M. 5,133
*Abel Penfold, M. 4,660
D. Marsh, P. 4,364
Dr. Albert Lindow, P. 4,041

NOTE.—Members of the last Council are marked with an asterisk.
† The Earl of Dunraven has resigned (see p. 341).

ALPHABETICAL LIST OF ALDERMEN AND COUNCILLORS.

Name.	Electoral Division.
Allen, A. A. (P.)	Bermondsey.
Antrobus, Robert C., J.P. ...	Alderman till 1904.
Arnold, Sir Arthur, D.L., J.P.	Alderman till 1904.
Baines, J. A.	Alderman till 1904.
Baker, J. A. (P)	East Finsbury.
Balian, C. (P)	St. George-in-the-East
Barratt, C. (P)	St. George-in-the-East
Bayley, Edric (P).............	West Southwark.
Beachcroft, R. Melvill (M)...	Central Finsbury.
Benn, John Williams (P) ...	Kennington.
Benson, J. (P)	East Finsbury.
Blake, W. F.	Alderman till 1904.
Bond, Edward, M.P. (M)......	Hampstead.
Boulnois, E., M.P. (M)	East Marylebone.
Branch, James, J.P. (P)......	S.-W. Bethnal Green.
Browne, E. (P)	South Hackney.
Bruce, William Wallace (P)	Bow & Bromley.
Bull, Wm. J. (M)	Hammersmith.
Burns, John, M.P. (P)	Battersea.
Campbell, C. H., J.P. (M) ...	South Kensington.
Campbell, Col. F. (M)	Norwood.
Carrington, Earl, G.C.M.G. (P)	West St. Pancras.
Clarke, C. Goddard (P)	Peckham.
Clarke, Henry, J.P. (M)	City of London.

Name.	Electoral Division.
Cohen, Benj. L., M.P. (M) ...	City of London.
Collins, W. J., M.D., J.P. (P)	West St. Pancras.
Cooper, B. (P)	Bow and Bromley.
Cooper, G. J. (P)	Bermondsey.
Corbett, T. L., J.P. (M)	Clapham.
Cornwall, E. A., J.P. (P) ...	N.-E. Bethnal Green.
Costelloe, B. F. C. (P)........	S.-W. Bethnal Green.
Cousins, J. R. (M.)	Dulwich.
Crooks, William (P)	Poplar.
Davies, W., J.P. (P)...........	Battersea.
Dew, G.	Alderman till 1904.
Dickinson, W. Hyett	Alderman till 1901.
Dimsdale, Sir J. C. (M)	City of London.
Dodson, G. E. (M)	Lewisham.
†Dunraven, Earl of, K.P. (M)	Wandsworth.
Easton, E. G. (M)	Fulham.
Elliott, G. S. (Ind.)	South Islington.
Emden, T. W. L., J.P. (M)...	Strand.
Farquhar, Lord (M)	East Marylebone.
Fletcher, S. J., J.P. (M)	Hampstead.
Ford, Lieut.-Col. C. (P)	North Lambeth.
Forman, E. Baxter, J.P. (M)	North Hackney.
Freak, Charles (P)	N.-E. Bethnal Green.
Fryer, G. E. S. (M)	North Kensington.

Name.	Electoral Division.
Gilbert, J. D. (*P*)	*West Newington.*
Glanville, H. J. (*P*)	*Rotherhithe.*
Goodman, Wm. (*P*)	*West Islington.*
Gosling, H.	*Alderman till 1901.*
Goulding, E. A., M.P. (*M*)	*Hammersmith.*
Grant, Bryce (*M*)	*Dulwich.*
Harben, H. A. (*M*)	*South Paddington.*
Hardwicke, Earl of (*M*)	*West Marylebone.*
Harris, Sir G. D., J.P. (*M*)	*South Paddington.*
Harris, H. P. (*M*)	*North Paddington.*
Haydon, W. (*M*)	*Brixton.*
Hayter, L. H. (*M*)	*Westminster.*
†Hoare, Alfred	*Alderman till 1904.*
Horniman, E. J. (*P*)	*Chelsea.*
Hubbard, N. W.	*Alderman till 1901.*
Hughes, Col. Edwin, M.P. (*M*)	*Woolwich.*
Hunter, Thomas (*P*)	*West Southwark.*
Hutton, Sir John (*P*)	*South St. Pancras.*
Idris, T. H. W., J.P. (*P*)	*North St. Pancras.*
Jackson, R. S. (*P*)	*Greenwich.*
Jeffery, J. (*P*)	*Chelsea.*
Jerome, C. (*M*)	*Brixton.*
Johnson, W. C. (*P*)	*Whitechapel.*
Lampard, G. (*P*)	*North Hackney.*
Laughland, J. (*P*)	*East Islington.*
Lawson, H. L. W., J.P. (*P*)	*Whitechapel.*
Lefevre, Rt. Hon. G. J. Shaw- (*P*)	*Haggerston.*
Legge, Col. the Hon. H. (*M*)	*St. George, Hanover Sq.*
Leon, A. L., J.P. (*P*)	*Limehouse.*
Longstaff, G. B., J.P. (*M*)	*Wandsworth.*
McDougall, John (*P*)	*Poplar.*
Maple, Sir J.B., Bt , M.P. (*M*)	*South St. Pancras.*
Meath, Earl of	*Alderman till 1901.*
Monkswell, Lord (*P*)	*Haggerston.*
Napier, T. B., LL.D., J.P. (*P*)	*North Islington.*
Organ, T. A. (*P*)	*Kennington.*
Parker, R. (*P*)	*Walworth.*
Parkinson, W. C. (*P*)	*North Islington.*
Payne, W. H. C. (*M*)	*St. George, Hanover Sq.*
Pearce, William, J.P. (*P*)	*Limehouse.*
Penfold, A. (*M*)	*Woolwich.*
Peppercorn, J. (*P*)	*Greenwich.*
Phillimore, R. C. (*P*)	*Deptford.*
Piggott, J. (*P*)	*West Newington.*
Poland, Sir H. B., Q.C.	*Alderman till 1901.*
Pomeroy, A. (*P*)	*Rotherhithe.*

Name.	Electoral Division.
Porter, J. B. (*M*)	*North Kensington.*
Porter, Sir W. H. Bart.	*Alderman til'l 190'.*
Poynder, Sir J. Dickson-, Bt., M.P. (*M*)	*Holborn.*
Probyn, Lt.-Col. C., J.P. (*M*)	*Strand.*
Purchese, F. (*P*)	*East St. Pancras.*
Radford, G. H. (*P*)	*West Islington.*
Remnant, J. F. (*M*)	*Holborn.*
Robinson, Nathan (*P*)	*East St. Pancras.*
Robinson, R. A. (*M*)	*South Kensington.*
Rotton, Lt.-Col. A., R.A., J.P. (*M*)	*Clapham.*
Russell, Earl	*Alderman till 1904.*
Rutland, P. J. (*M*)	*Central Finsbury.*
Sawell, H. T. (*P*)	*Hoxton.*
Seager, J. Renwick (*P*)	*Mile End.*
Smith, Alfred (*P*)	*South Hackney.*
Smith, Frank (*P*)	*North Lambeth.*
Smith, R. W. Granville-, (*M*)	*Westminster.*
Spokes, R. (*P*)	*Walworth.*
Steadman, W. C., M.P. (*P*)	*Stepney.*
Straus, B. S. (*P*)	*Mile End.*
Strong, R., J.P. (*P*)	*North Camberwell.*
Stuart, James, M.P. (*P*)	*Central Hackney.*
Taylor, H. R. (*P*)	*North Camberwell.*
Thynne, Lord Alexr. (*M*)	*City of London.*
Torrance, A. M., J.P. (*P*)	*East Islington.*
Tweedmouth, Lord	*Alderman till 1904.*
Urquhart, Wm. (*M*)	*North Paddington.*
Verney, F. W. (*P*)	*Peckham.*
Ward, Henry (*P*)	*Hoxton.*
Waterlow, D. S. (*P*)	*North St. Pancras.*
Webb, Sidney (*P*)	*Deptford.*
Welby, Lord, G.C.B.	*Alderman till 1901.*
West, Rt. Hon. Sir Algernon E., K.C.B.	*Alderman till 1901.*
Westacott, T. B., J.P.	*Alderman till 1901.*
White, Edward (*M*)	*West Marylebone.*
White, James, LL.D. (*M*)	*Norwood.*
Whitmore, C. A., M.P.	*Alderman till 1901.*
Williams, Rev. C. Fleming	*Alderman till 1904.*
Williams, H. J. (*P*)	*South Islington.*
Williams, T. W., J.P. (*M*)	*Lewisham.*
Wolverton, Lord (*M*)	*Fulham.*
Wood, T. McKinnon (*P*)	*Central Hackney.*
Yates, W. B. (*P*)	*Stepney.*

NOTE.—The italic capital letters (*M*), (*P*), (*I*) stand for the Party whose candidate the Member was at the election—viz., (*M*) Moderate; (*P*) Progressive; (*I*) Independent; (*IL*) Independent Labour.

† The Earl of Dunraven and Alderman Hoare have resigned their seats, but up to the date of going to press, no successors had been elected.

CHIEF OFFICERS OF THE COUNTY COUNCIL.

Clerk of the Council, C. J. Stewart £2,000
Engineer, Sir Alexander Binnie, Kt. £2,000
Architect, W. E. Riley £2,000
Valuer, A. Young £1,500
Comptroller, H. E. Haward £1,152
Solicitor and Deputy Clerk, W. A. Blaxland £1,200
Assistant Solicitor (Conveyancing), G. P. Jackson £1,000
Medical Officer, Shirley Forster Murphy, M.D. £1,250
Public Control Dep., Alfred Spencer £900

Statistical Officer, G. Laurence Gomme £900
Chemist, F. Clowes, D.SC. £800
Parliamentary Agent, H. L. Cripps £1,100
Parks Dep., Lt.-Col. J. J. Sexby £600
Chief of Fire Brigade, Comm. L. de L. Wells £900
Manager Works Dep., W. Adams £1,500
Tramways Manager, Alfred Baker £1,000
Clerk Asylums Com., R. W. Partridge £1,000
Secretary, Technical Education Board, W. Garnett, M.A., D.C.L. £1,250

London City Libery Companies.

THE CITY COMPANIES, NUMBER OF LIVERYMEN (1898), CORPORATE AND TRUST INCOMES, MASTERS, CLERKS, AND HALLS.

As will be seen from the following table, many of the London Livery Companies are possessed of great wealth. Of some portion of the property they are merely trustees, and no doubt render periodical accounts to the Charity Commissioners; but of the "Corporate" property they are the sole owners, are not bound to render any account, and may dispose of the income as they please. Fifteen of the Companies have more than ten thousand pounds a year; some of them are very liberal in their charities, especially in the way of education. Some of the Companies invite fresh members to join, others do their utmost to repel. Corrections have been made from time to time by most of the Companies; those marked ¶ have revised this year's list, but others withhold information. Where the return was incomplete, the Editor allowed the old figures to remain.

Company.	No. of Livery.	Corporate Income. £	Trust Income. £	Total Income. £	Master or Warden 1899–1900.	Clerk.	Hall.*
Mercers	183	48,000	35,000	83,000	Greville H. Palmer	John Watney	4 Ironmonger Lane.
Grocers	183	37,500	500	38,000		R.V.Somers-Smith	Princes St.
Drapers	300	50,000	28,000	78,000		W. P. Sawyer	Throgmorton St.
Fishmongers ¶	347	44,807	7,139	51,946	R. B. Martin, M.P.	J. W. Towse	AdelaidePl.,Lond.Br.
Goldsmiths ¶	140	43,000	16,000	54,000	Sir R. E. Webster, Q.C., M.P.	Sir W. S. Prideaux	Foster Lane.
Skinners ¶	200	27,000	13,660	40,660	Jeremiah Colman	E. H. Draper, B.A.	8 Dowgate Hill.
Merchant Taylors ¶	306	37,000	13,000	50,000	J. Ewart	Edward Nash	30 Threadneedle St.
Haberdashers	345	9,000	29,000	38,000	Capt. J. A Hunt	J. H. Townend	33 Gresham St.
Salters ¶	182	19,600	1,945	21,500	Capt. P. Perceval-Clark, M.A.	E. L. Scott	St. Swithin's Lane.
Ironmongers ¶	40	12,000	11,000	23,000	Janus F. Firth, Jr.	R. C. A. Beck	Fenchurch St.
Vintners	214	9,500	1,500	11,000	Frederic Stutfield	C. Lomas	68½ Upper Thames St.
Clothworkers ¶	150	42,000	18,000	60,000	A. C. Cronin	Sir Owen Roberts.	41 Mincing Lane.

The above are the Twelve "great" London Companies in order of Civic precedence.

Company.	No. of Livery.	Corporate Income. £	Trust Income. £	Total Income. £	Master or Warden 1899–1900.	Clerk.	Hall.*
Apothecaries ¶	150	...	600	...	J. S. Stocker	J. R. Upton	Water Lane.
Armourers and Brasiers	86	7,940	60	8,000	Charles G. Hale	Marshall Pontifex	81 Coleman St.
Bakers ¶	187	1,580	320	1,900	Joseph Rock	H. Grose-Smith	16 Harp Lane.
Barbers	115	...	...	...		Do.	Monkwell St.
*Basketmakers ¶	30	...	None.	...		J. G. White	[91 Cannon St.]
*Blacksmiths ¶	98	684	Nons.	684	John Conquest	W. H. Garrett	6 St. Mary at Hill, E.C.
*Bowyers	25	550	40	590	W. H. Glazier	C. B. Arding	[22 Surrey St., W.C.]
*Broderers	35	...	...	...	Geo. T. Robinson	G. W. Barber, J.P.	[13 St.Swithin's Ln., E.C]
Brewers ¶	45	2,500	15,000	17,500	Edward Mann	W. Higgins	Addle St., E.C.
Butchers ¶	146	1,233	800	2,018	W:lliam Haydon	H. J. V. Philpott.	Bartholomew Close.
Carpenters ¶	150	10,682	956	11,638	A. Jacob	S. W. Preston	Throgmorton Av.
*Clockmakers ¶	63	...	...	...	J. W. Abbott	H. C. Overall	[Guildhall.]
Coachmakers ¶	108	976	None.	976	R. Downs, F.R.G.S.	P. de L. Long	Noble St., E.C.
*Cooks ¶	85	1,850	150	2,000	Samuel Cawston	G. C. Sherrard, jr.	[34 Gresham St., E.C.]
Coopers ¶	200	2,400	5,000	7,400	T. Barnes-Williams	John Boyer	71 Basinghall St.
Cordwainers ¶	100	7,700	1,600	9,300	H. Robinson	H. Garrard Clarke	7 Cannon St.
Curriers ¶	81	1,410	62	1,172	Joseph Mann	E. H. Burkitt	5 London Wall.
Cutlers ¶	100	5,350	50	5,400	J. A. Rhodes	W. C. Beaumont	4 Warwick Lane, E.C.
*Distillers ¶	55	...	None.	...	R. Cooper	T. G. Vickery	[Gui dhall, E.C.]
Dyers	66	6,000	1,000	7,000		R. F. Brunskill	10 Dowgate Hill, E.C.
*Fanmakers †¶	90	150	None.	150	Al H.G.Smallman	Col. T. D. Sewell	[Guildhall, E.C.]
*Farriers ¶	95	72	None.	72	T. A. Dollar	W. E. Baxter	[9 Lawrence Putny. Hill.]
*Feltmakers ¶	65	...	126	...	J. C. Wells	Alfred Peachey	[17 Salisbury Sq., E.C.]
Fletchers	19	100	None.	100	Chas. Brock Hunt	B. Shepheard	[6 Finsbury Circus].
Founders ¶	92	1,855	102	1,957	J. Willis Dixon	A. G. Wells	13 St. Swithin's Lane.
*Framework Knitters ¶	100	310	130	440	Henry Pocock	James Funston	[93 Finsbury Pavement.]
*Fruiterers ¶	98	90	...	...	J. C. Dawson	John Eagleton	[40 Chancery Lane.]
Gardeners ¶	46	...	...	...	Philip Crowley	R.Gofton-Salmond	[7a Cheapside, E.C.]
Girdlers ¶	76	3,000	1,300	4,300	Ald. A. J. Norton	W. D. Smythe.	39 Basinghall St.
*Glass-sellers ¶	42	nil.	21	21	T. H. Green	R. H. Evans	[58 Gracechurch St.]
*Glasiers	60	260	40	300	S. Woodbridge	W. J. B. Tippetts	[11 Maiden Lane.]
*Glovers ¶	77	56	48	104	Alderman Bell	A. W. Burn.	[2 Moorgate St. Bldgs.]

COMPANY.	No. of Livery.	Corporate Income.	Trust Income.	Total Income.	Master or Warden 1898–9.	Clerk.	Hall.*
		£	£	£			
* Gold & Silver Wiredrawers ¶	130	35	3	38	B. L. Cowen, M.P.	W. E. Baxter ...	[9 Lawrence Pntny. Hill].
Gunmakers ¶	28	2,500	None.	2,500	A. S. Purdey	F. T. Aston	46 Commercial Rd., E.
Horners ¶	48	89	None.	89	H. E. Foster, F.S.I.	Howard Deighton	44 King William St., E.C.
Innholders ¶	80	1,700	227	1,927	H. W. Ball	J. A. Druce	College St., Dowgt. Hl.
Joiners ¶	111	1,300	None.	1,300	B. Turner	H. L. Bedford	[St. Sepulchre's Ch.,E.C.]
Leathersellers ¶	151	18,000	5,000	23,000	William Peart	W. A. Hepburn	St. Helen's Place, E.C.
* Loriners ¶	430	1,200	None.	1,200	Henry Clarke	Col. T. D. Sewell	[Guildhall, E.C.]
* Masons ¶	51	550	None.	550	T. S. Pest	R. L. Hunter	[9 New Sq. Linc. Inn,W.C.]
* Musicians ¶	50	400	None.	400	J. S. Collard	J. T. Theobald	[35 Bedford Row, W.C.]
* Needlemakers ¶	66	230	None.	230	Sir F. Seager Hunt	J. K. Farlow	[1 Church Ct., E.C.]
Painters ¶	130	700	2,300	3,000	William Rome	H. & T. Pritchard	9 Little Trinity Lane.
* Pattenmakers ¶	40	50	13	63	J. Welford, F.R.H.S.	Charles Fitch	[Guildhall, E.C.]
Paviors	none				E. T. Rody. Wilde	William P. Neal	[Pinner's Hall, Old Broad St., E.C.]
Pewterers ¶	108	4,400	167	4,567	T. R. Bone	C. W. Sawbridge	15 Lime St., E.C.
* Plaisterers ¶	51	1,100	30	1,130	S. Walker	Henry Mott	[22 Bedford Row, W.C.]
Pl. Card Makers ¶	100	50	£5 5s.	55	W. B. M. Bird	W. Hayes	[Guildhall, E.C.]
* Plumbers ¶	40	880	20	900	W. R. E. Coles	[1 Adelaide Bgs.Lond.Br.]
Poulters ¶	110	1,020	430	1,450	W. C. Parsons	A. W. Sadgrove	[1 Gt. Tower St., E.C.].
Saddlers ¶	82	11,200	1,000	12,200	Chas. G. Smithers	J. W. Sherwell	141 Cheapside, E.C.
* Scriveners ¶	50				H. Weatherall	J. C. Wootton	[2 Finsbury Circus, E.C.].
* Shipwrights ¶	200	830	None.	830	Sir W. H. White	W. E. Baxter	[9 Lawrence Pntny. Hill].
Spectaclemakers ¶	320	1,100	45	1,145	Ald. Sir R. Hanson, Bart., M.P.	Col. T. Davies Sewell, F.R.A.S.	[Guildhall, E.C.].
Stationers ¶	262	3,100	1,600	4,700	J. Hunt	C. R. Rivington	Stationers' Hall Ct.
Tallowchandlers ¶	102	...	220	220	Geo. S. Sapsworth	{ M. F. Monier-Williams ... }	5 Dowgate Hill, E.C.
* Tin Plate Wkrs. ¶	103	4 12 4	6 10 4	11 3 8	C. J. Wilkinson-Pimbury	{ E. A. Ebble-white, F.S.A. }	Coll., E.C.] [Somerset's Off., Heralds'
* Tylers & Bklrs. ¶	73	670	170	840	J. Barrow Ward	A. Bird	[6 Bedford Row, W.C.].
* Turners ¶	200	64	None.	64	H. W. Hunt	W. M. Shirreff	[53 Gresham Ho., E.C.].
* Upholders ¶	27	284	20	304	G. Fish	W. J. Crump	[10 Philpot Lane, E.C.].
Waxchandlers ¶	27	1,370	230	1,600	H. M. Gregory	A. J. Wood	Gresham St., E.C.
* Weavers ¶	102	1,150	994	2,144	F. R. Y. Radcliffe	C. A. Bannister	[70 Basinghall St., E.C.].
* Wheelwrights ¶	120	300	None.	300	F. M. Mercer	J. B. Scott	[32 Coal Exchange, E.C.].
Wire Workers ¶		(See Tin Plate Workers.)					
* Woolmen ¶	20		376	None.	376	T. J. Carless	P. C. C. Francis	[19 Gt. Winctsr St.,E.C

* In case of a Company having no Hall, the address of the Clerk is given in brackets.

The rateable value of the Halls of the London Companies is about £55,000, and that of their Schools and Almshouses about £18,000 a year. The value of their Plate and Furniture is about £320,000, and the annual income of the livings in their gift —several of the "great" Companies are patrons of livings—about £12,300. In 1880 the Companies were indebted to the extent of about £270,000.

The above information is mainly derived from the report, in 5 vols., published in 1884, of the City Livery Companies' Commission appointed in 1880, of which the late Earl of Derby was chairman.

LONDON WITHIN VARIOUS BOUNDARIES.	AREA IN STATUTE ACRES.	POPULATION,		
		1881.	1891.	1896.
Within the Registrar-General's Tables of Mortality	74,672	3,815,544	4,211,743	4,411,710
Within the Limits of the County of London	75,442	3,834,194	4,232,118	4,433,018
London School Board District	75,442	3,834,194	4,232,118	4,433,018
City of London within Municipal and Parliamentary Limits...	671	50,658	37,705	31,148
Central Criminal Court District	269,140	4,475,752	5,260,680	*
Metropolitan Parliamentary Boroughs (exclusive of the City).	74,771	3,783,536	4,194,413	4,401,870
Metropolitan Parliamentary Boroughs (including the City) ...	75,442	3,834,194	4,232,118	4,433,018
Metropolitan Police District (not including City)	442,750	4,716,003	5,596,101	*
Metropolitan and City Police Districts	443,421	4,766,661	5,633,806	*

The Metropolitan Police District extends over a radius of 15 miles from Charing Cross, exclusive of the City of London, with a rateable value in 1897-98 of £40,581,444, and embraces an area of upwards of 688 square miles. The number of new houses built since 1849 up to and including the year 1897 is 633,615, with 6,090 in course of erection: the new mileage since 1849 being 2,155.
* Not shown in the Census.

THE following list of Life Offices, with two or three unimportant exceptions, contains the names of all the British offices, of four Colonial companies, and of four offices founded in New York.

DATE OF FORMATION.—This is of considerable importance, inasmuch as the normal rate of mortality is not fully experienced until the company has been doing business for five-and-twenty or thirty years. Any company established more recently than this must be judged largely by its prospects instead of by its results.

CLASS OF BUSINESS.—The second column shows whether the company is conducted on the Mutual system, whereby the whole of the surplus or profits are allotted to the participating policyholders, or whether the company has proprietors or shareholders by whom part of the surplus is received. Many of the life offices also transact other insurance business as well. These are indicated by letters in the column headed "Class." In such cases the life funds are kept separately, and are not liable for the claims of other departments. The Share Capital, however, is usually liable for the claims of all branches. The companies in the first part of the Table all transact "ordinary" life business; the companies doing Industrial business are stated separately.

FUNDS.—The Funds as stated in the table are in all cases taken from the Revenue Accounts deposited by the offices with the Board of Trade. The Paid-up Capital of Proprietary Offices that transact Life business only is included in the Funds. Paid-up capital of offices transacting other classes of business as well is excluded from the Funds as stated in the Table, because such capital is available for other claims than those of the Life Branch. The Funds as well as the premium income are derived from the latest annual accounts published by the offices, the date in the majority of cases being December, 1898. The amount of the funds taken alone affords no indication of the financial stability of a company, which cannot be judged unless its liabilities are known as well as its assets.

PREMIUM INCOME.—The annual premium income is in all cases taken after deduction of the amount paid to other companies for reassuring parts of such risks as the offices do not feel justified in retaining in their entirety.

EXPENSES.—The expenses of a life office include not only the salaries of officials, rents of offices, cost of advertising, &c., but also in all cases where it is paid the commission paid to agents for the introduction of business. The amount of expenses as so understood is less important in itself than in relation to premium income, consequently we have stated in the table the percentage of the premium income absorbed in commission and expenses. The average percentage of the whole of the British Offices is about $14\frac{1}{4}$%, of which $5\frac{1}{2}$% is expended on commission and 9% on other expenses. This ratio taken by itself is frequently misleading, because a large proportion of a company's expenditure is incurred in obtaining new business. If the proportion of new business to total business is large, the percentage of the total premiums absorbed in expenses is also large; but when the expenses are distributed between new business and old, or renewal, business, a fair indication is obtained of the real expenditure that an office is incurring.

Perhaps the most satisfactory way to split up this expenditure is to assume that the percentage of new premiums absorbed in expenses is ten times as much as the percentage of renewal premiums absorbed in expenses. The expenses per cent. of new premiums given in the table means therefore that if, as in the case of the Atlas, 81.9% of the new premiums goes in expenses, one-tenth of this percentage or 8.19% of the renewal premiums is the cost of managing the renewal business. These two percentages taken together exactly amount to the total expenditure of the office. The relative economy or extravagance of the various offices may therefore be better judged by the percentage of new premiums absorbed in expenses than by the percentage of total premiums. The average annual expenditure of British offices is 80% of new premiums and 8% of renewal premiums.

VALUATIONS.—The last three columns of the table are derived from the valuation returns made by the companies to the Board of Trade usually every three, five, or seven years. These returns contain a great deal of information, and show the real position of a life office in a very complete manner. It is not possible in the space here available to give anything but a very small part of the information supplied by these returns. A valuation consists of a calculation of the present liability of an office under its existing policies after making allowance for the amounts it will have to pay and to receive. In making this calculation it has to be assumed that deaths will occur in accordance with a mortality table, and that interest will be earned at a certain rate. Various mortality tables are employed, those most frequently used being published by the Institute of Actuaries. These are called the Healthy Males (H^m) and the Healthy Males excluding from observation the mortality in the first five years of assurance ($H^{m(5)}$). If a company assumes that it will earn a high rate of interest in the future, the net liability will appear less than if it assumes that only a low rate of interest will be earned, while the liability on account of mortality appears greater by some tables than by others. Consequently the position of an office is very strong and satisfactory when a stringent basis of valuation is adopted, because the margin between the calculated liability and the experienced liability is larger, and the surplus available for bonuses is larger also. As an approximate guide in this matter we may state that the H^m and $H^{m(5)}$ tables in conjunction are more stringent than the H^m table alone, that the H^m is more stringent than English No. 3; English No. 3 more stringent than Northampton, and Northampton more stringent than American, and that with every table the lower the rate of interest assumed the more stringent the valuation. For comparison with the rate of interest assumed in the valuation we give the average rate of interest actually earned during the last valuation period. The greater the margin between the rates of interest earned and assumed the greater is the surplus, and, speaking generally, the larger the bonus, though bonuses may fall at the time when a more stringent basis is first adopted. The rate of interest earned upon the total funds is stated wherever possible; sometimes only the rate earned upon the investments alone can be ascertained, and in such cases the rate earned appears higher than it would if the total funds, had been employed in calculating the rate yielded.

LIFE ASSURANCE COMPANIES.

Established.	Class.	Name of Office.	Funds.	Annual Premium Income.	Expenses. % of. Total Prem.	Expenses. % of. New Prem.	Mortality Tables employed in Valuation.	Rate of Interest. Assumed.	Rate of Interest. Earned.
								£ s. d.	£ s. d.
1894	P	Absolute	29,713	4,924	98·72	—	Hm	3 10 0	2 13 10
1883	P I	Abstainers & Gen. (Ord.)	108,951	24,194	25·26	93·5	Hm	3 10 0	4 0 10
1824	P F	Alliance	3,125,359	322,944	10·00	45·9	Hm & Hm(5)	3 0 0	3 18 6
1808	P F	Atlas	1,611,071	140,265	15·3?	81·9	Hm & Hm(5)	2½ & 3	4 5 5*
1847	M	British Empire	2,725,339	271,581	15·94	91·0	Hm	3 5 0	4 5 10
1854	P	British Equitable	1,718,605	135,893	27·27	166·9	Hm	3 10 0	4 2 11
1896	P	British Life	26,389	4,988	90·76	e	—d	—	—
1891	P I	British Natural Premium	170,550	50,917	76·47	e	—d	—	—
1833*	P F	Caledonian	1,645,364	186,151	15·49	80·9	Hm	3 0 0	3 17 3
1838	P	City of Glasgow	2,491,989	225,430	18·68	92·1	Hm	3 0 0	3 14 10
1829	M	Clergy Mutual	4,128,712	249,957	6·53 f	48·0	Hm & Hm(5)	2 10 0	4 1 6
1824	P	Clerical, Medical & Gen.	3,533,405	288,325	12·44	73·3	Hm & Hm(5)	2 10 0	3 19 8
1873	M	Colonial Mutual	2,261,656	320,49?	24·77	137·0	Hm & Hm(5)	4 0 0	5 10 11
1861	P Fm	Commercial Union	2,058,849	210,524	13·14 a	59·2	Hm	3 0 0b	4 4 9
1807	P	Eagle	2,655,667	168,919	18·73 a	105·6	Hm	3 0 0	4 3 7
1823	M	Economic	3,996,933	233,708	13·15	76·1	Hm	3 0 0	4 0 9
1823	P	Edinburgh	3,402,516	278,958	13·19	71·0	Hm	3 0 0	3 19 2
1839	P	English & Scottish Law	2,321,068	208,248	17·06	81·6	Hm & Hm(5)	3 0 0	4 2 8
1762	M	Equitable	4,506,436	193,625	6·75 f	32·9	N'hampton*	3 0 0	3 18 2
1859	P	Equitable United States	53,445,840	8,050,105	22·58	110·4	Amer.&Act	4,3½ & 3	4 6 11
1844	P	Equity & Law	3,436,328	315,623	9·94	47·4	Hm & Hm(5)	2 15 0	4 2 4*
1832	M	Friends' Provident	2,677,713	176,508	9·71	59·2	Spécial	3 0 0b	4 1 10
1837	P	General	1,667,706	198,751	19·30	98·3	Hm	3 0 0	4 0 3
1848	P	Gresham	6,885,433	968,362	21·29	104·5	Hm&Special	3 10 0	4 1 8
1821	P FS	Guardian	2,958,999	210,565	13·56	80·2	Hm & Hm(5)	3 0 0	4 1 0
1836*	M F	Hand-in-Hand	1,323,354*	186,681	12·31 a	75·1	Hm & Hm(5)	2 0 0b	3 15 8
1820	P	Imperial	2,332,504	227,684	14·84	79·5	Hm & Hm(5)	3 & 3½	4 3 11
1852	P	Lancashire	1,078,086	99,017	15·48	80·8	Hm	3 10 0	4 2 10
1823	P	Law Life	4,968,264	262,049	11·48	62·0	Hm	3 0 0	4 4 2
1825*	P FS	Law Union & Crown*	3,713,202	322,234	13·32	73·5	Hm	3 0 0	4 4 0
1836	P	Legal & General	3,409,319	283,368	11·86 a	47·6	Hm	2 10 0	4 4 6
1838	P	Life Assoc. of Scotland	5,035,648	399,000	14·32	85·8	Hm	3½ & 3¾	3 19 7
1836	P F	L'pool & London & Globe	5,220,710	241,283	10·00	57·1	Hm & Hm(5)	3 0 0	3 17 10
1862	P S	London & Lancashire	1,306,448	240,917	25·03	108·4	Hm	3½ & 4	4 3 3
1720	P Fm	London Assurance	2,147,480	156,088	12·09	71·8	Hm	3 0 0	4 4 11
18?1	P I	London, Edin. & Glasgow	101,645	35,834	20·03*	64·7	Hm	3 10 0	3 5 9
1806	M	London Life	4,538,626	355,291	4·50 f	31·6	Hm	3 & 3½	3 18 3
1852	M*	Marine & General	941,839	94,667	19·70*	97·5	Hm & Hm(5)	3 0 0	4 5 8
1867	P	Methodist & General	37,456	59,687	78·46	—	Govt. 1883	4 0 0	3 17 1
?835	M	Metropolitan	2,055,508	163,124	7·85 f	57·4	Hm	3½ & 3	3 17 10
1869	M	Mutual of Australasia	1,257,604	153,168	27·75	124·5	d	—	—
1842	M	Mutual, New York	56,711,425	8,275,453	26·07	83·7	17 Offices	4 0 0	4 11 4
1881	M	Mutual Reserve Fund	612,163	1,634,618	35·55	e	American	4 0 0	4 18 6
1830*	M	National Mutual	2,600,428	186,382	14·36	100·0	Hm	4 0 0	4 1 0
1869	M	Natnl. Mutual of Austral.	2,765,571	341,619	25·29	113·4	Hm	4 0 0	4 18 5
1822	P FS	National of Ireland	252,858	18,582	13·46	e	Hm	3 10 0	3 19 5
1835	M	National Provident	5,206,584	421,131	11·83	78·7	Hm	3 0 0	3 19 5
1845	M	New York Life	44,051,384	7,124,285	25·93	100·8	Combined	4 0 0b	4 12 4
1823	P F	North Brit. & Mercantile	10,507,010	751,296	13·24	75·2	Hm	3 0 0	4 1 10
1836	P F	Northern	3,505,873	254,784	10·00	59·0	Hm & Hm(5)	3 0 0	4 0 0
1808	M	Norwich Union	3,645,691	384,140	15·50	56·8	Hm	3 0 0	4 3 9
1824	P FS	Patriotic	179,417	19,965	20·22	e	Hm	3 0 0	3 17 1
1797	P	Pelican	1,423,746	119,688	14·25	68·9	Hm	3 0 0	4 2 9

* For references see next page.

LIFE ASSURANCE COMPANIES—*continued.*

Established	Class	Name of Office.	Funds.	Annual Premium Income.	Expenses % of — Total Prem.	Expenses % of — New Prem.	Mortality Tables employed in Valuation.	Rate of Interest. Assumed.	Rate of Interest. Earned.
								£ s. d.	£ s. d.
1891	P S	Pioneer	3,882	9,756	65·72	e	Hᵐ & Hᵐ(5)	3 10 0	3 0 8
1896	P	Provident	3,220,909	233,752	14·80	95·3	Hᵐ	3 0 0	3 18 9
1840	M	Provident Clerks	1,955,647	146,431	16·87a	103·8	Hᵐ	3 0 0	3 18 4
1848	P I	Prudential (Ordinary)	17,156,394	2,967,502	10·00	48·3	Hᵐ	3 0 0	3 5 11
1864	P I	Refuge "	795,719	257,885	9·94	29·2	Hᵐ	3 0 0	3 1 11
1806	P S	Rock	3,227,773	150,735	19·00	90·1	Hᵐ	3 & 3½	3 17 0*
1845	P F	Royal	5,830,494	462,732	12·89	69·6	Hᵐ & Hᵐ(5)	3 0 0	3 19 2
1720	P Fm	Royal Exchange	2,456,894	205,222	15·48	65·7	Hᵐ & Hᵐ(5)	3 0 0	4 2 7
1864	P	Sceptre	773,664	66,183	13·85	87·1	Hᵐ & Hᵐ(5)	3 0 0	4 3 7
1896*	P S	Scottish Accident	5,845	5,920	30·12	...	—d*	—	—
1826	M	Scottish Amicable	3,974,605	238,644	14·49	53·7	Hᵐ & Hᵐ(5)*	2 10 0	4 6 1
1831	M	Scottish Equitable	4,203,187	358,601	13·60	80·2	Hᵐ	3 0 0	4 5 7
1865	P	Scottish Imperial	548,378	55,601	18·92	109·8	Hᵐ	3 10 0	3 16 5
1881	P	Scottish Life	465,591	63,281	17·59	67·7	Hᵐ	3 5 0	4 4 4
1876	P S	Scottish Metropolitan	386,993	66,875	19·76	85·5	Hᵐ	3 15 0	4 4 7
1837	M	Scottish Provident	10,942,258	641,448	10·97	53·6	Hᵐ	3 10 0 ob	4 6 6
1883	P S	Scottish Temperance	441,755	85,892	17·80	75·5	Hᵐ	3 10 0	4 0 5
1824	P F	Scottish Union & Nat.	3,855,829	315,059	13·74	85·3	Hᵐ & Hᵐ(5)	3 10 0	4 2 7
1815	M	Scottish Widows	14,544,766	998,702	9·79	66·7	Hᵐ & Hᵐ(5)	3 10 0 ob	4 4 4
1885	P S	Sickness, Accident & Life	12,068	2,612	38·44	38·4	d	...	...
1825	P	Standard	8,989,725	820,320	18·32	97·1	English	3 & 3½	4 2 8
1843	P	Star	4,684,168	551,747	16·76	79·7	Hᵐ	3 0 0	3 15 9
1810	P S	Sun Life	3,770,355	432,261	15·15	78·7	Hᵐ & Hᵐ(5)	3 0 0	3 13 0
1865*	P	Sun Life of Canada	1,658,170	372,220	35·24	109·8	Hᵐ	4 0 0	5 12 10
1813*	P F	Union	2,245,492	344,885	16·94	86·3	Hᵐ	3 0 0	3 16 2
1824	P	United Kent	667,538	40,827	15·67	80·6	Special	3 0 0	4 3 7
1840	M	United Kingdom Temp.	6,838,770	471,040	11·41	75·2	Hᵐ & Hᵐ(5)	2 10 0	3 17 9
1834	P	Universal	942,184	76,442	15·06	112·2	Hᵐ	3 0 0	4 0 0
1825	P	University	1,086,707	57,663	13·71	...	Hᵐ & Hᵐ(5)	3 0 0	4 2 11
1860	M	Victoria Mutual	93,128	11,223	24·43a	e	Hᵐ	3 0 0	3 18 5
1836	P	Westminster & General	650,873	57,353	18·32a	119·6	Hᵐ	3 0 0	4 2 0
1824	P FS	Yorkshire	861,127	73,789	16·41	71·3	Hᵐ & Hᵐ(5)	3 0 0	4 2 6*

INDUSTRIAL COMPANIES.

Established	Class	Name of Office.	Funds.	Annual Premium Income.	Total Prem.	New Prem.	Mortality Tables.	Assumed.	Earned.
1883	P O	Abstainers & General	18,480	11,059	56·95	e	Eng. No. 3	3 & 3½	4 0 11
1863	P	British Legal	182,670	99,473	51·27	e	Eng. No. 3	3 0 0	3 9 10c
1866	P O	British Workman's	448,857	606,343	43·06	e	Eng. No. 3	3 5 0	3 9 10
1881	P O	London, Edin. & Glasgow	109,891	283,950	47·10	e	Eng. No. 3	4 0 0	4 9 1
1869	P	London & Manchester	162,957	94,103	47·13	e	Eng. No. 3	3 0 0	2 7 3
1864	P O	Pearl	813,108	622,783	48·50	e	Eng. No. 3	3 0 0	3 9 9
1848	P O	Prudential	14,538,953	4,960,756	41·17	e	Eng. No. 3	3 0 0	3 14 4
1864	P O	Refuge	495,487	930,999	52·86	e	Eng. No. 3	3 0 0	2 14 3
1841	M O	Wesleyan & General	373,756	364,321	47·25	e	Eng. No. 3	3 10 0	3 18 8
1870	P	Yorkshire Provident	5,863	10,103	62·32	e	Eng. No. 3	3 10 0	3 10 11

P = Proprietary.
M = Mutual.
F = Transact Fire Business also.
S = Transact Sickness or Accident Business also.
O = Transact Ordinary Life Business also.
I = Transact Industrial Life Business also.
a = Expenses include cost of Valuation.
b = Special Reserve in addition to provide for assuming lower rate of interest in future, or for other purposes.
c = Rate of Interest earned is on Invested (not Total) Funds.
d = No valuation yet filed with Board of Trade.
e = New Premiums not stated.
f = Does not pay Commission.
m = Transact Marine Business also.
* Atlas. Interest earned excludes Reversions.
* Caledonian. Fire business commenced 1805.
* Equitable. With additional reserve of one-third of clear surplus.

* Equity and Law. Interest earned excludes Reversions.
* Hand-in-Hand. Fire Business commenced 1696. Funds stated exclude General Accumulated Funds. £1,512,457.
* Law Union and Crown amalgamated 1891.
* London, Edin., and Glasgow. Expenses exclude amount charged to Capital.
* Marine and General. Also insures Mariners, &c., effects. Expenses include those of Marine Branch.
* National Mutual. Amalgamated 1896.
* Rock. Interest in last year of valuation period £4 os. 4d.
* Scot. Acc. Accident Business commenced 1877.
* Scot. Amicable. Net premiums valued at 3½ per cent. so strengthening Reserves by £200,000.
* Sun of Canada. Commenced in Great Britain in 1893.
* Sun of India. Now taken over by Sun Life.
* Victoria Mutual. Accepts monthly payments.
* Union Fire Business commenced 1714.
* Yorkshire. Interest earned excludes reversions.

ANNUAL PREMIUMS FOR WHOLE LIFE ASSURANCE.

Life assurance may be effected either with or without participation in profits. If the policy does not participate in profits, both the sum assured and the premium remain unchanged. If the policy does participate in profits, a higher premium is charged and bonuses are declared from time to time. The bonuses may usually be used either to increase the sum assured or to reduce the premium, or they may be taken in cash. It is usually to the advantage of an assurer to take a policy that participates in profits, but to overcome the objection of the higher premium that participation in profits usually involves, a plan has been adopted in recent years whereby future bonuses are anticipated and used to reduce the premiums from the outset. This is called the "Discounted Bonus" or "Cost Price" system. If the bonuses actually declared exceed the bonuses anticipated, the difference is paid to the policyholder; if however the anticipated bonuses exceed the declared bonuses, the difference has to be paid by the policyholder or to remain as a debt upon the policy. We give below the average premiums charged by British offices for the three classes of policies. The rates quoted are the amounts payable annually for the whole of life to assure £100 at death.

AVERAGE ANNUAL PREMIUMS FOR WHOLE LIFE ASSURANCE OF £100.

Age at Entry.	With Profits.	Without Profits.	Discounted Bonus.	Age at Entry.	With Profits.	Without Profits.	Discounted Bonus.	Age at Entry.	With Profits.	Without Profits.	Discounted Bonus.
	£ s. d.	£ s. d.	£ s. d.		£ s. d.	£ s. d.	£ s. d.		£ s. d.	£ s. d.	£ s. d.
21	1 19 6	1 13 8	1 12 2	31	2 10 0	2 2 9	2 0 2	41	3 6 9	2 17 10	2 13 11
22	2 0 3	1 14 4	1 12 9	32	2 11 3	2 3 11	2 1 2	42	3 8 8	2 19 10	2 15 9
23	2 1 2	1 15 1	1 13 4	33	2 12 8	2 5 2	2 2 4	43	3 10 11	3 1 11	2 17 9
24	2 2 1	1 15 11	1 14 0	34	2 14 1	2 6 5	2 3 6	44	3 13 3	3 4 2	2 19 9
25	2 3 1	1 16 7	1 14 9	35	2 15 8	2 7 9	2 4 10	45	3 15 9	3 6 7	3 1 11
26	2 4 1	1 17 6	1 15 5	36	2 17 3	2 9 3	2 6 2	46	3 18 5	3 9 0	3 4 3
27	2 5 2	1 18 5	1 16 3	37	2 18 11	2 10 10	2 7 6	48	4 4 1	3 14 5	3 9 3
28	2 6 6	1 19 5	1 17 3	38	3 0 8	2 12 5	2 9 0	50	4 11 6	4 0 7	3 15 0
29	2 7 6	2 0 6	1 18 2	39	3 2 7	2 14 2	2 10 7	55	5 12 0	5 0 3	4 13 1
30	2 8 9	2 1 7	1 19 1	40	3 4 6	2 15 11	2 12 3	60	7 0 8	6 6 8	5 16 3

The rates in the above table are the average of the rates of all the offices that quote these three classes of policies respectively. The next table shows the annual premiums payable throughout life for the assurance of £100 at death with participation in profits in the different offices. Premium rates alone are not sufficient for judging the relative merits of life offices for participating policies. An office charging a high premium is more likely to give large bonuses than an office charging a low premium, and therefore the bonuses as well as the premiums have to be taken into account. But the details of bonuses are too voluminous to be given here; they may be obtained from various insurance annuals. Some offices only allow bonuses to be taken in reduction of premium, and on this plan the rates are usually high to commence with, but are greatly reduced after a few years. The offices that make a special feature of this sort of policy are the London Life, the Metropolitan, and (under one class of policy) the Hand-in-Hand.

ANNUAL PREMIUMS FOR ASSURANCE OF £100 PAYABLE AT DEATH. WITH PROFITS.

NAME OF OFFICE.	Age 21.	Age 25.	Age 30.	Age 35.	Age 40.	Age 45.	Age 50.	Age 55.	Age 60.
	£ s. d.	£ s. d.	£ s. d.	£ s. d.	£ s. d.	£ s. d.	£ s. d.	£ s. d.	£ s. d.
Absolute	1 16 6	2 0 7	2 7 3	2 15 4	3 5 10	3 19 7	4 13 4	5 13 9	7 4 6
Abstainers General	1 13 9	1 16 2	2 0 11	2 7 3	2 15 10	3 7 4	4 2 3	5 2 11	6 11 4
Alliance	2 0 9	2 3 6	2 8 9	2 15 7	3 4 5	3 16 0	4 10 9	5 10 6	6 17 1
Atlas	2 2 5	2 4 8	2 9 3	2 15 5	3 3 7	3 14 6	4 8 8	5 8 0	6 14 3
British Empire	1 19 1	2 1 10	2 7 2	2 14 3	3 3 9	3 16 2	4 12 3	5 14 2	—
British Equitable	1 19 0	2 3 0	2 9 0	2 16 0	3 6 0	3 18 2	4 14 3	5 16 4	—
British Life	1 16 6	2 2 10	2 9 1	2 16 3	3 5 8	3 16 4	4 12 0	5 15 9	7 7 8
Brit. Workman's Gen.	1 16 11	2 0 6	2 6 2	2 13 2	3 2 1	3 13 11	4 9 6	5 10 7	—
Caledonian	2 0 2	2 3 6	2 8 9	2 15 6	3 4 6	3 14 6	4 8 6	5 9 6	6 15 9
City of Glasgow	2 1 6	2 4 6	2 9 0	2 15 6	3 4 6	3 14 10	4 9 10	5 12 9	—
Clergy Mutual	1 16 0	2 0 2	2 6 4	2 13 0	3 2 2	3 12 4	4 7 4	5 10 4	7 1 6
Clerical, Med. & Gen.	1 18 7	2 2 9	2 8 7	2 16 4	3 6 9	3 19 2	4 16 3	6 0 1	7 11 3
Colonial Mutual	1 18 4	2 2 1	2 7 4	2 14 10	3 3 2	3 15 2	4 9 9	5 12 0	7 3 8
Commercial Union	1 19 8	2 3 8	2 9 5	2 15 9	3 4 2	3 13 10	4 7 5	5 9 2	6 17 8
Eagle	2 2 4	2 5 7	2 10 8	2 17 1	3 5 5	3 16 6	4 11 4	5 10 11	6 17 4
Economic	1 15 5	1 19 0	2 4 4	2 11 1	2 19 6	3 10 9	4 5 5	5 3 3	6 12 3
Edinburgh	1 18 2	2 2 0	2 7 7	2 14 9	3 3 2	3 14 2	4 9 0	5 9 3	6 15 8
English & Scot. Law.	2 1 3	2 4 6	2 9 6	2 16 4	3 5 2	3 16 4	4 10 11	5 10 0	6 15 5
Equitable	2 4 6	2 8 1	2 13 5	2 19 10	3 7 11	3 17 11	4 10 8	5 6 4	6 7 4
Equitable, U.S.	1 19 9	1 19 9	2 5 5	2 12 9	3 2 7	3 15 11	4 14 4	5 19 10	7 15 3
Equity and Law	2 0 7	2 3 2	2 8 10	2 15 10	3 4 6	3 15 7	4 10 9	5 12 6	7 2 5
Friends' Provident	1 18 2	2 1 3	2 5 9	2 11 2	2 18 1	3 7 0	3 19 3	4 16 8	6 1 9

NAME OF OFFICE.	Age 21.	Age 25.	Age 30.	Age 35.	Age 40.	Age 45.	Age 50.	Age 55.	Age 60.
	£ s. d.	£ s. d.	£ s. d.	£ s. d.	£ s. d.	£ s. d.	£ s. d.	£ s. d.	£ s. d.
General	2 0 0	2 4 0	2 9 10	2 16 6	3 5 4	3 16 8	4 12 8	5 11 8	6 18 0
Gresham	1 19 8	2 3 3	2 9 0	2 16 3	3 5 8	3 18 0	4 14 3	5 16 3	7 6 5
Guardian	1 18 2	2 2 4	2 8 10	2 16 7	3 4 6	3 15 2	4 9 3	5 8 4	6 14 6
Hand-in-Hand	2 4 5	2 7 11	2 13 7	3 0 8	3 9 10	4 1 2	4 16 2	5 15 7	7 1 1
Imperial	1 19 4	2 1 11	2 6 11	2 13 6	3 2 1	3 13 2	4 7 5	5 6 6	6 14 3
Lancashire	1 18 4	2 3 0	2 8 6	2 15 0	3 3 6	3 15 0	4 10 6	5 10 6	6 17 10
Law Life	2 0 1	2 3 8	2 9 4	2 16 2	3 4 10	3 16 3	4 11 0	5 10 9	6 17 6
Law Union & Crown	1 18 6	2 2 6	2 8 4	2 15 2	3 4 0	3 15 5	4 9 10	5 10 6	6 16 0
Legal and General	2 1 2	2 5 1	2 10 9	2 17 7	3 5 11	3 16 7	4 10 9	5 11 6	6 19 5
Life Assoc. of Scot.	1 19 8	2 4 0	2 10 0	2 17 0	3 5 4	3 17 4	4 13 4	5 13 8	7 2 4
L'pool & Lond. & Gl.	1 18 7	2 2 11	2 9 3	2 16 3	3 5 6	3 16 0	4 11 3	5 14 8	7 5 11
London & Lancashire	1 16 9	2 0 10	2 6 10	2 13 7	3 2 4	3 12 5	4 6 10	5 9 1	6 18 11
London Assurance	2 0 8	2 4 0	2 9 6	2 16 3	3 4 11	3 16 5	4 11 5	5 11 5	7 2 11
Lnd., Edin., & Glas.	1 19 11	2 3 4	2 8 11	2 15 10	3 4 7	3 16 5	4 12 0	5 13 0	7 2 0
*London Life	2 10 6	2 14 0	3 0 4	3 8 6	3 18 10	4 12 0	5 8 4	6 9 4	7 16 0
Marine & General	1 19 0	2 3 1	2 8 10	2 16 4	3 5 11	3 17 7	4 11 11	5 12 5	7 0 0
Metropolitan	2 0 5	2 4 0	2 9 9	2 17 5	3 6 4	3 18 11	4 12 0	5 14 0	7 2 10
Mutual of Australasia	1 18 0	2 2 0	2 7 0	2 14 0	3 3 0	3 15 0	4 11 0	5 12 0	7 1 0
Mutual of New York	1 19 1	2 2 8	2 8 4	2 15 9	3 5 6	3 18 9	4 16 9	6 1 8	7 16 2
National Mutual	2 0 9	2 3 4	2 8 4	2 14 11	3 3 7	3 14 11	4 9 6	5 9 4	6 16 2
National Mut of Aust.	1 17 7	2 1 3	2 6 8	2 13 3	3 3 1	3 16 2	4 4 7	5 2 9	6 18 10
National of Ireland	1 19 8	2 3 1	2 8 7	2 15 5	3 4 3	3 16 0	4 11 7	5 12 9	7 1 8
National Provident	2 0 3	2 4 3	2 10 2	2 17 5	3 6 3	3 17 4	4 11 1	5 8 8	6 11 10
New York	1 17 2	2 1 0	2 6 7	2 14 2	3 4 5	3 18 2	4 17 0	6 3 2	7 19 10
Nth. Brit. & Mercan.	1 19 1	2 3 5	2 9 10	2 17 0	3 6 1	3 16 7	4 11 11	5 11 2	6 16 10
Northern	2 1 2	2 3 10	2 9 0	2 15 9	3 4 8	3 16 2	4 10 10	5 10 8	6 17 4
Norwich Union	2 3 5	2 6 8	2 11 9	2 18 2	3 6 6	3 17 7	4 12 5	5 12 6	7 2 0
Patriotic	1 19 1	2 2 11	2 8 8	2 15 9	3 4 5	3 15 10	4 10 4	5 9 10	6 16 4
Pearl	1 19 10	2 3 7	2 9 0	2 16 0	3 5 0	3 16 11	4 10 4	5 12 10	7 6 2
Pelican	1 19 7	2 3 2	2 8 11	2 15 11	3 4 9	3 16 5	4 11 7	5 11 8	6 19 2
Provident	2 0 4	2 4 2	2 10 2	2 17 6	3 6 4	3 17 4	4 12 10	5 13 6	7 2 0
Provident Clerks	1 16 10	2 0 1	2 6 4	2 13 5	3 2 8	3 16 1	4 12 2	5 17 4	7 11 7
Prudential	1 18 10	2 3 2	2 9 6	2 16 8	3 5 11	3 16 4	4 11 11	5 15 4	7 6 11
Refuge	1 18 8	2 3 0	2 9 3	2 16 6	3 5 9	3 16 6	4 11 9	5 15 2	7 6 8
Rock	2 4 6	2 8 1	2 13 5	2 19 10	3 7 11	3 17 11	4 10 8	5 6 4	6 7 4
Royal	2 0 3	2 4 2	2 9 9	2 16 2	3 4 1	3 14 6	4 8 3	5 10 6	7 1 3
Royal Exchange	2 1 2	2 3 9	2 8 11	2 15 10	3 5 0	3 17 0	4 12 7	5 13 9	7 2 6
Sceptre	1 18 2	2 2 4	2 8 8	2 15 8	3 4 9	3 16 0	4 10 6	5 13 4	7 4 6
Scottish Amicable	2 3 0	2 6 5	2 11 9	2 18 2	3 6 3	3 16 3	4 10 1	5 11 0	7 0 0
Scottish Equitable	2 2 6	2 5 3	2 10 3	2 16 10	3 5 5	3 16 6	4 10 9	5 9 10	6 15 5
Scottish Imperial	1 16 7	2 0 6	2 6 7	2 14 1	3 3 3	3 15 8	4 11 7	5 12 10	7 1 8
Scottish Life	2 0 0	2 3 6	2 9 6	2 16 1	3 4 6	3 15 10	4 10 6	5 13 6	6 16 6
Scottish Metropolitan	1 15 1	1 16 10	2 0 8	2 6 7	2 14 7	3 5 4	3 19 7	4 19 0	6 6 1
Scottish Provident	1 16 3	1 18 0	2 1 6	2 6 10	2 14 9	3 5 9	4 1 7	5 1 11	6 6 7
§Scot. Temperance	1 19 1	2 3 0	2 8 2	2 15 3	3 3 9	3 15 0	4 9 10	5 9 8	6 16 10
Scottish Union & Nat.	1 19 0	2 3 2	2 10 0	2 17 0	3 5 0	3 16 0	4 10 0	5 11 0	7 0 0
Scot. Widows	2 3 1	2 6 2	2 11 9	2 18 2	3 6 3	3 16 4	4 10 7	5 13 8	7 4 9
Sickness, Acc. & Life	2 2 5	2 5 0	2 10 0	2 16 8	3 5 4	3 16 7	4 11 0	5 10 5	6 16 6
Standard	1 18 9	2 2 11	2 8 11	2 15 8	3 4 5	3 14 6	4 9 0	5 11 2	7 1 0
Star	1 18 3	2 2 7	2 8 9	2 15 11	3 4 11	3 15 0	4 10 8	5 13 7	7 4 9
Sun Life	1 17 11	2 2 6	2 9 2	2 16 8	3 6 0	3 17 8	4 14 2	5 19 11	7 14 11
Sun Life (of Canada)	1 13 6	1 17 6	2 4 0	2 12 1	3 2 7	3 16 7	4 15 4	6 0 7	7 15 6
Union	1 19 3	2 2 11	2 8 9	2 15 9	3 4 6	3 16 0	4 10 10	5 11 7	7 0 9
United Kent	2 0 9	2 4 3	2 9 8	2 16 3	3 4 3	3 15 11	4 10 5	5 9 6	6 16 7
United King. Temp.	1 18 4	2 2 7	2 8 10	2 15 7	3 4 11	3 15 5	4 10 6	5 13 8	7 4 6
Universal	1 19 9	2 3 4	2 9 0	2 16 1	3 5 0	3 16 10	4 12 3	5 13 1	7 1 6
University	2 2 0	2 4 10	2 9 11	2 16 8	3 5 4	3 16 7	4 11 5	5 11 2	6 18 0
Victoria	1 19 2	2 3 4	2 9 3	2 16 6	3 5 7	3 17 2	4 13 0	5 16 0	7 7 1
Wesleyan & General	1 19 1	2 2 10	2 8 9	2 16 6	3 6 6	3 19 5	4 16 3	5 18 3	7 7 4
Westminster & Gen.	1 18 3	2 2 7	2 8 10	2 15 10	3 5 0	3 15 5	4 10 6	5 13 8	7 4 4
Yorkshire	2 0 4	2 3 10	2 9 1	2 15 11	3 4 9	3 16 4	4 11 7	5 12 0	6 19 11
Assessment, etc.									
†Absolute	1 5 6	1 5 6	1 5 6	1 7 7	1 10 8	1 14 5	2 1 11	2 12 1	3 9 5
‡Brit. Natural Prem.	1 5 9	1 8 8	1 11 5	1 15 0	1 19 5	2 5 7	2 13 0	3 4 2	4 7 2

* London Life. These rates are for nearest age and are subject to reductions—anticipated to be not less than 55%;—in the eighth year and thereafter.   † Renewable Term Insurance without profits.
‡ Entrance Fees charged in addition.   § Scottish Temperance. Abstainers Rates are 10% less.

ANNUAL PREMIUMS FOR ENDOWMENT ASSURANCE OF £100. WITH PROFITS.

Under endowment assurances the sum assured is paid after a given number of years, or on the attainment of a fixed age. Should the assured however die during the endowment period, the sum assured is paid at death. The annual premiums payable throughout the endowment period, or till death if previous, for the assurance of £100 at various ages of entry and maturity, are given in the next table. Endowment assurance may be taken either with or without participation in profits; it is usually advantageous to take participating policies. The discounted bonus system described above is also applied to endowment assurance policies.

Each cell is given as £ s. d.

Name of Office	Sum Assured Payable at Age 55 or at Death if Previous					Sum Assured Payable at Age 60 or at Death if Previous				
	Age 25	Age 30	Age 35	Age 40	Age 45	Age 25	Age 30	Age 35	Age 40	Age 45
Absolute I	3 4 9	4 1 2	5 5 10	7 6 11	...	2 15 4	3 7 5	4 4 2	5 9 5	7 11 7
*Abstainers & Genrl.B	2 19 5	3 14 1	4 15 6	6 10 5	9 17 ...	2 11 2	3 2 1	3 17 0	4 19 0	6 14 11
Alliance I	3 3 9	3 18 7	5 1 0	6 18 8	10 15 0	2 15 7	3 6 4	4 1 6	5 4 7	7 3 2
Atlas I	3 5 7	4 0 5	5 2 11	7 0 8	10 17 2	2 17 5	3 8 3	4 3 5	5 6 4	7 5 2
British Empire ......B	3 4 3	3 19 4	5 2 10	7 2 10	10 19 2	2 15 4	3 6 1	4 1 1	10 5 2	7 7 0
British Equitable ...B	3 5 6	4 1 2	5 4 10	7 4 4	...	2 16 9	3 8 1	4 4 2	5 8 4	7 8 3
British Life I	3 1 4	3 15 10	4 17 5	6 15 10	...	...	3 2 9	3 19 4	5 2 5	6 19 3
British Workman's ...B	3 4 3	3 19 5	5 2 3	7 0 6	...	...	3 6 10	4 2 4	5 5 8	7 4 11
Caledonian I	3 3 1	3 17 10	4 19 8	6 15 7	10 7 2	2 14 7	3 5 6	4 0 6	5 2 9	6 19 10
City of Glasgow I	3 6 4	4 2 0	5 4 0	7 0 0	10 10 11	2 18 0	3 9 0	4 4 6	5 7 0	7 4 6
Clergy Mutual ....B	3 3 11	3 18 7	5 0 5	6 16 4	...	2 14 4	3 5 1	4 0 2	5 2 6	6 19 3
Clerical, Med. & Gen..	3 5 2	4 1 11	5 7 7	7 7 10	1 ...	2 15 7	3 7 3	4 4 5	5 10 11	11 14 7
Colonial Mutual........	3 1 0	3 14 6	4 15 6	6 13 7	...	2 13 6	3 3 3	3 17 11	4 18 10	6 18 1
Commercial Union ...B	3 6 2	4 2 7	5 6 1	7 5 7	...	2 17 7	3 9 2	4 5 1	5 9 0	7 7 11
Eagle I	3 5 10	3 19 4	4 19 10	6 14 3	10 3 6	2 18 0	3 7 9	4 1 7	5 2 9	6 18 3
Economic I	3 1 8	3 16 0	4 17 6	6 13 6	10 5 2	2 13 6	3 4 0	3 18 8	5 0 0	6 17 5
Edinburgh ....B	3 4 2	3 19 8	5 2 10	7 1 11	11 0 0	2 15 8	3 6 10	4 2 6	5 6 2	7 5 6
English & Scot. Law..B	3 6 7	4 0 0	5 2 0	6 17 2	10 6 2	3 2 18 0	3 8 4	4 3 2	5 5 0	7 0 9
Equitable	3 4 7	3 19 2	5 1 1	7 6 9	10 10 15	6 2 16 1	3 6 10	4 1 8	5 4 6	7 3 3
+Equitable (U.S.) ...I	3 1 3	3 16 4	4 19 7	6 19 0	10 18 2	...	3 3 7	3 19 4	5 3 3	7 7 4
Equity and Law I	3 5 3	4 0 4	5 3 1	7 0 10	...	2 16 8	3 7 9	4 3 2	5 6 4	7 5 2
Friends' Provident..B	3 5 3	3 17 3	4 18 2	6 13 5	10 4 5	2 15 2	3 4 10	3 18 10	4 19 11	6 15 4
General I	3 5 7	4 1 10	5 6 4	7 7 2	11 8 11	2 18 4	3 10 0	4 5 9	5 9 6	7 11 0
+Gresham ....B	3 2 0	3 16 11	5 0 5	6 19 10	...	2 14 6	3 5 5	4 4 0	5 4 10	7 5 6
Guardian ....B	3 4 5	3 17 10	5 1 7	7 1 0	...	2 17 0	3 6 9	4 0 10	5 5 0	7 5 6
Hand-in-Hand I	3 11 8	4 5 10	5 7 4	7 2 3	10 10 8	3 2 11	3 12 11	4 8 4	5 10 7	7 5 11
Imperial I	3 0 8	3 14 3	4 15 6	6 10 11	10 1 6	2 11 8	3 1 3	3 15 9	4 17 8	6 14 0
Lancashire I	3 4 6	3 19 6	5 1 6	6 17 0	10 10 0	2 16 6	3 7 0	4 2 0	5 3 10	7 1 0
Law Life I	3 4 0	3 18 2	4 19 3	6 14 4	10 4 7	2 16 1	3 6 7	4 1 0	5 2 2	6 18 7
Law Union & Crown..I	3 5 0	4 0 0	5 2 8	6 19 1	...	2 16 6	3 7 6	4 3 0	5 5 6	7 3 6
Legal and General ...I	3 5 3	4 0 4	5 3 1	7 0 10	...	2 16 8	3 7 9	4 3 2	5 6 4	7 5 2
Life Assoc.of Scotland I	3 4 7	3 19 1	5 0 9	6 16 10	10 9 2	2 15 6	3 7 4	4 2 1	5 4 2	7 1 4
L'pool & Lond. & Gl..I	3 5 10	4 0 11	5 3 7	7 0 5	10 14 10	2 17 4	3 8 5	4 3 9	5 6 8	7 4 11
London & Lancashire..I	3 4 7	4 0 8	5 4 0	7 3 9	11 0 0	2 15 6	3 7 3	4 2 11	5 6 11	7 4 10
London Assurance ...I	3 5 4	4 0 5	5 3 3	7 1 4	...	2 17 6	3 8 7	4 3 10	5 7 1	7 6 3
Lond.,Edin.,& Glasg.I	3 5 1	3 19 7	5 1 6	6 18 5	10 13 2	2 17 1	3 7 8	4 2 5	5 4 10	7 2 10
‡London Life ......L I	4 0 2	4 16 2	5 19 0	7 13 10	...	3 10 4	4 2 4	4 18 10	6 2 4	7 17 6
Marine and General ..I	3 5 5	4 0 6	5 3 4	7 1 9	10 18 1	2 16 9	3 7 8	4 3 5	5 5 7	7 2 6
+Mut of Australasia I	3 0 0	3 14 0	4 16 0	6 10 0	10 0 0	2 13 0	3 3 0	3 16 0	4 19 0	6 14 0
+Mutual of New York I	3 5 5	4 0 0	5 4 3	7 3 10	11 3 3	3 3 3	3 6 7	4 3 7	5 8 0	8 10 0
National Mutual I	3 4 9	3 18 8	5 0 0	6 16 5	10 9 0	2 16 4	3 6 4	4 4 0	5 3 1	7 0 1
Nat. Mutual of Aust..I	3 0 10	3 15 11	4 18 3	6 15 0	10 5 0	2 12 6	3 3 3	3 18 9	5 1 4	6 18 4
National Provident B	3 6 4	4 1 1	5 2 5	6 19 1	10 9 0	2 18 8	3 9 11	4 5 4	5 7 10	7 4 3
+New York I	3 2 10	3 18 2	5 1 5	7 2 0	11 2 0	2 14 0	3 5 2	4 1 2	5 6 0	7 7 7
NorthBrit.& Mercan. I	3 6 2	4 1 1	5 3 0	6 18 10	...	2 17 6	3 8 4	4 3 9	5 6 1	7 2 11
Northern I	3 5 8	3 19 8	5 1 1	6 16 11	10 9 8	2 17 2	3 7 4	4 1 11	5 4 1	7 0 8
Norwich Union I	3 4 4	3 17 3	4 19 5	6 15 6	10 6 9	2 16 0	3 6 7	4 1 1	5 1 3	6 19 3
Patriotic I	3 4 10	3 19 8	5 0 10	6 16 2	10 7 9	2 16 1	3 7 3	4 2 2	5 3 8	6 19 10
Pearl I	3 6 1	4 1 4	5 5 1	7 5 5	11 0 0	2 17 4	3 8 10	4 5 1	5 9 5	9 9 2
Pelican ....B	3 6 5	4 0 10	5 2 5	7 0 6	...	2 18 4	3 8 10	4 4 5	5 6 5	7 4 2
Provident I	3 8 4	4 3 3	5 5 0	7 1 10	10 15 8	3 0 4	3 11 2	4 6 6	5 8 4	6 6 6
*Provident Clerks'..B	3 11 3	3 18 8	5 0 7	6 16 10	10 9 0	2 15 7	3 6 5	4 1 1	5 3 1	10 7 1 2
Prudential	3 7 9		4 3 5	7 10 7	9 5	2 18	3 13 10	5 4 7	8 10 10	7 12 9
Refuge I	3 4 3	4 0 6	5 2 9	7 6 2	...	2 14 10	3 6 9	4 4 0	5 8 6	7 10 4
Rock I	3 3 9	3 19 6	5 2 9	7 1 1	10 17 8	2 16 4	3 8 1	4 3 8	5 4 4	7 8 4

NAME OF OFFICE	Sum Assured Payable at Age 55 or at Death if Previous.					Sum Assured Payable at Age 60 or at Death if Previous.				
	Age 25.	Age 30.	Age 35.	Age 40.	Age 45.	Age 25.	Age 30.	Age 35.	Age 40.	Age 45.
	£ s. d.	£ s. d.	£ s. d.	£ s. d.	£ s. d.	£ s. d.	£ s. d.	£ s. d.	£ s. d.	£ s. d.
Royal ....B	3 5 8	4 0 8	5 2 8	7 0 0	10 14 0	2 17 4	3 8 0	4 3 4	5 6 0	7 4 0
Royal Exchange I	3 5 9	4 0 3	5 2 11	7 1 1	...	2 17 3	3 7 6	4 2 8	5 6 1	7 5 0
*Sceptre	3 4 9	4 0 10	5 4 2	7 3 10	11 0 6	2 15 7	3 7 4	4 3 1	5 7 2	7 5 0
+Scottish Accident ...B	3 6 8	4 0 5	5 1 2	6 16 11	10 8 7	2 17 8	3 7 4	4 1 8	5 3 7	7 0 2
Scottish Amicable ...I	3 6 9	4 1 5	5 3 0	6 18 6	10 12 0	2 18 3	3 9 1	4 4 1	5 6 0	7 2 7
Scottish Equitable ...I	3 6 0	3 19 5	5 0 0	6 14 7	10 3 4	2 17 11	3 7 8	4 1 8	5 2 11	6 18 1
Scottish Imperial...B	3 2 7	3 17 1	4 19 0	6 15 11	10 10 0	2 14 7	3 5 2	3 19 11	5 2 4	7 0 4
Scottish Life I	3 6 5	4 1 1	5 2 3	6 16 6	...	2 17 10	3 8 10	4 3 9	5 4 7	7 0 3
Scot. Metropolitan...B	3 2 5	3 16 0	4 18 6	6 17 4	10 15 10	2 13 11	3 5 3	18 5	5 2 0	7 1 11
§ScottishTemperance B	3 4 11	3 19 7	5 1 10	6 19 4	10 17 0	2 16 7	3 7 2	4 3 3	5 4 11	7 3 6
Scottish Un. & Nat. B	3 5 6	4 1 6	5 4 0	7 3 6	...	2 16 0	3 7 0	4 3 0	5 6 6	7 5 0
Scottish Widows'......I	3 11 6	4 5 3	5 5 9	...	...	3 2 10	3 12 10	4 6 10	5 8 0	...
Sickness, Acc. & Life B	3 5 11	3 19 6	5 0 0	3 6 15	1 10 4	2 17 9	3 7 7	4 1 9	5 3 3	6 18 9
Standard I	3 6 4	4 1 4	5 3 7	7 0 0	...	2 17 8	3 8 0	4 3 11	5 6 2	7 2 10
Star I	3 4 8	4 1 2	5 3 0	7 1 0	...	2 15 4	3 7 4	4 3 5	5 5 11	7 5 5
Sun Life.................I	3 4 0	4 0 0	5 2 7	7 0 0	1 10 11 7	2 15 8	3 7 9	4 3 4	6 11 7	3 5
Sun of Canada	2 18 10	3 14 1	4 17 2	6 16 0	10 14 5	2 9 10	3 1 10	3 17 6	5 1 1	7 1 0
Union I	3 2 8	3 17 5	4 19 8	6 16 3	...	2 14 5	3 3 5	3 14 0	5 5 3	3 7 1
United Kent	3 5 6	4 0 6	5 2 11	7 0 3	...	2 17 0	3 8 0	4 3 3	5 6 4	4 4 7
+United King.Temp. B	3 1 3	3 16 1	4 18 4	6 15 2	...	2 12 7	3 3 7	3 18 9	5 1 5	6 19 3
University I	3 6 6	4 0 7	5 2 7	6 19 7	...	2 18 0	3 8 6	4 3 9	5 6 7	7 4 9
Victoria.................B	3 7 5	4 3 6	5 7 4	7 7 1	...	2 18 3	3 9 11	4 6 2	5 10 3	7 10 2
Wesleyan & General...	3 5 8	4 2 3	5 7 8	7 10 7	...	...	3 8	9 4 6	5 12 3	7 16 0
*Westminster & Gen...	3 4 8	4 0 9	5 4 1	7 3 9	...	2 15 7	3 7 3	4 2 11	5 6 11	7 4 10
Yorkshire ....B	3 5 6	4 0 2	5 2 7	7 0 0	1 10 15 8	2 17 3	3 7 3	4 2 5	5 5 5	6 7 3 10

* In the cases marked thus the rates are quoted for Assurances payable at ages 55 and 60, without mention being made as to the number of premiums payable. Thus it *may* in these cases be necessary to pay one more premium than in the case of those not marked *. For instance, a person Assuring at age 35 next birthday for a sum payable at age 60 *may* have to pay 26 premiums in an office marked *, while he would only pay 25 premiums in an office not so marked. In the latter case the sum Assured is sometimes paid on the anniversary of the day on which the Assurance was effected, sometimes on the anniversary of birth.   ‡ London Life, see note p. 349.
† With Tontined or Deferred Bonuses.   B Matures on birthday of assured.   I Matures on anniversary of issue.
§ Scottish Temperance, Abstainers rates are 2s. 6d. less.

LIFE ASSURANCE PROGRESS.

The business of foreign and Colonial companies doing business in the United Kingdom is not included in the following table :—

INCOME.	Ordinary Life Companies.		Industrial Life Companies.	
	1882.	1899.	1882.	1899.
	£	£	£	£
Premiums (less re-assurances)	11,658,319	20,199,386	1,941,994	7,570,150
Consideration for Annuities	590,911	1,985,892	...	1,635
Interest and Dividends (less Income Tax)	5,369,007	8,198,530	45,716	523,361
Increase in value of Investments.................	238,573	282,031	...	1,788
Fines, Fees, &c..	6,157	11,055	141	1,149
Miscellaneous..	44,571	68,211	1,832	152,447
Total Income	17,907,538	30,745,105	1,989,683	8,250,530
Claims (including Reversionary Bonuses)	9,850,259	13,176,900	697,778	2,912,046
Cash Bonuses and Reduction of Premium	854,297	1,028,396	...	288
Surrenders	734,051	930,339	2,533	37,836
Annuities	512,214	1,504,225	15	5,142
Commission and Expenses.......	1,572,816	2,899,497	935,180	3,272,538
Dividends and Bonuses to Shareholders	706,658	361,919	2,661	386,771
Loss or Depreciation.................................	101,844	112,591	422	4,041
Miscellaneous..	7,631	483,051	345	100,053
Increase in Funds	3,567,777	10,248,187	350,749	1,531,815
Total	17,907,538	30,745,105	1,989,683	8,250,530
Life and Annuity Funds	128,659,580	224,372,455	1,529,965	16,969,333

	Ordinary Life Assurances.		Industrial Life Assurances.	
	No.of Policies.	Net Sum Assured.	No.of Policies.	Net Sum Assured.
		£		£
Assurances in Force as shown by the latest Returns issued by the Board of Trade	1,698,043	587,907,816	17,230,712	165,988,493

THE following Table shows the amount of Annuity granted by the undermentioned Companies for every £100 paid. The age last birthday is that upon which the payment is based, but many offices quote intermediate rates for every half or quarter year of age. By a few Companies a proportionate amount of Annuity is payable to *day of death*.

The Annuity is calculated as payable half-yearly; the annual payment is in nearly all cases higher if paid annually and less when paid quarterly.

OFFICE.	MALES.				FEMALES.				
	Age 55.	Age 60.	Age 65.	Age 70.	Age 50.	Age 55.	Age 60.	Age 65.	Age 70.
	£ s. d.	£ s. d.	£ s. d.	£ s. d.	£ s. d.	£ s. d.	£ s. d.	£ s. d.	£ s. d.
British Empire	7 14 6	8 18 10	10 12 2	12 17 2	6 5 2	7 0 2	8 1 2	9 11 2	11 15 4
Caledonian	7 13 10	8 18 1	10 11 0	12 15 10	6 4 4	6 18 9	7 18 10	9 6 11	11 8 7
City of Glasgow	7 13 10	8 18 0	10 11 2	12 16 0	6 3 10	6 19 6	8 0 6	9 10 2	11 14 2
Eagle	7 15 0	8 18 10	10 11 2	12 14 6	6 5 10	7 0 8	8 1 6	9 10 8	11 13 6
Economic	7 16 0	9 0 4	10 14 2	12 18 6	6 6 4	7 1 6	8 2 10	9 12 10	11 16 6
Edinburgh	7 13 8	8 18 6	10 12 0	12 14 0	6 3 6	6 19 0	8 0 8	9 11 0	11 12 6
English & Scottish Law	7 9 6	8 12 6	10 3 10	12 7 2	5 19 10	6 14 0	7 13 4	9 1 2	11 1 0
Equitable	7 13 4	8 18 8	10 13 0	12 17 6	6 2 10	6 18 6	8 0 6	9 11 4	11 16 0
Equitable (U.S.)	7 18 2	9 3 4	10 19 0	13 0 10	6 7 6	7 3 0	8 4 10	9 15 2	11 14 6
Friends' Provident	7 10 4	8 10 7	9 18 10	11 18 6	6 5 8	6 19 11	7 19 11	9 7 1	11 4 7
General	7 13 6	8 19 0	10 15 0	12 17 6	6 3 0	6 19 0	8 1 0	9 11 0	11 15 0
Gresham	7 14 9	8 18 6	10 11 2	12 15 3	6 5 10	7 0 8	8 1 2	9 10 7	11 13 9
Guardian	7 9 2	8 13 4	10 6 0	12 9 8	6 0 0	6 15 0	7 16 0	9 5 6	11 8 8
Hand-in-Hand	7 8 2	8 11 6	10 4 2	12 9 2	6 0 4	6 14 8	7 15 6	9 5 8	11 8 2
Imperial	7 9 10	8 12 10	10 4 2	12 6 2	6 1 8	6 16 0	7 16 2	9 4 4	11 5 10
Lancashire	7 9 11	8 13 8	10 5 8	12 8 9	6 1 1	6 15 11	7 16 7	9 5 6	11 8 0
Law Life	7 13 4	8 17 0	10 9 0	12 11 11	6 4 7	6 19 3	7 19 10	9 8 8	11 11 2
Law Union and Crown	7 11 8	8 15 6	10 8 0	12 12 4	6 2 8	6 17 4	7 18 2	9 7 6	11 10 10
Legal and General	7 10 0	8 14 4	10 7 0	...	6 0 8	6 15 3	7 17 0	9 6 4	...
Life Assoc. of Scotland	7 11 8	8 15 6	10 8 2	12 12 4	6 2 8	6 17 6	7 18 2	9 7 6	11 10 10
Livrpl. & Lndn. & Globe	7 13 4	8 18 10	10 14 0	13 1 8	6 2 8	6 18 4	8 0 6	9 12 0	11 18 6
Lndn., Edin & Glasgow	7 14 10	9 0 8	10 14 4	13 0 0	6 4 8	7 1 0	8 2 10	9 13 0	11 17 10
Marine and General	7 13 3	8 14 9	10 10 0	12 12 0	6 4 3	6 18 9	7 19 6	9 8 3	11 10 6
Methodist & General	7 16 8	9 0 8	10 13 2	12 16 8	6 4 7	7 2 4	8 3 2	9 12 8	11 15 8
Mutual of Austral.	8 1 0	9 5 0	10 18 0	13 1 0	6 12 0	7 7 0	8 7 0	9 17 0	12 0 0
Mutual of New York	7 18 2	9 3 4	10 19 0	13 0 10	6 7 6	7 3 0	8 4 10	9 15 2	11 14 6
National Mutual	7 15 4	8 19 10	10 13 2	12 18 4	6 5 8	7 0 8	8 2 0	9 12 0	11 16 6
Nat. Mut. of Aust.	8 2 8	9 7 2	11 0 6	13 6 0	6 12 10	7 7 10	8 9 2	9 19 2	12 3 10
National Provident	7 10 4	8 10 6	9 18 10	11 18 6	5 8 6	6 19 10	7 19 10	9 7 0	11 4 6
New York	7 18 2	9 3 4	10 19 0	13 0 10	6 7 6	7 3 0	8 4 10	9 15 2	11 14 6
Nrth. Brit. & Mercantile	7 13 0	8 18 0	10 11 0	12 15 10	6 3 2	6 18 8	8 0 4	9 10 0	11 14 2
Northern	7 15 4	8 18 2	10 9 2	12 10 10	6 7 4	7 1 8	8 1 4	9 9 6	11 10 6
Norwich Union	7 13 11	8 19 0	10 12 1	12 17 6	6 3 10	6 19 5	8 1 1	9 11 3	11 15 6
Pearl (Ord.)	7 18 0	9 3 0	10 17 2	13 4 2	6 8 0	7 3 2	8 4 8	9 15 4	12 1 2
Pioneer	7 19 8	9 4 4	10 19 0	13 3 6	6 9 0	7 5 0	8 6 4	9 16 6	12 1 4
Provident Clerks'	7 11 9	8 15 1	10 6 10	12 9 5	6 3 3	6 17 10	7 18 1	9 7 0	11 8 7
Prudential	7 13 6	8 18 0	10 12 0	12 17 0	6 3 0	6 19 0	8 0 6	9 11 0	11 15 0
Rock	7 14 9	8 19 1	10 13 0	12 19 3	6 3 6	6 19 6	8 0 6	9 11 4	11 16 0
Royal	7 9 5	8 11 2	10 1 10	12 1 4	5 16 4	6 10 4	7 10 0	8 17 0	10 16 0
Royal Exchange	7 3 8	8 6 0	9 15 8	11 14 8	5 16 4	6 10 4	7 10 0	8 17 0	10 16 0
Scottish Amicable	7 12 0	8 15 6	10 10 6	12 16 0	6 3 0	6 17 0	7 17 0	9 5 0	11 3 6
Scottish Life	8 0 6	9 5 2	10 18 0	13 1 8	6 7 0	7 2 2	8 3 6	9 12 0	11 14 4
Scottish Metropolitan	8 1 3	9 2 6	10 14 11	12 18 11	6 5 6	6 19 8	7 18 2	9 5 2	11 4 5
Scottish Provident	7 12 10	8 16 11	10 9 2	12 14 4	6 3 8	6 18 7	7 19 6	9 8 11	11 12 8
Scottish Temperance	7 12 3	8 16 3	10 7 6	12 9 2	6 2 5	6 16 8	7 16 1	9 3 8	11 2 9
Scottish Union Nat.	7 12 0	8 15 6	10 8 6	12 12 6	6 3 0	6 17 6	7 18 6	9 7 6	11 11 0
Scottish Widows'	7 2 2	8 1 0	9 7 10	11 8 6	5 13 8	6 7 0	7 5 10	8 12 0	10 10 8
Sickness, Acc. & Life	7 13 10	8 18 0	10 11 2	12 14 10	6 4 4	6 19 4	8 0 6	9 10 0	11 13 10
Standard	7 15 1	8 18 5	10 10 3	12 7 9	6 9 8	7 4 4	8 5 1	9 14 5	11 7 1
Star	7 18 0	9 0 10	10 11 3	12 13 7	6 7 7	7 2 0	8 1 5	9 8 7	11 3 10
Sun Life	7 11 8	8 16 2	10 9 8	12 14 10	6 2 2	6 17 4	7 18 6	9 6 8	11 13 0
Sun Life of Canada	8 6 2	9 10 0	11 2 10	13 5 0	6 17 0	7 11 7	8 12 2	9 19 10	11 12 7
Untd. Kgdm. Tempnce.	7 10 3	8 12 5	10 2 0	12 0 11	6 2 11	6 16 11	7 16 4	9 3 4	11 2 3
Univer-al	7 9 6	8 12 6	10 3 10	12 7 2	5 19 10	6 14 0	7 13 4	9 1 2	11 1 0
Yorkshire	7 18 0	9 0 6	10 11 0	12 15 0	6 8 0	7 2 0	8 2 6	9 12 0	11 12 0
Post Office (Gov. Anns.)	7 9 10	8 14 0	10 6 10	12 10 0	6 0 6	6 15 2	7 16 8	9 6 4	11 9 6

ABBREVIATIONS.—A = Accident ; Bo = Boiler ; Bu = Burglary ; Ca = Horse and Cattle ; E = Employers' Liability ; F = Fire ; G=Guarantee ; Ha = Hailstorm ; L = Life ; Li = Licences ; Ma = Machinery ; M = Marine ; Mo = Mortgage ; P = Plate Glass.

Est d	Fire, Accident, Life, &c.	Name of Company.	Address of Head and London Offices.
1894	L	Absolute	87, St. James's-street, S.W.
1883	L, A	Attainers and Gen. (Ord)	City-bldgs., Carr's-lane, *Birmingham.*
1849	A, E, P, G, Bu	Accident	10, St. Swithin's-lane, E.C.
1824	F, Ha, L	Alliance	Bartholomew-lane, E.C.
1808	F, L	Atlas	92, Cheapside, E.C.
1865	G	Bankers' Guar. and Trust	86, King William-street, E.C.
1847	L	British Empire	4 & 5, King William-street, E.C.
1854	L	British Equitable	Queen-street-place, E.C.
1888	F	British Law	5, Lothbury, Bank, E.C.
1863	L	British Legal	1, Richmond-street, *Glasgow.*
1896	L	British Life	101, St. Vincent-street, *Glasgow.*
1891	L	British Natural Premium	56, Ludgate-hill, E.C.
1866	L	British Workman's	Broad-st.-crnr., *Bmgham.*; West-st, Finsbury-circ.
1881	A, E	Builders' Accident	31 and 32, Bedford-street, Strand.
1805	F, L	Caledonian	19, George-st., *Edin.* ; 82, King William-st., E.C.
1838	L	City of Glasgow	30, Renfield-st., *Glasgow*; 12, King William-st., E.C.
1829	L	Clergy Mutual	2 & 3, Sanctuary, Westminster.
1824	L	Clerical, Medical, and Gen.	15, St. James's-square, S.W.
1873	L	Colonial Mutual	33, Poultry, E.C.
1867	F, G, L	Co-operative	Long Millgate, *Manchester.*
1861	F, L, M	Commercial Union	24, Cornhill, E.C.
1807	F	County	50, Regent-street.
1807	L	Eagle	79, Pall Mall, S.W.
1890	F, Bu A	Eastern Counties	63, Market-place, *Hull.*
1887	F, Bu, P	Ecclesiastical	11, Norfolk-street, Strand.
1823	L	Economic	6, New Bridge-street, Blackfriars.
1823	L	Edinburgh	22, George-st., *Edinb.* ; 11, King William-st., E.C.
1830	A, E, G	Employers' Liability	84, King William-street, E.C.
1898	Bo	Engine Boiler & Emp. Liab.	12, King-street, *Manchester.*
1839	L	English and Scottish Law	12, Waterloo-place, S.W.
1762	L	Equitable	Mansion-house-street, E.C.
1873	F, A, E	Equitable Fire and Accident.	St. Ann-st., *Manchester* ; 12 & 13, Nicholas-la., E.C.
1859	L	Equitable, United States	*New York* ; 6, Princes-street, Bank, E.C.
1844	L	Equity and Law	18, Lincoln's Inn-fields, W.C.
1802	F	Essex and Suffolk	High-street, *Colchester.*
1890	F, A, E, Bu	Fine Art and General	90, Cannon-street, E.C.
1832	L	Friends' Provident	45, Darley-st., *Bradfd., Yks.*; 17, Gracechch.-st. E.C.
1886	A, E, Bu, G	General (Perth)	42, Tay-street, *Perth* ; 115, Cannon-street, E.C.
1837	L	General	103, Cannon-street, E.C.
1890	A, E, Bu, P	Globe Accident	1, York-street, *Manchester* ; 13, Cullum-st., E.C.
1891	Bu	Goldsmiths' and General	85, Gresham-street, Guildhall, E.C.
1848	L	Gresham	St. Mildred's-house, E.C.
1821	F, A, E, L	Guardian	11, Lombard-street, E.C.
1840	G	Guarantee Society	19, Birchin-lane. E.C.
1696	F, L	Hand-in-Hand	26, New Bridge-street, E.C.
1868	Ca	Horse, Carriage, and General	17, Queen Victoria-street, E.C.
1803	F	Imperial	1, Old Broad-street, E.C.
1820	L	Imperial	1, Old Broad-street, E.C.
1878	A, Ca	Imp. Acc., Live Stock, & Gen.	17, Pall-mall East, S.W.
1802	F	Kent	High-street, *Maidstone* ; 124, Cannon-street, E.C.
1852	F, A, E, L	Lancashire	Exchange-st., *Manc.* ; 14, King William-st., E.C.
1877	A, E, G	Lancashire and Yorkshire	37, Princess-street, *Manchester.*
1845	F	Law Fire	114, Chancery-lane, W.C.
1823	L, A	Law Life	187, Fleet-street, W.C.
1894	A, Bu	Law Accident	215, Strand, W.C.
1888	Mo, Li, G	Law Guarantee and Trust	49, Chancery-lane, W.C.
1825	F, A, E, L	Law Union and Crown	126, Chancery-lane, W.C.
1836	L	Legal and General	10, Fleet-street, E.C.
1891	Li	Licences	24, Moorgate-street, E.C.
1838	L	Life Assoc. of Scotland	82, Princes-st., *Edinburgh* ; 5, Lombard-st., E.C.

Estd.	Fire, Accident, Life, &c.	Name of Company.	Address of Head and London Offices.
1879	F	Lion	83, Queen-street, E.C.
1836	F, L	L'pool & London & Globe	1, Dale-street, *Liverpool* ; 7, Cornhill, E.C.
1838	G, Mo	Liverpool Mortgage	6, Castle-street, *Liverpool*.
1720	F, M, L	London Assurance	7, Royal Exchange, E.C.
1862	F	London and Lancashire Fire	43, Dale-street, *Liverpool* ; 73, King William-st.
1862	L, A	London and Lancashire	66 & 67, Cornhill, E.C.
1859	L	London and Manchester	Southwark Exchange, S.E.
1861	P	London and General	19, Haymarket, S.W.
1881	A, L, E, G, Bu	London, Edin. & Glasgow	Insurance-buildings, Farringdon-street, E.C.
1869	A, E, G	London Guarantee and Acc.	61, Moorgate-street, E.C.
1806	L	London Life	81, King William-street, E.C.
1716	M	Lloyds	Royal Exchange, E.C.
1824	F	Manchester	98, King-street, *Manchester* ; 96, Cheapside, E.C.
1854	Bo	Manchester Steam Users	9, Mount-street, *Manchester*.
1875	Ma	Machinery	Temple-chambers, Temple-avenue, E.C.
1852	L	Marine and General	14, Leadenhall-street, E.C.
1867	L	Methodist and General	107, Queen Victoria-street, E.C.
1835	L	Metropolitan	13, Moorgate-street, E.C.
1869	L	Mutual of Australasia	*Sydney* ; 5, Lothbury, E.C.
1842	L	Mutual, New York	*New York* ; 17 & 18, Cornhill, E.C.
1881	L	Mutual Reserve Fund	*New York* ; 79, Cannon-street, E.C.
1864	Bo	National Boiler	22, St. Ann's-square, *Manchester*.
1892	Bu	National Burglary	10, Moorgate-street, E.C.
1863	G	National Guaran. & Suretyship	67, George-street, *Edinburgh*.
1822	F, L	National of Ireland	3, College-green, *Dublin* ; 47, Cornhill, E.C.
1830	L	National Mutual	30, King-street, Cheapside, E.C.
1869	L	National Mutual of Austral.	*Melbourne* ; 75 & 76, Cornhill, E.C.
1835	L	National Provident	48, Gracechurch-street, E.C.
1854	P, G	National Provincial	66, Ludgate-hill, E.C.
1845	L	New York Life	*New York* ; Trafalgar-bldgs.. Trafalgar-sq., W.C.
1809	F, L	North British & Mercantile	61, Threadneedle-street, E.C.
1836	F, L	Northern	1, Moorgate-street, E.C.
1882	A, E, G	Northern Accident	19, West Nile-st., *Glasgow* ; 23, Coleman-st., E.C.
1797	F	Norwich Union	Surrey-street, *Norwich* ; 50, Fleet-street, E.C.
1808	L	Norwich Union	*Norwich* ; 50, Fleet-street, E.C.
1856	A, E, Ha, G, Bu	Norwich and London Acc.	St. Giles-street, *Norwich* ; 114, Cannon-st., E.C.
1871	A, E, Mo G Bu	Ocean Accident	40, Moorgate-street, E.C.
1886	F, A, E, G	Palatine	32, Brown-street, *Manchester* ; 101, Cheapside, E.C.
1824	F, A, E, L	Patriotic	9, College-gn., *Dublin* ; 69, King William-st., E.C.
1864	L	Pearl	London-bridge, E.C.
1797	L	Pelican	70, Lombard-street, E.C.
1782	F	Phœnix	19, Lombard-street, E.C.
1891	F, A	Pioneer	11, Dale-street, *Liverpool*.
1806	L	Provident	50, Regent-street.
1840	L	Provident Clerks	27 & 29, Moorgate-street, E.C.
1876	A, E	Provident Clerks' Acc.	61, Coleman-street, E.C.
1855	G	Provident Clerks' Guarantee	61, Coleman-street, E.C.
1848	L	Prudential (Ordinary)	Holborn-bars.
1849	A, E, G	Railway Passengers	64, Cornhill, E.C.
1864	L	Refuge	Oxford-st., *Manchester* ; 29, New Bridge-st., E.C.
1806	A, E, L	Rock	15, New Bridge-street, E.C.
1845	F, L	Royal	Royal Insur.-bdgs., *L'pool* ; Lombard-st., E.C.
1720	F, L	Royal Exchange	Royal Exchange, E.C.
1864	L	Sceptre	40, Finsbury-pavement, E.C.
1877	A, G, L	Scottish Accident	115, George-st., *Edinburgh* ; 27, Nicholas-lane, E.C.
1888	F, G	Scottish Alliance	151, St. Vincent-st., *Glasgow* ; 76, Queen-st., E.C.
1826	L	Scottish Amicable	St.Vincent-pl., *Glasgow* ; 1, Threadneedle-st., E.C.
1881	Bo	Scottish Boiler	111, Union-street, *Glasgow*.
1881	A, E, G	Scottish Employers' Liability	9, King-street, *Aberdeen* ; 88, Cannon-street, E.C.
1831	L	Scottish Equitable	26,St.Andrew-sq., *Edinb.*;19,KingWilliam-st.,E.C.
1865	L	Scottish Imperial	183,W.George-st., *Glasg.*;15,KingWilliam-st.,E.C.
1881	A, L	Scottish Life	19, St. Andrew-sq., *Edin.* ; 13, Clement's-lane.
1876	A, E, L	Scottish Metropolitan	25, St. Andrew-sq., *Edinburgh* ; 8, King-st., E.C.

Estd.	Fire, Accident, Life, &c.	Name of Company.	Address of Head and London Offices.
1837	L	Scottish Provident	6, St. Andrew-sq , *Edinb.*; 17, King William-st., E.C.
1883	A, L	Scottish Temperance	105, St. Vincent-st., *Glasgow* ; 96, Queen-st., E.C.
1824	F, L	Scottish Union and Nat.	35, St. Andrew-sq., *Edin.*; 3, King Wm.-st., E.C.
1815	L	Scottish Widows	9, St. Andrew-sq., *Edinburgh*; 28, Cornhill, E.C.
1889	G, Bu	Security	63, St. James's-street, S.W.
1885	A, E, G, L	Sickness, Accident, & Life	24, York-place, *Edin.*; 35. Moorgate-stre et, E.C.
1825	L	Standard	3, George-st., *Edinburgh*; 83, King William-st, E.C.
1843	L	Star	32, Moorgate-st., E.C.
1891	F	State	Exchange-bdgs., *L'pool.*; 13, Abchurch-lane, E.C.
1710	F	Sun	63, Threadneedle-street, E.C.
1810	A, L	Sun Life	63, Threadneedle-street, E.C.
1865	L	Sun Life of Canada	93, Queen Victoria-street, E.C.
1714	F	Union	81, Cornhill, E.C.
1824	L	United Kent	High-street, *Maidstone;* 124, Cannon-street, E.C.
1840	L	United Kingdom Temp.	1, Adelaide-place, London-bridge.
1834	L	Universal	1, King William-street, E.C.
1825	L	University	25, Pall-mall, S.W.
1860	L	Victoria Mutual	Memorial Hall-buildings, Farrington-st., E.C.
1859	A, E, G, Bo	Vulcan Boiler	67, King-street, *Manchester* ; 3, Eastcheap, E.C.
1841	L	Wesleyan and General	Corporation-st., *Birm'ham*; 18, New Bridge-st., E.C.
1717	F	Westminster	27, King-street, Covent-garden, W.C.
1836	L	Westminster and General	28, King-street, Covent-garden, W.C.
1824	F, A, L	Yorkshire	St. Helen's-square, *York* ; 82, Old Broad-st., E.C.
1870	L	Yorkshire Provident	10, Corporation-street, *Manchester*.

Fire Insurance Rates.

RATES.—For merchandise at the principal ports, and for mills and manufactories and other leading industries throughout the United Kingdom, all the tariff or associated offices charge an identical minimum. Non-tariff and some class offices advertise that they assess individual risks on their merits. The following is a digest of the scale put forward by some of the oldest companies, and the rates and classification are those which are generally adopted.

Common Insurances.—At 1s. 6d. to 2s. per cent. per annum, with certain exceptions :—

1. Buildings covered with slates, tiles, or metals, and built on all sides with brick or stone, or separated by party-walls of brick or stone which are carried through the roof, and used for residence, or non-hazardous purposes.

2. Goods in buildings as above, such as household goods, plate, wearing apparel, and printed books, liquors in private use, and personal effects not comprised in the following categories.

Hazardous Insurances.—At 2s. 6d. to 3s. 6d. per cent. per annum, with certain exceptions :—

1. Buildings of timber and plaster, or not separated by partition walls of brick or stone, or not covered with slates, tiles, or metals, and thatched barns and outhouses, having no chimney, nor adjoining to any building having a chimney ; and buildings falling under the description of common insurances, but in which hazardous goods are deposited, or hazardous trades are carried on.

2. Goods.—The stock and goods of bread-bakers, tallowchandlers (not melters), drapers, stationers, also chemists and grocers not dealing in mineral oils.

Doubly Hazardous Insurances.—At 4s. 6d. to 5s. per cent. per annum, with certain exceptions :—

1. Buildings.—All thatched buildings having chimneys, or communicating with or adjoining to buildings having one, although no hazardous trade shall be carried on, nor hazardous goods deposited therein, and all hazardous buildings in which hazardous goods are deposited, or hazardous trades carried on.

2. Goods.—All hazardous goods deposited in hazardous buildings, and in thatched buildings having no chimney ; also china, glass, mathematical and musical instruments, pictures, and jewels in private use.

Much depends upon the surroundings of the building insured ; for a printer's or bookbinder's workshop, in a narrow lane, with old wooden houses near it, the premium would possibly be from 10s. to 15s.

Special Insurances.—5s. per cent. per annum and upwards :—

Buildings and contents among others of workers in wood, dealers in mineral oils, large drapers, some mills, warehouses, and factories ; in the case of some theatres the rate is as high as 31s. 6d. per cent.

Close proximity to, or communication with, any building containing very hazardous goods or used for any specially hazardous trade will, of course, also increase the risk.

The most recent returns of 46 British Fire Offices give a premium Income of £19,244,867 ; Losses, £11,471,139 ; Expenses, £6,694,549. Funds exclusive of Capital, £30,172,789 ; Paid-up Capital, £8,474,475. The losses amount to 59·61 per cent. of the premiums and the expenses to 34·79 per cent., making together 94·4 per cent. of the premiums. In the previous year the losses were 56·12 per cent., expenses 33·61 per cent., together 89·73 per cent. of the premiums.

Rules by which the Personal Estates (including leaseholds) of English Persons, and the Movable Estates of Scottish, Persons Dying Intestate are Distributed.

IN EACH INSTANCE IT IS SUPPOSED THERE ARE NO NEARER RELATIONS THAN THOSE NAMED.

[* *Where this is prefixed the Regulation applies to Scotland only.*]

By the Intestates' Estates Act, 1890, passed in the Session 53 & 54 Vict. c. 29, a very important change is made in the law as regards provision for widows of men who die intestate and without issue after the first of September, 1890, whereby it is enacted that the real and personal estate of an intestate so dying, passes absolutely to the widow as far as the first £500 in value is concerned. If under £500 she takes the whole; if above £500 she takes £500 in addition to what she was entitled to under the law previously in force. This Act is not applicable to Scotland.

If the Intestate die, leaving	*His representatives take in the proportion following :—*
Wife only, no blood relations	Half to wife, other half to the Crown.
Wife, no near relations	Half to wife, rest to next-of-kin in equal degree to intestate.
Wife and child, or children, and children of a deceased child	One-third to wife, rest to child or children; and if children are dead, then to their lineal descendants, subject to this, that such child or children as had estate by settlement of intestate, or were advanced by him in his lifetime, shall bring such estate or advancement into account (but heir does not bring real estate into account). *One-third to wife; one-third to living children in equal shares (but the heir must collate the heritable estate, and those children who have been advanced by intestate in life must collate the advances); one-third equally among living children *per capita* (see NOTE A, next page), and issue of dead children *per stirpes.*
Wife and father	Half to wife, and half to father.
Wife and mother	Half to wife, and half to mother. *Half to wife, one-sixth to mother, two-sixths to Crown failing kin.
Wife, brother, or sister and children of a deceased brother or sister	Half to wife, one-fourth to living brother or sister, one-fourth to deceased brother's or sister's children. *Half to wife one-sixth to brother two-sixths equally among children of dead brother or sister.
Wife, mother, nephews, and nieces	Half to wife, one-fourth to mother, and other fourth to nephews and nieces *per stirpes.* *Half to wife, one-sixth to mother, two-sixths among nephews and nieces *per stirpes.*
Wife, mother, brothers, sisters, and nephews and nieces (children of deceased brothers and sisters)	Half to wife, residue to mother, brothers, sisters, and nephews and nieces (as to nephews and nieces *per stirpes*). *Half to wife, one-sixth to mother, two-sixths among the brothers and sisters (who take *per capita*), and the nieces who take *per stirpes.*
No wife or child	All to next-of-kin of equal degree.
Children by one or more wives and the issue of deceased children	All children equally *per capita*, issue of deceased children *per stirpes*; no difference between children of different wives. *One-half equally amongst all living children; the other half equally amongst living children *per capita*, and issue of dead children *per stirpes.*
Husband and children	Whole to husband.
Mother, but no wife, child, father, brother, sister, nephew, or niece	The whole to mother. *One-third to mother, two-thirds to the Crown failing kin.
Mother and brother or sister	Equally between them. *Mother one-third, brother two-thirds.
Mother, and brothers and sisters	Whole to mother equally. *Mother one-third, brothers and sisters two-thirds equally *per capita.*
Father, and brothers and sisters	Whole to father. *One-half to father, the other half equally amongst brothers and sisters *per capita* (see NOTE B).

Child and grandchild by deceased child...............	Half to child, half to grandchild, who takes by representation.
	*Three-fourths to child, one-fourth to grand-child.
If no child, children, or representatives of them...	All to next-of-kin in equal degree to intestate.
Brother or sister, and children of a deceased brother or sister	Half to brother or sister *per capita*, half to children of deceased brother or sister *per stirpes*.
Brother and grandfather........................	Whole to brother.
Brother's grandson, and brother's or sister's daughter	All to daughter.
Brother and two aunts..............................	All to brother.
Brother and wife..............................	Half to brother, half to wife.
Grandfather, no nearer relation	All to grandfather.
Father's father, and mother's mother...............	Equally to both.
Grandmother, uncle, or aunt.....................	All to grandmother.
	*All to uncle or aunt if paternal.
Uncle, and deceased uncle's child...............	All to uncle.
Uncle by mother's side, and deceased uncle or aunt's child	All to uncle.
	*Child of deceased paternal uncle or aunt takes in exclusion of maternal uncle.
Two aunts, nephew, and niece	Equally to all.
	*Nephew and niece.
Uncle's or aunt's children, and brother's or sister's grandchildren	Equally to all.
	*Brother's or sister's grandchildren.
Nephew by brother, and nephew by half-sister ...	Equally *per capita* (see Note A).
	*All to nephew by brother.
Nephew by deceased brother, and nephews and nieces by deceased sister	Each in equal shares *per capita*, and not *per stirpes*.
	*The same, having regard to Note B.

NOTE A.—*Per capita*, that is, taking individually, and not by representation. Thus, if A. die leaving three brothers or sisters, they each take an equal part of his effects in his or her own right But if either of them die, leaving children, his children would take his share *per stirpes*, that is *through him*, and not in their own rights.

NOTE B.—By English Law, brothers and sisters of the half blood, whether by the mother's or father's side, share equally with the whole blood. By the Scottish Law, brothers and sisters german (that is, by the same father and mother) and their issue take in exclusion of brothers and sisters consanguinean (that is, by the same father) and their issue. And brothers and sisters consanguinean and their issue take in exclusion of brothers and sisters uterine (that is, by the same mother) and their issue.

NOTE C.—Posthumous brothers and sisters take equally with those born in lifetime of father.

Intestates' Estates—Real Property.

(N.B.—Leaseholds are Personal Property.)

TABLE of Descent of Real Property in England on death of an intestate and also showing the persons entitled to administer personal estate. No illegitimate child is capable of inheriting real estate. Custom of Gavelkind (descent to all sons alike) still exists in Kent, and custom of Borough English (descent to youngest son) in divers ancient boroughs. Custom of London for Administration of Personal Estate abolished in 1856. Leaseholds are Personal Estate. The Dower (viz., widow's thirds) of widows married since 1833 is in the majority of cases barred by the purchase deed. Generally put in by Solicitors to avoid the inconvenience of dower attaching.

In each instance it is supposed that there are no nearer relations than those named.

The persons named within brackets are those who are entitled to administer.

If Intestate die, leaving	*Real Property would descend to—*
Wife only, no blood relations ...	One-third to wife for life, rest to Crown; copyholds to lord of manor. [*Wife*.]
Wife and child, or children, and children of a deceased child ...	One-third to wife for life; rest to eldest son or his issue. [*Wife*.]
	One-third to wife for life in any case. [*Wife*.]
	Rest to eldest son or his issue, such son and his issue, whether male or female, being preferred to any other son and his issue, and all sons and their issue, whether male or female, being preferred to all daughters and their issue, whether male or female.
	If no son, rest to daughters equally. [*Either daughter, or not exceeding three.*]
	If daughters and grandchildren (sons and daughters of deceased daughter) rest to daughters and eldest son of deceased daughter.
Wife and father........................	One-third to wife for life; rest to father, if deceased purchased same, or had it left him by will. [*Wife*.]
Wife and mother	One-third to wife for life; rest to mother, there being no heirs on father's side. [*Wife*.]

Wife, brother, or sister, and children of a deceased brother or sister	One-third to wife for life in any case; rest to eldest brother or his issue. (*See above*, "Rest to eldest son or his issue," under head "Wife and child," &c.) [*Wife.*]
	Sister and children of deceased sister, rest equally between sister and nephew (eldest). [*Ditto.*]
	Sisters and nieces, only, children of deceased sister, rest equally between nieces. [*Ditto.*]
Wife, mother, nephews, and nieces	One-third to wife for life; rest to nephew (eldest), or nieces, if brother left no son. [*Wife.*]
Wife, mother, brother, sisters, and nieces (children of deceased brothers and sisters) ...	One-third to wife for life in any case; rest to eldest brother. [*Wife.*]
	Rest to nieces, equally, if children of elder brother deceased.
No wife or child or issue of a deceased child	Lineal ancestor paternal, males of whole blood first. [*Father or grandfather, as case may be.*]
Children by one or more wives, and the issue of deceased children	All to eldest son, or his issue. (*See above*, "Rest to eldest son or his issue," under head "Wife and child," &c. [*Either sons or daughters, not exceeding three.*]
	Daughters equally.
Husband and child or children ...	Husband for life; afterwards to only child or to eldest son or issue of a deceased eldest son. [*Husband.*]
	If all daughters, to them equally.
Mother, but no wife, child, or issue of a child, father, brother, sister, nephew, or niece, or more distant descendants of father...	All to mother in default of lineal ancestors on the father's side, issue of such ancestors. [*Mother.*]
Mother, and brothers and sisters	All to eldest brother. [*Mother.*]
Mother and sisters	All to sisters. [*Mother.*]
Father, and brothers and sisters	All to father. [*Father.*]
Child and grandchild by deceased child	*See above*, "Rest to eldest son or his issue," under head "Wife and child," &c. [*Child.*]
Brother and grandfather............	All to brother. [*Brother.*]
Brother's grandson, and brother or sister's daughter	All to great-nephew, if eldest brother's grandson. [*Niece.*]
	All to brother's daughter if child of eldest brother.
Brother and two aunts..............	Brother, all. [*Brother.*]
Brother and wife	One-third to wife for life; rest to brother. [*Wife.*]
Grandfather (no nearer)	All to grandfather. [*Grandfather.*]
Father's father, & mother's mother	All to father's father. [*Either, or both.*]
Grandmother & uncle, or aunt on father's side (no nearer)	All to uncle or aunt. [*Grandmother.*]
Uncle, and deceased uncle's child	Uncle, unless deceased uncle was elder brother, when his child takes all. [*Uncle.*]
Uncle by mother's side, and deceased uncle or aunt's child ...	Child of deceased uncle on father's side, or (if none) child of deceased aunt on father's side. [*Deceased uncle or aunt's children, not exceeding three.*]
Two aunts, nephew, and niece, children of deceased brother ...	Nephew. [*Two aunts.*]
Uncle or aunt's children, and brother's grandchildren through a son	Eldest brother's grandson, or if granddaughters between them equally. [*Either, not exceeding three.*]
Nephew by brother, and nephew by half-sister	Nephew by brother. [*Either, or both.*]
Nephew by deceased brother, and nephews and nieces by deceased sister.....................	All to eldest nephew, son of deceased brother. [*To either of the nephews and nieces, not exceeding three.*]

INSTRUCTIONS FOR OBTAINING PROBATE OR ADMINISTRATION WITHOUT EMPLOYING A SOLICITOR.

THE entrance to the office for personal applications is in the south-east corner of the Quadrangle of Somerset House, Strand, Room 37. The applicant should bring the registrar's certificate of the death of the deceased, or an official certificate of burial, and the will, if there be one, and full details of the property and debts of the deceased.

If there be no will or no executor be appointed, or the executor will not act, two sureties must also attend and enter into a bond for the faithful administration of the estate, unless the whole personal estate does not exceed £50, or the husband is the applicant, when one surety only will be required.

The scale of probate duty as remodelled under the Finance Act of 1894, will be found in detail on pp. 430-431.

In no case can any correspondence be entered into; nor can an interview be given to any agent. The business of the department can be transacted only with the applicant in person.

Where the deceased resided within the district of one of the District Probate Registries (see Appendix), application may be made at that registry instead of at Somerset House.

Where the whole real and personal estate, without the deduction of debts or funeral expenses, does not exceed £500, application may be made at one of the Inland Revenue Offices.

Where the deceased has left no will, and the whole personal estate does not exceed £100, and the widow resides at more than three miles from any Probate Registry, application may be made to the Registrar of the County Court.

When the Session opened, the Government laid before Parliament a heavy programme of domestic legislation, and although most of the proposals were of an unexciting character, several of the measures contained controversial details, still the Opposition, both in debate and committee, did not score with effect. Possibly the chief of these was the London Government Bill, which created subordinate municipalities in the places of existing vestries and district boards, thereby solidifying local administrations. The powers of both the City of London and the London County Council, however, were not interfered with. In Committee a fight took place, in which the House of Lords ultimately vetoed the inclusion of Women Councillors and Aldermen.

The Tithe Rent-Charge Rating Bill aroused a somewhat acrimonious discussion, arising from the controversy over the crisis of so-called Ritualistic practices in certain churches. The second reading, however, was carried by 314 votes to 176. The Board of Education Bill, introduced in the House of Lords, was accepted in the lower chamber after some debating; but the same fate did not attend Lord James' Money Lending Bill —a much needed reform.

Although the Budget statement of the Chancellor of the Exchequer showed a big and continuous growth of revenue, proposals had to be made for raising additional taxation. This was done by augmented stamp and wine duties. As in former years many of the Government bills, after passing through their preliminary stages, were dropped. Among the most important of these were the Limited Liability Bill, the Food and Drugs Bill, the Factory Acts Amendment Bill, and the Agricultural Holdings Bill.

Owing to hostilities supervening a political crisis in the Transvaal an autumn session of Parliament was called for the purpose of voting supplies. It met on the 15th of October and sat till the 27th of the same month.

February 7.—Lords. The Duke of Bedford moved and Lord Cawdor seconded the Address. In reply to Lord Kimberley's criticisms of the Government's policy Lord Salisbury defended the action taken in upholding the Egyptian power in the Soudan.

Commons. Col. Bagot moved and Mr. W. D. F. Smith seconded the Address. Sir H. Campbell-Bannerman, as leader of the Opposition, made his first speech in that rôle. Replying, Mr. A. J. Balfour complimented him. The debate was continued by Sir J. Lubbock, Sir H. Vincent, Sir H. Wedderburn, Sir C. Dilke and Mr. Brodrick.

February 8.—An amendment on China by Sir E. Ashmead Bartlett discussed and withdrawn. Mr. S. Smith moved an amendment regretting the lawlessness prevailing in parts of the Protestant Church of England.

February 9.—After a reply by Mr. Balfour, Mr. Smith's amendment defeated by 221 to 89.

Lords. Discussion on Church discipline initiated by the Bishop of Winchester. The Archbishop of Canterbury advocated the exercise of a spirit of conciliation.

February 10.—Lord Dudley's Companies Bill again read a second time.

Commons. An amendment to the Address by Mr. E. J. C. Morton on the subject of the taxation on Ground values defeated, a lively discussion by 157 votes to 123.

February 13.—Mr. Herbert Lewis's amendment on the subject of Welsh legislation after debate, negatived by 194 votes to 154. Mr. Labouchere's amendment in favour of abolishing the veto of the House of Lords, rejected by 223 votes to 105.

February 14.—A question of privilege raised on the question of Peers at election meetings. Debates on the Scotch Crofters Question and the Calcutta Municipal Bill.

February 15.—Mr. McNeill's amendment relating to Ministers of the Crown as company directors rejected by 247 votes to 143.

February 16.—Mr. Seton Karr's amendment on the dependence of this country on Foreign food stuffs negatived without a division. Home Rule amendment rejected by 300 votes to 43.

February 17.—Debates on amendments relating to Irish railways and Distress in Ireland.

February 20.—Mr. Chaplin introduced a bill to require the Metropolitan Water Companies to supply each other with water in emergency.

Lords. Lord James of Hereford introduced the Money-Lender's Bill which was read a first time.

February 21.—Commons. The Address agreed to. Mr. Herbert Lewis's resolution about Bishops in the House of Lords rejected by 200 to 129.

February 23.—Mr. Balfour introduced the London Government Bill with an explanatory speech.

Lords. Her Majesty's reply to the Address brought up.

February 24.—Commons. Committee of Supply. The question of the recent expedition in the Soudan discussed, and an amendment by Mr. J. Morley negatived by 119 votes to 51.

February 27.—Supplementary estimates.

February 28.—Second reading of the London Improvement Bill.

March 1.—Mr. Robson's bill relating to "half-timers," read a second time.

March 2 and 3.—Army estimates in Committee of Supply.

March 6.—Mr. Hanbury explained the Government proposals with regard to acquiring the telephones. Second reading of the bill dealing with the restriction and prevention of the adulteration of foods and drugs.

March 8.—The second reading of a bill, introduced by Sir J. B. Maple, to extend the franchise, carried.

March 9.—The Navy Estimates submitted. The Sale of Food and Drugs Bill read a second time, as also was the London Water Bill.

March 10.—Civil Service estimates vigorously debated in Committee of Supply. Mr. Chamberlain announced the decision of the Government to establish a school of tropical medicine in England.

March 13.—Debate on the Navy and new programme of the Government.

March 14.—A bill for the amalgamation of the South Eastern and the London, Chatham and Dover Railway Companies read a second time by 288 votes to 82. Mr. Chamberlain introduced a bill for enabling local authorities to assist working men to purchase the houses in which they reside. Army Estimate considered in supply.

March 15.—A bill for raising the flash point of petroleum from 73 degrees to 100 degrees, rejected by 244 votes to 159.

Lords. The Duke of Devonshire introduced a bill to make better provision for secondary education.

March 16.—Navy estimates discussed.

LORDS. The Money-Lending Bill read a second time.

March 17.—COMMONS. Army estimates in Supply.

March 20.—On going into Committee of Supply Mr. Chamberlain made a statement with regard to the Transvaal in which he said that the Government regretted that President Kruger had not kept his promises.

March 21.—Mr. Balfour moved the Second reading of the London Government Bill. A debate followed in which Mr. H. Gladstone, Mr. Whitmore, Mr. Haldane, Lord Percy, Mr. Holland and Mr. A. Gibbs took part.

March 22.—Mr. L. Holland's Old Age Pension Bill discussed. Mr. Chamberlain explained the position of the Government on the question.

March 23.—Debate on the London Government Bill continued by Sir J. B. Maple, Mr. Asquith, The Solicitor-General, Mr. Courtney, and Sir E. Clarke.

March 24.—The London Government Bill read a second time after speeches by Mr. Burdett Coutts, Sir H. Campbell-Bannerman and Mr. Balfour.

March 27.—The Sale of Food and Drugs Bill referred to the Standing Committee on Trade.

March 28. — The House adjourned for the Eastern recess till April 10th.

April 10.—In Committee of Supply on the Civil Service estimates, the management of the Royal Parks discussed. The Metropolitan Water Companies Bill passed through Committee.

April 11.—Discussion on lawlessness in the Church of England.

April 12.—A bill for the re-instatement of evicted Irish tenants rejected by 167 votes to 69.

April 13.—Budget Statement by the Chancellor of the Exchequer.

April 14. — Navy Estimates discussed. The future of Wei-hai-Wei as a secondary naval base to Hong Kong explained by Mr. Goschen.

April 17.—The bill for enabling local authorities to assist working men to purchase their houses was read a second time by 249 votes to 69, and referred to the Standing Committee on Law.

April 19.—A bill to repeal the Irish Crimes Act, introduced by Mr. Dillon, negatived by 220 votes to 141.

April 20.—The Budget Proposals debated.

LORDS. The Lord Chief Justice introduced the Secret Commissions bill.

April 21.—COMMONS. Army estimates considered in Committee of Supply.

April 24.—A Select Committee appointed to inquire into the old age pension question.

LORDS. Debate on the second reading of the Education Bill.

April 24. COMMONS. The London Government Bill in Committee.

April 26.—The Ecclesiastical Assessments (Scotland) Bill read a second time.

April 27.—Consideration of the London Government Bill in Committee, the question of women as aldermen discussed.

April 28.—The Education estimates laid before the House.

LORDS. The Metropolitan Water Companies Bill and the Copyright (artistic) Bill read a second time.

May 1.—LORDS. Announcement by Lord Salisbury as to the agreement between Russia and England, with regard to operations in China. Money Lending Bill passed through Committee.

COMMONS. On the second reading of the Finance Bill Sir H. Fowler strongly criticised the Government Budget proposals.

May 2.—Debate on the Finance Bill continued by Sir W. Harcourt, Mr. Goschen, and the second reading carried by 283 votes to 155.

LORDS. The Duke of Devonshire introduced the Board of Education Bill.

May 3.—COMMONS. Private Bill to control the liquor Traffic in Scotland, rejected by 217 votes to 143.

May 4.—London Government Bill in Committee.

May 5.—Civil Service Estimates.

May 8.—London Government Bill reported for third reading.

May 10.—Mr. C. McArthur's Church Discipline Bill discussed and the second reading defeated by 310 votes to 156.

May 11. The Budget Bill discussed and certain wine duties lowered.

May 12.—The Budget Bill passed through Committee.

May 15 and 16.—The London Government Bill in Committee.

May 17.—LORDS. The Metropolitan Water Companies Bill and the Money-Lending Bill, read a third time and passed.

May 18.—COMMONS. The London Government Bill passed through Committee.

May 18.—House adjourned for Whitsun recess.

June 1.—Mr. Dillon moved adjournment of the House to call attention to Religious rioting in Belfast. Post Office votes and Customs votes agreed to in Committee of Supply.

June 2.—Vaccination discussed on the Vote for the Local Government Board.

LORDS. Message from the Queen read recommending the grant of £30,000 to Lord Kitchener.

June 5.—COMMONS. The grant to Lord Kitchener carried by 393 votes to 51.

June 6.—The London Government Bill passed the report stage.

LORDS. Lord Russell of Killowen's Prevention of Corruption Bill read a second time.

June 8.—Lord Kitchener and his troops thanked in both Houses for the success in the Soudan.

June 9.—COMMONS. Debate on the Foreign policy of the Government initiated by Sir Charles Dilke. Speech by Lord Charles Beresford on China.

June 13.—Mr. Chamberlain stated the instructions given to Sir A. Milner with regard to the crisis in the Transvaal.

June 15.—Sir H. Fowler's vote of Censure on the Government upon the importation of bounty fed sugar defeated by 293 votes to 152.

June 16.—Scottish estimates in Supply.

June 21.—Motion by Mr. G. Wyndham authorising an expenditure of four millions sterling upon Military works agreed to after discussion by 241 votes to 66.

June 22.—The Tithe Rent-Charge (Rates) Bill, (to relieve the poorer clergy) introduced.

June 23.—Debate on the establishment of a Roman Catholic University in Ireland.

June 26.—The Board of Education Bill read a second time.

LORDS.— By 182 votes to 63 expunged from the London Government Bill the clause inserted in the House of Commons qualifying women for election to the new councils.

June 27.—Conclusion of the Committee stage of the London Government Bill.

COMMONS. Discussion on the second reading of the Clerical Tithes Bill, Mr. George Whiteley, Unionist member for Stockport, announced his resignation.

June 28.—The Telephone Bill referred to a Grand Committee.

June 29.—The Clerical Tithes Bill after an acriminious debate read a second time.

June 30.—Irish estimates in Committee of Supply.

July 3.—Resolution passed by 223 votes to 101, transfering territories of the Royal Niger Company to the Imperial Government on the payment of £865,000.

LORDS. The London Government Bill reported as amended and the "Half-Timers" Bill passed through Committee.

July 4.—The London Government Bill read a third time.

July 5.—COMMONS. A bill to create a new department of Agriculture and Technical Instruction in Ireland read a second time.

July 6.—LORDS. The "Half-Timers" Bill read a third time.

Ju y 7.—The Militia Ballot Bill read a first time.
COMMONS. Mr. Balfour made a statement with regard to the Transvaal crisis.

July 10.—The Clerical Tithes Bill in Committee.

July 11.—A lively discussion in Committee on the Clerical Tithes Bill.

July 13.—All-night sitting of the House. The Tithes Bill passed through Committee.

July 14.—Scotch Estimates in Committee of Supply.

July 18.—LORDS. A resolution brought forward by Lord Inchiquin calling on the Government to give immediate attention to the question of compensating Irish landowners for injuries inflicted on them by recent legislation, carried against the Government by 39 votes to 34.

July 20.—COMMONS. The third reading of the Tithes Bill carried by 182 votes to 117.

July 21.—Navy Estimates in Committee.

July 24.—LORDS. After a discussion the Tithes Bill read a second time by 113 votes to 23.
COMMONS. Debate on the Irish Industries Bill and the Telephone Bill.

July 25.—The Sale of Food and Drugs Bill read a third time and the Naval Works Bill a second time.

LORDS. Lord Kitchener of Khartoum took his seat.

July 26.—COMMONS. The Niger (Acquisition of) Bill considered in Committee.

July 27.—The Niger Bill read a third time.
LORDS. The Tithes Bill passed through Committee.

July 28.—Debate on the South African Crisis.
COMMONS. Colonial Office Vote discussed in Committee of Supply and agreed to.

July 31.—The Telephone Bill read a third time by 132 votes to 29.

August 2.—The Colonial Loans Bill read a third time.

August 3.—Civil Service estimates in Supply.

August 4.—The report of Supply agreed to, and the Appropriation Bill brought in.

August 7.—The Appropriation Bill read a second time. The Government policy in the Transvaal criticised by Sir W. Lawson and Mr. Scott.

August 8.—Indian Budget discussed.

August 9.—Parliament Prorogued by Royal Commission.

October 15.—The Sixth Session of the Fourteenth Parliament of the present reign opened by Royal Commission.

LORDS. The Marquis of Granby moved and Lord Barnard seconded the Address. Lord Salisbury made a speech in which he defended the action of the Government in commencing hostilities against the Transvaal Government. The Address agreed to.

COMMONS. The address moved by Sir A. Acland Hood and seconded by Col. Royds. Sir H. Campbell-Bannerman, although supporting the Government in the present crisis, absolved himself from agreeing with their action which led up to the diplomatic rupture. Mr. Balfour replied. Mr. Dillon proposed an amendment, which was seconded by Mr. Labouchere, and supported by Mr. Davitt and Mr. W. Redmond. It was negatived by 322 votes to 54.

October 18.—Debate continued by Mr. Stanhope and Sir W. Harcourt.

October 19.—Mr. Chamberlain replied defending policy of the Government. Sir E. Clarke explained his attitude. Mr. Morley and Mr. Courtney also spoke.

October 20.—A vote of ten millions assented to, and the militia and reserves called out. Mr. W. Redmond suspended.

October 23.—During the discussion on the proposals of the Government Mr. P. O'Brien suspended.

October 24.—The Appropriation Bill read a first time.

October 25.—The Appropriation Bill read a second time after Mr. Chamberlain had made a very spirited defence of the Government policy. Mr. M. Davitt announced his intention of resigning his seat.

October 27.—Both Houses formally prorogued to January 15th, 1900.

TABLE OF THE STATUTES

Passed in the Fifth Session of the Twenty-Sixth Parliament of the United Kingdom of Great Britain and Ireland (62 & 63 Vict.—A.D. 1899).

1. An Act to change the Date of the Season for Partridge Shooting in Ireland.
2. To apply certain sums out of the Consolidated Fund to the service of the years ending on the 31st day of March, 1898, 1899, and 1900.
3. To provide, during twelve months, for the Discipline and Regulation of the Army.
4. To amend the Solicitors Acts.
5. To amend the Public Libraries (Scotland) Acts.
6. To amend the Law with respect to the hearing of Appeals and Motions by the Court of Appeal.

7. To enable and require the Metropolitan Water Companies to supply each other with Water in cases of emergency.

8. To extend the Infectious Disease (Notification) Act, 1889, to Districts in which it has not been adopted.

9. To grant certain duties of Customs and Inland Revenue, to alter other duties, and to amend the Law relating to Customs and Inland Revenue, and to make other provision for the financial arrangements of the year.

10. To enable Parish Councillors to hold Office for Three Years.

11. To assimilate the Law of Scotland and of Ireland as to Imprisonment in default of Payment of Fines to that of England.

12. To amend the Law with regard to Reformatory Schools.

13. To amend the Law respecting the Employment and Education of Young Children.

14. To make better provision for Local Government in London.

15. To amend the provisions of the Metropolis Management Acts with respect to Bye-laws.

16. To give powers to the Executive Committee of the Gordon Memorial College at Knartoum to invest Trust Funds in certain Securities.

17. To amend the Law with respect to the Payment of Rates on Tithe Rentcharge attached to a Benefice.

18. To amend certain provisions of the Land Law (Ireland) Act, 1896, affecting the Congested Districts Board, and to make further provision for the expenses of that Board out of money provided by Parliament.

19. For incorporating in one Act certain provisions usually contained in Provisional Orders made under the Acts relating to Electric Lighting.

20. For enabling Bodies Corporate to hold Property in Joint Tenancy.

21. To provide for Seats being supplied for the use of Shop Assistants.

22. To amend the Summary Jurisdiction Act, 1879.

23. To simplify and amend the Law relating to the Testing and Sale of Anchors and Chain Cables.

24. To amend the University of London Act, 1898, with respect to Holloway College.

25. To appoint additional Commissioners for executing the Acts for granting a Land Tax and other Rates and Taxes.

26. To amend the Law with respect to the Salaries and Allowances of the Commissioner, Receiver, and Assistant Commissioners of the Metropolitan Police.

27. To remove doubts as to the Validity of certain Marriages.

28. To amend Section Twenty of the Parish of Manchester Division Act, 1850.

29. To amend the Baths and Washhouses Acts.

30. To amend the Inclosure Acts, 1845 to 1882, and the Law relating to Commons and Open Spaces.

31. To grant Money for the purpose of certain Local Loans and for other purposes relating to Loans out of the Local Loans Fund.

32. To make better provision for the Elementary Education of Defective and Epileptic Children in England and Wales.

33. To provide for the Establishment of a Board of Education for England and Wales, and for matters connected therewith.

34. To continue various Expiring Laws.

35. To amend the Inebriates Act, 1898.

36. To authorise certain Public Loans to certain Colonies and Places.

37. To amend Section One of the Poor Law Act, 1889, and Section Four of the Pauper Inmates Discharge and Regulation Act, 1871.

38. To make further provision for the Improvement of Telephonic Communication, and otherwise with respect to Telegraphs.

39. To amend the Law with respect to Customs Duties in the Isle of Man.

40. To amend the Law relating to the Reserve Forces.

41. To make further provision for defraying the Expenses of certain Military Works and other Military Services.

42. To make further provision for the construction of Works in the United Kingdom and elsewhere for the purposes of the Royal Navy, and to amend the Law with respect to the construction and use of Tramways for Naval purposes.

43. To make provision for certain Payments to be made in connection with the Revocation of the Charter of the Royal Niger Company.

44. To empower Local Authorities to Advance Money for enabling Persons to acquire the Ownership of Small Houses in which they reside.

45. To amend the Patriotic Fund Act, 1881, and the Patriotic Act, 1886.

46. To amend the Enactments relating to the Improvement of Land.

47. To provide for improving and extending the Procedure for obtaining Parliamentary Powers by way of Provisional Orders in matters relating to Scotland.

48. To constitute the Divisions of Lincolnshire separate Counties for all the purposes of the Coroners Acts.

49. To apply a sum out of the Consolidated Fund to the service of the year ending on the 31st day of March, 1900, and to appropriate the Supplies granted in this Session of Parliament.

50. For establishing a Department of Agriculture and other Industries and Technical Instruction in Ireland, and for other purposes connected therewith.

51. To amend the Law relating to the Sale of Food and Drugs.

Remarkable Occurrences, &c., 1898-1899.

DECEMBER, 1898.

BANK RATE 4 per cent.

1. Meeting at the Mansion House in support of Lord Kitchener's proposal to found a Gordon Memorial College at Khartoum.

3. The Queen visited sick and wounded men from the Soudan campaigns in the wards at Netley Hospital.

5. The Prince of Wales opened the Centenary Exhibition of the Smithfield Cattle Club at Islington.

— Meeting of Congress at Washington; the President's message foreshadowed the occupation of Cuba until the inhabitants should be capable of self-government, and recommended the increase of the permanent army to 100,000 officers and men.

6. The Imperial Navy Contribution Bill read a third time in the Cape Assembly without division.

8. Sir William Harcourt addressed a letter to Mr. John Morley (which was published on December 15) resigning the leadership of the Liberal Party in the House of Commons.

— The Johnston Line *Vedamore* arrived at Baltimore, U.S.A., and reported the loss of *s.s. Londonian.*

— Convention signed in Paris prolonging for six months from December 14 the "Niger Convention" between United Kingdom and France.

9. The 1st battalion Gordon Highlanders arrived in Edinburgh from India, and met with a most enthusiastic reception.

— Bye-election Kirkdale Division of Liverpool.

— The prosecution of Col. Picquart, which was instituted on account of his espousal of the cause of Captain Dreyfus, ordered to be suspended by the *Cour de Cassation.*

10. Lord Curzon of Kedleston sailed for Calcutta to assume office as Viceroy of India.

— Treaty of Peace signed in Paris by plenipotentiaries of Spain and U.S.A.

11. Major Marchand, the French explorer, evacuated Fashoda (whither he had penetrated from the West Coast of Africa) by order of the French Government.

13. The Empress Dowager, for the first time in the history of China, received in audience the ladies of the various foreign embassies at Peking.

16. The Queen left Windsor for Osborne.

20. The Prince of Wales presided at Marlborough House over a meeting of the National Association for the Prevention of Consumption.

21. Prince George of Greece enthusiastically received at Canea, where he arrived to assume office as Governor-General of Crete.

25. CHRISTMAS DAY.—The Imperial Penny Post came into operation.

— Lord Charles Beresford arrived at Hong Kong on a commercial mission to China.

26. Col. Lewis defeated the Dervish Emir Ahmed Fedil, at Gedaref.

27. The secret *dossier* on the Dreyfus case was communicated to the *Cour de Cassation* for examination during the revision of the trial of Captain Dreyfus.

Consols, highest, 111⅛; lowest, 109⅞.

JANUARY, 1899.

1. Foundation of the "League de la Patrie Française" to combat the movement for a revision of the Dreyfus case.

2. In the list of New Year's honours Lord Cromer, the British Agent at Cairo, was created a Viscount.

3. Lord Curzon of Kedleston arrived in Calcutta and assumed office on 6th.

5. Viscount Cromer laid the foundation-stone of the Gordon Memorial College at Khartoum.

6. Fatal boiler explosion at Barking, six deaths.

— Bye-election Aylesbury Division of Buckinghamshire.

8. Resignation of M. Quesnay de Beaurepaire, President of the Civil Chamber of the *Cour de Cassation* on account of his certainty that the verdict would be in favour of revision.

14. Launch of White Star Line *Oceanic*, the largest steamer in the world (see September 6).

16. Bye-election Newton Division of Lancashire.

19. Anglo-Egyptian agreement signed at Cairo defining the principles upon which the Soudan Provinces are to be administered.

— Bank rate lowered from 4 to 3½ per cent.

21. The Senate of U.S.A. passed the Nicaragua Canal Bill.

22. By the death of Earl Poulett rival claimants arose for the succession to the title and estates.

23. T.R.H. the Duke and Duchess of Saxe-Coburg-Gotha celebrated their silver wedding.

— Bye-election Epsom Division of Surrey.

24. Mr. E. T. Hooley applied for discharge to Mr. Registrar Hope; the Official Receiver opposed the application.

— Parr's Bank, Bartholomew Lane, E.C., robbed of bank notes to the amount of £60,610.

26. The Federal Council of Australia met at Melbourne, and before dissolving in February agreed in principle to Federation, the question to be submitted to a referendum in each individual colony.

28. In accordance with the Anglo-Egyptian agreement of January 19, the British flag was hoisted at Atbara and Wady Halfa.

Consols, highest, 111½; lowest, 110¼.

FEBRUARY.

1. Conference at Dublin on the Roman Catholic University question.

2. The Bank rate lowered from 3½ to 3 per cent.

4. Fighting in the Philippine Islands between American troops and Filipinos.

6. Death of H.R.H. Prince Alfred, Hereditary Duke of Saxe-Coburg-Gotha, grandson of Queen Victoria.

— The American Senate ratified the treaty of peace with Spain.

— Sir Henry Campbell-Bannerman unanimously elected Leader of the Liberal Party.

— Lord Elgin arrived in London on completion of term of Vice-Royalty.

7. Fifth session of the Queen's 14th Parliament opened by Royal Commission.

8. Two Brahmins, who had been principal witnesses in the trial of the murderer of Mr. Rand and Lieut. Ayerst assassinated at Poona.

9. From this date Mr. G. R. Birt, Chairman of the Milwall Docks Company, absented himself from his duties; it subsequently transpired that a large sum (£200,000 in all) had been paid in dividends to the shareholders, but never actually earned.

10. Funeral of H.R.H. the Hereditary Prince of Saxe-Coburg-Gotha at Gotha.

12. The Duke of Connaught laid the foundation stone of the Nile reservoir at Assouan.

14. The Queen returned from Osborne to Windsor.

— Bye-election in North Birmingham.

16. Sudden death in Paris of heart disease of François Félix Faure, President of the French Republic.

— Bye-election Londonderry City.

17. The Cunard Line *Pavonia*, after terrible trials in severe hurricanes, arrived safely at the Azores.

18. Emile Loubet elected President of the French Republic by Congress assembled at Versailles; 483 votes were cast for M. Loubet, against 279 for M. Méline.

— Resignation of the Hungarian (Banffy) Ministry; M. Szell succeeded as Premier.

20. The Anglo-American Commissioners assembled at Washington to settle the Canada-Alaska boundary question were unable to agree, and adjourned the meeting until August 2nd, when it subsequently adjourned *sine die.*

21. Bye-election in North-West Lanark.

22. Ruskin Hall opened at Oxford.

23. Bye-election Rotherham Division of Yorkshire.

24. The Hamburg-American Line *Bulgaria* safely reached the Azores after terrible trials in the severe weather.

25. Bye-election North-West Antrim.

28. The French Senate decreed that the report on the 1894 trial of Captain Dreyfus should be communicated to the whole body of the *Cour de Cassation*, and not to the Criminal Department only.

Consols, highest, 111½; lowest, 110⅞.

MARCH.

1. Sudden death at Washington of Lord Herschell, President of the Anglo-American Boundary Commission.

— The R.M.S. *Labrador* wrecked on the Mackenzie Rock, New Hebrides; no lives lost.

— Bye-election Hythe.

2. Mr. Rudyard Kipling, who had been very dangerously ill with double pneumonia, was reported to be on the road to recovery.

5. The Lagouban Naval Magazine at Toulon blown up; over 50 lives lost.

6. The Lord Mayor presided at a meeting to provide for a fitting celebration of the Millenary of King Alfred.

7. Appearance at Khartoum of No. 1 of the "*Sudan Gazette.*"

8. Bye-election Elland Division of Yorkshire.

— Lord Charles Beresford returned from China, and subsequently published his impressions in book form.

9. Opening of the Great Central Railway.

11. Mr. Cecil Rhodes had an interview with the German Emperor in connection with the extension through German territory of the Cape to Cairo Railway.

— The Queen left Windsor for Cimiez *viâ* Folkestone and Boulogne.

15. The Gordon Memorial College fund closed at £   , but subsequently additional sums were received.

— An Adventurer's Share in the New River Company sold for £122,500.

16. Bye-election North Norfolk.

17. Fatal fire at the Hotel Windsor, New York; 14 killed. 51 injured. 50 missing.

20. The Indian Budget statement showed a deficit for 1897-8, but a surplus for 1898-9 and 1899-1900.

21. A convention signed by Great Britain and France delimiting their respective spheres in Central Africa.

23. Mr. Henniker-Heaton received the freedom of Canterbury, which city he represents in the House of Commons, in recognition of his efforts in obtaining reforms in the Postal System, and in bringing about Imperial Penny Postage.

25. Heavy fighting in the Philippines; success of U.S.A. forces at Caloocan.

— Cambridge won the University Boat Race by 3¼ lengths.

27. Press message received at South Foreland from Wimieux (France) by the Marconi system of wireless telegraphy.

— Mr. L. W. Longstaff, F.R.G.S., placed the sum of £25,000 at the disposal of the Royal Geographical Society to enable co-operation with the German Antarctic Expedition.

28. Man hunting trials with blood-hounds held near Aylesbury.

30. Total loss of *s.s. Stella* from Southampton to Channel Islands on the Casquets off Alderney; of 180 passengers and crew over 70 were drowned, the remainder being saved owing to the admirable conduct of all on board.

31. The Paris *Figaro* commenced a series of articles, detailing the evidence given during the revision of the Dreyfus case before the *Cour de Cassation.*

Consols, highest, 111⅜; lowest, 110.

APRIL.

1. A British-American column, landed on account of local disturbances, fell into an ambush near Apia, Samoa, and was forced to retreat with loss.

3. Mr. John Roberts retained the Billiard Championship.

5. Bye-election Harrow Division of Middlesex.

6. First elections under the Irish Local Government Act; of the County Councillors elected 546 were Nationalists and 113 Unionists.

11. Funeral of Mr. T. E. Ellis, M.P., the chief whip of the Liberal Party.

— Mr. G. R. Birt, late Chairman and Managing Director of the Milwall Docks, committed for trial.

— The Duke and Duchess of York visited the Punchestown Races during their visit to Ireland.

14. Herr von Bülow announced in the Reichstag that Germany, U.S.A., and Great Britain, were appointing a commission to deal with Samoan affairs.

15. Sheffield United won the Association Football Cup.

19. Conclusion of the *Tourmaline* case; the accused, Major Spilsbury, being acquitted by Court-martial at Gibraltar.

20. Marriage of the Earl of Crewe to Lady Peggy Primrose at Westminster Abbey.

22. The King and Queen of Italy reviewed the British Channel Squadron in Aranci Bay.

24. The Duke and Duchess of York returned from Ireland and visited North Wales.

24-26. Three days' heavy fighting in the Philippines round Calumpit.

25. Ter-centenary of the birth of Oliver Cromwell.

26. Celebration of the 700th year of corporate life by Kingston-on-Thames.

26. The business portion of Dawson City, Canada, entirely destroyed by fire.

— The Duke of Westminster's *Flying Fox* won the Two Thousand Guineas.

— A detachment of New South Wales Lancers arrived in England for six months' training at Aldershot.

29. Aston Villa beat Liverpool, and secured the Association Football League Championship.

Consols, highest, 110⅞; lowest, 110¼.

MAY.

1. First train of Cape to Cairo Railway entered Salisbury, Mashonaland.

2. Mr. Cecil Rhodes addressed a crowded meeting of shareholders of the British South Africa Company at the Cannon St. Hotel, and explained his financial proposals for completing sections of the Cape to Cairo Railway.

— Bye-election Merionethshire.

4. The Queen returned to England from the Continent.

— Strike of postmen in Paris; the letters delivered by privates of infantry regiments quartered in Paris.

6. Colonel Hector Macdonald, C.B., A.D.C., entertained at a banquet, and presented with a sword of honour by the Highland Association of London.

— Resignation of the French Minister for War (Freycinet).

9. The Duchess of York visited Pembroke and christened the new Royal yacht.

— Colonel Evatt defeated the mutineers and captured the rebel chiefs Kabareega and M'wanga, of Uganda.

13. Essex defeated the Australians by 126 runs.

17. The Queen laid the foundation-stone of the Victoria and Albert Museum in South Kensington.

18. The Peace Conference assembled at the Hague; the British Commissioners were Sir Julian (now Lord) Pauncefote and Sir Henry Howard, with Sir John Fisher and Sir John C. Ardagh as naval and military expert advisers.

21. The American Liner *Paris* went ashore on the Manacle Rocks, near Falmouth, near the spot where the *Mohegan* foundered Oct. 14, 1898; no lives were lost, and the *Paris* was refloated and towed into Falmouth (see July 6).

22. International Miners Congress met at Brussels.

24. Eightieth birthday of Her Majesty the Queen.

25. The Duke and Duchess of York opened the Royal Military Tournament at the Agricultural Hall.

30. M. Ballot de Beaupré made his report on the Dreyfus case to the *Cour de Cassation*.

— Major Marchand, the African explorer, arrived at Toulon.

— Bye-election, Southport Division of Lancashire.

31. Conference at Bloemfontein, O.F.S., between President Krüger, of the S.A.R., and Sir Alfred Milner, High Commissioner of Cape Colony, the matters involved being mainly the representation and admission to the franchise of British subjects resident in the Transvaal. The proposals of President Krüger were coupled with an assertion of his country's complete independence, and the Conference broke up on June 5 without result.

— The Duke of Westminster's *Flying Fox* won the Derby; Holocauste, a French horse, which had been made second favourite, broke a fore leg when leading, and had to be destroyed.

Consols, highest, 110½; lowest, 109⅝.

JUNE.

1. CRICKET: The first of the five test matches between England and Australia commenced at Nottingham, ending on 3rd in a draw favouring the latter team.

2. Opening of the Cortes at Madrid; the Carolinas, Ladrones, Pelaos, and Marianne Islands ceded to the German Empire in return for a cash payment of £837,500.

3. The *Cour de Cassation* unanimously decided that Captain Dreyfus be given a new trial by Court-martial.

4. Assault on the French President at the Auteuil racecourse.

5. Sudden death, after an attack of apoplexy while speaking in the House, of Dr. Robert Wallace, M.P. for the Eastern Division of Edinburgh.

7. An International Congress of Publishers assembled in London.

8. The thanks of both Houses of Parliament voted to Lord Kitchener and his officers for their conduct of the recent campaign in the Soudan; £30,000 voted to the former in recognition of his brilliant service.

9. Captain Dreyfus embarked on the French cruiser *Sfax* at the Ile du Diable for conveyance to Rennes.

10. Lord George Hamilton unveiled a memorial to the Kentish martyrs at Canterbury.

11. Fire at the Elswick works, Newcastle-on-Tyne; damage estimated at over £125,000.

12. Defeat of the French Ministry (Dupuy) on account of their vigorous repression of attempted disturbances.

— Conference of Members of Parliament interested in the Irish Channel Tunnel project.

13. The charges against Col. Picquart dismissed.

14. Issue of a Parliamentary "Blue Book" containing Sir Alfred Milner's views on the Uitlanders' position and treatment in the Transvaal.

15. Sir Richard Webster opened the British case before the Arbitration Court at Paris on the Venezuela–British Guiana boundary dispute.

16. Reciprocity Treaty, affecting U.S.A. and Barbados, signed by Great Britain and U.S.A.

17. In the second test match at Lord's the Australians defeat the English team by 10 wickets.

20. 62nd anniversary of the accession of Queen Victoria.

— The referendum in New South Wales resulted in 107,274 votes being recorded for and 72,701 votes against Federation.

— Bye-election in South Edinburgh.

21. Oxford University conferred the degree of D.C.L. upon Lord Elgin, Lord Kitchener of Khartoum, and Mr. Cecil Rhodes.

— A bazaar at the Hotel Cecil in aid of the Charing Cross Hospital resulted in a net profit of over £15,000.

22. M. Waldeck-Rousseau formed a new French Cabinet.

23. The Prince of Wales laid the foundation-stone of the new Royal School of Art Needlework at South Kensington; and on 24th of the new buildings of the Post Office Savings Bank at Hammersmith.

— Bye-election in East Edinburgh.

26. The Queen reviewed the Divisional Troops under the command of Sir Redvers Buller at Aldershot.

— Launch of Sir T. Lipton's yacht *Shamrock*, built to compete for the America Cup.

— International Congress of Women opened at Westminster under the presidency of the Countess of Aberdeen.

27. Masque at Guildhall by the Art Workers' Guild.

28. Serious Socialist riots in Brussels.

30. The Duke of Albany announced in the Diet at Coburg to be heir presumptive to his uncle the reigning Duke of Saxe-Coburg-Gotha.

Consols, highest, 109⅞; lowest, 107¼.

JULY.

1. The Queen reviewed the Honourable Artillery Company at Windsor.

— The third test match between England and Australia at Sheffield resulted in a draw in favour of the former.

— Captain Dreyfus landed at Quiberon (Brittany), and taken to Rennes for his re-trial.

3. The Niger Territories Bill passed the House of Commons, by which the lands of the Niger Company became Crown property at the price of £865,000.

5. Bye-election in the Osgoldcross Division of Yorkshire, and on 6th in the borough of Oldham.

6. The American liner *Paris* refloated from Manacle Rocks, where she had gone aground on May 21.

— The Duke of Cambridge opened the new buildings of King's College School at Wimbledon.

7. General Zurlinden removed from his post as Military Governor of Paris.

8. The Prince of Wales reviewed 27,000 Volunteers in Horse Guards' Parade.

11. Dr. W. G. Grace, playing for the Gentlemen *v.* the Players at Lord's, scored 78 runs, and thus totalled 50,000 runs for 36 years' play ; the 1.223 completed innings yielding an average of over 40 runs per innings.

12. Bye-election in East St. Pancras.

13. President Krüger submitted his franchise proposals to the Volksraad.

— Esterhazy confirmed the statement that he was the author of the famous *bordereau* which secured the condemnation of Dreyfus.

— Bank-rate raised from 3 to 3½ per cent.

14. Lt.-Col. Klobb and Lieut. Meunier assassinated near Sindar, in the Niger-Soudan region, by Capt. Voulet, whom the former officers had been sent to supersede in his command.

— BISLEY : The English team won the Kolapore Cup, and on 15th the Elcho Challenge Shield also fell to England ; on 21st the Scottish team secured the National Challenge Trophy.

15. The Queen presented a state colour to the regiment of Scots Guards.

— Seventy-one whales captured in the Shetlands.

18. The Transvaal Volksraad adopted a motion for giving the Uitlanders a 7-year retrospective franchise.

19. The fourth test match at Leeds between England and Australia ended in a draw.

20. Mr. Henniker-Heaton, M.P., presented with the freedom of the City of London in recognition of his work in reforming the postal system.

21. Explosion on H.M.S. *Bullfinch* in the Solent; 13 lives lost.

22. International athletics at Queen's Club. The united Oxford and Cambridge team defeated that made up from Harvard and Yale Universities by five events to four.

— Private Priaulx, of Guernsey, won the Queen's Prize at Bisley.

25. The reformatory school-ship *Clarence* destroyed by fire in the Mersey.

— Surrey beat the Australians at the Oval by 104 runs.

29. Close of the Peace Conference at the Hague after the establishment of a permanent Court of Arbitration and the modification of certain rules of warfare, but without any definite conclusion in the disarmament proposals for which it had been summoned.

31. The Archbishop of Canterbury gave a decision at Lambeth Palace against the ceremonial use of incense and processional lights.

Consols, highest 108 ; lowest 105¾.

AUGUST.

1. At the R.Y.S. Regatta at Cowes the German Emperor's yacht *Meteor* won the Queen's Cup.

3. The naval manoeuvres ended in the safe arrival of " B " fleet (Admiral Domvile) with convoy at Milford Haven.

6. M. Delcassé arrived at Petersburg on a visit to the Tsar ; according to the special correspondent of the *Times*, this visit was made in order to dissuade the Tsar from abdicating, which otherwise he would have done.

7. Opening of the Dreyfus Court-martial at Rennes under the Presidency of Col. 'ouast, the counsel for Dreyfus were Maîtres Labori and Demange.

— Further disastrous hurricane in the West Indies ; the island of Montserrat completely devastated.

8. The torpedo gunboat *Leda* captured a French trawler fishing within the territorial limit, but before the surrender a member of the French crew was shot.

— J. A. Jarvis (the amateur champion) established a new world swimming record for the mile (25m. 13⅜s.).

11. The German Emperor opened the Dortmund-Ems Canal.

12. Ter-centenary celebration at Antwerp of the birth of Vandyk.

— M. Deroulède and others arrested in Paris on a charge of being concerned in a Royalist plot ; one of the accused, M. Guérin, shut himself up with some companions in a newspaper office in the Rue de Chabrol, whence he was not dislodged until September 20.

— The Australians suffered their third defeat of the tour at the hands of Kent at Canterbury.

14. Attempted assassination of Maître Labori, counsel for Dreyfus. at Rennes.

16. Defeat of the Imperial German Ministry on the Rhine-Elbe Canal question.

— The fifth and last test match at the Oval resulted in a draw (England 576, Australia 352 and 254 for 5 wickets.)

17. Up to this date 13 deaths had occurred at Oporto from bubonic plague.

18. Fatal colliery explosion near Bridgend ; 21 lives lost.

— Arrival at New York of Sir T. Lipton's yacht *Shamrock*, the challenger for the America Cup.

19. On this date and on 21st the Transvaal Government offered the five years' franchise for

Uitlanders as asked for by Mr. Chamberlain, but coupled it with the abolition of the suzerainty.

20. Serious Anarchist riots in Paris; 380 persons injured in conflict with the military and police.

22. Maître Labori reappeared in the Dreyfus trial after his attempted assassination.

23. At the annual general meeting of the Royal Niger Company the transfer of dominion to the British Government was approved.

25. Publication of Parliamentary "Blue Book" dealing with the Transvaal question.

— Celebration at Frankfort-on-Main of the 150th anniversary of the birth of Göethe.

26. Lord Kitchener formally opened the railway bridge over the River Atbara.

— Mr. Chamberlain addressed a Liberal-Unionist meeting at Highbury, Birmingham, on the Transvaal question.

27. An attempted Mahdist insurrection at Shukaba, on the Blue Nile, quelled by Capt. N. M. Smyth, ꝟ℃.

28. The "Kaffir Kraal" at Earl's Court Exhibition closed to inspection for ladies after much correspondence and comment by the Press.

30. Mr. Chamberlain replies to the Boer proposals of Aug. 19 and 21 and maintained the suzerainty of the Queen over the Transvaal, which was not as claimed, a "Sovereign International State."

— Examination in bankruptcy of Mr. James Colquhoun, solicitor, of Glasgow; the examination aroused great interest owing to the debtor being under arrest on a charge of embezzlement of trust funds, stated to amount to £50,000.

— Collapse of steel framework of the Coliseum, a building in course of erection in New York; 30 killed and injured.

Consols, highest, 106⅝; lowest, 105¼.

SEPTEMBER.

2. The Transvaal Government withdrew its proposals for the franchise given out on August 19 and 21.

5. Owing to the introduction, as witness for the prosecution, of a foreign subject, Maître Labori requested that an application be made to the Governments at Vienna and Rome for the taking of the evidence of Cols. Schwartzkoppen and Panizzardi (formerly Austrian and Italian attachés at Paris), either personally or on commission. This request was abruptly refused by Col. Jouast.

6. The Duke of Westminster's *Flying Fox* won the St. Leger Stakes.

— The White Star liner *Oceanic*, the largest vessel in the world, left Liverpool on her maiden trip across the Atlantic.

8. At a Cabinet Council it was decided to immediately increase the Natal garrison, and to inform President Krüger that Her Majesty's Government absolutely repudiated his view of the status of the Transvaal, and that they were quite unable to consider any proposals coupled with the acceptance of this view. They were prepared, however, to accept the proposals of August 19, after appointing Commissioners to enquire into their effect; and if the reply to this note should be negative or inconclusive Her Majesty's Government would consider the whole question *de novo*.

— Severe hurricane in the West Indies.

— Mr. Clinton Dawkins introduced the Currency Bill to the Legislative Council at Simla.

9. Captain Dreyfus convicted of communicating the documents enumerated in Esterhazy's *bordereau* to the agent of a foreign Power and sentenced to ten years' imprisonment; this verdict aroused intense and universal indignation outside France, the Press of all countries maintaining that it was directly in opposition to the evidence and returned by judges (four to two), intimidated by the General Staff of the French army.

11. Fatal accident at the Exchange station, Manchester, owing to the collision of an excursion train with one standing in the station; 35 persons injured, one of whom died on 12th.

12. Violent cyclone in Bermuda; no lives lost.

— The sloop *Martha* picked up at sea near King Charles' Islands a buoy dropped by the Andrée expedition; when opened, however, it was found to contain no message of any kind.

13. Annual meeting of the British Association at Dover.

17. A demonstration took place in Hyde Park and expressed the deepest sympathy with Captain Dreyfus and his wife in their misfortunes.

18. The Prince of Wales presented new colours to the Gordon Highlanders.

19. Railway collision at Perth station; no lives lost.

20. Captain Dreyfus, who had been pardoned on the 19th, was released from prison.

22. Her Majesty's Government expressed to Sir Alfred Milner their regret at receiving no reply to their note of Sept. 8, and now declared that the whole question would be reconsidered. With regard to the charge of breach of faith directed against Mr. Conynghame Greene, the British Agent at Pretoria, by the State Attorney of the Transvaal, Her Majesty's Government entirely refuted this charge.

24. Her Majesty's reign exceeded by three years that of King George III.

25. Serious earthquake and landslip in Darjeeling; 80 lives lost.

— End of the State trial in Servia in connection with the attempted assassination of ex-King Milan.

26. Admiral Dewey, the hero of Manila, arrived at New York on board the cruiser *Olympia*, and was accorded a most enthusiastic reception.

27. It was announced in the *Times* that the mosquito, to which the spread of the malarial fever in the West African Colonies is supposed to be due, had been traced and identified by Dr. Ross.

29. The Queen presented new colours to the Seaforth Highlanders.

Consols, highest, 105½; lowest, 103¾.

OCTOBER.

3. The Arbitration Tribunal (appointed under the provisions of the Anglo-American treaty of Feb. 2, 1897), sitting at Paris to adjudicate on the British and Venezuelan territorial claims delivered its award; this was in the nature of a compromise and was regarded as satisfactory both in England and America.

— An attempt was made to sail the first race between *Shamrock* and *Columbia* for the America Cup off the coast of New Jersey, U.S.A.; owing to the absence of wind the yachts were unable to complete the course within the prescribed limit, and the race was declared off. Further unsuccessful attempts were made on 5th, 7th, 10th, 12th and 14th.

3. Bank Rate raised to 4½ per cent.
4. In response to an enquiry by Sir Alfred Milner, President Steyn, of the Orange Free State, declared that in the event of war the Orange Free State would fulfil its treaty obligations to the Transvaal.
— Dr. James Colquhoun sentenced to five years' penal servitude for embezzlement of moneys entrusted to him by clients—the amount exceeded £50,000.
5. Bank rate raised to 5 per cent.
— The Duke of Westminster laid the foundation of the Gladstone memorial library at Hawarden.
6. Serious landslip at Dover in the new harbour works.
7. Proclamation issued convening Parliament on 17th Oct., and calling out the Army Reserve on permanent service.
8. A Bull fight, organized and carried out at Boulogne, aroused much comment in English newspapers.
9. The Transvaal Executive forwarded an ultimatum to the British Government requiring an immediate acquiescence to (1) arbitration, (2) removal of troops from Transvaal borders, (3) cessation of reinforcements. If the terms be not accepted by 8 a.m., on Oct. 11, the Transvaal would consider Her Majesty's Government to declare war against the Transvaal. Her Majesty's Government notified to Sir Alfred Milner their regret at this despatch, and directed him to state that it was impossible to discuss; Mr. Greene was also directed to apply for his passports and to hand over his duties to the Consul of the United States of America at Pretoria.
— Railway collision at St. Paul's station; the guard of one of the trains injured.
14. Gen. Sir Redvers Buller, V.C., left England to assume command of the 1st Army Corps in South Africa.
16. The first race for the America Cup ended in a victory for *Columbia.*
17. A special session of Parliament met, and after debate voted a credit of £10,000,000 for the military operations in South Africa; after the winding-up of the business Parliament was prorogued to Jan. 15, 1900.
— The second race for the America Cup. *Columbia* was again victorious, *Shamrock* breaking her topmast and retiring.
20. Sir Wm. Penn Symons, K.C.B., attacked the Transvaal Boers outside the town of Glencoe, in Northern Natal; the operations were entirely successful and conducted with great gallantry, but Sir Wm. Symons was mortally wounded when leading the infantry attack and died of his wound Oct. 23, after being promoted Major-General for distinguished service; the British losses were about 43 killed and 180 wounded with 80 missing.
— The third race for the America Cup decided the series in favour of *Columbia.*
21. Further successful engagement between Sir George White's advance posts, and the O. F. S. Boers at Elaands Laagte, near Ladysmith, the movement being made in order to cover the retirement of Gen. Yule (who succeeded Gen. Symons), from Glencoe; British losses, 257 killed and wounded. Generals White and Yule joined forces in the evening.
24. During a successful engagement with the enemy, at Rietfontein, the British losses amounted to over 100.

27. Bye-election, Bow and Bromley Division.
29—30. General White unsuccessfully attempted to bring about a general engagement with the Boers who had concentrated round Ladysmith; part of the British force (about 850 strong) was cut off and forced to surrender, and the main body fell back on Ladysmith after receiving reinforcements from the Durban fleet.
Consols, highest, 104½; lowest, 101¾.

NOVEMBER.

1. The Transvaal War Relief Funds amounted to £90,000, and the Refugees Fund to £152,000.
2-3. Successful reconnaisance under General Brocklehurst south-west of Ladysmith.
6. Bye-election at Exeter.
8. Publication of the Anglo-German agreement respecting the Samoan Archipelago.
— The Tsar of Russia visited the German Emperor at Potsdam.
9. Sir Redvers Buller received a pigeon message from Gen. White that all was well at Ladysmith.
11. The Queen arrived at Windsor Castle from Balmoral and reviewed the composite regiment of Household Cavalry for service in South Africa.
11. Major Cabell, of the U.S.A. Army Medical Dept., granted special leave of absence in order that he might act as surgeon of the American Hospital Ship *Maine* which had been fitted out by American ladies for the use of British wounded.
14. Lord Kitchener left Cairo for Khartoum on receipt of news of the whereabouts of the Khalifa.
15. The Hamburg-Amerika Liner *Patria* forced to land her passengers at Dover owing to the discovery of fire in the hold.
15. The Queen visited Bristol and opened the Diamond Jubilee Convalescent Home.
17. Statue of de Lesseps unveiled at Port Said.
18. Railway collision at the Central Station, Manchester; about 30 passengers injured.
— M. Deroulède during his trial for high treason by the French Senate, insulted President Loubet and was sentenced to imprisonment.
20. The German Emperor and Empress with two of their sons arrived at Portsmouth on a visit to the Queen.
— Death of the Marchioness of Salisbury, wife of the Prime Minister.
22. The Prince and Princess of Wales visited the Red Cross Society's hospital ship at Tilbury.
23. Lord Methuen, advancing with his Division (including the Brigade of Guards and a Naval Brigade) encountered a force of O.F.S. Boers at Belmont and occupied their position.
24. Lord Methuen's advance further opposed at Gras Pan.
— Col. Sir F. R. Wingate came up with the fugitive Khalifa at Om Debrikat and totally annihilated his forces. Among the slain were the Khalifa and his principal Emirs, the survivors being captured with 9,000 fighting men, and women and children.
28. Lord Methuen's Division fought a 10-hours' fight at the Modder River with 8,000 Boers.
29. The German Emperor and Empress left Sheerness for Flushing where they were met by the Queen of Holland.
30. The Transvaal War Funds amounted to £341,000 and the Refugees Fund to close on £170,000.
— Bank rate raised to 6 per cent.
Consols, highest, 103⅝; lowest, 102⅛.

The amounts appended are those proved by the executors ; for a further list, see pp. 372-73.

Abdy, His Honour John Thomas, LL.D., late Recorder of Bedford and County Court Judge for Essex, aged 77.—*Sept.* 25.

Alexander, Maj.-Gen. Sir Claud, 1st Baronet of Ballochmyle (Crimea), M.P. for S. Ayrshire 1874-85, aged 68.—*May* 23.

Allen, Grant, novelist and scientific writer, aged 51.—*Oct.* 25.

Alleyne, Maj.-Gen. Sir James, K.C.B., R.A. (Red River, South Africa, and Soudan), aged 56.—*April* 23.

Allison, Col. James John, C.B., aged 72.—*March* 25 (estate £33,695).

Allman, James, M.D., LL.D., Emeritus Professor of Natural History at Edinburgh, aged 87.—*Nov.* 25, 1898, (£10,577).

Anderson, Sir William, K.C.B., F.R.S., Director-Gen. of Ordnance Factories, aged 64.—*Dec.* 11, 1898 (£6,981 net).

Antelme, Sir Célicourt Auguste, K.C.M.G., M.E.C. of Mauritius, aged 80.—*June* 6.

Antrobus, Sir Edmund, 3rd Baronet, formerly M.P. for East Surrey and Wilton, aged 80.—*April* 1 (£25,597 net).

Arbuthnot, Gen. Sir Charles George, G.C.B., R.A. (Crimea and Afghanistan), aged 74.—*April* 17 (£14,001 net).

Arbuthnot, Lieut.-Gen. George Alexander (Indian Mutiny), aged 68.—*Feb.* 11.

Archdale, William Humphreys, M.P. for Fermanagh 1874-85, aged 84.—*June* 23.

Armstrong, Sir Alexander, K.C.B., R.N., F.R.S. (Russian War and N.W. Passage), aged 81.—*July* 4.

Armytage, Sir George, 5th Baronet, aged 79.—*March* 9 (£23,520 net).

Ascroft, Robert, M.P. for Oldham, aged 52 (his colleague, Mr. Oswald, thereupon resigning).—*June* 19 (£29,739 net).

Aspinall, James Perronet, Q.C.—*Nov.* 29, 1898.

Barnett, Lt. R. C., K.R.R.C., killed at Glencoe.—*Oct.* 20.

Bassett, Francis, M.P. for Beds. 1872-4, aged 79.—*June* 9 (£103,791 net).

Bates, Harry, A.R.A., well-known sculptor.—*Jan.* 30.

Beaufort, Henry Charles FitzRoy, 8th Duke of, K.G., was M.P. 1846-53 and A.D.C. to the Duke of Wellington and Visc. Hardinge, aged 75.—*April* 30 (£8,687 net).

Berry, Dr. Charles Albert, distinguished Congregational minister.—*Jan.* 31 (£8,339).

Bingham, Gen. George William Powlett, C.B. (Persia and Mutiny), aged 81. — *March* 25 (£22,729).

Binns, Hon. Sir Henry, K.C.M.G., Premier of Natal.—*June* 5.

Black, William, distinguished novelist, formerly on the staff of the *Morning Star* and *Daily News*, aged 57.—*Dec.* 10, 1898 (£25,379 net).

Bloemfontein, Rt. Rev. John Wale Hicks, 4th Lord Bishop of, aged 59.—*Oct.* 12.

Blomfield, Sir Arthur William, A.R.A., architect to the Bank of England, aged 70.—*Oct.* 30.

Bolingbroke and St. John, Henry, 5th Viscount, aged 79.—*Nov.* 7.

Bonheur, "Rosa" (Marie Rosalie), famous French painter, aged 77.—*May* 26.

Borlase, William Copeland, formerly M.P. for East and Mid Cornwall, aged 50.—*March* 31.

Bourke, Hon. Charles, C.B., uncle of 7th Earl of Mayo, aged 66.—*April* 4 (£11,849 gross).

Bowen, Rt. Hon. Sir George Ferguson, G.C.M.G., formerly Governor of Queensland and other Colonies, aged 77.—*Feb.* 21 (£16,270).

Boyd, Rev. Andrew Kennedy Hutchison, D.D. ("A.K.H.B."), author of "Recreations of a Country Parson" and of many other books and papers, aged 73.—*March* 1 (£13,253).

Boyle, Maj.-Gen. Robert, C.B. (Nicaragua 1848, and China), aged 76.—*Oct.* 31.

Boynton, Sir Henry Somerville, 11th Baronet, aged 54.—*April* 11 (£65,620).

Bradbury, Lt. L. B., Gord. Highs., killed at Elaands Laagte.—*21 Oct.*

Bradshaw, Vice-Adm. Richard, C.B. (Abyssinia, Ashanti, &c.), aged 70.—*June* 22.

Bree, Rt. Rev. Herbert, D.D., 5th Bishop of Barbados, aged 70.—*Feb.* 26 (£335).

Bright, Rt. Hon. Jacob, formerly M.P. for Manchester, a brother of the Rt. Hon. John Bright, aged 78.—*Nov.* 8.

Brise, Col. Sir Samuel Brise Ruggles-, K.C.B., M.P. for East Essex 1868-84, aged 73.—*May* 28 (£22,125 gross).

Broughton, Sir Henry Delvès, 9th Baronet, aged 90.—*Feb.* 26 (£167,871 net personalty).

Bruce, Rev. Alexander Balmain, D.D., theological author and Professor of Apologetics in Glasgow Free Church College, aged 68.—*Aug.* 7.

Bruce, Lt.-Gen. Sir Henry Le Geyt, K.C.B., R.A. (Gwalior, Sutlej, Punjab, and Mutiny), aged 75.—*April* 15.

Bruce, Col. Robert, C.B. (Crimea and Indian Mutiny), late Inspector-Gen. of Roy. Irish Constabulary, aged 74.—*Sept.* 1.

Buchan, David Stuart, 13th Earl of, aged 83.—*Dec.* 3, 1898.

Bulgaria, H.R.H. Maria Louisa, Princess of, aged 29.—*Jan.* 31.

Bulwer, James Redfoord, Q.C., a Master in Lunacy, formerly M.P. for Ipswich, aged 78.—*March* 4 (£19,597).

Burrell, Sir Charles Raymond, 6th Baronet, aged 51.—Sept. 6 (£38,883).

Cadbury, Richard, a Birmingham philanthropist, of the well-known cocoa-manufacturing firm, aged 63.—*March* 22 (£42,817 gross, £40,000 is left to charities).

Campbell, Lt. J. A., Gord. Highs., killed at Elaands Laagte.—*Oct.* 21.

Candy, George, Q.C., aged 58.—*Oct.* 25.

Cartwright, Sir Henry Edmund, F.S.A., formerly a Judge in the Bahamas, aged 76.—*March* 30.

Chalmers, Sir David Patrick, late Chief Justice of British Guiana.—*Aug.* 5 (£18,162 net).

Chamberlain, Richard, M.P. for West Islington 1885-92, aged 58.—*April* 2 (£136,821 net .

Chisholm, Lt.-Col. J. J. Scott-, commanding Imperial Light Horse, killed at battle of Elaands Laagte, aged 48.—*Oct.* 21.

Chitty, Rt. Hon. Sir Joseph William, Q.C., a Lord Justice of the Court of Appeal, M.P. for Oxford 1880-1, aged 70.—*Feb.* 15 (£159,341 net).

Clarke, Rev. Sir Charles, 2nd Baronet of Dunham, aged 86.—*April* 25 (£55,272 net).

Clifden, Leopold George Frederick, 5th Viscount, formerly M.P. for Kilkenny, aged 70.—*Sept.* 10 (£3,896 net).

Clowes, Samuel William, formerly M.P. for N. Leicestershire and S. Derbyshire, aged 77.—*Dec.* 31, 1898 (£151,518 net).

Cobbe, Sir Alexander Hugh, K.C.B. (Indian Mutiny and Afghanistan), aged 74.—*Sept.* 13 (£5,683 gross).

Cocks, Thomas Somers, M.P. for Reigate 1847–57, aged 84.—*Aug.* 30.—(£3,670 net).

Colomb, Vice-Adm. Philip Howard, F.R.G.S. (China, Burma, Baltic, and Arctic Expedition 1854), aged 65.—*Oct.* 14.

Connor, Capt. F. H. B., R. Irish Fus.; died of wounds received at Glencoe.—*Oct.* 20.

Cook, John Mason, head of the tourist agency known by his name, aged 64.—*March* 4 (£345 396).

Coote, Rev. Sir Algernon, 11th Baronet of Ballyfin and Premier Baronet of Ireland, aged 82.—*Nov.* 20.

Cotton, Gen. Sir Arthur Thomas, K.C.S.I. (Burma 1824, followed by long engineering service in Southern India), oldest officer in H.M.'s service, aged 96.—*July* 24 (£125 net).

Cox, Robert, M.P. for South Edinburgh, aged 54.—*June* 2.

Cripps, Henry William, Q.C., Recorder of Lichfield, aged 84.—*Aug.* 14 (£41,521).

Curtis, Sir Arthur Colin, 3rd Bart. of Gatcombe, aged 40.—*June* 10, 1893 (disappeared at Klondyke and was in 1899 adjudged deceased). (£2,099).

Daly, Augustin, dramatist, aged 61.—*June* 7.

Darbhanga, H. H. the Maharaja of, G.C.I.E., aged 52.—*Dec.* 16, 1898.

Daunt, Maj.-Gen. William, C.B. (Crimea and Afghanistan), aged 68.—*Nov.* 27.

Dawson, Sir John William, C.M.G., F.R.S., eminent geologist, aged 79.—*Nov.* 19.

Deane, Sir Thomas Newenham, C.E., R.H.A., distinguished architect, aged 71.—*Nov.* 8.

De Longuetil, Charles Colmore, 7th Baron (Canadian title), aged 54.—*Dec.* 13, 1898.

De Reuter, Paul Julius, 1st Baron (of Saxe-Coburg), founder of Reuter's Agency, aged 82.—*Feb.* 25 (£117,653 net).

Denne, Maj. H. W., Gord. Highrs., killed at Elaands Laagte.—*Oct.* 21.

Dingley, Nelson, Chairman of Committee of Ways and Means to U.S. House of Representatives, aged 66.—*Jan.* 9.

Dryden, Sir Henry Edward Leigh, 7th Baronet, aged 81.—*July* 24 (£4.862 net).

Dunboyne, James FitzWalter, 24th Baron (15th by patent), aged 60.—*Aug.* 17.

Dunkin, Edwin, F.R.S., Past Pres. Roy. Astron. Soc., aged 77.—*Nov.* 26, 1898.

Dunsany, John William, 17th Baron and an Irish Representative Peer, M.P. for Thornbury Division of Gloucestershire 1886–92, aged 45.—*Jan.* 14 (£8,629 gross), net *Nil.*

Edgar, Hon. Sir James David, K.C.M.G., Q.C., Speaker of the Canadian House of Commons, aged 60.—1899.

Ellis, Thomas Edward, M.P. for Merionethshire and First Whip of the Liberal Party, aged 39.—*April* 5 (£11,097 net).

Erckmann, Emile, renowned novelist in conjunction with the late M. Chatrian (who died 1890).—*March* 13.

Esher, William Baliol, 1st Viscount, P.C., late Master of the Rolls, M.P. for Helston 1866–8, aged 83.—*May* 24 (£81,463 net).

Exmouth, Edward Fleetwood John, 4th Viscount, aged 38.—*Oct.* 31.

Farrell, Dep. Surg.-Gen. George Elias, C.B. (Afghanistan and Burma), aged 67.—*April* 28.

Farrer, Thomas Henry, 1st Baron, aged 80.—*Oct.* 11.

Faunce, Lieut.-Gen. Edmund, C.B., I.S.C. (Ind. Mutiny and Upper Burma), aged 60.—*Sept.* 15.

Faure, François Félix, President of the French Republic from 1895, aged 58.—*Feb.* 16.

Field, Gen. Sir John, K.C.B. (Afghanistan 1841–4, Mutiny, and Abyssinia), aged 78.—*April* 16 (£3,119).

Flower, Sir William Henry, K.C.B., F.R.S., Pres. Zool. Soc., aged 67.—*July* 1 (£36,835).

Foli, Signor (Allen James Foley, of Tipperary), distinguished bass singer.—*Oct.* 20.

Fooks, William Cracroft, Q.C.—*Aug.* 2.

Ford, Rt. Hon. Sir Francis Clare, G.C.B., G.C.M.G., late Ambassador at Rome, aged 70.—*Jan.* 31 (£29,657 net).

Forrest, Sir James, 4th Baronet, aged 46.—*Sept.* 18.

Foster, Myles Birket, distinguished water-colour painter and illustrator of various works, aged 74.—*March* 27 (£30,538 net).

Foster, William Orme, formerly M.P. for South Staffordshire, aged 84.—*Sept.* 29 (£1,000,000).

Fowler, Sir John Arthur, 2nd Baronet of Braemore, aged 44.—*March* 25.

Frankland, Sir Edward, K.C.B., M.D., F.R.S., formerly analyst of waters, President of Chemical Society, &c., aged 74.—*Aug.* 9. (His wife died *Jan.* 20 preceding.) (£126,472 net.)

Galton, Capt. Sir Douglas, K.C.B., F.R.S., formerly Director of Public Works and Buildings, Assistant Under Secretary for War, &c., aged 76.—*March* 10 (£91,557).

Genge, Lt. C. J., R. Dub. Fus., killed at Glencoe.—*Oct.* 20.

George, Grand Duke, heir presumptive to the Russian throne, aged 28.—*July* 10.

Gill, J. Frederick, Northern Deemster, I. of Man, aged 57.—*Oct.* 15.

Gooch, Sir Alfred Sherlock, 9th Baronet of Benacre, aged 47.—*Feb.* 24 (£35,958 net).

Gordon, Surg.-Gen. Sir Charles Alexander, K.C.B., M.D. (Indian Mutiny and China), aged 78.—*Sept.* 30.

Gordon, Gen. John, C.B. (Sutlej and Mutiny), aged 81.—*Jan.* 1.

Gowing, Richard, formerly editor of the *Gentleman's Magazine* and the *School Board Chronicle.*—*Jan.* 12.

Grant, Albert, Baron (Italian title; real name Gottheimer), twice M.P. for Kidderminster, known as a promoter of unfortunate companies and also as the improver of Leicester Square and other public places, aged 68.—*Aug.* 30.

Gregory, Sir William Earle Welby-, 4th Baronet, aged 69.—*Nov.* 25, 1898 (£15,093 net).

Grosvenor, Hon. Norman de l'Aigle, son of 1st Baron Ebury, M.P. for Chester 1869 till 1874, aged 53.—*Nov.* 21, 1898 (£30,841 net).

Gunning, Lt.-Col. Robt. H., commanding 3rd K.R.R.C., killed at battle of Glencoe.—*Oct.* 20.

Hambro, Lt. N. J., K.R.R.C., killed at Glencoe.—*Oct.* 20.

Hamilton, James Winterbottom, Q.C., Recorder of Oldham, aged 49.—*Oct.* 18.

Hannah, Lt. W. M. J., Leic. R., killed at Glencoe.—*Oct.* 20.

Hardcastle, Joseph Alfred, M.P. for Colchester 1847–52, afterwards twice for Bury St. Edmunds, aged 83.—*Aug.* 8.

Hawes, Col. Alexander James Donnelly, D.S.O. (Jowaki, Afghanistan, Zhob Valley, &c.), aged 58.—*March* 2.

Hay, Admiral John (Morea Castle 1828, China War 1840–1), aged 94.—*Jan.* 19 (£20,836).

Hay, Maj.-Gen. John Crosland, C.B. (Mutiny, Afghanistan, and S. Africa), aged 61.—*June* 25.

Hayward, Sir William Webb, Mayor of Rochester in 1846 and again in 1896, aged 81.—*March* 18 (£1,554 net).

Henley, Anthony Henley, 3rd Baron, M.P. for Northampton 1859-74, aged 73.—*Nov.* 27, 1898 (£4,985 not personally).

Herschell, Farrer, 1st Baron, P.C., G.C.B., twice Lord Chancellor in Liberal Ministries and M.P. for Durham 1874-85, aged 61.—*March* 1 (£149,041 net).

Heureaux, General Ulisses, President of the Dominican Republic.—Assassinated *July* 26.

Hill, Lt. A. H. M., R. Irish Fus., killed at Glencoe.—*Oct.* 20.

Hirst, Col. Henry Sagar, C.B., V.D., aged 69.—*May* 4 (£53,801 net).

Holburn, John Goundry, M.P. for N.W. Lanark.—*Jan.* 23.

Hornby, Admiral. Sir William Windham, K.C.B. (Jamaica 1832), late a Commissioner of Prisons, aged 86.—*June* 28 (£10,001).

Houlton, Sir Edward Victor Lewis, G.C.M.G., formerly Chief Secretary to Govt. of Malta, aged 76.—*Aug.* 24 (£15,065).

Howard de Walden, Frederick George, 7th Baron (3rd Baron Seaford), aged 69.—*Nov.* 3.

Hulse, Sir Edward, 5th Baronet, aged 90.—*June* 11 (£1,428).

Hylton, Hedworth Hylton, 2nd Baron, M.P. for Wells 1855-68, aged 70.—*Oct.* 31.

Irwin, Sir George, aged 66.—*June* 11.

Jee, Dep. Insp.-Gen. Joseph, C.B., V̄C̄, M.R.C.S. (Persia and Mutiny), aged 80.—*March* 17.

Jenner, Sir William, 1st Bart., G.C.B., M.D., F.R.S., the eminent physician, aged 83.—*Dec.* 11, 1898 (£375,333 net).

Johnston, Rev. David, D.D., Professor of Biblical Criticism at Aberdeen University, aged 67.—*Aug.* 6.

Kershaw, Sir Louis Addin, Q.C., Chief Justice of High Court, Bombay, aged 53.—*Feb.*17 (£2,903).

Lacon, Sir Edmund Broughton Knowles, 4th Baronet, aged 57.—Aug. 11 (£91,374 gross).

Lahore, Rt. Rev. Henry James Matthew, D.D., 2nd Bishop of.—*Dec.* 2, 1898 (£16,292).

Lampson, Sir George Curtis, 2nd Baronet, aged 66.—*Nov.* 7.

Larpent, Sir George Albert De-Hochepied-, 3rd and last Baronet, aged 52.—*May* 18.

Ledgard, Frederic Thomas Durell, Q.C., aged 63.—*July* 21.

Leiningen, H. G. D. H., Princess Marie of, aged 65.—*Nov.* 21.

Leyland, Sir Herbert Scarisbrick Naylor-, 1st Baronet, M.P. for the Southport Division, aged 34.—*May* 7 (£22,530 gross).

Limerick, Rt. Rev. Charles Graves, D.D., 51st Lord Bishop of (also of Ardfert and Aghadoe), aged 86.—*July* 17 (£22,415 net).

Lindsey, Montague Peregrine, 11th Earl of, aged 83.—*Jan.* 29.

Lisburne, Ernest George Henry Arthur Malet, 6th Earl of, aged 37.—*Sept.* 4.

Lithgow, Surg.-Maj.-Gen. Stewart Aaron, C.B., D.S.O. (Mutiny, Afghanistan, and Nile), aged 66.—*Sept.* 20.

Lloyd, Rt. Rev. Daniel Lewis, D.D., late Lord Bishop of Bangor (1890-08), aged 56.—*Aug.* 4.

Lloyd, Sampson Samuel, formerly M.P. for South Warwickshire, and chairman of Lloyds Banking Co., aged 78.—*March* 3 (£37,586 net).

Longworth, Francis T. Dames-, Q.C., Lieutenant of Westmeath, aged 64.—*Dec.* 3, 1898 (£24,603 net).

Maberly, Maj. Gen. Evan, C.B. (Indian Mutiny), aged 84.—*Nov.* 16.

McCoy, Sir Frederick, K.C.M.G., F.R.S., Professor of Natural Science in Melbourne University, aged 65.—*May* 15.

MacFarlan, Lieut.-Gen. David, C.B. (Mutiny, Frontier, and Afghanistan), aged 65.—*June* 23.

MacKinnon, Gen. George Henry (Kaffir Wars of 1846-7 and 1851-2), aged 92.—*Sept.* 16 (269,964 net).

Malmesbury, Edward James, 4th Earl of, aged 57.—*May* 19 (£36,411 net).

Manfield, Sir Moses Philip, late M.P. for Northampton, head of a large boot-manufacturing firm, aged 80.—*July* 31 (his wife having died July 12).

Marryat, Florence (Mrs. Francis Lean), novelist and magazine writer.—*Oct.* 27.

Mathews, Mrs. Charles, widow of the famous actor.—*Jan.* 4.

Matthews, William, a representative for Dulwich on L.C.C. (his colleague retiring on his death), aged 65.—*May* 10 (£22,865 net).

Mexborough, Agnes, Countess of.—*Dec.* 23, 1898 (£163,047 net).

Mexborough, John Charles George, 4th Earl of, M.P. for Gatton 1831, and for Pontefract 1835-47, aged 89.—*Aug.* 17.

Michell, Thomas, C.B., late Consul-General for Norway, aged 64.—*Aug.* 5.

Michie, Hon. Sir Archibald, K.C.M.G., Q.C., formerly Attorney-General and Minister of Justice in Victoria, aged 85.—*June* 21.

Milbanke, Sir Peniston, 9th Baronet, aged 52.—*Nov.* 28.

Miller, Adm. Thomas, F.R.G.S. (Borneo, Benin, &c.), aged 80.—*April* 22 (£14,747).

Monro, Lt C. G., Gord. Highrs., killed at Elaands Laagte, *Oct.* 21.

Monroe, Rt. Hon. John, Q.C., late Judge of Landed Estates Court (Ireland), aged 60.—*Sept.* 28.

Moon, Sir Richard, 1st Baronet of Copsewood, many years Chairman of L. & N.W. Railway, aged 85.—*Nov.* 17.

Mouat, Surg.-Gen. Sir James, K.C.B., V̄C̄, F.R.C.S. (Crimea and New Zealand), aged 83.—*Jan.* 4 (£26,570 net).

Mowbray, Rt. Hon. Sir John Robert, 1st Baronet, M.P. for Oxford University and Father of the House of Commons, aged 83.—*April* 22 (£184,554 net).

Murray, Col. John, C.B. (Zululand, 1879), aged 65.—*March* 17 (£19,573).

Murray, Lt. J. G. D., Gord. Highrs. killed at Elaands Laagte, *Oct.* 21.

Nairne, Gen. Sir Charles Edward, K.C.B. (Indian Mutiny, Afghanistan, and Egypt), aged 62.—*Feb.* 19 (£12,743).

Napier of Merchistoun, Francis, 10th Baron, created also 1st Baron Ettrick, aged 79.—*Dec.* 19, 1898 (£11,018 net).

Newton, William John, 1st Baron, formerly M.P. for S. Lancashire and Cheshire, aged 70.—*Dec.* 15, 1898 (£25,271 net).

Nicholson, William Newzam, M.P. for Newark 1880-5, aged 84.—*May* 17 (£19,675 gross).

Noel, James Gambier, C.B., late of the Admiralty aged 73.—*Aug.* 7 (£5,460).

Norbury, Col. Thomas Coningsby Norbury, C.B. (Crimea), aged 70.—*Oct.* 16.

Northcott, Lt.-Col. Henry Ponting, C.B., killed at Modder River, aged 43.—*Nov.* 28.

Northumberland, Algernon George, 6th Duke of, K.G., P.C., M.P. for Beeralston 1831-2, and for N. Northumberland 1852-65, aged 88.—*Jan.* 2 (£50,950 net).

Novara, Franco (F. Naish), bass singer.—*Jan.* 8.

Nubar Pacha, G.C.S.I., G.C.M.G., late President of the Council to the Khedive, aged 73.—*Jan.* 15.

Nugent, Col. Sir Charles Butler Peter Nugent Hedges, K.C.B. (Baltic), aged 74.—*Oct.* 7.

Nugent, Sir John, M.D., late Commissioner of Lunacy in Ireland, aged 90.—*Jan.* 26 (£38,870).

Nulty, Rt. Rev. Thomas, D.D., R.C., Bishop of Meath.—*Dec.* 24, 1898.

O'Beirne, Col. Francis, formerly M.P. for Co. Leitrim, aged 56.—*April* 11 (£17,540).

Osborn, Sir Melmoth, K.C.M.G., late British Resident in Zululand, aged 64.—*June* 1.

Ouvry, Col. Henry Aimé, C.B. (Punjab and Mutiny), aged 85.—*Feb.* 12 (£4,206).

Palmer, James Dampier, late M.P. for Gravesend, aged 48.—*Oct.* 16.

Papillon, Philip Oxenden, M.P. for Colchester 1859-65, aged 73.—*Aug.* 16.

Pechell, Capt. M.R.H., K.R.R.C., killed at Glencoe, *Oct.* 20.

Peel, Sir Charles Lennox, G.C.B., late Clerk to the Privy Council, aged 66.—*Aug.* 19 (£97,963 net).

Pipon, Capt. John Pakenham, R.N., C.B., C.M.G. (Malays, Alexandria, and Burma), aged 50.—*May* 6 (£953).

Playfair, Sir Robert Lambert, K.C.M.G., late Consul-General for Algeria, aged 70.—*Feb.* 18.

Poulett, William Henry, 6th Earl, aged 71.—*Jan.* 22.

Price, Rev. Bartholomew, D.D., Master of Pembroke College, Oxford, aged 80.—*Dec.* 29, 1898 (£88,091 net.)

Price, Edwin Plumer, Q.C., formerly Recorder of York and a County Court Judge, aged 81.—*Aug.* 1 (£1,903 net).

Price, Sir Rose Lambart, 3rd Baronet, aged 61.—*April* 17 (£1,455).

Pyke, Lionel Edward, Q.C., aged 44.—*March* 25 (£3,839 net).

Rainals, Sir Harry Thomas Alfred, formerly in Consular Service, aged 83.—*Nov.* 25.

Randolph, Rev. Edward John, Chancellor of York Minster, aged 84.—*Dec.* 9, 1898.

Rawson, Sir Rawson William, K.C.M.G., C.B., late Gov.-in-Chief of the Windward Islands, aged 87.—*Nov.* 20.

Redington, Rt. Hon. Christopher Talbot, Commissioner of National Education, Ireland, aged 51.—*Feb.* 4 (£17,411 gross).

Rees, Sir Josiah, F.R.A.S., Chief Justice of the Bermudas, aged 78.—*Nov.* 4.

Ritherdon, Gen. Augustus, I.S.C. (Pegu), aged 75.—*May* 6.

Roberts, Sir Alfred, M.R.C.S. of Sydney, N.S.W., aged 75.—*Dec.* 19, 1898.

Roberts, Sir Randal Howland, 4th Baronet, an officer in the Crimea and Indian Mutiny, and war correspondent of the *Daily Telegraph* in the Franco-German War, aged 62.—*Oct.* 10.

Roberts, Sir William, M.D., F.R.S., aged 69.—*April* 16 (£44,210 net).

Rothschild, Baron Ferdinand James de, M.P. for the Aylesbury Division, aged 59.—*Dec.* 17, 1898 (£1,488,128 gross; £100,000 left to Evelina Hospital).

Routledge, Col. Robert Warne, late Managing Director of Messrs. George Routledge and Sons, the well-known firm of publishers, aged 61.—*July* 3.

Routledge, Edmund, of the same firm of publishers, aged 56.—*Aug.* 21.

Rutherfurd Clark, Lord, late of Scottish Court of Session, aged 70.—*July* 26 (£96,775).

Rutland, Janetta, Duchess of (formerly Lady Jno. Manners).—*July* 11 (£1,316).

Salisbury, Marchioness of, V.A., C.I.—*Nov.* 20.

Salmon, Ven. Edwin Arthur, Archdeacon of Wells.—*Sept.* 20.

Saxe-Coburg, H.R.H. Alfred, Hereditary Prince of, aged 24.—*Feb.* 6.

Sealy, Sir John, K.C.M.G., formerly Attorney-General of Barbados, aged 91.—*Feb.* 13.

Selwyn, Very Rev. Arthur Edward, Dean of Newcastle, N.S.W., formerly Canon of Gloucester, aged 76.—*June* 27.

Severne, John Edmund, M.P. for South Shropshire 1876-85.—1899 (£14,953 net).

Sherston, Lt. Col., John, D.S.O., killed at Glencoe, *Oct.* 20.

Sinclair, Sir Robert Charles, 9th Baronet of Stevenson, aged 78.—*May* 5.

Skene, Felicia Mary Frances, authoress and philanthropical worker, one of Miss Nightingale's helpers, aged 78.—*Oct.* 6.

Smart, John, R.S.A., painter of Highland scenery and genre subjects.—*June* 1.

Smith, Surg.-Gen. Alexander, C.B., M.D. (Crimea and Afghanistan), aged 74.—*Nov.* 26, 1898.

Smith, William Bickford, formerly M.P. for the Helston Division, aged 71.—*Feb.* 24 (£47,245 net).

Somers, Philip Reginald, 5th Baron, aged 84.—*Sept.* 30.

Spence, Maj.-Gen. Frederick, C.B. (Crimea and China), aged 84.—*Jan.* 10.

Spinks, Thomas, Q.C., ecclesiastical lawyer, aged 79.—*Jan.* 14 (£21,328 gross).

Spooner, Very Rev. Edward, Co-Dean of Bocking, aged 77.—*Jan.* 25.

Spottiswoode, George Andrew, Vice-Chairman of the House of Laymen in the Convocation of Canterbury and head of a well-known printing firm, aged 71.—*Feb.* 8 (£85,583 net).

Staples, Sir Nathaniel Alexander, 8th Baronet, aged 81.—*March* 12.

Stapleton, Sir Francis George, 8th Baronet, formerly Capt. Gren. Guards, aged 68.—*Oct.* 30.

St. John of Bletso, Dowager Lady.—*Nov.* 28.

Stockwell, Maj.-Gen. Charles Montizambertt, C.B. (Crimea, Afghanistan, and Egypt), aged 60.—*June* 22.

Stokes, Capt. Sir Robert Baret, C.B. (Indian Mutiny), late a Resident Magistrate in Ireland, aged 66.—*Sept.* 5.

Stopford, Lt.-Col. Horace Robert, 2nd Coldstream Guards, killed at Modder River, aged 44.—*Nov.* 28.

Storey, Sir Thomas, a well-known philanthropist of Lancaster, of which town he was four times Mayor, aged 73.—*Dec.* 13, 1898 (£178 net).

Strafford, Henry William John, 4th Earl of, K.C.V.O., C.B., aged 67 (held the title only 13 months).—*May* 16 (£16,536 net).

Struthers, Sir John, M.D., F.R.C.S.E., aged 76.—*Feb.* 24.

Sullivan, Rt. Rev. Edward, retired Bishop of Algoma.—*Jan.* 6.

Sullivan, Sir Edward Robert, 4th Baronet, of Thames Ditton, a frequent writer on political subjects, aged 72.—*July* 22 (£24,412 net).

Suther, Gen. William Grigor, C.B. (Syria and Japan), aged 78.—*July* 23 (£2,033).

Swanwick, Anna, authoress and translator, aged 86.—*Nov.* 2.

Sykes, Christopher, formerly M.P. for Beverley, the East Riding, &c., aged 67.—*Dec.* 15, 1898. (£53,125 gross—net *nil*).

Sykes, Sir Frederic Henry, 5th Baronet of Basildon, aged 72.—*Jan.* 20 (£42,510).

Symons, Lieut.-Gen. Sir William Penn, K.C.B. (Burma, Tirah, &c., mortally wounded at Glencoe, Natal), a descendant of Wm. Penn of Pennsylvania, aged 56.—*Oct.* 23.

Taylor, Lt. J., K.R.R.C., killed at Glencoe, *Oct.* 20.

Tennyson, Arthur, brother of the late Poet Laureate and sixth son of Dr. Tennyson, aged 85.—*June* 27.

Tennyson, Horatio, eighth and last of the above sons, aged 80.—*Oct.* 2.

Thompson, Gen. Thomas, I.S.C. (Kurnool Fd. Force), aged 81.—*March* 24.

Townshend, John Villiers Stuart, 5th Marquess, many years an earnest philanthropical worker, aged 68.—*Oct.* 28.

Tozer, Rt. Rev. William George, formerly Bishop of Central Africa, Jamaica, and Honduras.—*June* 21 (£10,449).

Traill (Mrs.) Catherine Parr (*née* Strickland), once a distinguished authoress and naturalist, aged 98.—*Sept.*

Trench, Hon. Power Henry Le-Poer-, late British Minister Plenipotentiary at Tokio, aged 57.—*April* 30 (£36,077).

Truro, Thomas Montague Morrison, 3rd and last Baron, aged 42.—*March* 8 (£15,599).

Upington, Hon. Sir Thomas, K.C.M.G., Q.C., formerly Premier and a Puisne Judge of Cape Colony, aged 54.—*Dec.* 10, 1898.

Vanderbilt, Cornelius, American financier.—*Sept.* 12.

Verner, Sir Edward Wingfield, 4th Baronet, formerly M.P. for Lisburn and for Armagh, aged 68.—*June* 21 (£43,521 gross).

Vernon, George William Henry, 1st Baron, P.C., aged 44.—*Dec.* 15, 1898 (£61,208).

Vogel, Sir Julius, K.C.M.G., formerly Premier in New Zealand, aged 63.—*March* 12.

Walker, Sir James Robert, 2nd Baronet of Sand Hutton, formerly M.P. for Beverley, aged 69.—*June* 12 (£86,177 gross.)

Wallace, Maj.-Gen. Hill, C.B. (Abyssinia 1868), aged 75.—*June* 5.

Wallace, Robert, D.D., M.P. for East Edinburgh, aged 67.—*June* 6 (£953 net).

Warburton, Col. Sir Richard, K.C.I.E., C.S.I. (Abyssinia, Afghanistan, and Tirah), aged 56.—*April* 22 (£4.395 net).

Watson, William, Baron, a Lord of Appeal, formerly Lord Advocate, M.P. 1875-80 for Glasgow and Aberdeen Universities, aged 74.—*Sept.* 14.

Way, Col. George Augustus, C.B., I.S.C. (Waziri Expedition), aged 62.—*Oct.* 19.

Weare, Lieut.-Gen. Sir Henry Edwin, K.C.B. (Punjab, Crimea, and New Zealand), aged 73.—*Dec.* 31, 1898 (£42,832).

Welby, Rt. Rev. Thomas Earle, D.D., 2nd Bishop of St. Helena, aged 88.—*Jan.* 6.

Weldon, Capt. G. A., R. Dub. Fus., killed at Glencoe, *Oct.* 20.

Wharncliffe, Edward Montagu Stuart Granville, 1st Earl of, aged 71.—*May* 13 (£114,439 net).

White, Adm. Richard Dunning, C.B. (St. Jean d'Acre and Baltic), aged 85.—*July* 29.

Wilford, Lt. Col. Edmund P., commanding 1st Glosr. Regt., killed at Reitfontein, *Oct.* 24.

Williams, Sir Monier Monier, K.C.I.E., Professor of Sanscrit at Oxford, aged 79.—*April* 11 (estate £15,816).

Willis, Lieut.-Gen. Sir Frederic Arthur, C.B. (Indian Mutiny and Hazara 1868), aged 69.—*May* 28.

Wilson, Isaac, formerly M.P. for Middlesbrough, aged 77.—*Sept.* 22.

Wright, Sir James, C.B., formerly Engineer-in-Chief R.N., aged 75.—*April* 17 (£4,300).

Wright, Rev. William, D.D., Editorial Superintendent for the British and Foreign Bible Society, aged 62.—*July* 31.

Wynford, William Draper Mortimer, 3rd Baron, aged 73.—*Aug.* 27.

Younghusband, Lieut.-Gen., Charles Wright, C.B., F.R.S. (Crimea), aged 78.—*Oct.* 28.

Wills Proved, 1898–99.

Wills disposing of estates over £100,000 each and some others of interest. The gross amount of the whole of the estate and the net value of the personalty only appear upon the official records. The net value of the whole including realty is not ascertainable.

Ailsa, Julia Marchioness of, Pont Street (*Jan.* 11), £34,582 net.

Allen, Harry, 45, Sheffield, steel manufacturer (*April* 3), £133,435 net.

Allen, Thomas Newland, 87, The Vache, Chalfont (*March* 11), £214,497 gross.

Andrew, Charles, 77, Coughton Court, Redditch (*Jan.* 5), £148,244 gross, £139,948 net.

Anglesey, Henry, 4th Marquess of, 64, Plas Newydd (*Oct.* 13, 1898), £535,395 gross, £22,978 net.

Antrobus, Sir Edmund, 80, 3rd Bart., formerly M.P. (*April* 1), £62,818 gross, £25,597 net.

Antrobus, Hugh Lindsay, 76, of Coutts & Co., banker (*March* 11), £354,340 gross, £290,916 net.

Armitage, John Ramsden, —, Bradford, dyer, (*Jan.* 30), £210,795 gross, £120,045 net.

Arran, Elizabeth Marianne, Countess of, widow of 4th Earl (*April* 27), £45,310 net.

Barclay, Miss Jane Mary, 80, of Walthamstow, (*Jan.* 27), £105,957 net.

Baxter, Frederick, 77, of Woolton Heys, Liverpool (*Aug.* 30), £234,033 gross, £136,918 net.

Bayliss, Samuel, 78, engineer and contractor (*Nov.* 27, 1898), £545,850 net.

Bell, Rev. Canon Charles Dent, 80, of Ambleside (*Nov.* 11, 1898), £30,023 net.

Bentall, Edward Hammond, 84, of Maldon Iron Works, M.P. for Maldon 1868-74 (*Aug.* 7, 1898), £174,503 net.

Bevan, James Johnstone, 80, of the Bury and Suffolk Bank (*Nov.* 5, 1898), £30,982 gross, £24,850 net.

Beverley, Mrs. Susan, of Hamilton Terrace (*July* 11), £123,240 net.

Bibby, John, 59, of Garston, copper works (*Aug.* 2, 1898), £220,039 gross, £135,198 net,

Binks, Benjamin, 78, of Headingley, Leeds (*March* 25), £105,215 gross, £61,738 net.

Blackall, Dr. Thomas, 82, of Exeter (*May* 4), £62,414 gross, £133,569 net.

Blades, Rowland Hill, 72, Abchurch Lane, printer (*Nov.* 1, 1898), £21,486 net.

Bradshaw, William, 70, of Moorgate Street, solicitor (*Feb.* 8), £168,348 gross, £130,300 net.

Bramley-Moore, John Arthur, 59, of Liverpool, merchant (*July* 10), £103,057 gross, £93,353 net.

Brandreth, Thomas, 82, of Wimbledon (*May* 27), £138,122 net.

Broadwood, Walter Stewart, 79, of John Broadwood and Sons, £103,3²3 net.

Bromilow, David, 79, Bitteswell Hall, Leicester (*Oct.* 10, 1898), £221,505 gross.

Bulpett, William Whitear, 92, of Alresford, banker (*Jan.* 20), £402,473 gross, £261,547 net.

Burkitt, Samuel, 67, of Chesterfield, corn merchant (*June* 13, 1898), £129,447 gross, £104,707 net.

Burton, Edward, 73, of Eaves Hall, Bradford (*Sept.* 23, 1898), £274,750 net.

Campbell, Andrew, 79, of Marden, retired jeweller (*Nov.* 30, 1898), £100,471 gross, £14,769 net.

Cave, Lawrence Trent, 75, of Ditcham Park, Hants. (*Aug.* 17), £541,540 gross, £490 302 net.

Chalmers, Frederick, 62, of Brown, Shipley, & Co. (*Dec.* 28, 1898), £147,804 net.

Christie, Charles Peter, 69, of Hoddesdon, brewer (*Oct.* 5, 1898), £457,073 gross, £137,325 net.

Clark, Norman, 29, of Paisley, thread manufacturer (*Dec.* 3, 1898), £326,000 net.

Clarke, John Sleeper, 66, retired comedian, a native of Baltimore, U.S.A. (*Sept.* 25), £63,757 gross, £2,382 net.

Clonmell, Thomas Charles, 5th Earl of, 56 (*June* 18, 1896), £30,927 net.

Clutterbuck, Thomas, 89, Stanmore, brewer, (*March* 18, 1898), £601,090 net.

Cochrane, Charles, 63, of Greenroyde, Worcester, iron-master (*May* 11, 1898), £121,068 net.

Cockayne, William, 65, Sheffield, draper, (*Oct.* 7, 1898), £171,153 gross, £31,885 net.

Congreve, Richard, 80, of Palace Gardens Terrace, director for 40 years of the Church of Humanity in England (*July* 5), £5,597 net.

Cox, George Addison, 78, of Cox Brothers, Ltd., jute manufacturers (*May* 6), £224,352 net.

Cunliffe, Thomas Potter, 85, of Manchester, solicitor (*Sept.* 14, 1898), £273,740 net.

Davies, Herbert Ernest Matthew, 43, director of gold mining companies (*July* 4), £734,311 gross, £332,695 net.

Davis, Frederick, 72, of 147, Old Bond Street, dealer in works of art (*Feb.* 18), £254,847 gross, £145,451 net.

Delves-Broughton, Sir Henry, 90, Staffords and Chester, 9th Bart. (*Feb.* 26), £766,747 gross, £167,872 net.

Derby, William Hodgson, Tong Park, Otley (*May* 20), £247,437 net.

Desart, William Ulick, 4th Earl of, 53 (*Sept.* 15, 1898), £3,313 gross).

De Stern, Julia Baroness, of Hyde Park Gate (*Jan.* 3), £209,178 gross, £193,185 net.

Dresden, Edward Zadok, 85, merchant (*March* 15), £600,205 net.

Duncanson, Edward Ford, 66, of T. A. Gibb & Co., merchant (*April* 17), £188,325 gross, £99,347 net.

Edwards, Harry Smith, of South Shields (*Oct.* 7, 1898), £190,160 gross, £32,622 net.

Eglington, William, 79, Southborough, Surbiton (*March* 24), £199 973 gross, £116,425 net.

Evans, Henry Jones, 75, of the Brecon Old Bank (*Dec.* 9, 1898), £167,030 gross, £149,665 net.

Farley, Alderman Reuben, 73, West Bromwich, iron founder (*March* 11), £167,735 gross, £136,174 net.

Findlay, John Ritchie, 74, chief proprietor of *The Scotsman* newspaper (*Oct.* 16, 1898), £299,332 net.

Fletcher, Professor Banister, 66, architect, M.P., North-West Wilts, 1885-86 (*July* 5), £75,844 gross, £39,166 net.

Forwood, Sir Arthur Bower, 62, 1st Bart., M.P. for Ormskirk, 1885-98, Secretary to Admiralty, 1885-92 (*Sept.* 27, 1898), £87,322 gross, £74,333 net.

*Foster, William Orme, 84, Opley Park, Salop, iron-master, M.P. for Staffords, 1857-63 (*Sept.* 29), £1,000,000 gross, "so far as can at present be ascertained."

*Fowler, Sir John, 81, of Braemore, 1st Bart., engineer (*Nov.* 30, 1898), £179,330 gross, £153,650 net.

Frankland, Professor Sir Edward, 74, M.D., F.R.S. (*Aug.* 9), £138,627 gross, £126,472 net.

Gassiot, John Peter, 78, of Carshalton, F.R.G.S., and formerly of Martinez, Gassiot & Co., wine shippers (*July* 26), £273,765 gross.

Gibson, Alexander, 70, of Ayton, N.B., formerly of Ceylon (*June* 10, 1898), £173,940 net.

Giles, John Edward, 86, Temple, barrister (*July* 20), £352,004, £336,969.

Gjers, John, of Middlesbrough, ironworks (*Oct.* 6, 1898), £128514 net.

Gray, Sir William, 75, of West Hartlepool, shipbuilder (*Sept.* 12, 1898), £1,500,423 gross, £1,397,483 net.

Greaves, George Richard, 54, of Winslow, Bucks (*Feb.* 25), £119,567 net.

Greg, Arthur, 63, Eagley Mills, Bolton (*May* 11), £202,745 gross, £140,826 net.

Grey, Sir George, 86, K.C.B., Colonial Governor (*Sept.* 19, 1898), £605 net.

Gurney, Richard Hanbury Joseph, 44, of Northrepps Hall, Norfolk (*May* 6), £110,311 gross.

Hainsworth, Edwin, 66, of Pembridge Gardens, formerly of Liverpool (*Nov.* 23, 1898), £121,645 net.

Hall, John, 74, of Newcastle-on-Tyne, shipowner (*June* 26), £564,198 net.

Harrington, Elizabeth William, Countess of, 70, widow of the 5th Earl (*Dec.* 24, 1898), £226,018 net.

Harris, Henry, 79, of Coleman Street, solicitor (*Jan.* 22), £129,987 net.

Harrison, Lawrence, of Sutton Place, Guildford (*Feb.* 19), £113,637 net.

Harvey, Charles, 81, of Barnsley, linen manufacturer (*Oct.* 31, 1898), £215,558 net.

Hawkins, Charles Henry, 80, of Maitlands, Colchester (*Dec.* 3, 1898), £148,733 net.

Hays, Alfred, 61, of Royal Exchange Buildings, theatrical agent (*May* 11), £36,114 gross, £24,025 net.

Head, Jeremiah, 63, of Middlesbrough, civil engineer (*March* 10), £22,920 net.

Heape, Benjamin, 82, of Prestwich-cum-Oldham (*Sep'.* 16), £106,657 gross, £81,399 net.

Hignett, John, 68, of Liverpool, tobacco manufacturer (*Sep'.* 15, 1898), £400,457 net.

Hindley, Frederic, 78, retired cabinet maker (*Nov.* 11, 1898), £102,529 gross, £61,061 net.

Hoare, Robert Gurney, 54, of Newcastle-on-Tyne, banker (*May* 22), £62,149 net.

Hodgkins, Henry, of Cheltenham, and late of Stockton, U.S.A. (*June* 30), £111,166 gross, £80,508 net.

Hodgson, James Stuart, 72, formerly of Baring, Bros. & Co. (*July* 14), £327,676 gross, £255,562 net.

Howard de Walden, Lucy John, Baroness, 92, daughter of the 4th Duke of Portland (*July* 27), £176,306 gross, £146,795 net.

Jackson, Peter Rothwell, 85, of the Salford Rolling Mills (*Feb.* 8), £108,737 gross, £88,401 net, personalty.

Jarvis, John Samuel, 77, of Devon House, Clapham (*Dec.* 15, 1898), £104,075 net.

Jenkins, Peter, ———, St. Leonards-on-Sea (*June* 27), £160,893 gross, £16,817 net.

Jones, Owen Glyndyr, 89, of Oswestry (*March* 18), £115,748 net.

Joseph, Alexander Gedalje, 51, diamond merchant (*Aug.* 11), £167,555 net.

Joynson, Peter, 86, of Southport (*Jan.* 8), £149,875 net.

Keeley, Mrs. Mary Anne, 93, of Pelham Crescent, retired actress (*March* 15), £17,645 net.

Keiller, John Mitchell, 48, marmalade manufacturer (*Jan.* 21), £435,368 net.

Keiller, William, marmalade manufacturer (*Jan.* 25), £100,533 net.

Kelso, John Robert, 82, of North Shields (*Feb.* 14), £218,031 net.

King, John, 87, of Queen's Gate (*Feb.* 26), £166,567.

Kirkhope, John, 90, of West Coats, N.B., wine-merchant (*March* 27), £106,930 net.

Knill, Alderman Sir Stuart, 74, 1st Bart., Lord Mayor, 1892-93 (*Nov.* 19), £100,722 gross, £20,223 net.

Laird, William, 68, of Birkenhead, ship-builder (*Feb.* 7), £307,873 gross, £250,525 net.

Lamond, James, 86, of Edinburgh, solicitor (*Oct.* 27, 1898), £101,560 net.

Lane, Mrs. Sarah, 78, of the Britannia Theatre, Hoxton (*Aug.* 16), £122,320 net.

Langworthy, Edward Martin, 50, of Guy's House, Holyport (*Oct.* 27, 1898), £145.

Langworthy, Mildred Sabine Palliser, 42, of Folkestone (*Oct.* 27, 1898), £1,422 gross.

Lathom, Edwd., 1st Earl of, 60, three times Lord Chamberlain (*Nov.* 10, 1898), £147,537 gross, £127,882 net.

Lawrie, Thos., 58, of Gorringe's, Buckingham Palace Road (*June* 1), £64,101 net.

Layton, Alfred Thos., 73, of Birchin Lane, stationer, C.C., Alderman of Croydon (*Aug.* 3), £95,189 net.

Lean, Vincent Stuckey, 78, of the Middle Temple (*March* 24), £414,786 net.

Lightbown, Hy., 80, of Pendleton, paper stainer (*Aug.* 16), £162,109 gross, £142,516 net.

Lindner, Maximilian, 87, of Birmingham, merchant (*Oct.* 17, 1898), £224,658 net.

Lloyd, Herbert, of Coombe Farm, Croydon, and of Edward Lloyd, Limited (*May* 12), £103,963 gross, £90,802 net.

Lloyd, Sampson Saml., junr., 53, of The Priory, Warwick (*April* 15), £100,962 gross, £87,528 net.

Long, Cecil, 77, of Sherrington Manor, Sussex, son of the late Thomas Chantless, Q.C., and grandson of Sir William Long (*Sept.* 30), £275,878 gross, £245,028 net.

Lowe, Chas., Reddish and Bradford, manufacturing chemist (*Nov.* 1, 1898), £173,347 gross, £148,978 net.

Lowe, Henry, 89, of Edgbaston (*April* 20), £272,620 net.

Lowe, Jas., 73, of Manchester, M.A., draper and author (*April* 24), £106,052 gross, £48,753 net.

Maofie, Robert, 87, of Airds House, N.B., and of Liverpool, sugar refiner (*Feb.* 22), £108,666 net.

Maddy, Edwin Davis, of Queen's Gate Terrace (*April* 11), £125,877.

Mansfield, Wm. David, 4th Earl of, 92, of Scone Palace, N.B. (*May* 2, 1898), £137,243 net.

Marlborough, Frances Anne Emily, Duchess of, widow of 7th Duke, 77 (*April* 16), £7,053 net.

Marriott, Wm. Thos., 77, of Wakefield, colliery proprietor (*Feb.* 2, 1899), £211,753 gross, £192,720 net.

Marshall, Walter Gore, 53, of the Cannon Brewery (*May* 21), £199,783 gross, £124,768 net.

Martin, Dame Helena Fawcit, 82, of Bryntisilio, Llangollen (*Oct.* 31, 1898), £27,978.

Martin, Henry Daniel, 87, of Halbery, I.W. (*Sept.* 25, 1898), £108,246.

Mathews, Mrs. Elizabeth (Lizzie Davenport), widow of C. J. Mathews (*Jan.* 4), £15,368 net.

Mathieson, Thos. Adam, of the Saracen Tool Works, Glasgow (*March* 10), £138,637 net.

Maxted, Geo. Wm., 79, of Lancaster, solicitor (*Dec.* 13, 1898), £156,093 gross, £143,284 net.

Medley, Geo. Webb, 72, of the Stock Exchange, and of the Cobden Club (*Nov.* 29, 1898), £252,038.

Micholls, Henry, 84, of Prince's Gardens (*May* 13), £116,989 net.

Miller, Brice Alan, of Queen's Gate Gardens and Valparaiso (*Oct.* 27, 1898), £150,943 net.

Mills, Arthur, 82, of Bude Haven, M.P. for Taunton, 1857-65, and for Exeter 1874-80, £38,959 net.

Mills, John, 63, of Bistern, Hants (*Feb.* 24), £116,769 gross, £23,700 net.

Mogg, William Henry, 84, of Bristol (*March* 24), £152,779.

Mowbray, Dame Elizabeth Gray, 76, wife of Sir J. R. Mowbray, M.P. (*Feb.* 16), £2,040 net.

Naylor, John Wm., 71, Leeds, engineer (*June* 4), £455,159 gross, £448,119 net.

Neill, Robt., 82, Manchester, contractor (*March* 5), £254,735 gross, £222,266 net.

Nelson, Henry, 84, Leeds, solicitor to the G.N. Ry. Co. (*May* 20), £84,409 gross, £59,403 net.

Neve, Wm. Tanner, 84, of Cranbrook, surveyor (*March* 8), £169,334 gross, £157,662 net.

Nickalls, Tom, 70, of the Stock Exchange, many years Master of the Surrey Staghounds (*May* 10), £141,219 gross, £82,322.

Nicol, Geo. 78, of Gordon House, Clapham (*Feb.* 14), £127,941 gross, £115,662 net.

Nixon, John, 84, Nixon's Navigation Co. (*June* 3), £1,145,658 net.

Norton, Henry Elland, 84, retired solicitor (*July* 27), £133,960 net.

Orr, James, 87, Harviestown, N.B. (*March* 1), £787,035 gross, £217,350 net.

Orgill, Jno. Jas., 83, brewery valuer (*May* 2), £75,100 gross, £52,212.

Oxenbridge, Wm. Jno., 69, 1st Viscount (*April* 16, 1898), £6,505 gross, £302 net.

Parker, Thos., of Manchester, confectioner (*Sept.* 20, 1898), £133,704 gross, £115,430 net.

Paul, Dr. Jno. Hayball, 83, of Camberwell House Asylum (*Jan.* 26), £138,080 gross, £100,053 net.

Pawley, Chas. 69, of Upper Norwood (*July* 7, 1898), £151,850 gross, £59,252 net.

Pease, Arthur, 61, of Darlington, M.P. for Whitby, 1880-85; for Darlington, 1892-98 (*Aug.* 27, 1898), £439,036 gross, £239,449 net.

Pechell, Hervey Chas., 57 of Maresfield Park, Sussex (*Dec.* 28, 1898), £163,139 gross, £93,264 net.

Peck, Robert, 54, Howbury Hall, Beds., trainer and breeder of horses (*Aug.* 17), £13,663 gross, £8,550 net.

Peel, Sir Chas. Lennox, G.C.B., clerk to Privy Council (*May* 19), £104,380 gross, £97,963 net.

Phillips, Acton Francis, —, of the Lyric Opera House, Hammersmith (*May* 17), £48,508 gross, £38,909 net.

Plevins, Chas. Hy., 75, of Thrapston (*May* 8), £764,607 gross, £473,062 net.

Potter, Thos., Bayley, 80, founder of the Cobden Club, M.P. for Rochdale, 1865-95 (*Nov.* 6, 1898), £98,326 gross, £88,091 net.

Pritt, William, 83, of Rampsbeck, Cumberland (*Feb.* 22), £110,493 gross, £52,432 net.

Ralli, Ambrose Pundia, 47, of Ralli Bros., Greek merchant (*March* 13), £115,270 net.

Raphael, Henry Lewis, 67, of the Stock Exchange (*May* 4), £1,520,380 net.

Ratcliff, Richard, 68, of Bass, Ratcliff, and Gretton, Ltd., brewer (*Nov.* 24, 1898), £1,116,190 gross, £1,007,362 net.

Restell, Thos. Miles, 59, of Mark Lane, wine broker (*June* 24), £120,458 gross, £97,573 net.

Ridley, Saml. Wm., 82, of Islington, oil cloth manufacturer (*Feb.* 6), £443,868 gross, £355,164 net.

Righton, Thos. Edwd. Corrie, of Gloucester Place, comedian (*Jan.* 1), £5,564 net.

Rookwood, Eden, Baroness, 80, wife of the 1st Lord Rookwood (*April* 1), £54,765 net.

Ross, Capt. Wm. Walter, 92, formerly Madras Native Infantry (*July* 6), £100,284 net.

Roundell, Chas. Selborne, 26, of Gledstone, Yorks (*Jan.* 6), £105,702 net.

Ryland, Frederick, of Harborne, Birmingham (*Feb.* 11), £120,575 gross, £59,017 net.

Satow, Mrs. Marie M. H. P., of Folkestone (*April* 14), £204,173 net.

Schwind, Chas., 77, of Morley, Derby (*April* 2), £190,962 gross, £162,841 net.

Scott, John, 87, of Cannon Street, shawl manufacturer (*May* 12), £212,536 gross, £107,554 net.

Scott, Walter, 78, of Weybridge and Dumfries (*March* 14), £223,938 gross, £166,252 net.

Sefton, Cecil Emily, Countess of, widow of Wm. Philip, 4th Earl (*Feb.* 25), £13,164 gross, £4,734 net.

Senior, Guy, 64, of the Oakwell Brewery, Barnsley (*Dec.* 8, 1898), £112,566 gross, £71,953 net.

Shakerley, Sir Chas. Watkin, 66, of Somerford Park, 2nd Bart. (*Oct.* 20, 1898), £128,461 gross, net *nil*.

Shaw, Joseph, 80, of Wakefield, wine merchant (*May* 30), £245,172 gross, £165,772.

Shelley, Dame Jane, of Boscombe Manor, Hants, widow of Sir Percy Florence Shelley, 3rd Bart., (*June* 24), £115,990 gross, £55,992 net.

Shrubb, Chas. Peyto, 62, of Worplesdon (*Feb.* 4), £156,067 gross, £107,372 net.

Silva, Edwd., 58, of Silva and Cosens, wine merchant (*May* 23), £147,819 gross, £136,885 net.

Simon, Henry, 64, Manchester, engineer (*July* 22), £176,306 gross, £146,795 net.

Skinner, John Holt, of Moray House, I. W. (*July* 20), £92,471 net.

Smith, George, 91, of the Reform Club and formerly of Chicago (*Oct.* 7), £59,257 net.

Snow, Thos. Maitland, 81, of the City Bank, Exeter (*Jan.* 21), £118,026 gross, £89,097 net.

Sowler, Thos., 31, of the *Manchester Courier* (*April* 4), £80,522 net.

Spurgeon, Rev. Dr. Jas. Archer, of West Croydon Baptist Church (*March* 23), £36,378 gross, £5,877 net.

Stevens, Wm., 54, proprietor of the *Family Herald* (*June* 30), £272,095 gross, £205,460 net.

Stirling, Wm. Rogers Arthur, 71 of Cambridge Terrace, actor (*Dec.* 2, 1898), £15,228.

Swarbrick, Saml., 79, formerly manager Great Eastern Ry. (*Jan.* 22), £18,567 net.

Swire, Jno. Saml., 72, of Billiter Street, merchant (*Dec.* 1, 1898), £218,867.

Tankard, John Wm., 46, of Birkdale and Bradford, worsted spinner (*Dec.* 6, 1898), £74,357 net.

Taylor, Thos., 89, of Burleigh, Salop (*Jan.* 12), £110,186 gross.

Taylor, Wm., —, of Southport and Oldham, cotton spinner (*Jan.* 26), £132,620 net.

Teacher, Adam, of Glasgow, wine and spirit merchant, £440,164 net.

Thellusson, Peter, 49, Brodsworth Hall, Yorks (*May* 17), £136,897 gross, £27,812 net.

Tindall, Wm. Hy., 78, of Eastcheap, merchant and shipowner (*Feb.* 9), £74,058 gross, £61,505 net.

Trower, Hy., 84, of St. Mary-at-Hill, wine merchant (*Jan.* 9), £194,910 net.

Tufnell, Hy. Archd., 44, of The Grove, Wimbledon (*Sept.* 21, 1898), £219,772 gross.

Usher, Andrew, 72, of Johnstownburn, N.B., wine merchant (*Nov.* 1, 1898), £612,716 gross, £466,005 net.

Vereker, Hon. Jane Charlotte, 78, of Somers Place (*July* 10), £18,758 net.

Vlasto, Alex. Anthony, 66, of Ralli Bros., Greek merchants ( ), £332,357 net.

Wakefield, Hy., —, of 11, Adam Street, Adelphi, engineer (*April* 19), £119,433 gross.

Walker, Isaac Donnithorne, 54, brewer and cricketer (*July* 6, 1898), £195,483 net.

Wallop, Hon. and Rev. Arthur Geo. Edwd., 32, of Stockbridge (*Dec.* 22, 1898), £13,270 net.

Warburg, Frederick Elias, 66, of Jonas, Simonsen, and Co. (*Feb.* 9), £200,978 net.

Watson, Sir John, of Earnock, N.B., 1st Bart., 79 (*Sept.* 26, 1898), £121,797 gross, £90,023 net.

Webb, Wm. Fredk., 70, of Newstead Abbey, Notts. (*Feb.* 24), £165,538 gross, £58,135 net.

Wedd, Geo., 77, of the Stock Exchange (*Oct.* 30, 1898), £121,797 gross, £90,023 net.

Weir, Jas., of Blackrock, Dublin, wine merchant (*Oct.* 30, 1898), £165,805 net.

Wheler, Chas. Wheler, 65, Lestow Hill, Normanby (*May* 6), £174,327 gross, £65,580 net.

Whitaker, John, 69, of Winsley Hall, Westbury, Salop (*July* 7), £257,247 gross, £171,978 net.

Whitmore, Mrs. Adelaide Anna, widow of Henry Whitmore, M.P., £92,035 gross, £80,789 net.

Wiggins, Capt. Arthur, 47, of Sandhills, Christchurch (*Nov.* 30, 1898), £212,262 net.

Wilder, Fredk., 66, of Purley Hall, Berks (*May* 13), £104,790 gross, £76,025 net.

Wilson, Fredk. Thos., 32, of Newent, Gloucester (*April* 12), £165,107 net.

Winchilsea and Nottingham, Murray Edward Gordon, 11th Earl of, 47 (*Sept.* 7, 1898), £106,404 gross, net *nil*.

Wood, Dr. James, 54, of Southport (*Feb.* 15), £161,021 net.

UNDER 466 of the wills reported during the eight years 1891-98, disposing of personal estate in the United Kingdom to the aggregate amount of £75,968,905, there were pecuniary bequests for charitable, religious, and educational purposes, amounting to about £10,119,671, in the proportion of not quite 13¼ per cent. of the amount of estate. The charitable bequests under the wills of 150 ladies were equal to 25¾ per cent. of the personal estate over which they had power of disposal, and those of the 316 testators were in the proportion of 11¼ per cent. The annual average of the bequests for charities during the eight years was altogether about £1,250,000. The large bequests were for the most part those of childless persons. The wills proved each year exceed 50,000 in number, and only a small proportion of these are reported, but it seems probable that not many bequests of considerable amount for charitable purposes escape notice, and, approximately, it may be estimated that, including those of which no reports are published, the total sum bequeathed for charitable, religious, and educational purposes, under wills proved in the United Kingdom, is, on an average, about £2,000,000 a year. This does not include specific legacies for public uses to the British Museum, the National Gallery, the Universities, and scientific and other institutions. Perhaps the most important bequest of this kind during recent years was that of Lady Wallace, who, in 1897, left, upon certain conditions to trustees for the Nation, the Hertford House collection of pictures and other works of art, formed chiefly by the fourth Marquess of Hertford and inherited from him by Sir Richard Wallace. This collection is supposed to be now worth at least £1,000,000. Amongst charitable bequests, that of Clare Baroness Hirsch Gereuth, widow of Baron Meritz Hirsch, is noteworthy. Under his will, proved this year, a sum of nearly £2,700,000 is bequeathed to Jewish and other charitable institutions, mostly in France, Austria, and the United States of America, but including £160,000 to the London Jewish Board of Guardians. There is also a contingent reversion for certain charities to further £2,000,000 from Baroness Hirsch's estate.

The following is a list of some of the bequests for charitable and other public uses in the United Kingdom, under wills reported in 1899:—

	Value of Personality £	Amount of Bequest about. £
Clare, Baroness Hirsch Gereuth	51,277	160,000
Baron Ferdinand J. A. De Rothschild, M.P.	1,488,128	150,000
Vincent Stuckey Leon	414,786	129,000
John Hall, of Newcastle-on-Tyne	564,828	110,000
Miss Emma Lacy Fleming, of Westbourne Park	103,488	70,000
Julia Baroness de Stern	193,185	66,000
James Brown Thomson, of Glasgow	178,113	60,000
Joseph Shaw, of Wakefield	165,772	57,500
Thomas Lockwood, of Harrowgate	46,416	55,000
Rev. Lancelot Capel Bathurst	74,924	50,000
Richard Cadbury, of Birmingham	42,817	44,000
Charles Cochrane, of Pedmore, Worcester	121,067	40,000
David Aitchison, of Maidenhead Thicket	115,535	31,500
John William Naylor, of Allerton House, Leeds	448,120	31,250
Mrs. Sarah Beach, Westbourne Terrace	31,745	30,000
Francis Heathcoat, of Margate	38,635	30,000
William Roberts, of Manchester	15,967	24,000
James Orr, of Harviestown, N.B.	783,035	23,100
Miss Jane Mary Barclay, of Walthamstow	105,957	20,000
John Mitchell Keiller, of Aberdeen	435,367	20,000
John Holt Skinner, of Moray House, I.W.	92,335	17,000
Herbert Lloyd, of the *Daily Chronicle*	99,802	16,000
Dr. Charles Drury Edward Fortnum, of Stanmore	39,522	16,000
Dr. John Say, of Ryde, I.W.	20,420	14,000
Robert Macfie, of Airds House, N.B.	108,665	14,000
Thomas Miles Restell, of Mark Lane	97,573	12,000
George Smith, late of Chicago	59,435	12,000
Lady Howard de Walden, of Portland Place	170,673	10,700
Thomas Brandreth, of Wimbledon	152,511	10,600
Sir William Gray, of Hartlepool	1,397,483	10,000
Miss Harriet Spike, of Lymington	28,565	10,000
Edward Goddard Towell-Ellis, of Inverness Terrace	13,834	9,000
Mrs. Peacock, of Hest Bank, Lancaster	43,755	6,000
Joseph Graham, of Maida Vale	15,773	6,000
John Peter Gassiot, of Carshalton	273,765	5,000
Miss Elizabeth Browne, of Cirencester	35,298	4,700
Miss Emma Charrington, of Englefield Green	44,780	4,500
Miss Elizabeth Rolland, of Weybridge	26,203	4,100
Miss Emma Poitch, of Bristol	57,666	4,000
Mrs. Ellen Barclay, of Reigate	14,228	4,000
	£8,202,600	£1,486,950

EXHIBITIONS, PUBLIC BUILDINGS, THEATRES, AND OTHER PLACES AND OBJECTS OF INTEREST IN THE METROPOLIS AND SUBURBS.

THE following List comprises some of the Objects of Interest to persons visiting the Metropolis, also some of the Suburban Resorts frequented by Londoners. The daily papers, however, will generally, in their advertisement columns, supply the necessary particulars of times of opening, fares, terms of admission, &c. Except where otherwise stated, "Open Daily" means every Week-day, and not on Sundays.

EXHIBITIONS, &c.

ACADEMY, ROYAL, Burlington House, Piccadilly. —Exhibition of works by living artists, open from 1st Monday in May to 1st Monday in August, from 8 to 7; Admission, 1s.; Catalogue, 6d. Evening Exhibition, last week, from 7.30 to 10.30; Admission, 6d.; Catalogue, 6d. Exhibition of works by Old Masters and deceased British artists, 10 weeks from 1st Monday in January, from 9 till 6; Admission 1s.; Catalogue, 6d. Gibson and Diploma Galleries, free, daily, from 11 to 4.

AQUARIUM, ROYAL, Westminster. — Entertainments, dog, pigeon, chrysanthemum, and other shows; yachting and fishing exhibitions, at various dates, &c. Open 10 a.m. to 11.30 p.m. Admission, 1s.

ART EXHIBITIONS.—*Royal Society of Painters in Water Colours*, 5A Pall Mall East, admission 1s. Exhibitions confined to the works of members and associates are held in May and December; open for 3 months. *Royal Institute of Painters in Water Colours*, 191 Piccadilly; exhibitions open to all artists; March 25 to middle of July, 1s. *Royal Society of British Artists*, Suffolk Street, Pall Mall East, 1s., open to all artists, April to July and Oct. to Feb., 10 to 6. *Grafton Galleries*, 8 Grafton St., W., *Sec.* H. Bishop. *New Gallery*, 121 Regent St. Jan. to Apr., exhibition of works by deceased artists; May to Aug., annual summer exhibition of works by living artists; Sep. to Nov., Royal Photographic Society; Nov. and Dec., Socy. of Portrait Painters, 10 to 6, 1s. *Doré Gallery*, 35 New Bond Street. Daily, 10 to 6, 1s. *French Gallery*, 120 Pall Mall, open all the year: admission, 1s. *Hanover Gallery*, 47 New Bond Street, 1s. Those not specially mentioned in the preceding or following lists are open at uncertain seasons. The usual period is between the beginning of May and the end of August. There are also some Winter Exhibitions. *The Society of Oil Painters*, 191 Piccadilly, open from Nov. 1 to end of January, 1s.

CRYSTAL PALACE, Sydenham, S.E.—Open 10 a.m. to 11 p.m. Sunday concerts, afternoon and evening. Beautiful gardens and park of 200 acres, fine art courts containing examples of ancient and modern statuary and architecture; annual exhibitions of modern pictures; children's and shows during year, viz:—horses, kennel club, ponies, poultry, cage birds, cats, flowers and fruit, national cycle, co-operative and others; grand firework displays during summer; oratorio performances by Handel Festival Choir; Saturday classical concerts during winter; polo, football and cricket matches; cycle track and other sports; grand electric fountains, concerts and entertainments daily. Access from all suburban railway stations by means of the London and Brighton, and Chatham and Dover lines at cheap fares, including admission. Admission (unless otherwise advertised), 1s. Annual season tickets, one guinea, or half-a-guinea to employés and students.

MADAME TUSSAUD'S EXHIBITION, Marylebone Road, N.W. (adjoining Baker Street Station).—

Portrait models of celebrities past and present. Napoleon, Wellington, Nelson, and other relics. Open from 10 to 10. Admission, 1s.; children half-price; 6d. to the extra rooms.

NATIONAL GALLERY, Trafalgar Square.—National collection of pictures, open free on Monday, Tuesday, Wednesday, and Saturday, from 10 to 4 or 6; Students' days, Thursday and Friday. Admission after 11 a.m. on Students' days, 6d.; Sunday, Apr. to Oct. inclusive, from 2 to 5 or

NATIONAL GALLERY OF BRITISH ART (Tate Gallery), Millbank, S.W. National Collection of Modern British Pictures. Hours when open, Students' days and Sunday opening, same as *National Gallery*.

NATIONAL PORTRAIT GALLERY.—St. Martin's Place, Charing Cross. Open free on Monday, Tuesday, Wednesday, and Saturday, from 10 to 4, 5, or 6, according to the season; on Sundays from 2.30 to 5.30, free, Apr. to Oct. inclusive. Students' day, Thursday and Friday, from 10 to 4 or 5, according to the season.

WALLACE COLLECTION —Hertford House, W.

GARDENS.

BOTANIC, Regent's Park.—Accessible daily at 9. On Mondays and Saturdays, 1s.; other days by orders from Fellows. On Sundays at 10.30 a.m.

HOME PARK, HAMPTON COURT.—Open free, to pedestrians only.

KENSINGTON GARDENS.—Free every day. At the west of Hyde Park.

KEW, ROYAL BOTANIC GARDENS.—Accessible by railway, omnibus, and steamboat. Open daily free. Weekdays 12 to sunset; Sundays 1 to sunset; Bank Holidays 10 to sunset. Closed on Christmas Day.

TEMPLE, near Fleet St. & Thames Embankment.

ZOOLOGICAL, Regent's Park.—Admission from 9 a.m. till sunset, on Monday, 6d.; the rest of the week, 1s.; to children under twelve, all days, 6d.; on Sunday only by an order from a Fellow.

MISCELLANEOUS.

BRIDGES.—*London, Southwark, Blackfriars, Waterloo, Charing Cross* (foot and railway), *Westminster, Lambeth, Vauxhall, Chelsea, Albert, Battersea, Hammersmith* (suspension), &c., *Tower* (opened 1894), and the various *railway* bridges.

HOSPITALS.—For list, see page 285.

PARKS.—*St. James's*, near Charing Cross, 83 acres; the *Green Park*, adjacent to St. James's, 71 acres; *Hyde Park*, 400 acres (this should be visited between 11 and 1 and 5 and 7 during the season); *Kensington Gardens*, 300 acres (Albert Memorial, opposite Royal Albert Hall); *Victoria Park*, Hackney, 300 acres; *Battersea Park*, 250 acres; *Regent's Park and Primrose Hill*, 450 acres; *Finsbury Park*, Hornsey, 115 acres; *Peckham Rye Park*, Southwark Park, 62 acres; *West Ham Park, Kennington Park*; *Waterlow Park*, Highgate, 30 acres; *Highbury*

Fields, Islington ; *Deptford Park,* 17 acres, and *Clissold Park,* Stoke Newington—all accessible from the centre of the metropolis at the cost of a 2d. or 3d. ride by omnibus, railway, tramway, or steamboat. *Hampstead Heath,* 240 acres, *Greenwich Park,* 180 acres; *Bushey Park,* horse-chestnut-trees ; *Highgate Woods, Hadley Common,* near " Barnet Field ; " *Clapham, Streatham, Mitcham, Peckham Rye, Hackney, Plumstead,* and small parks or re-creation grounds in several other parts.

SCHOOLS, PUBLIC. - *Westminster,* near the Abbey; *St. Paul's,* Kensington, *Christ's Hospital (Bluecoat School),* in Newgate Street; *Merchant Taylors',* at the Charterhouse; *City of London,* on the Victoria Embankment.

THAMES EMBANKMENTS.—Magnificent public promenades, City of London School ; Sion College ; London School Board ; Somerset House ; Hotels Cecil and Savoy; Central Police Offices, among other fine buildings ; Cleopatra's Needle ; between Blackfriars Bridge and Westminster on the north, and Vauxhall and Westminster Bridge on the south, of the Thames.

MUSEUMS.

BETHNAL GREEN.—Branch of Victoria and Albert Museum. Collections of pictures, art objects, animal and waste products, food, entomology, boots and shoes, loan collection of English pottery, &c. Free daily: On Mondays, Thursdays and Saturdays, from 10 to 10 ; Tuesdays, Wednesdays, and Fridays, from 10 to 4, 5, or 6, according to the season ; Sundays, from 2 till dusk.

BRITISH, Bloomsbury.—Fine collections of ancient sculpture, &c. Exhibition of specimens of early printed books, bindings, manuscripts, autograph letters, and prints and drawings ; of Egyptian, Assyrian, Etruscan, Greek and Roman, Cyprian, British and Mediæval and other antiquities ; coins, gold ornaments, gems, nielli, &c. Entirely free. Open every week-day throughout the year except Good Friday and Christmas from 10 to 6, but in winter months certain galleries are closed at 4 or 5 ; also open on Sunday afternoons. *Reading-Room* open daily to readers, January to April, and September to December, 9 till 8 p.m. ; May to August, till 7 p.m.; lighted after dusk by electric light. Closed for cleaning first four week-days in March and Sept. For permission to see it, apply in the great hall. Tickets of admission to the reading-room, print room, or sculpture gallery, for purposes of research, reference, or study, are granted to persons not under twenty-one on written application to the Principal Librarian. The applicant must state abode, business or profession and purpose, and must send a recommendation from a householder, who must be a person of recognised position. *Print-Room* open daily to persons holding tickets, 10 to 5. *Sculpture Galleries,* open to students holding tickets (for copying statues, &c.), daily from 9 till hour of closing.

BRITISH MUSEUM OF NATURAL HISTORY.—The departments of Zoology, Geology, Mineralogy, and Botany have been removed from Great Russell Street to Cromwell Road, South Kensington. Open free daily at 10; Sundays, from May to Aug. inclusive, from 2.30 to 7 ; other months, 2 p.m to weekday closing time. The hours of closing are:— Jan., Nov., and Dec., 4 ; Feb. 4.30 ; Mar. and Sept., 5.30 ; April to Aug. (inclusive), 6 ; Oct., 5 ; also on Mon. and Sat. only, from May 1 to the middle of July, 8 ; and onwards to end of Aug., 7. The collections comprise all branches of natural history. An index-museum; galleries of mam-

mals, including whales, osteological specimens, birds and their nests, fishes, reptiles, insects, shells, corals, sponges, &c.; galleries of fossils of all kinds; a botanical gallery ; and an extensive gallery of minerals and meteorites, with a series of specimens forming an introduction to the study of mineralogy. Students are admitted daily for the special study of the collections, and to draw from specimens, under regulations to be obtained of the Director.

HORNIMAN MUSEUM, London Rd., Forest Hill. Open free, Mon Wed. and Sat., 2 to 9; Sundays, 2 to 5. The new Museum in course of erection is expected to be open this year.

IMPERIAL INSTITUTE of the United Kingdom, the Colonies, and India, South Kensington. Permanent collections of Colonial and Indian commercial and economic products. Open from 11 to 5 in summer, 11 to 4 in winter, free ; also Commercial Reading Room. In winter season, illustrated lectures on Monday evenings, free ; on certain Wednesdays, concerts, by ticket only, value 1s. 6d. ; to be obtained from Fellows. BRANCH, 112 Cannon Street, E.C. Open 10 to 5 daily, for supplying commercial information.

INDIAN, South Kensington.—Free all the week. Open from 10 to 10, Mon., Tu. and Sat.; 10 to dusk, Wed., Th. and Fri ; Sundays, from 2 till dusk.

PARKES MUSEUM of the Sanitary Institute, 74A Margaret Street, W., contains various sanitary appliances and various exhibits relating to Health and Hygiene ; there is a large library of sanitary literature. The Museum is open free daily from 10 to 6, and on Mondays to 8.

PRACTICAL GEOLOGY, Jermyn Street, Piccadilly. —Open every week-day, free, from 10 to 4, Nov., Dec., Jan., and Feb., and 10 to 5 during other months; on Mondays and Saturdays from 10 to 10; on Sundays, from 2 till 7 in summer, rest of year from 2 till dusk ; closed from the 10th of August to the 10th of September.

ROYAL ARCHITECTURAL, 18 Tufton St., Dean's Yard, S.W., 10 to 4. *Curator,* Francis Ford.

ROYAL COLLEGE OF SURGEONS, Lincoln's Inn Fds. —Admission to the Museum by order of members, or on application to the Secretary, 1st four days of the week, from 10 to 5 in summer, and 10 to 4 from November to February inclusive. Closed Sept.

ROYAL UNITED SERVICE INSTITUTION, Banqueting House, Whitehall.—Rubens' celebrated ceiling, Models of Trafalgar and Waterloo; interesting Naval and Military Relics ; models of ancient and modern war vessels. Admission to the Museum 6d., daily. Soldiers and Sailors in uniform, free. April to Sept., 11 to 6 ; Oct. to Mar., 11 to 4.

SIR JOHN SOANE'S, 13 Lincoln's Inn Fields.— Contains pictures by Hogarth, Turner, Sir J. Reynolds, Canaletti, Ruysdael, Watteau, and Callcott. Alabaster sarcophagus of Seti father of Rameses II. amongst other art treasures. Open free from 11 to 5 on Tuesdays, Wednesdays, Thursdays, and Fridays from first Tuesday in March to last Friday in August. Monday and Saturday reserved for students. Cards for private days during the recess, and for students, are to be obtained from the Curator at the Museum.

SOCIETY OF ARTS, Adelphi.—Barry's Pictures in the Great Hall. Admission free, daily, 10 to 3 ; Saturdays, 10 to 1. Not open on Sunday.

VICTORIA AND ALBERT, South Kensington.— Open daily. Containing works of decorative art, modern pictures, sculpture, Art and Science libraries, architectural illustrations. Free Mondays, Tuesdays, and Saturdays, from 10 to 10; on other week-days from 10 to 4, 5, or 6, on payment of 6d.; Sundays, from 2 till dusk. Naval, mechanical, and scientific models, and Scientific Collections, free all the week.

WESLEY'S HOUSE MUSEUM, 47 City Road.—Open from 10 to 4, 3d.

CHURCHES AND PLACES OF WORSHIP

ST. PAUL'S CATHEDRAL.—The masterpiece of Sir Christopher Wren. Splendid architecture; monuments to celebrated men; magnificent reredos. Nave and transepts free; choir closed except during divine service. Fees to the following parts: library, whispering gallery, and stone gallery, 6d.; golden gallery, 1s.; crypt, 6d.; ball, 1s.; total, 3s. Service on Sundays at 8, *10.30, *3.15, and *7. Week days at 8, *10, 1.15, *4, and 7. (*Services are choral.)

WESTMINSTER ABBEY, near the Houses of Parliament.—Open on Weekdays at 9 30 a.m. Chapel of Henry VII., Chapter House, and Cloisters. Free to body of the Abbey; to other parts by fee of 6d., except on Mondays and Tuesdays. Services on Sundays: Holy Communion at 8; choral at 10, 3, and 7. Daily-School Service at 9.15; choral at 10 and 3. Communion, Thursday at 8.30 a.m. in St. Faith's Chapel. St. Edward's Shrine, tombs of kings, and many other monuments and objects of interest, especially Poets' Corner. St. Margaret's Church, close by, is also worth visiting.

ST. SAVIOUR'S COLLEGIATE CHURCH, Southwark.—Future Cathedral for South London. Finest mediæval building in London after the Abbey. Known as St. Mary Overie previous to 1540. Burial place of Gower, Massinger, and Bp. Andrewes, &c. Open 7 a.m. to dusk, free. Sunday services; Communion, 8 and 11. Week days; 7.30, 8, and 5 p.m.

TEMPLE, South side of Fleet Street.—The Hall and Church very interesting, as also the Gardens; these are generally open to the public during the summer months after 6, and are thoroughly appreciated by the wives and children of working men. Church open to strangers on week days from 11 to 1, and from 2 to 4; service on Sundays at 11 a.m. and 3 p.m.

ST. BARTHOLOMEW'S Priory Church, Smithfield, the oldest church in London (1123).—Fine old Norman building, with tomb of the first prior, Rahere. N. transept restored, and re-opened in June, 1893, by H.R.H. the Prince of Wales. Crypt and Lady Chapel now open. Services daily 11 and 4.32; Sunday 8, 11, 4, and 7. Open free daily, 9.30 to 5.

ST. ALBAN'S, Brooke Street, Holborn (Ritualistic).—Vicar, Rev. R. A. J. Suckling. Services on Sundays: Holy Eucharist at 7 and 8; choral at 9.15; solemn, with sermon, at 11; matins, 10.30; Litany, baptisms, and churchings at 2.15; children's service and catechising, 3.15; sermon at 4.15; evensong and sermon at 7 p.m. Open daily, 6.45 to 9 p.m.

CONGREGATIONAL.

CITY TEMPLE, Holborn Viaduct. — Rev. Dr. Parker. Sunday morning at 11; evening at 7. Thursdays at 12.

UNION CHAPEL, Islington.—Rev. W. H. Harwood. Sunday morning at 11; evening, 6.30; Wednesday evening, 8.

BAPTIST.

METROPOLITAN TABERNACLE, Newington. Mr. Spurgeon's. —(Destroyed by fire—re-building.) Services in large new Hall under Tabernacle—Sunday, 11 and 6.30; Monday and Thursday 7.30.

WESTBOURNE PARK, Porchester Rd., Bayswater. —Rev. Dr. Clifford. Sundays 11 a.m. and 7 p.m. Wednesdays 8 p.m.

WESLEYAN.

WESLEY'S CHAPEL, CITY ROAD.—Sunday morning at 11; evening at 6.30; Tuesdays, 8; John Wesley's tomb in graveyard behind chapel.

GREAT QUEEN ST.— Rev. William Gooderidge. Sundays at 11; evening, 6.30; Wednesdays, 8 p.m.

ROMAN CATHOLIC.

THE ORATORY, Brompton.—Sundays: Low Masses, 6.30, 7, 8, 9, 10; High Mass and Sermon, 11; Vespers and Benediction, 3.30; Evening Service and Benediction, 7. Week-days: Low Masses, 6.30, 7, 7.30, 8, 8.30, 9, 10; Holidays: High Mass and Sermon, 11; Evening Service, except Saturday, 8; Thursdays and Saturdays, 4.30, Benediction. Great Day—St. Philip's, 26 May, High Mass 11: Solemn Vespers, 4.30; Benediction, 8.

WESTMINSTER CATHEDRAL— building. *Altogether, the Metropolitan Churches and Chapels are about 1,400 in number.*

HALLS FOR PUBLIC MEETINGS, CONCERTS, &c.

AGRICULTURAL HALL, Upper St., Islington, N. —Cattle Show in December; World's Fair in Dec. and Jan.; Dog Show in Feb.; Horse Shows in Feb. and March; Military Tournament in May; Dairy Show in Oct.; and many exhibitions throughout the year, including the following trades:—Furnishing, in Mar.; Motor Cars, in Apr.; Laundry, in Apr., May; Tramways and Light Railways, in June and July; Confectioners, in Sept.; Grocers, Sept.; Brewers, Oct.; Leather, in Nov.; Cycle, in Nov.; &c. *The Mohawk Minstrels* perform in the large Concert Hall every evening at 8, except in summer vacation, and during the Cattle Show.

ALBERT HALL, South Kensington.—Concerts, &c. R.A.H. Choral Society, Mr. Wm. Carter's Choir, Operatic, National, and Military Concerts, Masonic and Public Meetings. Concerts every Sunday at 3.30.

EGYPTIAN HALL, 171 Piccadilly.—Mr. Maskelyne's magical performances daily, 3 and 8. In same building, Dudley Gallery, occasional exhibitions of pictures, &c. Small Hall, billiard matches.

EXETER HALL, 372 Strand.—Headquarters of the Central Young Men's Christian Association. Chief place for "May Meetings."

FREEMASONS', 59 Great Queen Street. —Headquarters of Freemasonry in England. Public meetings, dinners, &c.

MEMORIAL HALL, Farringdon Street.—Headquarters of Congregational Denomination. Historically interesting as the site of the old Fleet Prison. Halls and public rooms let for meetings.

OLYMPIA, Addison Road, Kensington, W.

PRINCES' HALL, 191 Piccadilly.—Picture gallery concerts, meetings, dinners, &c.

QUEEN'S HALL, Langham Place, W.

STEINWAY HALL, Lower Seymour Street, W.

ST. GEORGE'S HALL, Langham Place, W.

ST. JAMES'S HALL, 28 Piccadilly.—Public meetings, &c. The "Richter" Concerts, Mon. and Sat. Popular, St. James's Hall Ballad and Sarasate Concerts, &c.; Small Hall, Moore & Burgess Minstrels.

ST. MARTIN'S HALL, Charing Cross Road.

PUBLIC AND PRIVATE BUILDINGS.

BREWERIES.—The great breweries of Messrs. Barclay & Perkins in the Borough; of Messrs. Whitbread in Chiswell Street; of Hanbury in Spitalfields, and some others, are well worthy of a visit, but special permission must be obtained.

BURLINGTON HOUSE, Piccadilly.—Royal; Antiquarian; Astronomical; Linnean; Chemical; Geological Societies; Royal Academy Exhibition.

BUCKINGHAM PALACE.—Not open to the public.

CEMETERIES.—*Abney Park*, Stoke Newington, N.; *Brompton* (formerly West London), Brompton Road; *Bunhill Fields*, City Road, N. (tombs of Bunyan, Defoe, &c.); *Chingford*, Chingford Mount, ESSEX: *City of London*, Little Ilford; *Colney Hatch*, New Southgate, N.; *Crystal Palace*, near Beckenham; *Dulwich*, S.E.; *Highgate*, N.; *Kensal Green*, W.; *Lee*, S.E.; *Norwood*, West Norwood, S.E.; *Nunhead*, S.E.; *Tower Hamlets*, Mile End Road, E.; *Woking*,and many others—all within easy access by omnibus, tramway, and railway.

CUSTOM HOUSE.—On the north bank of the Thames, east of London Bridge; Long-room, free. View of the river from the terrace.

DOCKS.—*St. Katharine's, London, East and West India, Commercial, Victoria*, &c.—All accessible by steamboat, tramway, or railway at about 4*d*. All free. Wine-tasting orders may be obtained through the leading wine-merchants.

GOVERNMENT OFFICES.—Magnificent new *Home Colonial, Foreign*, and *India* Offices, Whitehall and St. James's Park; *Admiralty, Horse Guards, Treasury, War Office*, &c., interior free, by order from heads of departments.

GUILDHALL, King Street, City.—Grand Civic Hall; Library and Reading Room, 10 a.m. to 9 p.m., Museum, Art Gallery, 10 to 5, April to Sept.; 10 to 4, Oct. to March. Special exhibitions held in summer months, which are open on Sundays 3 to 6 p.m. Admission free. *Librarian and Curator*, Charles Welch, F.S.A.

HOUSES OF PARLIAMENT, Westminster.—Open to visitors on Saturdays, unless either House is sitting, and on Easter and Whit Mondays and Tuesdays, from 10 to 4. Admission by tickets, obtainable near the Victoria Tower. House of Lords, on the above menti ned days, from 10 a.m. to 3.30 p.m. Admission to the Strangers' Gallery of the House of Commons, during session, by member's order.

INNS OF COURT.—These are the *Inner Temple* and *Middle Temple*, Fleet Street; *Gray's Inn*, Holborn; and *Lincoln's Inn*. They are governed by Benchers, under whose superintendence lie the admission and education of students for the Bar, the Calling of Barristers, and regulation of the profession. The following are Inns of Chancery, but have no functions:—*Clement's Inn*, Strand; *Clifford's Inn*, 187 Fleet Street; *New Inn*, 21 Wych Street; and *Furnival's Inn, Staple's Inn, Barnard's Inn*, Holborn.

KENSINGTON PALACE.— The birthplace of the Queen. Open to the public every day (except Wednesday) including Sunday, free.

LAMBETH PALACE.—The official residence of the Archbishop of Canterbury, on south bank of Thames, Lambeth.

LAMBETH PALACE LIBRARY.—On Mondays, Wednesdays, Thursdays, and Fridays, 10 to 4; Summer, 10 to 5, and forenoon of Tuesday. Modern works lent under certain conditions to clergy and residents in Lambeth, Southwark, and Westminster. Closed Easter week, Christmas, and for six weeks from 1st September.

LAW COURTS.—*Royal Courts of Justice*, Strand, *Central Criminal Court*, Old Bailey; *London County Sessions, Sessions House*, Clerkenwell Green; *Surrey Sessions*, Newington Causeway.

LONDON COUNTY COUNCIL.—Spring Grdns., S.W.

MANSION HOUSE, City.—The official residence of the Lord Mayor; the Egyptian Hall and ball-room are the chief attractions. Admission by order and a small fee.

MARKETS.—*Central Meat, Fish, and Poultry Markets*, Smithfield; *Leadenhall Market* (Poultry); *Billingsgate* (Fish), Thames Street; *Covent Garden* (Fruit, Flowers, &c.); *Farringdon, Borough*, and *Spitalfields* (Vegetables, &c.); *Cattle Market* (Mon. and Th.) *and Abattoirs*, Caledonian Road; *Foreign Cattle Depôt*, Deptford; *Hay Market*, Smithfield, Wed. and Sat.; and *Cumberland Market*, Regent's Park; *Shadwell* (Riverside Fish-market).

MONUMENTS.—ALBERT, South Kensington, finest in the country. LONDON, to commemorate Great Fire, near London Bridge; fine views of the City; admission, 3*d*. DUKE OF YORK'S, St. James's Park; NELSON'S, Trafalgar Square; GUARDS', Waterloo Place; CRIMEAN, Broad Sanctuary.

PEOPLE'S PALACE, Mile End, E.

POST OFFICE, St. Martin's-le-Grand.

PUBLIC RECORD OFFICE, Chancery Lane.—Contains a collection of the National Records since 1100. Search rooms open daily, with certain exceptions, from 10 to 4.30; Saturdays, 10 to 2.

ROYAL EXCHANGE, Cornhill.—Free. Statues of the Queen, Wellington, Peabody, Queen Elizabeth, Sir Thomas Gresham, and others; Frescoes by Leighton and others. 'Change, the busy time from 3 to 4 p.m.

ROYAL MINT.—Tower Hill, where gold, silver, and bronze are coined. Admission by order, application for which should be made some days in advance.

ST. JAMES'S PALACE, in Pall Mall.—*Levées* held here during the season. York House, residence of the Duke of York.

SOMERSET HOUSE, Strand.—Free. Now devoted to Inland Revenue Office, Exchequer and Audit, Registry of Wills, Births, Deaths, &c.

THE TIMES and the DAILY TELEGRAPH PRINTING OFFICES.—By special orders only.

TOWER.—Regalia, Armouries, &c. Admission 6*d*. to see the Armouries and the Beauchamp Tower; and 6*d*. to the Jewel House. Mondays and Saturdays free by tickets issued at the office at gateway. Not open on Sundays. *Keeper of Regalia*, General Sir Hugh H. Gough, VC, G.C.B.

WESTMINSTER HALL, adjacent to the Houses of Parliament.—For admission, see regulations as to Houses of Parliament. Contains Portrait Statues of kings. One of our largest and oldest buildings.

WHITEHALL, opposite Horse Guards.—Erected by Inigo Jones, intended for a banqueting-house. King Charles I. was beheaded here. Now occupied by the Royal United Service Institution.

ELECTRIC GENERATING STATION, Stowage Wharf, Deptford, by special order from London Electric Supply Corporation, Limited.

SUBURBAN RESORTS.

BURNHAM BEECHES. — Magnificent sylvan scenery, purchased by the City of London for the benefit of the public. During the summer months omnibus runs daily, Sundays included, from Slough, and cheap through tickets are issued from London and Suburban Stations by G.W.R.

CHESHUNT.—Temple Bar (at entrance to Theobald's Park), Cheshunt Great House, Cromwellian relics, &c.

DULWICH.—By Chatham and Dover Railway. Large Public School. Fine Gallery of paintings at the old College, daily, from 10 to 4, 5, or 6, according to season, free. Not open on Sunday.

ENFIELD LOCK.—By G. E. Railway. Royal Small Arms Factory. Visiting days, Monday and Thursday; other days by order.

EPPING FOREST, LOUGHTON, BUCKHURST HILL, CHINGFORD, HIGH BEECH, on Great Eastern Railway.—Fare, 1s. Beautiful forest scenery. A favourite resort for picnic parties, beanfeasts, &c.

GRAVESEND.—Access from London by steamboat (20 miles), and railway; fares 1s. to 1s. 6d. Windmill Hill, Springhead Gardens, Cobham Park, fine views of the Thames (here a mile wide), shipping, &c. Near are *Rosherville Gardens*, admission 6d. Opposite are *Tilbury Fort and Docks*.

GREENWICH.—Royal Naval College, commonly known as *Greenwich Hospital*. The Painted Hall, Nelson's Relics, &c., free on week-days from 10 till 4 or 6, according to time of year, and from 2 on Sundays. *Naval Museum*, interesting Collection of Models, &c., open daily, except Friday and Sunday, from 10 till 4 or 6. *Chapel* closed on Fridays and Sundays. *Observatory* only by permission of the Astronomer Royal. Blackheath and Shooter's Hill are close by.

HAMPTON COURT.—Built by Cardinal Wolsey, 15 miles from London; railway fare, 1s. 2½d.; 1s. 10d. return. Steamboats in summer, with beautiful view of river. Gardens and splendid collection of pictures, daily, except Friday, summer 10 to 6, winter 10 to 4; and every Sunday, summer 2 to 6, winter 2 to 4. Free.

RICHMOND.—The *Park*, and adjacent villages, &c., as Twickenham. *Pope's Villa*, Sheen, Mortlake, Teddington, Thames Ditton; boating, fishing, &c. By rail, boat, or omnibus. Fare, 1s.

RYE HOUSE, at Hoddesden, on the River Lea. Scene of the celebrated plot. Great resort for Londoners who include feasting and fishing in their day's enjoyment.

ST. ALBANS.—Abbey recently restored. Ruins of ancient City of Verulam, and St. Michael's Church, with tomb of Lord Bacon.

WALTHAM ABBEY.—By Great Eastern Railway. The Abbey, powder-mills, fishing, &c.

WEMBLEY PARK. (Tower in course of erection.)

WINDSOR.—22 miles from London; by Great Western and South Western Railways. The State Apartments of the Castle (shown during the absence of the Queen) are open gratuitously Mondays, Tuesdays, Thursdays, Fridays, and Saturdays, April 1 to Oct. 31, from 11 to 4; Nov. 1 to March 31 from 11 to 3, and on Wednesdays, from April 1 to October 31, from 11 to 4. Tickets obtained only at the Lord Chamberlain's Stores in the Castle Yard. Official Guide Books only to be had where tickets are issued. Round Tower closed during winter months. Private Apartments are not shown to the public.

WOOLWICH.—*Extensive Barracks for Royal Artillery, Army Service Corps, &c.* Common for military evolutions. *Rotunda* daily, Sundays excepted, free, from 1 April to 30 Sept., 10 to 5; 1 Oct. to 31 March, 10 to 4. *Royal Arsenal*, Royal Ordnance Factories, and Ordnance Store Dépôt, admission on Tuesdays and Thursdays, 10 to 12 a.m. and 2 to 4 p.m., by order obtained at War Office, Pall Mall, or from the Director-General of Ordnance Factories, Royal Arsenal, Woolwich, for British subjects only; foreigners must apply through their respective Embassies. South Eastern Dockyard Station for Barracks, Rotunda, &c., and the Arsenal Station for Royal Arsenal.

LONDON SWIMMING BATHS.

CHELSEA, 171 King's Road, S.W.
HAMPSTEAD, 175 Finchley Road, N.W.
KENSINGTON, Lancaster Road, W.
LAMBETH, 156 Westminster Bridge Road, S.E.
METROPOLITAN, Shepherdess Walk, City Rd., N.
PADDINGTON, Queen's Road, Bayswater.
POPLAR, East India Dock Road, E.
ROTHERHITHE, Lower Road, S.E.
ST. GEORGE'S, { 88 Buckingham Palace Road, (2nd. Cl.) Eccleston St. East, S.W.
ST. MARYLEBONE, 181 Marylebone Road, N.W.
ST. PANCRAS, { Whitfield St. Tottenham Ct. Rd. 70A King St. Camden Town.
ST. SAVIOUR'S, Lavington St., Southwark, S.E.
WENLOCK, 20 Wenlock Street, City Road, N.
WESTMINSTER, Great Smith St., S.W.

LONDON THEATRES AND MUSIC HALLS.

THEATRES.

ADELPHI, 411 Strand, W.C.
AVENUE, Northumberland Avenue, W.C.
BRITANNIA, Hoxton, N.
COMEDY, Panton Street, S.W.
COURT, Sloane Square, S.W.
COVENT GARDEN, Bow Street, W.C.
CRITERION, Piccadilly Circus, W.
DALY'S, Leicester Square, W.C.
DRURY LANE, Catherine Street, W.C.
DUKE OF YORK'S, St. Martin's Lane, W.C.
GAIETY, 345 Strand, W.C.
GARRICK, Charing Cross Road, W.C.
GLOBE, Newcastle Street, Strand, W.C.
GRAND, Upper Street, Islington, N.
HAYMARKET, Haymarket, S.W.
HER MAJESTY'S (TREE'S), Haymarket, S.W.
LYCEUM, Wellington Street, Strand, W.C.
LYRIC, Shaftesbury Avenue, W.
OLYMPIC, Wych St., W.C.
OPERA COMIQUE, 209 Strand, W.C.
PRINCE OF WALES'S, Coventry Street, W.
PRINCESS'S, 152 Oxford Street, W.
ROYALTY, Dean Street, Soho, W.
SAVOY, Victoria Embankment, W.C.
ST. JAMES'S, King Street, S.W.
SHAFTESBURY, Shaftesbury Avenue, W.
STANDARD, Bishopsgate, E.
STRAND, 168 Strand, W C.
SURREY, Blackfriars Road, S.E.
TERRY'S, 105 Strand, W.C.
VAUDEVILLE, 404 Strand, W.C.
WYNDHAM'S, Cranbourne Street, W.C.

MUSIC HALLS.

ALHAMBRA, Leicester Square, W.C.
CAMBRIDGE, 136 Commercial Street, E.
CANTERBURY, 143 Westminster Bridge R1.
COLLINS'S, Upper St., Islington
EMPIRE, Leicester Square, W.C.
METROPOLITAN, Edgware Road, W.
MIDDLESEX, Drury Lane, W.C.
OXFORD, 14 Oxford Street, W.
PALACE, Cambridge Circus, W.C.
PARAGON, Mile End Road, E.
PAVILION, LONDON, Piccadilly Circus, W.
ROYAL, 242 High Holborn, W.C.
SOUTH LONDON, London Road, S.E.
TIVOLI, 65 Strand, W.C.

THE Italics following the name of the Town denote the Market Days.

ABBREVIATIONS.—*b* butter, *c* cattle, *ch* cheese, *clo* cloth, *cy* cherry, *fl* flannel, *gen* general, *gr* grain, *gt mt* great market, *h* horse, *har* hardware, *hi* hiring, *la* lamb, *lea* leather, *p* pigs, *ped* pedlery, *pl* pleasure, *sh* sheep, *stk* stock, *w* wool.

Much trouble has been taken to make the List as complete and accurate as possible, but in no case will the Editor be held responsible for any loss or inconvenience arising from inaccuracy.

If the date falls on a Saturday or Sunday the fair is usually held on the following Monday.

BEDFORDSHIRE—
Ampthill—*Thurs.* May 4, Sept 29 pl hi, Nov 30 c
Bedford—*Sat.* Cattle markets every S, every M p, Apl 21 c pl, 1st T in Jy w, Oct 12 c pl
Biggleswade—*Wed and Sat.* Auction stk sales every W. Feb 14 h, East S c, Nov 8 c sh, 3rd F and S in Nov. pl
Dunstable—*Wed.* Cattle markets every W, Ash W c h sh, 2nd W in May, Aug and Nov h c sh, M aft 4th F in Sept pl
Elstow—May 15 h c pl, Nov 5 c h ch
Leighton Buzzard—*Tues.* Cattle markets every T, Feb 5, 2nd T in Apl, Whit T. 1st F in Jy w, Jy 26 cy, Oct 24 c, 1st T aft 10 Dec hi Xmas stk, 3rd T in Dec mt
Luton—*Mon* and *Sat.* c mt and stk sale every M, 3rd M in Apl c pl, 3rd M in Oct c
Markyate Street—4th F aft 1st M in Sept pl
Potton—*Sat.* 3rd M and T aft Jan 12 (Old New Year) gt h fair, Oct 22 c
Shefford—*Fri.* Oct 11 pl
Toddington—*Sat.* Apl 25, 1st W in Oct hi pl, Nov 2 h c sh pl, Dec 6 c
Woburn—*Fri.* Jan 1 c, Mar 23 c, Jy 13 chv, Oct 6 pl

BERKSHIRE—
Abingdon—*Mon.* Cattle & corn market every M except Bank holidays; 1st M in Lent h, May 6 h, Ju 20 h, Aug 5 w la, h, M bef and aft Oct 11 hi, Dec 11 h
Blewbury—Th aft Sept 29 pl.
Bracknell—Cattle market every Th; Apl 25, Aug 22, Oct 1 c and pl at each
Didcot—*Tues.* 1st T in Jy w
East Ilsley—*Mon.* Feb 7, 21, Mar 7, 21 c sh, Apr 4, 18, Easter Fair, May 2, 16, 30, Whit Fair, June 6, 20, July 4, Aug. fair, Aug, 1 and 29 W. aft Sep. 29, Oct 13 hi, W aft Oct 16 sh, W aft Nov. 12 sh
Farringdon—*Tues.* 1st T month c sh p, Feb 13, Whit Tu, T aft Oct 11 hi
Hungerford—*Wed.* Last T and W in Apl c sh, Ju 26 w, 3rd M in Aug, Nov 10 sh
Lambourn—*Fri.* May 12 hi, Oct 2 sh c pl, 4 Dec sh c h
Maidenhead—*Wed.*
Mortimer—Apl 27 h c, Nov 6 h c
Newbury—*Thurs.* Holy Th h c; July 5 pl ; Sept 4 & 5 pl. Th aft Oct 11 hi
Reading—*Mon, Wed.* and *Sat.* Cattle market every M fat stk, every S store stk Jan 31, Feb 1 and 2 c h ch, Apl 30, May 1 and 2 c h pl; Jy 24, 25 and 26 c h ch; Sept 20, 21 and 22 c h pl hops hi
Wallingford—Stk sales every alternate F commencing 1st F in Jan, Sept 29 hi
Wantage—*Wed.* Stk sale 1st and 3rd W in every month, 1st S in Mar and May, 8 aft Oct 11 hi
Windsor—*Wed* and *Sat.* Cattle markets every S c sh
Wokingham—*Tues.* Stk sales every T, Nov 2 pl

BUCKINGHAMSHIRE—
Amersham—*Tues.* Whit M c, Sept 19
Aylesbury—*Sat.* Cattle markets every

S, every W fat stk. 3rd S in Jan. S bef Palm Su, 2nd S in May; 3rd S in Ju; 2nd W in Jy w; 1st S in Aug rams. 4th S in Sept, 2nd S in Oct hi stk, and W in Dec (Xmas mt). Horses and store stock at each fair, rams at Aug fair, hi at Sept fair
Beaconsfield—*Wed.* Feb 13, May 10 pl
Brill—Whit M pl ; W aft Oct 11 c
Buckingham—*Sat.* Cattle markets every S c sh p ; every M calves ; 1st S in Sept sh, 1st S aft Oct 11 pl ; 3rd S in Ju w, S bef London Xmas mkt (fat stk fair)
Colnbrook—Apl 5 c ; Oct 16 c pl
Chesham—*Wed* and *Sat.* Auction sales each W. Apl 21, Jy 22, Sept 28 c sh
Fenny Stratford—*Tues.* Cattle markets alternate Th comm Jan 4
Great Marlow—*Sat.* Oct 29, h c sh pl
High Wycombe—*Fri.* M and T bef Sept 29 hi
Ivinghoe—*Sat.* May 6 pl, Oct 17 pl
Lavenden—*Tues.*
Newport Pagnell—*Wed & Sat.* Cattle markets every W c sh p ; Ju 22 pl
Olney—*Thurs.* Ju 29 pl
Penn—Sept 17 c pl
Princes Risborough—*Thurs.* May 6 c pl, Oct 21 pl
Slough—Auction sales each Tu fat and store stk
Stony Stratford—*Fri.* Auction sales 1st M in every month. 1st M in Aug pl ; F aft Oct 11 hi
Wendover—*Mon.* May 13 c pl, Oct 2 pl
Winslow—W corn, 1st and 3rd W each month c, 1st W bef and aft Oct 11 pl
Wooburn—May 4, Nov. 12, c pl
Wolverton—M c and corn, F genl

CAMBRIDGESHIRE—
Butt's Green (Cambridge)—*Wed & Sat.* c mt every M c sh p Midsummer fair; Ju 22 and 3 following days pl, Ju 24 h c, Sept 24 h c
Chatteris—*Fri.* Stock sale every F c pigs. Last F in Apl c h ; last F in Oct h
Ely—*Th.* Cattle market every Th c sh p ; last Th and days following in May h c sh p pl; last Th and days following in Oct h c sh p pl
Ickleton—Jy 22 and 23 h
Linton—Jy 16, and 17 pl
March—*Wed* and *Fri.* Cattle markets every W c p. 3rd W in Sept hi
Newmarket—*Tues.* Cattle market every T ; Whit T stk ; Nov 8 c
Reach—Rogation M h c wood
Royston—*Wed.* East W, Ash W. Whit W, 1st W in Jy stk; W aft Oct 11 ch stk
Soham—*Fri.* May 9 c h
Sturbridge—Sept 25 h onions hops wood
Thorney—*Tues.* Jy 1, Sept 21 c h
Whittlesea—*Fri.* Stock sale every F c p, Whit T p, Ju 13 h
Wisbech—*Thurs* and *Sat.* Cattle market every Th fat stk, every S lean stk and corn ; 1st and 2nd S in Mar pl, and Th in May h c, Jy 25 h, 1st Th in Aug c

CHESHIRE—
Altrincham—*Tues.* Apl 29, Aug 5 and 6, Nov 22 c h, Oct 26 c h sh p. Old Wakes Su on or aft Sept 18, and during the week, Agricultural Show Th in Wake week
Beeston Castle—Cattle auctions every M c sh p
Budworth—Feb 13, Oct 2, Apl 15, cows (nearly defunct)
Chester—*Wed* and *Sat.* Sales by auction—every T fat stk (commencing at 11 a.m.). Horse-fairs: Jan 4, Feb 1, Mar 1, 29, Apl 26, May 24, Ju 21, Jy 19, Aug 16, Sept 13, Oct 11, Nov 8, Dec 6. Cattle fairs are now held every Th. Cheese fairs; 3rd W in every M at 9 30 a.m. in the Public Market adjoining the Town Hall
Congleton—*Sat.* 1st W in Jan h c, Th bef Shrove T c h sh p ; May 12 c h sh p ; Jy 13 h c, 3rd W in Sept h c ; Nov 22 c h sh p. Cattle are shown every S, from 1st aft Shrove T until May 12
Crewe—Cattle market every M, fat and stores ; great bull sale Mar and sales of horses twice quarterly, dates not fixed. Xmas fat cattle Dec 6, pigs and calves Dec 10, great sp'l horse sales dates not fixed.
Frodsham—*Wed.* Cattle auction every alt T, last T in Apl, last Th in Oct fairs
Hooton—Cattle auctions every W, c sh p
Hyde—May 16 c, Nov 15 c
Knutsford—*Sat.* Apl 23, Whit M c May 1 pl, Nov 8 c
Lymm—Apl 5, Nov 5 c p, nearly defunct
Macclesfield—*Tues* and *Sat.* 3rd T in Feb, Mar 6, Apl 4 c, May 6, Ju 22. Jy 11, Aug 12, Sept 4, Oct 4, 3rd T in Oct, Nov 11 c h sh p hi, 3rd T in Dec h c. Auction sales every alternate M commencing 2nd M in Jan, 1st M in each mo. at 9.30 ch
Malpas—*Wed.* Cattle sales alternate T, commencing Jan19 c sh p Special sale T bef East
Middlewich—*Tues.* Last T in Feb, Apl, and Oct, c
Mottram—Apl 27, Oct 31 c p
Nantwich—*Sat.* S aft Feb 2, 1st Thurs in Apl, June, Sept and Dec c. sh p. Store pigs every S, Cheese fairs: 1st Th in every month except Jan
Northwich—*Fri.* Apl 10, Aug 2, Dec 6, c cows.
Over—*Wed.* 1st W aft May 12, 1st W aft Sept 21, c sh
Runcorn. Whit M pl
Sandbach—*Thurs.* East Th c sh, Th aft Sept 21 c, Dec. 28 c sh hi
Stockport—*Fri.* Jan 1, 1st F in Feb. Mar 4 and 25, May 1, 1st F in Ju, Jy 9, 1st F in Aug and Sept, Oct 23, 1st F in Dec h c p at each. Cattle and pig market every F (except fair days)
Tarporley—*Thurs.* May 1,
Tarvin—Apl 20 c p cabbage plants, Dec 2 c p nearly defunct
Tattenhall—*Fri.* May 18 c sh p, Nov 21, c sh p
Tattenhall Road—Stock sales at Aldersey Arms every alternate W c sh p calves
Wilmslow—3rd M in Apl, 3rd M in Oct c p at each

Winsford—*Sat.* May 8, Nov 25 cows
Wrenbury—Stk sales every alt M comm Jan 2

CORNWALL—

Blisland—M aft Sept 22
Bodmin—*Sat.* Cattle markets 1st M in every month except Feb, May and Jy, also Jan 25, Jy 8, Dec 6 T and W bef Whit Su, 1st day sh, 2nd c and pl
Boscastle—May 7, Aug 5, Nov 23
Bude—Sept 22
Callington—*Wed.* Cattle markets 1st W in every month c sh p genl
Camborne—*Sat. Wed.* Cattle market every M. Fairs, Mar 7, Whit T, Ju 29, Nov 11 h c pl at each
Camelford—*Fri.* 1st Fri aft Mar 10, c sh p May 26. July 17 and 28, Sept 6 c 1a, 1st F in Oct, and F in Nov
Canworthywater—June 3, Sept 28
Constantine—Apl 10, Ju 26, Oct 1
Copperhouse (Phillack)—Sept 15 pl, h and c occasionally shown
Doladon—Ju 24, Oct 1
East Looe—*Sat.* Feb 13, Jy 10, Sept 4, Oct 10
Endellion—3rd W in Sept
Falmouth—*Tues. Thurs.* and *Sat.* Cattle markets 8 each month h c sh p genl, Jy 29, Oct 30
Five Lanes—July 6, Sept 28
Fowey—*Sat.* Shrove T, May 1, Sept 10. c
Goldsithney—Apl 30, Aug 5 h pl
Grampound—*Sat.* Cattle markets 4th M each month h c sh p genl. Fairs have become absorbed by the cattle markets
Hallworthy—2nd M in Jy, Oct 5, Nov. 18
Hayle—Sept 17
Helland—Jan 8
Helston—*Sat.* Cattle mkts and & 4th W in every month h c sh genl, Jan 21, Mar 25, Ju 3, Jy 22, Sept 9, Oct 28, and 3rd and 3rd S bef Xmas
Kilkhampton—Tues bef Holy Thurs 1st Thurs in July, Aug 26
Landrake—1st W in Feb c, Ju 29, 1st W in Sept
Lanivet—Ju 17
Lanreath—Mar 19, May 2, Nov 18
Launceston—*Sat.* Cattle markets last W in every month c h sh la, Dec 21 (Giglet)
Lelant—Aug 15 h pl
Liskeard—*Sat.* Cattle markets and M each month excepting Oct gt mt; Oct 2 c
Little Petherwick—Ju 14
Lostwithiel—*Fri.* Cattle markets 2nd T in every month h c sh p genl. T aft Mid-Lent Su, May 6, Jy 10, Sept 4, Nov 13 c h sh
Ludgvan—Oct 8
Marazion—*Sat.* Sept 30 sh h pl c
Marham Church—*Sat.* Thurs bef Lady Day, Aug 12
Menheniot—Apl 23, Ju 11, Jy 28 c; 1st F in Dec
Millbrook—May 1, Sept 29
Mitchell—Oct 15 large stock fair
Mullion—May 4, Sept 28
Newlyn—Nov 8 c gr sh
Northill—Sept 8, Nov 4
Padstow—*Sat.* 1st Tu in May c
Pelynt—1st T in Feb. Ju 24
Penrhyn—*Sat.* Mar 9, May 12, Jy 7, Oct 8, Dec 21 c
Penzance—*Tues. Sat.* Cattle markets every Th c sh p Mar 28, May 23, Ju 13, Sept 5, Nov 28
Perranarworthal—Apl 23, Ju 7, Sept 27
Perrazabuloe—Mar 16
Phillack—June 18
Pillaton—Whit T h c sh
Polbathie (St Germans)—Cattle markets 3rd M in every month
Polperro—*Fri.* Jy 10

Poundscross—Ju 24, last M in Nov
Poundstock—1st M in Jy
Praz (Crowan)—Jy 15 h c
Quethrock—Jan 28
Redruth—*Fri.* East T h c, May 2 h c Whit M pl, Aug 3 h c, Oct 12 h c
Roche—Jy 19, Oct 11
Ruan Minor—Apl 6, Nov 11
St. Austell—*Fri. c.* Cattle markets 3rd M in every month h c sh p genl. Maundy Th. Whit Th, F aft Jy 26, F aft Oct 16, Dec 2, fairs nearly defunct
St. Blazey—Feb 2, Jy 4
St. Buryan—Mar 3 pl
St. Column Major—*Thurs.* and *Sat.* Cattle markets 3rd M in every month, except Mar and Nov, c sh p genl. Th aft Mid-Lent Su, Th aft Nov 12
St. Column Minor—Ju 9 c unless it falls on Sat, when it is held following Mon
St. Eval—1st T in Ju
St. Ewe—Apl 8, Oct 14
St. German—*Fri.* May 28 h c sh p
St. Issey—Ju 3, Oct 7
St. Ives—*Sat.* and *Wed.* Nov 30
St. Keverne—T aft Jan 6, 1st T in Mar, T nearest Ju 24, 1st T in Oct
St. Kew—1st Th in Apl
St. Lawrence—Aug 21 h c sh, Oct 29 and 30, 1st day sh, 2nd day c. If either date falls on Sat or Su the fair is carried forward to M and Tu
St. Mabyn—Feb. 14
St. Martin—Feb 13, and M in Nov
St. Mawgan in Pydar—Ju 24.
St. Mellion—Mar 26
St. Merryn—Ju 17
St. Mewan—Ju 3, Oct 21
St. Neot—3rd T in Apl, 2nd T in Nov
St. Stephen's—May 14, Sept 10
St. Stephen's by Saltash—Apl 1, Sept 2
St. Teath—Feb 25, Jy 7
St. Tudy—May 20, Sept 16
St. Veep—Ju 19
St. Winnon—2nd T in Jan, Feb 23
Saltash—*Sat.* Cattle markets 1st M and 3rd Tues in every month c sh p
South Petherwin—2nd T in May, and T in Oct
Stokeclimbsland—Last M in May, h c sh
Stratton—*Tues.* May 19, Nov. 8, Dec. 11 c sh
Summercourt—Sep. 25 c, large fair
Tintagel—M aft Oct 18, on M if 19
Tregonatha—May 6, Aug 1
Tregoney—*Sat.* Cattle markets 3rd M in Jan, Mar, Apl, Ju, Aug, Oct and Dec, Shrove T, May 3, Jy 25, Sept 2, Nov 6 c
Tresillian Bridge—M aft Feb 2, M bef Whit S
Trewen—May 1, Oct 12
Truro—Cattle markets every W c h sh p genl. Whit T and W h csh p
Tywardreath—Ju 10
Wadebridge—*Fri.* Cattle markets and T each month c h sh p. Mar 13, May 13, Ju 20, Oct 10, fairs nearly defunct
Wainhouse Corner—*Tues.* and *Sat.* M bef Mar 25, Ju 24, Jy 28, Sept 29, 1st M in Nov. stk
Week St. Mary—Jy 29, Sept 15, W bef Xmas Day stk
Wendron—May 20, Jy 29
West Looe—*Sat.* May 6 c
Withiel—Oct 5

CUMBERLAND—

Abbey Holme—*Wed.* T bef Whit Su, Oct 29 c h sh
Alston—*Sat.* 3rd S in Mar c &c, last Th in May c h sh. 8 on or bef Sept 27 rams; S on or bef Oct 18 c; 1st Th in Nov c h
Arlecdon Hill (Rowrah Station), Apl 24 c, 1st F in Ju c h, Sept 17 c h

Boonwood. Apl 25 and W in Aug 1a Oct 18 c
Bootle—*Sat.* Apl 27, c F bef Whit Sunday, Aug 3 c, Sept 24 c corn; F bef Nov 11 hi
Braithwaite—1st Th in Oct sh
Brampton—*Wed.* Apl 20 c sh; 2nd W aft Whit Su w c sh; 2nd W in Sept c sh; F bef 3rd S in Oct c h sh p, W on or aft Nov 11 hi. Sales of la and sh last W in Aug unless Carlisle fair falls on that day, in which case it is carried forward to the following W, 1st W in Oct
Broughton—Apl 27 c, Wbit W hi, Aug 1 c sh. Oct 6 hi c, W on or aft Nov 11 hi, Nov 24 c sh w
Carlisle—*Wed.* and *Sat.* Cattle markets every M fat stk ; every S h mt and lean stk. Large sales of lambs and sheep commence on Aug. 21 and are held every Saturday until end of Oct. Horse sale 1st Th in each month except Oct, when held on 2nd Th. Horse fairs: 8 bef Feb 13 and 3 following Sats, Aug 26, Sept 19. Cattle fairs Apl 22, 8 bef Whit Su hi genl. Aug 26, Sept 19, last 3 S in Oct. 2 S nearest Nov. 11 hi. East Cumberland Agricultural Show 1st Thurs in July. Large c and sh sales are held every fair day. Large special sales of care held weekly at both mts from last weeks in Sept till middle of Nov Large sales of colts and h are held in the weeks before Appleby June and Brough Hill Sept fairs. If the c fairs fall on Su or M, held on previous S.
Cockermouth—*Mon.* and *Sat.* Stock sales every M, c sh p, Feb 18, h fair: W after Mar 12 c sh p, and every alternate W for 8 W's c ; Whit M, hi ; Aug 2, hi; last F in Aug and Sept c sh 1a; and W in Oct h, c, sh ; Nov 11 if M, hi: if it falls on Tu or W it will be held M before, if it falls later in the week it will be held on following M. M after Apl 5, show of entire horses, Feb 2 & Aug 2, if M hi (if not M, M after). Horse fairs 1st 8 each month except Jan, Feb and Oct, Feb 17, Oct 6. Special Sales:—Mar 23 young bulls, Apl 18, May 2, 16, & 28 c sh; Aug 24 la, Sept 28 rams, Oct 11 c sh ; on or about Oct 26 young bulls, Nov 13 c sh, Dec 10 Xmas show.
Croglin (Lazonby)—Aug 18 h c sh pl
Egremont—*Sat.* S bef Whit Su hi ; S nearest or on Nov 11 hi, 3rd S in Feb c, April 24 c, 3rd F in May c sh, Sept 18 (Crab fair sports) c sh. When the 24th or 18th falls on Sun the fair is held on the preceding Sat. Feb and Apl fairs nearly defunct
Hesket New Market (Penrith or Dalston Stations)—1st F in May and every alt F till Whit S c sh, last Th in Aug c sh, and Th in Oct c sh
Ireby—*Thurs.* F nearest Apl 20 c sh, 1st F in Oct c h sh and Agricultural Show
Keswick—*Sat.* 1st S in Jan hi ; Th aft April 12 c sh; 3 alt Th's in May aft the 1st ; S bef Whit Su hi ; 1st S in Oct c sh ; S aft Oct 29 c h ; S nearest to Nov 11 hi
Kirk Oswald—*Thurs.* Th bef Whit Su, Aug 5 c
Lazonby—Cattle auctions alt M's, com 2nd M in Jan
Longtown—*Thurs.* 3rd Th in June W. Th after Xmas day h. If Xmas day happens on a Th the fair is held on the next Th.
Maryport. F bef Whit Su hi, F on or bef Nov 11 hi
Netherwasdale. Sept 7 sh
Penrith—*Tues.* Fat stock sales every M, Feb 21 and 3 T's following h. Apl 23 c, sh. Apl 24 c sh and young bulls. If 23 is S, the fair is held on

23 and 25. If 23 is Su, it is held on 24 and 25, Whit T c hi, and 6 alternate T's aft c, and T aft Whit T pl, Martinmas T c hi, and every T until Xmas c. Special sales of store c and sh every T from the middle of Sept to Martinmas.

Penruddock. 8 bef the 1st Th in Sept c sh

Ravenglass—*Wed.* May 6, Ju 9 c sh; Aug. 5 c sh; Oct 3 sh

Red Dial—Aug 1 sh la

Renwick—Th on or bef Sept 26 c h sh p

Rosley Hill—Apl 21, Whit M and every alternate M till Aug 1; Sept 30 sh la ; 3rd M in Oct c

Threlkeld—1st Th in Sept c sh w. Principally for Herdwick and Half-bred sh and la

Uldale—Fair for sh and la in Aug, the date of which is fixed about three weeks previous

Whitehaven—*Thurs* and *Sat.* Cattle sales every Th hi Whitsuntide and Martinmas

Wigton—*Tues.* Horse sale about Feb 19, Feb 20 h, T after Whit Su hi pl; Whit T hi, T on or aft Nov 1, hi. Fat stk sales every T. Shorthorn cattle sales in Apl and Oct.

Workington—*Wed & Sat.* Stock sales every W c sh p, special sales and W in Apl c sh, 1st W in May c sh, last W in Aug la and store sh, and every alternate W to Nov. Autumn cattle sales 1st W in Oct and every W until 2nd W in Nov.

DERBYSHIRE—
Alfreton—*Mon.* Jy 31 h, Oct 7 ch, Nov. 24 hi

Ashbourne—*Sat.* Cattle markets alternate Th's fat and store stock c h sh, commencing 1st Thurs. in January ; 8 aft Jan 6 (New Market), Feb 12 h, Feb 13 c sh, May 21 c h sh, Aug 15 h, Aug 16 c sh, Oct 19 h, Oct 20 c sh, Nov 29 c h sh. Cheese fairs and T in Mar, 1st T in Sept, T bef Nov. 11. Should any of the dates fall on a Su the fair is held on the following day, except on Nov 29, which in such case is held the day previous. 8 aft Xmas day pl. St aft Aug 16 wakes

Ashover—Apl 25 c, Oct 15 hi.

Bakewell—*Fri.* Cattle markets every M c s'h p. East M, Whit M, M bef or on Aug 26 c sh h p ch, M aft Oct 10, M aft Nov 11

Belper—Th and F nearest Oct 30 h c ch p

Bolsover—Last F in Apl, 1st F in Oct ch p

Buxton—*Sat.* M bef the Th preceding Old Candlemas Day h c sh, Apl 1, May 2, M bef and W in Sept, Oct 28 c

Castleton—3rd W in Mar, Apl 21, 1st W in Oct, 3rd W in Nov c sh

Chapel-en-le-Frith—*Thurs.* Cattle markets 1st and 3rd Th in every month, Jy 7 w pl

Chesterfield—*Sat.* Cattle markets every S. Jan 27, Feb 28, 1st S in Apl, May 4, Jy 5, Sept 25 c h, Nov 25

Derby—*Tues* and *Fri.* Cattle markets, fat stock every T, lean stock every F, F in East week c ped pl, F in Whit week c ped pl. Cheese fairs, 1st T in Feb, Apl, Ju, Aug, Oct, and Dec

Dronfield—*Thurs.* Jan 10, W aft Mar 12 Apl 25 c, Jy 15, Th aft Oct 12, Nov 3

Duffield—*Thurs.* Th aft Jan 1, Mar 1

Glossop—*Sat.* May 6 c pl, 1st W on or aft Oct 10 c pl. New wakes: 1st Su on or aft Aug 1 and 3 following days. Old wakes: 1st Su aft Sept 12 and three following days.

Hathersage (Sheffield)—F aft Oct 11. New Cattle market on W.

Hayfield—May 12 c pl, Oct 10 c. Old wakes: Su aft Sept 19 and 6 following days

Higham—1st W after Jan 1 c

Kirk Ireton—2nd W in Apl h c, W aft Oct 11 h c

Matlock—*Mon.* and *Sat.* Cattle markets alt Th c sh p. Feb 25, Apl 2, May 9, Oct 24

Measham—M nearest Nov 5 pl

Newhaven—Oct 30 c

Pleaseley—May 6, Oct 29 c h sh

Ripley—*Sat.* East W, Oct 23 c

Tideswell—*Wed.* May 15, last W in Jy, and W in Sept, Oct 29 c ch

Whaley Bridge—Apl 26 c, Oct 26 c

Wirksworth—*Tues.* Shrove T, T nearest May 12, East T, T nearest Sept 8, 3rd T in Nov hi c ped

DEVONSHIRE—
Ashburton—*Sat.* Cattle markets 3rd S in every month c sh implements &c. ; Fairs: 1st Th in Mar and Ju, and Th in Aug & Nov c sh

Ashreigney—Feb 6

Axminster—Cattle markets every alternate Th c, sh p, commencing 2nd Th in Jan, T aft Apl 25. W aft Oct 10 hi and c

Bampton—*Sat.* Last Th in Oct c h sh. Great fair for Exmoor ponies.

Barnstaple—*Fri* and *Tues.* c mt every F, except Good F & Xmas day, then day previous. Fair; W, Th, and F c sh h pl, bef Sept 20 h c sh. Great markets ; F bef 3rd S in month c sh, F bef Apl 31, F bef last S in Jy, and F in Dec.

Bideford—*Tues.* Cattle markets every Thurs.

Bishop's Nympton—W bef Oct 25

Blackawton—Cattle mkt 4th T. in every month

Blackmoor Gate—Auction sales 3rd W every month'

Bow—*Thurs.* Stock Sales at Railway Station. 3rd M in Jan, Mar, May, Jy, Sept, and Nov. Fair and Tues in Apl h c sh.

Bradninch—*Thurs.*

Bradworthy—1st Mon after June 9, Sept 9. Great mkts 1st M in Feb, June and Nov c s h

Bratton-Fleming—*Aug* 19 c sh. Stk sales in spring and autumn

Brent—*Sat.* Last T in Apl, last T in Sept. Great mts Feb 26, Aug. 27

Bridestowe—1st W in Ju, last M in Jy

Broadclyst—Live Stk sale, 3rd M in every month

Broadhembury—2nd M in Dec

Brushford—1st T in every month c

Buckfastleigh — *Sat.* 3rd Th in Ju, 2nd Th in Sept pl

Buckland Mona—Ju 10

Budleigh East—Apl 16

Budleigh (Salter)—Whit Tues. Nearly defunct.

Burlescombe—Cattle mkts last M in every month

Burrington—June 10

Chagford—*Thurs.* Last Th. in Mar, 1st Th. in May, Sept and Oct c sh

Chapmanswell—Apl 17, Jy 22

Chawleigh—May 6, Oct 29, Dec 11

Chittlehampton—Jy 2

Chudleigh—*Sat.* East T c sh

Chumleigh—*Wed.* Mch 14, East W, last W. in Jy

Churchingford—Jan 25 h, Jan 26 c, last F in Apl

Coleford—Jy 15

Colyford—*Wed.* W aft Mar 11, May 8

Colyton—*Thurs.* 3rd T in Apl, and T in Oct

Copplestown—Cattle mkts, Jan 28, Mar 4, May 6, Jy 1, Oct 7, Dec 9

Crediton—*Sat.* Cattle mkts 3rd Th in Jan, Feb, Mar, May, Ju, Jy, Sept, Oct, and Nov. Xmas mkt 1st Th in Dec. Sat bef last W in Apl gt c mt. Aug 22nd (if that date is T, W, or Th ; if not following T) c pl

Crediton (Yeoford Station) — Cattle mkts 2nd M in Jan, Apl and Oct, also 1st M in Ju

Cullompton — *Sat.* Cattle markets every W h c sh p. 1st W in May and Nov c

Culmstock—3rd M in May c

Dalwood—*Wed.* Aug 17

Dartmouth—Cattle mkt 2nd T in every month

Dawlish—Cattle sales 3rd M in every month

Denbury—Sept 19 pl

Dodbrook—Cattle mt. 3rd W in every month c sh, Apl 3

Dolton—Stock sales 2nd week in Feb and 3rd week in Apl

Down St. Mary—2nd M in Ju

Drewsteignton—Feb 8

Dunsford—M aft Sept 8 c

Eggesford—Cattle mkts 2nd W in every month c pl p

Exeter—*Tues, Fri* and *Sat.* Cattle markets every F c h sh p. 2nd F in every month gt mt for c h sh p ; 2nd W in Feb c genl ; 1st Th in May h ; 3rd W in May c gnl, 3rd W in Jy c genl ; 1st Th in Oct h, 2nd W in Dec c genl

Exmouth—*Tues* and *Sat.* Apl 28 pl, Oct 28 pl. Cattle markets 2nd and last T in each mont'1

Galpton (Dartmouth) — Cattle Auctions 4th M in every month c sh p

Georgenympton—1st W in Jy

Hartland—*Sat.* 2nd S in Mar, Easter W, Sept 25 c se ; Sept 26 pl

Hatherleigh – *Tues.* 3rd T in May, 4th T in Ju, Sept. 4, Nov 8 or T aft, c genl

Hemyock (Collompton) — Cattle mkt 3rd M in every month

High Bickington—M aft May 14 c sale

Highbridleigh—Good F pl

Holsworthy — *Wed* and *Sat.* — Cattle markets 3rd W in every month except Jy, c sh p. Mar 13, Apl 17, Jy 9, 10 & 11, c, Oct 16. Gt mkts Feb 6, Nov 6

Honiton—*Sat.* Cattle mkt every S, 2nd S in Apl gt mt, W aft Jy 19 c, Th aft Jy 19 h, 3rd S in Oct 18 gt mt

Ilfracombe—*Sat.* (Principal) and *W*
Ivy Bridge—Cattle markets 3rd M in every month c sh p genl

Kilmington—1st W in Sept

Kingsbridge—*Sat.* Cattle mkt 3rd W in every month. Fair 1st Th after Jy 20. If 20th is Th fair is held on that date h

King's Nympton—Jy 29

Kingsteignton—Whit T pl and h show

Lapford—Jy 15

Lew Down—3rd W in Apl

Lifton—Feb 12, 1st T in Ju

Lydford—4th T in Jy

Lynton—Fair (Aug 16) obsolete. Stk sales on fair day

Milton Abbott—Jy 24 c rh

Modbury—*Thurs* and *Sat.* Cattle mkt 2nd M in every month except May. Fair May 4 except it falls on F, S or Su, when it is fixed by the Portreeve, h c sh p, May 7 h

Morchard Bishop—Stock sale 3rd W in Apl. Fair 1st M after Sept 8 c pl

Morchard Road Station—Stock sale M before and W in Jul

Morebath—M aft Aug 24

Morton Hampstead — *Sat.* Cattle markets 4th T in every month c h sh p genl

Newton Abbot — *Wed.* Cattle mts every W. W bef Midsummer day h c pl. W aft Sept 12 pl

Newton Poppletord—3rd W in Apl, W on or aft Oct 17

Newton St. Agnes—M bef Ju 24

North Bovey—M aft Ju 24

North Molton—W ait May 12, last W in Oct, c h sh

North Tawton—3rd T in Apl, 2nd T in Oct, 1st T in Dec, gt c mt last Th in Feb, Ju, and Aug

Norton—Mar 10, Oct 10

Okehampton—*Sat.* Cattle market every 8. Gt mkts 1st 8 in every month. Fair and Th after Mar 11 c pl

Otterton—*Thurs.* Cattle market

Ottery St. Mary—*Thurs.* 3rd Tu in every month, last T in Mar, 3rd T in Sept

Parracombe—Aug 18 c.

Plymouth—*Tues, Thurs, and Sat.* Cattle market every M fat stk, every Th stores. 1st M in Apl & Nov.

Plympton—*Sat.* Cattle market 1st M in every month c sh p.

Prince Town—*Sat.* 1st Th in Sept

Sampford Courtney—1st T in Jy pl

Sampford Peverell—M bef last W in Apl h c sh.

Sandford—M aft Jy 26 c pl.

Sherwell—*Fair*, Tu bef Sep 20 c sh

Sheepwash—*Fri.* Mar 28, Th bef Oct 10

Shobrooke—3rd M in Jy

Sidbury—3rd W in Sept c pl

Sidmouth—*Tues* and *Sat.* East M, 3rd M in Sept pl

Silverton—2nd Th in Feb, 1st Th in Jy nearly defunct.

South Brent—Cattle market last T in Feb, Jy, & Nov. *Fairs* last T in Apl & Sept h c s

South Molton—*Sat.* Cattle mkts 1st Th in every month, 3rd W in Ju, W aft Aug 25 c

South Zeal (South Tawton)—Th aft St. Thomas-a-Becket day in July c, two following days la

Sutcombe—Last Th in Ju

Tavistock—*Tues* and *Fri.* Cattle markets 2nd W in every month c h sh p, and W in Oct h c pl, large h fair goose and Jy previous

Tedburn—Last M in Sept

Thorncombe—Mar. Apl 16

Thorverton—Last M in Feb sh, M aft Jy 18 la

Tiverton—*Tues* and *Sat.* Cattle markets and T in every month h c sh p genl. 1st Th in Ju stk. 1st Th in Oct stk w. Great mkts, 2nd & last T in every month

Torquay—*Tues* and *Fr.* East M pl

Torrington—*Sat.* 3rd S in Mar gt mt. 1st Th in May c. Agricultural Show pl, 1st Th Oct c pl. Cattle markets last S in every month

Totnes—*Sat.* Cattle markets 1st & 3rd T in every month c sh p. *Fairs*, May 12, Oct 28

Two Bridges—3rd M in Aug

Uffculme—*Wed.* Great markets 1st M in Mar, Ju, Sept, and Dec h c sh p

Uppottery—T bef Lady Day pl, Oct 24 pl

West Country Inn (Hartland)—1st W in Aug c, and M in Oct c

Whimple—M bef Sept 29 pl

Witheridge—Last Th but one in Apl, Th aft Ju 4, Th aft Sept 21, 1st Th in Nov

Wo·da Bay—Auction sales 1st W in every month

Woolardisworthy—Trinity M, 1st W in Oct

Yealmpton—Cattle markets 4th W in each month c p genl, 4th W in May

Yeoford—Cattle mts 3rd Th in every month

DORSETSHIRE—

Beaminster—*Thurs.* Sept 19 c h stk

Blandford—*Sat.* Mar 7 pl, 10, Jy 7 Aug 4, Sept 1 h c sh, 9 pl, Oct 13 h c sh, Nov 8 pl, 10 h c sh

Bridport—*Wed.* and *Sat.* Apl 6 c h, Oct 10 h ch

Broadwinsor—Trin M, p

Cerne Abbas—*Wed.* Oct 2 c h p

Corfe Castle—*Thurs.* May 12 pl, Oct 30 ch p

Cranbourne—Aug 24, Dec 6 c

Dorchester—*Wed* and *Sat.* Feb 14 c h, Jy 6 c sh h, Aug 6 c sh h, last Th in Sept sh, Oct 25 c sh h. If any of the dates happen on Su, the fair is held on previous day c p

Evershot—*Sat.* May 12 (if S then M aft) c p

Farnham—Aug 21 ch

Gillingham—*Alternate Mon.* Oct 19 c h ssh

Lambert Castle—3rd W and Th in Ju c, 2nd W in Sept p

Leigh—Mar 25, May 1 c, Sept 3

Lyme—*Tues* and *Fri.* 1st T aft Feb 2, 1st T aft Sept 29

Maiden Newton—2nd Th in Mar, May c

Martinstown—Nov 22 sh, Nov 23 c h

Milborne St. Andrew—Nov 30 c ch

Poole—*Thurs.* May 1, Nov 1

Portland—Nov 5 h sh stk

Shaftesbury—*Sat.* 8 bef Palm Su, last 8 in Aug c &c. Nov 23 c sh

Sherborne—*Thurs.* Jy 26, M aft Oct 10 c sh h p w

Shroton—Sept 25 & 26

Stalbridge—*Tues.* Cattle mt alternate Th, May 6, Sept 4 c h

Sturminster—Cat mkts alternate M, May 12, Oct 24 c

Sydling—Dec 6 p

Thorncombe—East T, Oct 20 c h

Toller Down—May 18, Sept 7 c h sh

Verwood—Dec 8

Wareham—*Tues.* 3rd T in Apl, and T in Sept c p sh

West Down—Cattle fair in Sept, date advertised fortnight bef

Wimborne—*Fri.* No fairs

Woodbury Hill—Sept 21 sh pony

Woodlands—Jy 5 pl

Wool—May 14

Yetminster—Apl 27, T aft Oct 5

DURHAM—

Barnard Castle—*Wed.* Cattle markets and sales every alternate W c sh p; East W h c; Aug 1 h c sh W bef Sept 30 h c sh; 1st and 2nd W bef May 13 hi; 1st and 2nd W bef Nov 23 hi

Bents, Weardale—*Sat.* Last F in Sept.

Bishop Auckland—*Thurs.* Two Th's preceding May term day and Martinmas hi

Chester-le-Street—Stock sales alternate M's commencing 1st M in Jan c sh p. Horse sale 1st W in Oct. Sp'l store stock sales: Mch 22, Apl 13, May 19, June 7, July 3, Aug 10, 24, Sept 9, 19, 25, Oct. 13, 23, Nov 6.

Darlington—Mon and Fri. Cattle markets every M c sh p; 1st M in Mar h c genl; East M h c genl; two M's preceding Old May Day (May 13) hi, Whit M h c genl; 2nd M after Whit M h c genl; Nov 10 h c genl; 2 M's preceding Old Martinmas Day (Nov 23) hi; latter fair also for h c genl; and M's ft. Old Martinmas Day h c genl. When Xmas Day, New Year's Day, or any genl Thanksgiving day shall fall on midday, the respective markets shall be held on the preceding Friday; and when on Friday or Saturday, on the preceding day. If on Good Friday on the day following

Durham—*Sat.* Last F in Mar b c, and 4 previous days h; F bef or on May 13 c sh; Whit Th sh; F bef or on Sept 15 c sh la; F bef or on Nov 23 c sh. Hiring fairs: 2 S's before May 13, if May 13 is S then May 6 and 13; 2 S's bef Nov 23; if Nov 23 is S then Nov 16 and 23

Ferryhill—Stock sales alternate M's commencing 1st M in Jan c sh p

Gateshead (Red Heugh Bridge)—Sales of fat stock every M; dairy cows every Fri; sp'l store stk sales 1st Fri ea month.

Hartlepool—*Sat.* May 14, Aug 21, Oct 9, Nov 27

Houghton-le-Spring—Fri. Oct 8 and 9

Middleton-in-Teesdale—*Sat.* 3rd Th in Apl and Sept

Rookhope—F bef Aug 24

St. John's Ch-pel—3rd W in Apl. and W in Sept fair and hi, 2nd S in May, 2nd S in Nov

Sedgefield—*Fri.* 1st F in Apl and Oct

Shotley Bridge—Th bef East, and M bef May 13 and Nov 11, F nearest Oct 18

South Shields—*Sat & Mon.* W bef and aft May 1, and bef and after Nov 11

Stanhope—*Fri.* W bef East, 2nd F in Sept, Dec 21

Stockton—*Wed* and *Sat.* Cattle mts and stk sales every W. Hirings:—2 clear W bef May 14; 2 clear W bef May 14 and Nov 23

Sunderland—*Sat.* May 11 and 12, Oct 10 and 11, or near those dates

Westgate, Wearsdale—Last Th in Feb, Th bef Newcastle Oct fair

Wolsingham—*Tues.* May 12, St. Matthew's Day (Sept 21) ped, T bef Mar 1 and 31, and bef May 12, Sept 15, Oct 2 and 29, Nov 23

ESSEX—

Billericay—*Tues.* Aug 2 and 3 h, Oct 7 and 8 c

Braintree—*Wed.* cattle markets every W c h sh la May 8 and 9 pl, Oct 2, 3, and 4 c h sh hops pl

Brentwood—Oct 15 and 16 c h

Chelmsford—*Fri.* May 12, Nov 12 c

Chipping Ongar—*Sat.* Stock sales alt T

Coggeshall—*Thurs.* Whit Tu c

Colchester—*Sat.* Oct 20 ch

Dedham—East T

Epping—*Fri.* Fair-Lop pl fair, held in Jy, also Wanstead Flats pl fair 1st M in Aug. Oct 12 hi, Nov 13 and 14 c h sh

Fingrinhoe—East M

Great Bardfield—*Mon.* Ju 22 h c pl

Great Chesterford—1st F in Jy pl

Great Dunmow—*Tues.* Stk sales T

Halstead—*Tues.* May 6, Oct 29 c

Harlow—Nov : 8 c h 29 pl

Harwich—*Tues* and *Fri.* May 1, Oct 18 pl

Hatfield Peveril—Whit T

Ingatestone—Dec 1 c

Maldon—*Thurs.* 1st Th in May, and Th in Sept c

Manningtree—Whit T

Rochford—*Thurs.* Stk sales T h c sh p. Special sale in Oct

Romford—*Wed.* Jy 24 c

Saffron Walden—*Sat.* 8 bef Mid Lent and M after c h pl, Nov 1, 2 c pl, stk sale T

Stanstead Montfichet—May 1 c

Stebbing—Jy 10 c h sh

Thaxted—May 28 c, 29 pl, Aug 10 stk pl

Thorpe—Sept 29 pl

Tilbury (Chadwell St. Mary)—Cattle mkt T, stk sales alt M c sh p

Waltham Abbey—*Tues.* May 14 c, Sept 25 c hi

Witham—*Tues.* M bef Whit Su, Sept 14

Writtle—Whit M

GLOUCESTERSHIRE—

Andoversford—Stk sales 1 & 3 F each mo c sh p Gt. ewe sale Sept 17 or near that date

Berkeley—*Wed.* 1st W in every mo ch, May 14 pl, 1st W in Dec pl

Berkeley Road—Stk sales last W each mo c sh p

Birdlip—May 8 c

Bisley—*Thurs.* May 4, Nov 12 pl

Blakeney—*Wed.* May 12, Nov 12c sh p

Bridge Yate—Stk sales last W each month c sh p

Bourton-on-the-Water—Stk sales la M each month except Sept, when it is held on the last Tues c sh p

Bristol—*Thurs.* Cattle Markets every Th c h sh p; 1st Th in Mar h c, and W in Mar lea, day following w, 1st Th in Sept h c, and W in Sept lea w, day following w, Th bef Jy 25 c colts

Charfield—3rd W each month g8 mt stk sales 1st & 3rd W each month c sh

Cheltenham—*Thurs* and *Sat.* Auc sale ev alt Th, com Jan 12, and Th in Apl, Holy Th, Aug 5, Th bef and aft Oct 11, 3rd Th in Dec prize show. Horse sales every altnate Thurs

Chipping Camden—Cattle Mkts last W in every month

Chipping Sodbury—Stk mkts 1st & 3rd Tu each mo, c sh p, F bef Mar 25 pl, Sep 29 pl

Cinderford—Ju 15, Oct 24 c pl

Cirencester—*M & Sat.* 1st M in May c sh p; 1st T in Aug sh; 1st M in Sept sh ; M bef and after Oct 11 pl; 1st M in Nov c; 1st and 3rd M each month g8 mt

Coleford—*Fri.* Ju 20 pl, Dec 5 c pl

Durnley—*Thurs.* May 6, Dec 4 pl

Fairford—*Thurs.* Cattle mkt 2nd T each mo

Frampton—3rd T in Feb, 3rd T in Sept

Gloucester—*Wed* and *Sat.* Cattle auctions every M c sh p. Store stk S. Great markets —W bef Candlemas day and W bef St.Thomas' day. Cheese markets:—3rd M in every month. Wool fairs :—3rd M in Feb, June and Sept. Stock fairs :—1st S in Apl h c sh. 1st S in Jy h c sh, last S in Nov h c sh.—Sept 28 (Barton fair) pl. Hiring fairs:—1st and 2nd M in Oct, last s in Nov

Hampton—Trin M, Oct 27

Honeybourne—1st W in every month c

Iron Acton—Apl 25, Sept 13 h c pl

Lechlade—*Fri.* Cattle mkts last T in every month c sh p

Little Dean—Whit M, Nov 26 c

Lydney—*Wed.* May 4, Ju 25, w pl Nov 8 c. Gt mkt 1st each month

Marshfield—*Tues.* May 24 c ; Oct 24 c ch sh

Minchinhampton—Oct 27 h c sh

Mitcheldean—*Tues* and *Fri.* Oct 10 c hi

Moreton-in-Marsh—*Tues.* 2nd T in each month c

Nailsworth—last T in each month g8 mt

Newent—*Fri.* F aft Sept 19 onions and pl

Newnham—*Fri.* Ju 11, Oct 18 c pl

Northleach—*Wed.* W bef Oc 11 hi, W aft Oct 11 hi, May 12, Oct 24

Painswick—*Tues.* Whit T pl Sept 12 c

Stonehouse—*Wed.* May 1 Oct 11, c pl

Stroud—*Fri.* May 10, Aug 21 c p

Stow-on-the-Wold—*Thurs.* May 12, Oct 24 h c ch

Tetbury—*Wed.* and W in each month Ash W pl W bef Apl 4 pl, Jy 22 hl, W bef and aft Old Michaelmas Day pl

Tewkesbury—*Wed* and *Sat.* Oct 10

Thornbury—*Sat.* 2nd W each month c

Westerleigh—Sept 19 pl

Winchcombe—*Sat.* Last S in Mar h, May 6 c, Jy 28 h, S bef & aft Oct 11 hi

Wooton-under-Edge—*Fri.* T bef Mar 25, Sept 25 pl

Yate—Stock sales 2nd and 4th T c sh p

HAMPSHIRE—

Alresford—*Thurs.* Last Th in Jy sh la, Th aft Oct 11 pl

Alton—*Tues.* S bef May 1 sh pl, Jy 12 la, Sept 29 c pl

Andover—*Sat.* Nov 17 sh

Appleshaw—Nov 4 c

Basingstoke—*Wed* and *Sat.* Auc sales ev W c sh p. Horse sales 1st W iu ev month. Last T Whit W last Th in May ch Sep 1 2 3 c sh, Oct 11 hi. last Th in Nov Ch

Beaulieu—*Tues.* Apl 15, Sept 4

Blackwater—Nov 8 and 9 c h

Brading—May 12, Oct 2

Eling—July 5

Fair Oak—June 9 pl

Fareham—*Alt Mon.* Ju 30 pl

Giles Hill—Sept 12 ch h

Gosport—*Tues, Thurs,* and *Sat.* May 4, Oct 10 pl

Hartley Row—Dec 4 c h

Havant—*Tues.* c sh p

Kingsclere—*Tues.* 2nd T in Oct pl

Lyndhurst—Aug 9, Ponies

Newport—*Sat.* Stock alt W and every Sat

Odiham—*Tues.* Mid-Lent Sat pl

Overton—*Mon.* Jy 18 sh

Petersfield—*Wed.* Cattle Mkt alternate W comm Jan 3, Oct 6 c

Ringwood—*Wed.* July 10 and Dec 11 h c sh p

Romsey—*Thurs.* Every Th c, alt Th corn, East T ch sh, Aug 26, Nov 8 ch sh p

Southampton—*Wed.* (F corn) Trin M h sh pl

Stockbridge—*Thurs.* Jy 10 sh

Weyhill—2nd Th in Apl, last F in Jy sh, Oct 10 & 5 following days c h sh hops p

Wherwell—Sept 24 c sh

Wickham—May 20 c pl

Wilton—May 4, Sept 12, Nov 13

Winchester—*Wed* and *Sat.* Last S in Feb c sced, Mar 1 ch sh p seed, Oct 23 and 24 ch ch sh p

Woodbury Hill—Sept 21 c sh

Yarmouth—*Fri.* Jy 25 hi

Yarnborough Castle—Oct 4 c

HEREFORDSHIRE—

Brampton Bryan—Ju 21, 22. 1st day sh c, 2nd day h and ponies

Bromyard—*Mon.* May 1 hi. Cattle Auctions alternate Th commencing Jan 11 c sh p.

Eardisley—Mar 22, F bef 3rd W in Oct c, May 15

Ewias Harold—1st M in May, 1st M aft Oct 10

Hereford—*Wed.* Cattle markets every W c sh p calves, 1st W aft Feb 2, 1st W in Apl, W aft May 2, 1st W in Jy, 3rd W in Aug and Oct, and W in Dec h c sh p at each fair. Horse sales 1st and 3rd W in every month. Special sh sale on mkt days in Sep

Huntingdon—Jy 18, Nov 13

Kingsland—Oct 11 h c

Kington—*Wed.* T bef Feb 2, 2nd T in Mar h, T bef East Week hi pl, May 11, 1st T in Ju, 2nd T in Jy, and T in Aug, Sept 18 19, T bef Oct 10, T bef Nov 13, and T in Dec

Ledbury—*Tues.* Cattle mkts every alt T c sh p, 2nd T in Oct b ch hi

Leintwardine—May 7 pl

Leominster—*Fri.* Auc sales altnate T commencing Jan 9, Feb 13, T aft Mid-Lent Su, May 2, and F in Ju, Jy 10, Aug 4, Sept 4, M bef 3rd W in Oct, Nov 8, F aft Dec 11

Longtown—Apl 29, Sept 21

Orleton—Apl 23

Pembridge—May 13

Peterchurch—M bef Feb 2 ; M bef Mar 12 h ; May 16, pl ; last M in Ju; 1st M in Sept; 1st M in Oct pl last M in Nov

Ross—*Thurs.* Cattle markets every alternate Th commencing 2nd Th in Jan c sh p. *Fairs:* 1st Th in Mar, 2nd Th in May, Ju, Oct, and Dec

Weobley—*Thurs.* May 8 hi pl

Wigmore—May 6 c sh p pl, Aug 5 c sh p

HERTFORDSHIRE—

Aldbury—Jy 12 pl

Ashwell—*Thurs.* 1st Th in Nov stk

Baldock—Mar 7, last Th in May, Aug 5 h, Oct 2 and 3 h pl, Dec 11 c h

Barkway—Jy 20 ped

Barnet—*Wed.* Cattle market every W c sh p, Apr 8 and 9 c h sh, Sept 4, 6 great fair c h sh p

Berkhampstead—*Sat.* Stock sales Jy 19 c sh p

Bishop's Stortford—*Thurs.*

Braughing—Whit M

Buntingford—East M, Whit M, Ju Nov 30

Hatfield—*Thurs.* Apl 23, Oct 18

Hemel Hempstead—*Thurs.* Cattle market every Th c sh p, Holy Th h c sh, last F in Ju w, 3rd M in Sept pl

Hertford—*Sat.* Cattle market every S c sh p, 3rd S bef East h c sh pl, May 12, Jy 5 h c sh, Nov 8 h c sh pl

Hitchin—*Tu.* East T. Whit T sh, Oct 12

Hoddesdon—*Th.* Ju 29 pl

Pirton—4th Th aft Apl 5, 4th Th aft Oct 10

Preston—*Sat.* 1st W in May, last W in Oct sh

Redbourn—1st W in Jan sh

Rickmansworth—*Sat.* Nov 24 c h sh

Royston — *Wed.* Ash W, East W, 1st W in Jy h c, W aft Oct 11 c ch h sh

St. Alban's—*Sat.* Cattle Mkt ev W. Christmas show 2nd W in Dec

Sawbridgeworth—Apl 23, Oct 20 pl

Standon—Apl 25

Stevenage—Sept 22 c ch

Tring—*Fri.* Stock sales every M c sh p, East M p, Oct 11 hi

Ware—*Tu.* 1st T in Apl, T bef Sept 21. Sale of pedigree sheep 4th M in July

Watford—*Tu.* Cattle markets every T. Also Auc sales c sh p

HUNTINGDONSHIRE—

Alconbury—Jy 24

Earith—May 4, Jy 25, Nov 1 c h sh

Godmanchester — *Wed.* East T sh h c (large horse fair)

Huntingdon—*Sat.* 1st W in Jy w

Kimbolton—*Fri.* East F sh ped, Whit F, F aft Oct 11, Dec. 11 c p

Leighton—May 1 pl

Ramsey—*Wed.* Jy 22 23 and 24 pl

St Ives—*Mon.* Cattle markets every M, Whit M c h sh, Oct 11 c h sh

St. Neots—*Th.* Cattle mkt every Th c sh p, Holy Th h c. 3 weeks aft Holy th stk, Th aft Oct 11, 4th Th aft Dec 17 c h

Yaxley—*Th.* Ascension Day pl

ISLE OF MAN—

Ballasalla—*Sat.* 4th W in Jan, Ju and Nov h c, 1st W in Mar and Oct, 2nd W in Apl and Aug h c

Ballaugh—*Sat.* 3rd T in May h c, 4th W in Aug h c

Colby—*Sat.* Dec 6 h c

Douglas—*Sat.* Nov 12 h c

Laxey—*Sat.* 2nd T in May h c, 1st W in Aug h c

Peel—Mar 28

Ramsey—*Sat.* 2nd W in Feb h c, 3rd W in Mar h c, T aft Nov 1 h c, 2nd W in Dec h c

St. John's—*Sat.* 1st and 4th W in Feb h c, 2nd W in Mar hi, 4th W Mar and Apl h c, 3rd W in M h c, Jy 5 h c, 1st and 3rd W in Nov h c

St. Marks—*Sat.* 2nd W in May h c

St. Michael—*Sat.* 3rd W in Ju h c hi, 2nd W in Oct h c hi

Santon—*Sat.* 4th W in May h

Sulby—*Sat.* 1st W in Apl c hi, 1st W in May and Ju c, 3rd W in Jy c

KENT—

Ashford—*Tu.* 2nd T in Apr. sh, 2nd T in Aug la, 1st T in Sept la, last T in Oct c sh, May 17 and 18 and Oct 11 12 pl

Badelsmere—Nov 17

Bapchild—Aug 21

Benenden—May 15 c sh pl

Bethensden—3rd M in Apl, Jy 31

Biddenden—Nov 8 h c, Nov 9 pl

Brasted—Ascension Day, Sept 25

Bromley—*Th.* Feb. 14 c, Aug 5 c

Brompton—May 29

Brookland—Aug 1

Canterbury—*Wed* and *Sat.* Cattle market every S, lean stk, fat stk every 4th M, Oct 11 and three following days p

Charing—Apl 29, Oct 29 c h

Chatham—*Sat.* May 15 pl, Sept 19 c

Chislehurst—Whit M pl

Cranbrook — Alternate W corn and hops, May 30 c hops, Sept 29 c h sh hops

Crayford—Aug 21

Dartford—*Sat.* First T each month gt mt, cattle every Tues c sh p

Deal—*Tu* and *Sat.* Apl 6, Oct 1

Dover—*Wed* and *Sat.* Nov 22

Eastry—Oct 2 c ped

Edenbridge—*Tu.* May 6 c, Oct 16 c, and 4th T each month gt mt

Farningham—Oct 15 c h sh

Faversham—*Wed* and *Sat.* Oct 11, 12 and 13 pl, Cattle markets alternate T's c sh

Folkestone—*Wed* and *Sat.* Ju 28 pl, East Th

Greenstreet—May 1 c

Gravesend—*Sat.* Oct 24 c h sh p

Hamstreet—Last Th in Aug sh

Hawkhurst—Aug 10 pl

Hythe—*Th.* Jy 10 and 11 pl, Dec 1 sh

Lamberhurst—Apl 6 c sh

Maidstone—*Th* and *Sat.* Feb 13 c h, May 12 c h sh la, 13 pl; Jy 20 c h, Oct 17 c h sh hops, 18 pl, every T stk mt, Th corn mt

Malling, West—*Sat.* Aug 12, Oct 2, Nov 17 c h

New Romney—Aug 21 h c la

Orpington—Holy Th

Pembury—Whit T

Preston—May 1

Queensboro'—Aug 6

Rochester—*Tu* c, *Fri.* May 30 pl, Dec 11 pl, 1st, 3rd, an 4th T each month stk mt

Romney—*Sat.* Aug 11 sh

Sandhurst—May 25 sh c pl

Sandwich—*Wed* and *Sat.* Dec 4

Sevenoaks—*Sat.* Jy 10 cy, Oct 12 c

Sittingbourne—*Wed* and *Fri.* Whit M, Oct 11 c pl, 3rd T each month gt mkt

Smeeth—May 13, Sept 29

Staplehurst—1st and 3rd M each month c sh p and implements.

Stelling—Holy Th, Nov 12

Strood—Aug 26 pl

Tenterden—*Fri.* 1st M in May pl

Tunbridge—Ash W, Jy 5, Oct 11 pl, last F in Oct c h sh, 1st and 3rd T each month gt mt

Tunbridge Wells—*Fri.* Ju 5

Westerham—*Wed.* May 3 stk pl

West Wickham—East M c

Whitstable—Th bef Whit Su

Wingham—May 12, Nov 12 c h

Wrotham—*Mon.* May 4

Wye—May 29, Sept 30

Yalding—Whit M, Oc 15 c

LANCASHIRE—

Accrington—*Tues.* 1st Th in Apl c h pl, 1st Th in Aug c h pl

Ashton-under-Lyne—*Sat.* Cattle markets 2nd Th in each month, Mar 23 c, Jy 25 c h g, Nov 21 ch

Aspull Moor (Wigan)—1st W in May c

Blackburn — *Wed* and *Sat.* Cattle markets every W May 12 c, 2nd M in Ju h, 2nd M in Oct h, Oct 17 h c p

Bolton—*Mon* and *Sat.* Cattle market every M, 2nd W in Jan cows, Shrove M cows, East M pl, last W in Jy cows, and next day h, 2nd W in Oct cows, and next day h, Dec 31, Jan 1, 2 and 3 pl

Broughton-in-Furness—*Wed.* Apl 27 c, Whit W hi, Aug 1 c sh, Oct 6 c sh, W on or aft Nov 11 hi

Burnley—*Mon.* Cattle market alternate Th commencing 2nd Th in Jan, Mar 6, 3rd M in Jy c h

Bury—*Sat.* Cattle markets on 2nd and 4th W in every month. Fairs: Mar 5 h c p, May 3 h c p, Sept 18 h c p, Wakes : last S in Aug

Carnforth—Auction sales every T c sh p, Apl 29 c

Cartmel—Whit M pl, Nov 5 c sh

Chipping—Apl 23 c sh, 1st W in Oct c h sh

Chorley—*Tues* and *Sat.* Mar 26 c p, May 5 c, Aug 20 c h, Sept 4, 5 and 6 pl, Oct 21 c t h

Churchtown (North Meols)—1st S in Mar, last S in Oct

Clitheroe—*Tu.* Cattle mt alternate M's, Auction sales every M c sh p, Mar 24, 3rd Th in May c h sh, Aug 1, Th bef the 4th S aft St. Michael's Day (Michaelmas fair) c h sh, Dec 7

Cockerham—Annual horse sales on or about Apl 30 and July 28, also Apr, Jy, Dec, Fri bef the 1st full week in Jan

Colne—*Wed* and *Sat.* Cattle market last W in every month. 2nd W in March c, two following days pl, 2nd W in May h c, two following days pl, 2nd W in Oct h c, two following days

Coniston—3rd S in Sept c sh

Croston—M bef Shrove T c p; W aft Oct 12 c h sh p

Dalton-in-Furness—*Sat.* Apl 28 c ch hi, Ju 6 c h, Oct 23 c h hi

Darwen—*Sat.* 1st Th in Apl and Oct

Garstang—*Th.* Nov 22 c, Nov 23 h, hi

Great Eccleston—Apl 14, Trin M c Nov 4 c h sh

Great Harwood—Aug 21 h c sh, Whit T agricultural show

Haslingden—*Tues* and *Sat.* Feb 2 c h p, May 8 c h sh, Jy 4, Oct 2 c h sh p

Hawkshead—*Mon.* East M, M bef Holy Th, Oct 2 c h ped

Heywood—1st F in Apl and Oct h p

Hindley—2nd W in Sept h c

Hornby—Alternate T in Jy, Aug, and Sept (same week as Kirkby Lonsdale) la, Ju 20 c, Jy 30 and 31 c

Inglewhite—Apl 25 sh, M and T aft Rogation Su c sh

Kirkham—*Tues.* Feb 4 c h, Apl 28 c, Oct 28 c

Lancaster — *Wed* and *Sat.* Cattle auctions every T fat stk and dairy cows, every S from 1st in Aug, to 3rd in Nov store stk, F bef the 1st Su in the new year h, May 1 c, May 2 sh h, Jy 5 c, Jy 6 sh h w, Oct 10 c, 11 sh h Cheese Fairs : 1st W in Feb, May, Jy, Aug, Oct, and Dec. Special Sales :— Last Th in Sept store c, 3 days during Oct fair, Highland c sh chiefly Scotch ewes, unbroken horses rd S in Nov.

Leigh—Apl 24 c h ped, Dec 7 c h ped. Pleasure fairs S and M aft above dates; if either fall on S the pl fair is also held on that day

Leyland—Mar 24 c, Oct 20 c

Liverpool— *Wed*, *Fri*, and *Sat.* Cattle market every M (fairs held in New Haymarket), M aft Feb 5, M aft May 1, last M in Aug, M aft Nov 20 c and h at each fair. Repository horse sales, every W hea horses every S light horses and ponies

Select sales altnate Ths commencing Jan 11, Canadian and American horses at Stanley Station every T

Longridge—Feb 16 c sh, Mar 10 c sh, Apl 16 c sh, Nov 5 c

Lytham—A great three days' horse sale is held in Aug

Manchester—*Tues, Wed, Th.* and *Sat.* Cattle market every T, pig market every M and W

Mossley—Ju 21, last M in Oct

Newburgh (Ormskirk)—Ju 20 and 21 c p

Newton-le-Willows—May 17 c, h, Aug 11 c sh p, Aug 12 h

Oldham—1st Th aft Feb 2 h c, May 2 h c, Jy 8 h c, 1st W aft Oct 11 h c

Ormskirk — *Thurs.* Whit M cows Whit T h, Sept 10 cows, Sept 11 h

Prescot—*Tu* and *Sat.* Cattle markets commence on Shrove T and every alt T till 1st T in May. Trin Th c

Preston—*Wed* and *Sat.* Cattle markets, fat stk every W, calving cows ev F—T, W, and Th aft 1st Su in new year h, F following c, Feb 15 c h, Mar 5 c, Mar 27 c, Mar 28 h, Apl 15 c, 2nd W in May c, day aft h, Aug 25 c, Aug 26 h, Oct 3 c, Oct 4 h, Nov 6 c, Nov 7 h. If the 15th falls on Su, the fair will be held day previous. A pork market every F during season at 8 a.m., from 1st F in Sept. Store stk sales alt W, also spl horse sales on Jan 2, and on the Mon, May, Aug. and Nov h fair days

Preston Cheese Fairs — Last T in every month except Dec, commencing 9.30 a.m. Pot Fairs—Mar 27, 3 days, Aug 25, 8 days, Nov 7, 5 days

Rawtenstall—*Mon.* 1st T in Jan h c sh p, 1st T in Apl and Ju h c sh p, Ju 21 p har ped pl, 1st T in Sept h c sh p

Rochdale—*Mon* and *Sat.* Cattle markets 1st and 3rd M in each month, May 14, Nov 7 h c sh p

Skerton (Lancaster)—Apl 30 c sh

Staleybridge — *Sat.* Cattle market last M in every month h c sh p. Fairs, last M in Jan, Apl, Jy and Oct h c sh p genl, S nearest May 20 pl

Standish—Whit M pl

Todmorden—*Sat.* Cattle markets 1st Th in every month. Th bef East c, last Th in Sept c

Turton (Bolton-le-moors)—Sept 4 h c sh

Ulverstone—*Thurs.* Cattle auctions every Th, T preceding the 1st full week in Jan h, Whit Th ped hi, 1st Th aft Nov 11 hi

Upholland (Wigan)—East M h c sh p

Warrington—*Wed* & *Sat.* Auction sales every M, Jy 17 c, Jy 18 h, and 9 following days pl, Nov 29 c Nov 30 h, and 9 following days pl

Weeton (Kirkham)—1st M aft Trin Su c

Whalley—1st Tu in Oct c sh

Wigan—*Mon, Fri,* and *Sat.* W bef Holy Th c, Holy Th h, Last Wed in Ju (Scholes fair) h c, Oct 21 c, 22 h, 24 and 26 pl

LEICESTERSHIRE—

Ashby-de-la-Zouch—*Sat.* Shrove M, East T, Whit T c sh, T aft Sept 21 hi, Nov 10 stk

Belton—M aft Trin M c

Billesdon—*Fri.* Last M in Feb, 1st M in May, last M in Aug, 1st M in Oct, last M in Nov stk

Bosworth Husband—*Fri*

Castle Donington—*Sat.* Mar 17, Jy 25, Sept 29 c ch

Hallaton—*Th.*

Harrow Inn—1st Th each month

Hinckley—*Mon.* East M pl, Whi M pl, Aug 26 c ch, Th aft Sept 28 hi pl

Kegworth—Feb 18, East M, Apl 30, Jy 29, Oct 10 pl

Loughborough—Th. Cattle markets every M fat stk, every Th store stk, Feb 14, Mar 24, Mar 28 ch, Apl 25 c h sh, Holy Th c pl, Aug 12, Sept 30 ch, and Th in Nov h c, next day hi y

Leicester—Wed. and Sat. Cattle markets every W fat stk, every 8 lean stk. Cheese: 2 Th's in Mar and Oct. Pleasure: May 12 and 6 following days. Oct 10 and 9 following days ; 2 F in Mar, May, and Jy, ch s, 2 Th in Oct sh and h, 2 F in Oct c and h, 2 F in Dec c h sh, horse sales every S in Nov sh

Lutterworth—Th. Apl 2 h c, Holy Th h c sh, Sept 16 h c sh

Market Bosworth—Wed. Stock sales every alternate M, comm Jan 1, c sh p, May 8 c sh and bulls, last W in Sept sh, 3rd W in Oct foals and h

Market Harborough—Tues. Cattle markets every T, Apl 29 c, Oct 15 and 16 h, Oct 19 c

Melton Mowbray—Tu. Cattle market every T c sh p Fairs: M and T aft Jan 17 h c, 2nd T in Apl c, Whit T c, Aug 21 c, Sept 29 h c, Oct 24 h c, Dec 8 Xmas stk, and and 4th T in Sept rams, Sept 24 rams pl. Cheese fairs : 2d Th in Apl, 4th Th in Sept, 1st Th in Dec

Mount Sorrel—Mon. Jy 9 pl, Jy 29

Waltham-on-the-Wold—Sept 18 h, Sept 19 c h. Very large fairs

Welford—Stk sales alternate Th

LINCOLNSHIRE—

Alford—Tu. Whit Tu c sh pl, Jy 31 la, Aug 4 sh, Sept 17 ch sh foals, 2nd W in Oct c sh, Nov 8 c sh pl

Barton—Mon. Trin Th c hi, W aft May 12 hi

Belton—Sept 25 flax

Bollingbroke—Jy 10 c

Boston—Wed and Sat. Cattle markets every W, May 4 sh, May 5 c, May 6 pl, and W aft May 5 c sh hi, Aug 5 c, Sept 15 c sh foals, Nov 18, 19 and 20 h, Dec 21 c

Bourn—Thurs. Stk fairs : 1st Th in Apl, Th aft May 5, last Th in Sept and Oct

Brigg—Tu. Cattle markets, store stk every Th, F stk sales every alternate Tu comm Jan 9, 11 a.m, F bef May 11 hi. Aug 5 c sh h

Burgh—Th. Cattle markets alternate Th, and Th in May c, and Th in Aug c, Sept 26 c sh h

Burton-on-Stather—Th. 1st M in May, M aft Nov 11 c

Burwell—May 14, Oct 11 pl

Caistor—Sat. F and 8 bef Palm Su sh, 8 bef Palm Su c h, F and 8 bef Whit Su sh, 8 bef Sept 18 sh, S aft Oct 11 ch sh. Largeish fairs

Caythorp—and F aft Good F stk

Corby—Wed. Aug 26 pl, M bef Oct 11 c sh

Crowland—Th.

Crowle—Fri. Last M in May, Nov 22 c flax hemp

Donington—Sat. May 26 c h, Sept 4 c h, Oct 17 c h

Epworth—Thurs and Sat. Th aft May 1 c flax &c. Th aft Sept 29 c p

Falkingham—Thurs. May 13 c, June 15 c, Jy 13 c, Nov 22 c

Gainsborough—Tues and Sat. Cattle market. every T c sh p, East T c, East W, T on or aft Oct 20 c sh, W aft Oct 20 c h sh la gnl. Hirings : May day and Martinmas

Grantham—Mon and Sat. Cattle mt and sales every M c sh p, Holy Th c, East twe c, 5th M in Lent c and two following days pl, 1st and and 8 aft May 11 hi, Jy 13 cy, Oct 26 c sh, Dec 18 fat stk

Grimsby—Fri. Cattle markets every

M c sh p, 2nd M in Apl c h sh, May 14 pl, M bef Oct 11 c h sh

Haxey—Jy 6 pl

Heckington—Oct 10 c sh

Holbeach—Thurs. Pig sales every Th, May-day week statute fair for hi, May 17 h c, Sept 17 h c, Oct 11 c h

Horncastle — Sat. Cattle markets every alt Th, 4th in Lent c sh, Ju 21 h, Ju 22 c sh, 2nd M in Aug and during week h, Th sh, F c, and Th in Sept c h sh, Oct 28 h sh, Oct 29 c

Kirton—Sat. Jy 18, Dec 21 c h sh

Lincoln—Fri. Cattle markets every T fat stk, every F lean stk. Last whole week in Apl 1st 3 days h, 4th day sh, 5th and last day c, all the week pl, 1st F in Jy foals, last F in Sept h, 3rd F in Oct h sh la, 3rd F in Nov h c sh. The foal fair in Jy is nearly defunct

Long Sutton—Fri. Cattle auctions every F, May 13 c, F aft Sept 24 c

Louth—Wed and Sat. Cattle markets every F fat and lean stk, 4th F in Lent c, Apl 29 sh, and 30 c h genl, F bef Sept 18 c, F bef Oct 28, Nov 23 c. Wool markets commence 1st W in Jy

Ludford—Aug 2 hi, Nov 30 hi

Market Rasen—Thurs. 4th T in Lent c, Sept 25 c h sh p

Messingham—Thurs. Trin M pl

Navenby—Th bef Good F pnd, Oct 17 sh h p onions

New Bolingbrook—Tues. Jy 10 c pl

Partney—Aug 1 sh. Aug 25 sh, Sept 18 and 19 h c sh, W and Th aft Oct 11 h c sh. Large sh fairs

Saltfleetby—Oct 3 foals

Skegness—Cattle markets alt Th

Sleaford—Mon. Cattle mts and stk sales every M, Plough M c, 2nd M in New Year c sh, East M c sh, Whit M c, Oct 20 c pl

Spalding—Tues. Cattle markets every T, fat and lean stk. T aft Lincoln Apl fair c h sh, last T in Ju c h, last T in Aug c h, Sept 25 c h sh, 26 pl, F bef London Xmas market fat stk. Hirings : two T's in Mid-Lent and a few days prior to May 14

Spilsby—Mon. M bef and aft Whit M, M aft Jy 12 stk p

Stamford—Mon and Fri. Cattle mts every M and F. Toll Free Fairs: Feb 6 h c sh, Mar 19 h, Mar 26 (? own Fair), Apl 9 (Spring Fair), May 7, Ju 28 (Corpus Christi), Jy 23, Nov 8 h sh, Nov 9 card cheese, onions, vegetables

Stow Green—J 112 h ponies, 1st W and Th in Jy pl, Oct 10 c foals

Swineshead—2nd Th in Ju ch, Oct 2 h sh p c

Torksey—Whit M pl

Tetney—M aft Ju 12 pl

Wainfleet—Sat. Cattle markets alternate Th from Jy to Sept, 3rd S in May c sh, Aug 24, Oct 24 ch

West Stockwith—Sept 4 c h

Winteringham—Jy 14 pl

Winterton—Wed. T bef Palm Su c, Jy 26 pl, Sept 23

Wragby—Thurs. May 1 sh, Holy Th sh, Sept 28

MIDDLESEX—

Brentford—Tues. May 17, 18 and 18 c sh pl, Sept 12, 13 and 14 h c sh pl

Edgware—1st M in Aug c sh p

Harefield—East M c sh h

Hounslow—Trin M, M aft Sept 29

Isleworth—1st M in Jy

Islington—M in the first full week in Dec and 4 following days Xmas cattle show in Agricultural Hall. M aft the first full week in Dec Xmas cattle market

Southall—East W, W aft Oct 11

Staindrop—F oly Th

taines—Fri. May 11 c Sept 19 c h Sonions

Sunbury—Shrove T, Whit W

Twickenham—Holy Th

Uxbridge—Thurs corn, Sat. Mar 25 Jy 31 c h sh, Aug 1 w, Sept 29, Oct 11

MONMOUTHSHIRE—

Abergavenny—Tues. 3rd T in Jan and Mar, May 14 and 15 c, 3rd T in Ju, last T in Jy, Sept 25, 3rd T in Nov

Blaenavon—Apl 16, Jy 8, Sept 16 c p pl at each fair except Jy, which is for p sh la and pl

Bishton—2nd T in Sept

Caerleon—May 1, Jy 20, Sept 21

Castletown—May 6, Aug 4, Nov 26

Chepstow—2nd and last T in every month c, Ju 22 w pl

Christchurch—Nov 29

Grosmont—East M, Aug 10, F bef 3rd W in Oct c sh p

Maesycwmmer—Apl 3, Oct 6

Magor—T bef Apl 17, and T bef Oct 17

Monmouth—Sat. Cattle markets 2nd and 4th M in every month and M in May c hi pl, Ju 18 w, 2nd M in Feb and Sept c, Nov 22 c ch

Newport—Wed and Sat. Cattle markets every W, 2nd W in Apl, W in Whit week, Ju 23 w, 2nd W in Aug, 1st W in Nov

Pontypool—Apl 2 and 22, Jy 5, Oct 10 c ch

Redwick—1st T in Sept

Raglan—Mar 31, M bef 3rd W in Oct stk, &c., 3rd M in each month c sh p

Tredegar—2 M in Apl c, 1st M in Sept c

Usk—Fri. Apl 20 c, Trin M c, Oct 29 c genl h ped, F bef Ju 18 w pl, Dec 16 c fat stk

NORFOLK—

Acle—Stock sales every Th c sh p

Aldborough—Ju 21 live stk sale, 22 pl

Attleborough—Thurs. Last Th in every month from Jan to Apl fat stk. Last Th in Mar h. Xmas show and week in Dec. Cattle auct alt Th commencing 2nd Th in Jan c sh p

Aylsham—Tues. Cattle auctions every alternate M from Jan to Jy c sh p, Mar 23 h, last T in Sept pl

Banham—Ju 21 pl

Binham—Jy 26 h c pl ponies. If 26 is S or Su the fair is held on M—only a small fair

Briston—Tues. Last Th in May h c sh pl

Burnham—Stk sales alternate M, commencing 2nd M in Jan, Aug 1 and 2 pl

Castle Acre—May 1 pl, Aug 3 pl

Cley-next-the-Sea—Last F and S in Jy c pl

Cawston—Feb 1 pl, last W in Aug sh show at "Woodrow" Inn

Coltishall—Whit M pl

Cromer—Whit M pl

Diss—Fri. Stock sales every F c sh p, last Th in Ju great sale of lambs

Downham—Sat. Mar 1, 2 and 3 h, last day for c, 1st F in May c sh. 3rd F in Sept h c, Horse sales on Fair days ; 2nd F in Nov c sh

East Dereham—Fri. Cattle markets every F c sh p. Pleasure fairs:- F bef Jy 6, F bef Sept 28

East Harling—Tues. May 4 h c p, 1st T aft Sept 11 h c sh rams, Oct 24 h c pl. Very large hogget sale in Apl and h sale about 1st week in Jy

Fakenham—Thurs. Cattle auctions every Th fat and lean stk,also stk sales

Hempton Green (nr. Fakenham)— Whit M pl, Whit T c sh. 1st W in Sept rams and ewes, Nov 22 c

Feltwell—Nov 20 & 21 h c pl

Forncett—Cattle auctions every T c sh p

Foulsham—Thurs. 1st T in May pl

Harleston—*Wed.* Cattle auctions every W h c sh p meat &c
Heacham—Ju 20 pl
Hingham—*Tues.* Cattle markets every Tc sh p, Mar 7 h c, Oct 11 h c pl
Hockham—East M pl
Hockwold—Jy 25 pl
Holt—Cattle auc every F Jan to Jy, Apl 25 c h sh pl, Nov 25 c sh pl
Ingham (nr Stalham)—M following Whit week c h
Kenninghall—*Mon.* Jy 18 la, Sept 30 c h sh
Loddon—*Tues.* Pig market every F, sometimes a few sheep
Long Stratton–Sept 28 & 29 pl
Lynn—*Tues.* Cattle markets every T c sh p, Feb 14 and 5 following days pl, 2nd T in Apl hoggets sh, 2nd T in Nov c genl
Martham—1st T in Jy pl
Methwold—*Mon.* Cattle auctions every M c sh p, Apl 23 c sh p pl
New Buckenham—*Sat.* Last Th in May, Nov 21 h c sh p
North Walsham—*Thurs.* Cattle auction sales every Th from Nov to Ju c sh p. Holy Th pl
North Wold (Brandon)—Nov 30 pl
Norwich—*Wed* and *Sat.* Cattle markets every S. Th bef East Su (Tombland fair) sh h c pl, East M and T pl, two days following Xmas pl
Oxborough—East T pl
Reedham—Stock sales every T and W, Ju 29 pl
Reepham—Auc sales every W c s p
Shouldham—Sept 19, Oct 11 c sh h foals
Sitcham—Whit T pl, Nov 1 pl
Southrepps—3rd T aft Whit Su, and day following pl
Stoke Ferry—*Fri.* 1st F in Jy (feast), Th bef Oct 11 hi. Dec 6 h c
Stow Bridge—Whit S stock &c
Swaffham—*Sat.* Cattle auctions every S c sh p, 2nd W in May h c sh pl, 3rd W in Jy h c sh, 1st W in Nov h c sh
Thetford—*Sat.* Gen mt
Walsingham—2nd M aft Whit M pl, also small show of ponies and donkeys
Watton—*Wed.* Corn mt. Cattle auction every alternate W commencing 2nd W in Jan c sh p
Wells—Stk sales alternate M commencing 1st M in Jan, Shrove T pl and small show of ponies, donkeys &c
Winfarthing—Ju 22 pl
Winnold (Downham)—Mar 1 to 6 very large horse fair
Worsted—*Sat.* May 12 & 13 pl
Wymondham—Stock sales alternate F from Jan. to Jy. Feb 14 c pl, May 17 c pl, Oct 22 pl
Yarmouth—*Wed* and *Sat.* Cattle markets every alternate W c sh p, F and S aft East pl, also fat and store stock sales every W

NORTHAMPTONSHIRE—

Boughton Green—Ju 24 and 25 pl w, Ju 26 c sh h
Brackley—*Wed.* Dec 11 c h sh. T nearest Ju 17 w
Brigstock—Apl 25, Sept 4, Nov 22 c sh
Daventry—*Wed.* 2nd T in each month c, except Oct, Oct 3 and 2t ch onions, W on or aft Oct 11 an 2 following W's hi
Fotheringhay—M aft Jy 19 c h
Kettering—*Fri.* Cattle markets every F, Th bef East, F bef Whit Su, Th bef. Oct 11, Th bef Dec 11 c s
Long Buckby—*Tues.* May 1, Oct 11 c
Northampton—*Wed* and *Sat.* Cattle markets every W fat stk and store p, every S store c and sh also h. Horse and cattle fairs: 2nd T in Jan, Feb 20, 3rd M in Mar, Apl 5, May 4, Ju 19, Aug 5, Aug 26 Sept 19. S aft Oct 11 hi, 1st Th in Nov hi, Nov 28, Sept 19 an-

nual sale of rams and ewes. Xmas mt. F bef London Xmas mt. Wool Fairs: Wk aft Leicesterw fair. Horse sales 1st Sat in every month except Apl, Ju, Jy, Sept and Dec, when on 2nd Sat
Oundle—*Thurs.* Feb 25 c h, Whit M, Aug, Oct 21 pl
Peterborough—*Wed* and *Sat.* Cattle markets every W fat stk. every S lean stk; 2nd M in Mar and 5 following days pl, and M in Jy (proclaimed day previous and continued day following) h c sh 1st W in Sept rams and foals, 1st W and Th in Oct (proclaimed day previous) h c sh rams wood onions pl
Rockingham—*Thurs.* Sept 25 c h sh
Rothwell—*Mon.* Trin M, T and W stk genl
Thrapstone—*Tues.* Cattle markets every T, 1st T in May c sh, Aug 5 pl, T aft Oct 11 c sh
Towcester—*Tues.* Stock sales every alternate T commencing and T in Jan c sh p, Shrove T c, May 12 c, T bef Oct 12 hi, Oct 29 c
Weldon—Jy 14 c
Welford Wharf—Stock sales every alternate T commencing 2nd Th in Jan c sh
Wellingborough—*Wed.* Cattle markets every W c sh p, Oct 29 pl
West Haddon—*Fri.* Last F in Sept hi
Yardley—Whit T

NORTHUMBERLAND—

Allendale—Aug 22 cheviot and black-faced la
Alnwick—*Mon.* Stock sales every M. fat stk. Cattle market every S, 1st S in Mar hi, May 12 hi c, 1st S aft Jy 5 w, 1st M in Jy, S aft Sept 15 c h sh, 1st T in Oct h c, 1st S in Nov hi
Belford—*Tues.* Jy 2, Sept 25 ewes. Hiring fairs: 1st W in Mar, last W in Apl. 1st W in Oct
Bellingham—*Sat.* S bef May 13, 1st S aft Jy 20 w, 4th S in Aug la, 3rd S in Oct ewes and wethers
Berwick—*Sat.* Cattle market every S, May 29 c h sh. Hiring fairs: 1st S in Mar, May, Aug, and Nov
Blanchland—Aug 21 genl, Oct 4 ewes
Corn Mill (Allendale)—3rd F in Sept
Elsdon—1st T in May and Oct 21
Felton—1st M in May and Nov
Framlington—2nd T in Jy great la fair
Glanton—1st W in Mar and last W in Oct hi
Haltwhistle—*Thurs.* May 14, Sept 17 Nov 22
Harbottle—Jy 8, Sept 19
Hexham—*Tues.* Last T in Feb, Mar 24, Aug 6, Nov 9. Cattle markets alternate T from last T in Feb till last T bef Midsummer. Hiring fairs: 1st T in Apl, May 13, Nov 11. Cattle sales: fat stk every M, store stk every T
Morpeth—*Wed.* Stk sales alternate M. commencing 1st M in Jan c sh p, M bef last W in Mar and Oct h c; 1st W in May and Trin W c. Hiring fairs: 1st W n May and Nov (single servants) 1st and 2nd W in Mar (hinds)
Newcastle—*Tues* and *Sat.* Cattle markets every T fat stk ; every S calving and dairy cows. Last W in Mar and Nov c h; 2nd W in Aug and last W in Oct genl fairs, which last about three days. There is a fair for the best kind of horses three or four days previous to the general fairs in Aug and Oct. Horse sales every Sat. Hiring fairs : 1st W in Apl (hinds), 1st M in May and Nov (single)
Norham—3rd Th in May, 3rd Th in Ju, and 2nd Th in Oct
North Shields—Last F in Apl, 1st F in Nov
Ovingham—Apl 26
Ponteland—Special sales of store c and sh, Apl, Oct, dates not fixed

Rothbury—Fairs: F in East week, Whit M, Nov 1 Stock sales, fat stock every alt M, com and M in Jan c sh p. Large spl sales of c and sh in Spring and Aut, dates not fixed
Scotswood—Stk sales alternate M, commencing 1st M in Jan c sh p
Stagshawbank—May 6 c sh, Whitsun Eve, Jy 4, Aug 5 la, Sept 26, Oct 24
Stamfordham—Th bef Apl 26 h c sh. Th bef Aug 26 c sh la. Hiring fairs: Last Th in Mar (hinds). Th bef May 12 and Nov 13 (single)
St. Ninian's—Sept 27 great ewe fair
Warkworth—Th bef Nov 22
Whitsun B mk—3rd M in May
Whittingham—Aug 24
Wooler—May 4, Oct 17 great sh fair

NOTTINGHAMSHIRE—

Bawtry—Whit Th, Nov 11
Bingham—*Thurs.* T and W bef Feb 13 h, 1st Th in May, May 31, Whit Th pl, last Th in Oct hi, Nov 8 and 9
Dunham—Aug 12 c ch
Eastwood—1st M in May, M aft Oct 11, Nov 4
Farnsfield—M aft Oct 11
Gringley—Dec 13
Lenton—Whit W, Nov 11 c h sh p
Mansfield—*Thurs.* Cattle markets every M c sh p stores and fat. 2nd Th in Apl c, 2nd Th in Jy c h pl, 2nd Th in Oct c h ch hi, 1st F in Nov hi
Marnham—Sept 12
Newark—*Wed.* Cattle market every T fat stk, every W lean stk. Fair: Fortnight bef Good F h c, May 14 and 15 h c hi pl, Whit T h c, Aug 2 h c, 2nd W in Sept rams, W bef Oct 2, h c ch, Nov h c, M bef Dec 11 h c
Nottingham—*Wed* and *Sat.* Cattle market every W fat stk, every S lean stk. F aft Jan 13 h c, Mar 7 and 8 c h ch, Th bef East c, 1st Th. F and S in Oct c ch geese and h, Martinmas S hi. Horse sales 3rd F in every month
Retford—*Sat.* Cattle markets every M fat stk, every S lean stk and p, Mar 23 c h ch, Oct 2 h c sh pl ch hops
Southwell—*Sat.* M aft Palm Su c, Whit M c, Trin M c, Nov 11 c hi
Stockwith—Sept 4 c h
Tuxford—*Mon.* May 12 c sh p, M bef Oct 2 hops
Warsop—*Mon.* Sept 29 c sh, Nov 17 stk
Worksop—*Wed.* Mar 31, 2nd W in Apl and Oct c, Dec 13 c.

OXFORDSHIRE—

Bampton—*Wed.* Aug 26 h
Banbury—*Thurs.* Cattle markets alternate Th, commencing 1st Th in Jan. Fairs: 1st Th aft Old Twelfth day (Jan 18) c, three preceding days of Old Michaelmas (Oct 11) c ch hi, and Th bef Xmas ft stk
Bicester—*Fri.* Cattle markets every alternate F commencing 1st F in Jan. Cattle fairs: East F c, 1st F in Ju c, 1st F in Jy c w, Aug 5 c pl, Aug 6 pl, F bef Oct 11 & 2 following F's pl, F aft Dec 11 c
Binford—Apl 26
Burford—*Sat.* Last S in Apl c ch, last S in Jy cy, Sept 25 hi, 1st S in Dec
Charlbury—*Fri.* 3rd M in each month mt, Jan 1, and F in Lent, and F aft May 3 stk, Oct 20 hi
Chipping Norton—*Wed.* 1st W in each month, bef and aft Oct 13 hi
Deddington—*Tues.* Stock sales every month. Aug 12, Oct 12, Nov 22 c
Dorchester—East T
Henley—*Thurs.* May 7, Holy Th, Th aft Trin Su c, Th aft Sept 21 hi
Heyford—Last M in Jan, Ap, May, Jy and Sept pl

Hook-Norton—Jy 29, Nov 28

Nettlebed—M aft Oct 18

Oxford—*Wed* and *Sat.* Cattle markets 2nd and last W in every month c sh p, May 3 jt, and W in Aug rams, M aft 1st Sun aft Sept 1 pl (St Giles's Fair), Th bef Sept 29 pl

Stoken Church—Jy 10

Thame—*Tues.* Cattle mkt every T, East T c h, T bef Whit Su, Oct 11 h hi

Watlington—*Sat.* Apl 6, S bef Oct 11 c, S aft Oct 11 hi

Wheatley—Sept 30

Witney—*Thurs.* East. Th, Th aft Jy 9, Aug 24, M and T after Sept 8 hi pl, Th aft Sept 8 ch, Th bef Oct 11, Dec 4

Woodstock — *Tues.* 1st T in every month c sh p, 1st T in Oct pl

Woodstock Road Station—Stock sales 4th W in each month c sh p

RUTLAND—

Oakham—*Thurs.* 2nd M in Jan, and M in Feb, Mar 15 c sh, 1st M in Apl, May 6 c h pl, 2nd M in Ju, Jy, and Aug, Sept 9 c sh p, Oct 1 c h sh p, Nov 5 c sh p, 2nd M in Dec c h sh p

Rockingham—Sept 25 c h

Uppingham—*Wed* and *Sat.* Mar 7 c h sh, Jy 7 c h

SHROPSHIRE—

Baschurch—Cattle sales alternate M c sh p, commencing Jan 8

Bishop's Castle—Cattle markets on the 2nd F in every month, except Mar and May ; horse markets in Mar and Oct also, Mar 26 and 1st F aft May-Day, c auction every 4th F commencing Jan 6 c sh p

Bridgnorth—Pleasure Fair: May 1st. Sales :—Jan 1, 15, 29, Feb 12, 26, Mar 12, 26, Apl 9, 23, May 1, 7, 21, Ju 4, 18, Jy 2, 16, 30, Aug 13, 27, Sept 10, 17 sh, 24, Oct 8, 22, 29. (St. Luke's fair) Nov 5, 19, Dec 3, 17 (Xmas stk), 31. Horse sales:—1st S in Feb, Apl, Ju, Aug, Oct, Dec. Bull sale, Mch 12.

Brosley—Apl 28 pl

Burford—Auction sales every alt T com Jan 2, or day aft Ludlow

Church Stretton—2nd Th in Jan c h sh, 3rd Th in Mar c h sh, May 14 c sh hi, Jy 3 w, Sept 25 sh and colts, last Th in Nov c h sh

Cleobury Mortimer—Apl 21 c p sh, May 2 hi pl, Trin M c sh p, Oct 27 c h sh. Monthly sales on W

Clun—Last F in Jan, Mar, June, Aug, Sept and Nov c & sh, May 11 hi pl

Craven Arms—Stock sales every alternate M, commencing Jan 8. *Fairs*· last M in every month c sh p

Ditton Priors—Fairs and stock sales, May 10, Oct 25.

Dorrington—Sept 22 p colts

Ellesmere—Cattle markets and sales · Jan 2, 16, 30 Feb 13, 27, Mar 13, 27, Apl 10, 24, May 8, 22, Ju5 19, Jy 3, 17, 31, Aug 14, 28, Sept 11, 25 Oct 9, 23. Nov 6, 20, Dec 4. 18.

Hadnall—Auction sales every alt F c sh p

Hodnet—Cattle sales in Smithfield every alt T commencing Jan 9

Ironbridge—May 29 pl

Llanymynech—Apl 1, May 29, Sept 23 c sh p

Ludlow—Cattle sales alt M's commencing Jan 1, c sh p. *Fairs*: 2nd M in every month c sh p, May 1st pl. Horse Fairs:—2nd M in Jan, Mar, Ju and Oct Special sh Fairs:—2nd M in Aug and Sept

Market Drayton—Cattle markets every W. *Fairs*: Sept 17, Oct 24 c sh

Minsterley—2nd M in every month c sh, May 3 hi

Much Wenlock—Cattle auctions every alternate M commencing Jan 1, v.

day before Ellesmere. Special Sheep Sales, Sept ; Special Horse Sales, Ju, Oct.

Nesscliffe—Last M in Apl c

Newport—Cattle sales alternate M commencing Jan 1. Hiring fairs: May 28, 1st S aft Xmas

Oswestry—Cattle markets every W c sh p genl. 1st W in every month h b ch bacon, &c. First W in Jy w

Pulverbach—Sept 21 c sh

Shifnal—*Tues.* Nov 22 c sh. Cattle sales every alt M, com Jan 8

Shrewsbury—Cattle markets T. 2nd W ev month b ch and bacon. 1st T aft 1st M ev month h, Mar 6 and 7 great h fair. Horse Sales last F and S ev month. Great monthly sales of store c and sh Pedigree Shropshire sh sales in Aug Sept and Oct.

Tenbury—Cattle sales alt T, com Jan 2 c sh p, May 1 pl, about Sept 26 and 27, gt sale of rams and ewes

Wellington—Cattle markets every M c sh p. The bulk of the stock is sold by auction. Monthly horse sales are also held on the 2nd S in each month.

Wem—Cattle mkts at M, com Jan 1, sh p

Westbury—Sept 27 c

Whitchurch—Cattle markets Jan 8, 22. Feb 5, 19, Mar 1, 19, Apl 2, 16, 30, May 14, 28, June 11, 25, Ju 9, 23, Aug 6, 20, Sept 3, 17, Oct 1, 15, 29, Nov 12, 26, Dec 10, 24. Cheese fairs :—Nth W in every month except Dec Nov. 23, 24 (also Dairy Show). Monthly horse sales on last F

Worthen—Last Th in Mar c, May 2 c hi, last Th in Ju, Sept colt show and Nov c

Wrenbury—Stock sales every alternate M c sh p, comm Jan 1

SOMERSETSHIRE—

Ashbrittle—M before last T in Feb, 3rd M in Oct

Ashcott—Jan 9 stk p

Ashill—East W, Sept 12, if W then W aft

Axbridge—*Thurs.* Feb 4, Mar 25 and 26 c genl, and T in Oct, last S each month gt mt

Backwell—Sept 21 stk p, Sept 22 pl

Bagborough—May 23

Bagborwest—May 13

Banwell—Jan 18 c, Jy 18 c

Bath—*Wed* and *Sat.* Feb 14 c, T aft Dec 9 c, ch mt and W in every month

Binegar—Whit W and Th large h fair

Bishops Lydeard—Last F in Mar

Blagdon—Last F in Aug

Bridgwater—*Wed.* Last W in Jan and Mar c gnl, last W in Ju c h clo last W in Sept c sh h pl. Gt mkt Dec 5

Bristol—*Wed, Thurs, Fri,* and *Sat.* Cattle markets every Th c sh p. *Fairs:* 1st Th in Mar h c, 2nd W in Mar lea w, day following w, 1st Th in Sept h c, 2nd W in Sept lea w, day following w. Th bef Jy 25 c colts

Broadway—W aft Sept 10 stk p onion-

Broomfield—Nov 13

Bruton—*Sat.* Apl 23, Sept 17

Buckland—Oct 10

Buckland St. Mary—T W and Th after Sept 20

Burnham—Trin M c sh p

Burtle—Aug 9

Castle Carey—*Tues.* T bef Palm S, May 1, Whit T, 4th T in Sept, alt M c

Chard—*Mon.* 1st W in May and Aug stk, 1st W in Nov stk ch. Great mkts:—1st M in Jan, Feb, Mar, Apl, Oct, Nov and Dec

Cheddar—May 4, Oct 29 c h sh

Chislehorough—4th Th in Oct

Congresbury—W aft Sept 8 h c pl

Coombe St. Nicholas—Ju 19, W aft Dec 10

Crewkerne—*Sat.* Sept 4 c h la ch,

Great mkts ; 4th S in Mar, Ju, Sept. 3rd S in Dec. Sheep mkts :—On seven S after Mar 4t 1st

Crowcombe—*Tues.* 1st F in May, M aft Aug 1, Oct 31

Curry Rivel—Last F in Feb. M aft Aug 2 c

Cutcombe—Sept 19 (if Th, if not then Th bef Sept 19)

Draycott—2nd M in Sept

Dulverton—*Sat.* Great mkts :—2nd S in Mar, 4th S in Sept

Dundry—Sept 12

Dunster—*Fri.* Whit-M. Great mkts :—and F in Feb, 3rd M in Nov

East Brent—Last T in Aug

Exford—Aug 14

Froshford—Sept 6

Frome—*Wed* and *Sat.* Great market last W in every month ch genl. Cattle fairs last W in Feb, last W in Sept, W bef Xmas

Glastonbury—*Mon.* Oct 11 c sh, 2nd M each month except Oct c h sh

Highbridge—Cattle markets 1st and 3rd M in every month. Cheese, 1st M

Hinton St. George—Apl 23

Holloway—May 2

Huntspill—Ju 29, 1st and 3rd M each month gt mt

Ilchester—*Wed.* M bef Palm Su c, Jy 2, Aug 2 c

Ilminster—*Sat.* Last W but one in Feb gt mt, last W in May gt mt, last W in Aug c h sh p, last W in Nov gt mt. Last W in July w

Keynsham—*Thurs.* 4th M in Apl, 3rd M in Aug c h sh

Kilmington—Aug 20

Kingsbrompton—1st Th in Aug, 3rd Th in Oct c

Langport—*Tues.* M bef Lent, 2nd W in Aug. Last M in Nov. Sept 3 h colts

Lansdown—Aug 10 c

Lydford Green—Holy Th, Aug 12

Lyng—2nd M in Aug

Mark—T bef Whit S. 3rd M in Au and Sept c

Martock—Cattle mkt last M in every month. Aug 21 c

Mells—M aft Trin M c c ch, last M in Sept p

Midsomer Norton—Easter M

Milborne Port—Ju 5, Oct 28

Milverton—*Fri.* East T, Jy 25, Oct 1

Minehead—*Wed.* Whit W ped

Moorlinch—Aug 20

Montacute—Mar 9, Sept 27

North Curry—*Tues.* 1st T in Sept c sh

North Petherton—*Tues.* May 1 toys. M bef Nov 13

Norton St. Phillip—*Thurs.* 3rd Th n Mar c, last Th in Aug c, May 1 pl

Nunney—Nov 21 c

Otterford—Last W in Oct

Pensford—*Tues.* May 6 c h sh, Nov 8 h sh Oct, last Th in Aug c mt

Porlock—*Thurs.* 2nd Th in May and Oct, last Th in Aug c mt

Priddy—Aug 21, Dec 21 h c pl

Queen Camel—Trin Th, Oct 25

Redlynch—Ju 29

Road—M aft Sept 9

Ruishton—Whit-M

Shepton Mallet—*Fri.* May 8, June 21, Aug 3, Nov 11 gt mt

Shipham—Apr 27, Nov 17,

Somerton—Alternate T p. Last M in Jan, Palm T, 3rd, 6th, 9th, and 12th T aft Palm T, Sept 30, Nov 8 ch sh p

South Brent—2nd M in Oct c sh p

South Petherton—*Thurs.* Jy 6 c la

St. Decumans—Aug 24, Sept 17

Stockhambdon—Apl 25

Stogumber—1st Th in May, 2nd Th in Sept

Stogursey—Last W in Apl and Sept

Stoke under Hamdon—Apl 25

Stolford—Ju 11, Sept 28

Stowey—*Tues.* Sept 18

Sucklebridge—F bef Holy Th, W aft Oct 10

Taunton—*Wed* and *Sat.* Great mar-

ket last 8 in every month. Ju 17 c h,
Jy 8 and 9 pl
Ubley—Oct 4
Watchet—*Sat.* Last M in Aug pl
Wedmore—Last M in July and Sept
Wellington—*Thurs* and *Sat* c. Shw
c, W bef Holy Th c, 1st Th in month
gt mt, 2nd Wed in Mar pl, 1st W in
Ju, pl
Wellow—May 20, Oct 17
Wells—*Sat.* Great markets 1st 8 in
each month. Fairs : 1st Tu in Jan,
May, Jy, Nov and Dec
West Pennard—1st M in Aug
Weston Zoyland—Sept 9
Whitedown—Whit-M and T
Williton—Ju 10
Wincanton—*Wed.* East T, Sept 29 c
Winsford—Aug 20
Winsham—Whit-W
Wiveliscombe—*Tues.* Last T in May,
Ju, Jy, and Sept c sh
Woolavington—Oct 18 c
Wootton Courteney—Sept 19
Yarlington—Aug 26
Yeovil—*Fri* and *Sat.* Great c mt
every alternate F, last F in Ju c sh,
3rd F in Nov c stk, corn, flax

STAFFORDSHIRE—
Betley—*Tues.* Last T in Apl, Jy 31,
last T in Oct
Brewood—*Tues.* 2nd Th in May, Sept
19
Biddulph Moor (New Inn)—May 11
h c sh p
Burslem—S bef Shrove T, S bef
Easter, S bef Whit S, S on or after Ju
24 to follow S, S bef Xmas day c p
Burton-on-Trent—*Thurs.* Cattle auc-
tions alt M, com Jan 2, Holy Th pl,
Oct 28 and 29, unless Su intervenes,
then 28 ; or 29 and 30, Candlemas Toll
Free Fair Feb 2 c, Apl 5 c ch, Holy
Th b pl, M after Sept 29 hi pl
Calton Moor—Aug 15, Sept 20
Cannock—Last M in Oct c
Celler Head—*Sat.* May 6, Th after
Nov 1 stk
Cheadle—Jan 6, Mar 25, Holy Th, Jy 4,
Aug 21, Oct 18 c. These fairs are
gradually declining
Ecclesshall—*Fri.* Cattle auctions alter-
nate M's, commencing 1st M in Jan
Fazeley—M and T nearest Oct 13; 1st
day h c sh ; 2nd day hi and pl
Flash—Sept 29 c sh
Gnosall—May 7, Sept 23
Great Barr—Stock sale every alternate
T commencing 1st T in Jan
Grindon—T on or nearest Nov 1st c
Hanley — *Wed* and *Sat.* Cattle
Markets every T, Mar 4, Apl 22, Ju
10, Aug 3 pl
Ipstones—M nearest Nov 6
Leek—*Wed* and *Sat.* Cattle Markets
alt W's commencing 1st W in Jan.
Fairs : W bef Feb 13, East W, May
18, Whit W, Jy 3, 28, W aft Oct 10,
Nov 13 c hi, W aft Xmas day unless
Xmas day falls on a W, then on Dec
26. Cheese fairs: Last W in Feb,
Aug, and Oct.
Lichfield—*Fri.* Cattle sales alt M's
commencing 2nd M in Jan, Ash W,
May 12. Great w sale, Ju 30. Horse
sales 1st F in every month. Sales of
Shropshire sh and W and Th in Sept,
Oct 6 Foal Show 3rd F in Oct.
Longnor—*Tues.* East T. Whit T c
Newcastle-under-Lyme—*Wed* and *Sat.*
Jan 8 (new market), c Ju, Jan 29, Feb
26 h c (shrove fair), Mar 12, Apl 16
(Easter fair), May 7, June 4 (Whit
fair), Jy 9 (wool fair), Aug 6, Sept
17 (wakes fair), Oct 8, Nov 5 (cold
fair), Dec 3 h c. Cattle mts alternate
M commencing 2nd M in Jan
Pattingham—Last T in Apl
Penkridge—*Sat.* Cattle auctions alt
M's, commencing 1st M in Jan, Apl
30 c. Oct 10 c

Rugeley—*Thurs.* Stock sales every
alternate T commencing 1st T in Jan,
Ju 1 to 6 ch, gt h f air, Ju 6 c sh, Oct
21 and 22 h c sh, Th aft Xmas day hi
Sandon—East Th. Nov 14
Shenstone—Last M in Feb
Stafford—*Mon* and *Sat.* Cattle markets
alt T, commencing Jan 9, bef Shrove
bef Shrove T, Apl 3, May 14, S bef Ju
29, Oct 20 ch. Dec 4c h
Stone—*Sat.* Cattle auctions every T,
Horse sales every month
Tamworth—*Sat.* Jy 26 c h, 1st M in
Oct hi. Stock sale alternate M com-
mencing 1st M in Jan c sh p
Tutbury—Oct 8 c p; declining in
recent years.
Uttoxeter — *Wed.* Cattle markets
alternate W, commencing Jan 10.
Cattle fairs :—May 6, Oct 19 foals and
h, Nov 11, 27. Cheese fairs : Th
aft and T in Mar, 1st Th in Sept, and
Th in Nov
Walsall—*Tues* and *Sat.* Feb 24, Whit
T, T bef Sept 29 h
Wetley Rocks—May 3, Oct 2
Wheaton Aston—Oct 26, Nov 1
Wolverhampton — *Wed* and *Sat.*
Cattle markets every W, horses are
also shown, it being considered the
best market for that class of animals
in the kingdom. Whit M T and W pl

SUFFOLK—
Beccles — *Fri.* Feb 11 Ju 11, and
Whit-M, Oct 11
Bergholt—Last W and Th in Jy
Bildeston—Ash W, Holy Th pl
Boxford—East M and T, Dec 21
Boxted—Whit T
Brandon—*Thurs.* corn
Bungay—*Thurs.* May 14 h c, Sept 25
p hi
Bury St Edmunds — *Wed.* Cattle
markets every W, fat and lean stock,
also corn. Horse sales last W in
every month, 1st T in Sept c sh, 1st
T in Dc h
Cavendish—Ju 11 and 12 pl
Clare—*Mon.* Corn and genl
Cowlinge—Jy 31 and Aug 1, Oct 17
and 18 ped and gipsies
Dunwich—Jy 25 ped
Earl Soham—Jy 23
Elmset—Whit-T
Eye—*Mon.* Sale by Auction of fat
and store c sh swine, fortnightly
special sales of grazing c, May and
Nov, Xmas stock Dec 12
Framlingham—*Sat.* Repository sale
generally on last S in Month. Ann : d
sale in connection with the Framling-
ham Live Stock Association gene-
rally on 3rd or 4th F in Jy.
Framsden—Holy Th
Glemsford—Jy 24 and 25 pl
Great Thurlow—Oct 11
Hacheston—Nov 13 ped
Hadleigh—*Mon.* Whit-M, M nearest
Sept 20 c sh, Oct 10 sh
Halesworth—*Tues.* Whit T, pl
Haverhill—*Fri.* May 12, Oct 10 c
Horningsheath—Sept 4 sh
Hundon—Holy Th ped
Ipswich—*Tues* & *Sat*—Cattle mts every
T, 1st and 3rd T May c h sh p pl,
Aug 22 (ram fair) h sh pl la, second
largest fair in the Eastern Counties ;
sale by auction every mt day. Sp'l
sales : Apl 3 red poll c, May 1, 16 c,
Ju 15 w, Jy 14 w, Aug 21 la. Horse
sales, Jan 30, Mar 13, Apl 10, May 15,
Ju 5, Sept 11, 25, Oct 23, Nov 20.
Ixworth—May 13 pl
Kersey—East-M
Lakenheath—Last Th in Ju h c
Lavenham—*Tues.* Shrove-Th, Oct 11
b ch
Laxfield—May 12, Oct 25
Lowestoft—*Wed.* May 12, Oct 12
Melford—Whit-T ped, Whit-W c sh
Nayland—*Fri.* W aft Oct 2 c

Needham Market—Oct 12 pl
Newmarket—*Tues* and *Sat.* Stock
sales every T c sh p, Nov 8 h
Saxmundham — *Wed.* Stock sales every
alt W c sh p. Annual lamb sales in
Jy
Southwold—*Thurs.* Trin M pl
Stoke—W aft May 13
Stowmarket—*Thurs.* Jy 10 pl, Aug 12
c sh la
Sudbury—*Thurs.* Mar 12, Jy 10 pl,
Sept 4
Sutton nr. Woodbridge—2nd F in Ju.
1st and 3rd F in Jy, 2nd F in Aug
Sp'l la sales Jy 7, Aug 4.
Woodbridge—*Thurs.* Sales by auction
every mt day of fat c sh swine
Woolpit—Sept 16 h c pl

SURREY—
Bletchingley—May 10, Nov 2 c h
Bookham—Nov 29
Chertsey—*Wed.* 1st M in Lent c,
May 14 c sh, Aug 6, Sept 25 c h
Cobham—May 1, Dec 11 pl
Croydon—*Sat.* Oct 2 and h c
Dorking—*Thurs.* Holy Th & day bef
c h
Epsom—*Wed.* Aug
Ewehurst—Aug 5
Ewell—May 12 c, Oct 29 c sh
Farnham—*Thurs.* May 10, Ju 23, Nov
10 c h sh
Frogerheath—Ju 16
Godalming—*Wed.* corn *Sat.* Feb 13
c h
Godstone—Jy 22 c pl
Guildford—May 4, Nov 22
Haslemere—*Tues.* May 13 c, Sept 25
Hounslow—Trin M, M aft Sept 29
Kingston—*Thurs* and *Sat.* Aug 2, Nov
13 c
Knaphill—Nov 10 c
Leatherhead—Oct 10 c h
Lingfield—Ju 29 c, Oct 11 hi
Mitcham—Aug 12
New Richmond—May 29
Oxted—*Alt Wed.* c
Reigate—*Tues.* Whit-M c, Sept 14 pl,
Dec 9 c h sh
Thorpe—May 29 c pl

SUSSEX
Arundel—*Alt Mon* corn and c, May 4,
25 pl
Balcombe—Apl 13
Battle—Sept 8 c h sh, Nov 22 c h, and
T in month stk and corn
Bodiam—Ju 6
Bognor—*Tues, Thurs.* and *Sat.*
and 6 pl
Burwash—*Tues.* May 12 c sh p, Oct,
pl
Burgess Hill—Ju 5 h c pl
Chailey Common—*Wed.* Cattle auctns.
alt M comm Jan 8,
Chichester—*Wed* c corn. Oct 20 h
hops gr, cattle mkt alternate W
comm Jan 10
Chiddingly—Jy 23 h c sh pl
Crawley—*Alt. Fri* corn. May 8, Sept
9 c sh h
Cross-in-hand—Nov 19 h c
Crowborough—Apl 25 c
Dicker—Holy Th c sh
Eastbourne—Oct 11 c sh
East Grinstead—*Thurs,* corn. Apl 21,
Dec 11 h c sh p pl, cattle-market alt
Th comm Jan 4
East Hoathley—Apl 8 h c sh
Findon—Holy Th c, Jy 12 c h la, Sept
12 h c sh
Flimwell—Nov 26 c
Forest Row—Nov 8 c h sh
Hailsham—*Alt. Wed* c corn. Aug 12
h c sh
Harefield—May 9. Th aft Trin
Hassocks Gate—*Alt Th* c
Hastings—*Sat* com. Whit-T pl, Ju
26, Oct 1, Nov 23
Hayward's Heath—*Tues* c, *Wed* com
Apl 23, Nov 18

Heathfield—*Thurs* c. Apl 14 h c
Henfield—Live stk sales alternate M
Hooe—May 1 c
Horsebridge—May 9, Sept 29
Horsham—Red c corn, Apl 5 c sh, Jy 18 h c sh la, Nov 17 h c sh, Nov 27 h c sh
Horsted Keynes—*Fri.* Mar 27, Sept 12
Lamberhurst—Apl 6 h c sh
Lewes—*Tues.* Jy 26 w, Sept 21 h, Sept 28 c h
Lindfield—Apl 1 c sh, May 12 c, Aug 8 c h sh la, Sept 23 sh
Littlehampton—*Alt Tues.* Oct 26 pl
Maresfield—Sept 4, Nov 18
Mayfield—May 30, Nov 13 c
Midhurst—*Thurs.* Apl 6, Whit-T c sh pigs, Oct 30 c
Newick—Apl 30 c pl
Peasemarsh—Trin Th
Pett—May 27, Jy 16
Petworth—*Sat.* Sept 20 pl
Pulborough—*Fri* corn. Alt M comm Jan 8 c sh p
Rackham—May 20, Oct 14
Robertsbridge—*Fri.* Sept 25 hops, alternate M gt mt
Rotherfield—*Alt Tues.* Ju 18, Oct 20
Rye—*Alt Wed* c. Aug 3, 22 pl
Selmestone—Sept 29
Slangham—East T, Sept 29
South Harting—Ju 4, Oct 28
Steyning—*Wed* c corn. Oct 11 c h
Storrington—*Alt Wed.* May 13, Nov 11 stk
Thakeham—Whit T
Uckfield—*Fri* c. May 14, Aug 29 c h sh
Wadhurst—*Tues.* Apl 29, Nov 1 c h sh, alternate M c mt
West Preston—Ju 23
Wilmington—Sept 17

WARWICKSHIRE—
Alcester—*Tues.* T bef Jan 29 c, T bef Mar 29 c hi, 3rd T in Apl c, 3rd T in May c pl, last T in Jy c, 3rd T in Sept c, T bef and aft Oct 11 hi, T aft Oct 16 c corn pl, 1st T in Dec c h sh
Bedworth—*Sat.* Apl 6, Whit W c, Aug 25
Birmingham—*Tues, Thurs, and Sat.* Cattle market every T and Th, p daily, 1st Th in Ju, Th aft Whit M c, last Th F & S in Sept c h pl onions. Horse sales 1st Tu in month
Bingley Hall (Birmingham)—Stock sales periodically
Brailes—East T
Coleshill—*Wed.* 1st M in Jan c, Shrove M h, May 7 c, Jy 9 stk, Oct 1 c
Coventry—*Wed and Fri.* Cattle markets every M fat stk, every S lean stk and h, May 2 h c sh p, F in Whit week h c sh p, M to F in Whit week pl, Nov 1 h c sh p
Dunchurch—3rd M in Jan c, last M in Feb, 3rd M in Mar c, 3rd M in Apl, M bef May 24 c, M bef Ju 24 c, 3rd M in Jy c, T bef Aug 21 c, Sept 15 c, bef Oct 20 c, 3rd M in Nov c h hi, Nov 13 & 14 h, T bef Dec 22 c sh
Hampton in Arden—Cattle auctions 3rd M every month
Henley in Arden—*Mon.* Mar 25 hi, Oct 11 hi
Kineton—*Tues.* Feb 5, Oct 2 hi
Leamington—Stock sales 1st and 3rd W in every month c sh p, except Dec Xmas sale and W in Dec
Nuneaton—*Sat.* Cattle auctions every T c sh p, May 1 h c sh, Oct 11 h pl
Rugby—*Sat.* Cattle markets every M fat stk. Last M in Jan c, Feb 17 c, last M in Mar and Apl c, May 15 c, last M in Ju and Jy c, Aug 21 c, M bef Sept 29 c, M bef Oct 27 c, M bef Nov 10 and 4 following days great h fair, Nov 22 great cattle fair, M in Dec c, 1st M aft Xmas c
Solihull—*Wed.* Last W in Apl c, last W in Sept c hi

Southam—*Mon.* 1st M each month c sh p, 1st M on or aft Oct 11 hi
Stratford on Avon—*Fri.* Cattle market and stock sales every T. Hiring fairs :—Oct 12. last F in Oct
Studley—Sept 28
Sutton Coldfield—*Mon.* Stock sales 1st T in every month c sh p
Warwick—*Sat.* Cattle markets and stock sales on 2nd and 4th M in every mo c sh p, 2nd M in Apl ch, and M in Jy w, Oct 12 pl hi, and M in Nov h

WESTMORLAND—
Ambleside—*Wed and Sat.* Whit W c sh, and W aft Whit W c sh, Oct 13 sh, Oct 29 c
Appleby—*Sat.* Cattle auctions every alternate M with Kirkby Stephen c sh p, and W in Ju and day before h c sh pl, Aug 21 c sh, S aft Oct 1 pl, Whit M hi pl. S on or aft Nov 11 pl, hi
Brough—2nd Th in Feb, Mar and Apl c sh, Th bef Whit Su
Brough Hill—Sept 30, Oct 1 h c sh (very large fair)
Burton—3rd W in April
Grasmere—1st T in Sept c sh
Kendal—*Sat.* Cattle markt and stock sales every M Feb 22 h, Mar 22 c, Apl 29 c, Nov 8 c, Nov 9 h, 1st and 2nd S aft Martinmas pl and hi, p market every S
Kirkby Lonsdale—*Thurs.* Apl 5, Holy Th c clo, 3 weeks aft Holy Th, Th bef East, Oct 5, Dec 21 c clo. Alt Tu from 2nd Tu in Ju to end of year la sh
Kirkby Stephen—*Mon.* Cattle auctions alt M's commencing 1st M in Jan, M bef Shrove T h, M bef Apl 25 h, Sept 29 h c, Oct 27 c sh, Aug 20 ch. M bef Whit M hi, last M in Ju hi. 1st M in Jy hi, M on or bef Nov 11 hi
Low Borrow Bridge (Tebay)—2nd W in Sept c sh
Milnthorpe—May 11 and 12, Oct 17 c h sh
Orton—*Fri.* May 3, 1st W in Sept, 2nd Fri after Oct 11 c and sh
Patterdale—Sept 23 c sh
Pooley Bridge—3rd M in Sept c sh, principally half-bred and herdwick h
Shap—May 4, Sept 23 h c sh
Staveley—*Wed.* Oct 7 c sh
Temple Sowerby—Last Th in Jan, Feb and Mar, 2nd Th in May c sh, last Th in Oct

WILTSHIRE—
Amesbury—*Fri.* May 17, Ju 22, Oct 6, Dec 18
Barwick—Nov 10 c
Barwick St. Leonards—Nov 6 sh h
Bradford—*Tu and Sa.* Trin M c h d
Bradford Leigh—*Fri.* M aft A   ch p
Britford -Aug 12 sh
Calne—*Wed.* May 6 c, Jy 22. Sept
Castle Combe—May 4 c sh
Chilmark—Jy 30
Chippenham—*Fri.* Cattle mkts 2nd and last F each month. Cheese 2nd F. Last F in Ju w
Clack—Apl 5, Oct 10 c h
Collingbourne Ducis—Dec 11
Corsley Heath—Whit T, 1st M in Aug
Cricklade—*Sat.* Sept 21 pl, 3rd T in each month h c
Devizes—*Thurs.* Feb 14, Apl 20, Oct 20 c, 1st Th each month gt mt
Dilton March—Sept 24
Downton—Apl 23 sh sh, Oct 2 c sh p
Great Bedwin—*Tues.* Jy 26 pl
Heytesbury—May 14
Highworth—*Wed.* Aug 13 c, Oct 11 c sh. Gt mkt 4th W in every month
Hindon—*Thurs and Sat.* May 27, M before Whit Su pl, Oct 29 pl
Kingsdown—W bef Sept 21 (St. Matthew's day) h c sh p pl
Laycock—Jy 7, Dec 20
Ludgershall—*Wed.* Jy 25 pl

Maiden Bradley—May 6, Oct 2
Malmesbury—*Sat.* Gt mkt 3rd W in every month, Mar 28 c h, Apl 28 ch, Ju 5 c h, Dec 15 c corn ch
Marlborough—*Sat.* Aug 22 h sh, c bef and aft Oct 11 hi, Nov 23 h sh
Melksham—*Mon.* Great market last T in every month c sh p, Jy 27 c h sh, and M in Aug h, alternate T corn
Mere—*Tues.* May 17 c, Oct 10 c ch p
Norleaze—Apl 23
North Bradley—May 13, M aft Sept 14
Pewsey—*Tues.* Sept 15
Purton—T bef May 6, F aft Sept 19
Ramsbury—May 14 c pl, Oct 11 hi
Salisbury—*Tues and Sat.* Cattle markets 2nd Th in every month h c sh p. Gt.mkts a t T com 1st T in Jan. 2nd T aft Jan 6 sh ch poultry, Jy 15 sh, T aft Oct 17 ch h onions Live stk T. Sp'l n sale last F in Oct
Sherston—May 12, Oct 2
Steeple Ashton—Sept 19 c
Swindon—*Mon.* Cattle markets and last M in month, M bef Apl 5 hi, M aft Sept 11 p hi
Tan Hill—Aug 6 c
Trowbridge—*Thurs and Sat.* Cattle market every Th, Aug 5, 6 7 c ch h pl
Uphaven—Oct 29
Warminster—*Sat.* Apl 22 c h ch, Aug 11 c ch, Oct 26 sh
Westbury—*Fri.* 1st T in Sept c sh, Sept 24 c sh (Dilton's Marsh).
Westbury Hill—Sept 6 c h sh, 1st T in Dec c
Wilsbury—Nov 17
Wilton—*Wed.* May 4 stk, Sept 12 sh
Wootton Bassett—*Tues.* 1st W in every month c, T bef Apl 6 hi. T bef Oct 11 hi
Yarnborough Castle—Oct 4

WORCESTERSHIRE—
Alvechurch—1st W in May and 1st W in Oct statute
Bewdley—*Sat.* Apl 23 pl
Bromsgrove—*Tues.* Cattle market every alternate T, commencing 1st T in Jan. Ja 24 c pl h
Dudley—*Sat.* 1st M in Mar, May, and M in Aug, 1st M in Oct h p pl
Evesham—*Mon.* 1st M in Feb, 1st M aft East, M aft Whit M, and M Aug, 1st M Sept, h c sh, F bef and aft Oct 10 hi
Hagley—Stock sales every M c sh p, 1st M in May c sh p
Hales Owen—East M and T pl, M nearest Oct 10 statute hi
Hanbury—Mar 25, Sept 29 statute
Kidderminster—*Thurs.* Cattle markets every alternate T, commencing 1st T in Jan, 3rd Th in Ju and two following days pl
King's Norton—1st M in Oct h
Pershore—*Tues.* Ju 26 h
Redditch—*Sat.* 1st M in Aug, 3rd M in Sept pl
Shipston-on-Stour—*Sat.* 3rd T in Apl h, Ju 22 h pl. T aft Oct 10 hi, 1st T in Dec, last W but one in Jan, Feb, Mar, May, Jy, Aug, Sept & Nov c mkts
Stourbridge—*Fri.* Last M in Mar
Tenbury Wells—*Tues.* Cattle mkts every alternate T fat and store c sh p. *Fairs:* Apl 22 c, May 1 pl
Upton-on-Severn—*Thurs.* Cattle sales 2nd Th in every month. Th att Mid-Lent Su, Th in Whitsun-week, Jy 10, Th bef Oct 2 hi
Worcester—*Wed and Sat.* Cattle markets every M h c sh p, Sept 19 (annual) ch, Dec 16, Xmas stk

YORKSHIRE—
Addingham—(Skipton) Mar 22 c, Ap 28 c, Oct 3 ch
Adwalton—Feb 6, Mar 9, East Th h c Whit Th h, Nov 5 c hi, Dec 23 c

Apperley Bridge—Auction sales c sh p

Askrigg—*Thurs.* Jy 1 and 2 gt sh fair, 2nd Th in Jy hi, Oct 28 c sh w

Austwick—Th bef Whit Su c

Aysgarth—Oct 30 c sh

Barnoldswick—Tu bef last w in Apl c, 2nd T in Sept c

Barnsley—Every T c sh by auction, every W p mt. Last W in Feb h, May 13 h, Oct 11 h and c fair, 1st S in Nov statutes hi pl

Bawtry—*Thurs.* Th aft Whit Sunday h c, Nov 23 h c hi pl

Bedale—*Tues.* Stock sales every alternate T. East T c sh, Whit T c sh, Jy 6 c, Jy 7 h, Oct 11 c, Oct 12 sh, M aft Dec 10 c sh

Bentham—Feb 5, Good F, East Eve. Ju 22, Jy 22, Oct 25 c sh

Beverley—*Sat.* Cattle market alt W c sh p, Th bef Feb 25, Holy Th, Jy 5, Nov 5 h c, Nov 6 hi, about Nov 29 hi (date fixed by Mayor).

Bingley—Stock sales every T c sh p, 1st T in Apl, and T in Oct h c sh

Bolton-by-Bowland—Ju 28 hi

Boroughbridge—*Sat.* Stk sales every alternate T c sh p, Apl 27 and 28 c sh, M aft and W in Ju and all the week (Barnaby Fair) h, Ju 21 and 22 c sh, pl, Oct 23 and 24 c sh (very large fair)

Bradford—*Mon* and *Thurs.* Cattle markets every Th. Mar 3, Ju 17 c h sh, Dec 9 c h sh p, 1st M in Jan and Jy pl

Buckden (Skipton)—2nd M in Sept, Oct 12 sh

Cast'eton—M bef Oct 10 rams, F aft Oct 20 ch

Catchall (Linton)—Nov 3 c sh

Catterick—Auction sales alt on. commencing Jan 1

Clapham—Sept 27 la sh, Oct 2 c sh

Cross Hills (Skipton)—Sept 24 sh

Dacre Banks—Auct sales alt. Tu com Jan 9 c sn p.

Denholme—M aft Aug 6 pl.

Dewsbury—2nd W in May p, F and S bef 1st M in Aug pl, 2nd W in Oct onions

Doncaster—*Tues* and *Sat.* Every T fat stk. every S corn c produce Fairs for h and c : 1st Th in Feb, Apl, Aug and Nov. Wool mts commence either on last S in May or 1st S in Ju and continue every S until the fair day (Aug. 3), 1st S in Sept and Oct

Driffield—*Thurs.* Auction sales every Mon. East M, Whit M, Aug 26, Sept 19 h sh

Easingwold—N Apl 2 c p, Jy c sh, Sept 26 c s F aft Nov 5 hi

East Wilton—May 3, Nov 20 c sh

Egton—2nd T in Jan c h sh, T bef Feb 14 c h, T bef Palm Su c h, 2nd T in Apl, T bef May 13, and every T till 9 mts are held, and T in Aug c h, Sept 4, T bef Oct 11 c h, Nov 5 h, T bef Nov 23, and T in Dec c h

Emley—1st W aft May 15 pl

Farsley—Sept 4, 5, 6 pl

Ford Inn—1st S aft Apl 11, 1st S aft Oct 5 c

Gargrave—2nd T in Oct c sh h, Dec 11 and 12 calving cows and store c

Giggles ick—Mar 12c

Gisourn—Cattle markets alternate M, East M, 2nd and 4th M aft East, Sept 18 and 19 c bed

Goole—*Wed* and *Sat.* M aft Oct 11 hi

Grassington—Mar 4, Apl 24 c sh, Sept 26 c sh

Guisborough—*Tues.* Last T in Apl hi pl stall, last T in Ju w, and T in Nov pl hi. Stock sales every alternate T c sh p

Halifax—*Sat.* Cattle markets every S, Ju 24 c h sh p and pl fair all week, 1st S in Nov c h p

Harewood—2nd and last M in Oct c sh

Hawes—*Tues.* Cattle mts and stk sales alternate T, commencing 2nd T in Jan, Whit T clo c sh, F aft 2nd W in Ju h c hogs, Aug 30 la, Sept 14 la, 28 h c, T aft Oct 12 rams sh, T bef Nov 5 c, T bef Dec 11 c

Heckmondwike—1st M in May c, 1st M in Nov c

Hedon—*Sat.* Cattle markets alternate M, Feb 14, Aug 2, Sept 22, Nov 17 hi, Dec 6 c

Hellfield—Cattle auctions every W, store c calving cows and dairy stk every Th

Helmsley—*Fri.* Jy 16 c h sh, Oct 1 sh, Oct 2 c, 5 sh. Nov 6 c h, May 19 c h

Holmfirth—S bef Mar 31, S aft May 4, last S in Oct c

Howden—*Sat.* Cattle markets alternate T, 2nd M, T and W in Apl h, Th foll c, M T and W foll Doncaster races. Great horse fair, Th foll c, Nov 24 hi. If on Su held day previous

Huddersfield—*Tues* and *Fri.* Cattle markets every T, Mar 31, May 14, Oct 4 c h p, Ju 20 pl

Hull—*Tues, Fri,* and *Sat.* Cattle markets every M and T c sh p. 2nd T in Apl c h, Oct 11 c h pl, 12 and 13 pl. Annual feasts : "Drypool" 2nd M in Aug; "Pottery" East M and T. Wool sales: 2nd T in Ju, and every T to the end of Jy

Ilkley—W foll 1st W aft Sept 14 sh la

Ingleton—Nov 17 c

Keighley—*Wed* and *Sat.* May 8 c h, Nov 8 c h

Kettlewell (Skipton)—Jy 6 hi, Sept 2 la, Oct 23 sh

Kirkburton—W aft Whit week pl

Knaresborough—*Wed.* 1st W aft Jan 13, Mar 12, May 5, Oct 11, Nov 23, and Dec 10. Cattle markets alt W c sh p.

Lee Gap (Dewsbury—Aug 24 and Sept 17 (large horse fairs)

Leeds—*Tues, Wed,* and *Sat.* Every Tu calves and pigs, every T and F corn and p, every F c1o, p. Cattle markets every W calving cows, fat and store stock. Leather fairs: 3rd W in Jan, 1st W in Mar, 3rd W in Apl, 1st W in Ju, 3rd W in Jy, 1st W in Sept, 3rd W in Oct, 1st W in Dec. Jy 10 and 11 h pl, Nov 8 and 9 h hi pl Horse sales every Tues. Sp'l sale 1st Tues in every month

Leyburn—*Fri.* c mt alternate F, and F in Feb. May c sh, 2nd F in Oct sh, day aft c, 2nd F in Dec c sh

Long Preston—*Mon.* Ctl mkts alt M. Mar 1 hi, Sept 4 c, F bef and T in Oct great ewe fair, every Th calv c

Malham—Ju 30 la sh. 1st Th in Aug sh la, Oct 15 sh rams

Malton—*Tues* and *Sat.* Cattle markets every S ; stk sales every T c s hp calves. M to W bef Palm Su (great horse fair). Oct 11 and 12 c h sh, last 3 S in Nov hi, sh bef Whit Su, Jy 11, and Nov 23 c ch

Market Weighton—*Wed.* Stock sales alt T c sh p, May 14, Sept 25 ch, 26 pl

Marsden—Anl 25, Jy 10 c, Sept 25 c h sh

Masham—*Wed.* Easter W c sh, Sept 17 sh, 18 c

Meltham—1st S in Apl h c, 1st S aft Oct 11 c sh

Mid'leham—*Mon.* Mar 30 c sh

Middleham Moor—Nov 5 sh, Nov 6 c h

Mirfield—Last M in Apl and Oct h c

New Mill—M bef last S in Mar and Oct c

Northallerton—*Wed.* Cattle auctions alt T c sh p, comm and T in Jan c sh p, Feb 14 c h, May 1 to 4 (incl) h, May 5 h c hi, Sept 4 and 6 la, Oct 3 and 4 c

Northowram—Sept 21 h c

Otley—*Fri.* Cattle auctions alternate M & T c sh p M one week and T the next. Horse sales 2nd F in mo.

East W h c sh, and every alternate W until Whitsuntide c, M aft the Su following Aug 2 h c sh pl, F bef and aft Nov 23 hi

Pannal—Alt M comm Jan 1

Pateley Bridge—*Sat.* Cattle mkts every alt S comm Jan 13 c sh, S bef East Su c sh pl stallions, 2nd S in Oct c sh pl

Penistone—*Thurs.* Cattle mkt every Th, Th bef Feb 28, last Th in. Mar, Th bef May 12 c, Th aft Oct 11 ch

Pi'kering — *Mon.* Cattle markets alternate M. M aft Feb 3 c, eve of Palm Su h, M bef May 13 Jy 6, Sept 25 c h sh, M aft Nov 16

Pocklington—*Mon* Cattle auctions alternate T (same week as York) Feb 24 c h, Mar 7, May 6, Aug 5, Nov 7 hi, Dec 28 c h at each fair

Pontefract — *Sat.* Cattle markets alt S (same week as York), stk sales every Tu fat c sh sings. S aft Jan 14, S aft Feb 13, S bef Palm Su, May 5, Oct 5 c, Nov 30 c

Pudsey—Aug 28, 29, 30 pl

Richmond—*Sat.* Cattle markets alt S, S aft Feb 2 stk, S bef Palm Su stk, 1st S in Jy stk, Sept 25 stk

Richmond Moor—Nov 3 c h sh

Ripley—*Sat.* Aug 26 h c

Ripon—*Thurs.* Stock sales alternate M from Jan 1 and alternate T from Jan 9. Last Th in Jan h c, May 13 h c, May 14 sh hi, 1st Th in Ju c, day aft sh, 1st Th in Oct sh, 1st Th in Nov, Nov 23 c hi

Romaldkirk (Barnard Castle)—Th aft Brough Hill fair in Oct h c sh

Rotherham—*Mon* and *Fri.* Cattle auctions every M, Whit-M h, 1st M in Nov hi pl, Dec 1 or M aft ch

Santhorpe—Sales every M

Scarborough—*Thurs* and *Sat.* May 27 sh c, Holy Th, N v 22 c

Seamer Junction—Auction sales alt Mon comm Jan 1

Sedburgh—*Wed.* Jan 24 c. Feb 26 c, Mar 20 c, Apl 28 c sh, 3rd W in Mav c sh, Oct 29 c rams

Selby—*Mon.* Stock sales every M c, sh p, East T Ju 22, every F in Ju w, Oct 11 c

Settle—*Tues.* Cattle markets alt M from Ju to Nov. *Fairs :* Apl 26, Aug 19, 1st T aft Oct 27 c sh. T bef Palm Su c, Whit T c

Sheffield—*Tues* and *Sat.* Cattle markets every M fat stk, every T lean stk and calving cows, every F also p and calves, Whit T and W c h ch, T and W next following Xmas day, except when Xmas day falls on T or W, then winter fair is held on the two days next following. The horse fair is always on the first day

Shipley—East T, 3rd M in Oct c

Silsden—T aft Apl 23, T aft Sept 16 c

Skipton—*Sat.* Cattle markets and Sstk sales every M c sh p, Ju 19 genl ped, Aug 23 c h, Nov 23 genl ped, Dec 6 c sh p, Dec 26 c sh p. *Fair :* Aug 23

Slaidburn—T nearest Mar 20 c sh, 1st T in Oct c sh

Slaithwaite—Cattle mkts alt M comm Jan 1, Welsh calving cows and grazing stirks

Snaith—*Thurs.* Last Th in Apl c, Aug 10 c la h, Nov 15 hi, Nov 25 hi

Stanningley—Jy 31 and 2 foll days pl

Stokesley—*Sat.* Stock sales alt M c sh p, S bef Feb 14 c, S bef Palm Su c, S bef Trin Su sh, S aft Oct 11 c sh

Tadcaster—*Wed.* Cattle mts alternate M, last W in Apl and May c h sh, last W in Oct c h sh, Nov 1 hi

Thirsk—*Mon.* Stk sales every M : Shrove M c sh, Apl 4 and 5 c sh, May 31 c sh, Aug 4 and 5 c sh, Oct 28 and 29 c sh, Nov 11 hi, T aft Dec 11 c sh

Thorne—*Wed.* M, T, and W aft Ju 11 and Oct 11 c

Thornton—M aft 1st S in Nov h c sh p, Tu aft Aug 6 pl

Tickhill—*Fri.* Aug 21 c sh la, and F in Oct c sh

Topcliffe—*Jy* 17 sh, Jy 18 c h, Oct 1 c

Wakefield—*Wed.* and *Sat.* Cattle markets every W, fat stock, Jy 4 h, Jy 5 pl, Nov 11 c h, Nov 12 hi

West Burton (Aysgarth)—Mar 10 c sh, May 6 and 7 c sh

Wetherby—*Thurs.* Cattle mts alt Th c sh p. Sales every M. Th bef Martinmas hi, Th on or aft Martinmas hi

Whitby—*Sat.* Aug 25 c sh la, Nov 11. Nov 23 hi

Whitewell—W nearest Sept 20 sh (only)

Whitgift—Jy 22 and 23 c hi, Nov 15 hi

Whitkirk (Crossgates station)—Auct sales alt Mon comm Jan 1 fat and store c s p

Wibsey—Oct 5 h c pl, Oct 6 pl, Nov 25 h c

Yarm—*Thurs.* Th bef Apl 5 c, Holy Th c, Aug 2 c sh la, Oct 18 h, Oct 19 c, Oct 20 sh (large fairs), Oct 26 ch sh

York—*Thurs* and *Sat.* Cattle markets alternate Th commencing on the 2nd Th in Jan, Fat stk sales Tu, every W and S p, Th bef Palm S, Whit M, Ju 10, Aug 12, Nov 14 h. Nov 24 c h, last whole week bef Xmas day great h fair, Th bef Old Candlemas day. Live fairs: S bef Old Candlemas day, S bef Old Lady day, Whit M, Old St. Peter's day, Old Lammas Day, S bef Old Michaelmas, S bef Old Martinmas, S bef Xmas day. Leather fairs: 1st W in Mar, Ju, Sept and Dec. Auction sales on fair days, and special sales of sheep in Sept and Oct. Horse sales alt Th. except Oct and Nov, when the sales are held ev Th. Sp'l sales of hunters, May, Aug, and Dec. Bloomstock May and Aug.

PRINCIPAL FAIRS IN SCOTLAND AND IRELAND, AND WELSH HORSE FAIRS.

SCOTLAND.

MANY of the principal Fairs in Scotland have lapsed, and those that are still held have declined in a great measure in recent years, so much so in fact, that in a few more years we may expect to see them become defunct. This decadence is in consequence of the rapid growth of the Auction-mart system, which affords sellers and buyers certain facilities and advantages which formerly, under the old system, did not exist. Our object is to furnish such information as may be useful, particularly to English buyers who intend visiting Scotland for the purpose of purchasing the native cattle or sheep.

WEST HIGHLAND CATTLE:—Important special sales are held in May, June, Sept. Oct. and Nov., at Stirling, Oban, Perth, Inverness, and Fort William.

FAIRS :— Falkirk Trysts (Larbert Station), and Tues. in Aug. ; and Tues. and day before in Sept. and Oct. All the best cattle are sold on the first day at each of these fairs.

ABERDEEN POLLED ANGUS CATTLE :— The best quality of this remarkable beef producing breed of cattle is very much in private breeder's hands, and although some excellent stores can be bought in the Aberdeenshire and Forfarshire Auction marts in the Spring and Autumn, it is from the breeders that most English buyers draw their supplies.

GALLOWAY POLLED CATTLE :— Castle Douglas, Newcastleto and Lockerbie are the only Auctic. marts in Scotland where large sales of this class of cattle are held in the Spring and Autumn. Very large sales of pure-bred Galloway, and cross-bred (Blue Grey) cattle are also held on the Border, at the Carlisle Auction marts in the Spring and Autumn

BLACK - FACE (HORNED) SHEEP :— Practically, all the fairs where this class of sheep was formerly sold are now defunct, except, perhaps, Grantown in the Spring, where young sheep and lambing ewes are sold. For high-class quality, Lanark is the premier mart, and very large sales of young sheep are held in the Spring ; for lambs in Aug. and Sept. ; and for cast ewes in Oct. Lockerbie, Peebles, Ayr, Stirling, Perth and Inverness, Ayr, and Thornhill, Dumfriesshire are marts where large numbers of blackface sheep are sold during the Spring and Autumn.

CHEVIOT SHEEP:—Special sales are held, principally in the Autumn, for this class of sheep at Hawick, Newcastleton, and on the Border at Rothbury and Bellingham.

NORTH OF SCOTLAND CHEVIOT SHEEP (which are generally a larger kind than the Border sheep), are sold in large numbers in the Autumn at the Perth and Inverness marts.

CROSS-BRED SHEEP (Border, Leicester and Black-face) are mostly sold as lambs in Aug. and Sept. at all the South of Scotland marts, perhaps the best quality class being at Carlisle Auction marts at the fairs, Aug. 26 and Sept. 19. A good class of Cross-bred lambs, mostly by a Wensleydale (Yorkshire) ram out of a Black-face ewe, can be obtained at the Castle Douglas and Ayr marts. Three-parts-bred, and Half-bred (Border, Leicester and Cheviot) lambs are sold in July and Aug. at St. Boswells ; also at Hawick, Peebles, Rothbury, Newcastleton and Lockerbie marts.

KELSO GREAT RAM sales, and Fri. in Sept

CLYDESDALE HORSES :—These horses are sold in great numbers at all the South of Scotland fairs, and although cattle and sheep have gone into the Auction marts, the supply of horses at the fairs shows no appreciable falling off. The principal fairs are : Dumfries, Tues. and Wed. after Castle Douglas (Candlemas fair) in Feb. ; Wed. before May 26 ; Sept. 24 and 25, if Tues. and Wed., if not, Tues. and Wed. after ; Wed. before Nov. 22. Castle Douglas: Feb. 11 if Mon., if not, Mon. after (Candlemas fair) ; Sept. 23 if Mon., if not, Mon. after ; Mon. before Nov. 22. Glasgow : 2nd and 4th Wed. in Jan. ; every Wed. in Feb. and March ; 1st and 2nd Wed. in April ; 1st Wed. in May, June, July, Aug., Sept., Oct. and Dec. Rutherglen : Fri. after May 4 ; Tues. after June 4 ; Fri. after July 25 ; Fri. after Aug. 23 ; Wed. before 1st Fri. in Nov. Edinburgh : Tues. and Wed. after and Mon. (Hallow fair) ; 2nd Wed. after Hallow Fair (Big Wed.). St. Boswells : July 18. Falkirk Trysts : 2nd Tues. in Sept. and Oct. Clydesdale horses are also sold at the Ayr, Lanark, Edinburgh, Stirling and Perth Auction marts, also at the Border fairs held at Longtown (Cumb.), Carlisle, Stagshawbank, Newcastle, Wigton (Cumb.) and Cockermouth, dates of which are shown in the English List.

IRELAND.

DUBLIN HORSE SHOW usually on Tu and three following days in third full week in Aug.

PRINCIPAL HORSEFAIRS. — Armagh (co. Armagh), 1st Thurs. in each month. Athlone (co. Roscommon), 3rd Mon. in Jan. and March. Ballinasloe (co. Galway), 1st Tues. in Oct. and four following days. Ballinrobe (co. Roscommon), Aug. 25. Ballibay (co. Monaghan), 3rd Sat. in each month. Ballyboghan (co. Meath), Sept. 26. Banagher (Kings Co.), Sept. 15. Banbridge (co. Down) 1st Mon. in Jan. and Ju. Bandon (co. Cork), 1st W in every month except May and Nov. May 6 and 30, Oct. 29, Nov. 28. Boyle (co. Roscommon), Jan. 3, Feb. 3, March 6, April 3, May 9 and 30, July 9 and 25, Aug. 16, Oct. 1, Nov. 25. Cahirmee (co. Cork), July 12 and 13. Clones (co. Monaghan), last Thurs. in each month. Clonmel (co. Tipperary, 1st Wed. in each month. Drogheda (co. Louth), and Wed. in each month. Dundalk (co. Louth), 3rd Wed. in each month. Fermoy (co. Cork), and Tues. in Jan. May, Aug. and Oct. Frenchfurs (co. Kildare), July 26. Limerick (co. Limerick), last Thurs. in Jan, April, July, and Oct. Lisburn (co. Antrim). July 21, Oct. 5. Loughrea (co. Galway), February 11, May 25. Moy (co. Tyrone), 1st Fri. in each month. Mullingar (co. Westmeath), April 5, Aug. 29, Sept. 26. Rathsallagh (co. Wicklow), Sept. 5. Spancil Hill (co. Clare), June 23. Thurles (co. Tipperary), 1st Tues. in each month. Wicklow (co. Wicklow), Aug. 12.

WALES.

PRINCIPAL HORSEFAIRS.—Hay (Brecon), 1st Thurs. in March. Aberystwith, 1st Mon. in every month and day before Lampeter May Fair. Abergele, 3rd Wed. in May, Aug., and Oct. Criccieth, May 23, Sept. 25, Oct. 24. Lampeter, May 8, if 8th is Sun. held day before. Pwllheli, May 1 and 22, Sept. 24. Capel St. Silin, Feb. 7 (Ponies). Carnarvon, Sept. 23. Menai Bridge, Fri. after the 1st Tues. in Sept., Oct. 24. Llangefni, Thurs. after the 1st Tues. in Sept., and 2nd Thurs. after ; Thurs. after the 1st Tues. in Oct., and 2nd Thurs. after, subject to alteration by the County Council. Knighton, Fri. after March 3rd, 3rd Thurs. in April, May 17, Thurs. after Jy 10, Aug. 18, Sept. 14, Oct. 2. Talgarth, April 18, and Tues. in May, and May 31, July 10, Aug. 10, Sept. 23, Oct. 13, Nov. 2. Welshpool, 1st Mon. in March, April, May, Sept., Oct. and Nov. Machynlleth, 1st Wed. in March, May 16, Sept. 18, Oct. 21, Nov. 26. Brecon, 1st Tues. in March, May, July, Sept., Oct. and Nov. Abergavenny, 3rd Tues. in March, May 14, 3rd Tues. in June, Sept. 25, Nov. 19. Carmarthen, March 15, April 15, June 3, July 10, Aug. 12, Sept. 9, Oct. 9, Nov. 14. Denbigh, and Tues. in March, April, May, July, Aug., Sept., and Oct. Newbridge-on-Wye, 3rd. Thurs. in March, May 17, Oct. 17, Nov. 11. Tregaron, March 16, Whit. Tues. Wrexham, Gt. Horse Sls. twice a Quarter. Mothvey (Myddfai), May 18. Newtown (Mont.), last Tues. in March and May, Tues. after last Mon. in July. Builth, July 17, Oct. 16. Llanrhaiadr yn Mochnant, July 23 and 24 (Ponies). Haverfordwest, and Tues. in Aug., 3rd Tues. in Sept. and Oct., and Tues in Nov. Narberth, day after Haverfordwest in Aug., Sept., Oct., and Nov. Corwen, 3rd Tues. in Sept. and Oct. Llanrwst, Sept. 17, Oct. 25. Neath, 2nd Thurs. in Sept., last Wed. in Oct., 1st and 2nd Wed. and Nov. 12. Rhayader, Sept. 25, Oct. 14. Waen (Merthyr), Sept. 3, (Ponies). Four Crosses (Carnarvonshire), Oct. 21. Llanbedr (Conway), Oct. 3, Ponies. Penybont, Oct. 16.

Racing Calendar, 1900.

March.	No. of Days.
26 Lincoln Spring M.	
29 Liverpool Spr. M....	3

April.	No. of Days.
2 Northampton Sp. M.	2
4 Warwick..............	2
5 Croxton Park	1
6 Derby Spring M....	2
9 Nottingham........	2
11 Leicester Spring M.	2
14 Alexandra Park ..	1
16 Newcastle Spring ..	2
16 Kempton Park	2
16 Birmingham Easter	2
17 Windsor Spring M.	1
18 Newmarket Craven	3
19 Catterick Bridge ...	2
24 Epsom Spring M....	2
26 Sandown Pk. Sp. ...	2
26 Pontefract Sp. M....	2

May.	No. of Days.
1 Newmarket 1st Sp.	4
1 Carlisle Spring M. .	2
3 Thirsk	2
5 Hurst Park............	1
8 Chester	3
11 Kempton Pk. Jubil.	2
15 Newmarket 2nd Sp.	3
18 Gatwick Spring M.	2
18 Haydock Park	2
22 York Spring M. ...	2
22 Bath....................	2
23 Hamilton Park Sp.	2
24 Doncaster Spring...	2
24 Salisbury	2
26 Harpenden	1
29 Epsom Sum. M. ...	4

June.	No. of Days.
2 Kempton Pk. June	1
4 Hurst Park	1
4 Redcar 1st Summer	2
4 Wolverhampton ...	2
5 Lingfield	2
6 Manchester	4
12 Ascot	4
16 Windsor June M....	1
19 Beverley	2
19 Gatwick Summer...	2
21 Lincoln	2
22 Sandown Pk. 1st Sm.	2
25 Birmingham	1
25 Lewes	2
26 Newcastle Sum. M.	3
28 Brighton	2
30 Hurst Park............	1

July.	No. of Days.
3 Newmarket 1st July	4
3 Carlisle July M. ...	2
5 Worcester	2
7 Alexandra Park ...	1
9 Nottingham	2
10 Bibury Club	3
11 Pontefract Sum. M.	2
13 Lingfield Sum. M.	2
13 Hamilton Park	2
17 Newmarket 2nd July	3
20 Sandown Eclipse ...	2
24 Leicester Sum. M.	2
26 Liverpool July M.	2
27 Windsor	2
31 Goodwood	4

August.	No. of Days.
4 Alexandra Park ..	1
6 Birmingham Au. M.	2
6 Hurst Park	1
6 Ripon Aug. M.	2
7 Brighton	3
9 Paisley	2
10 Lewes Summer M.	2
10 Haydock Park	2
14 Kempton Pk. 2nd S.	2
14 Redcar 2nd Summer	2
17 Windsor Aug. M. ..	2
20 Wolverhampton ...	2
21 Stockton	3
21 Folkestone	2
24 Nottingham Aug. M.	2
24 Hurst Pk. Aug. M.	2
28 York Aug. M.	3
31 Hamilton Park	2

September.	No. of Days.
1 Sandown Pk. Sept.	1
3 Warwick	2
5 Derby Summer M.	3
8 Kempton Park	1
11 Doncaster Sept. M.	4
15 Alexandra Park ..	1
17 Birmingham	2
18 Yarmouth	1
18 Lingfield	2
18 Pontefract Aut. M.	2
19 Western M., Ayr ..	3
21 Manchester Sep. M.	2
22 Hurst Pk. Sept. M.	1
25 Newmarket 1st Oct.	4
25 Lanark...............	2
27 Edinburgh	2
29 Windsor	1

October.	No. of Days.
1 Nottingham Aut....	2
3 Leicester Oct. M. ..	2
5 Kempton Pk. Oct...	2
5 Haydock Park ..	2
9 Newmarket 2nd Oct.	4
13 Lingfield	1
16 Newcastle Autumn	2
16 Gatwick Oct. M. ..	2
18 Sandown Pk. Aut.	2
18 Thirsk Aut. M.......	2
22 Wolverhampton ...	1
23 Newmarket Ho. M.	4
25 Worcester Aut. M.	2
27 Hurst Park	1
30 Northampton Aut.	2
31 Lewes Autumn M.	1

November.	No. of Days.
1 Lingfield	2
1 Beverley Aut.........	2
3 Gatwick	1
5 Lincoln Aut. M. ..	2
7 Liverpool Aut. M...	4
13 Leicester Nov. M....	2
15 Derby Aut. M.	3
20 Warwick Aut. M....	2
20 Folkestone	2
22 Manchester Nov. M.	3

Winners of Races, 1890—1899.

DERBY.*—1m. 4f. 29y.

1890 Sir J. Miller's Sainfoin (J. Watts), 1; Baron de Rothschild's Le Nord (F. Barrett), 2; Duke of Westminster's Orwell (G. Barrett), 3 (8 ran); time, 2m. 49⅗s.

1891 Sir F. Johnstone's Common (G. Barrett), 1; M. E. Blanc's Gouverneur (J. Woodburn), 2; Sir J. Duke's Martenhurst (J. Fagan), 3 (11 ran); time, 2m. 56⅗s.

1892 Lord Bradford's Sir Hugo (Allsopp), 1; Baron de Hirsch's La Flèche (G. Barrett), 2; M. C. Blanc's Bucentaure (Chesterman), 3 (13 ran); time, 2m. 44s.

1893 Mr. H. McCalmont's Isinglass (T. Loates), 1; Mr. Rose's Ravensbury (H. Barker), 2; Duke of Portland's Raeburn (J. Watts), 3 (11 ran); time, 2m. 43s.

1894 Lord Rosebery's Ladas (J. Watts), 1; Lord Alington's Matchbox (M. Cannon), 2; Mr. T. Cannon's Reminder (G. Chaloner), 3 (7 ran); time, 2m. 45⅘s.

1895 Lord Rosebery's Sir Visto (S. Loates), 1; Mr. T. Cannon's Curzon (h-b) (G. Chaloner), 2; Mr. J. B. Maple's Kirkconnel (W. Bradford), 3 (15 ran); time, 2m. 43⅗s.

1896 H.R.H. the Prince of Wales's Persimmon (J. Watts), 1; Mr. L. de Rothschild's St. Frusquin (T. Loates), 2; Mr. H. E. Beddington's Earwig (F. Allsopp), 3 (11 ran); time, 2m. 42s.

1897 Mr. J. Gubbins's Galtee More (C. Wood), 1; Lord Rosebery's Velasquez (J. Watts), 2; Sir S. Scott's History (M. Cannon), 3 (11 ran); time, 2m. 44s.

1898 Mr. J. W. Larnach's Jeddah (O. Madden), 1; Duke of Westminster's Batt (M. Cannon), 2; Mr. W. Ward's Dunlop (F. Pratt), 3 (18 ran); time, 2 m. 47s.

1899 Duke of Westminster's Flying Fox (M. Cannon), 1; Mr. W. R. Marshall's Damocles (S. Loates), 2; Mr. J. A. Miller's Innocence (W. Halsey), 3 (12 ran); time, 2 m. 42⅕ s.

	ECLIPSE STAKES of £10,000. (SANDOWN PARK.)—(1¼ miles.)	OAKS. About 1½ miles.	ST. LEGER.† 1m. 6f. 132yds.	2,000 GUINS. 1m. 11yds.	1,000 GUINS. 1m. 11yds.
1890	Did not fill	Memoir	Memoir	Surefoot	Semolina
1891	Mr. A. Merry's Surefoot, 4y 10st 2lb (9)	Mimi	Common	Common	Mimi.
1892	Duke of Westminster's Orme, 3y 9st 1lb (7)	La Flèche	La Flèche	Bonavista	La Flèche
1893	Duke of Westminster's Orme, 4y 10st 2lb (6)	MrsButterwick	Isinglass	Isinglass	Siffleuse.
1894	Mr. H. McCalmont's Isinglass, 4y 10st 2lb (7)	Amiable	Throstle	Ladas	Amiable.
1895	Bn. Shickler's Le Justicier, 3y 9st 1lb (8)	La Sagesse	Sir Visto	Kirkconnel	Galeottia.
1896	Mr. L. de Rothsch'd's St. Frusquin, 3y 9st 4lb (4)	C'nt'b'y Pilgrim	Persimmon	St. Frusquin	Thais.
1897	H R H. P. of Wales's Persimmon, 4y 10st 2lb (5)	Limasol	Galtee More	Galtee More	Chelandry.
1898	Lord Roseberys' Velasquez, 4y 10st 2lb (9)	Airs and Graces	Wildfowler	Disraeli	Nun Nicer.
1899	D. of Westminster's Flying Fox, 3y 9st 4lb (5)	Musa	Flying Fox	Flying Fox	Sibola.

* 1865—Gladiateur, first French bred horse that won; 1867—snow fell during the day; 1869—second received 300 sovs. and the third 100 sovs. out of the stakes; 1872—start altered to New Level Post; 1876—Kisber, the first Hungarian bred horse that won. The Derby is now a stake of £6.000—£5,000 to the winner, £500 to the nominator of the same, £300 to the second, and £200 to the third horse. Best time, Persimmon's 2m. 42s.

† This race was established in 1776, but did not receive the name until 1778, when it was named out of compliment to Colonel St. Leger, and run for the first time on Doncaster Town Moor.

ASCOT CUP. 2½ miles.

1886	Althorp 4y 9st
1887	Bird of Freedom 5y 9st 4lb
1888	Timothy 4y 9st
1889	Trayles 4y 9st
1890	Gold 4y 9st
1891	Morion 4y 9st
1892	Buccaneer 4y 9st
1893	Marcion 3y 7st 7lb
1894	La Flêche 5y 9st 1lb
1895	Isinglass 5y 9st 4lb
1896	Love Wisely 3y 7st 7lb
1897	Persimmon 4y 9st
1898	Elf II. 5y 9st 4lb
1899	Cyllene 4y 9st

GOODWOOD CUP. 2½ miles.

1886	The Bard 3y 7st 7lb (w.o.)
1887	*Saville 3y 7st 7lb
1888	Rada 3y 7st 4lb
1889	Trayles 4y 9st 10lb
1890	Philomel 5y 8st 13lb
1891	Gonsalvo 4y 9st 6lb
1892	Martagon 3y 9st 10lb
1893	Barmecide, a., 3st 6lb
1894	Kilsallaghan 4y 8st 2lb
1895	Florizel II. 4y 9st 6lb
1896	Ct.Schomb'gay 3st 2st... (w.o.)
1897	C'nt. Schomburg 5y 10st 4lb
1898	King's Messeng~r 3y 7st 7lb
1899	Merman, a., 9st 5lb

DONCASTER CUP. 2 miles.

1886	The Bard 3y 8st 2lb
1887	Carlton 4y 8st 10lb
1888	Grafton 3y 7st 9lb
1889	Claymore 3y 7st 9lb
1890	Tyrant 5y 9st
1891	Queen's Birthday 4y 9st 4lb
1892	Chesterfield 4y 9st 4lb
1893	Prisoner 3y 8st 6lb
1894	Sweet Duchess 3y 9st 4lb
1895	Kilsallaghan 5y 10st 1lb
1896	Laodamia 6y 9st 4lb
1897	Winkfield's Pride 4y 9st 4lb
1898	Pinfold 3y 8st 1lb
1899	Calveley 4y 9st 4lb

QUEEN'S VASE. 2 miles.

1886	Bird of Freedom 4y 9st
1887	Quiip 3y 7st 8lb
1888	Exmoor 5y 9st 4lb
1889	Morglay 3y 7st
1890	Tyrant 5y 9st 4lb
1891	Mons Meg 3y 6st 12lb
1892	Martagon 5y 9st 4lb
1893	Convent 3y 7st 3lb
1894	Quæsitum 4y 9st
1895	Florizel II. 4y 9st 5lb
1896	Pride 4y 9st
1897	CountSchomberg 5y 9st 4lb
1898	Rush 6y 9st 4lb
1899	Did not fill

ALEXANDRA PLATE (ASCOT). 3 miles.

1886	Blue Grass 6y 9st 7lb
1887	Eurasian 5y 9st 6lb
1888	Timothy 4y 9st 5lb
1889	Trayles 4y 9st 5lb
1890	Netheravon 4y 8st 6lb
1891	Gonsalvo 4y 9st
1892	Blue Green 5y 9st 8lb
1893	Bushey Park 4y 9st
1894	Aborigine 4y 9st
1895	Ravensbury 5y 9st 11lb
1896	Pride 4y 9st
1897	St. Bris 4y 9st
1898	Piety 5y 9st 6lb
1899	Le Senateur 4y 9st

CHESTER CUP. 2¼ miles.

1886	Eastern Emperor 5y 8st 2lb
1887	Carlton 4y 7st 11lb
1888	Kinsky, aged, 8st 12lb
1889	Millstream 6y 7st 4lb
1890	Tyrant 5y 7st
1891	Vasistas 5y 8st 3lb
1892	Dare Devil 4y 7st 8lb
1893	Dare Devil 5y 7st 11lb
1894	Quæsitum 4y 8st
1895	Kilsallaghan 5y 8st 9lb
1896	The Rush 4y 8st 5lb
1897	C'nt. Schomberg 5y 8st 10lb
1898	Up Guards 4y 6st 13lb
1899	Uncle Mac 5y 7st 7lb

HUNT CUP (ASCOT). New mile (7fur. 166yds.).

1886	Despair, aged, 4y 7st 13lb
1887	Gay Hermit 4y 7st 13lb
1888	Shillelagh 3y 6st 3lb
1889	Whiteleys 4y 8st 6lb
1890	Morion 3y 7st 9lb
1891	Laureate II. 5y 7st 12lb
1892	Suspender 3y 7st 10lb
1893	Amandier 4y 7st 3lb
1894	Victor Wild 4y 7st 7lb
1895	Clorane 4y 9st 10lb
1896	Quarrel 5y 7st 11lb
1897	Knt. of the Thistle 4y 7st 5lb
1898	Jacquemart 4y 9st 5lb
1899	Refractor 3y 6st 3lb

STEWARDS' CUP (GOODWOOD). T.Y.C.

1886	Crafton 4y 7st 11lb
1887	Upset 4y 6st 3lb
1888	Tib 5y 6st 7lb
1889	Dog Rose 6y 7st 12lb
1890	Marvel 3y 7st 6lb
1891	Unicorn 3y 9st
1892	Marvel 5y 8st 8lb
1893	Medora 3y 6st 14lb
1894	Gangway 4y 9st 5lb
1895	Wise Virgin 3y 9st 6lb
1896	Chasseur 4y 8st 5lb
1897	Amphora 4y 8st 8lb
1898	Altesse 4y 8st 4lb
1899	Northern Farmer 5y 7st 6lb

CESAREWITCH. 2 miles afur. 35yds.

1886	Stone Clink 4y 7st 7lb
1887	Humewood 3y 7st 6lb
1888	Ténébreuse 4y 9st 12lb
1889	Primrose Day 4y 6st 4lb
1890	Sheen 5y 9st 4lb
1891	Ragimunde 3y 6st 10lb
1892	Burnaby 5y 6st 11lb
1893	{ Red Eyes 3y 7st 10lb / Cypria 3y 6st 5lb }
1894	Childwick 4y 7st 9lb
1895	Rockdove 4y 6st 10lb
1896	St. Bris 5y 6st 6lb
1897	Merman 4y 7st 5lb
1898	Chaleureux 4y 7st 5lb
1899	Scintillant 3y 7st

CAMBRIDGESH. 1 mile & distance. A.F.

1886	Sailor Prince 6y 7st 7lb
1887	Gloriation 3y 7st 6lb
1888	Veracity 4y 7st 6lb
1889	Laureate 3y 7st 6lb
1890	Alicante 3y 7st 9lb
1891	Comedy 3y 7st 3lb
1892	La Flêche 3y 8st 10lb
1893	MollyMorgan4y6st7lb
1894	IndianQueen 3y6st12lb
1895	Marco 3y 7st 9lb
1896	W'kf'd'sPride3y6st10lb
1897	Comfrey 3y 7st 2lb
1898	Georgic 6y 7st 8lb
1899	Irish Ivy 3y 7st 11lb

GRAND PRIX DE PARIS. 1 mile 7fur.

1886	Mr. R. C. Vyner's Minting
1887	M. P. Aumont's Ténébreuse
1888	M. P. Donon's Stuart
1889	M. H. Delamarre's Vasistas
1890	Baron Schickler's Fitz-Royal
1891	M. E. Blanc's Clamart
1892	M. E. Blanc's Rueil
1893	M. Webb's Ragotsky
1894	Bn. Schickler's Dolma-Baghtché
1895	M. E. Blanc's Andrée
1896	M. E. Blanc's Arreau
1897	M. J. Arnaud's Doge
1898	Bn. Rothschild's Le Roi Soleil.
1899	Mons. Caillault's Perth

LINCOLNSH. HDCP. 1 mile.

1886	Fulmen 6y 7st 13lb
1887	Oberon 4y 7st 8lb
1888	Veracity 4y 6st 10lb
1889	Wise Man 4y7 † lb
1890	Rejected 6y 8st
1891	Lord George 5y £s
1892	Clarence 3y 6st 8lb
1893	Wolf's Crag 3y 6st 7
1894	Le Nicham 4y 8st 7lb
1895	Euclid 6y 7st 12lb
1896	Clorane 6y 9st 4lb
1897	Winkfield's Pride 4y 8st 4lb
1898	Prince Barcaldine 5y7st5lb
1899	General Peace 5y 7st 5lb

GRAND NATIONAL. 4 miles 856yds.

1886	Old Joe, aged, 10st 9lb
1887	Gamecock, aged, 11st
1888	Playfair, aged, 10st 7lb
1889	Frigate, aged, 11st 4lb
1890	Ilex 6y 10st 5lb
1891	Come Away, aged, 11st 12lb
1892	Father O'Flynn, a., 10st 5lb
1893	Cloister, a., 12st 7lb
1894	Why Not, aged, 11st 5lb
1895	W'dM'n fr.B'noo,a.10st1lb
1896	The Soarer, aged, 9st 13lb
1897	Manifesto, aged, 11st 3lb
1898	Drogheda 6y 10st 12lb
1899	Manifesto aged 12st 7lb

CITY & SUBURBAN. 1¼ miles.

1886	Royal Hampton 4y 8st 4lb
1887	Merry Duchess 5y 7st 5lb
1888	Fullerton 3y 8st 4lb
1889	Goldseeker 4y 8st
1890	Rêve d'Or 6y 7st 13lb
1891	Nunthorpe 5y 8st 4lb
1892	Buccaneer 4y 7st 10lb
1893	King Charles 4y 6st 9lb
1894	Grey Leg 3y 7st
1895	Reminder 4y 8st 9lb
1896	Worcester 6y 8st 12lb
1897	Balsamo 4y 7st 4lb
1898	Bay Ronald 4y 7st
1899	Newhaven II. 6y 9st

NORTHUMB. PLATE. 2 miles.

1886	Stone Clink 4y 7st 8lb
1887	Exmoor 4y 8st 12lb
1888	Matin Bell 4y 6st 10lb
1889	Drizzle 5y 6st 10lb
1890	Houndsditch 4y 7st 11lb
1891	Queen's Birthday 4y 9st
1892	Newcourt 4y 7st 3lb
1893	Seaton Delaval 4y 7st
1894	Newcourt 6y 8st 6lb
1895	The Docker 4y 7st 6lb
1896	Dare Devil, aged, 8st 7lb
1897	Bradwardine 4y 8st 4lb
1898	King Crow 4y 8st 7lb
1899	Sherburn 4y 8st 5lb

L'POOL AUT'MN. 1 mile 3fur.

1886	Melton 4y 9st 3lb
1887	St. Mirin 4y 9st 3lb
1888	Lady Rosebery 3y 5st 12lb
1889	Philomel 4y 9st 3lb
1890	Lady Rosebery 5y 7st 8lb
1891	Made. d'Albany 4y 6st 6lb
1892	Windgall, 3y 8st 2lb
1893	La Flêche 4y 9st 6lb
1894	Son of a Gun 4y 8st 4lb
1895	The Rush 4y 6st 13lb
1896	C'nt. Schomberg 4y 9st 11lb
1897	Chiselhampton, 4y 8st 1lb
1898	Alt Mark 3y 7st
1899	Chubb 4y 7st 12lb

JUBILEE HANDICAP (KEMPTON PARK). 1 mile.

1889	Amphion 3y 7st 1lb (16)
1890	The Imp 3y 6st 1lb (17)
1891	Nunthorpe 5y 9st (19)
1892	Euclid 3y 7st 4lb (21)
1893	Orvieto 3y 9st 5lb (11)
1894	Avington 4y 8st 1lb (20)
1895	Victor Wild 5y 8st 4lb (18)
1896	Victor Wild 6y 9st 7lb (15)
1897	Clwyd 6y 7st 5lb (14)
1898	Dinna Forget 6y 7st 7lb (16)
1899	Kt of the Thist'e6y8st4lt (17)

NEW STAKES (ASCOT). For two-year-olds. 5 furlongs 136 yards.

1889	Surefoot 9st 3lb (10)
1890	Orvieto 8st 10lb (10)
1891	Goldfinch 8st 10lb (10)
1892	Isinglass 8st 10lb (10)
1893	Wedding Bell 8st 7lb (4)
1894	Kissing Cup 8st 7lb (8)
1895	Roquebrune 8st 7lb (11)
1896	Velasquez 8st 10lb (8)
1897	Florio Rubattino8st10lb(6)
1898	Flying Fox 8st 10lb (10)
1899	The Gorgon 8st 7lb (12)

MIDDLEPARKPLATE (NEWMARKET). 6 furlongs.

1889	Signorina 9st (9)
1890	Gouverneur 9st (9)
1891	Orme 9st 3lb (10)
1892	Isinglass 9st (14)
1893	Ladas 9st 3lb (7)
1894	Speedwell 8st 10lb (9)
1895	St. Frusquin 8st 3lb (12)
1896	Galtee More 9st (5)
1897	Dieudonne 9st 3lb (14)
1898	Caiman 9st (9)
1899	Democrat 9st (6)

DEWHURST PLATE (NEWMARKET). Last 7 f. of R.M.

1889	Le Nord 8st 13lb (8)
1890	Corstorphine 8st 6lb (5)
1891	Orme 9st 5lb (3)
1892	Meddler 9st 4lb (5)
1893	Matchbox 9st 2lb (5)
1894	Raconteur 8st 13lb (5)
1895	St. Frusquin 9st 5lb (5)
1896	Vesuvian 8st 9lb (5)
1897	Hawfinch 8st 9lb (6)
1898	Frontier 8st 9lb (7)
1899	Democrat 9st 3lb (3

* After a dead heat with St. Michael, 4y 9st 5lb.

HENLEY REGATTA.
GRAND CHALLENGE CUP (EIGHT OARS)

		M. S.
1888	Thames R. C.	7 1
1889	Thames R. C.	7 4
1890	London C.	7 4½
1891	Leander C.	6 51
1892	Leander C.	7 12½
1893	Leander C.	7 22
1894	Leander C.	7 30
1895	Cambridge, Trin. Hall	7 30
1896	Leander C. ‡	7 43
1897	New College, Oxford	6 51
1898	Leander C.	7 13
1899	Leander C.	7 12
	‡ Cornell, U.S., defeated.	
	† Yale, U.S., defeated.	

DIAMOND SCULLS.

		M. S.
1887	J. C. Gardner, C.U.B.C.	8 51
1888	G. Nickalls, O.U.B.C.	8 36
1889	G. Nickalls, O.U.B.C.	8 56
1890	G. Nickalls, O.U.B.C.	8 57½
1891	V. Nickalls, O.U.B.C.	w.o.
1892	J. J. K. Ooms, Neptunus R.C., Amsterdam	10 9½
1893	G. Nickalls, O.U.B.C.	9 12
1894	Guy Nickalls, O.U.B.C.	9 32
1895	Hon. R. Guinness, Lean.	9 31
1896	Hon. R. Guinness, Lean.	9 35
1897	F. H. Ten Eyck, U.S.A.	8 35
1898	B. H. Howell, C.U.B.C.	8 29
1899	B. H. Howell, T. R. C.	8 39
1835, First year of new course, finishing at the Point. † Record.		

ETON AND HARROW.

Yr.	Winner.
1886	Eton won by 6 wickets.
1887	Eton won by 5 wickets.
1888	Harrow won by 156 runs.
1889	Drawn ; rain 1st day.
1890	Harrow won by 9 wickets.
1891	Harrow won by 7 wickets.
1892	Harrow won by 64 runs.
1893	Eton won by 9 wickets.
1894	Drawn ; rain 1st day.
1895	Drawn.
1896	Drawn.
1897	Drawn.
1898	Harrow won by 9 wickets.
1899	Drawn.

Totals, Harrow 30,   28, drawn 16.

DOGGETT'S COAT & BADGE.

Yr.	Winner.
1886	H. Cole, Deptford.
1887	W. G. East, Isleworth.
1888	C. R. Harding, Chelsea.
1889	G. M. Green, Barnes.
1890	J. T. G. Sansom, Kew.
1891	W. A. Barry, Victoria Docks.
1892	G. Webb, Gravesend.
1893	J. Harding, jun., Chelsea.
1894	F. Pearce, Hammersmith.
1895	J. H. Gibson, Putney.
1896	R. J. Carter, Greenwich.
1897	T. Bullman, Shadwell.
1898	A. J. Carter, Greenwich.
1899	J. See, Hammersmith.

WINGFIELD SCULLS.
AMATEUR CHAMPIONSHIP OF THAMES. PUTNEY TO MORTLAKE.

		M. S
1869	A. de L. Long, L.R.C.	— 1
1870	A. de L. Long, L.R.C.	— 13
1871	W. Fawcus, Tynemouth	26 13
1872	C. C. Knollys, O.U.B.C.	28 30
1873	A. C. Dicker, C.U.B.C.	24 40
1874	A. C. Dicker, C.U.B.C.	25 45
1875	F. L. Playford, L.R.C.	27 6
1876	F. L. Playford, L.R.C.	24 46
1877	F. L. Playford, L.R.C.	24 41
1878	F. L. Playford, L.R.C.	24 50
1879	F. L. Playford, L.R.C.	24 50
1880	Alex. Payne, Molesey	— 5
1881	J. Lowndes, Derby	25 13
1882	Alex. Payne, Molesey	27 40
1883	J. Lowndes, Derby	w.o.
1884	W. S. Unwin, O.U.B.C.	24 12
1885	W. S. Unwin, O.U.B.C.	25 0
1886	F. J. Pitman, C.U.B.C.	24 12
1887	G. Nickalls, O.U.B.C.	25 23
1888	G. Nickalls, O.U.B.C.	23 30
1889	G. Nickalls, O.U.B.C.	w.o.
1890	J. C. Gardner, C.U.B.C.	26 20
1891	G. Nickalls, O.U.B.C.	w.o.
1892	V. Nickalls, O.U.B.C.	23 40
1893	G.E.B.Kennedy,Kingstn.	24 56
1894	V. Nickalls, O.U.B.C.	23 30
1895	V. Nickalls, L.R.C.	25 46
1896	Hon. R. Guinness, T.R.C.	24 11
1897	T. T. Blackstaffe, V.B.C.	23 53
1898	B. H. Howell, C.U.B.C.	22 56
1899	B. H. Howell, Thames R.C.	23 7 *
* Record.		

WORLD'S AQUATIC CHAMPIONSHIP.

Yr.	Winner.
1882	Hanlan beat Trickett.
1883	Hanlan beat Kennedy.
1883	Hanlan beat Wallace Ross.
1884	Hanlan beat Laycock.
1884	W. Beach beat Hanlan.
1885	W. Beach beat Hanlan.
1885	W. Beach beat Neil Matterson.
1886	W. Beach beat J. Gaudaur.
1886	W. Beach beat Wallace Ross.
1887	W. Beach beat Hanlan.
1888	P. Kemp beat T. Clifford.
1888	P. Kemp b. Hanlan (twice).
1888	H. Searle beat Kemp.
1889	H. Searle b. W. O'Connor.*
1890	P. Kemp b. Neil Matterson.
1891	J. Stanbury b. J. McLean.
1892	J. Stanbury b. J. Sullivan.
1896	J. Stanbury b. C.R. Harding.
1896	J. Gaudaur b. J. Stanbury.

After Trickett had carried off the Championship to Australia in 1876, a Championship of England Cup was instituted, which, after being held in turn by R. W. Boyd, J. Higgins, and W. Elliott, was finally won by Hanlan, when he defeated the latter in 1879.

* Searle died in December, 1889, and O'Connor in 1892. George Towns, of Newcastle, Australia, is the champion sculler of England.

CYCLISTS UNION CHAMPIONSHIPS.

		M.		H. M. S.
1897	25	W. P. Fawcett (Leeds) A.		1 3 42½
"	50	A. J. Cherry (Catford) A.		1 53 45
"	1	F. W. Chinn (Midlands) P.		0 33½
"	1	F. W. Chinn (Midlands) P.		0 24⅖
"	5	C. F. Barden (Putney) P.		0 14 3½
"	1	T. Summersgill (Leeds) A.		0 32½
1898	1	W. A. Edmonds (Catford)A.		3 8
"	1	A. S. Ingram (Polytech.) A.		0 14 11½
"	25	H. W. Payne (W. Roads) A.		1 4 52½
"	1	H. Chinn (Birmingham) A.		1 51 41½
"	2	F. Burnand (Catford) A. and		
		E. J. Callaghan (Poly.) A.		0 4 21
"	1	S. Jenkins (Noderl'd B.C.) P.		0 33⅖
"	1	F. W. China (Brmgham.) P.		0 2 51
"	1	H. E. Meyers (Dutch C.C.) P.		0 15 35¼
"	2*	T. J. Gascoigne & H. Brown P.		0 4 17⅗
1899	1	P. Albert (Hanover) A.		0 29
"	1	P. Albert (Hanover) A.		0 32½
"	5	A. S. Ingram (Poly. C.C.) A.		0 14 41½
"	25	H.W.Payne (W.Rds.C.C.)A.		1 11 15½
"	50	G. F. Payne (W.Rds C.C.)A.		2 3 36⅗
"	2*	A. S. Ingram and R. Janson (Poly. C. C.) A.		0 5 4½
"	1	J. Green, Northumberld. P.		0 33½
"	1	S. Jenkins (Catford C.C.) P.		0 24½
"	5	S. Jenkins (Catford C.C.) P.		0 12 39½
"	2*	Declared void. P.		
* Tandem.				

OLD BILLIARD CHAMPIONSHIP (SPECIAL TABLE).

Yr.	Winner.
1871	Roberts, jr. b. J. Bennett.
1871	W. Cook b. J. Roberts.
1872	W. Cook b. J. Bennett.
1872	W. Cook b. J. Roberts, jr.
1874	W. Cook b. J. Roberts, jr.
1875	J. Roberts, jr. beat Cook.
1875	J. Roberts, jr. beat Cook.
1877	J. Roberts, jr. beat Cook.
1880	J. Bennett beat W. Cook.
1881*	J. Bennett beat T. Taylor.
1885	J. Roberts, jr. beat Cook
1885†	Roberts, jr. b. J. Bennett.

* Bennett resigned. Cook d. 1883.
† Roberts made the largest break of these matches—155. This and the previous match were 3,000 up; the others, with the exception of the first, 1,000 up No match since 1885.
1st champion B A. rules C. Dawson 1899

LAWN TENNIS CHAMPIONSHIPS.

1895	W. Baddeley (G.)
"	Miss C. Cooper (L.).
1896	H. S. Mahony (G.)
"	Miss C. Cooper (L.).
1897	R. F. Doherty (G.)
"	Mrs. Hillyard (L.).
1898	R. F. Doherty (G.).
"	Miss C. Cooper (L.).
1899	R F. Doherty (G.)
"	Mrs. Hillyard (L.).

FOOTBALL.

RUGBY UNION.

ENGLAND v. SCOTLAND.

		g. t.	g. t.
1891	Scotland	3 0	1 0
1892	England	1 0	0 0
1893	Scotland	2 0	0 0
1894	Scotland	0 2	0 0
1895	Scotland	1 1	0 0
1896	Scotland	1 2	0 0
1897	England	2 1	1 0
1898	Drawn	0 1	0 1
1899	Scotland	1 0	0 0

COUNTY CHAMPIONSHIP.

Lancashire.
Yorkshire.
Yorkshire.
Yorkshire.
Yorkshire.
Yorkshire.
Kent.
Northumberland.
Devonshire.

ASSOCIATION.

ENGLAND v. SCOTLAND.

		g.	g.
England		2 to 1	
England		4 to 1	
England		5 to 2	
Drawn		2 to 2	
England		3 to 0	
Scotland		2 to 1	
Scotland		2 to 0	
England		3 to 1	
England		2 to 1	

ASSOCIATION CUP.

Blackburn Rovers b. Notts 3—1.
West Bromwich Albion b. Aston Villa 3—0.
Wolverhampton Wanderers b. Everton 1—0.
Notts County b. Bolton Wanderers 4—1.
Aston Villa b. West Bromwich Albion 3—0.
Sheffd. Wednesday b. W'hampton Wandrs. 2—1.*
Aston Villa b. Everton 3—2.
Notts Forest b. Derby County 3—1.
Sheffield United b. Derby County, 4—1.

RUNNING (AMATEURS).

Yds.	Name	Year	Time. H. M. S.
100	J. Owen [8]	1890	0 0 9 4/5
	B. J. Wefers [8]	1895	0 0 9 4/5
120	W. P. Phillips	1882	
	C. Bradley	1894	0 0 11 1/2
150	C. J. B. Monypenny	1892	0 0 14 4/5
	C. G. Wood	1887	
200	E. H. Pelling	1889	0 0 19 4/5
220	B. J. Wefers [8]	1896	0 0 21 1/5
250	E. H. Pelling	1888	0 0 24 1/5
300	B. J. Wefers [8]	1896	0 0 30 3/5
440	E. C. Bredin	1895	
	H. C. L. Tindall	1889	0 0 48 1/2
500	T. E. Burke [8]	1897	0 0 57 3/4
600	T. E. Burke [8]	1896	0 1 11
880	C. J. Kilpatrick [8]	1895	0 1 53 1/2
1,000	L. E. Myers [8]	1881	0 2 13
1,320	W. G. George	1882	0 3 8 1/4
Mls 1	F. E. Bacon	1895	0 4 17
2	W. G. George	1884	0 9 17 1/2
3	S. Thomas	1893	0 14 24
4	C. E. Willers	1893	0 19 33 3/4
5	S. Thomas	1892	0 24 53 1/5
10	W. G. George	1884	0 51 20
20	G. Crossland	1894	1 51 54
30	J. A. Squires	1885	1 37 36 1/2
40	G. A. Dunning	1879	4 50 12
50	J. E. Dixon	1885	6 18 26 1/2
100	J. Saunders [8]	1882	17 36 14

(PROFESSIONALS).

Name	Year	Time. H. M. S.
H. M. Johnson [1 8]	1886	0 0 9 1/2
H. Gent [1]	1887	0 0 11 1/2
C. Westhall [1]	1851	0 0 15
G. Seward [1]	1847	0 0 19 1/4
H. Hutchens [1]	1885	0 0 21 1/2
H. Hutchens [10]	1888	0 0 25 1/2
H. Hutchens	1884	0 0 30
R. Buttery	1873	0 0 48 1/4
E. C. Bredin	1899	0 0 59
J. Nuttall	1864	0 1 13
F. Newell [7]	1871	0 1 53 1/2
W. Cummings	1881	0 2 17
W. Richards	1866	0 3 7
W. G. George [2]	1886	0 4 12 3/4
W. Lang	1863	0 9 11 1/2
P. Cannon	1888	0 14 34 1/2
P. Cannon	1888	0 19 25 1/4
J. White	1863	0 24 40
H. Watkins	1899	0 51 5 1/4
J. E. Warburton	1881	1 56 38
G. Mason	1881	3 15 9
J. Bailey	1881	4 34 27
C. Cartwright	1887	5 55 4 1/2
C. Rowell	1882	13 26 30

Professional Records.—Greatest distance run in 1 hour 11m. 1286 yds., by H. Watkins, Sept. 16, 1899, at Rochdale, while J. Bailey (1881) ran 35 4/5 m. in 4 hours, and C. Rowell 89 m. 1,540 yds. in 12 hrs., and 150 m. 395 yds. in 23 hours, Feb., 1882.

Amateur Records.—W. G. George ran 11 m. 932 yds. 1 hour, July 28, 1884; G. Crossland, September 22, 1894, ran 20 miles and a half in 2 hours, both at Stamford Bridge T. P. Conneff in America, Aug. 21, 1895, ran 1 mile in 4m 15 secs., and 1320 yds., 3m. 2 4-5 secs., but not in an open race

---

WALKING (AMATEURS).[2]

Mls.	Name	Year	Time. H. M. S.
1	W. J. Sturges	1896	0 6 33 1/2
2	W. J. Sturges	1897	0 13 24 1/2
3	W. J. Sturges	1897	0 21 14
4	W. J. Sturges	1897	0 28 24 1/2
5	W. J. Sturges	1895	0 36 27
8	W. J. Sturges	1895	0 58 56
10	W. J. Sturges	1896	1 17 38 1/2
20	T. Griffiths	1870	2 47 52
50	A. W. Sinclair	1879	8 25 25 1/2
100	A. W. Sinclair	1881	19 41 50

(PROFESSIONALS)

Name	Year	Time. H. M. S.
W. Perkins	1874	0 6 23
J. W. Raby	1883	0 13 14
J. W. Raby	1883	0 20 21 1/2
J. W. Raby	1883	0 27 38
J. W. Raby	1883	0 35 10
J. Hibberd	1883	0 58 44
J. W. Raby	1883	1 14 45
W. Perkins	1877	2 39 57
J. Hibberd	1888	7 54 16
W. Howes	1880	18 8 15

The greatest distance walked in 1 hour was 8 m. 270 yds. by W. J. Sturges in 1895; in 2 hours W. Perkins (1877), 15 m. 824 yds.; in 3 hours H. Thatcher (1882), 22 m. 456 1/2 yds. and in 4 hours W. Franks (1882), 27 1/2 miles.

JUMPING (AMATEURS).[5]

Event	Name	Distance. ft. in.	Year
Running Long Jump	A. C. Kraenzlein [8]	24 4 1/2	1899
Standing Long Jump	R. C. Ewer [8]	11 0	1897
Running High Jump	M. Sweeney [5 8]	6 5 5/8	1895
Standing High Jump	A. P. Schwaner [8]	5 3 1/4	1892

(PROFESSIONALS).[6]

Name	Distance. ft. in.	Year
W. Davison	21 10	1895
E. A. Johnson	11 1	1881
E. A. Johnson	6 0 1/2	1881
E. A. Johnson	5 3	1878

Putting the Weight, 16 lbs, G. R. Gray, 47ft., 1893. Throwing the Hammer, 16 lbs., J. Flanagan 164ft. 1 in., 1899. Both in America from 7ft. circles, amateur world's records.

[1] These are the only records generally accepted, though it is certain that several professionals have travelled the distances a yard or two yards quicker. Geo. Seward's apocryphal 9 1/4 secs. is no longer accepted. On July 9, 1890, an American amateur, W. C. Downs, ran a straight 1-mile in 47 2-5th secs. at Boston.

[2] After becoming a professional in a match with Cummings, Aug., 1886, beating previous record by nearly 4 secs.

[3] In America F. P. Murray is credited with 1 mile in 6 min. 29 2-5th secs., 3 miles in 21 min. 9 1-5th secs.

[5] British amateur records:—100 yds., 10 secs., by A. Wharton, C. Bradley, A. R. Downer, F. W. Cooper, R. W. Wadsley, and C. R. Thomas; 220 yds., 21 4-5th secs. by C. G. Wood; 300 yds., 31 2-5th secs., by C. G. Wood; 500 yds., 58 1/4 secs., and 600 yds., 1 m. 11 2-5th secs., both by E'

C. Bredin. Half-mile, 1 m. 54 3-5th secs., by F. J. K. Cross. Broad Jump, 24ft. 1/2 in., by W. J. M. Newburn. High Jump, 6 ft. 4 1/4 in., by J. M. Ryan. Throwing the Hammer (16 lbs., 9 ft. circle), 132ft. 9in., by T. F. Kiely. Putting the Shot (16 lbs., 7ft. sq.), 46ft. 5 1/4 in., by D. Horgan.

[6] The pole-jumping record is held by an amateur, R. D. Dickinson, with 11 ft. 9 in. at Kidderminster, 1891.

[7] Made in New Zealand.

[8] Made in America. [10] Made in Australia.

[9] Not Music-hall exhibitions but all doubtful.

* Balls jammed in mouth of pocket.

N.B.—The following records (amateurs) are also authentic: 120 Yards Hurdles in England G. B. Shaw, 15 4-5th secs., on grass. In America, on cinders, S. Chase. 15 2-5th secs. Walk, London to Brighton, 52 1/2 miles, E. Knott, 8 h. 56 m. 44 secs., 1897. Throwing the cricket ball. 127yds. 1ft., by W. H. Game, at Oxford, 1873. Greatest distance in a six days professional contest, 623 m. 1,320 yds., by G. Littlewood, New York, 6th December, 1888.

BILLIARDS.

BEST "spot-in" break (exhibition match) 3,304, by W. J. Peall, 1890; match for money, 2,031, by W. J. Peall, 1888. Best spot-barred breaks, 1,392, by J. Roberts, 1894, and 1,467 by T. Taylor, 1891. Greatest number of spot-hazards in succession 633, by W. J. Peall, 1888. Longest run of successive nursery cannons 230, by J. Mack, 1898. Longest run of successive losing red hazards 98, by J. Roberts, 1894. Largest number of successive screwback red hazards 186, by J. G. Sala, 1888. Fastest 1,000 up game, all-in, W. J. Peall, 1884, 44 min. Fastest 1,033 spot-barred, J. Roberts, 1894, 59 1/2 min. Under Billiard Association Rules: A. R. Wisdom is the amateur champion, and C. Dawson the professional champion. Also the record break 1872 by C. Dawson, Oct. 21, 1899, with ivory balls, and 597, with bonzoline balls, by John Roberts, March 2, 1899.

SWIMMING.

CAPTAIN MATTHEW WEBB swam from Dover to Calais in 21 hrs. 45 mins., August 24 and 25. Fastest 100 yards, J. H. Derbyshire (amateur) 60 1-5 secs., Nov., 1898, Manchester. Longest time under water, Miss E. Wallenda, 4 min. 45 1/2 secs., in a tank, Alhambra, London, Dec. 14, 1898. Longest plunge (amateur), 82ft by Major W. Taylor, Bootle Baths, 1899, without time limit

BICYCLING WORLD'S PATH RECORDS.

Dist. Mles	Name.	Place.	Year	Time. H.	M.	S.
¼+	Major Taylor	Chicago	1899	0	0	19⅕
¼	J. Green	Crystal Palace ...	1899	0	0	27⅘
½+	Platt Betts	,, ,, ...	1899	0	0	44⅘
½	J. Green	,, ,, ...	1899	0	0	51⅕
1+	Major Taylor	Chicago	1899	0	1	22⅖
1	J. Green	Crystal Palace ...	1899	0	1	40⅖
5	H. Elkes	America	1899	0	7	38⅕
5	E. James and G. A. Nelson (tandem)..	Crystal Palace	1897	0	8	48⅗
25	H. Elkes—American	America	1899	0	40	33
50	E. Bouehours	Crystal Palace	1899	1	27	16⅗
100	M. Baugé	Paris...	1899	3	7	47⅕

Hrs.	Name.	Place.	Yr.	Distance. Mls.	Yds.	Kls. Mtrs.
1	E. Taylor	Auteuil	1899	36	1144	58 930
1	S. MacGregor & G. A. Nelson (tandem) ..	Crystal Palace	1896	31	1660	—
12	A. E. Walters	Auteuil [Paris	1899	341	629	—
*24	A. E. Walters	Princes Pk.,	1899	634	774	1 020 977

RECORDS CONTINENTAL MEASUREMENTS.

Dist. Kilo	Name.	Place.	Year.	Time. H.	M.	S.
1	Simar	Auteuil............	1899	0	1	8⅕
†1	Champion..............	Paris	1898	0	0	56
5	E. James and J. A. Nelson	Crystal Palace	1897	0	5	28⅕
5	E. Taylor	Auteuil...........	1899	0	5	7⅖
10	E. Bonhours	,, ...	1899	0	10	7⅘
20	Bor......................	,, ...	1899	0	20	28⅖
50	,, ...	,, ...	1899 27 Oct	0	51	24
100	E. Bonhours	Crystal Palace...	1899	1	48	50⅖
1,000	A. E. Walters........	Auteuil	1899	23	20	50⅗

All these records were made with motor pacing.

† Flying starts.

On Sept. 17-18, 1899, M. Cordang, at the Hague, Holland, rode 640 miles 196 yards in 24 hou s but owing to his suspension at the time by the U.V.F. the record is not rceognised. At Madison Square Gardens, New York, December, 1898, Charles Miller rode 2,007 miles 4 laps in 142 hours.

Road Records.

24 Hours.—Safety (F. R. Goodwin, 1898), 428 miles; ordinary bicycle, 312 miles (J. F. Walsh, 1891); single tricycle (F. T. Bidlake), 356½ miles, 1894; tandem tricycle, 333½ miles (Holbein and Bidlake, 1893); tandem safety (M. A. Holbein and J. A. Bennett), 397½ miles, 1895.

100 Miles.—Safety 4h. 16m. 35s. (A. A. Chase, 1897); ordinary bicycle 6h. 22m. 15s. (J. F. Walsh, 1891); tricycle 5h. 15m. 57s. (F. T. Bidlake, 1896); tandem tricycle 5h. 30m. 31s. (S. F. Edge and J. E. L. Bates, 1891). Tandem safety 4h. 45m. 1s. (A. and L. Ilsley), 1898.

The Land's End to John o' Groats record; safety (G. P. Mills), 3 days 5m. 49s., 1894; tricycle (G. P. Mills), 3 days 16m. 47s., 1893. London to Brighton and back; tricycle (J. Parsley), 6h. 18m. 28s.; safety (W. J. Neason), 5h. 6m. 42s., 1897; tandem safety (P. Wheelock and G. Fulford), 4h. 54m. 54s., 1899; London to York (J. R. Goodwin), 10h. 1m.: 1,000 miles (T. A. Edge), 4d. 9h. 19m., 1896; Bath to London and back (F. W. Barnes), 11h. 48m. 42s., 1897. Tricycle, J. G. Gibb, 14h. 8m. 37s., 1897.

12 Hours' Safety Road Record, 224 miles, Sept. 1, 1899, by J. R. Goodwin.

English 1 Hour Records (Path).

Safety, E. Bonhours, Aug. 7, 1899 (34m. 740yds.); ordinary, B. W. Attlee, 1891 (21m. 180yds.); tricycle, W. Ellis, 1894 (23m. 800yds.); tandem tricycle, 23m. 310yds. (L. Stroud and J. E. L. Bates, 1894); tandem safety (S. MacGregor and G. A. Nelson, 1896), 31m. 1,610yds. The amateur tandem safety record is 29m. 1,110yds. (C. Heydon and H. Thackthwaite), 1898.

Cricket.—Highest score, A. E. Stoddart, 485, Hampstead *v.* Stoics, 1886; A. E. J. Collins (*age* 13) 628 in house match at Clifton College, 1899, English Largest gross score, Orleans Club *v.* Rickling Green, 920, Aug. 3rd, 1882. In a first-class match, Yorkshire, 887, *v.* Warwickshire. May 8, 1896. Also in first-class cricket, highest individual score, A. C. MacLaren, 424, for Lancashire *v.* Somerset, at Taunton, July 1895. Lowest score in an innings, 12, by Oxford University (one man absent) *v.* M.C.C. and Ground, at Oxford, May 1877 Most runs made in a year in England, 3,159, by K. S. Ranjitsinhji, in 1899, in 55 innings (7 times not out) average 57·9. England *v.* Australia matches, 32 in Australia, 24 in England. England won 26, Australia 20, drawn 10, up to end of 1899. Total 56.

Trotting.—Fastest mile, in America, 2m. 3¾s. by Alix, 1894. Fastest pacing mile, 1m 59¼s., by Star Pointer, 1897.

SKATING RECORDS.

Dist. Yards.	Name.	Place.	Time. H.	M.	S.	Year.
100	G. D. Phillips ..	New York	0	0	10⅗	1883
200	J. S. Johnson....	Minneapolis	0	0	17⅗	1893
220	F. Hiam..	London	0	0	20⅘	1895
440	W. Lindahl......	London	0	0	42⅗	1895
880	J. S. Johnson .	Minneapolis ..	0	1	22	1893
880	P. Oestlund ..	Minneapolis ..	0	1	22	1895
Mls. 1	J. Nilsson	Montreal	0	2	41⅕	1897
2	Olaf Rudd	Red Bank, N.J..	0	5	42⅗	1895
3	Harold Hagen ..	Hamar	0	8	46⅗	1892
4	J. Nilsson	Minneapolis ..	0	12	0½	1894
4	A. Schiebe	Minneapolis ..	0	12	0½	1894
5	J. Nilsson	Montreal	0	14	47	1897
10	J. S. Johnson ..	Montreal	0	31	11⅕	1894
20	A. D. Smith	Minneapolis	1	6	36⅗	1894
100	J. F. Donoghue .	Stamford, U.S.A.	7	11	38⅕	1893
19 348y	C. Edgington....	Davos	1	0	0	1899

INTERNATIONAL SKATING RECORDS.

Dist. Metrs	Name.	Place.	Time. H.	M.	S.	Yea
500	A. Naess	Montreal	0	0	46⅕	1897
500	P. Oestlund	Trondhjem	0	0	46⅕	1897
1,000	P. Oestland	Daves..........	0	1	38⅖	1899
1,500	P. Oestlund	Davos Platz..	0	2	23⅘	1898
5,000	J. J. Eden	Hamar	0	8	37⅗	1894
0,000	J. J. Eden	Hamar	0	17	56	1895

Eden must have beaten several of the English measurement times in the above records.

All Foreign Records in miles are doubtful. With a wind, T. Donoghue, in 1887, skated 1 mile straightaway on the Hudsen River in 2 min. 12 3-5th secs. Our champion, Fish Smart, in 1881, skated 1 mile straightaway, with a flying start, in 3 min. dead, no wind; and in 1893, J. E. Aveling, at Lingay Fen, skated a quarter-mile in 38⅕ secs.

With the wind, or on doubtfully-measured tracks, much faster times than the above are recorded. H. Hagen, of Norway, a professional, on Feb. 28, 1892, skated a half-mile in 1 min. 20⅕ secs. In England, 1893, Marten Kigma, a Dutch professional, skated 1 mile with three turns in 3 min. 8 secs

COURSING.—WATERLOO CUP.

Year	Nominator.	Winner.	Runner-up.
1890	Col. North	Fullerton........	Downpour.
1891	Col. North	Fullerton........	Faster&Faster.
1892	Col. North	Fullerton........	Fitz Fife.
1893	Mr. R. L. Cotterel	Character.........	Button Park.
1894	Count Stroganoff	Texture	Falconer.
1895	R. B. Carruthers	Th'ghtl'ss Beauty	Fort'naFav'nte
1896	Mr. G. F. Fawcett	FabulousFortune	Wolfhill.
1897	Mr. T. P. Hale ..	Gallant..........	Five by Tricks
1898	Mr. J. Trevor ..	Wild Night	Lang Syne.
1899	J. B. Thompson..	Black Fury	Lapul.

UNIVERSITY BOAT RACE.

Yr.	Place of Rowing	Winner.	m.	s.	Won by
1836	Westm. to Putney	Camb....	36	0	1 min
1837	and 1838 not rowed	—	—		
1839	Westm. to Putney	Camb....	31	0	1 min. 45 sec.
1840	Westm. to Putney	Camb....	29	30	2-3rds length.
1841	Westm. to Putney	Camb....	32	30	1 min. 4 sec.
1842	Westm. to Putney	Oxford ..	30	45	13 sec.
1843	and 1844 not rowed	—	—		
1845	Putney to Mort..	Camb....	23	30	36 sec.
1846	Mortlake to Put..	Camb....	21	5	Two lengths.*
1847	and 1848 not rowed	—	—		
1849	Putney to Mort..	Camb....	22	0	Many lengths.d
	Putney to Mort..	Oxford ..	Foul		Foul.d
1852	Putney to Mort..	Oxford ..	21	36	27 sec.
1854	Putney to Mort..	Oxford ..	25	29	11 strokes.
1856	Mortlake to Put.	Camb....	25	50	Half length.
1857	Putney to Mort..	Oxford ..	22	50	35 secs.†
1858	Putney to Mort..	Camb. ..	21	23	22 secs.
1859	Putney to Mort..	Oxford ..	24	40	Camb. sank.
1860	Putney to Mort..	Camb....	26	0	One length.
1861	Putney to Mort..	Oxford ..	23	27	48 sec.
1862	Putney to Mort..	Oxford ..	24	40	30 sec.
1863	Mortlake to Put.	Oxford ..	23	5	43 sec.
1864	Putney to Mort..	Oxford ..	21	40	26 sec.
1865	Putney to Mort..	Oxford ..	21	0	Four lengths.
1866	Putney to Mort..	Oxford ..	25	48	15 sec.
1867	Putney to Mort..	Oxford ..	22	39	Half length.
1868	Putney to Mort..	Oxford ..	20	56	Six lengths.
1869	Putney to Mort..	Oxford ..	20	4	Three lengths.a
1870	Putney to Mort..	Camb....	22	6	1½ length.
1871	Putney to Mort..	Camb....	23	5	One length.
1872	Putney to Mort..	Camb....	21	14	Two lengths.b
1873	Putney to Mort..	Camb....	19	35	3¾ lengths.‡
1874	Putney to Mort..	Camb....	22	35	2½ lengths.
1875	Putney to Mort..	Oxford ..	22	2	Ten lengths.
1876	Putney to Mort..	Camb....	20	20	Eight lengths.
1877	Putney to Mort..	dead heat	24	8	§
1878	Putney to Mort..	Oxford ..	22	13	Ten lengths.
1879	Putney to Mort..	Camb....	21	20	2½ lengths.
1880	Putney to Mort..	Oxford ..	21	23	3 lengths.¶
1881	Putney to Mort..	Oxford ..	21	54	Three lengths.c
1882	Putney to Mort.	Oxford ..	20	12	Seven lengths.
1883	Putney to Mort..	Oxford ..	21	8	Four lengths.‖
1884	Putney to Mort.	Camb....	21	39	2½ lengths.¶
1885	Putney to Mort..	Oxford ..	21	37	Three lengths.
1886	Putney to Mort..	Camb....	22	29	2-3rds length.
1887	Putney to Mort..	Camb....	20	52	3½ lengths.
1888	Putney to Mort.	Camb....	20	48	Five lengths.
1889	Putney to Mort.	Camb....	20	14	Three lengths.
1890	Putney to Mort	Oxford ..	22	3	One length.a
1891	Putney to Mort..	Oxford ..	21	48	Half length.
1892	Putney to Mort.	Oxford ..	19	21	2¼ lengths.
1893	Putney to Mort..	Oxford ..	18	47	1 length 4ft.a
1894	Putney to Mort..	Oxford ..	21	39	3½ lengths.
1895	Putney to Mort..	Oxford ..	20	50	2¼ lengths.
1896	Putney to Mort..	Oxford ..	20	2	2-5ths length.
1897	Putney to Mort..	Oxford ..	19	12	2⅓rd lengths.
1898	Putney to Mort..	Oxford ..	22	15	13 lengths.e
1899	Putney to Mort..	Camb....	21	4	3¼ lengths.

* First race rowed in outriggers.
† First race in present style boats without keels.
‡ Sliding seats used for first time.
§ The Oxford bow-man caught a crab and sprung his oar when leading
e Rowed in a gale.
‖ Rowed on a Thursday. ¶ Rowed on a Monday.
a Rowed on a Wednesday. d Two races this year.
b Rowed in a snowstorm. c Rowed on a Friday.
Oxford 32; Cambridge 23; dead heat 1877.

THE CRICKET MATCH.

Yr.	Result.	Yr.	Result.
1835	Oxford won by 121 r	1854	Ox. won in 1 inn. by 8 r.
1838	Oxford won by 98 r.	1855	Oxford won by 3 wkts.
1839	C. won in 1 inn. by 125 r.	1856	Camb. won by 3 wkts.
1840	Camb. won by 63 runs	1857	Oxford won by 81 runs.
184	Camb. won by 8 runs	1858	Ox. won in 1 inn by 38 r.
1842	Camb. won by 162 r	1859	Camb. won by 28 runs.
1843	Camb. won by 54 runs	1860	Camb. won by 3 wkts.
1845	Camb. won by 6 wkts.	1861	Camb. won by 133 runs.
1846	Oxford won by 3 wkts.	1862	Camb. won by 8 wkts.
1847	Camb. won by 138 r.	1863	Oxford won by 8 wkts.
1848	Oxford won by 23 r.	1864	Oxford won by 4 wkts.
1849	Camb. won by 3 wkts.	1865	Oxford won by 114 runs.
1850	Oxford won by 127 r.	1866	Oxford won by 13 runs
1851	C. won in 1 inn. by 4 r.	1867	Camb. won by 5 wkts.
1852	O. won in 1 inn. by 77 r.	1868	Camb. won by 168 runs.
1853	Ox. won in 1 inn by 19 r	1869	Camb. won by 58 runs.

CRICKET—continued.

Yr.	Result.	Yr.	Result.
1870	Camb. won by 2 runs	1884	Oxford won by 7 wickets.
1871	Oxford won by 8 wickets.	1885	Camb. won by 7 wickets.
1872	Camb. won in 1 inn. by 166 r.	1886	Oxford won by 133 runs.
1873	Oxford won by 3 wickets.	1887	Oxford won by 7 wickets.
1874	Oxford won in 1 inn. by 92 r.	1889	Camb. won by 1 inns. & 105 r.
1875	Oxford won by 6 runs.	1890	Camb. won by 7 wickets.
1876	Camb. won by 9 wkts.	1891	Camb. won by 2 wickets.
1877	Oxford won by 10 wickets	1892	Oxford won by 5 wickets.
1878	Camb. won by 238 runs.	1893	Camb. won by 266 runs.
1879	Camb. won by 9 wickets.	1894	Oxford won by 8 wickets.
1880	Camb. won by 135 runs.	1895	Camb. won by 134 runs.
1881	Oxford won by 135 runs.	1896	Oxford won by 4 wickets.
1882	Camb. won by 7 wickets.	1897	Camb. won by 179 runs.
1883	Camb. won by 7 wickets.	1898	Oxford won by 9 wickets.

In 1827, 1844, 1888 and 1899 the matches were not finished.
Summary:—Cambridge, 32 Oxford, 29; drawn, 4.

ATHLETICS.

Year.	Result.
1866	Cambridge, 5½—3½.
1867	Cambridge, 6—3.
1868	Oxford, 5—4.
1869	Cambridge, 5½—3½.
1870	Oxford, 7½—1½.
1871	Oxford, 5½—3½.
1872	Cambridge, 5½—3½.
1873	Oxford, 6—3.
1874	Oxford, 5—4.
1875	Oxford, 6—3.
1876	Oxford, 6—3.
1877	Cambridge, 5—4.
1878	Cambridge, 5—4.
1879	Cambridge, 5—4.
1880	Cambridge, 6—3.
1881	Oxford, 5—4.
1882	Cambridge, 5—4.
1883	Cambridge, 6—3.
1884	Oxford, 6—3.
1885	Oxford, 5½—3½.
1886	Oxford, 6—3.
1887	Cambridge, 6—3.
1888	Cambridge, 5—4.
1889	Cambridge, 5½—3½.
1890	Cambridge, 6—3.
1891	Cambridge, 6½—2½.
1892	Cambridge, 5—4,
1893	Oxford, 7—2.
1894	Oxford, 6—3.
1895	Cambridge, 5—4.
1896	Cambridge, 5—4.
1897	Oxford, 4—3.*
1898	Oxford, 7—2.
1899†	A tie, 5—5.

* Ties in 100 and High Jump.
† Half Mile; and A.A.A. rules as to Shot and Hammer.
Oxford 15 Cambridge 19; 2 ties.

The best records in the series of sports are:—

100—10 secs., by J. H. Wilson (Oxford) in 1868-70, and G. H. Urmson (Oxford) in 1873.

440—49⅗ secs., by W. Fitz-Herbert (Camb.) in 1896.

1 Mile—4 min. 19⅘ secs. by W. E. Lutyens (Camb.) in 1894.

3 Miles—14 min. 44 secs., by F. S. Horan (Camb.) in 1893.

Hurdles—16 secs., by A. B. Loder (Camb.) in 1876, and W. R. Pollock (Camb.) in 1884, and Paget Tomlinson (Camb.) in 1899.

High Jump—M. J. Brooks (Oxford), 6 ft. 2½ in.

Long Jump—23 ft. 5 in., by C. B. Fry (Oxford) in 1892.

Putting the Weight, 16 lbs. (10 ft. square), 39 ft. 1 in., by J. H. Ware (Oxford) in 1886.

Throwing the Hammer, 16 lbs. (30 ft. circle), W. Lawrence (Oxford) 120 ft. 2 in. in 1881. The square and circle were first introduced in 1880.

Half Mile—1 min. 59⅗, by H. E. Graham (Cambridge

RUG FOOTBALL.

Year.	Result.
1875-6	Oxford, 1 try to nil.
1876-7	Camb., 1 g. 2 tr. to nil.
1877-8	Oxford, 2 tr. to nil.
1878-9	Drawn, 0—0.
1879-80	Cambridge, 2 g. to 1 g.
1880-1	Drawn, 1 try each.
1881-2	Oxford, 2 g. & 1 t. to 1 g.
1882-3	Oxford, 1 try to nil.
1883-4	Oxford, 3 g. & 4 t. to 1 g.
1884-5	Oxford, 3 g. & 1 t. to 1 t.
1885-6	Cambridge, 2 t. to nil.
1886-7	Cambridge, 3 t. to nil.
1887-8	Camb., 1 g. & 2 t. to nil.
1888-9	Camb., 1 g. & 2 t. to nil.
1889-90	Oxford, 1 g. & 1 t. to nil.
1890-1	Drawn, 1 goal each.
1891-2	Cambridge, 2 t. to nil.
1892-3	Drawn, nothing scored.
1893-4	Oxford, 1 try to nil.
1894-5	Drawn, 1 goal each.
1895-6	Cambridge, 1 g. to nil.
1896-7	Oxford, 2 g. (1 dr.) to 1 g. 1 t.
1897-8	Oxford, 2 tries to nil.
1898-9	Camb., 1 g. & 2 t. to nil.

Oxford, 10; Cambridge, 9; drawn, 7. Total, 26.

ASSOCIATION.

Year.	Result.
1875-6	Oxford, 4 to 1.
1876-7	Oxford, 1 to 0.
1877-8	Cambridge, 5 to 1.
1878-9	Cambridge, 1 to 0.
1879-80	Cambridge, 3 to 1.
1880-1	Cambridge, 2 to 1.
1881-2	Oxford, 3 to 0.
1882-3	Cambridge, 3 to 2.
1883-4	Cambridge, 2 to 0.
1884-5	Cambridge, 1 to 0.
1885-6	Cambridge, 5 to 0.
1886-7	Cambridge, 3 to 1.
1887-8	Oxford, 3 to 2.
1888-9	Drawn, 1 to 1.
1889-90	Cambridge, 3 to 1.
1890-1	Oxford, 2 to 1.
1891-2	Cambridge, 5 to 1.
1892-3	Oxford, 3 to 2.
1893-4	Cambridge, 3 to 1.
1894-5	Oxford, 3 to 0.
1895-6	Oxford, 1 to 0.
1896-7	Oxford, 1 to 0.
1897-8	Cambridge, 1 to 0.
1898-9	Cambridge, 3 to 1.

Cambridge, 15; Oxford, 10 with one drawn game in 1888-9

GOLF.

1899. Cambridge won by 18 holes. Of the 21 matches played, 11 have been won by Cambridge and 9 by Oxford one (1896) having been halved.

AND OTHER USEFUL INFORMATION.

BIRTHS.

When a birth takes place, personal information of it must be given to the Registrar, and the register signed in his presence, by one of the following persons:—1. The father or mother of the child. If they fail, 2. The occupier of the house in which the birth happened; 3. A person present at the birth; or, 4. The person having charge of the child. The duty of attending to the registration thereof rests firstly on the parents. One of them must, within 42 days of the birth, give to the Registrar by word of mouth the information needed to enable him to register, and must sign the register in his presence. If they fail to do this without reasonable cause, they will become liable to a penalty of forty shillings. In case of their failure, one of the other persons above named must give personal information and sign the register within the same period. If at the end of 42 days no one has given information and signed the register, the Registrar may write to any one of the above-mentioned persons, requiring him or her to come to him for that purpose, at a stated time and place. Any person who fails to comply with this requisition will become liable to a penalty of forty shillings. Not only will liability to a penalty be avoided, but the registration of a birth will be free of charge when it takes place within 42 days (but in *Scotland* the period is 21 days), unless either of the persons above named sends to the Registrar a written request to come and register at his or her residence, or at the house where the child was born, when the Registrar on so attending to register may claim a fee of one shilling. After three months a birth cannot be registered except in the presence of the superintendent Registrar, and on payment of fees to him and the Registrar. After twelve months a birth can be registered only on the Registrar-General's express authority, and on payment of further fees. It is important to persons of all classes to be able to prove their age and the place of their birth. The only legal proof of these is afforded by the civil registers, which the law now requires to be made as above described. The child's baptismal name, if changed, or not previously given, may be inserted in the register within twelve months after the registration of the birth.

DEATHS.

When a death takes place, personal information of it must be given to the Registrar, and the register signed in his presence, by one of the following persons:—1. The nearest relative of the deceased present at the death, or in attendance during the last illness. If they fail, 2. Some other relative of the deceased in the same (Registrar's) sub-district. In default of any relatives, 3. A person present at the death; or, the occupier of the house in which the death happened. If all the above-named fail, 4. An inmate of the house, or, the person causing the body to be buried. Relatives present or in attendance are first required to attend to the registration. One of them must, within five days of the death, give to the Registrar by word of mouth the information needed, and must sign the register; or must within the same time send him written notice of the death, accompanied by a certificate of the cause of death, signed by a registered medical practitioner, if any such attended the deceased. The written notice will be useless without a legal medical certificate. If notice is sent, information must nevertheless be given and the register signed within fourteen days from the death. If relatives present or in attendance fail without reasonable cause to carry out these provisions, they will become liable to a penalty of forty shillings. In case of their failure, one of the other persons above named must give personal information and sign the register in their stead. It is important that every death should be registered and a certificate of registry be obtained from the Registrar before the funeral. This certificate should be delivered to the clergyman or other person who performs the funeral or religious service. The penalty for not delivering this certificate is forty shillings. If at the end of fourteen days one of the persons above mentioned has not attended to the registration, the Registrar may, by written application, require any one of them to come to him and do so at a stated time and place. Any person failing to attend on this application will be liable to a penalty of forty shillings. Whenever the deceased has been attended by a registered medical practitioner, a certificate of the cause of death, signed by him, must be delivered to the registrar. Any person receiving such a certificate from the practitioner and not so delivering it will incur a penalty of forty shillings. The registration of a death is free of charge when it takes place within the above-mentioned periods, unless on request it is effected at an informant's house, or at the house where the death happened, when a fee of one shilling will be payable to the registrar. After twelve months a death can be registered only on the Registrar-General's express authority, and on payment of fees.

Coroners' Inquests are held in all cases of violent and unnatural deaths, such as the case of a person slain or drowned, or dying suddenly, and of any person dying in prison. Sudden deaths are supposed by the law to demand inquiry. Still, it often occurs that a medical man quite familiar with the case will give his certificate that the death arose naturally, from heart disease, apoplexy, &c., and in such case a coroner's inquest is dispensed with. Coroners do not obtrude into the houses of persons for the purpose of holding inquests, but are sent for by the peace officers, to whom it is the duty of those in whose houses violent or unnatural deaths occur to make immediate communication, whilst the body remains in the same situation as when the death occurred. Inquests are not to be held on Sunday. When the Coroner receives due notice of a violent death, casualty, or misadventure, he issues his warrant or precept to summon a jury to appear at a particular time and place for the purpose of instituting the inquiry, when, how, and by what means the deceased came by his death. The jury must consist of at least twelve lawful and honest men, "*probi et legales homines*," and the number is immaterial provided twelve agree. The jury is usually summoned from the householders residing in the neighbourhood in which the death took place. Any person having been duly summoned as a *witness* is bound to attend, or renders himself liable to be fined in any sum not exceeding forty shillings, the fine for defaulting *jurymen* being £5. The exemptions of persons from serving on juries contained in Jury Acts also apply to Coroners' inquests. There have been many instances of Coroners' inquests into the cause of fire, even where there is no loss of life, and this is an excellent practice.

VACCINATION.

The parent of every child born in England must within six months after the birth of the child, or the person having custody of a child must within six months after receiving it have the child vaccinated by a registered private medical practitioner or by the Public Vaccinator for the district. If the vaccination is performed by a private medical practitioner a certificate in the form prescribed by the Vaccination Order, 1898, of successful vaccination must be sent to the Registrar of Births within seven days. The Public Vaccinator is required on the request of the parent or guardian of a child to visit the home of the child and vaccinate it free of charge with glycerinated calf lymph or with such other lymph as may be issued by the Local Government Board at the option of the parent. If a child is not vaccinated within 4 months of its birth, the Public Vaccinator is required to give 24 hours' notice to the parent and to visit the home of the child and offer to vaccinate it. No parent or other person will be liable to any penalty under the Vaccination Acts if within four months from the birth of the child he satisfies two justices or a stipendiary or metropolitan police magistrate that he conscientiously believes that vaccination would be prejudicial to the health of the child and within seven days thereafter delivers to the Vaccination Officer for the district a certificate of such justices or magistrate of such conscientious objection. It will be seen that a conscientious objector to vaccination can thus escape all penalties, but a person who does not obtain this certificate of exemption will still be liable to penalties for not having a child vaccinated, and by the Vaccination Order, 1898, issued under the Vaccination Act, 1898, by the Local Government Board, the due vaccination of every child not exempted is secured by a very complete system of registration, and in future the Vaccination Officers will be able to undertake prosecutions without directions from Boards of Guardians, and the Boards will have no power to prevent such prosecutions.

MARRIAGE BY BANNS OR LICENCE.

BANNS OF MARRIAGE. — "Banns" formerly applied to any public kind of proclamation, and now refer only to marriages, so that the word signifies the public announcement in the parish church, the object being to ensure notoriety, and exclude clandestine marriages. Formerly banns might be proclaimed on Church holidays, but the Marriage Act, 26 Geo. II. c. 33, prescribes audible publication according to the rubric, on three Sundays preceding the ceremony. If there is morning service the right time for banns is after the Nicene Creed; and if there be afternoon or evening, and no morning service, then the right time is after the 2nd lesson. The law is now chiefly contained in the Marriage Act, 4 Geo. IV. c. 76, which repealed most of the laws then in force. Where the parties reside in different parishes, the banns must be published in both, the minister giving his certificate of the same to be handed to the minister of the parish where the marriage takes place. The law provides specially for the case where one of the parties resides in Scotland, the publication being then in the Established church of the parish. In like manner in Scotland the publication takes place in the parish church, even where the parties are married in the

Anglican or Episcopal church. It may be noted that, by Scottish law only, omission to publish the banns does not invalidate the marriage. The names by which the parties are known are sufficient for publication of banns, so that a variance from the strict baptismal name is not important. But where wrong names are designedly given, for the purpose of concealment or otherwise, the case is different, and the marriage may be null and void (*Wood's case*, 4 S. & T. 267). Where a wrong and fraudulent name is given by one party only, and the other party is innocent, the validity of the marriage is not affected.

The Bishop may license a Chapel of Ease for the celebration of marriages; but where a district has been assigned to a chapel, and it becomes a vicarage, or "ecclesiastical parish," the option ceases, and the banns must be proclaimed and marriage celebrated therein, and not in the "mother church" or that of the civil parish.

If three months be permitted to elapse, the banns become useless, and the parties must either obtain a licence, or submit to the republication of banns. The minister ought to satisfy himself that the parties are of full age, or that the consent of parents is obtained, and it is usually on the score of insufficiency of age that banns are "forbidden." By the Act 6 & 7 Will. IV. c. 85, a marriage may be performed in church on a registrar's certificate without banns.

Marriage licences are of two kinds—(1) the Common or Ordinary Licence granted by the Archbishops and Bishops for marriage in any church or chapel duly licensed for marriages; (2) the Special Licence granted by the Archbishop of Canterbury for marriage at any time or in any place on good reason being shown (see p. 403). The Act of 1823 is severe on the clergy, making it a felony for any clergyman to marry the parties in the absence of banns or licence; the penalty is far less severe on a Dissenting minister or registrar taking part in an irregular marriage. By a subsequent alteration in the law, the hours for marriage were extended, and they are now from 8 a.m. to 3 p.m.

The minister should be careful that there are two witnesses present, and that these witnesses attest the entries in the register books, which are kept in duplicate.

All civil jurisdiction over marriage was taken away from the Ecclesiastical Courts by the Act of 1857. An incumbent may under this Act refuse to marry a divorced person, but he must allow another clergyman of the diocese to perform the service.

Although the presumption of law is in favour of the validity of a marriage, great care should be taken to comply with the directions of the several statutes in every particular. Where it is impossible to comply literally, the parties must do all they can to comply with the law.

A marriage certificate is nothing more than a copy of the entry in the church register; and the customary fee is 2s. 6d., and a stamp duty of 1d. Searches on the register-books may be made on payment of small fees, viz., 1s. for a single year, and 6d. additional for every other year. There are small fees, regulated by custom, on the certificate given of banns in one parish for marriage in another. Marriage fees are not uniform, and if excessive there is power with the Diocesan Chancellor to moderate them. With those who are in a position to afford it, it is usual to pay a guinea to the clergyman, and 5s. to the clerk; and the usual fees are paid although a stranger-clergyman be invited to perform the service.

MARRIAGE LICENCES.

MARRIAGE LICENCES can be obtained in London by application at the Faculty Office, at the Vicar-General's Office, and at the Bishop of London's Registry, all within the old area known as Doctors' Commons, by one of the parties about to be married. In the country they may be obtained at the offices of the Bishops' Registrars, but licences obtained at the Bishop's Diocesan Registry only enable the parties to be married in the diocese in which they are issued; those procured at the Faculty Office, 23 Knightrider Street, or at the Vicar-General's Office, 3 Creed Lane, Ludgate Hill, E.C. (hours in both offices 10 to 4; Saturdays, 10 to 2), are available for London and all England and Wales. No instructions, either verbal or in writing, can be received, except from one of the parties; nor will any agent be allowed to interfere, either in procuring or paying for the licence. Affidavits are prepared from the personal instructions of one of the parties about to be married, and the licence is delivered to the party upon payment of fees amounting to about thirty shillings, in addition to the cost of stamps, 12s. 6d. The cost of licences through a clerical surrogate in the country varies, according to the diocese, from £1 15s. to £2 12s. 6d. By the 4th George IV. c. 76, it is enacted, " in order to avoid fraud and *collusion* in obtaining licences for marriage, that before any such licence be granted one of the parties shall make a declaration, on oath, that there is no legal impediment to the intended marriage; and also that one of *such parties hath had* his or her usual place of abode for the space of fifteen days immediately preceding the issuing of the licence within the boundary of the parish church, or the district parish in the church of which the marriage is to be solemnized."

It may be added that in the country there may generally be found a parochial clergyman who is also a surrogate, before whom the above-mentioned affidavit may be taken, and whose office it is to procure the licence from the Bishop's registry, this being the usual mode of obtaining a marriage licence, the surrogate delivering the same personally to the applicant.

SPECIAL MARRIAGE LICENCES.

SPECIAL LICENCES are granted by the Archbishop of Canterbury (after application at the Faculty Office, 23 Knightrider St., Doctors' Commons), under special circumstances, for marriage at any place with or without previous residence in the district, or at any time, &c.; but the reasons assigned must be such as to meet with his Grace's approval. Fees for licence stamp, &c., average £29 8s.

PROCEEDINGS AS TO A MARRIAGE BEFORE A REGISTRAR.

NOTICE AND DECLARATION. — In case of an intended marriage *by Certificate* at a register office (*i.e.*, the superintendent registrar's office), or a certified building (*i.e.*, usually a Roman Catholic or Nonconformist church or chapel), it is necessary for one of the parties to give notice under his or her hand (in the form prescribed by the 19 & 20 Vict. c. 119, schedule A.) to the superintendent registrar of the district within which the parties shall have dwelt for the space of seven days then next immediately preceding; or if the parties dwell in different superintendent registrars' districts, a like notice must be given to the superintendent registrar of each district: every form of notice contains solemn declarations that there is no lawful hindrance to such marriage, as to the necessary residence, the ages of the parties, and consent of parent in case of a minor; such notice and declarations must be signed before a registration officer of the district, namely, a superintendent registrar, or registrar of births and deaths or marriages or the deputy of some such registrar. If the marriage is intended to be had *by licence*, it is necessary for only one of the parties to give notice to the superintendent registrar, in manner before mentioned, in whose district he or she has resided for the space of fifteen days immediately preceding, and if the other party reside in a different superintendent registrar's district, it is not requisite that notice should be given to such last-mentioned superintendent registrar; but one of the parties must, for the space of fifteen days immediately preceding the giving of the notice, have had his or her usual place of residence within the district of the superintendent registrar to whom such notice is to be given. In case a minister did not happen to attend and the parties wished, they might be married before the registrar without any religious ceremony.

CERTIFICATE.—After the expiration of twenty-one days next after the day of the entry of notice of marriage which is to be had without licence, the superintendent registrar is required, provided there be no lawful impediment, to issue, upon the request of the party giving the notice, a certificate in the form prescribed by the 19 & 20 Vict. c. 119, schedule B. At any time within three calendar months next after the day of the entry of the notice of marriage the intended marriage may be solemnized under the authority of the certificate.

LICENCE.—In the case of marriage by licence the superintendent registrar is required, after the expiration of one whole day next after the day of the entry of the notice of marriage, provided there be no lawful impediment, to issue his certificate and also a licence to marry. At any time within three calendar months next after the day of the entry of the notice of marriage the intended marriage may be solemnized under the authority of the licence.

MARRIAGE CEREMONY.—After the expiration of twenty-one days after the entry of the notice if the marriage is intended to be had without licence, or of one whole day if by licence, the marriage may be contracted at the register office and in the presence of the superintendent registrar and some registrar of the district, and in the presence of two witnesses, between the hours of eight a.m. and three in the afternoon, with open doors. Each of the parties is required to declare as follows :—" I do solemnly declare that I know not of any lawful impediment why I, *A. B.*, may not be joined in matrimony to *C. D.* :" and each of the parties shall say to the other, "I call upon these persons here present to witness that I, *A. B.*, do take thee, *C. D.*, to be my lawful wedded wife [*or* husband]." A wedding-ring is usually required. In case a minister does not happen to be present, and the parties wish it, they may be married in any chapel or building certified for marriages, the registrar only being present with the two witnesses. The marriage laws of Scotland are peculiar, and cannot here be set out; but it may be mentioned that "Gretna Green weddings" are obsolete, a period of residence being now required by law. Provision is made in the Marriages and Registration Act, 1837, sect. 23, for the declaration and form of words to be used in Welsh in Wales and in all places where the Welsh tongue is commonly used. If both parties are of the Jewish persuasion, they must give notice to the registration officer, in manner before mentioned, and may marry according to their usages in a synagogue or private dwelling-house, and at any hour of the day; the marriage must be registered by the secretary of the synagogue to which the husband belongs. If both parties are members of the Society of Friends, they must give notice to the registration officer in manner before mentioned, and may be married in a Friends' meeting-house, and the marriage must be registered as soon as conveniently may be after its solemnization by the registering officer of the Society appointed to act for the district in which the meeting-house is situated. The presence of a registrar of marriages is not requisite at such marriages of Jews or members of the Society of Friends. The provisions as to Notices and Licences given above do not apply to Ireland. [Marriages *before a Registrar* in that country are regulated by 7 & 8 Vict. c. 81, and 26 & 27 Vict. c. 27; the Act regulating marriages in that country *in places of Worship* is 33 & 34 Vict. c. 110.]

CERTIFICATE OF BIRTH, DEATH, OR MARRIAGE. —On giving the name and date this can be obtained at Somerset House on payment of 3s. 7d. made up as follows : 2s. 6d. for certificate, 1s. for search, and 1d. for stamp. Enquiries by post from residents in the Metropolis will not be considered; attendance in person or by agent is necessary. Certificates are also obtainable from the superintendent registrar of the district in which the birth, death, or marriage took place at the above rate.

FEES FOR MARRIAGE AT REGISTRY OFFICE.

	s.	d.
For entering notice of a marriage without licence into the marriage notice-book ...	1	0
For entering notice of a marriage by licence into the marriage notice-book, 1s. ; stamp duty, 2s. 6d.	3	6
For every certificate of notice of a marriage without licence	1	0
For every certificate of notice of a marriage by licence	1	0
For every licence for marriage	30	0
Stamp duty on licence for marriage	10	0
For every marriage solemnized in the presence of the Registrar without licence...	5	0
Ditto, by licence	10	0
For every certificate of marriage	2	6
Stamp duty on ditto	0	1

MARRIAGES OF BRITISH SUBJECTS ABROAD.

AN Act was passed on the 27th June, 1892, to consolidate enactments relating to the marriage of British subjects outside the United Kingdom. This Act came into force on the 1st January, 1893. An Order in Council was passed on the 28th October, 1892, laying down Regulations for Marriages under the Act.

British subjects desirous of being married at an embassy, legation, or consulate, must give seven days' notice of the intended marriage, but one of the parties at least must have resided for that time in the district immediately preceding the giving of such notice. After the suspension of such notice for fourteen days the marriage may take place, provided one or both parties have resided for three weeks immediately preceding within the consular district. In cases where one of the parties only has dwelt within the district of the officer by whom the marriage is to be solemnized, the non-resident party, if resident abroad, must give notice to the Consular Officer for the district in which he or she resides; or, if

resident in a place in the United Kingdom, the same notice must be given as if that party were about to be married at that place, and in England or Ireland shall be given to the superintendent registrar, or registrar and in Scotland shall be given by proclamation of banns. A Consular Officer holding a warrant for a district can only solemnize a marriage at his own official house. He cannot solemnize a marriage at the office of any subordinate consular officer, or elsewhere. No marriages performed at any other place are valid under the Foreign Marriage Act. Parties residing within a consular district who may wish to be married under the Act must go to the consular officer provided with a warrant for that district; two or more witnesses are required to be present; and an oath, declaration, or affirmation must be made by both parties with reference to their age, and parents' consent, if minors.

The following fees for marriages under the Foreign Marriage Act are leviable under the Consular Fees Order in Council of 18th August, 1892, and are payable to Her Majesty's Government :—

	£	s.	d.
For receiving notice of an intended marriage	0	10	0
For receiving notice of a caveat	1	0	0
For every marriage solemnized by or in the presence of a Marriage Officer and registered by him	0	10	0
For certificate by a Marriage Officer of notice having been given and posted up, in case of one of the parties residing outside the consular district in which the marriage is to take place	0	5	0
For attendance by consular officer at a marriage solemnized in accordance with the local law and for registration of the same	1	0	0

Marriages may be solemnized between the hours of 8 a.m. and 3 p.m.

The ceremony, if a marriage under the Foreign Marriage Act, may be performed by, or in the presence of, any Ambassador, Minister, Chargé d'Affaires, or any of the Secretaries authorized for that purpose, or by any Consul-general, Consul, Vice-consul, Consular agent (or any person duly authorized to discharge their duties), or Pro-consul, provided that such consular officer is furnished with a warrant signed by the Secretary of State for Foreign Affairs. No religious ceremony is required, but any form according to the creed of the contracting parties may be used. The presence of the duly authorized Marriage Officer is, however, necessary to render the marriage valid. If the ceremonial be that of the Church of England, it can only be performed by a clergyman of that Church. If the service be not that of the Church of England, the contracting parties must make a declaration before the Marriage Officer to the effect that they know not of any lawful impediment why they may not be joined in matrimony, and that they call upon the persons present to witness that they take each other respectively to be lawful wedded husband and wife In the absence of any religious ceremony, such declaration is sufficient.

Marriages solemnized under the Foreign Marriage Acts are legal by English law when both parties are British subjects, and also when only one of them is a British subject, but such marriages are not necessarily valid out of Her Majesty's dominions. In cases where one of the parties is a subject of the country where the marriage is proposed to take place, or of a third country, the party in question must previously comply with the requirements of the marriage law of the country to which he or she belongs, so far as it may be possible to do so, in order to render such marriage also valid by the law of that country.

An Englishwoman married to a foreigner follows the nationality of her husband.

In Germany marriages by any foreign consular officer are, in the absence of any treaty stipulations, strictly prohibited. A consular officer is authorized to register, at the consulate at which he is appointed to reside, marriages solemnized in accordance with the *local law* between parties of whom one at least is a British subject, provided that he be satisfied by personal attendance that the marriage has been so solemnized ; he cannot be required to attend at the solemnization of a *lex loci* marriage beyond the place at which he is appointed to reside.

A marriage which would not be valid if solemnized in England would be equally invalid if solemnized in one of Her Majesty's embassies, legations, or consulates abroad. For instance, marriages within the prohibited degrees of consanguinity or affinity (such as that between a man and his deceased wife's sister) would not be valid in England even if valid in the country where the marriage was contracted.

Marriages may also be solemnized under the "Foreign Marriage Act, 1892," before any governor, high commissioner, or resident, who may be duly authorized to that effect, and also before the commanding officers of any of Her Majesty's ships on a foreign station.

BRITISH NATIONALITY AND NATURALIZATION.

NATIONALITY.—The following are, by the law of England, deemed to be British subjects :—

1. All persons born in Her Majesty's dominions, whether of British or of Foreign parents.
2. Children of natural-born British subjects, wherever born.
3. Grandchildren of natural-born British subjects, wherever born.
4. Persons naturalized (*a*) By Special Act of Parliament, (*b*) Under the provisions of the "Naturalization Act, 1870."

The above does not apply to married women, who are deemed to be subjects of the state of which their husbands for the time being are subjects.

Natural-born British subjects can only deprive themselves of British nationality, (1) If they happen to be born in the British dominions of foreign parents in which case they may, if of full age and if under no disability, make a declaration of alienage ; (2) If they voluntarily become naturalized in a foreign state.

British subjects born in foreign countries sometimes become, by the law of the country of their birth, subjects or citizens of that country. In such case they may, by the law of England, when of full age, and if under no disability, make a declaration of alienage, and they then cease to be British subjects. Should they retain their British nationality, and continue to reside in the country of their birth, their British nationality will not avail them if claimed as subjects or citizens of the country in question.

NATURALIZATION.—Although in rare instances aliens are naturalized by special Act of Parliament, the ordinary way of becoming naturalized as a British subject is by fulfilling the requirements of the "Naturalization Act, 1870." The

applicant must either have resided in the United Kingdom for a term of not less than five years, or have been in the service of the Crown for a similar period. He must also furnish evidence of his intention, when naturalized, either of residing in the United Kingdom, or of serving under the Crown. All applications for certificates of naturalization should be addressed to the Secretary of State for the Home Department.

The privileges of naturalized British subjects are thus stated in the "Naturalization Act" :

"An alien to whom a certificate of naturalization is granted shall in the United Kingdom be entitled to all political and other rights, powers, and privileges, and be subject to all obligations, to which a natural-born British subject is entitled or subject in the United Kingdom, with this qualification, that he shall not, when within the limits of the foreign state of which he was a subject previously to obtaining his certificate of naturalization, be deemed to be a British subject unless he has ceased to be a subject of that state in pursuance of the laws thereof, or in pursuance of a treaty to that effect."

With reference to the last paragraph of the foregoing extract, it may be mentioned that the only country with which Great Britain has yet concluded a treaty on the subject of naturalization is the United States of America. In all other countries, therefore, it is incumbent on the person concerned, if he wishes to have British protection in the country of which he was previously a subject, to show that he has ceased to be a subject of that state.

A natural-born British subject, who has become naturalized in a foreign country, may obtain a certificate of re-admission to British nationality on fulfilling the conditions required in the case of aliens applying for a certificate of naturalization.

The children of naturalized British subjects, if born in the British dominions, are by the law of England deemed to be British subjects. If born abroad, they are only deemed to be naturalized British subjects provided that their father was naturalized under the Naturalization Act, 1870, and that during infancy they became resident with their father, or mother being a widow, in any part of the United Kingdom.

British colonies have power to legislate on the subject of naturalization. Colonial naturalization is, however, only operative within the limits of the particular colony in which the naturalization may have been granted.

The following fees are leviable under the Naturalization Act, 1870 :—

	£	s.	d.
On grant of certificate of naturalization...	5	0	0
For registration of declaration, with or without oath of allegiance	0	10	0
For certified copy of any declaration or certificate with or without oath	0	10	0

STATUS OF ALIENS.—Real and personal property of every description may be taken, acquired, held, and disposed of by an alien in the same manner in all respects as by a natural-born British subject, but the acquisition of a title to such property does not confer any right on an alien to hold real property out of the United Kingdom, or qualify him for any municipal, parliamentary, or other franchise.

Aliens are not entitled to be tried by a jury *de mediatatæ linguæ*, but are triable in the same manner as if they were natural-born subjects.

NOTIFICATION OF INFECTIOUS DISEASES.

By the Infectious Disease (Notification) Extension Act, 1899, the provisions of the Infectious Disease (Notification) Act of 1889 was extended to the whole of England and Wales on the 1st January, 1899. It became necessary from that date henceforth for every case of infectious disease, as defined by the Act, to be notified to the Medical Officer of Health of the district in which it occurs. The notice may be by letter or even verbal, and must be given by the head of the family to which the patient belongs, or by the nearest relatives present in the building or in attendance on the patient, or any other person in attendance, or by the occupier of the building. In addition to this, the medical man in attendance is required to send a certificate concerning the case to the Medical Officer of Health. Failure to send the notice or certificate renders the defaulter liable to 40s. fine. No payment is made for the notices required to be given by persons in the house, but the medical man gets 2s. 6d. for every case in his private practice and 1s. for every case in a public institution of which he is medical officer.

The diseases to which the Act applies are small-pox, cholera, diphtheria, membranous croup, erysipelas, scarlatina or scarlet fever, and the fevers known by any of the following names: typhus, typhoid, enteric, relapsing, continued, or puerperal. The local authority may by resolution order that the Act shall apply to any infectious disease other than those just mentioned, but such an order must be approved by the Local Government Board. In over 100 cases the Act has been extended to measles, in 7 to röthaln, or German measles, in 26 to whooping cough, in 8 to chickenpox, and in 1 each to mumps, hydrophobia, yellow fever, and plague. In the case of an epidemic of such a common malady as measles or whooping cough, it has been found that the local authority has to pay very large sums to medical practitioners for certificates without deriving any corresponding advantage. Hence in a large number of cases the addition of these diseases has been revoked. The Local Government Board have refused to allow consumption or phthisis to be added to the list. In the case of London the provisions of the Public Health (London) Act, 1891, are similar to those now extended to the rest of the country.

INFECTIOUS DISEASES.

PRECAUTIONS NECESSARY TO BE OBSERVED.—By the Public Health Act, 1875, it is provided that any person who—(1) While suffering from any dangerous infectious disorder wilfully exposes himself without proper precautions against spreading the said disorder in any street, public place, shop, inn, or public conveyance, or enters any public conveyance without previously notifying to the owner, conductor, or driver thereof that he is so suffering; or, (2) Being in charge of any person so suffering, so exposes such sufferer; or, (3) Gives, lends, sells, transmits, or exposes, without previous disinfection, any bedding, clothing, rags, or other things which have been exposed to infection from any such disorder, shall be liable to a penalty of £5. A person suffering from such disorder who enters a public conveyance without previously notifying to the owner or driver that he is so suffering, shall be ordered by the Court to pay the owner and driver the amount of any loss and expense they may incur in respect of the disinfection of the conveyance. Every owner or driver of a public conveyance must provide for the disinfection of such conveyance after it has conveyed any person suffering from dangerous infection; but he cannot be required to convey any person so suffering until he has been paid a sum sufficient to cover any loss or expense incurred in disinfecting the conveyance. No person may knowingly let for hire any house, room, or part of a house in which any person has been suffering from any dangerous infectious disorder without having the same and all articles liable to retain infection, disinfected to the satisfaction of a legally qualified medical practitioner, as testified by a certificate signed by him. Any person letting for hire, or showing for the purpose of letting for hire, any house or part of a house, who, on being questioned by any person negotiating for the hire of such house as to the fact of there being, or within six weeks previously having been therein, any person suffering from any dangerous infectious disorder, knowingly makes a false answer to such question, is liable to a penalty not exceeding £20, or to imprisonment with or without hard labour for a period not exceeding one month. Where the Infectious Disease (Prevention) Act, 1890, is in force, the occupier of a house, or of any part in which there has been a case of infectious disease within six weeks before he ceases to occupy it, must have the premises disinfected and inform the owner of the disease. If the outgoing occupier gives false information to the owner or to an intending tenant as to the occurrence of the infection he is liable to heavy penalties and to an action for damages. Where, on the certificate of the Medical Officer of Health, or of any two medical practitioners, it appears to any District Council that any house, or part thereof, is in such a filthy or unwholesome condition that the health of any person is affected or endangered thereby, or that the whitewashing, cleansing, or purifying of any house, or part thereof, would tend to prevent or check infectious disease, they may give notice in writing to the owner or occupier of such house to whitewash, cleanse, or purify the same, and such person is liable to a penalty of 10s. for every day during which he fails to comply with the notice, and the Council may cause the work to be done, and recover the expenses from the person in default. A District Council may direct the destruction of any bedding, clothing, or other articles which have been exposed to infection from any dangerous infectious disorder, and may give compensation for the same. Where any suitable hospital or place for the reception of the sick is provided, any person who is suffering from any dangerous infectious disorder, and is without proper lodging or accommodation, or is lodged in a room occupied by more than one family, may, on a certificate signed by a legally qualified medical practitioner, and with the consent of the superintending body of such hospital or place, be removed by order of any justice to such hospital or place. Similar provisions apply to the Metropolis.

REASONS FOR MAKING A WILL.—Every man having a wife and family should make his will. However small his estate, however remote may seem the probability of death, however confident that his property will pass to those he most wishes to benefit, it is an imperative duty in most cases, and is safer in every case, to protect the interest of the survivors by means of a will, and by the appointment of one or more trustworthy persons to carry his wishes into effect. When persons die intestate, having foolishly put off making a will until it is too late, their negligence may deprive those for whom they were most anxious of the very benefits which had demanded a life-long struggle to provide. Thus a widow may find, to her grievous disappointment, that the estate, a life policy perhaps, or a few hundreds in Consols, is not all hers, but has to be shared with a distant cousin of her husband's, whose name perhaps she had never before heard. Or it may be the eldest son of an intestate ousting all his brothers and sisters from possession of the real estate, or an improvident or unbusinesslike nearest relative may claim to administer the estate. Instances might be multiplied in which negligence, or unreasoning dislike to making a will, becomes an irreparable crime against those who have the first claim to protection. The help of a lawyer in making a will is not in every case essential, but it is always advisable, particularly where there is a desire on a testator's part to provide for his property being "settled" as it is called—*e.g.* the income being paid to his widow for her life, or until remarriage, and on her death or remarriage the capital being divided among his children equally. The tying-up or postponing the enjoyment of income or capital requires the skill of a practised lawyer. Assuming that a lawyer is not employed, a person having resolved to make a will must not regard it as a light matter, to be got rid of in a few minutes, like writing a letter, but one demanding the most serious attention. It is only after a person is dead, and cannot explain his meaning, that his will can be open to dispute. It is the more necessary, therefore, to express what is meant in language of the utmost clearness, avoiding the use of any word or expression that seems to admit of another meaning than the one intended. The lawyers have a maxim that the unforeseen (*i.e.*, the event not provided for) always happens. It is better to be prolix than to leave the smallest room for doubt or uncertainty, although the same name or word be repeated over and over again. Sounding phrases are entirely out of place. Avoid the use of "legal terms," such as "heirs" and "issue," when the same thing may be expressed in plain language. If in writing the will a mistake be made, it is better to rewrite the whole. Before a will is executed, that is, *signed by the testator in presence of two witnesses*, an alteration may be made by striking through the words with a pen, but opposite to such alteration the testator and witnesses should write their names or place their initials. Never scratch out a word with a knife or other instrument, and no alteration *of any kind whatever* must be made after the will is executed. If the testator afterwards wishes to change the disposition of his estate, it is better to make a new will, revoking the old one, or to add a codicil to the first, which must be duly executed and attested in the same manner as the original will. *A will should be written in ink and very legibly on a single sheet of paper.* Although, of course, forms of wills must vary to suit different cases, the following directions may be found useful to those who, in cases of emergency, are called upon to draw up wills, either for themselves or others:—

TESTATOR OR TESTATRIX.—The person who makes the will is the testator, or if the will-maker be a woman, the testatrix.

ESTATE.—By this word is to be understood property of all kinds, both real and personal. Real property includes tithes and advowsons, as well as freehold lands and houses; while personal property includes debts due, arrears of rents, money, leasehold property, house furniture, goods, assurance policies, stock in public companies, and the like.

RESIDUARY LEGATEES.—It is well in all cases to leave to some person or persons "the residue of my estate and effects," although it may be thought that the whole of the property has been disposed of in legacies already mentioned in the will. It should be remembered that a will operates on property acquired after it has been made.

TO BEGIN A WILL.—A form in which a will may be commenced is:—"This is the last will of me, Thomas Smith, of Vine Cottage, Silver Street, Reading, in the county of Berks."

TO END A WILL.—After disposing of the property, the will may be ended as follows:—"And I revoke all former wills and codicils. Dated this tenth day of December, 1890."

EXECUTION OF A WILL.—The testator should sign his name at the foot or end of the will, in presence of two witnesses, who will immediately sign their names in his and in each other's presence. A person who has been left a legacy or share of residue in the will, or whose wife or husband has been left a legacy, should not be an attesting witness. Their attestation would be good, but they would forfeit the legacy. It is better that a person named as executor should not be a witness. Husband and wife may both be witnesses, provided neither is a legatee. If a solicitor be appointed executor, it is lawful to direct that his ordinary fees and charges shall be paid; but in this case he (as an interested party) must not be a witness to the will.

ATTESTING EXECUTION.—Opposite to or beneath the testator's signature should be written the attestation clause. The following form of attestation will be found sufficient:—

Signed by the testator [or testatrix, as the case may be], in the presence of us, both present at the same time who in his [or her] presence and in the presence of each other have hereunto set our names as witnesses.

   THOMAS SMITH [Signature of Testator.]

William Jones, of Vine Cottage, Silver Street, Reading, Tailor. Henry Morgan, of North Street, Reading, Esq.

It is desirable that the witnesses should be fully described, as they may possibly be wanted at some future time. If the testator should be too ill to sign, even by a mark, another person may sign the testator's name to the will for him, in his presence and by his direction, and in this case it should be shown that the testator knew the contents of the document. The attestation clause should therefore be worded: "Signed by Thomas Brown, by the direction and in the presence of the testator, Thomas Smith in the joint presence of us, who thereupon signed our names in his presence and in the presence of each other, the will having been first read over to the testator, who appeared fully to understand the same." If the testator be blind the will should be read aloud to him in the presence of the witnesses, and the fact mentioned in the attestation clause. If by inadvertence the testator should have signed his will without the witnesses being present, then the attestation should be :—" The testator acknowledged his signature already made as his signature to his last will and testament, in the joint presence," &c. Any omission in the observance of these details causes delay and expense, and sometimes great difficulty is experienced in procuring an affidavit by one of the attesting witnesses before the will can be admitted to Probate.

CODICIL.—When any change is required to be made in the disposition of property as stated in the will, the change should be embodied in a codicil. A codicil should begin :—" This is a codicil to the will of me, Thomas Smith, of Vine Cottage, Silver Street, Reading, in the county of Berks, the said will bearing date," &c. A codicil must be dated at the end, and signed and witnessed with exactly the same formalities as the will.

EXECUTORS.—It is usual to appoint two executors, although one is sufficient. The name and address of each executor should be given in full, as follows :—" I appoint John Jones, of number twenty-one, London-street, Ipswich, and Edward Matthews, of number seventeen, Market Street, Lincoln, executors of this my will." An executor may be a legatee under the will. Thus a child or wife to whom the whole or a portion of the estate is left may be appointed sole executor, or one of two executors. The addresses of the executors are not necessary if it is well known who are the persons intended ; but it is desirable, here as elsewhere, to avoid ambiguity or vagueness.

APPOINTMENT OF TRUSTEES.—The form of appointment of executors will also serve when the estate is left in care of trustees, except that the persons should be designated "executors and trustees."

TRUSTS OF THE WILL.—When the estate is wholly for the children, the will may read, after the appointment of the executors and trustees :— " I give and devise all my estate and effects, real and personal, of which I may die possessed or entitled to, unto the said John Jones and Edward Matthews, upon trust in equal shares for all or any my children or child living at my death who being sons or a son attain the age of 21 years or being daughters or a daughter attain that age or marry. And for all or any the children or child living at my death who being male attain the age of 21 years or being female attain that age or marry of any child of mine who dies in my lifetime leaving children or a child living at my death, such last-mentioned children or child to take the share or shares which their parent would have taken if living at my death, and so that no grandchild of mine shall take whose parent is living and capable of taking." Where the widow is to have a life-interest use the following words : "upon trust for my wife during her life [or during her widowhood] and after her death [or second marriage, which first happens] upon trust in equal shares for all or any my children or child " &c. as before. The

words in square brackets will only be used where the widow is to lose her interest if she marries again.

WHO CANNOT MAKE A WILL.—A minor cannot make a will. A woman married before the 1st of January, 1883, can make a will with her husband's consent ; but without such consent she can only (under the Married Women's Property Act) bequeath property accruing to her after that date except in certain circumstances, respecting which it is advisable to consult a solicitor. But a woman married after that date can dispose by will of all property belonging to her at the time of her marriage, and of all property acquired thereafter, in all respects as if she were an unmarried woman.

REVOCATION.—A will is revoked by a subsequent will (but only so far as such subsequent will operates as a virtual revocation, as by making other provisions inconsistent with the previous will ; for this reason a will should always have a clause revoking previous testamentary dispositions), or by burning, tearing, or otherwise destroying the same. It is not sufficient to obliterate the will with a pen. Marriage in every case acts as the revocation of a will : so that after marriage the old will should be re-acknowledged, or a new one made.

LAPSED LEGACIES.—If a legatee die in the lifetime of the testator, the legacy or share of residue lapses and falls into the residue, excepting only in cases where the legatee is a child or "other issue" of the testator and leaves issue living at the testator's death, and the will does not provide for the class of children or issue being ascertained at some period other than the death of the testator. For instance, if a share of residue is left to "all my children living at my wife's death," the share of a child who died in the wife's lifetime would lapse even though the child should leave issue.

TO ONE PERSON ABSOLUTELY.—When it is the intention to leave all the property to one person, as for instance a wife or child, the will may read :—" I devise and bequeath all my estate and effects, real and personal, which I may die possessed of or entitled to, unto my wife Mary Smith, absolutely."

TO CHILDREN UNDER AGE.—When estates are left wholly or in part to children under the age of 21 years, trustees should be appointed to hold the property in trust for those to whom it will ultimately belong. The trustees will have power to apply the annual income for their maintenance. A wife may be appointed a trustee, or may be sole trustee. It is also usual to appoint the executors, or some near relative, guardians of children under age. By the Guardianship of Infants Act, 1896, the mother of a child, if she survives the father, becomes the guardian of such child, either alone, if no guardian is appointed, or jointly with any guardian appointed by the father.

ALL PROPERTY TO BE INVESTED.—Executors and trustees may be empowered to sell and dispose of an estate, and after the payment of all just debts and expenses to invest the remainder. For this purpose the section headed " Trust Investments" should be consulted.

The stringency of the law as to the due execution of wills is only relaxed in favour of sailors and soldiers while on service. The law of wills is mostly contained in the Wills Act. 1 Vict. c. 27.

DUTIES OF EXECUTORS.—After the death of the testator, the duties of the executor may be stated briefly as follows:—The first duty of the executors, or of one of them, is to see that the funeral takes place in a suitable and becoming way; then to make lists or schedules of the debts and the assets or property. For purposes of duty it is necessary to estimate the value of the real and personal property left, or get it valued. Under the Finance Act, 1894, duties are charged on *all* property in which the testator had a life interest, even though the property may not have been under his personal control. The executor must take the will to the Probate Registry, Somerset House, or to the Probate Registry of the district in which the testator had a fixed place of abode, or to a solicitor, and prove the will; to collect all the property of the deceased and pay all his just debts, and before distributing the estate, if it be a large one, it is necessary in order to relieve the executors from personal liability to duly advertise in certain London and local newspapers for all claims against the estate to be sent in before a specified date. Pay the legacy or succession duty. Dispose of the residue of the property as directed in the will. By the Land Transfer Act, 1897, all the testator's real estate becomes vested in the executors, who hold the same as trustees for the persons beneficially entitled under the will or otherwise, and such persons can only acquire a title to the estate through the executors, after payment of all charges and liabilities to which the same is subject. Executors are not obliged to act, neither is it necessary that all the executors should act: one alone is competent to prove a will and carry out its provisions. In small estates, probate and letters of administration may be obtained through an Inland Revenue Office.

ADMINISTRATORS.—If an executor has not been appointed in the will, or if the executor be dead, or does not wish to act, the residuary legatee nearest of kin to the deceased, or a legatee under the will, is entitled to act and administer the will, and is called administrator.

NEW ESTATE DUTY.—The Finance Act of 1894 imposes a graduated duty, for which see p. 430.

LEGACY DUTY, varying according to the relationship, is payable excepting where the legatee is the wife or husband of the testator or testatrix, or intestate. (See p. 432).

ILLEGITIMACY.—A man may be summoned to petty sessions on the application of the mother of a bastard child, or by the Guardians of the Poor where the child becomes chargeable to the Union or parish; and the Justices, on his being proved to be the father of the child, may make an order requiring him to pay for its maintenance and education a sum not exceeding 5s. a week. The mother has the custody of her bastard children. No person is required as father of an illegitimate child to give information concerning the birth of such child, and the registrar is forbidden to enter in the register the name of any person as father of such child unless at the joint request of the mother and father. Such person is in that case required to sign the register, together with the mother. A menial servant found to be *enceinte* may be peremptorily dismissed without notice; but any attempt to examine without her consent a servant supposed to be *enceinte* renders the employer liable to an action. A man who is adjudged the father of a bastard child may be peremptorily discharged by his employer. In case any living new-born child is found exposed, it is the duty of any person finding such child, and of any person in whose charge such child may be placed, to inform the Registrar of Births.

Population, Births, and Deaths.

CITIES AND BOROUGHS.	POPULA-TION.	Rate per 1,000.	
		BIRTHS.	DEATHS.
London	4,504,766	29·7	19·2
West Ham	286,654	30·9	15·3
Croydon	124,421	25·4	14·1
Brighton	122,310	25·1	16·2
Portsmouth	186,618	26·7	15·7
Plymouth	99,136	29·5	19·1
Bristol	316,900	28·4	17·6
Cardiff	177,770	31·5	14·8
Swansea	102,001	29·3	18·1
Wolverhampton	88,051	36·4	21·4
Birmingham	510,343	33·9	20·4
Norwich	111,699	29·9	19·4
Leicester	208,662	29·9	17·1
Nottingham	236,137	28·9	17·5
Derby	104,834	26·9	16·9
Birkenhead	113,189	29·9	17·7
Liverpool	633,645	35·0	23·9
Bolton	121,495	31·5	19·7
Manchester	539,079	32·8	21·4
Salford	215,702	34·7	21·9
Oldham	148,288	25·2	17·9
Burnley	109,546	27·5	17·2
Blackburn	133,228	27·2	18·7
Preston	116,356	31·1	19·6
Huddersfield	102,454	23·2	16·7
Halifax	96,729	23·0	18·4
Bradford	233,737	24·1	17·5
Leeds	410,618	31·1	19·9
Sheffield	355,478	33·8	20·6
Hull	229,887	33·8	18·2
Sunderland	143,849	35·2	22·0
Gateshead	103,775	36·2	20·4
Newcastle	223,021	31·9	20·8
Edinburgh	295,628	27·5	19·5
Glasgow	724,349	33·5	21·5
Dublin	349,594	30·5	26·2
Calcutta	466,460	*	28·9
Bombay	821,764	13·0	64·1
Madras	452,518	42·0	42·8
Paris	2,511,629	23·8	19·9
Brussels	551,011	25·2	17·0
Amsterdam	508,266	29·4	16·1
Rotterdam	303,878	36·8	18·6
The Hague	196,325	29·8	16·7
Copenhagen	345,000	29·3	17·5
Stockholm	283,550	26·6	17·4
Christiania	203,337	25·5	16·5
St. Petersburg	1,132,677	32·6	29·2
Moscow	988,610		30·8
Berlin	1,773,003	26·8	17·3
Hamburg	661,015	32·2	17·4
Dresden	385,300	*	19·1
Breslau	392,795	35·2	24·6
Munich	430,000	35·6	23·0
Vienna	1,590,295	30·4	20·5
Prague	382,029	28·8	23·4
Buda Pesth	648,104	35·2	21·5
Trieste	165,177	32·0	27·9
Rome	499,861	23·0	17·8
Turin	344,203	20·8	16·6
Venice	169,545	23·9	22·6
Cairo	570,062	*	··
Alexandria	319,765	*	*
New York (including Brooklyn)	3,438,899	22·4	19·0
Philadelphia	1,240,266	*	

* Rate not stated.

It will be observed that some of the populations given in this table differ from those shown in other parts of the Almanack.

Architects' Fees.

The custom is to charge 5 per cent. on the cost of new work, if exceeding £1,000. Below that sum, an increased scale is usual. An increased charge is also made for alterations to existing buildings, and for designs for decorations, fittings, and furniture. If PLANS, &c., are prepared for works which are never carried out, the charge is one-half the above, with a further half per cent. if tenders have been invited and received. These charges do not include negotiations for purchase of site, &c., nor settlement of difficulties with adjacent owners and public authorities, nor taking out quantities. For repetitions a modified charge is usually arranged. The minimum charge per day is three guineas. In all cases, travelling and other out-of-pocket expenses are paid by the employer in addition to the fees. For furnishing or checking a Schedule of Dilapidations and Estimate the usual charge is 5 per cent. on the estimate, but in no case less than two guineas. For valuing and negotiating the settlement of claims under the Lands Clauses and similar Acts the charge is on Ryde's Scale.

Surveyors' Fees.

SURVEY with plain plan—100 acres and under —by arrangement, according to work required. Over 100 acres, 2s. per acre and expenses; if with finished map, according to amount of embellishment.

VALUATION to fix rent—5 per cent. on first £200, and 2½ on remainder of one year's rental value, and expenses.

TIMBER valuation—5 per cent. on first £100, and 2½ on the excess, and out-of-pocket expenses.

CROPPING—5 per cent. up to £100, and 2½ on the excess, and out-of-pocket expenses.

VALUATION for probate—2 per cent. on first £500, and 1¼ on the excess, and out-of-pocket expenses. But it is now usual to make a bargain for a fixed and moderate sum.

VALUATION of land—6d. per acre, and out-of-pocket expenses. No fee less than 5 guineas.

Auctioneers' and Estate Agents' Fees.

FOR THE SALE OF FREEHOLD AND COPYHOLD ESTATES AND HOUSES AND GROUND LEASES, BY PRIVATE TREATY.—£5 per cent. on the first £100; £2½ per cent. up to £5,000; and on the residue above that sum £1½ per cent.; and the usual commission of £5 per cent. in addition on the amount paid for fixtures, furniture, and effects, and in addition for any disbursements.

FOR LETTING UNFURNISHED HOUSES, OR DISPOSING OF LEASES OTHER THAN GROUND LEASES BY ASSIGNMENT OR OTHERWISE.—Where the term is for three years or less, £5 per cent. on one year's rent; where for more than three years, £7½ per cent on one year's rent, and (in either case) upon the premium or consideration, £5 per cent. up to £1,000, and 2½ per cent. on the residue, and the commission on any sum obtained for fixtures, furniture, or effects of any kind, of £5 per cent. up to £500, and 2½ per cent. on the residue.

FOR LETTING FURNISHED HOUSES, IN TOWN OR COUNTRY.—When let for a year or less period, £5 per cent. on the rental. When let for more than a year, £5 per cent. on first year's rent, and £2½ per cent. on rent for remainder of term. Where a property is let, and the tenant afterwards purchases, the commission for selling will then become chargeable, less the amount previously paid for letting furnished or unfurnished.

FOR VALUATIONS OR SALE OF FURNITURE, FIXTURES, AND OTHER EFFECTS BY AUCTION OR OTHERWISE.—£5 per cent. up to £500, and 2½ per cent. on the residue.

FOR VALUATION OF FURNITURE AND EFFECTS, FOR PROBATE OR ADMINISTRATION.—£2½ per cent. on the first £100, and £1½ per cent. on the residue.

FOR VALUATION OF PROPERTIES.—£1 per cent. up to £1,000, 5s. per cent. beyond, on full amount of valuation. In valuations for Mortgage, if an advance is not made, one-third of the above scale, the minimum fee to be £3 3s.

FOR NEGOTIATING THE PURCHASE OF ESTATES, HOUSES, AND GROUND LEASES.—£2½ per cent. up to £500, and £1 per cent. beyond that amount.

FOR NEGOTIATING THE TAKING OF FURNISHED OR UNFURNISHED HOUSES.—Half the scale for letting.

FOR LETTING BUILDING LAND.—Amount of one year's ground rent, or by agreement.

FOR MAKING AND EXAMINING INVENTORIES, and making catalogue for auction sale—From one guinea, according to length, exclusive of expenses.

MAKING schedule of fixtures to attach to lease —From 1 to 4 guineas, or about 3 guineas per day.

FOR MAKING schedule of dilapidations, and serving notice to repair—From 2 to 5 gs. per day.

FOR SETTLING amount of dilapidations—5 per cent. on amount, and out-of-pocket expenses.

RAILWAY, School Board, Corporation. Board of Works. and other compensations—SCALE :—

If the award be for £1,000 the fee chargeable is 18 gs. and for £1,200 19 gs. and so on, each £200 additional earning a further guinea.

But no fee less than 7 guineas, and a fee of 3 guineas per day for London valuers, and 5 guineas per day for valuers outside the London area, for attendance in London before jury or arbitrator.

MANAGEMENT of estates, including collection of rents—Tithe-rent charges, ground rents, &c., from 3 to 5 per cent. ; cottage property, from 5 to 10 per cent., according to special agreement.

Allowances under Bankruptcy Acts, 1883 and 1890.

The following charges are to be subject to reduction by agreement with the Official Receiver or the trustee, or to increase with the sanction of the Committee of Inspection and the Receiver:—

Brokers.—For inventory not exceeding 5 folios, 10s. 6d. ; additional per folio to 20 folios, 1s. 6d.; each folio after 20, 1s. For inventory and valuation :—On the first £100, £2 10s. ; for the next £400, £1 5s. ; above £400 up to £10,000, £1 ; above £10,000, 10s. Travelling expenses in addition

Auctioneers.—For sales by private contract half the above charges for inventory and valuation ; for sales by auction (in addition to certain out-of-pocket expenses) of chattel property, 5 per cent. on first £50, 4 per cent. on next £500, above £1,000 2½ per cent.; and of estates in land, including prior valuations for determining amount of reserve bids, on first £300 5 per cent., on next £1,600 2½, above up to £5,000 1¼, and above £5,000 1 per cent. Cost of surveys, dilapidations and specifications, £2 to £5.

Accountants.—For preparing balance-sheet, investigating accounts, &c., principal's time, exclusively so employed, per day of seven hours, including necessary affidavit, £1 1s. to £5 5s. Chief-clerk's time, 10s. 6d. to £1 11s. 6d. Other clerk's time, per day of seven hours, 7s. 6d. to 16s. These charges to include stationery, except forms used.

MEDICAL FEES.

UNLIKE those in most other businesses or professions, the charges made by medical men are assessed upon a sliding scale. All engaged in the profession are supposed to be equal in point of skill, and therefore entitled to charge alike, the tariff depending chiefly upon the residence of doctor or patient. A medical man living in the eastern suburbs of London will perhaps charge but half a crown or three-and-sixpence if waited upon by a patient, but, when he removes to the neighbourhood of Cavendish Square, the fee charged for the first visit will be two guineas, and one guinea for the second and every subsequent visit.

Patients are charged according to their supposed incomes, the income being indicated by the rental of the houses in which they reside. The following are the charges usually made by general practitioners :—

GENERAL PRACTITIONERS.	RENTALS.		
	£10 to £25.	£25 to £50.	£50 to £100.
Ordinary Visit	2s. 6d. to 5s.	3s. 6d. to 7s.	5s. to 10s. 6d
Night Visit	Double an ordinary visit.		
Mileage beyond two miles from Home..	1s. 6d.	2s.	2s. 6d.
Detention per ¼ hour	2s. 6d. to 5s.	3s. 6d. to 7s.	5s. to 10s 6d
Letters of Advice	Same charge as for an ordinary visit		
Attendce. on servants	2s. 6d.	3s. 6d.	3s. 6d. to 5s.
Midwifery	21s.	21s. to 63s.	63s. to 105s.
Adminstrng. Chlfrm.	10s. 6d.	21s.	42s.
CONSULTANTS.			
Advice or Visit alone	21s.	21s.	21s.
Advice or Visit with another Practitioner	21s.	21s. to 42s.	21s. to 42s.
Mileage beyond two miles from Home..	10s. 6d.	10s. 6d.	10s. 6d.

Special visits—i.e., of which due notice has not been given before the practitioner starts on his daily round, are charged at the rate of a visit and a half. Patients calling upon the doctor are charged at the same rate as if visited by him.

When the ordinary medical attendant is called upon to meet another in consultation, he is entitled to charge double his ordinary fee. When he himself is called in, in consultation, he is entitled to the minimum fee of 21s.

When more members of one family are ill at the same time, half a fee is charged for each beyond the first.

In midwifery cases the fee generally covers all charges for visits, &c., if all goes well, but if the illness be protracted, or if any special operation has to be performed, there is an extra charge.

If attendance on servants is paid for by employer, or if *he* send for the doctor, the charge is the same as to himself.

Certificates of health are to be charged for same as visits, except where special investigation is needed, as in certificates for lunacy, insurance offices, &c., when the charge may be from half a guinea to two guineas.

Vaccination is usually charged for according to the number of visits required.

Medical bills are commonly rendered once or twice a year, and contain but one amount—"Attendance and medicine," from date to date, so much. The patient has no means of checking the correctness of the charge, although medical men, like all others, are liable to err; they, however, are always willing to show their ledgers when requested.

THESE are now usually regulated in conveyancing and non-contentious business by the Solicitors' Remuneration Act, 1881, and the Scale thereunder—we say "usually" because that Act allows an option to a solicitor of declining to adopt it. In practice, most solicitors (although some old-established firms are found to prefer the old system) are willing to adopt the Scale, and especially on mortgages and sales. Looking first at the old system, we find that an Act of 1843 made solicitors' charges on conveyancing liable to taxation by a public official; and in 1870 a further Act enabled the taxing officer to have regard to "skill, labour, and responsibility" as well as to mere length of documents. The Act of 1881 enabled the high legal authorities, with the consent of certain representative solicitors, to frame a Scale, and this has been done. It chiefly relates to sales, purchases, and mortgages, and is based upon the value of the property or amount of the money involved. It is too lengthy for insertion here, but a copy of the Remuneration Act, and the "General order made thereunder," with judgments bearing thereon up to the end of the Hilary sittings, 1889, is obtainable of the Incorporated Law Society, Chancery Lane, W.C., price 5s. Vol. I. contains a concise table of charges, which table is in daily use among solicitors themselves. Besides this, it is legal for a client to make a bargain beforehand for a fixed sum. The amount coming to the solicitor, whether under Scale or agreement, is intended to cover the services of himself and his clerks, while it is, of course, exclusive of actual outlay for stamps, &c. On purchase, or mortgage-money exceeding £300 and not exceeding £1,000, the Scale charge for each party's solicitor is 1½ per cent.; this does not apply to sales by auction. Where a negotiation fee is chargeable, in addition, by the vendor's, purchaser's, or mortgagee's (not mortgagor's) solicitor, the Scale charge on sums exceeding £300 and not exceeding £3,000 is 1 per cent. It should be noted that if the solicitor *negotiates* the purchase or mortgage, he is entitled to an additional fee of substantial amount under the Scale referred to.

TRUST FUNDS AND INVESTMENTS.

BY RULE OF THE SUPREME COURT, DATED NOVEMBER, 1888, trustees may invest trust funds in the following securities :—

2¾ per Cent. Consols; to be reduced, 5th April, 1903, to 2½ per cent. Consols and Reduced 3 per cent. Annuities. 2¾ per Cent. and 2½ per Cent. Annuities. Exchequer Bills. Bank Stock. India 3½ per Cent. and 3 per Cent. Stocks. Indian Guaranteed Railway Securities. Colonial Government Stocks guaranteed by Imperial Government. Mortgage of freehold or copyhold estates in England or Wales. 3 and 3½ per Cent. Metropolitan Consolidated Stock.

Debenture, preference, guaranteed, or rentcharge stocks of railways in Great Britain or Ireland having for ten years next before the date of investment paid a dividend on ordinary stock or shares.

Nominal stocks or nominal debenture stocks issued under the Local Loans Act, 1875, provided in each case that such stocks shall not be liable to be redeemed within a period of fifteen years from the date of investment.

Local Loans Stock under the National Debt and Local Loans Act, 1887.

THE RULE OF COURT OF NOVEMBER, 1888, will be little referred to now that all the foregoing items in more extensive, and in some cases slightly different, language, are authorized by the Trustee Act, 1893, the more important clauses of which, especially where the Rule of Court is varied, may be summarized as follows :—This Act, which consolidates the enactments relating to trustees, authorizes mortgages on freeholds, or property equivalent to freehold, not only in England and Wales, but also (where not prohibited) in Ireland and Scotland. A very few leaseholds, viz., terms of 200 years, at a nominal rent, are also authorized by the Trustee Act, 1893.

THIS ACT ALSO AUTHORIZES investments by trustees upon any securities guaranteed by Parliament, and these include the following :—Certain Canada Government stocks, the Turkish Loan of 1855, the Egyptian 3 per cent. guaranteed Loan, a Jamaica 4 per cent. Loan, and one or two others of small amount. In addition to Metropolitan Stock, any stocks of the London County Council are now authorized; also any Corporation or Municipal stocks of the cities or boroughs (about 60 in number) having at the last census a population exceeding 50,000. Also stocks, &c., under certain conditions, of Waterworks Companies and of Water Commissioners. Another very important addition to the list of trust securities is this : Preference, Debenture, Guaranteed, or Rentcharge Stocks of British Railway Companies which have paid 3 per cent. on their ordinary stocks for ten years. This includes all the great lines in England, Ireland, and Scotland, except a few, *e.g.*, the North British, Great Eastern, and Chatham and Dover, which have not, for the whole period of ten years, paid regular dividends to their ordinary shareholders.

THE ACT FURTHER AUTHORIZES trust investments in certain Indian Railways guaranteed by the Indian Government, which can be found on reference to the Stock Exchange official lists. But with regard to the entire list, a trustee cannot invest in anything which is (directly or by implication) prohibited by the terms of his trust. It remains to add (1) that by this Act a trustee may buy at a premium under fixed conditions, but not where the stock is redeemable within 15 years at par, "or some other fixed rate." (2) The last power, as well as every other, is to be used at the "discretion of the trustee"—a phrase which can only be taken in a technical sense, as the Court expects him to show a prudent and cautious discretion, and forbids him, for instance, to favour the tenant for life at the expense of those to follow after. (3) A trustee must consider what is directed, and what is forbidden, by the terms of his trust, before resorting to any of the securities authorized by the Rule of Court, or by the new Act. (4) The Settled Land Act of 1882 also gives a list of securities on which "capital money" arising from sales of property under that Act may be invested—it does not materially differ from the above. The safest plan for a trustee to adopt is this : after looking to his trust, to see that nothing is prohibited, to turn his attention solely to the Act of 1893, sect. 1, and take his choice of the securities therein mentioned. Nearly all of them are at a high price, and he can hardly make sure of obaining 2¾ per cent. for trust money.

If the deed or will under which he is acting authorizes Colonial or Foreign Government Securities, but not otherwise, he may consult the list of such securities, and select one or more, so as to obtain a slightly higher return on the capital invested.

Regulations for Motor Cars.

APPLICABLE TO ENGLAND AND WALES.

THE following is a summary of the regulations issued by the Local Government Board, supplementary to the Locomotives on Highways Act :—

A light locomotive means a vehicle propelled by mechanical power, under three tons in weight unladen; only used for the purpose of drawing one vehicle, such vehicle and its locomotive together not exceeding in weight unladen four tons; not emitting any smoke or visible vapour, except from any temporary or accidental cause.

In calculating the weight of a vehicle unladen, the weight of any water, fuel, or accumulators used for the purpose of propulsion shall not be included.

It must be capable of being worked either forwards or backwards. The tyre of each wheel must be smooth, with a breadth varying according to the weight of the vehicle, from four inches to two and a-half inches. There must be two independent brakes, each capable of preventing two wheels on the same axle from revolving. If a vehicle is drawn by the locomotive, it, too, must have an efficient brake, controlled by a competent person ; or else, the brakes on the locomotive must be able to control the vehicle. The width of a locomotive must not exceed six and a half feet. A lamp is to be carried during the period between one hour after sunset and one hour before sunrise, exhibiting a white light forwards and a red light in the reverse direction. If drawing another vehicle, it must have the name of its owner and his address conspicuously painted on it, together with its weight on the right or off-side in letters white on black, or black on white, not less than one inch in height. The weight must also be painted on every locomotive weighing unladen a ton and a-half and upwards.

Greatest possible speed is fixed at twelve miles an hour. If the weight be one ton and a-half, and does not exceed two tons, the speed shall be not more than eight miles an hour. If the weight exceeds two tons, the speed shall be not more than five miles an hour. Whatever the weight, if used to draw any vehicle, the speed shall not exceed six miles an hour.

This regulation has effect for six months, from Nov. 9, 1896, and thereafter until the Local Government Board direct otherwise.

GENERAL REGULATIONS.—The police are to regulate speed and stoppages for the convenience of the general traffic. A bell or other instrument shall give warning of the approach or position of the light locomotive. The ordinary rules of the road shall be observed. The name of owner shall be given whenever demanded by a constable, or on the reasonable request of any other person.

A breach of any regulation may, on summary conviction, be punished by a fine not exceeding ten pounds.

SCOTTISH REGULATIONS.

The limit of speed is fixed at ten miles an hour if the locomotive be under one and a-half tons *unladen*: if over this but under two tons, the limit is eight miles, and from two tons onwards the maximum is fixed at five miles an hour. Whatever the weight if used to draw any vehicle the maximum speed must not exceed six miles an hour.

Fares by Distance: If hired and discharged *within* the Four-Mile Radius, for any distance not exceeding two miles .... *s.* 1 *d.* 0

For every additional mile or part of a mile ... 0 6

If hired *outside* the Four-Mile Circle, wherever discharged, for the first and each succeeding mile or part of a mile 1 0

If hired *within* but discharged *outside*, the Four-Mile Circle, whole distance not exceeding one mile, 1s.; exceeding one mile, then for each mile *ended* within the circle, 6d.; and for each mile or part of a mile *ended* outside 1 0

Fares by Time: *Inside* the Four-Mile Circle. Four-wheeled Cabs, for one hour or less, 2s.; two-wheeled Cabs 2 6

If above one hour, for every quarter hour or part of a quarter of the whole time, four-wheeled Cab, 6d.; if a two-wheeled Cab...... 0 8

If hired *outside* the Circle, wherever discharged, for one hour or less 2 6

If above one hour, then for every quarter hour or part of quarter of the whole time... 0 8

If hired *within*, but discharged *outside*, the Four-Mile Circle, the same.

Extra Payments.—*Hirers of Cabs should be particular in noticing these regulations, as disputes generally arise from their not being clearly understood.*

Whether hired by **Distance or by Time**.

Luggage.—For each package carried outside the carriage .... *s.* 0 *d.* 2

Extra Persons: For each above two (two children under 10 years of age count as one person) 0 6

Waiting—By distance: for every 15 minutes completed—if hired within the Four-Mile Circle, four wheels, 6d.; two wheels ... 0 8

If hired without Circle, 2 or 4 wheels...... 0 8

General Regulations.—Fares are according to distance or time, at the option of the hirer, *expressed at the commencement of the hiring;* if not otherwise expressed, the fare to be paid according to distance; but driver can refuse to be hired by time between 8 p.m. and 6 a.m.

Driver, if hired by distance, is not compelled to drive more than six miles, nor more than one hour if hired by time; further, if hired by time, the driver may be required to drive at any rate not exceeding four miles an hour; if required to drive more than four miles within the hour he may demand, in addition to the fare regulated by time, for every mile or any part exceeding four miles, the fare regulated by distance.

Agreement to pay more than legal fare is not binding.

If the driver agree beforehand to take any sum less than the proper fare, the penalty for demanding more than the sum agreed upon is 40s.

The driver of every hackney carriage shall have with him, and when required produce, the Authorized Book of Distances, and every driver of any hackney carriage shall, if so required, deliver to the hirer a printed ticket, showing fares, &c.

Driver may demand a reasonable sum as a deposit from persons hiring and requiring him to wait at any place, over and above the fare to which the driver is entitled for driving thither. Penalty 40s., if driver, having received such deposit, refuse to wait, or go away before the expiration of the time for which the deposit shall be a sufficient compensation; or if the driver shall refuse to account for such deposit.

The London Cab Act, 1896, enacts that if any person hires a cab, knowing, or having reason to believe, he cannot pay the fare; or, fraudulently endeavours to avoid payment of a fare; or, having failed, or refused, to pay a fare, refuses or gives a false address, is liable, in addition to the fare, to a penalty of 40s.

The fares legally demandable by a stage carriage are those painted in a conspicuous manner on the inside of every such carriage, and they are recoverable in a summary way before a Justice of the Peace, in the same way as fares for a hackney carriage.

All property left in any hackney carriage shall be deposited by the driver (and in the case of a stage carriage, by the conductor, or driver if no conductor) at the nearest Police Station within twenty-four hours, if not sooner claimed by the owner; such property to be returned to the person who shall prove to the satisfaction of the Commissioner of Police that the same belonged to him, on payment of all expenses incurred, and of such sum to the driver as the Secretary of State has by order prescribed. Property found in a stage carriage by a passenger must be given up to the conductor under a penalty of £10.

All inquiries, &c., relating to public carriages should be addressed to the Public Carriage Office, New Scotland Yard; but inquiries as to property left in a hackney or stage carriage should be made at the Lost Property Office, New Scotland Yard.

On the 31st December, 1898, there were licensed public carriages:—Hansoms, 7,899; clarences, 3,648; omnibuses, 3,423; tram-cars, 1,295; total, 16,265. Drivers and conductors:—Hackney drivers, 13,475; stage drivers, 7,498; conductors, 8,753; total, 29,726.

Hackney and Stage Carriage Drivers before obtaining a licence are required to pass an examination as to their ability to drive, and hackney carriage drivers, in addition, have to pass an examination as to their knowledge of town. It extends to a knowledge of the principal squares, streets, and public buildings in London. During 1898, of 972 men examined, 776 were successful. The annual average number of applicants who passed the examination during the past five years was 855. The proportion of drivers to carriages is 11·65 drivers to 10 carriages: 169 of the drivers are over 70 years of age. In 1870 the accommodation of the Metropolitan public was provided for at the rate of one stage carriage to 2,917 people; in 1892 the proportion was one to 1,724.

Of lost property, 38,201 articles were deposited, of which 19,391 were claimed by the owners, and £2,762 awarded to the drivers and conductors.

Streets and Footpaths.—The scavenging of streets and the cleansing of footways and pavements is generally undertaken by the sanitary authority of each district, but under certain circumstances the cleansing of footways and pavements adjoining premises, and the removal of filth and ashpit refuse, may be imposed upon occupiers. It is, however, unlawful in any Urban Sanitary District to place or leave on any footway any furniture, goods, wares or merchandise, or any cask, tub, basket, pail, &c.; or to place over any footway any blind, shade, covering, awning, or other projection less than eight feet in height from the ground; or to place any goods, wares, merchandise, matter, or thing whatsoever, so that the same project in such a manner as to obstruct or incommode the passage of any person over or along a footway; or to roll any cask, tub, hoop, or wheel upon any footway, except for the purpose of crossing the footway; or to throw or lay down any materials in any street, or beat or shake any carpet, rug, or mat in any street after the hour of eight in the morning.

THE tithe of produce, the ancient provision for the maintenance of the clergy, a large amount of which is now the property of laymen, was, after various attempts at modification and composition, commuted in 1836 by Act of Parliament to a payment in money. The land was valued, and a modus fixed, based upon the average value of corn for the preceding seven years, and payments, collected half-yearly by the clergy or lay-owners, have since been made on a septennial average. The value fixed amounted in some cases to as much as ten shillings per acre. The better the land for corn-growing, the larger was the sum to be paid, as it was a direct charge upon the corn grown. The prices upon which the Act was based being per quarter—wheat at 56*s.* 2*d.*; barley, 31*s.* 8*d.*; and oats, 22*s.* Consequently much land, not being worth the tithe, is now out of cultivation, or let at a price which just covers the charge. An Act passed in 1891 makes it compulsory for the owners of the land, instead of the occupiers, to pay the tithe, which amounts in the aggregate to about four millions annually, of which sum £766,334 is paid to 2,096 lay-owners or impropriators. Extraordinary tithes were an additional charge made, when the Commutation Act was passed, upon hop, fruit, and market-garden grounds. These special industries were so affected by the tax, which in some cases amounted to thirty shillings an acre, that serious resistance against the payment ensued, and an Act was passed in 1886 providing that it should not be levied on land brought under such cultivation after the passing of the Act, but land under these crops at the time was permanently burdened with the impost. The tithe map and apportionment for each parish is deposited with the incumbent and churchwarden. Any one interested therein may have access to the same and obtain extracts by paying 2*s.* 6*d.* for inspection, and 3*d.* for every 72 words contained in the extract. Tithe may, upon the joint application of the land-owner and tithe-owner to the Board of Agriculture, be redeemed for a sum *not less* than 25 times its amount. This is dependent upon the consent of the Board, and sometimes on that of the Bishop and patron. Town property and building land is often redeemed, agricultural land rarely, the cost being too great. Since the Commutation Act of 1836 £26,414 16*s.* 10*d.* has been redeemed, the redemption money being £665,574 2*s.* 2*d.*

The average for the past seven years is computed to the Thursday next before Christmas Day; it is taken every year, and the result published in January.

The average Tithe Rent Charge for the first fifty years from 1836 was £102 9*s.* 9½*d.*, and for the past seven years (1893-1899) £71 10*s.* 11½*d.*

Years.	Wheat. *s.*	*d.*	Barley. *s.*	*d.*	Oats. *s.*	*d.*	Tithe Rent-charge.		
1836	*56*	*2*	*31*	*8*	*22*	*0*	*100*	*0*	*0*
1863	44	9	33	9	21	2	107	5	2
1864	40	2	29	11	20	1	103	3	10¾
1865	41	0	29	9	21	10	98	15	10½
1866	49	11	37	5	24	7	97	7	9¼
1867	64	5	39	11	26	0	98	13	3
1868	63	9	43	0	28	1	100	13	8
1869	48	2	39	5	26	0	103	5	8¼
1870	46	11	34	7	22	10	104	1	0¼
1871	56	8	36	2	25	2	104	15	1
1872	57	0	37	3	23	2	108	4	0¼
1873	58	8	40	5	25	5	110	15	10¼
1874	55	9	44	11	28	10	112	7	3
1875	45	1	38	5	28	8	112	15	6¾
1876	46	2	35	2	26	3	110	14	11
1877	56	9	39	8	25	11	109	16	11½
1878	46	5	40	2	24	4	112	7	5¼
1879	43	10	34	0	21	9	111	15	1½
1880	44	4	33	1	23	1	109	17	9¼
1881	45	4	31	11	21	9	107	2	10½
1882	45	1	31	2	21	10	102	16	2
1883	41	7	31	10	21	5	100	4	9¾
1884	35	8	30	8	20	3	98	6	2¼
1885	32	10	30	1	20	7	93	17	3
1886	31	0	26	7	19	0	90	10	3½
1887	32	6	25	4	16	3	87	8	10
1888	31	10	27	10	16	9	84	2	8¾
1889	29	9	25	10	17	9	80	19	8½
1890	31	11	28	8	18	7	78	1	3½
1891	37	0	28	2	20	0	76	3	3¾
1892	30	3	26	2	19	10	75	18	3¼
1893	26	4	25	7	18	9	74	15	2¾
1894	22	10	24	6	17	1	74	3	9½
1895	23	1	21	11	14	6	73	13	0½
1896	26	2	22	11	14	9	71	9	6¾
1897	30	2	23	6	16	11	69	17	11½
1898	34	0	27	2	18	5	68	14	11
1899	...		...		...		68	2	4¾

AVERAGE PRICES OF WHEAT, BARLEY, AND OATS PER IMPERIAL QUARTER FROM 1785.

Yrs.	Wheat *s.*	*d.*	Barley. *s.*	*d.*	Oats. *s.*	*d.*	Yrs.	Wheat *s.*	*d.*	Barley. *s.*	*d.*	Oats *s.*	*d.*
1785	43	1	24	9	17	8	1825	68	6	40	0	25	8
1786	40	0	25	1	18	6	1826	58	8	34	4	26	8
1787	42	5	23	4	17	2	1827	58	6	37	7	28	2
1788	46	4	22	8	16	1	1828	60	5	32	10	22	0
1789	52	9	23	6	16	6	1829	66	3	32	6	22	9
1790	54	9	26	3	19	5	1830	64	3	32	7	24	5
1791	48	7	26	10	18	1	1831	66	4	38	0	25	4
1792	43	0	27	7	16	9	1832	58	8	33	1	20	5
1793	49	3	31	1	20	6	1833	52	11	27	6	18	5
1794	52	3	31	9	21	3	1834	46	2	29	0	20	11
1795	75	2	37	5	24	5	1835	39	4	29	11	22	0
1796	78	7	35	4	21	10	1836	48	6	32	10	23	1
1797	53	9	27	2	16	3	1837	55	10	30	4	23	1
1798	51	10	29	0	19	5	1838	64	7	31	5	22	5
1799	69	0	36	2	27	6	1839	70	8	39	6	25	11
1800	113	10	59	10	39	4	1840	66	4	36	5	25	8
1801	119	6	68	6	37	0	1841	64	4	32	10	22	5
1802	69	10	33	4	20	4	1842	57	3	27	6	19	3
1803	58	10	25	4	21	6	1843	50	1	29	6	18	4
1804	62	3	31	0	24	3	1844	51	3	33	8	20	7
1805	89	9	44	6	28	4	1845	50	10	31	8	22	6
1806	79	1	38	8	27	7	1846	54	8	32	8	23	8
1807	75	4	39	4	28	4	1847	69	9	44	2	28	8
1808	81	4	43	4	33	4	1848	50	6	31	6	20	6
1809	97	4	47	0	31	5	1849	44	3	27	9	17	6
1810	106	5	48	1	28	7	1850	40	3	23	6	16	5
1811	95	3	42	3	27	7	1851	38	6	24	9	18	7
1812	126	6	66	9	44	6	1852	40	9	28	6	19	1
1814	74	4	37	4	25	8	1853	53	3	33	2	21	0
1816	78	6	33	11	27	2	1854	72	5	36	0	27	11
1817	96	11	49	4	32	5	1855	74	8	34	9	27	5
1818	86	3	53	10	32	5	1856	69	2	41	1	25	2
1819	74	6	45	9	28	2	1857	56	4	42	1	25	0
1820	67	10	33	10	24	2	1858	44	2	34	8	24	6
1821	56	1	26	0	29	6	1859	43	9	33	6	23	2
1822	44	7	21	10	28	1	1860	53	3	36	7	24	5
1823	53	4	36	6	22	11	1861	55	4	36	1	23	9
1824	63	11	36	4	24	10	1852	55	5	35	1	22	7

Stock.	Dividends Payable.*
Bank Stock	April 5 and October
2¾% Consols (until 5th April, 1903)	Jan.5, Apl.5, July Oct.5
2½ per Cents. (1905)	„ „ „ „
2¾ per Cents. (1905)	„ „ „ „
Local Loans 3% (1912) ...	„ „ „ „
Metrop. Police 3% (1920)	January 1 and July 1
India 3½ per Cents. (1931)	Jan.5,Apl.5,July 5,Oct.5
India 3 per Cents. (1948)	„ „ „ „
India 2½ per Cents. (1926)	„ „ „ „
Annuities for Terms of Years	Jan.5,Apl.5,July 5,Oct.5
Red Sea&IndiaTelegraph (1908)	Feb. 4 and August 4
Metrop.3½perCent.(1929)	Jan.5,Apl.5,July 5,Oct.5
„ 3 per Cent. (1941)	Feb.1,May 1,Aug.1,Nv.1
„ 2½perCent.(1949)	Mar.1,Jn.1,Sept.1,Dec.1
Lond. Cty. 2½% Consold. Stock (1932)	„ „ „ „
Birkenhead 2¾ per Cent. (1919-1959)	April 1, October 1
Birmingham 2½ (1926) 3½ (1946) & 3 per Cent. (1947)	January 1 and July 1
Hampshire 3 per cent. County Stock	March 1 and Sept. 1
Corporn. of London 2½% Deb. Stock (1957)	Jan. 1 and July 1
Liverpool 3½ per Cent. .	Jan.1,Apl. 1,July 1,Oct.1
Manchester 3 % (1941) ...	Feb. 1 and August 1
Ramsgate 3% Stock..........	„ „
West Sussex 3% County St.	„ „
Swansea and Hull 3½% ..	January 1 and July 1
Swansea 3%	„ „
Middlesex 3% County Stk.	„ „
Wolverhampton 3½ per Cent. (1932)	March 1 and Sept. 1
Nottingham 3 per Cent. .	May 1 and Nov. 1
New Zealand 4 per Cent. Consols (1929)	„ „
„ 3½%(1940)	January 1 and July 1
„ 3% (1945)	April 1 and Oct. 1
N. S. Wales 4 per Cent. (1933)......	January 1 and July 1
„ 3½perCent. (1924)......	April 1 and October 1
„ 3½perCent. (1918)......	March 1 and Sept. 1
„ 3 per Cent. (1935)......	April 1 and Oct. 1
Queensland 3½ and 4 per Cent. (1915-1947)	January 1 and July 1
Eastern Bengal Rail."A" and "B" (1957)	April 1 and October 1
Eastern Bengal Rail. (4%) Irredeemable	January 1 and July 1
Scinde, Punjaub, & Delhi Rail. "A" & "B" (1958)	„ „
E. I. Railway (4½%) Irredeemable	April 1 and October 1
Egyptian 3½% Preference	April 15 & October 15
S. Ind. Rail. Perp. 4½%...	January 1 and July 1
Thames Conservancy A & B 3% (1954)	„ „
Chinese 5%Gold Loan(1895)	April 1 and October 1
„ 4½% „ (1898)	March 1 and Sept. 1
Greek 2½% Gold Loan ...	April 1 and October 1

* When the due date of the Dividends falls on a Sunday or Bank Holiday, the Dividends are payable on the business-day next ensuing.

MISCELLANEOUS BONDS, &c., WITH COUPONS PAYABLE AT THE BANK OF ENGLAND.

Bonds.	Dividends Payable.
Turkish 4 % Loan (1855) Guaranteed	Feb. 1 and August 1
City of London Bonds ...	Various dates
East Indian Railway 2½% Debentures	Various dates
Egyptian Preference 3½% Bonds	April 15 and October 15
Egyptian Unified 4% Bonds	May 1 and November 1
Egyptian Govt. Irrigation Trust, 4%	Jan. 1 and July 1
Greek Guaranteed Gold Loan 2½% (1898).........	Apri 1 and October 1

INVESTMENT OF DIVIDENDS ON GOVERNMENT STOCKS 2½% CONSOLIDATED STOCK AND LOCAL LOANS STOCK—Holders of amounts of less than £1,000 may instruct the Bank to receive and invest their dividends by filling up forms, to be obtained at the Head Office, at any of the Branches, or at any Money Order Office. A commission is charged of 1d. per £, or part of a £, with 3d. additional for each advice of a purchase, should such advice be required.

STOCK CERTIFICATES TO BEARER can be obtained in exchange for 2¾ per Cent. Consolidated Stock, 2½ per Cent. and 2¾ per Cent. Annuities, Local Loans 3 per Cent. Stock, and Metropolitan Police Debenture Stock; India 2½, 3, and 3½ per Cent. Stocks; Metropolitan and London County Stocks; New Zealand, New South Wales, and Queensland Stocks; and the various Corporation Stocks. The charge for Issue is 2s. per Cent., and for Reinscription 1s. per Certificate, except Metropolitan and County Stocks, where no charge for issue.

DIVIDENDS are paid in one of the following modes :—
I. In person at the head office, or at a country branch, by arrangement with the agents, to stockholders, or to their attorneys, or in a Joint account to one of the stockholders.
II. By transmission of dividend warrants by post to stockholders, their attorneys or nominees, at the risk of the stockholder, under the following regulations :—
1. Any stockholder residing within the United Kingdom who desires to have his dividend-warrant sent to his address by post, must fill up a form of application, to be obtained at the Bank, or at any of its branches, and for English Government Stocks at any Money Order Office.
2. In the case of joint accounts, to the first stockholder upon his sole request, provided the Bank have not received any written notice to the contrary from any other of the stockholders.

TRANSFER DAYS, any day but Saturday, from 11 to 3; for buying and selling, 11 to 1; for accepting, 9.30 to 4. Dividends are payable from 9 to 4; on Saturdays, 9 to 2. Transfers made on Saturdays are charged a fee of 2s. 6d.

GENERAL HOLIDAYS.—Banks of England and Ireland, and the Exchequer : Good Friday, Easter Monday, Whit Monday, First Monday in August, Christmas Day and following day, or if that be Sunday, then the Bank is closed on Monday. The Stock Exchange, in addition to the Bank holidays, is also closed on May 1 and November 1. In Scotland : New Year's Day, Good Friday, First Monday in May, First Monday in August, and Christmas Day.

To ascertain the Weight of Paper.

Lbs. per Ream.	Weight of a Sheet in Grains, per Ream of			Lbs. per Ream.	Weight of a Sheet in Grains, per Ream of		
	480 Sheets	500 Shts.	516 Sheets		480 Sheets	500 Shts.	516 Sheets
10	145·8	140	135·7	47	685·4	658	637·6
11	160·4	154	149·2	48	700·0	672	651·2
12	175·0	168	162·8	49	714·6	686	664·7
13	189·6	182	176·4	50	729·2	700	678·3
14	204·2	196	189·9	51	743·7	714	691·9
15	218·7	210	203·5	52	758·3	728	705·4
16	233·3	224	217·1	53	772·9	742	719·0
17	247·9	238	230·6	54	787·5	756	732·6
18	252·5	252	244·2	55	802·1	770	746·1
19	277·1	266	257·8	56	816·7	784	759·7
20	291·7	280	271·3	57	831·2	798	773·3
21	306·2	294	284·9	58	845·8	812	786·8
22	320·8	308	298·4	59	860·4	826	800·4
23	335·4	322	312·0	60	875·0	840	814·0
24	350·0	336	325·6	61	889·6	854	827·5
25	364·6	350	339·1	62	904·2	868	841·1
26	379·2	364	352·7	63	918·7	882	854·7
27	393·7	378	366·3	64	933·3	896	868·2
28	408·3	392	379·8	65	947·9	910	881·8
29	422·9	406	393·4	66	962·5	924	895·3
30	437·5	420	407·0	67	977·1	938	908·9
31	452·1	434	420·5	68	991·7	952	922·4
32	466·7	448	434·1	69	1006·2	966	936·0
33	481·2	462	447·7	70	1020·8	980	949·6
34	495·8	476	461·2	71	1035·4	994	963·2
35	510·4	490	474·8	72	1050·0	1008	976·7
36	525·0	504	488·4	73	1064·6	1022	990·3
37	539·6	518	501·9	74	1079·2	1036	1003·9
38	554·2	532	515·5	75	1093·7	1050	1017·4
39	568·7	546	529·1	76	1108·3	1064	1031·0
40	583·3	560	542·6	77	1122·9	1078	1044·6
41	597·9	574	556·2	78	1137·5	1092	1058·1
42	612·5	588	569·8	79	1152·1	1106	1071·7
43	627·1	602	583·3	80	1166·6	1120	1085·3
44	641·7	616	596·9	90	1312·5	1260	1220·9
45	656·2	630	610·5	96	1400·0	1344	1302·3
46	670·8	644	624·0	100	1458·3	1400	1356·6

SIZES OF WRITING AND DRAWING PAPERS.

	Dimensions.		
Emperor	72	×	48
Antiquarian	53	×	31
Double Elephant	40	×	26¾
Atlas	34	×	26
Colombier	34½	×	23½
Imperial	30	×	22
Elephant	28	×	23
Super Royal	27	×	19
Royal	24	×	19
Medium	22	×	17½
Large Post	20¾	×	16¾
Copy or Draft	20	×	16
Demy	20	×	15½
Post	19	×	15¼
Foolscap	17	×	13½
Brief	16½	×	13¼
Pott	15	×	12½

SIZES OF BROWN PAPERS.

	Dimensions.		
Casing	46	×	36
Double Imperial	45	×	29
Elephant	34	×	24
Double Four Pound	31	×	21
Imperial Cap	29	×	24
Haven Cap	26	×	21
Bag Cap	24	×	19½
Kent Cap	21	×	18

A quire of paper contains 24 perfect sheets; an outside quire 20, some of which may be torn.

Sizes of Type.

ALL founders cast their type nearly to one uniform height, though the letters may vary considerably in their breadth.

The type chiefly used in this Almanack is named *Nonpareil*. The column contains 75 lines, and is, technically, 12 Pica ems wide; on an average every column actually contains about 3,000 letters. The compositor in making out his bill reckons that the column contains so many (1,800) ems; he then, doubling that number, charges as so many (3,600) ens.

A very minute type, used only occasionally, is:—

Brilliant. A column the size of this in the Almanack if set in Brilliant would contain 124 lines, and about 7,500 letters.

Printing is the art of producing impressions, from characters or figures, on pap

Diamond is the next size; the column would contain 107 lines, and about 6,000 letters.

Printing is the art of producing impressions, from characters or figures, o

Pearl, 95 lines, 4,370 letters—

Printing is the art of producing impressions, from charac

Ruby, 87 lines, 3,740 letters—

Printing is the art of producing impressions, from cha

Nonpareil, 75 lines, 3,000 letters—

Printing is the art of producing impressions, from

Minion, 64 lines, 2,360 letters—

Printing is the art of producing impressions

Brevier, 58 lines, 1,970 letters—

Printing is the art of producing impressio

Bourgeois, 53 lines, 1,590 letters—

Printing is the art of producing impre

Long Primer, 47 lines, 1,360 letters—

Printing is the art of producing imp

Small Pica, 43 lines, 1,120 letters—

Printing is the art of producing i

Pica, 37 lines, 890 letters—

Printing is the art of produci

English, 34 lines, 680 letters—

Printing is the art of pro

Great Primer, 27 lines, 430 letters—

Printing is the art o

Double Pica, 22 lines, 280 letters—

Printing is the

SIZES OF PRINTING PAPERS.

Post	19½	×	15½
Demy	22½	×	17½
Sheet and Half Post	23½	×	19½
Medium	24	×	19
Royal	25	×	20
Double Foolscap	27	×	17
Super Royal	27½	×	20½
Double Crown	30	×	20
Imperial	30	×	22
Double Post	31¼	×	19¾
Double Demy	35	×	22½
Double Royal	40	×	25

Per Year. £ s.	Per Month s. d.	Per Week. s. d.	Per Day. s. d.	Per Year. £ s.	Per Month. £ s. d.	Per Week. s. d.	Per Day. s. d.	Per Year. £ s.	Per Month. £ s. d.	Per Week. £ s. d.	Per Day. £ s. d.
0 10	0 10	0 2¼	0 0¼	8 0	0 13 4	3 1	0 5¼	18 0	1 10 0	0 6 11	0 0 11¾
1 0	1 8	0 4½	0 0¾	8 8	0 14 0	3 2¾	0 5½	18 18	1 11 6	0 7 3¼	0 1 0½
1 10	2 6	0 7	0 1	8 10	0 14 2	3 3¼	0 5½	19 0	1 11 8	0 7 3¾	0 1 0½
2 0	3 4	0 9	0 1¼	9 0	0 15 0	3 5½	0 6	20 0	1 13 4	0 7 8¼	0 1 1¼
2 2	3 6	0 9½	0 1½	9 9	0 15 9	3 7½	0 6¼	30 0	2 10 0	0 11 6½	0 1 7¾
2 10	4 2	0 11½	0 1¾	10 0	0 16 8	3 10¼	0 6½	40 0	3 6 8	0 15 4½	0 2 2¼
3 0	5 0	1 1¾	0 2	10 10	0 17 6	4 0½	0 7	50 0	4 3 4	0 19 2¾	0 2 9
3 3	5 3	1 2½	0 2	11 0	0 18 4	4 2¾	0 7¼	60 0	5 0 0	1 3 1	0 3 3½
3 10	5 10	1 4¼	0 2¼	11 11	0 19 3	4 5¼	0 7½	70 0	5 16 8	1 6 11	0 3 10
4 0	6 8	1 6½	0 2¾	12 0	1 0 0	4 7½	0 8	80 0	6 13 4	1 10 9¼	0 4 4½
4 4	7 0	1 7½	0 2¾	12 12	1 1 0	4 10¼	0 8¼	90 0	7 10 0	1 14 7½	0 4 11¼
4 10	7 6	1 8¾	0 3	13 0	1 1 8	5 0	0 8½	100 0	8 6 8	1 18 5½	0 5 5¾
5 0	8 4	1 11	0 3¼	13 13	1 2 9	5 3	0 9	200 0	16 13 4	3 16 11	0 10 11½
5 5	8 9	2 0¼	0 3½	14 0	1 3 4	5 4½	0 9¼	300 0	25 0 0	5 15 4½	0 16 5¼
5 10	9 2	2 1½	0 3¾	14 14	1 4 6	5 7¾	0 9¾	400 0	33 6 8	7 13 10¼	1 1 11
6 0	10 0	2 3¾	0 4	15 0	1 5 0	5 9¼	0 9¾	500 0	41 13 4	9 12 3¾	1 7 4¾
6 6	10 6	2 5	0 4¼	15 15	1 6 3	6 0¾	0 10¼	600 0	50 0 0	11 10 9¼	1 12 10½
6 10	10 10	2 6	0 4¼	16 0	1 6 8	6 1¾	0 10½	700 0	58 6 8	13 9 2¾	1 18 4¼
7 0	11 8	2 8¼	0 4½	16 16	1 8 0	6 5½	0 11	800 0	66 13 4	15 7 8¼	2 3 10
7 7	12 3	2 10	0 4¾	17 0	1 8 4	6 6½	0 11¼	900 0	75 0 0	17 6 1¾	2 9 3¾
7 10	12 6	2 10½	0 5	17 17	1 9 9	6 10½	0 11¼	1000 0	83 6 8	19 4 7¼	2 14 9½

A TABLE SHOWING THE CORRESPONDING WEIGHTS PER REAM OF WRITING AND PRINTING PAPERS OF DIFFERENT SIZES.

Foolscap. 16½ × 13¼. lbs. oz. dwt.	Post. 18¾ × 15¼. lbs. oz. dwt.	Large Post. 20¾ × 16½. lbs. oz. dwt.	Demy. 17¾ × 22½. lbs.	Dbl. Foolscap. 17 × 27. lbs. oz. dwt.	Royal. 20 × 25. lbs. oz. dwt.	Sup. Royal. 20 × 28. lbs. oz. dwt.	Dbl. Crown. 20 × 30. lbs. oz. dwt.	Imperial. 22 × 30. lbs. oz. dwt.
6 9 0	8 9 9	10 4 11	12	13 12 10	15 0 6	16 13 3	18 0 7	19 13 4
7 10 12	10 0 7	12 0 0	14	16 1 6	17 8 7	19 10 1	21 0 8	23 2 2
8 12 2	11 7 5	13 11 9	16	18 6 3	20 0 8	22 6 15	24 0 9	26 7 0
9 13 13	12 14 3	15 6 17	18	20 10 15	22 8 9	25 3 13	27 0 10	29 11 15
10 15 3	14 5 2	17 2 6	20	22 15 12	25 0 10	28 0 11	30 0 12	33 0 13
13 2 4	17 2 18	20 9 3	24	27 9 5	30 0 12	33 10 7	36 0 14	39 10 9
15 5 4	20 0 15	24 0 1	28	32 2 13	35 0 14	39 4 2	42 1 0	46 4 5
17 8 5	22 14 11	27 6 18	32	36 12 7	40 1 0	44 13 14	48 9 2	52 14 1
19 11 6	25 12 7	30 13 15	36	41 5 15	45 1 2	50 7 10	54 1 5	59 7 14
21 14 3	28 10 4	34 4 12	40	45 15 8	50 1 4	56 1 6	60 1 7	66 1 10
24 10 2	32 3 8	38 8 14	45	51 11 7	56 5 6	63 1 9	67 9 11	74 5 13
27 5 18	35 2 15	42 13 6	50	57 7 6	62 9 9	70 1 12	75 1 14	82 10 1

From the above table it will be seen that a sheet of 24 lb. Demy is about the same substance as a sheet of Royal of 30 lbs.

GENERAL COUNCILS.

		A.D.
Jerusalem	Against Judaisers	51
Arles	Against the Donatists	314
**Nicæa*	First Œcumenical Council	325
Antioch	Founded Canon Law of Greek Church	341
Sardica	Against Arianisers	343
**Constantinople*	Second Œcumenical	381
**Ephesus*	Third do.	431
**Chalcedon*	Fourth do.	451
**Constantinople*	Fifth do.	553
**Constantinople*	Sixth do.	680
Nicæa	Seventh do.	787
Constantinople	Eighth do. (Roman reckoning)	869
	(Greek reckoning)	879
Rome	First Lateran	1123
Rome	Second do.	1139
Rome	Third do.	1197
Rome	Fourth do.	1215
Lyons	Emperor Frederick deposed	1243
Lyons	Temporary reunion of Greek and Latin Churches	1274
Vienne	Fifteenth Œcumenical	1312
Pisa	Popes elected and deposed	1409
Constance	Huss condemned to be burnt	1414
Basle	18th Œcumenical	1431 to 1449
Florence	Last attempt at reunion of Greek and Latin Churches	1449
Rome	Fifth Lateran	1512 to 1517
Trent	19th Œcumenical	1545 to 1563
Rome	Last Œcumenical	1870

* Only the six thus marked were indisputably General or Œcumenical.

Annual Production of Gold and Silver in the World from 1889 to 1898.

YEAR.	BRITISH EMPIRE.		OTHER COUNTRIES.		TOTAL.	
	Gold.	Silver.	Gold.	Silver.	Gold.	Silver.
1889	£9,279,000	£2,179,000	£16,131,000	£33,885,000	£25,410,000	£36,064,000
1890	9,154,000	2,697,000	15,300,000	35,131,000	24,454,000	37,828,000
1891	10,789,000	3,153,000	16,094,000	37,998,000	26,883,000	41,151,000
1892	13,387,000	4,186,000	16,820,000	41,760,000	30,207,000	45,946,000
1893	14,810,000	5,587,000	17,560,000	43,558,000	32,379,000	49,145,000
1894	18,403,000	5,752,000	18,926,000	43,137,000	37,329,000	48,889,000
1895	20,197,000	4,325,000	21,005,000	45,662,000	41,202,000	49,987,000
1896	19,969,000	6,786,000	23,442,000	48,524,000	43,411,000	55,310,000
1897	25,837,000	6,833,000	23,222,000	47,299,000	49,061,000	54,132,000
1898	33,938,000	6,498,000	25,485,000	50,177,000	59,423,000	56,675,000
Totals ...	£175,764,000	£47,996,000	£193,995,000	£427,131,000	£369,759,000	£475,127,000

The figures given in the above table are based mainly on Returns prepared by the Director of the United States Mint and published in his annual Reports. Under "British Empire" are included Australasia, Great Britain, Canada, British Guiana, British India, and Africa. The mines of the South African Republic, however, from 1889 to 1898 produced about £59,000,000 or 18·7 per cent. of the total gold output of the world, and the increase under "British Empire" in recent years is mainly attributable to those mines.

Gold has been valued in the table at the legal rate of £3 17s. 10½d. per troy ounce standard, and silver at its *coining* value in this country, namely 5s. 6d. per troy ounce standard.

The Imperial Coinage.

The authorised Coinage of the United Kingdom consists of the following pieces, some of which are issued only on special occasions :—

Denomination.	Standard Weight.	Least Current Weight.	Remedy of Weight.
	Grains.	Grains.	Grains.
GOLD :			
Five Pound	616·37239	612·500	1·00000
Two Pound	246·54895	245·000	0·40000
Sovereign	123·27447	122·500	0·20000
Half-Sovereign .	61·63723	61·125	0·15000
SILVER :			
Crown	436·36363	—	2·000
Double Florin ...	349·09090	—	1·678
Half-Crown	218·18181	—	1·264
Florin	174·54545	—	0·997
Shilling	87·27272	—	0·578
Sixpence.........	43·63636	—	0·346
Groat or 4d. ...	29·09090	—	0·262
Threepence	21·81818	—	0·212
Twopence	14·54545	—	0·144
Penny	7·27272	—	0·087
BRONZE :			
Penny	145·83333	—	2·91666
Halfpenny	87·50000	—	1·75000
Farthing	43·75000	—	0·87500

STANDARD GOLD contains eleven-twelfths of fine metal and one-twelfth of alloy; fineness, 916·66. Twenty troy pounds of standard gold are coined into 934 sovereigns and one half-sovereign; one troy ounce is, therefore, intrinsically worth £3 17s. 10½d., and one ounce of pure gold, on the same basis, £4 4s. 11½d.

STANDARD SILVER consists of thirty-seven-fortieths of fine metal and three-fortieths of alloy; fineness, 925. One troy pound of standard silver is coined into 66 shillings. [Another Standard, called the "New Sterling" or Britannia, of the fineness 11 oz. 10 dwt. (958·33), is practically obsolete. It is occasionally used, however, for high-class plate.]

*BRONZE is an alloy of copper 95 parts, tin 4 parts, and zinc 1 part.

THE "REMEDY" is the amount of variation permitted in fineness and in weight of coins when first issued from the Mint.

TOKENS.—No person is allowed to coin any token to pass for, or as representing, bronze or other money, under a penalty of £20.

LIGHT GOLD.—Any person to whom it is tendered may break, cut, or deface any gold coin below the least current weight, but, under the provisions of the Coinage Act, 1891, light gold coin which has not been illegally dealt with is received by the Bank of England on behalf of the Mint at its full nominal value.

BANK OF ENGLAND NOTES are issued for sums of £5, £10, £20, £50; also for £100, £200, £500, and £1,000.

BANK POST BILLS are drawn for any sum from £10 to £1,000, and made payable to order at seven days' date, or at sixty days'. No charge is made for bills so drawn : they may be obtained at the Chief Office in London, or at any of the branches.

LEGAL TENDER OF MONEY.—The tender of Bank of England Notes is legal in England and Wales for every purpose, and by anyone (except by the Bank of England). No one can be compelled to give change. Gold, if above the least current weight, is a legal tender to any amount. Silver is not a legal tender for sums over two pounds, nor bronze, including farthings, for sums over one shilling.

OLD MONEYS.—Guinea, 21s.; Carolus, 23s.; Moidore, 27s. 6d.; Angel, 10s.; Noble, 6s. 8d.; Tester, 6d.; Groat, 4d.

SCOTS MONEY.—Merk=1s.1½d.; Pound=1s.8d.; Shilling=1d.; Plack=2 Bodles=4d. Scots.

* It is interesting to note that the weight of a penny is one-third, of the half-penny one-fifth, and of the farthing one-tenth of an ounce avoirdupois, *approximately*. Further, the half-penny is one *inch* in diameter.

For some countries not included in this list, see note below.

Country.	Money of Account.	Circulating Value. (See note.)		Number of Coins receivable for £1 at par. (See note.)
Argentine Republic	Peso of 100 centesimos	3s.	11½d.	5·05
Austria-Hungary	Florin or gulden of 100 kreutzer	1	11½	10·2
" "	Crown (new unit) of 100 hellers	0	10	24·0
Belgium	Franc of 100 centimes	0	9½	25·2
Brazil	Milreis	2	3	8·9
Bulgaria	Leva of 100 stotinkis	0	9½	25·2
Chile	Peso of 100 centavos	3	11½	5·05
China	Tael of 1,000 cash	6	6¼	3·07
Denmark	Crown of 100 öre	1	1¼	18·2
Egypt	Pound of 100 piastres	20	3¾	0·985
Finland	Markka of 100 penni	0	9½	25·2
France	Franc of 100 centimes	0	9½	25·2
German Empire	Reichsmark or mark of 100 pfennige	0	11¾	20·4
Great Britain and Ireland	Pound or sovereign of 20 shillings	20	0	1·0
Greece	Drachma of 100 lepta	0	9½	25·2
Holland and Java	Florin or guilder of 100 cents	1	8	12·0
India	Rupee of 16 annas	1	4	15·0
Indo-China	Piastre	4	2	4·8
Italy	Lira of 100 centesimi	0	9½	25·2
Japan	Yen of 100 sen	2	0½	9·76
Mexico	Peso of 100 centavos	4	3¾	4·64
Norway	Crown of 100 öre	1	1¼	18·2
Persia	Khran of 20 shahis (varies)	0	7	34·0
Portugal	Milreis	4	5¼	4·50
Roumania	Ley of 100 banis	0	9½	25·2
Russia	Rouble of 100 kopecks	3	2	6·30
Servia	Dinar of 100 paras	0	9½	25·2
Siam	Tical	2	5	8·3
Spain	Peseta of 100 centimos	0	9½	25·2
Sweden	Crown of 100 öre	1	1¼	18·2
Tunis	Piastre	0	6	40·3
Turkey	Pound of 100 piastres	18	0¾	1·107
United States	Dollar of 100 cents	4	1¼	4·87

In Belgium, Bulgaria, Greece, Italy, Roumania, Servia, Spain, and Switzerland the money of account is identical with that of France—the franc—the names alone differing. Nearly all the South American States issue standard coins corresponding to the peso of Chile, which is identical with the 5-franc piece of France. The principal circulating medium of Austria-Hungary, Russia, Argentine Republic, and Brazil is paper, but, in the first-named country, the paper is in process of being withdrawn, and the currency placed on a gold basis, with the crown (see above) as a new unit of account. In Russia the gold Imperial is now rated at 15 instead of 10 roubles, and the paper currency is being replaced by silver and bronze. The currency of Japan is now on a gold basis, silver bearing a ratio to that metal of 1 to 32·348. In British Honduras the money of account is now the United States gold dollar of 100 cents, subsidiary coins being specially struck for the Colony. Ceylon and Mauritius also possess special subsidiary currencies on the basis of the rupee. By an Order in Council passed in 1894 a British dollar was authorised to be issued for circulation in the East. It is identical in weight and fineness with the Japanese yen, and has been made legal tender in Hong Kong, the Straits Settlements, and Labuan. The last two columns of the Table are calculated on the supposition that the relation between the values of gold and silver remains fixed at 15½ to 1; in other words, that the price of standard silver is 60⅞d. per oz. troy. They give therefore the full metallic values on that basis, not the values for purposes of exchange, which are very variable, and depend mainly on the price of silver (see Table below).

Price of Silver, 1889-98.

The Average yearly Price of Silver per standard Troy Ounce in the London Market during the last ten years was as follows :—

1889.	1890.	1891.	1892.	1893.	1894.	1895.	1896.	1897.	1898.
d.	d.	d.	d.	d.	d.	d.	d.	d.	d.
42¹¹⁄₁₆	47¾	45¹⁄₁₆	39¹³⁄₁₆	35⅝	29	29⅞	30¾	27⁹⁄₁₆	26¹⁵⁄₁₆

In the United States the price of silver is quoted in cents per Troy ounce *fine*. In order to convert an English quotation into cents per ounce fine, first express the pence as a whole number and decimal fraction and then multiply by 2·192 ; to express a United States price on the English system multiply the cents by 0·4562.

Equivalent Investments.

A Table showing the Profits upon Investments in the various Government Funds, Banks, Railways, &c., at the Undermentioned Prices.

Return Per Cent.	2½ Pr. Ct.	2¾ Pr. Ct.	3 Pr Ct.	3¼ Pr Ct.	3½ Pr Ct.	4 Pr Ct.	4½ Pr Ct.	5 Pr. Ct.	5½ Pr. Ct.	6 Pr Ct.	7 Pr. Ct.	7½ Pr. Ct.	8 Pr. Ct.	9 Pr. Ct.	10 Pr Ct.
£2 10 0	100	110	120	130	140	160	180	200	220	240	280	300	320	360	400
2 12 6	95¼	104¾	114²⁄₇	123⁶⁄₇	133⅓	152⅓	171⅓	190⅓	209½	228½	266⅔	285¾	304⅔	342⅔	381
2 13 9	93	102⅓	111⅔	121	130⅓	149	167½	186	204⅔	223⅓	260⅔	279⅓	298	335	372
2 15 0	90⅚	100	109	118	127⅙	145⅓	163½	181⅔	200	218	254⅓	272⅔	290⅔	327	363⅓
2 17 6	87	95⅝	104⅓	113	121⅔	139	156½	174	191¼	208⅔	243⅓	260⅔	278	313	347⅔
3 0 0	83⅓	91⅔	100	108¼	116⅔	133⅓	150	166⅔	183⅓	200	233⅓	250	266⅔	300	333⅓
3 0 7	82½	90¾	99	107¼	115½	132	148½	165	181½	198	231	247½	264	297	330
3 1 6	81¼	89⅜	97½	105¾	113¾	130	146¼	162½	178¾	195	227½	243¾	260	292¾	325
3 2 6	80	88	96	104	112	128	144	160	176	192	224	240	256	288	320
3 3 6	78¾	86⅝	94½	102¼	110¼	126	141¾	157½	173¼	189	220½	236¼	252	283½	315
3 4 6	77½	85¼	93	100¾	108½	124	139½	155	170½	186	217	232½	248	279	310
3 5 7	76¼	83⅞	91½	99¼	106¾	122	137¼	152½	167¾	183	213½	228¾	244	274½	305
3 6 8	75	82½	90	97½	105	120	135	150	165	180	210	225	240	270	300
3 7 10	73¾	81⅛	88½	95¾	103¼	118	132¾	147½	162¼	177	206½	221¼	236	265½	295
3 9 0	72½	79¾	87	94¼	101½	116	130½	145	159½	174	203	217½	232	261	290
3 10 2	71¼	78⅜	85½	92¾	99¾	114	128¼	142½	156¾	171	199½	213¾	228	256½	285
3 11 5	70	77	84	91	98	112	126	140	154	168	196	210	224	252	280
3 12 9	68¾	75⅝	82½	89⅓	96¼	110	123¾	137½	151¼	165	192½	206¼	220	247½	275
3 14 1	67½	74¼	81	87¾	94½	108	121½	135	148½	162	189	202½	216	243	270
3 15 6	66¼	72⅞	79½	86¼	92¾	106	119⅓	132½	145⅔	159	185½	198¾	212	238½	265
3 16 11	65	71½	78	84½	91	104	117	130	143	156	182	195	208	234	260
3 18 5	63¾	70⅛	76½	82¾	89¼	102	114¾	127½	140¼	153	178½	191¼	204	229½	255
4 0 0	62½	68¾	75	81¼	87½	100	112½	125	137½	150	175	187½	200	225	250
4 1 7	61¼	67⅜	73½	79⅔	85¾	98	110¼	122½	134¾	147	171½	183¾	196	220⅔	245
4 3 4	60	66	72	78	84	96	108	120	132	144	168	180	192	216	240
4 5 1	58¾	64⅝	70½	76½	82¼	94	105¾	117½	129¼	141	164½	176¼	188	211½	235
4 6 11	57½	63¼	69	74¾	80½	92	103½	115	126½	138	161	172½	184	207	230
4 8 11	56¼	61⅞	67½	73¼	78¾	90	101¼	112½	123¾	135	157½	168¾	180	202½	225
4 10 11	55	60½	66	71½	77	88	99	110	121	132	154	165	176	198	220
4 13 0	53¾	59⅙	64½	69¾	75¼	86	96¾	107½	118⅙	129	150½	161¼	172	193½	215
4 15 3	52½	57¾	63	68¼	73½	84	94½	105	115½	126	147	157½	168	189	210
4 17 7	51¼	56⅜	61½	66¾	71¾	82	92¼	102½	112¾	123	143½	153¾	164	184½	205
5 0 0	50	55	60	65	70	80	90	100	110	120	140	150	160	180	200
5 2 7	48¾	53⅝	58½	63⅓	68¼	78	87¾	97½	107¼	117	136½	146¼	156	175½	195
5 5 3	47½	52¼	57	61¾	66½	76	85½	95	104½	114	133	142½	152	171	190
5 8 1	46¼	50⅞	55½	60¼	64¾	74	83¼	92½	101¾	111	129½	138¾	148	166½	185
5 11 1	45	49½	54	58½	63	72	81	90	99	108	126	135	144	162	180
5 14 3	43¾	48⅛	52½	56¾	61¼	70	78¾	87½	96¼	105	122½	131¼	140	157½	175
5 17 8	42½	46¾	51	55¼	59½	68	76½	85	93½	102	119	127½	136	153	170
6 0 0	41⅔	45⅞	50	54¼	58⅓	66⅔	75	83⅓	91⅔	100	116⅔	125	133⅓	150	166⅔
6 2 5	40⅚	44⅞	49	53	57⅙	65⅓	73½	81⅔	89⅔	98	114⅓	122½	130⅔	147	163⅓
6 5 0	40	44	48	52	56	64	72	80	88	96	112	120	128	144	160
6 7 8	39⅙	43⅛	47	50¾	54⅚	62⅔	70½	78⅓	86⅙	94	109⅔	117½	125⅓	141	156⅔
6 10 5	38⅓	42⅙	46	49¾	53⅔	61⅓	69	76⅔	84⅓	92	107⅓	115	122⅔	138	153⅓
6 13 4	37½	41¼	45	48¾	52½	60	67½	75	82½	90	105	112½	120	135	150
6 16 4	36⅔	40⅓	44	47¾	51⅓	58⅔	66	73⅓	80⅔	88	102⅔	110	117⅓	132	146⅔
6 19 6	35⅚	39⅜	43	46½	50⅙	57⅓	64½	71⅔	78⅚	86	100⅓	107½	114⅔	129	143⅓
7 2 10	35	38½	42	45½	49	56	63	70	77	84	98	105	112	126	140
7 6 4	34⅙	37½	41	44½	47⅚	54⅚	61½	68⅓	75⅙	82	95⅔	102½	109⅓	123	136⅔
7 10 0	33⅓	36⅔	40	43⅓	46⅔	53⅓	60	66⅔	73⅓	80	93⅓	100	106⅔	120	133⅓
7 13 10	32½	35¾	39	42¼	45½	52	58½	65	71½	78	91	97½	104	117	130
7 17 11	31⅔	34⅞	38	41	44⅓	50⅔	57	63⅓	69⅔	75	88⅔	95	101⅓	114	126⅔
8 2 2	30⅚	33⅞	37	40	43⅙	49⅓	55½	61⅔	67⅚	74	86⅓	92½	98⅔	111	123⅓
8 6 8	30	33	36	39	42	48	54	60	66	72	84	90	96	108	120
8 11 5	29⅙	32⅛	35	37¾	40⅔	46⅔	52½	58⅓	64⅙	70	81⅔	87⅚	93⅓	105	116⅔
8 16 6	28⅓	31⅙	34	36¾	39⅔	45⅓	51	56⅔	62⅓	68	79⅓	85	90⅔	102	113⅓
9 1 10	27½	30¼	33	35¾	38½	44	49½	55	60½	66	77	82½	88	99	110
9 7 6	26⅔	29⅓	32	34¾	37⅓	42⅔	48	53⅓	58⅔	64	74⅔	80	85⅓	96	106⅔
9 13 7	25⅚	28⅖	31	33½	36⅙	41⅓	46½	51⅔	56⅚	62	72⅓	77½	82⅔	93	103⅓
10 0 0	25	27½	30	32½	35	40	45	50	55	60	70	75	80	90	100

UNIFORMITY.—An edict of King Edgar decreed that there should be but one Standard Measure, that kept at Winchester; and by the 27th section of Magna Charta there was to be one Weight or all England. Nevertheless numerous customary weights and measures have continued in use—custom was stronger than law, especially with regard to land, corn, and wool. In 1824, however, an Act was passed rendering uniformity compulsory from the 1st of January, 1826, since which time the Imperial Statute System of Weights and Measures has been in general use, although some remains of the older form still linger.

Avoirdupois Weight.

Drachm...... dr. = 27½ grains (27·34375).
Ounce ...... oz. = 16 drachms, 437·5 grains.
Pound ...... lb. = 16 oz., 256 dr., 7,000 grains.
Customary Stone, st., Butcher's Meat = 8 lbs.
Legal Stone...st. = Horseman's weight = 14 lbs.
Quarter ......qr. = 28 lbs.
Cental or Quintal, cent. = 100 lbs.
Hundredweight, cwt. = 4 qrs., 112 lbs.
Ton ...... T. = 20 cwt., 2,240 lbs.

Avoirdupois weight is used in almost all commercial transactions and common dealings, but in addition to the above there are special weights for various articles, the chief of which are :—

A Quartern Loaf .... = 4 lbs.
A Peck of Flour, 2 Gallons .... = 14 „
A Firkin of Butter .... = 56 „
A Firkin of Soft Soap .... = 64 „
A Box of Fish, about .... = 90 „
A Barrel of Gunpowder .... = 100 „
A Barrel of Raisins .... = 112 „
A Seam of Glass, 24 stones of 5 lbs. = 120 „
A Barrel of Butter—4 firkins .... = 224 „
A Barrel (or pack) of Soft Soap ...... = 256 „
A Faggot of Steel .... = 120 „
A Pig of Ballast .... = 56 „
A Fodder of Lead, London and Hull = 19½cwt.
A do. Derby=22½ cwt.; Newcastle = 21½ „
A Cask of Blacklead .... = 11½ „
A Sack—Flour, 280 lbs.; Coals, 224 lbs.; a ton of Coals, 10 sacks.

The Metrical System of weights is used in Belgium, France, Germany, Italy, Portugal, Spain, Sweden and Norway, and some other countries, the unit of which is the Gramme=15·432 grains; the chief multiple of the Gramme is the Kilogramme=2·2046 lbs.: in practical use this is found inconvenient for small purchases, and nearly all commodities are sold by the demi or half kilo. The Centner of 50 kilos=110¼ lbs., very nearly represents the English cwt.; but heavy goods are sold by the Tonneau of 2204·621 lbs., about 19 cwt. 77 lbs., the Myriagramme being ignored. See p. 424.

In the United States and in Canada the cwt. is generally reckoned as 100 lbs., and the ton of 20 cwt.=2,000 lbs.

In Russia the Pood of 36 lbs. is the commercial weight : 63 Poods=1 English ton.

Indian Weights (Bengal).

Tola, unit of postage=180 grains.
Chittak=5 Tolas; Seer (16 Chittaks)=2·1/14 lbs.
Imperial or Indian Maund=82½ lbs.

Madras.

Viss=3·09 lbs., Maund=25 lbs., Candy=500 lbs.

Troy Weight.

Carat .... = 3·17 grains.
Pennyweight...... dwt. = 24 grains.
Ounce.............. oz. = 20 dwts., 480 grs.
Pound ....lb. = 12 oz., 240 dwts., 5,760 grs.
Hundredweight . cwt. = 100 lbs.

TROY is the weight used by goldsmiths and jewellers. The grains Troy, Apothecaries', and Avoirdupcis are equal, and the same in England, France, the United States, Holland, and in most other countries; but the carat varies: in France it is 3·18 grains, in Holland, 3·0 grs., and in the U. S. 3·2 grs. In the U. K. the jewellery ounce is divided into 151½ carats or 600 pearl grains.

The oz. Troy and Apothecaries'= 1·09714 oz. avoirdupois; but the lb. Troy and lb. Apothecaries' = only 0·82286 lb. avoirdupois; while 175 lb. Troy and Apothecaries'= 144 lb. avoirdupois.

Apothecaries' Weight.

Scruple ℈ = 20 grains .... = 20 grs.
Drachm ℨ = 3 Scruples .... = 60 „
Ounce ℥ = 8 Drachms .... = 480 „
Pound ℔ = 12 Ounces .... = 5760 „

The avoirdupois oz. of 437½ grains, and the lb. of 7,000 grains are the weights named in the British Pharmacopœia; drugs are purchased by avoirdupois, but compounded by apothecaries' weight. The apothecaries' oz. and lb. may now be considered obsolete.

Hay and Straw.

Truss of Straw, 36 lbs. Truss of Old Hay, 56 lbs.
Truss of New Hay (to September 1st), 60 lbs.
Load, 36 Trusses—Straw, 11 cwt. 2 qrs. 8 lbs.;
Old Hay, 18 cwt.; New Hay, 19 cwt. 1 qr. 4 lbs.

Wool.

Clove, cl. = 7 lbs.
Stone, st: = 2 Cloves 14 lbs.
Tod, td. = 2 Stones 1 qr.
Wey, wy. = 6½ Tod 1 cwt. 2 qrs. 14 lbs.
Pack, pk. = 240 lbs.
Sack, sk. = 2 Weys 13 qrs.
Last, la. = 12 Sacks 39 cwt.

Since the advent of SHODDY, some of the above weights have become nearly obsolete, although the terms are still in use with different values : thus 16 lbs. = 1 st.; 28 lbs. = 1 Tod; 20 lbs. = 1 Score; 12 Score or 240 lbs. = 1 Pack.

Worsted Yarn.

Wrap, 80 yards; Hank=560 yards=7 Wraps.
Counts or Numbers are the number of hanks in a lb.

Cotton Wool.

Cotton Wool, Bale variable; U.S.A. average 477 lbs.; Egyptian, 719 lbs.; East Indian, 396 lbs. Brazilian, 220 lbs.

Cotton Yarn.

Thread = 1½ yards.
Lea, or Skein, skn. = 120 Yards. }
Hank, hk. = 7 Skeins, or Leas. } Also same
Spindle, spdl. = 18 Hanks. } for silk.

Counts=the number of Hanks in 1 lb.
Bundle Hanks, either of 5 lbs. or 10 lbs.
Reels of Cotton vary from 30 to 1,750 yards, but by the new Act must be marked correctly.
Bundles of Cotton are chiefly made up for export.

Liquid Measure.

The Gill contains 8·665 cubic inches.
The Pint contains 4 gills or 34·660 inches.
Quart = 2 pints = 8 gills.
Gallon = 4 quarts = 32 gills.
Pin = 4½ Gallons or ⅛ Barrel.

	Gals.	Qts.	Pts.
Firkin or Quarter Barrel	9	36	72
Anker (10 gallons)	10	40	80
Kilderkin, Rundlet, or ½ Barrel ...	18	72	144
Barrel	36	144	288
Tierce (42 gallons)	42	168	336
Hogshead of Ale (1½ barrel)	54	216	432
Puncheon	72	288	576
Butt of Ale (3 barrels)	108	432	864

Practically, the only measures in use are gallons, quarts, pints, and gills, the others are merely nominal; *e.g.*, the hogshead of 54 gallons, *old measure*, contains but 52 gallons, 1 quart, 1 pint, and 3·55 gills imperial measure; and of wine six nominal quart bottles go to the gallon. Of wines imported in casks the following are the usual measurements:—

Pipe of Port or Masdeu	=	115 gallons.
„ Teneriffe	=	100 „
„ Marsala	=	93 „
„ Madeira and Cape	=	92 „
„ Sherry and Tent	=	108 „
Butt of Lisbon and Bucellas	=	117 „
Aum of Hock and Rhenish	=	30 „

Hogshead of Claret, 46; Port, 57; Sherry, 54; Madeira, 46 gallons.

In the United States the old British or "Winchester" wine gallon of 231 cubic inches is in use; the names of measures are the same, but the capacity of the gill is only 7·21875 cubic inches.

Apothecaries' Fluid Measure. Marked

60 Minims ♏ (drops)	=	1 Fluid Drachm	f ʒ
8 Drachms	=	1 Ounce	f ℥
20 Ounces	=	1 Pint	O
8 Pints	=	1 Gallon	C., or Cong.

1 Drachm = 1 Tea-spoonful.
2 Drachms = 1 Dessert-spnful.
4 Drachms = 1 Table-spoonful.
2 Ounces = 1 Wineglassful.
3 Ounces = 1 Teacupful.

Prescribing medicine by the spoon, glass, or cupful, is unsafe, as all those vessels vary in size. Graduated glass measures may be purchased for a few pence.

Dry or Corn Measure.

Quart... = 2 Pints.		Strike ... = 2 Bushels.	
Pottle... = 2 Quarts.		Coomb... = 4 Bushels.	
Gallon . = 4 Quarts.		Quarter. = 8 Bushels.	
Peck ... = 2 Gallons.		Load ... = 5 Quarters.	
Bushel . = 4 Pecks.		Last ...... = 10 Quarters.	

Boll of Meal = 140 lbs.; 2 Bolls = 1 Sack.

Wheat and other cereals are commonly sold by weight, the bushel being thus reckoned:—

Wheat, English, 63 lbs. Foreign, 62 lbs.

Barley, English, 52 and 56 lbs. French, 52½ lbs. Mediterranean, 50 lbs.

Oats, English, 40 & 42 lbs. Foreign, 38 & 40 lbs.

Rye and maize, 60 lbs.

Buckwheat, 52 lbs. to the bushel.

Grain of all kinds is frequently sold by the stone of 14 lbs.

Coals were formerly sold by measure: 3 heaped bushels = 1 sack, 12 sacks = 1 chaldron. Coke, apples, potatoes, and some other goods are still sold by heaped measures and the sack of three bushels; of coke, four bushels are usual.

Fruit—The Covent Garden bushel basket is 17½ inches in diameter at top, 10 inches at the bottom, and is 10 inches deep. The smaller market baskets are said to vary in size according to the season and the supply.

Cubic or Solid Measure.

Cubic Foot	=	1,728 Cubic Inches.
Cubic Yard	=	27 Cubic Feet, 21·033 bushels.
Stack of Wood	=	108 Cubic Feet.
Shipping Ton	=	40 Cubic Feet merchandise.
Shipping Ton	=	42 Cubic Feet of Timber.

Ton of displacement of a Ship = 35 Cubic Feet.

Measures of Length.

Mile Geographical, Admiralty Knot, or Nautical Mile, 6,080 Feet = 1·1 Mile Statute.

League = 3 Miles.

Degree = 60 Geographical, or 69·121 Statute Miles.

Inch, *in.*	=	72 Points, or 12 Lines.
Nail, $\frac{1}{16}$	=	2¼ Inches.
Palm	=	3 Inches.
Hand	=	4 Inches.
Link	=	7·92 Inches.
Quarter (or a Span)	=	9 Inches.
Foot	=	12 Inches.
Cubit	=	18 Inches.
Yard	=	36 Inches.
Pace, Military	=	2 Feet 6 Inches.
Pace, Geometrical	=	5 Feet.
Fathom	=	6 Feet.
Rod, Pole, or Perch	=	5½ Yards.
Chain (100 Links)	=	22 Yards (4 Poles).
Cable's Length	=	100 Fathoms, 600 Feet.
Furlong	=	40 Rods, 220 Yards.
Mile	=	8 Furlongs, 80 Chains, 320 Rods, 1,760 Yards, 5,280 Feet, 63,360 Inches.

Although no longer sold by that measure, Calicos, &c., are sometimes said to be "Ell wide"—the English Ell being 1¼ yard, the Flemish Ell ¾ yard, and the French Ell 1½ yard.

The old *Scottish Mile* was 5,920 feet: ten Scots Miles being about equal to 11¼ Statute Miles. Eleven *Irish Miles* were equal to 14 Statute Miles.

Square, Surface, or Land Measure.

The Square Foot contains 144 Square Inches.
Yard = 9 feet = 1,296 inches.
Rod, Pole, or Perch = 30¼ yards = 272¼ feet.
Chain = 16 rods = 484 yards = 4,356 feet.
Rood = 40 rods = 1,210 yards = 10,890 feet.
Acre = 4 roods = 160 rods = 4,840 yards.
Yard of Land = 30 acres = 120 roods.
Hide = 100 acres = 400 roods.
Mile = 640 acres = 2,560 roods = 6,400 chains = 102,400 rods, poles, or perches, or 3,097,600 square yards.

An Acre *roughly* stated has four equal sides of 69½ yards: *accurate* measurement gives each side 208·71 feet.

The sides of a square half-acre would be 147·581 feet, and of a square quarter-acre, 104·355 feet.

The above Imperial Measure is now employed in the United Kingdom, in Canada, Australia, and the Colonies generally, also in the United States; but occasionally some older measurements are referred to, of these—

The Lancashire Acre of 160 perches, each containing 49 square yards = 7,840 square yards.

The Cheshire Acre of 160 perches, each containing 64 square yards = 10,240 square yards.

The Irish Acre, equal to 1·619835 Statute; or 1 Statute equal to 0·617347 Irish.

The Cunningham Acre, equal to 1·291322 Statute; or 1 Statute Acre is equal to 0·7744 Cunningham.

The Scottish Acre = 1·261183 Statute (nearly 6,104 square yards).

Measures of Time.

60 Seconds	=	1 Minute.
60 Minutes	=	1 Hour.
24 Hours	=	1 Day.
(23*h.* 56*m.* 4*s.*	=	1 Sidereal Day.)
7 Days	=	1 Week.
28 Days	=	1 Lunar Month.
28, 29, 30, or 31 Days	=	1 Calendar Month.
12 Calendar Months	=	1 Year.
365¼ Days	=	1 Common Year.
366 Days	=	1 Leap Year.
365*d.* 5*h.* 48*m.* 46*s.*	=	1 Tropical Year.

The Astronomical Day commences at noon, and is computed from 1 to 24 hours.

In 400 years 97 are Leap-years and 303 common, Leap-year being omitted every 100th year, but *not* omitted every 400th. (1900 is not a Leap year.)

Angular Measure.

60 Seconds ″ .... = 1 Minute.
60 Minutes ′ .... = 1 Degree.
30 Degrees ° .... = 1 Sign.
90 Degrees .... = 1 Quadrant.
4 Quadrants, or 360° ... = 1 Circumference, or Circle.

The Earth rotates at a velocity of 15 degrees an hour (about 17·366 miles a minute at the Equator); 1° is therefore equal to 4 minutes.

Circular Measure.

Diameter of a Circle × 3·1416 gives Circumference.
Diameter Squared × ·7854 gives Area of Circle.
Diameter Squared × 3·1416 gives Surface of Sphere.
Diameter Cubed × ·5236 gives Solidity of Sphere.
One Degree of Circumference × 57·3 gives Radius.
Diameter of Cylinder × 3·1416, and product by its length, gives the Surface.
Diameter Squared × ·7854, and product by the length, gives Solid Contents.

A Circular Acre is 235·504 feet, a Circular Rood 117·752 feet in diameter. The Circumference of the Globe is about 24,855 miles, and the Diameter about 7,900 miles.

Electrical Measures.

It is customary among electricians to express all measurements in terms of the centimeter, gramme, second (C.G.S.) system, either as force or work according to their nature, and, due allowance being made for the effect of gravitation, these units are called "absolute." To understand the basis of this system requires a great deal of very careful study, and more space than we have at our disposal; but it is fair to mention that the accuracy aimed at has not, and probably never will be, attained.

For practical and commercial purposes the chief units are the—

	For the measure of
VOLT	Electromotive force = about 92·6% of that given by one Daniell's battery cell.
OHM	Resistance = the resistance offered to the passage of a current of electricity by a thread of mercury 106 cm. long and 1 mm. cross section at the temperature of melting ice.
AMPÈRE	Current = the current 1 volt will drive through 1 ohm.
COULOMB	Quantity = 1 ampère flowing for 1 second of time.
MICROFARAD .	Capacity = ·000,001 coulomb at 1 volt pressure.
WATT...........	Power = 44 ft. lbs. per minute.

Board of Trade Unit = 1,000 Watts 1 hour.
746 Watts = 1 horse-power.

In incandescent lamps of 16-candle power (nominal) about four watts are required per candle power to give good economical results for domestic purposes.

One Board of Trade unit will keep a 16-candle incandescent lamp alight for about 16 hours.

Fish Measure.

Herrings are sold by the *Cran*, containing 26⅔ imperial gallons, on the East Coast of Scotland from Shetland to Berwick, also at Castle Bay and Stornoway; but on the West Coast, Isle of Man, and in Ireland, by the *Maze*, which contains 5 long hundreds of 123 each. On the East coast of England they are sold by the *Last*, which contains 13,200 fish. They are counted by the *Warp*, which is 4. 33 Warps = 1 Long Hundred, 132; 10 Hundred = 1 Thousand, 1,320; 10 Thousand = 1 Last, 13,200.

Timber and Wood.

40 cubic feet rough, 50 cubic feet squared = 1 load.
50 cubic feet of planks = 1 load.
100 superficial feet = 1 square of flooring.
120 Deals = 100.
Width of Battens 7 inches; Deals, 9 inches; Planks are 2 to 4 inches thick, and 10 or 11 inches wide.

Carpenters', Bricklayers', and Builders' Measurements.

Stock or kiln bricks	8¾	inches	×4¼	×2¾
Welsh fire-bricks	9	„	×4½	×2¾
Paving bricks	9	„	×4½	×1¾
Square tiles	9¾	„	×9¾	×1
„	6	„	×6	×1
Dutch clinker bricks.........	9¼	„	×3	×1½

A Rod of Brickwork 16½ feet × 16½ feet × 1½ brick thick = 306 cubic feet, or 11⅓ cubic yards, and contains about 4,500 bricks with about 75 cubic feet of mortar.

A Square of Flooring is 100 square feet.

Ordinary bricks weigh about 7 lbs. each; a load of 500 weighs over 1½ ton.

Sizes of Slates.

	in. in.		in. in.
Empress	26×16	Ladies	16×10
„ Small ...	26×14	„ Small	16× 8
Princesses.........	24×14	„ Large	14×12
Duchesses.........	24×12	„ „	14× 8
Marchionesses...	22×12	Plantation	13×11
„ Small	22×11	Doubles	13×10
Countesses	20×10	„	13× 7
„ Wide	20×12	Smalls	12× 8
Viscountesses ...	18×10	Ditto	12× 6
„ Small	18× 9	Ditto	11×5½

Water.

Cubic inch .... = ·0361 lb.
Gallon .... = 10·0000 „
Cubic foot = 62·3210 lbs. or 6·2321 gallons.
35·943 cubic feet (224 gallons) = 1 ton.

The gallon is = 277¼ cubic inches, = 0·16 cubic feet, = 10 lbs. distilled water.

Water for Ships: Ton, 210 gals., Butt 110, Puncheon 72, Barrel 36, Kilderkin 18.

Cisterns: 1 cubic foot is equal to about 6¼ gallons, or 62·321 lbs. A cistern 4 feet by 2½ and 3 deep will hold about 187 gallons, and weigh nearly 16 cwt. in addition to its own weight.

A TON WEIGHT OF THE FOLLOWING WILL AVERAGE IN CUBIC FEET

Earth	21	Coal, Newcastle ...	43
Clay	18	Pit Sand	22
Chalk	14	River ditto	19
Thames ballast......	20	Marl	18
Coarse gravel	19	Shingle	23
Coal, Welsh	40	Night Soil	18

A cubic foot of pure gold weighs 1,210 lbs., pure silver 655 lbs., cast iron 450 lbs., copper 550 lbs., lead 710 lbs., pure platinum 1,220 lbs., tin 456 lbs., aluminium 163 lbs.

Old Scottish Measures.

LIQUIDS.

4 Gills... = 1 Mutchkin.	2 Pints ... = 1 Quart.
2 Mutchkins = 1 Choppin.	4 Quarts . = 1 Gallon.
2 Choppins = 1 Pint.	8 Gallons = 1 Barrel.

CORN MEASURE.

4 Lippies... = 1 Peck.	4 Firlots = 1 Boll.
4 Pecks ... = 1 Firlot.	16 Bolls = 1 Chalder.

Old Scottish Weights.

16 Drops 1 Ounce, 16 Ounces 1 Pound, 16 Pounds 1 Stone.

Metrical Weights and Measures.

THE French Metrical System is based upon the (assumed) length of the fourth part of a terrestrial meridian. The ten-millionth part of this arc was chosen as the unit of measures of length, and called a *Mètre*. The cube of the tenth part of the mètre was adopted as the unit of capacity, and denominated a *Litre*. The weight of a litre of distilled water at its greatest density was called a *Kilogramme*, of which the thousandth part, or *Gramme*, was adopted as the unit of weight. The multiples of these, proceeding in decimal progression, are distinguished by the employment of the prefixes *deca, hecto, kilo*, and *myria*, from the Greek, and the subdivisions by *deci, centi*, and *milli*, from the Latin :—

MEASURES OF LENGTH (UNIT MÈTRE).

EQUAL TO	Inches.	Feet.	Yards.	Fathms.	Miles.
Millimètre	0·03937 ...	0·003 ...	0·001 ...	0·000 ...	0·000
Centimètre	0·39371 ...	0·032 ...	0·010 ...	0·005 ...	0·000
Décimètre	3·93708 ...	0·328 ...	0·109 ...	0·054 ...	0·000
MÈTRE	39·37079 ...	3·280 ...	1·093 ...	0·546 ...	0·000
Décamètre	393·70790 ...	32·808 ...	10·936 ...	5·468 ...	0·006
Hectomètre.........	3937·07900 ...	328·089 ...	109·363 ...	54·681 ...	0·062
Kilomètre	39370·79000 ...	3280·892 ...	1093·633 ...	546·816 ...	0·621
Myriamètre........	393707·90000 ...	32808·991 ...	10936·330 ...	5468·165 ...	6·213

CUBIC, OR MEASURES OF CAPACITY (UNIT LITRE).

EQUAL TO	Cub. In.	Cub. Feet.	Pints.	Gallons.	Bshls.
Millilitre, or cubic centim.	0·06103 ...	0·000 ...	0·001 ...	0·000 ...	0·000
Centilitre, 10 cubic do. ...	0·61027 ...	0·000 ...	0·017 ...	0·002 ...	0·000
Décilitre, 100 cubic do. ...	6·10271 ...	0·003 ...	0·176 ...	0·022 ...	0·002
LITRE, or cubic Décimètre	61·02705 ...	0·035 ...	1·760 ...	0·220 ...	0·027
Décalitre, or Centistère...	610·27052 ...	0·353 ...	17·607 ...	2·200 ...	0·275
Hectolitre, or Décistère...	6102·70515 ...	3·531 ...	176·077 ...	22·009 ...	2·751
Kilolitre, or Stère	61027·05152 ...	35·316 ...	1760·773 ...	220·096 ...	27·512
Myrialitre, or Décastère 610270·51519	...·353·165 ...	17607·734 ...	2200·966 ...	275·120	

MEASURES OF WEIGHT (UNIT GRAMME).

EQUAL TO	Grains.	Troy oz.	Avoir. lb.	Cwt.=112 lb.	Tons=20 cwt.
Milligramme	0·01543 ...	0·000 ...	0·000 ...	0·000 ...	0·000
Centigramme	0·15432 ...	0·000 ...	0·000 ...	0·000 ...	0·000
Décigramme	1·54323 ...	0·003 ...	0·000 ...	0·000 ...	0·000
GRAMME	15·43235 ...	0·032 ...	0·002 ...	0·000 ...	0·000
Décagramme	154·32349 ...	0·321 ...	0·022 ...	0·000 ...	0·000
Hectogramme......	1543·23489 ...	3·215 ...	0·220 ...	0·001 ...	0·000
Kilogramme	15432·34880 ...	32·150 ...	2·204 ...	0·019 ...	0·000
Myriagramme	154323·48800 ...	321·507 ...	22·046 ...	0·196 ...	0·009

SQUARE, OR MEASURES OF SURFACE (UNIT ARE).

EQUAL TO	Sq. Feet.	Yards.	Perches.	Roods.	Acres.
Centiare, or sq. mètre ...	10·764299 ...	1·196...	0·039 ...	0·000 ...	0·000
ARE, or 100 sq. mètres ...	1076·429934 ...	119·603...	3·953 ...	0·098 ...	0·024
Hectare, or 10,000 sq. m. 107642·993419 ...	11960·332...	395·382 ...	9·884 ...	2·471	

TABLE FOR CONVERTING METRIC WEIGHTS AND MEASURES.

For the use of this table the following explanation is necessary: The figures in heavier type represent either of the two columns beside them as the case may be, viz., with Hectares and Acres in the first set of columns, 1 Acre = 0·405 Hectare, and *vice versa* 1 Hectare = 2·471 Acres, and so on.

Hectare.		Acre.	Kilomtr.		Eng. mil.	Square Kilomtr.		Eng. mil.
0·405	1	2·471	1·609	1	0·621	2·592	1	0·386
0·809	2	4·942	3·219	2	1·243	5·184	2	0·772
1·214	3	7·413	4·828	3	1·864	7·776	3	1·158
1·619	4	9·885	6·438	4	2·486	10·368	4	1·544
2·023	5	12·356	8·047	5	3·107	12·960	5	1·930
2·428	6	14·827	9·656	6	3·728	15·552	6	2·316
2·833	7	17·298	11·265	7	4·350	18·144	7	2·702
3·237	8	19·769	12·879	8	4·971	20·736	8	3·088
3·642	9	22·240	14·484	9	5·592	23·328	9	3·474
4·047	10	24·711	16·093	10	6·214	25·920	10	3·860
8·093	20	49·423	32·186	20	12·428	51·840	20	7·720
12·140	30	74·134	48·279	30	18·641	77·760	30	11·580
16·187	40	98·846	64·373	40	24·855	103·680	40	15·440
20·234	50	123·557	80·466	50	31·069	129·600	50	19·300
24·286	60	148·268	96·559	60	37·283	155·520	60	23·160
28·327	70	172·980	112·652	70	43·497	181·440	70	27·020
32·373	80	197·692	128·746	80	49·710	207·360	80	30·880
36·420	90	222·903	144·839	90	55·924	233·280	90	34·740
40·467	100	247·114	160·932	100	62·138	259·200	100	38·601

Time and Watch on Board Ship.

WATCH.—For purposes of discipline, and to divide the work fairly, the crew is mustered in two divisions: the Starboard (right side, looking forward) and the Port (left). The day commences at noon, and is thus divided:—

Afternoon *Watch*	noon to 4 p.m.
First Dog " ...	4 p.m. to 6 p.m.
Second Dog " ...	6 p.m. to 8 p.m.
First " ...	8 p.m. to midnight.
Middle " ...	12 a.m. to 4 a.m.
Morning " ...	4 a.m. to 8 a.m.
Forenoon " ...	8 a.m. to noon.

This makes seven WATCHES, which enables the crew to keep them alternately, as the *Watch* which is on duty in the forenoon one day has the afternoon next day, and the men who have only four hours' rest one night have eight hours the next. This is the reason for having *Dog Watches*, which are made by dividing the hours between 4 p.m. and 8 p.m. into two *Watches*.

TIME.—Time is kept by means of "Bells," although there is but one bell on the ship, and to strike the clapper properly against the bell requires some skill.

First, two strokes of the clapper at the interval of a second, then an interval of two seconds; then two more strokes with a second's interval apart, then a rest of two seconds, thus :—

BELL, ONE SECOND; B., TWO SECS.; B. s.; B. ss.; B.
B. s.; B. ss.; B.

1 Bell is struck at 12.30, and again at 4.30, 6.30, 8.30 p.m. ; 12.30, 4.30, and 8.30 a.m.

2 Bells at 1 (struck with an interval of a second between each—B, B.), the same again at 5, 7, and 9 p.m. ; 1, 5, and 9 a.m.

3 Bells at 1.30 (B. s, B. ss, B), 5.30, 7.30, and 9.30 p.m. ; 1.30, 5.30, and 9.30 a.m.

4 Bells at 2 (B. s, B. ss, B. s, B.), 6 and 10 p.m. ; 2, 6, and 10 a.m.

5 Bells at 2.30 (B. s, B. ss, B. s, B. ss, B.) and 10.30 p.m. ; 2.30, 6.30, and 10.30 a.m.

6 Bells at 3 (B. s, B. ss, B. s, B. ss, B. s, B.) and 11 p.m. ; 3, 7, and 11 a.m.

7 Bells at 3.30 (B. s, B. ss, B. s, B. ss, B. s, B. ss, B.) and 11.30 p.m. ; 3.30, 7.30, and 11.30 a.m.

8 Bells (B. s, B. ss, B. s, B. ss, B. s, B. ss, B. s, B.) every 4 hours, at noon, at 4 p.m., 8 p.m., midnight, 4 a.m., and 8 a.m.

METRICAL CONVERSION—*continued.*

Metre.		Yard.	Kilogr.	lb. avoir.		Litre.		Gallons.
0·914	1	1·093	0·454	1	2·20	4·54	1	0·22
1·829	2	2·187	0·907	2	4·41	9·09	2	0·44
2·743	3	3·281	1·361	3	6·61	13·63	3	0·66
3·658	4	4·374	1·814	4	8·82	18·17	4	0·88
4·572	5	5·468	2·268	5	11·02	22·72	5	1·10
5·486	6	6·562	2·722	6	13·23	27·26	6	1·32
6·401	7	7·655	3·175	7	15·43	31·80	7	1·54
7·315	8	8·749	3·629	8	17·64	36·35	8	1·76
8·229	9	9·843	4·082	9	19·84	40·89	9	1·98
9·144	10	10·936	4·536	10	22·05	45·43	10	2·20
18·288	20	21·873	9·072	20	44·09	90·87	20	4·40
27·432	30	32·809	13·608	30	66·14	136·30	30	6·60
36·576	40	43·745	18·144	40	88·18	181·74	40	8·80
45·719	50	54·682	22·679	50	110·23	227·17	50	11·00
54·863	60	65·618	27·215	60	132·28	272·61	60	13·20
64·007	70	76·554	31·752	70	154·32	318·04	70	15·40
73·151	80	87·491	36·288	80	176·37	363·48	80	17·60
82·295	90	98·427	40·823	90	198·42	408·91	90	19·80
91·438	100	109·363	45·359	100	220·46	454·35	100	22·01

To convert degrees CENTIGRADE or RÉAUMUR into degrees FAHRENHEIT, or *vice versâ*, use one of the following formulæ:—

Let F = Number of degrees Fahrenheit, C = Number of degrees Centigrade and R = Number of degrees Réaumur, then—

Freezing point = 32° F = 0° C = 0° R; Boiling point = 212° F = 100° C = 80° R.

$$F = O + R + 32 \qquad R = \frac{4(F-32)}{9}$$

$$F = \frac{9R}{4} + 32 \qquad O = \frac{5(F-32)}{9}$$

THERMOMETER.
Comparison between Scales of Fahrenheit, Réaumur, and the Centigrade.

Cent.	Fah.	Rmr.	Cent.	Fah.	Rmr.
100 B.	212 B.	80 B.	25	77	20
99	210·2	79·2	24	75·2	19·2
98	208·4	78·4	23	73·4	18·4
97	206·6	77·6	22	71·6	17·6
96	204·8	76·8	21	69·8	16·8
95	203	76	20	68	16
94	201·2	75·2	19	66·2	15·2
93	199·4	74·4	18	64·4	14·4
92	197·6	73·6	17	62·6	13·6
91	195·8	72·8	16	60·8	12·8
90	194	72	15	59	12
89	192·2	71·2	14	57·2	11·2
88	190·4	70·4	13	55·4	10·4
87	188·6	69·6	12	53·6	9·6
86	186·8	68·8	11	51·8	8·8
85	185	68	10	50	8
84	183·2	67·2	9	48·2	7·2
83	181·4	66·4	8	46·4	6·4
82	179·6	65·6	7	44·6	5·6
81	177·8	64·8	6	42·8	4·8
80	176	64	5	41	4
79	174·2	63·2	4	39·2	3·2
78	172·4	62·4	3	37·4	2·4
77	170·6	61·6	2	35·6	1·6
76	168·8	60·8	1	33·8	0·8
75	167	60	Zero	32	Zero
74	165·2	59·2	1	30·2	0·8
73	163·4	58·4	2	28·4	1·6
72	161·6	57·6	3	26·6	2·4
71	159·8	56·8	4	24·8	3·2
70	158	56	5	23	4
69	156·2	55·2	6	21·2	4·8
68	154·4	54·4	7	19·4	5·6
67	152·6	53·6	8	17·6	6·4
66	150·8	52·8	9	15·8	7·2
65	149	52	10	14	8
64	147·2	51·2	11	12·2	8·8
63	145·4	50·4	12	10·4	9·6
62	143·6	49·6	13	8·6	10·4
61	141·8	48·8	14	6·8	11·2
60	140	48	15	5	12
59	138·2	47·2	16	3·2	12·8
58	136·4	46·4	17	1·4	13·6
57	134·6	45·6	18	0·4	14·4
56	132·8	44·8	19	2·2	15·2
55	131	44	20	4	16
54	129·2	43·2	21	5·8	16·8
53	127·4	42·4	22	7·6	17·6
52	125·6	41·6	23	9·4	18·4
51	123·8	40·8	24	11·2	19·2
50	122	40	25	13	20
49	120·2	39·2	26	14·8	20·8
48	118·4	38·4	27	16·6	21·6
47	116·6	37·6	28	18·4	22·4
46	114·8	36·8	29	20·2	23·2
45	113	36	30	22	24
44	111·2	35·2	31	23·8	24·8
43	109·4	34·4	32	25·6	25·6
42	107·6	33·6	33	27·4	26·4
41	105·8	32·8	34	29·2	27·2
40	104	32	35	31	28
39	102·2	31·2	36	32·8	28·8
38	100·4	30·4	37	34·6	29·6
37	98·6	29·6	38	36·4	30·4
36	96·8	28·8	39	38·2	31·2
35	95	28	40	40	32
34	93·2	27·2	41	41·8	32·8
33	91·4	26·4	42	43·6	33·6
32	89·6	25·6	43	45·4	34·4
31	87·8	24·8	44	47·2	35·2
30	86	24	45	49	36
29	84·2	23·2	46	50·8	36·8
28	82·4	22·4	47	52·6	37·6
27	80·6	21·6	48	54·4	38·4
26	78·8	20·8	49	56·2	39·2

PRESENT VALUE OF A LEASE, FREEHOLD ESTATE, OR ANNUITY.

Per £100 clear Annual Rental or Value, without any deduction whatever.

In the following Table, compound interest at the rates of 3, 4, 5, 6, and 7 per cent. is reckoned.

Years.	3%	4%	5%	6%	7%	Years.	3%	4%	5%	6%	7%
½	49	48	48	48	47	44	24 25	20 55	17 55	15 38	13 56
1	97	96	95	94	93	45	24 52	20 72	17 77	15 46	13 61
2	1 91	1 89	1 86	1 83	1 81	46	24 77	20 88	17 88	15 52	13 65
3	2 83	2 78	2 72	2 67	2 62	47	25 02	21 04	17 98	15 59	13 69
4	3 72	3 63	3 55	3 47	3 39	48	25 26	21 20	18 08	15 65	13 73
5	4 58	4 45	4 33	4 21	4 10	49	25 50	21 34	18 17	15 71	13 77
6	5 42	5 24	5 08	4 92	4 77	50	25 73	21 48	18 26	15 76	13 80
7	6 23	6 00	5 79	5 58	5 39	51	25 95	21 62	18 34	15 81	13 83
8	7 02	6 73	6 46	6 21	5 97	52	26 16	21 75	18 42	15 86	13 86
9	7 78	7 44	7 11	6 80	6 51	53	26 37	21 87	18 49	15 90	13 89
10	8 53	8 11	7 72	7 36	7 02	54	26 58	21 99	18 56	15 95	13 91
11	9 25	8 76	8 31	7 89	7 50	55	26 77	22 11	18 63	15 99	13 94
12	9 95	9 39	8 86	8 38	7 94	56	26 96	22 22	18 70	16 03	13 96
13	10 63	9 99	9 39	8 85	8 36	57	27 15	22 32	18 76	16 06	13 98
14	11 29	10 56	9 90	9 29	8 75	58	27 33	22 43	18 82	16 10	14 00
15	11 94	11 12	10 38	9 71	9 11	59	27 50	22 53	18 87	16 13	14 02
16	12 56	11 65	10 84	10 11	9 45	60	27 67	22 62	18 93	16 16	14 04
17	13 16	12 17	11 27	10 48	9 76	61	27 84	22 71	18 98	16 19	14 05
18	13 75	12 66	11 69	10 06	62	28 00	22 80	19 03	16 22	14 07
19	14 32	13 13	12 08	11 16	10 34	63	28 15	22 89	19 07	16 24	14 08
20	14 88	13 59	12 46	11 47	10 59	64	28 30	22 97	19 12	16 26	14 10
21	15 41	14 03	12 82	11 76	10 84	65	28 45	23 04	19 16	16 29	14 11
22	15 94	14 45	13 16	12 04	11 06	66	28 59	23 12	19 20	16 31	14 12
23	16 44	14 86	13 49	12 30	11 27	67	28 73	23 19	19 24	16 33	14 13
24	16 93	15 25	13 80	12 55	11 47	68	28 87	23 26	19 27	16 35	14 14
25	17 41	15 62	14 09	12 78	11 65	69	29 00	23 33	19 31	16 37	14 15
26	17 87	15 98	14 38	13 00	11 83	70	29 12	23 39	19 34	16 38	14 16
27	18 33	16 33	14 64	13 21	11 99	71	29 24	23 45	19 37	16 40	14 17
28	18 76	16 66	14 90	13 41	12 14	72	29 36	23 51	19 40	16 41	14 17
29	19 19	16 98	15 14	13 59	12 28	73	29 48	23 57	19 43	16 43	14 18
30	19 60	17 29	15 37	13 76	12 41	74	29 59	23 63	19 46	16 44	14 19
31	20 00	17 59	15 59	13 93	12 53	75	29 70	23 68	19 48	16 45	14 19
32	20 39	17 87	15 80	14 08	12 65	76	29 81	23 73	19 51	16 47	14 20
33	20 76	18 15	16 00	14 23	12 75	77	29 91	23 78	19 53	16 48	14 21
34	21 13	18 41	16 19	14 37	12 85	78	30 01	23 82	19 55	16 49	14 21
35	21 49	18 66	16 37	14 50	12 95	79	30 10	23 87	19 57	16 50	14 22
36	21 83	18 91	16 55	14 62	13 03	80	30 20	23 91	19 59	16 51	14 22
37	22 17	19 14	16 71	14 74	13 12	85	30 63	24 11	19 68	16 55	14 24
38	22 49	19 37	16 87	14 85	13 19	90	31 00	24 27	19 75	16 58	14 25
39	22 81	19 58	17 02	14 95	13 26	95	31 32	24 40	19 80	16 60	14 26
40	23 11	19 79	17 16	15 05	13 33	100	31 60	24 50	19 85	16 62	14 27
41	23 41	19 99	17 29	15 14	13 39						
42	23 70	20 19	17 42	15 22	13 45		IN PERPETUITY.				
43	23 98	20 37	17 55	15 31	13 51		33 33	25 00	20 00	16 66	14 28

EXAMPLE 1.—What is the present value of a Lease having 37 years to run of the net annual value of £100, interest being reckoned at 4 per cent. ANSWER :—19 14 years' purchase or £1,914.

EXAMPLE 2.—A man, aged 54, in the receipt of a pension or annuity of £100 a year net, wishes to commute that for a present payment, interest being reckoned at 5 per cent. How much will he receive? ANSWER :—Looking at the Table of Expectation of Life on p. 357, it will be seen that the expectation for age 54 is about 17 years; and from the above table an annuity certain for 17 years, interest at 5 per cent., is worth 11 27 years' purchase. The present payment required would therefore be £1,127 approximately.

Note to Example 2.—This method is only approximate. The values of annuities which depend on lives of a given present age, when properly calculated according to a given mortality table and a given rate of interest, are always somewhat less than those given by the method used in this example.

THE ENGLISH MILE COMPARED WITH OTHER EUROPEAN MEASURES

	English Mile.	English Geog. M.	French Kilom.	German Geog. M.	Russian Verst.	Austrn. Mile.	Dutch Ure.	Norweg. Mile.	Swedish Mile.	Danish Mile.	Swiss Stunde.
English Statute Mile......	1·000	0·867	1·609	0·217	1·508	0·212	0·289	0·142	0·151	0·213	0·335
English Geog. Mile	1·150	1·000	1·855	0·250	1·738	0·245	0·333	0·164	0·169	0·246	0·386
Kilomètre	0·621	0·540	1·000	0·135	0·937	0·132	0·180	0·088	0·094	0·133	0·208
German Geog. Mile	4·610	4·000	7·420	1·000	6·953	0·978	1·333	0·657	0·694	0·985	1·543
Russian Verst	0·663	0·575	1·067	0·144	1·000	0·141	0·192	0·094	0·100	0·142	0·222
Austrian Mile	4·714	4·089	7·586	1·022	7·112	1·000	1·363	0·672	0·710	1·006	1·578
Dutch Ure	3·458	3·000	5·565	0·750	5·215	0·734	1·000	0·493	0·520	0·738	1·157
Norwegian Mile	7·021	6·091	11·299	1·523	10·589	1·489	2·035	1·000	1·057	1·499	2·350
Swedish Mile	6·644	5·764	10·692	1·441	10·019	1·409	1·921	0·948	1·000	1·419	2·224
Danish Mile	4·682	4·062	7·536	1·016	7·078	0·994	1·354	0·667	0·705	1·000	1·567
Swiss Stunde	2·987	2·592	4·808	0·648	4·505	0·634	0·864	0·425	0·449	0·638	1·000

TABLE I.—Showing the Sum to which an Annuity of One Pound accumulating at Compound Interest will amount in from One to Fifty Years at Rates varying from 2½ to 5 per Cent.

Yr.	2½ Per Ct.	3 Per Ct.	3½ Per Ct.	4 Per Ct.	4½ Per Ct.	5 Per Ct.
1	*1·000	1·000	1·000	1·000	1·000	1·000
2	2·025	2·030	2·035	2·040	2·045	2·050
3	3·076	3·091	3·106	3·122	3·137	3·153
4	4·153	4·184	4·215	4·246	4·278	4·310
5	5·256	5·309	5·362	5·416	5·471	5·526
6	6·388	6·468	6·550	6·633	6·717	6·802
7	7·547	7·662	7·779	7·898	8·019	8·142
8	8·736	8·892	9·052	9·214	9·380	9·549
9	9·955	10·159	10·368	10·583	10·802	11·027
10	11·203	11·464	11·731	12·006	12·288	12·578
11	12·483	12·808	13·142	13·486	13·841	14·207
12	13·796	14·192	14·602	15·026	15·464	15·917
13	15·140	15·618	16·113	16·627	17·160	17·713
14	16·519	17·086	17·677	18·292	18·932	19·599
15	17·932	18·599	19·296	20·024	20·784	21·579
16	19·380	20·157	20·971	21·825	22·719	23·657
17	20·865	21·762	22·705	23·698	24·742	25·840
18	22·386	23·414	24·500	25·645	26·855	28·132
19	23·946	25·117	26·357	27·671	29·064	30·539
20	25·545	26·870	28·280	29·778	31·371	33·066
21	27·183	28·676	30·269	31·969	33·783	35·719
22	28·863	30·537	32·329	34·248	36·303	38·505
23	30·584	32·453	34·460	36·618	38·937	41·430
24	32·349	34·426	36·667	39·083	41·689	44·502
25	34·158	36·459	38·950	41·646	44·565	47·727
26	36·012	38·553	41·313	44·312	47·571	51·113
27	37·912	40·710	43·759	47·084	50·711	54·669
28	39·860	42·931	46·291	49·968	53·993	58·403
29	41·856	45·219	48·911	52·966	57·423	62·323
30	43·903	47·575	51·623	56·085	61·007	66·439
31	46·000	50·003	54·429	59·328	64·752	70·761
32	48·150	52·503	57·335	62·701	68·666	75·299
33	50·354	55·078	60·341	66·210	72·756	80·064
34	52·613	57·730	63·453	69·858	77·030	85·067
35	54·928	60·462	66·674	73·652	81·497	90·320
36	57·301	63·276	70·008	77·598	86·164	95·836
37	59·734	66·174	73·458	81·702	91·041	101·628
38	62·227	69·159	77·029	85·970	96·138	107·710
39	64·783	72·234	80·725	90·409	101·464	114·095
40	67·403	75·401	84·550	95·026	107·030	120·800
41	70·088	78·663	88·510	99·827	112·847	127·840
42	72·840	82·023	92·607	104·820	118·925	135·232
43	75·661	85·484	96·849	110·012	125·276	142·993
44	78·552	89·048	101·238	115·413	131·914	151·143
45	81·516	92·720	105·782	121·029	138·850	159·700
46	84·554	96·501	110·484	126·871	146·098	168·685
47	87·668	100·397	115·351	132·945	153·673	178·119
48	90·860	104·408	120·388	139·263	161·588	188·025
49	94·131	108·541	125·602	145·834	169·859	198·427
50	97·484	112·797	130·998	152·667	178·503	209·348

* When the annuity is payable at the beginning instead of at the end of the year, the amount for the following year, less £1, must be taken. Thus, for £1 at 2½ per cent. for 25 years, take 26 years, £36·012, and deduct £1=£35·012.

TABLE II.—Showing the Amount which One Pound accumulating at Compound Interest will reach in from One to Fifty Years at Rates varying from 2½ to 5 per Cent.

Yr.	2½ Per Ct.	3 Per Ct.	3½ Per Ct.	4 Per Ct.	4½ Per Ct.	5 Per Ct.
1	1·0250	1·0300	1·0350	1·0400	1·0450	1·0500
2	1·0506	1·0609	1·0712	1·0816	1·0920	1·1025
3	1·0769	1·0927	1·1087	1·1249	1·1412	1·1576
4	1·1038	1·1256	1·1475	1·1699	1·1925	1·2155
5	1·1314	1·1593	1·1877	1·2167	1·2462	1·2763
6	1·1597	1·1941	1·2293	1·2653	1·3023	1·3401
7	1·1887	1·2299	1·2723	1·3159	1·3609	1·4071
8	1·2184	1·2668	1·3168	1·3686	1·4221	1·4775
9	1·2489	1·3048	1·3629	1·4233	1·4861	1·5513
10	1·2801	1·3439	1·4106	1·4802	1·5530	1·6289
11	1·3121	1·3842	1·4510	1·5395	1·6229	1·7103
12	1·3449	1·4258	1·5111	1·6010	1·6959	1·7959
13	1·3785	1·4685	1·5640	1·6651	1·7722	1·8856
14	1·4130	1·5126	1·6187	1·7317	1·8519	1·9799
15	1·4483	1·5580	1·6753	1·8009	1·9353	2·0789
16	1·4845	1·6047	1·7340	1·8730	2·0224	2·1829
17	1·5216	1·6528	1·7947	1·9479	2·1134	2·2920
18	1·5597	1·7024	1·8575	2·0258	2·2085	2·4066
19	1·5987	1·7535	1·9225	2·1068	2·3079	2·5270
20	1·6386	1·8061	1·9898	2·1911	2·4117	2·6533
21	1·6796	1·8603	2·0594	2·2788	2·5202	2·7860
22	1·7216	1·9161	2·1315	2·3699	2·6337	2·9253
23	1·7646	1·9736	2·2061	2·4647	2·7522	3·0715
24	1·8087	2·0328	2·2833	2·5633	2·8760	3·2251
25	1·8539	2·0938	2·3632	2·6658	3·0054	3·3864
26	1·9003	2·1566	2·4460	2·7725	3·1407	3·5557
27	1·9478	2·2213	2·5316	2·8834	3·2820	3·7335
28	1·9965	2·2879	2·6202	2·9987	3·4297	3·9201
29	2·0464	2·3566	2·7119	3·1187	3·5840	4·1161
30	2·0976	2·4273	2·8068	3·2434	3·7453	4·3219
31	2·1500	2·5001	2·9050	3·3731	3·9139	4·5380
32	2·2038	2·5751	3·0067	3·5081	4·0900	4·7649
33	2·2589	2·6523	3·1119	3·6484	4·2740	5·0032
34	2·3153	2·7319	3·2209	3·7943	4·4664	5·2533
35	2·3732	2·8139	3·3336	3·9461	4·6673	5·5160
36	2·4325	2·8983	3·4503	4·1039	4·8774	5·7918
37	2·4933	2·9852	3·5710	4·2681	5·0969	6·0814
38	2·5557	3·0748	3·6960	4·4388	5·3262	6·3855
39	2·6196	3·1670	3·8254	4·6164	5·5659	6·7048
40	2·6851	3·2620	3·9593	4·8010	5·8164	7·0400
41	2·7522	3·3599	4·0978	4·9931	6·0781	7·3920
42	2·8210	3·4607	4·2413	5·1928	6·3516	7·7616
43	2·8915	3·5645	4·3897	5·4005	6·6374	8·1497
44	2·9638	3·6715	4·5433	5·6165	6·9361	8·5572
45	3·0379	3·7816	4·7024	5·8412	7·2482	8·9850
46	3·1139	3·8950	4·8669	6·0748	7·5744	9·4343
47	3·1917	4·0119	5·0373	6·3178	7·9153	9·9060
48	3·2715	4·1323	5·2136	6·5705	8·2715	10·4013
49	3·3533	4·2562	5·3961	6·8333	8·6437	10·9213
50	3·4371	4·3839	5·5849	7·1067	9·0326	11·4674

REPAYMENT OF PUBLIC LOANS.

Large sums of money are every year advanced to County or District Councils and other public bodies, for improvements, building of workhouses, schools, harbours, bridges, &c., to be repaid in a given number of years, including interest. The following scheme of tables for the repayments of Loans was compiled under the Local Government Act, 1858, and examined by the actuary of the National Debt Office. It gives the sums needed as the annual amount of principal combined with interest required for the liquidation of a debt of £100, at the stated percentage, in 10, 20, 30, 40, and 50 years:—

Years	3 per Ct.			3½ per Ct.			4 per Ct.			4½ per Ct.			5 per Ct.		
	£	s.	d.	£	s.	d.	£	s.	d.	£	s.	d.	£	s.	d
10	11	14	5¼	12	0	5¾	12	6	7	12	12	9	12	19	0
20	6	14	5½	7	0	8¾	7	7	2	7	13	9	8	0	5¾
30	5	2	0½	5	8	9	5	15	8	6	2	9½	6	10	1¼
40	4	6	6½	4	13	7¾	5	1	0½	5	9	8½	5	16	6¾
50	3	17	8¾	4	5	3¼	4	13	1¼	5	1	2½	5	9	6¾

If the loan be for £1,000, each annual instalment as shown above must be multiplied by 10; if for £2,000, then by 20, and so on.

No.	¼d.	½d.	¾d.	1d.	2d.	3d.	4d.	5d.	6d.	7d.	8d.	9d.	10d.	11d.	No.
1	0 0¼	0 0½	0 0¾	0 1	0 2	0 3	0 4	0 5	0 6	0 7	0 8	0 9	0 10	0 11	1
2	0 0½	0 1	0 1½	0 2	0 4	0 6	0 8	0 10	1 0	1 2	1 4	1 6	1 8	1 10	2
3	0 0¾	0 1½	0 2¼	0 3	0 6	0 9	1 0	1 3	1 6	1 9	2 0	2 3	2 6	2 9	3
4	0 1	0 2	0 3	0 4	0 8	1 0	1 4	1 8	2 0	2 4	2 8	3 0	3 4	3 8	4
5	0 1¼	0 2½	0 3¾	0 5	0 10	1 3	1 8	2 1	2 6	2 11	3 4	3 9	4 2	4 7	5
6	0 1½	0 3	0 4½	0 6	1 0	1 6	2 0	2 6	3 0	3 6	4 0	4 6	5 0	5 6	6
7	0 1¾	0 3½	0 5¼	0 7	1 2	1 9	2 4	2 11	3 6	4 1	4 8	5 3	5 10	6 5	7
8	0 2	0 4	0 6	0 8	1 4	2 0	2 8	3 4	4 0	4 8	5 4	6 0	6 8	7 4	8
9	0 2¼	0 4½	0 6¾	0 9	1 6	2 3	3 0	3 9	4 6	5 3	6 0	6 9	7 6	8 3	9
10	0 2½	0 5	0 7½	0 10	1 8	2 6	3 4	4 2	5 0	5 10	6 8	7 6	8 4	9 2	10
11	0 2¾	0 5½	0 8¼	0 11	1 10	2 9	3 8	4 7	5 6	6 5	7 4	8 3	9 2	10 1	11
12	0 3	0 6	0 9	1 0	2 0	3 0	4 0	5 0	6 0	7 0	8 0	9 0	10 0	11 0	12
13	0 3¼	0 6½	0 9¾	1 1	2 2	3 3	4 4	5 5	6 6	7 7	8 8	9 9	10 10	11 11	13
14	0 3½	0 7	0 10½	1 2	2 4	3 6	4 8	5 10	7 0	8 2	9 4	10 6	11 8	12 10	14
15	0 3¾	0 7½	0 11¼	1 3	2 6	3 9	5 0	6 3	7 6	8 9	10 0	11 3	12 6	13 9	15
16	0 4	0 8	1 0	1 4	2 8	4 0	5 4	6 8	8 0	9 4	10 8	12 0	13 4	14 8	16
17	0 4¼	0 8½	1 0¾	1 5	2 10	4 3	5 8	7 1	8 6	9 11	11 4	12 9	14 2	15 7	17
18	0 4½	0 9	1 1½	1 6	3 0	4 6	6 0	7 6	9 0	10 6	12 0	13 6	15 0	16 6	18
19	0 4¾	0 9½	1 2¼	1 7	3 2	4 9	6 4	7 11	9 6	11 1	12 8	14 3	15 10	17 5	19
20	0 5	0 10	1 3	1 8	3 4	5 0	6 8	8 4	10 0	11 8	13 4	15 0	16 8	18 4	20
21	0 5¼	0 10½	1 3¾	1 9	3 6	5 3	7 0	8 9	10 6	12 3	14 0	15 9	17 6	19 3	21
22	0 5½	0 11	1 4½	1 10	3 8	5 6	7 4	9 2	11 0	12 10	14 8	16 6	18 4	20 2	22
23	0 5¾	0 11½	1 5¼	1 11	3 10	5 9	7 8	9 7	11 6	13 5	15 4	17 3	19 2	21 1	23
24	0 6	1 0	1 6	2 0	4 0	6 0	8 0	10 0	12 0	14 0	16 0	18 0	20 0	22 0	24
25	0 6¼	1 0½	1 6¾	2 1	4 2	6 3	8 4	10 5	12 6	14 7	16 8	18 9	20 10	22 11	25
26	0 6½	1 1	1 7½	2 2	4 4	6 6	8 8	10 10	13 0	15 2	17 4	19 6	21 8	23 10	26
27	0 6¾	1 1½	1 8¼	2 3	4 6	6 9	9 0	11 3	13 6	15 9	18 0	20 3	22 6	24 9	27
28	0 7	1 2	1 9	2 4	4 8	7 0	9 4	11 8	14 0	16 4	18 8	21 0	23 4	25 8	28
29	0 7¼	1 2½	1 9¾	2 5	4 10	7 3	9 8	12 1	14 6	16 11	19 4	21 9	24 2	26 7	29
30	0 7½	1 3	1 10½	2 6	5 0	7 6	10 0	12 6	15 0	17 6	20 0	22 6	25 0	27 6	30
31	0 7¾	1 3½	1 11¼	2 7	5 2	7 9	10 4	12 11	15 6	18 1	20 8	23 3	25 10	28 5	31
32	0 8	1 4	2 0	2 8	5 4	8 0	10 8	13 4	16 0	18 8	21 4	24 0	26 8	29 4	32
33	0 8¼	1 4½	2 0¾	2 9	5 6	8 3	11 0	13 9	16 6	19 3	22 0	24 9	27 6	30 3	33
34	0 8½	1 5	2 1½	2 10	5 8	8 6	11 4	14 2	17 0	19 10	22 8	25 6	28 4	31 2	34
35	0 8¾	1 5½	2 2¼	2 11	5 10	8 9	11 8	14 7	17 6	20 5	23 4	26 3	29 2	32 1	35
36	0 9	1 6	2 3	3 0	6 0	9 0	12 0	15 0	18 0	21 0	24 0	27 0	30 0	33 0	36
37	0 9¼	1 6½	2 3¾	3 1	6 2	9 3	12 4	15 5	18 6	21 7	24 8	27 9	30 10	33 11	37
38	0 9½	1 7	2 4½	3 2	6 4	9 6	12 8	15 10	19 0	22 2	25 4	28 6	31 8	34 10	38
39	0 9¾	1 7½	2 5¼	3 3	6 6	9 9	13 0	16 3	19 6	22 9	26 0	29 3	32 6	35 9	39
40	0 10	1 8	2 6	3 4	6 8	10 0	13 4	16 8	20 0	23 4	26 8	30 0	33 4	36 8	40
41	0 10¼	1 8½	2 6¾	3 5	6 10	10 3	13 8	17 1	20 6	23 11	27 4	30 9	34 2	37 7	41
42	0 10½	1 9	2 7½	3 6	7 0	10 6	14 0	17 6	21 0	24 6	28 0	31 6	35 0	38 6	42
43	0 10¾	1 9½	2 8¼	3 7	7 2	10 9	14 4	17 11	21 6	25 1	28 8	32 3	35 10	39 5	43
44	0 11	1 10	2 9	3 8	7 4	11 0	14 8	18 4	22 0	25 8	29 4	33 0	36 8	40 4	44
45	0 11¼	1 10½	2 9¾	3 9	7 6	11 3	15 0	18 9	22 6	26 3	30 0	33 9	37 6	41 3	45
46	0 11½	1 11	2 10½	3 10	7 8	11 6	15 4	19 2	23 0	26 10	30 8	34 6	38 4	42 2	46
47	0 11¾	1 11½	2 11¼	3 11	7 10	11 9	15 8	19 7	23 6	27 5	31 4	35 3	39 2	43 1	47
48	1 0	2 0	3 0	4 0	8 0	12 0	16 0	20 0	24 0	28 0	32 0	36 0	40 0	44 0	48
49	1 0¼	2 0½	3 0¾	4 1	8 2	12 3	16 4	20 5	24 6	28 7	32 8	36 9	40 10	44 11	49
50	1 0½	2 1	3 1½	4 2	8 4	12 6	16 8	20 10	25 0	29 2	33 4	37 6	41 8	45 10	50
51	1 0¾	2 1½	3 2¼	4 3	8 6	12 9	17 0	21 3	25 6	29 9	34 0	38 3	42 6	46 9	51
52	1 1	2 2	3 3	4 4	8 8	13 0	17 4	21 8	26 0	30 4	34 8	39 0	43 4	47 8	52
53	1 1¼	2 2½	3 3¾	4 5	8 10	13 3	17 8	22 1	26 6	30 11	35 4	39 9	44 2	48 7	53
54	1 1½	2 3	3 4½	4 6	9 0	13 6	18 0	22 6	27 0	31 6	36 0	40 6	45 0	49 6	54
56	1 2	2 4	3 6	4 8	9 4	14 0	18 8	23 4	28 0	32 8	37 4	42 0	46 8	51 4	56
58	1 2½	2 5	3 7½	4 10	9 8	14 6	19 4	24 2	29 0	33 10	38 8	43 6	48 4	53 2	58
60	1 3	2 6	3 9	5 0	10 0	15 0	20 0	25 0	30 0	35 0	40 0	45 0	50 0	55 0	60
63	1 3¾	2 7½	3 11¼	5 3	10 6	15 9	21 0	26 3	31 6	36 9	42 0	47 3	52 6	57 9	63
66	1 4½	2 9	4 1½	5 6	11 0	16 6	22 0	27 6	33 0	38 6	44 0	49 6	55 0	60 6	66
69	1 5¼	2 10½	4 3¾	5 9	11 6	17 3	23 0	28 9	34 6	40 3	46 0	51 9	57 6	63 3	69
70	1 5½	2 11	4 4½	5 10	11 8	17 6	23 4	29 2	35 0	40 10	46 8	52 6	58 4	64 2	70
72	1 6	3 0	4 6	6 0	12 0	18 0	24 0	30 0	36 0	42 0	48 0	54 0	60 0	66 0	72
76	1 7	3 2	4 9	6 4	12 8	19 0	25 4	31 8	38 0	44 4	50 8	57 0	63 4	69 8	76
80	1 8	3 4	5 0	6 8	13 4	20 0	26 8	33 4	40 0	46 8	53 4	60 0	66 8	73 4	80
84	1 9	3 6	5 3	7 0	14 0	21 0	28 0	35 0	42 0	49 0	56 0	63 0	70 0	77 0	84
90	1 10½	3 9	5 7½	7 6	15 0	22 6	30 0	37 6	45 0	52 6	60 0	67 6	75 0	82 6	90
100	2 1	4 2	6 3	8 4	16 8	25 0	33 4	41 8	50 0	58 4	66 8	75 0	83 4	91 8	100

NOTE.—The instruments for which the use of Postage (Unified) adhesive stamps is "permitted" under the Stamp Act, 1891, are :—

Agreements liable to the duty of 6d.—s 22. Bills of exchange for payment of money on demand—s. 34 (1). Certified copies of or extracts from registers of births, &c—s. 64. Charter-parties—ss. 49, 50. Contract-notes where the value is less than £100—s. 52. Delivery orders—s. 69 (3). Lease or tack—s. 78 : i of a dwelling-house, or part of it, for a definite term not exceeding a year, at a rent not exceeding the rate of £10 per annum ; ii.. of any furnished dwelling-house or apartments for any definite term less than a year, where the rent for such term exceeds £25. Letter of renunciation s. 79 (2), and 62 & 63 Vic., c. 9, s. 9 (3). Notarial Acts—s. 90. Policies of Insurance (not life or marine)—s. 99. Protests of bills of exchange and promissory notes—s. 90. Proxies liable to the duty of 1d.—s. 80. Receipts—s. 101 (2). Transfers of shares in Cost-book min s—s. 110. Voting papers—s. 80. Warrants for goods—s. 111 (2).

	£	s.	d.
ADMISSION to the degree of a barrister	50	0	0
As solicitor or proctor, or W.S.	25	0	0
Any Inn of Court or Student of King's Inn, Dublin	25	0	0
As Fellow of College of Physicians...	25	0	0
As Burgess, by birth, apprenticeship, or marriage	1	0	0
Ditto on any other ground	3	0	0
Faculty as a Notary Public, England	30	0	0
Ditto, Ireland or Scotland	20	0	0
As a Burgess in Scotland	0	5	0
AFFIDAVIT, or statutory declaration	0	2	6
AGREEMENT, or memorandum of agreement, under hand only, not otherwise charged	0	0	6
Ditto, for less than a year of a furnished house, the rent exceeding £25	0	2	6
ALKALI WORKS, Cert. of Registration...	5	0	0
APPOINTMENT of a new trustee and in execution of a power of property, not being by a will...	0	10	0
APPRAISEMENT OR VALUATION of any estate or effects where the amount of the appraisement shall not exceed £5	0	0	3

APPRAISEMENT (cont.)	£	s.	d.		£	s.	d.
Not exc. £10	0	0	6	Not exc. £50	0	2	6
„ 20	0	1	0	„ 100	0	5	0
„ 30	0	1	6	„ 200	0	10	0
„ 40	0	2	0	„ 500	0	15	0

	£	s.	d.
Exceeding £500	1	0	0
Appraisers and House Agnts., ann. U.K.	2	0	0
APPRENTICESHIP INDENTURES...	0	2	6
ARMORIAL BEARINGS, annual licence, Great Britain	1	1	0
If used on any carriage, do.	2	2	0
Arms, grant of, stamp duty on	10	0	0
ARTICLES of clerkship to solicitor, in England or Ireland	80	0	0
In Superior Courts, in Scotland, or Counties Palatine of Lancaster and Durham	60	0	0
AUCTIONEER's Annual Licence, U.K....	10	0	0
May act as Appraisers or House Agents without further licence.			
AWARD—Where the amount or value awarded does not exceed £5	0	0	3

AWARD (cont.)	£	s.	d.		£	s.	d.
Not exc. £10	0	0	6	Not exc. £100	0	5	0
„ 20	0	1	0	„ 200	0	10	0
„ 30	0	1	6	„ 500	0	15	0
„ 40	0	2	0	„ 750	1	0	0
„ 50	0	2	6	„ 1,000	1	5	0

	£	s.	d.
Exceeding £1,000, and also in all other cases not above provided for	1	15	0
BANK NOTE for money payable on demand :—			

Not exceeding £1		5d.	Not exceedng £20		2s.		
„ £2		10d.	„ £30		3s.		
„ £5..18.3		1½d.	„ £50		5s.		
„ £10.18.9		2d.	„ £100 8s. 6d.				

	£	s.	d.
BANKER's Annual Licence, U.K.	30	0	0
Bankers' Cheques	0	0	1
BEER—per barrel of specific gravity of 1055 (55° of gravity)	0	6	9

	£	s.	d.
BEER-DEALERS' AND BREWERS' annual licences :—			
Beer-dealers, wholesale, not brewers, United Kingdom	3	6	1
Beer-dealers to sell in any quantity, additional, not to be consumed on the premises, England and Ireland	1	0	0
Brewers brewing beer for sale, U.K....	1	0	0
Other brewers, U.K., annual value of house exceeding £8 but not exceeding £10	0	4	0
The annual value exceeding £10 but not exceeding £15	0	9	0
Ditto in every other case in addition to the duty on the beer made...	0	4	0
*Retailers of beer, cider, and perry :—			
For consumption on the premises (United Kingdom)	3	10	0
Not to be consumed on premises (England)	1	5	0
Retailers of table-beer (off) (U. K.)	0	5	0
Retailers of beer (Scotland) (off-licences) rated under £10	2	10	0
Do. at £10 or upward	4	4	0
Retailers of beer and wine (U.K) :—			
* For consumption on the premises...	4	0	0
*Not to be consumed on the premises	3	0	0
*For Early-closing and Six-day Licences, see PUBLICANS.			
BILL OF LADING	0	0	6
BILLS OF EXCHANGE, Inland or Foreign, payable on demand, or within 3 days after date or sight, 62 & 63 Vict., c. 9, s. 10 (2), for any amount	0	0	1
Bills of Exchange of any other kind, and also Promissory notes not exceeding £5	0	0	1
Exc. £5 and not exceeding £10	0	0	2
„ 10 „ 25	0	0	3
„ 25 „ 50	0	0	6
„ 50 „ 75	0	0	9
„ 75 „ 100	0	1	0
Every £100, and also for any fractional part of £100, of such amount	0	1	0
Bill of Exchange (Foreign drawn and expressed to be payable out of U.K) exceeding £50 and not exceeding £100	0		6
Ditto £100, 6d. for every £100 or fractional part of £100 (62 & 63 Vict., c. 9, s. 10).			
BOND for payment of money. See MORTGAGE BOND, &c.			
Ditto, for securing an annuity :—			
1. Where the total amount is ascertainable. Same as MORTGAGE BOND, &c.			
2. Where the payments are for the term of life, or other indefinite period :—			
For every £5, and every fractional part of £5 payable—			
If as primary security	0	2	
If as collateral security	0	0	

	£	s.	d.
BOND for Customs or Excise duties, same as MORTGAGE BOND, &c. (but not to exceed 5s.).			
Ditto, not specifically charged (including Fidelity Bonds) same as MORTGAGE BOND, &c. but not to exceed 10s.			
On obtaining letters of administration, &c. (not exceeding £100 exempt)	0	5	0
CAPITAL DUTY (Share).—Companies and Corporations with limited liability, on every £100 of the nominal capital	0	5	0
CAPITAL DUTY (Loan). On issues by Local Authorities, Companies, and Corporations, &c., on every £100 of amount secured (62 & 63 Vict., c. 9. s. 8)	0	2	6
CARD (Playing) makers, to sell (U.K.)	1	0	0
„ for every pack, duty	0	0	3
CARRIAGES, annual licence (Great Britain).—Hackney Carriages	0	15	0
For every other carriage with four wheels, and drawn or adapted or fitted to be drawn by two or more horses, or by mechanical power	2	2	0
If with four wheels, and drawn or fitted or adapted to be drawn by one horse only	1	1	0
If with less than four wheels	0	15	0
Half these rates only charged on licences taken out between 1st October and 31st December.			
MOTOR CARS.—For every light locomotive, in addition to the carriage licence duty as above, a further excise duty is chargeable as follows:—			
If the weight exceed one ton, but not two tons, *unladen*	2	2	0
If the weight exceed two tons *unladen*	3	3	0
N.B.—In calculating the weight of a vehicle *unladen*, the weight of water, fuel, or accumulator shall not be included.			
CERTIFICATE—to be taken out yearly by every attorney, solicitor, proctor, writer to the signet, notary public, and sworn clerk, practising within 10 miles of the General Post Office, London; or either in the city or shire of Edinburgh, or in the city of Dublin, or within 3 miles thereof	9	0	0
If practising elsewhere	6	0	0
(During first three years one half only.)			
CERTIFICATE:—Of goods, being duly entered inwards, for drawback	0	4	0
Of birth, baptism, marriage, death, or burial	0	0	1
CHARTERPARTY	0	0	6
CHEQUES, or drafts, payable on demand or to order	0	0	1
CHICORY, per cwt., raw or kiln-dried	0	12	1
CIDER AND PERRY (England), annual licence, retailers of. *See also* PUBLICANS*	1	5	0
COFFEE MIXTURES or substitutes, per ¼lb.	0	0	½
COLLATERAL SECURITY, for every £100	0	0	6
COMMISSION to any Officer in the Army or Royal Marines	1	10	0
To any Officer in the Navy	0	5	0
Of Lunacy	0	5	0
CONTRACT NOTE for the sale or purchase of any stock or marketable security of the value of £5 and under £100	0	0	1
Of the value of £100 or upwards	0	1	0
Contract or Grant for payment of a Superannuation Annuity: for every £5 or fractional part of £5	0	0	6

	£	s.	d.
CONVEYANCE OR TRANSFER:—Of Bank of England Stock	0	7	9
Of any Colonial debenture stock or funded debt for every £100, or fractional part of £100, of nominal amount transferred	0	2	6
CONVEYANCE or transfer on sale of any property except such stock as aforesaid:—where the purchase-money shall not exceed £5	0	0	6
Exceeding £5 and not exceeding £10..	0	1	0
„ 10 „ 15..	0	1	6
„ 15 „ 20...	0	2	0
„ 20 „ 25...	0	2	6
For every additional £25 up to £300..	0	2	6
If exceeding £300, then for every £50	0	5	0
Of any kind not otherwise charged	0	10	0
Proviso for composition for transfer duty see 54 & 55 Vict. c. 39, *and* 57 & 58 Vict. c. 39.			
COPY OR EXTRACT (attested or authenticated), the same duty as original, but not to exceed	0	1	0
COPYHOLD AND CUSTOMARY ESTATE:—If on sale, mortgage, or demise, the *ad valorem* duties under those heads. Not upon sale, mortgage, or demise. Surrender, or grant made out of court, or the memorandum thereof, and copy of court-roll of any surrender or grant made in court	0	10	0
CORPORATE AND UNINCORPORATE BODIES. Upon the *net* annual value, income, or profits accrued in respect of all real or personal property vested in such bodies...per cent.	5	0	0
(Subject to certain exceptions laid down in the Act 48 & 49 Vict. c. 51.)			
COVENANT, deed of, *ad valorem* duty, but not to exceed	0	10	0
DEBENTURE or Certificate for drawback, or goods exported, &c., not exc. £10	0	1	0
Exceeding £10 and not exc. £50........	0	2	6
Exceeding £50	0	5	0
DECLARATION, *see* AFFIDAVIT.			
DELIVERY ORDER of goods of the value of 40s. or upwards, lying in any dock, port, warehouse, or wharf, or rent, or hire, on the sale or transfer of goods...	0	0	1
DEMISE, *see* LEASE.			
DISTILLER's Annual Licence, U.K.	10	10	0
DOGS of any kind (annually), Great Britain	0	7	6
Dogs under 6 months of age, and those kept solely for the purpose of tending sheep or cattle on a farm, or by shepherds; or by blind persons, for their guidance, exempt.			
DUPLICATE OR COUNTERPART: Same duty as original, but not to exceed	0	5	0
ECCLESIASTICAL LICENCES:—To hold the office of lecturer, &c.	0	10	0
For licensing a building for divine service, &c., and any chapel for solemnising marriages	0	10	0
Licence not otherwise charged	2	0	0
EQUITABLE MORTGAGES under hand only. For every £100 or part thereof	0	1	0
ESTATE DUTY: In the case of every person dying after 1st August, 1894 (prior to which date Probate, Affidavit, or Inventory Duty is payable), where the principal value of all property, real or per-			

sonal, settled or not settled, passing on the death of such person, per cent. exceeds :

			£	s.
£100 and does not exceed		£500	1	0
500	,,	1,000	2	0
1,000	,,	10,000	3	0
10,000	,,	25,000	4	0
25,000	,,	50,000	4	10
50,000	,,	75,000	5	0
75,000	,,	100,000	5	10
100,000	,,	150,000	6	0
150,000	,,	250,000	6	10
250,000	,,	500,000	7	0
500,000	,,	1,000,000	7	10
1,000,000		—	8	0

In calculating duty the net value of an estate where the death occurred between 2nd August, 1894, and 30th June, 1896, is raised to the next complete £10; and on deaths after that date any fraction of £100 is ignored, such adjusted value determining both the rate and amount of duty.

Gifts made by the deceased within a twelvemonth of death are subject to aggregation with the rest of the estate.

In addition to the above, where property liable to Estate Duty is settled by the will of the deceased, or having been settled by some other disposition passes under that disposition on the death of the deceased to some person not competent to dispose thereof, a further duty is payable at the rate of £1 per cent. on the settled property, but from that payment the *ad val.* stamp duty charged on the settlement may be deducted.

But where the net value of the property, real and personal, does not exceed £1,000, Estate Duty only is payable, and the property is exempt from Settlement Estate Duty, and from Legacy or Succession Duties.

Small estates up to £300 and £500 gross, are charged at the option of the accounting parties, either by the preceding scale or with fixed duties of 30s. and 50s., and are exempt from all other death duties.

Where the net value exceeds £100, but does not exceed £200 the *ad valorem* duty amounts to £1 only, provided that the death occurred on or after 1st July, 1896.

Interest at 3 per cent. per annum is also payable on the Estate Duty on Personalty from the date of the death up to that of delivery of the affidavit or account.

The Estate Duty on real property may be paid, if desired, by eight yearly or sixteen half-yearly instalments, and that on certain annuities may at option be paid in 4 yearly instalments and 3 per cent. interest is charged on all unpaid portions of duty in these cases from 12 months after death.

FACULTY OR DISPENSATION :
In England, in all cases, £30.

In Scotland or Ireland, in some cases £20, in others £25.

	£	s.	d.

FEES are taken in all Public Departments by means of Stamps: such payments are accounted for to the Exchequer under the heading of Miscellaneous Revenue.

	£	s.	d.
GAME LICENCES. United Kingdom, if taken out after 31st July and before 1st Nov., to expire on 31st July following	3	0	0
After 31st July, to expire following 31st October	2	0	0
After 31st Oct., to expire 31st July	2	0	0
Licence for a continuous period of fourteen days	1	0	0
Gamekeepers (Great Britain), to expire 31st July	2	0	0
Ditto, Deputation of, Stamp Duty	0	10	0

Gamekeepers, Ireland, same as Game Licences.

	£	s.	d.
Game-Dealer's Licence, U.K., to expire 1st July, annually	2	0	0
GUN LICENCES (gun or pistol)	0	10	0

Payment is now rigidly enforced, even to the carrying of a revolver. Persons holding game licences, soldiers and volunteers are exempt; but the licence cannot be transferred to a son or to a servant. U.K., expire 31st July.

	£	s.	d.
HAWKER'S Annual Licence, U.K. (*see* Pedlars)	2	0	0
HOUSE AGENTS, letting furnished houses at a rent above £25 a year, annual licence, United Kingdom	2	0	0

HOUSE DUTY.—On inhabited houses, occupied as farm-house, public-house, coffee-shop, shop, warehouse, or lodging-house *of the annual value of £20,*

	£	s.	d.
and not exceeding £40	0	0	2
Exceeding £40 and not exc. £60	0	0	4
Exceeding £60	0	0	6

in the £

Other houses *of the annual value of £20, and not exceeding £40* ...

	£	s.	d.
£20, and not exceeding £40	0	0	3
Exceeding £40, and not exc. £60	0	0	6
Exceeding £60	0	0	9

INCOME TAX.—See Property and Income Tax.

	£	s.	d.
INEBRIATES' RETREATS Licences	5	0	0

(10s. additional is payable for every patient over 10 in number.)

INSURANCE POLICIES—LIFE :

	£	s.	d.
For any sum not exceeding £10	0	0	1
Exc. £10, and not exc. £25	0	0	3
Exc. £25, and not exc. £500, for every £50 or fractional part of £50	0	0	6
Exc. £500, and not exc. £1,000, for every £100 or fractional part of £100	0	1	0
Exc. £1,000, for every £1,000 or any fractional part of £1,000	0	10	0

Policies of Indemnity against loss under the Employers' Liability Act, 1880 and the Workmen's Compensation Act 1897:

	£	s.	d.
Annual Premium not exceeding £1	0	0	1
Ditto exceeding £1 under hand	0	0	6
Ditto Ditto under seal	0	10	0
—ACCIDENTAL DEATH, or Personal Injury, or on periodical payments during sickness, or loss or damage upon Property	0	0	1

Proviso for Composition for Insurance Duty, see 52 & 53 Vict. c. 42, s. 20, and 59 & 60 Vict. c. 28, s. 13.

		£	s.	d.
INSURANCE POLICIES—SEA:				
Where the premium does not exceed 2s. 6d. per cent.		0	0	1
In other cases, for every £100, or fraction thereof, insured		0	0	3
For every policy *for Time*, for every £100, and any fractional part of £100 thereby insured, for any time not exc. 6 months, 3d. ; not exc. 12 mos.		0	0	6

INVENTORY DUTY. *See* ESTATE DUTY.

LAND TAX.—The quota payable by each Parish as fixed in the year 1798 (less the amount redeemed) is raised by an equal pound rate, the rate of Assessment not to exceed 1s. in the £. Where the income of the owner of the land does not exceed £160 he is exempt from payment of land tax, and if the owner's income does not exceed £400 one half of the tax is remitted.

LEASES :—Lease or tack of any dwelling-house or part thereof for any definite term not exceeding a year at a rent not exceeding £10 per annum, 1d. ; for any definite term less than a year of any furnished dwelling-house or apartments where the rent for such term exceeds £25, 2s. 6d. ; of any lands, tenements, &c., at a yearly rent :—

Exceed.	Not Exceed.	Not exceeding 35 years.			Between 35 years and 100.			Exceeding 100 years.		
	£5	0	0	6	0	3	0	0	6	0
£5	10	0	1	0	0	6	0	0	12	0
10	15	0	1	6	0	9	0	0	18	0
15	20	0	2	0	0	12	0	1	4	0
20	25	0	2	6	0	15	0	1	10	0
25	50	0	5	0	1	10	0	3	0	0
50	75	0	7	6	2	5	0	4	10	0
75	100	0	10	0	3	0	0	6	0	0
100, for £50, or frct. part of £50		5	0	0	1	10	0	3	0	0

Agreement for lease not exceeding 35 years, same as actual lease.

LEGACY AND SUCCESSION DUTIES :—*Also see* "*Estate Duty.*"

If the deceased died on or after the 1st June, 1881, every pecuniary Legacy or Residue, or share of Residue, although not of the amount or value of £20, is chargeable with Duty by the 44 Vict. c. 12, s. 42.— Except in the cases of small estates, see note to Estate Duty.

No succession duty is payable where the principal value of all the successions on the same death does not amount to £100: 16 & 17 Vict. c. 51, s. 18.)

Rates of duties payable on legacies, annuities, and residues (£1 *per cent. Legacy Duty practically abolished since* 1881), and of Succession Duties where deceased died before 1st July, 1888, or where Estate Duty, Finance Act, 1894, is payable (*in which latter case* 1 *per cent. is also practically abolished*).

To Children of the Deceased, or their Descendants, or to the Father or Mother or other Lineal Ancestor of the Deceased (see above) ....£1 per cent.

To Brothers and Sisters of the Deceased, or their Descendants ....£3 per cent.

To Brothers and Sisters of the Father or Mother of the Deceased, or their Descendants ....£5 per cent.

To Brothers and Sisters of the Grandfather or Grandmother of the Deceased, or their Descendants ....£6 per cent.

To any Person in any other degree of collateral Consanguinity, or to a Stranger in Blood to the Deceased ....£10 per cent.

Where deceased died on or after 1 July, 1888, and Probate or Estate Duty is not payable, Succession Duties for the relationships above are at rates of 1½, 4½, 6½, 7½, and 11½ respectively.

The Husband or Wife is chargeable with Estate Duty, but not Legacy or Succession Duty ; and the Husband or Wife of a relation is chargeable at the rate at which the relation would be charged.

Penalties.—Persons paying or receiving any Legacy, Residue, or Share of Residue liable to Duty, without taking or signing the proper Receipt for the same. Persons not giving notice of a succession, or not delivering an account, are subject to certain Penalties.

	£	s.	d.
LETTERS OF ALLOTMENT AND OF RENUNCIATION			
Less than £5			1d.
£5 and upwards			6d.
6. & 63 Vict. c. 9, s. 9 (3).			
LETTERS OF MARQUE AND REPRISAL			£5

LETTERS PATENT, GRANT OF, to any honour or dignity, viz. : Duke, £350 ; Marquis, £300 ; Earl, £250 ; Viscount, £200 Baron, £150 ; Precedence, £100 ; Baronet, £100 ; *Congé d'élire* to elect an Archbishop or Bishop, £30 ; any other honour, dignity, or franchise, £30. Change of surname or arms, in accordance with will, £50 : upon voluntary application (£10).

LOAN CAPITAL DUTY (*v.* Capital Duty (Loan)).

	£	s.	d.
MALE SERVANTS, ANNUAL LICENCE.— Great Britain. Every male servant	0	15	0

MARKETABLE SECURITIES (transferable by delivery):—
(1) (*a*) Colonial Government Securities
(*b*) Securities dated between 3rd June, 1852 and 7th August, 1885 (Interest payable in U. K.) same duty as on *mortgage Bond, &c.*, (q.v.).

	£	s.	d.
(2) Of any other description, for every £10 or fractional part of £10	0	1	0
(3) Foreign Share Certificates (secs. 4 (2) and 6 of Finance Act, 1899) for every £25 or fractional part of £25	0	0	3
MARRIAGE LICENCE, special, England and Ireland	5	0	0
Not special (*see* pages 402-404)	0	10	0

MEDICINES (Patent) Great Britain only :—

	£	s.	d.		£	s.	d.
Not exc. 1s.	0	0	1½	Not exc. 20s.	0	2	0
„ 2s.6d.	0	0	3	„ 30s.	0	3	0
„ 4s.	0	0	6	„ 50s.	0	10	0
„ 10s.	0	1	0	Exceed. 50s.	1	0	0

	£	s.	d.
Medicines (Patent), dealers, &c., Annual Licence (Great Britain), for each set of premises	0	5	0
MORTGAGE BOND, &c., not exceeding £10	0	0	3

	£	s.	d.		£	s.	d.
Not exc. £25	0	0	8	Not exc. £200	0	5	0
„ 50	0	1	3	„ 250	0	6	3
„ 100	0	2	6	„ 300	0	7	6
„ 150	0	3	9				

	£	s.	d.
Exceeding £300, for every £100 and fractional part of £100	0	2	6
Transfer of Mortgage (except marketable securities) for every £100	0	0	6
Reconveyance, Release, &c., for every £100	0	0	6

MOTOR CAR LICENCES, *vide* CARRIAGES.

	£	s.	d.
NOTARIAL ACT of any kind (except protests)	0	1	0

OCCASIONAL LICENCES, per day :—

	£	s.	d.		£	s.	d.
Publicans		2	6	Wine retailers .	0	1	0
Beer retailers .	1	0		Tobacco dealrs.	0	0	4

PASSENGER VESSELS, on board which exciseable liquors and tobacco are sold { Licence for a Year ... 5 0 0 / 1 day 1 0 0

PASSPORT 0 0 6
PATENT (LETTERS) for inventions :—
On application for provisional protection 1 0 0
On filing complete specification 3 0 0
Application for certificate of payment of renewal :—
Before the expiration of the 4th year from the date of the patent, and in respect of the—

	£	s.	d.		£	s.	d.
5th year	5	0	0	10th year	10	0	0
6th ,,	6	0	0	11th ,,	11	0	0
7th ,,	7	0	0	12th ,,	12	0	0
8th ,,	8	0	0	13th ,,	13	0	0
9th ,,	9	0	0	14th ,,	14	0	0

Other small fees are also payable of such amount as may be from time to time prescribed by the Board of Trade with the sanction of the Treasury.

PAWNBROKERS, ANNUAL LICENCE, U.K. 7 10 0
,, trading in plate without regard to weight, an additional 5 15 0
PEDLARS (Police Licence) 0 5 0
PLATE: Dealers in, annual licence, U.K.
Above 2 dwts. and under 2 oz. gold, or above 5 dwts. and under 30 oz. silver, in one article 2 6 0
2 oz. gold, or 30 oz. silver, or upwards 5 15 0
Refiners of gold or silver, annual licence, United Kingdom 5 15 0
POWER OF ATTORNEY, &c., receiving prize-money or wages......... 0 1 0
For sale, transfer, or acceptance of any of the Government funds not exceeding £100 (nominal amount)... 0 2 6
In any other case......... 0 10 0
For the receipt of dividends or interest of any stock, if for one payment only 0 1 0
In any other case......... 0 5 0
Proxy to vote at a meeting 0 0 1
Power of attorney of any other kind... 0 10 0
PROCURATION, Deed or other Instrument of 0 10 0
PROPERTY AND INCOME TAX. *In the £*
Schedule A, Lands, Tenements, &c. 0 0 8
Payable by Owner of property.
Relief is given in certain cases in respect of Income Tax under Sch. A to the extent of either $\frac{1}{8}$ or $\frac{1}{6}$ part of the assessment (57 & 58 Vict. c. 35). *In the £*
Schedule B, Nurseries & Mrkt. Grdns. ... 0 0 8
,, In respect of the Occupation of Farms, &c., on $\frac{1}{3}$rd of Annual Value (59 & 60 Vict. c. 28, s. 26).
Schedule C D, and E, Income......... 0 0 8

EXEMPTION AND ABATEMENTS.

Income exced.		Income not exceeding.	
	...	£160 Exempt from Taxation.	
£160	...	400 Abatement of £160	
400	...	500 ,,	150
500	...	600 ,,	120
600	...	700 ,,	70

When the total joint income of a husband and wife does not exceed £500, a wife can separate her claim for exemption or abatement from that of her husband on account of profits derived from any profession, employment, or vocation under Sch. D, or from any office or employment under Sch. E (57 & 58 Vict. c. 30, s. 34, s.s. 2), or from any business carried on by means of her own personal labour (60 & 61 Vict. c. 24, s. 5) provided the husband is assessable under Sch. D

PROTEST of any Bill of Exchange—
Where the duty on the Bill or Note does not exceed 1s., the same duty as the Bill or Note. £ s. d.
In any other case......... 0 1 0

PUBLICANS, Annual Licences, U.K., for Spirits, Beer, and Wine, to be consumed on the premises :—
If annual value is under £10 .... 4 10 0

	£	s.	d.		£	s.	d.
Under £15	6	0	0	Under £200	30	0	0
,, 20	8	0	0	,, 300	35	0	0
,, 25	11	0	0	,, 400	40	0	0
,, 30	14	0	0	,, 500	45	0	0
,, 40	17	0	0	,, 600	50	0	0
,, 50	20	0	0	,, 700	55	0	0
,, 100	25	0	0	£700&upwds.	60	0	0

Hotels and Theatres of the value of £50 and upwards pay no higher amount of licence duty than £20, and
Restaurant Keepers pay no higher amount than £30 under certain conditions.
*Publicans keeping their premises closed the whole of Sunday, or closing one hour sooner than otherwise required on week-days, pay only six-sevenths of the above amounts; and keeping closed on Sunday, and also closing one hour earlier each day through the week, only five-sevenths of the above amounts.

RAILWAYS, on passenger receipts per £100 (in Great Britain, but subject to an exemption in respect of fares not exceeding the rate of one penny a mile) :— £ s. d.
Urban District traffic 2 0 0
Other traffic 5 0 0
RECEIPTS, £2 or upwards 0 0 1
Penalty for not stamping 10 0 0
REFRESHMENT HOUSES, annual licence, England and Ireland, under £30 rent 0 10 6
,, ,, £30 or above 1 1 0
SCRIP CERTIFICATE, OR SCRIP 0 0 3
SETTLEMENTS.—Any deed whereby any definite sum or share is settled upon or for the benefit of a person, for every £100 or part of £100 .... 0 5 0
SHARE WARRANT and STOCK CERTIFICATE to Bearer :—
1. Of any Company in the U.K. *on issue*, per cent. on nominal value 1 15 0
2. Of any Foreign or Colonial Company *on first delivery* in U.K., for every £10 or fractional part of £10 .... 0 1 0
SPIRITS, home-made, per proof gallon ... 0 10 5
,, imported from Channel Islands, per proof gall. 0 10 10
SPIRITS, Annual Licences, U.K., rectifiers and compounders 10 10 0
,, Dealers not retailers, ditto 10 10 0
,, ,, to sell in bottles, add.(E.) 3 3 0
,, ,, or to sell foreign liqueurs only in bottles .. 2 2 0
,, (Methylated), makers of 10 10 0
,, ,, retailers of 0 10 0
,, Retailers of.—See Publicans.

		£	s.	d.
SPIRITS, SCOTLAND, Grocers (*including sale of beer*), not to be consumed on premises :—				
Premises under value of £10		4	4	0
Of value of £10 and under £20		5	5	0
,, 20 ,, 25		9	9	0
,, 25 ,, 30		10	10	0
,, 30 ,, 40		11	11	0
,, 40 ,, 50		12	12	0
,, 50 and upwards		13	13	0

SPIRITS, IRELAND, Grocers, selling spirits not to be consumed on premises :—

		£	s.	d.
If rated under £25		9	18	5
If rated at £25 and under £30		11	0	6
,, 30 ,, 40		12	2	6
,, 40 ,, 50		13	4	7
,, 50 and upwards		14	6	7

The sale of methylated spirits is prohibited between the hours of 10 o'clock on Saturday evening and 8 o'clock on the following Monday morning under penalty of £100 (52 & 53 Vict. c. 42).

		£	s.	d.
STILLS or RETORTS, annual, U.K.— Chemists and others, keeping or using		0	10	0
SWEETS, dealers in, annual licence, U.K.		5	5	0
,, *Retailers of, annual, U.K. ...*		1	5	0

See also PUBLICANS.

SUCCESSION DUTIES—*see* LEGACY DUTIES.

		£	s.	d.
TOBACCO and Snuff, U.K., annual :— Dealers in		0	5	3
Tobacco Manufacturers, not exceeding 20,000 lbs.		5	5	0
Exc. 20,000 lbs. and not exc. 40,000		10	10	0
40,000 ,, 60,000		15	15	0
60,000 ,, 80,000		21	0	0
80,000 ,, 100,000		26	5	0
100,000		31	10	0

Beginners to pay £5 5s. and a surcharge on renewal.

TRANSFER OF STOCK.—*See* CONVEYANCE.

		£	s.	d.
Transfer of Share in Cost-Book Mines...		0	0	6
VALUATION, *see* APPRAISEMENT.				
VINEGAR-MAKERS, annual licence, U.K.		1	0	0
VOTING PAPER or PROXY		0	0	1
WARRANT FOR GOODS		0	0	3
WINE, annual licences, U.K. :— Dealers (wine only)		10	10	0
Retailers, selling for consumption on the premises. (*See also* PUBLICANS)		3	10	0
Wine retailers (or grocers), England and Ireland, selling wine not to be consumed on the premises		2	10	0
Do., grocers, Scotland (off)		2	4	1

SPOILED STAMPS.

ALL applications for allowance must be made within two years from the time of spoilage of unexecuted instruments, or within two years of the date or of the first execution of others.

The hours of attendance for the allowance of spoiled stamps at Somerset House are from 11 to 3; Saturday, 10 to 1. At Telegraph Street, E.C. for the allowance of sea policy and general spoiled stamps, are from 11 to 3 on Monday Wednesday, and Friday.

DEEDS STAMPED AFTER EXECUTION.

REGULATIONS under which the Commissioners as a general rule allow deeds and other instruments to be stamped after execution.

WITHOUT PENALTY, ON PAYMENT OF THE DUTY ONLY :—

Agreements under hand only, liable to the duty of 6d.—Agreements for letting furnished houses for less than a year.—Appraisements.

—Attested copies, within 14 days of *first* execution.

Life policies, within one month of *first* execution.

Foreign sea policies, within 10 days of arrival in U.K.

Deeds and instruments not otherwise excepted, within 30 days of *first* execution.

NOTE.—Where the deed or instrument has been wholly executed *abroad*, the period within which it may be stamped begins to reckon from the date of its arrival here.

WITH PENALTY IN ADDITION TO PAYMENT OF THE DUTY :—

Articles of clerkship.

Bills of exchange upon stamps of sufficient amount but of improper denomination.

Charter-parties. Receipts, within certain limits of time.—*Vide* Table of Penalties.

Contract notes. Delivery orders.

Letters of allotment. Scrip certificates.

Share warrants. Warrants for goods.

Policies of insurance liable to fixed duty of 1d.

INSTRUMENTS WHICH CANNOT BE LEGALLY STAMPED AFTER EXECUTION :—

Bills of exchange (except as before mentioned).—Bills of lading.

Marine policies executed in the United Kingdom. Proxies.—Voting papers

TABLE OF PENALTIES USUALLY ENFORCED :—

	£	s.	d.
Agreements under hand only. Attested copies or extracts : after the expiration of 14 days from their first execution	10	0	0
Charter-parties, within 7 days from their first execution	0	4	6
Charter-parties after the expiration of 7 days, but within one month	10	0	0
Receipts, within 14 days after they have been given	5	0	0
Receipts, after 14 days, but within one month (beyond this period receipts cannot be stamped under any conditions)	10	0	0
Other instruments not enumerated, excepting those which cannot be legally stamped after execution	10	0	0

In addition to these penalties certain documents are also liable by way of further penalty on stamping to a forfeiture of an amount equal to the stamp duty deficient.

All applications for the remission, mitigation, or return of penalties must be made by memorial, addressed to the Commissioners of Inland Revenue, Somerset House, and supported by statutory declaration, such declaration being exempt from stamp duty.

EXEMPTION FROM ALL STAMP DUTIES :—

Transfers of shares in the Government or Parliamentary Stocks or Funds.

COMPANIES ACT, 1862.

FEES TO BE PAID BY STAMPS.

On registration, with a capital of £2,000, £2; £3,000, £3; £4,000, £4; £5,000, £5.

Five shillings extra per £1,000 above £5,000 up to £100,000; 1s. extra per £1,000 above £100,000; but no fee higher than £50.

Deed stamp 10s. to be put both upon Memorandum and Articles of Association.

For ad valorem stamp on capital see p. 430

HOURS AT SOMERSET HOUSE.

Inland Revenue Office, 10 to 5. No money received after 4 (Saturdays, 2).

Stamp Office. Stamps issued from 10 to 4 (Saturdays, 10 to 2).

Impressed Stamps, 10 to 4 (Saturdays, 10 to 2).

INLAND POSTAL RATES.

THE prepaid postage of Letters, Books, and Parcels to any part of the United Kingdom, including the Orkney and Shetland Islands, the Channel Islands, Isle of Man, and the Scilly Islands, is as follows:—

LETTER POST.

Not exceeding 4 oz.	1d.
For every additional 2 oz.	½d.

BOOK POST.

Not exceeding 2 oz.	½d.

PARCEL POST.

Not exceeding.	s.	d.	Not exceeding.	s.	d.
1 lb.	0	3	6 lb.	0	8
2 ,, ...	0	4	7 ,, ...	0	9
3 ,, ...	0	5	8 ,, ...	0	10
4 ,, ...	0	6	9 ,, ...	0	11
5 ,, ...	0	7	11 ,, ...	1	0

NEWSPAPERS.—A prepaid postage of one halfpenny is charged for the inland transmission of any daily or weekly *registered* newspaper, the weight being disregarded. If more than one paper be included in a packet, the charge is as by an insufficiently paid letter, or transferred to the Parcel Post, whichever charge is the lower, with a fine of 1a. in addition to any deficient postage.

WEIGHTS AND DIMENSIONS.

LETTERS.—The weight is unlimited. Maximum length 2 ft.; width 1 ft.; depth 1 ft., unless sent to or from a Government office.

NEWSPAPERS.—Not over 5 lbs. in weight, 2 ft. in length or 1 ft. in width or depth.

BOOK POST.—Packets exceeding 2 oz. now pass unconditionally at the rate of 1d. for the first 4 oz., and ½d. for every additional 2 oz. The limits of length, width, and depth are the same as those of letters.

PARCELS.—The limit of weight is 11 lbs. The parcel must not be more than 3 ft. 6 ins. in length, or length and girth combined, more than 6 ft. A short parcel may be thicker: thus, if it measure no more than 3 ft. in length, it may measure as much as 3 ft. in girth, *i.e.*, round its thickest part.

GENERAL REGULATIONS.

If the postage of letters, books, or newspapers be not paid in advance, *double postage* will be demanded on delivery; and if the postage be insufficient, *double the deficiency* will be charged. Parcels are not accepted for transmission unless the charges are prepaid.

No advertisement, decoration or printed matter, beyond the address, is permitted on the right hand half of the address side of envelope or wrapper.

BOOK POST.—Packets not exceeding 2 oz. in weight may be sent for ½d. if the following conditions are complied with.

Any matter wholly printed on paper (paper sent as stationery not admissible), books and periodicals, manuscript, invoices, deeds and agreements, circulars produced in identical terms by any mechanical process (but not to include typewriting or imitations thereof) prints or photographs (when not on glass, or in cases containing glass, or any like substance), together with the legitimate binding or mounting, and anything necessary for safe transmission. The packet must be open at the ends, but may be tied with string, or in an unfastened envelope, or cover easily removed, and must contain no communication in the nature of a letter.

CONVEYANCE OF SINGLE LETTERS BY RAIL.—On payment of 2d. to a servant of the railway, in addition to the usual 1d. stamp, *Inland* letters not exceeding 4 oz. may be forwarded by the next available train or steamship by those companies in agreement with the Post Office, to be called for at the station to which the letter is addressed, or to be transferred thence to the nearest letter-box for postal delivery. The letter must be taken to a passenger station of the railway company. Railway letters may be handed in at any express delivery post office for immediate conveyance to the railway station by special messenger on payment of the express fee of 3d. per mile.

EXPRESS DELIVERY SERVICE.— Letters and parcels are now forwarded immediately in the London postal area, and at almost all provincial postal-telegraph offices, by special messengers, at the following rates:—Not exceeding 1 lb. in weight, inclusive of railway, omnibus, or tramcar charges, for every mile or part of mile, 3d. If the distance exceeds two miles and a public conveyance is not available, a special conveyance must be paid for. Ordinary postage is not charged. If the packet exceeds 1 lb. in weight, for each lb. or part beyond first lb., 1d., maximum charge, 1s. Maximum weight 20lbs; or if a public conveyance is not available, 15lbs. Cabs may be used if specially paid for. Fees to be paid in stamps. Express mail letters may not be posted in any letter box, but must be handed in over the counter, and clearly marked *Express Delivery* above the address on the left-hand corner of the cover. No Express Delivery on Sundays, Good Friday (except in Scotland), and Christmas Day. Articles of a dangerous or offensive nature are prohibited.

NEWSPAPERS.—No writing in the nature of a letter is permitted, but the wrapper may bear the name and address of the sender, and a reference to any page of its contents to which it is desired to draw attention.

NOTICE OF REMOVAL and for the re-direction of letters must be given on printed forms, to be obtained from the local postmaster or from postmen. A separate form must be filled in for the re-direction of parcels. The notice holds good for twelve months.

PARCEL POST.—The parcel should be distinctly marked in the left-hand top corner "Parcel Post," and handed across the counter of the receiving houses or given to a rural postman. It must not be posted in a letter-box, and the postage must be prepaid by stamps, affixed by the sender. The hours for Parcel Post business are the same as for general postal business. Money is received at the District Offices in London, at the offices at Charing Cross, Gracechurch Street, Lombard Street, Mark Lane, Ludgate Circus, and Battersea, and at the head offices at Edinburgh and Dublin, and in certain large provincial towns when the postage of a number of parcels amounts to 20s. These parcels must be presented at the offices between 9 a.m. and 3.30 p.m. (Battersea to 3 p.m.), and must be tied up in bundles representing a postage of 5s. each. Money payments as above are also received at the Chief Office till 4 p.m. Parcels will be collected in London and a few large towns when the number reaches 10 at a time, or 50 a week. The name and address of sender should be on the outside of every parcel. A greater weight than 11 lbs. must not be accepted from one person by a rural postman on foot, or 21 lbs. by a mounted postman, unless he shall have received notice on the day previous that a greater weight would be sent; and either of them may refuse parcels if already loaded.

Parcels left "to be called for" are charged **1d.** a day after they have lain in the office one clear day, the maximum charge being **1s. 5d.**

Parcels addressed to, or sent from the Channel Islands, are liable to customs duty, and the sender must make a declaration of contents at the office of posting. Parcels for the Isle of Man are treated as those for the British Isles generally.

No parcels are *received* on Sundays, Christmas Day, or (except in Scotland) Good Friday. For Bank Holidays, see page **440**.

Insurance.—Compensation to the amount of **£2** can be claimed for loss or damage. To secure compensation where no insurance fee is paid, a certificate of posting should be filled up and handed in for the signature of the post-office official. The insurance fee in stamps can be paid only at a post office. *See also* REGISTRATION *below.*

(No compensation will be granted for loss or damage of parcels containing money, watches, or jewellery, unless registered, or for damage done to a fragile or perishable article.

POSTE RESTANTE.—This is intended solely for the accommodation of strangers and travellers who have no permanent abode in the town. Letters and parcels may be addressed to the Poste Restante at every Head Post Office in the United Kingdom and to all Branch Post Offices in London. Letters or parcels to be called for should have the words "Poste Restante" included in the address. No initials, or fictitious names, or Christian name only, will be taken in, but are at once sent to the Returned Letter Office for disposal; and all persons applying for "Poste Restante" letters must prove their identity. Foreigners must produce their passports. Poste Restante letters from abroad are not kept more than two months; at Provincial Post Offices only one month; letters posted in London, for one fortnight. After these intervals they are sent up to the Returned Letter Office. When, however, letters addressed "to be called for" bear a request for their return within a specified time, if not delivered, they are dealt with in accordance with such request.

RE-DIRECTION.—*Letters* re-posted unopened more than a day after delivery are charged with postage at the prepaid rate. If re-posted the same day no charge is made, provided they do not appear to have been opened or tampered with. *Parcels* may be re-directed free of charge if the original address and the corrected address are both in a delivery from the same office, otherwise they are charged again at the ordinary prepaid rate. *Post-cards, book-packets, and newspapers* are permitted to be re-directed, under the same conditions as those relating to *letters.*

REGISTRATION.—The fee for registering an inland letter, newspaper, or postal packet (including parcels) is 2*d.* in addition to the postage. These must be handed to an agent of the Post Office, and a receipt taken. By prepayment of a fee of **2*d.*** in addition to the postage and registration fee, the sender of a registered letter may obtain an acknowledgment of its due delivery. The latest time for registering for the night mails is usually half an hour before the box closes for letters; in the case of parcels, half an hour before the latest time for posting ordinary parcels. If an inland packet marked "Registered" be put in a letter-box it will be liable on delivery to a charge of **4*d.***, less any amount prepaid for registration. The payment of the registration fee effects an insurance on the packet against loss or damage up to £120, at the following rates:—Fee 2*d.*, compensation £5; **3*d*, £10; 4*d.*, £20; 5*d.*, £30; 6*d.*, £40; 7*d.*, £50; 8*d.*, £60; 9*d.*, £70; 10*d.*, £80; 11*d.*, £90; 1*s.*, £100; 1*s.* 1*d.*, £110; 1*s.* 2*d.*, £120.**

RETURNED AND MISSING LETTERS.—Inland letters undelivered, bearing full name and address of sender, are returned unopened; others are opened and returned if possible to senders, a registration fee of **2*d.*** being charged should anything of value be inside. If without an address, and containing nothing of value, they are at once destroyed. Undelivered foreign letters are returned, unopened, to the countries whence received. If senders of ½*d.* packets place a request for their return, in the upper left hand corner of the outside cover, in case of non-delivery, a second postage is charged the sender on their return, otherwise they are disposed of at the Head Office. Inquiries for missing letters should be made at the Secretary's office, G. P. O. North, St. Martin's-le-Grand, between **10** a.m. and **5** p.m.; Saturdays between **10** a.m. and **1.30** p.m. The Returned Letter Office is at Mount Pleasant, E.C.

SOLDIERS' AND SEAMEN'S LETTERS.—Letters to or from non-commissioned officers, private soldiers and seamen serving abroad, the Cape Mounted Rifles, and enrolled pensioners in Canada, not exceeding ½ oz., are forwarded for 1*d.* If posted for a place abroad unpaid, or insufficiently paid, or the description of the soldier, &c., be not given, it will be detained and returned to sender for payment of the postage.

STAMPS, ENVELOPES, ETC.

POSTAGE STAMPS (used also for receipts, telegrams, and certain Inland Revenue duties up to **2*s.* 6*d.***) are sold of the respective values of ½*d.*, 1*d.*, 1½*d.*, 2*d.*, 2½*d.*, 3*d.*, 4*d.*, 4½*d.*, 5*d.*, 6*d.*, 9*d.*, 10*d.*, 1*s.*, 2*s.* 6*d.*, 5*s.*, 10*s.*, 20*s.*, and £5. These may be purchased at most offices between 8 a.m. and 8 p.m., and at any office during the hours that attendance is given for telegraph business. Rural postmen are authorised to sell 1*d.* stamps and registered letter envelopes.

The perforation of stamps with *initials* is recommended. The perforation of the stamps on post-cards, newspaper wrappers and embossed envelopes is also not objected to. Stamps perforated otherwise than with initials, embossed stamps, or stamps cut from envelopes, wrappers or post-cards, are not available for postage.

EMBOSSED ENVELOPES.—Embossed Halfpenny Envelopes are in two sizes, Commercial, in packets of 10 for 5½*d.*, and Foolscap, 10 for 6*d.*; they are also sold singly. Penny Envelopes of the following sizes are kept in stock:—**A**, 4¾ × 3$\frac{11}{16}$, in packets of 20 for **1*s.* 10*d.***; **C**, 5¼ × 3, **24** for 2*s.* 2*d.*; and a cheaper quality (Commercial), 20 for **1*s.*** 9*d.*; but all may be had in smaller numbers. Envelopes embossed with a twopence-halfpenny stamp (sizes **L**, 5½ × 3$\frac{1}{16}$, and **M**, 5½ × 4⅜ ins.) are sold at the following rates:—**L**, 1 for 2¾*d.*, 10 for 2*s.* 2½*d.*; **M**, 1 for 2¾*d.*, 10 for 2*s.* 3*d.*

REGISTERED LETTER ENVELOPES, for foreign and inland letters, bearing a twopenny stamp embossed on the flap for the payment of the registration fees, are of five sizes, and are sold: **F**, 5¼ ins. × 3¼ ins.; **G**, 6 ins. × 3¾ ins., 2¼*d.* each, or 12 for 2*s.* 2½*d.*; **H**, 8 ins. × 5 ins., **H²**, 9 ins. × 4 ins., 2¾*d.* each, or 12 for 2*s.* 7*d.*; **K**, 11½ ins. × 6 ins., 3*d.* each, or 12 for 2*s.* 10*d.*

LETTER CARDS are sold thus:—**1** for **1¼*d.***, and **8** for **9*d.***, also in packets of **96** for **9*s.***

POST-CARDS impressed with a halfpenny stamp are sold at the rate of 10 for 5½d., or 11s. per parcel of 240; a thicker quality being 10 for 6d., or 5s. per parcel of 100. They can also be had in sheets of 42 cards at £11 8s. and £12 6s. per quarter ream (120 sheets) respectively. Reply Post-cards are about double the rates for single cards, but are not sold in sheets.

COLONIAL AND FOREIGN POST-CARDS are supplied in packets of 10, price 10d.; singly, 1d.

Private cards, bearing an adhesive ½d. stamp and corresponding as nearly as possible to the size and weight of the official card, may be used.

Private Post Cards are also admissible for foreign and colonial post provided they have "Post Card" printed on them and are in conformity with the official cards in size and weight.

WRAPPERS bearing a halfpenny stamp may be had at ¾d. each or 7 for 4d.; 5s. 8½d. per parcel of 120. With a penny stamp the price is, singly 1¼d., or 4 for every 4¼d.; 10s. 7½d. per parcel of 120. Uncut sheets of *halfpenny* wrappers, 14 on each sheet, may be obtained in quarter reams of 120 sheets for £3 18s.

LONDON POSTAL ARRANGEMENTS.

FOR the purpose of facilitating the collection and delivery of letters, the Metropolis is divided into eight districts, marked:—

East Central (E.C.)	South Eastern (S.E.)
Eastern (E. and N.E.)	South Western (S.W.)
Northern (N.)	Western (W.)
North Western (N.W.)	West Central (W.C.)

Of these the E.C.—comprising the whole of the City, the W.C.—the district between Temple Bar and Charing Cross, and the S.W.—containing nearly all the Government Offices, are the most important. In the E.C. or City district there are twelve deliveries daily. By appending the initials the sorting of letters is facilitated, and frequently two or more hours saved in the delivery. In the other districts there are from six to eleven collections and deliveries. Letters properly directed, and properly posted, should be delivered within from two to four hours.

FOR THE COUNTRY AND ABROAD.—Letters and cards to go the same evening should be posted at Chief District offices, Branch offices, Receiving houses, and Pillar boxes before 6; in suburban places, half an hour to an hour and a half earlier.

LATE INLAND LETTERS.—Inland letters and post-cards bearing an extra ½d. stamp are forwarded by the night mails if posted at the town Branch offices and Receiving houses before 7 p.m., and at St. Martin's-le-Grand before 7.45. At certain District offices the hour for posting with the late fee is 7.30 and 8, when the letters are to go from the railways in their immediate neighbourhoods. Letters having an extra ½d. stamp may also be posted at the sorting carriage or platform barrier at the various railway termini up to the time of the departure of the train bearing the mails, varying from 5.15 a.m. to 10 p.m.

NIGHT POSTING.—Country letters too late for the ordinary mails, but posted in the London districts before the 9 o'clock collection, are delivered by the first post next morning if for places (about 250) within the range of the supplementary night and midnight despatches. Later collections are made in London and the suburbs—mostly between 11 and 12—the letters, &c., for the provinces being despatched by the early morning trains, and those for London and suburban districts coming within the first morning delivery. For early trains and the same delivery a collection is made from 2 to 3 a.m. on certain main routes; also at many places in the N.W., S.W., W., and W.C. districts; and at 3.15 in the E.C. district. At all the Chief District Offices the boxes are cleared at 6 a.m. for the first delivery in London districts, and at 7 a.m. for local letters.

LATE FOREIGN LETTERS, with an extra 1d. stamp, may be posted till 7 o'clock at Aldermanbury, Barbican. Finsbury Square, Lombard Street, Gracechurch Street, Mark Lane, Eastcheap, Leadenhall Street, Throgmorton Avenue, Threadneedle Street, Fleet Street, Ludgate Circus, Charing Cross, Cannon Street, the District offices, and St. Martin's-le-Grand; with an extra 1d. at the latter office till 7.15, or till 7.30 with an extra 3d.

FOREIGN AND COLONIAL POST.

IMPERIAL PENNY POSTAGE.—The charge for letters to nearly all British Colonies and Possessions is 1d the half-ounce—the exceptions being the Australian Colonies, Tasmania, New Zealand. To these places and to all foreign countries the charge is 2½d. the half-ounce.

The Foreign Post-card Rates to all places to which Post-cards are available is 1d. single, 2d. return.

Inland cards are transmissible abroad if the additional postage be supplied by adhesive stamp.

BOOKS, NEWSPAPERS, &c.

NEWSPAPERS, BOOKS, PRINTED PAPERS, AND COMMERCIAL PAPERS generally, ½d. per 2 ozs.

PATTERNS AND SAMPLES, ½d. per 2 ozs.; but with a minimum charge of 1d.

COMMERCIAL PAPERS, ½d. per 2 ozs.; but with a minimum charge of 2½d.

The limits of size in British Possessions or non-Union countries* are—length 2 ft., width or depth 1 ft., and must not exceed 5 lbs. in weight. To countries in the Postal Union the length is limited to 18 in.; weight not to exceed 4 lbs. If in the form of a roll, the limits of size in either case are 30 in. in length and 4 in. in diameter.

The above-named rates should in all cases be prepaid; no packet can be sent forward wholly unpaid, but, if by inadvertence the postage is insufficiently prepaid, double the deficit will be chargeable on delivery.

MAILS for Canada are made up every Monday and Wednesday evening, and Saturday morning and afternoon; to the United States every Sunday, Wednesday afternoon, and Saturday morning and afternoon, and various other days; and to Newfoundland alternate Monday and Friday evenings.

To the West Indies alternate Wed. mornings.

To Australasia, every Monday evening, and various other days

To India, every Friday evening.

To China, Japan, Hong Kong and Ceylon, Monday evening, and various other days.

To Portugal, Morocco and Tangier, every morning; to Roumania every morning and evening; to Greece, Sunday, Monday and Thursday mornings, and every Friday evening.

To Egypt, Sunday; Monday morning, and Monday and Friday evening, and various other days; to Cyprus, Friday evening, and alternate Wednesday mornings; to Malta, every afternoon.

To the Cape and Rhodesia every Saturday afternoon; to West Coast of Africa every Tuesday and Friday evening; to Abyssinia, every Friday evening.

* Abyssinia, Afghanistan, Africa (Native possessions on the West Coast), Arabia, Bechuanaland Protectorate, British Central Africa, China, Friendly Islands, Madagascar, Morocco, Niger Protectorate, Samoa, Sierra Leone Protectorate, Society Islands.

To Buenos Aires, Monte Video, and Rio Janeiro, alternate Monday mornings and Saturday evenings.

To Mexico, Wednesday evening and Saturday afternoon; to Chile, alternate saturdays, morning and evening, and various other days, with U. S. mails.

To other parts of the world, the places and rates are too numerous for insertion; particulars may be obtained at every Receiving house.

PARCEL POST.

The rules and regulations to be observed are similar to those relating to inland parcels, with the addition that every parcel must have a Customs declaration respecting the contents. This must be on a form obtainable at any Post Office. The sender may arrange to prepay all charges to certain British possessions and foreign countries by paying a fee of 6*d.*, making a deposit of 1*s.* for each 4*s.* value of the parcel and signing an undertaking to pay all Customs and other charges on demand; otherwise they are collected on delivery. Certain articles are prohibited; among them letters nearly everywhere; gold, silver, jewellery, and firearms to many places; opium to Hong Kong, Siam and India; and pork and bacon to some places. The "Triple system" of 3lbs. 1*s.*, 7lbs. 2*s.* and 11lbs 3*s.*, is charged to the following Colonies:—Ascension, Bahamas, Bermuda, Brit. East Africa, Brit. Guiana, Brit. Honduras, Ceylon, Cyprus, Falkland Islands, Gambia, Gibraltar, Gold Coast, Grenada, Lagos, Leeward Islands, Malta (viâ France, 3lbs. 2*s.*, 7lbs. 3*s.*, 11lbs. 4*s.*), Mauritius (viâ France. 3lb. 3*s.* 2*d.*, 7lbs. 3*s.* 9*d.*, 11lbs. 4*s.* 4*d.*), Newfoundland, Niger Coast, St. Helena, St. Lucia, St. Vincent, Sarawak, Seychelles, Sierra Leone, Straits Settlements, Trinidad, Tobago, Zanzibar. The charges for India, other Colonies and for Foreign Countries are as follow:—

	Per lb. to 1 lb. 11 lbs.	Per lb. to 1lb. 11lbs.
	s. d. s. d.	*s. d. s. d.*
Australasia	1 0 .. 0 6	India & Aden, 1 lb. 1*s.* ;
*Bechuanaland		3lb. 2*s.* 4*d.* ; 11lb. 3*s.*
Protectorate	2 9 .. 2 9	Jamaica........ 0 9 ..0 9
*British Central		Labuan ...... 0 11 ..0 8
Africa	1 6 .. 1 6	Natal .... 0 9 ..0 9
Canada	0 8 .. 0 6	North Borneo . 0 11 ..0 8
Cape Colony ..	0 9 .. 0 9	*Rhodesia ...... 2 9 .. 2 9
Fiji	1 0 .. 0 8	St. Thomas, 3 lbs. 1*s.* 9*d.* ;
Hong Kong ..	0 9 .. 0 6	7 lbs. 3*s.* 0*d.* ; 11 lbs. 4*s.* 3*d.*

Foreign Countries.	3 lb.	7 lb.	11 lb.
	s. d.	*s. d.*	*s. d.*
Algeria	1 9	2 2	2 7
Annam	3 10	4 3	4 8
Argentine	2 4	3 7	4 10
Austria H., *viâ* Hamburg ..	1 5½	1 11½	2 4
,, *viâ* Belgium	1 9	2 2	2 7
Azores	2 5	2 10	3 3
Belgium	1 3	1 8	2 2½
†Bulgaria, *viâ* Cologne.....	2 3	3 0	..
,, *viâ* Hamburg ...	2 5	3 0	..
Cameroons	2 3	2 10	3 3
Cape Verd Is.	2 5	2 10	3 3
Cayenne	3 1	3 6	.. 11
Chili	3 9	4 2	4 7
,, *viâ* France	3 10	4 3	4 8
China (some places). 1 lb. 9*d.*, then 6*d.* per lb. to 11 lbs.			
Cochin China	3 10	4 3	4 8
Colombia	2 0	3 0	4 0
Congo	2 7	3 0	3 5
Costa Rica	2 4	3 10	5 6

* The limit of weight to Bechuanaland Protectorate, British Central Africa and Rhodesia is 7 lbs.

† Parcels over 6½ lbs. (3 kilograms) are subject to surtax on delivery.

Foreign Countries—*continued.*	3 lb.	7 lb.	11 lb.
	s. d.	*s. d.*	*s. d.*
Denmark, *viâ* Hamburg.......	1 5	2 0	2 5
,, *viâ* Belgium	1 9	2 2	2 7
Dutch East Indies	3 11	4 4	4 9
,, Guiana	3 6	4 0	4 6
,, West Indies	3 6	4 0	4 6
Egypt, *viâ* P. & O.	1 0	2 0	3 0
,, *viâ* France	2 0	3	4 0
Finland (*viâ* Sweden)	2 3	2 9	3 ;
France	1 4	1 9	2 2
French Congo	3 1	3 6	3 11
German E. Africa	4 2	4 7	5 0
,, S.W. ,, *viâ* Walfisch Bay..	3 10	4 5	4 10
,, ,, *viâ* Cape Town ..	5 7	6 2	..
Germany	1 0	1 7	2 0
,, *viâ* Belgium	1 4	1 9	2 2
Greece	2 3	2 9	3 3
Guadaloupe	3 1	3 6	3 11
Hawaii. 1 lb. 1*s.* 0*d.*, then 1*s.* per lb. to 11 lbs.			
Holland	1 0	1 8	2 3
Honduras	2 4	4 0	5 8
Italy, *viâ* France	1 8	2 1	2 6
,, *viâ* Belgium	2 4	2 9	3 2
Japan, *viâ* Canada	1 10	3 6	5 2
Java	3 11	4 4	4 9
Liberia	1 10	3 6	5 2
Luxemburg	3 1	3 8	5 0
Madagascar	3 1	3 8	3 11
Madeira	2 0	2 5	2 10
Martinique	3 1	3 6	3 11
§Mexico	1 0	2 6	3 6
Montenegro, *viâ* Hamburg	2 3	2 10	3 3
,, *viâ* Cologne	2 7	3 0	3 5
¶Morocco, *viâ* France	1 10	2 3	2 8
,, *viâ* Hamburg	2 3	2 10	3 3
Norway	0 10½	1 5½	2 1
Obock	2 3	2 8	3 1
Orange Free State. 1 lb. 1*s.* 0*d.*, then 1*s.* per lb. to 11 lbs.			
Paraguay	2 8	4 0	..
Persia, *viâ* Gibraltar. 1 lb. 4*s.* 4*d.*			
,, *viâ* Marseilles	5 8	6 10	..
Peru	6 4	7 10	..
,, *viâ* France. 6½ lbs. 2*s.* 6*d.*	4 5	5 0	5 5
Portugal	1 7	2 0	2 5
Portuguese W. Africa .... {	2 5	2 10	3 3
	3 3	3 8	4 1
Reunion	3 1	3 6	3 11
‡Roumania, *viâ* Cologne	2 4	2 9	3 2
,, *viâ* Hamburg	2 0	2 7	3 0
Salvador	3 6	5 3	7 0
Samoa, *viâ* Hamburg	3 10	4 5	4 10
,, *viâ* N. Z. 1 lb. 1*s.* 2*d.*, then 10*d.* per lb. to 11 lbs.			
Senegal	2 3	2 8	3 1
Servia, *viâ* Cologne	2 2	2 7	3 0
,, *viâ* Hamburg	1 10	2 5	2 10
Siam. 1 lb. 1*s.* 0*d.*, then 6*d.* per lb. to 11 lbs.			
Spain, Ry. Stns. only. 6½ lbs. 2*s.* 1*d.*			
Sweden	1 2	2 3	2 11
Switzerland, *viâ* France	1 6	2 0	2 5
,, *viâ* Belgium ...	1 9	2 2	2 7
Tahiti	5 6	5 11	6 4
Tangier. 1 lb. 8*d.*, then 5*d.* per lb. to 11 lb.			
Tonquin	3 10	4 3	4 8
Transvaal. 1 lb. 1*s.* 0*d.*, then 1*s.* per lb. to 11 lbs.			
Tripoli	1 10	2 3	2 8
Tunis	2 3	2 8	3 1
Turkey, Austrian & French Agencies only, see foot of next page	2 3	2 8	3 1
Uruguay	..	..	4 6
Venezuela	3 8	4 1	4 6

To India and the Colonies generally and to Constantinople, Beyrout, Smyrna, and Egypt the maximum length is 3 feet 6 inches, or length and girth combined 6 feet; Canada, length 2 feet, depth or width 1 foot; to Italy, Spain, Greece, and parts of Turkey, length 2 feet, length and

‡ Parcels for Greece and Roumania must be packed in some stronger material than paper or cardboard.

§ Must be packed for opening by Customs.

¶ See also Tangier.

girth combined 4 feet; other places in Europe, 2 feet in any direction.

INSURANCE OF COLONIAL PARCELS.—Insurance may be effected for parcels to the following Colonies and possessions, up to either £50 or £120, according to destination, at the following rates:—
5d. for £12; 7½d. for £24; 10d. for £36; 1s. 0½d. for £48; 1s. 3d. for £60; 1s. 5½d. for £72; 1s. 8d. for £84; 1s. 10½d. for £96; 2s. 1d. for £108; 2s. 3½d. for £120. The parcels insured must comply with the regulations of the Colonial Parcel Post.

Aden	Gambia	Niger Coast
Antigua	Gibraltar	St. Helena
Ascension	Grenada	St. Kitts
Australia	Hong Kong	St. Lucia
Bahamas	India	St. Vincent
Barbados	Labuan	Sarawak
Bermuda	Lagos	Sierra Leone
British North	Mauritius	Straits Settlements.
British India	Montserrat	Tasmania
Ceylon [Borneo	Nevis	Tobago
Cyprus	Newfoundland	Tortola
Dominica	New Zealand	Trinidad
Falkland Islands		Zanzibar

MONEY AND POSTAL ORDERS.

MONEY ORDERS, INLAND.—The highest amount granted in one order is limited to £10. The commission charged is:—
For sums not exceeding £1, 2d.; £3, 3d.; £10, 4d. No order may contain a fractional part of 1d.

Money orders will under no circumstances be paid on the day of issue. The rules and regulations are on the forms issued.

TELEGRAPH MONEY ORDERS.—These are issued between all post offices authorised to transact telegraph and money order business. They are limited to £10, and the commission is for sums not exceeding £3, 4d.; above this, to £10, 6d., in addition to the charge for an advice to the postmaster and its repetition, the minimum being 6d. If the order is to be delivered at payee's address any charge for porterage must be prepaid.

POSTAL ORDERS.—Unlike Money Orders they are issued for fixed sums; those of 1s. and 1s. 6d., at a charge of ½d.; of 2s., 2s. 6d., 3s., 3s. 6d., 4s., 4s. 6d., 5s., 7s. 6d., 10s., and 10s. 6d., 1d.; those of 15s. and 20s., 1½d. These orders must be presented for payment within 3 months from last day of the month of issue, or a fresh commission will be charged. Stamps to the amount of 5d., but not fractions of 1d., may be affixed to the *face* of an order, so that practically any odd sum can be transmitted by means of postal orders. The name of the payee must be inserted by the purchaser before parting with it. Payment may be deferred for a period not exceeding ten days, by writing across the order the words "Payable after ——— days," and by inserting the name of the office of payment. Postal Orders are issued at all offices in the United Kingdom, and at Constantinople, Malta, and Gibraltar; they are issued, but not paid, in India, Straits Settlements, Hong Kong, and Newfoundland; they are payable at all Money Order Offices in the United Kingdom and Constantinople; also in Malta and Gibraltar, provided they were issued in the U. K. or Constantinople.

The Chief Money Order Office in London is at Mount Pleasant, E.C.

MONEY ORDERS, FOREIGN AND COLONIAL.—These are issued in the United Kingdom on the undermentioned places, the commission being for sums not exceeding £2, 6d.; £6, 1s.; £10, 1s. 6d.:—

*Aden	Fiji	Newfoundland
Amoy	*Finland	*New Guinea
Australasia	Foochow	(German)
*Austria	France and	Niger Coast P.
*†Austrian	Algeria	Ningpo
Agencies	Gambia	North Borneo
Bagdad	*Germany	*Norway
*Bahrain	*German E. & Orange Free St.
*Bassorah	S.W. Africa	Panama
*Belgium	Gibraltar	Pondicherry
Bermuda	*Goa	*Portugal (with
Brit Bechuanald	Gold Coast	Madeira and
British Columb.	*Guadur	the Azores)
British Guiana	Hankow	Rhodesia
Brit. Honduras	Hawaii	*Roumania
*Bulgaria	Hoihow	St. Helena
*Burma	*Holland	*Salvador
*Bushire	Hong Kong	Sarawak
*Cameroons and	*Hungary	*Servia
Togo	*Iceland	Seychelles Isls.
Canada	*India	Shanghai
Canton	*Italy	*Siam
Cape of Good	Japan	Sierra Leone
Hope	*Jask	Smyrna
Ceylon	Korea	Straits Settlemts
Chili	Lagos	Swatow
*Congo Free St.	*Linga	*Sweden
Constantinople	*Lux-mburg	*Switzerland
Cyprus	Malta	Tangier
*Danish West	Mauritius	Transvaal
Indies	*Mohammerah	*Tunis
*Denmark and	Mombasa	United States
Faroe Islands	*Muscat	West Indies
*Dutch E. Indies	Natal	Zanzibar
*Egypt	New Brunswick	Zululand
Falkland Islds.		

TELEGRAMS.

INLAND.—Telegrams may be sent to all parts of the United Kingdom at the rate of 6d. for the first twelve words, and one halfpenny for every additional word; stamps in payment to be affixed to the form by the sender. The address of the receiver is charged for, but not that of the sender when written on the *back* of the telegram form. Five figures are counted as one word. The charge includes delivery within the town postal limits, or within three miles of a head office—beyond that limit the charge is 3d. per mile from the office door. Porterage to be paid by sender. Telegram forms are of two kinds—one issued gratis; the other (A1), embossed with a stamp, may be purchased singly, or interleaved with carbonic paper, in books of 20, price 10s. 2d.

FOREIGN TELEGRAMS are subject to a code of 33 rules, too lengthy to be transcribed. The charges vary from 2d. a word to Belgium, France, Germany, and Holland, 2½d. to Luxembourg, 3d. to Algeria, Denmark, Italy, Switzerland, Austria H., Norway, and Tunis, 3½d. to Gibraltar, Morocco, Sweden, Portugal and Spain, 4d. to Bosnia-Herzegovina, Montenegro, Roumania, and Servia, 4½d. to Bulgaria, 5d. to Tangier, 5½d. to Russia and Spain *via* France, 6d. to Malta, 6½d. to Turkey, Cyprus and Greece, 8½d. to Tripoli, 9d. to the Azores and Canaries, 11d. to Turkish Islands, 1s.

* Orders issued for the places marked thus * are retained by the remitter.
† Austrian agencies are Adrianople, Beyrout, Candia, Canea, Chios, Dardanelles, Dédé Agatch, Durazzo, Gallipoli, Ineboli, Jaffa, Janina, Jerusalem, Kaifa, Kavala, Kerassonde, Lagos (Turkey), Mitylene Prevesa, Retimo, Rhodes, Salonica, Samsoun, Santi Quarante, Trebizond, Valona, Vathy-Samos.
French Agencies *for Parcels only*, are Alexandretta, Latakia, Mersina, and San Giovani de Medua.

to 1s. 6d. to Canada and United States, 3s. 8d. upwards to India. 4s. 7d. upwards to Australasia, and 3s. 6d. to 6s. 9 i. to South America.

SUNDAY TELEGRAMS.—In most provincial towns the Telegraph Offices are open from 8 to 10 a.m. in England; in Scotland and Ireland from 9 to 10 a.m. In London the following offices are always open:—G.P.O. Central; G.N.R., King's Cross (except from 1.30 to 2.30 p.m. on Sundays); G. E. R., Liverpool Street and Stratford; London Bridge (S. E. R.), Paddington, St. Pancras, Victoria (L. C. & D.), Waterloo and Willesden Stations, and West Strand Post Office, the offices at Birmingham; Bradford and Brighton (except between midnight Saturday and 8 a.m. Sunday); Bristol, Cardiff Docks, Derby, Devonport, Dover, Exeter, Falmouth, Holyhead, Hull, Leeds, Liverpool, Manchester, Newcastle-on-Tyne, Norwich, Nottingham, Penzance, Plymouth, Portsmouth, Sheffield, and Southampton; as also are those at Aberdeen, Dundee, Edinburgh, and Glasgow, in Scotland; and Belfast, Cork, Dublin, Londonderry, and Queenstown, in Ireland.

LONDON-PARIS TELEPHONE.—Public Call Offices, G. P. O., West (Bath Street), West Strand Branch, open always, and Threadneedle Street Branch (week days, 8 a.m. to 8 p.m). Fee—8s. per conversation of three minutes. Two *consecutive* conversations are permitted. NOTE.—Paris time is 10 minutes earlier than London time.

SUNDAY AND HOLIDAY ARRANGEMENTS.

At all offices in the PROVINCES which are open on Sunday, postage stamps are sold, and letters may be registered, during the time such offices are open. The same regulation applies to CHRISTMAS DAY and GOOD FRIDAY. In LONDON, letters cannot be registered on Sunday, except at certain railway stations, but on Good Friday and Christmas Day postage stamps are sold and letters may be registered at all offices which are open. The hours at which telegraph business is attended to are, as a rule, from 8 to 10 a.m.; but no Money Order, Savings Bank, Insurance, or Annuity Business is transacted on these days, nor in Scotland on Sacramental Fast Days.

BANK HOLIDAYS AND FAST DAYS.—Where Bank Holidays are observed as public holidays, the counters of the head office and branch offices are closed at 12 noon (in some small places they are not even opened) *except* for telegraph business, the reception of parcels, the sale of postage stamps, and the registration of letters. At no provincial town in England or Ireland is there more than one delivery of letters on Sunday, Christmas Day, or Good Friday; nor in Scotland on Sunday or the Sacramental Fast Days; and any person is at liberty to prevent even this delivery so far as relates to himself.

In London the holiday arrangements are of an exceptional character, and due notice of them is given by means of bills at the various offices.

THE DISTRICT MESSENGER SERVICE : Head Office, 100 St. Martin's Lane, W.C.

Originated in 1890 for the purpose of supplying electrical call boxes by means of which "messengers," "cabs," "police," "fire brigade," and "doctor" can be electrically summoned. By this system, messages, letters, parcels, &c., are conveyed under licence from the Postmaster-General from various stations to all parts of London, the Provinces and the Continent. Messengers are supplied for almost any purpose, and tickets for theatres can be obtained from any of the Company's offices, which are as follows:—

78 Park St., Mayfair, W.
Torrington Place Lodge, Torrington Sq., W.C.
Sloane Sq., S.W. (4 Holbein Place).
193 Piccadilly, W.
269 Regent St., Regent Circus, W.
27 Chancery Lane, E.C.
85A Brompton Rd., Albert Gate, S.W.
121 Finchley Rd., Swiss Cottage, N.W.
17 London St., Paddington, W.
Hotel Cecil, Strand, W.C.
2 Shorter's Court, Stock Exchange, E.C.
118 High St., Kensington, W.

Whitehall Court, S.W.
Holborn Restaurant.
Trafalgar Sq., S.W. (4 Charing Cross).
Artillery Mansions, 73A Victoria St., S.W.
82 Gloucester Rd., S. Kensington.
Charing Cross District Railway Station.
Westminster Bridge   ,,   ,,
Mansion House   ,,   ,,
Victoria St.   ,,   ,,
Broad St. House, Wormwood St., E.C.
66 Queen Victoria St., E.C.
120 Leadenhall St., E.C.

The charges are:—Half a mile and under, 4 i.; including reply 6d.; over half a mile to one mile (including reply), 6d.; over one mile to one mile and a half (including reply), 9d.; beyond this distance, special rates. Messengers can also be engaged at 8d. per hour, exclusive of railway or omnibus fares. The district offices are open day and night, including Sundays and Bank Holidays (except in City). The company holds itself responsible up to £20 for articles entrusted to its messengers, provided the value has been previously declared.

POST OFFICE SAVINGS BANKS.

These are established at all Money Order Offices, and are opened for the receipt of deposits during the hours appointed for the sale of stamps, commencing at 8 a.m. Every such office is also open for the payment of withdrawals on week days during certain hours, which are specified in a notice exhibited at the office.

Deposits can be made from 1s. to £50 in one year, the total never to exceed £200 including interest, which is at 2½ per cent.

ANNUITIES AND LIFE ASSURANCE.—Immediate or deferred annuities from £1 to £100 may be purchased through the Post Office on the life of any one over 5 years old. These are payable by equal half-yearly instalments.

Life insurances, from £5 to £100, are granted to persons between 14 and 65 years of age. Children between 8 and 14 can be insured for £5.

If the amount of the annuity or insurance purchased is less than £100, further amounts may be bought, until the total sum amounts to £100.

The Post Office Savings Bank is at 144A, Queen Victoria Street, E.C.

BRADBURY, AGNEW, & CO., LIMITED, PRINTERS, LONDON AND TONBRIDGE.

THE EMPIRE OF INDIA.

THE BRITISH EMPIRE IN INDIA extends over a territory larger than the Continent of Europe without Russia. Afghanistan, Nepal and Bhutan are within the sphere of its influence. Baluchistan (130,000 square miles) and Kashmir with its dependencies of Chitral, Hunza, Nagar, are within its frontier. On the north-west and on the north-east there are also tracts of tribal territory under the political influence though not yet under the administrative rule of the "Indian" government. The political boundary of India marches with Persia from the sea to near Zulfikar on the Harirud; then with the Russian Empire along the frontier laid down by agreement in 1885 as far as the Oxus at Khamiab; thence along the Oxus by the Panjah branch up to the Victoria lake, and from the east end of the Victoria lake by the line demarcated in 1895 up to Chinese territory on the Taghdumbash Pamir. From this point the frontier, in many parts not yet clearly defined, touches the Chinese Empire, mainly along the crests of the Himalayas, till the limits of French control are reached on the Upper Mekong. The Indian frontier leaving the Mekong marches with Siam till it reaches the sea half way down the Malay peninsula. Beyond the sea the Indian Empire includes the Andaman and Nicobar Islands, and the Laccadive Islands, Aden and Perim, and protectorates over Socotra, Bahrein, and various Chiefships along the coast from Aden to the Persian Gulf. The British protectorate over the Somali Coast, opposite Aden, has since October, 1898, formed part of the charge of the Foreign Office. Continental India, including Baluchistan, reaches from the 8th to the 37th degree of north latitude, and from the 61st to the 100th degree of longitude east of Greenwich; Calcutta itself lying in 88° E. long. Its total area may be taken to be 1,700,000 square miles, of which 750,000 square miles are under Native and the remainder under British administration. The population of India, shown by the census in February, 1891, if we include the population (computed or estimated) of Manipur, Sikkim, and the Shan States, but not the protected territory of Baluchistan, was 288,350,000, of which 66,750,000 belonged to the Native States. The increase of the population of the Indian Empire in the decade 1881 to 1891 was 33½ millions, of which 5½ millions were added by the inclusion of tracts, particularly Upper Burma, not enumerated in 1881, while the remainder of the increase being at the rate of over 10 per cent. in the decade, represents the ordinary growth of population. By 1900 the population of India may be taken to have increased to about 312 millions, of which 73 millions would belong to the Native States. The languages spoken in India, excluding European tongues and those which are spoken by less than 1,000 persons, are 78 in number, grouped in a dozen different families; of which 20 languages belonging to five families are spoken by not less than one million persons each. Other particulars regarding the population will be found on pages 467–468. Excluding the Province of Burma, which lies to the east of the Bay of Bengal and forms no part of the Indian Peninsula, we may broadly divide the country, for geographical purposes, into three sections, viz. :—the Himalayan region, the northern river-plains, and the southern table-land. The first of these includes the mountain-range of the Himalayas and their offshoots to the southward. This region, lying mainly beyond the limit of British administration, must be considered as the natural northern boundary of India, and may be described as consisting of two giant mountain-ranges running from north-west to south-east, with a series of great valleys between. The southern range, which rises precipitously from the belt of swampy land lying to the north of the Ganges and parallel to its course, springs up to a height of 20,000 feet above the plain, and culminates in the loftiest peaks yet measured on the globe—Mount Everest, 29,002 feet; KunchinJunga, 28,176 feet; and Dwhalagiri, over 27,000 feet, near the centre of the range, and Mount Godwin Austen (K. 2), 28,250 feet, near its junction with the Hindu Kush Moun-

The principal Government publications relating to India, presented to Parliament in 1899 were :—Statistical Abstracts, 1888-89 to 1897-98, C. 9,519; Moral and Material Progress Report, 1897-98, No. 211; Trade of British India, 1893-94 to 1897-98, C. 9,120; Sanitary Measures in India, 1897-98, Vol. xxix.; Financial Statement for 1899-1900, No. 254; Home Accounts, 1897-98, with Estimates 1898-99, No. 192; Explanatory Memorandum regarding the Accounts and Estimates of 1899-1900, C. 9,399; Return of Net Income and Expenditure for eleven years 1887-88 to 1897-98, No. 80; Administration Report of Railways in India for 1898-99, C. 9,369; Education in India, 1892-93 to 1896-97, C. 9,190; Famine Commission Report, C. 9,178; with Appendices, C. 9,252 to 9,258; Indian Currency Committee, Evidence Vol. II. C. 9,222, Index and Appendices, C. 9,376, Report, C. 9,390, Secretary of State's despatch thereon, C. 9,421; Staff Corps Officers: Correspondence, No. 82: Sugar, Countervailing Duties in India, Correspondence and Act, C. 9,287; Sugar Importation and Cultivation in India, Return No. 181; Military Bullets, Reports No. 264.

tains. The Himalayas, however, are not only a rampart of defence, but also serve to collect and store up a supply of water for the tropical plains below them. The sides of the Himalayas afford an admirable simultaneous representation of the various natural belts of the earth's surface, being divided into the tropical, the temperate, and the arctic zones as the upward journey is taken from the plains below. The vegetation of the Himalayan region includes such varied species as the tree-fern, the deodar or native cedar, numerous rhododendrons, the ilex, orchids, barley, oats, millet, and many common vegetables of domestic use. In the way of trade this region produces large quantities of timber, charcoal, barley, millet, and honey. The fauna are no less varied than the flora, and include the bison, musk-deer, yak, wild sheep and goat, bear and ounce, eagles, partridges, and a large number of pheasants. The native tribes afford examples of both the Aryan and the Turanian races, together with an intermingling of the two. The northern river-plains, lying at the foot of the Himalayas, and stretching from sea to sea, comprehend the rich alluvial plains watered by the Indus, the Ganges, the Lower Brahmaputra, and their tributaries. At no great distance from each other, four rivers take their rise in the Himalayas. Of these, two are on the north side of the mountains—the Indus, which flows westward, and the Sang-po or Brahmaputra, which flows eastward. The other two, on the southern slope, are the Sutlej, which, after flowing west and south-west for 900 miles and collecting to itself various other waters, joins the Indus; and the Ganges, which, during a south-east and easterly journey of nearly 1,600 miles, drains almost the whole of the Bengal plain. Meanwhile the Brahmaputra, which runs close along by the mountains on the northern side, having reached the eastern extremity of the Himalayas, turns sharply to the south, then to the west, and finally joins the Ganges, the two rivers discharging themselves together into the Bay of Bengal. The Indus is 1,800 miles long; the Brahmaputra nearly 1,500 miles long. It will be seen from this that the Himalayas send to India the water gathered on both their northern and southern slopes: this result is due to the peculiar *lie* of the land, and this it is which has not only given great abundance and wealth to the country, but has also made it the prey of the spoiler and invader for many centuries. The richest, the most populous, and the most prosperous part of India is to be found in the basins of these three great river-systems, which include in the aggregate an area of 1,125,000 square miles. Each of these rivers is of inestimable value to the country it drains, but particularly is this so with the Ganges. The Ganges is not only the great highway of Bengal, it is also the water-carrier and the fertiliser; without it traffic, where not impossible, would be enormously dear, and the province almost a desert. So rich is the Ganges valley that a wholly agricultural population of nearly 60 millions finds support on the soil at a density of over 700 persons to the square mile (the average density of the population of England and Wales being 500 to the square mile). There are several agricultural districts with a population exceeding 900 to the square mile. There are three harvests in Lower Bengal each year: pease, pulse, and various oil-seeds are reaped in April and May, the early rice crop in September, and the great rice crop two or three months later. The chief vegetable products of N.W. Bengal are the mango, the banyan, the wild cotton-tree, and the tamarind: while the delta region gives rice, the bamboo, and a large variety of palms (cocoanut, date, areca, &c.). In the north, again, we also find wheat, Indian corn, millet, and barley; while to the south, indigo, cotton, sugar-cane, tobacco, and many different dyes, drugs, and spices are also produced. These include the aloe, castor-oil tree, resins, and gums; but there are also grown the melon, pumpkin, tea-plant, yams, the opium poppy, the mulberry, and jute. Just as the Himalayas on the north and the Suleiman Mountains on the north-west form natural barriers of defence for Hindustan, so do the Vindhya Mountains, running almost due east and west from the head of the Gulf of Cambay, form a firm southern boundary to the river-plains of Northern India. Southern India, or the Deccan, is a plateau of triangular shape and very old geological formation, bounded on two sides by the Malabar and Coromandel Coasts, which converge at Cape Comorin, and on the third by the Vindhya Mountains, north of the Nerbudda River. The Eastern and Western Ghauts all but complete the triangle of mountain ranges with which this region is surrounded. As the Western Ghauts lie so close to the coast, and afford no exit for rivers, we find no streams on the Malabar Coast south of the Tapti River: all the rivers—and they are both numerous and of great size—flow eastwards, and passing through gaps or defiles in the Eastern Ghauts, discharge their waters into the Bay of Bengal. The four chief rivers are the Mahanuddy, in the extreme N.E. (520 m.), the Godavery (900 m.), the Kistna (800 m.), and the Cauvery (472 m.) at intervals further to the south; in the extreme N.W., too, south of the Vindhyas, and parallel to them, but north of the Western Ghauts, we find the Nerbudda and the Tapti flowing westwards. The division line of the basins of these last two rivers is sharply defined by the Satpura Mountains, which lie midway between them. The physical geography of S. India has given it much of its history : the S.W. coast, shut in by the mountains, is very primitive and moves slowly ; the S.E., open and easy of access both from within and without, has advanced with rapid strides in commerce and all other civilising influences. The mountain slopes of this region, those of the Western Ghauts in particular, are still covered with the splendid vegetation of primeval forests of the tropics : teak, ebony, ironwood, and Indian mahogany abound, so also do the jackwood, blackwood, sandalwood, and the ubiquitous bamboo. Coffee is now largely cultivated there, and tea and cinchona are also grown. The elephant, tiger, bison, leopard, deer, sheep, and various smaller game afford limitless sport to the hunter. In the valleys and on the higher plains many crops are raised in profusion, chiefly the same as those grown in the lower basin of the Ganges. The southern table-land has in past times furnished considerable supplies of different minerals, including gold : those found and worked now are mainly lime, coal, iron and gold : the output of the gold mines of Mysore is steadily increasing. To the west of the peninsula the Indian Empire includes the mountainous, barren, and thinly populated region of Baluchistan ; its coal and petroleum have not hitherto repaid working. East of the peninsula is the large province of Burma, watered by the Irawaddi and its tributaries and by the Salween. The delta region is flat ; further inland the country is one of hills and rolling downs ; and in the north the province loses itself in the mountains. Rice is the chief staple ; cotton, sesamum, and tobacco are also extensively grown. The forests, particularly of teak, make a very large contribution to the exports. Among the industries still to be developed in the province is that of tea-cultivation, the tea-plant being indigenous. In the Shan Hills the growth of wheat is being encouraged. Burma is rich in minerals. Rubies, sapphires, and jade are mined. Gold and silver undoubtedly exist ; wells for the production of petroleum have long been in operation ; coal, copper, tin, lead, are also found. Three-fifths of the Indian Empire are under the direct rule of the British Government, and are divided for administrative purposes into eight principal Provinces—viz., Madras, Bombay, Bengal, the North-West Provinces and Oudh, the Punjab, Burma, the Central Provinces, and Assam, and five minor administrations. The remaining two-fifths are made up of a large number of Native States, whose chiefs are, as it is termed, in subordinate alliance with, or under the suzerainty of, Her Imperial Majesty, KAISAR-I-HIND. Her Majesty's representative is styled the Viceroy and Governor-General, his relations with the Home Government being regulated by Act 21 & 22 Vict. c. 106, which substituted the authority of a Secretary of State for India, aided by a Council of fifteen members, for that of the East India Company and the Board of Control. By an Act of 1889, the Secretary of State is permitted to leave five of the seats on his Council unfilled. For the present members of Council see page 160.

For the knowledge we possess of the period that preceded the commencement of connected history in India we are chiefly indebted to the sacred books of the Hindus, the accounts of Greek and Chinese writers, the records of inscriptions and coins, and the evidences of race and language. The existence of various races in India speaking languages not cognate, proves that the country has been subject to successive invasions in remote ages. The first of which we possess direct evidence is that of the ARYANS, who, coming from north of the Hindu Kush, overspread Persia in one direction and Northern India in the other. The *Vedas*, which are the most ancient and venerated of the sacred writings of the Indian Aryans, and are written in Sanskrit of the earliest type, are supposed to date from 1400 B.C. In the early Vedas all classification and ranking of the gods is absolutely wanting ; something of the kind, however, is done in the Upanishads, which form a kind of commentary on the Vedas, and make some attempt to solve the problems of creation, the nature of the Deity, and the human soul. The Upanishads, in fact, founded admittedly on the Vedas, contain the germs of those great systems of Hindu philosophy which, in their later development, brought about the separation of the creed of the vulgar from that of the educated. The *Mahabhárata* and *Rámdyana* are epic poems of later date, abounding in extravagant myths, from which, however, the learned have succeeded in gaining a general knowledge of the habits and condition of the people and of the course of events during the dark period of Aryan conquest. Themselves a branch of the Indo-European race, by whom Europe had already been colonised, the Aryans are believed to have entered India some 2,000 years B.C. They were then a pastoral and agricultural people ; their form of government was patriarchal, and the offices of prince and priest were united in the same person. Their conquest seems to have been confined at first to the country south of the Himalayas on the west of the Jumna, where they long remained, before they began their advance southwards and eastwards down the Gangetic valley. The enemies they met, who had preceded them in the occupation of the country, were a yellow-skinned, serpent-worshipping race in the Himalayan districts, and in the south a dark-skinned population, short in stature, treacherous, and degraded. The condition of the people, as well as the progress of their wars with the older inhabitants of the country, can be clearly traced in the sacred poems. It appears that when Oudh and Bengal had been subdued, the deified hero Ráma effected the conquest of Southern India, and afterwards that of Ceylon. By this time a great change had come over the Aryan invaders. Their primitive simplicity had disappeared. Patriarchs had become luxurious princes, whose priestly duties were deputed to the sect of Brahmans; and by the fifth century, when, it is supposed, the *Laws of Manu*, a digest of the current customary laws, were compiled, this caste had succeeded in establishing its superiority over the Kshetriyas, or military caste, to whom it had been at first subordinate. The *Laws of Manu* give a good idea of what the priestly caste wished Indian society to be at the period when they were composed. In them we find mention made of the existence of caste and village communities. In the sixth century B.C. a new religion arose, called Buddhism. Its founder was Sákya Muni, or Gautáma, a prince of the Kshetriya caste, who took the name of Buddha, the "awakened," and died at a great age in 543 B.C. His tenets are contained in the *Tripitaka*, the Buddhist gospel. Buddhism was, in India itself, mainly a social reform, a revolt against the pride of caste and the exclusiveness of the Brahman priesthood; and within three centuries from the death of its founder it had been accepted as the national religion. For more than a thousand years it existed in India side by side with Brahmanism, which it never succeeded in ousting. But either from internal dissensions of its own, or from persecution without, Buddhism became practically extinct in India before the twelfth century, though it still flourishes not only in China and Japan, but also in Nipal, Burma, and Ceylon. Its decline in India was accompanied by a revival of Brahmanism, much modified. One branch of it, however, survived in the distinct sect of the Jains, whose religion was a combination of Buddhism and Brahmanism. The followers of this creed, of which the antiquity and relations with Buddhism are much disputed, are still very numerous in Guzerat, and may be found in many parts of India.

With Alexander's invasion (327 B.C.) we reach the first landmark in the political history of India. Herodotus tells us that the twentieth satrapy of Persia had previously included part of the north-west of India. Alexander himself did not penetrate beyond the tributaries of the Indus, though he sailed down the river; his Indian possessions fell to Seleucus, whose ambassador, Megasthenes, has left an account of the country under the rule of Chandragupta, the Greek Sandracottus. Megasthenes describes the democratic village-communities of the Punjab, and speaks of the peoples as brave and truthful, and averse to litigation, and of the women as chaste; and he notes the absence of slavery. Asoka (B.C. 260-220), the grandson of Chandragupta, whose edicts throw light upon this period, was the great patron of Buddhism, which became for a time the State religion throughout the greater part of India. Our last contributors to a knowledge of India before the period of authentic history are the Buddhist pilgrims from China, who visited the country between the fifth and tenth centuries. The influence of the Greek conquest was swept away by the Scythians, who poured in many waves, between 126 B.C. and 544 A.D., over Northern India. Their inroads, as well as the existence of ancient aboriginal tribes in India, left a lasting influence on the character of the population, and profoundly modified the religious beliefs and domestic institutions of the Hindus.

So early as A.D. 664 Arabs began to make predatory expeditions against Guzerat and Sind. The conquest of Persia, towards the middle of the seventh century, at length brought the successors of Mohammed to the Indus, and in the N.W. of India they made some temporary acquisitions during the ensuing hundred years. However, two centuries more were to pass before the foundations of a durable Mohammedan empire were laid. It was in the year 999 that Mahmud declared the independence of the kingdom of Ghazni in Afghanistan—a proceeding which he followed up by at least twelve expeditions into India, one of which carried him beyond the Jumna, and another ended in the occupation of Guzerat. Later, in 1024, he conquered and annexed to his kingdom the provinces of Lahore and Mooltan. The succeeding dynasties of Afghan kings held power in India for 500 years; but the advance of their power was gradual, for it was not till 1206 that Delhi was taken, and the greater part of Hindustan annexed by Kutb-ud-din, with whose memory is connected the Kutb Minar, near Delhi; and the first Mohammedan invasion of the Deccan took place in 1294.

From this time onward the history of India is the history of invasion, dynasty following dynasty, while the Mongol hordes again and again swept into the country. At length, during the reign of the last monarch of the Toghlak line, the famous Tamerlane burst into India at the head of a mighty host, and captured and sacked Delhi in 1398: he left behind him Khizr Khan, who thenceforward held the reins of power. A period of misrule, tyranny, and anarchy ensued, and fittingly paved the way for the total conquest of the country by the Mogul emperors.

THE MOGUL EMPIRE.—The Mongols, or Moguls, a Mohammedan Power, after overrunning Central and Western Asia, arrived in 1219, under Genghis Khan, on the frontiers of India, and, as has been stated, again and again invaded that country. In 1398, during the invasion of Tamerlane, or Teimur, a great part of Hindustan was laid waste. In 1526 *Sultan Baber*, a descendant of both these Tartar chiefs, overthrew the last of the Afghan kings at Panipat, and founded the MOGUL EMPIRE. *Humayoon* (1530-56) lost the whole of the territory conquered by Baber, but recovered a portion of it shortly before his death. *Akbar*, his son (1556-1605), being a minor, the Government was for five years under a regency, but it was a much longer time before Akbar's many opponents were subdued and his Empire firmly established, embracing Cabul, Candahar, all Hindustan, and a portion of the Deccan. The Mogul Empire thus absorbed not only the Afghan kingdom in Hindustan, but also the independent Mohammedan kingdoms of Bijapur, Golconda, Ahmednagar, Berar, and Bidar, in the Deccan. Akbar followed up his conquests by important financial reforms; he was tolerant in religion, and just to all classes of his subjects. Among the great men whom he drew around him were Raja Todar Mall, his able finance minister; Abul Fazl, the historian of his reign; and Faiz, the poet; nor should we overlook Bairam Khan, Akbar's faithful guardian in his youth. The revenue of Akbar's empire is estimated to have been 19 millions sterling; and this gradually increased till under Aurangzeb, at the close of the 17th century, the imperial revenue amounted to £43,500,000. *Jehangir* (1605-28) received in 1615 an embassy despatched by James I., under the conduct of Sir Thomas Roe. His empress was the famous Nur Mehal. Under *Shah Jehan*

(1628–58) the Mogul Empire reached its zenith. Many public works and grand buildings testify to his magnificence and taste, amongst others the Taj Mahal at Agra, which is said to have been the work of a French architect—Austin of Bordeaux. The close of *Shah Jehan's* reign was embittered by the rivalries of his four sons. *Aurangzeb* (1658–1707) defeated his brothers and put them to death; his father he kept a prisoner for the rest of his life. *Aurangzeb* had great ability and courage, and was a master of dissimulation; but bigotry and distrust were the bane of his policy, and the decline of the Mogul Empire dates from his reign. Four sons disputed the right of succession: at last *Bahadur Shah* gained the coveted crown, but only for five years. Dying in 1712 he was succeeded by his son, *Jehundar Shah*, who was cruelly murdered by one Farokshir, a great-grandson of the famous Aurangzeb, who seized on the crown. He in turn was himself put to death six years later, and *Muhammad Shah*, grandson of Bahadur, came to the throne. The viceroys of his own appointment grew uneasy and rebellious, and all unconsciously aided in the growth of the Mahratta power. One of them refused his aid to his sovereign, and the Mahrattas in consequence subdued the Deccan. In 1738, to avenge an alleged insult, Nadir Shah of Persia invaded India, captured Delhi, and gave the city over to the mercy of his terrible followers, who are said to have slain more than 100,000 of the inhabitants, and to have levied as contribution and carried off as plunder, treasure equal to more than £50,000,000 sterling. In spite of this enormous sacrifice, peace was only obtained by giving up to the conqueror all the country west of the Indus. On the death of Muhammad, in 1748, the country was fast going to decay—it was, in fact, only waiting for a fresh conqueror. The Mahrattas were there ready for the work to be done. About 1724 the Deccan, Oudh, and Bengal became practically independent under Nizam-ul-Mulk (ancestor of the present Nizam), Sadat Khan, and Aliverdi Khan respectively.

THE MAHRATTAS.—Simultaneously with the decline of the Moguls rose the power of the Mahrattas. They were Hindus, and the country from which they came may be roughly described by drawing two lines from Nagpur to Surat and Goa on the west coast. The founder of their power was *Sivaji* (1627–1680), a chieftain of the family of Bhonslah. *Balaji Vishvanath* (1712–1720), Peishwa, or Prime Minister, succeeded in making that office of paramount importance and hereditary in his family, Sivaji's descendants thenceforth holding a merely nominal position as Rajas of Satara. Under the Peishwas, aided by Scindia, Holkar, and the Gaekwar, who formed independent States about this time, the Mahrattas rapidly extended their territory and influence. In 1760 Delhi was in their hands, and though they suffered a disastrous defeat at Panipat in 1761, at the hands of Ahmed Shah, the Afghan invader, they remained for some time the first Power in India, and were the most dangerous opponents of the English. Their system, however, was one of organised plunder rather than of settled government. Like the Pindaris, a horde of freebooters who followed in their train, they were a scourge to the country. It was not until both Pindaris and Mahrattas were finally overthrown in 1818, that India enjoyed the blessings of internal peace. The Mahratta empire, containing within itself the seeds of disintegration, was fated to bend before the superior sway of European adventurers, who, either from love of

adventure or thoughts of gain, had been attracted in increasing numbers to the shores of India.

EUROPEAN ADVENTURE.—From time immemorial the trade of Europe with India and the farther East has been the most lucrative branch of the world's commerce, and has enormously enriched in turn each nation that has carried it. In the 15th century it was mainly possessed by the Venetians at its European end, and by the Arabs, the successors of the old Phœnicians, in its Eastern portion; the chief centres of the trade of the Arabs were Calicut, Ormuz, Aden and Malacca. Seeing the large profits to be derived from this trade, the rising nations of Europe in the 15th century sought to obtain a share. Hence the ardour of the navigators who set out to discover an ocean route to India. The sea route round the Cape of Good Hope was discovered by Vasco da Gama, who anchored before Calicut on 20th May, 1498. From that time until they lost their naval supremacy the *Portuguese* may be considered to have enjoyed the monopoly of Indian trade. The first Portuguese viceroy, Francis of Almeida (1505–1509), established numerous factories and fortresses, and took possession of Ceylon and the Maldive Islands; while his successor, Alfonso de Albuquerque, captured Goa (1510), and extended the Portuguese dominion in various places, but notably on the Malabar and Malacca coasts. This dominion had, in 1542, practically amounted to an entire regulation of the Asiatic coast trade with Europe from the Persian Gulf to Japan, and for nearly sixty years afterwards the King of Portugal was the virtual suzerain of the southern coast of Asia. When the Portuguese crown fell into weak hands its power in the Eastern seas began to decline; and it was almost annulled in 1580, when the crowns of Spain and Portugal were united under Philip II., and the Asiatic interests of Portugal were subordinated to the European interests of Spain. The Portuguese were content to bring the exports of India to Lisbon; they left it to the Dutch to carry them thence to the other ports of Europe. But when Philip II., on account of the revolt of the United Provinces, shut the harbour of Lisbon against them, the *Dutch* (1580) were driven either to forego the trade or seek it in the East themselves. The enterprise of the nation decided the question, especially as the Spanish naval supremacy had been shattered by the defeat of the "Invincible Armada" in 1588. In 1602 "The Dutch East India Company" was formed by the amalgamation of the previously existing trading societies, and between 1602 and 1620 the principal Portuguese settlements in the East were captured. In 1661 the Portuguese possessed only those remnants of their Indian possessions which they still hold. The Dutch Eastern Empire, situated mainly in the Malayan Peninsula and contiguous islands, passed with the Mother Country under the dominion of the French in 1810. Attacked in consequence and conquered by the English in 1812, it was surrendered again to the Dutch in 1816, since which date it has remained in Dutch hands.

ENGLISH DOMINION.—At the close of the 16th century the English also began to feel the necessity of freeing themselves from dependence on others for the supply of Indian produce, and to desire a share in the profits of Indian commerce. After the success of some smaller ventures, the English East India Company was incorporated by Queen Elizabeth by royal charter on the 31st December 1600; there were 125 shareholders, the capital was £70,000, and the official title was "The Governor and Company of Merchants of London trading to the East Indies." When voyages to India—and almost profitless voyages they proved to be—were first undertaken on the joint-stock account, the company's capital was raised to £400,000. Quarrels with the Portuguese ensued; and no footing of any kind was obtained until the year 1615, when Captain Best, with four English ships, won a great victory over the Portuguese squadron off Surat, where a settlement was established, and a satisfactory treaty concluded with the Emperor Jehangir. Under the terms of this treaty, King James I. sent out as ambassador Sir Thomas Roe, who was not only granted various trading concessions, but was also permitted to reside at the Court of the Great Mogul. When Charles I. was in need of money he granted a second charter to a new Company. Confusion was the result; and piratical and other acts dishonourable to Europeans followed. The Protector Cromwell, however, was equal to the crisis; the rival companies were merged into one, the famous Navigation Act was passed, a reign of order was established, and the English traders gained a reputation for general honesty which—in spite of individuals and solitary cases—they have ever since maintained. In 1639 the English, who had acquired a narrow strip of land, six miles in length and one mile inland, on the coast just below Masulipatam, built a factory there and having surrounded it with a wall, mounted it with guns, and named it Fort St. George; fourteen years later (1653) this settlement of Madras became an independent Presidency. When, in 1661, Charles II. was married to Katharine of Braganza, a part of her dowry from Portugal was the Island of Bombay: five years afterwards it was formally made over to the English monarch, who in his turn, in 1668, transferred all his rights over it, together with the responsibilities connected with it, to the East India Company for an annual payment of £10. In 1687 the factory at Surat was given up by the Company, and Bombay was made the seat of the Western Presidency. Although in 1634 the Company had obtained certain treaty rights concerning Bengal from the Mogul, and six years afterwards a factory had been established at Hooghly, near the mouth of the Ganges, yet in that part of the country they held no territorial possessions as in Bombay and Madras. In 1688 the exactions of the Mohammedan authorities forced them to abandon their settlement. They were, however, invited to return, and in 1689 were laid, amid swamp and jungle, the foundations of Fort William, afterwards destined to develop into the modern city of Calcutta. In 1698 a rival company called "The English East India Company," to distinguish it from the old "London Company," was started with a capital of two millions. The competition resulted in over-trading; the home markets were glutted with all kinds of Indian produce, and the English manufacturers were loud in their complaints. In 1702 the two rival companies were united, and in 1708, thanks to the prudence and tact of Lord Godolphin, the whole of the English companies were at last amalgamated under the charter granted by Queen Anne to "The United Company of Merchants Trading to the East Indies." England having entered upon the war of the Austrian succession in 1744, the rival companies of England and France first came into collision in 1746, the immediate result being the capture of Madras in that year. Had Dupleix received continuous support from home, he might have succeeded in founding a French Empire in India. The first reverses of the English were retrieved by *Clive*, whose gallant defence of Arcot (1751) was followed up by a series of brilliant movements, culminating in the utter defeat of the French army at Wandewash in 1760, and in the capture of Pondicherry in 1761, which completed the ruin of the French. The territory retained by the French in India since that date is insignificant; and in these possessions they are forbidden by treaty to hold any considerable military force. The tragedy of the Black Hole of Calcutta (1756) summoned Clive from Madras, and the victory of Plassey in the following year made British influence predominant in Bengal. Clive was appointed first Governor of Bengal in 1758. In 1762, in his absence, the English were again embroiled in Bengal, but completely defeated their opponents at Buxar (1764). As a result of this battle, they received from the Emperor at Delhi the *diwani* or fiscal administration of Bengal, Behar, and Orissa, and the jurisdiction over the Northern Circars. Clive returned a second time to Bengal as Governor, and before he left finally in 1767, he succeeded in reforming the services, in which great abuses existed. After an interval of misrule *Warren Hastings* (1772–85) was appointed President of Calcutta, and then Governor-General in 1774, on the creation of that office under the Regulating Act of 1773. He not only greatly increased the power and territory of the Company, notwithstanding the opposition of a hostile Council, of which Sir Philip Francis, the reputed author of *Junius*, was a member, but was also the first great administrative organiser of the British possessions in India. He repelled Hyder Ali's memorable invasion of the Carnatic (1780), and defeated the triple alliance of the Nizam, the Mahrattas, and Hyder Ali. In so doing he probably saved British India. The first reign of *Lord Cornwallis* (1786–93) was marked by the complete reform he effected in the Company's Civil Service, by the introduction of the Permanent Settlement of the Land Revenue in Bengal, and by the Second Mysore War. After the uneventful rule of *Sir John Shore*, afterwards Lord Teignmouth (1793–98), came the administration of the *Marquess Wellesley* (1798–1805), of which the events were numerous and important. Mysore in 1760 had been seized by Hyder Ali, a Mussulman adventurer, and a powerful and inveterate enemy of the English. His son and successor, Tippoo, equally courageous and equally hostile to the English, was in 1798 in secret correspondence with the French, who had then the predominant influence in the military councils of the Nizam and of Scindia, were strongly established in the islands of Mauritius and Bourbon, and under Napoleon, then engaged in his Egyptian campaign, were aiming at a great Eastern Empire. Lord Wellesley saw the necessity of crushing this dangerous Power, and the Fourth Mysore War ended in the capture of Seringapatam (1799), the death of Tippoo, and the restoration of Mysore to a representative of the family of Hindu Rajas whom Hyder Ali had dethroned. The Treaty of Bassein (1802) broke up the Mahratta Confederacy. The campaigns of Lord Lake and Sir Arthur Wellesley, in the Second and Third Mahratta Wars, curtailed the power of Scindia and Holkar, and added to the strength and extent of the Company's dominions. Lastly, Lord Wellesley developed, if he did not establish, a system of subsidiary alliances with Native States, which promised to give greater security than the balance of power attempted by Lord Wellesley's predecessors. *Lord Minto* (1807-13) established peaceful relations with the Sikhs, Cabul, and Persia, through the mediation of Metcalfe, Mountstuart Elphinstone, and Malcolm respectively, occupied the Mauritius, and extended British influence in the Eastern Seas. Under the *Marquess of Hastings* (1814-23) the Bombay Presidency, hitherto the smallest of the three, attained its present dimensions on the annexation, in 1818, of the territory of the Peishwa, whose power had lasted a little over 100 years. By his wars in Central India, Lord Hastings also delivered the country from the ravages of the *Pindaris*, freebooters who organised bands, sometimes many thousands strong, and devastated the country in all directions; and he settled on their existing basis the relations of the Supreme Power with the feudatory States of Rajputana and Central India. A war with Nepaul also occurred during Lord Hastings' *régime*. In 1823 *Lord Amherst* succeeded the Marquess of Hastings, and marked his period of office by a conquest in another direction. The King of Ava had been not only guilty of great insolence to the Governor-General, but was ever making encroachments on British territory. The result was the First Burmese War, which cost us 20,000 lives and nearly £14,000,000, but gave us the fertile provinces of Aracan and Tenasserim, and, practically, Assam. While *Lord William Bentinck* was Governor-General (1828-35), steam communication with India was introduced, Suttee (or widow-burning) was abolished, educated natives were admitted more largely into the service of the Company, and various measures were passed affecting education, economy, and justice. The Charter of the East India Company was in 1833 renewed for twenty years, on condition that the Company should altogether abandon its trading, and allow of the settlement of Europeans in the country. *Lord Auckland's* resolution to support Shah Shuja against Dost Mohammed brought on the First Afghan Expedition (1839-42), and the serious disaster attendant on the fatal Retreat from Cabul. This was atoned for in the administration of *Lord Ellenborough* (1842-44), which also saw the Conquest of Sind by Sir Charles Napier. *Lord Hardinge* (1844-48) conducted in person the First Sikh War, and fought a series of severely-contested battles, ending with Sobraon (1846). *Lord Dalhousie's* administration (1848-56) was fruitful in events. The Second Sikh War resulted in the submission of the Sikhs, who at Chillianwallah and Goojerat gave further proof of their bravery. The annexation of their country was followed by that of Tanjore; and the Second Burmese War (1852) deprived the King of Burma of his sea-board provinces. Lord Dalhousie promoted the introduction of Railways and the Telegraph. He established cheap postage; promoted steam navigation with England *viâ* the Red Sea; and opened the Ganges Canal, still the largest irrigation work in India. His annexation policy was much criticised at home: it proceeded on the principle that British being preferable to Native rule in the interest of the subject populations, gross misrule or a break in the natural succession justified the transfer of a Native State to the British Government. In 1849 Satara, and in 1853 Jhansi, thus became British territory; and after the death of the last of the Mahratta Princes of Nagpur, his territory was annexed, and became the Central Provinces in 1853. In 1856, after long and painful hesitation on the part of the Direc-

torate, and after repeated warnings to the Government of Oudh—a Government marked by tyranny and oppression—that kingdom was also added to the list of annexations. The proclamation was made on February 13, 1856, and the transfer took place without the shedding of blood or the striking of a single blow. *Earl Canning* (1857-62), who succeeded Lord Dalhousie, left England pledged to pursue a policy of peace. It was, however, his fate to meet the greatest crisis that has threatened the British Empire in India. A Mutiny of the Native troops broke out on the 10th of May, 1857, at the station of Meerut, and spread through the whole Bengal Army. Delhi was for some months in the possession of 40,000 of the rebels, and many chiefs joined the revolt. The siege of Delhi, the massacre at Cawnpore, the relief of Lucknow, the Central India campaign of Sir Hugh Rose (Lord Strathnairn), and all the heroism displayed during that momentous time, will never be forgotten. The Great Mutiny proved the deathblow to the East India Company, whose glorious annals were brought to a close by the transfer of its entire authority and administration to the Crown.

THE BRITISH INDIAN EMPIRE.—The Act for the better government of India established the authority of the Crown; and a Proclamation to the Princes, Chiefs, and People of India, dated the 1st of November, 1858, announced the resolution of Her Majesty to assume the government of the territories in India "heretofore administered in trust by the Honourable East India Company." *Lord Canning* was succeeded in 1862 by *Lord Elgin*, who, however, died November 20th, 1863. The attention of *Sir John* (*Lord*) *Lawrence* (1864-69) was directed to the necessity for financial retrenchment, which arose chiefly from increased military expenditure. His rule was also marked by the Bhutan War and by the terrible Orissa Famine of 1866. *Lord Mayo* (1869-72) succeeded in carrying out a number of measures for the reform of the administration and for the development of the resources of the country, of which perhaps the chief was the introduction of the system of provincial finance, a large measure of decentralisation since extended. He was assassinated on the 8th of Feb., 1872, while on a visit to the convict settlement at Port Blair, in the Andamans. During the time of *Lord Northbrook* (1872-76), H.R.H. the Prince of Wales visited India, and received a loyal welcome from all classes. In the same period occurred a famine in the Lower Provinces of Bengal, and the deposition of the Gaekwar of Baroda for misrule and disloyalty. *Lord Lytton's* Viceroyalty (1876-80) was made eventful by the terrible Famine in Southern India, by the Second Afghan War, and by the Queen's assumption of the title of EMPRESS OF INDIA. He was succeeded by the *Marquess of Ripon* (1880-84), whose peaceful rule was marked by the extension of local self-government. He, in his turn, gave place to the *Marquess of Dufferin* (1884-88), whose *régime* was remarkable for the Third Burmese War, by which Upper Burma and its dependent Shan States were added to the Empire. In this Administration, too, the north-western frontier of Afghanistan was delimited, the frontier of India strengthened, and the army increased; and the Jubilee of Her Majesty's reign (1887) was enthusiastically celebrated by all classes and races throughout India. The *Marquess of Lansdowne* (1888-93) succeeded Lord Dufferin. He continued his predecessor's policy of strengthening the army and extending and consolidating

British influence on the frontier. Hunza and Nagar, feudatories of Kashmir, were brought under more direct control: an arrangement was made with the Amir relative to the boundary of Afghanistan: and an outbreak in Manipur, where British officers were murdered, was suppressed. In domestic policy he took the first step in currency reform by closing the Indian mints to the free coinage of silver, thus cutting away the rupee currency from its silver basis. He also reconstituted the Legislative Councils by the introduction of a more popular element. The viceroyalty of the *Earl of Elgin and Kincardine* (1894-98) was full of events: there was an earthquake, the most disastrous on record, which devastated Assam on June 12th, 1897 : there were military operations on a larger scale than any since the Afghan war; and there was the great famine and the outbreak of plague. In 1895 a rising in Chitral made necessary a formidable military expedition which was conducted with rapidity and success. A decision of the Government to abandon Chitral was on a change of Ministry reversed in favour of a policy of holding that position and maintaining British control by the opening of the direct road from Peshawar by the Lowari route and by posting garrisons on the Malakand pass and at Chakdara. For two years the peace of the country was maintained. But in 1897 the tribes on this frontier, simultaneously with those along almost the whole border southwards to Baluchistan rose against the British garrisons. A series of military expeditions had to be rapidly organised, in which more than 60,000 troops were employed. The territories of the Bunerwals and Swatis, of the Mohmands, of the Afridis and Urakzais, and of the Waziris were invaded; their opposition was broken after some severe fighting, and fines in money and arms inflicted upon them. The final arrangements for the maintenance of peace and order on the frontier were not concluded till after the arrival of Lord Elgin's successor. Another feature of Lord Elgin's *régime* was the number of frontier settlements and demarcations. The Pamir boundary was delimited with Russia. The frontier between Baluchistan and Persia, and almost the whole of the border of Afghanistan on the side of Baluchistan and of India were delimited. The Mekong was accepted as the line of division of British and French territory north of Siam. The Burma-China boundary was defined in a Convention of 1894 and further modified by an agreement in 1897. The British protectorate on the Somali coast, after being delimited, was transferred to the charge of the Foreign Office. In 1897 Lord Elgin had to face, in addition to troubles on the frontier, the internal calamities of famine, earthquake, and plague. The rains of 1896 failed and famine set in. At its height in June, 1897, 4½ millions were in receipt of relief, and relief works were in operation over an area of over 570,000 square miles containing a population of nearly 130 millions. In actual relief the State spent 7½ crores; its loss of revenue by famine is said to have amounted to an additional 9 crores. The experience of the famine was examined by a specially appointed Commission. The summary of their Report states "that while the areas over which intense and severe distress prevailed in the famine of 1896-97 were greater than in any previous famines, the success actually attained in the relief of distress and saving of human life was, if not complete, far greater than any that has yet been recorded in famines that

are at all comparable with it in point of extent, severity, or duration; and that this result has been achieved at a cost which, when compared with the expenditure in previous famines, and with other standards that we have had before us, cannot but be regarded as very moderate." The Commission recommend the rapid extension of irrigation, and various alterations, chiefly of detail, in the famine codes which prescribe the measures to be taken in each province in the event of famine. They point out also the remarkably uniform level of prices all over the country, due to the network of railways, a result of which is the extension of the area of distress with a diminution of its intensity. In September, 1896, came the first reports of bubonic plague in Bombay; it has continued to rage ever since in the Bombay Presidency, and for shorter periods it has appeared in other localities. Up to 22 Sept., 1899, the recorded deaths from plague numbered 270,000, of which all but 23,000 were in the Bombay Presidency. Bombay (with about 44,000 deaths), Poona (18,000), and Karachi (8,000) have been the worst sufferers. No doubt there were very many more deaths from plague than those actually so reported. The epidemic has tended to expand in the wet weather and to die down in the hot months. The measures taken by the Government to stamp out the epidemic caused much apprehension and irritation, particularly in 1897, and more especially in Poona where the Native press became very virulent, and popular feeling was excited. Writers and editors of seditious papers were prosecuted and convicted; and the sedition law itself modified to render prosecution more effectual. Other noticeable measures of Lord Elgin's Viceroyalty were the abolition of the Presidential army system, the imposition of the cotton duties, the elevation of Burma to a Lieutenant-Governorship, the creation of Legislative Councils for Punjab and Burma, an extended programme for the construction of railways, and the celebration of the Queen-Empress's Diamond Jubilee. Lord Elgin was succeeded as Governor-General by the *Right Hon. Lord Curzon of Kedleston* in December, 1898. Two important departures in legislation mark his first year of office, one adopting the recommendation of the Currency Committee, to establish the gold sovereign as the standard of currency in India, and to make it legal tender in India concurrently with rupees at the exchange of 15 rupees to the sovereign (1s. 4d. the rupee), the other to place countervailing duties on the import of such sugars as have enjoyed the benefit of bounties on export from their country of manufacture. Another important bill introduced has been one to check the alienation of land by the agricultural classes of the Punjab. In his first year of office Lord Curzon has been called on to despatch nearly 6,000 British troops belonging to the army in India to South Africa for the maintenance of imperial interests; he has also had to face a continuance of plague in a virulent form, and to provide against the recurrence of famine now severe in Rajputana, the Central Provinces, Sind, and the northern division of Bombay, and adjoining parts of the Punjab, N.W.P., and Berar. In laying down the lines of frontier policy he has decided to increase the Local Militia and tribal levies, and to entrust them with the task of holding, as far as possible, outlying positions, while the regular troops on the frontier are being concentrated in strong central positions, and organised so as to be ready to move rapidly to their support on any emergency. Lord Curzon's first budget in March, 1900, promises to give scope for important financial measures, notwithstanding the heavy expenditure thrown upon his government by plague and famine.

IMPERIAL LEGISLATION.—The original charter of the East India Company was granted by Queen Elizabeth at the end of the year 1600. *The Regulating Act* (1773), which created the first Governor-General, created also his Council, and was the first that recognised the East India Company as a ruling body. It was followed, in 1784, by *Pitt's India Bill*, which, while leaving the Government of India nominally to the Court of Directors, in reality transferred it to a *Board of Control*, whose President represented Indian affairs in the House of Commons; and in 1788 by the *Declaratory Act*, which expressly affirmed this important fact. The Act of 1784 also established the supremacy of the Presidency of Bengal, authorising the historic phrase "The Governor-General in Council." In 1793 the Company's Charter was renewed for 20 years, and its

exclusive privileges were continued. In 1813 an Ecclesiastical Establishment was formed, and the trade to India was thrown open; in 1833 the China monopoly was likewise abandoned; a legal member was at the same time added to the Governor-General's Council, and the North-West Provinces were made a separate Administration. In 1853 the Company's Charter was renewed for the last time. Bengal was put under a Lieutenant-Governor, and the Indian Civil Service was thrown open to competition. Act 21 & 22 Vict. c. 106, "An Act for the Better Government of India," received the Royal Assent on the 2nd of August, 1858. By it all the territories heretofore under the Government of the East India Company were transferred to Her Majesty the Queen, who in 1877 (Act 39 & 40 Vict. c. 10) formally assumed the title of Empress of India; and all the powers hitherto exercised by the East India Company, or by the Board of Control, were vested in the Secretary of State for India, assisted by a Council. The number of members of this Council, who are appointed by the Secretary of State, may not fall short of 10 or exceed 15.

The Government of India.

THE expenditure of the revenues of India is subject to the control of the Secretary of State for India in Council, who also conducts Indian business transacted in England. In matters requiring secrecy (*e.g.*, foreign policy) the Secretary of State can act on his own authority without consulting his Council, and in most other matters can overrule the majority of his Council. In all matters the Secretary of State, as the representative of Her Majesty's Government, can impose his orders on the Government of India. The Crown or the Secretary of State appoints the Viceroy and Governor-General, the Governors of Madras and Bombay, the Commander-in-Chief, the Ordinary Members of the Councils of the Governor-General and of the Governors of Madras and Bombay, and the Judges of the Presidency High Courts. The appointments of Lieutenant-Governor are made by the Governor-General, subject to the approval of the Secretary of State. The term of these appointments, except judgeships, is usually for five years. The four Lieutenant-Generals commanding the forces are appointed, two from the British and two from the Indian service, on the recommendation of the Commander-in-Chief at home. Subject to the Secretary of State's control, the Supreme Executive Authority in India is the Governor-General in Council. The Governor-General's Executive Council consists of seven members, including the Commander-in-Chief, who is an Extraordinary Member, and the Public Works Member, whose post may be left vacant at the option of the Crown. Governors and Lieut.-Governors also become Extraordinary Members when the Council meets within their Province. All acts of the SUPREME GOVERNMENT IN INDIA run in the name of "The Governor-General in Council"; but the Governor-General himself has the power of overruling the opinions of the majority of his Council. The Viceroy's Council, when it meets for purposes of Legislation, consists of the above members and of "Additional Members" for making Laws and Regulations." There are similar Legislative Councils in Madras, Bombay, Bengal, the North-West Provinces (with Oudh),

the Punjab and Burma. The business of the Government of India is divided into the Departments of Finance and Commerce, Home Affairs, Revenue and Agriculture, Military Administration, Legislation, Public Works, and Foreign Affairs. Each Department is under the charge of a Secretary, and is also the special care of a Member of the Supreme Council, who has authority to deal with affairs of routine and minor importance, and to select what is worthy of the consideration of the Governor-General and his collective Council. The Governor-General specially superintends the political business of the Foreign Office. The *Department of Finance and Commerce* looks to questions of Finance, to Stamps, Excise, the Post Office, and anything involving a permanent charge on the State; also to questions bearing on the commerce of the country. The most important subject coming under the attention of the *Department of Revenue and Agriculture* are the Land Revenue, Forests, and the Agricultural development of the country. The *Home Department* deals with th Educational, Medical, Sanitary, Ecclesiastical, and Judicial affairs, Municipalities, Local Government Boards, Police, and other matters, and has charge of the penal settlement of Port Blair. The *Foreign Department* conducts our relations with Afghanistan, Nepal, and other conterminous countries, and through its Political Residents and Agents in the various Native States supervises their administration and directs their relations with the paramount power. The *Public Works Department* deals with matters connected with Railways, Telegraphs, Roads, Canals, Buildings, &c. The Marine Service, as well as the Army, is under the *Military Department*. The Legal Member takes charge of Government Bills in the *Legislative Council*.

Separate *High Courts* have been established for the Presidencies of Madras and Bombay and for the Lieutenant-Governorship of Bengal (with jurisdiction also over Assam), and of the North-West Provinces. The Punjab has a Chief Court; the Central Provinces, Oudh, and Mysore have each a Judicial Commissioner, and Burma has two Judicial Commissioners (for Upper and Lower

Burma respectively) and a Recorder of Rangoon. A proposal to give Burma a Chief Court is now under consideration.

The division of India into Presidencies is now misleading. The expression is a relic of the time when the three settlements of Fort William, Fort St. George, and Bombay, each under the management of a President and Council, comprised, or were supposed to comprise, the whole of British India. British India is now really divided into *thirteen Local Governments and Administrations,* viz.:—Under Governors, Madras and Bombay, also termed Presidencies; under Lieutenant-Governors, Bengal, North-West Provinces with Oudh (of which the Lieutenant-Governor is Chief Commissioner), the Punjab, and Burma; under Chief Commissioners, Assam, Central Provinces, Berar (of which the Resident at Hyderabad is Chief Commissioner, Ajmere Merwara (the Governor-General's Agent in Rajputana being Chief Commissioner), Coorg (of which

the Resident at Mysore is Chief Commissioner), British Baluchistan (of which the Governor-General's Agent in Baluchistan is Chief Commissioner), and the Andaman Islands. These several Local Governments and Administrations enjoy a large measure of financial and administrative independence. The Governors of Madras and Bombay have greater independence than the others, being alone permitted to communicate on certain minor matters direct with the Secretary of State.

The unit of administration throughout British India is the District, at the head of which is an executive officer, called Collector-Magistrate or Deputy-Commissioner, as the case may be. In subordination (in most Provinces) to a Commissioner, who corresponds direct with the Provincial Government, he has control in every department of administration, and is the responsible head of his jurisdiction. There are 250 Districts in British India.

For India Office Establishment, see p. 160.

THE SUPREME GOVERNMENT, CALCUTTA.

[Indian revenue figures are stated in tens of rupees under the denomination Rx.]
[Indian salaries are the substantive salaries (excluding allowances) stated in rupees *per mensem.*]

Viceroy and Governor-General (Rs. 20,833 *per mensem*), His Excellency the Right Honourable the Lord Curzon of Kedleston, P.C., G.M.S.I., G.M.I.E., *b.* 1859, *m.* Mary Victoria Leiter. (6 January, 1899.)

Private Secretary, Walter Roper Lawrence, C.I.E. ....Rs. 2,000
Assistant Private Secretary, F. W. Latimer.
Military Secretary ....Rs. 1,500
Aides-de-Camp, [Lieut. F. L. Adam, Scots Guards;] Capt. R. G. T. Baker-Carr, Rifle Brigade; Capt. R. J. Marker, Coldm. Gds.; Lieut. C Wigram, I.S.C.
Extra Aides-de-Camp, The Earl of Suffolk, Lieut. H. N. Holden, 5th Bengal Cavalry.
Native Aides-de-Camp, Risaldar-Maj. Bahauddin Khan, Sardar Bahadur, 1 C. I. H., and Risaldar Wali Muhammad, Sardar Bahadur, Gov.-Genl.'s Bodyguard.
Surgeon, Lieut.-Col. E. H. Fenn, C.I.E., R.A.M.C. ....Rs. 1,200

COUNCIL OF THE GOVERNOR-GENERAL.

Extraordinary Member, H.E. General Sir. Wm. S. A. Lockhart, G.C.B., K.C.S.I., Commander-in-Chief in India (1898) ....Rs. 8,333
Ordinary Members (5), Maj.-Gen. Sir E. H. H. Collen, K.C.I.E.; Sir Arthur Charles Trevor, K.C.S.I.; Chs. M. Rivaz, C.S.I.; Clinton Ed. Dawkins (to be succeeded in March 1900 by Sir Ed. FitzGerald Law, K.C.M.G.); Thomas Raleigh ....each Rs. 6,666
Extraordinary Members, the Governors of the other Presidencies when the Council shall assemble within their territory.
Additional Members for Making Laws and Regulations:— *Official*, J. J. D. La Touche, C.S.I.; J. K. Spence, C.S.I.; G. Toynbee; D. M. Smeaton, C.S.I.; J. D. Rees, C.I.E.; Rai Bahadur Protul Chandar Chatterjee. *Non-Official*, Sir G. H. P. Evans, K.C.I.E.; R. B. Pandit Suraj Kaul, C.I.E.; Gangadhar Rao Madhav Chitnavis, C.I.E.; Allan Arthur; Phirozeshah Mervanji Mehta, C.I.E.; Nawab Mumtaz-ud-Dowlah Muhammad Fayaz Ali Khan; Maharaja of Durbhanga; Nawab Bahadur Sir Khwaja Ahsanuella, K.C.I.E.; M.R.Ry. P. Ananda Charlu Vidia Vinodha Avargal, C.I.E.
Sec. to Council and Sec. to Government Legislative Department, J. M. Macpherson, C.S.I....Rs. 3,500
SECRETARIES TO THE GOVERNMENT OF INDIA.
HOME.—John P. Hewett, C.I.E. ....Rs. 4,000
REVENUE AND AGRICULTURE.—T. W. Holderness, C.S.I. ....Rs. 4,000
FINANCE AND COMMERCE.—James Fairbairn Finlay, C.S.I. ....Rs. 4,000
FOREIGN.—Sir W. J. Cuningham, K.C.S.I....Rs. 4,000
MILITARY.—Maj.-Gen. P. J. Maitland, C.B.

PUBLIC WORKS.—F. R. Upcott.
Advocate-General, Sir Gregory C. Paul, K.C.I.E.
Agents to Gov.-Gen. (Rs. 4,000): *Central India,* Lt.-Col. D. W. K. Barr, C.S.I. (Rs.4,250); *Rajputana,* A. H. T. Martindale (Rs. 4,250); *Baluchistan,* H. S. Barnes, C.S.I. (Rs. 4,750).
Residents: Hyderabad (Rs. 5,000), Sir T. J. C. Plowden, K.C.S.I.; *Mysore* (Rs. 4,500), Lt.-Col. Donald Robertson, C.S.I.; *Cashmere* (Rs. 2,750), Lt.-Col. SIR A.C. Talbot, K.C.I.E.; *Baroda* (Rs. 2,500), Lt.-Col. N. C. Martelli; *Nepal,* Col. H. Wylie, C.S.I. (Rs. 2,250); *Gwalior,* Lieut.-Col. J. H. Newill (Rs. 2,150).
Political Residents: Persian Gulf, Lieut.-Col. M. J. Meade (Rs. 2,750); *Aden,* Brigadier-Gen. O'M. Creagh, V.C. ....Rs. 3,500
Political Agent and Consul-General, Bagdad, Major P. J. Melvill ....Rs. 2,500
MILITARY DEPARTMENT, GOVERNMENT OF INDIA.
Director-General of Ordnance in India, Maj.-Gen. R. Wace, R.A., C.B.
Director-General of Military Works, Maj.-Gen. S. C. Turner, R.E.
Commissary General-in-Chief, Maj.-Gen. T. F. Hobday, C.B., I.S.C.
Director-General Indian Medical Service, Surg.-Gen. R. Harvey, C.B.

HEADQUARTERS STAFF OF ARMY OF INDIA.
COMMANDER-IN-CHIEF IN INDIA, H.E. Gen. Sir Wm. S. A. Lockhart, G.C.B.; 1898 ....Rs. 8,333
Milit. Sec., Col. F. S. Gwatkin, I.S.C.
Adjutant-General, Maj.-Gen. Sir W. G. Nicholson, K.C.B.
Quartermaster-General, Major-General A. R. Badcock, C.B.

Principal Medical Officer, H.M.'s Forces in India, Surg.-Gen. W. Taylor, C.B.

Judge Advocate-General in India, Lt.-Col. W. H. F. Macmullen.

Principal Veterinary Officer in India, Vety.-Col. H. Thomson.

Director of Military Education in India, Col. H. D. Hutchinson.

Lieutenant-Generals Commanding the Forces (4).

Lt.-Gen. Sir G. B. Wolseley, K.C.B., Madras Commd.

Lt.-Gen. Sir R. C. Low, G.C.B., Bombay Commd.

Lt.-Gen. Sir G. Luck, K.C.B., Bengal Commd.

Lt.-Gen. Sir A. P. Palmer, K.C.B., Punjab Commd.

First Class District Commanders (10).

Maj.-Gen. Sir B. Blood, K.C.B., Meerut.

Maj.-Gen. Sir G. de C. Morton, K.C.I.E., Lahore.

Maj.-Gen. C. E. Egerton, C.B., Punjab Frontier Force.

Maj.-Gen. M. H. Nicolson, C.B., Mhow.

Maj.-Gen. Sir A. Hunter, K.C.B., Quetta (temporarily in S. Africa).

Maj.-Gen. B. A. Coombe, C.B., Rawal Pindi.

Maj.-Gen. M. Protheroe, C.B., Burma.

Maj.-Gen. C. Tucker, C.B., Secunderabad.

Maj.-Gen. C. J. Burnett, C.B., Poona.

Maj.-Gen. R. M. Jennings, C.B., Oudh.

Second Class District Commanders (19).

Brigdr.-Gen. O'M. Creagh, V.C., Aden.

Maj.-Gen. G. C. Hogg, C.B., Deesa.

Maj.-Gen. D. J. S. McLeod, C.B., Bangalore.

Brigdr.-Gen. E. J. Lugard, Southern (Madras).

Brigdr.-Gen. Sir E. R. Elles, K.C.B., Peshawar.

Brigdr.-Gen. J. T. Cummins, D.S.O., Madras.

Brigdr.-Gen. Sir R. C. Hart, V.C., Belgaum.

Brigdr.-Gen. J. H. Barnard, C.B., A.D.C., Mandalay.

Brigdr.-Gen. Sir R. Westmacott, K.C.B., Nagpore.

Brigdr.-Gen. S. E. Rolland, Rangoon.

Brigdr.-Gen. F. Ventris, Bombay.

Brigdr.-Gen. Sir J. H. Wodehouse, C.B., Presidency.

Brigdr.-Gen. P. D. Jeffreys, C.B., Narbudda.

Brigdr.-Gen. Sir A. Gaselee, K.C.B., A.D.C., Bundelkhand.

Brigdr.-Gen. Sir W. H. Meiklejohn, K C.B., Rohilkhand.

Brigdr.Gen. A. J. F. Reid, C.B., Allahabad.

Brigdr.-Gen. St. J. F. Michell, Assam.

Brigdr.-Gen. H. A. MacDonald, C.B., A.D.C., Sirhind.

Vacant, Sind.

Maj.-Gen. Sir M. G. Gerard, K.C.S.I., Hyderabad Contgt.

Colonels on the Staff Commanding Stations (10).

Col. G. Henry, Rawal Pindi.

Col. C. R. Macgregor, C.B., Ferozepore.

Col. Henry S. Tandy, Nusserabad.

Col. N. F. FitzG. Chamberlain, Delhi.

Col. E. B. Anderson, Southern Shan States.

Col. W. J. Vousden, C.B., Sialkot.

Col. G. H. More-Molyneux, Cawnpore.

Col. R. A. Gilchrist, Bellary.

Col. G. H. C. Dyce, C.B., Mooltan.

ECCLESIASTICAL.

Bp. of Calcutta, Metropolitan of India and Ceylon, Most Rev. Jas. Edward Cowell Welldon, D.D.

Archdeacon and Commissary, Ven. A. E. Stone.

Bp.'s Commissary in England, Rev. Brook Deedes, Hawkhurst, Kent.

Bp. of Madras, Most Rev. Henry Whitehead, M.A.

Archdeacon and Commissary, Ven. W. W. Elwes.

Bp.'s Commissary, Rev. Canon W. Benham, B.D.

Bp. of Bombay, Rt. Rev. James MacArthur, D.D.

Archdeacon and Commissary, Ven. W. E. Scott.

Bp.'s Commissary in England, Rev. H. G. Daniell-Bainbridge, Minor Canon of Westminster.

Bp. of Lahore, Rt. Rev. George Lefroy.

Archdeacon and Commissary, Ven. A. N. W. Spens.

Bp. of Rangoon, Rt. Rev. John M. Strachan, D.D.

Archdeacon, Ven. C. H. Chard.

Bp. of Travancore and Cochin, Right Rev. E. N. Hodges.

Bp. of Chota Nagpur, Rt. Rev. Jabez Cornelius Whitley.

Bp. of Lucknow, Rt. Rev. Alfred Clifford.

Archdeacon, Ven. O. D. Watkins.

Abp. of Calcutta (Rom. Cath.), The Most Rev. Dr. Paul Goethals, S.J.

Abp. of Madras (Rom. Cath.), The Most Rev. J. Colgan, D.D.

Abp. of Bombay (Rom. Cath.), Most Rev. T. Dalhoff.

Abp. of Agra (Rom. Cath.), Most Rev. Dr. Emmanuel Vanden Bosch.

PROVINCIAL GOVERNMENTS AND ADMINISTRATIONS.

(1) MADRAS (area,* 141,189 sq. miles; pop.* 35,630,440), was the scene of our struggle with the French, whose principal settlement, Pondicherry, is 90 miles south of the city of Madras. Though the most important of the three Presidencies until Clive's conquest of Bengal, it was small in extent till 1801, when the annexation of the Carnatic raised it to nearly its present dimensions. It is larger than Great Britain and Ireland together, and has a population equal to that of Italy. With a coast-line of 1,730 miles the province has not one good natural harbour; a large artificial harbour has been completed at Madras at great expense. The province is not naturally fertile, and possesses little mineral wealth. The irrigation systems in the river deltas of this province have enormously increased the produce of the soil, and have yielded a large profit to the State. Its trade is served by South Indian, Madras, and East Coast railways, while the Great Indian Peninsula

and Southern Mahratta lines connect it with the Bombay Presidency. The Governor of Madras is assisted by a Council ordinarily of two members, to whom are added, for legislative business, other members not to exceed 21 (including the Advocate-General *ex officio*), of whom the first seven have been appointed on the recommendations of the Madras Corporation (1), of other Municipal Councils (2), of District Boards (2), of the Chamber of Commerce (1), and of the University (1); the rest are selected by the Government.

CHIEF CITY, Madras. Population, 452,518.

Governor, Sir Arthur Elibank Havelock, G.C.M.G. (18 March, 1896) ....Rs. 10,000

Priv. Sec., H. A. Sim ....Rs. 1,500

Mil. Sec., Maj. J. W. Currie, I.S.C.   Rs. 1,000

Aides-de-Camp, Capt. W. McL. Campbell, Black Watch; Lieut. Hon. G. E. Mills (*extra*), and Lieut. Wm. A. Fetherstonhaugh, 20th Madr. Inf. (*extra*).

Native Aide-de-Camp, Subadar-Major Shaikh Farid Bahadur.

Medical Officer, Maj. W. B. Browning, I.M.S., C.I.E. ....Rs. 1,000

* The areas and populations of the separate provinces are for British territory only, and do not include the Native States subordinate to the provinces in question: the populations are taken from the census returns of 1891.

COUNCIL OF THE GOVERNOR.

The Hons. Arundel Tagg Arundel, C.S.I., and Henry Martin Winterbotham, Rs. 5,333 each.

Additional Members for Making Laws and Regulations :—Official, Geo. Hy. Stuart ; John Sturrock ; Gabriel Stokes ; Geo. Stuart Forbes ; James Thomson ; D. Duncan, D.SC. ; P. Rajaratna Mudaliar, Diwan Bahadur ; F. A. Nicholson, C.I.E. *Non-Official*, N. Subha Rao Pantulu ; C. Jambalingam Madaliyar, Rao Bahadur ; C. Vijaraghava Chariyar ; P. Ratnasabhapati Pillai ; S. Shangra Subbayar, C.I.E. ; Ghulam Muhammad Sahib Bahadur ; H. P. Hodgson ; V. Bashyam Aiyangar, C.I.E. ; Raja of Bobbili, K.C.I.E. ; Lt.-Col. Sir G. M. J. Moore, C.I.E. ; Chas. E. P. Vans Agnew ; E. J. Norton.

SECRETARIES TO GOVERNMENT.

Chief Secretary, Gabriel Stokes...............Rs. 3,750
Revenue Dept., Geo. S. Forbes ....Rs. 3,125
Local and Municipal, J. H. A. Tremenheere Rs. 2,500
Public Works Department, Walter B. de Winton Rs. 2,000

HIGH COURT OF JUDICATURE.

Chief Justice, Hon. C. A. White......... Rs. 5,000
Judges, Hons. Horatio Hale Shephard ; S. Subramanya Aiyar, C.I.E. ; J. A. Davies ; R. S. Benson ; Hungerford T. Boddam ...Rs. 4,000
Advocate-Gen. (vacant) ....Rs. 1,800

(2) BOMBAY.—The Island of BOMBAY was part of the dowry of the Infanta of Portugal (1661), and was made over by Charles II. to the East India Company in 1668. The Province (exclusive of Native States, but including *Sind*, *Aden*, and *Perim*) contains 125,144 sq. miles (nearly equal in size to Prussia), with a population of 18,901,123 : it is 1,050 miles in length, and has many fine natural harbours, Bombay and Karachi being by far the most important. Native States occupy about one-third of the Presidency ; Sind, conquered in 1843, a non-regulation province, one-fourth ; and Bombay proper the remaining 82,000 square miles. The greater portion of the people (76 per cent.) are Hindus, and 17 per cent. are Mohammedans. The greater part of the territory was obtained by annexations from the Mahratta powers, and by the lapse of the Satara State. Sind was conquered by Sir Charles Napier in 1843. Its administration is in some respects separate from that of the rest of the Presidency. Aden, occupied in 1839, and Perim (1857), having together an area of 85 square miles and a population of 41,912, belong to the Government of Bombay. Cotton is largely produced for export and for manufacture in the constantly growing cotton mills of Bombay itself. The chief railway systems of Bombay are the Bombay Baroda and the lines worked by it to the north, and the Great Indian Peninsula eastwards ; south-eastwards is the Southern Mahratta system ; while Karachi is the outlet for the North Western railway, the old Scinde Punjaub and Delhi line. The Governor is assisted by a Council similar to that in Madras, already described, except that the first eight of the additional members are appointed on the recommendation of Bombay Corporation (1), of other Municipal Corporations (1), of District Boards (1), of Sardars of the Deccan (1), of Jaghirdars and Zamindars of Sind (1), of Bombay and Karachi Chambers of Commerce (1 each), and of Bombay University (1).

CHIEF CITY, Bombay. Population, 821,764.

Governor, Lord Sandhurst, G.C.I.E. (2nd Feb., 1895) (to be succeeded in Feb. 1900 by Sir Henry Stafford Northcote, Bt.) ....Rs. 10,000
Private Sec., A. M. T. Jackson...........Rs. 1,500
Military Sec., Maj. Richard Owen, 21st Lancers.
Aides-de-Camp, Capt. A. D. Young, R.H.A. ; Lt. J. G. Greig, 28 Bo. Inf. ; Lt. H. B. D. Wilkinson, 2nd Durham L.I. *(extra)* (*Native A.-de-C.*). Risaldar Shaikh Abdul Karim, Govr's. Body Guard.
Medical Officer, Maj. H. Martin, I.M.S., M.B. Rs.1,000

COUNCIL OF THE GOVERNOR.

John Nugent, C.S.I. ; Sir E. C. K. Ollivant, K.C.I.E. ....Rs. 5,333
Additional Members for Making Laws and Regulations, The Hons. Basil Lang (*Advocate-General*) ; Mir Allahbakshkhan walad Mir Alibakshkhan Shahvani Talpur ; Narayan Ganesh Chandavakar ; Gokuldas Kahendas Parekh ; Meherban Narayanrao Govind ; Fazulbai Visram ; Dhondo Shamrao Garud ; Phirozeshah M. Mehta, C.I.E. ; Vribhukandas Atmaran ; E. Giles ; Chunilal Venilal, C.I.E. ; W. C. Hughes ; Achynt Bhaskar Desai ; P. C. H. Snow, C.I.E. ; F. S. P. Lely ; A. Abercrombie ; T. L. F. Beaumont ; Shripat Anant Chatre ; J. Tate ; H. F. Aston ; J. W. P. Muir-Mackenzie ; Bamanji Dinshaw Petit ; L. C. Crump, *Secy.*

SECRETARIES TO GOVERNMENT.

Chief Secretary, Revenue, Financial, and Separate Departments, Jas. Monteath, C.S.I. ......Rs. 3,750
Educational, General, &c., J. DeC. Atkins. Rs. 2,500
Public Works, John Tate ....Rs. 2,500
Political, Judicial, Legislative, Steyning W. Edgerley, C.I.E...................................Rs. 3,125

HIGH COURT OF JUDICATURE.

Chief Justice, Sir Lawrence Hugh Jenkins, Kt., Rs. 5,000
Judges, Hons. Henry James Parsons ; Edward Townshend Candy ; R. B. Mahadeo Govind Ranade, C.I.E. ; Badrudin Tyabji ; Edmund McG. H. Fulton ; L. P. Russell....each Rs. 4,000
Commissioner in Sind, Henry E. M. James, C.S.I. Rs. 4,000
Political Resident at Aden, Brig.-Gen. O'M. Creagh, V.C..............................Rs. 3,500

(3) BENGAL (area 151,543 sq. miles ; pop. 71,346,987) was placed under a Lieutenant-Governor in 1854, having previously been part of the charge of the Governor-General. With a population nine millions in excess of that of the United States of America, it is spread over an area 1-23rd of that country. It occupies the Valley of the Ganges eastward of Benares, and extends from the Himalayas to the mouth of the Mahanuddy. For the most part the province is a great alluvial plain, producing rice, and is the most populous and productive in all British India. Orissa and Chota Nagpur, to the west and south-west, are ill-watered and liable to drought. The chief products, besides rice, are opium, indigo, and jute. In the hills bordering the great alluvial plain, coal measures are also being largely worked. The East Indian line is the great railway artery of the Ganges Valley. The Eastern Bengal railway also terminates in Calcutta. Other important systems are the Bengal and North-Western in the north and the Bengal Nagpur in the south of the province. The Assam Bengal line, which will make Chittagong the port of Assam, is under construction. The Lieutenant - Governor is assisted by a Council for the purposes of making Laws and Regulations, of not more

than 20 members. Of the following list seven members have been appointed on the recommendations of the following bodies:—Calcutta Corporation (1), other Municipal Corporations (2), District Bodies (2), Bengal Chamber of Commerce (1), and Calcutta University (1).

Chief City, CALCUTTA (pop., including suburbs, 978,370).

Lieutenant-Governor (Rs. 8,333), Hon. Sir John Woodburn, K.C.S.I. (7 April, 1898).

   Private Secretary, Capt. J. Strachey ...... Rs. 950
   Aide-de-Camp,   Rs. 452

COUNCIL OF THE LIEUT.-GOVERNOR FOR MAKING LAWS AND REGULATIONS.

The Lieut.-Governor (*President*), The Honourables Sir Gregory Ch. Paul, K.C.I.E. (*Adv.-Gen.*); Nawab Syud Ameer Hossein, C.I.E.; W. B. Oldham; R. B. Buckley; C. W. Bolton, C.S.I.; E. N. Baker; M. Finucane, C.S.I.; Durga Gati Banerjee, C.I.E.; J. Pratt; C. E. Buckland, C.I.E.; Saligram Singh; Kali Charan Banerjee; Maharaja Bahadur of Darbhanga, G.C.I.E.; Surendranath Banerjee; Jatra Mohan Sen; T. W. Spink; Raja Shashi Shakhareswar Roy Bahadur; Raja Ranjit Sinha, Bahadur of Nashipur; Sahibzada Mahomed Bakhtyar Shah, C.I.E.; D. F. Mackenzie.

SECRETARIES TO GOVERNMENT.

Chief Secretary, C. W. Bolton, C.S.I. ......Rs. 3,333
General, Revenue, and Statistical, M. Finucane, C.S.I. ....Rs. 2,916
Financial and Municipal, Herbert Hope Risley, C.I.E. ....Rs. 2,916
Public Works, Col. A. D. McArthur, R.E. Rs. 2,500

HIGH COURT OF JUDICATURE.

Chief Justice, Hon. Sir Francis W. Maclean, Kt., K.C.I.E. ....Rs. 6,000
Puisne Judges, The Hons. Sir Henry Thoby Prinsep (Rs. 4,166); William Macpherson; Chunder Madbub Ghose; Dr. Gooroo Das Banerjee; Amir Ali, C.I.E.; Charles H. Hill; Robert F. Rampini; Stephen George Sale; John Foster Stevens; John Stanley; C. A. Wilkins.
                        each Rs. 4,000
Adv.-Gen., Sir Gregory Charles Paul, K.C.I.E.
                             Rs. 3,135

(4) The NORTH-WEST PROVINCES and OUDH (area, 107,503 sq. miles; pop. 46,905,085), with a population as large as that of the German Empire on less than one-half its area, form the upper part of the great plain of the Ganges to the west of Bengal, lying between the Himalayan Mountains and the hilly border of the central plateau. Originally the North-West Provinces formed part of the Bengal Presidency. In 1833 it was intended (Act 3 & 4 Will. IV. cap. 85) to establish a separate Presidency of Agra. The idea was dropped in 1835 (Act 5 & 6 Will. IV. c. 52), when, however, a Lieutenant-Governor was appointed for the separate administration of these provinces. OUDH, equal in size to Holland and Belgium, was annexed in 1856 and placed under a Chief Commissioner, but since 1877 the offices of Lieutenant-Governor of the North-West Provinces and Chief Commissioner of Oudh have been combined in the same person. In 1887 a Council was established for making Laws and Regulations for the combined Provinces. Of the following list six members have been appointed on the recommendations of the following bodies:—Municipal Corporations (2), District Bodies (2), Chamber of Commerce of Upper India (1), and Allahabad

University (1). The maximum number on the Council is 15. The character of the province resembles that of Bengal. The chief staple is wheat, and indigo, cotton, sugar, opium, and oilseeds are sown largely for commerce. Tea is also cultivated in the sub-Himalayan districts. The province is well served with railways, belonging to the East Indian, Oudh and Rohilkhand, and Rohilkhand-Kumaon systems. The *Chief City* of the North-West Provinces is ALLAHABAD (pop. 175,246); that of Oudh is LUCKNOW (pop. 273,028).

Lieut.-Gov., Sir Antony P. MacDonnell, G.C.S.I. (6 Nov. 1895) ....Rs. 8,333
   Priv. Sec., Capt. E. C. Bayley, I.S.C....... Rs. 725
   Aide-de-Camp, Maj. H. L. Pennall ....Rs. 890
Chief Sec. to Govt., J. O. Miller .... Rs. 3,000
2nd Sec. to Govt., L. M. Thornton......... Rs. 2,250
3rd Sec. to Govt., J. S. Meston.

COUNCIL OF THE LIEUT.-GOVERNOR AND CHIEF COMMISSIONER FOR MAKING LAWS AND REGULATIONS.

The Lieutenant-Governor (*President*). The Hons. Raja Rampal Singh; Babu Sri Ram, Rai Bahadur; Lt.-Col. W. E. Cooper, C.I.E.; J. O. Miller; C. W. Odling, C.S.I.; J. Hooper; Pandit Bishambar Nath; H. F. Evans, C.S.I.; T. Conlan; Raja Balwant Singh, C.I.E.; Nawab Mumtaz-ud-Daula Mahammad Faiyaz Ali Khan; Maharaja Sir Partab Narayan Singh, K.C.I.E.; R. H. Macleod; J. S. Meston; D. T. Roberts.

HIGH COURT OF JUDICATURE (WITH JURISDICTION IN THE NORTH-WEST PROVINCES ONLY).

Chief Justice, Hon. Sir Arthur Strachey...Rs. 5,000
Puisne Judges, The Hons. George Edward Knox, Harrison F. Blair, Babu Pramoda Charan Banarji, William Robert Burkitt, Robert Smith Aikman ....each Rs. 4,000
Judicial Commissioner of Oudh, Joseph Deas
                          Rs. 3,500
Add. Judl. Commrs., George T. Spankie; Wm. Blennerhasset...........................Rs. 3,333

(5) The PUNJAB (area, 110,667 sq. miles; pop. 20,866,847), with a larger population than Spain and Portugal together, occupies the north-western angle of the great northern plain of India, and receives its name from "Five Rivers" which, descending from the Himalayas, cross the plain and unite in the Indus. It was annexed in 1849, and up to 1853 was administered by a Board of Administration. This Board was then superseded by a Chief Commissioner, who in 1859 was raised to the rank of Lieutenant-Governor. The division of Delhi was at the same time transferred to the Province from the North-West Provinces. In April 1897 the Indian Councils Act was extended by proclamation to the Punjab and a Legislative Council for the Province constituted, to consist of 9 nominated members, 5 being officials and 4 non-officials. Besides the territory under British Administration, which is about as large as the Kingdom of Italy, there is an area of one-third that size belonging to 34 Feudatory Native States, with a population of more than 4¼ millions. Thirdly, there are the frontier tribes, split up into numerous clans with divergent interests, whose fighting strength is estimated at 130,000 men. The province is mainly agricultural, and depends largely for its harvests on artificial irrigation works which in the Punjab are on a vast scale and highly remunerative. It

possesses rich deposits of rock-salt, which, with wheat and other grains and cotton, form its principal exports. The various branches of the North Western system of railways serve the Punjab.

CHIEF CITY, Lahore. Population, 176,854.

Lieut.-Governor, Sir W. Mackworth Young, K.C.S.I...Rs. 8,333

Private Sec. & A.-de-C., Capt. J. M. Stewart. Rs. 724

Council of the Lieutenant-Governor for making Laws and Regulations, Sir Baba Bedi Khem Singh, K.C.I.E.; S. S. Thorburn; Haji Nawab Fatteh Ali Khan; Saiyid Muhammad Hussain, Khalifa, Khan Bahadur; J. S. Beresford; Rai Babadur Madan Gopal; C. L. Tupper, C.S.I., H. C. Fanshawe, L. W. Dane, E. W. Parker, *Secretary*.

Chief Sec. to Govt., L. W. Dane .... Rs. 2,500

Revenue Sec. to Govt., N. W. Fenton.

Sec. to Govt., Judl. and Genl. Depts., H. J. Maynard.

Financial Commissioner, S. S. Thorburn.. Rs. 3,500

Settlement Commissioner, Lt.-Col. Jas. A. L. Montgomery...Rs. 3,000

Chief Court:—Chief Judge, W. O. Clark.. Rs. 3,750

Judges, A. H. S. Reid ; Protul Chunder Chatterji, Rai Bahadur; T. G. Walker; J. A. Anderson ....each Rs. 3,500

(6) The Province of BURMA is bounded by China and by Chinese subordinate tribes, by Siam, by our provinces of Bengal and Assam, and by the sea. The area of Lower Burma is 87,957 square miles; that of Upper Burma, 83,473 square miles. Tenasserim and Arakan were annexed after the first Burmese war in 1826, Pegu after the second war in 1852, and Upper Burma and the Shan States after the third war of 1885. The province is thinly peopled. The population of Lower Burma was 4,658,627 in 1891; that of Upper Burma 2,946,933. The delta country of Lower Burma is flat, but above Prome it is an upland, hilly country. Rice is the main product of the delta region, and is very largely exported. The principal export besides rice is teak, which comes from the forests of both Upper and Lower Burma, and from the Shan States and Siam. The Upper Province is also rich in minerals, including rubies, jade, iron, lead, tin, coal, and petroleum ; gold and silver are also known to exist. The Irrawaddy and its chief tributaries, the Chindwin, the Shweli, and the Myitnge, supply important navigable waterways. The main river is itself navigable beyond the town of Bhamo, 900 miles from its mouth. Manufactured goods are exported by land to the Shan States and to China. There is a large traffic by river and by the Burma railway, which has reached Myitkina on the upper Irrawaddy while a branch is being built to the Kunlon Ferry on the Salween. The inhabitants—of the common Indo-Chinese stock—belong to numerous different tribes, who are distinguished by a variety of manners, languages, and religions. The most general religion is some form of Buddhism. The Lieutenant-Governor of Burma has a Local Legislative Council of 9 nominated members (5 official and 4 non-official).

CHIEF TOWN OF LOWER BURMA, Rangoon. Pop. 180,324.

CHIEF TOWN OF UPPER BURMA, Mandalay. Pop. 188,815.

Lieut.-Governor, Sir Frederic William Richards Fryer, K.C.S.I...Rs. 8,333

Private Sec.,

A.-de-C., Capt. E. S. Jackson, 6th Dgns.

COUNCIL OF THE LIEUT.-GOVERNOR FOR MAKING RULES AND REGULATIONS.

The Lieut.-Governor (*Presid nt*); J. E. Bridges; E. S. Symes, C.I.E.; C. G. Bayne ; A. Pennycuick, C I E.; J. Macgregor; U Gaung, C.S.I., Ex-Kinwun Mingyi ; Hkun Saing, C.I.E., Sawbwa of Hsipaw; C. E. Fox; H. J. Richard.

Chief Sec., Edward Spence Symes, C.I.E. Rs. 3,000

Revenue Sec., C. G. Bayne ....Rs. 2,000

Sec., F. C. Gates.

Sec. P. W. Dept., H. J. Richard.

Financial Commissioner, Donald Mackenzie Smeaton, C.S.I. ....Rs. 3,000

Judicial Commissioners (*Upper Burma*), H. Thirkwell White, C.I.E. ....Rs. 3,000

(*Lower Burma*) F. S. Copleston .... Rs. 2,880

Recorder of Rangoon, Sir Wm. Fischer Agnew Rs. 2,880

Rangoon by the mail route is 7,663 miles from London ; transit 18 to 21 days.

Mandalay is 386 miles from Rangoon by railway ; transit 18 hours.

Telegrams to Burma, per word by Eastern or Indo-European Cos., 4s. 2d. ; *vid* Turkey, 3s. 10d. Post and parcel rates same as India.

(7) The CENTRAL PROVINCES (area, 86,501 sq. miles; pop. 10,784,294), containing a population equal to that of Holland and Belgium combined on an area 3½ times that of those countries, were formed in 1861, out of territory taken from the North-West Provinces and Madras, but originally belonging to the Mahratta Kingdom of Nagpur. These provinces contain a large population of aboriginal tribes. Much has been done, by constructing railways (belonging to the Indian Midland, Bengal Nagpur, and Great Indian Peninsula systems) and roads, to open up the country, which possesses large coal-fields, as well as excellent iron ores, and is an important producer of rice, wheat, and cotton for export.

CHIEF CITY, Nagpur. Population, 117,910.

Chief Comm., Denzil C. J. Ibbetson, C.S.I. Rs. 4,666

Chief Sec. to Chief Com., M. W. Fox Strangways Rs. 2,000

Judicial Commissioner, S. Ismay ....Rs. 3,166

(8) ASSAM (area, 49,004 sq. miles; pop. 5,476,833), was constituted a separate administration in 1874. out of Bengal districts, most of which had been ceded by Burma in 1825. A range of mountains divides the province into the Surma and Brahmaputra Valleys. The *chief City* of the Brahmaputra Valley is GAUHATI (pop., in 1891, 10,817), and of the Surma Valley SYLHET (pop., in 1891, 14,027). The revenue is comparatively small. The staple crop is rice. But Cachar, Sylhet, Sibsagar, and Lakhimpur are the most important tea-growing districts in India. The mineral resources, consisting mainly of coal, petroleum, iron, and limestone, have only begun to be utilized. The construction of an important system of railways (the Assam-Bengal line) for the development of Assam is in progress.

SEAT OF GOVERNMENT, Shillong. Pop., 2,185.

Chief Comm. (Rs.4,166),Hy.J.StedmanCotton,C.S.I.

Sec. to Ch. Comm. (Rs.2,000), Francis John Monahan.

(9) BERAR, also termed the *Hyderabad Assigned Districts* (area, 17,718 sq. miles; pop. 2,897,491), which lies to the north of Hyderabad, was placed in our hands by the Nizam in 1853, in payment of arrears due to the British Government and to meet for the future the cost of the Hyderabad contingent. The laws of British India do not run as

such in Berar; they are, however, generally in force as regulations which the Governor-General has directed shall be followed in those districts. The province is fertile, and yields the finest cotton grown in India. It forms part of the charge of the British Resident at Hyderabad. The revenue and expenditure of the Hyderabad Assigned Districts, amounting respectively to Rx. 992,346 and Rx. 1,004,708 in 1897-98, are excluded from the Accounts of the Government of India. The surplus revenues, after defraying the cost of administration and the charges for the Hyderabad Contingent, go to the Nizam's Government. There was no surplus in 1897-98. The amounts paid over to the Nizam on account of the Berar surplus since the transfer of the province to British administration make up a total of Rx. 3,342,000. *Chief City*, ELLICHPUR (pop., in 1891, 36,240). The administration is under the *Resident at Hyderabad*, Sir Trevor J. C. Plowden, K.C.S.I. (Rs. 4,000).

(10) AJMERE-MERWARA (area, 2,711 sq. miles, pop. 542,358), ceded in 1818, lies within Rajputana. The Governor-General's Agent in Rajputana is *ex officio* Chief Commissioner of Ajmere-Merwara and the chief executive and judicial authority.
Agent to the Governor-General in Rajputana and Chief Commissioner of Ajmere-Merwara, A. H. T. Martindale (Rs. 4,000).

(11) COORG (area, 1,583 sq. miles, pop. 173,055), annexed in 1834. The Resident at Mysore is *ex officio* Chief Commissioner and the chief executive and judicial authority.
Resident at Mysore and Chief Commissioner of Coorg, Lt.-Col. Donald Robertson, C.S.I. (Rs. 4,000).

(12) BRITISH BALUCHISTAN was constituted a separate administration in 1888, under the Governor-General's Agent in Baluchistan as *ex officio* Chief Commissioner. The districts comprised in this administration were partly acquired from Afghanistan by the treaty of Gundamuck, partly by arrangement with the Khan of Kalat. The Governor-General's Agent also supervises and controls, by advice, by arbitration, and if necessary by direct interference, the affairs of the rest of Baluchistan to the Persian frontier. The area and population of the Agency are not known. The population of British Baluchistan is 145,417.
Agent to the Governor-General for Baluchistan and Chief Commissioner of British Baluchistan, H. S. Barnes, C.S.I. (Rs. 4,750).

(13) The ANDAMANS (area, 2,508 square miles), a chain of islands in the eastern part of the Bay of Bengal, divided into two groups known as the Great and Little Andamans, are of tertiary formation, covered with a luxuriant vegetation, and inhabited by a tribe of Nigritos. The race is dying out. Since 1858 these islands have been used as a penal settlement by the British Government of India; Port Blair, with its safe and spacious harbour, on South Andaman, constituting the civilised portion. Much valuable timber is obtained from the jungles. Tea, rice, Indian corn, manioc, Otaheite potatoes, and artichokes are successfully cultivated, and experiments in Liberian coffee, cacao, and indigo are being persevered in. Of the entire population (about 15,000) four-fifths comprise the convict element. Convict labour is at present mainly devoted to the construction of cellular jails for future newly-arrived convicts and bad characters.

The *Nicobar Islands* (635 sq. miles) lie almost due south of the Andamans and to the north-west of Sumatra. They formerly belonged to Denmark, but were first occupied by the British in

1869, since when they have been affiliated to the Chief Commissionership of the Andamans. They consist of twelve inhabited and seven uninhabited islands, of which the most important is the northernmost (Car Nicobar), containing half the entire population of the group, and supplying more than half the export trade; while the southernmost island (Great Nicobar) contains more than half the entire area, and presents a rich field for colonial enterprise. The principal products are cocoanuts. The inhabitants, numbering about 7,000, are strong, thickly-built men of the Malay type. Their chief characteristic is laziness. Their race in the central and southern islands is dying out. Attempts at colonisation made by the Danes in 1754 and 1831 failed.
Chief Com. & Superintdt., Lt.-Col. R. C. Temple, C.I.E. (Rs. 2,600).

Portuguese India.—The city of *Nova Goa*, capital of the territory of the same name, and indeed of all the Portuguese possessions east of the Cape of Good Hope, is situated on the Malabar Coast, about 265 miles S.S.E. of Bombay. Old Goa, five or six miles inland, is fast falling to decay, and New Goa, or Panjim, at the head of the harbour, a walled and strongly-fortified city, is now the centre of trade and government. It is connected by the Portuguese West of India railway (51 miles) with British territory to the East. The principal imports are piece-goods, ivory, raw silk, sugar, woollens, &c.; the principal exports are hemp, cowries, betelnut, toys, &c. The whole territory of *Goa*, 60 miles long by 30 miles broad, contains an area of 1,080 square miles, and a population of 561,384 (1891). The other Portuguese possessions in Western India are *Damaun* (pop. of town, 26,964; pop. of territory, 63,284, area 384 square miles), to the north of Bombay; and *Diu*, a town and fort on an island off the Guzerat coast (pop. 12,758, area 52 square miles). The revenue of the Portuguese possessions falls rather short of, and the expenditure exceeds, £200,000.
Governor-General, Duke of Oporto.

French India.—Pondicherry, the capital of the French possessions in Hindustan, is on the Coromandel Coast, 85 miles S. by W. from Madras. The fortifications were once strong, but in the war with England they were destroyed, and a clause in the Treaty of Paris forbids their being rebuilt or the place being garrisoned by a French force beyond what is required for police purposes. Rice, indigo, tobacco, betelnut, and cotton are cultivated. The chief exports are oilseeds; the imports consist of lace, fancy goods, furniture, and jewellery. There is no harbour to the place, though the roadstead is as good as any along this coast. The area of the French possessions in India is 205 square miles; the population is increasing. In 1891 it numbered 282,923. The chief settlement is Pondicherry, with an area of 115 square miles, and a population of 172,941. The other settlements are *Chandernagore*, on the banks of the Hooghly, 17 miles north of Calcutta (area 4 square miles, population 24,281); *Karikal*, in the Cauvery delta (area 53 square miles, population 70,526); *Yanaon*, in the Godavery delta (area 5 square miles, pop. 5,327); and *Mahee*, a small town on the opposite coast of India (area 26 square miles, pop. 9,978). There are 22 miles of railway, of which 14 (Peralam to Karaikal) were opened in 1898. The trade of French India amounted to 32½ million francs in value in 1886; it had fallen to 15 millions in 1895; and in 1898 it was less than 5 millions, of which exports were

3⅓ millions. The expenditure of France 297,000 francs, and from local revenues 1.210,000 francs.

NATIVE STATES OF INDIA.

The administration of the Native or Feudatory States of India, with few temporary or unimportant exceptions, is not under the direct control of British officials. But it is subject to the control of the Supreme Government, which is exercised in varying degrees. The chiefs have no power of making war and peace, or of sending ambassadors to each other or to external States; the military force they maintain is strictly limited; no European is allowed to reside at any of their courts without special sanction, and in case of misgovernment the Supreme Government can dethrone the Chief or temporarily suspend him from the exercise of his powers. Some pay tribute, some do not. Generally speaking, the States are governed by their native Princes, Ministers, or Councils, with the help and under the advice of a political officer of the Supreme Government. A common characteristic of all Native States, important or insignificant, is that in their territory British Indian law does not run. For them the Legislative Councils of the Governor-General or of the Provincial Governments cannot legislate; and over them the High Courts and Chief Courts of the Provinces have no jurisdiction. The Assigned Districts of Hyderabad (Berar), Mysore (Bangalore), of Kalat (Quetta and Pishin), are still technically foreign, or Native States territory. The Shan States are on the other hand technically part of British India, though they are administered by their local Sawbwas or petty chiefs.

Afghanistan, Nepal, and Bhutan are considered as independent States, though within the British sphere of influence. For these States, however, see pages 470, 471.

Excluding these countries and that of the trans-Salween Shan States, of which the area is not defined, the Native States of India may be said to cover an area of 750,000 square miles, and to contain a population of over 70 millions. The gross revenues of the chiefs come to about Rx. 21,000,000, out of which an annual tribute of about Rx. 900,000 is paid to the British Government, and they maintain troops to the aggregate number of 80.000 men in addition to their Imperial Service troops. The States vary greatly in size and importance. Hyderabad, for instance, is as large as the kingdom of Italy, and the Nizam enjoys a gross revenue of Rx. 4,000,000. On the other hand, in Kattywar and elsewhere, where family custom has led to minute subdivision, there are many chiefs of a single village. In the case of such petty estates, it is not correct to speak of Native rule; the nominal chief may have some very limited magisterial powers, though this is not always the case, but the administration is regulated and carried on by the British Government in its executive capacity. The amount of control exercised by the British Government over a Native State in its internal affairs depends upon a number of considerations, and varies from State to State. Although the number of Native States, large and small, amounts to as many as 650, only about 200 are of any real importance. Most of these States are of more recent origin than the British power in India. They may be classed under fifteen heads: 1. The Indo-Chinese group of States, and the numerous hill tribes of the North-East Frontier. 2. The aboriginal Gond and Kole tribes, under petty princes of aboriginal

or Rajput blood, in Chota Nagpur, Orissa, the Central Provinces, and the Jaipur (Vizagapatam) Agency. 3. The Himalayan Hill States, west of Nepal (including Cashmere). 4. The numerous Afghan and Baluch tribes of the North-West Frontier, inhabiting the mountains from the north of Peshawar to the base of the Suleiman range, a distance of 800 miles. 5. Kalat, with the other Baluch Chiefships which are more or less subordinate to Kalat. 6. The Sikh States, in the Sirhind plain, south of the Sutlej. 7. The three Northern Mohammedan States of Khairpur in Sind, Bahawalpur to the north-east of it, and Rampur, from which Warren Hastings expelled the Rohillas in 1774. 8. The ancient sovereignties of Rajputana, lying to the south of the Punjab, and between Sind and the North-West Provinces. 9. The States of Central India, lying to the north of the Nerbudda, and to the south and east of Rajputana. 10. Guzerat, including Kutch and the numerous petty chiefships of Kattywar. 11. The Southern Mahratta States. 12. Baroda. 13. Hyderabad. 14. Mysore. 15. The Malayalim States of Travancore and Cochin, lying together in the far south.

Hyderabad is the premier State in India. The present Nizam was installed in 1884. *Kashmir* was granted to Gholab Sing by Lord Hardinge, after the First Punjab War. The present Maharaja came to the throne in 1885, since which date the administration of the State has been much improved under the advice of the British Resident. Kashmir is important as a frontier State. A British force stationed at Gilgit watches the northern passes and controls the feudatory chiefships of Hunza and Nagar; while on the west the subordinate chiefship of Chitral is also occupied by British troops, depending for their support on the Peshawar border. Of the Sikh States the most important is *Patiala*. *Rajputana* measures some 460 miles from north to south, and 530 miles in breadth; it has a population of twelve millions. Of its nineteen principalities, the most important are *Jodhpur (Marwar)*, *Udaipur (Meywar)*, and *Jaipur*. The Rajput dynasties are very ancient, and resemble feudal monarchies. A large part of the area of Jodhpur, Bikaner, and Jaisalmir is desert. The Governor-General's Agent's headquarters are at Ajmir; he has under him a staff of twenty officers, distributed among the States to overlook the administration, and give advice when it is needed or asked for. The *Central India States*, which are one-third less in extent than Rajputana, are split up into nearly four times as many States. The two most important are *Gwalior* and *Indore*, which include between them one-half of the whole area. The opium grown in Malwa is a valuable, though diminishing, source of revenue to the Maharaja of Indore and to the Indian Government. *Bhopal*, one of the principal Mohammedan States in India, has for three generations prospered under female rule. In 1875 the reigning Gaekwar of *Baroda* was deposed, but the Native administration was continued under an adopted heir. In 1881 the province of *Mysore*, which had been administered by the British Government since 1834, was restored to Native rule. The present Maharaja is a minor and the State is under a regency.

The salutes enjoyed by the Native Princes may be taken to indicate their relative importance. Those with eleven guns or more are addressed with the title of His Highness. Some of the chiefs who by their enlightened administration or for other causes have earned the special approbation of Government have had their salutes increased; but such increase is personal and lapses on the death of the particular chief. The following is a list of the Chiefs having salutes of thirteen guns or more, with some particulars as to their States. In each group the States are given in alphabetical order. In addition to the list given below there are 35 Chiefs having salutes of eleven guns, of whom six have two additional guns in their salutes personal to the present ruler, and there are 26 Chiefs with salutes of nine guns; in one of these cases the present ruler has a personal addition of two guns to his salute.

TABLE OF PRINCIPAL INDIAN CHIEFS, SHOWING SALUTES TO WHICH THEY ARE ENTITLED, AND AREA, POPULATION, AND REVENUE OF THEIR STATES.

Salute and Title of Chief.	Area in sq. miles.	Population in 1891.	Revenue actual for last year recorded or approximate.	Date of Succession.
Salutes of 21 Guns.				
Baroda, The Maharaja of (Gaekwar)	8,226	2,415,396	Rx.1,681,000	27 May, 1875.
Hyderabad, The Nizam of	82,698	11,537,040	3,819,000	26 Feb., 1869.
§Mysore, The Maharaja of	27,936	4,843,523	1,779,000	1 Feb., 1895.
Salutes of 19 Guns.				
*Bhopal, The Begum (or Nawab) of	6,784	954,901	400,000	31 Oct., 1868.
*Gwalior, The Maharaja (Sindhia) of	29,047	3,378,774	1,502,000	3 July, 1886.
*Indore, The Maharaja (Holkar) of	8,400	1,091,689	712,000	12 July, 1886.
*Jammu and Kashmir, The Maharaja of	80,900	2,543,952	651,000	12 Sept., 1885.
Kalat, The Khan of	106,000	220,500	80,000	15 Aug., 1893.
Kolhapur, The Raja of	2,855	913,131	428,000	17 Mar., 1884.
Meywar (Udaipur), The Maharana of	12,753	1,863,126	375,000	21 Dec., 1884.
+Travancore, The Maharaja of......................	6,730	2,557,736	892,000	19 Aug., 1885.
Salutes of 17 Guns.				
Bahawalpur, The Nawab of.........................	17,285	650,042	160,000	25 Mar., 1866.
Bharatpur, The Maharaja of	1,982	640,303	270,000	15 Feb., 1894.
Bikanir, The Maharaja of...........................	23,173	831,955	215,000	19 Aug., 1887.
Bundi, The Maharao Raja of	2,220	295,675	70,000	28 Mar., 1889.
Cochin, the Raja of..................................	1,362	722,906	207,000	Sept., 1895.
+Jaipur, The Maharaja of	15,579	2,823,966	670,000	18 Sept., 1880.
Karauli, The Maharaja of	1,242	156,587	40,000	14 Aug., 1886.
Kotah, The Maharao of	3,784	526,267	278,000	11 June, 1889.
Kutch, The Rao of	6,500	558,415	252,000	1 Jan., 1876.
Marwar (Jodhpur), The Maharaja of	34,963	2,582,178	582,000	11 Oct., 1895.
Patiala, The Maharaja of............................	5,951	1,583,521	657,000	14 April, 1876.
Rewah, The Maharaja of	13,000	1,503,176	165,000	4 Feb., 1880.
Tonk, The Nawab of	2,552	380,069	170,000	30 Dec., 1867.
Salutes of 15 Guns.				
Alwar, The Maharaja of	3,144	767,786	279,000	5 June, 1892.
Banswara, The Maharawal of.......................	1,946	211,641	25,000	1842.
Datia, The Maharaja of	836	185,728	90,000	10 Dec., 1880.
Dewas, The Senior Raja of	155	77,922	35,000	1861.
Dewas, The Junior Raja of	134	65,723	37,000	23 May, 1892.
‡Dhar, The Raja of	1,739	167,504	90,000	May, 1860.
Dholpur, The Maharaj Rana of	1,154	279,890	125,000	9 Feb., 1873.
Dungarpur, The Maharawal of	1,447	165,400	22,000	28 Sept., 1846.
Idar, The Maharaja of	1,900	302,134	63,000	26 Dec., 1868.
Jaisalmir, The Maharawal of	16,062	115,701	16,000	12 April, 1891.
Khairpur, The Mir of.................................	6,109	131,937	114,000	April, 1894.
Kishengarh, The Maharaja of	858	125,516	57,000	25 Dec., 1879.
+Orchha, The Maharaja of...........................	1,933	333,389	90,000	15 Mar., 1874.
Partabgarh, The Maharawal of	886	87,975	40,000	18 Feb., 1890.
Sikkim, The Maharaja of	2,702	30,500	10,000	April, 1874.
Sirohi, The Maharao of..............................	1,964	190,836	42,000	16 Sept., 1875.
Salutes of 13 Guns.				
‡Benares, The Raja of (not a Ruling Chief)				
Jaora, The Nawab of	872	112,280	175,000	30 April, 1865.
Kuch Behar, The Maharaja of	1,307	578,054	216,000	Aug., 1863.
Rampur, The Maharaja of	945	537,055	298,000	27 Feb., 1889.
+Tipperah, The Raja of	4,086	137,442	50,000	31 July, 1862.

* Within their own territories these chiefs have salutes of 21 guns permanently.
† The present chief has a salute with two additional guns as a personal salute, or, in the case of Jaipur, of four additional guns.
‡ The present chief enjoys the title of Maharaja as a personal distinction.
§ The Maharani Regent of Mysore enjoys also a personal salute of 19 guns.

INDIA IN PARLIAMENT,
AND INDIAN LEGISLATION IN 1898-99.

There was no legislation in Parliament relating particularly to India : the two principal debates on India were on the Indian Budget and on a proposal to disallow the Indian Act imposing countervailing duties on bounty-fed sugar. The "Dum Dum" bullet formed the subject of discussion and condemnation at the Peace Conference. The Parliamentary Commission on Indian Expenditure appointed in 1895 issued no report or volume of evidence during the year.

The closing Acts of the Indian legislature in 1898 included (Acts XI. and XII.) a Tenancy Act and a Land Revenue Act for the Central Provinces, a Burma Laws Act (No. XIII.) declaring the laws and regulations in force in that province, an Act No. IX. regulating the importation of live stock so as to prevent the entry of diseased animals into India.

Of the Acts in 1899 the most controversial was No. XIV. amending the Indian Tariff Act by the imposition of an additional import duty on bounty-fed articles, sugar being particularly aimed at. The law relating to stamps was amended and consolidated by Act II.; that relating to Petroleum by Act VIII. The Indian Evidence Act, 1872, was amended by Act V. No. IX. amended the law relating to Arbitration. A Glanders and Farcy Act (No. XIII.) consolidated the law on this subject. No. VI. was an amendment of the Indian Contract Law designed to check the use of undue influence by money-lenders. Other Acts were I. amending the Indian Marine Act (1887); IV. the Government Buildings Act, exempting such buildings from municipal taxation; VII. an amendment of the Inland Steam Vessels Act of 1884; No. X. the Carriers Act; XI. amending the Court Fees Act; and XII. entitled The Currency Notes Forgery Act. Important Acts passed in the Autumn of 1899 were the Currency Law, to carry out the Currency Committee's recommendations to make the gold sovereign legal tender at the ratio of 15 rupees to the sovereign, and an Act of the Bengal Legislative Council remodelling the constitution of the Calcutta Municipality. There were also Bills under consideration to prevent the alienation of land in the Punjab away from the agricultural classes, and to revise the power of appeal in civil suits in the Punjab.

INDIAN APPOINTMENTS.

The civil administration of British India is recruited from four sources—1. Competitive examination in England; 2. The Indian Staff Corps; 3. The patronage of the Secretary of State; 4. The patronage of the local Governments. The next examination of candidates for appointments in the *Covenanted Civil Service* of India will commence in London on 1st August, 1900, the number of appointments varying with the requirements of the local Governments. Inquiry on the subject at the India Office or the Civil Service Commission. The appointments are distributed between (1) Upper Provinces, &c.; (2) Lower Provinces and Assam; (3) Madras; (4) Bombay; (5) Burma, according to their requirements. The number of appointments to be offered in 1900 will probably be 54. Successful candidates may express their preference for the provinces in which they wish to serve. But their allotment will depend upon a consideration of all the circumstances, especially the requirements of the public service. The candidates for this examination must be over 21 and under 23 on 1st January preceding. The selected candidates will be on probation in England for one year only, and will receive an allowance of £100 if they pass their probation at one of the Universities or Colleges approved by the Secretary of State for India, and show due diligence. Application for admission to the examination must be made on or before the 2nd July, on forms that can be obtained at any time after 1st December preceding, from "The Secretary, Civil Service Commission, London, S.W." Examination fee is £6. Seniority in the service depends on the order of the list resulting from the combined marks of the competitive and final examinations. Within a certain time of the candidate's arrival in India, he must elect to serve in the executive or the judicial branch of the administration, the summit of the profession in one branch being the Lieutenant-Governorship of a Province, in the other a Judgeship of the High Court. The salary of a covenanted civil servant commences at Rs. 4,800 a year. The number of covenanted civilians at present in the Indian Service is about 1,000. The Native Army absorbs the larger proportion of the *Indian Staff Corps;* but out of a total of about 2,500 officers some 380 are attached to the Police or the Public Works Department, or are in Civil or Political departments. Thirty-five appointments in the *Indian Staff Corps* are offered to successful candidates for admission to the Royal Military College, Sandhurst, at each competitive examination, viz. in June and November. Upon receiving his commission a successful candidate is provided with a passage to India, and is attached for a year to a British regiment, and then transferred to a Native regiment. Till he has passed certain language and professional tests, which must be passed before the end of the third year from appointment to the Indian Staff Corps, he is practically on probation. Nominations to Indian cadetships and Honorary Indian cadetships, giving special facilities for entrance into the army, with choice of appointment to the Indian Staff Corps, are also given by the Secretary of State for India. Applications should be made to the Military Department of the India Office. Any officers who may from time to time be required to supplement the direct supply from Sandhurst will be drawn from R. A. or Line regiments serving in India, subject to certain conditions. A Lieutenant's Staff Corps pay commences at Rs. 2,700 a year.

The *Public Works Department* is recruited from the Royal Indian Engineering College at Coopers Hill (President Col. J. W. Ottley, C.I.E., R.E.; for staff see page 263). from the corps of Royal Engineers, and, in respect of Natives, from the Civil Engineering colleges in India. About 50 students are admitted yearly to Coopers Hill College. Candidates must be between 17 and 21 on 1st July of the year of admission. The course begins in September. Applications for admission should be made not later than 15 June. After three years, during which the annual charge is £183, the students undergo a competitive examination, and the highest obtain appointments in India (commencing at Rs. 4,200 a year), the number of these being generally twelve each year. One appointment in the Accounts Branch Indian Public Works Department (commencing salary Rs. 3,600 a year), and one in the Traffic Department, Indian State Railways (commencing salary Rs. 3,000 a year), will also be offered to students of the College in 1900. Candidates for the *Telegraph Department* enter the college in the same manner. but their competitive examination is at the end of two years, and the number of appointments offered in 1900 will probably b four. The commencing salary is Rs. 3,600 a year. The *Forest Department* of India is recruited from this country; the examination is held, usually in June, conjointly with that for the Indian Police Department. In 1900, seven appointments will be offered for competition, the limits of age being 17 and 20 on the 1st of June, 1900. Applications should be made to the Revenue Department of the India Office before 1st May, 1900. In the entrance examination good sight, good hearing, and good powers of physical endurance are insisted on. The course of study extends over about three years, divided into seven terms, to be passed mainly at Coopers Hill, and a period of study under supervision in continental forests. The charge for each of the seven terms spent at the college is £61, and for the period of foreign study is £150. Probationers who acquit themselves creditably during their college course will begin on arrival in India as Assistant Conservators of Forests, on a salary of Rs. 4,200 a year. In June, 1900, an examination, which is the same as that for Forest appointments, is to be held in England for ten appointments to the Indian *Police*, for Madras and Bombay two each, Bengal. Punjab. and Central Provinces one each. and North-W st Provinces and Oudh three. Candidates must be between 19 and 21 on 1st June, 19c0, and applications must be sent before 1st May, 1900, to the Secretary, Judicial and Public Department, India Office, to whom also any inquiries should be addressed. Selected candidates will be allotted as probationers to provinces "upon a consideration of all the circumstances, including their wishes." Initial salary of a probationer is Rs. 3,000 a year. On passing the necessary examinations, which must be done within two years of arrival in India, the probationer will be appointed an Assistant-Superintendent on Rs. 300 a month. Examinations for the *Indian Medical Service* take place generally in February and August. The number of appointments made after each examination has usually been about 12. The examination will be conducted together with that for admission to the Army Medical Staff. Candidates must be between the ages of 21 and 28 at the date of examination, and must possess a diploma or diplomas entitling them under the Medical Acts to practise both medicine and surgery. No candidate may compete more than three times. Successful candidates are required to attend a course for not less than four months at the Army Medical School at Netley, during which period they receive an allowance of 8s. a day, to cover cost of maintenance. The commencing salary in India is Rs. 3,810 a year; the highest medical appointment in India carries a salary of Rs. 32,400. The greater part of the medical service is in civil employ, but liable to be recalled to medical duty. The *patronage of the Secretary of State for India* is very small, and is chiefly dependent on the uncertain requirements of the Government of India in the Ecclesiastical, Judicial, or Educational Departments. *Chaplains*, on appointment, will, for the first three years, be on probation only. Applications for appointment should be made to the Secretary of State. Appointments, usually of distinguished graduates of the Universities of the United Kingdom, are made to the Indian *Educational Service* by the Secretary of State. No limits of age are fixed. Appointments are in the first instance usually for five years, the salary beginning at Rs. 500 a month, with annual increments of Rs 50 a month. The number of appointments varies year by year and is not large. The Local Governments have many appointments in their gift, but no one who is not a Native, a covenanted civilian, or an officer of the Staff Corps can be appointed to a post of over Rs. 200 a month without the sanction of the Government of India—the departments excepted from this rule being: *Opium, Salt, Customs, Survey, Mint, Public Works Department, Police.* Appointments are also made by the India Office to the Royal Indian Marine (limits of age 17 and 22), the Bengal Pilot Service (age 18 to 22), and the Indian Nursing Service.

The *Ecclesiastical Establishment* in India, which forms a Civil, not a Military department, consists of three Bishops (others whose names will be found at page 451 are not Bishops on the Establishment), and 160 Chaplains. Certain allowances are also paid from Indian revenues to other clergymen, and to priests and ministers of other denominations when ministering to British regiments.

Pay, Leave, and Pension Regulations of the Indian Services are contained in the Civil Service Regulations, of which a partial summary will be found in the India List, published by Messrs. Harrison, 59 Pall Mall, S.W.

THE FINANCES OF INDIA FOR THE YEARS ENDED 31ST MARCH, 1897 AND 1898.

The notation Rx. signifies ten Rupees. (A Rupee was equivalent to 1s. 2'451d. in 1896-97; to 1s. 3'354d. in 1897-98; thenceforth it may be taken approximately to equal 1s. 4d.)

REVENUE AND RECEIPTS.

	1896-97	1897-98
Principal Heads of Revenue:		
Land Revenue	Rx.23,974,489	Rx.25,683,642
Opium	6,409,238	5,179,772
Salt	8,421,705	8,594,225
Stamps	4,777,742	4,837,043
Excise	5,614,200	5,489,454
Provincial Rates	3,536,855	3,723,290
Customs	4,491,477	4,641,205
Assessed Taxes	1,872,809	1,895,465
Forest	1,733,869	1,739,514
Registration	458,271	486,544
Tributes (Nat. States)	901,753	884,029
Total	Rx.62,192,408	Rx.63,154,273
Interest	Rx.1,082,555	Rx.872,241
Post Office, Telegraph, Mint:		
Post Office	Rx.1,783,474	Rx.1,879,163
Telegraph	1,071,524	1,300,330
Mint	156,635	182,055
Total	Rx.3,011,633	Rx.3,370,548
Receipts by Civil Departments:		
Law and Justice	Rx.664,917	Rx.663,193
Police	436,916	448,330
Marine	160,477	200,724
Education	220,782	217,518
Medical	93,715	90,209
Minor Departments	101,761	103,537
Total	Rx.1,678,568	Rx.1,723,511

REVENUE AND RECEIPTS—contd.

Miscellaneous:	1896-97.	1897-98.
In aid of pensions, &c.	Rx.357,968	Rx.343,285
Stationery & Printing.	86,400	80,003
Exchange	144,233	43,970
Miscellaneous	477,973	473,736
Total	Rx.1,066,574	Rx.940,994

Railways:		
State Railways (Gross Receipts)	Rx.17,639,604	19,044,525
Guaranteed Companies (Net Traffic Receipts)	2,634,164	2,201,392
Subsidised Cos. (Interest)	24,052	14,969
Total	Rx.20,297,820	Rx.21,260,836

Irrigation:		
Majr. Wks.: Direct Repts.	Rx.2,067,961	Rx.2,377,744
„ Port. of Land Rev. due to Irrigation	871,808	964,738
Minor Works & Navigtn.	210,870	227,382
Total	Rx.3,150,639	Rx.3,569,864

Buildings and Roads:		
Military Works	Rx.61,268	Rx.52,561
Civil Works	634,946	615,262
Total	Rx.696,214	Rx.667,823

Receipts by Military Depts.:		
Army: Effective	Rx.838,379	Rx.697,163
„ Non-effective..	114,951	111,078
		73,623
Total	Rx.953,330	Rx.881,864
Total Revenues	Rx.94,129,741	Rx.96,442,004

EXPENDITURE.

Direct Demands on the Revenues:	1896-97.	1897-98.
Refunds & Drawbacks	Rx.327,540	Rx.284,344
Assignments&Cmpens.	1,562,079	1,541,748
Collection Charges, viz.:		
Land Revenue	4,109,603	4,187,601
Opium	2,486,692	2,389,117
Salt	523,352	473,747
Stamps	164,781	154,027
Excise	212,855	240,463
Provincial Rates	54,301	52,530
Customs	203,386	211,379
Assessed Taxes	30,323	32,278
Forest	993,955	1,001,689
Registration	240,824	247,890
Total	Rx.10,909,691	Rx.10,816,813

Interest:		
On Debt (excl. Rlwys. and Irrigation Wks.)	Rx.2,995,742	Rx.2,957,024
On other Obligations...	458,211	515,236
Total	Rx.3,453,953	Rx.3,472,260

Post Office, Telegraph, & Mint:		
Post Office	Rx.1,703,111	Rx.1,729,474
Telegraph	946,759	1,051,494
Mint	61,823	88,557
Total	Rx.2,711,693	Rx.2,869,525

Salaries & Expenses of Civil Debts:		
Gen. Administration...	Rx.2,019,630	Rx.1,990,902
Law and Justice	4,179,139	4,255,894
Police	4,156,560	4,233,923
Marine (inc. RiverNvgn.)	720,266	679,040
Education	1,576,150	1,581,072
Ecclesiastical	189,385	173,962
Medical	1,076,696	1,351,417
Political	1,003,401	933,820
Minor Departments ...	523,969	535,517
Total	Rx.15,445,196	Rx.15,739,547

EXPENDITURE—cont.

Miscellaneous Civil Charges:	1896-97.	1897-98.
Territrl. & Pol. Pensions	Rx.437,397	Rx.442,458
Civil Furlough and Absentee Allowances ...	375,734	294,057
Superannuation Allowances and Pensions...	4,119,225	4,021,249
Stationery & Printing.	679,523	724,093
Miscellaneous	244,830	234,959
Total	Rx.5,856,709	Rx.5,716,825

Famine Relief & Insurance:		
Famine Relief	Rx.2,079,525	Rx.5,325,608
Cons. of Protective Rys.	...	...
„ „ Irrig. Wks.	46,830	37,517
Total	Rx.2,126,355	Rx.5,363,125

Construction of Railways (in addition to that under Famine Insurance)	Rx.12,750	Rx.3,792

Railway Revenue Account:		
State Rys. (Wkg. Exp.)	Rx.8,819,553	Rx.9,201,202
„ „ (Int. on Debt)	5,452,514	5,509,138
„ „ (Annuities in pur. of Rys.)	2,844,343	2,676,715
„ „ (Int. chargble. agst. Cos. on advances)	404,708	429,873
„ „ (Int. on Cap. depsd. byCos.)	1,215,145	1,243,288
Guar. Cos. (Srpls. Profits)	475,385	125,213
„ „ (Interest) ...	3,597,232	3,377,084
Subsidised Companies (Land, &c.)	85,020	113,760
Miscellaneous Ry. Exp.	63,901	16,229
Total	Rx.22,957,801	Rx.22,623,502

Irrigation:		
Major Wks.: Wkg. Exp.	Rx.871,180	Rx.892,119
„ Int. on Debt	1,253,479	1,284,249
Minor Wks. & Navigtn.	1,126,350	967,717
Total	Rx.3,251,009	Rx.3,144,085

Buildings and Roads:		
Military Works	Rx.1,157,006	Rx.1,168,385
Civil Works	4,626,289	4,250,551
Total	Rx.5,783,295	Rx.5,418,936

Army Services:		
Army: Effective	Rx.19,414,806	Rx.18,412,441
„ Non-effective..	4,840,532	4,697,077
Military Operations ...	...	3,887,256
Total	Rx.24,255,338	Rx.26,996,774

Special Defence Works:	Rx.94,610	Rx.23,708

	1896-97.	1897-98.
Total Expenditure	Rx.96,858,400	Rx.102,258,893
Add (+) or *deduct* (−) net amount added to or *withdrawn from* Provincial Balances, as total Prov. Exp. fell short of or *exceeded* total Prov. allotments	− Rx.*1,023,637*	Rx. − *457,678*
Total Expenditure charged against Revenue	Rx.95,834,763	Rx.101,801,215

In addition to the above expenditure from revenue there was a capital outlay in 1897-98, not charged to revenue, of Rx. 3,632,005 on State Railways, and of Rx. 692,431 on Irrigation Works, and on Miscellaneous Public Improvements Rx. 4,105, making a total of Rx. 4,328,541.

The total revenue and expenditure for the year 1897–98 may be classified in the following manner:

Receipts:		Expenditure:	
In India—		In India—	
Imperial....Rx.	69,795,232	Imperial ...Rx.	50,137,336
Provincial..	22,255,297	Provincial..	21,925,041
Local	4,088,758	Local	4,419,014
In England ..	302,717	In England ..	25,319,824
Total ..Rx.	96,442,004	Total....Rx.	101,801,215

RECEIPTS AND EXPENDITURE IN THE SEVERAL PRO-
VINCES FOR THE YEAR ENDED MARCH 31, 1898.

PROVINCES.	Receipts.	Expenditure.
India	Rx.17,249,537	Rx.25,088,712
Bengal	20,288,493	10,324,105
N.-W. Provinces & Oudh	11,183,480	6,702,003
Punjâb................	9,015,123	5,069,422
Burma	6,368,294	4,185,849
Central Provinces...	2,120,483	2,932,356
Assam	1,341,107	986,998
Madras	14,142,046	10,203,315
Bomb. (with Sind)	14,430,724	10,982,631
England	Rx.302,717	Rx.25,319,824
Total	Rx.96,442,004	Rx.101,801,215

In this statement the cost of the troops in the Madras and Bombay commands is included in the expenditure in those Presidencies; the remaining military expenditure is given under India.

The following is a Table of Revenue and Expenditure for 1842–43, and for each tenth year since, and for 1897–8, together with the totals of 56 years between 1842–3 and 1897–8, the values being stated in the notation of Rx. (Rx.=Rs. 10). It should be borne in mind that the area of British territory in India has risen since 1842 from 626,000 to 965,000 square miles:—

REVENUE.

	Land.	Opium.	Taxes.	Public Works.	Tribute & other	Total.
	Mil. Rx	Mil. Rx	Mil. Rx	Mil. Rx	Mil. Rx	Mil. Rx
1842-43	13·56	2·09	5·75	—	1·20	22·60
1852-53	16·19	5·09	5·82	—	1·51	28·61
1862-63	19·57	8·06	13·55	·44	3·52	45·14
1872-73	21·37	8·69	16·25	3·90	6·34	56·55
1882-83	21·87	9·50	17·66	13·05	8·19	70·27
1892-93	24·90	7·99	25·36	22·15	9·77	90·17
1897-98	25·68	5·18	29·18	25·50	10·90	96·44
Total 56 ys.	1120·95	390·95	821·95	401·74	321·11	3056·74

EXPENDITURE.

	Collection.	Civil Admin.	Interest.	Army.	Public Works.	Famine, Rel.&Ins.	Miscellaneous.	Total.
	Mil.Rx	Mil.Rx	Mil.Rx	Mil.Rx	Mil.Rx	M.Rx	Mil.Rx	Mil.Rx
1842-53	5·28	5·32	2·47	10·61	·19	—	·00	23·87
1852-53	6·56	6·48	3·30	11·09	·55	—	—	27·58
1862-63	8·49	7·39	5·47	14·89	5·97	—	1·11	43·12
1872-73	7·34	9·57	5·86	15·50	10·33	—	6·18	54·78
1882-83	8·49	11·04	4·77	18·30	20·31	1·50	5·13	69·70
1892-93	9·46	14·26	4·37	23·42	32·08	1·50	5·97	91·00
1897-98	9·00	15·74	3·47	26·00	31·26	5·36	9·97	101·00
Total 56 Yrs.	445·46	544·73	241·93	961·20	575·48	39·75	199·95	3108·56

During these 56 years there have been 24 years of surplus and 32 of deficit, the net deficit amounting to 51·82 millions of tens of rupees. During the 15 years previous to the Mutiny there had been 11 years of deficit and 4 years of surplus, the net deficit amounting to 11·42 millions. The Mutiny years 1857 to 1862 added 36·28 millions to the total of deficits. Since 1862, there have been 20 years of surplus and 15 of deficit, yielding a net deficit of 4·12 millions, or a net surplus of 1·11 millions if we count as surplus 5·33 millions charged against the revenues but not spent otherwise than in reduction of debt, under the head of Famine Insurance. Under this head has also been charged expenditure on construction of railways and irrigation works designed to protect the country against famine to the amount of 11·78 millions. With the passing away of famine, the year 1898–99 was originally estimated to give a surplus of Rx. 891,400; but in August, 1899, Lord G. Hamilton was able to say that the surplus had grown to Rx. 4,759,000, the largest Indian surplus on record. The Budget for 1899–1900 estimated for a surplus of Rx. 3,933,000, on the basis of a comparatively low rate of exchange. An actual surplus nearly equal to that of 1898–99 might therefore be anticipated but for the exceptional outlay that may be necessitated by the recrudescence of famine. The annual burden of taxation in India is calculated to be less than Re. 1, 4½ annas per head of population, if the land revenue demand which is of the nature of rent be excluded. Including land revenue it would slightly exceed Rs. 2, 6½ annas.

The INDIAN DEBT stood on the 31st March, 1899, at Rx. 112,650,000. plus £124,259,000 adding Rx. 18,898,000 for other obligations, the liabilities of the Indian Government are shown at Rx. 131,548,000 ÷ £124,259,000. On the side of assets there are Rx. 100,643,000 for railways constructed by the State, £59,236,000 for purchased railways, £7,700,000 for advances to Railway Companies, Rx. 33,362,000 for Irrigation Works, Rx. 12,481,000 lent to Corporations, &c., and cash balances amounting to Rx. 17,072,000 and £4,304,000, making altogether totals of Rx. 193,558,000 and £71,240,000. The liabilities uncovered by assets stand at £53,029,000 in sterling, diminished by Rx. 32,010,000, the amount of net assets in rupees. In 1898–99 a 3½ p. c. loan of Rx. 1,200,000 was raised in India at 94⅝s. In England £6,000,000 of 2½ p. c. stock was issued at £88 10s. 5d. Out of £6,000,000 India sterling bills falling due 4½ millions were replaced. Debt discharged amounted to Rx. 245,000 and £3,385,000. So far no loan is expected to be raised in 1899–1900 either in England or in India, while it is proposed to discharge debt to the amount of Rx. 190,000.

The charge for *Interest* on debt and other obligations is distributed in the statement of expenditure on the previous page in the following manner:—

For Railways	Rx.5,939,011
,, Irrigation	1,284,249
,, Ordinary Debt	2,957,024
,, Other obligations	515,235
Total	Rx.10,695,520

EXCHANGE.—The net sterling expenditure of the Indian Government was, in 1898–99, about 16 millions. The less the value of the Indian silver coinage relatively to gold, the greater the number of rupees required to meet this sterling expenditure. With low exchange also a larger number of rupees is required to meet the pay of the European soldier in India, and to compensate officers for the loss they suffer on remittances to England. Ten rupees used approximately to be equivalent to each £1 sterling. Excess expenditure caused by the fall of the rupee below this rate is the "loss by exchange." Previous to 1872–73 the average value of the rupee was about 1s. 11d., its highest value having been slightly above 2s. 2d. in 1860–61, and its lowest almost as low as 1s. 9d. in 1848–49. In 1871–72 the value of the rupee relatively to gold began to fall rapidly; in five years it had sunk from over 1s. 11d. to 1s. 8½d. The next five years it remained fairly steady at something under 1s. 8d. During the last sixteen years the following are the figures, together with the actual loss thrown on the Indian Exchequer by the depreciation of the rupee below its former value of £1 = Rs. 10.

Year.	Average Rate.	Loss by Exchange.
	s. d.	Rx.
1883–84	1 7·536	3,359,000
1884–85	1 7·308	3,536,000
1885–86	1 6·254	4,290,000
1886–87	1 5·441	5,632,000
1887–88	1 4·898	6,049,000
1888–89	1 4·379	6,383,000
1889–90	1 4·566	6,758,000
1890–91	1 6·090	5,468,000
1891–92	1 4·733	7,201,000
1892–93	1 2·985	10,287,000
1893–94	1 2·547	11,523,000
1894–95	1 1·101	15,045,000
1895–96	1 1·638	13,991,000
1896–97	1 2·451	12,116,000
1897–98	1 3·354	10,552,000
1898–99	1 4·000	9,254,000

CURRENCY: The principal coin in use in India is the silver rupee, which contains 165 grains of fine silver and 15 grains alloy. With silver at 60 pence the oz. the value of the rupee would be 1·858s. With silver at 28 l. to 27d. the oz. (as in 1899) and the rupee at 1s. 4d. rupees are valued at 50 to 60 per cent. beyond the value of the silver of which they consist. Previously to June 1893, when the Indian Mints were open by law to the free public coinage of silver into rupees, the rupee circulated at its intrinsic value. The legislation of that date closed the mints, with a view to eventually fixing the exchange. For a time, however, the rupee continued to fall, going in 1894 even as low as 1s. 1d., with silver at 23¾d. per oz. It has since risen, and from January 1898 it has been practically stable at 16d.

The Indian Currency Committee reported (C. 9,390) in July 1899. They were unanimously opposed to reverting to the silver standard, and advised measures for the effective establishment of a gold standard. They did not approve the special proposals of the Government of India, but recommended that the British sovereign should be made legal tender in India, and that Indian mints should be opened to the unrestricted coinage of gold, the Government of India however retaining the right to coin rupees, the profit on such coinage to go to a special reserve and not to be used as revenue. They did not approve any of the suggested schemes for ensuring immediate convertibility, as it was inadvisable to impose on

Government the obligation to give gold for rupees on demand, but they advised that Government should obtain a gold reserve to be made available for foreign remittances when it was necessary to support exchange. They recommended that the permanent rate for the rupee under the gold standard should be 1s. 4 l.—two of the Committee would have preferred 1s. 3d. Three of the Committee recorded their strong opinion against sterling borrowing for currency purposes, and one added a particular recommendation in favour of the improvement and concentration of banking facilities in India. The Secretary of State in Council accepted the views of the Committee and authorised the Government of India to adopt the measures suggested. There are some technical and legal difficulties which for the time delay the introduction of legislation to allow the Indian mints to coin a gold sovereign; but an Act has already been passed in India to make the British sovereign legal tender in India at the ratio of 15 rupees to the sovereign (=1s. 4d. the rupee); the rupee, however, remaining also legal tender to any amount.

THE OPIUM REVENUE.—Poppy is grown in parts of Bengal and of the North-West Provinces and Oudh and in the Central India Native States. The area of opium cultivation in the Ganges Valley in 1897–98 was 540,000 acres. The manufacture is a Government monopoly. The price paid to the cultivators for their produce is Rs. 6 for a seer, or 2 lbs. At the Government Agencies at Ghazipur and Patna, the juice which has been sent in, is dried to a certain consistency, and packed in chests containing about 140 lbs. each. It is then sent down to Calcutta, disposed of by auction at monthly sales, and exported to China and the Straits Settlements. In face of the competition of the drug grown in China the imports of Indian opium, which is heavily taxed on entrance into China have much declined. In the year ending 31st March, 1898, 39,000 chests were thus sold for export, at a rate of Rs.1,020 per chest. The sales realised Rx. 3,991,000. The cost of production of Government opium in 1897–98 was Rx. 2,389,000, and the net revenue Rx. 1,602,000, to which, however, may be added Rx. 218,000 as the value of opium issued for the use of the Excise Department in India.

A large quantity of opium is also grown in the Native States of Central India, and pays duty on its entry into the Bombay Presidency. This opium is called Malwa opium, and is also exported for the most part to China, after paying a duty of Rs.500 per chest. The revenue derived by the Indian Government from this duty amounted in 1897–98 to Rx.971,000.

SALT.—The duty on salt is Rs. 2, 8 annas a maund (82⅔lbs.) in the whole of India, excepting Burma, where it is 1 rupee a maund. The total consumption of salt in British India in 1898–99 is stated at 35,123,000 maunds, yielding a net revenue of Rx. 8,120,000. The consumption was more than before the famine.

RAILWAYS, &c.—Excluding the 73 miles of lines in French and Portuguese territory, the number of miles open for traffic on 31st March, 1899, was 22,418; 13,070 miles on the standard (5 ft. 6 in.) gauge, 8,927 on the metre gauge, and 420 miles on other gauges. In addition to the open lines there were 3,568 miles of line then under construction, or already sanctioned for construction. Of these 632 miles were sanctioned in 1898–99. The total amount of capital expended on the open Railways (including steamboat service and ferries) up to 31st December, 1898, was Rx. 266,141,000, of which Rx. 201,975,000 represented the cost of standard gauge lines and Rx. 62,817,000 lines on the metre gauge; the percentage of working expenses on gross earnings averaged 45 on standard gauge lines and 51½ on the metre gauge lines, and the percentage of net earnings on total capital outlay on open lines 5·63 and 5·07 respectively. The year's net receipts on the Indian railways in 1898 were Rx. 14,114,000, or a return of 5·30 per cent. on the capital sunk (as measured in rupees), against Rx. 13,101,000, or a return of 5·08 per cent. in 1897; the number of passengers increased slightly to 151½ millions, but the goods traffic increased from 33¾ to 35½ million tons. The apparent net loss to the State on the working of the railways in India is calculated at Rx. 1,287,000 in 1897-98, and at Rx. 620,000 in 1898-99. The loss accrues owing to payments to Companies at contract rates of exchange above the actual rate. The net loss in 1898-99 would be reduced Rx. 212,000 if interest on capital outlay of lines still under construction, and contributions to sinking funds for redemption of railway debt were excluded. Moreover, it should be remembered that the railway account is charged with interest on outlay at the rate of 4 per cent., whereas the Government can now raise money in England at less than 3 per cent. The capital expenditure on railways in India in 1898-99 exceeded 10 crores, of which about half was expended by the State and half by Companies guaranteed or subsidized by the State. In 1899 notice was given that the Great India Peninsula Railway would be purchased in the following year by the issue of annuities. On *Irrigation* works the Government up to 31 March, 1898, have laid out a capital of Rx. 39,423,000, which, apart from the advantages to cultivators and protection against famine, gave a return to the State in 1897-98 of about 7 per cent. In this year over 13 million acres were irrigated from Government canals. The capital outlay on irrigation is to be increased in future years.

There are more than 80,000 square miles of *Forests* reserved and scientifically worked by the State in British India, besides about 30,000 square miles of forests managed by the State which may hereafter be reserved. The forests yielded in 1897-98 a net revenue of Rx. 738,000. The length of *Telegraph* lines in India on 31st March, 1898, was 50,306 miles, on which the number of messages was nearly 5¾ millions. They yielded in 1897-98 a revenue of 7·19 per cent. on their capital cost of Rx. 6,294,000. In addition the Indo-European Telegraph Department gave a profit of 6·57 per cent. on its capital of Rx. 1,153,000. The *Post Office,* which conveyed 465 millions of letters, post-cards, and newspapers, &c., was worked at a net profit to Government of Rx. 149,000.

Army.—The actual strength of the *Army of India* on the 1st April, 1898, is shewn in the statement on the next page.

For police duties and frontier service the regular military is supplemented by about 170,000 Native Police, officered mainly by Europeans. In addition, the Native Army Reserves numbered 17,000 men (infantry), and the Imperial Service Troops furnished by Native States contributed 18,000, of whom 8,000 were cavalry, besides transport corps and sappers. Further, there were European and Eurasian volunteers to the number of 30,000, of whom 28,000 were declared efficient. On the frontier there were also considerable numbers of frontier militia and local levies, the numbers of which have been considerably increased of late years, and are to be still further increased under the frontier policy recently adopted by Lord Curzon. The year 1897-98 was an important one to the Indian army. In the military operations on the frontier 53,000 men were employed, viz., 7,000 in the Tochi valley, 8,000 for the Malakand force, 7,000 against the Mohmands, and 31,000 for the Tirah campaign. The total casualties (including those of camp followers) numbered 533 killed, 537 died of disease, 1,460 wounded and 129 missing. The army is now under a single Commander-in-Chief, and is divided, as is shown on next page, into four Lieutenant-Generals' commands :—

GROSS AMOUNT OF THE REVENUE AND EXPENDITURE (excluding Capital Expenditure on Public Works not charged to Revenue) IN INDIA AND IN ENGLAND, SHOWING SURPLUS OR DEFICIENCY IN EACH OF THE TEN UNDERMENTIONED OFFICIAL YEARS.

(Throughout this statement Rx. represents ten Rupees, or their equivalent, whether the transactions have taken place in England or in India.)

Official Years ended 31 March.	GROSS REVENUE.			EXPENDITURE.			Net Revenue in India. Col. 1-4.	Net Expenditure in England. Col. 5-2.	Surplus.	Deficiency.
	In India.	In England (including Exchnge)	Total. Cols. 1+2.	In India.	In England (including Exchange)	Total. Cols. 4+5.				
	1.	2.	3.	4.	5.	6.	7.	8.	9.	10.
	Rx.	Rx.	Rx.	Rx.	Rx.	Rx.	Rx.	Rx.	Rx.	Rx.
1889..	81,212,210	484,468	81,696,678	59,705,003	21,954,657	81,659,660	21,507,207	21,470,189	37,018	—
1890..	84,598,760	486,443	85,085,203	60,960,805	21,512,305	82,473,170	23,637,955	21,025,922	2,612,033	—
1891..	85,221,551	520,098	85,741,649	61,397,459	20,656,019	82,053,478	23,824,092	20,135,921	3,688,171	—
1892..	88,773,360	369,923	89,143,283	65,763,836	22,911,912	88,675,748	23,009,524	22,541,989	467,535	—
1893..	89,819,707	352,731	90,172,438	64,844,035	26,161,815	91,006,850	24,975,672	25,809,084	—	833,412
1894..	90,246,041	319,173	90,565,214	66,000,101	26,112,111	92,112,212	24,245,940	25,792,938	—	1,546,998
1895..	94,814,831	372,598	95,187,429	65,718,671	28,775,648	94,494,319	29,093,160	28,403,050	693,110	—
1896..	97,977,005	393,162	98,370,167	69,377,831	27,458,338	96,836,169	28,599,174	27,065,176	1,533,998	—
1897..	93,586,471	543,270	94,129,741	69,600,508	26,234,255	95,834,763	23,985,963	25,690,985	—	1,705,022
1897-8..	96,139,287	302,717	96,442,004	75,481,391	25,319,824	101,801,215	19,657,896	25,017,107	—	5,359,211
Total for 10 years.	902,389,223	4,144,583	906,533,806	659,849,640	247,096,944	906,946,584	242,539,583	242,952,361	9,031,865	9,444,643 Net 4 12,778

ACTUAL STRENGTH OF THE ARMY OF INDIA.

PUNJAB COMMAND.				
British.				
Cavalry (3 regiments)	1,887			
Artillery (22 batteries and companies)	3,227			
Infantry (15 battalions)	15,223			
Native.		20,337		
Cavalry (15 regiments)	9,217			
Artillery (5 batteries)	1,118			
Infantry (40 battalions)	33,897			
		46,232		66,569
BENGAL COMMAND.				
British.				
Cavalry (2 regiments)	1,379			
Artillery (27 batteries and companies)	4,225			
Engineers	43			
Infantry (17 battalions)	17,605			
Native.		23,252		
Cavalry (11 regiments)	6,908			
Artillery (2 batteries)	494			
Sappers and Miners (8 companies)	1,312			
Infantry (25 battalions)	23,108			
		31,822		55,074
MADRAS COMMAND.				
British.				
Cavalry (2 regiments)	1,261			
Artillery (15 batteries and companies)	2,356			
Engineers	52			
Infantry (8 battalions)	8,778			
Native.		12,447		
Cavalry (3 regiments)	1,773			
Sappers and Miners (9 companies)	1,480			
Infantry (32 regiments)	26,157			
		29,410		41,857
BOMBAY COMMAND.				
British.				
Cavalry (1 regiment)	622			
Artillery (24 batteries and companies)	3,855			
Engineers	54			
Infantry (10 battalions)	10,105			
Native.		14,636		
Cavalry (7⅝ regiments)	4,708			
Artillery (2 batteries)	575			
Sappers and Miners (5 companies)	824			
Infantry (31 regiments)	23,996			
		30,103		44,739
Hyderabad contingent (6 Regts. Cav., 4 Batt. Art., 6 Battns. Inf.); Bodyg., etc.	......	......		8,021
TOTAL .... { British Troops	......	73,050	}	
Miscellaneous Officers	......	892	}	219,566
Native Troops	......	145,624	}	

The ROYAL INDIAN MARINE consists of four troopships of 1500 to 4000 tons each, three other steamers of about 1000 tons each, and a number of smaller craft for harbour and river navigation. Another ship of large tonnage was ordered in 1899, to replace the "Warren Hastings," wrecked three years ago. The trooping service between England and India is carried out by hired steamers. The principal officers and ships of the R.I.M. are as follows :—

Director of the Royal Indian Marine and Resident Transport Officer, Bombay, Capt. W. S. Goodridge, R.N., A.D.C.

Assist. ditto, Capt. W. Chandler.

Deputy ditto (Calcutta), Capt. A. Gwyn.

The business of the Indian Troop Service is under the superintendence of the Director of Transports at the Admiralty.

[*The R.I.M. Troopships carry no armament: the figures below denote tonnage and indicated horse-power*].

Canning, 2246 (1077), troopship, Bombay. *Comm.* A. J. G. Piffard.

Clive, 2722 (2304), troopship, Bombay. *Comm.* E. J. Beaumont.

Dalhousie, 1524 (2202), troopship, Rangoon. *Comm.* St. L. S. Warden.

Lawrence, 4 guns (6 pdr.) 902 (1277), despatch vessel, Persian Gulf. 1st Lieut. C. J. C. Kendall (*in command*).

Mayo, 1125 (2157), Port Blair. *Commander*, C. F. Fletcher.

Minto, 960 (2028), Bombay. Lieut. C. R. Ford (*in command*).

BOMBAY DOCKYARD (7 docks).—*Staff-Officer, Comm.* G. E. Holland ; *Constructor*, R. Watson ; *Inspector of Machinery*, F. O. Gadsden.

CALCUTTA DOCKYARD (9 docks).—*Staff-Officer, Comm.* T. A. L. de Berry ; *Constructor*, T. Avery ; *Inspector of Machinery*, C. Fuller.

EDUCATION, instead of making the usual progress, suffered in 1897-98 a perceptible falling off owing to the famine and plague, the institutions numbering less than 150,000 and the scholars 4,285,000, of which only 400,000 were females. Of the institutions, about three-quarters are maintained by the State, or aided by grants; the remainder being private and unaided. There are five Universities in India, founded on the model of the University of London, viz., those of Calcutta, Madras, Bombay, and Allahabad, and the Punjab University. Of the total expenditure on education of 356 lakhs, 105 came from fees, and 65 from provincial revenues, or local and municipal funds. A Parliamentary paper (C. 9,190) issued in 1899 reviews the progress of education in India between 1892-93 and 1896-97. The figures for the last year were affected by famine and plague which caused the attendance of pupils to fall away, and reduced the funds available for schools. For the year 1896-97 the increase for all India was 1 per cent. in the number of institutions and 1 per cent. in pupils as compared with a uniform yearly increase in the four previous years of 2 per cent. in institutions and 3 per cent. in pupils. The percentage of pupils to the estimated population of school-going age in 1896-97 was 22·3 for males and 2·3 for females. The corresponding percentage in 1885-87 were 19·3 and 1·7.

The INDIAN MUNICIPALITIES in 1897-98 were 760 in number, with a total population of 16,045,000, and an income from taxation of over 2¾ millions (Rx.), and from other sources of 3½ millions. In almost all districts in British India there are local district boards, partly representative, for the management of local interests. The large increase of expenditure in the year occurred almost wholly in Bombay, and is due to the measures that had to be taken against plague.

MAILS for India are made up and despatched from London *viâ* Brindisi, every Friday evening. Letters reach Bombay in 17, Madras in 19, Calcutta in 20, and Rangoon in 22 to 25 days. The postage rate for letters to any part of India or Burma is 1*d.*, and for cards 1*d.*; newspapers, not exceeding 4 oz. 1*d.*; books, magazines, &c., every 2 oz. ½*d.*

The PARCEL POST (to Aden and Burma also) is made up every Wednesday morning, the limit is 11 lbs., and the charge—first lb. 1*s.*, and every subsequent lb. 8*d.*

TELEGRAPHS.—Two lines of telegraphic communication are open. The charges by the Indo-European Company or by the Eastern Company per word are—to India, 4*s.* ; Burma, 4*s.* 2*d.* *Vid* Turkey the rates are—for India, 3*s.* 8*d.*, and for Burma, 3*s.* 10*d.*

The P. and O. Company convey parcels to India at the rate of 1*s.* per lb. (limit 50 lbs.) for any post-town or district in British India ; books at the rate of 6*d.* per lb. There are various regulations and restrictions, which may be learnt from the notice issued from the P. and O. Company's offices, 122 Leadenhall Street, and 25 Cockspur Street.

For Indian Weights and Measures see p. 700.

N.B. A lac (lakh) is 100,000 ; a crore is 100 lacs.

FRONTIER LAND TRADE.

The registration of the trade which crosses the land frontier of British India is defective, but constant efforts are made to render it more complete and accurate.

The following is a table showing the land trade of India with the neighbouring regions, some of which, such as Kashmir and the Shan States, are not, politically, foreign countries; Zimmé (Chiengmai) is a province of Siam :—

	1897-98.		1898-99.	
	Imports.	Exports.	Imports.	Exports.
	Rx.	Rx.	Rx.	Rx.
Lus Bela	96,713	41,241	60,759	26,538
Khelat	87,077	41,424	70,005	50,497
Kandahar	309,299	163,785	357,705	268,756
Zhob & Loralai	16,937	41,068	11,084	55,659
Kabul	129,109	285,623	217,236	312,266
Tirah..........	10,123	13,067	16,287	20,297
Bajaur	247,993	323,238	310,072	426,375
Kashmir	810,510	644,698	881,453	903,577
Ladakh.........	52,662	45,635	76,016	45,686
Thibet	124,388	100,848	191,478	153,603
Nepal	2,056,529	1,828,810	2,140,981	1,606,350
Sikkim.........	49,404	36,496	56,864	42,298
Bhutan.........	14,685	15,882	16,187	17,883
Western China	147,853	209,085	166,907	199,953
Siam	131,832	112,757	79,998	68,755
N. Shan States	365,709	277,265	434,630	295,249
S. Shan States	473,610	462,351	456,371	491,692
Karenni	158,272	109,921	190,214	63,270
Zimmé	288,802	150,304	275,336	169,996
Total (including other countries)	5,634,610	4,931,697	6,092,943	5,289,725

SEA-BORNE TRADE OF INDIA.*

The *course of trade* with India is shewn by the fact that in the last 49 years Indian exports of merchandise have exceeded the imports by 1,109 million Rx., while in the same period the net imports of treasure have amounted to 515 millions. Compared with the two previous years the trade of 1898-99 was markedly prosperous ; the exports were, indeed, in excess of any previous year, but the imports did not exceed the average of the last seven years. The famine, plague, and monetary stringency of 1896-97 and 1897-98 had been prejudicial to commerce. The balance of trade for the past 3 years is as shown on the following page:—

* Aden is not a part of India for purposes of trade statistics. The trade of Aden in 1897-98 was valued at 815 lakhs ; viz. Imports 440 lakhs, Exports 375 lakhs. The trade of the Somali coast amounts to about 100 lakhs. Aden is a great emporium for the commerce of the Arabian and African coasts.

	1896—97.	1897—98.	1898—99.
	Rx.	Rx.	Rx.
Exports of Merchandise	103,984,000	97,633,000	112,831,000
„ Gold....................................	2,200,000	2,372,000	2,337,000
„ Silver	2,737,000	4,776,000	5,075,000
Total	108,921,000	104,781,000	120,213,000
Imports of Merchandise	76,104,000	73,666,000	72,111,000
„ Gold..................................	4,491,000	7,281,000	8,840,000
„ Silver	8,593,000	13,249,000	9,056,000
Total	89,188,000	94,191,000	90,007,000
Net Exports of Merchandise	27,880,000	23,972,000	40,690,000
„ Imports of Gold	2,291,000	4,909,000	6,503,000
„ „ Silver	5,856,000	8,473,000	3,981,000
Excess of Exports	19,733,000	10,590,000	30,206,000
Rupee paper enfaced for payment of interest in England	−1,379,000	−2,535,000	−89,000
Total surplus Exports	18,354,000	8,055,000	30,117,000
Remittances by the Government :—			
Payments in India for Council Bills, &c.	25,228,000	14,795,000	28,386,000
Bills drawn on India for interest on enfaced rupee paper ...	839,000	708,000	710,000
	26,067,000	15,503,000	29,096,000
Excess of surplus Exports over remittances by Government ...	−7,713,000	−7,448,000	1,021,000
Equivalent of amount borrowed in sterling to meet charges not defrayed by India	—	13,102,000	—

By the Tariff Act of 1896 cotton yarn and cotton sewing thread are exempted from duty ; the tax on other cotton goods is 3½ per cent ; most other articles pay a 5 per cent. duty. There are special import duties on arms and ammunition which are taxed mainly for police purposes. Liquors pay duty, generally at Rs. 6 a gallon L.P. ; and salt pays Re. 1 a maund (82 lbs.) in Burma, and Rs. 2·8 annas in the rest of India. Iron and steel goods, however, pay 1 per cent., and machinery, coal, raw cotton, jute and wool, grain and pulse, oilcake, manures, living animals, unmanufactured tobacco, quinine, gold, precious stones and pearls, and a few other unimportant items are free from duty. Under Act XIV. of 1899, bounty-fed sugars pay on import into India countervailing duties calculated according to the amount of the bounty given. Opium grown in the Native States pays duty on crossing the land frontier into British Indian territory ; and opium not covered by a Government pass pays Rs. 24 per seer of 80 tolas.

The Indian sea-borne trade was shared by the various maritime provinces as follows, the figures being lakhs of rupees for imports and exports of merchandise respectively :—Bengal, 27·95 and 45·95 ; Bombay, 25·65 and 34·94 ; Madras, 5·27 and 11·18 ; Burma, 5·61 and 11·72 ; Sind, 3·98 and 8·93.

In 1898-99 3,508 vessels engaged in foreign trade, with a tonnage of 3,303,627, entered, and 4,360 with a tonnage of 4,402,593 cleared from Indian ports. These figures show little increase in numbers, but a large increase in tonnage over the previous year. Large steamers are replacing sailing ships of less bulk.

The value of the coasting trade, imports and exports being added together, amounted to Rx. 68,200,970 in 1896-97, Rx. 75,859,000 in 1897-98, and Rx. 70,834,950 in 1898-99.

The following statement exhibits the principal articles of the foreign trade of India in 1898-99, Government transactions being excluded :

IMPORTS.	Lakhs Rs.
Cotton goods and yarn	27,24·0
Metals (excluding hardware and cutlery)	5,17·9
Sugar	4,01·7
Oils	3,55·2
Machinery, &c.	3,25·8
Railway plant .	2,88·7
Liquors	1,64·7
Provisions ...	1,53·2
Woollen goods	1,52·4
Hardware and cutlery ...	1,43·5
Apparel	1,38·0
Silk (man.) ...	1,35·2
Spices	88·9
Drugs, narcotics, &c. ...	1·2
Silk (raw) ...	79·8
Dyes, &c. ...	77·7
Coal, &c.	69·8
Glass	66·2
Salt	66·1
Chemicals ...	42·5
Governmt. Stores	3,65·7

EXPORTS, (excluding re-exports, amounting to 3,39,9 lakhs.)	Lakhs Rs.
Rice	15,31·4
Seeds	11,84·7
Cotton	11,18·5
Wheat	10,21·6
Tea	8,04·5
Cotton yarns and cloth ...	7,78·8
Hides and skins	7,45·0
Opium	7,12·6
Jute	6,94·1
Jute manufacts.	5,79·8
Indigo	2,97·0
Coffee	1,75·0
Wool(raw&man.)	1,48·2
Pulse, &c. ...	1,16·7
Teak	95·5
Lac	85·6
Oils	80·1
Spices	61·9
Provisions ...	61·0
Silk(raw & man.)	58·6
Fodder, &c. ...	44·9
Manures	40·4

The following table shows the distribution of Indian sea-borne trade among other Countries in 1898-99.

Countries	Merchandise only. Imports and Exports.
	Lakhs Rs.
United Kingdom	79,38·6
China { Hong Kong.............	9,23·0
Treaty Ports...........	5,31·6
Germany	9,98·3
France	8,85·8
Straits Settlements...........	7,98·0
Egypt..........................	6,99·1
Belgium	6,98·0
United States	5,75·0
Japan.........................	5,78·3
Ceylon	5,61·2
Austria-Hungary	4,52·6
Italy	3,87·7
Mauritius	3,28·5
Russia.........................	2,18·3
Persia.........................	2,14·6
Arabia.........................	2,00·0

For the five months April to August 1899 the foreign trade of India shows the following variations as compared with 1898-99:—

Imports of merchandise, increase 307 lakhs, or 12 per cent.; treasure, decrease 62 lakhs, or 7 per cent.

Exports of merchandise, decrease 272 lakhs, or 6 per cent.; treasure, decrease 50 lakhs, or 13 per cent.

The output of the 147 collieries in India in 1897 was 4,063,000 tons. The 154 cotton mills at work contained 3,976,300 spindles, and produced 421,539,000lbs. of yarn and 82 321,000lbs. of woven goods ; the 32 jute mills contained 254,000 spindles. There were also 5 woollen and 10 paper mills, and 26 breweries. With regard to other industries particulars are not so precise.

The *Home Charges* amounted in 1897-98 to £16,004,601 (Rx. 25,017,107), thus : — Railway Revenue Account, including Railway Debt, £5,840,000 ; Interest and Management of Debt, other than that for Railways, £2,908,000 ; Stores, £937,000, of which £55 000 were Marine. and £511,000 Military ; Army Effective charges at home, including trooping service. amounted to £999,000, and non-effective charges to £2,996,000 ; Civil and Marine non-effective charges aggregated £1,218,000 : Furlough payments amounted to £524,000, of which £287,000 were under the head of Military. The cost of the India Office was £189,000. The Home charges for 1898-99 are estimated at £16,091,000, and for 1899-1900 at £16,324,000. The *Royal Commission*, appointed in 1895 to enquire into Indian expenditure and into the question of the division of certain charges between the Indian and English treasuries, had produced no Report up to the time of going to press.

PARTICULARS REGARDING POPULATION ACCORDING TO CENSUS OF 1891.

—	Total Population.	By Sex.		By Religion (minor religions omitted).			
		Males.	Females.	Hindus.	Mohammedans.	Buddhists.	Christians.
British India ...	221,172,952	112,542,739	108,630,213	155,171,943	49,550,491	7,095,398	1,491,662
Native States ...	66,050,479	34,184,557	31,865,922	52,559,784	7,770,673	35,963	792,718
Total India ...	287,223,431	146,727,296	140,496,135	207,731,727	57,321,164	7,131,361	2,284,380

LARGE CITIES WITH POPULATIONS EXCEEDING 150,000 (INCLUDING CANTONMENTS) IN 1891.

—	Total population	Hindus.	Mohammedans.	Christians.	Others.
Calcutta, including Howrah and all Suburbs ...	978,370	657,347	283,837	32,367	4,819
Bombay City and Island ...	821,764	543,276	155,247	45,310	77,931
Madras City	452,518	358,998	53,184	39,742	594
Hyderabad and Suburbs ...	415,039	226,840	172,861	13,829	1,509
Lucknow	273,028	161,896	104,198	5,715	1,219
Benares	219,467	168,691	49,405	1,206	165
Delhi	192,579	108,058	79,238	1,700	3,583
Mandalay	188,815	7,892	15,514	2,996	162,213
Cawnpore	188,712	141,031	44,199	2,994	488
Bangalore Town	180,366	125,258	34,364	20,327	417
Rangoon	180,324	57,845	28,836	12,678	80,965
Lahore	176,854	62,077	102,280	4,697	7,800
Allahabad	175,246	118,819	50,174	5,858	395
Agra	168,662	111,295	49,369	4,015	3,983
Patna.........................	165,192	124,506	40,077	541	68
Poona.........................	161,390	128,333	19,990	8,185	4,882
Jeypore	158,905	109,861	38,953	244	9,847

AREA AND POPULATION OF BRITISH INDIA ACCORDING TO CENSUS OF 1881 & 1891.

PROVINCES, ETC., UNDER THE ADMINISTRATION OF:	Area in Square Miles.	NUMBER OF OCCUPIED HOUSES. 1881.	1891.	POPULATION. 1881.	1891.	Incrse. per ct. since 1881.	NUMBER PER SQUARE MILE. 1881.	1891.
The Gov.-Gen. of India—								
Ajmere and Mhairwara...	2,711	64,118	101,654	460,722	542,358	17·72	170	200
Berar	17,718	466,027	591,008	2,672,673	2,897,491	8·41	151	163
Coorg	1,583	22,357	26,806	178,302	173,055	−2·94	113	109
Andaman Is. (P. Blair only)	(?)	2,938	2,997	14,628	15,609	6·70	—	—
Baluchistan Cantonments	(?)	—	4,543	—	27,270	—	—	—
Governors—								
Madras	141,189	5,641,914	6,709,990	30,827,113	35,630,440	15·58	215	252
Bombay (inc. Sind & Aden)	125,144	2,830,723	3,380,640	16,505,967	18,901,123	14·51	132	151
Lieutenant-Governors—								
Bengal	151,543	10,531,228	13,592,154	66,750,520	71,346,987	6·89	445	471
North-West Prov. & Oudh	107,503	6,866,503	8,225,191	44,150,507	46,905,085	6·23	416	436
Punjâb	110,667	2,707,091	3,127,823	18,843,186	20,866,847	10·74	170	188
Burma { Lower	87,957	677,362	869,132	3,736,771	4,658,627	24·67	43	53
Upper	83,473	—	554,472	—	2,946,933	—	—	35
Chief Commissioners—								
Assam	49,004	859,388	1,118,885	4,881,426	5,476,833	11·3	105	112
Central Provinces........	86,501	2,336,976	2,158,668	9,838,791	10,784,294	9·61	116	125
Total British India...	964,993	33,009,068	40,463,963	198,875,079	221,172,952	9·70	229	230
NATIVE STATES—								
Hyderabad..................	82,698	1,859,600	2,283,787	9,845,594	11,537,040	17·18	120	139
Baroda......................	8,226	479,463	538,967	2,185,005	2,415,396	10·54	255	294
Mysore......................	27,936	733,200	894,446	4,186,188	4,943,604	18·09	169	177
Kashmir.....................	80,900	—	447,993	1,534,972	2,543,952	63·34	19	31
Rajputana Agency	130,268	2,101,451	2,177,425	9,959,012	12,016,102	20·22	79	92
Central India Agency	77,808	1,680,394	1,961,771	9,387,119	10,318,812	9·92	123	133
Bombay	69,045	1,348,599	1,596,132	6,926,464	8,059,298	16·35	100	116
Madras	9,609	685,447	726,966	3,344,849	3,700,622	10·63	353	385
Bengal	35,834	505,546	584,912	2,786,446	3,296,379	18·30	78	92
Central Provinces	29,435	375,283	409,096	1,709,720	2,160,511	26·36	59	73
North-West Provinces ...	5,109	125,907	132,815	741,750	792,491	6·84	144	155
Punjâb	38,299	655,215	713,735	3,860,761	4,263,280	10·42	101	111
Total Native States ‡ ...	595,167	10,550,285	12,468,045	56,467,880	66,047,487	15·52	96	111
Grand Total India	1,560,160	43,559,353	52,932,006	255,372,959	287,223,431	10·96	174	184

‡ To these may be added the following population figures; for Sikkim (area 2,702 sq. m.) 30,458 ; Manipur (area 8,000 sq. m.) 250,000 (estimated); British Baluchistan 145,417 ; Cis-Salween Shan States (area 44,000 sq. m.) 375,962; Burma Frontier Tracts 116,493 ; and Rajputana Hill Tracts 204,241 : making a total of 1,122,571. To this again may be added for French possessions 282,923, and for Portuguese possessions 561,384 ; making a grand total for all India of 289,187,316.

DISTRIBUTION of the POPULATION of INDIA according to SEX, RELIGION, and EDUCATION, in 1891.

RELIGION.	TOTAL POPULATION. Males.	Females.	MALES. Learning.	Literate.	Illiterate.	FEMALES. Learning	Literate.	Illiterate.
Hindu	95,970,162	92,978,518	2,124,787	7,976,605	85,868,770	103,208	277,491	92,597,819
Sikh	1,070,124	824,599	14,784	88,350	966,990	410	2,585	821,604
Jain	481,008	428,707	44,562	212,261	224,185	2,010	3,846	422,851
Buddhist.........	3,479,300	3,543,591	219,086	1,428,323	1,831,891	15,035	76,210	3,452,346
Zoroastrian (Parsis) ... }	45,639	43,932	8,857	26,619	10,163	4,498	17,492	21,942
Mussulman	27,772,718	26,181,585	492,784	1,473,909	25,806,025	28,760	58,608	26,094,217
Christian.........	1,193,318	1,089,675	83,211	325,465	784,642	42,408	105,200	942,067
Jews	8,646	8,545	1,149	3,337	4,160	493	1,338	6,714
Animistic	3,346,452	3,365,425	8,305	18,942	3,319,205	825	672	3,363,928
Minor	149	36	6	103	40	5	13	18
Religion not returned ... }	3,485	3,312	27	121	3,337	10	40	3,262
Total	133,371,001	128,467,925	2,997,558	11,554,035	118,819,408	197,662	543,495	127,726,768

Note.—The populations of Aden and Andaman Islands are not included in these columns.

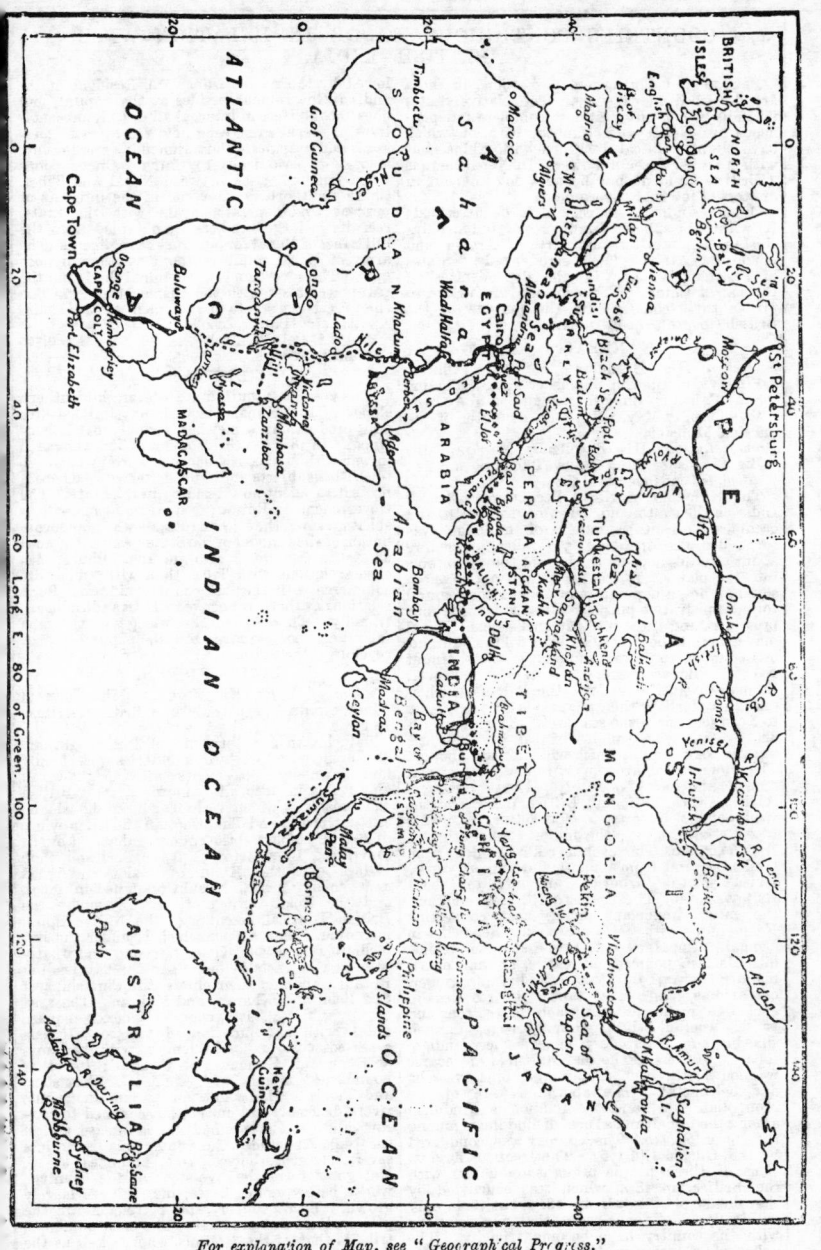

For explanation of Map, see "Geographical Progress."

WHITAKER'S ALMANACK, 1900.

FRENCH and Portuguese possessions in India are described on page 455. The Native States in India which enjoy almost complete independence are Nepal and Bhutan, both of which have slight political relations with China, but with no other foreign Power. In Nepal there is a British Resident, but he does not interfere in matters of internal government.

Outside India there remain to be described; (1) within the sphere of influence of India, Baluchistan, Afghanistan and parts of Arabia and north-east Africa ; (2) the independent States of Persia and Siam; (3) the dependencies of Russia, of China, of France, and of Turkey, so far as these come within the purview of the British Government in India.

NEPAL.

Sovereign, His Highness Maharaja Dhiraj, Pirthivi Bir Bikram Shamsher Jang Bahadur, Sah Bahadur Shamsher Jang, *b.* 8 August, 1875 ; *suc.* 17 May, 1881 ; *m.* a daughter of the Prime Minister.

Prime Minister, His Excellency Maharaja Sir Bir Shamsher Jang Rana Bahadur, G.C.S.I., *appointed* 22 November, 1885.

The Kingdom of Nepal lies between British India on the south and Tibet on the north, and occupies the southern ranges of the Himalayas for a distance of about 500 miles, extending about 20 miles beyond the base of the mountains into the plains. It has an area of about 54,000 square miles, a population of about 2,000,000, and for administrative purposes it is divided into four provinces, and these into fifteen districts. Nepal may generally be described as a wild, mountainous country, containing, amongst others, Mount Everest. Between the sterile ranges, however, lie many beautiful valleys, the soil of which is extremely fertile ; their elevations are from 2,000 to 6,000 feet above the sea level. The lower hills are covered with jungles of sal, pine, spruce, mimosa, oak, &c., in which wild animals abound. The chief minerals are copper, iron, sulphur, jasper, marble, and rock crystal. Nepal has commercial relations with Tibet and British India, and the value of its exports to the latter in 1898–9 was Rs. 2,14,10,000 ; the imports amounting to Rs. 1,63,63,000. The revenue, realised chiefly from land rent, and from export and import duties levied at the frontier, amounts to about Rs.1,50,00,000. The trade routes are numerous, the most important being that connecting Katmandu with Motihari and Segowli, in Bengal. Nepal exports rice and other grains, oilseeds, *ghi*, ponies and cattle, opium, musk, madder, borax, jute, hides and furs, ginger, cardamoms, and yaks' tails. It receives in exchange raw and manufactured cotton and twist, woollen cloth, shawls, rugs, flannel, silk brocade, embroidery, sugar, spices, indigo, tobacco, salt, &c. The manufactures are coarse woollen cloth, iron, copper and brass vessels, and bell-metal. The aborigines are of the Mongolian type, and the religion is Hinduism among the upper, and a form of Buddhism among the lower classes. The country was conquered by the Gurkhas in 1767. The frequent aggressions of these people brought on a war with the British, in 1814, which was concluded by the Treaty of Segowli in 1815, but it is only within the last forty years that our relations with the country have become friendly. The policy of seclusion is, however, consistently followed by the native rulers. A Resident of the Indian Government resides at the capital, but does not interfere in internal affairs. Representatives of Nepal greet each new Viceroy with messages and presents. Complimentary missions are also sent periodically to China. On occasions when friction arises between Nepal and Tibet. Chinese authorities intervene in the interests of peace. Under arrangements with the State, recruits in large numbers are obtained from the hill tribes of Nepal for our Gurkha regiments. The army of Nepal numbers about 35,000 with 1,000 guns. The sovereign is the nominal chief ; but the real power rests with the Prime Minister. The chief receives a salute of 21 guns in British India.

Khatmandu (Pop. 53,000)*—British Resident,* Lt.-Col. W. Loch ....Rs. 2,500
Transit, 20 days.

BHUTAN.

This is another outlying State on the southern slopes of the Himalayas with physical features and productions somewhat similar to those of Nepal. In 1863 the Government of India engaged in war with it in consequence of certain outrages to British subjects and representatives. There is no British agent now residing in the State. The Government of Bhutan is dual in form, with a spiritual chief, the Dherma Raja—who is an incarnation of the founder of the State—and a temporal chief, the Deb Raja, who governs. Bhutan has closer relations with Tibet than with India ; its commerce with the latter is insignificant. Such relations as there are between Tibet and India are friendly. There is no knowledge of the area (about 20,000 square miles), population, or revenue of the State.

BALUCHISTAN.

Khan of Kalat, His Highness Mir Mahmud Khan, G.C.I.E., 1893. Salute in British territory 19 guns.

Baluchistan is a term of political geography. Its northern and western boundaries were finally laid down by agreements with Afghanistan and Persia in 1896. It comprises, (1) "British Baluchistan," which includes the assigned districts of Pishin and Thal Chotiali and is a province of British India ; (2) the country inhabited by the Marri and Bugti tribes ; (3) the Bori and Zhob valleys and the Khan of Kalat's assigned districts of Quetta, Nushki (assigned in 1899), and the Bolan, which are directly under the British Political Agent ; (4) the Native State, including Kalat proper which is under the immediate rule of the Khan, Sarawan and Jhalawan, or the tracts belonging to the two leading Brahui clans and their chiefs, the Chiefships of Las Bela, and Kharan, and Makran. The area of division (4) is given at 106,000 square miles, with a population of 220,500. It has a sea-coast 600 miles in length, with harbours at Sunmiani, Kalmat, and Gwadur ; its other boundaries march with India, Afghanistan, and Persia. The country is mountainous, the rivers deficient, and cultivation confined to narrow valleys. The summer heat is intense, and in the higher altitudes the winter cold is no less severe. Camels, horses, kine, buffaloes, sheep, and goats form the live-stock of the country ; wheat, barley, millet, dates, and fruit are largely grown. Lead, copper, and petroleum are the principal mineral products. The most numerous tribe is that of the Brahuis, who, as well as the Baluchis, are Sunni Mohammedans. The Khan

Afghanistan—Persia. 471

of Kalat is the head of a rather loose confederacy; and till his treaty with the British Government in 1876, he received a rather spasmodic obedience from his feudal inferiors. The principal feudatories are the Jam of Las Bela and the Khan of Karan. Mir Khudadad Khan, G.C.S.I., who was Khan of Kalat from 1857 to 1893, was deposed in the latter year. The influence of the British Political Agent is extensive though undefined, and the State cannot be considered as independent, even in regard to internal administration. It has no relations with other foreign Powers, and British troops occupy the strong fortress of Quetta commanding the Bolan Pass, and have the treaty-right to occupy any other position in the State. A trade route from Quetta to Persian Seistan along the north of Baluchistan has recently been opened up. Its permanent value has yet to be proved.

Khan's Capital, Kalat. Head-Quarters of the British Administration, Quetta.

Agent to the Governor-General in Baluchistan and Chief Commissioner of British Baluchistan, Hugh S. Barnes .... Rs. 4,750 per mensem.
Telegrams 3s. 7d. or 3s. 3d. a word.

AFGHANISTAN.

Amir, His Highness Abdur Rahman Khan, Ziaul-Millat-wad-Din, G.C.B., G.C.S.I., s. 1880, b. 1845; has four sons, of whom Sardar Habibulla Khan, G.C.M.G., is the eldest, and Sardar Nasrullah Khan, G.C.M.G., the second, and Umar Jan the youngest, but born of a mother of higher rank than his half brothers. Salute in British territory 21 guns.

By agreement with the Amir, Afghanistan has no foreign relations with other Powers except the Government of India. In all other respects Afghanistan is independent, and the rule of the Amir despotic.

The country lies on the north-west frontier of India, between the parallels of 60° 40′ and 74° 30′ E. longitude, and 30° and 38° 20′ N. latitude, bounded on the west and south by Persia and Baluchistan, and north by the Russian provinces and dependencies in Central Asia. The whole northern boundary from Persia to China has been settled in agreement with Russia and demarcated, the Oxus from Lake Victoria (Wood's Lake) to Khamiab forming part of this frontier. Within these limits Afghanistan has a breadth from north to south of about 500 miles, and a length from east to west of about 600 miles. The area may be estimated at 270,000 sq. miles. Geographically its three divisions are the Oxus basin, the Kabul (or Indus) basin, and the Helmand basin. The country is divided into five provinces, Kabul, Kandahar, Herat, Turkestan, and Badakshan with Kafiristan and Wakhan. The country is generally rugged and mountainous, the elevation being, with few exceptions, more than 4,000 feet above the sea; the climate is severe, cold in winter, hot in summer. The population is estimated to number 4 or 5 millions, who are divided into a number of tribes,—Ghilzais, Tajiks, Duranis, Hazarahs, Aimaks, Uzbegs, &c. All are Sunni Mohammedans except the Hazarahs and Kizilbashes, who belong to the Shiite sect, and the Kafirs, who are idolators, except in so far as the Amir has recently succeeded in converting them to Islam. The Amir has by degrees reduced all the tribes to subordination. In the cultivable parts of the country there are generally two crops in the year, one of

wheat, barley, or lentils, the other of rice, millet, &c.; wheat, however, being the staple food. Afghanistan is also rich in fruits of many kinds. The mineral wealth of the country is reputed considerable, but few mines are worked. The roads are unsuitable for wheeled traffic, there being only one good road in the country—that made by the English from Peshawar to Kabul through the Khaibar pass, the route by which India has so often been invaded. The Amir has recently taken measures to improve the roads, particularly towards his northern and eastern provinces. Goods are conveyed by beasts of burden, mostly by camels. In the 11th and 13th centuries the Afghan empires of the Sultans of Ghazni and Ghor, and in the last century that of Ahmed Shah, extended over the Punjab. In 1838 the country was occupied by British troops, but three years later a national revolt broke out at Kabul, which resulted in the destruction of an English army, and the abandonment of the country to its Native rulers. A second invasion by the English in 1879 led to the temporary occupation of Kabul and Kandahar. In 1881 they passed into the hands of the present Amir, only the chief passes between Afghanistan and India being retained under British control. The trade of Afghanistan with India is valued at about Rx. 1,150,000. It is restricted by the Amir's oppressive trade policy. The Amir's revenue is unknown, and consists largely of payments in kind. It may amount to one crore (10 million) rupees. He receives a subsidy of Rs. 18,00,000 a year from the Government of India, and has received from the same source considerable quantities of arms. The Amir has a large army; his regular troops numbering perhaps 60,000 men; with the help of English engineers he has started factories for the manufacture of guns, rifles, and cartridges. He also engages in other industrial and commercial enterprises. The Amir has an agent with the Government of India, an agent at Peshawar, and a business agent.

CAPITAL, Kabul. Other cities, Khulum, Kandahar, Herat, all famous commercial cities.

Letters require stamps of P. O. Kabul for transmission beyond the Indian frontier. Postage from Peshawar to Kabul, letters and newspapers weighing ⅓ of a tola, 6d.

British Agent at Kabul, vacant.

PERSIA.

Sovereign, Shah Muzaffer-ed-Din Mirza, b. 25 March, 1853; succeeded 1 May, 1896.
Heir-Apparent, (or Vali Ahd), Mohammed Ali Mirza, Gov. of Azerbaijan, b. 1872: procld. 12 June, 1896.
Prime Minister (Sadr Azam), H.H. Ali Asghar Khan, Amir Sultan, Sadr Azam.
Min. for Foreign Affairs, H.E. Mushir-ed-Dowleh.
Interior, H.E. Dahir-ul-Mulk.
War, H.H. Amir Khan, Sardar.
Justice and Commerce, H.E. Amin Khalvat.
Envoy Extry. and Min. Pleny. in London, Gen. Mirza Mohamed-Ali-Khan Ala-es-Sultané, Amir Tooman, 30 Ennismore Gdns., S.W.
Secretaries, Mirza Hussein Kuli Khan, Mirza Mehdi Khan, and Mirza Abdul Ghuffar Khan.
Consul-General, Harry Seymour Foster, M.P.
Persia, called by the natives Iran, is situate between 25° 10′—39° 50′ N. lat. and 44° 15′—53° E. long., extending about 700 miles from north to south, and about 900 miles from east to west, and comprising an area of 630,000 square miles. The Caspian Sea, which bounds it

on the north, is wholly under Russian influence; the Persian Gulf on the south is dominated and policed by the British Government. The northern frontiers of Persia are in contact with Russian provinces; its eastern with Afghanistan and Baluchistan, which are within the British sphere of influence; and its western with Turkey. The population was estimated in 1881 at 7,653,600, possibly increased to 9,000,000. The greater part of the country is an elevated table-land, encircled, except on the east, by mountains. The northern mountain ranges rise to 12,000 feet above the sea, and the peak of Demavend to over 19,000 feet. The central and eastern portion of the plateau is a vast salt desert. With the exception of the Karun it has scarcely a river that can be termed navigable, though some of the rivers are several hundred miles in length, and possess great volume of water. The Karun from Mohamerah to Ahwaz has been thrown open to foreign navigation. Messrs. Lynch Bros. run a fortnightly steamer to Ahwaz. The Upper Karun from Ahwaz to Schuster is also navigable, but its navigation is reserved to the Persian flag. Railways are practically non-existent, and the Shah has bound himself not to allow the construction of railways in Persia for several years to come. Cart-roads are being made between Tehran and Tabriz, Tehran and the Caspian, and between Tehran and Ahwaz on the Karun. A carriage-road also exists between Meshed and Askhabad in Russian territory. Travelling is mostly done by post-horses and caravans, and transport by pack-animals. The whole country is divided into provinces, of which the chief are Azarbijan, Ghilan, Mazanderan, Astrabad, Ardelan, Kermanshah, Irak-Ajemi, Khorassan, Fars, Luristan, Kerman, and Laristan, which are under Governors - General. The chief products are wheat, barley, and other cereals, cotton, sugar, rice, tobacco, and opium. Its minerals are salt, iron, and coal; copper, lead, antimony, sulphur, &c., also turquoises and some other precious stones are found. The most important manufacture is that of silks, of the richest and most gorgeous kind. The Persians excel in their dyes, also in brocade and embroidery. Arms, carpets, shawls, felts, cotton and woollen fabrics are among the manufactures. The royal treasury is reputed to contain immense wealth in gold and other valuables, but the administration of the state is corrupt, and suffers frequently from a want of means. The commerce of Persia with Russia is chiefly through ports on the Caspian Sea, or by the Trans-Caspian railway, and with British India by way of the Persian Gulf. European goods also reach Persia from the Black Sea, *viâ* Trebizond and Tabriz; the imports of Great Britain by this route were valued at £297,000 in 1898. The trade through Afghanistan between Persia and India has been quite ruined by the Amir's fiscal policy, but a new route has been recently opened up from Quetta through Baluchistan to Persian Seistan, which avoids Afghan territory and the exactions of the Amir's officials. Of the foreign trade of Persia half passes north through Russia and Turkey, half south by the Persian Gulf. The Persian Gulf trade, exclusive of what passes up the Shat-ul-Arab to Basra, is mainly with India and the United Kingdom. In 1898 it amounted to nearly 5¼ millions sterling in value, of which nearly 3 millions represented the share of India and the United Kingdom, most of the remainder being local. The exports consist of silk, tobacco, wool,

carpets, opium, gums, hides, dates, &c. Protection to British trade is secured by the Treaty of 1841. The Imperial Bank of Persia is an English Company, which has its head office at Tehran and branches in the chief cities. These are, with their populations, Tehran (210,000), Tabriz (180,000), Ispahan (60,000), Meshed (60,000), &c. The regular army numbers about 80,500 (of whom 24,000 with the colours), with 200 field guns; the militia 70,000 men. There are 4,150 miles of telegraph, the greater part managed by the Indo-European telegraph department of the Government of India. The Persians are mostly Mohammedans of the Shiah sect. There are also a considerable number of Armenian Christians. The Government is an absolute despotism; the laws are based on the precepts of the Koran; the dispensation of justice is summary. For several years past Persian trade and revenues have suffered from a series of bad harvests. The total revenue has been calculated at 55,369,516 krans (=£1,652,820), and the expenditure at 42,233,472 krans (=£1,260,700) for the year 1888. The sea customs receipts of the southern ports in 1897 was valued at 2,145,000 krans. The kran is a silver coin weighing 71 grains, and has depreciated relatively to gold with the fall in silver. In 1898 the exchange was about 53 krans to the £1. 10 krans = 1 tuman. The weights and measures in use in the country are not uniform.

Direct imports from U. Kingdom, 1898…£338,017
Direct exports to ditto, 1898 ………… 193,791

CAPITAL, Tehran. Population, 210,000.

Envoy Extraordinary & Minister Plenipo-
tentiary & Consul - General, Sir Henry
Mortimer Durand, K.C.S.I., K.C.I.E.……£5,000
Sec. of Legation, C. A. Spring Rice ………… 750
Military Attaché and Oriental Secretary,

Asst. Mil. Attaché, Capt. C. V. Schneider, I.S.C.	450
2nd *Secs.,* E. A. Rennie (£400); T. G. Ford	315
Physician, T. F. Odling, C.M.G. ………………	600
Vice-Consul, C. Grahame …………………	350
Fars, &c.—Cons.-Gen., Lt.-Col. M. J. Meade.……………………Rs. 2,750 *per mensem*	
Bushire—Vice-Consul, John C. Gaskin …… Rs. 350 *per mensem*	
Mohammerah—Vice-Con., Wm. McDouall…	£350
Ispahan—Consul, John R. Preece, C.M.G. …	560
Yezd—Vice-Consul, M. M. Ferguson ………	
Kerman—Consul, Major Percy M. Sykes …	
Meshed—Political Agent and Cons.-Gen., Lt.-Col. Henry M. Temple …… Rs. 3,000 *per mensem*	
Assist. to Polit. Agent, Khorassan, and Consul, Capt. J. F. Whyte ……… Rs. 700 *per mensem*	
Resht & Asterabad—Consul (vacant) …………	£600
Tabreez—Cons.-Gen., Cecil G. Wood………	650

Parcels, not exceeding 1 lb. 4s. 4d.; for each additional lb. up to a limit of 7 lbs., 8d.; telegrams, per word, 1s. 6d. to 2s. 5d.

SIAM.

King, Khoulalonkorn, *b.* 21 Sept., 1853; *succeeded* 1 Oct., 1868.
Crown Prince, Prince Somdetch Chowfa Maha Vajiravudh, *b.* 1880; *procl.* 17 Jan. 1895.
Chief Minister, H. R. H. Krom Luang Dewawongse.
Legal Adviser, Robert J. Kirkpatrick.
Envoy Extr. and Min. Plen. in London, Phya Prasiddhi Salakar, 23 Ashburn Place, South Kensington, S.W.
Councillor of Legation, Fredk. Verney, 6 Onslow Gdns., S.W.

Interpreter, Edward H. Loftus.

Attaché, Luang Prakitch.

Consul, James Riches, 6 Great Winchester St., E.C.

The Kingdom of Siam lies between the British Indian province of Burma and its dependencies on one side, and the territory of French Indo-China on the other. By the Anglo-French agreement of May, 1896, the main central part of Siam, including the basins of the Rivers Menam, Petcha Bouri, and Petriou, was neutralised, the two governments agreeing not to send troops into it or to obtain any exclusive advantages in it. Freedom of action was retained by the two powers in regard to the portions of Siam west and east of the neutralised zone. The western portion includes the Malay States dependent on Siam which are adjacent to the British protected Malay States under the Governor of the Straits Settlements. The eastern portion, including the provinces of Battambong and Angkor, are in close connection with the French protected State of Cambodia and the territories acquired by France by the treaty with Siam of 1893. By this treaty France also acquired a certain right of interference with the Siamese administration west of the Mekong to a distance of 25 kilometres from that river. The area of Siam may be taken at 220,000 square miles, with a population variously estimated between 7½ and 38 millions, but probably numbering about 12 millions, of whom about 4 millions are Siamese, the rest being Chinese, Shans, Laos, Malays, Burmese, and hill tribesmen. Bangkok is the only much-frequented port; Chantaboon, which was occupied by the French as a guarantee for the fulfilment of the treaty to which Siam assented in 1893, is still in their possession. Siamese trade, which centres at Bangkok, is very largely in the hands of British firms, or of Chinese trading from Singapore and Hongkong. The chief products are rice, teak, sandalwood, rosewood, and fruits and garden products. Of merchandise the chief export is rice; teak and other woods, marine products, pepper and cattle are also exported in considerable quantities. Among imports are cotton and piece goods and yarn, silks, gunny bags, kerosine, sugar, opium, hardware and cutlery, steel and iron goods, machinery, &c. The Government is monarchical; the King appoints the successor. There is a new Legislative Council of State consisting of the ministers, six Royal Princes, and from 10 to 20 members appointed by the King. A number of Europeans, principally English, Belgians, Danes, and Germans, are employed in the service of the Siamese State. There is an army of 8,000 men, and a few small gunboats. A telegraph connects Bangkok with Saigon (Cochin-China), and with Burma. Bangkok is connected with Paknam by rail; an important line to Korat is nearly completed, and a line northwards to Chieng-mai is under contemplation.

The currency is the Mexican dollar, valued in 1897 at 2s. In the north-west of Siam the Indian rupee is current.

Revenue and expenditure…each about	£2,000,000
Imports from United Kingdom, 1898…	215,440
Exports to United Kingdom, 1898 ……	63,749
Total Imports at Bangkok, 1898 ………	2,622,183
Total Exports at Bangkok, 1898 ………	3,491,270

Over 80 per cent. of this trade is with Singapore, Hong Kong and Bombay; 77 per cent. of the entire steam tonnage at Bangkok (463,244 tons) is under the British flag; but during 1899 a large difference in favour of Germany was made by the transfer to the German flag of the ships of a large British shipping firm trading to Bangkok.

Indian land trade with Siam was valued in 1898–99 at Rs 44,00,000.

CAPITAL, Bangkok. Population, 600,000.

Minister Resident & Consul-Gen., George Greville, C.M G.	£1,600
Consul, W. J. Archer	800
Vice-Consuls, C. E. W. Stringer, John Stewart Black	£450 & 400
1st Assistant, T. H. Lyle	400
2nd Assistant, T. F. Carlisle	350
Student Interpreters, G. H. Moor, £300; W. A. R. Wood, £300; W. N. Dunn, £300	
Medical Attendant, P. A. Nightingale, M.D.	300
Chiengmai—V.-Consul, W. R. D. Beckett.	600
Kedah—Consul, C. W. Kynnersley, C.M.G.	

Parcels (Bangkok only), per lb. 10*d.*; telegrams, per word, 4*s.* 4*d.* to 5*s.* 7*d.*

RUSSIA IN CENTRAL ASIA.

The Russian provinces of Central Asia are Trans-Caspia, with an area of 383,618 square miles, and a population of 352,0000; and Turkestan, with an area of 409,414, and a population of 3,341,913. The population of 1897 gave a total for both provinces of 4,175,100. The Trans-Caspian Railway, starting from Krasnovodsk on the Caspian, goes through Merv, crosses the Oxus at Charjui, and passes through Bokhara to Samarcand. Since 1895 it has been continued to Andijan and Tashkent. A branch from Merv on the Transcaspian line to Kushk on the Afghan frontier (180 miles in length) was also opened in 1899. It brings the Russian system of railways within 80 miles of Herat, and about 450 miles from the Chaman terminus of the Indian railway system. The connection of Tashkent with the main Russian system by a line to Orenburg or one to Omsk is under contemplation. The Central Asian railway has been the means of greatly increasing the Russian trade and has led to an immense increase of cotton cultivation in Central Asia for export to Russia (*see also* map p. 469, and Article, p. 605). Trans-Caspia is in contact with Persia and Afghanistan, while Turkestan stretches into the Pamir region. Its southern boundary was fixed by the Pamir agreement between Russia and England. The Russian forces in Turkestan and Trans-Caspia number about 45,000 men, besides a few native irregulars. The provinces do not pay the charges of occupation and administration.

Governor-General of Turkestan, Baron Vrevsky.

Besides these provinces directly administered by Russian officials, the Russian Empire in Central Asia includes the two vassal States of Bokhara and Khiva.

BOKHARA.

Amir, Syed Abdul Ahad, succeeded Nov. 12, 1885. Once the most famous State in all Central Asia, but since the capture of Samarkand by the Russians, in May, 1868, a vassal State of Russia. By the treaty of 1873 no foreigner may be admitted into Bokhara without a Russian passport. Steps have been taken to incorporate the Bokhara customs administration with that of the Russian provinces. Bokhara, with Karategin, has an area of 92,300 square miles, and a population of 2,130,000. The Amir retains an ill-trained native army of about 10,000 men. The Uzbegs, of Turkish extraction, are the dominant race, but the Aryan Tajiks or Sarts are the aboriginal inhabitants of the country. The people are fanatical Mohammedans of the Sunni sect. Slavery has been abolished through the influence of Russia. The country produces corn and fruit, cotton, silk, wine, tobacco, and hemp. Sheep, horses, goats, and camels are numerous; gold, salt, alum, sulphur, and coal are among the mineral productions. The foreign trade is valued at 32,000,000 roubles, imports slightly exceeding the exports. The Amu-Darya, or Oxus, which forms the southern frontier of the country, is now navigated by Russian steamers. The Russian paper rouble is current. The capital, Bokhara, has 70,000 inhabitants.

Telegrams, per word, 1s. 11d.

Russian Political Resident, Major Ignatieff.

KHIVA.

Khan, Syed Mohamed Rahim Khan, *suc.* 1865.

A Russian vassal State in Western Turkestan, on the western side of the Lower Amu-Darya, or Oxus, which here flows into Lake Aral. The Russians captured Khiva on May 20th, 1873, abolished slavery, and compelled the Khan to acknowledge himself a vassal of the Czar. The area is 22,320 square miles, with about 700,000 inhabitants, dominant among whom are the Uzbegs. The people are Mohammedan of the Sunni sect. The fields and gardens are irrigated by canals, derived from the Oxus; all the surrounding country being a barren wilderness, affording but little pasturage. Wheat, melons and other fruits, silk, cotton, and wool are among the productions. The State has no external relations except with Russia. The Khan's military force is limited by treaty with Russia to 2,000 men, and he pays tribute to Russia to the amount of 150,000 roubles a year, out of a yearly revenue of 500,000 roubles.

CAPITAL, Khiva. Population, 6,000.

CHINA IN CENTRAL ASIA.

YUNNAN, TIBET, CHINESE TURKESTAN.

India is in contact with three provinces of China. On the north-east of Burma is the province of *Yunnan* (area 107,969 square miles, population 11,721,576). In 1897 an agreement was made between Great Britain and China, supplementing the frontier Convention of March, 1894, which laid down a boundary between Burma with its dependencies and Yunnan, and made arrangements for trade, extradition, &c. The question of access to Yunnan and Szechuen is one of great importance to the commercial nations of Europe. The shortest route to Yunnan-fu is through French territory by the Red River. In 1899 the Chinese Government is reported to have agreed with the French Government to build a railway from the French frontier to Yunnan-fu, the French Colonial Government themselves constructing a line from Haiphong, the capital of Tonkin, to the frontier town of Laokay on the Red River. There are competing routes through Burma. A part of Yunnan is most easily reached from Bhamo. The Indian railway system is being extended to Kunlong Ferry, on the Salween, from which a route to Yunnan-fu and thence into Szechuen, with a branch to Talifu, is said to be practicable. Another route for a railway has been suggested through Chiengmai and Northern Siam. More important routes at present are by river up the Canton or West River, or by the Yang-tze-kiang. By the agreement of 15 January, 1896, Great Britain and France agreed to share equally all privileges or advantages that might be conceded by China in the provinces of Yunnan and Szechuen. Both provinces are reputed to be rich in minerals, and the latter has a large and busy population. The chief imports into Yunnan are raw cotton, cotton yarn and piece goods. British Consuls have been lately appointed to Ssumao and Momein (Têng-yuëh) in Yunnan. Opium and tin are the chief exports. Next to Yunnan is *Chinese Tibet*, or *Bodyul*, as it is named by its inhabitants, which may perhaps be called a province of China, though it is in internal matters practically independent. Tibet forms the northern frontier of India, from Burma to Kashmir; but, separated by the gigantic range of the Himalayas, the intercourse between the two countries is of the slenderest description. It contains the sources of almost all the great rivers of India and China. It is itself a plateau of extraordinary altitude, seldom lower than 10,000 feet, and protected by the vast mountain ranges of the Kuenlun in the north and the Himalayas on the south. The capital, Lhassa, is the religious centre of a special form of Buddhism, contains a large population with a great number of Buddhist monasteries, and continues to be out of the reach of European travellers. The country is, no doubt, very rich in minerals, but these are little worked; cultivation is carried on under extreme climatic difficulties; and the whole country is still shrouded in mystery. Steps are being taken to improve the Indian trade with Tibet, which is valued at about 35 lakhs of rupees. There are as yet no British representatives in Tibet, but a treaty port has been opened at Yatung, beyond the Sikkim frontier. *Chinese Turkestan*, including Yarkand and Kashgar, was re-occupied by China in 1878, on the suppression of the revolt of Yakub Beg. Little is known of its area and population. Russia has special treaty rights in the north, and a Russian consul is at Kashgar. A representative of the Indian Government also resides at that place, but without the title of consul. Trade between India and Chinese Turkestan has to pass by the lofty pass of Karakoram (18,500 feet), or by the very difficult routes through Kashmir and Hunza, and by almost as lofty passes across the Hindu Kush. Leh is the centre in Kashmir through which this trade passes.

Consul: Momein, Têng-huën: P. F. Hausser £800.

Ssumao: J. N. Tratman, £800.

Special Assistant to Resident in Kashmir: Kashgar: Mr. G. Macartney.

FRENCH POSSESSIONS.

French India. See page 455.

French Indo-China.—These possessions, which have three times the area of France, consist of Cochin-China, Cambodia, Tonquin, Annam, and the Laos country. The administration is in the hands of a civil governor-general, assisted by a colonial secretary (for Tonquin principally), a lieutenant-governor for Cochin-China, and residents in Annam, Cambodia, and Laos. Affairs are directed by a permanent Commission consisting of the governor-general, the general commanding, the lieutenant-governor, the director of finance, the procureur-general, and the directors of customs and of commerce and agriculture. The first cession of Cochin-China was in 1862; its western provinces were occupied in 1867. Cambodia recognised the French protectorate in 1863; its present status is, however, regulated by a convention of 17 June, 1884; the effective protectorate over Annam dates from 1874, but present relations are determined by a convention of 6 June, 1884. Tonquin may be said to have been finally conquered when peace had been concluded with China in 1885. The Lao country up to the Mekong was added to the French protectorate as a result of the dispute with Siam in 1893, and the Mekong was finally fixed as a boundary between French and British dominions in 1896. Cochin-China is wholly annexed and directly administered by French officials. Annam is governed by a king, with his court at Hué. Subject to the control of the French Resident, the Annamese kingdom is an absolute despotism, after the Chinese type, and the administration is in the hands of the king's officials; the customs are, however, under the management of French officers. In Cambodia the French Resident presides over the State Council, and French interference in internal administration is greater than it is in Annam: but government is carried on in the name of the King of Cambodia. In Tonquin the direction of affairs is in the hands of the French Resident and his subordinate officials. The French possessions extend northwards to 25° 20', and march with China as far west as the Mekong, which river forms the western boundary along almost the whole length of the French Colony. The area and population are estimated as below:—

	Area. Square miles.	Pop.
Cochin-China	23,082	2,252,034
Cambodia	38,600	1,500,000
Annam and Laos	100,000	6,000,000
Tonquin	34,740	12,000,000
Total	196,422	21,752,034

The Budget for 1899 was for 30,699,604 dollars, the dollar being equivalent to 2½ francs.

The deltas of Cochin-China and Tonquin are fertile; Annam, connecting them, is a long mountainous tract, with a narrow littoral on one side, and a wild sparsely populated hill tract stretching to the Mekong on the other. Rice, cotton, sugar, seeds, tobacco, spices, and fish, are the principal productions of the alluvial districts. The principal mineral production is coal, which is largely mined at Tourane, on the coast of Annam, and at Hongay and Kebao on the Tonquin coast. Other minerals, including gold, silver, tin, copper, lead, &c., are said to exist in the protectorate. The principal harbours are Haiphong in Tonkin,

Tourane and Thuanan (for Hué) in Annam, and Saigon. The Saigon river is navigable to the capital, and small craft can reach Hué by the Hué river. But the chief routes of inland navigation are the Mekong, which, notwithstanding obstructions and rapids, has been navigated as far as Chinese territory; but it is not likely to develop into an important commercial route; the Red River, which is ascended by steamers as far as Laokai on the Chinese frontier, and which carries an increasing trade with Yunnan and the Black River. Much has been done towards improving the canal and road communications in the deltas, and two small lines of railway have been built, of which the most important connects Hanoi with Langson. In 1899 the French Chamber voted a loan of 200 million francs for the construction of the following railways:—Haiphong to Laokai (300 miles); Hanoi to Vinh (240 miles); Tourane to Hué (150 miles); Saigon to Tanhoa (160 miles). China is said also to have been induced to agree to build a railway with the help of French engineers from Laokai to Yunnan-fu. Encouraged by protection, French exports to Indo-China have trebled in 10 years, and amounted in 1897 to 30,734,000 francs, imports from that colony to France amounting to 21,880,000 francs. The export trade of Indo-China was valued in 1896 at 35 million dollars (about £3,600,000) about four-sevenths consisting of rice and two-sevenths of fish. The imports are half the exports. Imports from the United Kingdom have declined from £235,000, in 1893, to £73,000 in 1897. The subsidised French shipping accounted for 280,000 tons. The foreign shipping, of which half was under the British flag, amounted to 434,000 tons. The French army of occupation numbers about 8,000, in addition to 12,000 native troops.

Imports from the United Kingdom in 1897, £73,325; Exports to ditto, £360,229.

CAPITAL of Cochin-China, Saigon. Pop., 17,235.
Gov.-Gen. of Indo-China—M. Paul Doumer.
Lieut.-Gov. of Cochin-China—M. Picanon.
H. B. M.'s Consul—C. F. Tremlett.
Telegrams, 5s. 1d. a word (*via* Turkey, 4s. 11d.).
Parcels, 3 lbs., 3s. 10d. ; over 3 and under 7 lbs., 4s. 3d. ; over 7 and under 11 lbs., 4s. 8d.

CAPITAL of Cambodia, Pnom Penh. Population, 50,000.
King—Norodom (1889).
Résident-Supérieur—M. Ducos.

CAPITAL of Annam, Hué. Population, 30,000.
King—Tkunthai.
Résident-Supérieur—M. Brière.
Telegrams, 5s. 10d. a word (*via* Turkey, 5s. 8d.).
CAPITAL of Tonquin, Hanoi. Population, 70,000.
Regent—Hoang-lao-Khai.
Résident-Supérieur—M. Fourès.
Telegrams, 6s. 3d. a word (*via* Turkey, 6s. 1d.).
Parcels, 3 lbs., 4s. 3d. ; over 3 and under 7 lbs., 4s. 8d. ; over 7 and under 11 lbs., 5s. 1d.

Other French possessions with which India is in contact are: (1) *Jibuti* on the Somali coast, and the adjoining protectorate which includes the old headquarters, now almost deserted, of Obok. The coast line of the protectorate extends for 200 miles; the limits inland at a distance of about 25 miles have been recently fixed by an agreement with King Menelek of Ethiopia. This agreement also included a concession for a railway from Jibuti to Harrar and on to Adis Abeba. This railway is now under rapid construction. The population of the protectorate is perhaps 50,000. There is an Anglo-French agreement which determines the boundary of the French and English spheres of influence in the direction of Harrar, which place neither party is at liberty to annex. (2) *Réunion,* in which there is a large number of Indian coolie immigrants; area, 700 square miles, population, 167,847; and (3) *Madagascar,* for which see page 556.

Jibuti: Gouverneur—M. Martineau; *Envoy to the Court of the Emperor Menelik of Ethiopia,* M. Lagarde.

Réunion: Gouverneur—M. Danel.

        British Consul—C. W. Bennett....£1,100

ARABIA AND TURKISH DEPENDENCIES.

The whole peninsula of *Arabia* may be considered to have an area of 1,220,000 square miles, and a population of five or six millions, of which perhaps three are in the Turkish province of Yemen. A large portion is desert, but in the interior, which is elevated, are many extensive tracts affording good pasturage. The inhabitants are Bedouins (Bedawi) and Muhammadans, with the exception of a small Jewish population; their wealth consists largely of horses, camels, asses and mules, for which Arabia is famous. Millet is cultivated for home consumption. Dates and coffee are largely exported. The climate is healthy; but the insanitary condition of the holy cities is a source of contamination, and in some years, of the spread of cholera or plague among Muhammadan pilgrims. The European Governments are accordingly interested in the improvement of the sanitary condition of the pilgrimage.

British Possessions. Aden, Perim, and protected chiefships.—Of old time Aden has been an important trade centre, lying on the Red Sea trade route between Europe and the East. Its scanty rainfall require 1 a spec al system of water supply; its water reservoirs date from B.C. 1720. Aden trade flourished before the Portuguese discovery of the Cape route. Its greatest decadence was before the British occupation in 1839. With the opening of the Suez Canal it has acquired more than its old importance; it is now a great coaling station, a great emporium for the whole trade of Southern Arabia, its imports and exports being valued at nearly 100 million rupees a year, and one of the strongest fortified naval stations commanding the Red Sea route. Aden and Perim—a small island in the narrow strait leading into the Red Sea. which was occupied in 1857—are legally part of British India (see page 452). Aden is the centre of a British protectorate over the neighbouring Arab tribes from Perim to Muscat territory at Ras Sair, which are in subordinate treaty alliance with the Government of India. In this sphere of protectorate are also the *Kooria Mooria* Islands—valuable for their guano—and the island of *Sokotra,* with an area of 1,000 square miles and a population of 5,000. In the Persian Gulf is the Island of Bahrein, which is under British protection. It is the chief centre of the pearl fisheries of the Gulf. The independent tribes on the coast itself are bound together under treaties with the Indian Government to maintain a maritime truce for the prevention of piracy and the slave trade and for the cessation of hostilities at sea. Their chiefs are in consequence sometimes referred to as the "Trucial" chiefs. The British Political Resident in the Persian Gulf, who resides ordinarily at Bushire, is the recognised arbiter in the quarrels of these tribes, and the peace of the Gulf is maintained by the British flag. Between Ras Sair and the Persian Gulf lies the territory of the Sultan of *Muscat (Oman),* who is in treaty relations with the Government of India, and has a

political agent of that Government at his cour . Muscat, with its commercial suburb of Muttra, a town of 60,000 inhabitants, is the centre of a considerable trade, mostly British and British Indian valued at 5½ million dollars. Behind Muscat territory and the semi-independent Arab tribes on the littoral of the Gulf lie the districts of El Hasa and Nejd, which form part of the *Turkish Pashalik of Basra,* with detached garrisons at El Bidaa and some other ports. This Turkish province extends northwestwards as far as Ali Garbi on the Tigris and Kalat-al-Daraj on the Euphrates. The higher basins of these rivers form the *Pashalik of Baghdad,* which extends to Syria and Kurdistan. Not far from Baghdad itself is the town of Kerbela, the most sacred centre of pilgrimage for the Shia (Persian) Mohammedans. The trade of the Shat-el-Arab and its branches is considerable; much of it is carried by the vessels of the Euphrates and Tigris Steam Navigation Company. The trade in 1898 was valued at £640,000 for exports and £1,270,000 for imports at Baghdad, and at £833,000 for exports and £1,178,000 for imports at Basra. The Pashaliks of Basra and Baghdad were incorporated together previously to 1871; then they were separated for four years, again incorporated, and again in 1884 separated. In the Pashalik of Basra are now included the districts of Amara, Muntafik, and Hasa, each under a subordinate Mutasarrif. The province extends over Central Arabia, as far as the Nefud and Syrian deserts. Beyond these deserts are the Turkish provinces of *Hejaz,* in which are included the sacred cities of Mecca and Medinah, the home of Muhammad, with the port of Jeddah, and *Yemen,* with its chief port at Hodeida, and towns at Sanaa, Assir, and Taiz. The Sinai peninsula and the old land of Midian belong to Egypt. The Jeddah trade, almost wholly imports, was valued at £665,000 in 1897, that of Hodeida at £1,418,000.

Aden: Political Resident—Brig.-Gen. Charles A. Cuningham, *per mensem.*...................... Rs.3,000

Muscat: Political Agent & Consul—Capt. P. Z. Cox. Rs.1,150 *per mensem* + £80 *per annum.*

Persian Gulf, Bushire: Political Resident & Consul-General for Fars, &c.—Lieut.-Col. M. J. Meade, *per mensem* Rs.2,750

Baghdad: Polit. Res. & Cons.-Gen. in Turkish Arabia —Major P. J. Melvill, *per mensem* Rs.2,500

Bussorah (Basra): Consul — A. C. Wratislaw £700

Jeddah: Consul—G. P. Devey £700

    V. - Con. — Shaikh Muhammad Hussein, *per mensem* Rs.400

Hodeida: Vice-Consul—Ahmed Tamiz-ud-din.

Telegrams, per word, Aden and Hejaz, 3s. 9d.; Yemen, 4s. 4d.; Bushire, 2s. 5d. (or 2s. 1d. *via* Turkey). Parcels, to Aden, 1st lb. 1s.; then per lb. 8d. to 11 lbs.

Greater Britain in the East.

(*Other than the Empire of India.*)

THE following accounts of the different British Colonies and Possessions have been revised by the Local Governments, to whom the Editor begs to return his warmest thanks. He is also indebted to the "Colonial Office List," which contains information upon every subject connected with Greater Britain.

Postage:—Except to the Australasian Colonies the rate is 1d. the half-ounce to almost all of the British Colonies and Possessions.

Parcels:—A new system has been adopted for many of the Colonies known as the "Triple Scale," viz., 3 lbs., 1s.; 7 lbs. 2s.; 11 lbs., 3s. Full particulars of the rates are given on pp. 438, 439.

Imports and Exports:—In the statistics denoting the value of the trade from the home country, the term "Domestic Imports," means Produce and Manufactures of the United Kingdom, and is exclusive of Foreign and Colonial merchandise re-exported.

CEYLON,

an island in the Indian Ocean, to the south-east of the peninsula of Hindustan, is situated between 5° 53′—9° 51′ N. lat. and 76° 42′—81° 55′ E. long. Its area is about 25,365 square miles, or more than three-fourths of that of Ireland. Its greatest length is, from north to south, 266 miles; and its greatest width 140 miles.

The climate varies with the altitude of the district; but on the whole, although tropical, it is healthy, except in the low-lying jungle. There are no great extremes of temperature, and throughout the low country the thermometer varies little in the course of the year, the mean temperature at Colombo being nearly 81° F. The coolest months are December and January; the hottest are April and May.

The population of Ceylon numbers (est. 1896) 3,298,342, the most important element being the Singhalese, descendants of colonists from the valley of the Ganges, who first settled in the island about B.C. 543. According to the 1891 census, the population then consisted of Singhalese, 2,041,158; the Tamils, a race of Southern India, 723,853; the Moormen and other races, 216,156; the Burghers or Eurasians, 21,231; and the Europeans, 6,068. There is also a sprinkling of Veddahs, who are perhaps the aboriginal race of the island; and of Afghans and of Malays. In 1507 the Portuguese landed in Ceylon and formed settlements along the coast; but about 150 years later they were dispossessed by the Dutch. In 1796 the British took possession of the Dutch settlements on the island, and annexed them to the Presidency of Madras; but six years after, in 1801, Ceylon was erected into a separate Crown colony. In 1815 the King of Kandy was deposed and banished; and his dominions, which had up to that time maintained their independence of European rule, were annexed to the British Crown.

The staple products of the island are agricultural. The most important for home consumption is rice in its two forms of padi and dry grain. Of the exports, coffee is still important, but tea has in the last few years entirely usurped the place held by the former as the principal export. Other products are cinchona, cocoa, cardamoms, vanilla, and cinnamon, which was in Dutch times a Government monopoly and the most important product of the island. In 1898, the chief exports were coffee 1,421,574 lbs., tea 122,395,517 lbs., cinchona 977,760 lbs., and cinnamon 4,481,165 lbs.

About one-fifth of the island is under cultivation, and the leading areas in 1898, in acres, were rice, 647,510; other grain, 105,962; tea, 424,856; coffee, 19,023; cocoanuts, 854,296; cinchona, 749; cinnamon, 45,119. Among the more important native industries are gold, silver, ivory and tortoise-shell work, pottery, mats, fans, and wood-carving. Ceylon is famous for precious stones, especially catseyes, rubies, &c.; and the pearl fishery in the Gulf of Manaar, off the N.W. of the island, is in some years a valuable source of revenue. The manufacture of salt is a Government monopoly, and yielded in 1898 a revenue of Rs. 1,079,852.

There are 298 miles of railway open, and in 1897 the post and telegraph offices numbered 364, there being 1,727 miles of telegraph wire.

The Government of Ceylon is administered by a Governor, aided by an Executive Council of 5 members, and a Legislative Council of 18 members including the Governor and the Executive Council. The Legislative Council contains representatives of the principal races and interests in the island.

For administrative purposes the island is divided into nine provinces, at the head of each of which is a government agent. The larger towns have municipalities or local boards; and in the country districts the natives retain their village councils and tribunals for matters of minor importance.

Public revenue, 1898	Rs.25,138,669
Public expenditure, 1898	22,843,852
Public debt, 1898	£3,470,821 and Rs. 3,256,212
Total imports, including specie, 1898	Rs.97,893,058
Total exports, including specie, 1898	85,372,622

Domestic Imports from U. K., 1898:—

Apparel, etc.	£35,452	Machinery	£94,704
Coal and Fuel	147,179	Metals	201,393
Cottons	245,835		
			£1,177,132

Exports to United Kingdom, 1898:—

Cocoa	£138,521	Plumbago	£198,033
Nuts for Oil	164,469	Cinnamon	62,951
Oil	180,402	Tea	3,694,123
			£4,847,721

CAPITAL, Colombo. Population, 120,000.

Governor, Col. Rt. Hon. Sir Joseph West Ridgeway, K.C.B.	Rs.80,000
Priv. Sec.,	3,000
Commg. Forces, Maj.-Gen. F. T. Hobson	23,480
Lieutenant-Governor and Colonial Secretary, Sir Edward Noel Walker, K.C.M.G.	24,000
1st Assistant do., H. L. Crawford	12,000

2nd do., H. White	Rs.7,500
Auditor-Gen., W. T. Taylor, C.M.G.	18,000
Treasurer, L. F. Lee	18,000
Govt. Agent, W. Prov., F. R. Ellis	16,000
,, ,, Central ,, A. Bailey	18,000
,, ,, Northern ,, R. W. Ievers	18,000
,, ,, N. West ,, H. H. Cameron	16,000
,, ,, Southern ,, H. Wace	14,000
,, ,, Eastern ,, C. A. Murray	15,000
,, ,, N. Cent. ,, E. M. D. Byrde	12,000
,, ,, Uva ,, G. A. Baumgartner	12,000
,, ,, Sabaragamuwa, L. W. Booth	12,000
Surveyor-General, F. H. Grinlinton	12,000
Director Pub. Wks., F. A. Cooper	15,000
Postmaster-General, C. E. D. Pennycuick	15,000
Collector of Customs, H. L. Moysey	15,000
Chief Justice, Sir John Winfield Bonser	25,000
Senior Puisne Judge, A. C. Lawrie	18,000
Junior do., George Henry Withers	18,000
District Judge, Colombo, D. F. Browne	16,000
,, ,, Kandy, J. H. de Saram	16,000
,, ,, Galle, J. F. de Livera	15,000
,, ,, Jaffna, C. E. Wilmot	14,500
Attorney-General, Chas. Peter Layard	18,000
Solicitor-General, P. Rama Nathan, C.M.G.	10,000
Registrar-General, P. Arunáchalan	11,000
Director Public Instruction, S. M. Burrows	12,000
Princ. Med. Offi , Maj. A. Perry, R.A.M.C.	12,000
Prisons & Police, Major L. F. Knollys, C.M.G.	16,000
Manager Railways, W. T. Pearce	15,000

The MALDIVE ARCHIPELAGO lies to the S.W. of Ceylon, a few degrees north of the equator. Malé, the seat of government, is about 400 miles distant from Ceylon, to which the islands have always been nominally tributary. The Sultan acknowledges his allegiance by sending an annual embassy to Colombo. The natives are Mohammedans. The islands are poor and unhealthy, and the main exports are dried fish, cowry shells, cocoanut coir, and tortoiseshell.

Colombo, distant 6,300 miles ; transit, 20 days. Telegrams per word, by Eastern Co., 4s. 1d. ; via Turkey, 3s. 9d.

STRAITS SETTLEMENTS.

This is the name given to the British possessions on the west coast of the Malay Peninsula, of which the whole southern portion, comprising about 25,000 square miles, is now under the protection, and a large portion under the direct control, of the British Government in Singapore. The importance of this portion of H.M.'s dominions has rapidly increased of late years, and it is now, in point of trade, revenue, and general prosperity, in the front rank among the Crown Colonies.

The name is derived from the Straits of Malacca, on which the Settlements are situated. The settlements forming what is known as the Colony of the Straits Settlements are Singapore ; Penang, or Prince of Wales's Island, with Province Wellesley and the Dindings ; and Malacca. The Cocos or Keeling Islands, a coral group in the Indian Ocean, on the route from Ceylon to Australia, have since 1886 been a dependency of the Straits Settlements. The colony has an entire area of about 1,472½ square miles. The population in 1891 was 512,342 (Singapore, 184,554 ; Penang, Prov. Wellesley and Dindings, 235,618 ; Malacca, 92,170). The great bulk of the population consists of Chinese and Malays.

The climate of the colony is almost uniform throughout the year, and foliage is perennial. The rainfall in 1898 amounted in Singapore to 106·19 inches, and in Penang to 124·51 inches.

Public revenue in 1898	$5,071,282
Public expenditure in 1898	4,587,367
Public Debt	nil
*Total imports, 1898	248,110,547
*Total exports, 1898	212,308,029
Imports from United Kingdom, 1898	31,904,164
Exports to United Kingdom, 1898	28,385,028

The exports comprise—gutta-percha, gambier, pepper, india-rubber, horns, hides, canes, sugar, rice, sago, tapioca, spices, dye-stuffs, tea, coffee, tobacco, gums, tin, &c.

The Government consists of a Governor, assisted by an Executive Council of 8 members, and a Legislative Council of 8 official and 7 unofficial members, appointed by the Crown. Two of the unofficial members are nominated by the Chambers of Commerce at Singapore and Penang. The Resident Councillors of Penang and Malacca have seats in both Councils. The law of the colony is the common and statute law of England as it was in 1826, qualified by Indian Acts until 1867 and since then by local ordinances. The Supreme Court consists of the Chief Justice and three puisne judges, and constitutes also a court of appeal from which there is yet another appeal in certain cases, viz. to the Privy Council. There is also in Singapore and Penang a Vice-Admiralty Court ; and in each settlement there are ordinary magistrates' courts, together with Courts of Requests.

Governor and Commander-in-Chief, Lt.-Col. Sir Chas. B. H. Mitchell, G.C.M.G. (with entertainment allowance)	$33,800
A.-de-C., Capt. A. A. Duff	3,000
Comm. Troops, Maj.-Gen. J. B. B, Dickson, C.B.	
Colonial Secretary, Hon. Sir James Alexander Swettenham, K.C.M.G.	10,800
Resident Councillor of Penang, Hon. Charles Walter Sneyd Kynnersley, C.M.G.	9,600
Do., Malacca, Hon. J. K. Birch	7.800
Attorney-General, W. R. Collyer	7,800
Solicitor-General, J. A. Harwood	5,400
Treasurer, Hon F. G. Penney	7,800
Auditor-General, Hon. E. C. H. Hill	7,800
Colonial Engineer, Hon. A. Murray, C.E.	7,200
Chief Justice, Sir William Henry Lionel Cox	13,500
Puisne Judge, A. J. Leach (Singapore)	8,400
Do. A. Fitzgerald Law (Penang)	8,400
Do. W. H. Hyndman-Jones	8,400
Assistant Colonial Secretary and Clerk of Councils, E. M. Merewether	6,000
Insp.-Gen. of Police, Lt.-Col. E. G. Pennefather	5,400
1st Magistrate, W. Egerton (Singapore)	6,000
Do. A. T. Bryant (Penang)	6,000
Princ. Civil Medical Off , M. F. Simon, M.D.	7,200
Protector of Chinese, W. Evans	6,000
Master Attendant, Commander C. Q. G. Craufurd, R.N. (retd.)	5,400

SINGAPORE is an island situated off the southern extremity of the Malay peninsula, from which it is separated by a narrow strait about three-quarters of a mile in width : its length is about 27 miles, and its breadth 14 miles ; it comprises, with the adjoining islets, an area of 206 square miles. It was first occupied in 1819, and formally ceded to the British Government by the Sultan of Johore in 1824. The seat of government, for all the settlements, is the town of Singapore, situated on the south side of the island in lat. 1° 16′ N. and long. 103° 53′ E., with 162,547 inhabitants in 1891. The harbour, in the extent

* Exclusive of coasting traffic.

of its shipping, is one of the greatest ports in the world, being a point of call for vessels trading between Europe or India and the far East, the North of Australia, and the Netherlands Indies. For its defence several batteries to carry heavy guns have been constructed, at a cost of nearly £100,000, paid by the colony, for which the Imperial Government has furnished guns. The trade returns for 1898 (including inter-settlement trade), amounted to $361,788,795, the value of exported tin being $22,390,055.

The number of merchant vessels entered and cleared in 1898, exclusive of native craft, was 9,717 with a tonnage of 8,287,184. The total for the whole colony was 17,837, with a tonnage of 12,661,442. The total native craft entered at all three ports during the same year was 15,509 (tonnage, 604,751). The climate is fairly healthy for Europeans, except for the absence of any marked change of temperature throughout the year. There are excellent docks. It is a free port; no duties are levied upon anything except wines and beer ; the opium and spirit trades are farmed out to Chinese, and the Chinese element is conspicuous among the trading classes.

PENANG is the northernmost of the Settlements. It includes Pulo Penang or Prince of Wales's Island (on the eastern side of which is Georgetown, the port and capital, population 1891, 84,948), and the strip of mainland opposite, known as Province Wellesley (population 1891, 108,117). The DINDINGS, 80 miles to the South of Penang, have also been included in the Settlement for administrative purposes under the Resident Councillor, who also has Consular authority over the Siamese Tributary States on the west coast of the peninsula between Province Wellesley and British Burma. Penang island, about 15 miles long and 9 broad, is situated off the west coast of the Malay Peninsula, in lat. 5° 18′ N., long. 100° 21′ E., and was ceded to the Government of India in 1786 by the Raja of the neighbouring territory, Kêdah. Area, 107 square miles. At the time it was founded, Penang was the only British settlement in further India; now it is the emporium for all the trade of the northern and more prosperous parts of Sumatra and the Malay Peninsula. Its aggregate trade for 1898 (including inter-settlement trade), amounted to $114,831,346 ; the export of tin from the port being $10,665,339 in 1898. Population (1891), 235,618.

PROVINCE WELLESLEY is a strip of coast about 45 miles in length with an area of 288 square miles, ceded by the Raja of Kêdah in 1798, with some land S. of the Krian river acquired more recently. The province is in a high state of cultivation as compared with the neighbouring territory, containing rice, sugar, spices, and tapioca plantations.

The Dindings are at present little developed; but they contain what is considered the best port on the western side of the peninsula, named Lumut, where a District Officer is stationed, and steamers call regularly at Pulo Pangkor. They comprise a group of islands (of which Pulo Pangkor is the largest) ; and a strip of the mainland on the west coast of the peninsula cut out of the State of Pérak, and measuring about 22 miles long by about 10 miles in width.

MALACCA, the largest of the Settlements, situated on the western coast of the peninsula, between Singapore and Penang, and about 110 miles to the N.W. of Singapore, comprises an area of about 659 square miles. It is one of the oldest European settlements in the East, having been taken possession of by the Portuguese in 1511, and held by them till 1640, when the Dutch drove them out. In 1795 it was captured by the English, and retained till 1818, when it was restored to the Dutch ; it finally became a British possession, in pursuance of the treaty with Holland, 17th March, 1824, being exchanged for the British settlements in Sumatra.

Revenue (1875, $118,000) 1898 .... $392,747
Aggregate trade, 1898 .... $4,089,409

Singapore, distant 8,700 miles ; transit, 24 days. Penang and Malacca, 24 days. Telegrams 4s. 6d. (or viâ Turkey) 4s. 3d. per word.

THE FEDERATED MALAY STATES

are closely connected with the Straits Settlements; they are the States of Pêrak, Sêlângor, Negri Sembilan, and Pahang, which have by treaty (1895) renewed their engagements with the British Government administered under the advice of a British Resident-General, who controls the Residents subject to the instructions of the High Commissioner, who is also Governor of the Straits Settlements.

The first two States extend from the border of Province Wellesley to that of Negri Sembilan, Pahang is on the East Coast, and Negri Sembilan inland near Malacca. All are governed by their native rulers under the above-mentioned control. Under the Colonial Loans Act. 1899, the sum of £500,000 was advanced for the purpose of railway construction in these states.

High Commissioner, Lieut.-Col. Sir Charles Bullen Hugh Mitchell, G.C.M.G.

British Resident-General, Sir Frank Athelstane Swettenham, K.C.M.G. (*Selangor*) ...$12,000

Judicial Commissioner, Laurence C. Jackson, Q.C. $9,600

(1) *Pêrak* has an area of 10,000 square miles, and in 1891 the population numbered 214,254. The chief industry is tin-mining ; but rice, sugar, and coffee have been largely cultivated. Revenue, 1897, $3,837,558. The chief town is Taiping, in the district of Larut. Railways are in operation : Port Weld to Taiping 8 miles ; Taiping to Ulu Sapetang 9 miles, and from Teluk Anson viâ Ipoh to Suggor 68 miles, with an extension under construction to Taiping and Prai, about 70 miles ; with a further extension of 50 miles to join the system of Pêrak and Selangor.

British Resident, W. H. Treacher, C.M.G......$9,600

(2) *Selangor,* with an area of 3,500 square miles, and a population of over 150,000, lies immediately south of Pêrak, and, like that State, depends largely for its prosperity upon its tin-mining. Liberian coffee, cocoanuts and pepper are being planted with success. The revenue in 1897 was $3,688,390 ; and a railway, 22 miles long, from the capital, Kwala Lumpor, to the port of Klang, was opened in July, 1886, and this has since been extended inland to Kwala Kubu, a distance of 38¼ miles, with a branch line from Kwala Lumpor to Kajang 16 miles long. Fresh sections to connect Klang with Kwala Klang, and from Kuala Kubu to Tapali in Pêrak (65 miles) are under construction. Imports (1896), $9,131,195, exports, $12,006,108.

British Resident, John Pickersgill Rodger, C.M.G. $8,400

(3) *Negri Sembilan* is the name of a confederacy of small States in the interior of the peninsula, the affairs of which have been placed under a British Resident residing at Seramban. The confederacy comprises Sri Menanti, Rem-

bau, Johol, Tampin, Sungei Ujong, Jelébu, and other small States, comprising about 3,360 square miles, with a population of 41,617 in 1891. Revenue (1897), $572,546. Twenty-three miles of railway connect Seramban, the administrative centre of the confederation, with Port Dickson on the Malacca coast, and 24 miles are building to connect with the Selangor system. The cultivation of Liberian coffee is attracting considerable attention. *British Resident*, E. W. Birch... $6,000

(4) *Pahang* is a large State on the east coast, to which, in 1888, a British Resident was sent at the request of the Sultan. The country is of great extent, exceeding 12,000 square miles, and is already full of tin-mining and gold-mining enterprise. Pop., 1891, 57,542. Rev., 1897, $198,193.

British Resident, Hugh Clifford $6,000

HONG KONG.

The Crown Colony of Hong Kong consists of an island situate off the south-eastern coast of China, at the mouth of the Canton River, in 22° 10'—22° 17' N. lat. and 114° 6'—114° 18' E. long, and of a portion of the mainland of China leased by the British Government for 99 years, the lease dating from June 9, 1898. The island is about eleven miles long and from two to five miles wide, with an area of 30½ square miles; the whole colony comprises an area of about 252½ square miles. The island lies close to the mainland, being separated at one point by a narrow strait (the Li-ü Mun Pass) not more than ¼ of a mile wide. The city of Victoria lies along its northern shore, facing the mainland; and between the mainland and the city is the harbour, which is one of the finest in the world, with a water area of some ten square miles. The port is free. It possesses excellent docks, capable of holding the largest vessels, and is fortified.

The island is broken in shape and mountainous, the highest point being Victoria Peak, which is over 1,800 feet high. This peak is a favourite place of residence in the hot season, which lasts from March to October. During the winter months, from November to February, the climate is cooler and invigorating. The thermometer ranges from a minimum of 32° in February to a maximum of 93° in August. The average annual rainfall is 85 in., of which not less than 70 in. are received between May and September, when the S.W. monsoon prevails.

Hong Kong was first taken possession of by Great Britain in January, 1841, and was formally ceded by the Treaty of Nankin in 1842, British Kaulung being subsequently acquired by the Peking Convention of 1860; and the Kwangtung peninsula, being the southern part of the province of that name, by a lease signed June 9, 1898. It is a military and naval station for the protection of British commerce, and it is the centre of a vast trade in many kinds of produce—chiefly opium, sugar, flour, oil, amber, cotton, ivory, betel, sandalwood, rice, tea, woollens, silks, salt, &c.

It is calculated that, exclusive of the traffic which merely passes through the harbour without breaking bulk, the actual trade of the colony amounts to over £20,000,000 sterling per annum. In the year 1898 shipping to the extent of 8,453,983 tons entered the port.

The population of the island in 1898 was estimated at 254,500, of whom about 240,000 were Chinese. The white residents, including the garrison, numbered about 14,000.

Much encouragement is given by the Government to education in the colony, and the Chinese are fully alive to the advantages arising therefrom. In 1898 there were 109 schools subject to Government supervision, attended by 8,522 pupils. There were also many private schools, attended by about 2,900 pupils.

Hong Kong is a Crown colony, and its government is administered by a Governor, aided by an Executive Council of 8 members, together with a Legislative Council of 14 members including himself.

CAPITAL, Victoria. Population (1898), 248,710.

Public revenue in 1893	$2,918,159
Public expenditure, 1898	2,841,805
Public debt, 1 Jan., 1898	£341,799
Domestic imports from U. K., 1898 ...	£225,115
Exports to United Kingdom, 1898	£726,637

Governor, &c., Sir H. A. Blake, G.C.M.G. ...$32,000
    A.-de-C., Capt. Viscount Suirdale.
Commander of the Forces, Maj.-Gen. W. J.
    Gascoigne, C.M.G.
Colonial Secretary and Registrar-General,
    Hon. J. H. Stewart Lockhart, C.M.G. ... 9,720
Treasurer, &c., Hon. A. M. Thomson 4,800
Attorney-General, Hon. W. M. Goodman... 8,400
Director of Public Works, Hon. R. D. Ormsby 6,660
Chief Justice, Sir J. W. Carrington, C.M.G. 12,000
Puisne Judge, His Honour A. G. Wise 8,400
Registrar Supreme Ct., J. Norton-Kyshe ... 5,400
Police Magistrate, T. Sercombe Smith 6,000
Captain Supt. Police, Hon. F. H. May, C.M.G. 5,760
Principal Civil Medical Officer, J. R. Atkinson, M.B. 4,800
Harbour-Master, R. Murray Rumsey, R.N... 5,400

Hong Kong, 9,834 miles, *viâ* Suez Canal; transit, 36 days. Telegrams, 5s. 6d. and 5s. 9d. or (*viâ* Turkey) 5s. 5l. and 5s. 7d. per word.

WEI-HAI-WEI.

Owing to the occupation by the Russian Government of Port Arthur, Great Britain obtained the lease (for so long a period as this Russian occupation should last) of a port in the Shantung province named Wei-hai-wei, situated in about 37° N. and 122° E. This port is opposite Port Arthur in the gulf of Pechili, and included in the lease is the island of Liu-Kung and a strip of land round the mouth of the harbour ten miles in breadth. An infantry regiment of Chinese, with British officers, is being raised for the defence of the port.

Col. on the Staff for R.E., Col. A. R. F. Dorward, R.E., D.S.O.
Comdt. Chinese Regt., Lt.-Col. H. Bower, I.S.C.

BORNEO.

Next to Australia and New Guinea, this is supposed to be the largest island in the world. It was discovered by the Portuguese in 1521, and is situated in the Eastern Archipelago, extending from lat. 7° 4' N. to 4° 10' S., and from long. 108° 50' to 119° 20' E. It is about 850 miles in length and 600 in breadth, and contains an area of 280,000 square miles, divided by the equatorial line into two nearly equal portions. The population is probably about 1,846,000, consisting chiefly of Dyaks, Malays, Kyans, Papus or Negritos, Chinese, and Bugis (the aboriginal Celebes). Formerly the greater part of the island was independent under a Sultan of Borneo, now represented by the dependent Sultan of Brunei. British intercourse with the Sultan was marked in 1848 by a treaty ceding to Great Britain the island of Labuan, which at that time formed part of his dominions. In 1842 a British subject obtained the concession of a tract on the west coast round the town of Sarawak, and various extensions were obtained in after years. About 1830, the Dutch East India Company, which had previously established trading settlements in the island, commenced to extend its territory, and rather more than two-thirds of the island is now included within the Dutch possessions in the East Indies. Over the remainder of the island a British Protectorate has been established; the whole of the northernmost corner forms the territories of the British North Borneo Company: on the north-west is the dependent kingdom of Brunei, and the western and south-western portion forms the dependent kingdom of Sarawak. The mineral kingdom includes gold, silver, diamonds, antimony, quicksilver, iron, tin, and coal, the latter abundant. The principal imports are opium, tea, cottons, cloths, hardware, brass, iron, &c.; exports, sago, beeswax, edible birds-nests, camphor, hides, rattans, tortoiseshell, tre-pang, cinnabar, antimony, coal, diamonds, and gold. The principal towns of Dutch Borneo are Banjermassin in the south and eastern administrative districts and Pontianak in the western.

Imports from the United Kingdom, 1898 £20,750
Exports to the United Kingdom, 1898 ... 1,601

THE BRITISH NORTH BORNEO COMPANY.

The territories of the British North Borneo Company extend over the northern part of the island, from the Sipitong River on the west to 4° 10′ on the east coast, together with all the islands within three leagues. By an arrangement with the British Government, dated 1 Jan., 1890, the administration of the neighbouring British island, Labuan, was transferred from the Colonial Office to the Company. The total area of the Company's territories is about 30,000 square miles, and the population is estimated at 150,000. The inhabitants are Mohammedan Malays with an infusion of Chinese and Arab blood on the coast, and various aboriginal tribes resembling Dyaks in the interior. The original concession was made to a company by the Sultans of Brunei and Sulu in 1877-8, and was subsequently transferred to the British North Borneo Company, to whom a royal charter was granted 1st November, 1881. The territory ceded has a coast-line of some 987 miles, with many excellent harbours. The soil is rich, producing rice, sago, sugar-cane, coffee, cocoa, gambier, pepper, tea, tobacco (1897, $1,636,173), hemp, cinchona, gutta-percha, india-rubber, beeswax, edible birds' nests, camphor, gum, and timber. About 700,000 acres of land have at present been taken up by agricultural companies on cultivation leases. Gold, copper, coal, and other minerals have been found. The company does not itself engage in trade. The revenue is derived from opium and other farms, sales of land, royalties on exports, and duties. The principal places are Sandakan, the headquarters of the administration, Gaya on the west coast, Kudat in the north, Silam on the east, and Mempakol in Brunei Bay.

The government is administered by a Governor, assisted by a Council and by Residents of districts. The mode of government adopted is similar to that of a British colony, with modifications to meet native customs and local circumstances. A metre gauge railway (52 miles) is constructing from the west coast to the interior.

CAPITAL, Sandakan; population of Sandakan Bay, 6,319.
Public revenue, 1898 ....$457 820
Public expenditure, 1898 642,178
Total imports, 1898, $2,419,087. Exports, $2,881,851
High Commissioner and Consul-General for the Territories of the British North Borneo Company and f r Brun i and Sarawak, Sir Charles Bullen Hugh Mitchell, G.C.M.G. (Singapore).
Consular Agent, Sandakan, Alexander Cook
Governor, Hugh Charles Clifford $9,850
Resident, Kudat, E. Barrault $4,200
Principal Medical Officer, Dr.G.M. Harrison 4,278
Office of the British North Borneo Company, 15 Leadenhall Street, E.C. *Sec.* H. G. Forbes.
Sandakan is distant 9,500 miles. Transit. average 35 days. Telegrams, 4s. 10d. to 5s. and 5s. to 5s. 3d. per word.

BRUNEI.

Sultan, His Highness Hasim Jalilal Alam Akamaddin, ebni Almarhom Sri Paduka Maulana, al Sultan Omar Ali Saefuddin, *succeeded* May, 1885.
A native state on the west coast of the island of Borneo. The total area is about 3,000 square miles. The territory was placed under British protection in 1888. The chief town, Brunei, has a population of about 5,000, and is built entirely on the water, communication being possible only by boat. A trading steamer calls monthly on its way between Labuan and Singapore.
H.B.M. Consul at Brunei, Arthur L. Keyser.
Medical Officer, R. E. Adamson, M B.
Postmaster, W. Boyd.

Brunei is 5 hours by steamer from Labuan. Telegrams *sent by post* from Labuan.

SARAWAK.

Raja, H.H. Sir Charles Johnson Brooke, G.C.M.G. *born* 3 June, 1829; *suc.* his uncle, the Raja Sir James Brooke, 11 June, 1868; *m.* 1869, Margaret Alice Lily de Windt, of Highworth, Wilts.
Heir, Charles Vyner Brooke (Raja Muda), *b.* 26 Sept. 1874.
Resident, 1st Div., Hon. C. A. Bampfylde... $6,000
  ,,   *3rd Division,* Hon. H. F. Deshon ... 5,400
Commandant, Maj. G. L. B. Killick £400
Treasurer, H. C. Brooke-Johnson (*acting*) $2,640
Postmaster-General, A. K. Leys 3,000
Supt. of Surveys, &c., H. D. Ellis £500
Principal Medical Officer, A. J. G. Barker $4,800
The Sarawak territory lies on the west coast of Borneo, with a seaboard of 400 miles, an area of about 50,000 square miles, and a population of about 500,000, composed of various races. The government of this district was obtained in 1842 from the Sultan of Borneo by the late Sir James Brooke, who became well known as Raja Brooke of Sarawak, and was uncle of the present Raja. Other concessions have been made in 1861, 1882, 1885, and 1890, when the Limbang River was obtained, the transfer being approved by H.M. Government, August, 1891. The country produces sago, gutta-percha, india-rubber, beeswax, birds' nests, gold, silver, diamonds, antimony, quicksilver, tobacco, rice, rattans, coal, gambier, and pepper.
Revenue, 1898, $638,188; Expenditure...$543,506
Imports, 1898, $2,906,143; Exports $3,367,141
CHIEF TOWN, Kuching. Distance from London 8,700 miles; transit 30 to 35 days. Telegrams *sent by post* from Labuan.

LABUAN
is an island of the Malayan Archipelago, situated about six miles off the north-west coast of Borneo, in 5° 16′ N. lat. and 115° 15′ E. long. Its area is about 31 square miles; and its population is 5,853. It was ceded to Great Britain by the Sultan of Borneo in 1846, being at that time uninhabited. A British settlement was established in 1848, the first Governor being the late Sir James Brooke. The island has a fine harbour, and possesses extensive coal-measures, which are now being developed, the annual export being about 50,000 tons. The trade consists in the exchange of cloth, rice, crockery, ironware, &c., for the produce of Borneo and the neighbouring islands (gutta-percha, india-rubber, birds' nests, canes, bêche-de-mer, wax, sago, &c.). There are four manufactures in the island where the raw sago imported from the coast of Borneo is converted into flour, and then exported to Singapore. Victoria Harbour, in the south-east, is the principal inlet, and affords good anchorage; a rifle range is often utilized by passing ships of the Royal Navy.

The government is administered by the Governor of the British North Borneo Company's territory.

CHIEF CITY, Victoria. Population, 5,853.

Public revenue, 1898, $53,106; Expenditure, $69,617; Total imports, 1898, $928,329; Exports, $797,615

Governor, Hugh Charles Clifford.
Police Magistrate and Treasurer, G. M. O'B. Horsford.

Labuan is distant 9,100 miles, *via* Suez Canal; average transit 30 days.

Telegrams, 4s. 10d. and 5s. per word.

Dates of some Events in the History of the British Colonial Empire.

Newfoundland discovered	*Circa* 1500	Mutiny commenced at Meerut, 10th May	1857
Virginia taken possession of by Raleigh	1584	India transferred to the Crown, 1st Sept.	1858
India; First Adventure from England	1591	Slavery abolished in U.S.A.	1862
British E. I. Company Incorporated	1600	Confederation of Canada	1867
Barbados first settled	1605	Abyssinian War	1868
Massachusetts founded by English Puritans	1620	Transportation of convicts abolished	1868
Nova Scotia settled by the Scottish	1632	Ashantee War	1873–74
Maryland settled by Eng. Roman Catholics	1634	Queen proclaimed Empress of India	1876
Madras founded	1640	Cyprus occupied	1878
Jamaica taken from the Spaniards	1655	First Transvaal Campaign	1881
Bombay ceded to Charles II. by Portugal	1662	End of Afghan War (cost £23,500,000)	1882
New York conquered from Dutch & Swedes	1664	British Occupation of Egypt	1882
Pennsylvania settled by the Quakers	1682	Military Operations in the Soudan	1884–91
William Dampier landed in Australia	1686	Burmese Empire entirely annexed	1886
Calcutta purchased	1698	Jubilee of Queen Victoria	1887
Gibraltar taken from the Spaniards	1704	Zululand became a British possession	1887
Canada taken from the French	1759	British South Africa Co. chartered	1889
Bengal, Berar, and Orissa ceded	1765	Western Australia a self-governing colony	1890
Captain Cook landed at Botany Bay	1770	First Matabele War	1894
United States; first so styled 9 Sept.	1776	British Guiana-Venezuela dispute	1895
New South Wales settled	1787	The Pamir Convention	1895
Impeachment of Warren Hastings	1788	Chitral Expedition	1895
United States' independence acknowledged	1793	Ashantee Campaign	1895
Battle of Seringapatam; death of Tippoo	1799	Dr. Jameson's Raid	1896
Malta acquired by conquest	1800	Second Matabele War	1895
Tasmania (Van Diemen's Land) organized	1803	Dongola Expedition	1896
Cape of Good Hope taken from the Dutch	1806	Diamond Jubilee of Queen Victoria; Colonial Premiers entertained	1897
Mauritius taken from the French	1810	Discovery of Gold in the Klondyke	1897
Ceylon acquired	1815	Re-conquest of the Soudan	1898
West Australia formed into a province	1829	The Fashoda inc'dent	1898
Slavery in British Colonies abolished	1833	Occupation of Wei-hai-Wei	1898
South Australia formed into a province	1834	"Cape to Cairo" line reached Bulawayo	1898
Accession of Queen Victoria	1837	Anglo-Russian Chinese Treaty	1898
Electric Telegraph first constructed	1838	Anglo-French Niger Convention	1898
Aden captured and settled	1839	Lord Kitchener Governor of Sudan	1899
New Zealand made a separate colony	1841	Australian Federation Bills passed	1899
Hong Kong taken from the Chinese	1841	Anglo-French Sudan Convention	1899
The Punjaub formally annexed	1849	Second Transvaal Campaign; Colonial Contingents sent	1899
Queensland formed into a province	1850	Anglo-German Samoan Agreement	1899
Victoria formed into a province	1850	Defeat and death of the Khalifa	1899
First International Exhibition	1851	Sudan Railway extended to Khartoum	1899
Second Burmese War; Pegu annexed	1852–53		
Oude annexed; Lord Canning Viceroy	1856		

THE British Possessions in North America include the whole of the northern part of that continent, excepting Alaska, and the small islands of St. Pierre and Miquelon, in the Gulf of St. Lawrence, and extend from the United States boundary to the Arctic Ocean. From a physical point of view the whole region may be divided into an eastern and a western division, the Red River Valley, in long. 97°, forming the separating line. The eastern division comprises three areas, presenting radically distinct aspects :— (1) The south-eastern area, bounded by the line of the Gulf and River St. Lawrence, from Belle Isle to Quebec, thence by a line running directly south to Lake Champlain, which is generally hilly, and sometimes mountainous, with many fine stretches of agricultural and pastoral lands. (2) The southern and western area, presenting, in the main, a broad, level, and slightly undulating expanse of generally fertile country, with occasional step-like ridges or rocky escarpments. The main hydrographical feature is the chain of lakes, with an area of 150,000 square miles, contributing to the great river system of the St. Lawrence. (3) The northern area, embracing nearly two-thirds of the Dominion, with an average elevation of 1,000 feet above the level of the sea, preeminently a region of waterways, and including the great Laurentian mountain range. In this area are found the other great river systems, the Nelson and the Mackenzie. The western division referred to is divided into two divisions, equally distinct in character. The first stretches from the Red River Valley to the Rocky Mountains. Here, between lat. 49° and 54°, is the great Prairie Region, rising to the west in three terrace-like elevations, the lowest of which is 700 feet, and the third about 3,000 feet above the level of the sea. North of the 54th parallel the country passes again into forest. The second division, from the western edge of the Prairie to the Pacific coast, is a distance of 400 miles, and contains the Rocky Mountains and the Gold and Cascade Ranges, whose summits are from 4,000 to 16,000 feet high, the country being on the whole densely wooded. The climate in the eastern and central portions of the Dominion presents greater extremes of cold and heat than in corresponding latitudes in Europe, but in the south-western portion of the Prairie Region and the southern portions of the Pacific slope the climate is milder. Spring, summer, and autumn are of about seven to eight months' duration, and the winter four to five months. The country possesses great mineral wealth, and coal, gold, silver, copper, nickel, lead, petroleum and asbestos are produced, while iron, phosphates, salt, graphite, &c., occur ; the total value of the minerals produced in 1898 was about $38,000,000. The soil is generally fertile, and all the products of the temperate zone are cultivated.

THE DOMINION OF CANADA.

THE Dominion of Canada includes the various Provinces of North America formerly known as Upper and Lower Canada (now Ontario and Quebec respectively), New Brunswick, Nova Scotia, Prince Edward Island, British Columbia, and the extensive regions long under the quasi-government of the Hudson Bay Company, now styled Manitoba, the North-West Territories, and the Yukon Territories ; in fact, the whole of British North America except Newfoundland and Labrador. This territory, nearly as large as Europe, stretches from the Atlantic to the Pacific Ocean, and is estimated to contain a total area of 3,315,647 square miles, exclusive of the great lakes and rivers. The total population of the Dominion is about 5,250,000, a number which is rapidly increasing, and notwithstanding its diversity of origin, is fast being welded into one harmonious and homogeneous whole. The descendants of the French Colonists reside chiefly in the Province of Quebec, where out of a total population of 1,400,000 above 1,000,000 are Roman Catholics, the majority of whom still very generally use the French language. A Religious Census of Canada was taken in 1891, and the numbers were :— Roman Catholics 1,992,017, Methodists 839,815, Presbyterians 754,193, Church of England 646,059, Baptists 302,565, Congregationalists 28,157, and Lutherans 63,982. Canada possesses an Active Militia numbering 38,000 men (including infantry, cavalry, and artillery), and a reserve estimated at 1,030,000. During the military operations in South Africa 1899 a Canadian Contingent, 1,000 strong, was sent by the Dominion Government to fight for the Mother Country in line with contingents from the Australasian Colonies.

Few possessions of Great Britain have made greater strides of late years in wealth, trade, and general advancement than the Dominion of Canada. The population has increased very rapidly : in 1841 it was about 1,538,500 ; in 1851, 2,380,988 ; in 1861 it was 3,182,418 ; in 1871, 3,635,024 ; in 1881, 4,324,810 ; and in 1891, 4,833,239. In 1881 there were 35 cities and towns of 5,000 inhabitants and upwards, having a total population of 660,040 ;

in 1891 there were 47 of such cities and towns, and their total population was 1,030,250. Montreal, the largest city in the Dominion, has a population of nearly 300,000 (or with suburbs 350,000), and Toronto, the capital of Ontario, has over 200,000 inhabitants. Ottawa, the political capital, has doubled its population in the last 15 years and now has 60,000 inhabitants; Winnipeg, in Manitoba, from 241 in 1871 has grown to 39,000 in 1898, and Vancouver, in British Columbia, which had no existence in 1885, numbers over 20,000. The city of Dawson, the "business centre" of the Klondyke gold region, was a barren waste in 1897 and in 1899 had a population of 4,500. The general rate of increase throughout the Dominion in the last decade was 11·74 per cent.

Canada was originally discovered by Sebastian Cabot in 1497, but its history dates only from 1534, when the French took possession of the country. The first settlement (Quebec) was founded by them in 1608. In 1759 Quebec succumbed to the British forces under General Wolfe, and in 1763 the whole territory of Canada became a possession of Great Britain by the Treaty of Paris of that year. Nova Scotia was ceded in 1713 by the Treaty of Utrecht, the Provinces of New Brunswick and Prince Edward Island being subsequently formed out of it. British Columbia was formed into a Crown colony in 1858, having previously been a part of the Hudson Bay Territory, and was united to Vancouver Island in 1866. By the British North America Act, passed in 1867, the Provinces of Canada (Ontario and Quebec), Nova Scotia, and New Brunswick were united under the title of DOMINION OF CANADA, and provision was made in the Act for the admission at any subsequent period of the other provinces and territories of British North America. In 1870 the Province of Manitoba was formed, and, with the remainder of the Hudson Bay Territory, now called the North-West Territories, admitted into the Dominion. British Columbia followed in 1871, and Prince Edward Island in 1873, Newfoundland alone remaining a separate colony.

OTTAWA is 3,540 miles from London; letters are nine to eleven days in transit. Mails despatched from London on the evenings of Wednesday, Friday, Saturday, and Sunday. Telegraph charges from 1s. to 1s. 6d. per word.

The Dominion has entered into the "Imperial Penny Postage" scheme, and letters are transmitted at the rate of 1d. the half-ounce.

*Ordinary public revenue, 1898 .... $40,555,233	Imports from United Kingdom, 1898... $32,866,007
*Ordinary public expenditure, 1898 ... 38,832,526	Exports to United Kingdom, 1898...... 104,998,838
Net public debt, July 1, 1898 263,956,339	Total gold output, 1898 13,760,000
Total value of imports, 1898 140,323,053	Sea-going shipping entered and cleared,
Total value of exports, 1898............... 164,152,683	1898 ....tons 24,746,116

* Consolidated fund.

POLITICAL CAPITAL and Seat of Government. Ottawa. Pop. (1899), 58,000 (with suburbs 70,000).

CIVIL ESTABLISHMENT.

Governor-General, Right Hon. the Earl of Minto, G.C.M.G. (appointed 1898 for five years) ... £10,000
Governor-General's Secretary and Military Secretary, Major L. G. Drummond, Scots Guards 750
Aides-de-Camp, Capt. W. F. Lascelles, Scots Gds.; Lieut. H. J. C. Graham, Scots Gds...each 205
Commanding the Forces (Halifax), Lieut.-Gen. Lord William F. Seymour 1,384
Commanding the Militia, Major-General Edward Thomas Henry Hutton, C.B. 820

The Executive Government and authority are vested in the Queen, and exercised in her name by the Governor-General, aided by a Privy Council. The legislative power is a Parliament, consisting of an Upper House, styled the Senate, and a House of Commons. The Senate consists at present of 81 members, distributed between the various provinces thus: 24 for *Ontario*, 24 for *Quebec*, 10 for *Nova Scotia*, 10 for *New Brunswick*, 4 for *Prince Edward Island*, 3 for *British Columbia*, 4 for *Manitoba*, and 2 for the *North-West Territories*. The members of the Senate are appointed for life by the Crown on the nomination of the Ministry for the time being; each nominee must be thirty years old, a resident in the province for which he is appointed, a natural-born or naturalised subject of the Queen, and the owner of a property qualification amounting to $4,000. The House of Commons is chosen every five years at longest, and consists at present of 213 members; 92 being elected for *Ontario*, 65 for *Quebec*, 20 for *Nova Scotia*, 14 for *New Brunswick*, 7 for *Manitoba*, 6 for *British Columbia*, 5 for *Prince Edward Island*, and 4 for the *North-West Territories*. The House of Commons is also com-

posed of natural-born or naturalised subjects of the Queen, no property qualification is necessary, and its members are elected upon a very wide suffrage. For electoral purposes each province is divided into districts, each of which returns a member on a majority of votes taken by ballot. The members of the House themselves elect their Speaker, and twenty, including the Speaker, form a quorum. Each province has also a separate Legislature and Administration, with a Lieutenant-Governor, appointed by the Governor-General, at the head of the Executive. Justice is administered as in England by judges, police magistrates, and justices of the peace, of whom the first named are appointed by the Governor-General, for life, from among the foremost men at the bar in the several provinces. The highest court is the Supreme Court of Canada, composed of a Chief Justice and five puisne judges, and holding three sessions in the year at Ottawa. The only other Dominion Court, viz., the Exchequer Court of Canada, is presided over by a separate judge, and its sittings may be held anywhere in Canada. The Provincial Courts include the Court of Chancery, Court of Queen's Bench, Court of

Error and Appeal, Superior Courts, County Courts, General Sessions, and Division Courts. The duties of coroners are generally analogous to those in force in England, as are also methods of civil and criminal procedure; and trial by jury prevails everywhere throughout the Dominion. The Queen's Privy Council is at present composed of 14 Ministers and two Members without portfolio.

The number of industrial establishments in 1891 was 75,968, with an invested capital of $354,620,750, employing 370,256 hands (273,424 men, 70,280 women, 19,476 boys, and 7,706 girls under 16 years of age), and producing goods to the value of $476,258,885. The amount paid in wages amounted to $100,663,650. $31,466,324 were invested in land, $60,303,043 in buildings, $81,401,247 in machinery and tools, and $181,450,136 other than fixed.

The principal articles of trade between Canada and the home country in 1898 were as follows:—

Exports from Dominion to United Kingdom.

Animals	£2,015,646	Fish	£380,390
Bacon	995,625	Fruit (Apples)	448,515
Butter	661,935	Hams	213,272
Cheese	2,943,725	Leather	182,565
Corn : Wheat	1,918,147	Linseed	156,732
Oats	702,232	Pulp for Paper	171,490
Pease	3:9,290	Skins & Furs	285,099
Maize	1,533,749	Wheatmeal	1,057,927
Eggs	251,710	Wood & Timber	4,484,355

Domestic Imports from United Kingdom.

Apparel, &c.	£391,699	Linens	£234,942
Chemicals	121,145	Machinery	105,849
Cottons	825,948	Spirits	147,926
Earth & Chinaware	172,148	Telegraph Wire, &c.	91,125
Hats	127,547	Woollens	1,238,532
Jute Manufactures	132,576	Wrought Iron, &c.	459,127

Premier and President of Privy Council, Rt. Hon. Sir Wilfrid Laurier, G.C.M.G., P.C.	£1,644
Clerk of the Privy Council, John J. McGee	657
Min. Trade and Commerce, Hon. Sir Richard John Cartwright, G.C.M.G.	1,440
D-p. Min. do., W. G. Parmelee	657
Sec. of State, Hon. R. W. Scott, Q.C., LL.D.	1,440
Under do., Joseph Pope	657
Railways & Canals, Hon. A. G. Blair	1,440
Dep. Min. do. and Chief Engineer of Govt. Rys., Collingwood Schreiber, C.M.G.	1,232
Finance, Hon. William S. Fielding	1,440
Dep. Min. do., John M. Courtney, C.M.G.	863
Justice, Hon. David Mills, Q.C.	1,440
Dep. do., E. L. Newcombe, Q.C.	657
Interior, Hon. Clifford Sifton, Q.C.	1,440
Dep. Min. do., James A. Smart	657
Public Works, Hon. Joseph Israel Tarte	1,440
Dep. Min. do., Antoine Gobeil	657
Agriculture, Hon. Sydney Arthur Fisher	1,440
Dep. Min. do., W. B. Scarth	657
Militia, Hon. Fred. W. Borden, B.A., M.D.	1,440
Dep. Min. do., Lt.-Col. L. F. Pinault	657
Marine & Fisheries, Hon. Sir Louis Henry Davies, K.C.M.G., Q.C.	1,440
Dep. Min. do., François F. Gourdeau	657
Postmaster- Gen., Hon. Wm. Mulock, M.A., Q.C.	1,440
Dep. do., R. M. Coulter, M.D.	657
Customs, Hon. William Paterson	1,440
Do. Commissioner, John McDougald	740
Inland Revenue, Hon. Sir Henri Gustave Joly de Lotbinière, K.C.M.G.	1,440
Do. Commissioner, E. Miall,	863
Without Portfolio, Hon. Richard Reid Dobell and Hon. James Sutherland	
Solicitor- Gen., Hon. Chas. Fitzpatrick, Q.C.	1,232
Chief Justice, Supreme Court, Rt. Hon. Sir Samuel Henry Strong, P.C.	1,644
Puisne Judges, Hons. Henri E. Taschereau, J. W. Gwynne, Robert Sedgwick, LL.D., Geo. King, Désiré Girouard, each	1,440

Judge of the Court of Exchequer for the Dominion, Hon. George W. Burbidge	£1,232

High Commissioner in London for the Dominion of Canada :—*Offices,* 17 Victoria Street, London, S.W.

Rt. Hon. Lord Strathcona and Mount Royal, G.C.M.G.

Secretary, Joseph G. Colmer, C.M.G.

ONTARIO AND QUEBEC.

The area of these provinces is 568,928 (Ontario, 222,000, Quebec, 346,928) square miles (including the portions of the great lakes within the boundary), comprising all the basin of the St. Lawrence on the north side of that river and the great lakes, and on the south side N. of the parallel of 45°, and extends from 42° to 55° N. lat. and 57° to 90° W. long. The Province of Ontario, formerly called Upper Canada, and the Province of Quebec, formerly Lower Canada, are separated from each other by the River Ottawa. Quebec also comprises the Isle of Anticosti and the Magdalen Islands, in the Gulf of St. Lawrence. Nearly 80 per cent. of the inhabitants of Quebec are of French descent, preserving their original language, religion, and customs; 95 per cent. of those of Ontario are British.

The timber trade, the original occupation of the people, is still of great commercial value, although fast yielding to those of agriculture, dairy-farming, and cattle-raising. The fisheries are increasing in importance, and yield a considerable annual revenue; a recent decision of the Privy Council has given the control to the Provinces of the confederation, it having been formerly administered by the Dominion Government. The mineral resources of the country are scarcely yet developed. Great part, however, especially the regions north of Lakes Huron and Superior and around Lake of the Woods and Rainy Lake, are valuable for their mineral products, such as iron, zinc, lead, copper, nickel (deposits of nickel ore in the Sudbury district of Ontario are found over an area of about 3,000 sq. miles, and mining and smelting operations are actively carried on), silver, cobalt, &c., and in the eastern, northern, and western districts of Ontario gold has been discovered in quartz veins over extensive areas; in 1897 a number of mills were completed, and these are now working. Phosphate of lime, corundum, and asbestos are abundant, and sandstone, limestone, slate, and marbles of every colour are also found in many parts. Petroleum and salt are produced in large quantities, During the last thirty years agriculture has made vast progress, both in Ontario and Quebec. The land is generally very fertile, and produces all the varieties of cereals, fruits, roots, &c. Cattle-raising and dairy-farming are also very important industries, and at present large exports are principally from these provinces—Montreal, Toronto, and Quebec being the great centres of distribution. These provinces, doing 82 per cent. of all the manufacturing of the Dominion, contain the chief manufacturing centres of Canada, which are becoming very important, employing considerable capital and labour. Montreal and Toronto command a vast overland system of communication, by canal and railway, both with Canada and the Eastern and Western parts of the United States. The educational system in force in these provinces, and in fact throughout the Dominion, provides practically free instruction, and gives successful pupils the chance of acquiring the highest education at a moderate cost.

The returns collected by the Bureau of Industries in Ontario, show that in that province in 1897 the total area of cleared land was 12,853,081 acres, of which 8,701,705 acres were under crop, the total value of the land being \$554,054,553. The total area under pasture was 2,658,245 acres, with 326,341 acres of orchards and gardens. The average production of the principal field crops in Ontario in 1897 was, in bushels per acre : fall wheat, 25·2 ; spring wheat, 15·1 ; barley, 26·6 ; oats, 35·5 ; rye, 18·0 ; peas, 15·5 ; corn, 73·6 ; buckwheat, 22·8 ; beans, 19·4 ; potatoes, 95·0 ; mangolds, 440·0 ; carrots, 369·0 ; turnips, 457·0 ; hay (tons), 1·63. The total wool clip amounted to 5,139,984 lbs., the average weight of the fleeces being 5·79 lbs. The total quantity of cheese made in 1,147 factories (in 1896) was estimated at 104,393,985 lbs., valued at \$8,646,735. There were 170 creameries in operation, which made 6,033,241 lbs. of butter, valued at \$1,101,066. The returns of live stock show that there were 613,670 horses, 2,182,326 cattle, 1,690,350 sheep, 1,284,963 pigs, and 8,435,341 poultry in the province in 1897. Fruit growing is here engaged in on a very extensive scale ; there are vineyards and peach orchards of 50 or 60 acres in extent, and innumerable apple orchards. The Ontario Agricultural College at Guelph is the best place of its kind in Canada, and supplies a general education together with a technical training in agriculture. The students meet part of their expenses by the labour they perform on the Experimental Farm attached to the College, the annual balance of cost for board, washing, and tuition (payable by the students' guardians) being from £10 to £15 for natives of Ontario and from £20 to £30 for students from other parts. A central experimental farm has been established by the Dominion Government at Ottawa, and branch farms in connection with it have been established in the several provinces, and in the North West Territories. Free grants of land are obtainable in this province, and improved farms can also be bought at advantageous rates.

In the Province of Quebec the lumber industry is still by far the most important trade, but the settled portion of the country has been too much denuded of wood, and the provincial Government has found it necessary to establish two great national parks (Laurentides National Park, containing about 1,600,000 acres, and the Trembling Mountain Park) to favour the planting of trees along highways and on farms, and to organize an effective service of rangers to prevent the destruction of trees by forest fires. The forest lands cover an area of 62,000,000 acres, of which 32,000,000 are under licence to cut timber. The wood pulp industry is assuming great importance ; several large factories have recently been built, and the value of the output, which was only \$800,000 at the last census, is now probably ten times that amount. Improved farms may often be obtained in the Eastern townships, largely occupied by settlers from Great Britain, at from £4 to £6 per acre, including dwelling-house, outbuildings, and fencing ; while unimproved lands may be bought from the Government at from 20 to 60 cents per acre, and the purchase-money paid in five instalments. The area of land subdivided for the purposes of settlement unsold on 30 June, 1896, was 6,931,978 acres. In 1895 there were 1,471 cheese factories and 302 butter factories, forming a total of 1,773.

ONTARIO. Population (Census 1891), 2,114,321. The Government is vested in a Lieutenant-Governor and Legislative Assembly composed of 92 members elected for four years (no property qualification being necessary), representing 91 electoral districts into which the province is divided, but which differ from those sending members to the Dominion Parliament. The Executive Council consists of eight members, acting as the Ministry of the province ; the legislature meets every year at Toronto. The principal cities are Toronto, the capital of the province, with great shipping interests on the Lakes, and the chief centre of industrial and commercial activity (population, 200,000) ; Hamilton, the Birmingham of Canada (48,980) ; Ottawa, the Federal Capital, with a large lumber trade and woodenware manufactories (60,000) ; London (31,977), Kingston (19,264), Belleville (9,914), Chatham (9,000), Stratford (9,501), Guelph (10,539), St. Catharine's (9,170), Brantford (15,000), St. Thomas (10,370), Windsor (10,000).

Lieut.-Governor, Hon. Sir Oliver Mowat,	
G.C.M.G., P.C., LL.D., D.C.L. £2,000	
A.D.C., Capt. H. M. Mowat	hon.
Official Sec., Commander F. C. Law, R.N.	£250
Premier and Treas., Hon. G. W. Ross, LL.D.	1,400
Assist. Treas., W. N. Anderson	460
Atty.-Gen., Honble. Lt.-Col. J. M. Gibson,	
LL.B., Q.C.	800
Deputy, J. R. Cartwright, Q.C.	600
Education, Hon. Richard Harcourt, Q.C......	800
Deputy, John Millar, B.A.	460
Agriculture, Hon. John Dryden	820
Deputy, C. C. James, M.A.	460
Crown Lands, Hon. E. J. Davis	800
Assistant, A. White	534
Provincial Secretary, J. R. Stratton	800
Assistant, G. E. Lumsden	450
Public Works, F. R. Latchford	800
Secretary, W. Edwards	400
Without Portfolios, J. T. Garrow, Hon. W. Harty.	
Director, Bureau of Mines, A. Blue	500

Chief Justice, Hon. Sir G. W. Burton	1,400
Puisne Judges, Court of Appeal, Hons. F. Osler, James Maclennan, Charles Moss, and James F. Lister ....each	1,200
C. J. Queen's Bench, Hon. J. D. Armour ...	1,400
Puisne Judges, Q.B , Hons. William G. Falconbridge, and Wm. R. Street ..each	1,200
Chief Justice Common Pleas, Hon. Sir W. R. Meredith	1,400
Puisne Judges, Com. Pleas, Hon. John Edw. Rose, and Hugh MacMahon ....each	1,200
Chancellor, Hon. Sir John Alexander Boyd	1,400
(Hon. R. M. Meredith ...	1,200
Vice-Chancellors, { Hon. Thos. Ferguson...	1,000
(Hon. T. Robertson.........	1,000
Master in Ordinary, Thomas Hodgins	800
Registrar Supreme Ct., Ct. of Appeal, A. Grant	450
Master in Chambers, J. Winchester	620

Emigration Agent in England, P. Byrne, Nottingham Buildings, 19 Brunswick Street, Liverpool.

QUEBEC. Population (Census 1891), 1,488,535. The Government of this province is vested in a Lieut.-Governor and an Executive Council, consisting of 24 members appointed for life, and a Legislative Assembly of 74 members elected for five years to represent the same number of electoral districts in the province. The principal cities are Quebec (population, 63,090), the capital of the province, with a large export timber trade and the great seaport town of Canada ; and Montreal (population, Census 1891, 216,650), the commercial metropolis, and the principal centre of the grain export trade north of New York, situate at the confluence of the Ottawa and St. Lawrence rivers. Other important towns are Three Rivers (8,334), Levis (7,301), Hull (11,265), Sherbrooke (10,110), St. Hyacinthe (7,016). Ocean-going steamers ascend the St. Lawrence as far as Montreal. The tonnage of sea-going vessels that arrived at and departed from the ports of Montreal and Quebec in 1892 was 1,440,481 tons and 945,403 tons respectively.

Lieut.-Gov., Hon. Louis A. Jetté, LL.D.	...£2,000
Aide-de-Camp, Captain Sheppard, C.A.	
Premier & Treasurer, Hon. F. G. Marchand	1,000
Provincial Secretary, Hon. J. E. Robidoux	800
Attorney-General, Hon. Horace Archambault	800
Agriculture, Hon. F. G. M. Dechêne	800
Lands, Forests & Fisheries, Hon. S. N. Parent	800
Colonisation & Mines, Hon. Adélard Turgeon	800
Public Works, Hon. H. Thos. Duffy	800
Without Portfolio, Hons. Joseph Shehyn, G. W. Stephens, J. J. Guerin	
Ch. Just. Queen's Bench, Hon. Sir A. La Coste	1,200
Puisne Judges, Hons. J. G. Bossé; Jean Blanchet; R. N. Hall; J. S. C. Wurtele, D.C.L.; J. A. Ouimet	each 1,000
Chief Just. Sup. Court, Sir L. N. Casault ...	
Puisne Judges, A. B. Routhier; L. Belanger; L. B. Caron; J. B. Bourgeois; H. T. Taschereau; M. Mathieu; E. Cimon; Fred. A. Andrews; J. E. La Rue; L. O. Loranger; C. H. Pelletier; Sir M. M. Tait; C. P. Davidson, LL.D.; Ch. C. de Lorimier, LL.D.; S. Pagnuelo; Louis Tellier; W. W. Lynch; L. A. de Billy; A. N. Charland; C. J. Gill; J. A. Gagné; C. J. Doherty, D.C.L.; J. S. Archibald; W. White; J. J. Curran; F. Langelier; F. X. Lemieux; F. Aug. Choquette	each £800

Quebec is 2,634 nautical miles from London.

NOVA SCOTIA, a province of the Dominion, is a peninsula between 43° 30'—46° N. lat. and 61° —66° 15' W. long., and is connected with New Brunswick by a low fertile isthmus about sixteen miles wide. It comprises an area (with Cape Breton Island) of 20,600 square miles, one-fifth part of which consists of lakes, rivers, and inlets of the sea; of the whole, about 5,000,000 acres are fit for tillage, that is, nearly half the entire area, and the soil in the western half of the province, particularly in the Annapolis Valley and around the Basin of Minas, is unsurpassed for fertility, owing to the rich marine deposits left on the shore-land by the tides of the Bay of Fundy The climate is delightful, and the winter is not so cold as in other parts of the Dominion. The population of the entire Province in 1891 was 450,396. In 1891 there were 6,080,695 acres of land occupied (1,993,697 improved), of which 969,548 acres were under crop, 994,113 acres in pasture, and 30,036 acres in gardens and orchards, the remainder being woodland. Hay is the most important crop of the Province, occupying one-fourth of all the improved land, and yielding 600,000 to 700,000 tons. Fruit cultivation is making wonderful progress; apples especially are claimed to be the best in the world; in 1898 the product was about 2,000,000 bushels, and many new orchards are coming into bearing. Halifax, the capital of the province, has a magnificent harbour covering 10 square miles. It is the principal winter port of Canada, and is the *entrepôt* of a large trade with the West Indies and South America. It is the principal naval station of North America, and the British Government have an extensive dockyard there. The Dry Dock can accommodate the largest vessels afloat for repairs. The coal deposits are extensive and of good quality, 2,262,696 tons being the output in 1898; iron-ores are plentiful, and gold mines are now being profitably worked, £2,606,000 representing the product of the past 37 years. The principal fisheries are upon the eastern coast. In 1893 the total value of their produce was $6,407,279. The fish of which the largest catches in value are made are cod, halibut, haddock, mackerel, herring, salmon, and lobsters. The manufacturing interest is also a growing one. In order to give an impetus to farming, the Government have established an agricultural college and experimental farm near Truro, where both men and women can receive a good practical education in agriculture and domestic economy. The Annapolis Valley is one of the greatest apple-growing regions in the Dominion. Improved farms of 100 to 250 acres, with house and buildings, may be obtained at from £100 to £1 000, whilst the Government offer uncleared Crown lands at £8 16s. per 100 acres, and 1s. 10d. per acre for any additional quantity. Hunting, shooting, and fishing abound; among wild animals there are bears, foxes, moose deer, otter, mink, sable, musquash, hares, racoons, and squirrels; and among the feathered game are the woodcock, plover, snipe, partridges, ducks, geese, and curlew.

Nova Scotia has a Provincial Government, administered by a Lieutenant-Governor, aided by an Executive Council, a Legislative Council of 21 members, and a Legislative Assembly of 38 members.

CAPITAL, Halifax. Population, about 47,000. Principal towns, Dartmouth (6,249), Truro (5,102), Windsor (2,838), Sydney (2,426), Annapolis Royal (2,832), Yarmouth (6,089), Amherst (3,781), Pictou, New Glasgow, Lunenburg.

Lieut.-Gov., His Honour M. B. Daly	£1,800
Private Sec., Lieut.-Col. H. W. Clerke ...	250
Prov. Sec., Hon. G. H. Murray (*Premier*) ...	800
Assist. Sec., E. C. Fairbanks ...	360
Commissioner, Public Works and Mines, Hon. Charles E. Church	640
Deputy Comm. of Mines, &c., E. Gilpin	360
Attorney-Gen., Hon. J. W. Longley	640
Without Office, Hons. Thomas Johnson, A. H. Comeau, Angus McGillivray, Thos. R. Black, W. T. Pipes, and David McPherson	
Chief Justice, Hon. James McDonald	1,000
Judge in Equity, Hon. J. Wallace Graham	1,000
Puisne Judges, Hons. N. H. Meagher, Robt. L. Weatherbe, J. Norman Ritchie, Charles J. Townshend, and H. McD. Henry	each 800
Judge, Vice-Admiralty Court, Hon. James McDonald	123

Agent-General for Nova Scotia in London, John Howard, 143, Cannon Street, E.C.

Halifax is 2,463 miles from Liverpool. Telegrams, 1s. per word.

CAPE BRETON ISLAND, formerly a distinct Colony, now incorporated with Nova Scotia, contains an area of 3,125 square miles, with a population of 86,794 inhabitants. The chief town is

Sydney, on the eastern coast, having valuable collieries in the neighbourhood, other towns being North Sydney, Sydney Mines, and Port Hawkesbury.

NEW BRUNSWICK is situated between 45°—48° N. lat. and 63° 47'—69° W. long., and comprises an area of 28,200 square miles, with a population in 1891 of 321,263. It was first colonised by British subjects in 1761, and in 1783 by disbanded troops from New England. The chief industrial pursuits arise from the produce of the forests, the fisheries, and the shipbuilding trade. Coal is found; also silver, lead, antimony, copper, iron, manganese, and other valuable minerals in considerable quantities. With reference to the agriculture of the province, according to the Census of 1891 the occupied land amounted to 4,471,250 acres, of which 1,509,790 acres were improved, 1,018,704 acres being under crop, 479,607 acres in pasture, and 11,479 acres devoted to gardens and orchards. Free grants of land are offered, and settlement encouraged. Improved farms are obtainable at reasonable rates. Sport of all kinds is abundant. The fisheries include salmon, cod, mackerel, herring, and shad, and were in 1895 of the value of $4,403,158, ranking second in importance to those of Nova Scotia. ST. JOHN is also a winter port of Canada; and new railway connections tapping the Intercolonial Railway at Rivière du Loup are now completed, adding to its importance and trade.

The Provincial Government of New Brunswick is administered by a Lieutenant-Governor, assisted by an Executive Council, and a Legislative Assembly of 46 members elected by the people.

CAPITAL, Fredericton. Pop. (1891) 6,502; chief cities, St. John and Portland (39,179), and Moncton (8,765).

Lieut.-Governor, Hon. Abner Reid McClelan	£1,800
Aides-de-Camp, Lt.-Col. R. A. Call;	
Lieut. A. G. Blair.	
Commissioner of Public Works, Hon. Henry R. Emmerson (*Premier*)	420
Attorney-Gen., Hon. Albert S. White......	420
President of Council and Provincial Sec., Hon. Lemuel J. Tweedie	420
Dep. Prov. Sec., R. W. L. Tibbits............	$1,700
Surveyor-Gen., Hon. Albert T. Dunn	1,700
Dep. Surveyor-Gen., W. P. Flewelling ...	1,600
Sec., T. B. Winslow	300
Agriculture, Hon. Charles H. La Billois......	280
Without Portfolio, Hons. Lauchlan P. Farris, and Ambroise D. Richard	
Chief Justice, Hon. W. H. Tuck	1,250
Judge, Vice-Admiralty, Hon. E. McLeod.	

Puisne Judges, Daniel L. Hanington, Fredk. E. Barker, Pierre A. Landry, James A. Vanwart, Ezekiel McLeod.

Agent-General in London, Hon. Charles A. Duff Miller, 17, Leather Market, Bermondsey, S.E.

Fredericton is 2,748 miles from Liverpool *via* Cape Race, or 2,535 miles *via* Belleisle and Chatham, N.B.

MANITOBA, formerly the Red River Settlement, was formed into a distinct Province in 1870, and admitted into the Confederation on 15th July in the same year. It is situated in about the centre of the continent, between 49°—53° N. lat. and 90°—101° W. long. (these parallels and meridians forming its boundaries), and the Canadian Pacific Railway connecting the Atlantic and Pacific coasts, entirely through British territory, is sure to give an important impetus to the rapid development of this Province. Its area is 116,021 square miles, somewhat smaller than Great Britain and Ireland. Its population, census 1891, was 152,506, being an increase of 145 per cent. since 1881, and in 1899 was estimated at about 250,000. The Red River intersects the province, which appears destined to become a great agricultural country. The soil is fertile and productive, emigration is invited and encouraged, and liberal grants of land are made to settlers. According to the census returns of 1891, there were 6,000,000 acres of land occupied, 1,696,583 being cultivated (1896). The acreage under wheat in 1899 was 1,629,995. The crop of 1899 was 33,504,766 bushels of wheat, 23,003.126 oats, 5,532.972 barley, and 388,458 fl.x, rye and peas. The main line of the Canadian Pacific Railway traverses Manitoba, and there are several other lines in operation. The Red and Assiniboine rivers are also navigable throughout their entire course in the Province.

The Government of the Province is administered by a Lieutenant-Governor, assisted by an Executive Council of 5 members and a Legislative Assembly of 40 members.

CAPITAL, Winnipeg. Population (1897), 42,000. Other towns, Portage la Prairie, [pop. 4,000; and Brandon, pop. 5,500.

Lieut.-Gov., Hon. James C. Patterson	£2,000
Agriculture and Immigration, President of the Council & Railway Commr., Hon. Thomas Greenway (*Premier*)	630
Attorney-Gen., Commissioner of Lands and Municipal Commr., Hon. J. D. Cameron	510
Public Works, Hon. Robert Watson	540
Provincial Secretary, Hon. C. J. Mickle ...	540
Prov. Treas. and Commr. of Lands, Hon. D. H. McMillan	540
Chief Justice, Hon. Albert Clements Killam	1,000
Puisne Judges, Hons. Joseph Dubuc. J. F. Bain, and Albert Elswood Richards..each	800

NORTH-WEST TERRITORIES.—These Territories comprise that portion of British North America from the boundary of the United States (lat. 49° N.) to the most northerly part of the continent, and from the western shores of Hudson's Bay to the Rocky Mountains, and have a total area of about 2,497,427 square miles—until recently very sparsely populated. During the last decade immigration considerably augmented the number of settlers.

Out of this vast territory, the Dominion Government formed in 1882, for the convenience of settlers in the southern part of the Territories and for postal purposes, four provisional districts, named Assiniboia (89,535 square miles), Saskatchewan (107,092 square miles), Alberta (106,100 square miles), and Athabasca (104,500 square miles). In October, 1895, the unorganized and unnamed part of the Territories to the north was divided into four similar districts, named Ungava, Franklin, Yukon, and Mackenzie, while the district of Athabasca was enlarged to an area of 265,000 square miles. Three of these districts are now represented in the Dominion Parliament; Assiniboia returning two members, and Alberta and Saskatchewan one each.

Over 150,000 square miles have been reported favourable for stock-raising and agriculture, the former being largely followed in Alberta, where the climate is milder, owing to the influence of the Chinook winds from the Pacific. Both Assiniboia and Alberta are traversed by the Canadian Pacific Railway, and settlement thereby favoured; local railways are also being developed.

There are large deposits of iron, coal, and gold; the most notable discovery of gold was made in 1897 in the tributaries of the Klondyke river in the Yukon district, almost within the Arctic circle, and the beds of all rivers on the eastern slope of the Rockies are being successfully examined; coal is abundant in Alberta, where mines are now being largely worked.

The territories are watered by some of the finest rivers on the American continent, and it is estimated that there are about 10,000 miles navigable. The fur trade was till recently almost the sole commercial occupation of the inhabitants, but agriculture is being developed and grants of 160 acres of land are given to settlers free of cost, and other lands can be bought at prices from 2s. 6d. per acre upwards, according to location.

On the ranches in the districts of Alberta, Assiniboia, and Saskatchewan, there were 31,222 cattle, 60,639 horses, and 64,920 sheep. The southern half of the district of Alberta is specially adapted for stock-raising of all kinds, animals being able to graze at large during the winter; and it is estimated that there are now over 145,000 head of cattle in this district alone. Assiniboia, Saskatchewan and the northern part of Alberta are more particularly adapted to mixed farming, but some districts are altogether confined to agriculture, in which case wheat is generally the only crop grown.

A large tract of land, enclosing hot mineral springs of remarkable curative powers, has been reserved by the Dominion Government at Banff, in the Rocky Mountains, as a national park; the grounds are being laid out under Government superintendence, and the place is becoming one of the most popular and beneficial health resorts on the continent.

A census of the three Provisional districts of Assiniboia, Alberta, and Saskatchewan, was taken in August, 1894, by the North-West Mounted Police, when the population was found to be 66,851, of whom 13,345 were Indians. The population of the other portions of the Territories, not included in the above census, in 1891 was 32,168, making a total population of 99,967. According to the census returns of 1891 there were in the three districts 2,910,144 acres occupied, and 194,773 acres cultivated.

In 1870 the Territories were included in the Dominion, previous to which they had been held by the Hudson's Bay Company.

The Government consists of a Lieut.-Governor and a Legislative Assembly of 31 elected Members, advised by an Executive Council of 3 members of the Assembly. The three provisional districts of Alberta, Assiniboia, and Saskatchewan are now divided into 31 electoral districts, thereby securing an entire representation to its population.

CAPITAL, Regina. Population (1895), 1,583.

Lieut.-Governor, Hon. Amédée Emanuel
  Forget (1898) £1,400
Premier and Attorney-General, Hon. F. W.
  Haultain.
Commissioner of Works, Hon. J. Ross
*Commissioner of Agriculture and Territorial
  Sec.*, Hon. G. H. V. Bulyear.
Clerk to Council, J. A. Reid.
Clerk of the Legislative Assembly, R. B.
  Gordon.
Supreme Court, Hons. Hugh Richardson,
  C. B. Rouleau, E. L. Wetmore, Thos.
  H. McGuire, and D. L. Scott ....each   1,000

Comm. of the North-West Mounted Police,
  L. W. Herchmer £520
Registrars, W. H. Newlands, Horace Harvey,
  George Roy, R. F. Chisholm...   400
Sheriffs, J. H. Benson, D. J. Campbell,
  P. W. King, Grahame Neilson, G. B.
  Murphy..   400

Regina is 4,750 miles from London, *via* Liverpool, Montreal, and Canadian Pacific Railway.

PRINCE EDWARD ISLAND, the last admitted province, lies in the southern part of the Gulf of St. Lawrence, between New Brunswick and Cape Breton, that is to say, between 46°—47° N. lat. and 62°—64° 30′ W. long. It is about 140 miles in length, and from 4 to 34 miles in breadth; its area is 2,000 square miles (about equal to that of the English county of Norfolk), and its population (census 1891), 109,078. The history of the island is somewhat strange: it was discovered simultaneously with the neighbouring countries, and was first settled by the French, who held it for many years, but only as a fishing station. The English took it from them in 1745, but afterwards restored it; they seized it again, however, during the Seven Years' War (1756—1763), and compelled the greater part of its French inhabitants to leave. From that time it has remained, without intermission, in the hands of the English. By an Act passed in 1798, which came into operation 1st February, 1799, the island received its present name from Prince Edward, Duke of Kent, having been previously known as St. John's Island. The island is divided into three counties (King's, Queen's, and Prince), each of which elects 10 representatives. The freehold of the island was originally held by a number of absentee landlords, who were finally bought out under the Land Purchase Act of 1875. Its inhabitants are almost exclusively engaged in agriculture, considerable attention, however, being devoted to the fisheries and to the breeding of horses and sheep. There were (1891) 718,092 acres of improved land, of which 536,175 acres are under crop, 178,072 acres of pasture land, and 3,845 acres of gardens and orchards. The soil consists for the most part of a rich red loam, uniform in character and peculiarly suited to the growth of grasses. The rivers, too, contain extensive deposits of what is known as mussel mud, which is raised in the winter by a dredging machine worked on the ice, and afterwards used on the land as a fertiliser, where it helps largely in producing excellent crops of hay. The conditions obtaining on the island are favourable for the rearing of live stock, of which a large number are exported to other parts of the Dominion and the New England States of America. Nearly the whole of the land is now cleared, and improved farms can be bought at about 20 dollars an acre.

The Provincial Government is vested in a Lieut.-Governor and an Executive Council, and a Legislative Assembly of 30 members elected by the people.

CAPITAL, Charlottetown, on the shore of Hillsborough Bay, which forms a good harbour, is distant from Liverpool 2,630 miles, transit about 8 days. Population, 11,373. Summerside (pop. 2,882) and Georgetown (pop. 1,060), on the east coast, are also ports of considerable size, and the centres of shipbuilding trade.

Lieut.-Gov., Hon. Peter Adolphus McIntyre $7,000
Premier, Hon. Donald Farquharson   1,200
*Prov. Sec. & Treas. and Commr. of Public
  Lands*, Hon. Angus McMillan   1,200

Attorney-Gen., Hon.	$1.200
Com. for Pub. Works, Hon. James R. Maclean	1,200
Provincial Auditor, Benjamin Balderston ...	1,000
Supt. Education, Donald J. McLeod	1,200
Assist. Sec. and Treas., Arthur Newbery ...	1,000
Sec. Public Works, Richard Smith	900
Official Court Stenographer and Librarian, W. H. Crosskill	1,000
Registrar of Deeds, W. C. White	1,000
Prothonotary, John A. Longworth	800
Deputy do. and Clerk of the Crown, W. A. Weeks	1,100
Without Portfolio, Honbles. Peter Sinclair ; James W. Richards ; Anthony McLaughlin ; Peter McNutt ; Benjamin Rogers.	
Chief Justice and Judge of Vice-Admiralty Court, Hon. W. W. Sullivan	4,000
Assistant Judge of Superior Court & Master of the Rolls, Hon. Edward J. Hodgson ...	3,200
Assist. Judge & V.-C., R. R. Fitzgerald ...	3,200

BRITISH COLUMBIA occupies the western frontier of the Dominion of Canada extending from the summit of the Rocky Mountains and the 120th meridian of longitude, west by the 60th parallel of north latitude to the boundary of Alaska; thence southward and along the Pacific coast (including QUEEN CHARLOTTE ISLANDS and VANCOUVER ISLAND) to the Straits of Fuca; thence easterly along those straits and the 49th parallel of latitude to the summit of the Rockies. The area of the mainland is calculated at 383,300 square miles; Queen Charlotte Islands at 6,000 sq. miles; and Vancouver Island at 14,000. Coal (output 1898, 1,117,915 tons) is obtained from the latter; in the Queen Charlotte group of islands on the north-west coast; and in the south-eastern parts of Kootenay district near the Crow's Nest Pass, through which a railway runs. In addition to the main line of the Canadian Pacific Railway which enters the Province through the Kicking Horse Pass and penetrates it to the coast at Burrard Inlet upon the outlet of which Vancouver City is built, and the Esquimalt and Nanaimo Railway from Victoria to Wellington on Vancouver Island, four branch lines of the former have been constructed. Communication is afforded from the termini of the Nakusp and Robson branches with the main line by steamboats. The Nelson and Fort Sheppard, an independent line of railway, runs south from Nelson, connecting on the American side of the line with the Spokane Northern; the Kaslo and Slocan Railway connects the mines of the Slocan district with Kaslo on Kootenay Lake, on which steamboats ply from Nelson southward, calling at Pilot Bay, Ainsworth and Kaslo, connecting with the Great Northern at Bonner's Ferry. The Columbia and Western Railway has been built from Trail to Rossland in the Trail Creek mining district, and thence to Midway, in the Yale district. A short line of railway runs from Victoria to Sidney on Haro Strait: the Westminster Southern from New Westminster connects with the Great Northern at Seattle, *via* Blaine; Vancouver and New Westminster cities are connected by an electric tramway. A line is proposed to run from Vancouver *via* New Westminster, the Fraser Valley, and Hope, direct to the mines of southern Kootenay, with an ultimate outlet at Crow's Nest Pass, and a British Pacific Railway is projected from Victoria along the east coast of Vancouver Island to Seymour Narrows, where it is proposed to cross to the mainland and run from Bute Inlet through the interior to Yellow Head Pass. The entire area of the Province is supposed to be

highly mineralised and is interspersed with fertile valleys, which are capable of sustaining a large farming population. The climate of the coast is mild, while the interior is subject to great extremes of temperature. The southern end of Vancouver Island, the New Westminster district, the north and south Thompson valleys, and the valleys of the Okanagan are already partially settled, and all the land capable of cultivation is adapted for the growth of the products of the temperate zone. There is a very extensive reserve of timber on the coast, consisting of Douglas fir, spruce, red and yellow cedar, and hemlock, the present available supply of which is variously estimated at from 40,000,000,000 to 100,000,000,c00 feet. Some 60 mills are in operation, with an annual capacity of about 550,000,000 feet. The mines and fisheries are the chief sources of wealth, the principal centres of the former being Trail, Slocan, and Toad Mountain in Kootenay Boundary in Yale, Alberni, and Clayoquot on Vancouver and Texada Islands, and the old placer diggings in Cariboo. The output of the fisheries is valued at about $4,000,000 per annum, and give employment to between 8,000 and 10,000 persons, salmon canning (total pack 1898, 496,529 cases) on the Fraser River and the coast inlets is the principal branch of the fishing industry, but deep-sea fishing is rapidly growing in importance.

The history of British Columbia is comparatively recent. From about 1810 to 1846 the Caledonia and Oregon territory was occupied by the Hudson Bay Co. as a fur preserve. Vancouver Island was exclusively the possession of that company from 1849 to 1859, with a Governor dating from 1850 and a Parliament from 1856. The Mainland, as British Columbia, and Vancouver Island each became independent Crown Colonies in 1858, when the gold excitement began, and continued so until 1866, when they were united under one government. In 1871 British Columbia entered the Confederation.

The population of the Province in 1891 was classified as follows :—Whites, 65,266; Indians, 23,257; Half-Breeds, 214; Chinese, 9,091; Japanese, 306; Negro, 36; total 98,170. Four lines of steamships ply to and from the Orient and one to Australia. There are a number of coast lines to San Francisco and Alaska.

Capital of the province, VICTORIA, population (1898) 22,000. VANCOUVER CITY, 80 miles from Victoria; population (1899) about 30,000. NEW WESTMINSTER, 8,000; NANAIMO, 5,000; and ROSSLAND, 5,000.

Revenue, 1897-8	$1,439,623
Expenditure, 1897-8	$2,001,031
Public Debt, 1898	$4,845,413
Exports, 1898-9	$14,748,025
Imports, 1898-9	$8,414,733
Customs Collections, 1898-9 ...	$2,350,738
Gold produced in 1898	$2,844,563
Silver „ „	$2,375,841
Lead „ „	$1,077,581
Copper „ „	$874,781

The Government of the Province consists of a Lieut.-Governor and an Executive Council, together with a Legislative Assembly of 38 members, 5 of them being the Executive Council.

CAPITAL, Victoria. Population (1897), 22,000.

Lieut.-Governor, Hon. T. R. McInnes	£1,800
Secretary, T. R. E. McInnes	240
Premier and Prov. Sec., Hon. C. A. Semlin ..	1,000
Finance, Agriculture, Lands and Works, Hon. F. L. Carter-Cotton	800

Attorney-General, Hon. Alexander Henderson	£800
Mines, Hon. J. Fred. Hume	800
Without Portfolio, Hon. R. E. McKechnie, M.D.	unp.
Chief Justice, Hon. Angus J. McColl	1,150
Puisne Judges, Hons. G. A. Walkem; M. W. T. Drake; P. Æ. Irving; Archer Martin ...each	800

CANADIAN RAILWAYS.

The CANADIAN PACIFIC stretches across the entire continent, from Montreal to Vancouver on the coast of British Columbia, a total distance of 2,906 miles. Starting from the seaports of Quebec and St. John's, N.B., the lines run to Montreal (the headquarters of the Company), where the trans-continental line proper begins, passing through Ottawa, Carleton Junction, Renfrew, North Bay, Sudbury Junction, Port Arthur, Fort William, Rat Portage, Keewatin, Ignace, Winnipeg, Carberry, Brandon, Moosomin, Qu'Appelle, Regina, Moose Jaw, Swift Current, Maple Creek, Medicine Hat, Crowfoot, Calgary, and Stephen—the last-named on the summit of the Rocky Mountains—and then through the Selkirk Range to Vancouver, on the Pacific coast. The share capital amounts to $142,324,882. Chairman, Sir William C. Van Horne. President, Thos. G. Shaughnessy. Secretary, Charles Drinkwater. The total length of the Canadian Pacific Railway system is 7,785 miles, 300 of which are cut through the solid rock. The last spike was driven on the 7th November, 1885, and the road was opened for general traffic on 28th June, 1886, since which time there has been a daily mail service between the Atlantic and Pacific coasts. The time occupied in making the road was four years six months, an average of 2·6 miles per day. The distance from China, Japan, and the Pacific coast generally to Liverpool is from 1,000 to 1,200 miles less by the Canadian Pacific Railway than by other routes.

The Imperial and Dominion Governments having granted the Canadian Pacific Railway annual subsidies of £45,000 and £15,000 respectively, a mail service has been established between England and China over this line, the distance being shortened by several days, and the overland journey being entirely through British territory. Steamers have been built in England specially for this service,* and mails have been landed in London within twenty-one days from leaving Yokohama.

THE GRAND TRUNK was originally formed in 1853 by an Act of the Legislature, and in 1893 the following lines were consolidated, viz.—Grand Trunk, Great Western, Midland, Georgian Bay, London, Huron and Bruce, Wellington, Hamilton, Northern and North-Western, North Simcoe, Montreal and Champlain, Beauharnois, Jacques Cartier, Waterloo Junction, and Cobourg, Blairton and Marmora, thus forming a continuous line through the provinces of Quebec and Ontario. The total loan and share capital of the company amounts to over £65,000,000 sterling. The mileage of the lines owned and leased is 3,512 miles, in addition to which the company controls 674 miles in the States of Michigan, Indiana and Illinois, making the mileage of the entire system 4,186 miles. The eastern extremities of the line are Quebec and Portland, Maine, and it extends westward to Detroit, Chicago, Grand Haven and Mus-

kegon, supplying the means of communication with Montreal, Toronto, Hamilton, Niagara, Buffalo, Detroit, and all the principal cities and towns in the provinces of Quebec and Ontario. President, Sir Charles Rivers Wilson, G.C.M.G., C.B.; Vice-President, Joseph Price; Secretary, Walter Lindley. London office, Dashwood House, New Broad Street, E.C.

NEWFOUNDLAND.

This island, the twelfth largest island in the world, is situated between 46° 37′—51° 39′ N. lat. and 52° 35′—59° 25′ W. long., on the north-east side of the Gulf of St. Lawrence. It is about 317 miles long, and 316 miles broad, and contains about 42,200 square miles, and at the end of 1891 it had a population of 197,934, not including those resident in the portion of Labrador (4,106) within the jurisdiction of Newfoundland. Of these 72,342 are Roman Catholics, 68,075 Church of England, 52,672 Methodists, 1,447 Presbyterians, and 3,398 various. This is the oldest English Colony. It was discovered by John Cabot in 1497; the first land seen was hailed as Primo Vista—the present Cape Bona Vista. The inhabitants are chiefly located on the coast-line of the shore and bays, and the greater part are engaged in fishing; for cod in summer, and seal fishing in winter and spring; these are the two main industries of the island. Lakes and rivers abound; it is estimated that about one-third of the surface is covered with water. The interior is practically in a state of nature; but a railway has opened up large tracts of rich agricultural, mineral, and timber lands hitherto of small value. There are about 633 miles of railway; the Government has completed a trans-insular line to Port-aux-Basques, viâ Exploits River and Bay of Islands, with branch connections to Placentia (the principal settlement in Conception Bay), and to Burnt Bay (in Notre Dame Bay). The Colonial Government have entered into an agreement with a railway contractor whereby the railways, docks, telegraphs, and steam service of the entire colony were transferred to him and extensive grants of public lands made in return for the immediate commencement and future development of public works and railway, dock, and telegraph extension. A steamer runs from the terminus at Port-aux-Basques to Cape Breton, the nearest point of the mainland, making the passage in six hours. The climate is salubrious, and the people are a strong, healthy, hardy, industrious race. The thermometer seldom falls below zero in winter, and ranges in the shade in summer from 70° to 80°.

The principal exports of the Colony are codfish, value $3,640,392; cod and seal oil, value $577,689; sealskins, $372,063; tinned lobsters, $376,711; copper, copper ore, iron pyrites and other minerals, $568,294; and Labrador exports, $657,307; besides which there is a prospect of a coal-mining industry being developed.

LABRADOR, a dependency of Newfoundland, forms the most easterly part of America, and extends from Blanc Sablon in the Straits of Belleisle on the south to Cape Chudleigh at the entrance of Hudson's Straits on the north; it possesses valuable cod, herring, trout, and salmon fisheries. There are a few Moravian missionary settlements on the coast, and also some posts of the Hudson Bay Company.

The Government is a responsible one, administered by a Governor, appointed by the Crown; a responsible executive of seven, a legislative council of not over fifteen, appointed for life, and a

* See article "Our Ocean Mail."

House of Assembly of thirty-six, elected by the people every four years. The first general election, under the "ballot system" and "Manhood Suffrage Acts," passed in the 1889 session of the Legislature, and in 1890 the franchise was given to all males of 21 years and over.

Gross public revenue, incl. loans, 1897	$1,610,788
Gross public expenditure ,, ,, 1897	1,866,811
Public debt, 1897	16,639,944
Total imports, 1897	5,938,335
Total exports, 1897	4,925,789
Imports from United Kingdom, 1898 ..	£366,283
Exports to United Kingdom, 1898	351,032

The CAPITAL, St. John's (population 31,142), contains two cathedrals, several banks, and numerous public buildings.

Governor, Lt.-Col. Sir H. E. McCallum, R.E., K.C.M.G. ...	£1,438
A.-d.-C., Capt. G. D. Timmis.	
Premier and Minister of Justice, *Hon. Sir James Spearman Winter, K.C.M.G.	411
Colonial Secretary, *Hon. J. Alex. Robinson	411
Finance and Customs, *Hon. W. J. S. Donnelly	411
Agriculture and Mines, Thomas Duder	411
Auditor-General, F. C. Berteau	411
Public Works, Wm. Woodford	411
Postmaster-General, J. O. Fraser...............	411
Chief Justice, Hon. J. I. Little	1,027
Assist. Judge, Hon. George Emerson	822
Do., Hon. Donald Morison	822

The ministers with an asterisk before their names, together with the Hons. C. Dawe, George Shea, M. H. Carty, and A. Kean, form the Executive Council.

Commissioners to inquire into French Treaty Rights (1898), Sir John Bramston, K C.M.G.; Admiral Sir James Elphinstone Erskine, K.C.B. *Secretary*, the Earl of Westmeath.

St. John's, 2,500. miles; transit, seven days. Telegrams, 1s. a word.

BRITISH GUIANA.

(See also map, p. 609.)

which includes the settlements of Demerara, Essequibo, and Berbice, is situated on the north-east coast of South America, and comprises a vast area, the boundaries of which were definitely determined by the award of the Arbitrators in the Venezuela-British Guiana boundary question (1899) (see page 609). The definite settlement of this long-standing difficulty should give a great impetus to the development of the colony. It has a seaboard of more than 300 miles. The Essequibo River intersects the country in its entire length; the Corentyne River separates it from Dutch Guiana; the Cuyuni is the great waterway on the west. The colony is bounded on the south by Brazil, on the west by Venezuela, and on the north and N.E. by the Atlantic Ocean. The two towns are Georgetown, population 53,176, and New Amsterdam, population 8,903. The climate is hot, but not generally unhealthy; the country is now almost free from the epidemics of yellow fever which were once prevalent. The cultivated portion of the country, amounting to 83,000 acres (of which 70,873 acres are in sugar-cane), is confined to the sea-coast and to a short distance from the rivers. It is very like Holland, being below the level of the sea and intersected with canals constructed by its former Dutch owners. The seasons are divided into dry and wet, the two dry seasons lasting from the middle of February to the end of April and from the middle of August to the end of November. The temperature ranges between 75° and 90° F. The chief product is sugar, which forms 82 per cent. of the export trade of the colony. Good coffee is also produced. The other principal products are rum, molasses, rubber, timber, and gold. The returns of the leading exports for the year 1898-9 were as follow:—Sugar, value £1,040,982; rum, £144,712; molasses, £11,968; timber, 250,463 cubic feet, value £16,884; gold, 112,464 oz., valued at £414,447. The population, April, 1891, was 278,328 (1898, est. 286,484), of whom about one-third were Indian immigrants. There are about 10,000 aboriginal Indians, belonging chiefly to Arawak, Acawoi, Carib, and Warau tribes; they are occupied largely in fishing, hunting, and raising crops of cassava. The territory now forming the Colony of British Guiana was first partially settled by the Dutch West India Company in 1580, and was from time to time held by Holland and France; it was finally surrendered to this country at the Peace of 1814. It was stipulated that the Dutch laws and institutions should be maintained.

The Government consists of a Governor and a Court of Policy of 15 other members, 7 official and 8 elected by the direct vote of the people—in which the Governor has an original and a casting vote, and a veto on any measure at any stage. The Court of Policy discharges the functions of a Legislative Council, except as to levying taxes, which is the prerogative of what is called the Combined Court, composed of the Court of Policy and of 6 Financial Representatives elected directly by the people. There is, besides, the Executive Council, consisting of the Governor, 6 official and 3 unofficial members nominated by the Crown, which exercises all the executive and administrative functions of government other than those before mentioned. An elective member of the Court of Policy must be the owner of 80 acres of land in the colony, of which 40 at least must be under cultivation, or of immovable property value £1,562 10s., or of house and land of an annual rental of £250. The qualification for the general electors, who number only about 2,928, is, *Country*—Ownership of 3 acres of land under cultivation, or tenancy of 6 acres, do.; tenancy of a house of £40 rental; income of £100 a year; payment of £4 3s. 4d. taxes. *Town*—Ownership of house, value £104 3s. 4d.; tenancy of house, rental £25 a year; income and taxes as above. The general electors also choose the Financial Representatives, who must have a similar qualification, or an annual income of £300. There are 1,153 miles of Post Office telegraph and telephone lines, and 17 cables, and 74 post-offices; also Post-office Telephone Exchanges in Georgetown and New Amsterdam, with over 600 subscribers. There is a line of Railway along the sea coast from Georgetown to Mahaica, 21 miles in length, owned by the Demerara Railway Company, constructed at a cost of £280 000, and extensions east and west are being rapidly constructed, part of the western extension being now open; another line has been opened connecting the Essequibo and Demerara rivers. The depression in the sugar market causes much apprehension, and it is feared that many estates will go out of cultivation unless a revival takes place. Attention is in consequence being given to other industries such as farming and rice-growing, and there is good prospect of a development of gold mining in the interior, for which purpose railways are being projected to the richer districts, and roads are in course of construction.

CAPITAL, Georgetown. Population, 1891, 53,176.

Public revenue in 1898-9	£525,865
Public expenditure, 1898-9	525,387
Total debt, 1898-9	975,791
Total imports, 1898-9	1,371,412
Total domestic exports, 1898-9	1,673,013
Gold produced, 1898-9, 112,464 ozs.	414,447
Imports from United Kingdom, 1898-9	723,456
Exports to the United Kingdom, 1898-9	575,714

Governor, Sir Walter Joseph Sendall, G.C.M.G.	£4,000
(With allowance for contingencies, £1,000.)	
Government Sec., Sir Cavendish Boyle, K.C.M.G.	1,500
Assistant Government Secretary (vacant)	700
Attorney-Gen., H. A. Bovell, Q.C.	1,500
Auditor-Gen., N. Darnell Davis, C.M.G.	1,000
Immigration Agent-Gen., A. H. Alexander	1,200
Government Emigration Agent in India, Robert W. S. Mitchell, C.M.G.	1,600
Receiver-General, C. B. Hamilton, C.M.G.	1,000
Compt. of Customs, James Stewart, C.M.G.	800
Commndg. Militia, Col. E. B. McInnis, C.M.G.	300
Assist. Receiver-Gen. at Berbice, P. Hemery	500
Col. Civil Engineer, G. W. Dickson, B.A., C E.	1,000
Assist. do. do., M. K. North	600
Postmaster-General, F. W. Collier	700
Surgeon-Gen., David Palmer Ross, M.D., C.M.G.	1,100
Medical Insp., J. E. Godfrey, M.D.	900
Insp.-Gen. of Police, Col. McInnis, C.M.G.	750
Admin.-Gen., W. F. Bridger	800
Solicitor-Gen., C. S. Dawson, LL B.	400
Registrar of the Supreme Court. M. P. Olton	750
Inspector of Prisons, Capt. A. W. Baker	800
Sup. Penal Settlement, Capt. B. V. Shaw	500
Resident Surg. ditto, G. Ozanne, M.D.	300
Crown Solicitor, J. A. King	300
Chief Justice, Sir William James Smith	2,000
Puisne Judges, Alfred Kingdon, Q.C.	1,500
Alfred van Waterschoodt Lucie-Smith	1,250

Georgetown, 3,963 miles; transit, 13½ days by R. Mail steamer on alternate Wednesdays from Southampton. Telegrams, per word, 7*s*. 2*i*.

BRITISH HONDURAS.

This colony comprises about 7,562 square miles of territory in Central America, extending from 18° 29′ 5″ to 15° 53′ 55″ N. latitude, and from 89° 9′ 22″ to 88° 10′ W. longitude. Its extreme length and breadth are 174 m. and 68 m. respectively; it abuts on the Atlantic, and is bounded on the north by Yucatan and Mexico, on the west and south by Guatemala, and on the east by the Caribbean Sea. The climate generally is damp and hot, but not unhealthy. The temperature ranges from 56° to 96°. The average lies between 75° and 80°, but this is considerably tempered by the prevailing sea-breezes. The country consists chiefly of primeval forest, with savannahs and so-called "pine-ridges," which are open sandy plains covered with a wiry grass and dotted with pine-trees, affording fair runs for cattle. The ground is level and swampy along the coast-line, and generally flat for about ten to twenty miles inland ; after which hills from 500 ft. to 4,000 ft. high succeed each other to the western boundary. The Census (1891) gives the population at 31,471 (males, 16,268 ; females, 15,203).

The staple products are the natural woods of the colony, principally mahogany and logwood ; the export of mahogany, of which the cost ready for shipment, is $40 to $50 per 1,000 ft. amounted in the year 1898 to 7,630,252 ft., that of

logwood ($10 to $15 per ton) being 23,579 tons in 1898. There are some sugar estates, and coffee plantations have been started. Fruits, including bananas, plantains, cocoanuts, pineapples, oranges, and mangoes, grow well, while inland there are extensive regions of good pasturage, and there are indications that gold and other minerals exist. Other exports are: Sugar, rum, cedarwood, india-rubber and bananas. The latest returns show that about 15,000 acres are under cultivation. The best description of cocoa trees grow wild in the bush. Crown lands can be purchased at $1 per acre, or leased at an annual rental of 10c. to 30c. per acre.

On the 15th October, 1894, the gold dollar of the United States was made the standard coin, with a subsidiary silver coinage, and a paper currency. The sovereign and half-sovereign are legal tender at $4.85 and $2.43 respectively.

There are forty-nine schools in the colony, all but one of which are denominational, and in receipt of Government aid.

British Honduras is governed as a Crown colony. The Executive Council consists of the Colonial Secretary, the Treasurer, the Attorney-General, the Inspector Commandant of Constabulary, and three unofficial members appointed by the Sovereign. The Legislative Council includes the following members :—the Colonial Secretary, the Treasurer, the Attorney-General, and not less than five unofficial members appointed by the Sovereign.

CAPITAL, Belize ; population (1891), 5,767.

Public revenue, 1898	$274,690
Public expenditure, 1898	301,413
Public Debt, 1898	168,815
Total imports, 1898	1,243,910
Domestic Exports, 1898	955,264
Transit Exports, 1898	327,329
Imports from the United Kingdom, 1898	420,127
Exports to the United Kingdom, 1898	853,193

Gov., Col. Sir David Wilson, K.C.M.G., V.D.	$8,748
Private Sec., C. Wilson	840
Colonial Sec., Francis Jas. Newton, C.M.G.	3,500
Colonial Treas., W. J. McKinney, C.M.G.	2,916
Inspector of Constab., A. L. M. Mitchell	1,500
Surveyor-General, C. R. Usher	1,944
Colonial Engineer, B. W. Baber	1,944
Colonial Surgeon, C. H. Eyles	2,187
Supt. of Police, D. D. Barnes	1,500
Postmaster, W. B. Gutteron	1,500
Chief Justice, Sir Wm. John Anderson, Knt.	4,860
Attorney-General, F. M. Maxwell	2,430
Registrar-General, A. J. K. Young	1,944
Clerk to Councils, A. G. Clayton	1,800

Belize is distant about 5,701 miles ; transit, seventeen days. Telegrams *sent by post* from New Orleans.

BERMUDA.

The Bermudas, or Somers Islands, are a cluster of about 100 small islands (15 or 16 only of which are inhabited, the rest being mere rocks) situated in the west of the Atlantic Ocean, in 32° 15′ N. lat. and 64° 51′ W. long., comprising an area of about 19 square miles, and containing (1897) an estimated population of 16,098, of whom 6,184 are white, exclusive of army and navy. These islands derive their name from Bermudez, a Spaniard, who sighted them in 1527 ; but they were first colonised by Admiral Sir George Somers, who was shipwrecked here in 1609, on his way to Virginia. The nearest point of the mainland is Cape Hatteras, in North Carolina, 580 miles distant. Bermuda possesses a strongly-fortified dockyard, where the British North American squadron refits.

These islands have become a favourite winter resort for visitors from the neighbouring States of America and the Dominion of Canada. Numbers repair thither from November until April to escape the cold of the North American Continent: large hotels have been erected for their accommodation. The climate during this period is most salubrious, the range of thermometer being 60° to 70°, and invalids derive great benefit from the mildness of the winter.

The soil is, on the whole, poor. The products of the island chiefly consist of onions and potatoes, which are grown in large quantities for the spring supply of the New York market, a few melons and pumpkins, and arrowroot of a very fine quality. Lily bulbs, especially the Bermuda Easter Lily, are grown for export, chiefly to the United States. The sea abounds with fish; a few turtles are taken.

The Government is administered by a Governor, who is also Commander-in-chief of the military forces. He is advised by an Executive Council of 6 members, appointed by the Crown. There is also a Legislative Council, composed of 9 members appointed by the Crown; and a representative House of Assembly consisting of 36 members, four of whom are elected by each of the nine parishes. There are 1,112 electors, whose individual qualifications are the possession of freehold property of not less value than £60. Hamilton, on the coast of Long Island, is the chief

town and the seat of government: population (1891), 1,854. The churches and chapels are all endowed under a temporary Act: the sum of £10 is paid for every hundred of the denomination.

Public revenue in 1898	£38,943
Public expenditure in 1898	39,102
Public debt, 31 Dec., 1898	45,600
Imports from the United Kingdom, 1898	114,487
Exports to the United Kingdom, 1898	1,815

Governor and Commander-in-Chief, Lt.-Gen.

George Digby Barker, c.b.	£2,946
Assist. Mil. Sec., Capt. O. D. Hickman...	
Aide-de-Camp, Lieut. H. E. Platt..........	
Colonial Secretary, Archibald Alison	400
Receiver-General, F. W. Major	500
Chief Justice, Sir Josiah Rees	700
Assistant Judges, T. N. Dill	} *......Paid by fees.*
C. V. Ingham	
Attorney-General, S. Brownlow Gray, c.m.g.	£500
Solicitor-General, Richard D. Darrell........	
Postmaster, Allan F. Smith	300

Naval Officer in Chge., Capt. T. MacGill, c.b.
Inspector of Machinery, J. A. Lemon ....
Naval Storekeeper, H. C. Maule ....
Commanding R.E., Lt.-Col. E. J. Bor, r.e.
Do. R.A., Lt.-Col. H. C. M. Woods, r.a.
Ordnance Stores, Lt.-Col. R. T. Stainforth...
District Paymaster, Maj. J. W. T. S. Smythe
Senior Medical Officer, Brig.-Surg.-Lt.-Col.
G. D. N. Leake

Hamilton, 2,970 miles; transit, 14 days. Telegrams, per word, 2s. 6d.

Immigration and Emigration, 1880—1898.

The following tables give the number of persons who entered or left the British Isles during the period of nineteen years 1880-1898. In the first case the countries from which the Immigrants set out is given, and, in the second (which deals with British and Irish Emigrants only), the destinations of those who left this country:—

	IMMIGRANTS.					EMIGRANTS.				
	NATIONALITY.					DESTINATION.				
Year.	British and Irish.	Foreigners.	Not distinguished.	Total.	Year.	To North American Colonies.	To the United States.	To Australia and New Zealand.	To other Places.	Total.
1880	47,007	21,309	—	68,316	1880	20,902	166,570	24,184	15,886	227,542
1881	52,707	24,398	—	77,105	1881	23,912	176,104	22,682	20,304	243,002
1882	54,711	22,582	5,511	82,804	1882	40,441	181,903	37,289	19,733	279,365
1883	73,804	26,699	—	100,503	1883	44,185	191,573	71,264	13,096	320,118
1884	91,356	32,007	103	123,466	1884	31,134	155,280	44,255	11,510	242,179
1885	85,468	27,006	1,075	113,549	1885	19,838	137,687	39,395	10,724	207,644
1886	80,018	28,474	387	108,879	1886	24,745	152,710	43,076	12,639	232,900
1887	85,475	32,008	1,530	119,013	1887	32,025	201,526	34,183	13,753	281,487
1888	94,133	33,895	851	128,879	1888	34,853	195,896	31,127	17,962	279,928
1889	103,070	43,122	1,206	147,398	1889	28,269	168,771	28,294	28,461	253,795
1890	109,470	44,663	1,777	155,910	1890	22,520	152,413	21,179	22,004	218,116
1891	103,037	47,197	1,135	151,369	1891	21,578	156,395	19,547	20,987	218,507
1892	97,780	44,673	1,294	143,747	1892	23,254	150,339	15,950	20,799	210,042
1893	102,119	37,634	1,301	141,054	1893	24,732	148,949	11,203	23,930	208,814
1894	118,309	66,129	1,361	185,799	1894	17,459	104,001	10,917	23,653	156,030
1895	109,418	64,803	1,453	175,674	1895	16,622	126,502	10,567	31,490	185,181
1896	101,742	56,509	1,662	159,913	1896	15,267	98,921	10,354	37,383	161,925
1897	95,221	57,994	1,899	155,114	1897	15,571	85,324	12,061	33,504	146,460
1898	91,248	46,362	1,735	139,345	1898	17,640	80,494	10,693	31,817	140,644

AUSTRALASIA, that is, Austral or Southern Asia, comprises the great island-continent of Australia, the islands of New Zealand and Tasmania, and a vast number of smaller islands, chiefly in the Southern Hemisphere, between the Pacific and Indian Oceans, together with a portion of the island of Papua or New Guinea.

The whole of the British Possessions in this area, including Fiji and a portion of New Guinea, is estimated to contain 3,173,882 square miles, and a population of 4,975,000.

AUSTRALIA is the largest island on the face of the globe, extending from 10° 39' to 39° 11½' S. lat., and from 113° 55' to 153° 16' E. long, with a coast line of 8,850 miles. Its boundaries on the N. are Torres Straits, the Sea of Timor, and the islands of New Guinea (Papua), Timor, Flores, &c. ; on the E., the South Pacific Ocean ; on the S., Bass's Strait, Tasmania, and the South Pacific Ocean ; and on the W., the Indian Ocean. Its nearest point to Asia is situate at a distance of 1,600 miles S.E. of Singapore, the extremity of the continent in this direction ; the intervening space being occupied by the East Indian Archipelago, chiefly in the possession of Holland. The area of this vast island-continent is estimated at 2,944,628 square miles. The greatest dimensions are in length from E. to W. 2,400 miles, and in breadth from N. to S. 1,971 miles. There is a rapidly-increasing population, estimated at 4,566,336 in 1899 for all the colonies. The continent itself is divided into five colonies—New South Wales, Victoria, Queensland, South Australia, and Western Australia. There are many excellent and spacious harbours in various parts of the coast ; at an average distance of sixty miles a range of steep mountains runs along the E. coast, but the greater part of the shore on the N., the W., and S. is low and sandy. A large part of the interior, particularly in the west, consists of sandy and stony desert, covered with spinifex and containing numerous salt-marshes, though reaches of grass-land occur here and there. The geological formation of Australia is remarkable for its simplicity and regularity ; the *strike* of the rocks is, with a single exception, coincident with the direction of the mountain-chains, from N. to S. ; and the tertiary formation to be found in the N., S., and W. develops in the S.E. into a gigantic tertiary plain, watered by the Darling and the Murray rivers. Nearly all round the coast, however, and in the eastern portion of the island, is a rich grazing country, admirably adapted to the rearing of sheep, of which there were (1899) in New South Wales, 41,241,004 ; Victoria (1894), 13,180,943 ; Queensland (1899), 17,552,608 ; South Australia, 5,076,696 ; Western Australia, 2,244,888. Sheep-farming is the pre-eminent branch of industry, and it is chiefly as a wool-producing country that Australia has risen into importance. Years of drought occasionally occur, constituting the greatest impediment to the progress of the colonies, often followed by years of flood. The commencement of the seasons is as follows: Autumn, about March 21; Winter, June 21; Spring, September 23 ; and Summer, December 22. The principal rivers are the Murray, with its tributaries, the Murrumbidgee, Lachlan, and Darling, in the S.E. part of the island, which fall into the sea on the south coast; on the east coast, the Hunter, Hawkesbury, Clarence, Richmond, Macleay, Brisbane, Fitzroy, and Burdekin ; on the west, the Swan, Murchison, Gascoyne, Ashburton, the Fortescue, De Grey, and Fitzroy ; and the Victoria, the Flinders, and Mitchell, which debouch into the Gulf of Carpentaria, on the north; but they are of little service in facilitating internal traffic. The most extensive mountain system on the Australian continent takes its rise near the S.E. point, and includes a number of ranges known by different names in different places, none of them being of any great height. The chief ranges of the system are the Australian Alps in Victoria and New South Wales, the Blue Mountains and the Liverpool Range in New South Wales, and the Craig Range in Queensland, the highest point being Mount Kosciusko (7,328 ft.), 327 miles from Sydney, N.S.W. In 1898 there were 11,285 miles of Government railways in operation : New South Wales owned 2,691 ; Victoria, 3,047 ; Queensland, 2,635 ; South Australia, 1,870 ; Western Australia, 992. There were also 728 miles of private lines.

Speaking generally, it may be said that one of the most marked characteristics of the whole continent is the scarcity of rivers and fresh-water lakes. There are few rivers of any considerable size along the whole coast-line ; indeed, for 1,500 miles along the S. coast there is not a single watercourse. Lakes are numerous, but nearly all are salt, and even those barely merit the name, as they are dependent for their supplies of water upon the rivers and floods; at one time they are immense reedy swamps ; at another time they are areas of submerged levels, with broad mud banks for shores that render the water absolutely unapproachable. But the scarcity of the natural water supply has been, to a great measure, mitigated by successful borings, of which there are 350 in Queensland alone, yielding upwards of 180,000,000 gallons daily. Minerals comprise gold, silver, copper, iron, and coal in large quantities, antimony, mercury, tin, zinc, &c. The settled portions are intersected by railways, already extending to 12,013 miles, as shown above, and with about 49,992 miles,(excluding telephone lines) of telegraphic lines, connecting together all the principal towns on the continent. Direct steam communication is established with England and the Continent by means of the Peninsular and Oriental, the Orient, Messageries Maritimes, the North German Lloyd, and other lines; there is a weekly mail from London. (See p. 437). "The Great South Land" is believed to have been first seen by De Gonneville, a French navigator, in 1503, and was inserted in a map constructed by Le Testu of Dieppe about the year 1542. Portions of the coast on the north-west and south were sighted by the Dutch and English at different times, but practically speaking, the Island Continent was made known to the world by Captain Cook in 1770, when he saw the land to the west of Cape Howe, and explored the whole eastern coast to Torres Strait. Subsequently Flinders sailed round it, in 1802, and gave it the name of "Australia." Following the favourable report of Cook, the first British settlement was formed at Port Jackson (Sydney) in 1788. The aborigines are rapidly becoming extinct; the present number being under 200,000.

POSTAGE.—The Australasian Colonies joined the Postal Union on the first of October, 1891, and the postal rate is 2½d. the half-ounce.

Australian Federation :—After many years of discussion and thought, a scheme for the federation of the Australasian Colonies has been adopted, and submitted to a plébiscite in the several Colonies. Of the five continental Colonies, New South Wales, Victoria, Queensland and South Australia have agreed to join, but Western Australia stands aloof; while Tasmania is included, but New Zealand, on account of its distance from the continent, will remain separated as before. The *Commonwealth of Australia* will be similar in its constitution to the Dominion of Canada, with the Queen (represented by a Governor General) and two Houses of Parliament as a governing body; but the powers of the Central Parliament will be limited by the Provincial bodies, and not *vice versâ*, as in the Dominion Constitution. Another point of divergence is that in matters involving the interpretation of the Constitution appeal to the Privy Council is not provided for. Each Colony contributes the same number of Senators to the Upper House, but membership of the House of Representatives is dependent on population, the ratio being fixed at one member for every 50,000, with a minimum of five members from each Colony. This scheme has been submitted to the Queen for her sanction, and if this be obtained the Federation will come into operation on 1st January, 1901.

GENERAL STATISTICS OF AUSTRALASIA.

ALL THE COLONIES, EXCEPT FIJI AND NEW GUINEA.

Gross amount of public revenue, 1898-9 £32,683,583	Ocean ships entered and cleared...tons 21,822,177
Gross amount of expenditure, 1898-9 ... 31,791,653	Total gold output, 1898 .... ozs. 3,551,761
Public debt, June, 1899 233,494,940	Imports from United Kingdom, 1898 ..£26,151,685
Value of total imports, 1898 68,651,078	Exports to United Kingdom, 1898 32,151,812
Value of total exports, 1898 78,636,190	Gold exports to U.K., 1898 7,566,249

THE AUSTRALIAN NAVY.

NEW SOUTH WALES.—**Acheron** and **Avernus**, torpedo steam launches. *Captain commanding Naval Forces,* Francis Hixson (late master R.N.) ; *Paymaster,* F. Rule ; *Engineer,* W. Ames ; *Commanders,* G. S. Lindeman, R.N. ; E. R. Connor, R.N.

QUEENSLAND. — **Gayundah,** twin-screw steel ship, 4 guns, 360 tons, 400 h.p.—**Otter,** gunboat, steel, 2 guns, 220 tons, 460 h.p.—**Paluma,** twin-screw iron ship, 2 guns, 360 tons, 400 h.p. ; with one torpedo-boat. *Acting Naval Commandant, Q.D.F., Commander* Walton Drake, late R.N.

SOUTH AUSTRALIA.—**Protector,** cruiser, 9 guns, 920 tons, 1641 h.p. *Commander and Naval Commandant,* W. R. Creswell, R.N., C.M.G. ; *Ch. Eng. and Eng.-in-Charge of Submarine Mine Defences and Torpedo Corps,* W. Clarkson.

VICTORIA.—**Cerberus,** double-screw iron armour-plated turret ship ; with two first-class and three second class torpedo-boats. *Comm.* F. Tickell, R.N., £500 ; *Fleet Eng.* J. L. Breaks, £450 ; *Staff-Surg.* C. A. Stewart, £150.

TASMANIA.—One torpedo boat.

Australian Auxiliary Squadron :—

(The ships of the Royal Navy, given in the following list, were constructed by the Home Government under an agreement with the seven colonies, and when in commission are stationed in Australian waters, the cost of maintenance and interest on cost of construction being borne by the seven Colonies, and paid in the form of an annuity to the Home Government. For further particulars concerning the vessels, see pp. 218-230).

Boomerang (735 tons), **Karrakatta** (735), **Katoomba** (2,575), **Mildura** (2,575), **Ringarooma** (2,575), **Tauranga** (2,575), **Wallaroo** (2,575).

NEW SOUTH WALES.

The whole of the eastern part of Australia, including the several colonies of New South Wales, Victoria, and Queensland, received the name of NEW SOUTH WALES from Captain James Cook, in 1770. The present colony of New South Wales originated in a penal settlement formed by the British Government, when Captain Arthur Phillip, R.N., its first Governor, arrived at Botany Bay, in H.M.S. *Sirius*, in January, 1788, with an armed tender, six transports and three store-ships, where they anchored, but subsequently proceeded to Port Jackson, which was found to be more suitable than Botany Bay for the new settlement: he there landed the 756 "persons" under his charge, and the British ensign was for the first time hoisted on the shores of Sydney Cove, now the capital and seat of government.

The colony is situated between the 29th and 36th parallels of S. lat. and 141st and 153rd meridians of E. long., and comprises an area of 310,700 square miles—*i.e.*, more than six times the area of England, and nearly three times the size of Great Britain and Ireland—with a population, Census 1891, of 1,132,234, and 1,357,050 on June 30, 1899; made up (1891) of 612,562 males and 519,672 females. The estimated number of aborigines is 6,891, of whom 2,187 are adult males, 1,675 adult females, and 3,029 children. The first Governor, Capt. Phillip, remained from Jan. 26, 1788, to Dec. 10, 1792, and was succeeded by Capt. Grose, Dec. 11, 1792, to Dec. 12, 1794; Capt. Paterson, Dec. 13, 1794, to Sept. 1, 1795, when a duly appointed Governor, Capt. Hunter, R.N., arrived, and remained from Sept. 7, 1795, to Sept. 27, 1800. Capt. P. G. King followed, Sept. 28, 1800, to August 12, 1806, when he was followed by the unfortunate Capt. Bligh, whose rule came to an abrupt termination by a general revolt; and after an interregnum of nearly two years, Major-General L. Macquarie arrived, and, Jan. 1, 1810, assumed the governorship, which he retained for nearly eleven years, since which time there has been a regular succession of governors. In 1813 the interior of the country was explored, and the great plains being found admirably adapted for sheep-farming, several breeds of sheep, including the celebrated merino, were introduced. In 1792 there were but 23 head of cattle, 11 horses, 105 sheep, and 43 pigs. On the 31st December, 1898, there were 491,553 horses, 2,029,516 cattle, 41,241,004 sheep, and 247,061 pigs. In 1898, 271,864,306lbs. of wool, valued at £8,361,721, were produced.

Minerals.—The gold fields were discovered in 1851. Copper, silver, tin, iron, antimony, asbestos, cinnabar, and kerosene shale are also found; and in small quantities, diamonds, rubies, opals, and other precious stones. The total value of minerals raised up to the end of 1898 was £119,853,429, coal accounting for £34,321,205; £4,794,928 was added in 1897.

Agriculture is one of the principal industries of the colony. About 2,204,500 acres are under cultivation (excluding 348,829 under permanent artificial grasses), producing during the year ended 31st March, 1899, 15,728,496 bushels of wheat, maize, and other kinds of grain, with 61,900 tons of potatoes, and 12,706 cwt. of tobacco. Sugarcane to the extent of 289,206 tons was produced; also 845,232 gallons of wine, and 7,839,216 dozens of oranges, and almost every kind of fruit and vegetable may be grown. The total extent of land alienated or in process of alienation at the end of 1898 was 46,388,590 acres, while the area of

land leased for pastoral occupation and homestead, mining, and other purposes at the same date was 127,609,598 acres. At Sydney the mean temperature in the shade for 39 years averaged 63°; the mean temperature in the shade for the Table Lands is 58°—the Coastal District 64°—and the Western Plains 65°.

The western portion of the country is not well watered, the Darling and the Murrumbidgee, both tributaries of the Murray, which divides the colony from Victoria, are only navigable for part of the year; the coastal districts are watered by the Richmond, Clarence, Macleay, Manning, Hunter, Hawkesbury, and Shoalhaven, which empty their waters into the Tasman Sea.

Religion.—All religions are free, there is no establishment, and all payments are voluntary, with the exception of such as remain due by the State, under former arrangements. About two-thirds of the people are Protestants, the members of the Church of England in New South Wales, according to the Census of 1891, numbering 502,980, There were (1891) 286,911 Roman Catholics. Presbyterians and Methodists come next, and almost every sect is represented. The number of places of worship in the colony was 5,004 in 1899.

Education.—Education is compulsory, the total enrolment in 1898, in 2,602 State schools, being 227,561, and the average daily attendance 141,723; the State expenditure was £764,841, including £15,556 received from Government by university affiliated colleges, and Sydney Grammar School. The University of Sydney was incorporated in 1851. In addition to the State schools there are 956 colleges and schools with 58,179 scholars.

"Responsible government" was established by the Constitution Act, 18 & 19 Vict. c. 54, and is vested in a Governor appointed by the Crown, and a Legislative Council consisting of not less than 21 members; the Council at present consists of 58 members. The Legislative Assembly consists of 125 members, representing 125 electoral districts, elected under an Act assented to on June 13, 1893, and receiving a salary of £300 per annum. With few exceptions all natural-born or naturalised males, 21 years of age, who have resided 12 months in the Colony and three months in the district, are entitled to the franchise.

Communications.—Railways, roads, and bridges have their several departments. There were open on June 30, 1899, 2,707 miles of Government railway, upon the construction of which £37,992,276 have been spent; and 84½ miles of private railway lines; there are also 66 miles of Government tramways (upon which £1,516,343 were spent), and 7 miles of private tramways. There were (Dec. 31, 1898) 35,637 miles of telegraph-wire with 916 stations.

Postal.—The Post Offices and receiving offices numbered 2,098, the number of letters conveyed being 75,119,595; newspapers, 42,570,850; packets and book parcels, 16,497,334; and parcels, 596,433.

Shipping.—In 1898 the number of vessels entered and cleared was 6,579, with a total tonnage of 6,919,928.

Banking, &c.—There were (31 Dec., 1898) 13 banks of issue, with a paid-up capital of £18,092,428; assets £42,638,224, and liabilities £31,311,293. The savings bank deposits amounted to £4,454,875, in addition to 512 Post Office savings banks with deposits amounting to £5,026,069. The Public Debt was mostly incurred for public works.

Defences.—In December, 1898, there were enrolled in the permanent and volunteer naval and military service of the colony 9,288 men: 1,283 artillerymen, 116 engineers, 128 submarine miners, 74 electricians, 4,357 infantry, 737 mounted rifles, 388 lancers, 50 army service corps, 142 medical staff corps, 1,500 rifle club reservists, and 111 staff, &c. The naval brigade and naval artillery volunteers comprise 579 officers and men. The "Soudan contingent" and the "South African contingent" were chiefly selected from these forces. The cost of defence for the year ended 30th June, 1899, was £298,651, and the expenditure up to end of June, 1899, from Consolidated Revenue, £5,053,625; from Loans, £1,326,571; volunteer land orders, £168,045; total, £6,548,241 (which is exclusive of the cost of the Seudan contingent, £121,630).

SYDNEY, the chief city and Capital, stands on the shore of Port Jackson, surrounded by scenery of surpassing beauty. It extends four miles north and south by three miles east and west; and contains 117 miles of streets with 23,185 houses, and a population of about 98,250, or, including suburbs, 1,533 miles of streets, 90,935 houses, and 3,100 acres of park, &c., with a population of 426,950. In addition to the Government buildings, there are the Royal Mint, the University, National Art Gallery, Free Public Library, Observatory, two cathedrals, and numerous churches. Other towns are Newcastle, 16,070; Broken Hill, 22,570; Bathurst, 9,450; Goulburn, 10,560; Parramatta, 13,000; Maitland, E. & W., 11,000; Wickham, 6,500; Grafton, and South Grafton, 5,930; Albury, 5,750; Hamilton, 5,510; and Tamworth, 5,740.

Total revenue 1898-9		£9,754,185
Total expenditure 1898-9 £9,734,417		11,769,810
From loans	2,035,384	
Public debt (30 June), 1899		63,761,666
Mineral output, 1898		4,794,928
Value of total imports, 1898		24,453,560
Value of total exports, 1898		27,648,117

Domestic Imports from U.K. 1898 :—

Apparel	£734,103	Leather	£177,934
Arms, &c	106,258	Linens	138,253
Beer and Ale	151,746	Machinery	253,931
Books	109,218	Painters gds.	101,609
Cotton goods	941,466	Paper	144,804
Hardware	104,271	Pickles, &c.	116,232
Hats & Caps.	135,936	Spirits	219,274
Iron & Steel	767,720	Woollens	672,377
			6,630,789

Exports to United Kingdom, 1898 :—

Butter	£167,618	Meat, Extract	388,548
Copper, Ingts.	435,404	Fresh Mutton	641,720
Lead	231,476	Tallow, &c.	506,676
Leather	320,116	Wool	5,406,135
			9,281,740

Governor, The Rt. Hon. Earl Beauchamp, K.C.M.G. (appointed 1899) £7,000
Private Sec. (vacant)
Clerk, H. H. Lewis.......................... 275
A.-D.-C., Capt. W. R. A. Smith, Lt. Hon. R. H. Lindsay
Lieut.-Gov., Hon. Sir F. M. Darley, Kt. ...

EXECUTIVE COUNCIL.

Premier & Colonial Treas., Hon. William John Lyne	£1,370
Chief Secretary, Hon. John See	1,820
Attorney-General, Hon. B. R. Wise, Q.C.	1,820
Lands, Hon. Thomas Henry Hassall	1,370
Public Works, Hon. Edw. Wm. O'Sullivan	1,370
Mines and Agriculture, Hon. John L. Fegan	1,370
Justice, Hon. William Herbert Wood	1,370
Public Instruction, Labour and Industry, Hon. John Perry	1,370
Postmaster-General, Hon. William P. Crick	1,370
Vice-Pres., Hon. James Alex. Kenneth Mackay, M.L.C.	

UNDER SECRETARIES.

Principal Under Secretary, Critchett Walker, C.M.G., J.P.	£1,010
Treasury, Francis Kirkpatrick, J.P.	920
Lands, W. Houston, J.P.	920
Public Works, R. R. P. Hickson	1,100
Justice, G. Miller	920
Mines and Agriculture, D. C. McLachlan	920
Post Office (Deputy Postmaster-Gen.), S. H. Lambton, J.P.	920
Public Instruction, J. C. Maynard, J.P.	920
President of the Legislative Council, Hon. Sir John Lackey, K.C.M.G.	1,100
Clerk of the Parliaments, John J. Calvert, J.P.	740
Speaker Leg. Assem., Hon. Sir Jos. Palmer Abbott, K.C.M.G.	1,370
Clerk of Assembly, F. W. Webb, C.M.G.	960
Defence (Military Secretary), Colonel C. F. Roberts, C.M.G., A.D.C.	920
Maj.-Gen. Commanding Military Forces, G. A. French, C.M.G., R.A.	1,250
Public Service Board, J. Barling, J.P., George A. Wilson, J.P. (chairman), T. A. Coghlan, J.P. each	1,000
Mint, Dep. Master, E. H. S. von Arnheim	1,100
Railways, Chief Commissnr., C. N. J. Oliver	2,500
" *Commissioners*, W. M. Fehon, David Kirkaldie ....each	1,500
" *Engineer-in-Chief for existing Lines*, Thomas R. Firth	1,060
Eng.-in-Chief for Railway Construction, Henry Deane	1,100
" *for Public Works*, C. W. Darley	1,100
Registrar-General, W. G. Hayes-Williams	1,000
Statistician, T. A. Coghlan	900
Auditor-General, E. A. Rennie	920
Collector of Customs and First Commissioner for Taxation, N. Lockyer	920
Taxation and Stamp Duties, R. N. Johnson.	800
Astronomer, H. C. Russell, B.A., C.M.G.	800
Government Architect, W. L. Vernon	1,064
Inspector-Gen. of Police, Edmund Fosbery.	920
" *of Insane*, Eric Sinclair, M.D.	974
Chief Justice, Hon. Sir F. M. Darley, K.C.M.G.	3,500
Puisne Judges, Hon. M. H. Stephen, Hon. William Owen, Hon. G. B. Simpson (Divorce), Hon. Henry Emanuel Cohen, Hon. A. H. Simpson (Ch. Judge in Equity), Hon. W. G. Walker (in Bankruptcy and Probate) each	2,600
Crown Solicitor, G. Colquhoun	1,640
Agent-Gen. in London, Sir Julian Salomons, Q.C., 9, Victoria Street, S.W.	
Secretary, Samuel Yardley, C.M.G.	830

[NORFOLK ISLAND, the residence of the descendants of the Mutineers of the *Bounty*, removed from Pitcairn Island, is attached to New South Wales, and was given a constitution with a resident magistrate and elective council in 1896. Pop. about 850. *Resident Magistrate*, C. McA. King.]

Lord Howe Island (450 miles north-east of Sydney), (pop. 55) and Pitcairn Islands are also dependencies.

Sydney, *via* Suez Canal, is 12,043 miles from London; transit from 30 to 43 days. Telegrams, 4*s.* 9*d.* and 4*s.* 11*d.* per word.

VICTORIA.

This territory originally formed part of New South Wales (known as the Port Phillip district), from which it was severed, and erected into a separate colony in the year 1851. It comprises the south-east corner of Australia, at that part where its territory projects farthest into the southern latitudes : it lies between the 34th and

39th parallels of south latitude, and the 141st and 150th meridians of east longitude. Its extreme length from east to west is about 490 miles, its greatest breadth is about 300 miles, and its extent of coast line nearly 700 miles. The entire area comprises 87,884 square miles, or 56,245,760 acres, of which 3,877,922 were under cultivation in 1899.

Population.—Its population on the 30th June, 1899, was 1,176,824, including about 9,500 Chinese and aborigines. At the census of 1891 the native Victorians numbered about 713,000; natives of other Australian colonies about 80,000; English, 163,000; Irish, 85,000; Scottish, 51,000; Chinese, 8,000; and other nationalities about 40,000. The Victorian aborigines at the time of the first colonisation of the district were about 15,000 in number; in 1851 the official return gave 2,693; in 1891 only 565 (325 males and 240 females). The birth-rate of Victoria for 1898 was 25·72 per 1,000; the death-rate was 15·94 per 1,000.

Religion.—Nearly four-fifths of the population are Protestants, while the Roman Catholics number about 250,000.

Minerals.— Victoria is the principal gold-producing colony of Australia, to which it owes its very rapid progress: from the discovery of gold in 1851 to the end of the year 1898, the quantity raised—62,610,217 ozs., estimated at £4 per oz.—amounted in value to £250,440,868, the amount produced in 1898 being 837,257 ozs. The value of other minerals raised to the end of 1898, consisting principally of tin, copper, coal, and antimony, is estimated at about £2,046,394.

Communications.—There were 3,129 miles of railway completed at the end of June, 1898, all of which belonged to the Government, the capital cost amounting to £38,593,205, or an average of about £12,399 per mile. Of this amount £2,803,740 was paid from general revenue, the remainder being raised by taxes. The net income was £952,842, or 2½ per cent. There were 782 stations for electric telegraphs, extending over 6,599 miles (poles), which produced a revenue of £97,565 in 1898, the total mileage of wire being 14,729, and the telegrams transmitted numbering 1,806,184. There were also 11,425 miles of telephone wire.

Trade and Industry.—Wool, gold (including specie), wheat, flour, biscuit and butter are the staple productions of the colony. In 1898 the chief exports were, wool, £4,036,968; gold (including specie), £5,921,775; butter, £736,325; wheat, flour, and biscuit, £502,461; leather, £301,145; skins and hides, £373,054; and live stock, £259,950. A trade is also springing up in preserved and frozen meats, the value of the exports (excluding bacon and hams) being £226,759 in 1898. The principal imports of the colony in 1898 were wool (from across the border), £1,808,492; live stock, £732,001; sugar and molasses, £665,014; gold (including specie), £2,624,993; cottons, £1,140,393; woollens, £602,255; and timber, £344,024.

The estimated number of sheep in 1894-95 was 13,180,943. Agriculture has of late years much improved, wheat and oats being chiefly cultivated; the dairy industry has also made marked progress. Of the 3,877,922 acres under cultivation in 1898-99, 2,154,163 were wheat crops, and 266,159 oats. In 1897-98, 1,919,389 gallons of wine were produced 2,822,263 in 1896-7). There were (1897) 25,790 dairy farms with 399,617 milch cows producing over 34,000,000 lbs. of butter and 4,312,507 lbs. of cheese. In 1898 there were 2,869 manufactories, employing 54,778 hands.

Shipping.—The shipping statistics of the colony furnish abundant evidence of the magnitude and value of its trade. In 1898, 4,051 vessels, 4,956,737 tons, with 182,754 men, entered and cleared.

Public revenue, 1898-99	£7,378,842
Public expenditure, 1898-99	7,027,415
Public debt, 30th June, 1898	49,264,277
Gold output, 1898	ozs. 837,257
Total imports, 1898	£16,768,904
Total exports, 1898	15,872,246

Imports from U. K., 1898. (*B. of Trade.*)

Apparel, &c.	£329,157	Metals, Iron	£494,483
Books	138,278	Paper	164,040
Cottons	927,577	Spirits	170,408
Machinery	168,675	Woollens	490,114
			4,633,455

Exports to U. K., 1898. (*B. of Trade.*)

Butter	£605,611	Skins & Furs	£153,404
Gold & Specie	2,954,153	Tallow and	
Copper	235,193	Stearine	135,298
Leather	251,743	Wool	2,929,192
Mutton, Fresh	99,864		
			5,021,477

MELBOURNE, the chief city and seat of government, is an episcopal see, and is distinguished for its University, Museum, Mint, Public Gardens, Observatory, Public Library, Hospital, its churches and other institutions: with its suburbs it contained on 31 December, 1898, an estimated population of 469,680 inhabitants, being the most populous city in Australasia. Other towns are Ballarat, 46,137; Bendigo (Sandhurst), 43,975; Geelong, 24,807; Castlemaine, 6,932; Warrnambool, 6,600; and Stawell, 5,556.

The Government is vested in a Governor appointed by the Crown, aided by an Executive Ministry consisting of 10 members, and a Parliament consisting of a Legislative Council of 48 members elected for 14 provinces, and a Legislative Assembly of 95 members for 84 districts.

Governor and Commander-in-Chief, The Rt. Hon. Lord Brassey, K.C.B. (1895)	£7,000
Private Secretary, Capt. A. Pakenham	
Aides-de-Camp, Capt. Lord Richard Neville, Capt. A. W. J. Cecil, Lord Hindlip, Comm. W. Colquhoun, Capt. E. W. Wallington, *hon.*	
Lt.-Gov. Hon. Sir J. Madden, K.C.M.G.	
Premier & Colonial Treasurer, Rt. Hon. Sir George Turner, P.C., K.C.M.G.	£1,400
Attorney.-Gen., Hon. I. A. Isaacs	1,000
Min. of Defence, Hon. W. McCulloch, M.L.C.	1,000
Chief Sec. & Min. of Educ., Hon. A. J. Peacock	1,000
Postmaster-General, Hon. J. G. Duffy	1,000
Min. of Customs & Lands, Hon. R. W. Best	1,000
Solicitor-General, Hon. Sir Henry Cuthbert, K.C.M.G.	1,000
Railways & Health, Hon. H. R. Williams	1,000
Minister of Mines and Water Supply, Hon. Henry Foster	1,000
Minister of Public Works and Agriculture, Hon. J. W. Taverner	1,000
Without Portfolio, Hon. S. Williamson, M.L.C.	

JUDGES AND HEADS OF DEPARTMENTS.

Chief Justice, Hon. Sir John Madden, K.C.M.G., LL.D.	£3,500
Judges, Their Honours Sir Hartley Williams, Knt., E. D. Holroyd, T. A'Beckett, H. E. A. Hodges, Joseph H. Hood...each	3,000
County Court Judges, Hons. J. J. Casey, C.M.G., A. W. Chomley, E. B. Hamilton, W. H. Gaunt, H. Molesworth......each	1,500
Master in Equity and Lunacy, and Income Tax Commissioner, T. Prout Webb	1,800

Queen's Prosecutors, J. T. T. Smith, £860; W.S. Garnett, C. B. Finlayson each £660; J. A. Gurner	£600
Crown Solicitor, E. J. D. Guinness	1,000
President Legislative Council, Hon. Sir W. A. Zeal, K.C.M.G.	750
Speaker Legislative Assembly, Hon. F. C. Mason	1,000
Commissioners of Audit & Public Service Bd., J. W. Fosbery, A. Morrah, and A. W. Howitt ....each	1,000
Clerk Executive Council, Thomas Brisbane...	450
Chief Secretary's Department, Under-Secretary, C. A. Topp	1,000
Under-Treasurer, H. W. Meakin	852
Public Instruction, J. Bagge	750
Law Department, M. Byrne	750
Commissioner of Titles, E. T. de Verdon, Q.C.	1,250
Defence, Capt. R. M. Collins, R.N.	900
Lands and Land Tax, T. F. Morkham	800
Trade and Customs, H. N. P. Wollaston, LL.D., J.P.	1,000
Deputy P.-M.-Gen., F. L. Outtrim, J.P. ...	750
Mines, J. Travis, F.G.S.	450
Engineer Water Supply, Stuart Murray, C.E.	1,200
Public Works and Agriculture, D. Martin ...	800
Pub. Health, Chairman, D. A. Gresswell, M.D.	1,000
Victorian Rails. Commissioner, J.Mathieson	3,500
Engineer-in-Chief, F. Rennick	1,250
Secretary, R. G. Kent	1,000
Statists, J. J. Fenton, £485; R. N. D. Treacey	350
Penal and Gaols, Capt. J. Evans, R.N.	750
Industrial Schools, T. M. Millar	600
Chief Commissioner of Police, H. M. Chomley	900
Public Librarian, E. La Touche Armstrong	455
Astronomer, P. Baracchi	400
Botanist, (vacant)	800
Curator of Estates of Deceased Persons, T. F. Bride, LL.D. ....*paid by fees*	
Parliamentary Draftsman, E. Carlile	1,300

Agent-Gen.in London, Lt.-Gen.Hn.Sir Andr. Clarke, R.E., G.C.M.G.,15 Victoria St.,S.W. 1,500 *Ch. Clerk & Acct.,* H. Myddleton.

Melbourne, distant 11,267 miles; transit, 32 to 37 days. Telegrams, 4s. 8d. to 4s. 10d. a word; press, per word, 1s. 10d.

SOUTH AUSTRALIA.

South Australia was established as a British Province by 4 & 5 Will. IV., cap. 95, but not proclaimed until 28th Dec., 1836, so that its history falls within Queen Victoria's reign. Originally it comprised 300,000 square miles, but with the addition of the Northern Territory in 1853, and by other extensions, the area is now 903,690 square miles, or twice that of Germany and France combined, and fifteen times greater than England and Wales. The Province is situated between 11° and 37° S. lat. and 129° and 141° E. long., and covers 12° of longitude and 27° of latitude. The total length is 1,850 miles, the extreme breadth 650 miles, with about 2,000 miles of seaboard.

Population.—The population at the 1891 census was 320,431, and on 31 Dec. 1898, 362,897 [187,251 males and 175,646 females]; birth rate 24·98, death rate 13·06, and marriage rate 6·18 per 1,000.

Meteorology.—The mean temperature of the original colony is 74°, with a mean rainfall of 16 inches on the plains and 42 inches in the hills, the 60 years' average at Adelaide being 21 inches. The winter temperature averages 53° with 100° for summer, but the climate is so dry that the inconvenience is comparatively slight. The settled portions may not unfairly be compared to Southern France and Italy in respect of climate.

Water Supply.—The source of the Torrens and Onkaparinga rivers provides the capital with an abundant water supply; the reservoirs have a total capacity of 4,000,000,000 gallons.

Government.—The Government is administered by a Governor, the Legislative Council with 24 members, and the House of Assembly with 54 members. There are 6 Cabinet Ministers, members of the Legislative and *ex officio* members of the Executive Council, of which the Governor is president. Election is by ballot, with universal adult suffrage for the House of Assembly for all British subjects male and female; there is a small property qualification for electors to the Legislative Council, who numbered 47,151 (9,121 women) in 1898, those for the Assembly numbering 151,143 (67,953 women).

Local Government.—There are 33 Municipalities and 141 District Councils, the aggregate assessment of property within their boundaries being £2,518,668 and the revenue (1898) £282,855, and expenditure, (1898) chiefly on roads, £272,735.

Law and Justice.—The Supreme Court is presided over by the Chief Justice and two Puisne Judges; there are Courts of Vice-Admiralty and Insolvency, as well as Local Civil Courts, with stipendiary magistrates and the usual Police Courts. The Supreme Court convictions average about 103 annually, which is at the rate of 1 in every 3,523 of the population. The Real Property Act (1858) simplifies the transfer of land, and since the passing of the Act, land to the value of £15,316,907 has been dealt with.

Religion.—About 85 per cent. are Protestants, the remainder being Roman Catholics.

Education.—There is an endowed university at Adelaide, founded in 1881 with 301 undergraduates; all classes are open to women. A State school of mines and industries has also been established. Primary education is provided by the State, and controlled by a responsible minister : it is secular, compulsory, and free; there are 670 State schools with 1,253 teachers and 61,763 scholars; the expenditure in 1898 was £144,805, the total outlay on school buildings amounting to £459,947. The Public Library, Museum, Art Gallery and local Institutes are supported or assisted by the State at an annual cost of £10,329.

Finance and Banking.—There are 8 Banking Institutions in Adelaide with 133 branches, having a total liability of £5,821,303 and assets £6,809,603 in 1898; their note issue amounted to £347,201. The Government Savings Bank has 132 agencies with 96,401 depositors (£3,069,752 bearing interest at 3 per cent.). The Public Debt is at the rate of £66 per head, and bears an average interest of 4 per cent.

Commerce in 1898.—Total value £12,980,579, or £36 per head of the population :—

	Imports from.	Exports to.
United Kingdom	£1,974,818	£2,306,202
British Colonies	3,542,451	3,897,753
Foreign Countries	667,536	591,819
	£6,184,805	£6,795,774

Shipping.—The total tonnage inwards and outwards in 1898 was 3,682,525 tons; 2,903,727 tons were British, and 573,798 tons Foreign.

Railways.—The length of Government lines open in 1898 was 1,724 miles. The total cost to 31 Dec. 1898, was £12,833,572 or £7,449 per mile: the working expenses in 1898 were £590,558 and the net receipts £426,874 or 3·3 per cent. on the cost.

Posts and Telegraphs.—The Adelaide and Port Darwin line, total length 1,975 miles, was laid in 1872, the whole cost (£515,000) being borne by the colony; this completed intercommunication with the outside world, and the wire is being duplicated at the cost of £50,000. There are 5,874 miles of total lines and 268 stations, the number of messages being 1,062,503, (of which 125,512 were international) in 1898. Postal and Telegraph receipts (1897-8) £248,614.

Agriculture.—Of the total area about two-thirds are farmed or grazed, and 2,967,370 acres cultivated, under wheat 1,788,770 acres, hay 316,413, oats, barley, and potatoes, with 734,610 acres lying fallow. The quantity of wheat produced in 1898-99 was 8,778,900 bushels. English fruit, oranges, lemons, almonds, and olives are successfully grown, and fruit drying is profitable.

In 1898 there were 19,159 acres of vines, the export of wine being 513,065 gallons in 1898. Brandy and other spirits are also produced.

Sheep and Cattle.—There were 5,012,620 sheep in 1898, and 35,118,644 lbs. of wool (valued at £945,589) were exported; cattle number 250,343, and horses 161,774.

Minerals.—Copper and gold, silver, lead, manganese, bismuth, iron and coal are found.

Defences.—The cavalry, artillery, and infantry, number 1,186. Land batteries, at Glanville and at Largs Bay, have been constructed to resist attacks by sea; and there is one gun-boat.

Revenue (1896, £2,628,049), 1898		£2,612,730
Expenditure (1896, £2,615,860), 1898		2,590,390
Public Debt, 30 June, 1898		24,309,035
Total imports, 1898		6,184,805
Total exports, 1898		6,795,774
Imports from United Kingdom, 1898		1,974,818
Exports to United Kingdom, 1898		2 306,202

CAPITAL, Adelaide. Population — 31st Dec. 1898, inclusive of suburbs, 147,6.6.

Governor, Lord Tennyson, K.C.M.G. (appointed 1899)	£4,000
Privat Sec., Capt. E. W. Wallington.	
Aide-de-Camp, Capt. G. R. Lascelles.	
Premier and Attorney-Genl., Rt. Hon. Charles Cameron Kingston, P.C., Q.C., M.P.	1,000
Chief Secretary, Hon. J. V. O'Loghlin, M.L.C.	1,000
Treasurer, Hon. F. W. Holder, M.P.	1,000
Commr. of Crown Lands, Hon. L. O'Loughlin, M.P.	
Com. Public Works, Hon. J. G. Jenkins, M.P.	1,000
Agriculture & Education, Hon. Richard Butler, M.P.	1,000
Lieut.-Governor, Chief Justice & Judge of Vice-Admiralty, Rt. Hon. Sir Samuel James Way, Bart., P.C., D.C.L.	2,000
Second Judge, Hon. Sir J.P. Boucaut, K.C.M.G.	1,700
Third Judge, Hon. William Henry Bundey	1,700
Pres. Legislative Council, Hon. Sir R. C. Baker, K.C.M.G.	600
Speaker, House of Assembly, Hon. Sir Jenkin Coles, K.C.M.G.	600
Under Secretary, L. H. Sholl	600
Secretary, Attorney-General, C. C. Cornish.	600
Under Treasurer, T. Gill	550
Secy. Commr. of Crown Lands, T. Duffield	550
Secy. Commr. of Public Works, J. Gardiner	550
Secy. Minister of Education and Agriculture, James Bath	600
Surveyor-General, Wm. Strawbridge	900
Engineer in Chief, A. B. Moncrieff	1,100

Postmaster General & Superintendent of Telegraphs, Sir Chas. Todd, K.C.M.G.	£1,000
Collector of Customs, T. N. Stephens	700
Agent-General in London, Hon. John Alexander Cockburn, M.D. LOND., 1, Crosby Sq., Bishopsgate Street Within, E.C.	£1,500
Secretary, T. Fred. Wicksteed	

Adelaide, 11,100 miles; transit, 35 days. Telegrams, 4s. 7d. and 4s. 9d. a word.

QUEENSLAND.

This colony, situated in lat. 10° 40′—29° S., and long. 138°—153° 30′ E., comprises the whole north-eastern portion of the Australian continent. Its eastern seaboard was discovered by Captain Cook in 1770; some years afterwards its coast was visited by Capt. Flinders; but the first attempt to explore and settle any portion of the interior was made by Oxley, the Surveyor-General of New South Wales, who, in 1823 entered the River Brisbane, and selected the site of its future capital city of that name on a spot about 20 miles from its mouth, in Moreton Bay.

Queensland proper possesses an area of 668,497 square miles (*i.e.*, equal to more than 5½ times the area of the United Kingdom), of which the Government have parted with the fee simple of 13,043,806 acres; under a system of deferred payment, 2,033,651 more are in process of alienation out of the total of 427,838,080 acres, but an additional area of 256,690,698 acres has been leased out for sheep and cattle runs and grazing farms. The population, Dec. 31, 1898, numbered 498,523, of whom 279,670 were males, and 218,853 females. Wheat, oats, and barley flourish on the downs; while a still larger area is devoted to maize, which yields an average crop of about 25 bushels per acre. Both English and sweet potatoes are cultivated; as also are coffee cotton, oranges, peaches, pineapples, grapes bananas, and various English fruits. In the year 1898, 153 734 tons of sugar were produced. The chief articles of export, the produce of the Colony, in 1898, were: — Wool, £3,009,162, gold, £2,830,553; silver, £49,825; tin, £31,871; pearl and tortoise-shell, £111,975; meat, £941,308; extract of meat, £216,640; green fruit, £96,286; oysters, bêche-de-mer, ; sugar, £1,329,876; timber, hides and skins, £466,265; tallow, £323,531; live stock, £898,818. At Brisbane the average temperature for 1898 was 68·1°; the maximum in the shade was 105·4 and the minimum 40·1°. Wool is at present the staple production; rich gold, copper, tin, lead, quicksilver, antimony, and coal deposits are found in several districts; timber also of fine quality for cabinet manufacture, the Moreton Bay pine and the *Dammara robusta*, together with the cedar of Queensland, forming valuable products for export. At the end of 1898 the horses numbered 480,469, cattle, 5,571,292, sheep, 17,552,603, and pigs 127,081.

At the end of 1898 there were 2,742 miles of railway open; the length of telegraph wire being 18,565 miles, and the number of post-offices 1,165. In 1898 there were 843 State schools in operation, with 1,924 teachers and an average daily attendance of 58,296 children; and 181 private schools, with an average attendance of 11,541.

The banking deposits on the 31st Dec. 1898 were £12,166,842, apart from the £2,807,705 in the hands of the Government savings bank.

The number of sea-going vessels entered inwards during 1898 was 615 (tonnage, 602,006), and the number outwards 598 (tonnage, 596,313). An Act of Parliament was passed in 1884, under which a force of about 3,000 men are at present enrolled. These comprise 3 classes, "Permanent Defence," numbering about 150; "Defence" (paid for each day's drill) some 2,000 strong, the rest being "Volunteers." Besides these, however, every male above 18 and under 60 helps to form one of four lines of "Reserves." The marine defences include a battery at Lytton commanding the entrance to the Brisbane River, and at Thursday Island commanding the Torres Straits, and some torpedo works carried out under the advice of Sir W. Jervoise. The colony possesses a torpedo boat, two gun-boats, and a picket-boat; also four Naval Brigade corps.

Public revenue in 1898	£3,891,767
Public expenditure, 1898	3,802,795
Public Debt, 31st December, 1898	33,598,414
Gold output, 1898	ozs. 920,048
Total imports, 1898	£6,007,265
Total exports, 1898	10,856,127

Domestic Imports from U. K. 1898 :—

Apparel, &c.	£147,625	Machinery	£97,734
Cottons	293,171	Iron	321,625
			1,950,185

Exports to the United Kingdom, 1898 :—

Beef, Fresh	£738,413	Tallow and	
Meat, Preserved	147,146	Stearine	£123,387
Shells	116,074	Wool	1,585,975
			3,002,802

The contour of the Queensland coast-line and the relative position of its inland parts operate against any centralisation similar to that at Melbourne, Sydney, or Adelaide, and numerous ports of considerable size extend along the coast :—Brisbane (pop. 107,840), Rockhampton (19,650), Maryborough (14,000), Townsville (16,500), Port Douglas, Mackay, Thursday Island, Cooktown, and Bundaberg. Other places of importance are Ipswich (14,500), Toowoomba (15,000), Charters Towers (26,000) and Gympie (15,000).

The Constitution was slightly altered by an Act of 1869, but is now very similar to that of the other Australian colonies, and comprises a Governor, Legislative Council, and Assembly—the former consisting of 41 members, nominated for life by the Crown, and the latter of 72 members elected by the people. There is a Supreme Court, with a Chief Justice, and four puisne judges; and inferior courts, as in New South Wales.

CAPITAL. Brisbane. Population within 5-mile radius (1898) 107,840.

Governor, Rt. Hon. Lord Lamington, K.C.M.G. (appointed 1895)	£5,000
Private Sec., P. W. G. Stuart	400
A.-de-C., Capt. C. H. A. Pelham	300
Lieut.-Gov., Sir S. W. Griffith, G.C.M.G.	
Pres. of Legis. Council, Rt. Hon. Sir Hugh Muir Nelson, P.C., K.C.M.G., D.C.L.	1,000
Premier & Chief Sec., Hon. J. R. Dickson, C.M.G.	1,300
Post Master General & Public Instruction, Hon. W. H. Wilson	1,000
Sec. for Lands, Hon. D. H. Dalrymple	1,000
Treas. & Sec. for Mines, Hon. Robt. Philp.	1,000
Sec. for Agriculture & Pub. Lands, Hon. J. V. Chataway	1,000
Home Secretary, Hon. J. F. G. Foxton	1,000
Attorney-Gen., Hon. A. Rutledge	1,000
Sec. for Railways and Public Works, Hon. John Murray	1,000

Without Portfolio, Hon. G. W. Gray	
Chief Justice Supreme Court, Sir Samuel Walker Griffith, G.C.M.G.	£3,500
Puisne Judges, Hon. Patrick Real, Hon. Pope A. Cooper, Hon. C. E. Chubb (Northern), V. Power (Central) each	2,000
District Court Judges, George W. Paul, Granville G. Miller, Arthur B. Noel, Edward Mansfield each	1,000

UNDER SECRETARIES.

Chief Sec.'s Dept., H. S. Dutton	£600
Home Sec.'s Dep., W. H. Ryder	700
Public Instruction, J. G. Anderson	800
Treasury, T. M. King	800
Public Lands, F. X. Heeney	800
Mines, P. F. Sellheim	750
Public Works, R. Robertson	600
Agriculture, P. McLean	500
Postal & Tel. Dept., R. T. Scott (acting)	800
Dept. of Justice, W. Cahill	700

Registrar-General, J. Hughes	
Commis. for Railways, Robt. John Gray	1,500
Commandant Land Forces, Maj.-Gen. Howel Gunter	700
Sheriff, H. Pinnock	700
Registrar, Supreme Court, J. L. Blood-Smyth	700
Crown Solicitor, J. H. Gill	700
Curator in Intestacy and Insanity, and Official Trustee in Insolvency, J. B. Hall	600

Agent-Gen. in London, Hon. Sir Horace Tozer, K.C.M.G. (1898), Westminster Chambers, 1, Victoria Street, S.W.	1,500
Secretary, Charles Shortt Dicken, C.M.G.	800

Transit from London. 44 days. Telegrams, 4s. 11d. and 5s. 1d. a word.

WESTERN AUSTRALIA

includes all that portion of the continent west of 129° E. long., the most westerly point being in 112° 52′ E. long., and from 13° 30′ to 35° 8′ S. lat. Its extreme length is, from north to south, 1,480 miles, and 1,000 from east to west, and its total area 975,920 square miles. The jarrah (Eucalyptus marginata), sometimes erroneously called mahogany, covers immense tracts of land in the S.W. portion of the colony: its timber is extraordinarily durable, and as it resists the white ant and the "Teredo navalis," it is admirably adapted for railway sleepers, and for piles for bridges and harbour works. The sandalwood (Santalum cygnorum) has long been an article of export; the tuart (Eucalyptus gomphocephala) and karri (Eucalyptus diversicolor), eucalypti of enormous size, are valuable timber trees. The occupied portion of the colony extends along the western coast for about 1,200 miles, while the mining population has penetrated over 500 miles into the interior, and the population, June 30th, 1899, was 168,129. The average temperature of Perth (lat. 32° S.), for the past twenty-three years, was 64·9°, while the mean for the barometer for fourteen years was 30·053 inches. The climate is one of the healthiest and most enjoyable in the world. There are two seasons, the wet and the dry, the former lasting from May to October. The total rainfall at Perth during 1898 was 31·76, the average for the past 23 years being 32·957. The chief products are gold, wool, timber, pearls and pearl-shells, lead, copper, tin, horses, and cattle. Cultivation has in the past been retarded by want of sufficient labour and means of transport; large tracts of fertile soil, in the south-western districts, where sandalwood and other trees grow abundantly, are suitable for the culture of the vine, olive, and fig. The climate and soil are admirably adapted for silk-growing and for vintage purposes, and there are at present 2,952 acres of vineyards in the colony. Good wheat-growing soils also exist in the southern division, and 74,732 acres were under cultivation in 1898. Magnetic iron, lead, copper, and tin ores exist in large quantities.

Gold Statistics.—The groups of the Coolgardie goldfields (covering a vast portion of the interior and extending to the 125th meridian), as well as other fields, are being rapidly developed, the export of gold being 231,512 ozs. in 1895, 281,265 ozs. in 1896, 674,994 ozs. in 1897, 1,050,184 ozs. in 1898, and 847,777 ozs. in the first seven months of 1899; 531,164 ozs. have already been obtained from the Coolgardie, and 835,637 ozs. from the East Coolgardie fields. Gold is also found in the Kimberley, Pilbarra, Ashburton, Murchison, and Peak Hill districts. The total amount exported from the colony from 1886 to 31 December, 1898, is 2,692,804 ozs.

There are 1,768 miles of railway open (31 Dec., 1898); the Great Southern Railway connects Perth, the capital of the colony, with Albany (King George's Sound), and the Eastern connects the capital with Fremantle and Kalgoorlie, and also with Kanowna and other towns on the goldfields. The Midland and Northern lines join Perth to Cue. There is direct telegraphic communication with England by the Eastern Extension Telegraph Co.'s cable from Roebuck Bay on the N.-W. coast, in addition to the line through Eucla to Adelaide. The two principal ports are Albany and Fremantle. The imports chiefly consist of provisions, sugar, tea, tobacco, spirits, beer, soap, machinery, ironmongery, clothing of various kinds, &c. The exports are of wool, gold, jarrah and karri timber, tin, copper ore, guano, sandal-wood, pearls and pearl-shells, kangaroo skins, &c. The estimated value of the exports for 1898 was :—Wool, £287,731; timber, £326,195; sandal-wood, £31,812; pearls, £20,000; pearl-shells, £78,784; gold, £3,990,698. The stock returns of the colony are as follows :—Horses, 62,442; cattle, 245,907; sheep, 2,244.838; and pigs, 39,234. In 1898 the vessels entered inwards numbered 633 (tonnage, 1,199,894); and those outwards 631 (tonnage, 1,189,732).

Revenue (1888, £357,004) 1898-9 ....£2,478,811
Expenditure (1888, £385,130) 1898-9 ... 2,539,358
Public Debt, 30 June, 1899 10,488,363
Imports (1888, £786,250) 1898 5,241,965
Exports (1888, £680,345) 1898 4,960,006
Gold exports, 1898.....................ozs. 1,050,184
Imports from United Kingdom, 1898... £2,051,872
Exports to United Kingdom, 1898 2,293,652

Under an Act of the Imperial Parliament, 53 & 54 Vict. c. 26, the colony is ruled by a Governor appointed by the Crown, a Legislative Council, and a Legislative Assembly. This Act was proclaimed and came into operation 21st Oct. 1890. Of the population one-half belong to the Church of England, one-fourth are Roman Catholics, and the remaining fourth belong to various other denominations. The Bishop of Perth is assisted by a Synod (established in 1872), in which the lay element forms a prominent feature. The educational system is compulsory, numerous elementary schools are under the control of the Minister of Education. There is a school in Perth

for the higher education of boys. The total amount expended on education during the year ended 30th June, 1899, was £56,949.

The principal towns in the colony are :—Perth (pop. about 33,600), on the right bank of the Swan River estuary, 12 m. from Fremantle; Fremantle (15,700); Albany (3,200), and Geraldton (2,500); Coolgardie (11,000), Kalgoorlie (20,000), Kanowna (2,500); Southern Cross (5,000), and York, Menzies. Northam, Bunbury, Broad Arrow, Claremont, and Guildford (from 1,000 to 3,000 each). There are, also, numerous smaller townships scattered throughout the colony, *e.g.*, Busselton, Bridgetown, Pinjarra, Newcastle, Marble Bar, Cossack, Rocbourne, Cue, Esperance, Norseman, &c.

	£
Governor, Col. Sir Gerard Smith, K.C.M.G.	4,000
A.-de-C., Lt. G. Marsden	250
Private Sec., D. B. Ord	350
Premier & Colonial Treasurer, Rt. Hon. Sir John Forrest, K.C.M.G.	1,200
Under Treasurer, L. S. Eliot	650
Collector of Customs, C. T. Mason	700
Harb.-Master, Capt. C. R. T. Russell, R.N.	550
Commiss. of Police, Lt.-Col. G. B. Phillips	750
Commdt. Defences, Lt.-Col. J. H. Chippendall	600
Chief Protector of Aborigines, H. C. Prinsep	550
Railways and Public Works, Hon. F.H.Piesse	1,000
Und. Sec. Railways, A. F. Thomson	550
Engr. in Chief, C. Y. O'Connor, C.M.G.	1,500
Under S c. Works, M. E. Jull	700
Genl. Ry. Manager, J. Davies	1,250
Crown Lands, Hon. G. Throssell	1,000
Under Sec., R. C. Clifton	600
Mines, Hon. H. B. Lefroy	1,000
Secretary for Mines, H. S. King	500
Wardens of the Gold Fields, F. A. Hare, J. M. Finnerty, A. Ostlund, E. P. Dowley, V. Black, A. S. Hicks, L. R. Davis, W. L. Owen, A. G. Clifton, P. L. Gibbons, A. E. Burt, C. U. Bagot, P. Troy, A. Phelps, J. Young, D. W. Green......... *and allowances*, each £250 to 750	
Attorney-Gen., Hon. R. W. Pennefather	1,000
Sec., Law Dept., W. F. Sayer	650
Crown Solicitor, R. B. Burnside	750
Chief Justice, Sir Alexander C. Onslow	1,700
Puisne Judges, E.A.Stone, A. P.Hensman, each	1,400
Sheriff & Inspector of Prisons, James B. Roe	700
Comm. of Titles, (vacant)	700
Colonial Sec., Hon. G. Randell	1,000
Under Sec., Octavius Burt	650
Colonial Surgeon, T. H. Lovegrove	550
Govt. Printer, R. Pether	550
Registrar-General, M. A. C. Fraser	500
Insp. Gen. of Schools, C. Jackson	650
Postmaster-General, R. A. Sholl	650
Auditor-General, Frederick Spencer	700
Govt. Astronomer, W. E. Cooke	500
Deputy Master of the Mint, J. F. Campbell	900
Superintendent, A. Ventris	£550 to 700
Chief Clk. & Acctt., F. E. Allum	£500 to 650
Agent-Gen. in London, Hon. E. H. Wittenoom, 15, Victoria Street, S.W.	1,500
Secretary, Reginald C.Hare.	650

Transit from London to Perth, 28 days. Telegrams, 4s. 7d. and 4s. 9d. a word.

NEW ZEALAND,

a colony in the South Pacific Ocean, consisting of three islands, known as the North, Middle (or South), and Stewart Islands, situate about 1,200 miles E. of New South Wales, between 33°—50° S. lat. and 162° E. long.—173° W. long. Portions of them were explored by Tasman, under the direction of the Dutch East India Company, in 1642, and visited at various times during the 18th century, and in 1777 by Captain Cook. The first settlement of Europeans was made in 1814, but no colonisation took place until 1839. In 1841 New Zealand was, by letters patent, erected into a separate colony distinct from New South Wales. The entire area (inclusive of the Auckland and Kermadec Islands) is stated at 104,471 square miles, or 66,710,320 acres (being a little smaller than Great Britain and Ireland), of which two-thirds are fitted for agriculture and grazing. The North Island comprises about 44,468 sq. miles; Middle Island, 58,525; Stewart Island, 665, with only 252 inhabitants; and an adjacent group, named the Chatham Islands, contain 375 sq. miles.

The European population on 12th April, 1896, was 703,360 (371,415 males and 331,945 females). The native population (Maoris) in February, 1896, was 39,854 (21,673 males and 18,181 females), chiefly in the North Island, making the total population of the colony, including Maoris, 743,214 persons. In 1840 a treaty was concluded at Waitangi with the native chiefs, whereby the sovereignty of the islands was ceded to Great Britain, while the chiefs were guaranteed the possession of their lands, forests, &c., the right of pre-emption being reserved to the Crown if they wished to alienate any portion. This right was abolished by legislation in 1862, when the Crown relinquished its right of pre-emption, whilst at the same time the purchase of native lands for the Crown did not abate, but continued side by side with the private purchases until 1894, when the right of private purchase was withdrawn. The seat of government was at first fixed at Auckland, but was removed to Wellington in 1865.

New Zealand in many parts is very mountainous; a mountain chain traverses the west side of the South Island, culminating in Mount Cook, 12,349 feet in height. The extremes of daily temperature vary throughout the year only by an average of 20°: London is 7° colder than the North Island and 4° colder than the South Island. The mean annual temperature of the whole colony for the different seasons is:—Spring, 55°; Summer, 63°; Autumn, 57°; and Winter, 48°; and the climate is admirably adapted for raising every fruit, flower, and edible that flourishes in Great Britain. Amongst the productions are the Kauri pine (found only at the northern extremity of the islands), most valued for ship building, and for its resin (Kauri gum); and the native flax, which is used for the manufacture of ropes and twine. The principal exports in 1898 were wool (£4,645,804), frozen meat (£1,698,750), gold (£1,080,691), Agricultural products, tallow, Kauri gum, and timber. Gold mining, both alluvial and quartz, is an important industry in many districts, and a rich iron ore, in the form of ironsand, has been found in Taranaki. Coal and copper are also found.

The total extent of land under all kinds of crop (excluding lands in artificial grasses), and of land broken up but not under crop, is (1899) 1,688,703 acres, while there are 11,244,739 acres of land in sown grass of which 6,178,879 acres had not been previously ploughed. In 1898, the number of sheep was 19,673,725; horned cattle, 1,203,024; and horses, 258,115. In March, 1899, there were 2,009 miles of Government railway lines in working order, and 81 under construction; and 167 miles of private lines, together with an excellent coaching system. The shipping trade is considerable, and regular lines of steamers run between the numerous ports, besides direct steam communication with England. During 1898 the vessels entered inwards numbered 620 (tonnage, 765,255); and those entered outwards 622 (tonnage, 765,793).

Public Revenue, 1898-9	£5,258,228
Public Expenditure, 1898-9	4,858,511
(and from loan accounts, £1,543,683)	
Public debt (gross), 31 March, 1899	46,938,006
Accrued sinking fund, 31st Mar., 1899	857,2 9
Total imports, 1898	18,232,600
Total exports, 1898	10,517,955
Gold Export 1898 (ozs. 230,175)	1,080,691

Domestic Imports from U.K., 1898:—

Apparel, &c.	£427,554	Iron & Steel	£534,942
Carriages	82,893	Machinery	225,132
Cotton Goods	525,632	Spirits	135,261
Leather	121,038	Woollens	312,254

     4,020,677

Exports to U.K., 1898 (B. of Trade):—

Beef (fresh)	£146,010	Rabbits	£153,315
Butter	338,400	Skins & Hides	309,456
Cheese	99,774	Tallow, &c.	321,480
Kauri Gum	321,884	Wool	4,735,206
Mutton	2,108,477		

     9,015,540

The General Government consists of a Governor, aided by a Ministry, a Legislative Council appointed by the Governor (prior to 1891 the appointments were for life; since that date for seven years only), at present consisting of 48 members, and a House of Representatives, consisting of 74 members elected for three years. Four of the members are Maoris elected by the natives. Women are entitled to register as electors and to vote at the elections for Members of the House of Representatives, but are not qualified for election, nor for appointment to the Legislative Council.

The State system of education is free, secular, and compulsory. There were (December, 1898) 1,624 public primary schools, with 3,664 teachers and 131,621 scholars; there are also 294 private schools, with 14,782 scholars, and, in addition, 80 village schools for the Maoris. The higher education of boys and girls in the cities and large towns is carried on in 25 endowed colleges and grammar schools. The University of New Zealand has power to confer degrees. The annual postal circulation of the colony was (1898 , 37,134,911 letters and post-cards, 15,095,487 newspapers, and 16,822,704 books and packets, and the work is effected by 1,561 post-offices. There are 6,766 miles of telegraph line carrying 18,745 miles of wire. The administration of the law is carried out by a Supreme Court, consisting of a Chief Justice and four puisne judges, and by district judges, stipendiary magistrates, and justices of the peace.

Defences.—New Zealand has 4 torpedo-boats; the Calliope Dock, capable of docking two warships, was subsidised by the Imperial Government in 1898.

Capital, Wellington, in the North Island.

The population of the chief cities and towns on 31st Dec., 1898, was as follows:—Wellington (and suburbs), 47,207; Auckland (and suburbs), 63,203;

Dunedin (and suburbs), 49,492; Christchurch (and suburbs), 54,500; Invercargill (and suburbs), 10,191; Napier, 9,399; Nelson, 7,064; and Oamaru, 5,372.

Governor and Commander-in-Chief, Rt. Hon. the Earl of Ranfurly, K.C.M.G.	£5,000
Private Sec. and A.-de-C., Capt. Dudley Alexander; Lieut. H. D. O. Ward, R.H.A.	
Assist. Sec., Hon. C. E. Hill-Trevor	

EXECUTIVE COUNCIL, Sept., 1898.

His Excellency the Governor presides.

Premier, Col. Treas., Trade & Customs, Postmaster-Gen., Electric Telegr., Labour, and Native Affairs, Rt. Hon. Richd. J. Seddon	1,000
Min. of Lands, Agricult., Forests, and Min. in Charge of Advances to Settlers Office, Hon. J. McKenzie	800
Min. of Rail. & Mines, Hon. A. J. Cadman	800
Comm. of Stamp Duties, Col. Sec. (actg.), and Member of Executive Council representing Native Race, Hon. J. Carroll	400
Min. of Immigration, Education, Hosps., and Charitable Aid, Hon. W. C. Walker	800
Min. of Public Works, Marine, and in Charge of Printing-office, Hon. W. Hall-Jones ...	800
Min. of Justice, Defence, & Industries & Commerce, Hon. T. Thompson	800
Chief Justice, Hon. Sir Robt. Stout, K.C.M.G.	1,700
Puisne Judge, Wellington, W. B. Edwards...	1,500
Do., Auckland, E. T. Conolly	1,500
Do., Canterbury, J. E. Denniston	1,500
Do., Dunedin, J. S. Williams	1,500
Solicitor-General, W. S. Reid	1,000
Controller & Auditor-Gen., J. K. Warburton	1,000
Commissioner Govt. Life Insurance Dept., J. H. Richardson	800
Public Trustee, J. C. Martin	800
Inspector of Lunatic Asylums, Hospitals and Charitable Institutions, D. MacGregor, M.B.	1,200

UNDER SECRETARIES, &c.

Colonial Secretary, Hugh Pollen	£450
Treasury, J. B. Heywood	700
Customs and Marine, W. T. Glasgow	650
Education, George Hogben, M.A.	600
Justice, F. Waldegrave	475
Public Works, H. J. H. Blow	600
Crown Lands and Surv.-Gen., S. P. Smith	750
Registrar-General, E. J. von Dadelszen......	450
Govt. Printer, John Mackay	420
Commissioner of Taxes, Supt. Advances to Settlers Office and Valuer-Gen., John McGowan	850
General Manager Railways, T. Ronayne ...	850
Secretary Gen. Post Office, W. Gray............	700
„ *Stamps,* C. A. St. G. Hickson............	500
Chief Judge of Native Land, Court, and Registrar-Gen. Land & Deeds, G. B. Davy.	800
Under Secretary Mines, H. J. H. Eliott......	550
Director Geological Survey, Museum and Observatories, Sir J. Hector, K.C.M.G., M.D., F.R.S.	800
Secretary for Agriculture, J. D. Ritchie	525
Secretary for Labour, Edward Tregear	375
Under Secretary for Defence, Major Sir A. P. Douglas, Bart	400
Secretary to Cabinet and Clerk of the Executive Council, A. J. Willis	500

Agent-General in London, Hon. W. P. Reeves, Westminster Chambers, 13 Victoria St., S.W.

Secretary, Walter Kennaway, C.M.G.

Wellington, 16,000 miles; transit, 38 days. Telegrams, 5s. and 5s. 2d. a word.

TASMANIA

is an island in the South Pacific Ocean, off the southern extremity of Australia, from which it is separated by Bass Straits, in which are situated the Furneaux Group and King Island, included within the colony. It lies between 40° 33'—43° 39'S. lat. and 144° 45'—148° 30' E. long., and contains an area of 26,215 square miles, or 16,778,000 acres of land, of which, on 1st March, 1899, 258,542 acres were under crop, and 283,799 under artificially-sown grass; wheat 85,287, acres were leased from the Crown principally for pastoral purposes, in 1898; the terms of purchase are £1 an acre for cash, or a £1 6s. 8d. in 14 yearly instalments. The estimated population, 30th June, 1899, was 178,792, half of whom belong to the Church of England, and about one fifth to the Roman Catholic Church. The aboriginals have become quite extinct, the last, a female, "Truganini," having died in 1876. The island was first discovered by Tasman, in December, 1642, and named by him "Van Diemen's Land," in honour of his patron, the then governor of the Dutch possessions in India. It was subsequently partially explored by Captain Cook, and in 1803 Lieut. Bowen, despatched from Sydney with a few soldiers and convicts to form a penal settlement, fixed upon the spot where Hobart now stands. In 1825 it was severed from New South Wales and formed into a distinct colony. Transportation of criminals was abolished in 1853, and the name officially changed from Van Diemen's Land to Tasmania. The climate is fine and salubrious, and well suited to European constitutions, and the hot winds of Australia do not reach the island. At Hobart in 1898 the mean annual temperature was 54°, the mean summer temperature being 62·6°, and that of winter 47·1°, the average rainfall was 20·404 inches. The surface of the country is generally undulating forest land with mountains from 1,500 to 5,000 feet in height, and wide expanses of level, open plains. The chief products of the colony are wool, gold, silver, copper, timber, tin, and fruit, and sheep farming is the principal industry. The amount of stock on 1st March, 1899, was, sheep (and lambs), 1,493,638; cattle, 148,538; horses, 29,797; and pigs, 45,274. The forests of Tasmania abound in the most beautiful cabinet woods and the largest-size timbers, adapted for every variety of purpose. The fauna include the Tasmanian devil and native tiger, and the curious duck-billed platypus; while the wombat, the wallaby, and the opossum supply valuable skins. There are silver fields on the west coast; over 63,000 acres have been taken on mineral leases, and mines of both lode and stream tin, are being worked in the north; the value of tin exported in 1898 was £141,439, of silver £169,618, and of copper £378,565. Iron-ore exists and gold has been found, the amount exported in 1898 being £188,478. Coal, of a good quality, and in easily-accessible positions, is very generally distributed over the island. There are in all 508 miles of railway open, including the main line running from Hobart to Launceston, through the island, and 258 telegraph stations, with 3,578 miles of wire, a submarine cable (427 miles) communicating with the Universal Telegraph System; 705 miles of telephone; 344 post-stations, and 2,067 miles of post roads. On Dec. 31, 1898, the total registered shipping for the year was 43 steamers and 156 sailing vessels, with a total tonnage of 15,154 tons. The inward entries during 1898 were

739 (tonnage, 574,964); and the outward entries 786 (tonnage, 584,029). The present military defence is mainly composed of volunteers, who number 1,945. On the Derwent and the Tamar, batteries have been constructed, and the colony possesses a torpedo-boat.

A Department of Agriculture was formed in 1892. Primary education is administered by a Department, and there are 296 State schools.

Public revenue, 1898	£908,223
Public expenditure, 1898	830,168
Public debt, 31 December, 1898	8,412,904
Total imports, 1898	1,652,018
Total exports, 1898	1,503,369
Imports from United Kingdom, 1898	465,544
Exports to United Kingdom, 1898	431,518

The Constitution of Tasmania was settled by Local Act (18 Vict., No. 17). By this Act the Legislative Council and House of Assembly are constituted "The Parliament." The former consists of 18 members, elected for six years; and the latter of 37 members, elected for 3 years. The Governor, who is appointed by the Crown, is aided by a Cabinet of responsible Ministers. For local purposes the island is divided into municipal, police, and road districts, which elect their own councillors and trustees.

CAPITAL, City of Hobart. Population, with suburbs, 40,450. Other towns are Launceston, pop. 25,771, Zeehan, Ulverstone, E. Devonport, Latrobe, Waratah, Westbury, Longford, and Queenstown.

Gov., Rt. Hon. Visct. Gormanston, G.C.M.G.	£3,500
Private Secretary, J. F. A. Rawlinson	250
Premier and Attorney-Gen., Hon. N. E. Lewis	950
Chief Secretary, Hon. G. T. Collins	750
Treasurer, Hon. B. S. Bird	750
Under-Treasurer, A. Reid	550
Lands, Works, and Mines, Hon. E. Mulcahy	750
Minister without Portfolio, Hon. F.W. Piesse	
Under-Secretary, G. C. S. Steward	450
Auditor-General, J. W. Israel	550
Clerk of Legislative Council, E. C. Nowell.	475
Pres. of Legis. Council, Hon. Adye Douglas	350
Speaker of H. of Assem., Hon. N. J. Brown	350
Clerk of do., J. K. Reid	325
Registrar-General, R. M. Johnston	600
Collector of Customs, J. Barnard	500
Secretary to Law Dept., W. O. Wise	375
Chief Justice, John Stokell Dodds, C.M.G.	1,500
Puisne Judge, A. T. Clark	1,200
" J. McIntyre	1,200
Solicitor-General & Crown Solicitor, Hon. Alfred Dobson	500
Registrar Supreme Court, P. S. Seager	450
Judges Associate, G. Browne	350
Post Office & Telegraphs, H. V. Bayly	500
Collector of Taxes, C. Mitchell	350
Secretary of Mines, W. H. Wallace	350
Commissioner of Police, G. Richardson	500
General Manager of Railways, F. Back	1,100
Director of Education, J. Rule	400
Deputy Surveyor-General, E. A. Counsel	500
Commdt. Defence Force, Col. H. B. Cox	
Recorder of Titles, J. W. Whyte	510
Recorder of Launceston, E. D. Dobbie	450

Agent-Gen. in London, Hon. Sir P. O. Fysh, K.C.M.G., 5 Victoria St., S.W.	
Secy., Herbert W. Ely.	

Hobart, 13,250 miles; transit, 36 to 40 days. Telegrams, 5s. 3d. and 5s. 5d. a word.

FIJI

is a group of 200 to 250 islands in the South Pacific Ocean, about 1,100 miles north of New Zealand, which extend 300 miles from east to west, and 300 north to south, between 15° 45′–21° 10′ S. lat. and 176° E.–178° W. long. The gross area of the group is about 7,451 square miles. The islands are of volcanic origin, with lofty mountains, and well wooded. The principal are Viti Levu (Great Fiji), and Vanua Levu (Great Land). The area of Viti Levu is 4,112 square miles, and that of Vanua Levu 2,432 square miles. The island of Rotumah (pop. 2,143) was annexed in 1881. The climate is equable and remarkably healthy for Europeans; the average temperature in the shade in the cool season is 72°, rising to 84° in the hot season, extremes lying between 60° and 94°. Vegetation is remarkably luxuriant, the chief productions being the breadfruit tree, banana, plantain, pea-nuts, yams, and dalo (taro), cocoanut, sugar-cane, tea, cotton, maize, tobacco, and arrowroot. Sugar, pearl-shells, maize, bêche-de-mer, and copra and cocoanut oil, were for some time the chief exports, but the cultivation of fruit, especially bananas and pine-apples, for export to Australia and New Zealand, has extended rapidly of late years, and the value of this export has of late been second only to that of sugar. Fiji was ceded by its chiefs to the British Crown, and the islands were formally annexed by Sir Hercules Robinson, on Oct. 10, 1874. Sir Arthur Gordon (now Lord Stanmore), the first Governor, landed in the colony in June, 1875. The Governor is appointed by the Crown, and is assisted by an Executive Council, consisting of three official members. Laws are passed by a Legislative Council, of which the Governor is president, and which contains six official and six unofficial members, all nominated by the Crown. Native administration is carried on through the chiefs under the Governor's supervision. The population in Dec., 1897) was 121,798; comprising 99,773 native Fijians, 12,025 Indian immigrants, 3,401 Europeans, and some Polynesians, half-castes, and Chinese.

In 1899 a European battalion of volunteers was raised, armed with the Martini-Enfield rifle.

Public income, 1897	£74,492
Public expenditure, 1897	73,232
Public debt, 1896	213,256
(of which £97,556 is to the Imperial Government, bearing no interest)	
Imports from British Colonies, 1897	242,106
Exports to British Colonies, 1897	415,836
Total imports, 1897	248,748
Total exports, 1897	431,860

CAPITAL, Suva, in the island of Viti Levu.

Governor and Colonial Secretary, Sir George Thomas Michael O'Brien, K.C.M.G. (and £300 as High Comm. of Western Pacific)	£2,200
Chief Justice, Hon. Sir Henry S. Berkeley (and £500 as Chief Judicial Commr., Western Pacific)	900
Attorney-Gen., Hon. John Symonds Udal	500
Receiver-General and Assist. Col. Sec., Hon.	600
Chief Med. Officer, Hon. Bolton G. Corney	600
Commissioner for Lands, Hon. John Berry	500
Native Commissioner, Hon. W. L. Allardyce	450
Agent-Gen. of Immigration, John Forster	375
Chief Police Magistrate, H. Hunter	400
Registrar of Supreme Court, John Langford	400
Collector Customs, J. K. M. Ross	400
Sheriff & Command. of armed Constabulary, Col. Claude Francis .... and fees	400

Postmaster, L. J. Walker £300
Registrar-Gen. and of Titles, M. Dods 300

Suva is 11,000 miles from London : transit from London *via* Vancouver, about 33 days.

Telegrams *sent by post* from Sydney or Auckland.

BRITISH NEW GUINEA

Papua or New Guinea, the largest island in the world after Australia, extends for 1,490 miles from N.W. to S.E. between the equator and lat. 12° S. and between E. long. 130° 50' and 154° 30'. Its greatest breadth is 430 miles, and its area about 306,000 sq. miles. The N.W. half, to the W. of 141° E. long., belongs to Holland, which annexed it in the 16th century. The E. portion was independent until 1884, when it was divided between Great Britain and Germany. The colony of British New Guinea comprises the southern and south-eastern shores of the island, from the 141st meridian of east longitude eastward as far as East Cape, and thence north-westward as far as the 8th parallel of south latitude in the neighbourhood of Mitre Rock, together with the territory lying south of a line from Mitre Rock, proceeding along the said 8th parallel to the 147th degree of east longitude, then in a straight line in a north-westerly direction to the point of intersection of the 6th parallel of south latitude and of the 144th degree of east longitude, and continuing in a west-north-westerly direction to the point of intersection of the 5th parallel of south latitude and of the 141st degree of east longitude, together with the Trobriand, Woodlark, D'Entrecasteaux, and Louisiade groups of islands, and all other islands lying between the 8th and the 12th parallels of south latitude, and between the 141st and the 155th degrees of east longitude, and not forming part of the Colony of Queensland ; and furthermore, including all islands and reefs lying in the Gulf of Papua to the northward of the 8th parallel of south latitude.

The extent of territory is about 90,000 square miles, about half as large again as England, with a small population, the number of which is at present unascertained, but is probably not over 150,000. All tropical trees and fruit grow abundantly. The most important export is bêche-de-mer ; pearl-shell, copra, gum, and sandal-wood are also exported, and alluvial gold has been found.

The territory was at first taken over as a Protectorate under the management of a Special Commissioner ; but on the Colonies of Queensland, New South Wales, and Victoria undertaking to guarantee £15,000 a year for the cost of administration, which was further secured by a Queensland Act, the Queen's sovereignty was formally proclaimed on the 4th Sept. 1888, and the territory was constituted as a colony under the name of British New Guinea. It is governed by a Lieut.-Governor, with a nominated Legislative Council consisting of not less than two other persons.

The ports of entry are Samarai, Port Moresby, and Daru.

CAPITAL, Port Moresby. Pop., about 1,500.
Revenue, 1895–6, £6,547 ; Expenditure, £15,000
Imports, 1895–6, £34,521 ; Exports, 19,401
Imports from United Kingdom, 1898 1,937
Exports to United Kingdom, 1898 190
Lieut.-Gov., Geo. Ruthven Le Hunte,C.M.G. 1,500
Chief Judic. Officer, Hon. F. P. Winter,C.M.G. 1,000
Government Sec., Hon. Anthony Musgrave 700
Treasurer & Customs, Hon. D. Ballantine . 350
Resident Magistrate and Medical Officer, Port Moresby, Hon. Dr. J. A. Blaney 400

Resident Magistrates : Central Div., Dr. J. A.
Blaney, £375 ; *Western*, B. A. Hely, £500 ; *Eastern*, M. H. Moreton, £400 ; *Louisiades*, A. M. Campbell £300
Commandant of Constabulary, Capt. A. W.
Butterworth 3 0

Port Moresby is 12,000 miles from London.

PACIFIC ISLANDS.

British Protection has been declared at various times over islands and groups of islands in the Pacific Ocean, the general government thereof being vested in a High Commissioner (the Governor of Fiji) who is assisted by Deputy Commissioners. The principal groups are : —

(1) *The Cook Islands Federation*, a group of 6 islands, with a few islets, situate in the Eastern Pacific between 18° 15' to 21° 47' S. lat. and 157° to 160° W. long. The population numbers about 8,000 Natives, and 150 to 200 of European and other nationalities. The chief island is Raratonga, about 23 miles in circumference, with a population of 2,500. The chief products are coffee, copra, and lime-juice, oranges and other tropical fruits. The Exports in 1896 were £23,709—the Imports £23,068. The Chief of the Federal Government is Makea Takau—Ariki Vaine (Queen) of Avarua in Raratonga. *British Res.*, Col. Gudgeon (Raratonga).

(2) *The British Solomon Islands*, protected since 1893, and consisting of Guadalcanar, Malayta, and other islands situated in about 8° S. and 120° W., with a total area of about 8,500 sq. miles. The revenue in 1898-9 was £1,257 and the expenditure £1,030 ; the exports were valued at £16,818. The seat of government is Tulagi. Under the Anglo-German Agreement of 1899 respecting Samoa those of the German Solomon Islands east and south-east of Bougainville were ceded to the United Kingdom. This acquisition consists of the islands of Choiseul and Ysabel, Lord Howe's Group, and many smaller islands. *Resident Commissioner*, Charles M. Woodford............ £500

(3) *The Gilbert Group*, situated round the Equator in about 173° E, and consisting of 15 islands (Makin, Taritari, Apia, Tarawa, Maiana, Apamana, Kuria, Nonouti, Peru, Byron, Aurai, Tamana, Drummond, Ocean, and Pleasant). Their total area is about 166 sq. miles, with a population of about 35,000. *Resident Commissioner*, W. Telfer Campbell £400

(4) *The Tonga, or Friendly, Islands*, the possession of which came about in 1899 under a treaty with Germany (whereby all claims to the Samoan archipelago were withdrawn by Great Britain).

These islands are situated in the Southern Pacific to the E.S.E. of Fiji, and 390 miles therefrom, with an area of 385 square miles, and 17,500 inhabitants. The limits of the group are between 15° and 23° 30' south, and 173° and 177° west, and it consists of three divisions, called Tongatabu, Haapai, and Vavau. At the former is the seat of government, the king being Jioaji Tubou II., who was born 18 June, 1874. Soil generally is fertile ; the principal exports are copra, green fruit, kava, and whale oil. Most of the imports come from British ports, whilst the majority of the export trade is shipped in foreign bottoms.

The imports in 1895 amounted to £87,240, and the exports to £113,240, the share of British Colonies being £79,119 and £23,249 respectively. *Deputy Commissioner*, R. B. Leefe £440

(5) *The Ellice Islands*, eight in number (St. Augustine's, Speiden or Lynx, Hudson, Nether-

land, De Peysten, Ellice, Mitchell and Sophia), with some islets in 6° and 11° S. and 176° to 180° E.

(6) *The Phœniz Islands,* seven in number (Wilkes, Gardner, Birnie, Hull, Enderbury, Phœnix, and Sidney) between 2° 30′ and 4° 30′ S. and 171° and 174° W.

(7) *The Union Group* of six islands and some islets (Duke of York, Duke of Clarence, Bowditch, Swain, Danger and Nassau).

(8) There are also a large number of scattered groups and isolated islands.

The functions of the High Commissioner, in addition to the government of the Protected Islands, are to carry out the provisions of certain Acts of the Imperial Parliament; the New Hebrides and various other ·small groups come under his jurisdiction.

High Commissioner, The Governor of Fiji	£300
Chief Judicial do., The Chief Justice of Fiji...	300
Sec. to High Oommission, Merton King	400
Registrar, J. Langford	500

The British Customs Tariff (1899–1900).

IMPORT DUTIES to countervail EXCISE DUTY upon BRITISH BEER.

	£	s.	d.
Beer called mum, spruce, or black beer and Berlin white beer, and other preparations, whether fermented or not fermented, of a character similar to mum, spruce, or black beer, the worts of which were before fermentation of a specific gravity not exceeding 1,215°, for every 36 gallons	1	8	0
Exceeding 1,215° for every 36 gallons	1	12	10
Beer of any other description the worts of which were before fermentation of a specific gravity of 1,055°, for every 36 gallons	0	7	0
And so in proportion for any difference in gravity.			

IMPORT DUTIES to countervail EXCISE DUTY upon BRITISH SPIRITS.

	£	s.	d.
Spirits and strong waters: For every gallon, computed at hydrometer proof, of spirits of any description (except perfumed spirits), including naphtha or methylic alcohol purified so as to be potable, and mixtures and preparations containing spirits ... proof gal.	0	10	10
Additional on spirits imported in bottle, enumerated and tested, and sweetened spirits imported in bottle, unenumerated and tested ... proof gal.	0	1	0
Liqueurs, cordials, or other preparations containing spirits, in bottle, entered in such a manner as to indicate that the strength is not to be tested ... gal.	0	15	8
Perfumed spirits ... ,,	0	17	3
Additional if imported in bottle ..... ,,	0	1	0
Spirits, methylated in bond .. proof gal.	0	0	4
Chloroform ... lb.	0	3	1
Chloral hydrate ... ,,	0	1	3
Cocoa and chocolate, in the manufacture of which spirit has been used, in addition to any other duty to which such cocoa or chocolate is at present liable	0	0	0½
Collodion ... gal.	1	5	0
Confectionery, in the manufacture of which spirit has been used, in addition to any other duty to which such confectionary is a present liable ...lb.	0	0	0½
Ether, Acetic ... ,,	0	1	10
,, Butyric ... gal.	0	15	8
,, Sulphuric ... ,,	1	6	2
Ethyl, Bromide ... lb.	0	1	0
,, Chloride ... gal.	0	15	8
,, Iodide of ... ,,	0	13	7
Methylic alcohol, purified so as to be potable, *see* Spirits and strong waters.			

Naphtha alcohol, purified so as to be potable, *see* Spirits and strong waters.

	£	s.	d.
Soap, transparent, in the manufacture of which spirit has been used ...lb.	0	0	3

IMPORT DUTY to countervail STAMP DUTY on BRITISH-MADE ARTICLES.

	£	s.	d.
Playing Cards ...doz. packs.	0	3	9

ORDINARY IMPORT DUTIES.

	£	s.	d.
Cocoa, raw... ...lb.	0	0	1
,, husks and shells ...cwt.	0	2	0
,, or chocolate, ground, prepared, or in any way manufactured...lb.	0	0	2
,, butter ...lb.	0	0	2
Coffee, raw... ...cwt.	0	14	0
,, kiln-dried, roasted, or ground, lb.	0	0	2
Chicory, raw or kiln-dried ...cwt.	0	13	3
,, roasted or ground ...lb.	0	0	2
,, (or other vegetable substances) and coffee roasted and ground, mixed ...lb.	0	0	2
Fruits, dried : currants ...cwt.	0	2	0
,, ,, figs, fig-cake, plums not preserved in sugar, prunes and raisins ...cwt.	0	7	0
Tea ... ...lb.	0	0	4
Tobacco, unmanuf., containing 10 lbs. or more of moisture in every 100 lbs. weight thereof...lb.	0	2	8
,, unmanuf., containing less than 10 lbs. of moisture in every 100 lbs weight thereof...lb.	0	3	0
,, manufactured, Cigars ... ,,	0	5	0
,, Cavendish or Negrohead ... ,,	0	3	10
,, Snuff, containing in every 100 lbs weight thereof more than 13 lbs. of moisture...lb.	0	3	2
,, Snuff. containing in every 100 lbs. weight thereof not more than 13 lbs. of moisture lb.	0	3	10
,, Other manufactured tobacco, and Cavendish or Negrohead manufactured in bond from unmanufactured tobacco . lb.	0	3	5
Wine, not exc. 30° of proof spirit...gal.	0	1	3
,, exc. 30°, but not exc. 42° ...gal.	0	3	0
Every degree or part of a degree beyond the highest above charged an additional duty of ...gal.	0	0	3
Degree not to include fractions of the next higher degree.			
Wine includes lees of wine.			
Additional duty on sparkling wine imported in bottle ...gal.	0	2	6
,, ,, on still wine imported in bottle ...gal.	0	1	0

THE West Indies are an immense number of islands and islets, some of them mere rocks, extending from 10° to 27° North, and from 59° 30′ to 85° West. They are divided by geographers into (1) the Bahamas, (2) the Greater Antilles, and (3) the Lesser Antilles, of which the last named are subdivided into the Leeward and Windward Islands. The islands lying off the coasts of South America and Central America respectively form two separate groups in addition to those already mentioned. The total area of the West Indies is probably about 95,000 square miles, of which the Greater Antilles occupy not less than 83,000 square miles. The prevalent character of the islands is bold and mountainous. The highest points are about 8,000 feet above the sea-level, and several of the islands contain active volcanoes, while nearly all of them show signs of volcanic action. The mean yearly temperature of the islands is about 78°, but that of the higher lands is often much less. The seasons alternate from drought to moisture, and in most parts of the archipelago there are two wet and two dry seasons. On the whole it may be said that the climate is generally healthy, and between the months of November and May in many of the islands it is delightful. The vegetable productions are both varied and abundant, the principal articles of commerce including sugar, bananas, oranges, coffee, cocoa, cotton, pimento, nutmegs, indigo, tobacco, maize, guava, ginger, cocoa-nuts, annotto, aloes, sassafras, the castor-oil tree, cabbage-tree, and medicinal drugs. Of the more common fruits there are the pine-apple, pomegranate, cocoa-nut, oranges, lemons, limes, citrons, the mango, shaddock, papaw, banana, and plantain. Yams, sweet potatoes, and manioc also grow freely. The mountains in the greater islands furnish a varied abundance of timber, including mahogany, cedar, lignum-vitæ, iron-wood, Indian-fig, well adapted for cabinet-work, shipbuilding, and other arts. Indian corn yields abundant crops almost everywhere, and rice in the island of Trinidad. The total population is nearly 4,000,000, of whom above half are negroes, while the remainder are chiefly mulattoes. The islands at the time of their discovery, were inhabited partly by the Caribs, a fierce and warlike race, and partly by a less savage race known as the Arrowauks ; but both these native Indian races are now practically extinct. By far the largest of the West Indies are the magnificent islands of Cuba (see p. 590), and Hispaniola (see pp. 550, 565).

The first spot on which Columbus landed in the New World in 1492 was San Salvador, one of the Bahamas. On the same voyage Cuba and Hispaniola were discovered, and the other islands very shortly afterwards. For some time the West Indies remained in the undisputed possession of Spain, subject only to occasional visits from French and English ships. At the commencement of the 17th century, however, the English French, and Dutch began to form settlements, and to import negroes from West Africa to work the plantations ; and whenever war broke out in Europe it spread to the West Indies. They are now divided as follows :—*British :* Jamaica, Turks and Caicos Is. ; all the Bahamas ; Antigua, Montserrat, Nevis, St. Christopher, Dominica, the Virgin and the Cayman Islands, Grenada, St. Vincent, St. Lucia, Barbados, Trinidad, Tobago (which is now a ward of Trinidad) ; and the islands off the coast of British Honduras. *Spanish :* Isle de Pinos, Bieque, and Culebra. *French :* Martinique, Guadaloupe, Deseada, Marie Galanta, Les Saintes, St. Bartholòmew, and St. Martin (the last partly Dutch). *Dutch :* St. Eustatius, Saba, Bonaire, Curaçao, Aruba. *Danish :* Santa Cruz, St. Thomas, St. John. *U.S.A. :* Cuba and Puerto Rico. *Venezuelan :* Coche Cuagua, Tortuga, and Margarita. *Independent :* Hispaniola, divided into Hayti and San Domingo. The British Islands have an area of about 13,750 square miles, and a population of 1,350,000. In 1898 a most disastrous hurricane swept over the group of islands, almost all of which were affected, while St. Vincent, Barbados, St. Lucia, and Trinidad were practically devastated. On August 7th, 1899, a further hurricane devastated the island of Montserrat, doing damage also to St. Kitts, Nevis, and Antigua. The island of Puerto Rico (U.S.A.), Guadaloupe (French), and Santa Cruz (Danish) also suffered severely. Relief Funds were opened at the Mansion House, London, in 1898 and 1899, and sums of money were also received from parts of Greater Britain. A Parliamentary Grant-in-aid, to the amount of £65,000, was made in the Supplementary Estimates for the Civil Services, and under the Colonial Loans Act, 1899, certain sums were advanced to cope with the depression which the distress following upon the hurricanes had so greatly increased.

Domestic imports from United Kingdom, 1898 :		Total exports to United Kingdom, 1898 :	
Apparel, &c. ..£203,533	Machinery .. 44,210	Cocoa........£446,498	Rum 106,223
Cottons 450,244	Metals 125,138	Coffee 92,379	Spices 97,614
Leather 82,974	Woollens .. 65,202	Dye-Woods .. 33,820	Sugar 229,211
	——£1,839,980		——£1,283,413

JAMAICA,[*]

aboriginally Xaymaca, or Land of Wood and Water—an island situate in the Caribbean Sea, about 90 miles to the south of Cuba, within 17° 43′—18° 32′ North lat. and 76° 11′—78° 21′ W. long. It is the largest and the most valuable of the British West Indian Islands, being 144 miles in length and 49 in extreme breadth, containing an area of 4,193 square miles, and a population, in April, 1891, of 639,491, shewing an increase during the previous decade of 58,687; in 1891 the whites numbered 14,692; coloured, 121,955; blacks, 488,624, and there were a number of Coolies and Chinese. The estimated population on March 13, 1899, was 730,000.

Jamaica was discovered on May 3, 1494, by Columbus, who called it St. Jago. It was taken possession of by the Spaniards in 1509; but in 1655 a British expedition, sent out by Oliver Cromwell, under Penn and Venables, attacked the island, which capitulated after a trifling resistance. In 1670 it was formally ceded to England by the Treaty of Madrid.

From the sea-level on all sides of Jamaica a series of ridges gradually ascend towards the central ranges, dividing the large rivers, and attaining, in the culminating Western Peak of the Blue Mountains, an elevation of 7,360 feet. From these mountains at least 70 streams descend to the north and south shores, but none are navigable except the Black River, and that only for small craft. There are several excellent harbours, and the island is intersected by good roads. There are 185 miles of railway open. Telegraph stations and post-offices are established in every town and in very many villages; the number of accounts open in the savings banks was 31,870 (1899). Most of the staple products of tropical climates are raised. Sugar and rum are manufactured and exported; the latter is still counted the best in the world; and the coffee raised in certain districts of the Blue Mountains fetches the highest price that is given in the London market. There is an extensive trade in fruits, chiefly bananas and oranges, with the United States. Maize and Indian corn grow luxuriantly. The Guinea grass, from four to six feet in height, grows wild, and is superior to any other for pasturage, while the woods furnish an abundance of rich dye-stuffs, drugs, and spices, and the forests abound in the rarest of cabinet woods. The Governor is assisted by a Privy Council not to exceed 8 members; the Legislative Council consists of the Governor, the senior military officer, the Colonial Secretary, Attorney-General, Director of Public Works, and the Collector-General (all *ex-officio*), and of such other persons, not exceeding 10, as the Queen or the Governor provisionally may appoint, called Nominated Members, and 14 elected by the people, being one for each parish of the island. The island is divided into three counties, Surrey in the east, Middlesex in the centre, and Cornwall in the west. The principal city is Kingston, the seat of government and the largest port and town, with Port Royal, the naval station, pop. 46,542; the next in importance are Spanish Town, pop. about 5,000, and Montego Bay, 4,803.

Under the Colonial Loans Act the sum of £453,000 was allocated to the Colony; of this amount £150,000 was advanced in aid of revenue;

[*] The Government of Jamaica publishes annually a Handbook of the Island, full of information respecting the history and *personnel* of the island.

£190,000 for railway purposes: £40,000 for waterworks, and £65,000 for public works.

Public revenue, 1897–98	£672,535
Expenditure from income, 1897–98	765,948
Expenditure from loans, 1897–98	30,801
Public debt in 1898	1,994,184
Total imports, 1898–99	1,814,793
Total exports, 1898–99	1,662,543

The chief articles of export in order of importance are: Fruit, 41·4; coffee, 10·5; sugar, 9·8; dye-woods, 8·8; and rum, 6·1. The chief customers are the U.S.A., 59·1, and the U.K., 20·6, the imports being from the U.K. 44·7, U.S.A. 45·1.

Captain-General and Governor-in-Chief, Sir Augustus W. L. Hemming, K.C.M.G.	£5,000
Private Sec., Eyre Hutson.	
Comdg. Troops, Mj.-Gen. H. J. Hallowes.	
Colonial Secretary, Hon. Fredk. Evans, C.M.G.	1,300
Assist. Colonial Secretary, Philip C. Cork	620
Auditor-Gen., L. J. Bertram	800
Director Pub. Wks., Val. G. Bell, C.E.	1,200
Director Pub. Gardens, Wm. Fawcett, B.SC.	600
Emigration Agent in India, A. Stewart	500
Insp.-Gen. Police and Prisons (vacant)	850
Inspector of Schools, Thomas Capper, B.A.	700
Sup. Medical Officer, C. B. Mosse, C.B.	1,200
Protector of Immigrants, E. W. Pigou	400
Treasurer, Hon. Samuel Paynter Musson	800
Postmaster, G. H. Pearce	700
Collector-General, Hon. James Allwood	825
Collector of Customs, Kingston, Chas. Goldie	750
Government Printer, J. C. Ford	500
Chief Justice and Keeper of Records, His Hon. Sir Fielding Clarke	2,000
Puisne Judge, Hon. Ernest A. Northcote, LL.D	1,200
Second ditto, Hon. Chas. F. Lumb, LL.D.	1,000
Registrar Supreme Court, O'Con. de Cordova	600
Attorney-Gen., H. R. Pipcon Schooles, LL.B.	1,500
Solicitor-Gen., Thos. Bancroft Oughton	500
Crown Solicitor, A. W. Farquharson	820
Administrator-Gen. and Trustee in Bankruptcy, John Nethersole	400
Registrar-Gen. and Deputy Keeper of Records, S. P. Smeeton	700

Kingston, 5,000 miles; transit, 16 days. Telegrams, 3s. per word.

TURKS AND CAICOS (Cayos or Keys).

These islands geographically form a sort of annexe of the Bahama group, from which Government they were separated in 1848. In 1874 they were annexed to Jamaica, from the north-west of which they are distant about 430 miles. They have an area of about 223 square miles. The population in 1891 was 4,744, of which the principal island, Grand Turk, contains 2,500.

A Commissioner administers the affairs of the Settlement, assisted by a Legislative Board. This Board has sole control of local finance, and passes local ordinances; but the supreme legislative body is the Legislative Council of Jamaica.

Revenue, 1897-8 (excluding surplus 1897 £2,458)	£7,232
Expenditure, 1897-8	8,061
Total imports, 1897-8, £27,067; exports	24,811

Commissioner, Edward J. Cameron	600
Judge Sup. Court, G. P. St. Aubyn	500

THE BAHAMAS,

a chain of islands lying between 21° 42′—27° 34′ N. lat. and 72° 40′—79° 5′ W. long. The group consists of about twenty inhabited islands, and an immense number of islets and rocks, comprising an area of about 5,794 square miles, and a population in 1895 of 50,599, the most part black, whites, and the rest descendants of liberated Africans. The principal islands are: New Providence (containing the capital, Nassau), San Salvador, Abaco, Grand Bahama, Long Island, Eleuthera, Mayaguana, Harbour Island, Great Inagua, and Andros Islands. Originally settled by Englishmen, the Bahamas were, in 1781, surprised by the Spanish, but at the Peace of Versailles were restored to the English. The climate is salubrious, and in winter Nassau, which is outside the tropics, is frequented by many Americans. The chief industry is spongegathering; the exports of sponge in 1898 were valued at £97,512. The fruit trade, principally with the United States, is also important, the total value of pineapples exported in 1898 being £24,360; bananas, cocoanuts, tomatoes, and other fruit and vegetables are also exported. Mahogany, lignum-vitæ, mastic, iron-wood, ebony, logwood, and satinwood are found throughout the islands; tobacco, castor-oil plants, and cotton flourish, but enterprise is lacking to encourage these industries. The fibre industry may now be considered as fairly established, the estimated land under cultivation of the fibre plant being about 20,000 acres. The imports are chiefly food-stuffs, wines, spirits, cotton, silk and worsted fabrics, and hardware.

The Government is vested in a Governor, aided by an Executive Council of 9 members, a Legislative Council of 9 members, and a Representative Assembly of 29 members.

CAPITAL, Nassau.

Amount of public revenue in 1898	£74,367
Amount of public expenditure in 1898	64,672
Public debt, 1898	118,426
Total imports, 1898, £238,336; exports	174,850
Governor, Sir Gilbert T. Carter, K.C.M.G.	£2,000
Priv. Sec. H. Mostyn.	
Colonial Sec., J. K. G. T. Spencer-Churchill	700
Chief Justice, Sir Ormond Drimmie Malcolm	800
Receiver-Gen., Hesketh H. J. Bell	500
Postmaster, J. A. Thompson	300
Surveyor-Gen., William Miller	400
Provost-Marshal & Commandt. of Constabulary, C. A. Fraser	500
Attorney-Gen., W. R. Davies	400
Stipendiary & Circuit Magistrates, J. M. Rae; R. S. Johnston each	500

Nassau is distant 4000 miles; transit, 14 days. Telegrams 2s. 5d. per word.

THE LEEWARD ISLANDS.

The Leeward Islands under British authority consist of the 5 presidencies of (1) Antigua, with Barbuda and Redonda; (2) St. Christopher and Nevis, with Anguilla. (3) Dominica under Administrators; (4) Montserrat; and (5) the Virgin Islands, each having their own local legislature. These five presidencies make up the colony of the Leeward Islands, which is administered by a Governor, to whom the Administrators and Commissioners are subordinate, and which has also a general Legislative Council possessing concurrent legislative powers with the local Legislatures on certain subjects. The federal colony in 1891 contained 127,723 inhabitants (58,780 males and 68,943 females). The General Legislative Council consists of 10 nominated and 10 elective members.

Public revenue in 1898	£112,577
Expenditure, 1898 (excluding expenditure from Loans for Public Works)	138,612

Public debt, 1898	£300,121
Imports, 1898, £299,973; exports, 1898	286,493
Governor, Sir Francis Fleming, K.C.M.G.	£3,000
Private Sec.,	300
Colonial Sec., George Melville, C.M.G.	800
Chief Justice, Sir Henry Thomas Wrenfordsley, Knt.	1,500
Puisne Judge, John Martin Danavall	750
Do., C. Major (*acting*)	700
Attorney-General, William Henry Stoker	500
Assist. do., *St. Kitts*, G. K. J. Purcell	200
,, ,, *Dominica*, E. St. J. Branch	200
Auditor-General, E. A. Foster	600

Transit, 13 to 16 days. Telegrams, per word, to Antigua, 4s. 7d., Dominica 4s. 5d., St. Kitts-nevis, 4s. 11d.

(1) ANTIGUA (AND BARBUDA).

Antigua is the seat of government and residence of the Governor-in-Chief. It lies in 17° 6' N. lat. and 61° 45' W. long., and is about 70 miles in circumference. Its area is nearly 108 square miles, equal to 68,980 acres, of which nearly 20,000 are under cultivation. The population (with Barbuda) in 1891 was 30,699, including 17,124 males and 19,575 females. Settled by the English in 1632, and granted to Lord Willoughby by Charles II., this is one of those islands which has always been more distinctively English. It was at one time a naval and military station of some importance. It is much less hilly and wooded than the other Leeward Islands. It is almost entirely given up to the cultivation of sugar, the export amounting to £101,106 in 1897; but it also exports rum, molasses, tamarinds, and arrowroot. In March, 1899, the Crown Colony system of government was instituted.

Public revenue in 1898	£39,663
Expenditure in 1898	55,586
Public debt, 1898	137,471
Imports, 1898, £43,829; exports, 1898	79,178
CAPITAL, St. John's, population	10,000
President & Island Sec. (the Col. Sec. of the Leeward Islands), George Melville, C.M.G.	£50
Auditor-Gen., E. A. Foster	600
Treasurer, W. D. Auchinleck	500
Magistrate, W. H. Whyham	400
Do., G. C. Evelyn	400

Barbuda is situated 30 miles N. of Antigua, of which it is a dependency, in lat. 17° 35' N., long. 61° 45' W. Area, 75 square miles. Population, 580. The island is flat and fertile, producing corn, cotton, pepper, and tobacco. It was formerly a possession of the Codrington family.

Magistrate, J. F. Smyth (*acting*)	£150

Redonda, a small island with a phosphate industry, has a population (1891) of 120.

(2) ST. CHRISTOPHER (ST. KITTS) AND NEVIS (WITH ANGUILLA).

These two islands, with their dependency of Anguilla, were severely visited by the hurricane of 1899. They were united in 1882 to form one presidency, and taken together they had a population (1891) of 47,062. St. Christopher, popularly called St. Kitts, is situated in lat. 17° 18 N. and long. 62° 48' W., about 46 miles to the west of Antigua: it comprises an area of 68 square miles, its greatest length being 28 miles, and greatest breadth about five and a half miles. It is one of the most effectively cultivated sugar islands in the West Indies, a continuous line of green estates sweeping up all round the coast from the sea towards the central cone, which rises to a height of nearly 4,000 feet. Sulphur is found in the mountains, but is not made an article of commerce.

CAPITAL, Basseterre, population (1891), 9,097 (males 4,110, females 4,987).

Nevis (separated from St. Kitts by a strait some 3 miles wide) is but a single mountain rising 3,200 feet above the sea, and has an area of 50 square miles, with a population in 1891 of 13,087. Sugar, rum, and molasses are the only exports, but some proprietors have extensive plantations of the lime, and coffee is being grown. Chief town, Charlestown. Population (1891) 838.

Anguilla (or Little Snake) is about 60 miles N.W. of St. Kitts, 16 miles in length, and varies in breadth from 3 to 1½ miles, containing an area of 35 square miles. Population, 1891, 3,699, of whom hardly any are white. Salt, obtained from a small lake in the centre of the island, and phosphate of lime are the principal productions, besides cattle and garden stock.

Public revenue in 1898	£40,430
Expenditure in 1898	44,659
Public debt, 1899	74,450
Imports, 1898, £122,968; exports 1898	138,222
Administrator, C. T. Cox	£700 to 900
Assistant Treasurer, H. Lockhart	250
Magistrates, { F. S. Wigley	400
St. Kitts { Captain A. Roger	350
Nevis R. B. Roden	250
Anguilla, N. Rat	220

(3) DOMINICA,

The largest island of the colony, and the loftiest of the Lesser Antilles, is situate between 15° 20'—15° 45' N. lat. and 61° 13'—61° 30' W. long., 95 miles S. of Antigua, and is about 29 miles long and 16 broad, comprising an area of 291 sq. miles, or 186,240 acres, of which about 55,000 acres are cultivated, the major part being difficult of access. It is of volcanic origin and very mountainous and picturesque, abounding in rivulets well stocked with fish. Sulphur, thrown out of the soufrières, is very plentiful; and good game is abundant. Land may be purchased at about 10s. an acre. Population (1891), 26,841 (males 12,059, females 14,782). The natives still speak a French patois, resulting from their former connection with France. The soil is good and the principal productions are cocoa, sugar, coffee, molasses, rum, lime-juice, fruit, spices, and cabinet woods. The climate varies greatly according to the altitude: on the high lands it is excellent, but in the lowlands and the coast districts the mass of vegetable matter of various kinds keeps it unduly moist. There is a Legislative Assembly which controls local finance, and administration, half the members of which are elective. The principal town is Roseau, on the south-west coast; population (1891) 5,186.

Public revenue in 1898	£24,569
Public expenditure in 1898	24,643
Public debt raised or authorised, 1898	70,900
Imports, 1898, £31,346 ; exports, 1898	63,912
Administrator, H. J. Hesketh-Bell	£700 to 900
Treasurer, W. H. Porter	300
Colonial Engineer, C. V. Bellamy	350
Magistrates, W. Coull ; W. H. Roper ; and R. F. Garraway	each 300

(4) MONTSERRAT

which was almost entirely devastated by the hurricane of Aug, 7, 1899, is situated in 16° 42' N. lat. and 62° 13' W. long., 26 miles S.W. of Antigua. It is about 12 miles in length and 8 in breadth, comprising an area of 47 square miles, and in 1891 a population of 11,762 (5,331 males, 6,431 females). It was settled by Englishmen, but conquered and held by the French, and only finally assigned to Great Britain in 1784. It is justly considered one of the most healthy and beautiful of the Antilles : it contains an active soufrière and several hot springs. About two-thirds of the island are mountainous, the rest well cultivated. The lime-tree is largely grown ; the Montserrat company alone has a plantation of 600 acres, and annually exports about 100,000 gallons of lime-juice, valued at £7,426. Sugar is the crop of greatest importance, the export in 1897 reaching £5,087, but there are no first class sugar estates. The chief town is Plymouth, with a population (1891) of 1,475.

Public revenue, 1898, £6,199; expenditure, £11,935	
Public debt, 1898	17,300
Total imports, 1898, £15,161 ; exports, 1898	13,849
Commr. & Treasurer, W. M. Gordon (*acting*)	500

(5) THE VIRGIN ISLANDS,

a group of islands belonging chiefly to Great Britain and Denmark, form a connecting link between the Greater and Lesser Antilles. They form a thickly studded archipelago of islands and rocks, the majority of which are mountainous. Such of the islands as are British became so in 1666; the principal are—Tortola (the largest), situate in 18° 27' N. lat. and 64° 40' W. long., Virgin Gorda, and Anegada. The area of the British possessions is 58 square miles, and the population in 1891 was 4,639. There is good pasturage for cows, sheep, and goats. Sugar and cotton are raised in small quantities, and fishing and poultry-rearing are also carried on. A valuable mine of copper has been worked at Virgin Gorda in past years. The capital of the group is Roadtown, on the south side of Tortola; population (1891) 403.

Public revenue, 1898, £1,715; expenditure, £1,783	
Imports, 1898, £3,943 ; exports, 1898	3,855
Commissioner & Treasurer, N. G. Cookman	308

THE WINDWARD ISLANDS.

The Windward, or Southern, group of the West Indian islands includes Barbados, St. Lucia, St. Vincent, the Grenadines, Grenada, and Tobago. Of these, Barbados is a separate colony with its own governor, and Tobago is attached to Trinidad. The Government of the Windward Islands is made up of the three colonies of Grenada (the seat of government), St. Vincent, and St. Lucia, with their dependencies, the Grenadines being divided between Grenada and St. Vincent. There is one governor for the three islands ; but there is no General Legislative Council as in the Leeward Islands, and no common tariff or treasury. There is a Court of Appeal, consisting of the judges of the three colonies and of Barbados, a common Audit, and a common Lunatic Asylum ; but, with this exception, each island retains its own institutions, and in the governor's absence is governed by an Administrator subordinate to him. The aggregate population (1891) was 135,976; and the total area 508 sq. miles.

Governor and Commander-in-Ch., Sir Alfred Moloney, K.C.M.G.	£2,500
Private Secretary, and Clerk of the Councils, Grenada, M. H. De la Poer Beresford	425
Aide-de-Camp, Lieut. F. Owen-Lewis I.S.C.	

Transit, about 14 days. Parcels, 3 lbs., 1s. ; 7 lbs., 2s. ; 11lbs., 3s. : telegrams, per word. Grenada, 4s. 11d.; St. Lucia, 4s. 9d.; St. Vincent, 4s. 9d.

GRENADA (AND THE GRENADINES).

Grenada is situated between the parallels of 12° 30'—11° 58' N. lat. and 61° 20'—61° 35' W. long., and is about 21 miles in length and 12 miles in breadth ; it is about 95 miles north of Trinidad, 63 miles S.S.W. of St. Vincent, and 100 miles S. W. of Barbados. It contains about 85,120 acres, of which about 20,418 are cultivated, and a population (including some of the Grenadines) of 53,209 (1891). The country is mountainous and very picturesque, and the climate is healthy. The Grand Etang, a lake on the summit of a mountain ridge about 1,740 feet above the level of the sea, and Lake Antoine, are the most remarkable natural curiosities. Grenada was discovered by Columbus in 1498, and, named Conception. The colony was founded by the French in 1650, and surrendered to the British in 1762 ; in 1779 it was retaken by the French but in 1783 it was ceded by the Treaty of Versailles to Great Britain, in whose possession it has since remained. The soil is very fertile, and cocoa, spices, sugar, rum, cotton, coffee, and large quantities of fruit are grown. The export of cocoa (or cacao) was 83,150 cwts. (value £227,654) in 1898, and of nutmeg 3,842 cwts. (value £19,740) with 528 cwts. of mace (value £2,344). The forests are rich in many valuable timbers, particularly bullet wood, locust, mahogany, white cedar, and galba; and vanilla and several varieties of gum-yielding trees are indigenous. Turtle are caught and exported, and whales are met with, especially among the Grenadines. The imports chiefly comprise dry goods, bread-stuffs, hardware, &c. The Legislative Council consists of 14 members, seven of whom are officials.

St. George's, on the south-west coast, is the chief town, and possesses a good harbour and coaling station.

Public revenue in 1898	£62,875
Expenditure in 1898	57,612
Public debt, 1898	127,670
Total imports, 1898	210,783
Total exports, 1898	257,274

Colonial Secretary, Edward Rawle Drayton ... £600
Treasurer and Postmaster, C. Falconer Anton 450
Chief Justice, Charles James Tarring 1,000
Attorney-General, Leslie Probyn 700
Registrar, (vacant) 350

The GRENADINES are a chain of small islands lying between Grenada and St. Vincent (within which Governments they are included), comprising an area of 8,462 acres. The largest island is Carriacou, attached to the Government of Grenada, pop. 6,031.

ST. LUCIA,

the largest and most picturesque of the Windward group, situated in 13° 50' N. lat. and 60° 58' W. long., at a distance of about 90 miles W.N.W. of Barbados, 21 miles N. of St. Vincent and 21 miles S.E. of Martinique, is 24 miles in length with an extreme breadth of 12 miles ; it comprises an area of 233 square miles, with a population (in 1898) of 47,976. It possibly possesses the most interesting history of all the smaller islands. Fights raged hotly around it, and it constantly changed hands as between the English and the French. It is mountainous, its highest point being 3,145 feet above the sea, and for the most part is covered with forest and tropical vegetation. The principal exports are—Sugar (8,403,750 lbs. in 1898), molasses, cocoa—which is now being extensively cultivated—fuel and sticks.

St. Lucia at present stands alone amongst British sugar islands in having inaugurated the Central Factory system of sugar-growing. The chief places are Castries, the capital (pop. 1891, 8,000), and Soufrière (pop. 2,300).

Port Castries, one of the finest in the W. I., is the second naval station of the empire in these parts, and a coaling dépôt. In 1898, 557 steamers (tonnage, 757,170) entered Port Castries, and many British and foreign war ships coaled.

Public revenue in 1898	£67,628
Expenditure in 1898	60,975
Public debt, 1898	189,580
Total imports, 1898	271,595
Total exports, 1898	166,508

Administrator & Col. Sec., C. A. King-Harman, c.m.g. (and allowance £100) £800
Treasurer, D. G. Garraway 500
Chief Justice, Arthur Child 700
Attorney-General, E. G. Bennett.................. 400

ST. VINCENT,

an island about 95 miles west of Barbados, situate in 13° 10' N. lat. and 60° 57' W. long., is 18 miles in length and 11 in breadth, comprising an area of 140 square miles, and a population (in 1891), including dependencies, of 41,054. In 1846 a large number of Portuguese labourers, amounting to 2,400, immigrated hither, and proved a valuable acquisition to the island. St. Vincent is more thoroughly English than the two other islands of the group, though it has been the scene of warfare. In 1783 it was secured to Great Britain.

The chief products are sugar, molasses, rum, arrowroot, cassava, cocoa, coffee, cotton, and spices. The St. Vincent arrowroot has a specially good name in London. Its chief imports are linen, cotton, and woollen manufactures, American flour, fish, &c. The upset price of Crown lands is 20s. per acre, cash, or £2 if spread over 5 years, and steps are being taken to settle the labouring classes on lands specially acquired for the purpose. CAPITAL, Kingstown (pop. 1891, 4,547). Under the Colonial Loans Act (1899) the sum of £50,000 was advanced to aid in the development of the resources of the island ; a free grant of £25,000 was also made in the same year.

Public revenue in 1896	£26,487
Expenditure in 1896	27,591
Total imports, 1896	71,489
Total exports, 1896	67,392

Administrator, Colonial Sec., Registrar. Treas. & Collector of Customs, Harry L. Thompson, c.m.g. (and £100 table allowance) ... £700
Chief Justice & Vice-Chan., and Police Magistrate of Kingstown, J. B. Walker 800
Attorney-Gen., C. Ormond Hazell.

BARBADOS,

the most windward of the West India Islands, is situated in 13° 4' N., and longitude 59° 37' W. It is nearly 21 English miles long by 14 broad at the widest part, and comprises an area of 106,470 acres (about 166 square miles), about 100,000 acres being cultivated. The population in 1896 was estimated at 182,285, being about 1,114 to the square mile. The principal exports are sugar, molasses, and rum, and the imports rice, salted meat, corn, salted fish, butter, flour, and Indian corn meal. The island is the headquarters of H.M. forces in the West Indies, and a station of the West India and Panama Telegraph Company ; there is a railway across the island, a tramway through town and suburbs, and telephonic communication throughout the island. The deposits in the savings bank on Dec. 31, 1898, were £218,575. Liberal provision is made for elementary education, and Harrison's College, a school organised on the lines of the English public schools, places Barbados in the front of the West Indies as regards higher education. Unlike most of the neighbouring islands, Barbados has always remained in the possession of Great Britain, by which it was settled in 1625. In 1885 it was constituted a distinct government, with a Governor, aided by an Executive Council and an Executive Committee, a Legislative Council of nine members appointed by the Sovereign, and a House of Assembly of twenty-four members elected yearly on the basis of a moderate franchise.

The CAPITAL and port is Bridgetown (pop. about 21,000), on the shores of an open roadstead known as Carlisle Bay; Speightstown, on the west coast, is further to the north.

A free grant was made by the Imperial Government in 1899 to the amount of £40,000, and by the Colonial Loans Act the sum of £50,000 was advanced for the development of the resources of the island.

Revenue in 1898	£182,682
Expenditure in 1898	185,840
Public debt, 1898	414,000
Total imports, 1898	1,058,885
Total exports, 1898	789,231
Imports from the United Kingdom, 1898	428,063
Exports to United Kingdom, 1898	35,207

Governor, Sir James Shaw Hay, K.C.M.G.... £3,000
  (and table allowance, £600).
  Private Secretary & Aide-de-Camp, Lieut.
  A. H. Bathurst (R Berks. R.) 200
  Extra A.D.C., Lieut. H. Street (20 Hrs.)
Colonial Sec., Hon. Ralph C. Williams...... 750
Commander of Forces, Maj.-Gen. R. F. Butler.
  D.A.A.G., Maj. R. E. Hill, Lt.-Col.
  L. E. B. Booth.
  Commg. R.A., Maj. A. L. Molesworth.
  Commg. R.E., Lt.-Col. J. J. Leverson, C.M.G.
  Senior Medical Officer, Lieut.-Col. E. A. Roche, R.A.M.C.
Chief Judge, Sir William Conrad Reeves ... 1,500
Pres. of Legis. Council, Sir G. C. Pile, Knt.
Speaker, House of Assembly, Hon. F. J. Clarke
Attorney-General, W. H. Greaves, B.A., Q.C. 1,000
Solicitor-General, G. A. Goodman .... nil.
Treasurer, W. L. C. Phillips 600
Auditor-General, E. T. Grannum 600
Controller of Customs, P. L. Dillon 600
Inspector of Police, Maj. A. B. R. Kaye 400
Colonial Postmaster, W. P. Trimingham...... 600

Barbados, distant 3,635 miles; transit, 11 days. Telegrams, 5s. 0d. per word.

TRINIDAD AND TOBAGO.

TRINIDAD is the most southerly of the West India Islands. It is close to the north coast of the continent of S. America, the nearest point of Venezuela being 7 miles distant. It lies between 10° 3′—10° 50′ N. lat. and 61° 39′—62° W. long., and is about 55 miles in length by 40 in breadth, with an area of 1,750 square miles (200,000 acres cultivated), and an estimated population (1898) of 260,000. The island was discovered by Columbus in 1498, was colonized in 1588 by the Spaniards, and capitulated to the British under Abercromby in 1797. The chief town and port of entry, "Port of

Spain," is one of the finest towns in the West Indies. Other towns of importance are San Fernando (pop. 6,570), about 30 miles south of the capital; Princestown (pop. 4,197), and Arima (pop. 3,653). A remarkable phenomenon is the pitch lake near the village of La Brea, 110 acres in extent, containing an apparently inexhaustible supply; in 1898, 100,208 tons (£113,829) were exported. The soil is rich and productive, its most important products being sugar, cocoa, molasses, rum, and cocoa-nuts, and various kinds of timber and fruits. The chief exports (1898) were:—Sugar, 113,578,304 lbs.; rum, 86,513 gals.; molasses, 660,535 gals.; bitters, 33,989 gals.; and cocoa, 28,195,224 lbs. Coal is found in Manzanilla, and is indicated in other parts of the island. There are 81 miles of railway open, and harbour improvements, waterworks and sewage operations are being undertaken. The island is crossed by the telegraph wire of the West India and Panama Company, and by Government telegraph and telephone wires. Thirty-two steamers from Europe arrive every month, and four from the United States and Canada. The Government is vested in a Governor, an Executive Council, and a Legislative Council, all of whom are nominated by the Crown.

Under the Colonial Loans Act (1899) the sum of £110,000 was advanced by the Imperial Government to aid in the development of the resources of the island.

Revenue, 1898, £615,372; expenditure...	£640,952
Public debt, 1898	911,211
Total imports, 1898, £2,283,056; exports	2,310,133

Tobago, originally settled by the British, was held for some time by the French, and eventually was ceded to England in 1763. For many years it was included in the government of the Windward Islands; but in 1889 it was annexed to the Government of Trinidad, and on Jan. 1, 1899 it was constituted a ward of that island. It is between 11° 9′ N. lat. and 60° 43′ W. long., about 75 miles southeast of Grenada, 18 miles north-east of Trinidad, and 120 miles S.S.W. of Barbados; is 26 miles long and from 6 to 7½ broad, and has an area of 114 square miles, with a population (31st Dec. 1891) of 18,692. It is one of the most healthy of the West Indies; the temperature varies from 81° in February to 88° in September.

There are two towns in the island, viz., Scarborough (population 1,370) and Plymouth.

CAPITAL, Port of Spain, pop. 33,273. Transit, 13 days. Telegrams, per word, 5s. 3d.

Governor, Sir H. E. H. Jerningham,
  K.C.M.G. £5,000
Colonial Sec., Sir C. C. Knollys, K.C.M.G.,,, 1,200
Attorney-General, N. Nathan, Q.C. 1,300
Commandant Local Forces and Inspector-
  Gen. of Police, Sir F. Scott, K.C.B., K.C.M.G. 1,200
Auditor-General, H. C. Bourne 800
Chief Justice, Sir John Tankerville Goldney 1,800
Director of Public Works, W. Wrightson 1,000
Solicitor-General, Vincent Brown, Q.C. ... 582
First Puisne Judge, W. Llewellyn Lewis, M.A. 1,000
Second Puisne Judge, Thomas Baynes...... 1,000
Collector of Customs, R. H. McCarthy 900
Sub-Intendant, Crown Lands, G. F. Bushe 700
Receiver-Gen., D. B. Horsford 900
Protector of Immigrants, W. H. Coombs 1,000
Registrar-Gen., E. C. M. Stone 550
Postmaster-Gen., J. A. Bulmer 550
Harbour Master, Capt. J. B. Saunders...... 500
Surgeon-Gen., Fras. Hy. Lovell, C.M.G. ... 1,100
Inspector of Schools, R. G. Bushe, M.A. ... 700

THERE are two leading groups of British Colonies in Africa:—the South African colonies, which occupy the southern extremity of the continent, and are generally healthy and well adapted for European settlement; and the West African colonies, situated upon the tropical, fever-stricken coast to the north of the Equator. There are also the island of Mauritius and its dependencies, which are usually regarded as belonging to Africa, and the islands of Ascension and St. Helena in the Atlantic. And, besides the colonies, there are now large portions of the continent under British protection, viz., the Protectorates of Northern and Southern Nigeria, the Lagos Protectorate, and the Sierra Leone Protectorate on the West Coast; those of the East Africa Protectorate upon the East Coast; the British Central Africa Protectorate; the Uganda Protectorate, the Zanzibar Protectorate; the Witu Protectorate; the Bechuanaland Protectorate; and the territories of the British South Africa Company generally known as "Rhodesia." A portion of the Somali coast is a British Protectorate, and is administered by the Foreign Office; while the Port of Aden in Arabia and the Island of Socotra, also British, are comprehended in the Empire of India (see p. 476). The territories of the Royal Niger Company, whose administrative rights are taken over by Her Majesty's Government on Jan. 1, 1900, will from that date be divided between two administrations, to be termed Northern and Southern Nigeria; the former to include the Company's territories, north of Ida on the Niger, the latter to consist of the Company's Southern territories, together with what has hitherto been known as the Niger Coast Protectorate.

SOUTH AFRICA.

The South African Colonies are the Cape of Good Hope or Cape Colony, Natal, and Basutoland; and Her Majesty exercises a Protectorate over part of Bechuanaland, and the territories of the British South Africa Company. The first among the colonies in wealth and importance is the great self-governing colony of the Cape. Further along the coast to the north-east is the self-governing colony of Natal, which, since Dec. 30, 1897, includes the former Crown Colony of Zululand and the territory of Amatongaland, which extends to the Portuguese territory of Delagoa Bay. Inland, to the west of Zululand and Delagoa Bay, is Swaziland, the administration of which is under the Government of the South African Republic in accordance with the convention of 1894 between Great Britain and the Republic. Then, further to the westward, and extending for some 400 miles from north to south and about the same distance from east to west, is the South African Republic or Transvaal, which is under the suzerainty of Great Britain as regards its foreign relations, but is otherwise independent. Between the Transvaal and the Cape Colony is the Orange Free State; and between the Free State, Natal, and the Cape Colony is the small British colony of Basutoland. To the westward of the Transvaal is British Bechuanaland, now a part of the Cape Colony, beyond which, upon the west and north, is a British Protectorate, extending westward to the boundary of the German Protectorate. Upon the north, the interior as far as the Lakes Moero, Tanganyika, and Nyasa is also under British protection. To the west of the 20th meridian the whole country from the Orange River to the Cunene River, with the exception of the Walfisch Bay territory, which forms part of the Cape Colony, is under the protection of the German Empire. The eastern coast from Delagoa Bay northwards to Cape Delgado belongs to Portugal.

The total area of the British Colonies, excluding territory which is only protected, is more than 300,000 square miles. The white population as at the 1891 census was, Cape Colony, 376,987; Natal, 46,788; Bechuanaland, 5,211; Basutoland, 578.

The Cape of Good Hope was discovered in 1486 by Bartholomew Diaz, the commander of one of the many expeditions sent out by successive Kings of Portugal to discover an ocean route to India. Diaz merely doubled the Cape and returned home. Eleven years later, in 1497, Vasco da Gama not only doubled the Cape and landed in what is now Natal, but successfully accomplished the voyage to India. The Portuguese, however, did not make any permanent settlement at the Cape, although it was used by their vessels, and subsequently also by those of England and Holland, as a place of call in going to and from the East Indies. In 1652 the Dutch East India Company took possession of the shores of Table Bay, established a fort, and occupied the lands adjacent, in order to be always ready with supplies for their passing ships. Until 1796 the Cape remained in the hands of the Dutch, when it was captured by an English force; but in 1803 it was restored to the Batavian Government. In 1806 it was for the second time occupied by a British force, and at the general peace of 1814 it was formally ceded to the British Crown.

The history of the subsequent expansion of the Colony, and the formation of the various States and Colonies which have grown out of it, will be found under the separate headings.

The long and patient efforts of Her Majesty's Government to secure by negotiation with the Government of the South African Republic the equitable treatment of the very large population of "Outlanders," principally British, resident within the Transvaal, came to an unsuccessful conclusion in October 1899. Earlier in the year it had been found necessary to provide for possible eventualities by strengthening the British forces at the Cape and in Natal. On October 7th the Reserves were called out ; on the 10th an Ultimatum was received from the Transvaal Government demanding the recall of the British troops stationed near their frontiers, and also of any that were at that date on the way to South Africa. The terms of this communication were, of course, totally unacceptable, and the period fixed for their acceptance having expired, a state of war began at 5 P.M., Transvaal time, on October 11th. On the following day Natal was invaded by the Transvaal Boers acting in co-operation with the Boers of the Orange Free State, the Government of which had a short time previously notified their intention of throwing in their lot with their neighbours on the North. Very shortly after the opening of hostilities an Army Corps, under the command of General Sir Redvers Buller, V℃, was despatched to the scene of action. At the time of writing military operations are in progress, and it would be premature to anticipate what may be the intentions of Her Majesty's Government as regards their policy towards the two Republics when hostilities have been brought to a successful conclusion.

The main geographical feature of South Africa is the great mountain range which begins near the Orange River, and stretches for more than 1,000 miles, right through the Cape Colony and Natal, towards the north-east. Its direction coincides with that of the sea-coast, from which it is never more than from 100 to 150 miles distant. Viewed from the seaward side it is a veritable mountain range, rising in places to the height of 10,000 ft. ; but when surmounted it is seen to be properly but the broken edge of the great table-land, between 3,000 and 4,000 ft. high, which occupies the whole of the interior of South Africa. From the mountains to the sea the ground descends, not regularly, but by a series of terraces or steps ; and, as the British possessions also extend for some miles from south to north, the differences of elevation and latitude produce in them many varieties of climate. As a general rule South Africa is dry and well suited to Europeans. It is also suitable to the members of the great Bantu family, to which the Kafirs, Zulus, Bechuanas, Hereros, and other tribes now inhabiting South Africa belong. These tribes have been gradually coming down by land from the north-east, while Europeans have been coming in by sea from the south ; and between the two invading streams the aboriginal Hottentots and Bushmen have been almost crushed out of existence. The Bantus have shown no signs of dying out from contact with civilization ; and in comparing South Africa with Canada or Australia as a field for colonization, it must always be borne in mind that in South Africa there are three distinct elements in the population—the Dutch, the British, and the Kafir or (as it is usually, though not quite correctly, termed) Native, element. To reconcile the divergent interests of these separate elements, and to secure that the whole population shall live peacefully together, is the great problem of South African administration.

POSTAGE.—The Cape Colony and Natal entered the Postal Union on Jan. 1, 1895, and the postal rate is 2½*d.* the half ounce to and from all countries outside the British Empire. To and from the United Kingdom, and British Colonies, the rate is 1*d.* the half-ounce.

CAPE COLONY.

The CAPE OF GOOD HOPE, strictly speaking, is a small promontory near the S.W. extremity of the continent of Africa ; but the extensive colony of that name, in which are now included the Diamond Fields, the Transkei territories, Bechuanaland, and Pondoland, is washed by the Atlantic and Indian Oceans on the west and south and south-east, while upon the north and north-east it is bounded by the German Protectorate and each of the other colonies and states of South Africa. It reaches in S. lat. from 26° to 34° 50', and in E. long. from 16° 25' to 30°. Its extreme length from E. to W. is nearly 600 miles, and its breadth 452 miles, with a coast-line of nearly 1,200 miles, and an area of 277,151 square miles, or 177,376,640 acres, according to the latest estimate (1899), of which 49,564,606

acres were not disposed of in 1898. The territory of Walfisch Bay on the west coast is also a portion of the colony. The principal events in the history of the colony since it came under British rule have been the following :—Introduction of British settlers into the eastern districts as a barrier against the Kafirs, 1820 ; first Kafir war, 1834 ; commencement of the trekking of the Dutch Boers, which resulted eventually in the colonization of Natal and the Free States, 1836 ; second Kafir war, ending in the extension of the boundary to the Kei River, 1847 ; introduction of representative government, 1853 ; first diamond discovered, 1867 ; Griqualand West proclaimed a colony, 1871 ; introduction of responsible government, 1872 ; Gaika and Galeka rebellion, 1877-8 ; Basuto war, 1879-81 ; amalgamation of Griqualand West with the Colony, 1880 ; separation of Basutoland from the Colony, 1883; establishment of German Protectorate on the west coast to the north of the Orange River, 1884 ; incorporation of all the Transkeian territories, except part of Pondoland, with the Colony completed, 1885, annexation of Pondoland, 1894, and Bechuanaland, 1895. In 1899 a fresh crisis in the history of the Colony was reached by the declaration of war by the Presidents of the Transvaal and Orange Free State against British rule in South Africa.

The Colony is divided, geographically, into two parts by the main range of mountains, which, as already mentioned, follows the line of the South African coast at a distance of 100 to 150 miles from the sea ; and the southern portion is divided again by two other ranges which run across from W. to E., and are not quite so high as the first. Between the mountains and the sea, in the south-western portion of the Colony, are the chief grain and wine producing districts ; in the south there are extensive forests ; and along the south-eastern coast, where there are summer rains, tobacco and maize are successfully cultivated. Between the two upper ranges of mountains is an elevated tract known as the Great Karroo, which extends from W. to E. for 300 miles, and has a breadth of 70 miles. During a great portion of the year the Karroo is, as its name implies, a dry and barren district, but after rain it is covered with luxuriant vegetation, and supports countless flocks of sheep and many cattle and horses. It is here also that the important industry of ostrich-farming is carried on. The country to the north of the mountains is still more elevated, forming part of the great South African table-land. It supports, like the rest of the Colony, large numbers of sheep, and contains the chief mineral districts. The rivers of South Africa are numerous, but practically useless for either irrigation or navigation. Most of them flow in deep and precipitous ravines, and, except when swollen by the rains, are mere shallow torrents, even the largest having only sufficient water for the smallest craft, or bars at their mouths which render entrance both difficult and dangerous. The climate is healthy, and its peculiar dryness and the uniformity of the temperature causes it to be much favoured by Europeans suffering from pulmonary complaints. The vegetation of South Africa has a peculiar and distinctive character ; flowers of great variety abound everywhere. The principal native flora are heaths, proteæ, and stapelias (or carrion flowers), and dense thorny thickets of what is called *bush*, in which are several species of aloe. The native animals are either disappearing altogether or retreating northward owing to the rapid spread of civilization. But elephants and buffaloes are still found on the south coast, and springboks abound.

The *Population* of the whole Colony (Census of 1891) was 1,599,960, of whom the Europeans or whites were 382,198 (not including the population of Pondoland, *circ.* 200,000, and Bechuanaland, *circ.* 76,000, 1897). The birth-rate of the Colony Proper (*i.e.*, excluding Native Territories) was 33·99 per 1,000, and the death-rate 24·71 per 1,000 in 1898. The Dutch preponderate in the western, and the English in the eastern, districts.

Education.—The number of schools in operation (1898) was 2,588, attended by about 96,500 children, of whom 41·27 were white and 58·73 coloured. The expenditure under the Education Vote in 1898 was £235,000.

Commerce and Industry.—The principal indus-

tries are the production of wool and wine, and the rearing of horses, cattle, and ostriches, but great attention is paid to the culture of wheat, barley, and oats. The external trade amounted in 1898 to £16,601,354 for imports (textiles, £4,367,027 ; food stuffs, £3,791,849 ; and building materials, £1,881,214) and £24,423,413 for exports (animal and vegetable substances, £3,790,544 ; minerals and metals, £15,663,961 ; and diamonds, £4,568,897).

Minerals, &c.—There are important mines of copper in Namaqualand, the ores being of the richest kind, and yielding a percentage of from 32 to 36. Gold is found in the Knysna and Prince Albert divisions, and manganese in the Paar. Coal is also raised of considerable value, the output in 1898 being 191,858 tons. But by far the most valuable export is that of diamonds, which are chiefly found at Kimberley, the garrison of which town was closely besieged by the Transvaal Boers during the earlier part of the war of 1899.

Railways.—The railways are mostly the property of the Government, which on June 30, 1899, owned and worked 1,990 miles. There are also 653 miles of privately owned railways worked by Government, and 224 miles privately owned and worked ; in addition to which 219 miles are under construction for private companies. The *Cape to Cairo* Railway scheme places Capetown in communication with Buluwayo, the commercial centre of Rhodesia. To the 31st Dec., 1898, the capital expended by Government was £20,222,263, in which amount is included the money expended upon the Kimberley line. The returns for 1898 show a profit of £4 13s. 11d. per cent. per annum on the capital expended. There are 7,224 miles of telegraph open, carrying 21,767 miles of telegraph wire.

Defence.—The Colonial Forces in December, 1898, consisted of Cape Mounted Riflemen (1,003 officers and men) ; and horse and foot volunteers (6,953 officers and men). There is also a body of Mounted Police with about 1,900 officers and men. In cases of emergency every able-bodied man between 18 and 50 years of age may be called upon to defend the Colony, and there is a large Imperial garrison stationed at Cape Town. For purposes of external defence a Cape and West African Squadron is stationed in these waters, having a naval depôt in the Colony itself at Simon's Bay.

Extensive harbour works are being constructed at Table Bay (Cape Town), Port Elizabeth, and East London. On the works at Table Bay alone no less than £2,623,928 has been spent up to 31st December, 1898, and further works are in progress. There are electric tramways in Capetown, Port Elizabeth and East London.

Receipts (1847, £222,014) ; 1897–98		£7,327,975	
Payments (1847, £193,689) ; 1897–98		8,613,659	
Expended under vote, £7,082,255.			
Public debt (1878, £7,449,109):—			
General Government, 31 Dec., 1898		25,277,445	
Corporate Bodies, 31 Dec., 1898		3,166,477	
*Imports (1847, £1,152,018) ; 1898		16,021,354	
*Exports (1847, £512,778) ; 1898		24,423,413	

Domestic imports from U.K., 1898 :—

Apparel, &c.	£1,476,174	Leather	£493,189
Arms, &c. ..	203,050	Machinery ..	651,899
Books	138,855	Iron & Steel	1,031,526
Carriages ..	207,383	Paper	131,398
Cycles	120,366	Pickles, &c.	137,139
Coal, &c. ..	168,427	Soap	107,122
Cottons......	799,592	Spirits	121,513
Furniture ..	100,454	Stationery..	114,254
Hardware ..	152,986	Woollens ..	515,176
			£9,144,420

* Excluding specie.

Domestic exports to United Kingdom, 1898:—

Copper Ore,&c.	£400,447	Skins, Goat.	£128,875
Diamonds	4,583,815	,, Sheep.	456,813
Feathers	760,559	Wool, Sheep.	2,209,6c6
Hides	455,399	,, Goats.	464,393

£9,618,187

The Colony is under responsible government. There is a Governor appointed by the Crown, a Legislative Council of 23 elected members, and a House of Assembly of 95 elected members. The Ministers comprised in the Cabinet, who are responsible to the Colonial Legislature, are the Colonial Secretary (Premier), the Secretary for Agriculture, the Commissioner of Public Works, the Treasurer, and the Attorney-General.

CAPITAL, Capetown. Pop., 1891, 51,251 (including suburbs, 83,898); Grahamstown, 10,498; Port Elizabeth, 23,266; Kimberley, 28,718; Beaconsfield, 10,478.

Governor, High Commissioner, and Commander-in-Chief, Sir Alfred Milner, G.C.M.G. (1897)	£8,000
Secretary to High Commissioner, George Vandeleur Fiddes	1,200
Private Secretary, M. S. O. Walrond	410
Military Secretary, Lt.-Col. John Hanbury-Williams, C.M.G.	460
Aide-de-C., Lieut. R. Chester-Master	220
Clerk to Executive Council, C. H. Pennell	600
Naval Commander-in-Chief, Rear-Admiral Sir Robert Hastings Harris, K.C.M.G	
Commanding Troops, Lt.-Gen. Sir F. W. E. Forestier-Walker, K.C.B.	
Commanding 1st Army Corps, South Africa, General Sir Redvers H. Buller, V.C., G.C.B.	
Premier and Colonial Secretary, Hon. William Philip Schreiner, Q.C., C.M.G	1,750
Secretary, Sydney Cowper	700
Treasurer, Hon.John Xavier Merriman, M.L.A.	1,500
Commissioner Public Works, Hon. Jacobus Wilhelmus Sauer, M.L.A.	1,500
Sec. for Agriculture, Hon. Albertus Johannes Herholdt, M.L.C.	1,500
Attorney-Gen., Hon. Richard Solomon, Q.C.	1,500
Without Portfolio, Hon. Thomas Nicholas German Te Water, M.L.A.	
Speaker House of Assembly, Hon. W. B. Berry, M.L.A.	1,500
Clerk, E. F. Kilpin	850
Sec. to Native Affairs Dept., W. E. M. Stanford, C.M.G. (and £100 allowance)	1,000
Chief Magistrate (Tembuland, Pondoland, and Transkei), Maj. Sir H. G. Elliot, K.C.M.G.	1,350
Do. (E. Griqualand), J. H. Scott	1,000
Under Col. Sec. & Acctg. Officer, N. Janisch	850
Secretary for Defence, Lt.-Col. P. Homan-Ffolliott	700
Sup.-Gen. of Education, Dr. T. Muir	1,200
Assistant Treasurer, H. de Smidt, B.A., F.S.S.	1,000
Controller & Aud.-Gen., Hon. C. A. Smith	1,200
Collector of Customs, A. R. Orpen	1,000
Postmaster-General, S. R. French, C.M.G.	1,000
Sec. to Law Department, J. J. Graham, C.M.G.	1,000
Assist. Law Adviser, J. D. Sheil	80c
Chief Justice & Pres. of Legislative Council, Rt. Hon. Sir J. H. de Villiers, K.C.M.G.	3,000
Clerk, Legislative Council, S. le Sueur	850

Puisne Judges, Hons. Ebenezer J. Buchanan, C. G. Maasdorp, Sir Jacob D. Barry (Judge President of E. D. Ct.), each £2,000: S. T. Jones and W. H. Solomon, each £1,750; P. M. Laurence (Judge President of High Ct. of Griqualand West), £2,000; W. M. Hopley, J. H. Lange, each £1,750.

Reg., High Sheriff, & Taxing Off., H. Tennant	£900
Master of Sup. Ct., George Reynolds	800
Secretary for Public Works, C. L. Mansergh	700
Ch. Insp. of Public Works, J. Newey, M.I.C.E.	1,200
Gen. Man. of Railways, C. B. Elliott, C.M.G.	1,300
Under Sec. for Agriculture, C. Currey	900
Surveyor-General, J. Templer Horne	1,000
Agent-Gen. in London, Hon. Sir David Tennant, K.C.M.G., 112 Victoria St., S.W.	2,000
Secretary, Spencer Brydges Todd, C.M.G.	800

Cape Town is 5,979 miles from Southampton; transit, 18 days. Telegrams, per word, 4s.

BASUTOLAND.

Basutoland is an inland colony, being completely hemmed in by the Cape Colony, the Orange Free State, and Natal. It lies between 28° 45' and 30° 40' South latitude and 27° and 29° 30' East longitude, and has a computed area of 10,293 square miles. The population in 1891 was 218,324 natives and 578 Europeans; the latter are not allowed to settle without special permits (estimated pop. 1896, 250,000).

The territory is well watered, and enjoys a delicious climate. It is one of the finest grain producing districts in South Africa, and the abundant grass enables the Basutos to rear immense herds of cattle. The Maluti Mountains, forming a part of the great Drakensberg chain, occupy most of the country, which is elevated, broken, and rugged. The Basutos were first formed into a single tribe by a chief named Moshesh, about 1818. In 1852 they fought against the British Government and were defeated, but their country was not annexed. In 1856 disputes, resulting in hostilities, arose between Moshesh and the Orange Free State. These disputes continued more or less until 1868, when the Basutos, being hard pressed by the Free State, were saved from destruction by being taken under British protection. In 1871 their country was annexed to the Cape, but was not made subject to the general law of the Colony. In 1879 a chief named Moirosi rescued his son from justice, and it was only after severe fighting that his stronghold was taken by the Colonial forces. In the following year, owing to the extension to Basutoland of a Cape Act providing for a general disarmament, the whole tribe rebelled, and, after much negotiation, it was arranged that the Imperial Government should take over the country, receiving a subsidy of £20,000 (reduced to £18,000) from the Cape Government towards the cost of the administration. This arrangement was carried out in 1884, and Basutoland thus became a separate Colony. Basutoland entered the customs union in 1891, and a share of the dues is paid over to the Cape as a set off against the £18,000.

The territory is governed by a Resident Commissioner under the direction of the High Commissioner for South Africa, the latter possessing the legislative authority which is exercised by proclamation. The chiefs adjudicate on cases between natives, with a right of appeal to the magistrates' courts, where all cases between Europeans and natives are brought. The Revenue arises from the Cape contribution, the Post-office, native hut-tax, and the sale of licences. Telegraph offices have been opened at Maseru and Mafeteng, in connection with the Cape Colonial system. There are 163 schools, with 9,714 scholars, nine-tenths being in the schools of the French Protestant Mission. There are two small

Government schools, and grants in aid of education were made to the extent of £4,449 in 1898-9.
Revenue, 1898-99, £46,847; expenditure..£46,417
Imports, 1898-99, £93,683; exports £82,615

During the hostilities between the forces of the Boer Republics and the British Army Corps and force in Natal (October 1899), a Proclamation was issued by the Orange Free State annexing the northern territories of Basutoland; this increased the difficulties of the Commissioner in his efforts to restrain the Basutos from taking part in the war.

CAPITAL, Maseru. Pop., 763 (99 Europeans).

Resident Commissioner, Sir Godfrey Yeatman Lagden, K.C.M.G. £1,500
Govt. Sec., & Accountant, H. C. Sloley 675
Assistant Commissioners, S. Barrett, £650;
  T. P. Kennan, J. W. Bowker, L. Wroughton, J. C. Macgregor, £575;
  F. Enraght-Moony, C. Griffith... 500
Accounting Clerk, C. Y. Brabant............... 290
Medical Officers, E. C. Long (£568), N. M. Macfarlane, W. R. Nattle, D. M. Tomory ....each 350

Maseru is distant from London 7,668 miles; transit through the Cape about 22 days. Telegrams, per word, 4s.

THE BECHUANALAND PROTECTORATE.

The Protectorate is bounded on the east by the South African Republic and Matabeleland, on the south by Cape Colony, on the west by German South-West Africa, and extends northwards to the northern boundaries of the Bamangwato territory. It is about 400 miles long and 450 miles broad, and its area is about 400,000 square miles.

The climate is healthy, but there is a great scarcity of water, and much of the country is thick bush. The natives have suffered much from the rinderpest and a bad harvest, and cattle-raising, the chief industry, has been almost entirely checked in consequence. The exports consist mainly of maize or mealies, wool, hides, cattle, and wood, for the Kimberley market. The local revenue is derived chiefly from customs, and the greater part of the expenditure will be met by a special grant in aid.

The High Commissioner (Cape) has the power of making laws by proclamation for the Protectorate, where he is represented by a Resident Commissioner and two Assistant Commissioners. The population is almost entirely a native one, the principal tribes being those of Khama (Bamangwato), of Linchwe (Bakathla), of Sebele (Bakweni), of Bathoen (Bangwaketsi), and of Ikaneng (Bamalete).

The railway from Kimberley to Vryburg and Mafeking has been opened for traffic as far as Bulawayo, Rhodesia. There is a telegraph line from Cape Colony through from Mafeking, *vid* Gabarones Palapye, Tati and Maeloutsie to Bulawayo and Salisbury.

The chief European centres are Gaberones Palapye and Tati.

Governor, Sir Alfred Milner, G.C.M.G.
(Governor of Cape Colony).
Resident Commissioner, Major Hamilton John Goold-Adams, C.B., C.M.G. £1,000
Accountant, Barry May 400
Clerk, Albert Russell 250
Assist. Comm. and Magistrates in Lower Protectorate, W. H. Surmon 800
Clerk, J. Ellenberger 300

Assistant Commissioner and Magistrate in Upper Protectorate, J. A. Ashburnham. £700
Clerk, F. A. Douglas 250
Commandant of Police, Sir Richard Rowley Martin, K.C.B., K.C.M.G.
Commanding B. B. P., J. Walford.
    ,,   *Native Police,* C. Griffith.

Palapye is distant from London about 7,000 miles; transit, *via* Cape Town, about 23 days. Telegrams, per word, 4s.

NATAL.

The colony of Natal derives its name from the fact of its discovery by the celebrated Portuguese navigator Vasco da Gama, on Christmas Day, 1497. The Portuguese did not attempt to make any settlement, and two attempts made by the Dutch, in 1688 and 1721, were both unsuccessful. The country was occupied solely by natives until 1824, when the first European settlement was formed by a small party of Englishmen, who came by sea and established themselves on the coast where Durban now stands. Natal was then a part of the great Zulu Kingdom under T'Chaka. Between 1835 and 1837 another settlement was formed by a large body of Dutch Boers, who came with their waggons overland from the Cape Colony, and settled in the northern districts, where to this day the Boers preponderate, although the bulk of the whole white population of the Colony is British. The Boers attempted to set up an independent government at Pietermaritzburg; but the Governor of the Cape took military possession of the district, and in 1843 Natal was proclaimed as British and annexed to the Cape Colony. In 1856 it was erected into a separate colony, with representative institutions, and in 1893 acquired responsible government. It lies on the south-east coast of Africa, Durban or Port Natal being about 800 miles from Cape Town. Speaking roughly, it is in 30° E. long. and 30° S. lat. It comprises an area of 29,434 square miles (including 10,521 square miles for Zululand), with a seaboard of 376 miles (including 210 for Zululand). The population in 1898 was estimated at 902,365, consisting of Europeans, 53,688; natives (Zulu-Kafirs), 787,574; Indian Coolies, 61,103. The scenery is in parts picturesque in the extreme. The country is well watered, no less than 35 distinct rivers running through it into the Indian Ocean, but not one of them is navigable. On the N.W., Natal is bounded by the Drakensberg Mountains, a portion of the great range extending from Cape Town; and, as in the Cape Colony, the country rises from the sea to the mountains by a series of terraces. The coast region, extending about 15 miles inland, is highly fertile, and has a tropical climate. Sugar, coffee, indigo, arrowroot, ginger, tobacco, rice, and pepper thrive there, and the pine-apple ripens in the open air. Tea is also grown. The midland district is more adapted for cereals and other European crops. The upper district is chiefly grazing land, and sheep-farming is the principal occupation of the inhabitants; horses and cattle are also reared in large numbers. The coalfields of the colony are of large extent, and are now connected by rail with the seaport of Durban; the output for the year ended 31 Dec., 1898, was 387,811 tons. The advantages accruing to the colony from this industry are considerable, but they depend in great measure on the export trade, which is rapidly being developed. Some attempts have been made to utilize the rich beds of iron ore which have been found in many parts of the colony. Large forests of valuable timber abound in the kloofs of all the mountain ranges, and many tracts along the coast are also well wooded. The chief exports in 1898 were wool, £565,479; gold, £40,635; sugar, £18,153; hides, £160,176; angora hair, £36,545; skins, £24,674; bark, £30,929; coal, £124,523.

In Durban, or Port Natal, the Colony has the only harbour of any importance on the south-east coast. The bar, which hitherto has prevented large vessels from entering, is now in course of removal. *Railways:*—There are 524 miles of railway open (1899), all of which, except the North Coast Extension from Verulam to Tugela (50 miles), were constructed by the Government, and the whole system is Government worked. The main line runs from Durban through Pieter-maritzburg (the capital), and *via* Ladysmith and Glencoe Junction to Charlestown (309 miles inland), where it connects, by means of a tunnel passing under the Drakensberge mountains, at Laing's Nek, with the Netherlands South Africa Company's line to Johannesburg and Pretoria. A branch runs from Ladysmith (on the main line at the 190 mile post) to the western border at Van Reenen's Pass (36 miles), and thence over the Drakensberge in O.F.S. territory to Harri-smith (23½ miles). At Glencoe Junction a short line connects with Dundee. From Durban a branch runs northwards along the coast to Tugela (70 miles), and from Durban there is a coast line southwards to Park Rynie (36 miles), which is to be extended to Port Shepstone to open up a part of the colony, with large natural resources and valuable deposits of marble. Other exten-sions will lead from Pietermaritzburg to Grey-town (65 miles), and from Coalfields (Dundee) to Buffalo river, and across the northern border to Vryheid. The total amount expended on railway construction up to 31 December, 1898, was £6,950,621, the revenue in 1898 being £986,417 gross, and £395,602 net, a return of £5 14s. 1½d. on the capital expended on lines now open. There is a weekly mail service with Eng-land; and a telegraph cable to Zanzibar, Aden, and Europe, besides land lines to all parts of South Africa. There are Government High Schools at Pietermaritzburg and Durban; and 22 elementary schools; there are also 495 private aided, government aided, European, native, and Indian schools. The climate of the middle and upper districts is singularly beneficial to those suffering from pulmonary complaints. That of the coast district is, as already stated, tropical.

The Government consists of a Governor, a Legis-lative Council, and a Legislative Assembly. The former consists of 12 members, nominated by the Governor in Council, one half of whom retire every 5 years. The latter consists of 39 members elected by popular vote. There are 11,115 electors on the register, and there is a property qualification.

PIETERMARITZBURG, the capital and seat of government, is situated about 50 miles inland from Port Natal. Population (1898), 24,595.

Public revenue in 1898	£2,121,036
Expenditure in 1898	1,923,977
Public debt, 31st Dec., 1898	8,019,143
Imports (1843, £11,712), 1898	5,323,216
Exports (1843, £1,348), 1898	1,263,354

Domestic imports from U.K., 1898:—

Apparel, &c.	£689,834	Leather	£186,432
Carriages	5,061	Machinery	165,235
Cottons	107,258	Metals	204,525
Furniture	74,221	Woollens	84,249
			£3,055,390

Domestic exports to the U.K., 1898:—

Angora Hair..	£36,090	Skins	£23,885
Coal	11,378	Wool, Sheep.	565,470
Hides,&c.	155,145	Wattle Bark..	23,781
			£922,949

PROVINCE OF ZULULAND.

Under letters patent passed by Royal warrant 1 Dec., 1897, and in accordance with an Act of the Natal Parliament (No. 37 of 1897), the Territory of Zululand was proclaimed annexed to, and as forming part of, the Colony of Natal from 31 Dec., 1897. The Province comprises about two-thirds of the country formerly under Zulu kings, and is bounded on the south and south-west by the Tugela river; on the south-east by the Indian Ocean; on the north by the Portuguese posses-sions; and on the west by the S. A. R. and Swazi-land. By the Zululand Laws Consolidation Act (No. 17 of 1898), all the laws of Natal, which were applied to Zululand by proclamation of 21 June, 1897, and all the subsequent proclama-tions declaring the law of Zululand, which were made before its annexation to Natal, were extended to the Province of Zululand, with the exceptions and limitations specified in the schedules of that Act, and the Province is now administered as an integral part of the Colony of Natal. The Amaputaland Protectorate, created by proclamation of 22 Nov., 1897, was annexed to Zululand on Dec. 27, 1897, and now forms the Maputa District of the Province.

In October, 1899, the neighbouring Boer States of the Transvaal and Orange Free State declared war against Great Britain, and invaded the Colony by way of Laing's Nek and Van Reenen's pass. Actions were fought on October 20, at Glencoe Junction, by a British force under Sir W. P. Symons (who was mortally wounded, and died on October 23), and on October 21 and 23, near Ladysmith, by Sir George White's force; in each case the British were successful, but, upon the arrival of reinforcements for the enemy round Glencoe, General Yule (who succeeded General Symons) retired southwards, and effected a junction with Sir George White at Ladysmith. The military operations were thenceforward con-fined to a resistance to the opposing forces from within the entrenchments at Ladysmith; but at the time of going to press a considerable body of men had been landed at Durban and were about to advance under the direction of General Buller and Gens. Hildyard and Clery.

Gov. and Comm.-in-Chief, Hon. Sir Walter

Francis Hely-Hutchinson, G.C.M.G.	£5,000
Private Secretary, H. W. B. Robinson	250
Prime Minister, Minister of Lands and Works,	
The Honble. Lt.-Col. A. H. Hime, C.M.G.,	
late R.E.	1,000
Attorney-Gen.& Education, Hon. Hy. Bale, Q.C.	800
Colonial Sec., Hon. Charles John Smythe	800
Treasurer, Hon. William Arbuckle	800
Sec. for Native Affairs, Hon. F. R. Moor	800
Agriculture, Hon. H. D. Winter	800

Commanding Natal Field Force, Lieut.-Gen.
  Sir George S. White, V.C., G.C.B.

President Legislative Council, The Hon. J. T.	
Polkinghorne	400
Speaker Legislative Assembly, The Hon. J. L.	
Hulett	400

Chief Justice, **Sir Michael Henry Gallwey**, K.C.M.G., Q.C.	£1,500
1st Prisne Judge, Arthur Wier Mason, B.A.	1,000
2nd do., R. I. Finnemore	1,000
Judge of Native High Court H. C. Campbell	900
Auditor-General, W. E. Goldby	600
Gen. Manager of Railways, D. Hunter, C M.G.	1,200
Engineer-in-Ch. of Railways, J. W. Shores	1,000
Chief Com. of Police, Col. J. G. Dartnell, C.M.G.	900
Sec., Law Dept., J. F. W. Bird	800
Collector of Customs, George Mayston	800
Postmaster-General, W. G. Hamilton	700
Principal Under-Secretary, C. Bird	800
Superintendent of Education, R. Russell	750
Surveyor-General, J. L. Masson	650
Ch. Engineer of Public Works, J. F. E. Barnes	800
Registrar-General, G. Lamond	675

Agent-General in London, Sir Walter Peace, K.C.M.G., 26, Victoria Street, Westminster.

Secretary, Robert Russell, B.C.L.

Natal, 6,800 miles ; transit, 22 days. Telegrams, per word, 4s.

RHODESIA.

THE BRITISH SOUTH AFRICA COMPANY

(Incorporated by Royal Charter, 29th October, 1889.)

Directors: The Duke of Abercorn, K.G. (*President*) ; Earl Grey (*Vice-President*) : the Rt. Hon. Cecil John Rhodes ; Lord Gifford, V.C.; Sir Sidney Shippard, K.C.M.G.; Rochfort Maguire ; P. Lyttelton Gell.

Head Office, 15, St. Swithin's Lane, E.C.

Manager, H. Wilson Fox ; *Secretary,* J. F. Jones ; *Registrar,* E. C. Clegg.

Senior Administrator of Rhodesia, W. H. Milton (Salisbury).

Administrator of Ma'abeleland, Captain Hon. Arthur Lawley (Buluwayo).

Deputy Administrator of Northern Rhodesia, R. Codrington (Blantyre).

Deputy Administrator of Barotsiland, R. T. Coryndon.

Resident Commissioner, Lt.-Col. Sir Marshall J. Clarke, K.C.M.G. (Salisbury).

Commandant-General, Col. J. S. Nicholson, D.S.O. (Salisbury).

Cape Town Agency, J. A. Stevens, *Secretary.*

RHODESIA, so called after the Right Honourable Cecil Rhodes, whose policy secured this vast and important inland territory to the British Empire, has an area of about 750,000 square miles, thus exceeding the whole of Central Europe between the Pyrenees, the North Sea and the Russian frontier. By the Royal Charter of 1889, the British South Africa Company was entrusted with the administration and development of this Province, which established an uninterrupted British dominion from the Cape to Lake Tanganyika and British Central Africa. It is bounded on the south by Bechuanaland and the Transvaal, from which it is separated by the Limpopo or Crocodile River; on the east by the Portuguese dominions and British Central Africa (see p. 529): on the northeast by German East Africa ; and on the north and north-west by the Congo Free State. The eastern boundary of Rhodesia follows generally the north-easterly trend of the African seaboard, from which it is separated by a wide belt of Portuguese territory falling rapidly to the Indian

Ocean. The western frontiers are still somewhat undefined. The River Zambesi divides the territory into Northern and Southern Rhodesia.

NORTHERN RHODESIA.

This territory, first opened to British influence by Dr. Livingstone, is still entirely occupied by the Native tribes living under their own chiefs. It has been hitherto administered, together with Barotsiland, by the Chartered Company under the African Order in Council, for which hereafter the provisions of the North-Eastern Rhodesia and North-Western Rhodesia Orders in Council of 1899 are to be substituted. Now that the tyranny of the Arab slave raiders has been finally suppressed, and the territory has been opened up from south to north by the African Transcontinental Telegraph, the steady development of its resources may be anticipated. Here, as in Southern Rhodesia, Missions of various denominations are at work, and are generally successful when associated with industrial education.

SOUTHERN RHODESIA.

The political and industrial development of Southern Rhodesia has been far more rapid. In latitude it is sub-tropical, but being situated upon the plateau which constitutes the watershed between the Limpopo and the Zambesi, 3,000 ft. to 5,000 ft. above the sea level, it is well suited for British occupation, and the high, bracing air is especially invigorating in the dry winter months. It is now traversed by public roads, of which about 3,000 miles have been opened, by about 2,000 miles of telegraph, and a telephone system which connects the chief townships and stations of the police.

Railways.—The main arteries of communication are the Mashonaland and the Rhodesian Railways. The finished portion of the latter (originally constructed as the Bechuanaland Railway) represents the first section of Mr. Rhodes' gigantic "Cape to Cairo" project, and runs almost due north-east from Mafeking at the northern extremity of Cape Colony, entering Rhodesia at Ramaquabane, more than 1,200 miles from Cape Town. Bulawayo, the chief town of Matabeleland, 1,360 miles from Cape Town, is the terminus for the moment. The Mashonaland Railway runs westward from the Portuguese frontier near Umtali. It reached Salisbury in 1899, connecting the Mashonaland goldfields with the excellent harbour of Beira, 380 miles distant, on the Indian Ocean. The Beira Railway through the Portuguese territory, is now being widened to the general "Cape to Cairo" gauge (3 ft. 6 in.), which has been adopted alike in Egypt and South Africa. This identity of gauge enabled Mr. Rhodes to expedite Lord Kitchener's advance on Khartoum in 1898, by handing over to Egypt at a time of great urgency, four engines constructed for the Rhodesian traffic. The Railway system is now being extended from Bulawayo in various directions, to the Gwanda goldfields on the south-east, to the Wankie district on the north-west, and above all, it is progressing northwards (taking the Gwelo goldfields and coal deposits on the road), towards the Zambesi, which it will strike between the junctions of the Kafue and Loangwa streams with that great continental waterway. Simultaneously, the line from Beira through Salisbury will be pushed on to meet this northern extension, thus connecting the two systems which start respectively from Cape Town and Beira. All the chief Rhodesian centres will thus be brought within three weeks of England. An Agreement between Germany and the Chartered Company was signed in 1899 providing also for the future construction of a westward extension to the Atlantic coast, which would still further reduce the journey.

The *Telegraph System* of Southern and Northern Rhodesia similarly forms a link in Mr. Rhodes' line from the Cape to Cairo which is being rapidly constructed by the African Transcontinental Telegraph Company. That line has now reached Lake Tanganyika 2,800 miles from the Cape, and 2,170 miles from the Egyptian terminus, serving Southern and Northern Rhodesia on its way, so that British settlers in every township can now communicate with England within a few hours.

Rivers.—With the exception of the Zambesi, there are no streams of any value for purposes of transit, though it is known that the River Sabi was formerly used as a means of access to Mashonaland. The marked alternation of the rainy and dry seasons renders the smaller rivers unreliable. There is, however an adequate rainfall for all purposes of cultivation, and schemes for water storage and irrigation have been taken in hand.

The Natives, estimated at 509,000, have now settled down, apparently content with their unwonted prosperity and immunity from tyranny and pillage, while others are flocking in from the Portuguese and Transvaal borders. Matabeleland is divided into fifteen Native Districts, Mashonaland into fourteen, and for each District there is a Native Commissioner whose duty it is to protect and control the natives through their own Indunas. The most trusted of the latter receive small salaries from the Company. The B.S.A. Mounted Police, about 1,200 strong, have posts throughout the territory. They are maintained by the Company at an annual cost of nearly £300,000, their Commandant being nominated by the Crown.

Industrial Progress.—Southern Rhodesia is rich in mineral deposits (its identity with the ancient land of Ophir is practically established), and it abounds in traces of the ancient goldworkers. Though the climate is sub-tropical the average altitude makes it well suited to European fruit-trees, cereals, and vegetables, in addition to the indigenous products of the country, *e.g.*, tobacco, india-rubber, indigo, cotton, and all kinds of grain.

The extraordinary series of misfortunes which has overtaken the whole of South Africa during the last ten years has delayed the development of the well-ascertained resources of the territory. Rinderpest and locusts devastated the country in 1896. The Natives impoverished, starved, and only half subdued, broke out into rebellions which, with no railway and no transport cattle, were not extinguished without heroic efforts.

The South African War of 1899-1900 and the Boer irruptions into Natal, Cape Colony, Bechuanaland, and Rhodesia have again checked the returning flood of development. The railway and telegraph communications were broken, and men and capital alike diverted from the work in hand. The defence of Mafeking, when left exposed to the Boers by Cape Colony, was largely due to B.S.A. Police and Rhodesian Volunteers under Col. Baden-Powell.

In spite, however, of these crises, extensive progress has been accomplished in the first decade of the Chartered Company's history. A territory which, but ten years ago was barbarous, inaccessible, and to most men all but mythical, has

been settled, pacified, and opened up for rapid development. The country is being restocked, and inoculation upon a large scale is stamping out various descriptions of veterinary disease. Native cultivation is extending, and in the vicinity of the towns and mining centres, there is a steady demand for market and dairy produce at very remunerative prices. The wages of all skilled artizans are high.

Among the mineral products of Rhodesia, gold, silver, copper, iron, coal, tin, plumbago, and kieselguhr have already been localised. So far, it is only the goldfields which have received much attention; nor have they as yet been adequately explored outside the lines of ancient workings.

The first regular crushing returns began with 2,346 ozs. from three mines in September, 1898, and by August 31, 1899, about 63,000 ozs. had been recovered from 116,000 tons of quartz, valued at about £225,000. The goldfields at present actually producing are those of Gwanda, Selukwe, and Bulawayo; but development work is in full progress in the gold belts of Sebakwe, Belingwe, Msiza, Hartley, Lo Maghonda, Mazoe, Abercorn, Manica, Victoria, and elsewhere. The present scarcity and inadequacy of Native labour are the sole impediments to a much larger output.

Constitution.—Southern Rhodesia is administered by the Company under the Charter of 1889, as amended by the Orders in Council of 1894 and 1898. The Senior Administrator is now advised by an Administrative Council of seven, and a Legislative Council of eleven members, the latter comprising two elected representatives from each Province.

The proceedings and enactments of both Councils are subject to the sanction of the High Commissioner at Cape Town, as representing the Crown, and his Deputy, the "Resident Commissioner," is present (without a vote) at their sittings. The laws in force in the Cape Colony up to June 10th, 1891, have continued in force in Southern Rhodesia, so far as they are applicable; whilst from 1891 to 1899, when the Legislative Council was first convened, laws were amended or enacted by the ordinances of the Directors, the regulations of the Administrator in Council, and the proclamations of the High Commissioner. Municipal self-government has been established for Bulawayo and Salisbury under mayors and town councils. Justice is administered by resident magistrates and judges, the sanction of the Crown, as represented by the High Commissioner, being required for all judicial appointments of every rank. Trial by jury was established in 1899. There is an appeal to the High Court at Cape Town and thence to the Privy Council.

The political capital is SALISBURY, 4,700 ft. above sea level, the chief town of Mashonaland, and the residence of the Senior Administrator. It has a white population of 2,000. BULAWAYO, 4,400 ft. above the sea level, the chief town of Matabeleland and, until 1893, the Kraal of Lobengula, is the commercial centre, with a white population of 7,500. These towns are 280 miles apart. Both possess daily newspapers, clubs, hotels, theatres, parks, and public hospitals, together with schools and churches of the Church of England and many other Religious bodies. Townships are also growing up at Umtali, Selukwe, Tuli, Melsetter, Gwanda, Gwelo, Victoria, Filabusi, Hartley, and Abercorn.

Telegrams to Northern Rhodesia, 4s. 5d. per word; Southern Rhodesia, 4s. 2d. per word.

WEST AFRICA.

(See also Map, page 608.)

The West African Colonies are the Gambia, Sierra Leone, the Gold Coast, and Lagos, which are all situated upon the coast of North-Western Africa between the mouths of the rivers Senegal and Niger. These were not originally colonies in the strict sense of the word, but merely trading settlements, in which the products of the neighbouring countries were collected and exchanged for European goods with as little outlay as possible ; but of late years a great part of the revenue has been expended on the advancement of the scholastic and technical education of the native and on the encouragement of the cultivation of natural produce instead of its spoliation. The climate is such that Europeans cannot live there permanently, and even the negro inhabitants suffer greatly from malarial fever. The West Coast of Africa has, however, been eagerly frequented by European traders since it was first explored by the Portuguese in the latter part of the 15th century, just before the discovery of America by Columbus. In the 17th century all the chief maritime nations of Europe, except the Spaniards, had forts or factories established on the coast, from which they used to supply slaves to their plantations in the West Indies and on the mainland of America. The importance of the coast was much diminished when these same nations agreed, at the commencement of the present century, to join in putting down the slave trade. The Dutch and the Danes relinquished their possessions ; and although the French and the Portuguese maintained their positions, the English were practically without any serious rivalry in the development of a legitimate trade in tropical products, of which palm oil was the most important, to take the place of the trade in slaves. Within the last few years, however, the French have been spending large sums, and making strenuous efforts, with the avowed intention of founding a great French Empire in North-Western Africa. The Germans possess the territory of the Cameroons and Togoland, in the immediate neighbourhood of the British possessions; and, more to the south, the Congo Free State has been founded by the King of the Belgians. British authority has been extended, not only by means of the colonies, but also by means of Protectorates over the Niger Coast and over territory adjacent to the Colonies of Sierra Leone, the Gold Coast and Lagos, and through the Royal Niger Company, which has exercised under a charter from the British Crown, all the functions of government ceded to it by various rulers and peoples. The arrangements made for the revocation of the Company's Charter, on January 1st, 1900, and for the future administration of the territories hitherto under their control, have already been referred to on page 515. By agreement with Germany (14 November, 1899), the greater portion of the territory previously known as "The Neutral Zone" in the rear of the Gold Coast, was allotted to Great Britain (see map, p. 608), this being part of the arrangement whereby this country abandoned in favour of Germany and the United States any claim over the Samoan Islands. The partition of West Africa among the various European Powers is now complete, and it only remains to proceed with the demarcation on the spot of the frontiers arrived at by international conventions—a task which, in some cases, will be one of some difficulty.

GAMBIA.

The river Gambia rises in the mountains at the back of Sierra Leone ; it flows first towards the north, and then turning towards the west, empties itself into the Atlantic about 100 miles south of Cape Verde. The chief town, Bathurst, is situated on an island at the mouth of the river in 13° 24′ N. lat. and 16° 36′ W. longitude. The Gambia is the only West African river which is navigable by ocean-going steamers, having 26 feet of water on the bar at low tide. Vessels drawing 10 feet can go up it for 250 miles. It was discovered by the Portuguese in 1447 ; and in 1588, the year of the Spanish Armada, Queen Elizabeth, being then at war with Spain and Portugal, gave a charter to a British Company to trade with the Gambia, and as early as 1618 an effort to do so was made, but it was not successful. In 1686 a fort was built upon a rocky island, and, in honour of the new King, was named Fort James ; but the English merchants had formidable rivals in the Portuguese and French, and it was not until 1783 that the river was recognized, by the Treaty of Versailles, as British. It had no regular political institutions until 1807, when it was put under the Colony of Sierra Leone. The Colony of the Gambia was created in 1843, and was constituted a separate government in 1888.

The Colony now consists of the Island of St. Mary, British Combo Albreda, the Ceded Mile, McCarthy's Island, and various other islands and territories on the banks of the river The estimated population on 31 December, 1898, was 14,266. The climate is as unhealthy as that of any other part of West Africa during the rainy season, viz., from June to October ; but during the rest of the year it is fairly healthy. The chief export is ground-nuts, which forms nearly nine-tenths of the total exports. They are sent chiefly to Marseilles, where the oil is extracted and used for the same purposes as olive oil. Beeswax, rubber, and hides are also exported ; and rice, cotton, maize, and a kind of millet called *kous* are produced in the countries bordering the Gambia, but not in sufficient quantities for export. The chief imports are cotton goods, Kola nuts, rice and tobacco. The colony has no debt, but, on the contrary, an amount of money invested. There is an armed police force in the settlement (numbering about 100 men), which performs both civil and military duties. The government, which is that of a Crown Colony, is now vested in an Administrator, assisted by an Executive Council, and by a Legislative Council consisting of 3 official members (besides the Administrator) and 2 unofficial members, nominated by the Crown.

Public revenue in 1898 ....£46,717
Public expenditure, 1898 29,035
Total imports, 1898, £246,091 ; exports ... 247,831
Imports from U.K., 1898, £127,464 ; exports 35,023
  Chief Town, Bathurst.   Pop. (1896), 6,239.
Administrator, Sir R. B. Llewelyn, K.C.M.G.
  (and £600 allowances) £1,500
Treasurer, H. M. Brandford-Griffith...£500 to 600
Chief Magistrate A. D. Russell, M.A., LL B. ... 600
Collector of Customs, T. E. Peirce 460
Colonial Engineer, H. Reeve 500
Colonial Surgeon, R. M. Forde..................... 400
Superintendent of Police, J. Brown 350
Travelling Commissioners, J. H. Ozanne, C.M.G.,
  £400 ; C. Sitwell, £400 ; P. Wainewright, £300 ;
  H. L. Pryce, £300.
Transit, 14 days.   Telegrams, 4s. 7d. a word.

THE GOLD COAST COLONY.

(See also Map, p. 608.)

This colony comprises the coast of the Gulf of Guinea from about 3° W. to 1° 10′ E. of Greenwich, with a protectorate extending inland to an average distance of 300 miles, bounded on the West and North by the French colonies of the Ivory Coast and French Soudan, and on the East by the German Colony of TOGOLAND. The population of the Colony is estimated at 1,500,000 (exclusive of Ashanti and the northern territories), of whom 200 are Europeans. The natives are almost all Pagans ; but the number of Mohammedans and Christians is steadily increasing. The Castle and settlement of Elmina was founded by the Portuguese and taken from them by the Dutch. In 1618, some English merchants built a fort at Cormantyne, and subsequently many forts and factories were established, not only by the English and Dutch, but also by the French, the Danes, and the Germans, for the purpose of supplying slaves to their West Indian and American possessions. The first English Company to trade with the Gold Coast was chartered in 1662. This was succeeded in 1672 by the Royal African Company, which enlarged and strengthened Cape Coast Castle until it was the best on the Coast, and also built forts at Dixcove, Secondee, Commendah, Anamaboe, Winnebah, and Accra. This was again succeeded in 1750 by the African Company of Merchants, which was constituted by Act of Parliament, with liberty to trade and form establishments on the West Coast of Africa between 20° N. and 20° S. lat. The settlements were in 1821 transferred to the Crown, and placed under the Government of Sierra Leone, from which they were finally separated in 1874 under the title of Gold Coast Colony. The Dutch and English forts were intermingled until 1867, when an exchange was effected which gave all those on the West of the Swat River to Holland and those on the East to Great Britain. In 1872 the Dutch transferred all their forts to Great Britain, which had previously, in 1850, bought the Danish forts.

It was out of this transfer that the Ashanti war of 1873–4 arose, as the King of Ashanti, who had always been on good terms with the Dutch, feared that he would be cut off from the sea. The result of the war was that the Ashanti power was completely shattered, and the British possessions were left free for development without fear of native aggression or hindrance from European rivalry.

In 1894, however, Prempeh, the King of Ashanti, having successfully fought against the Nkoranzas who had revolted against his rule, threatened to attack the Attabubus, who had been given protection in 1890. This attack was averted by the despatch of an armed force, and an ultimatum was then sent to Prempeh warning him not to enter British territory, and suggesting that he should acquiesce in the establishment of a Residency at Kumasi. No definite reply could be obtained, and a military expedition to Kumasi, to compel compliance with the demands of Her Majesty's Government, was therefore decided upon. The expedition entered Kumasi without resistance, January, 1896, and Prempeh made submission, but, failing to comply with the terms dictated, was brought to the coast as a political prisoner and now lives in banishment in Sierra Leone. A Resident was at the same time installed at Kumasi, and thus has commenced an entirely new departure in the relations of the Gold Coast Colony with Ashanti.

Within the last few years the French have begun to extend and develop their Colony of the Ivory Coast, which adjoins the British Colony on the West ; and the German settlement adjoining the Colony on the East, called Togoland, is rapidly increasing in commercial importance. Disputes with France having arisen as to the respective spheres of influence of Great Britain and that country in the hinterland of the colony, a convention was signed in Paris (14 June, 1898) definitely settling all matters in dispute. A considerable amount of territory in the north was acquired, and this is now known as the Northern Territories.

By an agreement with Germany, in November, 1899, the greater portion of the territory previously regarded as Neutral, and known as "The Neutral Zone" in the hinterland of the Gold Coast was allotted to Great Britain (see p. 608).

The produce of the Gold Coast is chiefly sent to Great Britain. Gold is found in considerable quantities, and ivory, gumcopal, monkey-skins, cotton, camwood, Guinea grains, and oil, are also exported to England. The principal exports, and their value in 1898, are rubber £551,667, palm oil £114,288, timber £110,331, and palm kernels £66,378. The chief imports are textiles, alcohol, and hardware. The climate is damp, hot, malarious, and unhealthy. Very little was done for the natives for 400 years, but the Government is now assisting the Roman Catholic, Methodist, and German missionaries in educational matters, and great efforts are being made to improve the sanitary condition of the Coast towns. The Government has established schools of its own ; the towns are lighted and policed, 700 miles of telegraphs have been established in the colony, and a considerable mileage recently constructed in the Northern Territories. A government railway from the coast to Tarkwa, the centre of the gold-mining industry, is now in course of construction.

Under the Colonial Loans Act, 1899, the sum of £578,000 was advanced for the purpose of railway developement, and £98,000 for harbour works at Accra.

The seat of Government is Accra (population 16,276). The other principal towns are Cape Coast (11,614), Elmina (10,530), Addah (7,530), Saltpond, and Quitta. The Legislative Council consists of 6 official and 3 unofficial members.

Revenue, 1898 (including grant £45,000) £303,822
Expenditure, 1898 377,972
Imports from United Kingdom, 1898...... 726,197
Exports to United Kingdom, 1898 713,335
Total imports, 1898 960,336
Total exports, 1893 992,998

Governor, Sir Frederic Mitchell Hodgson,
K.C.M.G. (and £500 table allowance) ... £3,000
Col. Sec., W. Low £1,250
Chief Assist. Sec. G. B. Haddon-Smith £600 to 700
Assistant Secs. C. H. Hunter, H. M. Hull,
each £400 to 500

Treasurer, C. Riby Williams.................. 700
Comptroller of Custom, G. Attrill 700
Chief Justice, Sir Wm. Brandford Griffith.. 1,500
Puisne Judges, Francis Smith, £1,000; Wm.
Nicoll, LL.D., S. W. Morgan ...... each 800
Attorney-General, W. Clark.......... £800 to 1,000
Inspect.-General Constabulary, (vacant)...... 700
Administrator of Northern Territories, Col.
H. P. Northcott, C.B. (*at present with
Army Corps in South Africa*)
Director of Works, A. M. Anderson £850 to 1,000
Chief Medical Officer, W. R. Henderson,
M.D. £800 to 1,000
British Res., Kumasi, D. W. Stewart, C.M.G.
£700 to 1,000

Distant from Liverpool, 3,920 miles; transit, 21 30 days. Telegrams, 6s. 3d. to 6s. 5d. per word.

SIERRA LEONE.

The peninsula of Sierra Leone (Lion Mountain) was ceded to Great Britain in 1787 by the native chiefs, to be used as an asylum for the many destitute negroes then in England; and great numbers of liberated Africans from North America and the West Indies, besides those taken in slavers on the coast, have from time to time been settled there. In this respect Sierra Leone is really a colony and so differs from the other Colonies on the West African coast (which were all formed as merely trading stations), while it is also of commercial importance. The route from Freetown to the great central African plateau is shorter and easier than that from the navigable head of the Gambia, and there is an excellent harbour strongly fortified as a coaling-station for the Royal Navy on the Cape route to India. In addition to the peninsula, the colony now comprises Sherbro Island, and various other territories extending along the coast from the French Colony known as the "Guinée Française" upon the North to the Republic of Liberia on the South. The extreme length is about 185 miles, with an estimated area of 4,000 sq. miles. The population in 1893 amounted to 136,000, of whom 210 were resident Europeans. Of the rest, more than half were liberated Africans and their descendants, while the remainder belonged to the neighbouring tribes. The liberated Africans were brought from all parts of Africa, and as the result no less than 60 different languages are said to be spoken in Freetown. Almost every Christian denomination is represented in Freetown, and there are also many Pagans and Mohammedans. Education, though not compulsory, is in an advanced state. The climate is humid and enervating to Europeans, and malarial

fevers are prevalent, especially at the beginning and end of the rains, which last from May to October. The peninsula itself produces hardly anything. The inhabitants are almost all employed in exchanging the products of the interior for European goods. The exports consist chiefly of palm-kernels and kola nuts; but benni-seed, cocoa-nuts, ginger, ground-nuts, india-rubber, gum-copal, hides, beeswax, and rice are also exported. The principal imports are cotton goods, coals, apparel, hardware, provisions and tobacco. The taxation consists of specific duties on wine, spirits, ale and porter, tobacco, gunpowder, guns, kerosine oil, lumber, hardware, salt, and sugar; and of a 10 per cent. ad valorem duty on other goods. Under the Colonial Loans Act, 1899, the sum of £310,000 was advanced for railway construction in the Colony.

Public revenue, 1898 ....£117,681
Public expenditure, 1898 121,112
Total imports, 1898 606,348
Total exports, 1898 290,991
Imports from U.K., 1898, £512,098; exports 117,726

The Governor is aided by Executive and Legislative Councils, the latter consisting of 5 official and 3 unofficial members.

Freetown, the capital and seat of government, had, in 1895, a population of over 30,000; it is the greatest seaport and has the finest harbour in West Africa.

Governor, Col. Sir Fredk. Cardew, K.C.M.G.£2,500
Chief Justice, His Hon. George Stallard ... 1,200
Colonial Sec., the Hon. Lt.-Col. J. C. Gore,
£750 to 800
Assistant Colonial Sec., T. F. Meagher 350 to 400
Col. Treasurer, E. O. Johnson...................... 550
Attorney-Gen., Hon.P. Crampton Smyly, B.L. 700
Solicitor-Gen., Arthur Hudson, B.L. 500
Master Supreme Court & Registrar-General,
D. F. Wilbraham 400
Collector of Customs, Hon. W. J. P. Elliott. 750
Colonial Surgeon, W. T. Prout, M.B............. 591
Director of Public Works, T. E. Laing, C.E. 500
Police Magistrate, R. de Groot 450
Inspector-General Frontier Police, Capt. S.
Moore 450
Bishop of Sierra Leone, Right Rev. John
Taylor Smith, D.D.
Mayor of Freetown, Hon. Sir S. Lewis, C.M.G.

THE SIERRA LEONE PROTECTORATE.

A Protectorate was proclaimed over the territories adjacent to the Colony of Sierra Leone on August 31, 1896. The region has long been recognised as within the British sphere of influence, and lies between 7° and 10° N., and 11° and 13° W., being bounded on the N. and N.E. by French Guinea, and on the S. and S.E. by Liberia. It has an area of about 30,000 square miles and a population roughly estimated at 500,000.

For administrative purposes the Protectorate is divided into 5 districts under District Commissioners, the principal peoples being the Limbas and Kurankos in the North, the Tinmenis and Susus in the centre, and the Mendis in the South. The principal products are rubber, gum, and palm trees, benni seed, rice, ground and kola nuts, while sheep and cattle thrive.

Freetown, 3,078 miles from Liverpool; transit, 14 days. Telegrams, 5s. 5d. per word.

LAGOS.

The Colony and Protectorate of Lagos, formerly one of the great centres of the African slave trade, is situated on the Bight of Benin between Dahomey and the Niger Coast Protectorate (Southern Nigeria). Its sphere of influence extends northwards over the Yoruba country, a large and fertile region, and one of the most successful fields of missionary enterprise. Lagos Island was permanently occupied by Great Britain in 1861. Until 1886 it formed a dependency first of Sierra Leone and later of the Gold Coast, but is now a separate Crown Colony and Protectorate. The Protectorate comprises the kingdoms of Pokra, Okeodan, Ilaro, Addo, Igbessa, Awori, Jebu Remo, Mahin, Ogbo, and Jakri. Lagos island has an area of 3¾ square miles, and the whole Colony and Protectorate includes 1,500 square miles, with perhaps 2,000,000 inhabitants, of whom about 200 are of European birth. A railway has been constructed to Abeokuta 60 miles inland, and Lagos is now connected by telegraph with Jebba on the Niger.

Rubber, palm-oil and palm-kernels constitute the most important natural products of the Colony. A flourishing trade in timber has recently sprung up. The value of the palm-oil exported in 1898 was £97,337, kernels £362,539, and rubber £285,409. The imports are chiefly cotton-goods (£339,778), spirits (£76,931), and kola nuts (£23,052).

Public revenue, 1898 ....£206,444
Public expenditure, 1898 203,802
Total imports, 1898, £908,355 ; exports ... 883,229
Imports from United Kingdom, 1898 723,650
Exports to U.K., 1898 1,129,543

LAGOS, the capital and seat of government, has about 33,000 inhabitants.

Governor, Sir W. MacGregor, K.C.M.G., C.B. £2,500
   (and entertainment allowance £1,000)
Chief Justice, His Hon. Sir T. C. Rayner .. £1,200
Colonial Secretary, The Hon.Capt. Geo. C. Denton,
  C.M.G. £1,000
  Assists., Mark Kerr, £500 ; F. B. Archer £400
Queen's Advocate, Hon.Francis Oswald Edlin... 700
Treasurer, Hon.C. H. Harley Moseley...£500 to 700
Inspect.-Gen. of Houssas, J. G. O. Aplin (Capt.)
                          £600 to 700
Collector of Customs, E. A. Lovell, M.A. £500 to 700
Director Public Works, H.B.Chapman£800 to 1,000
Chief Medical Off. Hy. Strachan ....£800 to 1,000
Harbour-Master, Capt. W. C. Speeding 450

Lagos is 4,279 miles from Liverpool ; transit 22 to 26 days. Telegrams, 6s. 3d. per word.

THE NIGER COAST PROTECTORATE, OR SOUTHERN NIGERIA.

H.M. Commissioner and Consul-General, Sir Ralph
  Dinham Rayment Moor, K.C.M.G. £2,500
Dep. Commr. & Consul, Major H. L. Gallwey,
  C.M.G., D.S.O...............................£800 to 900
Vice-Consuls & Dep. Commrs.,A. G. Leonard, R. F.
  Locke ....£600 to 700
District Commissioners, C. E. Harrison, A. B. Harcourt, A. A. Whitehouse, N. Burrows, F. T.
  Bartwell H. Bedwell, E. M. Murray........£500
17 *Assist. District Commrs.*.......... each £300 to 400
Travelling District Commissioners, F. S. James,
  W. C. G. Heneker £500
Resident, Benin City, W. F. W. Fosbery...... £500
  Assist. do., R. K. Granville............ £300 to 400
Director Gen. Customs & Postmaster General, T. A.
  Wall ....£650 to 800
Commandant of Forces, Maj.C. H. P. Carter
Supt. Marine Dept., H. A. Child ......£600 to 700
Treasurer, C. E. Dale....................£600 to 700
Judicial Officer, M. R. Menendez ......£700 to 800

Principal Medical Officer, R. Allman £1,000
Agents, London, Crown Agents for the Colonies.

This Protectorate, formerly called the "Oil Rivers Protectorate," includes the whole of the maritime region lying between Lagos and the Rio del Rey. The coast region was secured by treaties with the native chiefs, concluded by E. H. Hewett, C.M.G., in 1884, and was placed, in 1891, under an Imperial Commissioner, appointed by the Secretary of State for Foreign Affairs. The Protectorate was announced in the *London Gazette* of June 5, 1885, Oct. 18, 1887, and May 16, 1893. Centres of trade are Old Calabar, the capital (pop. about 15,000), Opobo, Bonny, New Calabar, Brass, Benin, Warri and Sapele and Akassa, the last named being situated at the Nun mouth of the Niger, which will pass on January 1st 1900 from the Administrative Court of the Royal Niger Company to that of "Southern Nigeria," as the Protectorate will in future be called.

The leading exports are palm-oil, palm-kernels, rubber, ebony, and ivory. The leading imports are cotton-goods, cooper's stores, hardware and cutlery, and spirits.

Revenue, 1898-9 ....£169,567
Total Imports, 1898-9 732,639
Total Exports, 1898-9 774,647
Imports from United Kingdom, 1898-9 583,067
Exports to United Kingdom, 1898-9.........500,367

Steamers of the "British and African" and "African" lines run regularly between Liverpool and the principal ports. Headquarters, Old Calabar. Transit about 22 days.

Telegrams, Bonny 8s. 3d., and Brass, 7s. 10d. per word.

NORTHERN NIGERIA.
(See also p. 608.)

This Protectorate will include, from January 1st, 1900, the northern portion of the territories hitherto administered by the Royal Niger Company. The Governor of this new Protectorate will be Lieut. Col. F. D. Lugard, C.B., D.S.O., and the headquarters of the administration will probably be fixed at Lokoja, the junction of the Niger and the Benne. It is impossible to furnish details with regard to the staff, &c., as the formation of the administration is not yet (Nov. 1898) completed. Lokoja and Jelba, some 220 miles higher up the Niger, are connected by telegraph with Lagos.

THE ROYAL NIGER COMPANY.
(See also p. 607.)

Governor,Rt.Hon.Sir G. Taubman-Goldie, K.C.M.G.
Deputy Gov., Rt. Hon. the Earl of Scarborough.
Secretary, Henry Morley.
Office, Surrey House, Victoria Embankment.
Agent-General, Joseph Flint.
Chief Justice, H. G. Kelly.
Principal Medical Officer, E. E. Craster.

The Royal Niger Company was the result of the amalgamation or buying up between 1879 and 1886 of all the various trading concerns in the Niger districts, including two powerful French societies inaugurated by the French Colonial Party. By its means a vast district has been subdued and secured for the British crown, for on 1 Jan., 1900, the dominion over the Company's territories passes to the Crown (see page 608).

The most prominent feature of the Company's administration has been the remarkable success of all their military operations. At the close of 1896 war broke out with the Emir of Nupe, the most powerful province of the Foulah Empire and a force (strengthened by the addition of Imperial Service officers) acting in concert with an armed fleet on the Middle Niger, routed the enemy in the southern districts and, advancing northwards, defeated and crushed a hostile force 30,000 strong after a two days' battle, 27-28 Jan., 1897. The capital, Bida, was thus secured and war declared on the Foulah province of Ilorin, the chief town being captured (16 Feb., 1897), and the Sultan deposed, to be afterwards re-instated as the vassal of Great Britain.

EAST AND CENTRAL AFRICA.
(See also Map, p. 607.)

THERE are no British *Colonies* on the East Coast of Africa to the north of Natal (already treated of under the head of "South Africa"). But a large portion of the Continent, both on the coast and inland, is under British protection and is administered directly by the Imperial Government, through the Foreign Office. Just as on the West Coast, the rivalry of European Powers has resulted in the division of the territory on the East into "spheres of influence," the definition of whose boundaries has given rise to much diplomatic negotiation, and is not yet finally completed. From the boundary of Amatongaland northward to Cape Delgado is *Portuguese*; from Cape Delgado to the river Umba is *German East Africa*; the islands of Zanzibar and Pemba form a British Protectorate; and the East Africa Protectorate (together with the little Witu Protectorate) extends from the Umba to the river Juba, which forms the southern boundary of the *Italian Sphere* extending northward as far as the British Protectorate on the Somali Coast. It will be observed that on this portion of the African Continent the French have made no acquisitions, but their recent annexation of the great island of Madagascar places them in a position of importance on the East Coast, although their influence does not extend to the mainland. The history of the European occupation of East Africa may be briefly stated thus :—the Portuguese acquired their rights by discovery and conquest. The Germans obtained a footing on the mainland opposite Zanzibar between 1880 and 1885, at which latter date the Sultan of Zanzibar recognized their Protectorate over Usagara, and in the same year the Germans declared a Protectorate over Witu. In 1888 the Imperial British East Africa Company received a Royal Charter, having been granted a few years previously by Seyyid Barghash, Sultan of Zanzibar, administrative rights over his mainland possessions. In 1890 the respective spheres of Great Britain and Germany were settled by agreement. Zanzibar became a British Protectorate, and Germany withdrew from her Protectorate over Witu in favour of Great Britain. The boundaries of the *Italian Sphere* were agreed upon in 1891. The Imperial British East Africa Company transferred the administration of their territories to the Imperial Government in 1895, having done much to promote the advance of civilization in the large tract of country now known as the "East Africa Protectorate."

The term "British Central Africa" is rather misleading to the unofficial mind. It must be understood as not applying to Uganda, although that country is, properly speaking, the most "Central" of the British Colonies or Protectorates in the Continent, but as the name given to a territory of more than 500,000 square miles in extent, north of the Zambesi, the greater part of which is under the administration of the British South African Company; the rest, which is under direct Imperial control, being called the "British Central Africa Protectorate." (See page 529.) The respective limits of British and Portuguese possessions or protectorates in East Africa were determined by the Treaty signed at Lisbon on June 11, 1891.

THE SOMALILAND PROTECTORATE.
In 1884 a Protectorate was declared over part of Somaliland, a country now subject (except where reserved by Great Britain and Italy) to Abyssinia, and forming the north-eastern horn of the African continent. The British Protectorate contains about 90,000 sq. miles. The population, mainly consisting of Somalis, a Mohammedan tribe, has not yet been estimated. The boundaries are defined by treaty with Abyssinia and Italy; the northern coast as far as 49° E. and the 8th parallel of N. latitude are the limits on the north and south.

The PRINCIPAL TOWNS are Berbera, Bulhar, and Zeyla.

The protectorate was transferred in 1898 from the administration of the India Office to that of the Foreign Office.

Consul General, Lt.-Col. J. Hayes Sadler, £1500
Consul at Zeyla, Capt. J. L. Harrington
   (*also Br.tish Agent in Abyssinia*)...... 650
Vice-Consul Berbera, Lieut. C. F. Harold 500

THE EAST AFRICA PROTECTORATE.
Commissioner & Consul-Gen., Sir A. H. Hardinge, K.C.M.G., C.B. (*See Zanzibar.*)
Members of Protectorate Council, Sir A. H. Hardinge; W. B. Cracknall, C.M.G.
Secretary, A. Alexander.
Sub-Commissioner and Consul, C. H. Craufurd £750
Sub-Commissioner and Vice-Consuls, J. Ainsworth, £500; A. S. Rogers, £700; and A. C. W. Jenner 500
Judicial Officer, R. S. P. Cator 700
Treasurer, E. Bradbridge............ .... £550 to 700

Chief of Customs and Vice Consul and Governor of Mombasa Gaol, A. Marsden £700
Commandant of Forces, Colonel G. P. Hatch. 900
Principal Med. Off., W. H. B. Macdonald 500
Agents in London, Crown Agents for the Colonies.

The Imperial British East Africa Company was incorporated by Royal Charter, dated September 3, 1888; and under the control of the Secretary of State for Foreign Affairs, exercised sovereign jurisdiction over the territories leased to it by the Sultan of Zanzibar, or acquired by treaties entered into with native Chiefs. A British Protectorate was announced over these territories on June 18, 1895, and the Company handed over the administration on July 1, 1895.

These territories are now comprised under the name of "The East Africa Protectorate," and include the whole of the coast from the Umba to the Juba River, granted on a 50 years' lease by the Sultan of Zanzibar, as also the vast territories in the interior bounded in part by international conventional lines. The southern boundary was defined by the Anglo-German conventions of 1886, 1890, and 1893; that on the east (along the Juba) and north-east, by an agreement with Italy (1891). On the west the Protectorate adjoins that of Uganda. The administration of the Protectorate is carried on under the Foreign Office, and the Commissioner, Sir A. Hardinge, is also H.M. Agent and Consul-General at Zanzibar.

A great portion of this vast region consists of pasture lands, or barren wastes, but there are not lacking extensive districts of great natural fertility on the coast, as well as in the interior. The Protectorate is divided for administrative purposes into four districts: (1) The Coast Province; (2) Ukamba; (3) Tanaland; and (4) Jubaland, of which the centres of administration are respectively Mombasa, Machakos, Lamu, and Kismayu. Of the four districts Ukamba is the only one which, generally speaking, is suitable to colonization by Europeans. There is also a considerable region within the boundaries of the Protectorate which is still undeveloped and has not yet been included in any administrative district.

Mombasa, which is connected with Europe by telegraph, is the capital of the Protectorate, and possesses, perhaps, the finest harbour on the east coast of Africa (population, about 24,000). There is also telegraphic communication along the coast between Mombasa and Lamu. The Uganda Railway has its terminus at Mombasa, which is connected with the mainland by a railway bridge 1,732 feet in length.

The principal exports are ivory, rubber, grain, live stock, gums, orchella weed, sesame, ebony, borities (poles and rafters), rhinoceros horn, hippopotamus teeth, &c.; the principal imports, on which is charged an *ad valorem* duty of 5 per cent. are piece goods, rice, grain and flour, building materials, European provisions, &c.

The importation of arms and ammunition is prohibited, except under the most stringent regulations, and the introduction and local manufacture of spirits is also heavily checked.

CAPITAL, Mombasa; transit about 21 days. Telegrams, Mombasa, 5s. per word, other places, 5s. 5d.

THE WITU PROTECTORATE.

Sultan, Omari bin Hamed, *succeeded* 1895.
British Resident, A. S. Rogers. (See East Africa Protectorate.)

This Protectorate is a small tract of country extending about 65 miles along the coast, and 30 miles at furthest inland, at the mouth of the river Tana. The Germans proclaimed a protectorate over it in 1885, which they resigned to Great Britain by the agreement of 1890. (See introductory note.) The British Protectorate was proclaimed Nov. 19, 1890. In March, 1891, the Imperial British East Africa Company undertook the administration of the country, from which they withdrew on July 31st, 1893. Witu is now regarded, for administrative purposes, as part of *Tanaland*, one of the districts into which the British East Africa Protectorate is divided.

Parcels, same as E. Africa Protectorate.

THE UGANDA PROTECTORATE.

(See also p. 607.)

Special Commissioner and Consul-General, Sir H. H. Johnston, K.C.B.................. £
Deputy Commissioner, Consul and Commandant of Forces, Lt.-Col. T. P. B. Ternan, D.S.O. 1000
Vice-Cons., F. J. Jackson, C.B., R. Macallister 650
Legal Vice-Consul, E. de L. Collinson......... 600
Senior Medical Officer, Dr. R.U. Moffat, C.M.G. 650
Director of Transport, A. D. Mackinnon ... 600
Agents in London, The Crown Agents for the Colonies, Downing Street, S.W.

A British Protectorate over the territory of Uganda was proclaimed in the "London Gazette" of June 19, 1894, and included only the country subject to King Mwanga, known as Uganda proper, bounded by the territories known as Usoga, Unyoro, Ankoli and Koki. This Protectorate has since been extended over Unyoro and Usoga—(see notice in "London Gazette," July 3, 1896). *Uganda proper* lies on the N.W. shore of Lake Victoria, between 500 and 600 miles in a direct line from the nearest point on the East Coast of Africa. It is situated on, and to the N. of the Equator. *Usoga* lies further to the East, on the N. shore of the Lake. *Unyoro* is to the N.W. of Uganda and extends to Lake Albert. *Koki* is to the S.W. of Uganda. The total population of the Protectorate may be roughly estimated at between 2 and 3 millions.

The capital town of Uganda is Mengo, but the centre of the Protectorate Administration is the neighbouring settlement of Kampala. The population of Uganda is estimated at over 300,000. The exports are at present almost confined to ivory. Principal imports are cotton cloths, prints, beads, &c.

In July, 1897, Mwanga left Uganda and headed an insurrectionary movement in Buddu, which was suppressed. He then fled to the neighbouring German territory, and his infant son was declared King of Uganda, with a native council of regency. In Sept. 1897, a mutiny broke out among the Soudanese troops in the Protectorate, which was only suppressed after several months' fighting, in circumstances of great difficulty and danger in which several British Officers lost their lives (Parly. Paper, Africa, No. 10, 1898). The military forces have since been completely reorganized.

The Uganda Railway.—A survey of the route to be followed by a railway to connect Uganda with the coast at Mombasa was made in 1892. In 1895 H.M. Government decided to proceed with the construction of the railway, and in September of that year a Committee was formed with the late Sir Percy Anderson, Assistant Under-Secretary of State for Foreign Affairs, as Chairman, to supervise the undertaking and organise details, under the authority of the Secretary of State for Foreign Affairs. The Committee meets regularly at the Foreign Office, and since the death of Sir Percy Anderson, the chair has been taken by the Hon. Francis Bertie, Assistant Under-Secretary of State. The gauge adopted for the railway is one metre. The chief engineer and staff arrived at Mombasa in December, 1895, and a large number of labourers have been imported from India for the work of construction, in addition to such local labour as can be engaged. The total length of the line to be constructed is about 560 miles, and 362 miles were completed in November, 1899. A telegraph line is also in process of construction. The necessary funds for the construction of the railway were provided by the Uganda Railway Act, 1896 (59 & 60 Vict. ch. 38) by which the issue of £3,000,000 was authorized from the Consolidated Fund.

CAPITAL, Kampala. Parcels must be sent to care of an agent at Mombasa.

THE ZANZIBAR PROTECTORATE.

Sultan, Hamud bin Muhamad bin Said, *succeeded* his cousin, Hamed bin Thwain, 27th Aug., 1896.

H. B. M. Agent and Consul-General, Sir A. H. Hardinge, K.C.M.G., C.B. £1,800

Consul, Basil S. Cave, C.B. 700

Judge of H. B. M. Court, W. B. Cracknall, C.M.G. 1,000

Assistant Judge, F. J. Collinson, Esq. ... 700

Vice-Consuls, V. K. Kestell-Cornish, £500; D. Mackenann, £500; J. H. Sinclair, £400.

President of Ministry, General Sir Lloyd William Mathews, K.C.M.G. (October, 1891).

Officer in Command of Native Troops, Brigadier-General A. E. Raikes.

The Zanzibar Dominions became independent in 1856 under the rule of Seyyid Majid, a son of Seyyid Said, Sultan of Muscat and Zanzibar. They formerly extended along the mainland as far South as Tanghi Bay and North as Warsheikh; but since the cession of the coast line from Ruvuma to Wanga, including the island of Mafia, to Germany in 1890, they are now confined to the islands of Zanzibar and Pemba (985 sq. m., and 165,000 inhabitants), and a ten-mile coast line from Wanga to Kipini, together with the islands of Lamu, Manda, and Patta, and the ports of Kismayu, Brava, Merka, Magdisho, each with a radius of 10 miles, and the port of Warsheikh, with a radius of 5 miles. As far as the mouth of the Juba, the Zanzibar dominions on the mainland are under the administration of H.M. Government through the Commissioner and Consul-General in the East Africa Protectorate (see p. 525), and the remainder, known as Benadir, is leased to the Italian Government. Zanzibar has been a British Protectorate since November, 1890.

On the sudden death of the late Sultan, Hamed bin Thwain, in August, 1896, Said Khaled, a member of the reigning family, seized the palace and held it with a large number of armed followers, in defiance of the protecting power. He proclaimed himself Sultan, but was not recognized as such by any of the foreign Consular representatives. Khaled having refused to quit the palace, it was found necessary to resort to force to compel his submission. After a bombardment of half-an-hour from the British warships in the harbour, Khaled fled to the German Consulate, whence he was eventually deported to German East Africa, and remains there under German supervision.

By a decree of Sultan Hamud (1897) the legal status of slavery ceased to be recognized in the islands of Zanzibar and Pemba.

The City of Zanzibar, on the island of the same name, is the largest in East Africa, and possesses a magnificent harbour, which presents great facilities to shipping and trade generally. The population of Zanzibar is about 250 000.

The principal imports, which amounted in 1898 to a total value of £1,555,070, are piece-goods, ivory, cloves, rice and coal; the exports are piece-goods, ivory, cloves, copra, rubber, gum-copal, and many minor articles amounting in 1898 to a total value of £1,497,883. The largest proportion of imports (£467,352) comes from British India, £93,516 from Germany, £26,631 from France, and £121,211 from Great Britain. The largest exports are made to German East Africa, which in 1898 accounted for £476,680, the principal other participators being British East Africa (£202,581), British India (£140,934), and Great Britain (£114,716). These figures refer to the port of Zanzibar, and not to the trade of the Zanzibar dominions. The large quantities of goods which pass through Zanzibar in mail and other steamers, and those which are transhipped to and from the coasting vessels in the harbour without being landed, are not included in the statistics from which the above figures are taken, which do not, therefore, give an adequate idea of the importance of the port of Zanzibar as the centre of trade in E. Africa. There is no direct steam communication with the United Kingdom, passengers, mails, and goods having to tranship at Aden. There are through steamers of French and German Companies.

The number of ocean-going vessels which entered the port in 1898 was—British 62, German 88, French 25, other nationalities 8, the total tonnage being 286,209. This does not include the coasting and dhow traffic, which is a very large one, extending to Bombay, Arabia, the Comoro Islands, and Madagascar.

Zanzibar is distant 8,064 miles, transit 20 days. Telegrams, 5s. 2d. a word.

BRITISH CENTRAL AFRICA

PROTECTORATE.

H.M. Commissioner and Consul-General, Alfred Sharpe, C.B. £1,400

Deputy Commissioner, Consul, and Commandant of British Central Africa Rifles, Lieut.-Col. W. H. Manning 800

Assist. Dep. Commr., Capt. F. B. Pearce ... 700

Vice-Consul and Agent at Chinde, E. Mac-Donell ....£450 to 600

Comm. Naval Forces, P. Cullen .....£520 to 700

Chief Judicial Officer and Vice-Consul, G. B. Piggott ....£600 to 700

Senior Medical Officer, Dr. D. Gray......£400 to 500

Agents in London, The Crown Agents for the Colonies, Downing Street, S.W.

This country, which was formerly termed *Nyassaland*, was proclaimed a British Protectorate on May 14, 1891. The Protectorate comprises the eastern portion of British Central Africa, and is administered directly by the Imperial Government through the Foreign Office. The remainder of the territory is administered by the British South Africa Company.

The population of the Protectorate is estimated at 845,000, of whom about 350 are Europeans and

260 British Indian subjects. The principal exports are coffee, ivory, and rubber; the total value being £37,964 in 1898-9. The cultivation of coffee is largely on the increase, and there are prospects of a steady development of this industry. Rice, tobacco, cotton, and tea are grown. The principal imports are soft goods, provisions and hardware, amount n to £108,383 in 1898-9, exclusive of specie. On Lake Nyassa there are seven British steamers (two of which are gunboats) and one German Government steamer. There are also gunboats and other steamers on the upper and lower Shiré river. At Chinde, situated in Portuguese territory at the mouth of Zambesi, is a piece of land leased from the Portuguese Government, where goods intended for the Protectorate may be transhipped free of duty.

Chief towns:—Blantyre (population about 100 Europeans and 6,000 natives) and Zomba, the headquarters of the administration. Communication is maintained between Chiromo (at the junction of the rivers Ruo and Shiré), and Chinde by the African Lakes Company's steamers, the Zambesi Traffic Co., and the African International Flotilla Company.

Between Chinde and Europe, the means of communication are Messrs. Rennie's line viâ Natal, the Union Steam Ship Co., the German East Africa S.S. Co., and the Portuguese Royal Mail steamers.

The construction of a railway to connect Chiromo with Blantyre is under consideration. The Protectorate is connected by telegraph overland with the Cape, viâ Fort Salisbury ; and, with the Portuguese wires, to Chinde and Quilimane. The African Trans-Continental Telegraph Company's line has now been extended northwards as far as Lake Tanganyika.

Telegrams, 4s. 5d. per word.

MAURITIUS.

Mauritius is an island lying in the Indian Ocean, 500 miles east of Madagascar, between 57° 18'–57° 49' E. long. and S. lat. 19° 58'–20° 32', and comprising an area of 705 square miles. The resident population on the 31st December, 1898, was 378,872, of whom 261,222 were Indians (the majority originally Coolies imported for working the sugar estates), and the remainder mainly of French or mixed descent. The whole island is practically given up to producing sugar for export, and the necessaries of life have all to be imported from abroad. Rice and grain are obtained from India, flour from Australia, oxen from Madagascar, and minor imports from South Africa and elsewhere. The chief trade of the island is with India. Being just within the tropics it has a hot climate; but, except in Port Louis and some of the low-lying districts, it is not unhealthy. The island is subject to cyclonic disturbances, and a hurricane in 1892 was particularly severe.

Mauritius was discovered in 1505 by the Portuguese, but they never formed any settlement on it. The Dutch visited it in 1598, and named it Mauritius, in honour of the Stadtholder, Count Maurice of Nassau. In 1644 they established a small colony on the shore, but in 1712 they abandoned the island, and in 1715 the French took possession of it. Under the French it became a great centre of trade, and in 1789 the seat of French Government in the East was removed to it from Pondicherry. In the war between England and France it was a base for privateering expeditions, which inflicted serious damage on British trade, until it

was taken by a British force in 1810. The French called it the Isle of France, and the French language and French law have been preserved under British rule. Its past greatness, and much of its present value, are due to the excellent harbour on the N.W. coast, on which the capital, Port Louis, stands. In 1898 there were 103 miles of railway and 60 post-offices in the island, with 135 miles of telegraph. A cable to Zanzibar was opened in 1893, bringing Mauritius and the Seychelles into telegraphic touch with the world. The annual trade of the island passes almost entirely through Port Louis.

The Government is more representative than that of an ordinary Crown Colony, being administered by a Governor, aided by an Executive Council of five officials, and two elected members of the Council of Government, and a Legislative Council of twenty-seven members, of whom eight are ex-officio, nine nominated by the governor, and ten elected for the various districts into which the island is divided. Port Louis has two members, and each of the country districts one.

The inhabitants of European descent are mostly Roman Catholic. The department of public instruction comprises two branches—the Royal College for higher education, and the Schools' Department for primary education. The College, which is affiliated to the London University, is under the control of a Rector, who is assisted by a staff of professors. The Schools' Department is under the direction of a superintendent, aided by two inspectors. The government schools are supported wholly by the State, the grant schools only partially so. The total expenditure on education in 1898 amounted to Rs. 486,836. Of the pupils in the government and aided schools 70·52 per cent. are Roman Catholics, 2·96 per cent. belong to the Church of England, and 1·33 per cent. to other Christian denominations ; 25·19 per cent. are Hindoos and Mohammedans to whom no assistance is given. The troops in the Colony on 31 December, 1898, numbered 2,096.

Under the Colonial Loans Act (1899) the sum of £32,820 was advanced for public works in the colony.

CAPITAL, Port Louis. Population, 1898, 54,223.

Public revenue in 1898	Rs : 7,620,318
Public expenditure in 1898	8,131,465
Public debt, 1898	£1,195,691
Paper money in circulation, 1898	Rs : 3,404,250
Total imports, 1898	28,325
Total exports, 1898	31,866,437
Imports from United Kingdom, 1898	5,443,934
Exports to United Kingdom, 1898 ...	1,171,359

Governor and Commander-in-Chief, Sir Charles Bruce, K.C.M.G.	£6,000
Commanding Forces, Major-General J. Talbot Coke	
Colonial Sec., Commander Sir John Graham-Bower, K.C.M.G., R.N. (ret.)	Rs : 13,500
Assist. do., Douglas Young	7,200
Procureur & Adv.-Gen., F. T. Piggott ...	13,500
Receiver-General, J. J. Brown	10,000
Registrar-Gen., G. A. L. Banbury *and fees,*	7,000
Auditor-General, George R. Dick, M.A. ...	10,000
Collector of Customs, G. Lumgair	9,000
Protector of Immigrants, J. F. Trotter ...	10,000
Surveyor-General, G. de Coriolis	8,000
Clerk of Councils, W. C. Rae	4,000
Chief Judge, Hon. Victor Delafaye	1,500
Puisne Judges, Hons. F. C. Moncreiff, Oliver Smith, E. Didier St. Amand, each	12,000

Bishop of Mauritius, Rt.Rev.W. Pym,D.D. Rs : 7,200
Do. Pt. Louis, R. C., Rt. Rev. P. A.
O'Neill, O.S.B. 7,200

(1.) RODRIGUES, 350 miles almost due east of Mauritius. Population in 1898 estimated at 2,870. Area, between 80 and 90 square miles. Cattle, beans, salt fish and goats are the principal exports. The ssland suffers much from hurricanes; and the revenue usually h as to be supplemented by a grant from Mauritius. *Magistrate,* B. H. Colin, Rs. 5,120.

(2.) OTHER DEPENDENCIES. Most of the scattered groups of coral islands belonging to Great Britain in the Indian Ocean are administered by the Mauritius Government, being visited periodically by a magistrate, whose duty it is to enquire into the condition of the labourers, and settle any disputes which may be referred to him. The chief product is cocoa-nut oil. The most important is Diego Garcia, one of the Chagos Archipelago, which lies on the direct route from the Red Sea to Australia, and, as it possesses a good harbour, has been much used of late years as a coaling station.

Transit: Mauritius, 27 days. Telegrams, 5s. per word.

THE SEYCHELLES ISLANDS.

These islands, which are about 30 in number, though still called dependencies of Mauritius, were practically made independent of the Mother Colony by letters patent issued in 1897. The principal islands of the group are Mahé, Praslin, and Ladigue, and their total area is estimated at about 150 square miles, of which, according to a recent survey, Mahé occupies nearly 56 square miles. The seat of Government is at Victoria, the capital, on the N.E. side of Mahé, which has an excellent harbour, and is constantly visited by men-of-war and steamers of the British India Company. The Admiralty have recently made Victoria a coaling station. The Seychelles Islands were originally discovered by the Portuguese, were occupied by the French about 1742, captured by a British ship in 1794, and were finally assigned to Great Britain in 1814. Although only 4° S. of the Equator, the islands are very healthy, the death-rate in 1896 being but 16 per 1,000, and the decennial average 1887-96, about 15 per 1,000. The estimated population of all the islands on December 31, 1897, was 18,639 (Mahé 14,000, Praslin 1,300, and Ladigue 900), an increase since the census of 1891 of nearly 2,500. There are 28 Roman Catholic and Church of England Primary Schools, and a grant-in-aid of Rs 9,000 (Roman Catholics Rs.6,343, Church of Eng. and Rs.1,656) was made

in 1897. In addition there is a Government School, maintained at an annual cost of Rs.3,864, where an education of a higher class is provided. This School was, until recently, affiliated to the Royal College of Mauritius, and will probably be again affiliated when there is regular communication between Seychelles and Mauritius.

The principal exports are vanilla, coconut oil and tortoise-shell, and recently the production of vanilla has greatly increased. Aldabra, one of the islands, is famous for the gigantic land tortoises, whilst the unique double cocoa-nut, *Coco de Mer*, is found in Mahé, and, in larger quantities, in Praslin. Mahé is in telegraphic communication with all important parts of the world *viâ* Mauritius and Zanzibar. It is proposed to enter into an agreement with the British India Steam Navigation Company for a fortnightly service of steamers, subsidised by the Imperial, Mauritius, and Seychelles Governments, between Colombo, Mauritius and Seychelles, and between Seychelles, Zanzibar, Aden and Bombay, and this service will take effect from the 1st January, 1900, and should prove of great benefit in developing the resources of the Seychelles Islands. The Government, which is that of a Crown Colony, is vested in an Administrator, assisted by an Executive Council, composed of three *ex-officio* members in addition to the Administrator, and by a Legislative Council, consisting of three officials, besides the Administrator, and three unofficial members. The Administrator is President of both Councils.

Revenue (1887, Rs.171,171), 1897 .... Rs.296,171
Expenditure, 1897 259,056
Imports (1887, Rs.431,201), 1897 1,122,411
Exports (1887, Rs.621,709), 1897 1,503,701
Savings Bank Deposits, 1897 63,624

Administrator, E. Bickham Sweet-Escott, C.M.G. Rs.15,000
Clerk to Administrator and Clerk of Councils, G. Gemmell Rs.1,500
Judge, R. M. Brown Rs.8,500
Treasurer and Collector, S. M. Bennett.. Rs.4,000
Auditor and Inspector of Schools, L. O. Chitty .... Rs 3,000
Conservator of Mortgages, Magistrate and Legal Adviser, A. Herchenroder Rs.5,000
Government Medical Officer, Mahé, R. Denman, M.R.C.S. Rs.4,000
Superintendent of Public Works and Government Surveyor, S. Baty Rs.3,000

The capital, Victoria, is 30 days distant from London. Telegrams, 5s. per word.

Greater Britain in the Southern Atlantic.

ASCENSION,

an isolated Island in the South Atlantic (3,417 miles from Plymouth, 690 from St. Helena, and 900 from Cape Palmas on the African coast), is of volcanic origin, the peak rising to the height of 2,820 feet, situated 7° 55' 55" S. lat., and 14° 25' 5" W. long. It is said to have been discovered by a Portuguese named João de Nova Gallego, on Ascension Day, and two years later was visited by Alphonse d'Albuquerque, who gave the island its present name. Its extreme length is 7½ miles, and extreme breadth 6 miles, with a circumference of 22 miles and an area of about 38 square miles,

and being situated in the heart of the S.E. trade winds, its climate is dry and salubrious. It remained uninhabited till 1815, when the English took possession of it. It now possesses a steam factory, naval and victualling yards, and a coaling dépôt. There are also excellent hospitals. Rabbits guinea-fowl, partridges, and goats, are being preserved for sporting purposes. The island is visited by the sea-turtle from January to May, which lay their eggs in the sand; as many as 276 being "turned" during the season of 1897, their weight being from 500 to 800 lbs., and their average price £2 15s.; the sooty tern, or "wide awake," use the island as a nesting-place about every eighth month, their eggs being collected in vast quantities, and much appreciated by the inhabitants. In 1896 there were about 16 acres of ground under cultivation, producing vegetables and bananas. The island is under the Board of Admiralty, by whom a naval officer is appointed as Captain in charge. There are no inhabitants except officers and their families, seamen, marines, and Kroomen; a limited number of men also have their families with them, the full complement of the island being 380 with about 60 women and children. Georgetown, the garrison settlement, is situated in a small bay on the N.W. coast. The island is of importance as a coaling station, and as a health resort for crews of vessels serving on the west coast division of the Cape station; it has recently been strongly fortified, and is being connected by the Eastern Telegraph Co. with the Cape, St. Helena, and Sierra Leone.

Domestic imports from U. K., 1897 ....£7,365
Officer in Charge, Capt. G. N. A. Pollard, R.N. £800
Fleet Paymaster, Abraham Turner, R.N.
Staff Surgeon, Charles W. Sharples, R.N.

Transit, about 28 days outward through St. Helena, and 14 days homeward. Telegrams *forwarded by post* from Cape Town.

TRISTAN D'ACUNHA

is the chief of a group of islands lying in lat. 37° 6′ S. and long. 12° 2′ W. These islands are of volcanic origin, and were discovered in 1506 by a Portuguese admiral, after whom they are named, and are very healthy. The population numbers about 100, and the inhabitants are said to be very long lived.

INACCESSIBLE ISLAND is a lofty mass of rock with sides 2 miles in length: the island is the resort of penguins and sea-fowl.

THE NIGHTINGALE ISLANDS are three in number, of which the largest is 1 mile long and ¾ m. wide, and rises in two peaks, 960 and 1,105 ft. above the sea-level respectively. The smaller islands, Stoltenhoff and Middle Isle, are little more than huge rocks. These islands are visited by large numbers of seals and sea-elephants.

FALKLAND ISLANDS.

These, the only considerable cluster in the South Atlantic, lie about 300 miles east of the Straits of Magellan, between 51° 15′—53° S. lat. and 57° 40′—62° W. long. They consist of East Falkland (area 3,000 sq. miles), West Falkland (2,300 sq. miles), and upwards of 100 small islands (islets, rocks, and sandbanks), comprising in the aggregate 6,580 sq. miles, and a population in 1897 of about 2,050. Mount Adam, the loftiest peak in the colony, rises 2,315 feet above the level of the sea. The Falklands were discovered by Davis in 1592, and visited by Hawkins in 1594. After having successively belonged to France and Spain, they were given up to Great Britain about 1771, but not actually occupied. In 1820 the Republic of Buenos Aires established a settlement in these islands, which was destroyed by the Americans in 1831. In 1833 they were again taken possession of by the English for the protection of the whale-fishery, and colonized, and from that time to the present have so continued, being, as a whole, the most southerly organized colony of the British Empire. The climate, though somewhat bleak, is usually considered healthy; and the temperature is on

the whole equable, the thermometer ranging in winter from 30° to 50°, and in summer from 40° to 65°. The islands are chiefly bog-land, and have proved very suitable for sheep; kitchen-gardens occupy the only cultivated part. The population is entirely British, and is engaged mainly in sheep-farming and seafaring industries. The chief exports in 1898 were wool £92,205, sheep-skins and tallow. The total tonnage of vessels entered and cleared in 1898 was 124,147. There are three places of worship (one Church of England, one Roman Catholic, and one Baptist). The only important settlement is Port Stanley, at the head of Port William, on the coast of East Falkland.

There is a volunteer force of about 100 men.

SOUTH GEORGIA, an island 800 miles east-south-east of the Falkland Group, with an area of 1,000 square miles, and several other small uninhabited islands, are comprised within this colony.

Public revenue, 1898	£13,039
Expenditure, 1898	14,278
Total imports, 1898	72,987
Total exports, 1898	106,984
Domestic imports from the U. K., 1898	64,992
Domestic exports to the U. K., 1898	103,700

The Government is vested in a Governor, aided by an Executive Council of three members, and a Legislative Council, the members of both being appointed by the Crown.

Governor and Chief Justice, William Grey-Wilson, C.M.G. ....(and fees) £1,200	
Colonial Secretary, &c., Frederick Craige-Halkett ....(and quarters)	500
Colonial Treasurer, &c., C. W. Hill	300
Colonial Surgeon, S. Hamilton, F.R.C.S.I.	300
Bishop, Rt. Rev. W. H. Stirling, D.D.	
Colonial Chaplain, The Very Rev. Dean Brandon, M.A.	300

CHIEF TOWN, Port Stanley.

Port Stanley is distant about 8,130 miles; transit, 30 days. Telegrams *sent by post* from Monte Video.

ST. HELENA,

probably the best known of all the solitary islands in the world, is situated in the South Atlantic Ocean, 955 miles S. of the Equator, 760 S.E. of Ascension, 1,140 from the nearest point of the African Continent, and 1,800 from the coast of S. America, in 15° 55′ S. lat. and 5° 42′ W. long. It is 10½ miles long, 6½ broad, and encloses an area of 47 square miles, with a population in 1891 of 4,116, including 1,986 males and 2,130 females. It is of volcanic origin, and consists of numerous rugged mountains, the highest rising to 2,700 feet, interspersed with picturesque ravines. The climate vies with that of Madeira in point of salubrity and evenness of temperature. Although within the tropics, the south-east "trades" keep the temperature mild and equable. The thermometer goes up to 84° in the town at the sea level; but in the country, 1,800 feet above the sea, the maximum is about 74°, and the mean temperature ranges from 57° in September to 66° in March, there being very little difference between night and day; the lowest temperature in winter is 51°, and the total rainfall (1898) 31 inches. St. Helena was discovered by the Portuguese navigator, Juan de Nova Castella, on 21st May, 1501 (St. Helena's Day), and remained unknown to other European nations until 1588, when it was visited by Captain Cavendish on his return from his voyage round the world. It remained uninhabited until the Dutch colonized it *circ.* 1645. The English East India Company seized it in 1651; but it was retaken by the Dutch in 1672. In 1673 it was again taken from the Dutch by Capt. Munden, of the English Navy, and was held by the East India Company, who had obtained a charter for its possession from Charles II., until 1834 (with the exception of the period 1815 to 1821, during which the British Government held it as a residence for Napoleon Bonaparte, who died there 5th May, 1821), when it was ceded by them to the Crown. It was formerly an important station on the route to India, but its prosperity received a fatal blow by the cutting of the Suez Canal, and it is now frequented only by a few sailing ships homeward bound from the East Indies. The tonnage dues on calling ships was abolished in 1882, and the port is now free to all ships except when bringing or taking cargo to and from the port : the number which called in 1898, excluding 192 boarded by island boatmen when passing, was 147. It is of strategical importance as a coaling station, and

has recently been fortified by the Imperial Government. St. James's Bay, on the north-west of the island, possesses a good anchorage.

The government is administered by a Governor, with the aid of an Executive Council of 4 members, the Governor alone making all ordinances.

CAPITAL, Jamestown. Population, 2,233.

Public revenue, 1898	£9,152
Expenditure, 1898	12,319
Amount of public debt, 31 December, 1899	(*Nil*)
Total imports, 1898	62,985
Total exports, 1898	4,391
Imports from the United Kingdom, 1898	16,416
Exports to the United Kingdom, 1898	581
Governor, Robert Armitage Sterndale (and table allowance £200)	£500
Police Magistrate, &c., J. Homagee	420
Harbour Master (Naval) and Emigration Agent, Commander Hewetson, R.N. ...... (*and fees*)	300
Colonial Surgeon, F. E. Welby	230
Comdg. Troops, Lt.-Col. A. Bor, W.I.E.	

Distance, 4,477 miles; transit, 17 days. Telegraph, inland only; foreign messages *sent by post* from Teneriffe, 1 s. 3 d. per word.

Greater Britain : In the Mediterranean.

CYPRUS,

is an island in the Mediterranean Sea, between N. lat. 34° 30′ and 35° 41′, and E. long. 32° 15′ and 34° 35′. It is about 60 miles distant from the nearest point of Asia Minor ; and 41 miles from Latakia on the Syrian coast, with which it is connected by a submarine telegraph cable. The distance to Port Said, at the entrance of the Suez Canal, is 238 miles. The larger part of the island is an irregular parallelogram, 100 miles long and 60 to 30 broad ; from which a narrow peninsula, 5 or 6 miles wide, runs out for 40 miles towards the north-east. The area is about 3,584 square miles. The population in 1891 was 209,286 persons (the latest estimate 1899 being 228,000), of whom about 23 per cent. were Mohammedans, and the remainder mostly members of the Orthodox Greek Church. The principal productions are grain of various kinds, sesame, linseed, wine and spirits, silk, olives, locust-beans, cotton, wool, and hides. The fertility of the soil has for centuries been proverbial. In 1898 the wine export was 1,272,756 gals., and that of spirits 79,594 gals., the bulk going to Turkey and Egypt. The climate varies in different localities. In the plains the summer heat is very great, and the British troops suffered severely when first stationed in the island. Excellent summer quarters were, however, found in the hills ; and, owing to the enforcement of various sanitary measures, the death-rate of the whole island is nearly as low as that of any European country.

Cyprus still forms part of the Ottoman Empire ; but by virtue of a treaty made between England and the Porte, dated 4th June, 1878, the government is administered by England for so long a time as Batoum and Kars may be kept by Russia. The inhabitants have been granted a political franchise, every man paying direct taxes having a vote. The government is administered, under the Colonial Office, by a High Commissioner, assisted by a Legislative Council composed of eighteen members, six being official and twelve

elected. The island is divided into three electoral districts, each returning one Mohammedan and three Christian members.

For administrative and legal purposes it is divided into six districts. In each district the executive government is represented by a commissioner ; and each has a Court of Law presided over by an English barrister, who is assisted by two native judges, one being a Christian and the other a Mohammedan. There is also a Supreme Court for the whole island, consisting of two English judges.

The amount payable to the Sublime Porte yearly is £87,800 for revenue, £5,000 in compensation for State lands, and 4,166,220 okes of salt in kind (an oke=2·8 lbs.). This sum is not actually paid to the Sultan, but is retained as part payment of the loss sustained by England and France in paying the deficiency on the Guaranteed Turkish Loan of 1855.

Under the Colonial Loans Act 1899 the sum of £314,000 was advanced for Harbour and Railway works and for the purposes of irrigation.

The capital is Nicosia (Lefkosia), near the centre of the island, with a population of 12,515 in 1891 ; the other principal towns are Larnaca (population 7,593), Limassol (7,388), Famagusta, Kyrenia, and Papho.

Public revenue, 1898-9	£210,284
Public expenditure, 1898-9	132,975
Imports from United Kingdom, 1898	a86,705
Exports to ditto, 1898	a94,531
Total imports, 1898	a288,258
Total exports, 1898	a343,687
a Exclusive of specie.	
High Commissioner, Sir William Frederick Haynes Smith, K.C.M.G.	£3,000
Priv. Sec. and A.-de-C., Lord Langton	150
Chief Sec., Capt. Arthur H. Young, C.M.G.	800
Assistant Secretary, W. H. Bennett	350
Receiver-General, A. M. Ashmore	750
Inland Treasurer (vacant)	360

Chief Justice, Sir Joseph Turner Hutchinson £1,000
Puisne Judge, J. P. Middleton 750
Queen's Advocate, A. G. Lascelles............ 750

Distance, 3,030 miles; transit, 8 to 11 days.
Telegrams, 6½d. a word, by Eastern Co. 1s. 7d.

MALTA,

an island in the Mediterranean Sea, 58 miles from
Sicily and about 180 from the African coast, about
17 miles in length and 9 in breadth, and having
an area of 9½ square miles. The colony includes
also the adjoining island of Gozo, with an area of
24¾ square miles ; COMINO — the site of the
Sultan's disaster in 1889, and several islets. The
population of the whole group, 31 Dec., 1898, was
180,328, exclusive of the British troops, who
numbered 11,317. In religion the Maltese are
Roman Catholics. The lower orders are mainly
Punic in race. The Maltese dialect, which
is generally spoken, is of Semitic origin, and
is held by some to be derived from the Car-
thaginian and Arabic tongues. The upper
classes are mostly descendants from families who
sought the protection of the Order of St. John
during the Middle Ages, from all parts of Southern
Europe, and usually speak Italian. There is a
native order of nobility consisting of 29 families.
The islands are highly cultivated. The chief
products are cotton, corn, oranges, melons, grapes,
cumin seed, and early potatoes for the London
market ; figs and honey are plentiful. It was estimated that in 1891 the area under cultivation in the
three islands was about 37,896 tumuli. From
4,000 to 5,000 women and children, chiefly in Gozo,
are employed in making lace. The principal occupation of the people is, however, in connection
with the shipping. In 1898 there were 59,823 persons living in Valletta, Floriana, and the "Three
Cities" on the other side of the harbour, and
many persons from the neighbouring villages
come in daily to work at the Port. The harbour
is one of the finest in the world, with such a depth
that the largest vessels can anchor alongside the
very shore. It is a most important port of call
for the many vessels passing to and from the East
and Australasia by the Suez Canal, being just
half-way between Gibraltar and Port Said. There
is also an extensive arsenal and important dockyard, Malta being the headquarters of the Mediterranean Fleet ; and an additional graving dock
was opened on Feb. 12, 1892. The island is strongly
fortified, and has a garrison of 11,317 (including 761 Royal Malta Artillery and a Maltese
regiment of militia 1,741 strong). The climate,
although not actually tropical, is very hot in
summer. In the two hottest months (July and
August) the average daily range of temperature is from 71° to 87° F., with an occasional
rise to 96° or fall to 65°. In winter the range
is from 48° to 58°, with an occasional fall to
41° or rise to 64°. Citta Vecchia, the former
capital of the island, is a handsome old town of
8,135 inhabitants, and contains the ancient palace
of the courts of justice, the Cathedral, and the
Seminary. It has, however, been entirely eclipsed
in importance by the modern fortified capital of
Valletta, which was founded in 1566. Malta is
well provided with an educational system. It
possesses a University and Lyceum at Valletta ;
and 89 elementary schools, 2 secondary schools,
and 31 night schools for boys, are maintained by
Government at a cost of £21,846 in 1898 ; in addition to which there are Garrison schools and a
Dockyard school, while 229 private schools at-

tended by 3,990 pupils in Malta and Gozo, receive
no aid from the government.

In ancient times, Malta was occupied in
succession by Phœnicians, Greeks, Cartha-
ginians, Romans, and Byzantine Greeks, as
each nation secured the command of the
Mediterranean Sea. It attained to a high
degree of commercial prosperity, being especially noted in Roman times for its textile
fabrics. It is said to have been converted to
Christianity on the occasion of St. Paul's shipwreck in 58 A.D. In the Dark Ages it was taken
by the Moors, its commerce was destroyed, and
it was used mainly as a base for piratical expeditions. In 1090 it was again brought under
Christian rule, being conquered by the Norman
Count Roger, of Sicily. For the next 440 years
it followed the fortunes of that kingdom ; but in
1530 it was handed over to the Knights of St.
John, who proceeded at once to make it a
stronghold of Christianity against the Turks.
In 1565 it sustained the famous siege, when the
last great effort of the Turks was successfully
withstood by the Grand Master La Vallette.
The Knights freely expended their vast
revenues in fortifying the island and carrying
out many useful and magnificent works, until,
in 1798, they were expelled by Napoleon. The
Maltese, however, rose against the French garrison, and with some help from British and
Neapolitan forces, compelled it, in 1800, to
capitulate. They then ceded the islands to
Great Britain, and the cession was confirmed by
the Treaty of Paris in 1814. The government is
administered by a Governor, who is usually a distinguished General, assisted by an Executive
Council consisting of 7 official and 3 unofficial
members, and by a Legislative Council, called the
Council of Government—6 official and 13 elected
members. The Governor is President in both.

In 1898 the port of Valletta was entered by
3,890 vessels (tonnage, 3,563,728).

CAPITAL, Valletta. Population, 25,650 in 1891.

Public revenue, 1898	£332,488
Expenditure, 1898	339,082
Imports (actual), 1898	880,164
Exports (actual), 1898	51,597
Imports (in transit), 1898	9,144,967
Exports (in transit), 1898	9,327,543
Total imports from U. K. (actual), 1898	203,517
Total exports to U. K. (actual), 1898 ...	701

Governor and Comm. of the Troops, Gen. Sir Francis Wallace Grenfell, G.C.B., G.C.M.G.	£5,000
Assistant Military Secretary, Major H. M. Grenfell, 1st Life Guards	
Vice-Pres. of the Council of Govt., His Hon. Sir Joseph Carbone, K.C.M.G., LL.D.	150
Chief Secretary to Government, Sir Gerald Strickland, Count della Catena, K.C.M.G.	1,000
Crown Advocate, Hon. Alfredo Naudi, LL.D.	600
Collector of Customs and Superintendent of Ports, Hon. Francesco Vella, C.M.G.	572
Compt. of Charitable Instit., Hon. R. Micallef	570
Public Works, Hon. L. Gatt, C.E...	500
Rec.-Gen. & Dir. of Contracts, C. Gatt	400
Auditor-General, Hon. A. Sciortino	500
Postmaster-Gen., S. Camilleri	500
Superintendent of Police, Capt. C. La-primandaye, R.N.	500
Education, Napoleon Tagliaferro	500
Chief Justice & Pres. of Court of Appeal, Sir Joseph Carbone, K.C.M.G., LL.D.	1,000

Judges, Dr. L. Ganado ; Dr. Baron A. Chapelle ; Dr. P. De Bono ; Dr. Z. Roncali ; Dr. G. Pullicino .... each £600

Malta is 2,280 miles by sea, and *via* Naples about 1,995 ; transit, 4 days. Telegrams, per word, 6d.

GIBRALTAR,

a rocky promontory, 3 miles in length and ¾ of a mile in breadth, and 1,439 feet high at its greatest elevation, near the southern extremity of Spain, with which it is connected by a low isthmus. It is about 14 miles distant from the opposite coast of Africa. Gibraltar was captured in 1704, during the war of the Spanish Succession, by a combined Dutch and English force, under Sir George Rooke, and ceded by the Treaty of Utrecht, 1713. Since that time it has remained continuously in possession of the British. Of the many attempts to retake it, the most celebrated was the great siege in 1779-83, when General Elliott, afterwards Lord Heathfield, held it for 3 years and 7 months against a combined French and Spanish force. The town stands at the foot of the promontory on the N.W. side. Gibraltar is a free port, and enjoys the advantages of an extensive shipping trade. During the year 1898 3,794 vessels entered, with a total tonnage of 4,563,822. The chief sources of revenue are the port dues, the rent of the crown estate in the town, and duties on wine, spirits, tobacco, and beer. An enclosed harbour with three graving docks, capable of accommodating the largest battleships in the British Navy, is being built at an estimated cost of about £4,000,000 ; the works include a commercial and coaling mole. The estimated resident civilian population 31 Dec., 1898, was 18,155. The actual strength of the troops at that date was 4,963.

The Governor is in command of the garrison, and exercises all the functions both of government and legislation ; there being no executive or legislative council.

Amount of public revenue, 1898	£56,019
Amount of expenditure, 1898	48,878
Domestic imports from U. K. 1898	712,917
Exports to United Kingdom, 1898	64,325

Governor and Commdr.-in-Chief, Gen. Sir Robert Biddulph, R.A., G.C.B., G.C.M.G. £4,167
Assistant Military Secretary, Lt.-Col. W. B. Fletcher, R.A.
Commanding Royal Artillery, Major-Gen. F. G. Slade, R.A., C.B.
Commanding Infantry Brigade, Maj.-Gen. Sir H. E. Colvile, K.C.M.G., C.B.

Colonial Secretary, Sir H. M. Jackson, K.C.M.G. .... £500 to 1,000
Treasurer and Collector, A. C. Greenwood £400 to 600
Captain of the Port, Comm. L. A. W. Barnes-Lawrence, R.N. 370
Postmistress, Miss M. Creswell 600
Police Magistrate, A. M. Coll, D.C.L. .. £500 to 600
Chief of Police, J. Bennet .... £300 to 400
Surgeon, Colonial Hospital, W. Turner, M.D. 250
Chief Justice, Stephen H. Gatty 1,150
Attorney-General, A. W. Fawkes, Q.C....... 800
Registrar, Supreme Court, E. M. Hutton, M.A. 550

Distance 1,209 miles ; transit 4½ days. Telegrams, 3¼d. per word.

Shipping of the United Kingdom.

STATEMENT OF ADDITIONS AND DEDUCTIONS FROM OFFICIAL REGISTER DURING 1898. (Prepared by Lloyd's Register from information supplied by the Registrar-General of Shipping.) N.B. Vessels of however small tonnage (if registered under the Merchant Shipping Acts) are included in this statement.

ADDITIONS.

1898.	STEAM.		SAIL.	
	No.	Tons Gross.	No.	Tons Gross.
New Vessels built in U. K.	646	1,011,233	242	18,067
New Vessels built abroad	...	...	...	...
Other Vessels bought from abroad	44	62,307	16	2,257
Other Vessels added	39	38,228	92	8,729
Total ...	729	1,111,768	350	29,053

DEDUCTIONS.

1898.	STEAM.		SAIL.	
	No.	Tons Gross.	No.	Tons Gross.
Vessels lost, broken up, &c.	195	227,142	448	75,304
Vessels sold to foreigners	260	434,725	220	153,783
Other Vessels deducted	29	34,793	26	5,781
Total......	484	696,660	694	234,868

See also Indian Section, pp. 441–476; Geographical Progress and Territorial Changes, pp. 604–611, and Maps, pp. 469, 607, 608, 609.

A list of the Principal Foreign Countries, giving the Name of their Sovereign or Ruler and Statistics of their Area, Population, Products, Railway and Telegraph system, Navies and Armies and Commerce, distinguishing the Amount of Trade with this Country; the Names of Her Majesty's Ambassadors, Ministers, and Consuls are also given, together with their actual Salaries, and the names of the Foreign Ambassadors and Consuls resident in London.

To many Countries their distance from this country is given and, to nearly all, the time occupied in transit, and the cost of Telegrams.

POSTAGE.—There is a uniform rate to all countries of the world which do not form part of the British Empire; the charge for letters is 2½d. the half-ounce; for newspapers and books ½d. the two ounces; patterns and samples ½d. the two ounces, but with a minimum charge of 1d.: and commercial papers the same, but with a minimum charge of 2½d.

PARCEL RATES will be found on pp. 438, 439.

TELEGRAPHIC RATES are given at the end of each article.

Many of the following Statistics have been revised specially for the Almanack by direction of the various Governments. The Editor is also indebted to Her Majesty's Representatives at Foreign Courts, and to the British Consuls; he has also to thank several of the Foreign Ministers and Consuls in London for many particulars. In statistics of trade the term "Domestic" Imports signifies the produce and manufactures of the country in question whence they come, and does not include articles re-exported after having been already received there from abroad.

ABYSSINIA or ETHIOPIA.

Emperor (*Negus Negusti or King of Kings*) Menelek of Shoa, G.C.M.G., *b.* 1843, *procl.* 12th March, 1889.

King of Godjam and Dependencies, Negus Tekla Haimanot.

Governor of Harrar and Dependencies and of Tigré, Ras Makunan.

Governor of Wollo, &c., Ras Michael.

Governor of Kaffa, &c., Ras Walda Georgis.

Abyssinia proper consists of four provinces, Tigré, Amhara, Godjam, and Shoa. The area of these provinces, lying between 8° and 15° 30′ N. lat. and 36° and 40° E. long. may be reckoned at 100,000 square miles with a population of 3 or 4 millions. But the boundaries of the empire are indefinite except on the east where they touch the Italian colony of Massowah (Eretria) which is a narrow coast strip, the French colony of Obok or Djibuti, and the British Somali Coast Protectorate. Northwards the boundary is about 15° 30′ N. lat., falling just south of Kassala. The arrangement between England and Italy in 1891 when Italy claimed a protectorate over Abyssinia, by virtue of their treaty of 1889 with Menelek, drew the westerly limit of Abyssinia along the 35° of longitude and the southerly limit along the 6° of N. lat. as far as the Shebeli river. Recent travellers have found Abyssinians in the neighbourhood of Lake Rudolf and in the Borana country, and Abyssinian expeditions have been as far south as Bardera.

⁂ In 1891 the Emperor Menelek notified the Powers that his empire extended roughly from the 14th to the 2nd degree N., including the country between the Sobat and the Blue Nile up to the White Nile. The British advance from the north prevented Russian and French expeditions from establishing an anti-British dominion across the Nile from Djibuti through Abyssinia to the French Congo. M. Leontieff, a Russian, has been appointed Governor of "the Equatorial Provinces," which lie on the east of the Omo River and north of Lake Stephanie.

Abyssinia proper is volcanic and mountainous. It contains little mineral wealth, though iron and coal are not uncommon, gold is washed in various streams, and salt, saltpetre, sulphur, copper, silver, are also procurable. The lower country and deep valley gorges are very hot; the higher plateaus are well watered and have a genial climate. In the hotter regions, sugar cane, cotton, coffee, indigo, banana, &c. flourish; in the middle zone the vine, palm, maize, wheat, barley, orange, peach and other fruit trees, tobacco, potatoes, &c., are cultivated; and above 9,000 feet are excellent pastures with some corn cultivation. There are two seasons in the year, a dry winter and a rainy summer. The chief river is the Blue Nile, issuing from the Tsana lake; the Atbara and many other tributaries of the Nile also have their rise in the Abyssinian highlands. Horses, mules, donkeys, camels, oxen, goats and sheep, form a large portion of the wealth of the people, the wild game consists of elephant, rhinoceros, hippopotamus, zebra, giraffe, antelope, buffalo, hyena, lynx, &c. To the north-east the people are more akin to the Caucasian and the Semitic, to the south-east more akin to the negro; on the west are the plain dwellers who talk Amharac; on the east the mountaineers speaking Tigré, which is akin to ancient Arabic. Of the Galla tribes to the south, some are Pagan, some Mahomedan, and some Christian; the Somalis are Mahomedan, but the Abyssinians are Christian and their kings claim descent from Menelek, the son of Solomon by the Queen of Sheba. They themselves were converted to Christianity probably about 600 A.D. by monks from Egypt, but have long been isolated from the rest of the Christian world. At the end of the 15th century an attempt was made by the Jesuits under the Portuguese power to bring the Abyssinian Church under the Papacy. For a time this event seemed likely; but, before the middle of the 17th century, the Jesuit influence was overthrown and expelled, and the Abyssinian Church reverted to its eastern forms, and no trace of Jesuit influence remained. There is no popular literature, and no education; there is a legal code said to be derived from Constantine, but practically government is autocratic, qualified by the power of revolt. There is no standing army, but all are the National Guard of about 400,000. The military soldiers, and in the struggle against Italy, the Emperor's army probably numbered 100,000, there being certainly that number of modern rifles in the country. The principal pursuits are war, agriculture, cattle breeding and hunting; industry is looked upon; the chief exports are coffee, honey, civet, wax, gums, musk, vegetable oils, spices, hides, ivory, gold, mules, cattle, and horses. The currency is the Maria Theresa (Austrian) dollar but Indian rupees also find some circulation in Harrar. There is a demand for imported cloth, cotton and woollen goods, cheap hardware, and cutlery, beads and matches. The import duty on all goods at Harrar is 8 per cent. *ad valorem;* in the interior the duty is variable. There is a large trade between the British port of Zaila and Harrar. England came into conflict with Abyssinia in 1867-68, when the then capital, Magdala, was occupied by a British Army under Gen. Napier (Lord Napier of Magdala). In 1889 the Italians made a treaty with King Menelek, under which they claimed a protectorate over Abyssinia: this was repudiated by Menelek in 1893 and finally given up after the Italian defeat at Adowa (1st March, 1896). The subsequent treaty with Italy confined the Italian protectorate to a mere strip, 180 miles wide, along the coast, with possession of, and access to, the Italian Settlement of Lugh, on the Juba River. Since that date Russian, French, and English missions have visited King Menelek at his new capital Antoto or Adis Ababba; the French mission under M. Lagarde, and the English mission under Mr. Rennell Rodd. A concession has been given for the construction of a railway under French auspices from Djibuti to the capital, with a branch to Harrar; this has been opened for engines to the 50th kilometre, while the line is picketed for 100 kilometres, and surveyed as far as Harrar. When completed this will probably take the trade which now mainly passes through the British port of Zaila, from which the road to Harrar is easier and shorter and more secure than that from Jjibuti. The principal towns of Abyssinia, besides Adis Ababba, are Adowa, the capital of Tigré, Gondar, Basso, Aksum, Ankober, and Harrar, which is a dependency of Shoa. There are ancient architectural remains at Aksum, Gondar, and Ankober; modern architecture is very poor.

Imports from the United Kingdom, 1898 £9,832
Exports to the United Kingdom, 1898 ... 84

CAPITAL, Adis Ababba (population fluctuates, but is ordinarily about 10,000).
British Agent, Capt. John Lane Harrington, I.S.C. (1898).
Harrar,—Cons. Agent, J. Gerolimato.
Adis Ababba is 500 miles from Zaila, *viâ* Harrar; letters from London are from 22 to 23 days in transit if the mail connects with steamer service from Aden; caravans take from 35 to 60 days.

AFGHANISTAN. (*See* pp. 469 & 471.)
ALGERIA (*French Colony, see* p. 555).
ANDORRA.

A miniature Republic in the Pyrenees, with an area of 175 sq. miles, and a population of 6,000: it is under the joint suzerainty of France and Spain. There is a Council of Twenty-four, elected by certain of the inhabitants, a judge, and two vicars (priests) appointed in turn by France and the Bishop of Urgel.

ANNAM. (*See* p. 475.)
ARABIA. (*See* p. 476.)
ARGENTINE REPUBLIC.
(*See also* p. 609).

President, Dr. Julio A. Roca, *sworn in* 12th Oct., 1898, for six years $36,000
Vice-Pres., Dr. D. N. Quirno Costa ....$18,000.
Foreign Affairs, & Public Worship, Dr. A. Alcorta.
Justice and Public Instruction, Dr. O. Magnasco.
Interior, Dr. Felipe Yofre.
Finance, Dr. José Maria Rosa.
War, General Luis Maria Campos.
Marine, Rear-Admiral Martin Rivadavia.
Agriculture,
Public Works, Dr. Emilio Civit.

Minister in London, Florencio L. Dominguez 16 Kensington Palace Gardens, W.
1st Sec. of Legation, Vicente J. Dominguez.
2nd Secretary, Luis H. Dominguez.
Consul-Gen., Sergio Garcia Uriburu, Broad St. House, New Broad Street, E.C.
Consul, A. Lumb, Broad Street House, E.C.
Vice-Consul, F. Torromé.
Consul-General at Glasgow, T. F. Agar.
There are also Consulates at *Liverpool, Southampton, Cardiff, Manchester, Falmouth, Newcastle, Birmingham, Newport, Edinburgh, Dundee, Belfast,* and *Dublin,* with Vice-Consulates at *Dover, Liverpool, Nottingham, Manchester, Swansea,* and *Aberdeen.*

The Republic is composed of 14 provinces and 9 territories, with a large seaboard on the east coast of South America. It is estimated to contain 1,212,000 square miles, with a population estimated at 4,093,000. By the treaty of 23rd July, 1881, with Chile, Terra del Fuego has been divided between these two Republics. The country was discovered in 1517, and settled by the Spaniards in 1535. The principal productions are wool, hides, linseed, sugar, maize, wheat, and tobacco. The other products are tallow, Paraguay tea, and excellent European and indigenous fruits. The mineral products are copper, silver, coal, and salt. The export of frozen sheep to Europe is becoming of great importance: there are at present 5 factories in working operation. The chief articles of export in the year 1897 were pastoral, or agricultural and forest products, and minerals.

The principal imports from the United Kingdom are machinery, hardware, and cotton, woollen, and linen goods. The total trade was distributed in 1896 as follows: with the U.K. £11,883,800; France £7,400,000; Belgium £4,650,000; Germany £5,400,000.

In 1897 there were 9,026 miles of railways in working order, connecting the principal cities of the Republic with the capital. Telegraphs, 21,000 miles, mostly government lines. Immigration is encouraged, the arrivals in 1889 reaching the unprecedented number of 218,744, mostly Italians, and in 1897 the total number of immigrants was 105,143: the language in ordinary use is Spanish. The Buenos Aires port works and the new port at the Ensenada have been opened for traffic, while two graving docks have been constructed at Buenos Aires and a naval port at Bahia Blanca; 651 British ships (1,010,350 tons) entered Buenos Aires port in 1897.

The Argentine Republic is connected by cable with all the cities in the world. The Army consists of 749 officers and 10,905 men, in addition to school has 150 cadets, and the school for non-commissioned officers, 120. Navy (1897): 30 vessels, including 6 armoured vessels, 4 cruisers, 3 gunboats, 4 destroyers, 3 transports, 26 torpedo boats, and 2 vessels under construction. The naval school has 60 cadets, and the school of gunners, 80. Public instruction is much developed: there are 2 universities, 2 schools of engineering, 2 colleges of agriculture, 27 training colleges, 3,751 public schools, and a school for deaf-mutes; with 9,035 teachers and 330,961 pupils in 1896. The climate of the Argentine Republic is temperate and healthy.

Revenue 1899 (budget) ....gold $26,453,973
　　　　　　　　　　　　paper 101,135,479
Expenditure, 1899 (budget)........gold 42,133,232
　　　　　　　　　　　　paper 67,972,000
Internal debt, Nov. 1898—paper (circ.) £8,500,000
　　　　　　　　　　　　gold 32,200,000
External debt, Nov. 1898 63,280,000
Paper and nickel in circulation..... : $295,165.957
Total Imports, 1898 ....gold 107,428,990
Total Exports, 1898 ....gold 133,829,458
Imports from U. K., 1898 .... £5,812,770
Exports to U. K. in 1898 7,788,332

CAPITAL, Buenos Aires. Pop., 1897, 656,198.
British Minister, Hon. W. A. C. Barrington...£3,000
Secretary of Legation, Frederick S. Clarke ... 500
Second Secretary, Hon. Theo. Russell ....
Consul, Alfred Grenfell 1,000
　Vice-Consul, Montagu Hankin 400
　Bahia Blanca — Vice-Consul, Charles C.
　　Cumming ....
　La Plata, Vice-Consul, E. T. Puleston ...
Rosario—Consul, Hugh M. H. Mallet 400
　Concordia—Vice-Consul, Oliver Budge ...
　Cordoba—Vice-Consul, D. M. Munro ......
　Parana—Vice-Consul, Oliver Bury ......
　Santa Fé—Vice-Consul, J. W. Richards...

Buenos Aires is 7,160 miles from Southampton; transit 22 days. Telegrams, 4s. and 4s. 6d. a word.

AUSTRIA-HUNGARY.

I.—THE JOINT MONARCHY.

Reigning Sovereign, Francis Joseph, Emperor of Austria, &c., and Apostolic King of Hungary, *born* 18 August, 1830 ; *succeeded* (as Emperor of Austria) 2 Dec., 1848 ; *crowned* King of Hungary at Ofen, June 8, 1867 ; *married* April 24, 1854, Elizabeth, daughter of Maximilian Joseph, Duke in Bavaria (*born* 24 Dec. 1837, *assassinated* in Geneva 10 Sept., 1898), and has issue 2 daughters.
Heir Presumptive, his nephew (son of the late Archduke Charles Louis), Archduke Francis Ferdinand of Este, *born* 18 Dec., 1863.

Minister of Foreign Affairs and of the Imperial and Royal House, Count A. Goluchowski.
Minister of Finance, M. Benjamin de Kállay.
Minister of War, Edler von Krieghammer.
Navy (department of War Office), Commander, Vice-Admiral Baron von Spaun.
Ambassador to Germany, L. de Szögyèny-Marich ; *Italy*, Freiherr von Pasetti Friedenburg ; *France*, Graf Wolkenstein Trostburg ; *Russia*, Baron d'Arenthal ; *Turkey*, Freiherr von Calice ; *U.S.A.*, Ladislaus Hengelmüller von Hengervar.

Ambassador in London, Count Franz Deym, 18 Belgrave Square, S.W.
Councillor and 1st Sec., Count Albert Mensdorff-Pouilly-Dietrichstein.
Secs.,Coun. Berchtold; Count K.Trauttmansdorff.

Attaché, Margrave Karl Pallavicini.
Naval Attaché, Capt. Ladislaus Sztranyavszky.
Military Attaché, Lieut.-Gen. H.S.H. Prince Louis Esterhazy.
Chancellor, Eduard K. Rüti.
Consul-General, Baron Alfred de Rothschild ; F. Stockinger, *acting*.
Secretary, J. Kohn. Office, 11 Queen Victoria Street, E.C.

The largest State, next to Russia, on the continent of Europe, situated between 42°—51° N. lat. and 9° 30′—26° 20′ E. long. It embraces an area of 261,649 English square miles, and a population (1896) of 44,901,036. Among the population (43,310,000 without Bosnia and Herzegovina) there were in 1896 about 19,145,000 Slavs, 10,591,000 Germans, 7,486,000 Magyars, 2,813,000 Roumanians and 696,000 Italians. According to religion (1890), nearly 32,312,000 Roman Catholics, 3,888,000 Protestants, 3,190,000 Greeks and Armenians, and 1,872,000 Jews.

The head of the Austro-Hungarian Monarchy is the Emperor of Austria and Apostolic King of Hungary who has three Imperial advisers in the Ministers of Foreign Affairs, Finance and War. The control of the official actions of these ministers and the voting of the common budget is exercised by Delegations consisting of 60 members chosen from the Upper House of Austria (Herrenhaus) and Hungary (Förendihaz) and from each Lower House (Abgeordnetenhaus and Kepviselöhar). The union between the two states is personal through the Emperor and also constitutional and commercial by reason of the *Ausgleich* or Agreement (literally "compromise") entered into by the Reichsrath of Austria and the Parliament of Hungary. This agreement is renewable every ten years, and was so renewed in 1877—1887, but not in 1897, so that the monarchy is at present held together by the personal tie alone.

The State is divided into the Austrian State and the Hungarian State, each having its own Parliament, Ministry, and Administration, the official denomination being Oesterreichische-Ungarische Monarchie (the Austro-Hungarian Monarchy).

The soil produces grain of all kinds, potatoes, beetroot, and wine. Austria-Hungary ranks next to France, Italy, and Spain as a wine-growing country, but from its inland position and other causes the wines are not well known in England. 797,138 tons of beet-sugar were manufactured in 1895-96. Industry is almost wholly confined to Austria, and more especially to Vienna, Bohemia, Moravia, Silesia, and Styria, the great centre of the iron trade. Brünn is famed for its woollens, Reichenberg for woollens and cottons, Trautenau for linen, Bohemia for glass, and Vienna and Pilsen for lager beer. The mineral riches are great, comprising gold, silver, copper, iron, quicksilver, lead, tin, zinc, and coal; petroleum is also found in Galicia.

The Joint Monarchy possesses a powerful army, amounting, on the peace footing, to 382,659 men, with 14,657 officers, and the war establishment, exclusive of the Landsturm, consists of 1,240,000 officers and men, with 2,192 field guns. Military service is compulsory on all. The navy consists of 142 vessels, of which 13 are line-of-battle ships, 18 cruisers, 2 hochseeboote, and 62 torpedo boats. Pola is the naval arsenal.

The principal articles exported from Austria-Hungary in 1898 were cereals, animals, and mill produce £12,300,000; sugar £5,587,000; raw material for agricultural and industrial purposes, £16,600,000; manufactured goods, £28,500,000; semi-manufactured goods, £10,600,000. Commerce is carried on principally with Germany, Italy, Roumania, and Russia, and through the ports of Trieste and Fiume, also direct with the transmarine world, including England. In 1897 20,536 miles of railway were open for traffic. The commercial marine consisted in 1897 of 266 vessels (exclusive of coasting and fishing vessels), burthen 431,430 tons.

Duality extends to the annual budgets. Towards the common expenses contained in the Imperial Budget, Austria contributes 68·6 per cent. and Hungary, 31·4 per cent. These common expenses, which are mainly those incurred for the maintenance of the Army, Navy, and Foreign Office, were estimated for 1897 at £13,666,000.

Common Debt, December, 1897........£230,260,000
Total exports, A. & H., 1898 69,242,000
Total imports, A. & H., 1898 67,391,000
Direct imports from U. K., 1898 2,287,395
Direct exports to U. K., 1898 1,135,482

[In calculating the above amounts the *florin* is reckoned at the rate of 12 to the £.]

British Ambassador, His Excellency The Right
  Hon. Sir Horace Rumbold, Bart., G.C.B.,
  G.C.M.G. £8,000
Sec. of Embassy, Ralph Milbanke, C.B. ... 850
Military Attaché, Col. F. M. Wardrop, C.B. 500
Naval Attaché, Capt. H. P. Williams, R.N. 500
    "   Comm. D. A. Gamble 500
Commercial Attaché, A. Percy Bennett...... 800
2nd Secs., M. de C. Findlay 400
    "   H. G. M. Rumbold 345
    "   Hon. Hugh Grosvenor 345
3rd Sec., F. O. Lindley (acting) ....
Chaplain, Rev. William H. Hechler 300
Consul-General, P. von Schoeller.................
Consul, Moriz Feldscharek ....
Prague—Consul, Capt. A. W. Forbes.
Innsbruck—Vice-Cons., Rev. R. E.Macdonald.
Trieste—Consul, Harry L. Churchill 600
  Vice-Consul, Jacob A. Nathan ......
  Chaplain, Rev. C. F. Thorndike ......
  "   (asst.) Rev. J. L. Davies ......
Lissa—Cons. Agent, Serafino Topich ....

II.—AUSTRIA.

President of the Council and Minister of the Interior and Agriculture, Count Clary-Aldringen.
Defence, Count Welser von Welsersheimb.
Railways, Dr. Chevalier de Wittek.
Justice, Chevalier de Kindinger.
Public Worship and Instruction, Chevalier de Hartel.
Finance, Chevalier de Kniaziolucki.
Commerce, Dr. Franz Stibal.
Without Portfolio, Dr. Chevalier de Chledowski.

Austria contains an area of 115,914 sq. miles, and a population of 24,972,056, giving a density of population of 215 to the square mile. The Central Government of the Kingdom is conducted by the Reichsrath, consisting of an Upper (Herrenhaus) and Lower House (Abgeordnetenhaus). There are 17 provinces, viz.:—Lower Austria, Upper Austria, Salzburg, Styria or Steiermark, Carinthia or Kärnten, Carniola or Krain, Coast Districts (Görtz, Gradisca-Trieste, and Istria), Tyrol, Vorarlberg, Bohemia, Moravia, Silesia, Galicia, Bukowina, and Dalmatia, each possessing a separate Diet (Landtage) and also sending representatives to the Reichsrath. Of

the inhabitants about 8,500,000 are Germans, 3,400,000 Bohemians, Moravians and Slovates, 3,750,000 Poles, and 3,000,000 Ruthenians with about 1,000,000 Slovenes. In addition to Vienna there are four cities with over 100,000 inhabitants and six in addition with over 50,000. There are about 19,000,000 Roman Catholics. 2,750,000 Orthodox, and over 1,000,000 Jews in the country.

Education is compulsory, and in 1896 there were 19,441 elementary schools with about 72,000 teachers and 4,000,000 children in attendance; the secondary schools, colleges, and technical schools numbered 190, with over 5,000 teachers and about 90,000 pupils. There are also universities at Vienna, Prague, Gratz, Cracow, Lemberg, Innsbruck and Czernowitz.

The principal industry is agriculture, in which nearly 14,000,000 were employed in 1891; trade and manufactures accounting for about 6,000,000, while mining occupied nearly 1,250,000. The chief products are grain, cereals, wine (76,704,068 gallons in 1896), and minerals (coal, iron, lead, zinc, silver, quicksilver, and copper); the manufactures being woollens, cottons, and glass. During the year 1896 the exports amounted to not quite one-third, and the imports to a little less than one-fourth, of the total for the monarchy.

Austrian revenue, 1898 (estimate) ... £60,342,000
Austrian expenditure, 1898 62,363,000
Austrian Special Debt, 1898 :—
  Consolidated £122,397,166
  Floating 331,750
                      —————— 122,728,916
Austrian imports, 1896 (estimate) ... 13,067,583
Austrian exports, 1896   "   ... 19,100,333

Capital, Vienna. Population, 1897, 1,594,129.
Vienna is 955 miles from London, transit 31 hours. Telegrams, per word, 3d.

III.—HUNGARY.

President of the Ministry, Coloman de Széll.
Minister a latere, Count Manó Szechényi.
Interior, Coloman de Széll.
Finance, M. Ladislaus Lukács.
Instruction and Religion, M. Julius Wlassics.
Commerce, Sandor Hegedüs.
Agriculture, Ignatius Darányi.
Justice, Sandor Plósz.
National Defence, Gen. Baron Géza Fejérváry.
Minister for Croatia, Erwin Cseh.

Hungary, with its dependent states, has an area of 322,310 sq. kilometres, about 124,448 sq. miles, that is, rather larger than the United Kingdom, with a population of 17,463,791 at the census of 1890: to this Fiume contributes 30,337, and Croatia and Slavonia 2,201,927. The country is divided into 72 counties with 474 districts for those of Hungary. Hungarian is the official language, except in Croatia and Slavonia, where Croatian is spoken. Croatia and Slavonia form an annexe of the Crown of Hungary, with autonomy in home affairs, justice and public instruction. At the head of the Croatian Government is the Banus (Viceroy) Khuen Héderváry, who is responsible to both the Diet of Croatia and to the Hungarian Prime Minister. The Croatian Diet sends 40 members to the Hungarian Parliament, and the Hungarian Ministry contains a Croatian member. Parliament consists of a Lower House of 453 members, elected for five years; of these Croatia sends 40, but they have no vote on matters connected with justice, education, and home affairs. There is also an Upper House, consisting of the *Barones regni,* prelates, such members of the magnate families who contribute more than 3,000 florins to the landtax, the *Banus*, with three members of Croatia sent by the Diet, and fifty members nominated by the Crown.

Of the inhabitants about 8,000,000 are Magyars, 2,500,000 Roumanians, and 2,000,000 Saxons. In addition to Buda Pest, which has about 600,000 inhabitants, there are six cities, with over 50,000 inhabitants.

All the great plains produce grain of excellent quality. The returns for 1895 (excluding Croatia and Slavonia) give 52,843,883 hectolitres of wheat, 17,055,120 of rye, 20,383,461 of barley, 24,643,183 of oats, and 45,412,645 of Indian corn. The cattle number 5,829,018, sheep 7,526,685, horses 1,972,448, and swine 6,446,573. The exports are chiefly cereals, live stock, and raw materials ; wheat figures for £4,223,000, barley £2,965,000, rye £1,453,000, and wheaten flour £6,800,000. The imports are chiefly manufactured goods, textile fabrics alone being valued at £13,650,000. The chief mineral products are gold, silver, copper, lead, quicksilver, antimony, iron, coal, and sulphur. The mines, however, are not well worked, and might be made a much greater source of income. Salt, which is a Government monopoly, produced £1,137,000 in 1895.

Hungarian revenue, 1897 .... £45,414,000
Hungarian expenditure, 1897 43,678,000
*Hungarian Special Debt, 1893 :—
  Consolidated £99,752,750
  Annuities 83,228,333
  Treasury Bonds 1,240,916
  Miscellaneous 5,434,500
  Arrears 20,838,916
                      205,495,403
Hungarian imports, 1896 45,748,000
Hungarian exports, 1896.............. 45,392,000

CAPITAL, Budapest. Population, 1896, 600,000.

British Cons.-Gen., C. Conway Thornton ...£1,000
  ,, *Consul,* Ignatz Brüll .... unp.
Fiume—Consul, George Louis Faber 300
  ,, *Vice-Consul,* Arthur Steinacker .... unp.

Budapest is distant 1,126 miles from London, transit 2 days. Telegrams, per word 3*d.*

* In the expenditure of the Kingdom of Hungary the sum of £2,525,916 is set aside annually as a contribution to the service of the Special Debt of Austria contracted before 1867.

IV.—CROWN LANDS.

Austria is charged with the administration of the Turkish Provinces of Bosnia and Herzegovina. These are situated between 42° 40′ to 40° 15′ N. lat. and 33° 22′ to 38° 45′ E. long. The Austrian garrison consists of 22,944 men, with a native army of 3,528, and a gendarmerie of 2,359. An entirely Austrian administration has been established. The local Revenue (1894 : £1,047,310) suffices for the cost of administration, but not for the maintenance of the army of occupation.

CAPITAL, Sarajevo (Bosna-Serai). Population (1895), 38,083.

Brit. Cons.-Gen., Edwd. Bothamley Freeman£700.
Telegrams 4*d.* per word.

BALUCHISTAN. (*See* p. 470.)

BELGIUM.

King, Leopold II., *born* 9 April, 1835; *suc.* 10 Dec., 1865 ; *mar.* 22 August, 1853, Marie Henriette, daughter of the late Archduke Joseph of Austria, *b.* 23rd Aug., 1836 ; issue three daughters.

Heir Presumptive, his brother Philippe, Count of Flanders, *born* 24 March, 1837 ; *mar.* 25 April, 1867, Princess Marie of Hohenzollern-Sigmaringen, *born* 17 Nov., 1845 ; issue one son, Albert, *born* April 8, 1879, and two daughters.

Premier and Minister of Finance and Public Works, M. De Smet De Naeyer.
Foreign Affairs, Paul de Favereau,
Interior and Public Instr., M. De Trooz.
Agriculture Baron van den Bruggen.
Industry & Labour, M. Liebert.
Justice, M. van den Heuvel.
Railways, Posts & Telegraph; ad int., M. Liebert.
War, General Cousebant d'Alkemade.

Minister in London, Baron Whettnall, 18 Harrington Gardens, South Kensington, S.W.
  Councillor, Viscount de Beughem.
  First Secretary, E. van Grootven.
  2nd do., A. Delcoigne.
Consul-Gen., François H. Lenders, 118 Bishopsgate Street Within, E.C.
Vice-Consul, Henri de Grelle Rogier, 130 London Wall, E.C.
Consul at Dover, Sir Wm. H. Crundall.
Vice-Consul at Harwich, William Groom.

A Kingdom of Central Europe, anciently inhabited by the Belgæ (a Celtic-speaking German tribe), and part of the *Gallia Belgica* of the Romans. In 1815 the country was joined to the Kingdom of the Netherlands, an arrangement which was upset by the Revolution of 1830. On Oct. 4, 1830, a National Congress proclaimed its independence, and on June 4, 1831, Prince Leopold of Saxe-Coburg was chosen hereditary King.

Belgium has a frontier of 831 miles, and is bounded on the north and east by the Netherlands (268 miles), on the south and west by France (381 miles), on the east by Germany (60 miles), and the Grand Duchy of Luxemburg (80 miles), with a seaboard of 42 miles. The Meuse and its tributary the Sambre divide it into two distinct regions, that in the west being generally level and fertile, whilst the table-land of the Ardennes, in the east, has for the most part a poor soil. The total area is 11,373 square miles, about equal to the four counties of Hertford, Lancashire, York, and Lincoln ; its great harbour and commercial *entrepôt* is Antwerp, a strongly fortified city on the Schelde. The other harbours are Ostend, Nieuport, and Blankenberg.

The "polders" near the coast, which are protected by dikes against floods, cover an area of 193 square miles. The highest hill, Baraque Michel, rises to a height of 2,230 feet, but the mean elevation of the whole country does not exceed 536 feet. The principal rivers are the Schelde (Escaut) and the Maas (Meuse). Brussels has a mean temperature of 50° F. (summer 63°, winter 37°).

The population was 6,659,732 on 31 Dec., 1898, or 586 to the square mile; it is consequently one of the most densely peopled countries of the world. The decennial increase is about 10 per cent, and since 1861 there has been an annual excess of immigrants over emigrants, the totals in 1896 being emigrants 21,830 ; immigrants 26,878. There are 3,343,542 females to 3,325,190 males ; and annually 29 births and 20 deaths to every 1,000 inhabitants. There are nine provinces, Antwerp, Brabant, Flanders (E. and W.), Hainaut, Liège, Limburg, Luxemburg, and Namur. BRUSSELS (with suburbs, 531,011 inhabitants), is the capital. Other towns with over 100,000 inhabitants are Antwerp, the chief port (267,902 exclusive of suburbs), Ghent (159,218), and Liège (165,404).

French is the chief official language and that of the upper classes, but Flemish is spoken by the majority, preponderating in Flanders and Brabant, including Antwerp. In 1890, 45 per cent. spoke Flemish, 41 per cent. French, and only 11 per cent. both tongues. Nearly all the inhabitants are at least nominally Roman Catholics, and in 1890 there existed 1,775 convents, inhabited by 4,120 monks and 21,242 nuns. Education is backward, for in 1890 29 out of every hundred inhabitants of 5 years of age and upwards were unable to read; and of the recruits levied in 1890, 13·45 per cent. were in a similar condition. There are four universities—Ghent (with 427 students), Liège (979), Brussels (1,265), and Louvain (1,179)—3,850 students in the academic year 1895-96, besides a famous Academy of Art at Antwerp, a Conservatoire of Music at Brussels, Ghent, Liège and Antwerp, and numerous technical schools.

Belgium is essentially a manufacturing country, and it is largely dependent upon foreign supplies for its food. The soil was divided (1889) among 1,173,169 proprietors. Of the total area 58 per cent. is under cultivation, 13 per cent. consists of meadows and pastures, 17 per cent. of forest. The mineral kingdom yields coal (1895, 20,451,000 tons), iron, zinc, lead, and copper. The leading manufactures are fire-arms (Liège), machinery (Seraing), iron and steel, glass (Charleroy), woollens (Verviers), cottons and linen (Ghent), lace (Brussels, Mechlin, and Bruges), hosiery (Tournai), beet-sugar (Hainaut), paper, and beer. The exports include, in addition to manufactures, corn, butter, eggs, vegetables, coal, building-stone, hides, tallow, and rabbits: they are taken principally by the United Kingdom, Germany, and France. The exports to the United Kingdom in 1898 were :—

Boots and Shoes	£205,770	Linen yarn	£480,397
Clocks & watches	745,951	Oil seed	226,805
Cotton manufacts.	1,674,534	Silk manufactures	2,119,965
Eggs	730,898	Sugar Refined	292,286
Embroidery & Lace	425,075	„ Unrefined	699,114
Flax	833,191	Wool	423,731
Glass	1,127,159	Woollen manufs.	428,014
Gloves	519,973	Do. yarn	931,413
Hides	217,085	Zinc	507,255
Iron manufactures	1,271,651		

The imports of British produce and manufacture included—

Animals (horses)	£289,739	Leather	£202,541
Arms &c.	282,552	Linen yarn & mfs.	223,386
Caoutchouc	116,234	Machinery	828,291
Coals, &c.	324,952	Manure	148,689
Cotton yarn & mfs.	1,570,858	Metals & hardware	254,229
Fish	213,163	Woollen yarn & mfs.	607,077

Most of the maritime trade of Belgium is carried on in foreign bottoms, the mercantile marine only consisting (1898) of 65 vessels, in addition to which there were about 600 fishing boats. In 1898 there were 2,850 miles of railway (2,057 being the property of the State, with a net revenue of about £1,320 per mile); the telegraphs had a length of 3,953 miles, and the post-office carried 4r·4 956,118 letters, post-cards, &c., in 1897. The navigable rivers and canals have a length of 1,370 miles.

The Belgian constitution of 1831 jointly vests the legislative power in the King, the Senate, and the Chamber of Representatives. The 102 senators (with the exception of 26 elected by the provincial councils), and 172 representatives are elected by the people, the former for 8, the latter for 4 years. Universal male suffrage, with plural voting up to 3 votes by property and educational qualifications, was introduced by the Electoral Law of 1894, and the united constituencies numbered about 1,407,000 voters, with 2,170,000 votes in 1897. There are in addition representative Provincial and Communal Councils, elected on a somewhat more liberal franchise.

The army, on a peace footing, numbers 47,361 men with the colours (1896), the total war strength being about 140,000. It is recruited by conscription, from which exemption can be purchased for 1,600 francs, the term of service being thirteen years, of which from 28 months to four years are passed with the colours. There is also a *Garde civique* of 43,647 men. Antwerp is the principal fortress, and new forts are being constructed on the Meuse: from the designs of Gen. Brialmont. Belgium has neither a navy nor colonies; but the King of the Belgians is at the same time "Sovereign" of the Congo Free State.

Public revenue, 1898	£17,567,938
Public expenditure, 1898	17,236,555
Public debt, 1898, of all kinds	104,551,487
Total imports, 1898 (excluding Transit)	81,788,000
Total exports, 1898 „	71,480,000
Imports from United Kingdom, 1898	13,850,902
Exports to United Kingdom, 1898	21,534,313

CAPITAL, Brussels. Pop., with suburbs, 531,611.

British Minister, Hon. Sir Francis Richard Plunkett, G.C.M.G.	£3,230
Sec. of Legation, Arthur S. Raikes	500
Military Attaché, Lt.-Col. Charles à Court	
2nd Secretary, Count de Salis	390
3rd Secretary, J. W. R. Macleay	250
Vice-Consul, Thomas E. Jeffes	
Antwerp—Consul-Gen., Gerald R. de Courcy Perry, C.M.G.	900
Vice-Consul, W. Lydcotte	
do. H. C. Venables	
Ghent—Vice-Consul, George H. Hallett	
Liège—Vice-Consul, R. S. Menzies	
Ostend and Bruges—Vice-Consul, W. G. E. Hervey	
Spa—Vice-Consul, H. Hayemal	

Brussels, 224 miles from London; transit, 10 hours. Telegrams, per word, 2d.

See also CONGO FREE STATE, pp. 545, 600, 603.

BHUTAN. (See p. 470.)

BOKHARA. (See p. 473.)

BOLIVIA, REPUBLIC OF.

President, Severo Fernandez Alonso, *proclaimed* Aug. 20, 1896 (until 1900).
Foreign Affairs, Señor Gomez.
Finance, Señor Gutierrez.
War, Señor Oblitas.
Justice, Señor Pinilla.
Interior, Señor Sanguines.

Envoy Extraordinary and Min. Plen., Señor F. A. Aramayo, 3 Roland Houses, S.W.
Consul, A. Ballivian, 12 Fenchurch St., E.C.

This and Paraguay are the only States of South America without a seaboard, Antofagasta, its former port, having been ceded to Chile in 1884. It was formerly comprised in the Spanish Viceroyalty of Colombia under the name of "Peru," and derives its present name from its great liberator, Simon Bolivar. It extends between lat. 8° and 23° S. and long. 57° 30′ and 73° W., and its area is said to be 570,000 square miles. Its population is estimated at about 2,000,000. In the war against Chile, 1879, it equipped an army of about 6,000 men. The mineral productions are very valuable: the silver mines of Potosi are believed to be almost inexhaustible, while gold, partly dug and partly washed, is obtained on the Eastern Cordillera of the Andes: copper, lead, tin, salt, and sulphur are also found. Its agricultural produce consists chiefly of rice, barley, oats, maize, cotton, coca, indigo, india-rubber, cacao, potatoes, the choicest fruits, cinchona bark, medicinal herbs, &c., which with gold, silver and copper are its principal exports; its chief imports being iron, hardware, and silks. There are about 500 miles of railway and 150 miles of telegraph.

Public revenue, 1898 (estimate)	£432,812
Public expenditure, 1898	476,158
Total exports, 1897, over	2,125,000
Total imports, 1897, about	2,038,000
Interior debt, 1898, about	300,000
Exterior debt, 1898, about	90,379

In the above statistics the *boliviano* is reckoned at 12 to the £.

CAPITAL, Sucre. Population, 12,000.

No British diplomatic or consular representative.

Sucre, 8,386 miles from London. Telegrams, 6s. 2d. per word.

BRAZIL, REPUBLIC OF.
(See also p. 609–610.)

President, Mansel Ferraz de Campos Salles, Nov. 15, 1898.

Vice-President, Francisco de Assis Rosa é Silva.

Foreign Affairs, Olyntho de Magalhaês.

Marine, Rear-Admiral José Pinto de Luz.

War, General de Medeiro Mallet.

Finance, A. Murthinho.

Agriculture, Severino Vieira.

Interior, Epitano Pessoa.

Minister in London, A. de Souza Corrêa, 55 Curzon St., Mayfair, W.

1st Secretary, M. de Oliveira Lima.

2nd Secretary, Silvyno Gurgel do Amaral.

Consul in London, F. Alves Vieira, 6 Great Winchester Street.

Consul-General in Liverpool, Capt. J.C. de P.Pinto.

The Republic of the United States of Brazil was founded on the 15th of November, 1889, by a bloodless revolution which drove Dom Pedro from the throne. A provisional government was immediately formed, upon the model of that of the United States of America, under the presidency of Marshal Deodoro da Fonseca, and on February 24, 1891, a new Constitution was voted by the Constituent Assembly by which the President's term of office was fixed at four years. Everything went on much as usual ; but the Church and the State were separated, civil marriages only made valid, and education secularised. A second revolution broke out in 1891 by which President Fonseca was unseated.

Brazil, the most extensive State of South America, discovered in 1500 by Pedro Alvarez Cabral, Portuguese navigator, is bounded on the north by the Atlantic Ocean, Guiana, and Venezuela; on the west by Ecuador, Peru, Bolivia, Paraguay, and Argentina ; on the south by Uruguay ; and on the east by the Atlantic Ocean. This immense country extends between lat. 4° 22' N. and 33° 45'8. and long. 34° 40' and 73° 15' W., being 2,600 miles from north to south, and 2,500 from west to east ; with a coast-line on the Atlantic of 3,700 miles. It comprises an area of 3,218,166 square miles, and contained a population of 17,000,000 in 1891, the greater part of mixed blood. In 1871 there were 1,800,000 slaves, but in that year the work of emancipation was commenced ; children were born free, but under certain regulations were compelled to serve with their mother until they reached the age of 21. On the 13th of May, 1888, a bill was passed for the immediate and unconditional manumission of all slaves, and now not one is to be found throughout the States. There are about 1,000,000 "wild" Indians, and other uncivilised tribes ; 100,547 immigrants, mostly Italians, Portuguese, and Spanish arrived at Rio in 1896. In 1896 the army consisted of 28,000 men, and the navy of 3 iron-clads, 5 cruisers, 3 torpedo boats, and 1 torpedo-catcher ; in 1898 the Republic sold their 3 ironclads to the U.S.A. for £470,000, and in the Budget of 1899 the naval expenditure is reduced from £1,286,339 (1896) to £74,365. Brazil contains 20 states, 16 of which lie along the coast, and 4 in the interior. There are 42 ports along the coast, of which the principal is Rio with a shore line of 123 miles. It is unequalled for the number and extent of its rivers : the Amazon, the largest, though not the longest, in the world, with its immediate tributaries ; and the Tocantins, San Francisco, and others. The minerals are very considerable and valuable, comprising gold, silver, iron, diamonds, topazes, and other precious stones. Its forests are immense, abounding in the greatest variety of useful and beautiful woods, adapted for dyeing, cabinet-work, or ship-building ; among these are mahogany, logwood, rosewood, brazilwood, &c. In the extreme south towards the interior the land rises by gentle gradations to the height of from 2,000 to 5,000 feet above the level of the sea, and in those regions European fruits and grain are reared in abundance, while the intermediate valleys are found extremely favourable for the raising of sugar, coffee, cotton, cocoa, india-rubber, tobacco, and tropical products. Its agricultural produce is abundant ; maize, beans, cassava-root, and nuts are very generally cultivated ; also, in some parts, wheat and other European cereals. Cotton also is being largely cultivated for export. Sugar-cane is grown in large and increasing quantities in the northern provinces, Pernambuco being the centre of the sugar-producing zone. India-rubber comes from the more northern provinces, especially Pará ; and coffee, though also grown in the north, comes chiefly from the central portions of the country, Rio de Janeiro, Minas, and Sao Paulo. Tobacco is grown largely, especially in Bahia. The exports consist solely of the raw produce of the soil, and owing to the vast extent of the country, and the consequent very different peculiarities of the soil and climate, their nature varies considerably. The imports consist of every description of manufactured articles, but there are 149 cotton-mills, giving employment to 30,000 hands, and representing an invested capital of 200,000 of contos of reis. The enormous protective duties were again increased in 1887, 1893, and 1896. In 1897 there were 9,072 miles of railway open, and about 3,500 miles in course of construction. Length of telegraph wires in 1897 about 11,375 miles ; number of post offices, 2,862.

Estimated Revenue, 1898	*£9,484,916
Estimated Expenditure, 1898	*10,873,699
Total Imports, 1897	*21,567,560
Total Exports, 1897	*26,752,223

Coffee produced 1897-8 ....bags 15,710,000
Public Debt, Dec. 31st, 1897 :—
External (£34,697,300 as per =)*Milreis 308,420,444
Internal *637,425,600
Govt. Paper Money........................ *439,614,276
Bank Notes *315,344,330
Floating Debt *299,473,041
Western Minas Loan .... £ 3,605,000
Imports from United Kingdom, 1898.. 6,449,903
Exports to United Kingdom, 1898 4,601,773

Number of foreign vessels entered and cleared at Rio in 1897—1,274 (2,146,854 tons), of which 887,824 tons were British.

CAPITAL, Rio de Janeiro. Population, 674,972.
Brit. Minister, E. Constantine H.Phipps,C.B. £4,000
Sec. of Legation, Sir B. Boothby, Bart. 700
  Consul-General, Wm. Geo. Wagstaff, C.M.G. 1,100
  Vice-Consul, C. B. Rhind 450
  Translator, J. R. Hancox 300
  Corumba—Cons. Agent, C. C. Cooper ......
Bahia—Consul, Ernest C. A. Nicolini........ 800
  Chaplain, ...
Fará—Consul, W. A. Churchill.................. 900
  Manáos—Vice-Consul, ... 400
  Maranham—Vice-Consul, Henry Airlie ...
Pernambuco—Consul, Adolph F. Howard ... 800
  Vice-Consul, A. L. G. Williams .... unp.
  Chaplain, Rev. Wm. E. Macray, M.A.
  Ceará—Vice-Consul, William Studart......
  Maceio—Vice-Consul, Charles Goble ......
  Paraiba—V.-Jons., A. T. Connor ....
  Penedo—Consular Agent, Henry B. Cox ...
  Rio Grande do Norte—V.-Con.,
Rio Grande do Sul—Con., P. J. F. Staniforth 600
  Porto Alegre—Vice-Con., Ambrose Archer
  St. Catherine's—V.-Cons., W. B. Chaplin
Santos—Consul, Francis W. Mark 850
  Curitybá.—V.-Cons., J. F. Murray.
  Paranagua—Vice-Con.,Joaquim S. Gomes.
  Sao Paulo—Vice Cons., P. C. P. Lupton.
Rio Janeiro, 5,750 miles distant; transit, 17 days. Telegrams, per word, 3s. 6d. to 6s.

BULGARIA.

Prince, H.R.H. Prince Ferdinand of Saxe-Coburg, born 26 Feb., 1861 ; elected 7 July, 1887 ; m., 20 April, 1893, Princess Marie Louise of Bourbon, d. of Robert, Duke of Parma ; (born 17 Jan. 1870, died 31 Jan. 1899) ; and has issue—Heir Apparent, Boris, Prince of Tirnovo, b. 30 Jan., 1894 (Prince Cyril, b. 17 Nov., 1895: Princess Eudoxie, b. 17 Jan., 1898; Princess Nadejda, b. 30 Jan., 1899).
President of the Council, Minister of Foreign Affairs and Public Worship, Ivántchof.
Minister of Finance, Ténef.
Minister of Interior, Radoslávof.
Minister of War, Col. Páprikof.
Minister of Public Works, Ways and Communications, Tóntchef.
Minister of Public Instruction, Vátchef.
Minister of Commerce & Agriculture, Nátchevitch.
Minister of Justice, Péshef.

The Principality of Bulgaria is under the suzerainty of Turkey. It was created by the Treaty of Berlin, 13th of July, 1878, and is governed by a Prince elected by the National Assembly or Sobranie, with a popular legislature and constitutional government.

Eastern Roumelia, likewise a creation of the Berlin Treaty of 1878, has an area of 13,862 square miles, and 998,431 inhabitants; it was intended to form an autonomous province, bu since the successful revolution at Philippopolis, of September 18th, 1885, it has been incorporated with the principality, under the name of Southern Bulgaria, and the accomplished fact was recognised by the arrangement of April 5th, 1885, at Constantinople, whereby the Prince of Bulgaria was appointed at the same time Governor-General of Eastern Roumelia.

This Province, under the name of South Bulgaria, now forms an integral portion of the Principality, with the same rulers, laws, and mode of administration.

By modification of the Constitution 1893, there is now one deputy to each 20,000 inhabitants, 113 for the northern, and 51 for the southern province. Prince Ferdinand was elected on July 7, 1887, and is now recognised by the Six Great Powers as ruler.

United Bulgaria is bounded on the north by Roumania, from which it is separated by the Danube; on the west by Servia and Macedonia; on the east by the Black Sea; and on the south by the Turkish province of Adrianople. It has a regular army of about 40,000 officers and men on a peace footing, and about 250,000, with 350 guns, in time of war. The navy consists of a torpedo gunboat and a few small steamers. The exports consist principally of cereals (especially wheat), live stock, essence of roses, woollens, skins, cheese, eggs, timber, cocoons, and tobacco ; the principal imports being textiles, metal goods and machinery, colonial wares, leather, building materials, petroleum and other oils, paper. salt fish, rice, and coal. The great ports are Varna (661 vessels of 541,323 tons in 1898) and Bourgas (1,295 vessels of 483,288 tons). There are (1899) 835 miles of railway open and 130 under construction ; 3,259 miles of telegraph and 915 miles of telephone lines North Bulgaria has an area of 24,237 square miles, and South Bulgaria an area of 12,706 square miles. The estimated population (1895) is 3,376,467. Population according to language or nationality and religion (census of January 1st, 1893).

NATIONALITIES.		RELIGIONS.	
Bulgarians	2,505,326	Orthodox Greeks ..	2,606,786
Turks............	569,728	Mohammedans	643,258
Roumanians	62,628	Israelites............	28,307
Greeks	58,518	Roman Catholics..	22,617
Gipsies	52,132	Armenian Greg-	
Spanish speak'g Jews	27,531	orians............	6,643
Tartars	16,290	Protestants	2,384
Armenians	6,445	Unknown	718
Germans & Austrians	3,620		
Albanian	1,221		
Russians	928		
Czechs	905		
Servians	818		
Italians	803		
Various	3,820		
	3,310,713		3,310,718

Public revenue, 1899 (estimated) £3,363,888
Public expenditure, 1899 ,, ... 3,361,421
Public debt, September, 1899 8,281,960
Total imports, 1898.............................. 2,909,210
Total exports, 1898.............................. 2,661,486
Imports from the U. Kingdom, 1898 695,345
Exports to the U. Kingdom, 1898 413,568

CAPITAL, Sofia, pop. (1893), 46,593; Philippopolis (Capital of E. Roumelia), 41,068; Roustchouk. 37,174; Varna, 28,174: Tirnovo, 25,295 ; Gornia Oréhovitsa, 25,013; Shoumla, 23,517 ; Slivno, 23,210 ; Plevna, 23,178; Tatar Pazarjik, 22,056; Razgrad, 21,551; Vidin, 20,944; Orehovo, 20,054.

*Average exchange, 1898, one milreis =7$\frac{11}{10}$d.

British Agent & Consul-Gen.. F. E. H. Elliot £1,500
Sofia—Vice-Consul, F. G. Freeman 400
Philippopolis—Vice-Con., P. J. McGregor 450
Rustchuk—Vice-Consul, W. H. Dalziel..... 400
Varna—Vice-Consul, A. G. Brophy 400
Bourgas—Consular Agent, J. Bonnal

Sofia is 1,416 miles from London; Philippopolis, 1,505; transit, 3 days. Telegrams, per word, 4½d.

CAMBODIA. (See p. 475.)

CHILE, REPUBLIC OF.

President, Federico Errázuriz, *installed* 18 Sept., 1896.
Premier and Interior, Rafael Sotomayor.
Foreign Affairs, Rafael Errazuriz Urmeneta.
Finance, Manuel Salines.
Justice, Francisco Herboso.
War, Carlos Concha.
Public Works, Gregorio Pinochet.

Envoy Extr. and Min. Plen.. Domingo Gana, 29 Queen's Gate Terrace, S.W.
Consul, A. G. Kendall, 148 Leadenhall St., E.C.

A State of South America, of Spanish origin, lying between the Andes and the shores of the South Pacific, extending coastwise from the Rio Sama to Cape Horn south, between lat. 18° 28' and 56° 35' S., and long. 66° 30' and 75° 40' W. Extreme length of coast-line about 2,485 miles. Its extreme length is about 2,800 miles, with an average breadth, north of 41°, of 100 miles. The great chain of the Andes runs along its eastern limit, with a general elevation of 5,000 to 10,000 feet above the level of the sea; but numerous summits attain the height of 18,000 feet—the highest, Aconcagua, an extinct volcano, being 22,422 feet. The chain, however, lowers considerably towards its southern extremity. There are no rivers of great size, and none of them are of much service as navigable highways. In the north the country is arid. Chile is divided into 21 provinces and 3 territories, the aggregate area of which is estimated at 250,741 square miles, with a population (1896) of about 3,300,000, exclusive of Araucanians, Bolivian and American Indians, numbering about 50,000. The boundary with Argentina has been determined by a treaty concluded at Buenos Aires on July 23rd, 1881, and recently revised and confirmed, but the actual boundary line has still to be marked. The population increases but slowly, and immigration, although to some extent encouraged, is inconsiderable. The number of tribal Indians is small. The Araucanians on the mainland voluntarily submitted to government in 1883, but several tribes on the islands and in the densely-wooded territory of Magellanes are still virtually independent. More has been done for education than in any other State of South America. Agriculture and mining are the principal occupations. Wheat, maize, barley, oats, beans, peas, lentils, wines, tobacco, flax, hemp, Chile-pepper, and potatoes are grown extensively; the vine and all European fruit-trees flourish. The mineral wealth is considerable; some rich gold mines have been discovered. The rainless north yields more especially nitrate of soda, iodine, borate of soda, gold and silver, a large number of mines yielding both being in actual work in Tarapacá, Guanaco, and Cachinal in Atacama, and Caracoles in Antofagasta; the centre, copper and silver; and the south, iron and coal. There are smelting-works for copper and silver, tanneries, corn and saw mills, starch,

soap, biscuit, rope, cloth, cheese, furniture, candle, and paper factories, breweries and distilleries, and the domestic industry furnishes cloth, embroideries, baskets, and pottery. The many ports favour commerce, and six lines of steamers connect the country with Panama and the Magellan Strait direct with Europe, a passage to Liverpool occupying from 40 days. There are 1,801 miles of railway open, 8,346 miles of telegraph, 484 post offices, and 5,250 miles of telephone, the last worked by an English Company. Contracts have been entered into for 600 additional miles in order to extend the trunk line through Araucania, and open up some of the mineral districts in the north as far as Huasco and Vallenar. These lines will be all Government property. A Civil War broke out in January, 1891, between the Congressionalists and the Presidential party, terminating, on August 28th, in the capture of Valparaiso by the former. The commercial marine numbers 191 vessels (40 steamers) of 90,738 tons. The staple articles of export are nitrate of soda, iodine, &c., copper bars and ores, silver ores, corn, flour, hides, and guano. The imports include silks, woollens and other textiles, food, and machinery. About 40 per cent. of the foreign trade is carried on with England. The regular army annually authorised by Congress consists of 5,000 men and 600 officers; the navy consists of about 12 large and 10 small ships of war. In 1896, at the request of the governments of Chile and Argentina, Queen Victoria consented to act as arbitrator in the boundary contentions of these two countries. There is a metallic currency with a gold $ worth 1s. 6d.

Revenue, 1898 (estimate)	$83,000,000
Expenditure. 1898 (estimate)	76,000,000
External debt, June, 1896..................	£17,696,270
Internal debt. June, 1896	2,252,678
Imports from United Kingdom, 1898...	1,855,771
Exports to United Kingdom, 1898.......	3,633,552
Total imports (exclud. bullion), 1896 .	11,729,777
Total exports (exclud. bullion), 1896 .	11,773,573

CAPITAL, Santiago. Population, 189,322; Valparaiso, 104,452; Concepcion. 24,180; Iquique, 15,391.
Envoy Extraordinary and Minister Plenipotentiary,
   Audley C. Gosling £2,000
Hon. Attaché, Ronald F. Gosling.
Vice-Consul, Frederic W. Kerr.
Iquique—Consul, Charles N. Clarke.
Valparaiso—Consul - General, Sir Berry
       Cusack-Smith, K.C.M.G. 900
   ,,   *Vice-Consul,* Arthur Rowley............ 400
Ancud—Vice-Cons.,
Antofagasta—Vice-Consul, John Barnett.
Arica—Vice-Consul, David Simpson.
Caldera—Vice-Consul, H. B. Beazley.
Caleta Buena—V.-Consul, George P. James.
Carrizal—Vice-Consul, John King.
Chañaral—Cons. Agt., A. Tilly.
Coquimbo—Vice-Consul, G. L. Ansted.
Coronel—Vice-Con., Alfred J. Franklin.
Corral—V.-Cons., C. H. Howard.
Junin—V.-Cons, L. J. Garratt.
Lota—Vice-Cons., H. H. Maguire.
Pisagua—Vice-Con., G. J. Clarke.
Punta Arenas—Vice-Consul, Percy C. West.
Talcahuano—Vice-Consul, Alfred Steel.
Taltal—Vice-Consul, P. N. Schjolberg.
Tocopilla—V.-Consul, Wm. H. Williams.
Tomé—V.-Consul, M. S. Pasmore.
Traiguen—Vice-Cons., F. Anderton.

Santiago, distant 9,000 miles *via* Panama, and 11,000 *via* the Strait; transit, 34 to 39 days. Telegrams, per word, 6s. 2d.

CHINA.

(*See also* pp. 474, 605-5.)

Emperor, Kuang Hsü, *born* 15 August, 1871; *suc.* 12 January, 1875; married 26th Feb., 1889.

Ruling Queen, His aunt, widow of the Emperor Toai-shun, Ai-sin Kioh-lo Tung-Chi, who died in 1875; the Queen was *born* in 1834.

Head of Tsungli Yamên, Prince Chung.

Inspector-General of Customs & Posts, Sir Robert Hart, Bart., G.C.M.G.

Envoy Extr. & Min. Plen. in London, H. E. Sir Chihchen Lofêngluh, K.C.V.O., 49 Portland Place, W.

Councillor of Legation, Sir Halliday Macartney, K.C.M.G., 3 Harley Place, Regent's Park, W.

Secretaries, Chang Tek-yee; Lo Tsung-yao.

China Proper (or the Eighteen Provinces) contains an area of 1,534,953 square miles, its length from north to south being 1,860 miles by 1,520 in breadth. It is bounded on the north by Mongolia and Manchuria; on the west by Turkestan, Tibet, and Burma; on the south by Burma, Tongking and the China Sea; and on the east by the Pacific Ocean, the Yellow Sea, and Corea. The northernmost part of this area is in lat. 44° 50′ N., and the southernmost point, Yulin Bay, in the Island of Hainan, in 18° 10′ N. On the east it extends to long. 126° 10′ E., on the W. to 97° 30′ E. But the possessions of China extend far beyond these limits, and include Manchuria, Mongolia, and Dzungaria in the north, and Eastern Turkestan and Tibet in the west. To the area of China Proper must be added those of her dependent territories, the whole extending to about 4,468,750 square miles, or rather more than one-twelfth part of the entire land surface of the globe. To this should perhaps be added Manchuria, Mongolia, and Tibet, and some other dependencies more or less closely connected with the empire. Within these limits are four great mountain ranges, whence proceed some of the largest rivers in the world, and these, with their tributaries, furnish an unrivalled internal water-communication. The Yangtze Kiang is about 3,200 miles in length, and is navigable to Ping-shan, 1,800 miles from its mouth, while its numerous affluents afford water communication throughout one-half the area of China proper; the West River is navigable by boats as far as Posê on the Yunnan frontier, but the Huangho or Yellow River, aptly called "China's Sorrow," is of little value as a waterway, while the devastation wrought by the periodical overflow is one of the scourges of the country. The Amur River in Manchuria is navigated by light draught (Russian) steamers up to the town of Chita in Trans-baikal (Siberia). The most extravagant estimates of the population of this empire have been made at various times; it is generally thought that the so-called census returns of Chinese officials are untrustworthy, and that the population does not exceed a total of over 300,000,000, a recent official Yellow Book giving the number of people as 303,241,969. The density of population in some parts is very great, but the statements regarding this require to be treated with caution. Of the 10,855 foreign residents in 1896, 4,362 were British, 1,439 Americans, 933 French, 870 Germans, 871 Portuguese, and 852 Japanese; and of the 672 foreign firms in China, 363 were British, 99 German, and 87 Japanese.

The chief imports are opium, cotton and woollen stuffs, kerosene, ginseng, and rice, whilst tea, silk, and silk manufactures, camphor, and sugar constitute the bulk of the exports. Thirty-one "Treaty" ports and two towns in Yunnan are thrown open to foreign commerce, and the customs are managed by European officials.

The NAVY: Four new cruisers, and a few vessels of no fighting value, are now in the possession of China. The ARMY at its full strength would number about 1,200,000 men, but of these only about 100,000 can be described as soldiers in the European sense of the word.

A war broke out in 1894 between China and Japan, in which the latter were completely victorious, and Formosa island with an indemnity of $80,000,000 were the immediate fruits of their victory.

SHIPPING.—The mercantile marine (1897) consisted of 184 steam and 95 sailing vessels, with a total tonnage of 62,945; in 1896 the number of vessels entered and cleared at the treaty ports was 40,495, with a tonnage of 33,490,857; of these 19,711 were British (tonnage 21,847,032), and 2,090 were German (tonnage 1,945,019).

COMMERCE.—The total foreign trade of China in 1897 amounted to 385 millions of *Haikwan taels (£54,568,000), which was shared by the nations of the world as under in 1896 :—

Country.	Millions.	Country.	Millions.
Great Britain	55·8	U.S.A.	23·0
Hong Kong	145·4	Europe, except Russia	27·5
India	25·2	Russia	17·1
Singapore	4·9	Japan	28·7
Australasia	1·2	Macao	6·2
Mauritius	·3	Cochin China	1·4
Brit. America	2·5	Turkey in Asia	1·7
Great & Greater Brit.	**235·3**	Foreign Countries	105·6

The principal exports to this country from China in 1898 were tea (£943 619), silk (£773,537), skins and furs of all kinds (£404,155), straw for plaiting purposes (£219,130), and bristles (£173 224); while the chief articles exported to China from the United Kingdom were cottons and cotton yarn (£4,825,204), woollens and worsteds (£494,413), machinery and mill work (£254,453), and metals (£707,567).

EDUCATION.—Nearly all the inhabitants are able to read more or less, with the exception of the women, of whom about 90 per cent. are absolute illiterates. In Peking, Tientsin, and Canton there are schools where a moderate education on western lines may be obtained, but these are not much frequented. The national universities have a unique syllabus and confine themselves to the Chinese classics. The pioneer of advance in educational and all other matters is Li Hung Chang, G.C.V.O., and the western-style schools are under the direction of Sir Robert Hart, G.C.M.G.

RAILWAYS.—Two lines only are quite or nearly complete, with a total length of about 320 miles in 1897; 200 miles, from Tientsin to Shan-Hai-Kwan, are open and this line will shortly be completed as far as Newchwang; a line from Tientsin to Peking has been opened, another line, 80 miles long, connects Peking with Pastingfu, the capital of Chi-li province, being the first section of the great trunk line which is to connect Peking with Hankow on the Yangtse; and several other lines are authorised. An important agreement was signed by the United Kingdom and Russia on 28 April, 1899, in which the British

* The average exchange value of the Haikwan tael was (1887) 4s. 10½d.; (1896) 3s. 4d.; (1897) 2s. 11¼d.

Ambassador, at St. Petersburg, undertook not to seek for railway concessions north of the Great Wall, and not to oppose any concessions to Russia in that region; in return for this, the Russian Foreign Minister undertook not to oppose public or private concessions to Great Britain in the Yangtse Kiang basin. There are about 3,000 miles of telegraph.

CUSTOMS.—The Imperial Maritime Customs is the controlling board; this body consists of 854 Europeans, a large proportion of them British subjects, all under the control of Sir Robert Hart, G.C.M.G. In addition to the collection of dues at the Treaty Ports the board manages the lighting and navigation thereof, and keeps a small fleet of cruisers to enforce its regulations.

FINANCES.—Consul General Jamieson, C.M.G., estimates the annual revenue as follows: land tax, 25,088,000 taels; grain tax, 6,562,000 taels; salt gabel, 13,659,000; likin, 12,952,000; customs (foreign), 21,989,000; (native) 1,000,000; duty and likin on native opium, 2,229,000; miscellaneous, 5,500,000; total, 88,979,000 taels, or about £14,829,000.

Revenue and expenditure, 1896, about	£14,850,000
§Net customs revenue, 1898	3,100,000
*Total debt, 1899, about	54,500,000
*Yearly interest due, about	2,500,000
§Total imports, 1896	30,213,000
§Total exports, 1897	24,355,000
+Imports from the U. Kingdom, 1898	5,099,497
+Exports to the United Kingdom, 1898	2,668,084

CAPITAL, Peking. Population, 1,000,000.

British Minister, Sir Claude Maxwell MacDonald, K.C.B., K.C.M.G.	£5,000
Sec. of Legation, H. O. Bax-Ironside	800
Mil. Attaché, Col. G. F. Browne, D.S.O.	...
2nd Secretary, H. G. N. Dering	500
Chinese Sec., Henry Cockburn, C.B.	860
Commercial Attaché, J. W. Jamieson	1,000
Hon. Attaché, Clive Bingham	...
Physician, Dr. Wordsworth Poole	650
Chaplain (acting), Rt. Rev. Bishop Scott	200
Amoy—Consul, R. W. Mansfield	1,000
Canton—Consul, B. C. G. Scott	1,200
Chefoo—Consul, L. C. Hopkins	800
Chinkiang—Consul, E. D. H. Fraser	800
Chungking—Consul, M. F. A. Fraser	800
Foochow—Consul, G. M. H. Playfair	1,000
Pagoda Island—V.-Con., E. T. C. Werner	600
Hangchow—Acting-Cons., W. J. Clennell	...
Hankow—Consul-Gen., Pelham L. Warren	1,000
Ichang—Consul, William Holland	800
Kiu-kiang—Consul, Octavius Johnson	800
Kiungchow—Consul, E. L. B. Allen	800
Macao—Vice-Cons., (see Portugal)	400
Momein (Têng-yuch)—Consul, P. F. Hausser	800
Newchwang—Consul, H. E. Fulford	800
Ningpo—Consul, W. H. Wilkinson	800
Pakhoi—Consul, R. W. Hurst	800
Samshui—Consul, Herbert F. Brady	800
Shanghai—Chief Justice of Supreme Court, Sir Nicholas J. Hannen	2,100
Consul-General and Registrar of Shipping, Byron Brenan, C.M.G.	1,500
Consul & Assistant Judge, C. W. Campbell	900
Crown Adv., Hiram Parkes Wilkinson	400
Registrar and Chief Clerk, E. H. Burrows	450

* The tael reckoned at 3s. 4d.
§ The tael reckoned at 2s. 11½d.
‡ These figures only represent the *direct* trade with the U.K., exclusive of India and the Colonies; they should be trebled to represent approximately the actual value of commodities exchanged.

Vice-Consul, C. W. Campbell	£650
Shashih—Acting-Cons.,	...
Soochow—Acting-Cons., T. G. Carvill	...
Ssumao—Consul, J. N. Tratman	800
Swatow—Consul, J. Scott	800
Tientsin—Consul, W. R. Carles	1,100
Wenchow—Consul, P. E. O'Brien Butler	800
Wuchow—Cons., Alex. Hosie	800
Wuhu—Consul, R. H. Mortimore	800

Peking, distant 11,770 miles; transit, 39 days.
Telegrams, 5s. 5d. to 5s. 9d. per word.

COCHIN-CHINA. (See p. 475).

COLOMBIA, REPUBLIC OF.

President, Dr. L. Sanclemente (1898).
Foreign Affairs, General Cuervo Marquez.

Charge d'Affaires, Dr. Manuel M. de Narvaez, 51, Victoria St., S.W.
Cons.-Gen., Guillermo R. Calderon.
Vice-Consul, L. Schloss, 36 Mark Lane, E.C.
Consul in Liverpool, J. M. Pasos.
Consul at Southampton, Daniel Gutierrez.

Formerly New Granada—a Republic with Constitution, 5 August, 1886—consisting of 9 Departments—Antioquia, Bolivar, Boyaca, Cauca, Cundinamarca, Magdalena, Panama, Santander, and Tolima—in the most N.W. part of South America, and includes the isthmus connecting the two continents, having a coast-line on both the Atlantic and Pacific Oceans. It is situated between 2° 40′ S. to 12° 25′ N. lat. and 68° to 83° W. long., comprising an area of 502,000 square miles, and possessing an estimated population (1895) of about 5,000,000, of whom more than one-half are whites and half-castes. It has been subjected to several revolutionary changes and civil wars. The country is intersected by three great ranges of the Andes, known as the Western, Central, and Eastern Cordilleras; the latter is by far the largest, consisting of a series of vast table-lands, cool and healthy. This temperate region is the most densely-peopled portion of the Republic. Its forests are extensive; among the trees are mahogany, cedar, fustic, and other dye-woods and medicinal plants. Its mineral productions are gold (of which the output is estimated to exceed that of any of the South American Republics), silver, platinum, copper, iron, lead, coal, and precious stones. Its principal agricultural products are coffee, cotton, plantains, and bananas, while in some parts tobacco, which was largely grown in years gone by, is again receiving attention; also wheat and other cereals. Its manufactures, for home consumption, consist of woollen and cotton stuffs. The plains yield large quantities of hides, and jerked beef is obtained from the cattle feeding there. The chief exports are coffee (11,215 tons in 1895, value £857,800), the precious metals, and india-rubber. All religions are tolerated. The standing army consists of about 6,000 men, and the navy of 3 small gunboats and one cruiser. Railroads are in their infancy, only 346 miles being open in 1895, including the Panama line (47 miles), with about 6,500 (1894) miles of telegraph. The currency is paper, of which £2,571,863 was in circulation in 1895; the rate of exchange averages $12 to the £.

Revenue, 1899	$29,918,640
Expenditure, 1895	£1,571,873
Debt, foreign, 1898	1,913,500
Arrears of interest, 1879–1896	1,600,942
Debt, interior, 1899	$11,359,074

Total imports, 1898 .... £2,216,605
Total exports, 1898 3,831,557
Imports from United Kingdom, 1898... 815,925
Exports to United Kingdom, 1898 635,488

CAPITAL, Bogotá. Population, about 100,000.
British Minister Resident, George Earle
  Welby £2,000
Vice-Consul   500
  Cucuta—Cons. Agt., C. Molyneux.
  Honda—Vice-Consul, John Gillies.
  Medellin—Vice-Consul, William Gordon.

Distant 6,200 miles; transit, 35 days. Telegrams, per word, Buenaventura, 5s. 6d.; other places, 5s. to 5s. 9d.

PANAMA
is one of the nine Departments of Colombia; its area is 31,890 square miles, the population (1895) about 311,000. There are 92 primary schools, at which about 4,005 children attend; and 8 public and private colleges, with about 500 pupils. The once famous pearl-fisheries in the Gulf of Panama yield now but little, but other beds are being worked near the Chiriqui Islands, the production being about 15 tons of shells monthly. Each ton produces about £15 worth of pearls. In 1898 tax was paid on 44 gold and 17 manganese mines, but only 11 gold and 1 manganese are being worked, and the bullion shipments have not been encouraging. The prosperity of the State depends very largely upon its favourable geographical position, which facilitates transit from the Atlantic to the Pacific. The distance from Limon Bay to Panama on the latter is only 35 miles, and the highest elevation of the watershed does not exceed 278 feet. Until 1896 Panama and Colon were free ports, and from Jan. 1 1889 a general import duty is leviable of 15 per cent. silver on the gold value of all imports except liquors, which are provided for separately. A railway 47½ miles in length (fare first class, $5, second class $10 silver) joins the two oceans. The imports in 1898 were valued at £722,468 (one third from the United Kingdom), and the exports (principally bananas, indiarubber, live stock, cabinet woods, and medicinal plants) at £212,220.

The Panama Canal.—A ship canal was commenced in 1879 by Ferdinand de Lesseps, the diggings being begun in 1881, but in March, 1889, work ceased owing to lack of funds. An eight-lock canal has been decided upon and, with the work already done, the latest technical commission estimate it can be completed in 10 years, at an additional outlay of £20,000,000. Up to the date of stoppage nearly £60,000,000 had been spent, and, if this be added to the amount estimated to be necessary for completion, the canal will eventually cost at least £83,000,000. The total length will be 46½ miles; depth, 30 feet; width at bottom, 72 feet, and at surface of water, 124 feet.

A new company (Compagnie Nouvelle du Canal de Panamá) was formed in Paris with a capital of 65,000,000 fr., and work commenced at Culebra on 1st Oct., 1894. A large amount of this capital has been spent upon the wharf at La Boca, the Pacific terminus, which is now complete. The company's concession expires on October 31, 1904.

  Panama—Consul, Claude C. Mallet £800
  Vice-Consul, C. H. Dolby-Tyler.
  Barranquilla—V.-Con., E. Macgregor

Bocas del Toro—Cons. Agent, F. E. W. Jackson.
Buenaventura—Cons. Agent,
Carthagena—V.-Cons.,Thos.C.Stevenson.
Colon—Vice-Consul, Frederick P. Leay... £500
Pedregal—Cons. Agent, T. C. S. Preedy.
Santa Martha—Vice-Con., Mansel F. Carr.
Tumaco—Cons. Agent, A. J. Woodville.

Panama, 5,466 miles; transit from Liverpool direct every Thursday, 19 days. Telegrams 5s. per word from London to Panama, and 92 cents (U.S. gold) per word from Panama to London.

CONGO FREE STATE.
(See also p. 608.)

Sovereign, Leopold II., King of the Belgians.
Governor-General, Colonel Wahis.
Vice-Governor of Boma, M. Waugermée.
Secretary of State, Baron van Eetvelde.

Consul-General in London, M. Houdret, 13, London Wall, E.C.
Consul, J. T. Grein, 21 Mincing Lane, E.C.
The Congo Free State has sprung out of the discoveries of Sir H. M. Stanley, and the explorations carried on subsequently by an International Association founded at Brussels under the presidency of the King of the Belgians in 1876. The new State was in the course of 1884 and 1885 recognized by the leading Powers of Europe, and by the United States, conditional upon its maintaining the principles of Free Trade, and of only levying such dues upon shipping, or otherwise, for which there shall be returned an equivalent in facilitating the operations of commerce. The territory of this State includes the right bank of the Congo to within a few miles below Shonzo; both banks of the river thence to Manyanga; the left bank only as far as the Equator, and thenceforth both banks. In the east it extends to Lake Tanganyika. The total area included within its limits amounts to 802,000 square miles, with a population of probably not over 8,000,000. The mighty Congo, with its numerous navigable tributaries, constitutes the leading feature of this so-called State. It is navigable for large vessels from its mouth at Banana to Matodi (95 miles), where the European steamers discharge and recharge their cargo; but between that place and Leopoldville, on Stanley Pool, there occur rapids and falls, which it has been proposed to avoid by a railroad 300 miles in length. The railway was opened for traffic in July, 1898, to Stanley Pool, the first-class fare from Matadi being £20, and freight 10d. per kilo; a line of telegraph is being taken from Stanley Pool to Stanley Falls, and thence to Lake Tanganyika and Redjaf, the two branches being expected to reach their destinations in 1900. Above Leopoldville the river is navigable as far as the Stanley Falls, a distance of over 900 miles. The population of this vast territory consists of numerous negro tribes, of whom none have as yet attained a superior degree of civilization, whilst some still practise cannibalism. There are undoubtedly many fertile tracts, more especially along the rivers; but the barren mountain-land, which shuts out the coast from the more productive interior, necessitating as it does considerable expenses for the transportation of articles of commerce ill able to bear them, must always present a difficulty in developing the resources of the country. The exports consist mainly of rubber (three-fifths of whole), palm-kernels, palm-oil, ground-nuts, ivory, hides, and a few minor

articles. The coffee plant, sugar-cane, and cotton grow wild, and tobacco has been planted with success. Iron, copper, and other minerals have been found. The King of the Belgians has endowed this State out of his private fortune to the extent of £40,000 annually. There is a special import duty on Spirits; 10 per cent. *ad valorem* is charged on salt and arms and ammunition, and 6 per cent. on other goods.

Internal Revenue, 1897	£367,334
Total Expenditure, 1897	about 470,000
Total Imports, 1898	1,037,405
Total Exports, 1898	1,015,868
Imports from United Kingdom, 1898	126,238
Exports to United Kingdom, 1898	10,632

*Boma—Vice-Consul,*Maj.Wm. P. Pulteney, D.S.O.

COREA.

Emperor, Li Hsi (King, 1864, proclaimed himself Emperor, 1897).

Chief Comm. of Customs, M'Leavy Brown, C.M.G.

Corea, the bone of contention in the war between Japan and China (1894-5), is an Asiatic Kingdom consisting mainly of a peninsula lying to the north-east of China, between 34° and 43° N. lat. and 125° and 130° E. long., 600 miles from north to south, and 135 miles from east to west, with an area of about 80,000 square miles, and a population, according to the "last government census," of 10,528,937. Corea has only three neighbours, China, Japan, and Russia. It possesses several good natural harbours. Off its southern coast is the island of Port Hamilton, which was occupied by Great Britain in 1885, but subsequently evacuated, China at the time guaranteeing that it should not be occupied by any other power, and Russia undertaking not to occupy Corean territory under any circumstances whatsoever. The name Corea is derived through the Portuguese from *Ko-ri* (Chinese Kao-li), the title of the previous dynasty from 920-1392 A.D.; to the inhabitants themselves the country was known as Cho-sen until the autumn of 1897, when it was charged by Imperial edict to DAIHAN. Buddhism grafted on spirit and ancestor worship may be said to be the religion of the country. There are a number of American and British and other Protestant missionaries in Corea; but their following is small compared with the converts of the Roman Catholic missionaries. The people are tall, robust and good-looking, and belong to the Mongolian stock, their language being Turanian with the addition of many Chinese words; they are idle and unprogressive, so that the commerce of the country is falling into the hands of the Japanese and Chinese. The soil is very fertile, but only partially cultivated: rice, beans, and all kinds of grain are raised, as also tobacco, hemp, pea-cotton, &c.; ginseng, a medicinal root much affected by Chinese, is an important article of cultivation and revenue under Government monopoly. Gold, copper, coal, iron, and galena abound, and a concession was recently granted to an American syndicate to work the gold mines in the neighbourhood of Won San, in Ping-Yaug, and others to German and British syndicates. Native manufactures are in a very primitive condition; an excellent quality of paper is made from the bark of *Broussonetia papyrifera.* The country was by the Treaty of Shimonoseki declared independent of China. The *limions* of the country were placed on a *sound footing* under the direction of the Chief

Commissioner of Customs who has proved conclusively that Corea can exist on her own resources. The *army* has recently been reorganized under Russian superintendence, and consists of about 5,000 men. By recent Treaties of Commerce, the capital, Sëoul, and the ports of Chemulpo (Jen-chuan or Jinsen), Fusan, Wonsan (Yuen-san or Gen-san), Mokpo, Chinnampo, Kunsan, Masampo, and Songchia, are open to foreign trade; and a free trade mart is to be opened in Ping-Yang. The seaborne trade is almost wholly carried on in Japanese bottoms, the number of Japanese vessels cleared in 1898 being 2,117, with a tonnage of 502,145; only one British vessel (1,908 tons) visited Chemulpo in 1898. In 1898 the trade of Chemulpo amounted to £1,096,686, exclusive of the value of gold exported.

A railway from Chemulpo to Sëoul is under construction, 22 miles being open in 1899; other lines are contemplated from Fusan to Sëoul, and (narrow gauge) from Songdo to Sëoul. There are one or two lines of telegraph and an inland postal system. Chemulpo contains four banks.

Estimated revenue, 1898	£647,332
Customs Revenue, 1898	$1,000,451
Total Imports, 1898	£1,194.843
Total Exports, 1898 (excluding specie)	576,896

CAPITAL, Sëoul or Sûl. Population, 200,000.

British Chargé d'Affaires, John Newell Jordan, C.M.G. £1,200

Chemulpo—Vice-Cons., H. Goffe.

Sëoul is distant 11,560 miles; transit, 40 days; telegrams, 6*s.* 2*d.* to 10*s.* 5*d.* per word.

COSTA RICA, REPUBLIC OF.

President, Rafael Iglesias, *re-elected* 8 May, 1898.

Minister of Foreign Affairs,

Consul-Gen. in London, John A. Le Lacheur, 58 Lombard Street, E.C.

The Republic of Costa Rica, the most southern State of Central America, extending across the Isthmus, between 8° 17′ and 11° 10′ N. lat. and from 82° 30′ to 85° 45′ W. long., contains an area of about 23,000 English square miles, and a population (1892) of 243,205. The chief exports are coffee (264,138 bags weighing 13.793.293 kilogrammes in 1898-99), sugar, caoutchouc, metals, sarsaparilla, dye-woods, hides, cedarwood, tortoise-shell, and fruits. In 1898, 2,331,036 bunches of bananas were exported, valued at £184,618. The chief ports are Punta-Arenas, on the Pacific, and Port Limon, on the Atlantic. The imports are dry goods, hardware, provisions, and machinery for drying and cleaning coffee from the United States, Germany, and England. A railway from Limon, on the Atlantic, to San José, the capital, 118 miles, and from thence to Alajuela, a further distance of 13 miles, is now open, and the chief imports and exports of the Republic are now made at Port Limon. There is a further line of railway, about 12 miles, from Punta-Arenas to Esparta on the Pacific, and a small line (4 miles) from Limon to Rio Banano. An American firm is constructing a railway from San José to Tivives on the Pacific. The line from Alajuela to Port Limon belongs to an English company styled "The Costa Rica Railway Company," and besides this a considerable amount of English capital is embarked in large tracts of lands, mines, markets, tramways, and other industries.

Public income (Budget), 1898-9	£566,300
Public expenditure (Budget), 1898-9	554,170
Public debt, foreign (consolidated 1883)	2,000,000

Total imports, 1898, £851,780; exports, £1,131,844
Imports from U.K., 1898, £167,034; exports £484,472
$14 = £1.$

CAPITAL, San José. Population (1892), about 20,000.
British Minister, G. F. B. Jenner (Guatemala).
British Consul, Percy G. Harrison ....
  Port Limon—Vice-Consul, C. V. Lindo.
  Puntarenas—Vice-Consul, M. Amador.

San José is 5,687 miles from London; transit direct, 21 days; *via* New York, 18 days. Telegrams, per word, 4s. 2d.

CRETE (or CANDIA).
Sovereign, H.M. the Sultan of Turkey.
High Commissioner, H.R.H. Prince George of Greece, *appointed* 26 Nov., 1898, for 3 years.

Crete (or Candia) is an island about 148 miles long and 7 to 30 miles in breadth, with an area of 2,950 square miles; the population amounts to about 250,000, of whom quite four-fifths are Christians, the remainder being Mussulmans, speaking the Greek tongue. The island formed part of the early and later Roman Empire, and in 1669 was captured by the Turks, from whose rule it has been almost perpetually in revolt, there having been seven insurrections of note in 1821, 1855, 1868, 1877, 1889, and 1895.

A blockade was instituted by the Powers in 1897, and in November, 1898, vigorous action was taken by Great Britain, Italy, France and Russia, who remain responsible for the island. All Turkish troops have been withdrawn and the island has the prospect of impartial administration under the high suzerainty of Turkey, but independent of its suzerain under the High Commissioner appointed by the Powers. The climate is healthy, and a fine anchorage is presented by Suda Bay. The chief products are wheat and fruit; and wool, soap, olive oil, and cheese are the principal exports.

The chief towns are Candia (pop. 14,000), CANEA, the capital (pop. 22,000), and Retimo (pop. 9,000).

Canea—Consul-General, R. W. Graves, C.M.G. £920
  Vice-Consul,
Candia—Vice-Consul, L. A. Calocherino.
Retimo—Vice-Consul, Teodoro A. Trifilli.

Telegrams, 11d. per word.

CUBA. (See p. 590.)

DENMARK.
King, Christian IX., *born* 8 April, 1818; *suc.* 15 Nov., 1863; *married*, 26 May, 1842, Louise (*b.* 7 Sept., 1817, *d.* 29 Sept., 1898), daughter of William, Landgrave of Hesse-Cassel, and has issue, 3 sons and 3 daughters.
Heir Apparent, Crown Prince Frederik, born June 3, 1843; *married*, July 28, 1863, Louise, Princess of Sweden and Norway, *b.* 31 Oct. 1851; issue (1) Christian, *b.* 1870, *m.* 1898, Princess Alexandrine of Mecklenburg-Schwerin, and has issue a son *b.* 11 March, 1899; (2) Carl, *b.* 1872, *m.* 1896, Princess Maud (of Wales); and 6 other children.
Premier and Minister of Finance, H. E. Hörring.
Interior, H. Bramsen.
Justice and Minister for Iceland, H. E. Hörring.
Public Worship and Instruction, Bishop Sthyr.
War (ad interim), Col. Schnach.
Foreign Affairs & Marine, Vice-Admiral N. F. Ravn.
Agriculture, Alfred Hage.

Envoy Extraordinary and Min. Plenip. in London, F. E. de Bille, 24 Pont Street, S.W.
Secretary, Baron Otto Reedtz-Thott.

Attaché, C. C. A. Gosch, 21 Stanhope Gardens.
Consul-Gen. in London, Ernest Adolf Delcomyn, 5 Muscovy Court, Tower Hill, E.C.
Vice-Consul, J. Clan.
Consul—Hull, H. Pattinson.
Consul-General—Leith, W. O. Berry.
Consul—Liverpool, J. F. Caröe.
Ditto—Manchester, P. A. Paulsen.
Ditto—Belfast, A. M. Münster.

A Kingdom of Northern Europe, and the smallest of the Northern States, with a Constitution dated 28 July, 1866; consisting of the islands of Zeeland, Fünen, Lolland, &c., the peninsula of Jutland, and the outlying island of Bornholm in the Baltic. Denmark is situated between 54° 34'—57° 44' N. lat. and 8° 5'—12° 40' E. long.; its present contracted dimensions being the result of the Dano-German war of 1864, which stripped it of the Duchies of Schleswig-Holstein and Lauenburg. It comprises an area of 14,789 square miles, with a population in 1890 of (including Faröe Islands) 2,185,335, nearly one-half of whom live exclusively by agriculture, and one-fourth by manufactures and trade. The common products are wheat, rye, oats, barley, potatoes, cattle, horses, pigs, sheep, and butter; the value of the latter exported to the United Kingdom in 1893 being £7,329,831. Its manufactures are, for the most part, for home consumption. Its principal imports are coals, manufactured goods (woollens, silks, cottons), iron, hardware, wine, fruit, tea, maize, and colonial produce. Its chief exports are those of agricultural produce, including wheat and barley, bacon, hams, flour, butter, eggs, hides, skins, corn-meal and oil-cake, horses, and cattle, the latter principally to Great Britain. Denmark possesses an army of 50,522 men on the warfooting; a navy consisting of 37 steam-vessels (including 4 ironclads), mounting 227 guns, with 1,270 officers and men; and a mercantile marine of 3,695 vessels, with a tonnage of 356,108. There are (1897-8) 1,531 miles of railway and 3.534 miles of telegraph line. There is a free harbour (Frihavn) at Copenhagen, opened 9th November, 1894.

Revenue (Budget, 1899—1900)	£3,755,550
Expenditure, ,,	3,741,440
Reserve Fund	992,475
Public debt, 31st March, 1897	10,911,413
Total imports, 1897	23,115,000
Total exports, 1897	18,223,000
Imports from United Kingdom, 1898	3,919,325
Exports to United Kingdom, 1898	11,703,334

CAPITAL, Copenhagen. Population (1895) (including suburbs), 408,300.

British Minister, Sir Edmund Fane, K.C.M.G. £3,000
Sec. of Legation, Hon. Alan Johnstone 500
3rd Sec., Arthur W. Ponsonby 250
Chaplain, Rev. Mortimer E. Kennedy, M.A. ... 200
Consul, Captain James Boyle 500
  Vice-Consul, C. H. Funch.
  Aalborg—Vice-Consul, C. T. Malling.
  Aarhus—Vice-Consul, G. F. Stark.
  Elsinore—V.-Con., Lorenz M. F. Schmidt.
  Esbjerg—Vice-Consul, J. Nielsen.
  Frederici—V.-Con., H. M. E. Rasmussen.
  Frederikshavn—V.-Con., Wm. Schmidt.
  Kastrup—Vice-Con., Silvio Alfred Fugl.
  Korsöer—Vice-Consul, P. Jorgensen.
  Lemvig—Vice-Consul, Anthon Andersen.
  Nyborg—Vice-Consul, August Birch.
  Oleuse—Vice-Consul, Laurids B. Muus.
  Randers—Vice-Consul, A. Kraunsöe.
  Rönne (Bornholm)—Vice-Consul, C. P. Lund.
  Thisted—Vice-Con., Emil A. Bendixen.

Thorshavn—Vice-Consul, Louis Bergh.
St. Thomas & Ste. Croix—Consul, Herman W. McDougal.
   ,,   *Chaplain*, Rev. Eyre Hutson.
Bassin (Ste. Croix)—V.-Con., R. Armstrong.
Fredericksted—Vice-Consul, W. B. Woods.

The outlying possessions and colonies of Denmark have an area of 75,115 square miles, with 127,184 inhabitants. They include the Faröe or Sheep Islands (515 sq. m., pop. 12,955); Iceland (*See* p. 565); Greenland (34,000 sq. m., pop. 10,516), the trade of which is a government monopoly, and 3 islands in the West Indies, St. Croix, St. Thomas, and St. John (142 sq. m., pop. 32,786). These latter export sugar and rum.

Exports Danish Possessions to U. K., 1898 £23,332
Imports from United Kingdom, 1898 53,264

Copenhagen, distant 728 miles; transit,32 hours. Telegrams, per word, 3d.

DOMINICAN REPUBLIC.

President, Señor Jimenez, Nov. 1899.
Interior and Police, José Brache.
Minister for Foreign Affairs, Domingo Ferreras.
War and Marine, Aristido Patiño.
Finance, Samuel Moya.
Public Works, Arturo Zeno.
Justice, José Manuela Nonel.
Posts and Telegraphs, José F. Guzman.

Cons.-Gen., Miguel Ventura, 17 Coleman St., E.C.

San Domingo, formerly the Spanish portion of the island of Hayti, is the oldest settlement of European origin in America, having been founded in 1494 by Bartolomeo Columbus. The capital city contains the Cathedral and Columbus's residence. It comprises an area of about 20,596 square miles, with an estimated population of nearly 500,000. The chief products are tobacco, coffee, sugar, cocoa, mahogany, and a great variety of other furniture woods, wax, honey, logwood, fustic, turtle-shell, hides, and divi-divi. Sugar, the most recent industry, is now the most important. The minerals are gold, copper, and iron. There are about 100 miles of railway, and telegraphic communication has been established throughout the Republic, which is connected by cable with North and South America.

Capital, San Domingo. Population, 18,000.
Revenue and expenditure, 1898-9...about £680,000
National Debt, 1899, about 8,000,000
Imports, 1898-9 1,154,000
Exports, 1898-9 340,000
British Consul-General for Hayti and Dominican Republic, Augustus Cohen £1,000
San Domingo—Vice-Consul, H. H. Gosling.
Porto Plata—Vice-Cons., Charles McGrigor.

San Domingo is distant 4,560 miles; transit, 16 days. Telegrams, 6s. 6d. per word.

ECUADOR, Republic of.

President, General Eloy Alfaro (1895) $24,000
Vice-President, Carlos Freile Zaldumbide.
Interior & Foreign Affairs, Dr. Ruben Rivera.
Finance, Dr. Fidel A. Novoa.
Public Instruction, Dr. J. Frigueros.
War, General Nicanor Arellano.

Consul-General in London, Celso Nevares, 3 Copthall Buildings, E.C.

A State of South America, on its western side, being that portion of the original Republic of Colombia which lies on each side of the Equator, extending from lat. 1° 38' N. to 6° 26' S. (according to the Ecuadorian geography, but there are boundary disputes with Peru and Colombia), and between 70° and 81° W. long., comprising an area of 120,000 English sq. miles. It has a population of about 1,270,000, mostly descendants of the Spaniards, aboriginal Indians, and Mestizoes. The giant chain of the Andes here presents the Chimborazo, 21,525 feet, the Cotopaxi, 19,613 feet, the Antisana, 19,335 feet, Cayambe, 19,186 feet above the level of the sea, and others. Ecuador is watered by the Upper Amazon, and by the rivers Guayaquil, Mira, Santiago, Chones, and Esmeraldas on the Pacific coast. There are extensive forests, and the cinchona bark tree is common. Its chief products are cocoa, vegetable ivory, cotton, coffee, india-rubber, orchella weed, straw hats and hammocks, bark, yams, tobacco, fruits, sarsaparilla, wheat, &c. Its minerals consist of gold, quicksilver, lead, iron, and copper; emeralds and rubies are occasionally met with and sulphur is found in many parts. The chief exports are—cocoa, caoutchouc, silver specie and gold, cinchona bark, Panama hats, coffee, and cattle. Ecuador is divided into 16 provinces and one territory. In 1891 there were 57 miles of railway open. An arrangement was recently made with the bondholders for the conversion of the Debt, but the Dictator, in 1895, suspended payment pending a further and less onerous arrangement; meanwhile a 10 per cent. surtax upon import dues is being collected and deposited in a Guayaquil bank. Guayaquil is the chief port: population, 1896, about 50,000. In 1890 the customs duties amounted to £460,162.

The population of the other chief towns is approximately as follows: Quito, 40,000; Cuenca, 25,000; Riobamba, 12,000; Ambato, Loja, and Latacunga, 10,000.

The Galapagos Islands (2,400 square miles) belong to Ecuador; only about 200 miles are susceptible of cultivation.

Public revenue, 1893 .... $4,325,701
Public expenditure, 1893 4,433,450
Public debt, 1893 .... £750,000
Internal debt, 1893 264,000
Imports, 1893, $2,975,718; Exports, 1893, 533,769
Total receipts from Custom House, 1893   3,509,484
Imports from United Kingdom, 1898 ... £341,757
Exports to United Kingdom, 1898 267,164
Average currency exchange, 1898, $10·25 to $10·50 to the £. The $ is a paper Sucre.

Capital, Quito. Population, about 40,000.
British Minister, William Nelthorpe Beauclerk (*see* Lima, Peru).
Consul, Ludovico Söderström.
Guayaquil—Consul,
Vice-Consul, Alfred Cartwright.

Quito, 6,560 miles; transit, 35 days. Telegrams, 6s. 2d. a word.

EGYPT.

(*See also* pp. 607-8, and Map, p. 607.)

(A)—EGYPT PROPER.

Khedive or *Reigning Sovereign*, Abbas Pasha, G.C.B., G.C.M.G., b. 14 July, 1874; *suc.* 7 Jan., 1892.
Heir apparent, Abdul Mouheim Bey, only son of the Khedive, *born* 20 Feb., 1899.
President of Council and Minister of Interior, Mustapha Fehmy Pasha, G.C.M.G.
Foreign Affairs, Boutros Pasha Ghaly, K.C.M.G.
Minister of Justice, Ibrahim Fuad Pasha.
War and Navy, Abani Pasha.
Public Works and Instruction, Fakhry Pasha.

Minister of Finance, Mazloum Pasha.
Financial Adviser to the Khedive, J. L. Gorst.
Sirdar of the Egyptian Army, Major-General Lord Kitchener of Khartoum, G.C.B., K.C.M.G.
Judicial Adviser to the Khedive, M. McIlwraith.
Commanding British Troops, Maj.-Gen. Hon. R. A. J. Talbot, C.B.
President, Government Railways, Lt.-Col. E. P. C. Girouard, R.E., D.S.O.
Director - General of Customs, Alfred Caillard Pasha, C.M.G.
British Controller-General, Daira Sanieh Administration, Harry Crookshank Pasha, F.R.C.S.
Controller, Port of Alexandria, Sir George Morice Pasha, K.C.M.G.

A country in the north-east corner of the Continent of Africa, was made part of the Turkish Empire in the latter part of the 12th century. Its history became interwoven with that of Europe when the army of Napoleon the Great entered into possession in 1801. British successes drove out the invaders, and in 1803 the newcomers also evacuated the country, which they endeavoured to restore to the control of the Sultan of Turkey; but after the abandonment by Great Britain a struggle arose between two Turkish parties, the Albanians and the Ghuzz, the former being completely victorious under their leader *Mehemet Ali,* who in 1811, in spite of the attempted intervention of Great Britain, obtained the supreme power, and ruled the country. This ruler was sometimes the ally, sometimes the enemy, of his suzerain the Sultan, until in 1833, after a succession of victories by land and sea, he obtained from the Sultan the title of Vali or Governor, and was confirmed in his rule in return for the payment of an annual tribute to the Porte. His reign was marked by the grant of a constitution, and by a more or less just administration until his mind gave way in 1848, when his son *Ibrahim* succeeded. The new ruler only lived for two months after his accession, dying a short time before his father in 1849. *Abbas* (1848–1854), son of Mehemet's third child Tousoun, succeeded, but entirely neglected the affairs of government, being followed by *Said* (1854–1863), Mehemet's fourth son. This ruler attempted to restore the Government to the state of efficiency which had marked his father's rule, and carried out many reforms, his reign being marked by the concession for the Suez Canal. He was succeeded by *Ismail* (1863–1879), who by a firman of the Sultan (14th May, 1867) was granted the title of KHEDIV MISR, or Ruler of Egypt, the previous rulers having had the title of Vali or Governor. In the early years of his reign the government was most successfully administered, and the Egyptian dominions very largely extended, until in 1875 its territories comprised an area of nearly 1,500,000 square miles, with a population of about 16,000,000. But on the heels of annexation and conquest followed misgovernment and financial embarrassment, until in 1879 the expenditure (£10,500 000) exceeded the revenue (£8,500,000) by £2,000 000, the service of the debt (£80,500,000) accounting for more than three-fifths of the total expenditure. At this point the Governments of France and Great Britain intervened, and forced Ismail to abdicate, appointing his son *Mohamed Tewfik* (1879–1892) to succeed him. By a decree of the new Khedive (10th Nov. 1879) a *Controller-General* was appointed by each Power, M. de Blignières being nominated by France, and Major Evelyn Baring, C.S.I. (now Viscount Cromer, G.C.B., &c.) by

Great Britain, their principal duty being the supervision of the finances, towards which unsuccessful efforts had already been made under British advisers after 1875. In 1882, however, the work of reform was interrupted by a military revolt, headed by an officer of the Egyptian army (Arabi Pasha), and, the French Government declining to co-operate, a British expedition was despatched to re-establish the authority of the Khedive. The port of Alexandria was bombarded by Sir Beauchamp Seymour (July 11th), and the rebel army routed at Kassassin (Aug. 28th), to be completely annihilated at Tel-el-Kebir (Sept. 23rd) by Sir Garnet Wolseley. The Dual Control was abolished by a decree of the Khedive (18th Jan., 1883), and a British financial adviser appointed as a member of the Khedivial Government.

Immediate steps were taken to re-establish the Khedive's authority, and a force raised to replace the army which had been disbanded; but during the disturbances in the north a revolt had broken out in the southern provinces, headed by Sheik Mohamed Ahmed of Dongola, who proclaimed himself a Mahdi, or prophet, foretold by the Moslems. This revolt was at first unchecked, and the victorious Sheik advanced northward and threatened the security of the Khedivial Government. Col. Hicks, who had been appointed to command the newly formed and undisciplined Egyptian army, was defeated and killed at El Obeid (3rd Nov., 1883) when advancing to meet the rebels, and, upon receipt of this intelligence, part of the British troops, which were about to be sent home, were retained in the country. General Gordon, the hero of the Chinese rebellion, was despatched to Khartoum (Jan., 1884) as Governor-General of the Soudan, but this step was not followed by immediate movements of troops against the rebels, and in 1885 General Gordon fell at the capture of Khartoum (26th Jan.) before a relief expedition, sent down the Nile, reached him. From this point the rebels gained a complete hold on the southern Soudan, and, although checked by repeated defeats in their advance northward, no definite steps were taken at that time to recover the lost provinces.

Meanwhile the work of internal reform was being carried on, and in accordance with a decree of 1880 an International Commission investigated the financial affairs of the country, until in 1890, with the consent of the European Powers, a scheme of conversion and unification was carried out by which the annual charge of the Egyptian debt was reduced to nearly one-half its former proportions, the balance being freed to meet internal expenditure, while the revenue was increased by the efforts of successive financial advisers.

In 1883 the Khedive created a Legislative Council of 30 members, and a General Assembly, consisting of the Legislative Council, the six Ministers of State, and 46 members elected by the people. These bodies, however, were, and still are, mainly consultative, the real legislative power resting with the Khedive and his Ministers. In addition to the reforms in the civil administration the Egyptian army was taken in hand. In 1883 Sir Evelyn Wood, ΥΓ, was appointed *Sirdar,* or Commander-in-Chief, and, with a staff of British officers, the whole body was reorganised and trained. Sir Francis Grenfell became Sirdar in 1885, to be succeeded in 1892 by Brigadier-General Herbert Horatio Kitchener,

C.B., C.M.G. (now Lord Kitchener of Khartoum). The command of the army is made by Khedivial decree with the consent of the British Government.

In 1892 (7th Jan.), the Khedive Mohamed Tewfik died, and was succeeded by his elder son *Abbas*, the present ruler.

The position of Egypt is, therefore, as follows:—nominally a province of the Ottoman Empire it is actually autonomous under the Khedive, subject to the annual tribute (£682,092) payable to the Sultan; it is at the same time dependent for its existence as a sovereign State upon the will of stronger Powers, Great Britain being the dominant factor since the abolition of the Dual Control in 1883.

For the purposes of local government the country is divided into governorships, each split up into provinces, which again are sub-divided into districts. Justice is administered by (1) Religious Courts; (2) the Mixed Tribunals established in 1875, to deal with questions arising between foreign inhabitants of different nationality and civil suits between natives and foreign subjects; (3) the Consular Courts, by which criminal charges against foreign subjects are investigated; and (4) the Native Tribunals containing Egyptian and foreign judges, dealing with cases of first instance, and also with appeals from their own lesser courts. A British Judicial Adviser to the Khedive watches the proceedings of the latter.

The population in 1882 was 6,805,381, including 90,886 European foreigners (37,301 Greeks, 18,665 Italians, 15,716 French, 8,022 Austrians, 6,118 English, &c.), and by the census of 1897, Egypt Proper (*i.e.* up to Wady Halfa) contains 9,750,000 inhabitants, of whom 112,500 were foreigners (38,000 Greeks, 24,500 Italians, 14,000 British subjects, 5,000 British army, 14,000 French subjects, 7,000 Austrians, 1,400 Russians, and 1,300 Germans).

The cultivated portion of Egypt is confined to the country annually inundated by the Nile, or capable of being irrigated by canals. The great irrigation works, to which Egypt may be said to owe its existence, are being further extended by the construction of two dams across the Nile at Assuan and Assiut for the storage of water. These works will cost £2,000,000, and £1,180,000 will be spent upon subsidiary canals and drains.

Agriculture, &c.—Its products consist of cotton, millet, maize, wheat, rice, melons, gourds, sugar, hemp, &c. No metals have been worked within recent times in any considerable quantity; but salt, petroleum, nitre, marble, red granite, Oriental alabaster, turquoises, and limestone are found.

Trade.—The chief imports are cotton stuffs, coals, provisions, woollens, coffee, tobacco, indigo, hardware, timber, wine and spirits, and machinery. The exports consist mainly of cotton and cotton-seed (85 per cent.), beans, wheat, sugar, maize, rice, gums, hides, wool, barley, cigarettes, ivory, and ostrich-feathers. Of the entire trade over 53 per cent. is carried on with the United Kingdom, 9 per cent. with Turkey, 8 per cent. with France and Austria.

Railways and Telegraphs.—There is a railway from Cairo to Assuan, just below the first cataract, and an extension from Wadi Halfa, below the second cataract, to Khartoum is being rapidly pushed on and will probably be completed before the end of 1899. An extension from Berber to Suakim is contemplated. The total length of these lines was 1,209 miles on 31 Dec. 1898, and 11,081,739 passengers and 2,786,000 tons of goods were carried in 1898, the total receipts being £E2,031,569 and the working expenses £E917,536. From the terminus to Luxor the standard gauge is used, but thence the gauge is 3ft. 6in. as in the extensions from Wadi Halfa to Kerma and Wadi Halfa to Khartoum. There are (1898) 2,058 miles of telegraph with 9,487 miles of wire, over which 2,743,488 messages were transmitted in 1898.

Defence.—The British army of occupation numbers about 5,000 men, but in the battle of Omdurman 8,000 British troops were used. The Egyptian forces at that time were 17,000 strong.

Finance.—Under the able administration of Sir Elwin Palmer, until lately financial adviser to the Khedive, the finances of the country have assumed a thoroughly sound aspect, and since the year 1891 there has been a large net surplus of revenue over expenditure, that for 1898 amounting to £E1,225,641. The debt was converted in a very economical fashion in 1890, and reserve funds have been established. These funds are as follows: (1) Formed by the Conversion of the Debt, and only available for payments with the consent of the Powers; (2) The General Reserve Fund, which may be applied to certain specified objects by consent of the *Caisse de la Dette*; (3) the Special Reserve Fund which is at the free disposal of the Egyptian Government. The last named showed, at the end of 1897, a deficit of £570,849, whereas, at the end of 1898 there was an available balance of £478,233, chiefly owing to the abandonment of all claim to the advance of £E778,832, made to the Egyptian Government by the House of Commons which, until 1898, was regarded as repayable.

Public revenue, 1898	£E11,347,980
Public expenditure, 1898	£E10,122,319
Consolidated debt, 31 Dec., 1898	£93,851,240
Annual debt charge, 1898	£E3,493,087

Reserve Funds (31 Dec. 1898):—

(1) By Conversion	£E3,217,898
(2) General	£E3,893,134
(3) Special	£E 478,233
	£E7,589,265
Total imports, 1898*	£E11,033,219
Total exports, 1898*	£E11,805,179
Imports from United Kingdom, 1898*	£E3,872,452
Exports to United Kingdom, 1898*	£E5,523,204

THE SUEZ CANAL.

The Suez Canal was opened in 1869, the British Government acquiring by purchase, 25 Nov., 1875, shares to the amount of £4,000,000 (the present value being £26,451,000). The total length of the canal is 99 miles, with a width of 327 feet for 77, and 196 for the remaining 22 miles; the depth is 26 feet throughout. By a convention, signed on Oct. 29, 1888, the canal was exempted from blockade, and vessels of all nations, whether armed or not, are to be allowed to pass through it in peace or war.

Traffic Returns:—

Year.	No. of Vessels.	Nett Tons.	% British.
1869	10	6,576	—
1870	486	436,609	—
1890	3,425	6,783,187	77
1893	3,341	7,659,068	75
1894	3,352	8,039,175	74
1895	3,434	8,448,383	71
1896	3,409	8,560,283	68
1897	2,998	7,921,320	67
1898	3,503	9,238,603	68

The Receipts in 1869 were £2,178; in 1870, £205,273; in 1893, £2,826,692; in 1894, £2,951,072;

* Exclusive of specie.

in 1895, £3,124,148; in 1896, £3,255,061; in 1897, £2,913,221; and in 1898, £3,411,790.

CAPITAL, Cairo. Population (1897), 570,000. Alexandria, chief port, pop. 320,000; other towns being Tantah, 57,000; Zagazig, 36,000; Mansurah, 36,000; Port Said, 42,000; Suez, 17,000; Ismailia, 7,000. In Upper Egypt Assiut has 42,000 inhabitants and Keneh 24,000.

Cairo, British Agent, Consul-General, and Minister Plenipotentiary, Viscount Cromer, G.C.B., G.C.M.G., K.C.S.I., C.I.E.	£6,000
Sec. of Legation, Sir Rennell Rodd, K.C.M.G., C.B.	600
2nd Secretary, Ralph Paget	475
3rd Secretary, T. B. Hohler	250
Attaché, A. Akers-Douglas.	
Consul, Raphael Borg, C.M.G.	600
Medical Adviser, Alexander Murison, M.D.	
Alexandria—Con.-Gen. Edward B. Gould ...	1,000
,, *Vice-Consul*, A. D. Alban	500
,, *Chaplain (Scotch)*, Rev. Wm. Cowan	
,, *Surgeon*, A. Morrison, M.D.	375
Assouan—Cons. Agent, Boutros Sarkiss.	
Birket-es-Sab — Consul Agent, Alex. W. Murdoch.	
Mansourah—Cons.-Agent, Fredk. Murdoch.	
Tantah—Cons. Agent, Joseph Inglis.	
Thebes (Luxor)—Cons. Agent, Said Moustapha Ayyad.	
Zagazig—Vice-Consul, Salvatore Felice....	
Port Said—Consul, Donald Andreas Cameron	800
,, *Vice-Consul*, Frederick F. Maling	400
Suakin—Consul,	700
Suez—Vice-Consul, John Roper Norrish	450

Cairo is 2,520 miles from London; transit, 6 days. Telegrams, per word, to Alexandria, 1s. 7d.; Suakin, 2s. 6d., other places 1s. 10d. to 2s. 3d.

(B)—THE SOUDAN PROVINCES.

Governor-General, Major-General Lord Kitchener of Khartoum, G.C.B., K.C.M.G., R.E., *Ferik, and Sirdar of the Egyptian Army*.

Asst. Mily. Sec., Major J. K. Watson, D.S.O., K.R.R.C.

Aide-de-Camp, Lt. J. M. A. Graham, R.Lanc.R.

Governors of First-class Districts :—
Khartoum, Col. J. G. Maxwell, D.S.O.
Sennar, Col. D. F. Lewis, C.B.
Kassala, Lt.-Col. J. Collinson, C.B.
Berber, Lt.-Col. Jackson.
Dongola, Lt.-Col. Hickman, D.S.O.

Governors of Second-class Districts :—
Wady Halfa, Capt. F. G. Anley.
Suakin, Major H. T. Godden, D.S.O.
Assouan, Major O. H. Pedley.

[*Assouan* is an Egyptian and not Soudan district, but is under military control.]

The history of the conquest of the Soudan Provinces, and of part of Equatorial Africa, has been related in the above article, as also their abandonment by the British Government in face of the strong resistance offered by the religious fanatics under the Mahdi, Sheik Mohamed Ahmed of Dongola, at whose death Abdullah al Taashi was appointed to succeed, with the title of Khalifa. The rule of both was a military despotism, marked by horrible excesses, and the country, which had been brought into a certain state of cultivation, was laid waste, the headquarters of the despotism being Omdurman, a city built opposite the city of Khartoum, razed to the ground after its capture in 1885. The Egyptian Army had, in the years since its reformation (1883-96), been brought to a very high state of perfection by the successive occupants of the

Sirdarieh, and in 1896 Sir Herbert Kitchener, who had been appointed Sirdar in 1892 (after a series of victories over the rebels when Governor of the Red Sea Littoral, 1886-9), advanced from Cairo with an Anglo - Egyptian force, and after defeating the enemy in numerous engagements recovered the province of Dongola. In 1897 the province of Berber was recovered, and on 8th April, 1898, General Kitchener defeated and captured the Emir Mahmoud, one of Abdullah's Generals, at the battle of the Atbara river. After this reverse Abdullah retired to Omdurman, before which town General Kitchener gained a decisive victory (2nd September, 1898) against a force more than twice as numerous. The city of Khartoum was immediately occupied, and a religious service held in memory of General Gordon on the spot where he had fallen. The Sirdar subsequently carried the British and Egyptian flags down the river Sobat, a tributary of the Blue Nile, encountering on the way a French force at Fashoda, whither the commandant (Major Marchand) had penetrated from the west coast of Africa. After short negotiations between the two Governments the post was evacuated, and a convention signed by Great Britain and France, delimitating the respective spheres of influence. On 24 Nov., 1899, about 14 months after the victory at Omdurman, Col. Sir F. R. Wingate overtook the fugitive Khalifa at Om Debrikat and entirely annihilated the Dervish army; among the slain were Abdullah and his principal emirs.

During the period of abandonment, 1885-1896, certain portions of Egypt's former dependencies had been recovered from the Mahdi by other countries. The Italian Government proclaimed a protectorate over the kingdom of Ethiopia, and placed a garrison in the Egyptian town of Kassala, but a vigorous campaign was carried on against the new comers by Menelek of Shoa, who had established himself as king of all Ethiopia. The result of the campaign was unfavourable to Italian arms, and the protectorate was withdrawn and a treaty of peace concluded with Menelek. A treaty was also signed by Great Britain and the ruler of Ethiopia, defining and enlarging the boundaries of the latter kingdom. The Italian Government handed over the town and district of Kassala to an Anglo-Egyptian representative, and have now withdrawn into a portion of the north-east coast bordering on the Red Sea, which constitutes their colony of Erithrea, and a strip of the Somali coast.

The extent of the Soudan Provinces is defined in a convention signed, on 19th Jan., 1899, by Viscount Cromer and the Egyptian Minister for Foreign Affairs, laying down the principles which are to underlie the administration. The territories affected are all those lying south of the 22nd parallel of latitude, which have never been evacuated by Egyptian troops since 1882, and those which, if evacuated and temporarily lost, have since been, or shall henceforth be, reconquered by the two Governments acting in concert. The Government is to be administered by a Governor-General in supreme civil and military command, appointed and removable by Khedivial decree with the consent of the British Government. The Governor-General may legislate by proclamation with the consent of the Governments, and the territories do not fall under the jurisdiction of the Mixed Tribunals.

The seat of Government is Khartoum, which is to be rebuilt, and the foundation stone has been laid there (5th Jan., 1899) of the Gordon Memorial College, for the establishment of which Lord Kitchener obtained, by public subscription in the United Kingdom and Greater Britain, the necessary funds. The territories are divided into five first-class districts, Khartoum, Sennar, Kassala, Berber, and Dongola, and two second-class districts, Wady Halfa, and Suakin. Communication is effected by means of the railway, which reached Khartoum in 1899; and at the close of the military operations navigation was found possible of the river Sobat, a tributary of the Blue Nile, so that the outlying districts of the British Protectorate of Uganda, and of the East Africa Protectorate are made accessible from the north. In the course of time the railway contemplated by Mr. Cecil Rhodes from Cape Town, through Rhodesia and leased territory, may be expected to join the system coming downwards through Khartoum, and with the railway a line of telegraph will also be laid.

The cost of military operations in the Soudan in the years 1883-86 amounted to £7,091,310, and on the expedition by which these territories were recovered, the sum of £798,802 only was expended, excluding the sum of £215,000 provided in 1897-8 by the Egyptian Government.

The territories are not expected to provide an income equivalent to their cost for some few years, but with the peaceful settlement in towns by the inhabitants, and the good government that is assured them, a substantial revenue may be expected, the cost of administration being meanwhile borne by the Egyptian Government.

CAPITAL, Khartoum. Population, about 1,000, consisting of masons, &c., and a small garrison. The population of Omdurman is still about 30,000, most of whom are refugees who will probably disperse to their homes. Distant from London via Cairo, 4,196 miles. Telegrams, 1s. 10d. to 2s. 3d. per word.

FRANCE.
(See also pp. 606-8.)

President of the Republic, Emile Loubet, *born at* Marsanne (Drôme), 31 December, 1838; elected 18th February, 1899 (in place of Félix Faure, deceased). Formerly President of the Senate £24,000
Premier & Min. of Interior, M. Waldeck-Rousseau.
Minister of Finance, M. Caillaux.
Minister of Public Instruction, M. Georges Leygues.
Minister of Justice, M. Monis.
Minister of War, General de Galliffet.
Minister of Marine, M. de Lanessan.
Minister of Commerce, Industry, and Posts & Telegraphs, M. Millerand.
Minister of Public Works, M. Pierre Baudin.
Minister of Foreign Affairs, M. Delcassé.
Minister of Colonies, M. Decrais.
Minister of Agriculture, M. Jean Dupuy.
Ambassador to Russia, Comte de Montebello; *Austria-Hungary,* Marquis de Reverseaux; *Germany,* Marquis de Noailles; *Italy,* Monsieur Barrère; *Turkey,* M. Constans; *U.S.A.,* M. Jules Cambon.

Ambassador in London, M. Paul Cambon, Albert Gate House, Hyde Park.
Minister Plenipotentiary, M. Geoffray.
2nd Secretaries, M. D. de la Chaussée ; E. Daeschner ; Vicomte de Manneville.
3rd ditto, F. Couget ; M. R. de Billy.
Attachés, Vicomte A. d'Espeuilles ; E. Pelletier.
Military Attaché, Lieut.-Col. Le Comte Du Pontavice de Heussey.

Naval Attaché, Captain Fiéron.
Secretary Archiviste, M. Knecht.
Consulate-General, 38 Finsbury Circus,
Consul-General, M. André Lequeux.
Consul, M. de Coppet.
Chancelier, M. Nettement.

The most westerly State of Central Europe, extending from 42° 20' to 51° 5' N. lat., and from 7° 45' E. to 4° 45' W. long., bounded on the north by the Channel and Straits of Dover, which separate it from England. Its circumference is estimated at about 3,000 miles, and its present area at 204,146 square miles. The territory lost in 1871 amounted to 5,602 square miles. France is divided into 87 departments, including the island of Corsica, in the Mediterranean, off the west coast of Italy. The head of the Government is the President, elected septennially. The principal rivers are the Seine, Loire, Garonne, and Rhône; the principal forests, Ardennes, Compiègne, Fontainebleau, and Orléans, consisting chiefly of oak, birch, pine, beech, elm, chestnut, and the cork-tree in the south. Fruit trees abound, and are very productive, the principal being the olive, chestnut, walnut, almond, apple, pear, citron, fig, plum, &c. The vine is cultivated to a very great extent (710,211,298 gallons were produced in 1898, and 825,089,298, were produced in 1899 (estimated), as the names Bordeaux, Burgundy, Champagne, &c., universally testify; cider making is also an important industry (234,023,592 gallons in 1898). The chief agricultural products are wheat,[*] barley, rye, maize, oats, potatoes, beetroot for the manufacture of sugar, hops, &c. Its mineral resources are comparatively small. They include, however, coal (1897, 30,277,888 French tons), pig iron (1897, 2,472,143 French tons), copper, lead, silver, antimony, and salt. The most important manufactures are of metals, watches, jewellery, cabinet-work, carving, pottery, glass, chemicals, dyeing, paper-making, woollens, carpets, linen, silk, and lace. Its oyster fisheries are an important industrial feature. The increase of population is very slow, as will be seen from the following table :

Year.	Population.	Year.	Population.
1700	19,660,320	1881	37,672,048
1801	27,349,003	1886	38,218,903
1821	30,461,873	1891	38,343,192
1856	36,039,364	1895	38,133,385
1866	38,067,064	1896	38,517,975
1872	36,102,921		

France has always been attractive to foreigners, of whom (1896) 1,027,491 were resident there. There are about 517,000 Frenchmen in the Colonies and in various parts of the world, and a colonial population of (according to the estimates of the French Ministry of Commerce) 31,053,774 ; but with French protectorates 77,139,000, including France. Even the comparatively small increase of the population now shown is largely due to immigration from other countries, but, as the figures below show, there is a slight preponderance of births over deaths for 1896 :—

	Births.	Deaths.		Births.	Deaths.
1884	937,758	—	1894	855,000	815,000
1889	880,579	794,933	1895	834,173	851,986
1890	838,019	876,000	1896	865,586	771,886
1893	874,000	867,000			

In 1881 there were 650,000 Protestants and about 85,000 Jews, 50,000 of whom reside in Paris.

[*] France is the largest wheat-growing country in Europe, the average crop for the last six years amounting to 332,642,866 bushels (1894, 366,790,119 ; 1895, 329,911,299 ; 1896, 326,989,019 ; 1897, 256,429,182 ; 1898, 370,829,550) ; 1899 (estimated) 354,905,832.

The effective strength of the ARMY under the colours in 1897 was 576,859 (excluding a gendarmerie of about 25,861 men), with 140,000 horses and 3,200 field guns. On a war footing the army could be raised to over 3,000,000 men. The NAVY consisted in 1898 of 27 battleships (8 *building*), 9 armoured cruisers (10 *building*), 30 protected cruisers (10 *building*), 16 unprotected cruisers, 14 coast defence, 13 torpedo vessels (2 *building*), 211 torpedo boats (38 *building*), and 1 special vessel, with 2,084 officers and 43,451 men. The educational system is governmental, and presided over by a Minister of Instruction, part of the expense being defrayed by the State. In addition to the faculties of Theology, Law, and Medicine, the Lycées, the Colleges, the Naval and Military Schools, and the Ecole Polytechnique, the State supports numerous establishments for instruction in special branches of knowledge. The system of railways in France is very extensive; they are almost entirely *concédés*, and become State property after the expiration of the concession. The average length open for traffic in 1898 was 23,269 miles, the total receipts for 1898 from passenger and goods traffic, &c., being £54,375,346. The length of telegraphs is 62,862 miles. There is a mercantile marine (1897) of 15,536 vessels (14,301 sailing) of 894,071 tons.

The principal imports are wool, wines (the imports of which exceed the exports), silks, cereals, cottons, coal, and timber. The exports rank thus:— Silk tissues, woollen tissues, wines, woollen yarn, toys, &c., and cotton tissues.

The trade in 1898 was shared thus:—

Exports *to* (1898, 3,511,000,000 francs)—

Great Britain .. £40,961,603	U.S.A......... £8,385,300
Belgium......... 21,477,600	Algeria......... 8,978,051
Germany 15,706,700	

Imports *from* (1898, 4,472,000,000 francs)—

Great Britain .. £20,225,209	Belgium......£11,493,900
U.S.A......... 25,355,600	Algeria 9,021,416
Germany 13,043,400	

The chief articles exported to the United Kingdom in 1898 were valued in francs at:—

Silk tissues......128,554,000		Wool 20,365,000
Woollen „ 99,622,000		Toys, &c....... 26,645,000
Wines 76,776,000		Feathers 7,848,000
Raw Sugar 41,374,000		Fruit (Table)... 18,908,000
Refined „ 17,246,000		Eggs 12,068,000
Butter 54,895,000		Cotton Tissues .. 11,574,000
Millinery 48,150,000		Vegetables 12,278,000
Leather 31,949,000		Poultry 5,207,730
Copper 40,332,000		Parisian Articles 4,949,000
Dressed Skins .. 38,497,000		Clocks & Watches 4,300,000
Timber......... 22,095,000		Preserved Fruits,
Brandy,Liqueurs		Biscuits, &c. .. 1,949,807
&c.........23,954,000		Cereals & Flour.. 4,640,000
Raw Hides, &c. 12,943,000		

The chief articles imported from the United Kingdom in 1898 were valued in francs at:—

Coal 81,821,000		Machinery 28,972,000
Woollen Goods ..24,094,000		Steel, Iron, Cast
Cotton Goods .. 11,177,000		Iron 6,860,000
Cotton Yarn 6,551,000		Chemical product 23,952,000
Linen & made up		Jute Goods 723,000
Garments 1,982,000		Tools & Hardware 6,045,000
Leather & Hides.. t,533,000		

The National Debt is stupendous, the nominal capital of the Funded Debt amounting in 1899 to £1,200,333,252 (the total of the Floating Debt being £40,619,709 in 1899), the heaviest debt ever yet incurred by any nation in the world.

The Interest on the Funded Debt paid in 1898 was as follows:—

Perpetual 3 per Cents.....................	£18,255,638
Perpetual 3½ per Cents...............	9,505,536
Redeemable 3 per Cents.................	4,663,994
Total.................	£32,425,168

Revenue (Budget), 1899 ....£135,944,379
Expenditure (Budget), 1900 ....£138,018,861
(including Military ..£26,534,787
and Naval .... 12,600,510)

Total value of imports, 1898	178,880,000
Total value of exports, 1898	140,440,000
Imports from United Kingdom, 1898	20,225,209
Exports to United Kingdom, 1898 ...	40,961,603

CAPITAL, Paris. Population (1896), 2,534,834.

Ambassador Extraordinary and Plenipotentiary, His Excellency Rt. Hon. Sir Edmund J. Monson, G.C.B., G.C.M.G. (1895)........................	£9,000
Sec.of Embassy,Hon.Michael Herbert, C.B.	1,000
Mil. Attaché, Lt.-Col. D. F. R. Dawson, C.M.G.	500
Naval do., Capt. H. P. Williams, R.N. ...	500
Commercial Attaché and British Administrator of the Suez Canal Company, H. Austin Lee, C.B.	1,500
2nd Sec., Hon. Reginald Lister	405
„ C. M. Marling	375
„ Henry H. D. Beaumont	315
3rd Sec., C. de R. Barclay	250
„ G. D. Grahame	250
Attaché, Hon. Maurice Baring	
„ Eric Phipps	
Hon. Attaché, Hon. A. D. J. Monson.	
„ Sir B. Sheffield, Bart.	
Consul, A. Percy Inglis	700
Vice-Consul, G. Falconer Atlee	150
Ajaccio—Consul, William J. Holmes	450
Bastia—Vice-Cons., Arthur C. Southwell	
Algiers—Consul-General, F. Hay Newton..	800
„ *Vice-Consul*, F. E. Drummond-Hay...	250
Arzeu—Vice-Consul, Aimé Gautray, M.D.	
Bone—Vice-Consul, Abel de la Croix......	150
Oran—Vice-Consul, Thomas Barber	
Philippeville – V.-Cons., Herbt.Scratchley	
Antananarivo—Consul, T. P. Porter	200
Majunga—V.-Consul, Stratton C. Knott	
Bordeaux—Consul, W. R. Hearn	700
„ *V.-Con.*, W. P. S. Palmer-Sambourne	
Arcachon—Vice-Consul, F. Audap	
Bayonne—V.-Consul, Paul Schoedelin ...	
Biarritz—Vice-Consul, H. Bellairs	
Pau—Vice-Cons.,Capt. F. J.Newton-King	
Toulouse—Vice-Consul, Thomas Huggins	
Brest—Consul, Capt. Herbert Gye, R.N......	600
„ *Vice-Consul*, Frederick Bonar	
Calais—Consul, C. A. Payton	600
„ *Vice-Consul*, E. H. Blomefield	50
Boulogne—Vice-Consul, Henry F. Farmer	
Cayenne—Consul, J. R. W. Pigott	800
„ *Vice-Consul*, Leon Wacongne	
Cherbourg—Consul, Roger Gage	400
„ *Vice-Consul*, M. T. Langdon	
Granville—V.-Con., Gen. H. McLeod, R.A.	
St. Malo—Vice-Consul, Hon. E. Henniker-Major	
Dakar—Consul, Capt. L. R. S. Arthur ...	600
Dunkirk—Consul, Edward Taylor............	500
„ *Vice-Consul*, W. Sigerson	
Havre—Consul-Gen., E. Cecil Hertslet	800
„ *Vice-Consul*, John Soulsby Rowell ...	150
Caen—Vice-Consul, Frank Lethbridge ...	
Croix—Pro-Cons., Rev. Charles Falkner ...	
Dieppe—V.-Cons., H. W. Lee-Jortin ...	
Fécamp—Vice-Consul, G. Constantin......	
Honfleur—Vice-Cons.,J. R.D. Charlesson	
Tréport—Vice-Consul, Alan F. O'Neill ...	
Trouville—V.-Cons., Alex. G. B. Bax ...	
La Rochelle—Consul, R. S. Warburton ...	500
„ *V.-Cons.*, C. J. Hans Hamilton	
Sables d' Olonne—V.-C., T. Lelièvre	

St. Nazaire and Nantes — Vice-Consul,
Harry Elford Dickie..........................
Tonnay-Charente—Vice-Consul, E. Rizat
Marseilles—Consul, M. C. Gurney............... £800
" *Vice-Consul,* N. C. Haag ....
" *Chaplain,* Rev. T. C. Skeggs ....
Cette—Vice-Consul, Gustave Espitalier ...
Hyères—Vice-Consul, G. Corbett ....
Lyons—Vice-Consul, W. L. Nott ....
Toulon—Vice-Consul, L. J. B. V. Jouve... 50
Martinique—Consul, James Japp ....
Guadaloupe—Vice-Consul, J. E. Devaux
New Caledonia—Cons., John. G. Haggard... 800
" *Vice-Consul,* Robert Erskine ....
Nice—Con., Sir James Charles Harris, C.V.O. 500
" *Vice-Consul,* L. Wookey ....
Cannes—Vice-Consul, John Taylor ....
Mentone—Vice-Consul, A. B. Carpenter ...
Pondicherry and Karikal—Consular Agent,
R. G. de Vismes...........................
Réunion—Consul, Courtenay W. Bennett ... 1,000
Rouen—Consul, Montague E. Loftus 300
" *Vice-Consul,* Comm. H. Cutfield, R.N.
Saigon—Consul, Charles F. Tremlett ....
Tahiti—Consul, R. T. Simons 600
Vice-Consul, J. Hart ....
Tamatave—Consul, Anatole Sauzier 800

Paris is distant from London 267 miles; transit,
8 to 9 hours. Telegrams, per word, 2*d.*

FRENCH COLONIES AND DEPENDENCIES.

(*See also* MAPS pp. 606 to 608.)

The French Colonial Empire covers a total
area of about 3,642,140 square miles, with about
55,464,000 inhabitants ; in *Asia,* 285,000 square
miles, with 24,000,000 inhabitants ; in *Africa,*
3,300,000 square miles, with 31,000,000 inhabitants ; in *America,* 48,000,000 square miles,
with 384,000 inhabitants ; in *Oceania,* 9,140 square
miles, with 80,000 inhabitants. The total cost to
France of her Colonial Empire was about
£4,250,000 in 1898 ; their total trade in 1897 was
£33,752,297 (imports £16,153,099, exports
£17,609,198), the figures for the United Kingdom
in 1898 being £1,200,640 for imports, and
£1,250,778 for exports from the Colonies to the
United Kingdom.

I. African : The French African Empire consists
of the colony of Algeria and the protectorate of
Tunis in the north ; in the north-west of an immense tract of country, in four main divisions, on
the coast line (French Guinea, Dahomey, Ivory
Coast, and Senegambia), penetrating inwards to
meet a fifth division (French Soudan), which forms
a hinterland for all the colonies on the coast. In
West Central Africa the French Congo and
Gaboon join, through protected territory, the
French protectorate of the Sahara, which meets
the common hinterland of the north-western
possessions. This common hinterland also
stretches northwards, and stands in the same
relation to the colony and protectorate in the
north (Algeria and Tunis), so that the whole
north-western portion of the vast continent,
except where occupied by Morocco and Tripoli,
and Spanish, Portuguese, British, and German
possessions, is claimed by France. In the east
France possesses a portion of Somaliland and
the island of Madagascar in the Indian Ocean,
with certain dependencies. In 1899 a convention
was signed by Great Britain and France delimitating the boundaries of co-terminous territory
in the west, and, owing to the British advance in
the Nile region, delimitating their respective
spheres in East and Central Africa.

On the north of the Continent, between

Morocco and Tunis, is the colony of Algeria,
formerly inhabited by pirates, and for this reason
bombarded by Lord Exmouth in 1816. Slavery
and piracy were suppressed, and in 1830 the
French occupied the country, which is now a
province of France. The area, exclusive of the
Sahara district, is 122,910 sq. miles, with a population (1896) of 4,429,421, of whom 318,317 are
French and 446,343 other Europeans. The exports
are wheat and other cereals, wine (74,262,452
gallons exported to France in 1898), esparto
grass, olive oil, fruit, vegetable and tobacco;
iron, copper, quicksilver, zinc and lead mines are
being worked, and in the province of Constantine
deposits of phosphates have been discovered.
The imports in 1897 amounted to £11,076,057,
and the exports £11,829,118, 80 per cent. of the
total trade being with France and 5 per cent.
with the United Kingdom; the revenue
(£2,166,095 in 1899) does not balance the cost
of civil and military administration (£2,485,779
in 1899). At the end of 1895 there were 2,925
miles of railway open for traffic. Algiers, the
capital (pop., 1897, 150,000), is frequented as a
health resort, and is an important coaling
station ; in 1897 7,991 vessels (mainly British)
entered and cleared.

To the east of Algeria is the PROTECTORATE OF
TUNIS (see p. 584).

On the East Coast is FRENCH SOMALILAND,
with the two ports OBOCK and DJIBOUTI, and extending round the GULF OF TAJOURAH ; with its
dependencies the colony contains about 45,000
square miles and about 250,000 inhabitants. This
territory gives France intercourse with the
kingdom of Ethiopia, to a town of which country
(Harrar) a scheme for a railway from Djibuti is
projected. The United Kingdom exported goods
into the colony to the value of £30,000 in 1898.

Off the East Coast, in the Indian Ocean, is the
vast island of MADAGASCAR, the fourth largest
island in the world, being 975 miles long and 350
miles broad at its greatest width. The total area
is about 230,000 square miles, and the population
5,000,000 to 6,000,000, the Hova being the dominant
tribe. Christian missions have been active in the
island, and about 450,000 of the natives are
Protestants, and about 50,000 Roman Catholics.
A French colonial station was planted, under the
protection of Richelieu, in 1662, since when the
island has been almost continuously claimed by
the French. Active steps were taken in 1865 to
make their influence felt, and in 1894 a military
expedition captured the capital and deposed the
queen, the island being declared a French possession in 1896. A railway between Tamatave on
the coast and the capital (Antananarivo) is
projected. Minerals are found in large quantities, and in the lowlands rice, manioc, arrowroot,
sugar-cane, tobacco, hemp, cotton, vanilla, tea
and coffee are successfully grown ; caoutchouc
and gum-copal are indigenous, and there is a
wealth of timber. The exports (estimated at
£172,976 in 1897) are cattle, hides, indiarubber,
gum-copal, wax, sugar, vanilla, coffee, rice,
and lamba manufactures; the imports, largely
reduced since the high protective tariff of 1897,
are mainly-cotton goods, and were estimated in
1897 at £727,085. The trade with the United
Kingdom was valued at £34,604 for imports
into the island, and at £30,880 for exports
in 1898. The capital, Antananarivo, has about
100,000 inhabitants ; Tamatave is the chief port,
others being Majunga, Tolia, Faradofay, Manan-
jura, Mahanoro, and Vatomandry. Madagascar

has immediate dependencies in the islands of NOSSI BÉ and SAINTE MARIE, while further east (420 miles from Madagascar) is the island of RÉUNION (area about 970 square miles, population estimated at 170,000), with the islands of ST. PAUL and AMSTERDAM and KERGUELEN lying to the south-east of these.

Gov. Gen. of Madagascar, General Gallieni.

In the western half of Africa are (1) the FRENCH CONGO and GABOON with the Congo Free State on the south and east, and the German Cameroons on the north and west, but undefined to the north-east. The area of this colony is about 280,000 to 290,000 square miles, and its population between 4,000,000 and 6,000,000; the principal exports are cocoa, coffee, ebony and other wood, gum copal, palm oil and rubber, the chief town and trading station being Loango on the coast. To the north is (2) DAHOMEY, between the British colony of Lagos and German Togoland; it consists of about 95 miles of the Benin coast, where are the settlements of KOTONOU and GRAND POPO with the hinterland, and contains an area of about 4,000 or 5,000 square miles inclusive of the Protectorates. The capital of the colony is Abomey and the chief port Whydah. Between the British colony of the Gold Coast and the republic of Liberia is (3) the FRENCH IVORY COAST comprising the settlements of GRAND BASSAM and ASSINIE and the KROO country with the hinterland; and next in order comes (4) FRENCH GUINEA comprising the settlements of RIVIÈRES DU SUD (capital, Konakri) and FUTA JALLON, and extending up the whole of the north-west coast (save where intercepted by Portuguese Guinea and the British colony of the Gambia) to join the colony of (5) SENEGAL (capital, St. Louis, pop. about 22,000), the principal exports of which are gold, ground nuts, gum, palm nuts and oil, and rubber. The total area of French Guinea and Senegal is about 60,000 square miles with a population of over 1,000,000. A railway has been constructed from Dakar to Rufisque, and thence north-west to St. Louis, at the mouth of the Senegal River, and from Kayes, on the same river, a line is being constructed to Bamako, on the Niger, and about one-third was open for traffic in 1899. The territory watered by the rivers Senegal and Gambia forms the district known as SENEGAMBIA. The hinterland of the Senegal and Guinea colonies forms the vast tract of territory known as (6) the FRENCH SOUDAN, which embraces an area of about 300,000 square miles, and contains an estimated population of between 3,000,000 and 4,000,000. In addition to the foregoing the greater part of (7) the SAHARA is a French Protectorate on the southern verge of which is the town of TIMBUCTOO (pop. about 25,000). The area of this vast district is variously estimated but probably contains over 1,000,000 square miles; the population may number anything between 50,000 and 500,000.

II. **American** : France possesses two small groups of islands off the south-east coast of Newfoundland of which ST. PIERRE and MIQUELON are the largest respectively ; their combined area is about 95 square miles, with a total population of about 12,000, and they form an excellent basis for the French cod fishery. In the *West Indies* two of the most fertile of the Lesser Antilles belong to France, viz., MARTINIQUE (capital Port de France), area about 400 square miles, estimated population 190,000 (Total imports, 1897, £851,042, ex-

ports, £765,013) ; and GUADALOUPE (capital Pointe-à-Pître), area about 590 square miles, estimated population 170,000 (Total imports, 1897, £676,486, exports, £445,851). Guadaloupe Proper has six dependencies ; MARIE GALANTE and ILE DES SAINTES to the south and south-east, and PETITE TERRE on the east (part of the administrative island), with ST. BARTHOLOMEW and the northern half of ST. MARTIN, about 150 miles north-west and almost due south of Anguilla (British). In *South America*, CAYENNE or FRENCH GUIANA has an area of about 47,000 square miles, and an estimated population of about 26,000.

III. **Asiatic** : France retains only PONDICHERRY, CHANDERNAGORE, KARIKAL, YANAON and MATREE (see p. 455), of her former Indian Empire, but FRENCH INDO-CHINA consisting of Cochin-China, Tonquin, Annam, and Cambodia (see p. 475), extends over about 200,000 square miles with a population of about 22,000,000.

IV. In **Oceania** : France possesses the penal colony of NEW CALEDONIA (capital Noumea), a large island containing an area of 5,000 to 6,000 square miles, with its dependencies, Isle of Pines, Loyalty Islands, Huon Islands, Chesterfield Islands, and the Wallis Archipelago annexed in 1886 (Total imports, 1897, £343,731, exports, £279,010) ; and the SOCIETY ISLANDS, Tahiti, Moorea, &c. (imports, 1898, £118,698 ; exports, £117,240), the Low ARCHIPELAGO or Tuamotu, the MARQUESAS, and the AUSTRAL ISLES or Tubuai, and the GAMBIER ISLANDS, altogether amounting to about 1,400 square miles with about 20,000 inhabitants. CLIPPERTON in the N. Pacific is an isolated and desolate possession of about 2 square miles. By a convention with Great Britain, of 24 Oct., 1887, it was agreed that the protection of persons and property in the NEW HEBRIDES (5,105 square miles, population 70,000) should be secured by means of a mixed commission of naval officers belonging to the French and British naval stations in the Pacific.

See also FRENCH INDIA, p. 455 ; FRENCH ASIA, p. 475 ; Map of E. Africa, p. 607 ; and TUNIS, p. 584.

THE GERMAN EMPIRE.

(*See also* p. 608.)

Emperor, William II. (King of Prussia). son of the Emperor Frederick and the Empress Victoria, Princess Royal of Great Britain. *Born* 27th January, 1859 ; *succeeded* his father 15th June, 1888 ; *married* 27th February, 1881, Princess Auguste Victoria of Schleswig-Holstein, *b.* 22nd Oct., 1858 (*issue*, 6 sons and a daughter).
Heir Apparent, Crown Prince William, *born* 6 May, 1882.
Imperial Chancellor and Prussian Premier, Prince Clovis zu Hohenlohe-Schillingsfürst.
Foreign Affairs, Herr von Bülow.
Interior, Count von Posadowsky Wehner.
Navy, Vice-Admiral Tirpitz.
Justice, Herr Nieberding.
Finance, Baron von Thielmann.
Posts, General von Podbielski.
German Ambassador to Austria, Count Eulenburg ; *Italy*, Baron Saurma ; *France*, Count Münster ; *Russia*, Prince Radolin ; *Turkey*, Baron Marschall von Bieberstein ; *U.S.A.*, Baron von Holleben.
Ambassador in London, Graf von Hatzfeldt-Wildenburg, 9 Carlton House Terrace, S.W.
Councillor of Embassy, Count Carl von Puckler.

2nd *Secretary*, Count H. Hatzfeldt.
3rd *ditto*, Baron Ritter zu Grünstein.
Attachés, Herr von Oppell; Alexander Grunelius.
Military Attaché, Capt. Baron Lüttwitz.
Naval do., Capt. Coerper.
Technical do., Herr H. Muthesius.
Agricultural do., Dr. H. Gerlick.
Physician, Dr. H. Weber.
Consul-Gen., Baron G. von Lindenfels, 49 Finsbury Square.
Vice-Consul, Baron M. von Ostman von de Leye.
Councillor and Director of the Chancery of the Embassy, William Adolph Schmettau.
Chanceliers, F. R. Moebius, F. Spies, V. von Bojanowski.

The Empire, according to the Constitution of 16th April, 1871, is confederate, under the presidentship of the King of Prussia, who bears the hereditary title of German Emperor. He has the right and the duty of representing the Empire for all purposes of international law, of declaring war, making peace and treaties, &c. He is the commander-in-chief of the whole army and navy in peace as well as in war, except the military forces of Saxony, Bavaria and Würtemberg, which form —but in *peace* time only—separate corps under the command of their respective kings. He names and dismisses the officers and functionaries of the Empire. His edicts, made in the name of the Empire, must be countersigned by the Chancellor, who, as the First Minister of the Empire, is by his signature responsible for them. The third factor of Government is the *Bundesrath*, formed of delegates of the confederated governments, and the *Reichstag*, or legislative parliament, consisting of one deputy to about every hundred thousand inhabitants of the Empire.

The departments especially belonging to the legislation, administration, or control of the Empire and its government are—all matters connected with the navy, post, and telegraphy, passports, emigration, colonization, political laws of the citizens, the whole civil law, coinage, banking, commerce, navigation, the railways, &c. The bills promulgated by the *Bundesrath* and the *Reichstag* in accordance, and sanctioned by the Emperor, are compulsory on all Governments of the Empire, and annul *eo ipso* all possible regulations contradictory to them in the different States.

This large Empire of Central Europe, situate in lat. 47° 18'—55° 52' N. and long. 5° 50'—22° 50' E., comprises the following 25 States, and a Reichsland (*see* p. 560):—

	English sq. miles	Pop. 1895	Increase upon 1885-90 per cent.
1. Prussia	134,531	31,849,795	6·3
Heligoland	¾	2,086	
2. Bavaria	29,634	5,797,414	3·6
3. Saxony	5,856	3,783,014	8·0
4. Würtemberg	7,619	2,080,898	2·0
5. Baden	5,891	1,725,470	4·1
6. Hesse	3,000	1,039,388	4·7
7. Mecklenburg-Schwerin	5,197	596,883	3·2
8. Saxe-Weimar	1,404	338,887	3·9
9. Mecklenburg-Strelitz	1,144	101,513	3·6
10. Oldenburg	2,508	373,739	5·3
11. Brunswick	1,441	433,986	7·5
12. Saxe-Meiningen	964	234,005	4·5
13. Saxe-Altenburg	517	180,012	5·4
14. Saxe-Coburg and Gotha	765	216,624	4·0
15. Anhalt	917	293,123	7·8
16. Schwarzburg-Sondershausen	337	78,248	3·6
17. Schwarzburg-Rudolstadt	367	88,590	3·2
18. Waldeck	438	57,782	0·9
19. Reuss (elder line)	123	67,454	7·5
20. Reuss (younger line)	323	131,469	9·7
21. Schaumburg-Lippe	133	41,224	5·3
22. Lippe	475	134,617	4·8
23. Lübeck	116	83,324	8·9
24. Bremen	100	196,278	8·8
25. Hamburg	160	681,632	9·5
26. Alsace-Lorraine	5,601	1,640,986	2·4
Total German Empire	211,168	52,246,589	5·7

According to religious confessions there were (1890) 31,026,810 Protestants (62·8 per cent.), 17,671,929 Catholics (35·8 per cent.), 567,884 Jews (1·1 per cent.).

German is spoken by the bulk of the inhabitants, but there reside within the limits of the Empire over 3,240,000 persons of other nationalities, viz., 2,922,411 Poles and 121,345 Lithuanians in the eastern parts of Prussia: 117,883 Wends in Lusatia, 50,000 Czechians on the Bohemian frontier, 140,000 Danes in Schleswig, and 280,000 Wallones and French to the west of the Rhine. On the other hand, about 13,500,000 Germans live in Austria-Hungary, Switzerland, and Russia.

There are in Germany 26 towns of over 100,000 inhabitants — viz., Berlin (1,677,135), Munich (350,594), Breslau (355,186), Hamburg (568,666), Leipzig (385,308), Cologne (281,681), Dresden (322,953), Magdeburg (202,234), Frankfort-on-the-Main (180,130), Hanover (174,455), Königsberg (161,666), Düsseldorf (144,662), Altona (143,249), Nuremberg (142,590), Stuttgart (139,817), Chemnitz (138,954), Elberfeld (125,899), Bremen (125,684), Strassburg (123,500), Dantzig (120,338), Barmen (116,144), Stettin (116,228), Crefeld (105,376), Aix la Chapelle (103,470), Halle (101,401), Brunswick (101,047).

EMIGRATION.—Between 1871-91 1,992,188 Germans emigrated, of whom 1,896,963 went to the United States. In 1881 the number of emigrants reached the exceptional figure of 210,547 ; in 1886 it had sunk down to 79,875 ; in 1887 it rose to 99,712 ; sunk in 1890 to 91,925, reaching 115,392 in 1891, falling in 1892 to 112,208, in 1893 to 84,458, in 1894 to 40,964, in 1895 to 37,498, and in 1896 to 33,824.

EDUCATION.—There are (1895) 21 universities in the Empire, with 2,430 professors and teachers, attended by about 31,556 matriculated students. Education is general and compulsory.

Germany is becoming more and more a manufacturing country. In 1895, 36 per cent. of the population were supported by agriculture, 39 per cent. by mining and industries, 11 per cent. by commerce and transportation. Of the total area in 1883 48·7 per cent. are cultivated, 20·3 per cent. consist of meadows and pastures, 25·7 per cent. are covered with forest. The agricultural produce no longer suffices to support the population. The produce of the mines was valued in 1888 at £24,735,350, in 1889 at £27,790,000, and in 1897 at £42,964,000, and included (in 1898) 96,280,000 tons of coal, 31,648,000 tons of lignite, 15,893,000 tons of iron ore, 3,013,600 tons of mineral salts, besides copper, lead, zinc, &c. The Lower Rhine (Crefeld, Elberfeld-Barmen), Alsace (Mülhausen), Saxony (Chemnitz), Westphalia, and Silesia are the great centres of the textile industries.

The chief articles of export to the United Kingdom in the year 1898 were the following:—

Butter	£224,046	Hides & leather	£814,169
Caoutchouc	489,327	Iron manufactures	830,211
China, &c.	361,544	Musical instruments	677,216
Chemical manufs.	270,440	Oil-seed cake	401,805
Coffee (Raw)	407,143	Paper	448,494
Corn of all kinds	708,853	Seeds of all kinds	261,280
Cotton mfs. & yarn	814,953	Sugar, refined	6 956,089
Eggs	788,844	„ unrefined	2,582,136
Farinaceous	258,693	Wood & timber	1,270,210
Glass	898,005	Wool & manufacts.	1,801,725
Hemp	213,655	Zinc	394,658

During the same period the chief articles of import from the United Kingdom were:—

Chemical products	£284,614	Leather	£368,537
Coal, &c.	2,287,527	Linen (yarn, &c.)	442,101
Copper	412,889	Machinery	2,091,486
Cotton yarn	1,853,779	Manure	327,322
Cotton manufacts.	1,761,901	Wool & yarn	3,790,742
Herrings	1,233,872	Woollen manufs.	934,888
Iron	1,774,008	Yarn, Alpaca, &c.	1,109,207

The MERCANTILE MARINE in 1897 consisted of 3,693 vessels, with a tonnage of 1,555,371, manned by about 40,000 men ; of these 1,171 were steamers, with a tonnage of 959,800.

The total length of the RAILWAYS in the Empire on 31 March, 1897, extended to 28,637 miles, of which 90 per cent. belong to the State. At the same date the length of telegraph lines was 85,243, the number of telegraph offices being 22,199, and 40,196,254 telegrams being transmitted.

In 1896 there were 31,497 post-offices, with about 168,000 employés, and 2,253,000,000 letters, &c., were conveyed.

In 1899 (Aug. 10) a CANAL, 160 miles long, was completed between Dortmund and the river Ems ; the total cost was £3,971,500.

The NATIONAL DEBT, 1898, is £107,717,015, bearing interest at 3½ per cent.: the total charge is estimated at £3,636,250 for 1898-9.

The strength of the GERMAN ARMY on the peace footing amounted in the year 1895 to 585,440 (including the Bavarian Army), made up of —23,088 officers, 78,217 non-commissioned officers, 479,229 privates, 2,107 doctors, 1,078 paymasters, &c., 583 veterinary surgeons, 1,138 armourers, 93 saddlers, with 97,850 horses, and 1,914 guns. On a war footing the total can be raised to 3,975,000.

The IMPERIAL NAVY in 1898 consisted of 17 battleships (*and 5 building*), 3 armoured cruisers (*and 2 building*), 7 protected cruisers (8 *building*), 21 unprotected cruisers, 11 coast defence, 2 torpedo vessels, (*and 1 t.-b. d. building*), 113 torpedo boats (9 *building*), and 1 special service, with 22,774 men in 1897.

Estimated expenditure, 1898-99	£71,856,998
(Military, £30,566,352 ; Naval, £5,972,592)	
Estimated revenue, 1898-99	£71,856,998
National Debt. Dec. 31, 1898	107,717,015
Total imports (Zollverein), 1897	*229,453,350
Total exports (Zollverein), 1897	*176,030,200
Imports from the United Kingdom, 1897	*32,012,595
Exports to the United Kingdom, 1897	*26,189,469

British Ambassador, His Excellency the Rt. Hon. Sir Frank Cavendish Lascelles,

G.C.B., G.C.M.G.	£8,000
Sec. of Embassy, Viscount Gough	850
Mil. Attaché, Lieut.-Col. J. M. Grierson	800
Naval Attaché, Capt. H. P. Williams, R.N.	500
2nd Secretaries, W. B. Townley	405
Hon. L. D. Carnegie	390
Commercial Attaché, W. S. H. Gastrell	800
3rd Secretary, Hon. R. D. Acton	150
„ H. W. Gaisford	150
Attaché, R. S. Seymour	
Hon. Attaché, H. H. A. Kennard	

* Excluding specie.

Consul-General, Paul Schwabach	
Vice-Consul,	
Dantzig—Consul, Hy. T. Carew-Hunt	£600
„ *Vice-Consul,* Edward A. Grandt	
Breslau—Vice-Consul, Hermann Humbert	
Königsberg—Vice-Cons., E. C. Hay	
Memel—Vice-Consul, Heinrich Pietsch	
Pillau—Vice-Consul, R. Lietke	
Düsseldorf—Consul-Gen., Thos R. Mulvany	
„ *Vice-Consul,* F. W. Lucan	
Cologne—Consul, C. A. Niessen	
Frankfort—Con.-Gen., Sir Chas. Oppenheimer	
Vice-Consul, C. W. Schwarz	
Hamburg—Consul-Gen., W. Ward	1,000
„ *Vice-Consul,* George A. Pogson	400
„ W. R. K. Gandell	
Brake—Vice-Consul, Karl Gross	
Bremen—Vice-Consul, Robert Boyes	
Bremerhaven—V.-Con., H. C. Gurney	
Cuxhaven—Vice-Consul, George Starke	
Emden—Vice-Consul, Franz D. Ihnen	
Flensburg—Vice-Consul, Thos. Hollesen	
Harburg—Vice-Consul, Carl Renck	
Husum—Vice-Consul, Carl Christiansen	
Kiel—Vice-Consul, A. L. A. Sartori	
Lübeck—Vice-Con., Heinrich L. Behncke	
Papenburg—Vice-Consul, C. Bruns	
Rostock—Vice-Consul, H. Ohlerich	
Tonning—Vice-Consul, Carl Becker	
Wismar—Vice-Consul, Heinrich Podeus	
Stettin—Consul, Ralph Bernal	600
„ *Vice-Consul,* James Stevenson	
Swinemünde—Vice-Consul, Edward Rose	

PRUSSIA.

King, William II., German Emperor, *born* 27 Jan., 1859 ; *suc.* 15 June, 1888 ; *married,* 27 Feb., 1881, Augusta Victoria (*born* 22 Oct., 1858), daughter of the late Frederick, Duke of Schleswig-Holstein (*issue,* 6 sons and a daughter).

Heir Apparent, Prince Royal, William (German Crown Prince), *born* 6 May, 1882.

Premier & Minister for Foreign Affairs, Prince Clovis von Hohenlohe-Schillingsfürst.

Minister of State and Interior, Dr. Studt.
Vice-President and Finance, Dr. von Miquel.
War, General von Gossler.
Public Works, Herr Thielen.
Agric., Woods, & Forests, Freiherr von Hammerstein-Loxten.
Commerce and Mines, Herr Brefeld.
Justice, Dr. Schönstedt.
Instruction and Worship, Dr. Bosse.

Prussia is an extensive Kingdom of Central Europe, comprising the larger portion of Germany, situate in lat. 49° 7'—55° 52' N. and long. 5° 50'—22° 50' E. On the 14th June, 1895, the population was as follows:—

	Provinces.	Sq. miles.	English.	Population.
1.	East Prussia	14,281	...	1,979,387
2.	West Prussia	9,851	...	1,469,932
3.	Brandenburg	15,405	...	4,410,829
4.	Pomerania	11,626	...	1,574,950
5.	Posen	11,182	...	1,773,036
6.	Silesia	15,562	...	4,357,555
7.	Saxony	9,746	...	2,704,539
8.	Schleswig-Holstein	7,299	...	1,298,192
	Heligoland	¾		
9.	Hanover	14,855	...	2,406,546
10.	Westphalia	7,802	...	2,669,415
11.	Hesse-Nassau	6,060	...	1,736,961
12.	Rhenish Province	10,421	...	5,043,979
13.	Hohenzollern	441	...	65,888
	Total	134,531¾		31,439,795

Of the above 36·1 lived by agriculture and fishery.

Prussia possesses a large number of navigable rivers intersecting the country—viz., the Niemen, Pregel, Vistula, Oder, Elbe, Weser, and Rhine. The coasts of the Baltic and North Seas form a number of gulfs and bays. Its principal mountains are the Harz and the Riesen-gebirge, the latter reaching an altitude of 5,255 feet. The forests are extensive, occupying an area of nearly 10,000,000 acres, chiefly consisting of fir. Its minerals consist of iron, copper, lead, alum, nitre, zinc, cobalt, sulphur, nickel, arsenic, baryta, amber, agate, jaspar, onyx, &c., and, to a small extent, silver. Salt (from the brine springs of Prussian Saxony) is abundant, also coal. Metallic ores, salt, precious stones belong partially, and amber totally, to the Crown. Agriculture and the rearing of cattle constitute the principal sources of employment and wealth of the rural population of the entire monarchy. Wheat, rye, oats, barley, peas, millet, rape-seed, maize, linseed, flax, hemp, tobacco, hops, &c., are extensively cultivated and largely exported. The western division is noted for its excellent fruits and vegetables, and the Rhenish provinces stand pre-eminent for their wines. Prussia has upwards of 100 mineral springs, possessing various properties and qualities. Its manufactures consist chiefly of linens, for which Silesia, Saxony, and Westphalia have long been noted. The cotton wares are extensive. Besides these there are numerous manufactories of silk, woollen, mixed cotton and linen fabrics, including shawls, carpets, &c.; woollens are made in almost every town and large village. Next in importance are leather, earthenware, glass, paper, and tobacco manufactures, and working in metals. Brewing is a business of great importance. The principal imports comprise coffee, tea, cotton, and other produce of the colonies; wines, silk, fruit, manufactured goods, tin, furs, and dyestuffs. The principal exports comprise linens, woollens, hardware, corn, wool, timber, pitch, linseed, tobacco, mineral waters; to which may be added horses, horned cattle, hams, salt meat, &c.; and from the Rhenish provinces, wine.

For the work of education there are about 34,000 elementary schools, attended by about 4,900,000 scholars. There are also 547 high schools, in addition to numerous technical schools.

There are ten celebrated universities in Prussia, attended by about 14,635 matriculated students in 1892; and the whole of the educational establishments are under the immediate control of the "Minister of Public Instruction and Ecclesiastical Affairs." The Royal Family belong to the Evangelical Church ("Evangelical" is a sort of compromise between Lutheran and Calvinist); and the majority of the population consists of Evangelicals (Protestants), who numbered 19,232,449 in 1890; of Catholics there were 10,252,818, and of Jews 372,059.

Estimated public revenue, 1899-1900 £116,316,367
Estimated expenditure, 1899-1900 ... 116,316,367
Total debt, 31 March, 1898 324,261,103
Debt charge, 1898-99 13,269,891

CAPITAL, Berlin. Population, 1895, 1,677,135.
Berlin, transit, 24 hours. Telegrams, per word, 2d.

ALSACE-LORRAINE.
Statthalter, Prince Hermann Ernst von Hohen-lohe-Langenburg (1894), *b.* Aug. 31, 1832.
Minister of State, Herr von Puttkamer.

Alsace-Lorraine (Elsass-Lothringen), which was annexed by France from the old German Empire between 1648 and 1697, was restored to Germany,

after a sanguinary war with France, by the Treaty of Frankfort in 1871. It embraces the fertile plain between the Rhine and the Vosges, and stretches beyond these mountains as far as Luxemburg. Wine, tobacco, and hops, iron, and coal are among its leading productions, and the cotton industry is most flourishing.

The new province is called a "Reichsland," or imperial territory, and is governed by a "Statthalter," appointed by the Emperor. There is an elective Provincial Committee of 58 members. The area is 5,601 square miles. The population in 1895 was 1,640,986. French was spoken by about 210,000 persons.

The principal towns are Strassburg (135,608), Mülhausen (82,986), and Metz (59,794).
Revenue and Expenditure (1898-99) .. £2,988,289
Debt (1897-98) ....(Rentes £35,764) 1,205,750

ANHALT, Duchy of.
Duke, Frederick, *born* 29 April, 1831 ; *suc.* 22 May, 1871 ; *married*, 22 April, 1854, Princess Antoinette of Saxe-Altenburg, *born*, 17 April, 1838.
Heir Apparent, Prince Friedrich, *born* 19 August, 1856 ; *married*, 2 July, 1889, Princess Marie of Baden ; *born*, 26 July, 1865.
Prime Minister, Herr von Koseritz.

A Duchy of Central Germany, in two principal portions, surrounded by Prussian Saxony, containing 906 square miles and a population of 293,298. Budget, 1899-1900, £753,382 ; Credit (1898), £343,710.
CAPITAL, Dessau. Population, 48,294.

BADEN, Grand Duchy of.
Grand Duke, Frederick, *born* 9 Sept., 1826 ; *Regent*, 24 April, 1852 ; *Grand Duke*, 5 Sept., 1855 ; *mar.* 20 Sept., 1856, Louise, *born* 3 Dec., 1838, daughter of Emperor William I. of Germany.
Heir Apparent, Frederick, *born* 9 July, 1857 ; *m.* 20 Sept., 1885, Princess Hilda of Nassau, *born* 5 Nov., 1864.
President of Ministry, Dr. W. Nokk.

A State of the German Empire, situate in the south-western part. The Rhine forms its southern and western boundary, separating it from Switzerland and Alsace. A great part of the surface is mountainous, and includes the Black Forest and Odenwald. It is divided into eleven districts (Kreise), viz., Konstanz, Villingen, Waldshut, Lörrach, Freiburg, Offenburg, Baden, Karlsruhe, Mannheim, Heidelberg, and Mosbach, and comprises an area of 5,893 square miles, 3,330 of which are under cultivation—corn, wine, fruit, potatoes, tobacco, hemp, hops, and chicory being the chief produce. The population in 1895 was 1,725,464, nearly two-thirds of whom were Catholics, and more than one-third Protestants (Jews 25,903). One-half of the people are engaged in agriculture, the other half mostly in manufactures. The principal manufactures are cigars, cotton and silk stuffs, straw hats, brushes, trinkets, clocks, chemicals, paper, and machinery. Elementary instruction is compulsory. There are 1,625 elementary schools, 94 colleges, a technical academy, and two universities, in addition to several technical, agricultural, normal, and other schools, including 3 State establishments for art. There are 963 miles of railway, almost entirely belonging to the State, constructed at a cost of over £24,000,000.
Budget, 1898 ....£3,741,478
Debt Jan. 1, 1898 (only railways) 16,451,463
CAPITAL, Karlsruhe. Population, (1895) 84,030.
British Chargé d'Aff., G. Buchanan (Darmstadt).
Mannheim—Consul, Paul Ladenburg.

BAVARIA.

King, Otto, *born* 27 April, 1848; succeeded his late brother, Louis II., 13 June, 1886.

Regent and Heir Presumptive, Prince Luitpold, *born* 12 March, 1821, uncle of the late and present Kings; appointed Regent, 10 June, 1886; *mar.* 15 April, 1844, Archduchess Augusta of Austria-Tuscany, who *died* 26 April, 1864.

Ministers of State—President and Minister of Foreign Affairs, Baron von Crailsheim. Dr. Baron von Riedel (*Finance*), Baron von Feilitzsch (*Interior*), Baron von Leonrod (*Justice*), Lt.-Gen. Baron von Asch (*War*), Ritter von Landmann (*Instruction*).

The second Kingdom in size and population of the German Empire. It is divided into two unequal parts. The eastern portion, comprising eleven-twelfths of the whole, is situated between 47° 16'—50° 33' N. lat. and 9°—13° 48' E. long. ; the western part, forming the Palatinate, on the left bank of the Rhine. Bavaria is divided into eight circles (Upper Bavaria, Lower Bavaria, Palatinate, Upper Palatinate, Upper, Middle, and Lower Franconia, and Swabia), comprising an area of 29,632 square miles, and a population (in 1897) of 5,818,544 (4,112,623 were Roman Catholics, 1,640,133 Protestants, and 53,750 Jews). Bavaria contributes two *corps d'armée* to the forces of the German Empire, and a division at Metz, and a third *corps* is to be raised in 1900; their strength is fixed at 66,356 men on a peace footing. The rivers are the Danube, Rhine, Main, Lech, Isar, and Inn. Its forests are extensive, covering nearly a third of the country; the soil is highly productive, wheat, rye, oats, and barley being the chief products; buckwheat and maize are also grown, and tobacco is one of the staple articles. Wine is produced in Lower Franconia and in the Palatinate. The hop-plant is most extensively cultivated. The chief minerals are salt, coal, iron, copper, and pyrites; manganese is found in some places. Many important manufactures are carried on. The brewing of beer is carried to great perfection. The chief imports are sugar, coffee, woollens, silks, stuffs, drugs, hemp, cotton, tobacco, and flax; the chief exports are timber, grain, wine, hops, beer, leather, glass, jewellery, &c. There are three Universities, viz., Munich, Würzburg, and Erlangen.

Budget, 1900 and 1901 ....£21,064,847
Public debt 1899 (including railway debt
£55,768,740) 72,931,762
CAPITAL, Munich. Population (1899), 445,000.
British Minister Res., Victor Drummond,C.B. £1,500
2nd Secretary, F. D. Harford 405
Consul, Jacob Krapp ....

BRUNSWICK, Duchy of.

Regent, Prince Albrecht of Prussia, *born* 8 May, 1837; *elected* 21 Oct., 1885.

Minister of State, Dr. von Otto.

A State of Northern Germany, consisting chiefly of three detached parts, comprising an area of 1,441 English square miles, and a population (1895) of 434,213, of whom 411,377 are Protestants; 19,508 Roman Catholics, and 1,836 Jews. Budget, 1898-99, Income, £722,188; Expenditure, £737,250; debt, £3,052,119.

CAPITAL, Brunswick. Population, 115,138.

HESSE, Grand Duchy of.

Grand Duke, Ernest Louis, *born* 25 Nov., 1868; *suc.* 13 Mar., 1892; *m.* 19 April, 1894, Princess Victoria Melita of Coburg, *b.* 25 Nov., 1876.

President of Ministry, J. Rothe.

A central State in the west of Germany, comprising two disconnected territories, nearly equal in size, containing an area of 2,966 square miles, and a population (in 1895) of 1,039,020, of whom two-thirds were Protestants. The southern portion is traversed by the Rhine, and the Main forms part of its boundary. The surface of the eastern portion of both parts is mountainous. The country is fertile, and agriculture is in a flourishing condition. Fruit is abundant, and the vine highly cultivated. Giessen has a university, and there is a technical university at Darmstadt.

Budget, 1897-98 ....£2,026,682
Public debt, 1897 (mostly for railways) 8,170,000
CAPITAL, Darmstadt. Population (1895), 63,745.
British Chargé d'Affaires, George William
Buchanan (Darmstadt) £500
Consul-Gen., Sir Charles Oppenheimer (at Frankfort).

MECKLENBURG-SCHWERIN, Grand Duchy of.

Grand Duke, Frederick Francis, *b.* 9 April, 1882; *suc.* 10 April, 1897.

Regent, John Albrecht, *b.* 1857.

Minister of State, A. von Bülow.

A maritime State of Northern Germany, on the Baltic, comprising an area of 5,197 square miles, with a population of 597,436. The Legislative power is vested in representatives of the towns, and of the Knights' estates. Revenue, £1,259,300; debt (1899), £5,591,800.

CAPITAL, Schwerin. Population, 36,363.

MECKLENBURG-STRELITZ, Grand Duchy of.

Grand Duke, Frederick William, *born* 17 Oct., 1819; *suc.* 6 Sept., 1860; *mar.* 28 June, 1843, Princess Augusta of Cambridge, *b.* 19 July, 1822.

Heir Apparent, Adolphus Fred., *b.* 22 July, 1848; *married*, 17 April, 1877, the Princess Elizabeth of Anhalt, *born* 7 Sept., 1857.

A State of Northern Germany, consisting of two detached pieces, separated by Mecklenburg-Schwerin. Area, 1,144 square miles; population, 101,540. No proper budget. Finances in good condition.

CAPITAL, Neu-Strelitz. Population, 10,343.

OLDENBURG, Grand Duchy of.

Grand Duke, Peter, *born* 8 July, 1827; *suc.* 27 February, 1853; *married*, 10 February, 1852, Elizabeth (daughter of the late Prince Joseph of Saxe-Altenburg), *born* 26 March, 1826, *died* 2 Feb., 1896.

Heir Apparent, Frederic Augustus, *b.* 16 Nov., 1852; *married*, firstly, Feb. 18, 1878, to the late Princess Elizabeth (second daughter of the late Prince Frederick Charles of Prussia), who *died* 28 August, 1895; and secondly to Princess Elizabeth of Mecklenburg-Schwerin, *born* 10 August, 1869.

A maritime State of North Germany, situate on the North Sea and the Weser, with an area of 2,508 square miles and a population of 373,739. Revenue, 1898, £361,589; expenditure, £417,741; debt, 1898, £2,520,402.

CAPITAL, Oldenburg. Population, 23,118.

SAXE-COBURG AND GOTHA, Duchies of.

Duke, Alfred (H.R.H. Duke of Edinburgh), *born* 6 August, 1844; *suc.* 22 Aug., 1893; *mar.* Jan. 23, 1874, to the Grand Duchess Marie, only daughter of the late Alexander II., Emperor of Russia.

Children: 1. *Alfred*, *born* 15 Oct., 1874, *died* 6 Feb., 1899; 2. Princess Marie, *born* 29 Oct., 1875, *mar.* 11 Jan., 1893, to Prince Ferdinand of Roumania; 3. Princess Victoria Melita, *b.* 25 Nov. 1876, *mar.* 19 April, 1894, Ernest Louis, Grand Duke of Hesse; 4. Princess Alexandra, *b.* 1 Sept., 1878, *mar.* April 20, 1896, the Hereditary Prince of Hohenlohe-Langenburg; 5. Princess Beatrice, *b.* 20 April, 1884.

Heir Presumptive, H.R.H. The Duke of Albany, *born* 19 July, 1884.

A State consisting of two principal and several smaller detached portions, with an area of 765 English sq. miles, and a population (1895) of 216,603, of whom 212,514 are Protestants. The country is distinguished by beautiful forests and castles of the Duke (Reinhardsbrunn and Rosenau, favourite retreat of Queen Victoria). The capital, Gotha (population 31,670), is the seat of the oldest life assurance company in Germany; also of the famous Geographical Institute of Justus Perthes. Coburg (the other capital) has 18,688 inhabitants. The domain revenue for Coburg and Gotha was estimated for the 'period of 1897—1901 at £21,980 and £96,501 respectively, and the expenditure at £12,780 and £54,667.

British Minister Resident, Sir Alexander Condie Stephen, K.C.M.G., C.B. £950

SAXE-WEIMAR.

Grand Duke, Charles Alexander, *b.* 24 June, 1818; *suc.* 8 July, 1853; *married* 8 Oct., 1842, Princess Sofia of the Netherlands, *born* 8 April, 1824.

Heir Apparent, William, *born* 10 June, 1876.

Area, 1,388 sq. miles. Population (1895) 339,217. Income and expenditure, 1898-1901 £523,054.

CAPITAL, Weimar. Population, 1895, 26,670.

SAXONY.

King, Albert, *born* 23 April, 1828; *suc.* 29 Oct., 1873; *mar.* 18 June, 1853, Caroline, dau. of the late Prince Gustave de Wasa, *b.* 5 Aug., 1833.

Heir Presumptive, his brother, Field-Marshal Prince George, *b.* 8 Aug., 1832; *mar.* 11 May, 1859, Maria Anna Infanta of Portugal, who *d.* 5 Feb., 1884.

Ministers of State, Dr. Schurig, Herr von Metzsch, Herr von der Planitz, Herr von Seydewitz, Herr von Watzdorf.

A Kingdom of Germany, the third in importance and population of the German Empire, comprising an area of 5,856 English square miles, with a population of 3,787,688 (1895 census), among whom are 140,255 Roman Catholics, and 9,902 Jews. More than one-half of the surface is arable, and has always been in a high state of cultivation; its agricultural products consist of the usual cereals and leguminous plants, with rape, buckwheat, flax, and fruits of all kinds suited to the climate. The potato harvest in the year 1892 yielded 28,316,465 lbs. The forests supply timber of excellent quality, and in such abundance as to render them a great source of industry and wealth. The minerals are another great source of wealth, the ores being both rich and abundant. The mines consist of silver, tin, bismuth, cobalt, iron, zinc, lead, nickel, arsenic, &c., besides coal, marble, porcelain-earth, and various gems—as topazes, chrysolites, amethysts, cornelians, &c. The smelting is centralized in large establishments belonging to the State. Manufacturing industry has been greatly developed, and in some branches carried to a high degree of perfection. The special manufactures of Saxony are: Machinery, cottons, worsted yarns, soft wool tissues, carriages, furs, clothing, jute, furniture stuffs, hosiery, gloves, and other knitted goods, laces, embroideries, curtains, paper, wood and straw pulp, and bottle glass; to these may be added musical instruments, chocolates, sweets, and cigars. The government factory at Meissen continues to produce the famous Meissen porcelain. The great fairs of Leipzig, although well attended, have lost much of their former importance. The imports are chiefly corn, wine, salt, cotton, silk, flax, hemp, wool, coffee, tea, &c. Its chief towns are Dresden, Leipzig, the great book-market, with, next to those of Berlin and Munich, the most frequented University of Germany (having 3,270 matriculated students in 1899); Freiberg, in the mining district; Zwickau, and Chemnitz, the Manchester of Saxony.

Saxony furnishes the 12th and 19th Army Corps of 42,938 officers and men.

Revenue and expendit., Budget, 1898-9 £8,240,995
Amount of public debt (chiefly for railways), January, 1898 37,623,247

CAPITAL, Dresden. Pop. (1895), 336,440.

Brit. Minister Resident, Sir A. Condie Stephen, K.C.M.G., C.B. (see Saxe-Coburg).
 Consul, H. Palmié.
 Vice-Consul, H. J. Stanley.
Leipzig—Cons.-Gen., Baron C. C. B. von Tauchnitz.
 Vice-Consul', Dr. Curt Otto.
Transit, 32 hours.

WALDECK.

Prince, Frederick, Prince of Waldeck-Pyrmont, Count of Rappolstein, Seigneur of Hoheneck and Geroldseck, Wasziegen, &c., *born* 20 Jan., 1865; *suc.* 12 May, 1893. His sisters are :—Pauline, *b.* 19 Oct., 1855; *m.* 7 May, 1881, to the Prince of Benthèim-Steinfurt; Emma, *b.* 2 Aug., 1858, *m.* 7 Jan., 1879, to the late King (and until 1898 Queen-Regent) of the Netherlands; Helena F. Augusta, *b.* 17 Feb., 1861, *married* 27 April, 1882, the late Duke of Albany; Elizabeth, *born* 6 Sept., 1873; and a half-brother, *b.* 26 June, 1892.

A Principality in the north-west of Germany, with an area of 438 square miles, and 57,766 inhabitants. The Budget for 1897 gives an income and expenditure of £70,021 each. There is also a Debt of £101,850.

CAPITAL, Arolsen. Population, 2,768.

Brit. Chargé d'Affaires, Sir Alexander Condie Stephen, K.C.M.G., C.B. (Coburg).

WÜRTEMBERG.

King, William II., *born* 25 Feb., 1848; *succeeded* 6 October, 1891; *mar.* 15 Feb., 1877, Princess Marie of Waldeck, who *died* 30 April, 1882; *remar.* 8 April, 1886, Princess Charlotte of Schaumburg-Lippe.

Heir Presumptive, Duke Nicolaus of Würtemberg, *born* 1 March, 1833.

President of Ministry, Baron Dr. von Mittnacht.

A Kingdom of South Germany, with an area of 7,528 English square miles, and a population (in 1898) of 2,081,151, of whom 30 per cent. are Roman Catholics. Würtemberg furnishes the 13th Corps to the German Army, consisting of 23,260 men on a peace footing. It possesses rich cultivated fields, orchards, gardens, and hills covered with vines; the forest, grain, and pastureland being nearly equally distributed throughout. Spelt, wheat, rye, oats, barley, hemp, hops, potatoes, beans, maize, and turnips are the principal agricultural products. The minerals, consisting chiefly of salt, iron, granite, limestone, ironstone, fireclay, &c., abound in the kingdom; mineral springs are also numerous. The principal rivers are the Neckar and the Danube. The manufactures generally are linen, woollen and cotton fabrics, carpets, paper, leather, gunpowder, firearms, tobacco, iron and steel goods, pianos, clocks, pottery, cabinet work, &c. There are also many oil mills, breweries, and brandy distilleries. The principal exports are grain, cattle, wood, gunpowder, fire-arms, pianos, clocks, salt, oil, leather, woollen, hosiery, cotton and linen fabrics, stays, beer, wine, &c.

Revenue, 1899 .... £4,074,904
Expenditure, 1899 4,037,508
Total amount of public debt, April, 1899
(including £22,515,457 for railways) 24,261,500
CAPITAL, Stuttgart. Population, 158,321.

Brit. Min. Res. Victor A. W. Drummond, C.B. (Munich)
Consul, Dr. Frederick Rose.

THE HANSE TOWNS.

The Hanse Towns comprise the three Cities of Hamburg, Bremen, and Lübeck, each with a small rural territory, and are situated in the North of Germany, on the Elbe, Weser, and Trave respectively. Hamburg is the great emporium of Germany, and is 65 miles from Cuxhaven, to which port it is connected by railway. Bremen is much smaller, but very prosperous, and only second in commercial importance to Hamburg. It is connected by railway with the outport of Bremerhaven, 35 miles distant, and carries on a very extensive American trade. Lübeck is situate near the Baltic; its commerce is principally with Denmark, Norway, Sweden, and Russia.

The commerce between the Hanse Towns and Great Britain is very large; the imports from the United Kingdom to Hamburg alone in 1898 (excluding bullion) amounting to £20,340,000. In October, 1888, Hamburg and Bremen, following the example set by Lübeck several years previously, joined the German Customs Union. They retain, however, their sovereignty and local self-government, like the other States of the Empire.

HAMBURG possesses an area of 160 square miles, and had a total population in 1898 of 724,016.

Burgomaster, 1899, Dr. Mönckeberg.
Public revenue in 1898 .... £4,047,750
Public expenditure in 1898 4,064,880
Public debt, 1898 17,255,289
Total imports, 1898 (exclud. bullion) .. 162,220,000
Total exports, 1898 142,770,000
British Consul-Gen., William Ward £1,000
Vice-Cons., G. A. Pogson £400
  „ W. R. K. Gandell ....

Hamburg, transit, 21 hours.

BREMEN possesses an area of 99 square miles, with a population of 208,888.

Burgomaster, 1899, Fredk. A. Schultz.
Public revenue, 1898–99 .... £1,168,655
Public expenditure, 1898–99 1,611,496
Total value of imports, 1898 46,564,030
Total value of exports, 1898 44,366,403
British Vice-Consul, Robert Boyes.

Bremerhaven—Vice-Cons., H. C. Gurney.

LÜBECK possesses an area of 115 square miles, with a population in 1895 of 83,324.

Burgomaster, 1899–1900, H. Klug.
Public revenue, 1898 .... £250,941
Public expenditure, 1898 236,921
Public debt, Jan. 1, 1899 930,651
Total value of imports, 1898.............16,440,000
   do.   exports, 1898.............14,050,000
Brit. Vice-Consul, Heinrich Leo Behncke......

GERMAN COLONIES AND DEPENDENCIES.

(See also pp. 608 and 610.)

The German colonies and dependencies have a

total area of about 1,021,575 square miles, and a population (1899) of about 9,800,000. In 1896 there were 6,095 Europeans resident in the African Colonies, of whom 962 were German officers, 3,913 non-Germans, and the remaining 1,220 German officials and colonists.

I. The AFRICAN POSSESSIONS: (*a*) TOGOLAND (23,160 square miles, pop. 850,000), capital Little Popo, exports india-rubber and ivory; and the CAMEROONS (191,074 square miles, pop. 4,500,000), capital Cameroon, in the west. (*b*) GERMAN SOUTH WEST AFRICA consisting of DAMARALAND with GREAT NAMAQUALAND, capital Great Windhoek, in the south-west (326,117 sq. miles, pop. 250,000); a railway is being constructed from the newly made harbour Swakop-mund towards the capital. (*c*) GERMAN EAST AFRICA (area 383,079 square miles, pop. 3,750,000) a large tract of ountry between Lake Nyassa and the Victoria Nyanza bounded on the east by the African coast between Cape Delgado and the (British) East Africa Protectorate; a line of railway has been laid from Tanga southwards, and others are projected from Tanga to Kilima-Njaro, and from Bagamoyo right across the territory; the capital is Bagamoyo on the coast.

II. In the PACIFIC the northern portion of the eastern half of New Guinea called KAISER WILHELMSLAND was declared a German Protectorate in 1884; with its dependencies, Long Island, Dampier Island, and Rook Island, its area is about 69,000 square miles, with a population of about 115,000; capital Stephansort. In 1884 a protectorate was also declared over the New Britain Archipelago, now called the BISMARCK ARCHIPELAGO, which contains about 19,200 square miles and nearly 200,000 inhabitants in the various islands. The island of BOUGAINVILLE, in the Solomon Group (see also p. 527), is administered from Kaiser Wilhelmsland. To the north-east are the MARSCHALL ISLANDS (capital, Jabwor), occupied in 1885; the total area of the 24 islands is 154 square miles, with a population of 16,000. In 1899, the government purchased from Spain the CAROLINE, PELEW and LADRONE (or Marianne) ISLANDS; the area of the new acquisitions is about 950 square miles, and their population about 46,000. By treaty with the United Kingdom in 1899, Germany acquired the islands of Upolu and Savaii in the SAMOAN ARCHIPELAGO, the island of Upolu containing the harbour and town of Apia. The trade of this island amounts to about £90,000 annually, the exports going mainly to Germany, while about half the imports are from the United Kingdom.

III. CHINESE POSSESSIONS: In 1897, consequent upon the murder of missionaries, an armed force was sent to Kiao Chao Bay, which was in 1898 granted in usufruct by the Chinese government with mining and railway concessions in the Province of Shan Tung; the bay covers an area of 212 square miles, and the leased territory 143 square miles, the "sphere of influence" extending over 2,740 square miles. There is a German garrison in Kiao Chao of 1,500 officers and men.

The total cost of administration of these colonies in 1898–9 (exclusive of the purchase price paid to Spain £837,500) is estimated to be £1,190,750 which is met by a revenue of £184,505 and imperial grants of £1,005,245; Togoland alone is self-supporting, having a revenue and expenditure of about £20,000. The trade of the colonies is given in the following table:—

	Imports, 1896.		Exports, 1896.
Togoland	£ 98,797	......	£38,551
Cameroons	267,000	......	198,000
S.-W. Africa (1897)	244,366	......	62,337
East Africa	478,851	......	261,533
New Guinea, &c. (1897)	48,620	......	26,000
Kiao Chao	—	......	—
Carolines, &c.	—	......	—
	£1,137,634		£586,421

*Imports from Germany, 1897 ....£459,000
*Exports to Germany, 1897 226,000
Imports from United Kingdom, 1897...... 128,615
Exports to United Kingdom, 1897 68,452

GREECE.

King, George, second son of the present King of Denmark, *born* 24 Dec., 1845; *elected* King of the Hellenes, 30 (18) March, 1863; *married* 27 Oct., 1867, Olga, eldest daughter of the Grand Duke Constantine of Russia, *born* 3 Sept., 1851, issue 5 sons and a daughter.

Heir Apparent. Prince Constantinos, Duke of Sparta, *born* 2 Aug., 1868; *married* 27 Oct., 1889, to the Princess Sophia, sister of the German Emperor, *born* 14 June, 1870.

Prime Minister, and Interior (14 April, 1899), M. Theotoki

Foreign Affairs, M. Romanos.
Marine, M. Bourdouris.
War, Colonel Koumoundouros.
Justice, M. Carapaulos.
Finance, M. Simopoulos.
Education and Religion, M. Eutaxias.

Chargé d'Affaires in London, M. D. Metaxas, 31 Marloes Road, Cromwell Road, S.W.
Cons.-Gen., M. L. Messinesis, Eastcheap Bdgs, E.C.
Consul and Secretary, J. M. Joannides.

A maritime Kingdom in the south-east of Europe, situate in lat. 35° 40′–40° 10′ N. and long. 18° 20′–25° 50′ E., comprising an area of 24,977 square miles (inclusive of the territory lost by the rectification of the Thessalian frontier after the war with Turkey in 1897), with a population (in 1896) of 2,433,806. The country is composed of a continental portion, almost separated into two parts by the Gulfs of Patras and Lepanto on the west, and the Gulf of Ægina on the east, the Archipelago of the Ægean Sea and the Ionian Islands, and is divided into sixteen provinces, called Nomarchies. The surface is nearly all mountainous; the coasts are elevated, irregular, and deeply indented. The most important of the fruit trees are the olive, the vine, orange, lemon, fig, almond, citron, pomegranate, and currant-grape. The imports are cotton and other manufactures, corn, timber, cattle, hides, sugar, salt fish, and coal. Its exports consist of currants, figs, olive oil, wine, cognac, tobacco, hides, lead, magnesium, emery, marble, and sponges. The ARMY in 1899 consisted of 26,238 officers and men. The navy consisted in 1899 of 5 armoured vessels, 11 cruisers, 1 training ship, 51 torpedo vessels, and 3,922 officers and men. There are 582 miles of railway open for traffic. There is a ship canal, cutting through the Isthmus of Corinth. Telegraphs, 4,569 miles. The mercantile marine consists of 5,809 sailing vessels, tonnage 223,158, and 103 steamers, tonnage 58,237.

Finance.—The Public Debt amounted Sept. 1899 to 701,374,500 drachmai gold (£28,054,980) and

93,775,974 drachmai paper (average exchange 1899 39 drachmai to £); the charge in 1899 was 14,657,535 drachmai gold, and 5,083,485 drachmai paper. The Debt Service is in the hands of an International Commission sitting at Athens, and to them the salt, matches, petroleum, playing card, cigarette paper and emery monopolies, and tobacco and stamps have been handed over, as well as the Piræus Customs House, as a supplementary guarantee. The gross income from all these sources (except the last) is divided into the sum of 28,900,000 drachmai; a sum (equivalent to 18 per cent.) for the expenses of administration; and the residue (the latter being apportioned thus—30 per cent.) for improvement of interest, 30 per cent. to sinking fund, and 40 per cent. to the Hellenic Government.

Revenue, 1899	£4,283,416
Expenditure, 1899	4,131,731
Total imports, 1898	6,083,345
Total exports, 1898	3,577,524
Imports from United Kingdom, 1898 .	1,179,476
Exports to United Kingdom, 1898	1,070,532

CAPITAL, Athens. Population, 1896 (including the Piræus). 179,755.

British Minister, Sir E. H. Egerton, K.C.B.	£3,500
Sec. of Legation, Francis W. Stronge	500
2nd Secretary & British Delegate on International Financial Commission, Vincent E. H. Corbett	435
3rd Secretary, George Young	250
Chaplain, Rev. F. R. Elliot	100
Acting Vice-Consul and Translator, Anthony Martelaos	200
Corfu—Consul, Charles A. Blakeney	100
„ *Vice-Consul,* Otho Alexander	
Cephalonia—Vice-Consul, John Saunders..	
Zante—Vice-Consul, A. L. Crowe	
Patras—Consul, Frederick B. Wood	
„ *Vice-Consul,* George W. Crowe	
Calamata — Vice-Consul, Demetrius A. Leondaiitti	
Pyrgos—Vice-Consul, Charles Fauquier ...	
Piræus—Consul, Hon. Reginald Walsh ...	500
„ *Vice-Consul,* John Joannidis	
Ergasteria—Vice-Con., Spiridon Desposito	
Syra—Consul, W. H. Cottrell	
„ *Vice-Consul,* Edward Bonavia	
Milo—Consular Agent, Andrew Gialeraki..	
Santorin—Consular Agent, A. Baseggio ...	
Seriphos—Consular Agent, E. Grohmann.	
Zea—Consular Agent, G. Stephanson	
Volo—Consul, A. A. C. E. Merlin	200

Athens, transit, 5 days. Telegrams, per word, 6½d.

GUATEMALA, REPUBLIC OF.

President, Manuel Estrada Cabrera (25 Sept., 1898).
Min. of Foreign Affairs, Francisco Anguiano.
Consul-Gen., Señor Machado, 150 Leadenhall St.

Guatemala, the most northerly of the Republican States of Central America, is situate in N. lat. from 13° 40′ to 17° 40′, and in W. long. from 88° 15′ to 92° 30′, and comprises an area of 46,774 square miles, and a population in 1892 of 1,510,000. The Republic is divided into 22 departments, and is traversed from W. to E. by an elevated mountain chain, containing several volcanic summits rising to 13,000 feet above the sea: earthquakes are frequent. The country is well watered by numerous rivers; the climate is hot and unhealthy near the coast, but more temperate and salubrious in the higher regions. There are about 350 miles of railway open, and the Interoceanic Railway con-

* African Colonies only.

necting San José (Pacific) with Port Barrios (Atlantic) was commenced in September, 1892; when completed the capital, Guatemala, will be within 290 hours of London. There were 2,643 miles of telegraph working in 1895. The chief ports are San José de Guatemala, Champerico on the Pacific, and Livingston and Puerto Barrios on the Atlantic side. The principal export is coffee, valued at £1,004,471 in 1898; the other articles are hides and bananas.

Revenue, 1898 (£1=$14)	£695,618
Expenditure, 1895	1,743,745
Foreign bonded debt, 4%, 31 Dec., 1898	1,482,800
Consolidated Internal debt, 1898	242,147
Other liabilities, 1898	878,405
Exports, 1898, £1,098,390; imports (1898)	775,133
Imports from United Kingdom, 1898	129,689
Exports to United Kingdom, 1898	……

Exchange: Jan. 1, 1899, $14=£1.
June 30, 1899, $40=£1.

CAPITAL, Guatemala. Pop., 74,000.
British Minister Resident, Geo. F. B. Jenner £2,000
Consul, C. H. M. Trayner 500
Vice-Consul, C. Fleischmann ... ...
Livingston and Puerto Barrios—Vice-Consul, Joseph Michovsky.
Oc.s—Vice-Cons., F. H. Jamison.
Quezaltenango—Consul, Hugo Fleischmann.
San José—Vice-Consul, E. H. Melville.
Telegrams, 3s. 1d. to 3s. 4d. per word.

HAWAIIAN (OR SANDWICH) ISLANDS.
(See page 590.)

HAYTI, REPUBLIC OF.

President, Tirésias Augustin Simon Sam, *elect.* 31 March, 1896 ... ... £4,800
Minister of Foreign Affairs, Brutus St. Victor.

Minister in London, Louis Joseph Janvier, *Chargé d'Affaires*, 5 Albany Court Yard, W.
Consul, Maurice Erdmann, 32 Fenchurch Street.

The Republic of Hayti is the western or French portion of the island of San Domingo, which, next to Cuba, is the largest of the West India Islands. It contains 29,830 square miles, of which 9,242 square miles belong to Hayti. It lies in N. lat. between 17° 37′—20°, and in W. longitude between 68° 20′—74° 28′; and belongs to the group of the Greater Antilles. The portion belonging to Hayti contains a population of about 1,244,650. The mountains are richly and heavily timbered, and susceptible of cultivation nearly to their summits: it is probably the most fertile spot in the West Indies, whilst its harbours, especially Port-au-Prince, offer considerable facilities to foreign trade. The principal productions are coffee, logwood, cocoa, cotton, hides, sugar, honey, gums, these being the chief exports. It is said to contain mines of gold, silver, copper, tin, and iron. Its commercial prosperity has been almost annihilated by repeated revolutions. The principal foreign trade is carried on with the United States, Great and Greater Britain, France and Germany.

Revenue, customs only, 1896-97	£1,180,000
Expenditure, 1895-97	1,105,000
Debt (external, 1897)	2,750,000
,, (internal, 1897)	2,000,000
Paper money in circulation, 1897	1,438,000
Imports from U. K., 1897	187,000
Exports to U. K., 1897	73,070

CAPITAL, Port-au-Prince. Population, 70,000.

British Consul-Gen., Augustus Cohen ... £1,000
Aux Cayes—Vice-Consul, Ernest L. Dutton.
Transit, 15 days; telegrams 5s. 4d. to 7s. 5d. per word.

HONDURAS, REPUBLIC OF.

President, Terencio Sierra, 1 Feb., 1899.

The Middle State of Central America, stretching in N. lat. between 13° 10′ and 16°, and W. long. between 83° 10′ and 88° 40′; containing 42,658 English square miles, including a small portion of the Mosquito Territory, and the Bay Islands in the Gulf of Honduras. The population in 1897 was 398,877, mostly of aboriginal blood. It has a coast-line of nearly 400 miles on the Caribbean Sea, chief ports, Truxillo, Puerto Cortez, Omoa, Roatan, and La Ceiba; but only about 40 miles on the Gulf of Fonseca, on the Pacific side, chief port, Amapala. The country is mountainous, being traversed by the Cordilleras. The products are mahogany, fruit, cattle, cotton, sugar, tobacco, coffee, indigo, sarsaparilla, hides and skins, india-rubber, cedar, fustic, rose and Lima wood. Its mineral wealth is great. The only railway (42-inch gauge) runs from Puerto Cortez to Pimienta, 60 miles, which it is intended to develop into an inter-oceanic railway connecting the Atlantic with the Pacific.

Revenue, 1897-98	£217,288
Expenditure, 1897-98	215,129
Debt (internal), July, 1898	426,581
Debt (exterior) (no interest paid)	5,985,108
Exports, 1897-98	254,102
Imports, 1897-98	239,810
Imports from U.K., 1898, £21,363; exports, £2,384	

CHIEF TOWN, Tegucigalpa. Pop. (1897), 14,000.

Amapala—British Consul, Robert Motz.
Puerto Cortez (Omoa)—Cons., R. J. Maclachlan.
San Pedro Sula—Vice-Consul, William J. Bain.
Tegucigalpa—Consul, Colin W. Campbell.
Truxillo—Consul, William Melhado
Yuscaran—Vice-Consul (vacant).

Distance 5,930 miles; transit, 18 to 20 days.
Telegrams, per word, 3s. 9d.

HUNGARY (*see* p. 539).

ICELAND (*Danish Dependency*).

Governor, Magnus Stephensen.
Danish Minister for Iceland, H. E. Hörring.

Iceland is a large, volcanic, and treeless island in the North Atlantic Ocean, extending from 63° 23′ to 66° 33′ N. lat., and from 13° 22′ to 24° 35′ W. long., with an estimated area of 40,497 square miles, or greater than that of Ireland. The population was estimated in 1899 at 75,653.

The present constitution was granted in 1874, and the assembly (Al-thing) is more or less controlled by the Government at Copenhagen. The principal products of the island are sheep, cattle, ponies, and fish, and the imports consist of almost all the necessaries of life, the chief items being grain and meal, sugar, coffee, salt, cotton goods, tobacco, spirits, hardware, and timber.

Total Imports, 1897	£460,000
Total Exports, 1897	355,009

CAPITAL, Reykjavik. Population about 5,000.
Other towns are Isafjörður, Akureyri, and Seydisfjord.
Reykjavik—Consul, John Vidalin.
Seydisfjord—Vice-Consul, Jens M. Hansen.
Transit, 10 days.

ITALY.

King, Humbert, *born* 14 March, 1844; *succeeded* 9 January, 1878; *married*, 22 April, 1868, Princess Margaret of Savoy (*born* 20 November, 1851), daughter of the late Duke of Genoa.

Heir Apparent, Victor Emmanuel, Prince of Naples, *born* 11 November, 1869, *married*, 24 Oct. 1896, Princess Helen of Montenegro.

Premier & Minister of the Interior, General Pelloux.
Foreign Affairs, Marchése Visconti Venosta.
Justice, Conte Adeodato Bonasi.
War, General Giuseppe Mirri.
Marine, Admiral Bettolo.
Public Instruction, Signor Baccelli.
Treasury, Signor Paolo Boselli.
Finance, Signor Pietro Carmine.
Agriculture, Signor Salandra.
Public Works, Signor La Cava.
Posts and Telegraphs, Marchese Antonio di San Giuliano.

Ambassador to France, Conte Tornielli; *Russia*, Gen. Morra di Lavriano; *Germany*, General Lanza; *Austria*, Conte Nigra; *Turkey*, Comm. Pansa; *U. S. A.*, Barone Fava.

Ambassador in London, Baron de Renzis di Montanaro, 20 Grosvenor Square, W.
1st Secretary, Count F. Bottaro Costa.
Secretaries, Count A. Del Vaglio; Prince M. Ruspoli; Count V. di Carrobio.
Naval Attaché, Commander A. Bianco.
Archivist, Cavaliere G. Manetti.
Consul-General, Sir J. Monteflore, 44 Finsbury Sq.
Vice-Consul, Cavaliere P. Righetti.

A Kingdom in the South of Europe, consisting of a peninsula, the large islands of Sicily and Sardinia, the island of Elba, and about 66 minor islands. It is situate between lat. 36° 38′ 30″–46° 40′ 30″ N. and long. 6° 30′–18° 30′ E., and comprises a total area of 110,623 square miles (91,277 mainland, 19,346 islands), with a population (31 Dec., 1897) of 31,479,217. Formerly it was composed of the various States of Sardinia, the Two Sicilies, the Pontifical States, the Lombardo-Venetian provinces of the Austrian Empire, the Grand Duchy of Tuscany, and the Duchies of Parma and Modena. In 1870 the unity of the country was finally effected, and Rome became again the capital of Italy, which is now divided for administration into 69 provinces. The coast-line of the mainland is estimated at 1,999 miles; of Sicily, Sardinia, and Elba at 1,389 miles; of the minor islands at 557 miles; in all 3,945 miles, having several large bays and gulfs. The peninsula is traversed throughout its length by the chain of the Apennines: the Alps form its northern limits, dividing it from France. The chief rivers are the Po, the Adige, the Tiber, and the Arno. Its wines are numerous and celebrated, and olives and olive-oil are furnished by Tuscany, Liguria, and the province of Bari; while fruit abounds and is largely exported. The cultivation of silk forms an important agricultural industry. Among the principal minerals are iron, lead, zinc, copper, manganese and antimony ores, sulphur, gypsum, amianthus, alum, and boracic acid. Silver is found in Sardinia, and some gold in the Alps. Salt is a Government monopoly. The total mineral produce was valued at £2,576,813 (1897), of which raw sulphur absorbed £1,392,410. The railway system is making rapid progress throughout the kingdom: in 1897 there were 9,592 miles open for traffic, and 23,665 miles of telegraph wire. The commercial marine (1897) consists of 6,238 vessels (366 steamers), of 786,644 tons. The imports chiefly consist of cotton, wheat, coal, coke, chemicals, colonial produce, yarns, jute and manufactured goods, woollens, raw silk, silkworms' eggs and cocoons, machinery, iron and steel in bars, plates and rails, hardware, raw hides, horses and cows, fixed oils, salt fish, dye-stuffs, tobacco, earthenware, &c. The principal exports are olive-oil, wine, candied citron, sienne earths, pastes, coral, rags, boracic acid, raw and thrown silk, hemp, cattle, straw hats, rice, iron, zinc, and copper ores, sulphur, marble, fruit, vegetables, fresh and prepared meats, poultry, chemical products, woods, roots, &c., for dyeing and tanning, artistic works, &c. The manufactures are woollen, cotton, silk, hemp, and linen yarns and tissues, leathers, straw and felt hats, furniture, chemical products, paper, agricultural and other machinery, prepared meats, artistic works (such as mosaics, pottery, Venetian glass, alabaster ornaments), &c. There is a large settled and floating population of English and Americans with churches (one costing £40,000) and chapels belonging to Methodists, Baptists, and others. The army in 1898 numbered 185,000 on a peace footing, which would be raised to nearly 2,200,000 in time of war. The NAVY in 1898 consisted of 13 battleships (*and* 2 *building*), 3 armoured cruisers (*and* 2 *building*), 15 protected cruisers (*and* 3 *building*), 1 unprotected cruiser, 15 torpedo vessels, 1 destroyer (*building*), 142 torpedo boats (*and* 2 *building*), and 2 special vessels. Spezia, the chief naval and military port of the kingdom, is securely fortified.

Public revenue, 1897–98	£67,986,364
Public expenditure, 1897–98 (military, £10,920,660, and £3,987,404 naval)...	67,689,374
Public debt, 1898–9	516,322,979
Interest on debt, 1898–99	£23,284,847
Total imports, 1898	61,786,723
Total exports, 1898	54,042,833
Imports from United Kingdom, 1898...	9,155,200
Exports to United Kingdom, 1898	4,664,320

CAPITAL, Rome. Population (1897), 489,965.

British Ambassador, His Excellency The Rt. Hon. Lord Currie, G.C.B.	£7,000
Secretary of Embassy, Sir G. Bonham, Bart.	800
Milit. Attaché, Col. Charles Needham ...	500
2nd Secretary, Stephen Leech	390
„ Charles Alban Young	345
Attaché, George Jardine Kidston	
Hon. Attaché, Eric Bonham.	
Consul, C. Ceccarelli-Morgan	
Civita-Vecchia—V.-Cons., Dr. P. R. Mackenzie	
Brindisi, Consul, S. G. Cocoto	
Gallipoli—V.-Con., A. Zarb	100
Taranto—V.-Con., Hon. W. G. Thesiger	300
Cagliari—Consul, Henry R. Pernis...	
Carlo Forte, San Antico, and San Pietro—Vice-Consul, Antonio Armeni	
Sassari—V.-Cons., Chev. G. Sechi-Pieroni	
Terranova—V.-Con., Gerolamo Tamponi.	
Florence, Consul-General, Major W. Percy Chapman	700
„ *Vice-Consul*, Gennaro Placci	
Ancona—V.-Consul, Albert P. Tomassini	
Elba—Vice-Consul, Giuseppe Tonietti ...	
Leghorn—Vice-Consul, M. Carmichael ...	300
Genoa—Consul, W. Keene	600
„ *Vice-Consul*, R. G. Macbean ...	
Bordighera—Vice-Cons., E. E. Berry......	
San Remo—V.-Consul, Dr. L. E. Kay-Shuttleworth	
Savona—Vice-Consul, Ottavio Ponzone ...	
Spezia—Vice-Consul, Joseph H. Towsey...	300
Turin—Vice-Consul, Giacinto Cassinis ...	
Milan—Consul, F. Armstrong	300

Naples and Southern Italy—Consul, Edward Neville Rolfe	£600
„ *Vice-Consul,* Julius Wolffsohn	
Bari—Vice-Consul, Emil Berner	
Barletta—Vice-Consul, A. Reichlin	
Castellamare—V.-Cons., J. Drinkwater	
Catanzaro—V.-Cons., Pasquale Cricelli	
Gioja—Vice-Consul, Edward Briglia	
Manfredonia—V.-Consul, Carlo Cafarelli	
Reggio—Vice-Consul, E. R. Kerrich	
Salerno—Vice-Consul, Pio Consiglio	
Palermo (Sicily)—Consul, Sidney Churchill	600
„ *Vice-Consul,* E. M. de Garston	
Catania—Vice-Consul, Arthur W. Elford	
Girgenti—Vice-Consul, Edward A. Oates	
Licata—Vice-Consul, Alphonse Giglio	
Marsala—V.-Consul, C. F. Gray	
Mazzara—Vice-Consul, Vito F. Verderame	
Messina—Vice-Consul, Geo. Pignatorre	400
Milazzo—Vice-Consul, Stefano Trifiletti	
Syracuse—Vice-Consul, Nicola Bisani	
Terranova—Vice-Cons., Giuseppe Bresmes	
Trapani—Vice-Consul, Giuseppe Marino	
Venice—Consul, Edward de Zuccato	

COLONIES.—Italy possesses the colony of Eritrea, a protectorate over part of the Somali coast, and an isolated station on the Juba river in North East Africa. The commencement of Italian influence was made in 1880, when the district of Assab was transferred from a trading company to the Government; in 1885, the town of Kassala, which had been abandoned by the Egyptian Government, was occupied, and shortly afterwards the tract of land now known as Eritrea was taken over. ERITREA (" Red Sea ") consists of a triangular portion of barren and sandy lowland between 12° and 18° N., containing in all a coast line along the Red Sea of about 700 miles, with a total area of 85,000 to 90,000 sq. miles, and a population of about 400,000. The capital is Massowa, where there is a good harbour, and the principal product, salt, of great value as being the monetary currency of Southern Abyssinia. In 1889, protectorate was declared over the neighbouring kingdom of Abyssinia, which was repudiated in 1893 by the Negus, Menelek II.; after a campaign which ended in disaster, the Italian Government concluded a treaty (1896) withdrawing the protectorate from all parts, except from a portion of the Somali coast, now known as Italian Somaliland, a strip of the coast, 180 miles wide, between 8° 3′ N. and the river Juba, which is the northern boundary of British E. Africa. The isolated station of LUGH 400 miles inland on the Juba river, was also reserved to Italy. The total area is about 130,000 square miles, and the population about 300,000, Itala, a newly formed settlement, being the seat of government. In 1897, the town of Kassala was restored to Egypt, and the Italian possessions are now confined to the colony, protectorate, and town above mentioned.

ROME—*Sovereign Pontiff,* Leo XIII., *born* 2 March, 1810; *elected* 20 February, 1878.
Secretary of State to His Holiness, The Cardinal Rampolla del Tindaro, appointed 1887.

Rome, transit, 44 hours. Telegrams, 3*d.* per word.

JAPAN.

Emperor, Mutsuhito, *born* 3 Nov., 1852; *succeeded* 13 Feb., 1867; *crowned* 13 Oct., 1868; *mar.* Haruko, 9 Feb., 1869, and has issue 1 son and 4 daughters.

Heir Apparent, Prince Yoshihito, *born* 31st Aug., 1879; installed Crown Prince 3 Nov., 1889; came of age, and took his seat in Upper House, 1897.
Prime Minister, Marquis Yamagata.
Foreign Affairs, Viscount Aoki.
Agriculture and Commerce, Arasuke Sone.
Interior, Marquis Saigo.
Finance, Count Matsukata.
War, General Katsura.
Marine, Admiral Yamamoto.
Justice, Keigo Kiyoura.
Education, Admiral Kabayama.
Communications, Viscount Yoshikawa.
Imperial Household, Viscount Tanaka.

Minister in London, Takaaki Kato, 4 Grosvenor Gardens, W.
Secretary of Legation, Keishiro Matsui.
2nd Secretary, Shosaku Matsugata.
Naval Attaché, Commander R. Kawashima.
Military Attaché, Colonel K. Iditti.
Ataché, Chozo Koike.
Consul, Minoji Arakawa, 84 Bishopsgate Street.
Consul at Liverpool (vacant).
at Glasgow, A. R. Brown.

This ancient and extensive Empire, splendidly victorious (1894-95) in a war with China, consists of four large and many small islands, said to comprise in all above 4,223, the principal of which are Hondō (the name of the Empire being Nihon), Shikoku, Kiū-shū, and Hokkaïdō or Yéso, situate to the north of the main island, from which it is separated by the Tsugaru Straits, and Formosa. The Ainu, an uncivilised but harmless tribe, who in ancient times occupied the greater part of the country, are still found in Yezo. The Kurile Islands have belonged to Japan since 1875, and in 1876 she incorporated the Luchu (Riu-kiu) Islands under the name of "Prefecture of Okinawa." The empire comprises an area of 162,655 square miles, with a population of 43,228,863, according to the last census, there being 21,823,651 men and 21,405,212 women.

Japan is said to possess a written history extending over 2,500 years, and its sovereigns to have formed an unbroken dynasty since 660 B.C., the present Emperor being the 121st of his race; but the authentic history begins about 400 A.D. Within the last few years Japan has made unparalleled progress in civilisation and the adoption of Western manners and customs. The feudal system under which the country was governed by numerous Lords has been abolished, and the Mikado is now absolutely the Sovereign of the State, and since the revolution of 1858 she has shown a most remarkable power of adopting Western knowledge and experience. A wise and enlightened ruler is at the head of the nation, and the first national Parliament, the outcome of the constitution granted to the people by the Emperor, promulgated 11th Feb., 1889, met for the first time in November, 1890. The feudal lords, who have lost all their powers of government, still retain their high social positions, and a new aristocracy with these as its basis has been formed; it consists of five grades, corresponding to the European titles of Prince (not imperial), Marquis, Count, Viscount, and Baron. The islands are eminently volcanic, and 18 of the summits are still active; the chief of these, Fuji-san, or Fuji-yama, the loftiest and most sacred mountain of Japan, about sixty miles from Tôkiô, is 12,370 ft. high, dormant since 1707. Japan is liable to frequent and disastrous earthquakes. On October 28, 1891, an earthquake occurred by which 9,960 persons were killed, 20,000 injured, and 130,000 houses destroyed; again in 1896 a tidal wave destroyed 7,475 houses, and killed 26,990 people, in addition to 25,137 injured. The country is very mountainous, and not more than one-sixth of its area is available for cultivation. It possesses numerous fine harbours. The soil is productive, teeming with every variety of agricultural produce. Copper, iron, and sulphur abound, whilst agate, carnelian, and rock crystal are also found. Gold and silver mining is prosecuted on a small scale, and there is a fair supply of middling coal. Among the vegetable productions may be noted the camphor-tree, paper mulberry, vegetable wax-tree, and a lacquer-tree, which furnishes the celebrated "lacquer" of Japan. The principal timber trees are the Cryptomeria japonica, Pinus Massoniana, and Zelkowa Keaki; the maple is merely for ornament. Chestnut, oak, beech, and elm are comparatively rare and little used. The tobacco-plant, tea-shrub, potato, rice, wheat, and other cereals are all cultivated; agriculture, upon which the Japanese bestow great care, being their chief occupation. The coasts are extremely rich in fish. The floral kingdom is rich, beautiful, and varied. The fruits are abundant, but for the most part of inferior quality. The chief industries are conducted in factories for silk and cotton, cotton yarn, matches, paper, glass, japanned ware, porcelain, and bronze, and shipbuilding in the yards. The chief imports are raw cotton from China and India, and piece goods, metals, woollens, drugs, rails, locomotives, and machinery from Europe and the U.S.A. Sugar is largely imported from China, Formosa, and Germany. The chief exports are silk, rice, tea, fish, copper, and matches. There were 2,310 miles of private railway and 661 miles of Government lines open in 1899. The Tōkaidō, Shinano, and Echigo, and Oshiu and Dewa lines are the property of the Government, with a total length of 661 miles, and the work of duplicating Tōkaidō (East Coast route) is progressing. The net profit on these lines was estimated at £542,576 in the budget for 1897-98.

The Army consisted of 273,258 officers and men at the end of 1893. The Navy (1899) consisted of 3 first class battleships (and 1 building); 2 second class battleships; 2 first class cruisers; 9 second class cruisers; 5 third class cruisers; 10 third class coast defence ships; 2 first class gunboats; 15 second class gunboats; 4 despatch vessels, torpedo tender and a number of torpedo boats and torpedo-boat destroyers. It was manned by 14,852 officers and men.

The mercantile marine consisted (1899) of 797 vessels (454,036 tons), of which 626 are steamers.

Of the 5,799 vessels (tonnage 8,033,244) that entered Japanese ports (1898) 1,915 were British (tonnage 4,035,743). From Oct. 1, 1897, the currency was placed upon a gold basis, the unit being the gold $ of 8,333 gr. containing 75 grammes of fine gold; but there is no smaller gold coin than the 5 *yen* piece. The local exchange value of the *yen* was (Sept. 1899) 2s. 0⅞d.

Under treaties with Great Britain and several other powers, Yedo (Tōkiō), Kanagawa (Yokohama), Hiogo (Kōbé), and Osaka (on the Inland Sea), Hakodate (in Yezo), Niigata, and 22 additional ports are open to trade. The trade of Japan in 1898 was distributed thus:—

British Empire (incl. Australia, Canada, India, & Hong Kong) £17,424,638	United States .. £3,913,125	China 6,096,113	France 2,804,880	Germany 2,956,513

The principal articles imported by the United Kingdom from Japan in 1898 were:—

China, &c. £31,234	Silk £38,973
Copper 89,974	Do., manufactures 195,317
Jute 41,434	Straw plaits 181,270
Paper 33,573	

And the principal articles exported to Japan from this country in 1898 were:—

Arms £139,940	Cotton Manufs... £1,093,840
Carriages, Railwy. 142,293	Machinery 820,893
Chemicals &c. ... 160,933	Metals, &c. 639,411
Cotton Yarn...... 699,093	Woollens 427,173

CAPITAL, Tōkiō, formerly called Yedo, the residence of the Emperor; population (1897), 1,333,256. Other cities are—Osaka,753,375; Kiôto, the ancient capital, 333,374; Nagoya, 183,455; Kobé, 194,598; and Yokohama, 252,693.

The total cost of the war with China was about $225,000,000, of which $80,000,000 was repaid by indemnity.

Estimated public revenue, 1899-1900 ...£18,873,843
Estimated public expenditure, 1899-1900 (£7,860,717 for the navy, and £6,332,134 for the army in 1898-9)... 21,659,394
Total debt, July, 1899 51,701,042
Total imports, 1898 28,328,345
Total exports, 1898 16,920,694
Imports from United Kingdom, 1898 . 6,401,393
Exports to United Kingdom, 1898 791,580

British Envoy Extraordinary, Minister Plenipotentiary, & Consul-General, Sir Ernest Mason Satow, K.C.M.G. £4,000

Sec. of Legation, J. B. Whitehead 800
Military Attaché, Lt.-Col. A. G. Churchill.
2nd Sec. & Japanese Sec., J. H. Gubbins, C.M.G 900
2nd Sec., Joshua Milne Cheetham 400
Chaplain, Ven. Archd. Alex. Croft Shaw hon.
Medical Officer, Erwin Baelz 350
Hakodate—Consul, F. W. W. Playfair 700
Kobé—Consul, John C. Hall..................... 950
Vice-Consul, A. E. Wileman 600
Nagasaki—Consul, J. H. Longford 900
Yokohama—Consul, H. A. C. Bonar 900
Formosa: Tainan—Consul, W. J. Kenny ... 800
Tamsui—Consul, R. de B. Layard 800

Yokohama, 11,260 miles distant; transit, 38 days (or *via* Vancouver, 32 days). Telegrams, per word, from 6s. 2d. to 7s. 9d.

JERUSALEM—PALESTINE.

Turkish Governor, Tewfik Bey, appointed 26 October, 1897.

Palestine, which occupies so prominent a place in the history of human kind, and in the affections of the Christian world, is a country capable of considerable development, and, although her ancient glories are departed, still produces wine and olives, corn and the most varied fruits. Its population is not far short of 700,000, of whom 80,000 to 100,000 are Jews. In and about Jerusalem, the Jews number from 45,000 to 50,000.

Geographically Palestine consists of a maritime lowland, the mountain region of Judah, which forms its backbone, the remarkable depression through which the Jordan wends its course towards the Dead Sea, and the elevated region lying to the east of the Jordan. The popular notion that Palestine is a barren country, not capable of yielding rich harvests, is a mistaken one. Its appearance is barren only during the dry season, when the grasses which cover the greater part of it are dried up, and the herdsmen retire with their flocks of sheep and goats to the loftier mountains. The alluvial lowland to the south of Mount Carmel is as fruitful as ever, and it only needs an honest and vigorous administration to restore Palestine to its former fruitful condition. The entire area is computed to be about 11,000 square miles.

Palestine comprises the independent Mutessariflick of Jerusalem (el Kuds), together with districts belonging to two other provinces, viz. : the vilayets of Beyrut and Damascus. The stream Nahr el Auja, which enters the sea a few miles north of Jaffa, forms the boundary between the district of Jerusalem and the first-named vilayet, the country to the east of the Jordan and the Dead Sea being subordinate to the vilayet of Damascus. Arabic is the language commonly spoken, and 80 per cent. of the population are Mohammedans. There are, however, many Greeks, Jews, and Franks of all nations and denominations. A railway was opened connecting Jaffa (Joppa) and Jerusalem in 1892.

The principal ports of Palestine are Acre, Haifa, and Jaffa, and their exports amount annually to over £500,000, consisting principally of sesame, fruits, barley, olive oil, maize, and articles of Christian veneration, these latter weighing 2,700 cwts. The imports were valued at £650,000. Austria takes the lead in this commerce.
Jerusalem—Consul, John Dickson £800
Jaffa—Consular Agent, Haim Amzalak ....
Distant by overland route about 2,500 miles; transit, 8 days.
Telegrams, 6½d. per word.

KHIVA. (See p. 474.)

LIBERIA.
President, William David Coleman, 13 Nov. 1896.
Vice-President, Hon. J. J. Ross.
Secretary of State, Hon. G. W. Gibson.
Secretary of Treasury, Hon. A. Barclay.
Attorney-General, Hon. J. C. Stevens.
Postmaster-General, Hon. H. R. Johnson.

Consul-General and Chargé d'Affaires in London,
    H. Hayman, 3 Coleman St., E.C.
Consul, Sigismund Sinauer De Stein.

An independent Negro Republic of Western Africa, occupying that part of the coast of North Guinea which is between the river Cavalla, S.E., and Manna, N.W., a distance of about 350 miles, with an area of 48,000 square miles, and extending to the interior to latitude 8° 50', a distance of 250 miles from the seaboard. The population consists of 25,000 emigrants from America and their descendants, and aborigines, numbering in all nearly 1,500,000. The principal exports are coffee, cocoa, palm-kernels, palm-oil, ivory, prassava, rubber, and camwood. The chief imports are cottons, haberdashery, salt, rice, provisions, arms and ammunition, tobacco, hardware, glass, and earthenware, rum, gin, timber and beads. Liberia was founded by the American Colonization Society in 1820, and has been recognised by the United States and the European Powers since 1847 as an independent State. The executive power is vested in a President elected for two years, assisted by a ministry : there are two houses of Legislature, the Senate, with eight members elected for four years, and the House of Representatives with 13 members elected for two years. There is no army, but there are two small revenue gunboats. Foreigners are only allowed to trade at the ports of entry, of which there are nine along the 350 miles of coast, viz. : Cape Mount, Monrovia, Junk, Grand Bassa and

Edina, River Cess, Since, Manue Kroo, Cape Palmas, and Half Cavally.
Revenue, 1894... £53,096. Expenditure... £31,661
    CHIEF TOWN, Monrovia. Population, 6,000.
British Consul, Col. Sir Frederick Cardew, K.C.M.G. (Sierra Leone).
Monrovia—Vice-Cons., William A. Ring.
    Monrovia, 3,650 miles distant; transit, 21 days.
Telegrams *forwarded by post* from Sierra Leone.

LIECHTENSTEIN.
Prince, Johann II., *born* 5 Oct., 1840; *suc.* 12 Nov., 1858.
A Principality on the Upper Rhine, between the Tyrol and Switzerland. It has an area of 61 square miles, with (1896) 9,434 inhabitants, who are not liable to conscription.
Revenue (1896), £10,794; expenditure (1896), £9,976. There is no debt.

LUXEMBURG.
Grand Duke, Adolphus, Duke of Nassau, b. 24 July, 1817; *suc.*, 23 November, 1890; *mar.* (2ndly) 23 April, 1851, Adelaide Marie, daughter of Prince Frederick of Anhalt-Dessau, *born* 25 Dec., 1833.
Heir, William Alexander, *b.* 22 April, 1852; *m.* 21 June, 1893, Princess Maria Anna of Braganza.
Minister of State, M. Eyschen.
A Grand Duchy in Central Europe, bounded by Germany, Belgium, and France; it formed part of the Germanic Confederation, 1815-66, and is still included in the German "Zollverein." In 1867 the Treaty of London declared it a neutral territory under the sovereignty of the King of the Netherlands, on whose decease, Nov. 23rd, 1890, it passed to the Duke of Nassau. The area is 999 square miles; the population (1895) 217,583, nearly all Roman Catholics. The principality is rich in iron-ore. The revenue in 1897 was £539,456, expenditure £425,489; debt (Jan. 1, 1899) £465,872. There are 277 miles of railway. The army numbers about 325 men. The capital, Luxemburg (pop. 19,909), is a dismantled fortress.
British Envoy, Sir H. Howard, K.C.M.G. (The Hague).
Telegrams, per word, 2½d.

MADAGASCAR
(*French Possession*, see p. 556.)

MALACCA.
Malacca, or the Malay Peninsula, has a southerly extension of about 900 miles, an area of 81,800 square miles, and about 1,250,000 inhabitants, including large numbers of Chinese. The country is hilly, densely wooded, abounding in game, and famous for its tin mines. The Isthmus of Krah, in about 11° N. lat., has been examined with a view to the construction of a ship-canal, which would much shorten the passage between India and China; but competent authorities have declared the scheme to be impracticable. The greater portion of the peninsula owns allegiance to Siam. Along its western coast are the British "Straits Settlements," and the Federated Malay States (see p. 479). The independent portion of the Malay Peninsula is occupied by a number of Mohammedan Malay States.
Telegrams, per word, 4s. 3d. and 4s. 6d.

MEXICO, FEDERAL REPUBLIC OF.
President of the Republic, Porfirio Diaz, *acceded* 1 Dec., 1884 (re-elected 3rd time 1896 *until* 1900).
Minister of Foreign Affairs, Don Ignacio Mariscal.

Minister in England, Sebastian Mier, 87 Cromwell Road, S.W.

Chargé d' Affaires, Don Cayetano Romero.
Financial Agent, Don Luis Camacho, Bloomfield House, London Wall, E.C.
Consul, Don Adolfo Bulle, Broad St. House, E.C.
Liverpool---Consul-General, Don J. Garcia Conde.

A country in the southern part of the continent of North America, with an extensive seaboard to both the Atlantic and Pacific Oceans, situated between 15°—32° N. lat. and 87°—117° W. long., and comprising one of the richest and most varied zones in the world, but from various causes her resources have never been fairly developed. It comprises 27 states, 2 territories (Lower California, almost separated from the main portion by the Gulf of California), and the federal district of Mexico, making in all 30 political divisions, comprehending an area of 767,005 square miles, with an estimated population of (1895) 12,619,959, of whom "only about 3,500,000 are taxable." The surface consists of an elevated plateau, commencing at a few miles from the coast, and containing several volcanic summits, the highest of which, Ixtaccihuatl and Popocatepetl, rise to 17,879 and 19,784 feet above the sea. Vera Cruz, Progreso, and Tampico are the chief seaports on the Gulf of Mexico, Mazatlan and Guaymas on the Pacific. There were 7,700 miles of railway open in 1898, and 42,150 miles of telegraph. The railways have in a large measure been built by American and English companies. The "Mexican Central" joins El Paso (Texas) with the city of Mexico, by which passengers can travel in five days from New York without change of carriage. The National Railway *via* Laredo takes 4½ days to New York, and there is a third route *via* Eagle Pass (International Railway). The principal crops are maize, wheat, barley, pulse, Chile - pepper, sugar, potatoes, coffee, cotton, tobacco, vanilla, flax, indigo, grapes, and all kinds of fruit. The maguey, or Mexican aloe, yields a favourite beverage, "pulque"; other species of the same plant supply pita-flax and sisal-hemp (henequen). The forests abound in mahogany, rosewood, ebony, and caoutchouc trees. The mineral wealth is very great; silver and gold, copper, lead, and quicksilver, iron and coal, are the leading products of the mines. Woollen and cotton spinning and weaving, and other branches of industry, are encouraged by high protective duties. The imports, nevertheless, consist very largely of textile manufactures. Of the exports 70 per cent. consist of silver and gold; flax and hemp, coffee, hides and skins, timber, logwood, vanilla, tobacco, dye-stuffs, sugar and drugs ranking next in importance. The army in 1898 was composed of about 32,000 men. The navy is limited to 7 small vessels, of about 200 to 300 tons, used for the prevention of smuggling. The following figures have been officially supplied, the value of the Mexican $ being 22½d. to 23d. (Aug. 1898.)

Estimated revenue, 1899-1900 ....$54,913,000
Estimated expenditure, 1899-1900 54,836,755
Total exports, 1897-98 128,972,749
Total imports, 1897-98.............. 43,603,492
Public debt, Internal, 1899 £10,500,000
     External (1898) 21,555,300
                  ——————£32,155,300
Imports from United Kingdom, 1898... 1,917,672
Exports to United Kingdom, 1898 264,093

CAPITAL, Mexico. Pop. 344,377 (census 1895).
Envoy Extraordinary and Minister Plenipotentiary, Sir Henry Nevill Dering, Bt.,C.B. £3,000

Sec. of Legation, F. L. Cartwright	£500
Translator, A. J. J. Baker........................	300
Consul, Lucien J. Jerome	700
Acapulco—*Vice-Con.*, R. Fernandez	
Chihuahua—*Vice-Cons.*, E. C. Creel	
Ensenada—*Vice-Consul*, J. H. Packard...	
Guaymas—*Vice-Cons.*, A. Bustamante ...	
Mazatlan—*Vice-Consul*, Robt. Henderson	
Monterey—*Vice-Cons.*, J. C. Middleton ...	
Porfirio Diaz—*Vice-Cons.*	
San Blas & Tepic—*Vice-Consul*, F. J. Parkinson	
Soconusco—*Vice-Consul*, R. O. Stevenson	
Tampico—*Vice-Cons.*, G. W. E. Griffith	300
Vera Cruz—*Consul*, Arthur Chapman........	800
,, —*Vice-Consul*, D. B. van der Goot	
Coatzocoalcos—*Vice-Cons.*, T. Gemmill...	
Frontera—*Vice - Consul*, Michael Girard	
Laguna de Terminos—*V.-C.*,German Hahn	
Progreso—*Vice-Consul*, A. Pierce............	
Tuxpam—*Vice-Consul*, G. Johannsen	

Transit, 14 days. Telegrams, per word, 1s. 6d., 2s. 6d., and 2s. 7d.

MONACO.

Sovereign Prince, Albert, *born* 13 November, 1848; *suc.* 10 Sept., 1889; *mar.* 1869, Lady Mary Douglas-Hamilton, daughter of 11th Duke of Hamilton (the Pope declared the marriage a nullity, 1880); *2ndly*, Oct. 1889, the Duchesse de Richelieu, *born* 10 February, 1858.
Heir, Prince Louis, *born* 12 July, 1870.
Governor-General, Olivier de Ritt.

Consul-General in London, Theodore Lumley, 37 Conduit Street, Bond Street, W.
  Vice-Consul, Paul Crémien-Javal, J.P., 43, Hill St., Berkeley Sq., W.

A miniature Principality on the Mediterranean, between France and Italy, consisting of the old town of Monaco, La Condamine, and Monte Carlo, where is the gambling establishment, and comprising a narrow strip of country extending from the Monaco Cemetery on the west to St. Roman on the east; it is about 3 miles long and 1½ miles broad, with (1886) 12,548 inhabitants. The whole available ground is built over, so that there is no cultivation. There is an army of 126 men.
British Consul, Sir James Charles Harris (Nice).
  ,,   *Vice-Consul*, J. W. Keogh (Monaco).
English Chaplain (1895), Rev. F. Stewart.

MONTENEGRO.

Prince, Nicholas, *born* 7 October, 1841; *succeeded* his uncle, Prince Danilo, 14 Aug. 1860; *m.* 1860, Milena, daughter of Voyevod Peter Vukotich, *b.* 4 May, 1847; issue 3 sons, 6 daughters.
Heir Apparent, Danilo Alexander, *b.* 29 June, 1871 ; *m.* 1899 Princess Jutta of Mecklenburg-Strelitz.
Pres. of State Council, Voivode Bozo Petrovitch.
Foreign Affairs, Voivode Gavro Vukovitch.

A small Principality, which has always claimed to be independent, and recognised to be so by the Treaty of Berlin. It has an area of 3,486 square miles, and a population of about 227,000, of whom 13,000 are Mussulmans, 14,000 Roman Catholics, and the remainder Orthodox Slavs. The surface forms a series of elevated ridges with lofty mountain-peaks, many of which are covered with forests. Chief products are maize, potatoes, sumac, sardines, cattle, castradina (smoked mutton), hides, and tobacco. The only manufactures are coarse woollens. Agriculture is the principal occupation.

For military purposes the principality is divided into 8 brigade districts, furnishing 48 battalions, or 36,000 men; one battalion is always in barracks at Cettinje, and supplies the palace guard, &c. The two ports, Antivari and Dulcigno, have about 150 coasting vessels.

Revenue, 1898	about	£70,000
Public Debt, 1898	"	170,000
Total Imports, 1898	"	60,000
Total Exports, 1898	"	50,000

CAPITAL, Cettinje. Population (1897) 2,300 (exclusive of permanent garrison of 800 men).

British Minister, R. J. Kennedy, C.M.G. ..£1,500
Distant about 1,100 miles; transit, average 5 days. Telegrams, per word, 4*d*.

MOROCCO, EMPIRE OF.

Sultan, Müley Abdul Aziz, *b.* 1879, *s.* June, 1894.
Grand Vizier and Minister of For. Affairs, Sid Hamed Ben Musa.
Commissioner for Foreign Affairs at Tangier, Sid Hadji Mohammed Torres.

The largest of the Barbary States, situate in the N.W. of Africa, between 27°—36° N. lat. and 1°—11° 40′ W. long. The Empire, which is an absolute monarchy, consists of the Kingdom of Fez and Morocco, to the north of the Atlas, and the territories of Sûs, Drâ, Wadi Tafilet, Tuat, and others to the south, which are again sub-divided into 33 districts, each under the superintendence of a "Kaïd"; but the semi-independent tribes are ruled by their own chiefs, and scarcely acknowledge the authority of the Sultan. Morocco contains about 314,000 square miles, of which the "Tell," or fertile regions of the mountains and coast, contains 76,000, the steppe-land 26,000, and the Sahara 217,000, with a population variously estimated at from 4,500,000 to 8,000,000. The Jews number about 300,000, and reside chiefly in the cities. Among the chief products of the country are wheat, barley, maize, beans, peas, oil, esparto, and hemp; among fruits, the fig, almond, pomegranate, lemon, olive, orange, and date are common; but agriculture is greatly neglected. Morocco is said to be rich in mineral treasures: antimony, iron, coal, copper, lead, tin—the last three in considerable quantities. Gold and silver also are found, and wool is plentiful. It is a country of great natural resources, which only need developing. The chief ports are Tetuan, Tangier (where the Representatives of fourteen nations reside), El Araish (Laraiche), Rabat, Casa Blanca (or Dar-al-baida) Mazagan, Saffi, and Mogador. There are no railways, and telegraphic communication from Tangier is by submarine cable of Eastern Telegraph Company to Gibraltar, and by Spanish Government telegraph to Tarifa. The exports are almonds (£52,655 in 1897), maize, beans (£27,897 in 1897), peas (£71,063 in 1897), oil, wool (£156.109 in 1897), dates, oxen, fowls, eggs, carpets, slippers, goatskins, leather, grain, ostrich-feathers, gums, esparto; and the imports, cotton, linen, muslin, and woollen goods, tea, coffee, sugar, candles, cloth, silk, iron, brass, hardware, &c. The army consists of between 15,000 and 20,000, one-half of whom are negroes, Sultan's bodyguard, and a sort of militia, of various arms, amounting to 80,000 men. An English newspaper, *Al Moghreb-al-Aksa*, a French paper, *Le Réveil du Maroc*, and three newspapers in Spanish are published at Tangier. There are three capitals, of which Fez, population 120,000, is the principal; Morocco, 50,000; and Mequinez, 56,000.

Imports, 1897		£1,396,970
Exports, 1897		1,114,136
Imports from United Kingdom, 1898 ...		549,865
Exports to United Kingdom, 1898		386,088

British Envoy, Sir Arthur Nicolson,
K.C.I.E., C.M.G. £2,000
Consul, with local rank of 2nd Secretary,
Herbert E. White 600
Hon. *Attaché*, Hon. Oliver Howard.. ......
Vice-Consul, A. M. Madden ......
Interpreter and Dragoman, A. Irwin 400
Clerk, E. Bristow 150
Alcazar—Cons. *Agent*, E. P. Carleton.
Fez—*Vice-Consul*, James McIver Macleod 400
Laraiche—*Vice-Consul*, Lewis Forde ......
Tetuan—*Vice-Consul*, W. S. Bewicke 150
Dar-al-Baida—Cons., Allan Maclean 600
Vice-Consul, Charles L. M. Pearson 350
Mazagan—*Vice-Consul*, Robt. A. Spinney
Mogador—V.-Cons., R. L. N. Johnston
Rabat—*Vice-Consul*, G. E. Neroutsos......
Saffi—*Vice-Consul*, George P. Hunot ......
Tangier is distant by sea about 1,200 miles; transit, 5 days, or by the Sud Express, 3 days. Telegrams, per word, Tangier 5*d*.; some other places, 3½*d*.

MUSCAT. (See p. 476 and 573.)

NAVIGATORS' ISLANDS, OR SAMOA.
See Germany, and U.S.A.

NEPAL. (See p. 478.)

NETHERLANDS (OR HOLLAND, KINGDOM OF).

Queen, Wilhelmina Helena Paulina Maria, *born* 31st August, 1880, *succeeded* her late father, King William III., 23 Nov., 1890.
Queen-Mother, Emma, Princess of Waldeck and Pyrmont, *born* 2 August, 1858; *married* the late King 7 Jan., 1879, who died 23 November, 1890; acted as Regent 1890-1898.
Premier and Minister of Finance, N. G. Pierson.
Foreign Affairs, W. H. de Beaufort.
Interior, H. Goeman Borgesius.
Colonies, J. T. Cremer.
Justice, P. W. A. Cort van der Linden.
War, K. Eland.
Marine, J. J. A. Röell.
Waterways, Commerce, & Industry, C. Lely.

Minister in London, Baron van Gericke (from Jan. 1, 1900), 118 Eaton Square, S.W.
Secretary, Baron Schimmelpenninck van der Oye.
Chancellor, H. N. Brouwer.
Consul-Gen., H. S. J. Maas, 40 Finsbury Circus.

A maritime Kingdom of Central Europe, situate on the North Sea, in lat. 50° 46′—53° 34′ N. and long. 3° 22′—7° 14′ E., consisting of 11 provinces, and containing a total area of 12,582 square miles, with a population, on Dec. 31, 1896, of 4,859,451. The majority, about three-fifths, belong to the Dutch Reformed Church; and the remainder are Roman Catholics, and a small number of Jews, mainly in large towns, such as Amsterdam, where there are about 70,000. The land is generally flat and low, intersected by numerous canals and connecting rivers—in fact, a network of watercourses. The principal rivers are the Rhine, Maas, and Yssel, with the mouths of the Schelde. There are 2,686 miles of railway open (1897), and 20,226 miles of telegraph. The chief native products are cattle, sheep, potatoes, rye, barley, oats, wheat, buckwheat, chicory, clover, flax, hemp, tobacco, and dairy produce. The principal manufactures are shipping bricks, butterine, cocoa, chocolate, linen, rich damasks, cottons, woollens, silks, and "geneva." Diamond-cutting employs numerous hands in Amsterdam. The chief exports consist of refined sugar, flax, butter and margarine, cheese, cattle sheep, geneva. The royal navy consisted, on Jan. 1, 1897, of 131 men-of-war (25 of them iron-clads); and the army, on the war footing of 1,950 officers and 76,431 men, with a militia (Schuttery) numbering about 43,716 more. The mercantile marine, on the 1st Jan., 1897, consisted of 172 steamers, tonnage 556,000, and 440 sailing vessels, with 279,000 tonnage, employing 18,300 men.

Holland figures largely in the trade returns of this country, a quarter of the value of which is represented by agricultural produce, but much of the merchandise sent to Holland was for distribution in Germany and other parts. The following are the chief articles imported from the United Kingdom in the year 1898 :—

Chemical products	£168,553	Leather	£190,497
Coal, &c.	525,459	Linen	136,306
Cotton yarn	1,012,480	Machinery	631,303
Cotton manuftrs	1,071,386	Oil & Floor cloth ..	116,964
Grease, &c.	247,841	Woollen manufts	580,618
Metals	1,510,492	Woollen yarn	227,317

The chief exports to the U. K. for 1898 were:—

Butter	£1,329,438	Margarine	£2,209,809
Cheese	724,936	Meat	524,154
Chemical manuftrs.	303,094	„ Mutton..	584,779
China, &c.	214,784	„ Pork	474,967
Cocoa, &c.	548,916	Painters'colours,&c.	430,953
Cotton manftrs.,&c.	1,040,842	Paper	961,688
Dye stuffs, &c.	626,065	Sugar, refined	1,483,699
Farinaceous sub.,&c.	200,735	Silk manuftrs.,&c.	1,741,691
Fish	245,697	Tobacco	352,435
Glass manufts., &c.	410,352	Toys	225,785
Gloves	549,326	Wool manufactrs.	2,547,485
Hides and leather.	476,012	Wine	401,676
Iron and steel, &c.	1,169,321	Yeast, dried	207,733
Lace	373,880	Zinc manufts., &c..	647,802

Revenue, 1898-99, estimated £11,202,696
Expenditure, 1898-99, estimated 12,717,820
    (£1,882,158 army; £4,342.202 navy,
    and £108,391 for colonies.)
Public debt in 1899 .... £95,277,958
Total imports in 1898 149,645,535
Total exports in 1898 126,320,924
Imports from United Kingdom, 1898... 22,416,801
Exports to United Kingdom, 1898 ... 28,150,221

COMMERCIAL CAPITALS, Amsterdam, population (1898), 512,758; and Rotterdam, population (1898), 309,309.

COURT CAPITAL, The Hague. Pop. (1897) 196,325.

British Minister, Sir Henry Howard, K.C.M.G., C.B. £3,600	
Secretary of Legation, Arthur Leveson-Gower	500
2nd *Secretary,* A. R. Peel	390
Hon. Chaplain, Rev. H. Ratford, B.A.	
Vice-Consul, Rev. Edward Brine	
Amsterdam—Consul, Wm. Cherry Robinson	100
„ *Vice-Consul,* Charles Robinson ...	
Groningen—Vice-Consul, U. J. Schilthuis	
Harlingen—Vice-Consul, Dirk Fontein ...	
Helder—Vice-Consul, W. J. Van Neck ...	
Ymuiden—V.-Cons., S. C. L. Reygersberg	
Batavia (Java)—Consul, H. V. S. Davids...	
Samarang—Vice-Cons., D. D. Fraser	
Sourabaya—Vice-Consul, A. J. Warren	
Balik Pappan (Dutch Borneo)—Vice-Cons., M. Abrahams	
Curaçao—Consul, Jacob Jesurun..............	
*Paramaribo—*See Surinam.	
Rotterdam—Consul, Henry Turing	
„ *Vice-Consul,* A. J. van Dyk	
Brouwershaven — Cons. Agent, Joost de Kater	

Dordrecht—Vice-Consul, E. Boonen.........	
Flushing—V.-Con., P. L. de Bruyne, M.V.O.	£150
Hellevoetsluis and Brielle—Cons. Agent, Johannes Magdalenus Mes	
Maasluis—Cons. Agent, G. Dirkzwager ...	
Terneuzen—Cons. A., J. A. van Rompu...	
Surinam—Consul, J. R. W. Pigott	800
Nickerie—Vice-Consul, J. C. Weidner......	

Transit, 12 hours. Telegrams, per word, 2d:

DEPENDENCIES.—The Dutch possessions in the EAST INDIES are very considerable, comprising the whole of the SUNDA ISLANDS, with the exception of a small portion of Borneo and Eastern Timor, together with WESTERN NEW GUINEA, with an area of 738,000 square miles, and a population (1896) of 35,206,000, of whom as many as 26,125 000 live in the islands of Java and Madura. Included in this estimate are many districts in the interior of SUMATRA, BORNEO, CELEBES, and other islands, in which Dutch sovereignty is merely nominal. JAVA and MADURA (custom receipts, 1898, £1,047,235) produces a sufficient supply of food for a dense population, besides furnishing coffee and other products for exportation to Europe. The "outlying" islands are frequently administered by their own princes, subject to the directions of a Dutch Resident. There is a colonial army of 1,359 officers and 41,750 men. The colonial revenue for 1899 is estimated at £11,104.626, and is largely derived from the sale of coffee, salt, sugar, bark, and tin; whilst the estimated expenditure is £12,087,569. The exports, in addition to the above, include also tobacco, indigo, gums, and spices, and amounted in 1897, for Java, Madura, and the other outlying islands, to £17,952,417, while the imports for the same year amounted to £14,371,166.

In South America the colony of SURINAM, or Dutch Guiana, embraces 46,072 square miles and contains 68,972 inhabitants; and in the West Indies, CURAÇAO (Imports 1897, £223,317) and five other small islands belong to Holland, having an area of 436 square miles, with a population of 51,084.

Exports from colonies to U.K., 1898 £476,213
Imports to colonies from U.K., 1898 ... £2,256,615

NICARAGUA, REPUBLIC OF.

President, José Santos Zelaya, June, 1893.

The largest State of Central America, with a long seaboard on both the Atlantic and Pacific Oceans, situate between 9° 45'—15° N. lat. and 83° 40'—87° 38' W. long., containing an area of 51,660 English square miles, including a large portion of the Mosquito Territory, and a population of 310,000, of whom about three-quarters are mixed blood, and the rest Indians, besides the Mosquitos who are mostly in a savage state. In 1891 there were 93 miles of railway open, and several lines projected, with 1,591 miles of telegraph, connected with the Pacific cable from Mexico to Peru. A Ship Canal connecting the Pacific with the Atlantic was commenced in Oct., 1890. The interest on the foreign loan has been reduced to 4 per cent.

Public revenue, 1896	.........about	£400,000
Public expenditure, 1896	.... „	350,000
Public debt, 1897, internal.............	„	300,000
Do. external four per cent.	„	300,000
Imports. 1897, £528,384 ; Exports,		611,533
Imports from U.K.,1898,£113,565; exports,£71,088		

CHIEF TOWN, Managua. Population, 20,000; Leon, about 60,000; Granada, 30,000; Rivas, 10,000; Multagalpa, 8,000.

Managua—Consul, Chas. Ed. Nicol.
Greytown—Consul, Herbert F. Bingham.
    Bluefields—Vice-Consul, (vacant).
Granada—Consul, W. J. Chambers.
Corinto—Consular Agent, Henry Palazio.

Distant 5,800 miles; transit, 25 days. Telegrams, San Juan del Sur, per word, 3s. 11d.; all other places, 4s. 2d.

NORWAY. (See p. 582-3.)

OMĀN.

Sultan, or Sovereign, Seyyĭd Feysal bin Turkee, *suc.* 4 June, 1888.

Omān is a Mohammedan State in S.E. Arabia with a coast-line of about 1,500 miles along the Gulf of Persia the Gulf of Omān, and the Arabian Sea, an area of 81,000 square miles, and a population of 1,600,000. The small territory of Gwadar on the Mekran coast also belongs to it. Zanzibar, on the African coast, was a dependency of Omān until 1856. The country rises from a bare and burning coast until in Jebel Akhdar it attains an elevation of 10,000 feet. In the interior, however, among the Bedouins, the authority of the Sultan is hardly even nominal.

The population of Omān is chiefly Arab, but there is besides a considerable foreign element, consisting of Banians and Khojas from Western India, Persians, East Africans, and Nubians. The chief productions are dates, grain, fruit, and sugar; and the fisheries are very productive. The revenue is about 425,000 dollars. The exports consist of dates, cloth, salt, fruits, pearls, dried fish, and matting. The imports are—sugar, rice, piece-goods, coffee, wheat, raw silk, cotton, &c. Omān has no independent coinage except copper pice, coined in England, and introduced in 1898; the East India rupee and (Austrian) Maria Theresa dollar are the current coins, the latter being the most used. The rainfall is very scanty, averaging about 6 inches annually.

Muscat, the capital, with 60,000 inhabitants, trades with India, the Persian Gulf, Batavia, Zanzibar, and Yemen, but has little direct intercourse with Europe.

Total exports, 1898-99 ....$1,697,400
  ,, imports, 1898-99 .... 2,592,2C0
British Consul,

Transit, 24 days. Mails weekly *via* Bombay. Telegrams *sent by post* from Jask and Gwadur.

ORANGE FREE STATE. (See p. 593-96.)

PARAGUAY, REPUBLIC OF.

President, Emilio Aceval (25 Nov., 1898) . £1,900.
Foreign Secretary, José Segundo Decoud.
Minister Plenipotentiary to London and Paris, Señor Eusebio Machain.

Consul-General in England, Alfred James, 18, Eldon Street, E.C.
Consul in London, A. F. Baillie.
Consul-General, Glasgow, (vacant).

One of the most rising States of South America, and, except Bolivia, styled by some as the "Garden of South America," the only one without any seaboard, situate between 22° 4'–27° 30' S. lat. and 54° 32'—61° 20' W. long. Its area is computed at 145,400 square miles, or about one-fifth larger

than the United Kingdom, enclosed within the rivers Parana and Paraguay; and contains a population of about 600,000. Now that it has a settled government, Paraguay may be considered one of the most promising countries of South America; its capabilities are practically exhaustless, and the climate favourable to Europeans; the average of the thermometer for 1887 was 73°. The chief crops are maize, rice, coffee, manioc, tobacco, sugar-cane, and oranges. Among its principal trees are several species of dye-wood, and many yielding juices or gums, as the caoutchouc or india-rubber; there is also the valuable tree Quebracho, used for tanning, and the valuable shrub called "Yerba Maté," or Paraguay tea-plant—one of its principal articles of commerce; there are an immense number of hardwood and other timber trees; medicinal plants also are very numerous. Stock-raising is the chief industry, and, there being excellent pasturage, it is capable of great development. The chief articles of export are oranges, hides, tobacco, yerbamaté, and timber. The army, 60,000 men strong in the war of 1865-72, has been reduced to 30,000 men; there is no navy. A railway, 155 miles in length, belongs to an English Company; the total cost was £1,455.832, and the earnings in 1896-7 amounted to $897,556.

Revenue, 1896, $5,832,867; Expenditure, $7,109.581.
Imports. 1896. $2,786,335; Exports, $9,341,182.
Imports from United Kingdom, 1898, £8,987.

CAPITAL, Asuncion. Population, 35,000.
British Minister, Hon. W. A. C. Barrington (Buenos Aires).
Consul, Cecil W. Gosling £450

Telegrams, per word, 4s. and 4s. 6d.

PERSIA (See p. 479).

PERU, REPUBLIC OF.

President, Señor Romana, *installed* 8 Sept., 1899, for four years.
Premier and Foreign Affairs, Dr. Manuel Gálvez.
Public Works, Carlos Basadre y Forero.
Interior, Col. Parra.
Finance and Commerce, Mariano Belaunde.
War, Captain Carrillo.
Justice, Dr. Eleodora Romero.

Minister to England and France, Señor Don José F. Canevaro (*Legation :* 3 Park Place, S.W.).
Secretary, Don Wenceslao Melendez.
Consul-Gen. in London, Don Eduardo Lembcke, 237, Winchester House, Old Broad St., E.C.
Chancellor, Don Eduardo Higginson.
Consul-General at Southampton, H. Guillaume.
Do., Liverpool, Robert B. Crowe.

Peru is a maritime Republic of South America, situated between 1° 31' 29' and 19° 13' S. latitude and between 68° and 81° 20' 45' longitude W. On the west is washed by the Pacific Ocean, having a coast-line of 1,300 miles. It is bounded on the north by the Republics of Ecuador and Colombia, on the east by the Brazils and Bolivia, and on the south by Bolivia and Chile.

The boundaries between Peru and Bolivia are not definitely fixed, and there are also boundary questions with Columbia and Ecuador, while the provinces of Talna and Arica are still occupied by Chile.

The total area of Peru is about 455,000 square miles, being as large as England, France, Spain, and Portugal together; and its population, of which no census has been taken since 1876, is about 3,000,000, including 350,000 Indians. The country is traversed throughout its length by the Andes, running parallel to and about 60 miles distant from the Pacific coast. The region between is sandy desert, except where watered by transverse mountain-streams, but capable of cultivation in the highest degree by irrigation. The valleys running to the coast are very fertile, and the mountains are rich in minerals, among which silver, quicksilver, copper and coal are conspicuous; while in some of the departments along the coast, there are important beds of petroleum. The interior provinces, *i.e.*, those on the eastern side of the Andes, are of vast extent and fertility, with a climate ranging from temperate to tropical. The medicinal productions are of great value, comprising cinchona or Peruvian bark, sarsaparilla, copaiba, &c. Coffee, cocoa, india-rubber, &c., are indigenous to the country. Important mines of gold, silver, and copper exist, some of which are now being worked, and the Lobos and other islands on the Pacific coast provide the Peruvian guano.

The total length of the railways open (1893) was 849 miles. There is also water communication on Lake Titicaca with Bolivia; the navigation of the lake and of the river Desaguadero has been improved.

The army on a peace footing consists of about 2,800 men, with a police force of about 2,400, and there are 4 war-ships. The principal imports are cotton manufactures, ironware and cutlery, woollen goods, and machinery. The chief exports are guano, cotton, hides, goat-skins, sheep, and alpaca-wool, sugar, silver, coffee, cocoa, vanilla, rubbers, and cinchona.

An arrangement was concluded in January, 1890, by the Peruvian Government for the cancelling of its external debt, in pursuance of which the State railways, the guano, the large silver mines of Cerro de Pasco, and vast tracts of land are vested in the Peruvian Corporation.

Public revenue. 1897	$10,721,521
Public expenditure, 1897	11,308,240
Internal debt, 1897	£4,759,176
Total imports, 1897	3,102,538
Total exports, 1897	1,800,405
Imports from United Kingdom, 1898	920,024
Exports to the United Kingdom, 1898	1,537,428

CAPITAL, Lima. Population, 113 000.
British *Minister*, Wm. Nelthorpe Beauclerk 2,000
Vice-Consul, Robert A. Clay ......
    Arequipa—Vice-Consul, Alex. Hartley...
    Cerro de Pasco—Cons. Agent,Geo. E. Steel
    Lambayeque and Eten—Vice-Consul, William V. Fry.
    Mollendo—Vice-Consul, Geo.F.Robilliard
    Pacasmayo—V.-Cons., Arthur J. Jones
    Payta—Vice-Consul, Roland H. East ...
    Perené—Vice-Consul, Dr. W. E. S. Jones
    Pisco—Vice-Consul, J. J. Venn ....
    Salaverry—Vice-Consul, Robert Reid ...
    Callao—Consul, Alfred St. John £750
    ,, *Vice-Consul*, George G. Wilson 400
    Iquitos—Consul, David Adamson.

Lima, 7,020 miles; transit. 29 days, or *viâ* New York and Colon 23 days. Telegrams, per word, 6s 2d.

PORTUGAL.

King, Dom Carlos, *born* 28 September, 1863; *suc.* 19 Oct., 1889; *m.* 22 May, 1885, Amélie, dau. of the late Comte de Paris, *born* 28 Sept., 1865 (*issue*, 2 sons).

Heir Apparent, Prince Royal, Luiz Filippe, Duque of Braganza, *born* 21 March, 1887.
Premier, and Interior, José Luciano de Castro.
Foreign Affairs, Francisco A. de Veiga Beirão.
Finance, Manuel Affonso de Espregueira.
Justice, J. M. de Alpoim.
War, Sebastião Telles.
Marine and Colonies, Antonio Ed. Villaca.
Public Works, E. J. de Sousa Brito.
Envoy Extr. & Minister Plen. in London, Luiz de Soveral, G.C.M.G., 12 Gloucester Place, W.
1*st Sec.*, A. de Castro.
2*nd Sec.*, Dom F. Lobo d'Almeida.
1*st Sec. attached to Legation*, Gen. L. de Quillinan.
Attaché, Baron da Costa Ricci.
Financial Agent, Albilio Lobo.

The most westerly Kingdom of Europe, and a part of the great Iberian Peninsula; it lies in 37°–42° 8' N. lat. and 6° 15'–9° 30' W. long., being 360 miles in length from N. to S., and averaging about 100 in breadth from E. to W. Continental Portugal contains an area of 34,606 square miles, with a population in 1890 of 5,082,247, exclusive of the colonies. The Azores and Madeira (1,237 square miles, pop. 401,624) form part of the kingdom, which thus has a population of 4,708,178. The chief products are wheat, barley, oats, maize, flax, hemp, and the vine in elevated tracts; in the lowlands, rice, olives, oranges, lemons, citrons, figs, and almonds. There are extensive forests of oak, chestnuts, sea-pine, and cork, the cultivation of the vine and the olive being among the chief branches of industry; the rich red wine known to us as "port" is shipped from Oporto. Its mineral products are important—copper, lead, tin, antimony, coal, manganese, iron, slate, and bay-salt, which last from its hardness and purity is in demand. Its manufactures consist of gloves, silk, woollen, linen, and cotton fabrics, metal and earthenware goods, tobacco, cigars, &c. The exports consist to the extent of 50 per cent. of wine, which is the chief industrial product of the country; others are cork, cattle, copper-ore, fruits, oil, sardines, and salt. The imports are manufactured goods—hardware, cotton and woollen stuffs, machinery, wheat, sugar, dried fish, coal, &c. There is a commercial marine of 36 steamers and 433 sailing vessels, about 110,000 tonnage. Railways, 1,338 miles in extent, were open for traffic in 1896, and there are 8,079 miles of telegraph wire. For many years the national income has been considerably less than the expenditure; this deficiency has added to the national debt, which now amounts to about £31 a head of the population.

The army in 1896 consisted of about 30,000 men, on a peace footing, and of 125,057 men with 264 guns on a war footing; and the navy of 39 steamers and 16 sailing vessels, many scarcely seaworthy, and about 4,898 sailors.

Estimated revenue, 1897–98	Reis 52,865,478
Estimated expenditure, 1897–98	55,563,304
National debt, Consolidated 1896	£148,490,103
Floating debt, 1 Jan., 1897	Reis 36,826,421
Total imports, 1896	£8,894,000
Total exports, 1896	5,881,000
Imports from United Kingdom	2,085,564
Exports to ,, ,,	3,448,056

CAPITAL, Lisbon. Population (1890), 307,661.
Brit. Min., Sir H. MacDonell, G.C.M.G., C.B. £3,750
Secretary of Legation, Edward Thornton ... 500
3*rd Sec.*, H. E. MacDonell 250
    ,, W. E. O'Reilly (*acting*)............

Translator, James Duff	£300
Consul, Francis Henry Cowper	800
Belem—V.-Cons., Anthony Ffrench Duff	
Faro—Vice-Consul, Francisco J. Tavares	
Setubal—Vice-Consul, Francisco J. Pereira	
Tavira—Vice-Consul, José F. P. Padinha	
Villa Nova de Portimão—V.-Consul, J. D. Serpa	
Villa Real de San Antonio—Vice-Consul, Franci co José L. Tavares	
Funchal (Madeira)—Consul, J. B. Spence...	500
„ Vice-Consul, Henry Mercer Bell...	
Loanda—Consul, R. Casement	1000
„ Vice-Consul, A. Nightingale	
San Thomé—V.-Cons. (vacant)	
Macao (China)—V.-C., F. O. Seaton.	
Marmagao (Portuguese India)—Con., (vacant)	
„ Vice-Consul, E. S. Pemberton ..	
Mozambique—Consul, Ralph Belcher.........	600
Beira—Consul, J. E. McMaster	700
„ V.-Cons., Rev. W. H. Robins	
Chinde—Vice-Consul, E. MacDonell.	
Lorenço Marques—Consul, A. C. Ross...	900
„ V.-Cons., A. Parminter	
Quilimane—Vice-Con., R. C. F. Greville...	500
Oporto—Consul, M. H. Drummond	600
„ Vice-Consul, Honorius Grant............	150
Caminha—Vice-Con., J. B. Harrison.	
Figueira—Vice-Consul, Charles Laidley..	
Leixoes—Vice-Consul, T. Coverley.	
Vianno—Vice-Consul, João Castro.........	
St. Michael's (Azores)—Consul, Wm. Read.	
Fayal—Vice-Consul, A. W. R. Dart	100
Flores—Vice-Consul, James McKay	
Graciosa—Vice-Consul, Carlos Leão.........	
St. George—Cons. Agent, J. J. Cardozo...	
Terceira—Vice-Consul, J. N. de Freitas	
St. Vincent—Consul, W. Rice	
„ Vice-Consul, H. G. B. Langdon	
St. Jago—Cons. Agent, J. R. da Silva ...	

Lisbon, dist. 1,110 m.; transit, 50 hours. Telegrams, 3½d. word.

COLONIES AND DEPENDENCIES.

	Sq. Miles.	Population.
Cape Verde Is....................	1,490	111,000
West Africa :		
Guinea, &c.	14,370	1,500,000
St. Thomas and Principe	420	22,000
Landana and Cabenda ...	2,030	30,000
Angola	510,670	3,750,000
East Africa	297,750	1,500,000
Asia.............................	7,811	1,054,456
	834,541	7,917,456

THE AZORES and MADEIRA (imports 1897 £239,531; exports, £272,222) are an integral part of Portugal Proper ; the CAPE VERDE ISLANDS off the Cape of that name in Senegambia consist of St. Antonio, St. Nicolas, Fogo, Santiago, Boavista, Sal, and some smaller islands, having a total area of 1,490 square miles, and a population of about 111,000 ; the capital is St. Vincent. In West Africa a portion of the GUINEA Coast, with the BISSAGOS ISLANDS, was acquired in 1885 ; the capital is Cacheo, and the territory has an area of 14,370 square miles with about 1,500,000 inhabitants. In the Gulf of Guinea the two islands of ST. THOMAS and PRINCIPE were obtained in 1879 ; these islands are extremely fertile and have an area of 420 sq. miles (population about 22,000). Between the French Congo and the Free State are

the territories of LANDANA and CABENDA, area about 2,030 sq. miles (population 30,000) ; and extending from the left bank of the Congo river to the right bank of the Cumene river is the vast kingdom of ANGOLA, with about 1,350 miles of coast line and an area of 510,670 sq. miles, population about 3,750,000. The capital of Angola is St. Paul de Loanda, other important places being Benguela and Mossamedes : there are about 300 miles of railway open, and about 250 miles of telegraph wires. In South East Africa are the important colonies of LOBENZO MARQUES and MOZAMBIQUE, together constituting PORTUGUESE EAST AFRICA, which extends from Tongaland (British Colony) to the British Central Africa Protectorate in the North West, and German East Africa in the North East, and is bounded on the West by the S. A. Republic and Rhodesia ; and on the East by the Mozambique Channel ; the total area is about 297,750 sq. miles, and the population 1,500,000. In the southern province are the ports of Lorenzo Marques (Delagoa Bay) and Beira, and in the northern, Quilimane, Mozambique, and Ibo: the trade of Beira (pop. 31 Dec. 1897, 4,055) in 1897 was £578,500 for imports and £35,400 for exports, that of Lorenzo Marques being £754,416 for imports and £37,856 for exports, and for Mozambique exports £160,571 ; imports £151,823. Part of Mozambique is leased to the Mosambique Company, who administer the Manica and Sofala territories. The railways in operation are the Delagoa Bay Railway from Lorenzo Marques north-west to join the Transvaal system on the frontier, about 60 miles, and the Beira Railway, from Beira to Umtali on the borders of Rhodesia, about 180 miles. In Asia, Portugal possesses GOA, DAMAUN, and DIU (see p. 455), and TIMOR in the East Indian Archipelago, and MACAO, an island near the mouth of the Canton river, having a total area of 7,811 sq. miles, and an estimated population of 1,004,456.

Imports to Colonies from U.K., 1898...£1,894,573
Exports from Colonies to U.K., 1898......£358,228

ROUMANIA.

King, Charles, second son of Prince CharlesAntoine of Hohenzollern-Sigmaringen, born 20 April, 1839 ; elected Hereditary Prince 26 March, 1866 ; confirmed 24 Oct. 1866 ; proclaimed King by vote of both Chambers, 26 March ; crowned 22 May, 1881 ; mar. 15 Nov. 1869, Elizabeth (Carmen-Sylva), daughter of the late Prince Hermann von Wied, born 29 Dec., 1843.

Heir Presumptive (Nephew), Prince Ferdinand von Hohenzollern, born 24 August, 1865 ; proclaimed Heir Presumptive 26 Mar., 1889 ; mar. 10 Jan. '93 to Princess Marie of Edinburgh, and has issue Carol, born 15 Oct. 1893, and Elizabeth, b. 1894.

Premier and Interior, M. George Cantacuzene.
Foreign Affairs, M. John Lahovary.
Finance, General Mano.
War, General Jacob Lahorary.
Instruction, M. Take Jonesco.
State Lands, M. Fleva.
Public Works, Dr. Istradi.
Justice, M. Disesco.

Envoy Extraordinary and Minister Plenipotentiary, M. de Balaceano, 28 Victoria St., S.W.
Councillor of Legation, D. Nedeyano.
Consul-General in London, Capt. James Inman, 68 Basinghall Street, E.C.

The Kingdom of Roumania consists of the Moldo-Wallachian provinces formerly belonging to Turkey, but which by the Treaty of Berlin, 13 July, 1878, were recognised as an independent State, and the territory of the Dobruja added to them. On the 26th March, 1881, Roumania was raised to a Kingdom. The entire area is 46,314 square miles, with a population of about 5,500,500. The dominating religion is that of the Greek Church (4,529,000); Roman Catholics, 114,200; Protestants, 13,800; Jews, 400,000. The soil is among the richest in Europe, and, but for the fearful summer droughts, would be also the most productive. The climate is extreme, for summer heats and winter colds are intense. The agricultural produce consists of wheat, maize, millet, barley, rye, beans, and peas. Vines and fruits are abundant. The forests are of great extent and importance, but the riches of the country consist mainly in its cattle, sheep, and horses, of which immense numbers are reared on its far-stretching pastures. Minerals and precious metals are said to be abundant, but only salt and petroleum are obtained. The imports are chiefly the manufactured goods of Western Europe; the exports consist principally of wheat, barley, maize, rock-salt, spirits, hides, wood, and cattle. The total length of railways is about 1,700 miles, and there are 223 telegraph offices with 9,915 miles of wire.

An International Commission, created by the Treaty of Paris, 1856, and whose powers were enlarged by the Treaty of Berlin, 1878, has its seat at Galatz, and exercises sovereign powers over the navigation of the Danube: the British representative is Lieutenant-Colonel Trotter, Consul-General. Its income, principally derived from shipping dues, amounts to about £60,000 per annum. On November 10, 1892, a large dock was opened at Ibraila (Brahilov), and in 1896 a canal through the "Iron Gates" rendered the hitherto dangerous part perfectly navigable.

The field army consists, on the peace footing, of about 46,000 men, but in time of war this can be raised to 158,000, and there is a militia in addition. There is also a small navy of 12 steamers.

Public revenue, estimated 1897-98 ....£8,883,800
Public expenditure,   ,,   ,, ... 8,830,028
Public debt, 1897 .... about 48,000,000
Total imports, 1896 13,516,916
Total exports, 1896 12,962,266
Imports from United Kingdom, 1898 .. 1,383,002
Exports to U. K. (chiefly corn), 1898 ... 2,579,601
CAPITAL, Bucharest. Pop. (about) 250,000.

British Min., John G. Kennedy £2,400
2nd Sec., Translator & V.-Cons., H.E.Browne   150
Galatz—Con.—Gen., Lt.-Col. H. Trotter, C.B.   650
   ,, *Vice-Consul*, L. C. Liddell 400
Orajova—Vice-Consul, Michail A. Dimos
Ibraila—Vice-Consul, Wm. J. Norcop ... 400
Kustendjie—Vice-Con., Peter F. C. Zohrab   400
Sulina—Vice-Con., Robt. A. Profeit 400
Transit, 3½ days. Telegrams, per word, 4d.
ROUMELIA, EASTERN. *See* Bulgaria, p. 543.

THE RUSSIAN EMPIRE.

Emperor, Nicholas II., Tsar of all the Russians, *b.* 18 May, 1868; *suc.* 20 Oct., *O.S.* (1 Nov., *N.S.*) 1894; *m.* 14 (26) Nov., 1894, Princess Alix of Hesse (Alexandra Feodorovna), granddaughter of Queen Victoria, and has issue 3 daughters, Olga, *b.* 15 Nov. 1895, Tatiana, *b.* 10 June, 1897, and Marie, *b.* 26 June, 1899.
Heir Presumptive, Grand Duke Michel.
Minister of Imperial Household, General Baron de Freederickz.
President of the Council of Ministers, M. Dournovo.
Foreign Affairs, Count Mouravieff.

Finance, M. de Witte.
Interior, M. Sipiaguine.
Public Instruction, M. Bogolepoff.
Public Works, Prince Khilkoff.
War, General Kroupatkin.
Marine, Vice-Admiral Tyrtov.
Justice, M. Muravieff.
Agriculture and Crown Domains, M. Yermoleff.
Ambassador to France, Prince Urussoff; *Germany*, Count Ostensacken; *Austria Hungary*, Count Kapnist; *Italy*, M. Nelidoff; *Turkey*, M. Zinovieff; *U.S.A.*, Count Cassini.
Ambassador in London, Actual Privy-Councillor de Staal, Chesham House, S.W.
Councillor, M. P. Lessar.
1st Secretary, Baron Grewenitz.
2nd Secretaries, N. Gourko; E. Demidoff; Prince de San Donato.
Attaché, H.S.H. Prince Radziwill.
Military At aché, Colonel Yermoloff.
Naval Attaché, Captain Jean Ouspensky.
Consul-General, Baron Ungern Sternberg, 17 Great Winchester Street, E.C.
Agent of Ministry of Finances, M. de Tatischeff.
Assist. do., Gregory Wilenkin.

An Empire comprising one-sixth of the territorial surface of the globe, stretching over a large portion of its northern regions, and approaching very nearly in extent to the dominion under British rule. In addition to Russia in Europe (exclusive of the Caucasus), situate between lat. 44° 28'—76° 33' N. and 17° 40'—64° 30' E. long., and embracing more than half of that continent, it comprehends one-third of Asia, and until 1867 included also a large section of North America. The empire comprises:

European Russia:—	English Square Miles.	Population in 1897.
Russia Proper (50 Provs.)	1,187,043 ...	94,188,750
Poland (10 Provs.)	49,142 ...	9 442,590
Finland (Grand Duchy)	144,211 ...	2,527,801
Asiatic Russia:—		
Caucasia (11 Provs.) ...	182,449 ...	9,723,553
Siberia (8 Provs. and Regions)	4,823,112 ...	5,731,732
Central Asia (10 Provs. and Regions)	1,364,124 ...	7,590,275
Russian subjects in } Khiva and Bokhara }	... ...	6,412
	8,450,081	129,211,113

Of the total population 64,616,280 are men and 64,594,883 women.

In the European parts of Russia alone the population increases annually at the rate of nearly a million and a half. The largest towns are St. Petersburg (1,267,023), Moscow (988,610), Warsaw (614,752), Odessa (404,651), Lodz (514,780), Riga (284,943). Kieff (248,750), Kharkoff (170,682), Vilna (160,000), Saratov (133.000), Kazañ (131.000), Ekaterinoslav (121,000), Rostoff (119,000), Astrakhan (113 000), Tula (111 000), and Kishineff (108,000); whilst Nijni Novgorod, Nikolaieff, Samara and Minsk have populations between 90,000 and 95,000. In Asiatic Russia the Caucasus contains two towns with over 100,000 inhabitants, Tiflis (160,000), and Baku (112,000); Turkestan contains five large towns, Tashkend (156,000), Namangan, Samarcand and Andijan; in Siberia, Tomsk, Iskutsk, and Ekaterinburg have each about 50,000 inhabitants. Nijni Novgorod, though small, is a station on the Trans-Siberian Railway, and has annually the largest fair in the world. The various nationalities in 1882 were represented about as follows:—Russ, 69,770,000; Poles, 6,010,000; Lithuanians,

2.910,000 ; Germans, 1,120,000 ; Swedes, 270,000 ; Tajiks (Persians), &c., 1,125,000 ; Armenians, 800,000 ; Jews, 2,954,000 ; Caucasians, 2,850,000 ; Finns, 2,000,000 ; Turks and Tartars, 7,700,000 ; Mongols, 530,000 ; various, 584,000. The established religion of the empire is the Russo-Greek Church, officially called the Orthodox Catho ic Faith. According to religions there are : —Greek Catholics(including Dissenters),72,990,000; Roman Catholics, 8,910,000; Protestants, 4,766,000 ; Jews, 2,954,000 (a very competent authority gives the number of Jews as being nearer four millions) ; Mohammedans, 11,814,000 ; and Pagans, 430,000. European Russia consists mainly of an immense plain ; the Valdai hills in the west rise only to about 1,000 ft., and the Lublin hills in the south-west to about 1,500 ft., on the right bank of lake Imandra, in the Kola peninsula, is an elevation of 3,300 ft , the Timanski range in the province of Archangel to about 3,000 ft., and Mount Lujaur-Ort in Finland rises to about 3,400 ft. In the Crimea and Caucasus various heights are over 4,500 ft., and the Obdorsk and Ural mountains, which form the border-land between Europe and Asia, rise in many places to between 4,000 and 5,000 ft. In Siberia the principal ranges are the Altai, Sayansk, Baikal, Yablonoi and Verkhoiansk mountains, with a vo'canic chain in Kamtchatka. In Russian Turkestan are portions of the Thian Shan range, and in Bokhara are the Pamirs, the "Roof of the World," and in all these ranges are heights of over 5,000 ft. The principal rivers are the Volga, Ural, Dnieper, Dniester, Don, Dvina, Duna, and Neva. The Volga is the largest river in Europe, and is navigable almost to its source. In Siberia, the Ob, Yenisei, Lena, and Amur are each larger than the Volga, with many important tributaries. The river Amur, dividing Manchuria from Eastern Siberia, is navigable from its mouth to Chita, in the Trans-baikal province by shallow draught steamers, and is of importance, together with the Trans-Siberian Railway, in spreading Russian influence in the outlying portions of the Chinese Empire.

A great portion of Russian territory is unfit for cultivation; in the north the *tundras* are almost constantly frozen, but in a short summer provide good pasture, and certain berries fit for human food ; in the south, round the head of the Caspian Sea, is an immense sandy desert, steppe ; whilst some of the interior provinces (to the extent of about 460,000,000 acres), and nearly the whole of Siberia are clothed with forests, in which the fir, pine, birch, oak, lime, maple and ash predominate. The country b-tween the Baltic and Black Sea, however, is eminently fertile, producing abundance of grain. The chief cereal raised is wheat. of which Russia is the second largest grower in Europe, the triennial average harvest in the period 1896-8 being about 200,250,000 bushels; other cereals are barley, oats, buckwheat, millet, and especially rye, the staple food of the inhabitants. Hemp and flax are extensively cultivated, and of late years potatoes and tobacco. The Obdorsk and Ural Mountains (forming the boundary land between Europe and Asia), contain very great mineral riches, and, with the Altai range, are the principal seat of mining and metallic industry, producing gold, platinum, copper, iron of very superior quality, rock-salt, marble, and kaolin, or china-c'ay. Silver, gold, and lead are also obtained in large quantities from the mines in the Altai Mountains. The naphtha springs on

the Caspian are annually increasing in importance, and already flood certain European markets with petroleum. An immense bed of coal, both steam and anthracite, and apparently inexhaustible, has been discovered in the basin of the Donetz (between the rivers Donetz and Dnieper).

The principal ports are Petersburg, the naval depot and fortress Kronstadt, Narva, Riga, Libau, Pernau and Windau (Baltic), Uleaborg (gulf of Bothnia), Revel, Helsingfors and Wiborg (gulf of Finland), Archangel and Onega (White Sea), Odessa, Nicolaieff, Sevastopol and Batoum (Black Sea), Taganrog, Mariupol, Rostoff and Kertch (Sea of Azov), Astrakhan, Derbent and Baku (Caspian Sea), and Okhotsk, Nicolaieff-k, Vladivostok, and Petrapaulovsk in Kamtchetka (Pacific) ; whilst the Chinese possessions of Port Arthur and Talienwan (gulf of Pechili) have been occupied by the Russian government in accordance with the Russo-Chinese treaty of 17 March, 1898.

With metallurgical and engineering factories, Russia possesses many extensive manufacturing establishments for weaving, tanning, fur-dressing, &c. Linen is largely manufactured by handlooms, the chief operations consisting in spinning and weaving flax and hemp. Woollen and worsted stuffs, fine cloths, and mixed fabrics are also produced. The chief imports are cotton, tea, and other colonial produce, iron and machinery, wool, wine, fruits and vegetables, oil, &c. The chief exports are grain (56 per cent.), raw and dressed flax, linseed, timber, hides and skins, hemp, tallow, wool, spirits, tow, and bristles.

The exports in 1897 to the United Kingdom amounted to £22,284,865, the chief articles being:—

Butter........	£880,625	Flax and tow £1,935,970
Corn, wheat....	2,540,588	Hemp............	201,568
„ oats......	973.333	Oil-seed cake	578,052
„ barley ..	2,408,101	Petroleum	632,712
„ maize....	568,546	Seeds linseed,&c.)	544,589
Bristles	141,232	Wood,hewnorsawn4,810,320
Eggs	966,129	Wool, &c.........	673,844

The chief articles of import into Russia from the United Kingdom in 1898 were:—

Coals, &c........	£1,075,408	Implements & tools £150,129
Chemical products	105,021	Machinery 2,844,561
Cotton yarn and		Metals, all kinds . . 1,938,844
manufactures ..	339,041	Wool, yarn and
Herrings	360,068	manufactures .. 538,791

The ARMY contains on a peace footing over 860,000 men, with 3,400 guns; on a war footing it is capable of being raised to about 3,400,000 men with 3.500 guns, not including the last reserves.

The NAVY (for which an estimated expenditure of £9.303,749 was allowed for 1900 consisted in November 1893 of 12 battleships *(and* 10 *building)*, 10 armoured cruisers *(and* 1 *building)*, 3 protected cruisers *(and* 5 *building)*, 3 unprotected cruisers, 15 coast defence ironclads *(and* 1 *building)*, 17 torpedo vessels, 28 torpedo-boat destroyers *(building)*, 174 torpedo boats, and 5 special service vessels.

RAILWAYS, &c.—In European Russia 25,625 miles were open for traffic in 1898 and 7.312 miles under construction; in Asiatic Russia *The Siberian Railway* was commenced in 1891 to connect Vladivostok with the Russo-Siberian frontier (Ekaterinberg), a distance of about 4,000 miles; Irkutsk, on the west of Lake Baikal (and about 3.830 miles from St. Petersburg), was reached in March 1899, and the line is expected to be open as far as Chita early in 1900, whence it will proceed through the Trans-baikal province (Zabaikalskaya) and the maritime province of Amur to its final destination Vladivostock. A section from Vladivostock to Khabarovka is complete,' thus shortening the distance to be traversed by over 500 miles. A contemplated extension will join Vladivostock to Talienwan and Port Arthur, and the latter to Peking; while it is reported that a line may be laid from Omsk to join at Taskend with *The Trans-Caspian Railway* from Poti to Baku on the western side of the lake, and on the eastern side from Krasnovodsk, *via* Merv and Bokhara to Taskend, whence branches run to Khokand and Andijan, another branch running from Merv to Kushk, or about 80 miles east of Herat. With the idea of further opening up communications in Southern Russia, a scheme has been projected for a canal between the Baltic and Black Sea. In the budget for 1899, the whole of the extraordinary expenditure of 109,073,413 *roubles* (£12,825,820) is devoted to railway development.

There were (1895) 7,887 post-offices, carrying 30,667,424 letters, &c. Of telegraphs there are 3,790 offices, with 91,000 miles of line.

The sea-going commercial marine consisted in 1896 of 2,207 sailing vessels and 567 steamers, with a total tonnage of 577,207; the ocean shipping of the Russian Empire is comparatively insignificant, but the internal (lake and river) shipping is considerable.

*Revenue, 1898 (1,571,732,646 *roubles*) £174,636 960
   Ordinary (1,462,059,233 *roubles*).
   Extra-Ordinary (109,073.413 *roubles*).
*Expenditure (1,571,732 646 *roubles* , £174,636,960
   Ordinary (1,456,190,263 *roubles*).
   Extra-Ordinary (115.542,383 *roubles*).
Cash Reserve, Jan. 1,1899 (115,000,000
   roubles) £12,777,777
Debt, 1895 :—
  Gold (3 to 5 per cent.) £322,728,000
  Paper (3 to 6 per cent.) 6,374,000
  Paper (no interest) ... 359,296,000
       Total 798,398,000
Interest, &c., on total debt, 1897 29,154,308
Total imports, 1897 75,528,209
Total exports, 1897 79,991,167
Domestic imports from U. K. 1898 ... 14,387,208
Total exports to U. K. 1898 19,489,203

The Grand Duchy of Finland.

Grand Duke, The Emperor of Russia.
Governor General, Lt.-Gen., N. Bobrikov.
Secretary of State, Actual Privy Councillor, V. de Plehve (*acting*).

A Grand Duchy on the gulfs of Finland and Bothnia, which was conquered by Russia from Sweden, and finally annexed in 1808. The area is 144,254 square miles, with a population of about 2,595,000 in 1898, of whom about 2,230,000 are Finns, 350,000 Swedes, 12,000 Russians, 2,000 Germans and 1,000 Laps, leading a nomadic life in the north. Nearly all the inhabitants are Lutherans. There is a university at Helsingfors, with 2,400 students. Swedish is the language of the upper classes. The leading crops are rye, barley, oats, potatoes; but there are not sufficient cereals for home consumption, and large quantities are imported from Russia and Germany. The live stock, in addition to horses, cattle, sheep, pigs, and goats, includes also the reindeer in the extreme north. Iron lake and bog-ore, copper, lead, and graphite are found, but no salt. The iron industry is of importance, and spinning and weaving of cotton, flax, and wool, distilling, the making of matches, sugar-refining, ship-

building, saw mills, and other branches of industry are carried on with success. The forests are a great source of wealth, and immense quantities of timber are prepared for export. The exports include timber, wood-pulp, butter, textile fabrics, paper, and iron. There are 1,652 miles of railway; and (1898) a marine of 2,298 vessels, of 324,244 tons.

Finland is a constitutional monarchy of a somewhat antiquated type. The Diet consists of four estates :—nobles, clergy, burgesses, and peasants, and is convoked triennially, and the country is chiefly governed by the Imperial Finnish Senate, of 22 members. There are 9 battalions of Finnish Rifles, mustering 5,600 men, and one regiment of dragoons 900 strong, with a reserve of 30,000. The revenue in 1898 was £4,299,097, and the expenditure £3 665,916; the debt amounts to £4,508,000 (1899). The imports in 1898 were £9,481,740, and the exports £7,200,626. The capital is Helsingfors, population 86,000 (including Russian garrison).

CAPITAL OF THE RUSSIAN EMPIRE, St. Petersburg. Population, 1,267,023.

British Ambassador, His Excellency the Rt. Hon. Sir Charles S. Scott, G C.B., G.C.M.G.	£7,800
Secretary of Embassy, Hon. Charles Hardinge, C.B.	900
Milit. Attaché, Lt.-Col. C. E. de la Poer Beresford	800
2nd Secretaries, Charles L. des Graz	520
R. W. Graham	330
Attaché, John P. Burrell	
,, Hon. R. C. Lindsay	
Hon. Attaché, P. W. de Bathe.	
,, Walter F. Farquhar.	
Consul-General, John Michell...	1,000
Vice-Consul, J. Whishaw	
Abo—Vice-Consul,	
Archangel—Vice-Consul, Henry Cooke ...	
Björneborg—Vice-Consul,	
Borga—Consular Agent,	
Cronstadt—Vice-Consul, A. Fishwick .	
Fredrickshamn—Vice-Con., A. Ahlgoist.	
Gamla Karleby—Vice-Consul,	
Hango—Vice-Consul,	
Helsingfors—Vice-Consul,	
Kemi—Vice-Consul,	
Kotka—Vice-Consul,	
Lovisa—Vice-Consul,	
Moscow—Consul, Arthur F. H. Medhurst	
Narva—Vice-Consul, Edward Siricius ...	
Nicolaistadt—Vice-Consul, George Bucht	
Revel—Vice-C., Baron E. G. de Soucanton	
Uleaborg—Vice-Consul,	
Wiborg—Vice-Consul,	
Batoum—Cons., Patrick Wm. Joseph Stevens	700
Novorossisk—Vice-Consul, T. Sterne	
Poti—Vice-Consul, John Pavoni (*acting*)	
Odessa—Cons.-Gen., Lt.-Col. H. P. Picot	900
,, *Vice-Consul,* H. G. Mackie ...	300
Eupatoria—Consular Agent, Chas.Martin.	
Kieff—Consul, Harry Paton Smith	
Nicolaieff—V.-C., A. W. W. Woodhouse	400
Sebastopol—Vice-C., Chas. J.Cooke	400
Theodosia—Vice-Consul, William Rees...	
Riga—Consul, Arthur Woodhouse............	650
,, *Vice-Consul,* William Breslau ...	
Libau—Vice-Consul, C. J. Hill	
Pernau—Vice-Consul, J. E. Cattley ...	
Windau—Vice-Consul, Carl Schenck......	
Taganrog—Consul, H. W. Hunt............	600
,, *Vice-Consul,* W. H. Hunt,	
Berdiansk—Vice-Consul, H. R. Lowe	

Genichesk—*Cons. Agent*, P. G. Costalá.
Kertch—*Vice-Consul*, J. O. Wardrop £400
Mariupol—*Vice-Consul*, W. S. Walton 150
Rostov—*Vice-Consul*, W. R. Martin.
Warsaw—*Consul-Gen.*, Capt. Alex. Murray 800
   ,, *Vice-Consul*, R. Kimens ....
St. Petersburg, *via* Calais, is 1,709 miles from London; transit 3 days. Telegrams, per word, 5½*d.*

SAMOA (NAVIGATOR'S ISLANDS).
[Divided in 1899 by treaty between U.S.A. and Germany. See pp. 563 and 500]

SAN MARINO.
A small "Republic" in the hills near Rimini, on the Adriatic, founded, it is stated, by a pious mason of Dalmatia in the 4th century, and governed by a Council of 60 (20 nobles, 20 townsmen, and 20 peasants), of whom two jointly as Regents. The area is 33 square miles, the population 8,000. There is an "army" commanded by several "generals," and honorary ranks and titles are bestowed on foreigners for a consideration. The village of San Marino (pop. 1,500) occupies the slope of Mount Titan, and has a castle, fortified by King Berengar of Lombardy, a fine church, and a theatre. Agriculture and viticulture flourish. By a treaty concluded in 1872 the Republic has placed itself under the protection of Italy.

SAN SALVADOR (REPUBLIC OF).
President, Gen. Tomas Regalado, 19 Nov., 1898.
Foreign Affairs, General J. J. Cañas.
Public Instruction, Dr. F. Novoa.
War and Marine, Col. Jacinto Castro.
Finance, Dr. Nicolas Angulo.
Interior, Don Daniel Huezo y Paredes.

Consul-General, M. J. Kelly, 8, Idol Lane, E.C.
Consul, Manuel de Montes.

Salvador extends along the Pacific coast for 170 miles, with a general breadth of 43 miles and contains an area of about 7,228 English square miles, with a population estimated at 750,000. The principal exports are coffee, indigo, tobacco, sugar, silver, balsam (known as balsam of Peru), rice, hides, cedar, and fustic. Its mineral resources are being developed, and in Cabañas gold has been discovered, carrying 79 ounces of free-milling gold to the ton. *A railway 34½ miles in length connects Acajutla with Ateos, 21 miles from capital, and has been extended to Sta. Ana, the coffee centre. Another line has been commenced from the port of La Union to San Miguel. The only river of importance is the Lempa, over which a bridge was constructed in 1897 at the cost of £28,600 ; only to be destroyed by a hurricane at the end of the year. Earthquakes are frequent ; the capital (now rebuilt) was entirely destroyed by one in 1873.

Revenue, 1897	£584,613
Expenditure, 1897	690,875
Imports, 1897	349,654
Exports, 1897	753,850
Internal Public Debt, 1899	$8,650,000
*External Public Debt, 1899	£234,000

Imports from U.K.,1898, £114,802; exports,210,906
CHIEF TOWN, San Salvador. Pop. *circ.* 35,000.
Consul, Walter E. Coldwell ....
  Acajutla—*V.-Con.,* Herbert W. Smith.
  San Miguel and La Union—*V.-Cons.* (Vacant).
Salvador is 5,700 miles London ; transit 23 days. Telegrams, Libertad 3*s.* 6*d.* ; other places 3*s.* 9*d.*

---

* The external debt was extinguished in 1899 by a Financial Syndicate who also purchased the railway and obtained a concession to complete it as far as the capital, which is expected to be reached in May 1900.

SERVIA.
King, Alexander (Obrenovitch), *b.* (2) 14 August, 1876 ; succeeded his father, King Milan (who abdicated), 6 March, 1889. Took royal authority into his own hands (1st) 13th April, 1893.
Premier & Foreign Affairs, M. Vladan Georgevitch (October, 1897).
Interior, M. G. Ghentchitch.
Public Works, Colonel Atanackovitch.
Finance, M. Voukaschin Petrovitch.
Justice, M. G. Stefanovitch.
Public Instruction, M. Andra Georgevitch.
War, Colonel Vuchkovitch.
Commerce, M. Zivan Zivanovitch.

Envoy Ext. and Min. Plen. in London, M. Chedomille Mijatovitch, 7 Phillimore Gardens, W.
Consul-General in London, H. W. Christmas, 42A Bloomsbury Square, W.C.
Consul in Manchester, Otto Baerlein.

A Kingdom of Eastern Europe, governed by an hereditary sovereign. By the constitution of 1889 a "Skupstchina," a parliament elected by ballot, represented the people. This constitution was suspended 21 May, 1894, by Royal decree and that of 1869 provisionally restored. It is separated from Hungary by the Danube and Save. By the Berlin Treaty, 1878, it received a large accession of territory, and now has an area estimated at 18,757 square miles, with a population in 1895 of 2,344,153. The surface of the country is mountainous, containing the remains of formerly extensive forests and uncultivated heaths. Agriculture is carried on in a somewhat primitive fashion. The principal crops are maize for home consumption, and wheat for export; flax, hemp, and tobacco are also grown, and silk-culture is carried on to a limited extent. The production of wine has suffered severely from Phylloxera and bad seasons, and of late the country has been compelled to import grapes and wine from Macedonia. The cultivation of prunes is very extensive, and these are sent chiefly to Austria-Hungary, Germany, and the United States. The live stock (1899) included 169,928 horses, 915,428 cattle, 3,620,197 sheep and goats, and 904,446 pigs. Lead, zinc, quicksilver, antimony, copper, iron, and coal are found. Carpet-weaving and embroidery, and the making of jewellery and filigree work, are of some importance. The imports consist in the main of cottons, sugar, and colonial goods, hardware, woollens, &c.; the exports of dried prunes (11·6 per cent.), pigs and wool, besides wheat, wine, hides, cattle, and horses. The bulk of the trade is with Austria. The direct trade of Servia with the United Kingdom is small (imports, 1897, £259,259; exports nil). There were (1894) 624 kilometres of railway, and 3,174 kilometres of telegraph, with 111 post offices and 392 kils. of telephone. The army, on a peace footing, numbers 19,000 men, with 186 field guns. On a war footing it includes a *field force* of 73,000 rifles and 4,000 sabres with 276 field guns ; a first *ban* of 55,000 rifles and 1,000 sabres, a second *ban* of 35,000 rifles and 500 sabres and *dépôts* with 2,000 rifles, 500 sabres, and 32 field guns : the total of the war footing is therefore 165,000 rifles, 6,000 sabres and 308 field guns. Every man between 18 and 50 years of age can be called to arms. Education is compulsory and free, and has been making rapid strides of late years.

Revenue, 1899 (estimated)		£2,752,980
Expenditure, 1899	,,	2,752,902
Public debt, 1899		15,676,512

Total imports, 1898 ....£1,644,076
Total exports, 1898 2,279,659
Imports from United Kingdom, 1898.. 153,463
CAPITAL, Belgrade. Population, 1899, 60,000.
Brit. Minister, William Edward Goschen ...£1,800
Consul, Ranald D. G. Macdonald................. 400
Belgrade, 1,175 miles from London. Transit, 2½ days. Telegrams, per word, 4d.

SIAM. (See p. 480.)

SOCIETY ISLANDS.
(*French Possession ; see p.* 557.)

SPAIN.

King, Alfonso XIII., son of Alfonso XII. and of Queen Maria Christina, *born* 17 May, 1886 (after the death of his father, 25 Nov., 1885).
Regent, Queen Maria Christina, Archduchess of Austria, widow of King Alfonso XII., and mother of the King ; *born* 21 July, 1858 ; sworn in as Regent, 26 Nov., 1885.
Heiress Presumptive, The Infanta Dona Maria de las Mercedes (Princess of Asturias), *born* 11 September, 1880.
Premier and Foreign Affairs, Señor Silvela.
Interior, Señor Dato.
Justice, Conde de Torreanaz.
War, General Azcarraga.
Marine, Señor Gomez Isnaz.
Public Works, Marques de Pidal.
Finance, Señor Villaverde.

Ambassador in London, Conde de Rascon, 1 Grosvenor Gardens, S.W.
Sec. of Embassy, Don Pedro Joves.
2nd Secretary, Don Jose Soriano.
Attachés, Felix Vazquez de Zafra, O. Heeren, J. Perez del Pulgar.
Secretary Particular, Jacobo Laborda.
Military Attaché, Lt.-Col. José Rivera.
Naval Attaché, Marquis de Arellano.
Consul-Gen., Don Arturo Baldasano, 20 Mark Lane.
Financial Delegate, Nicasio E. Jauralde, 37 New Broad Street, E.C.

A Kingdom situate in the south-west of Europe, between 36°—43° 45′ N. lat. and 4° 25′ E.—9° 20′ W. long., bounded on the south and east by the Mediterranean, on the west by the Atlantic and Portugal, and on the north by the Bay of Biscay and France, from which it is separated by the Pyrenees ; and occupying the larger portion of the great Iberian Peninsula. Its coast-line extends 1,317 miles—712 formed by the Mediterranean and 605 by the Atlantic. It was formerly divided into 14 kingdoms (now forming 49 provinces) ; the ancient Provinces, still best understood, are New Castile, La Mancha, Old Castile, Leon, Asturias, Galicia, Estremadura, Andalusia, Murcia, Valencia, Aragon, Catalonia, Basque Provinces, with the Canary and Balearic Isles, comprising an area of 196,173 English square miles, and a population in 1887 of 17,550,216. The Constitution upon which the present government is formed is dated 30 June, 1876. The interior of the peninsula consists of an elevated table-land, surrounded and traversed by mountain ranges—the Pyrenees, the Cantabrian Mountains, the Sierra Guadarrama, S. Morena, S. Nevada, Montes de Toledo, &c. The principal rivers are the Douro, the Tagus, the Guadiana, the Guadalquivir, the Ebro, and the Minho. Spain is rich in minerals, especially iron, copper, and lead, and as capital is attracted its resources will be developed. The country is generally fertile, and well adapted to agriculture and the cultivation of heat-loving fruits—as olives, oranges, lemons, almonds, pomegranates, and dates. The agricultural products comprise wheat, barley, maize, oats, rice, with hemp and flax of the best quality. The vine is cultivated in every province ; in the south-west, Jeres, the well-known sherry and tent wines are made ; in the south-east, the Malaga and Alicante ; these are the best known, but there are many others which only require to be brought before the English public in order to secure a market. Now that the country is in a more settled condition, there is little doubt that it will attract travellers, and then become better known. Most of the principal towns now possess very fair hotel accommodation. The principal articles imported are raw cotton, spirits, fish, wheat and flour, sugar, coal, timber, woollen manufactures, machinery, and railway materials, hides, &c. The principal exports are wine, copper and copper ores, lead, iron ores, olive oil, cattle, raisins, oranges, cork, esparto grass, wool, salt, quicksilver, grapes, &c. ; trade was for many years mostly confined to France and Great Britain, but Germany and the United States are now competing for a share. Home trade is rigidly protected by high customs duties.

The principal exports to the United Kingdom in 1898 were :—

Copper	£1,106,012	Olive Oil	£344,854
Cork	136,952	Quicksilver	331,963
Oranges	1,648,772	Esparto, &c.	278,610
Iron ore	3,378,816	Onions	231,185
Lead	1,338,775	Silver ore.........	191,244
Raisins	1,648,772	Wine	798,357

And the chief imports from the United Kingdom :—

Coal and coke £795,804		Manure	£363,090
Cotton manufacts.	148,009	Metals, all sorts ..	204,478
Machinery,all sorts	342,537	Wool,&c.	171,418

The army is raised by conscription, but exemption may be purchased ; the terms of service are three years with the colours, 3 years with the first and 6 years with the second reserve. On a peace footing it consists of 3 annual contingents of 40,000 or 120,000 men in all. On a war footing it consists of 12 annual contingents or 480,000 men. The colonial forces, which, including militia, numbered about 250,000, have been almost entirely disbanded. The Navy was almost entirely destroyed during the war of 1897 with the U.S.A., and there now remain one battleship, the *Pelayo* (built in 1887), and a few small craft.

During 1897, 18,738 vessels (tonnage 14,235,254) entered, and 17,352 (tonnage 14,214,748) cleared at Spanish ports.

Nearly all the 49 Provinces are now connected by railways, of which about 6,070 miles have been completed, and there are 17,628 miles of telegraph.

Finance.—An extraordinary budget was passed in 1896 to provide for an expenditure of £8,814,146 above the ordinary expenditure, but this failed to raise the revenue estimated, and has been modified and extended for two years. The liquidation of the budget for 1897-8 showed a deficit of £1,976,823. The estimates for the financial year 1898-9 were balanced at £34,632,675.

Public revenue, 1896-7 (actual) £34,360,436
Public expenditure, 1896-7 (actual)...... 34,232,241
National debt, Jan. 1, 1898 :

Spanish	£304,106,700
Cuban	57,655,000
Philippine	7,884,000
	£369,645,700

Interest on debts, 1898 19,627,946

Total imports, 1897	£31,733,644
Total exports, 1897	36,997,441
Imports from U. K. to Spain, 1898	3,505,728
Exports from Spain to U.K., 1898	13,188,258

CAPITAL, Madrid. Population, including suburbs (1887), 508,405.

British Ambassador, Rt. Hon. Sir Henry Drummond Wolff, G.C.B., G.C.M.G.	5,500
Sec. of Embassy, C. F. Frederick Adam...	700
Military Attaché, Maj. Wm. Lewis White	800
2nd Secretary, Percy Wyndham	360
Commercial Attaché, H. W. B. Harrison...	725
3rd Secretary, D. E. M. Crackanthorpe ...	250
Hon. Attaché, C. Drummond Wolff.	
Vice-Consul, Arthur Jackson.	
Chaplain, Rev. F. Bullock-Webster	200
Barcelona—Consul, J. F. Roberts	600
„ *Vice-Consul*, Frederick Witty.	
Alicante—V.-Cons., Jasper W. Cumming	
Burriana—Vice-Cons., E. Harker	
Denia—Vice-Consul, Joseph R. Morand...	
Gandia, &c.—Vice-Consul, F. Romaguera	
Iviza—V.-Cons., John E. Wallis...	
Jabea—Vice-Consul, G. Guardiola	
Palamos—Vice-Consul, Pablo Matas	
Palma(Bal.Is.)—B.Cons., B. Bosch y Cerda	
Port Mahon—V.-Cons., B. Escudero	
Tarragona—Vice-Consul, T. Robinson...	
Torrevieja—Vice-Consul, Romualdo Perez	
Valencia—Vice-Consul, A. F. Ivens	
Villanueva—V.-Consul, John Webb Witty	
Bilbao—Consul, Lieut. C. S. Smith, R.N. ...	700
„ *Vice-Consul*, Victor de Larrea	unp.
Castro-Urdiales—Vice-Cons., R. V. Shade	
San Sebastian—Vice-Con., Maj. J. A. Nutt	
Santander — Vice-Consul, Winter Single	
Cadiz—Consul, A. H. Vecqueray	600
„ *Vice-Consul*, E. H. Andrewes.	
Algeciras—Vice-Consul, Capt. C. F. Cromie	450
Ayamonte—Vice-Consul, José T. Feria ...	
Cordoba—Vice-Consul, Richard E. Carr...	
Huelva—Vice-Consul, Edgar L. Ricketts...	
Jerez—Vice-Consul, Henry S. Davies	
Port St. Mary—Vice-Consul, Rbt.J. Pitman	
San Lucar—V.-Con., Adolph. J. Aparicio	
San Roque—Vice-Consul, Geo. F. Cornwell	
Seville—Vice-Consul, Edward F. Johnston	
Corunna—Consul, Capt. Chas. A. P. Talbot	600
„ *Vice-Consul*, Thomas Guyatt	
Carril and Villagarcia—V.-Cons., (vacant)	
Corcubion — Vice-Consul, Francisco del Rio	
Ferrol—Vice-Consul, Emilio Añton	
Gijon—Vice-Consul, William Penlington	
Marin (Ponte Vedra)—Vice-Consul, José Acuna y Santos	
Vigo—Vice-Consul, M. Barcena y Franco	
Vivero—Vice-Consul, Joaquin Muñiz	
Fernando Po—Cons., Sir R. D. R. Moor, K.C.M.G.	
Cons. Agent, J. E. Gibney.	
Malaga—Consul, Alexander Finn	600
„ *Vice-Consul*, Charles Cowan	
Adra—Cons. Agent, Henry Benet	
Aguilas—Vice-Consul, Thomas H. Naftel	
Almeria—V.-Cons., William May Lindsay	
Carthagena—Vice-Consul, John C. Gray...	
Garrucha and Villaricos—Vice-Consul, George Clifton Pecket	
Granada—Vice-Cons., C. E. S. Davenhill	
Linares—Vice-Consul, John M. Power.....	
Marbella—Vice-Consul, Miguel Calzado...	
Mazarron—Cons. Agent, E. G. Pearse.....	
Motril—Cons. Agent, A. de Villar	
Teneriffe—Consul, John E. Croker	500
„ *Vice-Consul*, R. C. Griffiths	

La Palma—Vice-Consul, Manuel Yanes
Las Palmas—Vice-Consul, Peter Swanston
Orotava—Vice-Consul, Peter S. Reid......
Puerto de la Luz—Consular Agent, A. H. Baylis

Madrid, 1,150 miles; transit, about 36 hours. Telegrams, per word, 3½d. and via Marseilles 5½d.

SPANISH COLONIES AND DEPENDENCIES.

Until the termination of the Spanish-American War of 1898, the Islands of Cuba and Puerto Rico, in the West Indies, and the Philippine Islands and the Sulu Archipelago in the Pacific, were part of the Spanish Empire. Under the terms of the treaty of Peace, signed 12th Dec., 1898, all the above, together with Guam, the largest of the Ladrone islands, were ceded to the United States of America. Spanish dominion was thus confined to the remaining islands in the Ladrone group, the Caroline and the Pelao islands, and the African possessions. In 1899 the German Government purchased the Ladrone, Caroline, and Pelao Islands, and the Spanish Colonial Empire came to an end, the office of Minister for the Colonies being abolished in the same year. The oversea possessions now consist of the following, which are administered as if part of Continental Spain, the head quarters of the local administration being Teneriffe, in the Canary islands:

In the Gulf of Guinea, the island of FERNANDO Po, and ANNOBOW, CORISO and ELOBY islands off the coast of French Congo. In 1891 Spain relinquished her claim to Coriso Bay, retaining, however, CAPE SAN JUAN and the right of navigation over the rivers Benito and Muni. Part of the Western Sahara forms the Spanish Protectorate of RIO DE ORO and ADRAR (230,160 square miles, population 100,000), to the north-west of which are the CANARY ISLES (area about 3,000 square miles, population 300,000), the capital being Teneriffe. In Morocco are several "Presidios"; IFRI near Cape Non, TETUAN and CEUTA (30 square miles, population 16,000) opposite Gibraltar, and the coast towns of Gomera, Alhucemas, Melilla, and the Zaffarin Islands. The total area of these possessions is about 244,000 sq. miles, with a population of about 135,000.

SWEDEN AND NORWAY.

King of Sweden and Norway, Oscar II., *born* 21 January, 1829; *suc.* 18 September, 1872; *married* 6 June, 1857, Sophia, daughter of the late Duke William of Nassau, *born* 9 July, 1836 (and has issue, 4 sons).

Heir Apparent, Oscar Gustaf Adolf, Duke of Wermland, Crown Prince, *b.* 16 June, 1858; *m.* 20 Sept., 1881, Victoria, dau. of Grand Duke of Baden, *born* 7 August, 1862.

Envoy Ext. and Minister Plenipotentiary in London, Count Carl Lewenhaupt, 52 Pont Street, S.W.

Secretary of Legation, Baron Ch. E. Ramel.

Attaché, Count Eugène von Rosen.

Consul-General, D. Danielsson, 24 Great Winchester-Street, E.C.

The Kingdoms of Sweden and Norway, now united under one sovereign, embrace between them the entire north-western peninsula of Europe, situate between lat. 55° 20'—70° 12' N. and long. 4° 37'—31° E., bounded by the Baltic Sea and Gulf of Bothnia on the east, and the Atlantic on the west. The total area is 299,377 square miles, and the population numbered 7,108,332 in December, 1896. (Sweden, 5,009,632; Norway, 2,098,700.)

British Minister, Hon. Sir Francis J. Pakenham, K.C.M.G. (Stockholm) £3,000

Sec. of Legation, Arthur J. Herbert £500
2nd Secretary, E. M. Grant Duff 360
Hon. Attachés, Alfred Bles, Shelley L. L. Scarlett.
Chaplain, Rev. Edward Shepherd, M.A....

I. SWEDEN.

Prime Minister, E. G. Boström.
Foreign Affairs (vacant).
Justice, P. S. L. Annerstedt.
Marine, G. Dyrssen.
Interior, J. E. von Krusenstjerna.
Instruction, N. O. A. Claëson.
Finance, Count H. H. Wachtmeister.
War, J. T. Crusebjörn.
Ministers sans portefeuille, S. H. Wikblad ; D. G. Restadius.

Sweden comprises the eastern half of the peninsula, and, except the capital, is divided into 24 governments, "Län," with an area of 172,877 square miles, and a population, 31 Dec. 1898, of 5,062,918 nearly all of whom are Protestants, and for the most part well educated. About 57 per cent. of the population are devoted to agriculture, about 277,000 being owners, and 49,000 tenants of the land they cultivate. The coast-line is about 1,550 miles in extent. The country for the most part is flat, with pleasant undulations, rising in the north-west to the Kölen Mountains, which separate Sweden from Norway, and may be divided into three separate districts ; the northern, forest ; central, mining ; the southern, agricultural. The lakes cover about one-twelfth of the surface. The climate in the south is favourable for producing grain. The principal articles of cultivation are the various cereals—oats, rye, barley, wheat—and potatoes ; a large quantity of oats are annually exported. The forests are very extensive, covering nearly one-half of the surface of the country, and consisting of pine. birch, fir ; these are of great importance, as supplying not only pitch and tar, but also the chief fuel. The mineral products are extremely rich ; iron of excellent quality, that known as the Dannemora iron being converted into the finest steel ; gold and silver in small proportions ; copper, lead. nickel, zinc, cobalt, alum, sulphur, porphyry, and marble. There is a railroad opening up the rich iron-ore districts of Lapland, and mineral trains run from Gellivare, to Lulea *i.e.*, about 130 English miles. Considerable mines of coal are being worked in Scania. The chief imports are coffee, wine, tobacco, and other ordinary colonial produce, coals, cloth, yarn, wool, cotton, hides, salt ; oils, wheat, rye, pork, and machinery. The chief articles of export are timber, oats, cattle, butter, iron, steel, paper, matches, iron and zinc ores, &c. The chief domestic exports to Great Britain in 1897 were butter, iron, paper and paper-making materials, and timber ; and the chief domestic imports from Great Britain in 1897 were coal, metals, wool and woollen manufactures.

Commercial travellers in Sweden are compelled to take out a licence costing 100 crowns a month, or they incur the risk of being fined.

Railways 6,433 miles in length (of which 2,283 are the property of the State) were open in January, 1899 ; and 5,442 miles of telegraph (exclusive of 3,307 railway telegraph), 178 stations, and 1,176 railway telegraph stations. There were in 1899 54,002 miles of telephone wires.

The field army of Sweden numbers 40,412 officers and men, with 240 guns and 6,891 horses ; the militia and Landstorm, 450,000 more. The navy consists of 65 steamers (314 guns), 19 being ironclads, with 6 sailing vessels. The officers and men of the navy number about 6,000, with a reserve of 121 officers, and about 20,000 men.

Revenue (estimate 1900) £7,560,958
Amount of public debt, 1 Jan., 1899 .. 15,624.625
[Expended in the construction of railways.]
Total imports, 1898 .... £25,068,797
Total exports, 1898   18,992,795
Imports from United Kingdom, 1898 7,662,138
Exports to the United Kingdom, 1898 .. 8,185,515

CAPITAL, Stockholm. Population (1898), 295,789
Consul, A. S. MacGregor 600
  Vice-Consul, C. A. E. Bolinder.
  Borgholm—Cons. Agent, G. E. Erichson
  Calmar—V.-Con., John Jeanson
  Gefle—Vice-Consul, Robert Carrick ......
  Gotland—Vice-Consul, Edward Cramér...
  Hernösand—V.-Con., Paul Burchardt ...
  Hudiksval—V.-Con., O. W. Wallberg
  Lulea—Vice-Con., A. J. Westerberg ......
  Norrköping—Vice-Cons., Gustaf Fredrik August Enhöræing ....
  Oland—Vice-Consul, Capt. Svante Olivier Theodor Matthiesen ....
  Ornsköldsvik – Vice-Consul, HenricÖhngren
  Oscarshamn—Vice-Consul, O. Wingren...
  Skelleftea—V.-Con. O. V. Vahlberg ......
  Söderhamn—Vice-Cons., J. P. Myhre......
  Sundsval—V.-Cons., Carl Emil Bredenberg
  Umea—Vice-Consul, Wilhelm Glas.........
  Westervik—Vice-Con., Johan C. Tenger..
  Gottenburg—Consul, John Duff ....
    ,,   *Vice-Consul*, Richard Duff ....
  Carlscrona—V.-Con., Adolf Palander ...
  Halmstad—V.-Con., T. Schéle ....
  Helsingborg—V.-Cons., Carl Westrup ...
  Landskrona—V.-Con., Fred. E. Neess ...
  Malmö—V.-Con., P. M. Flensburg ......
  Marstrand—V.-Cons., C. A. Christenson.
  Strömstad—Vice-Consul, Wilhelm Theodor Lundgren ....
  Uddevalla and Lysekihl—Vice-Consul, William Franklin Thorburn...............
  Warberg—V.-C. C. Robt., T. Jobsón ...
  Ystad—V.-Cons., Emil A. Borg ....
Stockholm, 1,132 miles ; transit, 2 days.
Telegrams, per word, 3½d.

.II. NORWAY.

Council of State at Christiania.

President of the Council of Ministers, Minister of State and Chief for the Department of Public Accounts, J. W. C. Steen.
Defence, Major-General, P. T. Holst.
Ecclesiastical Affairs and Public Instruction V. A. Wexelsen.
Justice and Police, E. Löchen.
Interior, O. A. Quam.
Public Works, H. H. T. Nysom.
Finance and Customs, E. Sunde.
State Secretary, H. Lehmann.

Delegation of the Council at Stockholm.

Minister of State, O. A. Blehr ; *Ministers*, G. A. Thilesen, J. G. Lövland.
General Secretary, H. Schlytter.

Norway, an independent kingdom, since 1814 united with Sweden under the same King of the House of Bernadotte (the fundamental law of the 17th of May (4th of November), 1814, the Act of Union with Sweden of the 6th of August, 1815). The Parliament of 114 members is called the "Storthing," which is divided into two sections, chosen by itself to discuss projected Bills, called "Odelsthing" and "Lagthing." The western and northern portion of the peninsula is about 1,100 miles in length, its greatest width about 250 miles. It is divided into 20 provinces, or amts, and comprises an area of 124,500 sq. miles, with a population (1898) of 2,168 000. The coast-line is extensive, deeply indented with numerous fiords, and fringed with an immense number of rocky islands. The surface is mountainous, consisting of elevated and barren table-lands, separated by deep and narrow valleys. The cultivated area is about one-thirtieth part of the country; forests cover nearly one-fourth; the rest consists of highland pastures or uninhabitable mountains. Agriculture, though pursued with some vigour of late, is unable to furnish sufficient produce for home consumption; hence it has been necessary to import considerable quantities of corn, meat, and pork. The fisheries give employment to a large part of the population throughout the year. The most important are cod and herring; the exports of these with other sea-products and fish-oil were valued at £2,495,585 in 1898. The mineral products are similar to, but far less valuable than, those of Sweden. Timber-dressing, mechanical engineering, textile manufactures, ship-building, and pulp-making are the principal departments of Norwegian industry. The exports of produce of the forests were valued at £2,209,983 in 1898, the value of wood-pulp alone being £953.590. The imports consist chiefly of the necessary articles of consumption. The chief exports consist of timber, fish, oil and other products of the fisheries, pulp, skins and furs, nails, minerals, ice, condensed milk, margarine, butter, cattle, &c. The principal domestic exports from Norway to the United Kingdom in 1898 were paper and paper-making materials and timber; and the principal domestic imports from the United Kingdom in 1898 were coal, steamships, Manchester goods, metals, and woollens.

The navy consists of 8 ironclads, 3 cruisers, 29 torpedo vessels, and 10 gunboats, with 5,150 officers and men. The mercantile marine, 31 Dec., 1898, consisted of 7,049 vessels, of 1,558,378 tons. The army by law consists of 18,000 men of the line, and cannot be increased without the consent of the Storthing, but the number of trained men and officers under different names is about 36,000. Military service is obligatory and personal after the completion of the twenty-third year. The period of service is five years in the line, four years in the "landværn," and four years in the "landsturm." The debt was incurred chiefly in the construction of railways (1,119 miles open). The length of telegraphs belonging to the state in January, 1899, was 7,485 miles.

*Revenue, 1898–99 .... Estimated £3,931,926
*Expenditure, 1898–99 .... do. 4,768,273
Public debt, 1 July, 1899.................... 10,938.0 12
Total imports, 1898 15,428,360
Total exports, 1898 8,774,725
Imports from United Kingdom, 1898 . 4,463,073
Exports to United Kingdom, 1898 3,650,016

CAPITAL, Christiania. Population (1899), 221,073.
Consul-Gen., Hon. Chas. Saunders Dundas £900
 Vice-Consul. Edward F. Grav 200
 Arendal—Vice-Consul, Morten Kallevig .
 Bergen—V.-Consul, Albert N. Gran .....
 Bodö—Vice-Consul, Nils Falck ......

* The revenue estimated for the nine months ended 31 March, 1900, was £3,330,380, and the expenditure £4,310,307.

Christiansand — Vice-Consul, Ferdinand Reinhardt ....
Christiansund—V.-Con., Gram Parelius
Drammen—Vice-Consul, Anders Sveaas ..
Egersund—Vice-Consul, O. M. Puntervold
Farsund—Vice-Consul, Peter I. Suhdt ...
Flekkefiord—Vice-Consul, J. P. M. Eyde
Frederickshald—V.-C., W. Klein ....
Fredericksdad—V.-C., Carsten Thiis ......
Hammerfest—V.-C., George Robertson ...
Haugesund—Vice-Cons., Johan Jacobsen
Kragerö—Vice-Consul, Tom Parker ......
Laurvig—Vice-Con., Frederick Dahm ...
Lofoten—Vice-Cons., Henry J. Church ...
Mandal—Vice-Con., Tönnes F. Andorsen
Molde—Vice-Consul, Peter F. Dahl........
Mosjöen—Vice-Consul, Erik Bathen ......
Moss—Vice-Consul, Jörgen H. Vogt .,,...
Namsos—V.-Con., Johan Sommerschield
Porsgrund.—V-C., James Franklin ......
Risör—Vice-Consul, A. F. Finne ....
Stavanger—Vice-Consul, Eric Berentsen
Tromsö—Vice-Consul, J. H. Giæver ......
Trondhjem—V.-Con.. Francis Kjeldsberg
Vadsö—V.-C., Bernhard Akermand ......
Vardö—V.-C., Karl J. Schelderup Holmboe ....

Christiania, 656 miles; transit, 59 hours. Telegrams, per word, 3*d*.

SWITZERLAND, REPUBLIC OF.

† *President* (1899), Col. Müller... .... £540
Vice-President (1899), W. Hauser.
Minister for Foreign Affairs, The President.
Commerce, Industry, &c., A. Deucher.
Pres. of National Council, F. Streiff.
Pres. of Council of States, Dr. A. Brüstleim.
Federal Chanc., G. Ringier, of Zofingen (*Aargau*).
Federal Tribunal (*Lausanne*), 14 members and 9 representatives. *President*, Dr. Ch. Soldan.
Director, International Posts, Edmond Höhn.
Direc., International Telegraphs, Emil Frey.
International Industry & Fine Arts. Henri Morel.
Director Internat. Railway Offices, Numa Droz.
Director-General of Posts, Henri Lutz.
 „ „ *of Telegraphs*, Conrad Fehr.
Department of War, E. Ruffy.
Interior, A. Lachenal.
Justice, E. Brenner.

Minister in London, Charles Daniel Bourcart, 52, Lexham Gardens, W.

The Helvetia of the Romans, a Federal Republic of Central Europe, situated between 45° 50′—47° 84′ N. lat. and 5° 58′—10° 30′ E. long. It is composed of 22 Cantons, of very dissimilar size, united under a Constitution dated 29 May, 1874, and comprises a total area of 15,469 square miles, with a population of 2,933,334 in 1888, who are divided between Roman Catholics, 41 per cent., and Protestants, 59 per cent., Jews numbering 7,400, and others 11,000. The population is formed by three nationalities, distinct by their language, as German 71 per cent., French 21 per cent., Italian 6 per cent., and Romanshe (in the Grisons), 1½ per cent. The most important cities are Zürich, pop. (1896) 147.877, Geneva, 80,778, and Basle, 88,853. It is the most mountainous country in Europe, having the Alps, covered with perennial snow and glaciers, rising from 5,000 to 15,213 feet in height, not only along the whole of its southern

† The President is elected on Dec. 21 of each year, and remains in office until the same day of the ensuing year; he is *generally* succeeded by the Vice-President.

and eastern frontiers, but throughout the chief part of its interior; and the Jura mountains in the north-west. Agriculture is followed chiefly in the valleys, where wheat, oats, maize, barley, flax, hemp, and tobacco are produced, and nearly all English fruits and vegetables are grown. The forests cover about one-sixth of the whole surface. The manufactures consist chiefly of silks, cottons, linen, lace, thread, woollens, &c.; clocks and watches have long been the staple products of Geneva and Neufchâtel, while leather, gloves, pottery, tobacco, and snuff, cheese, &c., are made. Being an inland country, the direct trade with the United Kingdom is comparatively small. In 1894 there were 2,407 miles of railway in working order, and 4,693 miles of telegraph.

The military establishment on a war footing, including landwehr, consists of 209,603 men—staff 1,035, infantry 160,966, cavalry 6,048, artillery 29,597, engineers 7,357, others 4,600. To this number must be added the landsturm, or final reserve, of 276,161 more.

The legislative power is vested in a Parliament, consisting of two Chambers, a National Council of 147 members, and a Council of States of 44 members; both Chambers united are called the Federal Assembly, and the members of the National Council are elected for three years, an election taking place in October. The executive power is in the hands of a Federal Council of 7 members, elected by the Federal Assembly, presided over by the President of the Confederation. The President has a salary of £540; the Vice-President and other members of the Federal Council £480 each. The members of the Federal Council are elected for three years; each year the Federal Assembly elects from this council the President and the Vice-President; they are elected for one year, the five other members for three years. Not more than one of the same canton may be elected member of the Federal Council.

Public revenue, 1897	£3,662,261
Public expenditure, 1897	3,492,694
National debt, 1895	2,987,600
Imports, 1897-8	42,231,405
Exports, 1897-8	28,938,333
Federal Reserve, 1890, £1,493,563; 1896	2,436,433
Imports from United Kingdom, 1897...	2,161,720
Exports to United Kingdom, 1897	5,842,840

CAPITAL, Berne. Population, 1896, 48,782.

British Minister, Frederick R. St. John	£1,450
2nd *Sec.*, H. C. Lowther	450
Chaplain, Rev. J. R. Dutton Thompson	
Berne—Consul, Gaston de Muralt	
Geneva—Consul, Sir George Phillippo	
,, *Vice-Consul*, Lewis Stein	
Lausanne—Consul, Alfred Galland	
Zürich—Consul-Gen. (to the German and Italian speaking Cantons), Henry Angst	
,, *Vice-Consul*, John C. Milligan	
Lucerne—Vice-Consul, L. Falck	

Berne, transit, 22 hours. Telegrams, per word, 3d.

TIBET (see p. 474).

TONQUIN (see p. 475).

TRANSVAAL (see pp. 593 to 596).

TRIPOLI.

Governor-Gen., Hashem Bey, *appointed* March, 1899.

A Vilayet, or province of the Ottoman Empire, on the northern coast of Africa, and the most easterly of the Barbary States, extending from the frontiers of Tunis to those of Egypt, a distance of about 900 miles, and inland to the south a distance of about 800 miles. Formerly (1713-1835) it was under a native (Karamanly) dynasty and passed under direct Turkish control in 1835. It comprises the four sub-provinces or Mutessariflicks of Tripoli, Khoms, Jabel-el-Sharb, Fezzan, and Benghazi or Cyrenaica, the latter being under the direct government of Constantinople since 1875. It has an area of 410,000 square miles, and a population of 800,000. There are no rivers in the country, and, the rainfall being precarious, a good harvest can only be reckoned on every four or five years. The military force of the country now numbers about 10,000 men. The revenue is chiefly raised by a poll-tax, regulated according to the wealth of each individual, and by tithes. Barley, dates, olives, oranges, lemons and vegetables are produced, and the principal imports are metals, British and other European manufactures, tea, beads, wines and spirits, besides a number of articles for barter in Wadai, Bornu, and the Western Soudan, whither caravans proceed regularly from Tripoli. The principal articles of export are ostrich feathers, ivory, skins, sponges, hides, esparto grass, cattle and horses. The ancient ruins in Cyrenaica, *i.e.*, at Cyrene, Ptolemais, and Apollonia are interesting to explorers as well as those at Leptis Magna, which is close to Khoms, or 70 miles from the city of Tripoli; agricultural colonies of Cretan Moslem refugees are being formed in the neighbourhood. The town of Benghazi has a population of about 15,000, consisting of Arabs, Greeks, Maltese, and a few Levantines. The commerce in cereals, wool, cattle for Malta, and other agricultural produce, is considerable, when a sufficient rainfall causes good harvests.

Total imports, 1898	£385,400
Total exports, 1898	401,500
Imports from U.K., 1898	131,100
Exports to U.K., 1898	157,000

CAPITAL, Tripoli. Population, about 40,000.

Consul-General, Thomas S. Jago	£800
Vice-Consul, Alfred Dickson	350
Hon. Physician, Dr. Angelo Mizzi	
Khoms—Vice-Consul, Joseph Tate	
Benghazi—Consul, Justin C. W. Alvarez...	500
Derna—Cons. Agent, G. Farrugia	

Telegrams, per word, 8½d.

TUNIS.

(*French Protectorate.*)

Bey, H.H. Sidi Ali Pasha; *born*, 1817; *suc.* 28 October, 1882.

Heir Presumptive,

French Resident General, M. Millet (14th Nov. 1894).

The Regency of Tunis, formerly a tributary dependency of the Ottoman Empire, may now be considered an informally annexed dependency of France, nominally under the dominion of the Bey, but in reality under the control of a French Resident. By treaty, 12 May, 1881, "the occupation is to cease when the French and Tunisian authorities recognize by common accord that the local government is capable of maintaining order." By a convention signed 10 July, 1882, France administers the country and collects the taxes in the name of the Bey, who is granted a civil list of £37,500, and the princess a sum of £30,000. It is in the north of Africa, situated on the Mediterranean, east of Algeria, between lat. 32° 20'—37° 25' N. and long. 70° 40'—11° 15' E. It comprises an area of 44,920 square miles, and has about 1,500,000 inhabitants, of which there are about 25,000 Europeans.

The chief town, Tunis, is the largest and most commercial city of Barbary, with a population of 145,000, of whom 45,000 are Jews and 28,000 Christians (8,000 Italians, 7,000 Maltese and 3,000 French). It possesses considerable manufactures of silk and woollen stuffs, shawls, carpets, mantles, fez caps, bernouses, also otto of roses and jessamin. The chief exports are grain, oil, wool, and esparto grass. N.E. of Tunis is the site of the ancient city of Carthage. There are 258 miles of railway and 1,245 of telegraph.

Revenue, 1894	£1,023,899
Expenditure, 1894	869,459
Debt	5,656,750
Total Imports, 1894	1,676,909
Total Exports, 1894	1,477,310
Domestic imports from U. K., 1898	299,409
Total exports to the U. K., 1898	231,064

Consul General, E. J. L. Berkeley, C.B.	900
V.-Cons., G. C. Lascelles	150
,, R. Schembri	

Hon. Physician Dr. Ettore Camilleri.
Bizerta—Cons. Agent, Hon. Terence Bourke
Gabes—Cons. Agent, F. Calleja
Galippia—Cons. Agent, ...
Genba—Cons. Agent, Joseph Pariente ......
Mehdieh—Cons. Agent, G. Violante ....
Monastir—Cons. Agent, Francesco Portelli
Sfax—Vice-Consul, Silvio Leonardi ......
Suza—Vice-Consul, William Galea ....
Tunis, 1,350 miles. Telegrams, per word, 3*d.*

TURKEY (THE OTTOMAN EMPIRE).

Sultan, Abdul Hamid II., *b.* 22 September, 1842; *proclaimed* 31 August, 1876.
Heir Presumptive, his brother, Mehemmed Reshad Effendi, *born* 3 Nov., 1844.
Prime Minister (Grand Vizier), Khalil Rifaat Pacha.
Foreign Affs. (Kharidjie-Naziri), Tewfik Pacha.
Interior, Memdouh Pacha.
Finance, Reshad Bey.
Justice, Abdurrahman Pacha.
Public Instruction, Zuhdi Pacha.
Marine, Hassan Pacha.
War, Riza Pacha.
Public Works, Zihni Pacha.
Pious Foundations (Evkafs), Ghalib Pacha.
President of Council of State, Said Pacha.
Mines and Forests, Selim Pacha Melhamé.
Turkish Ambassador to France, Salih Munir Bey; *Russia*, Husni Pacha; *Germany*, Tewfik Pacha; *Austria-H.*, Mahmoud Nedim Bey; *Italy*, Mehemed Reshid Bey; *U.S.A.*, Ali Ferrouh Bey.

Ambassador in London, Costaki Pacha Anthopoulo, 1 Bryanston Square, W.
Councillor of Embassy, Hamid Bey.
1st Sec., Edhem Bey.
2nd do., Faid Ibrahim Bey; Abdul Hak Hussem Bey.
Imam, Mehmed Redjaii Effendi.
Consul-General, Emin Effendi Férédjullah, 7 Union Court, Old Broad Street. E.C.
This Empire, consists of the following districts:—

I TURKEY IN EUROPE, formerly very extensive, is now reduced to 66,500 square miles, with a population of 4,668,000. (This, however, does not include Bulgaria, Eastern Roumelia, and Bosnia, which jointly have an area of 58,739 square miles,

and a population of 4,320,110.) The total population includes about 700,000 Turks. 1,500,000 Albanians, and 1,300,000 Greeks, Bulgarians, and Wallachians. About 2,000,000 are Mohammedans. A great part of the surface is covered with mountains of moderate elevation. Since the Balkans no longer lie within the limits of the empire (although Turkey is entitled to occupy their passes in case of war), the loftiest mountains are those of the Rhodope or Despoto Dagh (7,464 ft.) in the east, and the mountain-ranges of Albania in the west. To the latter belongs the Skhar Dagh (10,007 ft.), the culminating point of the whole Balkan peninsula. Rivers are numerous, the principal of which are the Vardar, the Struma, and the Maritza. The soil is for the most part fertile, but owing to various causes little progress has been made in agriculture The cultivated products are maize, rice, cotton, barley, millet, sesame and other oil-seeds, and tobacco; the natural products are the pine, beech, oak, lime, and ash, with the palm, maple, sycamore, walnut, chestnut, carob, box, myrtle, laurel, &c., south of the Balkans; large forests of pine and fir in the north-west; the olive, orange, citron, vine, peach, plum, and fruit trees in Albania. The breeding of sheep is carried on extensively, and wool constitutes an important article of trade. The mineral products are iron in large quantity, lead blended with silver, copper, sulphur, salt, alum, and coal. Its manufactures are almost entirely domestic, such as woollen and cotton stuffs, carpets, shawls, leather, firearms, with dyeing and printing works. In Europe, 838 miles of railway are being worked, and 1,136 in Asia, and about 1,000 miles are being constructed in Europe and Asia.

II. TURKEY IN ASIA, the larger of the two divisions, comprises Asia Minor, Syria, including Palestine, the greater part of Armenia (where the recent massacres and reprisals originated), and Kurdistan, Mesopotamia (the valley of the Euphrates and Tigris), and the western portion of Arabia, bordering the Red Sea, with the district of El Hasa on the eastern side of the Persian Gulf; having a total area of 680,000 square miles, and an estimated population of 16,333,000 inhabitants. To this number must be added the autonomous island of Samos (180 sq. miles, pop. 40,513), and Cyprus (see p 530), which pays an annual tribute. Of the total population about 6,800,000 are Turks, 5,300,000 Syrians and Arabs, 1,000,000 Greeks, and 12,000,000 Mohammedans.

In AFRICA, Turkey rules Tripoli and Barka (399,000 sq. miles, pop. 1,010,000), and levies a heavy tribute upon Egypt.

Nominally, therefore, the Turkish Empire has an area of 1,710,000 square miles, with about 39,500,000 inhabitants, but of the vast territories only 1,145,500 square miles, with 22,011,000 inhabitants, are under the direct rule of the Turks, the rest paying a tribute or merely acknowledging the suzerainty of the Porte.

It was arranged by the Berlin Treaty that Bulgaria, Servia, Montenegro, and Greece should take upon themselves a portion of the Turkish debt, but little appears to have been received from these emancipated or aggrandized States. The tribute from Eastern Roumelia, fixed by Organic Statute at £218,180, but since reduced to £138,200, is, as a rule, punctually paid by Bulgaria.

The TURKISH ARMY on a peace footing numbers

(actually) 10,000 officers and 170,000 non-commissioned officers and men, and is composed of 292 battalions of infantry, 202 squadrons of cavalry, 165 field batteries, 46 mountain batteries, 15 horse batteries, 39 companies of engineers, and 1,356 guns, besides 132 companies of garrison artillery. These are formed into seven army corps, with headquarters at Constantinople, Adrianople, Monastir, Erzingan, Damascus, Baghdad, and Sana (Turkish Arabia), an independent division at Tripoli, and another in the Hedjaz. In time of war these can be supplemented by twelve army corps of redifs, and an indefinite quantity of *mustahfiz*. It is also proposed to form 100 regiments of local militia (Hamidieh cavalry), of which 60 are already enrolled, and in case of emergency it is probable that over 1,000,000 men of all categories could be called to arms.

The NAVY consists of 102 steamers, all of a more or less obsolete type (including 18 ironclads), and 25 torpedo boats, with a total peace strength of about 15,000 men.

The commercial marine of Turkey consists of 106 steamers, 49,500 tons, and 169 sailing vessels, 44,471 tons (Oct. 14, 1897).

Commerce.—The exports include tobacco, cereals, fruits, silk, opium, mohair, cotton, coffee, skins, wool, oil-seeds, valonia, carpets, &c., and are largely derived from the Asiatic provinces. Recently large quantities of wine and raisins for the manufacture of wine have been exported. Among the imports, cotton and woollen manufactures take the foremost rank. Since the establishment of the Anatolian railway, by German enterprise, the export of cereals, chiefly malting barley, has largely increased. The British Chamber of Commerce was established at Stamboul, Constantinople, in 1887; *Pres.*, Sir Wm. Whitthall; *Sec.* H. E. Mountain.

The principal domestic exports to the United Kingdom in 1897 were corn, fruit, wool and woollens, and the chief domestic imports from the United Kingdom in 1897 were coal, Manchester goods, metals and woollens.

Navigation.—The total shipping in 1896-7 was 38,288,639 tons, of which 12,820,050, or one third, was British. No. of vessels 188,961.

Finance.—Sir Edgar Vincent's report of December, 1896, estimates an annual deficit of £1,253,070, but points out certain reforms by which this can be avoided. The total amount of the loans negotiated since the year 1854, and still outstanding, is £131,500,000, and additional debts bringing the total to £163,050,000 (Russian war indemnity outstanding £31,225,000, out of a total £32,100,000 originally owed; indemnity to Russian subjects £50,000 out of a total of £318,180, and £275,000 due to the Damascus Railway).

Revenue, 1897-98 (estimated) £16,050,270
Expenditure, 1897-98 ,, ... 16,578,360
Turkish Debt (Loans), 1896 131,500,000
Indemnities owed, 1896 31,550,000
Total Imports, 1893-4 20,157,335
Total Exports, 1893-4 11,727,787
Domestic imports from U. K., 1898 ... 6,530,070
Total exports to United Kingdom, 1898 4,880,792

CAPITAL, Constantinople. Pop. (1885), 871,561.
British Ambassador, His Excellency The Rt. Hon.
  Sir Nicholas Roderick O'Conor, G.C.B. £8,000
Sec. of Embassy, M. W. E. de Bunsen, C.B. 1,000
Military Attaché, Colonel J. G. Ponsonby... 800
Judge of Sup. Court, Sir E. L. O'Malley ... 1,000
  Assistant Judge, H. W. de Sausmarez ... 800

	£
2nd Secretary, G. H. Barclay, C.M.G.	405
Chief Dragoman, Adam S. J. Block, C.M.G.	925
2nd Secretary, H. J. O'Beirne	330
Commercial Attaché, E. Weakley	800
Consul, Harry Charles Augustus Eyres ...	800
Chaplain, Rev. H. K. Anketell	300
Physician, Edward Dalzel Dickson, M.D......	700
3rd Secretary, H. C. Norman	150
,, Hon. E. S. Scott	350
,, Claud Russell	250
Hon. Attaché, Jas. H. Monk.	
Dragoman at Consulate, C. G. Stavrides, C.M.G.	750
2nd Dragoman, H. Marinitch, C.M.G.......	750
Dragoman & Archivist, Edward C. Blech..	650
3rd Dragoman, G. H. Fitzmaurice, C.M.G ..	510
Vice-Cons. Interpreter, Alex. T. Waugh ...	400
Vice-Consul Philip C. Sarell...................	390
Brussa—*Vice-Consul,* E. Gilbertson (*actg.*)	
Dardanelles—*Vice-Consul,* F. E. Crow ...	400
Dede-Agatch—*Vice-Consul,* Jacques A. Missir	
Enos—*Vice-Consul,* John Rossy	400
Gallipoli—*Vice-Consul,* W. Grech	
Ineboli—*Cons. Agent,* Victor Velasti	
Ismidt—*Cons.-Agent,* Percy Wills	
Panderma—*Cons. Agent,* S. Christides ...	
Rodosto—*Vice-Consul,* Edmond Dussi......	
Scutari (Albania) — *Vice-Cons.,* C. M. Hallward	400
Aleppo—*Consul,* H. D. Barnham, C.M.G. ...	600
,, *Vice-Consul,* John Falarga	
Adana—*Vice-Cons.,* P. H. H. Massy........	
Alexandretta — *Vice-Consul,* Augustine Catoni	
Antioch & Swedia—*Vice-Consul,* Joseph Douëk	
Angora—*Consul,* H. S. Shipley, C.M.G.	600
Konieh—*Vice-Cons.,* Arthur D. Keun.	
Bagdad (Turkish Arabia)—*Consul-General,* Major P. J. Melvill. *Rs. 2,500 per month. Paid by India.*	
Basrah—*Cons.,* A. C. Wratislaw	700
Kerbala, &c.—*Cons. Agent,* Nawab Mohamed Ibrahim Khan..............	
Mosul—*Cons. Agent,* Nimrod Rassam ...	
Beyrut—*Cons.-Gen.,* R. Drummond Hay ...	1,000
,, *V.-Con.,* Walter J. Heathcote	400
Haiffa—*Vice-Cons.,* James H. Monahan......	400
Latakia—*Vice-Consul,* Nicholas Vitali ...	
Tripoli—*Vice-Consul.* Dr. J. Abela........	
Safid—*V.-Cons.,* J. Micklasiewitz	
Sidon—*Vice-Consul,* S. Abela	
Bosna-Serai—*Con.-Gen.,* Edwd. B. Freeman	700
Damascus—*Consul,* W. S. Richards	500
Erzeroum—*Consul,* Harry H. Lamb	700
Diarbekir—*Vice-Consul,* Jno. Fras. Jones	400
Bitlis—*Vice-Consul* (vacant)	400
Kharput—*Vice-Cons.,* (vacant)	400
Van—*V.-Cons.,* F. R. Maunsell	500
Jeddah—*Consul,* G. P. Devey..................	700
Vice-Cons., Shaikh Mohammad Hussain	
Hodeida—*Vice-Con.,* Ahmed Tamiz-ud-din	200
Jerusalem—*Consul,* John Dickson	800
Jaffa—*Cons. Agent,* Haim Amzalak	
Salonica—*Consul-Gen.,* Sir A. Biliotti, K.C.M.G.	900
Cavalla—*Vice-Cons.,* Stanislas Pecchioli..	
Drama—*Vice-Consul,*	
Janina—*Cons. Agent,* Charles Roberts ...	
Preveso—*Vice-Consul,*	
Serres—*Vice-Consul,* Constantine Capety	250
Stratoni—*Vice-Consul,* L. Chevallier	
Uscub—*Vice-Consul,* R. A. Fontana	400

Smyrna—Con.-Gen., H. A. Cumberbatch, C.M.G.	£900
,, *Vice-Consul*, Chas. S. Hampson...	400
,, *Clerk*, E. F. A. Eldridge	200
Adalia—Vice-Consul, Gustave A. Keun...	
Aidin—Vice-Cons., E. Hadkinson	
Aivali, &c.—Vice-Cons., Assimaki Eliopulo	
Mitylene—Vice-Consul, Fredk. Hadkinson	
Rhodes—Vice-Consul, T. C. E. Macaulay	400
Samos—Consul, Denys Louis Marc	
Scala Nuova—Vice-Consul, John Alexachi	
Scio & Tchesmé—Vice-Con., J. Quintana ...	
Vourlah—Cons. Agent, N. Crindiropulo...	
Trebizond—Cons., Henry Zohrab Longworth	500
Samsoon—Cons. Agent, H. de Cortanze...	
Sivas—V.-Cons., Capt. W. J. Anderson	500

Constantinople, 1,814 miles; transit, by ordinary daily train, 5 days; by express, twice weekly, 72 hours. A favourite route is *via* Marseilles per Messageries steamer, 5 to 8 days; from Liverpool by sea is 14 days. Telegrams, per word, 6½d. Smyrna, 6 days. Telegrams, per word, 6½d. and 11d.

UNITED STATES OF AMERICA.

(See also p. 609.)

President, William McKinley, *born* 29 Jan. 1843; came into office 4 March, 1897 (until 4 March, 1901)	£10,000
Vice-President, Hon.	1,600
Sec. of State, Hon. John Hay	1,600
,, *Treasury*, Hon. Lyman J. Gage ...	1,600
,, *War*, Hon. Elihu Root	1,600
,, *Navy*, Hon. John D. Long	1,600
,, *Interior*, Hon. Ethan A. Hitchcock.	1,600
,, *Agriculture*, Hon. James Wilson	1,600
Postmaster-General, Hon. C. Emory Smith	1,600
Attorney-General, Hon. John W. Griggs...	1,600
Chief Justice of Supreme Court, Hon. Melville Weston Fuller	2,000

American Ambassador to France, Horace Porter ; *Germany*, Andrew D. White *Italy*, William F. Draper ; *Russia*, Charlemagne Tower

Envoy Extr. to Austria-H., Addison C. Harris ; *Turkey*, Oscar Strauss. ...

Office of Embassy, 123 Victoria Street, S.W.	
Ambassador Extraord. & Plenipotentiary in London, Hon. Jos. H. Choate, *Address*, Carlton House Terrace, S.W.	3,500
Sec. to Ambassador, W. Bayard Cutting	
Secretary of Embassy, Henry White	525
2nd *Secretary*, John Ridgely Carter, 15, Chesham St., S.W.	400
3rd *Secretary*, Joseph H. Choate	240
Naval Attaché, Lieut.-Comm. J. C. Colwell	
Military Attaché, Maj.-General S. Sumner	
Consul-Gen. in London, William McKinley Osborne, 12 St. Helen's Place, E.C. ...	1,500
Vice & Deputy do., Richard Westacott	
Deputy Consul-General, Francis W. Frigout	
Consular Office, 12 St. Helen's Pl., Bishopsgate St. E.C.	
Despatch Agent, B. F. Stevens, 4 Trafalgar Sq., W.C.	

A Federal Republic, consisting of 45 partially independent States, 5 organized and 1 unorganized Territory, occupies the central portion of North America, between the Atlantic and Pacific Oceans, in lat. 25°—49° N. and long. 67°—124° 30′ W. The area is estimated at 3,581,885 square miles, of which rivers and lakes cover 38,400 square miles. This area includes the vast district of Alaska, in the extreme north-west of the continent, purchased from Russia, 18th October, 1867, comprising 577,390 square miles. About one-third of the country is estimated to be in a state of cultivation. The population of the whole of the States and Territories, according to the Census of 1890, was 62,622,250. In 1892 the Indians on reservation numbered 133,382 ; off reservation, 115,891 (not including 58,806 civilized Indians) ; Chinese, 107,475 ; Japanese, 2,039 ; and Alaska, 31,795 (23,274 Indians) ; in addition to which figures no official data will be given before the census of 1900. The increase in the ten years, 1880-1890, was 12,466,467.

Its coast-line on both oceans is reckoned to have a length of about 13,200 miles, excluding the numerous bays and sounds, besides 3,620 miles on the great lakes. The principal river is the mighty Mississippi-Missouri, formed by the confluence of these two noble streams, traversing the whole country from north to south, and having a course of 4,500 miles to its mouth in the Gulf of Mexico ; with many large affluents, the chief of which are the Yellowstone, Nebraska, Arkansas, Ohio, and Red rivers. The rivers flowing into the Atlantic and Pacific Oceans are comparatively small ; among the former may be noticed the Hudson, Delaware, Susquehanna, Potomac, and Savannah ; of the latter, the Columbia, Sacramento, and Colorado. The Mobile and Colorado of Texas fall into the Gulf of Mexico, also the Rio Grande, a large river partly forming the boundary with Mexico. The areas of the water-basins have been estimated as follows :—rivers flowing to the Pacific, 644,040 square miles ; to the Atlantic, 488,877 ; and to the Gulf of Mexico, 1,683,325 square miles, of which 1,257,547 are drained by the Mississippi-Missouri. The chain of the Rocky Mountains separates the western portion of the territory from the remainder, all communication being carried on over certain elevated passes, several of which are now traversed by railroads ; west of these, bordering the Pacific coast, the Cascade Mountains and Sierra Nevada form the outer edge of a high tableland, consisting in great part of stony and sandy desert, and in which occurs the Great Salt Lake, extending to the Rocky Mountains. Eastward, the country is a vast, gently undulating plain, with a general slope southwards towards the marshy flats of the Gulf of Mexico, extending to the Atlantic, interrupted only by the Alleghany Mountains, of inferior elevation, in the Eastern States. Nearly the whole of this plain, from the Rocky Mountains to some distance beyond the Mississippi, consists of immense treeless savannahs and prairies of luxuriant grass. In the Eastern States (which form the more settled and most thickly inhabited portion of the territory) large forests of valuable timber, as beech, birch, maple, oak, pine, spruce, elm, ash, walnut ; and in the south, live-oak, water-oak, magnolia, palmetto, tulip-tree, cypress, &c., still exist, the remnants of the wooded region which formerly extended over all the Atlantic slope, but into which great inroads have been made by the advance of civilization. The Mississippi valley is eminently fertile. The mineral kingdom produces in great abundance copper, iron, coal, lime, salt, and lead, which in Missouri, Colorado, and Idaho appear inexhaustible ; there are also rich lead-mines in Illinois and Wisconsin. California produces silver, copper, and lead, and gold in large quantities.

The financial condition of the United States of America exerts a great influence on that of other nations. The following is a statement of the debt on the 1st November, 1899:—

Two per cent. bonds	$25,364,500
Three per cent. bonds	198,678,720
Four per cent. bonds and certificates	722,005,800
Five per cent. bonds	100,000,000
Debt on which interest has ceased	1,210,030
Bonds issued to Pacific Railroads and not yet presented	53,000
Debt bearing no interest	388,762,071
Certificates and Treasury notes, offset by cash	656,664,903

Total debt	2,092,739,024
Less cash and reserve in Treasury	946,056,443

Actual indebtedness $1,156,682,581

On Oct. 1, 1898, the actual indebtedness was $1,101,535,205.

The total decrease in the debt since August 31, 1865, when, after deducting the cash in the treasury, it amounted to $2,756,431,571, to Nov. 1, 1899, has been $1,599,748,990.

Balance Sheet for Year ending June 30, 1899.

RECEIPTS.

Customs	$205,128,482
Internal Revenue	273,437,162
Miscellaneous sources	36,394,976

$515,960,620

EXPENDITURE.

Civil service and miscellaneous	$119,191,256
War department	229,841,254
Navy department	63,942,104
Indians	12,805,711
Pensions	139,394,929
Interest on public debt	39,896,925
For the sinking fund	34,567

$605,106,746

The total income for the previous year was $405,321,335; and the expenditure, including sinking fund, $443,408,333.

The NAVY of the United States on the 1st November, 1899, consisted of the *Regular Navy:*—First-class battleships, 12; first-class battleships (sheathed), 3; second-class battleship, 1; armoured cruisers, 2; armoured cruisers (sheathed), 3; armoured ram, 1; steel single-turret monitors, 4; double-turreted monitors, 6; iron single-turreted monitors, 9; protected cruisers, 13; protected cruisers (sheathed), 8; unprotected cruisers, 4; gun-boats, 12; light-draft gun-boats, 3; composite gun-boats, 6; training-ship (Naval Academy), 1; special class, 2; gun-boats under 500 tons, 19; torpedo-boat destroyers, 16; steel torpedo-boats, 36; submarine torpedo-boat, 1; wooden torpedo-boat, 1; iron cruising vessels, 5; wooden cruising vessels, 7; sailing vessels (wooden), 6; tugs, 17; wooden steam vessels unfit for sea service, 11; wooden sailing vessels unfit for sea service, 6; total, 215; and of the *Auxiliary Navy:*—Merchant vessels converted into auxiliary cruisers, 7; converted gun-boats, 25; converted tugs, 27; colliers, 17; special supply vessels, 12; total, 88. Enlisted men (active list), 14,501; commissioned officers (active list), 1,299; warrant officers (active list), 231.

Marine Corps: Commiss. officers (active list), 211; privates & non-comm. officers (do.), 6,062.

The REGULAR ARMY at present consists of 2,208 officers and 62,376 enlisted men, and the *Volunteer Army* of 1,524 officers and 33,050 enlisted men, making a total of 3,732 officers and 95,426 enlisted men and an aggregate of 99,158.

The Government of the United States is, by the Constitution, intrusted to three separate authorities—the Executive, the Legislative, and the Judicial. The Executive power is vested in a President, who is elected every four years, and is eligible for re-election. The mode of electing the President is as follows:—Each State appoints, in such manner as the legislature thereof directs, a number of electors, equal to the whole number of Senators and representatives to which the State may be entitled in the Congress; but no Senator or representative, or any one holding office under Government shall be appointed an elector. The Electors for each State meet at their respective State Capitals on a day appointed, and there vote for a President by ballot. The ballots are then sent to Washington, and opened by the President of the Senate in presence of Congress, and the candidate who has received a majority of the whole number of electoral votes cast is declared President for the ensuing term. If no one has a majority, then from the three highest on the list the House of Representatives elects a President, the votes being taken by States, the representation from each State having one vote. There is also a Vice-President, who, on the death of the President, becomes *ex-officio* President for the remainder of the term. In case of the removal or death of both President and Vice-President, a statute provides for the succession of the Secretary of State, Secretary of the Treasury, Secretary of War, and others, so that the State can never be without a Head or Ruler.

The Legislative power is vested in two Houses, the Senate and the House of Representatives, the President having a *veto* power, which may be overcome by a two-thirds vote of each House. Two Senators from each State are elected by the Legislature thereof for the term of six years; and Representatives are chosen in each State, by popular vote, for two years. The number of Representatives for each State is allotted in proportion to its population, at present 1 for 173,901. The Senate consists of 90 members, and the House of Representatives, 1896, of 357 representatives and territorial delegates.

The Supreme Judicial Authority is vested in a Chief Justice and eight Justices, who are appointed by the President by and with the advice and consent of the Senate, to hold their offices during good behaviour.

TRADE WITH THE UNITED KINGDOM.—The chief exports to the United Kingdom in 1898 were:—

Animals, living	£7,242,309	Iron & steel mfs.	£3,374,860
Bacon	6,438,239	Lard	2,796,308
,, (Hams)	3,051,414	Leather	3,036,811
Beef (fresh)	4,677,431	Meat (fresh and salt)	875,411
Cheese	1,006,586	Oil, &c.	1,119,478
Copper, &c.	2,627,814	Oil seed cake	858,731
Corn, wheat	15,294,766	Paper	515,234
,, Barley	794,867	Paraffin	777,335
,, Oats	2,290,368	Petroleum	3,023,786
,, Maize	7,314,935	Pork	780,803
,, Wheatmeal & flour	9,470,433	Skins and Furs	499,860
Cotton, raw	27,513,032	Sugar	978,555
Fish	613,843	Tallow & Stearine	838,243
Fruit	732,247	Tobacco	2,886,916
Hops	838,074	Wood, all kinds	3,385,650

And the chief imports of domestic produce from the United Kingdom in 1898 were:—

Books	£501,636	Linen, &c.	£2,164,102
Chemical products	542,904	Machinery	358,815
Cotton manuffrs	2,061,967	Metals, all kinds	1,358,931
Earth & chinaware	540,048	Silk and manuffrs.	342,611
Fish	227,701	Skins and furs	709,173
Jute manufactures	844,980	Woollen manuffrs	1,191,588

AREA AND POPULATION OF EACH STATE AND TERRITORY IN THE UNITED STATES,

States and Territories.	Date of Act of admission.	Area.	Population 1890, White and Coloured.
ORIGINAL STATES.		sq. m.	
New Hampshire (N.H.)		9,305	376,530
Massachusetts (Mass.)		8,315	2,238,943
Rhode Island (R.I.)		1,250	345,506
Connecticut (Conn.)		4,990	746,258
New York (N.Y.)		49,220	5,997,853
New Jersey (N.J.)		8,175	1,444,933
Pennsylvania (Pa.)		45,215	5,258,014
Delaware (Del.)		2,360	168,493
Maryland (Md.)		12,210	1,042,390
Virginia (Va.)		42,450	1,655,980
North Carolina (N.C.)		52,250	1,617,947
S. Carolina (S.C.)		30,570	1,151,149
Georgia (Ga.)		59,475	1,837,353
STATES ADMITTED.			
Kentucky (Ky.)	1791	40,400	1,858,635
Vermont (Vt.)	1791	9,565	332,422
Tennessee (Tenn.)	1796	42,050	1,767,518
Maine (Me.)	1820	33,040	661,086
Texas (Tex.)	1845	265,780	2,235,523
West Virginia (W.Va.)	1862	24,780	762,794
PUBLIC LAND STATES AND TERRITORIES.			
Ohio	1802	41,060	3,672,316
Louisiana (La.)	1812	48,720	1,118,587
Indiana (Ind.)	1816	36,350	2,192,404
Mississippi (Miss.)	1817	46,810	1,289,600
Illinois (Ill.)	1818	56,650	3,826,351
Alabama (Ala.)	1819	52,250	1,513,017
Missouri (Mo.)	1821	69,415	2,679,184
Arkansas (Ark.)	1836	53,850	1,128,176
Michigan (Mich.)	1837	58,915	2,093,889
Florida (Fla.)	1845	58,680	391,422
Iowa	1846	56,025	1,911,896
Wisconsin (Wis.)	1848	56,040	1,686,880
California (Cal.)	1850	158,360	1,208,130
Minnesota (Minn.)	1858	83,365	1,301,826
Oregon	1859	97,030	313,767
Kansas (Kans.)	1861	82,080	1,427,096
Nevada (Nev.)	1864	110,700	45,761
Nebraska (Nebr.)	1867	77,510	1,058,910
Colorado (Colo.)	1875	103,925	412,198
North Dakota (N.Dak.)	1889	70,795	182,719
South Dakota (S.Dak.)	1889	77,650	328,808
Montana (Mont.)	1889	145,030	132,159
Washington (Wash.)	1889	69,180	349,390
Idaho	1890	84,860	84,385
Wyoming (Wyo.)	1890	97,890	60,705
Utah	1896	84,970	207,905
TERRITORIES.			
New Mexico	1850	122,580	153,593
Arizona	1863	113,020	59,620
Alaska	1868	...	...
Indian Territory	1854	31,400	125,711
District of Columbia	1791	70	230,392
Oklahoma	1890	39,030	61,834
Total	......	3,025,600	62,630,250
Hawaiian Islands	1898	6,587	107,000
Puerto Rico	1898	5,300	800,000
Philippine Islands	1898	114,400	5,500,000
Guam	1898	...	10,000
Cuba	1898	42,000	1,600,000
Samoan Islands	1899	...	...

POSTAL.—The number of Post Offices in the United States, June 30, 1899, was 75,000. The postal revenue was $95,021,384·17. The number of inland money orders issued was 29,007,870, and the amount $211,213,592·84. Of international money orders the number issued was 968,501, and the value $13,744,770·37. The postal expenditure was $101,632,160·92.

RAILWAYS.—The total mileage of railways in the U. S. on June 30, 1898, was 186,396·32, being an increase during the year of 1,967·85 miles.

MERCANTILE MARINE.—On July 1, 1899, it consisted of 22,728 vessels, of which 6,837 were steamers, and 15,891 other than steamers, the total tonnage being 4,864,238.

MINES.—Amount of Gold and Silver in fine ounces produced 1897:—

	Gold.	Silver.		Gold.	Silver.
Alaska	86,011	116,400	Nevada	143,983	1,228,900
Arizona	140,089	2,239,900	Oregon	65,456	69,000
California	707,160	474,400	S. Dakota	275,491	147,600
Colorado	924,166	21,636,400	Utah	83,500	6,265,600
Idaho	82,320	4,901,200	All other States	55,739	1,112,700
Montana	211,563	15,667,900			

The total imports and domestic exports for fiscal years ending June 30 have been as follows:—

Total imports (merchandise) ...1899 $697,148,489 (1897, $764,730,412; 1898, $616,049,654).

Total domestic exports ....1899 $1,203,931,222 (1897, $1,032,007,603; 1898, $1,210,291,913).

Imports from U. K................ 1899 $118,488,867 (1897, $167,947,820; 1898, $108,945,185).

Domestic Exports to U.K........ 1899 $505,668,925 (1897, $478,448,592; 1898, $534,398,302).

COMMERCE OF THE UNITED STATES.

Merchandise only, 1792 to 1898.

YEAR.	EXPORTS.	IMPORTS.	TOTAL.
	Dollars.	*Dollars.*	*Dollars.*
1792			20,753,098
1872	444,177,586	626,595,077	1,070,772,663
1873	522,479,922	642,136,210	1,164,616,132
1874	586,283,040	567,406,342	1,153,689,382
1875	513,442,711	533,005,436	1,046,448,147
1876	540,384,671	460,741,190	1,001,125,861
1877	602,475,220	451,323,126	1,053,798,346
1878	694,865,766	437,051,532	1,131,917,298
1879	710,439,441	445,777,775	1,156,217,216
1880	835,638,658	667,954,746	1,503,593,404
1881	902,377,346	642,664,628	1,545,041,974
1882	750,542,257	724,639,574	1,475,181,831
1883	823,839,402	723,180,914	1,547,020,316
1884	740,513,609	667,697,693	1,408,211,302
1885	742,189,755	577,527,329	1,319,717,084
1886	679,524,830	635,436,136	1,314,960,966
1887	716,183,211	692,319,768	1,408,502,979
1888	695,954,507	723,957,114	1,419,911,621
1889	742,401,375	745,131,652	1,487,533,027
1890	857,828,684	789,310,409	1,647,139,093
1891	884,480,810	844,916,196	1,729,397,006
1892	1,030,278,148	827,402,462	1,857,680,610
1893	847,665,194	866,400,922	1,714,066,116
1894	892,140,572	654,994,622	1,547,135,194
1895	807,538,165	731,969,965	1,539,508,130
1896	882,606,938	779,724,674	1,662,331,612
1897	1,050,993,556	764,730,412	1,815,723,968
1898	1,231,482,330	616,049,654	1,847,531,984
1899	1,227,023,302	697,148,489	1,924,171,791

The following is a list of dutiable articles and the *ad valorem* duty imposed on their importation in 1899 :—

Article.	Duty.	Article.	Duty.
	%		%
Breadstuffs	33·25	Jewellery, &c....	13·32
Chemicals	31·69	Leather........	35·68
Cotton manufacts.	55·99	Liquors, Malt	51·09
Earthenware......	65·92	,, Distilled	140·40
Flax, hemp, & jute		,, Wine....	51·28
raw ...	15·16	Sugar, &c........	77·11
,, manufactd.	42·04	Tobacco leaf and	
Fruit and nuts....	47·14	manufactures ..	113·40
Glass	60·07	Wood, &c.	21·29
Iron and steel	43·58		

TERRITORIAL EXPANSION.

In the year 1898 the U.S.A. became involved in war with Spain on account of the unsettled state of affairs in the neighbouring island of Cuba. The result of the war was the freedom of that island from Spanish control and the cession of the Philippine Islands and the Island of Guam, the island of Puerto Rico, which was captured during the war, being retained : these conditions were confirmed by a Treaty of Peace signed at Paris (10 Dec., 1898) During the year the independent islands of the Hawaiian group were annexed by a resolution of Congress, and in 1899 under the provisions of the Samoan Convention, those islands of the Samoan Archipelago not annexed by Germany fell to the share of the U.S.A. In a few months, therefore, the U.S.A. assumed the responsibility of a considerable oversea dominion, with between 9,000,000 and 10,000,000 inhabitants.

The *Hawaiian, or Sandwich, Islands* consist of thirteen islands in the North Pacific Ocean in lat. 19° to 22° 15′ N. and long. 154° 48′ to 160° 20′ W. Of these eight are inhabited (Hawaii, Maui, Oahu, Kauai, Molokai, Lanai, Niihau, and Kaloolawe), the area of the entire group being 6,587 square miles with a population in 1896 of 107,000, of whom 75,000 were Hawaiians, 24,000 Japanese, 15,000 Chinese, 9,000 Portuguese, and about 14,000 of mixed and European descent.

The Capital and seat of administration is Honolulu, in the island of Hawaii, the population in 1896 of this town being 28,061. The trade of the islands was valued at $13,813,923 in 1896.

The Samoan Islands.—By the Anglo-German agreement of 14 Nov. 1889 the island of Tutuila and all other islands in the Archipelago east of 171° E. long. were reserved to the U.S.A.

In the *West Indies:* The Island of Cuba, the "Queen of the Antilles," was discovered by Christopher Columbus on 28th October, 1492 and first colonized by his son Diego, who founded Santiago and Trinidad in 1514, and Havana in 1519. In shape Cuba is long and narrow, lying at the entrance of the Gulf of Mexico (making with Yucatan and Florida the Yucatan and Florida channels on the south and north), between 74° and 85° W. long., and 19° and 23° N. lat., with a total length of about 750 miles, and an average breadth of 60 or 70 miles, the area being nearly 42,000 square miles. The population is composed of Spaniards, Creoles, and Mulattoes and Negroes.

The imports in 1892 amounted to £11,400,000, the exports being valued at £18,000,000. The principal products are sugar, coffee, tobacco

r250,000 bales exported in 1892), cigars and cigarettes, and mahogany and other woods ; the principal imports are rice, beef, and flour. The capital, Havana, has about 200,000 inhabitants; other important towns, Santiago de Cuba (70,000) which was captured during the war ; Puerto Principe (45,000), Holguin (35,000), Sancti Spiritu (30,000), Cienfuegos (28,000), and Cardenas (24,000).

Further to the east is the island of Puerto Rico, captured during the war, which has an area of about 5,300 square miles, and about 800,000 inhabitants; the capital, San Juan, has a population of 23,000, Ponce (38,000), and San German (31,000), being also towns of importance. The products are sugar, coffee, and tobacco.

In the *East Indies:* The Philippine Islands have an area of about 114,400 square miles, with 5,500,000 inhabitants. The capital is Manila, which capitulated to Admiral Dewey and Gen. Merritt after the peace protocol had been signed, in the island of Luzon (population about 160,000), other large towns being Lauag (31,000), Lipa (42,000), Banang (36,000), Batangas (34,000). The principal products are hemp, sugar, coffee, indigo, and copra, in addition to the tobacco plant, which is extensively grown in the island of Luzon. The total trade in 1896 was £2,150,000 for imports, and £7,500,000 for exports. The native population of these islands has not yet been brought under control. To the south-east of the Philippines is the Sulu Archipelago (area about 1,000 square miles, population about 60,000), which form part of the concession.

Guam, the largest island of the Ladrone (or Marianne) group, is situated in 145° E. and 14° N., and has an area of about 850 square miles, with about 10,000 inhabitants. The capital is Agaña.

Federal Capital, Washington (3,850 miles from London). Pop. (1890, including the District of Columbia) 230,392.

Ambassador Extraordinary and Plenipotentiary, His Excellency Rt. Hon. Lord Pauncefote, G.C.B., C.C.M.G.	£6,500
Sec. of Embassy, Gerald A. Lowther......	700
2nd Secretary, R. T. Tower................	405
,, C. N. E. Eliot, C.B.	390
,, W. G. Max Müller	330
Hon. Attachés, R. Bromley ; A. E. Humphreys Owen	
Baltimore, Md.—Consul, Gilbert Fraser ...	900
,, Vice-Consul, Abraham G. Coates	400
Newport News—V.-Cons., J. Haughton...	
Norfolk, Va.—Vice-Consul, Barton Myers	
Richmond, Va.—V.-Con., Phil. A. S. Brine	
Boston, Mass.—Consul, J. E. Blunt, C.B.....	1,200
,, V.-Cons., Willoughby Herbert Stuart	400
Portland, Me.—V.-Consul, J. B. Keating	
Charleston, S.C.—C., H. W. R. de Coëtlogon	900
Brunswick, Ga.—V.-C., Rosendo Torras .	
Darien—V.-Cons., R. Manson	
Port Royal, &c., S.C.—V.-C., Jn. E. Kessler	
Savannah, Ga.—V.-C., Alex. Harkness...	
Wilmington, N.C.—V.-C., James Sprunt .	
Chicago, Ill.—Consul, W. Wyndham	900
,, Vice-Cons.,	400
Denver, Colorado—Vice-Cons., R. Pearce.	
Kansas City, Mo.—V-C., P. E. Burrough	
Omaha, Nix—Vice-Cons., M. A. Hall	
St. Louis, Mo.—V.-Cons., W. Bascombe	
St. Paul, Minnes.—V.-C., E. H. Morphy .	
Galveston, Tex.—Consul, H. D. Nugent	800
,, Vice-Consul, Frederick W. Blake	
Sabine Pass—Vice-Cons., A. Roland	

Havana—Con.-Gen., L. E. G. Carden	£1,200
Vice-Consul, E. A. M. Laing	400
Cardenas—Vice-Consul, Thos. Fitzgibbon	
Cienfuegos—Vice-Consul, Geo. R. Fowler	
Matanzas—Vice-Consul, John J. D'Acosta	
Sagua la Grande—Vice-Cons., J. S. Harris	
Honolulu (Hawaii)—Cons., W. R. Hoare	1,000
Vice-Consul, T. R. Walker	
Manila—Consul,	1,100
Vice-Consul, H. A. Ramsden	400
Cebu—Vice-Consul, J. N. Sidebottom	
Iloilo—Vice-Consul, W. S. Fyfe	
Porto Rico—Consul, Wm. B. Churchward...	800
Vice-Consul, G. I. Finlay	
Aguadilla—Vice-Con., Auguste Gauslandt	
Arecibo—Vice-Consul, D. Wilson	
Arroyo de Guayama—Vice-Consul, John Charles McCormick	
Mayaguez - Vice-Consul, Gerhardt Monefeldt	
Naguabo & Fajardo—Vice-Consul, Antonio Roig	
Ponce—Vice-Consul, Fernando M. Toro	
Vièques (Crab Island) Vice-Cons.,	
Santiago de Cuba—Consul,	150
Guantanamo—Cons. Agent, T. Brooks(*actg.*)	
New Orleans, La.—Cons., A. G. Vansittart	1,100
„ *Vice-Cons.*, J. A. Donnelly	400
Apalachicola—V.-Cons., Thos. F. Porter..	
Biloxi—V.-Cons., J. J. Lemon	
Fernandina, Fla.—V.-Con., E. V. Nicholl	
Jacksonville, Fla.—V.-Con., E. Sudlow...	
Key West, Fla.—V.-C., Wm. J. H. Taylor	
Mobile, Ala.—Vice-Con.. A. S. Benn	
Pascagoula, Miss.—Vice-Con., W. O. Clark	
Pensacola, Fla.—V.-C., Osmond C. Howe	400
Port Tampa, Fla.—Vice-Con., J. Bradley	
Punta Gorda—V.-Con., Albert F. Dewey	
New York, N.Y.—C.-G., Sir P. Sanderson, K.C.M.G.	2,000
„ *Con.*, C. Clive Bayley	600
„ *Vice-Con.*, C. A. S. Perceval	400
„ „ J. P. Smithers	250
Providence, R.I.—V.-C., Geo. A. Stockwell	
Philadelphia, Penn.—Con., Wilfrid Powell	900
„ *Vice-Consul*, C. B. C. Clipperton	400
Portland, Oregon—Cons., J. Laidlaw	600
„ *Vice-Consul*, J. E. Laidlaw	
Astoria, Oregon—Vice-Consul, P. L. Cherry	
Port Townsend, Washington—Vice-Consul, Oscar Klöcker	
Seattle, Vice-Consul, Bernard Pelly	
Tacoma, Washington—Vice-Con., Rev. J. B. Alexander	
San Francisco, Cal.—Cons.-Gen., W. C. Pickersgill, C.B.	1,200
„ *Vice-Consul*, Wellesley Moore	400
Los Angeles, Cal.—V.-Con., C. W. Mortimer	
San Diego, Cal.—V.-C., Maj. W. T. Allen	

New York (Pop. 1,801,739), transit, 6 days (now frequently less); Philadelphia (Pop. 1,142,653), 5½ days; San Francisco (Pop. 298,997), 11 days; Chicago (Pop. 1,099,850), 8 days. Distance, New York to Liverpool, about 3,100 miles. Telegrams, 1s. per word; other places, from 1s. to 1s. 8d.

URUGUAY.

President, Juan Lindolfo Cuestas, *elected* 1 March, 1899.
Foreign Affairs, Manuel Herrero y Espinosa.
Interior, Saturnino Camp.
War and Marine, General Callorda.

Finance, Juan Campistequi.
Education and Public Works, Luis Pena.

Minister Plenipotentiary and Envoy Extraordinary, (vacant), 83 Victoria St., S.W.
Secretary of Legation, Dr. Alfonso S. de Zumaran. *Consul-Gen.*,

A Republic in South America, on the east coast of the Rio de la Plata, situate in lat. 30°—35° S. and long. 53° 25'—57° 42' W., containing an area of 72,172 square miles, and an estimated population of 787,053 (1894); was formerly a dependency of Spain. United to the Argentine Confederation early in the present century, it was afterwards annexed by Portugal, and became later a province of Brazil; but through the bravery of the patriotic "thirty-three" it succeeded in throwing off the Brazilian yoke and declared its independence 25th of August, 1825. A war in consequence ensuing between Brazil and the Argentine Confederation, both the Powers agreed, through the mediation of Great Britain, to recognize Uruguay as a sovereign and independent State. The imports from the U. K. are numerous, the principal being woollen and cotton goods, hardware, and coals. The chief exports are wool, hides, horn, hair, tallow, and jerked beef. Wheat, barley, and maize are cultivated, but the wealth of the country is obtained from its pasturage, which supports large herds of horned cattle (5,205,272 in 1895), and sheep (12,820,736 in 1895), the wool of which is of excellent quality. Gold mines exist at Cuñapirú. The principal river is the Uruguay and its affluents, of which the Rio Negro is the chief. There are 1,002 miles of railway open, and 4,025 miles of telegraph in 1891.

Total revenue, 1897	£3,191,500
Total debt, 31 Dec., 1898	26,473,000
Debt charge, 1897	1,314,750
Total imports, 1898	5,273,200
Total exports, 1898	6,292,900
Imports from United Kingdom, 1898	1,440,000
Exports to United Kingdom, 1898	600,000

CAPITAL, Monte Video. Pop. (1894), 216,000.

Brit. Min. Res. & Con.-Gen., Walter Baring	£1,600
Consul, Herbert A. R. Hervey	400
Chaplain, Rev. S. F. Handcock	
Colonia—Vice-Consul (vacant)	
Maldonado—V.-Consul, Hy. W. Burnett	
Paysandu—Vice-Consul, John Chaplin	
Salto—Vice-Consul, J. J. Armstrong	

Monte Video, 7,030 miles. Transit, 21 days.
Telegrams, per word, 4s. and 4s. 6d.

VENEZUELA, REPUBLIC OF.

(*See also map* p. 609.)

President, General Castro, assumed office 24 Oct. 1899, for four years.
Premier and Foreign Affairs, Andurgia Palacio.
Interior, Francisco Castello.
Finance, Tello Mendoza.
War and Marine, Ignacio Pulido.
Instruction, Clemente Urraneja.
Public Works, Victor Rodriguez.
Commerce, Manuel Hernandez.

Minister to Great Britain and France, José Andrade.
Consul-General in London, Carlos A. Villanueva.
Consul in London, N. G. Burch, 31/32 King Wm. St.
Vice-Consul, Walter White.
Consul at Southampton, H. L. Paredes.
Consul at Liverpool, D. Urbaneja Padron.

The most northerly Confederation of South America, situated between 1° 40′ S. lat. and 12° 26′ N. lat. and 59° 52′—73° 15′ W. long. It consists of 20 States, an area of 566,159 square miles, and a population, in 1891, of 2,323,527. The chief imports are manufactured goods, provisions and wine. The principal exports in 1894 were:—

Coffee	£3,680,000	Hides	£90,000
Cocoa	60,000	Other	110,000
Gold	180,000	Total	£4,120,000

The railways opened and under construction have a length of 370 miles. For the boundary settlement (British Guiana—Venezuela) see p. 609.

Revenue, 1897-98	£1,323,953
Expenditure, 1897-98	1,803,664

Public Debt, 31 Dec., 1898, Interior	3,155,124
Exterior	4,566,358
Imports from United Kingdom, 1896	£568,567
Exports to United Kingdom, 1896	63,382

CAPITAL, Caracas. Population (1893), 80,000.

British Minister, W. H. Doveton Haggard .. £2,000
Consul, William A. Andral (acting) ....
Bolivar—Consul, C. H. de Lemos ......
   La Guayra—Vice-Cons., Robert Schunck.
   Maracaibo—Vice-Consul, M. Bodecker ... ...
   Puerto Cabello—Vice-Consul, Ricardo Kolster
   Puerto Tablas—Cons. Agt., E. Mathison ...

Caracas, 4,760 miles; telegrams, per word. 7s. 2d. to 7s. 7d.

Regulations respecting Passports.

FOREIGN OFFICE PASSPORTS are granted only to natural born subjects, or to persons naturalized either in the United Kingdom or in the British Colonies or in India; they are not limited in point of time, and are available for any number of journeys. If the applicant be a "Naturalised British subject," he will be so designated in his Passport, which will be issued subject to the qualification mentioned in the 7th Clause of the Act 33 Vict. c. 14.

Applications for Foreign Office Passports must be made in writing, and enclosed in a cover addressed to "The Passport Department, Foreign Office, London."

The charge is 2s., whatever number of persons may be named in it. Passports are issued at the Foreign Office between the hours of 11 and 4 on the day following that on which the application for the Passport has been received, except on Sundays and Public Holidays, when the Passport Office is closed. If the applicant does not reside in London the Passport may be sent by post, and a Postal order for 2s. must accompany the application. *Postage stamps will not be received in payment.*

Passports are granted to all persons either known to the Secretary of State or recommended to him by some person who is known to him, or upon the application of any *Banking firm* established in the United Kingdom; or upon the production of a certificate of identity signed by any Mayor, Magistrate, J.P., Minister of Religion, Physician, Surgeon, Solicitor or Notary resident in the United Kingdom; the applicant's Certificate of Birth may also be required in addition to the certificate of identity.

If the applicant be a NATURALISED BRITISH SUBJECT, his certificate of naturalisation must be forwarded to the Foreign Office *with* the certificate of identity. If resident in London, or in the suburbs, he must apply *personally* for the Passport at the Foreign Office; if resident in the country, the Passport will be sent and the certificate of Naturalisation will be returned to the person who granted the certificate of identity in order that he may cause the applicant to sign the Passport in his presence.

A Passport cannot be issued by the Foreign Office, or by an Agent at an outport, on behalf of a person already abroad; such person should apply for one to the nearest British Mission or Consulate; a Passport cannot be issued abroad to a Colonial Naturalised British Subject, except for a direct journey to the United Kingdom or to the Colony in which he has been naturalized.

The bearer of every Passport granted by the Foreign Office *must* sign his Passport as soon as he receives it; without such signature either the *visa* may be refused, or the validity of the Passport questioned abroad.

Travellers who intend to visit the Russian Empire, the Turkish Dominions, or the Kingdom of Roumania in the course of their travels, must not quit England without having had their Passports *visés* at the Russian Consulate in London, 17 Great Winchester Street, E.C., at the Consulate-General of the Sublime Porte, 29 Mincing Lane, E.C., or at the Roumanian Consulate-General, 68 Basinghall Street, E.C., respectively. Travellers about to proceed to any other country need not obtain the *visa* of the Diplomatic or Consular Agents of such country resident in the United Kingdom, except as an additional precaution, which is recommended in the case of Passports of old date.

Although British subjects are now free to enter Belgium, France, Holland, Italy, Denmark, Sweden, and Norway without Passports, and the rules about Passports have been virtually relaxed in other countries, nevertheless, British subjects travelling abroad are advised to furnish themselves with Passports, for even in those countries where they are no longer obligatory, they are found to be useful as affording a ready means of identification, and more particularly when letters have to be claimed at a *poste restante*. For *residence* in certain districts of Germany and Switzerland, a Passport is indispensable.

THE TRANSVAAL.

President of the Republic and Chairman of the "Uitvoerend Raad" (Executive), Stephanus J. Paul Krüger, *b.* 10 Oct., 1825, *re-elected* February, 1898, for five years.

Vice-President, General P. J. Joubert.

Chairman of 1st Volksraad, F. G. Wolmarans.

Do. 2nd do. N. Steen Kamp.

Secretary of State, F. W. Reitz.

The larger portion lies to the west of the Drakenberge (Mt. Mauch 8,725 feet) and slopes down to the Limpopo river and Bechuanaland; a smaller section lies to the east of that range towards the Indian Ocean, and it is shut in by British territory on all sides, except along the greater part of its eastern frontier, where it is closed in by Portuguese territory from having direct access to the sea. The area (including Swaziland, 5,560 sq. m.) amounts to 119,200 sq. miles; the population probably exceeds 750,000, of whom only 150,000 are whites. The latter include 53,000 Transvaal Boers and 87,000 Uitlanders, 80 per cent. of whom are probably British subjects. In 1896, 451,801 natives paid the hut-tax.

Steppes and bush predominate and favour pastoral industries, whilst agriculture labours under many drawbacks. Gold, first discovered in 1871, constitutes the wealth of the country, coal and silver are also found, whilst iron ores and other metals are known to exist. Railways connect the Republic with Delagoa Bay, Durban and the Cape; the total length open for traffic in 1896 was 890 miles, with about 200 miles under construction. Of the commerce 70 per cent. is with Cape Colony.

The legislative power is vested in a First Volksraad, elected by first class burghers, and a Second Volksraad, of no actual power, elected by the second class burghers. The privileges of First Class burghers are confined almost exclusively to white persons who resided in the Republic prior to 1876, and their descendants. Naturalised aliens and their children enjoy the very restricted privileges of Second Class burghers, whilst the bulk of the white population are without political rights. The President is elected for 5 years by the First Class burghers.

The Transvaal was founded in 1840 by Boers who, dissatisfied with British rule, had migrated from Cape Colony, and its independence was recognised by the British Crown in 1852. In 1877, when Sekukuni had defeated the Boers, and it was feared that the whole of South Africa might become involved in a disastrous native war, Sir Theophilus Shepstone was despatched to the Transvaal. He found the public treasury empty, and the country in a state of anarchy; to save it from further disaster he proclaimed it British territory, but on Dec. 16, 1880, at Heidelberg, the Boers rose in revolt, and the flag of the Republic was once more hoisted, a provisional government, or triumvirate (Krüger, Joubert and Pretorius) being formed, and after the battle of Majuba Hill (Feb. 27, 1881) the United Kingdom once more recognised its practical independence in a Convention, which was modified in 1884. Owing to the rupture in October, 1899, the country reverted to the status it held previous to the Convention of 1881. and is once more in revolt against its suzerain. The number of burghers liable to service in defence of the State was about 27,000 in 1856, and in 1899 about 30,000 fully-armed burghers responded to the mobilisation orders, the available forces being considerably increased by the advent of foreign adventurers and mercenaries. Swaziland was placed under the administration of the Republic in 1894, the rights of the natives (who retain their King) being safeguarded.

In 1882 the revenue only amounted to £177,407; in 1893 this had increased to £1,702,685, and in 1897 to £4,480,218, owing to the increased prosperity of the gold-bearing districts; the expenditure was £4,394,066 in 1897, and the debt £2,675,690 in 1893. The trade of the country amounted in 1897 to about £24,500,000, of which £13,563,827 represented the value of imports. The output of gold in the year 1897 was valued at £11,653,727.

The Capital is POTCHEFSEROOM, and the seat of Government PRETORIA, which had in 1899 about 12,500 inhabitants. The principal town and the commercial centre is Johannesburg. which had a population in 1899 of over 105,000, of whom about 60,000 were Whites.

ORANGE FREE STATE.

President, M. T. Steyn, 19 Feb., 1896, for 5 years.

Government Secretary, P. J. Blignaut.

Chairman of the Volksraad, C. H. Wessels.

Chief Justice Supreme Court, M. de Villiers.

This country is bounded on the East by British Basutoland and Natal, N. by the Transvaal, and W. by Cape Colony; it has an area of 48,326 square miles, with a population (1890) of 207,503, of whom 77,716 are whites. It was founded by Dutch emigrants from the Cape Colony in 1836 and was proclaimed British territory by Sir Harry Smith in 1848, but, by the convention entered into on the 23rd of February, 1854, between Sir George Clerk, Her Majesty's special commissioner, and the representatives of the people, the inhabitants were declared "to all intents and purposes a free and independent people, and their Government to be treated thenceforth as a free and independent Government." Until quite recently there has been but little immigration and the territory has remained suited to its ancient and patriarchal institutions. The Government became involved in trouble with the British Government owing to a defensive alliance which had been made with that of the Transvaal, declaring its adhesion thereto on October 4, 1899.

It is essentially a pastoral country, but the eastern part is also admirably adapted for the cultivation of grain. Diamonds, garnets, and other precious stones are found, and rich coal mines exist, while there are indications of gold. The chief exports are wool, ostrich feathers, hides, diamonds, grain, &c.

The Volksraad comprises 58 members, elected by the various constituencies into which the State is divided.

In 1898 the revenue was £799,757, and the expenditure £956,752. The debt, incurred mainly for railway purposes. amounted in that year to £1,839,000. The trade was represented by £1,923,425 for exports, and £1,190,932 for imports, the amount to and from the United Kingdom not being ascertainable. BLOEMFONTEIN, the Capital, and seat of Government, had a population of about 4,000 in 1898.

The O.F.S. is supposed to have contributed about 20,000 armed burghers to the forces of the Transvaal.

The immediate cause of the present rupture is the grievances of the Uitlanders or non-Boer white residents; but to understand clearly the relations of the Boers to the English, the characteristics and earlier history of the Boers must be kept in mind. The Boers, who are descendants of the early Dutch, French Huguenots who adopted Dutch as their language, and German immigrants to the Cape, are, as their name implies, essentially "farmers," frugal and industrious in their habits, rigidly Calvinistic in their religious views, and distrustful of foreigners, especially the English, under whose rule they came in 1814, when the Dutch ceded South Africa to Great Britain. In these modes of life and thought, the majority are influenced rather by the ideas and manners of the last century than by the progressive spirit of the present day; hence their aversion to change, the developments of trade, the progress of education, and other adjuncts of advancing civilisation. The Emancipation Act of 1833, by which slavery ceased in the Cape Colony (1834), and subsequent laws passed for the protection of the Native races caused great dissatisfaction among the Dutch; the liberal policy of the British Government toward the Natives being really a most important factor in the hostile feeling of the Boers against the English. This and other causes led to the trekking of the Boers and the colonising of the Transvaal and the Orange Free State. The difficulties between the Boers of the Transvaal and the Uitlanders, had their origin in the discoveries of gold at "Moodies," and the Sheba mine at Barberton in 1885 and 1886. These "finds" brought great numbers of people to the Transvaal, some 10,000 or 12,000 arriving in the country before the end of 1887; the discovery of the Witwatersrand formation increasing the tide of prosperity and the influx of population. This increase of population and the prosperity of the auriferous districts greatly enriched the coffers of the State; and of the revenue, the Uitlanders contribute, it is estimated, 4-5ths, but although it was by their capital and industry that the resources of the Transvaal were developed, and its revenue capacity increased, they were denied political rights or means of control over the expenditure of the country. Sir Alfred Milner, High Commissioner for South Africa, and Governor of Cape Colony, stated their case on May 4, 1899, to Mr. Chamberlain: "A busy, industrial community is not naturally prone to political unrest. But they bear the chief burden of taxation, they constantly feel in their business and daily lives the effects of local chaotic legislation, and of incompetent and unsympathetic administration; they have many grievances, but they believe all this could be gradually removed if they only had a fair share of political power. This is the meaning of their vehement demand for enfranchisement. Moreover, they are mostly British subjects, accustomed to a free system and equal rights; they feel deeply the personal indignity involved in a position of permanent subjection to the ruling caste which owes its wealth and power to their existence. The political turmoil in the Transvaal Republic will never end until the permanent Uitlander population is admitted to a share in the Government, and while that turmoil lasts there will be no tranquillity or adequate progress in Her Majesty's South African dominions." An agitation for reform, the remission of certain taxes or security for stands and claims, took shape in a political association, the Transvaal Republican Union, formed at Barberton, 1887. Subsequently the

Transvaal National Union was founded at Johannesburg, the shareholders in the mines forming a voluntary business association, known as the Witwatersrand Chamber of Mines, to represent to the Volksraad the existence of abuses and grievances, the remedies required, and the measures necessary to the progress of the industry in particular, and the welfare of the State in general. In 1895, a petition signed by 35,483 persons was presented to the Raad, praying for the extension of the franchise. Nothing practical resulting from it, the reform movement was started, and in conjunction with Dr. Jameson, it was proposed to obtain by force the concessions demanded. This unfortunate and ill-judged enterprise ended in disaster to the irregular troops who entered the Transvaal from the territories of the British South Africa Company, and, owing to the extinction of the movement at Johannesburg before their arrival, and the knowledge gained by the Boer Government of the expected advance, entirely failed in its object, the little band surrendering to a superior force on January 1, 1896, at Krugersdorp. This movement only delayed the advent of reform, and redress of grievances being still refused by the Transvaal Government, on March 28, 1899, a petition to the Queen signed by 21,684 Uitlanders was presented through Sir A. Milner. The chief points of this petition may be thus summarised: (1) deprivation of political rights for voting in the election of President and first Volksraad, the highest authority in the State, and the only one whose decisions are not subject to veto or revision; (2) abolition of concessions or virtual monopolies, as that of dynamite, &c.; (3) the heavy burden of taxation, of which the greater part by far is borne by the Uitlanders, amounting to about £16 per head, the chief items of the revenue of the State being contributed by the Uitlanders, as (1898) Customs £1,066,994, prospecting licences £321,651, railway receipts £668,951, the total revenue for the year being £3,983,560; (4) the State system of education, state-aided schools being compelled to use Dutch; (5) the mal-treatment of Uitlanders and the arbitrary administration of justice, including the Edgar case, where a party of four policemen broke into the house of a Uitlander at midnight without a warrant, and, merely on the suspicion of his having committed an offence, shot him dead; (6) the corruption of officials, and the abuse of the Secret Service Fund, which, for 1899, is set down as £36,000, and in 1896 amounted to £191,837. The conditions of the liquor traffic and Native labour are also grievances of the Uitlanders. On May 10, 1899, Mr. Chamberlain, in a dispatch, suggested a meeting between Sir A. Milner and President Kruger to discuss the situation with the view to an amicable settlement and reasonable concessions to the demands of the Uitlanders. A conference took place on May 31 at Bloemfontein. Sir A. Milner's proposals were that the franchise should be granted to every Uitlander who (1) had been resident for five years* in the Republic; (2) had declared his intention to reside permanently; and (3) took an oath to obey the laws, to undertake all obligations of citizenship, and to defend the independence of the country; the franchise to be confined to persons of good character possessing a certain amount of property or income; (4) there should be some increase of seats in

---

* Previous qualification 14 years' residence.

the districts where the Uitlanders principally resided. The number of these was a matter for discussion, but it was essential that they should not be so few as to leave the new constituencies in a contemptible minority. To these proposals President Kruger, June 2, made the counter proposals: - Newcomers registering themselves within 14 days after arrival to obtain naturalisation after two years on complying with the following conditions: (1) six months' notice of intention to apply for naturalisation; (2) two years' continuous registration; (3) residence in the South African Republic during that period; 4) no dishonouring sentence: (5) proof of obedience to the laws, no act against the Government or independence of the State; (6) proof of full State citizenship and franchise, or title to it, in former country; (7) possession of fixed property to the value of £150, occupation of a house of annual value of £50, or yearly income of at least £200, the Government to have the power of granting naturalisation to persons not satisfying these conditions; (8) the oath to be similar to that of the Orange Free State (which does not require renunciation of allegiance to the British Crown). Persons so naturalised, five years after naturalisation, to obtain the full franchise on the following conditions: (1) continuous registration for five years after naturalisation; (2) continuous residence during that period; (3) no dishonouring sentence; (4) proof of obedience to the laws, &c.; (5) property qualification as above; (6) residents in the South African Republic before 1890 getting naturalised within six months from the promulgation of this proposed law, and giving six months' notice of their intention to apply for naturalisation, to obtain full franchise two years after naturalisation, on complying with conditions for full franchise mentioned above, substituting two for five years; those not getting naturalised within six months, to fall under the already-mentioned conditions for newcomers; (7) those already resident for two years or more to be allowed immediate naturalisation on the above-mentioned naturalisation conditions for newcomers, and to obtain the full franchise five years after naturalisation on compliance with the above-mentioned full franchise conditions; (8) those already naturalised to obtain the full franchise five years after naturalisation on the last-mentioned conditions. In return for the above proposals the assurance was to be given him that the "Suzerainty" was to be for ever dropped. The Conference broke up June 5, Sir A. Milner informing President Kruger that his proposals were unacceptable. On July 13, the new Franchise Law was submitted to the Volksraad, the vital difference between its provisions and the proposals of Sir A. Milner being that the latter required a five years period retrospective for Uitlanders who had already been five years in the country, and hampered by no other conditions than are usually imposed in all civilised countries; the main object of the High Commissioner being to secure the immediate and effectual redress of the Uitlanders' grievances. Mr. Kruger's bill offered a seven years' franchise, retrospective in certain cases only, and surrounded by ambiguous provisos that might be interpreted in many different senses, leading probably to frequent disputes. No mention was made in the Bill of the new Uitlander seats in the Volksraad. The practical result of the Boer scheme was to render it impossible to obtain the franchise (with the exception of a few persons who entered the country nine years previously) for at least two years. Children of non-burgher fathers to be naturalised at 16, and enfranchised at 21 years of age.

The proposals contained in the Bill did not appear likely to remove the causes for dissatisfaction, but a proposal was made by Mr. Chamberlain for a joint Commission of Inquiry to ascertain how they would work in giving the Uitlanders an immediate and reasonable representation. President Kruger made an offer (August 19) to recommend to the Volksraad the five years retrospective franchise proposed by Sir A. Milner; to give to the Raad eight new seats: to undertake that the representation of the goldfields should never be less than one-fourth of the whole; to give the new burghers a vote for the President and Commandant-General, and to take into consideration such friendly suggestions about the details of the Franchise Law as the British Government might wish to convey through their Agent adding the following conditions: (1) That there should be no further interference with the affairs of the Republic; (2) That the controversy about the suzerainty* should be allowed to drop; (3) That the principle of arbitration of further difficulties should be conceded as soon as the franchise scheme had become law. In reply, August 30, Mr. Chamberlain stated that as regards (1) Her Majesty's Government could not debar themselves from their rights under the Conventions nor divest themselves of the ordinary obligations of a civilised Power to protect its subjects in a foreign country from injustice; as regards (2) the Transvaal was referred to the despatch of July 13 (which maintains the British suzerainty); as regards (3) it was, to a certain extent, agreed to and enlarged so as to include a further conference at Cape Town. The Transvaal Government was reminded that there are other matters of difference between the two Governments which will not be settled by the grant of political representation to the Uitlanders, and that it was necessary for them to be settled concurrently with the questions under discussion, forming, with the question of Arbitration, proper subjects for consideration at the proposed Conference. The reply of the Transvaal Government, Sept. 2, was to the effect that it considered its proposals which were exceedingly liberal were annulled, and that it was therefore unnecessary to submit them to the Volksraad; the Government desired the British Government should abide by the London Convention of 1884 and International Law, and agreed to the appointment of a Commission of delegates selected by both Governments to discuss technicalities, and invited the Imperial Government to define the constitution of the Commission, and to name the place of meeting.

---

* The omission of the Preamble to the Pretoria Convention of 1881 is construed by the Boers as the result of an agreement to abolish the suzerainty of Great Britain. As pointed out by Mr. Chamberlain, the London Convention of 1884 contains specific and not implied amendments of the 1881 Convention "that the direct request for the abolition of the suzerainty was refused by Lord Derby; that the preamble, as the fundamental declaration, must be deemed to be in force; and that it not, the same reason which is adduced against the continued existence of the suzerainty would hold good against the independence of the Transvaal, for in the preamble of the 1881 Convention alone is any mention made of either the grant or the reservation."

On September 8 a Cabinet Council was held, at which it was resolved to reinforce the Natal garrison by 10,000 men, and to send a fresh despatch stating that the Government absolutely repudiated the view taken of the political status of the South African Republic by its Government in their Note of April 16, 1898, and May 9, 1899, in which they claimed to be a Sovereign International State, and they were, therefore, unable to consider any proposal which was made conditional on the acceptance of Her Majesty's Government of those views ; that the proposals made by the Transvaal Government of August 19 cannot be considered ; that the law of 1899 was insufficient to secure the immediate and substantial representation Her Majesty's Government have always had in view. The Government were still prepared to accept the offer of the Note of August 19, five years' franchise, ten representatives for the goldfields, and at least one-fourth of the Raad, and a vote for the President and Commandant-General, if the inquiry proposed by Her Majesty's Government showed the new scheme of representation not to be encumbered by conditions which would nullify the intention to give substantial and immediate representation to the Uitlanders, and that the new members must be allowed to use their own language. An immediate and definite reply was pressed for, on receiving which immediate arrangements would be made for a further conference between the President of the South African Republic and the High Commissioner. If the reply of the Transvaal Government should be negative or inconclusive, Her Majesty's Government reserved the right to consider the situation *de novo*, and to formulate their own proposals for a final settlement.

A further despatch (Sept. 22) expressed regret that the proposals of the Imperial Government had not been accepted, and stated that they would now formulate their own proposals for a final settlement. This was followed the same day by another despatch repudiating the insinuation of a breach of faith on the part of the British Agent, Mr. Greene, in his communications with the State Attorney. On October 9 an Ultimatum was presented by the Transvaal Government demanding (1) that all points of mutual difference between the South African Republic and the Imperial Government should be referred to arbitration, (2) that the Imperial troops on the border should be instantly withdrawn, (3) that all reinforcements of troops landed in South Africa be withdrawn, (4) that Her Majesty's troops now on the high seas should not be landed in any port of South Africa. In the event of no satisfactory answer being received by 5 o'clock on October 11, or any further movement of troops taking place, the Transvaal Government would be compelled to regard the action of Her Majesty's Government as a declaration of war. In reply, Sir A. Milner was informed that the British Government had received with great regret the peremptory demands of the Transvaal, and was directed to inform the Pretoria Government that the conditions demanded were impossible to discuss. Mr. Greene, the British Agent, was directed to hand over the protection of British interests to the United States Consul, and to ask for his passports. The President of the Orange Free State, Mr. Steyn, in reply to an inquiry by Sir A. Milner, October 4, declared that in case of war the State would fulfil its obligations to the Transvaal. Parliament was summoned and met on October 17, and, after voting £10,000,000 for the expenses of the war, was prorogued to January 15.

The Transvaal Boers, immediately after the declaration of war, proceeded to concentrate in the neighbourhood of Laing's Nek, a pass over the Drakensberge into Natal, similar movements being made in the vicinity of Van Reenen's Pass by the Boers of the Orange Free State. A British force was despatched to Dundee in north-east Natal, with headquarters and base at Ladysmith, the permanent camp of the British garrison. The Boer plan of campaign was to attack in force the advanced post at Dundee, and, after reducing that town, to concentrate round Ladysmith and compel its surrender before the arrival of reinforcements.

The first serious engagement took place near Glencoe Oct. 20, when General Symons, who was mortally wounded in the hour of victory, drove back the enemy, and so prevented the maturity of his plan of subsequent attack. The Boers appeared the next day in great strength with heavy siege guns, and General Yule, who succeeded General Symons, fell back on Ladysmith unobserved, General White diverting the enemy by an attack at Elands Laagte on October 21 and at Rietfontein on October 24. On October 30 an effort to bring about a general engagement was unsuccessful, and part of the British force (about 850 officers and men) was isolated and captured. The stubborn defence of the town completely disorganised the Boer general plans for an advance to the sea against Durban, and, in spite of their numerical superiority of perhaps more than 4 to 1, they were compelled to remain round the town until the arrival of reinforcements from England enabled Sir George White to make a forward move against them.

Meanwhile, the Western border had been stubbornly defended by a small garrison of irregulars at Mafeking under Col. R. S. S. Baden-Powell, and by a mixed garrison under Col. Kekewich at Kimberley, and no efforts to dislodge the defenders were successful.

At the time of going to press almost all the troops of the Army Corps ordered out had arrived at Cape Town or Durban.

On November 27 General Buller arrived in Natal, and a general advance was made under his supreme control, for the relief of the beleaguered garrison at Ladysmith. On the north of Cape Colony a Division under Lord Methuen, including the Brigade of Guards and a Naval Brigade, successfully engaged the Free State forces at Belmont, Gras Pan, and Honey Nest Kloof, all on the northern line of railway, at the latter of which places the English troops captured over 2,000,000 rounds of ammunition. The Guards, and also the Naval Brigade, lost heavily in killed and wounded in these engagements as the Free State Boers were strongly entrenched on hills commanding the line of route, which positions were gallantly carried by assault. News of the relief of Kimberley was hourly expected at the time of going to press, and on the southern border of the O.F.S. General Gatacre was preparing an advance to drive the invaders back across the Orange River.

The result of the operations has never been doubted, and before the publication of the thirty-third volume the civil administration of the reconquered territory will have been taken in hand.

The total amount of the year's Trade for 1898 was £764,392,571, against £745,203,078 for the year preceding, and £748,944,115 in 1890, which was the largest amount ever previously known. The exports of British produce amounted to £233,359,240, our chief customers being the United States £14,716,489, France £14,744,496, Holland, &c., £10,838,767, Germany £22,650,145, Belgium £8,802,075, India £29,729,589, Australasia £21,123,086, British North America £6,154,773, Cape Colony £9,144,420, Natal £3,055,390, Straits Settlements £2,773,312, Ceylon £1,177,138, Hong Kong £2,225,115, and the British West Indies £1,839,980.

The Imports amounted to £11 11s. 11¼d. per head of the population, and the Domestic Exports to £5 15s. 0¾d. per head.

Imports by Parcel Post in 1898 were £1,355,526, and the Exports £2,139,660, a total increase of £393,968.

The totals for the years 1897-98 were:—

Total Imports (1897)	£451,028,960
" " (1898)	470,378,583
Increase in 1898	£19,347,623
Total Exports (1897)	£294,174,118
" " (1898)	294,013,988
Decrease in 1898	£160,130
Total Imports and Exports (1897)	£745,203,078
" " " (1898)	764,392,571
An increase in 1898 of	£19,189,493

Total Imports.

FOREIGN.	1897.	1898.
Africa, Western	£4,690	£7,445
America, United States of	113,041,627	126,062,155
Argentine Republic	5,753,916	7,788,332
Austria-Hungary	1,276,585	1,135,482
Belgium	20,885,812	21,534,313
Brazil	3,736,419	4,601,773
Bulgaria	396,832	94,752
Chile	3,191,683	3,633,552
China, excl. of Hong Kong	2,684,722	2,668,064
Colombia, Republic of	556,560	635,488
Congo Free State	13,859	10,632
Costa Rica	333,310	575,610
Denmark and Colonies	10,988,519	11,726,716
Ecuador	92,412	267,164
France	53,346,883	51,396,793
Do. Colonial Possessions	1,439,522	1,169,898
Germany	26,189,469	28,534,159
Do. Colonial Possessions	68,452	35,203
Greece	1,638,995	1,448,353
Guatemala	375,858	299,999
Hayti & San Domingo	74,034	91,483
Holland	28,971,316	28,532,904
Do. Colonial Possessions	363,013	476,213
Honduras	1,590	13,198
Italy	3,317,292	3,332,213
Japan	1,283,165	1,158,134
Mexico	593,894	264,092
Morocco	211,928	385,088
Nicaragua	148,176	71,088
Norway	4,995,461	4,986,500
Pacific, Islands in the	188,331	147,283
Persia	197,778	193,291
Peru	1,453,627	1,537,428
Portugal	2,652,713	3,488,056
Do. Colonial Possessions	407,238	358,228
Roumania	2,258,503	2,579,601
Russia	22,284,365	19,489,514

	1897.	1898.
San Salvador	£154,589	£210,906
Siam	246,940	63,749
Spain	13,125,660	13,188,258
Do. Colonial Possessions	1,897,533	2,249,254
Sweden	9,839,136	9,736,931
Tripoli	264,989	167,745
Tunis	61,882	231,064
Turkey: European	1,793,198	1,352,385
" Asiatic	4,356,965	3,528,407
" Egypt	9,294,240	8,855,689
Uruguay	339,904	392,014
Venezuela	63,382	45,599
Whale Fisheries	12,004	14,610
Total, Foreign Countries	**£357,010,027**	**£370,944,628**

GREATER BRITAIN.	1897.	1898.
Aden and Dependencies	£173,319	£212,355
Australasia :—		
New South Wales	9,262,226	9,281,740
Victoria	5,590,662	5,021,477
South Australia	1,922,272	1,796,606
Queensland	3,320,418	3,002,802
Western Australia	361,370	471,706
New Zealand	8,666,745	9,015,548
Tasmania	289,369	260,270
Fiji Islands	9,067	135
Bermudas	1,691	1,815
British East Africa	851	2,068
British Guiana	523,596	575,714
British Honduras	227,808	244,953
Canada, Dominion of	19,217,918	20,403,610
Cape Colony	4,195,741	5,094,372
Ceylon	4,688,278	4,847,721
Channel Islands	1,327,111	1,553,065
Cyprus	103,046	137,934
Falkland Islands	145,387	184,710
Gambia	49,238	54,229
Gibraltar	59,365	64,325
Gold Coast	460,131	666,455
Hong Kong	606,314	726,637
India, The Empire of :—		
Bombay	3,473,438	5,530,971
Madras	3,462,374	3,212,963
Bengal	15,999,536	16,503,957
Burma	1,877,751	2,222,190
Lagos	1,100,943	1,129,533
Malta and Gozo	74,903	92,829
Mauritius	94,548	100,863
Natal	752,254	922,949
Newfoundland	321,080	351,032
Niger Protectorate	351,517	377,545
Sierra Leone	191,483	124,523
St. Helena and Ascension	785	652
Straits Settlements	3,643,224	3,941,509
West Indies, British	1,453,089	1,283,413
Zanzibar & Pemba	182,330	154,437
Total, British Possess.	**£94,018,933**	**£99,433,955**
Total Foreign Countries and Brit. Possessions	£451,028,960	£470,378,583

Total Exports.

FOREIGN.	1897.	1898.
Abyssinia	£16,805	£9,852
Africa, Western	16,867	18,109
America, United States of	37,933,917	28,534,477
Argentine Republic	4,995,661	5,812,770
Austria-Hungary	2,120,019	2,287,395
Belgium	12,788,520	13,850,902

	1897.	1898.
Brazil	£5,696,296	£6,449,903
Bulgaria	409,141	317,946
Chile	2,376,290	1,855,771
China (excl. Hong Kong)	5,179,767	5,099,497
Colombia, Republic of ...	1,221,216	815,925
Congo Free State	99,102	126,338
Costa Rica	210,122	140,105
Denmark and Colonies...	3,535,526	3,972,590
Ecuador	435,398	341,757
France	19,517,711	20,513,958
Do. Colonial Possessions	1,118,394	1,200,640
Germany	32,012,595	33,331,701
Do. Colonial Possessions	128,615	136,538
Greece	921,636	1,259,107
Guatemala	246,358	169,589
Hayti and San Domingo	310,397	203,294
Holland	13,260,214	13,046,026
Do. Colonial Possessions	2,212,724	2,256,615
Honduras	42,177	31,179
Italy	6,312,669	6,284,965
Japan	5,978,454	5,062,150
Mexico	1,731,838	1,917,672
Morocco	511,985	549,865
Nicaragua	116,908	113,565
Norway	2,780,019	3,193,430
Pacific, Islands in the	196,019	208,129
Persia	442,656	338,017
Peru	834,856	920,024
Portugal	1,906,674	2,085,564
Do. Colonial Possessions	1,921,312	1,894,573
Rounania	1,441,263	1,363,002
Russia	11,868,078	14,187,208
San Salvador	266,614	114,802
Servia	20,607	13,004
Siam	154,252	215,440
Spain	3,815,951	3,505,728
Do. Colonial Possessions	2,022,873	1,339,934
Sweden	4,767,154	5,311,291
Tripoli	63,070	83,723
Tunis	220,095	299,409
Turkey: European	3,029,012	3,015,854
„ Asiatic	3,852,815	3,514,216
„ Egypt	4,542,140	4,626,881
Uruguay	839,212	1,303,932
Venezuela	568,567	472,280
Total to For. Countries	**£207,209,749**	**£203,903,252**

GREATER BRITAIN.	1897.	1898.
Aden and Dependencies	£173,357	£265,888
Ascension	7,774	7,960
Australasia :—		
New South Wales	6,813,388	7,318,139
Victoria	5,250,596	5,273,342
South Australia	1,918,417	1,814,295
Queensland	2,177,839	2,125,684
Western Australia	2,573,427	1,920,076
New Zealand	4,489,062	4,465,626
Tasmania	445,600	494,709
Fiji Islands	27,641	18,135
Bermudas	205,526	126,862
British East Africa	191,843	149,646
British Guiana	659,430	723,456
British Honduras	92,830	90,551
Canada, Dominion of	6,111,931	7,174,820
Cape Colony	10,765,158	9,865,134
Ceylon	1,070,932	1,240,463
Channel Islands	1,303,259	1,299,111
Cyprus	86,262	77,883
Falkland Islands	38,669	36,978
Gambia	81,069	91,376
Gibraltar	677,781	775,967
Gold Coast	482,378	550,463
Hong Kong	2,079,951	2,347,689

	1897.	1898.
India : Bombay	£9,748,749	£11,493,190
Madras	2,869,774	2,342,310
Bengal	12,985,328	13,951,577
Burma	2,405,534	2,575,857
Lagos	521,204	578,196
Malta and Gozo	856,694	930,464
Mauritius	303,487	261,407
Natal	3,621,373	3,282,531
Newfoundland, &c.	352,949	366,283
Niger Protectorate	608,193	746,206
Sierra Leone	305,759	322,177
St. Helena	21,743	22,370
Straits Settlements	2,583,916	2,816,863
West Indies, British	2,050,067	2,098,557
Zanzibar and Pemba	101,814	122,072
Total British Possessions	**£86,964,369**	**90,110,736**
Total Foreign Countries	**207,209,749**	**203,903,252**
Total to Foreign Countries and Greater Britain	**£294,174,118**	**£294,013,988**

BRITISH PRODUCE AND MANUFACTURES.—Chief Exports during 1898 :—

	1898.
Alkali (soda chiefly)	£1,005,763
Apparel, ready-made	4,695,660
Arms, ammunition, &c.	2,477,574
Beer and Ale	1,623,183
Books, printed	1,336,549
India-rubber manufactures	1,328,102
Railway carriages, trucks, &c.	1,828,028
Chemicals and dye-stuffs	2,515,563
Coals, &c.	18,145,502
Naphtha, and similar products	1,524,446
Corn, grain, and meal	618,163—758,427
Cotton yarn	8,913,272
Cotton manufactures—	
„ White or plain	£28,575,660
„ Printed, &c.	19,332,027
„ Lace, &c.	2,258,997
Sewing Cotton	3,412,220
Hosiery and small wares	2,396,200
Total of all cotton manufactures, &c.	**55,977,505**
Cycles	960,939
Earthen and china ware	1,819,815
Herrings and other fish	2,588,380
Haberdashery, &c.	1,504,519
Hardware and Cutlery	1,988,692
Hats	1,059,739
Implements and tools of industry	1,314,676
Iron and steel (raw material)	6,983,272
Leather, tanned, unwrought	1,421,995
„ Boots, &c.	1,802,358
Linen manufactures and yarn	5,278,180
Jute manufactures, including yarn	2,323,732
Manures, including chemical manures	2,173,356
Medicines, drugs, &c.	1,103,934
Oil, seed	1,200,851
Painters' colours and materials	1,689,005
Paper and stationery	1,431,959
Pickles, vinegar, confectionery, &c.	1,342,969
Spirits	1,951,913
Sugar, refined	414,380
Steam-engines	3,626,452
Machinery (not steam-engines)	14,763,511
Other iron and steel manufactures	15,647,000
Copper, brass, lead, tin, zinc, &c.	5,229,038
Silk manufactures, yarn, &c.	1,862,261
Wool, sheep and lambs', flock, &c.	2,802,883
Woollen and worsted yarn	6,443,739
„ manufactures	13,699,435

	1897.	1898.		1897.	1898.
Animals, living—Oxen...	£10,375,192	£9,399,793	Metals, other kinds	£7,465,771	£7,321,577
„ „ Sheep and lambs...	919,016	984,863	„ lead	2,245,758	2,521,356
„ „ Horses ...	1,254,362	1,146,324	„ silver ore	1,429,822	1,145,905
Bacon and hams............	12,549,812	14,216,513	„ tin	1,623,758	1,389,601
Beef, fresh	6,989,568	5,915,705	„ zinc	1,845,912	1,922,291
Butter	15,916,917	15,961,783	Milk, condensed	1,398,363	1,435,951
„ margarine	2,485,370	2,384,384	Musical instruments	1,183,439	1,220,512
Caoutchouc	5,164,526	6,874,378	Mutton, fresh	4,827,868	4,502,179
Cheese	5,885,521	4,970,242	Oil, palm	1,001,368	975,427
Chemicals..................	1,356,359	1,387,650	Oil-seed cake	1,834,729	2,284,244
Cocoa......................	1,528,546	1,968,599	Paper	3,480,574	3,530,184
Coffee	3,585,675	3,589,988	„ materials for ...	3,150,240	2,984,705
Corn—Wheat	23,363,503	26,147,256	Petroleum.................	3,335,271	3,733,632
„ Other	19,739,325	23,816,567	Pork, fresh and salted...	...	1,485,158
„ Meal and flour ...	10,476,645	11,545,443	Potatoes	1,200,328	1,913,912
Cotton, raw	32,195,172	34,125,554	Rice	2,115,559	2,005,620
„ manufactured ...	3,627,537	4,383,493	Seeds, cotton	1,925,321	2,069,111
Drugs	1,201,379	863,728	„ flax or linseed ...	2,988,503	2,920,624
Dyes	1,470,574	2,386,788	Silk, raw	1,113,238	1,338,614
Eggs	4,356,807	4,457,117	„ manufactures	20,310,549	16,623,230
Farinaceous substances .	...	1,442,926	Skins, goat	1,091,306	1,195,959
Feathers	1,298,417	1,440,001	„ furs	2,311,041	1,406,945
Fish	3,421,314	3,562,601	Spirits—brandy	1,375,364	1,149,334
Flax	3,203,184	2,932,646	Sugar, refined and candy	9,727,973	10,168,832
Fruits—Oranges	2,266,920	1,986,960	„ unrefined	6,222,971	7,053,119
„ Apples	1,187,303	1,108,056	Tea	10,405,084	10,335,643
Glass	3,007,018	3,275,586	Tobacco, unmanufact'd ...	2,345,942	2,437,025
Hemp and tow	1,849,011	2,308,480	„ manufactured ...	1,716,281	1,448,489
Hides, raw	2,750,157	2,905,964	Toys	1,068,953	1,100,475
Jute	5,632,477	5,394,116	Wine	6,042,311	6,575,651
Lace	1,434,224	1,430,014	Wood and timber, hewn	5,780,639	4,820,539
Lard	1,993,143	2,887,801	„ sawn, &c.	16,639,931	18,592,507
Leather.....................	7,647,457	7,788,261	Wool, sheep and lambs'	24,436,871	23,437,188
„ gloves	2,144,619	2,014,398	„ goats' or mohair,&c.	1,428,450	1,350,973
Meat, preserved	1,702,315	1,802,440	Woollen manufactures...	11,003,118	9,914,129
Metals, copper.............	6,277,743	6,713,964	„ yarn	1,772,102	1,987,620
„ iron ore	4,536,004	4,034,648	Parcel Post	1,044,032	1,213,606

Food supplied from Abroad.

The United Kingdom obtains from abroad immense supplies of food *auxiliary* to those produced at home. The following tables shew the quantities and values of the principal articles of such food imported therein in each of the twelve years from 1887 to 1898, distinguishing the imports from foreign countries from the imports from Greater Britain—*i.e.*, British Possessions abroad. Rice, maize, sago, &c., not being grown in the United Kingdom, are not comprised within the term "auxiliary."

States and Russia, and the principal British possessions are the British East Indies and Canada. In the year 1898 the quantities imported therefrom were, in round figures, as follows :—United States, 37,800,000 cwt. ; Russia, 6,200,000 cwt. ; British East Indies, 9,500,000 cwt. ; Canada, 5,000,000 cwt. In 1897, however, the quantity imported from Russia was 15,000,000 cwt. In 1898 the average value of wheat imported from

WHEAT.

Year.	From Foreign Countries.		From Greater Britain.	
	Quantity.	Value.	Quantity.	Value.
	Cwt.	£	Cwt.	£
1887	41,922,802	16,172,940	13,879,716	5,164,978
1888	45,630,535	17,458,056	11,630,828	4,537,918
1889	46,756,950	18,022,882	11,794,937	4,487,620
1890	47,176,349	18,389,251	13,297,831	5,194,593
1891	48,047,516	21,522,735	18,265,446	7,925,469
1892	46,513,181	17,797,978	18,388,618	7,059,924
1893	53,518,949	17,194,051	11,943,039	3,875,977
1894	58,071,243	15,459,543	12,034,989	3,300,962
1895	67,615,785	18,617,377	14,134,170	3,913,799
1896	64,288,640	19,959,445	5,737,340	1,719,544
1897	57,345,820	21,246,962	5,393,360	2,116,541
1898	50,465,820	20,563,116	14,762,110	5,584,140

OTHER CEREALS.
(Viz.:—Barley, Oats, Rye, Peas, and Beans.)

Year.	From Foreign Countries.		From Greater Britain.	
	Quantity.	Value.	Quantity.	Value.
	Cwt.	£	Cwt.	£
1887	32,833,886	8,471,855	2,155,203	613,904
1888	45,486,166	12,234,778	1,370,491	387,864
1889	38,442,894	10,559,239	818,342	278,159
1890	33,722,846	10,178,192	1,446,858	489,642
1891	37,829,989	12,659,294	2,794,181	990,976
1892	32,725,673	10,195,213	4,719,379	1,551,924
1893	41,208,880	11,339,672	2,566,269	797,368
1894	52,950,113	12,663,136	1,812,229	535,904
1895	47,957,106	10,826,852	1,399,880	416,600
1896	44,630,069	11,167,916	2,538,330	693,289
1897	38,504,155	9,661,580	3,250,500	842,119
1898	41,415,708	11,627,817	4,149,504	1,197,485

The principal foreign places to which Great Britain is indebted for wheat are the United foreign countries was 8s. 2d. per cwt., and from Greater Britain 7s. 7d. per cwt., as compared with

7s. 9d. and 7s. 5d. respectively in 1887, and 6s. 2d. and 6s. respectively in 1896.

The articles included under the heading "Other Cereals" only partially enter into the food of man. In 1898 the respective quantities of barley and oats imported from foreign countries were 21,297,744 cwt. and 13,082,550 cwt., with a value of £6,749,564 and £3,672,993 respectively, and from Greater Britain the quantities were, barley, 153,260 cwt., and oats 2,495,350 cwt., with a value of £41,908 and £709,864 respectively.

WHEATEN FLOUR.

YEAR.	From Foreign Countries.		From Greater Britain.	
	Quantity.	Value.	Quantity.	Value.
	Cwt.	£	Cwt.	£
1887	17,091,345	9,487,650	971,889	540,234
1888	16,070,249	9,050,179	840,193	480,567
1889	13,469,698	7,902,444	1,202,384	641,464
1890	14,708,372	8,477,761	1,064,964	596,527
1891	15,530,977	9,474,057	1,192,026	710,830
1892	20,702,244	11,541,525	1,403,765	725,928
1893	19,293,391	9,238,848	1,114,777	522,662
1894	17,865,323	7,488,044	1,269,282	506,629
1895	15,951,270	6,645,868	2,417,140	1,033,145
1896	19,387,280	8,410,883	1,932,920	816,990
1897	17,140,549	8,792,836	1,540,120	806,820
1898	19,038,789	10,482,198	1,978 320	1,063,245

In the year 1898 no less than 17,400,000 cwt. of wheaten flour, valued at £9,500,000, were imported from the United States; in the same year 1,970,000 cwt., valued at £1,058,000, were imported from Canada. In 1898 the average value of wheaten flour imported from foreign countries was 11s. 0d. per cwt., and from Greater Britain 10s. 9d. per cwt., as compared with 11s. 1d. in each case in 1887, and 8s. 8d. and 8s. 5d. respectively in 1896.

BUTTER AND MARGARINE.

YEAR.	From Foreign Countries.		From Greater Britain	
	Quantity.	Value.	Quantity.	Value.
	Cwt.	£	Cwt.	£
1887	2,747,455	11,719,265	41,819	171,436
1888	2,774,666	12,034,541	36,510	146,817
1889	3,129,020	13,724,078	40,512	175,619
1890	3,049,433	13,444,753	58,140	237,336
1891	3,269,277	14,687,496	101,760	461,890
1892	3,340,424	14,945,100	147,935	732,974
1893	3,412,750	15,337,420	214,694	1,071,517
1894	3,369,534	14,976,916	314,626	1,524,593
1895	3,411,898	15,217,963	353,932	1,584,437
1896	3,654,174	16,408,951	309,478	1,433,838
1897	3,772,852	16,649,857	381,493	1,752,430
1898	3,714,627	16,524,384	395,741	1,821,783

In the year 1898 the quantity of butter imported from foreign countries was 2,813,736 cwt., with a value of £14,140,738, rather more than one-half of which was imported from Denmark; in the same year the quantity imported from Greater Britain was 395,417 cwt., with a value of £1,821,045. Practically the whole of the margarine imported comes from foreign countries: in the year 1898, 900,291 cwt. were imported from those countries, and of this 844,177 cwt. came from Holland. The average value of the butter imported in that year from foreign countries was

£5 per cwt., and from Greater Britain £4 12s. per cwt. The average value of the margarine imported was £2 13s. per cwt.

CHEESE.

YEAR.	From Foreign Countries.		From Greater Britain.	
	Quantity.	Value.	Quantity.	Value.
	Cwt.	£	Cwt.	£
1887	1,193,513	2,934,149	643,276	1,580,233
1888	1,222,240	2,954,680	695,376	1,591,728
1889	1,227,071	2,911,423	682,780	1,583,216
1890	1,277,708	2,995,715	866,907	1,980,369
1891	1,153,770	2,747,520	887,655	2,066,050
1892	1,168,575	2,859,113	1,064,253	2,557,692
1893	993,891	2,489,171	1,083,848	2,672,289
1894	1,069,123	2,647,239	1,197,140	2,827,849
1895	889,427	2,116,665	1,244,460	2,558,571
1896	953,818	2,193,202	1,291,128	2,707,858
1897	1,019,416	2,392,633	1,595,647	3,512,032
1898	872,555	1,950,071	1,477,062	3,035,458

In the year 1898, of the cheese imported from foreign countries, 485,995 cwt., valued at £1,006,556, were imported from the United States, and 292,925 cwt., valued at £724 936, from Holland; of that imported from Greater Britain, 1,432,181 cwt., valued at £2,943,725, came from Canada. The average value of the cheese imported in that year from foreign countries was £2 5s. per cwt., and from Greater Britain £2 1s. per cwt., as compared with £2 9s. in each case in 1887. This is one of the few articles included in the tables where the supply from Greater Britain in recent years exceeds that from foreign countries.

EGGS.

YEAR.	From Foreign Countries.		From Greater Britain.	
	Quantity.	Value.	Quantity.	Value.
	Nos.	£	Nos.	£
1887	1,088,203,320	3,080,377	1,885,920	5,304
1888	1,124,961,360	3,078,186	1,831,320	4,981
1889	1,129,811,760	3,120,955	2,089,680	6,595
1890	1,231,802,520	3,418,701	3,147,000	10,105
1891	1,240,720,560	3,411,519	34,677,120	94,003
1892	1,305,304,440	3,706,879	31,425,840	87,839
1893	1,297,493,880	3,791,094	28,024,440	84,553
1894	1,392,182,400	3,687,069	33,053,760	99,260
1895	1,470,800,640	3,835,425	55,909,680	168,021
1896	1,526,131,560	3,997,303	63,269,760	187,353
1897	1,610,207,160	4,148,653	73,603,320	208,154
1898	1,640,626,560	4,202,783	90,325,560	254,334

The principal foreign countries from which eggs were imported in 1898 were France, Germany, Russia, Belgium, and Denmark, the number and value of the eggs imported from those countries in that year being as follows:—France, 253,811,520, valued at £817,336; Germany, 338,535,360, valued at £788,844; Russia, 437,508,360, valued at £966,129; Belgium, 281,995,440, valued at £730,898; Denmark, 242,340,560, valued at £685,447. Practically the whole of the eggs imported from Greater Britain in that year came from Canada. The average value of the eggs imported in 1898 from foreign countries was about 7¼d. per dozen, and from Greater Britain about 8d. per dozen, as compared with 8d. per dozen in each case in 1887.

LARD.

Year.	From Foreign Countries.		From Greater Britain.	
	Quantity.	Value.	Quantity.	Value.
	Cwt.	£	Cwt.	£
1887	852,673	1,507.278	54.961	96,965
1838	847.971	1,741,007	37.065	78,126
1889	1,155.655	2,109.236	36.999	67,096
1890	1,266,037	2,075,877	21,914	37,227
1891	1,049,920	1,714 314	21,172	35,151
1892	1,258,875	2,248,288	17,167	31,731
1893	1,179 222	2,927,810	22,638	50,829
1894	1,429 277	2,799,726	19,213	36,616
1895	1,737,920	2,919,358	53,212	88.595
1896	1,667,661	2,176,187	111,365	140,042
1897	1,759,708	1,979,445	40,748	46,858
1898	2,146,304	2,908,471	45,021	68,355

In the year 1898 nearly the whole of the lard imported from foreign countries came from the United States, the quantity therefrom being 2,044,727 cwt. valued at £2,756,308, and the whole of that imported from Greater Britain came from Canada. The average value of lard imported in that year from foreign countries was £1 7s. 1d. per cwt., and from Greater Britain £1 10s. 4d. per cwt., as compared with £1 15s. 4d. and £1 15s. 3d. respectively in 1887.

BACON AND HAMS.

Year.	From Foreign Countries.		From Greater Britain.	
	Quantity.	Value.	Quantity.	Value.
	Cwt.	£	Cwt.	£
1887	3,641,830	8,092,051	285.772	641,725
1888	3.436,569	7,972,126	157,643	371,261
1889	4 186 813	9,163,594	297,295	631,698
1890	4,598,694	9,077,018	401,322	770,158
1891	4,480,215	8,961,329	234,797	480,432
1892	4,781,161	10,159,423	353,349	734,410
1893	3,935,721	10,702,676	251,577	607,391
1894	4,513,953	10,201,990	305 335	653,725
1895	5,000,454	10,133.543	354,482	690,454
1896	5,382,623	9,929,033	626,315	1,051,571
1897	6,320,704	11,765,100	410,086	784,712
1898	7,030,271	12,997,529	653,350	1,228,984

In the year 1898 5,175 404 cwt. of bacon valued at £9,325,972 were imported from foreign countries, of which about 79 per cent. came from the United States, and about 20 per cent. from Denmark; and 1,854,867 cwt. of hams valued at £3,661,557 were imported from foreign countries, nearly the whole of which came from the United States. In the same year 535,918 cwt. of bacon valued at £995,702, and 117,432 cwt. of hams valued at £233,282 were imported from Greater Britain, practically the whole of which came from Canada. The average value of the bacon imported in 1898 from foreign countries was £1 16s. 0d. per cwt., and from Greater Britain £1 17s. 2d. per cwt.; the average value of the hams imported from foreign countries in that year was £1 19s. 6d. per cwt., and from Greater Britain £1 19s. 9d. per cwt.

BEEF (Fresh).

Year.	From Foreign Countries.		From Greater Britain.	
	Quantity.	Value.	Quantity.	Value.
	Cwt.	£	Cwt.	£
1887	647,600	1,461,497	8,594	16 696
1888	795,212	1,832,884	41,447	86,422
1889	1,285,601	2,843,782	100,151	185,372
1890	1,716,761	3,670 770	137,832	252,245
1891	1,771,113	3.793,319	149,398	245,175
1892	1,960,850	4,222,674	118,787	190,474
1893	1,582,285	3,477,840	225,766	352,756
1894	1,799,417	3,773,830	304,687	439,858
1895	1,680,732	3,496,738	510,305	778,8 0
1896	2,126,813	4,289,542	532,587	738,685
1897	2,370,358	4,834,982	640,029	948,685
1898	2,454,862	4,921,176	645,959	994,529

In the year 1898 nearly the whole of the fresh beef imported from foreign countries came from the United States, and nearly the whole of that imported from Greater Britain came from Australia and New Zealand, the quantities therefrom being as follows:—United States, 2,301,956 cwt. valued at £4,677,431; Australia, 531,651 cwt. valued at £807,328; and New Zealand, 92,755 cwt., valued at £146,010. The average value of the fresh beef imported from foreign countries in 1898 was £2 0s. 1d. per cwt., and from Greater Britain £1 10s. 9d. per cwt., as compared with £2 5s. 2d. and £1 18s. 1d. respectively in 1887.

MUTTON (Fresh).

Year.	From Foreign Countries.		From Greater Britain.	
	Quantity.	Value.	Quantity.	Value.
	Cwt.	£	Cwt.	£
1887	321,500	607,753	461,614	964,976
1888	444,866	834 263	543,144	1,104,212
1889	614,447	1,287,423	610,611	1,287.973
1890	753,813	1,613,358	902,606	1,834 418
1891	588,756	1,157,548	1,074,238	2,124,453
1892	712,386	1,449,895	987,580	1,997,207
1893	774,642	1,555,983	1,196,858	2,317 880
1894	849,141	1,556,725	1,445,925	2,784,502
1895	928,867	1,476,640	1,682,568	3,119,033
1896	1,042,008	1,613.220	1,853,150	3,105,326
1897	1,181,834	1,787,586	2,009,093	3,040,282
1898	1,379,718	1,961,107	1,934,283	2,941,072

In the year 1898 nearly the whole of the fresh mutton imported from foreign countries came from the Argentine Republic and Holland, and practically the whole of that from Greater Britain came from Australia and New Zealand, the quantities therefrom being as follows:—Argentine Republic, 1,106,201 cwt. valued at £1,357,926; Holland, 265,543 cwt. valued at £584,779; Australia, 619,489 cwt. valued at £832.221; and New Zealand, 1,314,619 cwt. valued at £2,108,477. The average value of the fresh mutton imported in 1898 from foreign countries was £1 8s. 5d. per cwt., and from Greater Britain £1 10s. 5d. per cwt., as compared with £1 17s. 10d. and £2 1s. 1d. respectively in 1887. It will be noticed that the supply of fresh mutton from Greater Britain exceeds that from foreign countries.

PORK (FRESH).

YEAR.	From Foreign Countries.		From Greater Britain.	
	Quantity.	Value.	Quantity.	Value.
	Cwt.	£	Cwt.	£
1887	151,319	373,484	45	117
1888	243,814	559,542	28	71
1889	117,347	287,371	121	323
1890	45,217	109,700	32	64
1891	127,429	302,567	89	158
1892	131,978	309,909	129	256
1893	181,860	455,097	231	447
1894	179,796	435,339	587	1,187
1895	287,694	663,697	590	1,249
1896	298,771	686,014	640	1,227
1897	347,355	764,611	262	517
1898	547,472	1,146,567	10,130	18,813

Pork is not an article of large import, and nearly the whole of that imported comes from foreign countries. In the year 1898, 222,672 cwt. of fresh pork, valued at £474,462 came from Holland and 276,829 cwt., valued at £556,269, came from the United States. The average value of fresh pork imported in that year was £2 1s. 10d. per cwt., as compared with £2 9s. 4d. in 1887.

OTHER MEAT (SALTED, PRESERVED, &C.).

YEAR.	From Foreign Countries.		From Greater Britain.	
	Quantity.	Value.	Quantity.	Value.
	Cwt.	£	Cwt.	£
1887	793,494	1,592,329	262,098	593,667
1888	860,112	1,762,651	211,658	445,448
1889	1,110,137	2,232,994	146,130	336,913
1890	1,206,470	2,511,585	161,802	385,340
1891	1,212,426	2,444,357	151,749	351,556
1892	1,269,713	2,599,590	184,109	391,970
1893	964,176	2,095,547	191,548	418,150
1894	956,948	2,034,594	254,505	545,402
1895	1,065,190	2,184,474	468,555	902,522
1896	1,096,755	2,150,807	387,260	774,430
1897	1,049,761	2,083,836	396,887	815,346
1898	1,166,219	2,424,823	308,633	783,137

Under the head of other meat are included salt beef and pork, beef and mutton preserved otherwise than by salting, and meat not classified under any particular head. The following table shows some of the imports included above for the year 1898 :—

	From Foreign Countries.		From Greater Britain.	
	Quantity	Value	Quantity.	Value.
	Cwt.	£	Cwt.	£
Salt Beef	207,361	270,668	1,584	2,336
Salt Pork	258,334	340,740	17,659	19,038
Beef preserved otherwise than by salting	167,421	568,912	113,923	448,568
Mutton do.	3,086	5,285	115,228	189,964

The bulk of the salt beef and pork came from the United States, most of the preserved beef from United States and Australia, and most of the preserved mutton from Australia and New Zealand.

OXEN AND BULLS.

YEAR	From Foreign Countries.		From Greater Britain.	
	Quantity.	Value.	Quantity.	Value.
	Nos.	£	Nos.	£
1887	156,549	2,708,658	62,672	1,093,987
1888	228,375	4,091,028	58,891	1,040,189
1889	359,446	6,704,186	82,361	1,429,212
1890	426,782	7,940,084	109,736	1,742,694
1891	342,022	6,460,710	98,481	1,632,336
1892	400,161	7,600,931	90,120	1,460,611
1893	255,721	4,774,166	81,342	1,439,281
1894	391,191	6,906,080	80,603	1,318,987
1895	315,905	5,531,960	97,432	1,618,852
1896	459,001	7,661,838	99,360	1,579,617
1897	489,181	8,368,621	123,899	2,006,571
1898	458,460	7,583,777	105,930	1,738,096

In the year 1898 over 369,000 oxen and bulls came from the United States, and 105,000 from Canada; the average value in that year from foreign countries was £16 11s. each, and from Greater Britain £16 8s. each, as compared with £17 6s. and £17 9s. respectively in 1887.

SHEEP AND LAMBS.

YEAR.	From Foreign Countries.		From Greater Britain.	
	Quantity.	Value.	Quantity.	Value.
	Nos.	£	Nos.	£
1887	935,910	1,579,891	35,494	65,948
1888	910,871	1,651,277	45,339	89,272
1889	620,036	1,080,700	57,922	114,432
1890	315,808	612,538	42,650	83,774
1891	312,871	601,678	31,633	61,337
1892	63,305	94,300	15,743	31,359
1893	59,093	81,748	3,589	6,782
1894	347,865	567,078	136,732	237,745
1895	847,748	1,389,151	217,722	393,393
1896	685,295	1,006,666	84,297	126,568
1897	547,741	823,486	63,763	95,610
1898	609,484	904,563	54,263	80,300

In the year 1898 upwards of 147,000 sheep and lambs came from the United States, 430,000 from the Argentine Republic, and 42,000 from Canada; the average value in that year from foreign countries was £1 9s. 8d. each, and from Greater Britain £1 9s. 7d. each, as compared with £1 13s. 9d. and £1 17s. 2d. respectively in 1887.

APPLES (RAW).

YEAR.	From Foreign Countries.		From Greater Britain.	
	Quantity.	Value.	Quantity.	Value.
	Bushels.	£	Bushels.	£
1887	1,539,362	436,015	405,098	127,904
1888	2,876,510	753,767	920,082	276,393
1889	2,879,565	756,019	732,750	218,386
1890	1,855,257	536,701	719,700	249,371
1891	2,057,691	636,644	1,089,682	397,353
1892	3,041,913	875,630	1,472,787	478,182
1893	2,805,079	615,657	654,905	227,875
1894	3,743,549	1,005,287	1,225,120	384,134
1895	2,111,752	594,544	1,180,510	365,729
1896	3,362,653	851,566	2,814,303	730,929
1897	2,991,215	808,421	1,208,756	378,882
1898	1,848,146	574,539	1,610,370	533,517

In the year 1898 about 67 per cent. of the apples imported from foreign countries came from the United States, and about 90 per cent. of those from Greater Britain came from Canada. The average value of the apples imported from foreign countries in that year was 6s. 3d. per bushel, and from Greater Britain, 6s. 7d. per bushel, as compared with 5s. 8d. and 6s. 4d. respectively in 1887.

ONIONS (RAW).

YEAR.	From Foreign Countries.		From Greater Britain.	
	Quantity.	Value.	Quantity.	Value.
	Bushels.	£	Bushels.	£
1887	3,567,868	604,254	78,054	12,496
1888	3,409,468	626,127	75,522	15,955
1889	3,703,210	645,163	151,243	26,916
1890	3,753,704	698,480	117,491	25,540
1891	4,195,212	717,437	85,833	16,308
1892	4,314,258	706,231	100,018	17,809
1893	4,658,000	780,854	13,809	2,551
1894	5,233,847	757,161	54,665	7,879
1895	5,692,144	690,130	42,624	6,298
1896	6,014,738	673,494	72,167	8,455
1897	6,052,135	752,585	56,789	7,975
1898	5,924,199	783,699	78,316	9,210

In the year 1898 1,722,668 bushels of raw onions were imported from Spain, 1,487,202 bushels from Holland, and 1,196,650 bushels from Egypt. The average value of raw onions imported from foreign countries in that year was 2s. 8d. per bushel, and from Greater Britain 2s. 4d. per bushel, as compared with 3s. 5d. and 3s. 2d. respectively in 1887.

POTATOES.

YEAR	From Foreign Countries.		From Greater Britain.	
	Quantity.	Value.	Quantity.	Value.
	Cwt.	£	Cwt.	£
1887	1,655,428	417,855	1,107,929	557,049
1888	954,934	259,840	1,428,873	542,194
1889	662,677	206,061	1,201,749	529,978
1890	752,017	223,674	1,188,083	490,583
1891	1,860,295	554,219	1,332,541	642,605
1892	1,670,377	389,428	1,337,959	560,904
1893	1,632,697	356,447	1,195,428	500,505
1894	1,540,482	477,465	1,163,321	552,626
1895	2,731,996	671,005	1,026,160	498,917
1896	957,869	326,887	1,286,758	581,088
1897	2,833,746	681,142	1,087,459	519,186
1898	5,499,532	1,335,805	1,254,196	578,107

In the year 1898, of the potatoes imported from foreign countries 1,554,445 cwt. valued at £457,580 came from France, and 1,953,638 cwt., valued at £420,491, from Germany; the remainder came principally from Belgium, and Holland. Nearly the whole of those imported from Greater Britain came from the Channel Islands. The average value of the potatoes imported in 1898 from foreign countries was 4s. 10d. per cwt., and from Greater Britain, 9s. 3d. per cwt., as compared with 5s. 1d. and 10s. 1d. in 1887. It will be observed that in several of the years included in the table the quantity of potatoes imported from Greater Britain exceeds that imported from foreign countries.

FISH.

YEAR.	From Foreign Countries.		From Greater Britain.	
	Quantity.	Value.	Quantity.	Value.
	Cwt.	£	Cwt.	£
1887	1,416,066	1,648,404	188,601	384,019
1888	1,707,236	1,948,134	200,408	376,231
1889	1,790,858	2,209,943	197,171	378,680
1890	2,034,250	2,221,947	261,724	589,508
1891	2,091,208	2,213,519	261,162	596,430
1892	2,290,681	2,218,604	259,936	541,396
1893	2,088,639	2,178,993	231,199	503,758
1894	2,203,649	1,869,528	352,328	777,552
1895	2,101,292	2,231,981	357,351	746,490
1896	2,291,294	2,423,855	330,738	789,228
1897	2,059,053	2,546,773	390,677	874,541
1898	2,475,189	2,543,895	504,924	1,018,706

In the year 1898, out of a total of 966,394 cwt of fresh herrings imported, 960,091 cwt., with a value of £211,581, came from Sweden and Norway; out of a total of 194,795 cwt. of oysters imported, 135,037 cwt., with a value of £89,245, came from the United States, and 45,801 cwt., with a value of £97,395, came from France; out of a total of 239,273 cwt. of sardines imported, (practically all from foreign countries) 139,900 cwt., with a value of £287,499, came from Portugal and 72,126 cwt., with a value of £326,805, from France. Of the other kinds of fish included in the table, 326,706 cwt. were imported from Norway; 274,730 cwt. from the United States; 209,388 cwt. from Holland; 162,841 cwt. from Denmark; and 405,930 cwt. from Canada.

In the case of several of the articles included in these tables, a small portion thereof is not retained for home consumption, but is re-exported, but in nearly every case it is a very small proportion of the total quantity imported.

Speaking generally, only in the case of cheese and fresh and preserved mutton has the quantity imported in recent years from Greater Britain exceeded that from foreign countries, the proportions from Greater Britain in the year 1898 being as follows:—Cheese 63 per cent.; fresh mutton, 58 per cent.; and preserved mutton, 97 per cent. In the case of peas, raw apples, and beef preserved otherwise than by salting, the proportion from Greater Britain in the year 1898 exceeded 40 per cent.; but as regards many of the other articles included in the tables the proportion therefrom was very small.

The particulars below relate to a few articles of *auxiliary* food not included in the above comparative tables:—

Articles.	From Foreign Countries.		From Greater Britain.	
	Quantity imported in 1898.	Value.	Quantity imported in 1898.	Value.
	Cwts.	£	Cwts.	£
Oatmeal and Groats	857,440	549,510	132,040	66,415
Milk, Condensed	816,602	1,435,067	672	884
Poultry and Game	Not sp'd	615,776	Not sp'd	21,716
Rabbits (Dead)	109,465	297,368	204,933	275,235

There has been no cessation in the work of exploration in all parts of the world during 1899, but the nature of the exploration becomes year by year more scientific, the surveyor is more in evidence than the pioneer, and accurate maps, rather than books of adventure, express the best work of to-day. The more important steps in geographical progress and the chief changes of boundaries made or first published between November 15 1898, and November 15, 1899, are summarised below.

ANTARCTIC REGIONS.

Satisfactory news was received of the two expeditions which were in the field at the close of last year. The *Belgica*, a small steam whaler of 250 tons, left Europe in August, 1897, under the command of Captain de Gerlache, of the Belgian navy, and after some difficulties in the dangerous channels of Tierra del Fuego, sailed from the Bay of St. John, Staten Island, on January 14, 1898. From January 24 to February 12 an archipelago, which was discovered to be separated by a strait from Hughes Bay on the west side of Palmer Land, was explored, about twenty landings were made, and important scientific investigations carried out. The first evidence of a land fauna in the Antarctic regions was found in the existence of three species of small insects. On February 16, Alexander I. Land was sighted, and on the 28th, in 70° 20′ S., and 85° W., the *Belgica* entered the ice in the hope of pushing southwards, but only reached 71° 31′ S. before being blocked. It was then too late in the season to escape; she was frozen in the pack on March 10, 1898, and drifted about all the winter (the first winter spent by any human being within the Antarctic Circle) and all the next summer, the highest latitude attained being 71° 36′. Lieutenant Danco, one of the scientific staff, died on June 5, and symptoms of incipient scurvy appeared in many of the ship's company. A desperate effort was made in January, 1899, to saw a canal through the ice, but a movement of the floe closed it just as it was being completed, and not until March 14 could the *Belgica* gain the open sea. She reached Punta Arenas on March 28, whence most of the scientific staff returned by steamer to Europe, but Captain de Gerlache brought his ship home under sail, after repairs, to meet with a splendid welcome at Antwerp on his arrival in November. The oceanographical and meteorological results of the expedition have been partially published by M. H. Arçtowski in the *Geographical Journal.*

Sir George Newnes' expedition, under the command of Mr. Borchgrevink, has had an auspicious commencement, and if the first winter in the Antarctic ocean was spent under the Belgian flag, the first winter on the Antarctic land is being passed under the British. The *Southern Cross*, leaving the Thames in August, 1898, touched at Hobart and sailed thence on December 19. The first ice was met with on December 30 in 61° 56′ S., and a few days later the vessel was beset in the pack off the Balleny Islands for a month, but eventually got through and anchored in Robertson Bay near Cape Adare, Victoria Land, on February 17, 1899. Stores, houses, and dogs were put ashore under considerable difficulties on account of heavy gales, by which the ship was several times placed in great danger. Three of the party made an early attempt to climb a peak from which a view of

the top of the plateau, beneath which they are encamped, could be obtained. They reached 2,300 feet, and the land beyond seemed, as was expected, to be a vast expanse of glacier ice. The houses were completed on February 28. Mr. Borchgrevink and his companions (ten in all) landed, and the *Southern Cross* left at once, making a rapid passage through the pack and reaching Port Chalmers, N.Z., on March 16. The 75 Siberian dogs were landed in good condition, and there is no doubt that a bold attempt has been made to explore the interior of the Antarctic land. The *Southern Cross* returns to Cape Adare in January, 1900, to communicate with, and possibly to take off the members of the land party. The expedition was thoroughly equipped, and the scientific staff had not only been trained in their special work, but had practice in the use of *ski* on the ice-floes on the way out, so that good results may be looked for.

The proposed German Antarctic expedition, under the leadership of Dr. Erich von Drygalski, has been subsidised to the extent of £60,000 by the German Government, and will set out in 1901. The expedition is intended to be purely scientific in its aims, and a special ship has been designed and will be built. Thanks to the efforts of Sir Clements Markham and other British geographers, a national British Antarctic expedition will co-operate with the Germans in 1901; the difficulty as to funds has been overcome by the public subscription of £42,000, £25,000 of which is due to the munificence of Mr. Ll. W. Longstaff, and Government has agreed to give £45,000 towards the expedition if the subscriptions of the public reach the same amount. The organization of the expedition has been placed in the hands of a joint committee of the Royal Society and the Royal Geographical Society, but the details of their plan have not been made public at the time of writing.

ARCTIC REGIONS.

The work of the last Arctic season has been characteristically disappointing. Mr. R. E. Peary's ship, the *Windward*, was frozen in at Allman Bay, Grinnell Land, on August 18, 1898. From this position (79° 40′ N.) he set out along the coast northwards with the Eskimo, and, pursuing his plan of winter travel, reached Greely's old winter quarters at Lady Franklin Bay (81° 44′ N.) in December, finding the house undisturbed. Having been frost-bitten in the feet, Peary was obliged to return to the *Windward*, and several of his toes had to be amputated. On his recovery he explored and mapped a considerable part of Grinnell Land, and on the ice opening in 1899 sent back the *Windward* for supplies, intending to make another attempt to get north early in 1900. The *Windward*, after being refitted, will return with stores for three years and remain at the farthest north point it can reach.

The *Diana* which was sent north to communicate with Peary last summer, made a very rapid passage across Melville Bay, where there was little ice, and reached Peary at Etah (where he intends to winter) on August 12. On her return she coaled at Disco Island direct from the coal-seams, and reached Sydney, Nova Scotia, on September 12. The *Diana* landed Dr. Robert Stein and two companions at Cape Sabine on Ellesmere Land, but no definite arrangement seems to have been made for communicating with this party next year.

Captain Sverdrup, in the *Fram*, wintered in 1898 fifty miles farther south than the *Windward*, close to Cape Sabine, and some exploration was done in Ellesmere Land. The surgeon to the expedition died during the winter. On August 18, 1899, the *Fram* was off Littleton Island (78° 25′) with little prospect of getting much further before winter. Her experience amply confirms the wisdom of Nansen's principle on which her first voyage was planned, that a ship can approach the Pole easily from the Siberian side only.

No better fortune attended Mr. Walter Wellman in Franz Josef Land. He divided his small party, sending two Norwegian sailors to winter in an outpost north of the main camp, where one of them died. In the northward advance with dogs and sledges Mr. Wellman injured his leg so severely that he had to return to headquarters. whence he was taken back to Europe by the *Capella*, reaching Tromsö on August 17. The precise nature of his explorations, in the course of which some new land is said to have been discovered, has not yet been made public.

H.R.H. the Duke of the Abruzzi, with a large staff of assistants, started in the *Stella Polare* from Christiania on June 12 with the object of forcing his way to a high latitude by sea north of Franz Josef Land and wintering on board. On August 9 his ship was met by the *Capella* close to Franz Josef Land with all well on board.

The fate of Andrée still remains a mystery. Rumours of a balloon having been seen and bodies found have come both from Northern Asia and Northern America, but they are not substantiated. Several expeditions have searched the coast of Asia and of Greenland in vain, and the only direct evidence obtained has been the discovery north of Spitzbergen of a buoy which had been taken by Andrée in his balloon with the object of dropping it with a letter if he reached the pole. There was no letter inside, and the most probable conjecture is, either that the buoy was thrown out in a desperate attempt to keep the balloon up or that the balloon was lost in the sea, and the buoy floated away.

Professor Nathorst visited the east coast of Greenland in search of traces of Andrée, and, although unsuccessful in that object, he mapped a great extent of coast, completely altering the outline of Franz Josef Fjord, discovering a magnificent new fjord, which was named after King Oscar, and conducting valuable geological investigations.

The Danish expedition, under Lieut. Amdrup, has also done good work on the east coast of Greenland, and returned to Europe.

Spitzbergen has been again visited by the Prince of Monaco in his yacht *Princesse Alice*, and in addition to oceanographical work some excellent surveys were made of part of the coast.

Admiral Makaroff, of the Russian navy, has tested the great steel ice-breaker *Yermak* in the Arctic pack north of Spitzbergen, and is likely to establish an entirely new method of polar research. The vessel, a steamer of 8,000 tons displacement, readily cut her way through ice over six feet thick, and was able by degrees to overcome an ice-barrier 14 feet in total thickness. When certain improvements are made, Admiral Makaroff believes that a vessel of this description should be able to navigate any part of the Arctic

sea. Her ordinary work will be to keep the Baltic open in winter up to St. Petersburg.

It will be noticed that no British expedition has been at work in the Arctic region this year — the United States. Sweden, Norway, Denmark, Russia, Italy and Monaco being the nations represented.

EUROPE.

Geographical work in Europe has been, as is to be expected, mainly of the unexciting nature of official surveys of high accuracy, or scientific studies of the distribution of various phenomena, and there is no country which cannot show some progress in these respects. Mr. Cuttriss and others have been carrying on the exploration of the caverns of Yorkshire, revealing the unsuspected extent and depth of Gaping Ghyll and other difficultly accessible recesses; and similar speleological work has been vigorously carried on in France, Austria, and Italy. In default of Government surveyors being deputed to undertake the work, Sir John Murray and Mr. F. P. Pullar have carried out detailed bathymetrical surveys of a group of lakes in Scotland, and intend to extend their operations to the other lakes. Iceland still affords some scope for real exploration, and Mr. F. W. W. Howell states that he has succeeded in crossing the great glacier called Lang Jökull for the first time and at an altitude of 5,000 feet. This height is greater than that assigned by Dr. Thoroddsen.

ASIA.

(*See map, p.* 469.)

The great stretches of little-explored or totally-unknown country in Asia have never ceased to attract attention. The Andrée search expeditions which visited the north coast of Siberia found no traces of the object of their search, but collected some additional geographical information. The Russian Government has granted to the well-known explorer Baron Toll funds for the purchase of a suitable ship in which to continue his researches in the region of the New Siberian Islands.

Railway activity is the chief interest of the Siberia of to-day. The great railway has been opened all the way from Europe to Irkutsk, and the Manchurian railway, which will ultimately carry it to the coast of China, has been steadily proceeded with. In Russian Central Asia the Trans-Caspian line has been extended in two directions, from Samarkand, north-eastward to Tashkent, and eastward towards Kashgar. An important branch has also been opened from a point near Merv to Kushk, on the borders of Afghanistan within 95 miles of Herat. It has been pointed out that only 438 miles of railway would require to be constructed (from Kushk to Chaman) to allow of the journey from London to Karachi being made in one week, by rail all the way except for the Strait of Dover and the crossing of the Caspian. Political considerations suggested by this proposal of a junction of the Indian and Russian railways in Afghanistan are too serious to admit of any early settlement, but the proposal is in many ways very attractive. *These lines, and one proposed by Mr. C. A. Moreing, are shown on the map of Asia, p.* 469.)

Professor Futterer, of Karlsruhe, has successfully completed his journey across Asia, which was conducted mainly for geological purposes. He reached the great lake Koko-nor in August, 1898, and turning thence southward, crossed the South Koko-nor Mountains to Lake Dabassu, then turned east to the Hwang-ho, which he reached in the Djupar mountains. On the borders of China the party was attacked by Tibetan robbers, but their collections were saved, and after many difficulties Dr. Futterer reached Hankow on January 24, 1899.

Captain Deasy has returned to India after two years spent in explorations in Central Asia. In the summer of 1898 he discovered the source of the Khotan-daria in northern Tibet, finding that it is separated only by a range of snowy mountains from the source of the Keria-daria. In November, 1898, he left Yarkand, and spent the winter with an Indian surveyor mapping in Sarikol, and completely exploring the upper course of the Yarkand river. The altitudes were great, frequently exceeding 15,000 feet, and the cold severe, but much definite geographical information was obtained.

Lieutenant Olufsen and the Danish expedition spent the winter of 1898-99 in the Pamirs, and in spring moved southward to explore the upper valleys of the northern slope of the Hindu Kush.

Dr. Sven Hedin has returned to the scene of his successful explorations in northern Tibet, but his immediate objects and the auspices under which his new expedition has been organised have not been made public. Russian expeditions are at work in several parts of Chinese Turkistan and the northern border of Tibet, where the Russian influence is becoming stronger every year.

Several climbers have directed their attention this year to the giant ranges of southern Asia. Mr. D. W. Freshfield, the doyen of British mountaineers, and Mr. Garwood reached the upper valley of the Teesta river in Sikkim in September, with the intention of ascending some of the great peaks from the northern or Tibetan side. Dr. and Mrs. W. H. Workman, with the well-known guide, M. Zurbriggen, ascended some peaks above the Biafo glacier and Hispar Pass in the Karakorams in July and August.

China has swarmed with commercial and industrial missions from most of the trading nations of the world, and the country is rapidly being opened up. The first steam launch to make the voyage from Chungking to Ichang on the Yangtsekiang reached the latter port in October, the passage occupying 31 hours. M. Bonin is still engaged in his explorations in China and Tibet, but the most notable completed journey in China of a purely geographical kind was that of Captain A. M. S. Wingate, who started from Hankow in November, 1898, and crossed the country, following on the whole Margary's route of 1874. He made one or two detours to the south through country that has been rarely visited, and from Yunnan-fu he struck south-westward to Chung-tung, crossing the head-waters of the Red River and thence on across the Burmese frontier to Bhamo, traversing a good deal of country never before visited by a foreigner, as the route lay well to the south of the Yunnan-Bhamo trade road. This country was extremely rugged and difficult. The whole route was surveyed by plane-table. The western valleys of Yunnan were found to be very unhealthy from malaria. Bhamo was reached on April 20, 1899, the intention of proceeding direct to Mandalay having been frustrated by a savage tribe called Ke-wa, living in the upper Salwin valley. The whole journey from Hankow to Bhamo was 2,360 miles.

Mr. Carey, of the Chinese Consular Service, has added considerably to our knowledge of the Shan tribes on the Chinese borders, and of their country.

The work of delimitation by the British and Chinese Commission on the Burmo-Chinese border is proceeding, and is expected to be completed in the working season 1899-1900.

No farther territorial concessions have been made in China, the representations of the Italian government for a lease of a port in San-mun Bay not having been granted.

In Japan a change of great importance as regards foreigners has taken place in the abolition of extra-territoriality and consular courts. Now all foreigners resident in Japan are subject to the courts of the country; the treaties with the various Powers securing this concession are the first ever made with an Asiatic, or indeed a non-Christian country. As a result of the change, new free ports have been opened and foreigners are now permitted to travel through Japan without having to obtain a passport.

There has been great rivalry between British and Russian merchants in Persia, the routes from Russian territory to Teheran have been greatly improved, and an effort has also been made to encourage trade between India and eastern Persia by the Sistan route, important surveys having been made from India along the road. The question of European predominance in Persia may become acute at any time.

The United States government having found it impossible to come to terms with Aguinaldo, the Filipinos have reverted to their familiar attitude of insurrection, and it has now been decided by the United States to accept the responsibility of pacifying the islands and maintaining them for the present as colonial possessions. Spain has sold her rights in the Caroline and Marianne Islands to Germany, which has thus increased her interests in the Western Pacific; but the United States retains the important island of Guam captured during the war.

The Cambridge Anthropological Expedition, under Dr. A. C. Haddon, reached Borneo in December, 1898, and remained in Sarawak until April, collecting valuable geographical as well as anthropological information. Several other expeditions have been at work in Borneo, including those of gold-prospectors, who have penetrated into the centre of the island.

AFRICA.

The record of 1899 is dark and stormy for most of the European Powers holding possessions in Africa; but notwithstanding wars and revolts, explorations and organisations have been carried on from every side. The evacuation of Fashoda by Major Marchand at the close of 1898 led to a new Franco-British agreement (signed in March, 1899) as to spheres of influence in the Sudan. By this agreement France renounces all claim to territory within the basin of the Nile, while Great Britain recognises the French right to extend political influence over Wadai. The boundary accepted by both powers is shown in the accompanying map, and in addition to the political limits, which are clearly defined, the agreement provides for equality of treatment and trading rights for both nations in the central Sudan between the Nile and Lake Chad. Ownerless Africa has thus been entirely apportioned, and apart from questions of the interpretation of treaties and actual delimitation, difficulties between European Powers can now only arise over the two Native States of Morocco and

Abyssinia, and the uncertain vassalage of Tripoli.

When Major Marchand and his companions left Fashoda on November 4. 1898, they ascended the Sobat River and crossed the south of Abyssinia to Adis-Abeba, which was reached on March 10, 1899 ; thence the expedition went to Jibuti, where they arrived in the middle of May, and took ship for France Marchand's journey will be memorable as the first crossing of the greatest breadth of Africa, although its political object necessarily diminished its opportunities for geographical work. At Adis-Abeba the opportunity was taken of determining the latitude and longitude of that capital very accurately by astronomical observations. The position of

Menelik's palace was found to be 9° 0′ 4″ N., 38° 42′ 50″ E.

Parts of Abyssinia have been traversed by several British expeditions which, entering from the south or east, passed out by the Nile One of these was a sporting expedition led by Lord Lovat and Mr. Weld Blundell. Another was the expedition of Captain Welby, who, proceeding southward from Adis-Abeba, first explored the region round Lake Rudolf, proving definitely that the Omo flowed into that lake, and then marched northward to the Sobat, making a careful planetable survey and fixing points astronomically as he went, and finally reaching Omdurman in July. The journey was most successful, and many interesting observations on places and people were made.

The northern part of British East Africa has also been the scene of other important expeditions, and by the railway from Mombasa the interior region has been brought within a shorter journey of the coast than any other part of tropical Africa equally distant from the sea. The detailed surveys of the line have made it possible to deviate advantageously from the preliminary plan and the rate of progress has been such that trains run to Njabe, 370 miles from the terminus Major H. H. Austin, detached from Colonel J. R. L. Macdonald's expedition, explored and mapped the western shore of Lake Rudolf towards the end of 1898. Dr. Donaldson Smith, one of the pioneers in this region, has returned to complete his explorations. The reorganisation of Uganda after the recent revolts having been entrusted to the competent administration of Sir H. H. Johnston, the scientific geography of that region is sure to receive increased attention. Mt. Kenya was ascended for the first time in September by Mr. Mackinder and a party including two Alpine guides, and the elevation was found provisionally to be over 17,000 feet but under 18,000. Fifteen glaciers were observed descending from the snowfields which cap the mountain.

The reorganisation of the Sudan under Lord Kitchener has gone on steadily and quietly, and the railway along the Nile valley has been pushed southward with remarkable rapidity ; it is to be opened to Khartum in 1899 The military expedition sent out to capture the Khalifa was at first unsuccessful, but Col. Sir. F. R. Wingate, K.C.M.G., came up with the fugitive on 24 Nov. 1899, and annihilated his forces ; the Khalifa was among the slain. In Egypt itself the great engineering works for improving the irrigation of the lower valley and delta by barring the Nile at Assuan approach in magnitude to geographical changes. The geological survey has been employed in the Sinaitic Peninsula, which, although in Asia, is politically part of Egypt.

Several Europeans have made trips into Morocco, some of them leading to valuable scientific results. Dr. Weisberger was able to prepare a plan of the city of Fez and Professor Theobald Fischer obtained data for a more detailed geological description of the west of Morocco than was before possible.

Sokotra has been visited by two expeditions, neither of which was primarily geographical. One of these, an Austrian enterprise, under Count Landberg and Dr. David Müller, set out towards the end of 1898 with the view of making an archæological exploration of Hadramut, in Arabia ; but the leaders quarrelled, and Dr. Müller went to Sokotra. Dr. H. O. Forbes and Mr. Ogilvie Grant were in Sokotra at the same time on a biological expedition, in the course of which they did some excellent surveying.

In French West Africa the excitement of contested frontiers has given way to the much more serious difficulties of attempting to explore and control a vast area peopled by turbulent and independent natives. Four large expeditions have been endeavouring to converge at Lake Chad from different directions. Some important exploring work was done in the northern part of the Niger bend, especially in the region of the watershed between the Niger tributaries and the Volta, by Captain Chanoine, who, in January, 1899, joined forces with Captain Voulet on the Upper Niger on his way eastward to Lake Chad. Serious reports as to the ill-treatment of natives by these expeditions caused the colonial administration to send out a superior officer to take command and supersede the two captains. On hearing of the approach of Colonel Klobb, Capt.

Voulet refused to relinquish his command, and opened fire on the advancing party, killing Colonel Klobb and scattering his escort. This horrible crime met with a speedy and dramatic vengeance. The example of mutiny spread to the Native troops, who, in a quarrel with their white leaders, shot both the guilty officers.

The second expedition, under Captain Bretonnet, was sent out at the close of 1898 to approach Lake Chad from French Congo on the south and to carry French influence into Wadai. It has been massacred by the forces of the formidable chief Rabah, who threatens to become as serious an enemy as Samory was to European influence in the western Sudan. A private expedition of a commercial nature had already gone north under M. Béhagle, and there seems no reason to doubt the truth of the report that it also has been destroyed and that its leader has died as a prisoner in Rabah's hands.

M. Foureau, the famous Saharan explorer, with Count Lamy as military commander of the expedition, left Biskra in September, 1898, to cross the Sahara to Lake Chad and effect a meeting with the other expeditions. The caravan contained over 1,200 camels, and was splendidly equipped. The last letters received were written by him not far from Aïr in February, 1899. Subsequently reports of the massacre of the expedition by the Tuaregs at Aïr were received by caravans arriving in Tripoli. These reports were contradicted, and for a time it was feared that Foureau had escaped the Tuaregs only to fall before the mutinous French officers, Voulet and Chanoine. A messenger who arrived at Algiers from Ghadames in October reports that the Foureau-Lamy expedition had safely arrived at Sinder, about midway between Lake Chad and the Niger, but the fact that no news has come to the French posts on the upper Niger is very disquieting. M. Foureau was awarded the gold medal of the Royal Geographical Society in April last for his nine previous journeys in the Sahara, but the fact could not be communicated to him.

Rabah's empire now appears to include Bagirmi and Bornu, and probably stretches from Lake Chad to Wadai, ignoring the boundaries of the European spheres of influence. The dominant army appears to be many thousands strong, well-armed and including cavalry.

The expedition of M. Fourneau in French Congo for the selection of a route for a projected railway between Libreville, at the mouth of the Gabun and the navigable Congo, has been successful. The expedition left Brazzaville on Stanley Pool, and made their way northwards to Wesso on the upper Sangha, and thence westwards to the Gabun, in two divisions. The result is to recommend two alternative routes from Gabun *viâ* the valley of the Jadie to the Sangha, or *viâ* the valley of the Mambili to Mossaki.

An agreement between the British and German Governments in November settled the partition of the square of neutral territory north of the Gold Coast and Toogo so that Salaga falls within the British, and Yendi within the German sphere. (See map, col. 2).

In the Congo Free State telegraph and railway surveys of some importance have been carried on. M. Adam has been sent out to make a survey for a railway from Stanley Falls eastward through the forest country to the watershed of the great lakes, and there branching north to Lake Albert and south of Lake Tanganyika, a total length of 1,250 miles.

All the German colonies are the scene of steady development. The territory is being surveyed, a scientific meteorological service has been established, and experiments are being made in developing the resources, so that before long the German parts of Africa bid fair to be the most fully studied and best known. The railway in German South West Africa from Swakopmünde to Windhoek has been opened for traffic to Jackalswater, 61 miles from the coast.

British West Africa has at last commenced to develop a railway system, though as yet only short lines at Sierra Leone and Lagos have been constructed. The visit of Major Ronald Ross, A.M.S., to Lagos for the study of the species of mosquito which is now believed to be the chief carrier of malaria, suggests the possibility of

ultimately improving the deplorable hygiene of the coast. The most important fact in this region, however, is the assumption by the Imperial Government of the administration of the whole Niger territory, formerly governed by the Royal Niger Company, to which a large grant of public money has been made as compensation, and to which all its commercial privileges, apart from the monopoly in trading which it had succeeded in establishing, are preserved. The labours of Sir George Goldie, who has resigned the governorship of the Niger Company since it ceased to exercise the functions of a government, have enriched the British empire by a province of vast value, at an expense much less than that of even a trifling war. The British possessions on the Niger and its delta have now been organised as a single territory under the Colonial Office, and no customs barriers exist within it. But for administrative purposes three divisions are recognised—Lagos, Southern Nigeria (including the Niger Coast Protectorate), and Northern Nigeria, which contains the greater part of the former territory of the Royal Niger Company. The boundaries of these divisions had not been defined up to November, 1899.

In South Africa all the geographical changes of the year are overshadowed by the outbreak of the most serious war which has taken place in Africa in modern times, brought on by the evolution of historical causes, but precipitated by an ultimatum of the Transvaal Government ordering the British Government to refrain from moving troops in Natal and Cape Colony. This question is dealt with on pp. 593-6.

Before the war great progress had been made with the geodetic survey of Cape Colony, which was being extended northward; and, jointly with German surveyors, the boundaries between the British and German possessions are being delimited with great accuracy, both on the west of Rhodesia and the north-east of British Central Africa.

The well-known German explorer, Dr. Passarge, has been employed by a company acting under the auspices of the British South Africa Company, in the thorough exploration of the region round Lake Ngami.

Captain Gibbons has navigated the Zambezi in a steamer to the Molele rapids, 20 miles below the Guay confluence, and, proceeding towards the source of the river, he has constructed a more accurate map of its course than previously existed. Mr. Poulett Weatherley has continued his exploration of the Bangweulu marshes, and continued to the upper Luapula, the navigation of which he found to be blocked by vegetation on account of the sluggish current. He visited the Mombotuta Falls (which he states no white man has seen before), and was much impressed by their grandeur; the roar of the water being heard eight or nine miles away on a still night.

The tree under which Livingstone's heart was buried, at Chitambo's, south of Lake Bangweulu, was decaying, and Mr. Coorington has cut out and sent home the section of the trunk bearing the inscription. A durable monument is to be erected on the spot, which is meanwhile marked with an iron telegraph pole.

Mr. J. E. S. Moore has been engaged in the exploration of the great African lakes, especially with the view of studying their animal life. He finds that the greatest depth of Lake Nyasa is 430 fathoms, or 2,580 feet; in other words, the deepest point lies 1,000 feet below sea level.

The "Cape to Cairo" telegraph wire from Rhodesia is now open to Lake Tanganyika, and is being pushed northward through German East Africa under a special agreement with the German government.

AMERICA.

The rush of gold-seekers to Klondike and to Alaska has naturally led to many journeys through these inhospitable regions, and has not tended to reduce the difficulties regarding the uncertain Alaskan frontier. The international conference between the United States and Canada at the close of 1898 failed to solve the various problems submitted for consideration, and it was only in October, 1899, that a *modus vivendi* regarding the Alaskan frontier was settled between the United States and Great Britain. This provides that a provisional line shall be drawn round the head of the Lynn Canal, leaving the United States in possession of the ports of entry to the Yukon district, while the boundary will be held to run through the summit of the White Pass and of the Chilkoot Pass, and along the south bank of the Klehini River to a point

within ten marine leagues of the ocean. The feeling in Canada is strongly against allowing this *modus vivendi*—which shuts out the Yukon territory from its natural outlet to the sea—to become permanent.

In the West Indies Cuba was declared under United States protection, and Porto Rico proclaimed as United States territory on January 1; and in both islands the change has already produced most beneficial results, in the revival of industry and trade and the sanitation of towns.

The Court of Arbitration between Great Britain and Venezuela has delivered its judgment on the boundary between British Guiana and

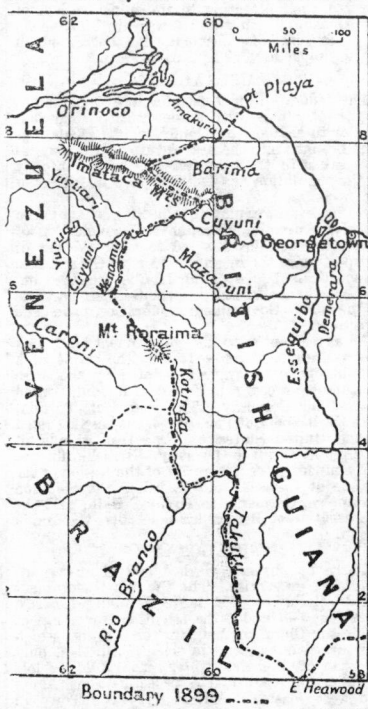

Boundary 1899 ___.

Venezuela at Paris. The new boundary, which is shown in the accompanying map, does not differ greatly from the well-known Schomburgk line. The British claim to the Cuyuni gold-fields was disallowed, and Venezuela has also obtained the land on the south of the Orinoco to 'its mouth; but no one can complain of the substantial fairness of the award.

The arbitration regarding the boundary between Argentina and Chile in the south, which was submitted to the British Government, has not yet been completed. Exploration in the disputed region has been carried on during the year from the Chilean side by Dr. Paul Krüger and Dr. Steffen. The former ascended the Rio Yelche by boat and found that it formed the lower course of the Futaleufa, a stream the destination of which had been much disputed; it drains a region of some importance, with several settlements to which the new route provided to the sea should prove advantageous.

Mr. J. B. Hatcher and Mr. O. A. Peterson have made a third scientific expedition, on behalf of Princeton University, in Patagonia, as a result of which they have accumulated data for a preliminary geological map of the territory south of 47° S., and east of the Andes, and made important collections of natural history specimens and photographs.

Dr. Hermann Meyer has continued his researches in Brazil, and several expeditions have devoted their attention to the upper valleys of the Amazon, which the U.S. warship *Wilmington*, of 1,300 tons displacement, has succeeded in navigating as high as Iquitos in Peru.

AUSTRALASIA.

The federation of Australia into a Commonwealth of States, with a constitution somewhat similar to that of the Dominion of Canada, has been brought into the near future by the general vote taken in the colonies. A large majority of the population has declared itself in favour of the measure.

No important exploring expeditions have taken place in Australia, although the exploitation of Western Australia has led to a great deal of prospecting in the interior. In New Guinea also a good deal of prospecting has been carried on, and both in the British and the German portions of the island Government exploration have been continued.

An agreement as to the government of Samoa has at last been arrived at as the result of a Commission of enquiry appointed by the three guardians powers, the United Kingdom, United States and Germany. The island of Tutuila, with the harbour of Pago-Pago, has been assigned to the United States, and the two islands of Upolu and Savaii to Germany. British influence is renounced on consideration of the cession of the islands of Choiseul and Isabel in the Solomon Group by Germany to Great Britain, and the confirmation of British influence over the Tonga group.

THE OCEANS.

There has been a marked revival in oceanographical enterprise. The German Government fitted out, in 1898, the large Hamburg-America liner *Valdivia* under the scientific leadership of Professor Chun, of Leipzig, for a cruise which has turned out second in scientific interest only to that of the *Challenger*. The *Valdivia* left Hamburg in August, 1898, proceeded south along the west coast of Africa, left Cape Town in November, re-discovered Bouvet Island in the South Atlantic, and steamed eastward for about 1,800 miles along the edge of the Antarctic ice-pack, reaching 64° 14' S. off Enderby Land. From this point, she crossed the Indian Ocean to Sumatra, and thence to Dar-es-Salaam, returning by the Suez Canal, and reaching Hamburg in April, 1899, with a splendid series of deep-sea soundings and valuable collections illustrating all branches of science.

A well-equipped Dutch deep-sea expedition on board the man-of-war *Siboga* has been at work in the interesting seas of the Malay Archipelago; and the United States' Fish Commission steamer *Albatross*, under the charge of Professor Alexander Agassiz, is exploring the Pacific, her cruise being intended to extend over 20,000 miles.

A conference of representatives of the maritime Powers bordering the North Sea met at Stockholm in the summer, and drew up plans for a complete oceanographical and biological study of the seas of north-western Europe, with a view to the improvement of fisheries.

GENERAL.

The seventh International Geographical Congress met at Berlin in September, under the presidency of Baron Richthofen, and the proceedings were carried on in surroundings of great magnificence, the Prussian Parliament House being placed unreservedly at the disposal of the Congress for its scientific meetings. The attendance exceeded 1,600, of whom, however, little over 200 were foreigners, seven-eighths of those present being Germans. One hundred and fifty papers were read, and seventeen resolutions bearing on the advancement of geography were adopted, most of these necessitating the election of international committees and the consultation of specialists. The work of the Congress was strongest in the departments of Polar, especially Antarctic, research, oceanography, and the geography of plants.

In this country one of the chief geographical events of the year has been the expansion of the teaching staff in Geography at the University of Oxford, by the appointment of Dr. A. J. Herbertson as assistant to Mr. Mackinder, the reader in geography, and Mr. H. N. Dickson and Mr. Grundy as lecturers. The Royal Geographical Society has subsidised this scheme to the extent of £400 per annum.

A curious example of posthumous honour to an explorer has occurred in consequence of the Spanish-American war. The remains of Columbus, which, after his death, were transferred from Valladolid to Seville, then removed to San Domingo, and subsequently, about a century ago, to Havana, were brought back to Spain in January, 1899, on the cession of Cuba, and deposited in the Cathedral at Seville with great ceremony.

GEOGRAPHICAL PUBLICATIONS.

The most important geographical publication of the year is the first instalment of "Bartholomew's Physical Atlas," which takes the form of an "Atlas of Meteorology, by J. G. Bartholomew and A. J. Herbertson, edited by Dr. A. Buchan." As a specimen of modern cartography, the work is satisfying, for it is not surpassed by the finest foreign productions, while as a repository of generalised observations on the climate of the world, it is monumental. Amongst books (disregarding mere popular narratives of travel, school-books, and works in languages other than English, French or German) one of the most important, in bringing information of practical utility into a scientific form, is Engelbrecht's treatise on the distribution of the chief crops of the temperate regions entitled "Die Landbauzonen der aussertropischen Länder," which is accompanied by an original atlas. Other books of a general character, although not designed for the general reader, are the first volume of the new edition of Professor Ratzel's great work "Anthropogeographie," which treats geography in its relation to man, and Prof. A. H. Keane's "Man, past and present," which is published in the Cambridge Geographical Series, but is more anthropological than geographical. Messrs. W. L. and P. L. Sclater have published a work on

"The Geography of Mammals," summarising the distribution of certain species, and Dr. R. F. Scharff, of Dublin, in his "History of the European Fauna," points out how the wild animals inhabiting the British Islands suggest the former distribution of land and water, and indicate the old land connections with the continent. The "Danish Ingolf Expedition" gives in English the results of an important Danish oceanographical expedition. The puzzling question of the transcription of geographical names in various languages and alphabets was studied by the late M. Christian Garnier, whose book was published after his death. Messrs. Beazeley and Prestage have translated Azurara's "Chronicle of the Discovery and Conquest of Guinea" for the Hakluyt Society, so that English readers may now have this famous historical work in their own language. Mr. Coolidge has practically re-written Ball's "Hints and Notes for Travellers in the Alps." Miss J. B. Reynolds gives many useful hints to teachers of geography in her report on "The Teaching of Geography in Switzerland." "The International Geography, by Seventy Authors," edited by the writer of this notice, is an attempt to produce, in one volume, a trustworthy epitome of geographical knowledge at the close of the nineteenth century. Geographical bibliography is provided for annually by two invaluable volumes—Baschin's "Bibliotheca Geographica," with the title of almost every book and paper of the year in question, produced by the Berlin Geographical Society, and Raveneau's "Bibliographie géographique annuelle," which gives an annotated selection of the best works.

The Arctic book of the year is F. G. Jackson's "A Thousand Days in the Arctic," in which the monotony of life near the North Pole appears in every page, without a word of complaint, however, and with high praise of the splendid set of fellows who shared the hardships which may be read between the lines.

"A Russian Province of the North" is the translation of an excellent account of Arkhangelsk by Governor Engelhardt. Mr. W. Z. Ripley, in his "Racial Geography of Europe," has made a most valuable contribution to the distribution of European peoples.

Books on matters Chinese have been legion, but Lord Charles Beresford's "Break-up of China" must be mentioned on account of the strong practical views and acute observations of the author, Mrs. Bishop's "The Yangtse Valley and Beyond" for the new ground it describes, and Mrs. Little's "Intimate China" because of her special knowledge of native life and thought. Arnot Reid's "From Peking to Petersburg" gives a straightforward and un-padded description of northern China and the great Siberian railway. Messrs. F. H. Skrine and E. D. Ross have produced in "The Heart of Asia" not only a history of Russian Turkistan, but a critical study of the present condition of that province. The Philippine troubles have produced a new edition of Mr. Foreman's standard work on the islands, and a lighter volume from Captain G. J. Younghusband.

Africa seems never likely to lose its interest for readers, and out of the multitude of fugitive writings called out by the events of the day a certain number of important works stand out prominently. Mr. A. Silva White, in his "Expansion of Egypt," treats the political history of Egypt on a geographical basis, and throws a glance at the future. Mr. Budgett Meakin publishes a detailed work on "The Moorish Empire." Mr. A. B. Lloyd has embodied the results of his recent crossing of Africa in "In Dwarfland and Cannibal Country," while Mr. Ansorge, in "Under the African Sun," has some things of importance to say about Uganda. H. Bindloss gives a startlingly vivid if not too attractive description of the West Coast in his "In the Niger Delta." So many books on the Transvaal have been hurriedly called out to meet the demands made by the war, that it is impossible to form an opinion as to their value before this list goes to press. The wide question of the colonisation of Africa by alien races forms the subject of Sir H. H. Johnston's "History."

Mr. E. J. Payne's second volume on "The History of the New World, called America," is one of those solid contributions to knowledge that are apt to find more admirers than readers. T. C. Porter's "Impressions of America," on the other hand, is an example of a slight sketch of travel without frivolity, and with some keen observations. So many of the "trippers" to the northern gold-fields have produced ephemeral notes of their experiences that the well-informed pages of Professor Angelo Hirlprin's "Alaska and the Klondike" are peculiarly welcome.

Fiske's "West Indies" and R. P. Porter's "Commercial Cuba" are trustworthy and practical books by Americans, called out in response to the demand for information on these islands in the United States. E. A. Fitzgerald's "The Highest Andes" is a fine record of an extremely plucky and successful piece of mountain exploration, in the course of which the summit of Aconcagua was reached.

An unusual number of good books have appeared on Australasia. J. E. Heeres' great folio on "The Part borne by the Dutch in the Discovery of Australia, 1606-1765," is a valuable contribution to the history of discovery. The translation of Professor Semon's "In the Australian Bush" gives the impressions and observations of a leading German naturalist on the coast of Queensland to English readers. Professor Baldwin Spencer and Mr. Gillen, in "Native Tribes of Central Australia," throw a flood of light on the curious customs of the black fellows, and Mr. Mathews' "Eagle Hawk and Crow," though less novel, has some bearing on the same questions. Mr. H. Ling Roth has produced a new edition of his "Aborigines of Tasmania," containing the most recent particulars of that lost people. Mr. D. W. Carnegie, in his "Spinifex and Sand," gives a good description of travelling in the interior of Western Australia, and in "The Long White Cloud" Mr. W. P. Reeves gives an excellent general account of New Zealand. Mrs. Edgeworth David's "Funafuti" sums up in popular form the results and the experiences of the coral-boring expedition in the Ellice group.

Count Pfeil's "Studien und Beobachtungen aus der Südsee" contains first-hand information regarding Melanesian island and people.

HUGH ROBERT MILL.

THE WEATHER IN THE BRITISH ISLANDS DURING THE YEAR ENDING
31ST OCTOBER, 1899.

THIS summary of the weather experienced in the British Islands during the year commencing November 1st, 1898, and ending October 31st, 1899, has been mainly compiled from data contained in the Daily and Weekly Reports issued by the Meteorological Office. It is hoped that the remarks on each month will be useful for purposes of reference and comparison, especially when considered in relation to the daily results of the Greenwich observations as given for each month in the Calendar of the Almanack.

MONTHS. 1898-9.	TEMPERATURE.		RAINFALL.			PRESSURE.		WIND.	SUNSHINE.
	Mean	Diff. from normal.	Mean days.	Mean amount.	Diff. from normal.	Mean.	Diff. from normal.	Resultant.	Percentage.
	°	°		inches.	inches.	inches.	inch.		hours.
1898 November..	48	4 above	23	4·47	0·35 more	29·77	0·10 below	SW	21
,, December...	47	5 ,,	24	4·15	0·04 less	29·86	0·01 above	WSW	18
1899 January ...	43	2 ,,	23	4·72	0·78 more	29·72	0·10 below	SWbS	22
,, February ...	43	2 ,,	15	3·52	0·43 ,,	29·77	0·09 ,,	SbW	26
,, March	43	1 ,,	16	2·42	0·24 less	30·02	0·18 above	W	41
,, April	47	nil	23	3·56	1·23 more	29·79	0·11 below	WbN	31
,, May	50	1 below	14	2·69	0·58 ,,	30·00	0·05 above	NW	43
,, June	57	1 above	9	1·53	0·69 less	30·06	0·11 ,,	NNW	44
,, July	60	1 ,,	14	2·34	0·65 ,,	30·04	0·12 ,,	WbN	36
,, August........	62	3 ,,	8	1·06	1·42 ,,	30·07	0·17 ,,	S	53
,, September..	56	nil	21	3·27	0·15 ,,	29·79	0·08 below	WNW	37
,, October......	51	1 above	17	3·31	0·88 ,,	29·97	0·15 above	SW	39

November, 1898.—The weather was very mild, with a fair duration of sunshine, normal rainfall, variable winds. The highest temperature, 66°, was reported at Killarney on the 2nd; the lowest, 9°, at Braemar on the 29th. At 8 A.M., Greenwich time, on the 6th, while the temperature at Scilly was 53°, it was only 34° at Loughborough; 9th, Scilly 51°, Nairn 31°; 10th, Scilly 56°, Nairn 33°; 23rd, Scilly 51°, Shields 31°; 29th, Belmullet 45°, Nairn 20°. At Stornoway the rainfall, measured at 8 A.M., amounted to 5·5 inches for the first five days; 1st, at Ardrossan 1·24; 23rd, Belmullet 1·00; 24th, Hurstcastle 1·33; 25th, Belmullet 1·00. The winds were from the east side on nine days. Rainfall exceeded the normal quantity in Ireland. Fog prevailed in east England on eight days. Hoar-frost formed in the mornings of fifteen days in the eastern and northern districts, less frequently elsewhere. The last decade was much cooler than the previous days. Thirteen cyclonic wind-systems passed over these islands, mostly raging over the northern parts; the most violent, on the 2nd, 22nd, 27th, caused wrecks and loss of life. Cold and harsh weather on the 22nd gave a snowstorm at night over Scotland, north and central England, and Wales. The snow was six inches deep at Southport. Snowdrifts were several feet deep in places. Sheep were lost and traffic interrupted. Snow fell in places on the 29th. Atmospheric pressure was greatest, 30·4 inches, on the 18th; lowest, 28·6, on the 25th. Bright sunshine, estimated in percentage of its possible duration, varied between 29 in the east England, and 15 in west Scotland.

During night 22nd, a quick fall in barometers occurred in the west and north-west, and next day a storm passed over Ireland from N.N.W., moved slowly to S. and S.S.E. till the 25th, then retrograded N. and retook the path southward to Brittany on the 26th.

The Autumn was one of the warmest of that season, had more than usual sunshine, normal rainfall, generally resembling that of 1897.

December, 1898.—The weather was exceedingly mild, with westerly winds, rain on many days but only in excessive quantity in the north of Scotland, very little fog, many storms. The temperature was warm enough for May. At Greenwich (*vide* Calendar) the 4th and 5th were the warmest on record. In the latter part of the month, some bright, frosty nights succeeded sunny days. The highest temperature, 61°, was reported at Llandudno on the 5th; the lowest, 16°, at Braemar on the 31st. At 8 A.M., 22nd, while Valentia had 50° Cambridge had only 29°, and the next morning 5° and 29° respectively; 24th, Pembroke 52°, Cambridge 32°; 29th, Pembroke 52°, Nairn 28°. At Stornoway on the 2nd, 1·4, inch of rain was measured; 4th, 1·35; 25th, 1·4; 26th, 1·5; 28th, 1·1; at Malin Head on the 5th, 1·01; Belmullet 1·2; 27th, Roche's Point 1·4, Pembroke 1·35; 28th Jersey 1·22. Aurora was seen in north Scotland on the 6th, 14th and 16th. Atmospherical pressure was greatest, 30·55 inches, on the 20th; least, 28·7, on the 29th. Fourteen cyclone storms reached these islands during this month, that on the 27th was the most extensive. The cores of these wind-systems skirted the west and north-west coasts; that of the 29th travelled across Ireland and England. The winds were violent or strong throughout the month. The wind-pressure was 29·8 lbs. on the square foot at Greenwich on the 27th. Bright sunshine varied between 26 per cent. in east England, and 8 in north Scotland.

January, 1899.—The weather was mild, especially in south-west England; stormy in the west and north districts; very rainy in the south-west and west; sunshine was generally much more than the average duration. The highest temperature, 57°, was reported at Greenwich on the 19th; the lowest, 10°, at Braemar on the 25th. At 8 A.M., 7th, while the temperature at Scilly was 51°, at Aberdeen it was only 27°; 15th, Valentia 54°, contrasted with Wick 31°; 18th, Valentia 53°; Sumburgh Head 31°; 26th, Roche's Point 47°, Loughborough 20°; 26th, Valentia 45°, York 23°; 27th, Sumburgh Head 43°, Aberdeen 18°; 29th, Sumburgh 45°, Nairn 25°. At 8 A.M., 2nd, 1·32 inch of rain was measured at Jersey; 10th, Pembroke 1·12; 21st, Roche's Point 1·35,

Pembroke 1·29. Atmospherical pressure was least, 28·6 inches, on the 2nd; greatest, 30·75. on the 26th: it was nearly as low on the 12th, 16th, 19th, 21st, 22nd, indicating the stormy character of the month. Disturbances came in quick succession from the Atlantic, and travelled northward or north-eastward over the western and northern coasts. An extensive and furious cyclone traversed Ireland and England on the 12th. Winds came from eastward on seven days. There was little or no fog or mist. Early in the month, a good deal of snow fell over north Scotland, and some fell locally in Scotland and north England on the 17th and 18th. Though bright, frosty weather prevailed during the last week, it merely whitened the land with hoar-frost. The week ending 28th had for the United Kingdom 42 per cent. of sunshine; south and west England 60; for the entire month bright sunshine varied between 34 in east England and 16 in west Scotland. Referring to the "Almanack," it will be seen that at Greenwich the wind attained a force of 22·5 lbs. on the 2nd, 32 on 12th, 17 on 16th, 28 on 21st; that north-easterly winds during the last nine days were attended by dry, bright weather—sunshine lasted 8·5 hours on the 28th, a remarkable duration as the sun was only 24 minutes longer above the horizon; that the 21st was the warmest day, highest 55·3°, lowest 50°, though commonly it is the coldest day.

February, 1889.—The weather of the first half of the month was very mild, with copious rain and fierce storms; during the latter part anti-cyclonic conditions were attended by frosty nights and misty mornings, followed by bright sunshine, notwithstanding the air was cold, dry and keen. The highest temperature, 66°, was reported at London on the 10th, the highest in a February for over 104 years; the lowest, 11°, at Braemar on the 5th. At 8 A.M., 4th, while the temperature at Scilly was 43° Loughborough had only 22°; 20th, Scilly 48°, Nairn 25; 22nd, Scilly 48°, Loughborough 25°, next morning 49° and 24° respectively; 24th and 25th, Scilly 50°, Cambridge 26°; 26th, Valentia 48°, Loughborough 22°; 27th, Roche's Point 46°, Loughborough 21°. Rain was scanty in east England, excessive in west Ireland. On the 17th 1·12 inch of rain was measured at Valentia. Snow fell on the early days but soon disappeared. Thunderstorms occurred 12th to 14th. Aurora was seen on the 12th in most parts of the kingdom, and in north Scotland on the 14th. Fog was noted on the 4th, 18th, 19th, 27th, 28th, mostly in east England, though the most overcast weather prevailed in the west of Ireland. The wind came from the east side on 10 days. Atmospherical pressure was least, 28·7 inches, on the 13th; greatest, 30·6, on the 28th. The wind attained a force of 33·4 lbs. on the square foot at Greenwich on the 13th. Bright sunshine varied between 34 per cent. in east England and 20 in west Scotland; the week ending 25th had 42 for the United Kingdom and 58 for north Scotland, and east and south England.

The *Winter's* chief features were extraordinary mildness, long sunshine, violent storms, and heavy rains producing floodings.

March, 1899.—The weather was variable, with normal temperature, few easterly winds. small rainfall in southern parts, large in northern, less than average in western and eastern. Till the 11th the atmosphere was dry, fine or fair. The next week was mostly dry and fine, though fog was prevalent in south-east England and snow fell on the north-eastern sea-board. The

succeeding week had inclement weather. abnormally cold, snow frequent and heavy on the east side. The last days were mild, rainy and unsettled. On the 19th atmospherical pressure was uniformly low, the air calm and the weather fine. Thence to 25th the conditions were peculiarly trying, very cold, keenly penetrating northerly winds. Fog prevailed, 14th to 17th chiefly over the eastern district, and was almost general on the 31st. A change of weather on the 25th favoured the Boat Race; afterwards geniality ruled with S.W. winds, showers, and mild and soft air. The 28th and 29th were stormy. The highest temperature was reported at Ochtertyre on the 12th, 68°; the lowest at Braemar on the 21st, 3°. At 8 A.M., 1st, Stornoway had 50°, while Parsonstown had only 29°; 5th, Scilly 44°, Parsonstown 23°; Scilly 47°, Cambridge 24°; 15th, Wick 49°, Loughborough 30°; 16th, Scilly 51°, Cambridge 29°; 20th, Valentia 45°, Loughborough 26°; 23th, Valentia 55°, Aberdeen 27°; 26th, Scilly 52°, Sumburgh Head 31°; 31st, Valentia 53°, Aberdeen 33°. An inch of rain was measured at Stornoway on the 29th. There were four inches of snow at Croydon on the 21st. Atmospherical pressure was greatest on the 1st, 30·7; least on the 9th, 29 inches. Bright sunshine varied between 48 per cent. in south-west and south England, and 26 in north Scotland. At Greenwich, the mean temperature of the week ending 25th was only 32°, that of the succeeding week 50°, which was more rainy and had less sunshine.

April, 1899.—The weather was variable, with normal temperature, scanty sunshine large rainfall, except south-west England, which had a normal amount of rain: in all parts numerous rainy days. The lowest temperature was reported at Braemar on the 22nd, 17°; the highest at Oehtertyre on the 28th, 65°. The least atmospherical pressure occurred on the 14th, 28·9; the greatest on the 23rd, 30·3 inches. On the morning of the 21st, 1·67 inch of rain was measured at Valentia, 1·1 at Roche's Point. Snow fell on several days in the north. Fog or mist was more than commonly prevalent in the south. Bright sunshine varied between 35 per cent. in south Ireland and 27 in central England. At London between 12.10 and 40 P.M., 8th, occurred a terrific squall, harsh and cold, with rain and snow.

May, 1899.—The winds and weather were variable, average warmth was not quite attained. excessive rain fell in the north of Scotland, a normal amount elsewhere. Till the 14th rain was scanty, frequent and locally heavy till the 25th, some snow in northern parts, dull skies, chilliness, frosty mornings, little sunshine: later on, brilliant sunshine with dry air. The lowest temperature was reported at Lairg on the 4th, 25°; the highest at Loughborough on the 31st, 75°. Temperature was low 8th to 14th, hoar frost at night, warm sunshine in keen air by day. Electrical storms occurred on the 1st in Ireland and south England; 12th west England; 16th south and south-east England; 23rd east England and west Ireland. At Sumburgh Head on the 16th, 1·34 inch of rain was measured; 17th, Stornoway, 1·0: 18th, Parsonstown, 1·0, Valentia, 1·36; 20th, Leith 1·1. The greatest atmospherical pressure occurred on the 6th and 28th, 30·5: the least on the 16th, 29 inches. The mean pressure was nearly uniform for the entire area of these islands, so that the resultant of the winds was very feeble and uncertain. Easterly winds, light but keenly harsh, prevailed on ten days. Bright sunshine varied between 51 per cent. in south England and 35 in north-east England. The week ending June 3rd gave 68 per cent. of sunshine to the United Kingdom, 85 in east, south, and south-west England.

Spring was a contrast to the genial winter, sombre and inclement. Wintry conditions prevailed until May, and then mere specimens of rather gloomy April weather.

June, 1899.—The weather for the most part of the month was hot and brilliant, the finish was stormy and changeable. The highest temperature was reported at Llandovery on the 5th, 85°; the lowest at Hillington on the 14th, 34°. Atmospherical pressure was greatest on the 8th, 30·5; least on the 20th, 29·2 inches. The winds came from eastward on eleven days. Rain fell on few days, and the amount was generally very deficient. On the 21st at Roche's Point 1·05 inch of rain was measured: the same amount at Valentia on the 28th; and an inch at Liverpool on the 29th. Little or no rain fell till the 17th; then showers or heavy local rains, consequently less sunshine, gloomy skies, with short intervals of brilliant hot weather. Electrical storms occurred on the 1st in west Ireland, 2nd, north Scotland, 21st, north Ireland, 28th and 29th in all parts, 30th, in central and east districts. They were variable in intensity, with large rainfall and some hail locally, causing temporary floodings in some districts. Bright sunshine varied between 56 per cent. in south-west England, and 30 in north Scotland.

July, 1899.—The sunshine was frequently intensely hot, though the mean temperature was not much above normal; rain was generally deficient, especially in Ireland, where, however, rainy days were numerous; sunshine was brilliant and of long continuance in England, scanty in Scotland, and deficient in Ireland. Commencing with showers, brisk winds, and low temperature, the month became brilliant and hot with intervals of cloudiness, several electrical storms, but fine throughout, the latter days splendid. The heat caused whirls of wind during the third week of frequent occurrence, manifested by the carrying away of hay, twisting standing crops. The lowest temperature was reported at Braemar on the 2nd, 37°; the highest at Cambridge on the 20th, 90°. Electrical storms occurred on the 3rd in north-west England; 7th, in most parts; 8th, in east England; 11th, 22nd, 23rd, in south England; 12th, in Great Britain; 17th, in England; 18th, in Scotland. On the 11th, 1·27 inch of rain was measured at Pembroke; 12th, 1·13 at Holyhead, 1·09 at Donaghadee, 1·02 at Scilly; 19th, 1·26 at Aberdeen; 21st, 3·36 at Holyhead; 23rd, 1·9 at Shaftesbury, 1·9 at Cullompton in two hours, 1·72 at Killarney in an hour and half. Heavy rains attending electrical storms must not be supposed to deprive the month of its general dry and brilliant character. Atmospherical pressure was least on the 1st, 30·4; greatest on the 31st, 30·45 inches. The winds were consistently quiet, and came from the east side on four days only. Fog was reported on seven days on the south-west coast and Irish Sea, on five west of Ireland. Bright sunshine varied between 57 per cent. in south England, and 19 in north Scotland.

August, 1899.—The weather was remarkably fine with much sunshine, very dry, temperature much above normal. The highest temperature was reported at Greenwich on the 15th, at Llandovery on the 25th, 90°; the lowest at Wick on

the 19th, 33°. At Valentia 2·22 inches of rain were measured on the 25th; nearly an inch at Liverpool on the 29th. Electrical storms occurred on the 3rd and 7th in Ireland; 15th in central England; 28th in north England; 25th and 29th in Scotland. The winds were light from eastward on half the number of days. Rainfall was normal only in west Ireland, greatly deficient in east England. The heavy rains of electrical storms being local, water was generally wanted, and roads were dusty. Atmospherical pressure was greatest on the 1st, 30·4; least on the 27th, 29·55 inches. Bright sunshine varied between 67 per cent. in south-west England, and 38 in north-east England. It was 71 in the Channel Isles. The week ending 26th had 67·6 for the United Kingdom.

The *Summer* was very brilliant, with sunshine, very hot and very dry. Central and south England was parched with drought, which, indeed was almost general to the whole state. It came to an end in the latter days of August. Its effect will be felt, even with adequate rainfall, far into the coming year, owing to the deficiency of subsoil water. The *Times* of September 26, stated that no summer so dry had been experienced in this country for fully 30 years. "With the exception of the summers of 1864 and 1868, the summer of 1899 has established its claim to be remembered as the hottest and driest of the last 60 years."

September, 1899.—The weather was stormy, especially in the north, and at the equinox; rain fell on many days, giving more than the normal quantity to the north, much less to the south, while intermediate latitudes had about the normal. The highest temperature was reported at London on the 5th, 80°; the lowest at Markree on the 30th, 29°. Atmospherical pressure was greatest on the 10th, 30.3; least on the 26th, 28·8 inches. Electrical storms occurred on the 2nd in east England; 17th, in north Ireland; 23rd, in north England; 27th, in south-east England. On the 6th, nearly an inch of rain was measured at Portland; 7th, 1·01 at London; 30th, 1·22 at Yarmouth. The rains were capricious, some districts having a scanty supply. The northern portion of Scotland had frequent and heavy rain. Aurora was seen in north Scotland on the 24th. Bright sunshine varied between 49 per cent. in south England, and 26 in north Scotland.

October, 1899.—The last two days of September and the first two of this month constituted a very stormy period, with much rain, causing floodings in places, while the wind at sea wrought much damage and the loss of many lives. Fine weather then set in and about the mid-month mists and fogs came as if to stay; copious rainfalls during the last week served to recall the typical character of the month, although the weather was mild and pleasant, with more than usual sunshine, though clear nights, with low temperatures, induced hoar frosts, and much mist and fog. The highest temperature was reported at Lairg on the 19th, 73°; the lowest at Glenlee on the 6th, 25°. Rain was scanty, except in the north of Scotland. Atmospherical pressure was greatest on the 24th, 30.5; least on the 12th, 29·2 inches; very nearly the same pressures occurred respectively on the 8th and 28th. On the 2nd, 1·09 inch of rain was measured at Shields, 1·11 at Holyhead; 28th, 1·06 at London. During the month diseases of the respiratory organs increased the death rate. Mist or fog prevailed in the east district on 11 days, other districts had less, and least was reported in the north. Bright sunshine varied between 48 per cent. in south England, and 24 in north Scotland.

The Year's Weather and the Crops, 1898-9.— During the fine sunshiny, soft, and balmy weather of November, wheat-sowing went on well till the last week, when wintry conditions prevailed with rain and snow. Fine weather enabled cleaning of the land to be done in the autumn. Wheat-sowing was well done, and the plants made good progress by the end of the year. Garden flowers lasted to late dates, there being no frosts to injure them till November 22. The frost imposed a check upon the precocity of vegetation, and destroyed the grubs of insect pests. After Christmas, tillage was prevented by the soddened state of the soil, but wintry conditions returned after January 22, short, however, for during the first part of February much rain fell, and tillages were again baffled. Fine, dry weather during the latter part of February allowed workable condition a return. No rain fell for a fortnight. The days were bright with sunshine; the nights favoured hoar-frost, and keenly-cool air. The first three weeks of March was the real winter; weather of Arctic severity, snow-storms, blizzard-like northerly winds, sharp frost, prevailed. The dry weather was favourable for spring sowing. The nights were cold, the mornings misty, the winds bitterly keen, even with warm sunshine. The searching winds, with the hot sunshine, were peculiarly unhealthy, increasing diseases of the respiratory organs. In each month, September to February, the temperature was above normal. April and May had normal temperature, with great fluctuations, and rain in excess. The general character of the weather was conducive to forwarding vegetation during the winter, with little maturing tendency in the spring. Throughout June, the weather was brilliant, dry, with abundance of sunshine. Wheat made rapid progress. The intense heat and drying winds affected adversely barley, oats, and root crops, which need moisture. For hay-making, the weather was perfect. The mown herbage having been both sun-cured and wind-dried, was soon secured. "The summer came in towards the end of May with an absolute drought, extending over the whole country, and lasting three or four weeks. It was accompanied by some high temperatures, much bright sunshine, and continuous dry winds, causing the maximum evaporation" (*Times*, July 17). After mid-June, rain fell abundantly in some districts, but July brought a return to high temperature, drought, and brilliant sunshine, which caused

cereals to ripen rapidly. The wheat harvest was favoured with fine weather, though the deficiency of rain was felt by other crops Root crops and grass fared badly from the drought and the scorching influence of August sunshine. Mangels throve, swedes and turnips languished. Hops were not troubled with insect pests. The crop was excellent in quality and quantity, estimated at the extraordinary yield of 12·76 cwts. per acre. For the British Islands, the general average yield of wheat was 32 bushels per acre; of barley, for Great Britain, 35 and oats 42. The following figures are taken from Sir J. B. Lawes' annual report on the wheat. The unmanured plot yielded 12 bushels per acre. The yield on the plot served with farmyard manure, was 42½; the mean of five plots, three of which had artificial manure, was 30½; the mean weight per bushel 61⅝ lbs ; 2¾ bushels above and 2 lbs. above the average of the 47 years 1852-98. The produce of straw, 36¾ cwts per acre, was 9¾ cwts. above the average. Upon the basis of his results, he has estimated the harvest in the United Kingdom available for food at seven and a-half millions of quarters of wheat. "The average population for the current harvest year is estimated at 40,807,717 ; and taking the consumption per head at six bushels of 60 lbs. per bushel, the total requirement for the harvest year will be 30,605,788 qrs. Deducting from this the available home produce, there remain 23 millions of quarters to be imported."

The most prominent relation of weather to health is exemplified by the deaths registered in London from diseases of the respiratory organs, which having been 266 for the week ending January 28, increased weekly till they attained 604 by March 25; the death rate due to all causes mounting from 16 to 24 in the interval per thousand per annum. The death rate rose again from 15 July 1 to 25·3 August 19, to which diarrhœa contributed largely. The greatest number of deaths, from the Registrar-General's classification of diseases, in any one week was: Scarlet fever 17, November 12, following rain and damp ; enteric fever 33, November 26, rain and damp; diphtheria 49, February 11, cold; whooping cough 90, diseases of respiratory organs 604, March 25, cold; phthisis 210, diseases of the circulatory system 198, March 18, cold; diarrhœa 481, August 19, maximum temperature above 70°.

The weather in October was well suited for work on the land, especially for sowing wheat.

Earthquakes and Volcanic Eruptions in 1898-9.

At the middle of September, 1898, telegrams from Naples stated a stream of lava from Vesuvius had destroyed a portion of the roadway leading from the Observatory to the lower station of the Funicular Railway. A mass of molten rock flowed down the mountain side in three imposing streams, one along the foot of Monte Somma, a second through the middle of the Vetrana zone, and a third along the Monte Corcella. The stream running round the base of Monte Somma burnt the chestnut wood and nearly reached the Observatory. The eruption was continued on succeeding days, and a stream of lava flowed down the immense valley of Vedrino

and nearly filled it. The volcano threw out stones and scoria, and seven new craters appeared to have formed round the central one, without, however, diminishing the activity of the latter. The violence of the outbreak soon after abated, and for the time removed the apprehensions of the people residing in the country at the foot of Vesuvius.

On Nov. 29, 1898, shocks of earthquake were felt at Patras, in Greece, and threw the inhabitants of the district into a state of panic, but there was no loss of life. On Dec. 31 another eruption of Vesuvius occurred, and two currents of lava, each twenty metres broad, soon reached the slopes of Monte Somma. A despatch from Port Antonio, Jamaica, on Jan. 21, 1899, stated that an earthquake had visited that island. The shock lasted 10 seconds, and was said to have been more severe than any other experienced for many years. On the same date, at half-past nine in the morning, a strong shock of earthquake was experienced throughout Peloponnesus, Greece, and especially in the S.W. departments. Great damage was done to house property, and many persons were severely injured by falling débris. In the town of Philiatra the inhabitants found it necessary to camp in the open, and in the vicinity of the place named two villages were completely destroyed. The houses in Kyparissia were shaken to their foundations, and many fell down; the village of Staso was also wrecked. At Navoun and Calamanta also severe damage was done to the buildings, and at Zante the shock was somewhat violent, though not serious. On Jan. 24 the earthquakes continued, but were less severe. The damage done was heaviest in the province of Kyparissia, where five villages were completely destroyed. On the same date an earthquake lasting three minutes was felt at Mexico. It seriously damaged more than 200 buildings, while 10 houses were totally wrecked. About 100 persons were injured, and a terrible panic prevailed among the inhabitants. On March 7 a severe shock was felt at Yokohama, in Japan, and chiefly affected the same districts as those which suffered from the earthquake of 1891. There were some loss of life and property. On April 15 several earthquake shocks were experienced in the Peloponnesus. On May 3 similar shocks were felt in the district south-east of the Peloponnesus. The town of Liquditsa was much damaged, the buildings in some cases being shaken down. On May 15 a violent undular earthquake was felt at noon at Sinj Turjake, Caporice, and other places in Dalmatia. It lasted about five seconds, and the direction of motion appeared to be from south-east to north-west. A considerable number of buildings were damaged. Two persons were seriously injured, and six others received slight hurt. The shocks were continued during the afternoon, and occasioned a panic amongst the inhabitants. On May 17, at Montserrat, one of the Leeward Islands, 45 earthquake shocks are reported to have occurred during a period of five hours. The first series was followed by isolated shocks at frequent intervals. A few persons met with severe injuries, and many of the houses were damaged so much as to be rendered uninhabitable. On July 14 a gallery in the Recklinghausen Mine in Westphalia collapsed in consequence of an earthquake shock which lasted twenty seconds. At Herne, two miles distant, houses were thrown down, the roofs fell in, chimneys and tiles were thrown

from others, and the people, panic stricken, fled into the open for safety. The earth tremors were felt at Munster. Nine persons were wounded by the falling buildings, and were attended to at the hospital at Herne. There were two shocks at 2.43 and 2.51 p.m., and each one lasted sixteen seconds, moving in the direction from east to west On July 19 in the morning, after a loud subterranean rumbling, an enormous column of smoke shot up from Mount Etna, followed by a pillar of sand. A violent shock of earthquake was felt at Rome in the afternoon. It lasted about twelve seconds. Bells rang, windows and furniture cracked, but there was no serious damage, and only a few persons were injured. A few of the churches had their walls cracked, and a portion of the town wall was shaken down. The people were terrified, and a correspondent of the *Daily News*, in describing the scene, says: "Nothing was heard but the shrieking of women and children and the cries of men. The prisoners in the gaol, partly from fear, partly to take advantage of the opportunity, threatened to mutiny, and it was necessary to send reinforcements to keep them under control. From some convents the nuns ran out into the streets. The panic was also very great in the hospitals and lunatic asylums. The earthquake was very violent along the villages on the Albanian Hills. Damage was done at Frascati, Marino, and Castelgandolfo. The phenomenon seems to have had its origin in the outburst of Etna. After the earthquake the eruption of the Sicilian volcano increased, a cloud of black smoke burst from the crater, accompanied by streams of fire and ashes. On subsequent days the earthquake shocks were repeated at Paterno and Belpasso, near Catania, and Etna continued to roar and to give frequent detonations. The great iron cupola on the Observatory was pierced by thirty red-hot stones from the crater, while other stones broke some of the steps of the great staircase, and damaged a few of the instruments. On July 21 a telegram from New York stated that a volcano called Mauna Loa, in the Hawaii Islands, had thrown up an extraordinary quantity of lava, which, flowing down the slopes of the mountain, threatened the coffee plantations and sugar lands with destruction. Another volcano, Kilcana, was working freely, and the whole island was enveloped in volumes of smoke. On July 28, in the department of Var, France, several shocks of earthquake were experienced. The disturbance moved from north to south. There was a slight shock at Toulon, but no serious damage resulted. On Sept. 15 an earthquake shock lasting some seconds occurred at Cape Colony, but no damage was done. The visitation was felt throughout the western portion of the colony, and the direction of motion was from a little east of south.

Storms and Floods in 1898-99.

During the year commencing November, 1898, and ending October, 1899, storms and floods may not have been so disastrous as they have been in former years; nevertheless, a vast amount of destruction has to be attributed to them. The record begins with the British Islands. By the 2nd of November, as the result of much rain, the Isle of Man experienced floods, so did the Rhonda Valley, likewise the valleys of Cumberland, while the Tay and the Esk overflowed. All

these localities sustained much damage and loss of stock. By the 5th, Windermere rose 18 ins. higher than had ever been known before. The floods in the Lake District were very destructive, the loss at Kendal alone being estimated at £10,000. About this date, the 7th, an appalling calamity happened in Shantung. The Yellow River flooded some 2,000 square miles of land, destroying crops, cattle, and villages. A million of people were considered more or less afflicted by the occurrence, some 10,000 camping out, winter approaching, famine imminent.

By the 24th, heavy rains brought floods to Dublin. The neighbouring fields became a vast lake. Snow fell in Tipperary on the 23rd. The district around Nenagh was flooded. Roads were impassable, and railway communication with Dublin was blocked. Three carriages were swept off the railway at Lispole. The gale acted very roughly with passenger steamers in the English Channel.

On the 27th, a terrific storm along the coast of New England wrecked six vessels, resulting in the loss of 180 lives; 109 persons were drowned by the wreck of the ss. *Portland*.

By January 16, 1899, the swollen state of the Rhone caused floods at several towns. By the 24th, the Thames was 30 inches above high-water mark, flooding the Windsor district. The Dee flooded the land between Bala and Chester. The Wye and Lugg were out for miles. The Severn inundated several thousand acres. The floods entailed drowning of sheep and pigs, as well as the washing out of trees and plants.

February 12, a S.W. gale driving in the spring tide caused the sea to rise at Newport, Monmouth, eight inches higher than the previous recorded highest. The water rose over the sea-wall, submerging thousands of acres. Many horses and cattle were drowned, much other property destroyed. Houses and two miles of railway were flooded at Llanelly.

New York reported a blizzard which raged in the United States from the 9th to the 13th. Railways and streets were blocked with snow; water-pipes and gas-pipes were frozen. Forty people were frozen to death. Freezing extended even to Florida.

March 7, a report from Buenos Ayres stated that heavy storms had destroyed 300,000 tons of wheat. On the 11th, a hurricane in Queensland caused the loss of 411 lives by drowning.

On April 27, a destructive tornado occurred at Kirkville, Missouri; numerous buildings were demolished, about 100 persons perished and at least 1,000 were injured. A large number of people were on the same day killed by the storm at Newtown, 40 miles north-west of Kirkville.

June 3, a storm was reported to have washed away six miles of the Wady Halfa-Abu Hamid Railway, interrupting the telegraphic communication. A report from Argentina on the 4th stated that floods in the valley of the Rio Negro caused much anxiety and destroyed much property. On the 9th, a terrible storm raged in Spain. About 6 p.m., for twenty minutes, an extraordinary quantity of hail fell at Madrid; the stones, the size of walnuts and some larger, collected in places to the depth of several inches and did much damage to vines and trees, killing several persons and injuring others. Houses were flooded, the train service stopped, and the mails delayed. At San Pedro, in Valladolid, 150 houses were destroyed, occasioning considerable loss of life. At Toledo great damage was done to buildings and the town was partially flooded. On the 13th, heavy floods in the district of Sylhet, Assam, produced serious damage to property. On the 13th, a great storm swept along the Upper Mississippi and its tributaries. New Richmond was almost destroyed, 200 people were killed and 1,000 injured, the town being crowded with visitors. Heavy rain destroyed the crops. On the 21st, a severe electrical storm broke over the district of Nenagh, Ireland,

causing damage and fatality, while the deluge of rain so swelled the streams that the rivers inundated and damaged standing crops and other property.

July 5, damage of an appalling character was reported in Texas. During six days, the Brazos River had flooded its valley to depths varying from 6 to 30 feet, making almost a wilderness. Hundreds of houses were water-logged and many swept away. The flooded district was estimated at 500 miles long and probably 50 wide. The deaths by drowning were variously reckoned between 100 and 300 persons.

In the afternoon of the 8th a furious hailstorm with lightning and thunder swept over Canterbury, England, damaging houses, plantations, crops, and glass-houses by falling hailstones and flooding. During an electrical storm in the afternoon of the 12th, over Lincolnshire, the West Riding, and Westmorland, several men were injured and many cattle killed. Darkness was intense; and, though the temperature was most oppressive, large pieces of ice fell in places. Rain flooded cellars and caused trouble and confusion. Streets were flooded, railways and telegraphs disorganised. On the 22nd, an electrical storm raged over South England and Ireland all night. At Newton Abbot some streets were flooded. Several orchards were ruined by torrents of rain. At Portsmouth the railway was under 2 ft. of water, and many streets were impassable. Damage was done by lightning in various localities.

On August 5th, a storm off Florida wrecked fifteen ships, by which some lives were lost and a million dollars' worth of property. On the 3rd a hurricane was experienced in latitude 12° 30′ N. longitude 35° W. This has been regarded as the origin of the hurricane which desolated the West Indies between the 7th and 12th. Its centre passed Antigua and Montserrat on the 7th, travelled south of Nevis and St. Croix, across Puerto Rico on the 8th, Haiti on the 9th, thence to the east of Cuba on the 11th, Nassau on the 13th, trended along the coast of the United States until the 19th, and was reported in latitude 40° N. longitude 60° W. on the 21st.[*] At Montserrat 100 persons perished, 1,500 were injured, 8,000 rendered homeless; buildings were overthrown, trees and crops uplifted, and the country had the appearance of fire having passed over it. The barometer went down to 27·3 inches. At St. Kitts and at Nevis the loss of life and the destruction of property were appalling. At Puerto Rico the torrents of rain caused the rivers to overflow. Towns were inundated by sea and rivers, causing immense destruction, and 2,000 persons were supposed to have perished. Much the same description applies to the destruction, destitution, and suffering in nearly all the islands. Estates, churches, houses, numerous lives of men and cattle were destroyed. At Guadaloupe two lighthouses were overturned and two villages obliterated. On the 10th, a telegram from Argentina reported disastrous floods in Chubat, which devastated many farms, the houses were swept away, goods and chattels lost, rendering

---

[*] NOTE.—Data collected by the Hydrographic Office of the United States have enabled this storm-system to be traced from August 3 to September 12. Leaving the American coast it moved eastward. August 24-30 its centre was almost stationary in mid-Atlantic. It then moved to the Azores by September 3; curved to the N.E., reaching Brest on the 7th, thence went S.E to Corsica on the 9th, about which region it caused strong gales and rough sea till the 12th.

the Welsh settlers destitute. During the afternoon of the 15th electrical storms occurred in central England. Torrents of rain caused temporary floodings, damaging crops, while lightning caused fires, destroying property and live stock. The sky was darkly overcast. Hailstones as large as marbles fell. A sudden gust of wind from northward passed over London at 5 p.m., very remarkable for its suddenness, short duration, and obnoxious from the dust it raised. About the end of August, a terrible gale in Behring Sea damaged H.M.S. *Pheasant.*

On September 3, a hurricane with excessive rain in the Azores, caused damage ashore, wrecks at sea, and loss of life. About mid-day of the 6th, a severe electrical storm raged over London, giving an inch of rain and utter darkness. Coming in the course of an hour, the quantity of water, none of which can percolate the well-paved ground, was too much for the sewers, so that many places became flooded. On the 12th, a hurricane at Bermuda damaged the dockyard and hundreds of houses, blew down thousands of trees, destroyed numerous boats, and damaged electric lines. This hurricane seems to have been encountered by the ss. *Lucania* on the 15th and 16th eastward of Newfoundland, in which region it wrought immense havoc, 400 fishing vessels being reported lost. On the 15th, the Danube reached eighteen and a-half feet above its normal level at Vienna, and low-lying streets were under water. The iron bridge over the Traun,

at Gmunden, was carried away, and nineteen men working on it perished. A dam burst at Kohavan, Buda-Pesth, putting nearly 40 square miles of land under water. During the night of the 25th, landslips on an extraordinary scale occurred at Darjiling, no less than 28 inches of rain having fallen within 38 hours. The destruction of property, including ten plantations, was enormous, said to exceed in value a million pounds sterling. More than 400 lives were lost.

On October 7, a typhoon swept over parts of central and eastern Japan, doing much damage to crops and other property. A train was blown from a bridge into the river near Utsunomiya, killing fifty persons and injuring many. On the 8th, a severe tempest broke over the Neapolitan district, and disastrous floods occurred in which about forty people perished in the province of Solerno. Several villages, bridges, mills, and houses were swept away, roads destroyed, vineyards ruined. On the 20th, serious damage was wrought by a storm in southern Italy. At San Giorgio the river overflowed, sweeping away a bridge and twenty houses. Lightning struck the church of Montemesola, killing three persons and injuring twenty; the Carosino Church was also struck. Jamaica, on the 30th, reported a severe storm which had raged since the 27th. Rainfall had been phenomenal, and wide-spread devastation was caused to public works and to cultivation by floods, and several persons perished.

Progress of Astronomical Science, 1899.

THE ASTEROIDS AND PLANETS.

In the past year fourteen new asteroids, which have received permanent numbers, have been added to the group, making a total of 444. There are also some others found on the photographic plates, provisionally called discoveries, which are awaiting confirmation. The planet seen by Palisa on March 9, and named Slatin, turns out to be identical with Lucia (222). Number 366, discovered by Charlois at Nice in March, 1893, has been named Vincentina; No. 433, by Herr G. Witt, Eros, and No. 439. by Coddington, Ohio. Hungaria (434) has a mean distance from the Earth less than that of any other of the asteroids excepting Eros (433). Calculating backwards, the places of this planet at the opposition for several years, and examining the photographs of those portions of the sky taken at Harvard and Arequipa, between the years 1893-6, impressions were found on 10 or 12 of the plates. The places thus obtained, together with the recent eye observations, will furnish the data for an accurate determination of the orbit. The opposition in November and December, 1900, will be the most favourable that will occur for many years and will no doubt be well observed in the northern hemisphere, but its great northern declination at that period, will make it rather difficult for observers in the southern observatories.

A telegram from America in March last, announced the discovery of a ninth Satellite to Saturn, discovered by Professor W. H. Pickering, on photographs taken at Arequipa, in August, 1898, with the Bruce telescope. It is estimated as somewhat fainter than Hyperion, having a period

of 17 months, and distant from the primary eight millions of miles. Further evidence is required before acknowledging this addition to the Saturnian family. At present it rests on somewhat slender testimony.

The Sun. In August and September last the disc of the Sun was free from spots, with the exception of one or two very small ones, which would seem to show that if the time of minimum has not already been reached, it cannot be far off. The autumn of 1900 was predicted as the time of minimum.

i (1898). This Comet, which was discovered by Brooks, was a very conspicuous object, ill-defined, and showing a somewhat eccentric condensation, with no trace of a tail. Its apparent motion was extremely rapid, owing to the Earth and comet moving in opposite directions. When at its brightest, it was just visible to the naked eye On the photographs taken with the Willard lens at Lick, a short, straight, and narrow tail was visible, extending 45′.

j (1898). A faint Comet, discovered by Chase on November 14. in R. A. 10ʰ. 7ᵐ. 4ˢ. and Decl. 22° 55′ N. A faint object and difficult to observe. Calculation of the elements shows that the orbit is parabolic with a period of about 33 years.

a (1899 . A bright Comet, discovered by Prof. Lewis Swift, on March 3, in R.A. 3ʰ. 15ᵐ. and Decl. 29° 8′. On May 6. it was described as very bright, with well-defined nucleus. On May 8, it was easily visible to the naked eye, though the tail (1° long) could not be made out. While visible, this Comet seems to have undergone many changes both in form and brightness. In the middle of May, the nucleus was observed to be eccentrically placed, and on the fine photographs taken at Lick the tail appeared 9° long. On May 10, this tail threw out side streamers and presented a contorted appearance. On May 19, the tail appeared curiously unsymmetrical. On June 5, it changed again, and showed five short cropped tails with streamer on each side.

b (1899). Tuttle's periodic Comet, re-discovered by Wolf, at Heidelberg, on March 5, and described as being of the 11th magnitude. In the middle of March, photographs were obtained at Greenwich with the 30-inch reflector telescope.

c (1899). Tempel's second periodic Comet, discovered on return, by Perrine on May 6. At this time, it was very faint, being estimated equal to a star of the 15th magnitude, increasing up to July 27, the time of perihelion passage, when it was at its maximum. Its place was found to agree very well with that of the ephemeris.

d (1899). Holmes' periodic Comet, discovered in 1892, was detected on its return to perihelion by Professor Perrine, of Lick, on June 10, and was then very faint, but slowly increased in brightness as it approached the Earth. It appeared a round nebulous mass 30″ in diameter. It was found in a position agreeing very closely with that given in the ephemeris.

e (1899). Tempel's first periodic Comet was looked for at Lick, in June and July, but without success. In July, some views were obtained of it by Mr. Denning, who described it as fairly bright in 10-inch telescope, with a faint, spreading tail pointing N.N.W. from the nucleus.

f (1899). A very faint Comet by Giacobini, on September 29, in R.A. 16h. 27m. and Decl. 5° 10 S., moving eastward 2′ and southward 10′.

Dr. T. D. Anderson, of Edinburgh, reports discovery of two new variable Stars. One in Hercules, varying to the extent of nearly one magnitude in R.A. 17h. 55m. 25s. and Decl. 19° 30′ N.; another in Cygnus, varying about three quarters of a magnitude; in R.A. 20h. 11m. 33s. and Decl. 30° 45′ N.

The period of the variable Star in Cygnus discovered by Madame Ceraski has been recently determined by Professor E. C. Pickering to be 4h. 13m. 45s., a value derived from the observations made at the Harvard College Observatory, together with an examination of the Draper Memorial photographic plates. The variation in brightness amounts to about three magnitudes.

OBSERVATORIES.—The new buildings at Greenwich are now completed, and the greater part of the staff, with the Astronomer-Royal, have moved into their new quarters, much to their comfort after the crowded experience of the last few years.

At the Melbourne Observatory all the catalogue plates of the International Photographic Survey of the Heavens have been taken, and the stars (3,500) contained on ten plates have been measured. The measures were made at first according to the Greenwich method, that is by means of a scale engraved on glass in the focus of the eye-piece. Mr. Barracchi considers that this method gives too large a probable error, and it was discarded in favour of the filar micrometer, the method adopted by Dr. Gill at the Cape Observatory. Many other observers, however, think that ample accuracy for the purposes of the Astrographic Catalogue can be obtained by the Greenwich method, and that it is a mistake to go back to the filar micrometer, as that will greatly prolong the time required for the measurements.

Owing to financial difficulties in the Colony, the observatory has for some time past been starved in the matter of money, but the recent improved condition of the finances which will materially increase the usefulness of the observatory to the Colony.

It is proposed to make the "City Observatory," Edinburgh, a teaching observatory, and arrangements are being made to give facilities to educational establishments in the City for the study of astronomy, by engaging a qualified assistant to deliver lectures at moderate fees. This use of the observatory seems a very wise one. It would be a waste of energy to attempt there work of the same kind as that done at the Royal Observatory on Blackford Hill.

The Egyptian government intend to establish an observatory on the Mokattam Hills, on the site occupied by the observers of the Transit of Venus (1874) under Captain Orde Brown. This site was also one of the stations used in the chain of longitudes connecting Greenwich with Madras.

M. Bischoffsheim, the founder of the Nice Observatory, is about to erect a mountain observatory on the summit of Mount Mounier, one of the peaks of the Maritime Alps lying to the north-east of Nice.

The magnetic work of the Vienna Observatory has been given up—the indications of the magnets having been rendered untrustworthy owing to the increased use of electricity in the neighbourhood for the purposes of traction and lighting. A new observatory will be erected at some distance from the city, and in a locality not likely to be so disturbed.

At the Royal Observatory, Cape of Good Hope, according to the last report, it is proposed to repeat the whole series of catalogue plates, so as to bring the epoch at which the plates were taken nearer to that at which the meridian observations of the comparison stars were made and also because it will permit suspected cases of large proper motion to be satisfactorily dealt with. A new measuring instrument has been ordered from the Messrs. Repsold in order to push on the work of measurement at a more rapid rate. An attempt was made to photograph the Leonid meteors, but without success. The geodetic survey of Rhodesia, and determination of the Anglo-German boundary between Bechuanaland and German South Africa, is being vigorously carried on under the direction of Dr. Gill, Her Majesty's Astronomer at the Cape.

Professor G. Rümker, having resigned the directorship of the Hamburgh Observatory. Professor F. Küstner, from the Bonn Observatory, has been appointed in his place.

Some time ago a Special Committee of the St. Petersburg Astronomical Society was appointed to examine and report upon the question of the reform of the Russian Calendar, and, after ascertaining the views of the various government departments, reported that in their opinion it is advisable to adopt the reform proposed at an early period. A difficulty in reconciling the dates of certain religious festivals in the Julian and Gregorian Calendars has led the committee finally to recommend that the dates according to the old and new style should appear on public documents, which amounts to saying that matters should remain as before.

The Superintendent of the United States Naval Observatory has issued a circular addressed to foreign observers who may wish to observe the total solar eclipse of May 28 next in America, that their instruments will be admitted free of charge. On receiving notification of intended port and date of arrival, the superintendent of the Naval Department will forward a letter to Consul at port, on receipt of which all possible facilities to the intending observers.

Professor Keeler, in a paper on a new form of photographic telescope, suggests that the most suitable ratio of focus to aperture lies between the limits 30 to 1 and 60 to 1, and that in no case should the focus exceed one hundred times the aperture.

The gold medal of the Royal Astronomical Society has been awarded to Mr. Frank McClean for his series of photographs of the spectra of all stars of the 3½ magnitude and upwards in both hemispheres.

The Lalande medal of the Paris Academy of Sciences has been given to Dr. S. C. Chandler for his contributions to Astronomy. The Damoiseau prize was presented to Dr. G. W. Hill, and the Prix Janssen to M. Bebopolsky, of the Imperial Observatory, St. Petersburg.

OBITUARY.—Latimer Clark, F.R.S., who died suddenly at Kensington on October 30, 1898, was distinguished chiefly as an electrician, but gave some attention to astronomy as an amateur. He was a Fellow of the Royal Astronomical Society, and the author of an elementary book on the transit instrument. Some years since, he designed a small portable instrument of this kind for the use of amateurs and country gentlemen, and in conjunction with the late Mr. Herbert Sadler, F.R.A.S., published (annually) transit tables for use with this instrument, to facilitate the determination of time.

Mr. Edwin Dunkin, F.R.S., late chief assistant at the Royal Observatory, died on the 26th of November, 1898, at Blackheath, and was buried at Charlton Cemetery on December 1 following. Mr. Dunkin was born in 1822, and, early in life, entered the Royal Observatory in the early days of Airy's reign. He was first engaged on the reduction of the lunar and planetary observations made at Greenwich from the time of Bradley to that of Pond. He was subsequently, for some years, attached to the magnetical and meteorological department of the observatory, and on the erection of the then new altazimuth instrument was transferred back to the astronomical department to superintend the observations and reductions with the new instrument.

Mr. Dunkin did much to popularise astronomy by his papers in the current magazines and other works. For many years a Fellow of the Royal Astronomical Society, he served in many offices, including that of Secretary, and was elected President in 1884. Mr. Dunkin was engaged in various scientific expeditions, among others that to observe the total solar eclipse in Norway in 1851, also the pendulum experiment in the Harton coal pit, South Shields, to determine the weight of the earth, and in telegraphic longitudes of Paris, Brussels, and Valentia. He retired from the service in 1884.

Mr. Herbert Sadler, F.R.A.S. (born in 1856, died suddenly on June 1, 1898), was an energetic amateur astronomer, who did much miscellaneous scientific work. In the field of astronomy he was the author of a "List of the Most Remarkable Objects visible with Small Telescopes," and was a frequent contributor to "Knowledge," "The Observatory," and other scientific publications. In conjunction with Mr. Neison he founded the Journal published by the Selenographical Society.

Professor Bunsen died at Heidelberg on August 16 last. Modern astronomy owes a debt of gratitude to him, who, with Kirchoff, put into the hands of astronomers such a powerful means of investigation as is provided by the discovery of spectrum analysis.

LOSS OF LIFE AT SEA (MERCANTILE MARINE ONLY) 1 JAN. TO 31 DEC., 1898.

| | Masters and Seamen Employed. | Lives Lost. | | | | | Percentages and Proportions. | | Total No. of Lives Lost in Merchant Ships Registered in the United Kingdom. | | |
| | | Drowned. | | | Masters and Seamen Lost by Accident other than Drowning. | Total Number lost by Drowning and other Accident. | Lives Lost by Drowning of Persons Employed. | Lives Lost by Drowning and other Accident of Persons employed | Crew. | Passengers (lost by Wreck only). | TOTAL. |
		Masters and Seamen Lost by Wrecks and Casualties.	Masters and Seamen lost when Vessel was not Damaged.	TOTAL.							
Sailing Vessels	46,553	317	148	465	71	536	1 in 100	1 in 87	536	7	543
Steam Vessels ...	172,830	385	284	669	147	816	1 in 258	1 in 212	816	79	895
TOTAL	219,383	702	432	1,134	218	1,352	1 in 193	1 in 162	1,352	86	1 438

To use this Table, take the Sun's declination in the left-hand column, and under the required latitude on the horizontal line will be found the apparent time of Sunset. Subtract the quantity found as above from 12h., and the remainder will be the apparent time of Sunrise.

This Table is arranged for Northern latitudes, but will serve equally well for Southern by changing the declination from North to South, and vice versâ.

Declination.	LATITUDE.														
	1°	14°	26°	35°	43°	49°	53°	56°	58°	60°	62°	63°	64°	65°	66°
	h. m.	h. m.	h. m.	h. m.	h. m.	h. m.	h. m.	h. m.	h. m.	h. m.	h. m.	h. m.	h. m.	h. m.	h. m.
24 N	6 4	6 28	6 53	7 16	7 42	8 7	8 30	8 51	9 8	9 29	9 57	10 15	10 38	11 13	...
23	6 4	6 27	6 50	7 12	7 37	8 1	8 22	8 41	8 57	9 16	9 40	9 55	10 13	10 36	11 12
22	6 4	6 25	6 48	7 9	7 32	7 55	8 14	8 32	8 47	9 4	9 25	9 38	9 53	10 12	10 35
21	6 4	6 24	6 46	7 5	7 27	7 49	8 7	8 24	8 37	8 53	9 12	9 23	9 37	9 51	10 10
20	6 4	6 23	6 43	7 2	7 23	7 43	8 0	8 15	8 28	8 42	8 59	9 10	9 21	9 34	9 49
19	6 3	6 22	6 41	6 59	7 18	7 37	7 53	8 7	8 19	8 32	8 48	8 57	9 7	9 18	9 32
18	6 3	6 21	6 39	6 55	7 14	7 31	7 46	8 0	8 10	8 22	8 37	8 45	8 54	9 4	9 16
17	6 3	6 20	6 37	6 52	7 9	7 26	7 40	7 52	8 2	8 13	8 26	8 34	8 42	8 51	9 1
16	6 3	6 18	6 35	6 49	7 5	7 21	7 33	7 45	7 54	8 4	8 16	8 23	8 30	8 38	8 48
15	6 3	6 18	6 32	6 46	7 1	7 15	7 27	7 39	7 46	7 56	8 6	8 13	8 19	8 27	8 35
14	6 3	6 16	6 30	6 43	6 57	7 10	7 21	7 31	7 39	7 47	7 57	8 3	8 9	8 15	8 23
13	6 3	6 15	6 28	6 40	6 53	7 5	7 15	7 24	7 31	7 39	7 48	7 53	7 59	8 5	8 11
12	6 3	6 14	6 26	6 37	6 49	7 0	7 9	7 18	7 24	7 31	7 39	7 44	7 49	7 54	8 0
11	6 3	6 13	6 24	6 34	6 45	6 55	7 3	7 11	7 17	7 23	7 31	7 35	7 39	7 44	7 49
10	6 3	6 12	6 22	6 31	6 41	6 50	6 58	7 5	7 10	7 16	7 22	7 26	7 29	7 34	7 39
9	6 3	6 11	6 20	6 28	6 37	6 45	6 52	6 58	7 3	7 8	7 14	7 17	7 21	7 25	7 29
8	6 3	6 10	6 18	6 25	6 33	6 41	6 47	6 52	6 56	7 1	7 6	7 9	7 12	7 15	7 19
7	6 2	6 9	6 16	6 22	6 29	6 36	6 41	6 46	6 49	6 53	6 58	7 1	7 3	7 6	7 10
6	6 2	6 8	6 14	6 19	6 25	6 31	6 36	6 40	6 43	6 46	6 50	6 52	6 55	6 57	7 0
5	6 2	6 7	6 12	6 17	6 22	6 26	6 30	6 34	6 36	6 39	6 42	6 44	6 46	6 48	6 51
4	6 2	6 6	6 10	6 14	6 18	6 22	6 25	6 28	6 30	6 32	6 35	6 36	6 38	6 40	6 41
3	6 2	6 5	6 8	6 11	6 14	6 17	6 19	6 21	6 23	6 25	6 27	6 28	6 30	6 31	6 32
2	6 2	6 4	6 6	6 8	6 10	6 12	6 14	6 16	6 17	6 18	6 20	6 20	6 21	6 22	6 23
1 N	6 2	6 3	6 4	6 5	6 6	6 6	6 9	6 10	6 10	6 11	6 13	6 13	6 13	6 14	6 15
0 S	6 2	6 1	6 0	6 0	6 0	5 59	5 58	5 58	5 58	5 57	5 57	5 57	5 57	5 56	5 56
1	6 2	6 0	5 58	5 57	5 55	5 54	5 53	5 52	5 51	5 50	5 49	5 49	5 48	5 48	5 47
2	6 2	5 59	5 56	5 54	5 52	5 49	5 48	5 45	5 43	5 42	5 40	5 41	5 40	5 39	5 38
3	6 2	5 58	5 55	5 51	5 48	5 45	5 42	5 40	5 38	5 36	5 34	5 33	5 32	5 31	5 29
4	6 2	5 57	5 53	5 49	5 44	5 40	5 37	5 34	5 31	5 29	5 27	5 25	5 24	5 22	5 20
5	6 2	5 56	5 51	5 46	5 40	5 35	5 31	5 26	5 23	5 19	5 11	5 17	5 15	5 13	5 11
6	6 1	5 55	5 49	5 43	5 37	5 31	5 26	5 22	5 19	5 15	5 11	5 9	5 7	5 5	5 1
7	6 1	5 54	5 47	5 40	5 33	5 26	5 21	5 16	5 12	5 8	4 55	4 53	4 49	4 46	4 42
8	6 1	5 53	5 45	5 37	5 29	5 21	5 16	5 10	5 5	5 1	4 55	4 53	4 49	4 46	4 42
9	6 1	5 52	5 43	5 34	5 25	5 16	5 10	5 5	4 59	4 55	4 49	4 46	4 42	4 39	4 34
10	6 1	5 51	5 41	5 31	5 21	5 12	5 4	4 57	4 52	4 46	4 39	4 35	4 31	4 27	4 22
11	6 1	5 50	5 39	5 28	5 17	5 7	4 57	4 50	4 44	4 38	4 31	4 27	4 22	4 17	4 12
12	6 1	5 49	5 37	5 25	5 13	5 2	4 52	4 44	4 38	4 30	4 23	4 18	4 13	4 7	4 1
13	6 1	5 48	5 34	5 22	5 9	4 57	4 47	4 37	4 30	4 23	4 13	4 8	4 3	3 56	3 50
14	6 1	5 47	5 32	5 19	5 5	4 52	4 41	4 31	4 24	4 14	4 4	3 59	3 53	3 46	3 39
15	6 1	5 46	5 30	5 16	5 1	4 46	4 34	4 24	4 15	4 6	3 55	3 49	3 42	3 35	3 27
16	6 1	5 45	5 28	5 13	4 57	4 41	4 28	4 17	4 8	3 57	3 45	3 39	3 31	3 23	3 14
17	6 1	5 44	5 26	5 10	4 53	4 36	4 22	4 10	4 0	3 48	3 35	3 28	3 20	3 11	3 0
18	6 1	5 43	5 24	5 7	4 48	4 30	4 15	4 2	3 51	3 39	3 25	3 17	3 8	2 58	2 46
19	6 1	5 41	5 22	5 4	4 44	4 24	4 9	3 54	3 43	3 29	3 14	3 5	2 55	2 43	2 30
20	6 1	5 40	5 19	5 1	4 39	4 19	4 2	3 46	3 34	3 19	3 2	2 52	2 41	2 28	2 12
21	6 1	5 39	5 17	4 57	4 35	4 13	3 55	3 38	3 24	3 9	2 50	2 38	2 25	2 10	1 52
22	6 1	5 38	5 15	4 54	4 30	4 7	3 47	3 29	3 15	2 57	2 36	2 23	2 8	1 50	1 27
23	6 1	5 37	5 12	4 50	4 25	4 1	3 40	3 20	3 5	2 45	2 21	2 7	1 49	1 26	...
24 S	6 1	5 37	5 12	4 50	4 25	4 1	3 40	3 20	3 5	2 45	2 21	2 7	1 49	1 26	...

Should the Sunrise and Sunset be required for any other latitude and declination within the limits of the Table, the required times may be easily found by proportion.

Tables for Determining the Latitude

FROM OBSERVATIONS OF THE ALTITUDE OF THE POLE STAR OUT OF THE MERIDIAN.

TABLE I.

Sidereal Time	Correction	Sidereal Time	Sidereal Time	Correction	Sidereal Time	Sidereal Time	Correction	Sidereal Time
H. M.	° ′ ″	H. M.	H. M.	° ′ ″	H. M.	H. M.	° ′ ″	H. M.
0 0	−1 8 23 +	12 0	4 0	−0 56 20 +	16 0	8 0	+0 12 3 −	20 0
0 10	−1 9 26 +	12 10	4 10	−0 54 15 +	16 10	8 10	+0 15 11 −	20 10
0 20	−1 10 21 +	12 20	4 20	−0 52 4 +	16 20	8 20	+0 18 17 −	20 20
0 30	−1 11 8 +	12 30	4 30	−0 49 47 +	16 30	8 30	+0 21 21 −	20 30
0 40	−1 11 47 +	12 40	4 40	−0 47 25 +	16 40	8 40	+0 24 22 −	20 40
0 50	−1 12 17 +	12 50	4 50	−0 44 57 +	16 50	8 50	+0 27 21 −	20 50
1 0	−1 12 40 +	13 0	5 0	−0 42 24 +	17 0	9 0	+0 30 16 −	21 0
1 10	−1 12 54 +	13 10	5 10	−0 39 45 +	17 10	9 10	+0 33 8 −	21 10
1 20	−1 13 0 +	13 20	5 20	−0 37 3 +	17 20	9 20	+0 35 57 −	21 20
1 30	−1 12 57 +	13 30	5 30	−0 34 16 +	17 30	9 30	+0 38 41 −	21 30
1 40	−1 12 47 +	13 40	5 40	−0 31 26 +	17 40	9 40	+0 41 21 −	21 40
1 50	−1 12 27 +	13 50	5 50	−0 28 31 +	17 50	9 50	+0 43 56 −	21 50
2 0	−1 12 0 +	14 0	6 0	−0 25 34 +	18 0	10 0	+0 46 26 −	22 0
2 10	−1 11 24 +	14 10	6 10	−0 22 33 +	18 10	10 10	+0 48 51 −	22 10
2 20	−1 10 40 +	14 20	6 20	−0 19 30 +	18 20	10 20	+0 51 10 −	22 20
2 30	−1 9 49 +	14 30	6 30	−0 16 25 +	18 30	10 30	+0 53 23 −	22 30
2 40	−1 8 49 +	14 40	6 40	−0 13 18 +	18 40	10 40	+0 55 31 −	22 40
2 50	−1 7 41 +	14 50	6 50	−0 10 10 +	18 50	10 50	+0 57 31 −	22 50
3 0	−1 6 26 +	15 0	7 0	−0 7 0 +	19 0	11 0	+0 59 26 −	23 0
3 10	−1 5 3 +	15 10	7 10	−0 3 49 +	19 10	11 10	+1 1 13 −	23 10
3 20	−1 3 32 +	15 20	7 20	−0 0 38 +	19 20	11 20	+1 2 54 −	23 20
3 30	−1 1 54 +	15 30	7 30	+0 2 33 −	19 30	11 30	+1 4 27 −	23 30
3 40	−1 0 10 +	15 40	7 40	+0 5 44 −	19 40	11 40	+1 5 53 −	23 40
3 50	−0 58 18 +	15 50	7 50	+0 8 54 −	19 50	11 50	+1 7 12 −	23 50
4 0	−0 56 20 +	16 0	8 0	+0 12 3 −	20 0	12 0	+1 8 23 −	24 0

TABLE II.

Sidereal Time	Altitude.															Sidereal Time
	0°	5°	10°	15°	20°	25°	30°	35°	40°	45°	50°	55°	60°	65°	70°	
H. M.	′ ″	′ ″	′ ″	′ ″	′ ″	′ ″	′ ″	′ ″	′ ″	′ ″	′ ″	′ ″	′ ″	′ ″	′ ″	H. M.
0 0	0 0	0 0	0 1	0 2	0 2	0 3	0 3	0 4	0 5	0 6	0 7	0 8	0 10	0 12	0 16	12 0
0 30	0 0	0 0	0 0	0 1	0 1	0 1	0 1	0 2	0 2	0 2	0 3	0 3	0 4	0 5	0 6	12 30
1 0	0 0	0 0	0 0	0 0	0 0	0 0	0 0	0 0	0 0	0 0	0 1	0 1	0 1	0 1	0 1	13 0
1 30	0 0	0 0	0 0	0 0	0 0	0 0	0 0	0 0	0 0	0 1	0 1	0 2	0 2	0 2	0 3	13 30
2 0	0 0	0 0	0 0	0 0	0 0	0 1	0 1	0 1	0 1	0 1	0 2	0 2	0 2	0 3	0 4	14 0
2 30	0 0	0 0	0 1	0 1	0 1	0 2	0 2	0 2	0 3	0 3	0 4	0 5	0 6	0 7	0 9	14 30
3 0	0 0	0 0	0 1	0 1	0 2	0 3	0 4	0 5	0 6	0 8	0 9	0 11	0 14	0 17	0 22	15 0
3 30	0 0	0 0	0 1	0 2	0 4	0 5	0 7	0 9	0 11	0 13	0 16	0 19	0 23	0 28	0 36	15 30
4 0	0 0	0 2	0 3	0 5	0 7	0 9	0 11	0 13	0 16	0 19	0 22	0 27	0 33	0 40	0 52	16 0
4 30	0 0	0 2	0 4	0 7	0 9	0 12	0 14	0 17	0 21	0 25	0 30	0 36	0 43	0 53	1 8	16 30
5 0	0 0	0 3	0 5	0 8	0 11	0 14	0 18	0 22	0 26	0 31	0 37	0 44	0 53	1 6	1 25	17 0
5 30	0 0	0 3	0 6	0 10	0 13	0 17	0 21	0 25	0 30	0 36	0 43	0 52	1 3	1 17	1 40	17 30
6 0	0 0	0 4	0 7	0 11	0 15	0 19	0 24	0 29	0 34	0 41	0 49	0 58	1 10	1 27	1 52	18 0
6 30	0 0	0 4	0 8	0 12	0 16	0 21	0 25	0 31	0 39	0 44	0 55	1 3	1 16	1 34	2 1	18 30
7 0	0 0	0 4	0 8	0 12	0 17	0 21	0 27	0 32	0 39	0 46	0 55	1 6	1 20	1 39	2 8	19 0
7 30	0 0	0 4	0 8	0 12	0 17	0 22	0 27	0 33	0 39	0 46	0 55	1 6	1 20	1 40	2 7	19 30
8 0	0 0	0 4	0 8	0 12	0 16	0 21	0 26	0 32	0 38	0 45	0 55	1 5	1 18	1 37	2 4	20 0
8 30	0 0	0 3	0 7	0 11	0 15	0 20	0 25	0 30	0 36	0 43	0 51	1 1	1 11	1 31	1 57	20 30
9 0	0 0	0 3	0 7	0 10	0 14	0 18	0 22	0 27	0 33	0 39	0 46	0 55	1 5	1 22	1 46	21 0
9 30	0 0	0 3	0 6	0 9	0 12	0 16	0 19	0 23	0 28	0 33	0 40	0 48	0 57	1 11	1 32	21 30
10 0	0 0	0 2	0 5	0 7	0 10	0 13	0 16	0 19	0 23	0 28	0 34	0 40	0 48	0 58	1 16	22 0
10 30	0 0	0 2	0 4	0 6	0 8	0 10	0 12	0 15	0 18	0 22	0 26	0 31	0 37	0 46	0 59	22 30
11 0	0 0	0 1	0 3	0 4	0 6	0 7	0 9	0 11	0 13	0 16	0 19	0 22	0 27	0 34	0 43	23 0
11 30	0 0	0 1	0 2	0 3	0 4	0 5	0 6	0 7	0 9	0 10	0 12	0 15	0 18	0 22	0 28	23 30
12 0	0 0	0 0	0 1	0 2	0 2	0 3	0 3	0 4	0 5	0 6	0 7	0 8	0 10	0 12	0 16	24 0

The local mean time of the observed altitude, when reduced to the corresponding Greenwich mean time, may be converted into sidereal time by means of the table on the next page. It will be observed that the sign on the left-hand side of the *correction* in Table I. is to be used when the argument is on the left, and *vice versâ* ; + means that the correction is to be added to the reduced altitude, and − that it is to be subtracted. The corrections derived from the double-entry Tables II. and III. are always added. In order to make the quantities taken out from Table III. additive they have been increased by 1′ ; this quantity must therefore be taken away from the final result.

TABLE III. (1900.)

Sidereal Time.	Jan. 1.	Feb. 1.	Mar. 1.	Apr. 1.	May 1.	June 1.	July 1.	Aug. 1.	Sept. 1.	Oct. 1.	Nov. 1.	Dec. 1.	Dec. 31.
H. 0	1 0	0 57	0 50	0 40	0 32	0 28	0 29	0 35	0 45	0 57	1 8	1 16	1 19
2	0 49	0 51	0 48	0 40	0 30	0 23	0 19	0 20	0 26	0 35	0 47	0 57	1 4
4	0 42	0 49	0 50	0 45	0 37	0 27	0 19	0 15	0 17	0 20	0 28	0 38	0 48
6	0 39	0 49	0 54	0 54	0 49	0 40	0 31	0 22	0 17	0 16	0 19	0 26	0 35
8	0 42	0 52	1 1	1 5	1 5	0 59	0 50	0 40	0 30	0 23	0 20	0 23	0 29
10	0 50	0 57	1 6	1 15	1 19	1 18	1 12	1 2	0 51	0 40	0 32	0 29	0 31
12	1 0	1 3	1 10	1 20	1 28	1 32	1 31	1 25	1 15	1 3	0 52	0 44	0 41
14	1 11	1 9	1 12	1 20	1 30	1 37	1 41	1 40	1 34	1 35	1 13	1 3	0 56
16	1 18	1 11	1 10	1 15	1 23	1 33	1 41	1 45	1 45	1 41	1 22	1 22	1 12
18	1 21	1 11	1 6	1 6	1 11	1 20	1 29	1 38	1 43	1 44	1 41	1 34	1 25
20	1 18	1 8	1 0	0 55	0 55	1 1	1 10	1 20	1 30	1 37	1 40	1 37	1 31
22	1 10	1 3	0 54	0 45	0 41	0 42	0 48	0 58	1 9	1 20	1 28	1 31	1 29
24	1 0	0 57	0 50	0 40	0 32	0 28	0 29	0 35	0 45	0 57	1 8	1 16	1 19

TO CHANGE INTERVALS OF MEAN SOLAR TIME INTO THE EQUIVALENT INTERVALS OF SIDEREAL TIME.

Hours of Mean Time.	Sidereal Equivalents.	Minutes of Mean Time.	Sidereal Equivalents.	Minutes of Mean Time.	Sidereal Equivalents.	Seconds of Mean Time.	Sidereal Equivalents.	Seconds of Mean Time.	Sidereal Equivalents.
	H. M. S.		M. S.		M. S.		S.		S.
1	1 0 9.86	1	0.16	31	5.09	1	1.00	31	31.08
2	2 0 19.71	2	0.33	32	5.26	2	2.01	32	32.09
3	3 0 29.57	3	0.49	33	5.42	3	3.01	33	33.09
4	4 0 39.43	4	0.66	34	5.59	4	4.01	34	34.09
5	5 0 49.28	5	0.82	35	5.75	5	5.01	35	35.10
6	6 0 59.14	6	0.99	36	5.91	6	6.02	36	36.10
7	7 1 9.00	7	1.15	37	6.08	7	7.02	37	37.10
8	8 1 18.85	8	1.31	38	6.24	8	8.02	38	38.10
9	9 1 28.71	9	1.48	39	6.41	9	9.02	39	39.11
10	10 1 38.56	10	1.64	40	6.57	10	10.03	40	40.11
11	11 1 48.42	11	1.81	41	6.74	11	11.03	41	41.11
12	12 1 58.28	12	1.97	42	6.90	12	12.03	42	42.12
13	13 2 8.13	13	2.14	43	7.06	13	13.04	43	43.12
14	14 2 17.99	14	2.30	44	7.23	14	14.04	44	44.12
15	15 2 27.85	15	2.46	45	7.39	15	15.04	45	45.12
16	16 2 37.70	16	2.63	46	7.56	16	16.04	46	46.13
17	17 2 47.56	17	2.79	47	7.72	17	17.05	47	47.13
18	18 2 57.42	18	2.96	48	7.89	18	18.05	48	48.13
19	19 3 7.27	19	3.12	49	8.05	19	19.05	49	49.13
20	20 3 17.13	20	3.29	50	8.21	20	20.05	50	50.14
21	21 3 26.99	21	3.45	51	8.38	21	21.06	51	51.14
22	22 3 36.84	22	3.61	52	8.54	22	22.06	52	52.14
23	23 3 46.70	23	3.78	53	8.71	23	23.06	53	53.15
24	24 3 56.56	24	3.94	54	8.87	24	24.07	54	54.15
		25	4.11	55	9.04	25	25.07	55	55.15
		26	4.27	56	9.20	26	26.07	56	56.15
		27	4.44	57	9.36	27	27.07	57	57.16
		28	4.60	58	9.53	28	28.08	58	58.16
		29	4.76	59	9.69	29	29.08	59	59.16
		30	4.93	60	9.86	30	30.08	60	60.16

To obtain the Sidereal Time corresponding to any given Mean Time, by means of the above tables, all that is required is to take the Sidereal Time at the preceding Mean Noon (which will be found on the second page of each month) and add to it the Sidereal Equivalents opposite to the hours, minutes, and seconds of the given Mean Time. If the sum of these numbers comes out more than twenty-four hours, twenty-four hours must be subtracted from it. For example:—

Let it be required to find the Sidereal Time corresponding to the Mean Time 14h. 3m. 40s. on October 10:—

		H. M. S.
Sidereal Time at Noon on October 10		13 14 32
Mean Time intervals and equivalents from table above { 14h. =		14 2 17.99
3m. =		3 0.49
40s. =		40.11
Corresponding Sidereal Time =		**3 20 30.59**

This table may also be used to show the acceleration of Sidereal on Mean Solar intervals, by subtracting the Mean Time arguments from their Sidereal Equivalents.

TO CHANGE INTERVALS OF SIDEREAL TIME INTO THE EQUIVALENT INTERVALS OF MEAN SOLAR TIME.

Hours of Sidereal Time.	Mean Time Equivalents.	Minutes of Sidereal Time.	Mean Time Equivalents.	Minutes of Sidereal Time.	Mean Time Equivalents.	Seconds of Sidereal Time.	Mean Time Equivalents.	Seconds of Sidereal Time	Mean Time Equivalents.
	H. M. S.		M. S.		M. S.		S.		S.
1	0 59 50·17	1	0 59·84	31	30 54·92	1	1·00	31	30·92
2	1 59 40·34	2	1 59·67	32	31 54·76	2	1·99	32	31·91
3	2 59 30·51	3	2 59·51	33	32 54·59	3	2·99	33	32·91
4	3 59 20·68	4	3 59·34	34	33 54 43	4	3·99	34	33·91
5	4 59 10·85	5	4 59 18	35	34 54·27	5	4·99	35	34·90
6	5 59 1·02	6	5 59·02	36	35 54·10	6	5·98	36	35·90
7	6 58 51·19	7	6 58·85	37	36 53·94	7	6·98	37	36·50
8	7 58 41·36	8	7 58·69	38	37 53·77	8	7·98	38	37·90
9	8 58 31·53	9	8 58·53	39	38 53 61	9	8·98	39	38·89
10	9 58 21·70	10	9 58·36	40	39 53·45	10	8·97	40	39·89
11	10 58 11·87	11	10 58 20	41	40 53·28	11	10·97	41	40·89
12	11 58 2·05	12	11 58·03	42	41 53·12	12	11·97	42	41 89
13	12 57 52·22	13	12 57·87	43	42 52·96	13	12·96	43	42·88
14	13 57 42·39	14	13 57·71	44	43 52·79	14	13·96	44	43 88
15	14 57 32·56	15	14 57·54	45	44 52·63	15	14·96	45	44·88
16	15 57 22·73	16	15 57·38	46	45 52·46	16	15·96	46	45·87
17	16 57 12·90	17	16 57·22	47	46 52·30	17	16·95	47	46·87
18	17 57 3·07	18	17 57·05	48	47 52·14	18	17·95	48	47·87
19	18 56 53·24	19	18 56·89	49	48 51·97	19	18·95	49	48 87
20	19 56 43·41	20	19 56·72	50	49 51·81	20	19·95	50	49·86
21	20 56 33·58	21	20 56·56	51	50 51·64	21	20·94	51	50·86
22	21 56 23·75	22	21 56·40	52	51 51·48	22	21·94	52	51·86
23	22 56 13·92	23	22 56·23	53	52 51·32	23	22·94	53	52·86
24	23 56 4·09	24	23 56·07	54	53 51·15	24	23·93	54	53·85
		25	24 55·90	55	54 50·99	25	24·93	55	54·85
		26	25 55·74	56	55 50·83	26	25·93	56	55·85
		27	26 55·58	57	56 50·66	27	26·93	57	55·84
		28	27 55·41	58	57 50·50	28	27·92	58	57·84
		29	28 55·25	59	58 50·33	29	28·92	59	58·84
		30	29 55·09	60	59 50·17	30	29·92	60	59·84

To obtain the Mean Time corresponding to any given Sidereal Time by means of the above tables, take the Mean Time at the preceding Sidereal Noon (which will be found on the second page of each month) and add to it the Mean Time Equivalents of the given Sidereal Time.

Let it be required to find the Mean Time corresponding to the Sidereal Time 3h. 20m. 31s. on October 10 :—

		H. M. S.
Mean Time at Sidereal Noon October 10		10 43 42
Sidereal intervals and Mean Time equivalents from table above { 3h. =		2 59 30·51
20m. =		19 56·72
31s. =		30·92
Corresponding Mean Time October 11 =		2 3 40·15 Morn.

SOME ELEMENTS OF THE PLANETARY SYSTEM.

Name.	Mean Distance from Earth in Millions of Miles.	Sidereal Period of Revolution round Sun.	Time of Axial Rotation.	Real Diameter in Miles.	Volume ⊕=1.	Density ⊕=1.
		D.	H. M.			
The Sun... ☉	92·9	......	607 48	866,400	1310000	0·25
Mercury... ☿	56·9	88	*24 5½	3,030	0·056	2·23
Venus...... ♀	25·7	225	*23 21⅓	7,700	0·920	0·86
Earth ...... ⊕	......	365	23 56	7,918	1·000	1·00
Mars ...... ♂	48·6	687	24 39⅓	4,230	0·152	0·72
Jupiter ... ♃	390·4	4,333	9 55½	86,500	1309	0·24
Saturn ... ♄	793·2	10,759	10 14½	71,000	849	0·13
Uranus ... ♅	1,689·0	30,687	9 30?	31,900	59	0·22
Neptune ... ♆	2,698·8	60,127	......	32,900	103	0·20

* The periods of rotation of Mercury and Venus are more probably equal to their periods of revolution.
N.B.—The numbers in the third column refer to the mean distances at inferior conjunctions for the inferior planets; at opposition, for the superior planets.

Summary of Celestial Objects and Phenomena for Observation, 1900

THE following is a description of the most interesting astronomical occurrences, and of the positions and configurations of the planets, in 1900. The information thus presented in a popular form will, it is hoped, afford a useful guide to all such persons who, either occasionally or habitually, apply themselves to the contemplation of the heavenly bodies, and find entertainment in witnessing their curious changes and attractive appearances. We have necessarily confined our descriptions to those particular objects and events which are capable of definite prediction. There are, of course, many others, which are irregular and occasional in their apparitions; amongst these may be included new comets, temporary stars, displays of Auroræ Boreales, and brilliant meteors or fireballs. Examples of some, if not of all, of these phenomena will be sure to offer themselves for observation in 1900, but it is not possible to specify the exact times and positions of their appearances. Those persons who are most vigilant in observing the sky are likely to be the most successful in detecting objects of the kind alluded to. We make reference to them in the hope that amateur astronomers will maintain a diligent watch of the firmament, and record and publish anything they may notice of special interest. New comets are usually announced in the newspapers a few days after they have been discovered, and such references are often accompanied with information which will enable any one to detect them; but a telescope is generally necessary in the observation of comets. Transitory objects, such as large meteors, confine their apparitions to a few moments of time; Auroræ are more lasting, and are sometimes displayed for several hours without intermission under a series of changeful aspects. It is obvious that spectacles of this character cannot be announced beforehand as they are irregular in their occurrence; they are therefore usually witnessed by such persons only as are favourably situated for such observations and maintain a frequent look-out for them.

Eclipses.—There will be two eclipses of the Sun and one of the Moon in 1900. On the afternoon of May 28 there will occur a total eclipse of the Sun, which may be observed as a partial eclipse at Greenwich. Nearly seven-tenths of the Sun will be hidden at the time of greatest obscuration (3h. 55m.), and it will prove much larger than any other eclipse visible in England since December 22, 1870, when about eight-tenths of the Sun were eclipsed. The eclipse of May 28, 1900, will be total across Spain, and several expeditions are now fitting out with the object of visiting the most suitable stations, and securing the necessary observations. In England the southern region of the Sun will be hidden, and at a time near the middle of the eclipse the solar orb will appear as a brilliant crescent with its concavity on the side nearest to the horizon. At stations north of Greenwich the magnitude of the eclipse will be less than in the southern part of England, while at places yet further south, such as France and Spain, the phenomenon will be of greater extent and duration.

It is well known that eclipses recur after intervals of 18 years and 11 days, which comprise 223 lunar months. The eclipse of May 28, 1900, is a return of that of May 17, 1882, May 6, 1864, April 25, 1846, &c. The next solar eclipse of importance visible in England after the one referred to will be that of August 30, 1905, when about eight-tenths of the Sun's lower limb will be obscured at 1h. in the afternoon.

On the morning of June 13, 1899, there will be a very small eclipse of the Moon. At 3h. 28m. A.M. about one-thousandth part of the Moon's surface will be involved in the Earth's shadow. The penumbra or fainter shadow will, however, cover a considerable part of the disc, and will be apparent, to anyone who carefully surveys the lunar disc, as a faint dusky veil moderating the silvery lustre of our satellite.

There will be an annular eclipse of the Sun on the morning of November 22, but it will be quite invisible to observers in England.

Occultations.—No occultations of very bright stars will take place in 1900, but there will be some very interesting planetary occultations during the year, as follows:—

Planet.	Date.	Disappearance.	Reappearance.
Neptune	Mar. 8	6h. 13m. P.M.	7h. 34m. P.M.
Saturn	,, 24	8h. 35m. A.M.	9h. 46m. A.M.
,,	June 13	9h. 4cm. P.M.	10h. 52m. P.M.
,,	Sept. 3	7h. 16m. P.M.	8h. 11m. P.M.

The occultation of Neptune will occur at the time of the Moon's first quarter and ought to be visible with moderately large telescopes, as the planet will disappear at the dark side of the Moon. The occultation of Saturn on March 24 will take place under circumstances which will preclude its observation by ordinary observers. The Sun will be shining brightly at the time if the air is clear, and a good telescope and a favourable position will be needed if it is to be witnessed satisfactorily, for the objects will be placed in a southern declination of 22°, and comparatively near the horizon. At the disappearances of Saturn on June 13 and September 3 the hour will be more convenient, and the conditions more suitable. With fine weather any small telescope will enable the event to be successfully witnessed on these occasions, but the observer must necessarily take up a position commanding a good view of the southern sky at a low altitude. Among the more conspicuous of the fixed stars which will suffer occultation during the year will be δ Scorpii (mag. 2.5) on July 8, ζ Tauri (mag. 3) on September 15 and October 13, and the times of occurrence are given in another portion of the "Almanack." Apart from their actual occultations, both Saturn and Neptune will make several very near approaches to the Moon during the year. Saturn will be in conjunction with our satellite on January 28, February 24, April 20, May 17, July 11, August 7, October 1 and 28, November 24. Neptune will be near the Moon on January 13, February 9, April 5, August 20, September 16, October 13, November 10, and December 7. The path of the Moon will also carry her near Uranus on several occasions during the year, viz., January 26, February 23, March 22, April 18, May 15, June 12, July 9, August 5, and September 2, and near Jupiter on April 18, May 15, June 11, July 8, and September 1 and 29. Occultations of one major planet by another are exceedingly rare, though near approaches of these bodies are comparatively frequent, and often singularly attractive in their visible aspect. Thus on August 7 Mars will be only 1° 27′ N. of Neptune, and there will be other phenomena of this kind which will be particularly alluded to in dealing with the individual planets.

Jupiter's Satellites.—To those amateur astronomers whose telescopes are of moderate dimensions, four of the satellites of Jupiter offer a most attractive group of objects for study. They can be distinctly perceived in any small glass, and the circumstance which, more than any other, renders them so interesting is that their relative places vary from hour to hour. The different configurations they successively assume are so entertaining that the observer experiences none of the monotony that would result from a stationary aspect. And the satellites not only change their positions at short intervals, but they frequently become eclipsed in the shadow of Jupiter or occulted by the large globe of the planet. They also make transits across the disc, and it is then they are sometimes visible as circular, dark spots projected on the bright surface of Jupiter. The shadows of the satellites are also to be seen on the face of the planet at such times, and a telescope will sometimes reveal the gratifying spectacle of two or three black spots coursing along the line of the Jovian belts and imparting quite an abnormal appearance to the planet's scenery. The satellites are not generally known by distinguishing names, it being customary to refer to them by the Roman numerals I., II., III., IV., and V. Satellite V. is the one nearest to Jupiter, and it is extremely faint and small as compared with the other four. It was discovered as lately as September 9, 1892, and is the most important addition to our knowledge with which the great 36-inch telescope at the Lick Observatory in California has supplied us. The satellites III. and IV. are the two outermost from Jupiter, and they are frequently seen transformed into dark spots when in transit. Under such circumstances they are fairly conspicuous objects even in small instruments. Appended are a few dates when satellite III. may be observed in transit:—

Date, 1900.	Ingress.	Egress.	Duration of Transit.
	H. M.	H. M.	H. M.
February 2	18 5	19 52	1 47
March 10 ..	14 18	15 59	1 41
April 22 ..	12 12	13 49	1 37
June 4 ..	8 5	9 49	1 44
,, 11	11 23	13 8	1 45
July 24	8 7	10 8	2 1

In this table astronomical time, counting from noon to noon, is employed. There will be no transits, eclipses or occultations of satellite IV. in 1900, owing to the inclination of the Jovian system, which will enable the satellite to pass clear of the northern or southern boundary of the planet. As it is an unusual and interesting spectacle to view one of Jupiter's Moons when situated precisely north or south of the disc of its primary, we give below some of the times when this curious spectacle may be witnessed :—

Date, 1900.	Satellite IV. South of disc.		Date, 1900.	Satellite IV. North of disc.	
	H.	M.		H.	M.
Feb. 19 .	19	9	April 2 .	13	2
Apr. 27 .	13	39	May 22 .	10	9
June 16 .	8	48	Aug. 30 .	9	25
Aug. 5 .	7	48			

Satellite III. is much the largest of the five satellites, and its transformation into a dark spot when in transit is very remarkable, and very obvious in any small telescope. The perfectly black shadow of the satellite is usually visible on the disc at the same time, though, when the planet is far from its opposition with the Sun, the difference in the times of transit of the satellite and its shadow are often very considerable. Before opposition (May 27, 1900) the shadow precedes the satellite, but after opposition the order is reversed and the satellite is in advance of its shadow. Thus on March 10, 1900, more than two months before opposition, the shadow of satellite III. enters on the disc of Jupiter more than *five* hours before the satellite itself. On July 24, about two months after opposition, the shadow passes on to Jupiter *four and a half hours* after the satellite. The shadow of this satellite, and of each of the others, is both darker and larger than the satellite itself, and may be identified from this circumstance and from the fact that the times of transit are different.

We have already intimated that satellite V. is an object far outside the boundary of popular observation. Its motion is very rapid, for it completes a revolution round Jupiter in 11h. 57m. 22.647s., which is less than half of a terrestrial day. The other four satellites are comparatively bright, and a good field-glass will exhibit them as tiny stars in the immediate vicinity of Jupiter. They are commonly seen to be arranged nearly in a line parallel with the belts and equator of Jupiter, but there are notable exceptions. Sometimes the four bright satellites are symmetrically placed, two on each side of the planet. At other periods they are grouped three on one side and one on the other, and occasionally they are all four placed on one and the same side. The following are some of the dates when they may be observed in this unusual position :—

Satellites on East side of Jupiter.	Satellites on West side of Jupiter.
January 24 a.m.	January 29 a.m.
March 15 ,,	February 12 ,,
,, 29 ,,	April 4 ,,
April 30 ,,	,, 11 ,,
May 20 p.m.	,, 24 ,,
July 9 ,,	May 30 p.m.
,, 23 ,,	June 13 ,,
August 6 ,,	,, 27 ,,
,, 13 ,,	August 2 ,,
	,, 16 ,,

A telescope will exhibit the satellites arranged in very close contiguity to the planet on the mornings of January 9, February 3, March 26, April 19 and 20, and evenings of May 13 and 14, June 15, July 2, 3 and 20, August 21, 22 and 29, and September 8. On occasions, which happen somewhat rarely, Jupiter is apparently attended by one satellite only, the three other bright ones being simultaneously in eclipse, occultation or transit. Thus on August 4 between 7h. 13m. and 7h. 42m. only one satellite (IV.) will be visible, for I. will be occulted, II. will be in transit, and III. will be eclipsed. This will, however, be the only occasion during the year when the phenomenon will be visible. A telescope of three or four inches aperture, mounted on a convenient stand, will exhibit excellent representations of these satellites, and all the attendant effects produced by their differences of motion. Observations of this character may be conveniently effected from a window having a good southern aspect. It will afford the observer some hours of agreeable recreation to notice these bodies on successive nights and delineate their positions in a series of diagrams. It often happens that two of the satellites approach each other very closely and are scarcely separable with moderate powers, the appearance being similar to that of a difficult double star. Sometimes there is a conjunction of three of these bodies, and the observation of these appearances never fails to prove entertaining to the possessors of small telescopes.

The Sun being the great central source of light and heat and the mainstay of planetary life, it is natural that every fact connected with so important an orb should receive marked attention. Many people have heard something about the "spots on the Sun," but comparatively few persons have ever seen these curious formations or learnt anything relating to their actual character. That an object so dazzlingly luminous as the Sun should exhibit dark markings is a circumstance which often excites surprise, and when it is stated that these markings are often of enormous size, and that they undergo exceedingly rapid changes, sometimes appearing or disappearing in a few hours, the attention becomes riveted on phenomena so strange. The spots are often sufficiently large to be detected with the unaided eye; indeed, they were occasionally seen many centuries prior to the invention of the telescope. When this instrument is directed to the Sun it becomes necessary to employ deeply-tinted glass in front of the eye-piece to limit the intense light and heat of the image, for unless a precaution of this kind is taken serious damage may result to the observer's eye. A very convenient plan of effecting solar observations is to detach the coloured glass from the instrument and to allow the Sun's image formed by the telescope to fall upon a piece of white cardboard. The details of the spots may be readily perceived in this manner, and the speckled appearance of the whole disc is brought out most satisfactorily. There is also no danger of injury to the eye. For critical examination of Sun-spot structure and variations we must, however, resort to the method of direct vision as the most effective in its results. The present is not a favourable epoch for watching solar phenomena, as the spots are likely to prove comparatively infrequent in 1900. They are displayed very abundantly at intervals of about eleven years, with intervening periods of minima when the solar surface is rarely variegated with conspicuous spots. We are now near a minimum of these phenomena, and may justly anticipate that during the few ensuing years the Sun-spots generally will be few and of small dimensions. There will, however, probably occur some notable exceptions. Though the last minimum of Sun-spot activity occurred in 1889 there were visible, some fine and interesting specimens of the objects alluded to. In 1889 a few fine groups presented themselves, though, in January and February, the solar disc was almost entirely free from them. A large spot came into view at the middle of March, and at the close of June a considerable group about 87,000 miles long was near its mid-transit. Various theories have been advanced to account for these solar outbursts, and there is no doubt that they represent extensive disturbances in the luminous atmosphere which involves the solid and probably dark body of the Sun. The spots are probably shallow depressions in the solar envelope, though this idea has been objected to in the light of some recent observations which are, however, indecisive, and much further evidence is required to settle this, and some other questions relating to the visible aspect of the Sun.

The Moon may be said without exaggeration to be the most varied, distinct and attractive object in the firmament. Her permanent features present a marked contrast to the evanescent formations in the luminous envelope of the Sun. The lunar landscape shows many apparent changes, it is true, but these are due to the constantly varying angle at which the sunshine falls upon them. We know that the manifold objects upon the Moon are permanent markings on her surface, and are liable to no rapid alterations of shape, though possibly undergoing slight modifications in a gradual way. Evidences of great activity in ages long past are scattered broadcast over the lunar orb, but the features as they are now displayed appear to be perfectly immutable. The most suitable period at which to view the craters and mountainous regions of the Moon is when her disc is only partly illuminated, and she is either in a crescent form, near first quarter, or slightly gibbous. At such times the shadows of the inequalities of landscape near the terminator are strikingly manifested, and the diversified character of the formations is pleasingly portrayed. This is far from being the case at the period of full Moon, for her features are then displayed under a high Sun and their shadows have disappeared, so that the inequalities of the landscape have lost their distinctive and varied character. The great refulgence of the full Moon is also an impediment to successful observation. Let the observer avail himself therefore of the period near the first quarter, for our satellite is then very conveniently presented in the evening sky, and other conditions are favourable. The Moon's surface has already been surveyed by several competent astronomers, but there remains much to be done in the re-examination and drawing of details in reference to which our knowledge is far from perfect. Observers should also search for evidences of active change, and compare reliable charts of the Moon with the actual objects as revealed in their telescopes. Indications of physical change have previously been discovered, but absolute proofs that any part of the lunar landscape has suffered material alteration have not yet been obtained. Our best charts of lunar scenery contain errors, and when a new observation proves discordant with features previously mapped it is usually indicative that the chart is wrong, and not that physical alterations have occurred on the lunar disc. This question of possible real changes on the surface of the Moon is a very attractive one, and may receive settlement by renewed application on the part of a really capable selenographer.

Though the epoch of rapid changes is probably long past there may occur minor disturbances during extensive periods of time. That these may be detected the observer must necessarily study the details of features with great accuracy and frequency. The proof of existing lunar activity would form an important discovery.

Planets.—Mercury. This planet will be presented to view under a very favourable aspect as an evening star during the first twelve days of March. He will attain his greatest eastern elongation (18° 16′ east) on the morning of March 8, and will become distinctly visible about an hour after sunset. The planet's times of setting and the intervals at which he follows the Sun will be as under :—

Date 1900.	Sun sets.	Mercury sets.	Interval.
	H. M.	H. M.	H. M.
March 1	5 38	7 9	1 31
,, 2	5 40	7 15	1 35
,, 3	5 41	7 20	1 39
,, 4	5 43	7 24	1 41
,, 5	5 45	7 29	1 44
,. 6	5 46	7 33	1 47
,, 7	5 48	7 37	1 49
,, 8	5 50	7 39	1 49
,, 9	5 52	7 40	1 48
,, 10	5 53	7 41	1 48
,, 11	5 55	7 42	1 47
,, 12	5 57	7 42	1 45

On clear evenings during this interval the planet may be observed shining like a bright-ruddy star over the western horizon. Venus will be brilliantly visible at the same period, but her position will be about 20° E. of that of Mercury. The former may be mistaken for the latter unless the observer is careful to identify both objects, and this may be done without much difficulty. In April, 1898, Mercury was well visible as an evening star, and being near Venus at the time many persons, including some regular astronomical observers, mistook Venus for Mercury. In March, 1900, the distance between the two objects will be much greater, but the mistake alluded to may possibly be repeated unless the observer remembers that Mercury sets before 8 P.M. while Venus sets at times varying from 9h. 17m. to 9h. 50m. between March 1 and 12. If clear weather should fortunately prevail, Mercury may be seen 4° 37' S. of the new Moon on the evening of March 2. This planet was satisfactorily observed by many persons in the last half of March, 1899. The weather was very clear on several successive evenings, and Mercury shone with a strong scintillating light over the west by north horizon. The early part of March, 1900, offers the most suitable occasion during the year for securing observations of the planet as an evening star, though at the end of June and early in July the planet will be set about 1½h. after the Sun. As a morning star he will come into prominent view during the third week of August, as he arrives at his greatest western elongation (18' 32') on the 19th of that month. His times of rising compared with the times of Sunrise will be as follows :—

Date, 1900.	Sun rises.	Mercury rises.	Interval.
	H. M.	H. M.	H. M.
Aug. 15	4 47	3 18	1 29
,, 16	4 49	3 15	1 34
,, 17	4 51	3 13	1 38
,, 18	4 52	3 11	1 41
,, 19	4 54	3 10	1 44
,, 20	4 55	3 10	1 45
,, 21	4 57	3 11	1 46
,, 22	4 58	3 13	1 45
,, 23	5 0	3 16	1 44
,, 24	5 1	3 18	1 43
,, 25	5 3	3 21	1 42

On clear mornings, about an hour before Sunrise, during this period, Mercury may be easily detected just above the east by north point of the horizon. The brilliant planet Venus will also be visible at the same time, situated about 25° to the west. No brilliant stars will be placed near Mercury at this period, the planet being in Cancer and close to the group of small stars known as Præsepe or "The Bee Hive." Again, at the early part of December, Mercury will make a conspicuous apparition in the morning sky and be even more favourably visible than in August. The times of his rising, &c., will be as follows :—

Date, 1900.	Sun rises.	Mercury rises.	Interval.
	H. M.	H. M.	H. M.
Nov. 28	7 41	6 5	1 36
,, 29	7 42	5 59	1 43
,, 30	7 44	5 56	1 48
Dec. 1	7 45	5 53	1 52
,, 2	7 46	5 51	1 55
,, 3	7 48	5 50	1 58
,, 4	7 49	5 50	1 59
,, 5	7 50	5 49	2 1
,, 6	7 52	5 50	2 2
,, 7	7 53	5 51	2 2
,, 8	7 54	5 53	2 1

At about this period the planet will be in the eastern region of Libra, and will not be near any bright stars or planets. It is not often that we get in the same year two such favourable opportunities of observing Mercury as a morning star. The view of Mercury is in itself sufficient recompense for any inconvenience the observation may occasion, for this orb is rarely seen by anyone outside the band of regular astronomical observers. The planet is so near to the Sun that he is generally obliterated in the glare from that luminary ; the greatest distance between the two bodies being 28'. It follows, therefore, that this planet can only be discerned when near the horizon about an hour before sunrise or the same interval after sunset, when the twilight is strong and the low sky seldom free from mist or fog. And it is only on a few succeeding days that this object admits of possible observation, for after reaching his greatest elongations from the Sun he quickly retraces his path, and is again lost amid the glare of the solar rays. It is often stated that Copernicus, who was one of the greatest astronomers of the sixteenth century, made many vain endeavours to obtain a view of Mercury, and it must be admitted that many difficulties bar the way to success. In a favourable climate, however, and from a position commanding good views of the E. and W. horizons, there is really no serious obstacle to prevent the planet being seen if the intending observer is careful to utilize good opportunities. Of course it is necessary to know just where to look, and the attempt must be made at a suitable time of the year and hour of the night. A celestial globe is of great assistance in work of this character, for the position of the planet can be obtained from an ephemeris and marked on the globe, and the latter being set for the hour of the intended observation, the place of the object relatively to the E. or W. horizon, and its altitude, can be readily determined. Preparation of this kind, and the assistance of an opera-glass, will enable the planet to be identified without much trouble. It can be safely said that there are few naked-eye observations which afford amateur astronomers more gratification than the view of this fugitive planet. He is usually seen at the evening apparitions, as the hour is more convenient than that preceding sunrise. It is hoped, however, that the particularly favourable apparition of Mercury in the mornings of December, 1900, may attract many observers to make some observations. And it may be useful to remember that this object appears in his greatest lustre a few evenings *before* his easterly elongations in the first half of the year, and on a few mornings *after* his westerly elongations in the last half of the year.

Venus.—This planet will be shining brightly as an evening star at the opening of 1900, and will set rather more than two hours after the Sun. As the year advances she will assume a still more favourable position until, on April 28, she reaches her greatest eastern elongation (45° 30') and sets 4½ hours after the Sun. Her greatest brilliancy will be exhibited at the close of May, and towards the end of June will have drawn so near to the Sun as to have become quite invisible. During the whole of the first half of the year she will form an attractive object in the evening sky, and her striking brilliancy will be sure to call for special remark even from observers not much interested in astronomical phenomena. Her path amongst the constellations during the period that she is favourably presented will be as follows:— At the beginning of January she will be in Capricornus, and moving rapidly eastwards during the first three months of the year she successively traverses Aquarius, Pisces and Aries. On April 3 she passes about 2° S. of the Pleiades. On April 27 her position will lie between the conspicuous stars β and ζ Tauri. On June 6 she will be situated about 5° S. of β Geminorum. Her conjunctions with the crescent Moon will be interesting though not very close except in April (when, however, the nearest approach of the two orbs will occur after they have set), and will happen on the following dates:— January 3, February 2, March 4, April 3. and May 2 and 31. In January her disc will be gibbous but becomes narrower as time progresses, so that at the close of April the planet will exhibit the same phase as the Moon in her first quarter. At the middle of June she will have become a slender crescent, but contemporary with this decrease in the illuminated portion of her disc her apparent diameter enlarges considerably, for while on January 1 it is only 11·5″, it is 18″ on April 1, 37″ on June 1, and 49″ on June 15. In the spring months of the year this spendid orb will be finely and conveniently displayed for telescopic study. Undoubtedly the most attractive feature is formed by the ever-varying phase of the planet, but there are no definite markings on her surface of the same prominent character as those which diversify the discs of Mars and Jupiter. Faint, cloudy spots of indeterminate outline are sometimes glimpsed on Venus, but they apparently represent slight differences in the reflective capacity of the planet's atmosphere, and it may be safely asserted that we know nothing of her actual surface markings. Certain recent observers have published some extraordinary diagrams of conspicuous spots which they allege to have been visible on the disc of Venus, but such objects owe their origin rather to the capacity of the imagination than to the

powers of the eye or telescope. Much further attention will be directed to this question during 1900, for the planet could scarcely be better placed for the sedulous and successful study of her surface. After June Venus will be invisible during several weeks, owing to the proximity of the Sun. In August, however, she brilliantly reappears, as a morning star, and on about the 14th the conditions will enable her to shine with the maximum degree of lustre. On September 17 she will reach her greatest western elongation (46° 1') and will rise more than four hours before the Sun. Right through the autumnal months, and until the close of the year, Venus continues a beautiful object in the morning twilight. Her position on August 10 will be in the south-western part of Gemini, and from thence her orbital motion will carry her eastwards successively through the constellations Cancer, Leo and Virgo. On October 7 she may be observed about 1° N. of the bright star Regulus (α Leonis). On October 30 she will be placed about 1° S. of β Virginis. She will be near the Moon on the mornings of August 21, November 19, and December 19. Appearing only as a narrow crescent early in August, the illumination of her disc will rapidly increase, so that at the middle of September she will be presented under the same aspect as our satellite when at the last quarter. By the close of the year her disc will appear nearly full, but it will be exceedingly small, for it declines from 45·6″ on August 1 to 16·2″ on November 1, and to 12·0″ at the end of December. To sum up, Venus will be incomparably better situated for observation in 1900 than any other bright planet, the conditions regulating her visibility being of the most favourable character possible. Shining with great splendour as an evening star during the first half of the year, she will be missing from the sky in July, but only to reappear with equal lustre in the mornings from August to December.

Mars. — Nothing can be seen of this planet during the first six months of 1900, for he will be constantly near the Sun and overpowered in his rays. But when, in July, the nights become a little darker and longer, a ruddy star will begin to show itself in the E.N.E just before sunrise. This will be Mars, which from this time onward, until his opposition in the early part of 1901, will continue to improve in position and increase in apparent diameter and brilliancy. On July 1 he will rise at 1ʰ. 30ᵐ. A.M., or 2¼ hours before the Sun, in September he rises at about midnight, and at the end of the year will appear above the horizon at 9ʰ. 23ᵐ. P.M., or about 5½ hours after sunset. His path in the firmament may be briefly described as under:—Early in July he will be situated between the Pleiades and Hyades in Taurus: he enters Gemini on about August 10, and Cancer towards the end of September. In later months he moves slower, and November and December will find him slowly wending his way eastwards amongst the stars of Leo. At the end of July his position will be 2¼° N. of ξ Tauri while on November 18 he will be 1½° N. of α Leonis (Regulus). He may be observed near the Moon on the mornings of July 23 and October 17. His apparent diameter will very slowly increase from 4·4″ on July 1 to 5·6″ on October 1, and to 10″ on December 31. On August 7 he will be 1½° N. of Neptune, and on about October 3 will be 1¼° N. of Vesta. As a telescopic object Mars will not offer us any prospective successes in 1900. Even at the best time (December) for observation his apparent diameter will be only 10″, and this is not sufficiently large to enable the more delicate features to be distinguished. Early in 1901 the conditions will be more suitable, as the planet will have increased in diameter and remain visible during the whole of the night. No planet of our system, except perhaps Jupiter, has incited more interest with regard to his surface configuration than Mars, and the discordances among the results of different observers have sometimes given rise to ardent discussion, without, however, clearing up the points in dispute. The problem is one which requires much further evidence to bring about its solution, and this will be obtained by careful observation in future years.

Minor Planets or Planetoids. Eros.—This small object, discovered by Witt in August, 1898, is a most important one, as it is the only minor planet yet discovered which revolves in an orbit, the mean position of which lies between the Earth and Mars. It will materially assist in the determination of the Sun's distance and with a degree of accuracy not to be attained by any other means. At the close of 1900 and beginning of 1901 the new planet may be seen with tolerably small telescopes, and it will be interesting to follow it as it rapidly traverses the stars of Cassiopeia and Andromeda. Its position on five nights will be as follows:—

Date.	R.A.			N. Dec.	Distance from Earth in millions of miles.	Magnitude.
1900.	H.	M.	S.	°		
Nov. 10 ...	1	56	24	... 54 23 ...	35 ...	9·38
„ 26 ...	1	30	40	... 51 52 ...	31 ...	9·07
Dec. 12 ...	1	29	22	... 46 23 ...	30 ...	8·88
„ 28 ...	1	54	28	... 39 39 ...	29 ...	8·78
1901.						
Jan. 13 ...	2	38	6	... 32 45 ...	30 ...	8·78

On December 29 the planet will be nearly 3° S. of γ Andromedæ. It will probably be fainter than about the 9th magnitude (given in the table), as no allowance has been made for the diminution in its light due to phase.

Ceres will reach opposition with the Sun on July 31, but will be scarcely observable in this country as her southern declination will be 29½°, and in August and September about 31°. At about this period she will appear to be as bright as an 8th magnitude star in the region south of Capricornus. *Pallas* will be most favourably visible in July, but will be fainter than a star of the 9th magnitude. In August the position of this object will be about 7° W. of α Aquilæ. *Juno* will be in opposition on September 27, at which date she will but slightly excel a star of 7th magnitude. She will be situated in a region of Pisces bare of conspicuous stars, but on October 17 may be observed in a place only 1¾° N. of ι Ceti (magnitude 3½). She will then move slowly westwards, but at the middle of November begins to retrace her steps, and on November 24 again makes a near approach to the star ι Ceti, being less than 1° S. of that object. A telescope with low power and large field of view, if turned upon this region on the latter date, could be so directed as to show both star and planet at the same time, Juno being at the S. edge and the star at the N. edge of the field. *Vesta* is much brighter than any of the other minor planets, and is in fact the only one of this numerous class of bodies visible to the naked eye. She will not be in opposition to the Sun in 1900, as she passed that position on

October 14, 1899, nor will she be perceptible to the unaided eye during the year, as her apparent magnitude will never exceed 7; but in a telescope she may be seen both at the early part and at the end of 1900. On February 12 she will be placed 4° N. of α Piscium (magnitude 3½). On December 21 she will be placed in the western region of Leo, and will be nearly stationary. The minor planets are usually disregarded by ordinary observers who have many more brilliant and larger objects with which to occupy themselves. But it is interesting to identify the fainter and smaller members of our system, and the identification of a minor planet from the stars surrounding it can be readily effected. The best method is to direct the telescope towards the point in which the object is situated, and then to make a diagram of the various stars in the field. On the next night, or on the first ensuing clear night, the diagram should be compared with the sky, and the planet sought for will be identified by its change of place relatively to the stars.

Jupiter.—At the opening of 1900 this planet will be prominently visible as a morning star, rising at 4h. 57m. A.M., or more than three hours before the Sun. As the year progresses he takes up a more favourable position, and on May 27 reaches opposition to the Sun, when he will be visible during the whole night. From this date, until the close of October, he will shine as a conspicuous evening star. His positions in 1900 curiously alternate with those of Venus, for while during the first half of the year Jupiter is a morning star, Venus is an evening star, and during most of the last part of the year the positions will be reversed. Speaking generally as to the presentation of Jupiter in 1900, it may be said that as compared with the few previous oppositions, he will not be so favourably exhibited on account of his more southern position, which will make telescopic observations of his surface rather difficult in northern latitudes. The following figures give the variation in his declination and diameter during the past five oppositions and the future one in May next:—

Opposition.		Declination of Jupiter.		Apparent Polar diameter.
		° ′		″
1894, Dec.	22 ...	23 13 north ...		44·4
1896, Jan.	24 ...	19 53 „ ...		42·4
1897, Feb.	23 ...	10 45 „ ...		41·2
1898, Mar.	25 ...	0 42 south ...		40·8
1899, Apl.	25 ...	11 57 „ ...		41·2
1900, May	27 ...	20 27 „ ...		42·0

Thus when passing the meridian in December, 1894, the planet's altitude was about 62° in the latitude of Greenwich, whereas in May, 1900, it will be only 18°. There will, however, be little change in the apparent diameter of the object, for when best visible he will present an expansive disc of 42″ on which all the principal belts and spots may be distinctly perceived. His position with reference to the stars will be as follows:— At the beginning of the year he will be close to β Scorpii (mag. 3), and afterwards moves slowly eastwards 10°, until on March 27 he becomes stationary and then retraces his path. On July 16 his position is only 4′ 36″ S. of that which he occupied on January 1. He will again be stationary on July 28, and thenceforward pursues an uninterrupted eastern course. Several times during the year will this planet be in conjunction with α and β Scorpii, and the dates and distances will be as follows:—

	Conjunction.	Distance.
α Scorpii	Feb. 7	5 28 Jupiter north
„	May 15	5 31 „
„	Oct. 6	5 5 „
β Scorpii	Jan. 4	0 12 Jupiter south
„	July 5	0 15 „
„	Aug. 22	0 26 „

The conjunctions with β Scorpii will be very close and interesting. That in January must necessarily be observed just before sunrise, Jupiter being a morning star, but the others in July and August may be conveniently witnessed in the evening sky. He will be in conjunction with the Moon on the following dates: January 26, February 23, March 22, April 18, May 15, June 11, July 9, August 5, and September 1. On October 19 10h. he will make a near approach to Uranus, the two objects being only 25′ distant. On this date, however, Jupiter sets at 6h. 49m., but just prior to this time he may be well observed in the same telescopic field as Uranus. As an object for telescopic study Jupiter is the most interesting of all the planets, from the facility with which his surface markings may be distinguished and their very diversified and changeable character. The belts and spots on the disc of this planet are very distinctly visible in moderately powerful telescopes. One spot has, during the last 30 years, by its durableness and definite oval outline, attracted a large amount of attention, and will doubtless continue to do so. It came under very general observation in July, 1878, when it was of an intensely red colour. This particular feature is now exceedingly faint, though there seems no reason to suppose that it is on the point of disappearance. It is probable that this object has been visible for a large number of years. Drawings by Schwabe between 1831 and 1856 show the hollow in the dark belt north of the spot, and subsequently to 1856 either the spot or its accompanying features has been figured by Dawes, Baxendell, Huggins, Gledhill, Lord Rosse, Copeland, Russell, and others. The comparison of a great number of these observations proves that during the 68 years from 1831 to 1899 the motion of the spot has varied from about 9h. 55m. 33s. to 9h. 55m. 42s. During the whole period from September 5, 1831, to February 26, 1899, the planet performed 59,587 rotations, and the mean period was 9h. 55m. 36·4s. The present rate of velocity is greater than this, for in 1899 the red spot gave a period of about 9h. 55m. 41.8s. For the guidance of those observers who may feel desirous of examining this extraordinary spot, we give a list of a few of the times when it may be expected to present itself on or very near the central meridian of the planet:

1900.	H.	M.	1900.	H.	M.
June 20	10	0	July 9	10	40
„ 22	11	38	„ 16	11	25
„ 27	10	46	„ 21	10	36
„ 29	12	24	„ 28	11	23
July 2	9	53	Aug. 2	10	33
„ 4	11	32	„ 9	11	19

The observer may readily compute for himself the times of transit for other nights, if he requires to know them, by adopting the rotation period of 9h. 55m. 42s., which is equivalent to the interval elapsing between successive transits of the same

spot. It is also useful to remember that every twelve days (which include twenty-nine rotations) the spot becomes central on Jupiter at nearly the same times as before. These remarks only have a special reference to the red spot, for it is found that different features furnish different periods of rotation. Some of the markings have exhibited a proper motion so rapid that they complete a circuit of Jupiter in 7¾ minutes less time than others. These features are doubtless of an atmospheric character, and are certainly influenced by currents of different velocity operating far above the sphere of Jupiter. As to the red spot, it is desirable that it should continue to be watched and its further changes of tint and motion duly recorded. Though it cannot be a formation cohering with the actual surface of Jupiter, it must be a feature possessing elements of remarkable permanency. Notwithstanding the large amount of observation which in past years has been given to the planet, there still remain a great number of interesting facts to be gleaned respecting his atmospheric currents and the many curious light and dark spots carried along at different velocities in them.

Saturn.—This planet is presented to view under nearly similar circumstances in any two succeeding years, as there is a difference of about 12 days only in the dates of his oppositions to the sun. Thus in 1899 he reached opposition on June 11, while in 1900 he arrives at the same aspect on June 23. In January, 1900, he will be perceptible as a morning star, rising on the 15th at 6h. 21m., or 1¾ hours before the sun. As the year advances he will assume a more favourable position, and at the close of April rises just before midnight. In June he will be displayed to the best effect, being visible during the whole night. Thereafter he will become an evening star, and remain perceptible as such until the early part of December. But the conditions will never be very favourable for telescopic observations of Saturn, as the planet is situated far south of the equator, and his altitude, even when passing the meridian, will be only 16° at Greenwich. The rings are now presented to us at a considerable inclination, and are visible with excellent effect. To show the variation in the declination of the planet, and also in the angle subtended by the outer minor axis of the ring and in the diameter of the globe of Saturn at the last four oppositions and that of 1900, the following figures may be quoted:

Opposition.	Planet's Declination South.		Minor axis, outer ring.	Diam. of globe.
	°	′	″	″
1896 May 5	14	9	15·70	17·4
1897 May 18	17	23	17·48	17·2
1898 May 30	19	55	18·66	17·0
1899 June 11	21	37	19·12	17·0
1900 June 23	22	27	18·89	17·0

Situated as he is at an enormous distance from the earth, the motion of this planet is apparently very slow, and in 1900 it will be limited to about 11° alternately forward and backward amongst the stars in the western part of Sagittarius. Three times during the year will the planet be in conjunction with the 4th mag. star μ Sagittarii, viz., February 8 (Saturn 1° 21′ S.), June 22 (Saturn 1° 21′ S.), and November 8 (Saturn 1° 40′ S.). On the morning of January 28 this planet will pass within 2′ of the Moon and narrowly escape occultation. On the morning of March 24, and evenings of June 13 and September 3, Saturn will be occulted, and the times of occurrence of these events are given on a preceding page. Saturn shines with a steady dull-yellowish light, and though far less lustrous than Venus and Jupiter, is always a fairly conspicuous object in a clear sky. In a telescope his luminous rings and the enclosed globe form a beautiful combination, and one which, so far as present knowledge extends, is absolutely unique in the solar system. But there is not much detail visible on the belts of Saturn, though occasional spots have been perceived by Dawes, Hall, and a few others. The opinion is gaining ground, and justly so, that much of the elaborate detail alleged to have been distinguished in small telescopes on the planet during the last few years has been due to the exercise of the imagination rather than to cuteness of vision. Saturn is precisely the object which, owing to his great distance, comparatively small diameter and the resulting feebleness of his light and surface markings, must induce mistaken impressions, and we need not be surprised to find that several observers have spoken far too confidently as to the existence of features which cannot be seen by some of the best observers using the most powerful telescopes. When the circumstances are considered, it need excite no surprise that much disputation has taken place in recent years as to the exact appearance of the markings both on Saturn and Mars. Saturn has eight satellites, but all of them cannot be seen, except in telescopes of the very largest kind. The brightest satellite, appropriately designated Titan, is visible in any small glass, and Iapetus is sometimes to be glimpsed with very small instruments, but Mimas and Hyperion require far greater power. Instances are recorded where these fainter satellites have been detected with telescopes apparently quite inadequate for the purpose, but such cases may be generally dismissed as pure efforts of the imagination. All observers of the phenomena of Jupiter and Saturn and of their satellites will find the ephemerides published annually in the "Monthly Notices of the Royal Astronomical Society" of the greatest utility to them in their studies.

Uranus will be in opposition to the Sun on the morning of June 1, and will be favourably visible during the summer months. This planet is, however, but faintly perceptible to the naked eye as a 5½ magnitude star, and seldom comes under the notice of anyone but a regular astronomical observer. The vast distance of Uranus causes him to move very slowly, so that his apparent position from one year's end to another varies very slightly. In 1900 his change of place amounts to only 6°, and his position is a few degrees N.E. of the bright star Antares. At the middle of August he will be placed less than ¾° south of the star ♋ Ophiuchi (magnitude 4½), and may be readily identified at about this period. If a telescope is directed to the region just south of the star named, Uranus will be easily seen, and if any doubt should remain as to his identity the positions of the various stars near should be jotted down, and subsequent observation will reveal the planet by his change of place. He will be close to the Moon on the night following May 15. June 11, July 9, August 5, September 1 and 29, and October 26. On October 19 he will be only 25' S. of Jupiter, and the configuration will be an interesting one, as the two planets may be observed in the same field of view. Uranus is not a difficult object to discern without telescopic aid

but the night must be dark and the atmosphere very clear to enable him to be seen to the best effect. The most suitable period for observations of this character will be July and August; in June the strong twilight will interfere with satisfactory views of a faint planet like this. His four satellites are too small to come within the powers of ordinary telescopes, but the two outermost, Titania and Umbriel, have occasionally been glimpsed with moderate appliances. The planet himself shines with a pale blue light, and telescopic power will immediately reveal the distinction between his disc and that of any one of the surrounding stars.

Neptune will be in opposition to the Sun on the morning of December 20, so that he will be visible to the best advantage in the first and last quarters of the year. This planet is, however, quite invisible to the naked eye, as he shines with a lustre not greater than that of a star of the 8th magnitude. His declination in 1900 being slightly more than 22° N. of the equator, he will remain above the horizon during periods of about 16 hours. He pursues his course on the extreme limits of the solar system, and his apparent motion is consequently extremely slow and limited to about 2¼° annually. His present position is between the constellations of Taurus and Gemini, and early in January he will be situated 2½° E.N.E. of the bright star ζ Tauri. At the end of 1900 and early in 1901 he will be placed about 2° N. of the stars 54 (mag. 4·7) and 57 (mag. 5·9) Orionis. He will be occulted by the Moon on the evening of March 8, and will pass very near to our satellite on February 9, April 5, August 20, September 16, October 13, November 10, and December 7. On August 7 he will be in conjunction with Mars. Everyone has seen and admired Venus, the brightest planet of our system, but few indeed have ever beheld Neptune, the faintest. It is true that no details can be traced on the tiny disc of Neptune, but the fact that he revolves on the outer boundary of the solar system and was discovered in a unique manner by the powers of the human intellect rather than by the capacity of the telescope, lends a special interest to the planet and attracts a few observers to gratify themselves with a view of his minute form. As to the satellite attending him, this, like the Moons of Mars and Uranus, and the fifth satellite of Jupiter, is beyond the grasp of all but the largest instruments and the keenest vision.

Periodical comets.—These objects form an interesting class, and our knowledge of them has increased rapidly in recent times. There is not a single year that passes but what is marked by the return of a periodical comet. The diligence of modern observers has enriched this branch with some important discoveries, but it appears that though new comets of short duration are being introduced by means of planetary perturbations (for which Jupiter is mainly responsible), there are others which encounter vicissitudes sufficiently forcible to endanger, if not to terminate, their existence. Biela's double comet appears to have been dissipated into a stream of shooting stars, and it is very probable that Brorsen's comet has disappeared, as it has not been redetected at its last few returns. The materials of which these presumably lost comets were formed probably still exists, though in a more scattered condition than formerly, and continue to obey the laws of gravitation; but under true cometary aspects they will never be recognisable again. The following is a table of the approximate dates of return of the chief periodical comets:—

Returns to Perihelion.	Period in Years.	Name of Comet.
1900. Feb.	6·627	Finlay.
August .	5·863	De Vico-Swift.
Sept. ..	5·398	Barnard (1884).
1901. Jan.	5·456	Brorsen.
Aug.	7·477	Denning (1894).
Sept.	3·303	Encke.
1902. Jan.	5·595	Brooks (1886).
Nov.	7·220	Swift (1895).
Dec.	5·534	Tempel – Swift.
1903. Apl.–May	6·411	Perrine (1896).
July	6·381	Spitaler (1890).
Oct.	7·556	Faye.
Dec.	7·073	Brooks (1883).

A few of these must be regarded as rather uncertain, as they have only been observed at a single apparition. In two or three cases the circumstances will be unfavourable (as in that of the return of Denning's comet in August, 1901), and the objects will probably escape observation. The majority of those included in the list will, doubtless, return at the computed times, and be suitably observed. It forms a most entertaining branch of astronomical work to trace a small comet threading its way amongst the neighbouring stars from night to night. Large comets appear promiscuously and with more or less suddenness, and in the present state of our knowledge it is impossible to definitely predict the times of their apparitions. The only intimation of their approach is that given by diligent observers who regularly sweep the firmament in quest of such objects, and are sometimes fortunate enough to sight them before they have visibly developed the conspicuous features which belong to comets of the largest class.

Meteoric Showers visible during the year. — Meteors, shooting stars, or falling stars as they are variously called, are visible on every clear night of the year, and at certain epochs are presented in such numbers as to form abundant and imposing showers. The year 1900, on November 15 before sunrise, will probably offer a special phenomenon of this kind, for a brilliant exhibition of meteors witnessed in 1799, 1833, and 1866, is due to return on the date mentioned. They are termed *Leonids*, as their flights are uniformly directed from a common centre amongst the stars forming the "sickle of Leo." The "shower" should not be looked for in the evening, as the point from which the meteors emanate does not rise above the horizon until 10.15 P.M., and the most favourable time at which to watch for the display will be after midnight on the night following November 14, or morning hours of November 15. It will also be advisable to watch for the display on the mornings of Nov. 14 and 16, as there is a little uncertainty as to the exact time of its recurrence. The Moon will unfortunately be nearly full, and exercise a detrimental influence upon the phenomenon. In regard to unusually large meteors or fireballs, which occasionally appear with brilliant and startling effects, and are often isolated, their paths amongst the stars should always be recorded with as much accuracy as circumstances permit. When this feature has been carefully noted at two or more stations, it affords the data for computing the heights, distances, and radiant point. Fireballs often approach much nearer to the earth than the ordinary shooting

stars, which usually descend from a height of eighty to fifty miles. The majority of the known meteoric systems are probably annual in their recurrences, but others are periodical, and are only displayed in their richest intensity after long intervals of time. The following is a list of the principal meteoric showers:—

No.	Epoch.	Radiant Point. R. A. Dec.	Name of Shower.
1	Jan. 2—3	230 +52	Quadrantids.
2	Jan. 14—20	295 +53	χ Cygnids.
3	Jan. 18—28	233 +31	θ Coronids.
4	Feb. 5—16......	74 +43	α Aurigids.
5	Feb. 15—20	236 +11	α Serpentids.
6	March 1—4	166 + 5	τ Leonids.
7	March 1—28....	308 +78	κ Cepheids,
8	March 24	161 +58	β Ursids.
9	April 17—25....	231 +17	β Serpentids.
10	April 17—20....	270 +32	Lyrids.
11	April 29—May 6	337— 2	η Aquarids.
12	May 5—June 17	254—21	α Scorpiids.
13	May 15	294+ 0	η Aquilids.
14	May 29—June 4	333 +27	η Pegasids.
15	June 10—28	335 +57	δ Coronids.
16	June 13—July 7	302 +24	Vulpeculids.
17	July 11—19	314 +48	α Cygnids.
18	July 12—17	255 +37	π Herculids.
19	July 19—27	271 +47	γ Draconids.
20	July 23—Aug. 4	48 +43	α—β Perseids.
21	July 27—29	339 —12	δ Aquarids.
22	August 9—11 ..	45 +57	Perseids.
23	August 5—16 ..	292 +53	κ Cygnids.
24	August 21—25..	291 +60	ο Draconids.
25	Aug. 21—Sep. 21	62 +37	ε Perseids.
26	Aug. 25—Sep. 22	5 +10	γ Pegasids.
27	Sept. 1—7.......	354 +38	ν Andromedids.
28	Sept. 7—24	64 +22	ε Taurids.
29	October 11—24..	40 +20	ε Arietids.
30	October 17—20..	92 +15	Orionids.
31	October	106 +23	δ Geminids.
32	Nov. 2—3	55+ 9	ε Taurids.
33	Nov. 10—23	133 +31	ν Cancrids.
34	Nov. 13—15	150 +23	Leonids.
35	Nov. 13—28	155 +40	Leo Minorids.
36	Nov. 20—28	63 +22	ε Taurids.
37	Nov. 26—27	23 +43	Andromedids.
38	Dec. 1—14........	108 +33	Geminids.
39	Dec. 7—10........	119 +29	α Geminids.
40	Dec. 22—29	194 +32	Canum Venaticids.

The Perseids, No. 22 in the foregoing list, display some singular characteristics, for they are probably visible for more than a month, during which period their radiant point is in constant motion to the eastward. The place of the radiant on alternate days during about four weeks of the chief activity of the shower is as follows:—

DATES AND RADIANTS OF PERSEIDS.

Date.	Radiant. R. A. Dec.	Date.	Radiant. R. A. Dec.
July 19	19·7 +50·9	Aug. 4	37·9 +55·5
,, 21	21·8 +51·6	,, 6	40·2 +56·0
,, 23	24·0 +52·2	,, 8	42·6 +56·5
,, 25	26·2 +52·8	,, 10	45·0 +57·0
,, 27	28·5 +53·3	,, 12	47·5 +57·5
,, 29	30·8 +53·8	,, 14	50·1 +58·0
,, 31	33·2 +54·4	,, 16	52·6 +58·5
Aug. 2	35·5 +55·0	,, 18	55·2 +58·9

As regards meteoric showers generally it may be safely said that we require many further observations, especially in reference to the shifting of certain radiants and the apparently stationary aspect of others.

Large meteors should be particularly looked for on the following nights:—

January 2, 21, 31; February 3, 7, 10; March 1, 2, 4; April 11-12, 19-20; May 2, 4, 15, 31; June 6-7, 22, 29-30; July 11, 20-21, 25-30; August 3, 5, 7-13, 15, 19-22; September 1-2, 6-7, 11-13, 25; October 13, 15, 17-18, 22, 24, 29; November 1-2, 4, 6-9, 11-15, 19, 27; December 8-9, 11-12, 21.

TELESCOPIC POWERS NECESSARY FOR OBSERVING CELESTIAL OBJECTS.

Comets, and large nebulæ such as those in Orion and Andromeda, require very low powers and an extensive field of view, so that the objects may be presented in their entirety, and their light sufficiently concentrated to display the fainter portions. If it is desired to critically examine the structure of a comet's nucleus or details of form in a nebula, then powers of 150 or 200 may be used. The cluster in Hercules (Messier 13) is splendidly resolved with 100 on a 10-in. reflector.

The spots on the Sun may be very distinctly seen in any small telescope, care being taken to protect the eye with deeply-tinted glass. A 3-in. refractor, powers 60 and 100, reveals the spots in great variety of detail and grouping. The craters, mountains, and plains of the Moon are satisfactorily seen with 100, though for very minute features powers of 300 and 400 are necessary on a 12-in. glass. Solar and lunar eclipses are best visible under powers of 50 and 75.

The phases of Mercury may be discerned with 75; those of Venus are plain with far less power. To see these planets well, observe them near the times of sunrise or sunset.

The chief spots on Mars, such as the Kaiser Sea, may be distinguished with 90 on a 2-in. refractor, but powers of 300 and 350, and an 8-in. refractor or 10-in. reflector, are desirable to exhibit the outlines of the fainter markings.

Jupiter's belts are visible in a 1½-in. telescope, power 40, but for studying their variable appearances and the different motions of the bright and dark spots 250 and 300 are requisite. The four bright satellites are visible in an opera-glass. Transits of satellites III. and IV. may be observed with a 3-in. refractor and power of 150.

The division in Saturn's ring and his principal dark belt are to be readily glimpsed with a 2½-in. glass, power 120. But magnifiers of 300 and 350, and a much larger aperture, are essential to reach the delicate features of the planet. A good 4½-in. refractor will show Encke's division in the ring, also the interior crape ring and five of the satellites, but the night must be good. Titan, the largest of the Saturnian moons, is visible in any small telescope; and Iapetus is also an easy object, though sometimes unduly faint; but Tethys, Rhea, and Dione are much more difficult, requiring care and attention.

Occultations of stars by the Moon may be well observed with a 3-in. glass, power 75, unless in the case of very small stars which will be quite overpowered if a much larger telescope is not employed.

For double stars the powers required will depend in a great measure upon the character of the object. For very close pairs, high powers, such as 300 or 400, and even more, are sometimes desirable, but in cases where the components are distant and the magnitudes differ considerably, as a Lyræ, then a moderate power, such as 100, will give excellent results. For showing variable stars a good field-glass is to be recommended. For groups of stars, a comet eyepiece, power 30 and field of 1½°, will be best.

It should always be remembered that on nights of good seeing, when the air is tranquil and planetary features very sharply defined, telescopes will bear much higher powers than on less favourable occasions when the images are more or less blurred and unsatisfactory.

The observer should regulate the eyepieces employed with his telescope in conformity with the character of the object, the state of the atmosphere, and the particular observations required. Experience is desirable in astronomical work, and will soon enable the amateur to apply such powers as are best under the prevailing conditions and for the particular object and purpose in view.

The most noteworthy dates are in larger type.

TABLE OF MEAN REFRACTIONS.

Apparent Altitude.	Mean Refraction.	Apparent Altitude.	Mean Refraction.
° '	' "	°	' "
0 0	34 55	15	3 32
0 10	32 49	16	3 19
0 20	30 52	17	3 7
0 30	29 4	18	2 56
0 40	27 23	19	2 46
0 50	25 50	20	2 37
1 0	24 25	21	2 29
1 20	21 56	22	2 22
1 40	19 52	23	2 15
2 0	18 9	24	2 9
2 30	16 1	25	2 3
3 0	14 15	26	1 58
3 30	12 49	27	1 53
4 0	11 39	28	1 48
4 30	10 40	29	1 44
5 0	9 47	30	1 40
5 30	9 2	32	1 32
6 0	8 23	34	1 25
6 30	7 50	36	1 19
7 0	7 20	38	1 14
7 30	6 53	40	1 9
8 0	6 30	45	0 58
8 30	6 8	50	0 48
9 0	5 49	55	0 40
9 30	5 32	60	0 33
10 0	5 16	65	0 27
11 0	4 49	70	0 21
12 0	4 25	75	0 16
13 0	4 5	80	0 10
14 0	3 47	85	0 5
15 0	3 32	90	0 0

This Table of Mean Refractions is derived from that by the late Professor Bessel. With the argument 'apparent altitude' it gives the correction to be applied to observed altitudes in order to free them from the effect of atmospheric refraction. As refraction causes all bodies to appear more elevated above the horizon than they really are, the quantities in the table must be *subtracted* from the observed altitudes.

For an altitude not in the Table, the value of the mean refraction may easily be obtained by interpolation. For example, let the mean refraction be required for 6° 35': here opposite to 6° 30' we have 7' 50", and opposite to the next argument, 7° 0', 7' 20" for the mean refraction, and we see that for an increase of 30' in the altitude, the refraction has decreased 30"; therefore a simple proportion shows us that the value corresponding to 6° 30' by 5", which will give 7' 45" as the mean refraction corresponding to 6° 35' of apparent altitude.

ATHLETICS.

As a general rule athletic meetings during 1899 were not quite so well supported by spectators as in many preceding years, although the Oxford and Cambridge sports, and other classic fixtures, seemed to be still very popular and attractive. It is difficult to account for this falling off in public interest, except that cycling, golf, and lawn-tennis are much more in evidence than formerly, and also that, except at a very few meetings, the class of competitor, both athletically and socially, was not of a very high status. Even this is not a very satisfactory explanation, as the London Athletic Club Meetings and the Inter-Hospital Gathering, when some of the very best athletes of the year were in evidence, failed to draw more than mere handfuls of spectators to Stamford Bridge. So far as racing is concerned, nearly all the chief handicaps of the year produced excellent finishes, indeed, the Amateur Athletic Association's system of licensed handicappers has certainly improved this department of athletics to a marvellous extent. The governing body, although keenly alive to its duties in the matter of punishing malpractices and various abuses, has anything but an easy task to discover and convict those so-called amateurs who manage by betting and obtaining expenses to make a very fair living out of the pastime. Wholesale suspensions appear to have very little effect, and before long the drastic measures of 1895 will have to be repeated, and some of the worst offenders ejected finally from the amateur ranks, even if absolute proof cannot be obtained to support what is common knowledge in the athletic world. No records of any importance were accomplished during the season, and the only visitors to the Championship Meeting were G. W. Orton, a Canadian, and Houdet, a Frenchman. The Oxford and Cambridge v. Harvard and Yale Meeting was undoubtedly the feature of the athletic year, and for once an International match was brought off without a single hitch or unpleasant incident. The Hon. Sec., of the Amateur Athletic Association, Mr. C. Herbert, was presented with a testimonial during the year to commemorate his seventeen years tenure of office. The offices of the Association are 10, John St., Adelphi, London, W.C.

In recording the cross-country events of the 1899 athletic season we must hark back to Dec. 3, 1898, when the annual cross-country match between the Oxford and Cambridge Universities took place at Roehampton over the Thames Hare and Hounds course, 8 miles. Cambridge were expected to win, but Oxford reversed the placing of the previous three years and scored a popular victory with 25 points, to the Cantabs' 30. E. A. Dawson, Oxford, was first man home in 46 min. $45\frac{4}{5}$ secs.; A. Hunter, Cambridge, finished second in 47 min. $23\frac{3}{5}$ secs.; and J. C. P. Kinsman, Oxford, was third. In February and March, 1899, the more important Cross-Country Associations held their championships. The Southern, Midland, and Northern were all held on the same day, viz., Feb. 18th. The Southern resulted as follows at, Wembley Park, C. Bennett, Finchley H., first; J. Pratt, Highgate H., second; T. Bartlett, Essex B., third; time, 61 min. $34\frac{4}{5}$ secs. Club placings, Highgate H., 42 points, first; Essex B., 81 points, second; Finchley H., 96 points, third. Northern, at Crewe Park, J. Hosker, Farnworth H., first; J. D. Marsh, Salford H., second; J. Tennant, West Cheshire H., third; time, 63 min. 37 secs. Club placings, Salford H., 49 points, first; Manchester H., 114 points, second; Farnworth H. 148 points, third. The Midland Championship, at Smethwick Cricket Ground, A. H. Meacham, Birchfield H., first; W. E. Stokes, Birchfield H., second; W. H. Tolley, Birchfield H., third; time, 65 min. 54 sec. Club placings. Birchfield H., 23 points, first; Small Heath H., 93 points, second; Derby and County A.C. and Leicester H.. a dead heat for third place, with 129 points each. The National Championship was decided at Wembley Park on March 4th. Eleven clubs competed. The race was won easily by C. Bennett, and the second position of the Haddington Harriers, a small Dublin Club, was the feature of the Championship. The result was as follows: C. Bennett, Finchley H., first; T. Bartlett, Essex B, second; J. G. Wood, Highgate H., third; time, 58 min. $35\frac{3}{5}$ secs. Club placings, Champions, Highgate H., 92 points; second, Haddington Harriers, Dublin, 124 points; third, Birchfield H., 138 points. All these four races were over supposed 10 mile courses. On the following day the Eleventh Cross-country Championship of France, at Ville d'Avray, near Paris, was won by Touquet first, Champoudry second, Marlius third. Time, for a course of about $9\frac{1}{2}$ miles, 61 min. 29 secs. The club placings were Société Athlétique de Montrouge, 61 points, first; Association Pédestre Française, 65 points, second. The Scottish Cross-country Championship, $10\frac{3}{4}$ miles, at Hampden Park, Crosshill, Glasgow, March 11th, gave the following result: J. Paterson (Watsonians), first; D. W. Mill (Clydesdale H.), second; A. R. Gibb (Watsonians), third; time 64 min. $36\frac{1}{5}$ secs. Club placings, Watsonians, 55 points, first; Maryhill H., Glasgow, 68 points, second. The Irish Cross-country Championship, at Dolphin's Barn, Dublin, on March 25, was won by the Ballinasloe H., 32 points, first; Haddington, H., with 58 points, second; and County Dublin H., 81 points, third; J. T. Joyce, Ballinasloe H., was first, in 33 min. $43\frac{3}{5}$ secs.; J. C. Hayes, H.H., second; and F. Curtis, H.H., third. The distance was not long enough for the Haddington team. Path athletics began at the Univerities at the end of January, but the College Meetings did not produce any very startling performances. Some, however, deserve notice. At Cambridge, Christ College Sports, H. E. Graham, of Jesus, won a Strangers' Mile from scratch in 4 min. $32\frac{1}{5}$ secs.; C. R. Thomas, of Jesus, Oxford, won the New College Strangers' Hundred Yards from scratch easily in $10\frac{1}{5}$ secs. H. E. Graham, with nine yards, won a Strangers' Half Mile Handicap at Trinity Hall Sports in 1 min. $58\frac{1}{2}$ secs. The Cambridge University Handicaps on Feb. 17 and 20, were rather too severe on the scratch men. The more important results were: Putting the Weight, G. W. Clark, Caius, 35 ft.; High Jump, W. G. Paget-Tomlinson, Trinity Hall, 5 ft. 7 in.; Quarter Mile Handicap, P. S. Stephens, Trinity, 16 yds.; time $49\frac{4}{5}$ secs.; One Mile, E. Bruce, Jesus, 95 yards, time 4 min. $21\frac{2}{5}$ secs.; One Hundred and Twenty Yards Handicap, P. M. Shanks, Christ's, 1 yard, time $12\frac{1}{5}$ secs.; Throwing the Hammer, L. O. T. Baines, Trinity Hall, 101 feet 10 in.; Half Mile, H. E. Graham, Jesus, scratch, 1 min. $58\frac{3}{5}$ secs.; Long Jump, W. G. Paget-Tomlinson, Trinity Hall, 20 ft. $8\frac{1}{2}$ in.; Three Miles, W. Winterbotham, King's, 200 yds., time 15 min. $14\frac{4}{5}$ secs; One Hundred and Twenty Yards Hurdles, E. Allcock, Trinity Hall, penalized 6 yards, time $17\frac{1}{5}$ secs. At Eton College about this time H. P. W. Macnaghten won the Senior

Mile in 4 min. 47 secs. easily, and also the Half Mile in 2 min. 11 secs. The Cambridge University Sports were held at Fenners, March 3, 4 and 6, the winners were: Putting the Weight, G. W. Clark, Caius, 34 ft. $5\frac{1}{2}$ in.; Quarter Mile, C. G. Davison, Sidney, in $51\frac{1}{5}$ secs., with P. M. Shanks, Christ, second; High Jump, W. G. Paget-Tomlinson, 5 ft. 6 in. He also won the Hurdles very easily in $16\frac{1}{5}$ secs. A. Hunter, of Trinity, won the Mile from H. E. Graham, of Jesus, in 4 min. $26\frac{2}{5}$ secs., Graham taking the Half in 2 min. $1\frac{2}{5}$ secs.; L. O. T. Baines, of Trinity Hall, won the Hammer, with 93 ft. 10 in., subsequently throwing 96 ft. 10 in.; H. A. Jones, the Framlinham Freshman, at Jesus, won the Long Jump with 21 ft. 8 in., and Paget-Tomlinson won the Hundred against the wind in $10\frac{3}{5}$ secs. The Three Miles was a hard win for H. W. Workman, of Pembroke, in 15 min. $24\frac{2}{5}$ secs. The Oxford University Athletic Club held their Meeting on March 6 and 8. C. R. Thomas, of Jesus, won the Hundred by four yards in 10 secs.; a record subsequently allowed him by the A.A.A. A. M. Hollins, of Hertford, won the Quarter in $50\frac{2}{5}$ secs.; S. A. Neave, the old Etonian, being second to him; H. R. Parkes, of Christchurch, the then Amateur Champion, won the Hurdles in $16\frac{1}{5}$ secs. The Half Mile went to T. Smith, of Magdalen, in 2 min. $1\frac{3}{5}$ secs., and the Mile was won by R. B. Arnold, of Magdalen, in 4 min. 35 secs. E. A. Dawson, of Worcester, the Inter-Varsity Cross-country winner, won the Three Miles in 15 min. 45 sec. G. C. Vassall, of Oriel, won the Long Jump, with 22 ft. 11 in., and E. V. J. Brooke, of Magdalen, took the High Jump with 5 ft. 8 in. The Hammer fell to J. B. Greenshields, of Oriel, with 96 ft., and J. B. Aspinall, of Christchurch, carried off the Weight with 33 ft. $6\frac{1}{2}$ in. On March 11, the C.U.A.C. met the L.A.C., at Fenners, for their annual match as a third and last trial before the all important Inter-Varsity fixture. The Cantabs won very decisively by seven events to three. The L.A.C. only won the Hundred (C. H. Jupp, time $10\frac{3}{5}$ secs.) The Weight (Nigel S. A. Harrison, 39 ft. 1 in.), and the Two Miles (M. Davie, in 9 min. $36\frac{4}{5}$ secs.). W. G. Paget-Tomlinson won the High Jump with 5 ft. $8\frac{1}{2}$ in., and the Hurdles in 16 secs., which ties the Fenners record. W. E. Lutyens, the old Cambridge blue, was beaten both in the One Mile by A. Hunter in 4 min. $24\frac{2}{5}$ secs., and also in the Half, by H. E. Graham in 1 min. $59\frac{3}{5}$ secs.; L. O. T. Baines, Hammer, 109 ft. 3 in., and H. A. Jones, Long Jump, 21 ft. $9\frac{1}{4}$ in., were the other Cambridge winners. The Oxford and Cambridge Sports were decided as usual at the Queen's Club on the day before the Boat Race, viz., March 24. The day was cold, and the path after several nights' hard frost not too fast. A long-standing argument between the two Clubs resulted in the introduction of a Half Mile into the programme, and also a wave of common sense induced "the powers that be" to consent to decide the Hammer and the Weight, under the universally recognized A.A.A. conditions. Strange to say, the alteration from nine to ten events immediately resulted in a tie, which has not occurred since the very first Meeting, thirty-six years ago. The Hurdles and the Long Jump were the most noticeable features of a very interesting afternoon's sport. The results were: Long Jump, G. C. Vassall, Oxford, 23 ft. 3 in., first; L. R. O. Bevan, Cambridge, 21 ft. $3\frac{1}{4}$ in., second; High Jump, H. S. Adair, Oxford, 5 ft. $8\frac{1}{4}$ in., first; W. G. Paget-Tomlinson, Cambridge, and E. V. J. Brooke, Oxford, a tie, second, at 5 ft. $7\frac{1}{8}$ in. Hammer (9 ft. circle), J. D. Greenshields, Oxford, 110 ft. 1 in., first; L. O. T. Baines, Cam., 106 ft. 5 in., second; Weight (7 ft. square), G. W. Clark, Cambridge, 34 ft., first; J. A. Campbell, Cambridge, 33 ft., $9\frac{1}{4}$ in., second. Hundred Yards, C. R. Thomas, Oxford, first; A. E. Hind, Cambridge, second; won by a yard and a-half, time $10\frac{2}{5}$ secs. Half Mile, H. E. Graham, Cambridge, first; C. H. W. Struben, Oxford, second; won by seven yards, time 1 min. $59\frac{3}{5}$ sec. One Hundred and Twenty Yards Hurdle, W. G. Paget-Tomlinson, Cambridge, first, H. R. Parkes, Oxford, second; won by two yards, time 16 secs., with the wind. Quarter Mile, A. M. Hollins, Oxford, first; C. G. Davison, Cam., second; won by six yards. time $51\frac{2}{5}$ secs. One Mile, A. Hunter, Cambridge first; R. B. Arnold, Oxford, second; won by thirty yards, time 4 min. 35 secs. Three Miles, H. W. Workman, Cambridge, first; A. R. G. Wilberforce, Oxford, second; won by sixty yards, time 15 min. $45\frac{2}{5}$ secs. In the same week, as the Inter-'Varsity Sports, the Eton College Quarter and Hundred were both won by Chute in $60\frac{1}{2}$ secs. and $11\frac{3}{5}$ secs. respectively. The next event of importance amongst the athletic fixtures of the year was the Ten Miles Championship of Scotland at Hampden Park, Glasgow, on April 7, won by a very moderate performer, W. M. Badenock, of the Edinburgh Harriers, in 58 min. $4\frac{1}{5}$ secs.; only two started, and the standard of 57 min. was not approached. The A.A.A. Ten Miles Championship was decided at the Vulcan Grounds, Derby, on April 15. The ground was absolutely unfitted for such an important event. The track was in no sort of order, and the attendance about 200. C. Bennett, of the Finchley Harriers, won easily in 54 min $12\frac{2}{5}$ secs., J. T. Rimmer, of the Liverpool H. being beaten one hundred yards for first place. An early date, April 8, saw the Public Schools Challenge Cup Meeting of the London Athletic Club at Stamford Bridge. The day was cold and wet, but the performances were decidedly good. The Challenge Cups were won as follow:—One Mile, D. C. Cowan, St. John's School, Leatherhead, time 4 min. $51\frac{3}{5}$ secs: Three Quarter Mile Steeplechase, J. Dickinson, Repton, w.o.; Quarter Mile. G. E. Barry, St. Paul's School, time $54\frac{4}{5}$ secs.; Half Mile, G. E. Barry, St. Paul's School, time 2 min. $6\frac{1}{5}$ secs.; Hurdles, G. F. Mortimer, Repton, time $17\frac{3}{5}$ secs., G. R. Garnier, of Sherborne, was second; Hundred Yards. S. C. Talbot, Cheltenham. time $10\frac{3}{5}$ secs.; High Jump, J. K. Macmeikan, Repton, 5 ft. 2 ins.; Long Jump, G. M. Spooner, of Milton Abbas, 18 ft $10\frac{1}{2}$ ins. W. E. Lutyens won the One Mile Club Challenge Cup, and G. C. Davison, the Quarter Mile Club Challenge Cup in 52 secs. During May and June, although plenty of athletic meetings were held, nothing resulted to throw very much light on the coming Championships, R. W. Wadsley and C. H. Jupp proved themselves far and away the best of the metropolitan sprinters. Outside the Universities no one seemed able to run a quarter mile in anything like decent time, and W. E. Lutyens was far and away the best man in the South at a mile or half a mile if we except C. Bennett at the longer distance. The Civil Service Sports in June were well attended as usual, but the performances, except in the sprint made from Jupp, were much below the high average of this meeting. The Championships fell to be held in the Midlands, and the executive with a very small choice of grounds to select from made an attempt to adapt the Molyneux Grounds, Wolverhampton, a cycle cinder track to the requirements of a good foot-racing path. The attempt failed, as it always will and must, and it is to be hoped that in the future these experiments will not be allowed by the ruling body. Also the day was cold and wet, and the enlarged and relaid portion of the track suffered severely. Fast times were out of the question. and the attendance was decidedly below the average. The sooner the Metropolis is selected as the sole venue of the Championships the better for everybody concerned. The results were:—The Mile, won by the holder, Hugh Welsh, of Watson's College, by a yard and a half from C. Bennett, of the Finchley Harriers, after a magnificent finish in 4 mins. 26 secs.; Hundred Yards, R. W. Wadsley, Highgate Harriers, won by two yards from C. H. Jupp, L.A.C., with the holder, F. W. Cooper, of Bradford a close third, time $10\frac{1}{5}$ secs., the sprint track being very fair going; Half Mile, A. E. Tysoe, Salford Harriers, beating W. E. Lutyens, L.A.C., by four feet in 1 min. $58\frac{3}{5}$ secs. after a magnificent race; Quarter Mile, R. W. Wadsley by two feet from H. W. P. Jones, of the Bath and Somerset A. C. in $54\frac{3}{5}$ secs., the holder, W. Fitzherbert, C.U.A.C., being beaten in his heat; Four Miles, C. Bennett, Finchley Harriers, the holder, won easily from A. E. Hutchings, Bexhill H. & H., in 20 min. $49\frac{3}{5}$ secs.; Two Miles Steeplechase, W. Stokes, Birchfield H., won easily, time 11 min. $16\frac{4}{5}$ secs.; Four Miles Walk, W. J Sturgess, holder, Polytechnic H., won easily in 29 min. 20 secs.; One Hundred and Twenty Yards Hurdles, W. G. Paget-Tomlinson, C.U.A.C., won by five feet from A. Trafford, of the Birmingham A. C. in $16\frac{2}{5}$ secs; D. Horgan, Irish A.A.A., won the Weight with a good put of 46 ft. $\frac{1}{2}$ in.; T. F. Kiely, another Irishman, and also the holder, won the Hammer with 136 ft. $4\frac{1}{2}$ ins. The High Jump again went to the Irish holder, P. Leahy, with 5ft. 10 ins., and another Irish holder, W. J. M. Newburn, won the Long Jump with 22 ft. 2 ins.; C. E. Pritchard, of Kidderminster, won the Pole Jump with 7 ft., afterwards clearing 9 ft. 1 in., the holder, J. Poole, being present but not being able to obtain a pole. The great meeting of the year, however, was yet to come. After a long period of negotiations Oxford and Cambridge combined issued a challenge to Yale and Harvard for an athletic competition to be decided in London, at the Queen's Club, on July 22. The programme was the English Inter-'Varsity one, less Putting the Weight, and with unfixed Hurdles on grass. The day was absolutely perfect for such a Meeting, the Prince of Wales was present, together with the Duke and Duchess of York, and the general attendance a bumper. The English Universities just won, T. E. Burke, an American certainty for the Half Mile, not coming off. The racing was excellent, the Hurdles and the Quarter being the chief features of the afternoon. The events were won as follows:—Throwing the Hammer, W. A. Boal, Harvard, first, 136 ft. $8\frac{1}{2}$ ins. from a 7 ft. circle and with a loop handle; H. G. Brown, Harvard, second, 122 ft. 9 ins.; J. D. Greenshields, Oxford, third, 109 ft. 6 ins. from a 9 ft. circle, A.A.A. rules. All used wire handles. Long Jump, G. C. Vassall, Oxford, first, 23 ft.; C. D. Daly, Harvard, second, 22 ft. 3 ins. High Jump, A. N. Rice, Harvard, first, 6 ft.; H. S. Adair, Oxford, second, 5 ft. 11 ins. One Hundred and Twenty Yards Hurdles, F. B. Fox, Harvard, first; W. G. Paget-Tomlinson, Cambridge, second, won by two yards, time $15\frac{3}{5}$ secs. One Hundred Yards, F. T. Quinlan, Harvard, first; C. R. Thomas, Oxford, second; won by a foot, time 10 secs. One Mile, A. Hunter, Cambridge, first; A. L. Danson, Oxford, second; won by 25 yards, time 4 min. 24 secs. Half Mile, H. E. Graham, Cambridge, first; C. F. W. Struben, Oxford, second; time 1 min. $57\frac{2}{5}$ secs. Quarter Mile, G. C. Davison, Cambridge, first; D. Boardman, Yale, second; won by seven yards, time $49\frac{2}{5}$ secs. Three Miles, H. W. Workman, Cambridge, first; C. H. Palmer, Yale, second; won by 150 yards, time 15 min. $24\frac{2}{5}$ secs. The American Ambassador was present at the dinner in the evening, when Lord Jersey presided, and the medals were presented. Nothing of any great importance occurred after this International fixture. C. R. Thomas won the Welsh Hundred Yards Championship at Newport on the August Bank Holiday, but as he did not compete for the Championship, and R. W. Wadsley was never subsequently beaten in a scratch race, the sprint honours of the year certainly belong to the Champion. It may be mentioned that Wadsley did not attempt another Quarter after his Wolverhampton victory. A. E. Relf, the 1898 Half Mile Champion, was *hors de combat* during the year, and Bennett retired after his Championship victory. St. Bartholomew's won the Inter-Hospital Challenge Shield on July 12 at Stamford Bridge, H. E. Graham's (St. Bart's.) Half in 1 min. $59\frac{3}{5}$ secs., and C. E. H. Leggatt's (St. Mary's) Long Jump of 23 ft. $4\frac{1}{2}$ ins. being records for the Meeting. Subsequently, in Dublin, Dublin University beat the United Hospitals easily. At Sandhurst R.M.C. Sports, May 11 and 12, the performances—perhaps owing to the Woolwich and Sandhurst Shield being still in abeyance—were not very brilliant, R. Worsley's Quarter in 55 secs., R. V. Simpson's Hundred in $11\frac{1}{5}$ secs., and R. Bullock's Hurdles in $17\frac{4}{5}$ secs., being perhaps the best. Bullock also cleared 21 ft. $\frac{1}{4}$ in. in the Long Jump, and Simpson's High Jump, 5 ft. $7\frac{3}{8}$ ins. was distinctly meritorious. At Woolwich R.M.A. on September 20, A. H. Du Boulay and W. M. Turner tied for the Challenge Bugle. The course was heavy going, and a very stiff breeze spoilt the times, Du Boulay's Quarter Mile in $55\frac{3}{5}$ sec. was perhaps the best performance. He also won the Hundred in $10\frac{2}{5}$ secs. with the wind. Lt. W. F. Reichwald, Royal Garrison Artillery, won the Half Mile Championship of the Army in 2 min. $5\frac{4}{5}$ secs. at the Aldershot Meeting. The other winners at the Army Meeting were:– Quarter Mile, Lieut. Reichwald, time $54\frac{4}{5}$ secs.; One Mile, Lieut. W. M. Freeston, 1st Somerset L.I., time 4 min. 36 secs.; Hundred, Lieut. H. H. Wade, 2nd Royal Lancaster Regt., time $10\frac{4}{5}$ secs.; Hurdles, Lieut. R. F. A. Hobbs, Royal Engineers, time $17\frac{3}{5}$ sees. At the Reading Meeting, August 26, A. Nelson, of the Goldsmith's Institute, won a Three Quarter Mile Handicap from scratch in 3 min. $11\frac{4}{5}$ secs. by a foot from the other scratch man, J. Binks, of the Unity A.C. This is the best authenticated time for the distance. Shortly afterwards Nelson again defeated Binks in a Half Mile Invitation Race on grass, at the S.L.H. Meeting at the Oval, September 9, in the very fast time of 1 min. $58\frac{2}{5}$ secs. C. Bennett at Stamford Bridge (L.A.C. Meeting) June 24, made a new record for One and a Half Miles, viz., 6 min. 51 secs.

BILLIARDS.

It may seem a paradox, but it is still perfectly true that the 1898-99 billiard season was both eventful, and at the same time, rather uninteresting. It certainly marked a new era in English billiards, because the new rules of the Billiard Association came into general use, and thus at last put a stop to the almost endless discussions and arguments as to the "spot-barred" and the "spot-in" games, to say nothing of the much debated "push" shot. For the future there can be no more push-barred champions, spot-in champions, and spot-barred champions, there is only one set of rules recognised as governing English Billiards, and the spot-stroke exponents and the push-shot exponents will now cease to trouble the compilers of records and the adherents of all round play. The Billiard Association has worked its way very carefully and well into its proper and governing position, and even the great champion, Roberts, appears to recognise its rulings—witness his dispute about ivory and bonzoline balls previous to the Roberts-Dawson match—and also now plays his matches under its rules and regulations. The Association has arranged in future to keep two sets of records, one set with ivory, and the other with bonzoline balls. Also the Association has passed a rule that none of its members shall play in public under any but B. A. rules without a special permit. The great and important features of the season were the Roberts-Dawson match, the first Billiard Association professional championship under the new rules, and also stirring contests for the Amateur Championship for the old spot-barred Challenge Cup of the Association. Although it was perfectly clear that age had at last begun to tell on John Roberts' incomparable play, nerve, and eyesight, he still proved himself able to give long starts and a beating to all the other professionals. His breaks were not quite so enormous as before, but between Dec. 9th and March, 1899, he made 514, 527, 548, 372 off the red ball alone. and on March 3rd 597, the then record break under the new rules, subsequently passed as correct by the B. A. This was generally quoted as the record until October, when Dawson, on a tested table, completely eclipsed it as given later on. He, Roberts, ran his usual Exhibitions at the Egyptian Hall up to March, and then toured in the North well into the summer. He continued to give away about the usual number of points, but not always successfully. H. W. Stevenson was defeated with 7,000 in 21,000, but just before his big match, Roberts entirely failed to give E. Diggle 5,500 in 21,000. Dawson clearly proved himself the next best player to the champion, with Diggle perhaps some 800 points in 18,000 behind him. Mitchell retained his form in a wonderful manner, his victory in the Roberts tournament was a marvellous exhibition of consistent play and nerve, with genuine money at issue. Stevenson certainly improved, and his 582 in November, 1898, was the first big break under the new rules and the record at the time. Peall played but seldom, and then only at times showed his best form. He very rarely played "spot-in." Harverson did not improve quite so much as was expected, and as some of the older players, North, Taylor, Spiller, and others, were not often seen in public, their places were not taken by any of the new aspirants for honours. Indeed, M. Inman seems to be the most likely man to push himself into the front rank. Except

at the Egyptian Hall, with Roberts on view, billiard entertainments were not as a rule profitable speculations. The great match of the season, John Roberts v. C. Dawson, level, began on March 20th. The points were 18,000 up for £100 aside. The first half of the match to be played at the Argyll Hall, and the second half at the Egyptian Hall The match was under B. A. rules, and on their ruling ivory balls had to be used. The match was admirably worked up by newspaper arguments, and so great was the interest, that the gate finally reached over £2,000, and this amount would have been increased had a larger hall been available. During the first week, Dawson had the best of it. The leads were on Monday, Roberts 110; Tuesday, Dawson 784; Wednesday, Dawson 510; Thursday, Dawson 872; Friday, Dawson 423; Saturday, Roberts 280; Monday, Roberts 882; Tuesday, Roberts 1,465. By Thursday night, Roberts was 2,078 points in front. On the last day but one, Dawson drew up to within 807 of the leader by means of some brilliant breaks of 243, 228. 212, 185, 155, 136, 126, and 112 ; Roberts best being 131 and 102. During that day Dawson scored 2,770 points to Roberts' 1,499 Roberts, however, in the last stage of the match went right away and won by 1,814 points. The best breaks in the first week were - Roberts 140, 172, 163, 182, 169, 180, 143, 266, 329, 151 ; Dawson 152, 150, 278, 156, 264, 186, 342. In the second week the best breaks were—Roberts 272, 155, 285, 316, 236, 188, 213, 207, 215 &c ; Dawson 170. 243. 228, 212, 185, 155. Mr. Rimington Wilson officiated as referee. The stakes and the gate subsequently became the subject of legal proceedings. The first Billiard Association Professional Championship under the new rules, which took place at the Gaiety Restaurant, January 9-14, could not be called a very brilliant inauguration. It clashed with the Roberts Handicap, which should certainly have been avoided, and doubtless in consequence there were only three entrants who put down their £20. Mitchell, Dawson and North. Of these, Mitchell withdrew, with the Roberts Handicap in view, and Dawson and North played an uninteresting game. The prizes were to the winner £100 per annum so long as he holds the title, three-fourths of the sweepstakes, and the gold medal of the Association. The gate money to be divided. The points were 9,000 up. Dawson went away from the start, and finally won easily by 4,285 points. The best breaks were—Dawson 337, 350, 282, 275. 152, 271, 276, 157, 179, 309, 320, 136, 221 ; North 207, 125, 167, 121, &c. Dawson certainly gave a wonderful exhibition of consistent play and large breaks on a Standard table, and even Roberts himself would not have been expected to win by more from North than did Dawson in the 9,000 up

The third great event of the Billiard Association's season was the competition for the Amateur Championship, decided at the National Sporting Club, on March 1st, and following days. The Challenge Cup was held by Mr. S. H. Fry under the spot-barred regulations, but he immediately consented to play for it under the new rules, when challenged by Messrs. E. C. Ogden, A. R. Wisdom, M. A. Oxlade, F. Wear, S. S. Christey, A. Vahid, and F. W. Payn; heats, 1,000 up. In the first heat, Mr. Ogden beat Mr. Christey by 135; Mr. Wear beat Mr. Payn by 198; Mr. Vahid beat Mr. Oxlade by 380. In the second round, Mr. Wisdom beat Mr. Ogden by 37. A 144 break by the loser being a then record for the

Amateur Championship. Mr. Vahid (with a best break of 75) beat Mr. Wear by 13 points. Mr. Wisdom in the final heat beat Mr. Vahid (with a best break of 82) by 53 points, and then met the holder, Mr. S. H. Fry, who had not been called upon to defend his title since 1895. The game was 1,500 up. Mr. Fry was led rapidly from the start. Mr. Wisdom with 81, leading by over 300 at 496 to 182. Mr. Fry then, with a splendid break of 168 (a record), closed up to within 37. But breaks of Fry, 63, 86 and 75 to Wisdom's 70, saw the totals, Fry 1,111, Wisdom 1,073. Finally, Mr. Wisdom, with 57, 43 and 56 unfinished, won the game and the Championship by 203 points. These two amateurs are evidently most evenly matched. Mr. Wisdom hails from Tonbridge. Mr. Maughan of Middlesbrough, a former champion before Mr. Fry, died during the year.

Shortly, the other events of the season have been as follows:—Messrs. Burroughes and Watts arranged, as usual, a tournament lasting about five months from October, 1898 to March 11th, 1899. The heats were 18,000 up, each game lasting a fortnight, and £100 was the prize. The 12 players engaged were C. Dawson scratch, E. Diggle 500, H. W. Stevenson 3,500, C. Harverson 4,000, W. Spiller 4,000, J. Mack 5,000, T. Taylor 5,500. T. Aiken 6,500, F. Bateman 7,000, J. Duncan, J. Meerton and W. Murray 7,500. Dawson and Stevenson were left in until the final heat, when Stevenson won easily by 2,162. Stevenson also made the best break of the tournament 524. Diggle was beaten easily by Stevenson in a semi-final heat.

At the end of 1898, the Billiard Association arranged a handicap under their rules, with £100 in prizes, at the Argyll Hall; heats 500 up. The handicap included C. Dawson scratch, W. Mitchell 40, H. W. Stevenson 50, W. J. Peall 40, J. North 80, W. Spiller 90, C. Harverson 90, W. Hardy 150, J. P. Mannock 140, J. Dunn 170, A. W. Morgan 170, W. Clark 190, B. Elphick 170, G. Collins 170, F. Copping 190, W. Cook 170, H. Barr 200, M. Inman 200, W. Critchell 210, C. Popkin 249, F. Dixon 253, J. Lloyd 120. J. North won the first prize of £50, beating J. Dunn two games off the reel in the final heat. Lloyd made the best break of 131.

Following the tournament, a most interesting match took place for £25 aside, between H. Barr and M. Inman, 1,500 up, B. A. rules. Barr, with a best break of 67 just getting home by 13 points.

The year opened with a big American tournament promoted by John Roberts, at the Egyptian Hall; heats, 600 up, Billiard Association Rules, bonzoline balls, and £410 in prizes. Seven heats were played each day, the handicap being John Roberts scratch, Diggle 150, W. Mitchell 175, W. J. Peall, H. W. Stevenson and J. G. Sala 200, C. Harverson 225, W. D. Courtney, T. Taylor and J. Mack 240, F. Bateman, W. Osborne, F. Copping and T. Aitken 260. But for the fact that four heats in the evening was far too large an order, the handicap was a great success. The veteran, Mitchell, won (playing most consistently all through) with 11 wins, taking the first prize of £200 and a £25 gold medal. J. G. Sala and Diggle tied for second place with 10 wins each, Sala eventually obtaining the second prize of £60. Roberts won 7 games; Mitchell ran out a winner in one of his heats with 248. He also made the best break of the tournament 254 unfinished. Diggle's 247 and Peall's 243 were amongst the chief breaks. In one game Diggle reached 584 to Roberts' 121, when the latter, with 135, 150 and

146 unfinished, won by 3 points. The table was passed as correct by the Billiard Association.

Messrs. Orme and Sons' Billiard Markers' Eighth Annual Tournament, B. A. rules and "Standard" table, and bonzoline balls, secured 128 competitors for the £120 prizes. The heats were 250 up. M. Inman of Brixton Hill won the final 500 up, with C. Popkin of Battersea Rise second. Inman also made the highest break of the competition, viz., 98.

Messrs. G. Wright and Co.'s Billiard Markers' Handicap for the Silver Challenge Cup and £154 in prizes at the Argyll Hall, heats 500 up, B. A. rules, was also won by young M. Inman (50), beating F. Storey of Ireland (190) two games out of three for the first prize of £40 and the Challenge Cup. Inman made a 94 in the very last heat, which he won by 186.

The London and Metropolitan Licensed Victuallers' Handicap, promoted by Messrs. Cox, Yemen, at the Gaiety Restaurant, obtained a record entry of 194. The heats were 250 up, B. A. rules and bonzoline balls. It began November 21st, 1898, and concluded on March 17th, 1899. Mr. Jesse Hill (30) beating Mr. I. R. Meyrick (112) by 74 points.

The London and Suburban L. V. Championship and Handicap, at Thurston's, also began on November 21st. Heats 250 up, B. A. rules, with 32 and 157 entries respectively. Mr. W. S. Jones proved the best of the challengers for the Championship. For the final heat he was only defeated by 7 points by the holder, Mr. W. S. Large, of the King's Head, Epsom, in 1,000 up. Mr. Jones made a break of 79 in the final heat. This was the third victory of Mr. Large for this Cup. Mr. H. Groom (35) won the first prize in the handicap.

The London Press Handicap, for the handsome 100 guinea Challenge Cup, was decided at Messrs. G. Wright and Co.'s, Argyll Hall. The heats were 300 up, B. A. rules, and no less than 67 entries were received. Mr. John Martin of the *Daily Telegraph* (80) won the final heat by 9 points from Mr. J. D. White of the Press Club (100).

The Oxford and Cambridge matches took place at Beechey's Rooms, Oxford, March 13th and 14th. In the single-handed game Messrs. B. Hargreaves (Oriel), Oxford, and M. W. Muir (Trinity), Cambridge, met. The Cantab reached 220 to Oxford's 163, and after a good game, the Oxonian, with a best break of 22, won by 49 points, 500 up. Mr. Muir's best was 45. In the four-handed match Messrs. Hargreaves and L. Mortimer of Magdalen, represented Oxford. Muir being partnered by W. E. Tucker of Christ's, for Cambridge, in the absence of G. L. Jessop. Oxford went right away and won by 208. Hargreaves 50, and Mortimer 39 were the best breaks. In both games the points were 500 up.

Ives, an American opponent of John Roberts some years ago, died during the year.

BOXING AND FENCING

The winners of the principal Championships for the year were as follows:—Oxford and Cambridge at the Corn Exchange, Cambridge, March 9, Oxford winning all but one event. Boxing: Feather Weights, F. G. White, Clare, Cambridge, beat Prince Maharaj K. Singh, Balliol, Oxford; Light Weights, A. Chatterton Sim, New, Oxford, w.o., H. A. Bishop, Emmanuel, Cambridge, being over weight; Middle Weights, J. Gordon-Jamieson, Balliol, Oxford, beat A. W. Wakefield,

Trinity, Cambridge ; Heavy Weights, H. W. C. Booth, Wadham, Oxford, beat D. McCraith, Trinity, Cambridge. Fencing : Count R. de Tracy, Grindle's Hall, Oxford, beat J. B. Leach, Christ's, Cambridge, and C. M. H. Howell, Trinity, Oxford, beat Baron G. R. De Manasce, Trinity Hall, Cambridge. Sabres : E. P. Garrett, Ch. Ch., Oxford, beat F. G. Bailey, Trinity, Cambridge. On March 18, the Amateur Gymnastic and Fencing Association's Amateur Championship was decided at Birmingham, A.W. Baker, Birmingham Dolobran A.C., winning the competition. On March 24-25, the Public Schools Gymnastic, Boxing, and Fencing Championships were held at the Queen's Avenue Gymnasium, Aldershot. The winners were :—Boxing, Heavy Weights, R. O C. Ward (Clifton). Middle Weights, C. H. Wolff (St. Paul's) ; Light Weights, P. P. Braithwaite (Felsted) ; Feather Weights, J. W. H. F. Douglas (Felsted) : Gymnastics Challenge Shield (32 schools), Cheltenham College (B. C. Footner and R. L. Haines) : Fencing, Foils, A. E. Bucknill (Charterhouse) : Sabres, H. W. Turner (Cranleigh). The Amateur Boxing Championships took place at St. James's Hall on March 28, the entries and the attendance being better than ever. The entry list ran up to 49 — a record. The results were :— Bantam Weights (8 st. 4 lbs.) A. Avent (Bristol A.C.) ; Feather Weights (9 st.), John L. Scholes (Athenæum Club, Toronto) ; Light Weights (10 st.), H. Brewer (Polytechnic B.C.) ; Middle Weights (11 st. 4 lbs.), R. C. Warnes (Lynn B.C.) ; Heavy Weights, T. Parks (Polytechnic B.C.). The A.G. and F. Association's Fencing Championships were held at the 2nd London Rifles' Drill Hall, April 14. B. C. Praed, London Fencing Club, won the Foils Championship, and T. P. Hobbins, of the C.S.R.V., won the Sabres, only five hits being recorded against him. Hobbins was second to Praed in the Foils Championship. The Army Fencing Championship at the Aldershot meeting, September 8 and 9, were won by Captain Edgeworth Johnstone, Royal Irish Regt., for Sabres, and by Captain H. P. Leader, 6th Dragoon Guards, for Foils. Major Hamilton, 6th Dragoon Guards, won the Swords (Mounted) Championship. The Army Boxing Championships were held at Aldershot, September 29-30 and October 2. The Officers' Competitions were won as follow :— Light Weights, Lt. H. H. Tudor, Royal Horse Artillery ; Middle Weights, Lt. R. H. M. C. Miers, 2nd Somerset Light Infantry ; Heavy Weights, Second Lieut. J. W. Ley, 2nd North Staffordshire Regt.

CRICKET.

Many things combined to make the cricket season of 1899 especially notable and interesting. The weather was exceptionally favourable both for the batsmen and for spectators. Another county, Worcestershire, entered for the first time into the charmed circle of the first class counties, and the tenth Australian team came to the old country with the reputation of being the most formidable combination yet opposed to our home cricketing talent. Directly the season began it became apparent that the International matches would quite overshadow the County Championship, and never before has so much interest been taken in Australia v. England matches. It is an open question whether the cricket of the year was of the very highest order notwithstanding the huge aggregate of runs compiled by the leading

batsmen, indeed many excellent judges consider the form of our most prominent players not up to the standard of a few seasons ago, and most certainly with one or two exceptions the bowling was not of a very superior class. Between the three best counties the championship gave most exciting matches towards the end of the season, and there was little to choose between them at the finish. It is to be hoped that no more candidates will be admitted. W. G. Grace after his long and marvellous career practically dropped out of first class cricket, much to the regret of his following of admirers all over the Kingdom. He, however, played in the first test match.

The County Championship worked out as follows :—

		Played.	Won.	Lost.	Drawn.	Points in Finshd. games.	Percentage
1	Surrey	26	16	2	14	8	66·66
2	Middlesex	18	11	3	4	8	57·14
3	Yorkshire	28	14	4	10	18	55·55
4	Lancashire	25	12	6	7	6	18	33·3
5	Sussex	22	7	5	10	2	12	16·16
6	Essex	20	6	6	8	0	12	—
7	Warwick	20	4	5	11	—1	9	—11·11
8	*Kent	19	6	8	5	—2	14	—14·28
9	Gloucester	20	5	8	7	—3	13	—23·07
10	Hampshire	20	5	8	7	—4	12	—33·33
11	Notts	16	2	4	10	—2	6	—33·33
12	Worcester	12	2	5	5	—3	7	—42·85
13	Leicester	18	2	8	8	—6	10	—60·00
14	Somerset	16	2	8	6	—6	10	—60·60
15	Derbyshire	18	2	9	7	—7	11	—63·63

* Exclusive of match at Whitsuntide abandoned without a ball being bowled.

The following table will show at a glance the result of every match in the Championship series.

County.	Derbyshire.	Essex.	Gloucester.	Hampshire.	Kent.	Lancashire.	Leicester.	Middlesex.	Notts.	Somerset.	Surrey.	Sussex.	Warwick.	Worcester.	Yorkshire.
Derbyshire		D	..	L	..	L	D	..	L	..	L	..	D	D	L
		W	..	W	..	L	D		L		L		D	D	L
Essex	L		..	W	..	W	L	D	..		L	W	D	..	L
	W		..	D	..	W	W	W			L	W	D		W
Gloucestershire .	..	W		..	D	L	..	L	D	D	D	W	D	..	..
	D	W		..	W	L	..	L	D	D	W	D	W		..
Hampshire......	L	D	..		..	L	..	..	D	W	L	L	D	D	..
	W	L	..		..	D	D	..	..	W	L	L	D	D	W
Kent	..	L	L	..		..	D	..	..	W	D	W	D	L	W
	..	L	D	..		A	..	L	W	D	L	W	L	..	L
Lancashire	W	D	W	D	A		..	L	D	W	W	L	D	..	..
	W	W	W	W	D		..	W	L	D	L	L	D	..	W
Leicestershire ..	D	L	..	D	..	L		D	..	L	..	L	W	L	..
	D	D	..	D	..	W		L	..	..	L	L	D	L	L
Middlesex	..	..	W	..	W	W	W		L	W	W	W	..	..	..
	..	..	W	..	W	W			W	W	D	L	W		..
Notts.	W	..	D	..	L	D	D			W	W	..	D	W	D
	W		D	..	L	D	D	..		D	D		D		D
Somerset	..	..	W	L	D	W	L	..	L		L	D	D	..	L
	..		W	L	D	W	..	..	D		L	D	D		D
Surrey	W	D	D	W	W	W	W	D	W	D		D	W	D	D
	W	W	W	L	D	W	D	L	D	D		D	W	D	W
Sussex	..	D	L	W	W	L	L	L	D	D	D		..	..	D
	L	L	D	W	W	L	L	L	D	D	D		..		D
Warwickshire ..	D	D	D	D	W	L	W	..	D	D	L	..		W	L
	D	D	D	W	L	W	..	..	D	D	L	..		D	D
Worcestershire ..	W	..	..	D	L	..	W	..	L	..	D	..	L		D
	D	..	L	..	L	..	W	..		..	D	..	D		D
Yorkshire	W	L	W	D	L	W	L	W	D	D	D	D	W	D	
	W	L	..	W	W	W	L	W	D	L	D	D	W	D	

w, won. L, lost. D, drawn. A, abandoned.

From the above tables it will be seen that Surrey has risen from fourth place in 1898 to be champion county once more, a position it has not occupied since 1895. Abel, Brockwell Hayward and Lockwood were answerable between them for a tremendous number of runs, and Abel's average of 64 from 35 innings and a total of 2,124 runs is a performance even that brilliant batsman must be decidedly proud of. Hayward's average with 29 innings is also over 60. Young Vivian Crawford, until his break down, played grand cricket for the county, and the bowling of Lockwood, Hayward and Brockwell, notwithstanding the falling off of Richardson, made the Surrey attack very dangerous indeed. At the commencement of the season Middlesex with six successive victories looked like obtaining the coveted position, but then they suffered defeat from both Notts and Kent. Towards the end of the season Yorkshire looked like retaining their honours, but then a collapse before the bowling of Kent shattered their hopes. Middlesex largely owe their position to the superb bowling of Trott. Their batting was of course weakened by the retirement of A. E. Stoddart but in August, when C. M. Wells and the brothers Douglas were available, the side was exceptionally strong all round. C. M. Wells heads the average of the county with 81·00, but P. F. Warner with 32 innings and an average of 33·4 must be considered a better performance. They had all the best of their two games with the Champions, and Trott, Wells, and Hearne bore the brunt of the bowling. Yorkshire with the heaviest list of engagements of any of the counties and although they did not manage to beat Surrey, Middlesex or Lancashire, were generally considered by good judges to be quite equal to the two counties in front of them on the M.C.C. ruling. F. S. Jackson comes out on top in his county average, and his batting all through the summer was of the most brilliant description. With 25 innings and a highest of 155, his average totals 45·96. Hirst whose average in 38 innings came out with 44 05 was conspicuous for sheer vigorous hard hitting, and Lord Hawke made, as usual, a most efficient captain and contributed several most valuable innings. Rhodes easily headed the bowling average, and with Haigh and Hirst took the brunt of the attack. Lancashire advanced from sixth to fourth place Up to the end of July they had a fair prospect of actually winning the Championship, but the fast wickets of the South at the end of their series of matches rather discounted their previous good form. They were very unlucky to lose Briggs after the Leeds test match when he was seized with a sudden illness which put all the burden of the bowling on to the shoulders of Mold and Cuttell. Ainsworth who headed the bowling averages with 114 overs and 11·94 average proved a great acquisition. Mold with 943 overs averaged 19·34. In the batting Tyldesley with a maximum of 40 innings topped the averages with 41 68 and a best innings for the county of 249. A. C. MacLaren and A. Ward also came out with capital averages. Sussex came with a bound into fifth place, Bland and Tate did most of the bowling, Tate's average being 21·78 with 953 overs. Ranjitsinhji, average 76·16, C. B. Fry, average 42·67, and G. Brann, average 32·21, contributed the bulk of the runs, and these three brilliant batsmen never played better county cricket. Essex goes down one in the list. F. L. Fane heads the batting averages with 61·08, P. Perrin contributing the highest total of runs. A. J. Turner stood second in both the batting and bowling averages, and

Mead with 1,046 overs and 17·12 average topped the bowling both in overs and average. Young and Bull were also most dangerous with the ball. Warwickshire took a very good position in the list for a side undoubtedly weak in bowling, Santall, Dickens and Field having to do nearly all the work with the ball. W. G. Quaife headed the batting averages with 35 innings. 1,480 runs average 54·81. Kent, mostly an amateur team, were rather an uncertain side. They beat Yorkshire, Middlesex, Notts and Sussex to say nothing of the Australians. W. M. Bradley and J. R. Mason took most of the bowling for either heading the averages with 18·77. A. H. Du Boulay, the Woolwich cadet, headed the batting averages with 74·50 but he only played in 6 innings. C. J. Burnup contributed the biggest quota of runs, viz., 1,568 with an average from 34 innings of 44·12. Gloucester without W. G. Grace dropped from third place to ninth although W. Troup made a most enthusiastic and capable captain. C. L. Townsend with nearly 1,700 runs, and seven times exceeding the century, topped the averages with 56·46. G. L. Jessop and F. H. B. Champain, the two varsity captains, played side by side for Gloucestershire and followed Townsend in the averages. Their new bowler Paish did nearly all the work for Gloucestershire and from 1,020 overs averaged 18 93. Hants and Notts tie for tenth place. The Hants season was chiefly remarkable for Major Poore's extraordinary batting, his average working out 116·58 with 16 innings and a grand total of 1,399 runs. Captain E. G. Wynyard comes next with 49·55 as an average. The bowling was weak, Baldwin and Heseltine doing most of the work, no less than 17 bowlers being tried during the season. Notts were weak in bowling, Attewell being off colour and J. Gunn and Wass left to do all the work. Shrewsbury and A. O. Jones with W. Gunn obtained most of the runs, Shrewsbury's record reading 22 innings, runs 1,150 average 56·50. A O Jones stood second on the list with 1,185 runs and an average of 53·85. Worcestershire, the new introduction to the first class counties, certainly did very well, and although only playing 12 matches managed to win two of them, a record which four other counties with a bigger list of engagements could not improve upon. They led off in a brilliant manner by only losing to Yorkshire by 11 runs. The brothers Foster were responsible for most of the runs, and in Wilson the county possesses a capital young professional bowler likely to make a name for himself in the near future. Leicestershire hardly improved upon their previous year's doings. Their best performance was beating Lancashire early in the season. Knight was a long way in front of their batsmen, with 33 innings, runs 1,231, and average 38 45. The bowling was very weak, Geeson having to do most of the work. Somerset with a strong batting team, the list being headed by S. M. J. Woods with 27 innings, 1,110 runs, and an average of 42·69, lost their matches owing to weakness in bowling. Tyler and Gill were chiefly responsible for the wickets taken, but Gill proved rather expensive. Somerset badly missed the services of the Palairets. Derbyshire, the last on the list, could only manage to defeat Essex and Hants. The death of G. Davidson was a most unfortunate blow to their bowling strength, and Hulme, with no one to support him except Bestwick, did nearly all of the work with the ball. Storer and L. G. Wright obtained most of the runs and topped the county batting averages.

S. H. Evershed only played in three innings, and Chatterton was quite out of form.

The Australian team and its doings require to be considered separately from the rest of the English 1899 Cricket season. It is an open question whether the 1899 eleven was or was not the very best one ever sent over here. Previously, the 1882 combination, the only other side which returned home victorious against England had been held up as the strongest Australian combination seen on English grounds, but although the 1882 Australians may have contained more bright particular stars, and more individual players of exceptional brilliancy, last year's lot for all round excellence would be very hard indeed to beat. In support of our argument the 1899 Australian visitors were the only team to leave these shores with only three defeats scored against them, their summary finally standing: matches won, 16; lost, 3; drawn, 16 total, 35 As regards the test matches, increased on this occasion to five as in Australia instead of three as formerly in this country, everyon mustregret that only one was played out to a finish, as the results were most unsatisfactory in the four unfinished drawn games. We were fairly and squarely defeated at Lord's after a very poor display on the part of England. At Nottingham nothing but time saved a second reverse for the home country. At Old Trafford and the Oval we, perhaps, held a slight advantage at the end of the three days' play, and at Leeds, nobody could forecast the probable result had the game been continued to a finish. The totals in the five test matches were:— June 1, 2, 3, Nottingham, Australia 252-230 (eight wickets down, innings declared closed), 482; England 193-155 (seven wickets down), 348—drawn. Lord's, June 15, 16, 17, Australia 421-28 (no wicket down), 449; England 206-240=446; Australia won by ten wickets. June 29-30, Leeds, Australia 172-224= 396; England 220-19 (no wickets down), 239—drawn, rain. Manchester, July 17, 18, 19, Australia 196-346 (seven wickets down, innings declared), 542; England 372-94 (three wickets down), 466—drawn. Oval, August 14, 15, 16, Australia 352-254 (five wickets down), 606; England 1st innings 576—drawn. Although the method of selection could not possibly have been improved upon, it cannot be said that the five English teams to do battle against the Australians gave complete satisfaction. The two elevens in the last, and perhaps the most interesting of all the five test matches were as follows:— England: F. S. Jackson 118, Hayward 137, Ranjitsinhji 54, C. B. Fry 60, A. C. Mac-Laren 49, C L. Townsend 38, W. M. Bradley 0, Lockwood 24, A. O. Jones 31, Lilley 37, Rhodes 16, extras 20=576. Australia, first innings: J Worrall 55, H. Trumble 24, V. Trumper 6. M. A. Noble 9, J. Darling 71, S. E Gregory 117. F. A. Iredale 9, J. J. Kelly 4, C. E. McLeod 31, E. Jones 0, W. P. Howell 4, extras 22=352 Second innings, Worrall 75. Trumble 3, Trumper 7, Noble 69. Darling 6, Gregory 2, McLeod 77, extras 15=254 for five wickets. The following also played for England in the other matches:— G. W. Quaife, Tyldesley, J. T. Hearne, W. G. Grace, Storer, W. Gunn, Young, G. L. Jessop, Mead, J. T. Brown, senior, G. Hirst, Brockwell Briggs played in one match, but did not bat through illness. In these five test matches, the best English batting averages were: Hayward, 7 innings, times not out 1, runs 413, best innings 137, average 68·83; Ranjitsinhji,

innings 8, not out 2, runs 278, best 93 not out, average 46·33; Lilley, average 45·25, with 5 innings; F. S. Jackson, 8 innings, 303 runs, best innings 118, average 43 28; A. C. MacLaren, 6 innings, 164 runs, average 32 80; C. B. Fry, innings 8, average 23 37. In the bowling, Lockwood comes out top: 2 innings, overs 55·3, maidens 24, runs 104, wickets 7, average 14 85; Young, with 111·1 overs, averaged 21·83; J. T. Hearne bowled 199·3 overs, with an average of 24·69; Rhodes, with 147·2 overs, averaged 26·23; and F. S. Jackson. 119·3 overs, averaged 56·80.

In the Test Matches, for the Australians, C. Hill (S.A.) came out at the head of the list of batting averages with—innings 5, not out 0, runs 301, best innings 135, average 60·20. M. A. Noble (N.S.W. was second with 9 innings, not out 2, runs 367, best innings 89, average. 52·42; J. Darling (S.A.) 10 innings, 1 not out, 232 runs, 71 best in an innings. average 25·77. In bowling, F Laver headed the averages with— innings 3, overs 32. maidens 7, runs 70. wickets 4, average 15 70; H Trumble came second with 192·3 overs, 78 maidens, runs 375, wickets 15, average 25·00; E. Jones was third. 255·1 overs, maidens 73, runs 657, wickets 26. average 25·26.

The final Test Match at the Oval was a magnificent display of cricket, in perfect weather, and with a tremendous attendance, the paying public for the three days numbering 18,000, 20,000, and 10,000 respectively. An attempt was made to arrange for this, the last match, to be played out to a finish. The Australians were quite willing, but the county engagement of the English players absolutely prevented this most desirable result. Another time when the Australians visit us again, most certainly arrangements for the Test Matches should include the possibility of five days being required to complete some of the games. As regards the whole tour of the Australians, which, owing to the weather, must have been a very big financial success, they sailed from Adelaide on March 23 in the *Ormuz*, and arrived in England towards the end of April. They began with a match against the South of England at the Crystal Palace. The English side was a strong one, but had the match been played out, Australia would certainly have won. The next venture against Essex, resulted in a defeat, and perhaps chiefly owing to Young's bowling, the Australians were beaten by 126 runs. Their following engagement conclusively proved their mettle, and by smashing Surrey by an innings and 71 runs, the visiting team at once established themselves as a most dangerous combination. It was in this match that Howell, the new bowler, played for the first time. and his feat of capturing the whole of Surrey's ten wickets for only 28 runs was one not easily forgotten. Surrey had their revenge in the return match, winning by 104 runs, in July, and at Canterbury, just before the final Test Match, Kent got the best of them by two wickets. The M C C (twice), Lancashire, Oxford University Past and Present, Cambridge University. Gloucestershire, Derbyshire, Leicestershire, Warwickshire, Middlesex, amongst the counties, were all defeated in turn. They were a very strong batting side, even without C. Hill, undoubtedly their best bat, who was not available for a considerable portion of the tour. Their fielding could hardly have been surpassed, and their bowling was always equal to any calls made upon it, and in J. Darling they had a captain who never made a mistake, and inspired the most thorough confidence in his men. They sailed for home before the end of September, and their manager, Major B. J. Wardill, must have been most thoroughly satisfied with the trip and its results.

Taking the year as a whole, the averages in first class cricket given below speak for themselves and they give a record of unprecedented scoring owing to the weather and the Australian fixtures. The batsmen had exceptional opportunities to add to the aggregates of their runs, but even apart from these advantages the all-round rise in averages is remarkable. Indeed, the big totals of runs caused plenty of suggestions, that the bat had too great a pull over the ball, and that the measurements of the bat or the wicket would have to be altered to meet the position. We fancy, however, that another season will prove that no such drastic measures need be taken. To come to figures. Scores exceeding 100 have been made in no less than 223 instances as compared with 151 in 1896. Abel's 357 not out for Surrey against Somerset tops the list, and then follow Major Poore 304, not out (hence his wonderful average), and V. Trumper, 300 not out. There were ten scores exceeding 200. No fewer than five players aggregated 2 000 runs, viz. Ranjitsinhji 3,159 (a record), Hayward 2,647, Abel 2,685, C. L. Townsend 2,440, C. B. Fry 2,366. In 1897 and 1898 only Abel reached 2,000 runs, and in 1896 only three, Ranjitsinhji, W. G. Grace and Abel, totalled the double thousand. Ranji's total is all the more remarkable because he was not helped by any exceptional innings and his runs always came when they were most wanted. Major Poore's performance makes it a matter of regret that he was not more often able to take part in first-class cricket. Hayward quite equalled the great expectations formed of this sterling batsman's merits. C. L. Townsend performed the W. G. Grace feat of making 2,000 runs and taking 100 wickets. W. G Quaife has not played up to his previous year's form. In the bowling, Trott with 1,772 overs and 239 wickets, to say nothing of his 1,175 runs from the bat, has set up a performance not very easy to equal. Rhodes has done remarkably well and Mead and Bradley were both reliable and even. J. T. Hearne is a long way under his last year's extraordinary average, and certainly did not do himself justice. W. G. Grace having retired from Gloucestershire cricket, after four matches, is very low down on the list, and for the great champion batsman of the age only to make a total of 515 runs and a best innings of 78 is indeed a remarkable occurrence. His new club at the Crystal Palace has not yet taken the high place in first-class cricket it was expected to do, but it may do so yet in the near future.

The leading batting averages of the year in all the first class matches were as follows:— Major R. M. Poore, 21 innings, 1,551 runs, highest score 304, not out 4, average 91·23; C. M Wells, 11 innings, 523 runs, highest 244, not out 3, average 65·37; K. S. Ranjitsinhji, 58 innings, 3,159 runs, highest 197, not out 8, average 63 18; Hayward, 49 innings, 2,647 runs, highest 273, not out 4, average 58·82; Abel, 53 innings, 2,685 runs, highest 357*, not out 3, average 53 70; Shrewsbury, 26 innings, 1,257 runs, highest 175, not out 2, average 52·37; C. L. Townsend, 54 innings, 2,410 runs, highest 224*, not out 7, average 51·91 F. L. Fane, 16 innings, 746 runs, highest 207, not out 0, average 46·62; P. Perrin, 36 innings, 1,491 runs, highest 196, not out 4, average 46·59;

F. S. Jackson, 44 innings, 1,847 runs, highest 155, not out 2, average 45·04 ; A. O. Jones, 38 innings, 1,603 runs, highest 250, not out 2, average 44·69; W. G. Quaife, 48 innings, 1,703 runs, highest 207*, not out 9, average 43·66 ; C. B. Fry, 55 innings, 2,356 runs, highest 181, not out 1, average 43·62; J. T. Brown, sen., 35 innings, 1,443 runs, highest 192, not out 1, average 47 44. Capt. E. G. Wynyard, 32 innings, 1,281 runs, highest 225, not out 1 average 41 32 ; V F S Crawford, 10 innings, 330 runs, highest 129 not out 2, average 41·25 S. M. J. Woods, 33 innings, 1,291 runs, highest 146, not out 1, average 40 34 A. J. Turner, 22 innings, 804 runs, highest 124, not out 2, average 40 20 C. J. Burnup, 42 innings, 1,565 runs, highest 171, not out 3, average 40·12 ; A. J. L. Hill, 18 innings, 672 runs, highest 168, not out 1, average 39 52 Also the following well-known men's averages were :—Tyldesley, 50 innings, 1,882 runs, highest 249, not out 2, average 39·20; C. A. Bernard, 24 innings, 847 runs, highest 94, not out 1, average 38·82; Hirst, 53 innings, 1,630 runs, highest 186, not out 7, average 35·43; Storer, 50 innings, 1,507 runs, highest 2 6*, not out 7, average 35·04; G. L. Jessop, 46 innings, 1,483 runs, highest 171*, not out 2, average 33·70; Brockwell, 48 innings, 1,542 runs, highest 167, not out 2, average 33·52; Denton, 50 innings, 1,595 runs, highest 113, not out 2, average 33·22; F. Mitchell, 56 innings, 1,748 runs, highest 194, not out 1, average 31·78 ; A. Hearne, 49 innings, 1,378 runs, highest 168, not out 5, average 31·31 ; Wainwright, 51 innings, 1,541 runs, highest 228, not out 1, average 30·82. Tunnicliffe, 53 innings, 1,434 runs, highest 85, not out 4, average 29·26 ; W. G. Grace, 23 innings, 515 runs, highest 78, not out 1, average 23·40.

* signifies not out.

The bowling averages were :—

	Overs.	Maidens.	Runs.	Wickets.	Average.
I'Anson	50	17	120	11	10·90
Woodcock	208·3	58	474	32	14·81
Griffin	119	41	217·4	14	15·50
J. L. Ainsworth	146	56	289	18	16 05
Trott	1772·4	587	4,080	239	17·09
Rhodes	1518·4	543	3,062	179	17·10
Mead	1378·2	515	2,634	146	18·04
Paish	1095·4	304	2,540	137	18·54
Mold	966·4	299	2,149	115	18 68
W. M. Bradley	1258	414	2,881	156	19·10
Briggs	667·1	247	1,150	60	19·16
Lockwood	860·3	228	2,284	117	19·52
J. R. Mason	795·3	319	1,635	83	19·69
J. T. Brown, jun.	431·4	121	1,133	57	19·89
C. M. Wells	217·3	64	459	23	19·95

Also we may notice—

F. W. Tate	1164·1	403	2,598	121	21·47
J. T. Hearne	1397·4	542	2,703	124	21·77
Cuttell	1132 3	476	1,961	90	21 78
Young	1250	382	3,030	139	21·79
Hayward	536·4	112	1,534	67	22 89
J. Gunn	584·1	156	1,290	56	23·3
C. B. Fry	84	23	261	11	23 72
W. G. Grace	214	66	482	20	24·10
Baldwin	1006	337	2.205	79	27·91
C. L. Townsend	1052·1	181	2,936	101	29·06
K. S. Ranjitsinhji	402 2	108	1,047	36	29 08

The first of the Gentlemen *v.* Players' matches at the Oval, in the Universities week, was certainly not really representative of the two classes. The Players, however, put up a huge total in their first innings, viz., 647; April 195, Hayward not out 134, Lockwood 84, Storer 53, being the biggest contributions to the aggregate. The Gentlemen contributed 303 and 308, being thus beaten easily. On the losing side the best scores were :—C. L. Townsend not out 112, A. G. Jones 71, W. G. Grace 28. In the second innings, B. J. T. Bosanquet 61, W. G. Grace 60, D. L. A. Jephson 59, were the chief items. Nine bowlers were tried on the Gentlemen's side, Townsend taking the lion's share. For the Players, Mead, Young and Brockwell, had most of the bowling. Strange to say, the return match was also a one innings victory, but this time for the Gentlemen. They totalled in their one effort 480 runs, Fry 104, W. G. Grace, 78, J R. Mason 72, C. L. Townsend 46, being the chief contributors. The Players' totals were 196 and 225, Hayward 77, Storer not out 44, Hirst 33, being the leading scorers. Major Poore, who played in both matches was not a success, and Ranji, in the Lord's match, did not come up to his usual quantum of runs. Bradley and Jephson did nearly all the bowling for the Gentlemen, and Lockwood, Trott, Rhodes and Mead were the chief exponents with the ball for the Players. It is, perhaps, curious that with such a tremendous amount of bowling talent the Players did not do better. The Eton v. Harrow match added another draw to the long list of 15, previously recorded in the history of this fashionable function. It must always be so with only two days' play on a good wicket and in fine weather. Eton put up 274 in their first innings against 283 for Harrow, Eton then made 264, and having only lost two wickets. H. R. Longman 81, and F. O. Grenfell 81, declared their innings closed. Harrow went in and added 133 for five wickets. The best scores for Eton in the first innings were:—O. C. S. Gilliat 53. H. K. Longman 14, and J. Wormald 43 For Harrow: E. M. Dowson not out 87, H. J. Wyld 57, E. W. Mann 41, were the chief batsmen. Dowson for Harrow and E. G Martin and A. C Barnard for Eton shared the brunt of the bowling. One of the most remarkable incidents of an exciting season was the performance of A. E. J. Collins, who, June 28, in a Junior House match, at Clifton College, compiled the greatest score ever made by an individual player, viz., 628 not out. He was batting for six hours and fifty minutes, his innings being continued in unequal instalments during five days. The previous best was 485 by A. E. Stoddart, in a club match. The Oxford v. Cambridge match, at Lord's, ended in a draw. Oxford were supposed to be the better side owing to their bowling being decidedly stronger than that of the Light Blues. The first day of the match was gloomy, but on the Tuesday and Wednesday, June 4th and 5th, the weather was perfect. Oxford went in first and scored 192, Cambridge followed with 241 ; 62 by S. H. Day, being the best score. Oxford in their second innings compiled 347; F. P. Knox not out 73, R. H. de Montmorency 62 and H. C. Pilkington 93, being the best individual totals. Cambridge only had 2¾ hours to make 299 runs, and when stumps were drawn their total was 229, four wickets only having fallen, and S. H. Day 50 and T. L. Taylor 52 both being not out. G. L. Jessop did most of the bowling for Cambridge, and S. H. End and E. R. Wilson also assisting ; F. W. Stocks and B. J. T. Bosanquet chiefly bowled for Oxford.

In the spring of the year Lord Hawke was touring in South Africa with a fairly strong team, and after the English season Ranjitsinhji, with an eleven, played a few matches in the United States. During the year a new rule was passed, giving more powers to the umpires in regard to "no balls," and the M.C.C. Committee have also recommended the following alterations in the laws of the game—(1) Six balls to constitute an over, (2) declaration permissible at or after the luncheon time on the second day, (3) the side that leads by 150 runs in a three days' match, 100 runs in a two days' match, or 75 runs in a one day match, shall have the option of calling on the other side to follow its innings.

CYCLING.

THAT cycling, as an amusement and recreation, still further increased in popularity during 1899, almost goes without saying, but as a racing sport it certainly did not add to its attractions, indeed public interest both in amateur and professional cycle racing, declined to such a degree in England, that cycle meetings pure and simple were very few and far between, and even these were anything but money-making speculations. By judicious selection of venues, the National Cyclists Union managed to ensure their Championships at New Brighton (on June 10), Guernsey (July 20), and Reading (September 23), being both successful and profitable, and on a Bank Holiday with a good mixed programme, an athletic and cycling meeting combined can and will draw a very big gate, but even the Union's own official organ recently confessed that "cycling as a sport has to some extent ceased to attract votaries both practical and spectacular." There are any number of reasons put forward for this state of things, but no doubt "loafing," "dishonest racing," and restrictive pacing legislation have most seriously affected the sport, and also that motor cycles with faster records than the man-driven machines have lowered the interest in the further pace development of the modern safety bicycle. Whatever may be the cause, the fact remains that amateur cycle racing nowadays is at a very low ebb, and that our best professional riders have either taken to motors or else gone on the Continent, where there is still plenty of money to be picked up. The National Cyclists Union, Offices, Lonsdale Chambers, 27 Chancery Lane, E.C., with a membership of 70,000, through its individual roll and affiliated clubs controls the sport in a most thorough and effectual manner, too thorough some people are inclined to suggest. The Union during the season promulgated a set of rules and regulations for bicycle polo, drafted very much on the so-called Irish rules. The possibilities of this game in reviving interest in cycling meetings are immense. The Union also wisely appear willing to hand over the government of motor racing to the Automobile Club, Offices, 4 Whitehall Court, London, S.W., whenever the latter body prepare a reasonable code of rules acceptable to the various governing bodies of amateur sport. The Cyclist Touring Club, with a membership of about 60,000, celebrated its coming of age during the summer. Motor pacing in the matter of road records, notably when F. R. Goodwin covered 245 miles in 12 hours, on September 1, caused the police on the North roads districts to practically put a stop to these clearly illegal practices by fining the riders heavily. On July 31, E. Hale, a well-known rider, commenced a year's ride of 100 miles per diem, Sundays being excluded. At the end of the year, he is stated to be going well but— *cui bono?* As usual, two big shows were held in November at the Agricultural Hall and the Crystal Palace, motors being a very conspicuous feature in both places.

At the end of 1898 came the news from New York that C. Miller, of Chicago, a German had won the Six Days Race at Maddison Square, New York, with a world's record of 2,007 miles. The general surroundings of this contest were so objectionable that the race is unlikely to be repeated under similar conditions. In England, the cycling year commenced with the coming-of-age dinner of the National Cyclist Union at the Trocadero, on March 24, with the Right Hon. Mr. A. J. Balfour, M.P., the president, in the chair. The function was a big success, and well worthy of the occasion. The racing season proper in England began as usual with the historic spring fixture of the Surrey Bicycle Club, at Kennington Oval, on April 8. The turf lap was quite spoilt by the heavy rains of the previous day, and the attendance suffered by reason of a drenching downpour just before the time fixed for the start. There was plenty of racing of a sort, but the class of the men competing was not quite up to Surrey form, and the times of course were slow. The mile handicap fell to E. J. Bass, 120 yds., in 2 mins. $38\frac{1}{5}$ secs., all the men in the final coming from the long-start brigade. The same thing happened in the half mile, F. Battersby, 75 yds., winning in 1 min 23 secs. The Half Mile Sydney Challenge Cup Trophy was carried off by a well-known rider, I. M. Bourke, in 1 min $38\frac{3}{5}$ secs. E. J. Callaghan in the previous autumn had won outright the sixth Ten Miles Challenge Cup. The Club, therefore, started a new trophy, the seventh. Callaghan, on some question of a licence, did not start. The best-known men Bourke, A. J. Cherry, H. W. Payne, and F. Burnand did not seem to like the heavy going, and a sturdy Bedford rider, A. Gell, won a rather stiff finish from C. A. Sedgwick in the very slow time of 33 mins. $53\frac{3}{5}$ secs. On April 23, in Paris, at the Prince's track at Auteuil, half-a-dozen professionals contested a fifty kilometres race, motor pacing alone being employed, T. Linton, A. E. Walters, Taylor, Champion, &c., were all engaged. Linton won rather easily, and the time for the distance, slightly over 31 miles, viz., 55 mins. $30\frac{3}{5}$ secs., a record, proved conclusively that motor pacing would give a new list of records during the season then commencing. On April 29, the powerful Polytechnic Cycling Club held a meeting at the Wood Green track, wet spoiling the attendance. Strange to say, not one single professional event was included in the programme. The amateurs, however, turned out in force. There were 30 entries for the One Mile Rucker Trophy, loafing tactics being strongly in evidence. A. S. Ingram, first, F. Burnand, and A. J. Cherry was the order of the final. Ingram winning for the second time after a very close finish in 3 mins. $8\frac{4}{5}$ secs., comment on the pace is needless. In the quarter mile handicap, R. J. Core, 50 yds., won in $28\frac{1}{5}$ secs.; J. E. Wells, 40 yds., won the half mile handicap from W. Holton, 20 yds., in 1 min. $10\frac{2}{5}$ secs.; and a one mile invitation tandem race fell to A. S. Ingram and R. Janson in 3 mins. $8\frac{4}{5}$ secs. On May 6, the Catford C.C. put a splendid programme before the public, containing amateur and professional events and motor pacing, but the attendance was very poor although the weather was perfect. A half mile professional handicap was won by W. T. Hall, 65 yds., in $57\frac{3}{5}$ secs. A one mile amateur handicap fell to A. Reed, 140 yds., in 2 mins. $5\frac{2}{5}$ secs. A third of a mile amateur level race, a miserable crawl, was won by A. S. Ingram in 1 min. $15\frac{3}{5}$ secs. Ingram and Janson, 20 yds., won a two mile amateur tandem handicap in 4 mins. 34 secs.; the time speaks for itself. Platt Betts and R. Palmer with motor pacing, engaged in a ten miles pursuit race, Betts winning with the better pacing in 19 mins. $39\frac{1}{5}$ secs. A one mile pursuit race, the men starting on opposite sides of the track, was won by T. J. Gascoyne beating J. Green in 2 mins. $8\frac{3}{5}$ secs. F. W. Chinn won a ten miles professional race, with sixteen starters, in 25 mins $4\frac{2}{5}$ secs. On May 7, in Paris, the Princes Park track saw the decision of a 100 kilometres race, Taylor winning in 1 hour 53 mins. $15\frac{1}{5}$ secs., Huret being second. In the same week, Taylor, mechanically paced, put on new records from 20 kilos up to 50 miles, the full time being 1 hour 28 mins. $34\frac{1}{5}$ secs., well inside the previous figures. Also in the same week, at Berlin, A. E. Walters won a 100 kilometres race in 2 hours 2 mins. $7\frac{3}{5}$ secs., and at Roubaix, Miller, of Chicago, won the 100 hours race by 30 miles with a score of 1,403 miles. In the following week, Taylor, in Paris, rode 100 kilometres in 1 hour 57 mins. $10\frac{1}{5}$ secs., and as a proof of the value of motor pacing J. Dupuy, a French amateur, under these conditions covered 51 kilos. 438 metres, or nearly 32 miles in the hour. No English amateur up to that time had ridden 30 miles in the hour. The English N.C.U. very wisely refusing to allow mechanical pacing in amateur events. On May 13 and 15, the Northern C.C. on the Celtic track, at Glasgow, held a big mixed meeting, T. Summersgill, J. Caldow, and T. Goss being the most successful of the amateurs, and J. Green and Bourillon, the Frenchman, amongst the professionals. In London on the Saturday, at Wood Green, A. J. Cherry beat A. S. Ingram in a five miles scratch race in 13 mins. $31\frac{3}{5}$ secs. On the Whit Monday Bank Holiday, no less than three big meetings were held in the Metropolitan district. At Wood Green, A. J. Cherry, 20 yds., won a one mile amateur handicap, in 2 mins. $19\frac{2}{5}$ secs. In a five miles amateur race, A. S. Ingram just beat A. J. Cherry in 12 mins. $50\frac{3}{5}$ secs., and H. B. Howard accounted for a ten miles profesional unpaced scratch race in 26 mins. $1\frac{3}{5}$ secs., and the same rider also won a pursuit race of five miles. At Catford, the handicaps were neither interesting nor fast, but P. W. Brown won a ten mile race in 24 mins. $51\frac{3}{5}$ secs. A bicycle polo match under Irish rules was by no means the least interesting portion of the programme. At the Crystal Palace, motor cycle racing was the attraction. A ten miles race, Class A., C. Jarrolt won in 21 mins. $43\frac{4}{5}$ secs., and in class B., in a twenty miles race, C. G. Wridgway won in 35 mins. $27\frac{1}{5}$ secs. In a match for the Century Cup, E. Bouhours, paced by motors, easily defeated Platt Betts in 1 hour 54 mins. 35 secs. for the distance about 62 miles. Most of the professionals, Reynolds, F. W. Chinn, Palmer, Chase, and Gascoyne, were competing at Aston Lower Grounds, near Birmingham, but rain and wet rather spoilt the times and performances. On May 27-28, the annual French road race from Bordeaux to Paris, of 594 kilometres (about 369 miles) was decided, and the pacing by large motors of practically unlimited speed resulted in the record being reduced by about four hours. The first time the race was held as an amateur contest,

G. P. Mills, the Englishman, won in 26 hour 34 mins. 57 secs. The 1899 contest was won by C. Huret in the remarkable time of 16 hours 35 mins. 47 secs., Fischer being second in 17 hours 21 mins. 26 secs., Rivierre, the previous holder of the record, was fourth, Cordang met with an accident early in the race and retired. On June 4, an attempt was made to revive the Hampton Court Meet, but the result was a dismal failure. On the same day, at New Brighton, on a three lap to the mile cement track, F. W. Chinn beat J. Green in a half mile in 1 min. 15⅕ secs., and Platt Betts beat Chinn in a five miles race in 11 mins. 49⅕ secs. Motor paced records were attempted by Betts, Palmer, and A. A. Chase, but all failed. At the same venue, on the following Saturday, the first batch of the N.C.U. championships were decided. The day was fine, there was no wind, and some 6,000 spectators were present. There were two amateur and four professional events. Loafing once more spoilt the racing. There were 23 in for the amateur mile, P. Albert the German, winner of the International amateur mile at Vienna, in 1898, was left in the final heat with T. Summersgill and J. Brooks. Albert won in 2 mins. 32⅗ secs., from Summersgill second; 2 mins. 25⅗ secs. was the best time done in any heat. The same two men were first and second in the amateur quarter, Albert again winning by a length in 29⅘ secs. The professional events were very poorly supported, only eight riders being engaged in four races. S. Jenkins won the one mile easily in 2 mins. 24⅘ secs from J. Green and T. J. Gascoigne. J. Green won the quarter-mile in 33⅕ secs. from F. W. Chinn and S. Jenkins in the order named. The same eight men started in the five miles, S. Jenkins being first in 12 mins. 39⅗ secs., with J. Green second and H. B. Howard third. Three pairs went for the tandem championship two miles—but they went so slowly that the time limit was exceeded and the race declared void. Previous to the racing the N.C.U. held a council meeting at Liverpool. Financially the position of the Union was most satisfactory the previous year's working showing a profit and the assets largely exceeding the liabilities. It was also very wisely decided to do away with the tandem championships after 1899. Before the end of the month Oxford University defeated the London Bicycle Club at Sheen House, winning the one and ten miles with D. Ritchie in 2 mins. 39⅕ secs. and 28 mins. 45⅕ secs. respectively, and the veteran L. Stroud won the four miles for the L.B.C. in 12 mins. 24⅕ secs. In Scotland at the Powderhall track Edinburgh J. Caldow won the ten miles amateur championship of Scotland in 26 mins. 39⅗ secs., and at Glasgow, Palmer, Platt Betts, and A. A. Chase made several attempts on records behind motors. In this month T. B. Marchant was unfortunately killed on the cement track at Herne Hill, a fall fracturing his skull. On the last Saturday in June the first All England Bicycle Polo Championship was decided at Sheen House, Sheen House (A team, four riders) winning the cup and medals in the final heat from the Royal Engineers (A team). Seven teams entered. On the same day at Wood Green, a five miles scratch race fell to H. W. Payne in 13 mins. 40⅘ secs., and Tommaselli an Italian, won the Grand Prix wheel race in Paris with a first prize of £32. Jaap Eden, Bourillon and Jacquelin were all defeated in previous rounds: Myers, a Dutchman was second. The time was 4 mins. 12⅗ secs. On July 1st the annual meeting between Oxford and Cambridge took place at Sheen House. The events, as usual, were one, four, and ten miles, each race being decided separately by points. All three events fell to Oxford on points, although P. Engleheart, Cambridge, won the one mile in 2 mins. 33 secs., and the ten miles in 26 mins. 4 secs. L. Martin, of Oxford, won the four miles in 11 mins. 17⅗ secs., Engleheart being second. On the same day, at Wood Green, H. W. Payne won the one mile Middlesex championship in 3 mins. 43⅘ secs.—how fast! and A. J. Cherry won a Middlesex twenty-five miles in 1 hour 5 mins. 1 sec. A veteran, C. B. Lawes, the old Cambridge stroke of 1865, at Canning Town about this time, with pacers — not motors — made three new amateur records during the last week of June, viz., 6 miles, 12 mins. 13⅗ secs., 11 miles, 22 mins. 22⅕ secs. and 12 miles, 24 mins. 25⅕ secs., and a crazy American is stated to have ridden one mile behind a locomotive in 57 secs. in the States the record however is doubtful. July 8th saw several very interesting events decided. At Sheen House the Amateur Cycling Association, not a very energetic body, held two championships, I. M. Bourke, of the United Hospitals winning them both. The one mile he took in 3 mins. 20 secs., H. B. Fitzherbert the Oxonian, being a dead heat with A. H. Bennett for second place. The ten miles Bourke carried off in 25 mins. 49⅗ secs., F. A. K. Stuart being second. So far the A.C.A. has not done very much to foster and improve genuine amateur racing. At the Crystal Palace F. C. Crowley won the 100 miles Carwardine Cup of the Anerley Bicycle Club in 3 hours 44 mins. 45⅗ secs. At Wood Green a big professional meeting and motor pacing, attracted nobody, and in a match between Platt Betts and Palmer both fell, Betts being again damaged. Just previously Betts had been riding so well that behind a motor at the Palace he tied the world's record for a flying mile in 1 min. 31⅗ secs. On the following day, at Auteuil, for the Bol d'Or the 24 hours' competition A. E. Walters, paced by motor tandems, put up the world's record of 1,020 kilometres 977 metres or nearly 634½ miles, in that period, his intermediate time being 100 miles 3 hours 13 mins. 12⅗ secs., 200 miles, 6 hours 48 mins. 53⅗ secs., and 300 miles 10 hours 27 mins. 15 secs. Cordang's previous record of 616 miles at the Crystal Palace was done with the aid of windsails. Directly afterwards, another notable performance took place in the same Parc des Princes track, Renaux riding a motor for one hour against time, and covering 61 kilometres 797 metres, about 38½ miles, in the period, the times being records from the tenth kilometre. The N.C.U.'s second instalment of championships came off on Thursday, July 20th, at Guernsey. The two events decided were the five and twenty-five miles for amateurs. A. S. Ingram won the five miles with I. M. Bourke second in the miserable time of 14 mins. 41⅕ secs. Nine men started for the twenty-five miles. A. J. Moore led at the last bend, but then the holder, H. W. Payne, went by and won fairly easily in 1 hour 11 mins. 15⅗ secs. For a small place like Guernsey the attendance of 4,000 spectators was remarkably good. Before the end of the month motor paced road record riding began in earnest. On the 19th F. R. Goodwin put on fresh figures from London to Edinburgh viâ York. From the G.P.O., London, to York he did the 199 miles in 10 hours 16 mins., 32 minutes better than Hunt's previous best behind tandems, and the Edinburgh time was 25 hours 26 mins for the 395 miles, as against Hunt's 26 hours 46 mins. Owing to a serious disagreement with the National Cyclist Union the Surrey Bicycle Club were unable to hold their usual autumn fixture at the Oval, and thus another genuine amateur race meeting followed the London County at Herne Hill, and dropped out of the list. This year that magnificently termed International Cyclist Association held their race meeting at Montreal, Canada, August 9th, 10th, and 12th Although so far away from Europe, the sport was good, and the attendances large. The amateur one mile championship in the final heat was left to T. Summersgill, England, E. Peabody, United States, and J. Caldow, Scotland. A miserable crawl and then a rush for the finish saw Summersgill the winner by a yard from Peabody, in the wretched time of 5 mins. 43⅗ secs. This may be scientific, but it is not racing. The 100 kilometres amateur championship on the second day, with motor pacing allowed, was won by J. A. Nelson (United States; he was the only man able to afford proper motor pacing, and he won by several miles from B. Goodson (Australia) and G. W. Riddle (Canada) in 2 hours 4 mins. 13⅕ secs. These two only had human pacemakers, and the fiasco of Vienna in 1898 in the way of pacing was repeated here. The coloured rider, Major Taylor (United States), won the one mile professional championship from T Butler (United States) in 3 mins. 3 secs. The professional 100 kilometres championship fell to H. Gibson in 2 hours 15 mins. 11⅘ secs. from a small field, the pacing being most unsatisfactory. The one mile match between the professional and amateur mile champions once more produced a fiasco, the nigger claiming a big fee to start, which not being forthcoming, Summersgill rode over, and yet some people consider amateur and professional cycle riding should be generally mixed up. The 1900 International Meeting is fixed to take place in Paris. On Saturday, September 2nd, the Catford C.C. Gold Vase was again put up for competition. As in previous years the professionals were not anxious to possess it, it reverted back to the amateurs last season, but the 100 miles contest was not too exciting, and W. B. Dudden won by two miles in 3 hours 52 mins. 55 secs. On the following Saturday, at the Crystal Palace, another rather ancient trophy, the Anchor Shield, after being in abeyance for four years, was once more put up for competition by the Anerley B C. It was a twelve hours contest for amateurs, and finally E. S Montgomery won by eleven miles, putting up a new record of 267 miles 400 yards. On the same day at the Oval, S.L.H. Autumn Meeting, a scratch five miles race was won by W. Holton, of the Putney A.C., in 14 mins 47⅖ secs. The last instalment of N.C.U. championships were decided at Palmer Park, Reading, September 23. The fifty miles went to G. F. Payne, of the West Roads C.C., in the slow time of 2 hours 3 mins. 36⅘ secs., and A. S. Ingram and R Janson, of the Polytechnic C.C, won the last of the series of tandem championships in 5 mins. 4⅕ secs. Finally, a weary and uninteresting English season concluded with the Amateur Cycling Association's fifty miles championship, at Sheen House. In the previous year the race was a terrible fiasco, and this season I. McW. Bourke, the hon. sec of the Association, won it by four yards in 2 hours 5 mins. 15⅗ secs., but the second man, P. Engleheart, the Cantab, lodged an objection for a foul early in the race, and Bourke was disqualified. The history of the records of the year is a very tangled skein, what with paced, unpaced, flying, and standing starts, motor-paced, cycle-paced, road, grass, and track records, singles, tandems, tricycles, &c. With motor pacing the whole of the world's records have been altered from those of 1898, and English riders, except Walters, have not very much to do with these figures. Before the lists came to be finally made up, some of the earlier performances were as follows, all being made under motor-pacing conditions. On the Auteuil track, in a hundred miles race, M. Bauge covered 50 miles in 1 hour 28 mins. 12⅕ secs., and 100 miles in 3 hours 7 mins. 47⅕ secs, the last remained, and is now a world's record. E Taylor, a French professional, then rode 56 kilos 966 metres or 35 miles 698 yards in one hour. Also on the Auteuil track Osmond, on a motor cycle, covered 62 kilometres 841 metres, or just over 39 miles in one hour. In the States, T. Linton rode 10 miles in 16 mins 29⅗ secs., and Pierce rode five miles in 8 mins. 2⅘ secs. J. Green, at the Palace, rode a standing start mile in · min 4⅗ secs., also placing the quarter, half, and three-quarter records to his credit en route. Platt Betts also scored flying-start quarter (21⅕ secs.), and ditto half-mile (44⅘ secs.). On the August Bank Holiday, for the Century Cup, at the Crystal Palace, E. Bouhours, motor-paced, defeated R. Palmer, the distance being 100 kilometres, or 62 miles 246 yards, and the time, a record, 1 hour 48 mins. 50⅘ secs. On the same day and place S. F. Edge, in a one hour's motor race, covered the distance of 35 miles 1,026 yards. A full list of world's records will be found in our record tables, but it may be mentioned that H. Elkes only just missed beating E. Taylor's one hour record owing to an accident in the last half-minute when in front of Taylor's time. Up to one mile there is no doubt Major Taylor, the black, is the fastest rider in the world. From six to twenty-four hours A. E. Walters tops the tree, as very grave doubts are cast on Cordang's latest whole day performance. In fact, all these record-cutting feats are open to more or less suspicion, with the possibilities of slight mistakes in track measurement, lap scoring, and time keeping. Perhaps the most wonderful record of the year came on October 9th, when, on the Auteuil track, Beconnais, on a motor tricycle, rode 67 kilometres 901 metres, 42 miles 337 yards, in one hour. Yet this is certain to be beaten in 1900.

FOOTBALL.

Football under both codes had nothing to complain about in 1899 as regards gates, popularity, and prominence in the newspapers, but that the premier winter pastime improved as a healthy and pure sport is very doubtful. The Association game has long ago resolved itself into a money-producing exhibition, with the result that possibly the standard of play is higher than formerly owing to the fact that it pays better now-a-days to be a first-class footballer than say a skilled mechanic But the genuine amateur player is gradually leaving the game owing to its demoralising associations, and hockey, golf, and lacrosse, are rapidly drawing away from football its best and most valuable exponents. The Upas-tree of Northern Union professionalism is killing the best interests of the Rugby Union in the North of England, and it is entirely owing to this that England and Wales have both been beaten by Ireland and Scotland, where the professional is unknown and the true amateur and the public school boy can indulge in the splendid pastime without any imputation of other motives beyond healthy exercise and sport-loving instincts. This may be rather a pessimistic view to take of the noble game as now practised, but, except at International and the very best clubs' Rugby matches, the same class of spectators do not attend the grounds as formerly, and in the Association League and Cup ties abusing referees and insulting the other officials is the usual and ordinary amusement of the crowds which Saturday after Saturday surround the various fields of play in the North, the Midlands and the South. These things are no secret and must be well known to everyone who is in the habit of attending big football matches in any part of the country.

The English Rugby season of 1899 was a distinct failure from the International Matches side of the question, England losing all three games, and showing a distinctly inferior style of play as regards the form of Scotland, Ireland, and Wales. This is the first time on record that such a thing has occurred, and the reasons for the utter rout of the English players are not far to seek. Forward play, as it used to be known at Rugby, Clifton, Marlborough, and our leading nurseries of the game, has undergone a complete change. The introduction of four three-quarter backs, and an attempt to copy the Welsh mechanism and heeling out, have together quite done away with the hard, dashing scrummaging of the old style of forwards. Nobody could accuse Vassall's celebrated Oxford fifteen of want of science, but Vassall was always a firm believer in the forwards playing for all they were worth, leaving the backs to make their own openings and look after themselves. One reason why the English team was a weak one was because the two 'Varsities were below their usual strength, and whenever this is the case, an English fifteen is certain to be moderate. Also there were no individually brilliant players at half or three-quarters. The first trial match of the season at Richmond, on November 30, saw the Combined Universities beaten by London by two goals and a try to one goal and one try, Rotherham, P. Stout, P. Royds, and Gamlin all playing splendidly. The first North v. South match at Bristol, on December 17, ended in a victory for the South by a penalty goal and a try to one try. The first International, Wales v. England, at Swansea, on January 7, was a regular smashing defeat for England by no less than four goals and two tries to a try. The brothers James, the Welsh halves, completely out-manœuvred Rotherham and Livesay, and with the English pack demoralised, the Welsh combination tactics were worked to perfection. On March 4, at Dublin, the English fifteen remodelled, were completely non-plussed by the dashing, hard play of the Irish forwards, and Ireland won by a penalty goal and a try to nil. A second North v. South match, at Newcastle, on February 25, gave another victory for the South by a goal and two tries to nil, a good many countrymen being played for the South. The last International match, England v. Scotland, was played at Blackheath on March 11. The sides were:—England—H. T. Gamlin (Somerset), back; E. F. Fookes (Yorks), W. L. Bunting (Richmond), J. C. Matters (Devon), and P. W. Stout (Gloucester), three-quarter backs; A. Rotherham (Richmond) and R. O. Schwarz (Richmond), half-backs; H. W. Dudgeon (Richmond), James Davidson (Cumberland), Joseph Davidson (Cumberland), R. F. Oakes (Durham),

F. M. Stout (Gloucester), J. P. Shooter (Yorkshire), A. O. Dowson (Midlands), and N. F. A. Hobbs (Blackheath), forwards. Scotland:—H. Rottenburg (London Scottish), back; H. T. S. Gedge (Fettes Loretto), G. A. W. Lamond (Kilvinside Academicals), D. P. Moneypenny (London Scottish), and T. L. Scott (Langholm), three-quarter backs; J. W. Simpson (Royal High School) and J. Gillespie (Edinburgh Academicals), half-backs; M. Morrison (Royal High School), W. McEwan (Edinburgh Academicals), H. O. Smith (Watsonians), G. C. Kerr (Durham), A. Mackinnon (London Scottish), J. B. Dykes (London Scottish), R. S. Stevenson (Northumberland) and W. J. Thompson (Oxford University), forwards. England played well; far better than in any of the previous matches. There was very little to choose between the three-quarters, but the Scottish halves, as a pair, were distinctly superior to their opponents. The Scotch forwards were faster and more dashing than the English, and time after time they carried the ball all down the field with a run. Scotland won by a goal to nothing, and were clearly the better team. Ireland won all their matches. They led off with a great victory over England, as before mentioned. The Irish team being chiefly recruits, no less than seven new caps appearing in the field. Owing to various causes, Ireland had to meet Scotland with 6 substitutes, but nevertheless they (Ireland) won by three tries to a goal, Scotland being outplayed all round. In their last match at Cardiff against Wales, Ireland won by a try to nothing securing the triple crown with three straight victories as in 1894. The team were a very young lot, and L. M. Magee, the captain, was a long way the best British half-back of the season. We have now only to deal with Wales. After their crushing defeat of England they expected to run round Scotland easily, but they calculated without remembering Northern Union professionalism. The Welsh two halves, the brothers James, who ought never to have been reinstated, suddenly sold themselves to Broughton, leaving their own club and country in the lurch; S. Biggs and L. Lloyd were selected in their places, but the change naturally weakened the side. Eventually Scotland won by three goals and three tries to two goals, or 21 points to 10, a most unexpected result. This left the International contest as below:—

	P.	W.	D.	L.	Pts.	Goals. For	Agst.
Ireland	3	3	0	0	6	18	3
Scotland	3	2	0	1	4	29	19
Wales	3	1	0	2	2	36	27
England	3	0	0	3	0	3	37

For the second time since the institution of the Cup, the County Championship came south, Devon going up to Newcastle and beating Northumber and on April 8th by a goal to nothing. The Metropolitan Counties, except Kent, did not perform very grandly in this competition, Northumberland won all their matches in their own particular group. The game is taking a very firm hold in Devon and Cornwall, and the County Championship is likely to still further take up the Rugby enthusiasm of the Devonians. The University match at the Queen's Club on December 14th, 1898, was for once in a way not interfered with by the fog. The non-favourite, Cambridge, by hard forward play, quite broke up the Oxford three-quarters and won by a goal and two tries to nil. The teams were—Cambridge: H. Rottenburg (back); G. M. Bennett, F. H. Jones, A. Hacking, and G. F. Collett (three-quarter backs); F. H. Fasson and M. A. Black (half-backs); A. J. L. Darley, J. A. Campbell, R. W. Bell, A. S. Pringle, N. C. Fletcher, J. Daniell, J. R. C. Greenless, and J. G. Fordham (forwards). Oxford: T. O. Jones (back); P. L. Nicholas, T. A. Nelson, L. J. Orpen, and J. E. Crabbe (three-quarter backs); F. H. B. Champain and J. Kershaw (half-backs); C. P. Evers, C. Harper, J. F. A. Swanston, C. E. Barry, H. Alexander, A. J. Chadwick, W. Rogers, and W. H. Peat (forwards). Blackheath was undoubtedly the strongest club in the London District, but the London Scottish and Richmond were as usual the most dangerous opponents of the red and black. Cardiff and Newport, however, were both able to defeat Blackheath. In Wales Newport at last had to come down from their high position, A. J. Gould, T. C. Graham, A. W. Boucher and other sterling Internationals having at last given up active play. Cardiff's record stands: Matches 28, won 22, lost 3. Newport: Matches 24, won 17, lost 6. Swansea: Matches 33, won 28, lost 2; Gloucester had a very good season, playing 34 matches and winning 27; Devonport Albion, with a big match list of 41, won 32 and only lost 6; Sowerby Bridge won the final tie in the Yorkshire Cup and Guy's won the Inter-Hospital Cup, beating London Hospital by 3 tries to nothing. A fairly strong team of Rugby players went out to Australia in the summer under the captaincy of the Rev. Mullineux, an old Cambridge footballer. They played a series of matches, some 21, winning 18 and only losing 3. In four matches against Australia, England won 3 of them. Queensland, however, defeated the English team.

The Northern Union, with an acknowledged professional system, and freely buying up good Welsh and other players where possible, certainly added to its adherents and attracted good gates. They are carrying out very strictly their rule that their professionals must have some regular employment, and at the end of 1899 fined one of the clubs £100 for playing a man not properly employed, outside his football salary. Batley came out at the head of the Yorkshire Senior Competition, with Hull second, and the Broughton Rangers, helped by the Brothers James, topped the Lancashire Senior Competition, with Oldham second. Financially the leading clubs in the Northern Union are not in a too flourishing condition as the expenses of keeping a team of fifteen together are very heavy, and even in Yorkshire the best clubs cannot attract the enormous gates of the Association League and Cup ties. The Hon. Sec. of the Rugby Union is Mr. G. Rowland Hill, Conduit Vale, Greenwich, S.E.

From a playing point of view the Association season was most successful, and one of the very best judges, and in his day one of the best exponents of the game, considers that English "soccer" has reached almost its highest possible standpoint. England in 1898 won all three of its International matches, and in 1899 the victory was repeated, England indeed winning fairly easy on all three occasions. All her three matches were played in England, which was of course in her favour, but even had this advantage not been present the result would certainly have been the same. England beat Ireland by 13 goals to 2, the Irish Association for the first time claiming the services of their native players engaged with

English clubs. England then at Bristol defeated Wales by 4 goals too, and then in heavy rain, which quite spoilt the game, at Birmingham, England beat Scotland by 2 goals to 1. Ireland had scored 1 goal to nothing against Wales, Scotland worsted Wales by 6 goals to 2. Just before the crucial match, England v. Scotland, the latter defeated Ireland by 9 goals to 1, so that there could be no question as to superiority of the Rose and Thistle over the other two countries. The relative positions of the four work out as follows:

		W.	D.	L.	Pts.	Goals. For	Agst.
1st	England	3	0	0	6	19	3
2nd	Scotland	2	0	1	4	16	3
3rd	Ireland	1	0	2	2	4	22
4th	Wales	0	0	3	0	11	

The England v. Scotland teams were—England: Robinson (Southampton), goal; Thickett (Sheffield United) and Crabtree (Aston Villa), backs; Howell (Liverpool), Frank Forman (Notts Forest), and Needham (Sheffield United), half-backs; Athersmith (Aston Villa), Bloomer (Derby County), G. O. Smith (Corinthians) (captain), Settle (Bury) and Fred Forman (Notts Forest), forwards. Scotland: Doig (Sunderland), goal; N. Smith (Rangers) (captain), and Storrier (Celtic), backs; Gibson (Rangers), A. J. Christie (Queen's Park), and Robertson (Southampton), half-backs; Campbell (Rangers), Hamilton (Rangers), R. McColl (Queen's Park), Morgan (Liverpool), and Bell (Celtic), forwards. After an interval of eight years, the old fixture, North v. South, was revived, and it proved an interesting game, a valuable trial of different styles of play, and a win for the North by 3 goals to 1. Inter Association football has fallen from its once high estate. League fixtures and Cup ties leave but little time and opportunity for these once thoroughly amateur and genuinely sporting fixtures. Middlesex 12 and Suffolk and Surrey 8 each were the largest number of matches played. The Oxford and Cambridge match, at the Queen's Club, was somewhat spoilt by the fog, Cambridge on form were supposed to have the best chance, and so the result proved, Cambridge won by 3 goals to 1, and were all round the faster team. The sides were—Cambridge: W. Campbell, goal; A. R. Wilson and W. S. Masterman, backs; A. T. Coode, F. D. Cautley, and H. Vickers, half-backs; A. R. Haig-Brown, L. J. Moon, R. N. R. Blaker, T. S. Gosling, and L. H. Wace, forwards. Oxford: S. H. J. Russell, goal; W. Blackburn and L. Wallace, backs; E. R. Turnbull, S. E. Osborne, and M. M. Morgan Owen, half-backs; E. M. Jameson, F. H. Hollins, C. F. Ryder, R. E. Foster, and G. C. Vassall, forwards. The Association Cup as usual formed the staple interest of the season, and towards the end of the competition, the ties produced mammoth gates and intense excitement. In the semi-final ties, Sheffield United, the ultimate winners, had to meet Liverpool no less than four times before a definite result could be arrived at. The final, at the Crystal Palace, gave the largest gate, viz., 73,831, ever attracted to a football match, and it may be reasonably supposed that nearly every one of these people visited the game. Derby County and Sheffield United were the two teams engaged. Derby led at half time by 1 goal to none, but then Sheffield went right away and won by 4 goals to 1. The teams were—Sheffield United: W. Toulke, goal; H. Thickett and P. Boyle, backs; W. H. Johnson, T. Morren, and

E. Needham, half-backs; W. Bennett, W. Beers, G. A. Hedley, J. Almond, and A. E. Priest, forwards. Derby County: J. S. Fryer, goal; J. Methven and J. Staley, backs; J. D. Cox. R. Paterson and J. May, half-backs; J. A. Arkesden, S. Bloomer, J. Boag, W. J. Macdonald, and H. Allen, forwards. The Amateur Cup as usual was a very poor affair, Stockton beating Harwich and Parkeston in the final by 1 goal to nothing. The other principal Cups of the season were won as follows:—Scottish, Celtic; Welsh, Druids; Irish, Linfield; Sheffield Charity, Aston Villa; London Charity, Clapton; London Senior, Old Carthusians; Middlesex Senior, London Caledonians; Army, 1st South Lancs. Regt.; Irish, Army, King's Royal Rifles; Devon, Royal Welsh Fusiliers; Inter-Hospital, London Hospital. The League Championship with 18 clubs engaged was won by Aston Villa with 45 points out of a possible 78, Liverpool was 2nd with 43, and Burnley 3rd with 39. Aston Villa played their last winning match against Liverpool on the last Saturday in April, 41,357 spectators were present, and the gate at Aston totalled up to £1,558 1s., both records for a League tie. Aston Villa altogether had a most successful season but an expensive one. Their income amounted to £15,263, and far exceeded that of any other club. Their profits were £3,225. Manchester City left off head of the Second Division of the League with 52 points, Glossop North End being second with 46 points. These two clubs this season will oust Bolton Wanderers and Sheffield Wednesday from the First Division. Southampton for the third successive year carried off the championship of the Southern League, Thames Ironworks heading the Second Division. The Rangers were champions of the Scottish and Distillery of the Irish Leagues. In the spring an Oxford Association team toured in Austria and in November the F.A. sent a team to Berlin and the continent. The Annual General of the Football Association at the end of May was interesting upon two or three points. The powers of the Executive were still further increased, the right of appeal from the decision of the Council to a General Meeting being abolished, a piece of legislation very likely to lead the F.A. into a regular mess some of these days, and a most tremendous mistake as regards policy. The balance sheet proved, if indeed, proofs were wanted, that as a money-making business Association football was a most flourishing speculation. The gates of the Cup ties accruing to the F.A. produced £7,000, Sheffield United, the winners, taking £2,000 of this, the Association retaining £2,700. The profit on International matches amounted to £1,800, and the Association up to date had some £11,000 in hand. The ultimate destination of such a huge total must, before long, be considered. Lord Kinnaird, a brilliant Etonian player in his day, is president of the F.A., and F. J. Wall, 61, Chancery Lane, W.C., is the Secretary.

PEDESTRIANISM.

It was not until the very end of the season that any real public interest could be detected in the various matches and contests amongst our professional pedestrians. The boom of the previous years had evidently died out, and as Downer, Bredin, Bacon, Crossland and Watkins had all met one another at their respective distances the relative form of each man was so well known that any genuine match with at all a doubtful result was quite hopeless. Downer from one hundred yards to a quarter of a mile was absolutely paramount. From 500 to 880 yards Bredin—until November—could find no one to challenge his championship. Bacon's waning powers left Tincler master of the situation at a mile and Watkins beyond that distance. However, in July, the advent of H. Cullum into the professional ranks at once set the ball rolling again, and before the end of the year the ex-amateur had wrested the half-mile championship from the ageing Bredin, and there should be some good and genuine contests in 1900 between the new champion and Tincler at any distance between the half and the mile, Cullum being quite equal to a very fast mile when properly trained. Exhibition races for fictitious stakes and purses must, however, be avoided if genuine matches are to be profitable speculations. In 1897 a big match at the Rochdale ground could and did produce between £400 and £500 in gate money. In 1899 at the same ground not one single contest gave £200 for division between the competitors. A very large proportion of our modern amateur athletes require very little persuasion to join the professional ranks if only the game can be proved worth the candle, and a few big matches with proportionate gates would speedily induce some of our present amateur champions to cross the rubicon, to the distinct benefit of both amateur and professional foot-racing. The chief events of the year follow. Christmas, 1898 and the New Year found most of the small professional army in the field. At Cliftonville, Belfast, M. O'Neill, of Limerick, defeated J. J. Mullen, of Armagh, both ex-amateurs, for the Four Mile Championship of Ireland and £50. The time was slow, viz., 21 min. 13 secs. Also at Christmas F. E. Bacon made an unsuccessful attempt on W. Cumming's 1885 ten miles record of 51 min. 6¼ secs. The trial took place at Ashton-under-Lyne, the track being heavy; and Crossland, Walsh, and Harrison acted as pacemakers. Bacon lost ground from the start, and finally completed the distance in 53 min. 49 secs. This performance proved conclusively that the ex-amateur mile champion had lost his old pace and stamina. On December 26, 1898, E. C. Bredin and A. R. Downer met for the second time at 500 yards; Bredin had won the previous match at Rochdale, and now when the pair ran at Barrow for £50 a side on a cold day and on a bad track Bredin again won in 59 secs., 1½ secs. outside world's record—a magnificent performance. It must, however, be remembered that this is Bredin's best distance. The gate was miserably small. Directly afterwards, at Sheffield, Bredin (15 yards) won a 130 yards sweepstake by a foot from H. Hutchens (13), with A. R. Downer (7) third; time, a yard worse than 12 secs. The Edinburgh Powderhall Ground New Year's handicap was won by D. Roberts, of Leith (16 yards in 130), from Downer. As Roberts could do at least "4 yards worse than evens" no wonder with such a start. The two days' gate at this meeting is worth something like £1,000. On February 18 Bredin and G. B. Tincler met at Rochdale for £50 a side and the half-mile championship of the world. The gate was a fairly good one, and after a magnificent race Bredin won by a yard in 1 min. 56½ secs, possibly, considering the time of year, the best performance Bredin has ever done at the distance. On February 25, at Leeds, J. W. Raby, of Elland, and D. Fenton, of London, both ex-amateurs, walked for the so-called ten miles championship and £50. The veteran Raby went right away, and after completing 7½ miles in the hour Fenton the favourite gave up, and Raby was allowed to stop. Early in April Bredin was foolishly induced to meet Tincler at 1,000 yards at Belfast for £25 a side. At this distance Tincler's staying powers told, and he won easily in 2 min. 26 secs. Tincler, however, had just before signally failed to give H. Watkins 80 yards start in two miles at Rochdale. This led up to Watkins and Bacon meeting at Rochdale on April 15 for £100 and the ten miles championship. On a bitterly cold day Watkins led all the way and at seven miles Bacon was so far behind that he retired, and Watkins, after completing seven miles in 35 min. 56⅖ secs., was allowed to stop at 7½ miles in 38 min. 33⅗ secs. On the following Saturday, April 22, perhaps the most important sprint race of the year took place, A. R. Downer, at Oldham, giving C. Harper, ex-sprint champion of England, 1½ yards in 130 for £50 a side. Downer ran magnificently and won by half-a-yard in "two yards inside evens," on a rather cold day. Once again, on May 6, at Rochdale, Downer and Bredin met for £50 a side. This time the distance was a compromise between the two men's favourite courses, viz., 470 yards. Downer, however, made the pace so hot for the first half of the distance that he just got home by two yards in 56⅕ secs. In May, at the Glasgow Northern C.C. sports, Tincler decisively beat Bacon at 1,000 yards in 2 min. 26⅖ secs., but the race was hardly of the genuine money-match order. A match of some interest took place at Rochdale on June 17, when Downer ran 130 yards against a 22-year-old mare, Old Polly. The mare won by five yards; time, "6 yards inside evens." Once again Bacon had to put up with defeat at ten miles, Len Hurst beating him at Hanley in June by 15 yards. The stakes were supposed to be £50 a side. Subsequently Downer went to America, but he failed to make much profit out of his visit; and C. Harper conclusively proved the merit of Downer's victory in April by defeating the American Sheffield handicap winner, T. F. Keane, by a yard in a 130 yards match at Oldham in July. In the middle of the summer a little life was infused into the professional arena by H. Cullum, of Cardiff, after suspension by the A. A. A. promptly joining the ranks of the money racers. Cullum led off in his new sphere by a reported performance of 1,000 yards in 2 min. 9⅕ secs. at Aberavon on August 5th. Of course the track was subsequently found to be decidedly short. Bredin in July and August appeared in several so-called matches for reputed big stakes. The races were all perfectly genuine so far as he was concerned, and he won them all, but these exhibition races all tend to spoil public interest in genuine money matches, which in the halcyon days of the profession were the backbone of the sport. At Milford, Derby, Bredin (7 yards) just won a 200 yards race from C. Harper (scratch), with H. Hutchens (7 yards) third; time, 20 secs. At Bristol City F.C. sports, August 12, Bredin defeated Bacon at 1,000 yards in 2 min. 34⅖ secs., and T. F. Keane defeated C. Harper at 200 yards. Bredin also gave Cullum 12 yards in 600 at Cardiff and defeated him. Cullum's next engagement was at Bristol on September 9, two miles on grass at the Bristol City F.C. ground against Bacon, Cullum fairly breaking up his opponent in 9 min. 58 secs., but the race was only for one of those mysterious purses. Towards the end of the year, on September 16, certainly the most important event of the season took place, H. Watkins, of Coventry, at Rochdale, making an attempt on the one-hour record of Bacon, made in 1897, viz., 11 miles 1243 yards. The evening was fine and calm, and paced and sheltered by a cyclist and several runners, Watkins not only made a new record for the one hour, viz., 11 miles 1286 yards, but *en route* also put up fresh figures for ten miles, viz., 51 min. 5⅕ secs., beating W. Cumming's 51 min. 6⅗ secs., made in 1885. The attendance of spectators was about 5,000, and Watkins must have profited fairly well by his brilliant running. Bredin and Cullum brought off two important matches before the end of the year. At Cardiff on September 30 the pair met for £50 a side before a very poor gate at 1,000 yards, Cullum winning easily in 2 min. 20 secs. This led up to a half-mile match at Rochdale for £100 a side on November 4, and here at last Bredin, the champion of the world at the distance, met his match, the younger man, Cullum, winning by a yard in 2 min. dead on a rather soft path with a strong breeze and with only a mere handful of spectators present. Finally, on November 11, M. O'Neill and Len Hurst met at Ashton for £50 a side to run five miles. After a capital race up to the final straight O'Neill won easily in 26 min 45⅕ secs.

RACKETS AND TENNIS.

There was certainly an increased interest in the ancient game of Rackets in 1899, and all the usual annual competitions filled well and produced exciting if rather moderate play. The Racket year commenced with the Grand Military Championship (100 guineas) Challenge Cup at the Prince's Club, Knightsbridge, London, on Monday, February 27, with seven entries. In the previons week the holders of the Cup, the 12th Lancers (Major J. C. B. Eastwood and Captain M. T. Tristram), played a match against Eton College (Messrs. De la Rue and S. M. Macnaghten), the Lancers winning easily. The scores were: 15-5, 15-10, 15-12, 15-3. The King's Shropshire Light Infantry, (Lt.-Col. Spens and Mr. E. M. Sprot) fought out the final heat with the Royal Scots Fusiliers (2nd Batt.), (Capt. A. W. Thorneycroft and Mr. M. McConaghey), the King's winning four games right off the reel at 15-10, 15-2, 15-0, 15-6. The winners of the final then met the holders, and after a most interesting game the King's S.L.I. won the Cup by four games to one, as follows: 10-15, 15-7, 15-6, 15-12, 15-10, 70 aces to 50; time, 48 minutes. Since the institution of the trophy, the 12th Lancers had proved successful on six occasions out of eight. Lt.-Col. Spens had several times competed for the Amateur Championship, and he sailed with his Regiment to South Africa in the autumn. On March 29, the Amateur Championship, both Doubles and Singles, were decided at the Queen's Club, H. K. Foster and Percy Ashworth winning by four games to nil against W. L. Foster and Ivor L. Johnston at 15-10, 15-6, 17-15, 15-11. E. H. Miles having beaten Capt. S. H. Sheppard in the final round of the singles, played for the Championship against the holder H. K. Foster, who had held the title since 1894. Miles, who has rather a weak service, was beaten by three games to nil at 15-10, 15-8, 15-12. In the week following the Boat Race, the Oxford and Cambridge matches took place at the Queen's Club. In the Doubles, all the players were new to the competition, and a most interesting match saw Cambridge (E. M. Baerlein, Eton and Trinity, and E. B. Noel, Winchester and Trinity) defeat Oxford (R. A. Williams, Winchester and University, and R. H. de Montmorency, St. Paul's and Keble) by four games to three at 15-13, 15-1, 10-15, 15-11, 3-15, 7-15, 15-1. In the Singles, strange to say, the Winchester pair for the 1898 Public Schools Cup represented Oxford and Cambridge respectively, Noel, the Cantab, winning by 3 games to 0 at 15-5, 15-10, 15-10 in 25 minutes. Noel had certainly improved and Williams rather deteriorated since the previous year. Cambridge thus won both matches. The Public Schools Challenge Cup competition was held at the Queen's Club, April 11-14, with eleven entries, Eton, Harrow, Clifton, Charterhouse, Wellington, Marlborough, Winchester, Haileybury, Rugby, Malvern, Tonbridge. The last-named scratched. The two crack Schools met in the final round, and Eton (S. M. Macnaghten and I. De la Rue) beat Harrow (F. B. Wilson and S. J. G. Hoare) by four games to one ; 15-11, 10-15, 15-9, 15-12, 15-7. The play on the whole was good. Harrow had won in the two previous years. Altogether, since 1868, when the competition was started, Harrow have won three Cups outright (three successive wins being necessary to do this). Eton have only been successful on seven occasions. The Woolwich v. Sandhurst Racket match took place April 19, Luther and Lee (Rugby) for Woolwich, beat the Sandhurst pair, Curling and Mackintosh (Eton), in the Doubles by three games to love, at 15-8, 18-13, 15-7, 15-5. Woolwich also won the Singles by 3 games to 2, with Luther against Curling at 15-1, 14-17, 15-8, 15-18, 15-7.

As regards Tennis, although there was no match during the year to equal in interest the great contest between Peter Latham and T. Pettitt in 1898, the various Championships and matches gave excellent play, and secured plenty of spectators. The Spring Handicap at the Queen's Club closed with 13 entries, Mr. H. B. Chapman being at scratch, A. D. Whatman meeting E. G. Raphael on level terms in the final tie, defeated him by two sets to nil, 13 games to 6. The winner played a remarkably good game. In the very first big exhibition match of the season, Mr. E. H. Miles, the holder of the gold prize, beat the Champion, Peter Latham, at the Queen's Club. The latter in his own court failed to concede the amateur odds of half-thirty, Mr. Miles proving himself to be in excellent form by winning by 3 sets to 1, 21 games to 15. There were 13 entries for the Amateur Championship, Mr. E. H. Miles won the final round, beating Mr. J. B. Gribble by 3 sets to 1, 19 games to 15; 6-5, 6-1, 1-6, 6-3, 123 strokes to 112. Mr. Miles had defeated Mr. P. Ashworth in an earlier round. As Mr. H. E. Crawley, the 1898 winner of the second prize, did not defend his position, Mr. E. H. Miles played Sir Edward Grey for the Championship at the Queen's Club on June 3. On a very hot day, Mr. Miles won rather easily in 1 hour 14 minutes, by 3 sets to nil, 18 games to 9, 101 strokes to 79, and became Champion for the year, and after several ties between the men defeated by Mr. Miles, Mr. J. B. Gribble became the holder of the second prize. The Oxford and Cambridge Tennis matches, giving a full blue to the competitors, took place July 10 and 11, at Prince's Club, Knightsbridge. Oxford in the Doubles against Messrs. E. A. Biedermann and T. Page against Messrs. E. M. Baerlein and J. C. Tabor, for Cambridge. Oxford won by 3 sets to 1 ; 3-6, 6-4, 6-3, 6-5, although at starting 3 to 1 on Cambridge had been laid by good

judges. In the Singles, Mr. Baerlein won easily for Cambridge against Mr. Biedermann for Oxford, by 3 sets to nil, 18 games to 7; 6-1, 6-4, 6-2. For the M.C.C. Gold Prize, played for at Prince's, the new court at Lord's not being quite ready, on a very hot day, July 26, Sir Edward Grey having beaten all the other challengers, met the holder Mr. E. H. Miles. The latter won by 3 sets to 2, 27 games to 18, 163 strokes to 149. Mr. Miles by this victory becomes the only double winner of the Championship and the Gold Prize in one season except Sir Edward Grey himself. The latter, of course, is the holder of the Silver Prize for the year.

ROWING.

As regards amateur oarsmanship the season of 1899 was in every way a great success. All the regattas, with hardly an exception, secured entries in excess of previous averages, and the magnificent summer weather which prevailed from June to the end of August contributed in no small degree to make every aquatic fixture equally pleasurable to both spectators and competitors alike. The Amateur Rowing Association reigned supreme at every important fixture, and its far-reaching amateur definition prevented the slightest suspicion of the professional taint creeping into this, almost the only absolutely pure sport we have left. The National Amateur Rowing Association ceased to trouble its omnipotent opponent and confined its attention to its own proper constituents where the latter declined the services of the Tradesmen's Rowing Association, with which body, sooner or later, the N.A.R.A. must amalgamate if they, the latter, wish to secure any support at all or have any oarsman to govern. Taking the season as a whole the standard of amateur rowing was certainly of a very high standard, and the "Grand" winners at Henley, the winning Cambridge crew, in the Inter-Varsity race at Putney, and the best London Rowing Club eight, were all splendid expositions of good training, coaching, and science combined. With the exception of the Stewards' Cup crew at Henley, four-oared rowing was not quite so polished as it should be, and scratch crews were the order of the day. Pair-oared rowing, even at Henley, produced quantity, but not quality, and after the Goblets came chaos and awful mediocrity. Our two best scullers of the previous year, Howell and Blackstaffe, remained a long way in front of everyone else, Howell, perhaps, coming on a trifle, and Blackstaffe slowing somewhat with advancing age. Skiff rowing and punting certainly increased their adherents during the season, and regattas of the picnic order, helped by the fine weather, became more popular than ever.

Rowing—amateur rowing—began for the year with the early stages of practice for the Oxford and Cambridge Boat Race, Cambridge, under the presidency of Mr. R. B. Etherington-Smith, and coached by Mr. W. A. L. Fletcher, the Oxford Ch. Ch. blue, started on January 9th, J. H. Gibbon rowing stroke. The Oxonians followed a week later; on Jan. 16th, Mr. Harcourt G. Gold, being the president of the Boat Club. By Feb. 4th, the two Eights had settled down, J. A. Tinné, in the Oxford boat, and W. B. Rennie in the Cambridge crew, being the only men subsequently displaced. Both the Torpids at Oxford—six days' racing—and the Lent races at Cambridge, four days racing, were decided during February. At Oxford, the three divisions of the Torpids ended as follows :— First division, Balliol ; second division, Balliol II. ; third division, Oriel; being the respective head boats. At Cambridge the leaders were left:—First division, First Trinity; second division, Caius II.; third division, St. Catharine. Both the last-named crews were bumped on the closing day of the races, a clear proof that four days is not sufficient for a division to settle down. The Clinker, or Gig Fours, are now, both at Oxford and Cambridge, decided during the first term of the year. At Oxford, Magdalen easily proved the best of four rather poor crews. At Cambridge, Peterhouse, a strong crew, won after a hard race from Trinity Hall and five other Fours. On the Saturday before the Oxford and Cambridge Boat Race, March 25th, R. Benson's crew defeated T. S. Kelly's crew for the annual Eton College Trial Eights. In the meantime the two Varsity eights, after a short stay up river, Oxford at Hedsor, near Cookham, with their president's father, and the Cantabs at Bourne End, with Mr. R. C. Lehmann, arrived at Putney, Cambridge on March 7th and Oxford on the following day. Messrs. Fletcher and D. H. Mc Lean coached during their tideway practice. Mr. Fletcher's mentorship had produced an exceptionally powerful and finished Eight, and but for the fact that their stroke, Gibbon, was practically a novice compared to the brilliant veteran Gold, the Light Blues would have been even better favourites than they were. As it was, after Cambridge had rowed the course up in practice in 18 min. 56 secs., the best trial ever accomplished during training, and Oxford's best time under almost exactly similar conditions, and on the succeeding day, was 19 min. 34 secs., odds of 3 to 1 on Cambridge were freely laid on the morning of the race, March 25th. Cambridge won the toss, and after a desperate race to Hammersmith Bridge, where Cambridge only led by half a length, Gibbon went right away and won easily by three-and-a quarter lengths in 21 min. 4 secs., 1889 being their last previous win. The crews were :—*Cambridge:* W. H. Chapman (bow) (Third Trinity) ; N. L. Calvert (Trinity Hall) ; °C. J. D. Goldie (Third Trinity) ; J. E. Payne, (Peterhouse); ° R. B. Etherington-Smith (First Trinity) ; R. H. Sanderson (First Trinity) ; °W. Dudley Ward (Third Trinity) ; J. H. Gibbon (Third Trinity) (st.) ; G. A. Lloyd (Third Trinity) (cox). Of these Chapman, Goldie, Dudley Ward and Gibbon were all Etonians. *Oxford:* *R. O. Pitman (New) (bow); C. W. Tomkinson (Balliol); A. H. D. Steel (Balliol); H. J. Hale (Balliol) ; C. E. Johnston (New) ; °J. W. Warre (Balliol) ; *A. T. Herbert (Balliol) ; *H. G. Gold (Magdalen) (stroke) ; G. S. Maclagan (Magdalen) (cox). C. J. M. Adie (First Trinity), Cambridge, and F. S. Le B. Smith (University), Oxford, were the spare men. In the Oxford crew all but Steel and Herbert were Etonians. (°Old Blues). The Cantabs rowed in a boat by George Sims, of Putney, and the Oxonians in one built for Balliol College by the Brocas Company, Eton. About this time Mr. H. G. Gold, the Oxford stroke, was elected Captain of the Leander Club, and the Skiff Club, under the captaincy of W. F. Folliott, promulgated a universal code to govern skiff races at Regattas, the A.R.A. definition of an amateur being included. Early in May rowing was once more in full swing at both the Universities. The O.U.B.C. officials were: F. W. Warre, Balliol, president, and C. E. Johnston, New, hon. secretary. At Cambridge, C. J. D. Goldie took over the presidency, and Dudley Ward, the hon. secretaryship; both hail from the Third

Trinity Boat Club. On May 13th, W. Dudley Ward and R. B. Etherington-Smith (stroke) won the Cambridge University or Magdalen Pairs after a very close race with a very much lighter Third Trinity pair, S. F. Cockerell and J. H. Gibbon (stroke), the two ex-presidents being no less than 3 stone 2 lbs. the heavier pair. Three days later R. H. Sanderson and R. B. Etherington-Smith (stroke) won the C.U.B.C. Lowe Double Sculls easily from H. T. W. Farquharson, Trinity Hall, and H. D. Crofton, First Trinity (stroke). Surely these Double Sculls might be confined to pairs drawn from one College club only. On May 18th, the O.U.B.C. Summer Eights commenced. New College started head of the river, with Magdalen second and Balliol third. Magdalen were probably the fastest eight, but during the six days' racing New managed to retain their place for the fourth successive year indeed, there was no change in the first six places ; Worcester made five bumps and finished seventh on the river, Hertford finished head of the second division. On May 31st, St. George's Hospital won the Senior Fours of the United Hospitals R.C., the crew being identical with the Caius Four, winners of the C.U.B.C. Fours in 1895 and the Henley Visitors' Cup in 1896. On June 7th, the C U.B.C. June races began, First Trinity starting head boat and Caius II. top of the second division. During each of the four days' racing, with a shorter distance than usual between the crews, First Trinity managed to keep away from Third Trinity, although overlapped at times. First Trinity remained head of the river, and Clare left off at the top of the second division. The O.U.B.C. Pairs were won by R. O. Pitman and C. E. Johnston of New College, beating E. L. and F. W. Warre of Balliol, and C. V. Fox, of Pembroke won the O.U.B.C. Sculls very easily. Henley Regatta took place on Wednesday, Thursday, and Friday, July 5th, 6th, and 7th. The entries numbered 53, one less than in 1898. Canada, Hamburg, and the Delft Students' R.C. were the only foreign representatives. For the first time the course on the Bucks side was boomed between the piles from above the winning post to beyond Remenham Rectory, with twelve openings in pairs which were closed during the racing. The length of the Grand Stand enclosure on the Berks side was also boomed out. This new arrangement proved in every way a big success, and the straight line of nearly a mile of skiffs inside the booms just before a race presented a most picturesque and pretty effect. The course as before was one mile 550 yards in length.

All three days were gloriously fine, with not too much wind, and the attendances on the first and last days were certainly records. The exigences of the draw necessitated a couple of trial heats being decided on the Tuesday afternoon. The following were the ultimate winners of the prizes ; Grand Challenge Cup, Leander Club, R. O. Pitman (bow), E. A. Beresford-Peirse, H. M. Willis, H. A. Game, C. D. Burnell, R. Carr, C. K. Phillips, H. G. Gold (stroke), G. S. Maclagan (cox) ; Stewards', Magdalen College, Oxford, M. C. Thornhill (bow), R. Carr, C. D. Burnell, H. G. Gold (st.), Favourite Hammonia R.C., Hamburg, being second; Silver Goblets, C. K. Phillips and H. M. Willis (stroke), Leander Club; Diamond Sculls, B. H. Howell, Thames R.C.; Ladies' Plate, Eaton College, C. A. Willis (bow), E. G. St. Aubyn, H. J. Bruce, C. H. Taylor, Lord Grimston, Hon. W. E. Guinness, R. H. Nelson, J. F. Kelly (stroke), H. Rose (cox) ; Visitors,

Cup, Balliol College, Oxford, C. N. Dyer, F. W. Warre, A. T. Herbert, C. W. Tomkinson (st.) ; Thames Cup, First Trinity, Cambridge (not the head boat on the Cam.) ; Wyfold Cup, Trinity Hall, Cambridge. An amalgamation of Third and First Trinity rowed for the Grand as Trinity College, Cambridge. After Henley, Regattas came thick and fast, the London Rowing Club easily keeping premier position as in the previous year ; indeed, its best eight was undefeated during the year, except by the Grand winners. At the Metropolitan Regatta, July 11, London won the Champion Eights and Metropolitan Eights. The Vikings won the Thames Cup Senior Fours, H. T. Blackstaffe, Vesta R. C., retained the London Cup for the Senior Scullers, E. Isler, of the Vesta, won the Junior Sculls. At Kingston, on July 15th, London won the Senior Eights and just lost the Senior Fours on a foul to Thames. H. W. Stout, London, won the Senior Sculls and de Meyier, of the Kingston, the Junior Sculls. Kingston also won the Senior Pairs. In the same week, C. V. Fox, O.U.B.C., won the Eblana Cup and Sculling Championship of Ireland at the Dublin Metropolitan Regatta. At Staines Regatta, on July 20th, London won the Senior Eights and Fours and also the Senior Sculls, while F. A. Boyton, Thames, won the Pairs and C. M. Steele, Trinity Hall, the Junior Sculls. On July 22nd, at Walton Regatta, London again won the Senior Eights and Fours, C. V. Fox, O.U.B.C. won the Senior Sculls, Kingston the Pairs, and S. C. Smith of the Thames the Junior Sculls. At Goring and Streatley, on July 26th, Thames won the Senior Eights, the Fieldhead B.C. the Senior Fours, F. A. Boyton, of the London, the Senior Sculls, and M. A. Sands and J. H. Gibbon, of the Vikings, the Challenge Pairs. On July 28th and 29th at Molesey Regatta, a two days' fixture, for the first time Thames won the Senior Eights against London's Thames Cup crew. London won the Senior Fours, the Vikings the Senior Pairs, F. A. Boyton, of the London, won the Senior Sculls and E. H. Good, of the Kingston, the Junior Sculls. Reading and Windsor and Eton brought the Regatta season proper to a close. At Reading, on Bank Holiday, Kingston won the Grand Challenge Cup for Eights, the Vikings the Challenge Cup for Fours, G. Bailey, of the Kensington R.C., the Junior Sculls, and St. George Ashe, of the Thames R.C., the Senior Sculls. On the previous Saturday, at Windsor, H. T. Blackstaffe won the Senior Sculls, A. H. Cloutte the Junior Sculls, and the Vikings the Challenge Fours. Marlow Rowing Club Regatta, on August 12th, has now

attained almost the importance of the old post Henley fixture. The Senior Sculls were won by St G. Ashe, of the Thames R.C., L. J. Wethered, of the Iris R.C., won the Junior Sculls. The Vikings won the Pairs and also the Fours. All these races were for Challenge Cups. The Wingfield Sculls, or Amateur Championship of the Thames, took place on July 27th. The holder, B. H. Howell was opposed by H. T. Blackstaffe, of the Vesta, in a 25-feet boat, and C. V. Fox, of Pembroke College, Oxford. The last named had no chance. Blackstaffe led Howell to Chiswick Church, but there the old Cantab went away and won easily in 23 min. 7 secs. Subsequently, in September, Blackstaffe won the Amateur Sculling Championship of the Netherlands, at Amsterdam, and on October 1st, C. V. Fox, the O.U.B.C. Sculls holder, won the Amateur Sculling Championship of France at Neuilly-sur-Marne, an International Championship for the Coupe de

Paris. In the country the Nottingham Rowing Club, G. W. & L. H. King, E. G. Horn, and R. H. Bouden (st.), won the Senior Fours at Burton, Chester, Stourport, and Hereford, (West of England) Challenge Cups, also the Nottingham Gold Challenge Vase. Burton Leander won the Toddington Vase at Tewkesbury. Eastbourne R.C. once more won the South Coast Challenge Cup for Senior Fours. Mr. R. C. Lehmann, Fieldhead, Marlow, is the Hon. Secretary of the Amateur Rowing Association. In America, Harvard defeated Yale, on June 29th, in Senior Eights and Fours, also in the Freshmen's Eights, all at New London, U.S.A.

Punting races, as in the previous year, were frequent and popular. At the Thames Punting Club's Annual Regatta, at Shepperton, August 3rd, N. M. Cohen won the Amateur Championship from the holder, W. C. Romaine, and W. C. Romaine and C. R. Mullings won the Championship Doubles. At Sunbury Regatta, in the following week, C. R. Mullings punted over for the Championship of the Lower Thames. At Maidenhead Regatta, in Bray Reach, on July 27th, the Amateur Champion, N. M. Cohen, won the Championship of the Upper Thames. The Professional Punting Championship was won, on August 11th, at Maidenhead, by G. Haines, of Old Windsor, in 10 min. 28 secs. for the mile course out and home.

It almost goes without saying that the professional rowing season was dull and uninteresting, and that no new native talent could be found with any pretentions to first-class style or pace. Indeed W. A. Barry, of Putney, who in the previous year had, by good luck, just managed to become the holder of the Championship of England Challenge Cup, was very easily defeated by the Australian, who in 1898 sank when apparently easily holding Barry. Until professional regattas are revived, and four-oared races between Thames and Tyne once more inaugurated, it is quite hopeless to expect the advent of that sculler who may restore England's lost supremacy on the river. Curiously enough, both in Australia and America, the days of Beach and Hanlan also appear to be over, and professional rowing is at a very low ebb. At any rate in this country there is not any amalgamation of the amateur and professional elements to be urged as a reason, whatever may be the cause in Australia and America, where certainly the two classes are only divided by a very fine line of demarcation. Evidently, at the present day, there is not so much money in the game as compared to cycling, golf, and football, and it must be remembered that in the palmy era of professional oarsmanship these three best paying athletic professions were practically non existent. The events of 1899 are soon recorded. On March 11th, over the Tyne half-mile course, from Redheugh to the High Level Bridge, J. Wray, of Australia, defeated W. Haines, of Old Windsor, in open boats for £50 aside, Wray, the favourite at 11 to 8 on, won by a length, after being astern for more than half way. The match arose out of the annual Christmas Tyne open boat handicap. After this nothing occurred until May 1st, when W. A. Barry, of Putney, was called upon to defend his Championship of England Cup, by George Towns, of Newcastle, Australia. The stakes were £200 aside, and an enormous crowd lined the banks for the full distance of the Thames Championship course, from Putney to Mortlake, Towns sculled in a short 25-feet boat, built on very full lines, Barry used an ordinary 30-

feet wager boat. Odds of 5 to 2 were laid on Barry, who, led by a length for nearly half-a-mile, and then, after a capital race to Hammersmith Bridge, where Barry held a trifling advantage, the rough water along Chiswick Eyot told, and Towns went right away and won by six lengths in 24 min. 2 secs. James Wray, of New South Wales, issued a challenge to row the winner, but nothing came of it, and the two Australians did not appear to be particularly anxious to meet. The only other event of any consequence in 1899, as regards professional rowing, took place on May 15th, a fortnight after the Championship match, when Tom Sullivan, late of New Zealand, an ex-champion of England, met William Haines, of Old Windsor, for £200 aside, over the Putney to Mortlake course. Sullivan rowed in a 25-feet boat, and after being led to Craven Steps, the veteran ex-champion went right away—very rough water off Chiswick suiting his boat to perfection—and finally won by 36 secs., in 26 min. 21 secs. Before the end of the month, on May 26th, T. Bullman, of Shadwell, and A. J. Carter, of Greenwich, the respective winners of Doggett's Coat and Badge in 1897 and 1898, sculled a match over the Thames Championship Course for £50 a side. Bullman led to the Crab Tree, but then Carter went right away and won easily in 24 min. 31 secs. On July 10th, on the Tyne Championship Course, S. Emmett, of Wandsworth, beat G. Drummond, of Newcastle, very easily for £50 aside, in 25 min. 7 secs. On October 15th, J. J. Corcoran and J. Baker sculled in open gigs for £50 aside, from the Tunnel Pier to Corbett's Raft, Greenwich, Corcoran failed to give 5 seconds start by three parts of a length. John See, of Hammersmith won Doggett's Coat and Badge in 27 min. 34 secs. During the year an ex-champion, Tom Blackman, died, aged 42, and also Bob Cooper and Wallace Ross. A big subscription list was opened for the veteran ex-champion and waterman, Harry Kelly, then living in poor health and straitened circumstances at Newcastle-on-Tyne.

SKATING.

For the second year in succession, England was not favoured during the winter with any sufficiently long periods of frost to enable the National Skating Association to decide their series of championships and competitions. Indeed, except in Scotland for one short week, there was no ice in this country during the winter of 1898-99. The Continent was hardly any better off in this respect, and all the European and World's Championships at Berlin, Vienna and Davos had to be altered from their original dates on account of rapid thaws and heavy snow storms. Peder Oestlund again proved himself the fastest amateur skater of the world, although the ice and the arrangements at Berlin were both so bad that the speedy Norwegian had no chance of lowering any of the existing records. There does not appear to be very much use for the professional skater nowadays in Europe, so probably Oestlund will not follow the example of Axel Paulsen, Sensburg, &c., and leave the amateur ranks. It is certainly a most unexpected honour, considering the few opportunities Englishmen have for practising at home, that the one-hour world's record should stand to the credit of a Britisher. The National Skating Association are to be commended for their activity and energy in putting skating (both the figure and speed departments) in good order, so that whenever we do happen to get a few days' hard frost no time will be lost in getting to work at once. The question of obtaining speed badges in the clear air and with the hard ice of Davos and St. Moritz, as compared to the much more difficult surroundings in the way of atmosphere and ice encountered by skaters in England when testing speed, is about to be dealt with. There is no decrease in the popularity of the Niagara Rink as a fashionable resort, and frequently the figure skating seen there is up to the very highest standard of Continental experts. The new year had barely turned before the various skating champions began to muster at Davos to prepare for the European figure and speed championships, amongst them Peder Oestlund, of Trondjhem. On the N.S.A. speed course, a mile with three turns, the Russian E. Vollenweider skated the distance easily in 3 mins. 14⅘ secs. Messrs. E. Gwynne Evans and C. Edgington both qualified for first-class gold badges with 3 mins. 26⅕ secs. and 3 mins. 17⅗ secs. The latter is the fastest time ever accomplished by an Englishman, and beats the record of 3 mins. 22 secs. by J. Aveling, former amateur champion. Also on Sils Lake, St. Moritz, the Cantab Mr. G. Bramson secured the Gold Medal with 3 mins. 26⅖ secs. On January 9th, over the course prepared for the European championships, Mr. C. Edgington, of Oxford, went for the World's 1-Hour Record, then held by W. Sensburg, the German amateur champion. The latter had turned professional since his wonderful performance in 1898, and Edgington, notwithstanding a fall which dislocated his shoulder, and another which put the shoulder in again, managed to beat the record with 30,896 mètres, or 19 miles 348 yards. The course was oblong, and 400 mètres to the lap. The European Figure and Speed Championships fixed for the 14th and 15th of January at Davos, owing to snow, had to be postponed to the 16th and 17th. The ice, however, was soft, and a blinding snowstorm came on at the end of the second day. This, of course, prevented any records being altered, but Peder Oestlund skated wonderfully well and added the title of European champion to that of the world to his name. In an extra race at the rather unusual distance of 1,000 mètres he made a world record of 1 min. 38 secs. C. Edgington, very sore after his fall the previous week, was unable to do himself justice, and Messrs. Bramson and A. E. Tebbitt, the British amateur champion, both returned home before the races. Oestlund won all four events, the 500 mètres in 47⅗ secs., the 5,000 mètres in 9 mins. 2⅗ secs., the 1,500 mètres in 2 mins. 27⅕ secs., and the 10,000 in the snow in 18 min. 38⅓ secs. G. Estlander, of Helsingfors, was second in the 1,500 and 5,000 mètres to the Trondjhem champion, and J. Greeve, of Amsterdam, and J. Seyler, of Munich, second in the 10,000 and 500 mètres respectively. The Figure Skating Championship was won by Herr Ulrick Salchow, of Stockholm, the last year's European champion, with 250⅘ points to Herr Hügel's, of Vienna, 240⅘ secs. Previously to these championships, on Thursday, 12th January, Davos beat St. Moritz, at bandy, by 6 goals to 2. Captain E. G. Wynyard was in goal for the winners, and C. K. Phillips, the Oxford rowing Blue, goal for St. Moritz, teams eight a-side. The English Skating Bowl on the 16th January was won by A. L. Duin with a total of 164 to E. Gwynne Evans's 157 out of a possible 200 points. At the time fixed for the world's championships January 21, 22 and 29, at Vienna and Berlin, there was no ice at either of those places, or even at Moscow or Buda Pesth, and Davos seemed likely to be ultimately selected. On January 28—30, the Scottish Branch of the N.S.A. were enabled to bring off one or two races during a short spell of frost which visited Scotland at that time. At Castle Semple Loch, the one-mile championship of Renfrewshire was won by J. Hemler, of Lochwinnoch, in 4 mins. 2$\frac{1}{5}$ sec. On Loch Leven the Club Skating One-Mile Championship was won by J. Bayne, of Kinross, in 3 mins. 42 secs., who also skated half a mile in 1 min. 42 secs. On Monday, the 30th, Bayne won the Scottish One-Mile Championship on Loch Leven in 3 mins. 39$\frac{3}{5}$ secs. On a fairly good quarter-mile track on the following Saturday, on Castle Semple Loch, A. E. Tebbitt, of Cambridge, won a mile-and-a-half championship of the Scottish Branch in 4 mins. 55 secs. The American Championships were decided at Spring Lake, Poughkeepsie, New York, Jan. 26—28. The distances were altered to those of the International Union for purposes of comparison. The ice was soft on the first day, but afterwards smooth and hard. The times (very poor) and winners were: 500 mètres E. A. Thomas, Newburg, 59$\frac{3}{5}$ secs.; 1,500 mètres, E. A. Thomas, 3 mins. 6$\frac{2}{5}$ secs.; 5,000 mètres, J. Drury, Montreal, 10 mins. 22$\frac{3}{5}$ secs.; 10,000 mètres, C. McClave, New York A.C., 21 mins. 36 secs. The World's Speed Championships eventually took place at Berlin, February 4th and 5th. The Berlin Skating Club held the first day's meeting in the Friedenau Sport Park, Berlin, and on the second day on the West Eisbahn in Charlottenburg; both were very thin ice sheets over rink surfaces. The track was small, and owing to the thaw their Norwegian blades were liable to go through into the earth beneath. The whole arrangements were disgraceful, and the championships were only so in name. However, the best man certainly won, so not much harm was done. P. Oestlund won the 500 mètres, time 50$\frac{1}{2}$ secs.; 5,000 mètres, time 9 mins. 54$\frac{3}{5}$ secs.; 1,500 mètres, time 2 mins. 45 secs. These victories gained him the World's Championship, and in the 10,000 mètres he was beaten by J. Seyler, Davos. But J. C. Greeve, of Amsterdam, won, with the fastest time of 4 mins. 36$\frac{1}{5}$ secs. In addition to the World's Championships, a German Centenary 1,500 mètres race was won by J. Seyler, of München, very easily in 2 mins. 50$\frac{3}{5}$ secs., for now that Kleeberg and Sensburg are both professionals there is no German amateur in Seyler's class. An International Figure Skating contest was also held, and G. Hügel, Vienna, turned the tables on V. Salchow, of Stockholm, winning with 188 points to 181$\frac{3}{5}$ out of a total of 210. E. Fellner of Vienna also competed. The result of this competition added to the interest in the Figure Skating Championship of the World contest, originally fixed to take place at Vienna, but, owing to want of ice, eventually transferred to Davos. The date was February 12th. There were only three competitors, Hügel, Salchow and an Englishman, Mr. Syers, of the N.S.A. The ice was soft, owing to a recent thaw, but the Austrian and the Swede gave a magnificent exhibition of the art of figure skating, the judges awarding the championship to Hügel with 341$\frac{3}{5}$ marks against 338$\frac{2}{5}$ to Salchow out of a possible 375, the average of the total points awarded by the five judges being given. Grenander, the 1898 champion, was not present. As a wind up to a by no means successful season, the annual competition for the combined Figure Skating Challenge Shield took place at Niagara, London, on March 7th. Four teams were engaged, and the judges awarded the shield to Mr. Bell's team with 73 marks, the Davos first team being second with 69$\frac{2}{5}$ marks. Miss M. Cave, in the winning team, was the only lady entered. The judging and verdict subsequently gave rise to a good deal of discussion in the papers. Mr. H. Ellington, London Rowing Club, Putney, is Hon. Secretary of the speed department of the National Skating Association.

SPORTING RETROSPECT.

Winners of the Oxford and Cambridge Competitions for 1899.

Cross Country	Oxford	30 points 25
*Rugby Football	Cambridge	11 points nil
*Association Football	Cambridge	3 goals 1
Hockey	Cambridge	5 goals 2
Boxing and Fencing	Oxford	5 events 1
Billiards (Single)	Oxford	49 points
Billiards (Double)	Oxford	208 points
Point-to-point Steeplechase	Oxford	easily
*Athletic Sports	Draw	5 events all
*Boat Race	Cambridge	easily
Chess	Cambridge	5$\frac{1}{2}$ games 4$\frac{1}{2}$
Golf	Oxford	18 holes
Rackets (Single)	Cambridge	4 games 3
Rackets (Double)	Cambridge	3 games love
Polo	Oxford	11 goals 1
Swimming	Cambridge	2 events 1
Lawn Tennis (Single)	Oxford	6 matches 3
Lawn Tennis (Double)	Cambridge	5 matches 4
Cycling	Oxford	10 points
*Cricket	Draw	
Tennis (Single)	Cambridge	3 sets love
Tennis (Double)	Oxford	3 sets 1

Total, Oxford, 10 events; Cambridge, 10 events; 2 draws.

* Events marked with an asterisk are supposed to be the five major ones, hence Cambridge can claim supremacy for the year, although on points Light and Dark Blues are exactly level.

SWIMMING.

The year 1899 was in every way a successful swimming year. Club entertainments attracted more spectators and more entries than before, and judging by the all-round improvement in records our best exponents of the art have arrived almost at the very highest pitch of perfection in skill, speed, and stamina. The Amateur Swimming Association, the controlling body of the sport, certainly never lose an opportunity for legislating for every branch and description of swimming; and if they are inclined to rather overburden their constituents with rules and regulations no one can deny that the A.S.A. has done a national service in fostering and improving swimming, and inducing thousands to learn how to save themselves and others from drowning, to say nothing of the great benefits to the community at large by increased and increasing bathing accommodation in our inland and over-populated towns, for which the A.S.A. is in a great measure responsible. The Life-Saving Society, a branch of the parent body, is doing most excellent work, and increasing its branches all over the world. In a few years there will be very few Englishmen not able to swim, and also very few who are not acquainted with the correct and proper methods to restore animation to the partially drowned. The championships of the A.S.A. may be, and, indeed, are, simply the stepping stones to the professional ranks, and the touring exhibitions of some of those champions may not be conducted quite on strictly amateur lines; but perhaps in swimming the end justifies the means, and it is not wise to look too closely at the methods by which we are rapidly becoming a nation of swimmers, and which will soon make swimming baths and swimming instruction a prominent feature in every town, college, and school in the kingdom. Professional swimming, except for the usual Devon and Cornwall August matches and a race in the Seine, were almost a dead letter in 1899. This is perhaps a natural result of the super-excellence of the amateurs of the present day.

The racing of the year may be briefly summed up as a long run of brilliant victories for J. A. Jarvis, who has now quite eclipsed the fame and reputation of the once invincible J. H. Tyers, now a professional, who at the end of 1897 held every amateur record from 100 yards to one mile. It is true that Derbyshire and Lane the Australian are both better than Jarvis at any distance from a quarter-mile and under, but then both have better records than even Tyers at these short distances. That Jarvis is the best long-distance racing swimmer that we have ever seen, either amateur or professional, goes without saying, and his mile and half-mile records are likely to stand for many a long day. Derbyshire is still so young that he may be expected to improve, and should ere long accomplish that ambition of all sprint champion swimmers—100 yards in one minute. All A.S.A. records for distances up to 500 yards must be made in a bath not less than 25 yards long, and from 880 yards to one mile in open water, with the course not less than 220 yards in length. The racing season may be said to open with the Oxford and Cambridge annual Swimming and Water Polo matches at the Bath Club in London on June 24th. The new Water Polo rule as to a penalty throw being awarded for a foul within four yards of the goal-line was very wisely not adhered to. The 50 Yards was won by H. A. Powell, Trinity, Cambridge, O. C. C. Nicholls, Keble, Oxford, being second, the Cambridge captain winning by inches in 33 2-5 secs. On points, a tie. The 120 Yards Powell also won, J. D. Adams, Balliol, Oxford, being second; time, 1 min. 20 2-5 secs. On points Cambridge won—four points to six. The Quarter Mile Adams won, D. C. Patterson, Christ's, Cambridge, being second; time, 7 min. 12 2-5 secs. On points a tie. Team race, seven a-side, Oxford won easily. In the Water Polo match Cambridge won easily, their third victory since the inauguration of these matches in 1891. In Swimming, the half blue is now granted at Cambridge. On July 1st the Thames swimming meeting at Surbiton was notable from the fact that in the Half Mile F. C. V. Lane, the Australian champion, easily defeated R. G. F. Cohen, of the Otter, and A. A. Green, of the same club, in 10 min. 5 4-5 secs. The 220 Yards Public Schools race was won by A. S. Good, of Laneing College, in 4 min. 7 secs. F. C. V. Lane, the Australian amateur champion, arrived in this country on May 11th, having entered for all the Amateur Championships. He was the holder of two World's records, viz., 300 Yards in 3 min. 46 3-5 secs., February 3, 1899, and 220 Yards in 2 min. 38 1-5 secs. J. H. Derbyshire began well for the season with a record at Burslem, viz., 1 min. 38 4-5 secs. for the Northern Counties A.S.A. 150-Yards Championship. The Southern Counties A.S.A. 100-Yards Championship at

Tunbridge Wells, was won by J. H. Hellings in 65 secs., A. A. Green being second. These two performances led up to the Long-Distance Amateur Championship, from Kew Railway Bridge to Putney Pier, on July 8th. J. A. Jarvis, of Leicester, the holder, led all the way, and won easily in 1 hour 9 min. 45 secs., T. Wildgoose, of Hyde Leal, being second; time, 1 hour 13 min. 4 secs. Twelve entered; all started and finished. On Saturday, July 15, Jarvis, at Walsall, added the 1,000 Yards record to his other laurels by swimming the distance in 14 min. 15 secs., as against Tyers' record of 15 min. 2 secs., a truly marvellous performance. On the same day at Highgate Ponds the Life Saving Society gave a display, attended by same 20,000 spectators. The principal racing items were: National Graceful Diving Contest, won by the holder, H. S. Martin; National 150-Yards Breast Stroke Championship, won by G. Smith, of Greenwich, in 2 min. 26 secs., and National 100-Yards Back Stroke Championship, won by F. Battersley, of Stockport, in 1 min. 40 secs. On July 22nd Jarvis, in the Southwick Canal, Brighton, won the A.S.A. Half-Mile Championship from F. C. V. Lane, of Australia, very easily in the new record time of 12 min. 45 3-5 secs., which puts in the shade his own previous record of 12 min. 52 secs. In the following week M. A. Holbein, the cyclist, performed a wonderful feat of swimming in the Thames from Blackwall to Gravesend and back in 12 hours 27 min. 42¾ secs., out and home, with the tide. The distance is 43 miles. Nothing of the sort has ever been attempted or accomplished before, and later in the season both Holbein and F. Holmes, of Birmingham, were at Dover, with an idea of making the Channel swim, but although the temperature of the water was highly favourable for the trial neither swimmer essayed the task. Both promise to emulate the late Captain Webb during the present year. A swimming match in the Seine, at Puteaux Bridge, for the Professional Championship of France, saw the four well-known Englishmen competitors—Greasley, P. Cavill, J. Nuttall, and A. Cavill. These four finished in the order named in the final heat, in front of all the Frenchmen. Sixty-eight swimmers started. The distance was 547 yards, and the first prize £40. On the Saturday before the August Bank Holiday the A.S.A. 220-Yards Championship, in the absence of the holder, J. H. Derbyshire—in the doctor's hands—was won by the Australian, F. C. V. Lane, in the Corporation Baths, Brighton, in the record time of 2 min. 38 1-5 secs., W. H. Lister, of the Osborne, being second. On the following Monday Jarvis, in the river Soar, near Abbey Park, added the A.S.A. One-Mile Championship, and also a new record, to his credit; T. Wildgoose, of Hyde Leal, was second to him. The time beat all records, amateur or professional, viz., 25 min. 13 2-5 secs. He won as he liked, and left the water perfectly fresh. Also during August Holbein, off Portsmouth, swam for twelve hours as a trial for the Channel trip, and T. Wildgoose won the Northern Counties 1,000-Yards Championship at Southport in 15 min. 10 secs., a long way behind Jarvis's new record. Derbyshire competed, but was still far from well. In a handicap race on August 24th Jarvis from scratch won in 5 min. 50 2-5 secs. at the Camberwell Baths. The time is a record, but it is not in conformity with the A.S.A. regulations for being accepted by that body. On the last Saturday in August at Blackpool F. C. V.

Lane and Jarvis met for the Salt Water Quarter-Mile Championship, and for once Jarvis was beaten, Lane winning by five yards from the Leicester man in 6 min. 30 secs., Wildgoose being third. Jarvis subsequently won the Midland Counties Half-Mile (12 min. 36 secs.) and Quarter-Mile (6 min. 1·5 sec.) Championships, and C. V. Lane at Blackpool swam 300 yards in 3 min. 47. 4·5 secs., which beats anything previously done in this country. Immediately before the A.S.A. Plunging Championship, which was won by the holder, Major W. Taylor, with a plunge of 73 ft. 9in., at St George's Baths, on September 21st, Taylor, at Bootle, without a time limit, accomplished 82 ft., after reaching the 78 ft. mark in the 60 seconds' limit. The Ulph Challenge Cup, swum from pier to pier at Great Yarmouth, was won on Sept. 18th by J. A. Jarvis, who won as he liked, G. Sharp, of Leicester, being second. The time was a record (9 min. 8 secs.). On the same day at Sunderland the A.S.A. 100-Yards Championship, " the blue ribbon of the bath," was won again by the holder, J. H. Derbyshire, beating Lane, the Australian, by four yards in 60 2·5 secs., only 1·5 sec. outside record. W. H. Lister was third in the final heat. On September 23rd, at Nottingham, the last of the A.S.A. championships, the 500 Yards, was won easily by J. A. Jarvis in 6 min. 51 secs. P. H. Lister was his only opponent, Lane being unwell and unable to compete. The Ravensbourne S.C. entertainment at the Westminster Baths on Sept. 30th was, as usual, a very varied and interesting function. The prizes were, if anything, too valuable, and provoked in certain quarters considerable discussion as to the advisability of rewarding amateurs with such a lavish hand. In a mixed distance team race, England (Derbyshire and Jarvis) *versus* Australia (Hellings and Lane), Australia with Lane won by a touch. The Ladies' 100-Yards Challenge Cup was won by Miss I. B. Cudlipp, of Portsmouth. Before the end of the season, at Paisley, on October 2nd, J. A. Jarvis put in some marvellous swimming, covering 1,000 yards in 13 min. 43 secs., and also *en route* beat the 500-yards amateur record with 6 min. 38 secs. On the following Wednesday at Edinburgh Jarvis swam 440 yards in 5 min. 51 3·5 secs., a record. Subsequently Jarvis made two more attempts on the 500 yards record, but failed. Water Polo flourished amazingly during the year, the results of the principal matches being :—

Scotland beat Ireland at Belfast, 4 goals to 1 ;
England beat Wales at Warrington, 8 goals to 1 ;
Wales beat Scotland at Penarth, 6 goals to 4 ;
Wales beat Ireland at Swansea, 6 goals to 3 ;
England beat Ireland at Westminster (Ravensbourne Gala), 12 goals to 0 ; and finally, on October 7, at Aberdeen, England, with Lister, Jarvis, and Derbyshire, beat Scotland, 5 goals to 1. Lancashire beat Middlesex for the County Championship, 4 to 2, and the North beat the South, 9 to 5. For the English Club Championship Manchester Osborne (with Lister and Derbyshire) beat St. Helens, 5 to 1. E. A. Fry, of Penarth, is the Welsh 100 yards champion, his time being 1 min. 11 secs. The Hon. Sec. of the Amateur Swimming Association is G. Pragnell, 22, St. Paul's Churchyard, E.C.

THE TURF.

THE turf year 1899 was chiefly remarkable for the wonderful success of Lord William Beresford's horses and the American jockeys. It was certainly a one-horse year so far as the three-year-olds were concerned, there being not a single animal able to really extend Flying Fox at even weights, and Cyllene, the champion four-year-old of the season, only ran twice, and then retired for good. The two-year-olds, with two exceptions, were not generally considered of a very high class, and one of these exceptions is a gelding. Turf legislation has been unusually quiet, but at last a final decision from the very highest legal authority in the land —the House of Lords—has been given in the Kempton Park case, the point being whether or not the Betting House Act could be applied to the rings and enclosures on our racecourses. The case went up from the Court of Appeal, which had almost unanimously decided that the " place " of the Betting House Act did not apply to a racecourse enclosure. The House of Lords thereupon heard the appeal argued in May, 1898, when the question was regarded as so important that nine judges were called in to sit with the law lords. The judgment of the law lords, delivered in March, 1899, was in the same direction as that of the Court of Appeal, and overwhelmingly so—by seven against two—Against : Lord Chancellor, Lord Chancellor of Ireland, Lord Watson, Lord Macnaghten, Lord Morris, Lord Shand, and Lord James. For : Lord Hobhouse and Lord Davey. The appeal was accordingly dismissed with costs. The grounds of this final decision, as stated by the Lord Chancellor, were to the effect that the Betting House Act of 1853 prohibited the opening of a house, office, room, or other place for the purpose of the owner or occupier betting with persons resorting to the house, etc., so opened. The Act did not prohibit betting, nor affect to deal with the betting of people unconnected with the house betting. The betting man using the particular place differed with regard to this question in no way from any other member of the public who entered it, and who neither did nor intended to bet. It was nothing to the purpose that there were a great many betting men who might be found in the enclosure ; there was no business being conducted by a keeper or owner in the enclosure. It was upon this word " use " that the whole question turned, and he thought here there was no such betting establishment at all as was aimed at by the Legislature, and no keeper or owner who betted with anyone. It seemed to him that the thing against which the enactment was levelled was any place used in the sense he had explained.

The starting gate is to have a real and genuine trial this season, although the Americans are said to be very much opposed to the Colonial plan.

The classic racing of the year—the Two Thousand, Derby, and St. Leger— resulted in adding another triple crown winner, the most appropriately-named Flying Fox, by Orme—Vampire, to the select list of these equine wonders. Early in January Caiman and Flying Fox were backed at evens against the field for the Two Thousand Guineas, but with Caiman not engaged in the Derby, Flying Fox at 4½ to 1 was always favourite for the great Epsom event, St. Gris and Holocauste being his nearest companions at 6 to 1 and 8 to 1 respectively. A defeat in the Column Produce Stakes at Newmarket, April 12th, soon settled St. Gris's pretensions, and a still more indifferent performance in the Newmarket Stakes (£3,196), won by Dominie II., May 10th, completely put the Galopin colt out of court. Flying Fox, ridden by M. Cannon, made his début for the year in the Two Thousand Guineas, value £4,250, with 6 to 5 laid on his chance, and he won by two lengths from Caiman, with Sloan up. The latter was reported beaten in his trial, and he was not backed to any great extent except by the then persistent backers of the American jockey. So great a certainty did the Derby appear for him that Flying Fox started at 2½ to 1 on, and he won very easily, Damocles being second, and Innocence third. Stakes value £5,450. The Frenchman, Holocauste, ridden by Sloan, and heavily backed at 6 to 1, broke a fetlock below Tattenham Corner, and had to be destroyed, Sloan fortunately escaping without injury. Flying Fox, by a couple of victories between the Derby and St. Leger, conclusively proved his title to be considered the very best of his year, but six successive victories by Caiman over one-mile courses established the American firmly in the St. Leger betting at 4 to 1, Flying Fox on the day being backed freely at 3½ to 1 on. If anything, M. Cannon beat Sloan more easily than in the Derby, Scintillant being third. The victory added £4,050 to the Duke of Westminster's account. Three times more Flying Fox appeared on a racecourse, on each occasion winning easily. Carrying 9st. 5lb. he won the Princess of Wales' Stakes at Newmarket, June 29th, value £7,190, Royal Emblem, 3 years, 8st. 2lb., being second, and Ninus, 4 years, 9st. 11lb., third ; 6 to 4 on was the price of the winner. Notwithstanding the hard ground he next started for the Eclipse Stakes, £9,285, at Sandown, July 14th, and won easily from Frontier, 3 years, 9st. 1lb., second, 100 to 14 being laid on the Derby winner's chance. This last effort for the season was in the Jockey Club Stakes (£7,190), at Newmarket, Sept. 28. Here, with 8 to 1 on, he won very easily, Scintillant, receiving 11lbs., being second, with Jeddah, the 1898 Derby winner, amongst the beaten lot. As he retired perfectly sound and is heavily engaged this season he should again sweep the board in 1900. Sibola, by Sailor Prince— Saluda, who ran six times, winning four races, and being second twice, won the One Thousand (£3,800), ridden by Sloan, with Fascination second, and Musa third. Sibola was favourite at 13 to 8. In the Oaks, Musa, by Martagon—Palmflower, and ridden by O. Madden, a 20 to 1 chance, just beat the favourite Sibola, 7 to 4 on, Sloan's mount, by a head ; Musa, however, did not win another race. The Cup Races of 1899 were hardly more successful than in 1898. Cyllene, by Bonavista—Arcadia, won the Gold Cup at Ascot, value £3,340, Lord Edward II. being second, and the French crack, Gardefeu, third. Previously, on the opening day at Ascot, Cyllene won the Forty-fifth Triennial Stakes (£672), over a two-miles course. This and the Cup distance of 2½ miles on the Thursday, on the terribly hard and badly kept Ascot course, may or may not have injured his legs. Any way, he did not run again, and after a match between Cyllene and Flying Fox had almost been arranged in the autumn Cyllene was withdrawn for stud purposes. A race between these two magnificent animals would have been an event of the century. Merman, a regular veteran, won the Goodwood Cup (£490), from King's Messenger and Newhaven II. Caverley won the Doncaster Cup, from St. Ia and Innocence. The ten thousand pound stakes and rich handicaps over short distances appear to have quite spoilt Cup racing amongst the better class of animals. Indeed, the

Queen's Vase, at Ascot, failed to fill, and the Three Miles Alexandra Plate (£1,395), at Ascot, was won by the Frenchman, Le Sénateur, Grace Skelton and Nouveau Riche being his only opponents. The handicaps of the year were mostly very successful from all points of view. General Peace, 5 years, 7st. 5lb., O. Madden up, at 100 to 7, won the Lincolnshire (£1,440), Knight of the Thistle being second, Sloan riding. Manifesto won the Liverpool Grand National (£1,975), at 5 to 1, a second favourite. King's Messenger, 4 years, 7st. 10lb., favourite at 4½ to 1, won the Great Metropolitan (£925), at Epsom, and Newhaven II., top weight, 9st., ridden by M. Cannon, won the City and Suburban Handicap (£1,665). The Chester Cup (£2,030), 2½ miles, fell to Uncle Mac, ridden by Finlay, at 12½ to 1. A splendid field started for the Kempton Park Great Jubilee Handicap (£2,215), Knight of the Thistle, 6 years, 8st. 4lb., the favourite at 4½ to 1, and ridden by Sloan, being a most popular victory. The Ascot Stakes (£1,680) fell to Tom Cringle, 4 years, 7st. 9lb., and the Hunt Cup (£2,520), another good field of horses, was won by Refractor, 3 years, 6st. 3lb., at 25 to 1. At Goodwood, the Stewards' Cup (£672) was won by Northern Farmer, 5 years, 7st. 6lb., at 20 to 1. At York the Great Ebor (£925) went to Cassock's Pride, 6 years, 8st., at 100 to 6. The Cesarewitch (£1,030) was as usual one of the— if not the most important handicap of the season. Scintillant and Irish Ivy were equal favourites at 6 to 1, and the former, 3 years 7st., won by a head in the hands of F. Wood. Scintillant, in March, had been backed at 20 to 1, for the Derby. Irish Ivy made up for this defeat by winning the Cambridgeshire, value £1,620, fairly easily at the much more remunerative price of 20 to 1. Chubb, 4 years, 7st. 12lb., won the Liverpool Autumn Cup, value £1,075, starting at 100 to 6, and ridden by K. Cannon, who also had had the mount on Irish Ivy. The last handicap of the year, the Manchester November £(1,375), was a complete surprise, Sloan winning on Proclamation, 3 years, 7st. 7lbs., including 10lbs. extra for winning the Derby Cup, subsequently to the weights for the Manchester race being published. For 25 to 1 to be laid against Sloan's mount was a most remarkable occurrence, and his thick-and-thin supporters must have been well rewarded, even after Sloan's long run of previous defeats. The American jockeys won all the races but one, on this the last day of the season, November 25. Proclamation had also run second to Chubb for the Liverpool Autumn Cup. In Australia, Mr. H. Power's Merriwee won the Victoria Derby, at Flemington, on November 4, and the same animal followed this up by also landing the Melbourne Cup over two miles—Australia's champion race ; a very smart performance for a three-year-old. Merriwee is by Bill of Portland.

As regards the two-year-olds, the racing of the season proves Lord William Beresford's Democrat, an American gelding by Sensation— Equality and Forfarshire by Royal Hampton— St. Elizabeth, to be far and away the pick of the youngsters. The last-named, after two defeats, won four races right off the reel. Democrat won six out of nine engagements. It is a difficult case between these two animals, as at Sandown in July Democrat gave Forfarshire nine pounds and beat him, but at Kempton Park subsequently, in October, Forfarshire gave the American 3 lbs. and beat him a head. Democrat's performances were as follows. He was beaten by Emotion for the

Royal Two-Year-Old Plate at Kempton (£2,660), on May 5, by O'Donovan Rossa for the Bedford Plate (£762), at Newmarket, May 11, and again at Epsom on June 1 in the Great Surrey Breeders' Foal Plate (£1,149) by the same colt, Forfarshire only obtaining third place, with Democrat fourth, the two latter meeting at even weights. At Ascot, Democrat won the Coventry Stakes (£1,826), Diamond Jubilee being fourth behind him, at even weights. At Hurst Park, July 1, Democrat won the Foal Plate (£1,135) from a weak field, and then at Sandown, on July 15, for the National Breeders' Produce Stakes (£4,357) he gave Forfarshire 9 lbs. and beat him a neck, O'Donovan Rossa being behind the pair. The classic Champagne (£1,310) at Doncaster, September 5, was the next victory of the American, a big field of previous winners being behind him. The Rous Memorial (£568) at Newmarket, September 29, followed—a 10 to 1 on victory; and then at Kempton, October 6, in the Imperial Stakes (£2,777), 6 furlongs, came Democrat's crucial test. Forfarshire, with 3 lbs. the worst of the weights, beat the Yankee by a head, the finish between S. Loates and Sloan being very fine indeed. Forfarshire did not appear again, and Democrat added the Middle Park Plate and the Dewhurst Plate to his victories, Diamond Jubilee being second on both occasions. Forfarshire, after his defeat by Democrat at Sandown in July, was not again compelled to lower his colours. At Goodwood, he won the Rous Memorial (£1,095), the Kempton Park International Breeders' Two-Year-Old Stakes (£935), the Derby Champion Breeders' Foal Stakes (£1,025), and then came the defeat of Democrat. Democrat is well shaped, and of the long and low order, and evidently as sound as a bell. Forfarshire is a big, upstanding, chesnut colt. He is rather high in the leg for the Epsom gradients, but he certainly retired for the season in a sound condition. Pephaps the third best two-year-old is the Prince of Wales's Diamond Jubilee by St. Simon —Perdita II. He ran six times, finishing second to Democrat in both the Middle Park and the Dewhurst Plate, his previous race and solitary win being in the Boscawen Stakes at Newmarket, September 27, value £1,220. He was beaten by Epsom Lad for the Prince of Wales Stakes at Goodwood, value £2,400, and before that, he suffered defeat in the Coventry Stakes at Ascot, won by Democrat, and also in the July Stakes at Newmarket. Diamond Jubilee will probably considerably improve on his two-year running, as there is plenty of room for him to fill out and he ran rather unkindly in several of his early efforts.

Owing to the remarkable career of Flying Fox, the Duke of Westminster heads the list of winning owners with the respectable total of £43,965, the Fox being responsible for £37,415 of this sum. Lord William Beresford comes second with £42,736 10s. his two-year-old crack Democrat only accounting for £13,000 of this amount. Sir R. W. Griffith, the third winning owner, is a long way behind the leading pair with £14,805. Mr. L. de Rothschild is fourth with £11,444, as against his last year's total of £30,267, when he stood first on the list. Mr. A. James is fifth with £10,655. The other big winners are Mr. D. Baird, £8,410; Prince Soltykoff, £8,196; Mr. Russel, £8,034; Lord Ellesmere, £6,979; Duke of Portland, £6,654; Lord Rosebery, £6,579; Mr. T. R. Dewar, £6,405. It may be noticed that the Duke of Westminster's total was obtained by six horses only, whereas Lord W. Beresford's

amount of prize money required thirty horses to win 69 races. The Prince of Wales won only the very small total of £2,189.

The table of winning jockeys of the season is always an interesting study, and the first dozen jockeys work out as follows:—1st, S. Loates, mounts 731, lost 571, won 160; 2nd, O. Madden, mounts 807, lost 677, won 130; 3rd, M. Cannon, mounts 468, lost 348, won 120; 4th, T. Ioates, mounts 693, lost 581, won 112; 5th, J. T. Sloan, mounts 345, lost 237, won 108; 6th, T. Weldon, mounts 374, lost 299, won 75; 7th, F. Allsop, mounts 688, lost 615, won 73; 8th, F. Rickaby, mounts 477, lost 405, won 72; 9th, L. Reiff, mounts 184, lost 129, won 55; 10th. F. Finlay, mounts 467, lost 419, won 48; 11th, J. H. Martin, mounts 168, lost 125, won 43; 12th, J. Fagan, mounts 280, lost 247, won 33. J. Reiff, another Yankee jockey, aged 14, has done very well with 140 mounts, 113 lost and 27 wins. In the order of winning percentages the four American jockeys, Sloan L. and J. Reiff, and J. H. Martin work out grandly, the order being—Sloan, 31·30, 1st; L. Reiff, 29·88, 2nd; M. Cannon, 25·64, 3rd; J. H. Martin, 25·59, 4th; S. Loates, 21·87, 5th; F. Weldon, 20·05, 6th; J. Reiff, 19·28, 7th. The investment of £1 per mount during the season would have given to the backers of S. Loates £55, Sloan £36, his last win on the last day of the season at 25 to 1 after 8 consecutive losing rides making all the difference. M. Cannon's backers would have lost £1 17s. 8d.; Madden's, £159 loss; and T. Loates, £163 loss. Sloan retired for a time in the middle of the summer, or his average would have been better no doubt.

J. Porter's stable was the most successful of the year, the total amount won by this trainer being £56,546 with 42 races, but the American trainer, Huggins, although only second as regards the aggregate sum won, viz., £42,793, easily tops the list as regards races won, viz., 72. Orme, by Ormonde, heads the list of winning sires of the season, his total wins 29, producing £46,703; Sensation comes next with 20 wins, value £20,188; St. Simon £17,505; Royal Hampton, £13,530; Donovan, £11,120; and St. Serf, £10,852, being the only five-figure winners.

YACHTING.

The season of 1899 will, of course, always be notable from the fact of another effort being made to bring the America Cup back to the Mother country. Sir Thomas Lipton's challenge, and the subsequent building of the *Shamrock*, provoking a more wide-spread interest and enthusiasm than has probably ever before been witnessed in the yachting history of this country.

In the earlier part of the year, there were indications that the big class would not furnish much sport.

Satanita, in her yawl rig, won 12 prizes in the Mediterranean Regatta, including the "First prize, objet d'art," the "Goelet-Bennett International Cup," and cup presented by the Due d'Abruzzi, for all three of which she sailed over.

The 20-rater *Eldred*, renamed *Mildred*, and the new *Laura*, built at Cowes for Mr. E. Hore, sailed many interesting matches, in which *Laura* scored 14 wins, including prizes presented by T.M. King and Queen of Italy; while the *Mildred* won the Goelet-Bennett Cup in her list of 12 wins.

The English season commenced with the New Thames Club matches on May 27. *Rainbow* and *Bona* were the only two of the big class to take part in the earlier fixture, but excellent sport was provided throughout the season by the 65-feet and 52-feet classes—formerly the 40 and 20-raters,—the competitors in both these classes being very evenly matched.

The handicap class brought out *Creole, Maid Marion, Brynhild,* and *Namara* amongst others, the yawl *Brynhild* proving a grand weather boat.

Britannia was re-purchased by H.R.H. Prince of Wales, and fitted out to act as "trial-horse" for *Shemrock* in two test matches on the Solent. She subsequently competed in the Solent Regattas, and went westward as far as Weymouth, but never won a race, although her inclusion, together with the German Emperor's *Meteor* (yawl-rigged), *Rainbow, Bona,* and *Satanita* created much more interest in the big class at Cowes.

The most prominent feature of the Solent Regattas was the remarkable success of *Meteor.* In her yawl-rig, her sail area had been reduced 514 feet from that which she carried as a cutter. In all, she started nine times, and won eight first prizes, value £690, and the Queen's Cup in the R.Y.S. Regatta. The only occasion on which she did not win, was when she carried away her bobstay and gave up.

The German Emperor's Cup, sailed for by schooners and yawls at the Royal Squadron Regatta, was won by the schooner *Roseneath,* 52 tons, Mr. A. W. Fulcher.

The third annual race, from Dover to Heligoland, for the German Emperor's Gold Cup was won by *Charmian,* schooner, 175 tons, Mr. F. B. Atkinson, and the North Sea Cup, sailed for over the same course by smaller yachts, was won by *Dianthus,* 35 tons, Mr. C. J. Salaman.

The races for the Coupe de France were sailed off at Ryde on July 29 and 31, under the flag of the Royal Temple Yacht Club. This trophy had been won by *Gloria* at Cannes. The challenging yacht on this occasion was the *Anna,* built specially for the purpose by M. Chevreux, for Comte Boni de Castellane. *Laurea,* designed and built at Summer and Paynes', Southampton, for Mr. E. Hore, was the defender. There was a large gathering of French yachts to witness the matches. *Laurea* won the first match by 53 secs. after losing about 12 minutes by leaving a mark on the wrong side, and having to return. In the second match, *Anna* lost her rudder and had to give up. The trophy therefore remains in England.

In addition to those already mentioned, the principal prize winners were : Big class, *Bona,* Mr. J. H. Taylor, Queen's Cup at Royal Cork Regatta, and £1,240; *Rainbow,* Mr. C. L. Orr-Ewing, M.P., £100 Cup, presented by Mr. G. L. Watson, and £180.

65-feet class : *Astild,* Mr. P. M. Inglis, £412 ; *Senta,* Mr. A. Busing, £387; *Tatty,* Carl von Siemens, £695; *Eelin,* Capt. J. Orr-Ewing, £287.

52-feet class : *Senga,* Mr. W. F. Cook, £456 ; *Caprice,* Sir H. Seymour King, Queen's Cup at Royal Thames Regatta, and £299 ; *Forsa,* Mr. C. A. Allan, £72; *Penitent,* Mr. W. P. Burton, £282; *Morning Star,* Mr. A. Coats, £77.

The interest in the America Cup matches was intensified by the absolute secrecy which was maintained in regard to the design and construction of *Shamrock* the Challenger. She was designed by W. Fife, junior, of the Clyde, this being the first America Cup Challenger designed by him. It was originally intended that she should be built at Messrs. Harland and Wolff's yard, Belfast, but with that firm's concurrence she was eventually constructed by Messrs. Thorneycroft, on the Thames at Chiswick. Aluminium entered largely into her composition, even her deck being laid in this metal. Her mast and boom were of hollow steel. She was commanded by Archie Hogarth, assisted by Wringe. She was launched on June 26, and towed round to Southampton to fit out. Two test matches were sailed in the Solent against the *Britannia* on July 18 and 19, when the Challenger's performances were such as to make the majority of yachtsmen very sanguine as to the achievement of her ultimate object, whilst her owner, designer and those more closely interested in her, appeared satisfied and confident. On her arrival in American waters, the general consensus of expert opinion was that their defending yacht *Columbia* had a big task set her to retain the Cup on that side of the Atlantic, although American yachtsmen naturally expressed confidence in their own boat and laid odds on her accordingly. Notwithstanding that the victorious Admiral Dewey return celebrations clashed with the International yacht race, the interest in the latter event by no means suffered.

Exceptional precautions were observed to prevent any interference with the yachts during the race by excursion steamers. The first of the

Year.	Yachts.	Nationality.	Rig.	Tons.	Owners.
1870	*Magic* (winner).	American.	*Schooner.*	98	Mr. F. Osgood.
	Cambria (challenger).	British.	*Schooner.*	198	Mr. J. Ashbury.
1871	*Columbia* } (winners).	American.	*Schooners.* }	220	Mr. F. Osgood.
	Sapphc			310	Mr. W. P. Douglas.
	Livonia (challenger).	British.	*Schooner.*	280	Mr. J. Ashbury.
1876	*Madeline* (winner).	American.	*Schooner.*	152	Mr. J. Dickerson.
	Countess of Dufferin (challenger).	Canadian.	*Schooner.*	139	Mr. C. Gifford.
1881	*Mischief* (winner).	American.	*Sloop.*	79	Mr. J. R. Busk.
	Atlanta (challenger).	Canadian.	*Sloop.*	84	Mr. A. Cuthbert.
1885	*Puritan* (winner).	American.	*Cutter.*	140	Mr. J. M. Forbes.
	Genesta (challenger).	British.	*Cutter.*	80	Sir R. Sutton.
1886	*Mayflower* (winner).	American.	*Cutter.*	161	Genl. Payne.
	Galat a (challenger).	British.	*Cutter.*	90	Lieut. W. Henn, R.N.
1887	*Volunteer* (winner).	American.	*Cutter.*	152	Genl. Payne.
	Thistle (challenger).	British.	*Cutter.*	149	Mr. J. Bell.
1893	*Vigilant* (winner).	American.	*Cutter.*	178	Mr. Morgan.
	Valkyrie II. (challenger).	British.	*Cutter.*	155	Lord Dunraven.
1895	*Defender* (winner).	American.	*Cutter.*	202	Mr. Iselin.
	Valkyrie III. (challenger).	British.	*Cutter.*	210	Lord Dunraven.

series of five races was set for decision on October 2, but not being completed within the time limit (five and a-half hours) through want of wind, was declared off, and owing to unfavourable weather conditions—calms and fogs—it was not until the eighth attempt that the first race was actually sailed off, when *Co'umbia* won by 11 minutes.

In the second race, *Shamrock* was unfortunate enough to carry away her topmast, and *Columbia* finished the course alone.

The third race was won by *Columbia*, who came home 6 minutes 34 seconds ahead of the Challenger, thus leaving the Cup still in the possession of the Americans.

The *Columb a* was designed by Mr. A. G. Herreshoff, of the Herreshoff Manufacturing Company. She is owned by Mr. J. Pierpont Morgan and Mr. C. Oliver Iselin. The Captain of the *Columbia* was Charles Barr, formerly of Gourock — a naturalised American. All the matches were sailed in the vicinity of Sandy Hook Lightship, eight miles outside New York. The distance sailed in each match was about thirty miles.

The principal dimensions of the competitors were: —

	Columbia.		*Shamrock*
Sailing length	102·135 ft.	...	101·92 ft.
Water line	89·68 ft.	...	87·69 ft.
Sq. root of sail area ..	114·61 ft.	...	116·15 ft.
From tip of bowsprit to tip of boom	181·62 ft.	...	189·13 ft.
Height, including topmast	134·75 ft.	...	128·28 ft.

It is generally anticipated that *Columb a* may be expected to come across here and enter at some of our regattas in 1900, when a grand class would be formed with *Shamrock*, *Meteor*, and the new cutter now building on the Clyde for Mr. C. D. Rose—a former owner of *Satanita* –from designs by G. L. Watson.

Dramatic Summary, 1898-9.

Nov. 2, 1898.—YOUNG MR. YARDE, ith Mr. Weedon Grossmith in the title rôle, put on at the Royalty.

Nov. 3.— THE MUSKETEERS, founded on Dumas' novel, presented at Her Majesty's. The principal characters were acted by Messrs. Beerbohm Tree, Lewis Waller, and McLeay, H. Ross, F. Mills, L. Calvert, G. du Maurier; Mesdames Tree, Brown-Potter, and Mabel Love.

Nov. 5.—THE BROAD ROAD, by Robert Marshall, produced at Terry's.

Nov. 10.—An original play by Louis N. Parker and Murray Carson, entitled THE JEST, produced at the Criterion, with Messrs. C. Wyndham, K. Bellew, A. Bishop; Mesdames Mary Moore. Cynthia Brooke, and M. Talbot in the principal parts.

Nov. 30.— A comedietta, A GOLDEN WEDDING, by Eden Phillpotts and Charles Groves, put on at the Haymarket.

Dec. 1.—ON AND OFF, produced at the Vaudeville with Messrs. G. Giddens, Paul Arthur, A. Godfrey; Mesdames E. Chester, E. Page, and L. Milner in the principal parts.

Dec. 3.—CUPBOARD LOVE, a farce by H. V. Esmond, produced at the Court.

Dec. 6.—THE BRIXTON BURGLARY, presented at Terry's.

Dec. 15.—MILORD SIR SMITH, with Mr. Arthur Roberts in the title rôle, given for the first time at the Comedy.

Dec. 22.—ALICE IN WONDERLAND, put on at the Opera Comique.

Dec. 24.—THE CRYSTAL GLOBE, a drama adapted from the French by Sutton Vane, brought out at the Princess's. The caste included Messrs. L. Irving, A. Playfair, J. D. Saunders, Oscar Adye, O. Yorke; Mesdames Bella Pateman, Ethel Hope, and Lena Ashwell.

Dec. 26.—THE FORTY THIEVES, pantomime by Arthur Sturgess and Arthur Collins, produced at Drury Lane, with Messrs. Dan Leno, Herbert Campbell, H. Fischer, Johnny Danvers; Mesdames Nellie Stewart, Rita Presano, Maud Fowler. and Lillie Belmore in the principal parts.

—— DICK WHITTINGTON, pantomime by Horace Lennard, presented at the Adelphi. The leading parts were played by Messrs. O. E Lemmon, S. Harcourt, F. Eastman, E. Lewis; Mesdames Amy Augarde, Marie Montrose, Jessie Danvers, and Millie Legarde.

Dec. 31.—A LITTLE RAY OF SUNSHINE, produced at the Royalty by Mr. W. S. Penley.

Jan. 3, 1899.—A farcical comedy, by Alfred Maltby and Frank Lindo, entitled MY SOLDIER BOY, presented at the Criterion, the principal parts being played by Messrs. Weedon Grossmith, A. Maltby, Ivan Watson, R. Spyers; and Mesdames Ellis Jefferies, Helen Ferrers, and Margaret Halstan.

Jan. 7.—THE LUCKY STAR, an adapted French comic opera, put on at the Savoy. The caste included Messrs. Walter Passmore, H. A. Lytton, S. Paxton; Mesdames Ruth Vincent, Isabel Jay, and Emmie Owen.

—— SCHOOL, revived at the Globe by Mr. John Hare, who was supported by Messrs. Frank Gilmore, W. H. Day, Gilbert Hare, and Fred. Kerr; Mesdames Mabel Terry-Lewis, and Mary Hersey.

Jan. 9.—THE AMBASSADOR, revived at the St. James's Theatre by Mr. G. Alexander.

Jan. 17.—Miss Annie Hughes gave a special Matinée of MATCHES.

Feb. 7.—Mr. H. V. Esmond produced his play, GRIERSON'S WAY, at an afternoon performance at the Haymarket Theatre. He was supported by Messrs. Fred. Terry, J. H. Barnes, G. S. Titheradge; Miss Pattie Bell and Miss Lena Ashwell.

Feb. 11.—A comic opera, THE COQUETTE, put on at the Prince of Wales's. The principal parts were played by Messrs. J. Le Hay, Courtice Pounds, W. Edouin; Mesdames A. D'Orme, S. Gastelle, A. Newton, and N. Cadiz.

Feb. 16.—THE ONLY WAY, an adaptation of The Tale of Two Cities, produced at the Lyceum by Mr. Martin Harvey, who was supported by Messrs. H. Blinn, J. G. Taylor, H. Sleath, and B. Webster; Mesdames Grace Warner, Marriott, and de Silva.

Feb. 18.—Robertson's OURS, revived by Mr. Hare at the Globe.

Feb. 22.—SWEET LAVENDER, revived at Terry's Theatre with Miss Nina Boucicault in the title rôle.

Feb. 28. — A REPENTANCE, by John Oliver Hobbs, produced at the St. James's. The caste included Messrs. G. Alexander, H. B. Irving, C. A. Smith, and H. Brown; Mesdames Julie Opp, and Kate Sergeantson.

March 2.—A comedy-farce, THE CUCKOO, adapted from the French DÉCORÉ by C. H. Brookfield, brought out at the Avenue. The principal parts were played by Messrs. C. Hawtrey, A. Williams, C. E. Stevens; Mesdames Fanny Ward, Vane Featherstone, and C. Collier.

March 8.—A LADY OF QUALITY, dramatised from Frances Hodgson Burnett's novel, put on at the Comedy.

March 11.—THE MAN IN THE IRON MASK, produced at the Adelphi. The principal characters were acted by Messrs. Norman Forbes, C. Sugden, W. H. Vernon, W. L. Abingdon, and G. W. Anson; Mesdames Genevieve Warde, D. Drummond, H. Hanbury, and Kate Rorke.

March 16.—A one act drama, by H. Woodville, entitled A WOMAN'S LOVE, put on at the Vaudeville.

March 18.—CASTE revived, by Mr. John Hare at the Globe.

April 1.—THE ONLY WAY removed from the Globe to the Prince of Wales's Theatre.

April 5.—L'AMOUR MOUILLÉ or CUPID AND THE PRINCESS, comic opera, adapted from the French by William Yardley and H. Byatt, produced at the Lyric, the principal parts being played by Mesdames Erie Greene, Jessie Hudleston, Kate Cutler, Messrs. John le Hay, Eastman and Cairn, James.

April 6.—A COMEDY OF TEMPERAMENT by Haddon Chambers, entitled THE TYRANNY OF TEARS, produced at the Criterion, with Messrs. Charles Wyndham, F. Kerr, A. Bishop; Mesdames Maude Millett and Mary Moore in the principal characters.

April 8.—THE GAY LORD QUEX, by Arthur Pinero, played for the first time at the Globe Theatre. The caste included Messrs. John Hare, Gilbert Hare, C. Cherry, F. Gilmore; Mesdames Irene Vanbrugh, Mono Oram, M. Terry Lewis, and L. McGilvray.

April 12.—A new play by H. A. Jones, called CARNAC SAHIB, produced at Her Majesty's. The leading characters were played by Messrs. Tree, L. Waller, F. P. Stevens, F. Mills, J. D. Beveridge, G. du Maurier; Mesdames Brown-Potter, Eva Moore, Vynor and Cardoza.

April 15.—ROBESPIERRE, rendered into English by Laurence Irving from Victorien Sardou's play, put on at the Lyceum, with Sir H. Irving in the *title rôle*. Other parts were played by Messrs. K. Bellew, Cooper Cliffe, Fuller Mellish, L. Calvert, L. Irving, C. Dodsworth, P. Johnson; Mesdames Ellen Terry, W. Fraser, Maud Milton and Edith Craig.

April 25.—CHANGE ALLEY, by Louis N. Parker and Murray Carson, brought out at the Garrick. The principal characters were acted by Messrs. Fred Terry, J. H. Barnes, E. Lewis, J. Billington, Murray Carson; Mesdames Julia Neilson, L. Waller, J. Ferrar and Hall Caine.

April 26.—IN DAYS OF OLD, by Edward Rose, produced at the St. James's, with Messrs. G. Alexander, H. B. Irving, H. V. Esmond, K. Douglas, A. Calvert, S. Brough; Mesdames Fay Davis, V. Vanbrugh, Esme Beringer and Julie Opp, in the principal parts.

April 27.—A GOOD TIME, a musical farce, put on at the Opera Comique.

May 1.—WHY SMITH LEFT HOME, put on at the Strand; characters by Messrs. M. Arbuckle, F. Peters, M. B. Snyder, W. Thomas; Mesdames Smith, Eberle, R. Snyder, D. Usher and Annie Yeamans.

May 2.—Lydia Thompson's farewell benefit at the Lyceum.

May 8.—The Opera Season opened at Covent Garden with a performance of Lohengrin.

May 9.—THE ORDEAL OF THE HONEYMOON, a duologue by Estelle Burney, played at the Prince of Wales's', by Miss Winifred Emery and Mr. Cyril Maude.

May 15.—A matinée performance of JUDY, by P. Pickering, given at the Prince of Wales's.

May 23.—An original comedy by R. C. Carton, entitled WHEELS WITHIN WHEELS, produced at the Court; principal parts by Messrs. Eric Lewis, Dion Boucicault, T. Thalberg, A. Bourchier; Mesdames Lena Ashwell, Pattie Brown and Miss Compton.

June 6.—Revival of H.M.S. PINAFORE, at the Savoy, with Messrs. W. Passmore, H. A. Lytton, R. Evett, R. Temple; Mesdames Ruth Vincent, E. Owen and R. Brandram, in the leading parts.

June 5.—THE COWBOY AND THE LADY, put on at the Duke of York's Theatre.

June 10.—HALVES, by A. Conan Doyle, produced at the Garrick, the principal parts being played by Messrs. B. Thomas, C. Maltby, F. Morgan; Mesdames Nellie Thorne and Geraldine Oliffe.

June 12.—Madame Sarah Bernhardt appeared as Hamlet at the Adelphi Theatre.

June 19.—AN AMERICAN CITIZEN, put on at the Duke of York's Theatre, with Mr. N. C. Goodwin and Miss Maxine Elliott in the principal parts.

June 26.—M. Coquelin appeared at the Adelphi in CYRANO DE BERGERAC.

June 27.—THE JEWELS, by S. H. Mosenthal, given at a morning performance at the Shaftesbury.

June 29.—THE WEATHER HEN, given at a matinée at Terry's Theatre.

July 5.—THE LADY OF OSTEND, a farce, put on at Terry's, with Messrs. Weedon Grossmith, C. Groves, E. Gurney; Mesdames E. Jeffreys, M. A. Victor, and Ethel Clinton in the principal parts.

July 20.—EL CAPITAN, put on at the Lyric, with an American company, headed by Mr. De Wolf Hopper.

July 25.—THE WILD RABBIT, a farcical comedy, by George Arliss, produced at the Criterion, under the management of H. A. Lytton and Stanley Cooke.

Aug. 19.—WITH FLYING COLOURS, by Seymour Hicks and Fred Latham, played for the first time at the Adelphi; principal characters by Messrs. Robert Pateman, W. L. Abingdon, H. Vibant, H. Nicholls, Clarence Holt; Mesdames Cecil Raleigh, Florence Lloyd, H. Leigh, and M. Hyde.

Aug. 24.—GOING THE PACE, put on at the Princess's.

Aug. 31.—An original comedy by Sydney Grundy, THE DEGENERATES, produced at the Haymarket. The principal parts were acted by Mesdames Langtry, Lily Hanbury, Lottie Venne, Lily Grundy; Messrs. C. Hawtrey, E. Maurice, G. Grossmith, jun., L. Kenyon and H. Beatty.

Sept. 1.—A TRIP TO MIDGET-TOWN, put on at the Olympic.

Sept. 2.—Mr. Wilson Barrett revived THE SILVER KING at the Lyceum.

Sept. 4.—THE LAST CHAPTER, by G. H. Broadhurst, presented at the Strand.

Sept. 6.—THE GHETTO, put on at the Comedy, with Mrs. Brown-Potter, Mr. Kyrle Bellew, and Miss Constance Collier, in the leading parts.

———. THE ELIXIR OF LIFE, produced at the Vaudeville; the leading parts being played by Messrs. George Giddens, G. Arliss, F. Eastman; Mesdames F. Jeffreys, Millie Legarde and Juliette Nesville.

Sept. 16.—HEARTS ARE TRUMPS, by Cecil Raleigh, produced at Drury Lane. The caste included Mesdames Violet Vanburgh, Beatrice Ferrar, Dora Barton, D. Drummond, Mary Brough; Messrs. E. Dagnall, Lionel Brough, J. Treasahar and Cooper Cliffe.

Sept. 20.—Mr. Beerbohm Tree revived KING JOHN, at Her Majesty's; himself in the title rôle, and Miss Julia Neilson as Constance.

Sept. 21.—THE MOONLIGHT BLOSSOM, a Japanese romance, produced at the Prince of Wales's, the principal parts being played by Mesdames Patrick Campbell, E. Calhoun, Rosina Filippi and Mr. J. Forbes Robertson.

Sept. 23.—AN INTERRUPTED HONEYMOON, produced at the Avenue.

Sept. 27.—MY DAUGHTER-IN-LAW, put on at the Criterion; principal characters by Messrs. Seymour Hicks, H. Standing, A. Bishop; Mesdames Ellaline Terriss, Fanny Brough and Cynthia Brooke.

Sept. 30.—ALONE IN LONDON, revived at the Princess's.

Oct. 7.—MAN AND HIS MAKERS, a drama, by Wilson Barrett and Louis N. Parker, produced at the Lyceum.

Oct. 9.—THE SACRAMENT OF JUDAS, put on at the Prince of Wales's, with Mr. J. Forbes Robertson and Mrs. Patrick Campbell, in the leading parts.

Oct. 14.—A ROYAL FAMILY, a comedy of romance, presented at the Court Theatre.

Oct. 16.—THE CHRISTIAN, by Hall Caine, put on at the Duke of York's, with Mesdames Evelyn Millard, Lizzie Ecobie, Lily Hall Caine; Messrs. H. Waring, A. Aynesworth, C. Fulton, B. Webster and C. Groves, in the principal characters.

Oct. 19.—THE SIGN OF THE CROSS, revived by Mr. Wilson Barrett at the Lyceum.

Oct. 21.—SAM TOY, a musical play by E. Norton, produced at Daly's Theatre; the leading parts being played by Messrs. Hayden Coffin, Rutland Barrington, Fred Kaye, Scott Russell, Cohn Coop; Mesdames Marie Tempest, Hilda Moody, Gracie Leigh and Gladys Homfray.

Oct. 28.—A dramatic version of Dumas' BLACK TULIP, by Sydney Grundy, produced at the Haymarket. The caste included Messrs. F. Harrison, Cyril Maude, M. Kinghorne, S. Valentine; Mesdames Winifred Emery and E. H. Brooke.

Nov. 6.—THE WRONG MR. WRIGHT, put on a' the Strand.

Scientific and Engineering Summary for 1899.

MOTOR CARS.—There has been a great development of motor cars during the year, especially in France, Belgium, and America. They do not compete so successfully with horses in the United Kingdom, but they are gradually coming into fashion. The most favoured are those worked by the Daimler and Denz petroleum motors, and by electricity, but the former are by far the most numerous. An idea that they are unmanageable and dangerous, or break down easily, has been prejudicial to them, but long journeys and races are giving people confidence in them. Motor car races have become a stirring form of sport. It is not unusual for country gentlemen to visit friends 40 or 50 miles distant by motor car and breakfast or dine with them instead of going by train. Farmers are also learning the advantage of sending their produce by motor car instead of by rail. The Parisian fire brigade has adopted the motor car for horse vehicles, and the French military are about to do the same, for transporting baggage and guns. Sportsmen at the moors, tourists and other pleasure seekers are pressing it into their service, and in addition to these light or heavy cars the motor cycle is coming into general use. It is more and more evident that the motor car is destined to a great future.

THE "ERMAK."—The new ice-breaking steamer "Ermak," built for the Russian Government to keep their Baltic ports clear of ice in winter, has been tried north of Spitzbergen with a view to test its capability for crushing a way to the North or South Pole, and has forced a passage through ice 14 feet thick, so that we may expect to hear of a Polar expedition of the kind. Another advance

in shipbuilding is the "Oceanic," a vessel larger than the "Great Eastern," which is now on the trans-Atlantic service.

STEAM PILOT BOATS.—The pilots of New York and Liverpool have adopted small screw steamers in lieu of the old pilot boats. These vessels are well found, and are to pilots what shelters are to cabmen. They are expected to diminish the mortality in this arduous profession.

SMOKE IN TUNNELS.—Professor Mosso, of Turin, has found by experiment that compressed air carried on the locomotive and allowed to escape as the train passes through a tunnel blows the smoke back and purifies the atmosphere. When compressed oxygen is let into the furnace of the locomotive the combustion is so complete that little smoke is discharged; but the compressed air being cheaper is that to be adopted by the railway company for whom he made his experiments.

TRANS-AFRICAN RAILWAYS.—A line is in progress from the Cape to Cairo and another from the east to the west coast by way of Ujiji and Uganda. These railways are, of course, accompanied by telegraph lines, for which a light iron post, made in two sections, has been designed.

FUELS.—A "smokeless coal" has been brought out in the United Kingdom. It burns like coals with intense heat, and is composed of coal dust with about 7 per cent. of pyroligneous tar and caustic lime, pressed into briquettes. At Stratford, Ontario, peat is now compressed into small cylinders, hard as anthracite, which give nearly as much heat as coal. A return to coke as a smokeless fuel for locomotives has been made by a Boston and Maine railway at a great saving of damages through starting forest fires by the sparks of the locomotives.

ACETYLENE.—This gas is growing in favour and many new lamps for burning it have come into use. Improved methods of generating it have also been introduced. It is found better not to employ the naked carbide of calcium to yield the gas, but to saturate it with petroleum or a mixture of tar and petroleum residues as in the "orlyte" of the Russian Orlowsky. An English firm have also brought out a convenient preparation of the carbide known as "acetyloid."

AN ELECTRIC STREET BROOM.—The municipality of Paris have adopted a motor car electric street brush which does very well. A tank of water before the rotary brush waters the street, and the brush is driven by an electric motor. A second motor propels the machine and the power is derived from accumulators. Another electric street brush has been introduced in St. Louis, U.S.

THE WIRELESS TELEGRAPH.—The Marconi system of wireless telegraphy has been tried successfully between the East Goodwin lightship and the South Foreland, between Boulogne and Wimereux in France, a distance of about 30 miles, between ships from 50 to 80 miles apart in the Naval manœuvres, and also between Chelmsford and Wimereux a distance of about 90 miles. It is therefore good for about 100 miles at a stretch, but a chain of relays, ships, or stations, would carry it across the Atlantic or other great distances. The apparatus is to be used in the Transvaal War. A number of rival systems are springing up in different countries The Rev. J. M. Bacon and Mr. J. N. Maskelyne have sent messages to a free balloon and exploded cartridges on the latter by electric waves, an advance which, however, is the subject of an English patent of earlier date. Communication has been established by wireless telegraphy between Chamounix and the observatory of M. Vallory on Mont Blanc. It was found that whilst the weather did not affect it the electrical installations at Chamounix disabled it. Sir W. H. Preece made experiments with his induction system across the Menai Straits using a telephone to receive the signals.

ELECTRIC RAILWAYS.—Great activity has been manifested in making electric railways and tramways of late, both at home and abroad. A line over 100 miles long has been projected through the mountains of northern India to Cashmere, water power being used to manufacture the electricity. This will be the longest yet made, but it will not keep the record for many years.

A FAST TELEGRAPH.—Advices from Vienna speak of a telegraph which can send 100,000 words an hour; experimentally at least. The receiver is a telephone, with a mirror on the diaphragm which throws a beam of light on a moving photographic film. The signal currents vibrating the diaphragm record the message on the film. In actual practice on long lines induction regarding the signals has to be taken into account.

SEEING BY WIRE.—A Polish inventor, Herr Jan Szezepanck, has devised an apparatus for transmitting pictures of moving objects by electricity, but it is too complicated to describe here, and is moreover only in the experimental stage A method of weaving by electricity, patented by the same inventor, is more successful, but also too intricate for description. It enables a piece of tapestry to be worked in five hours which by hand would require two or three years to finish.

AN ELECTRIC SIREN.—A fog siren worked by electricity was recently tried at Ottawa, and is to be installed on the coast of British Columbia. The sound is produced by a number of hammers worked by electromagnets, and striking a gong so as to make a boom which can be heard distinctly for several miles across the water. It is also stated that Signor Marconi has devised an arrangement of his wireless telegraph by which electric signals can be sent from rocks and coasts to warn ships.

DARK LIGHTNING.—Lord Kelvin while on the Continent distinctly saw a "dark" flash of lightning similar to a bright flash which preceded it, and on turning his eye to a bright wall still saw the dark streak. He therefore concluded that the dark lightning flash is a dazzlement of the eye, and not an objective reality. Dark flashes are sometimes seen on photographs, however, and their appearance there is a mystery, but according to the experiments of Mr. W. J. Lockyer with electric sparks, they are only due to a chemical effect on the plate.

THE AVION.—Experiments have been made at the military camp of Satory, in France, with a new flying machine, the "Avion," invented by M. Ader. It is of the aeroplane sort, but the aeroplanes or floating surfaces are great wings of bamboo and silk which can be altered in size at will. Two fan propellers drive it through the air. They are worked by a steam engine of great power for its weight and size The aeronaut sits on a chair and works the machine by levers It is designed to reconnoitre in warfare and to drop explosives on the enemy.

THE ZEPPELIN AIR-SHIP, now in construction on an island of the Boden See, is a cylindrical frame of aluminium in partitions, each holding a gas-bag. Two cars are suspended from it. The ship is propelled by two pairs of four-bladed screws, at bow and stern, and steered by two vertical rudders. The power is derived from a 15-horse power steam engine on board, and the speed attainable in a calm or a light wind is over 20 miles an hour. The buoyancy can be regulated by filling or emptying small gas-bags.

THE FASTEST BALLOON VOYAGE.—Last September, M. Hermite, a French aeronaut, travelled from St. Denis to the mouth of the Rhone in 15 hours, thus travelling as fast as an express train, although the balloon did not escape from clouds all the way, and even encountered a whirl-wind that sent it spinning round. The aeronaut scattered printed bills instructing the finder to let M. Hermite know where and when he picked it up.

SOLIDIFICATION OF HYDROGEN.—Prof. Dewar, by evaporating liquid hydrogen and thus producing intense cold, has succeeded in freezing liquid hydrogen into a clear glassy solid. Its freezing point is a temperature of 257 degrees Centigrade below zero (the freezing point of water) and therefore within 5 or 8 degrees of the "absolute" zero, a theoretical temperature not yet attained in practice.

MAKING OZONE.—M. Moissan has discovered another method of preparing ozone. It is obtained by the action of a current of flourine on water at the temperature of freezing point. He produces in this way a current of oxygen containing 12 to 15 per cent. of ozone which is exempt from nitrous vapour. His experiments described to the Académie des Sciences may become the source of industrial applications.

STERILISING WATER BY OZONE.—The Municipality of Lille have made experiments which demonstrate the success of ozone as a steriliser of water on a large scale. Not only does the gas kill all the microbes noxious to life, but it makes the water agreeable to drink.

RADIATION OF STARS.—Mr. Nichols, of the Chicago Observatory, has invented a very delicate radiometer, based on that of Crookes, by which he can detect the heat of a candle 18 miles distant. In measuring the heat of stars with it, he finds that Vega is equivalent to a candle 8 miles away.

ACAPNIA.—Asphyxia is caused by an excess of carbonic acid in the blood, and Professor Mosso of Turin has invented the term "Acapnia" for its opposite, that is for a deficiency of carbonic acid in the blood. According to his experiments what we call "mountain sickness" is due not merely to physical exhaustion and lack of oxygen in the blood but to lack of carbonic acid, and he recommends balloonists or mountain climbers to carry a supply of carbonic acid for breathing purposes at very high altitudes.

RYTHMIC TRACTION OF THE TONGUE.—In a paper to the Académie de Medicine, M. Laborde discussed fourteen new cases of persons restored to life from apparent death by the method of drawing out the tongue rythmically. One of these had been apparently dead for 3 hours, a fact which shows that life may be latent in the body for that time. Drowned persons can certainly be brought back to life after an immersion of 30 or 40 minutes.

HUMAN WAX.—Professor Ranvier, Member of the Académie des Sciences, Paris, has found that wax is secreted by our skin and serves to keep it from chapping and make it waterproof. Unguents supply the deficiency of the natural wax and prevent the skin from chapping in cold weather.

WEATHER AND MADNESS.—Dr. Mercier and others have shown from statistics that in the hot dry months of July and August mental derangements, crime, and suicide attain a maximum. Apparently the dryness of the air, as well as the heat, have a disturbing influence on the mind; but the general health is improved in the summer season.

DREAMS.—According to M. Vaschide, in a paper to the Académie des Sciences, Paris, we always dream in sleep, whether we remember it or not, and sleep is not the "brother of death," as Homer called it, but the "brother of life." The more the sleep is light the more our dreams are occupied with recent events, and the more profound the sleep the more they are concerned with the remoter past, or with the solution of problems which have puzzled us in waking hours. Another observer, Signor De Sanctis, in his work "I Sogni," finds that women dream more vividly than men and remember their dreams better. Criminals seldom remember their dreams, and apparently seldom dream of their crimes. When they do, it is with little or no emotion.

MUSIC AND GESTURE.—M. Albert de Rochas has made some interesting studies on the expression of the emotions by means of hypnotised subjects. He finds that music evokes the attitude and facial expression of the emotion it suggests. Thus the piece "Angels ever bright and fair" played to Mdlle. Lina, one of his subjects, causes her to raise her arms and look to heaven ecstatically, whilst in the hypnotic trance. She also makes the gestures traditionally associated with certain dances when the music is played to her, although, as in the case of the Spanish "fandango," these dances are quite strange to her actual experience.

THE RED MAN.—It was long claimed by archæologists and others that the American aborigines were of the same type and a distinct race of man. Anthropologists, however, by careful observations have recognised several types or groups, namely, the Eskimo, the northern and central or "Indian" type, the north-western brachycephalic (broadheaded) type, the south-western dolichocephalic (longheaded) type, the Toltecan brachycephalic type, the Antillean type, with probably the ancient Brazilian, the Fuegian, and the pre-Inca types of South America. Each of these types is found in its purity in a limited region, and more or less mixed in the surrounding country. According to Professor E. W. Putnam, of Harvard University, the pre-Incan or older Andean civilisation of Lake Titicaca is more like that of the early Mediterranean or Eurafrican race than any other American arts and customs, and he asks whether this is mere coincidence, or did the Eurafricans cross the Atlantic and settle in America. This hypothesis of a transatlantic migration from the north of Africa, though not exactly new, has much in its favour. The Incas were probably allied to the Toltecs or Mexicans. These brachycephalic people of Mexico spread their civilisation southwards into Honduras and South America, and northwards to the Mississippi, Ohio, and Atlantic coast. Their art resembles that of Asia and Egypt. There are physical resemblances between the brown type of eastern Asia and the ancient Mexican. A question arises, did this type pass from Asia to America, or is it a Eurafrican type which passed from America to Asia? The art of the "mound-builders" is evidently similar to that of ancient Mexico, and is much higher in quality than that of the Indians who subsequently mixed with them.

A NEW DINOSAUR.—Professor Reed, of the University of Wyoming, has unearthed the fossil of a dinosaur from the Laramie beds which far surpasses the biggest animal known to science. It must have been 120 to 130 feet long in the flesh, and about 35 feet high at the haunches. Its weight would be about 40 tons. Its neck would run to 30 feet and its tail to 50 feet, but the head was comparatively small. One of its lesser bones can scarcely be lifted by a man.

THE NEOMYLODON.—The curious skin of a mammal, plated with circular pieces of bone and having long hairs, which Moreno found at Hope Inlet, Patagonia, belongs, it is thought, to an extinct or nearly extinct mammal of the myloden species, whose fossils are found in Patagonia. The "Neomylodon" as it is called, may not be extinct altogether, and a Swedish expedition of Herr Nordensajold found a skin of the animal in a cave of Terra del Fuego, along with hay or straw. Dr. Moreno, of the La Plata Museum, thinks it has been used for bedding by the primitive men of Patagonia, but there is some hope that the animal is extant in Patagonia even now.

A WHITE SALAMANDER.—At San Marcos, Texas, there is an artesian well in the limestone rock from which curious blind animals are ejected with the water, and are thought to come from an underground lake in communication with the well. One of these is a little salamander 4½ inches long, with a disproportionately large head and eyes covered with skin. It is of a dirty white colour, and its tail has a fin like that of an eel. Living specimens are now in the aquarium of the Fish Commission, at Washington, U.S.

THE MALARIAL MOSQUITO.—Major Ross and his party who went from Liverpool to Sierra Leone to find the mosquito which is believed to infect those whom it stings with malaria fever, succeeded in his object. It is a speckled mosquito of a special kind, which breeds in small pools, but is not very common, and may perhaps be easily destroyed.

THE TRUE PEARL.— It appears from the researches of M. Leon Diguet that pearls are of two sorts, one the "nacre" pearl, which is generally a grain of sand or foreign body or some kind intruced into the shell, and coated with mother of pearl or nacre by the mollusc. The fine or orient pearl, however, has another origin. It is formed in any part of the body of the animal except the mantle, and is a calcification or "stone" from a collection of gelatinous humour, which comes, it is thought, from the irritation of a parasite. Remains of an organism are sometimes found in the heart of the pearl. Briefly, the common or "nacre" pearl is the result of an accident, and the fine pearl of a malady.

A NEW INDIARUBBER.—M. Jumelle finds that the "piralahy" of Madagascar, a kind of liana, yields a good rubber fit for industrial purposes. The Sakalaves extract a clear rubber from it containing only 5 per cent. of resin. The liana belongs to the Landolphia family, and it is expected that a rubber trade from this family will be established in the south of the Soudan.

A HARDY GUTTA-PERCHA TREE.—The Eucomia ulmoides is a tree whose fruit yields gutta-percha of good quality. It grows in temperate climes, for example the north of China, and it has been acclimatised in France. Fruit grown in the open air at Nogent-sur-Marne, yields about 30 per cent. of the gum by the Jungfleisch process. It is probable that the tree might flourish in the south of England.

A PARA-HAIL.—In Styria and the Carniole, the vine growers have combined against the hail storms, and provided a system of "para-hail" in the form of conical mortars, with which they fire blank charges into the hail clouds, thus dispersing them. The mortars are stationed from half to one mile apart

THE NATIONAL PHYSICAL LABORATORY.—The General Board and Executive Committee of the National Physical Laboratory has been formed under the Chairmanship of Lord Rayleigh, and the institution is to be established by extending the Kew Observatory in the Old Deer Park, Richmond.

The London Government Act, 1899.

ONE of the most important matters taken up by Her Majesty's Government in the session of 1899 was a bill dealing with the local government of London. The Local Government Act of 1888, which called into being the county councils throughout England and Wales and incidentally gave London, within the boundaries laid down by the Metropolis Management Act of 1855, a county council, has always been regarded as a first instalment only in the remodelling of London government. Ever since 1888, a scheme of district councils has been looked for, and such a scheme was actually drawn up by the "Unification" Commission in 1894, but owing to the defeat of the Liberal Government in the following year the recommendations of the Commission were not acted upon. The Local Government Act of 1894, which created urban district councils and rural district councils in the towns and villages throughout the country, gave to the London vestries the powers of urban district councils and extended the franchise. But what has been long felt to be wanted was a re-arrangement of local areas, and a concentration of duties hitherto variously performed, which should make for simplification in various matters of local government and at the same time give to the bodies charged with the administration of the new areas increased dignity and importance. The Act of 1899 does not, of course, satisfy all parties, especially those who desired to see an alteration in the status of the City Corporation, but it is admitted on all hands to be a most useful contribution towards the solution of the London government problem. It would be impossible here to enter into all the provisions and detailed arrangements of the Act, but the following is a brief general outline of it.

London is to be divided into 28 metropolitan boroughs, exclusive of the City, which is little affected. Fifteen of the larger parishes are scheduled as areas which are to be boroughs, and in some other cases parliamentary boroughs and divisions have been adopted. Smaller parishes are to be joined to form appropriate areas. One notable borough will consist of the ancient parliamentary borough of Westminster, comprising the parishes of St. Margaret and St. John, Westminster, the parishes of St. George, Hanover Square, St. James, Westminster, and St. Martin-in-the-Fields, the district of the Strand Board of Works, the Close of the Collegiate Church of St. Peter and the Liberty of the Rolls. For each borough is to be incorporated a council consisting of a mayor (who will be ex-officio a Justice of the Peace), aldermen and councillors, no woman being eligible for either office. The number of councillors is to be fixed in each case by an Order of the Privy Council, who are also to fix the number and boundaries of the wards, and to assign the number of councillors to each ward. The Privy Council will also make such adjustments in the boundaries of the various boroughs as appear to them expedient for simplification or convenience of administration. The number of aldermen is to be one-sixth of the number of councillors, and the total number of each council is not to exceed seventy. The aldermen will be elected, as in the case of county councils, by the councillors for a term of six years, one-half of them retiring at the end of three years. The mayor is to be elected by the aldermen and councillors. The first elections of borough councillors are to be held on the 1st November, 1900, or on such later day as may be fixed by the Lord President of the Council. Subsequent elections may be annual (for one-third of the total number) or triennial, as each borough council, with the approval of the Local Government Board, may determine.

Vestries and district boards will cease to exist on the day (to be appointed by an Order in Council) on which the borough councils for the respective districts first meet. Their powers and duties, property and liabilities, will be transferred to the borough councils. The powers of Commissioners of Baths and Libraries and of Burial Boards will also pass to the new councils. Certain minor duties are to be transferred from the London County Council, and in some other matters the borough councils are to have powers concurrently with the County Council, the most important, perhaps, being the power to adopt Part III. of the Housing of the Working Classes Act, for the provision of working-class dwellings. It is also provided that other powers may be transferred to or from the county council and the borough councils on the application of the former and a majority of the latter, if the Local Government Board see fit and make a provisional order to that effect. In the same way powers may be transferred between the county council and the common council of the city. Main roads are to vest in and be maintained by the borough councils, and the county council may call upon them to maintain any highway of a bridge or embankment at present maintained by the County Council upon payment of an annual sum to be agreed or determined by the Local Government Board. Borough councils will have the power to stop up streets for paving works, &c., without getting the sanction of the county council, as now; they will have to enforce the bye-laws as to dairies and slaughterhouses, knacker's-yards and offensive businesses, with power to the county council to act in default. An important power conferred upon the new councils is that of promoting and opposing bills in Parliament and of prosecuting and defending legal proceedings similar to borough councils outside London, subject to the provisions of the Borough Funds Act, 1872. All transfers of powers and duties are to be accompanied by contributions, whether capital or annual, to be fixed by agreement, or failing agreement by the Local Government Board.

Borough councils may delegate certain duties to committees subject to report to the council, but cannot delegate the raising of money by loan or rate; and a committee must not spend any money beyond the sums allowed by the council. Each council is to have a finance committee for regulating and controlling its finance, and "any costs, debt, or liability exceeding fifty pounds shall not be incurred except upon a resolution of the council passed on an estimate submitted by the finance committee." All payments to and by the borough council are to be made to and by the borough treasurer, and all payments by the council, unless they are required specifically by Act of Parliament or by order of a competent court, are to be made on an order of the council signed by three members of the finance committee present at the council meeting, and countersigned by the town clerk (the clerk of the council).

The provisions of the Act as to rating are important, and mark a distinct advance in the direction of simplification, which the bewildered ratepayer will doubtless appreciate. The borough councils will in future be the rating authorities, and the rate for all the expenses of the council and the poor rate are to be assessed, made, levied and collected as one "general rate." Rates (including the county council or other precepts) are to be levied as far as possible in one demand.

note in form to be approved by the Local Government Board, and stating the rateable value of the premises, the rate in the pound, the period for the rate, the purposes and the amount in the pound required for each purpose (including costs and losses in collection), and any other matter required to be stated by the Equalisation Act, 1894, or other Act. The council of each borough will be the overseers of every parish in the borough, and the town clerk is to be responsible for the preparation of the lists of voters and of the jury lists in the borough.

The accounts of borough councils and their committees are to be audited like the accounts of the London County Council, that is to say, by Local Government Board auditors, and any ratepayer or owner of property may attend the audit and object to any item in the accounts. At the conclusion of the audit an abstract of the accounts will have to be published.

The remaining sections are chiefly concerned with the machinery for giving effect to the Act. Commissioners have already been appointed "to prepare such orders and schemes as are required for carrying the Act into effect," and the orders and schemes so prepared may be settled by a committee of the Privy Council, but the draft orders forming any area into a borough are to be laid before both Houses of Parliament for thirty days during a session, and either House may petition against an order or any part of it, and in that event a new order will have to be prepared. The expenses are to be paid by the county council out of the county fund.

There are several parishes in London, parts of which are detached and situate in another parish. These detached parts of parishes are all to be annexed to or divided between the boroughs which they adjoin. In similar fashion detached parts of parishes in the county of London wholly surrounded by another county, and detached parts of parishes in another county wholly surrounded by the county of London, are to be transferred to the county in which they are situated. Thus, the detached portion of Clerkenwell at Muswell-hill will go to the county of Middlesex, and the detached portions of South Hornsey in the county of London will come to London. The whole of South Hornsey may come into London, forming with the parish of Stoke Newington one of the metropolitan boroughs. In the South, detached portions of Putney and Mitcham are to be dealt with in the same way. Penge, which is in the county of London, but attached to the Croydon Union for poor-law purposes, and which has hitherto been one of the most striking anomalies of the London government system, is now to be dealt with in an intelligible manner, though its exact position is left to be determined by the Privy Council. It may be left in the county of London and annexed to the borough of Lewisham or to the borough of Camberwell, or it may be transferred to the county of Kent or to the county of Surrey, being either constituted an urban district, or added to an adjoining county borough or urban district. Transfers of areas will be accompanied by the necessary financial adjustments of property, debts, and liabilities between the various county and borough councils concerned.

The Act contains numerous incidental provisions relating to Church affairs and charities, appointment of deputy town-clerks, transfer of existing officers, alterations of the number and boundaries of wards or apportionment of members of borough council among wards, and sundry other matters of detail.

The Parliamentary boroughs will remain as before. The boundaries of parliamentary and county boroughs and school-board and poor-law districts will still in many instances follow different lines. The rating of parishes within a metropolitan borough may vary, as each parish is to bear its own special rate, if any, for baths or libraries or for the purposes of the Burial Acts, and also the losses arising in its own area in the collection of rates.

During its passage through Parliament, the Bill underwent a great deal of alteration, and some of the most useful provisions now in the Act are the outcome of criticism which the measure freely received from both sides of the House. Anything which is likely to awaken Londoners to an increased interest in the affairs of local government cannot but be regarded as beneficial, and for this reason, as well as for the many good points which it contains, the Act is welcome.

The Growth of Joint Stock Companies.

THE present joint stock system dates from such a recent period that it would be of little practical utility to quote any detailed statistics regarding the subject prior to the passing of the Companies Act of 1862. Companies as they exist to-day, under the law of limited liability, were not known a century or more ago. The term was applied literally. Any association of individuals was a company, but it was only in the form of an enormous partnership of which each member was individually responsible for any debts or liabilities contracted by the company. Those privileged associations in which the members were irresponsible were better termed corporations, inasmuch as they were incorporated by charter or statute. Indeed, it may be said that any undertaking conducted in the manner of our present-day limited liability company was an indictable offence, the Bubble Act having particularly declared that "the acting or presuming to act as a corporate body or bodies, the raising or pretending to raise transferable stock or stocks, the transferring or pretending to transfer or assign any share or shares in such stock or stocks . . . . shall for ever be deemed to be illegal or void, and shall not be practised or otherwise put in execution." The stocks which were quoted on 'Change and in the Daily Share List for over 100 years after the passing of this Act were of the nature of stock of chartered companies or corporations working under special Acts of Parliament. In 1845, for instance, there were over 200 railway companies (a larger number, by-the-way, than exists at the present time, owing to the consolidation of interests forced upon the weaker undertakings by the decline of the railway mania), and an almost similar number of insurance and banking companies, docks, canals, and waterworks. During the following decade the necessity of legislation was urged upon the Government by the ever-pressing needs of the big trading partnerships, and from being an illegal nuisance they soon came to be regarded as having a legitimate right to trade as corporations, and various Acts were passed in their interests. The basis of the present legislation originally introduced from America, is found in the consolidation of these numerous Acts in 1862. From October 3, 1862, when the Act became operative, to the end of the year, 165 companies were registered, with a total nominal share capital of £57,006,620. The following year witnessed the registration of 790 companies with a total nominal share capital of £139,988,242, an indication that the new facilities were early taken advantage of by a large number of small capitalists. Whereas the average nominal capital of the companies registered in

1862 amounted to £343,000, it was only £20,000 in the following year.

It will be useful to record at the outset the figures showing the number and total nominal share capital of the companies which have been registered under the Companies Act, 1862, in England, Scotland, Ireland, and the Stannaries respectively, during the period from the commencement of the Act to December 31, 1899. The figures for the last two years I have estimated from various sources:—

There are four interesting periods covered by the table on p. 670 —the company-floating mania of 1862-54, the period of depression from 1874 to 1879, the gold mining mania of 1888-90, and the industrial boom of 1896-98.

The company-floating mania of 1862-64 commenced upon the passing of the Companies Act of 1862, and culminated in the famous Overend-Gurney crisis of 1866, the number of companies registered rising to over 1,000 in 1865, and falling to 497 in 1867. The crisis aroused Parliamentary intervention, and the Companies Amendment Act of 1867 was put into force. It is to this legislative hurry that we owe most of the evils of the present joint stock system. For many years the public did not take kindly to limited liability undertakings, and the country had entered upon the memorable decade of depression in the seventies before company formation had returned to its normal condition.

During the five years from 1874 to 1879 the total nominal share capital of companies registered amounted to only £340,000, or only a fifth of the amount recorded within a similar period of years subsequently. Trade was almost at a stand-still, and all new applications for capital were viewed with suspicion. There was a semi-recovery in 1880, but it only lasted for two years, and trade again relapsed into its depressed condition, accentuated by financial troubles in South America.

A gradual recovery occurred during the eighties, and in 1888 the boom in "Kaffir" mining shares swept all before it. The reduction by one-twelfth of the interest on the old Three per Cents, caused a great movement in investment stocks, and was partly responsible for the kindly reception given to the glowing applications for capital for the Witwatersrand mining industry. In 1888 a record amount of share capital was registered, viz., £353,781,594. Large loans raised on behalf of Argentina and our colonies accounted for a fair proportion of this sum, but South African mining ventures were mainly responsible for the sudden increase. In the following two years the number of companies registered was

Highest price of Consols.	Year of Registration.	In England. No. of Companies.	In England. Nominal Share Capital.	In Scotland. No. of Companies.	In Scotland. Nominal Share Capital.	In Ireland. No. of Companies.	In Ireland. Nominal Share Capital.	In the Stannaries. No. of Companies.	In the Stannaries. Nominal Share Capital.	In the United Kingdom. Total No. of Companies	In the United Kingdom. Total Nominal Share Capital.	Remarks.
94¾	1862 { Oct. 3 to Dec. 31	152	51,098,120	8	5,867,500	5	41,000	—	—	155	57,006,020	Companies Act (1862) became law.
94	1863	724	37,454,861	31	1,825 893	20	250,2 0	15	447,288	790	139,988.242	}
92	1864	914	232 236, 55	26	2,834,448	34	1,852,800	23	313 78	997	237,237.083	} Company-floating mania.
91½	1865	935	107.925.527	37	2,962,811	43	3,72 ,000	19	783,480	1 034	205.391,818	}
90⅜	1866	670	68.569 903	36	4.951,620	38	2,966,100	12	337,200	702	76,8 4,823	Overend-Gurney crisis.
96⅜	1867	435	28,86 .390	18	633,400	16	1,841,000	10	129,152	479	31,464 98	Companies Act (1867) Amendment Act passed.
95⅛	1868	411	33,971,342	25	719,200	16	1,713,960	9	123,200	46	36,527,702	Failure of Life Assurance Companies
94¼	1869	431	138.726.301	18	788,550	14	1,570,90	12	82,500	475	141,274.251	A company registered with capital of £100,000,000, but paid-up capital never exceeded £20.
94½	1870	439	36,913,364	9	474 350	15	410,920	22	445.740	59	38,252 374	}
94	1871	698	65,141,633	47	1,895,600	32	1,649,783	44	841,300	821	69,528,319	} Life Assurance Companies Acts of 1870-72.
93⅜	1872	941	120,200,239	84	8 474.920	29	1,787,600	62	2,579,2 6	1,116	133,041.393	}
94	1873	1,089	143 345 695	63	5 878,800	42	1,808 450	40	1,023,600	1,234	154,056,545	}
93¾	1874	1,124	102,918,2 3	64	6,221.250	18	356,000	35	1,044,000	1,241	110,540, 6	}
95¾	1875	1,078	76, 45,380	48	4.612,5	25	1,118,300	21	571.000	1,172	82,4 7,180	} Severe industrial depression.
97½	1876	939	41,196 725	69	5,288,260	31	1, 84,100	27	64 ,000	1 066	48,314.085	}
97⅜	1877	846	52,790,296	88	11 632,900	47	2,146,45	9	23 ,540	990	66,8 0,180	}
98	1878	778	59,505,142	64	4,835.100	30	3 012.900	14	503,83	886	67,856.975	City of Glasgow Bank collapse.
99⅝	1879	923	69.426.920	65	4.097,452	35	1,861,675	11	184,000	1.034	75.568,047	Companies Act 1879 passed.
100¾	1880	1,1 0	159,6 8 432	70	6,424,240	33	1,486,150	39	937,500	1,302	168, 66,322	}
103	1881	1.446	189,056 8 7	76	16,084,750	32	4,242,500	27	1,327,600	1,581	210 711,637	} Revival of business.
102½	1882	1.476	22 .243,521	114	33,319.410	40	1,134,40	2	47 000	1, 32	254.744,331	}
102¾	1883	1,533	143.787 257	118	8.314 980	110	15,287,950	5	290,000	1,766	167,680,187	
102⅝	1884	,37	125,2 6,458	113	11.587.820	55	1.569,150	3	78,000	1.541	138,491,428	Blakeway frauds and failure of Oriental Banking Corporatn
103⅜	1885	1,344	11 . 284,947	77	4,803,584	54	2,940,030	7	141,400	1,482	119,222.961	Financial crisis in Argentina.
102¼	1886	1,738	138.077,329	92	6,084,920	53	1,344.453	9	346,000	1,8 1	145,850,7 2	Guinness's Company (£6,000,000) floated.
1 3⅝	1887	1 8 3	160,616,454	97	7.442.35	52	1,968,870	8	145,000	2,050	170 172,074	} Kaffir mining "boom" commenced, and Salt Union formed.
103⅜	1888	2,346	339,858,866	125	11,053,053	69	2,694,075	10	175,000	2,550	353.781,594	}
99¼	1889	2,578	229.406,624	137	8,889,604	70	2,916,140	3	65,100	2 738	241,277,468	Directors' Limited Liability Act and Companies' Winding-Up Act.
98¾	1890	2,542	223,253,4 2	149	12,437.690	97	4,058,380	1	10,000	2,789	238,759,472	}
97½	1891	2 446	126,363,028	156	5,3 5,295	83	2,583.350	1	10,000	2,686	134.261,073	} Baring crisis and Liberator failures.
98¼	1892	2,371	95,683 168	164	6,748.413	7	971.750	—	—	2,607	103.403,331	}
99½	1893	2,332	84.720,623	189	9,059,738	96	2,873.800	—	—	2,617	96,654.161	}
103⅝	1894	2,668	08,818.965	208	6,630,960	92	2,927 595	2	54,050	2,97	118,431,570	Speculation in mining shares resumed.
108⅛	1895	3,517	216 259,010	201	11.283,912	93	3 774,255	1	50,000	3,892	231,368,077	}
113⅜	1896	4.291	285.261,077	308	19.160,655	136	5,111,215	—	—	4,735	309,532,947	} Conversion of big commercial houses.
113⅞	1897	4 75	169.391,715	332	17,801,624	147	3,864,220	—	—	5,229	291,117,559	}
113⅛	1898*	5,05	250,000,000	—	—	—	—	—	—	—	—	Hooley failure.
111½	1899*	4,800	243 000,000	—	—	—	—	—	—	—	—	Transvaal crisis.

* The totals for these years are estimated from published unofficial figures of the number of companies registered and total share capital. The official figures for 1899 are not available until late in 1900.

† 2¾ per Cent

still greater, although the average capital of undertakings was smaller. Nevertheless in 1889, of 500 prospectuses which were issued 44 were of companies capitalised at over a million sterling. There was a heavy falling off in 1891 public confidence having been again shaken by a "rig" in the shares of the company owning "Warner's Safe Cure," but the decrease in the number of registered companies is chiefly attributable to the Baring crisis, which at that time paralysed the stock markets and the financial world. From bad, things went to the worst, and in 1893 the total capital of companies registered was less than 100 millions sterling, only 30 millions of this sum being offered to the public.

In 1895 and 1896 the big commercial houses began to invite capital, and met with a remarkable response from the public. The Kaffir mining boom had collapsed, whilst the West Australian mining industry had not come up to expectations, and the public were willing to favourably consider commercial speculations as distinct from the hazardous risks of mining. The success which attended the conversion of some well-known businesses led to a wholesale application of the joint stock system to commercial undertakings throughout the United Kingdom. A fair indication of the general rush upon the part of the smaller industrial houses to take advantage of the limited liability system is to be gained from a comparison of the average capital of the companies registered during the past four years.

Av. capital of 3,537 Cos. formed in 1895 = £61,800
    ,,   ,, 4,291   ,,   ,, 1896 = £65,300
    ,,   ,, 4,750   ,,   ,, 1897 = £57,200
    ,,   ,, 5,050   ,,   ,, 1898 = £51,200
    ,,   ,, 4,800   ,,   ,, 1899 = £50,500

Leaving out of consideration the closing year, for which the figures are only estimated, we find that although the number of companies registered in 1896, 1897, and 1898 was increasingly larger the average capitalisation was much smaller.

For the year 1899 it is likely to be exceedingly small in comparison with previous years, both with regard to the number of companies registered and also in the amount of share capital. This falling off may be attributed to many causes, among which may be reckoned the nervousness created by the disclosures attending the Hooley failure in the previous year, and the general depression in the money and stock markets created by political uneasiness.

From the following comparative figures —

Years.	Total nominal Share Capital.	Increase or Decrease.
	£	£
From 1862 to 1869	925,715,521	—
,, 1870 ,, 1879	844,405,166	— 81,310,355
,, 1880 ,, 1889	1,070,399,324	+1,125,994,158
,, 1890 ,, 1899	2,022,528,790	+ 52,129,466

it would appear that the most satisfactory period —from a numerical point of view—in connection with joint stock enterprise was the decade 1880-89. There has to be remembered, however, in comparing this period with the following decade, that the Companies Act of 1879 had just been put into force. This Act provided chiefly for the registration of banks as limited liability companies, prompted by the disastrous collapse of the City of Glasgow Bank in the previous year, and a large number of these institutions took advantage of the new legislation. Particularly is the effect noticeable in relation to the figures for Scotland, where the amount of share capital registered increased from six to 33 million pounds within two years—

In the following table statistics are supplied showing the total number and paid-up capital of all registered companies having a share capital and believed to be carrying on business at the undermentioned dates :—

Year ending April.	Registered in England (including the Stannaries).		Registered in Scotland.		Registered in Ireland.		Total.	
	No.	Paid-up Capital.	No.	Paid-up Capital.	No.	Paid-up Capital.	No.	Paid-up Capital.
		£		£		£		£
1884	7,589	427,594,349	728	36,439,875	375	11,517,070	8,692	475,551,294
1885	8,119	442,099,549	805	39,815,676	420	12,994,637	9,344	494,909,861
1886	8,159	471,716,077	838	43,544,114	474	14,377,493	9,471	529,637,684
1887	9,091	528,671,858	895	46,948,125	508	15,888,709	10,494	591,508,692
1888	9,507	544,447,145	949	50,255,054	545	16,728,172	11,001	611,430,371
1889	10,375	604,239,039	1,017	50,387,974	566	17,243,171	11,968	671,870,184
1890	11,608	705,669,347	1,102	52,182,679	613	17,257,527	13,323	775,139,553
1891	13,032	813,445,671	1,192	58,546,874	649	19,511,567	14,873	891,504,112
1892	14,198	905,145,765	1,279	62,118,501	696	22,019,377	16,173	989,283,634
1893	15,431	925,025,647	1,382	65,687,129	742	22,406,574	17,555	1,013,119,352
1894	16,104	942,689,164	1,481	68,058,535	776	24,272,115	18,361	1,035,019,835
1895	16,988	862,141,029	1,619	75,113,251	823	25,479,541	19,430	1,062,733,821
1896	18,524	1,035,551,703	1,804	82,508,882	895	27,342,368	21,223	1,145,402,903
1897	20,720	1,160,251,535	2,038	93,393,989	970	31,36,497	23,728	1,283,012,021
1898	21,987	1,248,038,344	2,255	102,875,480	1,025	32,679,338	25,267	1,383,593,162

It will be gathered from an inspection of this table that in no case in any year since 1884 has there been a reduction in the number of companies carrying on business at April 1 in each year owing to removal (from liquidation or other causes) of companies from the register. The chances of this occurring appear to have been still more lessened in recent years, owing to the rapid increase of companies registered. The total number of unsuccessful companies during 1895 was in proportion to the new companies registered 57 per cent. as against 66 per cent. during previous years ; in 1896 it was 54 per cent. ; and in 1897, 44 per cent. The percentage of compulsory to total liquidations has fallen from 14 per cent. in 1891 to 7 per cent. in 1897 due to a general desire to escape the investigations provided for by the Companies (Winding Up) Act of 1890. and by the additional facilities for doing so afforded by the increased amount of vendors' capital. These points have been dwelt upon at length for many years in the annual report by the Inspector-General in Companies' Liquidation. Indeed, through this gradual reduction in the number of compulsory liquidations one is able by a little inquiry to strike at the root of much of the evil arising out of the present application of the joint stock laws. The following figures (extracted from an official table) indicate the amount of capital paid up on shares subscribed by the public or issued as fully-paid to vendors or promoters: —

Year.	In Compulsory Cases.		In Supervision Cases.		In Voluntary Cases.		Total.	
	Public.	Vendor.	Public.	Vendor.	Public.	Vendor.	Public.	Vendor.
	£	£	£	£	£	£	£	£
1892	3 069 328	1,320,768	1,485,239	2,984,956	22,663,653	10,936,136	27.218,220	15,261,860
1897	658 538	2,940.306	839 639	1,112,953	25,249,657	22 746,635	26 747.784	26,799,854

It was not until the Companies (Winding Up) Act of 1890 was passed that it was possible to examine and compare the character of the liquidations. Nine years later the available statistics clearly demonstrate the easy method by which promoters have put into liquidation doubtful undertakings which it would have been desirable for the court to examine. In 1892 it will be noticed the subscribed capital of the public in compulsory cases was nearly three times as large as that of the vendor, and in voluntary cases half as large, thereby enabling the public to enforce its opinion should it deem compulsory or voluntary liquidation necessary. During the succeeding five years the position has been reversed, and in compulsory cases the vendor capital is nearly five times larger than the public interest, and in voluntary cases it now ranks almost equal. The allotment of shares to vendors has been enormously increased, and the power to order a voluntary liquidation under their own control is thus placed in their hands by mere voting strength. Unfortunately there are at present no means of obtaining accurate data on the subject, and the extent and fluctuations of insolvency under the Companies Act must therefore remain largely a matter of conjecture.

Whilst the average capitalisation of companies registered thirty years ago was much more than it is to-day (about £50,000 capital per company), there is little doubt, after a lengthy examination of the figures, that the tendency during the past decade has been towards increased capitalisation. The average has been lowered owing to the remarkable number of "one man companies" which have grown up under the present joint stock system, having a paid-up capital of a few pounds, and intended merely as a working alias for a merchant or promoter, and in many cases for men who, as undischarged bankrupts, could not otherwise obtain credit for carrying on business. Otherwise the average capitalisation of companies would be considerably higher, owing to the creation of fictitious capital represented by fictitious assets, a point which was dwelt upon by the Inspector-General in his last Report (No. 337, 1898), and led him to suppose that a large proportion of the apparent increase of capital registered during the past few years in the books of the Registrar of Joint Stock Companies is based upon a more or less artificial foundation.

In the Companies Bill which has been before Parliament, and has been considered by a special committee, there are several provisions which will undoubtedly tend to correct many of the present abuses of the limited liability system One of the most important of these, and probably the most welcome to the trader and investor, is an obligation which will be imposed upon every company to prepare annual balance sheets, which shall be certified by directors and auditors as exhibiting in their opinion a correct view of the company's position, and to file a copy thereof (or of a statement of assets and liabilities based thereon) with the Registrar. This would, of course, be open to public inspection upon the same conditions as are the files containing statements of capital, copies of agreements, articles, share registers, &c., of the various companies now lodged with the Registrar at Somerset House. There are other provisions in the new Bill which it will be necessary to enforce more rigidly than has hitherto been the case with regard to the existing Acts. It has been submitted in some quarters, and with a very good show of reason, that were the penalties of the present Acts more strongly enforced there would be less necessity for new laws. There is, however, a consensus of opinion, both in the financial and the outer world, that a general reconstruction of the laws relating to the formation, working, and liquidation of joint stock companies is necessary, even if solely because of the immense strides made in the use of the system as indicated by the statistics tabulated, and the haste with which the construction and amendment of the present Companies Acts was undertaken.

HERBERT H. BASSETT.

CLOSE SEASON FOR GAME, WILD BIRDS &c.

The following Table gives the "close" time for different kinds of Game for England, Scotland, and Ireland, during which it is illegal to pursue the game mentioned, all dates inclusive :—

GAME.	ENGLAND.	SCOTLAND.	IRELAND.
Black Game or Heath Fowl.	11th Dec. & 19th Aug., 11th Dec. & 31st Aug., in Somerset, Devon, and New Forest.	11th Dec. & 19th Aug.	11th Dec. and 19th Aug.
Bustard......	2nd Mar. & 31st Aug.	None.	11th Jan. & 31st Aug.
Deer, Male .	None.	None.	1st Jan. & 9th June.
„ Fallow Male	None.	None.	Michaels. & 9th Jne.
Grouse or Red Game	11th Dec. & 11th Aug.	11th Dec. & 11th Aug.	11th Dec. & 11th Aug.
Hare*........	None.	None.	21st Apr. & 11th Aug.
Heath or Moor Game	None.	As "Muirfowl."	11th Dec. & 11th Aug.
Landrail ...	As "Wild Birds."	As "Wild Birds."	11th Jan. & 19th Sep.
Muirfowl or Ptarmigan	None.	11th Dec. & 11th Aug.	11th Dec. & 19th Aug.
Partridge ...	2nd Feb. & 31st Aug.	2nd Feb. & 31st Aug.	11th Jan. & 19th Sep.
Pheasant ...	2nd Feb. & 30th Sept.	2nd Feb. & 30th Sept.	2nd Feb. & 30th Sep.
Quail	As "Wild Birds."	As "Wild Birds."	11th Jan. & 19th Sep.

It is unlawful to kill pheasants, partridges, grouse, moor game, or hares on a Sunday or Christmas Day. Sand Grouse may not be killed at any time.

In England hares, rabbits, woodcock, snipe, quail, landrail, and heath or moor game (and the eggs of swan, wild duck, teal, and widgeon) are protected under the Game Laws, though no close-time is fixed for them by those laws. In Scotland the same remarks apply to deer and hares, to the first four birds, and to wild duck; in Ireland to all these five birds, with the further addition of widgeon, teal, and plover. The close-time for these birds (except quail and landrail in Ireland, for whose close-time see above) is, under the Wild Birds Protection Acts, 1880, 1881, and 1894, from 2nd March to 31st July, both inclusive, throughout the United Kingdom, except the Island of St. Kilda. The penalty for killing any wild bird in such close-time, or for selling or having in possession between the 16th March and the 31st of July, both inclusive (unless the killing can be proved to have occurred at a time and place to which the Act does not apply), is a reprimand and costs for the first offence, and 5s. and costs for each bird for every subsequent offence. In the case, however, of the undermentioned birds, the penalty is £1 for each bird for each offence :—

American quail.	Colin.	Dotterel.
Auk.	Cornish chough.	Dunbird.
Avocet.	Coulterneb.	Dunlin.
Bee-eater.	Cuckoo.	Eider-duck.
Bittern.	Curlew.	Fern-owl.
Bonxie.	Diver.	Fulmar.

See also below ' Seasons for hunting and ground game shooting.'

Gannet.	Owl.	Sheldrake.
Goatsucker.	Ox-bird.	Shoveller.
Godwit.	Oyster-catcher.	Skua.
Goldfinch.	Peewit.	Smew.
Grebe.	Petrel.	Snipe.
Greenshank.	Phalarope.	Sol n Goose.
Guillemot.	Plover.	Spoonbill.
Gull (except Black-backed).	Ploverspage.	Stint.
	Pochard.	Stone Curlew.
Hoopoe.	Puffin.	Stonehatch.
Kingfisher.	Purre.	Summer snipe.
Kittiwake.	Razorbill.	Tarrock.
Lapwing.	Redshank.	Teal.
Lark.	Reeve or Ruff.	Tern.
Loon.	Roller.	Thicknee.
Mallard.	Sanderling.	Tystey.
Marrot.	Sandpiper.	Whaup.
Merganser.	Scout.	Widgeon.
Murre.	Sealark.	Wild duck.
Night-hawk.	Seamew.	Willock.
Night-jar.	Sea parrot.	Wimbrel.
Nightingale.	Sea swallow.	Woodcock.
Oriole.	Shearwater.	Woodpecker.

Offenders refusing their names and addresses are liable to a further penalty of 10s., but the Act does not apply to any person shooting on his own land, or authorizing anyone so to shoot, any wild bird not included in the above list.

On the application of the local authorities, the Secretary of State in England and Wales, the Secretary for Scotland in Scotland, or the Lord Lieutenant in Ireland, has power to vary or abolish the close-time for any bird or birds in any county by order to be published in the *Gazette*. They may also direct that the above enactments shall apply to any wild bird not specified in the list, and may further prohibit the taking of the eggs of any wild bird in any county or part thereof. The Secretary of State in England and Wales, or the Secretary for Scotland, may also on the application of the local authorities make an order, providing that in any specified area the taking or killing of any particular kinds of wild birds shall be illegal during any period specified in the order. These various powers have been exercised in many cases—too numerous to recapitulate here.

SEASONS FOR HUNTING AND GROUND GAME SHOOTING.

There is no statutory close-time for fox-hunting or rabbit-shooting, nor is there, except in Ireland, for deer or hares; but there is an "unwritten law" which the sportsman respects as much as he does the enactments of Parliament. November 1st is the recognized date for the opening of the fox-hunting season, which continues till the following April. Otter-hunting lasts from mid-April to mid-September. The period for deer-hunting or stalking varies from about Aug. 12 to Oct. 12 for stags, and from Nov. 10 to the end of March for hinds. By an Act passed in 1892 the sale of hares or leverets in Great Britain is prohibited from March to July inclusive under a penalty of a pound. This does not apply to foreign hares. The statutory close season for hares in Ireland has been varied for some counties by order of the Lord Lieutenant, and it is now mostly from April 1st to August 12th.

CLOSE-TIME FOR SALMON.

I. ENGLAND AND WALES.

Under the Salmon Fishery Acts, salmon—(the word "Salmon" includes all migratory *salmonidæ*)—are protected, and a close-time is fixed for England and Wales, including the Esk in Dumfries, during which fishing for salmon is prohibited. The close-time for nets begins on 1st September, and ends on 1st February; and for rods it begins on 2nd November, and ends on 1st February. The commencement and termination of the close season may be varied by a bye-law by the local boards of conservators (see p. 675), but it must never begin for nets later than 1st Nov., nor be less than 154 days. For rod and line the minimum close-time is 92 days, which must commence not later than 1st December. For putts and puchers the annual close season is from 1st September to 1st May, which cannot be altered by bye-law. The following are the cases in which these dates have been varied:—

Close-time for	Nets.	Rods.
Adur	1 Sept. to 2 Feb.	1 Oct. to 2 Feb.
Avon & Stour	31 July to 1 Feb.	2 Oct. to 1 Feb.
Taff and Ely	31 Aug. to 30 Apr.	15 Nov. to 30 Apr.
Teify	—	1 Nov. to 1 Feb.
Dart	—	16 Oct. to 28 Feb.
Ayron	—	15 Nov. to 14 Feb.
Yorkshire	—	16 Nov. to 29 Feb.
Exe	1 Sept. to 1 Mar.	20 Oct. to 1 Mar.
Ribble	,, to ,,	,, to ,,
Teign	,, to 1 Mar.	1 Nov. to 2 Mar.
Towy	,, to 1 Apr.	2 Nov. to 1 Apr.
Dee	,, to 31 Mar.	,, to 31 Mar.
Ouse (Sussex)	,, to 1 Apr.	1 Nov. to 1 Apr.
Usk & Rumney	,, to 1 Apr.	2 Nov. to 1 Apr.
Stour (Kent)	,, to 1 May	,, to 1 May.
Severn†	,, to 15 Jun.	—
Lune	,, to 1 Mar.	2 Nov. to 1 Mar.
Eden	‡10 Sep. to 10 Feb.	16 Nov. to 15 Feb.
Dovey	14 Sep. to 30 Apr.	30 Nov. to 30 Apr.
Kent & Lev n.	15 Sep. to 31 Mar.	15 Nov. to 31 Mar.
Seiont	,, to 1 Mar.	15 Nov. to 1 Mar.
Dwyfach	,, to ,,	,, to ,,
Derwnt. (Cum.)	,, to 10 Mar.	,, to 10 Mar.
Cleddy	,, to 15 Mar.	1 Nov. to 1 Feb.
Coquet	,, to 25 Mar.	,, to 31 Jan.
W. Cumberlnd.	,, to 31 Mar.	14 Nov. to 10 Mar.
Conway	,, to 30 Apr.	15 Nov. to 30 Apr.
Ogmore	,, to ,,	,, to ,,
Clwyd & Elwy.	,, to 15 May	,, to 15 May
Axe	20 Sep. to 30 Apr.	20 Nov. to 30 Apr.
Taw & T'rridge	21 Sep. to ,,	16 Nov. to 31 Mar.
Avon & Erme…	‖30 Sep. to 1 May	30 Nov. to 1 May
Camel	21 Sep. to 4 Apr.	1 Dec. to 30 Apr.
Fowey	‡1 Nov. ,,	,, ,,

No fresh salmon may be sold between 3rd September and 1st Feb., except such as can be proved to come from parts beyond the seas, or to have been taken, if in the United Kingdom, in legal netting season and in legal manner. During that period all packages containing salmon consigned by any common or other carrier must be clearly marked with the word "Salmon." Salmon, dried, pickled, or cured abroad, or, if within the United Kingdom, between 1st February and 3rd November may be sold after that date. The onus of proof that the fish were caught out of the United Kingdom, or, if within the kingdom, that they were caught during the legal netting season by legal means, or that, if pickled, they were pickled between 1st Feb. and 3rd Nov., lies with the person selling or exposing for sale. The exportation of salmon from any part of the United Kingdom is prohibited between 3rd September and 30th April, unless it can be proved

† In Borough of Shrewsbury only.
‡ Below Old Sandsfield.   § Below Lostwithiel only.
‖ Except R. Erme, 30 Sept. (rods 30 Nov.) to 4 April.

that the salmon exported or entered for exportation was caught at a time at which its sale in the place where it was caught would be legal, if in the United Kingdom: the *onus probandi* lies on the person exporting. The capture and sale of "unclean" salmon, *i.e.*, salmon recently spawned or full of spawn, are prohibited under heavy penalties. Roe may not be used as a bait in salmon angling.

A weekly close season, during which net-fishing for salmon is prohibited, is fixed in England from noon on Saturday to 6 a.m. on Monday. This close-time may be varied by the Local Conservancy Boards, provided it is not less than 42 hours, nor more than 48 hours, and that it is fixed between Friday at midnight and noon on Monday.

II. Scotland.

In Scotland the annual close-time must not be less than 168 days. It is, for nets, from 27th August to 10th February, and, for rods, from 1st November to 10th February, except as follows:—

Close-time for	Nets.	Rods.
Add, Aray, Eckaig, N. & S. Esk, Fyne, Ruel, Shira.	1 Sept. to 15 Feb.	1 Nov. to 15 Feb.
Beauly, Dunbeath, Lossie, Ness, Spey.	—	16 Oct. to 10 Feb.
Halladale, Strathy, Naver, Borgie, Helmsdale.	—	1 Oct. to 10 Jan.
Girvan	10 Sept. to 24 Feb.	1 Nov. to 24 Feb.
Bervie, Carradale, Fleet, Garnock, Inner, Iorsa, Irvine, Laggan, Luce, Sorn, Ugie, Ythan, and rivers of Orkney, Harris, & Uist.	10 Sept. to 24 Feb.	1 Nov. to 24 Feb.
Nith	ditto	15 Nov. to 24 Feb.
Annan, Stinchar …	ditto	16 Nov. to 24 Feb.
Rivers of Shetland	ditto	16 Nov. to 31 Jan.
Urr	ditto	1 Dec. to 24 Feb.
Rivers of Bute	1 Sept. to 15 Feb.	16 Oct. to 15 Feb.
Thurso	—	15 Sept. to 10 Jan.
Hope, Polla	—	11 Sept. to 10 Jan.
Tay	—	16 Oct. to 10 Jan.
Tweed	15 Sept. to 14 Feb.	1 Dec. to 31 Feb.

The weekly close-time for nets is between 6 p.m. Saturday and 6 a.m. Monday; and, for rods, on Sundays. The Esk, in Dumfries, is included under the English Salmon Acts.

In Scotland the law as to the sale of salmon differs somewhat from that in force in England.

III. Ireland.

In Ireland the close-time for salmon applies also to trout. The netting close-time must never be less than 168 days. Many variations of the close season have been made, of which it is impossible to specify all the details here; the following list, however, shows the general close-time in force in the different districts, in parts of some of which, however, it is different (all dates inclusive). The second column gives the point of delimitation on the coast between the various districts, which include all rivers, &c., within their respective coast-limits.

District	Coast Limits	Cl.-T.Net.	Cl.-T.Rod.
Dublin	Skerries	16 Aug. to 1 Feb.	1 Nov. to 31 Jan.
Wexford	Wicklow	16 Sept. to 19 Apr.	1 Oct. to 14 Mar.
Waterford	Kiln Bay	16 Aug. to 31 Jan.	1 Oct. to 31 Jan.
Lismore	Helvick Head	31 July to 1 Feb.	30 Sept. to 1 Feb.
Cork	Ballycotton H.	16 Aug. to 14 Feb.	13 Oct. to 14 Feb.
Skibbereen	Galley Head	30 Sept. to 30 Apr.	1 Nov. to 1 Feb.
Bantry	Mizen Head	1 Oct. to 30 Apr.	1 Nov. to 16 Mar.
Kenmare	Crow Head	16 Sept. to 31 Mar.	1 Nov. to 31 Mar.
Killarney	Lamb Head	1 Sept. to 30 Apr.	1 Nov. to 31 Mar.
Limerick	Dunmore Head	1 Aug. to 11 Feb.	1 Oct. to 31 Jan.
Galway	Hags Head	1 Sept. to 15 Feb.	16 Oct. to 31 Jan.
Connemara	Cashla Coast-Guard Stn.	6 Aug. to 31 Jan.	16 Oct. to 31 Jan.
Ballinakill	Slyne Head	1 Sept. to 15 Feb.	1 Nov. to 31 Jan.
Bangor	Pigeon Point	1 Sept. to 15 Feb.	1 Oct. to 30 Apr.
Ballina	Benwee Head	13 Aug. to 15 Mar.	16 Sept. to 31 Jan.
Sligo	Coonamore	16 July to 31 Dec.	1 Oct. to 31 Jan.
Ballyshannon	Mullaghmore	19 Aug. to 28 Feb.	10 Oct. to 28 Feb.
Letterkenny	Rossan Point	20 Aug. to 3 Feb.	2 Nov. to 31 Jan.
Londonderry	Malin Head	1 Sept. to 14 Apr.	11 Oct. to 2 Apr.
Coleraine	Downhill	20 Aug. to 3 Feb.	1 Oct. to 28 Feb.
Ballycastle	Portrush	20 Sept. to 16 Mar.	1 Nov. to 31 Jan.
Dundalk	Donaghadee	16 Sept. to 31 Mar.	1 Oct. to 2 Feb.
Drogheda	Clogher Head	5 Aug. to 11 Feb.	16 Sept. to 11 Feb.

In Ireland the weekly close-time is fixed at 48 hours, from 6 a.m. Saturday till 6 a.m. Monday. Salmon and trout must not be sold in Ireland in the close season.

CLOSE-TIME FOR TROUT AND CHAR.

The capture of trout and char in England and Wales is prohibited between 2nd October and 1st February, except (1) in Norfolk and Suffolk, where, under a local Act (the Norfolk and Suffolk Fisheries Act, 1877), the conservators have fixed the close-time for trout, for nets only, at from 10th September to 25th January; (2) in the Thames, where the close season is from 11th Sept. to 31st March; and (3) in the cases noted below, where, under an Act passed in 1876, the trout and char close-time has been varied by bye-law by local boards of conservators. In the districts marked * the close-time, as altered, applies only to trout. The *sale* of trout and char, however, is absolutely prohibited throughout England and Wales from 2nd October to 1st February :—

*Eden ... 2 Sept. (rods 2 Oct.) to 28 Feb.
Tyne...... 1 Oct. to 21 Mar. (for rods and nets).
*Severn ... 2 Oct. to 1 Mar. (ditto)
*Taf & Ely 20 Sept. to 1 Feb. (ditto)
*Cleddy ... 29 Sept. to 1 Mar. (ditto)
*Ogmore.. 30 Sept. to 28 Feb. (ditto)
*Teign ... 1 Oct. to 2 March (ditto)
*Ayron ... 1 Oct. to 15 Mar. (ditto)
Derwent (Cumb.) { 15 Sept. to 10 Mar. (ditto) — Except Char in Crummock and Buttermere, 1 Nov. to 30 June.
W. Cumberland.. } 2 Sept. to 10 March (rods and nets).
*Teify, *Avon & Erme } 1 Oct. to 28 Feb. (ditto)
*Tees ...... 1 Oct. to 1 March (ditto)
Adur, Cuckm're, *Avon & Stour } 1 Oct.† to 31 Mar. (ditto)
Usk ...... 2 Oct. to 14 Feb. (ditto)
Clwyd and Elwy .... } 2 Oct. to 28 Feb. (ditto)
Camel, Fowey §§ } 1 Oct. to 15 March. (ditto)
*Esk ......
Seiont,&c. { Trout, 2 Oct. to 1 Mar.‡ (ditto) — Char, 22 Oct. to 1 Mar. (ditto)
*Wye, Towy, *Lune, Kent } 2 Oct. to 1 Mar. (ditto)
Ribble }
*Dart ...... 2 Oct. to 28 Feb. (ditto)
*Ouse and Nene .... } 2 Oct. to 31 Mar. (ditto)
Yorks .... 2 Oct. to 15 Mar. (ditto
Wear .... 2 Oct. to 1 Mar. (ditto)
*Suffolk & Essex. } 2 Oct. to 10 Apr. (ditto)
*Dee ...... 14 Oct. to 14 Feb. (for rod & line only).
*Coquet .. 1 Nov. to 3 Mar. (for rod & line only).

In Scotland there is no close-time for trout and char. In Ireland the close-time for trout is the same as for salmon. This may be altered, but not shortened, by the Inspectors. For pollen, however, the close-time is fixed by the Pollen Fishery (Ireland) Act, 1881, from 1st Nov. to 31st Jan.

Between Sept. 3 and Feb. 1 all packages in England and Wales consigned by any common or other carrier and containing trout or char must be distinctly marked with the word "Trout" or "Char" as the case may be.

CLOSE-TIME FOR FRESHWATER FISH.

By the Freshwater Fisheries Act, 1878, a close-time for "freshwater fish" (which are defined for this purpose to include all kinds of fish, other than pollen, trout, and char, which live in fresh water, except those kinds which migrate to or from the open sea) is fixed from 15th March to 15th June, both inclusive, for all parts of England and Wales except parts of Norfolk and Suffolk. The penalty for taking or selling freshwater fish in that period is £2 for a first and £5 for a subsequent conviction. The close-season, however, does not

† 15 Oct. above Amesbury.
‡ Rivers Braint and Cefni, 15th Oct. to 1st March.
§ 2 Oct. to March 31 for Windermere and Coniston and R. Duddon; and 1 Sep. to 15 Feb. for R. Bela.
§§ April 30 between Lostwithiel and St. Winnow.

apply to eels taken otherwise than by angling or to fish taken in private waters by leave of the owner, in public waters by leave of a Board of Conservators, or taken (with the leave of the owner if in private waters) for bait or for scientific purposes. Fishery districts may be wholly or partially exempted from this close-time with the sanction of the Board of Trade, and the Avon and Stour, Avon and Erme, Wye, Eden, and Towy fishery districts have been so exempted ; also the Kent and Leven, Severn and Yorkshire districts, as regards pike ; the Usk as regards eels ; and certain parts of the Severn as regards other fish than grayling. In the navigable rivers of Norfolk and Suffolk and the broads connected therewith, close-times have been fixed for various fish under the Norfolk and Suffolk Fisheries Act, 1877, from March 1 to June 30. For eels a separate close-time exists (so far as fixed engines in salmon rivers are concerned) in England from January 1 to June 24 ; in Ireland, with one or two exceptions, from January 11 to June 30. In the Severn, elvers, or the fry of eels, are protected between 1 Jan. and the last day of Feb., and between 26 April and 24 June.

PROTECTION OF CRABS AND LOBSTERS.

Under the Fisheries (Oyster, Crab, and Lobster) Act, 1877, it is prohibited to buy or sell crabs under 4¼ inches, measured across the largest diameter of the back, or lobsters under 8 inches, measured from tip of beak to end of tail when spread out flat.

CLOSE-TIME FOR OYSTERS.

By the Fisheries (Oyster, Crab, and Lobster) Act, 1877, a close-time for the capture and sale of "Deep-Sea Oysters" is fixed from the 15th June to 4th August ; and for all other kinds of oysters

—except oysters taken in the waters of a foreign state—from 14th May to 4th August. By a recent decision foreign oysters temporarily deposited on English oyster layings for purposes of storage only do not come within this close season. This Act applies to England and Scotland, but not to Ireland. By the Sea Fisheries Act, 1868, fishing for oysters is prohibited from the 16th June to 31st August inclusive, in that part of the English Channel comprised between a line drawn from the North Foreland Light to Dunkirk, and a line drawn from the Land's End to Ushant—the territorial seas of England and France alone being excepted. This close-time, however, cannot be enforced till the Convention between England and France, included in the Act, is ratified ; and until that is done, the Convention concluded in 1839, which prohibits oyster-fishing in those limits from 1st May to 31st August, is to remain in force so far as French fishermen are concerned. It is customary, however, for both Powers to agree to suspend the operation of this close season till June 16 in each year. In Ireland, the Act 5 & 6 Vict. cap. 106, prescribes that no oysters may be taken between 1st May and 1st September, though this close season has been varied by the Inspectors of Fisheries in the following cases :—

Tralee Bay	11th Mar. to 31st Oct.
Galway Bay	1st Jan. to 30th Nov.
Strangford Lough	1st Mar. to 31st Aug.
Achil Sound, Clew Bay	2nd April to 30th Sept.
Sligo, Ballisodare and	
Drumcliffe Bays ...	30th April to 1st June.

Taking oysters from licensed beds is made larceny.

Licences for Shooting and Fishing.

GAME AND GUN LICENCES.—A licence is required by every person who hunts, shoots, or takes game, except persons (in Great Britain) taking woodcock and snipe with nets or springes ; rabbit-warren proprietors, or others, on enclosed land, killing rabbits ; persons hunting deer, or hares, with hounds ; owners or occupiers, or their servants, killing deer on their own land ; beaters and others, not holding guns, attending holders of game licences. Occupiers of enclosed land, or owners, having the right to kill game, may themselves kill hares, or authorize others to do so, without a licence, but such authority must be limited to one person at a time in any one parish, and must be registered with the clerk of the Justices of the Petty Sessional Division in which the land is situate. Even when the quarry is not what is legally known as "game," a "gun" licence is necessary. A game licence, however, covers a gun licence, and soldiers, sailors, volunteers, or constables on duty, or at practice, or occupiers of land scaring birds or killing vermin on such land, or persons so acting under the orders of occupiers holding a licence, need not take out a gun licence. Unless, however, the occupier is himself licensed, he cannot authorize any unlicensed person to carry a gun. "Scaring" birds is not to be regarded as including killing of any birds, and "vermin" does not include rabbits. The rates of duty are given at p. 431.

SALMON LICENCES.—It is not so generally known that in salmon fishery districts in England and Wales, and in Ireland, it is necessary to take out a licence to fish for salmon, and, in most rivers, for trout or char. In Scotland no such licence is needed. A licence is available only in the district,

and for the season, in which it is issued, except that in Ireland one rod licence is available in all parts of that country. The rates on nets and other like instruments range from £20 downwards in England and Wales, and from £30 downwards in Ireland. In the latter country the rate on draft nets, the kind most commonly used, is £3 ; in England and Wales it varies from about £5 to £2. The licence duty on a rod and line is £1 in Ireland.—In England and Wales different rates are charged in different districts as follows (an asterisk signifies that lower rates of duty are chargeable for short periods, or for certain parts of the district) :—

*Derwent	*West Cumberland ...	10/6
*Lune	*Eden	
*Ribble	*Seiont	
*Dee	Dwyfach .... }	21/-
Clwyd & Elwy...	Towy	
*Conway	*Taw and Torridge...	
*Teifi	*Camel	12/-
Usk... .... } 20/-	*Kent and Leven ...	
*Wye	*Dovey	
Avon and Erme	*Ayron	
*Dart	Severn .... }	10/-
*Teign	Fowey................	
Exe	Axe	
Frome	Trent	
Avon and Stour	*Esk (Yorkshire) ...	
Stour (Kent) ...	Avon, Brue, & Parret }	7/6
Yorkshire.........	Tamar and Plym ... }	
Tees	Ouse (Sussex)	
*Tyne.............	Wear	
Cleddy............ } 10/6	Coquet .... }	5/-
Taff and Ely ...	Cuckmere	
Rumney............	Adur	
Ogmore		

ENGLAND AND WALES. — The administration of the laws of close season, &c., for salmon and trout is placed by the Salmon and Freshwater Fisheries Acts, 1861 to 1896, in the hands of local boards of conservators appointed for the purpose, with the Board of Trade as the central authority. Districts may be formed, and Boards of Conservators appointed, for waters containing salmon, or freshwater fish.

Such Boards have been appointed for 53 Districts' [The districts generally include all rivers running into the sea between the points named, and in the cases marked + also include the sea for a distance of three miles from the shore, or to the mid-channel in estuaries.]

These Boards of Conservators consist of three classes of members — those appointed annually by the County Councils of the various counties

NAME OF DISTRICT.	COAST LIMITS OF DISTRICT.	ADDRESS OF CLERK.
+Eden	Sark Foot to Seaton	J. B. Slater, Carlisle.
+Derwent	Seaton to St. Bees Head	T. C. Burn, Papcastle, Cockerm'uth.
+West Cumberland	St. Bees Head to Haverigg Point	J. Webster, Whitehaven.
+Kent, &c.	Haverigg Point to Warton	S. H. Jackson, Ulverston.
+Lune	Warton to Blackpool	J. T. Sanderson, Lancaster.
+Ribble	Blackpool to Formby Point	H. Backhouse, Blackburn.
+Dee	New Brighton to near Meliden Church	Henry Jolliffe, Chester.
+Elwy and Clwyd	Meliden Church to Rhos Bay	F. Wallis, Rhyl.
+Conway	Rhos Bay to R. Aber	C. T. Allard, Llanrwst.
+Seiont	{ Garth Point to Llanaelhaiarn Pt., and to Twyn y Parc Pt., in Anglesey }	J. T. Roberts, Carnarvon.
+Dwyfach	Llanelhaiarn Point to Criccieth	David Jones, Portmadoc.
Dovey	Criccieth to Cynvelin	W. R. Davies, Dolgelly.
+Ayron	Carreg Tipog to New Quay Head	E. L. Jones, Aberayron.
+Teify	New Quay Head to Dinas Head	H. W. Howell, Lampeter.
Cleddy	Dinas Head to St. Goven's Head	R. T. P. Williams, Haverfordwest.
+Towy, Loughor, & Taf	St. Goven's Head to Worm's Head	W. M. Griffiths, Carmarthen.
+Ogmore and Ewenny.	Porthcawl to Cold Knap	S. H. Stockwood, Bridgend.
+Taff and Ely	Cold Knap to Bute Dock	A. Waldron, Cardiff.
+Rhymney	Bute Dock to Ty ton y Pill	Colonel Lyne, Newport (Mon.).
+Usk and Ebbw	Ty ton y Pill to Collister Pill	Horace Lyne, Newport (Mon.).
+Wye	Collister Pill to Cone Pill	E. T. Owen, Builth.
+Severn	Cone Pill to Avon Battery	J. Stallard, junior, Worcester.
Avon, Brue & Parret.	Avon Battery to County Boundary	T. F. Barham, Bridgwater.
Taw and Torridge	North Coast of Devon	W. H. Toller, Barnstaple.
+Camel	West Boundary of Devon to Peel Point	J. H. Gameson, Bodmin.
+Fowey	Peel Point to Rame Head	W. Pease, junior, Lostwithiel.
+Tamar and Plym	Rame Head to Stoke Point	W. W. Matthews, Tavistock.
+Avon (Devon)	Stoke Point to Start Point	W. Beer, Kingsbridge.
+Dart	Start Point to Hope Ness	E. Windeatt, Totnes.
+Teign	Hope Ness to Clerk Rock	H. Michelmore, Newton Abbot.
Exe	Clerk Rock to Ottermouth	H. Ford, junr., Exeter.
Otter	Ottermouth to Beer Head	
+Axe	Beer Head to Portland Bill	W. Forward, Axminster.
Frome	Portland Bill to Hampshire Boundary	P. E. L. Budge, Wareham.
Avon and Stour	W. Boundary of Hants to Hurst Castle	R. D. Sharp, Christchurch.
+Adur	West Tarring to Portobello	E. W. Oxborrow, Brighton.
+Ouse (Sussex)	Portobello to Seaford Head	F. Holman, Lewes.
+Cuckmere	Seaford Head to Fairlight	H. J. Woodhams, Berwick, Polegate.
+Rother	Fairlight to Dungeness	T. J. Smith, Rye.
Stour (Kent)	North to South Foreland	
+Suffolk & Essex	Dovercourt Light to Covehithe Coastgd. Sn.	A. T. Cobbold, Ipswich.
Norfolk and Suffolk		H. Brittain, Norwich.
+Ouse and Nene	{ West Boundary of Norfolk to Lapwater Hall }	Joseph Miller, Bedford.
Welland	Lapwater Hall to Western Point	S. B. Sharpe, Market Deeping.
+Witham	Western Point to Gibraltar	H. Snaith, Boston.
+Trent	Ingoldmell's Point to Trent Falls	C. K. Eddowes, Derby.
+Yorkshire	Trent Falls to Hayburn Wyke	J. E. Jones, Market Street, York.
+Esk (Yorkshire)	Hayburn Wyke to Skinningrove Beck	W. Brown, Whitby.
+Tees	Skinningrove Beck to Hardwick Hall	M. B. Dodds, Stockton.
+Wear	Hardwick Hall to Souter Point	W. Halcro, Sunderland.
+Tyne	Souter Point to Newbiggin Point	J. Gibson, Hexham.
+Coquet	Newbiggin Point to Hawick Burn	C. Percy, Alnwick.

through which the rivers flow; *ex-officio* members, or those qualified by ownership of lands or fisheries of a certain value; and representative members, elected annually by the persons who have paid licence duty on instruments other than rod and line, used for salmon fishing in public waters.

There are also certain bodies created by local statutes, having authority over the fisheries, *e.g.*, the Thames Conservancy Board, Lee Conservancy Board, and Conservators of the Medway.

These Boards have power to make bye-laws, not only for the regulation of the fisheries for salmon and freshwater fish, but also, in certain cases, for the regulation of other kinds of fishing which are prejudicial to such Fisheries. They are also empowered to issue licences for fishing for salmon, trout, &c. (see p. 676.).

SCOTLAND.—In Scotland there are 105 Fishery Districts, nearly each separate river forming a district of itself, but only 31 Boards of Conservators. The powers of these Boards are limited to the Salmon Fisheries.

IRELAND.—In Ireland there are 23 districts, embracing between them the whole country, each with a separate Board of Conservators.

SEA FISHERIES DISTRICTS.—Under the Sea Fisheries Regulation Act, 1888, the Board of Trade has power to form sea fisheries districts within the territorial waters of England and Wales, and to appoint local Fisheries Committees. These committees may be appointed either for a single county or borough, or for several jointly. They have power to make bye-laws, to be confirmed by the Board of Trade, regulating or prohibiting the use of instruments for the capture of sea fish (including shell fish and crustaceans, but excluding salmon), the deposit of rubbish on fishing grounds, &c. The following districts have been created—including in each case the coast and territorial seas adjoining between the points respectively mentioned:—1. Northumberland (coterminous with that county). 2. North Eastern, from Northumberland to Donna Nook in Lincolnshire. 3. Eastern, from Donna Nook to Happisburgh. 4. Kent and Essex, from Dovercourt to Dungeness, and including the Thames estuary to London Stone near Yantlet Creek. 5. Sussex (coterminous with that county). 6. Southern, from the western boundary of Dorset to Hayling Island. 7. Devon. 8. Cornwall (each coterminous with the respective counties). 9. Glamorgan, from Nash Point to Worms Head. 10. Milford Haven, from Worms Head to Cemmaes Head. 11. Western, from Cemmaes Head to eastern boundary of Carnarvonshire. 12. Lancashire, from Carnarvonshire to Haverigg Point. 13. Cumberland, Haverigg Point to Sark Foot.

Similar districts are being formed in Scotland under the Sea Fisheries Regulation (Scotland) Act, 1895.

Seasonable and Unseasonable Fish.

THE following table shows the periods when the different kinds of edible fish mostly in use are "in season" and "out of season."

The asterisk (*) signifies that the fish are then in their prime; the dagger (†) signifies that the fish may be obtained, but are not at their best; the double dagger (‡) signifies that it is "close-time" as fixed by statute.

Name of Fish.	Jan.	Feb.	Mar.	Apl.	May	June	July	Aug.	Sept.	Oct.	Nov.	Dec.
Barbel	*	-	‡	‡	‡	‡	-	-	†	-	-	*
Bass	-	-	-	-	-	-	*	†	-	-	-	-
Bream	*	-	‡	‡	‡	-	†	-	*	*	*	*
" (sea)	-	-	-	†	-	†	†	*	*	*	*	-
Brill	*	*	*	†	*	*	*	*	*	*	*	*
Carp	*	*	‡	‡	*	-	-	†	*	*	*	*
Catfish	†	*	*	*	*	*	†	-	-	*	*	*
Char	‡	‡	†	*	*	*	*	*	*	‡	‡	‡
Chub	†	†	‡	‡	‡	‡	†	-	-	*	†	†
Coal fish or Saithe	-	-	-	†	†	-	-	-	-	-	*	*
Cockle	*	*	*	-	-	†	†	†	*	*	*	*
Cod	*	*	*	-	-	-	†	†	*	*	*	*
Conger	-	†	†	*	*	*	*	*	*	*	†	-
Crab	†	†	†	†	*	*	*	-	†	†	†	*
Crayfish (a)	†	†	†	†	*	*	*	-	†	-	-	-
Dab	*	*	*	*	-	†	-	*	†	†	†	†
Dace	*	*	‡	‡	‡	‡	-	†	*	*	*	*
Dory	*	*	*	*	*	*	*	*	*	*	*	*
Eel	*	*	*	*	-	†	†	*	*	*	*	*
Flounder	†	*	*	*	*	-	-	-	-	*	†	*
Grayling	†	†	‡	‡	‡	‡	‡	-	*	*	*	*
Gudgeon	†	†	‡	‡	‡	‡	-	†	*	*	*	*
Gurnard (red)	*	*	†	-	-	-	-	†	*	*	*	*
" (grey)	†	-	-	-	-	-	-	-	-	*	*	*
Haddock	*	*	*	‡	†	-	-	†	*	*	*	*
Hake	*	*	-	-	†	†	*	*	*	*	*	*
Halibut	*	*	*	†	*	-	†	-	*	*	*	*
Herring	†	†	†	-	-	-	-	*	*	*	*	*
Lampern	*	*	‡	‡	‡	‡	-	-	†	-	*	*
Lamprey	†	*	‡	‡	-	†	-	-	-	-	*	*
Ling	*	*	*	*	-	-	-	-	†	*	*	*
Lobster	†	*	*	†	*	*	*	*	*	*	†	†
Mackerel	-	-	†	†	*	*	*	*	†	†	†	-
Mullet (red)	-	-	†	-	*	*	*	*	*	†	†	†
" (grey)	†	-	-	-	†	†	*	*	*	*	†	†
Mussel	*	*	*	†	-	-	-	-	-	*	*	*
Oyster (b)	*	*	*	‡	‡	‡	‡	‡	*	*	*	*
Perch	*	*	‡	‡	‡	‡	-	†	*	*	*	*
Periwinkle	*	*	*	*	*	*	*	*	*	*	*	*
Pike	*	*	‡	‡	‡	‡	†	*	*	*	*	*
Pilchard	-	-	-	-	-	-	†	*	*	*	-	-
Plaice	*	*	*	†	-	†	†	†	*	*	*	*
Pollack	*	*	†	-	-	†	†	*	*	*	*	*
Prawn	*	*	*	*	*	*	*	*	*	*	*	*
Salmon & Sea Trout (c)	‡	*	*	*	*	*	*	*	‡	‡	‡	‡
Shad	-	-	-	†	-	*	†	-	-	-	-	-
Shrimp (d)	*	*	*	*	*	*	*	*	*	*	*	*
Skate	*	*	*	†	-	-	†	†	*	*	*	*
Smelt or Sparling	*	*	*	*	*	*	*	*	*	*	*	*
Sole	*	*	*	†	*	*	*	*	*	*	*	*
Sprat	*	*	-	-	-	-	-	-	-	-	†	*
Sturgeon	-	-	-	†	*	*	*	†	-	-	-	-
Tench	*	*	‡	‡	‡	‡	-	†	*	*	*	*
Thornback	†	†	*	*	*	*	-	†	*	*	*	*
Torsk or Tusk	*	*	*	-	-	-	-	†	*	*	*	*
Trout	‡	‡	†	*	*	*	*	*	*	*	‡	‡
Turbot	*	*	*	†	*	-	†	-	*	*	*	*
Whelk	*	*	*	*	*	*	*	*	*	*	*	*
Whitebait	-	†	-	-	*	*	*	†	-	-	-	-
Whiting	*	*	*	†	†	-	-	†	*	*	*	*
Wrasse	*	*	*	*	*	*	*	*	*	*	*	*

(a) This is for sea crayfish. River crayfish can be obtained in the spring, summer, and autumn. It is a moot point whether it is legal to take freshwater crayfish from March to June.

(b) Foreign oysters can be sold in the close season, and are to be had almost all through the year, even though they have been laid down in English beds for storage.

(c) In the close season salmon from Holland and also from certain British rivers where net fishing is permitted later in the year than usual, are largely sold.

(d) For the first six months the bulk of our London supply of shrimps comes from Holland, but Dutch shrimps are far inferior to the English, which are plentiful from July to December.

THE year 1899 will remain famous for a long while in the home educational world if only for the passage of the first serious attempt that has been made to deal with the organization of secondary education viz., the Board of Education Act. As an outline of the new Act, and brief notes as to its various stages, are given below, further reference is unnecessary here except, perhaps, to add that, in the opinion of some very competent critics, the measure is likely to rank among the most important achievements of the present Government. What direction the next development of this work may take it is impossible to say, though the re-introduction of the much-needed Registration of Teachers Bill is a step by no means unlikely. Another measure of real, though not perhaps of very obvious importance is what is generally known as the Half-Timers' Act, the value of which was cordially recognised alike by the special facilities afforded it by the Government, and by the cordial reception it met with at the hands of both Houses of Parliament. Other measures, beneficent and useful — the Reformatory Schools Amendment Act, the Defective and Epileptic Children Act, &c — have also been placed on the Statute book during the recent parliamentary session. In the elementary grade, "draft rules" for the carrying out of the Teachers' Superannuation Act (1898) have now been issued by the Education Department, and the measure may be described as in operation; and various other questions — such as the education of blind and deaf children, feeble-minded children, and deaf-mutes, evening continuation schools, the working of the recent Voluntary Schools' Act, and the suitability of the curriculum of elementary schools in rural districts — are engaging the attention of educationists, and a good deal is likely to be heard of them before long. In the domain of higher education, two matters are just now to the fore. The London University question is in course of settlement, under the powers conferred on the Statutory Commission in 1898; it is, however, already definitely decided that the new University will be housed in the buildings of the Imperial Institute, for the purchase and alterations of which a sum of £60,000 has been voted by the Commons. The second matter referred to is Mr. Chamberlain's proposal for the establishment of a Birmingham University, which shall have as one of its foremost aims the promotion of commercial education in all its branches. The appeal for subscriptions necessary for such a foundation is being liberally responded to; a quarter of a million has already been promised, and a sum of about £200,000 will also be available from the endowments of the present Mason College, which will, for manifest reasons, form one of the constituent colleges of the new university.

GENERAL CHRONICLE.

November, 1898.—Death of the Rev. Preb. A. Wilson, formerly secretary of the National Society; Annual Conference of the National Federation of Assistant-Teachers; Annual meeting of the Association of Head-masters of Higher Grade and Organised Science Schools. *January*, 1899.—Mr H. E. Oakeley receives knighthood on retiring from the Chief Inspectorship of Schools; Duke of Devonshire opens the new Municipal College erected at Derby at a cost of £40,000; second Annual Conference of the National Federation of Head Teachers' Association; Annual General Meeting of the Royal Drawing Society of Great Britain and Ireland. *February*.—Annual Meetings of the Sloyd Association of Great Britain and Ireland; Draft rules issued under the Elementary School Teachers' (Superannuation) Act, 1898. *March*.—Annual Meeting of the National Association of Voluntary Teachers. *April*.—Annual Conference of the National Union of Teachers held at Cambridge; Mr. T. Clancy (president N.U.T.) and Mr. J. H. Yoxall, M.P. (general secretary N.U.T.) receive the Cambridge M.A. *honoris causa*; Professor G. G. A. Murray resigns the Greek Chair in the Glasgow University; the new scheme of the Charity Commissioners for the management of St Paul's School issued; Second Annual Conference of the National Association of Manual Training Teachers; Miss M. G. May and Miss C. T. M'Millan graduate with first-class honours at Glasgow University. *May*.—Mr. Rudyard Kipling receives the LL.D. degree of M'Gill University, Montreal; Annual Congress of the General Association of Church School Managers and Teachers held at Canterbury; Bishop of London lays the foundation stone of a new school and technical institute (to cost £45,000) in connection with the Sir John Cass Foundation (Aldgate). *June*.—Jubilee celebrations of Bedford College. *July*.—University of Wales confers its M.A. upon Miss B. Edgell, lecturer at Bedford College; Viscountess Cranborne lays the foundation stone of St. Gabriel's Training College, Kennington; Miss W. M. Slater wins the Gold Medal in Classics at the London University M.A. examination; Roman Catholic reformatory ship *Clarence* destroyed by fire in the Mersey. *August*.—Rev. R. S. De Coorcy Laffan retires from the Principalship of Cheltenham College; Mr. Richardson retires from the Second Mastership of Winchester College; Agricultural Education Committee formed under the chairmanship of Sir William Hart Dyke. *September*.—Death of Dr. Robert Ogilvie, H.M. Chief Inspector of Schools for Scotland; death of Mr. Francis Peek, well-known educationist; Prof. Dicey, M.A., new Principal of the Working Men's College, Great Ormond Street, delivers his inaugural address to the students. *October*.—Shoreditch Technical Institute (formerly Haberdashers' Schools, Hoxton) opened for pupils; Death of Mr. E. J. Marshall, head-master of Brighton Grammar School. *December*.—Annual preliminary examination (Dec. 4 and 5) for London School Board scholarships.

PARLIAMENTARY.

February, 1899.—The Queen's speech announces "A measure for the establishment of a board for the administration of primary, secondary, and technical education in England and Wales"; Mr. Robson's Half-Timers Bill read a first time. *March*.—Second reading of the Half-Timers Bill in the Commons; first reading of the Board of Education Bill in the Lords. *April*.—Second reading of the Board of Education Bill in the Lords. *May*.—Board of Education Bill in committee in the Lords; third reading of the Board of Education Bill in the Lords. *June*.—Half-Timers Bill in committee in the Commons; second reading of the Reformatory Schools Amendment Bill in the Lords; third reading of the Half-Timers Bill in the Commons; first reading of Half-Timers Bill in the Lords; first reading of the Defective and Epileptic Children Bill in the Lords; second reading of the same Bill in the Lords; third reading of the Reformatory

Schools Amendment Bill in the Lords; second reading of the Board of Education Bill in the Commons. *July.*—Second reading of the Half-Timers Bill in the Lords; Board of Education Bill in committee in the Commons; Reformatory Schools Amendment Bill finishes its passage through both Houses; Half-Timers Bill read a third time in the Lords; third reading of the Defective and Epileptic Children Bill in the Commons. *August.*—Third reading of the Board of Education Bill in the Commons; Board of Education Bill and Defective and Epileptic Children Bill pass the Lords.

I.—HALF-TIMERS ACT.

This Act comes into force on January 1, 1900, and enacts that the earliest time at which a child may be permitted to leave school shall henceforward be at the age of twelve years instead of eleven years. But the enactment will not apply to children already legally exempt at the end of the present year, and some modifications are provided in the case of (1) children employed in agriculture and (2) children who have made a certain minimum number of attendances in each of the preceding five years.

II.—BOARD OF EDUCATION ACT.

This Act comes into force on April 1, 1900, and does not extend to Scotland nor Ireland. It provides for the establishment of a Board of Education, to take the place of the present Education Department and the Science and Art Department, and to superintend all "matters relating to education in England and Wales." This Board may be entrusted with the powers relating to education at present exercised by the Charity Commissioners (exclusive of the determination of endowments to educational purposes or otherwise) and by the Board of Agriculture; it will also, either by its officers or after taking the advice of a Consultative Committee (appointed by Her Majesty in Council and representatives of the universities and other bodies interested in education), undertake the inspection of secondary schools. It may appoint paid secretaries and a staff of paid officials, subject to the sanction of the Treasury, which will also determine the salary in each case. The President of the Board (who need not, but probably will, be the Lord President of the Council) will be a Crown appointment. He will hold office during Her Majesty's pleasure, and he will receive an annual salary not exceeding two thousand pounds.

III.—TECHNICAL EDUCATION.

Whatever room there may still be for variety of opinion as to the actual and comparative value of the technical education that is now being given in Great Britain and Ireland, there can be no question but that genuine progress is being made. Organisation that is really worth the name is only just coming into existence; the effectiveness of the work is not so great as it ought to be, the official bodies directing and controlling the movement are too numerous and unequal. In about two years from the present time (if the recent rate of increase be maintained) the country will be spending a million pounds per annum on its public technical education, yet there would be few to hazard the statement that it is now deriving advantages worth that sum from its expenditure, the simple fact being that in this, as in so many other forward movements, the real fruits will not be apparent until many years after the sowing of the seed. Still, considering that

legislation giving important financial support to technical education is no more than a dozen years old, it is cause for much satisfaction that distinct progress has been made, as is evident from the very full and detailed Return now issued by the Science and Art Department each year, "showing the extent to which, and the manner in which, Local Authorities in England, Wales, and Ireland have applied, or are applying, funds to the purposes of Technical Education (including Science, Art, Technical and Manual Instruction)." The leading figures from this Return were incorporated in the tables given on pp. 683-4 in the ALMANACK for 1899. But it will probably be found of interest to supply here a few further particulars as to the action of the various local bodies with whom the control of technical education at present largely rests, though it must of course be borne in mind that the Science and Art Department, by means of its money grants-in-aid, exercises a greater or less influence over the instruction that is given. Thus in England (excepting the county of Monmouth) thirty-eight out of forty-nine county councils are applying the whole of the "residue" to technical education, and ten are applying a part of it to the same purpose; and, of the sixty-one county borough councils, fifty-four are devoting the whole, and seven a part, of the residue to technical education. Again, one county council and the councils of sixteen county boroughs, seventy-five boroughs, and one hundred and forty-six urban districts in England are making grants out of the rates under the Technical Instruction Acts; and fourteen local authorities are devoting funds to technical education out of the rate levied under the Public Libraries Acts. Twenty-five local authorities raised sums by loan on the security of the local rate under the Technical Instruction Acts during the year 1896-7, and eighteen in the following year. In Wales and the county of Monmouth the thirteen county councils and the councils of the three county boroughs are devoting the whole of the residue grant to intermediate and technical education, chiefly under the Welsh Intermediate Education Act, 1889; while the councils of nine counties, two county boroughs, four boroughs, and eight urban districts are making grants out of the rates under the Technical Instruction Acts. In Wales and Monmouth no amounts were raised by loan on the security of the local rate under the Technical Instruction Acts during the two years 1896-7 and 1897-8: during the latter year, however, the halfpenny rate under the Welsh Intermediate Education Act of 1889 was levied, wholly or in part, in all the sixteen counties and county boroughs. The case of Ireland is altogether different, the residue grant there not being applicable to technical education. Grants are being made by twelve local authorities out of the rates under the Technical Instruction Acts; and one of these authorities is also applying to technical education part of the rate levied under the Public Libraries Acts. Moreover, one other local authority had decided (at the date of the Return) to put the Technical Instruction Acts in force. In conclusion, it may be stated that the whole amount of the residue grant received by the councils of counties and county boroughs in England and Wales in respect of the financial year 1896-7 was £845,259 11s. 2d., of which £741,364 10s. 7d. was appropriated to educational purposes, and £103,895 0s. 7d. to the relief of rates.

Those Titles having living representatives are marked with an asterisk (*).

*Aberdour—Morton
Aboyne—Huntly
Acheson—Gosford
Adare—Dunraven
Alexander—Caledon
Alford—Brownlow
Altamont—Sligo
Althorp—Spencer
Amberley—Russell
Andover—Suffolk
Anson—Lichfield
Apsley—Bathurst
Ardee—Meath
Armagh—Cumberland
Arundel—Norfolk
Ashley—Shaftesbury
Ava—Dufferin and Ava
Balcarres—Crawford
*Balgonie — Leven and Melville
Baring—Northbrook
Bective - Headfort
Belfast - Donegall
Belgrave—see Grosvenor
Bennet—see Ossulston
Bernard—Bandon
Berriedale—Caithness
Bertie--Lindsey
*Bingham—Lucan
*Binning—Haddington
*Blandford—Marlboro'
Boringdon—Morley
Bowmont—Roxburghe
*Boyle—Shannon
*Brackley—Ellesmere
*Brecknock—Camden
Brooke—Warwick
Bruce—Elgin
*Burford—St. Albans
*Burghersh—Westmlnd.
Burghley—Exeter
Burke—Clanricarde
*Bury—Albemarle
*Campden—Gainsboro'
Cantelupe—De la Warr
*Cardigan—Ailesbury
Cardross—Buchan
Carlow—Portarlington
Carlton—Wharncliffe
Carmarthen—Leeds
Carnegie—Southesk
Cassillis—Ailsa
Castle Cuffe—Desart
Castlereagh—Londndry.
*Castlerosse—Kenmare
Chelsea—Cadogan
Chewton—Waldegrave
Clements—Leitrim
Clifton—Darnley
*Clive—Powis
Clonmore—Wicklow
Cochrane—Dundonald
Coke—Leicester
Cole—Enniskillen
Compton—Northampton
Corry—Belmore
Courtenay—Devon
Cranborne—Salisbury
Cranley—Onslow
Cremorne—Dartrey
Crichton—Erne
Crowhurst—Cottenham
*Curzon—Howe
*Dalkeith—Buccleuch

*Dalmeny—Rossebery
Dalrymple—Stair
Dalzell—Carnwath
Daugan—Cowley
De Grey—Ripon
Deerhurst—Coventry
Delvin—Westmeath
Douglas—Hamilton
*Douglas of Hawick and Tibbers — see Drumlanrig
Doune—Moray
Douro—Wellington
Drumlanrig — Queensberry
*Dumfries—Bute
Duncan—Camperdown
*Duncannon—Bessboro'
Dungarvan—Cork
Dunglass—Home
*Dunluce—Antrim
Dunwich—Stradbroke
*Dupplin—Kinnoull
Dursley—Berkeley
Earlsfort—Clonmell
*Ebrington—Fortescue
Ednam—Dudley
*Elcho—Wemyss & March
Eliot—St. Germans
Elmley—Beauchamp
*Emlyn—Cawdor
Encombe—Eldon
Enfield—Strafford
Ennismore—Listowel
*Erskine—Mar & Kellie
Eslington—Ravensworth
*Euston—Grafton
*Falconer—Kintore
*Feilding and Callan—Denbigh
*Fincastle—Dunmore
FitzClarence—Munster
FitzHarris—Malmesbry.
*Folkestone—Radnor
Forbes—Granard
Fordwich—Cowper
Forth—Perth & Melfort
*Garioch—Mar
Garlies—Galloway
Garmoyle—Cairns
*Garnock—Lindsay
*Gifford—Tweeddale
Goillird—Clanwilliam
*Glamis—Strathmore
Glandine—Norbury
*Glentworth—Limerick
*Glerawly—Annesley
Graham—Montrose
*Granby—Rutland
Greenock—Cathcart
*Grey de Wilton—Wilton
Grey of Groby—Stamfd.
Grimston—Verulam
Grosvenor—Westminster
*Guernsey—Aylesford
*Haddo—Aberdeen
*Hamilton—Abercorn
Hartington—Devonshire
Hastings—Huntingdon
Hawarden—De Montalt
*Helmsley—Feversham
*Herbert—Pembroke
*Hillsborough — Downshire

Hinckingbrooke—Sand-
Hinton—Poulett [wich
Hobart—Buckinghamshire.
Holmesdale—Amherst
*Hope—Hopetoun
Houghton—Crewe
Howard of Effingham—Effingham
*Howick—Grey
Huntingtower—Dysart
*Hyde—Clarendon
Ikerrin—Carrick
Ingestre—Shrewsbury
Inverurie—Kintore
Jedburgh—Lothian
Jermyn—Bristol
Jocelyn—Roden
*Kelburne—Glasgow
Kerry—Lansdowne
*Kilconnel—Clancarty
*Kilcoursie—Cavan
Kildare—Leinster
*Killeen—Fingall
*Kilmarnock—Erroll
Kilworth—Mount Cashell
*Kingsborough—Kingston
Kirkwall—Orkney
Knebworth—Lytton
*Kynnaird—Newburgh
Lambton—Durham
*Langton — Temple of Stowe
Lascelles—Harewood
Leslie—Rothes
Leveson—Granville
*Lewes—Abergavenny
Lewisham—Dartmouth
Lincoln—Newcastle
Loftus—Ely
*Lorne—Argyll
*Loughborough—Rosslyn
Lowther—Lonsdale
Lumley—Scarborough
Lymington—Portsmouth
Macduff—Fife
*Mahon—Stanhope
*Maidstone—Winchilsea
Maitland—Lauderdale
*Malden—Essex
Mandeville—Manchester
*March—Richmond
*Marsham—Romney
Mauchline—Loudoun
*Medway—Cranbrook
*Melgund—Minto
Milton—Fitzwilliam
Molyneux—Sefton
*Montgomerie—Eglinton
*Moore—Drogheda
*Moreton—Ducie
*Morpeth—Carlisle
Mount Charles — Conyngham
Mulgrave—Normanby
Naas—Mayo
*Newark—Manvers
Newport—Bradford
*Newry and Morne—Kilmorey
*Newtown - Butler—Lanesborough
*Norreys—Abingdon
North—Guilford
*Northland—Ranfurly

Ookham—Lovelace
*Ogilvy—Airlie
Ossory—Ormonde
Ossulston—Tankerville
*Oxmantown—Rosse
Pakenham—Longford
Parker—Macclesfield
Pelham—Chichester
Perceval—Egmont
*Percy—Northumberland
Petersham—Harringt n
Pevensey—Sheffield
Pollington—Mexborough
*Porchester—Carnarvon
Proby—Carysfort
*Raincliffe—Londesboro'
Ramsay—Dalhousie
Raynham—Townshend
Reidhaven—Seafield
*Rocksavage—Cholm'ley
*Ronaldshay—Zetland
*Ross of Belvoir—Granby
Rosehill—Northesk
Royston—Hardwicke
Russborough—Milltown
St. Asaph—Ashburnham
*St. Cyres—Iddesleigh
St. Lawrence—Howth
Salford—Egerton
Sandon—Harrowby
*Settrington—March
Seymour—Somerset
*Skelmersdale—Lathom
Somerton—Normanton
*Stafford, M.—Sutherland
Stanhope, Ld.—Chester-
*Stanley—Derby [field
*Stavordale—Ilchester
*Stopford—Courtown
Stormont—Mansfield
Stuart, v.—Castlestewart
*Sudley—Arran
*Suirdale—Donoughmore
Tamworth—Ferrers
Tarbat—Cromartie
*Tavistock—Bedford
*Tewkesbury—see Fitz-Clarence
Throwley—Sondes
*Titchfield—Portland
*Trafalgar—Nelson
*Tullibardine—Atholl
*Turnour—Winterton
Tyrone—Waterford
*Uffington—Craven
Uxbridge—Anglesey
*Valletort—Mount Edgcumbe
Vaughan—Lisburne
Villiers—Jersey
Walpole—Orford
Warkworth—Percy
*Wendover—Carrington
*Weymouth—Bath
*Whitchester—Dalkeith
*Willoughby de Eresby—Ancaster
Wilmington—Compton
Wiltshire—Winchester
*Wodehouse—Kimberley
Wolmer—Selborne
Worcester—Beaufort
*Worsley—Yarborough
*Yarmouth—Hertford

Abbot—*Colchester*
Abbott—*Tenterden*
Abney-Hastings — *Loudoun*
Acheson—*Gosford*
Adderley—*Norton*
Addington—*Sidmouth*
Agar—*Normanton*
Agar - Robartes (and Agar-Ellis)—*Clifden*
Alexander—*Caledon*
Allans n-Winn — *Headley*
Allsopp—*Hindlip*
Anderson-Pelham—*Yarborough* [*Annesley*]
Annesley—*Valentia* (and
Anson—*Lichfield* [*bury*
Ashley-Cooper—*Shaftes-*
Astley—*Hastings*
Bailey - *Glanusk*
Baillie-Hamilton - Arden —*Haddington*
Bampfylde—*Poltimore*
Baring—*Ashburton*
Baring—*Cromer*
Baring—*Northbrook*
Baring—*Revelstoke*
Barnewall—*Trimlestown*
Bass—*Burton* [*Bateman*
Bateman — Hanbury —
Beauclerk—*St. Albans*
Beckett—*Grimthorpe*
Bennet—*Tankerville*
Beresford—*Waterford*
Berkeley—*Fitzhardinge*
Bernard—*Bandon*
Bertie—*Abingdon*
Bertie—*Lindsey*
Best—*Wynford*
Bethell—*Westbury*
Bethune—*Lindsay*
Bingham—*Clanmorris*
Bingham—*Lucan*
Blake—*Wallscourt*
Bligh—*Darnley* [*thom*
Bootle-Wilbraham—*La-*
Borthwick—*Glenesk* (and *Borthwick*)
Boscawen—*Falmouth*
Bourke—*Connemara*
Bourke—*Mayo* [*more*
Bowes - Lyon — *Strath-*
Boyle—*Cork*
Boyle—*Glasgow*
Boyle—*Shannon*
Brabazon—*Meath*
Brand—*Hampden*
Brett—*Esher*
Bridgeman—*Bradford*
Brodrick—*Midleton*
Brooks—*Crawshaw*
Browne—*Kenmare*
Browne—*Kilmaine*
Browne—*Sligo* [*more*
Browne-Guthrie—*Oran-*
Brownlow—*Lurgan*
Bruce—*Aberdare*
Bruce—*Balfour*
Bruce—*Elgin* [*bury*
Brudenell-Bruce—*Ailes-*
Burns—*Inverclyde*
Burrell—*Gwydyr*
Butler—*Carrick*
Butler—*Mountgarret*

Butler—*Ormonde*
Butler—*Lanesborough*
Byng—*Strafford*
Byng—*Torrington*
Campbell—*Argyll*
Campbell—*Blythswood*
Campbell—*Breadalbane*
Campbell—*Cawdor*
Campbell—*Stratheden*
Canning—*Garvagh*
Capell—*Essex*
Carleton—*Dorchester*
Carnegie—*Northesk*
Carnegie—*Southesk*
Cary—*Falkland*
Caulfeild—*Charlemont*
Cavendish—*Chesham*
Cavendish—*Devonshire*
Cavendish—*Waterpark*
Cavendish - Bentinck — *Portland*
Cecil—*Exeter* (See Gascoyne-Cecil)
Charteris—*Wemyss*
Chichester—*Donegall*
Chichester—*Templemore*
Child-Villiers—*Jersey*
Cholmondeley — *Delamere* (and *Cholmondeley*)
Clegg-Hill—*Hill*
Clements—*Leitrim*
Clifford - Butler — *Dunboyne*
Clifton—*Grey de Ruthyn*
Cochrane—*Dundonald*
Cochrane-Baillie—*Lamington*
Cocks—*Somers*
Coke—*Leicester*
Colborne—*Seaton*
Cole—*Enniskillen*
Collier—*Monkswell*
Compton—*Northampton*
Constable - Maxwell — *Herries*
Courtenay—*Devon*
Crewe-Milnes—*Crewe*
Crichton—*Erne*
Crichton-Stuart—*Bute*
Cubitt—*Ashcombe*
Cuffe—*Desart*
Cunliffe-Lister—*Masham*
Curzon—*Scarsdale*
Curzon—*Zouche*
Curzon-Howe—*Howe*
Cust—*Brownlow*
Dalberg-Acton—*Acton*
Dalrymple—*Stair*
Daly—*Dunsandle*
Dalzell—*Carnwath*
Dawnay—*Downe*
Dawson—*Dartrey*
Dawson - Damer — *Portarlington* [*Clanricarde*
De Burgh - Canning —
De Courcy—*Kingsale*
De Grey—*Walsingham*
De Montmorency — *Frankfort de Montm.*
De Montmorency — *Mountmorres*
De Worms—*Pirbright*
De Yarburgh-Bateson *Deramore*

Deane - Morgan — *Muskerry*
Denison—*Londesborough*
Devereux—*Hereford*
Dillon—*Clonbrock*
Dillon-Lee—*Dillon*
Dodson—*Monk Bretton*
Douglas—*Morton*
Douglas—*Queensberry*
Douglas - Hamilton — *Hamilton and Brandon*
Douglas-Home—*Home*
Douglas-Pennant — *Penrhyn*
Douglas-Scott-Montagu —*Montagu of Beaulieu*
Drummond—*Perth*
Drummond—*Strathallan*
Duff—*Fife*
Duncombe—*Feversham*
Dundas—*Melville*
Dundas—*Zetland*
Dutton—*Sherborne*
Eaton—*Cheylesmore*
Eden—*Auckland*
Edgcumbe—*M-Edgcumbe*
Edwardes—*Kensington*
Egerton—*Ellesmere*
Egerton—*Wilton*
Eliot—*St. Germans*
Elliot - Murray - Kynynmond—*Minto*
Ellis—*Howard de Walden*
Erskine—*Buchan*
Erskine—*Mar & Kellie*
Evans-Freke—*Carbery*
Eveleigh - de - Moleyns—*Ventry*
Fane—*Westmorland*
Feilding—*Denbigh*
Fellowes—*De Ramsey*
Finch - *Aylesford*
Finch - Hatton — *Winchilsea*
Fitzalan - Howard — *Howard of Glossop*
Fitzalan - Howard — *Norfolk*
FitzClarence—*Munster*
FitzGerald—*Leinster*
FitzGerald de Ros — *De Ros*
Fitzmaurice (Petty-) — *Lansdowne*
FitzMaurice—*Orkney*
FitzPatrick—*Castletown*
FitzRoy—*Grafton*
Fitzroy—*Southampton*
Flower—*Ashbrook*
Flower—*Battersea*
Foljambe—*Hawkesbury*
Forbes—*Granard*
Forbes—*Sempill*
Foster - Skeffington — *Massereene*
Fox - Strangways — *Ilchester*
Fraser—*Lovat*
Fraser—*Saltoun*
Fremantle—*Cottesloe*
French—*De Freyne*
Gammell - Forbes — *Forbes*
Gardner — *Burghclere* (and *Gardner*)

Gascoyne - Cecil — *Salisbury* [*brook*
Gathorne-Hardy—*Cran-*
Gibbs—*Aldenham*
Gibson—*Ashbourne*
Giffard—*Halsbury*
Giustiniani - Bandini—*Newburgh*
Glyn—*Wolverton*
Goodeve-Erskine—*Mar*
Gordon—*Huntly*
Gordon - Lennox — *Richmond*
Gore—*Arran* [*mond*
Gore-Langton—*Temple*
Gough - Calthorpe —*Calthorpe*
Graham—*Montrose*
Graham-Toler—*Norbury*
Grant-Ogilvie—*Seafield*
Greville—*Warwick* and *Greville*
Grey—*Stamford & Grey*
Grimston—*Verulam*
Grosvenor—*Ebury*
Grosvenor—*Stalbridge*
Grosvenor—*Westminster*
Guest—*Wimborne*
Guinness—*Ardilaun*
Guinness—*Iveagh*
Gurdon—*Cranworth*
Haldane-Duncan—*Camperdown*
Hamilton—*Abercorn*
Hamilton—*Belhaven*
Hamilton—*HolmPatrick*
Hamilton - Gordon — *Aberdeen* and *Stanmore*
Hamilton - Russell — *Boyne*
Hamilton - Temple - Blackwood—*Dufferin*
Hanbury-Tracy—*Sudeley*
Handcock—*Castlemaine*
Harbord—*Suffield*
Hare—*Listowel*
Harris—*Malmesbury* (and *Harris*)
Hastings—*Huntingdon*
Hawkins—*Brampton*
Haworth-Leslie—*Rothes*
Hay—*Erroll*
Hay—*Kinnoull*
Hay—*Tweeddale*
Heathcote - Drummond-Willoughby—*Ancaster*
Hely-Hutchinson — *Donoughmore*
Henniker - Major — *Henniker*
Hepburn-Stuart-Forbes-Trefusis—*Clinton*
Hepburne-Scott — *Polwarth*
Herbert—*Carnarvon*
Herbert—*Pembroke*
Herbert—*Powis*
Hervey—*Bristol*
Hewitt—*Lifford*
Hill—*Downshire*
Hill-Trevor—*Trevor*
Hobart - Hampden — *Buckinghamshire*
Holland—*Knutsford*
Holmes - A'Court — *Heytesbury*

Holroyd—Sheffield
Hood—Bridport (& Hood)
Hope—Hopetoun
Hore-Ruthven—Ruthven
Horsley - Beresford — Decies
Hovell - Thurlow - Cumming-Bruce—Thurlow
Howard—Carlisle
Howard—Effingham
Howard—Suffolk
Howard—Wicklow
Hozier—Newlands
Hubbard—Addington
Innes-Ker—Roxburghe
Irby—Boston
James—Northbourne (and James of Hereford)
Jerningham—Stafford
Jervis—St. Vincent
Jocelyn—Roden
Jolliffe—Hylton
Keith-Falconer—Kintore
Kennedy—Ailsa
Keppel—Albemarle
Kerr—Lothian
King-Tenison—Kingston
Knatchbull - Hugessen—Brabourne
Knox—Ranfurly
Lambart—Cavan
Lambton—Durham
Lascelles—Harewood
Law—Ellenborough
Lawless—Cloncurry
Lawley—Wenlock
Le-Poer-Trench — Clancarty
Leeson—Milltown
Legge—Dartmouth
Legh—Newton
Leslie—Rothes
Leslie-Melville—Leven
Leveson-Gower — Granville
Liddell—Ravensworth
Lindsay—Crawford
Lister—Ribblesdale (and Lister)
Littleton—Hatherton
Lloyd-Mostyn—Mostyn
Loftus—Ely
Lopes—Ludlow
Lowry-Corry—Belmore
Lowry-Corry—Rowton
Lowther—Lonsdale
Loyd-Lindsay—Wantage
Lumley—Scarbrough
Lumley-Savile—Savile
Lygon—Beauchamp
Lysaght—Lisle
Lyttelton—Cobham
McClintock - Bunbury — Rathdonnell
McDonnell—Antrim
M'Garel-Hogg—Magheramorne
Mackay—Reay
Mackenzie—Cromartie
Maitland—Lauderdale
Manners—Rutland (and Manners)
Manners - Sutton — Canterbury
Mansfield—Sandhurst
Marjoribanks — Tweedmouth
Marsham—Romney

Massey—Clarina
Matthews—Llandaff
Maude—De Montalt
Maxwell—Farnham
Meade—Clanwilliam
Milbanke—Lovelace
Milles—Sondes
Mills—Hillingdon
Milman—Berkeley, Bnss.
Molyneux—Sefton
Monckton or Monckton-Arundell—Galway
Monsell—Emly
Montagu—Manchester
Montagu—Sandwich
Montagu-Douglas-Scott—Buccleuch
Montagu - Stuart-Wortley - Mackenzie — Wharncliffe
Montgomerie—Eglinton
Moore—Drogheda
Mo(o)re—Mount Cashell
Moreton—Ducie
Morgan—Tredegar
Morgan-Grenville—Kinloss
Mostyn—Vaux
Mulholland—Dunleath
Murray—Dunmore
Murray—Elibank
Murray—Mansfield
Needham—Kilmorey
Nevill—Abergavenny
Neville - Braybrooke
Noel—Gainsborough
Noel-Hill—Berwick
North — Guilford (and North)
Northcote—Iddesleigh
Norton—Grantley
Nugent—Westmeath
O'Brien—Inchiquin
O'Grady—Guillamore
Ogilvy—Airlie
Orde-Powlett—Bolton
Ormsby-Gore—Harlech
Osborne—Leeds
Paget—Anglesey
Pakenham—Longford
Pakington—Hampton
Palk—Haldon
Palmer—Selborne
Parker—Macclesfield
Parker—Morley
Parnell—Congleton
Parsons—Rosse
Paulet—Winchester
Pelham—Chichester
Pelham - Clinton — Newcastle
Pellew—Exmouth
Pennington—Muncaster
Pepys—Cottenham
Perceval—Egmont
Percy—Northumberland
Pery—Limerick
Phipps—Normanby
Pierrepont—Manvers
Pleydell-Bouverie—Radnor [Plunket]
Plunket—Rathmore (and Plunket)
Plunkett—Dunsany
Plunkett—Fingall
Plunkett—Louth
Pomeroy—Harberton
Ponsonby—Bessborough
Ponsonby—De Mauley

Powys—Lilford
Pratt—Camden
Preston—Gormanston
Primrose—Rosebery
Prittie—Dunalley
Proby—Carysfort
Ramsay—Dalhousie
Rice—Dynevor [don
Rice—Monteagle of Brandon
Robinson—Ripon
Robinson—Rosmead
Roche—Fermoy
Rolls—Llangattock
Roper-Curzon—Teynham
Rous—Stradbroke
Rowley—Langford
Russell—Ampthill
Russell—Bedford
Russell—De Clifford (also two Russells)
Ryder—Harrowby
Sackville—De la Warr
Sackville-West—Sackville
St. Aubyn—St. Levan
St. Clair—Sinclair
St.-Clair-Erskine—Rosslyn
St. John — Bolingbroke (and St. John of Bletsoe)
St. Lawrence—Howth
St. Leger—Doneraile
St. Maur—Somerset
Sandilands—Torphichen
Saumarez—De Saumarez
Savile—Mexborough
Scarlett—Abinger
Sclater-Booth—Basing
Scott—Clonmell
Scott—Eldon
Scudamore - Stanhope — Chesterfield
Selwin-Ibbetson—Rookwood
Seymour—Hertford
Shirley—Ferrers
Shore—Teignmouth
Sidney—De L'Isle
Sinclair—Caithness
Smith—Hambleden
Smith—Strathcona
Smith-Gray—Gray
Somerset—Beaufort
Somerset—Raglan
Somerville—Athlumney
Spencer—Churchill
Spencer - Churchill — Marlborough
Stanhope — Harrington (and Stanhope)
Stanley—Derby (and Stanley of Alderley)
Stapleton—Beaumont
Stapleton-Cotton—Combermere
Stephen—Mount Stephen
Stern—Wandsworth
Stewart—Galloway
Stewart-Murray—Atholl
Stonor—Camoys
Stopford—Courtown
Stourton—Mowbray and Segrave
Strutt—Belper
Strutt—Rayleigh
Stuart—Blantyre
Stuart—Moray
Stuart - Richardson — Castlestewart

Sturt—Alington
Sugden—St. Leonards
Sutherland-Leveson-Gower—Sutherland
Talbot—Shrewsbury
Taylour—Headfort
Thellusson—Rendlesham
Thesiger—Chelmsford
Thomson—Kelvin
Thynne—Bath
Tollemache—Dysart (and Tollemache)
Townsend - Farquhar — Farquhar
Trench—Ashtown
Trollope—Kesteven
Tufton—Hothfield
Turnour—Winterton
Twisleton - Wykeham - Fiennes—Saye & Sele
Tyrwhitt (-Wilson)—Berners
Tyssen-Amherst — Amherst of Hackney
Upton—Templetown
Vanden-Bempde-Johnstone—Derwent
Vane—Barnard
Vane - Tempest - Stewart—Londonderry
Vanneck—Huntingfield
Vaughan—Lisburne
Venables - Vernon—Vernon
Vereker—Gort
Verney—Willoughby de Broke
Verney-Cave—Braye
Vernon—Lyveden (and Vernon)
Vesey—De Vesci
Villiers—Clarendon
Villiers (Child-)—Jersey
Vivian — Swansea (and Vivian)
Waldegrave—Radstock (and Waldegrave)
Wallop—Portsmouth
Walpole—Orford
Walsh—Ormathwaite
Ward—Bangor
Ward—Dudley
Weld-Forester—Forester
Wellesley—Cowley
Wellesley—Wellington
Wentworth-Fitzwilliam—Fitzwilliam
Westenra—Rossmore
White—Annaly
White—Overtoun
Wilde—Penzance
Wilde—Truro
Williamson—Ashton
Willoughby—Middleton
Windsor-Clive—Windsor
Wingfield—Powerscourt
Winn—St. Oswald
Wodehouse—Kimberley
Wood—Halifax
Wyndham—Leconfield
Wyndham - Quin—Dunraven and Mount Earl
Wynn—Newborough
Wynn-Carrington—Carrington
Yarde-Buller—Churston
Yelverton—Avonmore
Yorke—Hardwicke

In Almanacks previous to 1886 tables were given showing the EXPECTATION OF LIFE, and the numbers of survivors out of a given number of births at each successive year of life. Those tables were constructed by the late Dr. Farr, of the General Register Office, and were calculated on the death-rates of 1838–54; but since that time very important changes have occurred in the death-rates at different ages, and consequently new tables have been constructed by Dr. W. Ogle, who succeeded Dr. Farr, on the basis of the death-rates of 1871–80. The following table gives the results both of the older and the later calculations; the first two columns in the male and female parts, respectively, giving the survivors at each year of life out of a million born of the corresponding sex, by the older and the newer calculation; and the two other columns giving similarly the expectation of life at each year :—

AGE.	MALES.				FEMALES.				AGE.
	OF 1,000,000 BORN, THE NUMBER SURVIVING AT THE END OF EACH YEAR OF LIFE.		MEAN AFTER-LIFETIME (EXPECTATION OF LIFE).		OF 1,000,000 BORN, THE NUMBER SURVIVING AT THE END OF EACH YEAR OF LIFE.		MEAN AFTER-LIFETIME (EXPECTATION OF LIFE).		
	1838–54.	1871–80.	1838–54.	1871–80.	1838–54.	1871–80.	1838–54.	1871–80.	
Col'mn	1.	2.	3.	4.	5.	6.	7.	8.	Col'mn
0	1,000,000	1,000,000	39·91	41·35	1,000,000	1,000,000	41·85	44·62	0
1	836,405	841,417	46·65	48·05	865,288	871,266	47·31	50·14	1
2	782,626	790,201	48·83	50·14	811,711	820,480	49·40	52·22	2
3	754,849	763,737	49·61	50·86	782,990	793,359	50·20	52·99	3
4	736,845	746,587	49·81	51·01	764,060	775,427	50·43	53·20	4
5	723,716	734,068	49·71	50·87	750,550	762,622	50·33	53·08	5
6	713,881	726,815	49·39	50·38	740,584	755,713	50·00	52·56	6
7	706,156	721,103	48·92	49·77	732,771	750,276	49·53	51·94	7
8	699,688	716,309	48·37	49·10	726,116	745,631	48·98	51·26	8
9	694,346	712,337	47·74	48·35	720,537	741,727	48·35	50·53	9
10	689,857	708,990	47·05	47·60	715,769	738,382	47·67	49·76	10
11	685,982	706,146	46·31	46·79	711,581	735,405	46·95	48·96	11
12	682,512	703,595	45·54	45·96	707,770	732,697	46·20	48·13	12
13	679,256	701,200	44·76	45·11	704,155	730,122	45·44	47·30	13
14	676,057	698,864	43·97	44·26	700,581	727,571	44·66	46·47	14
15	672,776	696,419	43·18	43·41	696,917	724,956	43·90	45·63	15
16	669,296	693,695	42·40	42·58	693,050	722,084	43·14	44·81	16
17	665,529	690,746	41·64	41·76	688,894	718,993	42·40	44·00	17
18	661,402	687,507	40·90	40·96	684,378	715,622	41·67	43·21	18
19	656,868	683,941	40·17	40·17	679,463	711,946	40·97	42·43	19
20	651,903	680,033	39·48	39·40	674,119	707,949	40·29	41·66	20
21	646,502	675,769	38·80	38·64	668,345	703,616	39·63	40·92	21
22	641,028	671,344	38·13	37·89	662,474	699,141	38·98	40·18	22
23	635,486	666,754	37·46	37·15	656,509	694,521	38·33	39·44	23
24	629,882	661,997	36·79	36·41	650,463	689,759	37·68	38·71	24
25	624,221	657,077	36·12	35·68	644,342	684,858	37·04	37·98	25
26	618,503	651,998	35·44	34·96	638,148	679,822	36·39	37·26	26
27	612,731	646,757	34·77	34·24	631,891	674,661	35·75	36·54	27
28	606,906	641,353	34·10	33·52	625,575	669,372	35·10	35·83	28
29	601,026	635,778	33·43	32·81	619,201	663,959	34·46	35·11	29
30	595,089	630,038	32·76	32·10	612,774	658,418	33·81	34·41	30
31	589,094	624,124	32·09	31·40	606,296	652,747	33·17	33·70	31
32	583,036	618,056	31·42	30·71	599,769	646,957	32·53	33·00	32
33	576,912	611,872	30·74	30·01	593,196	641,045	31·88	32·30	33
34	570,716	605,430	30·07	29·33	586,575	635,003	31·23	31·60	34
35	564,441	598,860	29·40	28·64	579,908	628,842	30·59	30·90	35
36	558,083	592,107	28·73	27·96	573,192	622,554	29·94	30·21	36
37	551,634	585,167	28·06	27·29	566,431	616,144	29·29	29·52	37
38	545,084	578,019	27·39	26·62	559,619	609,599	28·64	28·83	38
39	538,428	570,656	26·72	25·96	552,758	602,924	27·99	28·15	39
40	531,657	563,077	26·06	25·30	545,844	596,113	27·34	27·46	40
41	524,761	555,254	25·39	24·65	538,876	589,167	26·69	26·78	41
42	517,734	547,288	24·73	24·00	531,849	582,104	26·03	26·10	42
43	510,567	539,161	24·07	23·35	524,765	574,919	25·38	25·42	43
44	503,247	530,858	23·41	22·71	517,617	567,612	24·72	24·74	44

AGE.	MALES. Of 1,000,000 Born, the Number Surviving at the End of Each Year of Life. 1838-54. 1.	1871-80. 2.	MALES. Mean After-Lifetime (Expectation of Life). 1838-54. 3.	1871-80. 4.	FEMALES. Of 1,000,000 Born, the Number Surviving at the End of Each Year of Life. 1838-54. 5.	1871-80. 6.	FEMALES. Mean After-Lifetime (Expectation of Life). 1838-54. 7.	1871-80. 8.	AGE.
45	495,770	522,374	22·76	22·07	510,403	560,174	24·06	24·06	45
46	488,126	513,702	22·11	21·44	503,122	552,602	23·40	23·38	46
47	480,308	504,836	21·46	20·80	495,768	544,892	22·74	22·71	47
48	472,306	495,761	20·82	20·18	488,339	537,043	22·08	22·03	48
49	464,114	486,479	20·17	19·55	480,833	529,048	21·42	21·36	49
50	455,727	476,980	19·54	18·93	473,245	520,901	20·75	20·68	50
51	447,139	467,254	18·90	18·31	465,372	512,607	20·09	20·01	51
52	438,099	457,022	18·28	17·71	457,814	504,188	19·42	19·34	52
53	428,801	446,510	17·67	17·12	449,966	495,645	18·75	18·66	53
54	419,256	435,729	17·06	16·53	442,027	486,973	18·08	17·98	54
55	409,460	424,677	16·45	15·95	433,331	477,440	17·43	17·33	55
56	399,408	413,351	15·86	15·37	424,239	467,443	16·79	16·69	56
57	389,088	401,740	15·26	14·80	414,761	456,992	16·17	16·06	57
58	378,481	389,827	14·68	14·24	404,895	446,079	15·55	15·45	58
59	367,570	377,591	14·10	13·68	394,636	434,695	14·94	14·84	59
60	356,330	365,011	13·53	13·14	383,974	422,835	14·34	14·24	60
61	344,744	352,071	12·96	12·60	372,895	410,477	13·75	13·65	61
62	332,789	338,820	12·41	12·07	361,387	397,644	13·17	13·08	62
63	320,451	325,256	11·87	11·56	349,436	384,319	12·60	12·51	63
64	307,720	311,368	11·34	11·05	337,031	370,495	12·05	11·96	64
65	294,588	297,156	10·82	10·55	324,165	356,165	11·51	11·42	65
66	281,064	282,638	10·32	10·07	310,833	341,326	10·98	10·90	66
67	267,160	267,829	9·83	9·60	297,048	325,988	10·47	10·39	67
68	252,901	252,753	9·36	9·14	282,819	310,170	9·97	9·89	68
69	238,328	237,487	8·90	8·70	268,177	293,899	9·48	9·41	69
70	223,490	222,056	8·45	8·27	253,161	277,225	9·02	8·95	70
71	208,453	206,539	8·03	7·85	237,822	260,207	8·57	8·50	71
72	193,297	190,971	7·62	7·45	222,230	242,934	8·13	8·07	72
73	178,114	175,449	7·22	7·07	206,464	225,497	7·71	7·65	73
74	163,003	160,074	6·85	6·70	190,620	208,003	7·31	7·25	74
75	148,076	144,960	6·49	6·34	174,800	190,566	6·93	6·87	75
76	133,453	130,227	6·15	6·00	159,126	173,316	6·56	6·51	76
77	119,251	115,986	5·82	5·68	143,722	156,392	6·21	6·16	77
78	105,592	102,359	5·51	5·37	128,711	139,927	5·88	5·82	78
79	92,587	89,449	5·21	5·07	114,229	124,065	5·56	5·50	79
80	80,343	77,354	4·93	4·79	100,394	108,935	5·26	5·20	80
81	68,946	66,153	4·66	4·51	87,323	94,662	4·98	4·90	81
82	58,471	55,842	4·41	4·26	75,119	81,305	4·71	4·63	82
83	48,970	46,489	4·17	4·01	63,862	68,966	4·45	4·37	83
84	40,471	38,132	3·95	3·58	53,615	57,723	4·21	4·12	84
85	32,979	30,785	3·73	3·56	44,419	47,631	3·98	3·88	85
86	26,476	24,436	3·53	3·36	36,284	38,710	3·76	3·66	86
87	20,926	19,054	3·34	3·17	29,202	30,958	3·56	3·46	87
88	16,268	14,870	3·16	2·99	23,135	24,338	3·36	3·26	88
89	12,428	10,926	3·00	2·82	18,027	18,788	3·18	3·08	89
90	9,321	8,015	2·84	2·66	13,802	14,225	3·01	2·90	90
91	6,859	5,748	2·69	2·51	10,376	10,553	2·85	2·74	91
92	4,946	4,025	2·55	2·37	7,650	7,698	2·70	2·58	92
93	3,492	2,749	2·41	2·24	5,526	5,429	2·55	2·44	93
94	2,411	1,828	2·29	2·14	3,963	3,786	2·42	2·30	94
95	1,628	1,183	2·17	2·01	2,704	2,533	2·29	2·17	95
96	1,071	742	2·06	1·90	1,827	1,661	2·17	2·11	96
97	688	452	1·95	1·81	1,204	1,057	2·06	2·03	97
98	430	266	1·85	1·72	774	653	1·96	1·83	98
99	262	151	1·76	1·65	483	389	1·86	1·73	99
100	134	82	1·68	1·61	295	225	1·76	1·62	100

Up to the year 1858 the probate and safe custody of wills was entirely within the jurisdiction of the Ecclesiastical Courts. Complaints of the carelessness and insecurity to which the documents were exposed at the hands of sinecurists and absentee officials became very rife, culminating perhaps in the vigorous onslaught on the system which was made by Charles Dickens in "David Copperfield" and "Household Words." The result was the establishment throughout the country of forty District Registries. To find a will proved before 1st January, 1858, the date on which the Court of Probate Act, 1857 (20 & 21 Vict. c. 77), came into operation, it is best to search first—if the testator was a man of substance—the index to the wills proved in the Prerogative Court of Canterbury, which is kept at Somerset House. Failing this, the will is probably to be found in the registry of the district in which it was proved. The wills proved prior to 1858 were all distributed among the district registries when these institutions came into existence. This is the only broad rule which can be laid down to guide a searcher. To find a will proved since 1858 is a far simpler task. It must have been proved either at the Principal Registry at Somerset House, or in the registry of the district in which the testator lived. In the former case the original will itself is carefully preserved at Somerset House, the copy of which probate has been granted is in the hands of the executors who proved the will, and another copy for Parliament is bound up in a folio volume of wills made by testators of that initial and date; the indices to these volumes fill a room of considerable size at Somerset House, which is freely open to the public. In the latter case, the original will, proved in the District Registry, is there kept, but a copy is sent to and filed at Somerset House, and may there be seen. Any will may be read by anybody who is ready to pay a search fee of one shilling; but the reader may not copy any part of the will except the names and addresses of the executors, and the date and private number of the will. If he desires a copy, he can order one to be made, for which he will pay according to the length of the will, at the rate of sixpence a folio (ninety words) for an ordinary copy, and ninepence a folio for a certified copy, which, with a shilling stamp impressed thereon, can be produced and read in any court of law. The District Registries established by the Act of 1857 are the following:—

Districts.	Registrar.	Registries.
Northumberland...	H. E. Edwards	Newcastle-upon-Tyne.
Durham	Joshua Earles..	Durham.
Cumberland and Westmorland ...	Wm. C. Butler	Carlisle.
Yorkshire, West Riding	G. Bridgeman ...	Wakefield.
,, N. Riding ,, E. Riding, inc. York.	Henry Arthur Hudson	York.
Lancashire, except Salford and West Derby Hundreds, Manchester .	J. G. Douglas-Willan	Lancaster.
Manchester and H of Salford .	Oswald H. Hardy .:.....	Manchester.
West Derby Hund.	T. E. Paget ...	Liverpool.
Chester	H. A. Jenner...	Chester.
Carnarvon & Anglesey	H. B. Roberts	Bangor.

Districts.	Registrar.	Registries.
Flint, Denbigh, & Merioneth	J. P. Lewis ...	St. Asaph.
Derbyshire	C. T. E. Wilde	Derby.
Nottinghamshire..	W. G. Vincent	Nottingham.
Leicestershire and Rutlandshire	G. H. Nevinson	Leicester.
Lincolnshire.......	John Swan ...	Lincoln.
Salop and Montgomery	F. R. B. Walton	Shrewsbury.
Northants, N. Huntingdon, & Cambridge	Henry William Gates	Peterboro'.
Norfolk	G. R. Harman	Norwich.
Suffolk, East	W. H. Walpole	Ipswich.
Essex, North		
Suffolk, W.	C. Wodehouse	Bury St. Edmunds.
Bedford & South Northants	C. C. Becke ...	Northampton
Warwickshire	W.G.Middleton	Birmingham.
Staffordshire	T.W.H. Oakley	Lichfield.
Radnor, Brecknock, and Herefordshire	T. C. Paris	Hereford.
Cardigan, Carmarthen, Pembroke, etc.	W. Morgan Griffiths	Carmarthen.
Glamorgan and Monmouthshire	Clemt.Waldron	Llandaff.
Worcestershire ...	H. A. Franklin	Worcester.
Gloucestershire, except Bristol.	R. Fuller.........	Gloucester.
Bristol and Bath.	Wm. H. Clarke	Bristol.
Oxford, Berks, & Bucks	Thomas M. Davenport	Oxford.
Somerset, East, except the Bath C. C. District.	John Raymond Holligan ...	Wells.
Somerset, West ...	E. T. Alms......	Taunton.
Devonshire	W. H. Bailey...	Exeter.
Cornwall	W. H. Shadwell	Bodmin.
Wiltshire	H. Elliot Fox	Salisbury.
Dorsetshire	H. F. C. de Crespigny	Blandford.
Hampshire	C. Wooldridge	Winchester.
Sussex, East.........	J. W. Heisch...	Lewes.
Sussex, West	Sir R. G. Raper	Chichester.
Kent, East	H.M. Chapman	Canterbury.

DEPOSITORY FOR THE WILLS OF LIVING PERSONS.—It is unfortunate for the success of this institution that its existence is so little known. It may be added that the formalities and expense attendant upon depositing a will in Somerset House for safe custody do little to recommend that safety to the public. Since 1857 this depository has been provided by the State under sect. 91 of the Act 20 & 21 Vict. c. 77; but the provision has been almost a dead letter, for in three recent years there were only seven, nine, and seventeen testators found to place their wills in Somerset House. This may be done through the Registrar of a District Registry, who will transmit the will to London in a registered letter on receiving a fee of 10s. for the deposit, of 2s. 6d. for entering a minute thereof, and 2s. for filing the affidavit which is required. A will once deposited will not be given up to anybody, but must remain in the registry until the testator dies, unless he goes to the registry with the original minute of deposit and other proof of his identity, and destroys his will in the presence of the Registrar,

In 1895 a Parliamentary Commission was appointed to enquire into the management and methods of distribution of the various sums of money which have from time to time come under the control of the Commissioners of the Royal Patriotic Fund This Fund, inaugurated in 1854, under the presidency of H.R.H. the late Prince Consort, was to provide relief to the widows and orphans of soldiers killed in the Crimean War, and it soon reached very considerable proportions. Since that time, various other philanthropic funds have been placed in the hands of the Royal Commissioners, such as the "Victoria Relief Fund," the "Captain Fund," and many others, until in 1896 the total capitalised amount was over £1,000,000. The following table gives the various funds administered by the Patriotic Commissioners; the date of foundation of each; amount invested in 1895, capital amounts, receipts and expenditure in 1898.

Description of Fund.	Date when Founded.	Value of assets, June, 1896 *	Capital amounts Dec. 31, 1898.	Receipts, 1898.	Expenditure, 1898, Payments to Widows, Orphans, &c.	Management, &c.
		£	£	£	£	£
Russian War Fund .... } Patriotic General Fund .... }	1854	481,422	†324,762	13,558	25,193	1,464
Rodriguez Fund.................	1864	18,700	16,023	565	291	12
Captain Fund	1870	39,630	32,162	1,310	1,018	46
Eurydice Fund	1878	19,746	14,396	521	429	19
Royal Naval Relief Fund	1878	8,962	8,007	272	275	12
Zulu War Fund	1879	27,884	26,507	1,098	837	36
Atalanta Fund	1880	7,811	7,400	292	232	9
Soldiers' Effects Fund............	1884	161,277	155,033	5,476	1,279	57
Ashanti War Fund	1873	2,073	2,000	80	89	3
Zeroudachi Fund	1883	1,954	1,831	62	55	2
Balaclava Fund	1891	2,977	2,500	113	199	6
County of Forfar Fund	1892	856	800	32	20	1
Victoria Fund....................	1893	94,284	60,511	2,130	3,500	99
Indian Army (European) Effects Fund	...	...	600	24	...	...
Royal Victoria Patriotic Asylum........	...	179,380	157,667	6,753	6,031	243
Thurlow Fund	...	745	670	25	2	...
Roman Catholic Orphans' Fund	...	41,184	35,504	1,420	1,318	26
		1,085,935	846,373	33,731	40,835	2,035

£42,870

* Report of Royal Commission.
† In addition to this amount there is a sum of £43,494, the income from which is paid to the governing bodies of various schools for the education and maintenance of 47 children of naval, military, and marine officers and men.

Among other Funds which occupied the attention of the Parliamentary Commission of 1896 were "Lloyd's Patriotic Fund" (founded in 1803 and amounting in 1895 to £162,000); the "Imperial War Fund," formed in 1882; the "Soldiers' and Sailors' Families Association," which had a capital of £37,000 in 1896; the "Royal Naval Fund" (1893), formed with a surplus of £47,658 from the Naval Exhibition of 1893; the "Indian Military Relief Fund" (£46,000), and the "Military Tournament Fund," which obtains a yearly income from the tournament held at the Agricultural Hall. None of these Funds is administered by the Patriotic Commissioners.

Relief (War) Fund in 1899.

The Funds opened at the Mansion House, in connection with the War in South Africa, are four in number.

1. For the widows, orphans and other dependants of soldiers killed during the Campaign.
2. For sick and wounded soldiers, sailors and marines.
3. For soldiers, sailors and marines who may have to leave the Service disabled by wounds.
4. For the benefit of wives, children and dependants left at home during the Campaign.

At the time of going to press, the amount raised stood as follows :—

Fund 1 .... £220,000
,, 2 25,000
,, 3 31,000
,, 4 50,000
Total received .. £341.000

Fund No. 1 is to be administered by the Commissioners of the Royal Patriotic Fund, who have stated their intention not to invest the money, but to divide it as required ; No. 2 comes under the management of the Red Cross Society ; No. 3 will be distributed by Lloyd's Patriotic Fund ; No. 4 will be administered by the Soldiers' and Sailors' Families Association.

The Transvaal Refugees Fund, also subscribed at the Mansion House, amounted to nearly £170,000.

Another very successful Fund is that inaugurated by the proprietors of the *Daily Telegraph*, and managed by themselves. This Shilling Fund (formed for the benefit of soldiers' relatives), at the time of going to press amounted to 1,287,012 shillings, which is *immediately* distributed through skilful agencies to the beneficiaries.

For Police purposes London is divided into two jurisdictions, that of the Metropolitan and that of the City Police. The former force superseded the "Night Watchmen" in 1830, when a Bill introduced by Sir Robert Peel authorised the establishment of a Metropolitan Police under the control of the executive government. The night watch system continued in the City itself until 1839, when a force of City Police was established under the control of the Common Council.

The City Police* district comprises an area of 671 statute acres, and contains two courts of justice, those of the Guildhall and Mansion House, where the Lord Mayor and the Aldermen are the magistrates. Although the area is comparatively small, the rateable value is enormous, and there are 31,148 night residents to be protected.

The Force comprises 1 Superintendent, 1 ditto, Detective Department, 3 Chief Inspectors, 15 District Inspectors, 23 Station Inspectors, 12 Detective Inspectors, 74 Sergeants, 7 Detective Sergeants, and 865 Constables; also 57 Constables on private service duty.

The Metropolitan Police* district embraces an area of 440,518 statute acres, with a population of between six and seven millions. There are within this area fifteen Police Courts, viz., Bow Street, Clerkenwell, Marlborough St., Greenwich, Lambeth, Marylebone, North London (Stoke Newington Rd.), South Western (Lavender Hill), Southwark, Thames (Stepney), West Ham, West London (Vernon St.), Westminster, Woolwich, and Worship St.

The Force on Nov. 20, 1899, consisted of 31 Superintendents, 572 Inspectors, 1,947 Sergeants, and 13,202 Constables, making a total of 15,752, with 313 horses.

It is scarcely possible to form an accurate estimate of the enormous actual value of the property under police protection, but the mean rateable value of the metropolitan area for

Metropolitan Police purposes for the year 1898-9 was £41,419,302. The Police Rate is now fixed by 31 & 32 Vict. c. 67 at 9d. in the £, of which 4d. in the £ is payable out of the Local Taxation Account under the Local Government Act, 1888. The total amount of Police Rate levied on the Parishes for the year ending 31 March, 1899, was £863,068, and the Local Taxation Account (including £4,389 under the Agricultural Rates Act, 1896) contributed £691,069 to the Police Fund during the year. The pay of the Force, including Chief Constables, Superintendents, Inspectors, Sergeants and Constables, was £1,293,137. During the year 1898, the criminal offences reported to the Metropolitan Police amounted to 19,656; an increase of 1,232 as compared with the preceding year. The proportion of felonies relating to property was only 2·637 per thousand of the population. Of burglaries, 498 were committed in 1898, an increase of 76 over 1897, and the estimated value of the property stolen in these burglaries was £5,269, of which £1,215 was recovered. Housebreakings numbered 1,374, and the value of the property lost was £12,509. Murder cases in 1898 numbered 18; there were eight death sentences; in four cases the homicides were made amenable but found insane, and in three cases the murderer committed suicide. Of manslaughter there were 39 cases in 1898 as compared with 30 in 1897. The number of Penal Servitude Convicts liberated on licence in the Metropolitan Police District was 750—23 less than in 1897.

* For the official staff of the two Forces, see p. 160.

Metropolitan Fire Brigade.

Previous to the formation of the Metropolitan Fire Brigade, under an Act passed in 1774, the churchwardens and overseers of every parish had been compelled to maintain an engine for putting out all fires occurring within their own boundaries; though, independently of this provision, for more than thirty years before 1866 the leading fire insurance companies had jointly organized and worked a fire-engine establishment of their own. On Jan. 1, 1866, the Metropolitan Board of Works took over these responsibilities. On Jan. 1, 1867, the Board also took over from the Royal Society for the Protection of Life from Fire (founded 1844), the service of the saving of life from fire.

By the passing of the Local Government Act, 1888, the London County Council assumed control of the Fire Brigade, and there is no limit as regards the amount of rate to be assessed.

The total expenditure for the year ended March 31, 1899, was, on capital account, all of which was borne by the ratepayers, £38,737, and on rate account £195,123. Of this latter amount the Treasury and the various insurance companies contributed £40,548. The amount raised from the ratepayers was £148,012.

The strength of the Brigade on 31 Dec , 1898, was as follows: 61 Land Fire-Engine Stations, 4 Floating or River Stations, 1 Sub-station, 17 Street Stations, 46 Hose Cart Stations, 137 Fire Escape

Stations, 31 Horsed Escape Duties, 8 Steam Fire-Engines on Barges, 9 Hose and Ladder Truck Stations, 60 Land Steam Fire-Engines, 39 Six-inch Manual Fire-Engines, 7 Under-six-inch Manual Fire-Engines, 40 Miles of Hose, 113 Hose Carts, 7 Steam Tugs, 12 Barges, 12 Skiffs, 230 Fire Escapes, 11 Long Fire Ladders, 12 Hose and Ladder Trucks, 6 Hose Tenders and Fire-Escapes combined, 42 Vans for carrying Fire-Escapes, Hose, Coal, and Stores, 1 Canteen Van, 2 Waggons for Street Stations, 6 Vehicles for use of Officers when inspecting Stations, &c , 133 Watch Boxes, 912 Firemen, including Chief Officer, Second Officer, and Third Officer (appointed February, '99), Superintendents, and all ranks. 32 men under Instruction, 17 Pilots, 125 Coachmen, 211 Horses, 108 Telephones between Fire Stations, 59 Alarm circuits round Fire Stations, with 600 call-points, 16 Telephones to Police Stations, 116 Telephones, and 8 Bell-ringing Fire Alarms and 1 Speaking Tube to public and other buildings.

The total number of calls for fires was 4,654, of which 830 were false alarms; of the latter no fewer than 270 were maliciously sent through the call-posts, unfortunately only 9 of the offenders being arrested.

During 1898 there were 3,585 fires in the metropolis, and at 85 of them lives were lost.

Headquarters, Southwark Bridge Road, S.E. *Chief Officer*, Commander L. de L. Wells, r.n. £900

THE FRENCH ACADEMY is composed of 40 members, elected for life, and is the highest of the five Academies constituting the *Institut de France*. The special object of this institution is the composition of the historical Dictionary of the French Language. It was founded in 1635, by Cardinal Richelieu, and re-organized in 1816. The other Academies are as follows:—

ACADÉMIE DES INSCRIPTIONS ET BELLES-LETTRES, founded 1663, 40 members.

ACADÉMIE DES SCIENCES, founded 1666, divided into 11 sections, each of which comprises 6 members.

ACADÉMIE DES BEAUX-ARTS, 5 sections, comprising 40 members, as follows—painting, 14 members; sculpture, 8; architecture, 8; engraving, 4; musical composition, 6.

ACADÉMIE DES SCIENCES MORALES ET POLITIQUES (for the study of questions of social and political economy), founded in 1832, 40 members, 5 sections.

All the Academies, with the exception of the Académie Française, elect a certain number of honorary members and of foreign correspondents.

MEMBERS OF THE ACADÉMIE FRANÇAISE.

Legouvé, Ernest Wilfred Gabriel Jean Baptiste, *born* in Paris, 1807, *elected* March, 1855, *predecessor* Ancelot.

Broglie, Duc de, Jacques Victor Albert, *b.* in Paris, 1821, *e.* 20 Feb., 1862, *p.* Lacordaire (father).

Ollivier, Olivier Emile, *b.* at Marseilles, 2 July, 1825, *e.* 7 April, 1870, *p.* De Lamartine.

Mézières, Alfred Jean François, *b.* in Paris, 1826, *e.* 29 Jan., 1874, *p.* St. Marc-Girardin.

Boissier, Marie Louis Antoine Gaston, *b.* at Nîmes, 1823, *e.* 8 June, 1876, *p.* Patin.

Sardou, Victorien, *b.* in Paris, 7 Sept., 1831, *e.* 7 June, 1877, *p.* Autran.

Audiffret-Pasquier, le Duc d', Edmond Armand Gaston, *b.* in Paris, 1823, *e.* 24 Dec., 1878, *p.* Bishop Dupanloup.

Rousse, Aimé Joseph Edmond, *b.* in Paris, 1817, *e.* 13 May, 1880, *p.* Jules Favre.

Sully-Prudhomme, René François Armand, *b.* in Paris, 1839, *e.* 8 Dec., 1881, *p.* Duvergier de Hauranne.

Perraud, Adolphe Louis Albert, Cardinal Bishop of Autun, *b.* at Lyons, 1828, *e.* 8 June, 1882, *p.* Auguste Barbier.

Coppée, François Edouard Joachim, *b.* in Paris, 1842, *e.* 21 Feb., 1884, *p.* De Laprade.

Bertrand, Joseph Louis François, *b.* in Paris, 1822, *e.* 4 Dec., 1884, *p.* J. B. Dumas.

Halévy, Ludovic, *b.* in Paris, 1834, *e.* 4 Dec., 1884, *p.* Le Comte d'Haussonville.

Gréard, Vallery Clément Octave, *b.* at Vire, 1828, *e.* 18 Nov., 1886, *p.* Le Comte de Falloux.

Haussonville, le Comte Othénin Paul Gabriel de Cléron d', *b.* at Gurey-le-Châtel (Seine and Marne), 21 Sept., 1843, *e.* 26 Jan., 1888, *p.* Caro.

Claretie, Jules Arnaud Arsène, *b.* at Limoges, 3 Dec., 1840, *e.* 26 Jan., 1888, *p.* Cuvillier-Fleury.

Vogüé, le Vicomte Eugène Marie Melchior de, *b.* at Nice, 24 Feb., 1848, *e.* 22 Nov., 1888, *p.* Désiré. Nisard.

Freycinet, Charles Louis de, *b.* at Foix, 14 Dec. 1828, *e.* 10 Dec., 1890, *p.* Emile Augier.

Viaud, Jean (Pierre Loti), *b.* at Rochefort, 4 July, 1850, *e.* 21 May, 1891, *p.* Octave Feuillet.

Lavisse, Ernest, *b.* at Nouvien-en-Thiérache (Aisne), 17 Dec., 1842, *e.* 2 June, 1892, *p.* Jurien de la Gravière.

Bornier, le Vicomte Etienne Charles Henri de, *b.* at Lunel, 25 Dec., 1825, *e.* 3 Feb., 1893, *p.* Xavier Marmier.

Thureau-Dangin, Pau Maria Pierre, *b.* at Paris, 12 Dec., 1837, *e.* 2 Feb., 1893, *p.* Camille Rousset.

Brunetière, Marie Ferdinand, *b.* at Toulon, 19 July, 1849, *e.* 8 June, 1893, *p.* Lemoinne.

Heredia, José Maria de, *b.* at Santiago de Cuba, 22 Nov., 1842, *e.* 22 Feb., 1894, *p.* de Mazade.

Sorel, Albert, *b.* at Honfleur, 13 Aug., 1842, *e.* 31 May, 1894, *p.* Taine.

Bourget, Paul Charles Joseph. *b.* at Amiens, 21 Nov., 1852, *e.* 31 May, 1894, *p.* Maxime Du Camp.

Houssaye, Henri, *b.* 1858, *e.* 6 Dec., 1894, *p.* Leconte de Lisle.

Lemaître, Jules, *b.* at Vennecy (Loiret), 27 April, 1853, *e.* 20 June, 1895, *p.* Duruy.

France, Anatole-François Thibault, *b.* at Paris, 16 April, 1844, *e.* 23 Jan., 1896, *p.* F. de Lesseps.

Costa de Beauregard, le Marquis Marie-Charles-Albert, *b.* at Nyotte-Servolex (Savoie), 24 May, 1839, *e.* 23 Jan., 1896, *p.* Camille Doucet.

Paris, Gaston Bruno Paulin, *b.* at Avenay (Marne), 9 Aug., 1839, *e.* 23 May, 1896, *p.* Pasteur.

Theuriet, Claud Adhemar, *dit* André, *b.* at Marly-le-Roi, 1833, *e.* 10 Dec., 1896, *p.* Alexandre Dumas.

Vaudal, Louis Jules Albert, *b.* at Paris, 1851, *e.* 10 Dec., 1899, *p.* Léon Say.

Mun, Adrien Albert Marie, Comte de, *b.* at Luimguy, 1841, *e.* 1 April, 1897, *p.* Jules Simon.

Hanotaux, Gabriel, *b.* at Beaurevoir, 1853, *e.* 1 April, 1897, *p.* Challemel-Lacour.

Guillaume, Claude Jean Baptiste Eugène, *b.* at Montbard, 4 July, 1822, *e.* 26 May, 1898, *p.* Duc d'Aumale.

Lavedan, Henri Emile Léon, *b.* in Orléans, 1859, *e.* 8 Dec , 1898, *p.* Meilhac.

Deschanel, Paul Eugène Louis, *b.* in Brussels, 1857, *e.* 18 May, 1899, *p.* Hervé.

And 2 fauteuils vacant (Pailleron, Cherbuliez).

Permanent Secretary and Treasurer, Marie Louis Antoine Gaston Boissier.

Chef du Secrétariat et Agent Spécial, M. Julia Pingard.

Offices: Palais de l'Institut, 23 Quai Conti, Paris.

THE ACADEMICAL HOOD, as now in use, is the direct representative of an article of dress, called by various names, worn upon the *cappa*, or *cope*, in order to protect the head and neck in the unwarmed schools and churches of mediæval times. It was not exclusively clerical, nor was it confined to graduates. It seems probable that the material of the hood denoted the owner's degree or status, while the colour of his cope or gown (to use the modern word) showed the faculty in which he was a student. Thus, bachelors of all faculties wore hoods of lamb's wool or rabbit's fur, masters, of minever, and doctors, of minever or lamb's wool. The use of silk for hoods probably dates from the fourteenth century, when the masters seem to have adopted it as a summer substitute for fur. The oldest hood now in use in this country is the white ermine or minever worn by the Oxford Proctors, which is simply the hood of the mediæval masters of arts. Those who desire further information concerning the history of academic dress should consult Dr. Rashdall's "Universities of Europe in the Middle Ages"

As now worn, hoods consist of two principal shapes, which will be evident if we compare the hood worn for the Arts degrees of Oxford, Edinburgh, or Glasgow with that adopted for the corresponding degrees at Cambridge, Aberdeen, or Victoria. The former, commonly called the Oxford shape, is simply an enlarged cowl, while the Cambridge shape includes a tippet upon the cowl. Nearly all Universities, however, use the Cambridge shape for their higher degrees.

Owing to the multiplicity of Universities and degrees it is difficult to frame general rules by which a hood can at once be identified. The following hints may, however, prove useful : dark blue often denotes a Dublin degree ; purple, a Durham one. A hood with fur on it is probably a Bachelor's in some faculty. The same is true of a silk edging. Cloth generally denotes a Doctor. The same is true of scarlet. No London hood has fur upon it. Black cloth generally shows an Edinburgh degree, white satin a St. Andrew's one. Hoods used in Church generally belong to degrees in Arts, Divinity, or Law, those used in School to Arts or Science

The following is a list of the principal Degrees, with a description of the corresponding hoods : —

B.A., or (more rarely) **A.B.** *Bachelor of Arts.* Granted by all Universities except those of Aberdeen, Edinburgh, and St. Andrew's. The normal type of hood is of black stuff or silk, edged with white fur. The following distinctions may be noted : *Oxford* is a simple hood ; *Cambridge*, a hood and tippet combined, square corners to the base of the hood ; *Durham* has a larger tippet ; *Dublin* and the *Royal University of Ireland* have a hood like Cambridge, but with rounded corners to the base and white edging to the neck-ribbon.

The modern type of hood is of black silk or stuff with a silk edging. The following distinctions may be noted : *London*, edged inside with russet brown silk (if owner is a member of Convocation also lined with white silk) ; *Victoria*, edged with pale blue silk ; *Wales*, edged with blue and green shot silk ; *Glasgow*, edged with bell-heather red.

B.C.L. *Bachelor of Civil Law.* Granted by Oxford and Durham. *Oxford*, light blue silk edged with white fur ; *Durham*, palatinate purple silk, bound with white fur.

B.D. *Bachelor of Divinity.* Granted by all Universities except London, Victoria, and the Royal University of Ireland. Hood : *Oxford*, *Cambridge, Dublin*, and *Durham*, plain black silk : *Lampeter*, black silk lined with violet silk, edged with white silk ; *St. Andrew's*, violet purple silk, lined with white satin, with white fur border ; *Aberdeen*, black silk, lined with purple silk ; *Edinburgh*, black silk, lined with purple silk, bordered with white fur ; *Glasgow*, black silk, lined with light cherry-coloured silk, bordered with scarlet cloth.

B.L. *Bachelor of Law.* Granted by Edinburgh and Glasgow. (This is a lower degree than LL.B., *Bachelor of Laws.*) *Edinburgh*, black silk edged with blue silk, trimmed with white fur ; *Glasgow*, black silk, with an inside border of Venetian red silk (colour of clove carnations).

B.Lit. or **Litt.B.** *Bachelor of Literature or Letters.* Granted by Oxford and Durham. Hood : *Oxford*, same as B.C.L. ; *Durham*, old gold satin, edged with fur.

B.Sc. *Bachelor of Science.* Granted by most Universities. *Aberdeen*, black silk, lined with green silk ; *Edinburgh*, black silk, lined with green silk, bordered with white fur ; *Glasgow*, black silk, bordered with scarlet cloth, and lined with gold-coloured silk ; *London*, black silk (lined with white silk, by members of Convocation), edged inside with gold-coloured silk ; *Oxford*, same as B.C.L. ; *Durham*, palatinate purple silk, bound with white fur ; *Victoria*, black cloth or silk edged with pale red silk ; *Royal University of Ireland*, black silk, lined with gold-coloured silk

D.C.L. *Doctor of Civil Law.* Granted by Oxford and Durham. Hood : *Oxford*, scarlet cloth, lined with crimson silk ; *Durham*, scarlet cassimere, lined with white silk.

D.D. or (more rarely) **S.T.P.** *Doctor of Divinity.* Granted by all Universities except London, Victoria, and the Royal. Hood : *Oxford*, scarlet cloth, lined with black silk ; *Cambridge*, scarlet cloth, lined with pink and violet shot silk ; *Dublin*, same as Oxford ; *Durham*, scarlet cassimere, lined with palatinate purple silk ; *Aberdeen*, scarlet cloth, lined with purple silk ; *Edinburgh*, black cloth, lined with purple silk ; *Glasgow*, scarlet cloth, lined with white silk ; *St. Andrew's*, violet-purple silk or cloth, lined with white satin.

D.Litt. *Doctor of Literature or Letters.* Granted by many Universities. Hood : *Cambridge*, same as LL.D. ; *Durham*, scarlet cassimere, lined with old gold satin ; *London*, scarlet cloth, lined with russet brown silk ; *Victoria*, gold-coloured velvet or satin serge, lined with silk of a lighter shade ; *Dublin*, and *Royal University*, scarlet cloth, lined with white silk ; *Edinburgh*, black cloth, lined wit royal blue and maize shot silk ; *Aberdeen*, same as Dublin.

D.Phil. *Doctor of Philosophy.* Granted by Edinburgh, Aberdeen, and the Royal University. This Degree has been lightly esteemed in this country, owing to the fact that in time past some of the smaller German Universities conferred the Degree for money, without regard to the qualification of the recipient. At the present day a German D Ph. is the mark of considerable learning. Hood : *Edinburgh*, black cloth, lined with Vesuvius and white shot silk ; *Aberdeen*, same as D.Litt.

D.Sc. *Doctor of Science.* Granted by most Universities. Hood : *Cambridge*, same as LL.D. ; *London*, scarlet cloth, lined with gold-coloured silk ; *Victoria*, same as D.Litt. ; *Durham*, palatinate purple cassimere, lined with scarlet silk; *Dublin* and *Royal University*, scarlet cloth, lined with blue silk; *Aberdeen*, scarlet cloth, lined with green silk; *Edinburgh*, black cloth, lined with green silk; *Glasgow*, scarlet cloth, lined with gold-coloured silk; *St. Andrew's*, amaranth silk or cloth, lined with white satin.

LL.B. *Bachelor of Laws.* Granted by all Universities except Oxford and Durham. Hood: *Aberdeen*, black silk, edged with pale blue silk; *Cambridge*, same as B.A.; *Dublin and Royal University*, black silk, faced with white; *Edinburgh*, black silk, lined with blue silk, edged with white fur; *Glasgow*, black silk, lined with Venetian red silk, bordered with scarlet cloth; *London*, black silk (lined with white silk if member of Convocation), edged with blue silk; *Victoria*, black silk, with broad edging of violet silk.

LL.D. *Doctor of Laws.* Granted by all Universities except Oxford and Durham. Hood: *Cambridge*, *Dublin, and Royal University*, scarlet cloth, lined with pink silk; *London*, scarlet cloth, lined with blue silk; *Victoria*, same as D.Litt.; *Aberdeen*, scarlet cloth, lined with pale blue silk; *Edinburgh*, black cloth, lined with blue silk; *Glasgow*, scarlet cloth, lined with Venetian red silk; *St. Andrew's*, scarlet silk or cloth, lined with white silk.

M.A. or (more rarely) **A.M.** *Master of Arts.* Granted by all Universities. Hood: *Oxford* and *St. Andrew's*, black silk, lined with red silk; *Cambridge, Aberdeen*, and *Edinburgh*, black silk, lined with white silk; *Dublin*, and *Royal University*, black silk, lined with blue silk; *London*, black silk, lined with russet-brown silk; *Durham*, black silk, lined with palatinate purple silk; *Victoria*, black silk, lined with pale blue silk; *Glasgow*, black silk, lined with bell-heather red silk.

M.B. *Bachelor of Medicine.* Granted by all Universities. Hood: *Oxford*, dark blue silk, trimmed with white fur; *Cambridge*, black silk, lined with dark pink silk; *Dublin*, black silk, lined white fur; *Royal University*, black silk, faced with scarlet silk; *Edinburgh*, black silk, lined with crimson silk, edged with white fur; *Aberdeen*, black silk, lined with crimson silk; *Durham*, scarlet silk, lined with palatinate purple silk, and edged with white fur; *London*, black silk (lined with white silk, by members of Convocation), edged with violet silk; *St. Andrew's*, crimson silk, lined with white satin, edged with white fur; *Glasgow*, black silk, lined with scarlet silk, bordered with scarlet cloth; *Victoria*, black silk, with a broad edging of red silk.

M.D. *Doctor of Medicine.* Granted by all Universities. Hood: *Oxford*, same as D.C.L.; *Cambridge*, scarlet cloth, lined with dark cherry-coloured silk; *Dublin, Glasgow* and *Royal University*, scarlet cloth, lined with scarlet silk;

Aberdeen, scarlet cloth, lined with scarlet silk; *Durham*, scarlet cassimere, lined with scarlet silk, and faced with palatinate purple; *London*, scarlet cloth, lined with violet silk; *Edinburgh*, black cloth, with appended cape faced and lined with crimson silk; *Victoria*, same as D.Litt.

Mus.B. *Bachelor of Music.* Granted by most Universities. Hood: *Oxford*, same as B.C.L.; *Cambridge*, dark cherry-coloured satin, lined with white fur; *Dublin* and *Royal University*, blue silk, lined with rabbit skin; *Durham*, same as B.Sc.; *London*, blue silk, lined with white watered silk; *Edinburgh*, scarlet silk, lined with white silk, edged with white fur; *St. Andrew's*, blue silk, lined with white satin, edged with white fur.

Mus.Doc. *Doctor of Music.* Granted by most Universities. Hood: *Oxford*, white silk, lined with crimson; *Cambridge*, cream-coloured silk, lined with cherry-coloured silk; *Dublin*, crimson cloth, lined with white silk; *Durham*, brocaded white satin, lined with palatinate purple silk; *London*, same as Mus.B., or, if member of Convocation, scarlet cloth lined with white silk; *Edinburgh*, scarlet cloth, lined with white corded silk; *St. Andrew's*, cerulean blue silk or cloth, lined with white satin; *Royal University*, white figured silk, lined and faced with rose-coloured satin.

It remains for us to add that the Archbishop of Canterbury has the right (in virtue of his former office of Legate of the Pope) of conferring Degrees in any faculty. These, which are commonly called Canterbury or Lambeth Degrees, are sometimes conferred *honoris causâ* upon persons of learning and eminence, but more often after an examination, which is kept up to the honours standard of the Universities. Those who have received such Degrees wear the gown and hood of the corresponding Degree in the University to which the Archbishop who conferred them belonged.

Besides these hoods, which belong to graduates, a number of hoods are worn in Church by non-graduates, in virtue of the 58th Canon, which directs them to wear "a decent tippet of black, so it be not silk." This black stuff hood is really the hood of the mediæval undergraduate, which was worn in the Oxford Schools till within living memory. The Upper House of Convocation has authorised members of theological colleges to add to the black stuff a distinctive edging of coloured silk. Those most commonly seen are: *King's College, London*, violet; *London College of Divinity*, red; *St. Aidan's*, slate. With them we may also note the hood of black stuff, bound with velvet and faced with purple silk and velvet, which marks the Licentiate in Theology (L.Th.) of Durham University.

ONE of the revivals of the past half century has been that of the taste for ancient gold and silver ware, but especially of silver. With the revival of this taste there has also grown up with it the very laudable desire to know something of the history of the manufacture and manufacturers of the plate itself. The literature of the subject is not large, but it is almost exhaustive, and for the materials of this Article readers of the Almanack are indebted to Mr. Wilfred Cripps, whose volume on "Old English Plate" contains nearly all that can be said upon the subject. Readers are also further indebted to that gentleman for the loan of some of the following illustrations, without which this paper would scarcely be intelligible.

It must be premised that *pure* gold and *pure* silver in a manufactured state do not exist; both are *alloyed* with a coarser metal, gold sometimes with silver, but mostly with copper; and silver invariably with the latter metal: silver thus alloyed becomes less brittle and is more easily shaped by the workman's hammer. But mixed, the metal is of less value than when pure, and, as the uninformed public could have no means of testing its intrinsic value, the Government at a very early period took steps to insure uniformity in the quantity of base metal used as alloy. So far back as the year 1180 there appears to have been a test or check upon the manufacture, and in 1260 discreet men of the craft were appointed to watch over the ware produced for sale; but not till the year 1300 was there any actual legislation, the first ordinance being that the Leopard's Head should be *marked* upon all *sterling* articles of gold and silver. The Company of Goldsmiths of London was incorporated by Edward III. in the year 1327, and the leopard's head has ever since been borne on the company's shield. In addition to London and the six others mentioned there have been Assay Offices at Bristol, Exeter, Newcastle-on-Tyne, Norwich and York, all of which are now closed. In Scotland, Edinburgh and Glasgow have this privilege: in Ireland, Dublin alone One of the duties imposed upon the Goldsmiths Company is to test all articles of gold and silver, except certain small articles, and having tested them, to impress the HALL MARK thereon. Sterling silver is one invariable standard, viz., 11 oz. 2 dwts. of fine silver to 18 dwts. of alloy, which, when thus mixed, becomes *standard*, and a pound troy coined into sixty-six shillings gives the nominal value of 5s. 6d. to the troy ounce. There is, however, a higher standard, viz., 11 oz. 10 dwts. of fine silver to 10 dwts. of alloy, and this was the only legal standard for the manufacture of plate from March 1697, to June 1720; after that date the old standard was again adopted, but the higher standard (commonly known as "Britannia" standard, from the figure of Britannia on all such plate) still remained in use, and is used, though to a very limited extent, at the present day. The Britannia standard is denoted by a lion's head erased, as well as by the figure of Britannia, the latter in place of the leopard's head and lion passant seen on silver of the sterling standard. In *sterling* gold there are twenty-two carats fine to two of alloy, the value of which is £3 17s. 10½d. In order to encourage the home jewellery trade, other degrees of fineness are permitted, but these degrees are marked on articles sent to the "Hall" for the purpose. The value of the various *standards* per ounce troy are—

		£	s.	d.
Pure gold, 24 carats		4	4	11½
Standard, 22 carats		3	17	10½
2nd ditto, 18 carats		3	3	8½
3rd ditto, 15 carats		2	13	1
4th ditto, 12 carats		2	2	5¾
5th ditto, 9 carats		1	11	10½

An ordinary piece of English silver plate has the following marks:

1. That of the maker, which must be the first letters of his Christian and Surname.

2. That of the Company, the Leopard's Head (this in London only).

3. That which is supposed to be the Sovereign's mark, the lion passant.

4. A letter denoting the year in which the plate is made, e.g. .... **A**

[And, in the case of those articles which were chargeable with duty, the Sovereign's Head; this is now no longer impressed, the duty having been abolished in June 1890.]

The maker's mark is placed upon the article by the manufacturer himself. The Sovereign's Head does not appear upon plate manufactured prior to the year 1784. And for the first year or so after its introduction it appeared in intaglio with the profile turned to the left; subsequently it appeared in relief like the other assay marks with the head turned to the right, although Queen Victoria's head is turned to the left again. The leopard's head is without crown from 1823.

In respect to gold plate we have precisely the same marks, with the exception of a crown in place of the lion passant and the degree of fineness as above stated; although previous to 1798 there was absolutely no distinguishing mark between gold of 18 carats and silver-plate, nor until 1844 for 22-carat gold. To prevent the importation of foreign plate of a lower standard than that required of English plate, all such plate of recent manufacture must be assayed and marked in the same way as that of home production, but with the addition of the letter F to denote its foreign origin.

Though there is now no duty upon gold and silver plate, the Hall marking is compulsory; no one can complain of this, as the charge for assaying and marking at Goldsmiths' Hall is little more than nominal, that for a dozen tea-spoons being but 3d., and for a dozen table spoons or forks and other wares weighing 5 oz. each and upwards one halfpenny per oz.

By the following table of date-marks the age of any piece of plate manufactured in London and assayed at Goldsmiths' Hall may be ascertained:

	Lombardic, simple	1438-9 to 1457-8
	Lombardic, external cusps	1458-9 " 1477-8
	Lombardic, double cusps	1478-9 " 1497-8
	Black letter, small	1498-9 " 1517-8

Lombardic	1518-9 to 1537-8
Roman and other capitals	1538-9 „ 1557-8
Black letter, small	1558-9 „ 1577-8
Roman letter, capitals	1578-9 to 1597-8
Lombardic, external cusps	1598-9 „ 1617-8
Italic letter, small	1618-9 „ 1637-8
Court hand	1638-9 „ 1657-8
Black letter, capitals	1658-9 „ 1677-8
Black letter, small	1678-9 „ 1696-7
Court hand	1697 .. 1715-6 From *March* 1697 on y, see col. 1 of p. 691.
Roman letter, capitals	1716-7 „ 1735-6
Roman letter, small	1736-7 „ 1755-6
Old English, capitals	1756-7 „ 1775-6
Roman letter, small	1776-7 „ 1795-6
Roman letter, capitals	1796-7 „ 1815-6
Roman letter, small	1816-7 „ 1835-6
Old English, capitals	1836-7 „ 1855-6
Old English, small	1856-7 to 1875-6
Roman letter, capitals	1876-7 „ 1895-6
Roman letter, small	1896-7 „ 1915-6

Each Assay Office has its distinguishing mark in lieu of the Leopard's Head of Goldsmiths' Hall, and its own cycle and chronological alphabet. The type and the shape of shield on which the letters are impressed change with each cycle.

The collector with even limited experience will find but little difficulty in distinguishing a letter of one cycle from that of another, presuming his knowledge to be insufficient to judge by the style and period of the article itself, *e.g.* :

An article marked with the letter F 1721-2 can be distinguished from letter F 1801-2 by the difference in the shape of the respective shields; as also those containing the crowned leopard's head and the lion passant; the absence of the sovereign's head in the former as against its presence in the latter case; the different form of the leopard's head; and lastly, the irregularity of the stamp in the first case as compared with the uniformity of the latter stamp. These again can be distinguished from F 1831-2 as before, by the different shield of the date letter only (the shields of the remaining marks being the same as those of F 1801-2); the absence of crown on leopard's head, and the presence of the Queen's *vice* the King's head.

The London Goldsmiths' letter for the year ending 29th May, 1900, is d, on a shield shaped like that of the last specimen shown above: that for 1901 is the letter e.

ASSAY OFFICES OUT OF LONDON.

Assay Office.	Distinguishing Mark.	*Letter for 1900-01.	Cycle.
Birmingham	An Anchor	a	Years. 25
Chester	The City Arms (3 garbs and a sword)	Q.R.	25 or 20
Sheffield	A Crown	g h	Vari'b'le [20 to 25]
Edinburgh	A Castle	t	25
Glasgow	Tree, Fish, and Bell	CD.	26
Dublin	A Harp, crowned	Œ	25

* The date letters are changed in the middle of each year.

THE following is a list of the Public Libraries in London, with the hours when open and the names of the Librarians; those marked with an asterisk (*) have been, or are about to be, opened in accordance with the Public Libraries Act, and in their case the date in brackets denotes the year in which the Acts were adopted.

*BARKING.—(1888), Local Board Buildings. 10 A.M. to 10.30 P.M. *Librarian*, George Jackson.

*BATTERSEA.—(1887), *Central Library*, Lavender Hill. *Branches*, Lurline Gdns., Victoria Rd., and Lammas Hall, Bridge Rd. West. 8 A.M. to 10 P.M.; Sundays, 3 to 9 P.M. *Librarian*, L. Inkster.

*BERMONDSEY.—(1887), Spa Rd. 9 A.M. to 9.30 P.M.; Sundays (Winter months), 3 to 9 P.M. *Librarian*, John Frowde.

BETHNAL GREEN.—London Street, E. 10 A.M. to 10 P.M. *Librarian*, G. F. Hilcken.

BISHOPSGATE INSTITUTE.—62 Bishopsgate Street Without, 10 to 7; Sat. 10 to 2. *Lib.*, C.W.F.Goss.

*BOW.—(1896).

*BRENTFORD.—(1889). 10 A.M. to 9 P.M.

BRITISH MUSEUM.—Great Russell Street, Bloomsbury. Reading Room, 9 A.M. to 8 P.M. (Closes at 7 from May to August.) *Dir. and Prin. Librarian*, Sir E. Maunde Thompson, K.C.B.

BROMLEY-BY-BOW.—(1891), 126 Brunswick Rd.

*BROMLEY, KENT.—(1892). *Lib.*, J. Harrison.

*CAMBERWELL.—(1889), *Central Library*, Peckham Road. *Branches*, 682 Old Kent Road; 130 Lordship Lane; Gordon Rd., Nunhead: Minet (jointly with Lambeth), Knatchbull Rd., Camberwell. 9 A.M. to 10 P.M. *Librarian*, E. Foskett.

*CHELSEA.—(1887), *Central Library*, Manresa Road. *Branch*, Harrow Rd., Kensal Town. 9 A.M. to 10 P.M.; Sundays, 3 to 9. *Lib.*, J. H. Quinn.

*CHISWICK.—(1890), 9 A.M. to 10 P.M.; Sundays 3 to 9. *Librarian*, H. J. Hewitt.

*CHRIST CHURCH, SOUTHWARK.—(1889), 178 Blackfriars Road, S.E. 9 A.M. to 9.30 P.M. *Lib.* R.Austin.

*CLAPHAM COMMON.—(1887), 1 North Side. 10 to 8; Sun. 3 to 9 (Oct. to May). *Lib.*, J. R. Welch.

*CLERKENWELL.—(1887),Skinner St., E.C. 8 A.M. to 10 P.M.; Sun., 3 to 9 (Oct. to May).

CRIPPLEGATE INSTITUTE.—Golden Lane, E.C. 10 A.M. to 8 P.M.; Sat. till 4. *Lib.*, H. W. Capper.

*CROYDON.—(1888), *Central Library*, Town Hall. *Branches*, South Norwood, Thornton Heath and Shirley. 9 A.M. to 10 P.M. *Lib.*, L. S. Jast.

*EALING.—(1883), 9 A.M. to 10 P.M. *Lib.*, T. Bonner.

*EAST HAM.—(1895), 9 A.M. to 10 P.M.; Sun. 3 to 9. *Librarian*, Wm. Bridle.

EAST HAM, NORTH WOOLWICH.—10 to 10; Sat. to 1. *Lib.*, W. Phipps.

*EDMONTON.—(1891). *Lib.*, P. W. Farnborough.

*FULHAM.—(1886), *Central Library*, 592 Fulham Road, S.W. *Branch*, Wandsworth Bridge Road. 9 A.M. to 10 P.M.; Sundays, 3 to 9. *Lib.*, F.T. Barrett.

GUILDHALL.—10 A.M. to 9 P.M., Sat. 10 to 6 (Summer months). *Lib.*, Charles Welch.

*HAMMERSMITH.—(1887), *Central Library*, Ravenscourt Park. *Branches*, Uxbridge Road, and College Pk., N.W. 9 A.M. to 10 P.M.; Sun. 6 to 9 P.M. *Lib.*, S. Martin.

*HAMPSTEAD.—(1893), *Central Library*, Finchley Road, 8.30 A.M. to 10.30 P.M.; *Belsize Branch*, Antrim St.; *Kilburn Branch*, Priory Rd., N.W. 9 A.M. to 10 P.M.; Sun. 3 to 9. *Reading Room*, Prince Arthur Road.

*HOLBORN.—(1891), 10 John Street, Bedford Row, W.C. 9 A.M. to 10 P.M. *Lib.*, Harry Hawkes.

*KENSINGTON.—(1887), *Central Library*, High Street, Kensington. *Branches* (open the Sun.), 108 Ladbroke Grove and Old Brompton Road, S.W. 9 A.M. to 10 P.M. *Lib.*, H. Jones.

*KINGSTON-ON-THAMES. — (1881), 8.30 A.M. to 10 P.M.; Sun Oct. to Apr. 6 to 9. *Lib.*, B. Carter.

*LAMBETH.—(1886), *Central Library*, Brixton Oval. *Branches*, South Lambeth Road; Knight's Hill Road, West Norwood; Kennington Cross; 74 Lower Marsh; Minet (jointly with Camberwell). 9 A.M. to 10 P.M. *Lib.*, F. J. Burgoyne.

*LEWISHAM.—(1890),*Cent. Lib.*, Perry Hill. 10.30 A.M. to 9 P.M.

*LEYTON.—(1891), 10.30 to 9.30. *Lib.*, Z. Moon.

*MILE END.—(1896).

*NEWINGTON.—(1890), 155 and 157 Walworth Road, S.E. 9 A.M. to 10 P.M., also on Sunday evenings. *Librarian*, R. W. Mould.

PADDINGTON.—7 Bishop's Road, W. Mon. 3.30 to 7 P.M.; other week days 11 A.M. to 1.30 P.M. and 3.30 to 7. *Lib.*, Miss Stace.

*PENGE.—(1891), Oakfield Rd., 9 A.M. to 10 P.M.; Sundays 3 to 6 P.M. *Librarian*, S. J. Clarke.

PEOPLE'S PALACE.—Mile End Road. 8.30 to 5, and 6 to 10; Sundays, 3 to 10.

*POPLAR.—(1890), *Central Library*, 126 High St., Poplar, E. 9 A.M. to 10 P.M. *Branch*, Wharf Rd., Cubitt Town, E. 5.30 to 9 30 *Lib.*, H. Rowlatt.

*PUTNEY.—(1887),9 A.M. to 10 P.M. *Lib.*, C.F.Tweney.

*RICHMOND.—(1879), 9 A.M. to 10 P.M.; Sun. (winter months) 6 to 9. *Lib.*, Albert A. Barkas.

*ROTHERHITHE.—(1890), Lower Road, S.E. 9 A.M. to 10 P.M. *Librarian*, Leonard Hobbs.

ST. BRIDE FOUNDATION INSTITUTE.— Bride Lane, E.C. 10.30 to 3, and 5 to 8; Saturday, 10.30 to 2.

*ST. GEORGE, HANOVER SQUARE.—(1890), *Central Lib.*, Buckingham Palace Road. *Branch*, South Audley Street. 9 A.M. to 10 P.M. *Lib.*, F. Pacy.

*ST. GEORGE THE MARTYR, SOUTHWARK.—(1896), Borough Rd. 9 A.M. to 10 P.M. *Lib.*, T. Aldred.

*ST. GEORGE-IN-THE-EAST.—(1896), 9 A.M. to 10 P.M.; Sun. 3 to 9. *Librarian*, F. M. Roberts.

*ST. GILES.—(1891), 198 High Holborn. 9 A.M. to 10 P.M. *Librarian*, W. A. Taylor.

ST. MARTIN IN THE FIELDS (1887), and ST. PAUL, COVENT GARDEN.—(1893), 115 St. Martin's Lane, W.C. 9 A.M. to 10 P.M. *Lib.*, T. Mason.

*ST. SAVIOUR'S, SOUTHWARK.—(1894), Southwark Bridge Road, S.E. 7.30 A.M. to 9.30 P.M.; Sun. 3 to 9. *Librarian*, H. D. Roberts.

*SHOREDITCH.—(1891), *Haggerston Library*, Kingsland Road, N.E. *Hoxton Library*, Pitfield St., N. 9.30 A.M. to 10 P.M.; Sun. 5 to 9. *Lib.*,

*SOUTHWARK.—See Christ Church, St. Saviour's, and St. George the Martyr.

*STOKE NEWINGTON.—(1890), Church Street. 9.30 A.M. to 10 P.M. *Librarian*, George Preece.

*STREATHAM.—(1889), Streatham Hill. 10.30 A.M. to 9 P.M. *Librarian*, Thomas Everatt.

*TWICKENHAM.—(1882), 10 to 9. Closes at 5 Fri.

*WANDSWORTH.—(1883), *Central*, 38 West Hill. *Branch*, Allfarthing Lane. 9 A.M. to 10 P.M.

*WEST HAM.—(1890), *Central Library*, Romford Road, E. *Branch*, Barking Road, Canning Town. Open on Sundays. *Lib.*, A. Cotgreave.

*WESTMINSTER.—(1856), *Chief Library*, Gt. Smith St., S.W. *Branch*, 3 Trevor Sq., Knightsbridge, S.W. 9 A.M. to 9 P.M. *Librarian*, H. E. Poole.

*WHITECHAPEL.—(1889), 77 to 80 High Street, Whitechapel. 9 A.M. to 10 P.M.; Sundays. 11 A.M. to 10 P.M. *Librarian*, A. Cawthorne.

*WILLESDEN.—(1891), Kilburn Library, Salusbury Road. 9 A.M. to 10 P.M. *Lib.*, J. A. Seymour. —Harlesden Library, Craven Pk. Rd. *Librarian*, Harry S. Newland.—Willesden Green Library, High Road. *Librarian*, Frank E. Chennell.

*WIMBLEDON.—(1883), 9 A.M. to 10 P.M.; Sun. 6 to 9. *Librarian*, H. W. Bull.

*WOOLWICH.—(1896). (Building.)

Academy—43 Chancery Lane, W.C.
Admiralty and Horse Guards Gazette—Savoy House, Strand, W.C.
African Review—10 Basinghall St.E.C.
African Times—121 Fleet Street, E.C.
Agricultural Gazette—9 New Bridge Street, E.C.
Architect—175 Strand, W.C.
Army and Navy Gazette—3 York St. Covent Garden, W.C.
Athenæum — Bream's Buildings, Chancery Lane, W.C.

Baptist—61 Paternoster Row, E.C.
Bazaar, Exchange, and Mart—170 Strand, W.C.
Bell's Weekly Messenger—150 Strand.
Bicycling News—25 Bouverie St., E.C.
Birmingham Post—138 Fleet St., E.C.
Black and White—63 Fleet Street, E.C.
Board of Trade Journal—East Harding Street, E.C.
Bookseller—12 Warwick Lane, E.C.
Bradford Observer—5 Austinfriars.
Bradford Telegraph—6a Ludgate Hill.
Bristol Mercury—74 Fleet Street, E.C.
Bristol Western Daily Press—61 Fleet Street, E.C.
British Medical Journal—429 Strand.
British Review—37 Essex Street, W.C.
Broad Arrow—Temple Avenue, E.C.
Builder—46 Catherine Street, W.C.
Building News—32 Strand, W.C.
Bullionist—27 Throgmorton St., E.C.

Canadian Gazette — Belle Sauvage, Ludgate Hill, E.C.
Catholic Times—9 Fleet Street. E.C.
Chemical News—3 Boy Court, Ludgate Hill, E.C.
Christian Globe—185 Fleet Street, E.C.
Christian Million—20 St. Bride St. E.C.
Christian World—13 Fleet Street, E.C.
Church Bells—12 Southampton Street, Strand, W.C.
Church Family Newspaper—111 Fleet Street, E.C.
Church Review—11 Burleigh Street, Strand. W.C
Church Times—32 Little Queen Street, Holborn, W.C.
Citizen—10 Throgmorton Avenue, E.C.
City Press—148 Aldersgate St., E.C.
Civil Service Gazette—12 Fetter Lane.
Colliery Guardian—49 Essex Street, Strand, W.C.
Commerce—Norfolk St., W.C.
County Gentleman—149 Strand, W.C.
Court Circular—213 Piccadilly, W.
Court Journal—13 Burleigh Street, Strand, W.C.
Critic—157 Leadenhall Street

Daily Chronicle—80 Fleet Street, E.C.
Daily Graphic—Milford Lane, Strand
Daily Mail—Carmelite Street, Temple, E.C.
Daily News—20 Bouverie Street, Fleet Street, E.C.
Daily Telegraph—135 Fleet St., E.C.

Echo—22 Catherine St., Strand, W.C.
Economist—340 Strand, W.C.
Educational Times — 89 Farringdon Street, E.C.
Electrician—Salisbury Court, Fleet Street, E.C.
Engineer—33 Norfolk St., Strand, W.C.
Engineering — 35 Bedford Street, Strand, W.C.
England—291 Strand, W.C.
English Churchman—8 Salisbury Court, W.C.
English Mechanic—332 Strand, W.C.
Era—49 Wellington St., Strand, W.C.
European Mail—Imperial Buildings, Ludgate Circus, E.C
Evening News—12 Whitefriars St.,E.C.

Family Churchman — 8 Salisbury Court, W.C.
Family Doctor—18 Catherine Street, Strand, W.C.
Farmer—190 Fleet Street, E.C.

Field—Bream's Buildings, Chancery Lane, W.C.
Finance—Norfolk St., W.C.
Financial News—11 Abchurch Lane.
Financial Times—52 Coleman St., E.C.
Financial World—12 Bow Lane, E.C.
Fishing Gazette—Bream's Buildings, Chancery Lane, W.C.
Freeman's Journal—211 Strand, W.C.
Freemason—16 Great Queen Street, Holborn, W.C.
Fun—27 Bouverie Street, E.C.

Gardeners' Chronicle—41 Wellington Street, Strand, W.C.
Gardening—37 Southampton St., W.C.
Gentlewoman—Arundel Street, W.C.
Glasgow Herald—65 Fleet Street, E.C.
Globe—367 Strand, W.C.
Graphic—190 Strand, W.C.
Guardian—5 Burleigh St.,Strand,W.C.

Hearth & Home—6 Fetter Lane, E.C.
Home News (for India)—55 Parliament Street, S.W.
Homœopathic World—12 Warwick Lane, E.C.
Hospital—28 Southampton Street, Strand, W.C.

Illustrated London News—198 Strand
Illustrated Sporting and Dramatic News—148 Strand, W.C.
Insurance, Banking, and Financial Review—23 Craven St., W.C.
Invention—54 Fleet Street, E.C.
Iron and Coal Trades Review—222 Strand, W.C.

Jewish Chronicle—2 Finsbury Sq.,E.C.
Judy—291 Strand, W.C.

Knowledge—326 High Holborn, W.C.

Labour News—10 Farringdon Avenue.
Ladies' Field—Southampton Street.
Lady—39 Bedford Street, Strand, W.C.
Lady's Pictorial—172 Strand, W.C.
Lancet—423 Strand, W.C.
Land and Water—58 Pall Mall, S.W.
Law Journal—5 Quality Court, Chancery Lane, W.C.
Law Times—Bream's Buildings, Chancery Lane, W.C.
Leeds Mercury—65 Fleet Street, E.C
Literary World—13 Fleet Street, E.C.
Literature—Printing House Sq., E.C.
Live Stock Journal—9 New Bridge Street, E.C.
Liverpool Courier—81 Fleet St., E.C.
Liverpool Post—130 Fleet Street, E.C.
Lloyd's Weekly News—12 Salisbury Square, E.C.
London—125 Fleet Street, E.C.
London Commercial Record—11 Jewry Street, E.C.
London Gazette—47 St. Martin's Lane, W.C.

Manchester Courier—27 Fleet St.,E.C.
Manchester Guardian—26 Charing Cross, S.W.
Mark Lane Express—1 Essex St., W.C.
Medical Press—20 King William Street, W.C.
Melbourne Argus—80 Fleet St., E.C.
Methodist Recorder — 161 Fleet Street, E.C.
Methodist Times—125 Fleet St., E.C.
Mining Journal—18 Finch Lane, E.C.
Money—Bishopsgate Street, E.C.
Money Market Review—2 Royal Exchange Buildings, E.C.
Moonshine—5 Bouverie Street, E.C.
Morning—19 St. Bride Street, E.C.
Morning Advertiser — 127 Fleet Street, E.C.
Morning Leader—Stonecutter St.,E.C.
Morning Post—346 Strand, W.C.
Musical Times—1 Berners Street W.
Nature—29 Bedford Street, W.C.
Navy and Army—Southampton Street
Newcastle Chronicle—22 Essex St,W.C.
News of the World—9 Whitefriars Street, E.C.

North British Daily Mail—
Notes and Queries—Bream's Buildings, Chancery Lane, W.C.
Observer—396 Strand, W.C.
Outlook—199 Fleet Street, E.C.
Overland Mail—65 Cornhill, E.C.

Pall Mall Gazette—18 Charing Cross Road, S.W.
People—Milford Lane, Strand, W.C.
Penny Illustrated Paper—10 Milford Lane, Strand, W.C.
Photographic News — 21 Furnival Street, E.C.
Primitive Methodist—4 Wine Office Court, E.C.
Public Opinion — 30 Maiden Lane, Strand, W.C.
Publishers' Circular — 108 Fetter Lane, E.C.
Punch—85 Fleet Street, E.C.

Queen—Bream's Buildings, Chancery Lane, W.C.

Railway Journal (Herapath's)—Savoy House, Strand, W.C.
Railway News—3 Whitefriars St., E.C.
Railway Times—2 Exeter St., W.C.
RailwayWorld—Temple Avenue,E.C.
Record—8 Red Lion Court, E.C.
Referee—Victoria Ho., Tudor St.
Regiment—Southampton Street.
Reynolds'Newspaper—313Strand,W.C.
Rock—12 St. Bride Street, E.C.

St. James's Gazette—Dorset Street, Whitefriars, E.C.
St. Paul's—Arundel Street, W.C.
Saturday Review — 38 Southampton Street, W.C.
Science Gossip—110 Strand, W.C.
Scotsman (Edinburgh) — 45 Fleet Street, E.C.
School Board Chronicle—72 Turnmill Street.
Shipping Gazette—54 Gracechurch Street, E.C.
Shipping List—13 St. Mary Axe, E.C.
Sketch—Arundel Street, W.C.
Society—173 Strand, W.C.
Speaker—115 Fleet Street, E.C.
Spectator—1 Wellington Street, W.C
Sporting Life—148 Fleet Street, E.C.
Sporting Times—139 Fleet Street, E.C.
Sportsman—139 Fleet Street, E.C.
Stage—46 York Street, W.C.
Standard—104 Shoe Lane, E.C.
Star—Stonecutter Street, E.C.
Stationery Trades Journal—12 Warwick Lane, E.C.
Statist—51 Cannon Street, E.C.
Sun—Temple Avenue, E.C.
Sunday School Chronicle—57 Ludgate Hill, E.C.
Sunday Times—46 Fleet Street, E.C.
Sydney Morning Herald—78 Queen Victoria Street, E.C.

Tablet—19 Henrietta Street, W.C.
Temperance Record—33 Paternoster Row, E.C.
Times—Printing House Square, E.C.
Times of India (Bombay)—121 Fleet Street, E.C.
Truth—Carteret Street, Queen Anne's Gate, S.W.

Vanity Fair—182 Strand, W.C.
Volunteer Service Gazette—121 Fleet Street, E.C.

War Cry—98 Clerkenwell Road, E.C.
Weekly Budget—Red Lion Ct., E.C.
Weekly Dispatch—Tudor Street, E.C.
Weekly Times and Echo—332 Strand.
Western Morning News—47 Fleet Street, E.C.
Westminster Gazette—Tudor St.,W.C.
Whitehall Review—Savoy House, Strand, W.C.
World—1 York Street, Covent Garden.

Yorkshire Post—171 Fleet St., E.C.

Name of Club.	Established.	Club-Houses.	No. of Members	Subscriptn. Entr.	Ann.	Secretary.	Remarks.
Albemarle	1875	13, Albemarle Street	..	5 Gs.	5 Gs.	Miss L. Brabrook	Ladies and gentlemen.
Alexandra	1884	12, Grosvenor St., W.	900	5 Gs.	5 & 4 Gs	Miss Eleanor M. Boyd	Ladies of position only.
Alpine	1857	23, Savile Row, W.	No limit	4 Gs.	2 Gs.	W. A. Wills (Hon.)	Intrstd. in mntn. explortn.
Army and Navy	1837	36, Pall Mall	2,400	£40	7 & 10 G	Gilbert J. Smallpeice	Officers of Army and Navy.
Arthur's	1765	69, St. James's Street	600	30 Gs.	10 G. & 11 Gs.	} Aubrey Hopwood	Social.
Article							
Arts	1863	40, Dover St., W.	600	£10	6 Gs.	Duncan Irvine	Art, literature, and science.
Arundel	1860	1, Adelphi Terr., W.C.	None		6 Gs.	G. F. Williams (Hon.)	Literary and artistic.
Athenæum	1824	107, Pall Mall	1,200	30 Gs.	8 Gs.	H. R. Tedder	Literary, scientific, artistic.
Authors		3, Whitehall Court.	390		5 & 2 Gs	G. Herbert Thring	Literary and Social
Automobile	1897	4, Whitehall Ct., S.W.	510	2 Gs.	4 Gs.	C. Johnson	Intrstd. in motorlocomotn.
Bachelors	1881	8, Hamilton Pl., W.	920	30 Gs.	10 Gs.	E. A. Smith	Social. Ladies adm. as vstrs.
Badminton	1876	100, Piccadilly, W.	1,000	10 Gs.	8 Gs.	P. M. Buchanan	Sporting & coaching club.
Baldwin	1887	79A, Pall Mall	225	5 Gs.	5 Gs.	W. S. Fyler (Hon.)	Social, whist small pts.
Bath	1894	{ 34, Dover Street, W. { (Berkeley St., Ladies)	1,500 500	10 Gs. None	10 & 6 G 7 Gs	} J. Wilson Taylor	{ Social, swimming, and { gymnastics.
Boodle's	1762	28, St. James's Street	650	30 Gs.	11 Gs.	Capt. H. Wombwell	Social.
Brooks's (Arts	1764	St. James's Street	600	25 Gs.	11 Gs.	Maj. J. F. Wegg-Prosser	Liberal. Social. [tors of art.
Burlingt'n Fine	1866	17, Savile Row	800	5 Gs.	5 Gs.	J. Beavan	Amateurs, artists, & collec-
Camera	1885	Charing Cross Road	700	£1	5 & 2 G	F. Seyton-Scott	Amateur photogra. Social, [scientific.
Carlton	1832	94, Pall Mall	1,809	£30	{ 10 G { & { 10 G	A. N. Streatfeild	Conservative.
Cavalry	1890	127, Piccadilly, W.	1,100	20 Gs.	10 & 7 G	Capt. H. R. Darley	Mounted Forces.
City Carlton	1868	St. Swithin's Lane	1,000	{ 21 G { 10 G	{ 10 G	G. T. Lawrence	Conservative.
City Liberal	1874	Walbrook	932	..	10 Gs.	W. T. Deverell	Liberal.
City of London	1832	19, Old Broad St., E.C.	800	30 Gs.	10 Gs.	E. Luscombe-Browne	Merchants, bankers, &c.
Cobden	1866	*6, Raymond Bldgs.	950	None	5 Gs.	Harold Cox	Free trade.
Cocoa Tree	1746	64, St. J'mes's St., S.W	500	4 Gs.	6 Gs.	John Graham	Social.
Colonial	1899	Whitehall St., S.W	..			Albert G. Berry	Social
Conservative	1840	74, St. James's Street	1,300	30 Gs.	10 Gs.	John Walter Knaggs	Strictly Conservative.
Constitutional	1883	Northumberland Av.	6,500	{ 15 Gs. { or 10 G	{ 5 Gs { 3 Gs	Hon. A. E. Henniker Major	} Political, Constitutional.
Crichton	1891	39, King St., W.C.	250	None	3 & 1 G	P. S. Levi (Hon.)	Social, musical, and lite-
Devonshire	1875	50, St. James's Street.	1,200	15 Gs.	10 Gs	Edgar W. Brodie	Liberal. [rary.
East India } United Serv. }	1849	16, St. James's Square	2,500	£22 or £15	8 Gs. 4 Gs.	{ A. D. Mc. Arthur, { Fleet Paym., R.N. ret.	Officers of Indian Mil. & Civ Serv. and of A. & N.
Eighty	1880	*3, Hare Ct., Tmpl., E.C.	600	1 G.	1 G.	R. C. Hawkin	Strictly Liberal.
Eldon	1879	40, Chancery Lane	200	2 Gs.	{ 5 G { 4 G	Maj. J. L. Steavenson.	Legal and social.
Farmers'	1842	Salisbury Sq. Hotel.	500	None	4 Gs.	S. B. L. Druce	Agricultural and social.
Garrick	1831	15, Garrick S. Cov. Gar.	650	20 Gs.	10 Gs.	Charles J. Fitch	Theatrical, literary, &c.
Golfers	1893	Whitehall Ct., S.W.	1,000	..	5, 7, G	Major W. F. Branston.	Social, golf.
Green Park	1894	10, Grafton Street, W.	600	2 Gs.	3 Gs.	Mrs. Luther Munday	Ladies, social and music.
Green Room	1877	20, Bedford St., Cov. Gar.	325	6 Gs.	4 Gs.	Geo. A. Delacher (Hon.)	Dramatic, artistic, &c.
Gresham	1843	1, Gresham Place, E.C.	475	25 Gs.	10 Gs.	L. R. Wynter	Merchants, bankers, &c.
Grosvenor	1883	135, New Bond St., W.	3,000	None	10 & 6 G	W. Cleather Gordon	Social. Non-political.
Grosvenor Crnt		Grosvenor Cr. S.W.	..	4 & 3 Gs	4 & 3 Gs	Miss Hewat	Ladies, Social
Guards'	1813	70, Pall Mall	102	30 Gs.	£11 & £10	} W. H. Hurnell	Offs. Past & Pres. of 3 rgt. of [Gds.
Gun Club, The	1861	Wood L., Notting H.	No limit	£15	2 Gs.	G. A. Battcock	Pigeon shooting.
Hurlingham	1868	Fulham, S.W.	1,600	20 Gs.	5 Gs.	J. K. Hurrell	Polo, and pigeon shooting.
Isthmian	1882	105, Piccadilly	1,600	None	5 Gs.	C. H. Jackson	Uvs. Pblc. schls., Army, Nvy
Junior Army } & Navy }	1869	10, St. James's Street.	2,000	10 Gs.	{ 8 Gs { 5 Gs	Sir N. R. Pringle, Bart.	{ Officers of Arm. Nav. Mar. { Yeomanry & Militia.
Jnr. Athenæum	1864	116, Piccadilly	1,200	None	10 Gs.	Henry de Carteret	Social, non-political.
Junior Carlton	1864	30 to 35, Pall Mall	2,100	37	10 Gs.	Charles Martin	Strictly Conservative.
Jr. Conservtve	1889	43, 44, Albemarle St.	5,500	..	3 & 1 Gs	Com.-Gen. Humley, C.B.	Conservative and social.
Jr. Constitutnl.	1887	101, Piccadilly	5,800	6 Gs.	3 & 5 Gs	Com. R. Ff. Powell, R.N.	Strictly Conservative.
Jnr. Untd. Serv.	1827	Charles St. St. James's	2,000	£40	8 Gs.	L. Cl. A.S. Baird-Douglas	Officers of Army & Navy.
Kennel	1874	27, Old Burlington St.	300	5 Gs.	5 Gs.	W. W. Aspinall	For imprvng. breed of dogs.
Law Society	1832	103, Chancery Lane.	450	5 Gs.	6 & 3 Gs	Arch. Keen	Mmbs. of the Incorp. Law
M.C.C. (Lord's)	1787	St. John's Wood Rd.	4,500	£5	£3	F. E. Lacey	Headqrs. of Cricket. [Soc.
Marlborough	1869	52, Pall Mall, S.W.	500	30 Gs.	10 Gs.	C. H. Stone, R.N.	Social.
National	1845	1, Whitehall Gardens	600	None	7 Gs.	Col. W.G. Robinson, C.B.	Protestant.
National Liberl.	1882	Whitehall Place, S.W.	6,000	None	6 & 3 Gs	Donald Murray	Strictly Liberal
Natnl. Sportg.	1891	Covent Garden	700	5 Gs.	4 & 6 Gs	A. F. Bettinsen (Mngr.)	Social and athletic.
Nav. & Military	1862	94, Piccadilly	2,000	40 Gs.	10 Gs.	S. C. Walrole.	Army, Navy, and Marines.
New Club		4, Grafton Street, W.	900	20 G Nil.	{ 10 G { 14 Gs	Kyrle G. Wright	Social.
New Oxf. & Cam.	1884	68, Pall Mall, S.W.	900	10 Gs.	10 Gs.	James Strange	Membs. of Ox. & Camb Univ.
New University	1863	57, St. James's Street	1,100	30 Gs.	8 Gs.	Major W. P. Thring	Membs. of Ox. & Camb. Univ.
N'w Victorian } (Ladies) }		30A, Sackville St., W.	400	2 Gs.	3 Gs.	Miss Johnston	Social.
Nimrod	1894	12, St. J'mes's Sq., S.W.	2,100	None	10 & 6 Gs	Cecil Maxwell-Lyte	Sporting.
Oriental	1824	18, Hanover Sq.	800	£21	9 Gs.	C. J. Pratt-Barlow	Social.
Orleans	1877	29, King St., St. J'mes's	500	20 Gs.	10 Gs.	Aubrey Coventry	Social.
Oxford & Camb.	1830	71, Pall Mall	1,270	40 Gs.	8 Gs.	W. Woodstock	Membs. of Ox. & Camb. Univ.
Palace	1882	9, Bridge Street, S.W.	250	None	2 Gs.	J. Williams	Social.
Piccadilly	1893	126, Piccadilly, W.	1,150		10 Gs.	A. Wallis	Social, ladies as visitors.
Portland	1816	9, St. James's Sq., S.W	300	10 Gs.	10 Gs.	A. S. Hincks	Non-political.
Press	1882	7, Wine Office Court E.C	365	1 G.	1 G.	Frank Palmer	Strictly journalistic.
Primrose	1886	4, St. Prk Pl., St. J'mes's	5,500		3 & 2 G		Conservative.
Prince's Racq. and Tennis }	1853	Knightsbridge	1,500	7 Gs.	7 Gs.	J. H. Saunders	For practice of these games.

* Address of Secretary; has no Club House.

Name of Club.	Established.	Club-House.	No. of Members.	Subscriptn. Entr.	Ann.	Secretary.	Remarks.
Queen's	1886	West Kensington	1,300	5 Gs.	5 Gs.	Henry Becks	Rackets, tennis, &c.
Raleigh	1853	16, Regent St., S.W.	800	15 Gs.	10 Gs.	Ernest Whitehead	Social.
Ranelagh	1894	Barn Elms, S.W.	1,710	10 Gs.	10 Gs.	Geo. A. Williams. M.A.	Polo, golf, &c.
Reform	1837	104, Pall Mall, S.W.	1,400	£40	10 Gs.	Lt.-Col. W. Newbigging	Strictly Liberal.
Royal Societies	1894	St. James's St., S.W.	1,500	None	6&4G.	D. Lewis-Poole (Hon.)	Memb. of learned societies.
R. Watercolour	1884	5a, Pall Mall East	250	1 G.	1 G.	Aubrey Stewart, M.A.	Art conversazione, &c {can
St. George's	1894	4, Hanover Sq., W.	3,000	None	2&5G.	J.Leigh Rowley	Social.Colonial,Cosmopol.
St. Geo.'s Chess	1826	37, St. James's Street	No limit	2 Gs.	3 Gs.	H. A. Richardson	For cultivation of chess.
St. James'	1857	106, Piccadilly	650	25 Gs.	11 Gs.	L. A. Baker	Diplomatic.
St. Stephen's	1870	1, Bridge St.Westmstr.	1,250	10 Gs.	10 Gs.	Alfred W. Gordon	Conservative.
Savage	1857	Adelphi Terr., W.C.	600	5 Gs.	5 Gs.	E. E. Peacock (Hon.)	Literary,art,music,drama.
Savile	1868	107, Piccadilly, W.	675	10 Gs.	6 Gs.	H. J. Hood (Hon.)	Social. and science.
Smithfd. Cattle	1708	12, Hanover Square	1,132	None	1 G.	E. J. Powell	Fat cattle & implemt. show.
Somerville	1878	19a, Hanover Sq.	No limit	1 G.	1 G.	Miss E. M. Kerr	Literary, social, ladies.
Sports	1893	8, St. James's Sq.	No limit	£8	6 & 3 Gs	Maj. F. A. B. Talbot	Social, sports, & athletics.
Thatched Hse.	1865	86, St. James's Street	750	—	10&5G	Frederic Propert	Non-political.
Travellers'	1819	106, Pall Mall	800	30 Gs.	10 Gs.	Maj. F. J. Carandini	Travellers.
Turf	1868	85, Piccadilly	550	30 Gs.	15 Gs.	Edward Parsey	Sporting and social.
Union	1822	Trafalgar Square	1,000	30 Gs.	7&3G.	Arthur Stirling	Social. Non-political.
United Service	1815	116 & 117, Pall Mall	1,600	{£38 £30}	{£8 £10}	S. G. Robson, R.N.	Combatant officers.
Untd. Unvrsty.	1822	1, Suffolk Street	1,050	40 Gs.	8 Gs.	Harry J. Hadow	Mmbrs. of Oxf.& Cam Univ.
University for Ladies.	1887	32, George Street, Hanover Sq., W.	No limit	1 G.	1 G.	Miss Brierley	Ladies of University education & medical women.
Victoria	1857	Wellington St., W.C.	450	10 Gs.	£6	W. Bowman (Mangr.).	Sporting and social.
Wellington	1885	1, Grosvenor Place	1,400	20 Gs.	10 Gs.	G. A. Hart Dyke	Social. Ladies as visitors.
Whitehall	1866	47, Parliament Street	600	20 Gs.	10 Gs.	W. R. Millar	Social.
White's	1730	37, St. James's Street	800	19 Gs.	11 Gs.	Mark Weyland	Non-political.
Windham	1828	13, St. James's Square	700	31 Gs.	£10	Lt. Col. H. A. Reid	Social.
Yorick	1888	29, Bedford St., W.C.	300	2 Gs.	1 G.	Louis Kent (Hon.)	Literature, drama, arts.

Yacht Clubs.

Name of Club.	Station.	Club-House.	Date of establishmt.	Date of Admty. Wrrnt.	Subscription. Entr.	Ann.	Commodore.
Royal Yacht Sqdn.	Cowes	Cowes	1812	1839	£100	£11	H.R.H. Prince of Wales, K.G.
— Albert	Southsea	Southsea	1864	1865	4 Gs.	4 Gs.	H.R.H. Duke of Coburg, K.G.
— Alfred	Kingstown	(2, Earlsfort Pl., Dublin)†	1864	..	2 Gs.	1G.	H.R.H. Duke of Coburg, K.G.
— Barrow	Barrow-in-F.	Barrow-in-Furness	1871	1872	1 G.	1 G.	Duke of Buccleuch, K.G., K.T.
— Channel Islands	Jersey	St. Helier's, Jersey	1863	1863	£1	£1	W. H. V. Vernon.
— Cinque Ports	Dover	Dover	1872	1872	3 Gs.	3 Gs.	H.R.H. Duke of Connaught.
— Clyde	Hunter's Qy.	Hunter's Quay	1856	1857	4 Gs.	2 Gs.	John Scott, G.B.
— Cork*	Queenstown	Queenstown	1720	1831	£7	£3 10s.	Rt. Hn. H. Smith-Barry, M.P.
— Cornwall	Falmouth	Falmouth	1871	1872	2 Gs.	2 Gs.	F. Layland Barratt.
— Dart	Dartmouth	Kingswear	1866	1870	1 G.	2 Gs.	H. Studdy.
— Dorset	Weymouth	Weymouth	1875	1875	7 Gs.	4 Gs.	H.R.H. Prince of Wales, K.G.
— Eastern	Firth of Forth	12, Queen St., Edinburgh	1826	1835	2 Gs.	None.	Duke of Buccleuch, B.T.
— Engineers	Chatham	Chatham	1845	1872	£1 10	£4 10	H.R.H. Duke of Cambridge.
— Forth	Granton	Granton	1868	1882	2 Gs.	2 Gs.	Sir Donald Currie, G.C.M.G.
— Harwich	Harwich	Harwich	1843	1845	1 G.	2 Gs.	H.R.H. Duke of York, K.G.
— Highland	Oban	Oban	1881	1881	5 Gs.	2 Gs.	Lord Malcolm of Poltalloch.
— Irish	Kingstown	Kingstown	1846	1846	£10	4 Gs.	The Marq. of Ormonde, K.P.
— London	Cowes	2, Savile Row, and Cowes	1838	1849	—	6 Gs.	Sir H.Seymour King K.C.I.E.
— Mersey	Liverpool	Mersey St., Birkenhead	1844	1844	1 G.	4 Gs.	Col. Sir D. Gamble, Bt., C.B.
— Munster	Monkstown	Monkstown, Co. Cork	1872	1892	1 G.	1 G.	A. F. Sharman-Crawford.
— Northern	Rothesay	Rothesay	1824	1831	£3	2 Gs.	Sir M. R. Shaw-Stewart, Bt.
— Portsmth.Corin.	Portsmouth	Portsmouth	1880	1880	None	3 Gs.	Pr.Edward of Saxe-Weimar.
— St. George	Kingstown	Kingstown	1838	1845	£15	£4	H.R.H. Duke of York, K.G.
— Southampton	Southampton	Southampton	1875	1877	3 Gs.	3&2 G.	F. Cox.
— Southern	Southampton	Southampton	1843	1848	4 Gs.	3& 4 Gs	Col. Hon. H. G. Crichton.
— South Western..	Plymouth	West Hoe, Plymouth	1890	1890	1 G.	2 Gs.	R.-Adm. J. H. Bainbridge.
— Temple	Thames and Ramsgate.	Hotel Cecil, Strand, and West Cliff, Ramsgate	1857	1898	None	2 Gs.	Lord C Beresford, C.B., M.P.
— Thames	Thames	7, Albemarle Street, W..	1823	1824	None	8&6 G.	H.R.H. Prince of Wales, K.G.
— Torbay	Torquay	Torquay	1875	1875	5 Gs.	4 Gs.	Major Boyle, R.E.
— Ulster	Bangor	Bangor, co. Down	1866	1870	2 Gs.	2 & 1G.	Marq. of Dufferin and Ava.
— Victoria	Ryde	Ryde	1844	1845	5 Gs.	6 Gs.	W. B. Paget.
— Welsh	Carnarvon	Carnarvon	1847	1847	3 Gs.	1 G.	Sir Llewelyn Turner.
— Wstrn. of Engld.	Plymouth	The Hoe, Plymouth	1827	1834	7 Gs.	£5	H.R.H. Prince of Wales, K.G.
— Windermere..	Bowness, Windermere	Bowness	1860	1887	2 Gs.	1to3Gs	W. Whitehead.
— Yorkshire	Hull	Vittoria Hotel, Hull	1847	1847	2 Gs.	1 G.	W. S. Bailey.
Alexandra	Southend	Southend	1873	1891	1&2 Gs.	2 Gs.	(Vacant)
Castle	Calshot	Calshot	1887	..	£3	£3	Earl of Dunraven, K.P.
Lond. Sailing Club	Hammsmith	Burnham-on-Crouch	1872	..	£1	1½ Gs.	Iltyd Nicholl.
Medway	Rochester	Sun Hotel, Chatham	1880	..	10s. 6d.	10s. 6d.	W. L. Wyllie, A.R.A.
New Thames	Gravesend	Gravesend	1867	1868	..	2 Gs.	Robert Hewett
Ocean Ycht. Sqdn.	None	(£50, Pall Mall, S.W.)	1888	..	..	3 Gs.	H.R.H. Duke of Coburg, K.G.
Solent	Yarmouth	Yarmouth, I. of W.	1879	..	2 Gs.	2 & 1G.	Sir Charles Seely, Bart.

* The R.C.Y.C. has an Admiral, not a Commodore.   † Secretary's address in brackets.   ‡ Office.
¶ Qualification—1,000 miles ocean voyage out and home in candidate's own yacht.

THE following are the values, according to the British standard, of the commoner measures of length, surface, capacity (dry and liquid), and weight in use in foreign countries. Those measures which appear in italics may be regarded as obsolete. It should be borne in mind that in the majority of semi-civilized lands the measures frequently vary with the locality, or with the species of thing to be measured. The chief authorities which have been consulted are Siegfried's "Münz-, Maass-, und Gewichts-Tabelle" (Leipzig, 1887), and Dr. W. A. Browne's "Merchants' Handbook" (Stanford, 1879). To the latter, inquirers may be referred for fuller information.

The Metrical System is fully given on p. 423.

Annam (Cochin China).

1 Tak	=	1·92 inches.
1 Thuok	=	19·2 inches.
1 Truon (2 Ngu)	=	16·0 feet.
1 Saö	=	24·0 feet.
1 Maö	=	240·0 feet.
1 Li, or Mile	=	486·0 yards.
1 Dam	=	972·0 yards.
1 square Saö	=	64·0 sq. yards.
1 Haö	=	6·222 gallons.
1 Shita, or Taö	=	12·444 gallons.
1 Fan (10 Li)	=	6·015 Tr. grains.
1 Luong (10 Dong)	=	601·562 Tr. grains.
1 Khan	=	1·375 lbs. av.
1 Yen	=	13·75 lbs. av.
1 Binah	=	68·75 lbs. av.
1 Ta	=	137·5 lbs. av.
1 Kwan	=	687·5 lbs. av.

Argentine Republic.

The Metrical System.

1 *Pie* (12 *Pulgada*)	=	11·365 inches.
1 *Vara* (3 *Pie*)	=	2·841 feet.
1 *Braza* (2 *Vara*)	=	5·682 feet.
1 *Ouadra* (150 *Vara*)	=	142·065 yards.
1 *Legua* (40 *Cuadra*)	=	3·228 miles.
1 *Quintal*	=	90·251 lbs. av.

Austria-Hungary.

Metrical, by compulsory law of Jan. 1, 1876.

1 *Faust, or Hand*	=	4·148 inches.
1 *Fuss* (12 *Zoll*)	=	1·037 feet.
1 *Elle*	=	30·613 inches.
1 *Vienna Klafter*	=	2·874 yards.
1 *Post Mile*	=	4·713 miles.
1 *square Fuss*	=	1·075 sq. feet.
1 *square Klafter*	=	4·301 sq. yards.
1 *Joch*	=	1·422 acres.
1 *Metze*	=	1·692 bushels.
1 *Muth* (30 *Metze*)	=	6·347 quarters.
1 *Mass*	=	1·246 quarts.
1 *Eimer*	=	12·463 gallons.
1 *Loth*	=	9·877 drams av.
1 *Pfund* (32 *Loth*)	=	1·234 lbs. av.
1 *Centner*	=	123·472 lbs. av.

Belgium.

The Metrical System.

1 *Pied* (10 *Pouce*)	=	11·811 inches.
1 *Aune* (4 *Pied*)	=	3·937 feet.
1 *Toise* (6 *Pied*)	=	5·905 feet.
1 *Perche* (10 *Pied*)	=	9·842 feet.
1 *Arpent*	=	38750·02 sq. feet.
1 *Pot*	=	·880 pint.
1 *Muid*	=	88·097 pints.
1 *Boisseau*	=	3·303 gallons.
1 *Livre*	=	1·102 lbs. av.
1 *Quintal*	=	110·231 lbs. av.

Bolivia.

As old Spanish (*q. v.*).

Brazil.

1 Pollegada (12 Linha)	=	1·093 inches.
1 Pé (12 Pollegada)	=	13·123 inches.
1 Covado	=	26·247 inches.
1 Vara	=	1·215 yards.
1 Braca	=	2·430 yards.
1 Estadio	=	285·235 yards.
1 Milha	=	1·296 miles.
1 Legoa	=	3·889 miles.
1 square Vara	=	1·476 sq. yards.
1 square Braça	=	5·906 sq. yards.
1 Geira	=	1·476 acres.
1 Oitavo	=	·360 gallon.
1 Alqueira (Bahia)	=	·825 bushel.
1 Alqueira (Rio)	=	1·1004 bushels.
1 Fanga	=	1·523 bushels.
1 Quartilho	=	·614 pint.
1 Canada (Rio)	=	2·44 quarts.
1 Almuda	=	3·684 gallons.
1 Oitavo	=	55·335 Tr. grains.
1 Onca	=	442·687 Tr. grains.
1 Arratel	=	1·0118 lbs. av.
1 Arroba	=	32·379 lbs. av.
1 Quintal (100 Arratel)	=	101·186 lbs. av.

And the Metrical System.

Bulgaria, As Turkish (*q. v.*).

The Metrical System is also used.

Burmah.

As Indian (*q. v.*); and,

1 Pulgat	=	1·0 inch.
1 Taim, or Maik (8 Thit)	=	5·5 inches.
1 Toung or Saading (4 Taim)	=	22·0 inches.
1 Lan (4 Toung)	=	88·0 inches.
1 Tha (7 Toung)	=	154·0 inches.
1 Okethapah	=	85·56 yards.
1 Tain	=	1069·44 yards.
1 Dain (4 Tain)	=	2·430 miles.
1 Uzena	=	15·555 miles.
1 Lamyet	=	1·0 gill.
1 Salay	=	1·0 pint.
1 Sah	=	1·0 gallon.
1 Saik	=	1·0 peck.
1 Teng	=	1·0 bushel.
1 Coyan (100 Teng)	=	12·5 quarters.
1 Large Ruay	=	3·937 Tr. grs.
1 Bai, or Anna	=	15·75 Tr. grs.
1 Moo	=	31·5 Tr. grs.
1 Mat	=	63·0 Tr. grs.
1 Tikal, or Kyat	=	252·0 Tr. grs.
1 Viss, or Piakthah	=	3·6 lbs. av.

Chile.

The Metrical System, and,

1 Vara (3 Pie)	=	33·367 inches.
1 Quadra	=	3·9 acres.
1 Arroba (wine)	=	7·742 gallons.
1 Quintal (100 Libra)	=	101·42 lbs. av.

Also as old Spanish (*q. v.*).

China.

1 Ts'un (10 Fan)............	=	1·41 inches.
1 Ch'ih (10 Ts'un)........	=	14·1 inches.
1 Chang (10 Ch'ih)........	=	141·0 inches.
1 Yin (10 Chang)	=	117·5 feet.
5 Ch'ih	=	1·0 Kung.
2 Kung	=	1·0 Chang.
1 sq. Chang (1 Ching) ...	=	121·0 sq. feet.
15 Ching (1 Chio)	=	1815·0 sq. feet.
4 Chio (1 Mou)	=	7260·0 sq. feet.
100 Mou (1 Ch'ing)	=	72600·0 sq. feet.
1 Ho	=	2·0 pints
1 Shêng (10 Ho)	=	*circ.* 20 pints.
1 Tou (10 Shêng)	=	*circ.* 100 pints.
1 Tael, or Liang	=	1·333 ozs. av.
1 Chin, or Chitty (16 Tael)	=	1·333 lbs. av.
1 Picul, or Tan (100 Chin)	=	133·333 lbs. av.

British weights and measures also are used at Hong Kong and other Treaty Ports.

Colombia.

The Metrical System since 1857. Previously, and still occasionally, the old Spanish.

Denmark.

1 Tomme (12 Linie) .	=	1·029 inches.
1 Fod (12 Tomme) ...	=	1·029 feet.
1 Alen (2 Fod)........	=	2·059 feet.
1 Favn (3 Alen)	=	6·178 feet.
1 Rode (2 Favn)	=	12·356 feet.
1 Mil (2000 Rode) ...	=	4·680 miles.
1 square Fod	=	1·060 sq. feet.
1 square Rode	=	16·965 sq. yards.
1 Tönde	=	1·363 acres.
1 Pægle	=	·4247 pint.
1 Flaske (3 Pægle)...	=	1·2743 pints.
1 Pot (3 Pægle)	=	1·5991 pints.
1 Kande.................	=	3·398 pints.
1 Viertel (4 Kande) .	=	1·6991 gallons.
1 Anker	=	8·0709 gallons.
1 Tönde (136 Pot) ...	=	23·885 gallons.
1 Oxehoved	=	48·425 gallons.
1 Fad	=	193·702 gallons.
1 Skeppe	=	·4778 bushel.
1 Fjerdingkar	=	·9557 bushel.
1 Tönde	=	3·823 bushels.
1 Læst	=	45·876 bushels.
1 *Liespfund*	=	17·63 lbs. av.
1 Pfund	=	16·00 Tr. ozs.
1 Centner	=	100·21 lbs. av.

Dutch Indies.—*Java.*

1 Duim	=	1·3 inches.
1 Foot	=	12·36 inches.
1 Ell	=	27·082 inches.
1 Djong (4 Bahn) ...	=	7·0149 acres.
1 Sack	=	61·034 lbs. av.
1 Pecul (2 Sack)	=	122·058 lbs. av.
1 Timbang (5 Pecul)	=	610·340 lbs. av.
1 Coyan (30 Pecul) ...	=	3662·042 lbs. av.
1 Kan	=	·328 gallon.
1 Leager	=	127·337 gallons.
1 Tael	=	·0848 lb. av.
1 Catty (16 Tael)......	=	1·356 lbs. av.
1 Pecul (weight)......	=	135·631 lbs. av.
1 Large Bahar.........	=	1831·021 lbs. av.
Commercial Pound...	=	7576 Tr. grains.

Sumatra.

1 Tempo...	=	4·5 ins.	1 Mailoh = 1·0 yard.
1 Junkal...	=	9·0 ins.	1 Tung... = 4·0 yards.
1 Etto	=	18·0 ins.	And as in Netherlands.

Ecuador.

Metrical since 1857, and as old Spanish (*q. v.*).

Egypt.

1 Kirat	=	1·125 inches.
1 Rub (6 Kirat)	=	6·75 inches.
1 Draâ, or Pike	=	27·0 inches.
1 Draâ Istambuli	=	26·654 inches.
1 Draâ Belendi	=	22·736 inches.
1 Endasch	=	25·134 inches.
1 Pike Nili	=	21·287 inches.
1 Nubian Draâ	=	26·654 inches.
1 Gasab	=	3·0 yards.
1 Feddan (400 sq. Gasab)...	=	1·1019 acres.
1 Ardeb (Alexandria)	=	7·4457 bushels.
1 Ardeb (Cairo)	=	4·9246 bushels.
1 Ardeb (Rosetta)	=	7·8131 bushels.
1 Ardeb (Nubia)	=	5·0069 bushels.
1 Mörrhi (12 Maud)	=	7·703 bushels.
1 Dirhem	=	47·661 Tr. grs.
1 Uckieh (12 Dirhem)	=	571·938 Tr. grs.
1 Rottolo (12 Uckieh)	=	·9804 lbs. av.
1 Cantar (100 Rottoli)	=	98·046 lbs. av.
1 Oka (400 Dirhem)	=	2·723 lbs. av.
1 Trade Oka (420 Dirhem) ...	=	2·859 lbs. av.
1 Kirat (jewels)	=	2·9783 Tr. grs.
1 Metikal	=	71·492 Tr. grs.

France.

Metrical System, and old "Système U suel."

1 *Pied* (10 *Pouce*)	=	11·8112 inches.
1 *Aune* (4 *Pied*)	=	3·937 feet.
1 *Toise* (6 *Pied*)	=	70·864 inches.
1 *Perche* (10 *Pied*)	=	118·1123 inches.
1 *Pot*	=	·8809 pint.
1 *Brande*	=	22·048 pints.
1 *Muid*	=	88·097 pints.
1 *Livre*	=	1·1023 lbs. av.
1 *Quintal*	=	110·231 lbs. av.
1 Barrique (Bordeaux)	=	401·28 pints.
1 Barrique (Marseilles) ...	=	394·24 pints.
1 Millerole	=	112·64 pints.
1 Pièce (Bordeaux)	=	668·8 pints.
1 Pipe	=	1091·2 pints.
1 Tonneau......................	=	2204·6 lbs. av.

Germany.

The Metrical System was legalized throughout the Empire, Jan. 1, 1872, but French nomenclature is as far as possible avoided. The millimètre is also called Strich; the centimètre, Neu Zoll; the mètre, Stab; the décamètre, Kette; the litre, Kanne; the half-litre, Schoppen; the hectolitre, Fass; the décagramme, Neu Loth; the half-kilogramme, Pfund. The Centner is 50, and the Tonne is 1,000 kilogrammes. The chief obsolete measures are:

Prussian Fuss (12 *Zoll*)......	=	1·0297 feet.
,, *Elle*	=	2·1881 feet.
,, *Ruthe*	=	4·1183 yards.
,, *Meile*	=	4·6805 miles.
,, *Morgen*	=	2·5207 roods.
,, *Hufe* (30 *Morgen*)	=	18·929 acres.
,, *Metze*...............	=	3·024 quarts.
,, *Scheffel* (4 *Viertel*)	=	1·512 bushels.
,, *Tonne*	=	·756 qr.
,, *Last* (60 *Scheffel*)...	=	11·340 qrs.
,, *Ossel*...............	=	1·007 pints.
,, *Anker* (60 *Ossel*) ...	=	7·559 gallons.
,, *Ohm* (2 *Eimer*) ...	=	30·237 gallons.
,, *Fuder*	=	181·422 gallons.
,, *Zollpfund* (30 *Loth*)	=	1·1023 lbs. av.

Germany—*continued.*

Prussian Old *Pfund*	=	7217·885 Tr. grs.
Saxon *Fuss*	=	11·1494 inches.
" *Stab*	=	44·5976 inches.
" *Scheffel*	=	2·892 bushels.
" *Kanne*	=	1·647 pints.
" *Fass* (2 *Oxhoft*)	=	88·937 gallons.
Hanoverian *Fuss*	=	11·5 inches.
" *Last*...............	=	10·284 qrs.
" *Anker* (4 *Viertel*) ...	=	8·570 gallons.
Brunswick *Fuss*	=	11·235 inches.
" *Anker* (10 *Stubschen*)	=	8·24 gallons.
Oldenburg *Fuss*	=	11·649 inches.
" *Anker* (26 *Kanne*) ...	=	7·850 gallons.
Baden *Fuss*	=	11·811 inches.
" *Maass*	=	1·320 quarts.
" *Pfund*	=	1·1023 lbs. av.
Würtemberg *Fuss*	=	·9399 foot.
" *Pfund* (32 *Loth*)	=	1·0311 lbs. av.
Hamburg *Fuss*	=	11·2825 inches.
" *Anker*	=	7·9735 gals.
" New *Pfund*	=	1·1023 lbs. av.
Bremen *Fuss*	=	11·3919 inches.
" *Anker*	=	7·8 gallons.
Lubeck *Fuss*	=	11·323 inches.
" *Anker*...............	=	8·006 gallons.
" *Pfund* (32 *Loth*) ...	=	1·0725 lbs. av.

Greece.

The Metrical System was introduced by an ordinance of Oct. 26, 1832. In Greece, gramme = millimètre ; daktylos = centimètre ; palame = décimètre ; pecheus = mètre ; stadion = kilomètre ; skionis = myriamètre ; stremma = are ; kybos = millilitre ; mystron = centilitre ; kotyle = décilitre ; litra = litre ; koilon = hectolitre ; kokkos = centigramme ; obolos = décigramme ; drachme = gramme ; mna = 1½ kilogramme.

Hayti, as in France.

India.—*Bengal.*

Under "The Indian Weights and Measures Act, 1870," the standard of weight is the Ser (Kilogramme) = 2·20462 lbs. av.: the standard of length is the mètre = 3·280899 feet; and the standard of capacity is the Ser (litre) = 1·760773 pints, or 61·027046 cubic inches.

1 Moot (4 *Ungulee*) ...	=	3 inches.
1 Háth (21 *Ungulee*)...	=	18 inches.
1 Hyderabad Háth ...	=	35·334 inches.
1 Guz	=	1 yard.
1 Coss	=	2000 yards.
1 Jojun	=	8000 yards.
1 Beegah	=	1600 sq. yards.
1 Beegah (N. W. Provs.)	=	3025 sq. yards.
1 Ser	=	2·20462 lbs. av.
1 Ser	=	1·76195 pints.
1 Tola	=	180 Tr. grains.
1 Seer (16 *Chittaks*) ...	=	2·059 lbs. av.
1 *Factory Maund*.........	=	74·66 lbs. av.
1 *Bazaar Maund*	=	72·33 lbs. av.
1 *Imperial Maund*	=	82·287 lbs. av.
1 *Masha* (8 *Ruttee*)	=	15·0 Tr. grains.
1 *Seer* (4 *Powah*)	=	1·961 pints.
1 *Maund* (40 *Seer*)	=	9·8098 gallons.

Bombay.

1 Guz (24 *Tussoo*)	=	27 inches.
1 Beegah (20 *Pund*) ...	=	3927 sq. yards.
1 Seer (72 *Tank*)	=	7 lbs. av.
1 Maund	=	28 lbs. av.
1 Candy	=	560 lbs. av.
1 Sattara Candy	=	3055 lbs. av.

Madras.

English measures, and,

1 Kole or Guz	=	33 inches.
1 Moolum	=	19½ inches.
1 Puddee	=	2·8852 pints.
1 Mercal	=	2·8852 gallons.
1 Parah	=	14·4261 gallons.
1 *Tola*	=	180 Tr. grains.
1 *Cutcha Seer*	=	4320 Tr. grains.
1 *Viss*	=	3·0857 lbs. av.
1 *Maund*	=	24·6857 lbs. av.
1 *Candy*	=	493·7142 lbs. av.

Italy.

The Metrical System.

1 Roman *Miglio* (1000 *Passo*) .	=	1627·783 yards.
1 Roman *Scorzo*	=	1381·648 sq. yds.
1 Roman *Quaterello*	=	1·012 bshls.
1 Roman *Foglietta*	=	·8015 pint.
1 Roman *Boccale*.............	=	3·2101 pints.
1 Roman *Denaro*	=	18·2 Tr. grs.
1 Roman *Oncia* (24 *Denaro*)...	=	436·2 Tr. grs.
1 Roman *Libbra* (12 *Oncia*) ...	=	·7477 lb. av.
1 Naples *Miglio*	=	1·1507 miles.
1 Naples *Oncia*	=	412·512 Tr. grs.
1 Sicilian *Miglio*	=	1625·793 yards.
1 Tuscan *Miglio*	=	1·0275 miles.
1 Lombard *Miglio*	=	1093·63 yards.

Japan.

1 Bu (10 *Ring*)	=	·1193 inch.
1 Sun (10 *Bu*)	=	1·1931 inches.
1 Shaku (10 *Sun*) ...	=	11·931 inches.
1 Ken (6 *Shaku*).........	=	5·965 feet.
1 Jo (10 *Shaku*)	=	3·314 yards.
1 Cho (60 *Ken*)	=	119·305 yards.
1 Ri (36 *Cho*)	=	2·44034 miles.
1 Kujirad Shaku	=	14·913 inches.
1 Chō	=	2·4507204 acres.
1 Tan	=	32·211526 sq. poles.
1 Se..........................	=	118·61486 sq. yds
1 Tsubo	=	3·9538239 sq. yards.
1 Shaku	=	·98845723 sq. ft.
1 Sai (10 *Sat*)	=	·003176 pint.
1 Shaku (10 *Sun*) ...	=	·0317627¹ pint.
1 Gō (10 *Shaku*)	=	·3176271 pint.
1 Shō (10 *Gō*)	=	3·176271 pints.
1 To (10 *Shō*)	=	3·703389 gallons.
1 Koku (10 *To*)	=	4·9629237 bushels.
1 Fun (10 *Rin*).........	=	5·797 Tr. grains.
1 Momme (10 *Fun*)...	=	57·97 Tr. grains.
1 Rin (10 *Mo*)	=	0·5797 Tr. grains.

Malta.

1 Piede	=	11·166 inches.
1 Palmo	=	10·2757 inches.
1 Misura	=	41·103 inches.
1 Canna	=	2·283 yards.
1 Salma (16 *Tumulo*)	=	4·964 acres.
1 Salma	=	7·9372 bushels.
1 Pint	=	·8331 pint.
1 Barrile (wine)	=	9·35 gallons.
1 Libbra (12 *Oncia*)	=	4886 Tr. grains.
1 Rotolo...................	=	1·745 lbs. av.

Mexico.

As old Spanish (*q. v.*).

Netherlands.

Since 1820 the Metrical System. Streep = millimètre; Duim = centimètre; Palm = décimètre; El = mètre; Roede = décamètre; Mijle = kilomètre; Wisse = stère; Vingerhoed = centilitre; Maatje = décilitre; Kan = litre; Vat = hectolitre; Korrel = décigramme; Wigtje = gramme; Lood = décagramme; Onze = hectogramme; Pond = kilogramme.

Norway.

The Metrical System since 1878.

Persia.

1 Zer (16 Gereh)	= 38 inches.
1 Fersakh (*Parasang*)	= 4·5 miles.
1 Chenica	= ·289 gallon.
1 Capicha	= ·578 gallon.
1 Collothun	= 1·809 gallons.
1 Artata	= 1·809 bushels.
1 Seer (16 Miscal)	= 284 Tr. grains.
1 Ratel	= 1·014 lbs. av.
1 Batman, or Maund	= 6·491 lbs. av.
1 Karwar	= 649·142 lbs. av.
1 Batman Rei	= 27 lbs. av.

Peru.

Metrical, old Spanish, and British; but Vara (3 pie) = 2·780 feet; Fanega (wheat) = 135 or 140 libra; Carga = 150 libra.

Philippine Islands.

1 Pulgada (12 Linea)	= ·927 inch.
1 Pie	= 11·125 inches.
1 Vara	= 33·375 inches.
1 Gantah	= ·8796 gallon.
1 Caban	= 21·991 gallons.
1 Libra (16 Onzo)	= 1·0144 lbs. av.
1 Arroba	= 25·360 lbs. av.
1 Catty (16 Tael)	= 1·394 lbs. av.
1 Pecul (100 Catty)	= 139·482 lbs. av.

Poland.

As in Russia, and,

1 *Cwierc* (6 *Cal*) = 5·606 in.	1 *Sznurow* = 47·245 yds
1 *Stopa* = 11·212 in.	1 *Mila* = 5·304 mls
1 *Loziec* = 22·425 in.	1 *Morgow* = 1·382 acs

Portugal, Roumania, and San Domingo.

The Metrical System.

Russia.

1 Stopa (8 Vershok)	= 14 inches.
1 Arschine (16 Vershok)	= 28 inches.
1 Saschen (3 Arschine)	= 7 feet.
1 Verst (500 Saschen)	= 1166·66 yards.
1 Desatine	= 13066⅔ sq. yards.
1 Vedro (100 Tscharkey)	= 2·704 gallons.
1 Anker	= 8·114 gallons.
1 Chetvert	= 46·2 gallons.
1 Sarokowaja	= 108·196 gallons.
1 Tschetwerik	= 2·885 pecks.
1 Pajak	= 1·442 bushels.
1 Last	= 11·540 quarters.
1 Zolotnick (96 Doli)	= 65·830 Tr. grs.
1 Funt (12 Lani)	= ·9028 lb. av.
1 Pood (40 Funt)	= 36·1127 lbs. av.
1 Berkowitz	= 361·273 lbs. av.
1 Packen	= 1083·382 lbs. av.

Servia.

The Metrical and Turkish Systems.

Siam.

1 Niw	= ·83 inch.
1 Kü'p (12 Niws)	= 10 inches.
1 Sawk (2 Kü'ps)	= 19½ inches.
1 Wah (4 Sok)	= 80 inches.
1 Sen (20 Wahs)	= 44·4 yards.
1 Yot (400 Sens)	= 9⅞ miles.
1 Röeneng	= 2·525 miles.
1 Thang	= 3·75 gallons.
1 Coyan	= 375 gallons.
1 Tael (4 Bat)	= 936·25 Tr. grains.
1 Chang, or Catty	= 2·675 lbs. av.
1 Hap, or Pecul	= 133·75 lbs. av.
1 Keean (20 Piculs)	= 1675 lbs. av.

Spain.

The Metrical System was made compulsory on July 1, 1868. In many countries that were colonized by Spain some of the old Spanish measures are still used, *e.g.*,

1 Pulgada (12 Linea)	= ·927 inch.
1 Sesma (6 Pulgada)	= 5·564 inches.
1 Vara (6 Sesma)	= 2·782 feet.
1 Estado (2 Vara)	= 5·564 feet.
1 Legua (of Castile)	= 4635·66 yards.
1 Fanegada	= 1·6374 acres.
1 Cuartillo (4 Capo)	= ·1109 gal.
1 Cuartilla (2 Azumbre)	= ·8879 gal.
1 Arroba Mayor (or Cantara)	= 3·5517 gals.
1 Mayor (16 Cantara)	= 56·276 gals.
1 Medio (2 Quartillo)	= ·0621 bushl.
1 Almude (2 Medio)	= ·1256 bushl.
1 Fanega	= 1·5076 bushls.
1 Cahiz	= 18·0919 bushls.
1 Tomin (12 Grano)	= ·02113 oz. av.
1 Onza	= ·0634 lb. av.
1 Libra (of Castile)	= 1·014 lbs. av.
1 Quintal	= 101·442 lbs. av.
1 Tonelada	= 1014·42 lbs. av.

Sweden.

The Metrical System since 1875.

1 *Fot* (10 *Tum*)	= 11·689 inches.
1 *Mil* (360 *Ref*)	= 6·6416 miles.
1 *Kanna*	= 4·608 pints.
1 *Skoalpund* (100 *Ort*)	= ·937 lb. av.

Switzerland.

The Metrical System since Jan. 1st, 1873.

1 *Fuss* (10 *Zoll*)	= 11·8112 inches.
1 *Stunde* (1600 *Ruthe*)	= 2·9826 miles.
1 *Malter* (10 *Viertel*)	= 4·126 bushels.
1 *Maass* (4 *Schoppen*)	= 2·641 pints.
1 *Pfund* (16 *Unze*)	= 1·1023 lbs. av.

Tripoli.

1 Pike	= 26·416 inches.
1 Draâ	= 19·13 inches.
1 Orbah	= 1·476 gallons.
1 Hueba (4 Temen)	= 2·952 bushels.
1 Secchie (4 Bozze)	= 2·361 gallons.
1 Oka (40 Uckieh)	= 2·69 lbs. av.
1 Centner (100 Rottoli)	= 107·66 lbs. av.

Turkey.

1 Pike or Arshen	= 27¼ inches.
1 Pike or Arshen (land)	= 29⅜ inches.
1 Halebi or Archim	= 27·9 inches.
1 Endazzch (Silk)	= 25¼ inches.
1 Agatsch (3 Berri)	= 3·1159 miles.
1 Jubbeh (11 Rottol)	= ·4851 bushel.
1 Fortin (4 Killow)	= 3·8809 bushels.
1 Rottol (12 Okiejeh)	= 2·513 pints.
1 Almud (8 Oka)	= 1·1519 gallons.
1 Cantar (100 Rottol)	= 31·417 gallons.
1 Cantar (dry)	= 124·08 av.
1 Okiejeh (100 Dirhem)	= ·70854 lb av.
1 Kèlé or Oke (4 Okiejeh)	= 2·1975 lbs. av.
1 Batman (dry)	= 16·92 av.

United States.

The Metrical System, authorized 1866; also weight, length, and surface measures as in England, and old Winchester measure.

1 Pint (dry)	= ·9694 pint.
1 Gallon (dry)	= ·9694 gallon.
1 Bushel	= ·9694 bushel.
1 Quarter	= ·9694 quarter.
1 Pint (wine or spirit)	= ·8331 pint.
1 Gallon (wine or spirit)	= ·8331 gallon.
1 Pint (beer)	= 1·017 pints.
1 Quintal or Centner	= 100 lbs. av.
1 Barrel (of flour)	= 196 lbs. av.
1 Barrel (of beef)	= 200 lbs. av.

Uruguay.

Metrical System, introduced 1864; also as in Argentine Republic. Venezuela, the Metrical System, since 1857; and old Spanish.

On the morrow of St. Martin (12th November) certain high officials, usually the Lord President of the Council, the Chancellor of the Exchequer, the Lord Chancellor, several Judges, the Clerk of the Council, and others, assemble in the Court of the Queen's Bench Division of the High Court of Justice, and after certain ceremonies have been gone through, three gentlemen are nominated for the office of Sheriff for every one of the counties of England and Wales ; Cornwall is nominated by the Prince of Wales as Duke of that county ; and Lancaster, by its Duke the Queen. The three names, engrossed upon a parchment roll, are afterwards brought before Her Majesty, who then, with a golden bodkin, pricks through the parchment against one name for every county. The name thus pricked is usually the first on the list, and they come into office after Hilary Term. The following is a list of the gentlemen thus nominated whose names stand first upon the roll :—

BEDFORDSHIRE.—Algernon Mercer, Morhanger Park. Sandy.

BERKSHIRE.—Frank Walters Bond, Parkfield, Hampton Wick.

BUCKINGHAMSHIRE.—Sir Robert Grenville Harvey, Bart., Langley Park, Slough.

CAMBRIDGE AND HUNTINGDON (SHIRES).—Charles Finch Foster, Pinehurst, Cambridge.

CHESHIRE.—Benjamin Chaffers Roberts, Oakfield, Chester.

CORNWALL.—

CUMBERLAND.—Charles Lacy Thompson, Farlamhall, Brampton.

DERBYSHIRE.—Sir Vauncey Harpur Crewe, Bart., Calke Abbey, Derby.

DEVONSHIRE.—John Smyth Smyth-Osbourne, Ash House, Iddesleigh.

DORSET.—Capt. Richard Baynton Foster, Lambert House, Dorchester.

DURHAM.—John Arundel Hildyard, Horsley House, Eastgate. Darlington.

ESSEX.—Henry Collings Wells, Broomfield Lodge, Broomfield.

GLOUCESTERSHIRE.—Peter Stubs, Blaisdon Hall, near Newnham-on-Severn.

HEREFORDSHIRE.—John Wood, Ryelands, Leominster.

HERTFORDSHIRE.— Sir George Faudel Faudel-Phillips, Bart., G.C.I.E., Balls Park, Hertford.

KENT.—William Marshall Cazalet, Fairlawn, Shiphourne, Tonbridge.

LANCASTER.—

LEICESTERSHIRE. — Richard Smith-Carrington, Ashby Folville Manor, Melton Mowbray.

LINCOLNSHIRE.—Arthur Cecil Tempest, Coleby Hall, near Lincoln.

LONDON, COUNTY OF.—John Verity, 18 Cadogan Place, S.W.

MIDDLESEX.— John Walker Ford, Enfield Old Park, N.

MONMOUTHSHIRE.—Hon. John Maclean Rolls, The Hendre, Monmouth.

NORFOLK.—Sir Edmund Charles Nugent, Bart., West Harling.

NORTHAMPTONSHIRE. — Thomas Francis Hazlehurst, Cold Ashby Hall.

NORTHUMBERLAND.—Lawrence William Adamson, Eglingham Hall, Alnwick.

NOTTINGHAMSHIRE.—Francis Abel Smith, Papplewick Hall, Nottingham.

OXFORDSHIRE.— Robert Hichens Camden Harrison, Shiplake Court.

RUTLAND. — Ernest Lucas Braithwaite, Edith Weston, Stamford.

SHROPSHIRE.—Frank Bibby, Sansaw Hall, near Shrewsbury.

SOMERSET.—Robert Neville Grenville, Butleigh Court, Glastonbury.

SOUTHAMPTON, COUNTY OF. — Herman Le Roy Lewis, Westbury House, Petersfield.

STAFFORDSHIRE.—Lachlan Andrew Macpherson, Wyrley Grove, Walsall.

SUFFOLK.—Roger Kerrison, Tattingstone Place.

SURREY.—Charles Hoskins Master, Barrow Green, Oxted.

SUSSEX. — Robert Lawrence Thornton, High Cross, Framfield.

WARWICKSHIRE.—Morton P. Lucas, Leamington.

WESTMORLAND. — Edward William Wakefield, Stricklandgate House. Kendal.

WILTSHIRE.—Mark Hanbury Beaufoy, Coombe House, Shaftesbury, Dorset.

WORCESTERSHIRE.—Sir Benjamin Hingley, Bart., Hatherton Lodge. Cradley.

YORKSHIRE.— William Henry Battie-Wrightson, Cusworth Park, Doncaster.

Wales (North and South).

ANGLESEY.—Richard Bennett, 6 Victoria Terrace, Beaumaris.

BRECONSHIRE.—Howel John James Price, Glynllech, Swansea Valley.

CARDIGANSHIRE.—Edward Walter David Evans, Camnant Hall, Llandyssil.

CARMARTHENSHIRE.—Benjamin Evans, Llwynderw Westcross, Swansea.

CARNARVONSHIRE.—Lt.-Col. Owen Lloyd Jones Evans, Broomhill, Chwilog.

DENBIGHSHIRE.—Robert William Wynne, Garthewin, Abergele.

FLINTSHIRE. — Henry Hurlbutt, Dee Cottage, Queensferry.

GLAMORGANSHIRE.—Hon. Ivor Churchill Guest, Sully, near Cardiff.

MERIONETHSHIRE. — Robert Charles Anwyl, Llugwy, Machynlleth.

MONTGOMERYSHIRE.—Captain Peter Audley David Arthur Lovell, Llanerchydol.

PEMBROKESHIRE.—John Evans, Welston, near Pembroke.

RADNORSHIRE.—J. Miller W. G. Watt, Doldowlod.

Foreign Moneys.

TABLE FOR CALCULATING THE VALUE OF ANY GIVEN WEIGHT OF STANDARD SILVER IN TROY OUNCES.

Market Price of Standard Silver in Pence per Troy Ounce.

Oz.	24	25	26	26½	27	27½	28	28½	29	29½	30
1	24	25	26	26·5	27	27·5	28	28·5	29	29·5	30
2	48	50	52	53·0	54	55·0	56	57·0	58	59·0	60
3	72	75	78	79·5	81	82·5	84	85·5	87	88·5	90
4	96	100	104	106·0	108	110·0	112	114·0	116	118·0	120
5	120	125	130	132·5	135	137·5	140	142·5	145	147·5	150
6	144	150	156	159·0	162	165·0	168	171·0	174	177·0	180
7	168	175	182	185·5	189	192·5	196	199·5	203	206·5	210
8	192	200	208	212·0	216	220·0	224	228·0	232	236·0	240
9	216	225	234	238·5	243	217·5	252	256·5	261	265·5	270

By means of the above table, taken in conjunction with the column of the opposite page headed "Equivalent Weight of Standard Silver in Troy Ounces," the intrinsic value of any coin can be easily calculated with silver at several prices other than those given. It will only be necessary to take the numbers representing tenths, hundredths, and thousandths of ounces in the first column, find the numbers opposite to them in the column of the above table giving the price of silver and add these together, taking care to move the decimal point successively one, two, and three places, to the left ; the result will be the coin's intrinsic value in pence.

Foreign Moneys and their English Equivalents.

EXPLANATORY NOTES.—France, Belgium, Italy, *Greece, and *Switzerland constitute what is known as the "Latin" Union, and their coins are alike in weight and fineness, occasionally differing, however, in name. The same system has been in part adopted by Spain, Servia, Bulgaria, Russia, and Roumania, but they have not joined the Union. Francs and centimes of France, Belgium, and Switzerland are respectively designated lire and centesimi in Italy; drachmai and lepta in Greece; dinars and paras in Servia; pesetas and centimos in Spain; leys and banis in Roumania; leva and stotinkis in Bulgaria. Similarly the Scandinavian countries, Norway, Sweden, and Denmark, employ coins of the same weight and fineness, their names being also alike. Most of the South American States possess a standard coin, equal in weight and fineness to the silver 5-fr. piece, generally termed a "peso." In Hayti the corresponding coin is a "gourde."

In most British Colonies, English money is current. The currency of Ceylon, Mauritius, and the East Africa Protectorate is, however, based on the rupee of British India, that of the Straits Settlements, Hong Kong, and Labuan on the Mexican dollar, and of Canada and British Honduras on the United States dollar. A British dollar, identical in weight and fineness with the Japanese "yen," was authorized by order in Council in 1894, and has been made legal tender in the Straits Settlements, Hong Kong, and Labuan. The exchange value of the moneys of those countries indicated by a * is determined by the rate of exchange for the day, and may be taken as approximately that given in the last column. The rate given in the daily papers generally represents the number of the standard coins (*see* page 419) that are equivalent to one sovereign. The Spanish rate is given in terms of pence per dollar (= 2 escudos), the Russian in pence per rouble, Portuguese in pence per milreis, and the United States rate in pence per dollar. The value of other silver coins must be sought in one of the columns headed "Intrinsic Value with Silver at per Troy Ounce." The exchange value of the rupee depends on the rate for "India Council Bills," but by an Act of 1898, the British sovereign was made legal tender and equivalent to 15 rupees, the rupee being thus rated at 1s. 4d. In "bimetallic" countries pure gold is generally taken as being worth 15½ times its weight of pure silver. This proportion corresponds to giving standard silver a constant value of 60⅞d., as in the last column of the table.

COUNTRY.	GOLD COINS. Denominations.	Legal Weight in Grains.	Sterling Value.	SILVER COINS. Denominations.	Legal Weight in Grains.	Equivalent Weight of Standard Silver in Troy Ounces.	Intrinsic Value with Silver at per Troy oz. 24d.	26d.	28d.	30d.	60⅞d., i.e. Gold to Silver as 15·5 is to 1.
			£ s. d.				s. d.	s. d.	s. d.	s. d.	s. d.
Argentine Republic	Argentino or 5-peso piece	124·44	0 19 10	Peso of 100 centesimos	385·8	0·782	1 6¾	1 8½	1 10	1 11½	3 11½
*Austria-Hungary	Ducat	53·85	0 9 4	Florin or gulden of 100 kreutzer	190·5	0·386	0 9¼	0 10	0 10¾	0 11½	1 11½
	8-florin or gulden piece	99·57	0 15 10½	¼-florin	82·4	0·097	0 2¼	0 2½	0 2¾	0 3	0 5¾
	10-krone piece	52·28	0 8 4	Krone of 100 hellers	77·2	0·144	0 3¾	c 3	0 3¼	0 4¼	0 8¾
Brazil	10 milreis	138·35	1 2 5½	1 milreis of 1,000 reis	190·8	0·406	0 9¾	0 10½	0 11¼	1 0¼	2 0¾
Chile, Columbia, Uruguay	doubloon or 5-peso piece	117·70	0 18 9	1 peso of 100 centavos	385·8	0·782	1 6¾	1 8½	1 10	1 11½	3 11½
China	....	....	....	Tael of 10 mace or 100 conderin or 1000 cash	583·3	1·288	2 7	2 9½	3 0	3 2¾	6 6¼
Denmark	10-krone piece	69·14	0 11 0½	1 krone of 100 ore	115·7	0·209	0 5	0 5½	0 5¾	0 6¼	1 0¾
Egypt	100-piastre piece (Egyptian £)	131·18	1 0 3½	1 piastre	21·6	0·041	0 1	0 1	0 1¼	0 1¼	0 2½
Finland	10-markkaa piece	49·78	0 7 11½	1 markka of 100 penni	80·0	0·156	0 3¾	0 4	0 4¼	0 4¾	0 9½
*France and Latin Union	10-franc piece	49·78	0 7 11½	5-franc piece	385·8	0·782	1 6¾	1 8½	1 10	1 11½	3 11½
				1 franc of 100 centimes	77·2	0·145	0 3½	0 3¾	0 4	0 4¼	0 8¾
*German Empire	Krone of 10 reichsmarks	61·4	0 9 9½	1 reichsmark or mark of 100 pfennige	85·7	0·174	0 4¼	2 4½	0 4¾	0 5¼	0 10½
*Great Britain	Sovereign of 20 shillings	123·27	1 0 0	Crown of 5 shillings	436·4	0·909	1 9¾	1 11½	2 1½	2 3¼	4 7¼
				Shilling of 12 pence	87·3	0·182	0 4¼	0 4¾	0 5	0 5½	0 11
*Holland and Java	Ducat	53·92	0 9 4½	Rixdaler of 2½ florins	385·8	0·821	1 7¾	1 9¼	1 11	2 0¾	4 2
	10-florin piece	103·71	0 16 6½	Florin of 100 cents	154·3	0·328	0 8	8½	0 9¼	0 9¾	1 8
India	Mohur of 15 rupees (obsolete)	180·00	1 9 2½	Rupee of 16 annas, 64 pice, or 192 pies	180·0	0·372	0 9	0 9¾	0 10½	0 11¼	1 10½
	Brit sovereign of 15 rupees										
Japan	20-yen piece	257·21	2 0 11¾	1 yen of 100 sen	416·0	0·843	1 8¼	1 10	1 11½	2 1¼	4 3¼
Mexico	10-peso piece	261·12	2 0 5½	1 peso of 100 centavos	417·8	0·849	1 8½	1 10	1 11¼	2 1½	4 3¾
*Netherlands	*See* Holland.										
*Norway and Sweden	*See* Denmark, and footnote.										
Ottoman Empire	Turkish pound of 100 piastres	111·36	0 18 0¾	1 piastre of 40 paras	18·6	0·035	0 0¾	0 1	0 1	0 1	0 2
Persia	Toman of 200 shahis	57·90	0 9 5	Khran of 20 shahis	71·0	0·142	0 3½	0 3¾	0 4	0 4¼	0 8½
Peru	Libra of 10-sols	123·27	1 0 0	Sol of 10 dineros or 100 cents	385·8	0·782	1 6¾	1 8½	1 10	1 11½	3 11½
*Portugal	Corôa of 10 milreis	273·70	2 4 4¾	Teston of 100 reis	31·6	0·080	0 2	0 2	0 2¼	0 2½	0 4¾
Roumania	*See* France, and footnote.										
*Russia	Imperial of 15 roubles	199·10	1 11 9	Rouble of 100 kopecks	308·6	0·626	1 3	1 4¼	1 5½	1 6¾	3 2
				Tchetvertak or ¼ rouble	77·1	0·156	0 3¾	0 4	0 4¼	0 4¾	0 9½
Servia and Bulgaria	*See* France, and footnote.										
*Spain	Doubloon of 10 escudos	129·43	1 0 7¼	5-peseta piece	385·8	0·782	1 6¾	1 8½	1 10	1 11½	3 11½
	25-peseta piece	124·46	0 19 10	Peseta of 100 centimos	77·2	0·145	0 3½	0 3½	0 4	0 4¼	0 8¾
Tunis	10-piastre piece	30·09	0 4 9½	Piastre	46·7	0·098	0 2¼	0 2½	0 2¾	0 3	0 6
Turkey	*See* Ottoman Empire.			Trade dollar	420·0	0·851	1 8½	1 10¼	1 11¾	2 1½	4 3¾
United States	Eagle of 10 dollars	258·0	2 1 1¼	Dollar of 100 cents	412·5	0·836	1 8	1 9¾	1 11½	2 1	4 2¾
				½ dollar of 50 cents	192·9	0·391	0 9½	0 10¼	0 11	0 11¾	1 11¾
*Uruguay	*See* Chile, and footnote.										

National Rifle Association.

OFFICES OF THE ASSOCIATION, 12, PALL MALL EAST.   *Secretary :* Lt.-Col. C. R. CROSSE.

THE QUEEN'S PRIZE. FIRST STAGE TO 1881.—**FIRST AND SECOND STAGES** FROM 1882.

THE N.R.A. SILVER MEDAL.

Conditions (1886) : 7 shots each at 200, 500, and 600 yds, 10 at 500, 15 at 600, and 10 each at 800 & 900 yds.

Year.	Winner.			Distances. Yards.	Shots.	Scores.	H.p.s.	Rifle used.
1876	Burgess	Pte.	1st Newcastle	2, 5, & 600	7	86 mks.	105	Snider B. L.
1877	Betts	Corp.	1st Norfolk	,,	,,	92 ,,	,,	,,
1878	Lowe	Pte.	Queen's Westmr	,,	,,	95 ,,	,,	Govt. Martini-Hen. B.L
1879	Macdonald	Qtrmr.	10th Forfar	,,	,,	36 ,,	,,	,, ,,
1880	Scott	Corp.	4th Cheshire	,,	,,	102 ,,	,,	,, ,,
1881	Ingram	Corp.	3rd Lanark	,,	,,	96 ,,	,,	,, ,,
1882	Smith	C.-Srg.	6th Surrey	,,	,,	174 ,,	205	,, ,,
1883*	Young	Capt.	2nd Renfrew	,,	,,	183 ,,	,,	,, ,,
1884	Taylor	Segt.	1st Lanark	,,	7 10 15	195 ,,	230	,, ,,
1885†	Simonds	Cr.-Srg.	14th Middlesex	,,	,,	189 ,,	,,	,, ,,
1886	Cortis	Capt.	2nd Sussex	,,	,,	194 ,,	,,	,, ,,
1887	Hill	Ar.-Srg.	5th Lanark	,,	,,	200 ,,	,,	,, ,,
1888	Noakes	L.-Crp.	1st Berks	,,	,,	201 ,,	,,	,, ,,
1889	Wattleworth	Pte.	2nd V. B. L'pool.	,,	,,	205 ,,	,,	,, ,,
1890	Murray	Pte.	3rd V.B.Gor.Hdrs	,,	,,	204 ,,	,,	,, ,,
1891	Milner	Sergt.	2nd V. B. Derby	,,	,,	200 ,,	,,	,, ,,
1892	Pollock	Major	3 V.B.A.&S.Hdrs.	,,	,,	201 ,,	,,	,, ,,
1893	Stocks	Pte.	2nd V. B. L'pool.	,,	,,	208 ,,	,,	,, ,,
1894	Bateman	Capt.	2ndTowr.H.Engs	,,	,,	208 ,,	,,	,, ,,
1895	Hogg	L.-Srg.	1st Rox. & Sel.	,,	,,	205 ,,	,,	,, ,,
1896	Foster	Capt.	4 V. B. W. Surrey	,,	,,	196 ,,	,,	,, ,,
1897	Scott	Ar.Serg.	1st Rox. & Selkirk	,,	,,	219 ,,	,,	Govt. Lee-Metford B L.
1898	Fletcher	Lt.	2nd V. B. L'pool.	,,	,,	214 ,,	,,	,, ,,
1899	Matthews	C.-Srg.	12th Middlesex	,,	,,	218 ,,	,,	,, ,,

* Fire 7 shots at 200, 500, and 600, and afterwards 10 shots at 500 and 600.
† Fire 7 shots at 200, 500, and 600, and afterwards 10 shots at 500 and 15 at 600.

QUEEN'S PRIZE. SECOND STAGE.

Year.	Winner.			Distances. Yards.	Shots.	Scores.	H.p.s.	Rifle used.
1870	Humphries	Pte.	6th Surrey	8, 9, & 1000	7	66 mks.	84	Govt. Whitworth M.L.
1871	Humphry	Ens.	Cambridge Univ.	,,	,,	68 ,,	,,	Govt. Martini-Hen. B.L
1872	Michie	C.-Srg.	London Scottish	,,	,,	65 ,,	,,	,, ,,
1873	Menzies	Srg.	Queen's Edinbrg.	,,	,,	60 ,,	,,	,, ,,
1874	Atkinson	Pte.	1st Durham	,,	,,	64 ,,	105	,, ,,
1875	Pearse	Capt.	18th Devon	,,	,,	73 ,,	,,	,, ,,
1876	Pullman	Srg.	South Middlesex.	,,	,,	74 ,,	,,	,, ,,
1877	Jamieson	Pte.	15th Lancashire	,,	,,	70 ,,	,,	,, ,,
1878	Rae	Pte.	11th Stirling	,,	,,	78 ,,	,,	,, ,,
1879	Taylor	Corp.	47th Lancashire	,,	,,	83 ,,	,,	,, ,,
1880	Ferguson	Pte.	1st Argyle	,,	,,	74 ,,	,,	,, ,,
1881	Beck	Pte.	3rd Devon	,,	,,	86 ,,	,,	,, ,,
1882	Lawrance	Srg.	1st Dumbarton	,,	,,	65 ,,	,,	,, ,,
1883	Mackay	Srg.	1st Sutherland	800 &900	10	79 ,,	100	,, ,,
1884	Gallant	Pte.	8th Middlesex	,,	15	110 ,,	150	,, ,,

THE QUEEN'S PRIZE. THIRD STAGE.—£250, AND THE N.R.A. GOLD MEDAL.

Year.	Winner.			Distances. Yards.	Shots.	Scores.	H.p.s.	Rifle used.
1892	Pollock	Major	3 V.B.A.&S.Hdrs.	200 to 900	66	277 mk.	330	Govt. Martini-Hen. B.L
1893	Davies	Serg.	1st V. B., Welsh.	,,	66	274 ,,	330	,, ,,
1894	Rennie	Pte.	3rd Lanark	,,	66	283 ,,	330	,, ,,
1895	Hayhurst	Pte.	Canada	,,	66	279 ,,	330	,, ,,
1896	Thomson	Lieut.	Queen's Edinb.	,,	66	273 ,,	330	,, ,,
1897	Ward	Pte.	1st V. B. Devon	,,	66	304 ,,	330	Service Rifle.
1898	Yates	Lt.	3rd Lanark	200 to 1000	76	327 ,,	380	,,
1899	Priaulx	Pte.	Guernsey	,,	76	336 ,,	380	,,

ELCHO CHALLENGE SHIELD. (Competitors, 8 from each Nationality.)

The Competing Teams were permitted to use any rifle, with 15 shots at (each distance) 800, 900, and 1,000 yards. From 1862 to 1873 highest possible score, 1,440 ; from 1874, 1,800.

1876	England	1,463 marks	1884	Ireland	1,583 marks	1892	Scotland	1,696 marks
1877	Ireland	1,568 ,,	1885	England	1,574 ,,	1893	England	1,688 ,,
1878	Ireland	1,610 ,,	1886	Ireland	1,571 ,,	1894	Scotland	1,627 ,,
1879	Scotland	1,505 ,,	1887	England	1,570 ,,	1895	England	1,503 ,,
1880	Ireland	1,638 ,,	1888	Ireland	1,652 ,,	1896	England	1,659 ,,
1881	England	1,642 ,,	1889	Ireland	1,689 ,,	1897	England	1,603 ,,
1882	England	1,536 ,,	1890	Ireland	1,646 ,,	1898	England	1,595 ,,
1883	Ireland	1,600 ,,	1891	England	1,670 ,,	1899	England	1,577 ,,

London Water Supply.

THE supply of water to London is in the hands of eight companies incorporated under private acts of Parliament. Five of them draw their water from the River Thames, two from the Lee, supplemented by springs and wells, and one from deep chalk wells in Kent. Considerable interest has been taken during late years in proposals to place the water supply in the hands of a public body, but one of the chief difficulties has always been to find the authority to which the control should be entrusted. A Royal Commission was appointed in 1897 to inquire whether, having regard to financial considerations and to present and prospective requirements as regards water supply, it is desirable in the interests of the ratepayers and water consumers that the undertakings of the eight water companies should be acquired, and, if so, by what authority or authorities, and, if not, whether additional powers of control should be exercised by local or other authorities.

The Commission, under the presidency of Lord Llandaff, commenced to take evidence on the 22nd November, 1897, and concluded on the 23rd March, 1899. Reference was made in last year's Almanack to the shortness of water in the district supplied by the East London Company. The Commission specially considered this matter, and on the 20th December, 1898, issued a preliminary report upon the practicability of connecting the mains of the water companies. The Government subsequently introduced a Bill providing for such connections, and the East London Company was thus enabled to give a constant service throughout the summer of 1899. The Commission has not yet issued any further report.

The summer of 1899 was again exceedingly dry, and the flow of water in the Thames was unprecedentedly low.

The London County Council has determined to again promote bills in the next session to authorise the purchase of the undertakings of the eight companies and the introduction of a new supply from the Welsh valleys. The Council contends that the latter is a more satisfactory and economical way of providing for the future than the counter proposals of the companies to construct huge reservoirs for storing the waters of the Thames and Lee.

The interests of the consumers in past years have been guarded by the London County Council, and its predecessor the Metropolitan Board of Works, and the Corporation of the City of London; and whenever application was made to Parliament by any of the Companies for further powers, their proposals were carefully watched, and, by the joint action of these two bodies and the Local Government Board, many restrictions in the consumers' interests have been placed upon the companies. No addition to share capital has been allowed since 1878 and the interest on debenture stock has, since 1894, been limited to such a rate as will, in the opinion of the Governor of the Bank of England, secure the issue of the stock at par. The additional debenture capital is, however, assumed to earn a considerably higher rate of interest namely, the average dividend and interest on the total capital, and, to prevent this going to swell the dividends already paid on the share capital, a clause, known as the "sinking fund clause," has been devised to intercept the difference between the interest paid and the interest earned; and the amounts, calculated as provided by the clause, which has been incorporated in all the recent acts, are paid over by the Companies to the Chamberlain of the City of London, to be held by him as trustee and invested to form a sinking fund to extinguish the capital of the Companies or otherwise, as Parliament may direct. The total amount of capital authorised subject to the sinking fund clause is now £7,470,000.

The following table summarises the financial position of the companies at the time of going to press:—

Name of Company.	Incorporat'd	Capital Called up.	Debenture and Preference. Amount.	Debenture and Preference. Rate of Interest per cent.	Ordinary. Amount.	Dividend. Max	Dividend. Paid 1899.	Latest Price per £100.	Yield on latest Dividends. £	s.	d.
		£	£		£				£	s.	d.
Chelsea	1723	1,318,590	538,191	2¾, 4½ & 5	780,399	10	*11	315½	3	10	6
East London	1807	3,015,300	1,294,740	3 & 4½	1,720,560	10	7	205½	3	8	3
Grand Junction	1810	1,580,000	310,000	4	846,000	10	7½	221	3	9	0
					154,000	7½	7½	204	3	14	3
					270,000	7	7	193	3	13	3
Kent	1809	990,000	122,000	3½, 4½ & 5	708,000	10	*14	352½	4	0	3
					160,000	7	7	210½	3	7	0
Lambeth	1785	1,950,000	500,000	3 & 4	1,043,800	10	*10¾	297½	3	11	6
					406,200	7½	*8	227½	3	11	0
New River	1619	3,759,958	1,740,000	3 & 4	2,019,958	—	§3	‡432½	3	3	6
Southwark and Vauxhall	1845	2,987,565	1,958,785	3, 4 & 5	902,300	10	7½	210½	3	12	0
					126,500	7½	7½	195½	3	17	9
West Middlesex	1806	1,655,066	500,000	3 & 4½	1,155,066	10	†10	300½	3	7	6
‖Staines Reservoirs Joint Committee	1896	703,500	703,500	3	—	—	—	—	—		

* Including payment on account of back dividends. † Claim to back dividends satisfied. ‡ New Shares.
‖ Grand Junction, New River, and West Middlesex Companies. § Actually £3 13s.

Local Taxation (England and Wales).—Poor Rate.

STATEMENT AS TO RATEABLE VALUE, RECEIPTS, AND EXPENDITURE, FOR EACH YEAR FROM 1861 TO 1898, INCLUSIVE, SHOWING THE PROPORTION OF EXPENDITURE CONNECTED AND UNCONNECTED WITH THE RELIEF OF THE POOR, THE RATES PER £ ON RATEABLE VALUE, AND PER HEAD OF POPULATION, ETC.

YEAR	RATEABLE VALUE £	RECEIPTS — From Poor Rates £	Rate in £ on Rateable Value s. d.	Rate per Head on Population s. d.	Receipts in Aid £	TOTAL £	EXPENDITURE CONNECTED WITH RELIEF OF POOR — In-Maintenance £	Out-Relief £	Maintenance of Lunatics in Asylums, &c. £	Salaries and Rations of Officers, and Superannuation £	TOTAL EXPENDITURE £	Rate per Head on Population s. d.	Rate in £ on Rateable Val. s. d.	EXPENDITURE UNCONNECTED WITH RELIEF OF POOR — County, Borough, and Police Rate £	Highway, Rural District, &c. Boards £	School Boards and Sch. Attendance Committee Expenses £	Registration of Births, &c., Expenses, Fees to Clergy, & Registrars £	Vaccination Fees and Expenses £	Parliamentary Registration, Jury Lists, School Fees, &c. £	Total Expenditure unconnected with Relief of Poor £	Total Expenditure with Relief of Poor £	Total Expenditure connected and unconnected with Relief of Poor £
1861	(a)	7,704,619	2 0 (a)	(a)	339,549	8,853,168	1,033,659	3,012,251	443,802	660,370	5,779,943	5 10		1,925,216			66,992	47,739	34,103	2,074,842		8,395,212
1862	(a)	8,511,161	(a)		337,829	8,838,990	1,133,286	3,155,820	482,425	660,257	6,027,036	6 0		1,975,668			60,133	53,163	35,586	2,223,645		8,866,071
1863	(a)	9,174,995			337,679	9,512,655	1,137,112	3,574,130	501,368	6,527,036	6 2			2,075,668			60,430	58,524	37,509	2,336,398		9,625,480
1864	(a)	9,448,319	(a)		425,250	9,874,459	1,095,814	3,466,392	524,166	705,529	6,443,381			2,163,200			72,946	55,818	37,715	2,856,625		9,792,558
1865	(a)	9,399,191			376,061	9,769,142	1,188,784	3,258,813	535,115	730,704	6,604,966			2,133,200			75,563	44,815	83,648	3,006,774		9,989,129
1866	93,638,403	9,573,772	2 0		388,478	9,958,250	1,375,640	3,196,685	567,994	747,550	6,439,527			2,571,551			74,239	50,087	37,175	3,265,901		10,995,173
1867	(a)	10,302,665	(a)		388,563	10,692,288	1,517,946	3,358,351	607,294	770,339	6,959,940			2,456,578			73,826	51,283	39,199	3,435,483		11,380,593
1868	100,653,698	11,054,513	2 1 (a)		418,330	11,472,843	1,546,526	3,677,379	650,794	777,653	7,658,000			2,554,735			71,213	54,378	71,293	3,579,557		11,773,909
1869	104,405,304	11,393,668	(a)		419,187	11,775,153	1,593,868	3,677,379	710,941	770,339	7,693,600			2,550,735			70,908	49,457	69,407	3,449,623		11,737,613
1870	107,308,342	11,610,920	2 2		470,520	11,932,668	1,524,640	3,583,577	745,113	818,456	7,335,000			2,508,344			72,383	73,533	59,997	3,044,783		12,692,741
1871	109,417,111	12,100,600	2 1 0		510,520	12,131,440	1,524,640	3,583,577	742,483	821,468	7,394,307			2,798,344			78,290	73,245	84,712	3,241,766		12,998,237
1872	112,392,352	12,190,600	2 0		568,448	12,123,449	1,549,403	3,583,177	780,987	901,231	7,664,967			3,041,185			100,557	81,579	85,205	3,244,783		13,615,490
1873	112,392,352	12,343,251	2 0 7		461,343	12,608,936	1,549,403	3,379,120	830,454	929,743	7,628,169			3,041,185			79,111	82,088	87,374	3,224,783		13,693,182
1874	115,646,631	12,483,133	2 0		461,343	12,657,943	1,577,596	3,379,120	859,073	972,481	7,488,481			3,252,056			81,579	88,400	91,623	4,595,154		14,390,240
1875	119,079,586	12,092,087	(a)		803,308	12,803,750	2,705,800	2,616,465	883,267	983,218	7,525,859			3,334,420			82,088	86,890	95,623	4,050,613		14,436,735
1876	123,158,442	13,049,046	1 11		801,528	12,995,395	1,613,757	2,616,465	911,426	997,308	7,409,036			3,334,420			88,400	89,868	87,374	4,943,906		15,098,237
1877	124,597,474	12,585,177	1 11 7		904,015	13,194,440	1,720,947	2,641,558	957,115	1,023,197	7,688,050			3,432,248			92,754	92,275	273,334	5,196,998		15,590,714
1878	127,948,360	13,013,591	(a)		957,821	13,489,714	1,720,947	2,544,558	986,350	1,094,184	7,829,619			3,433,248			95,745	96,500	257,477	5,415,973		15,995,951
1879	131,064,875	13,047,681	(a)		970,599	14,049,594	1,931,605	2,564,375	1,009,322	1,117,795	8,015,010			3,710,327			97,745	98,025	294,815	5,578,435		15,970,126
1880	135,645,417	13,202,354	(a)		970,599	15,238,111	1,931,605	2,565,375	1,098,322	1,117,795	8,334,177			3,846,534			99,861	93,618	297,336	5,573,325		17,735,574
1881	139,636,307	13,047,681	(a)		1,003,739	15,298,131	1,935,605	2,549,846	1,143,146	1,108,322	8,353,290			4,101,421			93,095	94,618	197,037	6,314,071		15,731,366
1882	140,991,686	14,097,519	(a)		1,050,824	15,387,647	1,994,592	2,517,603	1,188,012	1,093,226	8,491,600			4,301,590			95,547	99,618	191,750	6,556,678		15,356,791
1883	142,420,438	14,262,915	(a)		1,059,824	15,552,608	1,837,624	2,490,005	1,188,012	1,093,226	8,491,600			4,401,590			94,936	94,618	233,286	6,705,245		15,590,714
1884	145,527,041	14,501,844	(a)		1,070,693	15,816,095	1,865,304	2,498,450	1,159,750	1,175,107	8,176,708			4,516,060			94,057	93,475	247,906	6,705,245		15,356,791
1885	147,339,562	14,488,297	(a)		1,127,841	15,810,995	1,832,304	2,533,686	1,191,763	1,331,733	8,176,708			4,522,460			99,387	94,911	257,477	6,819,085		15,995,961
1886	148,907,727	14,771,132	(a)		1,421,842	15,810,995	1,886,000	2,513,688	1,293,095	1,344,074	8,340,637			4,526,360			94,057	94,911	294,819	6,819,085		15,970,122
1887	149,634,814	14,771,132	(a)		1,433,485	17,760,446	1,865,304	2,527,683	1,284,049	1,444,656	8,445,891			4,538,246			95,649	85,959	327,815	8,501,497		17,735,574
1888	149,771,139	15,240,564	(a)		2,094,284	18,358,078	1,951,486	2,374,986	1,284,656	1,454,820	8,847,078			6,171,117			83,446	78,408	394,896	8,833,031		19,411,807
1889	150,840,594	15,953,794	(a)		2,445,797	18,087,847	2,044,063	2,374,786	1,331,723	1,496,340	8,847,078			6,301,786			100,008	83,446	377,815	9,308,024		10,411,807
1890	152,116,006	15,042,060	(a)		2,445,797	20,180,594	2,105,676	2,370,613	1,393,061	1,566,500	9,672,505			6,739,017			98,419	87,981	330,638	10,053,030		21,402,031
1891	155,606,363	16,531,406	(a)		2,439,715	20,186,594	2,216,231	2,460,503	1,466,185	1,502,000	9,613,505			6,739,017			97,181	78,408	369,203	10,801,394		21,483,389
1892	157,722,913	17,743,664	(a)		2,483,058	21,046,951	2,226,357	2,529,574	1,502,000	1,656,958	9,860,605			7,868,362			94,200	78,408	309,203	10,801,394		24,473,560
1893	161,339,575	19,603,803	(a)		2,953,059	23,800,055	2,544,350	2,644,650	1,556,133	1,732,804	9,866,605			8,571,895			97,018	78,408	393,092	12,359,493		24,473,560
1894	164,850,925	20,603,803	(a)		2,944,284	23,625,616	2,216,231	2,784,650	1,612,505	1,784,509	10,215,974			9,299,672			100,018	97,018	393,092	12,359,493		24,473,560
1895	167,633,803	21,402,311	(a)		2,594,954	24,350,696	2,334,135	2,734,900	1,612,505	1,789,759	10,432,169			9,299,672			95,453	84,150	385,497	13,149,547		24,390,416
1896		21,410,311	90 13		2,594,395	24,650,696	2,334,135	2,734,135	1,691,505	1,789,759	10,885,278	6 11		8,930,572			96,453	84,150	394,481	13,149,547		24,390,416

(a) Not shown.

(b) Calculated on the Assessable Value for the purposes of the Agricultural Rates Act, 1896—that is, the Rateable Value reduced by an amount equal to one-half...

PREVIOUS to 1801 there existed no official return of the population of either England or Scotland; nor was it till 1813 that statesmen had anything more than surmise to guide them respecting Ireland, and the census then taken of that country was far from correct. The estimate formed of the English population at various periods, calculated from the numbers of baptisms, burials, and marriages, was in the years—

1570.....4,160,221	1670.....5,773,646
1600.....4,811,718	1700.....6,045,008
1630.....5,600,517	1750.....6,517,035

During the eighteenth century, manufactures attracted the rural population to towns, in consequence of which many villages were comparatively deserted. The American War and the French Revolutionary War carried off large numbers of men; and this, coupled with the removal of the rustic population, gave rise to the impression that the inhabitants of the country had decreased, and were rapidly decreasing. The first general Census in 1801 dispelled this idea, and showed that, notwithstanding all drawbacks, there were many more people than any one supposed. Since that time named there had been a fresh numbering every ten years, with the following results:—

	1801.	1821.	1831.	1841.	1851.	1861.	1871.	1881.	1891.
Eng. W.	9,334,549	12,289,331	14,156,988	15,914,148	17,927,609	20,066,224	22,712,266	25,974,439	29,002,525
Scotland.	1,608,420	2,091,521	2,364,386	2,620,184	2,888,742	3,062,294	3,360,018	3,735,573	4,025,647
Ireland.	*5,319,867	6,801,827	7,767,401	8,175,124	6,552,385	5,798,967	5,412,377	5,174,836	4,704,750
Islands	*82,810	89,508	103,710	124,040	143,126	143,447	144,638	141,260	147,842
Army, Navy, and Merchant Seamen Abroad.		....		202,954	212,194	250,356	216,080	215,374	224,211
U.K. &c.	16,345,646	21,272,187	24,392,485	27,036,450	27,724,056	29,321,288	31,845,379	35,241,482	38,104,975

* The population of Ireland and the Islands in the British Seas for 1801 is given by estimate.

POPULATION ENUMERATED IN ENGLAND AND WALES, AND SCOTLAND, AT EACH DECENNIAL CENSUS, 1801-91, IRELAND, 1821-91, AND ISLANDS IN THE BRITISH SEAS, 1851-91.‡

ENGLAND AND WALES.	POPULATION.			INCREASE.		FAMILIES.		INHABITED HOUSES.	
	Males.	Females.	Total.	Decennial.	Per Cent(a)	Number.	Persons in each.	Number.	Persons to each.
1801.	4,254,735	4,637,801	8,892,536	—	—	1,896,723	4·69	1,575,923	5·64
1811.	4,873,605	5,290,651	10,164,256	1,271,720	14·00	2,142,147	4·74	1,797,504	5·65
1821.	5,850,319	6,149,917	12,000,236	1,835,980	18·06	2,493,423	4·81	2,088,156	5·75
1831.	6,771,196	7,125,601	13,896,797	1,896,561	15·80	2,911,874	4·77	2,481,544	5·60
1841.	7,777,586	8,136,562	15,914,148	2,017,351	14·48	**	**	2,943,945	5·41
1851.	8,781,225	9,146,384	17,927,609	2,013,461	12·89	3,712,290	4·83	3,278,039	5·47
1861.	9,776,259	10,289,965	20,066,224	2,138,615	11·90	4,491,524	4·47	3,739,505	5·37
1871.	11,058,934	11,653,332	22,712,265	2,646,042	13·18	5,049,016	4·50	4,259,117	5·33
1881.	12,639,902	13,334,537	25,974,439	3,262,173	14·36	5,633,192	4·61	4,831,519	5·38
1891.	14,052,901	14,949,624	29,002,525	3,028,086	11·65	6,131,001	4·73	5,451,497	5·32
SCOTLAND.									
1801.	739,091	869,329	1,608,420	—	—	364,079	4·41	294,553	5·46
1811.	826,296	979,568	1,805,864	197,444	12·27	402,068	4·49	304,093	5·93
1821.	982,623	1,108,898	2,091,521	285,657	15·82	447,960	4·66	341,474	6·12
1831.	1,114,456	1,249,930	2,364,386	272,865	13·04	502,301	4·70	369,393	6·40
1841.	1,241,862	1,378,322	2,620,184	255,798	10·82	550,428	4·76	502,852	5·21
1851.	1,375,479	1,513,263	2,888,742	268,558	10·25	600,098	4·81	370,308	7·80
1861.	1,449,848	1,612,446	3,062,294	173,552	6·00	678,584	4·51	393,220	7·78
1871.	1,603,141	1,756,875	3,360,018	297,724	9·72	742,694	4·52	412,185	8·02
1881.	1,799,475	1,936,098	3,735,573	375,555	11·18	812,712	4·60	739,005	5·05
1891.	1,942,717	2,082,930	4,025,647	290,074	7·77	876,089	4·59	817,568	4·92
IRELAND.									
1821.	3,341,926	3,459,901	6,801,827	—	—	1,312,032	5·18	1,142,602	5·95
1831.	3,794,880	3,972,521	7,767,401	965,574	14·19	1,385,066	5·61	1,249,816	6·21
1841.	4,019,576	4,155,548	8,175,124	407,723	5·25	1,472,739	5·55	1,328,839	6·15
1851.	3,190,630	3,361,755	6,552,385	†1,622,739	+19·85	1,204,319	5·44	1,046,223	6·28
1861.	2,837,370	2,961,597	5,798,967	†753,418	+11·50	1,128,300	5·14	995,156	5·83
1871.	2,639,753	2,772,624	5,412,377	†386,590	+6·67	1,071,494	5·04	961,380	5·63
1881.	2,533,277	2,641,559	5,174,836	†237,541	+4·39	995,074	5·20	914,108	5·66
1891.	2,318,953	2,385,797	4,704,750	†470,086	+9·08	932,113	5·05	870,578	5·40
ISLANDS.									
1851.	66,854	76,272	143,126	—	—			21,845	6·55
1861.	66,140	77,307	143,447	321	0·22	31,530	4·55	23,012	6·23
1871.	66,222	78,416	144,638	1,191	0·83	—	—	23,982	6·02
1881.	66,081	75,179	141,260	†3,378	+2·34	—	—	24,197	5·84
1891.	69,555	78,287	147,842	6,582	4·66	—	—	25,824	5·72

(a) These rates have been corrected for the varying length of the intercensal periods.
‡ Exclusive of the Army, Navy, and Merchant Seamen Abroad, who numbered in 1801, 442,013; in 1811, 502,550; in 1821, 289,095; in 1831, 260,191; in 1841, 202,954; in 1851, 212,194; in 1861, 250,356; in 1871, 216,080; in 1881, 215,374; and in 1891, 224,211.   ** Incorrectly taken.   † Decrease.

Briefly the Census of 1891 showed an increase of 3,028,086 persons and 619,978 inhabited houses in England and Wales; in Scotland, increases of 290,074 and 78,563; in the Channel Islands and Man, an increase of 6,582 persons and of 1,627 houses; but in Ireland a decrease of 470,086 persons (or 62,961 families) and 43,530 inhabited houses; giving, after these deductions an increase of 2,854,656 persons and 656,638 inhabited houses.

THE history of canals in England dates from the time of the Romans, who constructed the Caer Dyke, 40 miles in length, connecting the rivers Nene and Witham, and the Foss Dyke, 11 miles which is still navigable. A series of Acts regulating the navigation of the Thames runs from the year 1423, of the Lea from 1424, and of the Severn from 1503. In the year 1539 the Corporation of Exeter obtained an Act under which a canal was constructed 3 miles in length, parallel to the river, but subject to the tide; this was lengthened in 1625, and again in 1820, the Act for the present ship-canal being obtained in 1829. It was, however, not till the introduction of locks in the 17th century, that canal development became possible; in 1625 an Act for rendering the rivers Aire and Calder navigable was rejected, but passed in 1699, the tolls being from May 1 to October 1, 10s. per ton, and from October 1 to May 1, 16s. per ton for the entire distance between Leeds and Wakefield. In 1737 powers were obtained for the construction of the Bridgewater canal, but lapsed; the work being finally carried out by the celebrated Duke of Bridgewater, and his engineer, James Brindley, under an Act of 1759, out of the Duke's private means. It was said to have cost £220,000, and was extraordinarily successful, her revenue it produced in the early part of this century being estimated at £130,000. The canal is now the property of the Manchester Ship Canal Company. The Trent and Mersey, or Grand Trunk canal, running across England, and connecting Liverpool with Nottingham and Hull, was commenced in 1766; in 1847 it was purchased by the North Staffordshire railway company. A period of canal enterprise followed the success of these undertakings, and by the year 1800 more than 100 canal and navigation Acts had been passed. It is noteworthy that prior to 1845, canal companies merely provided the waterway, and did not act as carriers; in that year, to meet growing railway competition, an Act was passed to enable canal companies to become carriers, and two years afterwards they were given power to borrow money for such purposes. Many companies availed themselves of these powers; but few now exercise them.

Prior to 1845 canals were subject to no general legislation, but were regulated by the provisions of their private Acts. In that year, besides the Act referred to above, an Act was passed giving to canal companies the same power of varying their tolls as possessed by railway companies. This was the era of railway and canal amalgamations, there being in 1846 upwards of 200 Bills containing such provisions. The Railway and Canal Traffic Act, 1854, aimed at checking the throttling of canals by the railway interest, and required companies to make arrangements to afford all reasonable facilities for receiving and forwarding traffic, and an Act of 1858, at preventing, without legislative sanction, the virtual amalgamation of canals with railways, which had been going on under the name of leases of independent canals by railway companies, who were also canal companies by virtue of previous purchases of canals. In 1873 the Railway Commission was created; the Act also providing that no agreement between a canal company and a railway company, by which a railway would obtain control over a canal, shall have any validity unless it is approved by the Railway Commissioners; and that where any canal is already the property of a railway company, or managed by a railway company, such company shall be required to keep it in good navigable condition. The Canal-Boats Acts of 1877 and 1884 provide for the registration of boats by the rural sanitary authority, the Local Government Board is also compelled to appoint inspectors of boats, with powers similar to those of poor-law inspectors. The last, and most important piece of legislation affecting canals, is the Railway and Canal Traffic Act of 1888. Its principal provisions are: the establishment of a new Railway and Canal Commission, consisting of two appointed and three ex-officio Commissioners (see p. 177), having jurisdiction as to the legality rates, power to order such reasonable facilities for traffic as may be required in the interest of the public, and under certain limitations, to fix through rates. Under this provision a uniform classification of merchandise, similar to that adopted for railways, has been fixed, and uniform tolls and rates (with some exceptions for special circumstances), which abrogate the varied charges hitherto made by canal companies under their private Acts. These came into operation on January 1, 1895. The following table shows the general scale of maximum tolls, rates, and wharfage charges for traffic in classes A and B of the classification, which include a very large proportion of the traffic carried on canals. The "rate" includes carriage, the "toll" does not.

There are in the United Kingdom 3,287 miles of canal. These figures are based on the return made to the Board of Trade in 1888, since which no official figures have been published; but the inclusion of partially canalised streams and disused canals would bring the mileage to over 4,000. 1,333 miles are owned or controlled by railway companies, and 2,494 miles are owned by 62 companies, having an outstanding capital (including Government grants to Scotch and Irish canals) of £30,545,000. The Manchester Ship Canal Co. owns 77 miles, with a capital of £15,412,000 : 61 companies therefore own 2,417 miles, or 40 miles each, and have a capital of £15,133,000, not including sums spent out of revenue on capital account, which would bring the capital of the free canals, excluding the Manchester Ship Canal, to considerably over £20,000,000. The capacity of inland canals is governed by that of the locks, which vary from 220 ft. long, 42 ft. wide, and 15 ft. deep, to 50 ft. long, 7 ft. wide, and 3½ ft. deep.

The Manchester Ship Canal is now excavated throughout to a depth of 26 ft.; the large docks

	Classes.	For the first ten miles.	For the next ten miles.	For the next ten miles.	For the remainder of the distance.	Maximum wharfage charge.
		Per ton per mile. d.	Per ton per mile. d.	Per ton per mile. d.	Per ton per mile. d.	Per ton. d.
Tolls	A & B	0·5	0·45	0·25	0·15	1·5
Rates	{ A	0·9	0·8	0·7	0·6	} 3
	{ B	1·15	1	0·9	0·75	

at Manchester to 26 ft., and the smaller docks to 20 ft. The bottom width is 120 ft., at the curve of the Weaver outfall 140 ft., and at the bend at Runcorn 150 ft.; for a distance of about 2½ miles between Latchford Locks and Partington Coal Basin, the width at present is 90 ft., and from Barton Aqueduct to Manchester Docks (3 miles) 170 ft. The fixed bridges are 75 ft. above the normal water level; but as the headway is necessarily a few feet less when high tides or floods occur, masts should clear the bridges at 70 ft. above the water level. The Manchester Docks are equipped with transit sheds of new design, hydraulic and steam cranes; a range of seven- and four-storied warehouses for cotton storage, and five-storied warehouses for general goods. The dock premises include 45 buildings containing 157 extensive depots. Oil tanks are also erected on the banks of the canal at Manchester and Eccles by various firms for the storage of oil. There is a commodious grain elevator built on the latest American principle capable of storing 40,000 tons grain, also fitted with drying apparatus.

The following canals enable direct communication to be maintained between the Ship Canal and all the inland navigations of the country:—Bridgewater, Leeds & Liverpool, Bolton & Bury, Rochdale, Ashton, Huddersfield, Stockport, Macclesfield, Calder & Hebble, Peak Forest, Aire & Calder, Trent and Mersey, Weaver Navigation, Shropshire Union. The company owns 85½ miles of railway. and is directly connected with the London and North Western, Great Western, Lancashire and Yorkshire, Great Northern, Midland, Great Central, and Cheshire lines.

The works in connection with the restoration of the Thames and Severn canal, from the Thames at Inglesham to Stroud, are completed. The restoration of the Thames Navigation between Oxford and Inglesham will shortly be completed. To facilitate trade between the Midlands and London, the Grand Junction Canal Company are erecting a lift at Foxton, on the Grand Union Canal, to take barges carrying 60 tons. in place of a flight of 10 narrow locks with a rise of 75 ft., this will be opened in the spring. The Grand Junction Canal Company have entered into agreements with the Oxford, Warwick and Neyston, and Warwick and Birmingham Companies, giving the entire control of the tolls between Birmingham and London to the Grand Junction Canal Company. This Company has also acquired control of the through tolls on the Leicester Loughborough, and Erewash Canals, enabling them to quote through rates from the Derbyshire coalfields to the Home Counties and London. The year 1898 has been one of abnormal drought in the East Midland portions of England, whereby inland navigation was seriously affected.

TABLE SHOWING THE MILEAGE, WIDTH OF LOCKS, CAPITAL, DIVIDEND, RECEIPTS, TONNAGE AND EXPENDITURE OF THE PRINCIPAL CANALS IN THE UNITED KINGDOM FOR THE YEAR 1898.

Name of Company.	Miles.	Min. width of Locks.	Total Capital.	Dividend.	Tonnage carried by Company or others.	Receipts from all sources.	Expenditure.
		ft. in.	£	%	Tons.	£	£
*Aire and Calder	93	18 0	2,686,051	—	2,412,051	276,697	160,399¶
†Birmingham	159	7 2	3,551,946	4	8,627,074	217,065	88,843
Coventry	33	7 2	50,000	9	381,740	—	—
*Grand (Ireland)§	361	13 6	665,900	4	—	84,000	62,000
Grand Junction	190	7 3	1,303,700	4	1,620,552	100,?05	51,171
Lee Conservancy Board	28	13 3	183,132	4	500,000	21,650	13,025
*Leeds and Liverpool	141	14 10½	1,912,832	2⅝	2,324,963	164,392	114,250
Manchester Ship§	35½	65 0	15,412,000	Nil	2,065,815	205,701	186,550
*Bridgewater§	42	14 9			2,378,186	281,402	239,333
North Metrop. (Regent's)	10¾	14 6	1,778,895	2⅛	1,041,506	84,992	40,973
*Rochdale	35	14 2	Loan 9,000 Deb. 48,000 Ord. 481,355	3½ 3½ 1	613,806	57,190	51,143
Sharpness New Docks &	16	60 0	1,249,500	1	1,000,000	73,311	24,763
Gloucester & Birmingham	37	7 1					
*Shropshire Union	200½	6 11	1,294,271	Leased by L. & N.W.R.		183,201	183,030
Staffordshire & Worcestersh.	51	7 0	Deb. 95,484 Ord. 210,000	3½ 3½	766,752	17,449	8,449
‡Trent and Mersey	119	7 4	1,461,672	4¼	1,215,540	48,866	33,346
Warwick and Birmingham	22½	7 2	150,000	2¾	354,022	10,022	5,537
Warwick and Napton	14¼	7 2	98,000	1¼	196,842	3,804	2,379
Weaver	20¾	42 0	220,308	Surplus paid to Co. of Chester	1,234,205	44,875	23,942
Totals§	1,610		32,635,140		26,439,062	1,856,594	1,271,881

* These companies are carriers.
† Railway controlled—dividend guaranteed by L. & N. W. R.
‡ Railway owned—purchased by North Staffordshire R. for £1,170,000 5% preference stock.
¶ Exclusive of Interest on Loans.
§ 1897 figures only.

Perpetual Calendar.

By H. F. L. MEYER.

EXPLANATIONS.

The old style ended in Italy on Oct. 4, 1582, and the new style began on Oct. 15, 1582; but in England the old style ended on Sept. 2, 1752, and the new style commenced on the following day, that day being called Sept. 14, 1752. Thus in that year the dates from Sept. 3 to Sept. 13 did not exist. In most other countries the change took place between 1582 and 1752, but Greece, Russia, and the Balkan States still adhere to the old style.

Examples:—To find the day of the week for 17 Nov., 1247. Under the year 47 in the line of the century 1900 stands Tu; take Tu above Nov., and in this line, over the 17th day, stands = Sunday.

On what day of the week was April 7, 1800? The letter for the century is W, which for Apr. stands in the second column of the central table, and in this line stands M for the 7th.

When will June 6 be on a Monday? The 6th day shows the M in a line, which for June gives Sa, and Sa for 1800 shows the year 98, and for 1900 the years 4, 10, 21, &c.

LEAP YEARS.

The years in heavier type are leap years, for which the two months January and February must be used. Examples below.

TABLE OF YEARS.

1	2	3	...	4	5	6
7	...	8	9	10	11	...
12	13	14	15	...	16	17
18	19	...	20	21	22	23
...	24	25	26	27	...	28
29	30	31	...	32	33	34
35	...	36	37	38	39	...
40	41	42	43	...	44	45
46	47	...	48	49	50	51
...	52	53	54	55	...	56
57	58	59	...	60	61	62
63	...	64	65	66	67	...
68	69	70	71	...	72	73
74	75	...	76	77	78	79
...	80	81	82	83	...	84
85	86	87	...	88	89	90
91	...	92	93	94	95	...
96	97	98	99	...	...	00

CENTURIES.

OLD STYLE.			NEW STYLE.									
...	700	1400	...	1700	2100	Sa	Su	M	Tu	W	Th	F
100	800	1500	...	...	...	F	Sa	Su	M	Tu	W	Th
200	900	1600	...	1800	2200	Th	F	Sa	Su	M	Tu	W
300	1000	1700	...	...	...	W	Th	F	Sa	Su	M	Tu
400	1100	...	1500	1900	2300	Tu	W	Th	F	Sa	Su	M
500	1200	...	1600	2000	2400	M	Tu	W	Th	F	Sa	Su
600	1300	...	...	...	...	Su	M	Tu	W	Th	F	Sa

1	2	3	4	5	6	7
8	9	10	11	12	13	14
15	16	17	18	19	20	21
22	23	24	25	26	27	28
29	30	31	...	...	...	...
Jan. 31 days	Jan. 31	...	...	Feb. 28	Feb. 29	...
...	Apr. 30	Sep. 30	Jun. 30	Mar. 31	Aug. 31	May 31
Oct. 31	Jul. 31	Dec. 31	...	Nov. 30	...	...

Examples for Leap Years.

When will Jan. 25 be on a Friday? The 25th day shows the F in the sixth line above it, and in this horizontal line stands Tu for Jan. and W for Jan. Now Tu for 1800 gave the year 95, and gives for 1900 the years 1, 7, 18, &c., and W is for the leap years in 1900, which are 24, 52, and 80.

In what years will Jan. 1 fall on a Sunday? The 1st day gives the Su for Jan. and Jan. in the 7th line of the week days, and these Su and M for 1800 show the year 99, and for 1900 the years 5, 11, 22, 28, 33, &c.

For further examples see the next column.

JOSEPH WHITAKER, F.S.A., was born on 4 May, 1820, and died 15 May, 1895. In the line of 1800, under the year 20, stands Su, and May shows the Su in a line which for the 4th has Thursday. 1895 began on a Tu, and the Tu above May has in that line a W for the 15th.

The first day of our era, the 1st January of the year 1 was a Saturday. The letter for the year 8 is M, therefore the 26 July of that year was a Thursday. The letter for 300 is Tu, therefore we use Tu for any of the months in that year, and find the 4 FEB. to be a Thursday. 1100 has M, 1101 has Tu, thus the 3 Aug. 1101 was a Saturday. February has 5 Sundays in the leap years 1824, 1852, 1880, 1920, 1948, 1976, &c. 1901, the first year of the next century, will have five Sundays in Mar., June, Sept. and Dec. There are 53 Sundays in 1899, 1905, 1911, 1916, &c. A week day with a fixed date is repeated at intervals of 5, 6, or 11 years, but with the leap day at 12, 28, or 40 years.

1900 is not a leap year, for it was found in the sixteenth century that three leap days must be omitted in every four centuries, since the length of the year is not 365d. 6h., but 365d. 5h. 48m. 46s., and it was decided that the secular years 1700·, 1800, and 1900 should be common years, but 2000 a leap year.

The Russian date "Dec. $\frac{7}{19}$ 1890," means the Friday which was the 7th in Russia and the 19th in England. The historical English date "Jan. 30, 1648-9" shows the old style year 1648, and the new style 1649, for the year 1648 ended on March 24.

The Solar year of 365 days could be divided into 13 months of 28 days each (excepting the last month, which would have 29, or in leap year 30), and the commencement of the year on the shortest day would make the calendar more consistent with astronomical events. The 1st, 8th, 15th, and 22nd days of each month would be on a certain day of the week. By this calendar the 1st day of 1900 was a Thursday (the 21 Dec., 1899), and the next leap day, that of 1904, would be the 30th of the 13th month (Tuesday the 20 Dec.).

Historical notes, references to foreign calendars, &c., appeared on pages 670 to 672 in the Almanack of 1897.

WE have been supplied with the following information by "Lloyd's Register of British and Foreign Shipping":—

MERCHANT AND OTHER VESSELS (not Warships) LAUNCHED IN THE UNITED KINGDOM DURING RECENT YEARS.

Year.	No.	Gross Tonnage.
1891	822	1,130,816
1892	681	1,109,950
1893	536	836,383
1894	614	1,046,508
1895	579	950,967
1896	696	1,159,751
1897	591	952,486
*1898	761	1,367,570

* In addition, there were launched in the United Kingdom, during 1898, 41 Warships of 191,555 tons displacement, of which 28 of 140,120 tons were for the British Government.

Of the merchant steamers (744 in all) launched in the United Kingdom during 1898, 4 vessels were over 10,000 tons, the largest being the "Afric" and "Medic," each 11,850 tons ; 15 were between 7,000 and 10,000 ; 64 were between 4,000 and 7,000 each ; and 289 were between 1,000 and 4,000 tons.

Except the "Inverclyde" of 1,634 tons gross, no sailing vessel of considerable size has been launched in the United Kingdom during 1898.

MERCHANT AND OTHER VESSELS (not Warships) UNDER CONSTRUCTION IN THE UNITED KINGDOM AT VARIOUS DATES. (Vessels not to be classed by Lloyd's Register are also included.)

30th September.	No.	Gross Tonnage.
1885	339	422,574
1886	255	349,120
1887	249	394,340
1888	400	698,995
1889	521	882,749
1890	406	552,248
1891	475	702,114
1892	385	678,780
1893	326	616,560
1894	327	653,331
1895	356	716,575
1896	355	659,641
1897	455	884,336
1898	598	1,354,250
1899	558	1,347,549

DESCRIPTION OF VESSELS BUILDING IN THE UNITED KINGDOM IN 1875 AND 1899 RESPECTIVELY.

Date.	STEEL.				IRON.				WOOD.				TOTAL.			
	STEAM.		SAIL.		STEAM.		SAIL.		STEAM.		SAIL.		STEAM.		SAIL.	
	No.	Tons Gross.	No.	Tons Gross.	No.	Tons Gross.	No.	Tons Gross.	No.	Tons Gross.	No.	Tons Gross.	No.	Tons Gross.	No.	Tons Gross.
30 Sept. 1875	...	...	...	...	126	157,466	114	106,521	6	1,065	203	51,122	132	158,531	317	157,643
30 Sept. 1899	471	1,331,215	9	3,620	61	11,060	1	110	1	110	16	1,544	533	1,342,385	25	5,164

These figures show that the average size of vessels built at the present time is nearly 3½ times that of vessels built twenty-four years ago. Then, steel was not used for shipbuilding purposes; now, it has all but supplanted iron. Then, the tonnage in hand was equally divided between steamers and sailing vessels; now, the proportion of sailing to steam tonnage is insignificant.

MERCHANT AND OTHER VESSELS (not Warships) LAUNCHED IN EACH OF THE PRINCIPAL SHIP-BUILDING DISTRICTS OF THE UNITED KINGDOM DURING 1898.

DISTRICT.	Steam.		Sail.	
	No.	Gross Tons.	No.	Gross Tons.
Barrow, &c.	10	15,696	2	300
Belfast, &c.	16	119,526	...	...
Clyde	231	389,340	2	1,965
Mersey	7	2,201	1	180
Tees, &c.	93	265,963	2	557
Tyne	120	238,551	...	...
Wear	84	258,754	...	...

OWNERSHIP OF MERCHANT AND OTHER VESSELS (not Warships) LAUNCHED IN THE UNITED KINGDOM DURING 1898.

Where Owned.	No.	Gross Tons.
United Kingdom	614	1,061,642
British Colonies	12	19,022
Denmark	22	44,691
France	10	10,972
Germany	9	37,045
Holland	17	26,654
Japan	7	30,191
Norway	16	44,338
Russia	24	38,330
Other Countries	30	54,685
TOTAL LAUNCHED	761	1,367,570

MERCHANT AND OTHER VESSELS (not Warships), OF 100 TONS AND UPWARDS, BUILT ABROAD DURING 1898, ACCORDING TO LLOYD'S REGISTER BOOK.

COUNTRY.	Steam.		Sail.		COUNTRY.	Steam.		Sail.	
	No.	Gross Tons.	No.	Net Tons.		No.	Gross Tons.	No.	Net Tons.
Austro-Hung.	9	5,365	...	...	Norway	25	21,552	4	2,034
*British Colonies	18	5,332	25	4,247	Russia	1	228	14	2,910
Denmark	11	9,176	9	1,353	Sweden	18	5,383	4	651
France	18	32,632	23	20,851	*U.S. of America	84	107,785	56	61,411
Germany	72	130,667	11	5,519	Other Countries	1	102	7	1,305
Holland & Belg.	16	15,098	12	4,764					
Italy	12	24,224	8	2,582	TOTAL	302	370,151	241	117,440
Japan	17	12,599	68	9,813	* Including steel vessels built on the Great Lakes.				

Shipping Owned in each Country of the World.

(Extracted from "Lloyd's Register of British and Foreign Shipping," 1899-1900.)

NUMBER, TONNAGE, AND DESCRIPTION OF VESSELS OF 100 TONS AND UPWARDS.

FLAG	STEAMERS								SAILING VESSELS								STEAMERS AND SAILING VESSELS	
	Wood & Comp.		Iron		Steel		Total		Wood and Comp.		Iron		Steel		Total			
	No.	Gross Tons	No.	Gross Tons	No.	Gross Tons	No.	Gross Tons	No.	Net Tons	No.	Net Tons	No.	Net Tons	No.	Net Tons	No.	Tons
British { United Kingdom	122	21,965	2,911	2,633,093	3,887	8,431,183	6,920	11,086,241	811	153,763	749	902,349	493	784,571	2,053	1,840,683	8,973	12,926,924
{ Colonies	275	76,791	342	226,926	300	329,189	917	633,006	1,039	379,300	54	35,457	15	13,821	1,108	428,578	2,025	1,061,584
Total	397	98,756	3,253	2,860,019	4,187	8,760,372	7,837	11,719,247	1,850	533,063	803	937,806	508	798,392	3,161	2,265,261	10,998	13,988,508
America (United States)	255	161,198	244	385,292	322	689,818	821	1,236,308	2,101	1,067,077	20	7,850	68	131,612	2,189	1,229,075	3,010	2,465,397
Argentine	4	915	44	26,451	47	31,996	95	59,365	64	16,804	20	7,850	19	4,649	103	29,303	198	88,668
Austro-Hungary	4	478	84	128,011	115	216,196	203	344,685	67	28,839	5	4,007	2	1,425	74	35,729	277	380,414
Belgian	4	454	56	64,016	53	86,952	113	151,422		426						420	113	151,842
Brazilian	10	3,630	70	47,477	19		99	141,062	112	28,898	7	4,007			119	32,905	347	273,967
Chilian			28	27,243			47	141,657	82	47,008	8	8,830			90	55,838	137	197,495
Chinese	3	2,376	17	22,999			35	64,558		573						573	49	65,131
Danish	7	1,961	161	132,441	192	268,936	361	403,333	361	65,826	48	7,149			436	108,573	796	511,958
Dutch	7	1,741	69	122,023	157	265,489	263	389,253	59	44,284	59				118	66,356	381	455,609
French	11	2,054	363	512,327	260	482,851	639	997,235	410	75,230	61	51,028	54	118,578	543	244,856	1,189	1,242,091
German	7	889	407	348,371	722	1,597,472	1,133	1,945,732	201	104,849	177	186,613	165	215,140	543	506,602	1,676	2,453,334
*Greek	4		68	62,669	56		128	155,598	273		6	7,024				78,045	404	233,643
Hawaiian	5	1,214	1	993	6		17	16,218		887						20,635	38	36,853
Italian	14	5,194	218	319,224	95	125,127	282	445,565	775	334,067	60	60,253	33	35,966	386	430,286	1,150	875,851
Japanese	258	59,593	124	172,367	339	241,744	477	473,704	363	58,732	1			945		59,677	841	533,381
Norwegian	99	35,832	351	282,097	329	419,493	779	731,414	1,567	777,699	142	135,279	40	43,840	1,749	956,818	2,528	1,594,239
Peruvian	2	221			2	2,769	45	4,869	33	9,056	1	761	1		34	9,817	37	14,686
Portuguese	2		22	18,069	21	33,961	17	57,271	119	35,135	11	9,167		185	131	44,497	177	101,778
*Roumanian			1	1,493	11	15,929	17	17,413		65					3	656	20	18,069
*Russian	39	4,731	243	98,775	252	289,479	438	392,935	732	215,298	25	29,837	4	5,407	76	250,544	1,218	643,527
Spanish	124	13,314	341	229,763	155	302,956	643	537,840	260	69,337	7	451	25	1,257	252	71,045	701	608,885
Swedish	341	25,785	83	23,434	177	125,024	643	380,572	736	202,356	25	19,099	5	3,964	766	225,419	1,408	665,991
*Turkish	83	5,081	2	705	33	9,338	143	97,743	170	48,810	1	102			170	48,810	313	140,553
Uruguayan	9	2,226	37	23,171	14	9,389	16	10,455	16	3,011	1		1	121	18	3,234	35	13,702
Other Countries	5	374			41	19,835	87	45,225	58	16,277	1	493			59	16,770	145	61,995
Total	1,315	429,122	5,502	6,194,102	7,507	14,254,532	15,334	20,877,746	10,417	3,843,257	1,439	1,532,511	1,000	1,421,014	12,856	6,795,782	28,180	27,673,528

* Note.—In the absence of satisfactory information, the records of numerous small sailing vessels (belonging chiefly to Greece, Turkey, Southern Russia, and the Dutch East Indies), have been omitted from the current edition of Lloyd's Register Book.

IN the early part of the 18th century the inventors were numerous who propounded schemes for applying steam-power to vessels to be run upon rivers and canals. Denis Papin, who made improvements in the steam engine—then in a crude state—fitted one to drive the paddle-wheels of a small boat on the river Fulda in 1707; Jonathan Hulls in 1736 patented designs embodying features similar to the modern paddle boat. For nearly 50 years little progress was made, but in 1769 James Watt patented a double-acting side-lever engine, the first one to be of any real service in the development of steam navigation.

After the Marquis of Jouffroy's attempts in 1783 came experiments independently carried on in America by James Rumsey and Robert Fitch; the former, in 1785, drove a boat along at 4 miles an hour by a jet of water steam-pumped through a pipe at the stern, an idea subsequently shelved as unsound. Fitch, in 1785, was trying steam-paddles, and fitted a boat on the Delaware, 1787, with a series of single canoe-paddles worked by a moving beam, which was America's earliest steamboat; another one in 1790 travelled for a short time at 7 miles an hour between Philadelphia and Burlington. Subsequent trials, including a propeller to a model, led to no practical results, and Fitch retired disgusted, his well-founded prophecies as to the future of steam navigation being only ridiculed. Miller of Edinburgh was experimenting in 1787 with primitive manual machinery, and in conjunction with Symington, the inventor of a locomotive for road purposes, an engine was fitted to a double-hull boat in 1788, developing a speed of 5 miles an hour, increased to 7 when the paddle-wheel was tried over the stern of a larger boat. When Miller abandoned these costly trials, Symington seized an opportunity to produce the *Charlotte Dundas* for Lord Dundas—which gave effect in part to Jonathan Hulls' ideas, hitherto untried—intended for towing barges on the Forth and Clyde canal, but she rusted away an idle spectacle, the proprietors in spite of satisfactory trials, fearing injury to their canal banks. The first sea voyage by steamer occurred two years later, when J. C. Stephens, with his screw boat *Phœnix*, fitted with a Watt's engine and tubular boiler, journeyed at 4 miles an hour from Hoboken to the Delaware. Robert Fulton and Henry Bell inspected the *Charlotte Dundas*. Fulton returned to America in 1806, having ordered a similar engine from Boulton and Watt for the *Clermont*, which he and Livingston built in 1807, her first trip from Albany to New York taking 32 hours; she was 133 × 18 × 7, the first passenger steamer continuously and profitably employed.

In 1809 the *Accommodation* was on the St. Lawrence, and in 1812 a steam-ferry connected New York with New Jersey, one year before the ferry *Etna* appeared at Liverpool. In 1814 Fulton built a frigate for the U. S. Government, but she only steamed 4 miles an hour. The *Washington*, in 1815, was the first to steam up as well as down the strong-running Mississippi, the side-wheeler *Ontario* being built on the Lakes, 1816, 25 years before the *Vandalia* intro-

duced the propeller there. The year 1819 brought a small instalment of the fulfilment of Fitch's predictions, when Scarborough and Isaacs purchased a sailing ship on the stocks at New York, and fitted her with auxiliary paddle-wheels; she sailed from Savannah, which she was called after, but only steamed 80 hours during her 30 days passage, which terminated at Liverpool, June 20th.

Bell, in Scotland—failing government support here or in America—had the *Comet* built in 1812, a twin-boat 25 feet long, going 5 miles an hour, with two paddle-wheels each side, increased to 6 miles with a new engine and only one pair of paddles. She ran between Glasgow and Helensburgh, the first passenger steamer regularly employed in Europe. The South Kensington Museum contains her engines, set up there by John Robertson, her maker. The *Marjory* in 1814 plied on the Thames, followed next year by the up-river steamer *Richmond*; the *Regent* starting in 1816 between London and Margate. In 1818 Denny built the *Rob Roy*, 90 tons, for Napier of Glasgow, who made her engines to run between Glasgow and Belfast, the first sea-trading steamer in the world. In 1819 the *Talbot*, 156 tons, inaugurated the Holyhead-Dublin steam service, when the passages of the sailing cutters averaged 20 hours. The *James Watt*, 448 tons, between Glasgow and Leith, was in 1822 the biggest steamer afloat, which year Napier got capitalists to build the *Robert Burns* and other steamers for the Liverpool and Glasgow trade.

Iron first superseded wood for building light inland craft; the *Vulcan* in 1818 being built on a Scotch canal. The *Aaron Manby* steamer was called after her designer, who built her at Tipton in 1821. The *Aglaia* appeared on the Clyde, and *Prince Albert* on the Tyne in 1832, in which year Laird and Co. built the *Elburkah* of iron for an expedition up the Niger; but ridiculous and imaginary objections long retarded its adoption for sea-going vessels. In 1837 the largest iron vessel was the *Rainbow*, 185 feet long, belonging to the General Steam Navigation Company.

1821 witnessed the birth in England of the railway system, which tended so much to promote trade, wealth, and general advancement. The Stockton and Darlington Railway was opened in 1825, a year bracketed with the names of George Stephenson and his famous locomotive *Rocket*. Vested interests hindered the movement until after 1840, when a railway mania succeeded the period of prejudice, and construction in all directions was hurried forward. With the introduction of the "iron horse" the General Steam Navigation Company arose to champion the adoption of steam; ocean trade was then carried on with sailing ships, mostly under 500 tons each, all the steamboats in the United Kingdom only numbering 109. The comprehensive area of the *Navy Co.'s* original programme is indicated by its title; its prospectus, which made a successful appearance in 1824, included amongst many influential names, Mr. John Hall, whose boats were trading between London and Hull, and Mr. Brocklebank, who was running the diminutive *Eagle* between London and Margate. The national benefits calculated to result from steam power, enabling vessels to enter and quit harbours regardless of wind and tide, were emphasised by the Directors, as well as the prospects of connecting the remotest parts of the earth, but the Company was too fully engaged with business near at hand to carry out that portion of the founder's views. The first operations were attended with remarkably profitable results; safer and quicker communications were established between the Capital and the Home Ports for passengers and goods in competition with the stage coaches and waggons ashore, and the smacks and "geordies" afloat. The Company soon extended its sphere of usefulness to maintaining express services between London and Continental ports, Her Majesty's mails being carried to Rotterdam and Hamburg long before the railway companies developed into running their own steamships. Queen Victoria and Prince Albert travelled from Scotland in the Company's *Trident*, 1000 tons, and were safely landed at Woolwich on September 30th, 1842.

The origin of the Propeller is lost in history, one, associated with Bernouli, dating back to 1762. Pettit Smith, John Ericsson, and Woodcroft, were the first to attain any success; Smith's culminating in the *Archimedes*, 237 tons, launched in 1838, which reduced the Dover-Calais passage, when tried there, under 2 hours. Commercial results, however, followed Ericsson's efforts. In 1837 he had the *Francis B. Ogden* built by Laird, and towed a vessel 7 miles an hour, and the Admiralty barge at 10 miles; but "my Lords" withheld encouragement, fearing the screw would impede steering. Others did not think so, notably an American, who at once ordered a boat fitted with Ericsson's propeller, named after himself *R. F. Stockton*; she sailed to America, the first iron vessel to cross the Atlantic, and was the first screw steamer ever used there, being employed as a tug-boat. Ericsson fitted a propeller to the U. S. warship *Princetown* in 1839, three years before a screw of an improved type by Woodcroft was used on H. M. S. *Rattler*, built by the Admiralty, 20 years after the first steamboat, the *Comet*, had been constructed in a Royal dockyard.

The earliest Atlantic steamers now claim attention. The first to steam across the Atlantic was the *Royal William*, launched at Wolfe's Cove, Quebec, 1831, her engines being sent from England. In 1833 she went from Pictou, N.S., to Gravesend, arriving Sept. 11th after 22 days' passage. She was bought by the Spanish government, re named *Isabella Segunda*, and was utilised as a warship at Sebastian against the Carlists.

The pioneer steamer from the old world to the new was the Cork-built *Sirius*, chartered by the British and North American Steam Navigation Company, whose vessels hailed from Portsmouth. Leaving Cork, April 5, 1838, she reached New York, April 23, having been compelled to burn everything available. On the same day the *Great Western*, the first specially built for the Atlantic service, paddled in, having left Bristol, April 8th —a wonderfully quick passage of 14½ days. The Great Western Steam Navigation Company patronised Bristol until 1846, and before the Royal Mail Company bought the *Great Western* in 1847 she reduced the westward record to 12 days 18 hours, and the one east to 12 days 7½ hours. In 1839 the company which had despatched the *Sirius* built and sent from Portsmouth, July 12, the *British Queen*, with 600 tons of coal, carrying a crew of 100 and a cargo valued at £1,500,000. After an outward run of 14 days 8 hours, she

made several voyages, but, failing to pay, was sold to the Belgian Government in 1841, which, with the loss the same year of her sister ship *President*—not heard of after leaving New York for Liverpool, March 10th—resulted in the retirement of her owners. A third company, called the Transatlantic Company, had selected Liverpool as their port, and started with the *Royal William*; she was the earliest steamer with watertight compartments, and was the first to cross from Liverpool, July 1838, taking 19 days. The Transatlantic Company built the *Liverpool*, which sailed first voyage, October 20th, 1838; she was eventually acquired by the Peninsular and Oriental Company, who called her the *Great Liverpool*.

The *Royal William* referred to before had been chartered from the City of Dublin Steam Packet Company, now the oldest steamship company in the world. It dates back to 1823, in which year the *Enterprise*, 479 tons, after ten stoppages *en route*, managed to reach Calcutta from London in 113 days. A voyage worth recalling here, by way of contrast, is that of the *City of Venice*, a full rigged ship which in 1867 sailed from the Clyde, over the same course as the *Enterprise*, in 65 days; she belonged to Messrs Geo. Smith & Sons, City Line of Glasgow, established 1840.

Messrs. Bourne & Co., the largest proprietors of the City of Dublin Steam Packet Company, were stage-coach contractors for the conveyance of mails in Ireland, and were instrumental in commencing several Continental trades. The Company was incorporated in 1833, and has carried the mails between Holyhead and Dublin during the whole of Her Majesty's reign.

One of their steamers, the *Royal Tar*, having been chartered to Dom Pedro, and then to the Queen Regent of Spain through their brokers Messrs. Willcox & Anderson, Messrs. Bourne & Co. were induced, in 1836, to put on steamers from Falmouth to Lisbon, which line was started by the *William Faucett*, 206 tons, and represented in London by Willcox & Anderson, the *Iberia* sailing September, 1837, being the first to carry the Peninsular mails. The original capital and directors were largely found by the Irish company, which was thus practically the godfather of the Peninsular and Oriental Company, so-called when the mail services upon this side of Egypt were combined in 1840, under the time-honoured flag of the "P. & O.," which received its charter in 1840.

The failure of the earliest Atlantic companies did not deter the establishment and development of the Cunard Company. Samuel Cunard, its founder, was the agent at Halifax, N.S., of the East India Company, and had been conducting with sailing ships the local services between Boston, Newfoundland, and Bermuda, which brought home to him the need for steam. As a director of the Canadian Company, which owned the first *Royal William*, he speedily made up his mind as to the possibilities and future of the new power, hence was well prepared to act promptly, when the opportune moment arrived for his memorable and successful mission. To the discomfiture and astonishment of the Great Western Company this enterprising gentleman's tender was accepted, which secured the subsidy of £80,000 a year for a monthly Atlantic service of 4 steamers. The gun brigs were thereupon superseded as mail carriers, and a brighter era was auspiciously commenced by the despatch of the *Britannia*, 1,139 tons, on July 4th, 1840.

In 1839, the Royal Mail Steam Packet Company was formed and incorporated by Royal Charter, and undertook the conveyance of mails to the West Indies at a time when a steam passage of even a fortnight's duration was to many a subject of wonder. In 1842 the *Thames*, 1889 tons, began the main line to the West Indies, smaller steamers being built to remain out there, and work the company's inter-colonial branch lines, in connection with the mail boats from Falmouth. Directly the feasibility of maintaining steam services across the Atlantic had been demonstrated, the Pacific Steam Navigation Company was formed to run a service between Panama and Valparaiso for the conveyance of the British mails along the shores of the Pacific, receiving them upon the other side of the Isthmus from the Royal Mail Steam Packet Company, who organised the necessary transport across it with mules and canoes. The Pacific Steam Navigation Co.'s *Chile* and *Peru*, each 700 tons, were sent out through the Straits of Magellan at the close of 1840, and were the first steamers to plough the waters of the Pacific, receiving a public welcome from the inhabitants of Valparaiso.

In 1847 the Pacific Mail Steamship Company was organised as an American line between Oregon and Panama, and the acquisition of California a year later by the United States hastened the necessity for improved communications with the Pacific. 1850 was memorable for the advent of the screw-steamers of Wm. Inman, who commenced his service from Liverpool to Philadelphia with the *City of Glasgow*, 1,600 tons, which had previously been run from Glasgow to New York by her builders, Tod and McGregor; two years later Messrs. Palmer & Co., of Jarrow, equipped the first steamer (a screw collier) with water tanks for ballast.

Here we are compelled to break off our early records, the chief modern developments being outlined briefly in the "Sketches" of the various companies dealt with later on; but Brunel's note-worthy creations, the *Great Britain* and *Great Eastern*, must be recorded.

Great Britain, 322 × 40 × 31, built at Bristol by the Great Western Co., was the first iron screw steamer. Leaving Liverpool Aug. 1845, she completed two Atlantic voyages, stranding upon her third outward passage at Dundrum Bay, 1846. She remained there intact until Aug. 1847, but the disaster necessitated her owners selling her and retiring. She ran in the Australian trade until 1874, long the only steamer on the Cape route: in 1882 was converted into a sailing ship, and soon after into a hulk at the Falkland Isles.

Great Eastern combined the declining paddle-wheel with the dawning propeller systems, but 1,700 horse-power for the former and but 1,000 for the latter, with which she was fitted, afforded nothing like enough power to manage and drive such a vast fabric, the hull of which was 680 feet long and 83 wide. She was begun at Millwall in 1854, and after several costly attempts at launching, floated herself in 1858. After some unremunerative voyages to America, she was in 1865 instrumental in laying the Atlantic cable, and subsequently other ones. She changed hands several times; and after vain efforts to employ the huge failure profitably, once even being tried as a coal hulk at Gibraltar, the leviathan was privately sold for £16,000 in 1887, and broken up after being on exhibition at Birkenhead.

Before the days of steamships the passage from England to the United States was an unknown quantity taking one or two months, but during the period the "side-wheels" were vainly struggling against the "propeller," some homeward runs were made by clippers of the Black Ball and other Lines, of sufficient interest to be chronicled here. The *Red Jacket* in 1854 crossed from New York to the Mersey in 13 days, and the *Lightning* did the passage in a little less time. In 1856 the *Staffordshire* made a run of 14 days, but the *Dreadnought*, 1413 tons, 220 × 45 × 26, eclipsed all previous runs and covered herself with renown in 1862, when she reeled off between Sandy Hook and Queenstown the enduring record of 9 days 17 hours. Mention must also be made of the celebrated clipper *Thermopylæ*, of the Aberdeen Line, between London and Australia, whose owners, Messrs. Geo. Thompson & Co., started business at Aberdeen in 1825. Her maiden voyage, in 1868, of 60 days between London and Melbourne remains the fastest ever known; but the *Thermopylæ* upon her next departure, Jan. 1, 1870, actually came within a few hours of her previous record, thus proving she had carved her name in the book of fame, upon her sailing merits. This swift vessel, built at Aberdeen by Messrs. Walter Hood and Co., was a full-rigged heavily-sparred ship, 991 tons, with a hull like that of a big yacht, 212 × 36 × 20. She travelled 2,000 miles in one week, and logged 380 miles in one day, from which can be formed some idea of her wonderful speed. In 1869 the *Patriarch*, 1,339 tons made for the same owners the record passage of 68 days between London and Sydney. Their ss. *Aberdeen*, built in 1881, was the earliest ocean steamer to demonstrate decisively the superior merits of triple expansion engines; and the favourite steamers of this Line, which follow the tracks of their former "flyers" round the Cape of Good Hope, are happily called after the picturesque packets of by-gone days.

The oldest sailing line is Messrs. Devitt & Moore's, dating back to the despatch of the *Conqueror* in 1836. Of late years this firm have made a speciality of the nautical instruction of youths desirous of becoming officers in the Merchant Service, two fine ships, the *Hesperus*, 1,777 tons, and *Macquarie*, 1867 tons, being arranged for this purpose.

The marvellous progress made by steam navigation can best be realised from the following figures. In 1814 the steamboats of all kinds registered in the United Kingdom amounted to less than 1,000 tons, increased to nearly 8,000 tons by 1820. When the Atlantic steam services were begun in 1838 there were 766 British merchant steamers afloat, which fell just short of 150,000 tons in all. In 1899 the steamship empire-builders of Greater Britain owned about 8,000 vessels, aggregating 12 millions of tons, and the dwindling disciples of time honoured canvas, with their 3,000 ships, swelled the magnificent total with 2½ millions more tons.

Lloyd's invaluable Register of British and Foreign Shipping, established 1834, shows that every other vessel met with upon the high seas flies the British Ensign; and the overwhelming proportions of Britannia's Mercantile Marine were strikingly demonstrated to friends and foes when the Government, in consequence of hostilities with the Transvaal, chartered over 140 vessels to convey an army corps 6,000 miles, with all its animals, munitions and stores, these 650,000 tons being speedily and easily placed at the disposal of the Admiralty, without interruption to maritime commerce, for the largest long-distance expedition on record.

FROM STEAM PACKET TO STEAM PALACE.

(1) Wood Paddle-boats.   (3) Iron Screw Steamers.
(2) Iron   „   (4) Steel „   „   (5) Steel Twin-Screw Steamers.

Date.	Name of Steamer.	Owners.	Remarks.
1833	Royal William ....(1)	Quebec & Halifax S. N. Co.	From Pictou (N.S.), 1st to cross the Atlantic.
1838	Sirius	British and Amer. S. N. Co.	From Cork. 1st departure from U.K.
„	Great Western	Great Western S. N. Co.....	„ Bristol, 1st built for Atlantic.
„	Royal William (2)	Transatlantic SS. Co.	„ Liverpool, 1st departure.
1840	Britannia	Cunard Line	„ Liverpool, 1st carried British Mails.
1849	Atlantic	Collins „	„ New York, 1st carried U.S. Mails.
1854	Canadian	Allan „	„ Glasgow, 1st steamer of Line.
1856	Tempest	Anchor „	„ 1st „ „
„	Borussia	Hamburg-American Line ...	„ Hamburg, 1st „ „
„	Adriatic	Collins „	Last sailing of Line.
1858	Bremen	Norddeutscher Lloyd	From Bremen to New York.
1856	Persia ....(2)	Cunard	First Cunard Iron Paddle Steamer.
1862	Scotia....................	„	Last „ „ „ „
1845	Great Britain.........(3)	Great Western S. N. Co. ...	1st Atlantic Iron Screw Steamer.
1850	City of Glasgow	Inman Line	1st to carry steerage passengers.
1858	GREAT EASTERN	East. & Aust'lian SS Co. ...	Paddle-wheels and propeller.
1868	Italy	National Line	1st Atlantic ss. with comp. engines.
1869	City of Brussels	Inman	1st „ „ steam steering gear.
1871	Oceanic (1st)	White Star Line	1st with mid-ship Saloon, &c.
1873	Pennsylvania	American „	1st sailing of line, to Liverpool.
1874	Britannic	White Star	1st to exceed 5 000 tons. G.E. excepted.
1875	City of Berlin	Inman	1st with Electric light.
1879	Arizona	Guion Line	Water T. Comps. floated her.
1882	Alaska	„ „ (1)	1st "Ocean Greyhound."
1883	Oregon	{ „ „ (1) .... } { Cunard „ (2) }	Sunk outside New York; every one saved by N. D. Lloyd ss. Fulda.
1879	Buenos Ayrean ....(4)	Allan	1st Atlantic Steel Steamer.*
1881	Servia	Cunard	1st Cunard „ „
„	City of Rome	{ Inman (1) } { Anchor (2) .... }	Fitted with three Funnels.
1884	America	National	1st and last express ss. of Line.
	{ Umbria .... } { Etruria .... }	Cunard	1st with 20 knots speed.
1886	Aller	Norddeutscher Lloyd	1st Triple expansion express ss.†
1888	{ City of New York ...(5) } { City of Paris .... }	Inman & International (1) } American Line (2) .... }	1st Twin-Screw Ocean expresses.‡ „ to exceed 10,000 tons.
1889	{ Teutonic .... } { Majestic .... }	White Star	Designed as Mercantile Cruisers.
1890	Furst Bismarck	Hamburg-American	1st under 6½ days from Southampton.
1892	La Touraine	Compagnie Générale Trans. .	Record Havre to New York 6¾ days.
1893	{ Campania .... } { Lucania .... }	Cunard	Lucania: highest day's run 562 kts. L'pool. to N. York records.
1895	{ St. Paul .... } { St. Louis .... }	American	Largest ever built in America.
1897	Kaiser Wilhelm der Grosse	Norddeutscher Lloyd	„ „ „ Germany.
1899	Oceanic	White Star	„ in the World. Balanced engines.
1900	Deutschland (building) ...	Hamburg-American	To be the fastest in the World.

* Union Co. of N. Z.'s Rotomahana 1,763 tons, was 1st Ocean Steel ss., 1879.
† Martello 2,432 tons, of Wilson Line, was first Atlantic cargo Triple expansion ss, 1884.
‡ Notting Hill 3,920 tons, of Twin-Screw Cargo Line, came out so engined, 1881.

REDUCTION OF PASSAGE.				PROGRESS IN LENGTH.			
	Days.		Tons.			Feet.	Tons.
1862.	Under 9 from Q'town. Scotia		3,871	1838	1st to exceed	200 Great Western	1,340
1869.	„ 8 „ „	City of Brussels	3,031	1845	„ „	300 Great Britain..	2,c84
1882.	„ 7 „ „	Alaska	6,400	1871	„ „	400 Oceanic (1)....	3,807
1889.	„ 6 „ „	*City of Paris	10,669	1881	„ „	500 Servia	7,392
1894.	„ 5¾ „ „	Lucania	12,950	1893	„ „	600 Campania	12,952
1897.	„ 6 „ S'ton.	+Kaiser Wilhelm		1899	„ „	700 Oceanic (2).....	17,247
	*Highest day's run 562 knots.	der Grosse.	14,349		Gt. Eastern	680 1858	18,918
	+Record day's run 580 knots.						

Table I.—First 10 in order of gross tonnage of each Fleet, showing sustained sea-speeds.

Owners.	Head Office.	20	19	18	17	16	15	14	13	12	Under 12 knots.	Total.
Hamburg-American Line *	Hamburg		1	1			2		7	6	55	73
Norddeutscher Lloyd †	Bremen	1		3	3	1	9	6	13	15	20	72
British India Steam Nav. Co. & Associated Steamers	London					1	3	3	4	10	87	108
Peninsular and Oriental Steam Navigation Co.	London	2	1	5	6	2	4	14	10	6	6	57
Elder, Dempster & Co.	Liverpool							1	1	7	66	85
Messageries Maritimes	Paris				7	4		1	27	8	15	62
Japan Mail Steamship Co.	Tokio						3	3	20	7	34	67
Ismay, Imrie & Co. (White Star Line) ‡	Liverpool	2			1	1	2	4	7	5	...	23
Thomas Wilson, Sons & Co., Limited	Hull						2	1	13	9	62	87
Navigazione Generale Italiana (Florio Rubattino)	Rome				4	3	1	5	9	12	60	94

* Also one 22-knots boat.   † Also one 22½-knots boat.   ‡ Also one 21-knots boat.

TABLE II.—REMAINDER IN ALPHABETICAL ORDER.

No. of vessels.

Owner	Office	No.	Owner	Office	No.
J. & A. Allan	Glasgow	32	Lamport & Holt	Liverpool	40
Austrian Lloyd	Trieste	68	F. Leyland & Co., Ld.	Liverpool	23
Bessemer SS. Co.	Cleveland, Ohio	25	Maclay & McIntyre	Glasgow	55
A. Bordes & Son	Paris	36	Pacific Steam Navigation Co.	Liverpool	35
Cayzer, Irvine & Co.	Glasgow	42	Royal Mail S. P. Co.	London	26
Chargeurs Réunis	Havre	28	Reading Co.	Philadelphia	59
China Navigation Co., Ld.	London	46	Rickmers Linie	Bremerhaven	19
Compania Trasatlantica	Cadiz	24	R. Ropner & Co.	W. Hartlepool	36
Comp. Gén. Transatlantique	Paris	56	Russian Steam Nav. Co.	Odessa	82
Cunard Steamship Co., Ld.	Liverpool	22	Shaw, Savill & Albion Co., Ld.	London	26
Donald Currie & Co.	London	25	George Smith & Sons	Glasgow	23
Forenede Dampskibs S.	Copenhagen	113	Union Steamship Co., Ld.	London	20
Hansa SS. Co.	Bremen	36	Union SS. Co. of New Zeald.	Dunedin	57
Hamburg S. American Co.	Hamburg	37	James Westoll	Sunderland	38
T. & J. Harrison	Liverpool	29	Watts, Watts & Co.	London	28
Henderson Bros.	Glasgow	28	West India & Pacific SS. Co.	Liverpool	18
Alfred Holt	Liverpool	38	Andrew Weir & Co.	Glasgow	41
Indo-China Navigation Co.	London	32			
International Navigation Co.	New Jersey	20			
Irrawaddy Flotilla Co.	Rangoon	109			
Wm. Johnston & Co., Ltd	Liverpool	25			
James Knott	N'otle.-on-Tne.	41			
Kosmos Co.	Hamburg	25			

The American Steel Barge Co., of New York, with 33 vessels; Robert M. Sloman & Co., of Hamburg, with 30; W. Wilhelmsen, of Norway, with 24; and Thos. Law & Co., of Glasgow, with 27, each own only a few tons less than the smallest Fleet in the above list.

TABLE III.—LARGEST SAILING SHIP OWNERS IN THE WORLD.

Owners.	Ships.	Tonnage	Belonging to.	Name and Tonnage of largest Ship.		Remarks.
A. D. Bordes & Son	37	66,306	Dunkirk	France	3942	
A. Weir & Co.	30	48,105	Glasgow	Cedar Bank	2825	Own 11 Steamers.
Thos. Law & Co.	27	40,350	Glasgow	Dumfriesshire	2522	
R. W. Leyland & Co.	16	33,351	Liverpool	Liverpool	3396	Own 1 Steamer.
B. Wencke & Söhne	16	28,626	Hamburg	Athene	2470	
Macvicar, Marshall & Co.	11	27,495	Liverpool	Dunstaffnage	3317	
F. Laeisz	15	27,402	Hamburg	Potosi	4027	Barque, 5 masts.
Aitken, Lilburn & Co.	17	26,502	Glasgow	Loch Nevis	2131	
Hampton & Bromehead	16	25,314	London	Forth	1829	Late Jas.Nourse (dec.).
P. Iredale & Porter	16	24,791	Liverpool	Mowhan	2873	

TABLE IV.—1898.

SHIPBUILDERS of over 50,000 Tons. In order of out-turn.

		Ships.	Tl. tons
Wm. Gray & Co.	W. Hartlepool	27	72,323
C. S. Swan & Hunter, Ld.	Wallsend	13	68,635
Harland & Wolff, Ld.	Belfast	7	67,993
Armstrong, Whitworth & Co.	Newcastle	15	54,379
Workman, Clark & Co.	Belfast	9	53,475

Russell & Co., of Port Glasgow; Ropner & Son, of Stockton; Palmer's Shipbuilding Co., Ld., of Jarrow; and Thompson & Sons, of Sunderland, each turned out over 40,000 tons.

ENGINEERS EXCEEDING 50,000 I.H.Power. In order of out-put.

		I.H.P.
R. & W. Hawthorn, Leslie & Co.	Newcastle	75,400
Fairfield Shipbuilding Co., Ld.	Govan	74,500
Clydebank Engineering Co., Ld.	Glasgow	72,300
Wallsend Slipway Co.	Newcastle	68,110

Earle's Shipbuilding Co., Ld., of Hull; The Central Marine Engine Works, West Hartlepool; and The North Eastern Marine Engineering Co. Ld., Newcastle, each put out over 40,000 I.H.P.

TABLE V.—LARGEST VESSEL BELONGING TO EACH COUNTRY.

Country.	Ship's Name.	Gross Tons.	Speed.	Owners.
Austria	Erzerzog F. F. ...	5,900	*	Austrian Lloyd.
Belgium	Friesland	6,409	15	Red Star Line.
Brazil	Brazil	2,003	*	Brazilian Lloyd.
Chile	Angamos	3,794	*	Chilian Government.
Denmark	Annam	5,300	*	East Asiatic Co. of Copenhagen.
France	La Loraine	11,220	20	Compagnie Gén. Transatlantique.
Germany	Deutschland	15,500	23½	Hamburg-American Line.
Great Britain	Oceanic	17,247	21	White Star Line.
Greece	Polymitis	3,191	*	A. A. Stathatos.
Holland	Ryndam	12,000	15	Holland-American Line.
Italy	Nord America	4,826	16½	La Veloce Navigazione Italiana.
Japan	Wakasa Maru	6,265	13	Nippon, Yusen, Kaisha K.
Norway	Guernsey	4,415	*	W. Wilhelmsen.
Spain	Alfonso XIII	5,125	16	Compania Trasatlantica.
Sweden	Oscar II.	3,519	*	A. Johnson.
United States	St. Louis	11,629	21	American Line.

* Under 12 knots.

TABLE VI.—VESSELS 10,000 TONS AND OVER. SPEED UNDER 20 KNOTS.

Names of Owners and Steamers.		Speed.	Under 11,000 Tons.	11,000 Tons. to under 12,000 Tons	12,000 Tons. and above.
FOREIGN.—*Hamburg-American Line.*					
Hamburg, Kiantschou		15	2	...	...
Patricia, Pretoria, Pennsylvania, Graf Waldersee		13½	...	...	4
Batavia, Belgravia, Belgia, Brasilia, Bulgaria		12	4	1	...
Norddeutscher Lloyd.					
Bremen Barbarossa. Fried. der Grosse, Königin Luise		15½	4	...	...
Prinzess Irene, König Albert		15	2	...	...
Grosser Kurfurst		14	...	...	1
Main, Rhein		13½	2	...	...
Holland-American Line.					
Statendam, Ryndam *		15	1	...	1
BRITISH.					
Briton, Saxon*	Union Steamship Co.	17½	2	...	...
Bavarian, Tunisian *	Allan Line	16	2	...	...
Ivernia,* Saxonia *	Cunard ,,	15½	...	...	2
Cymric	White Star ,,	15	...	...	1
Winefredan	Leyland ,,	14½	1	...	...
Georgic	White Star ,,	13	1	...	...
Afric, Medic Persic, Runic*, Suevic*	,, ,,	12½	...	5	...
New England	Richards, Mills & Co.	...	...	1	...
¶ N.B.—There are 341 steamers in the World over 5,000 tons each, of which 252 are British, 91 more are building in this country, 16 being not less than 10,000 tons each.	American Line 6*	...	...	...	...
	Austrian Lloyd 1*	...	...	...	...
	Pacific Mail SS. Co. 2*	...	...	...	...
	Richards, Mills & Co. 2*	...	...	...	...
	Totals		21	7	9

* Building.

TABLE VII.—OCEAN STEAMERS. 16 KNOTS AND OVER. Number belonging to each Country.

Country.	20 knots & above.	19 knots.	18½ kts.	18 knots.	17½ kts.	17 knots.	16 knots.	Total.
Austria	...	...	...	...	...	...	2	2
France	2	1	...	...	12	4	5	24
Germany	4	1	3	1	1	1	1	12
Great Britain	9	1	4	6	9	13	24	66
Italy	...	...	...	...	...	2	4	6
Japan	...	...	...	...	...	3	...	3
Russia	1	3	...	...	...	...	...	4
Spain	...	...	...	...	...	...	2	2
United States	4	...	...	...	...	2	6	12
Total	20	6	7	7	22	25	44	131

TABLE VIII.—SHORT TRIP STEAMERS (British and Foreign).   20 KNOTS AND OVER.

British Boats		Owners.
* Connaught, Leinster, Munster, Ulster all 23½ knots	4	City of Dublin Steam Packet Co.
Empress Queen 22, Prince of Wales 21, Queen Victoria 21	3	Isle of Man Steam Packet Co.
Waverley	1	North British Steam Packet Co.
France 21½, Sussex 21¼, Tamise 21¼, Manche 21¼ ...	4	London B. & S. C. Railway.
Banshee 21, Cambria	2	London & North-Western Railway.
Ibex, Reindeer, Roebuck	3	Great Western Railway.
Britannia, Cambria, Westward Ho	3	P. A. Campbell, Ltd.
La Marguerite 20½, Royal Sovereign	2	Fairfield S. & E. Co., Ltd.
Eagle	1	General Steam Navigation Co.
Total	23	
Foreign Boats.		
Belgian Government, 3, 22 kts.; 3, 21 kts.	6	Dover—Ostend Service.
Cie. des Chemins de Fer du Nord of France	2	Dover—Calais Service.
Zeeland Steamship Co. of Holland.....................	3	Queenborough—Flushing Service.
Total	11	

*The four fastest, short trip Steamers in the World.

TABLE IX.—OCEAN STEAMERS.   20 KNOTS AND OVER.   In order of Tonnage.

Built in	Names.	Owners.	Gross Tons.	Dimensions.	Speed.	Builders.
1899	Oceanic	White Star	17,247	685×68×44	21	Harland & W.
1900	Deutschland	Ham-American	16,000	666×67×44	23½	Stettin V. Co.
1897	Kaiser Wilhelm der Grosse	N. D. Lloyd............	14,349	627×66×35	22½	Stettin V. Co.
1893	Campania......................	Cunard	12,952	601×65×37	22	Fairfield.
1893	Lucania........................	"	12,950			
1897	Kaiser Friederich	Ham-American	12,480	581×63×44	22	Schichau.
1895	St. Louis......................	American	11,629	535×63×37	21	Cramp & Sons.
1895	St. Paul........................					
1900	La Lorraine..................	Com. Gén. Trans. ...	11,200	563×60×35	20	Owners.
1900	La Savoie......................					
1888	New York......................	American	10,674	527×63×39	20	Clydebank.
1889	Paris	"	10,669			
1889	Teutonic	White Star	9,984	565×58×39	20	Harland & W.
1890	Majestic	"	9,965			
1884	Umbria.........................	Cunard	8,128	501×57×38	20	Fairfield.
1884	Etruria........................		8,120			
1890	Kaiserin Maria Theresa ...	N. D. Lloyd............	7,840	528×51×36	20	Stettin V. Co.
1898	Moskva.........................	Russ. Vol. Ft. Assn.	7,267	487×58×26	20	Clydebank.
1898	Isis, and Osiris	P. & O.	1,728	300×37×17	20	Caird & Co.

FIRST FLEET OF TRANSPORTS CHARTERED OCTOBER, 1899, FOR TRANSVAAL WAR.

TABLE X. Owners.	Vessels	Tonnage.	Ports Vessels belonged to.							Various Ports.
			Dundee.	Glasgow.	Hull.	Livpool.	London.	Mnchstr.		
Allan Line	4	26,884	...	26,884	...	...	...	...		...
Anchor Line	4	20,829	...	20,829	...	...	...	...		...
Atlantic Transport Co.	3*	12,186	...	...	...	...	12,186	...		...
Asiatic S. N. Co.	4	20,357	...	...	...	20,357	...	...		...
Bibby Line	2	9,969	...	...	...	9,969	...	...		...
British India S. N. Co.	28	100,511	...	...	...	...	100,511	...		...
Castle Line	7	41,770	...	...	...	...	41,770	...		...
City Line	4	15,201	...	15,201	...	...	...	...		...
Cunard Line	6	36,294	...	...	...	36,294	...	...		...
Elder, Dempster & Co.	6	35,345	...	...	...	35,345	...	...		...
Houlder Bros............	5	22,531	...	...	...	...	22,531	...		...
Houston Line	3	9,651	...	...	...	9,651	...	...		...
Johnston Line...........	2	12,491	...	...	...	12,491	...	...		...
Manchester Liners ...	2	11,449	...	...	...	...	...	11,449		...
Moss Line	2	4,812	...	...	...	4,812	...	...		...
Nelson Donkin Co. ...	3	9,997	...	...	...	...	9,997	...		...
P. & O. Co.	8	40,172	...	...	...	...	40,172	...		...
Thomson & Co.	2	7,211	7,211	...	...	...	...	...		...
Union S. S. Co.	7	37,328	...	...	...	...	37,328	...		...
W. India P. S. S. Co.	4	20,226	...	...	...	20,226	...	...		...
White Star Line.........	3	22,738	...	...	...	22,738	...	...		...
Wilson Line	2	9,801	...	...	9,801	...	...	...		...
31 Shipowners	32	128,529	...	9,868	2,490	53,789	21,831	...		40,551
*1 Hospitalship gratuitously										
Totals	143	656,282	7,211	72,782	12,291	225,672	286,326	11,449		40,551

AFRICAN STEAMSHIP COMPANY, the earliest African line, traces its origin to a private expedition of the *Elburkah* up the Niger in 1832, its success leading to others for opening up the West Coast of Africa or suppressing the slave-trade. This Company, which owns 34 vessels, received its charter in 1852, with an annual subsidy of £30,000 for a monthly mail, passenger, and freight service, performed continuously ever since, the pioneer boats *Forerunner*, *Faith*, *Hope*, and *Charity* rendering valuable aid in the Crimean War. In 1891, the Company associated itself with the British and African Steam Navigation Company (see p. 721), under the conjoint management of Messrs. Elder, Dempster & Company, of Liverpool, and with first-class steamers designed and built to suit these trades maintain 7 distinct services from Liverpool, Hamburg, Rotterdam, and Antwerp to West and South-West Africa, the one from the last mentioned port being under contract with the Congo Free State.

London Office, 21, Gt. St. Helens, E.C.

ALLAN LINE.—The Allan Line Steamship Company, Limited, was originally called the Montreal Ocean Steamship Company, superseding McKean & Co.'s attempted line of steamers, of which the *Genova*, 800 tons, in 1853, was the first. When McKean gave up, a contract with the Canadian Government for a steam-link with the mother country was undertaken by the Allan Brothers, who, as sailing shipowners, had been connected with Canada since 1820. The *Canadian*, 1,700 tons, was despatched from Liverpool to Montreal and Quebec Sept. 20, 1854, but owing to the Crimean War the mail service did not begin until April, 1856, with the sailing of the *North American*, and the line has continued ever since to meet and promote the postal, commercial, and immigrational requirements of the colony, having been one of the chief factors in the rapid development of the now vast Dominion. Since 1859, sailings have been weekly, the steamers going to Halifax and Portland when the St. Lawrence is closed. The itinerary includes Glasgow, Liverpool, and London, embracing on the other side, in addition to several Canadian ports, Boston, New York, Philadelphia, and the River Plate. Among the most recent additions to the steamers, which aggregate 147,000 tons, are the *Sicilian*, 8,000 tons, and the twin-screw *Bavarian*, 10,376 tons; the latter, like her sister-ship *Tunisian*, accommodating 500 passengers. The Allan Line is not at the moment carrying the mails.

London Office, 103, Leadenhall Street, E.C.

AMERICAN LINE, which inherited the records of the noted Inman Line, alone of Transatlantic services flies the United States flag. The International Navigation Company, the proprietary organisation, was incorporated in Pennsylvania in 1871; a fortnightly service was established in 1873 between Antwerp and Philadelphia, with steamers under the Belgian flag, known as the Red Star Line; and the American Line was started with the American-built *Illinois*, *Indiana*, *Ohio*, and *Pennsylvania*; 1880 brought a weekly line between New York and Antwerp, this expansion being followed in 1885 by the important acquisition of the Inman Line with its five steamers and Liverpool-New York connections, Messrs. Richardson, Spence & Co. continuing their management on this side. The year 1888 and 1889 witnessed the enterprising appearance of the *City of New York* and *City*

of *Paris*, which vessels marked an advance in size as well as the adoption of twin-screws. In 1893 the Inman and International, as the line was then called, underwent another phase of re-organisation and extended into the American Line, the mail steamers exchanging Liverpool for Southampton, their names being all shortened to the bare titles of cities. The *New York* and *Paris* were, under a special Act of Congress, naturalised into the U.S. register providing two steamers of no less size or speed were produced for their owners upon American soil, which dramatic event was hailed as an auspicious omen for the reviving U.S. marine. The *St. Louis* and *St. Paul* in 1895, emanating from the busy yards at Philadelphia of Cramp & Sons, more than fulfilled the conditions of the memorable contract, each being 1,000 tons larger and one knot an hour quicker than their Clyde-built predecessors. The four boats are amongst the finest and fastest afloat (see p. 719), and gave a practical demonstration during the Spanish-American hostilities of their great value as mercantile armed cruisers to war-fleets in and out of action. Weekly New York mail lines are run to and from Antwerp, and also Southampton, the latter departures calling at Cherbourg. Philadelphia passenger and freight lines are maintained to and from Liverpool, as well as Antwerp. Six steamers over 10,000 tons each are in course of construction, 4 in the United Kingdom and 2 in the United States, which will bring the combined tonnage of the services to 170,000 tons.

London Office, 115 & 115, Leadenhall Street, E.C.

ANCHOR LINE.—In 1851 the Glasgow and New York Packet Service started a line with the ss. *Glasgow*, which continued until 1859. In 1856, the Anchor Line entered the Trans-atlantic trade with the *Tempest*, 1,500 tons, diverted from their South American and Indian sailing ships and converted into a screw steamer. When Messrs. Handyside and Henderson, the founders and owners, saw the American branch prospering they concentrated their attention upon it, and in 1863 put on two large steamers, the *Britannia* and *Caledonia*, and afterwards vigorously developed the Glasgow-New York trade with fine steamers, the sizes of which gradually increased to 5,000 tons, to cope with the growth of business. In 1879 the *Circassia* was carrying dead meat by the dry-air process of refrigeration. Besides the American service between Glasgow and New York, the line, which became a public company in 1899, maintains services between New York, New Orleans, and various Mediterranean ports; also runs one from Glasgow and Liverpool to Bombay, returning *vid* Marseilles and Gibraltar; and another to Calcutta, returning to London. It possesses a fleet of 29 steamers, which, with a 3000 tons hulk at Gibraltar, reaches 111,000 tons, and includes the *City of Rome*, 8,453 tons, *Furnessia*, 5,495 tons, *Algeria*, 4,510 tons, and *Astoria*, 5,049 tons.

London Office, 18 Leadenhall Street, E.C.

AUSTRIAN LLOYD STEAM NAVIGATION COMPANY, established in 1836, belongs to Trieste, whence seven services are kept up to and from Adriatic, Mediterranean, and Levant ports, served by three branch lines. Besides a line to the West as far as Brazil, there is an accelerated monthly mail service between Trieste, Brindisi, and Bombay; also an ordinary service as frequently between Trieste, Bombay, China, and Japan, in connection with a monthly branch between

Colombo, Madras, and Calcutta. Including a steamer exceeding 10,000 tons, which is being constructed by the company at their own shipyard, and 4 others building, the fleet will amount to 70 vessels with a total of 160,000 tons.

London Agents, Hickie, Borman & Co., 22, Billiter Street, E.C.

BIBBY LINE.—In 1807 Mr. Bibby, the founder of the line which bears his name, owned, amongst others, the sailing ship *Bispam,* and in 1821 established a regular line of ships to the East Indies, since which times succeeding generations of the family to whom the line belongs have conducted it through the various progressive stages of navigation. In 1851 the steam fleet was commenced with the *Tiber* and the *Arno.* Later, Mr. James Bibby ordered from Messrs. Harland & Wolff the *Syrian, Sicilian,* and *Venetian,* the pioneers of the present style of steamers, and which were the now famous shipbuilding firm's first order. In 1891 the *Lancashire,* whose passage of 23 days, 20 hours, in July, from Liverpool to Rangoon stands the fastest, started the present service, which runs to Colombo and Rangoon, *vid* Marseilles, from which port of call Ceylon is 18 days passage and Burmah 23. The fast and modern steamers of this Line, built by Harland & Wolff, are authorised by the Indian Government for officers returning on expiry of furlough, it being the recognised route to Burmah; and by the daily steam service between Colombo and Tuticorin easy connections are made with Southern India generally.

London Office, Dunster House, Mincing Lane, E.C.

BRITISH AND AFRICAN STEAM NAVIGATION COMPANY, Ltd., established in 1858, own a fleet of 24 modern mail, passenger, and cargo steamers, named after various African ports, trading stations, and rivers to which they run from Liverpool, &c. Some water-ways have been discovered, explored, and brought into prominence by their captains, one, the "*Jones,*" being so called after Alfred L. Jones, the presiding genius of the firm of Messrs. Elder, Dempster & Co., of Liverpool, who manage this Company conjointly with the African Steamship Company (see p. 720). The comprehensive and rapidly extending commercial operations of this Firm with the Canary Islands and the West Coast of Africa, as well as in the Canadian, United States, and other trades, are upon too large a scale to even recapitulate here, their existing tonnage already exceeding 282,000 tons.

London Office, 4, St. Mary Axe, E.C.

BRITISH INDIA STEAM NAVIGATION COMPANY.—In 1855 the founder of this Company, the late Sir William Mackinnon, arranged to establish the Calcutta and Burmah Steam Navigation Company for the performance of mail services for the East India Company, with which object it was incorporated in 1855, the *Baltic* and *Cape of Good Hope* being sent out in 1857 to start the business. The Company's vessels have often repeated the timely services rendered to the Government during the Mutiny that year, and during the Abyssinian War the compound engines of their steamers were serviceably employed condensing daily supplies of water for the troops. In 1862 a fresh mail service was entered into which included additional routes, and the name of the Company was officially altered to its present title—more in keeping with its business which strikingly benefited from the opening of

the Suez Canal, through which the Company's steamship *India* conveyed the first cargo of Indian produce. The Aden-Zanzibar mail service was put on in 1872, and from then until now new routes have been constantly added to its itinerary, the extent of which will not admit of more than a bare outline. The Company is under contract with the Home and Indian Governments for mail services to Arabia, Persia, India, Burmah, East India, the Mauritius and the Seychelles, and also runs other services to Batavia, Queensland, &c., the most noticeable extension in 1899 being a three-weekly line from Calcutta to Manila. To supply the 100 ports actually called at, a constantly recurring commercial game of "zig-zag" is played by 123 steamers under the management of Messrs. MacKinnon, MacKenzie & Co., in India, Messrs. Gray, Dawes & Co., having represented the Company in London since 1866. Including *Golconda* 5874, *Dunera* 5441, *Dilwara* 5413, *Avoca* 5327, and *Jelunga* 5190 tons, the fleet grosses 370,549 tons.

London Office, 9, Throgmorton Avenue, E.C.

CANADIAN-AUSTRALIAN LINE was established in 1893, and runs in connection with the Canadian Pacific Railway. The steamers *Aorangi,* 4,268 tons, *Miowera,* 3,345 tons, and *Warrimoo,* 3,326 tons (acquired last year by the New Zealand Shipping Company), are under contract with the Canadian, New South Wales, and Queensland governments for a monthly mail service between Vancouver, Victoria, B.C., Honolulu, Brisbane, and Sydney, N.S.W.

London Office, 138, Leadenhall Street, E.C.

CANADIAN PACIFIC RAILWAY runs all the way upon British soil from Quebec on the Atlantic to Vancouver on the Pacific, 3,050 miles. It was begun in 1875 by the Government, who handed it over in 1881 for completion to the more suitable Canadian Pacific Railway, which company, far ahead of contract time, laid the last rail Nov. 7, 1885, and by Midsummer, 1886, had the giant commercial enterprise equipped and working throughout a system of 4,315 miles, since increased to over 9,000 miles. Besides their Lake Route Steamships, the finest of their kind, the EMPRESS LINE, a three-weekly service between Vancouver and Japan and China, was established 1891, composed of magnificent twin-screw mail-boats, each 5,505 tons, and respectively named after *India, Japan* and *China,* and subsidised for service as cruisers. They call at Yokohama. Kobe, Nagasaki, Shanghai, and Hong Kong; the *Empress of India* went in 1887 from Vancouver to Yokohama in 10 days, 10 hours, 22 minutes, her total time to Hong Kong being 17 days, 16 minutes. By reducing the stopping-places, from 140 to 80, the Canadian Pacific Railway runs its Transcontinental Express, the "Imperial Limited," from Montreal to Vancouver in 100 hours, returning in 98, London being thus brought within three weeks of Japan.

London Office, 67, King William Street, E.C.

CASTLE LINE. — The original "Castles" belonging to Donald Currie were clippers trading to India, the present line of steamers being established by him in 1872. The postage to the Cape was then 1s. per ½ oz., and the Union Company had four years' unexpired contract for the mails; but the new line during the interval received valuable time-bonuses from the Home Government for the additional postage facilities they afforded. The pioneer steamers from London *vid* Dartmouth were the *Iceland* and *Gothland*, each but 1,400 tons, taking 32 to 34 days for passages now performed in under half that time by powerful steamers ranging up to 10,000 tons each. Communications are maintained with a fine fleet of vessels fitted with every modern improvement, which have carried the Royal Mails between England and South Africa jointly with the Union Line since 1876. The mail steamers sail fortnightly, with the intermediate boats making a weekly service, and have often distinguished themselves on important transport work for the Government. The object of the line—which has been successfully accomplished—is to ensure uniformly quick passages, with every regard to the comfort and safety of all classes of passengers, additional steamers being employed for South-African, Intercolonial and Mauritius connecting services. The *Dunottar* (5,625 tons), *Tantallon* (5,636 tons), and *Dunvegan* (5,958 tons) Castles have each come home under 15½ days, and the *Carisbrooke Castle*, 7,625 tons, which was added last year, has done so under 14½ days. The newest vessels are the *Kinfauns Castle*, 9,664 tons, with a sister-ship, *Kildonan Castle*, the tonnage of the fleet being 107 000 tons.

London Office, 3, Fenchurch Street, E.C.

CITY LINE.—Messrs. George Smith & Sons despatch 30 sailings every year from Glasgow and Liverpool to Calcutta and back to London ; as well as 13 to Bombay and Karachi, which return to Liverpool, all of these steamers carrying passengers regularly to and from Malta and Egypt, in addition to the above ports. The flag of the well-known City Line flies over 15 steamers and 8 sailing ships, its popularity and success having been fittingly hall-marked by a jubilee at Glasgow in 1889, fifty years after their *Constellation*, 344 tons, had sailed thence for Calcutta. The *Majestic*, a full-rigged ship of 560 tons, which appeared in 1845, was the first vessel specially built for the firm, who joined the ranks of steam in 1870, with the *City of Oxford*, 2,319 tons. The *City of Vienna*, 4,672 tons, steamed from Calcutta to London in 1891 in 26 days, whilst the *City of Sparta*, 5,179 tons, travelled over the same ground to London in 8 hours more in 1898. The sailing ships account for 10,000 tons out of a combined total of 69,000 tons.

London Agents, Montgomerie & Workman, 36, Gracechurch Street, E.C.

CLAN LINE began a fortnightly service from Glasgow and Liverpool to Bombay in 1878, adding one to Cape Colony and Natal in 1881, and another one to Colombo Madras, and Calcutta in 1882. The fleet of 41 "Clan" steamers grosses 150,000 tons, and includes 10 turret-deck steamers, of which the *Clan Farquhar*, 5,858 tons, and *Clan Urquhart*, 5,855 tons, are the largest. Over 50 boats of this kind have been built by Messrs. Doxford & Sons, the patentees, who claim for this type the largest possible carrying capacity on the smallest possible register. The line is under the management of Messrs. Cayzer, Irvine & Co., of Glasgow, &c., whose senior partner, Sir William Cayzer, M.P., is the founder of it.

London Office, 115, Leadenhall Street. E.C.

COMPAGNIE GÉNÉRALE TRANSATLANTIQUE, established 1862, is the second largest company in France, and is heavily subsidised by that government. *La Normandie*, 6,283 tons, *La Gascoigne*, 7,395 tons, and 8 others are over 16 knots, *La Touraine*, 8,893 tons, being 19. With its fine fleet of 56 boats, mostly fast ones, the Company maintains important connections between Havre (its head port), St. Nazaire, Bordeaux, Marseilles, etc., and various Mediterranean, African, West Indian, and North, Central, and South American ports. The *La Lorraine* and *La Savoie*, 20 knot boats, each 11,203 tons, are being built on French soil, according to terms of mail contract, at the Company's own shipyard, and will swell the total tonnage to 180,000 tons.

London Office, 36, Leadenhall Street, E.C.

COMPANIA TRASATLANTICA of Barcelona and Cadiz, the leading company in Spain, owns 24 steamers, the largest being *Reina Maria Christina*, 5,161 tons, and *A'phonso XIII.*, 5,125 tons, the Fleet grossing 73,000 tons.

Succeeding Messrs. A. Lopes & Co., the Company maintains regular mail and passenger services to the Antilles, River Plate, North Africa, Philippines, &c., the Liverpool Line being managed by Messrs. Larrinaga & Co.

CUNARD LINE.—As the history of this popular undertaking, which celebrated its jubilee in 1890, would fill an interesting volume, it must here suffice to chronicle the chief events from its establishment to its present position. The foundation stone was, and remains, *safety*; it has never lost the life of a single passenger. An important stepping-stone to sorely-tried sea-voyagers was *speed* : it made, and holds, the record each way between Liverpool and New York. Another consideration, which includes every luxury sea-travelling will admit of, is the *comfort* of its passengers (110,000 have been carried in one year), the total lists running into millions. Chief among the numerous rivals which vainly disputed its supremacy was the noted Collins Line of paddle steamers, built in the United States for the purpose of sweeping the Cunarders from the Atlantic. These fine but ill-fated boats beat the Cunard passages each way ; but their mission failed after a bitter fight, and the American Company's finances prevented it continuing a struggle with its steadily persevering antagonist after their Government withdrew all subsidies in 1857. The pioneer steamer, *Britannia*, left Liverpool July 4, 1840, carrying Charles Dickens to Boston in 14½ days. She was 207 by 34'2 by 22'4, 2,050 tons, 740 h.-p., and, like her three sister-ships, was specially built for the Company, then known as the British and North American Steam Packet Company. They were engined by D. Napier, of Glasgow, who, in conjunction with Burns of that city and MacIver of Liverpool, enabled Samuel Cunard to secure the first capital of £270,000. The first iron paddle steamer, the *Persia*, 3,300 tons, appeared in 1856: the *Scotia*, 3,871 tons, the Company's last paddle boat, was built in 1852, which year witnessed the *China*, 2,539 tons, their first Atlantic screw steamer. The *Russia*, 2,959 tons, took her place in the line in 1867, and before leaving it had traversed 630,000 miles and carried 26,076 cabin passengers, without experiencing an accident. The *Batavia*, 2,553 tons, in 1870, was followed with six steamers, the last being the *Gallia*, 4,808 tons, in 1879. all fitted with compound engines. The steel-built *Servia*, 7,392 tons, came in 1881, closely followed by the *Aurania*, and then the speedy *Oregon* joined the fleet. The *Etruria* and *Umbria*, each 8,127 tons, were in the foremost rank in 1884, the service being augmented in 1893 by the still swifter *Campania* and *Lucania*, each 12,950 tons. These long steps forward were the crowning glory of their builders, the Fairfield

Shipbuilding and Engineering Co., Ltd., and are subsidised by H.M. Government for service as fast armed cruisers, each steamer being provided with a duplicate set of triple expansion engines for driving twin-screws, capable of 30,000 h.-p. The best possible Ships, Crews, and Organisation are the Cunard life-secrets of sixty years' honourable records, which alone rendered possible 10,000 successive passages through the wreck-fields of the North Atlantic. How the Company's steamers pass the most exacting tests with immunity from loss of life, the storm-swept *Pavonia* strikingly demonstrated in 1899. A private company was formed in 1818, which the public participated in two years later. At the present time the Cunard Company owns 22 large steamers, exceeding a total tonnage of 140,000 tons, which include the two new twin-screw steamers *Ivernia* and *Saxonia*, each grossing 13,900 tons. The quickest crossings recorded to date are as follow:—

WEST.			EAST.			Average Sea Speed.	Highest Day's Runs.
d.	h.	m.	d.	h.	m.	knots.	knots.
Lucania 5	7	23	5	8	38	22	562
Campania 5	9	6	5	9	18	21¾	553
Etruria 5	20	35	6	0	40	20	509
Umbria 5	22	7	6	1	15	19¾	510

London Office, 93, Bishopsgate St. Within, E.C.

DOMINION LINE.—In 1870 some Liverpool and New Orleans cotton merchants formed the Mississippi and Dominion Steamship Company, Ltd., to run from Liverpool to Quebec and Montreal in summer, and to New Orleans in winter, but later on Portland (Maine) became the winter port. Since 1894 the proprietary company has been the British and North Atlantic Steam Navigation Company, Ltd., under the management of Messrs. Richards, Mills & Co. The *New England*, 11,394 tons, is the largest of the Company's nine steamers, which, in addition to a service to Canada, maintain a service from Boston, U.S., the passenger trade to and from which port will still more rival New York when the Boston route is further shortened by the new deep cut across the harbour to the wharves.

London Office, 22, Billiter Street, E.C.

GENERAL STEAM NAVIGATION COMPANY is essentially a London institution (see p. 713). Besides East Coast Services, Continental trades are served between Hamburg in the north and Bordeaux in the south, other lines extending to the Mediterranean, Adriatic, Levant, and Black Sea. The sea-going services include the *Shildreck*, 2,697 tons; *Adjutant*, 2,392 tons; *Preston*, 2,099 tons; whilst the *Eagle* and other fast paddle steamers run during the summer season to seaside resorts in Kent, Norfolk, &c. The fleet consists of 42 vessels with a total tonnage of 52,583 tons, of which 6 are popular pleasure boats.

London Office, 55, Great Tower Street, E.C.

HAMBURG-AMERICAN LINE, in point of carrying capacity, owns the largest fleet in the world, its 75 ocean steamers, 22 of which are large twin-screw passenger boats, amounting to 412,148 tons. The Packet Company began its Transatlantic service in 1847, with the *Deutschland*, 717 tons, and by 1853 possessed 5 more sailing vessels like her, all having a combined capacity for 4,000 tons of cargo, each accommodating 200 passengers. The entire fleet could then carry annually to New York only 12,000 tons of freight, which quantity the *Pennsylvania* can herself take in 12 days, a practical demonstration of the progress made in fifty years. The s.s. *Borussia*, 2,349 tons, appearing in 1853, was followed by other steamers, monthly departures being kept up until 1860 when the ships were sold, and enough steamers purchased to make fortnightly departures to New York, the sailings being increased to weekly ones in 1872. In 1888 the Company decided upon twin-screws, and the *Columbia*, *Auguste Victoria*, (*Normannia*), and *Furst Bismarck*, successively joined the ever-swelling fleet.

The very able administration of this prospering concern vividly represents the tendency of Continental shipping towards centralisation, the power to compete with British lines being correspondingly strengthened; its progressive policy boldly culminates in the *Deutschland*, 15,500 tons, the largest ever built in Germany, whose engines of 35,000 h.-p. are expected to take her across the Atlantic in the spring at 23½ knots an hour, and surpass all previous records. The routes of the Weekly Express steamers are Hamburg, Southampton, Cherbourg to New York, returning in reverse order. Another service leaves Hamburg every Sunday for New York *via* Boulogne-sur-Mer, in addition to which steamers run regularly to Boston, Baltimore, Philadelphia, New Orleans, Montreal, West Indies, Mexico, River Plate, China and Japan, a line to the Amazon, being started this year. Harmonious working arrangements exist with the North German Lloyd, whereby the earnings of both are augmented.

London Office, 22, Cockspur Street, W.

HAMBURG SOUTH AMERICAN STEAMSHIP COMPANY was established at Hamburg in 1871, the most recent additions being the *Cap Frio* and *Cap Roca*, each 5,600 tons, three similar boats being built. Regular passenger services are maintained from Germany, Portugal, and Spain, to Brazil, Uruguay and Argentine, and with the new boats the fleet of 33 steamers will be increased to 126,500 tons.

HANSA COMPANY of Bremen, established 1889, maintains regular cargo services between Bremen, Hamburg, Antwerp and Middlesbrough, and the chief ports in India, also a fortnightly service between Bremen and Antwerp, and the River Plate. The *Drachenfels*, 7,000 tons, heads the list of 33 steamers, which show a return of 77,000 tons.

London Agents, J. H. Wackerbarth & Co., 27, Leadenhall Street, E.C.

HARRISON LINE was established by Messrs. Thos. and Jas. Harrison, of Liverpool under the name of the Charente Steamship Company, Limited. The *Custodian*, 9,200 tons; *Collegian*, 7,237 tons; and *Politician*, 7,228 tons, are the largest of 29 steamers, totalling 121,000 tons, regularly engaged to and from West Indies, United States, Mexico, Brazil, East Indies, and South of France.

JOHNSTON LINE gradually entered the Mediterranean, Black Sea, American and Canadian trades. Including the *Quaramore*, 7,302 tons; *Maplemore*, 7,719 tons; and one, 9,100 tons building. Messrs. William Johnston & Co., Ltd., now own 28 steamers for freight and live stock, registering 124,609 tons.

London Office, 1, St. Mary Axe, E.C.

LAMPORT AND HOLT LINE.—The Liverpool, Brazil, and River Plate Steam Navigation Company, Limited, was formed in 1865, being popularly known as the Lamport and Holt Line, after its first and present managers. The steamers are run at regular intervals from Antwerp, London, Glasgow, Manchester, Liverpool, Havre and New York to Pernambuco, Bahia, Rio de Janeiro, Santos, Montevideo, Buenos Ayres, and Rosario; also to the ports of Chile, Peru, and Ecuador, on the West Coast of South America, likewise, a line from New York to Manchester. All the steamers are fitted with telescope masts, many have first-class accommodation for passengers, especially those running between New York and South America; others have been specially constructed to carry large numbers of horses, cattle, and sheep, having all the latest improvements for the safe-carriage of live-stock, and their well-being during transit. The *Canning*, 5,366 tons, is the largest; and with 4 vessels building grossing 21,000 tons, the number owned is brought up to 40, with a tonnage over 120,000 tons, steamers representing 20,000 tons more, running regularly under the "L. and H." flag.

London Office, 35, Lime Street, E.C.

LEYLAND LINE.—This old-established business was converted into a public company in 1892, after the death of its founder, Mr. F. R. Leyland. Owing to the enterprise and ability of the new management the company soon attained a solid and influential position, and now possesses a fine fleet including some of the largest vessels afloat. The *Winefredian* is 10,404 tons; with a similar boat and 4 others building, the total tonnage of the 33 vessels will amount to 145,000 tons, without counting the interest of the Company in the Wilsons and Furness-Leyland Line. In 1895, a new passenger service was established between Liverpool and the United States, and another line was started from Antwerp to Montreal in 1899. Besides their Transatlantic Services, regular lines are run to Portugal, Italy, Sicily, Malta, Alexandria, Constantinople, and Black Sea, which trades Mr. Leyland took up in succession to Mr. Bibby.

London Agents, T. Ronaldson & Co., Ltd., 34, Leadenhall Street, E.C.

MESSAGERIES MARITIMES DE FRANCE.—From a concern for inland mail carriage, the present noted company developed. In 1851, an over-sea contract was entered into for the French mails to Italy, Egypt, Syria, the Levant and Greece. There are five services to Mediterranean, Black Sea and Danube ports, the last two trades being taken up in 1857. The India and China Mail contract was secured in 1861. Besides a monthly line direct to Bombay, there is a service *vià* Bombay, and another *vià* Colombo, every month to China and Japan, with branches from Colombo, Singapore, and Saigon to Indian ports, Java, Tonquin and Cochin China. Departures to Australia and New Caledonia occur every four weeks, connecting at Colombo with China. main line. Two lines a month leave for Mauritius *vià* Djibouti, Zanzibar, Madagascar and Réunion, with a branch down South East Africa, between Diego-Suarez and Natal; also a Madagascar Coastal service between Nossi-Bé and Tullera. The foregoing, with a weekly cargo line to London *vià* Havre, sail from Marseilles. The mail service from Bordeaux to Brazil and River Plate, commenced in 1861, now leaves fortnightly, with a steamer once a month for cargo only. The *Tonkin*, 6,245 tons, *Indus*, 6,240 tons, *Sinai* 4,850 tons; *Annam* 6,250 tons; *Pacifique*, 2,000 tons, were recently added. With the *Polynesien*, 6,506

tons, at its head, the well-known fleet, including *Atlantique*, 6,000 tons, and two others building, records over 250,000 tons for the "M. M.," which successfully upholds its pride of place in France, with 66 splendidly appointed steamers, long distinguished for excellence in every department.

London Office, 97, Cannon Street, E.C.

NATAL LINE, established 1879 by Messrs Bullard King & Co., despatches steamers fortnightly from London *direct* to Natal, Delagoa Bay, Beira, and East African ports, which offer special facilities for passengers and cargo for those points. Besides a through service at regular intervals between South African ports and China and Japan; another fortnightly one, under contract with Natal Government, from Cape Colony and Natal *vià* East African ports to Madras and Calcutta, calls at Ceylon. The tonnages and draft of the 13 steamers composing the fleet, of which the largest is the *Umtata*, 2,800 tons, admit of their crossing the bar and discharging inside Natal harbour, avoiding risk and expense of transhipping.

London Office, 14, St. Mary Axe, E.C.

NAVIGAZIONE GENERALE ITALIANA.—Under this title were united the Lines which formerly belonged to Florio, of Palermo, and Rubattino, of Genoa, having the head office at Rome. The *Raffaele Rubattino*, 4,580 tons, heads a long list of 98 steamers, the tonnage of which fleet exceeds 180,000 tons. There are Lines from Italy to India, China, New York, New Orleans, and River Plate, in connection with the Company's Mediterranean, Adriatic, and Levant services. A weekly express runs between London and Cairo *vià* Naples and Alexandria, the sea passage occupying 63 hours; Cairo by this route being 4½ days from Berlin and 5 days 3 hours from London.

London Agents: A. Laming & Co., 8, Leadenhall Street, E.C.

NEW ZEALAND SHIPPING COMPANY, organised at Christchurch, New Zealand, in 1873, carried on business for ten years, with sailing ships specially built for passengers and the trade. The first direct steamer *Stad Harlem*, conveyed in 1879 600 emigrants to the enterprising Colony; four years later the *British King* began the Government Mail contract for which five steamers were built. Last year sailing ships vanished from the fleet which now consists of ten steamers, including the twin-screw *Paparoa*, 6,563 tons, two more like her of larger tonnage being built. New Zealand emphasises its British characteristics by sending here nearly all its produce, which the development of the frozen industries has multiplied. This Company's *Mataura* sailed from Port Chalmers in 1882, with 150 tons of mutton prepared on board in the absence of the necessary plant ashore. The passenger steamers sail from London every Thursday *vià* Plymouth, Teneriffe Cape Town, and Hobart, returning round Cape Horn *vià* Montevideo, or; Rio Janeiro. Rates are low compared with the conveniences, and table supplied to all classes. First-class fares being at 1⅜d. per mile, and third-class only ⅝d.

London Office: 138, Leadenhall Street, E.C.

NIPPON YUSEN KAISHA.—Since 1866 the Japanese have steadily improved their knowledge of navigation and added to their stock of sea-going vessels for purposes of war and commerce. Soon after the "Three Diamond" Company was organised with six coasting steamers a military expedition to Formosa was necessitated. Among the spoils of victory were some foreign-built steamers and ships, which were eventually handed over to the above Company by the Government, who also assisted it to acquire the Yokohama-Shanghai service and steamers therein from the Pacific Mail Steamship Company : thus by 1876 the Company possessed a mixed fleet of 42 vessels, only 12 of the steamers being over 1,000 tons each. In 1882 the Union Navigation Company was started, but in three years the proved inexpediency of having two State-aided concerns resulted in amalgamation. and the above, known as the Japanese Mail Steamship Company was established in 1885 Regular services were kept up from Kobe to Vladivostock, Tientsin, and Corean Ports ; a Line between Japan and Bombay being put on in 1892, when the development of the spinning industry increased the importation of raw cotton. The importance of the Company rose with the size of its fleet owing to the war with China in 1894, 50 of its steamers being engaged at one time transporting the 120,000 fighting men with their 100,000 attendant coolies, which were so efficiently despatched by the masterful rising Empire against the Dragon across the sea, whose hordes of millions were cramped by the weight of ages. Independent of a complete Japanese coastal system, services are maintained to China, Asiatic Russia, the Philippine Islands, Hawaii, the Straits Settlements, India, the Mediterranean, Europe, America, and Australia. The phenomenal progress of this Company, which has its head office at Tokyo, can be quickest realised in connection with the fact that during an era when the leading Companies have made enormous strides, the fleet belonging to the Kingdom of the Mikado, by the continual addition of 6,000 tons boats, the names of the largest being *Wakasa Maru*, 6,266 tons, *Bingo Maru*, 6,241 tons, and *Sado Maru*, 6,219 tons, now numbers 70 steamers, whose register of 208,000 tons places it amongst the first on the roll of the Conquerors of the Ocean.

London Office : 5, Fenchurch Avenue.

NORDDEUTSCHER LLOYD sprang into existence in 1856, initial operations taking the form of Lines to Hull and to London. On 19th June, 1858, the *Bremen*, 334 × 42 × 28, sailed to New York *via* Southampton with 52 cabin passengers, 92 steerage, and 150 tons of cargo, followed by the *Weser*, the service being made fortnightly in 1866. Extensions to Baltimore 1868, New Orleans 1869, West Indies 1871, Brazil and River Plate 1876, evidenced the growth towards front rank which was assumed in 1881 with fast mail-boats built for an Express Atlantic Service. The Imperal German Mail Service to Eastern Asia and Australia, with various branch lines, began in 1885, were followed in 1891, with an Express line between Italy and New York. In 1892, the first twin-screw steamer, *H. H. Meier*, joined the fleet, which from that date has been completely reorganised and renovated. Since 1894, the Company, which had expended millions in this country, have confined their orders to German firms. The startling result has no doubt been taken to heart by British shipbuilders. In 1897, the hands of the clock were substantially put forward by the *Kaiser Wilhelm der Grosse*, which glorification of German labour sallied forth from the Vulcan Works at Stettin. This superb display of the shipbuilder's art won and

retains the palm for ocean speed against all competitors, and in September, 1899, crossed from Cherbourg to Sandy Hook in 5 days 18 hours 5 min. The capacity of the fleet has been nearly doubled during the last ten years, and, counting 12 twin-screw boats (11 of them over 10,000 tons each), an array of 73 stately vessels supplies the Port of Bremen and the Fatherland with 358,000 tons.

London Agents: Keller, Wallis & Co., 2, King William Street, E.C.

OCEAN STEAMSHIP COMPANY.—The first to carry *high* pressure steam to sea successfully was Mr. Alfred Holt, who, with the *Cleator*, in 1864, and succeeding steamers, brought to light the previously half-known merits of the compound-engine system, which had been applied to many land engines, mainly in Cornwall, and used at sea by Messrs. Randolph and Elder, but only with *low* pressure. The successful performances of the *Cleator*, which ran for years on long voyages, resulted in the formation of the Ocean Steamship Company in 1865. The *Agamemnon* began the Line on April 19, 1866, sailing from Liverpool for Singapore and China *via* Mauritius, which port of call, as well as the Cape route, was given up on the opening of the Suez Canal. The Company maintains a ten - days' service from Liverpool to Singapore, China, and Japan ; also a fortnightly one from Amsterdam *via* Liverpool to Penang, Singapore, and Java. In conjunction with the West Australian Steam Navigation Company, Ltd., there is also a fortnightly line between Singapore and West Australian ports, the steamers of which have passenger accommodation. There are four steamers building, each 7,000 tons, viz., the *Ajax, Achilles, Agamemnon*, and *Deucalion*, bringing the total number of vessels to 40, and the gross tonnage to 165,000 tons.

London Agents: J. Swire & Sons, Billiter Buildings, E.C.

ORIENT LINE.—The Orient Line between England and Australia was really a development of the old-established lines of fast clipper ships run by the well-known firms of F. Green & Co. and Anderson, Anderson & Co., who are joint managers of the Orient Line, which they established as soon as trade with Australia required and could support such a first-class steam service. With the co-operation of the Pacific Steam Navigation Company (four of whose fine steamers run in the Line), monthly sailings were commenced with the *Lusitania* in 1877, but when the Orient Steam Navigation Company, Ltd., was formed in 1880 a fortnightly mail service each way was inaugurated, since regularly maintained under contract with the Government for an annual subsidy of £85,000. The steamers, which for the purposes of the Australian Trade are in all respects unrivalled, are timed to make uniform voyages without being pressed for isolated record passages. They sail from London on alternate Fridays for Sydney calling at Plymouth, Gibraltar, Marseilles, Naples, Port Said, Suez, Colombo, Albany, Adelaide, and Melbourne, returning homewards in the reverse order on alternate Saturdays. In addition to the magnificent twin-screw steamers *Ophir*, 6,910 tons, and *Omrah*, 8,500 tons (each 10,000 effective horse-power), another similar vessel, the *Ortona*, has just joined the service. The comfortable accommodation afforded by this Line to third-class passengers, whose requirements are made a special study of, strikingly testifies to the benefits conferred by steam navigation upon long-distance travellers able to pay only the cheapest fares. In addition to the mail service, the Orient Company were among the earliest to bring within easy reach of the public the advantages of pleasure yachting to foreign countries in ocean steamers, which are run frequently, the cruises varying from two to eight weeks in duration.

London Office: 5, Fenchurch Avenue, E.C.

PACIFIC STEAM NAVIGATION COMPANY, incorporated by Royal Charter in 1840, began business with the *Chile* and *Peru* (see p. 715), receiving a small subsidy. A bi-monthly service between Valparaiso and Panama necessitated four more steamers in 1852, the Pacific trade developing, and fresh branches of commerce being opened up. Compound engines were welcomed and adopted in 1856, thereby reducing the costly consumption of coal, the scarcity of which article had been the earliest difficulty. The Company's powers were enlarged in 1865, to run as far as the River Plate. In 1867, the capital was increased for the onerous performance of a monthly mail service from Liverpool, through the Straits of Magellan to Valparaiso, the *Pacific*, 1,630 tons, sailing from that port May, 1868. The success of the new line resulted in three sailings a month, and an extension to Callao, by 1870. Again, two years later, the capital was added to, the *Sorata*, 4,038 tons, starting in 1873 a weekly service from Liverpool to Callao *via* France, Spain, Portugal, Brazil, and River Plate. One of the finest and largest fleets was acquired, 54 steamers being employed in 1874, recording 120,000 tons, but trade with South America falling off, fortnightly departures were reverted to, and the requisite employment for some of the boats presented itself in 1877, when the *Lusitania* led the way to Australia for the Orient Line, in which service the Company have the *Ortona*, 8,000 tons, and three other vessels, viz: *Orizaba*, *Orcya*, and *Oruba*, each 6,000 tons; 35 steamers, fitted with every modern convenience and contrivance, now make up 120,000 tons, and the fleet triumphs over the perils of the sea, which are all met with upon such a voyage, winning for the "Pacific Company" a name for conveying its numerous passengers—safely, speedily, and comfortably.

London Office: 5, Fenchurch Avenue, E.C.

PENINSULAR & ORIENTAL STEAM NAVIGATION COMPANY.—Mr. Brodie McG. Wilcox began to sow the seeds in 1825, and from the *William Fawcett*, 206 tons: 60 h.-p. : $74 \times 15 \times 8$, blossomed the Peninsular Company, subsequently ripening into the above institution, which was incorporated 1840, and celebrated its Jubilee 1887. The company, universally known as the "P. & O.," glories in its motto, "Quis separabit," and its performances have always been in accordance with its traditions, grown old with Imperial significance.

The Log Book of the British Empire has been largely contributed to by our steamship owners, and we can only run through the head-lines of a few of the numerous pages, so handsomely filled by this famous company (see p. 714). Mails were conveyed by Post Office sailing packets from Falmouth to Lisbon before the contract was given to the Peninsular Company. The Indian Mails were at that time taken in Government Steamers from Bombay to Suez. Prior to the completion of the railway, 1857 (followed by the Suez Canal, 1870), everybody and everything had

to take the caravan route across the desert to Cairo, intimately associated with the name of Lieut. Waghorn, who organised quicker and better facilities, Nile steamers afterwards superseding the sailing boats between Cairo and Alexandria. From Alexandria, Home Government steam packets carried the mails to Gibraltar, where the Peninsular Company received them. They soon suggested and pressed a better service than this upon the Government, and eventually, a line from England *vid* Gibraltar and Malta to Alexandria, was begun by the *Oriental*, 1,600 tons, and *great Liverpool*, 1,540 tons, for which purpose, the above company was constituted. The P. & O. Company secured the contract for the mails between Suez and Calcutta in 1842, the first sailing being the *Hindustan*, 1,800 tons; but the East India Company obstinately refused to hand over their inferior Bombay-Suez Line until 1854, by which period the P. & O. had engaged to run to China and Singapore. The first service to Australia was interrupted by the Crimean War, 11 P. & O. boats being employed. The necessity growing for an independent Australian Mail Line, the government called for tenders in 1856, but the P. & O. declined the onerous conditions which were swallowed by the European and Australian Steam Navigation Company, who, when they got to work, demonstrated in two years, that to take a contract left alone by the prudently-managed P. & O. meant ruin to shareholders and inconvenience to the public. The Royal Mail Company stopped the breach but temporarily, and the Government, having learnt a lesson, accepted the tender of the P. & O. Company in 1859.

A history of the company from that date would embrace most of the salient features in one of Shipbuilding, Marine Engineering, and the Steam Transportation of Mails, Passengers, Specie, and Merchandise.

The Mails are invariably ahead of the contract times, which are as follows:—

Indian mails—Bombay	..	14½ days.
China ,, —Shanghai	33	,,
Australian ,, —Adelaide	30½	,,

The *Caledonia*, 7,558 tons, has landed the mails at Bombay within 12¼ days from London *vid* Brindisi, the steamer's own passage between Bombay and Plymouth having been less than 17 days. The *Isis* and *Osiris* running in the Brindisi-Port Said Express Service, deliver the Egyptian Mails within four days from the Metropolis of the Empire. An expression often heard from the mouth of a sailor, "as good as a P. & O. Boat" is equivalent to the landsman's pet phrase "as safe as the Bank of England," and the comparison is admirably in keeping with the solidity of this company, and the international esteem in which it is held. The fleet is being strengthened by the *Assaye*, *Sobraon*, and *Plassy*, each 7,240 tons; the *Persia*, 8,000 tons; and the *Banca*, 6,000 tons, £7,000,000 having been expended upon it during the last 20 years.

The above will bring the total of large and fast steamers to 57, amounting to 297,692 tons, a Flotilla of 30 steam tenders and tugs representing 3,000 tons more.

London Office: 122, Leadenhall Street, E.C.

PRINCE LINE, LIMITED, is the substantial handiwork of Mr. James Knott of Newcastle-on-Tyne, since he despatched the *Saxon Prince* in 1883. The fleet of 42 ubiquitous steamers reaches 94,000 tons, the *Dutch Prince*, with a dead weight capacity of 7,400 tons, being the largest. There are regular passenger and cargo services, but the Lines to West Indies, United States, Mexico, Brazil, Mediterranean, Syria, &c., are too numerous to detail. The recording of 13,587 emigrants conveyed from Italy to New York last year, and the carriage in bulk of 2,600,000 gallons of molasses by the *Russian Prince* tank steamer in four trips this spring, from Havana to Philadelphia, will illustrate the area the business ranges over.

London Office: 5, Fen Court, Fenchurch St., E.C.

ROYAL MAIL STEAM PACKET COMPANY was originated by Mr. James Macqueen, and received its charter in 1839, with a subsidy of £240,000 a year, essential for the conduct of operations to and from the West Indies, and the promotion of British interests therewith, as the coal needed left little space for even the small amount of freight then available. Beginning upon a big scale by building 14 steamers, the *Taames* started a fortnightly service from Falmouth, 1842, returning to Southampton, the Company's headquarters. In 1848 gold was discovered at Sacramento, the Californian fever greatly benefiting the Pacific Mail Steamship Company and its connections, including this Company. Owing to difficulties attendant upon the establishment of such a comprehensive system forthwith, instead of gradually, questions arose, chiefly concerning the Inter-Colonial services; but the Company successfully emerged from the ordeal of a Parliamentary enquiry, and secured a renewal of the subsidy in 1849, subject to the doubling of the service to Colon, and the performance of a monthly line to Brazil and River Plate, which was inaugurated 1851. The Royal Mail helped to finance the Panama railroad, which 47⅓ miles has been the highway for vast traffic, since its completion, 1855, and in 1857 added to its work by temporarily taking the mails *via* Suez to Australia. The abstraction of Messrs. Slidell & Mason from the *Trent* in 1861 created an international incident which aroused intense public excitement. In 1868 one of the main lines was extended to Colon, and next year the other one followed suit to Buenos Ayres, the latter growing into a fortnightly service by 1872. Passing slowly from one stage to another, and encountering varying vicissitudes, sometimes caused by hurricanes, the reputation of this distinguished company is now worthily sustained with 29 steamers exceptionally well adapted for tropical trades, the *Danube* and the *Nile*, each 5946 tons, helping to swell the total to 95,000 tons. The area of commerce covered by the fleet can be measured by its visits to 60 Ports, necessitating 4,000 departures and entrances annually, and 1¼ millions of mileage. (*See* p 715.)

London Office: 18, Moorgate Street, E.C.

SHAW, SAVILL AND ALBION COMPANY, LIMITED.—Messrs. Shaw, Savill and Company's London ships, and the Glasgow ones of Messrs. Patrick Henderson and Co., sailed monthly to New Zealand nearly 50 years ago, occupying 4 to 5 months, passages being subsequently reduced to 80 to 90 days by the Clippers. An amalgamated service of steamers was established in 1883, the vessels now ranging from 3,000 to 8,000 tons. Besides the 15,000 tons of 13 sailing ships, the company owns 13 steamers, making 75,000 tons in all. The *Karamea*, 5,464 tons; *Kumara*, 6,034 tons, and *Waiwera*, 6,237 tons, being latest additions. A first class monthly

service for mails, passengers, and merchandise is maintained, sheep and dairy produce figuring very largely homewards. Messrs. Ismay, Imrie and Company have associated with this Line their *Ionic, Delphic,* and *Gothic,* a passage of the last named having been under 35½ days. Outwards the passage is *via* the Cape of Good Hope, returning round Cape Horn, presenting a healthgiving and varied voyage of 25,000 miles.

London Office: 34, Leadenhall Street, E.C.

UNION STEAM SHIP COMPANY, LTD.—The original fleet—*Briton, Dane, Norman, Saxon,* and *Union*—belonging to the Union Steam Collier Company in 1853, totalled together but 2,327 tons; after making one or two voyages to Constantinople, the boats were all very profitably chartered in consequence of the Crimean War. As the fruits of sagacious and plucky management the directors can to-day point the finger of pride to the 114,715 tons of one of the finest fleets in the world, freighted in times of peace with mails, passengers, gold, diamonds, and merchandise from our ever-increasing and valuable South African dependencies, or crammed with all the paraphernalia of war when the foes of the Empire throw aside the mask, and in blind ignorance "ask for it." In 1857, the line secured a monthly mail contract with an annual subsidy of £30,000 to the Cape of Good Hope, St. Helena and Ascension becoming calling ports next year. In 1862, the mail contract was renewed, and another one entered into to Natal, the service being extended to Mauritius in 1864. Semi-monthly sailings in 1857, then three a month in 1873, with a branch service every four weeks between Cape Town and Zanzibar, and a fortnightly mail contract in 1876, were stepping stones to the present excellent services. In 1885, the *Moor,* during the Zulu War, was commissioned under a Naval officer, supplied with an armament of six guns and 110 officers and men, and cruised up the East coast of Africa. The *Scot,* nine years ago the largest boat in the trade, has gone out in 14 days 11 hours and returned in 14 days, both record passages. The cutting of the *Scot* into two for the addition of 54 feet to her length in 1896, was a brilliant engineering feat in the annals of those famous shipbuilders, Harland and Wolff, by which her tonnage was increased to 7,815 tons. Four wellknown "G.'s" were followed in 1894 by the *Norman,* 7,537 tons, four more "G.'s" afterwards strengthening the intermediate service. In 1898, the *Briton,* 10,248 tons, 550 × 60 × 40, joined the service, about to be further augmented by her sister boat the *Saxon,* bringing the fleet up to 22, including 13 twin-screw steamers, the *Galeka* having been added to the Intermediate Fleet. The mail steamers sail every alternate Saturday from Southampton *via* Madeira. Intermediate steamers leave Southampton every other Saturday (*via* Teneriffe) after calling at Hamburg and Antwerp every 14 days, and at Rotterdam every 28 days, and an extra boat goes every 28 days on Wednesdays from Southampton *via* Lisbon and Madeira.

London Office: 19, Bishopsgate St. Within, E.C.

UNION STEAM SHIP COMPANY OF NEW ZEALAND.—Prior to the opening of the gold fields in 1862, a solitary paddle-boat fulfilled the requirements of the district of Otago. Trade then increasing five more steamers were purchased for links with other Ports in the Middle Island, the undertaking developing by 1875 into the above concern. It is now the most important in the Southern Hemisphere and keeps busily and profitably employed the ss. *Moana*, 3,915 tons, and 54 other steamers fitted with every up-to-date improvement, the total tonnage of 75,000 tons testifying to the expansion of both Colony and Company.

London Office: 34, Leadenhall Street, E.C.

WEST INDIA AND PACIFIC STEAM SHIP COMPANY, LIMITED.—Mr. Alfred Holt entered the West Indian trade (from Liverpool) in 1857, with the steamer *Saladin*, 500 tons and conducted a Line which, as traffic increased, *via* the Panama route, attracted the attention of others. In 1863, the Line belonging to Messrs. Leech, Harrison and Forwood was formed into the above company, absorbing the others. The company's largest vessel in 1864 was 1,750 tons; now the *Atlantian* and *Indian* each exceed 9,000 tons. The fleet of 20 steamers aggregates 97,000 tons, and conveys passengers and cargo to the principal ports in the Spanish Main; to the West Coasts of North and South America, and the Gulf of Mexico. Since 1874, owing to the direct competition of Continental boats, which have of late years cut up the Transhipment Traffic *via* Liverpool, the steamers have been largely increased in carrying capacity to suit the cotton trade from New Orleans, the biggest boats each taking 28,000 to 30,000 bales.

London Office: Eastcheap Buildings, E.C.

WHITE STAR LINE.—The original line of clippers was taken over in 1867 by Mr. T. H. Ismay. Messrs. Ismay, Imrie & Co. soon saw how the tide was running, and wisely took the fortunate "turn" in 1869 by founding the Oceanic Steam Navigation Company, Ltd., better known as above, a project carried out by them with conspicuous success. They leapt immediately into prominence with the *Oceanic*, 3,807 tons, 420 × 42 × 31. in which vessel the genius of the late Sir Edward Harland introduced so many admirable features. A fleet was built of speedily-patronised steamers, whose names are too well known to need repetition, but not until 1875 did the line take the lead in point of speed with *Britannic*, 5,004 tons, and *Germanic*, 5,070 tons, the former running out in 7 days 10 hrs. 50 min., reducing by three hours the previous best on record. In 1895 *Germanic* received new boilers and engines, and in August, 1896, made her 229th westward passage in 6 days 21 hrs. 38 min.; her passenger accommodation having been re-arranged and re-decorated upon the improved plans and style of *Teutonic* and *Majestic*, another lease of popularity is ensured her. The *Teutonic*, 9,984 tons, came out in 1889, closely followed by *Majestic*, 9,965 tons, the first steamers designed for mercantile armed cruisers under arrangements with the Admiralty, upon whose list the line has five other steamers. *Teutonic* won golden opinions at Naval Review, 1889, and attended the Diamond Jubilee Review armed with 16 guns. The sister-ships soon enrolled their names on the honours list. In July, 1891, *Majestic* created a record of 5 days 18 hrs. 8 min (West), *Teutonic* lowering this the next month to 5 days 16 hrs. 31 min. In August, 1896, *Majestic* excelled her previous performance by 12 min., but the steamers of this line are notorious for improving with age, every one having been built by Harland & Wolff, a unique association; *Britannic* the same year actually completed a record of 1½ millions of miles, traversed with her

original boilers and engines, the passage terminating this feat being one of 7 days 7 hrs. 30 min. to New York. On January 14, 1899, a new chapter in the history of ship-building was grandly opened, when there glided from the famous yard of Harland & Wolff a giantess which put the *Great Eastern* in the shade, the tonnage of *Oceanic II*, reaching 17,247 tons and her displacement 30,000 tons. She considerably exceeds in size any vessel built or building, and sailed upon her maiden voyage Sep. 6, 1899. The *Medic*, 11,984 tons, with 85 passengers and a large cargo was despatched August 3, 1899, to inaugurate a Liverpool-Australian service with twin-screw steamers *via* the Cape, which will be conducted with the *Afric, Persic, Runic* and *Suevic*, all carrying only one class of passengers. The White Star Steam Expresses, models of comfort and luxury, have taken the United States mails since 1877, and, besides a cargo service to New York there is a Pacific line worked by the Occidental and Oriental Steamship Co. of San Francisco between San Francisco, Yokohama, and Hong-Kong, also a New Zealand service under the flag of Shaw, Savill & Albion Co., Ltd. The 24 noble steamships belonging to this Company approximately make up 188,000 tons; of these 17 are twin-screw vessels including some of the finest and largest cargo and live-stock carriers in existence.

London Office: 34, Leadenhall Street, E.C.

WILSON LINE.—The firm of Beckinton, Wilson, and Co., founded at Hull, about 1835, by Mr. Thos. Wilson, merged its proprietorship in the Wilson family a few years later, when the present style of the firm was adopted, and the business (which became a private Company in 1891) has been jointly conducted with remarkable energy and success by Messrs. Charles and Arthur Wilson. The first partners imported considerable quantities of Swedish and Russian iron, and ever since 1845, when they regularly sailed the *Patriot* and other ships, between Hull and Gothenberg, the firm has held the foremost position in the Baltic trade. In 1850, the present mail service between England and Sweden was started with the *Courier*, 400 tons, and soon developed into a large mail and passenger service to the principal Swedish and Norwegian ports. The St. Petersburg, Riga, and Stettin trades were gradually included, the *Dido*, 1,409 tons, in 1869 being the first departure to the Adriatic, the same year operations being extended to the Black Sea. A line from London to India was maintained from 1870 until 1875, when the steamers were required for the New York and Boston trade, which has developed into employing the most tonnage, the ss. *Idaho*, 5,974 tons, being the largest. In 1878 the steamers of Messrs. Brownlow, Marsden & Co. were purchased and the Hamburg, Antwerp and Dunkirk trades taken up. Connection with India was resumed in 1883, with a Line between Hull and Bombay, and in 1895, a service between London and Boston, U.S., was established in association with the Furness and Leyland Lines. Messrs. Thos. Wilson, Sons & Co., the largest private shipowning concern in the world, possess, with three vessels building, 85 steamers, grossing 175,000 tons, and maintain a series of regular services too voluminous to enumerate.

London Agents: W. E. Bott & Co., 1 E. India Av., E.C.

Thanks are due to the various Steam Ship Companies and others who have furnished information for this Article.

Railway Statistics of the World.

The following table has been compiled mainly from figures supplied by Messrs. Ackermann & Adamson, Civil Engineers, of Cape Town. The statistics of area and population will be found, in some instances, to differ from those given in other parts of the Almanack. The statistics refer to the year ended 31 December, 1898.

COUNTRY.	Population.	Area in sq. miles.	Miles of railway.	Sq. miles to 1 mile of railway.	Population to 1 mile of railway.	Density of population to 1 mile of railway.
United Kingdom	39,829,765	120,137	21,277	5⅔	1,872	331½
Empire of India	236,000,000	1,000,000	20,390	49	11,574	236
Dominion of Canada	5,250,000	3,315,647	11,404	290	460	1½
New South Wales	1,346,240	310,700	2,700	115	498	4⅓
Victoria	1,170,000	87,884	3,130	28	37	13⅓
Queensland	485,000	668,500	2,600	257	186	4⅔
South Australia	362,900	903,700	1,730	522	209	⅓
Western Australia	168,200	975,900	1,770	551	95	⅙
New Zealand	744,000	104,500	2,000	52	372	7
Tasmania	178,000	26,250	500	52	356	6¾
Cape Colony	1,765,960	276,567	2,495	111	708	6½
Rhodesia	22,500	750,000	714	105½	31	3/100
Natal	630,817	20,851	487	42½	1,295	31 1/5
Transvaal	750,000	119,200	1,090	110	688	6⅓
Orange Free State	207,503	48,326	700	69	297	4¼
United States	62,622,250	3,581,885	184,428	19⅛	339	17½
*Africa	202,446,420	10,264,918	4,909	2,091	41,240	20
†Asia	214,078,403	14,621,036	2,150	6,800	99,571	14½
Austria-Hungary	44,901,036	261,649	19,697	13¼	2,279	172
Belgium	6,586,593	11,373	2,839	4	2,320	580
Central America	18,660,055	1,424,497	8,564	166⅓	9,712	13
China	303,241,969	1,534,953	320	4,797	947,631	198
Denmark	2,185,335	14,789	1,389	10½	1,573	127¾
Finland	2,573,000	144,254	1,491	97	1,725	18
France	38,517,975	204,146	22,656	9	1,700	188½
Germany	52,246,589	211,168	28,071	7½	1,861	247
Greece	2,433,806	24,977	582	42¾	4,182	97½
Holland	4,859,451	12,582	2,686	4⅔	1,809	386
Italy	31,476,217	110,623	9,592	11½	3,282	284½
Japan	42,270,628	162,655	2,505	65	16,874	259
Norway	2,135,500	124,500	1,119	111	1,908	18
Portugal	5,082,247	34,606	1,420	24	3,580	150
Russia	106,159,141	2,080,396	25,898	80⅓	4,009	51
South America	32,345,570	6,649,638	27,592	24½	1,172	5
Spain	17,550,216	196,173	6,070	32	2,891	158½
Sweden	5,009,632	172,877	6,350	27	789	29
Switzerland	2,933,334	15,469	2,407	6½	1,218	189
Turkey	4,668,000	66,500	2,974	22	1,569	70
Europe	369,149,837	3,806,216	159,231	24	2,318	97
Asia	795,591,000	17,318,644	25,365	683	31,362	46
Africa	205,823,200	11,550,862	10,395	1,111	19,800	18
North & South America	100,415,400	15,806,154	231,988	68	433	6⅓
Australasia	5,631,093	3,425,075	16,157	212	348	1⅔
THE WORLD	1,476,610,530	51,906,951	443,136	117	3,084	28½

* Exclusive of Cape Colony, Rhodesia, Natal, Orange Free State, and Transvaal, given under separate heads.
† Exclusive of British India, China, and Japan, shown under those heads.

*** The following Table aims at exhibiting all Coal-mining properties employing 2,000 hands underground, as well as all individual mines employing over 1,000 (except a few, under 1,250 in all), the names of these latter being printed in *italics*; the other names are those of the largest pits in each group or property, to which the total number of working pits is appended in parentheses.

Inspector's District.	Owners.	Locality.	Leading Mine and Number in Group.	Hands employed. Below Grnd.	Hands employed. Above Grnd.
E. Scotland	Fife Coal Co.	Fifeshire	Cowdenbeath, &c. (9)	3,402	967
W. Scotland	Baird (Wm.) & Co.	Ayrsh., Lanarks., &c.	Common (Cummock) (32)	6,250	1,264
Newcastle. (Nthumb., Cumb., & N.E. Durham.)	Ashington Coal Co.	Morpeth	*Ashing'on, &c.* (3)	2,98c	646
	Bedlington Coal Co.	Bedlington, N'thbrld.	Bedlington, &c. (4)	2,728	453
	Bowes (Jno.) & Partners	Gateshead	Springwell, &c. (12)	3,758	1,007
	Cowpen Coal Co.	Blyth	North Seaton, &c. (4)	2,709	602
	Cramlington Coal Co.	Nr. Newcastle	Dudley, &c. (6)	2,138	601
	Harton Coal Co.	S. Shields	Whitburn, Boldon, &c. (4)	3,743	1,078
	Heworth Colliery Owners	Gateshead	*Heworth*	1,071	286
	Joicey (Jas.) & Co.	S. of Gateshead	Tantields (5), &c. (13)	3,533	918
	Perkins (Chas.) & Partners	Chester le-Street	Ravensworths (2), &c. (7)	2,075	469
	Seaton Delaval Coal Co.	Nr. Blyth	Seaton Delaval (7)	2,427	581
Durham (with N. Yorks).	Bolckow, Vaughan, & Co.	Bp. Auckland	Binchester, &c. (13)	4,390	1,475
	Consett Iron Co. (coal mines)	Nr. Lanchester	Derwent William, &c. (8)	2,544	601
	Hetton Coal Co.	Hetton-le-Hole	Eppletons, &c. (4)	2,089	944
	Lambton Collieries	Fence Houses	Houghton, &c. (15)	7,254	1,578
	Londonderry, Marq. of	Sunderland	Seaham and Silksworth (2)	3,243	817
	Pease & Partners	Nr. Durham	Esh, Ushaw Moor, &c. (10)	3,311	1,200
	Scott (Walter), Ld.	E. Durham	East Hetton, &c. (3)	2,051	595
	South Hetton Coal Co.	Sunderland	Murtons (3), &c. (4)	2,393	813
	Strakers and Love	Nr. Durham	Brancepeths (3), &c. (7)	2,345	959
	Weardale Iron Co. (coal mines)	Mid Durham	Tudhoe, &c. (10)	3,627	1,210
Yorks and Linc. (E. and W. Rdgs., &c.)	Acton Hall Co.	Pontefract	*Acton Hall*	1,424	475
	Briggs (H.), Son, & Co.	Normanton, Pont'fr't.	Silkstone, &c. (8)	2,68c	749
	Brown (Jno.) & Co.	Rotherham	Aldwarke Main, &c. (4)	2,863	913
	Charlesworth, J. & J.	Leeds and S. Yorks	Thorpbergh Hall, &c. (8)	3,453	774
	Denaby and Cadeby Main Cos.	Rotherham	Denaby Main and Cadeby, (2)	2,541	836
	Hickleton Main Coal Co.	"	*Hickleton Main*	1,103	267
	Newton, Chambers, & Co. (4 Ccs.)	Barnsley and Sheffield	Rockingham, &c. (4)	1,823	640
	Yorks. & Derby Coal & Iron Co.	Barnsley	*Carlton Main*	1,103	277
Manchester. (Lanc., N. & E., &Ireld.)	Bridgwater Trustees	S. Lanc.	Mosley Common, &c. (20)	2,939	518
	Clifton & Kersley Coal Co.	Nr. Manchester	Newtowns (2), &c. (6)	2,171	524
	Knowles (Andr.) & Sons	"	Pendlebury, &c. (7)	2,072	625
Liverpool. (S.W.Lanc., Dnb., &c.)	Evans (Richd.) & Co.	Nr. St. Helens	Princess, &c. (16)	3,250	473
	Pearson & Knowles Coal & Ir. Co	Wigan	Moss (1—5), &c. (8)	2,325	353
	Wigan Cl. & I. Co. (pt. M'ch'st'r)	Nr. Wigan	Hewlett, Crawford, &c. (27)	6,102	1,159
Midland (Derby, Notts,Leic., &c.	Annesley Colliery Co.	Nottingham	*Annesley*	1,058	238
	Babbington Coal Co.	Alfreton & Basford	Cinderhills, Tibshelfs, &c. (11)	2,876	873
	Barber, Walker, & Co.	Eastwood, Notts	Moor Green, &c. (5)	2,502	446
	Blackwell Colliery Co.	Alfreton, Derby	Blackwells (1—4), &c. (9)	2,175	444
	Butterley Iron & Coal Co.	Derby, Notts. & Staff.	Kirkby, Plumptre, &c. (21)	3,561	957
	Clay Cross Iron and Coal Co.	Clay Cross, Derb.	Park House, No. 7, &c. (7)	2,627	617
	Linby Colliery Co.	Nottingham	*Linby*	1,044	25c
	Newstead Colliery Co.	"	*Newstead*	1,203	283
	Sheepbridge Coal & Iron Co.	Chesterf'd. & Mansf'd	Langwith, &c. (4)	2,183	508
	Staveley Coal & Iron Co.	"	Markham No. 1, &c. (10)	5,093	753
	Wells, J. & G.	Eckington, Derby	Holbrooks, &c. (7)	2,115	456
Sth. Western (with Glos., Monm.,&c.)	Cardiff Steam Coal Colls.	Nr. Cardiff	*Llanbradach*	1,074	198
	Ebbw Vale Steel, &c. Co.	Monmouthshire	Waun Llwyd, &c. (10)	2,347	461
	Lancaster (Jno.) & Co.	Blaina, &c., Monm.	Griffins (3), &c. (6)	2,822	358
	Lancaster's Steam Coal Colls.	Cwmtillery, Monm.	*Rose Heyworth*	1,350	259
	Newport Blk. Vein Stm. Coal Co.	Abercarn	*Celynen*	1,450	260
	Tredegar Iron & Coal Co.	Tredegar, Monm.	Pochin, Bedwellty, &c. (7)	2,660	499
South Wales	Albion Steam Coal Co.	Pontypridd, Glam.	*Albion*	1,589	191
	Cambrian Collieries	Clydach Vale, Pontyp.	*Cambrian Navig., Nos. 1 & 2*	2,482	390
	Cory Bros. and Co.	" Glamorg.	Pentre, &c. (10)	2,642	532
	Davis (D.) & Sons	Pontypridd & Merthyr	Ferndales (8)	4,805	647
	Dowlais Iron Co. (coal mines)	Merthyr	Bedllnogs, &c. (10)	4,455	808
	Glamorgan Coal Co.	Pontyp. & Bridgend	Llwynypias (4), &c. (5)	2,457	341
	Insoles, Ld.	Pontypridd	*Cymmer, &c.* (2)	1,385	223
	Nixon's Navigation Coal Co.	Mnth. Ash & Merthyr	*Navign., Dp. Duffryn, Merthyr*	5,307	1,779
	North's Navigation Collieries	Bridgend & Maesteg	Coegnant, &c. (8) . [Vales, (6)	2,744	846
	Ocean Coal Co.	Merthyr and Bridgend	Dp. Navign., Park, &c. (9)	6,327	565
	Powell Duffryn Stm. Coal Co.	Glamorg. & Monm.	*New Tredegar, Ab'raman,&c.(10)*	4,982	840

SUMMARY.—The Coal produced in the U. K. in 1898 was valued at £64,169,382 (Durham, 10½ millions; Yorks, 9; Lanc., 7·8; Glamorg., 6·6; Lanark, 4·8; Staff., 4·2; Derby, 3·9; Northumb., 3·2; Monm., 2·4; Notts, 2·4; Fife, 1·4; Ayr, 1·1). A few of the above produce also Ironstone or Fireclay.

The total output of Coal for the United Kingdom in 1898 amounted to 202,054,516 tons, slightly less than last year, but some 4½ millions higher in value. There is a great decrease in Glamorg. and Monmouth, but an increase in the North and Scotld.; 12,273 tons came from open quarries.

*** Under the Metals information as to the extent of the output will be of more service than lists of the numbers of hands employed. Most, however, of the Iron, Stone, Slate, and Chalk mines or quarries are worked under either the Coal Mines or the Quarries Act, under which the former item is never supplied except in groups; in these cases the latter may have to be substituted.

Mineral.	Owners.	Locality.	Mine, or Leading Mine.	Weight of Output.	Val. at Mine.
					£
ARSENIC [1]	Devon Great Consols Co.	Tavistock	Devon Gt. Consols	1,723 tns.	24,210
BASALT, DIORITE, &c.[2]	Not given	Carnarv. (Diorite)	Various quarries	409,725 ,,	114,608
	,, ,,	S ropshire	,, ,,	241,651 ,,	28,325
CHALK [3]	,, ,,	Kent	,, ,,	2,904,422 ,,	112,200
CLAY [4]	,, ,,	Cornwall (China clay)	,, ,,	446,454 ,,	250,251
	,, ,,	Staffordsh. (Brick clay	,, ,,	1,709,611 ,,	174,666
COPPER [5]	Levant Mining Co.	St. Just, Penzance	Levant ......(Dressed)	2,981 ,,	12,057
GRANITE [6]	Not given	Leicest.	Various quarries	1,993,677 ,,	213,990
	,, ,,	Aberdeensh.	,, ,,	332,140 ,,	116,109
GRAVEL, &c.[7]	,, ,,	Lanark	,, ,,	208,473 ,,	17,219
GYPSUM [8]	,, ,,	Notts	,, ,,	74,667 ,,	31,603
IRON [9]	Barrow Hæmatite Steel Co.	Furness	Park, Stank, &c.	34‡,200 ,,	?173,000
	Bell Bros.	Guisbrough & Saltbn.	Skelton Pk., &c.	1,421 empd.	—
	Bolckow, Vaughan, & Co.	Middlesbro. & Saltbn.	Eston, &c.	1,685 ,,	—
	Gillfoot Pk. Mining Co.	Egremont, Cumbd.	Gillfoot Pk.	87,008 tns.	?45,000
	Harrison, Ainslie, & Co.	Lindal-in-Furness	Lindal Moor	154,477 ,,	?80,000
	Hodbarrow Mining Co.	Millom, Cumbd.	Hodbarrow	420,336 ,,	?229,000
	Kennedy Bros.	Dalton-in-Furness	Roanhead	139,558 ,,	?76,000
	Pease & Partners	Saltburn, N. Yorks	Loftus, &c.	1,506 empd.	—
	Wyndham Mining Co.	Egremont, Cumbd.	Wyndham	112,501 tns.	?61,000
LEAD [10] & SILVER [11]	Not given	Wanlockhead, Dumfries	Queensberry { Lead	1,456 ,,	} —
			{ Silv.	10,104 oz.	
	,, ,,	Holywell, Flint	Halkyn { Lead	3,643 tns.	} 41,851
			{ Silv.	29,584 oz.	
	,, ,,	Durham	{ Weardale Co.'s { Lead	1,571 tns.	} 17,551
			{ Mines { Silv.	10,761 oz.	
	,, ,,	Foxdale, I. Man	Foxdale { Lead	2,611 tns.	} 34,000
			{ Silv.	66,125 oz.	
	,, ,,	Durham	Teasdale Mines { Lead	1,904 tns.	} 15,618
			{ Silv.	20,173 oz.	
LIMESTONE [12]	,, ,,	Derbyshire	Various quarries	1,729,648 tns.	146,641
	,, ,,	Co. Durham	,, ,,	1,923,132 ,,	152,736
OIL SHALE [13]	,, ,,	W. & Mid Lothian	,, mines	2,031,909 ,,	508,000
SALT, ROCK [14]	Given collectively	Northwich, &c.	,, ,,	62,313 ,,	12,000
,, BRINE [15]	,, ,,	Chesh., with Staff.	,, pits and holes..	1,157,175 ,,	355,000
	,, ,,	Durham	,, ,,	194,379 ,,	87,174
SANDSTONE [16]	Not given	Yorks	Various quarries & mines	1,013,799 ,,	486,085
	,, ,,	Lanc.	,, ,,	824,893 ,,	248,344
SLATE [17]	Greaves (J. W.) & Sons	Blaenau Festiniog, Me-	Llechwedd	20,484 ,,	74,614
	Oakeley Slate Quarries Co.	,, ,,(rioneth	Oakeley	57,792 ,,	—
	Votty & Bowydd Sl. Quarries Co.	,, ,,	Votty & Bowydd	15,3‡8 ,,	—
	Not given	Carnarv.	Penrhyn, Dinorwic, &c.	318,012 ,,	967,999
TIN [18]	Bassett Mines, Ld.	Illogan, Cornwall	Bassett (Dressed)	356 ,,	14,001
	Carn Brea & Tincft. Mining Co.		Carn Brea & Tncft. ,,	618 ,,	24,361
	Dolcoath Mine, Ld.	Camborne	Dolcoath ,,	2,302 ,,	59,719
	Levant Mining Co.	St. Just, Penzance	Levant ,,	556 ,,	21,448
	West Kitty Mining Co.	St. Agnes, Penzance	West Wheal Kitty ,,	421 ,,	19,277
	Wheal Grenville Mining Co.	Camborne	Wheal Grenville ,,	877 ,,	39,110
ZINC [19]	Minera Mining Co.	Wrexham	Minera	2,917 ,,	18,209
	Various (Cumberland)	Alston and Keswick	,,	9,655 ,,	48,350

1 Total Arsenic from U.K. mines, £53,787 (Devon and Cornwall), also £8,144 Arsenical Pyrites (same cos.).
2 Total Basalt, &c., £465,543 (Carnarv., Dior. & Quartz-Porph.; Salop, Staff., Warw., Basalt; Yorks, Whinstone).
3 Total Chalk, £180,651 (chiefly Kent, but also Essex, Sussex, Hants, Surrey, Middlesex, Bedford, &c.).
4 Total Clays (Brick, China, Fire, Potter's, &c.), £1,615,358 (Cornw., Staff., Yorks., Lanc., Durham, Lanark, Leic., Worc., Derby, Warwick, &c.), including £13,552 Fuller's Earth (£7,063 Surrey, £6,695 Somerset).
5 Total Copper (ore and precipitate), £27,149 (Cornwall, Merioneth, Devon, Anglesea, &c.). Chief supply obtained from France, after that the United States, with some from Holland, Belgium, Germany, &c.
6 Total Granite £576,457 (Leic., largely Syenite. Aberd. Cumb., Cornw. Westmd. Kirkcudb., Argyle, &c.).
7 Total Gravel and Sand (besides shallow pits), £15,538 (Lanark. Staffs., Kent, Herts, Notts, Beds, Surrey, &c.).
8 Total Gypsum, £71,316 (Notts, Staff., Cumb., Derby, Sussex, and a little from Westmorld. and Somerset).
9 Total Iron, value as ore, £3,400,628 (Yorks., 0'98 million; Cumb., '76; Lanc. '41; Staff., '32; Linc., '25; Ayr, '15; Nthants, '14); value as pig iron, £14,740,043.
10 Total Lead, smelted (same for figures above), £332,995, or 25,355 tons (Flint, 5,313 tons; Derb., 4,062; Durh., 3,746 : I. Man, 2,900; Dumfries, 2,434; Westmorld, 1,115; Salop, 1,033).
11 Total Silver from British Lead mines, £23,728 for 211,404 oz. (I. Man, 76,419 oz.; Flint, 39,949; Durh., 34,199).
12 Total Limestone, £1,256,154 (Durh., Derb., Yks., Wilts., Dorset, Devon, Som. Lanc., Midloth., Glam., &c.).
13 Total Oil Shale £524,498 (W. & Mid Lothian, Lanark, Stirling, Yorks, Ayr., Flint, &c.).
14 Total Rock Salt £34,360 (Lanc., Chesh., and Antrim); in Antrim White Salt, value £4,44c, is made therefrom.
15 Total Brine Salt, £585,755 (Chesh., Durh., Worc., Lanc., Staff., and Yorks).
16 Total Sandstone £1,632,786 (Yorks., Lanc., Lanark., Dumf., Derby, Forfar, Ayr, Glamorg., Nthmb., Dur., &c.).
17 Total Slate, £1,900,228 (Carnarv. and Merioneth, also Argyle, Lanc., Cornw., Perth, Dentigh, Tipperary, &c.).
18 Total Tin, £288,325 (all Cornwall, except £69 Devon).
19 Total Zinc, £117,784, as Spelter £179,482 (Cumb., Denbigh, Flint, Cardigan, I. Man, Salop, Carnarv., &c.).
*** Total ANTHRACITE, £700,857; ARSENICAL PYRITES, £8,144; BARYTES, £23,253; CHERT and FLINT, £14,513; OCHRE, UMBER, &c., £13,003; SOPIUM, £12,750; WOLFRAM, £15,844. Also small quantities of Alum Clay (Bauxite), Alum Shale, Bluestone, Bog Ore, Fluor Spar, Gold (only £1,158 this year), Iron Pyrites, Magnesium, Manganese, Mica, Petroleum (£14 only), Phosph. of Lime, Potassium, Strontium, Sulphate, and Uranium.

RAILWAYS AND THEIR HISTORY.

TOTAL LENGTH, CAPITAL, PASSENGERS CONVEYED, RECEIPTS, AND WORKING EXPENSES OF RAILWAYS IN THE UNITED KINGDOM FOR THE PAST 50 YEARS, 1849–1898.

Year.	Length of Lines Open on 31st Dec.	Total Capital Paid up (Shares).	No. of Passengers (exclusive of Season Ticket Holders)	Total of Traffic Receipts.		Working Expenses.	Per cent. of Gross Receipts.	Net Traffic Receipts.
				Total.	Per Mile.			
	Miles.	£	Total.	£	£	£		£
1849	6,031	229,747,778	63,841,539	11,806,498	1,957			
1850	6,621	240,270,745	72,854 422	13,204.668	1,994			
1851	6,890	248,240,896	85,391,095	14,997.439	2,176			
1852	7,336	264,165,672	89,135.729	15,710,554	2.141			
1853	7,686	273,324 514	102,286,660	18,035,879	2,346			
1854	8,054	286,068,794	111,206,707	20,215,724	2,510	Cannot be given previous to 1860.		
1855	8,280	297,584,079	118,595,135	21,507,599	2,597			
1856	8,710	307,595,086	129,315,196	23,165,493	2,660			
1857	9,039	315,157,258	138,971,240	24,174,611	2,674			
1858	9,542	325,375,507	139,141,135	23,956,751	2,511			
1859	10,002	334,362,928	149,757,294	25,743,502	2,574			
1860	10,433	348,130,127	163,435,678	27,766,622	2,661	13,187,368	47	14,579,254
1861	10,865	362,327,338	173,721,139	28,565,355	2,629	13,843,337	48	14,722,018
1862	11,551	385,218,438	180,429,071	29,128,558	2,522	14,268,409	49	14,860,149
1863	12,322	404,215,802	204,635,075	31,156,397	2,529	15,027,234	48	16,129,163
1864	12,789	425,719,613	229,272,165	34,015,564	2,660	16,000,308	47	18,015,256
1865	13,289	455,478,143	251,862,715	35,890,116	2,701	17,149,073	48	18,741,040
1866	13,854	481,872,184	274,293,668	38,164,354	2,755	18,811,673	49	19,352,681
1867	14,247	502,262,887	287,688,113	39,479,999	2,771	19,848,952	50	19,631,047
1868*	14,628	511,680,855	—	—				
1869	15,145	518,779,761	312,759,953	41,075,321	2,712	20,780,078	49	21,915,849
1870	15,537	529,908,673	336,545,397	43,417,070	2,794	21,715,525	48	23,362,618
1871	15,376	552,661,551	375,220,754	47,107,558	3,064	23,152,860	47	25,739,920
1872	15,814	569,047,346	422,874,822	51,304,114	3,244	26,277,640	49	26,957,870
1873	16,082	588,320,308	455,320,188	55,675,421	3,462	30,752,848	53	26,989,152
1874	16,449	609,895,931	477,840,411	56,899,498	3,459	32,612,712	55	26,643,003
1875	16,658	630,223,494	506,975,234	58,982,753	3,541	33,220,728	54	28,016,272
1876	16,872	658,214,776	534,494,069	59,917,868	3,551	36,535,509	54	28,680,266
1877	17,077	674,059,048	549,541,325	60,644,057	3,551	33,857,978	54	29,115,350
1878	17,333	698,545,154	565,024,455	60,454,375	3,488	33,189,368	53	29,673,306
1879	17,696	717,003,469	562,732,890	59,395,381	3,356	32,045,273	52	29,731,430
1880	17,933	728,316,848	603,885,025	62,961,767	3,511	33,601,124	51	31,890,501
1881	18,175	745,528,162	623,047,787	63,908,353	3,516	34,602,616	52	31,954,826
1882	18,457	767,899,570	654,838,295	66,537,128	3,605	36,170,436	52	33,206,688
1883	18,681	784,921,312	683,718,137	68,210,052	3,651	37,368,562	53	33,693,708
1884	18,864	801,464,367	694,991,860	67,701,042	3,589	37,217,197	53	33,305,446
1885	19,169	815,858,055	697,213,031	66,644,967	3,477	36,787,957	53	32,767,817
1886	19,332	828,344,254	725,584,390	66,615,377	3,446	36,518,247	52	33,073,706
1887	19,578	845,971,654	733,678,531	67,914,586	3,469	37,063,266	52	33,880,110
1888	19,812	864,695,963	742,499,164	69,739,870	3,520	37,762,107	52	35,132,358
1889	19,943	876,595,166	775,183,073	73,717,057	3,696	40,094,116	52	36,930,901
1890	20,073	897,472,026	817,744,046	76,548,347	3,813	43,188,556	54	36,760,146
1891	20,191	919,425,121	845,463,668	78,361,633	3,881	45,144,778	55	36,731,624
1892	20,325	944,357,320	864,435,388	78,529,314	3,864	45,717,965	56	36,374,075
1893	20,646	971,323,353	873,177,052	76,844,086	3,722	45,695,119	57	34,936,773
1894	20,908	985,387,355	911,412,926	79,874,566	3,820	47,208,313	56	37,102,518
1895	21,174	1,001,110,221	929,770,909	81,396,047	3,844	47,876,637	56	38,046,065
1896	21,277	1,029,475,335	980,339,433	85,296,200	4,009	50,192.424	56	39,926,698
1897	21,433	1,089,765,095	1,030,420,201	88,375,236	4,123	53,083,804	57	40,653,250
1898	21,659	1,134,468,462	1,062,911,116	91,066,038	4,205	55,960,543	58	40,291,958

* Return for 1863 incomplete.

IN the first half of the seventeenth century (1633 has been cited as the best approach to a definite date) we meet with the earliest mention of the introduction of *rails* for the lessening of friction upon roads. Beams of wood, some six or seven inches in breadth, were about this time laid down to facilitate the draught of the waggons in the vicinity of some of the coal mines at Newcastle: and as a matter of necessity the addition of "sleepers" had speedily to follow. In 1738, at Whitehaven, it is stated that iron was first substituted as the material of the rails; and in 1767 it appears established that this revolution was adopted at Coalbrookdale, being followed nine years later at the Sheffield Colliery. As yet, however, only thick plates of iron were fastened to the surface of the wooden rails, and it was not till 1801 that "edge rails" were introduced, the credit of their adoption being assigned to Lord Penrhyn's slate quarries in Carmarthenshire. James Watt had conceived the idea of utilizing steam for locomotion, and there is a record of a steam locomotive having been used in Cornwall in 1784. George Stephenson, however, in the year 1825, was the first to bring the project fairly into practical shape.

The first Act obtained for the construction of a railway was that of the Surrey Iron Railway Company in 1801, for a line 6 miles long from Wandsworth to Croydon. In 1804 an Act was passed "for making and maintaining a railway or tramroad from the town of Swansea into the parish of Oystermouth, in the county of Glamorgan, and for the hauling or drawing of waggons or other carriages passing upon the said railway or tramroad with men, horses, or otherwise." On the 24th of February, 1804, Trevethick's patent locomotive steam engine was tried at Penydarran, near Merthyr, and conveyed along a tramroad 10 tons of bar iron. and about 70 persons, a distance of 9 miles, The application passed the third reading as a railway or tramroad. The word "otherwise" was evidently intended to cover the use of Trevethick's engine, and this Act may therefore be considered the first in which steam was contemplated as the motive power. The line is now known as the Swansea and Mumbles Railway. Then followed the Carmarthenshire, the Kilmarnock and Troon, the Severn and Wye, the Berwick and Kelso, the Gloucester and Cheltenham, and other small undertakings, about twenty in number altogether, with an aggregate of 250 miles, and an authorized capital somewhat under a million. It is almost unnecessary to add that animal power only was contemplated in their working. The Stockton and Darlington Act was obtained in 1821, with a capital of £102,000; and it is remarkable that, while animal power was to be relied upon for working the line, the clause in the Act states "with men and horses *or otherwise*." George Stephenson came upon the scene immediately after this Act was obtained, and was appointed engineer of the line; and at his urgent request, Edward Pease, the promoter, applied for a new Act empowering the company to work the railway with locomotive engines. Great opposition was encountered, but the bill finally passed in 1823, and the line, which was 25 miles in length, was opened on the 27th of September, 1825. A duplicate system of working was at first adopted, the passenger traffic being conducted by single one-horse coaches, while that of minerals was worked by a locomotive engine made under Stephenson's own directions and bearing the simple but significant designation of "No. 1." The first train consisted of 33 coal waggons with one passenger carriage in the rear; and during a portion of its journey it attained a speed of fifteen miles an hour. It appears to have been only a few weeks or months before horse-power was wholly displaced by steam locomotives. The above notable engine was long exhibited in front of the Darlington Station of the Stockton and Darlington line; but it is now placed under cover, mounted on stonework, in the large Central Station of the same town. This line, the germ, it may be called, of the railway system, proved a great success financially and otherwise. Nevertheless, the employment of locomotives remained almost unknown to the public at large until the opening of the Liverpool and Manchester line, five years later. The Monkland,

TABLE SHOWING THE HIGHEST AND LOWEST PRICES OF THE ORDINARY STOCKS OF THE PRINCIPAL RAILWAY COMPANIES, IN 1898 AND 1899 UP TO THE 6TH OCTOBER, TOGETHER WITH THE PRESENT PRICE AND THE YIELD THEREUPON, CALCULATED UPON THE BASIS OF THE DIVIDEND PAID FOR THE LAST TWELVE MONTHS ENDING 30TH JUNE, 1899.

RAILWAY.	1898.		Nine Months to Oct. 6, 1899		Last Two Half-Years Dividends, Rate per cent. per annum.		Twelve Months.	Present Price Oct. 5, 1899.	Yield at Present Price.		
	Highest.	Lowest.	Highest.	Lowest.	Dec '98	Jun '9					
Caledonian	161¾	144½	156	141¾	5	4¾	4⅞	143	£3	8	2
Glasgow and S. Western, Preferred	86½	78¾	84⅜	74	2½	2½	2½	77	3	4	11
,, ,, ,, Deferred	71½	60	74½	61½	2½	2½	2½	64	3	18	2
Great Central Preferred Ord.	77	57	66	48	Nil.	Nil.	Nil	52	—		
,, ,, Deferred Ord.	24 3/10	19¼	24⅛	18⅝	*Nil.		—	19	—		
Great Eastern	124⅝	114⅛	138	120¼	5¼	2½	3⅞	128	3	0	7
Great Northern, Deferred	61⅝	50¾	71⅞	57½	4½	—	2¼	59	3	16	3
Great Western	179⅛	162¼	175¼	160½	5½	4	4¾	163	2	18	3
Lancashire and Yorkshire	150½	144	152½	145	5½	5	5¼	146	3	11	11
London, Brighton, & S. Coast	191½	182¾	192	182¼	8¼	4¾	6½	185	3	10	3
,, ,, ,, ,, A	186¼	172½	185⅜	176⅛	*6¾	—	6¾	179¼	3	11	2
London, Chatham, and Dover	24	18	28⅝	21½	Nil.	Nil.	Nil.	24¾	—		
London and North Western	205½	195⅛	205¾	198	8	6½	7¼	199	3	12	8
London and S. Western Preferred	139	131	135	125¾	4	4	4	128	3	2	6
,, ,, ,, Deferred	98¾	87	94	74	*2½	—	2½	79	3	3	3
Metropolitan Consolidated	136⅞	123	127¾	112¾	3¾	3⅞	3 13/16	114	3	6	11
Metropolitan District	34¼	26½	42¾	29⅛	Nil.	Nil.	Nil.	30½	—		
Midland Preferred	88¾	82⅛	84¾	79½	2½	2½	2½	81½	3	1	4
,, Deferred	95⅞	83⅜	94¼	86⅛	4	3¼	3⅝	89¾	4	0	9
North British. Preferred	93⅜	86¾	92	88⅛	3	3	3	89¼	3	7	2
North Eastern	182⅜	172¾	185	175¼	7¼	6	6⅝	177	3	14	10
North London	232	219	223	215	7½	7½	7½	219	3	8	6
North Staffordshire	133⅝	123¼	129¼	124	4¾	4¼	4½	125	3	12	0
South Eastern	157	147	154	142½	6½	2½	4½	144	3	2	6
,, ,, A	117⅛	101	114⅝	104	*3	—	3	105½	2	16	10
Taff Vale	85⅝	73	87	75¾	2 2/5	3½	2 19/20	80	3	13	9

* For year 1898. Dividends declared annually in December.

opened in 1826, was really the first to follow the example of the Stockton and Darlington, and several other small lines—including the Canterbury and Whitstable, a remarkable undertaking, worked partly by fixed and partly by locomotive engines—quickly adopted the new traction power. The inauguration of the Liverpool and Manchester line in 1830, attended as it was with a tragic result, was the first to impress upon the people that a revolution in travelling had really taken place; but even then the aid of the Press, powerfully and influentially invoked, failed to arouse anything in the shape of enthusiasm. Royal patronage was not bestowed upon the opening ceremony, although eagerly solicited. To the great minds of the time, however, the event assumed more than ordinary importance, and it is reported that the impression made upon Lord Brougham's contemplative mind forced a tear from his eye. Leicester to Swannington came next, but that from London to Birmingham was the largest that had yet been projected. A great struggle took place with landowners and other influential personages, opposed not only to this Bill in particular, but to the introduction of railways generally. Undaunted courage and perseverance on the part of the promoters prevailed, and the Bill, which was rejected in 1832, passed in 1833, but not until landowners and others had been conciliated by having the price originally estimated for their land, &c., doubled and even trebled. The expenses of carrying this Bill, which was probably the most momentous parliamentary campaign in the history of railways, were over £70,000. The line was opened throughout in 1838, and the first train accomplished the distance at an average speed of over twenty miles an hour. The tide of public opinion was now fairly turned, and ran as strongly in favour of railways as it had before been against them. The London and Greenwich, London and Southampton, the Great Western, Birmingham and Derby, Bristol and Exeter, Eastern Counties, Manchester and Leeds, Midland Counties, North Midland, South Eastern, London and Brighton, Birmingham and Manchester, and Edinburgh and Glasgow, together with a large number of small Bills, were all passed in four years from the passing of the London and Birmingham Bill, and before that line was opened. Thus in four or five years was witnessed the laying of the foundations of nearly all the existing great trunk lines of railway in this country.

The expenditure incurred in securing legislative authority to construct railways was enormous. The Parliamentary costs of the Brighton Railway averaged £4,806 per mile; of the Manchester and Birmingham, £5,190 per mile; and of the Blackwall, £14,414 per mile! The solicitors' bill for the South-Eastern Railway contained 10,000 folios, and amounted to £240,000.

Up to 1840, inclusive, notwithstanding the delays and difficulties which surrounded railway projectors, even in the earliest stages of legislation, 299 Acts, authorizing the construction of 3,000 miles of line, had been passed. The inevitable reaction set in, and in 1841-2-3 only a few small Bills were passed by the Legislature; but as the Liverpool and Manchester, the London and Birmingham, and other leading concerns were paying ten per cent. dividends, and some of the smaller lines were yielding even larger returns, attention was naturally drawn to the remunerative character of this class of property, and the supply of railway shares became far below the demand. A flood of new projects appeared before the public, and the Legislature even, labouring apparently under the general excitement, encouraged promoters by relaxing or withdrawing the general opposition which had previously been offered. In 1844, 797 miles were authorized; in 1845, 2,883 miles; and in 1846, the prodigious total of 4,790 miles, under no less than 272 Acts, obtained Parliamentary sanction. The succeeding years saw some abatement, but still there were 1,663 miles passed in 1847, and 300 in 1848. These figures illustrate the rise and fall of the great fever known as the "railway mania." At least four times as many schemes came before the credulous and overweening public as ever came to receive legislative deliberation, and between the close of the 1845 session and the opening of that for 1846, no less than 1,300 projects were brought out, and it was calculated that even the small parliamentary deposits required to be lodged with each Bill would aggregate to nearly sixty millions. Gradually, however, it dawned upon the minds of reflecting people, that of the £600,000,000 required, a vast proportion were mere paper projects or competitive schemes, alike unnecessary and uncalled for, and the inevitable collapse soon followed.

General legislation relative to railways was

TABLE SHOWING THE FLUCTUATION IN THE RATE OF WORKING EXPENSES FOR EACH COMPLETE YEAR UPON THE PRINCIPAL RAILWAYS SINCE 1887.

COMPANIES.	Working Expenses per cent. of Earnings.											
	1887.	1888.	1889.	1890.	1891.	1892.	1893.	1894.	1895.	1896.	1897.	1898.
Caledonian	49·4	46·7	47·4	51·8	51·5	50·7	51·5	51·1	48·6	49·2	50·4	51·7
Glasgow and South Western	50·1	50·6	52·0	54·5	54·6	55·4	56·5	58·7	54·5	54·0	54·6	56·1
Great Central	51·7	50·5	49·8	52·0	52·5	52·6	59·5	53·9	53·2	55·4	56·4	58·3
Great Eastern	53·4	54·0	53·1	55·0	56·9	57·8	59·3	58·4	57·0	56·5	57·2	58·1
Great Northern	56·0	55·8	56·1	57·3	58·5	58·4	59·4	59·4	58·9	61·7	61·9	61·0
Great Western	48·9	48·8	49·5	51·6	53·1	53·9	55·1	55·2	55·4	55·3	56·5	60·4
Lancashire and Yorkshire	54·6	52·2	54·1	56·0	57·8	59·3	59·4	57·8	56·7	56·0	56·7	57·3
London, Brighton, and So. Coast	48·0	48·3	47·4	49·0	51·2	51·5	51·5	52·7	53·4	53·6	54·4	55·2
London, Chatham, and Dover	52·8	52·2	51·4	53·3	54·6	56·2	56·2	54·3	54·1	53·8	53·7	54·4
London and North Western	51·5	51·6	51·8	53·7	55·0	55·8	57·5	55·3	55·1	54·8	56·4	57·6
London and South Western	55·7	55·0	54·1	55·3	55·8	56·0	56·2	56·7	56·9	56·9	57·5	59·9
Midland	52·4	52·2	52·4	54·0	54·8	55·2	58·3	55·6	55·0	55·1	56·9	58·7
North British	48·3	47·0	47·5	51·4	53·0	52·8	49·9	50·9	49·6	49·8	49·8	50·1
North Eastern	53·7	53·2	52·9	55·6	57·0	59·3	57·2	57·5	57·6	57·1	58·3	59·3
North Staffordshire	46·6	46·0	48·2	48·4	49·9	51·3	51·4	52·4	52·6	53·3	54·1	55·1
South Eastern	47·4	48·1	49·2	50·7	53·1	53·3	53·7	53·0	53·5	52·1	53·3	56·1

introduced about 1840. The lines that had been constructed previous to this were established under Special Acts. More than anything else in the nature of public or private enterprise, it was beginning to be felt that the railways were instrumental in promoting the interests not only of the rich, but perhaps even in a greater degree the interests of the community at large. The enormous development of the trade of the country was ascribed to the instrumentality of railways. It is not wonderful, therefore, that a new branch of law for their regulation was introduced. The variety and repeated alterations in the railway laws showed the difficulty of dealing with the various and often conflicting interests concerned. The Railways Regulation Act of 1840, the first of the General Acts, provided for a month's notice being given to the Board of Trade before opening; for returns of traffic to be made by the companies, as also of accidents involving personal injury; for government inspection of works, for the approval of bye-laws, &c. Afterwards were passed Acts for their better regulation, and for the conveyance of troops, 1842, the Railways Further Regulation Act of 1844, the Railways Clauses Consolidation Act, 1845, and the Canal and Railway Carriers Act of the same session. Then followed legislation on the leasing and sale of railways, on the gauge, on cheap trains, passenger duty, &c. In their civil and commercial importance, and the enormous interests they represented, railways soon came to occupy the attention of leading minds of the day, and an active part in their administration was shared by members of the Government and of both Houses of Legislature, and the railway interest has continued powerfully represented.

RAILWAYS IN 1898.

The number of persons employed in working the railways of the United Kingdom in 1898 was 534,141. The number dependent upon this large body must also be very great; and if we take into account the vast numbers besides who are employed in branches of trade which administer to the requirements of railways, the social dependence upon their existence must be something enormous.

At the close of the year 1898 there were in use upon the railways 19,825 locomotive engines, 45 048 carriages for the conveyance of passengers, 17,817 other vehicles attached to passenger trains, 650,839 waggons for the conveyance of live stock, minerals, and general merchandise, and 16,437 miscellaneous vehicles.

TABLE OF DIVIDENDS PAID IN EACH COMPLETE YEAR UPON THE ORDINARY STOCKS OF THE PRINCIPAL RAILWAY COMPANIES IN THE UNITED KINGDOM, 1890–1898.

ENGLAND.	1890.	1891.	1892.	1893.	1894.	1895.	1896.	1897.	1898.
Furness	3¾	2¾	1½	1¼	1½	½	1½	1¾	2½
*Great Central (Pref.)	2¾	2⅛	1⅝	Nil.	¾	⅞	1¼	1½	½
Great Eastern	3	2⅝	2⅛	1	1⅝	2⅞	3⅛	3½	3⅝
Great Northern (Pref. Conv. Ord.)	4¾	4⅜	4⅛	4	4	4	4	4	4
Great Western	6½	6¼	5⅞	4¾	5¼	5⅛	6	6	3⅞
Lancashire and Yorkshire	4¼	3⅞	3⅝	3⅛	4	4½	5⅜	5⅛	5¼
London and North Western	7¼	7	6½	5⅜	6	6⅜	7⅛	7⅛	7⅛
London and South Western	6	6	6	6	6⅛	6⅛	6⅝	7	6½
London, Brighton, & S. Coast	7	6½	6½	5⅞	4	6	6⅜	6½	6⅜
London, Chatham, and Dover*	4½	4	$3\frac{19}{20}$	$3\frac{9}{20}$	3⅜	$3\frac{13}{20}$	4½	4½	4½
London, Tilbury, and Southend	3½	3¾	3⅞	3¾	6¼	4⅛	4⅜	4⅜	5
Maryport and Carlisle	8½	6¾	5¾	6⅛	5½	5¼	6	6¼	6½
Metropolitan	3	3¼	3¼	2⅞	2¾	$2\frac{15}{16}$	$3\frac{5}{16}$	3¾	3¾
Metropolitan District	Nil.	Nil.	Nil.	Nil.	Nil.	Nil.	Nil.	Nil.	Nil.
*Midland (Pref. and Def. Ord.)	6¼	6⅜	6	3⅞	5¼	5⅛	6	6½	5⅞
North Eastern	7¼	6½	4⅜	5⅞	5⅞	5⅝	6⅜	6⅜	6½
North London	7½	7½	7½	6¾	7⅛	6¾	7½	7½	7½
North Staffordshire	5	5	4⅝	4½	4¼	4¼	4½	4⅜	4⅜
South Eastern	4¾	4⅛	4	3¾	4	4⅛	$4\frac{11}{16}$	$4\frac{15}{16}$	4½
Taff Vale (including bonus)	3	2¼	3¼	2⅞	3¼	3⅛	3¼	3⅜	$1\frac{1}{5}$
SCOTLAND.									
Caledonian	4⅜	4¼	4⅛	4⅜	3⅝	5	5	5⅛	5
Glasgow and South Western (Pref. and Def. Ord.)	3¾	3¾	4⅛	3½	3⅛	4½	5⅛	5	5¼
Great North of Scotland (Pref. Conv. Ord.)	1⅝	3	3¼	3⅛	3¼	3½	3½	3¾	3
Highland	4	4⅞	4⅞	4⅞	4	2¾	1½	1¼	⅙
North British	3⅛	†2⅜	†3⅛	†3⅝	2¼	3	1⅛	1⅛	1¼
IRELAND.									
Belfast and Northern Counties	5¼	5½	5¼	5	5¼	5¾	6	6	5¾
Great Northern (Ireland)	4	5½	5¾	6	6¼	6½	6½	6½	6½
Great Southern and Western	4¾	5⅛	4⅞	5⅛	$5\frac{7}{16}$	5⅜	5¼	5⅜	5
Midland Great Western	4¾	5	4½	4¾	4¾	4¾	4	4¼	4
Waterford, & Western Limerick	Nil.	Nil.	Nil.	Nil.	Nil.	Nil.	Nil.	½	Nil.

* On Arbitration Preference Stock. † On Ordinary and Preferred Ordinary Stocks.

ALPHABETICAL LIST OF PRINCIPAL RAILWAYS OF UNITED KINGDOM, WITH OFFICERS AND OFFICIAL ADDRESSES.

Company.	Incorporated or pres. Title.	Chairman.	Deputy Chairman.	Secretary.	General Manager. T. Traffic Manager.	Goods Manager.	Head Office.
Belfast and County Down	1846	T. Andrews	James Barbour, J.P.	Thos. J. Brittain	J. Pinion	......	Queen's Qy., Belfast.
Belfast & Nortn. Counties	1850	Rt. Hon. J. Young	H. H. McNeile, D.L.	W. R. Gill	James Cowie	......	York Rd., Belfast.
Brecon and Merthyr	1859	H. F. Slattery ... D.L.	W. Bailey Hawkins	H. R. Price	John Gall (T.)	......	132.Palmerstn.Bdgs.
Caledonian	1845	J. C. Bunten	Sir James King, Bart.	Jno. Blackburn.	Sir J. Thompson	A. Hillhouse	Glasgow. E.C.
Cambrian	1864	J. F. Buckley	......	R. Brayne.	C. S. Denniss	W. Finchett.	Oswestry. E.C.
City and South London	1891	C. G. Mott.	......	W. F. Knight	T. C. Jenkin	......	46 King William St.,
Cork, Bandon,&SouthCoast	1845	{ J. W. Payne Sheares, J.P., D.L.	} Capt. Perry	R. H. Leslie.	E. J. O'B. Croker.	......	Albert Quay, Cork.
Dub., Wicklow, & Wexford	1860	Frederick W. Pim	J. L. Scallan ... [K.C.B.]	E. M. Cowan	John Coghlan (T.)	......	Dublin.
Furness	1844	Duke of Devonshire	Rt. Hn. Sir H. T. Hibbert,	Alfred Aslett	Alfred Aslett	Clement Mossop	Barrow-in-Furness.
Glasgow & South Western	1850	Sir Renny Watson	P. T. Caird	F. H. Gillies	David Cooper	Henry Evans	Glasgow.
Great Central	1897	A. Henderson, M.P.	Edward Chapman	O. S. Holt.	Sir W. Pollitt	C. T. Smith	Manchester.
Great Eastern	1862	Lord C. J. Hamilton.	Colonel Mr. C. Makins	W. Peppercorne	J. F. S. Gooday.	W. Gardner	L'pool St. Stn., E.C.
Great Nortnern	1846	Rt. Hn. W. L. Jackson.	Hon. R. A. Capel	William Latta.	Charles Steel	W. J. Grining.	King's Cross Stn., N.
Great Northern (Ireland)	1876	J. Gray .... [M.P.]	Sir W. Quartus Ewart, Bt.	T. Morrison	J. W. Philp	J. W. Philp	Dublin.
Great North of Scotland	1846	W. Ferguson, LL.D.	Earl of Aberdeen	W. Moffatt.	Henry Plews	A. M. Ross	Aberdeen.
Great Southern & Western	1844	J. J. Pim	W. Robertson ... [son.	G. B. Ormsby	R. G. Colhoun (T.)	R. W. Croker	Dublin.
Great Western	1835	Earl Cawdor	A. Hubbard, W. Robin-	F. K. Mills	J. L. Wilkinson.	H. W. Maiden	Paddington Stn., W.
Highland	1865	Sir G. Macph. Grant, Bt.	Earl of March	W. Gowenlock	T. A. Wilson	Geo. Thomson	Inverness.
Hull and Barnsley	1880	John Fisher	William Trotter	W. W. Hill	W. W. Hill	W. H. Wood	Hull.
Lanc., Derbysh., & E. Coast	1896	Emerson Bainbridge	Sir W. Birt	M. D. Hancock	H. Willmott	......	Chesterfield.
Lancashire and Yorkshire	1847	G. J. Armytage	W. Tunstill	R. C. Irwin	J. A. F. Aspinall.	B. Shaw	Manchester.
Lond., Brighton, & S. Coast	1846	Lord Cottesloe.	Rt.Hon.Sir A. Otway,Bt.	John J.Brewer	Wm. Forbes	G. W. Staniforth	Lond. Bge. Stn., S.E.
London & North Western	1846	Lord Stalbridge	J. P. Bickersteth	T. Houghton.	{ D. Greenwood (T.) F. Harrison	} Frank Ree	Euston Stn., N.W.
London & South Western	1839	Hon. H. W. Campbell	Sir Charles Scotter	GodfreyKnight	{ C. J. Owens C. T. White (T.)	} A. Malby	Waterloo Stn., S.E.
Lond., Tilbury,&Southend	1862	H. D. Browne	John Warren	H. Cecil Newton	A. L. Stride.	Edwin Chalk	Fenchurch St. Stn.,
Maryport and Carlisle	1837	Sir W. Lawson, Bt., M.P.	H. P. Senhouse	H. Carr	{ H. Carr J.Ellwood(T.)	}	Maryport. E.C.
Mersey	1866	James Falconer	......	G. H. Langham	J.A.Macaulay(T.)	......	{ Worcester House, Walbrook, E.C.
Metropolitan	1853	John Bell	J. J. Mellor, M.P.	G. H. Whissell	J. Bell	J. Bell	34, Westbourne Ter.
Metropolitan District	1864	Jas. Staats Forbes	Rt. Hon. Viscount Gort	W. Jones	A. Powell	......	Parliament Mansns.,
Midland	1844	Sir Geo. Ernest Paget.	Charles Thomas	A. L. Charles.	G. H. Turner	W. E. Adie	Derby. [S.W.
Midland Great Western	1845	Sir Ralph S. Cusack	C. J. Fergu'sson, J.P.	G. W. Greene	R. Morrison (T.)	Jos. Tatlow	Dublin.
North British	1862	Sir W. Laird	Sir Charles Tennant, Bt.	John Cathles	W. F. Jackson	A. Rutherford.	Edinburgh.
North Eastern	1854	SirJ.W.Pease,Bt.,M.P.	Sir Lowthian Bell, Bt.	C. N. Wilkinson	George S. Gibb	C. Jesper	York.
North London	1853	Rt. Hn. Lord Rathmore	......	G. B. Newton	G. B. Newton	G. N. Ford	Euston Stn., N.W.
North Staffordshire	1847	Thomas Salt.	F. Stanier	R. E. Pearce	W. D. Phillipps.	W. D. Phillipps.	Stoke-upon-Trent.
Rhymney	1854	W. Austin.	F. G. Evans.	W. Fairlamb	C. Lundie (T.).	CorneliusLundie	Cardiff.
South East. & L.C.D.Rlys.	1899	H. Cosmo Bonsor, M.P.	Sir Ed. Leigh Pemberton	{ Jn. Morgan Ch. Sheath	} A. Willis	G. Wallace	Lond. Bdge. Stn., S.E.
Taff Vale	1836	R. L. G. Vassall	Russell Rea	H. Clarke.	Ammon Beasley.	J. Tilley	Cardiff.
Watrfrd. Limk., & Wstn.	1845	P. B. Bernard, D.L.	Sir F. W. Brady, Bt.	J. J. Murphy	F. Vaughan (T.).	......	Waterford.

WHITAKER'S ALMANACK, 1900.

Capital embarked in Railways.—The total amount of capital authorized by Parliament to be raised for the construction of railways in the United Kingdom amounted on the 31st December, 1898, to £1,242,838,701. Of this sum, £1,134,468,462 (which includes £183,513,147 nominal capital caused by the consolidation or conversion of stocks) exists and forms the capital account of the various railway companies, and shows an increase over the year 1897 of £44,703,367, or 3·94 per cent. The £1,134,468,462 is composed of £110,379,595 guaranteed, £288,162,471 debenture, £290,913,869 preferential, and £433,429,544 ordinary stocks and shares, besides a sum of £11,582,983 raised by loans. The net receipts for the year amount to £40,291,958, equal to 3·55 per cent. on the total capital sunk, as compared with £40,653,250 in 1897, with a corresponding capital of £1,089,765,095, which gave a net receipt of 3·73 per cent. This percentage is considerably below the average of former years, and it will be interesting to railway proprietors to note a few of the causes of this decrease. During the first half of the year the engineers' strike seriously interrupted business, and the companies serving the cotton districts had to bear the effects of the great stagnation in the Lancashire cotton trade. The strike in the Welsh coal trade was also an unfavourable feature; but the two largest items which have affected the net revenue are the increased wages and curtailment of the hours of labour of railway servants and the rapid growth of local taxation, which is increasing in an alarmingly disproportionate ratio to the net profit, and to the benefits which the companies derive from the expenditure of the rates. That this burden shows a constant tendency to grow heavier year by year is illustrated by the fact that in 1888 the amount paid for rates and taxes was equal to 16 per cent. of the amount distributed as ordinary dividend, and in 1898 this percentage had increased to 20, or say 4*s.* in the £; yet with all these financial drawbacks the growing confidence of the public in railway stocks is evidenced by the appreciation in the market value of all descriptions of these securities, and it is interesting to note that it is but a few years since that railway companies, who were willing to give from 4 to 5 per cent. interest on their loans, can at the present time raise money at a little more than half that interest, and even at this low rate investors will pay an advance on the issue price of par.

Gross Earnings of the Railways.—The earnings for the year 1898 amounted to £96,252,501, as compared with £93,737,054 for the year 1897, which gives an increase of £2,515,447, equal to 2·68 per cent. The increase in the passenger receipts is £1,147,584, made up as follows:—

	1898. £	1897. £	Inc. or Dec. £
1st Class.........	3,200,867	3,210,482	−9,615
2nd ,, ...	2,585,627	2,306,318	+279,309
3rd ,, ...	26,216,247	25,491,880	+724,367
Seas. & Periodical Tk. Holders ...	3,180,743	3,027,220	+53,523
	35,183,484	34,035,900	+1,047,584

The numbers carried were:

	1898. No.	1897. No.	Inc. or Dec. No.
1st Class.........	33,037,190	32,497,673	+539,517
2nd ,, ...	66,199,930	62,762,650	+3,437,280
3rd ,, ...	963,673,996	935,159,878	+28,514,118
Seas. & Periodical Tk. Holders ...	1,283,045	1,286,508	−3,463
	1,064,193,161	1,031,706,709	+32,487,452

It will be seen that with the exception of receipts from 1st class traffic and in the number of season ticket holders there is an all round increase in numbers and receipts in all classes, including season ticket holders, and it is satisfactory to have to record, that whereas second-class traffic has hitherto been decreasing, it shows this year an increase of 3,437,280 in numbers and £279,309 in receipts. This increase is owing to the new plan, which is being generally adopted by railway companies who run second class carriages, of calculating the fares upon a scale of 2*d.*, 1¼*d.*, and 1*d.* per mile, according to the class of carriage, thus minimising the difference between the second and third class fare, and increasing the number of travellers in second class. The increase in numbers travelling by third class is 3·05 per cent. over 1897. The earnings for the conveyance of parcels, mails, and such other traffic as is generally carried by passenger trains, amounted in 1898 to £6,663,590, as compared with £6,482,164 in 1897, being an increase of £181,426 or 2·80. The total figures of traffic falling under the heading of "goods" are £49,218,964, as compared with £47,857,172 in 1897, an increase of £1,361,792, or 2·85. The aggregate is made up of £27,583,188 from merchandise; £20,256,373 from minerals; and £1,379,271 from live stock. The total quantity of goods carried in 1898 was 378,563,085 tons, as compared with 374,382,266 tons in 1897, showing an increase of 4,180,819 tons, or 1·12 per cent.

Expenditure.—The total working expenses of the whole of the railways for the year 1898

RAILWAYS OPENED IN 1898.

Railway.	From	To	Date.	Miles.
G. E., G. N. & Mid.	North Walsham........	Mundesley	July 1	5¼
Great Northern	Annesley	Skegby	Apr. 4	5
Great Western............	Plymstock	Yealpton	Jan. 15	6½
,, ,, ...	Newbury	Lambourn	Apr. 4	12½
London and South Western	Barnstaple	Lynton	May 11	20
,, ,, ...	Holsworthy	Bude............	Aug. 10	10¼
North British	Aberlady	Gullane	May 1	4½
North Sunderland	Chathill............	Seahouse............	Dec. 14	4
Port Talbot	Port Talbot	Cwmavon	Feb. 14	2
,, ...	Cwmavon	Tonmawr	Nov. 1	2
Waterloo and City	Waterloo	Mansion House............	July 11	1½

amounted to £55,960,543, equal to 58 per cent. of the gross earnings as compared with a total of £53,083,804 for the year 1897, equal to 57 per cent. The increase compared with 1897 amounts to £2,876,739 or 5·42 per cent. The total number of miles travelled by passenger and goods trains during the year 1898 was 380,255,340 or 12,379,417 more than in 1897. Analysing the expenditure we find the item £14,816,471 for locomotive power, £4,638,952 for repairs and renewals of carriages, &c.; £8,294,017 for maintenance of permanent way, stations, &c.; and £17,331,909 for traffic expenses. The locomotive expenses in 1898 amounted to 9·35d. per train mile.

Compensation.—The amount paid for compensation for personal injuries sustained during the year 1898 amounted to £161,842, as compared with £116,319 for the year 1897, resulting in an increase of £45,513, which is not a very serious item, seeing that the companies carried over 33 millions more passengers than in 1897. In the movement of goods the companies have paid for damages and losses £367,402, as compared with £315,088 in 1897, an increase of £52,314.

We subjoin a statement showing the amounts paid by the principal companies under both heads:—

COMPANY.	Passengers.	Goods.
Cheshire Lines Committee......	£1,242	£455
Great Central........................	4,445	7,001
Great Eastern........................	7,312	16,841
Great Northern.....................	5,643	23,570
Great Western.......................	8,585	48,885
Lancashire and Yorkshire ...	14,531	19,934
London and North Western ...	8,123	92,314
London and South Western ...	6,491	18,307
London, Brighton, and South Coast	1,739	13,329
London, Chatham, and Dover	1,513	4,204
Metropolitan	491	88
Midland	25,805	48,301
North Eastern	9,189	16,296
North Staffordshire	1,811	5,035
South Eastern	17,313	7,504
Taff Vale.............................	80	552
Total of all English Railways.	£125,766	£330,493

RAILWAY PASSENGER TRAFFIC.

Statement of the Receipts in each Class from Passengers upon the undermentioned Lines.
Exclusive of Season Tickets.

Year.	GREAT NORTHERN.			GREAT WESTERN.			LONDON & NORTH WESTERN.			MIDLAND. (No Second.)	
	First.	Second.	Third.	First.	Second.	Third.	First.	Second.	Third.	First.	Third.
	£	£	£	£	£	£	£	£	£	£	£
1889	164,273	78,725	972,869	280,592	426,828	2,357,205	518,637	336,549	2,575,329	243,662	1,663,877
1890	171,699	77,717	1,023,267	274,442	390,471	2,504,527	523,712	332,110	2,718,408	240,683	1,753,486
1891	170,981	68,748	1,052,966	265,678	343,294	2,687,322	508,850	322,977	2,773,001	237,361	1,809,428
1892	171,837	39,802	1,090,083	265,961	330,609	2,723,747	508,856	306,863	2,791,858	229,442	1,837,665
1893	164,349	23,779	1,115,204	249,406	291,980	2,718,825	498,469	257,782	2,813,434	214,771	1,832,322
1894	159,837	20,824	1,137,357	239,828	262,810	2,782,897	481,248	240,762	2,875,012	201,659	1,890,262
1895	164,831	19,745	1,136,428	245,461	245,593	2,816,402	501,152	236,330	2,962,025	202,441	1,936,805
1896	171,809	20,032	1,188,811	254,883	328,819	2,851,082	530,898	239,085	3,099,254	214,573	2,024,472
1897	178,044	20,112	1,237,129	265,240	419,127	2,882,389	529,038	289,021	3,163,208	222,615	2,114,584
1898	183,491	21,076	1,284,804	262,239	500,579	2,931,773	520,506	403,376	3,190,917	217,455	2,209,074

The Midland Railway Company took the initiative in passenger traffic reforms, having run third-class carriages by all trains from 1st April, 1872; afterwards, from 1st January, 1875, greatly reducing the first-class and abolishing second-class fares. From 1st November, 1891, the Great Northern Railway Company also abolished second-class fares to all stations north of Hatfield; from 1st January, 1893, the Great Eastern abolished it in the provinces; the Cambrian followed on 1st May of the same year, when it also disappeared from all journeys between London and Scotland, and on the 1st of July, 1897, the Furness Company discontinued second class accommodation.

ANALYSIS OF RAILWAY WORKING EXPENDITURE.

Year.	Maintenance of Way, Works, &c.	Locomotive Power and Carriage Repairs.	Traffic and General.	Rates, Taxes, and Government Duty.	Compensation.	Law & Parliamentary.	Steamboats, Canals, Harbours, &c.	Total Working Expenses.
	£	£	£	£	£	£	£	£
1889	6,565,578	14,281,400	14,036,106	2,557,993	429,867	269,047	2,006,597	40,094,116
1890	7,036,924	15,832,901	14,839,064	2,579,755	445,763	341,018	2,166,316	43,188,556
1891	7,285,884	16,732,769	15,670,944	2,567,690	423,023	321,010	2,197,587	45,144,778
1892	7,403,572	16,610,601	16,091,328	2,680,465	479,822	279,763	2,168,609	45,717,965
1893	7,486,739	16,195,285	16,216,707	2,874,493	372,752	241,837	2,304,284	45,695,119
1894	7,551,637	16,538,746	16,695,749	3,073,578	371,791	250,714	2,713,680	47,208,313
1895	7,658,136	16,558,757	17,054,195	3,266,824	353,184	260,751	2,725,655	47,876,637
1896	8,167,546	17,192,829	17,742,957	3,421,231	389,722	288,375	2,968,647	50,192,424
1897	8,619,686	18,083,839	18,765,687	3,294,094	431,417	328,149	3,254,573	53,083,804
1898	8,994,017	19,455,423	19,672,080	3,731,833	529,244	305,963	2,685,077	55,950,543

Company—	Passengers.	Goods.
Caledonian	£8,389	£14,498
Glasgow and South Western...	8,273	2,764
Great North of Scotland........	439	445
Highland	677	1,756
North British	4,491	11,929
Total of all Scottish Railways.	£22,296	£30,392
Dublin, Wicklow, & Wexford	£1,062	£275
Great Northern of Ireland......	5,616	1,414
Great Southern and Western...	416	2,513
Midland Great Western	689	626
Total of all Irish Railways .	£13,780	£6,517
Total of United Kingdom ...	£161,842	£367,492

Net Result of Working the Railways.—The gross receipts compared with those of the preceding year, show an increase from passengers (which includes season ticket, carriage, horse, dog and post office mail traffic) of £1,329,010; from goods, £1,361,792, and from rents, tolls, navigation and steamboats, &c., a decrease of £175,355, and a total increase from all sources of £2,515,447. The net receipts for 1898 on the capital outlay give a sum of 3·55 per cent., compared with 3·73 per cent. for the year 1897, and 3·88 per cent. for the year 1896. As may be seen, however, on page 732, 45 millions additional capital has been raised during the year 1898, a large proportion of which is "locked up" in works either unfinished or only partly finished, therefore unproductive. Increased working expenses, caused by diminished hours of labour and a proportionate increase in the number of men employed, and increased wages have also operated on the net profit. The increase in the amount of wages has for some years been gradually getting larger. A few

ACCIDENTS TO PASSENGER TRAINS IN 1898 INVOLVING LOSS OF LIFE OR SERIOUS PERSONAL INJURY.

1898.	Company.	Nature of Accident.	At	Passengers. Killed.	Passengers. Injur'd	Servants. Killed.	Servants. Injur'd
Jan. 3 ...	N. B.	Express train collided with de-railed goods waggons ...	Dunbar	1	21	—	2
Feb. 4 ...	G. & S. W.	Collision. Passenger & goods trains	Barassie............	4	7	3	1
Mar. 21 .	South East.	Passenger train, while stand-ing in station, was ran into in rear by another passenger train	St. John's.........	3	20	—	—
April 11 .	L. & S. W.	Light engine collided with special train	Bisley..............	—	30	—	—
June 2 ...	L. & Y. & L. & N. W.	Collision. Excursion trains.....	Leyland..........	2	37	—	2
June ...	G. Central.	Collision. Passenger trains........	Sheffield	—	13	—	—
July 13 ...	Belfast & N. C.	Collision. Passenger train with an empty carriage train	Larne.............	—	14	—	1
Aug. 2 ...	G. N. (Ir.)	Passenger train collided with buffer-stops	Inniskeen	1	14	—	—
Sept. 2 ...	Mid.	Express train came in contact with luggage-trolley which had fallen on to line.........	Wellingborough	5	60	2	5
Sept. 20 .	N. L.	Passenger train collided with buffer-stops	Broad Street ...	—	15	—	—
Sept. 23 .	L. & S. W.	Loaded 3rd class carriage ran into by light engine	Salisbury	—	12	—	—
Oct. 17 ...	G. Central.	Waggons laden with poles left the rails and fouled the main line, the down express from Cleethorpes to Retford dash-ing into them	Wrawby Junct..	8	26	—	1
Oct. 18 ..	G. W.	Connecting-rod of engine attached to passenger train broke............	Acton	—	—	2	—
Oct. 28...	N. B.	Collision. Goods train and light engine	Lunan Bay	—	—	2	2
Oct. 31..	G. W.	Passenger train left rails	Penryn	—	4	1	1
Nov. 10 .	Caledn.	Passenger train collided with light engine	Lesmahagow ..	—	3	—	3
Nov. 16 .	N. B.	Collision. Passenger and goods trains	Bellgrove	—	5	—	2
Nov. 19 .	L. & N. W.	Special goods train collided with light engine	Crewe.............	—	—	2	1
Nov. 24 .	Tralee & Dingle.	Passenger train left rails	Dingle	1	3	—	1
Dec. 15 ..	N. E.	Passenger train run into by light engine	Gateshead.........	—	7	—	1
Dec. 26...	S. E.	Horse-box propelled against passenger train with great violence	Appledore.........	—	8	—	—

years ago the amount paid as wages was less than 20 per cent., but now the wages bill represents 24 per cent. of the total. Rates and taxes are also yearly increasing in a disproportionate ratio to the net profit, but even with these increasing expenses a percentage of 3·55 on the net receipts for the year must be viewed as a very favourable result.

RAILWAY ACCIDENTS.

To the public generally, one of the most interesting points in connection with the working of the railways is the immunity from accidents, as evidenced for a considerable number of years past in the amount paid by the companies by way of compensation for personal injury to passengers. In 1897 the cost per passenger train-mile for personal injury was 0·14*d.*, and in 1898 0·18*d.* In loss and damage of goods, the cost in 1897 was 0·46*d.*, and in 1898 0·53*d.* per goods train-mile. The comparatively small amount paid by the companies for compensation is owing to the improved modes of working and the mechanical appliances which have been adopted to secure the safety of the travelling public, and it is in facilitating this security that some of the chief causes of increase of cost in railway working—such as the more general adoption of the block system, and the system of interlocking points and signals, and of improved continuous brakes, on which the Board of Trade have insisted—may

be accounted for. It is also very noticeable that on those lines where these improvements have not been carried out, the want of them has largely contributed to the accidents which have occurred. The general report to the Board of Trade for 1898 shows that although accidents and collisions of a serious nature have occurred during the year to passenger trains, yet the numbers (particularly in the case of the number killed) are very low when compared with the millions of passengers carried by the companies during the year.

The number of personal accidents on railways to passengers, railway servants, and others, reported to the Board of Trade during the year, show a total of 1,259 killed and 16,091 injured (as compared with 1,255 killed and 17,376 injured in 1897).

The increase since the year 1897 in the number injured is owing to an order recently made by the Board of Trade, regarding the mode in which the returns are to be compiled by the Railway Companies. Hitherto some Companies have only reported accidents of gravity, but they are now directed to report all accidents which prevent the servant injured from being employed for five hours on his ordinary work on one of the three working days next after the accident. We will now proceed to investigate under three distinct heads the various causes from which these accidents arose.

Accidents to Passengers.—Twenty-five passenger

RAILWAY SPEED.

THE FASTEST RUNNING, WITHOUT STOPPAGE, IS MADE BY THE COMPANIES AS UNDER :—

Company.	Train.	From	To	Time.	Distance.	Speed.
				H. M.	Miles.	
Caledonian	9.22	Forfar	Perth	0 33	32½	59·09
Great Northern	10.19	Grantham	York	1 31	82¾	54·52
Great Western	10.45	Paddington	Bath	2 2	107	52·72
Midland	11.29	Kettering	Kentish Town	1 19	70½	53·5
London and North Western	11.49	Rugby	Crewe	1 25	75¼	53·5
Great Eastern	1.30	Ipswich	Tivetshall	0 35	31¾	54·4
Great Central	4.4	Grantham	Sheffield	1 5	56½	52·15
North Eastern	1.55	York	Darlington	0 49	44¼	54·18
Cheshire Lines	8.59	Birkdale	Manchester	0 56	48½	51·96
Lancashire and Yorkshire	8.13	Southport	Salford	0 39	33½	51·53
Glasgow and South Western	5.15	Carlisle	Dumfries	0 39	33	50·77
London, Brighton, & S. Coast	11.0	Victoria	Brighton	1 0	50¾	50·75
London and South Western	11.16	Basingstoke	Vauxhall	0 55	46½	50·73
North British	9.9	Haymarket	Cowlairs	0 53	44½	50·38
London, Chatham, and Dover	5.10	St. Paul's	Margate	1 30	74½	49·46
South Eastern	6.42	Paddock Wood	Sandling Jun.	0 38	30½	48·16

THE LONGEST RUNS WITHOUT STOPPAGE ARE MADE BY THE COMPANIES AS UNDER :—

Company.	From	To	Time.	Distance.	Av. Speed.
			H. M.	Miles.	
Great Western	Paddington	Exeter	3 43	194	52·2
London and North Western	Euston	Crewe	3 5	158	51·0
Great Eastern	Liverpool Street	North Walsham	2 40	131	49·2
North Eastern	Newcastle	Edinburgh	2 23	124½	52·23
Midland	St. Pancras	Nottingham	2 23	123½	52·0
Great Northern	King's Cross	Newark	2 20	120	51·43
Caledonian	Carlisle	Stirling	2 23	117¾	49·41
London and South Western	Bournemouth	Vauxhall	2 12	106¼	48·29
North British	Carlisle	Edinburgh	2 20	98¼	42·10
Glasgow and South Western	Carlisle	Kilmarnock	1 49	91½	50·36
South Eastern	Cannon Street	Dover Pier	1 38	75½	46·22
London, Chatham, and Dover	Herne Hill	Dover Pier	1 32	74½	48·55
London, Brighton and S. Coast	London Bridge	Chichester	1 35	70¾	44·7

were killed and 632 injured from accidents to trains, rolling stock, permanent way, &c. (as compared with 18 killed and 324 injured in 1897), while 128 passengers were killed, and 1,238 injured from other causes—such as falling between carriages and platforms, or on to the platforms, on getting into or alighting from trains, passing over the line at stations, falling out of carriages during the travelling of trains, and is inclusive of 216 injuries resulting from the closing of carriage doors. In addition to the above may be recorded 9 killed and 489 injured by accidents in which the movement of railway vehicles was not concerned, viz.: ascending or descending steps at stations, falling off platforms, &c. and is inclusive of 73 injured by being struck by barrows or stumbling over packages.

Accidents to Servants in the employ of the railway companies or contractors.—The casualties under this head resulting from accidents to trains, or in which the movement of trains or vehicles used exclusively upon railways is concerned, show that 504 were killed and 4,149 injured during the year; of this number 16 deaths and 110 injuries were caused by collisions, 18 were killed and 481 injured in coupling or uncoupling vehicles, 6 were killed and 52 were injured by passing over or standing upon buffers during shunting, 32 were killed and 343 injured in getting on or off, or falling off, engines, waggons, &c.; 10 were killed and 319 injured whilst spragging or chocking wheels, 13 were killed and 365 injured by moving vehicles by capstans, turntables, props, &c., and 47 were killed and 501 injured during shunting operations; 99 were killed and 239 injured whilst working on the permanent way, sidings, &c., and 133 killed and 245 injured whilst walking, crossing, or standing on the line. In addition to these accidents, other casualties, in which the movement of vehicles used exclusively upon the railways are not concerned, have occurred, viz., 5 killed and 1,953 injured whilst loading, unloading, or sheeting waggons, 1 killed and 591 injured by the falling of waggon-doors, lamps, bales of goods, &c., 10 killed and 511 injured by falling off platforms, ladders, scaffolds, &c., in addition to a large number of accidents from various other causes, either the result of want of caution or misconduct.

Accidents to Persons other than Passengers or Servants.—Under this head is classed casualties whilst passing over railways at level crossings; this caused 64 deaths and 27 injuries in 1898 (as compared with 80 deaths and 25 injuries in 1897). There were 276 deaths and 147 injuries resulting from persons trespassing on the railways, 125 persons committed suicide upon the lines in 1898 (compared with 132 in 1897).

The above figures may appear formidable, but in analysing them it becomes necessary to review the business done by the railways of the United Kingdom during the year 1898. The companies carried over 1,000 millions of passengers holding ordinary tickets, and besides this number there were nearly one million and a half persons travelling with season or periodical tickets (the number of journeys made with these tickets can only be guessed at); still the companies must have carried over 1,500,000,000 of passengers (a number not very far short of the entire population of the globe), and also moved 379,000,000 tons of goods and minerals, and run 380,000,000 of train miles.

BLOCK SYSTEM.

There has been no relaxation during the past few years in the progress made for rendering railway working more safe, by the extension of the interlocking and absolute block systems over a larger railway mileage, and continual progress is reported in this matter, so essential to the safe working of the railways. The proportion in which the signal and point levers had been interlocked on railways was 99·7 per cent. in England and Wales, in Scotland 99, and 97·7 per cent. in Ireland, so that 99 per cent. is now given for the United Kingdom. At the end of the year the absolute block system had been adopted on 11,235 miles out of 11,252 miles of double lines open for traffic. When the orders made upon the railway companies under the Regulation of Railways Act, 1889, come into full force the absolute block and interlocking systems will have to be generally adopted.

CONTINUOUS BRAKES.

In several cases the good effects of continuous brakes have been specially mentioned, whilst in other cases the accidents and collisions might, according to the statements in the reports of inquiries, have been either prevented or their effects mitigated had the trains been fitted with quickly-acting continuous brakes, automatic in

CLASS OF SERVANTS.	Number Employed at the end of 1898.	Number Killed and Injured in 1898.		Proportion to the Number Employed.	
		Killed.	Injured.	Killed	Injured
Station-Masters	7,868	3	14	1 in 2,623	1 in 562
Brakesmen and Goods Guards	14,720	43	711	1 ,, 342	1 ,, 21
Permanent-way men	63,360	122	204	1 ,, 519	1 ,, 311
Gatekeepers	3,531	2	3	1 ,, 1,765	1 ,, 1,177
Engine-drivers	22,237	29	405	1 ,, 767	1 ,, 55
Porters	50,844	50	532	1 ,, 1,017	1 ,, 96
Shunters	9,244	47	616	1 ,, 197	1 ,, 15
Firemen	21,821	23	556	1 ,, 949	1 ,, 39
Inspectors	8,610	8	29	1 ,, 1,076	1 ,, 297
Passenger Guards	6,826	4	126	1 ,, 1,706	1 ,, 54
Pointsmen and Signalmen	26,599	13	61	1 ,, 2,046	1 ,, 436
Labourers	52,900	30	174	1 ,, 1,763	1 ,, 304
Ticket-Collectors, &c.	3,069	2	8	1 ,, 1,534	1 ,, 384
Mechanics	77,270	15	42	1 ,, 5,151	1 ,, 1,840
Other Classes	165,242	99	96	1 ,, 1,669	1 ,, 260
Total	534,141	490	4,117	1 in 1,090	1 in 130

their action, instead of those with which the trains were fitted. It appears that 99·4 per cent. of the vehicles used in passenger trains had been fitted with continuous brakes, leaving ·6 per cent. to be so fitted.

THE CHEAP TRAINS ACT.

The "Cheap Trains Act, 1883," is a measure which affects not only railway shareholders and the public generally, but especially the working classes whose domiciles have been interfered with by the extension of the railway systems into crowded centres of London and other large urban areas. The Act has been received by the railway companies with indifference, its provisions being regarded as partial so far as free and untaxed locomotion is concerned, and nothing less than total repeal of all taxation is the universal desire of the railway proprietors and authorities.

The Act, which took effect 1st October, 1883, provides that fares not exceeding the rate of one penny per mile shall be exempt from duty, but fares for return or periodical tickets shall be exempt from duty only where the ordinary fare for the single journey does not exceed that rate. Duty shall be payable at a reduced rate of two per cent. on fares exceeding the rate of one penny a mile between stations within one urban district. Such district will contain not less than one hundred thousand inhabitants, and must be of a continuous urban as distinguished from a rural or suburban character.

If at any time the Board of Trade have reason to believe that upon any railway a due and sufficient proportion of accommodation is not provided at fares not exceeding a penny a mile, or that such proper and sufficient trains are not provided for workmen going to and returning from their work, at such fares and at such times between six in the evening and eight in the morning as appear to the Board of Trade to be reasonable, steps may be taken to compel the company to provide such accommodation.

Provision is also made in the Act continuing the companies' powers as to special mileage and exceptional charges, and also enlarging their powers in dealing with the charges over distances which include fractions of a mile over a quarter of a mile. The Queen's forces, including officers or men in the navy or naval volunteers, or in the regular, reserve, or auxiliary forces of the army, or in any police force when conveyed by railway on any occasion for the public service, are, when travelling in bodies under one hundred and fifty in number, to be charged three-fourths the rates for ordinary passengers ; when over that number, at half rates. The Act does not extend to Ireland.

RAILWAY SERVANTS' RISKS.

Some idea of the relative amount of risk run by the different classes of railway servants is afforded by the table on p. 741, which shows the number of men employed in various occupations, and the number of fatal accidents and injuries to each class, in the year 1898.

The figures referring to goods guards and shunters are a very startling record of the dangers to which these men are exposed, necessarily in a few cases ; but in a great many instances they arise from indifference, or daring, which ordinary reason should be able to restrain. During the past year an attempt was made to grapple with

this class of accidents by introducing a Bill into Parliament, which, if it had passed, would have given the Board of Trade power to order the railway companies to apply certain safety appliances to rolling stock. The object of these appliances generally was to save men from the necessity of going between waggons to couple or uncouple, etc., but the railway companies and some owners of waggons felt it necessary to oppose the Bill, and it was withdrawn. The whole question, however of accidents to railway servants generally has been referred to a Royal Commission, whose report is expected shortly.

FURTHER LEGISLATION FOR RAILWAYS.

The report by the Board of Trade in accordance with section 24 of the Railway and Canal Traffic Act, 1888, on the classification of merchandize traffic and schedule of maximum rates applicable thereto, determined in respect of the various companies, shows that the proposed rates and the actual charges approach nearer than anticipated. The adoption of the New Schedules would result in a serious but not overwhelming loss, and there is no probability that the loss would be recouped by an increase of traffic, as the decrease in revenue would affect hundreds of thousands of rates, and the reduction for any particular class of goods would be too small to encourage new traffic. As to terminals for station accommodation, and charges for servants' labour, the Board of Trade have adopted a uniform maximum based on as fair an average as it is possible to attain, and have limited the charge to services for loading, unloading, covering, and uncovering. It is also proposed that in all cases there shall be a truck rate for the conveyance of animals. The Companies believe that, if they rightly understand the principle laid down in the report as to the revision of rates, no serious difference will be found to exist, but that it is the failure of these schedules to give due and fair effect to those principles that stands in the way of an agreement between the Board of Trade and the Companies. The new rates operated on and from January 1, 1893. The Workmen's Compensation Act, 1897. This Act, which received the Royal assent on August 6, 1897, and came into operation on July 1, 1898, is intituled " An act to amend the law with respect to compensation suffered in the course of their employment."

The Employers' Liability Act of 1880 only gives compensation in cases where the personal injury is caused by the negligence of the employer or his representatives, or by a defect in the works or machinery used in his business. The Act of 1897, entirely disregards the cause of the accident, with the exception of the wilful misconduct of the injured workman himself, and awards compensation to employés in all cases of personal injury by accident arising out of and in the course of their employment. It further provides that compensation for injuries received whilst performing duties involving considerable personal danger shall become a charge upon the profits of the undertaking, thus throwing a serious burden upon Railway Companies and other employers specifically enumerated in the 7th section of the Act. The new Act will in time cause the entire extinction of the Companies' Accident Insurance Societies, by whatever title they may be known.

STATEMENT OF CAPITAL, REVENUE, WORKING EXPENSES, DIVIDENDS, TRAIN MILEAGE, AND ROLLING STOCK OF THE PRINCIPAL RAILWAY COMPANIES OF THE UNITED KINGDOM, FOR THE YEAR ENDED 31ST DECEMBER, 1898.

Companies	Capital: Paid-up Sh. and raised by Loans (Thousands) £	Revenue: Miles in Work	Revenue: Gross Receipts £	Revenue: Per Mile £	Working Expenses: Amount £	Working Expenses: Per cent. on Gross Receipts	Net Receipts £	Dividend Ordinary Stock. Year 1898. £ s. d.	Train Mileage (Thousands)	Rolling Stock: Number of Engines	Rolling Stock: Number of Carriages	Rolling Stock: Number of Waggons
Cambrian	6,345	252	308,585	1,225	191,653	62	116,933		1,612	84	276	2,171
Furness	6,991	134	593,496	3,757	340,067	57	253,429	2 10 0	1,393	124	371	7,235
Great Central	40,153	479	2,774,672	5,793	1,617,868	58	1,156,804	0 0 0	10,286	**775	**1,123	**19,188
Great Eastern	49,376	1,110	5,172,802	4,660	3,004,415	58	2,168,387	3 12 6	20,949	993	4,711	22,102
Great Northern (Pref., Conv., Ord.)	53,568	819	4,975,570	6,075	3,033,658	61	1,941,412	3 17 0	23,202	1,151	3,146	35,396
Great Western	83,563	2,599	9,878,465	3,801	5,970,543	60	3,907,922	4 0 0	42,621	1,885	6,331	54,611
Lancashire and Yorkshire	61,286	556	5,201,016	9,354	2,979,548	57	2,221,468	3 5 0		1,330	4,173	26,617
Lancash., Derbysh., and East Coast.	2,524	55	68,296	1,242	40,091	59	28,205		286	17	75	805
London and North Western	117,269	1,908	13,155,925	6,895	7,572,692	57	5,583,233	7 2 6	47,549	2,900	8,731	63,675
London and South Western	42,196	894	4,548,084	5,087	2,726,962	60	1,821,122	6 6 7	17,058	702	3,748	12,091
London, Brighton, and South Coast.	24,951	438	3,114,475	7,102	1,774,080	57	1,340,395	6 10 0	10,457	465	3,001	9,420
London, Chatham, and Dover	27,543	188	1,673,071	8,899	910,299	54	762,772	6 7	4,851	210	1,240	2,085
London, Tilbury, and Southend	3,887	79	358,032	4,597	199,702	56	158,330	5 0 0	1,261	42	351	1,203
Maryport and Carlisle	887	41	107,645	2,626	54,048	50	53,597	6 15 0	450	27	35	1,847
Metropolitan	12,838	67	861,641	12,863	386,155	45	475,685	3 15 0	2,309	80	399	355
Metropolitan District	7,312	19	463,127	24,235	221,739	48	241,388		1,401	54	368	41
Midland	167,574	1,431	10,554,075	7,375	6,149,369	58	4,404,705	5 17 6	46,070	2,350	4,899	117,730
North Eastern	71,661	1,630	8,371,939	5,136	4,961,332	59	3,410,607	7 10 0	30,894	1,994	3,676	92,426
North London	3,941	12	543,354	45,279	291,475	54	251,879	7 0 0	2,178	112	760	506
North Staffordshire	10,079	193	857,853	4,445	479,872	56	377,981	4 10 0	2,294	154	416	5,605
South Eastern	25,709	421	2,733,562	6,493	1,532,218	56	1,201,344	4 0 0	9,145	459	2,478	7,302
Taff Vale	8,664	121	614,232	5,076	364,644	59	249,588	1 4	1,750	198	250	2,607
Total of all English & Welsh Railways	936,135	15,007	81,780,501	5,449	48,177,454	59	33,603,047	—	315,338	16,870	52,670	508,126
Caledonian	57,549	939	4,214,996	4,489	2,179,721	52	2,035,275	5 0 0	17,192	811	2,147	59,278
Glasgow and South Western†	21,200	394	1,587,993	4,030	890,984	56	697,009	5 5 0	6,914	345	1,151	15,793
Great North of Scotland	6,925	331	473,590	1,432	247,294	52	226,665	3 0 0	2,542	112	712	3,414
Highland‡	6,544	483	520,951	1,079	344,046	66	176,905	1 5	2,795	133	393	2,752
North British	56,003	1,240	3,947,787	3,184	1,978,546	50	1,969,241	1 5 0	17,248	752	2,776	59,446
Total of all Scottish Railways	158,983	3,476	10,873,318	3,128	5,712,866	53	5,160,452	—	48,189	2,155	7,235	149,709
Belfast and Northern Counties	2,714	249	304,004	1,221	186,304	61	117,700	5 15 0	1,553	73	350	2,221
Dublin, Wicklow, and Wexford§	2,523	144	270,908	1,881	161,561	60	109,347	Nil.	1,369	53	299	822
Great Northern (Ireland)	7,692	528	855,795	1,621	454,079	53	401,716	6 10 0	3,458	145	592	4,218
Great Southern and Western	8,672	671	912,942	1,361	516,495	57	396,446	6 0 0	4,068	188	616	4,636
Midland Great Western	6,324	538	554,775	1,031	295,726	53	259,049	4 0 0	2,457	127	382	2,711
Waterford, Limerick, and Western¶	2,706	342	252,257	732	153,176	61	97,081	Nil.	1,158	60	152	1,407
Total of all Irish Railways¶	39,350	3,176	3,542,378	1,115	2,070,223	58	1,528,459	—	16,729	800	2,960	18,441
Aggregate total	1,134,468	21,659	96,196,197	4,441	55,960,543	58	40,291,958	—	380,256	19,825	62,865	667,276

† For year ended January 31, 1899. ‡ For year ended December 31, 1899.

§ The reduction in receipts is almost entirely in passenger traffic, a result from the competition of the electric tramway, Dublin to Dalkey, opened May, 1896.

¶ Including Light Railways which are counted in the official aggregate total.

RAILWAY TUNNELS.
(OVER ONE MILE IN LENGTH).

		M.	Yds.
Severn	Great Western	4	624
Totley	Midland	3	950
Standedge	North Western	3	62
Woodhead	Great Central	3	17
Bramhope	North Eastern	2	225
Medway	South Eastern	2	220
Festiniog	North Western	2	206
Cowburn	Midland	2	182
Sevenoaks	South Eastern	2	80
Rhondda	Rhondda & Swans. B.	1	1683
Morley	North Western	1	1590
Box	Great Western	1	1467
Catesby	Great Central	1	1240
Dove Holes	Midland	1	1227
Littleborough	Lanc. & Yorks.	1	1177
Sapperton	Great Western	1	1040
Polehill	South Eastern	1	999
Mersey	Mersey	1	940
Bleamoor	Midland	1	867
Queensbury	Great Northern	1	742
Kilsby	North Western	1	663
Shepherd's Well	Chatham & Dover	1	572
Oxted	Brighton & S. E. Jt.	1	506
Wapping (L'pool)	North Western	1	490
Sydenham	Chatham & Dover	1	440
Clayton	Brighton & S. Coast	1	440
Drewton	Hull & Barnsley	1	356
Dronfield	Midland	1	264
Bradway	Midland	1	264
Sough	Lanc. & Yorks.	1	258
Abbot's Cliff	South Eastern	1	240
Corby	Midland	1	160
Honiton	South Western	1	121
Shambrook	Midland	1	100
Glaston	Midland	1	82
Merstham	Brighton & S. Coast.	1	70
Midford	South Western	1	53
Belsize	Midland	1	62
Glenfield	Midland	1	36
Claycross	Midland	1	11
Harecastle	North Staffordshire	1	3

LIST OF ENGINEERS OF THE PRINCIPAL RAILWAY CO.'S OF UNITED KINGDOM.

COMPANY.	NAME.
Belfast & County Down	G. P. Culverwell, C.E.
Belfast & Northn. Counties	B. D. Wise.
Caledonian	(Vacant)
Cambrian	Alfred J. Collin.
City & South London	P. V. McMahon.
Cork, Bandon & Sth. Coast	J. R. Keer, C.E.
Dub., Wicklow & Wexford	A. Shannon.
Furness	F. Stileman.
Glasgow & South Western	W. Melville. [M.I.C.E.
Great Central	C. R. Rowlandson,
Great Eastern	J. Wilson.
Great Northern	A. Ross, M.I.C.E.
Great Northern (Ireland)	W. H. Mills.
Great North of Scotland	P. M. Barnett, C.E.
Great Southern & Western	K. Bayley.
Great Western	J. C. Inglis.
Highland	W. Roberts, C.E.
Hull & Barnsley	R. Pawley.
Lanc. Derbysh. & E. Coast	T. B. Grierson, M.I.C.E.
Lancashire & Yorkshire	W. B. Worthington.
Lond., Bright. & Sth. Coast	C. L. Morgan.
London & North Western	F. Stevenson.
London & South Western	E. Andrews.
Metropolitan District	G. Estall.
Midland	J. A. McDonald.
Midland Great Western	W. P. O'Neill, C.E.
North British	James Bell.
North Eastern	C. A. Harrison.
North London	T. Matthews.
North Staffordshire	G.J.C.Dawson, M.I.C.E.
PortTalbot Rly. & DocksCo.	A. H. Case.
S. E. & C. D. Rlys.	P. C. Tempest.
Taff Vale	G. T. Sibbering.
Waterfd., Limk. & Western	J. Tighe.

THE RAILWAY CLEARING HOUSE.

This Institution was opened in Jan. 1842, and in addition to the work of clearing through bookings of passenger and luggage traffic, is the medium through which agreements relating to rates and fares, &c., are arrived at. *Chairman,* Lord Claud Hamilton ; *Secy.,* H. Smart ; *Offices,* Seymour Street, N.W.

Indian Railways.

The construction of Railways in India, which commenced in 1853, has been conducted on three different systems : first, the employment of companies under a system of guarantee ; secondly, by the State through its own officials ; and thirdly, by assisted companies either with or without guarantee or subsidy from the State, and working with capital wholly raised by themselves or partly with capital provided by the State. Out of eight lines constructed on the first system, five * have been purchased by the State. Two of these are worked by companies. The more important, the East Indian line, is carried on by the same company that constructed it in the first instance, on special terms as to the sharing of profits. The second, the South India line, is in the hands of a new company, whose capital was subscribed by the shareholders of the old one. The three remaining lines are worked by the State, and all five come into the category of State lines in the accounts of the Government of India.

In the following table, the annuities and stock created for the purchase of the lines, the yield on which does not depend on the profits of working, are excluded. The debenture stocks of the companies are also excluded. Some of the principal State lines worked by the State are given for purposes of comparison.

The figures of the Rajputana-Malwa line, which is worked by the Bombay-Baroda, are given separately, but in other cases the statistics of some minor undertakings are included in the totals of the railway by which they are worked.

The railways of India involve a yearly loss to the Indian revenues, amounting in 1898-99 to Rx. 878,100, and from the commencement to Rx. 57,734,761.

* East Indian ; * Eastern Bengal (part of the system now so called) ; * Oudh and Rohilkhund ; * Scinde, Punjab and Delhi (now part of North-western system) ; * South Indian ; Bombay, Baroda and Central India ; Great Indian Peninsula ; Madras.

Indian Railways.—STATEMENT OF CAPITAL, REVENUE, DIVIDENDS, Etc.

In the year 1894 an Act was passed making it legal for Indian Railway Companies to pay interest out of capital during construction, subject to the Secretary of State's specific sanction, and to certain other conditions.

Principal Railway Systems in India.	London Office of Company.	Date of first open'g of Line.	Year ended 31 December, 1898. Miles open. *	Total Capital Outlay, to end of Year.	Gross Receipts.	Working Expenses.	% on gross Receipts.	Net Receipts.	% on Capital outlay.	Total paid-up Capital of Company (excluding Debenture Stock and Annuities A, B and C) to Dec. 31, 1898.	Present minimum Government guarantee %.	Dividend % paid during last 12 months.	Price, 5th of £100 Capital	Yield %.
				Rx.	Rx.	Rx.		Rx.		£	£	£ s. d.		£ s. d.
Guaranteed Railways—														
[1] Bombay, Baroda & C. I.	45 Finsbury Circus ...	1860	686	10,936,855	1,586,272	712,052	44·89	874,220	8·05	7,550,300	5	5 0 0[9]	219	2 5 8
[1] Great Indian Peninsula	Copthall Avenue	1853	1,492	28,080,901	3,487,749	2,075,022	59·49	1,412,726	5·03	20,000,000	5	5 0 0[11]	172	2 18 2
[1] Madras	61 New Broad Street...	1856	858	13,979,229	1,096,855	536,603	48·92	560,251	4·54	10,257,630[8]	4½	5 1 0	140	3 12 4
											4¾		150	3 7 4
											5		160	3 3 2
State Lines worked by Companies—														
[3] Assam, Bengal [2]	Bishopsgate House ...	1895	304	4,432,732	130,812§	125,357	95·83	5,455	0·13	1,500,000	3†	3 5 0	101	3 4 4
[3] Bengal & N.-Western [6]	237 Gresham House ...	1875	928	6,705,569	647,603	280,855	43·37	366,747	5·47	2,750,000	—	5 0 0	146	3 8 6
[1] Bengal Central	199 Gresham House ...	1882	125	1,235,830	102,465	65,665	64·08	36,800	2·98	500,000	3½	4 13 0	120	3 17 6
[1] Bengal-Nagpur	132 Gresham House ...	1880	1,067	9,986,049	687,919	351,533	51·10	336,385	3·37	3,000,000	4	4 0 0	110	3 12 9
[3] Burma[7]	239 Gresham House ..	1877	936	7,865,818	899,143	520,292	57·87	378,852	4·82	—	—	—	—	—
[1] Delhi Umballa Kalka[5]	17 Victoria Street ... Worked by East Indian	1891	162	1,534,358	160,751	77,160	48·00	83,590	5·41	800,000	3¼	4 0 0	125	3 4 0
[1] East Indian	29–30 Nicholas Lane ...	1854	1,897	39,856,772	5,979,605	1,898,879	31·76	4,080,727	10·24	Ann. class D. 3,752,255	4	4 0 0[10]	151	2 13 0
[1] Indian Midland	Copthall Avenue	1893	973	10,177,367	678,314	374,694	55·24	303,619	2·66	3,000,000	4	4 0 0	110	3 12 9
[3] Rajputana-Malwa	W'rk'd by Bombay-Baroda	1873	1,838	13,275,734	2,099,039	899,076	42·83	1,199,963	9·04	State line.	—	—	—	—
Rohilkhund & Kumaon	237 Gresham House ...	1884	285	1,162,574	149,639	77,541	51·82	72,098	6·20	200,000	—	5 3 6	138	3 15 0
[3] South Indian	55 Gracechurch Street.	1861	1,094	7,509,041‡	849,941	463,266	54·51	386,674	5·15	1,000,000	3	5 0 0	119	4 4 0
[3] Southern Mahratta[5] ...	44 Finsbury Circus ...	1884	1,554	12,201,585	717,026	503,120	70·17	213,906	1·72	3,500,000	3½	5 0 0	117	4 5
Native State and Foreign	*Lines worked by Cos.—*													
[1] Nizam's (The)	50 Old Broad Street ...	1874	351	4,255,578	407,657	180,209	44·20	227,458	5·34	2,000,000	Nizam's Govt. 5	5 0 0	128	3 18 2
[3] W. of Ind. Portuguese[5]	9 Finsbury Circus ...	1887	51	1,629,744[5]	22,087	33,101	149·87	Loss 11,014	—	800,000	Portuguese Govt. 5	5 0 0	87	5 14 11
State Lines worked by the State—														
[4] Eastern Bengal	—	18[illegible]	860	11,707,088	1,471,787	638,281	43·37	833,506	7·12	—	—	—	—	—
[1] North-Western	—	1861	3,400	48,462,816	3,765,007	1,905,428	50·61	1,859,579	3·84	—	—	—	—	—
[1] Oudh & Rohilkhund ...	—	1867	1,033	11,395,836	985,159	454,387	46·12	530,772	4·56	—	—	—	—	—
Native State Lines—														
[3] Bhávnagar-Gondal......	—	1880	455	2,175,304	200,393	117,570	58·67	82,823	3·71	—	—	—	—	—
[3] Jodhpore-Bickaneer ...	—	1882	406	896,913	135,019	55,162	40·55	80,856	9·01	—	—	—	—	—

1 Standard Gauge. 2 Opened to traffic from July 1, 1895. 3 Metre Gauge. 4 Eastern Bengal Standard gauge and Northern and Behar sections Metre Gauge (including the Kaunia-Dharlia 2′ 6″ gauge branch), also Dacca section. 5 Decrease due to certain credits.
6 Although for convenience classed amongst State Railways, this line is the property of the Bengal Central Railway Company, to whom the working was made over on Jan. 1, 1897.
7 Working transferred to a Company from Sept. 1, 1896. 8 £8,757,670 at 5%, £500,000 at 4½%, £999,960 at 4¾%; these last two amounts have been lately converted into capital stock.
9 In addition to the guaranteed interest a bonus of £2 2s. 6d. for 1st half and £1 1s. 0d. second half year of 1898, was declared payable in following half years.
10 " " £1 10s. 6d. " £1 0s. 0d. " "
11 " " £0 8s. 9d. for 1898 was declared.
* Including Branch Lines worked. § The results are abnormal, chiefly owing to the undeveloped state of the traffic on the line and to the fact that certain portions of the open sections damaged by the earthquake in June, 1897, had to be temporarily closed. † 3½% to July 1, 1898. ‡ Decrease due to the transfer of the Nellore-Gudur section to the Ennúr-Bezwada Section.

County and Municipal Directory of England and Wales.

Containing a List of Counties, with the Acreage, Population, and Rental, the names of Lords-Lieutenant, High Sheriffs in office in January, Chairmen of Quarter Sessions and of County Councils, Clerks of the Peace and of County Councils, County Treasurers, Chief Constables (with the number of Officers), County Surveyors, Treasurers, Coroners, &c. Also of Cities and Municipal Boroughs, with their Poor Law valuation, the names of the High Stewards, Mayors, Recorders, Stipendiary Magistrates, Town Clerks, &c. The statistical figures as to area, population, &c., are given according to the alterations of the county boundaries effected pursuant to the Local Government Act of 1888, the County Boroughs being excluded from the Counties.

ABERAVON, Glamorg. Pop. 9,000. Val. £24,800
Mayor, Councillor Thomas D. Evans (*C*)
Town Clerk, Marmaduke Tennant

ABERYSTWYTH, Cardig. Pop. 6,696. Val. £32,285
Mayor, Counc. Caleb Morgan Williams (*L*)
Town Clerk, Arthur Johnson Hughes

ABINGDON, Berks. Pop. 6,557. Val. £23,592
High Steward, Earl of Abingdon
Mayor, Ald. John T. Morland (*C*)
Recorder, William Harry Nash
Town Clerk, Bromley Challenor

ACCRINGTON, Lanc. Pop. 43,105. Val. £156,675
Mayor, Counc. John Sharp Higham (re-elec.) (*L*).
Town Clerk, Arthur Henry Aitken

ALDEBURGH, Suffolk. Pop. 2,159. Val. £8,876
Mayor, George Herbert Garrett, J.P. (re-elec.) (*U*)
Town Clerk, Henry Clement Casley (Ipswich)

ANDOVER, Hants. Pop. 6,800. Val. £28,630
Mayor, Councillor S. G. Footner (*C*)
Recorder, Alexander John Mackey
Town Clerk, Thomas Edgar Longman
Clerk of the Peace, Thomas Lamb

ANGLESEY (COUNTY OF). Acres 175,836. Population 50,098. Rental £203,616
Lord Lieutenant (1896), *and Chairman of Quarter Sessions*, Sir Richard H. Williams Bulkeley, Bart., Baron Hill, Beaumaris
High Sheriff, Hon. Claud H. Vivian, Plasgwyn, Pentraeth.
Chairman of County Council, David Rees
Clerk of the Peace, J. Lloyd Griffith, Holyhead
County Treasurer, E. M. Roberts, Metropolitan Bank, Llangefni
Chief Constable, L. Prothero, Menai Bridge (30)
County Surveyor, W. E. Jones, Llanfair
Coroner, Robert Jones Roberts, Menai Bridge

APPLEBY, Westmorlnd. Pop. 1,776. Val. £9,222
Mayor, Richard Ernest Leach (*C*)
Town Clerk, William Hewitson (solicitor)

ARUNDEL, Sussex. Pop. 2,645. Val. £11,334
Mayor, John Nibloe Hare (*C*)
Town Clerk, Richard Holmes.

ASHTON-UNDER-LYNE. Lancashire. Estimated pop. 44,600. Val. £157,654
Mayor, Walter Newton (re-elected), (*C*)
Town Clerk, Frederick William Bromley

BACUP, Lancashire. Pop. 24,500. Val. £82,157
Mayor, Councillor Ben. Smith (re-elected), (*L*)
Town Clerk, W. L. Bown

BANBURY, Oxfordsh. Pop. 12,768. Val. £62,858
High Steward, Rt. Hon. Earl of Jersey, G.C.M.G.
Mayor, Councillor Hubert Bartlett, J.P. (*C*)
Recorder, Rt. Hon. Alex. Staveley Hill, Q.C., M.P.
Town Clerk, Oliver James Stockton

BANGOR, Carnarvon. Pop. 10,850. Val. £38,970
Mayor, Ald. John Evan Roberts, J.P. (re-elec.) (*L*)
Town Clerk, Richard Hughes Pritchard, M.A.

BARNSLEY, Yorks. Pop. 35,427. Val. £122,218
Mayor, Ald. Thomas Wilkinson (re-elected) (*C*)
Town Clerk Henry Horsfield

BARNSTAPLE, Devon. Pop. 14,000. Val. £49,615
High Steward, Hon. Mark Rolle.
Mayor, Joseph Green Hamlin (*C*)
Recorder, Sir George E. D. Sherston Baker, Bart.
Town Clerk, James Bosson
Clerk of the Peace, Wm. Henry Toller

*****BARROW-IN-FURNESS**, Lancashire. Pop. 57,387. Val. £235,676
Mayor, Counc. Leonard P. Chapman (re-elec.) (*C*)
Town Clerk, Charles Francis Preston

BASINGSTOKE, Hants. Pop. 10,000. Val. £46,567
Mayor, Thomas M. Kingdon (*L*)
Town Clerk, James A. Neville.

*****BATH**, Somerset. Pop. 52,600. Val. £305,446
Mayor, Robert Edmond Dickinson, J.P. (*C*)
Recorder, Henry Coleman Folkard
Town Clerk and Clerk of the Peace, Benj. Hick Watts

BATLEY, Yorks. Pop. 30,000. Val. £96,129
Mayor, Ald. John Illingworth (re-elected) (*L*)
Town Clerk, Joseph Hanson Craik (solicitor)

BEAUMARIS, Anglesey. Pop. 2,202. Val. £10,885
Mayor, Councillor W. R. Jones (re-elected) (*C*)
Town Clerk, John Rice Roberts, M.A.

BECCLES, Suffolk. Pop. 6,669. Val. £27,977
Mayor, Ald. Edward Masters (*U*)
Town Clerk, Tom Plowman Angell
Borough Treasurer, John Clarke, F.I.B., Barclay's Bank (1850)

BEDFORD, Beds. Pop. 35,500. Val. £139,437
Mayor, Hedley Baxter (*C*)
Recorder, William Russell Griffiths
Town Clerk, Thomas Sinnpson Porter
Clerk of the Peace, M. Whyley (County Coroner)

BEDFORDSHIRE. Acres 303,500. Population 160,704. Rental £940,921
Lord Lieut., Rt. Hon. Earl Cowper, K.G. (1861), Panshanger, Herts, and Wrest Park, Beds.
High Sheriff, Jas. Harold Howard, Kempston Grange, Bedford
Chairman of Quarter Sessions, Lord St. John of Bletsoe, Melchbourne Park
Chairman of County Council, Duke of Bedford, Woburn Abbey
Vice-Chairman of do., Viscount Peel, Sandy
Clerk of the Peace and of County Council, William Woodfine Marks
County Treasurer, Thomas Barnard, J.P.
Chf. Const., Lt.-Col. F. J. Josselyn, Bedford (100)
Surveyor, W. H. Leete, Bedford
County Coroner, Mark Whyley, Bedford
Coroner for Honor of Ampthill, Frederick Thomas Tanqueray, Woburn
County Analyst, T. Stevenson, M.D., Guy's Hosp. London

BERKSHIRE. Acres 458,272. Pop. 176,119. Rental £1,123,860
Lord Lieutenant, Col. Lord Wantage, K.C.B. V.C. (1886), Lockinge House, Wantage
High Sheriff, Charles Thomas Daniell Crews, Billingbear Pk., Waltham St. Lawrence, Twyford

Chairman of Q. S. and of County Council, Wm. George Mount, M.P.

Vice-Chairman of Q. S. and of County Council, Alb. Richard Tull, Crookham House, Newbury

Clerk of the Peace and of County Council, J. Thornhill Morland (*Deputy*, F. Morland), Reading

Treasurer, Henry Collins, Reading

Chief Constable, Col. A. Blandy, Reading (173)

Clerk to Lieuty., John T. Morland, Reading

Coroners: Bromley Challenor, Abingdon; Jas. Cockburn Pinniger, Newbury; Wm. Weedon, Reading; and Llewellyn Jotcham, Wantage

BERWICK-UPON-TWEED. Pop. 13,377. Val. £60,069

Mayor, Councillor David Herriot (*C*)

Recorder, H. B. Hans Hamilton

Sheriff, Major A. Tower Robertson, V.D.

Town Clerk, Robert Weddell

Clerk of the Peace, S. Sanderson

BEVERLEY, Yorks. Pop. 12,569. Val. £47,945

Mayor, Councillor Thomas Joseph Willis (*C*)

Town Clerk, James Willis Mills

BEWDLEY, Worcester. Pop. 2,876. Val. £8,186

High Steward, Viscount Cobham

Mayor, Langley Kitching, J.P. (4th time) (*L*)

Town Clerk, Stanley Hemingway

BIDEFORD, Devon. Est. Pop. 9,000. Val. £20,085

Mayor, Councillor Thomas Godman (*L*)

Recorder, Sir Geo. Sherston Baker, Bart.

Town Clerk, Charles William Hole

Clerk of the Peace, Henry Montague Bazeley

*BIRKENHEAD, Cheshire. Pop. 115,162. Val. £547,449

Mayor, James Gamlin (*C*)

Recorder, Clement Higgins, Q.C.

Town Clerk and Clerk of Peace, Alfred Gill

*BIRMINGHAM (City). Est. Pop. 514,956. Val. £2,348,858

Lord Mayor, Rt.Hon. Chs. G. Beale (third year) (*U*)

Recorder, John Stratford Dugdale, Q.C.

Stipendiary Magistrate, Thos. Milnes Colmore

Town Clerk, Edward Orford Smith

Clerk of the Peace, Charles Edward Mathews

Coroner, Isaac Bradley

BISHOP'S CASTLE, Salop. Pop. 1,586. Val. £6,514

Mayor, Councillor Selwyn Hale Puckle (*U*)

Town Clerk, Ernest Griffiths

*BLACKBURN, Lanc. Pop. 133,000. Val. £477,204

Mayor, Edwin Hamer, J.P. (*L*)

Recorder, Miles Walker Mattinson, Q.C.

Town Clerk & Clerk of Peace, Robert Eyes Fox

BLACKPOOL, Lanc. Est. Pop. 48,000. Val. £378,660

Mayor, Counc. Dr. Charles C. Kingsbury (*O*)

Town Clerk, Thomas Loftos

BLANDFORD FORUM, Dorset. Pop. 3,974. Val. £13,913

Mayor, Ald. Philip Abraham Barnes (re-elec.) (*C*)

Town Clerk, Edward Castleman Smith

BODMIN, Cornwall. Pop. 5,151. Val. £21,582

Mayor, William Arthur Bawden (*C*)

Town Clerk, Robert Phillips Edyvean

*BOLTON. Pop. 162,224. Val. £677,018

Mayor, Ald. J. Edwin Scowcroft, J.P. (*C*)

Recorder, Samuel Pope, Q.C.

Town Clerk, Robert Gudgeon Hinnell

Clerk of the Peace, Wm. Walter Cannon.

*BOOTLE, Lancashire. Pop. 53,544. Val. £477,424

Mayor, Councillor George Lamb (*L*)

Town Clerk, Joseph Henry Farmer

BOSTON, Lincolnshire. Pop. 14,593. Val. £47,637

Mayor, Councillor William Pooles (re-elctd.) (*L*)

Town Clerk, Robert William Staniland

BOURNEMOUTH. Pop. 37,781. Val. £380,602

Mayor, Councillor John Clark Webber (*O*)

Recorder, Robert Alexander Kinglake

Town Clerk, James Druitt

Clerk of the Peace, Clement John Haydon

BRACKLEY, Nthants. Pop. 2,591. Val. £11,143

Mayor, Alderman John Goffe Clarke (*C*)

Town Clerk, Walter Frederick Thomas

*BRADFORD (City). Yorks. Pop. 285,492. Val. £1,323,027

Mayor, William Charles Lupton, J.P. (*C*)

Recorder, Thomas Milvain, Q.C.

Stipendiary Magistrate, Charles Skidmore

Town Clerk, Frederick Stevens

BRECKNOCKSHIRE. Acres 454,536. Population 51,459. Rental £247,258

Lord Lieut. (1873) & *Chairman of Q. S.*, Lord Glanusk, Glanusk Park, Crickhowell

High Sheriff, Capt. D. Hughes Morgan, Brecon

Chairman of County Council, Charles Evan-Thomas, J.P., Gnoll, Neath

Vice-Chairman of County Council, Richard Digby Cleasby, J.P., Penyore, Brecon

Clerk of the Peace and of County Council, H. Edgar Thomas, Brecon

County Treasurer, John Tudor, Brecon

Chief Constable, E. R. Gwynne, Llanthetty Hall, Talybont-on-Usk

County Surveyor, William Williams, Brecon

County Coroners: Richard H. Arlingham Davies, Crickhowell; M. F. Thomas, Brecon; Dr. Wm. Rees Jones, Senny Bridge

BRECON, Brecknock. Pop. 5,794. Val. £22,963

Mayor, Counc. Col. John Morgan (8th time) (*C*)

Town Clerk, G. Hyatt Williams

BRIDGNORTH, Salop. Pop. 5,865. Val. £21,959

Mayor, Councillor Josiah William Steward (*C*)

Recorder, Rudolph Herries Spearman

Town Clerk, James Hughes Cooksey

Clerk of the Peace, Samuel Thos. Nicholls

BRIDGWATER, Som. Pop. 14,000. Val. £50,108

Mayor, Councillor Thomas Good (re-elected) (*L*)

Recorder, Wyndham Neave Slade

Town Clerk, William Thomas Baker

BRIDPORT, Dorset. Pop. 6,611. Val. £23,506

Mayor, John Cleeves Palmer (*C*)

Town Clerk, Charles George Nantes

BRIGHOUSE, Yorks. Pop. 20,666. Val. £76,925

Mayor, Councillor John Wm. Clay (re eletd.) (*C*)

Town Clerk, James Parkinson

*BRIGHTON, Sussex. Pop. 123,226. Val. £802,383

Mayor, Ald. John Edward Stafford, J.P. (*L*)

Recorder, Philip Chasemore Gates, Q.C.

Stipend. Magistrate, Chas. Gilbert Heathcote, M.A.

Town Clerk, Francis John Tillstone

*BRISTOL. Pop. 320,000. Val. £1,461,419

Lord Mayor, Rt. Hon. Sir Herbert Ashman (re-elected) (*L*)

High Steward, Duke of Beaufort, K.G.

Recorder, Edward James Castle, Q C.

High Sheriff, George Alfred Wills

Town Clerk, Daniel Travers Burges

Deputy Town Clerk, Edmund J. Taylor

BUCKINGHAM, Bucks. Pop. 3,364. Val. £16,790

High Steward, The Right Hon. Lord Addington

Mayor, Charles Aaron Bennett (*C*)

Town Clerk, Thomas Risley Hearn

BUCKINGHAMSHIRE. Acres 475,694. Population, 185,284. Rental £1,095,2:8

Lord Lieut.,

High Sheriff, Arthur Lasenby Liberty, The Lee, Great Missenden.

Chairman of C.C. and of Q. S., Lord Cottesloe

Vice-Chairman Quarter Sessions, C. A. Cripps, Q.C.

Clerk of the Peace, Wm. Crouch, Aylesbury

County Treasurer, C. E. Cobb, Aylesbury
Chf. Const., Maj. Otway Mayne, Aylesbury (151)
Coroners : Geo. Hanby De'Ath, Winslow ; H. Small, Buckingham; Geo. Fell, Aylesbury ; Geo. A. Charsley, Beaconsfield ; J. Worley, Newport Pagnell; F. T. Tanqueray, Ampthill.

BURNLEY, Lanc. Pop. 87,016. Val. £356,000
Mayor, Ald. William Dickinson, J.P. (re-elect.) (L)
First Recorder, Henry Gordon Shee, Q.C.
Town Clerk & Clerk of the Peace, W. T. Fullalove

BURSLEM, Stafford. Pop. 40,000. Val. £140,597
Mayor, Councillor Enoch Edwards (L)
Town Clerk, Arthur Ellis

BURTON, Stafford. Pop. 46,047. Val. £283,613
Mayor, Counc. George Littci Blackhall (C)
Town Clerk, T. N. Whitehead

*BURY, Lancashire. Pop. 62,000. Val. £250,054
Mayor, James Byron (L)
Town Clerk, John Haslam

BURY ST. EDMUNDS, Suffolk. Pop. 16,630. Val. £70,125
Steward of the Liberty, Marquess of Bristol
Mayor, Councillor Thomas Shillitoe (C)
Recorder, Edward Thomas E. Besley, Q.C.
Town Clerk, Charles Edward Salmon
Clerk of the Peace, Rowland Holt Wilson

CALNE, Wiltshire. Pop. 3,495. Val. £10,500
Mayor, Samuel W. Bennett (L)
Town Clerk, George Isaac Gough

CAMBRIDGE, Cambs. Pop. 36,983. Val. £226,507
High Steward, Duke of Rutland, K.G., G.C.B.
Mayor, Councillor A. J. Tillyard (L)
Recorder,
Town Clerk, John E. Ledsam Whitehead, M.A.

CAMBRIDGESHIRE. Acres 315,236. Population 120,236. Rental £748,261
Lord Lieutenant, Alexander Peckover, D.C.L. (1893), Bank House, Wisbech
High Sheriff (Cambs and Hunts), Capt. W. H. O. Duncombe, Waresley Park, St. Neots
Chairman of Q. S. and County Council, Arthur Sperling, LL.M., Lattenbury Hill, St. Ives
Clerk of Peace and to County Council, Samuel Reuben Ginn, D.L., Cambridge (*Deputy,* Arthur Wright, LL.M., Cambridge)
Treasurer, Edmd. H. Parker, M.A., Cambridge
Chief Constable, Chas. Stretten, Cambridge (71)
Coroner, Algernon Jasper Lyon, St. Andrew's Street, Cambridge
County Surveyor, W. M. Fawcett, M.A., Cambridge (See also ELY, ISLE OF.)

*CANTERBURY, Kent. Pop. 23,026. Val. £112,682
Mayor, Alderman Geo. Collard, J.P. (6th y.) (C)
Recorder, Frank Safford
Sheriff, Councillor Stephen Horsley
Town Clerk & Clerk of the Peace, Henry Fielding

*CARDIFF, Glamorg. Pop. 185,826. Val. £1,046,312
Mayor, Councillor S. A. Brain, J.P. (C)
Stipendiary Magistrate, Thomas William Lewis
First Recorder, Benj. Francis-Williams, Q.C.
Town Clerk & Clerk of Peace, Joseph Larke Wheatley

CARDIGAN (Boro'). Pop. 3,447. Val. £12,575
Mayor, Charles Evans Davis Morgan Richardson (3rd year) (U)
Town Clerk, David Morgan Jones

CARDIGANSHIRE. Acres 443,071. Population 63,467. Rental £283,226
Lord Lieutenant, Col. Herbert Davies-Evans (1888), Highmead
High Sheriff, Jas Jones, Cefenllwyd, Aberystwyth
Chairman of County Council, Rev. T. Mason Jones, Brow Trisant, Devil's Bridge.
Chairman of Quarter Sessions, John William Bund Willis-Bund, Wick Episcopi, Worcester

Clerk of the Peace, H. C. Fryer, Aberystwyth
County Treasurer, Jos. D. Perrott, Aberystwyth
Chief Const., Howell Evans, Aberystwyth (40)
County Surveyors, Roderick Lloyd, Tregaron ; David Davies, Brynhyfryd
Coroners : Abel Evans, Lampeter; John Henry Evans, Newcastle Emlyn ; John Evans, Aberystwyth

CARLISLE, Cumberland. Pop. 39,176. Value £193,258
Mayor, Councillor Christopher Ling, J.P. (L)
Recorder, Alexander Henry, M.A.
Town Clerk and Clerk of the Peace, Alfred Henry Collingwood

CARMARTHEN (Borough). Pop. 10,300. Value £39,728
Mayor, Councillor Walter Spurrell (C)
Recorder, Arthur Griffith Poyer Lewis
Sheriff, Councillor John Lewis
Town Clerk, Richard Macaulay Thomas
Clerk of the Peace, James John

CARMARTHENSHIRE. Acres 541,259. Population 120,266. Rateable value £517,271
Lord Lieutenant, Sir James Drummond, Bart., Edwinsford, Llandilo
Admiral of N. Wales, Lord Mostyn
High Sheriff, Gwilym Evans, Llanelly
Chairman of Quarter Sessions, Earl Cawdor
Chairman of County Council, Joseph Maybery
Vice-Chair. of do., John Lloyd, Abergwilly
Clerk of the Peace and of County Council, Thomas Jones, Llandovery (*Deputy,* D. T. M. Jones)
County Treasurer, R. Peel Price, Llandovery
Chief Constable, W. Philipps, Llandilo (90)
Coroners : Thomas Walters, Carmarthen ; Richard Shipley Lewis, Llandilo ; W. Buckley Roderick, Llanelly

CARNARVON (Boro'). Pop. 9,804. Val. £26,204
Mayor, Alderman W. J. Williams (L)
Town Clerk, John Hugh Bodvel-Roberts

CARNARVONSHIRE. Acres 365,930. Population 117,586. Rateable value £559,013
Lord Lieut. and Chairman of Q. S., John Ernest Greaves (1886), Bron Eifion, Criccieth
High Sheriff, John Robinson, Talysarn
Chairman of County Council, J. R. Pritchard, Carnarvon
Dep. Chairm. of Q. S., J. Bryn Roberts, M.P.
Clk. of the Peace, John Hugh Bodvel-Roberts (*Deputy,* Arthur Bodvel-Roberts), Carnarvon
County Treasurer, W. B. C. Jones, Criccieth
Chief Const., Lt.-Col. A. A. Ruck, Carnarvon (86)
County Surveyor, Evan Evans, Carnarvon
Coroners : John Hugh Bodvel-Roberts, Carnarvon ; Thos. Hunter Hughes, M.R.C.S., Pwllheli

CHARD, Somerset. Pop. 4,315. Val. £16,285. Acreage, 403
Mayor, Samuel Henry Dening, J.P. (L)
Town Clerk, Walter James Tucker

CHATHAM, Kent. Est. Pop. 35,000. Val. £123,900
Mayor, George Robbins Viney (C)
Town Clerk, Henry Philip Mann

CHELMSFORD, Essex. Pop. 12,000. Val. £53,187
Mayor, Councillor Adolphus G. Maskell (C)
Town Clerk, Thomas Dixon (solicitor)

CHELTENHAM, Glouc. Pop. 49,000. Val. £280,742
Mayor, Alderman George Norman (re-elected) (L)
Town Clerk, Edward Thomas Brydges

CHESHIRE (Administrative County). Acres 645,101. Population. 536 121. Rental £3,538,220
Lord Lieutenant, Duke of Westminster, K.G. (1883), Eaton Hall, Chester
High Sheriff, Thomas Hardcastle Sykes, Cringle House, Cheadle

Chairman of Quarter Sessions, His Hon. Judge Sir Horatio Lloyd, Chester
Chairman of County Council, George Dixon, Astle Hall, Chelford
Vice-Chairman of County Council, Thomas William Killick, Townfield, Altrincham
Clerk of the Peace and of County Council, Reginald Potts, Chester
County Treasurer, James R. Thomson, Chester
Ch. Const., Lt.-Col. J. H. Hamersley, Chester (439)
County Surveyor, Harry F. Bull, Chester
County Architect, Hy. Beswick, Chester
Medical Officer of Health, Francis Vacher, M.D., Glanmor, Birkenhead
County Coroners: J. C. Bate, Chester; Hercules Campbell Yates, Macclesfield; Francis Newton, Stockport; R. Dobson, Warrington

*CHESTER (City). Pop. 41,603. Val. £194,583
Mayor, Henry Thomas Brown (*U*)
Recorder, His Honour Judge Sir Horatio Lloyd
Sheriff, Robert Lamb
Town Clerk, Samuel Smith

CHESTERFIELD, Derby. Pop. 29,000. Val. £101,486
Mayor, William Spooner (*U*)
Town Clerk, John Middleton

CHICHESTER, Sussex. Pop. 10,808. Val. £52,500
Mayor, Richard Combe Miller, J.P. (*C*)
Recorder, Charles Frederick Gill
Town Clerk, J. W. Loader Cooper
Clerk of the Peace, Wm. Turgis Haines

CHIPPENHAM, Wilts. Pop. 4,618. Val. £19,134
Mayor, Councillor James Beaven (*L*)
Town Clerk, Francis Henry Phillips

CHIPPING NORTON, Oxn. Pp.4,222. Val.£11,527
Mayor, Albert Brassey, M.P. (*C*)
Town Clerk, Thomas Mace

CHORLEY, Lancashire. Pop.26,000. Val.£86,198
Mayor, Councillor B. A. E. Jackson (3rd time) (*U*)
Town Clerk, John Mills

CHRISTCHURCH, Hants. Pop.4,415. Val.£16,600
Mayor, Ald. Samuel Bemister (3rd year) (*L*)
Town Clerk, John Druitt

CINQUE PORTS. *See* Dover, Sandwich, Romney, Hythe, Hastings, Winchelsea, and Rye
Lord Warden, Most Hon. Marquess of Salisbury, K.G. (1895), Walmer Castle, Deal
Registrar, E. Wollaston N. Knocker, C.B.

CLITHEROE, Lanc. Pop. 10,828. Val. £39,356
Mayor, Ald. Hargreaves Tilletson (*C*)
Recorder, His Hon. Theoph. Hastings Ingham
Town Clerk, John Eastham

COLCHESTER, Essex. Pop.41,000. Val.£145,558
High Steward, Rt. Hon. Earl Cowper, K.G.
Mayor, Councillor Edward Thompson Smith (*L*)
Recorder, His Hon. Judge Philbrick, Q.C.
Town Clerk, Henry Charles Wanklyn
Clerk of the Peace, Edgar Church

COLNE, Lancashire. Pop. 25,250. Val. £80,000
Mayor, Alderman Robinson Foulds, J.P. (*L*)
Town Clerk, Alfred Varley

CONGLETON, Chesh. Pop. 10,744. Val. £38,274
High Steward, Gen. Sir Richd. Wilbraham, K.C.B.
Mayor, Ald. William Worrall (re-elected) (*L*)
Town Clerk, Alfred Steele Sheldon

CONWAY, Carnarvon. Pop. 3,436. Val. £22,100
Mayor, M. J. Morgan, M.D. (re-elected) (*L*)
Town Clerk, T. E. Parry

CORNWALL (COUNTY OF). Acres 868,208. Population 322,571. Rental £1,312,944
Lord Lieutenant, Vice-Admiral, & Chairman of County Council, Earl of Mount-Edgcumbe (1877), Mount Edgcumbe, Plymouth
High Sheriff, Sir Lewis William Molesworth, Bart., Trewarthenick

Chairman of Quarter Sessions and Vice-Chairman of County Council, Wm. Cole Pendarves, of Pendarves, Camborne; F. Buller Howell
Clerk of the Peace to County Council, Christopher L. Cowlard (solicitor), Bodmin
Treasurer, Consolidated Bank of Cornwall
Chief Constable, R. Middleton Hill (222)
County Surveyors, S. W. Jenkin, Liskeard; T. J. Hickes, Truro
Coroners: D. Thompson, Launceston; Edmund Gilbert Hamley, Bodmin; Edmund Laurence Carlyon, Truro; Geo. Pascoe Grenfell, Penzance; Albert C. L. Glubb, Liskeard

*COVENTRY, Warwick. Est. Pop. 71,500. Val. £262,939
Mayor, William Ranby Goate (*C*)
Town Clerk, Lewis Beard

COWBRIDGE, Glamorg. Pop. 1,377. Val. £4,233
Mayor, Alderman William Aaron James (*L*)
Town Clerk, William Thomas Gwyn (solicitor)

CREWE, Cheshire. Pop. 40,000. Val. £134,461
Mayor, Councillor James Henry Moore (*L*)
Town Clerk, Frederick Cooke

*CROYDON, E. Surrey. Pop. 128,600. Val. £787,065
Mayor, Nathaniel Page (*C*)
Recorder, Robert George Glenn, LL.B.
Town Clerk & Clerk of the Peace, E.Mawdesley,LL.B.

CUMBERLAND (COUNTY OF). Acres 968,136. Population 227,373. Rental £1,456,618
Lord Lieutenant, Lord Muncaster (1876), Muncaster Castle, Ravenglass
Vice-Admiral of the Coast, Earl of Lonsdale, Lowther Castle
High Sheriff, Wm. Parkin Moore, Whitehall, Carlisle
Chairman of Q. S., Richard Saul Ferguson
Chairman of County Council, Henry Charles Howard, of Greystoke Castle, Penrith
Vice-Chairman of ditto, Miles MacInnes, Rickerby, Carlisle
Clerk of the Peace and of County Council, Charles Bernard Hodgson, Carlisle
Chief Constable, Sir J. Dunne, D.L., Carlisle (201)
County Treasurer, George Agnew Main
County Financial Sec., Wm. Dobinson, Carlisle
County Surveyor, G. J. Bell, Carlisle
County Architect, G. D. Oliver, F.R.I.B.A., Carlisle
Coroners: James Blacklock Lee, Brampton; Joseph Hayton, Cockermouth; John Webster, Whitehaven; P. B. Stoney, Millom; and Gordon Falcon, Workington

DARLINGTON, Durham. Pop. 45,000. Val. £183,898
Mayor, Counc. Thos. Baker Swinburne, J.P. (*U*)
Town Clerk, Henry Gordon Steavenson

DARTMOUTH, Devon. Pop. 6,025. Val. £23,419
Mayor, William George Hellens Ellis (*L*)
Town Clerk, Onesimus Smart Bartlett

DARWEN, Lancs. Pop. 40,000. Val. £139,755
Mayor, J. W. Gillibrand, J.P. (*C*)
Town Clerk, Charles Costeker

DAVENTRY, Northants. Pop.3,939. Val.£14,714
Mayor, Councillor T. H. Reynolds (5th time) (*C*)
Town Clerk, Frederick Willoughby

DEAL, Kent. Pop. 9,500. Val. £43,323
Mayor, Ald. C. W. Thompson (3rd year) (*U*)
Recorder, James Fenning Torr
Town Clerk & Clerk of the Peace, Alf. Chas. Brown

DENBIGH (Boro'). Pop. 6,412. Val. £32,474
Mayor, Alfred Lloyd Jones (*L*)
Town Clerk, John Parry Jones

DENBIGHSHIRE. Acreage 425,038. Population 120,807. Rental £589,465
Lord Lieutenant, Col. William Cornwallis West (1872), Ruthin Castle, Ruthin

High Sheriff, Col. J. Higson, PlasMadoc, Llanrwst
Chairman of Quarter Sessions, Boscawen Trevor Griffith-Boscawen, Trevalyn Hall, Wrexham
Chairman of County Council, J. Watkin Lumley
Deputy Chairman of Q. S., Col. Arthur Mesham, Pontryffydd, Trefnant, R S.O.
Clerk of the Peace, W. R. Evans, Ruthin
County Treasurer, Marcell Conran, Brondyffryn, Denbigh
Chief Con., Maj. T. J. Leadbetter, Wrexham (82)
County Surv., R. Lloyd Williams, Denbigh (59)
Coroners: John Roberts Hughes, M.D., Denbigh; William Wynn Evans, Wrexham

*DERBY (County Boro'). Pop. 94,146. Val. £436,015
Lord High Steward, Duke of Devonshire, K.G.
Mayor, Councillor Thomas Fletcher (L)
Recorder, John Henry Etherington-Smith
Town Clerk and Clerk of the Peace, Harry Freckelton Gadsby

DERBYSHIRE. Acres 657,550. Population 520,914. Rental £2,198,438
Ld. Lt., Duke of Devonshire, K.G. (1892) Chatswth.
High Sheriff, Sir Arthur Percival Heywood, Bart., Duffield Bank, Derby
Chairman of County Council, Lord Waterpark, Doveridge, Derby
Vice-Chairman of C. C., G. Herbert Strutt, Makeney House, Derby
Chairman of Q. S., Tonman Mosley, Bangors Park, Iver, Uxbridge
Clerk of the Peace and of the County Council, Norton Joseph Hughes-Hallett, Derby
County Treasurer, John Farmer Thirlby, Derby
Chief Constable, Capt. H. C. Holland, Derby (321)
County Surveyor, J. Somes Story, Derby
Medical Officer of Health, S. Barwise, M.D., Derby
Coroners: William Harvey Whiston, Derby; Frederic Edward Leech, Derby; Godfrey Mosley, Derby; Charles George Busby, Chesterfield; Charles Davis, Glossop
County Analyst, John White, Derby

DEVIZES, Wiltshire. Pop. 6,426. Val. £24,298
Mayor, Alderman Herbert Biggs (C)
Recorder, Francis Reynolds Yonge Radcliffe
Town Clerk, Joseph Thornthwaite Jackson, B.A.
Clerk of the Peace, T. C. Hopkins

*DEVONPORT, Devon. Pop. 70,000. Val. £252,000
Mayor, William Hornbrook (re-elected) (L)
Recorder, His Hon. Henry Edward Duke
Town Clerk, A. B. Pilling
Clerk of the Peace, G. H. E. Rundle

DEVONSHIRE. Acres 1,666,579. Population 632,782. Rental £3,553,528
Lord Lieut. & Chairman of County Council, Lord Clinton (1887), Heanton Satchville, Dolton
Vice-Chairman of County Council, Earl of Morley
High Sheriff, Richard Bowerman West, Exeter
Chairmen of Q.S., Lord Coleridge, Q.C.; Viscount Ebrington; J. Graham, Q.C.
Clerk of the Peace, Henry Michelmore, Exeter
County Treasurers, Nat. Provl. Bank
Chief Constable, F. R. C. Coleridge, Exeter (421)
County Surveyors, E. H. Harbottle; C. G. Acock, Totnes; S. Ingram, Exeter
Coroners: C. E. Cox, Honiton; F. Burrow, Crediton; J. F. Bromham, Barnstaple; John D. Prickman, Okehampton; R. W. Prideaux, Dartmouth; Sidney Hacker, Totnes; T. Sanders, S. Molton; R. R. Rodd, East Stonehouse

DEWSBURY, Yorks. Pop. 29,847. Val. £122,290
Mayor, Councillor Robert Beattie, M.D. (C)
Town Clerk, G. Trevelyan Lee

DONCASTER, Yorks. Pop. 25,933. Val. £138,000
Mayor, Alderman Bentley, J.P. (C)

Recorder, His Honour Edgar John Meynell
Town Clerk, Thomas Babington Sugden

DORCHESTER, Dorset. Pop. 7,946. Val. £33,591
Mayor, Alderman George Davis (re-elected) (U)
Town Clerk, A. G. Symonds

DORSET (COUNTY OF). Acres 632,272. Population 194,517. Rental £1,095,665
Lord Lieutenant, Earl of Ilchester (1885), Melbury House, Dorchester
High Sheriff, William Colfox, Westmead, Bridport
Chairman of County Council, Viscount Portman
Vice-Chairman of C. C., Lord Stalbridge
Chairman of Q. S., Hastings Burton Middleton
Depy.-Chairman Q. S., Col. John R. P. Goodden
Clerk of the Peace and to County Council, Edward Archdall Ffooks, Sherborne
Clerk to Lieutenancy, Thomas Ffooks, Sherborne
County Treasurer, J. M. Lush, Dorchester
County Accountant, G. H. White. Sherborne
Chief Const., Capt. D. Granville. Dorchester (175)
County Surveyor, W. J. Fletcher, Wimborne
Coroners: John Comyns Leach, Sturminster Newton (North Dist.); Sir Rd. Nicholas Howard, Weymouth (South Dist.); Chas. H. Watts Parkinson, Wimborne (East Dist.); Charles Geo. Nantes. Bridport (West Dist.)

DOUGLAS (I. of Man) Pop. 23,000 Val. £137,000
Mayor, Alderman Samuel Webb, J.P. (re-elec.)
Town Clerk, Alexander Robertson

DOVER, Kent. Pop. 35,000. Val. £177,833
Lord Warden of the Cinque Ports and Constable of Dover Castle, Most Hon. The Marquess of Salisbury, K.G. (1895), Walmer Castle, Deal, and Hatfield House, Herts
Mayor, Councillor Sir William Henry Crundall, Knt. (10th time) (U)
Recorder, Sir Harry Bodkin Poland, Knt., Q.C.
Town Clerk, E. Wollaston Nadir Knocker, C.B.

DROITWICH, Worcest. Pop. 4,021. Val. £20,505
Mayor, Councillor Richard Paisthorpe Cully (C)
Town Clerk, Samuel John Tombs

*DUDLEY. Pop. 45,740. Val. £137,666
Mayor, Edward Grainger (L)
Deputy Mayor, George Henry Dunn
Town Clerk, Henry Cartright Brettell

DUNSTABLE, Beds. Est. Pop. 5,084. Val. £16,799
Mayor, Alfred James Perkins (L)
Town Clerk, Chas. Crichton-Stuart Benning

DURHAM (CITY). Pop. 14,863. Val. £50,335
Mayor, The Earl of Durham (U)
Recorder, His Hon. Francis John Greenwell
Town Clerk, Frederick Marshall

DURHAM (COUNTY PALATINE). Acres 647,281. Pop. 1,152,894. Rental £3,795,912
Lord Lieutenant, Earl of Durham (1884), Lambton Castle, Durham
High Sheriff and Deputy-Lieutenant, Ulrick A. Ritson, Jesmond, Newcastle-on-Tyne
Chairman of Quarter Sessions, Rt. Hon. John Lloyd Wharton, M.P., D.C.L.
Chairman of C. C., Samuel Storey
Depy. Ditto, Ald. Joseph Richardson, M.P.
Clk. of the Peace and to C. C., R. Simey, Durham
County Treasurer, J. E. Backhouse, Durham
Chief Const., Lt.-Col. J. H. Eden, Durham (625)
County Surveyor, William Crozier, Durham
Medical Officer of Health, T. Eustace Hill, Durham
Coroners: John Graham, Sunderland; John Thomas Proud, Bishop Auckland; Crofton Maynard, Durham; J. H. Bell, Stockton
Chancellor, Thomas Milvain, Q.C.
Attorney-General, John Forbes, Q.C.
Solicitor-General, Edwd. Tindal Atkinson, Q.C.

EAST RETFORD, Notts. Pop. 10,603. Val. £45,989
High Steward, Rt. Hon. Fras. J. Savile Foljambe
Mayor, Alderman Francis Huntsman (L)
Town Clerk, Samuel Jones

EASTBOURNE, Sussex. Pop.50,000. Val.£300,878
Mayor, Alderman H. W. Keay, J.P. (3rd time) (C)
Deputy, Councillor O'Brien Harding
Town Clerk, Henry West Fovargue

ECCLES, Lanc. Pop. 35,500. Val. £135,352
Mayor, Councillor Frederic Smith (L)
Town Clerk, William Henry Hickson

ELY (ISLE OF), Cambridgeshire. Pop. 63,340
Custos Rotulorum, Lord De Ramsey (1891), Ramsey Abbey, Hunts
High Sheriff, see CAMBRIDGESHIRE
Chairman of Quarter Sessions, Sir T. George Fardell, M.P., 26 Hyde Park Street, London
Chairman of County Council, Joseph Martin, Highfield House, Littleport
Vice-Chairman of C.C., Charles Bidwell, J.P., Ely
Clerk of the Peace and County Council, E. H. Jackson (*Depy.*, E. McD. C. Jackson), Wisbech
Treasurer, F. M. Bland, Wisbech
Chief Const., Col. W. Browne Ferris, Ely (65)
Coroners: William Welchman, Wisbech ; G. M. Hall, Ely

ESSEX (COUNTY OF). Acres 985,545. Population 784,258. Rental £3,454,803
Lord Lieutenant, Lord Rayleigh, F.R.S. (1892), Terling Place, Witham
High Sheriff, Edward Kensit Norman, Mistley Lodge, Manningtree
Chairman of Q.S., Right Hon. Lord Rookwood, Down Hall, Harlow ; and Andrew Johnston
Deputy Chairmen of Q.S., Hon. Charles Hedley Strutt, Wickham Hall, Witham ; (a vacancy)
Chairman of County Council, Andrew Johnston, Forest Lodge, Woodford Green
Clerk of the Peace & of C.C., H. Gibson,Chelmsford
Deputy, H. W. Gibson Chelmsford
County Treasurer, R. Woodhouse, Chelmsford
Chief Constable, Captain Edward Maclean Showers, Chelmsford (378)
County Surveyor, H. Stock, 9 Denman Street, London Bridge
Coroners: J. Harrison,Jun.,Braintree ; C. Edgar Lewis, Brentwood ; A. Ambrose, Loughton

EVESHAM, Worcestersh. Pop. 5,836. Val.£30,000
Mayor, Councillor Geoffrey New (re-elected) (U)
Town Clerk, Thomas Cox

*EXETER, Devon. Pop. 37,564. Val. £241,422
Mayor, Hubert Palmer Osborne Hamlin (C)
Recorder & Judge of the Provost Court, John Alderson Foote, Q.C.
Sheriff, George Frederick Gratwicke
Town Clerk & Clerk of th Peace, G. Roberts Shorto

EYE, Suffolk. Pop. 2,064. Val. £8,016
Mayor, Councillor Charles Tacon (5th year) (U)
Town Clerk, Major Francis Woolnough

FALMOUTH, Cornwall. Pop. 12,000. Val. £39,950
Mayor, Alderman Frederick James Bowles (C)
Town Clerk, John Henry Genn

FAVERSHAM, Kent. Pop. 10,478. Val. £46,202
Mayor, Counc. Charles Cremer (L)
Recorder, George Edwardes Dering
Town Clerk and Clerk of the Peace, Francis Frederick Giraud

FLINT (Boro'). Pop. 5,247. Val. £20,800
Mayor, E. J. Hughes (L)
Town Clerk, Henry Taylor, F.S.A.

FLINTSHIRE. Acres 163,954. Population 77,177. Rental £332,311

Lord Lieutenant, Hugh Robert Hughes (1874), Kimnel Park, Abergele
High Sheriff, Sir Edward Percy Bates, Bart., Gyrn Castle, Llanasa
Chairman of Quarter Sessions, Philip Pennant Pennant, Nantlys, St. Asaph
Chairman of C.C., Thomas Parry, Mold
Clerk of the Peace, Thos. T. Kelly, Mold
County Treasurers, North and South Wales Bank (Limited), Mold
Chief Constable, Major R. T. Webber, Mold (58)
Coroners: Richard Bromley, Rhyl ; William Alma Aylmer Lewis, Oswestry
Deputy Coroner, Fred. Llewellyn-Jones,Holywell

FOLKESTONE, Kent. Pop. 27,000. Val. £206,159
Mayor, Councillor Wm. Charles Carpenter (C)
Recorder, John Charles Lewis Coward
Town Clerk, Arthur Frederic Kidson
Clerk of the Peace, William Henry Harrison

*GATESHEAD, Durham. Pop. 106,552. Val. £334,314
Mayor, Councillor John Bradshaw, J.P. (L)
Town Clerk, William Swinburne

GLAMORGAN (County). Acres 504,376. Population 467,954. Rateable Value £2,595,044
Lord Lieutenant, Lord Windsor (1890), St. Fagan's Castle, Cardiff
High Sheriff, J. I. D. Nicholl, Bridgend
Chairman of County Council, John Blandy-Jenkins, J.P., Lanharan, Pontyclun, R.S.O.
Chairman of Quarter Sess., His Honour Judge Gwilym Williams
Clerk of the Peace and of County Council, Thomas Mansel Franklen, Cardiff
Depy. Clerk of the Peace and of C.C., W. E. R. Allen, Cardiff
Co. Treasurer, R. Wyndham Williams, Cardiff
Chief Const., Lionel Lindsay, Cardiff (453)
County Surveyor, T. Lloyd Edwards, Bridgend
Coroners: Edmund Bernard Reece, Cardiff ; R. J. Rhys, Aberdare ; H. Cuthbertson, Neath ; E. Strick, Swansea ; S. H. Stockwood, Bridgend
County Medical Officer, W. Williams, M.D., Penarth

GLASTONBURY, Som. Pop. 4,119. Val. £42,480
Mayor, Alderman John Baily (C)
Town Clerk, Stanley Austin

GLOSSOP, Derby. Pop. 22,414. Val. £60,978
Mayor, Counc. Samuel H. Wood, J.P., D.L. (re-elected) (C)
Town Clerk, Charles Davis

*GLOUCESTER (City). Pop.41,156. Val. £176,014
High Steward, Sir Michael E. Hicks-Beach
Mayor, Frank Treasure (C)
Recorder, His Honour Judge Alfred Young
Sheriff, Councillor Richard John Talbot
Town Clerk, George Sheffield Blakeway

GLOUCESTERSHIRE. Acres, 785,931. Population 325,688. Rental £2,051,346
Lord Lieutenant, Earl of Ducie (1857), Tortworth Court, Falfield (R.S.O.)
High Sheriff,Robert Ingham Tidswell, Gloucester
Chairman of County Council, Sir John Edward Dorington, Bt., M.P., Lypiatt Park, Stroud
Chairman of Quarter Sessions, Russell Jas. Kerr
Clerk of the Peace, Edwd. Theodore Gardom, Shire Hall, Gloucester
County Treasurer, J. P. Wilton Haines
Chief Constable, Admiral Henry Christian, R.N., Cheltenham (356)
County Architect, H. Medland, Gloucester
County Surveyor, Robt. Phillips, Gloucester
Coroners: Edward Mills Grace, M.D., Thornbury ; Alfred J. Morton Ball, Stroud ; John Waghorne, Cheltenham ; Maurice Fred. Carter, Newnham ; F. Moore, Tewkesbury

GODALMING, Surrey. Pop. 9,100. Val. £38,733
Mayor, Alderman Ebenezer Gammon (L)
Town Clerk, Thomas Percival Whately

GODMANCHESTER, Hunts. P.2,095.Val.£18,595
Mayor, Alderman T. B. Fordham (L)
Town Clerk, Gerald Hunnybun

GRANTHAM, Lincoln. Pop. 16,746. Val. £71,051
Mayor, Samuel Lamb Williamson (L)
Recorder, Thomas Spooner Soden
Town Clerk, Aubrey Henry Malim
Clerk of the Peace, F. W. Robinson

GRAVESEND, Kent. Pop. 24,067. Val. £111,417
Mayor, Councillor John Nathaniel Willis (C)
Recorder, Alexander D. O. Wedderburn, Q.C.
Town Clerk, Charles Edward Hatten
Clerk of Peace, George Edward Sharland

*****GREAT GRIMSBY**, Lincoln. Pop. 51,876.
Val. £198,000
High Steward, Rt. Hon. Lord Heneage, P.C.
Mayor, William Southworth (re-elected) (C)
Recorder, William Appleton
Clerk of the Peace, John Barker
Town Clerk, William Grange

GUILDFORD, Surrey. Pop. 14,316. Val. £87,059
High Steward, The Earl of Onslow, G.C.M.G.
Mayor, Councillor Henry Peak (L)
Recorder, Reginald More Bray, Q.C.
Town Clerk, Ferdinand Smallpeice

*****HALIFAX**, Yorks. Pop. 101,000. Val. £419,209
Mayor, Councillor William Brear (C)
Town Clerk, Keighley Walton

HAMPSHIRE (OR SOUTHAMPTON). Acres
949,376. Est. Pop. 418,927. Rental £2,167,124
Lord Lieutenant (1890) *and Chairman of County
Council*, Earl of Northbrook, G.C.S.I., Stratton,
Micheldever Station
High Sheriff, Sir R. N. Rycroft, Bt., Basingstoke
Vice-Chairman of Q. C. William W. Portal
Chairman of Q. S., Melville Portal (Civil), John
Lindsay Johnston (Judicial)
Clerk of Peace and County Council, Henry Barber
(Deputy, G. A. Webb), The Castle, Winchester
County Treasurer, G. E. Yonge, Winchester
Chief Constable, Major St. Andrew Bruce Warde,
West Hill, Winchester (381)
County Surveyor, W. J. Taylor, A.M.I.C.E.
Director of Technical Educn., David T. Cowan
County Coroners: P. E. J. Talbot, Andover; R.
Druitt, Christchurch; R. Hannen, Fording-
bridge; F. A. Johns, Ringwood; Edgar Goble,
Fareham; Hy. White, Winchester; Bernard
Harfield, Southampton; Spencer Clarke,
Whitchurch

*****HANLEY**, Stafford. Pop. 60,000. Val. £211,522
Mayor, Councillor George Ellis (re-elected) (C)
Recorder, Abel John Ram, Q.C.
Town Clerk and Clerk of Peace, Arthur Challinor
Assistant Town Clerk, J. B. Barrow

HARROGATE, Yorks. Pop. 21,000. Val. £141,643
Mayor, Councillor James A. Myntle, M.D., J.P.(C)
Town Clerk, Joseph Turner Taylor

HARTLEPOOL, Durh. Pop. 27,000. Val. £70,950
Mayor, Alderman John Horsley, J.P.(re-elec.) (U)
Recorder, John Thomas Belk, J.P.
Town Clerk, Herbert Wright Bell

HARWICH, Essex. Pop. 9,300. Val. £27,015
H. Steward, Edgar Walter Garland (Michaelstow)
Mayor, Alderman William Groom (6th time) (C)
Town Clerk, Arthur John Hanslip Ward

HASLINGDEN, Lancs. Pop. 18,225. Val. £74,491
Mayor, Alderman Aaron Holt (re-elected) (L)
Town Clerk, W. Musgrove

*****HASTINGS**, Sussex. Pop. 72,563. Val. £452,790
Mayor, Ald. F. Tuppenney, J.P. (re-elected) (L)

Recorder, Robert Henry Hurst
Town Clerk, Benjamin Frederick Meadows

HAVERFORDWEST (Town and County), Pemb.
Acres 1,436. Pop. 6,179. Val. £17,870
Lord Lieutenant (1875) *and Mayor* (1899-1900).
Sir Charles Edward Gregg-Philipps, Bart.,
Picton Castle (re-elected) (C)
Sheriff, Thomas Russell
Chairman of Q. S., His Honour Judge William
Stevenson Owen
Town Clerk, R. T. P. Williams
Clerk of the Peace, William Davies George

HEDON, Yorkshire. Pop. 979. Val. £3,327
Mayor, Robert Alan Park (C)
Town Clerk, Thos. Henry West

HELSTON, Cornwall. Pop. 3,198. Val. £9,075
Mayor, Alexander Pengilly (re-elected) (C)
Town Clerk, Joseph Walker Tyacke

HEMEL HEMPSTEAD. Pop. 11,000. Val.
£47,215
Mayor, Sir Astley Paston-Cooper,Bt.(re-elect.)(C)
Town Clerk, Lovel Smeathman

HENLEY-ON-THAMES. Pop.5,433. Val.£24,832
Mayor, Alderman Chamberlain (2nd time) (L)
Town Clerk, J. F. Cooper (Dep., A. Caldecott)

HEREFORD (City). Pop. 20,267. Val. £112,342
Chief Steward, Sir James Rankin, Bart., M.P.
Mayor, Councillor Wm.J.Humfrys (2nd time) (C)
Recorder, Arthur Gwynne-James, LL.B.
Town Clerk, Joseph Carless
Clerk of the Peace, Charles B. Beddoe

HEREFORDSHIRE. Acres 533,921. Popula-
tion 95,335. Rental £593,270
Lord Lieutenant, Lord Bateman (1852), Shobdon
Court, Leominster
High Sheriff, Arthur Wellesley Foster, Brock-
hampton, Ross
Chairman of Q. S., Sir Richd. Harington, Bt.
Chairman of County Council, Colonel Prescott
Decie, Bockleton Court, near Tenbury
Clerk of the Peace and of the County Council, James
Frederick Symonds, Hereford
County Treasurer, Henry C. Beddoe, Hereford
Ch. Const., Capt. the Hon. Evelyn Scudamore-
Stanhope, Hereford (79)
County Surveyor, A. G. Dryland, Hereford.
Coroners: Thomas Llanwarne, Hereford;
Charles E. Arthur Moore, Leominster

HERTFORD, Herts. Pop. 9,023. Val. £50,529
High Steward, Earl Cowper, K.G. (Panshanger)
Mayor, William Frampton Andrews (C)
Town Clerk, Thomas Joseph Sworder

HERTFORDSHIRE. Acres 404,429. Population
225,932. Rental £1,294,924
Lord Lieutenant, The Earl of Clarendon (1892),
The Grove, Watford
High Sheriff, Frederick Henry Norman, Moor
Place, Much Hadham
Chairman of County Council, Earl Cowper, K.G.,
Panshanger, Hertford
*Chairman of St. Albans Q. S. and Vice-Chairman
of County Council*, Sir John Evans, K.C.B., D.C.L.,
Nash Mills, Hemel Hempstead
Chairman of Hertford Quarter Sessions, Viscount
Cranborne, M.P.
Clerk of the Peace and of the County Council,
Charles Elton Longmore, Hertford
Deputy Clerk, Thomas J. Sworder. Hertford
County Treasurer, Barclay & Co., Hertford;
Ch. Const., Lt.-Col. Henry Daniell, Hatfield (248)
County Surveyor, U. A. Smith, 41 Parliament
Street, S.W.
Coroners: Thomas Joseph Sworder, Hertford;
Lovell Drage, M.D., Hatfield; Francis
Shillitoe, Hitchin; Walter Grover, Hemel

Hempstead; Henry Baker, Bishop Stortford; D. B. Balding, Royston; T. J. Broad, Watford
County Acct., W. B. Keen, 3 Church Ct., Old Jewry

HEYWOOD, Lanc. Est. Pop. 25,000. Val.£100,250
Mayor, Ald. Abraham C. Maden (re-elected) (L)
Town Clerk, John Henry Baldwick

HIGH WYCOMBE, OR **CHIPPING WYCOMBE**, Bucks. Pop. 16,000. Val.£41,120.
Mayor, Councillor Robt. Davenport Vernon (U)
Recorder, Edward John Payne, M.A.
Town Clerk, Arthur Joseph Clarke

HIGHAM FERRERS, Northants. Pop. 2,200. Val.£6,850
Mayor, Councillor C. S. R. Palmer (L)
Town Clerk, Wm. Hirst Simpson, B.A.

HONITON, Devon. Pop. 3,216. Val.£15,903
Mayor, Robert Henry Matthews (re-elected) (L)
Town Clerk, George Tash Tweed

HOVE, Sussex (1898). Pop. 35,397. Val.£337,604
Mayor, Alderman Jeremiah Colman (C)
Town Clerk, Henry Endacott

*****HUDDERSFIELD**, Yorkshire. Pop. 102,500. Val.£451,213
Mayor, Ald. George Wm. Hellawell (L)
Town Clerk, Frederick Charles Lloyd, LL.B.

*****HULL** (Kingston-upon-Hull) (City), Yorkshire. Pop. 234,270. Val.£916,729
High Steward, Marquess of Ripon, K.G.
Mayor, Counc. Wm. Alfred Gelder (re-elecd.) (L)
Recorder, John Forbes, Q.C.
Sheriff, Chas. H. Wellesley Wilson
Stipendiary Magistrate, Edward Curtis Twiss
Town Clerk, Edwin Laverack
Coroner, Alfred Thorney

HUNTINGDON (Boro'). Pop. 4,500. Val.£21,000
High Steward The Earl of Sandwich
Mayor, Alderman George Thackray (3rd time) (C)
Town Clerk, J. Percy Maule

HUNTINGDONSHIRE. Acres 234,162. Population 55,015. Rateable Val.£397,233
Lord Lieutenant and Chairman of County Council, Earl of Sandwich (1891), Hinchingbrooke, Huntingdon
High Sheriff, Capt. W. H. O. Duncombe, Waresley Park
Chairman of Q. S., J. Moyer Heathcote, Peterboro'
Vice-Chairman of C. C., George J. Coust, Huntingdon
County Treasurer, Ernest George Bevan, Hemingford Grey, St. Ives
Clerk of the Peace and of County Council, J. Percy Maule, Huntingdon
Chf. Const., Maj. H. G. Rooper, Huntingdon (54)
County Surveyor, E. Borissow, Huntingdon
Coroners: C.B.Margetts, Huntingdon and Herstingstone; C.R.Wade-Gery, St. Neots; Gerald Hunnybun, Hundred of Leightonstone; H. C. Gaches, Peterborough; F.R.Serjeant, Ramsey

HYDE, Cheshire. Pop. 30,670. Val.£117,139
Mayor, Counc. Thomas Carter Beeley (L)
Town Clerk, Thomas Brownson, B.A.

HYTHE, E. Kent. Pop. 6,019. Val.£24,466
Mayor, Counc. Henry Strachan, M.A. (C)
Recorder, Beaumont Morice
Town Clerk, George Wilks
Clerk of the Peace, Robert John Sidle

ILKESTON, Derbyshire. Pop. 19,744. Val.£63,637
Mayor, Councillor Charles Mitchell (L)
Town Clerk, Wright Lissett (barrister-at-law)

*****IPSWICH**, Suffolk. Pop. 57,360. Val.£257,607
High Steward, Lord Gwydyr (Stoke Park)
Mayor, William Alfred Churchman (C)
Recorder, Thomas Calthorpe Blofeld
Town Clerk, William Bantoft

ISLE OF WIGHT (Administrative County of). Acres 93,342. Pop. 78,672. Val.£433,624
Governor and Captain-General, H.R.H. Princess Henry of Battenberg, Osborne
Deputy Governor, Thomas B. H. Cochrane
Chairman of County Council, Godfrey Baring, Nubia House, Cowes
Vice-Chairman of County Council, Robey Frank Eldridge, Watergate Road, Newport
Chief Constable, Capt. H. G. A. Connor (55)
Clerk of the Council and Clerk of Peace (Registration), W. H. Wooldridge, Newport
County Surveyor, Francis Newman, Ryde
County Treasurer, William Pearce, Newport

JARROW-ON-TYNE, Co. Durham. Pop. 37,000. Estimated Val.£110,000
Mayor, Counc. John Evans (L)
Town Clerk, William Stephen Daglish
Deputy Town Clerk, William John Charlton

KEIGHLEY, Yorks. Est. pop. 40,000. Val.£126,059
Mayor, Henry Crofts Longsdon (C)
Town Clerk, George Burr

KENDAL, Westmorland. Pop. 14,430. Val.£63,469
Mayor, Gilbert Gilkes (L)
Town Clerk, John Bolton

KENT (COUNTY OF). Acres 995,392. Population 787,700. Rental £4,380,057
Lord Lieutenant, Earl Stanhope (1890), Chevening, near Sevenoaks
High Sheriff, James Taddy Friend, Northdown, Margate
Chairman of Q. S., His Honour Judge Sir William L. Selfe, East Kent; Rt. Hon. John G. Talbot, M.P., West Kent
Chairman of County Council, Sir John Farnaby Lennard, Bart., Wickham Court
Vice-Chairman of County Council, Geo. Marsham
Clerk of Peace & to C. C., Walter Byron Prosser
County Treasurers, H. Tasker and John Alfred Graham-Wigan, Maidstone
Chief Constable, Lieut.-Col. Henry Murray Ashley Warde, Maidstone (476)
County Surveyor, F. W. Ruck, Maidstone
Coroners: E. A. Carttar, Greenwich; Thomas Buss, Tonbridge; Reginald Mackenzie Mercer, Canterbury; Wm. J. Harris, Sittingbourne; C. D. Murton, Cranbrook; and Hy. Stringer, New Romney

KIDDERMINSTER, Worcestershire. Population 24,803. Val.£83,387
High Steward, Earl of Dudley, Witley Court
Mayor, Alderman Edward Parry (re-elected) (L)
Town Clerk, James Morton

KIDWELLY, Carmarth. Pop. 2,732. Val.£9,426
Mayor, Alderman Rowland Browne (L)
Town Clerk, Daniel Charles Edwards

KING'S LYNN, or **LYNN REGIS**, Norfolk. Pop. 18,265. Val.£82,533
Mayor, George Bristow (C)
Recorder, Hon. John Augustus de Grey
Town Clerk and Clerk of the Peace, Johnson William Woolstencroft

KINGSTON-UPON-THAMES, Surrey. Pop. Est. 34,500. Val.£172,089
Mayor, Alderman M. G. Moatt (L)
Recorder, Charles William Bardswell
High Steward, Lord Thring, K.C.B.
Town Clerk, Harold Albert Winser

LAMPETER, Cardigan. Pop. 1,569. Val.£4,025
Mayor, Counc. David Teifi Jones (re-elected) (L)
Town Clerk, David Lloyd

LANCASHIRE (County Palatine). Acres 1,208,154. Pop. 3,923,096. Rental £20,214,462

Lord Lieutenant, The Earl of Derby, K.G. (1897), Knowsley Park, Prescot, Lancs.

Chancellor of the Duchy, Right Hon. Lord James of Hereford, P.C.

Vice-Chancellor, Samuel Hall, Q.C.

Attorney-General, Wm. Ambrose, Q.C., M.P.

High Sheriff, William Charles Jones, Preston Brook, Warrington

Chairman of Q. S., John Fell, Lancaster; Henry Wilson Worsley-Taylor, Q.C., Preston; Sir Wm. Bower Forwood, Knt., Liverpool; William Goldthorpe, Manchester

Chairman of County Council, Right Hon. Sir John Tomlinson Hibbert, K.C.B., Hampsfield, Grange-over-Sands

Vice-Chairman of County Council, Sir William Henry Houldsworth, Bart., M.P.

Stipendiary Magistrate, Jos. Maghull Yates, Q.C., Manchester (suburban)

Clerk of Peace & to C.C., Harcourt E. Clare, Preston

County Treasurer, Henry Alison, Preston

Chief Constable, Lt.-Col. Henry M. Moorson, Preston (1,568)

Coroners: Henry John Robinson, Blackburn; John F. Price, Manchester; Fredk. Nassau Molesworth, Rochdale; Samuel Foster Butcher, Bury; Samuel Brighouse, Ormskirk; John Parker, Preston; Lawrence Holden, Lancaster; John Poole, Manor of Ulverston; W. Ascroft, Manor of Walton-le-Dale; H. Greenall, Manor of Hale; F. Smith, Manor of Prescot

LANCASTER, Lancs. Pop. 49,572. Val. £152,016
Mayor, Councillor Robert Preston, J.P. (L)
Town Clerk, Thomas Cann Hughes, M.A.

LAUNCESTON, Cornw. Pop. 4,345. Val. £17,488
Mayor, Councillor James Treleaven (L)
Town Clerk, Claude Hurst Peter

LEAMINGTON SPA, Warwickshire. Pop. 28,000. Rateable Value, £177,378
Mayor, Counc. James Murray Molesworth (C)
Town Clerk, Henry Consett Passman

LEEDS (City). Pop. 423,889. Val. £1,620,895.
Ld. Mayor, Rt. Hon. Alderman Gordon (C)
Recorder, Edward Tindal Atkinson, Q.C.
Stipendiary Magistrate, Chas. Milner Atkinson
Clerk of the Peace, Arthur Copson Peake
Town Clerk, William John Jeeves

LEICESTER (County Borough). Pop. 212,851. Val. £800,000. Acreage 8,586
Mayor, Alderman Thomas Windley (L)
Recorder, Marston Clarke Buszard, Q.C.
Town Clerk, James Bell
Clerk of the Peace, Alfred Howard Burgess

LEICESTERSHIRE. Acres, 532,786. Population 376,088. Rateable value £2,059,909
Lord Lieutenant, General Earl Howe, G.C.V.O. (1888), Gopsall, Atherstone
High Sheriff, Charles James Phillips, D.L., Old Dalby Hall, Melton Mowbray
Chairman of Quarter Sessions and Chairman of C. C., Hussey Packe, Prestwold Hall
Deputy Chairmen Qr. Sess., Sir A. R. Palmer, Bart., Wanlip Hall, Leicester; Thomas Cope, Obaston Hall
Deputy Chairman of County Council, Thomas Cope, Osbaston Hall, Nuneaton
County Treasurer, William Unwin Heygate
Clerk of Peace, to County Council, and Lieutenancy, Wm. Jesse Freer, 10 New Street, Leicester
Chief Constable, Edward Holmes, Leicester (166)
County Surveyor, (vacant)
Coroners: Geo. Edmund Bouskell, Leicester; Henry Deane, Loughborough; Arthur Henry Marsh, Melton Mowbray

LEOMINSTER, Hereford. Pop. 5,675. Val. £30, 23
Chief Steward, J. H. Arkwright, Hampton Court
Mayor, Councillor Henry Gosling, M.A. (C)
Town Clerk, William Thomas Sale

LEWES, Sussex. Pop. 10,997. Val £54,249
Mayor, Councillor Geo. Holman (re-elected) (C)
Town Clerk, Montague Spencer Blaker, B.A.

LICHFIELD, Stafford. Pop. 7,864. Val. £37,786
Mayor, Arthur Eyles, J.P. (re-elected) (L)
Recorder, Rupert Edward Cooke Kettle
Sheriff, Joseph Bamford
Town Clerk and Clerk of the Peace, Herbt. Russell

LINCOLN (Cty). Pop. 44,500. Val. £168,089
Mayor, Ald. Col. John George Williams, V.D. (L)
Recorder, George Sills
Sheriff, Edwin Brown
Town Clerk, John Thos. Tweed
Clerk of the Peace, Gilbert J. Dashper

LINCOLNSHIRE. Acres 1,693,547. Population 472,878. Rental £3,661,224
Lord Lieutenant, Earl Brownlow (1867), Belton House, Grantham
High Sheriff, T. Sherwin Pearson Gregory, Harlaxton Manor, Grantham
Chairmen of Q. S., Col. Charles T. John Moore, C.B., Boston; Rev. John Russell Jackson, Spalding (Parts of Holland); Earl of Ancaster, Sleaford and Bourne (Parts of Kesteven); Earl of Yarborough, Lincoln (Parts of Lindsey)
Chairmen of County Councils: Lindsey, W. E. Fox; Kesteven, Sir J. H. Thorold, Bart.; Holland, W. Upsall
Clerks of the Peace and to County Councils: Lindsey, Chas. Scorer, Lincoln; Kesteven, Joseph Phillips, Stamford; Holland, H. Chaderton Johnson, Boston; Lincoln City, Gil. J. Dashper
County Treasurers: B. Claypon Garfit, Boston; H. Ingoldby, Sleaford; A. S. Leslie-Melville, Lincoln
Chf. Const., Capt. P. B. Bicknell, Lincoln (305)
County Surveyors: Kesteven, W. Wright, Grantham; Lindsey, J. Thropp, Lincoln
Coroners: Walter Clegg, M.R.C.S., Boston; Charles Brown, Caistor; Geo. W. Glynne Beaumont, Grantham; George Mitchinson, M.D., Lincoln; Albert Iveson, Gainsborough; Frederick Sharpley, Louth; Joe George Calthrop, Spalding; V. G. Stapleton, Stamford

LISKEARD, Cornwall. Pop. 3,984. Val. £18,251
Mayor, William Alfred Jenkin (re-elected) (U)
Town Clerk, Henry Lyde Caunter

LIVERPOOL (City). Area 15,252 acres. Population 668,645. Val. £3,910,369
Lord Mayor, Rt. Hon. Louis Saml. Cohen (C)
Recorder, Charles Henry Hopwood, Q.C.
Police Magistrate, William John Stewart, J.P.
Assessor Court of Passage, Thos. H. Baylis, Q.C.
Coroner, Thomas Edward Sampson (solicitor)
Town Clerk, Edward Ralph Pickmere, M.A.
Clerk of the Peace, Henry Gutridge
Medical Off. of Health, Edward W. Hope, M.D.

LLANDOVERY, Carm. Pop. 1,742. Val. £5,753
Mayor, Councillor John Rhys James (L)
Town Clerk, John Thomas

LLANFYLLIN, Montgomery. Population 1,753. Val. £8,632
Mayor, John Marshall Dugdale (5th time) (C)
Town Clerk, William Anthony Pughe

LLANIDLOES, Montgomery. Pop. 3,800. Val. £7,350.
Mayor, Alderman Edward Davies (L)
Town Clerk, Arthur Davies

LONDON (City of): see p. 333.

LONDON (County of): see p. 336-341.

LONGTON, Stafford. Pop. 39,104. Val. £105, 50
Mayor, Alderman Aaron Edwards (5th time) (L)
Town Clerk, George Charles Kent
Stipendiary Magistrate, Harold Wright

LOSTWITHIEL, Cornw. Pop. 1,379. Val. £4,008
Mayor, Robert Barclay-Allardice (C)
Town Clerk, William Pease, jun.

LOUGHBOROUGH, Leicestershire. Pop. 18,196. Val. £82,443
Mayor, Councillor Thomas Mayo (C)
Town Clerk, John Jarratt

LOUTH, Lincoln. Pop. 10,040. Val. £36,357 ⁷⁸
High Steward, Wm. H. Smyth, D.L. (C), Elkington Hall
Mayor, Alderman Samuel Cresswell (C)
Town Clerk, Thomas Falkner Allison

LOWESTOFT, Suff. Pop. 27,000. Val. £121,514
Mayor, Ernest Edward Johnson (C)
Town Clerk, Robert Beattie Nicholson

LUDLOW, Salop. Pop. 4,460. Val. £15,352
Mayor, Robert Marston (C)
Recorder, Henry David Greene, Q.C., M.P.
Town Clerk, John Herbert Williams
Clerk of the Peace, Theophilus John Salwey

LUTON, Beds. Pop. 38,000. Val. £142,285
Mayor, Ald. Asher J. Hucklesby (4th year) (L)
Town Clerk, George Sell

LYDD, Kent. Pop. 2,070. Val. £8,982
Mayor, Alderman Edwin Finn (11th time) (C)
Town Clerk, Henry Stringer

LYME REGIS, Dorset. Pop. 2,364. Val. £9,105
Mayor, Ald. H. O. Bickley, J.P. (3rd year) (C)
Town Clerk, Matthew Colbeck Preston

LYMINGTON, Hants. Pop. 4,551. Val. £18,506
Mayor, Edw. Henry Pember, Q.C. (re-elected) (U)
Town Clerk, John Davis Rawlins

MACCLESFIELD, Cheshire. Pop. 36,009. Val. £104,062
Mayor, Ald. Frederick Hill (L)
Town Clerk, William Frederick Taylor

MAIDENHEAD, Berks. Pop. 10,607. Val. £72,826
High Steward, Wm. Henry Grenfell, Taplow Court
Mayor, Edwin Hewitt (C)
Town Clerk, John Kick

MAIDSTONE, Kent. Pop. 32,150. Val. £151,754
Mayor, Edmund Vaughan (L)
Recorder, Henry Fielding Dickens, Q.C.
Town Clerk, Herbert Monckton
Clerk of the Peace, Walter H. Day

MALDON, Essex. Pop. 5,397. Val. £18,186
Mayor, John Charles Float (3rd time), J.P. (L)
Recorder, William Willis, Q.C.
Town Clerk, Frederick Henry Bright

MALMESBURY, Wilts. Pop. 2,964. Val. £7,084
Mayor, Alderman Henry Garlick (L)
Town Clerk, Montagu Henry Chubb

MAN (ISLE OF): see p. 332

*MANCHESTER. Pop. 5-3,902. Val. £3,109,690
Lord Mayor, Rt. Hon. Thomas Briggs (C)
Recorder, Sir Joseph Francis Leese, Q.C., M.P.
Stipendiary Magistrate, Francis J. Headlam
Clerk of the Peace, Francis Ogden
Town Clerk, William Henry Talbot

MANSFIELD, Notts. Pop. 15,925. Val. £62,970
Mayor, Counc. William Jackson Chadburn (C)
Town Clerk, Richard Joseph Parsons

MARGATE, Kent. Pop. 18,662. Val. £149,232
Mayor, Counc. G. Moray Macfarlane (re-elect.) (L)
Recorder, Henry Bargrave Deane, Q.C.
Town Clerk, Edward Broeke

MARLBOROUGH, Wilts. Pop. 3,012. Val. £11,994
Mayor, James Morrison, J.P. (U)

Town Clerk, Edward Llewellyn Gwillim

MERIONETHSHIRE. Acres 427,810. Population, 49,212. Rental, £427,810
Lord Lieutenant and Chairman of Q. S., Wm. Robt. Maurice Wynne (1891), Peniarth, Towyn
High Sheriff, Richard E. Lloyd Richards, Caernwch, Dolgelly
Chairman of County Council, Evan Parry Jones, Festiniog
Vice-Chairman of County Council, H. Haydn Jones, Pontynewadd Towyn
Clerk of the Peace, Robert Jones, Portmadoc
County Treasurer, John Richards, Dolgelly
Chief Const., Major T. W. Best, Barmouth (35)
County Surveyor, J. M. Jones, Traws Fynydd
County Coroner, Wm. Robert Davies, Dolgelly

MIDDLESBROUGH, Yorkshire. Estimated pop. 95,000. Val. £318,606
Mayor, Counc. William Joseph Bruce (C)
Stipendiary Magistrate, Charles James Coleman
Town Clerk, Geo. Bainbridge (Deputy), Alf. Sockett

MIDDLESEX (COUNTY OF). Acres 148,847. Pop. 559,392. Rateable value £4,038,037
Lord Lieutenant, The Duke of Bedford (1898), 15 Belgrave Square, London, S W.
High Sheriff, Francis Augustus Bevan, Trent Park, Enfield
Chairman of Q. S., Ralph Makinson Littler, C.B., Q.C.
Dep. Chairm. of Q. S. and Chairman of County Council, Alderman Montagu Sharpe
Clerk of the Peace and of the Council, Sir Richard Nicholson, Guildhall, Westminster
Deputy Clerk of the Peace, &c., Alexander Geo. Austin
County Analyst, E. J. Bevan, 4 New Court, W.C.
Coroners: Western : W. Bruce Gordon Hogg, M.D., Chiswick ; Central : G. Danford Thomas, M.D., 87 Euston Rd., N.W.; Eastern : Alfred Hodgkinson, Solr., 13 Lansdowne Rd., Tottenham ; Duchy of Lancaster: Samuel F. Langham, Solr., Golden Lane, E.C.

MIDDLETON, Lanc. Pop. 26,500. Val. £73,047
Mayor, Robert Hilton, J.P. (L)
Town Clerk, F. Entwistle

MONMOUTH (Boro'). Pop. 5,470. Val. £24,239
Mayor, James Hayward Howse (C)
Town Clerk, Bickerton Deakin

MONMOUTH (Administrative County). Acres 342,548. Population 203,347. Rateable Value, £1,002,761
Lord Lieutenant, Lord Tredegar (1899), Tredegar Park, Newport
High Sheriff, C. W. E. Marsh, Newport
Chairman of Q. S., Samuel Courthope Bosanquet, Dingestow Court, near Monmouth
Chairman of County Council, Edwin Grove, Brendon View, Stow Park, Newport
Clerk of Peace & to County Council, Hen. Stafford Gustard, Newport
County Treas., W. C. A. Williams, Monmouth
Ch. Const., Victor Bosanquet, Abergavenny (178)
County Surveyor, William Tanner, Newport
County Coroners: M. Roberts Jones, Newport ; J. B. Walford, Abergavenny ; B. H. Deakin, Monmouth ; Fothergill Evans, Chepstow

MONTGOMERY (Boro'). Pop. 1,098. Val. £6,989
Mayor, Edward Rees James, J.P. (L)
Town Clerk, Charles Sidney Pryce

MONTGOMERYSHIRE. Acres 495,089. Population 58,003. Rental £497,173
Lord Lieutenant, Sir Herbert Lloyd Watkin Williams-Wynn (1891), Wynnstay, Ruabon
High Sheriff, Oliver Ormrod Openshaw, Llanfyllin

Chairman of Quarter Sessions, Capt. Devereux Herbert Mytton, Garth, Welshpool
Chairman of County Council, Arthur C. Humphreys-Owen, M.P., Glansevern, Berriew
Clerk of the Peace, G. D. Harrison, Welshpool
County Treasurer, T. Rowland Hughes, Welshpool
Chief Constable, W. J Holland, Newtown (35)
County Surveyor, G. A. Hutchins, Welshpool
County Coroners: Wm. A. Pughe, Llanfyllin; Edwd. Maurice Jones, Welshpool; John Rowlands, Machynlleth; R. Williams, Newtown

MORLEY, Yorkshire. Pop. 21,068. Val. £86,478
Mayor, Counc. Oliver Scatcherd, J.P. (re-elected)
Town Clerk, Richard Borrough Hopkins

MORPETH, Northumb. Pop. 5,219. Val. £21,101
Mayor, Councillor John Price (L)
Town Clerk, Francis Brumell

MOSSLEY, S.E. Lanc. Pop. 14,162. Val. £61,800
Mayor, William James Patten (L)
Town Clerk, Joseph Hyde

NEATH, Glamorg. Pop. 11,113. Val. £44,983
Mayor, Alderman H. P. Charles (C)
Town Clerk, Edwin Charles Curtis

NELSON, Lanc. Pop. 40,000. Val. £120,000
Mayor, Councillor Howard Dyson, J P. (L)
Town Clerk, R. M. Prescott

NEWARK, Notts. Pop. 14,457. Val. £65,338
Mayor, Frederick Henry Appleby (C)
Recorder, William James Noble
Town Clerk, Godfrey Tallents

NEWBURY, Berks. Pop. 11,002. Val. £40,381
High Steward, Earl of Carnarvon
Mayor, John Rankin (L)
Recorder, Frederic Coleridge Mackarness
Clerk of the Peace, J. C. Pinniger
Town Clerk, Francis Quekett Louch

NEWCASTLE-UNDER-LYME, Staffordshire. Pop. 18,452. Val. £56,850
Mayor, Councillor Wm. Needham Webster (U)
Recorder, Patrick Fleming Evans
Town Clerk and Clerk of the Peace, Joseph Griffith

*NEWCASTLE - UPON - TYNE. Pop. 228,625. Val. £1,131,145
Mayor, Councillor Riley Lord (L)
Recorder, Wm. Snowdon Robson, Q.C., M.P.
Sheriff, Councillor John James Forster
Town Clerk, Hill Motum
Clerk of the Peace, John Gibson Youll

NEWPORT, Isle of Wight. Pop. 10,216. Val. £41,270
Mayor, Councillor George Barnard Purkis (L)
Town Clerk, Henry Richard Hooper, B.A.

*NEWPORT, Mon. Pop. 70,000. Val. £350,000
Mayor, Counc. George Greenland, J.P. (L)
Town Clerk, Albert Augustus Newman

NORFOLK (COUNTY OF). Acres 1,302,882. Population 318,202. Rental £1,919,742
Lord Lieutenant, Earl of Leicester, K.G. (1846), Holkham Hall
High Sheriff, Henry Morris Upcher, East Hall, Feltwell, Brandon
Chairman of Q. S. and County Council, Lord Cranworth, Letton Hall, Thetford
Other Chairmen of Q. S., Lord Walsingham, LL.D.; Sir Wm. Hovell Browne Ffolkes, Bart. (also Vice-Chairman of County Counc.), Hamon le Strange, and Colonel Henry Elvin Hyde
Clerk of the Peace & to C. C., Chas. Foster, Norwich
Deputy Clerk of the County Council and Returning Officer, Geo. Christopher Davies, Norwich
County Treasurer, G. Fowell Buxton, Norwich
County Accountant, H. C. Bolingbroke, Norwich
Chief Constable, Paynton Pigott, D.L. (barrister-at-law), Norwich (239); *Supt. & Chief Clerk*, J. W. Lockett

County Surveyor, T. H. B. Heslop, Norwich
Coroners: Henry Read Culley, Norwich; Thos. Martin Wilkin, Lynn; Walter May Barton, East Dereham; H. E. Garrod, Diss; T. L. Reed, Downham Market; O.F. Read, Thetford

*NORTHAMPTON (County Borough). Pop. 61,778. Val. £215,863
Mayor, Councillor Joseph Jeffery, J.P. (L)
Recorder, Edward Philip Monckton
Town Clerk and Clerk of Peace, Wm. Shoosmith

NORTHAMPTONSHIRE. Acres 583,837. Population 203,281. Rateable Value, £1,386,136
Lord Lieutenant, Right Hon. Earl Spencer, K.G. (1872), Althorp Park, Northampton
High Sheriff, Reginald Bernard Loder, Cottesbrooke Hall, Northampton
Chairman of Q. S. and C. C., Sackville George Stopford Sackville, Drayton House, Thrapston
Vice-Chairman of County Council, James Rennie Wilkinson, Gt. Addington
Deputy Chairman Q. S., Christopher Smyth, Little Houghton, Northampton
Clerk of Peace and to C. C., Hy. P. Markham, D.L. (*Deputy*, C. A. Markham), Northampton
County Treasurer, Alfred Page, Northamptonshire Union Bank, Northampton
Chief Constable, Lieut. James Dalgleish Kellie MacCallum, Northampton (162)
County Surveyor, Edmund Law, Northampton
County Medical Officer, Charles E. Paget
Coroners: William Terry, Northampton; John Thos. Parker, Wellingborough; Thos. Mieres Percival, Towcester

NORTHUMBERLAND (COUNTY OF). Acres 1,289,756. Pop. 506,030. Rental £2,863,363
Lord Lieutenant, Earl Grey (1899), Howick, Lesbury
High Sheriff, William Armstrong Watson-Armstrong, Cragside, Rothbury
Chairman of Q. S. and Vice-Chairman of County Council, Watson Askew-Robertson, Ladykirk, Norham-on-Tweed
Chairman of County Council, Alderman the Duke of Northumberland, K.G., Alnwick Castle
Chairman of Standing Joint Committee, W. Hudspith, Greencroft, Haltwhistle
Clerk of the Peace and to Cty. Council, Stephen Sanderson, Moot Hall Courts, Newcastle-on-Tyne. (*Deputy*, Chas. Davison Forster)
County Treas., R. Clayton, Newcastle-on-Tyne
Chief Constable, Capt. H. D. Terry, Morpeth (233)
County Architect, J. Cresswell
County Surveyor, H. F. Sneyd-Kynnersley, A.M.I.C.E., Newcastle-on-Tyne
County Medical Officer, J. W. Hembrough, M.D., Moot Hall
Coroners: Joseph Richard Davidson Lynn; Charles Percy, Alnwick

*NORWICH (City), Norfolk. Pop. 112,000. Val. £357,172
Mayor, James W. Clabburn (L)
Deputy Mayor, George Henry Morse
Recorder, Thomas Richardson Kemp, Q.C.
Sheriff, Samuel Wainwright
Town Clerk, George Butler Kennett

*NOTTINGHAM (City). Estimated pop. 239,384 Val. £942,000. Area 10,935 acres
Mayor, Abraham Pyatt (L)
Recorder, Hon. Edwd. Chandos Leigh, Q.C., C.B.
Sheriff, James Black Roberts
Town Clerk and Clerk of the Peace, Sir Samuel George Johnson, Knt. (The Park)
City Coroner, Charles Lambert Rothera

NOTTINGHAMSHIRE. Acres 539,752. Population 445,823. Rental £2,617,015
Lord Lieutenant, Duke of Portland, G.C.V.O. (1898), Welbeck Abbey, Notts
High Sheriff, Sir G. Ernest Paget, Bart., Sutton Bonington, Notts
Chairmen of Q. S., Lord Belper, A.D.C., Nottingham; Major John Henry Becher, Newark; Rt. Hon. Fras. John Savile Foljambe, Retford
Deputy Chairmen of Q. S. (Nottingham div.), John Liell Francklin; (Newark div.), Col. James Thorpe, Coddington Hall.
Chairman of County Council, Lord Belper, A.D.C.
Clerk of the Peace, Jesse Hind, Nottingham
County Treasurer, F. A. Smith, Nottingham
Chief Constable, Capt. Wm. H. Tomasson, Nottingham (201)
County Surv., Edgar Purnell Hooley, Nottingham
Coroners: David Whittingham, Nottingham; F. B. Footitt, Newark; J. Housley, Retford

OKEHAMPTON, Devon. Pop. 1,879. Val. £4,550
Mayor, Councillor Robert F. Brealy (L)
Town Clerk, George L. Fulford

*OLDHAM, Lanc. Pop. 150,722. Val. £675,162
Mayor, Councillor John Hood, J.P. (L)
Recorder, George Xavier Segar
Town Clerk and Cl. of Peace, Abraham Nicholson

OSSETT, Yorks. Pop. 12,000. Val. £50,000
Mayor, Councillor Henry Wormald (L)
Town Clerk, Willie Brook

OSWESTRY, Salop. Pop. 9,000. Val. £46,179
Mayor, Richard Hopley Mason (L)
Recorder, Robert Lloyd Kenyon
Town Clerk, Joseph Parry-Jones
Clerk of the Peace, Charles H. Bull

*OXFORD (City). Pop. 52,800. Val. £339,401
Lord High Steward, Earl of Jersey, G.C.M.G.
Mayor, Councillor Frederic Parker Morrell, M.A. (O)
Recorder, Hon. Alfred Lyttelton, M.P.
Sheriff, Alderman John H. Salter, J.P.
Town Clerk, Richard Bacon

OXFORDSHIRE. Acreage 475,974. Population 143,753. Rateable value £792,048
Lord Lieut., Earl of Jersey, G.C.M.G. (1887), Middleton Park, Bicester
Chairman of County Council, Viscount Valentia, M.P., Bletchington Park, Oxford
High Sheriff, John Frederick Starkey, D.L., Bodicote House, Banbury
Chairman of Q. S., Sir William Reynell Anson, Bart., M.P., D.C.L., All Souls College, Oxford
Clerk of the Peace and of County Council, Thomas Marriott Davenport, M.A., Oxford
County Treasurer, John Parsons, Oxford
Chief Constable, Lieut.-Col. Hon. Edward A. Holmes-à-Court, Oxford (113)
County Surveyor, H. J. Tollit, Oxford
Coroners: William Wharton Robinson, Oxford; George Coggins, Deddington; Frederick Westell, Witney; Henry Dixon, M.R.C.S., Watlington

PEMBROKE (Boro'). Pop. 14,978. Val. £36,241
Mayor, Councillor John Rixon (L)
Town Clerk, William Odyerne Hulm

PEMBROKESHIRE. Acres 395,151. Population 89,133. Rental £426,947
Lord Lieutenant (1896), Earl Cawdor, Stackpole Court, Pembroke
High Sheriff, Edward Laws, Tenby
Chairman of Quarter Sessions, His Honour Judge William Stevenson Owen

Chairman of County Council, Sir Charles E. G. Phillips, Bart., Picton Castle, Haverfordwest
Clerk of the Peace and to County Council, William Davies George, Haverfordwest
County Treasurer, Jno. W. Cross, London and Provincial Bank, Haverfordwest
Chief Constable, T. Ince Webb-Bowen, Haverfordwest Castle (79)
County Surveyor, T. George, Pendine, St. Clears, R.S.O. (*Deputy*, Arth. H. Thomas, H'fordwest)
County Coroners: Ivor Evans, Cardigan; H. J. E. Price, Haverfordwest

PENRYN, Cornwall. Pop. 3,256. Val. £7,323
Mayor, Benjamin Williams Curgenven (O)
Town Clerk, George Appleby Jenkins

PENZANCE, Cornwall. Pop. 12,432. Val. £51,895
Mayor, Ald. Richd. Pearce-Couch (re-elected) (U)
Recorder (vacant)
Town Clerk, Thomas Henry Cornish
Clerk of the Peace, John Penn Milton

PETERBOROUGH, Northants and Hunts. Pop. 25,172. Val. £131,338
Mayor of Borough, Jno. Thos. Miller, J.P., C.C.(L)
Town Clerk, William Mellows
COUNTY OF THE SOKE. Acres 53,471.
Chairman of County Council, Col. C. I. Strong
Clerk C. C. and of the Peace, Leonard J. Deacon
Deputy Clerk C. C., &c., Walter J. Deacon

*PLYMOUTH, Devon. Pop. 100,000. Val. £427,000
Lord High Steward, H.R.H. the Prince of Wales
Mayor, Alderman John Pethick (re-elected) (C)
Recorder, Henry Edward Duke, Q.C.
Town Clerk and Clerk of the Peace, John H. Ellis

PONTEFRACT, Yorks. Pop. 9,702. Val. £42,092
Mayor, Alderman Francis W. Pease (C)
Recorder, Thomas Rowland Drake Wright
Town Clerk, William Haddock

POOLE, Dorset. Pop. 19,000. Val. £78,000
Mayor, John Arthur Cocker (C)
Recorder, George Pitt-Lewis, Q.C.
Sheriff, Walter Andrew
Town Clerk, Henry Salter Dickinson

*PORTSMOUTH AND SOUTHSEA, Hants. Estimated pop. 190,741. Val. £903,291
Mayor, Councillor Harold Rufus Pink (C)
Recorder, George Deedes Warry, Q.C.
Town Clerk, Alexander Hellard
Clerk of the Peace, Richard William Ford

*PRESTON, Lanc. Pop. 116,356. Val. £371,704
Mayor, Councillor James Yates Foster (C)
Recorder, Francis Hamilton Mellor
Town Clerk, Henry Hamer
Treasurer, James Carter

PWLLHELI, Carnarvon. Pop. 3,500. Val. £8,300
Mayor, Alderman Wynne-Griffith (L)
Town Clerk, Evan R. Davies

QUEENBOROUGH, Kent, Pop. 1,062. Val.£7,170
Mayor, Counc. Capt. Ed. Woodriff Jaffray (C)
Town Clerk, W. J. Harris

RADNOR (COUNTY OF). Acres 301,164. Population, 21,791. Rental, £117,369
Lord Lieutenant, Sir Powlett Charles John Milbank, Bart., M.P. (1895), Norton Manor, Presteign
Chairman of Q. S., John Corrie Carter, Cefnfaes, Rhayader
Chairman of County Council, C. C. Rogers, Stanage Park, Brampton Brian (R.S.O.)
High Sheriff, Col. Stephen Williams, Rhayader
Clerk of the Peace and to County Council, Edward

Wood, Rhayader and Presteign (*Deputy*, T. W. Harding)
County Treasurer, T. G. Sprague, Kington
Chief Constable, Capt. Fullarton James, Penybont (28)
County Surveyor, R. Wellings-Thomas, Llandrindod Wells
Coroners: Fred. L. Green, Knighton (East. Division); H. Vaughan Vaughan, Builth and Rhayader (Western Division)
RAMSGATE, Kent. Pop. 24,733. Val. £137,386
Mayor, Counc. J. Barnet Hodgson (re-elect.) (*C*)
Town Clerk, William Alexander Hubbard
RAWTENSTALL, Lanc. Pop. 32,000. Val. £111,938
Mayor, Henry Whittaker Trickett (*L*)
Town Clerk, James Whalley
*READING, Berks. Pop. 70,888. Val. £335,295
High Steward, H.R.H. Duke of York, K.G.
Mayor, William Poulton (*L*)
Recorder, Arthur Hewett Spokes, LL.B.
Town Clerk, Henry Day
Clerk of the Peace, Arthur Hugh Sherwood
REIGATE, Surrey. Pop. 22,639. Val. £175,246
Mayor, F. E. Barnes (3rd year) (*L*)
Town Clerk, Clair James Grece, LL.D.
RICHMOND, Surrey. Pop. 27,076. Val. £271,845
Mayor, James B. Hilditch (*C*)
Town Clerk, Frederick Bernard Senior
Deputy Town Clerk, Herbert A. Millington
RICHMOND, Yorks. Pop. 4,216. Val. £16,664
Mayor, Councillor H. W. Walton (*L*)
Recorder, William Norton Lawson
Town Clerk and Clerk of the Peace, Christopher George Croft, M.A.
RIPON, Yorkshire. Pop. 8,500. Val. £33,237
Mayor, Councillor Richard Wilkinson (*C*)
Town Clerk, M. Kirkley
*ROCHDALE, Lanc. Pop. 71,401. Val. £303,277
Mayor, William Cunliffe (*L*)
Town Clerk, James Leach
ROCHESTER, Kent. Pop. 26,290. Val. £113,680
Mayor, Counc. Percy John Neate (*LU*)
Recorder, Morton William Smith
Town Clerk, Apsley Kennette
Clerk of the Peace, F. C. Boucher
ROMNEY (NEW), Kent. Pop. 1,366. Val. £5,667
Mayor, Ald. Hy. Thos. Tubbs, J.P. (re-elect.) (*C*)
Town Clerk, James Bannon
ROMSEY, Hants. Pop. 4,276. Val. £19,503
Mayor, Rt. Hon. Evelyn M. Ashley (re-elect.) (*U*)
Town Clerk, Matthew Liddle Harle
ROTHERHAM, Yorks. Pop. 56,000. Val. £166,280
Mayor, Councillor George Gummer (*L*)
Town Clerk, Herbert Harry Hickmott
RUTHIN, Denbighshire. Pop. 2,760. Val. £12,608
Mayor, Edward Roberts (*L*)
Town Clerk, William Lloyd
RUTLANDSHIRE. Acres 94,889. Population 20,659. Rental £185,523
Lord Lieutenant, Earl of Dysart (1881), Buckminster Park, near Grantham
High Sheriff, Sir Arthur Richard de Capel Brooke, Bart., Great Oakley Hall, Kettering
Chairman of County Council, Earl of Gainsborough, Exton Park, Oakham
Chair. of Q. S., Sir Arthur John Fludyer, Bart., Ayston Hall
Clerk of the Peace and Clerk to County Council, Benjamin Addington Adam, Oakham
Chief Constable, William Keep, Oakham (15)
County Treas., Stamford & Spalding Banking Co.
County Surveyor, James Richardson, Stamford
Coroners: Ernest W. Phillips, Oakham; Valentine George Stapleton, Stamford
RYDE, Isle of Wight. Pop. 10,952. Val. £71,576

Mayor, Alderman James James, J.P. (*C*)
Town Clerk, Chas. G. Vincent. (*Deputy*, C.H. Collis)
RYE, Sussex. Pop. 3,871. Val. £12,400
Mayor, Councillor Frank Jarrett (*C*)
Recorder, Robert Henry Hurst
Town Clerk, Walter Dawes
Clerk of the Peace, William Dawes
SAFFRON WALDEN. Pop. 6,104. Val. £23,870
Mayor, Alderman Joseph Bell
Recorder, His Hon. William Willis, Q.C.
Town Clerk, William Adams
Clerk of the Peace, Chas. Stewart Douglas Wade
ST. ALBANS (City), Herts. Est. Pop. 15,900. Val. £57,948
Mayor, Henry Joseph Toulmin, J.P. (*C*)
Town Clerk, Alfred Herbert Debenham
*ST. HELENS, Lanc. Pop. 88,480. Val. £330,741
Mayor, Joseph Beecham (?)
Town Clerk, George William Barley
ST. IVES, Cornwall. Pop. 6,094. Val. £17,480
Mayor, Edward Hain, J.P., C.C. (*LU*)
Town Clerk, &c., Edward Boase
ST. IVES, Hunts. Pop. 3,037. Val. £12,346
Mayor, Herbert Ingle Hankin (re-elected) (*L*)
Town Clerk, George Dennis Day, M.A., LL.B.
*SALFORD, Lanc. Pop. 218,244. Val. £914,608
Mayor, Ald. Samuel Rudman (re-elected) (*C*)
Deputy Mayor, Ald. W. Robinson
Recorder (First), Joseph Maghull Yates, Q.C.
Stipendiary Magistrate, Joseph Makinson
Town Clerk, L. C. Evans.
Clerk of Peace, Samuel Brown.
SALISBURY, Wilts. Pop. 15,533. Val. £73,535
Mayor, David Stevens (*C*)
Recorder, Charles Willie Mathews
Town Clerk, William Charles Powning
SALTASH, Cornwall. Pop. 2,745. Val. £8,865
Mayor, Fred Avery Rawling (*U*)
Town Clerk, Frederick William Cleverton
SANDWICH, Kent. Pop. 2,796. Val. £10,934
Mayor, Ald Wm. James Hughes (9th year) (*C*)
Recorder, Montague Johnstone Muir-Mackenzie
Town Clerk and Clerk of the Peace, Dick Baker
SCARBOROUGH, Yorks. Pop. 33,776. Val. £217,034
Mayor, Counc. Capt. H. Darley, J.P. (re-elect.) (*C*)
Recorder, Charles Haigh
Town Clerk, John Edward Thorley Graham
Clerk of the Peace, George Taylor
SHAFTESBURY, Dorset. Pop. 2,122. Val. £5,785
Mayor, Councillor Robert Wm. Borley (*C*)
Town Clerk, John Kingsley Rutter
*SHEFFIELD (City). P. 361,169. Val. £1,325,668
Lord Mayor, Rt. Hon. Samuel Roberts (*C*)
Recorder, His Hon. Samuel Danks Waddy, Q.C.
Master Cutler, Robert A. Hadfield (Aug., 1899)
Stipendiary Magistrate, Edwd. M. Earle-Welby
Town Clerk, Henry Sayer
Clerk of the Peace, Joseph Binney
SHREWSBURY, Salop. Pop. 26,967. Val. £143,000
Mayor, Councillor Richard Scoltock Hughes (*C*)
Recorder, Arthur Richard Jelf, Q.C.
Town Clerk and Clerk of the Peace, Hy. C. Clarke
SHROPSHIRE. Acres 859,516. Population 236,339. Rental £1,668,081
Lord Lieutenant, Earl of Powis (1896), Powis Castle, Welshpool
High Sheriff, Hugh Ker Colville, Bellaport Hall, Market Drayton
Chairman of Q. S., Sir Offley Wakeman, Bart.
Chairman of County Council, J. Bowen-Jones.
Deputy Chairm. of do., R. G. Venables
Clerk of the Peace and to County Council, Edmund Cresswell Peele, Shrewsbury

Depy. Clerk, R. S. Clease, Shrewsbury
Chief Constable, Capt. G. Williams-Freeman(164)
County Surveyor, Alfred T. Davis, C.E.
Coroners: John Vernon T. Lander, Wellington;
Geo. Gordon Warren, Market Drayton; Henry
Thomas Weyman, Ludlow; R. E. Clarke,
Shrewsbury; R. F. Haslewood, Bridgnorth;
J. Herbert Williams, Ludlow; W. A. Lewis,
Oswestry
SOMERSET (COUNTY OF). Acres 1,037,329.
Population 355,275. Rateable val. £2,033,383
Lord Lieutenant, Earl of Cork and Orrery, K.P.
(1864), Marston House, Frome
High Sheriff, Col. W. Long, Woodlands, Congresbury, Axbridge
Chairman of Q. S. and of County Council, Rt.
Hon. Sir Richard Horner Paget, Bart., P.C.,
Cranmore Hall, Shepton Mallet
Clerk of the Peace and to C. C., Wm. Dunn, Frome
County Treas., W. C. King, Weston-super-Mare
Chf. Const., Capt. C. G. Alison, Glastonbury (339)
County Surveyor, W. J. Willcox, Bath
Coroners: Samuel Craddock, M.R.C.S., Bath;
Edward Queckett Louch, Langport; Thomas
Foster Barham, Bridgwater
*SOUTH SHIELDS, Durham. Pop. 102,312.
Val. £352,609
Mayor, Alderman John Donald, J.P. (L)
Town Clerk, John Moore Hayton, B.A.
*SOUTHAMPTON (County Borough). Pop.
(1897 est.) 100,000. Val. £413,521
Mayor, Counc. G. A. E. Hussey (re-elected) (C)
Recorder, J. Temple Cook
Clerk of the Peace, Henry Daniel Moody Page
Sheriff, Alderman Francis Henry Candy, J.P.
Town Clerk, Geo. Bellamy Nalder
SOUTHEND-ON-SEA, Essex. Pop. 26,000. Val.
£173,707
Mayor, Counc. Francis Ramuz (re-elected) (C)
Town Clerk, William Henry Snow
SOUTHMOLTON, Devon. Pop.3,126. Val.£13,583
Lord High Steward, Lord Poltimore
Mayor, Charles Pearce, J.P. (C)
Recorder, Charles Barrett Russell
Town Clerk and Clerk of the Peace, R. L. Riccard
SOUTHPORT, Lanc. Pop. 50,942. Val. £316,908
Mayor, Alderman T. P. Griffiths, J.P. (L)
Town Clerk, John Davies Williams, LL.D.
SOUTHWARK (Borough of), County of London
Steward and Judge, Court of Record, Sir Charles
Hall, K.C.M.G., Q.C., M.P. (Recorder of London)
High Bailiff and Parliam. Returning Officer, Thos.
Roderick, Guildhall, E.C.
Prothonotary, Henry Devereux Pritchard,
Painters' Hall, E.C.
SOUTHWOLD, Suffolk. Pop. 3,000. Val.£12,310
Mayor, Eaton Womack Moore (C)
Town Clerk, Ernest Read Cooper
STAFFORD (Boro'). Pop. 20,270. Val. £74,619
Lord High Steward, Earl of Shrewsbury and
Talbot (1892), Ingestre Hall
Mayor, Ald. W. C. T. Mynors (3rd year) (C)
Town Clerk, Matthew Folliott Blakiston
STAFFORDSHIRE. Acres 744,987. Population
1,086,240. Rental £4,469,589
Lord Lieutenant, Earl of Dartmouth (1891),
Patshull House, Wolverhampton
High Sheriff, Augustus Leveson Vernon, Hilton
Park, Wolverhampton
Chairman of County Council, Earl of Harrowby,
Sandon Hall, Stone
Vice-Chairman of County Council, Frank James
Silkmore, Stafford
Chairman of Q. S., Lord Hatherton, C.M.G.,
Teddesley, near Penkridge

Assistant do., Sir Reginald Hardy, Bart.
Clerk of the Peace and to County Council, Matthew
Folliott Blakiston, Stafford
County Treasurer, Perceval H. Harston, Stafford
Chief Constable, Capt. Hon. Geo. Aug. Anson,
Stafford (703)
County Surveyor, W. H. Cheadle, Stafford
Coroners: J. Booth, Talk-o'-th'-Hill; T. B.
Cull, Cheadle; William Morgan, Stafford;
H. A. Pearson, Handsworth: T. A. Stokes,
Wolverhampton; J. H. Joy, Tamworth
STALYBRIDGE, Cheshire. Estimated pop.
30,000. Val. £103,282
Mayor, Ald. Allwood Simpson (C)
Town Clerk, John Miller
STAMFORD, Linc. Pop. 8,358. Val. £32,526
Mayor, Councillor S. F. Halliday (3rd year) (C)
Recorder, James Corrie Carter
Town Clerk, James Edward Atter
Clerk of the Peace, D. J. Evans.
*STOCKPORT, Cheshire and Lancashire. Pop.
81,000. Val. £286,655
Mayor, Thomas Webb (re-elected) (L)
Town Clerk, Robert Hyde
STOCKTON-UPON-TEES, Durham. Pop. 56,000.
Val. £189,570
Mayor, Alderman John Hy. Nightscales (C)
Town Clerk, Matthew Bowser Dodds, M.A.,J.P.
STOKE-UPON-TRENT, Staffordsh. Pop. 24,027.
Val. £95,374
Mayor, Ald. Edward James Leadbeater, J.P. (L)
Stipendiary Magistrate, Harold Wright
Town Clerk, John Blow Ashwell
STRATFORD-UPON-AVON, Warwicksh. Pop.
8,318. Rateable value £37,920. Acreage 3,853
High Steward, Sir Arthur Hodgson, K.C.M.G.
Mayor, William Pearce (3rd year) (U)
Town Clerk, Robert Lunn
SUDBURY, Suffolk. Pop. 7,059. Val. £21,991
Mayor, Councillor Fred. Wheeler (re-elect.) (C)
Recorder, William Pinder Eversley
Town Clerk, William Bayly-Ransom
Clerk of the Peace, Thomas Bates
SUFFOLK (COUNTY OF). Acres 940,664. Population 304,828. Rental £2,041,583
Lord Lieut., Marquess of Bristol (1886),Ickworth,
Bury St. Edmunds, & 6 St. James's Sq., Lond.
Vice-Admiral, Earl of Stradbroke, Henham Hall
High Sheriff, Edwin J. Johnstone, Rougham Hall
Chairmen of Q. S., Lord Rendlesham and Thomas
Lomax, at Ipswich; Colonel Nathaniel Barnardiston and Colonel Frederic Pocklington,
at Bury St. Edmunds
Chairmen of County Councils: East Suffolk,
Lord Rendlesham; West Suffolk, Oliver
Denn Johnson
Clerk of the Peace and to County Councils, James
Cherry (*Deputy*, Alfred Townshend Cobbold),
County Hall, Ipswich
County Treasurers: Eastern Div., A. Gibb,
Ipswich; Western Div., Hervey Aston Oakes,
J.P., Bank, Bury St. Edmunds
Chief Constables: Eastern Division, Jasper G.
Mayne, Ipswich (174); Western Division, Maj.
A. F. Poulton, Bury St. Edmunds (115)
Treasr. of Suffolk Jt. Comm., W.S.Gurney,Ipswich
County Surveyors: Eastern Div., H. Miller,
M.I.C.E., Ipswich; Western Div., F. Whitmore,
Chelmsford
Coroners: C. W. Chaston, Mondham, Harleston; Arthur Fredk. Vulliamy, Ipswich;
Walter Brooke, Woodbridge; Henry Edwin
Garrod, Diss; Rowland Holt Wilson, Bury
St. Edmunds; Thomas Bates, Sudbury;
Geo. Owen Mead, Newmarket

*SUNDERLAND, Durham. Pop. 145,613. Val. £532,000
Mayor, Ald. Edwin Robert Dix (*C*)
Town Clerk, Francis Marshall Bowey

SURREY (COUNTY OF). Acres 485,129. Population 1,436,899. Rental £10,072,244
Lord Lieutenant, Viscount Midleton (1895)
Vice-Lieut., Edward Hugh Leycester Penrhyn
High Sheriff, Sir John Whittaker Ellis, Bart., Buccleuch House, Richmond
Chairman of County Council, Edw. Jos. Halsey, 104 Drayton Gardens, South Kensington
Deputy Chairman of County Council, Lord Ashcombe, Denbies, Dorking
Chairman of Quarter Sessions, &c., George Cave, Wardrobe Court, Richmond
Deputy Chairman Q. S., Henry Currie Leigh Bennett, M.P., Thorpe Place, Chertsey; Sir William Vincent, Bart., Ashtead
Clerk of the Peace and to County Council, Sir Richard Hy. Wyatt, D.L. (*Deputy*, Thos. W. Weeding), County Hall, Kingston-on-Thames
County Treasurer, Francis Henry Beaumont
Chief Constable, Capt. Mowbray Lees Sant (*Deputy*, Howard J. Page), Guildford (231)
County Surveyor, Frank G. Howell
County Coroners: Croydon District, W. Percy Morrison, Reigate; Kingston District, A. B. Hicks, 20 Lupus St., Pimlico, S.W.; Guildford Dist., G. F. Roumieu, Willey Park, Farnham

SUSSEX, EAST (COUNTY OF). Acres 522,065. Pop. 227,871. Rental £1,759,027
Lord Lieutenant, Marquess of Abergavenny, K.G. (1892), Eridge Castle, Frant, Tunbridge Wells
High Sheriff, Capt. R. H. Rawson, Woodhurst, Crawley
Chairman of Q. S., Earl of Chichester, Lewes
Chairm. of C.C., W. V. M. Steaning, E. Grinstd.
Clerk of the Peace and of the County Council, Frederic Merrifield, County Hall, Lewes
County Treasurer, Maj. H. P. Molineux, Lewes
Chief Constable, Maj. H. G. Lang, Lewes (187)
County Surveyor, Frederick J. Wood, Lewes

SUSSEX, WEST (COUNTY OF). Acres 402,909. Pop. 140,976. Rateable Val. £888,114
Lord Lieutenant. (See EAST SUSSEX)
High Sheriff. (See EAST SUSSEX)
Chairman of Quarter Sessions, Robert H. Hurst, Horsham Park, Horsham
Chairman of County Council, Duke of Richmond and Gordon, K.G., Goodwood, Chichester
Clerk of the Peace and of the County Council, Frederic Merrifield, County Hall, Lewes
County Treasurer, W. T. Haines, Chichester
Chief Constable, Capt. G. R. B. Drummond, Horsham (142)
County Surveyor, W. B. Purser, Horsham
County Coroners, F. W. Butler, Horsham; G. Vere Benson, Lewes; C. Sheppard, Battle; E. W. Skinner, M.D., Rye.

SUTTON COLDFIELD, Warwickshire. Pop. Estimated, 12,619. Val. £69,539
Mayor, Counc. Saml. C. Emery, J.P. (re-elect.)(*C*)
Town Clerk, Thomas Vincent Holbeche

*SWANSEA, Glamorg. Pop. 102,000.Val.£356,430
Mayor, Councillor William Watkins (*U*)
Recorder, Wm. Bowen Rowlands, Q.C.
Stipendiary Magistrate, John Coke Fowler
Town Clerk, John Thomas

TAMWORTH, Staff. Pop. 6,614. Val. £29,164
Mayor, Counc. Alfred M. Sculthorpe, M.R.C.S. (5th time) (*C*)
Town Clerk, John Matthews

TAUNTON, Somerset. Pop. 20,000. Val. £96,777
Mayor, Councillor Wm. Albert Wrenn, J.P. (*C*)
Town Clerk, George H. Kite

TENBY, Pembrokeshire. Pop. 4,542. Val. £22,027
Mayor, Clement John Williams (re-elected) (*C*)
Town Clerk, T. Aneuryn Rees

TENTERDEN, Kent. Pop. 3,429. Val. £17,508
Mayor, Obadiah Edwards (re-elected) (*C*)
Recorder, Henry Herbert Stephen Croft
Town Clerk, Joseph Munn Mace

TEWKESBURY, Glouc. Pop. 5,269. Val. £25,864
High Steward, Lord Sudeley (Toddington)
Mayor, Ald. William Evans Hayward (*C*)
Recorder, Laurence Morton Brown
Town Clerk, Harry Alexander Badham
Clerk of the Peace, Fred. James Brown

THETFORD, Norfolk. Pop. 4,300. Val. £17,560
Mayor, Counc. S. Oldman, Jun. (re-elected) (*L*)
Recorder, Charles Edward Malden
Town Clerk, J. Houchen
Clerk of the Peace, F. V. Houchen

THORNABY-ON-TEES, Yorks. Pop. 15,637. Val. £49,293
Mayor, Alderman John R. Crosthwaite, J.P. (*C*)
Town Clerk, William James Watson

TIVERTON, Devon. Pop. 10,892. Val. £62,293
Mayor, Edwin Harris Dunning (*C*)
Recorder (vacant)
Town Clerk & Clerk of Peace, Chas. Marshall Hole

TODMORDEN, W. Riding, Yorks. and Lancs. Pop. 25,000. Val. £109,728.
Mayor, Alderman William Ormerod, J.P. (*L*)
Town Clerk, Dan Sutcliffe

TORQUAY, Devon. Pop. 25,534. Val. £137,066
Mayor, Councillor W. Beavis (re-elected) (*U*)
Town Clerk, Frederick S. Hex

TORRINGTON, GREAT, Devon. Pop. 3,436. Val. £8,924
Mayor, William Vaughan (re-elected) (*L*)
Town Clerk, George Mark Doe

TOTNES, Devon. Pop. 4,016. Val. £19,100
Mayor, Thomas White Windeatt (*U*)
Town Clerk, Edward Windeatt

TOWER OF LONDON
Constable, General Sir Frederick C. A. Stephenson, G.C.B.
Lieutenant, General Godfrey Clerk, C.B.
Major, Lt.-Gen. Geo. Bryan Milman, C.B.
Coroner, Wynne Edward Baxter, J.P., D.L.

TRURO, Cornwall. Pop. 11,131. Val. £44,000
Mayor, Joseph Rogers (*C*)
Town Clerk, Robert Dobell

TUNBRIDGE WELLS, Kent. Pop. 31,000. Val. £250,000
Mayor, Frank William Stone (re-elected) (*C*)
Town Clerk, William Charles Cripps

TYNEMOUTH, Northumberland. Pop. 46,588. Val. £206,769
Mayor, Councillor Jonathan Eskdale (*C*)
Town Clerk, Horatio Alfred Adamson

WAKEFIELD, Yorks. Pop. 39,000. Val. £175,234
Mayor, Alderman Barron Kilner (*C*)
Town Clerk, Charles James Hudson

WALLINGFORD, Berks. Pop.2,989. Val. £10,225
High Steward, Edw. Wells (Hedges, Wells & Co.)
Mayor, Councillor Thomas Pettit (*L*)
Town Clerk, Francis Edward Hedges

*WALSALL, Staffordsh. Pop.71,789.Val.£246,560
Mayor, W. J. Pearman-Smith (*C*)
Recorder, Edward Annesley Owen
Town Clerk, John Richmond Cooper

WAREHAM, Dorset. Pop. 2,141. Val. £5,225
Mayor, William Crocker (2nd time) (*L*)
Town Clerk, George Clavell Filliter

WARRINGTON, Lanc. Pop. 64,000. Val. £220,000
Mayor, Alderman Henry Roberts, J.P. (L)
Town Clerk, James Lyon Whittle

WARWICK (Boro'). Pop. 11,905. Val. £57,820
Mayor, James Glover (3rd year) (C)
Recorder, Thomas Milnes Colmore
Town Clerk, Brabazon Campbell, M.A.

WARWICKSHIRE. Acres 577,462. Population 805,070. Rental £3,993,082
Lord Lieutenant, Lord Leigh (1856), Stoneleigh Abbey, Kenilworth
High Sheriff, Michael H. Lakin, Warwick
Chairman of Q. S. and of C. C., John Stratford Dugdale, Q.C., 29, Eaton Square, London.S.W.
Clerk of the Peace and of County Council, Algernon Sydney Field, Leamington
County Treasurer, Sam. Clarke Smith, Warwick
Chief Const., Capt. J. T. Brinkley, Warwick (301)
Bridgemaster and County Surveyor, John Willmot, Birmingham
Coroners: Charles Webb Iliffe, M.D., Coventry; W. W. Wilmshurst, Kenilworth; Theodore Christophers, Henley-in-Arden

WEDNESBURY,Staffs. Pop.25,311. Val.£89,736
Mayor, C. W. Davies Joynson, J.P. (re-elec.) (L)
Town Clerk, Thomas Jones

WELLS, Somerset. Pop. 4,822. Val. £20,010
Mayor, Councillor Robt. Norton (re-elected) (C)
Recorder, Thomas Englesby Rogers
Town Clerk, Reginald Lowbridge Foster

WELSHPOOL, Montgom. Pop.6,501. Val.£40,537
Mayor, David Jones (re-elected) (L)
Town Clerk, Edward Jones

WENLOCK, Shropsh. Pop. 15,703. Val. £51,118
Mayor, Lord Forester (re-elected) (C)
Recorder, William Edward Mirehouse
Clerk of the Peace, Edward B. Potts (Broseley)
Town Clerk, Godfrey Charles Cooper

*WEST BROMWICH, Staffordsh. Pop. 59,489. Val. £207,809
Mayor, Councillor Samuel Pitt (3rd year) (L)
Recorder, Reginald Chas. Edward Plumptre
Stipendiary, N. C. A. Neville
Town Clerk and C. of the Peace, Alfred Caddick

*WEST HAM, Essex. Pop.204,902. Val.£1,059,693
Mayor, Alderman John Henry Bethell, J.P. (L)
Recorder, Edward Morten
Stipendiary Magistrate, Ernest Baggallay
Town Clerk, Frederic Edward Hilleary, LL.D.
Clerk of the Peace, E. Harvey Cook

WEST HARTLEPOOL, Durham. Pop. 60,000. Val. £210,000
Mayor, Alderman Charles Macfarlane, J.P. (L)
Town Clerk, Higson Simpson

WESTMINSTER (City of), London
High Steward, The Duke of Westminster, K.G.
Deputy, John Charles Thynne, 3 Little Cloisters
High Bailiff, Harry Wilmot Lee. (*Deputy*, J. Troubbuck), Phillimore Cham., Gt. Smith St., S.W.
Town Clerk, William Mann Trollope, 31 Abingdon Street, Westminster

WESTMORLAND (COUNTY OF). Acres 500,451. Population 51,785. Rental £471,462
Lord Lieutenant, Lord Hothfield (1881), Appleby Castle, Appleby
High Sheriff, Frank Maude Taylor Jones-Balme, High Close, Ambleside
Chairman of Q. S., Montague Crackanthorpe, Q.C., Newbiggin Hall, (near Carlisle)
Chairman of County Council, James Cropper, of Ellergreen, Kendal
Clerk of the Peace, John Bolton, Kendal
County Treasurer, G. E. Cartmel, Kendal

Chief Constable,Sir John Dunne, D.L. Carlisle(36)
County Surveyor, J. Bintley, Kendal
Coroners: John Bolton Wilson, Kendal; Wm. Hewitson, Appleby: E. A. Heelis, Appleby

WEYMOUTH (and Melcombe Regis), Dorset. Pop. 21,000. Val. £93,000
Mayor, Benjamin Morris, J.P. (L)
Town Clerk, Sir Richard Nicholas Howard, J.P.

WHITEHAVEN, Cumberland. Pop. 20,000. Val. £73,659
Mayor, Ald. Jno. Raven Musgrave (re-elec.) (C)
Town Clerk, Thomas Brown

WIDNES, Lanc. Pop.30,011. Val. £150,723
Mayor, Alderman George Ingram Neil (C)
Town Clerk, Henry Samuel Oppenheim

*WIGAN, Lancashire. Pop. 62,787. Val. £191,553
Mayor, Counc. Joseph Thos. Gee (re-elected) (C)
Recorder, Joseph Walton, Q.C.
Town Clerk, John James Charnock

WIGHT, ISLE OF. *Vide* ISLE OF WIGHT

WILTON, Wiltshire. Pop. 2,300. Val. £8,748
Mayor, Earl of Pembroke, G.C.V.O. (C)
Town Clerk, Henry John King

WILTSHIRE. Acres 879,643. Pop. 249,464. Rental £1,129,322
Lord Lieutenant (1896), Marquess of Lansdowne, K.G., Bowood, Calne, Wilts
High Sheriff, Lt.-Col. Wyatt William Turnor, Pinkney Park, Malmesbury
Chairman of Q. S., Rt. Hon. Lord Ludlow
Second Chairmen of Q. S., Lord Edmond Fitzmaurice, Hon. Percy Wyndham, and the Earl of Radnor
Clerk of Peace and C.C., R. W. Merriman, Marlborough and Trowbridge
Deputy Clerk of C. C. & Commits., H. H. Copnall
County Treasurer, E. B. Merriman, Trowbridge
County Medical Officer of Health, Dr. John Tubb-Thomas, Trowbridge
Chief Const., Capt. R. Sterne, R.N., Devizes (227)
County Surveyor, Charles S. Adye, Trowbridge
Coroners: W. E. N. Browne, Chiseldon, Swindon; F. T. Sylvester, Trowbridge; R. A. Wilson, Salisbury; G. A. S. Waylen, Devizes

WINCHELSEA, Sussex. Pop. 670. Val. £4,500 (*Unreformed borough*, election Easter Monday)
Mayor, Major Robert Curteis Stileman (C)
Town Clerk, Walter Dawes

WINCHESTER, Hants. Pop. 19,073. Val. £90,839
Lord High Steward, Earl of Northbrook, G.C.S.I., Stratton, Micheldever Station
Mayor, Joseph Marks (L)
Recorder, William Blake Odgers, Q.C.
Town Clerk, Walter Bailey

WINDSOR, Berks. Pop. 12,327. Val. £79,847
Lord High Steward, H.R.H. Pr. Christian, K.G. Cumberland Lodge, Windsor Great Park
Mayor, Councillor Alfred Thompson Barber (C)
Recorder, Alfred Tristram Lawrence
Town Clerk, Philip Lovegrove
Clerk of the Peace, Charles William Last

WISBECH, Cambs. Pop. 9,395. Val. £40,411
Mayor, Councillor Wm. Shepherd Collins, J.P. (L)
Town Clerk, George Carrick

WOKINGHAM, Berks. Pop. 3,371. Val. £14,780
High Steward, Arth. Fraser Walter (Bearwood)
Mayor, Ald. T. Manley Westcott (3rd time) (C)
Town Clerk, James May

*WOLVERHAMPTON (County Borough), Staffordshire. Pop. 95,000. Val. £352,828
Mayor, Ald. Samuel Theodore Mander, B.A., J.P. (L)
Recorder, Frederick Albert Bosanquet, Q.C.

Stipendiary Magistrate, Nigel C. Alfred Neville
Town Clerk and Clerk of Peace. Horatio Brevitt

WOODSTOCK, Oxon. Pop. 1,628. Value £4,053
Mayor, Councillor John Banbury (3rd time) (*L*)
Town Clerk, Adolphus Ballard, B.A., LL.B.

WORCESTER (City). Pop. 42,908. Val. £193,116
Mayor, Ald. John Millington, J.P. (*C*)
Recorder, Richard Holmden Amphlett, Q.C.
Sheriff, William Arthur Campbell
Town Clerk, Samuel Southall
Clerk of the Peace, John Stallard, jun.

WORCESTERSHIRE. Acres 474,868. Population 296,603. Rateable Val. £1,757,499
Lord Lieutenant, Earl of Coventry (1891), Croome Court, Severn Stoke
High Sheriff, Charles William Dyson Perrins, Davenham, Malvern
Chairman of Q. S., County Council, and of Standing Joint Committee, John William Willis Bund, 15, Old Sq., Lincoln's Inn, London, W.C.
Deputy Chairman of Q. S., Richard Holmden Amphlett, Q.C., Wychfold Hall, Droitwich
Vice-Chairman of County Council, Robert Woodward, Arley Castle, near Bewdley
Clerk of the Peace and County Council and County Solicitor, Samuel Thornely, Worcester
County Treas., A. C. Cherry, Old Bank, Worcester
Chief Constable. Lieut.-Col. George Lynedoch Carmichael, Worcester (351)
County Surveyor, H. Rowe, Worcester
Coroners: Edwin Docker, Birmingham: Wm. Price Hughes, Worcester: W.H. Moore, Upton-on-Severn: Edward Percy Jobson, Dudley

WORKINGTON, Cumb. Pop. 26,000. Val. £83,000
Mayor, Alderman James Fletcher (*L*)
Town Clerk, John Warwick

WORTHING, Sussex. Pop. 21,500. Val. £121,030
Mayor, Ald. Frank Parish, M.R.C.S. (re-elected) (*C*)
Town Clerk, William Verrall

WREXHAM, Denbigh. Pop. 12,552. Val. £62,410
Mayor, Thomas Jones (*L*)
Town Clerk, Thomas Bury

YARMOUTH (GREAT), Norfolk and Suffolk. Pop. 49,334. Val. £300,000
High Steward, The Most Hon. Marquess of Salisbury, K.G., Hatfield House, Herts.
Mayor, Benjamin H. Press (*C*)
Recorder, Simms Reeve
Town Clerk, Arnold H. Miller

YEOVIL, Somerset. Pop. 9,648. Val. £52,346
Mayor, John Vincent (re-elected) (*L*)
Town Clerk, Henry Butler Batten

YORK (City). Pop. 73,474. Val. £352,130
Lord Mayor, Rt. Hon. Ald. Joseph S. Rymer (*C*)
Recorder, William Alfred Meek
Sheriff, Councillor Arthur Jones
Town Clerk, William Henry Andrew
Clerk of the Peace, Joseph Wilkinson

YORKSHIRE (EAST RIDING). Acres 741,827. Pop., 141,516. Rental £2,382,331. Rateable value £1,246,401
Lord Lieutenant, Lord Herries (1880), Everingham Park, York

High Sheriff, William Herbert St. Quintin, Scampston Hall, Rillington
Chairman of Q. S., Arthur Duncombe
Chairman of County Council, Sir Chas. Legard,Bt.
Clerk of Peace and to County Council, John J. Bickersteth (*Deputy*, J. R. Procter), Beverley
Treasurer, George A. Duncombe, Beverley
Chief Constable, Maj.W.H.Dunlop,Beverley (123)
Coroners: Luke White, Driffield; John Richardson Wood, York; Thomas Taylor, Wakefield; Jackson and Birks, Hull; Henry Green, Howden
County Surveyor, A. Beaumont, C.E., Beverley
Accountant, J. C. Kirk, Leeds

YORKSHIRE (NORTH RIDING). Acres 1,358,101. Pop. 284,837. Rental £2,550,936
Lord Lieutenant, The Most Hon. the Marquess of Ripon, K.G. (1873), Studley Royal, near Ripon
High Sheriff, see EAST RIDING
Chairman of Quarter Sessions, E. R. Turton, Upsall Castle, Thirsk
Chairman of C. C., John Hutton, M.P., Solberge, Northallerton
Clerk of the Peace and of County Council, W. C. Trevor, Guisbrough
Deputy Clerk of do.,
Ch. Const., R.L.Bower, C.M.G., Northallerton (267)
Surveyor, Walker Stead, Northallerton
Coroners: J. S. Walton, Northallerton; Wm. Richardson, Guisbrough; George Buchannan, Whitby; John Richardson Wood, York; Joseph Francis Porter, Helmsley; John Thos. Belk, Middlesbrough; Wm. Lowther Carrick, Stokesley

YORKSHIRE (WEST RIDING). Acres 1,684,848. Population 1,129,830. Rateable Val. £5,628,584
Lord Lieutenant, Earl of Scarbrough (1892), Sandbeck Park, Rotherham
High Sheriff, see EAST RIDING
Chairman of County Council, Charles Geo. Milnes-Gaskell, J.P., Thornes House, near Wakefield
Vice-Chairman of ditto, Frederick Bacon Frank, J.P., Campsall Hall, near Doncaster
Chairman of Q. S., Sir Thomas Brooke, Bart., Armitage Bridge, Huddersfield
Deputy-Chairmen of Q. S., Frederick Bacon Frank, and Sir Theophilus Peel, Bart.
Clerk of the Peace and County Council, Francis Alvey Darwin, Wakefield
Deputy do., William Vibart Dixon, Wakefield
Riding Treasurer, Percy Tew, Wakefield
Ch. Const., Capt. T. S. Russell, D.L., Wakefield (1,218)
Surveyor, J. Vickers Edwards, Wakefield
Riding Solicitor, Trevor C. Edwards, Wakefield
Coroners: Thos. Parkinson Brown, Skipton; J.R. Wood, York; J.S.Walton, Northallerton; Dossey Wightman, Sheffield; Fredk. Edwd. Nicholson, Doncaster; Wm. Barstow, J.P., Halifax; Thomas Taylor, J.P. and Pelham Page Maitland, Wakefield; Walter Brown Arundel, Pontefract; Arthur Ingram Robinson, Clitheroe; Charles Husband, Ripon

The County Boroughs named in the Third Schedule of the Local Government Act, 1888, are distinguished by having a * prefixed.

Directory of Scottish Burghs.

Giving the Population at the census of 1891, and Rateable Value of Property ascertained under 17 & 18 Vict. c. 91, and the name of the Provost and Town Clerk of each Burgh. Royal Burghs are distinguished thus (*)

∴ *For particulars of Scottish Counties see pages 324, 329.*

*ABERDEEN. Pop. 142,655. Value £753,802
Lord Provost, John Fleming
Town Clerk, William Gordon

AIRDRIE. Pop. 19,135. Value £60,958
Provost, David Martyn
Town Clerk, Gavin B. Motherwell

*ANNAN. Pop 3,475. Value £17,435
Provost, John Muir
Town Clerk, Murray Little

*ANSTRUTHER (Easter). Pop. 1,134. Value £4,992
Provost, William Martin
Town Clerk, William Thomson Jamieson and Archd. W. Jamieson

*ANSTRUTHER (Wester). Pop. 514. Value £1,736
Provost, John Porter
Town Clerks, W. T. Jamieson and Jno. Guthrie

*ARBROATH. Pop. 23,000. Value £92,229
Provost, Colin Grant
Town Clerk, W. K. Macdonald

*AYR. Pop. 24,900. Value £161,485
Provost, Thomas Templeton
Town Clerk, A. G. Young

*BANFF. Pop. 3,876 Value £13,031
Provost, Henry Munro
Town Clerk, John Allan

*BERVIE (or Inverbervie). Pop. 1,195. Val. £4,064
Provost, Alfred Gibb
Town Clerk, Arthur W. Kinnear

*BRECHIN. Pop. 9,000. Value £34,750
Provost, George Alex. Scott
Town Clerk, James Craig

*BURNTISLAND. Pop. 4,692. Value £29,271
Provost, John Connel
Town Clerk, Thomas A. Wallace

*CAMPBELTOWN. Pop. 8,235. Value £38,734
Provost, Hugh Mitchell
Town Clerks, D. and J. N. Mactaggart

COATBRIDGE (Municipal Borough of). Pop. 30,034. Value £165,258
Provost, Robert Sharp
Town Clerk, Jno. M. Alston

*CRAIL. Pop. 1,115. Value £4,924
Provost, George Sim
Town Clerks, W. T. Jamieson; John Guthrie

CROMARTY. Pop. 1,308. Value £2,630
Provost, Walter Johnstone
Town Clerk, Joseph Ritson

*CULLEN. Pop. 3,985. Value £3,778
Provost, Robert Gregor
Town Clerk, Alexander Sim

*CULROSS. Pop. 380. Value £2,263
Provost, John A. E. Cuninghame
Town Clerk, Alexander Fraser, Solicitor

*CUPAR-FIFE. Pop. 4,971. Value £24,072
Provost, David D. Watson
Town Clerk, John Lindsay Anderson

*DINGWALL. Pop. 3,300. Value £11,729
Provost, Colin Stewart
Town Clerk, Alex. Dewar

*DORNOCH. Pop. 515. Value £3,049
Provost, William Sutherland
Town Clerk, Hector M. Mackay

*DUMBARTON. Pop. 22,000. Value £76,000
Provost, Robert MacFarlan
Town Clerk, Alexr. Roberts

*DUMFRIES. Pop. 16,673. Value £75,013
Provost, Joseph Johnstone Glover
Town Clerk, John Grierson

*DUNBAR. Pop. 3,659. Value £22,747
Provost, John Gibb
Town Clerk, Charles Notman

*DUNDEE. Pop. 154,118. Value £829,389
Lord Provost, William Hunter
Town Clerk, Sir Thomas Thornton

DUNFERMLINE. Pop. 23,400. Value £91,232
Provost, Andrew Scobie
Town Clerk, William Simpson

*DYSART. Pop. 3,022. Value £11,715
Provost, Robert Livingstone
Town Clerk, James Herd

*EDINBURGH. Pop. 261,225. Value £2,648,061
Lord Provost, Rt. Hon. Mitchell Thomson
Town Clerk, Thomas Hunter
Chamberlain, Robert Paton

*ELGIN. Pop. 7,799. Value £39,414
Lord Provost, John Young
Town Clerk, Hugh Stewart

FALKIRK. Pop. 17,312. Value £69,939
Provost, John Weir
Town Clerk, A. Balfour Gray, Solicitor

*FORFAR. Pop. 12,057. Value £41,898
Provost, James McDougall
Town Clerk, Alexander MacHardy

*FORRES. Pop. 3,971. Value £18,114
Provost, James Lawrence
Town Clerk, Robert Urquhart

*FORTROSE. Pop 980. Value £4,580
Provost, William Spence Geddie
Town Clerk, John Henderson

GALASHIELS. Pop. 17,367. Value £67,392
Provost, John Dun
Town Clerk, Richard Lees

GLASGOW. Pop. 565,714. Value £4,780,000
Lord Provost, Samuel Chisholm
Town Clerk, Sir James David Marwick, LL.D.
City Chamberlain, James Nicol

GREENOCK. Pop. 70,000. Value £387,033
Provost, John Black
Town Clerk, C. MacCulloch

*HADDINGTON. Pop. 3,770. Value £20,613
Provost, Alexr. Mathieson Main
Town Clerk, Geo. Henderson Stevenson

HAMILTON. Pop. 24,863. Value £129,845
Provost, James Keith
Town Clerks, Wm. Pollok and P. M. Kirkpatrick

HAWICK. Pop. 19,204. Value £75,433
Provost, Robert Mitchell
Town Clerk, Robert Purdom

*INVERARY. Pop. 822. Value £2,514
Provost, James Wyllie
Town Clerk, Archibald Henderson

*INVERKEITHING. Pop. 1,663. Value £22,348
Provost, James Sim
Town Clerk, John Robert Menzies

*INVERNESS. Pop. 19,211. Value £118,845
Provost, William MacBean
Town Clerk, Kenneth MacDonald

*INVERURIE. Pop. 2,934. Value £14,235
Provost, George Jackson
Town Clerk, C. B. Davidson, LL.D.

*IRVINE. Pop. 9,027. Value £40,506
Provost, Charles Murchland
Town Clerk, James Dickie

*JEDBURGH. Pop. 3,397. Value £15,309
Provost, John Sword
Town Clerk, James Stedman

KILMARNOCK. Pop. 28,447. Value £131,533
Provost, David Mackay
Town Clerk, William Middlemas

*KILRENNY. Pop.2,610. Value £5,991
Provost, Peter Thomson
Town Clerks, T. Jamieson and J. Guthrie

*KINGHORN. Pop. 2,036. Value £7,965
Provost, John Sim
Town Clerk, W. Millie Dow

*KINTORE. Pop. 685. Value £2,695
Provost, Alexander Marshall
Town Clerk, David Edwards

*KIRKCALDY. Pop. 27,152. Value £141,303
Provost, Alexander Hutchison
Town Clerk, Wm. L. Macindoe

*KIRKCUDBRIGHT. Pop. 2,530. Value £10,150
Provost, William McEwen
Town Clerk, John Gibson

*KIRKWALL. Pop. 3,926. Value £14,252
Provost, Nicol Spence
Town Clerk, Wm. Cowper

*LANARK. Pop. 5,537. Value £18,208
Provost, Roderick Macleay
Town Clerks, Wm. and Jas. Annan

*LAUDER. Pop. 753. Value £2,483
Provost, William Moore
Town Clerk, Geo. Rankin

LEITH. Est. Pop. 77,385. Value £479,453
Provost, Richard Mackie
Town Clerk, T. B. Laing

*LINLITHGOW. Pop. 4,155. Value £15,868
Provost, Andrew Gilmour
Town Clerk, James Russell

*LOCHMABEN. Pop. 1,037. Value £2,998
Provost, Robert Johnstone
Town Clerk, Edward B. Rae

*MONTROSE. Pop. 13,048. Value £58,955
Provost, James Mitchell
Town Clerk, David Crombie Wills

MUSSELBURGH. Pop. 8,885. Value £42,660
Provost, David Whitelaw
Town Clerk, John Richardson

*NAIRN. Pop. 4,640. Value £17,494
Provost, William Dallas
Town Clerk, William Laing

*NEW GALLOWAY. Pop. 391. Value £1,316
Provost, Robert Garmory
Town Clerk, Robert Johnstone

*NORTH BERWICK. Pop. 3,038. Value £17,291
Provost, John Macintyre
Town Clerk, A. D. Wallace

OBAN. Pop. 4,902. Value £12,733
Provost, Hugh McCowan
Town Clerk, Alex. S. Black

PAISLEY. Pop. 66,418. Value £340,186
Provost, Archibald MacKenzie
Town Clerk, F. Martin

*PEEBLES. Pop. 3,059. Value £15,451
Provost, Henry Ballantyne, Junior
Town Clerk, William Buchan

*PERTH. Pop. 31,000. Value £181,185
Lord Provost, David MacGregor
Town Clerk, John Begg

PETERHEAD. Pop. 12,195. Value £46,678
Provost, William Hutchison Leask
Town Clerk, David Martin

*PITTENWEEM. Pop. 1,931. Value £5,747
Provost, James Christie
Town Clerk, Alexander C. Macintosh

PORT GLASGOW. Pop. 14,624. Value £60,585
Provost, Hugh McMaster
Town Clerk, Andrew Paton

*QUEENSFERRY. Pop. 1,531. Value £11,316
Provost, Robert Fairlie
Town Clerk, Peter Miller

*RENFREW. Pop. 9,000. Value £34,984
Provost, Andrew Brown
Town Clerks, Wm. Herron; Andrew R. Harper

*ROTHESAY. Pop. 9,034. Value £70,751
Provost, William McIntosh
Town Clerk, James Carse

*RUTHERGLEN. Pop. 13,361. Value £59,818
Provost, James Kirkwood
Town Clerk, George Gray

*ST. ANDREWS. Pop. 6,853. Value £53,223
Provost, James Ritchie Welch
Town Clerk, Stuart Grace

*SANQUHAR. Pop. 1,315. Value £4,543
Provost, Thomas Waugh
Town Clerk, George Birrell Carruthers

*SELKIRK. Pop. 5,783. Value £27,310
Provost, Alexr. Fowler Roberts
Town Clerk, John Pollok

*STIRLING. Pop. 16,974. Value £92,765
Provost, Archibald Forrest
Town Clerk, Thomas L. Galbraith

*STRANRAER. Pop. 6,193. Value £25,328
Provost, William M. MacRobert
Town Clerk, William Black

*TAIN. Pop. 1,632. Value £7,052
Provost, Donald Fowler
Town Clerk, John Mackenzie

*WHITHORN. Pop. 1,401. Value £3,787
Provost, Andrew McAdam
Town Clerk, W. C. Lawrie

*WICK. Pop. 2,962. Value £10,103
Provost, William Nicolson
Town Clerk, Hector Sutherland

*WIGTOWN. Pop. 1,509. Value £6,827
Provost, William Gardner
Town Clerk, William McClure

Directory of Irish Boroughs.

Giving the Population (1891) and Rateable Value of Property with the name of the Lieutenant and Custos Rotulorum, High Sheriff, Mayor or Chairman of the Town Commissioners, Clerks of the Crown and Peace and Town Clerk.

Parliamentary Boroughs are distinguished thus (*)

The Mayors and High Sheriffs are in some cases elected, in accordance with the terms of the Local Government (Ireland) Act, in the January of each year.

For particulars of Irish Counties, see page 331.

*ARMAGH (City). Pop. 7,800. Value £19,860
  Chairman of Urban District Council, Henry J. McKee, J.P.
  Town Clerk, T. G Peel

ATHLONE. Pop. 6,742. Value £10,256
  Chairman of Urban District Council, Robt. English, J.P.
  Town Clerk, P. Y. C. Murtagh

BANDON. Pop. 4,500. Value £6,450
  Chairman of Urban District Council, J. J. Calnan
  Town Clerk, John McDonnell

*BELFAST. Pop. 330,000. Value £1,064,000
  Lord Mayor, Ald. James Henderson, M.A., J.P.
  Town Clerk, Sir Samuel Black
  Recorder, His Hon. Henry FitzGibbon, Q.C.

*CARLOW. Pop. 7,000. Value £11,563
  Chairman of Urban District Council, Michael Governey
  Town Clerk, James Kelly
  Clerk of the Crown and Peace, James D. McCarthy

CASHEL (City). Pop. 3,216. Value £3,716
  Chairman of Urban District Council, M. McDevit
  Town Clerk, John O'Leary

CLONMEL. Pop. 10,520. Value £20,287
  Mayor, Edward Murphy
  Town Clerk, John F. O'Brien

COLERAINE. Pop. 6,845. Value £19,834
  Chairman of Urban District Council, Wm. J. Baxter
  Town Clerk, William Eccles, B.L.

*CORK (County of the City). Pop. 75,345. Value £165,383
  Lieutenant and Custos Rotulorum, The Earl of Bandon
  High Sheriff, A. M. Cole, J.P.
  Mayor, Eugene Crean, M.P.
  Town Clerk and Law Agent, Alexander McCarthy
  Recorder, His Hon. Sir Jas. C. Neligan, Q.C.

DROGHEDA. Est. Pop. 13,000. Value £24,079
  Lieutenant and Custos Rotulorum, Lord Bellew
  High Sheriff, Dr. J. B. Kelly
  Mayor, and Chairman of the Harbour Commission, Luke J. Elcock
  Town Clerk, J. B. Connolly
  Clerk of the Crown and Peace, S. O'Shaughnessy

*DUBLIN (City). Pop. 245,001. Value £690,864
  High Sheriff, Alderman Thomas D. Pile
  Lord Mayor, Daniel Tallon
  Town Clerk, Henry Campbell
  Recorder, His Hon. Sir Fredk. R. Falkiner

DUNDALK. Pop. 14,308. Value £28,804
  Chairman of the Urban District Council, John Hamill, J.P.
  Town Clerk, Mathew Comerford

DUNGANNON. Pop. 3,812. Value £9,781
  Chairman of Urban District Council, Hy. R. Kelly
  Clerk, James M. Hamilton

DUNGARVAN. Pop. 5,200. Value £9,880
  Chairman of Urban Dist. Council, H. W. Chambré, J.P.
  Town Clerk, Thomas McCarthy

ENNIS. Pop. 5,460. Value £7,402
  Chairman of Urban Dist. Council, P. J. Limane
  Town Clerk, Ernest Miniken

ENNISKILLEN. Pop. 5,570. Value £13,627
  Chairman of Urban District Council, W. Rutherford Cooney
  Town Clerk, William Cleland

*GALWAY (County of the Town). Pop. 16,959. Value £27,000
  Lieut. & Custos Rotulorum, Lord Clonbrock
  High Sheriff, Sir Thomas Moffett
  Recorder, His Honour Judge Anderson
  Clerk of the Crown and Peace, S. P. Redington
  Chairman of Urban District Council, Martin McDonagh, J P.
  Town Clerk, John Redington

*KILKENNY (County of the City). Pop. 13,722. Value £17,390
  Lieut. & Custos Rotulorum, Marq.of Ormonde, K.P.
  High Sheriff, Thomas Murphy
  Mayor, John Neale
  Clerk of the Crown and Peace, James Poe
  Town Clerk, Cornelius J. Kenealy

KINSALE. Pop. 4,500. Value £5,500
  Chairman of Urban Dist. Council, James O'Neill
  Clerk, R. A. Hegarty

*LIMERICK (County of the City). Pop. 37,155. Value £69,008
  Lieutenant and Custos Rotulorum, The Earl of Dunraven, K.P.
  High Sheriff (1899), T. H. Cleeve, J.P.
  Mayor, Alderman John Daly
  Town Clerk, William M. Nolan

LISBURN. Pop. 13,000. Value £28,191
  Chairman of Urban District Council, George St. George, M.D., J.P
  Clerk, Richard Young

*LONDONDERRY (City). Pop. 33,200. Val. £83,450
  Lieutenant and Custos Rotulorum, Sir H. H. Bruce
  High Sheriff, G. Knox Gillibrand
  Recorder, His Honour Judge Overend
  Clerk of the Crown and Peace, A. M. Munn
  Mayor, William McCearn
  Town Clerk, Sir Newman Chambers

*NEWRY (Borough). Pop. 13,623. Value £34,065
  Chairman of Urban District Council, Michael J. McCartan, M.D.
  Town Clerk, Robert H. Doherty

*SLIGO. Pop. 10,274. Value £23,518
  Mayor, P. A. McHugh, M.P.
  Town Clerk, Daniel MacGill

TRALEE. Pop. 9,400. Value £14,700
  Chairman of Urban District Council, Thomas Slattery
  Clerk, James Casey

*WATERFORD (County of the City). Pop. 27,713. Value £48,000
  Lieut. & Custos Rotulorum, Duke of Devonshire, K.G.
  High Sheriff, W. G. D. Goff, J.P.
  Mayor, Lawrence C. Strange
  Clerk of the Crown and Peace, Wm. J. Dennely, J.P.
  Town Clerk, J. J. Feely

*WEXFORD. Pop. 11,515. Value £16,647
  Mayor, Patrick Ryan
  Town Clerk, Wm. A. Browne

YOUGHAL. Pop. 5,722. Value £11,904
  Chairman of Urban District Council, Richard Carey, J.P.
  Town Clerk, James J. O'Shea

For the use of Parish Councils, Overseers, Churchwardens, Vestry Clerks, Magistrates' Clerks, Clerks of the Peace, and Town Clerks, Superintendent and District Registrars, Coroners, and County, Municipal, District, and Parochial Officers and Citizens generally, showing the days when certain Official Duties are to be performed; also the days when Inland Revenue Licences expire.

NOTA BENE.—1. *A rule of law is that Sunday is no day. Any act, therefore, which falls to be done on a Sunday should be performed the day previous unless statutory provision exists to the contrary. Every meeting or adjourned meeting of any vestry or corporation (other than Municipal, but including Parish, Rural, and Urban District Councils), or of any public company, for the nomination, election, or admission of any officer, or for the transaction of any affair of such vestry, corporation, or company, which according to any Act of Parliament, charter, prescription, or usage whatsoever, is or shall be required to be held on any day which shall happen to be a Lord's Day, shall, by* 3 & 4 *Will. IV. c.* 31, *be held on the Saturday preceding or on the Monday ensuing; and every matter transacted at any meeting or adjourned meeting held upon any Lord's Day shall be absolutely void. When no such nomination, election, or admission shall have taken place on the Saturday, every person whose term of office would have expired on any such Lord's Day shall continue in office, and exercise and enjoy all powers and privileges, until the Monday next ensuing.*

2. *By the Municipal Corporations Act,* 1882, *when a limited time from or after any date or event is appointed for the doing of any act, the time is exclusive of the day of that date or of the happening of that event, and as commencing at the beginning of the next following day; and the act is to be done on the last day of the limited time, unless that should be a Sunday, Christmas Day, Good Friday, Monday or Tuesday in Easter Week, or a day appointed for a public fast or thanksgiving, in which case the act will be done in due time if performed the day following. The same applies to any act directed to be done on a certain day, and that day falls on one of the days above mentioned. Further, if any act or proceeding is directed to be done within any time not exceeding seven days, the days above specified are not to be reckoned.*

3. *"Three clear days" means that three days must intervene between the day on which a notice is given and the day on which a meeting is held, and notices sent by post must be delivered three clear days before a meeting.*

4. *In regard to Bills of Exchange that fall due on a Sunday, Good Friday, Christmas Day, or a day appointed for a fast or thanksgiving, presentation for payment should be made on the preceding business day. Bills of Exchange falling due on a Bank Holiday are not payable until the following day, and when the last day of grace is a Sunday, and the second day of grace is appointed as a Bank Holiday, such bills are due and payable on the succeeding business day (see* 45 & 46 *Vict. c.* 61).

5. PARLIAMENTARY ELECTIONS.—*The times that must elapse between the receipt of the writ by the Returning Officer and the dates fixed for the various steps in the election are as follows:—Assuming that the writ is received on the* 1st *of any month, the notice of election must be issued on the* 2nd *in Boroughs, and* 3rd *in Counties. The nomination must take place on the* 4th *or* 5th *in Boroughs, and on any day between the* 5th *and* 10th *(both inclusive) in Counties.*

The poll (if any) must be fixed for some date between the 6th *and* 9th *(both inclusive) in all Boroughs, except those mentioned in Rule* 57, *Schedule I., to the Ballot Act,* 1872, *in which the date may be between the* 7th *and* 12th *(both inclusive).*

6. LOCAL GOVERNMENT AUDIT STAMP DUTY.— *The following is the scale of Stamp Duty payable by County and Urban and Rural District Councils and Parish Councils, and by the Chairmen of Parish Meetings on the Audit of their accounts by District Auditors:—*

Where the total of the expenditure comprised in the Financial Statement is—

			£	s.	d.
Under £20	the sum shall be		0	5	0
£20 and under £50	do.		0	10	0
£50 do. £100	do.		1	0	0
£100 do. £500	do.		2	0	0
£500 do. £1,000	do.		3	0	0
£1,000 do. £2,500	do.		4	0	0
£2,500 do. £5,000	do.		5	0	0
£5,000 do. £10,000	do.		10	0	0
£10,000 do. £20,000	do.		15	0	0
£20,000 do. £50,000	do.		20	0	0
£50,000 do. £100,000	do.		30	0	0
£100,000 and upwards	do.		50	0	0

January.

1 M.—The Land Tax, Income Tax, and the Duties on inhabited houses are due on this date. Under the Finance Act, 1898, any person (which term includes any corporate body) who is entitled to exemption from or abatement of income tax may obtain from the Surveyor of Taxes a certificate of exemption from or abatement of land tax. This provision is of great importance to Trustees, School Boards, Parish Councils, and others, who own small quantities of land. Licences for carriages, male servants, and to use armorial bearings fall due and must be taken out before the end of the month and thereafter within twenty-one days after a person becomes liable to duty. Dog licences must be taken out without delay: no grace can be claimed, but on *renewal*, if with other licences, they may be taken out any time during January.

The Registers of Parliamentary, Local Government and Parochial Electors come into force for the year.

By the Infectious Diseases (Notification) Extension Act 1899, the provisions of the Notification Act of 1889 are extended to the whole of England and Wales from this date.

The Parish Councillors (Tenure of Office) Act, 1899, comes into force on this day, making the term for which Parish Councillors are elected three years, and postponing the elections till 1901.

The Education Acts Amendment Act, 1899, comes into force, under which the age at which a child may be withdrawn from school to go to work is extended from eleven to twelve years.

The Seats for Shop Assistants Act, 1899, comes into force.

The Sale of Food and Drugs Act, 1899, comes into force, by which important new powers are conferred on the Board of Agriculture and the Local Government Board.

Watch Committee of Town Council to send to Secretary of State a copy of all rules made for the regulation and guidance of borough constables since the last quarterly return.

Between this date and the 31st March, the Medical Officer of the parish to visit every pauper lunatic not in an asylum; and before the 7th of this month make a report to the Clerk to the Guardians, or to the Overseers, of his visits during the preceding quarter, which report, within three days after its receipt, is to be transmitted to the Commissioners in Lunacy, and a copy sent to the Clerk to the Visitors of the asylum for the county or borough in which the union or parish is situate.

Clerk to Guardians and Overseers of parishes on this date, or as soon after as may be, to make out an annual list of all lunatics chargeable to the parish, and send copies before the 1st February to the Local Government Board, the Commissioners in Lunacy, Clerk to Visitors of Asylums, and to the Clerk of the Peace of the county, or Clerk to the Justices of the borough, to be by him laid before the Justices.

Return of Paupers relieved on 1st instant and of children boarded-out, to be made to Local Government Board.

On this date, or within ten days after (if no other day be prescribed), municipal corporations to appoint members of the council as trustees of corporate property.

Registrars, except of London districts, to post to the Registrar-General a correct return of births and deaths registered during the preceding quarter.

Coroners to send return of inquests for preceding year to Secretary of State during this month.

Within fifteen days after this date Registrars of Dioceses to send to the Registrar-General a list of all chapels wherein marriages may be lawfully solemnized.

Within fifteen days after this date bankers not registered under the Joint Stock Companies Act to deliver returns at the Stamp Office in London.

Medical Officers of Health are required to send their annual reports for the past year to the District Council for the district, to the County Council and to the Local Government Board as soon as possible.

Quarter Sessions to be held during this week. Under the Quarter Sessions Act, 1894, the Justices in General Quarter Sessions or at any adjourned or special meeting thereof, may at any time, when it may appear desirable for the purpose of not interfering with the Assizes then next ensuing, fix or alter the time for holding the then next General Quarter Sessions so that they shall be held not earlier than fourteen days before and not later than fourteen days after the week in which they would otherwise be held.

Within one week after the termination of Quarter Sessions the gaoler to send to the Secretary of State a calendar of the prisoners tried thereat.

Holiday on the Stock Exchange, and Bank Holiday in Scotland.

6 S.—Registrars of Births and Deaths to transmit to Overseers, on or before this date, a return of the names, ages, and residences of all male persons of full age, and also, when and as required by the Overseers, of all women who have died between the 8th September (or the date when the preceding return was made) and the 31st December.

Latest date for Medical Officers to send quarterly list of pauper lunatics visited by them to the Clerk to Guardians.

Solicitors, conveyancers, special pleaders, and draughtsmen in Equity in *Ireland* must renew their certificates between this date and Feb. 6.

9 Tu.—Latest date to pay Fire Insurances due at Christmas.

Latest date for Clerk to Guardians to send quarterly lists of lunatics to Commissioners in Lunacy, and to Clerk to Visitors.

Clerks of Courts of Summary Jurisdiction to send to the Home Secretary a statement of fines imposed during the last quarter.

11 Th.—Hilary Law Sittings commence.

13 S.—Latest date upon which notices of appeal against supplemental valuation lists in the Metropolis can be given.

Registrars to apply on or before this date to the officiating minister of every place of worship in which marriages may be solemnized within their sub-districts for certified copies of all entries of marriages solemnized, or for certificates of "No Registry," during the quarter ended 31st December last. Registrar to deliver these, on or before the 20th of this month, to the Superintendent Registrar.

Bankers' returns to be delivered at the Stamp Office not later than this date.

Latest date for Registrars of Dioceses to send to the Registrar-General a list of all chapels wherein marriages may be lawfully solemnized.

20 S.—On or before this date Registrars to personally deliver to Superintendent Registrars certified copies of all entries of Births, Deaths, and Marriages made during the quarter ended 31st December last. Last day for Local Authority to send to Local Government Board reports under Canal Boats Acts.

On or before this date returns to be sent to Mines Inspectors, giving particulars up to preceding 31st December, as required by s. 33 of Coal Mines Regulation Act, 1887.

Latest date for Savings Banks to send annual statement of affairs to Commissioners for Reduction of National Debt.

24 W.—Between this date and the 1st February, Companies, Corporations, and County Councils compounding for stamp duties with the Commissioners of Inland Revenue to deliver half-yearly accounts to the Commissioners.

31 W.—Latest date for Clerk to Visitors of Asylums to transmit report to Commissioners in Lunacy.

Last day for Local Authorities to send to Local Government Board Analysts' reports for preceding year.

Latest date for Superintendent Registrars to transmit to Registrar-General certified copies of the registers of Births, Deaths, and Marriages for the quarter ended 31st December last.

Railway Companies, on or before this date, if required, to send an abstract of their annual account to the Clerk of the County Council and the Overseers of the Poor of the counties through which the railway passes.

February.

1 Th.—Within 21 days after this date the Clerk of the Peace of every county, and the Town Clerk of every borough, to transmit to the Secretary of State a printed copy of the Register of Electors.

On or before this date borough Coroners to send to the Secretary of State returns in writing of inquests held by them or their deputies in the preceding year.

Latest date for Clerk to Guardians to transmit copies of annual list of pauper lunatics to Commissioners in Lunacy, Local Government Board, Clerk to Visitors of Asylums, Clerk to the Council of any County, and to the Town Clerk of any borough.

Reports of Medical Officers of Health for the past year should be sent to Local Government Board during this month.

Companies, Corporations, and County Councils compounding for stamp duties to deliver half-yearly accounts and pay duty to Commissioners of Inland Revenue not later than this date.

Four weeks at least before the 25th March Clerks to Board of Guardians to estimate the probable expenditure for the ensuing half-year and the probable balance due to or from each parish for the current half-year, and prepare contribution orders to be laid before the Guardians before the expiration of the current half-year. These estimates and the subsequent apportionments must be made on the "Assessable" value of Parishes as determined by s. 2 of the Agricultural Rates Act, and not on rateable value as formerly.

2 F.—Candlemas. Scotch Quarter Day.

3 S.—Latest date to renew certificates of Solicitors, Conveyancers, and Draughtsmen in Equity in *Ireland*.

17 S.—Nine days at least before the 1st March Town Clerk to publish a notice of the election of auditors.

21 W.—Latest day for delivery of nomination papers in election of Auditors in Boroughs.

Latest date for the Clerk of the Peace of every county, and the Town Clerk or other officer having charge of the register, to send a printed copy of the Register of Electors to the Secretary of State.

24 S.—Four days at least before the 1st March the Mayors of boroughs to publish notices of the situation of polling-places for the election of Auditors.

March.

1 Th.—Between this date and 1st August, persons shooting or taking wild birds are liable to penalties under the Wild Birds Protection Act, 1880, and persons selling or exposing for sale any hare or leveret (except a foreign hare) are liable to penalties under the Hares Preservation Act, 1892. Under the Wild Birds Protection Act, 1894, a Secretary of State may, on the application of any County Council, prohibit the taking of eggs within a county or any part thereof.

Ordinary day for election of elective Auditors in boroughs.

The Occupier of every Factory and Workshop must on or before this date send return of persons employed during year ending 31st December last, to Inspector of Factories, in pursuance of the Factory and Workshop Act, 1895.

Town Council of borough, on or before this date, to transmit to the Local Government Board a statement of receipts and expenditure up to last audit.

The Annual Parish Meeting is to be held in every Rural Parish on some day between 1st March and 1st April, to appoint Overseers.

Borough Treasurers to submit their accounts to audit within one month from this date, or that approved of by the Local Government Board for the making up of such accounts.

9 F.—Latest date for Returning Officers to publish Notice of Election for Urban and Rural District Councillors and Guardians.

15 Th.—After this date, and until the 1st August, any person having in his control or possession any wild bird killed or taken in the United Kingdom since the 1st of this month, is liable to a penalty under the Wild Birds Protection Act, 1880.

Nominations in Elections of Urban and Rural District Councillors and Guardians to be delivered by noon on this day.

20 Tu.—Within fourteen days after this date a special sessions may be held for appointment of the days for holding not less than eight nor more than twelve special sessions for executing the purposes of the Highways Act. This is liable to alteration by the County Council, and the fixing of these Sessions is no longer compulsory, as Highway business can be done at any Petty Sessions.

21 W.—Railway Companies to pay quarterly instalments of Income Tax on or before this date.

25 S.—Quarter Day. Union accounts to be made up to this date, or to the end of the Union week first completed after this date. Returns made to Local Government Board under Local Taxation Returns Act, 1877, by Corporations, and other local authorities to be made up to this date. (*See* 31st March.)

Half-yearly accounts of School Boards to be made up to this date.

Overseers of the Poor to be nominated and appointed within fourteen days after this date in Urban parishes.

Churchwardens and Overseers in Urban parishes and Overseers in Rural parishes, within fourteen days after other Overseers have been appointed to succeed them, to deliver to such succeeding Overseers a just, true, and perfect account in writing of all sums of money in their hands, as required by 17 Geo. II. c. 38, s. 1.

Medical Officer of Unions entitled to be paid any extra fees, to make out his quarterly account to this date, and lay the same before the Guardians; his claim to accrue at the expiration of one calendar month following this date, but the Guardians may pay it earlier.

The Overseers, and every Collector appointed for a Parish, to make up their accounts to this date, and deposit them for the free inspection of the ratepayers at some house within the parish for seven clear days at least before the audit.

Trustees of Parochial Charities to prepare accounts to be delivered to Parish Councils, and forward copy to Charity Commissioners within fourteen days.

District Medical Officers to notify at the commencement of this quarter to the Board of Guardians the paupers whose names have been inserted in the permanent medical relief list for a period of six months; advise as to the continuance of such paupers in such list, and take the direction of the Board thereon.

27 Tu.—Latest date for publication of Notice of Election of Urban and Rural District Councillors and Guardians.

31 S.—Under the Local Government Acts, 1888 and 1894, the local financial year ends on this date. All enactments relating to accounts of local authorities, or to meetings or other matters, are to be modified so far as is necessary to adapt them to the Act. The accounts of all County Councils, Urban and Rural District Councils, and of all Parish Councils and Parish Meetings, must be made up to this date.

Railway companies unincorporated to furnish statements of capital, traffic, and working expenditure to the Board of Trade not later than this date. Incorporated companies to send their returns within fourteen days after their first ordinary half-yearly meeting held in each year.

Quarter Sessions to be held the first week after this date. (*See* January 1.)

Hawkers', Refreshment-House Keepers', and Packet Boat liquor and tobacco licences expire on this date.

Watch Committee of Town Council to send to Secretary of State a copy of all rules made since 31st December for the regulation and guidance of constables.

Treasurer of Borough to submit his accounts for audit if made up to the 1st March.

April.

1 S.—The Board of Education Act, 1899, which provides for the establishment of a Board of Education for England and Wales, comes into force.

In the months of April and May, or one of them, Overseers to ascertain with respect to all property in their parishes, whether any man is entitled to be registered as a voter by reason of his being an inhabitant occupier, and enter in the Rate-book the name of every man so entitled, with a description of the dwelling.

Notice of intention to apply for an order under the Light Railways Act, 1896, must be advertised for two weeks during April or October.

Between this date and the 30th June, the Medical Officer of the parish to visit pauper lunatics not in asylums. (*See* January 1.)

The walls and ceilings of Common Lodging Houses to be limewashed in the first week of this month.

Registrars, except of London districts, to post to the Registrar-General a correct return of births and deaths registered during the preceding quarter.

District Councils to be elected this month.

During this and the two following months owners may be compelled to cut down oak-trees growing in hedges near highways ordered to be widened.

2 M.—Quarter Sessions to be held this week.

Elections of Urban and Rural District Councillors and Guardians take place on this day unless otherwise fixed by the County Council.

4 W.—On this day, unless otherwise provided by the County Council, all Parish Councils, Rural and Urban District Councils, and Boards of Guardians are to be elected where a poll is necessary under the Local Government Board's Election Orders, 1898.

5 Th.—Returns of assessed taxes made to this date.

6 F.—Commencement of the Financial year for Imperial purposes.

Within seven days before the 15th Clerks of the Peace and Town Clerks to send their precepts as to Registration to the Overseers.

The Fund for aiding the equalisation of Rates in London is to be based on the Rateable Value as at this date in each year.

Latest date for Medical Officers to send quarterly lists of lunatics to Clerk to Guardians.

Latest date for Clerk to Guardians to send quarterly lists of lunatics to Commissioners in Lunacy, and copies to Clerk to Visitors.

Registrars of Births and Deaths to transmit to Overseers, on or before this date, a return of all male persons of full age, and also, when and as required, of all women who have died during the three months ending 31st March.

9 M.—Latest date to pay Fire insurances due on Lady Day.

Clerks of Courts of Summary Jurisdiction to send to the Home Secretary a statement of fines imposed during the last quarter.

On this date, or within seven days before, Clerks of the Peace and Town Clerks to send precepts and copies of registers to Overseers.

11 W.—Hilary Law Sittings end.

13 F.—Registrars to apply to officiating ministers on or before this date for certified copies of all entries of marriages solemnized by them during the quarter ended 31st March.

15 S.—Guardians of Unions at their first meeting after this date to appoint the Union Assessment Committee, consisting of not less than six nor more than twelve.

Urban and Rural District Councillors and Guardians and Parish Councillors come into office.

Urban and Rural District Councils and Boards of Guardians must hold their Annual Meetings as soon as convenient after this date. Parish Councils must hold their Annual Meeting on or within seven days after this day.

20 F.—On or before this date Registrars to personally deliver to Superintendent Registrars copies of entries of Births, Deaths, and Marriages made during the previous quarter.

24 Tu.—Easter Law Sittings begin.

30 M.—Latest date for Superintendent Registrars to send to Registrar-General certified copies of entries of Births, Deaths, and Marriages made during the quarter ended 31st March.

May.

1 Tu.—Local Authorities in counties and boroughs to send to Secretary of State copies of orders made under Ballot Act as to polling districts.

Copies of draft orders and other documents under Light Railways Act, 1896, to be sent to County, District, and Parish Councils, and various Government departments, during May or November.

Overseers in the Metropolis to make and deposit supplemental valuation lists before 1st June.

Holiday at the Bank Transfer Office and Stock Exchange.

Bank Holiday in *Scotland*.

14 M.—Between this date and the 4th of August, no person to sell, expose for sale, or buy for sale any description of oysters other than those known as "deep-sea oysters."

15 Tu.—Scottish Quarter Day.

Licences for beer retailers, retailers of wine and spirits, and dealers in tobacco and snuff in *Scotland* expire.

18 F.—Within sixty days after this date the half-yearly receipts for interest to savings-banks are to be made out and allowed.

24 Th.—Queen's Birthday. The Custom House, Inland Revenue Offices, and other Government Offices and the Public Dockyards are closed on the day on which the birthday is appointed to be kept.

31 Th.—Before the 1st June Friendly Societies to make returns to the end of the preceding year to the Registrar of Friendly Societies.

Latest date for Overseers to enter names of inhabitant occupiers in rate-book for registration purposes.

Latest date for Overseers in the Metropolis to deposit supplemental valuation lists.

June.

1 F.—Annual returns of rates, taxes, tolls, and dues levied for local purposes, required by Local Taxation Returns Act, are to be furnished to the Local Government Board in this month.

Where any poor-rate due on the 5th of January last, from an occupier in respect of premises capable of conferring the franchise for a borough, remains unpaid on this date, the Overseers to give a notice, on or before the 20th of this month, to such occupier that he will not be entitled to have his name in the List of Voters in respect of his occupation unless he pays such rate on or before the 20th of July next.

Easter Law Sittings end.

2 S.—Where an owner of small tenements who has become liable to pay the poor-rates under the Poor-Rate Assessment and Collection Act, 1869, omits or neglects to pay before the 5th of June any rate due previously to the preceding 5th of January, he will not be entitled to any abatement, but must pay such rate in full.

12 Tu—Trinity Law Sittings begin.

15 F.—Sale of oysters prohibited. (*See* May 14.)

20 W.—On or before this date Overseers to publish the ownership portion of the register of county voters, and a notice to voters to send in claims to vote on or before the 20th July. Publication to be effected by affixing copies to churches and chapels, or to public buildings and post offices, there to remain for a period including two Sundays at least, but not later than the 20th July.

Overseers to publish notice that no person will be entitled to have his name in the list of Parliamentary £10 and inhabitant occupiers, or £10 Burgesses and County electors unless, on or before the 20th July, he has paid all rates due previous to the 5th January last. Notices of like effect are also to be served on occupiers who have not paid such rates.

Railway Companies to pay quarterly instalments of Income Tax on or before this date.

24 S.—Quarter Day. Medical Officers of Unions entitled to be paid any extra fees to make out their accounts quarterly to this date, and lay the same before the Guardians.

Sheriffs of London to be elected.

25 M.—Quarter Sessions to be held during this week.

District Medical Officers at the commencement of this quarter to notify to the Board of Guardians the paupers whose names have been inserted in the permanent medical relief list for a period of six months.

July.

1 S.—Watch Committee of Town Council to send to Secretary of State a copy of all rules made since 31st March for the regulation and guidance of constables.

On this date at the latest the Board of Trade to lay before Parliament a Report respecting the applications to them, and their proceedings under the Electric Lighting Act, 1882.

Between this date and the 30th of September, the Medical Officer of the parish to visit pauper lunatics not in asylums.

Special Meetings of Local Authorities for the granting of Licences to deal in Game to be held during this month.

Registrars, except of London districts, to post to the Registrar-General a correct return of Births and Deaths registered during the preceding quarter.

Return of paupers relieved on this date to be made to Local Government Board.

Before the expiration of this month County Councils are to appoint valuers for the purposes of the Finance Act, 1894, for the valuation of property for Estate Duty.

Licences to deal in Game expire.

5 Th.—The following licences expire on this date:—Appraiser, auctioneer, house agent, beer-dealer (retail) and retailer of table-beer to be drunk off the premises, dealer in plate, rectifier and compounder of spirits, dealer in spirits, for use of still or retort, retailer of and dealer in sweets and made-wines, manufacturer of and dealer (not a publican) in tobacco and snuff, manufacturer of vinegar, dealer in foreign wines.

9 M.—Medical Officers to send quarterly lists of lunatics to Clerk to Guardians before this date.

Latest date to pay Fire insurances due on Midsummer Day.

Latest date for Clerk to Guardians to send quarterly lists of lunatics to Commissioners in Lunacy, and to Clerk to Visitors.

Clerks of Courts of Summary Jurisdiction to send to the Home Secretary a statement of fines imposed during the last quarter.

13 F.—Registrars to apply to officiating ministers on or before this date for certified copies of all entries of marriages solemnized by them during the quarter ended 30th June.

20 F.—The Clerk of the Peace in every county, riding, or division must, before this date, issue his precept to the Overseers, requiring them to make out, before the 1st September next, a list of all persons qualified to serve on juries, and specify in the list those qualified as Special Jurors.

Within two days after this date Tax assessors and collectors to make out and deliver to Overseers a list of the persons who have not paid the assessed taxes due for the year preceding the 6th April last.

Latest date for Registrars to deliver to Superintendent Registrars copies of entries of Births, Deaths, and Marriages made during the previous quarter.

Latest date for Occupiers in counties and Householders in boroughs to pay poor-rates due in respect of the year preceding 5th January last, so as to be retained on the Register of Voters.

Registrars of Births and Deaths to transmit to Overseers, on or before this date, a return of all male persons of full age, and also when and as required, of all women who have died between 1st April and 15th July.

Latest date for tax-collectors to send to Overseers lists of persons who have not paid assessed taxes for the year preceding April 6.

On or before this date Overseers to make out list of persons disqualified as occupation voters by reason of the non-payment by the 20th of the poor-rates due on the preceding 5th January. Such list to be open to public inspection during the next fourteen days.

25 W.—On or before this date Overseers to remove copy of Register of Ownership voters from the places where published.

All persons on the Register of Voters in respect of lodgings, and desirous of remaining on the register in respect of the same lodgings, must send to the Overseers, on or before this date, their claims to be so retained.

Between this date and the 1st August, Companies, Corporations, and County Councils compounding for stamp duties with the Commissioners of Inland Revenue, to deliver half-yearly accounts to the Commissioners.

31 Tu.—On or before this date Overseers are to ascertain from the Relieving Officer acting for their parish or township the names of all persons disqualified from voting by reason of having received parochial relief.

On or before this date Overseers are to add on the margin of one copy of the ownership portion of the Register, and on the margin of the list of ownership claimants, the word "objected" before the name of every person therein whom they have reasonable cause to believe to be not entitled to be on the new Register; and the word "dead" before the name of every person whom they have reason, from the returns sent by the Registrars of Births and Deaths, or from their own knowledge, to believe to be dead. If it appears that any person is entered in the ownership portion of the Register for the parish or township in respect of a £50 rental qualification, the Overseers are to add the word "objected" before the name of such person, and to insert his name in the occupiers' list.

On or before this date Overseers to make out the occupiers' list in counties, the occupiers' list in boroughs, the old lodgers' list, and the non-resident list.

On or before this date Town Clerk to make out a list of freemen voters.

Latest date for Superintendent Registrars to transmit to Registrar-General certified copies of entries of Births, Deaths, and Marriages made during the quarter ended 30th June.

Pawnbrokers' licences expire on this date; also licences to kill game, and to carry a gun

August.

1 W.—Lammas Day. Scottish Quarter Day.
On or before this date Overseers are to sign one copy of the Register of ownership claimants, and of the lists specified under date 31st July. They are to cause a sufficient number of such lists to be printed, and to publish the Register with their marginal additions and signed by them. The Overseers are also to publish at the same time the corrupt and illegal practices list, and keep a copy of each of such lists, and of the ownership portion of the Register open to public inspection for fourteen days after publication. They are also to keep a copy of the list of defaulters in payment of assessed taxes, and allow it to be inspected, without fee, between 10 a.m. and 4 p.m. on any day except Sunday during the next fortnight; copies thereof to be delivered on payment.

On this date, or on any day until the 20th inclusive, a person desirous of having his name entered in the lodgers' list must send in his claim to the Overseers.

Overseers to make out lists of claims and objections of occupiers and lodgers.

Town Clerks to publish lists of freemen voters on or before this date, and keep copies thereof for inspection during the next fourteen days.

Companies, Corporations, and County Councils to deliver half-yearly accounts and pay duty to Commissioners of Inland Revenue not later than this date.

Clerks to Boards of Guardians are, four weeks at least before the 29th of September, to estimate the probable expenditure for the ensuing half-year and the probable balance due to or from each parish for the current half-year, and prepare contribution orders to be laid before the Guardians before the expiration of the current half-year.

5 S.—Latest date for inspection of lists of persons who have not paid poor-rates due January 5.

In boroughs in which there are ten acting justices, Licensing Committees are to be appointed in the fortnight preceding the 20th August.

6 M.—Bank Holiday, in *Scotland* also.

11 S.—Trinity Law Sittings end.

15 W.—Latest date for public inspection of the lists specified under date August 1.

Borough and county lists to be affixed to churches if published on the 1st inst.

20 M.—Latest date for Town Clerks and Overseers to receive notice of claims and objections, and of omissions from the Parliamentary Counties, Borough, and Parochial electors' lists and registers.

Latest date for lodgers to give notice of claims to Overseers.

Between this date and the 14th September the Justices in counties other than Middlesex and Surrey to hold the annual licensing meeting, and appoint special sessions for transferring publicans' licences.

On or before this date the Clerk to the Justices to give notice to Overseers of the time and place for holding petty sessions at which jury lists are to be produced.

25 S.—On or before this date Overseers to deliver to Clerks of the County Council and Town Clerks copies of corrupt and illegal practices lists.

On or before this date Overseers to make out lists of claims and objections. These lists are to be signed and published by the Overseers, who are to keep a copy, with the original notices of claims and objections, open to public inspection at any time between 10 a.m. and 4 p.m. on any day except Sunday during the next fourteen days; and copies are to be delivered on payment.

On or before this date Overseers to deliver to Clerks of the County Council or Town Clerks the following lists:—Ownership claimants, ownership portion of register, ownership electors' objections, two copies of occupiers' and old lodgers' lists, one each of occupiers' and lodgers' claims and objection lists, two copies of the non-resident list, and one each of claim and objection lists.

31 F.—Latest date for Overseers to make out list of persons qualified and liable to serve on Juries.

September.

1 S.—Licences for the manufacture and sale of playing cards and of patent medicines expire on this date.

List of Jurors and notice of special sessions to be affixed to doors of churches and other places of public worship on the first three Sundays of this month.

3 M.—Between this date and 1 Feb. next (both inclusive), salmon trout or char can only be sent by carrier if outside of package is marked with name of contents.

5 W.—On or before this date declarations as to misdescription, omission, or other error in registers or burgess lists to be sent to Town Clerks, and in the case of county lists to Clerks of the County Councils; such declarations to be open to public inspection on any day before the 8th inst.

7 F.—As soon as possible after this date, and between the 8th September and the 12th October (both inclusive) Courts for revision of lists of parliamentary voters, burgesses, and county electors to be held by Revising Barristers. Clerk of the Peace to attend Revising Barrister's first Court, and Overseers to attend courts for their respective districts and parishes, produce list of voters, and answer questions.

Last day for inspection of lists of claims and objections to voters.

On or before this date, or at such other time as shall be appointed by the Revising Barrister, Registrars of Births and Deaths to send to Overseers a return of all male persons of full age, and also, when and as required, of all women, who have died between the 16th of July and the time when such return is made.

20 Tu.—Railway Companies to pay quarterly instalments of Income Tax on or before this date.

22 S.—Within the last seven days of this month the Justices in every division in England and Wales are to hold a special sessions for receiving and examining the jury list, when the Overseers are required to attend, and the lists, when approved, are to be forwarded by the Justices' Clerk to the Clerk of the County Council.

Sheriffs of London to be sworn in.

29 S.—Quarter Day. Union accounts to be made up to this date, or to the end of the Union week first completed after this date.

Overseers' Accounts of Receipts and Payments to be made up to this date.

Half-yearly or yearly accounts of School Boards to be made up to this date.

District Medical Officers to notify, at the commencement of this quarter, to the Board of Guardians the paupers whose names have been inserted in the permanent medical relief list for a period of six months.

Within one month after this date annual returns of allowances granted under Poor Law Officers' Superannuation Act, 1896, to be sent to Local Government Board.

The Lord Mayor of London to be chosen.

30 ɔ.—Half-yearly accounts of Urban and Rural District Councils to be made up to this date, and Financial Statements prepared for audit duly stamped.

The following licences expire on this date:—
Brewer of beer (not for sale), maker of and retailer of methylated spirit.

October.

1 M.—On or before this date every body corporate or unincorporate chargeable with the duty of 5 per cent. on the annual value, income, or profits of its real and personal property, to deliver to the Commissioners of Inland Revenue a full account of all property in respect whereof such duty shall be payable, and of the gross annual value, income, or profits thereof accrued in the year ended the preceding 5th of April.

Notice of intention to apply for an order under the Light Railways Act, 1896, must be advertised for two weeks during April or October.

Watch Committee of Town Council to send to Secretary of State a copy of all rules made since 30th June for the regulation and guidance of constables.

Between this date and the 31st December, the District Medical Officer to visit pauper lunatics not in asylums.

Registrars, except of London districts, to post to the Registrar-General a correct return of Births and Deaths during the preceding quarter.

The Standing Joint Committee of every county, and the Watch Committee of every borough, on some day in this month, are to transmit to the Secretary of State, for the year ended 29th September last, a statement of the number of offences reported to the police, the number of persons apprehended, the nature of the charges against them, the result of the proceedings taken thereupon, and any other particulars relating to the state of crime within such county or borough.

In this month two or more of the justices having jurisdiction in a borough to appoint as many of the inhabitants not legally exempt as they think fit to act as special constables.

The walls and ceilings of Common Lodging Houses to be limewashed in the first week of this month.

7 S.—Latest date for Medical Officers to send quarterly list of lunatics to the Clerks to Guardians.

The following licences expire on this date:—Bankers', retailers of beer, cider, spirits in England and Ireland, and foreign wines; publicans retailing sweets and wines, and dealing in tobacco and snuff; and distillers of spirits.

Latest date for Clerk to Guardians to send quarterly lists of lunatics to Commissioners in Lunacy, and copies to Clerk to Visitors.

Clerks of Courts of Summary Jurisdiction to send to the Home Secretary a statement of fines imposed during the last quarter.

12 F.—The revision of the lists of parliamentary voters, burgesses, county and parochial electors to be completed not later than this date.

Registrars to apply to officiating ministers, on or before this date, for certified copies of all entries of marriages solemnized by them during the quarter ended 30th September.

13 S.—Latest date to pay Fire insurances due at Michaelmas.

15 M.—Quarter Sessions to be held this week. Music and dancing licences under 25 Geo. II. c. 36, to be granted and renewed.

19 F.—On or before this date Registrars to personally deliver to Superintendent Registrars copies of entries of Births, Deaths, and Marriages made during the previous quarter.

20 S.—On or before this date Town Clerks to complete burgess rolls, to come into operation for one year from 1st November next. County rolls to be completed by Clerks to County Councils by this date.

Nine days at least before the 1st November (*i.e.* on the 22nd) Town Clerks to publish a notice of election of Borough Councillors. All election notices must have the names and addresses of printer and publisher on their face.

24 W.—Nomination papers in the election of Borough Councillors to be delivered before five o'clock this day, *i.e.* seven days at least before the day of election.

Michaelmas Law Sittings commence.

26 F.—Mayor to attend at the town hall to decide on the validity of objections to nomination papers for Borough Councillors.

This day, *i.e.* four days at least before the day of election, Town Clerk to publish names and addresses of persons nominated for Borough Councillors, and Mayor to give notice of polling places.

31 W.—Latest date for Superintendent Registrars to transmit to Registrar-General certified copies of entries of Births, Deaths, and Marriages made during the quarter ended 30th September.

Certificates of Writers to the Signet, solicitors, agents, and notaries public in *Scotland*, and of conveyancers, special pleaders, and draughtsmen in equity in *England* expire on this date.

Short licences to kill game expire.

After the fourth day of Michaelmas Sittings courts to sit to hear appeals from Revising Barristers.

November.

1 Th.—Burgesses in England and Wales to elect Borough Councillors to supply the places of those going out of office. One-third of the Councillors, those longest in office without re-election, to go out. Municipal Borough Elections in Scotland are held on this day. On this date the first elections under the London Government Act, 1899, for the newly-created municipalities in the Metropolis will take place unless postponed by the Lord President of the Council.

Copies of draft orders and other documents under Light Railways Act, 1896, to be sent to County, District, and Parish Councils, and various Government departments during May or November.

Burgess-rolls come into operation for one year.

Holiday at Bank Transfer Office and Stock Exchange.

9 F.—Ordinary date of election of mayors of boroughs. The council of every borough being a county in itself, and the city of Oxford, to appoint a sheriff immediately after the election of the mayor, and elect borough aldermen to take the place of those retiring.

The Lord Mayor of London, having been chosen on St. Michael's Day, is, by 24 Geo. II. c. 48, to be presented at the Supreme Court of Judicature and sworn on this date, except the same shall fall on a Sunday, then on the day following.

11 S.—Martinmas. Scottish Quarter Day.

12 M.—High Sheriffs of England and Wales nominated in the Queen's Bench Division for appointment in January next.

15 Th.—Solicitors' Annual Certificates expire.

16 F.—Between this date and December 15th, solicitors, proctors, and notaries public in *England* must renew their certificates.

19 M.—End of Trustee Savings Bank year (26 & 27 Vict. c. 87).

Within sixty days the half-yearly receipts for interest from the National Debt Commissioners to savings banks to be made out and issued.

Trustee Savings Banks to make up accounts to this date, and within nine weeks publish annual statement.

26 M.—Municipal Elections in *Ireland* in Boroughs constituted under the Municipal Corporations Act, 1843, are held on this day.

30 F.—Latest date for depositing plans and books of reference in the Private Bill Office of the House of Commons and with Clerks of the Peace.

Latest date for Special Pleaders, Draftsmen in Equity, and Conveyancers in England to renew certificates. (*See* Oct. 30.)

December.

1 S.—Time expires for lodging declaration with Registrar of Solicitors for certificates.

Clerks of Union Assessment Committees to send in this month the totals of the gross estimated rental and rateable value of the property in the valuation lists of the several parishes to the Clerk or respective Clerks of the Council of the county or counties within which such parishes may be situate.

Chief Constables to transmit returns as to Constabulary force.

14 F.—Latest date for delivering notices, &c., to owners and occupiers affected by private bills.

Latest date for renewal of solicitors' certificates.

17 M.—Railway Companies to pay quarterly instalments of Income Tax on or before this date.

20 Th.—Clerk of the County Council to make up the "County Register," that is, the Register of County Electors for local government purposes, and also the Parochial Registers, so that it shall be completed before this date. It will come into force on the 1st January next. Michaelmas Law Sittings end.

21 F.—Common Councilmen in the City of London to be elected on this date.

Latest date for leaving petitions, declarations, &c., at Private Bill Office.

25 Tu.—Christmas Day. Quarter Day.

Medical officers of Unions entitled to be paid any extra fees, to make out their accounts quarterly to this date, and lay the same before the Guardians.

26 W.—Bank and General Holiday.

District Medical Officer to notify to the Board of Guardians at the commencement of this quarter the paupers whose names have been inserted in the permanent medical relief lists for a period of six months.

28 F.—Quarter Sessions to be held during the week following this date. (*See* Jan. 1.)

31 M.—Clerk of the Peace to deliver, on or before this date, County lists of voters to the Sheriff of the county, and Town Clerk to deliver Borough lists to the Returning Officer of the borough.

Railway Companies to prepare an annual abstract of receipts and expenditure for the year to this date, or some other convenient day in each year, and, if required, transmit a copy thereof, free of charge, to Overseers of parishes through which the railway runs.

Latest date for Assessment Clerks to send valuation returns to Clerks of the Peace.

Latest date for leaving estimates, lists of occupiers, &c., at Private Bill Office.

End of year for calculation of interest in Post Office Savings Banks.

End of the "official year" for the purposes of the Building Societies Act, 1894.

Annual Police Return to be made to Secretary of State as soon as possible after end of the year.

The following licences expire on this date :— Male servants, carriages, dogs, armorial bearings, and all "Establishment Licences."

. The following is an Index to the principal Articles or Paragraphs which, having appeared in the Almanack since its institution, have not been included in the present issue. Where the Article or Paragraph was repeated in two or more issues, the date given is that of the most recent edition in which it appeared.

BRADBURY, AGNEW & CO., LD., PRINTERS, LONDON AND TONBRIDGE.

INDEX TO ADVERTISEMENTS.

2

COST PRICE

LIFE

ASSURANCE.

A Guide to Offices yielding 3 and 4 per cent. (Compound Interest) on Ordinary and Endowment Policies respectively.

By T. G. ROSE.

SIXPENCE.

EFFINGHAM WILSON & CO.,

11, ROYAL EXCHANGE, E.C.

ALL BOOKSELLERS' AND BOOKSTALLS. [192

4

5

Literature.

EVERY SATURDAY,   Edited by H. D. TRAILL.
Price **6**d.   Published by THE TIMES.

A Weekly Journal devoted to International Literature.

TERMS OF SUBSCRIPTION.

	United Kingdom.		Abroad.
Three Months..	£0 7 1	....	£0 7 7
Six Months	0 14 1	....	0 15 2
Twelve Months	1 8 2	....	1 10 4

May be ordered of any Newsagent, or of the Publisher, THE TIMES *Office, E.C.*

The Times Atlas.

THE TIMES ATLAS consists of 118 pages of Maps, measuring 17 inches by 11 inches, and includes a large number of insets, making a total of 175 Maps.

The Index, consisting of about 130,000 names, has been compiled by a Fellow of the Royal Geographical Society, recommended by the late Secretary of the Society, and is believed to be more complete than any yet issued.

In accordance with the policy previously announced, THE TIMES ATLAS was carefully revised up to March, 1899. The constant advance in exploration, and the frequent changes resulting from political development made this task an exceedingly heavy one, but it has, nevertheless, been carried out with exceptional thoroughness. In this edition of the ATLAS, now issued from *The Times* Office, many alterations and additions have been made, including a new full-page map of NEW ZEALAND, with an inset map of TASMANIA, making a total of ONE HUNDRED AND EIGHTEEN pages. A SPECIAL INDEX to the new Map follows the last page of the General Index.

Many important additions have been made throughout the ATLAS. Many of the Maps have been added to and where necessary corrected, and various minor improvements effected.

The Prices of the ATLAS in its various forms are as follows, delivered post free within the United Kingdom:—

Bound in Cloth	**22s. 6d.**
Cloth, gilt edges	**23s. 0d.**
Half Morocco, very handsome, gilt edges ..	**26s. 0d.**

Orders may be given to any Bookseller, or may be sent direct to THE TIMES *Office, Printing House Square, London.*

NOTE.—The publication in Serial form of a New, Enlarged and Improved Edition of THE TIMES ATLAS commenced on October 24th, 1899, to be completed in 26 Weekly parts at 1s. each.

The Times

WEEKLY EDITION.

Every Friday.   *Price 2d.*

CONTAINS

A Careful Epitome of the Events of Interest during the Week

TOGETHER WITH

The Most Important LEADERS and SPECIAL ARTICLES from "THE TIMES" in extenso.

Parliament and Politics.	Trade, Money and Stocks.	Law and Police.
Colonial and Foreign News.	Ecclesiastical and Social Notes.	Home and Domestic Events.
Naval and Military Matters.	Reviews of Books.	Correspondence.

Chess by Special Expert.   News interesting to every class of reader.
And a Serial Work of Fiction.

May be had of all Newsagents.

TERMS OF SUBSCRIPTION.

	United Kingdom.		Abroad.
Three Months	2s. 9d.	....	3s. 3d.
Six Months	5s. 6d.	....	6s. 6d.
Twelve Months	11s. 0d.	....	13s. 0d.

Address THE PUBLISHER, Printing House Square, London, E.C. [174

CHATTO & WINDUS'S NEW BOOKS

THE SHIP: HER STORY. By W. CLARK RUSSELL. With 50 Illustrations by H. C. SEPPINGS WRIGHT. Small 4to, cloth, gilt top, 6s.

BOHEMIAN PARIS OF TO-DAY. Written by W. C. MORROW from Notes by EDOUARD CUCUEL. With 125 Illustrations by EDOUARD CUCUEL. Small 8vo, cloth, gilt top, 6s.

JUSTIN McCARTHY'S REMINIS-CENCES. SECOND EDITION (THIRD THOU-SAND). 2 Vols. Demy 8vo, cloth. With Portrait. 24s.

THINGS I HAVE SEEN IN WAR. By IRVING MONTAGU. With 16 Full-page Illustrations. Crown 8vo, cloth, 6s.

SOCIAL ENGLAND UNDER THE REGENCY. By JOHN ASHTON, Author of "Social Life in the Reign of Queen Anne." With 90 Illustrations. A NEW EDITION. Crown 8vo, cloth, gilt top, 6s.

The ANCIENT LEGENDS, MYSTIC CHARMS, AND SUPERSTITIONS OF IRELAND. With Sketches of the Irish Past. By Lady WILDE. A NEW EDITION. Crown 8vo, cloth, 3s. 6d.

LONDON SOUVENIRS: An Anti-quary's Note-Book. By C. W. HECKETHORN. Crown 8vo, cloth, gilt top, 6s.

THROUGH THE GOLD-FIELDS OF ALASKA TO BERING STRAITS. By HARRY DE WINDT. With Map and 33 Full-page Illustrations. A NEW EDITION. Demy 8vo, cloth, 6s.

JERUSALEM: The City of Herod and Saladin. By WALTER BESANT and E. H. PALMER. FOURTH EDITION. With a New Chapter, a Map, and 11 Illustrations. Small demy 8vo, cloth, 7s. 6d.

THE ORANGE GIRL. By Sir WALTER BESANT. With 8 Illustrations by FRED PEG-RAM. Crown 8vo, cloth, gilt top, 6s.

THE YOUNG MASTER OF HYSON HALL. By FRANK R. STOCKTON, Author of "Rudder Grange." With Illustrations by VIR-GINIA H. DAVISSON. Crown 8vo, cloth, 3s. 6d.

TERENCE. By B. M. CROKER, Author of "Beyond the Pale," &c. With Six Illustra-tions by SIDNEY PAGET. Crown 8vo, cloth, gilt top, 6s.

A CRIMSON CRIME. By GEO. MANVILLE FENN, Author of "A Fluttered Dovecote," &c. SECOND EDITION. Crown 8vo, cloth, 6s.

EUREKA. By OWEN HALL, Author of "The Track of a Storm," &c. Crown 8vo, cloth, gilt top, 6s.

AN ADVENTURESS. By L. T. MEADE, Author of "The Voice of the Charmer," &c. Crown 8vo, cloth, gilt top, 6s.

UNDER FALSE PRETENCES. By ADELINE SERGEANT, Author of "Dr. Endi-cott's Experiment," &c. THIRD EDITION. Crown 8vo, cloth, gilt top, 6s.

MRS. DUNBAR'S SECRET. By ALAN ST. AUBYN, Author of "The Old Maid's Sweetheart," &c. Crown 8vo, cloth, gilt top, 6s.

BRAVE MEN IN ACTION: Thrill-ing Stories of the British Flag. By STEPHEN J. McKENNA and JOHN AUGUSTUS O'SHEA. With Eight Illustrations by STANLEY L. WOOD. A NEW EDITION. Small demy 8vo, cloth, 5s.

LOVE'S DEPTHS. By GEORGES OH-NET. Translated by F. ROTHWELL. Crown 8vo, cloth, 3s. 6d.

A HONEYMOON'S ECLIPSE. By SARAH TYTLER, Author of "Mrs. Carmichael's Goddesses," &c. Crown 8vo, cloth, 3s. 6d.

A PLASTER SAINT. By ANNIE EDWARDES, Author of "Ought We to Visit Her," &c. Crown 8vo, cloth, 3s. 6d.

THE SIREN'S WEB: A Romance of London Society. By ANNIE THOMAS (Mrs. PENDER CUDLIP), Author of "Dennis Donne," &c. Crown 8vo, cloth, 3s. 6d.

South African Novels.

By BERTRAM MITFORD.
Crown 8vo, cloth, 3s. 6d. each.

THE GUN-RUNNER: A Romance of Zululand.

THE KING'S ASSEGAI.

The LUCK of GERARD RIDGELEY.

RENSHAW FANNING'S QUEST.

By ERNEST GLANVILLE.
Cr. 8vo, cloth, 3s. 6d. each; post 8vo, bds., 2s. each.

THE LOST HEIRESS: A Tale of Love, Battle, and Adventure.

THE FOSSICKER: A Romance of Mashonaland.

A FAIR COLONIST.

Crown 8vo, cloth, 3s. 6d. each.

THE GOLDEN ROCK.

TALES FROM THE VELD.

London: CHATTO & WINDUS, 111, St. Martin's Lane, W.C. [306

7

10

[301

Society for Promoting Christian Knowledge.

The Third and concluding volume of PROF. MASPERO'S great work on the
HISTORY of the ANCIENT PEOPLES of the CLASSIC EAST.

It is entitled—
"THE PASSING OF THE EMPIRES," 850 B.C.-330 B.C.

By Professor MASPERO. Edited by the Rev. Professor SAYCE, Translated by M. L. McCLURE. With Map, Three Coloured Plates, and Hundreds of Illustrations. Demy 4to, cloth boards, 25s.; half-morocco, gilt edges, 50s.

This Volume brings down the history of Egypt, Assyria, Babylonia, Persia, Media, etc., to the Victories of Alexander the Great. Among other things of interest to Bible Students, it deals with the circumstances attending the Captivities of Israel and Judah, and throws much light on the historic references in the Prophets.

THE HOLY GOSPELS.
With Illustrations from the Old Masters of the XIVth, XVth, and XVIth Centuries.

More than three hundred works, dealing exclusively with the events of our Lord's life, have been chosen from among the greatest examples of the Italian, German, Flemish and French Schools for the subject of these Illustrations. These Pictures, distributed, as they are, amongst the Churches and Galleries of the civilised world, are here for the first time collected together and presented in proximity to the Sacred Narrative which they were intended to illustrate. Notes dealing with the Pictures from the artistic standpoint are contributed by M. EUGENE MUNTZ, Member of the French Institute. The publication includes also a Chronological and Biographical Table of the Painters whose works are reproduced and a Classified List of the Engravings. The work contains 384 pages and over 350 illustrations, 48 of these being separate Plates printed in two tints. Half-bound, paste-grain roan, 47s. 6d.; whole-bound, paste-grain roan, 56s.

MATTER, ETHER, and MOTION. The Factors and Relations of Physical Science. By A. E. DOLBEAR, Ph.D. English Edition, edited by Professor ALFRED LODGE. Illustrated. Crown 8vo, cloth boards, 5s.

"Every page shows that the author is alive to the far-reaching consequences and implications of modern science."—*Literature.*

BRITISH BIRDS, SKETCH BOOK of. By R. BOWDLER SHARPE, LL.D., F.L.S. 272 pp., crown 4to. With Coloured Illustrations by A. F. and C. LYDON. Cloth boards, 14s.

"Briefly he has pronounced a most interesting and informing book, which has been admirably illustrated."—*Guardian.*

THE HISTORY OF INDIA. From the Earliest Times to the Present Day. By Captain L. J. TROTTER. Revised Edition, brought up to date. Demy 8vo, cloth boards, 6s.

THE ROMANCE OF SCIENCE.—OUR SECRET FRIENDS AND FOES. By PERCY FARADAY FRANKLAND, Ph.D., B.Sc.(Lond.), F.R.S. Fourth Edition, Revised and Enlarged, with several Illustrations. Small post 8vo, cloth boards, 3s.

** Eleven other Volumes have already appeared in this Series. List on application.

PAPERS AND ESSAYS. By the late Rev. GEORGE WILLIAM GENT, M.A. Edited by the Rev. JOHN HENRY BURN, B.D. With a Memoir by the Right Rev. E. S. TALBOT, D.D., Bishop of Rochester. Small post 8vo, cloth boards, 2s. 6d.

EARLY CHURCH CLASSICS. — BISHOP SARAPION'S PRAYER-BOOK. An Egyptian Pontifical, about A.D. 350. Translated from the Edition of Dr. G. WOBBERMIN, with Introduction and Notes, by JOHN WORDSWORTH, D.D., Bishop of Salisbury. Small post 8vo, cloth boards, 1s. 6d.

EARLY CHURCH CLASSICS. — THE EPISTLE OF ST. CLEMENT, BISHOP OF ROME. By the Rev. JOHN A. F. GREGG. Small post 8vo, cloth boards, 1s.

LONDON : NORTHUMBERLAND AVENUE, W.C. ;

43, QUEEN VICTORIA STREET, E.C. ; BRIGHTON : 129, NORTH STREET, [295

14

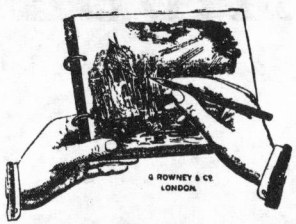

23

NATAL LINE OF STEAMERS.

LONDON TO NATAL DIRECT.

AND TAKING GOODS AND PASSENGERS FOR

DELAGOA BAY, BEIRA, CHINDE, &c.

The quickest and most direct service to JOHANNESBURG and PRETORIA.

CONGELLA.	UMFULI.	UMKUZI.	UMTALI.
PONGOLA.	UMGENI.	UMLAZI.	UMTATA.
UMBILO	UMHLOTI.	UMONA.	UMVOTI.
	UMZINTO.		

Sail every Fortnight from the East India Docks, calling alternately at Grand Canary (Las Palmas) and Teneriffe.

Also a Fortnightly Service, under contract with the Government of Natal, between Cape Colony, Natal, East Africa and India (Madras and Calcutta), calling at Ceylon, conveying goods and passengers; connecting at Calcutta a regular Through Service from China and Japan to South and East African Ports. Return Tickets issued to all Ports.

The Steamers of this Line have splendid amidship accommodation for Cabin Passengers at moderate rates, are fitted throughout with the electric light and bells, refrigerator, Ladies' Boudoir, Smoking Room, all modern appliances and a piano. High-class cuisine.

Surgeon and Stewardess carried. Saloons on Deck, of which inspection is invited by intending passengers. For freight or passage apply to the owners,

BULLARD, KING & CO., 14, St. Mary Axe, E.C.

AGENCIES:

BEIRA—SUTER & CO.	EAST LONDON—JAS. COUTTS.
CAPE TOWN—ATTWELL & CO.	CALCUTTA—ANDERSON, WRIGHT & CO.
DELAGOA BAY—L. COHEN & CO.	COLOMBO—DELMEGE, FORSYTH & CO.
JOHANNESBURG—KING & SONS.	HONG KONG, &c.—DODWELL & CO., LTD.
PORT ELIZABETH—KEITH & CO.	MADRAS—PARRY & CO.

Head Office for South Africa:—KING & SONS, Durban, Natal. [135

30

THE BANK OF ADELAIDE.

Incorporated by Act of Parliament, 1865.

Subscribed Capital	..	..	£500,000	**Reserve Fund** £165,000
Paid-up Capital	..	..	£400,000	**Reserve Liability of Shareholders** £600,000

Head Office—KING WILLIAM STREET, ADELAIDE.

DIRECTORS.

HENRY SCOTT, Esq., J.P., *Chairman.*

A. G. DOWNER, Esq. | JAMES HARVEY, Esq., J.P. | H. C. E. MUECKE, Esq., J.P.

The Honble. Sir JENKIN COLES, K.C.M.G.

JOHN SHIELS, *Manager.* R. S. YOUNG, *Accountant.*

BRANCHES.—Angaston (Agencies at Greenock, Nuriootpa and Truro), Caltowie (Agency at Georgetown), Gumeracha (Agency at Blumberg), Hammond (Agencies at Carrietown and Willowie), Hawker, Hindmarsh, Kapunda, Mannum, Mount Pleasant, Noarlunga (Agencies at Aldinga, McLaren Vale and Willunga), Port Adelaide, Port Augusta, Port Pirie (Agency at Crystal Brook), Quorn, Woodside (Agencies at Lobethal and Mount Torrens), Yankalilla, Yorketown (Agencies at Minlaton and Edithburg).

London Office—11, LEADENHALL STREET, E.C.

DIRECTORS—WILHELM LUND, Esq. ABRAHAM SCOTT, Esq.

PERCY ARNOLD, *Manager.* | ALEXANDER JOHNSTON, *Accountant.* | JOHN S. MURRAY, *Secretary.*

COLONIAL AGENTS.—IN VICTORIA:—The Colonial Bank of Australasia, Ltd.; The Bank of Victoria, Ltd. IN NEW SOUTH WALES:—The Commercial Banking Company of Sydney, Ltd. IN QUEENSLAND:—The Commercial Banking Company of Sydney, Ltd. IN WESTERN AUSTRALIA:—Western Australian Bank. IN NEW ZEALAND:—The Bank of New Zealand. IN FIJI:—Bank of New Zealand. IN TASMANIA:—The Commercial Bank of Tasmania, Ltd.

AGENTS AND CORRESPONDENTS.—IN ENGLAND:—Manchester and Liverpool District Banking Co., Ltd.; The Birmingham District and Counties Banking Co., Ltd.; The North Eastern Banking Co., Ltd.; S. Montague & Co.; Halifax Joint Stock Bank,Ltd.; The Bradford Old Bank, Ltd. IN SCOTLAND:—British Linen Company Bank; Union Bank of Scotland, Ltd. IN IRELAND:—Bank of Ireland. IN UNITED STATES AND CANADA:—Bank of Montreal; Bank of British North America; Bank of New York; First National Bank Chicago; Merchants Loan and Trust Company's Bank of Chicago; National Bank of North America; Union Trust Co. Bank, Chicago; also Zimmermann and Forshay, New York; IN SOUTH AFRICA:—Standard Bank of South Africa; the National Bank of the South African Republic. IN INDIA, CEYLON, CHINA, JAPAN, AND THE EAST:—Chartered Bank of India, Australia and China; National Bank of India, Ltd.; Credit Lyonnais, Nederlandsche Handel-Maatschappij. IN MAURITIUS:—Mauritius Commercial Bank. ON THE CONTINENT, &c.:—Credit Lyonnais, Paris and Branches; Deutsche Bank, Germany; Anglo-Egyptian Bank; Bank of Antwerp, Credito Italiano; Dresdner Bank, Germany; Credit Franco-Portugais, Lisbon; Niederosterreichische Escompte-Gesellschaft,Vienna; J. Betschen, Interlaken:—Banque Populaire Inter'aken : Banques d'Athens, Athens.

Drafts and Letters of Credit granted, and telegraphic remittances made.

Bills on the Colonies purchased or collected, and every other description of Banking and Exchange business transacted.

[207

The BANK OF AFRICA, Limited

Established 1879.

Incorporated under the Companies Acts, 1862 to 1877.

SUBSCRIBED CAPITAL, £2,250,000. In Shares of £18 15s. each.
PAID-UP AND CALLED, £750,000. RESERVE FUND, £463,000.

Head Office—No. 113, CANNON STREET, LONDON, E.C.

Branches.

CAPE COLONY.—Aliwal North, Cape Town, Cradock, East London, Grahamstown, Kimberley, King William's Town, Oudtshoorn, Paarl, Port Elizabeth, Queenstown. ORANGE FREE STATE.—Bethlehem, Bloemfontein, Fauresmith, Harrismith, Kroonstad, Ladybrand, Winburg. NATAL.—Durban, Durban Point, Pietermaritzburg. TRANSVAAL.—Barberton, Johannesburg, Pretoria, Vrijheid. EAST AFRICA.—Beira, Lourenço Marques. RHODESIA—Bulawayo, Salisbury, Umtali.

Board of Directors.

W. FLEMING BLAINE, Esq., *Chairman.*

A. BARSDORF, Esq. | A. A. FRASER, Esq.
A. CHAMBERLAIN, Esq., M.P. | ROCHFORT MAGUIRE, Esq.
OWEN R. DUNELL, Esq. | JOHN YOUNG, Esq.

General Manager (Resident at Cape Town)—JAMES SIMPSON.

Secretary—R. G. DAVIS.

Letters of Credit and Drafts issued.

Bills purchased and collected, and all other banking business transacted.

Remittances made by Telegraph.

The purchase and Sale undertaken of Colonial Government and other securities.

Deposits received for one, two or three years, at rates which may be ascertained on application.

[57

32

THE BRITISH BANK OF SOUTH AMERICA LTD.

Subscribed Capital, £1,000,000, in 50,000 Shares of £20 each, with power to increase.
Paid-up Capital, £500,000.   Reserve Fund, £320,000.

Head Office: 2a, MOORGATE STREET, LONDON E.C.

DIRECTORS.

HUGH KINSMAN BRODIE.
CHARLES CARRINGTON, Esq.
JOHN CONRAD IM THURN, Esq.

FREDERIC LUBBOCK, Esq.
FREDERICK WILLIAM LUNAU.
RICHARD HATT NOBLE, Esq.

ROSS PINSENT, Esq.

Manager—ALEXANDER DICK-CUNYNGHAM, Esq.
Sub-Manager—HENRY KIMBER GREGORY, Esq.
Secretary—WILLIAM HERBERT HOLLIS, Esq.

AUDITORS.

FREDERICK JOHN YOUNG, Esq.   FRANCIS MACKENZIE OGILVY, Esq.
PETER STEELE NICOLSON, Esq.

BANKERS.—**London**—THE BANK OF ENGLAND; LONDON JOINT STOCK BANK, Limited.
Paris—Messrs. HEINE & Co. **Hamburg**—Messrs. JOH. BERENBERG, GOSSLER & Co. **Portugal**—
BANK OF PORTUGAL. **Italy**—ROESTI & Co. **Spain**—Messrs. E. SAINZ e HIJOS.

BRANCHES.—RIO DE JANEIRO, SANTOS, SAÕ PAULO, BAHIA, PARA, BUENOS AYRES, ROSARIO
DE SANTA FÉ, and MONTE VIDEO.

AGENT IN NEW YORK—BANK OF NEW YORK, N.B.A.

Bills Negotiated, Advanced upon and sent for Collection.   Letters of Credit, Drafts and
Cable Transfers issued. [63

BRITISH MUTUAL BANKING COMPANY, Limited,
LUDGATE CIRCUS, LONDON, E.C.

Telegraphic Address—"BRIMFUL, LONDON."

CAPITAL £200,000, IN 40,000 SHARES OF £5 EACH.

DIRECTORS.

JOHN VIRET GOOCH, Esq., *Chairman.*
THOS. C. DEWEY, Esq.

SIR HENRY HARBEN.
EDGAR HORNE, Esq.

WM. E. HORNE, Esq.
T. WHARRIE, Esq.

Manager—EDWARD LEONARD.

Current Accounts are kept in conformity with the practice of London Bankers.   Interest *being
allowed on the minimum monthly balances of £50 and upwards at the rate of 2 per cent. per
annum, and credited to the Accounts half-yearly, on the 30th of June and 31st of December.*
No charge is made for keeping Accounts where a remunerative Balance is kept.
Present rate of Interest on Deposits 2½ per cent. per annum. [78

THE COLONIAL BANK.
(*Established and Incorporated by Royal Charter in* 1836.)

Subscribed Capital, £2,000,000, in 100,000 Shares of £20 each.
Paid-up, £600,000.   Reserve Fund, £150,000.

London Office: 13, BISHOPSGATE STREET WITHIN,

Secretary—GORDON WM. TURNER.   *Bankers*—LLOYDS' BANK, Limited.

Branches and Agencies.

ANTIGUA.
BARBADOS.
BERBICE.
DEMERARA.
DOMINICA.
GRENADA.
MARTINIQUE (Agency).

ST. KITT'S.
JAMAICA—KINGSTON.
And Agencies at—
FALMOUTH.
MONTEGO BAY.
SAVANNA-LA-MAR.

ST. CROIX.
ST. LUCIA.
ST. VINCENT.
ST. THOMAS.
TRINIDAD—PORT OF SPAIN.
SAN FERNANDO (Agency).

New York Agency—41, Wall Street.

LETTERS OF CREDIT, payable on demand, are granted on the several Establishments in the Colonies upon
payment of the amount at the London office.   **BILLS** are sent out for collection, and other monetary business transacted
in the above-named Colonies. [81

35

THE CAPITAL AND COUNTIES BANK, LIMITED.

Established 1834.

Subscribed Capital, £5,000,000. Paid-up Capital, £1,000,000. Reserve Fund, £750,000.

Directors.

MARQUIS OF AILESBURY.	HENRY KIMBER, Esq., M.P.
H. W. COBB, Esq.	W. A. LOMER, Esq.
Sir LIONEL E. DARELL, Bart.	EDWARD BAVERSTOCK MERRIMAN, Esq.
WILLIAM GARFIT, Esq., M.P.	WILLIAM REDMAN, Esq.
Sir GABRIEL GOLDNEY, Bart.	JOSIAH T. SMITH, Esq.
EDWIN HENTY, Esq.	WILLIAM WILLIAMS, Esq.

HEAD OFFICE—39, THREADNEEDLE STREET, LONDON.

G. A. HARVEY } *Joint General Managers.* R. C. HENDERSON, *City Manager.*
E. D. VAISEY } J. J. MACDONALD, *Chief Accountant.*
ARCHIBALD F. SIMPSON, *Chief Inspector of Branches.* | FRANK W. ROSE, *Secretary.*

Metropolitan Branches.

Covent Garden, 35, King Street, W.C.	Paddington, 195, Edgware Road, W.
Fore Street, 115, Fore Street, E.C.	Piccadilly, 35, Piccadilly, W.
Islington, 50, Upper Street, N.	Shoreditch, 145, High Street, E.
Ludgate Hill, 25, Ludgate Hill, E.C.	St. George's-in-the-East, 216, Commercial
Newington, 151 & 153, Newington Causeway, S.E.	Road, E.
Oxford Street, 125, Oxford Street, W.	Westminster, 89 & 90, York Street, S.W.

Current Accounts opened in London on Terms usual among London Bankers.

Deposit Receipts issued in London, and Interest allowed at rates as advertised from time to time.

At the Country Branches, Current and Deposit Accounts opened, Deposit Receipts and Drafts issued, and all other Banking business transacted on the usual terms.

Dividends and Coupons collected. Investments in and Sales of Home and Foreign Securities effected. Moneys received and advised for customers free of charge between all the offices.

Circular Notes and Letters of Credit are issued payable in the principal Cities and Towns of the Continent, and Letters of Credit are also issued payable in America, New Zealand, Australia and elsewhere.

The Agency of Foreign and Country Banks is undertaken.

The Officers of the Bank are bound to secrecy.

[65

Chartered Bank of India, Australia and China.

HATTON COURT, THREADNEEDLE STREET, LONDON.

Incorporated by Royal Charter.

CAPITAL, £800,000.   RESERVE FUND, £500,000.

COURT OF DIRECTORS, 1899-1900.

ALEXANDER PATRICK CAMERON, Esq.	HENRY NEVILLE GLADSTONE, Esq.
WILLIAM CHRISTIAN, Esq.	JOHN HOWARD GWYTHER, Esq.
Sir HENRY STEWART CUNNINGHAM, K.C.I.E.	EMILE LEVITA, Esq.
Sir ALFRED DENT, K.C.M.G.	JASPER YOUNG, Esq.

Joint Managers { WM. A. MAIN.
CALEB LEWIS.

AGENCIES AND BRANCHES:

BOMBAY.	THAIPING.	BATAVIA.	TIENTSIN.
CALCUTTA.	MEDAN (Deli, Sumatra).	SOURABAYA.	HANKOW.
RANGOON.	SINGAPORE.	HONGKONG.	MANILA.
COLOMBO.	BANGKOK.	FOOCHOW.	ILOILO.
PENANG.	KWALA LUMPOR.	SHANGHAI.	YOKOHAMA.
			KOBE.

BANKERS:

THE BANK OF ENGLAND. | THE LONDON CITY & MIDLAND BANK, Ltd

THE NATIONAL BANK OF SCOTLAND, Limited.

The Corporation buy and receive for collection Bills of Exchange; grant Drafts payable at the above Agencies and Branches; and transact general banking business connected with the East.

Deposits of money are received at rates which may be ascertained on application. [10

THE
COMMERCIAL BANKING COMPANY OF SYDNEY,
LIMITED.

Established 1834. Incorporated 1893.

CAPITAL SUBSCRIBED, £2,000,000.   PAID UP, £1,000,000.
RESERVE FUND, £1,010,000.

Sydney Board: HEAD OFFICE, SYDNEY, NEW SOUTH WALES.

Sir EDWARD KNOX, *Chairman.* | The Hon. H. E. KATER, M.L.C. | Hon. RICHARD JONES. M.L.C.
G. J. COHEN, Esq., *Deputy-Chairman.* | The Hon. H. MOSES, M.L.C. | T. A. DIBBS, *General Manager.*

London Board: OFFICE, 18, BIRCHIN LANE, LOMBARD STREET.

Sir JAMES ARNDELL YOUL, K.C.M.G. | F. H. DANGAR, Esq.
B. W. LEVY, Esq. | Hon. HENRY S. LITTLETON.

NATHANIEL CORK, *Manager.*

BRANCHES IN SYDNEY.—Eastern-Oxford Street. Exchange.—Pitt Street North, George Street West, King Street, Newtown, Paddington, Pitt and Bathurst Streets, Redfern, Southern-Haymarket, St. Leonards—North Sydney, Waterloo and Alexandria.

BRANCHES IN NEW SOUTH WALES.—Albury, Armidale, Ballina, Barraba, Bathurst, Bega, Bellingen, Berrigan, Berry, Bingara, Blayney, Bombala, Bourke, Bowral, Braidwood, Brewarrina, Camden, Campbelltown, Candelo, Canowindra, Carcoar, Casino, Chatswood, Cobar, Condobolin, Cooma, Coonamble, Cootamundra, Coraki, Corowa, Cowra, Cudal, Delegate, Dubbo, Dungog, Finley, Forbes, Germanton, Glen Innes, Goulburn, Grafton, Granville, Gundagai, Gunnedah, Gunning, Hay, Inverell, Kempsey, Kiama, Lismore, Lithgow, Liverpool, Lockhart, Maclean, Maitland, Manilla, Milton, Mittagong, Molong, Moree, Morpeth, Moruya, Moss Vale, Mudgee, Murrumburrah, Murrurundi, Murwillumbah, Mussellbrook, Narandera Narrabri, Narramine, Newcastle, Nowra, Nymagee, Nyngan, Orange, Parkes, Parramatta, Paterson, Penrith, Picton, Port Macquarie, Queanbeyan, Quirindi, Raymond Terrace, Richmond, Robertson, Shellharbour, Singleton, Tamworth, Taree, Tocumwal, Tumut, Wagga Wagga, Walcha, Walgett, Wallerawang, Warialda, Warren, Wee Waa, Wellington, Wilcannia, Windsor, Wingham, Wollongong, Yass, Young.

BRANCHES IN QUEENSLAND.—Brisbane, Bundaberg, Charleville, Childers, Cunnamulla, Dalby, Emerald, Fortitude Valley, Geraldton, Gladstone, Ingham, Longreach, Mackay, Maryborough, Rockhampton, Thargomindah, Toowoomba and Townsville.

The London Board of Directors grant Letters of Credit, payable on demand, and Bills of Exchange, upon all the branches of this Bank and cable Remittances. They also negotiate approved Bills upon the Australian Colonies, send out Bills for Collection, and transact every description of Banking Business with Australia through the above-named establishments of the Bank in New South Wales and Queensland, and its Agents in Victoria, South Australia, Western Australia, Tasmania and New Zealand.

No. 18, Birchin Lane, Lombard Street, E.C.   NATHANIEL CORK, *Manager.*   [200

COMPTOIR NATIONAL D'ESCOMPTE DE PARIS.
(FRENCH BANK.)

CAPITAL 100,000,000 francs .. £4,000,000.

Chairman—M. DENORMANDIE (late Governor of the Banque de France).
General Manager—M. ALEXIS ROSTAND.

HEAD OFFICE: 14, RUE BERGÈRE.

Principal Branch Office (Letter of Credit Department), 2, PLACE DE L'OPERA, PARIS.
Nineteen other Branches in various parts of Paris.

Suburban Branches { LEVALLOIS-PERRET, 3, *Place de la République.*
{ ENGHIEN-LES-BAINS, 47, *Grande Rue.*
{ ASNIERES, 8, *Rue de Paris.*

London Branch: 52, THREADNEEDLE STREET, E.C.
Manager—ERNEST LAZARUS.

Manchester Branch: 61, KING STREET.
Liverpool Branch: BANK CHAMBERS, CASTLE STREET.

Agencies in France:

Abbeville, Agen, Aix-en-Provence, Alais, Amiens, Angoulême, Arles, Avignon, Bagnères-de-Luchon, Bagnols-sur-Cèze, Beaucaire, Beaune, Bergerac, Béziers, Bordeaux, Bourboule (La), Caen, Calais, Cannes, Carcassonne, Castres, Cavaillon, Cette, Chagny, Chalon-sur-Saone, Chateaurenard, Clermont-Ferrand, Cognac, Condé-sur-Noireau, Dax, Dieppe, Dijon, Dunkerque, Elbeuf, Épinal, Firminy, Ferté-Macé (La), Flers, Gray, Havre (Le), Hazebrouck, Issoire, Jarnac, Lézignan, Libourne, Limoges, Luxeuil, Lyon, Manosque, Mans (Le), Marseille, Mazamet, Mont de Marsan, Mont Dore (Le), Montpellier, Nantes, Narbonne, Nice, Nîmes, Orange, Périgueux, Perpignan, Pont l'Evique, Remiremont, Rivesaltes, Roanne, Roubaix, Rouen, Royat, Saint-Chamond, Saint-Dié, Saint Etienne, Salon, Toulouse, Tourcoing, Trouville-Deauville, Vichy, Villefranche-sur-Saône, Villeneuve-sur-Lot, Vire.

(England) London, Manchester, Liverpool; (Africa) Tunis, Siax, Sousse, Gabés, Tanger; (Madagascar) Majunga, Tamatave, Tananarive, (Australia) Melbourne, Sydney; (U.S.A.) San Francisco, New Orleans; (India) Bombay, Calcutta.

The Bank conducts banking business of every description, upon terms to be ascertained at the Office.   [201

37

HONGKONG & SHANGHAI BANKING CORPORATION

*Incorporated by Special Ordinance of the Legislative Council of Hongkong, 20th July, 1867,
and confirmed by Her Majesty's Government.*

CAPITAL (All paid up) - - - - $10,000,000
RESERVE FUND $11,000,000.

*Of which $10,000,000 at Exchange of 2s. per $ = £1,000,000 Sterling, invested in Consols and other
Sterling Securities, which are held in London.*

RESERVE LIABILITY OF PROPRIETORS, $10,000,000.

Head Office and Board of Directors at HONGKONG.

Chief Manager........Sir THOMAS JACKSON.

Committee in London.

WM. ANASTASIUS JONES, Esq. (Director, London and County Banking Company, Ltd.)
F. D. BARNES, Esq. (Managing Director, Peninsular and Oriental Steam Navigation Company.)
G. E. NOBLE, Esq., 37, Inverness Terrace, Bayswater, W.

Managers in London.—EWEN CAMERON and JOHN WALTER.

Acting Sub-Manager.—H. T. S. GREEN.

London Bankers.—THE LONDON & COUNTY BANKING COMPANY, Limited.

Branches and Agencies.

AMOY—BANGKOK—BATAVIA—BOMBAY—CALCUTTA—COLOMBO—FOOCHOW—HAMBURG—HANKOW—
HIOGO—LONDON—LYONS—MANILA—NAGASAKI—NEW YORK—PEKING—PENANG—RANGOON—
SAIGON—SAN FRANCISCO—SHANGHAI—SINGAPORE—SOURABAYA—TIENTSIN—YLOILO—YOKOHAMA.

Drafts granted upon, and Bills negotiated or collected at any of the Branches or Agencies.

Letters of Credit and Circular Notes issued for the use of Travellers negotiable in the principal
Cities of Europe, Asia, Africa, Australia and America.

Deposits received for fixed periods at rates which can be ascertained on application.

Current accounts opened for the convenience of Constituents returning from China, Japan
and India.

The Agency of Constituents connected with the East undertaken. Indian and other Government Securities received for safe custody, and Interest and Dividends on the same collected as
they fall due.

Dividends on the Shares of the Corporation payable in London, on receipt of advice of the
meetings held in Hongkong in February and August in each year.

31, LOMBARD STREET, LONDON. *October*, 1899. [199

BANK OF LIVERPOOL Limtd.
LIVERPOOL, ENGLAND.

Established 1831.

**Subscribed Capital, £8,000,000. Paid-up Capital, £1,000,000.
Reserved Surplus Fund, £588,532.**

DIRECTORS.

HAROLD CUNNINGHAM, *Chairman.*	HUGH H. HORNBY, J.P., *Deputy Chairman.*
THOMAS BROCKLEBANK, J.P.	HELENUS R. ROBERTSON.
Sir W. B. FORWOOD, J.P.	WM. P. SINCLAIR, J.P.
R. D. HOLT, J.P.	H. L. SMYTH, J.P.
CHAS. LANGTON, J.P.	W. H. TATE, J.P.
A. T PARKER.	J. M. WOOD.

General Manager—J. H. SIMPSON. *Assistant General Manager*—JAMES MACDONALD.
Manager, Head Office—GEO. T. ADDIS.

London Agents—GLYN, MILLS, CURRIE & CO.; BARCLAY & CO., Ltd.; WILLIAMS,
DEACON & MANCHESTER & SALFORD BANK, Ltd.; and ROBARTS, LUBBOCK & CO.

Current and Deposit Accounts opened for Customers residing at home or abroad.
Interest allowed on sums remaining for one month at the rates for the time being of the
leading London Joint Stock Banks.

The Bank acts as Agent for Home and Foreign Banks, and through its Foreign
connection offers facilities for the transfer of money by cable.

Customers going abroad can have dividends received to their credit, and payments
attended to, during their absence; and documents of value may be left with the Bank
for safe custody, at the customer's risk. [66

49

LONDON & BRAZILIAN BANK, Limited.

CAPITAL, £1,500,000, in 75,000 Shares of £20 each.
PAID-UP CAPITAL, £750,000.   RESERVE FUND, £600,000.

Head Office: 7, TOKENHOUSE YARD, LONDON, E.C.

DIRECTORS.

Chairman—Hon. PASCOE CHARLES GLYN.   *Deputy Chairman*—CHARLES EDWARD JOHNSTON, Esq.

JOHN BEATON, Esq. (*Managing Director*).	WILLIAM WILTON PHIPPS, Esq.
EDWARD LONSDALE BECKWITH, Esq.	CHARLES DAY ROSE, Esq.
CHARLES SEYMOUR GRENFELL, Esq.	EDMUND D. SCHLUTER, Esq.
WILLIAM DOURO HOARE, Esq.	

JOHN GORDON, Esq., *Manager.*

BANKERS.
London: BANK OF ENGLAND; Messrs. GLYN, MILLS, CURRIE & Co.
Paris: Messrs. MALLET FRÈRES & Co.
Hamburg: Messrs. SCHRÖDER & Co.; JOH. BERENBERG, GOSSLER & Co.

BRANCHES.
Brazil—Rio de Janeiro, Pará, Pernambuco, Bahia, Santos, São Paulo, Campinas (Agency), Rio Grande do Sul, Pelotas, Porto Alegre. **River Plate**—Monte Video, Buenos Ayres, Rosario. **New York** (Agency). **Portugal**—Lisbon, Oporto.

CORRESPONDENTS.

The Bank has Agents in the principal Ports and Cities of the United States, Brazil, Uruguay, Argentina, and Portugal.

The Directors of this Bank grant Drafts on the Branches and negotiate or collect Bills payable at the above places on the most favourable terms.

They also issue Letters of Credit for the use of travellers in Brazil, the River Plate, and Portugal.

They undertake the Agency of parties connected with these countries; make Investments in the Public Funds, and other British and Foreign Securities; and receive Dividends and Interests free of charge to constituents.

Current Accounts opened at the Branches, where Money is also received on Deposit at rates of Interest varying according to the length of time for which the Deposit is made.

For further particulars apply at the Bank, 7, **TOKENHOUSE YARD**. Office hours, 10 to 4; Saturdays 10 to 1.   [70

LONDON & COUNTY BANKING COMPANY, Limited.

REGISTERED UNDER "THE COMPANIES ACTS." ESTABLISHED IN 1836.

CAPITAL £8,000,000, IN 100,000 SHARES OF £80 EACH.

PAID-UP CAPITAL ....£2,000,000 | **RESERVE FUND**................£1,275,000

DIRECTORS.

HANBURY BARCLAY, Esq.	WILLIAM EGERTON HUBBARD, Esq.
JOHN ANNAN BRYCE, Esq.	WILLIAM ANASTASIUS JONES, Esq.
JOHN JAMES CATER, Esq.	EDWARD HARBORD LUSHINGTON, Esq.
JOHN GREEN, Esq.	WILLIAM McKEWAN, Esq., *Honorary Director.*
CHARLES SEYMOUR GRENFELL, Esq.	WILLIAM GAIR RATHBONE, Esq.
WILLIAM JAMES HARTER, Esq.	JAMES DUNCAN THOMSON, Esq.
WILLIAM HOWARD, Esq.	

Auditors—ERNEST H. CUNARD, Esq., HENRY GRANT, Esq., THOMAS HORWOOD, ESQ.

Head Office Manager—HENRY DEAN.   *Deputy Head Office Manager*—GEORGE JOHN KODCLPH.

Country Manager—J. B. JAMES.   *Chief Inspector*—HENRY JOSLIN LEMON.

Chief Accountant—WILLIAM HALL   *Secretary*—JOHN HARRISON ATKINSCN.

Solicitors—Messrs. HARRIES, WILKINSON and RAIKES.

HEAD OFFICE—21, LOMBARD STREET.

THE LONDON AND COUNTY BANKING COMPANY, LIMITED,

Opens DRAWING ACCOUNTS with Commercial Houses and Private Individuals, upon the plan usually adopted by Bankers.

DEPOSIT ACCOUNTS.—Deposit Receipts are issued for sums of Money placed upon these Accounts, and Interest is allowed for such periods and at such rates as may be agreed upon, reference being had to the state of the Money Market.

CIRCULAR NOTES AND LETTERS OF CREDIT are issued payable in the principal Cities and Towns of the Continent. Letters of Credit are also issued payable in Australia, Canada, India, China, the United States, and elsewhere.

The *Agency* of Fore gn and Country Banks is undertaken.

The *Purchase and Sale* of Government and other Stocks, also of English and Foreign Shares are effected. *Dividends, Annuities, &c.,* are received for Customers of the Bank.

Great facilities are afforded to the Customers of the Bank for the receipt of money both from and in the Towns where the Company has Branches.

The Officers of the Bank are bound not to disclose the transactions of any of its Customers.

By Order of the Directors,

J. H. ATKINSON, *Secretary.*   [69

London & San Francisco Bank,

LIMITED.

Authorised Capital, 100,000 Shares of £7 each, £700,000.
Subscribed and Fully paid up, 70,000 Shares of £7 each, £490,000.

HEAD OFFICE: 71, LOMBARD STREET, LONDON, E.C.

Directors.

HENRY GOSCHEN, Esq.
CHARLES HEMERY, Esq.
BENDIX KOPPEL, Esq.

WILLIAM NEWBOLD, Esq.
ROBERT RYRIE, Esq.
ARTHUR SCRIVENER, Esq.

NORMAN DUNNING RIDEOUT, Esq. (San Francisco).
Manager—G. S. HEIN, Esq.   Secretary—D. HATCHER, Esq.

Bankers.

THE BANK OF ENGLAND. | THE LONDON JOINT STOCK BANK, LIMTD.
Auditors—TURQUAND, YOUNGS & CO.

BRANCHES.

SAN FRANCISCO, CALIFORNIA; PORTLAND, OREGON; TACOMA, WASHINGTON.

Agents at New York—Messrs. J. P. MORGAN & Co.

Usual Banking and Exchange Business, and the Agency of Foreign Banks undertaken at the Head Office in London.

The Branches in the United States of America transact every description of Banking Business throughout the Pacific States; Drafts and Cable Transfers granted on them.

Commercial Credits and Letters of Credit for Travellers issued, available in all principal cities of the world.

71, LOMBARD STREET, LONDON, E.C.   [263

LONDON & SOUTH WESTERN BANK LIMITED.

AUTHORISED CAPITAL, £3,000,000.   SUBSCRIBED CAPITAL, £2,000,000.
PAID-UP CAPITAL ...   £800,000.   RESERVE FUND ... ... £660,000.

Head Office: 170, FENCHURCH STREET, E.C.

London Branches:—

Acton, Addiscombe, Anerley, Balham, Barnes, Battersea, Battersea Park, Belgravia, Bermondsey, Bloomsbury, Bow, Brixton Hill, Brixton(North), Brixton (South), Brondesbury, Camberwell, Camden Town, Catford, Charlton, Chelsea, Chiswick, Clapham Clapham Junction, Clapton, Clerkenwell, Cricklewood, Crofton Park, Brockley, Croydon, Croydon (South), Dulwich, Dulwich (East), Ealing, Ealing Dean, Earl's Court, East Ham, Finsbury, Finsbury Park, Fleet Street, Forest Gate, Forest Hill, Fulham, Great Portland Street, Hackney, Hammersmith, Hampstead, Hampstead (South), Harlesden, Harrow Road, Highgate, Holland Park, Holloway, Hornsey, Ilford, Kennington, Kentish Town, Kew Bridge, Kilburn, Lavender Hill, Leyton, Merton and South Wimbledon, Mile End, Minories, Mortlake, New Cross, New Cross Gate, Norwood (South), Norwood (Upper), Norwood (West), Notting Hill, Oxford Street, Peckham, Poplar, Putney, Regent Street, St. John's Wood, Shepherd's Bush, Shoreditch, Southwark, Stepney, Stockwell, Strand, Streatham, Streatham Common, Stroud Green, Sydenham, Tooting, Tulse Hill, Upton Park, Vauxhall, Walham Green, Walthamstow (Hoe Street), Walthamstow (St. James Street), Walworth, Wandsworth, West Brompton, West Kensington, Willesden Green, Wimbledon, Wimbledon Common.

Sub-Branches:—Bushey (to Watford), Edgware (to Finchley, Church End), Honiton (to Ottery St. Mary), Stanmore (to Harrow), Wembley (to Harrow), Whetstone (to Finchley, Church End).

Country Branches:—Barking, Brighton, Bristol, East Molesey, Finchley (Church End), Finchley (East), Hanwell-Elthorne, Harrow, Hendon, Kingston-on-Thames, New Barnet, New Malden, Norbiton, Ottery St. Mary, Richmond, Sidmouth, Sutton, Twickenham, Wallington and Carshalton, Walton-on-Thames, Wanstead, Watford.

Every Description of Banking Business Transacted.

Joint General Managers .. .. JOHN WILLIAMS & ROBERT WOODHAMS.
Head Office Manager .. .. .. F. LUBBOCK JERMYN.
Chief Inspector .. JOHN A. ANDERSON.   Secretary .. HERBERT POTTER. [68

THE LONDON BANK OF AUSTRALIA, LIMITED.

SUBSCRIBED CAPITAL ... £1,645,020 | **PAID-UP** £914,915
UNCALLED, including Reserve Liability, £730,105.

LONDON OFFICE: 2, OLD BROAD STREET, CITY.

BOARD OF DIRECTORS.

Chairman—Sir JAMES FRANCIS GARRICK, Q.C., K.C.M.G.

Sir W. FOSTER, M.P. | ROBERT LANDALE, Esq. | ROBERT ROME, Esq.
A. C. GARRICK, Esq. | GEO. MILLER, Esq. | NICOL BROWN WATSON, Esq.

Secretary—W. N. TOMKINS. *Accountant*—F. J. CURTIS.

Auditors—Messrs. PRICE, WATERHOUSE & Co.
Bankers—BANK OF ENGLAND and LLOYDS' BANK, Limited.

ESTABLISHMENTS IN AUSTRALIA.

Inspector & General Manager—CHARLES GUTHRIE. *Branch Inspectors*—WM. REID, J. L. BALLANTYNE.
BRANCHES IN VICTORIA—**Melbourne:** also at 90, Bourke Street; 225, Swanston Street, and Flinders Street, Melbourne.

Other Branches in Victoria—Ararat, Ballarat, Ballarat East, Beeac (Ondit), Bendigo, Carisbrook (Agency), Carlton, Clifton Hill, Clunes, Dunolly, Echuca, Fitzroy, Geelong, Gordon, Horsham, Kerang, Majorca (Agency), Maldon, Maryborough, Northcote, St. Arnaud, Stawell, Swan Hill, with Agency at Lake Boga, Talbot, Wangaratta, Warragul.

IN NEW SOUTH WALES—**Sydney:** also at 192, Pitt Street, 62, Oxford Street, 198, Sussex Street, and Haymarket, Sydney and at Bourke, Broken Hill, Deniliquin, Goulburn, Hay, Newcastle, Wilcannia.

IN QUEENSLAND—**Brisbane,** Charters Towers, Townsville.

CORRESPONDENTS IN THE UNITED KINGDOM.

England—Lloyds' Bank, Ltd., and Branches, London and Provincial Bank and Branches.
Scotland—National Bank of Scotland and Branches.
Ireland—National Bank and Branches, and Ulster Bank, Limited.

Circular Notes are issued in sums of £10 and £20, negotiable by correspondents in the chief Cities of the Continent of Europe, North and South America, Africa and the East.

Letters of Credit and Drafts are granted on the foregoing Branches of the Bank. Bills negotiated or sent for collection. Telegraphic Transfers made, and Banking Business of every description transacted with the Australian Colonies.

Deposits received for fixed periods on terms which may be ascertained on application. [262

THE LONDON JOINT STOCK BANK LIMITED.

Established 1836. Registered 30th September 1882.
Subscribed Capital, £12,000,000. Paid-up Capital, £1,800,000. Guarantee Fund, £1,200,000.

	DIRECTORS.	
WILLIAM R. ARBUTHNOT, Esq.	The Right Hon. Lord HARLECH.	WILLIAM MÜLLER, Esq.
Sir EDWARD BLOUNT, K.C.B.	FRANCIS J. JOHNSTON, Esq.	E. M. RODOCANACHI, Esq.
WILLIAM T. BRAND, Esq.	HENRY J. JOURDAIN, Esq., C.M.G.	THOMAS RUDD, Esq.
JAMES DICKSON, Esq.	Sir ANDREW LUSK, Bart.	ROBERT RYRIE, Esq.
HOWARD GILLIAT, Esq.	DANIEL MEINERTZHAGEN, Esq.	HENRY WM. SEGELCKE, Esq.
ALEXANDER H. GOSCHEN, Esq.	FREDERICK MÜLLER, Esq.	JAMES STERN, Esq.
PAUL HARDY, Esq.		

Head Office—5, Princes Street, Mansion House, E.C.

LOTHBURY OFFICE, 6, Lothbury.
OLD BROAD STREET BRANCH, 55, Old Broad St.
LEADENHALL ST. BRANCH, 144, Leadenhall St.
FENCHURCH STREET BRANCH, 44, Fenchurch St.
LIMEHOUSE BRANCH, 680, Commercial Rd. East.
GREAT TOWER ST. BRANCH, 94, Great Tower St.
FINSBURY BRANCH, 17, Finsbury Pavement (*temporary premises*).
WOOD STREET BRANCH, 113, Wood Street.
CHARTERHOUSE ST. BRANCH, 89, Charterhouse St.
CHANCERY LANE BRANCH, 123, Chancery Lane.
RUSSELL SQUARE BRANCH, 1, Woburn Place.
OXFORD STREET BRANCH, 52, Oxford Street.
REGENT STREET BRANCH, 75, Regent Street.
PALL MALL BRANCH, 69, Pall Mall.
WESTMINSTER BRANCH, 22, Victoria Street.
VICTORIA BRANCH, 137, Buckingham Palace Rd.

ONSLOW SQUARE BRANCH, 1, Sydney Place.
SOUTH KENSINGTON BRANCH, 5, Bank Buildings, Gloucester Road.
PADDINGTON BRANCH, 2, Craven Road.
MARYLEBONE BRANCH, 15, Wigmore Street.
SOUTHWARK BRANCH, 28, Borough High Street.
MUSWELL HILL BRANCH, 11, Station Parade.
TOOTING BRANCH, The Broadway.
PECKHAM BRANCH, 69, High St. *Sub-Branch*—East Dulwich (52, Lordship Lane, S.E.).
WALTHAM ABBEY BRANCH, Waltham Abbey. *Sub-Branches*—Cheshunt, Waltham Cross, Enfield Highway, Lower Edmonton, Winchmore Hill, Palmers Green.
WOODFORD BRANCH, Woodford Green. *Sub-Branches* — Buckhurst Hill (Queen's Road), Loughton (High Road).

CHARLES GOW, *General Manager.*

Current Accounts are kept agreeably to the custom of London Bankers. Sums of £10 and upwards are received on Deposit at Interest from Customers and others, either at seven days' notice, or for fixed periods, as may be agreed upon. The Agency of Joint Stock Banks, Private Bankers, and Foreign Banks undertaken. Purchases and Sales of all descriptions of British and Foreign Securities, Bullion, Specie, &c., effected. Circular Notes and Letters of Credit are issued free of charge for the use of Travellers, payable in the principal Towns on the Continent of Europe, and in the chief Commercial Cities in the World. They may be obtained at the Head Office, or at the Branches. Dividends on English and Foreign Funds, and on Railway and other Shares and Debentures payable in this Country, received without charge to Customers.

EDWARD CLODD, *Secretary.* [195

THE LONDON CITY AND MIDLAND BANK, Limited.

ESTABLISHED 1836.

Authorised Capital	£12,000,000	Paid-up Capital	£2,202,400
Subscribed Capital	£10,571,520	Reserve Fund	£2,202,400

DIRECTORS:—

ARTHUR KEEN, Esq., Birmingham, *Chairman.*
WILLIAM GRAHAM BRADSHAW, Esq., London, *Deputy-Chairman.*

GEORGE FREDERICK BOLDING, Esq., Birmingham.	W. MURRAY FRASER, Esq., London.
WILLIAM BENJAMIN BOWRING, Esq., Liverpool.	JOHN HOWARD GWYTHER, Esq., London.
JOSHUA MILNE CHEETHAM, Esq., Oldham.	HARRY HEATON, Esq., Birmingham.
JOHN ALEXANDER CHRISTIE, Esq., Leamington.	E. H. HOLDEN, Esq., *Managing Director.*
JOHN CORRY, Esq., London.	ALEX. LAWRIE, Esq., London.
Sir JOSEPH CROSLAND, Huddersfield.	Sir THOMAS SUTHERLAND, G.C.M.G., M.P., Lond.
Sir F. D. DIXON-HARTLAND, Bart., M.P., London.	JAMES E. VANNER, Esq., London.
Sir G.F. FAUDEL-PHILLIPS, Bart., G.C.I.E., Lond.	WILLIAM FITZTHOMAS WYLEY, Esq., Coventry.

J. M. MADDERS, S. B. MURRAY, and D. G. H. POLLOCK, *General Managers.*
EDWARD J. MORRIS, *Secretary.*   H. W. LAMB, *Assistant Secretary.*

Head Office :—5, THREADNEEDLE STREET.
Registered Office :—52, CORNHILL, LONDON, E.C.

METROPOLITAN AND SUBURBAN BRANCHES.

THREADNEEDLE STREET.	CROYDON.	LEYTONSTONE.	ROTHERHITHE.
CORNHILL.	COVENT GARDEN.	LOUGHBOROUGH JUNC-	SHAFTESBURY AVENUE
ALDGATE.	DEPTFORD.	TION.	(Corner of Rupert Street).
BALHAM and TOOTING.	EALING.	LUDGATE HILL.	SHOREDITCH.
BECKENHAM.	EASTCHEAP.	MARYLEBONE.	STOKE NEWINGTON.
BEDFORD ROW.	FOREST GATE.	MILE END.	STREATHAM HILL.
BERMONDSEY.	FORE STREET.	NEW BOND STREET.	TOOLEY STREET.
BETHNAL GREEN.	HACKNEY.	NEWGATE STREET.	TOTTENHAM COURT
BISHOPSGATE STREET.	HACKNEY ROAD.	OLD STREET.	ROAD, City Bank Branch,
BLACKFRIARS.	HARRINGAY.	OLD BOND STREET.	Nos. 159 and 160.
BROMLEY (KENT).	HOLBORN.	OLD KENT ROAD.	TOTTENHAM COURT
CAMBRIDGE CIRCUS.	ISLINGTON (Metropolitan	OXFORD STREET.	ROAD, No. 237.
CHARING CROSS.	Cattle Market).	PADDINGTON.	WALHAM GREEN.
CHISWICK.	KNIGHTSBRIDGE.	PECKHAM.	WEST SMITHFIELD.
CLERKENWELL.	LEWISHAM.	QUEEN VICTORIA STREET.	WHITECHAPEL.
COLEMAN STREET.	LEYTON.	RICHMOND.	

COUNTRY BRANCHES.

Birmingham.	Manchester.	Leeds.	Liverpool.	Hull.
New Street.	King Street.	Park Row.	Dale Street.	Silver Street.
Aston Cross.	Ardwick.	Beeston Hill.	Everton.	Billingsgate.
Aston Road.	Bradford.	Bramley.	Islington.	Hessle Road.
Balsall Heath.	Chester Road.	Burley Road.	Old Haymarket.	
Cannon Street.	Corn Exchange.	Hunslet.	Scotland Road.	PONTYPRIDD.
Five Ways.	Deansgate.	Hyde Park.	St. Luke's.	PRESTON.
Handsworth.	Market Street.	Kirkgate.		ROCHDALE.
King's Heath.	Moss Side.	Kirkstall.	KEIGHLEY.	ST. ANNE'S-ON-SEA.
Moseley Road.	Stretford Road.	North Street.	KENDAL.	ST. HELENS.
Small Heath.	Swan Street.	Pudsey.	KENILWORTH.	SEAFORTH, near Liv-
Smethwick.		Roundhay Road.	KIRKBY LONSDALE.	erpool.
Smithfield.		Stanningley.	KIRKBY STEPHEN.	SEDBERGH.
Snow Hill.	BRADFORD.	Wellington Bridge.	KNOWLE.	SHAW.
Sparkbrook.	BRAMPTON.		LANCASTER.	SHEFFIELD.
Sparkhill.	BRIERLEY HILL.		LEAMINGTON.	SHIPLEY.
Warstone Lane.	BRIGHTON.	DERBY.	LEICESTER.	SILLOTH.
Waterloo Street.	BRISTOL.	DEWSBURY.	LICHFIELD.	SKIPTON.
	BURNLEY.	EASTBOURNE.	LYTHAM.	SOUTHAM.
ALSTON.	BURTON-ON-TRENT.	EGREMONT, Cheshire	MARGATE.	SOUTHAMPTON.
AMBLESIDE.	CARDIFF.	ERDINGTON.	MARYPORT.	SOUTHPORT.
BARNSLEY.	CARDIFF DOCKS.	FLEETWOOD.	MILNROW.	STOURBRIDGE.
BARRY DOCKS.	CARLISLE.	FOLESHILL.	MIRFIELD.	SUNDERLAND.
BATH.	CASTLEFORD.	GATESHEAD.	MORECAMBE.	SUTTON COLDFIELD
BATLEY.	CASTLETON.	GLOUCESTER.	MORLEY.	SWANSEA.
BEDFORD.	CHELTENHAM.	GOOLE.	NEWCASTLE - ON -	TAMWORTH.
BEWDLEY.	CHEPSTOW.	GUERNSEY.	TYNE.	ULVERSTON.
BLACKBURN.	CHESTERFIELD.	HALTWHISTLE.	NEWPORT (Mon.).	WAKEFIELD.
BLACKPOOL.	CHORLEY.	HASTINGS.	NORTHAMPTON.	WALSALL.
" South Shore.	CLECKHEATON.	HECKMONDWIKE.	NOTTINGHAM.	WARWICK.
BOLTON.	CLIFTON.	HEXHAM.	NUNEATON.	WATERLOO, near
BOOTLE.	CLITHEROE.	HOLMFIRTH.	OLDHAM.	Liverpool.
BOURNEMOUTH.	COCKERMOUTH.	HUDDERSFIELD.	ORMSKIRK.	WEDNESBURY.
BOWNESS - ON - WIN-	COLESHILL.	HYDE.	OSSETT.	WOLVERHAMPTON.
DERMERE.	COVENTRY.	JERSEY.	PONTEFRACT.	WORKINGTON.
ETC.	ETC.	ETC.	ETC.	ETC.

TERMS OF BUSINESS AT HEAD OFFICE AND BRANCHES.

Current Accounts conducted on the terms usual with London and Country Banks.
Deposits, at notice, of £10 and upwards received, and Interest allowed thereon at the rate advertised by the Bank
from time to time. Purchases and Sales of Stock effected, Circular Notes and Letters of Credit issued, Dividends received, and Coupons collected for Customers. Every description of Banking Business transacted. [193

46

METROPOLITAN BANK
(OF ENGLAND AND WALES) LIMITED.

Head Office:—60, Gracechurch Street, London, E.C. | Country Office:—Birmingham.

CAPITAL, £7,500,000, in 150,000 SHARES of £50 each.

PROPRIETORS' FUNDS, £898,142, viz.:—

Paid-up Capital, £500,000.	Bank Premises Redemption Fund, £33,387.
Guarantee Fund, £350,000.	Balance of Profits Carried Forward, £14,755.

DIRECTORS.

Sir THOMAS LEA, Bart., M.P., *Chairman.*
ALFRED BALDWIN, Esq., M.P.
JAMES TERTIUS COLLINS, Esq.
ROBERT FORREST, Esq.
Sir JOHN J. JENKINS, K.C., M.P.

MORGAN B. WILLIAMS, Esq., *Deputy-Chairman.*
ABRAM CRESWICKE RAWLINSON, Esq.
Lord ERNEST J. SEYMOUR.
WALTER E. WARDEN, Esq.
CHARLES H. WILLIAMS, Esq.

General Manager—F. W. NASH.
Secretary—JAS. SMITH WOOD.
London Manager—F. NALDER.

Assistant General Manager—F. J. HUGHES.
Chief Accountant—JOHN MENZIES.
London Sub-Manager—THOS. THOMSON.

BRANCHES.

ABERDARE	G. J. TUCKFIELD.		
ACOCK'S GREEN	W. H. OAKLEY.	LEAMINGTON	G. C. LAKE, and A. A. B. WILSON, Deputy Manager.
ALCESTER	J. H. HENDERSON.		
BANBURY	J. FINGLAND.	LLANBERIS	JOHN OWEN JONES.
BANGOR	WM. THOMAS.	LLANDUDNO	A. EVANS.
BARMOUTH	WM. WILLIAMS.	LLANDYSSUL	H. C. MORRIS.
BARRY DOCK	T. J. WILLIAMS.	LLANELLY	W. GRIFFITHS.
BATH	A. T. PERKINS.	LLANGEFNI	E. M. ROBERTS.
BETHESDA	WILLIAM THOMAS.	LLANRWST	W. BLEDDYN LLOYD.
BILSTON	J. E. BRIANT.	MAESTEG	D. J. GWYN.
BIRMINGHAM—		MAIDENHEAD	A. E. BONBERRY.
ASTON CROSS	H. W. SPONG.	MERTHYR TYDFIL	JOHN AUBREY.
BENNETT'S HILL	A. G. SAMPSON.	MORETON-IN-MARSH	S. F. HUNSTON.
MARKETS	THOS. GRIMLE	MUCH WENLOCK	F. SARJEANT.
SALTLEY	W. S. BUNN.	NEATH	C. E. S. THOMPSON.
STRATFORD ROAD	W. H. OAKLEY.	NEVIN	R. W. HUMPHREYS.
BLAENAU FESTINIOG	JOHN PARRY JONES.	NEWCASTLE EMLYN	H. C. MORRIS.
BLAENAVON	THOS. COOKE.	NEWPORT, MON.	F. GREENSLADE.
BLOXWICH	W. PRECEY.	OXFORD	G. HUGHES.
BRIDGEND	D. J. GWYN.	PONTYPRIDD	W. D. HODGES.
BRIDGNORTH	R. PILKINGTON.	PORTHMADOC	J. RICHARD PRICHARD.
BRIERLEY HILL	J. FINNEY.	PORT TALBOT	C. E. S. THOMPSON.
BRISTOL	D. LAING.	PWLLHELI	W. O. HUGHES.
BROMSGROVE	C. E. DAVENPORT.	READING	A. McNEIL.
CADOXTON	T. J. WILLIAMS.	REDDITCH	F. H. JOSCELYNE.
CARDIFF—		SHIPSTON-ON-STOUR	J. H. EVANS.
ST. MARY STREET		SLOUGH	J. CALDER.
CANTON	A. E. OLD.	STOURBRIDGE	H. JAMES.
CLIFTON STREET		STOURPORT	A. W. GABRIEL.
ROATH		STRATFORD-ON-AVON	C. E. MARTIN.
CARDIFF DOCKS	J. MARSHALL.	SWANSEA, High Street	T. W. ISLAY YOUNG.
CARDIGAN	J. W. NICHOLAS.	SWANSEA, WIND STREET	
CARNARVON	ROBERT WILLIAMS.	TIPTON	ALFRED T. PAGE.
CHEPSTOW	ARTHUR PRICE.	TREDEGAR	W. H. WOODLIFFE.
CHIPPING NORTON	T. H. BURBIDGE.	WALSALL, The Bridge	W. PRECEY.
COLWYN BAY	R. HUGHES-JONES.	WALSALL, Park Street	J. J. SHEDDEN.
CONWAY	DAVID JONES.	WARWICK	H. L. SOWDON.
COWBRIDGE	D. J. GWYN.	WEDNESBURY	H. E. PROCTOR.
DARLASTON	W. H. MARSHALL.	WEST BROMWICH	E. C. RICHARDSON.
DUDLEY	F. M. BAKER.	WILLENHALL	W. JOHNSON.
HAVERFORDWEST	JOHN SHETTLE.	WITNEY	H. W. SPRENGER.
HEDNESFORD	W. PRECEY.	WOLVERHAMPTON	W. S. ROWLAND.
HENLEY-IN-ARDEN	J. E. TURNER.	WORCESTER	F. R. LAURIE.
KIDDERMINSTER	E. C. NEWMARCH.		

SUB BRANCHES.

ABERGWYNFI	...Sub to	MAESTEG.	NEWBOROUGH ...Sub to	LLANGEFNI.
AMLWCH	"	LLANGEFNI.	PENCADER	" NEWCASTLE EMLYN.
BETHESDA	"	BANGOR.	PENRHIWCEIBER	" ABERDARE.
BLAENGARW	"	BRIDGEND.	PENRHYN-DEUDRAETH	" PORTMADOC.
BRITON FERRY	"	NEATH.	PENTRE	Sub to PONTYPRIDD.
BROWNHILLS	"	WALSALL, The Bridge.	PENYGRAIG	" PONTYPRIDD.
BRYNSIENCYN	"	LLANGEFNI.	PENYGROES	" CARNARVON.
BRYNMAWR	"	BLAENAVON.	PONTYCWMMER	" BRIDGEND.
BURRY PORT	"	LLANELLY.	PORTH	" PONTYPRIDD.
CRADLEY HEATH	"	STOURBRIDGE.	PORTHCAWL	" BRIDGEND.
CRICCIETH	"	PORTMADOC.	SARN MEILLTEYRN	" NEVIN.
DOWLAIS	"	MERTHYR TYDFIL.	STUDLEY	" REDDITCH.
EBBW VALE	"	TREDEGAR.	TALYSARN	" CARNARVON.
EBENEZER	"	BETHESDA.	TONYPANDY	" PONTYPRIDD.
FERNDALE	"	PONTYPRIDD.	TREFACH	" NEWCASTLE EMLYN.
FESTINIOG	"	BLAENAU FESTINIOG.	TREHARRIS	" ABERDARE.
LYE	"	STOURBRIDGE.	TREHERBERT	" PONTYPRIDD.
MILFORD HAVEN	"	HAVERFORDWEST.	TREORKY	" "
MORRISTON	"	SWANSEA.	TYNEWYDD OGMORE VALE	} " BRIDGEND.
MOUNTAIN ASH	"	ABERDARE.	YSTRADGYNLAIS	" SWANSEA.
MUMBLES	"	SWANSEA.	YSTALYFERA	" SWANSEA.

AGENCIES.

BAMPTON (OXON)	G. W. DUTTON.	GORING-ON-THAMES	H. A. L. SMITH.
BRAILES	A. ELLIOTT.	KINETON	C. F. BANCROFT.
CHARLBURY	T. G. SMITH.	PANGBOURNE	H. S. ADAMS.
CHIPPING CAMPDEN	A. WIXEY.	SHIPON-UNDER-WYCHWOOD	J. J. DANGERFIELD. [72

BANK OF NEW ZEALAND.

(Incorporated by Act of General Assembly, 29th July, 1861.) *Bankers to the New Zealand Government.*

Four per Cent. Guaranteed Stock £2,000,000 0 0		
Preferred Shares Issued to Crown 500,000 0 0		
Ordinary Capital called up under "Bank of New Zealand		
and Banking Act, 1895" £500,000 0 0		
Amount Paid to 31st March, 1899 .. .. 412,354 6 10	412,354 6 10	
		——————————
		£2,912,354 6 10

Nominal Reserve Liability on Shares £626,783 17 1

Head Office—WELLINGTON, NEW ZEALAND.

Directors:

J. R. BLAIR, Esq., *Chairman.*	HAROLD BEAUCHAMP, Esq.	F. DE CARTERET MALET, Esq.
MARTIN KENNEDY, Esq.	WILLIAM WATSON, Esq.	WILLIAM MILNE, Esq.

General Manager—C. G. TEGETMEIER.

London Office—1, QUEEN VICTORIA ST., E.C.—JAMES BAXTER, *Acting Manager.*
London Bankers—BANK OF ENGLAND and GLYN, MILLS, CURRIE & Co.

Branches and Agencies.—Akaroa, Alexandra, **Arrow**, Ashburton, Ashurst, **Auckland**, Balclutha, **Blenheim**, **Bluff**, Bulls, Cambridge, Carterton, **Christchurch**, Clinton, Clyde, Coromandel, Cromwell, Danevirke, **Dunedin**, Dunedin (N.), Eketahuna, Elsham, Featherston, Feilding, Fortrose, Foxton, **Gisborne**, Gore, **Greymouth**, Greytown, Halcombe, **Hamilton**, Hampden, Hastings, Hawera, Henley, **Hokitika**, Hunterville, Hutt, Inglewood, **Invercargill**, Kaiapoi, Kaikoura, Kaitangata, Kaponga, Kelso, Kimbolton, Kumara, Lawrence, Leeston, Levin, **Lyttelton**, Manaia, Manakau, Mangaweka, Marton, **Masterton**, Mataura, Midhirst, Millar's Flat, **Milton**, Mosgeil, Motueka, **Napier**, Naseby, **Nelson**, **New Plymouth**, Newton (Auckland), Ngaruawahia, **Oamaru**, **Ohinemuri**, Ophir, Opotiki, Opunake, Orepuki, Otautau, Outram, Oxford, Pahiatua, Palmerston, Palmerston (N.), Patea, Petone, Picton, Port Chalmers, Queenstown, Rakaia, Rangiora, Reefton, Riverton, **Rongotea**, Ross, Roxburgh, St. Bathans, Sanson, **Southbridge**, Stratford, Tapanui, Tauranga, **Te Aro**, Te Awamutu, Temuka, **Thames**, **Timaru**, Waikouaiti, Waimate, **Waipawa**, Waipukurau, Waitahuna, Waitara, **Wanganui**, Wellington, **Westport**, Whangarei, Winton, Woodville, Wyndham.
MELBOURNE (*Victoria*), SYDNEY (*New South Wales*), SUVA and LEVUKA (*Fiji*).

THE BANK OF NEW ZEALAND, LONDON.

Grants drafts on any of the above-named places in New Zealand, Australia and Fiji.
Opens Current Accounts for the convenience of its Colonial Constituents.
Negotiates and collects Bills payable in any part of the Australasian Colonies and Fiji.
Undertakes the Agency of persons connected with the Colonies; and receives for safe custody, on their behalf, Securities, Shares, &c., drawing interest and dividends on the same as they fall due.
Undertakes all other descriptions of Colonial Banking and Monetary Business, and affords every facility to persons in their transactions with the colonies. LONDON. [290

The QUEENSLAND NATIONAL BANK, LIMITED.

Incorporated under "The Companies Act, 1863," of the Legislature of Queensland.

Bankers to the Queensland Government.

Subscribed Capital, £800,000. Paid-up Capital, £412,644, 0s. 4d. (£459,091 2s. 4d., less Paid-up Capital on Forfeited Shares, £46,447 2s.)
Interminable Inscribed Deposit Stock, **£3,116,621 5s.**

Under Government Audit.

All New Business since 1893 Protected under Clause 9 of the Scheme of Arrangement.

COLONIAL BOARD.	LONDON BOARD.
JAS. MUNRO, Esq., *Chairman.*	Sir EDWYN SANDYS DAWES, K.C.M.G.
A. J. CALLAN, Esq., M.L.A.	ROBERT MUTER STEWART, Esq.
JOHN CAMERON, Esq.	REGINALD HOPE SPENS, Esq.
JAS. MILNE, Esq.	
FREDK. LORD, Esq., M.L.A.	

HEAD OFFICE, BRISBANE—*General Manager,* WALTER VARDON RALSTON.
LONDON OFFICE, 8, PRINCES STREET, E.C.—*Manager,* J. W. DICKINSON.
Bankers—BANK OF ENGLAND, LLOYDS' BANK, Limited.
Auditors—Messrs. JACKSON, PIXLEY, BROWNING, HUSEY & Co.

BRANCHES.

SYDNEY OFFICE—PITT STREET.

Albion, Allora, Barcaldine, Beaudesert, Blackall, Boonah, Bundaberg, Burketown, Cairns, Charleville, Charters Towers, Clifton, Clonscurry, Cooktown, Croydon, Cunnamulla, Dalby, Fortitude Valley, Geraldton, Gympie, Halifax, Herberton, Hughenden, Ingham, Ipswich, Isisford, Laidley, Longreach, Mackay, Maryborough, Mount Morgan, Muttaburra, Normanton, Pittsworth, Port Douglas, Ravenswood, Richmond, Rockhampton, Roma, Sandgate, South Brisbane, Thargomindah, Thursday Island, Toowoomba, Townsville, Warwick, Winton.

AGENCIES.

VICTORIA—National Bank of Australasia.	**SCOTLAND**—British Linen Company Bank.
SOUTH AUSTRALIA—National Bank of Australasia.	" Edinburgh: Messrs. Torrie, Brodie & Maclagan, 25a, St. Andrew Square. [Street.
WEST AUSTRALIA—National Bank of Australasia.	" Glasgow: Messrs. Wm. Ewing & Co., 45, Renfield
NEW ZEALAND—Bank of New Zealand.	" Dundee: Messrs. Andrew Hendry & Sons, 85, Murray-
TASMANIA—Bank of Australasia.	COPENHAGEN—Landmandsbank. [gate.
NEW YORK—Messrs. Laidlaw & Co.	BERLIN—Deutsche Bank.
SAN FRANCISCO—Bank of California.	**IRELAND**—Ulster Bank, Limited.
SCOTLAND—Royal Bank of Scotland.	" Dublin: Messrs. Guinness, Mahon & Co., 17, College [Green.

INDIA AND CHINA—Hongkong and Shanghai Banking Corporation, Chartered Bank of India, Australia and China, Mercantile Bank of India, Limited.

The Bank grants Drafts on all the above Branches and Agencies; also Telegraphic Transfers and transacts every description of Banking Business in connection with Queensland and other Australian Colonies on the most favourable terms.

The London Office receives Deposits for fixed periods at rates which can be ascertained on application. [74

THE UNION BANK OF LONDON, Ltd.

Established 1839.

DIRECTORS.

FELIX O. SCHUSTER, Esq., *Governor.* The Rt. Hon. Sir ALGERNON E. WEST, K.C.B., *Deputy-Governor.*

Sir S. H. WATERLOW, Bart.   H. G. DEVAS, Esq.   THEODORE BASSETT, Esq.
H. J. B. KENDALL, Esq.   P. BOSANQUET, Esq.   JULIUS WERNHER, Esq.
HERMAN HOSKIER, Esq.   The Rt.Hn.C.T. RITCHIE, M.P.   JOHN TROTTER, Esq.
W. O. GILCHRIST, Esq.   JOHN DENNISTOUN, Esq.   CHARLES H. R. WOLLASTON, Esq.

Principal Office: 2, PRINCES STREET, MANSION HOUSE.

Regent Street Branch, 14, Argyll Place.	Southwark Branch, 12, Southwark Street.
Charing Cross Branch, 66, Charing Cross.	Mayfair Branch, 12, Mount Street, W.
Chancery Lane Branch, 95, Chancery Lane.	South Kensington Branch, 18, Cromwell Place.
Holborn Circus Branch, Holborn Circus.	South Norwood Branch, 76, High Street.
Bayswater Branch, 67, Bishop's Road.	Bromley (Kent) Branch, 33, High Street.
Fenchurch Street Branch, 116, Fenchurch St.	Notting Hill Gate Branch, 8, High Street.
Tottenham Ct.Rd. Branch, 97,Tottenham Ct. Rd.	South Croydon Branch, 111, South End, Croydon.
Sloane Street Branch, 74, Sloane Street.	Bedford Row Branch 54, Theobald's Road, W.C.
Croydon Branch, High Street, Croydon.	

Manager—R. H. NUNN.   *Deputy-Manager*—J. E. W. HOULDING.   *Secretary*—F. V. HORNBY.
Assistant Secretary, H. R. HOARE.

The Capital of the Bank is £11,000,000 sterling, in 110,000 Shares of £100, on each of which £15 10s. have been paid, making the paid-up Capital £1,705,000, held by upwards of 5 200 Proprietors.

RESERVE FUND, £850,000; and Dividend for the last year at the rate of 10 per cent. per annum, and bonus of 3s., equal to a rate of about 2 per cent. per annum.

TERMS.

CURRENT ACCOUNTS.—These are kept according to the usual custom of London Bankers.
DEPOSIT ACCOUNTS.—Interest allowed on Money placed on Deposit at seven days' notice whether customers or the public generally, and receipts given for the sums so deposited.   If the money is withdrawn within fourteen days from the date of deposit no interest is allowed.

Notice of changes in the rate of interest will be given by advertisement only.

At the expiration of the seven days' notice of withdrawal of a deposit without the amount being withdrawn, the interest will cease, unless the depositor express his wish to continue the deposit, subject to further notice.

GENERAL BUSINESS.

The Agency of Country and Foreign Banks, whether Joint Stock or Private.   Circular Notes and Letters of Credit issued for all parts of the Continent of Europe or elsewhere.   Purchases and Sales effected in all the British and Foreign Stocks and Securities.   Dividends on Stocks and Shares, the Half-pay of Officers, Pensions, Annuities, &c., received for customers without charge.

The Officers and Clerks connected with the Bank are required to sign a declaration of secrecy as to the transactions of any of its customers.

[209]

THE BANK OF VICTORIA, Limited.

ESTABLISHED OCTOBER, 1852.   *Registered under the " Companies Act, 1890."*

Subscribed Capital—Preference	..	£416,760 0 0	
Ordinary	..	£2,400,000 0 0	£2,816,760 0 0
Paid-up Capital—On Preference Shares	..	£416,760 0 0	
On Ordinary Shares	..	£1,060,045 17 7	£1,476,805 17 7

Reserve Fund, £70,000 0 0

Head Office: MELBOURNE.

Directors.
The Hon. EDWARD MILLER, M.L.C., *Chairman.*
The Hon. GODFREY DOWNES CARTER, M.L.A., *Vice-Chairman.*
FREDERICK LLOYD, Esq., J.P.
GEORGE SHAW, Esq.
ROBERT MURRAY SMITH, Esq., C.M.G., M.L.A.

Auditors { THOS. BRENTNALL, Esq., F.I.A.V.
E. P. HASTINGS, Esq., F.I.A.V.
JAMES DONALDSON LAW, Esq., *General Manager.*
A. E. WALLIS, *Accountant.*
R. H. ANDREWS, *Inspector of Branches.*

London Office: 28, CLEMENT'S LANE, LOMBARD STREET, E.C.

DIRECTORS: HUGH LEWIS TAYLOR, Esq., *Chairman.* | GILBERT J. McCAUL, Esq.
HENRY FARNCOMBE BILLINGHURST, Esq.
WILLIAM FAIRCLOUGH, *Manager.*   T. A. STANLEY, *Accountant.*

BRANCHES IN VICTORIA —Ararat, Armadale, Avoca, Bairnsdale, Ballarat, Beaufort, Beechworth, Bendigo, Bruthen, Camperdown, Carlton, Casterton, Castlemaine, Charlton, Colac, Coleraine, Daylesford, Donald, Dunolly, Eaglehawk, Elmore, Fitzroy, Geelong, Hamilton, Harrow, Hawthorn, Heathcote, Heyfield, Horsham, Inglewood, Kaniva, Kerang, Kilmore, Kyabram, Kyneton, Maffra, Maldon, Maryborough, Mortlake, Murchison, Nathalia, Nhill, North Melbourne, Numurkah, Penshurst, Port Fairy, Portland, Prahran, Queenscliff, Rushworth, Rutherglen, Sale, Seymour, Shepparton, South Melbourne, St. Arnaud, Tatura, Terang, Walhalla, Warrnambool, Watchem, Wodonga, Yarram Yarram.

AGENCIES:

INDIA, CHINA, MAURITIUS, &c.	{ The Mercantile Bank of India, Ltd., and the Chartered Bank of India, Australia and China.
BATAVIA	The Chartered Bank of India, Australia & China, & Nederlandsche Handel Maatschapij.
NEW SOUTH WALES	The Australian Joint Stock Bank, Ltd., & the Commercial Banking Company of Sydney, Ltd.
NEW ZEALAND	The Bank of New Zealand.
NORTH AMERICA	The Hong Kong and Shanghai Banking Corporation.
QUEENSLAND	The Australian Joint Stock Bank, Ltd., & the Commercial Banking Company of Sydney, Ltd.
SCOTLAND	The National Bank of Scotland, Limited.
SOUTH AFRICA	The Standard Bank of South Africa, Limited.
SOUTH AUSTRALIA	The Bank of Adelaide.
TASMANIA	The Commercial Bank of Tasmania, Limited.
WESTERN AUSTRALIA	The Western Australian Bank.

The Bank conducts all ordinary Banking Business, issues drafts, negotiates and collects Bills at all its Branches.
Current accounts for the Colonial Constituents of the Bank are kept at the London Office.
Deposits are received upon terms which may be ascertained upon application.

WILLIAM FAIRCLOUGH, *Manager.* [203]

56

GENERAL REVERSIONARY AND INVESTMENT CO., Ltd.

Office: No. 26, PALL MALL, LONDON, S.W.
(Removed from No. 5, Whitehall.)

Established 1836. *Further empowered by Special Act of Parliament,* 14 and 15 *Vict., cap.* 130.

CAPITAL AND DEBENTURE STOCKS, £650,470.

DIRECTORS.

Chairman—HERBERT CHAS. MALKIN, Esq.   *Deputy-Chairman*—GEORGE BADHAM, Esq.

MARTIN J. K. BECHER, Esq.   JOHN COLES, Esq.
GEORGE E. COCKRAM, Esq.   Sir JAMES R. D. McGRIGOR, Bart.

WILLIAM STEBBING, Esq.

Auditors—CURLING HUNTER, Esq. ; ARTHUR L. SAVORY, Esq. ; WM. J. H. WHITTALL, Esq.

Bankers—UNION BANK OF LONDON, Limited, Charing Cross.

Solicitors—Messrs. SHOUBRIDGE & MAY, 32, Lincoln's Inn Fields.

This Company, established upwards of sixty years, PURCHASES or makes LOANS upon
REVERSIONARY INTERESTS, vested or contingent, in *well-secured Property* ;
also

LIFE INTERESTS in *Possession,* as well as in *Expectation.*

Loans upon Reversions may be obtained either at an Annual Interest, or in
consideration of redeemable deferred charges, payable upon the *Reversions* falling in.

PRESENT INCOMES are likewise granted upon the latter principle to persons
entitled to Reversionary Interests, who may thus obtain the means of support until their
property falls into possession, without being called upon for any payment until that event.

Prospectuses and Forms of Proposal may be obtained from the Secretary, to whom
all communications should be addressed.

D. A. BUMSTED, F.I.A., *Actuary and Secretary.*   [130

LAW REVERSIONARY INTEREST SOCIETY,
LIMITED.
ESTABLISHED 1853.

OFFICES :—No. 24, LINCOLN'S INN FIELDS, LONDON, W.C.

Capital, £400,000.   **Debentures and Debenture Stock, £201,380.**

DIRECTORS.

Chairman—JOHN CLERK, Esq., Q.C.   *Deputy Chairman*—C. R. RIVINGTON, Esq., J.P., D.L.

ERNEST BEVIR, Esq., Devereux Chambers.   L. W. N. HICKLEY, Esq., 10, King's Bench Walk.
EDWARD BULLOCK, Esq., Barrister-at-Law.   The Right Hon. J. W. MELLOR, Q.C., M.P.
The Hon. Mr. Justice CHANNELL.   RICHARD MILLS, Esq., 34, Queen's Gate Terrace.
EDWARD DALTON, Esq., 16, Porchester Square. JOHN HERBERT SECKER, Esq., Barrister-at-Law.
JOHN C. DEVERELL, Esq., 9, New Square.

Solicitors—Messrs. CAPRONS, HITCHINS, BRABANT & HITCHINS, Savile Place, Conduit Street.

PURCHASES.—The Society purchases Reversions and Remainders, whether absolute or contingent ; Life Interests, whether in possession or deferred, and generally all Interests (in approved
property) that depend upon the duration of human life.

LOANS.—The Society also grants Loans on the security of such Interests, either on Ordinary
Mortgage or by way of Reversionary Charge. The latter mode meets the convenience of borrowers
who do not wish to make any payment for either principal or interest until their Reversionary
Property falls into possession. The amount to which the Society will then be entitled is fixed at
the outset, and does not depend on the time elapsing between the grant of the Loan and its repay-
ment. The option of redeeming the Charge during the first three or five years can usually be
combined with this form of Loan.

Forms of Proposal and full information can be obtained at the Society's Offices.

W. OSCAR NASH, F.I.A., *Actuary and Secretary.*   [131

THE
London Property Investment Trust,
LIMITED.

Incorporated under the Companies Acts, 1862 to 1890.

CAPITAL **£100,000**

IN 20,000 SHARES OF £5 EACH, OF WHICH EIGHT ARE FOUNDERS' SHARES.

Directors.

GEORGE BAXTER, *Chairman and Managing Director.*

EDWARD ANGELL EADY. | WILLIAM LINDSAY COULSON.

Bankers.

PARR'S BANK, LIMITED, BARTHOLOMEW LANE, E.C.

Offices.

1, FREDERICK'S PLACE, OLD JEWRY, E.C.

This Trust is established for the purpose of acquiring Freehold and Leasehold Properties, primarily in the London District, solely for **investment** purposes.

It affords large and small capitalists opportunities for investment to great advantage, both as regards security and rate of interest. Transactions of a speculative character are studiously avoided, and only properties of sound commercial value are dealt with.

The Investments consist of Shop Properties situate in main thoroughfares and well-established neighbourhoods, the whole of which are let on full repairing leases, and over twenty-five per cent. of the present income is derived from freeholds, in which one-third of the entire funds of the Trust is invested.

The Directors, Solicitor and Secretary serve without remuneration, and as holders of the Founders' Shares, receive no share of profits until a dividend of 6 per cent. is paid to the Ordinary Shareholders, and one-fourth of the balance of profits is carried to a Reserve Fund **invested in Consols.**

The Ordinary Shareholders thus obtain a preferential dividend of 6 per cent. per annum, and their position is further assured by the Reserve Fund.

The Directors invite applications for Capital in fully paid Shares of £5 each, bearing 6 per cent. interest.

Applications can be made direct to the Secretary at the Offices of the Trust, No. 1, Frederick's Place, Old Jewry, E.C. [213

79

THE LONDON ASSURANCE,

Incorporated by Royal Charter, A.D. 1720.

For Fire, Life and Marine Assurances.

Head Office—No. 7, ROYAL EXCHANGE, LONDON.

Governor.—HOWARD GILLIAT, Esq.

Sub-Governor.	*Deputy-Governor.*
HENRY GOSCHEN, Esq.	CHARLES G. ARBUTHNOT, Esq.

Directors.

OTTO AUGUST BENECKE, Esq.
ROBERT HENRY BENSON, Esq.
WILLIAM THOMAS BRAND, Esq.
ARTHUR HENRY BRANDT, Esq.
COLIN F. CAMPBELL, Esq.
ALFRED CLAYTON COLE, Esq.
JOHN DENNISTOUN, Esq.
Sir ROBERT GILLESPIE.
CHARLES S. S. GUTHRIE, Esq.
GEORGE W. HENDERSON, Esq.
LOUIS HUTH, Esq.
HENRY J. B. KENDALL, Esq.

FREDERIC LUBBOCK, Esq.   [F.R.S.
Admiral Sir F. L. McCLINTOCK, K.C.B.,
SIR MONTAGU F. OMMANNEY, K.C.M.G.
GREVILLE H. PALMER, Esq.
SELWYN R. PRYOR, Esq.
GEORGE ROLFES, Esq.
ROBERT RYRIE, Esq.
Col. LEOPOLD R. SEYMOUR.
Field Marshal Sir D. M. STEWART, Bart.,
  G.C.B., G.C.S.I.
LEWIS A. WALLACE, Esq.
JOHN YOUNG, Esq.

Secretary.—CHARLES A. DENTON, Esq.

*Underwriter—*CHARLES GEORGE ELLIS, Esq.

Manager of the Fire and Life Departments.—JAMES CLUNES, Esq.

Actuary.—GEORGE KING, Esq.

The Corporation has granted Fire, Life and Marine Assurances for more than a Hundred and Seventy-five years; during that long period it has endeavoured to introduce into its practice all the real improvements that have from time to time been suggested, and to afford every facility for the transaction of business.

INCOME, 1898.

Life Premiums	..	..	..	..	..	..	£156,088 4 0
Fire Premiums	..	..	..	..	..	..	376,016 15 5
Marine Premiums	..	..	..	..	..	..	318,477 17 4
Interest	..	..	..	..	..	..	146,603 8 6
Other Receipts	..	..	..	..	..	..	402 10 4
							£997,588 15 7

FUNDS, 31st Dec., 1898.

Shareholders' Capital paid up	..	..	..	..	..	..	£448,275 0 0
General Reserve Fund	..	..	..	..	..	..	310,000 0 0
Life Assurance Funds	..	..	..	..	..	..	2,147,480 3 0
Fire Fund	..	..	..	..	..	..	675,051 18 5
Marine Fund	..	..	..	..	..	..	181,310 10 7
Profit and Loss	..	..	..	..	..	..	133,026 11 1
Provision for accrued liabilities	..	..	..	..	..	..	141,290 15 10
							£4,036,434 18 11

Prospectuses and copies of the Accounts can be had on application.   [87

92

93

97

99

196

THE CHILDREN OF SORROW.

MORE THAN 4,400 CHILDREN HAVE BEEN RESCUED BY

THE CHILDREN'S HOME & ORPHANAGE.

Founder and Principal—Rev. T. BOWMAN STEPHENSON, D.D., LL.D.
Vice-Principal—Rev. ARTHUR E. GREGORY.

Vice-Presidents.

The Bishop of WORCESTER.

The Dean of CANTERBURY.	Rev. Canon FLEMING.
Rev. Dr. CLIFFORD.	Right Hon. Sir H. H. FOWLER, M.P.
Rev. Dr. RIGG.	Rt. Hon. CHIEF JUSTICE WAY.
Rev. Dr. PARKER.	MARK WHITWILL, Esq., J.P.

Treasurers—J. E. VANNER, Esq.; T. B. HOLMES, Esq.
Secretary—Mr. JOHN PENDLEBURY, M.A.

Branches: LONDON, LANCASHIRE, FARNBOROUGH (Hants), BIRMING HAM, ALVERSTOKE, RAMSEY (Man), HAMILTON (Canada).

1,100 Children are now in Residence. Many are waiting to come in.
The Home receives Children of any Age or Denomination without Election. It is conducted on the family system and depends on Voluntary Contributions. Many are Crippled, Epileptic, or otherwise disadvantaged. About **£16** will maintain a child in the Home for a year. Collecting Books, Boxes, Cards, and Literature concerning the Home will be gladly forwarded to those who are willing to help.

Need not **Creed** decides the question of a child's admission.
Cheques should be crossed London, City and Midland Bank. Money Orders payable at G.P.O.
Remittances should be addressed: Rev. Dr. STEPHENSON, Bonner Road, London, N.E. [231

CITY OF LONDON HOSPITAL

FOR

DISEASES OF THE CHEST,

Victoria Park, E.

(Nearest Station: CAMBRIDGE HEATH, G.E.R.)

Telegrams—"PHTHISIS," LONDON.

Patron : Her MAJESTY the QUEEN.
President : H.R.H. the DUKE OF CONNAUGHT, K.G.

The Hospital contains **164** beds, and affords relief to the Poor and Working Classes afflicted with Consumption and Diseases of the Chest (including Heart Disease). The annual expenditure is about **£11,000**, and the reliable income is less than **£3,000**. The Institution has *No Endowment whatever*, and the support of the public is, therefore, earnestly solicited to sustain its operations, more especially in regard to the OPEN AIR TREATMENT, which has been adopted on the strong recommendation of the Medical Staff.

In-Patients under treatment, 1898 . . .	**691**
Out-Patients' attendances in 1898 . . .	**63,367**

HENRY T. DUDLEY RYDER, *Secretary.* [152

112

HAM COMMON, RICHMOND, SURREY.

Office: 12, Pall Mall, London.

Patrons:
THE DUKE OF CAMBRIDGE, PRINCESS CHRISTIAN, THE DUCHESS OF ALBANY, &c.

NATIONAL

A Cot for All Time may be had for £450.

Orphan Girls received, from 7 to 12 years, without distinction as to religion. They receive a plain English Education, and Practical Instruction in the Home, Kitchen and Laundry. Nearly 700 have been provided for. Seventy Children on the books; room for Eighty more. Lack of funds prevents them being received.

ORPHAN

This National Charity is in the greatest need of Annual Subscriptions, and the Secretary earnestly appeals to the charitable for help on behalf of the poor Orphans.

Reader, will you Help?

Subscriptions, Donations and Bequests gratefully received by the bankers,

HOME.

Lloyds Bank, Ltd., 16, St. James's Street,
And by E. EVANS CRONK, Secretary, 12, Pall Mall, S.W.   [167

NORTH EASTERN HOSPITAL FOR CHILDREN,
HACKNEY ROAD, SHOREDITCH, N.E.

Established 1867.

Patron—H.R.H. THE PRINCESS OF WALES.

Chairman—Lord FREDERICK FITZROY. | *Treasurer*—J. LISTER GODLEE, Esq.

VERY URGENT NECESSITY FOR IMMEDIATE EXTENSION.
Only Children's Hospital for Population of over 500,000. Now has only 57 Beds.

£20,000 still required to make up £25,000 (expected cost).

(1898) In-Patients, 764 (219 under 2 years of age).

Out-Patients, 15,554 (making 61,051 attendances).

Accident and Emergency Cases, 2,705. 1,509 operations were performed, and anæsthetics were administered 1,428 times.

Average Annual Expenditure, £5,758.

New Annual Subscriptions much wanted.

Bankers:—BARCLAY & CO., LTD.

T. GLENTON-KERR, *Secretary.*

City Office:—27, CLEMENT'S LANE, E.C.   [32

121

124

QUEEN CHARLOTTE'S LYING-IN HOSPITAL

MARYLEBONE ROAD, LONDON, N.W.

FOUNDED 1752. INCORPORATED BY ROYAL CHARTER, 1885.

Patron.—HER MAJESTY THE QUEEN.

Vice-Patrons { H.R.H. The PRINCESS OF WALES.
 H.R.H. The DUCHESS OF YORK.

President—THE VISCOUNT PORTMAN.

Treasurer—ALFRED C. DE ROTHSCHILD, ESQ.

Chairman—THE EARL OF HARDWICKE.

OBJECTS OF THE CHARITY.

1. To provide an Asylum for the delivery of Poor Married Women; and also of Deserving Unmarried Women *with their first child*.
2. To provide skilled Midwives to attend Poor Married Women in their *Confinements at their own homes.*
3. The Training of Medical Pupils, Midwives for the Poor, and Monthly Nurses.

Since the foundation of the Hospital 100,000 poor women have been relieved. Last year, 1,112 patients were received into the Hospital, and 1,070 were attended at their own homes.

Annual expenditure of the Charity exceeds £4,000; Reliable Income, £2,000 only.

An Annual Subscription of £3 3s., or a Donation of £31 10s., entitles the Contributor to recommend Two In-Patients and Three Out-Patients yearly, and qualifies for election as a Governor.

Contributions will be gratefully received by the Bankers, Messrs. Cocks, Biddulph & Co., 43, Charing Cross, S.W., or by

ARTHUR WATTS, Secretary. [151

REEDHAM ORPHANAGE

PURLEY, SURREY.

Patron—Her Most Gracious Majesty THE QUEEN.

Treasurer—H. COSMO O. BONSOR, Esq., M.P.

Bankers—Messrs. BARCLAY & CO., Limited, 54, Lombard Street, E.C.

Office—35, FINSBURY CIRCUS, E.C.

This Undenominational Institution is entirely dependent upon public benevolence, having *no endowment whatever.*

It was founded in 1844 for the Maintenance, Clothing and Education of Fatherless Children of both sexes.

Orphans are received from all parts of the Kingdom, at any age between *three months* and eleven years, and are retained until they are fifteen.

More than *2,000* children have already been admitted to its benefits, *300* of whom are still in the Orphanage.

Their requirements entail a yearly expenditure of at least *£8,000,* of which only *£2,300* is provided by annual subscriptions.

The large balance is dependent upon donations and legacies. Help from the benevolent public is therefore urgently needed and earnestly requested.

The Secretary will be pleased to give any further information.

J. ROWLAND EDWARDS, Secretary. [150

ROYAL FEMALE ORPHAN ASYLUM,

BEDDINGTON (Near CROYDON), SURREY.

Founded at Lambeth, 1758. Incorporated 1800. Removed to Beddington, 1866.

PATRON—HER MAJESTY THE QUEEN. PRESIDENT—H.R.H. THE DUKE OF CAMBRIDGE, K.G.
CHAIRMAN—SIR JOHN B. MONCKTON, F.S.A.

THIS Asylum maintains and educates Fatherless Girls from all parts of Great Britain. They are admitted between the ages of **7** and **10**, and at the age of **16** are placed out in respectable private families. They must in all respects be thoroughly sound and healthy. Elections half-yearly in June and December. Forms of nomination may be obtained at the offices. New Subscribers to this old Charity are most earnestly needed.

Life Subscription, 2 Votes .. £10 10 0 | Annual Subscription, 2 Votes .. £1 1 0
Ditto 1 Vote .. 5 5 0 | Ditto 1 Vote .. 0 10 6

A donation of **60** Guineas in one sum entitles the donor to the immediate presentation of one child. Fatherless girls are received and paid for at the rate of £12 12s. per annum, with an entrance fee of £2 2s. pending election or otherwise. Cheques crossed HOARE & CO.
Subscriptions most thankfully received and all information given on application to the Secretary.

Offices—32, Essex Street, Strand, W.C. BROUGH MALTBY, *Secretary.* [162

THE ROYAL HOSPITAL FOR INCURABLES,

WEST HILL, PUTNEY HEATH.

Sea-side House, 55, Marina, St. Leonards-on-Sea,

*Office—*106, QUEEN VICTORIA STREET, E.C.

The work of the Royal Hospital for Incurables is twofold: it affords a Home for the most necessitous, and grants a Pension of £20 a-year in cases where a home already exists. The Charity is National in its character; persons are received as Inmates and Pensioners from all parts of the United Kingdom. Present number of Beneficiaries:—INMATES, 217; PENSIONERS, 683. Total, 900.

AN ANNUAL SUBSCRIBER has One Vote for each Half-a-Guinea; A LIFE SUBSCRIBER has One Vote for Life for each Five Guineas. The ELECTIONS are held Half-Yearly, in the months of May and November.

The Hospital may be visited any week-day between the hours of 12 and 6, by the Governors and Friends of the Institution.

*Bankers—*Messrs. GLYN, MILLS, CURRIE & Co., 67, Lombard Street, E.C.
Post Office Orders payable at Queen Victoria Street, E.C.

FREDERIC ANDREW, *Secretary.* [239

ROYAL HUMANE SOCIETY.

Instituted 1774. Supported by Voluntary Contributions.

*Patron—*Her Most Gracious Majesty THE QUEEN.
Vice-Patrons— { H.R.H. the PRINCE of WALES, K.G., K.T., K.P.
{ H.R.H. the DUKE of CAMBRIDGE, K.G., G.C.M.G.
*President—*H.R.H. the DUKE of YORK, K.G., K.T., K.P.
*Chairman and Treasurer—*Colonel HORACE MONTAGU.
*Dep. Chairman—*Vice-Admiral GEO. DIGBY MORANT. *Secretary—*Maj. F.A.C. CLAUGHTON.

Honorary Rewards granted for Saving Life from Drowning in all British Possessions. Pecuniary Rewards granted within an area of Thirty Miles around the Metropolis.

During the Skating Season, experienced Icemen are provided to prevent loss of life in the various waters about London; and Boats are in daily attendance, morning and evening, to prevent fatal results attending Accidents to the enormous number of Bathers in the Serpentine.

Nearly Three Hundred Places in and around London are furnished with Life-Saving Apparatus to rescue persons from Drowning.

The Society, some years ago, with a view of encouraging swimming coupled with a knowledge of the method of restoring the apparently drowned, instituted competitions at many of the public schools and on training ships, a medallion being awarded for proficiency. These competitions are held annually, and are the means of imparting much useful knowledge and instruction.

The Society is known throughout all the civilised world, but the pecuniary support it receives is quite inadequate to its usefulness, and it is necessary to remind the inhabitants of London that during a severe winter the Society has to incur a large outlay in finding ice-boats, ladders and ropes, for the protection of those who venture on dangerous ice; also for the wages and equipment of Icemen.

Life Governor............TEN GUINEAS. Annual Governor.........ONE GUINEA.

Donations or Subscriptions will be thankfully received by Major F. A. C. CLAUGHTON, Secretary, at the Office, 4, Trafalgar Square, London, W.C.; or by Messrs. PRESCOTT, DIMSDALE, CAVE, TUGWELL & Co., Bankers, 50, Cornhill, E.C. [244

ST. THOMAS'S HOSPITAL,

LAMBETH, S.E.

President:
H.R.H. Duke of CONNAUGHT, K.G.

Treasurer;
J. G. WAINWRIGHT, Esq., J.P.

2 WARDS CLOSED

Bankers: **Union Bank of London, Charing Cross Branch**

Governor's Donation, £52 10s. Endowment of Bed, £1,000.

FUNDS

• URGENTLY NEEDED. •

[149]

S. THOMAS'S HOME,

S. THOMAS'S HOSPITAL,

ALBERT EMBANKMENT,

WESTMINSTER BRIDGE, S.E.

For Paying Patients.

Full particulars may be obtained on application to the Resident Medical Officer of the Home, who can be seen daily at 12 o'clock, or to the Steward, S. Thomas's Hospital.

[143]

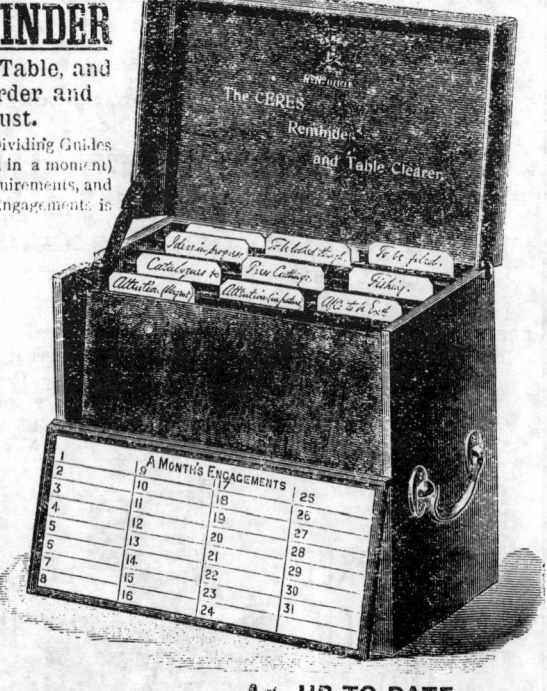
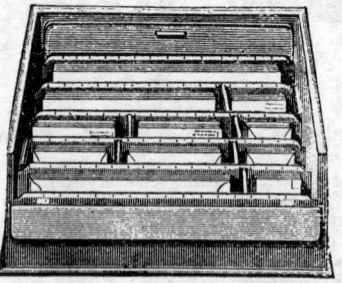

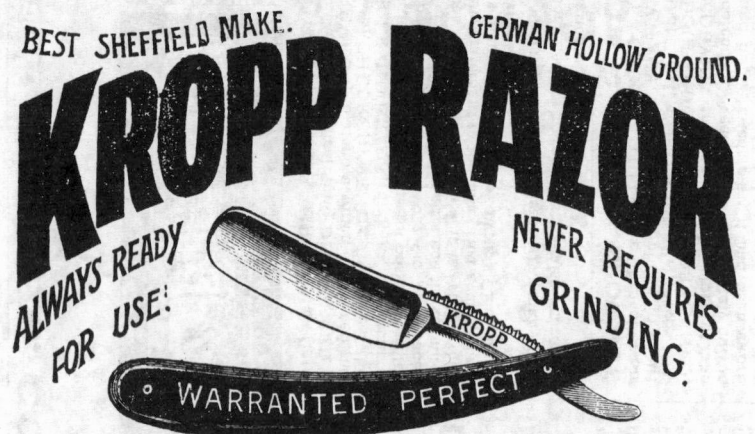

138

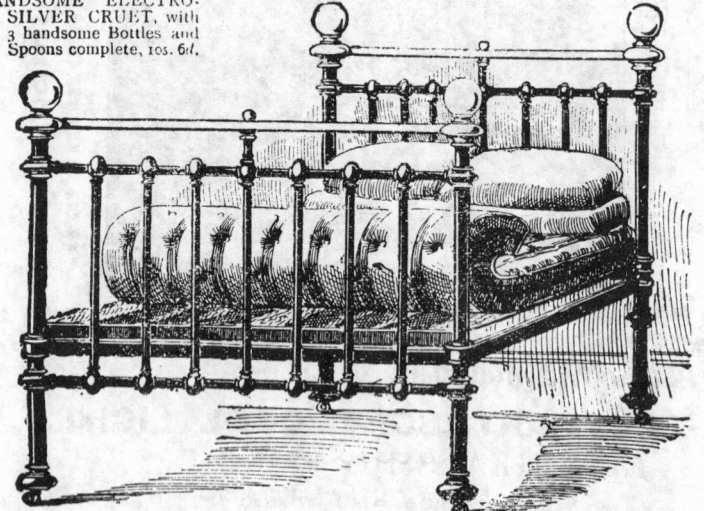

144

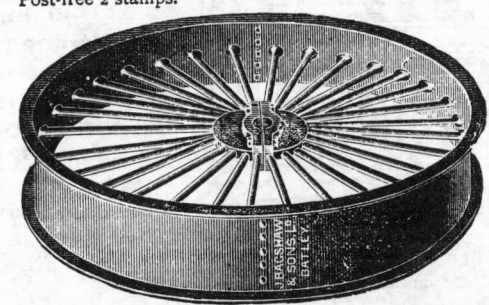

145

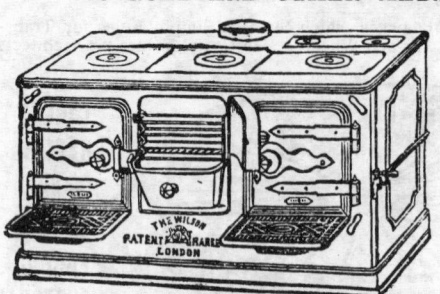

147

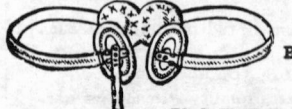 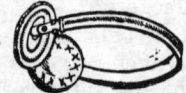

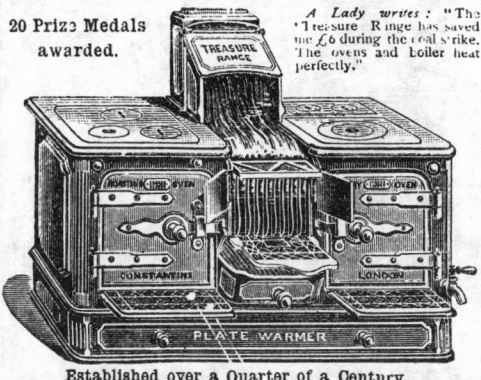

THE SAPPHIRE INKSTAND.

THIS Inkstand is without doubt the **Most Perfect**, and by far **the Cheapest**. It **Saves Time**, as washing is unnecessary; **Ink**, about two-thirds; **Breakages**, which mostly occur in washing; **New Ink-pots**, as a broken part can be replaced; **Dirty Fingers and Blots**, as clean ink is in sight and the dip adjustable; **Annoyance** by SPILLING, as very little can be spilled if upset. **Invaluable in Hot Climates.**

NEW PATTERN

No. 3 (Cut).

One-third Size.

NEW PATTERN

No. 3 (Cut).

One-third Size.

Trade Mark —

"SAPPHIRE."

Trade Mark —

"SAPPHIRE."

CONSTRUCTION AND ACTION.—The neck of the ink-well is clasped by an india-rubber collar, through which moves a stopper, compressing the air and forcing the ink into the dipping cup.

RETAIL PRICES.

No. 3.—Plain, strongly recommended.. **2 6** each. | No. 2.— Plain.. .. .. .. **2/-** each.
    Do.   Cut .. .. .. **5/-** ,, | Do. Cut .. .. .. **3/-** ,,

RACK 2d. extra. CATALOGUE ON APPLICATION.

EDWD. DARKE, Patentee and Sole Maker,
12, Pall Mall East, LONDON, S.W.

[25t

THE AUTOMATIC CYCLOSTYLE.

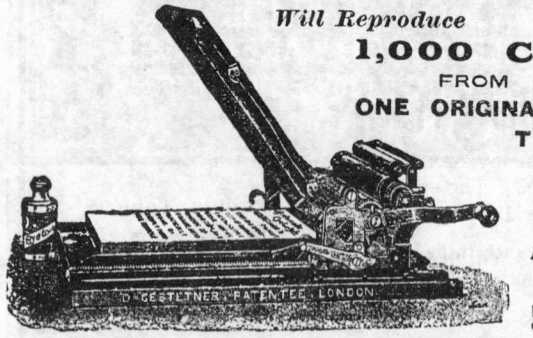

Will Reproduce

1,000 COPIES

FROM

ONE ORIGINAL HANDWRITING,
TYPEWRITING,
DRAWING, or
MUSIC.

A great advance on the Hand-Roller Apparatus.

Requires no skill to print perfect copies, and is quite clean in working.

THE LATEST AND BEST MACHINE

For Printing Circulars, Price Lists, Market Reports, Specifications, Returns, and Balance-Sheets, Freight Lists, Manifests, B/L, Examination Papers, Menus, Programmes, &c., &c.

THE AUTOMATIC CYCLOSTYLE,

Price Complete. { For Reproducing Handwriting Octavo size, £3 10s. Quarto size, £4 15s. Foolscap size, £5. Special Machine for Hot Climates, fitted with Hot Climate Rollers, 21s. extra. Outfit of Materials for reproducing Typewriting, 12s. 6d. extra each Machine.

For details and particulars apply to

THE CYCLOSTYLE CO., 79a, Gracechurch St., London, E.C., ENGLAND. [49

150

THE ÆOLIAN.

THE ÆOLIAN is an instrument upon which a person entirely without musical training can play artistically any piece of music ever composed. When we say artistically, we mean with perfect "technique," and with that which is the life and soul of all music, 'expression.'

A very small percentage of the many thousands of those who enjoy good music are able to play any instrument. There are many who possess a musical temperament who lack the technical skill necessary to play the piano or organ.

The best critics are seldom proficient performers. The keen appreciation of the true musician is born in a man—it can be cultivated or it can be neglected, but it never leaves him; it is a gift.

WILL RENDER ANY MUSIC EVER COMPOSED.

THE ÆOLIAN is the "true musician's" instrument. In **THE ÆOLIAN** he finds the medium by which he can express his musical conceptions.

He can play a sonata of Beethoven and impress it with his individual interpretation. The expression, the tempo, tone, colour and even the phrasing are directly under his control.

ANY ONE CAN PLAY IT.

The grandest symphony or the simplest song are instantly available without tiresome practice. The entire realm of music is his to command. His musical horizon is widened and his appreciation quickened.

THE ÆOLIAN entertains and instructs; it is the ideal home instrument. Prices from **£24** to **£600**.

THE ORCHESTRELLE CO.,
225, REGENT STREET.

THE ÆOLIAN is on Exhibition Daily at our Showrooms, and you should avail yourself of the opportunity of seeing it.

Catalogue 4 will be sent post free on application. [257]

Economy

PEARS' is the most economical of all soaps. It wears to the thinness of a wafer. Moisten and stick that soap=wafer on top of a fresh cake, then not a particle is lost. There is no waste in PEARS'. It is a clean soap, and it is a necessity for the clean. It is a comfort and a luxury.

PEARS' is the soap that lasts longest, and it is "a balm for the skin."